The Family Tree Sourcebook

Your Essential Directory of American County and Town Records

FROM THE EDITORS OF FAMILY TREE MAGAZINE

Cincinnati, Ohio FAMILY TREE BOOKS shopfamilytree.com

ONLINE ACCESS

★ Your purchase of this book includes 30 days of free access to the content of this book on Family Tree Magazine Plus, a members-only archive of thousands of expert genealogy articles on the *Family Tree Magazine* website.

To redeem your free one-month membership, go to **<www.familytreemagazine.com/secure/freepromo>**. Fill in the registration form with your account information, including a username and password, then enter the following code in the Promotion Code box:

FTSource

You can view the material from this book, along with bonus state maps, under the US Research category in the navigation bar.

If you wish to continue your Plus membership after 30 days, you can extend your subscription for $5.99/month or $39.99/year. In addition to this book's content, you'll get access to all newly published articles from *Family Tree Magazine*, America's #1 family history magazine.

fw media

EDITED BY
Diane Haddad

DESIGNED BY
Christy Miller

PRODUCTION COORDINATED BY
Mark Griffin

Published by Family Tree Books, an imprint of F+W Media, Inc., 4700 East Galbraith Road, Cincinnati, Ohio 45236. (800) 289-0963. Second edition.

For more genealogy resources, visit **<shopfamilytree.com>**.

14 13 12 11 10   5 4 3 2 1

Distributed in Canada by Fraser Direct
100 Armstrong Ave.
Georgetown, Ontario, Canada L7G 5S4
Tel: (905) 877-4411

Distributed in the U.K and Europe by F+W Media International
Brunel House, Newton Abbot, Devon, TQ12 4PU, England
Tel: (+44) 1626-323200,
Fax: (+44) 1626-323319
E-mail: postmaster@davidandcharles.co.uk

Distributed in Australia by Capricorn Link
P.O. Box 704, Windsor, NSW 2756 Australia
Tel: (02) 4577-3555

Library of Congress Cataloging-in-Publication Data
The Library of Congress has cataloged the first edition as follows:
The family tree resource book for genealogists / edited by Sharon DeBartolo Carmack and Erin Nevius.
789 p. : ill., maps ; 28 cm.
Includes bibliographical references.
ISBN: 1558706860 (alk. paper)
United States—Genealogy—Handbooks, manuals, etc.
CS47 .F36 2004
929/.1/072073 22

TABLE OF CONTENTS

INTRODUCTION

THE COUNTY COURTHOUSE. It's *the* place to find your ancestors. Today's genealogist is so accustomed to heading straight to the web for information about their ancestors that they often forget the wealth of information in the local courthouse.

Only a fraction of historical records are online. Records galore are waiting to be discovered in hundreds of brick-and-mortar sites across the nation. For example, here's just a sampling of the documents you might find in the county courthouse or town hall:

- adoptions
- apprenticeships and indentures
- bills of sale
- birth and death records
- bonds
- business and professional licenses
- civil court proceedings
- coroner's files and inquests
- criminal court records
- divorce petitions, cases, and decrees
- estate inventories
- insanity and commitment hearings
- jury lists
- justice of the peace records
- land deeds
- licenses and permits
- manumissions
- marriage bonds, licenses, and certificates
- military service discharges
- minute books
- name changes
- naturalization records
- oaths of allegiance
- prenuptial agreements
- relief, welfare and public assistance records
- subpoenas
- tax rolls
- voter registrations
- warrants
- wills and probate documents
- wolf-scalp bounties

Courthouse records are among the most richly detailed documents you'll find. And the best part? Most courthouse records are available to you even without making a trip to your ancestor's county. You can write to the county clerk to request copies of many documents, or you can find them on microfilm. We'll detail these options—as well as how to plan a visit—in the next section, How to Use This Book.

And don't stop there: You'll also want to explore the resources of the libraries, state archives, historical societies and published sources listed in the chapter for each state, as well as in the National Resources section on page 742. Finally, because there *is* great information online, we've listed the best websites for research in each state on page 739. So get ready for a whole new world of genealogical discovery!

» BY SHARON DEBARTOLO CARMACK

HOW TO USE THIS BOOK

For each state, you'll find an article featuring genealogy advice, a map of the state showing each county, fast facts such as statehood date and capital, a listing of state repositories and a listing of other resources for statewide records.

Following that, you'll find a directory of county, parish or town record-keeping offices. Here's an example:

Contact information for requesting records

County's date of formation

COOSA

★ Box 218, Rockford, AL 35136, (256) 362-5721, <www.rootsweb.ancestry.com/~alcoosa>
• **INCORPORATED:** Dec. 18, 1832 ★
★ • **PARENT COUNTY:** Creek Indian Treaty of Cusseta
• **BIRTH RECORDS:** start in 1878, kept by ★ Department of Health
• **MARRIAGE:** 1834, Probate Court ★
• **DEATH:** 1920, Department of Health ★
• **DIVORCE:** 1834, Probate Court ★
• **LAND:** 1832, Probate Court ★
• **PROBATE:** 1834, Probate Court ★
• **COURT:** 1834, Circuit Court Office ★
• **MILITARY:** 1834, Probate Court ★
• **NOTES:** Probate Court has a few ★ birth and death records 1920–1945.

Parent counties to search in if your ancestor's residence predates county formation

Research tips

Start dates and locations of important county records

Suppose you have an ancestor who was married in Teller County, Colo., in 1895. Turning to that county's listing in this book, you'll learn this county wasn't created until 1899, the same year marriage records began. You'll need to look in Teller's parent county of El Paso for your ancestors' marriage record. Turning to that page, you'll learn that El Paso marriage records began in 1861. To obtain the marriage record, you can see if it's online, search for microfilm at the Family History library or another repository, write to the courthouse at the address provided, or visit in person.

Look online: Not many courthouse records have been digitized and posted online, but it's worth checking. Try running a Google <google.com> search on the county name and court records. Study the county clerk's website for a link to historical or genealogical records. Also try the FamilySearch Pilot Record Search Site <pilot.familysearch.org>. Examine the database lists of subscription sites such as Ancestry.com <ancestry.com> and Footnote.com <footnote.com> (your local library may offer free access to institutional versions of these sites; inquire at the reference desk).

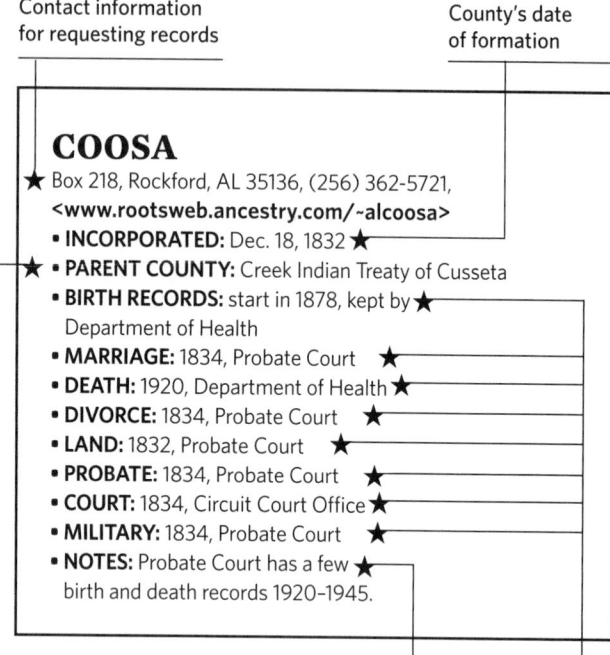

Search for microfilm: The Church of Jesus Christ of Latter-day Saints Family History Library (FHL) **<www.familysearch.org>** in Salt Lake City has microfilmed records at thousands of courthouses and town halls across the county. (Some records may be on microfiche, which is flat film rather than on a roll.) You can rent FHL microfilm by visiting one of the FHL's thousands of branch Family History Centers (FHCs). Follow these steps to find your film:

1 Go to the FHL online catalog **<www.familysearch.org/eng/library/fhlc/frameset_fhlc.asp>** and click Place.

2 Type the county name (don't include the word county). Type the state in the Part Of field. Click Search.

3 Scan the list of result headings for the records you need. For example, click Vital Records if you're looking for a marriage record.

4 You'll get a list of microfilm titles. Click each one to learn more about the records on that roll. If the title is a series, click the View Film Notes button for a list of microfilms within that series.

5 Print the catalog record or note the film numbers of microfilm rolls you'd like to rent. Take your list to the nearest FHC (search for one at **<www.familysearch.org/eng/library/fhc/frameset_fhc.asp>**), where a volunteer can help you request the roll from the FHL.

6 Staff will contact you when your film is available for viewing at the FHC

Most microfilm and microfiche readers have instructions, but ask a staff member for help if you're having trouble.

You also might find microfilmed courthouse records at state libraries and archives, and some large public libraries. Search each repository's online catalog or contact the reference desk to find out whether it has the microfilm you need. (This book focuses on county and state records, but for microfilm of federal records—such as censuses and military service papers—you'll start with the National Archives and Records Administration **<www.archives.gov>**.)

Write to the county clerk: An old-fashioned letter is still a good way to obtain records when the ones you need haven't been microfilmed or digitized. Be specific in your request, as the county clerk is busy and responding to letters from genealogists may not be high on her list of things to do. Provide only enough information so the clerk can help you.

Let's say you want to see if Great-great-grandpa William Shough, who died in 1878, left a will in Alleghany County, Va. First, turn to page 673 in this book and find the listing for that county. It will give you the year Orange County probate records begin, what court holds the records and the address for the clerk's office. You might word your letter like this:

> Alleghany County Clerk of Circuit Court
> 266 W. Main St.
> Covingtonn, VA 24426
>
> To Whom it May Concern,
> I am seeking the will of William Shough, who died in your county in 1878. Could you please check your index (please also check under the spelling "Show"), and let me know if you have a will recorded for him and what the cost would be to obtain a copy of the full record?
> Thank you for your assistance. I am enclosing a self-addressed, stamped envelope for your reply.
> Sincerely,
>
> *Your Name Here*

If you've consulted courthouse record indexes on microfilm or in a book, you'll make the clerk's job easier by including the volume and page number of the record, or even a photocopy of the index.

You may prefer to include a check for, say, $5, and say in the letter that you will send any additional fee. Keep in mind that most clerks will search only for what you ask. Although William Shough may have died in 1878, his will might not have been recorded until several years later, so it's a good idea to include a five- to 10-year search span. Also include common spelling variations of the name.

If you get a negative response, you may wonder how thorough the clerk's search was. This might be an item to recheck should you ever be able to visit the courthouse in person. Or you could hire a local genealogist to search for you; see a directory on the Association of Professional Genealogists website **<www.apgen.org>**.

Visit the courthouse or town hall: If you're lucky enough to visit your ancestral courthouse in person, you'll be able to scour the records to your heart's content. Note, though, that assisting genealogists isn't the primary duty of county and town clerks. When asking for help, it's best not to go into detail about your research. Give only enough information so that staff can help you find what you're looking for. Be as pleasant and friendly as possible.

Some researchers go the extra mile when they have a particularly helpful clerk and send a thank-you note. Next time, the clerk is likely to be even more helpful.

In some courthouses you'll be allowed to search the indexes and records yourself; in others, a clerk will do it for you. If the records have been transferred to the state archives or an off-site storage facility, you may be relegated to viewing records on microfilm. If you call ahead, the staff might have records brought to the courthouse or town hall for your use.

Visit the courthouse website or call prior to your visit to check on research hours and any special closures. Find answers to these questions:

- Is a photocopier available for public use?
- How much does it cost to obtain a certified and uncertified copy of a record?
- Can researchers take in briefcases and laptop computers?
- Is there a particular person I need to see about looking at a particular record?
- Does the office close for lunch?
- Are any records stored off site, and how can I get access to them?

Bring plenty of change for photocopiers, and make sure you have directions, parking information and an idea of where to get lunch. Take care when handling historical documents and records. Never tear, erase, mark or remove any document, book or microfilm.

ALABAMA

» BY EMILY ANNE CROOM

HISTORICAL OVERVIEW

Alabama's history is culturally diverse. Indians long inhabited the region and the Spanish explored there in the 16th century. France established the first permanent white settlement near Mobile Bay in 1702 as part of Louisiana. At the end of the French and Indian War (1763), France ceded to Britain lands east of the Mississippi River, including Alabama, as part of West Florida. However, Spain occupied coastal Alabama in 1780. At the end of the American Revolution, the 1783 Treaty of Paris gave the United States land north of the present Alabama-Florida boundary, the 31st parallel of latitude; Spain kept the Mobile Bay area as part of Spanish West Florida.

The US portion became part of Mississippi Territory in 1798, with most non-Indian residents living in Washington County. Although claimed by Georgia until 1802, the northern portion of the present state remained Indian lands. The Mobile Bay area was disputed territory after the Louisiana Purchase (1803), and US troops took the Spanish garrison at Mobile during the War of 1812. When Mississippi attained statehood in 1817, Alabama became a separate territory and two years later (1819) became the 22nd state.

Between 1805 and 1838, the US forced most Indians West and opened former Indian lands to white settlement. The land lured thousands of settlers, largely from Tennessee and Georgia, the Carolinas and Virginia. Numerous immigrants into central and southern Alabama used the Federal Road that stretched from Athens, Ga., to New Orleans.

Settlers found grasslands, forests and abundant wildlife, hills and plateaus in north and central counties, and coastal plains in the south. Agriculture, especially cotton and corn crops, dominated the economy until the 20th century.

Most of Alabama's navigable rivers eventually empty into Mobile Bay or the Gulf of Mexico, but the Tennessee River dips across northern Alabama before heading north to the Ohio River. Early planters in northern counties shipped cotton to New Orleans via the Tennessee, Ohio, and Mississippi rivers; those in central and southern counties, used the port of Mobile for exporting crops and importing supplies. These factors and the lack of north-south roads kept the northern part of the state fairly isolated from central and southern Alabama and helped create regional and political differences. Many Alabama farmers, planters, and townspeople were slaveholders. By 1860, of Alabama's nearly one million people, 55 percent were white and 45 percent were black, of whom less than 1 percent were free. Foreign-born people were about 1 percent. Ninety-five percent of the state's population was rural. Not until 1960 did the state's urban population surpass its rural population.

research tips

- Until 1850, probate courts were called orphans courts.
- Some probate courts have packets of loose case papers; many older probate records have been microfilmed.
- Ancestors reportedly born in Mississippi before 1817 or West Florida before 1813 may have been born in what is now Alabama.
- Alabama's federal censuses date from 1830.
- Much of Perry County's 1890 census survives.
- Explore resources in the Alabama Department of Archives and History (**<www.archives.state.al.us>**), Birmingham Public Library, Samford University, andthe University of Alabama.

CENSUS RECORDS

- Federal census population schedules: 1830, 1840, 1850, 1860, 1870, 1880, 1900, 1910, 1920, 1930
- State census: 1820, 1855, 1866
- Mississippi territorial census: 1810, 1816
- Federal mortality schedules for counties in existence: 1850, 1860, 1870, 1880
- Federal slave schedules: 1850, 1860 (schedules name slaveholders but rarely name slaves)

After Alabama seceded from the Union in January 1861, Montgomery was briefly the capital of the Confederate States of America. Confederate troops held Mobile almost until the end of the war, but the state saw about 200 engagements. Although most Alabamians supported the Confederate cause, a considerable number served in Union forces.

Left with widespread poverty after the war, Alabama didn't experience significant recovery until the 1900s. By the mid-20th century, the state's economy had diversified to include livestock, mining and steel, commercial forestry and related manufacturing, and production of consumer goods.

RECORD HIGHLIGHTS

The state health department **<www.adph.org/vitalrecords>** maintains birth and death records from 1908, marriage records from August 1936, and divorce records from 1950. Some county probate courts hold pre-1908 birth and death records. Before 1865, the state legislature had jurisdiction over most divorces.

A significant number of Alabama counties have lost records in courthouse disasters—few of which occurred during the Civil War. Since fires or storms rarely destroy everything, check for surviving records. Consult records in parent and neighboring counties, as well as colonial, local, state, and federal jurisdictions. Also use libraries, local historical societies, and the state archives.

Alabama is a federal land state. Its federal land patents are searchable at the Bureau of Land Management website **<www.glorecords.blm.gov>**. Subsequent land transactions between individuals were recorded at county courthouses.

Alabama-specific resources include territorial censuses; state censuses (1820, 1855, 1866); censuses of Confederate veterans (1907, 1921) and widows (1927); territorial militia and civil service appointments; state militia records; Confederate pensions; 1862 salt allotment lists; 1867 voter registrations; Mobile Municipal Archives; state legislative acts involving individuals and families; territorial and state tax records; *Territorial Papers of the United States* and *Territorial Papers of the United States Senate*; pre-1817 territorial records at the Mississippi State Archives; and records of depositors of the two Alabama branches of the Freedman's Savings and Trust Company (FHL microfilm 928571-72).

ARCHIVES, LIBRARIES, AND SOCIETIES

Alabama Department of Archives and History
624 Washington Ave., Montgomery, AL 36130, (334) 242-4435, **<www.archives.state.al.us>**

Alabama Department of Public Health Center for Health Statistics
Box 303017, Montgomery, AL 36103, **<www.adph.org/vitalrecords>**

Alabama Genealogical Society
Samford University Library, AGS Depository and Headquarters, 800 Lakeshore Drive, Box 2296, Birmingham, AL 35229, **<algensoc.org>**

Alabama Historical Association
Alabama Department of Archives and History, 624 Washington Ave., Montgomery, AL 36130, **<www.archives.state.al.us/aha/aha.html>**

Andalusia Public Library
212 S. Three Notch St., Andalusia, AL 36420, (334) 222-6612, **<www.andylibrary.com>**

Anniston Liles Memorial Library
Box 308, Anniston, AL 36202, **<www.rootsweb.ancestry.com/~alabgs>**

Roman Catholic Archdiocese of Mobile
Chancery Office, Box 1966, Mobile, AL 36633, (334) 434-1583

Auburn University Ralph Brown Draughton Library
231 Mell St., Auburn, AL 36849, (800) 446-0387, **<www.lib.auburn.edu>**

Autauga Genealogical Society
Box 680668, Prattville, AL 36068, **<www.rootsweb.ancestry.com/~alags>**

Barbour County Genealogy Group
Eufala Carnegie Library, 217 N. Eufala Ave., Eufala, AL 36027

Birmingham Genealogical Society
Box 2432, Birmingham, AL 35201, **<www.birminghamgenealogy.org>**

Birmingham Public Library
2100 Park Place, Birmingham, AL 35203, (205) 226-3610, **<www.bplonline.org>**

Birmingham-Southern College Charles Andrew Rush Library
900 Arkadelphia Rd., Birmingham, AL 35254, (205) 226-4740, **<library.bsc.edu>**

Bullock County Historical Society
Box 563, Union Springs, AL 36089

Butler County Historical and Genealogical Society
Box 561, Greenville, AL 36037, (334) 383-9564

Central Alabama Genealogical Society
Box 125, Selma, AL 36702

Chattahoochee Valley Historical Society, 3419 20th Ave., Valley, AL 36854, **< www.cvhistoricalsociety.org>**

Choctaw County Genealogical Society
4224 County Rd. 43, Butler, AL 36904, **<www.rootsweb.ancestry.com/~alccgs>**

Coosa County Historical Society
Box 388, Rockford, AL 35136

Cullman County Public Library
200 Clark St., NE, Cullman, AL 35055

Dale County Genealogical and Historical Society
Ozark-Dale County Public Library, 416 James St., Ozark, AL 36360, (334) 774-5480, **<www.odcpl.com>**

Dekalb County Genealogical Society
Box 681087, Fort Payne, AL 35968, **<dekalbsociety.freeservers.com>**

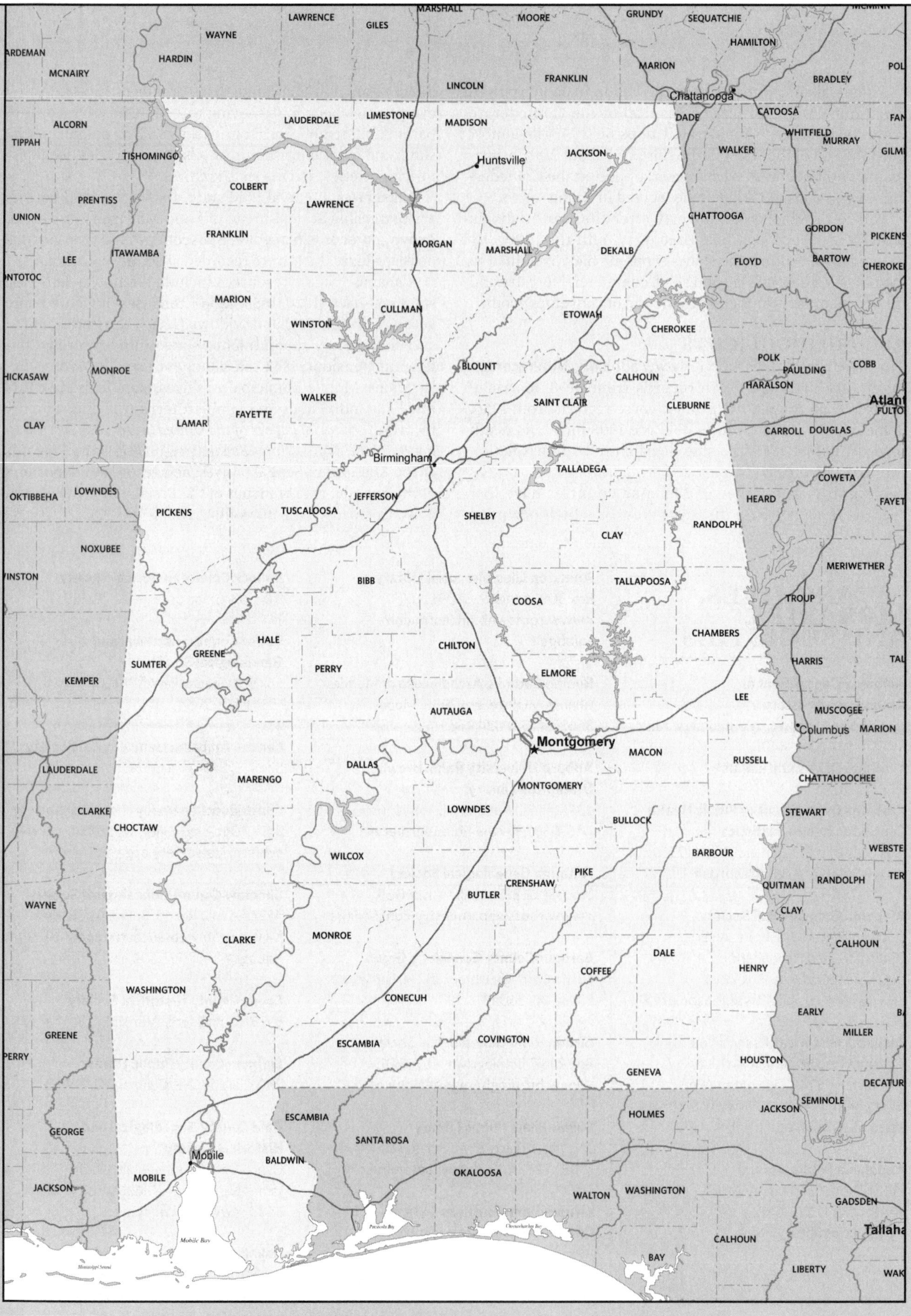
LAWRENCE
GILES
MARSHALL
MOORE
GRUNDY
SEQUATCHIE
HAMILTON
WAYNE
HARDIN
MCNAIRY
LINCOLN
FRANKLIN
MARION
BRADLEY
Chattanooga
LAUDERDALE
LIMESTONE
MADISON
DADE
CATOOSA
WHITFIELD
MURRAY
ALCORN
TIPPAH
TISHOMINGO
Huntsville
JACKSON
WALKER
COLBERT
LAWRENCE
PRENTISS
UNION
FRANKLIN
CHATTOOGA
GORDON
MORGAN
MARSHALL
DEKALB
FLOYD
BARTOW
LEE
ITAWAMBA
MARION
CULLMAN
WINSTON
ETOWAH
CHEROKEE
BLOUNT
POLK
PAULDING
COBB
MONROE
CALHOUN
HARALSON
SAINT CLAIR
CLEBURNE
WALKER
FAYETTE
LAMAR
CLAY
CARROLL
DOUGLAS
Birmingham
TALLADEGA
COWETA
LOWNDES
OKTIBBEHA
PICKENS
TUSCALOOSA
JEFFERSON
SHELBY
HEARD
RANDOLPH
CLAY
NOXUBEE
MERIWETHER
BIBB
TALLAPOOSA
COOSA
TROUP
CHAMBERS
HALE
CHILTON
GREENE
SUMTER
HARRIS
KEMPER
PERRY
ELMORE
LEE
AUTAUGA
MUSCOGEE
Columbus
MARION
Montgomery
MACON
LAUDERDALE
DALLAS
RUSSELL
MARENGO
MONTGOMERY
CHATTAHOOCHEE
CLARKE
CHOCTAW
LOWNDES
BULLOCK
STEWART
WILCOX
BARBOUR
PIKE
QUITMAN
RANDOLPH
CRENSHAW
BUTLER
CLAY
WAYNE
CLARKE
MONROE
DALE
CALHOUN
HENRY
COFFEE
WASHINGTON
CONECUH
EARLY
GREENE
MILLER
ESCAMBIA
COVINGTON
HOUSTON
GENEVA
SEMINOLE
JACKSON
ESCAMBIA
HOLMES
GEORGE
SANTA ROSA
Mobile
BALDWIN
MOBILE
OKALOOSA
JACKSON
WALTON
WASHINGTON
GADSDEN
CALHOUN
BAY
LIBERTY

Florence-Lauderdale Public Library
350 N. Wood Ave., Florence, AL 35630, (256) 764-6564, **<www.flpl.lib.al.us>**

Genealogical Society of East Alabama
Box 2892, Opelika, AL 36803

Hueytown Historical Society
Box 3313, Hueytown, AL 35023, **<www.hueytown.com/historical/index.html>**

Huntingdon College Houghton Memorial Library
1500 E. Fairview Ave., Montgomery, AL 36106, (334) 833-4421, **<library.huntingdon.edu>**

Huntsville Public Library
The Heritage Room, 915 Monroe St., Huntsville, AL 35801, (256) 532-5969, **<hmcpl.org/hhr>**

Jackson County Historical Association
Box 1494, Scottsboro, AL 35768

Lamar County Genealogical Society
Box 357, Vernon, AL 35592, **<www.fayette.net/carruth/genealogysociety.htm>**

Lawrence County Historical Commission
County Archives, Box 728, Moulton, AL 35650, **<www.lawrencecoarchives.com>**

Limestone County Historical Society
Box 82, Athens, AL 35611

Lowndes County Historical and Genealogical Society
5935 County Rd. 4, Minter, AL 36761,

Marion County Genealogical Society
Box 360, Winfield, AL 35594

Mary Wallace Cobb Memorial Library
110 First Ave. NW, Vernon, AL 35592, (205) 695-6123

Mobile Genealogical Society
1400 Joyce Rd., Mobile, AL 36618, (251) 414-1995, **<www.mobileroots.org>**

Montgomery County Historical Society
Box 1829, Montgomery, AL 36102, (334) 264-1837, **<www.montgomery historical.org>**

Montgomery Genealogical Society
Box 230194, Montgomery, AL 36123 **<www.rootsweb.ancestry.com/~almgs>**

Natchez Trace Genealogical Society
Box 420, Florence, AL 35631, **<www.rootsweb.ancestry.com/~alntgs>**

National Archives, Southeast Region
5780 Jonesboro Road, Morrow GA 30260, (770) 968-2100, **<www.archives.gov/southeast>**

North Central Alabama Genealogical Society
Box 13, Cullman, AL 35056

Northeast Alabama Genealogical Society
Box 8268, Gadsden, AL 35902

Ozark-Dale County Public Library
416 James St., Ozark, AL 36360, (334) 774-5480, **<www.odcpl.com>**

Pea River Historical and Genealogical Society
Box 310628, Enterprise, AL 36331, (334) 393-2901, **<www.rootsweb.ancestry.com/~alprhgs>**

Pike County Historical and Genealogical Society
<www.rootsweb.ancestry.com/~mspike/pikemain.html>

Samford University Harwell Goodwin Davis Library
800 Lakeshore Dr., Birmingham, AL 35229, (205) 726-2748, **<www.library.samford.edu>**

Shelby County Historical Society
Box 457, Columbiana, AL 35051, (205) 669-3912, **<www.rootsweb.ancestry.com/~alshelby/schs.html>**

Southeast Alabama Genealogical Society
Box 246, Dothan, AL 36302

Steward University System Library
RFD 5, Box 109, Piedmont, AL 36272

Tennessee Valley Genealogical Society
Box 1568, Huntsville, AL 35807, **<www.tvgs.org>**

Tennessee Valley Historical Society
Box 149, Sheffield, AL 35660

Tuscaloosa Genealogical Society
Box 020802, Tuscaloosa, AL 35402

University of Alabama, William Stanley Hoole Special Collections Library
University Libraries, Box 870266, Tuscaloosa, AL 35487, (205) 348-0500, **<www.lib.ua.edu/libraries/hoole>**

Walker County Genealogical Society
Box 3408, Jasper, AL 35502

Wallace State College Library
Box 2000, 801 Main St. NW, Hanceville, AL 35077 (256) 352-8000, **<www.wallacestate.edu/library.html>**

Washington County Historical Society
Box 456, Chatom, AL 36518

Wilcox Historical Society
Box 464, Camden, AL 36726, (334) 682-9825, **<www.wilcoxwebworks.com/history>**

Winston County Genealogical Society
Box 112, Double Springs, AL 35553, **<wcgs.ala.nu/wcgs.htm>**

GENERAL RESOURCES

Alabama Bible Records by Jeannette Holland Austin (J.H. Austin, 1987)

Alabama: The History of a Deep South State William Warren Rogers, et al. (University of Alabama Press, 1994)

Alabama, Her History, Resources, War Record, and Public Men, from 1540 to 1872 by Willis Brewer (Clearfield Co., 1995)

Alabama Research Outline by the Church of Jesus Christ of Latter-day Saints (online at **<www.familysearch.org/eng/search/RG/guide/alabama.asp>**)

The Federal Road Through Georgia, the Creek Nation, and Alabama, 1806-1836 by Henry deLeon Southerland Jr. and Jerry Elijah Brown (University of Alabama Press, 1989)

The Formative Period in Alabama, 1815-1828 by Thomas Perkins Abernethy (University of Alabama Press, 1990)

History of Alabama and Dictionary of Alabama Biography, 4 vols., Thomas McAdory Owen (Reprint Co., 1978)

Index to Colonel James Edmons Saunders' Early Settlers of Alabama by Lloyd F. Oliver (Genealogical Publications, 1978)

Indian Place Names in Alabama, revised edition, by William A. Read (University of Alabama Press, 1984)

Notable Men of Alabama: Personal and Genealogical, with Portraits edited by Joel Campbell DuBose (Reprint Co., 1976)

Place Names in Alabama by Virginia O. Foscue (University of Alabama Press, 1989)

Some Early Alabama Churches (Established Before 1870) compiled by Mabel Ponder Wilson, Dorothy Youngblood Woodyerd, and Rosa Lee Busby (Alabama Society, Daughters of the American Revolution)

Tracing Your Alabama Past by Robert Scott Davis (University Press of Mississippi, 2003)

☞ CENSUS RECORDS

1907 Alabama Census of Confederate Soldiers, 5 vols., from the Alabama Department of Archives and History (Gregath, 1982)

Alabama Census Returns, 1820, and an Abstract of Federal Census of Alabama, 1830 edited by the Department of Archives and History and Marie Bankhead Owen, (Genealogical Publishing Co., 1967)

Alabama Mortality Schedule 1850 by Marilyn Davis Hahn (Southern Historical Press, 1983)

Alabama Mortality Schedule 1860 by Marilyn Davis Hahn (Southern Historical Press, 1987)

Census of Confederate Veterans Residing in Southeast Alabama in 1907 compiled by Homer T. Jones (Pioneer Pub., 1998)

☞ IMMIGRATION RECORDS

Declarations of Intention, Naturalizations, and Petitions, 1855-1960 from the US District Court, Southern District of Alabama

Lists of Ships' Passengers, Mobile, Alabama, 2 vols., compiled by Lucille Mallon Connick (L.M. Connick, 1988)

Naturalization Records, Mobile, Alabama, 1833-1906 by Clinton P. King and merrem A. Barlow (Gateway Press, 1986)

☞ LAND RECORDS

English Land Grants in West Florida: A Register for the States of Alabama, Mississippi, and Parts of Florida and Louisiana, 1766-1776 by Winston DeVille (W. De Ville, 1986)

Old Cahaba Land Office Records and Military Warrants, 1817-1853 by Marilyn Davis Hahn (Old South Print & Publishing Co., 1981)

Old Huntsville Land Office Records and Military Warrants, 1810-1854 compiled by Marilyn Davis Barefield (Southern Historical Press, 1985)

Old Land Records of Colbert County, Alabama by Margaret Matthews Cowart (M.M. Cowart, 1985)

Old Land Records of Franklin County, Alabama by Margaret Matthews Cowart (M.M. Cowart, 1986)

Old Land Records of Jackson County, Alabama by Margaret Matthews Cowart (M.M. Cowart, 1980)

Old Land Records of Lauderdale County, Alabama by Margaret Matthews Cowart (M.M. Cowart, 1996)

Old Land Records of Lawrence County, Alabama by Margaret Matthews Cowart (M.M. Cowart, 1991)

Old Land Records of Limestone County, Alabama by Margaret Matthews Cowart (M.M. Cowart, 1984)

Old Land Records of Madison County, Alabama by Margaret Matthews Cowart (M.M. Cowart, 1979)

Old Land Records of Marshall County, Alabama by Margaret Matthews Cowart (M.M. Cowart, 1988)

Old Land Records of Morgan County, Alabama by Margaret Matthews Cowart (M.M. Cowart, 1981)

Old Sparta & Elba Land Office Records & Military Warrants, 1822-1860 by Marilyn Davis Hahn (Southern Historical Press, 1983)

Old St. Stephen's Land Office Records & American State Papers, Public Lands, Vol. I, 1768-1888 by Marilyn Davis Hahn (Southern Historical Press, 1983)

Old Tuscaloosa Land Office Records & Military Warrants, 1821-1855 compiled by Marilyn Davis Barefield (Southern Historical Press, 1984)

Private Land Claims, Alabama, Arkansas, Florida by Fern C. Ainsworth (F. Ainsworth, 1978)

Robert Armstrong's Survey Book of Cherokee Lands: Lands Granted from the Treaty of 27 February 1819 by James L. Douthat and Robert Armstrong (Institute of Historical Research, 1993)

☞ MAPS

Atlas of Historical County Boundaries, Alabama edited by John H. Long, and compiled by Peggy Sinko, compiler (Charles Scribner's Sons, 1996)

Dead Towns of Alabama by W. Stuart Harris (University of Alabama Press, 1977)

Handbook of Alabama, 2nd edition, by Saffold Berney (Reprint Co., 1975)

Historical Atlas of Alabama by Donald B. Dodd (University of Alabama Press, 1974)

A List of Nineteenth Century Maps of the State of Alabama by Sara Elizabeth Mason (Birmingham Public Library, 1973)

Yesterday's Faces of Alabama: A Collection of Maps, 1822-1909 edited by Society of Pioneers of Montgomery and John H. Napier III (Brown Print Co., 1978)

☞MILITARY RECORDS

Compendium of the Confederate Armies, 11 vols., by Stewart Sifakis (Facts on File, 1992-1995)

First Tennessee and Alabama Independent Cavalry, 1863-1864, Roster: Companies A, B, C, D, E, F, G, H compiled by John L.T.N. Potter and the US Army Alabama and Tennessee Cavalry, 1st, Vidette Cavalry (Mountain Press, 1995)

An Index to Alabama Society Sons of the American Revolution, Members and their Ancestors, 1903-1996 compiled by Clifford D. Black and the Sons of the American Revolution, Alabama (C.D. Black, 1996)

Law's Alabama Brigade in the War Between the Union and the Confederacy by J. Gary Laine and Morris M. Penny (White Mane Pub. Co., 1996)

Revolutionary Soldiers in Alabama by Thomas McAdory Owen and the Alabama Department of Archives and History (Genealogical Publishing Co., 1975)

Volunteer Soldiers in the Cherokee War, 1836-1839 by James L. Douthat (Mountain Press, 1995)

World War II: A Family Historian's Guide by Debra Johnson Knox (MIE Publishing, 2003)

☞PROBATE RECORDS

Index to Alabama Wills, 1808-1870 compiled by the Daughters of the American Revolution, Alabama Society (Genealogical Publishing Co., 1977)

☞VITAL RECORDS

Alabama Marriages Early to 1825: A Research Tool compiled by Liahona Research, Inc., Jordan R. Dodd and Norman L. Moyes (Precision Indexing, 1991)

Alabama Notes, 4 vols. by Flora Dainwood England (Genealogical Pub. Co., 1977-1989)

Bible and Cemetery Records, 2 vols., from the Birmingham Genealogical Society (1962-1966)

Divorces Copied from Printed Acts of Alabama, 1818-1864 by Donald F. Watson (Alabama Department of Archives and History, 1971)

Marriage Certificates, 1936-1992; Index, 1936-1959 from the Alabama Department of Health (filmed by the Genealogical Society of Utah, 1993)

Marriage & Death Notices from Alabama Newspapers and Family Records, 1819-1890 compiled by Helen S. Foley (Southern Historical Press, 1981)

Marriage, Death, and Legal Notices from Early Alabama Newspapers, 1819-1893 compiled by Pauline Jones Gandrud (Southern Historical Press, 1981)

COUNTY DETAILS

AUTAUGA

134 N. Court St. Suite 106, Prattville, AL 36067, (334) 361-3725
<www.autauga.org>

- **INCORPORATED:** Nov. 21, 1818
- **PARENT COUNTY:** Montgomery
- **LAND RECORDS:** start in 1809, kept by Probate Judge
- **PROBATE:** 1810, Probate Judge
- **COURT:** 1831, Circuit Court
- **NOTES:** Marriage records from 1829-1898, birth from 1871-1928 (delayed birth certificates), and death from March 1908-February 1916.

BAINE

- **INCORPORATED:** Dec. 7, 1866
- **PARENT COUNTIES:** Blount, Calhoun, Cherokee, DeKalb, Marshall, St. Clair
- **NOTES:** Abolished Dec. 3, 1867. Became Etowah County Dec. 1, 1868.

BAKER

- **INCORPORATED:** Dec. 30, 1868
- **PARENT COUNTIES:** Autauga, Bibb, Perry, Shelby
- **NOTES:** See Chilton County. Name changed to Chilton Dec. 17, 1874.

BALDWIN

1 Court Sq., Box 459, Bay Minette, AL 36507, (251) 937-0399,
<www.co.baldwin.al.us>

- **INCORPORATED:** Dec. 21, 1809
- **PARENT COUNTIES:** Washington, West Florida
- **BIRTH RECORDS:** start in 1908, kept by Department of Health
- **MARRIAGE:** 1819, Probate Court
- **DEATH:** 1908, Department of Health
- **LAND:** 1809, Probate Court
- **PROBATE:** 1810, Probate Court
- **COURT:** 1811, Circuit Court

BARBOUR

1800 Fifth Ave. N., Box 398, Clayton, AL 36016, (334) 775-8371,
<www.archives.state.al.us/counties/barbour.html>

- **INCORPORATED:** Dec. 18, 1832
- **PARENT COUNTIES:** Pike County, Original Territory
- **MARRIAGE RECORDS:** start in 1838, kept by Probate Judge
- **LAND:** 1832, Probate Judge
- **PROBATE:** 1833, Probate Judge
- **COURT:** 1832, Circuit Court
- **NOTES:** Birth records from 1891-1899 and 1906-1923 and Death records from 1906-1923

BENTON
- **INCORPORATED:** Dec. 18, 1832
- **PARENT COUNTY:** Creek Cession of 1832
- **NOTES:** See Calhoun County. Name changed to Calhoun Jan. 29, 1858.

BIBB
Centreville, AL 35042, (205) 926-4747
<www.archives.state.al.us/counties/bibb.html>
- **INCORPORATED:** Feb. 7, 1818
- **PARENT COUNTIES:** Monroe, Montgomery
- **MARRIAGE RECORDS:** start in 1818, kept by County Clerk
- **LAND:** 1818, County Clerk
- **PROBATE:** 1830, County Clerk
- **COURT:** 1830, Circuit Court
- **NOTES:** Formerly Cahawba County. Name changed to Bibb Dec. 2, 1820.

BLOUNT
220 Second Ave., E., Room 208, Oneonta, AL 35121, (205) 625-4153,
<www.hometownchronicles.com/al/blount/index.html>
- **INCORPORATED:** Feb. 6, 1818
- **PARENT COUNTIES:** Montgomery County and land acquired from the Creek Cession of 1814.
- **MARRIAGE RECORDS:** start in 1820, kept by County Archivist
- **LAND:** 1818, County Archivist
- **PROBATE:** 1829, County Archivist
- **BURIAL:** 1820, County Archivist
- **NOTES:** Clerk of Circuit Court has court records 1829-1852/1872.

BULLOCK
Box 71, Union Springs, AL 36089, (334) 738-2250,
<www.archives.state.al.us/counties/Bullock.html>
- **INCORPORATED:** Dec. 5, 1866
- **PARENT COUNTIES:** Barbour, Macon, Montgomery, Pike
- **MARRIAGE RECORDS:** start in 1819, kept by Probate Judge
- **LAND:** 1809, County Commissioner
- **PROBATE:** 1810, Probate Judge
- **COURT:** 1811, Circuit Court

BUTLER
700 Court Sq., Box 756, Greenville, AL 36037, (334) 382-3512
<theusgenweb.org/al/butler>
- **INCORPORATED:** Dec. 13, 1819
- **PARENT COUNTIES:** Conecuh, Montgomery
- **MARRIAGE RECORDS:** start in 1853, kept by Probate Judge
- **LAND:** 1853, Probate Judge
- **PROBATE:** 1853, Probate Judge
- **COURT:** 1853, Circuit Court
- **NOTES:** Courthouse burned 1853. County Health Department has birth records 1886-May 1891, March 1894-November 1919, delayed birth certificates 1870-1930, death records 1894-1919.

CAHAWBA
- **INCORPORATED:** Feb. 7, 1818
- **PARENT COUNTIES:** Monroe, Montgomery
- **NOTES:** See Bibb County. Name changed to Bibb Dec. 4, 1820.

CALHOUN
1702 Noble St., Suite 102, Anniston, AL 36201, (256) 236-8231
<www.calhouncounty.org>
- **INCORPORATED:** Dec. 18, 1832
- **PARENT COUNTY:** Creek Cession of 1832
- **MARRIAGE RECORDS:** start in 1834, kept by Probate Judge
- **LAND:** 1832, Probate Judge
- **PROBATE:** 1850, Probate Judge
- **COURT:** 1891, Circuit Court
- **NOTES:** Formerly Benton County. Name changed to Calhoun Jan. 29, 1858.

CHAMBERS
Court Square, Lafayette, AL 36862, (334) 664-1224,
<www.chambersco.com>
- **INCORPORATED:** Dec. 18, 1832
- **PARENT COUNTY:** Creek Cession of 1832
- **BIRTH RECORDS**: start in 1833, kept by Department of Health
- **MARRIAGE:** 1833, Probate Office
- **LAND:** 1833, Probate Office
- **PROBATE:** 1833, Probate Office
- **COURT:** 1833, Circuit Court

CHEROKEE
102 W. Main St., Centre, AL 35960, (256) 927-3363,
<www.cherokeecounty-al.gov>
- **INCORPORATED:** Jan. 9, 1836
- **PARENT COUNTY:** Cherokee Cession 1835
- **MARRIAGE RECORDS:** start in 1882, kept by Probate Judge
- **LAND**: 1882, Probate Judge
- **PROBATE:** 1882, Probate Judge
- **COURT:** 1882, Circuit Court
- **MILITARY:** 1882, Probate Judge
- **NOTES:** Records burned in 1882.

CHILTON
Box 557, Clanton, AL 35045, (205) 755-1555,
<www.chiltoncounty.org>
- **INCORPORATED:** Dec. 30, 1868
- **PARENT COUNTIES:** Autauga, Bibb, Perry, Shelby
- **MARRIAGE RECORDS:** start in 1870, kept by Probate Judge
- **LAND:** 1868, Probate Judge
- **PROBATE:** 1887, Circuit Court
- **COURT:** 1843, Circuit Court
- **NOTES:** Formerly Baker County. Name changed to Chilton Dec. 17, 1874.

CHOCTAW
117 S. Mulberry Ave., Butler, AL 36904, (205) 459-2417,
<www.archives.state.al.us/counties/Choctaw.html>
- **INCORPORATED:** Dec. 29, 1847
- **PARENT COUNTIES:** Sumter, Washington
- **MARRIAGE RECORDS:** start in 1873, kept by County Clerk
- **LAND:** 1873, County Clerk
- **PROBATE:** 1873, County Clerk
- **COURT:** 1871, Circuit Court
- **NOTES:** County Health Department has delayed birth records 1870-1900 and death records 1881-1893.

CLARKE
117 Court St., Box 548, Grove Hill, AL 36451, (334) 275-3251,
<www.clarkecountyal.com>
- **INCORPORATED:** Dec. 10, 1812
- **PARENT COUNTY:** Washington
- **BIRTH RECORDS:** start in 1908, kept by Health Clinic
- **MARRIAGE:** 1814, Probate Judge
- **DEATH:** 1908, Health Clinic
- **LAND:** 1812, Probate Judge
- **PROBATE:** 1810, Probate Judge
- **COURT:** 1813, Circuit Court

CLAY
Box 187, Ashland, AL 36251, (256) 354-2198,
<www.archives.state.al.us/counties/Clay.html>
- **INCORPORATED:** Dec. 7, 1866
- **PARENT COUNTIES:** Randolph, Talladega
- **MARRIAGE RECORDS:** start in 1872, kept by Probate Court
- **LAND:** 1875, Probate Court
- **PROBATE:** 1876, Probate Court
- **COURT:** 1875, Circuit Court
- **NOTES:** County Court has death records 1920-1940; County Health Department has birth records from 1920 and death records from 1920, and voting registry 1906-1936.

CLEBURNE
406 Vickery St., Heflin, AL 36264, (256) 463-5655,
<www.archives.state.al.us/counties/cleburne.html>
- **INCORPORATED:** Dec. 6, 1866
- **PARENT COUNTIES:** Calhoun, Raldolph, Talladega
- **MARRIAGE RECORDS:** start in 1819, kept by Probate Judge
- **LAND:** 1809, Probate Judge
- **PROBATE:** 1810, Probate Judge
- **COURT:** 1811, Circuit Court
- **NOTES:** Probate Judge has birth and death records 1911-1921, and County Health Department has birth/death records from 1908.

COFFEE
230 Court St., Elba, AL 36323, (334) 897-2211,
<www.coffee.us>
- **INCORPORATED:** Dec. 29, 1841
- **PARENT COUNTIES:** Dale
- **MARRIAGE RECORDS**: start in 1866, kept by Probate Judge
- **LAND:** 1887, Probate Judge
- **COURT:** 1811, Circuit Court

COLBERT
201 N. Main St., Tuscumbia, AL 35674, (256) 386-8500,
<www.colbertcounty.org>
- **INCORPORATED:** Feb. 6, 1867
- **PARENT COUNTY:** Franklin
- **BIRTH RECORDS:** start in 1881, kept by Department of Health
- **MARRIAGE:** 1867, Probate Judge
- **DEATH:** 1881, Department of Health
- **LAND:** 1867, Probate Judge
- **PROBATE:** 1867, Probate Judge
- **COURT:** 1867, Circuit Court
- **NOTES:** Abolished same year created, re-established 1869.

CONECUH
Box 347, Evergreen, AL 36401, (334) 578-2095,
<www.rootsweb.ancestry.com/~alconecu>
- **INCORPORATED:** Feb. 13, 1818
- **PARENT COUNTY:** Monroe
- **BIRTH RECORDS:** start in 1881, kept by Department of Health
- **MARRIAGE:** 1866, Probate Judge
- **DEATH:** 1881, Department of Health
- **LAND:** 1866, Probate Judge
- **PROBATE:** 1881, Probate Judge
- **COURT:** 1881, Circuit Court

COOSA
Box 218, Rockford, AL 35136, (256) 362-5721,
<www.rootsweb.ancestry.com/~alcoosa>
- **INCORPORATED:** Dec. 18, 1832
- **PARENT COUNTY:** Creek Indian Treaty of Cusseta
- **BIRTH RECORDS:** start in 1878, kept by Department of Health
- **MARRIAGE:** 1834, Probate Records
- **DEATH:** 1920, Department of Health
- **DIVORCE:** 1834, Probate Court
- **LAND:** 1832, Probate Court
- **PROBATE:** 1834, Probate Court
- **COURT:** 1834, Circuit Court Office
- **MILITARY:** 1834, Probate Records
- **NOTES:** Probate Court has a few birth and death records 1920-1945.

COTACO
- **INCORPORATED:** Feb. 6, 1818
- **PARENT COUNTY:** Cherokee Turkeytown Cession
- **NOTES:** See Morgan County. Name changed to Morgan June 14, 1821.

COVINGTON
Court Square, Andalusia, AL 36420, (334) 428-2520,
<covingtoncountyal.org>
- **INCORPORATED:** Dec. 7, 1821
- **PARENT COUNTY:** Henry
- **COURT RECORDS:** unknown start, kept by Circuit Court
- **NOTES:** Record loss in 1895. Probate Judge has marriage, land, and probate records 1895-1896. Clerk of Circuit Court has divorce records 1895-1896.

CRENSHAW
Box 227, Luverne, AL 36049, (334) 335-6568,
<www.archives.state.al.us/counties/crenshaw.html>
- **INCORPORATED:** Nov. 24, 1866
- **PARENT COUNTIES:** Butler, Coffee, Covington, Lowndes, Pike
- **BIRTH RECORDS:** start in 1889, kept by Department of Health
- **MARRIAGE:** 1895, Probate Judge
- **DEATH:** 1909, Department of Health
- **LAND:** 1896, Probate Judge
- **PROBATE:** 1896, Probate Judge

CULLMAN
500 Second Ave. SW, Cullman, AL 35055, (256) 739-3530,
<www.co.cullman.al.us>

- **INCORPORATED:** Jan. 24, 1877
- **PARENT COUNTIES:** Blount, Morgan, Winston
- **BIRTH RECORDS:** start in 1877, kept by Department of Health
- **MARRIAGE:** 1877, Probate Judge
- **DEATH:** 1877, Department of Health
- **DIVORCE:** 1877, Probate Judge
- **LAND:** 1877, Probate Judge
- **PROBATE:** 1877, Probate Judge
- **COURT:** 1877, Probate Judge

DALE
1702 Hwy. 123 S., Box 246, Ozark, AL 36361, (334) 774-6025,
<www.dalecountyal.org>
- **INCORPORATED:** Dec. 22, 1824
- **PARENT COUNTIES:** Covington, Henry
- **BIRTH RECORDS:** start in 1919, kept by Department of Health
- **MARRIAGE:** 1884, Probate Judge
- **DEATH:** 1920, Department of Health
- **DIVORCE:** 1885, Circuit Court
- **LAND:** 1884, Probate Judge
- **PROBATE:** 1895, Probate Judge
- **COURT:** 1884, Circuit Court
- **NOTES:** 1885 courthouse fire destroyed all records.

DALLAS
Box 997, Selma, AL 36702, (334) 874-2500,
<www.prairiebluff.com/algenweb/dallas>
- **INCORPORATED:** Feb. 9, 1818
- **PARENT COUNTIES:** Montgomery, Monroe
- **MARRIAGE RECORDS:** start in 1818, kept by Probate Judge
- **DIVORCE:** 1917, Probate Judge
- **LAND:** 1818, Probate Judge
- **PROBATE:** 1821, Probate Judge
- **COURT:** 1821, Circuit Court
- **NOTES:** County Health Department has birth records 1880-1930 (delayed birth certificates) and death records 1882-1888.

DEKALB
111 Grand Ave. SW, Fort Payne, AL 35967, (256) 845-8525,
<www.dekalbcountyal.us>
- **INCORPORATED:** Jan. 9, 1836
- **PARENT COUNTY:** Cherokee Cession of 1835
- **BIRTH RECORDS:** start in 1885, kept by Department of Health
- **MARRIAGE:** 1836, Probate Judge
- **DEATH:** 1885, Department of Health
- **LAND:** 1836, Probate Judge
- **PROBATE:** 1836, Probate Judge
- **COURT:** 1836, Circuit Court

ELMORE
Box 280, Wetumpka, AL 36092, (334) 567-1138, **<elmoreco.org>**
- **INCORPORATED:** Feb. 15, 1866
- **PARENT COUNTIES:** Autauga, Coosa, Montgomery, Tallapoosa
- **MARRIAGE RECORDS:** start in 1867, kept by Probate Judge
- **LAND:** 1867, Probate Judge
- **PROBATE:** 1867, Probate Judge
- **COURT:** 1876, Circuit Court
- **MILITARY**: 1919, Probate Judge
- **NOTES:** Probate Judge has birth and death records 1909-1913; County Health Department has birth records from 1884 and death records from 1927.

ESCAMBIA
Box 848, Brewton, AL 36427, (251) 867-0208,
<www.co.escambia.al.us>
- **INCORPORATED:** Dec. 10, 1868
- **PARENT COUNTIES:** Baldwin, Conecuh
- **MARRIAGE RECORDS:** start in 1879, kept by Probate Court
- **LAND:** 1868, Probate Court
- **PROBATE:** 1868, Probate Court
- **COURT:** 1882, Circuit Court
- **NOTES:** There was a record loss in 1868.

ETOWAH
800 Forrest Ave., Gadsden, AL 35901, (256) 546-2821,
<www.etowahcounty.org>
- **INCORPORATED:** Dec. 7, 1866
- **PARENT COUNTIES:** Blount, Calhoun, Cherokee, DeKalb, Marshall, St. Clair
- **BIRTH RECORDS:** start in 1894, kept by Department of Health
- **MARRIAGE:** 1867, Probate Judge
- **DEATH:** 1898, Department of Health
- **LAND:** 1867, Probate Judge
- **PROBATE:** 1867, Probate Judge
- **COURT:** 1867, Circuit Court
- **NOTES:** Formerly Baine County, abolished Dec. 3, 1867. Reestablished as Etowah County Dec. 1, 1868.

FAYETTE
Box 509, Fayette, AL 35555, (205) 932-4519,
<www.rootsweb.ancestry.com/~alfayett>
- **INCORPORATED:** Dec. 20, 1824
- **PARENT COUNTIES:** Marion, Pickens, Tuscaloosa
- **MARRIAGE RECORDS:** start in 1850, kept by Probate Judge
- **LAND:** 1824, Probate Judge
- **PROBATE:** 1851, Probate Judge
- **MILITARY:** 1919, Probate Judge
- **NOTES:** Probate Judge has birth records 1884-1941 and death records 1899-1941. There were record losses in 1866 and in 1916.

FRANKLIN
410 N. Jackson St., Russellville, AL 35653, (256) 332-1210,
<www.rootsweb.ancestry.com/~alfrankl>
- **INCORPORATED:** Feb. 6, 1818
- **PARENT COUNTIES:** Cherokee and Chickasaw Cession of 1816
- **MARRIAGE RECORDS:** start in 1890, kept by Probate Judge
- **LAND:** 1818, Probate Judge
- **PROBATE:** 1890, Probate Judge
- **COURT:** 1890, Circuit Court
- **NOTES:** Records burned 1890.

GENEVA
Box 430, Geneva, AL 36340, (334) 684-9300,
<www.genevacounty.net>
- **INCORPORATED:** Dec. 26, 1868
- **PARENT COUNTIES:** Dale, Henry, Coffee

- **MARRIAGE RECORDS:** start in 1898, kept by Probate Judge
- **LAND:** 1868, Probate Judge
- **PROBATE:** 1888, Probate Judge
- **MILITARY:** 1930, Probate Judge
- **COURT:** 1898, Circuit Court
- **NOTES:** Probate Judge has birth records 1909–1918 and death records 1909–1941. There was a record loss in 1898.

GREENE

Box 656, Eutaw, AL 35462, (205) 372-3349,
<www.archives.state.al.us/counties/greene.html>

- **INCORPORATED:** Dec. 13, 1819
- **PARENT COUNTIES:** Marengo, Tuscaloosa
- **MARRIAGE RECORDS:** start in 1823, kept by Probate Judge
- **DEATH:** 1881, Department of Health
- **LAND:** 1821, Probate Judge
- **PROBATE:** 1820, Probate Judge
- **COURT:** 1821, Circuit Court
- **NOTES:** County Health Department has birth records 1881–1896.

HALE

1001 Main St., Box 396, Greensboro, AL 36744, (334) 624-8740,
<www.archives.state.al.us/counties/hale.html>

- **INCORPORATED:** Jan. 30, 1867
- **PARENT COUNTIES:** Greene, Marengo, Perry, Tuscaloosa
- **MARRIAGE RECORDS:** start in 1867, kept by Probate Judge
- **DIVORCE:** 1868, Probate Judge
- **LAND:** 1867, Probate Judge
- **PROBATE:** 1867, Probate Judge
- **COURT:** 1867, Probate Judge

HANCOCK

- **INCORPORATED:** Feb. 12, 1850
- **PARENT COUNTY:** Walker
- **NOTES:** See Winston County. Name changed to Winston Jan. 22, 1858.

HENRY

101 W. Court Sq., Suite A, Abbeville, AL 36310, (334) 585-3257,
<www.henrycountyalabama.org>

- **INCORPORATED:** Dec. 13, 1819
- **PARENT COUNTY:** Conecuh
- **MARRIAGE RECORDS:** start in 1823, kept by Probate Judge
- **LAND:** 1819, Probate Judge
- **PROBATE:** 1822, Probate Judge
- **COURT:** 1822, Circuit Court
- **NOTES:** Probate Judge has birth records 1895–1922 and death records 1895–1906. County Health Department has birth and death records from 1931.

HOUSTON

Box 6406, Dothan, AL 36302, (334) 677-4700,
<www.houstoncounty.org>

- **INCORPORATED:** Feb. 9, 1903
- **PARENT COUNTIES:** Dale, Geneva, Henry
- **BIRTH RECORDS:** start in 1908, kept by Department of Health
- **MARRIAGE:** 1903, Probate Office
- **DEATH:** 1908, Department of Health
- **DIVORCE:** 1903, Reg. in Chancery
- **LAND:** 1903, Probate Office
- **PROBATE:** 1903, Probate Office
- **COURT:** 1903, Circuit Court

JACKSON

Box 397, Scottsboro, AL 35768, (256) 574-9320,
<www.jacksoncountyal.com>

- **INCORPORATED:** Dec. 13, 1819
- **PARENT COUNTY:** Cherokee Cession of 1816
- **MARRIAGE RECORDS:** start in 1851, kept by Probate Judge
- **DIVORCE:** 1895, Circuit Court
- **LAND:** 1819, Probate Judge
- **PROBATE:** 1866, Probate Judge
- **NOTES:** Record losses in 1860 and 1920.

JEFFERSON

716 N. 21st St., Birmingham, AL 35263, (205) 325-5300,
<jeffconline.jccal.org>

- **INCORPORATED:** Dec. 13, 1819
- **PARENT COUNTY:** Blount
- **MARRIAGE RECORDS:** start in 1818, kept by Probate Judge
- **LAND:** 1819, Probate Judge
- **PROBATE:** 1819, Probate Judge
- **COURT:** 1826, Circuit Court
- **NOTES:** Birth and death records are from 1871 and 1882 (partial) .

JONES

- **INCORPORATED:** Feb. 4, 1867
- **PARENT COUNTIES:** Marion, Fayette
- **NOTES:** Abolished Nov. 13, 1867. Reestablished as Sanford County Oct. 8, 1868. Name changed to Lamar Feb. 8, 1877.

LAMAR

Box 338, Vernon, AL 35592, (205) 695-9119,
<theusgenweb.org/al/lamar>

- **INCORPORATED:** Feb. 4, 1867
- **PARENT COUNTIES:** Marion, Fayette
- **LAND RECORDS:** start in 1967, kept by Probate Office
- **PROBATE:** 1967, Probate Office
- **COURT:** 1967, Circuit Clerk
- **NOTES:** Formerly Jones County. Abolished Nov. 13, 1867 and reestablished as Sanford County Oct. 8, 1868. Name changed to Lamar Feb. 8, 1877.

LAUDERDALE

Box 1059, Florence, AL 35631, (256) 760-5800,
<lauderdalecountyonline.com>

- **INCORPORATED:** Feb. 6, 1818
- **PARENT COUNTIES:** Cherokee and Chickasaw Cession in 1816
- **MARRIAGE RECORDS:** start in 1818, kept by Probate Judge
- **LAND:** 1818, Probate Judge
- **PROBATE:** 1818, Probate Judge
- **COURT:** 1821, Circuit Court

LAWRENCE

Courthouse, Moulton, AL 35650, (256) 974-0663,
<www.rootsweb.ancestry.com/~allawren>

- **INCORPORATED:** Feb. 6, 1818
- **PARENT COUNTIES:** Cherokee and Chickasaw in 1816
- **MARRIAGE RECORDS:** start in 1828, kept by Probate Judge
- **DIVORCE:** 1810, Probate Judge
- **LAND:** 1810, Probate Judge
- **PROBATE:** 1818, Probate Judge
- **COURT:** 1828, Circuit Court

LEE

215 S. Ninth St., Box 666, Opelika, AL 36801, (334) 749-7141,
<www.rootsweb.ancestry.com/~allee>

- **INCORPORATED:** Dec. 5, 1866
- **PARENT COUNTIES:** Chambers, Macon, Russell, Tallapoosa
- **MARRIAGE RECORDS:** start in 1867, kept by Probate Judge
- **LAND:** 1867, Probate Judge
- **PROBATE:** 1861, Probate Judge
- **COURT:** 1867, Circuit Court
- **MILITARY:** 1919, Probate Judge

LIMESTONE

310 W. Washington St., Athens, AL 35611, (256) 233-6404,
<www.co.limestone.al.us>

- **INCORPORATED:** Feb. 6, 1818
- **PARENT COUNTIES:** Cherokee and Chickasaw Cession in 1806 and 1816
- **NOTES:** County Archives has birth and death records 1881-1913. County Health Department has birth and death records from 1881; land, probate and court records 1818-1900; divorce records 1896-1947; marriage records 1832-1900; tax records 1861-1900. Record loss in 1862.

LOWNDES

Box 65, Hayneville, AL 36040, (334) 548-2331,
<www.rootsweb.ancestry.com/~allownde>

- **INCORPORATED**: Jan. 20, 1830
- **PARENT COUNTIES:** Butler, Dallas, Montgomery
- **MARRIAGE RECORDS:** start in 1830, kept by Probate Judge
- **DEATH:** 1832, Probate Judge
- **LAND:** 1830, Probate Judge
- **PROBATE:** 1830, Probate Judge
- **COURT:** 1830, Circuit Court
- **MILITARY:** 1919, Probate Judge
- **NOTES:** Birth records from 1881-1904, delayed birth certificates 1879-1911 are held by County Health Deparment.

MACON

101 E. Northside St., Tuskegee, AL 36083, (334) 727-1800,
<www.rootsweb.ancestry.com/~almacon>

- **INCORPORATED:** Dec. 18, 1832
- **PARENT COUNTY:** Creek Cession of 1832
- **MARRIAGE RECORDS:** start in 1832, kept by Probate Judge
- **LAND:** 1832, Probate Judge
- **PROBATE:** 1834, Probate Judge
- **COURT:** 1862, Circuit Court

MADISON

100 North Side Sq., Huntsville, AL 35801, (256) 532-3330,
<www.co.madison.al.us>

- **INCORPORATED:** Dec. 13, 1808
- **PARENT COUNTIES:** Cherokee and Chickasaw Cession of 1806
- **BIRTH RECORDS:** start in 1881, kept by Department of Health
- **MARRIAGE:** 1809, Probate Judge
- **DEATH:** 1881, Department of Health
- **LAND:** 1810, Probate Judge
- **PROBATE:** 1818, Probate Judge
- **COURT:** 1808, Circuit Court

MARENGO

101 E. Coats Ave., Linden, AL 36748, (334) 295-2210,
<www.rootsweb.ancestry.com/~almareng>

- **INCORPORATED:** Feb. 6, 1818
- **PARENT COUNTY:** Choctaw Cession of 1816
- **BIRTH RECORDS:** start in 1881, kept by Department of Health
- **MARRIAGE:** 1818, Probate Judge
- **DEATH:** 1906, Department of Health
- **LAND:** 1820, Probate Judge
- **PROBATE:** 1818, Probate Judge
- **COURT:** 1819, Circuit Court
- **NOTES:** Record loss in 1848 and 1965.

MARION

Box 460, Hamilton, AL 35570, (205) 921-3172,
<www.marioncountyalabama.org>

- **INCORPORATED:** Feb. 13, 1818
- **PARENT COUNTY:** Tuscaloosa
- **BIRTH RECORDS:** start in 1902, kept by Department of Health
- **MARRIAGE:** 1887, Probate Judge
- **DEATH:** 1902, Department of Health
- **LAND:** 1887, Probate Judge
- **PROBATE:** 1887, Probate Judge
- **COURT:** 1887, Circuit Court
- **MILITARY:** 1920, Probate Judge
- **NOTES:** Courthouse fire in 1883 destroyed all records.

MARSHALL

424 Blount Ave., Guntersville, AL 35976, (256) 571-7701,
< www.marshallco.org/index.php >

- **INCORPORATED:** Jan. 9, 1836
- **PARENT COUNTIES:** Blount, Cherokee Cession of 1836, Jackson
- **BIRTH RECORDS:** start in 1920, kept by Probate Judge
- **MARRIAGE:** 1836, Probate Judge
- **DEATH:** 1920, Probate Judge
- **LAND:** 1836, Probate Judge
- **PROBATE:** 1843, Probate Judge
- **COURT:** 1836, Probate Court

MOBILE

109 Government St., Mobile, AL 36602, (334) 690-8502,
<www.mobilecounty.org>

- **INCORPORATED:** Dec. 18, 1812
- **PARENT COUNTIES:** West Florida, Baldwin
- **BIRTH RECORDS:** start in 1820, kept by Department of Health
- **MARRIAGE:** 1814, Probate Judge
- **LAND:** 1812, Probate Judge
- **PROBATE:** 1814, Probate Judge
- **COURT:** 1814, Circuit Court

MONROE
Box 8, Monroeville, AL 35461, (334) 575-3778,
<www.rootsweb.ancestry.com/~almonroe>
- **INCORPORATED:** June 29, 1815
- **PARENT COUNTY:** Creek Cession 1814
- **BIRTH RECORDS:** start in 1881, kept by Department of Health
- **MARRIAGE:** 1833, Probate Judge
- **DEATH:** 1908, Department of Health
- **LAND:** 1833, Probate Judge
- **PROBATE:** 1833, Probate Judge
- **COURT:** 1833, Circuit Court
- **NOTES:** Courthouse fire destroyed records prior to 1833. 1816 Monroe County census published by *Monroe Journal*.

MONTGOMERY
Box 223, Montgomery, AL 36101, (334) 832-4950,
<www.mc-ala.org>
- **INCORPORATED:** Dec. 6, 1816
- **PARENT COUNTY:** Monroe
- **MARRIAGE RECORDS:** start in 1917, kept by Probate Judge
- **DIVORCE:** 1852, Clerk/Board/Revenue
- **LAND:** 1819, Probate Judge
- **PROBATE:** 1819, Probate Judge
- **COURT:** 1811, Circuit Court
- **NOTES:** Alabama Department of Archivists and History has marriage records 1817–1928.

MORGAN
302 Lee St. NE, Decatur, AL 35601, (256) 351-4600,
<www.co.morgan.al.us>
- **INCORPORATED:** Feb. 6, 1818
- **PARENT COUNTY:** Cherokee Turkeytown Cession of 1818
- **BIRTH RECORDS:** start in 1893, kept by Department of Health
- **MARRIAGE:** 1818, Probate Judge
- **DEATH:** 1893, Department of Health
- **LAND:** 1818, Probate Judge
- **PROBATE:** 1818, Probate Judge
- **COURT:** 1817, Circuit Court
- **NOTES:** Formerly Cotaco County. Name changed to Morgan June 14, 1821.

PERRY
Box 478, Marion, AL 36756, (334) 683-2210,
<www.usgennet.org/usa/al/county/perry>
- **INCORPORATED:** Dec. 13, 1819
- **PARENT COUNTIES:** Montgomery, Creek Cession of 1814
- **BIRTH RECORDS:** start in 1908, kept by Department of Health
- **MARRIAGE:** 1820, Probate Judge
- **DEATH:** 1908, Department of Health
- **LAND:** 1819, Probate Judge
- **PROBATE:** 1823, Probate Judge
- **COURT:** 1821, Circuit Court

PICKENS
Box 370, Carrollton, AL 35447, (205) 367-2010,
<www.rootsweb.ancestry.com/~alpicken/pcpage.htm>
- **INCORPORATED:** Dec. 20, 1820
- **PARENT COUNTY:** Tuscaloosa
- **BIRTH RECORDS:** start in 1903, kept by Department of Health
- **MARRIAGE:** 1876, Probate Judge
- **DEATH:** 1903, Department of Health
- **LAND:** 1876, Probate Judge
- **PROBATE:** 1876, Probate Judge
- **COURT:** 1876, Circuit Court
- **NOTES:** Record losses in 1864 and 1876, all records destroyed.

PIKE
Box 1008, Troy, AL 36081, (334) 566-1246,
<www.genrecords.net/alpike>
- **INCORPORATED:** Dec. 17, 1821
- **PARENT COUNTIES:** Henry, Montgomery
- **MARRIAGE RECORDS:** start in 1830, kept by Probate Judge
- **DEATH:** 1881, Department of Health
- **LAND:** 1830, Probate Judge
- **PROBATE:** 1830, Probate Judge
- **COURT:** 1830, Circuit Court
- **NOTES:** County Health Department has birth records from 1886. Courthouse fire in 1830, destroyed all records.

RANDOLPH
Box 249, Wedowee, AL 36278, (256) 357-4933,
<www.randolphcountyalabama.gov>
- **INCORPORATED:** Dec. 18, 1832
- **PARENT COUNTY:** Creek Cession 1832
- **BIRTH RECORDS:** start in 1886, kept by Department of Health
- **MARRIAGE:** 1897, Probate Judge
- **DEATH:** 1886, Department of Health
- **LAND:** 1897, Probate Judge
- **PROBATE:** 1897, Probate Judge
- **NOTES:** 1897 courthouse fire 1897, destroyed probate records. Probate Judge has military pensions 1904–1909.

RUSSELL
Box 969, Phenix City, AL 36868, (334) 298-7979,
<www.rootsweb.ancestry.com/~alrussel>
- **INCORPORATED:** Dec. 18, 1832
- **PARENT COUNTY:** Creek Cession 1832
- **BIRTH RECORDS:** start in 1893, kept by Department of Health
- **MARRIAGE:** 1928, Probate Judge
- **DEATH:** 1893, Department of Health
- **LAND:** 1832, Probate Judge
- **PROBATE:** 1832, Probate Judge
- **COURT:** 1832, Circuit Court

SANFORD
- **INCORPORATED:** Oct. 8, 1867
- **PARENT COUNTY:** Jones
- **NOTES:** See Lamar County. Formed from Jones County. Name changed to Lamar Feb. 8, 1877.

SHELBY
Box 1810, Columbiana, AL 35051, (205) 669-3760,
<www.shelbycountyalabama.com>
- **INCORPORATED:** Feb. 7, 1818
- **PARENT COUNTY:** Montgomery
- **MARRIAGE RECORDS:** start in 1819, kept by Probate Judge

- **LAND:** 1819, Probate Judge
- **PROBATE:** 1819, Probate Judge
- **COURT:** 1819, Circuit Court

ST. CLAIR

Box 397, Ashville, AL 35953, (205) 594-5114, **<www.stclairco.com>**

- **INCORPORATED:** Nov. 20, 1818
- **PARENT COUNTY:** Shelby
- **BIRTH RECORDS:** start in 1893, kept by Department of Health
- **MARRIAGE:** 1819, Probate Judge
- **DEATH:** 1908, Department of Health
- **LAND:** 1818, Probate Judge
- **PROBATE:** 1818, Probate Judge
- **COURT:** unknown, Circuit Court

SUMTER

Box 70, Livingston, AL 35470, (205) 652-2731
<www.archives.state.al.us/counties/sumter.html>

- **INCORPORATED:** Dec. 18, 1832
- **PARENT COUNTY:** Choctaw Cession of 1832
- **BIRTH RECORDS:** start in 1888, kept by Department of Health
- **MARRIAGE:** 1833, Probate Judge
- **DEATH:** 1881, Department of Health
- **LAND:** 1825, Probate Judge
- **PROBATE:** 1828, Probate Judge
- **COURT:** 1876, Circuit Court
- **NOTES:** Probate Judge has a few birth records 1888–1918.

TALLADEGA

Box 755, Talladega, AL 35160, (256) 362-4175,
<www.talladegacountyal.org>

- **INCORPORATED:** Dec. 18, 1832
- **PARENT COUNTY:** Creek Cession of 1832
- **BIRTH RECORDS:** start in 1897, kept by Department of Health
- **MARRIAGE:** 1834, Probate Court
- **DEATH:** 1897, Department of Health
- **LAND:** 1833, Probate Court
- **PROBATE:** 1833, Probate Court
- **COURT:** 1833, Circuit Court
- **MILITARY:** 1930, Probate Court
- **NOTES:** Chancery Court has Divorce records 1888–1892.

TALLAPOOSA

125 N. Broadnax St., Dadeville, AL 36853, (256) 825-4266,
<www.tallaco.com>

- **INCORPORATED:** Dec. 18, 1832
- **PARENT COUNTY:** Creek Cession of 1832
- **MARRIAGE RECORDS:** start in 1834, kept by Probate Judge
- **LAND:** 1832, Probate Judge
- **PROBATE:** 1838, Probate Judge
- **COURT:** 1835, Circuit Court
- **NOTES:** Tallapoosa and Coosa counties swapped 90 acres in 1963. Probate Judge has a few birth and death records 1881–1991.

TUSCALOOSA

714 Greensboro Ave., Tuscaloosa, AL 35401, (205) 349-3870,
<www.tuscco.com>

- **INCORPORATED:** Feb. 6, 1818
- **PARENT COUNTIES:** Cherokee and Choctaw Cession 1816
- **BIRTH RECORDS:** start in 1880, kept by Department of Health
- **MARRIAGE:** 1823, Probate Judge
- **DEATH:** 1880, Department of Health
- **LAND:** 1823, Probate Judge
- **PROBATE:** 1821, Probate Judge

WALKER

Box 1447, Jasper, AL 35502, (205) 384-7230,
<www.walkercounty.com>

- **INCORPORATED:** Dec. 26, 1823
- **PARENT COUNTIES:** Tuscaloosa, Blount, Jefferson
- **MARRIAGE RECORDS:** start in 1877, kept by Probate Judge
- **DEATH:** 1877, Department of Health
- **LAND:** 1877, Probate Judge
- **PROBATE:** 1877, Probate Judge
- **COURT:** 1877, Circuit Court
- **NOTES:** All court records burned in 1877.

WASHINGTON

Box 549, Chatom, AL 36518, (334) 847-2208,
<www.archives.state.al.us/counties/washingt.html>

- **INCORPORATED:** June 4, 1800
- **PARENT COUNTIES:** Mississippi Territory
- **BIRTH RECORDS:** start in 1908, kept by Probate Judge
- **MARRIAGE:** 1802, Probate Judge
- **DEATH:** 1908, Probate Judge
- **LAND:** 1786, Probate Judge
- **PROBATE:** 1820, Probate Judge
- **MILITARY:** 1919, Probate Judge

WILCOX

Box 668, Camden, AL 36726, (334) 682-4883,
<www.prairiebluff.com/algenweb/wilcox>

- **INCORPORATED:** Dec. 13, 1819
- **PARENT COUNTIES:** Monroe, Dallas
- **BIRTH RECORDS:** start in 1905, kept by Department of Health
- **MARRIAGE:** 1820, Probate Judge
- **DEATH:** 1905, Department of Health
- **LAND:** 1820, Probate Judge
- **PROBATE:** 1820, Probate Judge

WINSTON

Box 27, Double Springs, AL 35553, (205) 489-5219,
<www.winstoncountyalabama.org>

- **INCORPORATED:** Feb. 12, 1850
- **PARENT COUNTY:** Walker
- **MARRIAGE RECORDS:** start in 1891, kept by Probate Judge
- **DIVORCE:** unknown, Circuit Court
- **LAND:** 1891, Probate Judge
- **PROBATE:** 1891, Probate Judge
- **COURT:** 1892, Circuit Court
- **NOTES:** Formerly Hancock County. Name changed to Winston Jan. 22, 1858. Probate records lost in 1891 courthouse fire.

ALASKA

» BY DAVID A. FRYXELL

HISTORICAL OVERVIEW

Although Alaska didn't become part of the United States until 1959, joining as the 49th state, it was home to the very first Americans. Asians from Siberia crossed the Bering Strait between 21,000 and 42,000 years ago. Those who stayed became the precursors of Alaska's native peoples—the Athabascans, Haida, Tlingit and Inuit (often called "Eskimos"). Native American records include a collection of *Genealogical Records of Barrow Eskimo Families* and Juneau Area Agency records (1905–1964), both on microfilm at the Family History Library (FHL), and the Oregon Province Archives of the Society of Jesus Alaska Mission Collection (1853–1960) at Gonzaga University in Spokane, Wash., also on FHL microfilm.

The first Europeans came to Alaska from Russia with Vitus Bering's expedition in 1741, and sea-otter hunters arrived soon after. The Russian Orthodox church came to Kodiak in 1795, and remained dominant until the 20th century. Archives for the Diocese of Alaska were given to the Library of Congress in 1927; translated and microfilmed, these are available through the FHL.

Although the $7.2 million US purchase of Alaska from Russia in 1867 became known as "Seward's Folly," the Russians—strapped for cash after the Crimean War—knew the area was rich in gold, already found in 1861 near Telegraph Creek. A series of subsequent strikes sparked the Alaska Gold Rush, which brought 50,000 fortune-seekers between 1897 and 1920. Gold miners founded Nome in 1899 and Fairbanks in 1902. After a period under the jurisdiction of the War Department (1867–1877) and the Treasury Department (1877–1884), Alaska became a US District in 1884 and a territory in 1912.

World War II brought a fresh wave of migration to Alaska with 140,000 US military stationed there, some of whom stayed. Not long after statehood, Alaska's "black gold" rush began with oil at Prudhoe Bay in 1968. Even so, the largest state geographically remains the least densely populated.

RECORD HIGHLIGHTS

Unlike most states, Alaska has no counties; 14 "municipalities" and "boroughs" and 13 native corporations were formed post-statehood. Census takers from 1880 to 1900 created enumeration districts, and enumerators in 1910 used the four federal judicial districts. The 1870 census skipped newly acquired Alaska, and the 1880 and 1890 censuses have been lost. Various pre-territory local censuses are indexed in *Alaskan Census Records, 1870–1907*, edited by Ronald Vern Jackson and Gary Ronald Teeples (Accelerated Indexing Systems, ca. 1976). There are also 1870 and 1880 territorial censuses for Sitka. Federal census coverage begins with 1900.

Although Alaska didn't begin official recording of births, marriages and deaths until 1913, churches previously kept such records. The Bureau of Vital Statistics has microfilmed these church records and created delayed birth certificates. Note that in the absence of counties, vital records are kept almost entirely on the state level.

research tips

- It's crucial to understand the state's geography and history, including the dates of the various gold rushes.
- The National Archives in Anchorage has a large collection of records generated by the federal government since statehood (1959). Prior to statehood, the collections are divided between it and the state library and archives.
- Visit the Alaska and Polar Regions Department, Elmer E. Rasmuson Library, University of Fairbanks **<library.uaf.edu>**. The site links to the Alaska and Polar Periodical Index, which is an index to periodicals containing articles about Alaska and Alaskans.

CENSUS RECORDS

- Federal census 1900, 1910, 1920, 1930
- Territorial census: Sitka, 1870, 1880, 1881

Until statehood created the superior court, probate records were kept at the district courts in Juneau and Ketchikan (First District), Nome (Second District), Anchorage (Third District), and Fairbanks (Fourth District). Records are now at the state archives, as are many territorial court records.

Land records can offer clues. These are mostly at the Bureau of Land Management in Washington, DC, and the National Archives Pacific-Alaska Region in Anchorage. Mining claims are at the Department of Natural Resources in Fairbanks. You can also search for Gold Rush ancestors in the state archives' records from the Pioneers' Homes, state institutions in Sitka, Anchorage, Juneau, Fairbanks, Ketchikan, and Palmer.

Cemetery records can be hard to find for Alaska, given the remoteness of their locations. The Sitka National Cemetery has been indexed, however, as has the Clay Street and Birch Hill Cemetery in Fairbanks, which is online at Ancestry.com. The FHL has microfilm of remote Alaska cemeteries and those on the Kenai Peninsula.

Professional researcher Connie Malcolm Bradbury, coauthor with David Albert Hales of *Alaska Sources: A Guide to Historical Records and Information Resources* (HeritageQuest, 2001), emphasizes the importance of understanding the state's history and vast geography. If you're seeking a lost relative from the gold rush period, she says, know the dates of the strikes—and remember that the Klondike is in Canada, not Alaska. "The Klondike Stampede started in Alaska only because that is where the people disembarked from the ships bringing them north. Their destination was the Dawson, Yukon Territory, Canada area. As gold was prospected for on the creeks, some of the creeks extended to Alaska and the miners followed the creeks."

Whatever you're after in Alaska records, Bradbury says, you need to know exactly what you're looking for. The National Archives branch in Anchorage has a large collection of records generated by the federal government since statehood. Prior to statehood, the collections are divided between it and the state library and archives. "The Alaska State Library History Department has a wonderful collection," Bradbury adds. "They have good coverage of southeast Alaska but also have collections that are statewide or cover other areas. They have a website **<www.library.state.ak.us/hist/hist.html>** that will be helpful. The Alaska State Archives is a marvelous repository of records generated by the state government. The University of Alaska in both Anchorage and Fairbanks has archives. The Alaska and Polar Regions Department, Elmer E. Rasmusun Library, University of Alaska Fairbanks has the largest manuscript collection in the state, an excellent rare book collection, and a large Alaskana Collection of books. They also have an excellent website **<library.uaf.edu>**."

The site links to the Alaska and Polar Periodical Indexto periodicals containing articles about Alaska and Alaskans—a great place to start your search.

ARCHIVES, LIBRARIES, AND SOCIETIES

Alaska Historical Society
Box 100299, Anchorage, AK 99510
(907) 276-1596,
<www.alaskahistoricalsociety.org>

Alaska Moravian Church
3512 Robin St., Anchorage, AK 99504
(907) 868-3177

Alaska State Library and Historical Collections
Box 110571, 8th Floor, Juneau, AK 99811, (907) 465-2910, **<www.library.state.ak.us>**

Anchorage Genealogical Society
Box 242294, Anchorage, AK 99524,
<anchoragegenealogy.org>

Anchorage Museum of History and Art
121 W. Seventh Ave., Anchorage, AK 99501, (907) 343-4326,
<www.anchoragemuseum.org>

Anchorage Superior Courts
825 W. Fourth Ave., Anchorage, AK 99501,
<www.state.ak.us/courts/home.htm>

Archdiocese of Fairbanks, Catholic Bishop of Northern Alaska
1316 Peger Rd., Fairbanks, AK 99709
(907) 374-9500, **<www.cbna.info>**

Bethel Moravian Church
Box 312, Bethel, AK 99559, (907) 543-3174

Department of Health and Social Services, Bureau of Vital Statistics
Box 110675, Juneau, AK 99801 , (907) 465-3391, **<health.hss.state.ak.us/dph/bvs>**

Eagle Historical Society and Museum
Box 23, Eagle, AK 99738, (907) 547-2325,
<www.eagleak.org>

Elmer E. Rasmuson Library
310 Tanana Loop, University of Alaska Fairbanks, USA 99775, (907) 474-7481,
<library.uaf.edu>

Fairbanks Genealogical Society
Box 60534, Fairbanks, AK 99706,
<fairbanksgenealogicalsociety.com>

Gastineau Genealogical Society
3270 Nowell Ave., Juneau, AK 99801
(907) 586-3695, **<home.gci.net/~westjuneau/ggs/ggshome.htm>**

Genealogical Society of Southeastern Alaska
Box 6313, Ketchikan, AK 99901

Kenai Totem Tracers
Kenai Community Library, 163 Main St. Loop, Kenai, AK 99611, **<www.kenailibrary.org/Totemtracers_new.htm>**

National Archives, Pacific-Alaska Region
654 W. Third Ave., Anchorage, AK 99501
(907) 261-7820, **<archives.gov/pacific-alaska/anchorage>**

Palmer Historical Society
Box 1925, Palmer, AK 99645,
(907) 745-3703, **<www.palmerhistoricalsociety.org>**

Roman Catholic Archdiocese of Anchorage
225 Cordova St., Anchorage, AK 99501
(907) 297-7700, **<www.archdioceseofanchorage.org>**

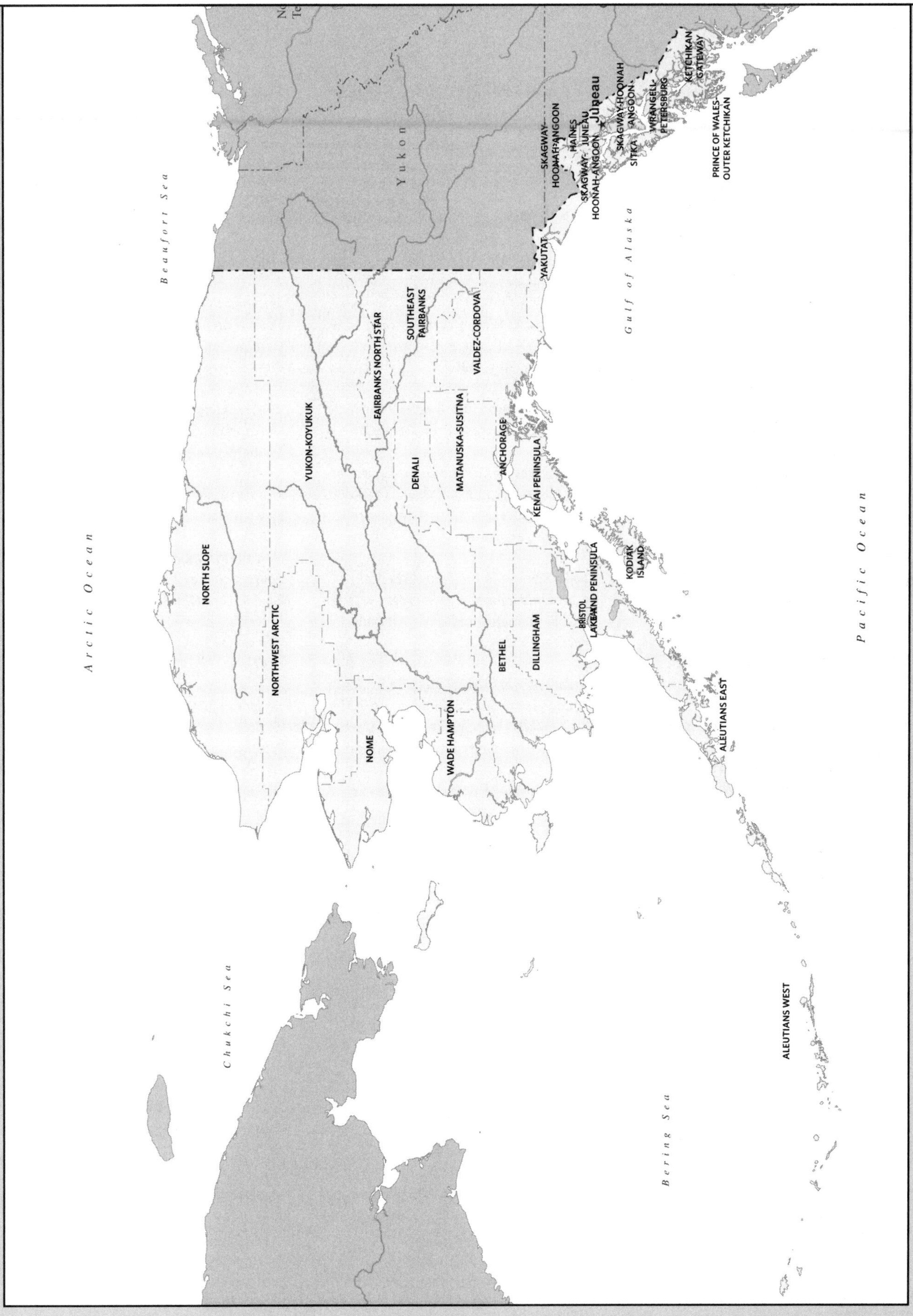
Beaufort Sea
Arctic Ocean
Chukchi Sea
Bering Sea
Pacific Ocean
Gulf of Alaska
Yukon
NORTH SLOPE
NORTHWEST ARCTIC
YUKON-KOYUKUK
FAIRBANKS NORTH STAR
SOUTHEAST FAIRBANKS
VALDEZ-CORDOVA
MATANUSKA-SUSITNA
DENALI
ANCHORAGE
KENAI PENINSULA
KODIAK ISLAND
BRISTOL BAY
LAKE AND PENINSULA
DILLINGHAM
BETHEL
WADE HAMPTON
NOME
ALEUTIANS EAST
ALEUTIANS WEST
YAKUTAT
HAINES
Juneau
SITKA
WRANGELL-PETERSBURG
KETCHIKAN GATEWAY
PRINCE OF WALES-OUTER KETCHIKAN

Roman Catholic Diocese of Juneau
415 Sixth St., Suite 300, Juneau, AK 99801
(907) 586-2227,
<www.dioceseofjuneau.org>

St. Herman's Theological Seminary, Russian Orthodox Church
414 Mission Rd., Kodiak, AK 99615
(907) 486-3524,
<www.sthermanseminary.org>

Sisters of Providence Archives
4800 37th Ave. SW, Seattle, WA 98126, (206) 937-4600, **<www.providence.org/phs/archives/default.htm>**

Sitka National Cemetery
803 Sawmill Creek Rd., Sitka, AK 99835
For information, contact Fort Richardson National Cemetery, (907) 384-7075.

State of Alaska Archives and Records Management
141 Willoughby Ave., Juneau, AK 99811
(907) 465-2270, **<www.archives.state.ak.us>**

US District Court, Anchorage Office
222 W. Seventh Ave., Rm. 229, Anchorage, AK 99513, (866) 243-3814,
<www.akd.uscourts.gov/default.htm>

US District Court, Fairbanks Office
101 Twelfth Ave., Rm. 332, Fairbanks, AK 99701, (866) 243-3813,
<www.akd.uscourts.gov/default.htm>

US District Court, Juneau Office
Box 020349, Juneau, AK 99802
(866) 243-3812, **<www.akd.uscourts.gov/default.htm>**

US District Court, Nome Office
Box 130, Nome, AK 99762, (907) 443-5216,
<www.akd.uscourts.gov/default.htm>

Wrangell Genealogical Society
Box 928EP, Wrangell, AK 99929

GENERAL RESOURCES

Alaska, 1741-1953 by Clarence Charles Hulley (Binfords & Mort, 1953)

Alaska, a Bicentennial History by William R. Hunt (Norton, 1976)

The Alaska Gold Rush by David Wharton (Indiana University Press, 1972)

The Alaska Handbook by R.K. Woerner (McFarland, 1986)

Alaska, a History of the 49th State, 2nd edition, by Claus M. Naske and Herman E. Slotnick (University of Oklahoma Press, 1987)

Alaska and Its History compiled and edited by Morgan B. Sherwood (University of Washington Press, 1967)

The Alaska Newspaper Tree by William R. Galbraith (Elmer Rasmuson Library, 1975)

Alaska Research Outline by the Church of Jesus Christ of Latter-day Saints (online at **<www.familysearch.org/eng/search/RG/guide/alaska.asp>**)

Alaska Sources: A Guide to Historical Records and Information Sources by Connie Malcolm Bradbury and David Albert Hales (Heritage Quest, 2001)

Alaska Women's Oral History Collection: Catalogue with Subject Index compiled by Maria Brooks (Learning Resources Center at Anchorage Community College, 1983)

The Alaska-Yukon Gold Book; A Roster of the Progressive Men and Women who were the Argonauts of the Klondike Gold Stampede ... (Sourdough Stampede Association, Inc., 1930)

Alaskan Census Records, 1870-1907 edited by Roland Vern Jackson and Gary Roland Teeples (Accelerated Indexing Systems, 1976)

Alaskan Maps: A Cartobibliography of Alaska to 1900 by Marvin W. Falk (Garland Pub., 1983)

The Alaskan Russian Church Archives by Antoinette Shalkop (Manuscript Division, Library of Congress, 1984)

Bibliography of Books on Alaska Published Before 1868 by Valerian Lada-Mocarski (Yale University Press, 1969)

Biographies of Alaska-Yukon Pioneers, 1850-1950 compiled and edited by Ed Ferrell (Heritage Books, 1994-2000)

The Dictionary Catalog of the Pacific Northwest Collection of the University of Washington Libraries, Seattle from the University of Washington Libraries (G.K. Hall, 1972)

Documenting Alaskan History: Guide to Federal Archives Relating to Alaska by George S. Ulibarri (University of Alaska Press, 1982)

The Founding of Juneau by R.N. DeArmound (Gastineau Channel Centennial Association, 1967)

History of Alaska, 1730-1885 by Hubert Howe Bancroft (A.L. Bancroft & Co., 1886)

How to Find Your Gold Rush Relative: Sources on the Klondike and Alaska Gold Rushes (1896-1914) compiled by R. Bruce Parham and the Alaska Gold Rush Centennial Task Force (National Archives, 1997)

An Index of Alaska Oral History Collections compiled by the Program for the Preservation of Oral History and Traditions, Alaska and Polar Regions Department, University of Alaska, Fairbanks (The Program, 1986)

Melvin Ricks' Alaska Bibliography: An Introductory Guide to Alaskan Historical Literature by Melvin Byron Ricks, edited by Stephen W. Haycox and Betty J. Haycox (Binford & Mort for the Alaska Historial Commission, 1977)

Russian America: A Biographical Dictionary by Richard A. Pierce (Limestone Press, 1990)

IMMIGRATION RECORDS

New Land, New Lives: Scandinavian Immigrants to the Pacific Northwest by Janet Elaine Rasmussen (University of Washington Press, 1993)

☞LAND RECORDS

Records of the Russian-American Company, 1802, 1817-1867 by Raymond H. Fisher and the National Archives (National Archives, 1971)

☞MAPS

Alaska Atlas and Gazetteer (DeLorme Mapping, 1992)

Alaska Place Names, 4th edition, by Alan Edward Schorr (Denali Press, 1991)

Alaska-Yukon Place Names by James Wendell Phillips (University of Washington Press, 1973)

Dictionary of Alaska Place Names by Donald J. Orth (Government Printing Office, 1967)

Geographic Dictionary of Alaska, 2nd edition, by Marcus Baker, prepared by James McCormick (Government Printing Office, 1906)

☞PROBATE RECORDS

District and Territorial Court System: Record Group Inventory Alaska State Archives (State Archives, 1987)

•-COUNTY DETAILS-•

ALEUTIANS EAST BOROUGH

Box 349, Sand Point, AK 99501, (907) 383-2669,
<www.aleutianseast.org>
- **INCORPORATED:** 1987
- **NOTES:** For vital records, contact the Department of Health and Social Services, Bureau of Vital Statistics, Box 110675, Juneau, AK 99801.

ALEUTIANS WEST CENSUS AREA

- **INCORPORATED:** unknown
- **NOTES:** This area has no form of county government. For vital records, contact the Department of Health and Social Services, Bureau of Vital Statistics, Box 110675, Juneau, AK 99801.

BETHEL CENSUS AREA

- **INCORPORATED:** unknown
- **NOTES:** This area has no form of county government. For vital records, contact the Department of Health and Social Services, Bureau of Vital Statistics, Box 110675, Juneau, AK 99801.

BRISTOL BAY BOROUGH

Box 189, Naknek, AK 99633, (907) 246-4224,
<www.theborough.com>
- **INCORPORATED:** 1962

DENALI BOROUGH

Box 480, Healy, AK 99743, (907) 683-1330,
<www.denaliborough.com>
- **INCORPORATED:** 1990

DILLINGHAM CENSUS AREA

- **INCORPORATED:** unknown
- **NOTES:** This area has no form of county government. For vital records, contact the Department of Health and Social Services, Bureau of Vital Statistics, Box 110675, Juneau, AK 99801.

FAIRBANKS NORTH STAR BOROUGH

809 Pioneer Rd., Box 71267, Fairbanks, AK 99707, (907) 459-1000,
<www.co.fairbanks.ak.us>
- **INCORPORATED:** 1964

HAINES BOROUGH

Box 1209, Haines, AK 99827, (907) 766-2231,
<www.haines.ak.us>
- **INCORPORATED:** 1968

JUNEAU, CITY AND BOROUGH

155 S. Seward St., Juneau, AK 99801, (907) 586-5278,
<www.juneau.org>
- **INCORPORATED:** 1963

KENAI PENINSULA BOROUGH

144 N. Binkley, Soldotna, AK 99669, (907) 262-4441,
<www.borough.kenai.ak.us>
- **INCORPORATED:** 1964

KETCHIKAN GATEWAY BOROUGH

344 Front St., Ketchikan, AK 99901, (907) 228-6625,
<www.borough.ketchikan.ak.us>
- **INCORPORATED:** 1963

KODIAK ISLAND BOROUGH

710 Mill Bay Rd., Kodiak, AK 99615, (907) 486-9300,
<www.kodiakak.us>
- **INCORPORATED:** 1963

LAKE AND PENINSULA BOROUGH

Box 495, King Salmon, AK 99613, (907) 246-3421,
<www.lakeandpen.com>
- **INCORPORATED:** 1989

MATANUSKA-SUSITNA BOROUGH

350 E. Dahlia Ave, Palmer, AK 99645, (907) 745-4801,
<www.matsugov.us>
- **INCORPORATED:** 1964

MUNICIPALITY OF ANCHORAGE

3601 C St., Anchorage, AK 99501, (907) 264-0514,
<www.ci.anchorage.ak.us>

- **INCORPORATED:** 1975
- **NOTES:** City of Anchorage and Greater Anchorage Area Bureau unified into the Municipality of Anchorage in 1975.

NOME CENSUS AREA

- **INCORPORATED:** unknown
- **NOTES:** This area has no form of county government. For vital records, contact the Department of Health and Social Services, Bureau of Vital Statistics, Box 110675, Juneau, AK 99801.

NORTH SLOPE BOROUGH

Box 69, Barrow, AK 99723, (907) 852-2611,
<www.co.north-slope.ak.us>

- **INCORPORATED:** 1972

NORTHWEST ARCTIC BOROUGH

Box 1110, Kotzebue, AK 99752, (907) 442-2500,
<www.nwabor.org>

- **INCORPORATED:** 1986

PRINCE OF WALES-OUTER KETCHIKA

- **INCORPORATED:** unknown
- **NOTES:**This area has no form of county government. For vital records, contact the Department of Health and Social Services, Bureau of Vital Statistics, Box 110675, Juneau, AK 99801.

SITKA BOROUGH

100 Lincoln St., Sitka, AK 99835, (907) 747-3294,
<www.sitka.org>

- **INCORPORATED:** 1971

SKAGWAY-HOONAH-ANGOON CENSUS AREA

- **INCORPORATED:** unknown
- **NOTES:** This area has no form of county government. For vital records, contact the Department of Health and Social Services, Bureau of Vital Statistics, Box 110675, Juneau, AK 99801.

SOUTHEAST FAIRBANKS CENSUS AREA

- **INCORPORATED:** unknown
- **NOTES:** This area has no form of county government. For vital records, contact the Department of Health and Social Services, Bureau of Vital Statistics, Box 110675, Juneau, AK 99801.

VALDEZ CORDOVA CENSUS AREA

- **INCORPORATED:** unknown
- **NOTES:** This area has no form of county government. For vital records, contact the Department of Health and Social Services, Bureau of Vital Statistics, Box 110675, Juneau, AK 99801.

WADE HAMPTON CENSUS AREA

- **INCORPORATED:** unknown
- **NOTES:** This area has no form of county government. For vital records, contact the Department of Health and Social Services, Bureau of Vital Statistics, Box 110675, Juneau, AK 99801.

WRANGELL-PETERSBURG CENSUS AREA

- **INCORPORATED:** unknown
- **NOTES:** This area has no form of county government. For vital records, contact the Department of Health and Social Services, Bureau of Vital Statistics, Box 110675, Juneau, AK 99801.

YAKUTAT BOROUGH

Box 160, Yakutat, AK 99689 , (907) 784-3323

- **INCORPORATED:** 1992

YUKON-KOYUKUK CENSUS AREA

- **INCORPORATED:** unknown
- **NOTES:** This area has no form of county government. For vital records, contact the Department of Health and Social Services, Bureau of Vital Statistics, Box 110675, Juneau, AK 99801.

ARIZONA

» BY DAVID A. FRYXELL

HISTORICAL OVERVIEW

Francisco Vasquera de Coronado came to Arizona in 1540 in search of the "seven cities of gold." The Zuni Indians pointed him west, hoping the Spanish would leave their area, which had already been inhabited by native people for some 12,000 years. Other tribes from Arizona include the Cochise, Anasazi, Mogollon, Apache, Navajo and Hopi. The Hopi village of Old Oraibi is the oldest continuously inhabited place in the United States, dating back more than 1,000 years.

Though the Zuni didn't entirely detour the Spanish, Arizona was slower to be colonized than neighboring New Mexico. Tucson wasn't founded until 1775, and the settlements were concentrated in the southern part of the state when Arizona became part of Mexico (as a part of the state of Sonora) with independence in 1821. The Treaty of Guadalupe Hidalgo in 1848 ended the Mexican-American War and closed the long chapter of Spanish-Mexican rule north of the Gila River in Arizona. The rest of present-day Arizona was added to the United States with the Gadsden Purchase in 1853. The Arizona Territory was split off from the New Mexico Territory in 1863, but statehood didn't follow until 1912—the last of the contiguous United States.

Today's Arizona largely sprang up after World War II, as Americans flocked to the sun. Between 1950 and 1990 the population of Phoenix increased from 100,000 to 980,000. In 1960, the Del Webb Corporation, created Sun City, launching Arizona as a retirement haven.

RECORD HIGHLIGHTS

Because settlement was later and thinner, Arizona's records from the Spanish and Mexican periods aren't as rich as those of neighboring New Mexico. The state archives in Phoenix and the Arizona Historical Society in Tucson do hold some documents from this era, such as the 1832 census of Santa Cruz County.

Territorial records begin with the 1860 census, in which Arizona was a county in the New Mexico Territory. A special census was taken in 1864 after the establishment of a separate Arizona Territory, with others in 1866, 1867, 1869, 1871, 1872, and 1882. (Note that what was called Pah-Ute County was included in Arizona Territory until 1866; thereafter it was part of the state of Nevada.) The new territory was included in the regular federal headcount beginning in 1870. Various "great registers" of voters, housed in the state archives, may also be used as census substitutes, generally covering 1882–1911.

Statewide birth and death records began in 1909, just before statehood. Because laws protect the privacy of birth records for 75 years and death records for 50 years, only family members with proof of relationship can access many records. But Arizona has a website **<genealogy.az.gov>** that lets you search for birth certificates (1887–1928) and death certificates (1878–1953), then view records in PDF format.

research tips

- Although Arizona is a large state, it's divided into just 15 counties.
- Several published indexes to Mexican censuses cover the area that's now Arizona: 1801 for Pimeria Alta; 1831 for Tucson, Tubac and Santa Cruz; and 1852 for Pimeria Alta.
- Check repositories for Arizona, New Mexico, and Mexico for early years.
- A good place to begin is the Arizona State Library, Archives, and Public Records website **<www.lib.az.us>**.

CENSUS RECORDS

- Federal census: 1860, 1870, 1880, 1900, 1910, 1920
- Federal mortality Schedules: 1870, 1880
- Territorial census: 1864, 1866, 1867, 1869, 1871, 1872, 1882

The Office of Vital Records also maintains a sampling of delayed birth records (from 1855) and death records (from 1877) from other sources. Marriage and divorce records, as well as probate records and any surviving information on pre–1909 births and deaths, are maintained by the clerk of the superior court in the county where the event occurred.

Obituaries and cemetery records can help fill in blanks when no death certificate is available. The state archives has a collection of cemetery records gathered by the Arizona Genealogical Society, as well as microfiche drawn from an index of obituaries covering 1865 to 1986.

Daniela Moneta, genealogy librarian for the Arizona State Archives, cautions researchers to remember that although Arizona is a large state, it's divided into just 15 counties. (Originally, only four counties were created: Yavapai, Mohave, Yuma and Puma.) Several Rhode Islands would fit into one of Arizona's counties. This makes travel from one county to the next time-consuming, especially if you want to visit historical societies and county courthouses.

You'll find a wealth of records post-1863, Moneta adds, but not much for the pre-territory years when Arizona was on the frontier. There are, however, several published indexes to Mexican censuses for the area that is now Arizona: 1801 for Pimeria Alta; 1831 for Tucson, Tubac, and Santa Cruz; and 1852 for Pimeria Alta. Remember to check repositories for Arizona, New Mexico, and Mexico for those early years.

For statewide information post-1863, Barbara B. Sayler, a professional genealogist and past president of the Arizona State Genealogical Society, says the state archives is the place to start. The collection includes records of marriage, civil and criminal cases, probates, insanity, inquests, wills and estates, naturalization, census, assessor rolls, the Great Register of voters, and real-estate deeds. You'll find an obituary index, a cemetery index, city directories, school yearbooks, maps and a 15,000-volume genealogy collection. The state library has the best collection of Arizona newspapers on microfilm, dating to 1864. To see holdings, go to **<www.lib.az.us>** and look under "Collections" for the Arizona Newspaper Project.

You can also try some unusual sources for clues to Arizona ancestors. Moneta mentions the archives' collection of more than 200 pioneer certificate applications, containing histories of families in Arizona before statehood. If your ancestors were ranchers, try the archives' cattle-brand books, in which families registered their unique marks. Arizona researchers are also lucky in having access to the second-largest Family History Center outside Salt Lake City, the Mesa Regional Family History Center **<www.mesarfhc.org/resources.htm>**.

Besides the state genealogical society, Sayler advises researchers to contact the genealogical or historical societies covering the area you're investigating. The Arizona Genealogical Advisory Board lists societies and professional researchers on its website, **<www.azgab.org>**. For specific county information, Sayler adds, contact societies and courthouses in that county, along with the libraries and special collections at the three state universities. Northern Arizona University in particular also holds a wealth of visual history; its online Image Database **<www.nau.edu/cline/speccoll/imagedb.html>** features 700,000-plus images.

ARCHIVES, LIBRARIES, AND SOCIETIES

Arizona Historical Foundation Hayden Library
Arizona State University, Box 871006, Tempe, AZ 85287, (480) 966-8331, **<www.ahfweb.org>**

Arizona Historical Society
949 E. Second St., Tuscon, AZ 85719, (520) 628-5774, **<www.arizonahistoricalsociety.org>**

Arizona Jewish Historical Society
122 E. Culver St., Phoenix, AZ 85004, (602) 241-7870 **<www.azjhs.org>**

Arizona State Library, Archives and Public Records
1700 W. Washington, Suite 200, Phoenix, AZ 85007, (602) 926-4035, **<www.lib.az.us>**

Arizona Sun Chapter, American Historical Society of Germans from Russia
2002 W. Sunnyside Drive #3105, Phoenix, AZ 85029, (602) 944-1684, **<www.ahsgr.org/arizona_sun_chapter.htm>**

Black Family Genealogy and History Society
Box 90683, Phoenix, AZ 90683, **<www.bfghs.net/aboutBFGHS.htm>**

Central Arizona Division, Arizona Historical Society
1300 N. College Ave., Tempe, AZ 85281

Cochise Genealogical Society
Douglas-Williams House, 1001 Ave. D, Douglas, AZ 85608, (520) 364-7370, **<www.mycochise.com/gene.php>**

Family History Society of Arizona
Box 63094, Phoenix, AZ 85082, **<www.fhsa.org>**

Genealogical Workshop of Mesa
Box 6052, Mesa, AZ 85216, **<members.cox.net/gwom>**

Green Valley Genealogical Society
Box 1009, Green Valley, AZ 85622, **<www.rootsweb.com/~azgvgs>**

Jerome Historical Society
Box 156, 407 Clark St., Jerome, AZ 86331, (928) 634-1066, **<www.jeromehistoricalsociety.org>**

Lake Havasu Genealogical Society and Library
Box 953 or 2126 N. McCulloch Blvd., Lake Havasu City, AZ 86405, (928) 854-5447, **<www.rootsweb.ancestry.com/~azlhgs>**

Mohave County Genealogical Society
400 West Beale St., Kingman, AZ 86401, (928) 753-3195, **<www.kindredtrails.com/AZ_Mohave.html>**

Mohave Valley Genealogical Society
Box 6045, Mohave Valley, AZ 86440

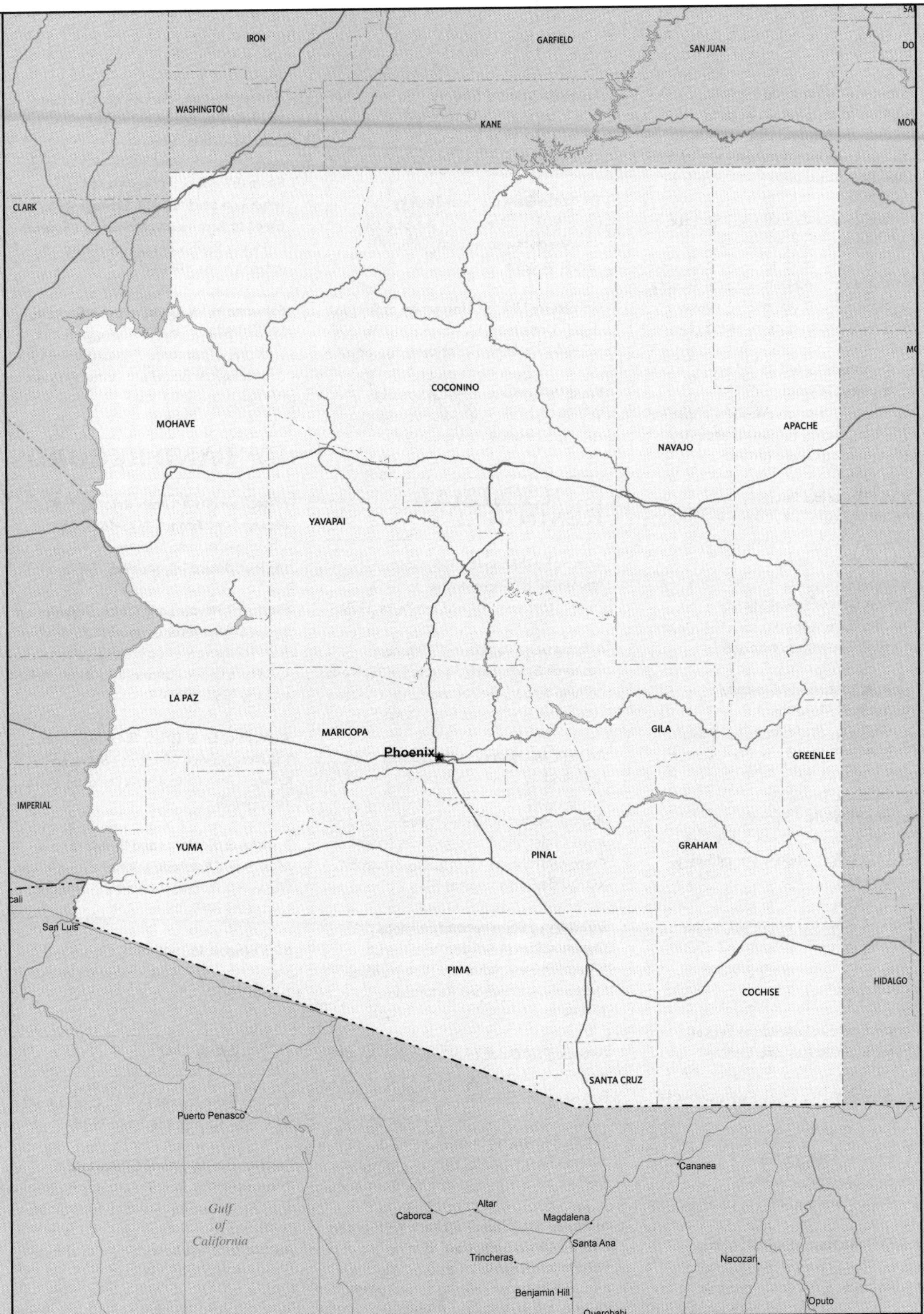
IRON
GARFIELD
SAN JUAN
WASHINGTON
KANE
CLARK
COCONINO
MOHAVE
APACHE
NAVAJO
YAVAPAI
LA PAZ
MARICOPA
Phoenix
GILA
GREENLEE
IMPERIAL
YUMA
PINAL
GRAHAM
San Luis
PIMA
COCHISE
HIDALGO
SANTA CRUZ
Puerto Penasco
Cananea
Gulf
of
California
Caborca
Altar
Magdalena
Santa Ana
Trincheras
Nacozari
Benjamin Hill
Oputo
Querobabi

National Archives and Records Administration, Pacific Region
23123 Cajalco Road, Perris, CA 92570, (951) 956-2000, **<www.archives.gov/pacific>**

Navajo County Genealogical Society
Box 1403, Winslow, AZ 86047

Northern Arizona Genealogical Society
Box 695, Prescott, AZ 86302, **<www.rootsweb.ancestry.com/~aznags>**

Northern Gila County Genealogical Society
302 E. Bonita, Payson, AZ 85541, (928) 474-2139, **<www.rootsweb.ancestry.com/~azngcgs/index.html>**

Oracle Historical Society
Box 10/Museum or 825 Mt. Lemmon Rd., Oracle, AZ 85623, **<www.oraclehistoricalsociety.org>**

Phoenix Genealogical Society
Box 38703, Phoenix, AZ 85069, (602) 274-8047, **<phxgensoc.org>**

Prescott Historical Museum/Sharlot Hall Museum
415 W. Gurley St., Prescott, AZ 86301, (928) 445-3122, **<www.sharlot.org>**

Rio Colorado Division, Arizona Historical Society
240 Madison Ave., Yuma, AZ 85364, (928) 782-1841, **<www.yumalibrary.org/ahs>**

Roman Catholic Diocese of Phoenix
400 E. Monroe St., Phoenix, AZ 85004, (602) 354-2000, **<www.diocesephoenix.org>**

Roman Catholic Diocese of Tucson, Bishop Moreno Pastoral Center
111 S. Church Ave., Box 31, Tuscon, AZ 85702, (520) 792-3410, **<www.diocesetucson.org>**

Sedona Genealogy Club
Box 4258, Sedona, AZ 86340, **<www.rootsweb.ancestry.com/~azsgc>**

Sierra Vista Genealogical Society
Box 1084, Sierra Vista, AZ 85636, **<www.rootsweb.com/~azsvgs>**

Tempe Historical Society
809 E. Southern Ave., Tempe, AZ 85282, (480) 350-5100 **<tempehistoricalsociety.org>**

Tri-State Genealogical Society
Box 21902, Bullhead City, AZ 86439, **<www.rootsweb.ancestry.com/~azcanvtsgs>**

University Library, University of Arizona
1510 E. University, Tucson, AZ 85721, (520) 621-6406, **<www.library.arizona.edu>**

West Valley Genealogical Society
WVGS, 12222 N. 111th Ave., Youngstown, AZ 85363 **<www.azwvgs.org>**

☞ GENERAL RESOURCES

Arizona Gathering II, 1950-1969; an Annotated Bibliography by Donald M. Powell (University of Arizona Press, 1973)

Arizona Genealogical and Historical Research Guide: Early Sources for Southern Arizona by Barbara Baldwin Sayer (Arizona State Genealogical Society, 2006)

Arizona, the History of the Frontier State by Rufus Kay Wyllys (Hobson & Herr, 1950)

Arizona Research Outline by the Church of Jesus Christ of Latter-day Saints (online at **<www.familysearch.org/eng/search/RG/guide/missouri.asp>**)

Directory of Churches and Religious Organizations in Arizona from the US Works Progress Administration (Arizona Statewide Archival and Records Project, 1940)

Genealogical Guide to Arizona and Nevada by Joyce V. Hawley Spiros (Verlene Publishing, 1983)

Farish, Arizona Historian, 8 vols., by Thomas Edwin Farish (The Filmer Brothers Electrotype Company, 1915-1918)

Mormons and Their Neighbors: An Index to Over 75,000 Biographical Sketches from 1820 to the Present, 2 vols., compiled by Marvin E. Wiggins (Harold B. Lee Library, Brigham Young University, 1984)

Newspapers and Periodicals of Arizona, 1859-1911 by Estelle Lutrell (University of Arizona, 1950)

Spanish & Mexican Records of the American Southwest: A Bibliographical Guide to Archive and Manuscript Sources by Henry Putney Beers (University of Arizona Press, 1979)

Surname Index for the Arizona Sentinel, 1875-1905 from the Genealogial Society of Yuma, Arizona, and *Arizona Sentinel* (Genealogical. Society of Yuma, Arizona, 1997)

☞ LAND RECORDS

Miscellaneous Archives Relating to New Mexico Land Grants, 1695-1842 from the US Bureau of Land Management (University of New Mexico Library, 1955-1957)

Record of Private Land Claims Adjudicated by the US Surveyor General, 1855-1890 from the New Mexico (Territory) Surveyor-General's Office (University of New Mexico Library, 1955-1957)

Records of Land Titles, 1847-1852 from the New Mexico (Territory) Secretary's Office (University of New Mexico Library, 1955-1957)

Spanish & Mexican Land Grants in New Mexico and Colorado edited by John R. Van Ness and Christine M. Van Ness (Sunflower University Press, 1980)

Vigil's Index, 1681-1846 by Donaciano Vigil (University of New Mexico Library, 1955-1957)

☞ MAPS

Arizona Place Names by Will Croft Barnes (University of Arizona Press, 1988)

Arizona Territory: Post Offices and Postmasters by John Theobald and Lillian Theobald (Arizona Historical Foundation, 1961)

Arizona's Names by Byrd Howell Granger (Falconer Publishing, 1983)

Ghost Towns of Arizona by James E. Sherman and Barbara H. Sherman (University of Oklahoma Press, 1969)

Historical Atlas of Arizona, 2nd edition, by Henry P. Walker and Don Bufkin (University of Oklahoma Press, 1986)

A History of Arizona's Counties and Courthouses edited by John J. Dreyfuss (National Society of the Colonial Dames of America in the State of Arizona, 1972)

☞MILITARY RECORDS

Arizona Frontier Military Place Names, 1846-1912, revised edition, by David V. Alexander and Daniel C.B. Rathbun (Yucca Tree Press, 2002)

Arizona's Memorial to Vietnam Veterans by Frances Arthur Hortsch (Phoenix Genealogical Society, 1987)

The Army in the West, A Guide to Microfilmed Records in the Library of the Arizona Pioneers' Historical Society from the Arizona Pioneers' Historical Society (W.C. Cox, 1974)

Chains of Command: Arizona and the Army, 1856-1875 by Constance Wynn Altschuler, Don Bufkin (Arizona Historical Society, 1981)

Frontier Military Posts of Arizona by Ray Brandes (Dale Stuart King, 1960)

The Rough Riders: A Brief Study and Indexed Roster of the 1st Regiment, US Volunteer Cavalry, 1898 by Howard Markland Gabbart with the US Army Volunteer Cavalry Regiment, 1st (Arizona State Genealogical Society, 1992)

The Transformation of Arizona into a Modern State by Charles Ynfante (Edwin Mellen Press, 2002)

☞PROBATE RECORDS

A Guide to Arizona Courts (Arizona Supreme Court, 1997)

☞VITAL RECORDS

Arizona Death Records: An Index Compiled from Mortuary, Cemetery, and Church Records, 3 vols. (Arizona State Genealogical Society, 1976-1982)

Northern Arizona Territorial Death and Burial Records, 1870-1910 by Dora M. Whiteside (D.M. Whiteside)

•-COUNTY DETAILS-•

APACHE
Box 365, St. Johns, AZ 85936, (928) 337-4364,
<www.co.apache.az.us>
- **INCORPORATED:** Feb. 24, 1879
- **PARENT COUNTY:** Yavapai
- **BIRTH RECORDS:** started in 1909, kept by Department of Health
- **MARRIAGE:** 1879, Superior Court
- **DEATH:** 1909, Department of Health
- **DIVORCE:** 1879, Superior Court
- **LAND:** 1879, Clerk of Courts
- **PROBATE:** 1879, Superior Court

CASTLE DOME
- **INCORPORATED:** 1860
- **PARENT COUNTY:** Original county
- **NOTES:** See Yuma County. Name changed to Yuma Nov. 8, 1864.

COCHISE
Box CK, Bisbee, AZ 85603, (520) 432-9364,
<www.co.cochise.az.us>
- **INCORPORATED:** Feb. 1, 1881
- **PARENT COUNTY:** Pima
- **BIRTH RECORDS:** start in 1909, kept by Department of Health
- **MARRIAGE:** 1881, Superior Court
- **DEATH:** 1909 Department of Health
- **DIVORCE:** unknown, Superior Court
- **LAND:** unknown, County Recorder
- **PROBATE:** unknown, Superior Court
- **NATURALIZATION:** unknown, Superior Court

COCONINO
100 E. Birch Ave., Flagstaff, AZ 86001, (928) 779-6536,
<www.coconino.az.gov>
- **INCORPORATED:** Feb. 19, 1891
- **PARENT COUNTY:** Yavapai
- **BIRTH RECORDS:** start in 1909, kept by Department of Health
- **MARRIAGE:** 1891, Superior Court
- **DEATH:** 1909, Department of Health
- **DIVORCE:** 1891, Superior Court
- **LAND:** unknown, County Recorder
- **PROBATE:** 1891, Superior Court
- **COURT:** 1891, Superior Court
- **NATURALIZATION:** 1891, Superior Court

EWELL
- **INCORPORATED:** 1860
- **PARENT COUNTY:** Original county
- **NOTES:** See Pima County. Name changed to Pima Nov. 8, 1864.

GILA
1400 E. Ash St., Globe, AZ 85501, (928) 425-3231,
<www.gilacountyaz.gov>
- **INCORPORATED:** Feb. 8, 1881
- **PARENT COUNTIES:** Maricopa, Pinal
- **MARRIAGE RECORDS:** start in 1881, kept by Superior Court
- **DIVORCE:** 1914, Superior Court
- **LAND:** unknown, County Recorder
- **BIRTH:** 1909, Department of Health
- **DEATH:** 1909, Department of Health

- **NOTES:** District Court has naturalization records 1894-1912. Clerk of the Superior Court has probate records 1880-1953.

GRAHAM

800 Main St., Safford, AZ 85546, (928) 428-3250,
<www.graham.az.gov>

- **INCORPORATED:** March 10, 1881
- **PARENT COUNTIES:** Apache, Pima
- **BIRTH RECORDS:** start in 1909, kept by Department of Health
- **MARRIAGE:** 1909, Department of Health
- **DEATH:** 1909, Department of Health
- **DIVORCE:** 1881, Superior Court
- **LAND:** unknown, County Recorder
- **PROBATE:** 1881, Superior Court
- **NATURALIZATION:** 1881, Superior Court
- **NOTES:** Clerk of the Superior Court has naturalization records 1903-1973.

GREENLEE

Webster St., Clifton, AZ 85533, (928) 865-3872,
<www.co.greenlee.az.us>

- **INCORPORATED:** March 10, 1909
- **PARENT COUNTY:** Graham
- **BIRTH RECORDS:** start in 1909, kept by Department of Health
- **MARRIAGE:** 1911, Superior Court
- **DEATH:** 1909, Department of Health
- **DIVORCE:** 1911, Superior Court
- **LAND:** 1911, County Recorder
- **PROBATE:** 1911, Superior Court

LA PAZ

1108 Joshua Ave., Parker, AZ 85344, (928) 669-6115,
<www.co.la-paz.az.us>

- **INCORPORATED:** Jan. 1, 1983
- **PARENT COUNTY:** Yuma
- **BIRTH RECORDS:** start in 1909, kept by Department of Health
- **MARRIAGE:** unknown, Superior Court
- **DEATH:** 1909, Department of Health
- **DIVORCE:** unknown, Superior Court
- **LAND:** unknown, County Recorder
- **PROBATE:** unknown, Superior Court
- **NATURALIZATION:** unknown, Superior Court

MARICOPA

201 W. Jefferson, Phoenix, AZ 85003, (602) 506-3204,
<www.maricopa.gov>

- **INCORPORATED:** Feb. 14, 1871
- **PARENT COUNTIES:** Pima, Yavapai, Yuma
- **BIRTH RECORDS:** start in 1909, kept by Department of Health
- **MARRIAGE:** 1871, Superior Court
- **DEATH:** 1909, Department of Health
- **DIVORCE:** 1871, Superior Court
- **LAND:** unknown, County Recorder
- **PROBATE:** 1916, Superior Court
- **NATURALIZATION:** 1912, Superior Court

MOHAVE

401 E. Spring St., Kingman, AZ 86401, (928) 753-9141,
<www.co.mohave.az.us>

- **INCORPORATED:** Nov. 8, 1864
- **PARENT COUNTY:** Original county
- **BIRTH RECORDS:** start in 1909, kept by Department of Health
- **DEATH:** 1909, Department of Health
- **DIVORCE:** unknown, Superior Court
- **LAND:** unknown, County Recorder
- **NATURALIZATION:** unknown, Superior Court
- **NOTES:** Clerk of Superior Court has marriage records 1919-1943 and probate records that include an estate register 1913-1922, minutes 1865-1915, letters of administration 1877-1921, and files of guardianships 1885-1951.

NAVAJO

Box 668, Holbrook, AZ 86025, (928) 524-6161,
<www.co.navajo.az.us>

- **INCORPORATED:** March 21, 1895
- **PARENT COUNTY:** Apache
- **BIRTH RECORDS:** start in 1909, kept by Department of Health
- **DEATH:** 1909, Department of Health
- **DIVORCE:** unknown, Superior Court
- **LAND:** unknown, County Recorder
- **PROBATE:** unknown, Superior Court
- **NATURALIZATION:** unknown, Superior Court
- **NOTES:** Clerk of Superior Court has marriage records 1895-1970.

PIMA

130 W. Congress St., Tucson, AZ 85701, (520) 740-8126,
<www.pima.gov>

- **INCORPORATED:** Nov. 8, 1864
- **PARENT COUNTY:** Original county
- **BIRTH RECORDS:** start in 1909, kept by Department of Health
- **DEATH:** 1909, Department of Health
- **DIVORCE:** unknown, Superior Court
- **LAND:** 1864, County Recorder
- **NATURALIZATION:** 1864, Superior Court
- **NOTES:** Clerk of Superior Court has marriage records 1908-1921 and probate records 1866-1909.

PINAL

Box 2730, Florence, AZ 85232, (520) 866-5300,
<www.co.pinal.az.us>

- **INCORPORATED:** Feb. 1, 1875
- **PARENT COUNTIES:** Pima, Yavapai
- **BIRTH RECORDS:** start in 1909, kept by Department of Health
- **DEATH:** 1909, Department of Health
- **DIVORCE:** 1883, Superior Court
- **LAND:** unknown, County Recorder
- **NATURALIZATION:** 1875, Superior Court
- **NOTES:** Clerk of Superior Court has marriage records 1874-1910 and probate records 1875-1949.

SANTA CRUZ

Box 1929, Nogales, AZ 85628,(520) 375-7730,
<www.co.santa-cruz.az.us>

- **INCORPORATED:** March 15, 1899

- **PARENT COUNTIES:** Cochise, Pima
- **BIRTH RECORDS:** start in 1909, kept by Department of Health
- **MARRIAGE:** 1899, Superior Court
- **DIVORCE:** unknown, Superior Court
- **LAND:** 1899, County Recorder
- **DEATH:** 1909, Department of Health
- **ADOPTION:** 1940, Superior Court
- **NOTES:** Clerk of Superior Court has military records 1907-1922 and Naturalization records 1888-1985.

YAVAPAI

120 S. Cortez, Prescott, AZ 86303, (928) 771-3312,
<www.co.yavapai.az.us>

- **INCORPORATED:** Nov. 8, 1864
- **PARENT COUNTY:** Original county
- **BIRTH RECORDS:** started in 1909, kept by Department of Health
- **MARRIAGE:** 1870, Superior Court
- **DEATH:** 1909, Department of Health
- **DIVORCE:** unknown, Superior Court
- **LAND:** 1864, County Recorder
- **PROBATE:** 1865, Superior Court
- **NATURALIZATION:** unknown, Superior Court

YUMA

168 S. Second Ave., Yuma, AZ 85364, (928) 329-2164,
<www.co.yuma.az.us>

- **INCORPORATED:** Nov. 8, 1864
- **PARENT COUNTY:** Original county
- **BIRTH RECORDS:** started in 1909, kept by Department of Health
- **DEATH:** 1909, Department of Health
- **DIVORCE:** 1863, Superior Court
- **LAND:** 1863, County Recorder
- **PROBATE:** 1876, Superior Court
- **NATURALIZATION:** 1863, Superior Court
- **NOTES:** Clerk of Superior Court has marriage records 1864-1927.

ARKANSAS

» BY EMILY ANNE CROOM

HISTORICAL OVERVIEW

In what is now Arkansas, 16th-century Spanish explorers found a considerable Indian population living in agricultural settlements. Between 1673 and 1740, French explorers, trappers and traders traversed the area. By the end of the Seven Years' War in 1763, France ceded to Spain all of Louisiana, the vast territory west of the Mississippi that included Arkansas. Later, as Napoleon prepared for retrocession of Louisiana to France, the Louisiana Purchase of 1803 made Arkansas US territory. By then, Osage, Caddo, and Quapaw Indians felt the push of Cherokee and white settlers moving into Arkansas.

Missouri and Arkansas were then part of the undefined district Upper Louisiana, and in 1805, became Louisiana Territory. For decades, Arkansas was a destination for white explorers and settlers, as well as a route for thousands of Indians forced from the Southeast to Indian Territory. The Caddo signed the last Indian land cession in Arkansas in 1835.

In 1812, Arkansas became part of Missouri Territory. Originally part of New Madrid County, Arkansas County was established in 1813. "Arkansaw" Territory, created in 1819, included most of Oklahoma as Indian lands; the present western boundary was established when Arkansas became the 25th state in 1836.

The state's numerous rivers drain into the Mississippi and were important transportation routes in the 19th century. Many settlers came via the Mississippi and its tributaries, but swampy and flood-prone plains along rivers in eastern Arkansas limited the growth of towns there. Major towns developed farther upriver. One early road that invited settlement along its route was the Southwest Trail across Arkansas, leading into Texas.

Despite mountainous terrain in the north and west and forests statewide, settlers saw agricultural opportunity in the availability of cheap federal land or, for some, bounty land due them for military service. Before the Civil War, settlers streamed into Arkansas from neighboring states—especially Tennessee—and from Alabama, other southern states, and the Ohio Valley.

Cotton, often cultivated with slave labor, became the dominant crop on farms and plantations in the east and south. By 1860, slaves were a quarter of the state's population. Wheat production was important in the north and west. Corn was a staple for people and livestock throughout the state.

Due largely to geography, settlement patterns and the state's regional economies, antebellum political power rested generally in the south and east. By 1861, many Arkansans were Unionists. Secession was hotly debated. Only after the war began did Arkansas join the Confederacy. The Union army occupied northwest Arkansas during much of the Civil War. Both pro-Union and -Confederate state governments operated in the last year of the war. Hostilities included both formal military operations and guerrilla warfare.

research tips

- Someone reportedly born in Missouri or Louisiana during either territorial period could have been born in what is now Arkansas.
- Arkansas is a federal land state, whose land patents are searchable at **<www.glorecords.blm.gov>**.
- Arkansas federal censuses date from 1830.
- Learn more about Arkansas History Commission records at **<www.ark-ives.com/research/materials.asp>**.

CENSUS RECORDS

- Federal census population schedules: 1830, 1840, 1850, 1860, 1870, 1880, 1900, 1910, 1920, 1930
- Federal mortality schedules: 1850, 1860, 1870, 1880
- Federal slave schedules: 1850, 1860 (schedules name slaveholders but rarely name slaves)
- Territorial sheriffs' censuses: 1823 (Arkansas County), 1829 (various counties)

Although the state rejoined the Union in 1868, reconstruction was difficult, with widespread poverty and discontent. Late-19th century economic development included railroads, logging and timber manufacturing. Post-Civil War decades also saw expansion of cotton farming, sharecropping and European immigration. In the early 20th century, Arkansas experienced growth in its textile, petroleum, and mining industries. But the economy remained generally rural and cotton-dominated until after World War II. By 1980, the rural population was slightly less than half the state total.

RECORD HIGHLIGHTS

Statewide vital records include birth and death records from 1914, evidence of marriage records from 1917, and evidence of divorce records from 1923. Check in the city or county for any vital records created prior to statewide registration. Request copies of divorce decrees or marriage licenses from the county court that issued the original documents; consult the Acts of Arkansas for legislature-granted divorces. For more information, see the Arkansas Department of Health website **<www.healthyarkansas.com/certificates/certificates.html>**.

A number of Arkansas counties have lost some records to floods or fires. Investigate surviving records, resources in parent and neighboring counties, and records of territorial, local, state and federal jurisdictions. These are some of the Arkansas sources available through the Family History Library (FHL) and/or the Arkansas History Commission:

- Territorial sheriffs' censuses, 1823 (Arkansas County), 1829 (various counties)
- Territorial and state tax lists for various counties and years
- Territorial Papers of the United States (National Archives microfilm M721) and Territorial Papers of the United States Senate (M200) for Orleans, Louisiana, Missouriand Arkansas territories; State Department Territorial Papers, Missouri (M1134)
- Records of depositors, Little Rock branch of the Freedman's Savings and Trust Company (FHL microfilm 928573)
- 1911 census of Confederate veterans in Arkansas
- Confederate pension applications
- Records of the Arkansas Confederate Home, 1890–1963, searchable at **<arkansashistory.arkansas.com/documenting/confederate_homes.asp>**

ARCHIVES, LIBRARIES, AND SOCIETIES

Arkansas Genealogical Society
Box 26374, Little Rock, AR 72221, **<www.agsgenealogy.org>**

Arkansas Historical Association
416 Old Main, University of Arkansas, Fayetteville, AR 72701, (479) 575-5884, **<www.uark.edu/depts/arkhist/home>**

Arkansas History Commission and State Archives
One Capitol Mall, Little Rock, AR 72201 (501) 682-6900, **<www.ark-ives.com>**

Ashley County Genealogical Society
Drawer R, Crossett, AR 71635

Ashley County Library
211 East Lincoln, Hamburg, AR 71646 (870) 853-8781

Batesville Genealogical Society
Box 3883, Batesville, AR 72503

Baxter County Historical and Genealogical Society
Box 2125, Mountain Home, AR 72654, **<www.baxtercountyonline.com/bchgs>**

Benton County Historical Society
Box 1034, Bentonville, AR 72712 (479) 273-3890, **<www.uark.edu/depts/globmark/bchsark>**

Bradley County Genealogical Society
Box 837, Warren, AR 71671, **<www.rootsweb.ancestry.com/~arbradle/bradcogensoc.shtml>**

Butler Center for Arkansas Studies, Central Arkansas Library
100 Rock St., Little Rock, AR 72201 (501) 320-5700, **<www.butlercenter.org>**

Carroll County Historical and Genealogical Society
Box 249, Berryville, AR 72616, (870) 423-6312, **<www.rootsweb.ancestry.com/~arcchs>**

Clark County Historical Association
Box 516, Arkadelphia, AR 71923, **<clarkcountyhistory.com>**

Clark County Library
609 Caddo St., Arkadelphia, AR 71923 (870) 246-2271, **<clark-library.com>**

Clay County Genealogical Club
Piggott Public Library, 361 West Main, Piggott, AR 72454

Cleburne County Historical Society
Box 794, Heber Springs, AR 72543 (501) 362-5225, **<www.cleburnehistory.info>**

Craighead County Historical Society
Box 1011, Jonesboro, AR 72403, **<www.craigheadhistorical.org>**

Crawford County Genealogical Society
Box 276, Alma, AR 72921, **<www.rootsweb.com/~arcrawfo>**

Crawford County Historical Society
929 E. Main St., Van Buren, AR 72956, **<www.rootsweb.ancestry.com/~arcrawfo>**

Craighead County Jonesboro Public Library
315 W. Oak Ave., Jonesboro, AR 72401 (870) 935-5133, **<www.libraryinjonesboro.org>**

Crowley Ridge Genealogical Society
Box 2091, State University, AR 72467

Dallas County Arkansas Genealogical and Historical Society
Dallas County Library, 501 E. Fourth St. Fordyce, AR 71742

Department of Arkansas Heritage
1500 Tower Bldg., 323 Center St., Little Rock, AR 72201, (501) 324-9150, **<www.arkansasheritage.com>**

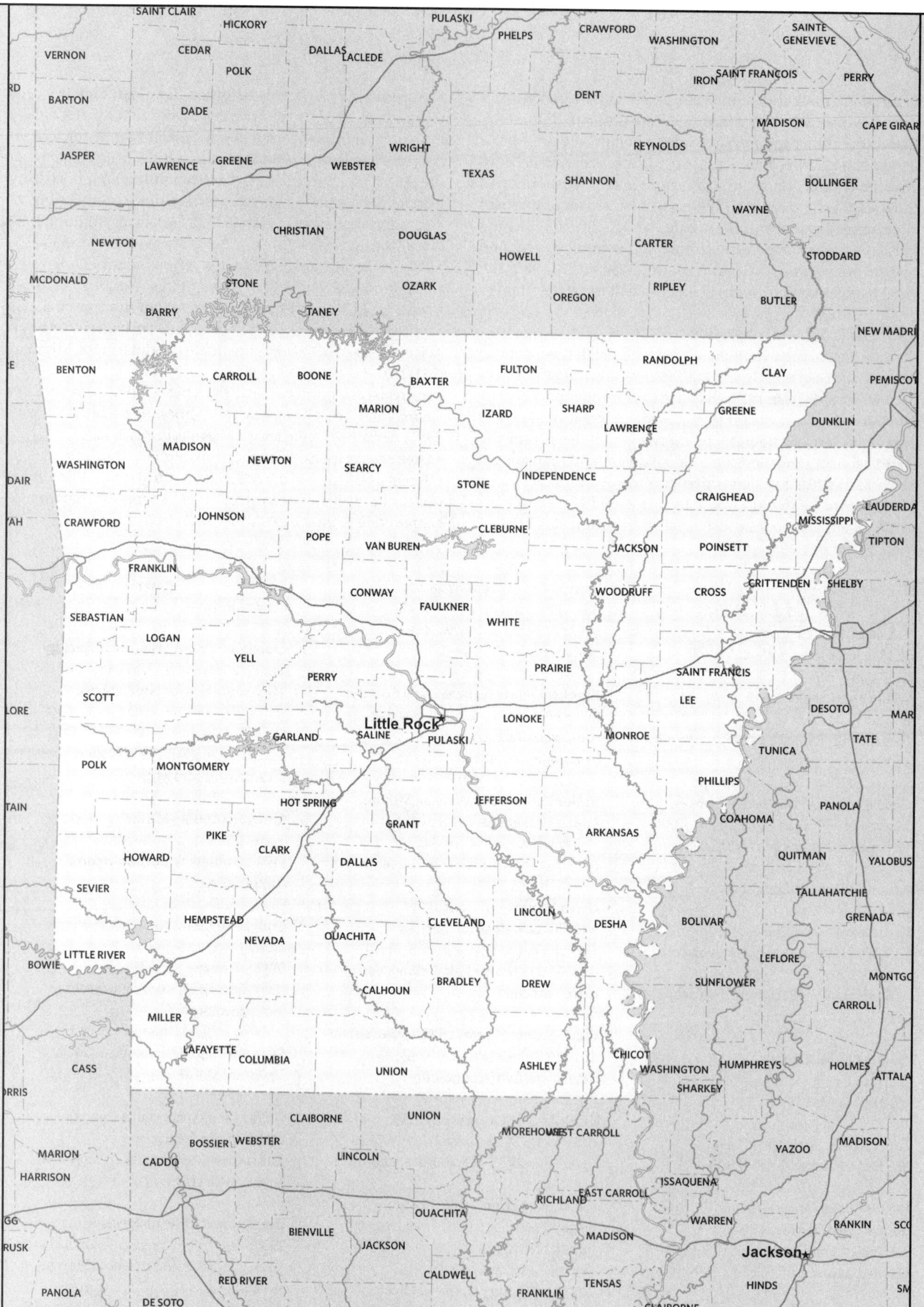
SAINT CLAIR
HICKORY
PULASKI
PHELPS
CRAWFORD
WASHINGTON
SAINTE GENEVIEVE
VERNON
CEDAR
DALLAS
LACLEDE
POLK
IRON
SAINT FRANCOIS
PERRY
BARTON
DADE
DENT
MADISON
JASPER
WRIGHT
REYNOLDS
LAWRENCE
GREENE
WEBSTER
TEXAS
SHANNON
BOLLINGER
WAYNE
CHRISTIAN
DOUGLAS
NEWTON
HOWELL
CARTER
STODDARD
MCDONALD
STONE
OZARK
RIPLEY
OREGON
BUTLER
BARRY
TANEY
BENTON
CARROLL
BOONE
BAXTER
FULTON
RANDOLPH
CLAY
MARION
IZARD
SHARP
GREENE
LAWRENCE
DUNKLIN
MADISON
WASHINGTON
NEWTON
SEARCY
STONE
INDEPENDENCE
CRAIGHEAD
CRAWFORD
JOHNSON
MISSISSIPPI
POPE
CLEBURNE
VAN BUREN
JACKSON
POINSETT
TIPTON
FRANKLIN
CONWAY
WOODRUFF
CROSS
CRITTENDEN
SHELBY
SEBASTIAN
FAULKNER
WHITE
LOGAN
YELL
PRAIRIE
PERRY
SAINT FRANCIS
SCOTT
LEE
DESOTO
Little Rock
LONOKE
GARLAND
SALINE
PULASKI
MONROE
TATE
TUNICA
POLK
MONTGOMERY
PHILLIPS
HOT SPRING
JEFFERSON
PANOLA
GRANT
COAHOMA
PIKE
ARKANSAS
CLARK
HOWARD
DALLAS
QUITMAN
SEVIER
TALLAHATCHIE
GRENADA
HEMPSTEAD
LINCOLN
CLEVELAND
DESHA
BOLIVAR
NEVADA
OUACHITA
LITTLE RIVER
BOWIE
LEFLORE
CALHOUN
BRADLEY
DREW
SUNFLOWER
CARROLL
MILLER
LAFAYETTE
COLUMBIA
CHICOT
CASS
UNION
ASHLEY
WASHINGTON
HUMPHREYS
HOLMES
SHARKEY
CLAIBORNE
UNION
MOREHOUSE
WEST CARROLL
BOSSIER
WEBSTER
MADISON
MARION
YAZOO
CADDO
LINCOLN
HARRISON
ISSAQUENA
EAST CARROLL
RICHLAND
OUACHITA
WARREN
RANKIN
BIENVILLE
MADISON
JACKSON
Jackson
CALDWELL
RED RIVER
TENSAS
HINDS
PANOLA
DE SOTO
FRANKLIN
CLAIBORNE

Desha County Historical Society
506 Henry Dr., Dumas, AR 76139,
<deshacountyhistorical.org>

Faulkner County Historical Society
Box 731, Conway, AR 72033,
<www.faulknerhistory.com>

Fayetteville Public Library
401 W. Mountain St., Fayetteville, AR 72701
(479) 571-2222, **<www.faylib.org>**

Fort Smith Historical Society
61 S. Eighth St., Fort Smith, AR 72901,
<www.fortsmithhistory.org>

Fort Smith Public Library
3201 Rogers Ave., Fort Smith, AR 72903
(479) 783-0229, **<www.fortsmith library.org>**

Frontier Researchers Genealogical Society
Box 2123, Fort Smith, AR 72902

Garland County Historical Society
328 Quapaw Ave., Hot Springs, AR 71901
(501) 321-2159, **<www.garlandcounty historicalsociety.com>**

Garland-Montgomery Regional Library
200 Woodbine St., Hot Springs, AR 71901

Grand Prairie Genealogical Society
Stuttgart Public Library, 2002 S. Buerkle St., Stuttgart, AR 72160, (870) 673-1966,
<www.rootsweb.ancestry.com/~ararkans/grandpra.htm>

Grand Prairie Historical Society
Box 122, Gillett, AR 72055

Greene County Historical and Genealogical Society
212 W. Court St., Box 121, Paragould, AR 72451, **<www.greenecountyargen.com>**

Hempstead County Genealogical Society
Box 1158, Hope, AR 71801

Heritage Seekers Genealogical Club
Box 532, North Little Rock, AR 72115

Historic Genealogical Society of Marion County
Box 761, Yellville, AR 72687

Hot Springs County Historical Society
Box 674, Malvern, AR 72104

Independence County Historical Society
Box 2722, Batesville, AR 72503,
<www.knology.net/~lizglenn/ichs.htm>

Izard County Historical Society
Box 110, Dolph, AR 72528, **<www.couch genweb.com/arkansas/izard>**

Jefferson County Genealogical Society
Box 2215, Pine Bluff, AR 71613,
<www.rootsweb.com/~arjcgs>

Johnson County Historical Society
Box 505, Clarksville, AR 72830,
<www.ar-johnsoncohistory.com>

Johnson County Public Library
Taylor Circle #2, Clarksville, AR 72830
(479) 754-3135

Lafayette County Historical Society
Box 758, Lewisville, AR 71845
(870) 921-5252

Logan County Historical Society
Box 40, Magazine, AR 72943

Madison County Genealogical and Historical Society
Box 427, Huntsville, AR 72740
(501) 738-6408

Marion County Public Library
309 W. Old Main St., Yellville, AR 72687
(870) 449-6015

Melting Pot Genealogical Society
Box 936, Hot Springs, AR 71902
(501) 624-0229 , **<www.rootsweb. ancestry.com/~armpgs>**

Montgomery County Historical Society
Box 520, Mount Ida, AR 71957

National Archives and Records Administration, Southwest Region
1400 John Burgess Drive, Fort Worth, TX 76140, (817) 831-5620, **<www.archives. gov/southwest>**

Nevada County Depot and Museum
403 W. First St. S., Prescott, AR 71857,
<www.depotmuseum.org>

Newton County Historical Society
Box 360, Jasper, AR 72641,
<newtoncountyar.com>

Northwest Arkansas Genealogical Society
405 S. Main St., Bentonville, AR 72712
(479) 273-3890, **<www.rootsweb. ancestry.com/~arnwags>**

Ouachita Baptist University, Riley-Hickingbotham Library
410 Ouachita St., Arkadelphia, AR 71998,
<www.obu.edu/library>

Ouachita-Calhoun Genealogical Society
Box 2092, Camden, AR 71711,
<www.rootsweb.ancestry.com/~arouachi/societie.htm>

Ouachita-Calhoun Genealogical Society Archives
Public Library of Camden & Ouachita County, 120 Harrison St., NW, Camden, AR 71701, (870) 836-5083

Ouachita County Historical Society
926 Washington St., Camden, AR 71701
(870) 836-9243, **<www.rootsweb. ancestry.com/~arouachi/mccullom.htm>**

Pike County Archives and History Society
Box 875, Murfreesboro, AR 71958,
<www.pcahs.org>

Pine Bluff and Jefferson County Public Library
200 E. Eighth Ave., Pine Bluff, AR 71601, (870) 534-4802,
<pbjclibrary.state.ar.us>

Polk County Genealogical Society
Box 1525, Mena, AR 71953,
<www.arkgenealogy.polk.org>

Polk County Library
410 Eighth St., Mena, AR 71953
(479) 394-2314

Pope County Historical Association
<popecountyarkansas.org>

Pope County Library System
116 E. Third St., Russellville, AR 72801, (479) 968-4368, **<www.popelibrary.org>**

Pulaski County Historical Society
Box 251903, Little Rock, AR 72225, **<www.pulaskicountyarkhistory.org>**

Randolph County Historical Society
111 W. Everett St., Pocahontas, AR 72455, **<www.rootsweb.ancestry.com/~arrandol>**

Saline County Historical Commission
Gunn Museum Saline County, 218 S. Market St., Benton, AR 72015

Saline County History and Heritage Society
Box 1712, Benton, AR 72018, (501) 778-3770, **<www.rootsweb.ancestry.com/~arschhs/index.html>**

Scott County Historical and Genealogical Society
Box 1560, Waldron, AR 72958, (479) 637-2466, **<www.argenweb.net/scott>**

Sevier County Historical Society
717 N. Maple Ave., De Queen, AR 71832, **<www.genealogyshoppe.com/arsevier>**

Southwest Arkansas Genealogical Society
1022 Lawton Circle, Magnolia, AR 71753

Southwest Arkansas Regional Archives
201 Hwy. 195 S., Box 134, Washington, AR 71862, (870) 983-2633, **<www.southwestarchives.com>**

Stone County Historical Society
Box 210, Mountain View, AR 72560, **<www.rootsweb.com/~arscgs>**

Stuttgart Public Library
2002 S. Buerkle St., Stuttgart, AR 72160 (870) 673-1966, **<www.stuttgartpubliclibrary.org>**

Tri-County Genealogical Society
Box 580, Marvell, AR 72366, **<www.rootsweb.ancestry.com/~artcgs>**

Union County Genealogical Society
Barton Library, 200 E. Fifth St., El Dorado, AR 71730

University of Arkansas Libraries
365 McIlroy Ave., Fayetteville, AR 72701 (479) 575-4101, **<libinfo.uark.edu>**

Van Buren Historical Society
Box 1023, Clinton, AR 72031, (501) 745-4066, **<www.rootsweb.ancestry.com/~arvanbur/VBHistSoc/historicalsociety.html>**

Washington County Arkansas Genealogical Society
Box 41, Fayetteville, AR 72702, **<www.rootsweb.ancestry.com/~arwcags>**

Washington County Historical Society
118 E. Dickson St., Fayetteville, AR 72701, (479) 521-2970, **<www.washcohistoricalsociety.org>**

William F. Laman Public Library
2801 Orange St., North Little Rock, AR 72114, (501) 758-1720, **<www.laman.net>**

Yell County Historical and Genealogical Society
Box 622, Dardanelle, AR 72834, **<www.argenweb.net/yell/yhs.htm>**

GENERAL RESOURCES

Abstracts of Arkansas Reports, January 1837 through January 1861 compiled by Joan Thurman Taunton (Arkansas Genealogical Society, 1988)

Arkansas Families: Glimpses of Yesterday Columns from the Arkansas Gazette by Lucy Marion Reaves, edited by Desmond Walls Allen (Arkansas Research, 1995)

Arkansas and Its People, a History, 1541-1930 edited by David Yancey Thomas (The American Historical Society, 1930)

Arkansas Links: A Comprehensive Guide to Genealogical Research in the Natural State by Rhonda S. Norris (Morris Publishing, 1999)

Arkansas Pensioners, 1818-1900 compiled by Dorothy E. Payne (Southern Historical Press, 1985)

Arkansas Research Outline by the Church of Jesus Christ of Latter-day Saints (online at **<www.familysearch.org/eng/search/RG/guide/arkansas.asp>**)

Arkansas Researchers' Handbook by Claudia Wagoner (Research Plus, 1986)

Biographical and Historical Memoirs of Eastern Arkansas (The Goodspeed Publishing Co., 1890)

The By-Name Index to the Centennial History of Arkansas compiled and edited by Lewis E. Roberts (L.E. Roberts, 1991)

Early Days in Arkansas by William F. Pope (F.W. Allsopp, 1895)

From Slavery to Uncertain Freedom: The Freedmen's Bureau in Arkansas, 1865-1869 by Randy Finley (University of Arkansas Press, 1996)

Genealogist's Guide to Arkansas Courthouse Research by Jack Damon Ruple, Sr. (J.D. Ruple, 1989)

History of the Arkansas Press for a Hundred Years and More by Frederick William Allsopp (Parke-Harper Publishing, 1922)

Lest We Forget, or, Character Gems Gleaned from South Arkansas by J.H. Riggin and W.F. Evans (Southern Historical Press, 1978)

Pioneers and Makers of Arkansas by Josiah Hazen Shinn (Genealogical Publishing Co., 1967)

They Sought a Land: A Settlement in the Arkansas River Valley, 1840-1870 by William Oates Ragsdale (University of Arkansas Press, 1997)

Union List of Arkansas Newspapers, 1819-1942, prepared by Historical Records Survey, Works Projects Administration (Historical Records Survey, 1942)

CENSUS RECORDS

1820 Census of the Territory of Arkansas (Reconstructed) by James Logan Morgan (Arkansas Research, 1992)

Arkansas 1850 Census Every-Name Index by Bobbie Jones McLane and Desmond Walls Allen (Arkansas Research, 1995)

☞ IMMIGRATION RECORDS

Cherokee Emigration Rolls, 1817-1835 transcribed by Jack D. Baker (Baker Publishing Co., 1977)

☞ LAND RECORDS

Arkansas Land Patents, Eastern Arkansas (Clay, Craighead, Crittenden, Cross, Greene, Lee, Mississippi, Monroe, Phillips, Poinsett, and St. Francis counties): Granted through 30 June 1908 by Desmond Walls Allen and Bobbie Jones McLane (Arkansas Research, 1991)

Arkansas Military Bounty Grants (War of 1812) compiled by Katheren Christensen (Arkansas Ancestors, 1971)

☞ MAPS

Arkansas Atlas & Gazetteer (DeLorme, 1997)

Arkansas Township Atlas: A History of the Minor Civil Divisions in Each Arkansas County by Russell Pierce Baker (Arkansas Genealogical Society, 1984)

Arkansas Township Digest: Minor Civil Divisions, 1820-1990 by Desmond Walls Allen (Arkansas Research, 1994)

The Atlas of Arkansas edited by Richard M. Smith (University of Arkansas Press, 1989)

Historical Atlas of Arkansas by Gerald T. Hanson and Carl H. Moneyhon (University of Oklahoma Press, 1989)

☞ MILITARY RECORDS

Arkansas 1911 Census of Confederate Veterans transcribed and edited by Bobbie J. McLane and Capitola Glazner (B.J. McLane,C. Glazner, 1977-1981)

Arkansas Confederate Veterans and Widows Pension Applications compiled by Frances Terry Ingmire (F.T. Ingmire, 1985)

Arkansas' Damned Yankees: An Index to Union Soldiers in Arkansas Regiments by Desmond Walls Allen (D.W. Allen, 1987)

Arkansas' Mexican War Soldiers by Desmond Walls Allen (Arkansas Research, 1988)

Arkansas' Spanish American War Soldiers by Desmond Walls Allen (Arkansas Research, 1988)

Arkansas Union Soldiers Pension Application Index compiled by Desmond Walls Allen (D.W. Allen, 1987)

Compendium of the Confederate Armies, 11 vols., by Stewart Sifakis (Facts on File, 1992-1995)

Confederate Arkansas: The People and Policies of a Frontier State in Wartime by Michael B. Dougan (University of Alabama Press, 1976)

First Arkansas Confederate Mounted Rifles by Desmond Walls Allen (Arkansas Research, 1988)

Forty-Fifth Arkansas Confederate Cavalry by Desmond Walls Allen (Arkansas Research, 1988)

The Fourteenth Arkansas Confederate Infantry by Desmond Walls Allen (Arkansas Research, 1988)

History of the Twenty-Seventh Arkansas Confederate Infantry by Silas Claiborn Turnbo, edited by Desmond Walls Allen (Arkansas Research, 1988)

Index to Arkansas Confederate Pension Applications compiled by Desmond Walls Allen (Arkansas Research, 1991)
Index to Arkansas Confederate Soldiers, 3 vols. by Desmond Walls Allen (Arkansas Research, 1990)

Rugged and Sublime: The Civil War in Arkansas edited by Mark K. Christ (University of Arkansas Press, 1994)

The Seventh Arkansas Confederate Infantry by Desmond Walls Allen (Arkansas Research, 1988)

Thirty-Eighth Arkansas Confederate Infantry by Desmond Walls Allen (Arkansas Research, 1988)

The Twenty-Seventh Arkansas Confederate Infantry by Desmond Walls Allen (D.W. Allen, 1987)

☞ PROBATE RECORDS

Index to Wills and Administrators of Arkansas from the Earliest to 1900 edited by Mrs. James Harold and Mrs. Edward Lynn Westbrooke (Vowels Print Co., 1986)

☞ VITAL RECORDS

Arkansas Death Record Index, 4 vols. by Desmond Walls Allen with the Arkansas State Department of Health (Arkansas Research, 1996-1999)

The Arkansas Gazette Obituaries Index, 1819-1879 by Stephen J. Chism (Southern Historical Press, 1990)

Arkansas Marriage Notices, 1819-1845 by James Logan Morgan (Arkansas Research, 1992)

Arkansas Marriage Records by James Logan Morgan (Arkansas Research, 1994)

Arkansas Newspaper Abstracts, 1819-1845 by James Logan Morgan (Arkansas Research, 1992)

Arkansas Newspaper Index, 1819-1845: Index to Obituaries, Biographical Notes and Probate and Chancery Notices from Arkansas Newspapers, 1819-1845 by James Logan Morgan (Morgan Books, 1981)

Guide to Vital Statistic Records in Arkansas: Volume II, Church Archives from the Arkansas Historical Survey Project, Work Projects Administration (Historical Records Survey)

Index to Sources for Arkansas Cemetery Inscriptions compiled by the Daughters of the American Revolution, Prudence Hall (DAR, 1976)

•-COUNTY DETAILS-•

ARKANSAS
101 Court Sq., DeWitt, AR 72042, (870) 946-4349,
<www.rootsweb.ancestry.com/~ararkans>
- **INCORPORATED:** Dec. 31, 1813
- **PARENT COUNTY:** Original county
- **BIRTH RECORDS:** start in 1914, kept by Department of Health
- **MARRIAGE:** 1838, County Clerk
- **DIVORCE:** 1803, Circuit Court
- **DEATH:** 1914, Department of Health
- **LAND:** unknown, Circuit Court
- **PROBATE:** 1809, County Clerk
- **COURT:** 1803, Circuit Court

ASHLEY
215 E. Jefferson St., Hamburg, AR 71646, (870) 853-5243,
<www.rootsweb.ancestry.com/~arashley>
- **INCORPORATED:** Nov. 30, 1848
- **PARENT COUNTIES:** Chicot, Drew, Union
- **BIRTH RECORDS:** start in 1914, kept by Department of Health
- **MARRIAGE:** 1848, County Clerk
- **DIVORCE:** unknown start, Circuit Court
- **DEATH:** 1914, Department of Health
- **LAND:** unknown, County Clerk
- **PROBATE:** unknown, County Clerk

BAXTER
Courthouse Sq., 1 E. Seventh St., Mountain Home, AR 72653, (870) 425-3475, **<www.baxtercounty.org>**
- **INCORPORATED:** March 24, 1873
- **PARENT COUNTIES:** Fulton, Izard, Marion, Searcy
- **BIRTH RECORDS:** start in 1914, kept by Department of Health
- **MARRIAGE:** unknown start, County Clerk
- **DIVORCE:** unknown, County Clerk
- **DEATH:** 1914, Department of Health
- **LAND:** unknown, County Clerk
- **PROBATE:** unknown, County Clerk
- **COURT:** unknown, County Clerk

BENTON
Box 699, Bentonville, AR 72712, (479) 271-1013,
<www.co.benton.ar.us>
- **INCORPORATED:** Sept. 30, 1836
- **PARENT COUNTY:** Washington
- **BIRTH RECORDS:** start in 1914, kept by Department of Health
- **MARRIAGE:** 1861, County Clerk
- **DIVORCE:** unknown start, Circuit Court
- **DEATH:** 1914, Department of Health
- **LAND:** unknown, Circuit Court
- **PROBATE:** 1859, County Clerk
- **COURT:** unknown, Circuit Court

BOONE
100 N. Main St., Harrison, AR 72601, (870) 741-8428,
<boonecountyar.com>
- **INCORPORATED:** April 9, 1869
- **PARENT COUNTIES:** Carrol, Madison
- **BIRTH RECORDS:** start in 1914, kept by Department of Health
- **MARRIAGE:** 1869, County Clerk
- **DIVORCE:** unknown start, Circuit Court
- **DEATH:** 1914, Department of Health
- **LAND:** unknown, Circuit Court
- **PROBATE:** 1869, County Clerk
- **COURT:** unknown, Circuit Court

BRADLEY
101 E. Cedar St., Warren, AR 71671, (870) 226-3853,
<www.rootsweb.ancestry.com/~arbradle>
- **INCORPORATED:** Dec. 18, 1840
- **PARENT COUNTY:** Union
- **BIRTH RECORDS:** start in 1914, kept by Department of Health
- **MARRIAGE:** 1846, County Clerk
- **DIVORCE:** unknown start, Circuit Court
- **DEATH:** 1914, Department of Health
- **LAND**: unknown, Circuit Court
- **PROBATE:** 1850, County Clerk
- **COURT:** unknown, Circuit Court

CALHOUN
Box 626, Hampton, AR 71744, (870) 798-2517,
<www.rootsweb.ancestry.com/~arcalhou>
- **INCORPORATED:** Dec. 6, 1850
- **PARENT COUNTIES:** Bradley, Dallas, Ouachita
- **BIRTH RECORDS:** start in 1914, kept by Department of Health
- **MARRIAGE:** 1851, County Clerk
- **DIVORCE:** 1880, County Clerk
- **DEATH:** 1914, Department of Health
- **LAND:** 1851, County Clerk
- **PROBATE:** 1880, County Clerk
- **COURT:** 1880, County Clerk

CARROLL
210 W. Church St., Berryville, AR 72616, (870) 423-2967,
<co.carroll.ar.us>
- **INCORPORATED:** Nov. 1, 1833
- **PARENT COUNTY:** Izard
- **BIRTH RECORDS:** start in 1914, kept by Department of Health
- **MARRIAGE:** 1870, County Clerk
- **DIVORCE:** 1870, Circuit Court
- **DEATH:** 1914, Department of Health
- **LAND:** 1870, Circuit Court
- **PROBATE:** 1870, County Clerk
- **COURT:** 1870, Circuit Court

CHICOT
108 Main St., Lake Village, AR 71653, (870) 265-8000,
<www.kindredtrails.com/AR_Chicot.html>
- **INCORPORATED:** Oct. 25, 1823
- **PARENT COUNTY:** Arkansas

- **BIRTH RECORDS:** start in 1914, kept by Department of Health
- **MARRIAGE:** 1839, County Clerk
- **DIVORCE:** unknown, Circuit Court
- **DEATH:** 1914, Department of Health
- **LAND:** unknown, Circuit Court
- **PROBATE:** 1839, County Clerk
- **COURT:** 1824, Circuit Court

CLARK

Courthouse Sq., 401 Clay St., Arkadelphia, AR 71923, (870) 246-4491, **<www.clarkcountyarkansas.com>**
- **INCORPORATED:** Dec. 15, 1818
- **PARENT COUNTY:** Arkansas
- **BIRTH RECORDS:** start in 1914, kept by Department of Health
- **MARRIAGE:** 1821, County Clerk
- **DIVORCE:** unknown, Circuit Court
- **DEATH:** 1914, Department of Health
- **LAND:** unknown, Circuit Court
- **PROBATE:** 1800, County Clerk
- **COURT:** unknown, Circuit Court

CLAY

Box 306, Piggott, AR 72454, (870) 598-2813, **<www.argenweb.net/clay>**
- **INCORPORATED:** March 24, 1873
- **PARENT COUNTIES:** Randolph, Greene
- **BIRTH RECORDS:** start in 1914, kept by Department of Health
- **MARRIAGE:** 1893, County Clerk
- **DIVORCE:** 1893, Circuit Court
- **DEATH:** 1914, Department of Health
- **LAND:** 1893, Circuit Court
- **PROBATE:** 1893, County Clerk
- **COURT:** 1893, Circuit Court
- **NOTES:** Formerly Clayton County. Name changed to Clay Dec. 6, 1875. Records were burned in 1893.

CLAYTON

- **INCORPORATED:** March 24, 1873
- **PARENT COUNTIES:** Randolph, Greene
- **NOTES:** See Clay County. Named changed to Clay Dec. 6, 1875.

CLEBURNE

300 W. Main St., Heber Springs, AR 72543, (501) 362-4620, **<www.rootsweb.com/~arclebur>**
- **INCORPORATED:** Feb. 20, 1883
- **PARENT COUNTIES:** White, Van Buren, Independence
- **BIRTH RECORDS:** start in 1914, kept by Department of Health
- **MARRIAGE:** 1883, County Clerk
- **DIVORCE:** 1883, County Clerk
- **DEATH:** 1914, Department of Health
- **LAND:** 1883, County Clerk
- **PROBATE:** 1883, County Clerk
- **COURT:** 1883, County Clerk

CLEVELAND

Box 348, Rison, AR 71665, (870) 325-6521, **<argenweb.net/cleveland/index.html>**
- **INCORPORATED:** April 17, 1873
- **PARENT COUNTIES:** Bradley, Dallas, Jefferson, Lincoln
- **BIRTH RECORDS:** start in 1914, kept by Department of Health
- **MARRIAGE:** 1880, County Clerk
- **DIVORCE:** unknown, County Clerk
- **DEATH:** 1914, Department of Health
- **PROBATE:** unknown, County Clerk
- **COURT:** unknown, County Clerk
- **NOTES:** Formerly Dorsey County. Name changed to Cleveland March 5, 1885.

COLUMBIA

1 Court Sq. #1, Magnolia, AR 71753, (870) 235-3774, **<www.countyofcolumbia.net>**
- **INCORPORATED:** Dec. 17, 1852
- **PARENT COUNTIES:** Lafayette, Hempstead, Ouachita
- **BIRTH RECORDS:** start in 1914, kept by Department of Health
- **MARRIAGE:** 1853, County Clerk
- **DIVORCE:** 1860, County Clerk
- **DEATH:** 1914, Department of Health
- **LAND:** 1853, County Clerk
- **PROBATE:** unknown, County Clerk
- **COURT:** 1860, County Clerk

CONWAY

117 S. Moose St., Morrilton, AR 72110, (501) 354-9621, **<www.rootsweb.com/~arconway>**
- **INCORPORATED:** Oct. 20, 1825
- **PARENT COUNTY:** Pulaski
- **BIRTH RECORDS:** start in 1914, kept by Department of Health
- **MARRIAGE:** 1858, County Clerk
- **DIVORCE:** unknown, Circuit Court
- **DEATH:** 1914, Department of Health
- **LAND:** unknown, Circuit Court
- **PROBATE:** unknown, County Clerk
- **COURT:** unknown, Circuit Court

CRAIGHEAD

511 S. Main St., Jonesboro, AR 72401, (501) 354-9621, **<www.craigheadcounty.org>**
- **INCORPORATED:** Feb. 19, 1859
- **PARENT COUNTIES:** Mississippi, Greene, Poinsett
- **BIRTH RECORDS:** start in 1914, kept by Department of Health
- **MARRIAGE:** 1878, County Clerk
- **DIVORCE:** 1878, Circuit Court
- **DEATH:** 1914, Department of Health
- **LAND:** 1900, Circuit Court
- **PROBATE:** 1878, County Clerk
- **COURT:** 1878, Circuit Court

CRAWFORD

300 Main St., Van Buren, AR 72956, (501) 474-1312, **<www.crawford-county.org>**
- **INCORPORATED:** Oct. 18, 1820
- **PARENT COUNTY:** Pulaski
- **BIRTH RECORDS:** start in 1914, kept by Department of Health
- **MARRIAGE:** 1877, County Clerk
- **DIVORCE:** unknown, Circuit Court
- **DEATH:** 1914, Department of Health

- **LAND:** 1877, Circuit Court
- **PROBATE:** 1877, County Clerk
- **COURT:** 1877, Circuit Court

CRITTENDEN

100 Court St., Marion, AR 72364, (870) 739-4434,
<www.rootsweb.ancestry.com/~arcritte>

- **INCORPORATED:** Oct. 22, 1825
- **PARENT COUNTY:** Phillips
- **BIRTH RECORDS:** start in 1914, kept by Department of Health
- **MARRIAGE:** unknown, County Clerk
- **DIVORCE:** unknown, Circuit Court
- **DEATH:** 1914, Department of Health
- **LAND:** unknown, County Assessor
- **PROBATE:** unknown, County Clerk
- **COURT:** unknown, Circuit Court
- **MILITARY:** unknown, Circuit Court

CROSS

705 Union Ave. E. #8, Wynne, AR 72364, (870) 238-5735,
<www.crosscountyar.com>

- **INCORPORATED:** Nov. 15, 1862
- **PARENT COUNTIES:** Crittenden, Poinsett, St. Francis
- **BIRTH RECORDS:** start in 1914, kept by Department of Health
- **MARRIAGE:** 1863, County Clerk
- **DIVORCE:** 1866, Chancery Circuit Clerk
- **DEATH:** 1914, Department of Health
- **LAND:** 1865, Circuit Court
- **PROBATE:** 1863, County Clerk
- **COURT:** 1865, Circuit Court
- **COUNTY COURT:** 1865, County Clerk
- **TAX:** 1865, County Clerk

DALLAS

206 W. Third St., Fordyce, AR 71742, (870) 238-5735,
<www.argenweb.net/dallas>

- **INCORPORATED:** Jan. 1, 1845
- **PARENT COUNTIES:** Clark, Bradley
- **BIRTH RECORDS:** start in 1914, kept by Department of Health
- **MARRIAGE:** 1855, County Clerk
- **DIVORCE:** unknown, County Clerk
- **DEATH:** 1914, Department of Health
- **LAND:** 1845, County Clerk
- **PROBATE:** unknown, County Clerk
- **COURT:** unknown, County Clerk

DESHA

604 Robert S. Moore Ave., Arkansas City, AR 71630,
(870) 877-2323, **<www.rootsweb.ancestry.com/~ardesha>**

- **INCORPORATED:** Dec. 12, 1838
- **PARENT COUNTIES:** Arkansas, Chicot
- **BIRTH RECORDS:** start in 1914, kept by Department of Health
- **MARRIAGE:** 1865, County Clerk
- **DIVORCE:** unknown, Circuit Court
- **DEATH:** 1914, Department of Health
- **LAND:** unknown, Circuit Court
- **PROBATE:** unknown, County Clerk
- **COURT:** unknown, Circuit Court

DORSEY

- **INCORPORATED:** April 17, 1873
- **PARENT COUNTIES:** Bradley, Dallas, Jefferson, Lincoln
- **NOTES:** See Cleveland County. Name changed to Cleveland March 5, 1885.

DREW

210 S. Main St., Monticello, AR 71655, (870) 460-6260, **<www.kindredtrails.com/AR_Drew.html>**

- **INCORPORATED:** Nov. 26, 1846
- **PARENT COUNTIES:** Arkansas, Bradley
- **BIRTH RECORDS:** start in 1914, kept by Department of Health
- **MARRIAGE:** unknown, County Clerk
- **DIVORCE:** unknown, Circuit Court
- **DEATH:** 1914, Department of Health
- **LAND:** unknown, County Assessor
- **PROBATE:** unknown, County Clerk
- **COURT:** unknown, Circuit Court
- **MILITARY:** unknown, Circuit Court

FAULKNER

801 Locust St., Conway, AR 72034, (501) 450-4910,
<www.faulknercounty.org>

- **INCORPORATED:** April 12, 1873
- **PARENT COUNTIES:** Conway, Pulaski
- **BIRTH RECORDS:** start in 1914, kept by Department of Health
- **MARRIAGE:** 1873, County Clerk
- **DEATH:** 1914, Department of Health
- **PROBATE:** 1873, County Clerk
- **COURT:** 1873, County Clerk

FRANKLIN

211 W. Commercial St., Ozark, AR 72949, (501) 667-3607,
<www.rootsweb.ancestry.com/~arfrankl>

- **INCORPORATED:** Dec. 19, 1837
- **PARENT COUNTY:** Crawford
- **BIRTH RECORDS:** start in 1914, kept by Department of Health
- **MARRIAGE:** 1850, County Clerk
- **DEATH:** 1914, Department of Health
- **LAND:** 1899, County Clerk
- **PROBATE:** 1838, County Clerk

FULTON

Box 278, Salem, AR 72576, (870) 895-3310,
<www.argenweb.net/fulton>

- **INCORPORATED:** Dec. 21, 1842
- **PARENT COUNTY:** Izard
- **BIRTH RECORDS:** start in 1914, kept by Department of Health
- **MARRIAGE:** 1887, County Clerk
- **DIVORCE:** 1891, County Clerk
- **DEATH:** 1914, Department of Health
- **LAND:** 1891, County Clerk
- **PROBATE:** 1891, County Clerk
- **COURT:** 1891, County Clerk

GARLAND

501 Ouachita Ave., Hot Springs, AR 71901, (501) 622-3600,
<www.garlandcounty.org>

- **INCORPORATED:** April 5, 1873
- **PARENT COUNTY:** Saline
- **BIRTH RECORDS:** start in 1914, kept by Department of Health
- **MARRIAGE:** unknown, County Clerk
- **DIVORCE:** unknown, Circuit Court
- **DEATH:** 1914, Department of Health
- **LAND:** unknown, Circuit Court
- **PROBATE:** unknown, County Clerk
- **COURT:** unknown, Circuit Court

GRANT

101 W. Center St. #106, Sheridan, AR 72150, (870) 942-2551, **<grantcountyar.com>**

- **INCORPORATED:** Feb. 4, 1869
- **PARENT COUNTIES:** Jefferson, Hot Springs, Saline
- **BIRTH RECORDS:** start in 1914, kept by Department of Health
- **MARRIAGE:** 1877, County Clerk
- **DIVORCE:** 1877, County Clerk
- **DEATH:** 1914, Department of Health
- **LAND:** 1877, County Clerk
- **PROBATE:** 1877, County Clerk
- **COURT:** 1877, County Clerk

GREENE

320 West Court St., Paragould, AR 72450, (870) 239-6311, **<www.greenecountyar.com>**

- **INCORPORATED:** Nov. 5, 1833
- **PARENT COUNTY:** Lawrence
- **BIRTH RECORDS:** start in 1914, kept by Department of Health
- **MARRIAGE:** 1876, County Clerk
- **DIVORCE:** unknown, Circuit Court
- **DEATH:** 1914, Department of Health
- **LAND:** 1876, County Clerk
- **PROBATE:** 1876, County Clerk
- **COURT:** 1876, County Clerk

HEMPSTEAD

Box 1420, Hope, AR 71801, (870) 777-2241, **<www.argenweb.net/hempstead>**

- **INCORPORATED:** Dec. 15, 1818
- **PARENT COUNTY:** Arkansas
- **BIRTH RECORDS:** start in 1914, kept by Department of Health
- **MARRIAGE:** 1823, County Clerk
- **DEATH:** 1914, Department of Health
- **LAND:** 1900, County Clerk
- **PROBATE:** 1823, County Clerk

HOT SPRING

210 Locust St., Malvern, AR 72104, (501) 332-2291, **<www.argenweb.net/hotspring>**

- **INCORPORATED:** Nov. 2, 1829
- **PARENT COUNTY:** Clark
- **BIRTH RECORDS:** start in 1914, kept by Department of Health
- **MARRIAGE:** 1825, County Clerk
- **DIVORCE:** unknown, Circuit Court
- **DEATH:** 1914, Department of Health
- **PROBATE:** 1834, County Clerk
- **COURT:** unknown, Circuit Court

HOWARD

421 N. Main St., Nashville, AR 71852, (870) 845-7502, **<www.genealogyshoppe.com/arhoward>**

- **INCORPORATED:** April 17, 1873
- **PARENT COUNTIES:** Pike, Hempstead, Polk, Sevier
- **BIRTH RECORDS:** start in 1914, kept by Department of Health
- **MARRIAGE:** 1873, County Clerk
- **DIVORCE:** 1873, Circuit Court
- **DEATH:** 1914, Department of Health
- **LAND:** 1873, Circuit Court
- **PROBATE:** 1873, County Clerk
- **COURT:** 1873, Circuit Court

INDEPENDENCE

192 E. Main St., Batesville, AR 72501, (870) 793-8828, **<www.independencecounty.com>**

- **INCORPORATED:** Oct. 23, 1820
- **PARENT COUNTIES:** Lawrence, Arkansas
- **BIRTH RECORDS:** start in 1914, kept by Department of Health
- **MARRIAGE:** 1826, County Clerk
- **DIVORCE:** unknown, Circuit Court
- **DEATH:** 1914, Department of Health
- **LAND:** unknown, Circuit Court
- **PROBATE:** 1839, County Clerk
- **COURT:** unknown, Circuit Court
- **BURIAL:** unknown, County Librarian

IZARD

Box 327, Melbourne, AR 72556, (870) 368-4328, **<backwardbranch.com/arizard/index.html>**

- **INCORPORATED:** Oct. 27, 1825
- **PARENT COUNTY:** Independence
- **BIRTH RECORDS:** start in 1914, kept by Department of Health
- **MARRIAGE:** 1889, County Clerk
- **DIVORCE:** 1889, County Clerk
- **DEATH:** 1914, Department of Health
- **LAND:** 1889, County Clerk
- **PROBATE:** 1889, County Clerk
- **COURT:** 1889, County Clerk
- **NOTES:** Border with Sharp County changed March 9, 1877.

JACKSON

208 Main St., Newport, AR 72112, (870) 523-7420, **<www.jacksoncountyar.org>**

- **INCORPORATED:** Nov. 5, 1829
- **PARENT COUNTY:** Independence
- **BIRTH RECORDS:** start in 1914, kept by Department of Health
- **MARRIAGE:** 1843, County Clerk
- **DIVORCE:** 1845, Circuit Court
- **DEATH:** 1914, Department of Health
- **LAND:** unknown, Circuit Court
- **PROBATE:** 1845, County Clerk
- **COURT:** 1845, Circuit Court

JEFFERSON

101 W. Barraque St., Pine Bluff, AR 71601, (870) 541-5360, **<www.rootsweb.ancestry.com/~arjeffer>**

- **INCORPORATED:** Nov. 2, 1829

- **PARENT COUNTIES:** Arkansas, Pulaski
- **BIRTH RECORDS:** start in 1914, kept by Department of Health
- **MARRIAGE:** 1830, County Clerk
- **DIVORCE:** unknown, Circuit Court
- **DEATH:** 1914, Department of Health
- **LAND:** unknown, Circuit Court
- **PROBATE:** 1845, County Clerk
- **COURT:** unknown, Circuit Court

JOHNSON

215 W. Main St., Box 57, Clarksville, AR 72830, (501) 754-3967,
<www.johnsoncountygenealogy.com>

- **INCORPORATED:** Nov. 16, 1833
- **PARENT COUNTY:** Pope
- **BIRTH RECORDS:** start in 1914, kept by Department of Health
- **MARRIAGE:** 1855, County Clerk
- **DIVORCE:** unknown, Circuit Court
- **DEATH:** 1914, Department of Health
- **LAND:** unknown, Circuit Court
- **PROBATE:** 1844, County Clerk
- **COURT:** unknown, Circuit Court
- **BURIAL:** unknown, Extension Office

LAFAYETTE

1 Courthouse Sq., Lewisville, AR 71845, (870) 921-4858,
<www.lafayettecounty.arkansas.gov>

- **INCORPORATED:** Oct. 15, 1827
- **PARENT COUNTY:** Hempstead
- **BIRTH RECORDS:** start in 1914, kept by Department of Health
- **MARRIAGE:** 1848, County Clerk
- **DIVORCE:** unknown, Circuit Court
- **DEATH:** 1914, Department of Health
- **LAND:** unknown, Circuit Court
- **PROBATE:** unknown, County Clerk

LAWRENCE

Box 553, 315 W. Main, Walnut Ridge, AR 72476, (870) 886-1111,
<www.arkansasgenealogy.com/lawrence>

- **INCORPORATED:** Jan. 15, 1815
- **PARENT COUNTY:** New Madrid, MO
- **BIRTH RECORDS:** start in 1914, kept by Department of Health
- **MARRIAGE:** unknown, County Clerk
- **DEATH:** 1914, Department of Health
- **PROBATE:** unknown, County Clerk

LEE

15 E. Chestnut St., Marianna, AR 72360, (870) 295-7715,
<www.rootsweb.ancestry.com/~arlee2/lee.htm>

- **INCORPORATED:** April 17, 1873
- **PARENT COUNTIES:** Phillips, Monroe, Crittenden, St. Francis
- **BIRTH RECORDS:** start in 1914, kept by Department of Health
- **MARRIAGE:** 1873, County Clerk
- **DIVORCE:** 1873, Circuit Court
- **DEATH:** 1914, Department of Health
- **PROBATE:** 1873, County Clerk
- **COURT:** 1873, Circuit Court
- **TAX:** 1873, County Clerk
- **MILITARY:** 1873, Circuit Court

LINCOLN

300 S. Drew St., Star City, AR 71667, (870) 628-4217,
<www.kindredtrails.com/AR_Lincoln.htm>

- **INCORPORATED:** March 28, 1871
- **PARENT COUNTIES:** Arkansas, Bradley, Desha, Drew, Jefferson
- **BIRTH RECORDS:** start in 1914, kept by Department of Health
- **MARRIAGE:** 1871, County Clerk
- **DEATH:** 1914, Department of Health
- **LAND:** 1871, County Clerk
- **PROBATE:** 1871, County Clerk
- **TAX:** unknown, County Clerk

LITTLE RIVER

351 N. Second St., Ashdown, AR 71822, (870) 898-7208,
<www.littlerivercounty.org>

- **INCORPORATED:** March 5, 1867
- **PARENT COUNTY:** Hempstead
- **BIRTH RECORDS:** start in 1914, kept by Department of Health
- **MARRIAGE:** 1880, County Clerk
- **DIVORCE:** unknown, Circuit Court
- **DEATH:** 1914, Department of Health
- **LAND:** unknown, Circuit Court
- **PROBATE:** 1880, County Clerk

LOGAN

25 W. Walnut St., Paris, AR 72855, (479) 963-3601,
<www.rootsweb.ancestry.com/~arlogan>

- **INCORPORATED:** March 22, 1871
- **PARENT COUNTIES:** Pope, Franklin, Johnson, Scott, Yell
- **BIRTH RECORDS:** start in 1914, kept by Department of Health
- **MARRIAGE:** unknown, County Clerk
- **DIVORCE:** unknown, Circuit Court
- **DEATH:** 1914, Department of Health
- **LAND:** unknown, Circuit Court
- **PROBATE:** unknown, County Clerk
- **COURT:** unknown, Circuit Court
- **NOTES:** Formerly Sarber County. Name changed to Logan Dec. 14, 1875.

LONOKE

Box 431, Lonoke, AR 72086, (501) 676-6403,
<www.rootsweb.ancestry.com/~arlonoke>

- **INCORPORATED:** April 16, 1873
- **PARENT COUNTIES:** Pulaski, Prairie
- **BIRTH RECORDS:** start in 1914, kept by Department of Health
- **MARRIAGE:** unknown, County Clerk
- **DEATH:** 1914, Department of Health
- **PROBATE:** unknown, County Clerk
- **NOTES:** Some Lonoke County records are in Des Arc, Prairie County.

LOVELY

- **INCORPORATED:** 1827
- **PARENT COUNTY:** Northwest Arkansas & Northeast Oklahoma
- **NOTES:** Lost to Oklahoma and abolished 1828.

MADISON
201 W. Main St., Huntsville, AR 72740, (501) 738-6721,
<www.argenweb.net/madison>
- **INCORPORATED:** Sept. 30, 1836
- **PARENT COUNTY:** Washington
- **BIRTH RECORDS:** start in 1914, kept by Department of Health
- **MARRIAGE:** 1901, County Clerk
- **DEATH:** 1914, Department of Health
- **PROBATE:** 1901, County Clerk

MARION
Box 545, Yellville, AR 72687, (870) 449-6226,
<www.argenweb.net/marion>
- **INCORPORATED:** Nov. 3, 1835
- **PARENT COUNTY:** Izard
- **BIRTH RECORDS:** start in 1914, kept by Department of Health
- **MARRIAGE:** 1888, County Clerk
- **DIVORCE:** 1888, County Clerk
- **DEATH:** 1914, Department of Health
- **LAND:** 1888, County Clerk
- **PROBATE:** 1888, County Clerk
- **COURT:** 1888, County Clerk
- **NOTES:** Formerly Searcy County. Name changed to Marion Sept. 29, 1836.

MILLER
400 Laurel St., Texarkana, AR 71854, (870) 744-1501,
<www.millercounty.arkansas.gov>
- **INCORPORATED:** December 1874
- **PARENT COUNTY:** Lafayette
- **BIRTH RECORDS:** start in 1914, kept by Department of Health
- **MARRIAGE:** 1875, County Clerk
- **DIVORCE:** unknown, Circuit Court
- **DEATH:** 1914, Department of Health
- **LAND:** 1875, County Clerk
- **PROBATE:** 1875, County Clerk
- **COURT:** unknown, Circuit Court

MILLER, OLD
- **INCORPORATED:** April 1, 1820
- **PARENT COUNTY:** Hempstead
- **NOTES:** Abolished 1836. Re-established December 1874 from Lafayette County.

MISSISSIPPI
200 W. Walnut, Blytheville, AR 72315, (870) 763-3212,
<www.rootsweb.com/~armissi2>
- **INCORPORATED:** Nov. 1, 1833
- **PARENT COUNTY:** Crittenden
- **BIRTH RECORDS:** start in 1914, kept by Department of Health
- **MARRIAGE:** 1850, County Clerk
- **DIVORCE:** 1866, Circuit Court
- **DEATH:** 1914, Department of Health
- **LAND:** 1865, Circuit Court
- **PROBATE:** 1865, County Clerk
- **COURT:** 1866, Circuit Court

MONROE
123 Madison St., Clarendon, AR 72029, (870) 747-3921,
<www.argenweb.net/monroe>
- **INCORPORATED:** Nov. 2, 1829
- **PARENT COUNTIES:** Phillips, Arkansas
- **BIRTH RECORDS:** start in 1914, kept by Department of Health
- **MARRIAGE:** 1850, County Clerk
- **DIVORCE:** 1839, Circuit Court
- **DEATH:** 1914, Department of Health
- **LAND:** 1829, Circuit Court
- **PROBATE:** 1839, County Clerk
- **COURT:** 1830, Circuit Court

MONTGOMERY
1 George St., Mount Ida, AR 71957, (870) 867-3521,
<www.rootsweb.ancestry.com/~armontgo>
- **INCORPORATED:** Dec. 9, 1842
- **PARENT COUNTY:** Hot Spring
- **BIRTH RECORDS:** start in 1914, kept by Department of Health
- **MARRIAGE:** 1845, County Clerk
- **DIVORCE:** 1845, County Clerk
- **DEATH:** 1914, Department of Health
- **LAND:** 1845, County Clerk
- **PROBATE:** 1845, County Clerk
- **COURT:** 1845, County Clerk
- **BURIAL:** unknown, County Agent

NEVADA
215 E. Second St. S., Prescott, AR 71857, (870) 887-3115,
<www.rootsweb.ancestry.com/~arnevada>
- **INCORPORATED:** March 20, 1871
- **PARENT COUNTIES:** Hempstead, Columbia, Ouachita
- **BIRTH RECORDS:** start in 1914, kept by Department of Health
- **MARRIAGE:** 1871, County Clerk
- **DIVORCE:** 1871, Circuit Court
- **DEATH:** 1914, Department of Health
- **LAND:** 1871, Circuit Court
- **PROBATE:** 1871, County Clerk
- **COURT:** 1871, Circuit Court

NEWTON
100 Court St., Jasper, AR 82641, (870) 446-5335,
<newtoncountyar.com>
- **INCORPORATED:** Dec. 14, 1842
- **PARENT COUNTY:** Carroll
- **BIRTH RECORDS:** start in 1914, kept by Department of Health
- **MARRIAGE:** 1866, County Clerk
- **DEATH:** 1914, Department of Health
- **LAND:** 1866, County Clerk
- **PROBATE:** 1880, County Clerk
- **COURT:** 1880, County Clerk

OUACHITA

145 Jefferson St., Camden, AR 71701, (870) 837-2220,
<www.rootsweb.ancestry.com/~arouachi>

- **INCORPORATED:** Nov. 29, 1842
- **PARENT COUNTY:** Union
- **BIRTH RECORDS:** start in 1914, kept by Department of Health
- **MARRIAGE:** 1875, County Clerk
- **DIVORCE:** unknown, Circuit Court
- **DEATH:** 1914, Department of Health
- **LAND:** unknown, Circuit Court
- **PROBATE:** 1875, County Clerk
- **COURT:** unknown, Circuit Court

PERRY

Box 358, Perryville, AR 72126, (501) 889-5126, **<www.rootsweb.ancestry.com/~arperry>**

- **INCORPORATED:** Dec. 18, 1840
- **PARENT COUNTY:** Conway
- **BIRTH RECORDS:** start in 1914, kept by Department of Health
- **MARRIAGE:** 1882, County Clerk
- **DIVORCE:** 1882, County Clerk
- **DEATH:** 1914, Department of Health
- **LAND:** 1882, County Clerk
- **PROBATE:** 1882, County Clerk
- **COURT:** 1882, County Clerk

PHILLIPS

600 Cherry St., Helena, AR 72342, (870) 338-5505,
<www.rootsweb.ancestry.com/~arphill2/phillips.htm>

- **INCORPORATED:** May. 1, 1820
- **PARENT COUNTIES:** Arkansas, Hempstead
- **BIRTH RECORDS:** start in 1914, kept by Department of Health
- **MARRIAGE:** 1831, County Clerk
- **DIVORCE:** 1820, Circuit Court
- **DEATH:** 1914, Department of Health
- **LAND:** 1820, Circuit Court
- **PROBATE:** 1850, County Clerk
- **COURT:** 1820, Circuit Court

PIKE

Box 219, Murfreesboro, AR 71958, (870) 285-2231,
<s239292887.onlinehome.us>

- **INCORPORATED:** Nov. 1, 1833
- **PARENT COUNTIES:** Clark, Hempstead
- **BIRTH RECORDS:** start in 1914, kept by Department of Health
- **MARRIAGE:** 1895, County Clerk
- **DIVORCE:** 1895, County Clerk
- **DEATH:** 1914, Department of Health
- **LAND:** 1895, County Clerk
- **PROBATE:** 1895, County Clerk
- **COURT:** 1895, County Clerk
- **MILITARY:** 1895, County Clerk

POINSETT

401 Market St., Harrisburg, AR 72432, (870) 578-4410,
<www.poinsettcounty.us>

- **INCORPORATED:** Feb. 28 1838
- **PARENT COUNTIES:** Greene, St. Francis
- **BIRTH RECORDS:** start in 1914, kept by Department of Health
- **MARRIAGE:** 1873, County Clerk
- **DIVORCE:** unknown, Circuit Court
- **DEATH:** 1914, Department of Health
- **LAND:** unknown, Circuit Court
- **PROBATE:** unknown, County Clerk
- **COURT:** unknown, Circuit Court

POLK

507 Church Ave., Mena, AR 71953, (479) 394-8123,
<www.argenweb.net/polk>

- **INCORPORATED:** Nov. 30, 1844
- **PARENT COUNTY:** Sevier
- **BIRTH RECORDS:** start in 1914, kept by Department of Health
- **MARRIAGE:** 1885, County Clerk
- **DIVORCE:** unknown, Circuit Court
- **DEATH:** 1914, Department of Health
- **LAND:** 1885, Circuit Court
- **PROBATE:** 1900, County Clerk
- **COURT:** 1885, Circuit Court
- **MILITARY:** unknown, Circuit Court

POPE

100 W. Main St., Russellville, AR 72801, (479) 968-6064,
<www.pope.countyservice.net>

- **INCORPORATED:** Nov. 2, 1829
- **PARENT COUNTY:** Crawford
- **BIRTH RECORDS:** start in 1914, kept by Department of Health
- **MARRIAGE:** 1831, County Clerk
- **DIVORCE:** unknown, Circuit Court
- **DEATH:** 1914, Department of Health; 1965, County Clerk
- **LAND:** unknown, Circuit Court
- **PROBATE:** 1831, County Clerk
- **COURT:** 1857, County Clerk
- **VOTER:** 1965, County Clerk
- **MILITARY:** unknown, Circuit Court

PRAIRIE

Box 278, Des Arc, AR 72040, (870) 256-3741,
<www.argenweb.net/prairie>

- **INCORPORATED:** Nov. 25, 1846
- **PARENT COUNTIES:** Pulaski, Monroe
- **BIRTH RECORDS:** start in 1914, kept by Department of Health
- **MARRIAGE:** 1885, see Notes
- **DIVORCE:** 1885, see Notes
- **DEATH:** 1914, Department of Health
- **LAND:** 1885, see Notes
- **PROBATE:** 1885, see Notes
- **COURT:** 1885, see Notes
- **MILITARY:** 1917, see Notes
- **NOTES:** Part of the county was taken from Monroe in 1869. Check Monroe County for earlier records. Monroe County Clerk has naturalizations 1907-1912, as well as the records noted above.

PULASKI

401 W. Markham St., Little Rock, AR 72201, (501) 340-8500,
<www.co.pulaski.ar.us>

- **INCORPORATED:** Dec. 15, 1818

- **PARENT COUNTY:** Arkansas
- **BIRTH RECORDS:** start in 1914, kept by Department of Health
- **MARRIAGE:** 1838, County Clerk
- **DIVORCE:** unknown, Chancery Court
- **DEATH:** 1914, Department of Health
- **LAND:** unknown, Circuit Court
- **PROBATE:** 1820, County Clerk
- **COURT:** unknown, Circuit Court
- **VOTER:** 1952, County Clerk
- **NOTES:** History Commission has Probate records before 1920. Real estate, personal property, and poll tax records from the mid-1800s are with the county clerk.

RANDOLPH

107 W. Broadway, Pocahontas, AR 72455, (870) 892-5822,
<www.randolphchamber.com>

- **INCORPORATED:** Dec. 18, 1832
- **PARENT COUNTY:** Creek Cession of 1832
- **BIRTH RECORDS:** start in 1914, kept by Department of Health
- **MARRIAGE:** 1837, County Clerk
- **DIVORCE:** 1836, County Clerk
- **DEATH:** 1914, Department of Health
- **LAND:** 1836, County Clerk
- **PROBATE:** 1837, County Clerk
- **COURT:** 1836, County Clerk
- **MILITARY:** 1836, County Clerk

SALINE

215 N. Main, Suite 9, Benton, AR 72015, (501) 303-5630,
<www.salinecounty.org>

- **INCORPORATED:** Nov. 2, 1835
- **PARENT COUNTIES:** Pulaski, Hempstead
- **BIRTH RECORDS:** start in 1914, kept by Department of Health
- **MARRIAGE:** 1836, County Clerk
- **DEATH:** 1914, Department of Health
- **LAND:** 1871, County Clerk
- **PROBATE:** 1836, County Clerk

SARBER

- **INCORPORATED:** March 22, 1871
- **PARENT COUNTIES:** Pope, Franklin, Johnson, Scott, Yell
- **NOTES:** See Logan County. Name changed to Logan Dec. 14, 1875.

SCOTT

100 W. 1 St., Suite 1, Waldron, AR 72958, (501) 637-2155, ,
<www.rootsweb.ancestry.com/~arscott/scott.htm>

- **INCORPORATED:** Nov. 5, 1833
- **PARENT COUNTIES:** Pulaski, Crawford, Pope
- **BIRTH RECORDS:** start in 1914, kept by Department of Health
- **MARRIAGE:** 1882, County/Circuit Clerk
- **DIVORCE:** 1882, County/Circuit Clerk
- **DEATH:** 1914, Department of Health
- **LAND:** 1882, County/Circuit Clerk
- **PROBATE:** 1882, County/Circuit Clerk
- **COURT:** 1882, County/Circuit Clerk

SEARCY

Courthouse Sq., Box 297, Marshall, AR 72650, (870) 448-3807,
<www.rootsweb.ancestry.com/~arsearcy>

- **INCORPORATED:** Dec. 13, 1838
- **PARENT COUNTY:** Marion
- **BIRTH RECORDS:** start in 1914, kept by Department of Health
- **MARRIAGE:** 1881, County Clerk
- **DIVORCE:** 1881, County Clerk
- **DEATH:** 1914, Department of Health
- **LAND:** 1866, County Clerk
- **NATURALIZATION:** 1881, County Clerk

SEBASTIAN

35 S. Sixth St., Fort Smith, AR 72901, (479) 782-5065,
<www.sebastiancountyonline.com>

- **INCORPORATED:** Jan. 6, 1851
- **PARENT COUNTIES:** Scott, Polk, Crawford, Van Buren
- **BIRTH RECORDS:** start in 1914, kept by Department of Health
- **MARRIAGE:** 1865, County Clerk
- **DIVORCE:** unknown, Circuit Court
- **DEATH:** 1914, Department of Health
- **LAND:** unknown, Circuit Court
- **PROBATE:** 1866, County Clerk
- **COURT:** unknown, Circuit Court

SEVIER

115 N. Third St., De Queen, AR 71832, (870) 642-2425,
<www.seviercounty-ar.gov>

- **INCORPORATED:** Oct. 17, 1828
- **PARENT COUNTIES:** Hempstead, Miller
- **BIRTH RECORDS:** start in 1914, kept by Department of Health
- **MARRIAGE:** 1829, County Clerk
- **DIVORCE:** unknown, Circuit Court
- **DEATH:** 1914, Department of Health
- **PROBATE:** unknown, Circuit Court
- **COURT:** 1829, County Clerk
- **NATURALIZATION:** unknown, Circuit Court

SHARP

Box 307, Ash Flat, AR 72513, (870) 994-7338,
<www.sharpcounty.org>

- **INCORPORATED:** Jul. 18, 1868
- **PARENT COUNTY:** Lawrence
- **NOTES:** Line between Sharp and Izard changed 1877.
- **BIRTH RECORDS:** start in 1914, kept by Department of Health
- **MARRIAGE:** 1880, County Clerk
- **DIVORCE:** 1880, County Clerk
- **DEATH:** 1914, Department of Health
- **LAND:** 1880, County Clerk
- **PROBATE:** 1880, County Clerk
- **COURT:** 1880, County Clerk

ST. FRANCIS

313 S. Izard St., Forrest City, AR 72335, (870) 261-1725,
<www.argenweb.net/stfrancis>

- **INCORPORATED:** Oct. 13, 1827
- **PARENT COUNTY:** Phillips
- **BIRTH RECORDS:** start in 1914, kept by Department of Health

- **MARRIAGE:** 1875, County Clerk
- **DIVORCE:** unknown, Circuit Court
- **DEATH:** 1914, Department of Health
- **LAND:** unknown, Circuit Court
- **PROBATE:** 1910, County Clerk
- **COURT:** unknown, Circuit Court
- **TAX:** 1910, County Clerk

STONE

Box 120, Mountain View, AR 72560, (870) 269-5550,
<www.rootsweb.ancestry.com/~arscg>

- **INCORPORATED:** April 21, 1873
- **PARENT COUNTIES:** Izard, Independence, Searcy, Van Buren
- **BIRTH RECORDS:** start in 1914, kept by Department of Health
- **MARRIAGE:** 1873, County Clerk
- **DIVORCE:** 1873, County Clerk
- **DEATH:** 1914, Department of Health
- **LAND:** 1873, Circuit Court
- **PROBATE:** 1873, Circuit Court
- **COURT:** 1873, Circuit Court
- **MILITARY:** 1873, Circuit Court

UNION

101 N. Washington St., El Dorado, AR 71730, (870) 864-1910,
<www.argenweb.net/union>

- **INCORPORATED:** Nov. 2, 1829
- **PARENT COUNTIES:** Hempstead, Clark
- **BIRTH RECORDS:** start in 1914, kept by Department of Health
- **MARRIAGE:** 1846, County Clerk
- **DIVORCE:** unknown, Circuit Court
- **DEATH:** 1914, Department of Health
- **LAND:** unknown, Circuit Court
- **PROBATE:** 1846, County Clerk
- **COURT:** unknown, Circuit Court

VAN BUREN

Box 180, Clinton, AR 72031, (501) 745-4140,
<www.rootsweb.com/~arvanbur>

- **INCORPORATED:** Nov. 11, 1833
- **PARENT COUNTIES:** Independence, Conway, Izard
- **BIRTH RECORDS:** start in 1914, kept by Department of Health
- **MARRIAGE:** 1859, County Clerk
- **DIVORCE:** 1874, County Clerk
- **DEATH:** 1914, Department of Health
- **LAND:** 1859, County Clerk
- **PROBATE:** 1860, County Clerk
- **COURT:** 1859, County Clerk

WASHINGTON

280 N. College Ave. #300, Fayetteville, AR 72701, (501) 444-1711,
<www.co.washington.ar.us>

- **INCORPORATED:** Oct. 17, 1828
- **PARENT COUNTY:** Crawford
- **BIRTH RECORDS:** start in 1914, kept by Department of Health
- **MARRIAGE:** 1845, County Clerk
- **DIVORCE:** unknown, Circuit Court
- **DEATH:** 1914, Department of Health
- **LAND:** unknown, Circuit Court
- **PROBATE:** 1828, County Clerk
- **COURT:** unknown, Circuit Court

WHITE

300 N. Spruce St., Searcy, AR 72143, (501) 279-6200,
<www.whitecountyar.org>

- **INCORPORATED:** Oct. 23, 1835
- **PARENT COUNTIES:** Pulaski, Jackson, Independence
- **BIRTH RECORDS:** start in 1914, kept by Department of Health
- **MARRIAGE:** unknown, County Clerk
- **DIVORCE:** unknown, County Clerk
- **DEATH:** 1914, Department of Health
- **LAND:** unknown, County Clerk
- **PROBATE:** unknown, County Clerk
- **COURT:** unknown, County Clerk
- **TAX:** unknown, County Clerk

WOODRUFF

500 N. Third St., Augusta, AR 72006, (870) 347-5206,
<www.rootsweb.ancestry.com/~arwoodru>

- **INCORPORATED:** Nov. 26, 1862
- **PARENT COUNTIES:** Jackson, St. Francis
- **BIRTH RECORDS:** start in 1914, kept by Department of Health
- **MARRIAGE:** 1865, County Clerk
- **DIVORCE:** unknown, Circuit Court
- **DEATH:** 1914, Department of Health
- **LAND:** unknown, Circuit Court
- **PROBATE:** 1865, County Clerk
- **COURT:** unknown, Circuit Court

YELL

<www.argenweb.net/yell>

- **INCORPORATED:** Dec. 5, 1840
- **PARENT COUNTIES:** Pope, Scott
- **BIRTH RECORDS:** start in 1914, kept by Department of Health
- **MARRIAGE:** 1865, County Clerk
- **DIVORCE:** 1865, County Clerk
- **DEATH:** 1914, Department of Health
- **LAND:** 1865, County Clerk
- **PROBATE:** 1865, County Clerk
- **COURT:** 1865, County Clerk
- **NOTES:** Yell County has two county courthouses: Box 219, Danville, AR 72833, (504) 495-2414 or Box 457, Dardanelle, AR 72834, (504) 229-4404.

CALIFORNIA

» BY DAVID A. FRYXELL

HISTORICAL OVERVIEW

California's vast territory and varied cultures make it seem more like a nation—which it was briefly in 1846—than a state. Eyed by England and Russia, California was first settled by the Spanish: Father Junipero Serra arrived at the future site of San Diego in 1769 and began a string of missions along *El Camino Real* (The Royal Highway). Missions would be crucial to the state's history under Spain and, after 1821, Mexico. The Spanish divided California into four districts—San Diego, Monterey, San Francisco, and Santa Barbara—each with a *presidio* (prison) and at least one mission.

Americans had begun crossing the continent to California in 1841, forming the "Bear-Flag Republic" in 1846. The breakaway republic was swept into the US war with Mexico, becoming an American protectorate. California was ceded to the United States in 1848 and became a state two years later.

The fast track to statehood was paved with gold, famously discovered at Sutter's Mill in 1848. More than 300,000 people—the most from New England, Pennsylvania and New York—followed the Gold Rush to California by 1854.

Also among early arrivals were Irish, Italians, and Chinese, whose numbers swelled from seven in 1848 to 20,000 in 1852. Many Chinese also worked on the transcontinental railroad, which linked California to the East in 1869. An 1880s real-estate boom attracted English, Germans, and transplants from the Midwest. After 1885, when Japanese could legally leave their native country, many came to California.

The Great Depression brought the "Okies," whose plight was immortalized by John Steinbeck in *The Grapes of Wrath*. After the industrial boom of World War II, California's population surged, including influxes of African Americans, Mexicans, and Southeast Asians. Today the "Golden State" is America's most populous.

RECORD HIGHLIGHTS

Pre-statehood censuses, called *padrones*, were taken for places including Los Angeles (1790, 1836, 1840), San Carlos (1769), San Luis Obispo (1797, 1798), San Antonio (1798), and Soledad (1798). An 1852 state census covered the entire household and listed each person's previous residence.

research tips

- The biggest challenge facing California researchers can be getting official vital records from the state. Instead, try contacting the county recorder's office where the document was recorded.
- The state library's death index, 1905 to 1997, and its marriage index, 1949 to 1986, are online from 1940 at **<vitals.rootsweb.ancestry.com/ca/death/search.cgi>**.
- An often-overlooked resource is the collection of the Daughters of the American Revolution transcriptions of records, which includes cemeteries, Los Angeles baptisms, pioneer obituaries, Bibles, early wills, and veteran grave registrations.
- Since California is such a large and populous state, some of its counties are enormous. You should always try to pin down the exact locality of your ancestors before contacting an office or society for records.
- Unorthodox resources, such as newspapers, family letters, county records, cemetery inscriptions, etc., can sometimes assist you more in California research than traditional genealogical records.

CENSUS RECORDS

- Federal census: 1850, 1860, 1870, 1880, 1900, 1910, 1920, 1930
- Federal mortality schedules: 1850, 1860, 1870, 1880
- State census: 1852
- Los Angeles census: 1790, 1816, 1836, 1844
- Early mission censuses: 1790s

Several cities took censuses from 1897 to 1938, including Los Angeles (1897), San Jose (1897), San Diego (1899), and Oakland (1902). The first federal census to cover California was in 1850. The state library has mortality schedules for the 1850, 1860, 1870, and 1880 censuses.

You can supplement censuses with the "Great Registers," county voting registers compiled roughly every two years. Early registers included naturalization data fand even physical descriptions. The state library has registers from 1866–1944, and they're on subscription site Ancestry.com.

Churches kept the first vital records, then counties, with statewide registration of births, deaths and marriages starting in 1905. Counties began delayed birth registration in 1943.

Land records can provide clues to early California ancestors. For example, the Spanish Archive Record Group, at the state archives and on Family History Library (FHL) microfilm, covers 1833 to 1845. The National Archives has Mexican land records from 1822 to 1846, as well as the papers of the US commission set up in 1852 to process claims based on Spanish and Mexican land grants. Later federal land records are at the National Archives branches in San Bruno and Riverside, and in the state archives. The FHL also has microfilm of many county deeds and mortgage filings.

You can find San Francisco ship passenger lists in the state library and the National Archives. Angel Island in San Francisco harbor became known as the "Ellis Island of the West," and was the gateway to America for many Chinese.

The biggest challenge facing California researchers, according to Nancy Hendrickson, San Diego genealogist and author of *Finding Your Roots Online* (Betterway Books, 2003), is getting official vital records from the state. The wait for marriage certificates, for example, can stretch to three years. A law combating identify theft further complicates obtaining birth and death certificates.

Frederick Sherman, director of research for the California Genealogical Society, recommends contacting the county recorder's office instead of the state. "It's much faster," he says, "and the cost is the same." Hendrickson suggests turning to published and online transcripts, often from local genealogy societies. Or try the state library's death index, 1905 to 1997, (searchable online from 1940 at **<uvitals.rootsweb.ancestry.com/ca/death/search.cgi>**) and its marriage index, 1949 to 1986. Hendrickson notes that many Californians went to Nevada to get hitched (or un-hitched); the state library also has Nevada marriage and divorce indexes on microfiche.

An often-overlooked resource, Hendrickson adds, is the collection of Daughters of the American Revolution (DAR) transcripts of records, which includes cemeteries, Los Angeles baptisms, pioneer obituaries, Bibles, early wills, and veteran grave registrations. You can access these at the state library or borrow many through the FHL.

Sherman cautions, "California is large and populous. Some of its counties, such as Los Angeles, are huge, so it pays off to make every effort to pin down the town or small locality in which your target persons lived, before you ask for help from a countywide or statewide office or society. This is especially true if you are searching for an obituary."

"Almost everybody in California arrived fairly recently, since 1850," Sherman goes on. "The population grew explosively before record-keeping systems became well-established and efficient. Many early arrivals came through San Francisco, which lost almost all civil records and many church records in the 1906 earthquake and fire. Reconstructing a picture of the early days depends more on scattered resources, such as newspapers, family letters, county records, cemetery inscriptions, etc., than traditional genealogical records."

The Internet can help, too: The Federation of East European Family History Societies' site **<feefhs.org>** includes an ambitious reconstruction of records from when San Francisco was home to so many European immigrants. The San Francisco GenWeb page **<www.sfgenealogy.com>** has an extensive list of links to pre-1906 information.

☞ ARCHIVES, LIBRARIES, AND SOCIETIES

African-American Genealogical Society of Northern California
Box 27485, Oakland, CA 94602,
(877) 884-2843, **<www.aagsnc.org>**

Alameda County Library
2450 Stevenson Blvd., Fremont, CA 94538,
(510) 745-1500, **<www.aclibrary.org>**

Alhambra Historical Society
Box 6687, Alhambra, CA 91802

Alhambra Historical Society Museum
1550 W. Alhambra Rd., Alhambra, CA 91802, (626) 300-8845,
<www.cityofalhambra.org/government/Parks_Recreation/Parks/historical_society.html>

Altadena Heritage
730 E. Altadena Dr., Altadena, CA 91003,
(626) 797-0054, **<www.altadenaheritage.moonfruit.com>**

Altadena Historical Society
730 E. Altadena Dr., Altadena, CA 91001,
(626) 797-8016, **<www.mtlowe.net/altadenahistoricalsociety.htm>**

Amador County Archives
12200-A Airport Rd., Jackson, CA 95642
(209) 223-6389, **<www.co.amador.ca.us/index.aspx?page=525>**

American Historical Society of Germans from Russia, Central California Chapter
3233 N. West Ave., Fresno, CA 93705
(559) 229-8287, **<www.ahsgr.org/fresno/cacentra.html>**

Angel Island Association
Box 866, Tiburon, CA 94920,
(415) 435-3972, **<www.angelisland.org>**

Antelope Valley Genealogical Society
Box 1049, Lancaster, CA 93584,
<www.avgenealogy.org>

Augustan Society
Box 771267, Orlando, FL 32877,
(407) 745-0848,
<www.augustansociety.org>

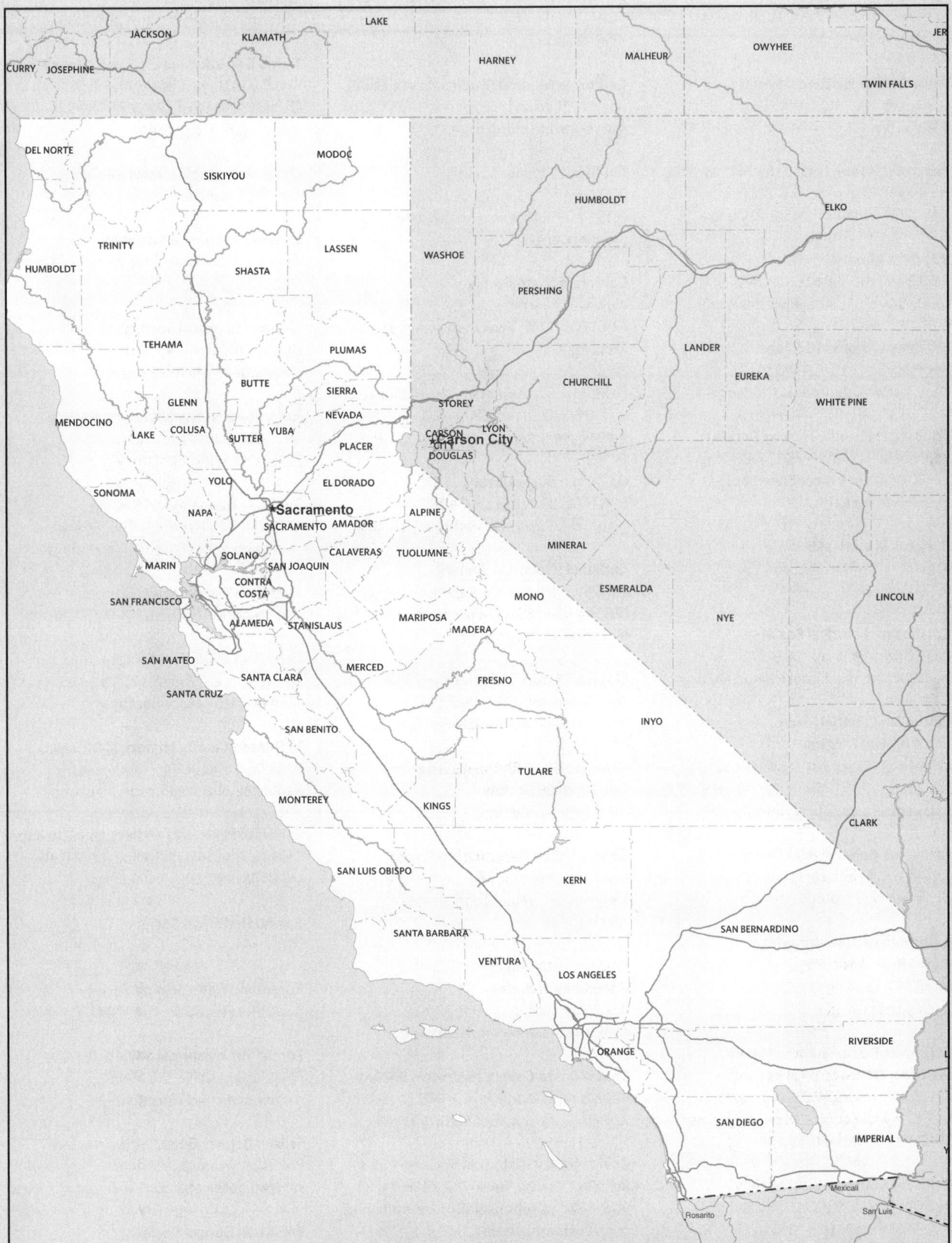
LAKE
JACKSON
KLAMATH
CURRY
JOSEPHINE
HARNEY
MALHEUR
OWYHEE
TWIN FALLS
DEL NORTE
MODOC
SISKIYOU
HUMBOLDT
ELKO
TRINITY
LASSEN
WASHOE
HUMBOLDT
SHASTA
PERSHING
TEHAMA
PLUMAS
LANDER
EUREKA
BUTTE
SIERRA
CHURCHILL
GLENN
STOREY
WHITE PINE
NEVADA
MENDOCINO
COLUSA
YUBA
LYON
LAKE
SUTTER
PLACER
CARSON CITY
Carson City
DOUGLAS
YOLO
EL DORADO
SONOMA
Sacramento
NAPA
ALPINE
SACRAMENTO
AMADOR
MINERAL
CALAVERAS
TUOLUMNE
SOLANO
MARIN
SAN JOAQUIN
CONTRA COSTA
ESMERALDA
MONO
LINCOLN
SAN FRANCISCO
NYE
ALAMEDA
STANISLAUS
MARIPOSA
MADERA
SAN MATEO
MERCED
SANTA CLARA
FRESNO
SANTA CRUZ
INYO
SAN BENITO
TULARE
MONTEREY
KINGS
CLARK
SAN LUIS OBISPO
KERN
SAN BERNARDINO
SANTA BARBARA
VENTURA
LOS ANGELES
RIVERSIDE
ORANGE
SAN DIEGO
IMPERIAL
Mexicali
Rosarito
San Luis

Azusa Historical Society
City Hall Complex, 213 E. Foothill Blvd., Azusa, CA 91702

Baldwin Park Historical Society
Box 1, Baldwin Park, CA 91706, (818) 338-7130

Bancroft Library, University of California
Berkeley, Berkeley, CA 94720, (510) 642-3781, **<bancroft.berkeley.edu>**

Bay Area Library
2471 Flores St., San Mateo, CA 94403, (650) 349-5538 **<baylibraries.org>**

Berkeley Historical Society
Box 1190, Berkeley, CA 94701, **<www.ci.berkeley.ca.us/histsoc>**

British Isles Family History Society
2531 Sawtelle Blvd., PMB 134, Los Angeles, CA 90064, **<www.rootsweb.ancestry.com/~bifhsusa>**

Burbank Historical Society
1015 W. Olive Ave., Burbank, CA 91506, (818) 841-6333

Calabasas Historical Society
Box 8067, Calabasas, CA 91372, **<www.calabasashistoricalsociety.org>**

Calaveras County Library, San Andreas Central
1299 Gold Hunter Rd., San Andreas, CA 95249, (209) 754-6510, **<www.co.calaveras.ca.us/libraryinfo.html>**

Calaveras Genealogical Society
Box 184, Angels Camp, CA 95222, **<calaverasgenealogy.com>**

California African-American Genealogical Society
Box 8442, Los Angeles, CA 90008, **<www.caags.org>**

California Department of Health Services, Office of Vital Records
M.S. 5103, Box 997410, Sacramento, CA 95899, **<www.cdph.ca.gov/programs/CHS/Pages/default.aspx>**

California Genealogical Society
2201 Broadway, Ste. LL2, Oakland, CA, 94612, (510) 663-1358, **<www.calgensoc.org>**

California Mennonite Historical Society
4824 E. Butler Ave., Fresno, CA 93727, **<calmenno.org>**

California Mission Studies Association
Box 420215, San Diego, CA 92142, **<www.ca-missions.org>**

California Pioneer Society
300 Fourth St., San Francisco, CA 94107, (415) 957-1849, **<www.californiapioneers.org>**

California State Archives
1020 O St., Sacramento, CA 95814, (916) 653-7715, **<www.sos.ca.gov/archives>**

California State Genealogical Alliance
Box 10195, Oakland, CA 94610, **<www.csga.com>**

California State Library
900 N St., Sacramento, CA 95814, (916) 654-0266, **<www.library.ca.gov>**

Carlsbad Historical Society
Box 252, Carlsbad, CA 92018, (760) 434-9189, **<www.carlsbadhistoricalsociety.org>**

Clayton Historical Society and Museum
Box 94, Clayton, CA 94517, (925) 672-0240, **<claytonhistory.org>**

Colorado River Blythe-Quartzsite Genealogical Society
411 S. Fifth St., Blythe, CA 92225

Conejo Valley Genealogical Society
Box 1228, Thousand Oaks, CA 91358, **<www.rootsweb.ancestry.com/~cacvgs>**

Contra Costa County Genealogical Society
Box 910, Concord, CA 94522, **<www.rootsweb.com/~cacccgs>**

Contra Costa County Historical Society
610 Main St., Martinez, CA 94553, (925) 229-1042, **<www.cocohistory.com>**

Covina Valley Historical Society
Box 1862, Covina, CA 91722, (626) 966-9871, **<firehousejailmuseum.tripod.com/covinamuseum>**

Dalton Genealogical Club
880 Ames Ct., Palo Alto, CA 94303

Davis Genealogical Club and Library
The Davis Senior Center, 646 A St., Davis, CA 95616, (530) 757-5696, **<davisgenealogy.org>**

Delta Genealogical Interest Group
Box 157, Knightsen, CA 94548

Downey Historical Society
Box 554, 12540 Rives Ave., Downey, CA 90241, (562) 862-2777

Duarte Historical Society
Box 263, Duarte, CA 91009, **<www.duartehistory.org>**

Eagle Rock Valley Historical Society
2225 Colorado Blvd., Eagle Rock, CA 90041, **<eaglerockhistory.org>**

East Bay Genealogical Society
Box 20417, Oakland, CA 94620, **<www.rootsweb.ancestry.com/~caebaygs>**

East Kern Genealogical Society
Box 961, North Edwards, CA 93523

Echo Park Historical Society
Box 26946, Los Angeles, CA 90026, **<www.historicechopark.org>**

El Dorado County Historical Museum
104 Placerville Dr., Placerville, CA 95667, **<www.co.el-dorado.ca.us/museum>**

El Monte Historical Society and Museum
3150 N. Tyler Ave., El Monte, CA 91731, (626) 580-2232

Encino Historical Society
16756 Moorpark St., Encino, CA 91436

Escondido Genealogical Society
Box 2190, Escondido, CA 92025

Forestville Historical Society
Box 195, Forestville, CA 95436, **<www.sonic.net/forestville>**

Fresno County Genealogical Society
Box 1429, Fresno, CA 93716, **<www.rootsweb.com/~cafcgs>**

Fresno Historical Society
7160 W. Kearney Blvd., Fresno, CA 93706,

(559) 441-0862, <www.valley history.org>

Genealogical Association of Sacramento
Box 292145, Sacramento, CA 95829, <home.surewest.net/bbetts/gas.htm>

Genealogical and Historical Council of the Sacramento Valley
Box 214749, Sacramento, CA 95821, <www.sacvalleygenes.net>

Genealogical Society of Coachella Valley
Box 124, Indio, CA 92202

Genealogical Society of the Morongo Basin
Box 234, Yucca Valley, CA 92284, <www.gsmb.info>

Genealogical Society of North Orange County
Box 706, Yorba Linda, CA 92885, <www.gsnocc.org>

Genealogical Society of Riverside
Box 2557, Riverside, CA 92516, <www.gsor.org>

Genealogical Society of Santa Cruz County
Box 72, Santa Cruz, CA 95063

Genealogical Society of Stanislaus County
Box A, Modesto, CA 95352, (209) 529-6467, <www.cagenweb.com/lr/stanislaus/gssc.html>

Genealogy Club of Sun City
Box 175, Sun City, CA 92586, <www.genealogyclub.org>

Genealogy Society of Hispanic Americans of Southern California
Box 2472, Santa Fe Springs, CA 90670 (310) 202-1122, <www.gsha.net>

Genealogy Society of Vallejo-Benicia
734 Marin St., Vallejo, CA 94590, <www.rootsweb.com/~cagsv>

German Genealogical Society of America Southern California Genealogical Society
417 Irving Dr., Burbank, CA 91504, (818) 843-7247, <www.scgsgenealogy.com/Germansig.htm>

Glendale Historical Society
Box 4173, Glendale, CA 91202, (818) 242-7447, <www.glendalehistorical.org>

Glendora Genealogical Group
Box 1141, Glendora, CA 91740, (909) 592-4030

Glendora Historical Society and Museum
314 N. Glendora Ave., Glendora, CA 91741, (626) 963-0419

Golden Gate Chapter, American Historical Society of Germans from Russia <www.ahsgr.org/golden_gate_chapter.htm>

Hayward Area Genealogical Society
Box 754, Hayward, CA 94543, <www.rootsweb.ancestry.com/~cahags>

Hemet-San Jacinto Genealogical Society
Box 2516, Hemet, CA 92546, <www.hsjgs.org>

Hi Desert Genealogical Society
Box 1271, Victorville, CA 92392, <www.cagenweb.com/hdgs>

Historical Society of Centinela Valley
7634 Midfield Ave., Los Angeles, CA 90045, (213) 649-6272

Historical Society of Long Beach
4260 Atlantic Ave., Long Beach, CA 90807, (562) 424-2220 <www.historicalsocietylb.org>

Historical Society of Monterey Park
781 S. Orange Ave., Box 172, Monterey Park, CA 91754

Historical Society of Pomona Valley
1460 E. Holt Ave., Pomona, CA 91767, <www.osb.net/Pomona/default.htm>

Historical Society of Southern California
200 E. Ave. 43, Los Angeles, CA 90031, (323) 460-5632, <www.socalhistory.org>

Historical Society of the Upper Mojave Desert
Box 2001, Ridgecrest, CA 93556, <www.maturango.org/Hist.html>

Holt-Atherton Church Archives
University of the Pacific, 3601 Pacific Ave., Stockton, CA 95211, (209) 946-2404

Hungarian/American Friendship Society
1035 Starbrook Dr., Galt, CA 95632, (209) 744-8099, <www.dholmes.com/hafs.html>

Humboldt County Genealogical Society
2336 G St., Eureka, CA 95501, <www.humboldthistory.org>

Humboldt County Historical Society
703 Eighth St., Box 8000, Eureka, CA 95502, (707) 445-4342, <www.humboldthistory.org>

Immigrant Genealogical Society
Box 7369, Burbank, CA 91510, <www.immigrantgensoc.org>

Jewish Genealogical Society of Los Angeles
Box 55443, Sherman Oaks, CA 91413, (818) 771-5554, <www.jgsla.org>

Jewish Genealogical Society of Orange County
11751 Cherry St., Los Alamitos, CA 90720

Jewish Genealogical Society of Sacramento
1935 Wright St., Sacramento, CA 95825, <www.jewishgen.org/jgs-sacramento>

Jewish Historical Society of Southern California
6505 Wilshire Blvd., Los Angeles, CA 90048, (323) 761-8950, <www.jewishhistoricalsociety.org>

Kern County Genealogical Society
Box 2214, Bakersfield, CA 93303, <www.rootsweb.ancestry.com/~cakcgs>

La Puente Valley Historical Society
Box 522, La Puente, CA 91744, (626) 336-7644

Lake County Genealogical Society
<www.cagenweb.com/lake/lakehistornetwork.htm>

Lake Elsinore Genealogical Society
Box 807, Lake Elsinore, CA 92531, <www.bakerfamily.org/legs>

Leisure World Genealogical Workshop
Leisure World Library, Box 2069, Club House 5, Seal Beach, CA 90740

Livermore-Amador Genealogical Society
Box 901, Livermore, CA 94551,
<www.l-ags.org>

Lomita Historical Society
24016 Benhill Ave., Lomita, CA 90717

Los Angeles City Historical Society
Box 41046, Los Angeles, CA 90041,
(213) 891-4600

Los Banos Genealogical Society
Box 2525, Los Banos, CA 93635

Lucerne Valley Genealogy Association
<www.lucernevalley.net/orgs/roots>

Madera County Genealogical Society
Box 495, Madera, CA 93639, (559) 675-7871, **<www.cagenweb.com/madera>**

Maidu Genealogical Society
Maidu Community Center, 1550 Maidu Dr., Roseville, CA 95661, (916) 786-0186

Marin County Genealogical Society
Box 1511, Novato, CA 94948,
<www.maringensoc.org>

Martinez Historical Society
Box 14, Martinez, CA 94553,
<www.martinezhistory.org>

Mendocino Coast Genealogical Society
Box 762, Fort Bragg, CA 95437

Mendocino County Historical Society
603 W. Perkins St., Ukiah, CA 95482,
<www.pacificsites.com/~mchs>

Merced County Genealogical Society
Box 3061, Merced, CA 95344,
<www.rootsweb.com/~camcgs>

Monterey County Genealogical Society
Box 8144, Salinas, CA 93912,
<www.mocogenso.org>

Monterey County Historical Society
Box 3576, Salinas, CA 93912, (831) 757-8085, **<www.mchsmuseum.com>**

Moraga Historical Society
1500 St. Mary's Rd., Moraga, CA 94556,(925) 377-8734,
<www.moragahistory.org>

Moravian Heritage Society
17907 Kuykendahl, Suite 202, Spring, TX 77379, (281) 251-7690

Mt. Diablo Chapter, American Historical Society of Germans from Russia
849 Camino Ricardo, Moraga, CA 94556, (925) 376-6374, **<www.ahsgr.org/mtdiablo_chapter.htm>**

Mt. Diablo Genealogical Society
Box 4654, Walnut Creek, CA 94596

Napa Valley Genealogical and Biographical Society
1701 Menlo Ave., Napa, CA 94558,
(707) 252-2252, **<www.napavalleygenealogy.org>**

National Archives and Records Administration, Pacific Region, Riverside
23123 Cajalco Road, Perris, CA 92570,
(951) 956-2000, **<archives.gov/pacific/riverside>**

National Archives and Records Administration, Pacific Region, San Francisco
1000 Commodore Dr., San Bruno, CA 94066, (650) 238-3501 , **<archives.gov/pacific/archives/san-francisco>**

Nevada County Genealogical Society
Box 176, Cedar Ridge, CA 95924, **<www.rootsweb.ancestry.com/~cancgs>**

North San Diego County Genealogical Society
Box 581, Carlsbad, CA 92018,
<www.cagenweb.com/nsdcgs>

Orange County Genealogical Society
Box 1587, Orange, CA 92856,
<www.occgs.com>

Pacific Palisades Historical Society
Box 1299, Pacific Palisades, CA 90272,
(310) 454-5037

Palm Springs Genealogical Society
Box 2093, Palm Springs, CA 92263

Paradise Genealogical Society
Box 460, Paradise, CA 95967,
<www.pargenso.org>

Pasadena Genealogical Society
Box 94774, Pasadena, CA 91109

Pasadena Heritage
651 S. St. John Ave., Pasadena, CA 91105, (626) 441-6333, **<www.pasadenaheritage.org>**

Pasadena Historical Society
470 W. Walnut St., Pasadena, CA 91103
(626) 577-1660

Patterson Genies
525 Clover Ave., Patterson, CA 95363

Peter J. Shields Library, University of California, Davis
100 NW Quad, Davis, CA 95616,
(530) 752-6561, **<www.lib.ucdavis.edu/ul/libcoll/shields.php>**

Pico Rivera History and Heritage Society
Box 313, Pico Rivera, CA 90666,
(213) 948-2408

Placer County Genealogical Society
Box 7385, Auburn, CA 95604,
<pcgs.pcgenes.com>

Plumas County Historical Society
Box 695, Quincy, CA 95971

Pocahontas Trails Genealogical Society
3628 Cherokee Lane, Modesto, CA 95356

Polish Genealogical Society of California
Box 713, Midway City, CA 92655,
<pgsca.org>

Pomona Valley Genealogical Society
Box 286, Pomona, CA 91769,
<www.pvgs.us>

Questing Heirs Genealogical Society
Box 15102, Long Beach, CA 90815,
<www.cagenweb.com/questing>

Redondo Beach Historical Society
Box 978, Redondo Beach, CA 90277,
(310) 372-0197, **<www.redondobeachhistorical.org>**

Redwood Genealogical Society
Box 645, Fortuna, CA 95540,
(707) 725-3791

Renegade Root Diggers
9171 Fargo Ave., Hanford, CA 93230

Roman Catholic Diocese of Los Angeles Archival Center
San Fernando Mission, 15151 San Fernando Mission Blvd., Mission Hills, California 91345, (818) 365-1501, **<www.archdiocese.la/about/archival>**

Roman Catholic Diocese of San Diego
3888 Paducah Dr., San Diego, CA 92117, (858) 490-8200, **<www.diocese-sdiego.org>**

Root Cellar, Sacramento Genealogical Society
Box 265, Citrus Heights, CA 95611, **<www.rootcellar.org>**

Roseville Genealogical Society
Box 459, Roseville, CA 95678, **<www.rgsca.org>**

Sacramento German Genealogy Society, **<www.sacgergensoc.org>**

Sacramento Valley Chapter, American Historical Society of Germans from Russia
<www.ahsgr.org/Sacramento_Valley_Chapter.htm>

San Bernardino Valley Genealogical Society
Box 911, San Bernardino, CA 92402, **<www.sbpl.org/genealogy.html>**

San Diego Genealogical Society
7343 Ronson Rd., Suite O, San Diego, CA 92111, (858) 279-7347, **<www.rootsweb.com/~casdgs>**

San Diego Historical Society
Box 81825, San Diego, CA 92138, **<www.sandiegohistory.org>**

San Fernando Valley Genealogical Society
Box 3486, Winnetka, CA 91396, **<www.rootsweb.ancestry.com/~casfvgs>**

San Fernando Valley Historical Society
Andres Pico Adobe, Box 7039, 10940 Sepulveda Blvd., Mission Hills, CA 91346, (818) 365-7810, **<www.sfvhs.com>**

San Francisco Bay Area Jewish Genealogical Society
Box 471616, San Francisco, CA 94147, **<www.jewishgen.org/sfbajgs>**

San Gorgonio Genealogical Society
1050 Brinton Ave., Banning, CA 92220

San Joaquin Genealogical Society
Box 690243, Stockton, CA 95269, **<www.rootsweb.com/~sjgs>**

San Luis Obispo County Genealogical Society
Box 4, Atascadero, CA 93423, **<kcbx.net/~slogen>**

San Luis Obispo County Genealogical Society Library
995 Palm St., San Luis Obispo, CA 93401, (805) 785-0383 **<kcbx.net/~slogen>**

San Luis Obispo County Genealogical Society
Box 4, Atascadero, CA 93423, **<kcbx.net/~slogen>**

San Luis Obispo County Library
Box 8107, San Luis Obispo,CA 93403, (805) 781-5989, **<www.slolibrary.org>**

San Marino Historical Society
Box 80222, San Marino, CA 91118, **<www.smnet.org/comm_group/historical>**

San Mateo County Genealogical Society
Box 5569, San Mateo, CA 94063, (650) 306-3423, **<www.smcgs.org>**

San Ramon Valley Genealogical Society
Box 305, Diablo, CA 94528 , **<srvgensoc.org>**

Santa Barbara County Genealogical Society
Box 1303, Goleta, CA 93116, (805) 884-9909, **<www.sbgen.org>**

Santa Clara County Public Libraries
14600 Winchester Blvd., Los Gatos, CA 95032, **<www.santaclaracountylib.org>**

Santa Clara County Historical and Genealogical Society
2635 Homestead Rd., Santa Clara, CA 95051, **<www.scchgs.org>**

Santa Clarita Valley Historical Society
Box 221925, Newhall, CA 91322, (661) 254-1275, **<www.scvhs.org>**

Santa Cruz Public Libraries
224 Church St., Santa Cruz, CA 95060, (831) 420-5790, **<www.santacruzpl.org>**

Santa Maria Public Library
421 S. McClelland St., Santa Maria, CA 93454, (805) 925-0994, **<www.ci.santa-maria.ca.us/210.html>**

Santa Maria Valley Genealogical Society and Library
Box 1215, Santa Maria, CA 93456

Santa Monica Historical Society Museum
1539 Euclid St., Santa Monica, CA 90404, (310) 395-2290, **<www.santamonicahistory.org>**

Sequoia Genealogical Society
Tulare City Library Genealogical Room, 113 N. F St., Tulare, CA 93274, (559) 685-2342, **<www.cagenweb.com/cpl/tulare>**

Shasta Genealogical Society
Box 493431, Redding, CA 96049, **<www.rootsweb.ancestry.com/~cascogs>**

Siskiyou County Genealogy Society
Box 225, Yreka, CA 96097

Siskiyou County Library
719 Fourth St., Yreka, CA 96097, (530) 841-4175, **<www.snowcrest.net/siskiyoulibrary>**

Slovak Genealogical Research Center
6862 Palmer Ct., Chino, CA 91710, **<www.slovakia.org/society-geneology.htm>**

Solano County Genealogical Society and Library
620 Main St., Vacaville, CA 95688, (707) 446-6869, **<www.rootsweb.ancestry.com/~cascgsi>**

Sonoma County Library, Central Branch
211 E St., Santa Rosa, CA 95404, (707) 545-0831, **<www.sonoma.lib.ca.us>**

Sonoma Genealogical Society
Box 2273, Santa Rosa, CA 95405, **<www.scgs.org/scgs.html>**

South Bay Cities Genealogical Society
Box 11069, Torrance, CA 90510, **<www.rootsweb.ancestry.com/~casbcgs>**

South Orange County Genealogical Society
Box 4513, Mission Viejo, CA 92690, **<www.rootsweb.ancestry.com/~casoccgs>**

Southern California Chapter, American Historical Society of Germans from Russia
16371 Silver Lane, Huntington Beach, CA 92647, **<www.ehrman.net/ahsgr/casocal.html>**

Southern California Genealogical Society
417 Irving Dr., Burbank, CA 91504, (818) 843-7247, **<www.scgsgenealogy.com>**

Spanishtown Historical Society
Box 62, Half Moon Bay, CA 94019, (650) 726-7084

St. Ives Historical Society
8648 Lupine Loop Dr. #5, California City, CA 93505, **<www.saintives.com>**

Stanislaus County Free Library
1500 I St., Modesto, CA 95354, (209) 558-7800, **<www.stanislauslibrary.org>**

Sutro Branch, California State Library
480 Winston Dr., San Francisco, CA 94132, (415) 731-4477, **<www.library.ca.gov>**

Tehama County Genealogical and Historical Society
Box 415, Red Bluff, CA 96080, **<www.tcghsoc.org>**

Temple City Historical Society
Box 1379, Temple City, CA 91780, (626) 279-1784

Topanga Historical Society
Box 1214, Topanga, CA 90290, (310) 455-1969, **<www.topangaonline.com/ths>**

Tracy Area Genealogical Society
1141 Adam St., Tracy, CA 95376, (209) 832-1106 , **<www.rootsweb.ancestry.com/~catags>**

Triadoption Library
Box 5218, Huntington Beach, CA 92646

TRW Genealogical Society
One Space Park S-1420, Redondo Beach, CA 90278

Tulare County Public Library
113 N. F St., Tulare, CA 93274, (559) 685-2341 , **<www.tularepubliclibrary.org>**

Tuolumne County Genealogical Society
158 W. Bradford Ave., Sonora, CA 95370, (209) 532-1317, **<www.tcgsonline.org>**

Vandenberg Genealogical Society
Box 814, Lompoc, CA 93438, (805) 736-9637

Ventura County Genealogical Society
Box 24608, Ventura, CA 93002, **<www.rootsweb.ancestry.com/~cavcgs>**

Ventura County Genealogical Society Library
Camarillo Library, 4101 Las Posas Road, Camarillo, CA 93010, (805) 388-5222, **<www.vencolibrary.org>**

West Covina Historical Society
Box 4597, West Covina, CA 91793

Whittier Area Genealogical Society
Box 4367, Whittier, CA 90607, **<www.cagenweb.com/kr/wags>**

Whittier Historical Society and Museum
6755 Newlin Ave., Whittier, CA 90601, (562) 945-3871, **<www.whittiermuseum.org>**

Workman and Temple Family Homestead Museum
15415 E. Don Julian Rd., City of Industry, CA 91745, (626) 968-8492, **<www.homesteadmuseum.org>**

Yolo County Archives
226 Buckeye St., Woodland, CA 95695, (530) 666-8010

Yolo County Historical Society
Box 1447, Woodland, CA 95776, (530) 662-2212, **<www.yolo.net/ychs>**

Yucaipa Valley Genealogical Society
Box 32, Yucaipa, CA 92399, **<www.yvgs.org>**

GENERAL RESOURCES

California Local History: A Bibliography and Union List of Library Holdings: Supplement to the 2nd Edition Covering Works Published 1961 through 1970 edited by Margaret Miller Rocq (Stanford University Press, 1976)

The California Locator: A Directory of Public Records for Locating People Dead or Alive in California by Laurie Nicklas (Nicklas Publishing Co., 1996)

California Pioneer Register and Index, 1542-1848. Including Inhabitants of Calfornia, 1769-1800, and List of Pioneers by Hubert Howe Bancroft (Regional Publishing Co., 1964)

California Research Outline by the Church of Jesus Christ of Latter-day Saints (online at **<www.familysearch.org/eng/search/RG/guide/california.asp>**)

Contemporary Biography of California's Representative Men, 2 vols., by Alonzo Phelps (Research Publications, Inc., 1968)

The Foreign-Born Voters of 1872 compiled by Jim W. Faulkinbury (J.W. Faulkinbury, 1994)

Genealogical Records of California by Sherman Lee Pompey (1968)

Gold! German Transcontinental Travelers to California, 1849-1851 by Clifford Neal Smith (Westland Publications, 1988)

An Index to the Biographies in 19th Century California County Histories by J. Carlyle Parker (Gale Research Co., 1979)

Index to the DAR Records of the Families of the California Pioneers by the Solano County Genealogical Society (The Society, 1988-1990)

The Spanish Borderlands; a Chronicle of Old Florida and the Southwest by Herbert Eugene Bolton (Yale University Press, 1921)

CENSUS RECORDS

The California 1890 Great Register of Voters Index, 3 vols., compiled by the California State Genealogical Alliance, edited by Janice G. Cloud (Heritage Quest, 2001)

☞IMMIGRATION RECORDS

Manifests of Alien Arrivals at San Ysidro (Tia Juana) California, April 21, 1908-December 1952 by the US Immigration and Naturalization Service and Claire Prechtel-Kluskens (National Archives, 1999)

San Francisco Passenger Departure Lists, 3 vols., by Peter E. Carr (Cuban Index, 1991-1993)

Sea Routes to the Gold Fields; the Migration by Water to California in 1849-1852 by Oscar Lewis (A.A. Knopf, 1949)

☞LAND RECORDS

California Ranchos: Patented Private Land Grants, Listed by County, 2nd edition, by Burgess McK. Shumway, edited by Michael and Mary Burgess (Borgo Press, 1988)

Index to the Spanish-Mexican Private Land Grant Records and Cases of California by J.N. Bowman (J.N. Bowman, 1958)

Spanish and Mexican Land Grants in California by Rose Hollenbaugh Avin´a (Arno Press, 1976)

Veterans Who Applied for Land in Southern California, 1851-1911 compiled by Judy A. Deeter (Gateway Press, 1993)

☞MAPS

California City and Unincorporated Place Names by the California Division of Highways (1971)

California County Boundaries by Owen C. Coy (Berkeley, CA: California Historical Survey Commission, 1923)

California, Index to Topographic and Other Map Coverage by the United States Geological Survey (US Geological Survey, National Mapping Program, 1983)

California Place Names, 3rd edition, by Erwin Gustav Gudde (University of California Press, 1969)

The Dictionary of California Land Names compiled by Phil Townsend Hanna (Automobile Club of Southern California, 1951)

Early California; Early Forts, Old Mines, Old Town Sites prepared by Ralph N. Preston (Western Guide Publishers, 1974)

Historical Atlas of California by Warren A. Beck and Ynez D. Haase (University of Oklahoma Press, 1974)

History of California Post Offices, 1849-1976 by Harold E. Salley (Postal History Associates, 1977)

History of California Post Offices, 1849-1990, 2nd ed., by Harold E. Salley, edited by Edward L. Patera; research by H.E. Salley and E.L. Patera (The Depot, 1991)

Patterns on the Land; Geographical, Historical, and Political Maps of California, 4th edition, by Robert W. Durrenberger (National Press Books, 1972)

Southern and Central California Atlas & Gazetteer, 2nd edition (DeLorme Mapping Co., 1990)

Spanish and Indian Place Names of California by Nellie Van de Grift Sanchez (Arno Press, 1976, ca.1930)

☞MILITARY RECORDS

California Conquered: War and Peace on the Pacific, 1846-1850 by Neal Harlow (University of California Press, 1982)

Honorable Remembrance: the San Diego Master List of the Mormon Battalion edited by Elmer J. Carr (Mormon Battalion Visitors Center, 1978)

Records of California Men in the War of the Rebellion, 1861 to 1867 by the California Adjutant General's Office and Richard H. Orton (Gale Research, 1979)

Sons of the Revolution in the State of California, Centennial Register, 1893-1993 by Richard Hoag Breithaupt Jr., and the Sons of the Revolution in the State of California (Walika, 1994)

Spanish Bluecoats: the Catalonian Volunteers in Northwestern New Spain, 1767-1810 by Joseph P. Sanchez (University of New Mexico Press, 1990)

☞PROBATE RECORDS

1860 California Census Index, 2nd edition, compiled by Bryan Lee Dilts (Index Publishing, 1984)

California County Courthouse Records: A Directory of Vital Records Found in Each County Office in California by Laurie Nicklas (L. Nicklas, 1998)

☞VITAL RECORDS

California Marriage Records Indexes, 1960-1985 by the California State Registrar (Office of the State Registrar, ca.1983)

California's Old Burying Grounds by Helen Marcia Bruner, prepared for the National Society of Colonial Dames of America (Portal Press, 1945)

Graves and Sites on the Oregon and California Trails by the Oregon-California Trails Association (Oregon-California Trails Association, 1991)

Guide to Public Vital Statistics Records in California by the Historical Records Survey (Northern California Historical Records Survey, 1941)

Northern California Marriage Index, 1850-1860 by Nancy Justus Morebeck (N.J. Morebeck, 1993)

Permanent Californians: an Illustrated Guide to the Cemeteries of California by Judi Culbertson and Tom Randall (Chelsea Green Publishing Co., 1989)

A Personal Name Index to Orton's Records of California Men in the War of the Rebellion, 1861 to 1867: index compiled by J. Carlyle Parker (Gale Research Co., 1978)

•-COUNTY DETAILS-•

ALAMEDA
1106 Madison St., Room 101, Oakland, CA 94607
(510) 272-6362 **<www.acgov.org>**
- **INCORPORATED:** March 25, 1853
- **PARENT COUNTIES:** Contra Costa, Santa Clara
- **MARRIAGE RECORDS:** start in 1854, kept by County Clerk
- **DIVORCE:** 1853, County Clerk
- **LAND:** 1853, County Clerk
- **PROBATE:** 1853, County Clerk
- **COURT:** 1853, County Clerk
- **NOTES:** County Clerk has birth records 1919-1988 and some from 1873, as well as death records 1905-1988, and some from 1876.

ALPINE
99 Water St., Box 158, Markleeville, CA 96120, (530) 694-2287, **<www.alpinecountyca.gov>**
- **INCORPORATED:** March 16, 1864
- **PARENT COUNTIES:** El Dorado, Amador, Calaveras, Mono, Tuolumne
- **BIRTH RECORDS:** start in 1900, kept by County Clerk
- **MARRIAGE:** 1900, County Clerk
- **DEATH:** 1900, County Clerk
- **DIVORCE:** 1900, County Clerk
- **LAND:** 1900, County Clerk
- **PROBATE:** 1900, County Clerk
- **COURT:** 1900, County Clerk

AMADOR
500 Argonaut Ln., Jackson, CA 95642, (209) 223-6468, **<www.co.amador.ca.us>**
- **INCORPORATED:** May 11, 1854
- **PARENT COUNTIES:** Calaveras, El Dorado
- **BIRTH RECORDS:** start in 1872, kept by County Clerk
- **DEATH:** 1872, County Clerk
- **DIVORCE:** unknown, Superior Court
- **PROBATE:** unknown, Superior Court
- **COURT:** unknown, Superior Court
- **NATURALIZATION:** unknown, County Archives

BRANCIFORTE
- **INCORPORATED:** Feb. 18, 1850
- **PARENT COUNTY:** Original county
- **NOTES:** See Santa Cruz County. Name changed to Santa Cruz April 5, 1850.

BUTTE
25 County Center Dr., Oroville, CA 95965, (530) 538-7691, **<buttecounty.net>**
- **INCORPORATED:** Feb. 18, 1850
- **PARENT COUNTY:** Original county
- **BIRTH RECORDS:** start in 1859, kept by County Recorder
- **MARRIAGE:** 1851, County Recorder
- **DEATH:** 1859, County Recorder
- **LAND:** unknown, County Recorder
- **NOTES:** Meriam Library, California State University, Chico has divorce, probate, and court records 1850-1879 and naturalization records 1850-1960. You can find probate and court records with the County Clerk 1850 along with divorce records 1850.

CALAVERAS
891 Mountain Ranch Rd., San Andreas, CA 95249, (209) 754-6376, **<co.calaveras.ca.us>**
- **INCORPORATED:** Feb. 18, 1850
- **PARENT COUNTY:** Original county
- **BIRTH RECORDS:** start in 1860, kept by County Recorder
- **MARRIAGE:** 1882, County Recorder
- **DIVORCE:** 1882, County Recorder
- **DEATH:** 1882, County Recorder
- **LAND:** 1852, County Recorder
- **PROBATE:** 1866, County Recorder
- **COURT:** 1866, County Recorder
- **MINING CLAIMS:** 1850, County Recorder

COLUSA
546 Jay St., Colusa, CA 95932, (530) 458-0500, **<www.countyofcolusa.com>**
- **INCORPORATED:** Feb. 18, 1850
- **PARENT COUNTY:** Original county
- **BIRTH RECORDS:** start in 1873, kept by County Clerk
- **MARRIAGE:** 1853, County Clerk
- **DEATH:** 1889, County Clerk
- **LAND:** 1851, County Clerk
- **PROBATE:** 1851, County Clerk
- **COURT:** 1851, County Clerk
- **GREAT REGISTERS:** 1866, County Clerk
- **MILITARY ROLLS:** 1879, County Clerk
- **ASSESSMENT ROLLS:** 1851, County Clerk
- **NOTES:** Colusa County was created in 1850 but attached to Butte County for administration until it was organized in January 1851.

CONTRA COSTA
730 Las Juntas St., Box 350, Martinez, CA 94553, (925) 646-2360, **<www.co.contra-costa.ca.us>**
- **INCORPORATED:** Feb. 18, 1850
- **PARENT COUNTY:** Original county
- **BIRTH RECORDS:** unknown start, kept by County Recorder
- **MARRIAGE:** unknown, County Clerk
- **DIVORCE:** unknown, County Clerk
- **DEATH:** unknown, County Recorder
- **PROBATE:** unknown, County Clerk
- **COURT:** unknown, County Clerk

DEL NORTE
981 H St., Crescent City, CA 95531, (707) 464-7216,
<www.co.del-norte.ca.us>
- **INCORPORATED:** March 2, 1857
- **PARENT COUNTY:** Klamath
- **BIRTH RECORDS:** start in 1873, kept by County Recorder
- **MARRIAGE:** 1873, County Recorder
- **DIVORCE:** 1848, County Clerk
- **DEATH:** 1873, County Recorder
- **LAND:** 1853, County Recorder
- **PROBATE:** 1848, County Clerk
- **COURT:** 1848, County Clerk
- **NOTES:** County Recorder has leases and agreements records 1857-1954.

EL DORADO
360 Fair Ln., Placerville, CA 95667, (530) 621-5490,
<www.co.el-dorado.ca.us>
- **INCORPORATED:** Feb. 18, 1850
- **PARENT COUNTY:** Original county
- **BIRTH RECORDS:** unknown start, kept by County Recorder
- **MARRIAGE:** unknown, County Recorder
- **DIVORCE:** unknown, County Clerk
- **DEATH:** unknown, County Recorder
- **LAND:** unknown, County Recorder
- **PROBATE:** unknown, County Clerk
- **COURT:** unknown, County Clerk
- **MILITARY:** unknown, County Recorder
- **BURIAL:** unknown, County Recorder

FRESNO
2221 Kern St., Fresno, CA 93721, (559) 488-3003,
<www.co.fresno.ca.us>
- **INCORPORATED:** April 19, 1856
- **PARENT COUNTIES:** Merced, Mariposa, Tulare
- **BIRTH RECORDS:** start in 1855, kept by County Clerk
- **MARRIAGE:** 1855, County Clerk
- **DEATH:** 1855, County Clerk

GLENN
526 W. Sycamore St., Box 391, Willows , CA 95988
(530) 934-6412 **<www.countyofglenn.net>**
- **INCORPORATED:** March 11, 1891
- **PARENT COUNTY:** Colusa
- **BIRTH RECORDS:** start in 1887, kept by County Recorder
- **MARRIAGE:** 1891, County Recorder
- **DEATH:** 1905, County Recorder
- **LAND:** 1891, County Recorder
- **PROBATE:** unknown, Superior Ct.
- **COURT:** unknown, Superior Ct.
- **MILITARY:** 1919, County Clerk-Recorder

HUMBOLDT
825 Fifth St., Eureka, CA 95501, (707) 476-2384,
<co.humboldt.ca.us>
- **INCORPORATED:** May 12, 1853
- **PARENT COUNTIES:** Trinity, Klamath
- **BIRTH RECORDS:** unknown start, kept by County Recorder
- **MARRIAGE:** unknown, County Recorder
- **DIVORCE:** 1853, County Clerk
- **DEATH:** unknown, County Recorder
- **LAND:** unknown, County Recorder
- **PROBATE:** 1853, County Clerk
- **COURT:** 1853, County Clerk
- **BURIAL:** unknown, County Recorder

IMPERIAL
940 W. Main St., El Centro, CA 92243, (760) 482-4220,
<www.co.imperial.ca.us>
- **INCORPORATED:** Aug. 6, 1907
- **PARENT COUNTY:** San Diego
- **BIRTH RECORDS:** start in 1907, kept by County Recorder
- **MARRIAGE:** 1907, County Recorder
- **MARRIAGE:** 1907, County Clerk
- **DIVORCE:** 1907, County Clerk
- **DEATH:** 1907, County Recorder
- **PROBATE:** 1907, County Clerk
- **COURT:** 1907, County Clerk

INYO
168 N. Edwards St., Box F, Independence, CA 93526,
(760) 878-0218 **<www.inyocounty.us>**
- **INCORPORATED:** March 22, 1866
- **PARENT COUNTIES:** Tulare, Mono
- **BIRTH RECORDS:** start in 1904, kept by County Clerk
- **MARRIAGE:** 1866, County Clerk
- **DEATH:** 1904, County Clerk
- **LAND:** 1866, County Clerk
- **MINING:** 1872, County Clerk

KERN
1655 Chester Ave., Bakersfield, CA 93301, (661) 868-6449,
<www.co.kern.ca.us>
- **INCORPORATED:** April 2, 1866
- **PARENT COUNTIES:** Tulare, Los Angeles
- **BIRTH RECORDS:** start in 1850, kept by County Recorder
- **MARRIAGE:** 1850, County Recorder
- **DIVORCE:** 1866, County Recorder
- **DEATH:** 1850, County Recorder
- **LAND:** 1850, County Recorder
- **PROBATE:** 1866, County Recorder
- **COURT:** 1866, County Recorder
- **VOTER REGISTRATION:** 1866, County Recorder
- **NOTES:** Exchanged territory with San Bernardino County in 1963.

KINGS
1400 W. Lacey Blvd., Hanford, CA 93230, (559) 582-3211,
<www.countyofkings.com>
- **INCORPORATED:** March 22, 1893
- **PARENT COUNTY:** Tulare
- **BIRTH RECORDS:** start in 1893, kept by County Clerk
- **MARRIAGE:** 1893, County Clerk
- **DIVORCE:** 1893, County Clerk
- **DEATH:** 1893, County Clerk
- **LAND:** 1893, County Clerk
- **PROBATE:** 1893, County Clerk

- **COURT:** 1893, County Clerk
- **NATURALIZATION:** 1893, County Clerk

KLAMATH
- **INCORPORATED:** April 25, 1851
- **PARENT COUNTY:** Original county
- **NOTES:** Dissolved March 28, 1874.

LAKE
255 N. Forbes St., Lakeport, CA 95453, (707) 263-2368,
<www.co.lake.ca.us>
- **INCORPORATED:** May 20, 1861
- **PARENT COUNTY:** Napa
- **BIRTH RECORDS:** start in 1867, kept by County Clerk
- **MARRIAGE:** 1867, County Clerk
- **DIVORCE:** unknown, Superior Court
- **DEATH:** 1867, County Clerk
- **LAND:** 1867, County Clerk
- **PROBATE:** unknown, Superior Court
- **COURT:** unknown, Superior Court
- **MINING:** unknown, County Clerk

LASSEN
220 S. Lassen St., Susanville, CA 96130, (530) 251-8216,
<www.co.lassen.ca.us>
- **INCORPORATED:** April 1, 1864
- **PARENT COUNTIES:** Plumas, Shasta
- **MARRIAGE RECORDS:** start in 1864, kept by County Recorder
- **DIVORCE:** 1864, County Clerk
- **LAND:** 1857, County Recorder
- **PROBATE:** 1864, County Clerk
- **COURT:** 1864, County Clerk
- **NATURALIZATION:** 1864, County Clerk
- **NOTES:** County Recorder has birth and death records, some prior to 1907 but incomplete before 1929.

LOS ANGELES
12400 E. Imperial Hwy., Box 1024, Norwalk, CA 90650
(562) 462-2137 **<lacounty.gov>**
- **INCORPORATED:** Feb. 18, 1850
- **PARENT COUNTY:** Original county
- **BIRTH RECORDS:** unknown start, kept by County Recorder
- **MARRIAGE:** unknown, County Recorder
- **DIVORCE:** 1880, County Clerk
- **DEATH:** unknown, County Recorder
- **LAND:** unknown, County Recorder
- **PROBATE:** 1850, County Clerk
- **COURT:** 1850, County Clerk

MADERA
209 W. Yosemite Ave., Madera, CA 93637, (559) 675-7700,
<www.madera-county.com>
- **INCORPORATED:** March 11, 1893
- **PARENT COUNTY:** Fresno
- **BIRTH RECORDS:** start in 1893, kept by County Clerk
- **MARRIAGE:** 1893, County Clerk
- **DIVORCE:** 1893, County Clerk
- **DEATH:** 1893, County Clerk
- **LAND:** 1893, County Clerk
- **PROBATE:** 1893, County Clerk
- **COURT:** 1893, County Clerk
- **NOTES:** County Clerk has some voting records.

MARIN
3501 Civic Center Dr., San Rafael, CA 94903, (415) 499-6094,
<www.co.marin.ca.us>
- **INCORPORATED:** Feb. 18, 1850
- **PARENT COUNTY:** Original county
- **BIRTH RECORDS:** start in 1863, kept by County Recorder
- **MARRIAGE:** 1856, County Recorder
- **DIVORCE:** 1900, County Clerk
- **DEATH:** 1863, County Recorder
- **LAND:** 1852, County Recorder
- **PROBATE:** 1880, County Clerk
- **COURT:** 1900, County Clerk

MARIPOSA
5100 Bullion St., Mariposa, CA 95338, (209) 966-5719,
<www.mariposacounty.org>
- **INCORPORATED:** Feb. 18, 1850
- **PARENT COUNTY:** Original county
- **BIRTH RECORDS:** unknown start, kept by County Recorder
- **MARRIAGE:** unknown, County Recorder
- **DIVORCE:** unknown, County Clerk
- **DEATH:** unknown, County Recorder
- **PROBATE:** unknown, County Clerk
- **COURT:** unknown, County Clerk
- **BURIAL:** unknown, County Recorder

MENDOCINO
501 Low Gap Rd., Room 1090, Ukiah, CA 95482, (707) 463-4221,
<www.co.mendocino.ca.us>
- **INCORPORATED:** Feb. 18, 1850
- **PARENT COUNTY:** Original county
- **BIRTH RECORDS:** unknown start, kept by County Recorder
- **MARRIAGE:** unknown, County Recorder
- **DIVORCE:** 1858, Superior Ct.
- **DEATH:** unknown, County Recorder
- **LAND:** unknown, County Recorder
- **PROBATE:** 1872, Superior Ct.
- **COURT:** 1858, Superior Ct.
- **NOTES:** Some old records are in Sonoma County.

MERCED
2222 M St., Merced, CA 95340, (209) 385-7627,
<www.co.merced.ca.us>
- **INCORPORATED**: April 19, 1855
- **PARENT COUNTY:** Mariposa
- **BIRTH RECORDS:** unknown start, kept by County Recorder
- **MARRIAGE:** unknown, County Recorder
- **DIVORCE:** 1855, County Clerk
- **DEATH:** unknown, County Recorder
- **PROBATE:** 1855, County Clerk
- **COURT:** 1855, County Clerk
- **BURIAL:** unknown, County Recorder

MODOC
204 Court St., Alturas, CA 96101, (530) 233-6205,
<www.modoccounty.us>
- **INCORPORATED:** Feb. 17, 1874
- **PARENT COUNTY:** Siskiyou
- **BIRTH RECORDS:** unknown, kept by County Recorder
- **MARRIAGE:** unknown, County Recorder
- **DIVORCE:** 1874, County Clerk
- **DEATH:** unknown start, County Recorder
- **PROBATE:** 1874, County Clerk
- **COURT:** 1874, County Clerk
- **VOTER REGISTRATION**: 1874, County Clerk

MONO
Bryant Annex 2, Box 537, Bridgeport, CA 93517, (760) 932-5241,
<www.monocounty.ca.gov>
- **INCORPORATED:** April 24, 1861
- **PARENT COUNTIES:** Calaveras, Fresno
- **BIRTH RECORDS:** start in 1861, kept by County Clerk
- **MARRIAGE:** 1861, County Clerk
- **DIVORCE:** 1900, County Clerk
- **DEATH:** 1900, County Clerk
- **LAND:** 1900, County Clerk
- **PROBATE:** 1900, County Clerk
- **COURT:** 1900, County Clerk
- **BURIAL:** 1900, County Clerk

MONTEREY
240 Church St., Box 29, Salinas, CA 93902, (831) 755-5041,
<www.co.monterey.ca.us>
- **INCORPORATED:** Feb. 18, 1850
- **PARENT COUNTY:** Original county
- **BIRTH RECORDS:** start in 1893, kept by County Recorder
- **MARRIAGE:** 1893, County Recorder
- **DIVORCE:** unknown, County Court
- **DEATH:** 1893, County Recorder
- **LAND:** unknown, Superior Court
- **PROBATE:** unknown, Superior Court
- **COURT:** unknown, County Court

NAPA
Box 298, Napa, CA 94559, (707) 253-4246,
<www.countyofnapa.org>
- **INCORPORATED:** Feb. 18, 1850
- **PARENT COUNTY:** Original county
- **BIRTH RECORDS:** start in 1873, kept by County Recorder
- **MARRIAGE:** 1850, County Recorder
- **DIVORCE:** 1850, Court Executive Officer
- **DEATH:** 1873, County Recorder
- **LAND:** 1850, County Recorder
- **PROBATE:** 1850, Court Executive Officer
- **COURT:** 1850, Court Executive Officer

NEVADA
950 Maidu Ave., Nevada City, CA 95959, (530) 265-1221,
<mynevadacounty.com>
- **INCORPORATED:** April 25, 1851
- **PARENT COUNTY:** Yuba
- **BIRTH RECORDS:** start in 1873, kept by County Clerk
- **MARRIAGE:** 1856, County Clerk
- **DIVORCE:** 1880, County Clerk
- **DEATH:** 1873, County Clerk
- **LAND:** 1856, County Clerk
- **PROBATE:** 1880, County Clerk
- **COURT:** 1880, County Clerk

ORANGE
12 Civic Center Pl., Santa Ana, CA 92701, (714) 834-2500,
<www.san-benito.ca.us>
- **INCORPORATED:** March 11, 1889
- **PARENT COUNTY:** Los Angeles
- **BIRTH RECORDS:** unknown start, kept by County Recorder
- **MARRIAGE:** unknown, County Recorder
- **DIVORCE:** 1964, County Clerk
- **DEATH:** unknown, County Recorder
- **LAND:** unknown, County Recorder
- **PROBATE:** 1964, County Clerk
- **COURT:** 1964, County Clerk

PLACER
2954 Richardson Dr., Auburn, CA 95603, (530) 886-5600,
<www.placer.ca.gov>
- **INCORPORATED:** April 25, 1851
- **PARENT COUNTIES:** Yuba, Sutter
- **BIRTH RECORDS:** start in 1873, kept by County Recorder
- **MARRIAGE:** 1873, County Recorder
- **DEATH:** 1873, County Recorder
- **LAND:** 1850, County Recorder
- **PROBATE:** 1851, County Clerk
- **COURT:** 1880, County Clerk

PLUMAS
520 Main St., Quincy, CA 95971 , (530) 283-6218,
<www.countyofplumas.com>
- **INCORPORATED:** March 18, 1854
- **BIRTH RECORDS:** start in 1860, kept by County Recorder
- **MARRIAGE:** 1860, County Recorder
- **DIVORCE:** 1860, County Clerk
- **DEATH:** 1860, County Recorder
- **LAND:** 1860, County Recorder
- **PROBATE:** 1860, County Recorder
- **COURT:** 1860, County Recorder

RIVERSIDE
2724 Gateway Dr., Box 751, Riverside, CA 92502, (951) 486-7000,
<www.countyofriverside.us>
- **INCORPORATED:** March 11, 1893
- **PARENT COUNTIES:** San Diego, San Bernardino
- **BIRTH RECORDS:** start in 1893, kept by County Recorder
- **MARRIAGE:** 1893, County Recorder
- **DIVORCE:** 1893, Superior Court
- **DEATH:** 1893, County Recorder
- **LAND:** 1893, County Recorder
- **PROBATE:** 1893, Superior Court
- **COURT:** 1893, Superior Court

SACRAMENTO
Box 839, Sacramento, CA 95812, (916) 874-6334,
<www.saccounty.net>
- **INCORPORATED:** Feb. 18, 1850
- **PARENT COUNTY:** Original county
- **BIRTH RECORDS:** unknown start, kept by County Recorder
- **MARRIAGE:** unknown, County Recorder
- **DIVORCE:** 1880, County Clerk
- **DEATH:** unknown, County Recorder
- **LAND:** unknown, County Recorder
- **PROBATE:** 1880, County Clerk
- **COURT:** 1880, County Clerk

SAN BENITO
440 Fifth St., Second Floor, Hollister, CA 95023, (831) 636-4029,
<www.san-benito.ca.us>
- **INCORPORATED:** Feb. 12, 1874
- **PARENT COUNTY:** Monterey
- **BIRTH RECORDS:** start in 1894, kept by County Clerk
- **MARRIAGE:** 1894, County Clerk
- **DIVORCE:** unknown, Superior Ct.
- **DEATH:** 1894, County Clerk
- **LAND:** 1894, County Clerk
- **PROBATE:** unknown, Superior Ct.
- **COURT:** unknown, Superior Ct.
- **NATURALIZATION:** 1894, County Clerk
- **BURIAL:** 1894, County Clerk

SAN BERNARDINO
222 W. Hospitality Ln., San Bernardino, CA 92415, (909) 387-8306,
<www.co.san-bernardino.ca.us>
- **INCORPORATED:** April 26, 1853
- **PARENT COUNTIES:** Los Angeles, San Diego
- **BIRTH RECORDS:** start in 1853, kept by County Recorder
- **MARRIAGE:** 1857, County Recorder
- **DIVORCE:** 1856, County Clerk
- **DEATH:** 1853, County Recorder
- **LAND:** 1854, County Clerk
- **PROBATE:** 1856, County Clerk
- **COURT:** 1853, County Clerk

SAN DIEGO
1600 Pacific Hwy., San Diego, CA 92101, (619) 238-8158,
<www.sdcounty.ca.gov>
- **INCORPORATED:** Feb. 18, 1850
- **PARENT COUNTY:** Original county
- **BIRTH RECORDS:** start in 1857, kept by County Recorder
- **MARRIAGE:** 1856, County Recorder
- **DIVORCE:** unknown, Superior Ct.
- **DEATH:** 1873, County Recorder
- **LAND:** 1850, County Recorder
- **PROBATE:** unknown, Superior Ct.
- **COURT:** unknown, Superior Ct.

SAN FRANCISCO
1 Dr. Carlton B. Goodlett Pl., San Francisco, CA 94102,
(415) 554-4950, **<www.ci.sf.ca.us>**
- **INCORPORATED:** Feb. 18, 1850
- **PARENT COUNTY:** Original county
- **BIRTH RECORDS:** unknown start, kept by Department of Public Health
- **MARRIAGE:** unknown, County Recorder
- **DIVORCE:** unknown, Superior Court
- **PROBATE:** unknown, Superior Court
- **COURT:** unknown, Superior Court

SAN JOAQUIN
24 S. Hunter St. #304, Box 1968, Stockton, CA 95201,
(209) 468-8075, **<www.co.san-joaquin.ca.us>**
- **INCORPORATED:** Feb. 18, 1850
- **PARENT COUNTY:** Original county
- **BIRTH RECORDS:** unknown start, kept by County Recorder
- **MARRIAGE:** unknown, County Recorder
- **DIVORCE:** 1851, County Clerk
- **DEATH:** unknown, County Recorder
- **LAND:** unknown, County Recorder
- **PROBATE:** 1851, County Clerk
- **COURT:** 1851, County Clerk

SAN LUIS OBISPO
1144 Monterey St. Suite C, San Luis Obispo, CA 93408
(805) 781-5080, **<www.slocounty.ca.gov>**
- **INCORPORATED:** Feb. 18, 1850
- **PARENT COUNTY:** Original county
- **BIRTH RECORDS:** start in 1873, kept by County Recorder
- **MARRIAGE:** 1850, County Recorder
- **DIVORCE:** unknown, County Clerk
- **DEATH:** 1850, County Recorder
- **LAND:** 1842, County Recorder
- **PROBATE:** unknown, County Clerk
- **COURT:** unknown, County Clerk

SAN MATEO
400 County Center, Redwood City, CA 94063, (650) 363-4712,
<www.co.sanmateo.ca.us>
- **INCORPORATED:** April 19, 1856
- **PARENT COUNTY:** San Francisco
- **BIRTH RECORDS:** start in 1866, kept by County Recorder
- **MARRIAGE:** 1866, County Recorder
- **DIVORCE:** 1880, County Recorder
- **DEATH:** 1866, County Recorder
- **LAND:** 1880, County Recorder
- **PROBATE:** 1856, County Recorder
- **COURT:** 1880, County Recorder

SANTA BARBARA
105 E. Anapamu, Room #204, Santa Barbara, CA 93101
(805) 568-2550, **<www.countyofsb.org>**
- **INCORPORATED:** Feb. 18, 1850
- **PARENT COUNTY:** Original county
- **BIRTH RECORDS:** start in 1850, kept by County Recorder
- **MARRIAGE:** 1850, County Recorder

- **DIVORCE:** unknown, Superior Ct.
- **DEATH:** 1850, County Recorder
- **LAND:** 1850, County Recorder
- **PROBATE:** unknown, Superior Ct.
- **COURT:** unknown, Superior Ct.
- **NATURALIZATION:** unknown, Superior Ct.

SANTA CLARA

70 W. Hedding St., First Floor, San Jose, CA 95110, (408) 299-2481, **<www.sccgov.org>**

- **INCORPORATED:** Feb. 18, 1850
- **PARENT COUNTY:** Original county
- **BIRTH RECORDS:** start in 1873, kept by County Recorder
- **MARRIAGE:** 1850, County Recorder
- **DIVORCE:** unknown, County Clerk
- **DEATH:** 1873, County Recorder
- **LAND:** 1846, County Recorder
- **PROBATE:** unknown, County Clerk
- **NATURALIZATION:** unknown, County Clerk
- **MILITARY:** 1920, County Recorder

SANTA CRUZ

701 Ocean St., Santa Cruz, CA 95060, (831) 454-2800, **<www.co.santa-cruz.ca.us>**

- **INCORPORATED:** Feb. 18, 1850
- **PARENT COUNTY:** Original county
- **BIRTH RECORDS:** start in 1905, kept by County Recorder
- **MARRIAGE:** 1850, County Recorder
- **DIVORCE:** unknown, Superior Court
- **DEATH:** 1905, County Recorder
- **LAND:** 1850, County Recorder
- **PROBATE:** unknown, Superior Court
- **COURT:** unknown, Superior Court
- **MILITARY:** 1930, County Recorder
- **NOTES:** Formerly Branciforte County. Name changed to Santa Cruz April 5, 1850.

SHASTA

Box 990880, Redding, CA 96099, (530) 225-5730, **<www.co.shasta.ca.us>**

- **INCORPORATED:** Feb. 18, 1850
- **PARENT COUNTY:** Original county
- **BIRTH RECORDS:** unknown start, kept by County Recorder
- **MARRIAGE:** unknown, County Recorder
- **DIVORCE:** 1880, County Clerk
- **DEATH:** unknown, County Recorder
- **PROBATE:** 1880, County Clerk
- **COURT:** 1880, County Clerk

SIERRA

100 Courthouse Sq., Suite 11, Downieville, CA 95936, **<www.sierracounty.ws>**

- **INCORPORATED:** April 16, 1852
- **PARENT COUNTY:** Yuba
- **BIRTH RECORDS:** start in 1857, kept by County Recorder
- **MARRIAGE:** 1852, County Recorder
- **DIVORCE:** 1852, Superior Ct.
- **DEATH:** 1862, County Recorder
- **LAND:** 1852, County Recorder
- **PROBATE:** 1852, Superior Ct.
- **COURT:** 1852, Superior Ct.
- **NATURALIZATION:** 1852, Superior Ct.

SISKIYOU

311 Fourth St., Box 8, Yreka, CA 96097, (530) 842-8065, **<www.co.siskiyou.ca.us>**

- **INCORPORATED:** March 22, 1852
- **PARENT COUNTIES:** Shasta, Klamath
- **BIRTH RECORDS:** unknown start, kept by County Recorder
- **MARRIAGE:** unknown, County Recorder
- **DIVORCE:** 1853, Court Services
- **DEATH:** unknown, County Recorder
- **PROBATE:** 1853, Court Services
- **COURT:** 1853, Court Services
- **BURIAL:** unknown, County Recorder
- **ELECTION:** unknown, County Clerk
- **NOTES:** County Clerk has board of supervisors minutes from 1860.

SOLANO

701 Texas St., Fairfield, CA 94533, (707) 421-6265, **<www.co.solano.ca.us>**

- **INCORPORATED:** Feb. 18, 1850
- **PARENT COUNTY:** Original county
- **BIRTH RECORDS:** unknown start, kept by County Recorder
- **MARRIAGE:** unknown, County Recorder
- **DIVORCE:** 1850, County Clerk
- **DEATH:** unknown, County Recorder
- **LAND:** unknown, County Recorder
- **PROBATE:** 1850, County Clerk
- **COURT:** 1850, County Clerk

SONOMA

2300 County Center Dr., LaPlaza Building B177, Santa Rosa, CA 95403, (707) 565-3800, **<www.sonoma-county.org>**

- **INCORPORATED:** Feb. 18, 1850
- **PARENT COUNTY:** Original county
- **BIRTH RECORDS:** unknown start, kept by County Recorder
- **MARRIAGE:** unknown, County Recorder
- **DIVORCE:** 1850, County Clerk
- **DEATH:** unknown, County Recorder
- **LAND:** unknown, County Recorder
- **PROBATE:** 1850, County Clerk
- **COURT:** 1850, County Clerk
- **BURIAL:** unknown, County Recorder

STANISLAUS

Box A, Modesto, CA 95352, (209) 525-6467, **<www.co.stanislaus.ca.us>**

- **INCORPORATED:** April 1, 1854
- **PARENT COUNTY:** Tuolumne
- **BIRTH RECORDS:** start in 1900, kept by County Clerk Recorder
- **MARRIAGE:** 1870, County Clerk Recorder
- **DIVORCE:** 1854, Superior Court
- **DEATH:** 1900, County Clerk Recorder
- **LAND:** 1854, County Recorder

- **PROBATE:** 1854, Superior Court
- **COURT:** 1854, Superior Court

SUTTER
433 Second St., Yuba City, CA 95992, (530) 822-7120,
<www.co.sutter.ca.us>
- **INCORPORATED**: Feb. 18, 1850
- **PARENT COUNTY:** Original county
- **BIRTH RECORDS:** start in 1873, kept by County Recorder
- **MARRIAGE:** 1850, County Recorder
- **DIVORCE:** unknown, Superior Court
- **DEATH:** 1873, County Recorder
- **LAND:** 1850, County Recorder
- **PROBATE:** 1850, Superior Court
- **COURT:** unknown, Superior Court
- **MILITARY:** 1850, County Recorder

TEHAMA
633 Washington St., Red Bluff, CA 96080, (530) 527-3350,
<www.co.tehama.ca.us>
- **INCORPORATED:** April 9, 1856
- **PARENT COUNTIES:** Colusa, Butte, Shasta
- **BIRTH RECORDS:** start in 1889, kept by County Clerk
- **MARRIAGE:** 1856, County Clerk
- **DEATH:** 1889, County Clerk
- **MILITARY:** 1944, County Clerk

TRINITY
101 Court St., Box 1258, Weaverville, CA 96093, (530) 623-1215,
<www.trinitycounty.org>
- **INCORPORATED:** Feb. 18, 1850
- **PARENT COUNTY:** Original county
- **BIRTH RECORDS:** start in 1905, kept by County Recorder
- **MARRIAGE:** 1905, County Recorder
- **DIVORCE:** 1881, Court Services
- **DEATH:** 1905, County Recorder
- **LAND:** unknown, Court Services
- **PROBATE:** 1887, Court Services
- **COURT:** 1881, Court Services
- **NOTES:** County Recorder has birth and death record indexes 1873-1905, marriage record indexes 1857-1905, and naturalization records 1850-1940.

TULARE
221 S. Mooney Blvd., Visalia, CA 93291, (559) 733-6418,
<www.co.tulare.ca.us>
- **INCORPORATED:** April 20, 1852
- **PARENT COUNTY:** Mariposa
- **BIRTH RECORDS:** start in 1852, kept by County Clerk Recorder
- **MARRIAGE:** 1852, County Clerk Recorder
- **DIVORCE:** unknown, Superior Court
- **DEATH:** 1873, County Clerk Recorder
- **LAND:** unknown, County Assessor
- **PROBATE:** unknown, Superior Court
- **COURT:** unknown, Superior Court
- **NATURALIZATION:** unknown, Superior Court
- **MILITARY:** 1919, County Clerk Recorder

TUOLUMNE
2 S. Green St., Sonora, CA 95370, (209) 533-5570,
<www.tuolumnecounty.ca.gov>
- **INCORPORATED:** Feb. 18, 1850
- **PARENT COUNTY:** Original county
- **BIRTH RECORDS:** start in 1858, kept by County Recorder
- **MARRIAGE:** 1850, County Recorder
- **DIVORCE:** 1850, County Recorder
- **DEATH:** 1859, County Recorder
- **LAND**: 1850, County Recorder
- **PROBATE:** 1850, County Recorder
- **COURT:** 1850, County Recorder
- **BURIAL:** 1916, County Recorder

VENTURA
800 S. Victoria Ave., Ventura, CA 93009, (805) 654-2267,
<www.countyofventura.org>
- **INCORPORATED:** March 22, 1872
- **PARENT COUNTY:** Santa Barbara
- **BIRTH RECORDS:** start in 1873, kept by County Recorder
- **MARRIAGE:** 1873, County Recorder
- **DIVORCE:** 1873, Superior Court
- **DEATH:** 1873, County Recorder
- **LAND:** 1850, County Recorder
- **PROBATE:** 1873, Superior Court
- **COURT:** 1873, Superior Court
- **NOTES:** Some land went to Kern and Los Angeles counties in boundary change.

YOLO
Box 1130, Woodland, CA 95776, (530) 666-8130,
<www.yolocounty.org>
- **INCORPORATED:** Feb. 18, 1850
- **PARENT COUNTY:** Original county
- **BIRTH RECORDS:** start in 1850, kept by County Clerk
- **MARRIAGE:** 1850, County Clerk
- **DIVORCE:** 1850, County Clerk
- **DEATH:** 1850, County Clerk
- **LAND:** 1850, County Clerk
- **PROBATE:** 1850, County Clerk
- **COURT:** 1850, County Clerk

YUBA
935 Fourteenth St., Marysville, CA 95901, (530) 741-6547,
<www.co.yuba.ca.us>
- **INCORPORATED:** Feb. 18, 1850
- **PARENT COUNTY:** Original county
- **MARRIAGE RECORDS:** start in 1865, kept by County Clerk
- **DIVORCE:** 1850, County Clerk
- **PROBATE:** 1850, County Clerk
- **COURT:** 1850, County Clerk
- **VOTER REGISTRATION:** 1866, County Clerk

COLORADO

» BY JAMES W. WARREN

HISTORICAL OVERVIEW

Zebulon Pike arrived in 1806 to explore the area that would become Colorado. Half a century later, the promise of gold brought early settlers to the mountains of Colorado.

In 1803, the Louisiana Purchase brought the part of Colorado north and east of the Arkansas River under US control. Government expeditions soon began mapping the area. By the 1820s, fur trappers and traders had begun moving in.

In the 1840s, Mexican land grants in Southwestern Colorado brought Hispanic settlers. In 1848, the United States acquired the rest of Colorado from Mexico and agreed to honor claims to earlier Spanish and Mexican land grants. Settlers from Spanish New Mexico settled in the San Luis Valley beginning in 1851. In 1852, Fort Massachusetts was built. Fort Garland was the second military outpost in Colorado.

Denver and many other mining towns were formed as the 1858 Pikes Peak Gold Rush brought a flood of settlers, primarily from the Midwest and Northeast, but there were some from almost every part of the United States, as well as many foreign immigrants.

Colorado Territory was organized in 1861. By the time of the 1870 census, the transcontinental railroad linked Denver with Cheyenne, Wyo., and Kansas City, Mo., providing direct connections to the East and West coasts. By then, the Plains Indian inhabitants, primarily Arapaho, Cheyenne, Kiowa and Comanche, had been forced to move to Indian Territory in Oklahoma, leaving only the Ute. In 1876, Colorado became the 38th state. The Ute were relocated to Utah reservations, and in 1881, western Colorado opened for settlement.

The gold rush era began to wane after the last major gold strike at Cripple Creek in 1890. By 1910, the midwestern states were the primary feeders for migration to Colorado, but many immigrants came from Germany, Russia, Italy, Austria, Sweden and England. Mining, ranching and later, oil and industry, continued to be prominent in the development of Colorado throughout the 20th century.

RECORD HIGHLIGHTS

On the 1860 federal population census, what would become Colorado is split among four territories: Kansas, Nebraska, New Mexico and Utah. The 1870 and 1880 censuses and a special 1885 federal census, all for Colorado Territory, are available. They include population, agricultural, manufacturing and mortality schedules. Social Statistics Schedules

research tips

- The Western History/Genealogy Department at the Denver Public Library is an indispensable resource for Colorado research **<history.denverlibrary.org>**.
- The Colorado State Archives has court records from most counties, with several online databases **<www.colorado.gov/dpa/doit/archives>**.
- The Colorado Department of Health (CDH) has statewide marriage and divorce indexes. The state archives or county courthouses have copies of the actual records.
- Early vital records can be obtained from county offices; see **<www.cdphe.state.co.us/certs/genealogy.html>** for instructions.

CENSUS RECORDS

- Federal census: 1880, 1885, 1900, 1910, 1920, 1930
- Federal mortality schedules: 1860 (with Kansas), 1870, 1880
- 1860 territorial census and mortality schedules: Nebraska 1860 (schedules designated "unorganized territory" which became northeastern Colorado), Arapahoe County, Kansas Territory 1860 (central eastern Colorado), Toas and Mora Counties of New Mexico Territory 1860 (southeastern Colorado)
- 1870 Colorado territory census and mortality schedules

survived for 1870, and the seven supplemental schedules for Defective, Dependent and Delinquent Classes ("DDD" schedules) are available for 1880. After statehood, available federal censuses are 1900, 1910, 1920 and 1930. The 1890 census, including the Union Veterans' and Widows schedule, was destroyed. Colorado didn't take state censuses.

Local vital-record keeping was mandated in 1876. Early records may be available at county courthouses or the Colorado Department of Health (CDH), Vital Records Section. Statewide registration began in 1907 and was generally complied with by the 1920s; request those records from CDH.

Marriage records are available from county courthouses, though many early ones have been turned over to the State Archives. CDH has statewide marriage indexes for 1900 to 1939 and 1975 to the present. CDH also has copies of marriage records for 20 of Colorado's 63 counties. CDH has statewide divorce indexes for the years 1900–1939 and 1968 to the present. Divorce records are available only from the county clerk where the divorce took place.

Court records are held by county and district courts. Probate records and wills are with the county clerk in each county except Denver, which has a separate probate court. Land records are in the office of the county recorder. The Family History Library (FHL) has a few microfilmed Colorado vital, probate, land and court records. Naturalization records for most counties are at the state archives.

Many local cemetery and church records or abstracts have been published or posted online. But in most cases, you'll need to contact the cemetery. Published abstracts of or indexes to other records and sources, as well as church or business histories, may be in local libraries, museums, and historical societies. One helpful guide is Kay R. Merrill's *Colorado Cemetery Directory* (Colorado Council of Genealogical Societies, 1985).

The Colorado Historical Society's collection of microfilmed newspapers is the most complete available. The society also has newspaper indexes and clipping files, along with extensive historical and genealogical materials.

The Western History/Genealogy Department at the Denver Public Library is a major national genealogical repository. Among the many resources are obituary indexes, Denver naturalization records (1877–1952), and the Colorado Index to Marriages and Divorces, 1900–1939 and 1975–present. The library offers online access to indexes to many records at **<history.denverlibrary.org/research/exclusive.html>**.

The Colorado State Archives houses court records from most counties. That includes naturalization records, probate cases, and civil and criminal cases. Often, indexes for civil and criminal case files will still be at the county courthouse, even though the case files themselves have been transferred to the Archives. The Archives has extensive collections of school records. You can search an index of some of its birth, death, divorce and other records in the Colorado Historical Records Index **<www.colorado.gov/dpa/doit/archives/hrd>**.

The Western Historical Collection in the Norlin Library at the University of Colorado at Boulder has an extensive map collection. The Colorado Genealogical Society (CGS) **<www.cogensoc.us>** has published many early Colorado county records in its journal, *The Colorado Genealogist*. The Colorado GenWeb Project **<cogenweb.com>** has an array of volunteer projects that provide information, indexes, transcriptions and actual record copies for Colorado research. It's always important to seek original records. For example, you can find the Denver Public Library's Reformatory Prisoner's Record Index (1887–1939) online. But to find out if the story had a happy ending for your ancestor, you'll have to use the original records collection at the State Archives: Parole Record With Index (1898–1951).

☞ARCHIVES, LIBRARIES, AND SOCIETIES

Ann Zugelder Library
307 N. Wisconsin Ave., Gunnison, CO 81230, (970) 641-3485, **<www.gunnisoncountylibraries.org>**

Archdiocese of Denver Archives
1300 S. Steele St., Denver, CO 80210, (303) 520-9986, **<www.archden.org/index.cfm/ID/5/OFFICES>**

Archuleta County Genealogical Society
Box 1611, Pagosa Springs, CO 81147, **<www.pagosamuseum.org/acgs.htm>**

Aspen Historical Society
620 W. Bleeker, Aspen, CO 81611, (970) 925 3721, **<www.aspenhistory.org>**

Aurora Genealogical Society of Colorado
Box 31732, Aurora, CO 80041, **<www.freewebs.com/uroragenealogysociety>**

Black Genealogy Search Group of Denver
Box 40701, Denver, CO 80204, **<www.bgsgden.com>**

Boulder Genealogical Society
Box 3246, Boulder, CO 80307, **<www.rootsweb.ancestry.com/~bgs>**

Boulder Public Library
1001 Arapahoe Ave., Boulder, CO 80302, (303) 441-3100, **<boulderlibrary.org>**

Brighton Genealogical Society
343 S. 21st Ave., Brighton, CO 80601

Bureau of Land Management, Colorado State Office
2850 Youngfield St., Lakewood, CO 80215, (303) 239-3600, **<www.co.blm.gov>**

Carnegie Branch Library
1125 Pine St., Boulder, CO 80302, (303) 441-3110, **<boulderlibrary.org/carnegie>**

Colorado Coalition for Women's History
2401 Welton St., Box 12566, Denver, CO 80212, (720) 865-2401, **<coloradowomenshistory.org>**

Colorado Council of Genealogical Societies
Box 40270, Denver, CO 80204, **<www.rootsweb.ancestry.com/~coccgs>**

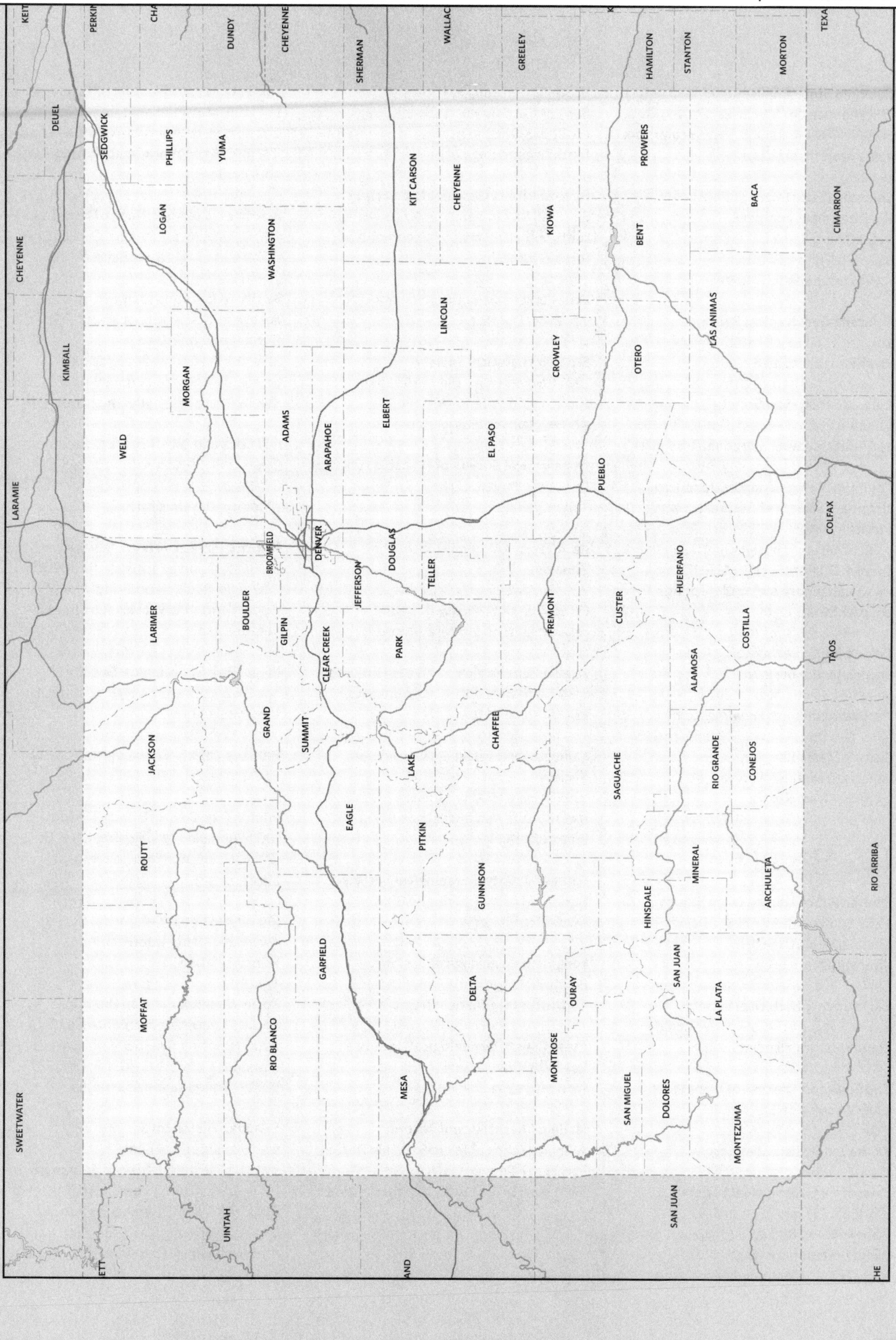
SEDGWICK
PHILLIPS
YUMA
LOGAN
WASHINGTON
KIT CARSON
CHEYENNE
KIOWA
PROWERS
BENT
BACA
LINCOLN
CROWLEY
OTERO
LAS ANIMAS
MORGAN
ADAMS
ARAPAHOE
ELBERT
EL PASO
PUEBLO
WELD
DENVER
BROOMFIELD
DOUGLAS
TELLER
JEFFERSON
BOULDER
LARIMER
GILPIN
CLEAR CREEK
PARK
FREMONT
CUSTER
HUERFANO
COSTILLA
ALAMOSA
GRAND
SUMMIT
JACKSON
LAKE
CHAFFEE
SAGUACHE
RIO GRANDE
CONEJOS
EAGLE
PITKIN
ROUTT
GUNNISON
MINERAL
ARCHULETA
HINSDALE
SAN JUAN
LA PLATA
GARFIELD
DELTA
OURAY
MOFFAT
RIO BLANCO
MONTROSE
MESA
SAN MIGUEL
DOLORES
MONTEZUMA
KEITH
PERKINS
CHASE
DUNDY
CHEYENNE
SHERMAN
WALLACE
GREELEY
HAMILTON
STANTON
MORTON
TEXAS
DEUEL
CIMARRON
CHEYENNE
KIMBALL
LARAMIE
COLFAX
TAOS
RIO ARRIBA
SWEETWATER
UINTAH
SAN JUAN

Colorado State Archives
1313 Sherman, St., Rm. 1B-20, Denver, CO 80203, (303) 866-2358, **<www.colorado.gov/dpa/doit/archives>**

Colorado Department of Public Health and Environment
4300 Cherry Creek Dr. S., Denver, CO 80246, (303) 692-2000, **<www.cdphe.state.co.us>**

Colorado Genealogical Society
Box 9218, Denver, CO 80209, **<www.cogensoc.us>**

Colorado Historical Society
1300 Broadway, Denver, CO 80203, (303) 866-3682, **<www.coloradohistory.org>**

Colorado Springs Chapter, American Historical Society of Germans from Russia
3330 Templeton Gap Rd. Unit, Colorado Springs, CO 80907, (719) 579 9711, **<www.ahsgr.org/colorado_springs_chapter.htm>**

Columbine Genealogical and Historical Society
Box 2074, Centennial, CO 80161, **<www.columbinegenealogy.com>**

Denver Metro Chapter, American Historical Society of Germans from Russia
2727 Bryant St., Room L4, Denver, CO, 80211, (303) 455-2727, **<www.ahsgr.org/denver/codenver.htm>**

Denver Public Library, Main Branch
10 W. Fourteenth Ave. Pkwy., Denver, CO 80204, (720) 865-1363, **<denverlibrary.org>**

Eagle County Historical Society
Box 192, Eagle, CO 81631, **<www.eaglecountyhistoricalsociety.com>**

The Episcopal Diocese of Colorado
1300 Washington St., Denver, CO 80203, (800) 446-3081, **<www.coloradodiocese.org>**

Estes Park Genealogical Society
Box 1687, 335 East Elkhorn Ave., Estes Park, CO 80517, (970) 586-8116, **<www.esteslibrary.org>**

Foothills Genealogical Society
Box 150382, Lakewood, CO 80215 (303) 935-9192, **<www.foothillsgenealogy.org>**

Fore-Kin Trails Genealogical Society
Box 802, Montrose, CO 81402, **<www.rootsweb.ancestry.com/~comontro/forekin.htm>**

Four Corners Genealogy Society
Box 2636, Durango, CO 81302

Frontier Historical Society
1001 Colorado Ave., Glenwood Springs, CO 81601, (970) 945-4448, **<www.glenwoodhistory.com>**

Genealogical Society of Hispanic America
Box 3040, Pueblo, CO 81005, **<www.gsha.net>**

Ira J. Taylor Library, Iliff School of Theology
2201 S. University Blvd., Denver, CO 80210 (303) 765-3173, **<www.iliff.edu/research/archives/default.htm>**

Jewish Genealogical Society of Colorado
5186 S. Shalom Park Circle., Aurora, CO 80015, **<jgsco.org>**

Lafayette and Louisville Genealogy Society
10689 Union Way, Broomfield, CO 80021, **<www.rootsweb.ancestry.com/~collgs/index.html>**

Larimer County Genealogical Society
Box 270737, Fort Collins, CO 80527, **<www.lcgsco.org>**

Longmont Genealogical Society
Box 6081, Longmont, CO 80501, **<www.rootsweb.ancestry.com/~colgs>**

Mesa County Genealogical Society
Box 1506, Grand Junction, CO 81502, **<www.gjmesa.com/mcgs>**

National Archives and Record Administration, Rocky Mountain Region
Box 25307, Denver, CO 80225, (303) 407-5700, **<archives.gov/rocky-mountain>**

Norlin Library, University of Colorado
184 UCB, 1720 Pleasant St., University of Colorado, Boulder, CO 80309, (303) 492-8705, **<ucblibraries.colorado.edu/norlin>**

Northeast Colorado Health Department
700 Columbine St., Sterling, CO 80751 (970) 522-3741, **<www.nchd.org>**

Northern Colorado Chapter, American Historical Society of Germans from Russia
22409 Weld County Road 46, LaSalle, CO 80645 , (970) 284-5301, **<www.ahsgr.org/conorthe.htm>**

Old Colorado City Historical Society
One S. 24th St., Colorado Springs, CO 80904-3319, (719) 636-1225, **<history.oldcolo.com>**

Penrose Public Library
Box 1579, Colorado Springs, CO 80901 (719) 389-8968, **<library.ppld.org/AboutYourLibrary/HoursLocations/penrose.asp>**

Pikes Peak Genealogical Society
Box 1262, Colorado Springs, CO 80901, **<www.ppgs.org>**

Prowers County Genealogical Society
Box 929, Lamar, CO 81052

Pueblo City-County Library District
100 E. Abriendo Ave., Pueblo, CO 81004, (719) 562-5600, **<www.pueblolibrary.org>**

Rio Blanco County Historical Society, **<www.meekercolorado.com/HSociety.htm>**

Rocky Mountain Jewish Historical Society Center for Judaic Studies
2000 E. Asbury Ave., Suite 157, University of Denver, Denver, CO 80208, (303) 871-3020, **<www.du.edu/cjs/rmjhs>**

San Juan Historical Society
Box 154, Silverton, CO 81433, **<www.silvertonhistoricsociety.org>**

Sedgwick County Genealogy Society
Box 86, Julesburg, CO 80737, **<www.rootsweb.com/~cosedgwi/society.htm>**

Sheridan Historical Society
4101 S. Federal Blvd., Sheridan, CO 80110-5399, **<www.rootsweb.ancestry.com/~coshs>**

Southern Peaks Public Library
423 4th St., Alamosa, CO 81101, (719) 589-6592, **<www.alamosalibrary.org>**

Summit Historical Society
Box 745, Breckenridge, CO 80424, (970) 468-2207, **<www.summithistorical.org>**

Tutt Library, Colorado College
1021 N. Cascade Ave., Colorado Springs, CO 80903, (719) 389-6662, **<coloradocollege.edu/library>**

Ute Pass Historical Society
Box 6875, Woodland Park, CO 80866, (719) 686-7512, **<www.utepasshistoricalsociety.org>**

Weld County Genealogical Society
Box 278, Greeley, CO 80632, **<www.rootsweb.com/~cowcgs>**

Weld County Public Library, Centennial Park Branch
2227 23rd Ave., Greeley, CO 80634, (970) 506-8600, **<www.mylibrary.us>**

GENERAL RESOURCES

Colorado Area Key: A Comprehensive Study of Genealogical Records Sources of Colorado, Including Maps and Brief General History compiled by Florence Runyan Clint (Eden Press, 1968)

Colorado Bibliography edited by Bohdan S. Wynar and Roberta J. Depp, assistant editor (Libraries Unlimited for the National Society of Colonial Dames of America in the State of Colorado, 1980)

Colorado Families, a Territorial Heritage (Colorado Genealogical Society, 1981)

Colorado Postal History: The Post Offices by William H. Bauer, James L. Ozment, and John H. Willard (J-B Publishing Co., 1971)

Colorado Research Outline by the Church of Jesus Christ of Latter-day Saints (online at **<www.familysearch.org/eng/search/RG/guide/colorado.asp>**)

Genealogical Index to the Records of the Society of Colorado Pioneers by the Society of Colorado Pioneers, the Colorado Genealogical Society, and Bette D. Peters (Colorado Genealogical Society, 1990)

Guide to Colorado Newspapers, 1859-1963 compiled by Donald E. Oehlerts (Bibliographical Center for Research, Rocky Mountain Region, 1964)

Pioneers of the Territory of Southern Colorado by the Territorial Daughters of Colorado, Southern Colorado Auxiliary (1980)

Subject Index to the Colorado Genealogist by Kay R. Merrill (Colorado Genealogical Society, 1982)

IMMIGRATION RECORDS

Colorado and its People: A Narrative and Topical History of the Centennial State compiled by LeRoy R. Hafen (Lewis Historical Publishing Co., 1948)

Naturalization Records: Index to US District Court—Denver, Colorado compiled by Patricia Crayne-Trudell, Joan Thomas and the US District Court (Foothills Genealogical Society of Colorado, 1997)

LAND RECORDS

Mercedes Reales: Hispanic Land Grants of the Upper Rio Grande Region by Victor Westphall (University of New Mexico Press, 1983)

Record of Private Land Claims Adjudicated by the US Surveyor General, 1855-1890 by the New Mexico (Territory) Surveyor General's Office (University of New Mexico Library, 1955-1957)

Spanish and Mexican Land Grants in New Mexico and Colorado edited by John R. Van Ness and Christine M. Van Ness (Sunflower University Press, 1980)

Spanish & Mexican Records of the American Southwest: A Bibliographical Guide to Archive and Manuscript Sources by Henry Putney Beers (University of Arizona Press, 1979)

Vigil's Index, 1681-1846 by Donaciano Vigil (University of New Mexico Library, 1955-1957)

MAPS

Colorado Ghost Towns and Mining Camps by Sandra Dallas; photographs by Kendal Atchison (University of Oklahoma Press, 1985)

Colorado Place Names: Communities, Counties, Parks, Passes with Historical Lore and Fact Plus a Pronunciation Guide by George R. Eichler (Johnson Publishing, 1980)

Crofutt's Grip-Sack Guide of Colorado by George A. Crofutt (Cubar Associates, 1966)

A Gazetteer of Colorado by Henry Gannett (Government Print Office, 1906)

MILITARY RECORDS

Colorado Volunteers in New Mexico, 1862 edited by Richard Harwell (R.R. Donnelley, 1962)

Confederate Soldiers Buried in Colorado by Sherman Lee Pompey (Historical and Genealogical Publishing, 1995)

Just Outside of Manila: Letters from Members of the First Colorado Regiment in the Spanish-American and Philippine-American Wars edited by Frank Harper (Colorado Historical Society, 1991)

PROBATE RECORDS

Abstract of Early Probate Records by Ella Ruland MacDougall (19-?)

☞VITAL RECORDS

Colorado Cemetery Directory edited by Kay R. Merrill (Colorado Council of Genealogical Societies, 1985)

Colorado Cemetery Inscriptions compiled by Lela O. McQueary (K.R. Merrill, 1985)

From the Grave: A Roadside Guide to Colorado's Pioneer Cemeteries by Linda Wommack (Caxton Press, 1998)

Guide to Vital Statistics Records in Colorado by the Historical Records Survey and the US Works Progress Administration (The Survey, 1942)

Marriages of Arapahoe County, Colorado, 1859-1901: Including Territory that Became Adams, Denver and Other Counties compiled by the Arapahoe County Marriage Committee (Colorado Genealogical Society, 1986)

Statewide Marriage Index, 1900-1939, 1975-1992 by the Colorado Department of Health (Colorado Department of Health, 1975-1992)

•-COUNTY DETAILS-•

ADAMS

450 S. Fourth Ave., Brighton, CO 80601, (303) 654-6026,
<www.co.adams.co.us >

- **INCORPORATED:** April 15, 1901
- **PARENT COUNTY:** Arapahoe
- **BIRTH RECORDS:** start in 1876, kept by Clerk/Recorder
- **MARRIAGE:** 1902, Clerk/Recorder
- **DIVORCE:** 1905, County Court Clerk
- **DEATH:** 1907, Clerk/Recorder
- **LAND:** 1902, Clerk/Recorder
- **PROBATE:** 1905, County Court Clerk
- **COURT:** 1905, County Court Clerk
- **NOTES:** County Clerk has some burial records, some land records from Arapahoe County prior to 1901, and school census 1902-1964. State Archives has naturalization records 1906-1954.

ALAMOSA

402 Edison Ave., Box 630, Alamosa, CO 81101, (719) 589-6681,
<www.alamosacounty.org>

- **INCORPORATED:** March 8, 1913
- **PARENT COUNTIES:** Costilla, Conejos
- **BIRTH RECORDS:** start in 1870, kept by County Clerk
- **MARRIAGE:** 1914, County Clerk
- **DIVORCE:** 1914, Clerk of District Court
- **DEATH:** 1902 County Clerk
- **LAND:** 1914, County Clerk
- **PROBATE:** 1914, Clerk of District Court
- **COURT:** 1914, Clerk of District Court
- **NOTES:** County Clerk has marriage records for Costilla and Conejos counties for late 1800s. State Archives has naturalization records 1915-1991.

ARAPAHOE

5334 S. Prince St., Littleton, CO 80166-0060, (303) 795-4200,
<www.co.arapahoe.co.us>

- **INCORPORATED:** Nov. 1, 1861
- **PARENT COUNTY:** Original county
- **BIRTH RECORDS:** start in 1876, kept by Clerk/Recorder
- **MARRIAGE:** 1902, Clerk/Recorder
- **DIVORCE:** 1903, Clerk of District Court
- **DEATH:** 1907, Clerk/Recorder
- **LAND:** 1902, Clerk/Recorder
- **PROBATE:** 1903, Clerk of District Court
- **COURT:** 1903, Clerk of District Court
- **NOTES:** First formed in 1855 as Territorial County. Clerk/Recorder has some incomplete Land records from late 1800s. See Kansas for 1860 census records.

ARCHULETA

Box 2589, Pagosa Springs, CO 81147, (970) 264-8350,
<www.archuletacounty.org>

- **INCORPORATED:** April 14, 1885
- **PARENT COUNTY:** Conejos
- **BIRTH RECORDS:** start in 1880, kept by County Clerk
- **MARRIAGE:** 1886, County Clerk
- **DIVORCE:** 1885, Clerk of Combined Courts
- **DEATH:** 1907, County Clerk
- **LAND:** 1886, County Clerk
- **PROBATE:** 1885, Clerk of Combined Courts
- **COURT:** 1885, Clerk of Combined Courts

BACA

741 Main Street Springfield, CO 81073, (719) 523-4372,
<www.springfieldcolorado.com/countygov.html>

- **INCORPORATED:** April 16, 1889
- **PARENT COUNTY:** Las Animas
- **BIRTH RECORDS:** start in 1910, kept by County Clerk
- **MARRIAGE:** 1889, County Clerk
- **DIVORCE:** ca. 1918, Clerk of Combined Courts
- **DEATH:** 1911, County Clerk
- **LAND:** 1889, County Clerk
- **PROBATE:** ca. 1918, Clerk of Combined Courts
- **COURT:** ca. 1918, Clerk of Combined Courts
- **NATURALIZATION:** unknown, Clerk of District Court

BENT

Box 350, Las Animas, CO 81054, (719) 456-2009,
<www.bentcounty.org>

- **INCORPORATED:** Feb. 11, 1870
- **PARENT COUNTIES:** Huerfano, Indian Reserve Lands
- **BIRTH RECORDS:** start in 1905, kept by Nursing Service
- **MARRIAGE:** 1888, County Recorder

- **DEATH:** 1908, Nursing Service
- **LAND:** 1888, County Recorder
- **PROBATE:** 1888, Clerk of Combined Courts
- **COURT:** 1888, Clerk of Combined Courts
- **NOTES:** Clerk of Combined Courts has divorce records 1907-1919.

BOULDER

1750 Thirty-Third St., Boulder, CO 80301, (303) 413-7770, **<www.co.boulder.co.us>**

- **INCORPORATED:** Nov. 1, 1861
- **PARENT COUNTY:** Original county
- **BIRTH RECORDS:** start in 1866, kept by Department of Health
- **MARRIAGE:** 1864, County Recorder
- **DEATH:** 1866, Department of Health
- **LAND:** 1865, County Recorder
- **PROBATE:** 1862, Probate Register
- **COURT:** 1862, Clerk of District Court
- **NOTES:** Clerk of District Court has divorce records 1904-1912. State Archives has naturalization records 1872-1958.

BROOMFIELD

One DesCombes Dr., Broomfield, CO 80020, (303) 464-5819, **<www.ci.broomfield.co.us>**

- **INCORPORATED:** Nov. 15, 2001
- **PARENT COUNTIES:** Adams, Boulder, Jefferson, Weld
- **BIRTH RECORDS:** start in 2001, kept by Department of Health
- **MARRIAGE:** 2001, Central Records Office
- **DIVORCE:** 2001, Clerk of County Court
- **DEATH:** 2001, Department of Health
- **LAND:** 2001, Central Records Office
- **PROBATE:** 2001, Clerk of County Court
- **COURT:** 2001, Clerk of County Court

CARBONATE

- **INCORPORATED:** Feb. 8, 1879
- **PARENT COUNTY:** Lake
- **NOTES:** See Lake County. Name changed to Lake Feb. 10, 1879.

CHAFFEE

104 Crestone Ave., Box 699, Salida, CO 81201, (719) 539-6913 not sure which office to list, **<www.chaffeecounty.org>**

- **INCORPORATED:** Feb. 10, 1879
- **PARENT COUNTY:** Lake
- **MARRIAGE RECORDS:** start in ca. 1890, kept by Clerk/Recorder
- **DIVORCE:** ca. 1880, Clerk of Combined Courts
- **LAND:** ca. 1890, Clerk/Recorder
- **PROBATE:** ca. 1880, Clerk of Combined Courts
- **COURT:** ca. 1880, Clerk of Combined Courts
- **NOTES:** Clerk/Recorder has very few birth and death records from early 1900s. State Archives has naturalization records 1881-1906.

CHEYENNE

51 S. First St., Box 567, Cheyenne Wells, CO 80810, (719) 767-5685, **<www.co.cheyenne.co.us>**

- **INCORPORATED:** March 25, 1889
- **PARENT COUNTIES:** Bent, Elbert
- **BIRTH RECORDS:** start in 1910, kept by County Vital Records Office
- **MARRIAGE:** 1906, Clerk/Recorder
- **DIVORCE:** ca. 1920, Clerk of Combined Courts
- **DEATH:** 1911, County Vital Records Office
- **LAND:** 1906, Clerk/Recorder
- **PROBATE:** ca. 1920, Clerk of Combined Courts
- **COURT:** ca. 1920, Clerk of Combined Courts

CLEAR CREEK

405 Argentine St., Box 2000, Georgetown, CO 80444 (303) 679-2339, **<www.co.clear-creek.co.us>**

- **INCORPORATED:** Nov. 1, 1861
- **PARENT COUNTY:** Mountain
- **MARRIAGE RECORDS:** start in 1882, kept by County Archives
- **DIVORCE:** 1862, Clerk of Combined Courts
- **LAND:** 1862, County Clerk
- **PROBATE:** 1862, Clerk of Combined Courts
- **COURT:** 1862, Clerk of Combined Courts

CONEJOS

Box 157, Conejos, CO 81129, (719) 376-5772, **<www.ccionline.org/index.cfm/ID/51 >**

- **INCORPORATED:** Sept. 9, 1861
- **PARENT COUNTY:** Original county
- **MARRIAGE RECORDS:** start in ca. 1940, kept by County Clerk
- **DEATH:** 1918, County Clerk
- **LAND:** 1900, County Clerk
- **NOTES:** Formerly Guadalupe County. Name changed to Conejos Nov. 7, 1861. Courthouse burned in 1980, destroying many records. County Clerk has birth records 1877-1910. Clerk of Combined Courts has court and probate records from early 1900s and divorce records 1899-1915. State Archives has naturalization records 1882-1948.

COSTILLA

Box 308, San Luis, CO 81152, (719) 672-3301, **<www.costillacounty-co.gov>**

- **INCORPORATED:** Nov. 1, 1861
- **PARENT COUNTY:** Original county
- **MARRIAGE RECORDS:** start in 1853, kept by County Clerk
- **DIVORCE:** unknown, Clerk of Combined Courts
- **LAND:** 1853, County Clerk
- **PROBATE:** 1874, Clerk of Combined Courts
- **COURT:** 1874, Clerk of Combined Courts
- **NOTES:** State Archives has naturalization records 1877-1931.

CROWLEY

631 Main St., Ordway, CO 81063, (719) 267-5225, **<www.crowleycounty.net>**

- **INCORPORATED:** May 6, 1911
- **PARENT COUNTY:** Otero
- **BIRTH RECORDS:** start in 1909, kept by County Registrar
- **MARRIAGE:** 1911, County Clerk
- **DIVORCE:** 1911, Clerk of Combined Courts
- **DEATH:** 1909, County Registrar
- **LAND:** 1911, County Clerk
- **PROBATE:** 1911, Clerk of Combined Courts
- **COURT:** 1911, Clerk of Combined Courts

CUSTER

Box 150, Westcliffe, CO 81252, (719) 783-0441, **<www.custercountygov.com>**

- **INCORPORATED:** March 9, 1877
- **PARENT COUNTY:** Fremont
- **MARRIAGE RECORDS:** start in 1876, kept by County Clerk
- **DIVORCE:** ca. 1900, Clerk of Combined Courts
- **LAND:** 1876, County Clerk
- **PROBATE:** ca. 1900, Clerk of Combined Courts
- **COURT:** ca. 1900, Clerk of Combined Courts
- **NOTES:** State Archives has naturalization records 1881-1927.

DELTA

501 Palmer St., Suite 211, Delta, CO 81416, (970) 874-2150, **<www.deltacounty.com>**

- **INCORPORATED:** Feb. 11, 1883
- **PARENT COUNTY:** Gunnison
- **BIRTH RECORDS:** start in 1897, kept by County Recorder
- **MARRIAGE:** 1883, County Recorder
- **DIVORCE:** 1883, Clerk of Combined Courts
- **DEATH:** 1883, County Recorder
- **LAND:** 1883, County Recorder
- **PROBATE:** 1883, Clerk of Combined Courts
- **COURT:** 1883, Clerk of Combined Courts
- **NOTES:** County Clerk has school census 1891-1964.

DENVER

Municipal Office Bldg., Department 101, 201 W. Colfax Ave., Denver, CO 80202, (720) 865-8400, **<www.denvergov.org>**

- **INCORPORATED:** March 18, 1901
- **PARENT COUNTY:** Arapahoe
- **BIRTH RECORDS:** start in 1906, kept by County Vital Records Office
- **MARRIAGE:** 1897, County Recorder
- **DIVORCE:** 1901, Clerk of District Court
- **LAND:** 1901, County Assessor
- **PROBATE:** 1901, Probate Administrator
- **COURT:** 1901, Clerk of District Court
- **NOTES:** Has annexed territory from Arapahoe, Adams, and Jefferson counties. State Archives has naturalization records 1862-1915.

DOLORES

Box 58, Dove Creek, CO 81324, (970) 677-2381, **<www.dolorescounty.org>**

- **INCORPORATED:** Feb. 19, 1881
- **PARENT COUNTY:** San Juan
- **BIRTH RECORDS:** start in 1887, kept by County Clerk
- **MARRIAGE:** 1887, County Clerk
- **DIVORCE:** 1881, Clerk of Combined Courts
- **DEATH:** 1887, County Clerk
- **LAND:** 1887, County Clerk
- **PROBATE:** 1881, Clerk of Combined Courts
- **COURT:** 1881, Clerk of Combined Courts
- **NOTES:** State Archives has naturalization records 1881-1906.

DOUGLAS

301 Wilcox St., Castle Rock, CO 80104, (303) 660-7469, **<www.douglas.co.us>**

- **INCORPORATED:** Nov. 1, 1861
- **PARENT COUNTY:** Original county
- **DIVORCE:** start in unknown, kept by Clerk of Combined Courts
- **LAND:** 1864, County Recorder
- **PROBATE:** unknown, Clerk of Combined Courts
- **COURT RECORDS:** unknown, Clerk of Combined Courts
- **NOTES:** County Clerk/Recorder has marriage records 1864-1925. State Archives has naturalization records 1903-1920.

EAGLE

Box 537, 500 Broadway, Eagle, CO 81631, (970) 328-8723, **<www.eaglecounty.us>**

- **INCORPORATED:** Feb. 11, 1883
- **PARENT COUNTY:** Summit
- **BIRTH RECORDS:** start in 1894, kept by Department of Health
- **DIVORCE:** 1883, Clerk of District Court
- **DEATH:** 1894, Department of Health
- **LAND:** 1883, County Recorder
- **PROBATE:** 1883, Clerk of Combined Courts
- **COURT:** 1883, Clerk of Combined Courts
- **NOTES:** Clerk of Combined Courts has naturalization records 1883-1928. County Clerk/Recorder has marriage records 1883-1940.

EL PASO

200 S. Cascade Ave., Colorado Springs, CO 80903 (719) 520-6200, **<www.elpasoco.com>**

- **INCORPORATED:** Nov. 1, 1861
- **PARENT COUNTY:** Original county
- **BIRTH RECORDS:** start in 1890, kept by Department of Health & Environment
- **MARRIAGE:** 1861, County Recorder
- **DEATH:** 1893, Department of Health & Environment
- **LAND:** 1861, County Clerk
- **PROBATE:** 1876, Clerk of Combined Courts
- **COURT:** 1876, Clerk of Combined Courts
- **NOTES:** Clerk of Combined Courts has divorce records 1903-1941. State Archives has naturalization records 1869-1970.

ELBERT

215 Comanche St., Box 7, Kiowa, CO 80117, (303) 621-3128, **<www.elbertcounty-co.gov>**

- **INCORPORATED:** Feb. 13, 1874
- **PARENT COUNTIES:** Douglas, Greenwood
- **MARRIAGE RECORDS:** start in 1816, kept by County Recorder
- **DIVORCE:** unknown, Clerk of Combined Courts
- **LAND:** 1816, County Recorder
- **PROBATE:** 1876, Clerk of Combined Courts
- **COURT:** 1876, Clerk of Combined Courts
- **NOTES:** State Archives has naturalization records 1886-1931.

FREMONT

615 Macon, Room 102, Cañon City, CO 81212, (719) 276-7330, **<www.fremontco.com>**

- **INCORPORATED:** Nov. 1, 1861

- **PARENT COUNTY:** Original county
- **MARRIAGE RECORDS:** start in 1861, kept by County Clerk
- **LAND:** 1861, County Clerk
- **NOTES:** Clerk of Combined Courts has court, divorce, and probate records from early 1900s. State Archives has naturalization records 1882–1966.

GARFIELD

109 Eighth St., Suite 200, Glenwood Springs, CO 81601
(970) 945-2377, **<www.garfield-county.com>**

- **INCORPORATED:** Feb. 10, 1883
- **PARENT COUNTY:** Summit
- **BIRTH RECORDS:** start in 1883, kept by County Recorder
- **MARRIAGE:** 1883, County Recorder
- **DEATH:** 1883, County Recorder
- **LAND:** 1883, County Recorder
- **PROBATE:** 1892, Clerk of Combined Courts
- **COURT:** 1892, Clerk of Combined Courts
- **NOTES:** Clerk of Combined Courts has divorce records 1906–1916.

GILPIN

203 Eureka St., Box 429, Central City, CO 80427, (303) 582-5321, **<http://co.gilpin.co.us>**

- **INCORPORATED:** Nov. 1, 1861
- **PARENT COUNTY:** Original county
- **MARRIAGE RECORDS:** start in 1850, kept by County Recorder
- **DIVORCE:** unknown, Clerk of Combined Courts
- **LAND:** 1850, County Recorder
- **PROBATE:** unknown, Clerk of Combined Courts
- **NOTES:** State Archives has naturalization records 1869–1917.

GRAND

308 Byers Ave., Box 120, Hot Sulphur Springs, CO 80451
(970) 725-3347, **<www.co.grand.co.us>**

- **INCORPORATED:** Feb. 2, 1874
- **PARENT COUNTY:** Summit
- **BIRTH RECORDS:** start in 1907, kept by Clerk/Recorder
- **MARRIAGE:** 1874, County Recorder
- **DIVORCE:** ca. 1880, Clerk of Combined Courts
- **LAND:** 1874, Clerk/Recorder
- **PROBATE:** ca. 1880, Clerk of Combined Courts
- **COURT:** ca. 1880, Clerk of Combined Courts

GREENWOOD

- **INCORPORATED:** Feb. 11, 1870
- **PARENT COUNTY:** Indian Lands
- **NOTES:** Abolished Feb. 6, 1874. Bent and Elbert counties formed from Greenwood.

GUADALUPE

- **INCORPORATED:** Nov. 1, 1861
- **PARENT COUNTY:** Original county
- **NOTES:** See Conejos County. Name changed to Conejos Nov. 7, 1861.

GUNNISON

221 N. Wisconsin Ave., Suite C, Gunnison, CO 81230, (970) 641-1516, **<www.gunnisoncounty.org>**

- **INCORPORATED:** March 9, 1877
- **PARENT COUNTY:** Lake
- **BIRTH RECORDS:** start in ca. 1880, kept by Department of Social Services
- **MARRIAGE:** 1877, County Recorder
- **DIVORCE:** 1877, Clerk of Combined Courts
- **DEATH:** ca. 1880, Department of Social Services
- **LAND:** 1877, County Recorder
- **PROBATE:** 1877, Clerk of Combined Courts
- **COURT:** 1877, Clerk of Combined Courts

HINSDALE

Box 9, 317 North Henson St. Lake City, CO 81235, (970) 944-2228 **<www.hinsdalecountycolorado.us/home.html>**

- **INCORPORATED:** Feb. 10, 1874
- **PARENT COUNTY:** Conejos, Lake, Costilla
- **BIRTH RECORDS:** start in 1900, kept by Clerk/Recorder
- **MARRIAGE:** 1880, County Recorder
- **DIVORCE:** 1874, Clerk of Combined Courts
- **LAND:** 1874, County Recorder
- **PROBATE:** 1874, County Court
- **COURT:** 1874, County Court

HUERFANO

401 Main St., Walsenburg, CO 81089, (719) 738-2380, **<www.huerfano.us>**

- **INCORPORATED:** Nov. 1, 1861
- **PARENT COUNTY:** Original county
- **MARRIAGE RECORDS:** start in 1870, kept by County Clerk
- **DIVORCE:** 1872, Clerk of Combined Courts
- **LAND:** 1874, County Clerk
- **PROBATE:** 1872, Clerk of Combined Courts
- **COURT:** 1872, Clerk of Common Pleas Court
- **NOTES:** State Archives has naturalization records 1882–1958.

JACKSON

Box 1019, Walden, CO 80480, (970) 723-4664, **<www.ccionline.org/index.cfm/ID/69>**

- **INCORPORATED:** May 5, 1909
- **PARENT COUNTY:** Larimer
- **BIRTH RECORDS:** start in 1909, kept by County Clerk
- **MARRIAGE:** 1909, County Clerk
- **DEATH:** 1909, County Clerk
- **DIVORCE:** 1909, Clerk of Combined Courts
- **LAND:** 1909, County Clerk
- **PROBATE:** 1909, Clerk of Combined Courts
- **COURT:** 1909, Clerk of Combined Courts
- **NOTES:** State Archives has naturalization records 1910–1940.

JEFFERSON

100 Jefferson County Pkwy., Golden, CO 80419, (303) 271-8186, **<co.jefferson.co.us>**

- **INCORPORATED:** Nov. 1, 1861
- **PARENT COUNTY:** Original county
- **BIRTH RECORDS:** start in 1907, kept by Department of Health
- **MARRIAGE:** 1868, County Recorder
- **DIVORCE:** 1863, Clerk of Combined Courts
- **DEATH:** 1868, Department of Health

- **LAND:** 1867, County Recorder
- **PROBATE:** 1863, Clerk of Combined Courts
- **COURT:** 1863, Clerk of Combined Courts
- **NOTES:** State Archives has naturalization records 1862-1955.

KIOWA
1305 Goff, Box 37, Eads, CO 81036, (719) 438-5421, **<www.kiowacountycolo.com>**
- **INCORPORATED:** April 11, 1889
- **PARENT COUNTY:** Bent
- **MARRIAGE RECORDS:** start in 1889, kept by County Clerk
- **DIVORCE:** 1889, Clerk of District Court
- **LAND:** 1908, County Clerk
- **PROBATE:** 1889, Clerk of District Court
- **COURT:** 1889, Clerk of District Court

KIT CARSON
251 Sixteenth St., Suite 203, Box 160, Burlington, CO 80807 (719) 346-8638, **<www.kitcarsoncounty.org>**
- **INCORPORATED:** April 11, 1889
- **PARENT COUNTY:** Elbert
- **BIRTH RECORDS:** start in unknown, kept by County Commissioner
- **MARRIAGE:** 1908, County Clerk
- **DIVORCE:** 1910, Clerk of Combined Courts
- **DEATH:** unknown, County Commissioner
- **LAND:** 1908, County Clerk
- **PROBATE:** 1910, Clerk of Combined Courts
- **COURT:** 1910, Clerk of Combined Courts

LA PLATA
98 Everett Street, Suite C, Durango, CO 81303, (970) 382-6280, **<co.laplata.co.us>**
- **INCORPORATED:** Feb. 10, 1874
- **PARENT COUNTY:** Conejos, Lake
- **BIRTH RECORDS:** start in unknown, kept by San Juan Basin Department of Health
- **MARRIAGE:** 1878, County Clerk/Registrar
- **DEATH:** unknown, San Juan Basin Department of Health
- **LAND:** 1876, County Recorder
- **NOTES:** Clerk of Combined Courts has court, divorce, and probate records from early 1900s. State Archives has naturalization records 1873-1908.

LAKE
505 Harrison Ave., Leadville, CO 80461, (719) 486-1410, **<www.lakecountyco.com>**
- **INCORPORATED:** Nov. 1, 1861
- **PARENT COUNTY:** Original county
- **MARRIAGE RECORDS:** start in 1869, kept by County Recorder
- **DIVORCE:** unknown, Clerk of Combined Courts
- **LAND:** 1876, County Recorder
- **PROBATE:** 1879, Clerk of Combined Courts
- **COURT:** 1879, Clerk of Combined Courts
- **NOTES:** Known as Carbonate County for two days Feb. 8-10, 1879. County Clerk has some burial records 1885-1903.

LARIMER
200 W. Oak St., Fort Collins, CO 80521, (970) 498-7860, **<www.larimer.org>**
- **INCORPORATED:** Nov. 1, 1861
- **PARENT COUNTY:** Original county
- **BIRTH RECORDS:** start in 1902, kept by Department of Health
- **MARRIAGE:** 1862, County Clerk/Registrar
- **DIVORCE:** 1862, Clerk of Combined Courts
- **DEATH:** 1902, Department of Health
- **LAND:** 1862, County Recorder
- **PROBATE:** 1862, Clerk of Combined Courts
- **COURT:** 1862, Clerk of Combined Courts
- **NOTES:** State Archives has naturalization records 1872-1958.

LAS ANIMAS
200 E. First St., Box 115, Trinidad, CO 81082, (719) 846-3314, **<www.tlac.net/county>**
Could not find site replacement
- **INCORPORATED:** Feb. 9, 1866
- **PARENT COUNTY:** Huerfano
- **MARRIAGE RECORDS:** start in 1887, kept by County Recorder
- **DIVORCE:** 1881, Clerk of Common Pleas Court
- **LAND:** 1883, County Recorder
- **PROBATE:** 1881, Clerk of Combined Courts
- **COURT:** 1881 Clerk of Combined Courts
- **NOTES:** County Health Department has birth and death records from late 1800s. State Archives has naturalization records 1881-1958.

LINCOLN
103 Third Ave., Box 67, Hugo, CO 80821-0067, (719) 743-2444, **<www.lincolncountyco.us>**
- **INCORPORATED:** April 11, 1889
- **PARENT COUNTIES:** Elbert, Bent
- **MARRIAGE RECORDS:** start in 1889, kept by County Recorder
- **DIVORCE:** 1889, Clerk of Court
- **LAND:** 1889, County Recorder
- **PROBATE:** 1889, Clerk of County Court
- **COURT:** 1889, Clerk of County Court
- **NOTES:** State Archives has naturalization records 1889-1947.

LOGAN
315 Main St., Sterling, CO 80751, (970) 522-1544, **<www.loganco.gov>**
- **INCORPORATED:** Feb. 25, 1887
- **PARENT COUNTY:** Weld
- **BIRTH RECORDS:** start in 1894, kept by Department of Health
- **MARRIAGE:** 1887, County Recorder
- **DIVORCE:** 1887, Clerk of District Court
- **DEATH:** 1894, Department of Health
- **LAND:** 1887, Clerk/Recorder
- **PROBATE:** 1887, Clerk of District Court
- **COURT:** 1887, Clerk of District Court

MESA

544 Rood Ave., Box 20000 Grand Junction, CO 81502, (970) 244-1607, **<www.co.mesa.co.us>**

- **INCORPORATED:** Feb. 14, 1883
- **PARENT COUNTY:** Gunnison
- **BIRTH RECORDS:** start in 1890, kept by Department of Health
- **MARRIAGE:** 1883, County Recorder
- **DIVORCE:** 1884, Clerk of District Court
- **DEATH:** 1890, Department of Health
- **LAND:** 1883, County Recorder
- **PROBATE:** 1884, Clerk of District Court
- **COURT:** 1884, Clerk of District Court
- **NOTES:** State Archives has naturalization records 1884-1994.

MINERAL

Box 70, Creede, CO 81130, (719) 658-2440, **<www.mineralcountycolorado.com >**

- **INCORPORATED:** March 27, 1893
- **PARENT COUNTIES:** Hinsdale, Rio Grande, Saguache
- **MARRIAGE RECORDS:** start in 1893, kept by County Clerk
- **DIVORCE:** 1893, Clerk of Combined Courts
- **LAND:** 1893, County Clerk
- **PROBATE:** 1893, Clerk of Combined Courts
- **COURT:** 1893, Clerk of Combined Courts
- **NOTES:** State Archives has naturalization records 1893-1905.

MOFFAT

221 W. Victory Way Suite 200, Craig, CO 81625, (970) 824-9104, **<www.co.moffat.co.us>**

- **INCORPORATED:** Feb. 27, 1911
- **PARENT COUNTY:** Routt
- **BIRTH RECORDS:** start in 1900, kept by Reg./Vital Records
- **MARRIAGE:** 1911, County Recorder
- **DIVORCE:** 1911, Clerk of Combined Courts
- **DEATH:** 1900, Reg./Vital Records
- **LAND:** 1911, County Clerk/Registrar
- **PROBATE:** 1911, Clerk of Combined Courts
- **COURT:** 1911, Clerk of Combined Courts
- **NOTES:** State Archives has naturalization records 1902-1959.

MONTEZUMA

109 W. Main St., Cortez, CO 81321, (970) 565-3728, **<www.co.montezuma.co.us>**

- **INCORPORATED:** April 16, 1889
- **PARENT COUNTY:** La Plata
- **BIRTH RECORDS:** start in 1879, kept by County Recorder
- **MARRIAGE:** 1889, County Recorder
- **DIVORCE:** 1889, Clerk of District Court
- **DEATH:** 1892, County Recorder
- **LAND:** 1879, County Recorder
- **PROBATE:** 1889, Clerk of District Court
- **COURT:** 1889, Clerk of District Court
- **NOTES:** State Archives has naturalization records 1889-1906.

MONTROSE

320 S. First St., Box 1289, Montrose, CO 81402, (970) 249-3362, **<www.co.montrose.co.us>**

- **INCORPORATED:** Feb. 11, 1883
- **PARENT COUNTY:** Gunnison
- **BIRTH RECORDS:** start in 1910, kept by County Recorder
- **MARRIAGE:** 1883, County Recorder
- **DIVORCE:** 1883, Clerk of Combined Courts
- **DEATH:** 1907, County Recorder
- **LAND:** 1883, County Recorder
- **PROBATE:** 1883, Clerk of Combined Courts
- **COURT:** 1883, Clerk of Combined Courts

MORGAN

231 Ensign St., Box 1399, Fort Morgan, CO 80701, (970) 542-3521, **<www.co.morgan.co.us >**

- **INCORPORATED:** Feb. 19, 1889
- **PARENT COUNTY:** Weld
- **BIRTH RECORDS:** start in 1906, kept by Northeast Colorado Health Department
- **MARRIAGE:** 1898, County Clerk
- **DIVORCE:** 1889, Clerk of District Court
- **DEATH:** 1900, NE Colorado Health Department
- **LAND:** 1898, County Clerk
- **PROBATE:** 1889, Probate Clerk
- **COURT:** 1889, Clerk of District Court

OTERO

13 W. Third St., La Junta, CO 81050, (719) 383-3020, **<www.oterogov.com>**

- **INCORPORATED:** March 25, 1889
- **PARENT COUNTY:** Bent
- **MARRIAGE RECORDS:** start in 1889, kept by County Recorder
- **DIVORCE:** 1889, Clerk of Combined Courts
- **LAND:** 1889, County Recorder
- **PROBATE:** 1889, Clerk of Combined Courts
- **COURT:** 1889, Clerk of Combined Courts
- **NOTES:** County Health Department has birth and death records from the late 1800s.

OURAY

Box C, 541 Fourth St., Ouray, CO 81427, (970) 325-4961, **<www.ouraycountyco.gov>**

- **INCORPORATED:** Jan. 18, 1877
- **PARENT COUNTY:** Hinsdale, Lake
- **BIRTH RECORDS:** start in 1880, kept by County Treasurer
- **MARRIAGE:** 1881, County Recorder
- **DIVORCE:** 1878, Clerk of Combined Courts
- **DEATH:** 1894, County Treasurer
- **LAND:** 1881, County Recorder
- **PROBATE:** 1878, Clerk of Combined Courts
- **COURT:** 1878, Clerk of Combined Courts
- **NOTES:** State Archives has naturalization records 1878-1918. Name changed to Uncompahgre County Feb. 27, 1883, renamed Ouray County March 2, 1883.

PARK

501 Main St., Box 220, Fairplay, CO 80440, (719) 836-4333, **<www.parkco.us>**

- **INCORPORATED:** Nov. 1, 1861
- **PARENT COUNTY:** Original county
- **BIRTH RECORDS:** start in 1875, kept by Clerk/Recorder
- **MARRIAGE:** 1881, County Recorder
- **DIVORCE:** 1861, Clerk of Combined Courts
- **DEATH:** 1903, Clerk/Recorder
- **LAND:** 1861, County Recorder
- **PROBATE:** 1861, Clerk of Combined Courts
- **COURT:** 1861, Clerk/Common Pleas Court
- **NOTES:** State Archives has naturalization records 1909-1930.

PHILLIPS

221 S. Interocean Ave., Holyoke, CO 80734, (970) 854-3131, **<www.cogenweb.com/phillips>**

- **INCORPORATED:** March 27, 1889
- **PARENT COUNTY:** Logan
- **BIRTH RECORDS:** start in unknown, City Registrar
- **MARRIAGE:** 1892, County Clerk
- **DIVORCE:** 1889, Clerk of Combined Courts
- **DEATH:** unknown, City Registrar
- **LAND:** 1892, County Clerk
- **PROBATE:** 1889, Clerk of Combined Courts
- **COURT:** 1889, Clerk of Combined Courts
- **NOTES:** State Archives has naturalization records 1889-1930.

PITKIN

530 E. Main St., first floor, Aspen, CO 81611, (970) 920-5180, **<www.aspenpitkin.com>**

- **INCORPORATED:** Feb. 23, 1881
- **PARENT COUNTY:** Gunnison
- **MARRIAGE RECORDS:** start in 1890, kept by County Recorder
- **DIVORCE:** unknown, Clerk of Combined Courts
- **LAND:** 1890, County Recorder
- **PROBATE:** unknown, Clerk of Combined Courts
- **COURT:** unknown, Clerk of Combined Courts

PROWERS

301 S. Main St., Suite 210, Lamar, CO 81052, (719) 336-8011, **<www.prowerscounty.net>**

- **INCORPORATED:** April 11, 1889
- **PARENT COUNTY:** Bent
- **BIRTH RECORDS:** start in 1908, kept by County Recorder
- **MARRIAGE:** 1889, County Recorder
- **DIVORCE:** 1889, Clerk of Combined Courts
- **DEATH:** 1908, County Recorder
- **LAND:** 1889, County Recorder
- **PROBATE:** 1889, Clerk of Combined Courts
- **COURT:** 1889, Clerk of Combined Courts

PUEBLO

215 W. Tenth St., Pueblo, CO 81003, (719) 583-6507, **<www.co.pueblo.co.us>**

- **INCORPORATED:** Nov. 1, 1861
- **PARENT COUNTY:** Original county
- **BIRTH RECORDS:** start in 1887, kept by Department of Health
- **MARRIAGE:** 1865, County Recorder
- **DIVORCE:** 1876, Clerk of Combined Courts
- **DEATH:** 1887, Department of Health
- **LAND:** 1865, County Recorder
- **PROBATE:** 1876, Clerk of Combined Courts
- **COURT:** 1876, Clerk of Combined Courts
- **NOTES:** State Archives has naturalization records 1878-1913, 1949-1983.

RIO BLANCO

555 Main St., Box 1067, Meeker, CO 81641, (970) 878-9460, **<www.co.rio-blanco.co.us>**

- **INCORPORATED:** March 25, 1889
- **PARENT COUNTY:** Summit
- **BIRTH RECORDS:** start in 1902, kept by County Recorder
- **MARRIAGE:** 1889, County Recorder
- **DIVORCE:** 1889, Clerk of Combined Courts
- **DEATH:** 1902, County Recorder
- **LAND:** 1889, County Recorder
- **PROBATE:** 1889, Clerk of Combined Courts
- **COURT:** 1889, Clerk of Combined Courts

RIO GRANDE

965 Sixth St., Box 160, Del Norte, CO 81132, (719) 657-3334, **<www.riograndecounty.org>**

- **INCORPORATED:** Feb. 10, 1874
- **PARENT COUNTY:** Conejos, Costilla
- **MARRIAGE RECORDS:** start in 1876, kept by County Recorder
- **DIVORCE:** 1876, Clerk of Combined Courts
- **LAND:** 1874, County Recorder
- **PROBATE:** 1876, Clerk of Combined Courts
- **COURT:** 1876, Clerk of Combined Courts
- **NOTES:** State Archives has naturalization records 1874-1906.

ROUTT

522 Lincoln Ave., Box 773598, Steamboat Springs, CO 80477 (970) 870-5556, **<www.co.routt.co.us>**

- **INCORPORATED:** Jan. 29, 1877
- **PARENT COUNTY:** Grand
- **MARRIAGE RECORDS:** start in 1877, kept by County Recorder
- **DIVORCE:** 1877, Clerk of Combined Courts
- **LAND:** 1877, County Recorder
- **PROBATE:** 1877, Clerk of Combined Courts
- **COURT:** 1877, Clerk of Combined Courts
- **NOTES:** State Archives has naturalization records 1885-1966.

SAGUACHE

501 Fourth St., Box 176, Saguache, CO 81149, (719) 655-2512, **<www.saguachecounty.net>**

- **INCORPORATED:** Dec. 29, 1866
- **PARENT COUNTY:** Costilla, Lake
- **MARRIAGE RECORDS:** start in 1885, kept by County Recorder
- **LAND:** 1885, County Recorder
- **NOTES:** Clerk of Combined Courts has court, divorce, and probate records from the late 1800s. State Archives has naturalization records 1878-1940.

SAN JUAN

Box 466, Silverton, CO 81433, (970) 387-5671,
<www.sanjuancountycolorado.us>

- **INCORPORATED:** Jan. 31, 1876
- **PARENT COUNTY:** Lake
- **BIRTH RECORDS:** start in 1880, kept by County Treasurer
- **MARRIAGE:** 1880, County Clerk
- **DIVORCE:** 1876, Clerk of Combined Courts
- **DEATH:** 1901, County Treasurer
- **LAND:** 1880, County Clerk
- **PROBATE:** 1876, Clerk of Combined Courts
- **COURT:** 1876, Clerk of Combined Courts
- **NOTES:** State Archives has naturalization records 1877-1926.

SAN MIGUEL

305 W. Colorado Ave., Box 548, Telluride, CO 81435
(970) 728-3954, **<www.sanmiguelcounty.org>**

- **INCORPORATED:** March 2, 1883
- **PARENT COUNTY:** San Juan
- **BIRTH RECORDS:** start in 1897, kept by County Treasurer
- **DIVORCE:** 1883, Clerk of Combined Courts
- **DEATH:** 1906, County Treasurer
- **LAND:** 1890, County Recorder
- **PROBATE:** 1883, Clerk of Combined Courts
- **COURT:** 1883, Clerk of Combined Courts
- **NOTES:** County Clerk/Recorder has marriage records from the early 1800s.

SEDGWICK

315 Cedar St., Suite 220, Julesburg, CO 80737, (970) 474-3346,
<www.sedgwickcountygov.net>

- **INCORPORATED:** April 9, 1889
- **PARENT COUNTY:** Logan
- **MARRIAGE RECORDS:** start in 1889, County Clerk
- **DIVORCE:** 1889, Clerk of Combined Courts
- **LAND:** 1889, County Clerk
- **PROBATE:** 1888, Clerk of Combined Courts
- **COURT:** 1888, Clerk of Combined Courts

SUMMIT

208 E. Lincoln Ave., Box 1538, Breckenridge, CO 80424
(970) 453-3470,**<www.co.summit.co.us>**

- **INCORPORATED:** Nov. 1, 1861
- **PARENT COUNTY:** Original county
- **MARRIAGE RECORDS:** start in 1900, kept by County Recorder
- **LAND:** 1861, County Recorder
- **NOTES:** Clerk of Combined Courts has court, divorce, and probate records form the late 1800s.

TELLER

101 W. Bennett Ave., Box 1010, Cripple Creek, CO 80813
(719) 689-2951, **<www.co.teller.co.us>**

- **INCORPORATED:** 23 March 1899
- **PARENT COUNTY:** El Paso
- **BIRTH RECORDS:** start in 1876, kept by County Recorder
- **MARRIAGE:** 1899, County Recorder
- **DIVORCE:** 1899, Clerk of Combined Courts
- **DEATH:** 1902, County Recorder
- **LAND:** 1899, County Recorder
- **PROBATE:** 1899, Clerk of Combined Courts
- **COURT:** 1899, Clerk of Combined Courts
- **NOTES:** State Archives has naturalization records 1899-1941.

UNCOMPAHGRE

- **INCORPORATED:** Feb. 27, 1883
- **PARENT COUNTY:** Ouray
- **NOTES:** Name changed to Ouray March 2, 1883.

WASHINGTON

150 Ash Ave., Box L, Akron, CO 80720, (970) 345-6565,
<co.washington.co.us >

- **INCORPORATED:** Feb. 9, 1887
- **PARENT COUNTY:** Weld
- **MARRIAGE RECORDS:** start in 1887, kept by County Clerk
- **DIVORCE:** 1887, Clerk of District Court
- **LAND:** 1887, County Clerk
- **PROBATE:** 1887, Clerk of District Court
- **COURT:** 1887, Clerk of District Court

WELD

1402 N. Seventeenth Ave., Greeley, CO 80631, (970) 304-6530,
<www.co.weld.co.us>

- **INCORPORATED:** Nov. 1, 1861
- **PARENT COUNTY:** Original county
- **BIRTH:** start in 1908, kept by Department of Health
- **MARRIAGE:** 1861, County Recorder
- **DIVORCE:** 1876, Clerk of Combined Courts
- **DEATH:** 1900, Department of Health
- **LAND:** 1861, County Recorder
- **PROBATE:** 1876, Clerk of Combined Courts
- **COURT:** 1876, Clerk of Combined Courts
- **NOTES:** State Archives has naturalization records 1871-1961.

YUMA

310 Ash St., Suite F, Box 467, Wray, CO 80758, (970) 332-5809,
<www.yumacounty.net>

- **INCORPORATED:** March 15, 1889
- **PARENT COUNTY:** Washington
- **MARRIAGE RECORDS:** start in 1889, kept by County Recorder
- **DIVORCE:** 1889, Clerk of Combined Courts
- **LAND:** 1887, County Recorder
- **PROBATE:** 1889, Clerk of Combined Courts
- **COURT:** 1889, Clerk of Combined Courts

CONNECTICUT

» BY MAUREEN A. TAYLOR

HISTORICAL OVERVIEW

Prior to European settlement, Native American tribes including the Mohegan, Nipmuc, and Pequot resided in the area that would become Connecticut. Connecticut towns founded in the early 17th century by European settlers include Windsor (1633), Wethersfield (1634), and Saybrook (1635). Congregational minister Reverend Thomas Hooker and his followers from Massachusetts, seeking political and religious freedoms, established Hartford in 1636 and became part of Connecticut Colony. Hooker's beliefs formed the foundation of The Fundamental Orders of Connecticut (1639), the first written constitution in the colonies that codified laws and allowed residents to elect public officials.

In 1662, King Charles granted Connecticut Colony a new charter that gave settlers land and control over their governance. Connecticut Colony merged with New Haven Colony, which included only six towns along Long Island Sound, in 1665. Colonial conflicts, such as the Pequot War of 1636 and King Philip's War of 1675-76, erupted between native populations and Europeans.

During the American Revolution, British troops captured Fort Griswold in New London and raided towns along the coastline. After the war, Connecticut delegates objected to the strong central government proposed for the new country. They lobbied for The Connecticut Compromise, the two-house legislature with equal representation in the Senate and population-based leadership in the House—the system still used today. Connecticut became the fifth state after ratifying the Constitution in 1788.

In 1818, a new state constitution allowed most men age 21 and over to vote and disestablished the Congregational Church. Connecticut outlawed buying and selling slaves in the state in 1784, completely abolishing slavery in 1848.

Until the early 18th century, most of the population farmed the rocky soil, but in the 1720s, they began migrating to the cities for work in mills, mines, and small factories. "Yankee Peddlers" traded the manufactured goods to other areas of the country. During the 19th century, immigrants from Italy, Germany, Canada, Ireland, and Poland sought employment in Connecticut's growing industrial economy.

research tips

- Many Connecticut vital records from 1650 are microfilmed or published, indexes for many are available at the Connecticut State Library **<www.cslib.org>**.
- If tracking colonial ancestors, check out *Connecticut Census of 1670* by Jay Holbrook (Holbrook Research Institute, 1977). It's a census substitute based on information from tax, land, church, probate, and freeman records from 1667 to 1673.
- Land records contain deeds, attachments, mortgages, tax liens, and other useful materials, and can be found in the town in which they were recorded.
- Records of military service for the colonial period from the Pequot War are published and can be found at the Connecticut Historical Society.

CENSUS RECORDS

- Federal census: 1790, 1800, 1810, 1820, 1830, 1840, 1850, 1860, 1870, 1880, 1900, 1910, 1920
- Federal mortality schedules: 1850, 1860, 1870, 1880
- Special military census: 1917

Transportation innovations improved the exportation of goods via the Farmington Canal (1828-1847) and rail lines between Providence and Stonington (1837) and between New Haven and New York City (1848), just two of the many operating in the state in the 19th century. Several towns along the southern coast built ships and participated in the whaling industry. Many early insurance companies formed in Hartford to insure goods being sent overseas.

Nearly 60,000 Connecticut soldiers fought in the Civil War, and its factories produced uniforms, weapons and ships. Connecticut men and women participated in all the major military conflicts of the 20th century and manufactured many of the weapons.

RECORD HIGHLIGHTS

"Connecticut's historic records are among the most complete and best kept in the nation," says certified genealogist Joyce Pendery. Many Connecticut records are microfilmed or published, with most indexes available at the Connecticut State Library. The University of Connecticut digitized the multivolume *Public Records of Colonial Connecticut* **<www.colonialct.uconn.edu>**. Like other New England states, Connecticut town clerks began recording vital records by 1650. In addition to the extensive Barbour Collection of Connecticut Vital Records to 1850, over a million tombstone inscriptions up to 1933 are in the Hale Collection of Connecticut Cemetery Inscriptions at the Connecticut State Library.

Tracking your colonial ancestors is easier due to *Connecticut Census of 1670* by Jay Holbrook (Holbrook Research Institute, 1977), a census substitute based on information from tax, land, church, probate, and freeman records that name heads of households from 1667 to 1673. With the exception of the federal census of 1890, a full set of US census records exists for Connecticut.

Look for tax lists and vital, probate, and land records on the town level. Land records contain deeds, attachments, mortgages, tax liens and more. Grantor/grantee indexes, maps, surveys, and zoning records are also with town clerks. While probate indexes and bound volumes with copies of the records are available in probate clerk offices in town halls, more towns exist than probate district offices. You may have to look in a town different from the one where your ancestor lived to find the records you need. Local tax lists exist for many cities and towns. The 1798 US Direct Tax, along with several early 19th century tax rosters, are on microfilm, with the originals at the Connecticut Historical Society (CHS).

Congregationalists helped settle Connecticut and established churches in most towns; their records can be quite extensive. Many churches sent records to the Connecticut State Library (CSL), where they've been partially indexed.

Find your ancestors in the pages of historical newspapers at both CSL and CHS. Some are indexed. Also available at CHS is a large collection of genealogical manuscripts.

Records of military service are published for the colonial period from the Pequot War. CHS maintains a collection of original and published military documents. A military census for 1917 was intended to count men between 20 and 30 years of age, but many towns included those between 16 and 60. A card index of deceased veterans and their places of burial is at the Connecticut State Library.

Connecticut researchers visiting Hartford can access even more records at CHS and the CSL. Probate, court, cemetery and some church records, as well as state papers, are centrally located at the CSL. The CHS maintains a general genealogical and historical library, loans books to members, and has an outstanding manuscript collection. You'll also find good documentation for Connecticut American Indians. Start research with resources in these two facilities, and then once you've determined the location of records, visit town halls, libraries and historical societies. Some town offices are open limited hours, so call ahead. Proof of membership in a genealogical society registered with the state is required to access birth records since 1900. Connecticut vital records information is available online at **<www.vitalrec.com/ct.html>**.

ARCHIVES, LIBRARIES, AND SOCIETIES

Abington Social Library
536 Hampton Road, Box 73, Pomfret Center, CT 06259, (860) 974-0415, **<www.abingtonsociallibrary.org>**

Amity and Woodbridge Historical Society
1907 Litchfield Turnpike, Woodbridge, CT 06525, (203) 387-2823, **<www.woodbridgehistory.org>**

Aspinock Historical Society of Putnam
206 School Street, Putnam, CT 06260, (860) 963-0092, **<aspinockhs-putnam.weebly.com>**

The Avon Historical Society
Box 448, Avon, CT 06001, (860) 678-7621, **<www.avonhistoricalsociety.org>**

Barkhamsted Historical Society
100 East River Road, Box 94, Pleasant Valley, CT 06063, (860) 738-2456, **<www.barkhamstedhistory.org>**

Beardsley and Memorial Library
40 Munro Place, Winsted, CT 06098, (860) 379-6043, **<www.beardsleyandmemorial.org>**

Cyrenius H. Booth Library
25 Main St., Newtown, CT 06470, (203) 426-4533, **<www.chboothlibrary.org>**

The Branford Historical Society, Harrison House
124 Main St., Box 504, Branford, CT 06405, (202) 488 4828, **<www.branfordhistory.org>**

Bridgeport Public Library
925 Broad St., Bridgeport, CT 06604, (203) 576-7403, **<www.bridgeportpubliclibrary.org>**

Bristol Public Library
5 High St., Bristol, CT 06010, (860) 584 7787, **<www.bristollib.com>**

Brookfield Museum and Historical Society
165 Whisconier Road, Box 5231, Brookfield, CT 06804, (203) 740-8140, **<www.brookfieldcthistory.org>**

Brooklyn Historical Society
25 Canterbury Road, Brooklyn, CT 06234 0090, (860) 774 7728, **<www.brooklynct.org>**

Burlington Historical Society
781 George Washington Turnpike, Box 1215, Burlington, CT 06013, (860) 675-3425, **<www.burlington history.org>**

Canterbury Historical Society
Box 2, Canterbury, CT 06331, **<www.canterburyhistorical.org>**

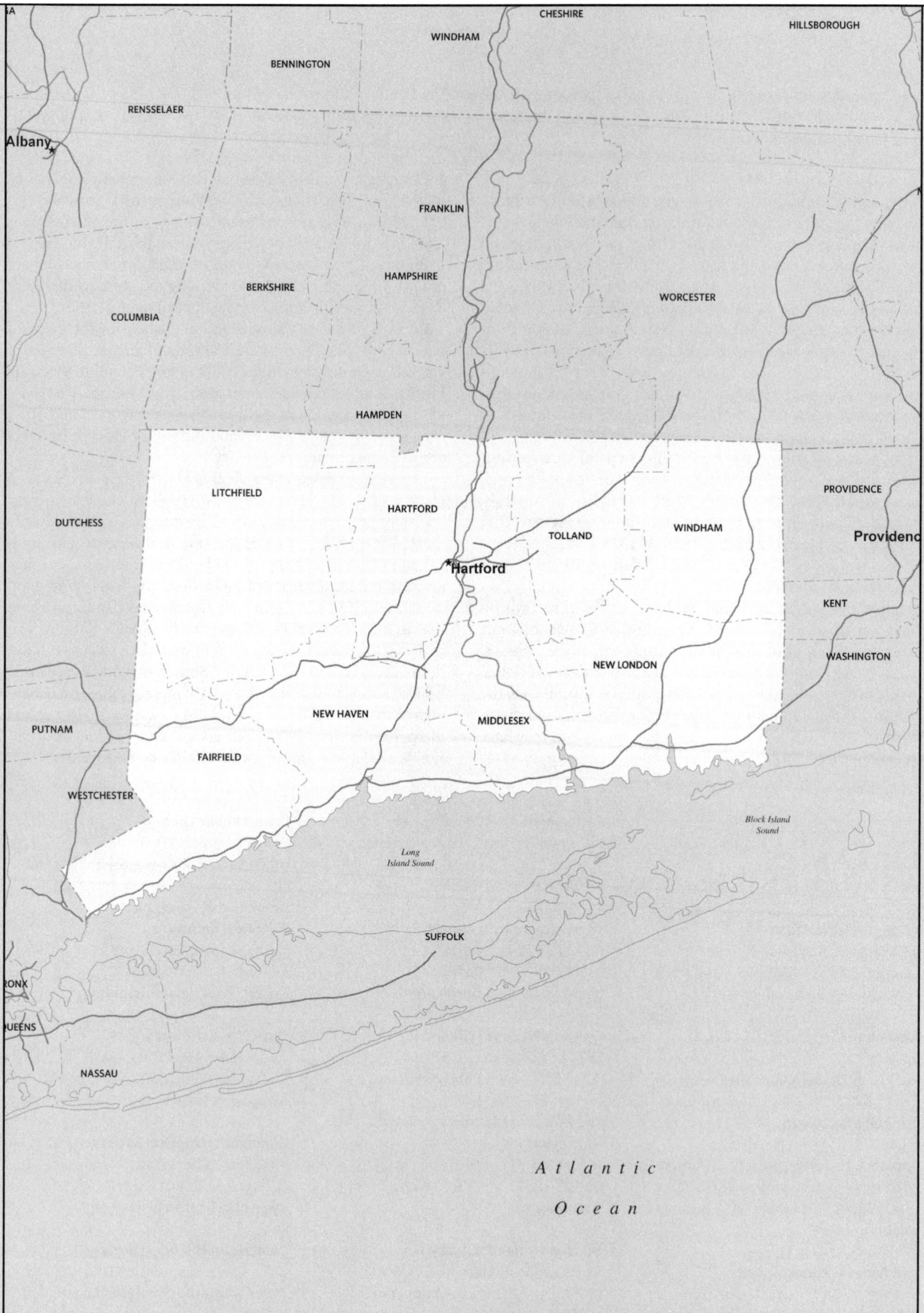
CHESHIRE
HILLSBOROUGH
WINDHAM
BENNINGTON
RENSSELAER
Albany
FRANKLIN
HAMPSHIRE
BERKSHIRE
WORCESTER
COLUMBIA
HAMPDEN
LITCHFIELD
HARTFORD
DUTCHESS
TOLLAND
WINDHAM
PROVIDENCE
Hartford
KENT
NEW LONDON
WASHINGTON
NEW HAVEN
MIDDLESEX
PUTNAM
FAIRFIELD
WESTCHESTER
Block Island Sound
Long Island Sound
SUFFOLK
NASSAU
Atlantic
Ocean

Canton Historical Society
11 Front St., Collinsville, CT 06019, (860) 693 2793, **<www.canton museum.org>**

Cheshire Historical Society
Box 281, Cheshire, CT 06410, (203) 272-2574, **<www.cheshirehistory.org>**

Chester Historical Society
9 West Main St., Box 204, Chester, CT 06412, **<www.chester historicalsociety.org>**

Colebrook Historical Society,
558 Colebrook Road, Box 85, Colebrook, CT 06021, **<www.colebrook historicalsociety.org>**

Columbia Historical Society
486 Rt. 66, Columbia, CT 06237, (203) 228 9385

Connecticut College Library
270 Mohegan Ave., New London, CT 06320, (860) 439-2655, **<www.conncoll.edu/is/info resources>**

Connecticut Commission on Art, Tourism, Culture, History and Film
1 Constitution Plaza, 2nd floor, Hartford, CT 06103, (860) 256-2800, **<www.cultureandtourism.org>**

Connecticut Historical Society
One Elizabeth St., Hartford, CT 06105, (860) 236-5621, **<www.chs.org>**

Connecticut League of History Organizations
940 Whitney Ave., Hamden, CT 06517, (203) 624-9186, **<www.clho.org>**

Connecticut Professional Genealogists Council
Box 4273, Hartford, CT 06147, **<www.rootsweb.com/~ctpgc>**

Connecticut State Archives at the Connecticut State Library
231 Capitol Ave., Hartford, CT 06106, (860) 757-6595, **<www.cslib.org/archives.htm>**

Connecticut State Library
231 Capitol Ave., Hartford, CT 06106, (860) 757-6580, **<www.cslib.org/handg/htm>**

Connecticut Trust for Historic Preservation
940 Whitney Ave., Hamden, CT 06517 (203) 562-6312, **<www.cttrust.org>**

Connecticut Valley Tobacco Historical Society
Box 241, Windsor, CT 06095, (860) 285-1888, **<www.tobaccohistsoc.org/connecti.htm>**

Cornwall Historical Society
7 Pine St., Box 115, Cornwall, CT 06753, (860) 672-0505, **<www.cornwallhistoricalsociety.org>**

Coventry Historical Society
Box 534, Coventry, CT 06238, (860) 742-9025, **<www.coventrycthistoricalsociety.org>**

Cromwell Historical Society
395 Main St., Cromwell, Box 146, CT 06416 (860) 635-0501, **<hometown.aol.com/cromwellhistory>**

Danbury Museum and Historical Society
43 Main St., Danbury, CT 06810, (203) 743-5200, **<www.danburymuseum.org>**

Danbury Public Library
170 Main St., Danbury, CT 06810, (203) 797-4505, **<danburylibrary.org>**

Darien Historical Society
45 Old Kings Hwy. N., Darien, CT 06820 (203) 655-9233, **<historical.darien.org>**

Derby Historical Society
Box 331, Derby, CT 06418, (203) 735-1908, **<derbyhistorical.org>**

East Granby Historical Society
9 Center St., Box 188, East Granby, CT 06026, **<www.eastgranby.com/HistoricalSociety>**

East Haddam Historical Society and Museum
264 Town St., East Haddam, CT 06423, (860) 873-3944, **<www.easthaddam.net>**

East Hartford Public Library
840 Main St., East Hartford, CT 06108, (860) 289-6429, **<www.ehtfdlib.info>**

East Haven Historical Society
200 Tyler St., Box 120052, East Haven, CT 06512

East Lyme Historical Society
Box 112, East Lyme, CT 06333, (860) 739-6070, **<www.eastlyme historicalsociety.org>**

East Windsor Historical Society
Box 363, E. Windsor Hill, CT 06028, **<members.cox.net/mjsalvatore/mjsalvatore>**

Easton Historical Society
Box 121, Easton, CT 06612, (203) 261-2090

Ellington Historical Society
70 Main St., Box 73, Ellington, CT 06029, **<www.ellingtonhistsoc.org>**

Enfield Historical Society
1294 Enfield St., Box 586, Enfield, CT 06083, (860) 745 1729, **<home.att.net/~mkm of enfct/EHS/EHSaboutUs.html>**

Episcopal Diocese of Connecticut
1335 Asylum Ave., Hartford, CT 06105, (860) 233 4481, **<www.ctdiocese.org>**

Essex Historical Society
Box 123, Essex, CT 06426, **<www.essexhistory.org>**

Fairfield Historical Society
370 Beach Road, Fairfield, CT 06824, (203) 259-1598, **<www.fairfield historicalsociety.org>**

Fairfield Public Library
1080 Old Post Road, Fairfield, CT 06824, (203) 256-3155, **<www.fairfield publiclibrary.org>**

The Falls Village-Canaan Historical Society
44 Railroad St., Box 206, Falls Village, CT 06031, (860) 824-8226, **<www.between thelakes.com/canaan/hist_society.htm>**

Farmington Historical Society
Box 1645, Farmington, CT 06034, **<www.farmingtonhistoricalsociety-ct.org>**

Ferguson Library
One Public Library Plaza, Stamford, CT 06904, (203) 964-1000, <www.futuris.net/ferg>

Finnish-American Heritage Society
Box 252, Canterbury, CT 06331, (860) 546-6671, <www.fahs-ct.org>

Franklin Historical Society
North Franklin, CT 06254

French-Canadian Genealogical Society of Connecticut
Box 928, Tolland, CT 06084, (860) 872-2597, <www.fcgsc.org>

Gaylordsville Historical Society
Box 25, Gaylordsville, CT 06755, (860) 350-0300, <www.gaylordsville.org>

Glastonbury Historical Society
1944 Main St., Box 46, Glastonbury, CT 06073, (860) 633-6890, <www.hsgct.org>

Godfrey Memorial Library
134 Newfield St., Middletown, CT 06457, (860) 346-4375, <www.godfrey.org>

Goshen Historical Society
21 Old Middle Road, Box 457, Goshen, CT 06756, (860) 491-9610, <www.goshenhistoricalct.org>

Greenwich Library
101 W. Putnam Ave., Greenwich, CT 06830, (203) 622-7900, <www.greenwichlibrary.org>

Groton Public Library
52 Newtown Road, Groton, CT 06340, (860) 441-6750, <www.town.groton.ct.us/library>

Haddam Historical Society
14 Hayden Hill Road, Box 97, Haddam, CT 06438, (860) 345-2400, <www.haddamhistory.org>

Miller Memorial Cultural Center
2901 Dixwell Ave., Hamden, CT 06518, <www.hamdenlibrary.org/Historical%20Society/historicalsociety.html>

Hampton Historical Society
Box 12, Hampton, CT 06247, (860) 455-0783, <www.hamptonct.org/Services/historical.htm>

Hartford Public Library
500 Main St., Hartford, CT 06103, (860) 695-6300, <www.hplct.org>

Harwinton Historical Society
Box 84, Harwinton, CT 06791

Hebron Historical Society
Box 43, Hebron, CT 06248, <www.hebronhistoricalsociety.org>

Historical Society of East Hartford
Box 380166, East Hartford, CT 06138, (860) 568-2884, <www.hseh.org>

Historical Society of the Town of Greenwich
39 Strickland Road, Cos Cob, CT 06807, (203) 869-6899, <www.hstg.org>

Indian and Colonial Research Center
39 Main St., Box 525, Old Mystic, CT 06372, (860) 536-9771, <www.theicrc.org>

Jewish Genealogical Society of Connecticut
134 Newfield St., Middletown CT 06457, (860) 346-4375, <www.jgsct-jewish-genealogy.org>

Jewish Historical Society of Greater New Haven
Box 3251, New Haven, CT 06515 (203) 392-6125, <jhsgnh.org>

Jewish Historical Society of Lower Fairfield County
Box 16918, Stamford, CT 06905, (203) 359-2196, <www.stamfordhistory.org/jhslfc.htm>

Kent Memorial Library
50 N. Main St., Suffield, CT 06078, (860) 668-3896, <www.suffield-library.org>

Killingly Historical and Genealogical Society
196 Main St., Box 6000, Danielson, CT 06239, (860) 779-7250, <www.killinglyhistory.org>

Lebanon Historical Society Museum and Visitor's Center
856 Trumbull Hwy., Lebanon, CT 06249, (860) 642-6579, <www.historyoflebanon.org>

Litchfield Historical Society
Box 385, 7 South St., Litchfield, CT 06759, (860) 567-4501, <www.litchfieldhistoricalsociety.org>

Madison Historical Society
Allis-Bushnell House, 853 Boston Post Road, Madison, CT 06443, (203) 245-4567, <www.madisoncthistorical.org>

Manchester Historical Society
106 Hartford Road, Manchester, CT 06040, <www.manchesterhistory.org>

Mansfield Historical Society/Museum
954 Storrs Road, Box, 145, Storrs, CT 06268, (860) 429-6575, <www.mansfieldct-history.org>

Meriden Public Library
105 Miller St., Meriden, CT 06450, (203) 238-2344,<www.cityofmeriden.org/services/library>

Middlebury Historical Society
Box 104, Middlebury, CT 06762, <www.middlebury-ct.org/historical_society.php>

Middlefield Historical Society
405 Main St., Middlefield, CT 06455, (860) 349-0665

Middlesex County Historical Society
151 Main St., Middletown, CT 06457, (860) 346-0746, <www.middlesexhistory.org>

Middlesex Genealogical Society
Box 1111, Darien, CT 06820, <mgs.darien.org>

Monroe Historical Society
31 Great Ring Road, Box 212, Monroe, CT 06468, (203) 261-1383, <www.monroehistoricsociety.org>

Mystic River Historical Society
74 High St., Box 245, Mystic, CT 06355, <www.mystichistory.org>

Mystic Seaport Museum
75 Greenmanville Ave., Box 6000, Mystic, CT 06355, <www.mysticseaport.org>

National Archives and Records Administration, Northeast Region
Frederick C. Murphy Federal Center, 380 Trapelo Road, Waltham, MA 02452, (781) 663-0130, **<www.archives.gov/northeast/boston>**

Naugatuck Historical Society
Box 317, 195 Water St., Naugatuck, CT 06770, (203) 729-9039, **<naugatuckhistory.com>**

New Britain Public Library
20 High St., New Britain, CT 06051, (860) 224-3155, **<www.nbpl.info>**

New Canaan Historical Society
13 Oenoke Ridge, New Canaan, CT 06840, (203) 966-1776, **<www.nchistory.org>**

New England Historic Genealogical Society
99 Newbury St., Boston, MA 02116, (888) 296-3447, **<www.nehgs.org>**

New Fairfield Historical Society
Box 8156, New Fairfield, CT 06812, (203) 312-5687

New Haven Colony Historical Society
114 Whitney Ave., New Haven, CT 06510, (203) 562-4183, **<www.newhavenmuseum.org>**

New Haven Free Public Library
133 Elm St., New Haven, CT 06510, (203) 946-8130, **<www.cityofnewhaven.com/library>**

New London County Historical Society
11 Blinman St., New London, CT 06320, (860) 443-1209, **<www.newlondonhistory.org>**

New London Public Library
63 Huntington St., New London, CT 06320, (860) 447-1411, **<www.plnl.org>**

New Milford Historical Society and Museum
Box 359, New Milford, CT 06776, **<www.nmhistorical.org>**

Newtown Historical Society
Box 189, Newtown, CT 06470, (203) 426-5937, **<www.newtownhistory.org>**

Norfolk Historical Society
13 Village Green, Box 288, Norfolk, CT 06058, (860) 542-5761, **<www.norfolkhistoricalsociety.com>**

North Haven Historical Society
27 Broadway, North Haven, CT 06473, (203) 239-7722, **<www.northhavenhistoricalsociety.org>**

North Stonington Historical Society
1 Wyassup Road, North Stonington, CT 06359, **<www.nostoningtonhistsoc.homestead.com>**

Norwalk Historical Society
2 E. Wall St., Box 335, 2 E. Wall St., Norwalk, CT 06852, (203) 846-0525, **<www.norwalkhistoricalsociety.org>**

Old Lyme Historical Society
Box 352. Old Lyme, CT 06371, (860) 434-0684, **<www.oldlymehistoricalsociety.org>**

Old Saybrook Historical Society
350 Main St., Box 4, Old Saybrook, CT 06475, (860) 388-2622, **<www.saybrookhistory.org>**

Orange Historical Society
Box 784, Orange, CT 06477, (203) 795-3106, **<www.orangehistory.org>**

Otis Library
261 Main St., Norwich, CT 06360, (860) 889-2365, **<www.otislibrarynorwich.org>**

Phoebe Griffin Noyes Library
2 Library Lane, Old Lyme, CT 06371, (860) 434-1684, **<www.oldlyme.lion org>**

Polish Genealogical Society of Connecticut and the Northeast
8 Lyle Road, New Britain, CT 06053, (860) 223-5596, **<www.pgsctne.org>**

Portland Historical Society
492 Main St., Box 98, Portland, CT 06480, **<www.geocities.com/portlandhistsoc>**

Preston Historical Society
<www.preston-ct.org/html/historical_soc.html>

Ridgefield Historical Society
4 Sunset Lane, Ridgefield, CT 06877, (203) 438-5821, **<www.ridgefieldhistoricalsociety.org>**

Rocky Hill Historical Society
785 Old Main St., Box 185, Rocky Hill, CT 06067, (860) 563-6704, **<www.rockyhillhistory.org>**

Roman Catholic Archdiocese of Hartford
134 Farmington Ave., Hartford, CT 06105 (860) 541-6491, **<www.archdioceseofhartford.org>**

Seymour Public Library
46 Church St., Seymour, CT 06483 (203) 888-3903, **<www.seymourpubliclibrary.org>**

Sharon Historical Society
The Gay-Hoyt House, 18 Main St., Sharon, CT 06069, (860) 364-5688, **<www.sharonhist.org>**

Shelton Historical Society
70 Ripton Road, Box 2155, Shelton, CT 06484, (203) 925-1803, **<www.electronicvalley.org/shelton/history.html>**

Simsbury Public Library
725 Hopmeadow St., Simsbury, CT 06070 (860) 658-7663 **<www.simsburylibrary.info>**

Somers Historical Society,
Box 652, Somers, CT 06071 (860) 749-5735, **<www.somersnow.com/HistoricalSociety>**

Southington Genealogical Society
Box 698, Plantsville, CT 06479

Southington Public Library
255 Main St., Southington, CT 06489 (860) 628-0947, **<www.southingtonlibrary.org>**

Stamford Historical Society
1508 High Ridge Road, Stamford, CT 06903, (203) 329-1183 **<www.stamfordhistory.org>**

State of Connecticut Department of Public Health
410 Capitol Ave., Box 340308, Hartford, CT 06134, (860) 509-7897, **<www.dph.state.ct.us/OPPE/hpvital.htm>**

Sterling Memorial Library, Yale University
120 High St., Box 208240, Yale University, New Haven, CT 06520, (203) 432-1775, **<www.library.yale.edu/rsc/sml>**

Stonington Historical Society
Box 103, Stonington, CT 06378, **<www.stoningtonhistory.org>**

Stratford Historical Society
967 Academy Hill, Stratford, CT 06615, (203) 378-0630, **<www.stratfordhistoricalsociety.com>**

Thompson Historical Society
Box 47, Thompson, CT 06277, (860) 923-3776, **<www.thompsonhistorical.org>**

Trumbull Historical Society
Box 312, Trumbull, CT 06611, **<www.trumbullhistory.org>**

United Methodist Archives Center,
Drew University Library, 36 Madison Ave., Madison, NJ 07940, (973) 408-3588, **<www.depts.drew.edu/lib/uma.html>**

Vernon Historical Society
734 Hartford Turnpike (Route 30), Box 2055, Vernon, CT 06066, (860) 875-4326, **<vhsvernonct.tripod.com>**

Watkinson Library, Trinity College
300 Summit St., Hartford, CT 06106 (860) 297-2268, **<library.trincoll.edu/research/watk>**

☞ GENERAL RESOURCES

Black Roots in Southeastern Connnecticut, 1650-1900 by Barbara W. Brown and James M. Rose (New London County Historical Society, 2001)

Burpee's The Story of Connecticut, 4 vols., by Charles W. Burpee (American Historical Co., Inc. 1939)

A Catalogue of the Names of the Puritan Settlers of the Colony of Connecticut by Royal Ralph Hinman (Printed by E. Gleason, 1846)

A Complete History of Connecticut by Benjamin Trumbull (Arno Press, 1972)

Connecticut, a Bibliography of its History Prepared by the Committee for a New England Bibliography, edited by Roger Parks (University Press of New England, 1986)

Connecticut Genealogical Resources compiled by Barbar S. Giles (Fiske Genealogical Foundation, 1991)

Connecticut Research Outline by the Church of Jesus Christ of Latter-day Saints (online at **<www.familysearch.org/eng/search/RG/guide/connecticut.asp>**)

Connecticut Researcher's Handbook by Thomas Jay Kemp (Gale Research, 1981)

Connecticut Sources for Family Historians and Genealogists by Kip Sperry (Everton Publishers, 1980)

Connecting to Connecticut by Betty Jean Morrison (Society of Genealogists, 1995)

Early Connecticut Marriages as Found on Ancient Church Records Prior to 1800, 7 vols., by Frederic William Bailey (Bureau of Ancestry, 1896-1906)

Encyclopedia of Connecticut Biography, Genealogical-Memorial; Representative Citizens, 10 vols., compiled by Samuel Hart et al. (American Historical Society, 1917-1923)

Families of Ancient New Haven compiled by Donald Lines Jacobus and Helen D. Love Scranton (Genealogical Publishing Co., 1974)

Founders and Leaders of Connecticut, 1633-1783 by Charles E. Perry (Books for Libraries Press, 1971)

A Genealogical Dictionary of the First Settlers of New England, 4 vols., by James Savage (Genealogical Publishing Co., 1965)

Genealogical and Family History of the State of Connecticut by William Richard Cutter, et al. (Clearfield Co., 1994)

Genealogical Research in New England edited by Ralph J. Crandall (Genealogical Publishing Co., 1984)

Genealogist's Handbook for New England Research by Marcia Melnyk (NEHGS, 1999)

The Greenlaw Index of the New England Historic Genealogical Society, 2 vols., by William Prescott Greenlaw and the New England Historic Genealogical Society

Guide to Archives in the Connecticut State Library (Connecticut State Library, 1981)

Guide to Vital Statistics in the Church Records of Connecticut by the Historical Records Survey (The Survey, 1942)

The History of the Episcopal Church in Connecticut by Eben Edwards Beardsley (1893)

Illustrated Popular Biography of Connecticut compiled and published by J.A. Spalding (Press of the Case, Lockwood Brainard Co., 1891)

Inventory of the Church Archives of Connecticut, Lutheran by the Historical Records Survey (The Survey, 1941)

Inventory of the Church Archives of Connecticut, Protestant Episcopal by the Historical Records Survey (The Survey, 1940)

List of Officials, Civil, Military and Ecclesiastical of Connecticut Colony: From March 1636 through 11 October 1677, and of New Haven Colony Throughout Its Separate Existence, Also Soldiers in the Pequot War who then or Subsequently Resided within the Present Bounds of Connecticut compiled by Donald Lines Jacobus (R.M. Hooker, 1935)

Men of Mark in Connecticut edited by Colonel N.G. Osborn (W.R. Goodspeed, 1906-1910)

New England Family Histories: State of Connecticut by Lu Verne V. Hall and Donald O. Virdin (Heritage Books, 1999)

Nutmegger Index: An Index to Non-Alphabetical Articles and a Subject Index to the Connecticut Nutmegger, volumes 1-28, 1968-1996 by Helen S. Ullmann (Picton Press, 1996)

The Public Records of the State of Connecticut, 7 vols., by Charles J. Hoadly et al. (Case, Lockwood & Brainard Co., 1894-1948)

The Refugees of 1776 from Long Island to Connecticut by Frederic Gregory Mather (Genealogical Publishing Co., 1972)

Report of the Temporary Examiner of Public Records, 1906 by the Connecticut Temporary Examiner of Public Records (Hartford Press, 1907)

The Rogerenes: Some Hithero Unpublished Annals Belonging to the Colonial History of Connecticut by John Rogers Bolles (Stanhope Press, F.H. Gilson Co., 1904)

Sketches of Church Life in Colonial Connecticut edited by Lucy Cushing Jarvis (Tuttle, Morehouse & Taylor Company, 1902)

Who's Who in Connecticut by Ward E. Duffy (W.C. Cox Co., 1975)

Women Before the Bar: Gender, Law, and Society in Connecticut, 1639-1789 by Cornelia Hughes Dayton (University of North Carolina Press, 1995)

☞CENSUS RECORDS

Connecticut 1670 Census by Jay Mack Holbrook (Holbrook Research Institute, 1977)

☞IMMIGRATION RECORDS

Copies of Lists of Passengers Arriving at Miscellaneous Ports on the Atlantic and Gulf Coasts and at Ports on the Great Lakes, 1820-1873 by the US Bureau of Customs (National Archives, 1964)

☞LAND RECORDS

Lyme Records, 1667-1730 compiled and edited by Jean Chandler Burr (Pequot Press, 1968)

☞MAPS

Connecticut Place Names by Arthur H. Hughes and Morse S. Allen (Connecticut Historical Society, 1976)

Connecticut Town Origins by Helen Earle Sellers (Pequot Press, ca. 1964)

Connecticut Towns and Counties: What was What, Where and When by Michael J. Denis (Danbury House Books, 1985)

A Gazetteer of the States of Connecticut and Rhode-Island by John Chauncey Pease (Printed and Published by William S. Marsh, 1819)

A Geographic Dictionary of Connecticut and Rhode Island by Henry Gannett (Genealogical Publishing Co., 1978)

Town and City Atlas of the State of Connecticut by D.H. Hurd and Co. (1893)

☞MILITARY RECORDS

Catalogue of Connecticut Volunteer Organizations (Infantry, Cavalry and Artillery) in the Service of the United States, 1861-1865 by the Connecticut Adjutant General's Office (University Publications of America, 1991)

Collections of the Connecticut Historical Society by the Connecticut Historical Society (The Society, 1860-1895)

Connecticut Soldiers of the Pequot War of 1637 by James Shepard (Journal Publishing Co., 1913)

Connecticut's Black Soldiers, 1775-1783 by David O. White (Pequot Press, 1973)

The Military and Civil History of Connecticut During the War of 1861-65 by W.A. Croffut and John M. Morris (Ledyard Bill, 1869)

Pension Records of the Revolutionary Soldiers from Connecticut by the US Pension Bureau (1919)

Record of Service of Connecticut Men in the Army and Navy of the United States During the War of the Rebellion compiled by the authority of the General Assembly under the direction of the Adjutants-General (Case, Lockwood & Brainard Co., 1889)

Record of Service of Connecticut Men in the I. War of the Revolution, II. War of 1812, III. Mexican War by the Connecticut Adjutant General's Office and Henry P. Johnston (Case, Lockwood & Brainard, 1889)

Register of Pedigrees and Services of Ancestors (Society of Colonial Wars in the State of Connecticut, 1941)

Revolutionary War Pension and Bounty-Land-Warrant Application Files by the US Veterans Administration (National Archives, 1969)

Roll and Journal of Connecticut Service in Queen Anne's War, 1710-1711 by Thomas Buckingham (The Tuttle, Morehouse & Taylor Press, 1916)

Rolls of Connecticut Men in the French and Indian War, 1755-1762 (Connecticut Historical Society, 1903-1905)

Rolls and Lists of Connecticut Men in the Revolution, 1775-1783 (Connecticut Historical Society, 1901)

☞PROBATE RECORDS

A Digest of the Early Connecticut Probate Records compiled by Charles William Manwaring (Genealogical Publishing Co., 1995)

Property and Kinship: Inheritance in Early Connecticut, 1750-1820 by Toby L. Ditz (Princeton University Press, 1986)

Records of the Particular Court of Connecticut, 1639-1663 by the Connecticut Particular Court (Heritage Books, 1987)

☞VITAL RECORDS

Early Connecticut Marriages as Found on Ancient Church Records Prior to 1800 by Frederic William Bailey (Bureau of American Ancestry, 1896-1906)

New England Marriages Prior to 1700 by Clarence Almon Torrey and the New England Historic Genealogical Society (Northeast Document Conversion Center, ca. 1983)

•-COUNTY DETAILS-•

FAIRFIELD

1061 Main St., Bridgeport, CT 06604, (203) 579-6527,
<www.rootsweb.ancestry.com/~ctfairfi>

- **INCORPORATED:** May 10, 1666
- **PARENT COUNTY:** Original county
- **BIRTH RECORDS:** start in 1700, kept by Town Clerk
- **MARRIAGE:** 1700, Town Clerk
- **DEATH:** 1700, Town Clerk
- **LAND:** 1649, Town/City Clerks
- **PROBATE:** 1648, Town Probate Clerks
- **VITAL:** 1640, Town/City Clerks
- **NOTES:** Towns organized before 1800: Brookfield 1788, Danbury 1687, Fairfield settled in 1639 incorporated in 1947, Greenwich settled in 1640 incorporated in 1955, Huntington (Shelton) 1789, New Fairfield 1740, Newtown 1711, Norwalk 1651, Redding 1767, Ridgefield 1709, Stamford 1641, Stratford 1639, Trumbull 1797, Weston 1787, Westport 1735.

HARTFORD

95 Washington St., Hartford, CT 06106, (860) 548-2700,
<www.munic.state.ct.us/hartford.htm>

- **INCORPORATED:** May 10, 1666
- **PARENT COUNTY:** Original county
- **BIRTH RECORDS:** unknown start, kept by Town/City Clerks
- **MARRIAGE:** unknown, Town/City Clerks
- **DEATH:** unknown, Town/City Clerks
- **LAND:** 1635, Town/City Clerks
- **PROBATE:** 1641, Town Probate Clerk
- **BURIAL:** unknown, Town/City Clerks
- **VITAL:** 1621 Town/City Clerks
- **NOTES:** Towns organized before 1800: Berlin 1785, Bristol 1785, Canton 1737 incorporated 1806, East Hartford 1783, East Windsor 1768, Enfield 1683, Farmington 1685, Glastonbury 1690, Granby 1664 incorporated 1786, Hartford 1635, Hartland 1761, Simsbury 1670, Southington 1779, Suffield 1674, Wethersfield 1634, Windsor 1633.

LITCHFIELD

Box 247, Litchfield, CT 06759, (860) 567-0885,
<www.litchfieldcty.com>

- **INCORPORATED:** Oct. 14, 1751
- **PARENT COUNTIES:** Hartford, Fairfield
- **BIRTH RECORDS:** unknown start, Town Clerk
- **MARRIAGE:** unknown, Town Clerk
- **DEATH:** unknown, Town Clerk
- **DIVORCE:** 1752, Clerk/Superior Court
- **LAND:** 1659, Town/City Clerks
- **PROBATE:** 1719, Probate Judge
- **COURT:** ca. 1800, Clerk/Superior Court
- **VITAL:** 1683, Town/City Clerks
- **NOTES:** Towns organized before 1800: Barkhamstead 1779, Bethlehem 1787, Canaan 1739, Colebrook 1779, Cornwall 1740, Goshen 1739, Harwinton 1737, Kent 1739, Litchfield 1719, New Hartford 1738, New Milford 1712, Norfolk 1758, Plymouth 1795, Roxbury 1796, Salisbury 1741, Sharon 1739, Torrington 1740, Washington 1779, Warren 1786, Watertown 1780, Winchester 1771, Woodbury 1674.

MIDDLESEX

1 Court St., 2nd Floor, Middletown, CT 06457, (860) 343-6400,
<www.rootsweb.ancestry.com/~ctmiddle/midlsxco.htm>

- **INCORPORATED:** May 2, 1785
- **PARENT COUNTIES:** Hartford, New London, New Haven
- **BIRTH RECORDS:** unknown start, kept by Town Clerk
- **MARRIAGE:** unknown, Town Clerk
- **DIVORCE:** 1800, Clerk/Superior Court
- **DEATH:** unknown, Town Clerk
- **LAND:** 1647, Town/City Clerks
- **PROBATE:** 1741, Town Probate Clerks
- **COURT:** 1639, Clerk/Superior Court
- **VITAL:** 1640, Town/City Clerks
- **NOTES:** Towns organized before 1800: Chatham 1767, Durham 1708, East Haddam 1734, Haddam 1668, Killingsworth 1667, Middletown 1651, Saybrook 1635.

NEW HAVEN

235 Church St., New Haven, CT 06510, (203) 503-6800,
<www.munic.state.ct.us/newhaven.htm>

- **INCORPORATED:** May 10, 1666
- **PARENT COUNTY:** Original county
- **BIRTH:** unknown start, kept by Town Clerk
- **MARRIAGE:** unknown, Town Clerk
- **DEATH:** unknown, Town Clerk
- **DIVORCE:** unknown, Clerk/Superior Court
- **LAND:** 1639, Town/City Clerks
- **PROBATE:** 1647, Town Probate Clerks
- **COURT:** na, Clerk/Superior Court
- **VITAL:** 1639, Town/City Clerks
- **NOTES:** Towns organized before 1800: Branford settled 1644 incorporated 1685, Cheshire 1780, East Haven 1785, Guilford 1639, Hamden 1786, Meriden incorporated 1806, Milford 1639, New Haven 1784, North Haven 1786, Oxford 1798, Seymour settled 1678 incorporated 1850, Southbury 1787, South Derby 1675, Wallingford 1670, Waterbury 1686, Wolcott 1796, Woodbridge 1784.

NEW LONDON

70 Huntington St., New London, CT 06320, (860) 443-5363,
<www.rootsweb.ancestry.com/~ctnewlon>

- **INCORPORATED:** May 10, 1666
- **PARENT COUNTY:** Original county
- **BIRTH RECORDS:** start in 1659, kept by Town Clerk
- **MARRIAGE:** 1659, Town Clerk
- **DIVORCE:** unknown, Clerk/Superior Court
- **DEATH:** 1659, Town Clerk
- **LAND:** 1646, Town/City Clerks
- **PROBATE:** 1675, Town Probate Clerks
- **BURIAL:** 1893, Town/City Clerks

- **VITAL:** 1640, Town/City Clerks
- **NOTES:** Towns organized before 1800: Bozrah 1786, Colchester 1699, Franklin 1786, Groton 1705, Lebanon 1700, Lisbon 1786, Lyme 1667, Montville 1786, New London 1648, Norwich 1662, Preston 1687, Stonington settled 1649 incorporated 1662, Voluntown 1721.

TOLLAND

69 Brooklyn St., Rockville, CT 06066, (860) 896-4920,
<users.rcn.com/lmerrell/tolland.html>

- **INCORPORATED:** Oct. 13, 1785
- **PARENT COUNTY:** Windham
- **BIRTH RECORDS:** unknown start, kept by Town Clerk
- **MARRIAGE:** unknown, Town Clerk
- **DEATH:** unknown, Town Clerk
- **LAND:** 1702, Town/City Clerks
- **PROBATE:** 1759, Town Probate Clerks
- **COURT:** unknown, Clerk/Superior Court
- **VITAL:** 1665, Town/City Clerks
- **NOTES:** Towns organized before 1800: Bolton 1720, Coventry 1711, Ellington 1786, Hebron 1708, Mansfield 1702, Somers 1749, Stafford 1719, Tolland 1715, Union 1734, Vernon settled 1726 incorporated 1808, Willington 1727.

WINDHAM

155 Church St., Putnam, CT 06260, (860) 928-7749,
<users.rcn.com/lmerrell/windham.html>

- **INCORPORATED:** May 12, 1726
- **PARENT COUNTY:** Hartford, New London
- **BIRTH RECORDS:** start in 1692, kept by Town Clerk
- **MARRIAGE:** 1692, Town Clerk
- **DEATH:** 1692, Town Clerk
- **DIVORCE:** unknown, Clerk/Superior Court
- **LAND:** 1686, Town/City Clerks
- **PROBATE:** 1719, Town Probate Clerks
- **BURIAL:** 1900, Town/City Clerks
- **VITAL:** 1665, Town/City Clerks
- **NOTES:** Towns organized before 1800: Ashford 1714, Brooklyn 1786, Canterbury 1703, Hampton 1786, Killingly 1708, Plainfield 1699, Ponfret 1713, Sterling 1794, Thompson 1785, Windham 1692, Woodstock (New Roxbury) 1690.

DISTRICT OF COLUMBIA

» BY JAMES W. WARREN

HISTORICAL OVERVIEW

In late 1800, President John Adams and Congress moved from Philadelphia to the almost uninhabited town of Washington, built from swampland to be the new seat of the US government. The staff of federal employees who accompanied them consisted of about 140 people. Today, more than 350,000 people staff federal offices in Washington alone.

The Federal District was formed over three years (1788-1791) from land Maryland and Virginia ceded to the United States. George Washington oversaw the surveying of the District. Originally a diamond-shaped area 10 miles on each side, the District's land was modified after the federal government relocated to Washington. In 1801, the District was divided into two counties: Washington County on the east (Maryland) side of the Potomac, and Alexandria County on the west (Virginia) side. The City of Washington was officially established in 1802.

During the war of 1812, the British captured Washington, and in 1814 burned much of the city and its records. In 1846, the portion of the District west of the Potomac was returned to the State of Virginia. DC grew slowly until the Civil War era, when the population more than doubled in just a few years. In 1871, Congress changed Washington City's status to that of a federal territory. In 1895 Congress merged Georgetown into the city of Washington, making the city's boundaries identical to the District's, which they still are today.

DC developed through the 20th century from a sleepy southern town into one of the most cosmopolitan and visited metropolitan areas in the country. The District is home to several of the nation's most significant genealogical collections. The National Archives and Records Administration (NARA), the Daughters of the American Revolution Library and the Library of Congress collections offer much about ancestors from every state. For those with DC ancestors, these repositories and others offer specific records and resources to help build your family history.

research tips

- The best available guide for researchers in DC is Erma Miller Angevine's *Research in the District of Columbia*, (National Genealogical Society).
- The Martin Luther King Jr. Memorial Library is an invaluable source for the history of the city and its people **<www.dclibrary.org>**.
- All the pre-1863 records and most of the later records of DC courts are in the custody of the National Archives **<www.archives.gov>**.
- To research people living in DC before 1800 or during the first half of the 19th century, your research needs to include the parent counties of the District: Alexandria County, Va., and Montgomery and Prince George counties, Md.

CENSUS RECORDS

- Federal census: 1790 (with Maryland), 1800, 1820, 1830, 1840, 1850, 1860, 1870, 1880, 1890 (only a small part of the 1890 census still survives), 1900, 1910, 1920, 1930
- Federal mortality schedules: 1850, 1860, 1870, 1880
- District census: 1867, 1878
- Police census: 1885, 1894, 1905, 1906, 1907, 1908, 1909, 1912, 1915, 1917, 1919

RECORD HIGHLIGHTS

The federal census population records for the District of Columbia begin with 1800. The 1810 census and almost all of 1890 were destroyed. The 1890 veteran's census for DC has survived. Slave schedules for 1850 and 1860 are also available, as are mortality schedules for 1850, 1860, 1870, and 1880. Police censuses were taken in 12 various years between 1885 and 1925, but contain only basic information similar to the

1820 census data. District censuses taken in 1803, 1807, and 1818 are also skimpy on details. Two other District censuses, 1867 and 1878, offer more information, including marital status, length of residence, occupation and parents' birthplace.

DC local courts have been identified by various names over time: Circuit Court from 1801-1863, Supreme Court from 1863-1928, and Superior Court from 1928 to the present. The federal court that serves the area has been identified as District Court since 1813. All the pre-1863 records and most of the later records of these courts are in the custody of NARA, and are inventoried as part of Record Group 21, Records of the District Courts.

For local court naturalization records, check with the Superior Court (500 Indiana Avenue NW). Federal District Court naturalizations (1802-1906) are held by NARA. Wills (1801-present) are with the Register of Wills and Clerk of Probate Court at the US Courthouse (500 Indiana Avenue NW). Other probate records are with NARA. Land records are available at the Recorder of Deeds (515 D Street NW). However, DC land records for 1792 to 1886 and a grantee/grantor index from 1792 to 1919 are microfilmed and available through the Family History Library (FHL). Land records for the surrounding counties (Alexandria County, Va,. and Montgomery and Prince George counties, Md.) are also available on FHL film up to the 1860s or later.

Birth and death registration was required in the District starting in 1874. Compliance with registration was generally upheld for births by 1915 and for deaths by 1880. One glaring gap is the Civil War era, when death records were not kept. Copies of the records are available from the Vital Records Section (4265 I Street NW). The FHL has microfilmed births from 1874 to 1897 and deaths from 1855 to 1949. Registration of marriages began in 1811, and those records are available from the Marriage License Bureau (500 Indiana Avenue NW). Most pre-1956 divorce records are with the Clerk of the US District Court (Constitution Ave. and John Marshall Place NW), though some have been turned over to NARA.

The nature of federal government employment meant that many people came to the area but did not remain. Church and cemetery records can be helpful in tracking such non-permanent residents and families, and can also provide clues for searches in court and vital records.

Federal records cannot be overlooked in dealing with DC research. This applies not only to District residents, but also the many people who lived in Virginia or Maryland and worked for the federal government in the District. Federal records and government publications are rich with detail about federal employees. *Preliminary Inventory of the Records of the Government of the District of Columbia, Record Group 351,* by Dorothy S. Provine, is a starting point. Many other federal record groups held by NARA give extensive information on government employees. For example, most agencies prepared annual reports to Congress that often listed all agency employees and included more details than just names. Information about records at NARA is available at **<www.archives.gov>**.

The Martin Luther King Jr. Memorial Library **<www.dclibrary.org>**, the District's main library at 901 G Street NW, is a great resource for the history of the city and the individuals who lived and worked here. It holds microfilmed DC newspapers from 1800 to the present, with indexes and subject clipping files. The Historical Society of Washington, found at 801 K Street NW, h"as a photograph, archives and library collection that can be of value as well (**<www.historydc.org>**).

To research people living in the area pre-1800 or during the first half of the 19th century, your research needs to include the parent counties of the District: Alexandria County, Va., Montgomery County, Md., and Prince George County, Md.

One facility whose valuable historical records are unfortunately difficult to access is the DC Records Center at 1300 Naylor Court NW. It opened in the mid-1980s under former mayor Marion Berry as the District's local archives. The facility was intended to house the District's historical federal records, which were to be transferred from NARA. It would showcase the DC residents' move to "Home Rule," symbolically reclaiming the District's history after more than a century of "Congressional rule." The plan never materialized, and the building, neighborhood, budget and priceless documents all suffer from neglect and deterioration.

While there have been many changes since it was written, the best available guide for researchers remains Erma Miller Angevine's *Research in the District of Columbia,* first published in March 1990 as an article in the *National Genealogical Society Quarterly*.

☞ARCHIVES, LIBRARIES, AND SOCIETIES

Afro-American Historical and Genealogical Society
Box 73067, Washington, DC 20056, **<www.aahgs.org>**

Arlington National Cemetery
Administrative Building, Arlington, VA 22211, (703) 607-8000, **<www.arlington cemetery.org>**

District of Columbia Superior Court, Family Court, H. Carl Moultrie Courthouse
500 Indiana Ave. NW, John Marshall Level, East Wing, JM 520, Washington, DC 20001, (202) 879-1212

District of Columbia Public Library
901 G St. NW, Washington, DC 20001, (202) 727-0321, **<dclibrary.org>**

Episcopal Diocese of Washington Archives
Massachusetts and Wisconsin Avenues NW, Washington, DC 20016
(202) 537-8981, rhewlett@cathedral.org

Historic Congressional Cemetery
1801 E St., S.E., Washington, DC 20003, (202) 543-0539, **<www.congressionalcemetery.org>**

Historiographer, Archdiocese of Washington
5001 Eastern Ave., Hyattsville, MD 20782, (301) 853-4500

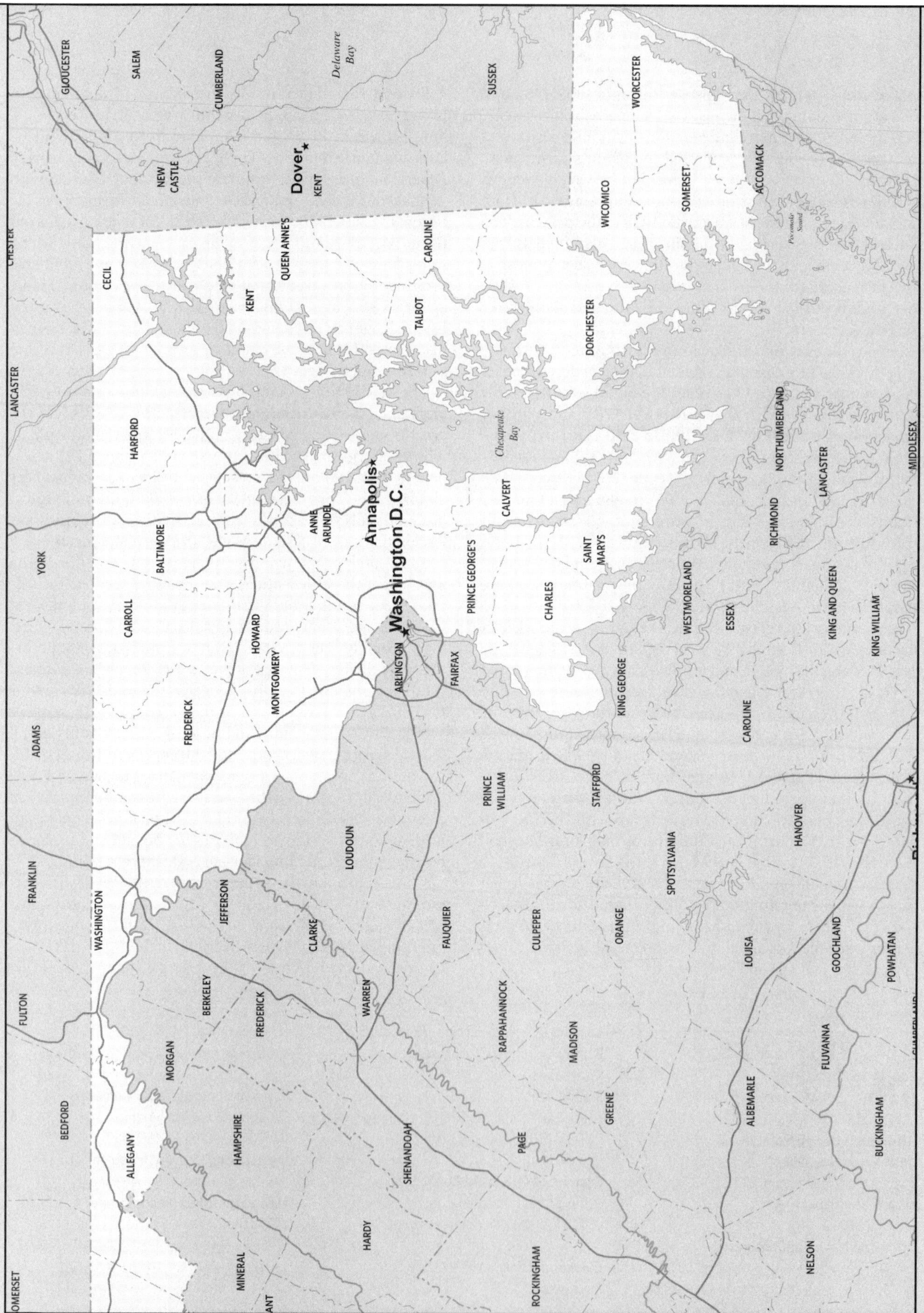
Washington D.C.
Annapolis
Dover
Delaware Bay
Chesapeake Bay
Pocomoke Sound
GLOUCESTER
SALEM
CUMBERLAND
SUSSEX
NEW CASTLE
KENT
WORCESTER
WICOMICO
SOMERSET
ACCOMACK
CHESTER
CECIL
QUEEN ANNE'S
CAROLINE
KENT
TALBOT
DORCHESTER
LANCASTER
HARFORD
YORK
BALTIMORE
ANNE ARUNDEL
CALVERT
PRINCE GEORGE'S
SAINT MARYS
CHARLES
ADAMS
CARROLL
HOWARD
MONTGOMERY
FREDERICK
ARLINGTON
FAIRFAX
KING GEORGE
WESTMORELAND
NORTHUMBERLAND
RICHMOND
LANCASTER
MIDDLESEX
ESSEX
KING AND QUEEN
KING WILLIAM
CAROLINE
PRINCE WILLIAM
STAFFORD
HANOVER
SPOTSYLVANIA
LOUDOUN
FRANKLIN
WASHINGTON
JEFFERSON
CLARKE
FAUQUIER
CULPEPER
ORANGE
LOUISA
GOOCHLAND
POWHATAN
FULTON
BERKELEY
FREDERICK
WARREN
RAPPAHANNOCK
MADISON
FLUVANNA
BEDFORD
MORGAN
HAMPSHIRE
ALLEGANY
SHENANDOAH
PAGE
GREENE
ALBEMARLE
BUCKINGHAM
HARDY
MINERAL
ROCKINGHAM
NELSON
OMERSET

Library of Congress
101 Independence Ave., SE, Washington, DC 20540, (202) 707-5000, **<www.loc.gov>**

Library of Virginia
800 E. Broad St., Richmond, VA 23219, (804) 692-3500, **<www.lva.lib.va.us>**

Maryland State Archives
Reference Department,
350 Rowe Blvd., Annapolis, MD 21401, **<www.msa.md.gov>**

Mt. Olivet Cemetery
1300 Bladensburg Rd. N.E., Washington, DC 20002, (202) 399-3000

National Society, Daughters of the American Revolution Library
1776 D St. NW, Washington, DC, 20006, (202) 628-1776, **<www.dar.org>**

Nation's Capital Area Chapter, American Historical Society of Germans from Russia
<www.ahsgr.org/nation_capital_area.htm>

Oak Hill Cemetery
3001 R St. NW, Washington, DC 20007, (202) 337-2835

Prospect Hill Cemetery
2201 N. Capitol St., N.E., Washington, DC 20002, (202) 667-0676

St. Alban's Episcopal Church
3001 Wisconsin Ave. NW, Washington, DC 20016, (202) 363-8286, **<www.st-albans-parish.org>**

Society of the Cincinnati Anderson House Museum
2118 Massachusetts Ave., NW, Washington, DC 20008, (202) 785-2040, **<www.hereditary.us/cin_anderson.htm>**

State Center for Health Statistics Administration, Vital Records Division
825 N. Capitol St. NE, 2nd floor; Washington, DC 20002, (202) 442-5865, **<www.app.doh.dc.gov/about/index_schs.shtm>**

US Court of Appeals for the District of Columbia Circuit
333 Constitution Ave. NW, Washington, DC 20001, (202) 216-7300

White House Historical Association
Box 27624, Washington, DC 20038, (202) 737-8292, **<www.whitehousehistory.org>**

GENERAL RESOURCES

A Biographical Congressional Directory With an Outline History of the National Congress, 1774-1911 by the US Congress (61st, 2nd Session: 1909-1911) (Government Printing Office, 1913)

Capital Collections: Resources for Jewish Genealogical Research in the Washington, DC Area edited by Sharlene Kranz (Jewish Genealogical Society of Greater Washington, 1995)

Centennial History of the City of Washington, DC by Harvey W. Crew (United Brethren Publishing House, 1892)

The Center: A Guide to Genealogical Research in the National Capital Area by Christina K. Schaefer (Genealogical Publishing Co., 1996)

The City of Washington, its Origin and Administration by John Addison Porter (Johnson Reprint Corp., 1973)

A Directory of Churches and Religious Organizations in the District of Columbia, 1939 by the Historical Records Survey (District of Columbia Historical Records Survey, 1939)

District of Columbia Ancestors by Wesley E. Pippenger (Family Line Publications, 1997)

District of Columbia: A Bicentennial History by David L. Lewis (New York: Norton, 1976)

District of Columbia Free Negro Registers, 1821-1861 compiled and edited by Dorothy S. Provine (Heritage Books, 1996)

District of Columbia Indentures of Apprenticeship, 1801-1893 compiled by Dorothy S. Provine (Willow Bend Books, 1998)

Early Days of Washington by Sally Somervell Mackall (The Neale Company, 1899)

Federal Assessment, 1790-1805, Maryland, District of Columbia by the US Congress (Maryland, Hall of Records Commission, 1965)

Guide to the Records of Your District of Columbia Ancestors by Eleanor Mildred Vaughan Cook (Family Line Publications, 1987)

Guide to Washington National Records Center Services by the National Archives and Records Administration (National Archives)

Historical Collections of Virginia ... To Which is Appended an Historical and Descriptive Sketch of the District of Columbia by Henry Howe (Regional Publishing Co., 1969)

Inventory of Church Archives in the District of Columbia: The Protestant Episcopal Church, Diocese of Washington by the Historical Records Survey (Historical Records Survey, 1940)

Lest We Forget: A Guide to Genealogical Research in the Nation's Capital by H. Byron Hall (Annandale Stake of the Church of Jesus Christ of Latter-day Saints, 1992)

Official Congressional Directory by the US Congress (US Government Printing Office, 1865)

Official Register of the United States: Containing a List of Officers and Employees in the Civil, Military, and Naval Service (US Government Printing Office, 1863)

The Postal History of Maryland, the Delmarva Peninsula, and the District of Columbia by Chester M. Smith Jr. and John L. Kay (The Depot, 1984)

Research in the District of Columbia by Erma Miller Angevine (National Genealogical Society, 1992)

Standard History of the City of Washington from a Study of the Original Sources by William Tindall (H.W. Crew & co., 1914)

Washington: A History of the Capital, 1800-1950 by Constance McLaughlin Green (Princeton University Press, 1964)

Washington DC: a Guide to the Nation's Capital edited by Randall Bond Truett (Hastings House, 1986, ca.1942)

Washington, Past and Present: A History, 4 vols., by John Proctor Clagett (Lewis Historical Company, Inc., 1930)

Washington; or, The Revolution. A Drama. (In Blank Verse.) Founded Upon the Historic Events of the War for American Independence by Ethan Allen and illustrated by Henry Kratzner (F.T. Neely, 1899)

☞CENSUS RECORDS

An Illustrated Genealogy of the Counties of Maryland and the District of Columbia as a Guide to Locating Records by Mary Ross Brown (French-Bray Print Co., 1967)

☞IMMIGRATION RECORDS

Copies of Lists of Passengers Arriving at Miscellaneous Ports on the Atlantic and Gulf Coasts and at Ports on the Great Lakes, 1820-1873 by the US Bureau of Customs (National Archives, 1964)

☞LAND RECORDS

District of Columbia Original Land Owners, 1791-1800 by Wesley E. Pippenger (Willow Bend Books, 1999)

Original Patentees of Land at Washington Prior to 1700 by Bessie Wilmarth Gahn (Genealogical Publishing Co., 1969)

☞MAPS

Atlas of Historical County Boundaries. Delaware, Maryland, and the District of Columbia edited and compiled by John H. Long (Charles Scribner's Sons, Simon & Schuster Macmillan, 1995)

District of Columbia Geographic Names by the US Office of Geographic Research, Branch of Geographic Names (US Branch of Geographic Names, 1981)

A New and Comprehensive Gazetteer of Virginia and the District of Columbia by Joseph Martin (J. Martin, 1836)

Round About the Nation's Capital with Descriptive Notes by the National Geographic Society Cartographic Division (The Society, 1956)

☞MILITARY RECORDS

Civil War Cemeteries of the District of Columbia Metropolitan Area compiled by Paul E. Sluby, Sr., edited by Stanton L. Wormley (Columbian Harmony Society, 1982)

Maryland and the District of Columbia Volunteers in the Mexican War by Charles J. Wells (Family Line Publications, 1991)

Roll of Honor: Names of Soldiers who Died in Defense of the American Union, Interred in the National Cemeteries by the US Quartermaster's Department (Genealogical Publishing Co., 1994)

Selected Final Pension Payment Vouchers, 1818-1864. District of Columbia abstracted by Alycon Trubey Pierce (Willow Bend Books, 1998)

☞PROBATE RECORDS

Abstracts of Wills in the District of Columbia, 1776-1815: Compiled From Records in the Office of the Register of Wills compiled by Mrs. Alexander H. Bell (1945-1946)

District of Columbia, DC Department of Corrections Runaway Slave Book, 1848-1863; US District Court for the District of Columbia Fugitive Slave Cases, 1862-1863 by Jerry M. Hynson (Willow Bend Books, 1999)

District of Columbia Probate Records: Will Books 1 Through 6, 1801-1852 and Estate Files, 1801-1852 compiled by Wesley E. Pippenger (Family Line Publications, 1996)

Indentures of Apprenticeship Recorded in the Orphans Court, Washington County, District of Columbia, 1802-1811 by the District of Columbia Orphans Court (National Archives, 2000)

Index to District of Columbia Wills, 1801-1920 prepared by Dorothy S. Province (Genealogical Publishing Co., 1992)

Index to District of Columbia Wills, 1921-1950 prepared by Dorothy S. Province (Willow Bend Books, 1998)

☞VITAL RECORDS

Blacks in the Marriage Records of the District of Columbia, Dec. 23, 1811-Jun. 16, 1870 by Paul E. Sluby and Stanton L. Wormley (Columbian Harmony Society, 1988)

District of Columbia Marriage Licenses: Register 1, 1811-1858 compiled by Wesley E. Pippenger (Family Line Publications, 1994)

District of Columbia Marriage Licenses: Register 2, 1858-1870 compiled by Wesley E. Pippenger (Willow Bend Books, 1996)

Historical Court Records of Washington, District of Columbia by Homer A. Walker (1956)

Historical Graves of Maryland and the District of Columbia, With the Inscriptions on the Tombstones in Most of the Counties of the State and in Washington and Georgetown by Helen W. Ridgely (Genealogical Publishing Co., 1967)

Marriage Licenses of Washington, DC, 1811-1830 by F. Edward Wright (Family Line Publications, 1988)

DELAWARE

» BY MAUREEN A. TAYLOR

HISTORICAL OVERVIEW

In 1638, two ships—the *Kalmar Nyckel* and the *Fogel Grip*—brought 30 people from Sweden to settle near present-day Wilmington, Del. They named their new home New Sweden. Ownership of the area changed several times during the 17th century. The Dutch took over the colony from the Swedish settlers, then the British captured the renamed New Netherland in 1664. The Dutch reasserted their ownership in 1673, but ended up returning the area to the British a year later. The three lower counties of the Colony—New Castle, Kent and Sussex—became part of William Penn's Pennsylvania, while Maryland also claimed part of the region.

The residents declared their independence from both Great Britain and Pennsylvania June 15, 1776, renaming the area Delaware. On Dec. 7, 1787, Delaware became the first state to ratify the Constitution.

Its central location, harbors and waterways made the state ideal for transportation systems. Steamboats carried passengers along the Delaware River, while the Chesapeake and Delaware Canal connected the two bays of the same names. In 1831, the New Castle and Frenchtown Railroad connected the eastern and western parts of the state.

Early in the 19th century, the du Pont family began manufacturing gunpowder. Their success made them the wealthiest family in Delaware, and their chemical research firm one of the largest in the world. Irish and German immigrants arrived to work in chemical manufacturing, shipbuilding and agriculture. Jews, Poles, Italians and Scandinavians immigrated later in the 19th century. Major industries in the 20th century included shipbuilding, chemicals (nylon for parachutes), textile mills and gunpowder factories in the northern part of the state, with agriculture and poultry farming in the southern half.

research tips

- The Historical Society of Delaware collects nongovernmental records such as genealogies, manuscripts, and church records.
- The Delaware Public Archives is the primary repository for state and local government records, including deeds, mortgages, probate records, court documents, and municipal papers **<www.state.de.us/sos/dpa/collections/guideintro.shtml>**.
- Be on the lookout for the land division "hundreds." While Delaware has only three counties, it has many hundreds—akin to townships in other states—that were created for taxation purposes.

CENSUS RECORDS

- Federal census: 1800, 1810, 1820, 1830, 1840, 1850, 1860, 1870, 1880, 1900, 1910, 1920, 1930
- Federal mortality schedules: 1850, 1860, 1870, 1880
- Reconstructed state census: 1790
- Slave schedules: 1850, 1860. Note that slave schedules generally don't list names of slaves, only the names of slave owners.
- Tax lists: 1700s-1915
- Militia records: 1765-1841

RECORD HIGHLIGHTS

Records for colonial Delaware are plentiful and varied. But according to the Historical Society of Delaware's website, "Delaware's rich and complex colonial history offers genealogists a special challenge. Early colonial documents might be found in many places, including the archives of New York State and Pennsylvania, as well as those of Sweden, the Netherlands, and Great Britain."

The Delaware Public Archives (DPA) has documents from the Swedish colonial period, 1638 to 1655; the Dutch settlement, 1655 to 1664; the Duke of York regime, 1664 to 1682; and the Penn Proprietorship, 1682 to 1776, with the majority of their holdings dating from statehood in 1776.

Use the Archive's online guide to the collections **<archives.delaware.gov>** and search the database, which is just a portion of the holdings, for types of records—not for your ancestors' names. For example, type in "birth records 1864" to find out where your ancestor's birth certificate may be located.

DPA has an index to marriages, births and deaths, from marriage bonds, church and Bible records, and newspapers from 1680 to the present. Statewide registration of Delaware births began in 1861, was discontinued in 1863 and resumed in 1881. Marriage records start as early as the 1700s for some towns; statewide registration began in 1847 and was generally complied with by 1913. Statewide death registration began in 1881 and was generally complied with by 1890. You can access birth records older than 72 years and marriages and deaths older than 40 years from the DPA. Look for microfilmed vital records at the Family History Library , too.

The 1790 US census was Delaware's first, but most schedules were destroyed. You'll find a reconstruction from tax and assessment records in *Reconstructed 1790 Census of Delaware* by Leon de Valinger Jr. (National Genealogical Society). Early tax records also can substitute for colonial censuses. Delaware didn't take state censuses.

During the colonial period, Presbyterians, English Quakers, Baptists, Catholics and Methodists settled in the area. Many church records have been published. Also look for original records and indexes at various repositories including the DPA and Historical Society of Delaware (HSD).

The DPA is the primary facility for noncurrent state and local government records, such as probate records, court documents (civil, criminal, naturalization, indenture) and municipal papers (minutes, accounts, reports). The collection inventory is online at **<www.state.de.us/sos/dpa/collections/guideintro.shtml>**. Original deeds and mortgages from 1680 are also there, as are miscellaneous genealogical manuscripts and a large collection of grave records known as the Tatnell Tombstone collection. Staff member Russ McCabe emphasizes that the archives has a "fairly large and growing library of printed and unpublished genealogies."

"Visit both the Historical Society of Delaware and the Delaware Public Archives," says Constance Cooper, librarian at the HSD. The HSD is a private, nonprofit organization that collects nongovernmental records such as genealogies, manuscripts and church records. Its website **<www.hsd.org>** features a Guide to Research in the Delaware Historical Society Library, an online instruction manual. Cooper says "a personal visit is the best way to research your Delaware families, because staff provides an orientation to the collection as well as assistance." One helpful on-site resource is the Genealogical Surname File, a card catalog of names and references arranged alphabetically by surname. The cards were compiled over the years from newspapers printed before 1850, books, journals, church records and other sources.

The Delaware Genealogical Society compiles information on Delaware research, including the *Delaware Genealogical Research Guide*, 3rd edition, by Thomas P. Doherty (Delaware Genealogical Society, 2002). Search the website **<delgensoc.org>** for names entered into the Delaware Families Project.

Delaware has only three counties—New Castle, Kent and Sussex—so research in the state initially appears simple. But William Penn decided to divide the colony into "hundreds" for taxation. This old English land division is explained by the Delaware Genealogical Society website as a "land division which is smaller than a county or shire and larger than a tithing. It comprises 10 tithings of 10 freeholder families each, or 100 families." Hundreds are roughly equivalent to townships in other states. Once used as judicial and legislative districts, they remain now only as the basis for property tax assessment.

ARCHIVES, LIBRARIES, AND SOCIETIES

Catholic Diocese of Delaware
Box 2030, Wilmington, DE 19899,
(302) 573-3100, **<www.cdow.org>**

Delaware Genealogical Society
505 N. Market St., Wilmington, DE 19801,
<delgensoc.org>

Delaware Legislative Council Library
Box 1401, Legislative Hall, Dover, DE 19903,
(302) 744-4308, **<www.delaware.gov>**

Delware Public Archives,
Vital Statistics Records
121 Duke of York St., Dover, DE 19901,
<www.state.de.us/sos/dpa/collections/vital.shtml>

Fort Delaware Society
Box 553, Delaware City, DE 19706, (302) 834-1630, **<www.fortdelaware.org>**

Hagley Museum and Library
Box 3630, Wilmington, DE 19807, (302) 658-2400, **<www.hagley.lib.de.us>**

Historical Society of Delaware
505 N. Market St., Wilmington, DE 19801,
(302) 655-7161, **<www.hsd.org>**

Jewish Federation of Delaware
100 W. 10th St., Suite 301, Wilmington, DE 19801, (302) 427-2100, **<www.shalomdelaware.org>**

Jewish Historical Society of Delaware
505 Market St. Mall, Wilmington, DE 19801, (302) 655-6232, **<www.hsd.org/jhsd.htm>**

National Archives and Records Administration, Mid-Atlantic Region
900 Market St., Philadelphia, PA 19107,
(215) 606-0100, **<www.archives.gov/midatlantic>**

University of Delaware Library
181 S. College Ave., Newark, DE 19717,
(302) 831-2965, **<www.lib.udel.edu>**

Wilmington Institute Library
10 E 10th St., Wilmington, DE 19801,
(302) 571-7400, **<www.wilmlib.org>**

GENERAL RESOURCES

Abstracts from the Pennsylvania Gazette, 1748-1755 by Kenneth Scott and Janet R. Clarke (Genealogical Publishing Co., 1977)

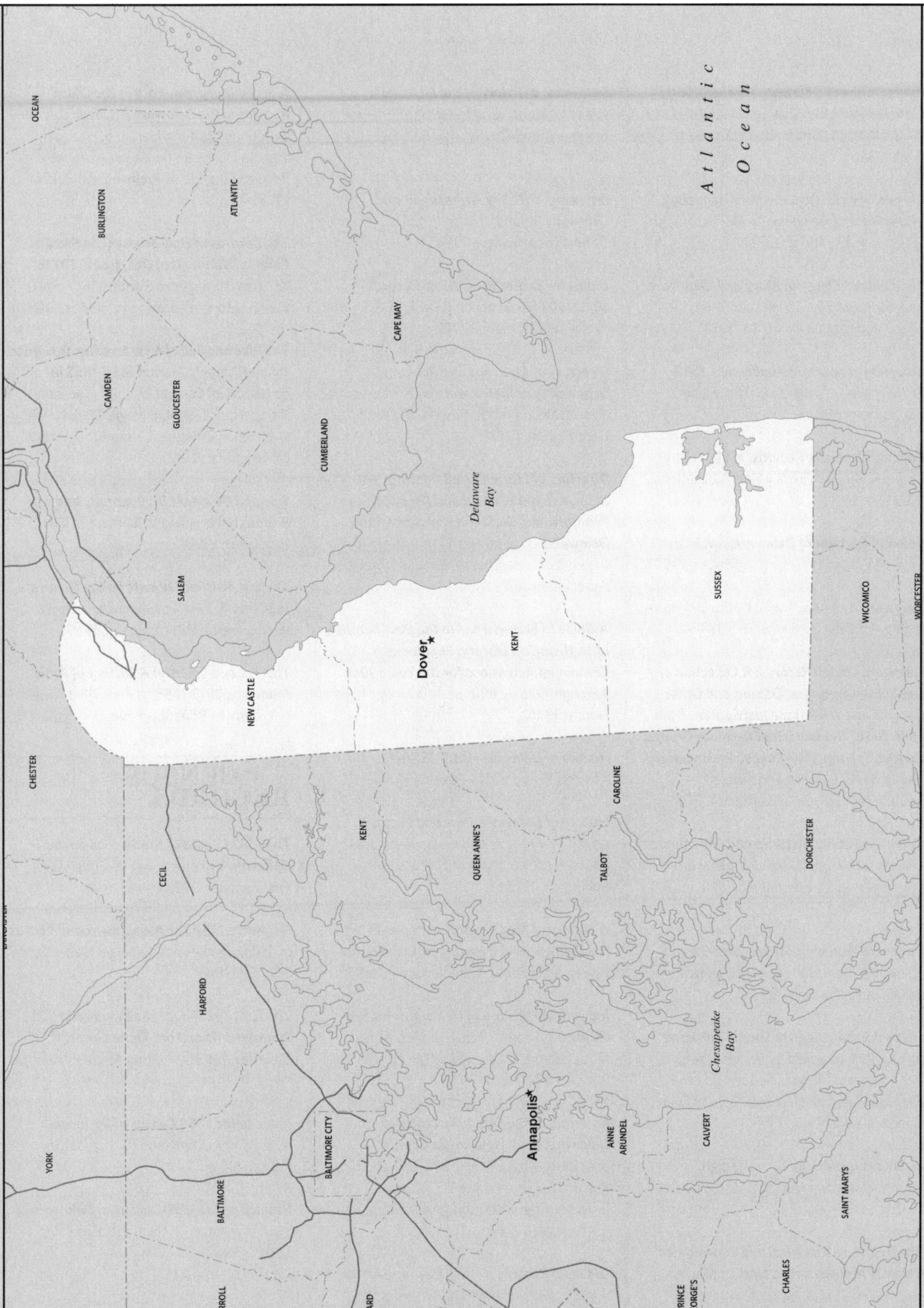
Atlantic Ocean
Delaware Bay
Chesapeake Bay
OCEAN
BURLINGTON
ATLANTIC
CAPE MAY
CAMDEN
GLOUCESTER
CUMBERLAND
SALEM
NEW CASTLE
Dover
KENT
SUSSEX
WICOMICO
WORCESTER
CHESTER
CECIL
KENT
QUEEN ANNE'S
CAROLINE
TALBOT
DORCHESTER
HARFORD
YORK
BALTIMORE CITY
BALTIMORE
Annapolis
ANNE ARUNDEL
CALVERT
SAINT MARYS
CARROLL
PRINCE GEORGE'S
CHARLES

Bibliography of Delaware Through 1960 compiled by Henry Clay Reed and Marion Bjornson Reed (University of Delaware Press, 1966)

Chronology and Documentary Handbook of the State of Delaware by Mary L. Frech (Oceana Publications, 1973)

The Colonial Clergy of Maryland, Delaware, and Georgia by Frederick Lewis Weis (Genealogical Publishing Co., 1978)

Colonial Delaware Assemblymen, 1682-1776 by Bruce A. Bendler (Family Line Publications, 1989)

Colonial Delaware Records, 1681-1713 by Bruce A. Bendler (Family Line Publications, 1992)

Colonial Families of Delaware, 4 vols. by F. Edward Wright (Willow Bend Books, 1999)

Delaware Archives, 4 vols. by the Delaware Public Archives Commission (1911)

Delaware Church Records: A Collection of Baptisms, Marriages, Deaths, and Other Records and Tombstone Inscriptions, from 1686-1880, Five Important Religious Groups: Baptist, Episcopal, Methodist, Presbyterian, and Quaker compiled and indexed by Raymond B. Clark Jr. (R.B. Clark, 1986)

Delaware Family Histories and Genealogies compiled by Donald Ordell Virdin, edited and published by Raymond B. Clark Jr. (R.B. Clark Jr., 1984)

Delaware Genealogical Research Guide edited by Thomas P. Doherty (Delaware Genealogical Society, 1997)

Delaware Genealogical Society Surname Index, 1995 compiled by Robert Joseph Redden, Barbara Fooks Redden, and the Delaware Genealogical Society (Delaware Genealogical Society, 1995)

Delaware Genealogy by Jean Foight Trumbore and the Hugh M. Morris Library (1979)

The Delaware Historical and Genealogical Recall of Matilda Spicer Hart by Matilda Spicer Hart (Delaware Genealogical Society, 1984)

Delaware, a History of the First State edited by Henry Clay Reed with Marion Bjornson Reed (Lewis Historical Publishing Co., 1947)

Delaware 1782 Tax Assessment and Census by Ralph D. Nelson, et al. (Delaware Genealogical Society, 1994)

Delaware Trails: Some Tribal Records, 1842-1907 transcribed by Fay Louise Smith Arellano (Clearfield, 1996)

Directory of Churches and Religious Organizations in Delaware by the Delaware Historical Records Survey (Public Archives Commission, 1942)

Directory of Libraries and Information Sources in the Philadelphia Area (Eastern Pennsylvania, Southern New Jersey and Delaware) edited by Barbara Ann Holley for the Philadelphia Chapter Special Libraries Association (1977)

A Guide to Manuscripts in the Eleutherain Mills Historical Library: Supplement Containing Accessions for the Years 1966 Through 1975 by John Beverley Riggs (The Library, 1978)

History of Delaware, 1609-1888 by John Thomas Scharf (W.C. Cox Co., 1974)

History of Delaware, Past and Present edited by Wilson Lloyd Bevan; associate editor, E. Melvin Williams (Lewis Historical Publishing, 1929)

A History of the Original Settlements on the Delaware—& a History of Wilmington by Benjamin Ferris (Gateway Press, 1987)

Index to the History of Delaware, 1609-1888 by J. Thomas Scharf, edited by Gladys M. Coghlan and Dale Fields (Historical Society of Delaware, 1976)

Inventory of the County Archives of Delaware, no. 1, New Castle County prepared by the Delaware Historical Records Survey and the US Works Progress Administration (Public Archives Commission, 1941)

Old Bible Records by the Daughters of the American Revolution (Daughters of the American Revolution, 1950-1973)

A Preliminary Inventory of the Older Records in the Delaware Archives compiled by Joanne Mattern, Harold B. Hancock and the Delaware Bureau of Archives and Records (Bureau of Archives and Records, 1978)

The Records of Holy Trinity (Old Swedes) Church, Wilmington, Del., from 1697 to 1773 translated from Swedish by Horace Burr (Historical Society of Delaware, 1890)

The Rise and Fall of New Sweden: Governor Johan Risingh's Journal 1654-1655 in its Historical Context by John Claesson Rising, Hans Norman, Marie Clark Nelson and Stellan Dahlgren (Almqvist & Wiskell International, 1988)

Selected Delaware Bibliography and Resources compiled by Barbara S. Giles (B.S. Giles, 1990)

The Swedish Settlements on the Delaware, 1638-1664, 2 vols. by Amandus Johnson (Genealogical Publishing Co., 1969)

This is Good Country: A History of Amish Delaware, 1915-1988 by Rev. Allen B. Clark (Gordonville Print Shop, 1988)

☞ CENSUS RECORDS

The 1693 Census of the Swedes on the Delaware by Peter Stebbins Craig (SAG Publications, 1993)

Delaware 1782 Tax Assessment and Census by Ralph D. Nelson (Delaware Genealogical Society, 1994)

The First Tax List for the Province of Pennsylvania and the Three Lower Counties, 1693 by Adams Apple Press (The Press, 1994)

Index to the 1850 Census of Delaware by Virginia L. Olmstead (Genealogical Publishing, 1977)

Reconstructed 1790 Census of Delaware by Leon Devalinger Jr. (National Genealogical Society, 1962)

The Reconstructed Delaware Census of 1782 by Harold B. Hancock (Delaware Genealogical Society, 1973)

☞IMMIGRATION RECORDS

Copies of Lists of Passengers Arriving at Miscellaneous Ports on the Atlantic and Gulf Coasts and at Ports on the Great Lakes, 1820-1873 by the US Bureau of Customs (National Archives, 1964)

Philadelphia Naturalization Records: An Index to Records of Aliens' Declarations of Intention and/or Oaths of Allegiance, 1789-1880, in United States Circuit Court, United States District Court, Supreme Court of Pennsylvania, Quarter Sessions Court, Court of Common Pleas, Philadelphia edited by P. William Filby (Gale Research Co., 1982)

Ship Passenger Lists: Pennsylvania and Delaware (1641-1825) edited and indexed by Carl Boyer (Boyer, 1980)

☞LAND RECORDS

Delaware's Fugitive Records: An Inventory of the Official Land Grant Records Relating to the Present State of Delaware by the Delaware Bureau of Archives and Records (Department of State, Division of Historical and Cultural Affairs, 1980)

Original Land Titles in Delaware, Commonly Known as the Duke of York Record (Family Line Publications, 1988)

Warrants and Surveys of the Province of Pennsylvania Including the Three Lower Counties, 1759 compiled by Allen Weinberg and Thomas E. Slattery, under the direction of Charles E. Hughes, Jr. (Department of Records, 1965)

☞MAPS

Atlas of Historical County Boundaries. Delaware, Maryland, and the District of Columbia edited and compiled by John H. Long (Charles Scribner and Sons, Simon & Schuster Macmillan, 1995)

Atlas of the State of Delaware by Daniel G. Beers (Pomery & Beers, 1868)

Delaware Geographic Names: Alphabetical Finding List (US Geological Survey Topographic Division, 1981)

Delaware Place Names by L.W. Heck (US Government Printing Office, 1966)

A Gazetteer of Maryland and Delaware by Henry Gannett and the US Geological Survey (Genealogical Publishing Co., 1976)

Maryland, Delaware Atlas & Gazetteer (DeLorme Mapping, 1993)

The National Gazetteer of the United States of America: Delaware, 1983 by the US Geological Survey and the US Board on Geographic Names (US Government Printing Office, 1984)

A Postal History of Delaware by Harvey Cochran Bounds (Printed by Press of Kells, 1938)

The Postal History of Maryland, the Delmarva Peninsula, and the District of Columbia: The Post Offices and First Postmasters From 1775 to 1984 by Chester M. Smith Jr., and John L. Kay (The Depot, 1984)

☞MILITARY RECORDS

Colonial Delaware Soldiers and Sailors, 1638-1776 by Henry C. Peden Jr. (Family Line Publications, 1995)

Delaware Archives, 5 vols. by the Delaware Public Archives Commission (1911)

Delaware, World War I Selective Service System Draft Registration Cards, 1917-1918 by the US Selective Service System (National Archives, 1987-1988)

Delaware's Role in World War II by William H. Conner and Leon deValinger Jr. (Delaware Heritage Press, 2003)

Index to Revolutionary War Service Records, 4 vols., transcribed by Virgil D. White (National Historical Publishing Company, 1995)

Revolutionary Patriots of Delaware, 1775-1783 by Henry C. Peden Jr. (Family Line Publications, 1996)

☞PROBATE RECORDS

A Calender of Delaware Wills, New Castle County, 1682-1800 abstracted and compiled by the Historical Research Committee of the Colonial Dames of Delaware (GenealogicalPublishing Co., 1969)

Calender of Sussex County, Delaware, Probate Records, 1680-1800 by the Delaware Public Archives Commission (1964)

Colonial Delaware Wills and Estates to 1800: An Index by Donald O. Virdin (Heritage Books, 1994)

Court Records of Kent County, Delaware, 1680-1705 edited by Leon deValinger Jr. (American Historical Association, 1959)

Delaware Papers, 2 vols. edited and translated by Charles T. Gehring, Edmund Bailey Callaghan, and the Holland Society of New York (Genealogical Publishing Co., 1977-1981)

Documents Relative to the Colonial History of the State of New York procured in Holland, England and France by John Romeyn Brodhead, edited by E.B. O'Callaghan (Weed, Parsons Printers, 1853-87)

The First Laws of the State of Delaware by John D. Cushing (Michael Glazier, Inc., 1981)

☞VITAL RECORDS

Delaware Marriages and Deaths From the Delaware Gazette, 1875-1879 edited by Mary Fallon Richards and John C. Richards (Willow Bend Books, 2000)

Delaware Tombstone Inscriptions: 700 Revolutionary Soldiers in Three Counties; 600 in Small Church & Family Cemeteries, Chiefly in Sussex County compiled and edited by Raymond B. Clark Jr. (R.B. Clark, 1989)

Souls in Heaven, Names in Stone: Kent County, Delaware, Cemetery Records, 2 vols. by Raymond Walter Dill, William Martin Dill and Elizabeth Ann Bostick Dill (Gateway Press, 1989)

COUNTY DETAILS

DEALE

- **INCORPORATED:** 1680
- **PARENT COUNTY:** Whorekill
- **NOTES:** See Sussex County. Name changed to Deale June 30, 1680. Name changed to Sussex Dec. 4, 1682.

KENT

555 Bay Rd., Dover, DE 19901, (302) 744-2366, **<www.co.kent.de.us/Departments/Administration/kc_complex.htm>**

- **INCORPORATED:** 1682
- **PARENT COUNTY:** St. Jones
- **MARRIAGE RECORDS:** unknown start, kept by the Clerk of Peace
- **DIVORCE:** unknown start, County Courthouse
- **LAND:** 1680, Count Courthouse
- Probate: 1680, State Archives
- **COURT:** 1680, State Archives
- **NOTES:** Formerly St. Jones County. Name changed to Kent 1682.

NEW CASTLE

87 Reads Way, New Castle, DE 19720, (302) 395-5555, **<www2.nccde.org>**

- **INCORPORATED:** 1664
- **PARENT COUNTY:** Original County
- **MARRIAGE RECORDS:** start in 1911, kept by the Clerk of Peace
- **DIVORCE:** unknown start, County Court
- **LAND:** unknown, Recorder of Deeds
- **COURT:** unknown, State Archives
- **WILLS:** 1682, State Archives
- **NOTES:** Once named New Amistel. Name changed to New Castle Dec. 31, 1674. State Archives has wills 1682-1800.

ST. JONES

- **INCORPORATED:** 1680
- **PARENT COUNTY:** Whorekill County
- **NOTES:** See Kent County listing. Name changed to Kent in 1682.

SUSSEX

Box 589, Georgetown, DE 19947, (302) 855-7700, **<www.sussexcountyde.gov>**

- **INCORPORATED:** 1670
- **PARENT COUNTY:** Deale
- **LAND RECORDS:** start in 1693, kept by the Recorder of Deeds
- **PROBATE:** 1680, State Archives
- **NOTES:** Formerly Whorekill, formed in 1670. Name changed to Deale in 1680. Name changed to Sussex in 1682.

WHOREKILL

- **INCORPORATED:** 1670
- **PARENT COUNTY:** Original county
- **NOTES:** See Deale County. Whorekill was divided into Deale and Saint Jones counties in 1680.

FLORIDA

» BY RHONDA R. MCCLURE

HISTORICAL OVERVIEW

Though Massachusetts and Virginia continue to duke it out over which founded the "new country," in actuality, the history of Florida predates both states: St. Augustine was founded in 1565. Perhaps the fact that Florida settlement didn't begin in earnest until the late 18th century makes researchers think of the state as a late bloomer.

Florida was long a pawn, traded back and forth between England and Spain until well after the American Revolution. In 1763, at the end of the French and Indian War, Britain had control of Florida. At this time the provinces of East Florida (land from the Atlantic Ocean to the Apalachicola River) and West Florida (from the Apalachicola River to the Mississippi River) were formed.

England didn't have Florida for very long. In 1783, Spain regained both provinces, and most British settlers moved out. In 1812, parts of West Florida were annexed to Louisiana and the Mississippi Territory. Seven years later, Spain ceded the remainder of West Florida and all of East Florida to the United States. By 1822, Florida was a territory, and it finally gained statehood on March 3, 1845.

All of this back and forth between Spain and England has resulted in the history of Florida being broken up into different periods: the first Spanish colonial period (1565-1763), British colonial period (1763-1783), second Spanish period (1784-1821), and territorial era (1821-1845). With each period came different records, and in the case of the Spanish periods, records in a different language.

RECORD HIGHLIGHTS

Before traditional land records, you'll find the Spanish Land Grants. These records, created from 1820 to 1822, were settlers' claims to the US government that they'd received land from Spain. You can search digitized versions at **<www.floridamemory.com/collections/spanishlandgrants>** and use the published five-volume transcript *Spanish Land Grants in Florida* (Florida State Library Board, 1940).

In addition to federal census records that begin in 1830 and continue decennially until the most recently released, 1930, a few fragments of colonial, territorial and state censuses have survived for Florida. Most can be found at the state Bureau of Archives and Records Management, 500 South Bronough Street, Tallahassee, Florida 32399, (850) 245-6700, **<dlis.dos.state.fl.us/barm/index.html>**. Ten of the Spanish colonial censuses are reproduced in *The Spanish Censuses of Pensacola, 1784-1820: A Genealogical Guide to Spanish Pensacola*

research tips

- Birth and death records at the state level are primarily available beginning in January 1917 and can be requested from the Bureau of Vital Statistics of the State Department of Health and Rehabilitative Services.
- The state vital statistics office has marriages, divorces, and annulments from June 6, 1927.
- A few fragments of colonial, territorial, and state censuses have survived, and can be found at the Florida Department of State, Division of Library & Information Services, Bureau of Archives and Records Management.
- A proven list of people in the state before March 3, 1845 is on the Florida State Genealogical Society Web site **<www.rootsweb.ancestry.com/~flsgs/pioneer_program.htm>**

CENSUS RECORDS

- Federal census: 1830, 1840, 1850, 1860, 1870, 1880, 1900, 1910, 1920, 1930
- State census: 1825 (Leon County), 1855 (Marion County), 1867 (Hernando, Madison, Orange, Santa Rosa Counties), 1875 (Alachua County), 1885 (all counties except Alachua, Clay, Nassau, and Columbia), 1935, 1945
- Mortality schedules: 1850, 1860, 1870, 1880

by William S. Coker and G. Douglas Inglis (Perdido Bay Press, 1980). Some of these censuses are also available online through subscription site Ancestry.com. One census often misidentified as a state census was taken in 1885. This was actually a census conducted by the federal government, but it is an excellent resource for filling the void left by the 1890 US census, which was destroyed due to fire.

Other useful land records include homestead applications from 1881 to 1905, housed at the Florida State Archives. These records, along with the Homestead Contest Dockets (1887-1891), Homestead Occupying Claimant Files (1881-1904), and Homestead Swampland Claim Files (1846-1918), are available on microfilm through the Family History Library (FHL).

Birth and death records at the state level are generally available beginning in January 1917 and can be requested from the Bureau of Vital Statistics of the State Department of Health and Rehabilitative Services, (Box 210, Jacksonville, Florida 32231) **<www.doh.state.fl.us/planning_eval/vital_statistics>**. Vital records before this time are incomplete, though you will certainly want to investigate in case your ancestor's records were filed. In addition, you may want to check with the health department in your ancestor's county, as some of earlier records may be found there. The state vital statistics office also has marriages, divorces and annulments from June 6, 1927. Look for marital events before then in county courts. For a copy of the marriage license application, then contact the county clerk where the marriage took place.

The Florida State Genealogical Society has a program to honor those descendants who can prove relationship to a resident who was living in Florida before March 3, 1845. A list of established pioneers is at **<www.rootsweb.ancestry.com/~flsgs/pioneer_program.htm>**. The packets for those descendants who applied before 1995 are on 54 rolls of microfilm through the Family History Library. These packets contain copies of original records to prove the applicant's descent from a Florida pioneer.

An often overlooked alternative to vital records is the WPA-compiled *Register of Deceased Veterans Buried in Florida* (Veterans' Graves Registration Project, 1940-1941). These volumes cover 51 of the 67 counties in Florida. Among other repositories, the Orlando Public Library has a complete set in its Genealogy Department. Staff can't do look ups for you, so you'll need to visit in person or hire a professional genealogist in the area.

ARCHIVES, LIBRARIES, AND SOCIETIES

Afro-American Historical and Genealogical Society, Central Florida Chapter
Box 1347, Orlando, FL 32802, **<www.rootsweb.ancestry.com/~flcfaahg/member.html>**

Alachua County Genealogical Society
Box 12078, Gainesville, FL 32604, **<www.afn.org/~acgs>**

Amelia Island Genealogical Society
Box 6005, Fernandina Beach, FL 32035 (904) 261-2139, **<www.aigensoc.org/aigs/index.asp>**

Apalachicola Historical Society, Inc.
Box 75, Apalachicola, FL 32329, **<mailer.fsu.edu/~rthompso/fchs_adr.html>**

Archer Historical Society
Box 1850, Archer, FL 32618, **<www.afn.org/~archer>**

Baker County Historical Society
Box 856, Macclenny, FL 32063, **<www.rootsweb.ancestry.com/~flbakehs>**

Big Lake Family History Society
Box 592, Okeechobee, FL 34973-0592

Bonita Springs Genealogy Club
Box 366471, Bonita Springs, FL 34136

Bonita Springs Public Library
26876 Pine Ave., Bonita Springs, FL 33923

Bowling Green Historical Council
Box 478, Bowling Green, FL 33834

Boynton Beach Historical Society
Box 12, Boynton Beach, FL 33425, (561) 742-6397

Brevard Community College Library
1519 Clearlake Rd., Cocoa, FL 32922, (888) 747-2802

Brevard County Genealogical Society
Box 1123, Cocoa, FL 32923, **<www.rootsweb.ancestry.com/~flbgs>**

Broward County Historical Commission
301 S.W. 13th Ave., Fort Lauderdale, FL 33312, (954) 357-5553, **<www.broward.org/history/Pages/Default.aspx>**

Cape Coral-Lee County Public Library
921 S.W. 39th Terrace, Cape Coral, FL 33914, (239) 533-4500, **<www.lee-county.com/library/library/branches/cc.htm>**

Central Florida Genealogical Society
Box 536309, Orlando, FL 32853, **<www.cfgs.org>**

Charlotte County Genealogical Society
Box 494707, Port Charlotte, FL 33949, **<www.charlottecountyfloridagenealogy.org/contact.php>**

Citrus County Genealogical Society
Box 2211, Inverness, FL 34451, **<www.rootsweb.ancestry.com/~flccgs2>**

Citrus Springs Memorial Library
1826 W. Country Club Blvd., Citrus Springs FL 34434, (352) 489-2313, **<library.citrussprings.org>**

Cocoa Public Library
430 Delannoy Ave., Cocoa, FL 32922

Collier County Public Library
Library Headquarters, 2385 Orange Blossom Dr., Naples, FL 34109, **<www.colliergov.net/index.aspx?page=108>**

Cooper Memorial Library
2525 Oakley Seaver Dr., Clermont, FL 34711, (352) 536-2275, **<www.lakeline.lib.fl.us/cmlintro.htm>**

DeLand Public Library
130 E. Howry Ave., DeLand, FL 32724

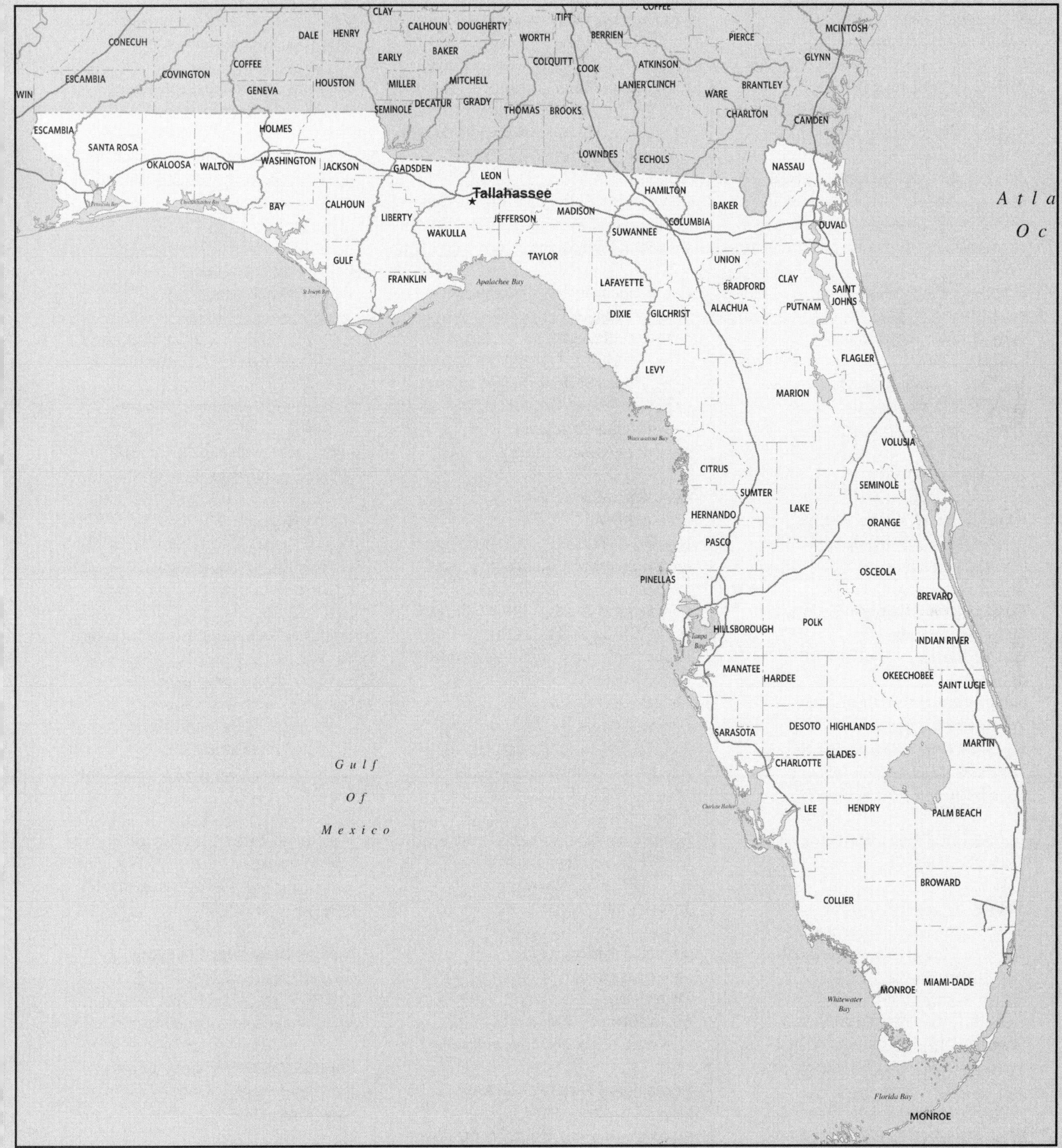
Tallahassee
ESCAMBIA
SANTA ROSA
OKALOOSA
WALTON
HOLMES
WASHINGTON
JACKSON
BAY
CALHOUN
GULF
LIBERTY
FRANKLIN
GADSDEN
LEON
WAKULLA
JEFFERSON
MADISON
TAYLOR
HAMILTON
SUWANNEE
LAFAYETTE
DIXIE
GILCHRIST
COLUMBIA
BAKER
NASSAU
DUVAL
UNION
BRADFORD
CLAY
ALACHUA
PUTNAM
SAINT JOHNS
FLAGLER
LEVY
MARION
VOLUSIA
CITRUS
SUMTER
LAKE
SEMINOLE
ORANGE
HERNANDO
PASCO
PINELLAS
OSCEOLA
BREVARD
HILLSBOROUGH
POLK
INDIAN RIVER
MANATEE
HARDEE
OKEECHOBEE
SAINT LUCIE
SARASOTA
DESOTO
HIGHLANDS
MARTIN
CHARLOTTE
GLADES
LEE
HENDRY
PALM BEACH
COLLIER
BROWARD
MONROE
MIAMI-DADE
MONROE
Apalachee Bay
Gulf
Of
Mexico
Atla
Oc
CONECUH
ESCAMBIA
COVINGTON
COFFEE
GENEVA
DALE
HENRY
HOUSTON
CLAY
CALHOUN
DOUGHERTY
EARLY
BAKER
MILLER
MITCHELL
SEMINOLE
DECATUR
GRADY
THOMAS
BROOKS
WORTH
TIFT
COLQUITT
COOK
BERRIEN
ATKINSON
LANIER
CLINCH
LOWNDES
ECHOLS
PIERCE
WARE
BRANTLEY
CHARLTON
MCINTOSH
GLYNN
CAMDEN
COFFEE
WIN

DeSoto Correctional Institution Library
Box 1072, Arcadia, FL 33821

DeSoto County Historical Society
Box 1824, Arcadia, FL 34265, **<www.historicdesoto.org>**

Dixie County Historical Society
Box 928, Cross City, FL 32628, (352) 542-0047, **<www.dixiehistory.org>**

East Hillsborough Historical Society
605 N. Collins St., Plant City, FL 33563, (813) 757-9226, **<www.rootsweb.ancestry.com/~flqgbac/ehhs.html>**

Elmer's Genealogy Library
Box 5, Pinetta, FL 32350, (850) 973-3282, **<www.elmerslibrary.com>**

Englewood Genealogical Society
Box 795, Englewood, FL 34295, **<www.rootsweb.com/~flegsf>**

Alma Clyde Field Library of Florida History
435 Brevard Ave., Cocoa, FL 32922, (321) 690-1971, **<www.florida-historical-soc.org>**

Florida Baptist Historical Society, Stetson University
Box 8353, DeLand, FL 32720

Florida Bureau of Archives and Records Management
500 S. Bronough St., Tallahassee, FL 32399, (850) 245-6700, **<dlis.dos.state.fl.us/barm>**

Florida Genealogical Society
Box 18624, Tampa, FL 33679

Florida Historical Society
1320 Highland Ave, Melbourne, FL 32935, (321) 254-9855, **<www.florida-historical-soc.org>**

Florida State Genealogical Society
Box 10249, Tallahassee, FL 32302-2249, **<www.rootsweb.ancestry.com/~flsgs>**

Florida Suncoast Chapter, American Historical Society of Germans From Russia
83 Spoonbill Lane, Ellenton, FL 34222, (941) 962-5095, **<www.ahsgr.org/florida_suncoast_chapter.htm>**

Fort Lauderdale Historical Society
219 S.W. Second Ave., Fort Lauderdale, FL 33301, (954) 463-4431

Fort Myers-Lee County Public Library
2050 Central Ave., Fort Myers, FL 33901, (239) 533-4600, **<www.lee-county.com/library/library/branches/fm.htm>**

Genealogical Group of Seminole County
Box 180993, Casselberry, FL 32718

Genealogical Society of Broward County
Box 485, Fort Lauderdale, FL, 33302, **<www.rootsweb.ancestry.com/~flgsbc>**

Genealogical Society of Collier County
Box 7933, Naples, FL 34101, **<www.naples.net/presents/gscc>**

Genealogical Society of Flagler County
Box 35-4671, Palm Coast, FL 32135, **<www.flaglerlibrary.org/genealogy/genstart.htm>**

Genealogical Society of Greater Miami
Box 161648, Miami, FL 33116-1648, **<www.rootsweb.ancestry.com/~flgsgm>**

Genealogical Society of North Brevard
Box 897, Titusville, FL 32781-0897, **<nbbd.com/npr/gsnb/index.html>**

Genealogical Society of Okaloosa County
Box 1175, Fort Walton Beach, FL 32549-1175, **<www.members.cox.net/youngjmy/GSOC.html>**

Genealogical Society of Okeechobee
Box 371, Okeechobee, FL 34972-0371, (863) 467-2674, **<www.rootsweb.ancestry.com/~flgso>**

Genealogical Society of Santa Rosa County
Milton Public Library Branch, 805 Alabama St., Milton, FL 32570, **<www.db229.com/aboutus.htm>**

Genealogical Society of Sarasota
Box 1917, Sarasota, FL 34230-1917, **<www.rootsweb.ancestry.com/~flgss>**

Genealogical Society of South Brevard
Box 786, Melbourne, FL 32902-0786, **<www.rootsweb.ancestry.com/~flgssb>**

Genealogical Society of Southeast Volusia County
c/o New Smyrna Beach Public Library 1001 S. Dixie Fwy., New Smyrna Beach, FL 32168, (386) 424-2910, **<www.rootsweb.ancestry.com/~flgssvc>**

Genealogy Club of Osceola County
Box 701295, St. Cloud, FL 34770.

Genealogy Society of Hernando County
Box 1793, Brooksville, FL 34605-1793, **<www.rootsweb.ancestry.com/~flhernan>**

Geneva Historical and Genealogical Society
Box 91, Geneva, FL 32732, **<www.usgennet.org/usa/fl/county/seminole/Geneva/society.htm>**

Gulf County Genealogical Society
Box 541, Port St. Joe, FL 32457, **<www.rootsweb.ancestry.com/~flcalhou/gulf/gcgs/index.htm>**

Halifax Historical Museum
252 S. Beach St., Daytona Beach, FL 32114, (386) 255-6976, **<www.halifax historical.org>**

Hamilton County Historical Museum
Box 929, Jasper, FL 32052, (386) 792-3850, **<www.rootsweb.ancestry.com/~flhchms/index.htm>**

Haydon Burns Library
122 N. Ocean St., Jacksonville, FL 32202, (904) 630-2665

Highlands County Genealogical Society
c/o Sebring Public Library, 319 W. Center Ave., Sebring, FL 33870, **<www.myhlc.org/spl<**

Historic Ocala/Marion County Genealogical Society
Box 1206, Ocala, FL 34478, **<mariongenealogy.tripod.com>**

Imperial Polk Genealogical Society
Box 10, Kathleen, FL 33849, **<www.ipgs.org>**

Indian River County Main Library
1600 21st St., Vero Beach, FL 32960, (772) 770-5060, **<www.irclibrary.org>**

Indian River Genealogical Society
Box 1850, Vero Beach, FL 32961-1850, **<www.irgs.org>**

Jackson County Florida Library
2929 Green St., Marianna, FL 32446, (850) 482-9631

Jacksonville Genealogical Society
Box 60756, Jacksonville, Duval Co., FL 32236, **<jaxgen.home.comcast.net>**

Jacksonville Public Library
303 N. Laura St., Jacksonville, FL 32202, (904) 630-2665

Jewish Genealogical Society of Broward County
Box 17251, Fort Lauderdale, FL 33318, **<www.jgsbc.org>**

Jewish Genealogical Society of Central Florida
Box 520583, Longwood, FL 32752

Jewish Genealogical Society of Greater Orlando
Box 941332, Maitland, FL 32794, **<www.rootsweb.ancestry.com/~fljgscf>**

Jewish Genealogical Society of Palm Beach County
<www.jgspalmbeachcounty.org>

Keystone Genealogical Society
Box 50, Monticello, FL 32344

Keystone Genealogy Library
695 E. Washington St., Monticello, FL 32345

Kinseekers Genealogical Society of Lake County
Box 492711, Leesburg, FL 34749, **<www.rootsweb.ancestry.com/~fllckgs>**

Largo Library
120 Central Park Dr., Largo, FL 33771, (727) 587-6715, **<www.largo.com/department/?fDD=11-0>**

Lee County Genealogical Society
Box 150153, Cape Coral, FL 33915, **<www.leecountygenealogy.org>**

Lehigh Acres Genealogical Society
Box 965, Lehigh Acres, FL 33970

Lemon Bay Historical and Genealogical Society
Box 236, Englewood, FL 33533

Levy County Genealogy Society
c/o Levy County Journal, Box 159, Bronson, FL 32621

Madison County Genealogical Society
Box 136, Madison, FL 32341-0136, **<www.madisongenealogy.com>**

Manasota Genealogical Society
3547 53rd Ave. W., PMB 269, Bradenton, FL 34210, **<www.rootsweb.ancestry.com/~flmgs>**

Manatee County Public Library
1301 Barcarrota Blvd. W., Badenton, FL 34205, (941) 748-5555, **<library.co.manatee.fl.us>**

Marco Island Historical Society
2282, Marco Island, FL 34146, (239) 394-5845, **<www.themihs.org>**

Martin County Genealogical Society
Box 275, Stuart, FL 34995, **<www.rootsweb.com/~flmcgs>**

Melbourne Public Library
540 E. Fee Ave., Melbourne, FL 32901, (321) 952-4514, **<www.mylibraryworld.com/pages/visit_your_library/melbourne>**

Micanopy Historical Society Museum
Box 462, Micanopy, FL 32667, (352) 466-3200, **<www.afn.org/~micanopy<**

Monroe County Genealogical Society
c/o Rachel J. Lowe
21 Ventana Ln., Big Coppitt Key, FL 33040

National Archives and Records Administration, Southeast Region
5780 Jonesboro Road, Morrow, GA 30260, (770) 968-2100, **<www.archives.gov/southeast>**

Northwest Regional Library System
Bay County Public Library, 898 West 11th St., Panama City, FL 32401, (850) 522-2100, **<www.nwrls.lib.fl.us>**

Office of Vital Statistics
Box 210, Jacksonville, FL 32231, (904) 359-6900 ext. 1029

Orlando Public Library
101 E. Central Blvd., Orlando, FL 32801, (407) 835-7323, **<www.ocls.info/Locations/MainLibrary/default.asp>**

Ormond Beach Public Library
30 S. Beach St., Ormond Beach FL 32174, (386) 676-4191

Osceola County Department, Genealogy Research
326 Eastern Ave., St. Cloud, FL 32769

Osceola County Historical Society
750 N. Bass Rd., Kissimmee, FL 34746, (407) 396-8644, **<www.osceolahistory.org>**

Palatka Public Library
601 College Rd., Palatka, FL 32177

Genealogical Society of Palm Beach County
Box 17617, 3650 Summit Blvd., West Palm Beach, FL 33416, **<www.pbcgs.org>**

Palm Harbor Library
2330 Nebraska Ave., Palm Harbor, FL 34683, (727) 784-3332, **<www.palmharborlibrary.org>**

Pasco County Genealogical Society
Box 2072, Dade City, FL 33526, **<www.rootsweb.ancestry.com/~flpcgs>**

Pastfinders of South Lake County
<www.rootsweb.ancestry.com/~flpslc>

Pinellas Genealogical Society
c/o Largo Library, 120 Central Park Dr., Largo, FL 33771-2110, **<www.rootsweb.ancestry.com/~flpgs>**

P.K. Yonge Library of Florida History
Box 117007, Gainesville, FL 32611-7001, **<web.uflib.ufl.edu/spec/pkyonge>**

Polk County Historical Association
Box 2749, Bartow, FL 33831, **<www.polkcountyhistory.org>**

Polk County Historical and Genealogical Library
100 E. Main St., Bartow, FL 33830, (863) 534-4380, **<library.mypclc.org/historical>**

Putnam County Genealogical Society
Box 35, Palatka, FL 32178

Putnam County Historical Society
Box 35, Palatka, FL 32178, **<www.rootsweb.ancestry.com/~flpchs>**

Quintilla Geer Bruton Archives Center
605 N. Collins St., Plant City, FL 33563, (813) 754-7031, **<www.rootsweb.ancestry.com/~flqgbac>**

Ridge Genealogical Society
Box 477, Babson Park, FL 33827

Roman Catholic Archdiocese of Miami Pastoral Center/Chancery
9401 Biscayne Blvd., Miami Shores, FL 33138, (305) 757-6241

Roots and Branches Genealogical Society
Box 612, DeLand, FL 32721

Sebring Historical Society
321 West Center Ave., Sebring, FL 33870, (863) 471-2522, **<www.sebringhistoricalsociety.org/contact.php>**

Slovenian Genealogical Society-Florida Chapter
12776 Maiden Cane Lane, Bonita Sprigs, FL 33923, **<www.sloveniangenealogy.org>**

South Hillsborough Genealogists
Rte. 1, Box 400, Palmetto, FL 33561

Southern Genealogist's Exchange Society
Box 2801, Jacksonville, FL 32203, **<www.sgesjax.com>**

St. Augustine Genealogical Society
c/o Southeast Branch, St. Johns County Public Library, 6670 US1 S., St. Augustine, FL 32086, **<www.stauggens.com>**

St. Johns County Public Library System
1960 N. Ponce de Leon Blvd., St. Augustine, FL 32084, (904) 827-6940

St. Lucie Historical Society
Box 578, Fort Pierce, FL 34954, **<www.stluciehistoricalsociety.org>**

State Library of Florida
500 S. Bronough St., Tallahassee, FL 32399, (850) 245-6600, **<dlis.dos.state.fl.us/stlib>**

Suwannee Valley Genealogical Society
Box 967, Live Oak, FL 32064, (386) 330-0110, **<svgsoc.org>**

Tallahassee Genealogical Society
Box 4371, Tallahassee, FL 32315, **<www.rootsweb.ancestry.com/~fltgs>**

Tarpon Springs Public Library
138 E. Lemon St., Tarpon Springs, FL 34689, (727) 943-4922, **<www.tblc.org/tarpon>**

Taylor County Historical Society
118 E. Main St., Perry, FL 32347-2739,

Treasure Coast Genealogical Society
Box 12582, Fort Pierce, FL 34979, **<www.rootsweb.ancestry.com/~fltcgs>**

University of Florida George A. Smathers Libraries
Department of Special Collections, Box 117005, Gainesville, FL 32611-7005, (352) 273-2755

University of Miami, Otto G. Richter Library
1300 Memorial Dr., Box 248214, Coral Gables, FL 33124-0320, (305) 284-3233, **<www.library.miami.edu/Richterlibrary.html>**

University of West Florida, John Chandler Pace Library
11000 University Pkwy., Pensacola, FL 32514-5750, (850) 474-2424

Villages Genealogical Society, **<www.villagesgenealogy.org>**

Volusia County Public Library
City Island, 105 E. Magnolia Ave., Daytona Beach, FL 32114, (386) 257-6036

Volusia Genealogical & Historical Society
Box 2039, Daytona Beach, FL 32015

Wakulla County Historical Society
Box 151, Crawfordville, FL 32326-0151, (850) 926-7405, **<www.psy.fsu.edu/~thompson/wchs/wchs_page.html>**

Washington County Genealogical Society
205 Wells Ave., Chipley, FL 32428

West Florida Genealogical Society
<www.rootsweb.ancestry.com/~flwfgs>

West Pasco County Genealogical Society
Box 1142, Port Richey, FL 34673, **<homepages.rootsweb.ancestry.com/~wpcgs/wpsgmember.htm>**

West Volusia Historical Society
137 W. Michigan Ave., DeLand, FL 32720, (386) 740-6813, **<volusia.com/delandhouse>**

GENERAL RESOURCES

1830 Private Land Claims in East Florida (Institute of Historic Research, ca. 1990)

The Black Experience: A Guide to Afro-American Resources in the Florida State Archives by Debra D. McGriff (Florida Department of State Division of Library and Information Services, 1991)

Catalog of the Florida State Archives (Department of State, 1975)

Church and State in the Spanish Floridas, 1783-1822 by Michael Joseph Curley (AMS Press, 1974)

The Cross in the Sand: The Early Catholic Church in Florida, 1513-1870 by Michael V. Gannon (University of Florida Press, 1965)

The Episcopal Diocese of Florida, 1892-1975 by George R. Bentley (University of Florida Press, ca. 1989)

Florida Connections Through Bible Records by Anne Wood Taylor (Florida State Genealogical Society, ca. 1993)

Florida: Historic-Dramatic-Contemporary, 4 vols., by Junius E. Dovell (Lewis Historical Publishing Co., 1952)

Florida Pioneers and Their Descendants by Anne Wood Taylor (Florida State Genealogical Society, ca. 1992)

Florida Prison Records, 1875-1900 by Carol Cox Bouknecht (C.C. Bouknecht, ca. 1993)

The Florida State Genealogical Society, Inc. Surname Directory, 1995 by Linda Pazics Kleback (The Society, ca. 1995)

Florida's Indians from Ancient Times to the Present by Jerald T. Milanich (University Press of Florida, ca. 1998)

Genealogy and Local History: A Bibliography, revised edition by Gill T. Bodziony (State Library of Florida, 1978)

Genealogy and Local History: A Bibliography (supplement) by Beverly Pittman Byrd (Department of State, Division of Library Services, 1983)

Guide to Depositories of Manuscript Collections in the United States: Florida by the Historical Records Survey (Florida Historical Records Survey Project, 1940)

A Guide to the History of Florida by Paul S. George and Samuel Proctor (Greenwood Press, ca. 1989)

Guide to the Microfilm Edition of the Records of the Diocese of Louisiana and the Floridas, 1576-1803 by Thomas Timothy McAvoy (University of Notre Dame Archives, 1967)

Guide to Public Vital Statistics Records in Florida by Historical Records Survey, Florida (Florida Historical Records Survey, 1941)

History of Florida, Past and Present, Historical and Biographical by Harry Gardner Cutler (Lewis Publishing Co., ca. 1923)

The History of Methodism in Georgia and Florida: From 1785 to 1865 by Geo. G. Smith Jr. (Jno. W. Burke & Co., 1877)

A History of the Timucua Indians and Missions by John H. Hann (University Press of Florida, ca. 1996)

Index to the Archives of Spanish West Florida, 1782-1810 by Stanley Clisby Arthur (Polyanthos, Inc., 1975)

Index to Florida Jewish History in the American Israelite, 1854-1900 by Yael Herbsman (University of Florida George A. Smathers Libraries, ca. 1992)

Inventory of the Church Archives of Florida Baptist Bodies by Historical Records Survey (Historical Records Survey, 1939-1940)

Missions of Spanish Florida by David Hurst Thomas (Garland, ca. 1991)

Names and Abstracts from the Acts of the Legislative Council of the Territory of Florida, 1822-1845 by William A. Wolfe and Janet B. Wolfe (Florida State Genealogical Society, ca. 1991, 1985)

Pioneers of Florida's First Coast by the Southern Genealogist's Exchange Society (Gregath, 1991)

A Preliminary List of Religious Bodies in Florida by Historical Records Survey (Historical Records Survey, 1939)

Searching in Florida: A Reference Guide to Public and Private Records by Diane C. Robie (Independent Search Consultants, Inc., 1982)

Seminole Indians of Florida by Raymond C. Lantz (Heritage Books, ca. 1994)

The Seminole and Miccosukee Tribes: A Critical Bibliography by Harry A. Kersey (Indiana University Press, ca. 1987)

The Spanish Borderlands: A Chronicle of Old Florida and the Southwest by Herbert Eugene Bolton (Yale University Press, 1921)

A Story of the Southern Synod of the Evangelical and Reformed Church, 1740-1968 by Banks J. Peeler (Southern Synod of the Evangelical and Reformed Church, ca. 1968)

The Story of Southwestern Florida by James Warren Covington (Lewis Historical Publishing Co., 1957)

The Trail of the Florida Circuit Rider: An Introduction to the Rise of Methodism in Middle and East Florida by Charles Tinsley Thrift Jr. (Florida Southern College Press, ca. 1944)

☞ CENSUS RECORDS

Florida Voter Registration Lists, 1867-68 (Tallahassee Genealogical Society, ca. 1992)

Florida Voters in Their First Statewide Election, May 26, 1845 by Brian E. Michaels (Florida State Genealogical Society, ca. 1987)

Florida's First Families: Translated Abstracts of Pre-1821 Spanish Censuses by Donna Rachal Mills (Mills Historical Press, ca. 1992)

☞ IMMIGRATION RECORDS

Havana, USA; Cuban Exiles and Cuban Americans in South Florida, 1959-1994 by Maria Cristina Garcia (University of California Press, ca. 1996)

Index to passenger lists of vessels arriving at miscellaneous ports in Alabama, Florida, Georgia, and South Carolina, 1890-1924 (US Immigration and Naturalization Service, 1957)

Passenger lists of vessels arriving at Key West, 1898-1920 (US Immigration and Naturalization Service, 1946)

☞ LAND RECORDS

English Land Grants in West Florida: A Register for the States of Alabama, Mississippi, and Parts of Florida and Louisiana, 1766-1776 by Winston De Ville (W. De Ville, ca. 1986)

Florida Land: Records of the Tallahassee and Newnansville General Land Office, 1825-1892 by Alvie L. Davidson (Heritage Books, ca. 1989)

Private Land Claims, Alabama, Arkansas, Florida by Fern Ainsworth (F. Ainsworth, 1978)

Spanish Land Grants in Florida by the Historical Records Survey (State Library Board, 1940-1941)

Spanish Plat Book of Land Records of the District of Pensacola, Province of West Florida, British and Spanish Land Grants, 1763-1821 by Billie Ford Snider (Antique Compiling, ca. 1994)

☞MAPS

A Chronology of Florida Post Offices by Alford G. Bradbury and E. Story Hallock (Florida Classics Library, 1993)
Florida Atlas and Gazetteer (DeLorme Mapping, ca. 1987)

Florida, Atlas of Historical County Boundaries by Peggy Tuck Sinko (Charles Scribner, ca. 1997)

Florida Place Names by Allen Covington Morris (University of Miami Press, ca. 1974)

Florida State Gazetteer and Business Directory by R.L. Polk and Company (R.L. Polk, 1907/08)

☞MILITARY RECORDS

Compendium of the Confederate Armies by Stewart Sifakis (Facts on File, ca. 1992-1995)

The Defenses of Spanish Florida, 1565 to 1763 by Verne E. Chatelain (Baltimore Press, 1941)

Index to compiled service records of volunteer Union soldiers who served in organizations from the state of Florida by the US Adjutant General's Office (National Archives, 1958)

Register of Florida CSA Pension Applications by Virgil D. White (National Historical Publishing Co., ca. 1989)

☞VITAL RECORDS

Cemetery Records of Florida by E.H. Hayes (Genealogical Society of Utah, 1946)

Guide to Public Vital Statistics Records in Florida by the Historical Records Survey (Florida Historical Records Survey, 1941)

Guide to Supplementary Vital Statistics from Church Records in Florida (preliminary) by the Historical Records Survey (Florida Historical Records Survey, 1942)

●COUNTY DETAILS●

ALACHUA
201 E. University Ave., Box 600, Gainesville, FL 32602, (352) 374-3636, <**www.clerk-alachua-fl.org/archive**>
- **INCORPORATED:** Dec. 29, 1824
- **PARENT COUNTIES:** Duval, St. Johns
- **PROBATE RECORDS:** start in 1840, kept by County Clerk
- **COURT:** unknown, County Clerk
- **LAND:** 1848, County Clerk
- **NOTES:** County Clerk has incomplete marriage records from 1837.

BAKER
339 E. Macclenny Ave., Macclenny, FL 32063, (904) 259-8113, <bakercountyfl.org>
- **INCORPORATED:** Feb. 8, 1861
- **PARENT COUNTY:** New River
- **MARRIAGE RECORDS:** start in 1877, kept by County Clerk
- **COURT:** 1880, Circuit Court
- **DIVORCE:** 1880, Circuit Court
- **PROBATE:** 1877, County Clerk

BAY
300 E. Fourth St., Box 2269, Panama City, FL 32402, (850) 763-9061, <**www.baycoclerk.com**>
- **INCORPORATED:** July 1, 1913
- **PARENT COUNTY:** Calhoun
- **BIRTH RECORDS:** unknown start, kept by Department of Health
- **DEATH:** unknown, Department of Health
- **MARRIAGE:** 1913, Circuit Court
- **PROBATE:** 1913, Circuit Court
- **DIVORCE:** 1913, Circuit Court
- **COURT:** 1913, Circuit Court
- **LAND:** 1913, Circuit Court

BENTON
- **INCORPORATED:** March 6 1844
- **PARENT COUNTY:** Alachua
- **NOTES:** See Hernando County. Name changed to Benton March 6, 1844. Name changed back to Hernando Dec. 24, 1850.

BRADFORD
945 N. Temple Ave., Drawer B, Starke, FL 32091, (904) 966-6280, <**www.bradford-co-fla.org**>
- **INCORPORATED:** Dec. 21, 1858
- **PARENT COUNTY:** Columbia
- **MARRIAGE RECORDS:** start in 1875, kept by County Clerk
- **PROBATE:** 1892, County Clerk
- **COURT:** 1892, County Clerk
- **LAND:** 1876, County Clerk
- **NOTES:** See New River County. Name changed to Bradford Dec. 6, 1861.

BREVARD
Clerk of Court, Box 219, Titusville, FL 32781, (321) 637-5413, <**www.brevardcounty.us/bcc/bccdeptindex.cfm**>
- **INCORPORATED:** March 14, 1844
- **PARENT COUNTY:** Mosquito
- **MARRIAGE RECORDS:** start in 1868, kept by Circuit Court
- **LAND:** 1871, Circuit Court
- **COURT:** 1879, Circuit Court
- **DIVORCE:** 1879, Circuit Court
- **PROBATE:** 1917, Circuit Court

- **MILITARY:** 1919, Circuit Court
- **DEATH:** 1985, Department of Health
- **BIRTH:** unknown, Department of Health
- **NOTES:** See St. Lucie County. Name changed to Brevard Jan. 6, 1855. Some records prior to 1885 were destroyed.

BROWARD

201 S.E. Sixth St., Ft. Lauderdale, FL 33301, (954) 765-4578, **<www.clerk-17th-flcourts.org/ClerkWebsite/welcome2.aspx>**

- **INCORPORATED:** April 30, 1915
- **PARENT COUNTIES:** Dade, Palm Beach
- **COURT:** start in 1915, kept by Circuit Court
- **PROBATE:** 1915, Circuit Court
- **LAND:** 1915, Circuit Court
- **MARRIAGE:** 1915, Circuit Court
- **DIVORCE:** 1915, Circuit Court

CALHOUN

425 E. Central Ave., Blountstown, FL 32424, (850) 674-4545, **<www2.myfloridacounty.com/wps/wcm/connect/calhounclerk>**

- **INCORPORATED:** Jan. 26, 1838
- **PARENT COUNTY:** Franklin
- **COURT RECORDS:** unknown start, kept by County Clerk
- **LAND:** unknown, County Clerk
- **DIVORCE:** unknown, County Clerk
- **MARRIAGE:** unknown, County Judge
- **PROBATE:** unknown, County Judge

CHARLOTTE

350 E. Marion Ave., Box 511687, Punta Gorda, FL 33951-1687, (941) 637-2199, **<www.co.charlotte.fl.us>**

- **INCORPORATED:** April 23, 1921
- **PARENT COUNTY:** DeSoto
- **MARRIAGE RECORDS:** start in 1921, kept by Circuit Court
- **DIVORCE:** 1921, Circuit Court
- **PROBATE:** 1921, Circuit Court
- **COURT:** 1921, Circuit Court
- **LAND:** 1921, Circuit Court

CITRUS

110 N. Apopka Avenue, Inverness, FL 34450, (352) 341-6400, **<www.bocc.citrus.fl.us>**

- **INCORPORATED:** June 2, 1887
- **PARENT COUNTY:** Hernando
- **PROBATE:** 1887, Office of Historical Resources
- **LAND:** 1887, Office of Historical Resources
- **COURT:** 1887, Office of Historical Resources
- **BIRTH:** unknown, Department of Health
- **DEATH:** unknown, Department of Health
- **NOTES:** Office of Historical Resources has marriage records 1887-1945 and military discharge records 1919-1969.

CLAY

Box 698, Green Cove Springs, FL 32043, (904) 284-6362, **<www.claycountygov.com>**

- **INCORPORATED:** Dec. 31, 1858
- **PARENT COUNTY:** Duval
- **MARRIAGE RECORDS:** start in 1872, kept by Circuit Court
- **PROBATE:** 1872, Circuit Court
- **COURT:** 1872, Circuit Court
- **LAND:** 1872, Circuit Court
- **DIVORCE:** 1859, Circuit Court
- **BIRTH:** 1973, Department of Health
- **DEATH:** 1973, Department of Health

COLLIER

3301 Tamiami Trail E., Naples, FL 33962, (239) 252-2646, **<www.colliergov.net>**

- **INCORPORATED:** May 8, 1923
- **PARENT COUNTY:** Lee
- **DIVORCE RECORDS:** start in 1923, kept by Circuit Court
- **COURT:** 1923, Circuit Court
- **LAND:** 1923, Circuit Court
- **MARRIAGE:** unknown, County Judge
- **PROBATE:** unknown, County Judge

COLUMBIA

Box 2069, Lake City, FL 32056-2069, (386) 758-1342, **<www.columbiacountyfla.com>**

- **INCORPORATED:** Feb. 4, 1832
- **PARENT COUNTY:** Alachua
- **MARRIAGE RECORDS:** start in 1875, kept by Circuit Court
- **LAND:** 1875, Circuit Court
- **DIVORCE:** 1892, Circuit Court
- **COURT:** 1892, Circuit Court
- **PROBATE:** 1895, Circuit Court
- **BIRTH:** unknown, Public Health Unit
- **DEATH:** unknown, Public Health Unit
- **BURIAL:** unknown, Public Health Unit

DADE

- **INCORPORATED:** Feb. 4, 1836
- **PARENT COUNTY:** Monroe
- **NOTES:** See Miami-Dade County. Name changed to Miami-Dade Dec. 2, 1997.

DE SOTO

115 Oak St., Arcadia, FL 33821, (863) 993-4876, **<co.desoto.fl.us>**

- **INCORPORATED:** June 19, 1887
- **PARENT COUNTY:** Manatee
- **COURT RECORDS:** start in 1887, kept by Circuit Court
- **DIVORCE:** 1887, Circuit Court
- **LAND:** 1887, Circuit Court
- **PROBATE:** 1887, County Judge

DIXIE

Box 1206, Cross City, FL 32628, (352) 498-1200 **<www.dixie.fl.gov>**

- **INCORPORATED:** April 25, 1921
- **PARENT COUNTY:** Lafayette
- **MARRIAGE RECORDS:** start in 1973, kept by Circuit Court
- **DIVORCE:** unknown, Circuit Court
- **PROBATE:** unknown, Circuit Court
- **COURT:** unknown, Circuit Court
- **LAND:** unknown, Circuit Court

DUVAL
330 E. Bay St., Jacksonville, FL 32202, (904) 630-2028, **<www.duvalclerk.com>**
- **INCORPORATED:** Aug. 12, 1822
- **PARENT COUNTY:** St. Johns
- **DIVORCE RECORDS:** start in 1921, kept by Circuit Court
- **COURT:** 1921, Circuit Court
- **LAND:** 1921, Circuit Court
- **MARRIAGE:** unknown, County Judge
- **PROBATE:** unknown, County Judge

ESCAMBIA
223 S. Palafox Pl., Pensacola, FL 32501, (850) 595-4310, **<www.co.escambia.fl.us>**
- **INCORPORATED:** July 21, 1821
- **PARENT COUNTY:** Original county.
- **MARRIAGE:** 1821, County Court
- **PROBATE:** 1821, County Court
- **COURT:** 1821, County Court
- **BIRTH:** unknown, Department of Health
- **DEATH:** unknown, Department of Health
- **LAND:** 1821, Comptroller

FLAGLER
Kim C. Hammond Justice Center, 1769 E Moody Blvd, Bldg 1, Bunnell, FL 32110, (386) 313-4400, **<www.flaglerclerk.com>**
- **INCORPORATED:** April 28, 1917
- **PARENT COUNTY:** St. Johns
- **MARRIAGE RECORDS:** start in 1917, kept by Circuit Court
- **DIVORCE:** 1917, Circuit Court
- **PROBATE:** 1917, Circuit Court
- **COURT:** 1917, Circuit Court
- **LAND:** 1917, Circuit Court

FRANKLIN
33 Market St., Suite 203, Apalachicola, FL 32320, (850) 653-8861, **<www.franklincountyflorida.com>**
- **INCORPORATED:** Feb. 8, 1832
- **PARENT COUNTY:** Jackson
- **DIVORCE:** unknown start, kept by Circuit Court
- **COURT:** unknown, Circuit Court
- **LAND:** unknown, Circuit Court
- **MARRIAGE:** unknown, County Judge
- **PROBATE:** unknown, County Judge

GADSDEN
10 E. Jefferson St., Quincy, FL 32351, (850) 875-8622, **<www.clerk.co.gadsden.fl.us>**
- **INCORPORATED:** June 24, 1823
- **PARENT COUNTY:** Jackson
- **MARRIAGE RECORDS:** unknown start, kept by County Judge
- **PROBATE:** unknown, County Judge
- **DIVORCE:** unknown, Circuit Court
- **COURT:** unknown, Circuit Court
- **LAND:** unknown, Circuit Court

GILCHRIST
112 S. Main St., Trenton, FL 32693, (352) 463-3170, **<www.co.gilchrist.fl.us>**
- **INCORPORATED:** Dec. 4, 1925
- **PARENT COUNTY:** Alachua
- **MARRIAGE:** start in 1926, kept by Circuit Court
- **DIVORCE:** 1926, Circuit Court
- **PROBATE:** 1926, Circuit Court
- **COURT:** 1926, Circuit Court

GLADES
500 Avenue J, Box 10, Moorehaven, FL 33471, (863) 946-6010, **<www.gladescofl.us>**
- **INCORPORATED:** April 23, 1921
- **PARENT COUNTY:** DeSoto
- **MARRIAGE RECORDS:** start in 1921, kept by Clerk of Courts
- **DIVORCE:** 1921, Clerk of Courts
- **LAND:** 1921, Clerk of Courts
- **PROBATE:** 1921, Clerk of Courts
- **COURT:** 1921, Clerk of Courts
- **BURIAL:** 1925, Clerk of Courts
- **BIRTH:** 1921, Department of Health
- **DEATH:** 1921, Department of Health

GULF
1000 Cecil G. Costin Sr. Blvd., Port St. Joe, FL 32456, (850) 229-6112, **<www.gulfcounty-fl.gov>**
- **INCORPORATED:** June 6, 1925
- **PARENT COUNTY:** Calhoun
- **MARRIAGE RECORDS:** start in 1925, kept by Circuit Court
- **PROBATE:** 1925, Circuit Court
- **DIVORCE:** 1925, Circuit Court
- **COURT:** 1925, Circuit Court
- **LAND:** 1925, Circuit Court
- **MILITARY:** 1925, Circuit Court

HAMILTON
207 N.E. First St., Jasper, FL 32052, (386) 792-1288, **<www.hamiltoncountyflorida.com>**
- **INCORPORATED:** Dec. 26, 1827
- **PARENT COUNTY:** Jefferson
- **DIVORCE RECORDS:** start in 1881, kept by Circuit Court
- **COURT:** 1881, Circuit Court
- **LAND:** 1837, Circuit Court
- **MARRIAGE:** unknown, County Judge
- **PROBATE:** unknown, County Judge

HARDEE
417 West Main St., Suite 105, Wauchula, FL 33873, (863) 773-4174, **<www.hardeeclerk.com>**
- **INCORPORATED:** April 23, 1921
- **PARENT COUNTY:** DeSoto
- **MARRIAGE RECORDS:** start in 1921, kept by Circuit Court
- **DEATH:** 1921, Circuit Court
- **DIVORCE:** 1921, Circuit Court
- **PROBATE:** 1921, Circuit Court
- **COURT:** 1921, Circuit Court
- **LAND:** 1921, Circuit Court

HENDRY
25 E. Hickpochee Ave., Box 1760, LaBelle, FL 33975, (863) 675-5217, **<www.hendryclerk.org>**
- **INCORPORATED:** May 11, 1923
- **PARENT COUNTY:** Lee
- **MARRIAGE RECORDS:** start in 1923, kept by Circuit Court
- **DIVORCE:** 1923, Circuit Court
- **LAND:** 1923, Circuit Court
- **PROBATE:** 1923, Circuit Court
- **COURT:** 1923, Circuit Court
- **BURIAL:** 1953, Circuit Court
- **BIRTH:** unknown, Department of Health
- **DEATH:** unknown, Department of Health

HERNANDO
20 N. Main St., Brooksville, FL 34601, (352) 754-4201, **<www.co.hernando.fl.us>**
- **INCORPORATED:** Feb. 24, 1843
- **PARENT COUNTY:** Alachua
- **MARRIAGE RECORDS:** start date unknown, kept by County Court
- **DIVORCE:** 1877, Circuit Court
- **PROBATE:** 1877, Circuit Court
- **COURT:** 1877, Circuit Court
- **LAND:** 1877, Circuit Court
- **NOTES:** Name changed to Benton March 6, 1844. Name changed back to Hernando Dec. 24, 1850.

HIGHLANDS
590 S. Commerce Ave., Sebring, FL 33870, (863) 402-6564, **<www.highlands-county.com>**
- **INCORPORATED:** April 23, 1921
- **PARENT COUNTY:** DeSoto
- **MARRIAGE RECORDS:** start in 1921, kept by Circuit Court
- **DIVORCE:** 1921, Circuit Court
- **PROBATE:** 1921, Circuit Court
- **COURT:** 1921, Circuit Court
- **LAND:** 1921, Circuit Court

HILLSBOROUGH
419 N. Pierce St., Tampa, FL 33602, (813) 276-8100, **<www.hillsboroughcounty.org>**
- **INCORPORATED:** Jan. 25, 1834
- **PARENT COUNTY:** Alachua
- **MARRIAGE RECORDS:** unknown start, kept by County Judge
- **PROBATE:** unknown, County Judge
- **DIVORCE:** ca. 1800, Circuit Court
- **LAND:** ca. 1800, Circuit Court

HOLMES
201 N. Oklahoma St., Bonifay, FL 32425, (850) 547-1100, **<www2.myfloridacounty.com/wps/wcm/connect/holmesclerk>**
- **INCORPORATED:** Jan. 8, 1848
- **PARENT COUNTY:** Jackson
- **MARRIAGE RECORDS:** unknown start, kept by Circuit Court
- **PROBATE:** unknown, Circuit Court
- **DIVORCE:** unknown, Circuit Court
- **COURT:** unknown, Circuit Court
- **LAND:** unknown, Circuit Court

INDIAN RIVER
1840 25th St., Vero Beach, FL 32960, (561) 567-8000, **<indian-river.fl.us>**
- **INCORPORATED:** May 30, 1925
- **PARENT COUNTY:** St. Lucie
- **MARRIAGE RECORDS:** start in 1925, kept by Circuit Court
- **DIVORCE:** 1925, Circuit Court
- **PROBATE:** 1925, Circuit Court
- **COURT:** 1925, Circuit Court
- **LAND:** 1925, Circuit Court
- **BIRTH:** unknown, Department of Health
- **DEATH:** unknown, Department of Health

JACKSON
Box 510, Marianna, FL 32447, (850) 482-9552, **<www.jacksoncountyfl.com>**
- **INCORPORATED:** Aug. 12, 1822
- **PARENT COUNTY:** Escambia
- **MARRIAGE RECORDS:** start in 1845, kept by Circuit Court
- **LAND:** 1824, Circuit Court
- **DIVORCE:** 1900, Circuit Court
- **PROBATE:** 1900, Circuit Court
- **MILITARY:** 1900, Circuit Court
- **COURT:** 1900, Circuit Court

JEFFERSON
County Courthouse, Room 10, Monticello, FL 32344, (850) 342-0218, **<www.co.jefferson.fl.us>**
- **INCORPORATED:** Jan. 6, 1827
- **PARENT COUNTY:** Leon
- **MARRIAGE RECORDS:** start in 1840, kept by Circuit Court
- **DIVORCE:** 1900, Circuit Court
- **PROBATE:** 1850, Circuit Court
- **COURT:** 1850, Circuit Court
- **LAND:** 1827, Circuit Court

LAFAYETTE
Box 88, Mayo, FL 32066-0088, (386) 294-1600, **<www2.myfloridacounty.com/wps/wcm/connect/lafayetteclerk>**
- **INCORPORATED:** Dec. 23, 1826
- **PARENT COUNTY:** Madison
- **DIVORCE RECORDS:** start in 1902, kept by Circuit Court
- **COURT:** 1907, Circuit Court
- **LAND:** 1893, Circuit Court
- **MARRIAGE:** unknown, County Judge
- **PROBATE:** unknown, County Judge

LAKE
315 W. Main St., Box 7800, Tavares, FL 32778, (352) 742-4100, **<www.lakegovernment.com>**
- **INCORPORATED:** May 27, 1887
- **PARENT COUNTY:** Orange
- **MARRIAGE RECORDS:** start in 1887, Circuit Court
- **DIVORCE:** 1887, Circuit Court
- **COURT:** 1887, Circuit Court
- **LAND:** 1887, Circuit Court
- **PROBATE:** 1893, Circuit Court
- **DEATH:** unknown, Department of Health

LEE

2115 Second St., Fort Myers, FL 33901, (941) 335-2283,
<www.lee-county.com>

- **INCORPORATED:** May 13, 1887
- **PARENT COUNTY:** Monroe
- **MARRIAGE RECORDS:** unknown start, kept by Circuit Court
- **DIVORCE:** unknown, Circuit Court
- **PROBATE:** unknown, Circuit Court
- **COURT:** unknown, Circuit Court
- **LAND:** unknown, Circuit Court

LEON

301 S. Monroe St., Box 726, Tallahassee, FL 32301, (850) 577-4000,
<www.leoncountyfl.gov>

- **INCORPORATED:** Dec. 29, 1824
- **PARENT COUNTY:** Gadsden
- **MARRIAGE RECORDS:** start in 1825, kept by Circuit Court
- **DIVORCE:** 1825, Circuit Court
- **PROBATE:** 1825, Circuit Court
- **COURT:** 1825, Circuit Court
- **LAND:** 1825, Circuit Court
- **MILITARY:** 1914, Circuit Court
- **BIRTH:** unknown, Department of Health
- **DEATH:** unknown, Department of Health
- **BURIAL:** unknown, Department of Health

LEVY

355 S. Court St., Box 610, Bronson, FL 32621, (352) 486-5229,
<www.levycounty.org>

- **INCORPORATED:** March 10, 1845
- **PARENT COUNTY:** Alachua
- **MARRIAGE RECORDS:** start in 1850, kept by Circuit Court
- **DIVORCE:** 1850, Circuit Court
- **PROBATE:** 1850, Circuit Court
- **COURT:** 1850, Circuit Court
- **LAND:** 1850, Circuit Court

LIBERTY

Box 399, Bristol, FL 32321, (850) 643-2237,
<www.libertycountyflorida.com>

- **INCORPORATED:** Dec. 15, 1855
- **PARENT COUNTY:** Gadsden
- **DIVORCE RECORDS:** unknown start, kept by Circuit Court
- **COURT:** unknown, Circuit Court
- **LAND:** unknown, Circuit Court
- **MARRIAGE:** unknown, County Judge
- **PROBATE:** unknown, County Judge

MADISON

Box 237, Madison, FL 32341, (850) 973-1500,
<www.madisonfl.org>

- **INCORPORATED:** Dec. 26, 1827
- **PARENT COUNTY:** Jefferson
- **MARRIAGE RECORDS:** start in 1838, kept by Circuit Court
- **PROBATE:** 1838, Circuit Court
- **COURT:** 1838, Circuit Court
- **LAND:** 1831, Circuit Court
- **DIVORCE:** unknown, Circuit Court

MANATEE

1115 Manatee Ave., West Bradenton, FL 34205, (941) 749-1800,
<www.co.manatee.fl.us>

- **INCORPORATED:** Jan. 9, 1855
- **PARENT COUNTY:** Hillsborough
- **MARRIAGE RECORDS:** start in 1857, kept by Circuit Court
- **DIVORCE:** 1857, Circuit Court
- **PROBATE:** 1857, Circuit Court
- **COURT:** 1857, Circuit Court
- **LAND:** 1857, Circuit Court

MARION

Box 1030, Ocala, FL 34478-1030, (352) 620-3904,
<www.marioncountyfl.org>

- **INCORPORATED:** March 14, 1844
- **PARENT COUNTY:** Alachua
- **LAND RECORDS:** unknown start, kept by Recording Office
- **DIVORCE:** unknown, Recording Office
- **PROBATE:** unknown, Recording Office
- **COURT:** unknown, Recording Office
- **BIRTH:** unknown, Department of Health
- **MARRIAGE:** unknown, Clerk of Courts
- **DEATH:** unknown, Department of Health

MARTIN

100 E. Ocean Boulevard, Suite 200, Stuart, Florida 34994, (772) 288-5576, **<www.martin.fl.us>**

- **INCORPORATED:** May 30, 1925
- **PARENT COUNTY:** Palm Beach
- **MARRIAGE RECORDS:** start in 1925, kept by Circuit Court
- **DIVORCE:** 1925, Circuit Court
- **PROBATE:** 1925, Circuit Court
- **COURT:** 1925, Circuit Court
- **LAND:** 1925, Circuit Court
- **BIRTH:** unknown, Department of Health
- **DEATH:** unknown, Department of Health
- **BURIAL:** unknown, Department of Health

MIAMI-DADE

111 NW First St., Suite 17-202, Miami, FL 33128, (305) 375-5126,
<miamidade.gov>

- **INCORPORATED:** Nov. 13, 1997
- **PARENT COUNTIES:** Monroe, Dade
- **DIVORCE RECORDS:** start in 1890, kept by Circuit Court
- **LAND:** 1890, Circuit Court
- **MARRIAGE:** unknown, County Judge
- **PROBATE:** unknown, County Judge
- **NOTES:** See Dade County. Name changed to Miami-Dade Dec. 2, 1997.

MONROE

500 Whitehead St., Key West, FL 33040, (305) 292-3540,
<www.co.monroe.fl.us>

- **INCORPORATED:** July 3, 1823
- **PARENT COUNTY:** St. Johns
- **MARRIAGE RECORDS:** start in 1853, kept by Circuit Court
- **DIVORCE:** 1853, Circuit Court
- **PROBATE:** 1853, Circuit Court

- **COURT:** 1853, Circuit Court
- **LAND:** 1853, Circuit Court

MOSQUITO
- **INCORPORATED:** Dec. 29, 1824
- **PARENT COUNTY:** St. Johns
- **NOTES:** See Orange County. Name changed to Orange Jan. 30, 1845.

NASSAU
416 Centre Street, Fernandina Beach, FL 32034, (904) 491-6430, **<www.nassauclerk.org>**
- **INCORPORATED:** Dec. 29, 1824
- **PARENT COUNTY:** Duval
- **MARRIAGE RECORDS:** start ca. 1800, kept by Circuit Court
- **DIVORCE:** ca. 1800, Circuit Court
- **PROBATE:** ca. 1800, Circuit Court
- **COURT:** ca. 1800, Circuit Court
- **LAND:** ca. 1800, Circuit Court

NEW RIVER 21 DEC. 1858
- **INCORPORATED:** Dec. 21, 1858
- **PARENT COUNTY:** Columbia
- **NOTES:** See Bradford County. Name changed to Bradford Dec. 6, 1861.

OKALOOSA
101 E. James Lee Blvd., Crestview, FL 32536, (850) 689-5000, **<www.co.okaloosa.fl.us>**
- **INCORPORATED:** June 3, 1915
- **PARENT COUNTY:** Santa Rosa
- **DIVORCE RECORDS:** start in 1915, kept by Circuit Court
- **COURT:** 1915, Circuit Court
- **LAND:** 1915, Circuit Court
- **MARRIAGE:** unknown, County Judge
- **PROBATE:** unknown, County Judge

OKEECHOBEE
312 N.W. Third St., Okeechobee, FL 34972, (863) 763-2131, **<www.co.okeechobee.fl.us>**
- **INCORPORATED:** May 8, 1917
- **PARENT COUNTY:** Brevard
- **MARRIAGE RECORDS:** start in 1917, kept by Circuit Court
- **DIVORCE:** 1917, Circuit Court
- **PROBATE:** 1917, Circuit Court
- **COURT:** 1917, Circuit Court
- **LAND:** ca. 1880, Circuit Court
- **BIRTH:** ca. 1900, Department of Health
- **DEATH:** ca. 1880, Department of Health

ORANGE
425 N. Orange Ave., Orlando, FL 32801, (407) 863-0517, **<www.orangecountyfl.net>**
- **INCORPORATED:** Dec. 29, 1824
- **PARENT COUNTY:** St. Johns
- **MARRIAGE RECORDS:** start in 1890, kept by Circuit Court
- **COURT:** 1869, Circuit Court
- **PROBATE:** 1869, Circuit Court
- **NOTES:** See Mosquito County. Name changed to Orange Jan. 30, 1845.

OSCEOLA
2 Courthouse Sq., Suite 2000, Kissimmee, FL 34741, (407) 343-3500 ext. 3517, **<www.osceola.org>**
- **INCORPORATED:** May 12, 1887
- **PARENT COUNTY:** Brevard
- **MARRIAGE RECORDS:** start in 1887, kept by Circuit Court
- **DIVORCE:** 1887, Circuit Court
- **PROBATE:** 1887, Circuit Court
- **COURT:** 1887, Circuit Court
- **LAND:** 1887, Circuit Court

PALM BEACH
205 North Dixie Highway, West Palm Beach, FL 33401 (561) 355-2996, **<www.co.palm-beach.fl.us>**
- **INCORPORATED:** April 30, 1909
- **PARENT COUNTY:** Dade
- **DIVORCE RECORDS:** unknown start, kept by Circuit Court
- **COURT:** unknown, Circuit Court
- **LAND:** unknown, Circuit Court
- **MARRIAGE:** unknown, County Judge
- **PROBATE:** unknown, County Judge

PASCO
38053 Live Oak Ave., Dade City, FL 33523-3894, (352) 518-4008, **<portal.pascocountyfl.net>**
- **INCORPORATED:** June 2, 1887
- **PARENT COUNTY:** Hernando
- **DIVORCE RECORDS:** start in 1887, kept by Circuit Court
- **COURT:** 1887, Circuit Court
- **LAND:** 1887, Circuit Court
- **MARRIAGE:** ca. 1890, Circuit Court
- **PROBATE:** ca. 1890, Circuit Court

PINELLAS
315 Court St., Clearwater, FL 33756, (727) 464-7000, **<www.co.pinellas.fl.us/bcc>**
- **INCORPORATED:** May, 23, 1911
- **PARENT COUNTY:** Hillsborough
- **MARRIAGE RECORDS:** start in 1912, kept by Circuit Court
- **DIVORCE:** 1912, Circuit Court
- **PROBATE:** 1912, Circuit Court
- **COURT:** 1912, Circuit Court
- **LAND:** 1912, Circuit Court

POLK
255 N. Broadway Ave., Bartow, FL 33830, (863) 534-4540, **<www.polk-county.net>**
- **INCORPORATED:** Feb. 8, 1861
- **PARENT COUNTY:** Brevard
- **MARRIAGE RECORDS:** start in 1861, kept by Circuit Court
- **DIVORCE:** 1861, Circuit Court
- **PROBATE:** 1861, Circuit Court
- **COURT:** 1861, Circuit Court
- **LAND:** 1861, Circuit Court
- **NOTES:** Boundaries changed 1871.

PUTNAM
410 St. Johns Ave., Palatka, FL 32177, (386) 329-0361,
<www.putnam-fl.com/bocc>
- **INCORPORATED:** Jan. 13, 1849
- **PARENT COUNTY:** Alachua
- **MARRIAGE RECORDS:** start in 1849, kept by Circuit Court
- **DIVORCE:** 1849, Circuit Court
- **PROBATE:** 1849, Circuit Court
- **COURT:** 1849, Circuit Court
- **LAND:** 1849, Circuit Court
- **NOTES:** Clerk of Circuit Court has naturalization records 1849-1914.

SANTA ROSA
6865 Caroline St., Milton, FL 32570, (850) 623-3159,
<www.co.santa-rosa.fl.us>
- **INCORPORATED:** Feb. 18, 1842
- **PARENT COUNTY:** Escambia
- **MARRIAGE RECORDS:** start in 1869, kept by County Archives
- **DIVORCE:** 1869, County Archives
- **PROBATE:** 1869, County Archives
- **COURT:** 1869, County Archives
- **LAND:** 1869, Main Courthouse
- **NOTES:** Courthouse burned in 1869.

SARASOTA
2000 Main St., Sarasota, FL 34237, (941) 362-4066,
<www.co.sarasota.fl.us>
- **INCORPORATED:** May 14, 1921
- **PARENT COUNTY:** Manatee
- **MARRIAGE RECORDS:** start in 1921, kept by Circuit Court
- **PROBATE:** 1921, Circuit Court
- **COURT:** 1921, Circuit Court
- **LAND:** 1921, Circuit Court
- **DIVORCE:** 1945, Circuit Court
- **BIRTH:** ca. 1920, Department of Health
- **DEATH:** ca. 1920, Department of Health

SEMINOLE
301 N. Park Ave., Sanford, FL 32771, 407) 665-4330,
<www.co.seminole.fl.us>
- **INCORPORATED:** April 25, 1913
- **PARENT COUNTY:** Orange
- **DIVORCE RECORDS:** start in 1915, kept by Circuit Court
- **COURT:** 1915, Circuit Court
- **LAND:** 1915, Circuit Court
- **MARRIAGE:** unknown, County Judge
- **PROBATE:** unknown, County Judge

ST. JOHNS
4010 Lewis Speedway Blvd., St. Augustine, FL 32084
(904) 819-3600, **<www.co.st-johns.fl.us>**
- **INCORPORATED:** July 21, 1821
- **PARENT COUNTY:** Original county.
- **DIVORCE RECORDS:** start in 1900, kept by Circuit Court
- **COURT:** 1821, Circuit Court
- **LAND:** 1821, Circuit Court
- **MARRIAGE:** unknown, Circuit Court
- **PROBATE:** unknown, Circuit Court

ST. LUCIE
2300 Virginia Ave., Fort Pierce, FL 34982, (772) 462-6928,
<www.stlucieco.gov>
- **INCORPORATED:** May 24, 1905
- **PARENT COUNTY:** Brevard
- **MARRIAGE RECORDS:** start in 1905, kept by Circuit Court
- **PROBATE:** 1905, Circuit Court
- **DIVORCE:** 1905, Circuit Court
- **COURT:** 1905, Circuit Court
- **LAND:** 1905, Circuit Court
- **DEATH:** unknown, Department of Health
- **BURIAL:** unknown, Department of Health

SUMTER
910 N. Main St., Bushnell, FL 33513, (352) 793-0200,
<www.sumtercountyfl.gov>
- **INCORPORATED:** Jan. 8, 1853
- **PARENT COUNTY:** Marion
- **LAND RECORDS:** start in 1853, kept by Circuit Court
- **DIVORCE:** 1900, Circuit Court
- **COURT:** 1913, Circuit Court
- **MARRIAGE:** 1853, Circuit Court
- **PROBATE:** 1856, Circuit Court
- **NOTES:** Clerk of Circuit Courts has delayed Birth records 1943-1972.

SUWANNEE
224 Pine Ave., Live Oak, FL 32064, (386) 364-3410,
<www.suwcounty.org>
- **INCORPORATED:** Dec. 21, 1858
- **PARENT COUNTY:** Columbia
- **MARRIAGE RECORDS:** start in 1859, kept by Circuit Court
- **DIVORCE:** 1859, Circuit Court
- **LAND:** 1859, Circuit Court
- **PROBATE:** 1859, Circuit Court
- **MILITARY:** 1859, Circuit Court
- **COURT:** 1859, Circuit Court
- **DEATH:** ca. 1900, Department of Health

TAYLOR
Box 620, Perry, FL 32348, (850) 838-3506,
<www.taylorcountygov.com>
- **INCORPORATED:** Dec. 23, 1856
- **PARENT COUNTY:** Madison
- **MARRIAGE RECORDS:** start in 1908, kept by Circuit Court
- **DIVORCE:** 1898, Circuit Court
- **LAND:** 1857, Circuit Court

- **PROBATE:** 1941, Circuit Court
- **COURT:** 1946, Circuit Court
- **MILITARY:** 1914, Circuit Court

UNION

55 W. Main Street, Room 103, Lake Butler, FL 32054, (386) 496-3711, **<www.myunioncounty.com>**

- **INCORPORATED:** May 20, 1921
- **PARENT COUNTY:** Bradford
- **DIVORCE RECORDS:** start ca. 1920, kept by Circuit Court
- **COURT:** ca. 1920, Circuit Court

VOLUSIA

123 W. Indiana Ave., DeLand, FL 32720, (386) 736-5915, **<www.volusia.org>**

- **INCORPORATED:** Dec. 29, 1854
- **PARENT COUNTY:** Orange
- **MARRIAGE RECORDS:** unknown start, kept by Circuit Court
- **DIVORCE:** unknown, Circuit Court
- **COURT:** unknown, Circuit Court
- **PROBATE:** unknown, Circuit Court
- **LAND:** unknown, Circuit Court

WAKULLA

3056 Crawfordville Highway, Crawfordville, FL 32327, (850) 926-0905, **<www.mywakulla.com>**

- **INCORPORATED:** March 11, 1843
- **PARENT COUNTY:** Leon
- **MARRIAGE RECORDS:** start in 1896, kept by Circuit Court
- **DIVORCE:** 1896, Circuit Court
- **PROBATE:** 1896, Circuit Court
- **COURT:** 1896, Circuit Court
- **LAND:** 1896, Circuit Court
- **NOTES:** Courthouse burned in 1896. County Health Department has some birth records.

WALTON

Box 1260, DeFuniak Springs, FL 32434, (850) 892-8118, **<www.co.walton.fl.us>**

- **INCORPORATED:** Dec. 29, 1824
- **PARENT COUNTY:** Escambia
- **MARRIAGE RECORDS:** start in 1885, kept by Circuit Court
- **PROBATE:** 1882, Circuit Court
- **DIVORCE:** 1905, Circuit Court
- **COURT:** 1905, Circuit Court
- **LAND:** 1905, Circuit Court
- **BIRTH:** unknown, Department of Health
- **DEATH:** unknown, Department of Health

WASHINGTON

711 Third St., Chipley, FL 32428, (850) 638-6200, **<www.washingtonfl.com>**

- **INCORPORATED:** Dec. 9, 1825
- **PARENT COUNTY:** Jackson
- **MARRIAGE RECORDS:** start in 1890, kept by Circuit Court
- **DIVORCE:** 1890, Circuit Court
- **PROBATE:** 1890, Circuit Court
- **LAND:** 1890, Circuit Court
- **COURT:** 1890, Circuit Court

GEORGIA

» BY EMILY ANNE CROOM

HISTORICAL OVERVIEW

After French and Spanish explorations in the 16th century, Spain claimed the Georgia-Florida area and established missions among coastal Indians. A century later, Britain chartered the Carolina colony. By the early 1700s, with Spanish settlements to the south and the French in greater Louisiana, Britain wanted to strengthen its presence and provide a buffer against attack on Carolina. Thus, in 1732 Britain chartered the Georgia colony to 20 trustees for 21 years, and the first settlers founded Savannah in 1733. Early immigrants included English, Welsh, Scottish, and Irish, with some Italian, Portuguese, Swiss, and German settlers. Protestants and Jews were welcome, but not Catholics. Slavery was prohibited until 1749.

When the Georgia trustees relinquished their charter in 1752, Georgia became a royal colony. More settlers arrived from other British colonies, especially Virginia and the Carolinas. In southern Georgia, flat-to-rolling coastal plains were ripe for plantation agriculture. The northern highlands and mountains remained largely Indian lands until the 1830s.

As the 13 colonies moved toward independence, loyalist feelings were strong in Georgia, and it was the last colony to send representatives to the Continental Congress. The Georgia delegation joined the other colonies in voting for independence in July 1776. During the Revolution, the British occupied both Savannah and Augusta and controlled most of the state. In 1787, Georgia ratified the US Constitution.

As the nation expanded, Georgians pushed into northeastern Indian lands. Although gold had been found periodically in Cherokee territory, a gold rush began with discoveries about 1828. The forced removal of thousands of Cherokee from northern Georgia in 1838, during which some 4,000 died, became one of several Trails of Tears.

Railroads came to Georgia in the 1830s and gave impetus to some industries, especially textiles. Before the Civil War, the core of the state's economy was agriculture, especially cotton cultivation using slave labor. By 1860, 44 percent of Georgia's million residents were slaves; 1 percent were immigrants.

In January 1861, Georgia seceded from the Union, despite a sizeable anti-secession minority. Deprivation and destruction characterized the Civil War years, and in September 1864, General Sherman's army destroyed Atlanta as it burned its way toward the coast. Reconstruction saw continued hardship and poverty. By the turn of the 20th century,

research tips

Georgia sources are available on microfilm at the state archives, and often, the Family History Library. They include:

- State tax digests, by county, from the 1780s
- Poor school and academy lists, fragmentary from the late 1820s to the 1860s
- Civil War salt allotments
- Men subject to military duty, March 1862: men from 16 to 60 who had not enlisted by the beginning of 1864
- Reconstruction registration oath books and returns of qualified voters, 1867–1868
- Register of "inmates," 1901–1941, and Confederate widows' applications for the Confederate Soldiers' Home of Georgia
- Confederate pension records from 1870

CENSUS RECORDS

- Federal Census Schedules: 1820 (except Franklin, Rabun and Twiggs Counties), 1830, 1840, 1850, 1860, 1870, 1880, 1890 (Washington County), 1900, 1910, 1920, 1930
- Federal Census Soundex: 1880, 1900, 1910, 1920, 1930
- Federal Mortality Schedules for all Georgia counties available at the Georgia Archives for the years: 1850, 1860, 1870, 1880
- Federal slave schedules: 1850, 1860. Schedules name slaveholders but rarely name slaves.
- State census: 1798 to about 1879, various years, various counties

Georgia's economy was slowly industrializing, with logging, mining and related industries stemming from the state's numerous natural resources. Cotton still fed Georgia's textile industry, but crop diversification encouraged food-processing industries. By the mid-20th century, the population and economy were no longer predominantly agricultural.

RECORD HIGHLIGHTS

Statewide birth and death records date from 1919. Check major cities and the state archives for earlier records. Most counties kept marriage records from the county's inception; statewide records date from 1952. For more information, see the Division of Public Health website **<health.state.ga.us/programs/vitalrecords>**.

Georgia had a unique system of distributing newly opened state land by lottery. Eligible state citizens registered in their home counties, and drawings in the state capital matched winners with newly surveyed lots. Winners paid a registration fee to claim the land, but many sold their claims. Lotteries were held in 1805, 1807, 1820, 1821, 1827 and 1832 (two drawings). Qualifications and land locations are on the Georgia archives website, **<sos.georgia.gov/archives/what_do_we_have/land_lottery/default.htm>**. Most lottery results have been published; indexes to the state's lottery records are available through the Family History Library (FHL).

Although the 1790 to 1810 federal censuses for Georgia are lost (except for Oglethorpe County in 1800), partial substitutes have been compiled from land, tax and other records. Because citizens eligible for the 1805 lottery had to have lived in Georgia before mid-1802, those lottery records act as a substitute for the 1800 census. From 1798 to about 1879, Georgia took septennial censuses of heads of household. Surviving records vary by year and county; some are published.

Special African-American resources include slave narratives, records of antebellum plantations and industries, and records of Georgia's three branches of the Freedman's Savings and Trust Co. (see FHL microfilm 928576-80).

Georgia was originally divided into districts and towns, then into parishes as a royal colony. In 1777, the parishes became the seven original counties. Before 1777 and during British occupation in the American Revolution, the districts and parishes were not governmental entities and did not create books of record. Deed, estate and other books of record were kept centrally in Savannah. Surviving colonial records have been microfilmed; some abstracts have been published.

Of Georgia's 159 counties, more than a third have suffered varying degrees of record losses due to fires and storms. Nevertheless, check for surviving county records along with family, colonial, local, state, federal, parent county and neighboring county sources.

☞ARCHIVES, LIBRARIES, AND SOCIETIES

African-American Family Historical Association
Box 115268, Atlanta, GA 30310

Alma-Bacon County Historical Society
406 Mercer St., Alma, GA 31510, (912) 632-8450

Alpharetta Historical Society
1835 Old Milton Pkwy., Alpharetta, GA 30004, (770) 475-4663, **<ahsga.org>**

Andrew College Archives, Pitts Library
501 College St., Cuthbert, GA 39840, (229) 732-5944, **<andrewcollege.edu/pittsinfo.html >**

Appling County Heritage Center
209 Thomas St., Box 87 Baxley, GA 3151, (912) 367-8133

Aragan Historical Society
Box 333, Aragon GA, 30104, (770) 684-3771

Ashantilly Center
Box 1449, Darien, GA 31305, (912) 634-0303, **<ashantilly.org >**

Athens-Clarke County Library
2025 Baxter St., Athens, GA 30606, (706) 613-3650, **<clarke.public.lib.ga.us>**

Athens Historical Society
Box 7745, Athens, GA 30604, (706) 543-6922, **<www.rootsweb.ancestry.com/~gaahs>**

Atlanta-Fulton Public Library
1 Margaret Mitchell Square, Atlanta, GA 30303, (404) 730-4636, **<af.public.lib.ga.us>**

Atlanta History Center
130 W. Paces Ferry Rd., Atlanta, GA 30305, (404) 814-4000, **<atlantahistorycenter.com>**

Augusta Genealogical Society
Box 3743, Augusta, GA 30914, (706) 722-4073, **<augustagensociety.org>**

Augusta Museum of History
560 Reynolds St., Augusta, GA 30901, (706) 722-8454, **<augustamuseum.org>**

Barnesville-Lamar County Historical Society
Box 805, Barnesville, GA 30204, (770) 358-0150, **<rootsweb.ancestry.com/~galamar/society.html>**

Bartow County Genealogical Society
101 N. Erwin St., Box 993, Cartersville, GA 30120, (770) 606-0706, **<barctygen.org>**

Bethesda-Union Society
Box 13039, Savannah, GA 31416-0039, (912) 351-2061

Bonaventure Historical Society
Box 5954, Savannah, GA 31404-4615, **<bonaventurehistorical.org>**

Brantley County Historical and Preservation Society, Inc.
Box 1096, Nahunta, GA 31553, **<rootsweb.ancestry.com/~gabrantl/branco-home.html>**

Bulloch County Historical Society
Box 42, Statesboro, GA 30459, (912) 681-1956, **<bullochhistory.org>**

Burke County Historical Society
536 Liberty St., Waynesboro, GA 30830, **<usgennet.org/usa/ga/state1/burke>**

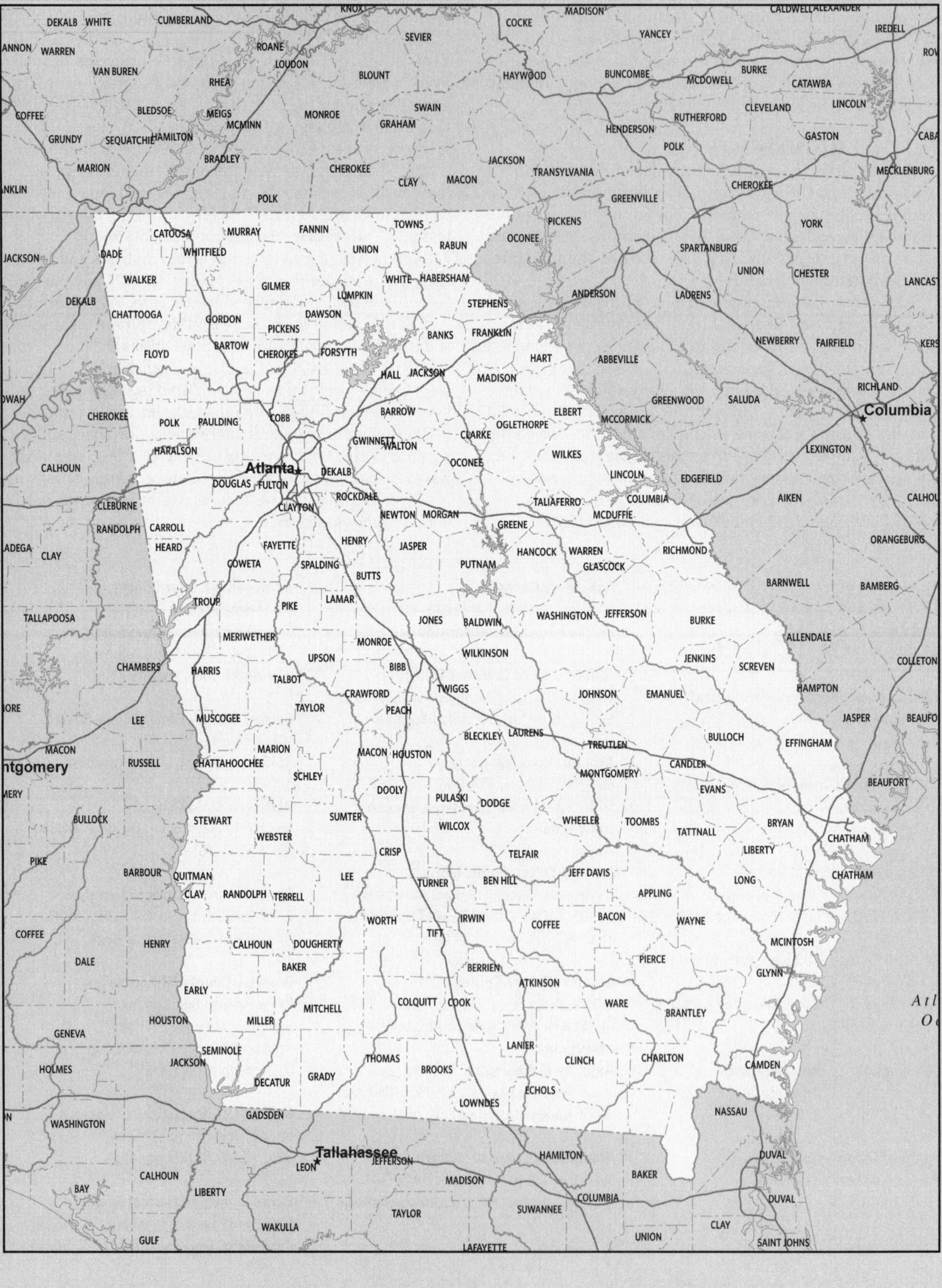
KNOX
MADISON
CALDWELL
ALEXANDER
DEKALB
WHITE
CUMBERLAND
COCKE
IREDELL
WARREN
SEVIER
YANCEY
ROANE
LOUDON
VAN BUREN
BLOUNT
HAYWOOD
BUNCOMBE
MCDOWELL
BURKE
CATAWBA
RHEA
LINCOLN
COFFEE
BLEDSOE
MEIGS
MONROE
SWAIN
GRAHAM
RUTHERFORD
CLEVELAND
MCMINN
HENDERSON
GASTON
GRUNDY
SEQUATCHIE
HAMILTON
POLK
MARION
BRADLEY
CHEROKEE
JACKSON
TRANSYLVANIA
CLAY
MACON
MECKLENBURG
POLK
GREENVILLE
CHEROKEE
PICKENS
YORK
TOWNS
CATOOSA
MURRAY
FANNIN
OCONEE
RABUN
SPARTANBURG
JACKSON
DADE
WHITFIELD
UNION
UNION
CHESTER
WALKER
GILMER
WHITE
HABERSHAM
LANCASTER
DEKALB
LUMPKIN
ANDERSON
LAURENS
STEPHENS
CHATTOOGA
DAWSON
GORDON
PICKENS
BANKS
FRANKLIN
NEWBERRY
FAIRFIELD
BARTOW
FLOYD
CHEROKEE
FORSYTH
HART
ABBEVILLE
HALL
JACKSON
MADISON
RICHLAND
GREENWOOD
SALUDA
Columbia
CHEROKEE
BARROW
ELBERT
POLK
PAULDING
COBB
OGLETHORPE
MCCORMICK
CLARKE
GWINNETT
WALTON
HARALSON
LEXINGTON
WILKES
CALHOUN
OCONEE
Atlanta
DEKALB
LINCOLN
EDGEFIELD
DOUGLAS
FULTON
ROCKDALE
COLUMBIA
AIKEN
CLEBURNE
TALIAFERRO
CLAYTON
NEWTON
MORGAN
MCDUFFIE
RANDOLPH
CARROLL
GREENE
HEARD
FAYETTE
HENRY
JASPER
HANCOCK
WARREN
RICHMOND
ORANGEBURG
CLAY
COWETA
SPALDING
PUTNAM
GLASCOCK
BUTTS
BARNWELL
BAMBERG
TROUP
LAMAR
PIKE
TALLAPOOSA
JONES
BALDWIN
WASHINGTON
JEFFERSON
BURKE
MERIWETHER
ALLENDALE
MONROE
WILKINSON
UPSON
JENKINS
COLLETON
CHAMBERS
BIBB
SCREVEN
HARRIS
TALBOT
TWIGGS
CRAWFORD
JOHNSON
EMANUEL
HAMPTON
TAYLOR
PEACH
LEE
MUSCOGEE
JASPER
BLECKLEY
LAURENS
BULLOCH
MACON
MARION
EFFINGHAM
TREUTLEN
MACON
HOUSTON
RUSSELL
CHATTAHOOCHEE
CANDLER
MONTGOMERY
SCHLEY
BEAUFORT
EVANS
DOOLY
PULASKI
DODGE
BULLOCK
STEWART
SUMTER
WHEELER
TOOMBS
BRYAN
WILCOX
TATTNALL
WEBSTER
CHATHAM
CRISP
LIBERTY
PIKE
TELFAIR
CHATHAM
JEFF DAVIS
BARBOUR
QUITMAN
LEE
LONG
TURNER
BEN HILL
CLAY
RANDOLPH
TERRELL
APPLING
IRWIN
COFFEE
BACON
WORTH
WAYNE
TIFT
COFFEE
HENRY
CALHOUN
DOUGHERTY
MCINTOSH
DALE
BAKER
PIERCE
BERRIEN
GLYNN
ATKINSON
EARLY
MITCHELL
COLQUITT
COOK
WARE
HOUSTON
BRANTLEY
MILLER
GENEVA
LANIER
SEMINOLE
THOMAS
CLINCH
CHARLTON
JACKSON
CAMDEN
HOLMES
BROOKS
GRADY
DECATUR
ECHOLS
LOWNDES
NASSAU
GADSDEN
WASHINGTON
Tallahassee
LEON
JEFFERSON
HAMILTON
DUVAL
CALHOUN
BAKER
MADISON
BAY
LIBERTY
COLUMBIA
DUVAL
TAYLOR
SUWANNEE
WAKULLA
CLAY
GULF
UNION
LAFAYETTE
SAINT JOHNS

Byron Area Historical Society
Box 755, Byron, GA 31008, (912) 956-2409

Candler County Historical Society
Box 325, Metter, GA 30439

Carroll County Genealogical Society
Box 576, Carrollton, GA 30112, (770) 832-7746, **<sites.google.com/site/ccgsga>**

Carroll County Historical Society
Box 1308, Carrollton, GA 30112, (770) 834-3081, **<carrollcountyhistory.org>**

Catoosa County Historical Society
Box 113, Ringgold, GA 30736, (706) 965-3056

Catoosa County Library
108 Catoosa Circle, Ringgold, GA 30736, (706) 965-3600, **<catoosacountylibrary.org>**

Central Georgia Genealogical Society
1600 Elberta Rd. Box 2024, Warner Robins, GA 31099, **<www.cggs.org>**

Chattahoochee Valley Historical Society
1213 Fifth Ave., West Point, GA 31833

Chattooga County Historical Society
Box 626, Summerville, GA 30747, **<rootsweb.ancestry.com/~gachatto>**

Cherokee County Historical Society
100 North St., Box 1287, Canton, GA 30114, (770) 345-2388, **<www.rockbarn.org>**

Clark Oconee Genealogical Society
Box 6403, Athens, GA 30604, **<rootsweb.ancestry.com/~gacogs>**

Clay County Library
208 Hancock St., Fort Gaines, GA 39851 (229) 768-2248, **<fortgaines.com/library.html>**

Clayton County Library System
865 Battlecreek Rd., Jonesboro, GA 30236, (770) 473-3850, **<clayton.public.lib.ga.us>**

Coastal Georgia Historical Society
Box 21136, St. Simons Island, A 31522, (912) 638-4666, **<saintsimonslighthouse.org>**

Cobb County Genealogy Society
Box 1413, Marietta, GA 30061, **<cobbgagensoc.org>**

Cobb County Public Library
266 Roswell St., Marietta, GA 30060, (770) 528-2320, **<library.cobbcat.org>**

Cobb Landmarks and Historical Society
30 Atlanta St. SE , Marietta, GA 30060, (678) 594-4994, **<cobblandmarks.com>**

Colquitt County Historical Society
214 Sixteenth Ave. SE, Moultrie, GA 31778, (912) 985-3413

Coweta County Genealogical Society
Box 427, Grantville, GA 30264, **<www.ccgsinc.org>**

Decatur County Historical Society
Box 682, Bainbridge, GA 39818, (229) 248-1719

Decatur-DeKalb Library
215 Sycamore St., Decatur, GA 30030, (404) 370-3070, **<www.dekalblibrary.org/branches/decatur.html>**

DeKalb Historical Society
101 E. Court Square, Decatur, GA 30030, (404) 373-1088, **<www.dekalbhistory.org>**

Delta Genealogical Society
504 McFarland Ave., Rossville, GA 30741 **<rootsweb.ancestry.com/~gadgs>**

Douglas County Genealogical Society
Box 5667, Douglasville, GA 30154, **<www.douglascountygensoc.org>**

Douglas County Historical Society
8562 Campbellton St., Box 2018, Douglasville, GA 30133

Early County Historical Society
Box 564, Blakely, GA 31723, (912) 723-4977, **<rootsweb.ancestry.com/~gaearly/misc/early_historical_society.htm>**

East Georgia Genealogical Society
Box 117, Winder, GA 30680, **<www.rootsweb.ancestry.com/~gaeggs>**

Eatonton-Putnam Historical Society
104 Church St., Eatonton, GA 31024, (706) 485-6442

Echols County Historical Society
814 Bethel Church Rd., Lake Park, GA 31636, (229) 559-5230

Elbert County Historical Society
1 Deadwyler St., Box 1033, Elberton, GA 30635

Emanuel County Historic Preservation Society
Box 353, Swainsboro, GA 30401, (478) 237-6924

Etowah Valley Historical Society
115 W. Cherokee Ave., Box 1886, Cartersville, GA 30120, (770) 606-8862, **<evhsonline.org>**

Evans County Historical Society
Box 6, Claxton, GA 30417, **<rootsweb.ancestry.com/~gaevans>**

Fannin County Ancestral Hunters
<homepages.rootsweb.ancestry.com/~fcgs>

Fayette County Historical Society
195 Lee St., Box 421, Fayetteville, GA 30214, (770) 716-6020, **<fayettehistoricalsociety.com>**

Flowery Branch Chapter of the Hall County Historical Society
Box 1994, Flowery Branch, GA 30542, (770) 641-2308

Foxfire Fund
Box 541, Mountain City, GA 30562-0541, (706) 746-5828, **<foxfire.org>**

Franklin County Historical Society
310 McFarlin Bridge Rd., Carnesville, GA 30521, **<rootsweb.ancestry.com/~gafrankl>**

Genealogy Unlimited Society, Lowndes County
Box 3013, Valdosta, GA 31604-3013, **<rootsweb.ancestry.com/~gagus>**

Georgia Genealogical Society
Box 550247, Atlanta, GA 30355, **<gagensociety.org>**

Georgia Historical Society
501 Whitaker St., Savannah, GA 31401, (912) 651-2125 or Library: (912) 651-2128, **<georgiahistory.com>**

Georgia Salzburger Society
2980 Ebenezer Rd., Rincon, GA 31326, (912) 754-7001, **<georgiasalzburgers.com>**

Georgia State Archives
5800 Jonesboro Rd., Morrow, GA 30260, (678) 364-3700, **<georgiaarchives.org>**

Georgia State University Library
100 Decatur St. SE, Atlanta, GA 30303 (404) 651-2422, **<www.library.gsu.edu>**

Georgia Trust
1516 Peachtree St. NW, Atlanta, GA 30309, (404) 881-9980, **<georgiatrust.org>**

Gordon County Historical Society
335 S. Wall St., Calhoun, GA 30701, (706) 629-1515, **<rootsweb.ancestry.com/~gagordon/index.html>**

Grady County Historical Society
586, Cairo, GA 31728, (229) 377-9728

Gilbert H. Gragg Decatur County Library
301 S. Monroe St., Bainbridge, GA 39819, (229) 248-2665

Greene County Historical Society
Box 238, Greensboro, GA 30642, (706) 453-7250

Griffin Spalding Historical Society
633 Meriwether St., Griffin, GA 30224, (770) 229-2432, **<griffinhistory.com>**

Guale Historical Society
Box 398, St. Marys, GA 31558, (912) 882-4587, **<gualehs.blogspot.com>**

Gwinnett County Library
1001 Lawrenceville Hwy., Lawrenceville, GA 30045-45707, (770) 978-5154, **<www.gwinnettpl.org>**

Gwinnett Historical Society
185 East Crogan St., Box 261, Lawrenceville, GA 30046, (770) 822-5174, **<gwinnetths.org>**

Hall County Historical Society
380 Green St. NE, Box 2999, Gainesville, GA 30501, (770) 503-1319

Hart County Historical Society
31 E. Howell St., Box 96, Hartwell, GA 30643, (706) 376-6330

Sara Hightower Regional Library
205 Riverside Pkwy. NE, Rome, GA 30161, (706) 236-4611, **<romelibrary.org>**

Historic Oglethorpe County
Box 1793, Lexington, GA 30648, **<www.rootsweb.ancestry.com/~gaogleth>**

Historical Society of Forsyth County
Box 1334, Cumming GA 3028, (678) 455-7260, **<historicforsyth.com>**

Historical Society of the Georgia National Guard
Box 17965, Atlanta, GA 30316, (678) 569-6061, **<www.hsgng.org>**

Huxford Genealogical Society
Box 595, Homerville, GA 31634, (912) 487-2310, **<huxford.com>**

Jefferson County Historical Society
Box 491, Louisville, GA 30434, (912) 625-3244

Jewish Genealogical Society of Georgia
1440 Spring St. NW, Atlanta, GA 30309, (678) 222-3700, **<jewishgen.org/jgsg>**

Johnson County Historical Society
Box 87, Wrightsville, GA 31096, (478) 864-0977

Kennesaw Historical Society
c/o Southern Museum of Civil War and Locomotive History, 2829 Cherokee St., Kennesaw, GA 30144, **<mindspring.com/~robertcjones/khs/khs.htm>**

Kennesaw Mountain Historical Association
900 Kennesaw Mountain Dr., Kennesaw, GA 30152, **<kmha.org>**

Ladson Genealogical Library
c/o Vidalia-Toombs County Library, 610 Jackson St., Vidalia, GA 30474, (912) 537-8186, **<www.ohoopeelibrary.org/userfiles/ladsoninfo.html>**

LaFayette-Walker County Library
305 S. Duke St., LaFayette, GA 30728, (706) 638-2992, **<walker.public.lib.ga.us/branches/lafaywalk.htm>**

Lake Blackshear Regional Library
307 E. Lamar St., Americus, GA 31709, (229) 924-8091, **<lbrls.org>**

Lake Park Area Historical Society
Box 803, Lake Park, GA 31636, (229) 559-5771, **<lakeparkga.com/hsociety.html>**

Laurens County Historical Society
Box 1461, Dublin, GA 31040, (478) 272-9242, **<laurenshistory.org>**

Lee County Historical Society
Box 393, Leesburg, GA 31763

Liberty County Historical Society
Box 982, Hinesville, GA 31310

Lincoln County Library
181 N Peachtree St., Lincolnton GA 30817, (706) 359-4014, **<lincolncountyga.com/Library.asp>**

Lincoln County Historical Society
147 Lumber St., Box 896, Lincolnton, GA 30817, (706) 359-1031

Lower Altamaha Historical Society
Box 1405, Darien, GA 31305, (912) 485-2251, **<loweraltamahahistoricalsociety.org>**

Lowndes County Historical Society
305 W. Central Ave., Valdosta, GA 31601, (229) 247-4780, **<valdostamuseum.org>**

Lumpkin County Historical Society
Box 894, Dahlonega, GA 30533, (706) 864-0743

Macon County Historical Society
N. Dooly St., Box 571, Montezuma, GA 31063

Middle Georgia Archives
Macon-Bibb County LIbraries, 1180 Washington Ave., Macon, GA 31201, (478) 744-0800, **<www.co.bibb.ga.us/library/mgarchives.htm>**

Madison County Heritage Association
Box 74, Danielsville, GA 30633, (706) 795-2017

Marble Valley Historical Society
Box 815, Jasper, GA 30143, **<marblevalley.org>**

McDonough, The Genealogical Society of Henry and Clayton Counties
Box 1296, McDonough, GA 30253, (770) 954-1456, **<rootsweb.ancestry.com/~gagshcc>**

McDuffie County Historical Society
635 Hemlock Dr., Box 1816, Thomson, GA 30824, (706) 595-5584

Meriwether Historical Society
Box 741, Greenville, GA 30222

Middle Georgia Historical Society
935 High St., Box 13358, Macon, GA 31208, (912) 743-3851

Monroe County Historical Society
E. Johnston St., Box 401, Forsyth, GA 31029, (912) 994-5070

Morgan County Historical Society
277 S. Main St., Madison, GA 30650, (706) 342-9627

Moultrie-Colquitt County Library
The Odom Library, 204 Fifth St. SE, Moultrie, GA 31768, (229) 985-6540, **<www.colquitt.k12.ga.us/public_lib>**

Murrell Memorial Library/ Dodge County Library
505 Second Ave., Eastman, GA 31023 , (478) 374-4711, **<www.orls.org/dodge.htm>**

Muscogee Genealogical Society
Box 761, Columbus, GA 31902, **<muscogeegenealogy.com>**

National Archives and Records Administration, Southeast Region
5780 Jonesboro Rd., Morrow GA 30260, (770) 968-2100, **<archives.gov/facilities/southeast>**

Newnan-Coweta Historical Society
c/o Male Academy Museum, 30 Temple Ave., Newnan, GA 30263, (770) 251-0207, **<nchistoricalsociety.org>**

Newton County Historical Society
Box 2415, Covington, GA 30015, (770) 786-7310

Northeast Georgia Historical and Genealogical Society
Box 907643, Gainesville, GA 30501, (770) 967-3808, **<rootsweb.ancestry.com/~ganehags>**

Northwest Georgia Historical and Genealogical Society
Box 5063, Rome, GA 30162, (706) 236-4607, **<rootsweb.ancestry.com/~ganwhags>**

Oconee County Library
1080 Experiment Station Rd., Watkinsville, GA 30677, (706) 769-3950, **<clarke.public.lib.ga.us/oconee/index.html>**

Okefenokee Heritage Center
1460 N. Augusta Ave., Waycross, GA 31503, (912) 285-4260, **<okefenokeeheritagecenter.org>**

Old Capitol Historical Society
Box 1177, Milledgeville, GA 31059, (478) 445-4545

Old Clinton Historical Society
RFD 5-Clinton, Box 143, Gray, GA 31032

Orphans Cemetery Association
Box 4411, Eastman, GA 31023, (478) 374-2180

Paulding County Historical Society
Box 333, Dallas, GA 30132, **<pchsm.org>**

Peach County Historical Society
Box 889, Fort Valley, GA 31030, **<rootsweb.ancestry.com/~gapchs>**

Piedmont Regional Library
189 Bellview St., Winder, GA 30680, (770) 867-2762, **<prlib.org>**

Pierce County Historical and Genealogical Society
Box 443, Blackshear, GA 31516, **<piercecounty.www.50megs.com>**

Pine Mountain Regional Library
218 Perry St., Box 709, Manchester, GA 31816, (706) 846-2186 , **<meriwether.public.lib.ga.us>**

Polk County Historical Society
Box 203, 205 S.College St., Cedartown, GA 30125, (770) 749-0073, **<polkhist.home.mindspring.com/home.htm>**

Quitman/Brooks County Historical Museum and Cultural Center
121 North Culpepper St., Quitman, GA 31643, (22ancestry.9) 263-7080

Rabun County Historical Society
Box 921, Clayton, GA 30525, **<www.rootsweb.ancestry.com/~garchs>**

Richmond County Historical Society
c/o Reese Library, Augusta State University 2500 Walton Way, Augusta, GA 30904, (706) 737-1532, **<thearchs.org>**

Richmond Hill Historical Society
Box 381, Richmond Hill, GA 31324, (912) 861-5444, **<richmondhillga.com/museum>**

Rockdale County Genealogical Society
954 Green St., Conyers, GA 30012

Rockdale County Historical Society
945 Green St., Conyers, GA 30012, (770) 483-4398, **<rockdalehistory.org>**

Rome Area History Museum Archives
305 Broad St., Rome, GA 30161, (706) 235-8051, **<romehistorymuseum.com>**

Roopville Historical Society and Archives
165 Old Highway 27 S., Box 285, Roopville, GA 30170, (770) 854-8099

Roswell Historical Society
617 Atlanta St., Roswell, GA 30075, (770) 992-1665, **<roswellhs.org>**

Satilla Regional Library
200 S. Madison Ave., Ste. D, Douglas, GA 31533, (912) 384-4667, **<srlsys.org>**

Savannah Area Genealogical Society
Box 15385, Savannah, GA 31416, **<savannahgenealogy.org>**

Schley County Historical Society
Box 326, Ellaville, GA 31806

Screven County Library
106 S. Community Dr., Sylvania, GA 30467, (912) 564-7526, **<sjrls.org>**

Seminole County Historical Society
Box 713, Donalsonville, GA 31759

Smyrna Historical and Genealogical Society
2861 Atlanta St., Smyrna, GA 30082, **<rootsweb.ancestry.com/~gashgs>**

South Georgia Genealogical Society
Box 246, Ochlocknee, GA 31773

Southwest Georgia Genealogical Society
Box 4672, Albany, GA 31706, **<swgs.org>**

Sparta-Hancock County Historical Society
526 Court St., Sparta, GA 31087, **<shchs.org>**

Statesboro-Bulloch County Library
124 S. Main St., Statesboro, GA 30458, (912) 764-1341, **<strl.info/statesboro-regional-library>**

Stephens County Historical Society
313 Pond St., Box 125, Toccoa, GA 30577, (706) 282-5055

Taliaferro County Historical Society
Box 32, Crawfordville, GA 30631, (706) 456-2776

Tattnall County Historical Society
Box 2012, Reidsville, GA 30453, (912) 557-4402

Taylor County Historical-Genealogical Society
Box 1925, Butler, GA 31006, (912) 862-3410, **<rootsweb.ancestry.com/~wvtaylor/tchgs.htm>**

Terrell County Restoration Society
Box 63, Dawson, GA 31742, (229) 995-2125

Thomas County Historical Society
725 N. Dawson St., Thomasville, GA 31792, (229) 226-7664, **<www.thomascountyhistory.org>**

Thomaston-Upson Archives
Box 1137, Thomaston, GA 30286, (706) 646-2437, **<home.windstream.net/tuarch>**

Thomasville Genealogical, History and Fine Arts Library
135 N. Broad St., Thomasville, GA 31792, (229) 226-9640, **<home.rose.net/~glibrary>**

Thronateeska Heritage Center
100 W. Roosevelt Ave., Albany, GA 31701, (229) 432-6955, **<heritagecenter.org>**

Toombs County Historical Society
Box 2825, Vidalia, GA 30474, (912) 537-3477

Towns County Historical and Genealogical Society
Box 1182, Hiawassee, GA 30546, **<townshistory.org>**

Treutlen County Historical Society
206 Second St. S., Soperton, GA 30457, (912) 529-6711

Troup County Historical Society and Archives
136 Main St., Box 1051, LaGrange, GA 30241, (706) 884-1828, **<trouparchives.org>**

Turner County Historical Society
233 E. College Ave., Box 766, Ashburn, GA 31714, (229) 567-3431

Tybee Island Historical Society
Box 366 Tybee Island, GA 31328, (912) 786-5801, **<tybeelighthouse.org>**

Union County Historical Society
Box 35, Blairsville, GA 30514, (706) 745-5493, **<ngeorgia.com/uchs.html>**

Upson Historical Society
Box 363, Thomaston, GA 30286, **<www.rootsweb.ancestry.com/~gauhs>**

Vienna Historic Preservation Society
Box 309, Vienna, GA 31092, (229) 268-3663, **<historicvienna.org>**

Walker County Historical Society
Box 707, LaFayette, GA 30728

Walton County Historical Society
Box 1733, Monroe, GA 30655, (770) 267-6663

Washington County Historical Society
129 Jones St. Sandersville, GA 31082, (478) 552-6965, **<usgennet.org/usa/ga/county/washington>**

Wayne County Historical Society
125 NE Broad St., Jesup, GA 31545, (912) 427-3233

West Georgia Genealogical Society
Box 1051, LaGrange, GA 30241

Whitfield-Murray Historical Society, Crown Garden and Archives
715 Chattanooga Ave., Dalton, GA 30720, (706) 278-0217, **<whitfield-murrayhistoricalsociety.org>**

Wilkinson County Historical Society
Box 476, Gordon, GA 31031, (478) 946-2723, **<netstarz.net/wilco>**

Wiregrass Genealogical Society
Rte. 1, Box 68G, Adrian, GA 31002, **<rootsweb.ancestry.com/~gawgs>**

Worth County Historical Society
Box 5073, Sylvester, GA 31791, (912) 776-4481

GENERAL RESOURCES

Ambiguous Lives: Free Women of Color in Rural Georgia, 1789-1879 by Adele Logan Alexander (University of Arkansas Press, 1991)

A Bibliography of the Writings on Georgia History, 1900-1970, revised edition, by Arthur Ray Rowland and James E. Dorsey (Reprint Co., 1978)

Biographical Souvenir of the States of Georgia and Florida (F.A. Battey and Company, 1889)

Checklist of Eighteenth Century Manuscripts in the Georgia Historical Society compiled by Lilla Mills Hawes and Karen Elizabeth Osvald (Georgia Historical Society, 1976)

Colonial Georgia Genealogical Data, 1748-1783 by William H. Dumont (National Genealogical Society, 1971)

The Colonial Records of the State of Georgia compiled by Allen D. Candler, et al. (State printer, 1904)

Confederate Imprints at the Georgia Historical Society by Richard Barksdale Harwell (Georgia Historical Society, 1975)

Dictionary of Georgia Biography edited by Kenneth Coleman and Charles Stephen Gurr (University of Georgia Press, 1983)

The Federal Road Through Georgia, the Creek Nation, and Alabama, 1806-1836 by Henry de Leon Southerland Jr. and Jerry Elijah Brown (University of Alabama Press, 1989)

The Fledgling Province: Social and Cultural Life in Colonial Georgia, 1733-1776 by Harold E. Davis (University of North Carolina Press, 1976)

Genealogical Material From Legal Notices in Early Georgia Newspapers by Folks Huxford (Southern Historical Press, 1989)

Georgia Baptists by Jesse H. Campbell (J.W. Burke and Co., 1874)

Georgia Bible Records compiled by Jeannette Holland Austin (Genealogical Publishing Co., 1985)

Georgia Biographical Dictionary (Somerset Publishers, 1994)

The Georgia Black Book: Morbid, Macabre & Sometimes Disgusting Records of Genealogical Value by Robert Scott Davis, Jr. (Southern Historical Press, 1982-1987)

Georgia Genealogical Gems: A Gathering of Articles Previously Published in the NGSQ (National Genealogical Society, 1981)

Georgia Genealogical Research by George K. Schweitzer (G.K. Schweitzer, 1987)

Georgia Genealogical Research: a Practical Guide by David H. Robertson (D.H. Robertson, 1989)

Georgia Genealogy and Local History: a Bibliography compiled by James E. Dorsey (Reprint Co., 1983)

The Georgia Gold Rush: Twenty-Niners, Cherokees, and Gold Fever by David Williams (University of South Carolina Press 1993)

Georgia Governor and Council Journal, 1761-1767 abstracted by Mary Bondurant Warren and Jack Moreland Jones (Heritage Press, 1992)

Georgia: a Guide to its Towns and Countryside by the Work Projects Administration (University of Georgia Press, 1940)

Georgia History: a Bibliography compiled by John Eddins Simpson (Scarecrow Press, 1976)

Georgia Indian Depredation Claims edited by Donna B. Thaxton et al. (Thaxton Co., ca. 1988)

Georgia Local and Family History Sources in Print, compiled by Marilyn Adams (Heritage Research, 1982)

Georgia Pioneers Genealogical Magazine, 24 vols. (Georgia Pioneers Publications, 1964-1987)

Georgia Sources for Family History compiled by Robert Holcomb Warnock (Georgia Genealogical Society, 1995)

Georgia Through Two Centuries edited by E. Merton Coulter (Lewis Historical Publishing Co., ca. 1966)

The Georgians: Genealogies of Pioneer Settlers compiled by Jeannette Holland Austin (Genealogical Publishing Co., 1984)

Georgians Past: Special Files of Georgia Settlers and Citizens, Subjects and Counties, 1722-1970s edited by Robert Scott Davis Jr. (Boyd Publishing Co., 1997)

The Germans of Colonial Georgia, 1733-1783 by George F. Jones (Genealogical Publishing Co., 1986)

Great Georgians by Zell Miller (Advocate Press, 1983)

A Guide to Native American (Indian) Research Sources at the Georgia Department of Archives and History by Robert Scott Davis Jr. (R.S. Davis, 1985)

Historical Collections of the Georgia Chapters, Daughters of the American Revolution, Vol. 1: Seventeen Georgia Counties (C.P. Byrd, state printer, 1926)

Historical Collections of Georgia by Rev. George White (Pudney & Russell, 1854)

History of the Baptist Denomination in Georgia (J.P. Harrison & Co., 1881)

History of Georgia, 4 vols. by Clark Howell (The S.J. Clarke Publishing Co., 1926)

An Index to Georgia Tax Digests, (Reprint Co., 1986)

Index to Georgia's 1867-1868 Returns of Qualified Voters and Registration Oath Books (White) compiled by John David Brandenburg and Rita Binkley Worthy (J.D. Brandenburg, 1995)

Joe Brown's Army: the Georgia State Line, 1862-1865 by William Harris Bragg (Mercer University Press, 1987)

Leon S. Hollingsworth Genealogical Card File (R.J. Taylor Jr., Foundation, ca. 1979)

A List of the Early Settlers of Georgia by E. Merton Coulter and Albert B. Saye (Univ. of Georgia Press, 1949)

Memoirs of Georgia; Containing Historical Accounts of the State's Civil, Military, Industrial, and Professional Interests, and Personal Sketches of Many of its People, 2 vols. (Southern Historical Association, 1895)

Men of Mark in Georgia; a Complete and Elaborate History of the State from its Settlement to the Present Time, 6 vols. by William J. Northen (A.B. Caldwell, 1907-1912)

Methodist Preachers in Georgia, 1783-1900 edited and compiled by Harold Lawrence (Boyd Publishing Co., 1984)

The Moravians in Georgia, 1735-1740 by Adelaide L. Fries (Edwards & Broughton, 1905)

Old Bible Records and Land Lotteries, Published Under the Auspices of the Lucy Cook Peel Memorial Committee compiled and edited by Lelia Thorton Gentry (Stein Printing Co., 1932)

Pioneers of Wiregrass Georgia, 11 vols., by Folks Huxford (1951-ca. 2002)

Research in Georgia compiled by Robert Scott Davis Jr. (Southern Historical Press, 1981)

A Researcher's Library of Georgia History, Genealogy, and Records Sources, 2 vols., by Robert Scott Davis Jr. (Southern Historical Press, 1987, 1991)

The Reuben King Journal, 1800-1806 edited by Virginia Steele Wood and Ralph Van Wood (Georgia Historical Society, 1971)

The Salzburgers and their Descendants: Being the History of a Colony of German (Lutheran) Protestants by Philip A. Strobel (T.N. Kurtz, 1855)

The Search for Georgia's Colonial Records edited by Lilla Mills Hawes and Albert S. Britt Jr. (Georgia Historical Society, 1976)

The Seed that was Sown in the Colony of Georgia, the Harvest and the Aftermath, 1740-1870 By Charles Spalding Wylly (The Neale Publishing Company, 1910)

Some Early Tax Digests of Georgia edited by Ruth Blair (Department of Archives and History, 1926)

Some Georgia County Records, 10 vols., compiled by Silas Emmett Lucas Jr. (Southern Historical Press, 1977-2002)

A Standard History of Georgia and Georgians by Lucian Lamar Knight (The Lewis Publishing Co., 1917)

The Story of Georgia and the Georgia People, 1732 to 1860, 2nd edition, by George Gillman Smith (Genealogical Publishing Co., 1968)

Whites Among the Cherokees: Georgia 1828-1838 edited by Mary B. Warren and Eve B. Weeks (Heritage Papers, 1987)

☞CENSUS RECORDS

1864 Census for Re-Organizing the Georgia Militia abstracted and compiled by Nancy J. Cornell (Genealogical Publishing Co., 2000)

The Reconstructed 1790 Census of Georgia compiled by Marie De Lamar and Elisabeth Rothstein (Genealogical Publishing Co., 1985)

☞IMMIGRATION RECORDS

The Bench and Bar of Georgia: Memoirs and Sketches by Stephen Franks Miller (J.B. Lippincott & Co., 1858)

Federal Naturalization Oaths, Savannah, Georgia, 1790-1860 compiled by Marion R. Hemperley (Georgia Historical Society Quarterly, Vol. 51, no. 4: 1967)

☞LAND RECORDS

1805 Georgia Land Lottery transcribed and indexed by Virginia S. Woof and Ralph V. Wood (Greenwood Press, 1964)

1832 Cherokee Land Lottery: Index to Revolutionary Soldiers, Their Widows, and Orphans Who were Fortunate Drawers compiled by Marian M. Richardson and Jessie J. Mize (Heritage Papers, 1969)

The 1832 Gold Lottery of Georgia: Containing a List of the Fortunate Drawers in Said Lottery compiled by Silas Emmett Lucas Jr. (Southern Historical Press 1988)

Abstracts of Georgia Land Plat Books A and B, 1779-1785 by Nathan and Kaydee Mathews (N. and K. Mathews, 1995)

Authentic List of all Land Lottery Grants Made to Veterans of the Revolutionary War by the State of Georgia, 2nd edition, compiled by Alex M. Hitz (Secretary of State of Georgia, 1966)

The Cherokee Land Lottery by James F. Smith (Southern Historical Press, Inc., 1991)

Colonial Plats and Warrants, 1755-1775, (Georgia Surveyor General Department: 1755-1775)

Entry of Claims for Georgia Landholders, 1733-1755 compiled by Pat Bryant (State Printing Office, 1975)

The First One Hundred Years of Town Planning in Georgia by Joan Niles Sears (Cherokee Publishing Co., 1979)

The Fourth or 1821 Land Lottery of Georgia compiled by Silas Emmett Lucas Jr. (Southern Historical Press 1986)

The Georgia Land Lottery Papers, 1805-1914 compiled by Robert S. Davis Jr. and Silas Emmett Lucas Jr. (Southern Historical Press, 1979)

Georgia Land Surveying History and Law by Farris W. Cadle (University of Georgia Press, 1991)

The Georgia Surveyor General Department: a History and Inventory of Georgia's Land Office by Marion R. Hemperley (State Printing Office, 1982)

Index to the Headright and Bounty Grants of Georgia, 1756-1909 (Georgia Genealogical Reprints, 1970)

Reprint of Official Register of Land Lottery of Georgia, 1827 (Walton-Forbes Co. 1929)

Revolutionary Soldiers' Receipts for Georgia Bounty Grants by the Georgia State Department of Archives and History (Foote and Davis Co., 1928)

The Second or 1807 Land Lottery of Georgia compiled by Silas Emmett Lucas, Jr. (Southern Historical Press, 1986)

The Third or 1820 Land Lottery of Georgia compiled by Silas Emmett Lucas, Jr. (Southern Historical Press, 1986)

☞MAPS

Atlas for Georgia History by James C. Bonner (Georgia Duplicating Department, 1969)

The Atlas of Georgia by Thomas W. Hodler and Howard A. Schretter (University of Georgia, 1986)

Cities, Towns, and Communities of Georgia Between 1847-1962: 8500 Places and the County in which Located compiled by Marion R. Hemperley (Southern Historical Press, 1980)

Georgia: Comprising Sketches of Counties, Towns, Events, Institutions, and Persons Arranged in Cyclopedic Form, 4 vols. edited by Allen D. Candler and Clement A. Evans (State Historical Association, 1906)

Georgia Counties, Their Changing Boundaries, 2nd edition, by Pat Bryant, revised by Ingrid Shields (State Printing Office, 1983)

Georgia Place-names, 1st edition, by Kenneth K. Krakow (Winship Press, 1975)

Hall's Original County Map of Georgia compiled by Hall Brothers, Civil and Mining Engineers, 1895 (Department of Archives and History, ca. 1980)

Nineteenth Century Maps in the Collection of the Georgia Surveyor General Department, 1800-1849 compiled by Margaret A. Johnsen (State Printing Office, 1981)

Placenames of Georgia: Essays of John H. Goff edited by Francis Lee Utley and Marion R. Hemperley (University of Georgia Press, 1975)

Pre-Nineteenth Century Maps in the Collection of the Georgia Surveyor General Department: a Catalog compiled by Janice Gayle Blake (State Printing Office, 1975)

☞MILITARY RECORDS

Colonial Soldiers of the South, 1732-1774 by Murtie June Clark (Genealogical Publishing Co., 1983)

Compendium of the Confederate Armies, 11 vols., by Stewart Sifakis (Facts on File ca. 1992-ca. 1995)

The Confederate Records of the State of Georgia, 6 vols., compiled by Allen D. Candler (C.P. Byrd, state printer, 1909-1911)

Georgia Citizens and Soldiers of the American Revolution by Robert S. Davis Jr. (Southern Historical Press, ca. 1979)

Georgia Civil War Sites by Jim Miles (J & R Graphics, ca. 1987)

Georgia Revolutionary War Soldiers' Graves, 2 vols., compiled by H. Ross Arnald Jr. and H. Clifton Burnham (Iberian Publishing Co., ca. 1993)

The Georgia State Memorial Book, Adopted as the Official Record by the Military Department, State of Georgia by Bert E. Boss (American Memorial Publishing Co.: 1921)

Georgia's Roster of the Revolution compiled by Lucian Lamar Knight (Genealogical Publishing Co., 1967)
Index to War of 1812 Service Records for Volunteer Soldiers from Georgia abstracted by Judy Swaim Kratovil (J. S. Kratovil, 1986)

Military Certificates of Georgia, 1776-1800, on File in the Surveyor General Department, semiquincentenary ed. compiled by Marion R. Hemperley (State Printing Office, 1983)

Militiamen, Rangers, and Redcoats: the Military in Georgia, 1754-1776 by James M. Johnson (Mercer University Press, 1992)

The Revolutionary Records of the State of Georgia compiled by Allen D. Candler (The Franklin-Turner Company, 1908)

Revolutionary Soldiers' Receipts for Georgia Bounty Grants issued by the Georgia State Department of Archives and History (Foote and Davies Co., 1928)

Roster of the Confederate Soldiers of Georgia, 1861-1865, 4 vols., by Georgia State Division of Confederate Pensions and Records (Longino & Porter, 1959-)

Roster of the Confederate Soldiers of Georgia, 1861-1865, 6 vols., compiled by Lillian Henderson (Longina and Porter, 1959-)
Roster of the Confederate Soldiers of Georgia, 1861-1865: Index compiled by Juanita S. Brightwell, Eunices S. Lee, Elise C. Fulghum (Reprint Co., 1982)

Roster of Revolutionary Soldiers in Georgia, 3 vols., compiled by Mrs. Howard H. McCall (Genealogical Publishing Co., 1968-1969)

A Roster of Spanish American War Soldiers from Georgia edited by Carlton J. Thaxton, Donna B. Thaxton, Stan Thaxton (Thaxton Co., 1984)

Volunteer Soldiers in the Cherokee War, 1836-1839 (Mountain Press, 1995)

☞PROBATE RECORDS

Abstracts of Colonial Wills of the State of Georgia, 1733-1777 indexed by Willard E. Wight (Reprint Co., 1981)

Georgia Intestate Records compiled by Jeannette Holland Austin (Genealogical Publishing Co., 1986)

Georgia Wills, 1733-1860 compiled by Ted O. Brooke (Pilgrim Press, 1976)

Index to Georgia Wills by Jeannette Holland Austin (Genealogical Publishing Co., 1985)

Index to Georgia's Federal Naturalization Records to 1950 (Excluding Military Petitions) by Linda Woodward Geiger (Heritage Books, 1995)

Index to Probate Records of Colonial Georgia, 1733-1778 (R.J. Taylor Jr., Foundation, 1983)

Statutes Enacted by the Royal Legislature of Georgia from its first Session in 1754 to 1768, 3 vols. compiled by Allen D. Candler (C.P. Byrd, state printer, 1910-1911)

☞VITAL RECORDS

30,638 Burials in Georgia by Jeannette Holland Austin (Genealogical Publishing Co., ca. 1995)

37,000 Early Georgia Marriages by Joseph T. Maddox (J.T. Maddox, 1975)
1850 Georgia Mortality Schedules or Census compiled by Aurora C. Shaw (Shaw, 1982)

Colonial Georgia Marriage Records from 1760-1810 by Frances T. Ingmire (F.T. Ingmire, ca. 1985)

Early Georgia Marriages, 4 vols., compiled by Joseph T. Maddox, and Mary Carter (J. T. Maddox, 1975)

Georgia Cemetery Directory and Bibliography of Georgia Cemetery Reference Sources by Ted O. Brooke (T.O. Brooke, ca. 1985)

Georgia Marriages: Early to 1800: a Research Tool by Liahona Research, Inc., edited by Jordan R. Dodd (Precision Indexing Publishers, ca. 1990)

Georgia Marriages 1811 Through 1820: Prepared from Extant Legal Records and Published Sources edited by Mary Bondurant Warren, abstracted by Frances H. Beckemeyer, et al. (Heritage Papers, ca. 1988)

Guide to Public Vital Statistics Records in Georgia by the Georgia Historical Records Survey (Historical Records Survey, 1941)

Marriages and Deaths, 1820 to 1830: Abstracted from Extant Georgia Newspapers by Mary Bondurant Warren with Sarah Fleming White (Heritage Papers ca. 1972)

Marriages and Obituaries from Early Georgia Newspapers abstracted by Folks Huxford (Southern Historical Press, ca. 1989)

Marriages and Obituaries from the Macon Messenger, 1815-1865 by Willard R. Rocker (Southern Historical Press, ca. 1988)

Obituaries Published by the Christian Index, 2 vols., abstracted and edited by Mary Overby (Georgia Baptist Historical Society, Mercer University, 1975-1982)

Some Early Epitaphs in Georgia compiled by the Georgia Society of the Colonial Dames of America (The Seeman Printery, Inc., ca. 1924)

•-COUNTY DETAILS-•

APPLING

69 Tippins St. Ste. 201, Baxley, GA 31513, (912) 367-8100,
<baxley.org/www.baxley.org/site/page5497.html>

- **INCORPORATED:** Dec. 15, 1818
- **PARENT COUNTY:** Creek Indian Lands
- **BIRTH RECORDS:** start in n/a, kept in Probate Court
- **MARRIAGE:** 1869, Probate Court
- **DEATH:** n/a, Probate Court
- **DIVORCE:** n/a, Superior Court Clerk
- **BURIAL:** n/a, Probate Court
- **LAND:** 1828, Superior Court Clerk
- **PROBATE:** 1879, Superior Court Clerk
- **COURT:** 1879, Superior Court Clerk
- **NOTES:** Records begin in 1879, some 1859.

ATKINSON

Box 518, Pearson, GA 31642,(912) 422-3391,
<atkinsoncounty.georgia.gov>

- **INCORPORATED:** Aug. 15, 1917
- **PARENT COUNTIES:** Coffee, Clinch
- **BIRTH RECORDS:** start in 1919, Kept by Department of Health
- **MARRIAGE:** 1919, Probate Court
- **DIVORCE:** 1919, Superior Court Clerk
- **DEATH:** 1919, Department of Health
- **LAND:** 1919, Probate Court
- **PROBATE:** 1919, Probate Court
- **COURT:** 1919, Superior Court Clerk

BACON

Box 356, Alma, GA 31510, (912) 632-5214,
<baconcounty.georgia.gov>

- **INCORPORATED:** 1914
- **PARENT COUNTIES:** Appling, Pierce, Ware
- **DIVORCE:** start in 1919, Superior Court Clerk
- **COURT:** 1919, Superior Court Clerk
- **LAND:** 1919, Superior Court Clerk
- **BIRTH RECORDS:** 1919, Health Department
- **MARRIAGE:** 1919, Probate Court
- **DEATH:** 1919, Health Department
- **PROBATE:** 1919 Probate Court

BAKER

Box 607, Newton, GA 39870, (229) 734-3000,
<bakercounty.georgia.gov>

- **INCORPORATED:** Dec. 12, 1825
- **PARENT COUNTY:** Early
- **BIRTH RECORDS:** start in 1919, kept by Health Department
- **MARRIAGE:** 1820, Probate Court
- **DIVORCE:** unknown, Superior Court Clerk
- **DEATH:** 1919, Health Department
- **LAND:** 1850, Superior Court Clerk
- **PROBATE:** 1868, Probate Court
- **COURT:** 1879, Superior Court Clerk

BALDWIN

121 Wilkinson St., Ste. 314, Milledgeville, GA 31061, (478) 445-4791,
<baldwincountyga.com>

- **INCORPORATED:** May 11, 1803
- **PARENT COUNTY:** Creek Indian Lands
- **BIRTH RECORDS:** start in 1919, kept by Health Department
- **MARRIAGE:** 1806, Probate Court
- **DEATH:**1919, Health Department
- **BURIAL:** unknown, Probate Court
- **PROBATE:** 1808, Probate Court
- **DIVORCE:** 1861, County Clerk
- **COURT:** 1861, Superior Court
- **LAND:** 1861, Superior Court

BANKS

144 Yonah Homer Rd., Homer, GA 30547, (706) 677-6200,
<bankscountyga.org>

- **INCORPORATED:** Dec. 11, 1858
- **PARENT COUNTIES:** Franklin, Habersham
- **BIRTH RECORDS:** start in 1919, kept by Health Department
- **MARRIAGE:** 1859, Probate Court
- **LAND:** 1859, Superior Court Clerk
- **PROBATE:** 1859, Probate Court
- **COURT:** 1859, Superior Court Clerk

BARROW

233 E. Broad St., Winder, GA 30680, (770) 307-3000,
<barrowga.org>

- **INCORPORATED:** July 7, 1914
- **PARENT COUNTIES:** Jackson, Walton, Gwinnett

- **BIRTH RECORDS:** start in 1919, kept by Health Department
- **MARRIAGE:** 1915, Probate Court
- **DIVORCE:** 1915, Superior Court Clerk
- **DEATH:** 1919, Health Department
- **BURIAL:** unknown, Probate Court
- **LAND:** 1915 Superior Court Clerk
- **PROBATE:** 1915, Probate Court
- **COURT:** 1915, Superior Court Clerk

BARTOW

135 W. Cherokee Ave. Cartersville, GA 30120, (770) 387-5030, **<bartowga.org>**

- **INCORPORATED:** Dec. 3, 1832
- **PARENT COUNTY:** Cherokee
- **BIRTH RECORDS:** start in 1919, kept by Health Department
- **MARRIAGE:** 1836, Probate Court
- **DIVORCE:** 1862, Superior Court Clerk
- **MILITARY:** unknown, Superior Court Clerk
- **LAND:** 1837, Superior Court Clerk
- **PROBATE:** 1853, Probate Court
- **COURT:** 1853, Superior Court Clerk
- **NOTES:** Formerly Cass County. Name changed to Bartow Dec. 3, 1832.

BEN HILL

402 A. E. Pine St., Fitzgerald, GA 31750, (229) 426-5100, **<benhillcounty.com>**

- **INCORPORATED:** July 31, 1906
- **PARENT COUNTIES:** Irwin, Wilcox
- **BIRTH RECORDS:** start in 1919, kept by Health Department
- **MARRIAGE:** 1906, Probate Judge
- **DIVORCE:** 1907, County Clerk
- **DEATH:** 1919, Health Department
- **BURIAL:** unknown, Probate Judge
- **LAND:** 1906, Superior Court Clerk
- **COURT:** 1906, Superior Court Clerk
- **PROBATE:** 1906, Probate Judge

BERRIEN

Box 446, Nashville, GA 31639, (229) 686-5421, **<rootsweb.ancestry.com/~gaberrie>**

- **INCORPORATED:** Feb. 25, 1856
- **PARENT COUNTIES:** Lowndes, Coffee, Irwin
- **BIRTH RECORDS:** start in 1919, kept by Health Department
- **MARRIAGE:** 1856, Probate Court
- **DIVORCE:** 1856, Superior Court Clerk
- **DEATH:** 1919, Health Department
- **LAND:** 1850, Superior Court Clerk
- **COURT:** 1856, Superior Court Clerk
- **PROBATE:** 1855, Probate Court

BIBB

Box 6518, Macon, GA 31201, (478) 749-6400, **<co.bibb.ga.us>**

- **INCORPORATED:** Dec. 9, 1822
- **PARENT COUNTIES:** Jones, Monroe, Twiggs, Houston
- **BIRTH RECORDS:** start in 1919, kept by Health Department
- **MARRIAGE:** 1823, Probate Court
- **DIVORCE:** 1823, County Clerk
- **DEATH:** 1919, Health Department
- **BURIAL:** unknown, Health Department
- **LAND:** 1823, Superior Court Clerk
- **PROBATE:** 1823, Probate Court
- **COURT:** 1823, Superior Court Clerk

BLECKLEY

306 SE Second St., Cochran, GA 31014, (478) 934-3200, **<Bleckley.org>**

- **INCORPORATED:** July 30, 1912
- **PARENT COUNTY:** Pulaski
- **BIRTH RECORDS:** start in 1919, kept by Health Department
- **MARRIAGE:** 1912, Probate Court
- **DIVORCE:** unknown, Superior Court Clerk
- **DEATH:** 1919, Health Department
- **LAND:** 1912, Superior Court Clerk
- **PROBATE:** 1912, Probate Court
- **COURT:** 1912, Superior Court Clerk

BRANTLEY

Box 398, Nahunta, GA 31553, (912) 462-5256, **<brantleycountyga.blogspot.com>**

- **INCORPORATED:** Aug. 14, 1920
- **PARENT COUNTIES:** Charlton, Pierce, Wayne
- **BIRTH RECORDS:** start in 1919, kept by Health Department
- **MARRIAGE:** 1921, Probate Court
- **DIVORCE:** 1921, Superior Court Clerk
- **DEATH:** 1919, Health Department
- **LAND:** 1921, Superior Court Clerk
- **PROBATE:** 1921, Probate Court
- **COURT:** 1921, Superior Court Clerk

BROOKS

Box 272, Quitman, GA 31643, (229) 263-5561, **<brookscounty.georgia.gov>**

- **INCORPORATED:** Dec. 11, 1858
- **PARENT COUNTIES:** Lowndes, Thomas
- **BIRTH RECORDS:** start in 1919, kept by Health Department
- **MARRIAGE:** 1859, Probate Court
- **DIVORCE:** unknown, Clerk of Courts
- **DEATH:** 1919, Health Department
- **LAND:** 1857, Superior Court Clerk
- **COURT:** 1859, Superior Court Clerk
- **PROBATE:** 1859, Probate Court

BRYAN

116 Lanier St., Pembroke, GA 31321, (912) 653-3819, **<bryancountyga.org>**

- **INCORPORATED:** Dec. 19, 1793
- **PARENT COUNTIES:** Effingham, Chatham
- **BIRTH RECORDS:** 1919, Health Department
- **MARRIAGE:** 1865, Probate Court
- **DIVORCE:** 1920, County Clerk
- **DEATH:** 1919, Health Department
- **PROBATE:** 1790, Probate Court
- **LAND:** 1793, Superior Court Clerk
- **COURT:** 1794, Superior Court Clerk

BULLOCH
Box 303, Statesboro, GA 30458, (912) 764-6245,
<bullochcounty.net>
- **INCORPORATED:** Feb. 8, 1796
- **PARENT COUNTIES:** Bryan, Screven
- **BIRTH RECORDS:** 1919, Health Department
- **MARRIAGE:** 1796, Probate Court
- **DIVORCE:** 1891, Superior Court Clerk
- **LAND:** 1796, Superior Court Clerk
- **PROBATE:** 1816, Probate Court
- **COURT:** 1806, Superior Court Clerk

BURKE
Box 89, Waynesboro, GA 30830, (770) 554-2324,
<www.burkecounty-ga.gov>
- **INCORPORATED:** Feb. 5, 1777
- **PARENT COUNTY:** Original county organized from St. George Parish
- **BIRTH RECORDS:** start in 1919, kept by Health Department
- **MARRIAGE:** 1855, Probate Court
- **DEATH:** 1919, Health Department
- **LAND:** 1843, Superior Court Clerk
- **COURT:** 1856, Superior Court Clerk
- **PROBATE:** 1856, Probate Court
- **NOTES:** Courthouse burned in January 1856; all records lost.

BUTTS
25 Third St., Jackson, GA 30233, (770) 775-820o,
<buttscounty.org>
- **INCORPORATED:** Dec. 24, 1825
- **PARENT COUNTIES:** Henry, Monroe
- **BIRTH RECORDS:** 1919, Health Department
- **MARRIAGE:** 1826, Probate Court
- **DIVORCE:** 1825, Superior Court Clerk
- **DEATH:** 1919, Health Department
- **LAND:** 1825, Superior Court Clerk
- **PROBATE:** 1826, Probate Court
- **COURT:** 1826, Superior Court Clerk

CALHOUN
111 School St., Morgan, GA 39866, (229) 849-4835,
<calhouncountyga.com>
- **INCORPORATED:** Feb.20, 1854
- **PARENT COUNTIES:** Baker, Early
- **BIRTH RECORDS:** start in 1919, kept by Health Department
- **MARRIAGE:** 1854, Probate Court
- **DIVORCE:** 1854, Superior Court Clerk
- **MILITARY:** 1854, Superior Court Clerk
- **DEATH:** 1919, Health Department
- **BURIAL:** unknown, Probate Court
- **LAND:** 1854, Superior Court Clerk
- **PROBATE:** 1854, Probate Court
- **COURT:** 1854, Superior Court Clerk

CAMDEN
2603 Osborne Rd., St. R, St. Marys, GA 31558, (912) 729-5840,
<co.camden.ga.us>
- **INCORPORATED:** Feb. 5, 1777
- **PARENT COUNTY:** Original county organized from St. Thomas and St. Mary parishes
- **BIRTH RECORDS:** 1919, Health Department
- **MARRIAGE:** 1819, Probate Court
- **DIVORCE:** unknown, Superior Court Clerk
- **DEATH:** 1919, Health Department
- **LAND:** 1773, Superior Court Clerk
- **PROBATE:** 1795, Probate Court
- **COURT:** 1790, Superior Court Clerk
- **NOTES:** Fire 1870, few records lost.

CAMPBELL ,
<rootsweb.ancestry.com/~gacampbe>
- **INCORPORATED:** Dec. 20, 1828
- **PARENT COUNTIES:** Carroll, Coweta, De Kalb, Fayette
- **NOTES:** See Fulton County. Merged into Fulton County Jan. 1, 1932.

CANDLER
705 N. Lewis St., Metter, GA 30439, (912) 685-2835,
<metter-candler.com>
- **INCORPORATED:** 1914
- **PARENT COUNTIES:** Bulloch, Emanuel, Tattnall
- **BIRTH RECORDS:** 1919, Health Department
- **MARRIAGE:** 1915, Probate Court
- **DIVORCE:** 1914, County Clerk
- **DEATH:** 1919, Health Department
- **LAND:** 1915, Superior Court Clerk
- **PROBATE:** 1915, Probate Court
- **COURT:** 1915, Superior Court Clerk

CARROLL
Box 338, Carrollton, GA 30112, (770) 830-5800,
<carrollcountyga.com>
- **INCORPORATED:** Dec. 11, 1826
- **PARENT COUNTY:** Creek Indian Lands
- **BIRTH RECORDS:** start in 1919, kept by Health Department
- **MARRIAGE:** 1827, Probate Court
- **DIVORCE:** 1900, Superior Court Clerk
- **DEATH:** 1919, Health Department
- **LAND:** 1827, Superior Court Clerk
- **PROBATE:** 1827, Probate Court
- **COURT:** 1827, Superior Court Clerk
- **NOTES:** Clerk of Superior Court has 1828 Confederate pension applications.

CASS
- **INCORPORATED:** 1832
- **PARENT COUNTY:** Cherokee
- **NOTES:** See Bartow County. Name changed to Bartow Dec. 6, 1861.

CATOOSA
7694 Nashville St., Ringgold, GA 30736, (706) 965-2500,
<Catoosa.com>
- **INCORPORATED:** Dec. 5, 1853
- **PARENT COUNTIES:** Walker, Whitfield
- **COURT:** 1853, Superior Court Clerk
- **DIVORCE:** 1853, Superior Court Clerk
- **LAND:** 1853, Superior Court Clerk

- **MARRIAGE:** 1853, Probate Court
- **PROBATE:** 1853, Probate Court

CHARLTON

100 S. Third St., Folkston, GA 31537, (912) 496-2549,
<charltoncounty.georgia.gov>

- **INCORPORATED:** Feb. 18, 1854
- **PARENT COUNTY:** Camden
- **BIRTH RECORDS:** start in 1919, kept by Health Department
- **MARRIAGE:** 1854, Probate Court
- **DIVORCE:** 1877, Superior Court Clerk
- **DEATH:** 1919, Health Department
- **BURIAL:** unknown, Probate Judge
- **LAND:** 1878, Superior Court Clerk
- **PROBATE:** 1878, Probate Court
- **COURT:** 1879, Superior Court Clerk
- **NOTES:** Courthouse burned in 1877.

CHATHAM

Box 8161, Savannah, GA 31412, (912) 652-7878,
<chathamcounty.org>

- **INCORPORATED:** Feb. 5, 1777
- **PARENT COUNTY:** Original county organized from St. Phillip and Christ Church Parishes
- **BIRTH RECORDS:** 1919, Health Department
- **MARRIAGE:** 1806, Probate Court
- **DIVORCE:** 1783, Superior Court Clerk
- **DEATH:** 1919, Health Department
- **LAND:** 1785, Superior Court Clerk
- **PROBATE:** 1777, Probate Court
- **COURT:** 1783, Superior Court Clerk

CHATTAHOOCHEE

Box 299, Cusseta, GA 31805, (706) 989-3602,
<chattahoocheecounty.georgia.gov>

- **INCORPORATED:** Feb. 13, 1854
- **PARENT COUNTIES:** Muscogee, Marion
- **BIRTH RECORDS:** 1919, Health Department
- **MARRIAGE:** 1854, Probate Court
- **DIVORCE:** 1854, Superior Court Clerk
- **DEATH:** 1919, Health Department
- **LAND:** 1854, Superior Court Clerk
- **PROBATE:** 1854, Probate Court
- **COURT:** 1854, Superior Court Clerk

CHATTOOGA

Box 211, Summerville, GA 30747, (706) 857-0700,
<chattoogacountyga.com>

- **INCORPORATED:** Dec. 28, 1838
- **PARENT COUNTIES:** Floyd, Walker
- **BIRTH RECORDS:** start in 1919, kept by Health Department
- **MARRIAGE:** 1839, Probate Court
- **DIVORCE:** ca. 1900, Clerk/Courts
- **DEATH:** 1919, Health Department
- **BURIAL:** unknown, Ordinary Office
- **LAND:** 1839, Superior Court Clerk
- **PROBATE:** 1839, Probate Court
- **COURT:** 1839, Superior Court Clerk

CHEROKEE

1130 Bluffs Parkway, Canton, GA 30114, (678) 493-6000,
<cherokeega.com>

- **INCORPORATED:** Dec. 26, 1831
- **PARENT COUNTY:** Cherokee Lands
- **BIRTH RECORDS:** start in 1919, kept by Health Department
- **MARRIAGE:** 1841, Probate Court
- **DIVORCE:** 1833, Superior Court Clerk
- **DEATH:** 1919, Health Department
- **BURIAL:** unknown, Probate Court
- **LAND:** 1833, Superior Court Clerk
- **PROBATE:** 1833, Probate Court
- **COURT:** 1832, Superior Court Clerk

CLARKE

325 E. Washington St., Room 215, Athens, GA 30601, (706) 613-3320, **<athensclarkecounty.com>**

- **INCORPORATED:** Dec. 5, 1801
- **PARENT COUNTY:** Jackson
- **BIRTH RECORDS:** start in 1919, kept by Health Department
- **MARRIAGE:** 1801, Probate Court
- **DIVORCE:** 1801, Superior Court Clerk
- **MILITARY:** 1922, Superior Court Clerk
- **DEATH:** 1919, Health Department
- **LAND:** 1801, Superior Court Clerk
- **PROBATE:** 1801, Probate Court
- **COURT:** 1801, Superior Court Clerk

CLAY

105 N. Washington, Fort Gaines, GA 39851, (229) 768-3238,
<claycountyga.org>

- **INCORPORATED:** Feb. 16, 1854
- **PARENT COUNTIES:** Early, Randolph
- **MARRIAGE:** 1854, Probate Court
- **DIVORCE:** unknown, Superior Court Clerk
- **LAND:** 1854, Superior Court Clerk
- **PROBATE:** 1854, Probate Court
- **COURT:** 1854, Superior Court Clerk

CLAYTON

112 Smith St., Jonesboro, GA 30236, (770) 477-3208,
<co.clayton.ga.us>

- **INCORPORATED:** Nov. 30, 1858
- **PARENT COUNTIES:** Fayette, Henry
- **BIRTH RECORDS:** start in 1919, kept by Health Department
- **MARRIAGE:** 1859, Probate Court
- **DIVORCE:** 1859, Superior Court Clerk
- **DEATH:** 1919, Health Department
- **LAND:** 1859, Superior Court Clerk
- **PROBATE:** 1859, Probate Court
- **COURT:** 1859, Superior Court Clerk

CLINCH

100 Court Square, Homerville, GA 31634, (912) 487-2667,
<clinchcounty.georgia.gov>

- **INCORPORATED:** Feb.14, 1850
- **PARENT COUNTIES:** Ware, Lowndes
- **BIRTH RECORDS:** start in 1919, kept by Health Department

- **MARRIAGE:** 1867, Probate Court
- **DIVORCE:** 1867, Superior Court Clerk
- **DEATH:** 1919, Health Department
- **LAND:** 1868, Superior Court Clerk
- **PROBATE:** 1867, Probate Court
- **COURT:** 1868, Superior Court Clerk
- **VOTERS LIST:** 1890, Superior Court Clerk
- **NOTES:** All records burned in 1856 and 1867.

COBB
100 Cherokee St., Marietta, GA 30090, (770) 528-1900,
<cobbcountyga.gov>
- **INCORPORATED:** Dec. 3, 1832
- **PARENT COUNTY:** Cherokee
- **BIRTH RECORDS:** start in 1919, kept by Health Department
- **MARRIAGE:** 1865, Probate Court
- **DIVORCE:** unknown, Superior Court Clerk
- **DEATH:** 1919, Health Department
- **LAND:** 1865, Superior Court Clerk
- **PROBATE:** 1865, Probate Court
- **COURT:** 1865, Superior Court Clerk
- **NOTES:** Fire in 1864, records lost.

COFFEE
101 S. Peterson Ave., Douglas, GA 31533, (912) 384-4799,
<coffeecounty.georgia.gov>
- **INCORPORATED:** Feb. 9, 1854
- **PARENT COUNTIES:** Clinch, Irwin, Ware, Telfair
- **BIRTH RECORDS:** start in 1919, kept by Health Department
- **MARRIAGE:** 1854, Probate Court
- **DIVORCE:** 1854, Superior Court Clerk
- **DEATH:** 1919, Health Department
- **PROBATE:** 1854, Probate Court
- **LAND:** 1854, Superior Court Clerk
- **COURT:** 1854, Superior Court Clerk
- **NOTES:** Clerk of Superior Court has some 1919 military discharges.

COLQUITT
Box 517, Moultrie, GA 31776, (229) 616-7400, **<ccboc.com>**
- **INCORPORATED:** Feb. 25, 1856
- **PARENT COUNTIES:** Lowndes, Thomas
- **BIRTH RECORDS:** start in 1919, kept by Health Department
- **MARRIAGE:** 1881, Probate Court
- **DIVORCE:** unknown, Superior Court Clerk
- **DEATH:** 1919, Health Department
- **LAND:** 1881, Superior Court Clerk
- **PROBATE:** 1881, Probate Court
- **COURT:** 1881, Superior Court Clerk
- **NOTES:** Fire in 1881, records lost.

COLUMBIA
Box 498, Evans, GA 30809, (760) 868-3300,
<columbiacountyga.gov>
- **INCORPORATED:** Dec. 10, 1790
- **PARENT COUNTY:** Richmond
- **BIRTH RECORDS:** start in 1919, kept by Health Department
- **MARRIAGE:** 1787, Probate Court
- **DIVORCE:** 1945, Clerk of Courts
- **DEATH:** 1919, Health Department
- **LAND:** 1790, Superior Court Clerk
- **PROBATE:** 1790, Probate Court
- **COURT:** 1790, Superior Court Clerk

COOK
209 N. Parrish Ave., Adel, GA 31620, (229) 896-2266,
<cookcountyga.us>
- **INCORPORATED:** July 30, 1918
- **PARENT COUNTY:** Berrien
- **BIRTH RECORDS:** start in 1919, kept by Health Department
- **MARRIAGE:** 1919, Probate Court
- **DIVORCE:** 1919, Superior Court Clerk
- **DEATH:** 1919, Health Department
- **LAND:** 1919, Superior Court Clerk
- **COURT:** 1919, Superior Court Clerk
- **PROBATE:** 1919, Probate Court

COWETA
22 E. Broad St., Newnan, GA 30263, (770) 254-2601,
<Coweta.ga.us>
- **INCORPORATED:** Dec. 11, 1826
- **PARENT COUNTY:** Creek Indian Lands
- **BIRTH RECORDS:** start in 1919, kept by Health Department
- **MARRIAGE:** 1828, Probate Court
- **DIVORCE:** 1828, Superior Court Clerk
- **DEATH:** 1919, Health Department
- **LAND:** 1827, Superior Court Clerk
- **PROBATE:** 1828, Probate Court
- **COURT:** 1828, Superior Court Clerk

CRAWFORD
Box 1059, Roberta, GA 31078, (478) 836-3782,
<crawfordcountyga.org>
- **INCORPORATED:** Dec. 9, 1822
- **PARENT COUNTY:** Houston
- **MARRIAGE:** 1823, Probate Court
- **DIVORCE:** 1850, Superior Court Clerk
- **LAND:** 1830, Superior Court Clerk
- **PROBATE:** 1830, Probate Court
- **COURT:** 1830, Superior Court Clerk

CRISP
210 Seventh St. S., Cordele, GA 31015, (229) 276-2672,
<www.crispcounty.com>
- **INCORPORATED:** Aug. 17, 1905
- **PARENT COUNTY:** Dooly
- **BIRTH RECORDS:** start in 1919, kept by Health Department
- **MARRIAGE:** 1905, Probate Court
- **DIVORCE:** 1905, Superior Court Clerk
- **DEATH:** 1919, Health Department
- **LAND:** 1905, Superior Court Clerk
- **PROBATE:** 1905, Probate Court
- **COURT:** 1905, Superior Court Clerk

DADE
Box 613, Trenton, GA 30752, (706) 657-4625,
<dadecounty.georgia.gov>

- **INCORPORATED:** Dec. 25, 1837
- **PARENT COUNTY:** Walker
- **MARRIAGE:** 1866, Probate Court
- **DIVORCE:** unknown, County Clerk
- **LAND:** 1849, Superior Court Clerk
- **COURT:** 1854, Superior Court Clerk

DAWSON
78 Howard Ave. E, Ste. 100, Dawsonville, GA 30534, (706) 344-3501, **<dawsoncounty.org>**

- **INCORPORATED:** Dec. 3, 1857
- **PARENT COUNTIES:** Lumpkin, Gilmer
- **BIRTH RECORDS:** 1919, Health Department
- **MARRIAGE:** 1858, Probate Court
- **DIVORCE:** 1857, Superior Court Clerk
- **DEATH:** 1919, Health Department
- **BURIAL:** 1858, Probate Court
- **LAND:** 1858, Superior Court Clerk
- **PROBATE:** 1858, Probate Court
- **COURT:** 1858, Superior Court Clerk

DE KALB
Courthouse, Decatur, GA 30030, (404) 294-2900, **<co.dekalb.ga.us>**

- **INCORPORATED:** Dec. 9, 1822
- **PARENT COUNTIES:** Fayette, Gwinett, Henry
- **MARRIAGE:** 1842, Probate Court
- **DIVORCE:** 1842, Superior Court Clerk
- **LAND:** 1842, Superior Court Clerk
- **PROBATE:** 1842, Probate Court
- **COURT:** 1842, Superior Court Clerk
- **NOTES:** Courthouse burned 1842 and 1916.

DECATUR
Box 726, Bainbridge, GA 31818, (229) 248-3030, **<decaturcountyga.org>**

- **INCORPORATED:** Dec. 8, 1823
- **PARENT COUNTY:** Early
- **MARRIAGE:** 1824, Probate Court
- **DIVORCE:** 1823, Superior Court Clerk
- **LAND:** 1823, Superior Court Clerk
- **PROBATE:** 1823, Probate Court
- **COURT:** 1823, Superior Court Clerk

DODGE
Box 818, Eastman, GA 31023, (478) 374-4361, **<eastman-georgia.com>**

- **INCORPORATED:** Oct. 26, 1870
- **PARENT COUNTIES:** Montgomery, Pulaski, Telfair
- **BIRTH RECORDS:** start in 1919, kept by Health Department
- **MARRIAGE:** 1871,Probate Court
- **DEATH:** 1919, Health Department
- **PROBATE:** 1871, Probate Court
- **DIVORCE:** unknown, Superior Court Clerk
- **COURT:** 1871, Superior Court Clerk
- **LAND:** 1871, Superior Court Clerk

DOOLY
Box 348, Vienna, GA 31092, (229) 268-4228, **<doolycounty.georgia.gov>**

- **INCORPORATED:** May 15, 1821
- **PARENT COUNTY:** Creek Indian Lands
- **BIRTH RECORDS:** start in 1919, kept by Health Department
- **MARRIAGE:** 1846, Probate Court
- **DIVORCE:** 1846, Superior Court Clerk
- **DEATH:** 1919, Health Department
- **BURIAL:** unknown, Probate Court
- **LAND:** 1847, Superior Court Clerk
- **PROBATE:** 1847, Probate Court
- **COURT:** 1847, Superior Court Clerk
- **NOTES:** Fire destroyed early records.

DOUGHERTY
222 Pine Ave., Albany, GA 31701, (229) 431-2121, **<dougherty.ga.us>**

- **INCORPORATED:** Dec. 15, 1853
- **PARENT COUNTY:** Baker
- **BIRTH RECORDS:** start in 1919, kept by Health Department
- **MARRIAGE:** 1854, Probate Court
- **DIVORCE:** 1856, Superior Court Clerk
- **DEATH:** 1919, Health Department
- **LAND:** 1854, Superior Court Clerk
- **PROBATE:** 1849, Probate Court
- **COURT:** 1854, Superior Court Clerk

DOUGLAS
8700 Hospital Dr., Douglasville, GA 30134, (770) 949-2000, **<co.douglas.ga.us>**

- **INCORPORATED:** Oct. 17, 1870
- **PARENT COUNTIES:** Carroll, Campbell
- **BIRTH RECORDS:** start in 1919, kept by Health Department
- **MARRIAGE:** 1871, Probate Court
- **DIVORCE:** 1870, Superior Court Clerk
- **DEATH:** 1919, Health Department
- **LAND:** 1871, Superior Court Clerk
- **PROBATE:** 1871, Probate Court
- **COURT:** 1871, Superior Court Clerk

EARLY
Box 693, Blakely, GA 31723, (229) 723-4432, **<blakelyearlychamber.com**

- **INCORPORATED:** Dec. 15, 1818
- **PARENT COUNTY:** Creek Indian Lands
- **NOTES:** Many records lost, first marriage book 1854.
- **MARRIAGE:** 1820, Probate Court
- **DIVORCE:** unknown, Clerk of Courts
- **CEMETERY:** unknown, Clerk of Courts
- **LAND:** 1821, Superior Court Clerk
- **PROBATE:** 1824, Probate Court
- **COURT:** 1820, Superior Court Clerk
- **MILITARY:** unknown, Clerk of Courts

ECHOLS
Box 190, Statenville, GA 31648, (229) 559-0190,
<echolscountygeorgia.com>
- **INCORPORATED:** Dec. 13, 1858
- **PARENT COUNTIES:** Clinch, Lowndes
- **NOTES:** Most records burned 1897.
- **MARRIAGE:** 1898, Probate Court
- **DIVORCE:** unknown, Superior Court Clerk
- **LAND:** 1897, Superior Court Clerk
- **PROBATE:** 1897, Probate Court
- **COURT:** 1898, Superior Court Clerk

EFFINGHAM
601 N. Laurel St.., Springfield, GA 31329, (912) 754-2123,
<effinghamcounty.org>
- **INCORPORATED:** Feb. 5, 1777
- **PARENT COUNTY:** Original county organized from St. Mathew and St. Phillip parishes
- **BIRTH RECORDS:** start in 1919, kept by Health Department
- **MARRIAGE:** 1791, Probate Court
- **DIVORCE:** 1777, Superior Court Clerk
- **DEATH:** 1919, Health Department
- **LAND:** 1786, Superior Court Clerk
- **PROBATE:** 1796, Probate Court
- **COURT:** 1791, Superior Court Clerk
- **NOTES:** Some records lost in Civil War and fire 1890.

ELBERT
10 W. Church St., Elberton, GA 30635, (706) 283-2005,
<elbertga.com>
- **INCORPORATED:** Dec. 10, 1790
- **PARENT COUNTY:** Wilkes
- **BIRTH RECORDS:** start in 1919, kept by Health Department
- **MARRIAGE:** 1791, Probate Court
- **DIVORCE:** 1790, Superior Court Clerk
- **DEATH:** 1919, Health Department
- **BURIAL:** unknown, Probate Court
- **LAND:** 1791, Superior Court Clerk
- **PROBATE:** 1791, Probate Court
- **COURT:** 1791, Superior Court Clerk
- **MILITARY:** 1922, Superior Court Clerk

EMANUEL
Box 787, Swainsboro, GA 30401, (478) 237-3881,
<emanuelcounty.georgia.gov>
- **INCORPORATED:** Dec. 10, 1812
- **PARENT COUNTY:** Montgomery, Bulloch
- **BIRTH RECORDS:** started in 1919, kept by Health Department
- **MARRIAGE:** 1812, Probate Court
- **DIVORCE:** 1812, Superior Court Clerk
- **DEATH:** 1919, Health Department
- **LAND:** 1812, Superior Court Clerk
- **PROBATE:** 1812, Probate Court
- **COURT:** 1810, Superior Court Clerk

EVANS
3 Freeman St., Claxton, GA 30417, (912) 739-1141,
<claxtonevanschamber.com>
- **INCORPORATED:** Aug. 11, 1914
- **PARENT COUNTIES:** Bulloch, Tattnall
- **BIRTH RECORDS:** start in 1919, kept by Health Department
- **MARRIAGE:** 1915, Probate Court
- **DEATH:** 1919, Health Department
- **BURIAL:** unknown, Probate Court
- **PROBATE:** 1915, Probate Court
- **DIVORCE:** 1915, Superior Court Clerk
- **COURT:** 1915, Superior Court Clerk
- **LAND:** 1915, Superior Court Clerk

FANNIN
171 Church St., Blue Ridge, GA 30513, (706) 632-2203,
<rootsweb.ancestry.com/~gafannin>
- **INCORPORATED:** Jan. 21, 1854
- **PARENT COUNTIES:** Gilmer, Union
- **BIRTH RECORDS:** start in 1919, kept by Health Department
- **MARRIAGE:** 1854, Probate Court
- **DIVORCE:** 1854, Superior Court Clerk
- **DEATH:** 1919, Health Department
- **LAND:** 1854, Superior Court Clerk
- **PROBATE:** 1854, Probate Court
- **COURT:** 1854, Superior Court Clerk

FAYETTE
140 Stonewall Ave W., Fayetteville, GA 30214, (770) 460-5730,
<admin.co.fayette.ga.us>
- **INCORPORATED:** May 15, 1821
- **PARENT COUNTY:** Creek Indian Lands
- **BIRTH RECORDS:** start in 1919, kept by Health Department
- **MARRIAGE:** 1823, Probate Court
- **DIVORCE:** unknown, Superior Court Clerk
- **DEATH:** 1919, Health Department
- **LAND:** 1823, Superior Court Clerk
- **PROBATE:** 1823, Probate Court
- **COURT:** 1823, Superior Court Clerk

FLOYD
Box 946, Rome, GA 30162, (706) 291-5110, **<floydcountyga.org>**
- **INCORPORATED:** Dec. 3, 1832
- **PARENT COUNTY:** Cherokee
- **MARRIAGE RECORDS:** start in 1834, kept by Probate Court
- **DIVORCE:** 1883, Superior Court Clerk
- **LAND:** 1840, Superior Court Clerk
- **PROBATE:** 1837, Probate Court
- **COURT:** 1840, Superior Court Clerk

FORSYTH
110 E. Main St., Cumming, GA 30040, (770) 781-2101,
<forsythco.com>
- **INCORPORATED:** Dec. 3, 1832
- **PARENT COUNTY:** Cherokee
- **BIRTH RECORDS:** start in 1919, kept by Health Department
- **MARRIAGE:** 1833, Probate Court
- **DIVORCE:** unknown, Clerk of Courts

- **DEATH:** 1919, Health Department
- **LAND:** 1832, Superior Court Clerk
- **PROBATE:** 1832, Probate Court
- **COURT:** 1832, Superior Court Clerk

FRANKLIN

141 Athens St., Carnesville, GA 30521, (706) 384-2483,
<franklin-county.com>

- **INCORPORATED:** Feb. 25, 1784
- **PARENT COUNTY:** Cherokee Indian Lands
- **MARRIAGE RECORDS:** start in 1806, kept by Probate Court
- **DIVORCE:** 1900, Superior Court Clerk
- **LAND:** 1786, Superior Court Clerk
- **PROBATE:** 1786, Probate Court
- **COURT:** 1786, Superior Court Clerk
- **NOTES:** Some records prior to 1850 in Georgia State Archives.

FULTON

141 Pryor St., Atlanta, GA 30303, (404) 730-4000,
<co.fulton.ga.us>

- **INCORPORATED:** Dec. 20, 1853
- **PARENT COUNTIES:** De Kalb, Campbell, Milton
- **MARRIAGE:** start in1854, kept by Probate Court
- **DIVORCE:** 1854, Superior Court Clerk
- **LAND:** 1854, Superior Court Clerk
- **PROBATE:** 1854, Probate Court
- **COURT:** 1854, Superior Court Clerk

GILMER

1 Westside Sq., Ellijay, GA 30540, (706) 635-4362,
<gilmercounty-ga.gov>

- **INCORPORATED:** Dec. 3, 1832
- **PARENT COUNTY:** Cherokee
- **BIRTH RECORDS:** start in 1919, kept by Health Department
- **MARRIAGE:** 1836, Probate Court
- **DIVORCE:** 1909, Superior Court Clerk
- **DEATH:** 1919, Health Department
- **LAND:** 1833, Superior Court Clerk
- **PROBATE:** 1833, Probate Court
- **COURT:** 1833, Superior Court Clerk
- **MILITARY:** 1902, Superior Court Clerk

GLASCOCK

Box 66, Gibson, GA 30810, (706) 598-2671,
<glascockcountyga.com>

- **INCORPORATED:** Dec. 19, 1857
- **PARENT COUNTY:** Warren
- **BIRTH RECORDS:** start in 1919, kept by Health Department
- **MARRIAGE:** 1858, Probate Court
- **DIVORCE:** unknown , Superior Court Clerk
- **LAND:** 1858, Superior Court Clerk
- **DEATH:** 1919, Health Department
- **PROBATE:** 1858, Probate Court
- **COURT:** 1858, Superior Court Clerk

GLYNN

1803 Gloucester St., Brunswick, GA 31520, (912) 554-7400,
<glynncounty.org>

- **INCORPORATED:** Feb. 5, 1777
- **PARENT COUNTY:** Original county organized from St. David and St. Patrick parishes
- **MARRIAGE RECORDS:** start in 1818, kept by Probate Court
- **DIVORCE:** 1792, Superior Court Clerk
- **PROBATE:** 1792, Probate Court
- **COURT:** 1810, Superior Court Clerk
- **NOTES:** Clerk of Superior Courts has land records. Records 1824-1829 burned, all records to 1818 damaged.

GORDON

Box 580, Calhoun, GA 30703, (706) 629-3795,
<gordoncounty.org>

- **INCORPORATED:** Feb. 13, 1850
- **PARENT COUNTIES:** Bartow (Cass), Floyd
- **BIRTH RECORDS:** start in 1919, kept by Health Department
- **MARRIAGE:** 1864, Probate Court
- **DIVORCE:** 1864, Superior Court Clerk
- **DEATH:** 1919, Health Department
- **BURIAL:** unknown, Probate Court
- **LAND:** 1850, Superior Court Clerk
- **PROBATE:** 1856, Probate Court
- **COURT:** 1850, Superior Court Clerk
- **NOTES:** Records destroyed 1864.

GRADY

250 N. Broad St., Cairo, GA 39828, (229) 377-1512,
<gradycounty.georgia.gov>

- **INCORPORATED:** Aug. 17, 1905
- **PARENT COUNTIES:** Decatur, Thomas
- **MARRIAGE RECORDS:** start in 1906, kept by Probate Court
- **DIVORCE:** 1906, Superior Court Clerk
- **LAND:** 1906, Superior Court Clerk
- **PROBATE:** 1906, Probate Court
- **COURT:** 1906, Superior Court Clerk

GREENE

1034 Silver Dr., Ste. 201, Greensboro, GA 30642, (706) 453-7716,
<greenecountyga.gov>

- **PARENT COUNTY:** Washington
- **INCORPORATED:** Feb. 3, 1786
- **BIRTH RECORDS:** start in 1919, kept by Health Department
- **MARRIAGE:** 1805, Probate Court
- **DIVORCE:** 1790, Superior Court Clerk
- **DEATH:** 1919, Health Department
- **LAND:** 1785, Superior Court Clerk
- **PROBATE:** 1785, Probate Court
- **COURT:** 1785, Superior Court Clerk

GWINNETT

75 Langley Dr., Lawrenceville, GA 30045, (770) 822-8000,
<gwinnettcounty.com>

- **INCORPORATED:** Dec. 15, 1818
- **PARENT COUNTY:** Cherokee Lands
- **MARRIAGE RECORDS:** start in 1871, kept by Probate Court

- **DIVORCE:** unknown, Superior Court Clerk
- **LAND:** 1871, Superior Court Clerk
- **PROBATE:** 1818, Probate Court
- **COURT:** 1858, Superior Court Clerk
- **NOTES:** Courthouse burned 1871, few records saved.

HABERSHAM

555 Monroe St. Unit 20, Clarkesville, GA 30523, (706) 754-6264, **<habershamga.com>**

- **INCORPORATED:** Dec. 15, 1818
- **PARENT COUNTY:** Cherokee Indian Lands
- **BIRTH RECORDS:** start in 1919, kept by Health Department
- **MARRIAGE:** 1824, Probate Court
- **DIVORCE:** 1819, Superior Court Clerk
- **DEATH:** 1919, Health Department
- **LAND:** 1819, Superior Court Clerk
- **PROBATE:** 1819, Probate Court
- **COURT:** 1819, Superior Court Clerk

HALL

711 Green St., Gainesville, GA 30501, (770) 535-8288, **<hallcounty.org>**

- **INCORPORATED:** Dec. 15, 1818
- **PARENT COUNTY:** Cherokee Indian Lands
- **MARRIAGE RECORDS:** start in 1819, kept by Probate Court
- **DIVORCE:** 1900, Superior Court Clerk
- **LAND:** 1819, Superior Court Clerk
- **PROBATE:** 1819, Probate Court
- **COURT:** 1819, Superior Court Clerk
- **NOTES:** Tornado destroyed courthouse in 1936, most records lost, except deeds.

HANCOCK

Courthouse Square, Sparta, GA 31087, (706) 444-5746, **<hancockcounty.georgia.gov>**

- **INCORPORATED:** Dec. 17, 1793
- **PARENT COUNTIES:** Greene, Washington
- **BIRTH RECORDS:** start in 1919, kept by Health Department
- **MARRIAGE:** 1806, Probate Court
- **DIVORCE:** 1919, Superior Court Clerk
- **DEATH:** 1919, Health Department
- **LAND:** 1794, Superior Court Clerk
- **PROBATE:** 1794, Probate Court
- **COURT:** 1794, Superior Court Clerk

HARALSON

Box 489, Buchanan, GA 30113,(770) 646-2002, **<haralsoncounty.georgia.gov>**

- **INCORPORATED:** Jan. 26, 1856
- **PARENT COUNTIES:** Carroll, Polk
- **BIRTH RECORDS:** start in 1919, kept by Health Department
- **MARRIAGE:** 1856, Probate Court
- **DIVORCE:** unknown, Superior Court Clerk
- **DEATH:** 1919, Health Department
- **BURIAL:** unknown, Probate Court
- **LAND:** 1856, Superior Court Clerk
- **PROBATE:** 1856, Probate Court
- **COURT:** 1856, Superior Court Clerk

HARRIS

104 N. College St., Hamilton, GA 31811, (706) 628-4958, **<harriscountyga.gov>**

- **INCORPORATED:** Dec. 14, 1827
- **PARENT COUNTIES:** Muscogee, Troup
- **BIRTH RECORDS:** start in 1919, kept by Health Department
- **MARRIAGE:** 1828, Probate Court
- **DIVORCE:** 1927, Superior Court Clerk
- **DEATH:** 1919, Health Department
- **LAND:** 1828, Superior Court Clerk
- **PROBATE:** 1828, Probate Court
- **COURT:** 1828, Superior Court Clerk

HART

800 Chandler St., Hartwell, GA 30643, (706) 376-2024, **<hartcountyga.org>**

- **INCORPORATED:** Dec. 7, 1853
- **PARENT COUNTIES:** Elbert, Franklin
- **BIRTH RECORDS:** start in 1919, kept by Health Department
- **MARRIAGE:** 1856, Probate Court
- **DIVORCE:** 1856, Superior Court Clerk
- **DEATH:** 1919, Health Department
- **BURIAL:** unknown, Probate Court
- **LAND:** 1856, Superior Court Clerk
- **PROBATE:** 1856, Probate Court
- **COURT:** 1856, Superior Court Clerk

HEARD

Box 40, Franklin, GA 30217, (770) 675-3821, **<heardcountyga.com>**

- **INCORPORATED:** Dec. 22, 1830
- **PARENT COUNTIES:** Carroll, Coweta, Troup
- **BIRTH RECORDS:** start in 1919, kept by Health Department
- **MARRIAGE:** 1886, Probate Court
- **DEATH:** 1919, Health Department
- **LAND:** 1894, Superior Court Clerk
- **PROBATE:** 1894, Probate Court
- **COURT:** 1894, Superior Court Clerk
- **NOTES:** Fire in 1894.

HENRY

140 Henry Pkwy., McDonough, GA 30253, (770) 954-2400, **<co.henry.ga.us>**

- **INCORPORATED:** May 15, 1821
- **PARENT COUNTY:** Creek Indian Lands
- **MARRIAGE RECORD:** start in 1822, kept in the Probate Court
- **PROBATE:** 1822, Probate Court
- **DIVORCE:** 1821, Superior Court Clerk
- **COURT:** 1822, Superior Court Clerk
- **LAND:** 1822, Superior Court Clerk

HOUSTON

200 Carl Vinson Pkwy., Warner Robins, GA 31088, (478) 542-2115, **<houstoncountyga.com>**

- **INCORPORATED:** May 15, 1821
- **PARENT COUNTY:** Creek Indian Lands
- **BIRTH RECORDS:** start in 1919, kept by Health Department
- **MARRIAGE:** 1822, Probate Court

- **DIVORCE:** 1822, Superior Court Clerk
- **DEATH:** 1919, Health Department
- **LAND:** 1822, Superior Court Clerk
- **PROBATE:** 1822, Probate Court
- **COURT:** 1822, Superior Court Clerk

IRWIN
207 S. Irwin Ave., Ocilla, GA 31774, (229) 468-9441,
<irwincounty.net>
- **INCORPORATED:** Dec. 15, 1818
- **PARENT COUNTY:** Creek Indian Lands
- **BIRTH RECORDS:** start in 1919, kept by Health Department
- **MARRIAGE:** 1838, Probate Court
- **DIVORCE:** 1821, Superior Court Clerk
- **DEATH:** 1919, Health Department
- **BURIAL:** 1920, Probate Court
- **LAND:** 1821, Superior Court Clerk
- **PROBATE:** 1821, Probate Court
- **COURT:** 1820, Superior Court Clerk
- **MILITARY:** 1900, Superior Court Clerk

JACKSON
67 Athens St., Jefferson, GA 30549, (706) 367-1199,
<jacksoncountygov.com>
- **INCORPORATED:** Feb. 11, 1796
- **PARENT COUNTY:** Franklin
- **BIRTH RECORDS:** start in 1919, kept by Health Department
- **MARRIAGE:** 1805, Probate Court
- **DEATH:** 1919, Health Department
- **LAND:** 1796, Superior Court Clerk
- **PROBATE:** 1796, Probate Court
- **COURT:** 1796, Superior Court Clerk
- **TAX:** 1800, Superior Court Clerk

JASPER
Courthouse, Monticello, GA 31064, (706) 468-4900,
<jaspercounty.georgia.gov>
- **INCORPORATED:** Dec. 10, 1807
- **PARENT COUNTY:** Baldwin
- **MARRIAGE RECORDS:** start in 1808, kept by Probate Court
- **DIVORCE:** 1900, Superior Court Clerk
- **LAND:** 1808, Superior Court Clerk
- **MILITARY:** 1900, Superior Court Clerk
- **PROBATE:** 1809, Probate Court
- **COURT:** 1808, Superior Court Clerk
- **NOTES:** Formerly Randolph County. Name changed to Jasper Dec. 10, 1812.

JEFF DAVIS
14 Jeff Davis St., Box 429, Hazlehurst, GA 31539, (912) 375-6615,
<hazlehurst-jeffdavis.com>
- **INCORPORATED:** Aug. 18, 1905
- **PARENT COUNTIES:** Appling, Coffee
- **MARRIAGE RECORD:** start in 1905, kept by Probate Court
- **DIVORCE:** 1905, Superior Court Clerk
- **LAND:** 1905, Superior Court Clerk
- **PROBATE:** 1905, Probate Court
- **COURT:** 1905, Superior Court Clerk

JEFFERSON
Box 658, Louisville, GA 30434, (478) 625-3332,
<jeffersoncounty.org>
- **INCORPORATED:** Feb. 20, 1796
- **PARENT COUNTIES:** Burke, Warren, Montgomery, Washington
- **BIRTH RECORDS:** start in 1919, kept by Health Department
- **MARRIAGE:** 1803, Probate Court
- **DIVORCE:** ca. 1900, Clerk of Courts
- **DEATH:** 1919, Health Department
- **LAND:** 1865, Superior Court Clerk
- **PROBATE:** 1796, Probate Court
- **COURT:** 1796, Superior Court Clerk
- **NOTES:** Records not complete.

JENKINS
City Hall, Walnut St., Millen, GA 30442, (478) 982-6100,
<jenkinscountyga.com>
- **INCORPORATED:** August 17, 1905
- **PARENT COUNTIES:** Bullock, Burke, Emanuel, Screven
- **MARRIAGE RECORDS:** start in 1905, kept by Probate Court
- **DIVORCE:** 1905, Superior Court Clerk
- **LAND:** 1905, Superior Court Clerk
- **PROBATE:** 1905, Probate Court
- **COURT:** 1905, Superior Court Clerk

JOHNSON
Box 269, Wrightsville, GA 31096, (478) 864-2218,
<johnsonco.org>
- **INCORPORATED:** Dec. 11, 1858
- **PARENT COUNTIES:** Emanuel, Laurens, Washington
- **MARRIAGE RECORDS:** start in 1859, kept by Probate Court
- **DIVORCE:** 1858, Superior Court Clerk
- **LAND:** 1859, Superior Court Clerk
- **PROBATE:** 1859, Probate Court
- **COURT:** 1859, Superior Court Clerk

JONES
Box 1359, Gray, GA 31032, (478) 986-6405, **<jonescounty.org>**
- **INCORPORATED:** Dec. 10, 1807
- **PARENT COUNTY:** Baldwin
- **BIRTH RECORDS:** start in1919, kept by Health Department
- **MARRIAGE:** 1811, Probate Court
- **DEATH:** 1919, Health Department
- **LAND:** 1808, Superior Court Clerk
- **PROBATE:** 1808, Probate Court
- **COURT:** 1808, Superior Court Clerk

KINCHAFOONEE
- **INCORPORATED:** Dec. 16, 1853
- **PARENT COUNTY:** Stewart
- **NOTES:** See Webster County. Name changed to Webster Feb. 21, 1856.

LAMAR
326 Thomaston St., Barnesville, GA 30204, (770) 358-5145,
<lamarcounty.georgia.gov>
- **INCORPORATED:** Aug. 17, 1920
- **PARENT COUNTIES:** Monroe, Pike

- **BIRTH RECORDS:** start in1921, kept by Health Department
- **MARRIAGE:** 1921, Probate Court
- **DIVORCE:** 1921, Superior Court Clerk
- **DEATH:** 1921, Health Department
- **LAND:** 1921, Superior Court Clerk
- **COURT:** 1921, Superior Court Clerk

LANIER

100 Main St., Lakeland, GA 31635, (912) 482-2088, **<laniercounty.georgia.gov>**

- **INCORPORATED:** Aug. 7, 1920
- **PARENT COUNTIES:** Berrien, Lowndes, Clinch
- **BIRTH RECORDS:** start in 1919, kept by Health Department
- **MARRIAGE:** 1921, Probate Court
- **DIVORCE:** 1921, Superior Court Clerk
- **DEATH:** 1919, Health Department
- **LAND:** 1921, Superior Court Clerk
- **PROBATE:** 1921, Probate Court
- **COURT:** 1921, Superior Court Clerk

LAURENS

Box 2011., Dublin, GA 31040, (478) 272-4755, **<laurenscoga.org>**

- **INCORPORATED:** Dec. 10, 1807
- **PARENT COUNTIES:** Wilkinson, Montgomery, Washington
- **BIRTH RECORDS:** 1919, Health Department
- **MARRIAGE:** 1809, Probate Court
- **DIVORCE:** 1807, Superior Court Clerk
- **DEATH:** 1919, Health Department
- **LAND:** 1807, Superior Court Clerk
- **PROBATE:** 1808, Probate Court
- **COURT:** 1808 Superior Court Clerk

LEE

Box 899, Leesburg, GA 31763, (229) 759-6000, **<lee.ga.us>**

- **INCORPORATED:** Dec. 11, 1826
- **PARENT COUNTY:** Creek Indian Lands
- **MARRIAGE:** 1867, Probate Court
- **DIVORCE:** unknown, Superior Court Clerk
- **LAND:** 1858, Superior Court Clerk
- **PROBATE:** 1858, Probate Court
- **COURT:** 1858, Superior Court Clerk
- **NOTES:** Courthouse fire 1858, all records lost.

LIBERTY

Box 829., Hinesville, GA 31310, (912) 876-2164, **<libertycountyga.com>**

- **INCORPORATED:** Feb. 5, 1777
- **PARENT COUNTY:** Original county organized from St. Andrew, St. James and St. John Parishes
- **BIRTH RECORDS:** start in 1919, kept by Health Department
- **MARRIAGE:** 1784, Probate Court
- **DIVORCE:** 1756, Clerk of Courts
- **DEATH:** 1927, Health Department
- **LAND:** 1784, Superior Court Clerk
- **PROBATE:** 1784, Probate Court
- **COURT:** 1784, Superior Court Clerk
- **NOTES:** Some early records lost.

LINCOLN

Box 340, Lincolnton, GA 30817, (706) 359-4444, **<lincolncountyga.com>**

- **INCORPORATED:** 20 Feb. 20, 1796
- **PARENT COUNTY:** Wilkes
- **BIRTH RECORDS:** 1919, Health Department
- **MARRIAGE:** 1796, Probate Court
- **DEATH:** 1919, Health Department
- **PROBATE:** 1796, Probate Court
- **DIVORCE:** 1796, Superior Court Clerk
- **COURT:** 1796, Superior Court Clerk
- **LAND:** 1796, Superior Court Clerk

LONG

49 S. McDonald St., Ludowici, GA 31316, (912) 545-2123, **<www.usgennet.org/usa/ga/county/long>**

- **INCORPORATED:** Aug. 14, 1920
- **PARENT COUNTY:** Liberty
- **BIRTH RECORDS:** start in 1919, kept by Health Department
- **MARRIAGE:** 1920, Probate Court
- **DIVORCE:** 1920, Superior Court Clerk
- **DEATH:** 1919, Health Department
- **BURIAL:** unknown, Probate Court
- **LAND:** 1920, Superior Court Clerk
- **PROBATE:** 1920, Probate Court
- **COURT:** 1920, Superior Court Clerk
- **ADOPTION:** 1920, Superior Court Clerk

LOWNDES

Box 1349, Valdosta, GA 31603, (229) 671-2400, **<lowndescounty.com>**

- **INCORPORATED:** Dec. 23, 1825
- **PARENT COUNTY:** Irwin
- **MARRIAGE:** 1870, Probate Court
- **DIVORCE:** 1858, Superior Court Clerk
- **LAND:** 1858, Superior Court Clerk
- **PROBATE:** 1862, Probate Court
- **COURT:** 1862, Superior Court Clerk

LUMPKIN

99 Courthouse Hill, Suite A, Dahlonega, GA 30533, (706) 864-3742, **<lumpkincounty.gov**

- **INCORPORATED:** Dec. 3, 1832
- **PARENT COUNTIES:** Cherokee, Habersham, Hall
- **BIRTH RECORDS:** start in 1919, kept by Health Department
- **MARRIAGE:** 1833, Probate Court
- **DIVORCE:** 1833, Superior Court Clerk
- **DEATH:** 1919, Health Department
- **BURIAL:** unknown, Probate Court
- **LAND:** 1833, Superior Court Clerk
- **PROBATE:** 1833, Probate Court
- **COURT:** 1833, Superior Court Clerk

MACON

Box 297, Oglethorpe, GA 31068, (478) 472-7021, **<maconcountyga.org>**

- **INCORPORATED:** Dec. 14, 1837
- **PARENT COUNTIES:** Houston, Marion

- **BIRTH RECORDS:** 1919, Health Department
- **MARRIAGE:** 1858, Probate Court
- **DIVORCE:** unknown, Superior Court Clerk
- **DEATH:** 1919, Health Department
- **LAND:** 1857, Superior Court Clerk
- **PROBATE:** 1857, Probate Court
- **COURT:** 1856, Superior Court Clerk
- **NOTES:** Courthouse burned 1857, all records were lost.

MADISON
Box 147., Danielsville, GA 30633, (706) 795-6300,
<madisoncountyga.us>
- **INCORPORATED:** Dec. 5, 1811
- **PARENT COUNTIES:** Clarke, Elbert, Franklin, Jackson, Oglethorpe
- **BIRTH RECORDS:** start in 1919, kept by Health Department
- **MARRIAGE:** 1812, Probate Court
- **DIVORCE:** 1812, Superior Court Clerk
- **DEATH:** 1919, Health Department
- **BURIAL:** unknown, Probate Court
- **LAND:** 1812, Superior Court Clerk
- **PROBATE:** 1811, Probate Court
- **COURT:** 1812, Superior Court Clerk

MARION
Box 481, Buena Vista, GA 31803, (229) 649-2603,
<marioncounty.georgia.gov>
- **INCORPORATED:** Dec. 14, 1827
- **PARENT COUNTIES:** Lee, Muscogee, Stewart
- **DIVORCE:** unknown, Superior Court Clerk
- **LAND:** 1846, Superior Court Clerk
- **COURT:** 1846, Superior Court Clerk
- **NOTES:** Courthouse fire 1845, all records lost.

MCDUFFIE
337 Main St., Thomson, GA 30824, (706) 595-2100,
<thomson-mcduffie.com>
- **INCORPORATED:** Oct. 18, 1870
- **PARENT COUNTIES:** Columbia, Warren
- **BIRTH RECORDS:** started in 1919, kept by Health Department
- **MARRIAGE:** 1871, Probate Court
- **DEATH:** 1919, Health Department
- **PROBATE:** 1871, Probate Court
- **DIVORCE:** 1872, Superior Court Clerk
- **COURT:** 1871, Superior Court Clerk
- **LAND:** 1871, Superior Court Clerk

MCINTOSH
Box 584, Darien, GA 31305, (912) 437-6641,
<mcintoshcounty.com>
- **INCORPORATED:** Dec. 19, 1793
- **PARENT COUNTY:** Liberty
- **MARRIAGE:** 1873, Probate Court
- **DIVORCE:** unknown, Superior Court Clerk
- **LAND:** 1873, Superior Court Clerk
- **PROBATE:** 1873, Probate Court
- **COURT:** 1873, Superior Court Clerk
- **NOTES:** Many records lost during Civil War, courthouse fire 1931.

MERIWETHER
Box 428, Greenville, GA 30222, (706) 672-1314,
<meriwether.ga.us>
- **INCORPORATED:** Dec. 14, 1827
- **PARENT COUNTY:** Troup
- **BIRTH RECORDS:** start in 1919, kept by Health Department
- **MARRIAGE:** 1828, Probate Court
- **DIVORCE:** 1827, Superior Court Clerk
- **DEATH:** 1919, Health Department
- **LAND:** 1827, Superior Court Clerk
- **PROBATE:** 1825, Probate Court
- **COURT:** 1828, Superior Court Clerk
- **MILITARY:** unknown, Superior Court Clerk

MILLER
155 S. First St., Colquitt, GA 39837, (229) 758-4104,
<millercounty.georgia.gov>
- **INCORPORATED:** Feb. 26, 1856
- **PARENT COUNTIES:** Baker, Early
- **BIRTH RECORDS:** start in 1919, kept by Health Department
- **MARRIAGE:** 1893, Probate Court
- **DEATH:** 1950, Health Department
- **PROBATE:** 1873, Probate Court
- **LAND:** 1873, Superior Court Clerk
- **DIVORCE:** unknown, Superior Court Clerk
- **COURT:** 1873, Superior Court Clerk
- **NOTES:** Courthouse fire 1873, all records lost.

MILTON
<rootsweb.ancestry.com/~gamilton>
- **INCORPORATED:** Dec. 18, 1847
- **PARENT COUNTIES:** Cherokee, Cobb, Forsyth
- **NOTES:** See Fulton County. Merged into Fulton Jan. 1, 1832.

MITCHELL
Box 187, Camilla, GA 31730, (229) 336-2000,
<mitchellcountyga.net>
- **INCORPORATED:** Dec. 21, 1857
- **PARENT COUNTY:** Baker
- **MARRIAGE:** 1867, Probate Court
- **DIVORCE:** 1857, Superior Court Clerk
- **LAND:** 1858, Superior Court Clerk
- **PROBATE:** 1858, Probate Court
- **COURT:** 1858, Superior Court Clerk
- **NOTES:** Courthouse fire 1869, some records saved.

MONROE
Box 189, Forsyth, GA 31029, (478) 994-7000,
<monroecountygeorgia.com>
- **INCORPORATED:** May 15, 1821
- **PARENT COUNTY:** Creek Indian Lands
- **BIRTH RECORDS:** start in 1919, kept by Health Department
- **MARRIAGE:** 1824, Probate Court
- **DIVORCE:** unknown, Superior Court Clerk
- **DEATH:** 1940, Health Department
- **LAND:** 1822, Superior Court Clerk
- **PROBATE:** 1824, Probate Court
- **COURT:** 1824, Superior Court Clerk

MONTGOMERY
415 Richardson St., Mount Vernon, GA 30445, (912) 583-2363, **<montgomerycountyga.gov>**
- **INCORPORATED:** Dec. 19, 1793
- **PARENT COUNTY:** Washington
- **BIRTH RECORDS:** start in 1919, kept by Health Department
- **MARRIAGE:** 1807, Probate Court
- **DIVORCE:** 1800, Superior Court Clerk
- **DEATH:** 1919, Health Department
- **LAND:** 1793, Superior Court Clerk
- **PROBATE:** 1806, Probate Court
- **COURT:** 1794, Superior Court Clerk
- **NOTES:** Most original records prior to 1890 are in State Archives.

MORGAN
Box 168, Madison GA 30650, (706) 342-0725, **<morganga.org>**
- **INCORPORATED:** Dec. 10, 1807
- **PARENT COUNTY:** Baldwin
- **BIRTH RECORDS:** start in 1919, kept by Health Department
- **MARRIAGE:** 1808, Probate Court
- **DIVORCE:** 1807, Superior Court Clerk
- **DEATH:** 1919, Probate Court
- **BURIAL:** unknown, Probate Court
- **LAND:** 1807, Superior Court Clerk
- **PROBATE:** 1808, Probate Court
- **COURT:** 1808, Superior Court Clerk

MURRAY
Box 1129, Chatsworth, GA 30705, (706) 695-2413, **<murraycounty.georgia.gov>**
- **INCORPORATED:** Dec. 3, 1832
- **PARENT COUNTY:** Cherokee
- **BIRTH RECORDS:** 1919, Health Department
- **MARRIAGE:** 1842, Probate Court
- **DEATH:** 1919, Health Department
- **PROBATE:** 1840, Probate Court
- **COURT:** 1833, Superior Court Clerk

MUSCOGEE
100 10th St., Columbus, GA 31901, (706) 653-4000, **<columbusga.org>**
- **INCORPORATED:** Dec. 11, 1826
- **PARENT COUNTY:** Creek Indian Lands
- **MARRIAGE:** 1838, Probate Court
- **DIVORCE:** 1838, Superior Court Clerk
- **LAND:** 1838, Superior Court Clerk
- **PROBATE:** 1838, Probate Court
- **COURT:** 1838, Superior Court Clerk

NEWTON
1124 Clark St., Covington, GA 30014, (770) 784-2000, **<co.newton.ga.us>**
- **INCORPORATED:** Dec. 24, 1821
- **PARENT COUNTIES:** Henry, Jasper, Walton
- **MARRIAGE:** 1822, Probate Court
- **DIVORCE:** 1822, Superior Court Clerk
- **DEATH:** 1819, Health Department
- **LAND:** 1822, Superior Court Clerk
- **PROBATE:** 1822, Probate Court
- **COURT:** 1822, Superior Court Clerk
- **MILITARY:** 1917, Superior Court Clerk

OCONEE
Box 145, Watkinsville, GA 30677, (706) 769-5120, **<oconeecounty.com>**
- **INCORPORATED:** Feb. 25, 1875
- **PARENT COUNTY:** Clarke
- **BIRTH RECORDS:** start in 1919, kept by Health Department
- **MARRIAGE:** 1875, Probate Court
- **DIVORCE:** 1875, Superior Court Clerk
- **DEATH:** 1919, Health Department
- **LAND:** 1875, Superior Court Clerk
- **PROBATE:** 1875, Probate Court
- **COURT:** 1875, Superior Court Clerk

OGLETHORPE
Box 261, Lexington, GA 30648, (706) 743-5370, **<onlineoglethorpe.com>**
- **INCORPORATED:** Dec. 19, 1793
- **PARENT COUNTY:** Wilkes
- **BIRTH RECORDS:** start in 1919, kept by Health Department
- **MARRIAGE:** 1795, Probate Court
- **DIVORCE:** 1794, Superior Court Clerk
- **DEATH:** 1919, Health Department
- **LAND:** 1794, Superior Court Clerk
- **PROBATE:** 1794, Probate Court
- **COURT:** 1794, Superior Court Clerk
- **NOTES:** Courthouse fire 1941.

PAULDING
120 E. Memorial Dr., Dallas, GA 30132, (770) 443-7550, **<paulding.gov>**
- **INCORPORATED:** Dec. 3, 1832
- **PARENT COUNTY:** Cherokee
- **MARRIAGE:** 1833, Probate Court
- **DIVORCE:** 1876, Superior Court Clerk
- **LAND:** 1848, Superior Court Clerk
- **PROBATE:** 1850, Probate Court
- **COURT:** 1859, Superior Court Clerk

PEACH
205 W. Church St., Fort Valley, GA 31030, (478) 825-2535, **<peachcounty.net>**
- **INCORPORATED:** July 18, 1924
- **PARENT COUNTIES:** Houston, Macon
- **BIRTH RECORDS:** start in 1925, kept by Health Department
- **MARRIAGE:** 1925, Probate Court
- **DIVORCE:** 1925, Superior Court Clerk
- **DEATH:** 1925, Health Department
- **LAND:** 1925, Superior Court Clerk
- **PROBATE:** 1925, Probate Court
- **COURT:** 1925, Superior Court Clerk

PICKENS
52 N. Main St., Jasper, GA 30143, (706) 253-8809, **<pickenscountyga.gov>**

- **PARENT COUNTIES:** Cherokee, Gilmer
- **INCORPORATED:** Dec. 5, 1853
- **BIRTH RECORDS:** start in 1919, kept by Health Department
- **MARRIAGE:** 1854, Probate Court
- **DIVORCE:** 1854, Superior Court Clerk
- **DEATH:** 1919, Health Department
- **BURIAL:** unknown, Probate Court
- **LAND:** 1854, Superior Court Clerk
- **PROBATE:** 1854, Probate Court
- **COURT:** 1854, Superior Court Clerk

PIERCE
Box 679, Blackshear, GA 31516, (912) 449-2022,
<piercecountyga.org>
- **INCORPORATED:** Dec. 18, 1857
- **PARENT COUNTIES:** Appling, Ware
- **BIRTH RECORDS:** start in 1919, kept by Health Department
- **MARRIAGE:** 1875, Probate Court
- **DIVORCE:** 1875, Superior Court Clerk
- **DEATH:** 1919, Health Department
- **LAND:** 1875, Superior Court Clerk
- **PROBATE:** 1875, Probate Court
- **COURT:** 1875, Superior Court Clerk
- **NOTES:** Courthouse fire 1874.

PIKE
Box 337, Zebulon, GA 30295, (770) 567-8734,
<pikecounty.ga.gov>
- **INCORPORATED:** Dec. 9, 1822
- **PARENT COUNTY:** Monroe
- **MARRIAGE:** 1822, Probate Court
- **PROBATE:** 1823, Probate Court
- **COURT:** 1824, Superior Court Clerk
- **LAND:** 1823, Superior Court Clerk

POLK
Box 268, Cedartown, GA 30125, (770) 749-2100,
<polkcountygeorgia.us>
- **INCORPORATED:** Dec. 20, 1851
- **PARENT COUNTY:** Paulding, Floyd
- **BIRTH RECORDS:** start in 1919, kept by Health Department
- **MARRIAGE:** 1852, Probate Court
- **DIVORCE:** 1852, Superior Court Clerk
- **DEATH:** 1919, Health Department
- **LAND:** 1852, Superior Court Clerk
- **PROBATE:** 1852, Probate Court
- **COURT:** 1852, Superior Court Clerk

PULASKI
Box 29, Hawkinsville, GA 31036-0029, (478) 783-4154,
<hawkinsville.org>
- **INCORPORATED:** Dec. 13, 1808
- **PARENT COUNTY:** Laurens
- **BIRTH RECORDS:** start in 1919, Kept by Health Department
- **MARRIAGE:** 1810, Probate Court
- **DIVORCE:** 1850, Superior Court Clerk
- **DEATH:** 1919, Health Department
- **LAND:** 1807, Superior Court Clerk
- **PROBATE:** 1810, Probate Court
- **COURT:** 1809, Superior Court Clerk

PUTNAM
108 S. Madison Ave., Eatonton, GA 31024, (706) 485-5826,
<putnamcountyga.us>
- **INCORPORATED:** Dec. 10, 1807
- **PARENT COUNTY:** Baldwin
- **BIRTH RECORDS:** 1919, Health Department
- **MARRIAGE:** 1919, Probate Court
- **DIVORCE:** 1807, Superior Court Clerk
- **DEATH:** 1919, Health Department
- **LAND:** 1806, Superior Court Clerk
- **PROBATE:** 1808, Probate Court
- **COURT:** 1807, Superior Court Clerk
- **NOTES:** Probate Court has tax digest records 1812-1848.

QUITMAN
Box 114, Georgetown, GA 39854, (229) 334-0903,
<quitmancounty.georgia.gov>
- **INCORPORATED:** Dec. 10, 1858
- **PARENT COUNTIES:** Randolph, Stewart
- **BIRTH RECORDS:** start in 1919, kept by Health Department
- **MARRIAGE:** 1879, Probate Court
- **DIVORCE:** 1923, Superior Court Clerk
- **DEATH:** 1919, Health Department
- **LAND:** 1879, Superior Court Clerk
- **PROBATE:** 1879, Probate Court
- **COURT:** 1879, Superior Court Clerk
- **NOTES:** Courthouse burned.

RABUN
25 Courthouse Sq., Box 8, Clayton, GA 30525, (706) 782-5271,
<rabuncounty.georgia.gov>
- **INCORPORATED:** Dec. 21, 1819
- **PARENT COUNTY:** Cherokee Indian Lands
- **MARRIAGE RECORDS:** start in 1820, kept by Probate Court
- **DIVORCE:** unknown, Superior Court Clerk
- **LAND:** 1821, Superior Court Clerk
- **PROBATE:** 1826, Probate Court
- **COURT:** 1829, Superior Court Clerk

RANDOLPH
Box 221, Cuthbert, GA 39840, (229) 732-6440,
<home.earthlink.net/~bwjohnson/rand_mn.htm>
- **INCORPORATED:** Dec. 20, 1828
- **PARENT COUNTY:** Lee
- **BIRTH RECORDS:** start in 1919, kept by Health Department
- **MARRIAGE:** 1835, Probate Court
- **DIVORCE:** 1835, Superior Court Clerk
- **LAND:** 1830, Superior Court Clerk
- **PROBATE:** 1835, Probate Court
- **COURT:** 1838, Superior Court Clerk

RANDOLPH, OLD
- **INCORPORATED:** Dec. 10, 1807
- **PARENT COUNTY:** Baldwin
- **NOTES:** See Jasper County. Name changed to Jasper Dec. 10, 1812.

RICHMOND

Box 1837, 600 Broad St., Augusta, GA 30911, (760) 821-1300,
<augustaga.gov>

- **INCORPORATED:** Feb. 5, 1777
- **PARENT COUNTY:** Original county created from St. Paul Parish
- **MARRIAGE:** 1785, Probate Court
- **LAND:** 1789, Superior Court Clerk
- **PROBATE:** 1782, Probate Court
- **COURT:** 1782, Superior Court Clerk

ROCKDALE

Box 289, Conyers, GA 30012, (770) 929-4000,
<rockdalecounty.org>

- **INCORPORATED:** Oct. 18, 1870
- **PARENT COUNTIES:** Henry, Newton
- **MARRIAGE:** 1871, Probate Court
- **DIVORCE:** unknown, Superior Court Clerk
- **DEATH:** 1919, Health Department
- **LAND:** 1871, Superior Court Clerk
- **PROBATE:** 1871, Probate Court
- **COURT:** 1871, Superior Court Clerk

SCHLEY

Box 352, Ellaville, GA 31806, (229) 937-2544,
<schleycounty.georgia.gov>

- **INCORPORATED:** Dec. 22, 1857
- **PARENT COUNTIES:** Marion, Sumter
- **BIRTH RECORDS:** start in 1919, kept by Health Department
- **MARRIAGE:** 1858, Probate Court
- **DIVORCE:** 1857, Superior Court Clerk
- **DEATH:** 1919, Health Department
- **BURIAL:** 1927, Probate Court
- **LAND:** 1857, Superior Court Clerk
- **PROBATE:** 1857, Probate Court
- **COURT:** 1857, Superior Court Clerk

SCREVEN

Box 159., Sylvania, GA 30467, (912) 564-7535,
<screvencounty.com>

- **INCORPORATED:** Dec. 14, 1793
- **PARENT COUNTIES:** Burke, Effingham
- **BIRTH RECORDS:** start in 1919, kept by Health Department
- **MARRIAGE:** 1817, Probate Court
- **DIVORCE:** 1816, Superior Court Clerk
- **DEATH:** 1919, Health Department
- **LAND:** 1794, Superior Court Clerk
- **PROBATE:** 1790, Probate Court
- **COURT:** 1811, Superior Court Clerk

SEMINOLE

Box 458, Donalsonville, GA 39845, (229) 524-2752,
<seminolecountyga.com>

- **INCORPORATED:** July 8, 1920
- **PARENT COUNTIES:** Decatur, Early
- **BIRTH RECORDS:** start in 1921, kept by Health Department
- **MARRIAGE:** 1921, Probate Court
- **DIVORCE:** 1921, Superior Court Clerk
- **DEATH:** 1921, Health Department
- **LAND:** 1921, Superior Court Clerk
- **PROBATE:** 1921, Probate Court
- **COURT:** 1921, Superior Court Clerk

SPALDING

Box 1087, Griffin, GA 30224, (770) 467-4200,
<spaldingcounty.com>

- **INCORPORATED:** Dec. 20, 1851
- **PARENT COUNTIES:** Fayette, Henry, Pike
- **MARRIAGE RECORDS:** start in 1852, kept by Probate Court
- **DIVORCE:** 1852, Superior Court Clerk
- **LAND:** 1852, Superior Court Clerk
- **PROBATE:** 1852, Probate Court
- **COURT:** 1852, Superior Court Clerk

ST. ANDREW PARISH

- **INCORPORATED:** 1758
- **PARENT COUNTY:** Creek Cession of 1733
- **NOTES:** See Liberty County. Organized as an early parish and became part of Liberty County Feb. 5, 1777.

ST. DAVID PARISH

- **INCORPORATED:** 1765
- **PARENT COUNTY:** Creek Cession of 1763
- **NOTES:** See Glynn County. Organized as an early parish and became part of Glynn County Feb. 5, 1777.

ST. GEORGE PARISH

- **INCORPORATED:** 1758
- **PARENT COUNTY:** Creek Cession of 1733
- **NOTES:** See Burke County. Organized as an early parish and became Burke County Feb. 5, 1777.

ST. JAMES PARISH

- **INCORPORATED:** 1758
- **PARENT COUNTY:** Creek Cession of 1733
- **NOTES:** See Liberty County. Organized as an early parish and became part of Liberty County Feb. 5, 1777.

ST. JOHN PARISH

- **INCORPORATED:** 1758
- **PARENT COUNTY:** Creek Cession of 1733
- **NOTES:** See Liberty County. Organized as an early parish and became part of Liberty County Feb. 5, 1777.

ST. MARY PARISH

- **INCORPORATED:** 1765
- **PARENT COUNTY:** Creek Cession of 1763
- **NOTES:** See Camden County. Organized as an early parish and became part of Camden County Feb. 5, 1777.

ST. MATTHEW PARISH

- **INCORPORATED:** 1758
- **PARENT COUNTY:** Creek Cession of 1733
- **NOTES:** See Effingham County. Organized as an early parish and became part of Effingham County Feb. 5, 1777.

ST. PATRICK PARISH
- **INCORPORATED:** 1765
- **PARENT COUNTY:** Creek Cession of 1763
- **NOTES:** See Glynn County. Organized as an early parish and became part of Glynn County Feb. 5, 1777.

ST. PAUL PARISH
- **INCORPORATED:** 1758
- **PARENT COUNTY:** Creek Cession of 1733
- **NOTES:** See Richmond County. Organized as an early parish and became Richmond County Feb. 5, 1777.

ST. PHILIP PARISH
- **INCORPORATED:** 1758
- **PARENT COUNTY:** Creek Cession of 1733
- **NOTES:** See Chatham and Effingham counties. Organized as an early parish. Became part of Chatham and Effingham counties Feb. 5, 1777.

ST. THOMAS PARISH
- **INCORPORATED:** 1765
- **PARENT COUNTY:** Creek Cession of 1763
- **NOTES:** See Camden County. Organized as an early parish and became part of Camden County Feb. 5, 1777.

STEPHENS
Box 386, Toccoa, GA 30577, (706) 886-9491, **<stephenscountyga.com>**
- **INCORPORATED:** Aug. 18, 1905
- **PARENT COUNTIES:** Franklin, Habersham
- **BIRTH RECORDS:** start in 1919, kept by Health Department
- **MARRIAGE:** 1906, Probate Court
- **DIVORCE:** 1906, Superior Court Clerk
- **DEATH:** 1919, Health Department
- **LAND:** 1906, Superior Court Clerk
- **PROBATE:** 1906, Probate Court
- **COURT:** 1906, Superior Court Clerk

STEWART
Box 157, Lumpkin, GA 31815, (912) 838-6769, **<stewartcounty.net>**
- **INCORPORATED:** Dec. 23, 1830
- **PARENT COUNTY:** Randolph
- **BIRTH RECORDS:** start in 1919, kept by Health Department
- **MARRIAGE:** 1828, Probate Court
- **DIVORCE:** 1830, Superior Court Clerk
- **DEATH:** 1919, Health Department
- **BURIAL:** 1927, Probate Court
- **LAND:** 1830, Superior Court Clerk
- **PROBATE:** 1830, Probate Court
- **COURT:** 1830, Superior Court Clerk

SUMTER
Box 295, Americus, GA 31709, **<sumter-ga.com>**
- **INCORPORATED:** Dec. 26, 1831
- **PARENT COUNTY:** Lee
- **BIRTH RECORDS:** start in 1919, kept by Health Department
- **MARRIAGE:** 1831, Probate Court
- **DIVORCE:** 1831, Superior Court Clerk
- **DEATH:** 1919, Health Department
- **BURIAL:** unknown, Health Department
- **LAND:** 1831, Superior Court Clerk
- **PROBATE:** 1831, Probate Court
- **COURT:** 1831, Superior Court Clerk

TALBOT
26 Washington Ave., Talbotton, GA 31827, (706) 665-3220, **<talbotcounty.georgia.gov>**
- **INCORPORATED:** Dec. 14, 1827
- **PARENT COUNTY:** Muscogee
- **BIRTH RECORDS:** start in 1919, kept by Health Department
- **MARRIAGE:** 1828, Probate Court
- **DIVORCE:** unknown, Superior Court Clerk
- **DEATH:** 1919, Health Department
- **LAND:** 1828, Superior Court Clerk
- **PROBATE:** 1828, Probate Court
- **COURT:** 1828, Superior Court Clerk

TALIAFERRO
Box 114, Crawfordville, GA 30631, (706) 456-2176, **<taliaferrocounty.georgia.gov>**
- **INCORPORATED:** Dec. 24, 1825
- **PARENT COUNTIES:** Green, Hancock, Oglethorpe, Warren, Wilkes
- **BIRTH RECORDS:** start in 1919, kept by Health Department
- **MARRIAGE:** 1826, Probate Court
- **DIVORCE:** 1826, Superior Court Clerk
- **DEATH:** 1919, Health Department
- **LAND:** 1826, Superior Court Clerk
- **PROBATE:** 1826, Probate Court
- **COURT:** 1826, Superior Court Clerk
- **CHURCH:** 1802, Probate Court

TATTNALL
Box 25, Reidsville, GA 30453, (912) 557-4335, **<tattnall.com>**
- **INCORPORATED:** Dec. 5, 1801
- **PARENT COUNTY:** Montgomery
- **BIRTH RECORDS:** start in 1919, kept by Health Department
- **MARRIAGE:** 1806, Probate Court
- **DIVORCE:** 1880, Superior Court Clerk
- **DEATH:** 1919, Health Department
- **LAND:** 1802, Superior Court Clerk
- **PROBATE:** 1802, Probate Court
- **COURT:** 1805, Superior Court Clerk

TAYLOR
Box 2044, Butler, GA 31006, (478) 862-3336, **<taylorcounty.georgia.gov>**
- **INCORPORATED:** Jan. 15, 1852
- **PARENT COUNTIES:** Macon, Marion, Talbot
- **BIRTH RECORDS:** start in 1919, kept by Health Department
- **MARRIAGE:** 1852, Probate Court
- **DIVORCE:** 1852, Superior Court Clerk
- **DEATH:** 1919, Health Department
- **LAND:** 1852, Superior Court Clerk
- **PROBATE:** 1852, Probate Court
- **COURT:** 1852, Superior Court Clerk

TELFAIR

128 E. Oak St., McRae, GA 31055, (229) 868-6525,
<telfaircounty.georgia.gov>
- **INCORPORATED:** Dec. 10, 1807
- **PARENT COUNTY:** Wilkinson
- **BIRTH RECORDS:** start in 1919, kept by Health Department
- **MARRIAGE:** 1810, Probate Judge
- **DIVORCE:** unknown, Superior Court Clerk
- **DEATH:** 1919, Health Department
- **LAND:** 1809, Superior Court Clerk
- **PROBATE:** 1831, Probate Judge
- **COURT:** 1810, Superior Court Clerk

TERRELL

Box 525, Dawson, GA 39842, (229) 995-4476,
<terrellcounty-ga.com>
- **INCORPORATED:** Feb. 16, 1856
- **PARENT COUNTY:** Lee, Randolph
- **MARRIAGE RECORDS:** start in 1856, kept by Probate Court
- **DIVORCE:** 1856, Superior Court Clerk
- **LAND:** 1856, Superior Court Clerk
- **PROBATE:** 1856, Probate Court
- **COURT:** 1856, Superior Court Clerk

THOMAS

Box 920, Thomasville, GA 31792, (229) 225-4208
<thomascountyboc.org>
- **INCORPORATED:** Dec. 23, 1825
- **PARENT COUNTIES:** Decatur, Irwin
- **BIRTH RECORDS:** start in 1919, kept by Health Department
- **MARRIAGE:** 1826, Probate Court
- **DIVORCE:** 1919, Superior Court Clerk
- **DEATH:** 1919, Health Department
- **LAND:** 1826, Superior Court Clerk
- **PROBATE:** 1826, Probate Court
- **COURT:** 1826, Superior Court Clerk

TIFT

Box 826, Tifton, GA 31793, (229) 386-7826, **<tiftcounty.org>**
- **INCORPORATED:** Aug. 17, 1905
- **PARENT COUNTIES:** Berrien, Irwin, Worth
- **BIRTH RECORDS:** start in 1919, kept by Health Department
- **MARRIAGE:** 1905, Probate Court
- **DIVORCE:** 1905, Superior Court Clerk
- **DEATH:** 1919, Health Department
- **LAND:** 1905, Superior Court Clerk
- **PROBATE:** 1905, Probate Court
- **COURT:** 1905, Superior Court Clerk

TOOMBS

Box 112., Lyons, GA 30436, (912) 526-3311,
<toombscounty.georgia.gov>
- **INCORPORATED:** Aug. 18, 1905
- **PARENT COUNTIES:** Emanuel, Tattnall, Montgomery
- **BIRTH RECORDS:** start in 1919, kept by Health Department
- **MARRIAGE:** 1905, Probate Court
- **DIVORCE:** 1905, Superior Court Clerk
- **DEATH:** 1919, Health Department
- **BURIAL:** 1905, Probate Court
- **LAND:** 1905, Superior Court Clerk
- **PROBATE:** 1905, Probate Court
- **COURT:** 1905, Superior Court Clerk

TOWNS

48 River St., Hiawassee, GA 30546, (706) 896-2276,
<townscounty.georgia.gov>
- **INCORPORATED:** unknown
- **PARENT COUNTY:** Rabun, Union
- **BIRTH RECORDS:** start in 1919, kept by Health Department
- **MARRIAGE:** 1856, Probate Court
- **DIVORCE:** 1865, Superior Court Clerk
- **DEATH:** 1919, Health Department
- **LAND:** 1856, Superior Court Clerk
- **PROBATE:** 1856, Probate Court
- **COURT:** 1856, Superior Court Clerk
- **MILITARY:** 1865, Superior Court Clerk

TREUTLEN

Box 88, Soperton, GA 30457, (912) 529-3664,
<treutlencounty.georgia.gov>
- **INCORPORATED:** Aug. 21, 1917
- **PARENT COUNTIES:** Emanuel, Montgomery
- **BIRTH RECORDS:** start in 1919, kept by Health Department
- **MARRIAGE:** 1919, Probate Court
- **DIVORCE:** 1919, Superior Court Clerk
- **DEATH:** 1919, Health Department
- **LAND:** 1919, Superior Court Clerk
- **PROBATE:** 1919, Probate Court
- **COURT:** 1919, Superior Court Clerk

TROUP

900 Dallis St., LaGrange, GA 30240, (706) 883-1610,
<troupcountyga.org>
- **INCORPORATED:** Dec. 11, 1826
- **PARENT COUNTY:** Creek Indian Lands
- **BIRTH RECORDS:** start in 1919, kept by Health Department
- **MARRIAGE:** 1828, Probate Court
- **DIVORCE:** 1827, County Archives
- **DEATH:** 1919, Health Department
- **BURIAL:** 1827, County Archives
- **LAND:** 1827, Superior Court Clerk
- **PROBATE:** 1827, Probate Court
- **COURT:** 1827, Superior Court Clerk
- **NOTES:** County Archives has military records 1890-1936 and naturalization records 1843-1908.

TURNER

Box 191, Ashburn, GA 31714, (800) 471-9696,
<turnercounty.com>
- **INCORPORATED:** Aug. 18, 1905
- **PARENT COUNTIES:** Dooly, Irwin, Wilcox, Worth
- **BIRTH RECORDS:** start in 1919, kept by Health Department
- **MARRIAGE:** 1906, Probate Court
- **DIVORCE:** 1906, Superior Court Clerk
- **DEATH:** 1919, Health Department
- **BURIAL:** unknown, Probate Court

- **LAND:** 1906, Superior Court Clerk
- **PROBATE:** 1906, Probate Court
- **COURT:** 1906, Superior Court Clerk

TWIGGS

425 Railroad St., Box 557, Jeffersonville, GA 31044, (478) 945-6563, **<twiggscounty.us>**

- **INCORPORATED:** Dec. 14, 1809
- **PARENT COUNTY:** Wilkinson
- **BIRTH RECORDS:** start in 1919, kept by Health Department
- **MARRIAGE:** 1901, Probate Court
- **DIVORCE:** unknown, Superior Court Clerk
- **DEATH:** 1919, Health Department
- **LAND:** 1901, Superior Court Clerk
- **PROBATE:** 1901, Probate Court
- **COURT:** 1901, Superior Court Clerk

UNION

114 Courthouse St., Box 1, Blairsville, GA 30512, (706) 439-6000, **<unioncountyga.gov>**

- **INCORPORATED:** Dec. 3,1832
- **PARENT COUNTY:** Cherokee
- **BIRTH RECORDS:** start in 1919, kept by Health Department
- **MARRIAGE:** 1833, Probate Court
- **DIVORCE:** unknown, Superior Court Clerk
- **DEATH:** 1919, Health Department
- **LAND:** 1860, Superior Court Clerk
- **PROBATE:** 1851, Probate Court
- **COURT:** 1854, Superior Court Clerk

UPSON

Box 889, Thomaston, GA 30286, (706) 647-7012, **<upsoncountygeorgia.com>**

- **INCORPORATED:** Dec. 15, 1824
- **PARENT COUNTIES:** Crawford, Pike
- **MARRIAGE RECORDS:** start in 1825, kept by Probate Court
- **DIVORCE:** 1825, Superior Court Clerk
- **LAND:** 1825, Superior Court Clerk
- **PROBATE:** 1825, Probate Court
- **COURT:** 1825, Superior Court Clerk

WALKER

Box 445, Lafayette, GA 30728, (706) 638-1437, **<co.walker.ga.us>**

- **INCORPORATED:** Dec. 18, 1833
- **PARENT COUNTY:** Murray
- **BIRTH RECORDS:** start in 1919, kept by Health Department
- **MARRIAGE:** 1883, Probate Court
- **DIVORCE:** 1883, Superior Court Clerk
- **DEATH:** 1919, Health Department
- **LAND:** 1883, Superior Court Clerk
- **PROBATE:** 1883, Probate Court
- **COURT:** 1883, Superior Court Clerk
- **NOTES:** Courthouse fire 1883.

WALTON

Box 585, Monroe, GA 30655, (770) 267-1370, **<waltoncountyga.gov>**

- **INCORPORATED:** Dec. 15, 1818
- **PARENT COUNTY:** Creek Indian Lands
- **BIRTH RECORDS:** start in 1919, kept by Health Department
- **MARRIAGE:** 1825, Probate Court
- **DEATH:** 1919, Health Department
- **DIVORCE:** 1900, Superior Court Clerk
- **LAND:** 1819, Superior Court Clerk
- **PROBATE:** 1820, Probate Court
- **COURT:** 1819, Superior Court Clerk

WARE

Box 1069, Waycross, GA 31502, (912) 287-4300, **<warecounty.com>**

- **INCORPORATED:** Dec. 15, 1824
- **PARENT COUNTY:** Appling
- **MARRIAGE RECORDS:** start in 1874, kept by Probate Court
- **LAND:** 1874, Superior Court Clerk
- **PROBATE:** 1879, Probate Court
- **COURT:** 1874, Superior Court Clerk
- **NOTES:** Records burned 1854.

WARREN

Box 46, Warrenton, GA 30828, (706) 465-2171, **<warrencountyga.com>**

- **INCORPORATED:** Dec. 19, 1793
- **PARENT COUNTIES:** Columbia, Richmond, Wilkes, Burke
- **BIRTH RECORDS:** start in 1919, kept by Health Department
- **MARRIAGE:** 1794, Probate Court
- **DIVORCE:** unknown, Superior Court Clerk
- **DEATH:** 1919, Health Department
- **LAND:** 1796, Superior Court Clerk
- **PROBATE:** 1794, Probate Court
- **COURT:** 1794, Superior Court Clerk

WASHINGTON

Box 308, Sandersville, GA 31082, (478) 552-2325 **<washingtoncounty-ga.com>**

- **INCORPORATED:** Feb.25, 1784
- **PARENT COUNTY:** Creek Indian Lands
- **BIRTH RECORDS:** start in 1919, kept by Health Department
- **MARRIAGE:** 1828, Probate Court
- **DIVORCE:** 1865, Superior Court Clerk
- **LAND:** 1865, Superior Court Clerk
- **PROBATE:** 1865, Probate Court
- **COURT:** 1865, Superior Court Clerk

WAYNE

Box 270, Jesup, GA 31598, (912) 427-5900, **<co.wayne.ga.us>**

- **INCORPORATED:** May 11, 1803
- **PARENT COUNTY:** Creek Indian Lands
- **BIRTH RECORDS:** start in 1919, kept by Health Department
- **MARRIAGE:** 1809, Probate Court
- **DIVORCE:** unknown, Superior Court Clerk
- **DEATH:** 1919, Health Department
- **LAND:** 1809, Superior Court Clerk
- **PROBATE:** 1809, Probate Court
- **COURT:** 1809, Superior Court Clerk

WEBSTER
Box 29, Preston, GA 31824, (229) 828-5775,
<webstercountyga.org>
- **INCORPORATED:** Dec. 16, 1853
- **PARENT COUNTY:** Stewart
- **BIRTH RECORDS:** start in 1919, kept by Health Department
- **MARRIAGE:** 1878, Probate Court
- **DIVORCE:** unknown, Superior Court Clerk
- **DEATH:** 1919, Health Department
- **BURIAL:** unknown, Probate Court
- **LAND:** 1860, Superior Court Clerk
- **PROBATE:** 1854, Probate Court
- **COURT:** 1854, Superior Court Clerk
- **NOTES:** Formerly Kinchafoonee County. Name changed to Webster Feb. 21, 1856.

WHEELER
209 W. Forest Ave., Alamo, GA 30411, (912) 568-7135,
<wheelercounty.georgia.gov>
- **INCORPORATED:** Aug. 14, 1912
- **PARENT COUNTY:** Montgomery
- **BIRTH RECORDS:** start in 1919, kept by Health Department
- **MARRIAGE:** 1913, Probate Court
- **DIVORCE:** 1913, Superior Court Clerk
- **DEATH:** 1919, Health Department
- **LAND:** 1913, Superior Court Clerk
- **PROBATE:** 1913, Probate Court
- **COURT:** 1913, Superior Court Clerk

WHITE
59 S. Main St. Ste. B, Cleveland, GA 30528, (706) 865-2613,
<whitecounty.net>
- **INCORPORATED:** Dec. 22, 1857
- **PARENT COUNTY:** Habersham
- **BIRTH RECORDS:** start in 1919, kept by Health Department
- **MARRIAGE:** 1858, Probate Court
- **DIVORCE:** 1858, Superior Court Clerk
- **DEATH:** 1919, Health Department
- **LAND:** 1858, Superior Court Clerk
- **PROBATE:** 1858, Probate Court
- **COURT:** 1858, Superior Court Clerk

WHITFIELD
Box 868, Dalton, GA 30720, (706) 275-7450,
<whitfieldcountyga.com>
- **INCORPORATED:** Dec. 30, 1851
- **PARENT COUNTY:** Murray
- **BIRTH RECORDS:** start in 1919, kept by Health Department
- **MARRIAGE:** 1852, Probate Court
- **DIVORCE:** 1852, Superior Court Clerk
- **DEATH:** 1919, Health Department
- **LAND:** 1852, Superior Court Clerk
- **PROBATE:** 1852, Probate Court
- **COURT:** 1852, Superior Court Clerk

WILCOX
103 N. Broad St., Abbeville, GA 31001, (229) 467-2640,
<wilcoxcounty.georgia.gov>
- **INCORPORATED:** Dec. 22, 1857
- **PARENT COUNTIES:** Dooly, Irwin, Pulaski
- **BIRTH RECORDS:** start in 1919, kept by Health Department
- **MARRIAGE:** 1858, Probate Court
- **DIVORCE:** 1900, Superior Court Clerk
- **DEATH:** 1919, Health Department
- **LAND:** 1858, Superior Court Clerk
- **PROBATE:** 1858, Probate Court
- **COURT:** 1858, Superior Court Clerk
- **MILITARY:** 1917, Superior Court Clerk

WILKES
23 E. Court St., Ste. 222, Washington, GA 30673, (706) 678-2511,
<washingtonwilkes.com>
- **INCORPORATED:** Feb. 5, 1777
- **PARENT COUNTY:** Creek and Cherokee Indian Lands
- **BIRTH RECORDS:** start in 1919, kept by Health Department
- **MARRIAGE:** 1790, Probate Court
- **DIVORCE:** 1778, Superior Court Clerk
- **DEATH:** 1919, Health Department
- **LAND:** 1777, Superior Court Clerk
- **PROBATE:** 1777, Probate Court
- **COURT:** 1778, Superior Court Clerk

WILKINSON
Box 161, Irwinton, GA 31042, (478) 946-2236,
<wilkinsoncounty.net>
- **INCORPORATED:** May 11, 1803
- **PARENT COUNTY:** Creek Indian Lands
- **MARRIAGE RECORDS:** start in 1854, kept by Probate Court
- **LAND:** 1855, Superior Court Clerk
- **PROBATE:** 1854, Probate Court
- **NOTES:** Courthouse fires in 1852 and 1924; land records saved in 1924. Clerk of Superior Court has some records from 1852.

WORTH
201 N. Main St., Sylvester, GA 31791, (229) 776-8200,
<worthcounty.com>
- **INCORPORATED:** Dec.20, 1853
- **PARENT COUNTIES:** Dooly, Irwin
- **BIRTH RECORDS:** start in 1919, kept by Health Department
- **MARRIAGE:** 1854, Probate Court
- **DIVORCE:** unknown, Superior Court Clerk
- **DEATH:** 1919, Health Department
- **LAND:** 1892, Superior Court Clerk
- **PROBATE:** 1879, Probate Court
- **COURT:** 1879, Superior Court Clerk

HAWAII

» BY DAVID A. FRYXELL

HISTORICAL OVERVIEW

No one who's visited the islands of Hawaii should be surprised that the world's great powers vied for this tropical paradise for centuries after its discovery by Europeans. Spanish sailors visited in 1627, but it was Captain James Cook who put Hawaii on the map with his third voyage; he was killed at Kealakekua Bay in 1779. Britain claimed Hawaii in 1794, though that didn't deter incursions by the Russians in 1815 and the French in 1849.

Missionary fervor rather than imperialism sparked early American visits. Protestant missionaries came in 1820 and eventually codified the written Hawaiian language. Mormon missionaries began making numerous converts after 1850.

King Kamehameha I established a monarchy in 1810 that survived until 1893. After a short-lived republic, Hawaii was annexed by the United States in 1898 and became a territory in 1900. The islands' modern face—sugar and pineapple crops, plus tourism—began to take shape soon after. Chinese laborers had been coming as early as 1852 to work on plantations, followed by Japanese beginning in 1865. The 1876 Reciprocity Act opened American sugar markets to Hawaiian growers. But James Drummond Dole's creation of a pineapple plantation in 1901 signaled a new day for Hawaii. In 1903, a Joint Tourism Committee began promoting Hawaii to the world; the first flight from San Francisco arrived in 1935.

Hawaii burst into the awareness of all Americans with the 1941 Japanese attack on Pearl Harbor. As the islands became a staging ground for the US response, the way was paved for Hawaii to become the 50th state in 1959. Today, Hawaii combines vibrant native culture with Western and Asian influences. Asian and Pacific populations added to this mix in the 1960s include Koreans, Filipinos, Tongans and Samoans.

RECORD HIGHLIGHTS

Parts of Hawaii were enumerated well before it became a territory, and microfilm of these censuses is available through the Family History Library (FHL), including 1840 to 1843 (index only), 1866 (fragment), 1878 (island of Hawaii), 1890 and 1896 (Oahu). The 1900 census was the first federal census to cover the new territory.

research tips

- Written records for native Hawaiians date only to the early 1800s, but some family histories contain traditional oral genealogies so it's possible, though rare, to link to pre-European contact ancestors.
- The 1900 census was the first federal census of the area, but parts of Hawaii were enumerated before it became a territory. Microfilm of these censuses is available through the FHL.
- Vital records at the state archives cover 1832 to 1949, and marriage records housed there cover 1826 to 1929.
- Land records didn't exist in Hawaii until 1840.

CENSUS RECORDS

- Federal census: 1900, 1910, 1920, 1930
- Royal census enumerations of the Kingdom of Hawaii: 1866 (mostly Maui), 1878, 1890, 1896 (part of Honolulu only)

You can fill in some blanks in 19th-century Hawaiian enumerations using two groups of files in the state archives loosely labeled "census." These files, covering 1840 to 1866 (available on FHL microfilm) and 1847 to 1896, include records such as school census statistics, population census statistics, and summaries of births, marriages and deaths.

For such a new state, Hawaii's vital records go back a long way, beginning with records kept by missionaries from 1826. Vital records at the state archives cover 1832 to 1949. Official birth and death records began in 1853, though records at the state health department are incomplete prior to 1896. Marriage records collected at the state archives cover 1826 to

1929 and are indexed to 1910. For copies of records held at the state level, write to the State Department of Health, Office of Health Status Monitoring, Vital Records Section, Box 3378, Honolulu, Hawaii 96801.

An important addition to Hawaii's vital records is the delayed birth record. Kathy McConnell DeFoster, librarian at the National Society Daughters of the American Revolution Aloha Chapter Memorial Library and treasurer of the Honolulu County Genealogical Society, calls these "an absolute gift" to researchers. As DeFoster explains it, a birth certificate could be created by the state for those lacking one through testimony from relatives, friends, and/or neighbors. These records are sometimes several pages long and may contain pictures and/or signatures of the applicant. "Many are veritable treasure troves of genealogical information—everything you wanted to know about your family in their own words," she says. Although the primary focus is on the applicant, these records often also include information on siblings and parents. Most are from the late 1890s to the 1920s. The FHL has 70 reels of microfilm of delayed birth records from 1859 to 1903, with indexes covering 1859 to 1938, plus 132 reels for 1904 to 1925.

Land records didn't exist in Hawaii until 1840; the king owned all the land. Foreign influences led to the 1845 creation of a land commission, which recorded almost 12,000 claims between 1848 and 1852. Many of these and subsequent records have been microfilmed by the FHL.

Hawaii also has its own immigration records, with passenger lists from 1843 to 1900 available on microfilm. Note that separate indexes as well as some entirely separate entry records exist according to nationality of origin: Chinese, Japanese and Portuguese.

Your challenges in tracing ancestors in Hawaii will vary depending on your ancestry, says to DeFoster. If you descend from Hawaiian royalty or early missionaries, who came mainly from New England and New York, the task is fairly simple, as most records have been preserved. If your search is for a Hawaiian commoner or for ancestors of Asian immigrants, however, DeFoster warns your search can be very difficult. In addition to the language barrier, she notes, you'll have to deal with the practice of changing names, in the case of many Asians, and the problem of not having surnames, in the case of Hawaiians before the latter part of the 1800s.

DeFoster cites an example of a woman of Japanese ancestry: When the woman's grandparents married in Hawaii, her grandfather took his wife's surname. She doesn't know the names of her grandmother's parents or her grandfather's original name. In such cases, DeFoster recommends the state library's collection of vital records in its Hawaiiana section. Since the woman knows when her grandparents married, information at the library may give her the record number that she can then take to the Department of Health for a copy of the marriage application.

When researching native Hawaiians, DeFoster says, keep in mind that written records on the native population date only to the early 1800s. Some family histories, however, contain traditional oral genealogies, so in rare cases it's possible to link to pre-European contact ancestors.

ARCHIVES, LIBRARIES, AND SOCIETIES

Bernice P. Bishop Museum Library
1525 Bernice St., Honolulu, HI 96817, (808) 848-4148, **<bishopmuseum.org>**

Bureau of Conveyances
1151 Punchbowl St., Room 120, Honolulu, HI 96813, (808) 587-0147, **<hawaii.gov/dlnr/boc>**

Friends of Moku'ula
505 Front St., Suite 221, Lahaina, Maui, HI 96761, (808) 661-3659, **<mokuula.com>**

Hawaii Chinese History Center
111 N. King St., Suite 410, Honolulu, HI 96817, (808) 536-5948

Hawaii County Genealogical Society
Box 831, Keaau, HI 96749

Hawaii Maritime Center
Pier 7, Honolulu Harbor, Honolulu, HI 96813, (808) 523-6151, **<holoholo.org/maritime>**

Hawaii State Archives
Kekauluohi Building, Iolani Palace Grounds, Honolulu, HI 96813, (808) 586-0329, **<hawaii.gov/dags/archives>**

Hawaii State Department of Health
Box 3378, Honolulu, HI 96801, (808) 586-4533, **<hawaii.gov/health/vital-records/vital-records/index.html>**

Hawaii State Library
478 S. King St., Honolulu, HI 96813, (808) 586-3500, **<librarieshawaii.org>**

Hawaiian Historical Society
560 Kawaiahao St., Honolulu, HI 96813, (808) 537-6271, **<hawaiianhistory.org>**

Honolulu County Genealogical Society
Box 235039, Honolulu, HI 96823, **<rootsweb.ancestry.com/~hihcgs>**

Kapi'olani Community College Library Char Asian-Pacific Study Room
4303 Diamond Head Rd., Honolulu, HI 96816, (808) 734-9757, **<library.kcc.hawaii.edu/main/char/index.htm>**

Kaua'i Historical Society
Box 1778, Lihue'e, HI 96766, (808) 245-3373, **<kauaihistoricalsociety.org>**

Kona Historical Society
Box 398, Captain Cook, HI 96704, (808) 323-3222, **<konahistorical.org>**

Land Court
777 Punchbowl St., Honolulu, HI 96813, (808) 539-4777, **<courts.state.hi.us/index.jsp>**

Lyman House Museum and Mission House
276 Haili St., Hilo, HI 96720, (808) 935-5021, **<lymanmuseum.org>**

Maui Genealogical Society
38A Alania Place, Kihei, HI 96753

HAWAII
Hawaii
Honuapo Bay
Kawaihae Bay
Alenuihaha Channel
Maui
Pailolo Channel
Kealaikahiki Channel
Kahoolawe
Lanai
Kalohi Channel
Molokai
MAUI
Kaiwi Channel
Honolulu
Oahu
HONOLULU
Kauai Channel
Pacific Ocean
Kauai
KAUAI
Kaulakahi Channel
Niihau

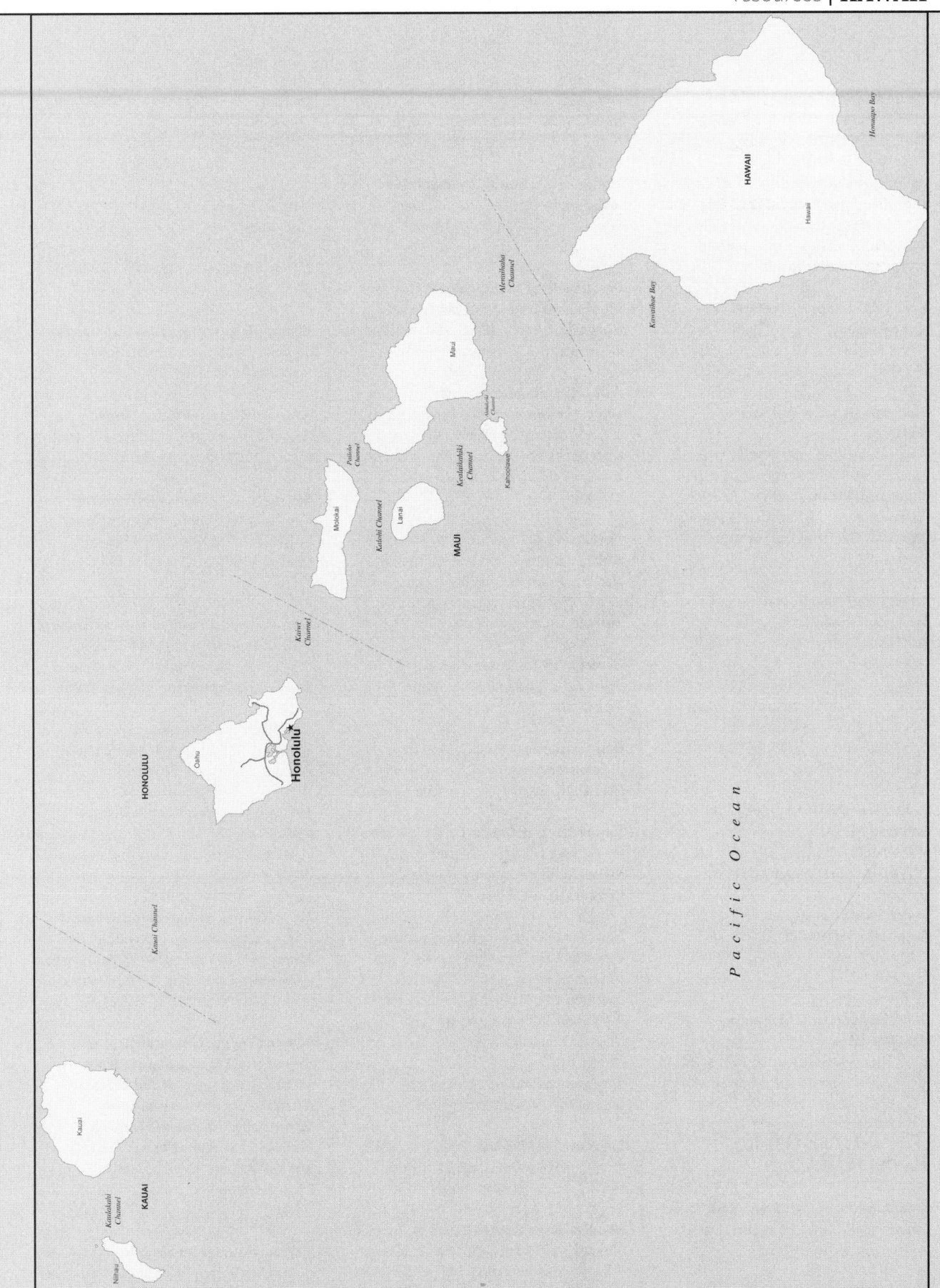

Maui Historical Society
2375-A Main St., Wailuku, HI 96793, (808) 244-3326, **<mauimuseum.org>**

National Archives and Records Administration, Pacific Region
1000 Commodore Dr., San Bruno, CA 94066, (650) 238-3500, **<archives.gov/pacific/san-francisco>**

National Memorial Cemetery of the Pacific
2177 Puowaina Dr., Honolulu, HI 96813, (808) 532-3720

Okinawan Genealogical Society of Hawaii
Hawaii Okinawa Center, 94-587 Ukee St., Waipahu, HI 96797, (808) 676-5400, **<huoa.org/kizuna/archives/clubs/okinawangenealogicalsocietyofhawaii/OkinawanGenealogicalSocietyOfHawaii.html>**

Portuguese Genealogical Society of Hawaii
2117 Doris Naumu., Pearl City, HI 96782,, (808) 845-1616

Roman Catholic Diocese of Honolulu
Chancery Office, 1184 Bishop St., Honolulu HI 96813, (808) 533-1791, **<catholichawaii.org>**

Joseph F. Smith Library, Bringham Young University-Hawaii
55-220 Kulanui St., Laie, HI 96762, (808) 675-3878, **<library.byuh.edu>**

United Puerto Rican Association of Hawaii
1249 N. School St., Honolulu, HI 96817, (808) 847-2751

University of Hawaii at Manoa, Hamilton Library
2550 The Mall, Honolulu, HI 96822, (808) 956-7214, **<library.manoa.hawaii.edu>**

GENERAL RESOURCES

Buddhism in Hawaii: Its Impact on a Yankee Community by Louise H. Hunter (University of Hawaii Press, 1971)

Chinese Genealogy and Family Book Guide: Hawaiian and Chinese Sources by Jean B. Ohai (Hawaii Chinese History Center, 1975)

The Chinese in Hawaii: an Annotated Bibliography by Nancy Foon Young (Social Science Research Institute, University of Hawaii, 1973)

Descendants of New England Protestant Missionaries to the Sandwich Islands (Hawaiian Islands), 1820-1900 compiled by R.G. Rigler (G.R. Greenwood, 1984)

A Directory of Libraries and Information Sources in Hawaii and the Pacific Islands, revised edition, compiled by Arlene DC Luster, edited by Yvonne Bartko and Beth Madinger (Hawaii Library Association, 1977)

The Filipinos in Hawaii: an Annotated Bibliography by Ruben R. Alcantara with Nancy S. Alconcel, John Berger, and Cesar Wycoo (Social Sciences and Linguistics Institute, University of Hawaii, 1977)

Genealogical Sources in Hawaii by Agnes C. Conrad (Hawaii Library Association, 1987)

Hawaii Genealogy Project: Directory of Secondary Sources by Jean Kadooka Mardfin (Office of Hawaiian Affairs, 1993)

Hawaii Research Outline by The Church of Jesus Christ of Latter-day Saints (online at **<www.familysearch.org/eng/search/RG/guide/hawaii.asp>**)

Hawaiian Genealogies: Extracted from Hawaiian Language Newspapers, 2 vols. by Edith Kawelohea McKinzie, edited by Ishmael W. Stagner, II (Institute for Polynesian Studies, Brigham Young University-Hawaii Campus, ca. 1986)

The Hawaiian Journal of History vols. 1, (Hawaiian Historical Society, 1967-)

The Hawaiian Kingdom, 3 vols.by Ralph S. Kuykendall (University of Hawaii, 1938-1967)

Hawaiian Newspapers by Esther K. Mookini (Topgallant Publishing Co., 1974)

Hawaiian Royal Genealogies: Charts and Comments by His Royal and Imperial Majesty, the Oukah, Emperor of Tsalagi, the Cherokee Nations (Triskelion Press, 1988)

Hawaii's People, 4th ed. by Andrew W. Lind (University Press of Hawaii, ca. 1980)

Hawaii's Religions by John F. Mulholland (C.E. Tuttle Co., 1970)

History Makers of Hawaii: a Biographical Dictionary by Arthur Grove Day (Mutual Publishing of Hawaii, 1984)

An Island Kingdom Passes: Hawaii Becomes American by Kathleen Dickenson Mellen (Hastings House, 1958)

The Japanese in Hawaii, 1868-1967: a Bibliography of the First Hundred Years by Mitsugu Matsuda (Social Science Research Institute, University of Hawaii, 1968)

Kanyaku Imin: a Hundred Years of Japanese Life in Hawaii edited by Leonard Lueras, designed by Kunio Hayashi (International Savings and Loan Association, ca. 1985)

Ke Au Okoa weekly newspaper, 8 vols. edited by J.M. Kapena 1870-1873 (Hale Paipalapala Aupuni, 1865-1873)

The Koreans in Hawaii: an Annotated Bibliography by Arthur L. Gardner (Social Science Institute, University of Hawaii, 1970)

Men of Hawaii: a Biographical Reference Library, Complete and Authentic, of the Men of Note and Substantial Achievement in the Hawaiian Islands, 9 vols. (Honolulu Star-Bulletin, limited, 1917-1972)

Men and Women of Hawaii: 1954, a Biographical Encyclopedia of Persons of Notable Achievement and Historical Account of the Peoples who have Distinguished Themselves Through Personal Success and through Public Service by Henry P. Judd, edited by Perry Edward Hilleary (Business Consultants, 1954)

Moramona: the Mormons in Hawaii by R. Lanier Britsch (Institute for Polynesian Studies, ca. 1989)

Notable Women of Hawaii edited by Barbara Bennett Peterson (University of Hawaii press, ca. 1984)

The Pacific Islands, 3rd edition by Douglas L. Oliver, illustrations by Sheila Mitchell Oliver (University of Hawaii Press, ca. 1989)

The Peopling of Hawaii by Eleanor C. Nordyke (University Press of Hawaii, ca. 1977)

Portraits of American Protestant Missionaries to Hawaii published by the Hawaiian Mission Children's Society (Hawaiian Gazette Co., 1901)

Portuguese-Hawaiian Memories by J. F. Freitas (Portuguese Genealogical Society of Hawaii, ca. 1992)

Target Your Hawaiian Genealogy, and Others as Well: a Family Guide by Maria Kaina (Hawaii State Public Library System, 1991)

Under Hawaiian Skies: a Narrative of the Romance, Adventure and History of the Hawaiian Islands by Albert Pierce Taylor (Advertiser Publishing Co., ltd., 1926)

Voyages to Hawaii Before 1860: a Record based on Historical Narratives in the Libraries of the Hawaiian Mission Children's Society and the Hawaiian Historical Society, Extended to March 1860 by Bernice Judd, edited by Helen Yonge Llind (University Press of Hawaii for Hawaiian Mission Children's Society, 1974)

LAND RECORDS

The Great Mahele: Hawaii's Land Division of 1848 by Jon J. Chinen (University of Hawaii Press, 1958)

Native American Estate: the Struggle Over Indian and Hawaiian Lands by Linda S. Parker (University of Hawaii Press, ca. 1989)

MAPS

Atlas of Hawaii, 3rd edition edited by Sonia P. Juvik and Hames O. Juvik, chief cartographer Thomas R. Paradise University of Hawaii Press, ca. 1998)

A Gazetteer of the Territory of Hawaii compiled by John Wesley Coulter (University of Hawaii, 1935)

Hawaiian Geographic Names compiled by W.D. Alexander (Government Printing Office, 1903)

Hawaiian Islands: Official Standard Names Approved by the United States Board on Geographic Names (US Office of Geography, 1956)

Place Names of Hawaii, revised edition by Mary Kawena Pukui, Samuel H. Elbert, and Esther T. Mookini (University Press of Hawaii, 1974)

Leslie's Official History of the Spanish-American War: a Pictorial and Descriptive Record of the Cuban Rebellion, the Causes that Involved the United States, and a Complete Narrative of our conflict with Spain on Land and Sea, Supplemented with Fullest Information Respecting Cuba, Porto Rico, the Philippines and Hawaii., (Leslie's Weekly, 1899)

MILITARY RECORDS

Unlikely Liberators: the Men of the 100th and 442d by Masayo Umezawa Duus, translated by Peter Duus (University of Hawaii Press, ca. 1987)

VITAL RECORDS

Hawaiian Cemetery Records, 2 vols., typed by Mrs. Jessie H. Lindsey, and the Hawaiian Mission, 1942-1954

Index to burial records of Lockview Cemetery: Pearl City, Island of Oahu, Hawaii, 1901-1937 compiled by Hawaii Archives Division (Hawaii State Archives, 1991)

Index to burial records of Makiki Cemetery: Honolulu, island of Oahu, Hawaii, 1896-1954 compiled by Hawaii Archives Division (Hawaii State Archives, 1991)

Tombstone Inscriptions from the Royal Mausoleum by George Olin Zabriskie (n.p., 1969)

COUNTY DETAILS

HAWAII

25 Aupuni St., Hilo, HI 96720, (808) 961-8255, **<hawaii-county.com>**

- **INCORPORATED:** 1905
- **PARENT COUNTY:** Original county
- **BIRTH RECORDS:** start in 1853, kept by Health Department
- **DIVORCE:** 1951, Health Department
- **DEATH:** 1853, Health Department
- **LAND:** unknown, Health Department
- **PROBATE:** unknown, Health Department
- **WILLS:** unknown, Health Department
- **NOTES:** State Health Department has marriage records 1826-1929.

HONOLULU

530 S. King St., Honolulu, HI 96813, (808) 547-7000, **<honolulu.gov>**

- **INCORPORATED:** 1905
- **PARENT COUNTY:** Original county
- **BIRTH RECORDS:** start in 1853, kept by Health Department
- **MARRIAGE:** unknown, Health Department
- **DIVORCE:** 1951, Health Department
- **DEATH:** 1853, Health Department
- **LAND:** unknown, Health Department
- **PROBATE:** unknown, Health Department
- **WILLS:** unknown, Health Department

KALAWAO

- **INCORPORATED:** 1905
- **NOTES:** Kalawao County was created in 1905 along with the other four original counties, but has been politically absorbed by Maui County. Maui does not claim jurisdiction over the villages of Kalaupapa, Kalawao, or Waikolu. Contact the State Health Department or Maui County for Kalawao records.

KAUAI

4444 Rice St., Ste. 235, Lihue, HI 96766, (808) 241-4900, **<kauaigov.gov>**

- **INCORPORATED:** 1905
- **PARENT COUNTY:** Original county
- **BIRTH RECORDS:** start in 1853, kept by Health Department
- **MARRIAGE:** unknown, Health Department
- **DIVORCE:** 1951, Health Department
- **DEATH:** 1853, Health Department
- **LAND:** unknown, Health Department
- **PROBATE:** unknown, Health Department
- **WILLS:** unknown, Health Department

MAUI

200 S. High St., Wailuku, HI 96793, (808) 270-7171, **<co.maui.hi.us>**

- **INCORPORATED:** 1905
- **PARENT COUNTY:** Original county
- **BIRTH RECORDS:** start in 1853, kept by Health Department
- **MARRIAGE:** unknown, Health Department
- **DIVORCE:** 1951, Health Department
- **DEATH:** 1853, Health Department
- **LAND:** unknown, Health Department
- **PROBATE:** unknown, Health Department
- **WILLS:** unknown, Health Department

IDAHO

» BY DAVID A. FRYXELL

HISTORICAL OVERVIEW

Though native peoples came to Idaho as long as 14,000 years ago, it wasn't until after the Louisiana Purchase in 1803 that Europeans and Americans to explored the area, beginning with Lewis and Clark in 1805. Fur traders dominated the early 19th century, establishing Fort Henry—the first American fur-trading post west of the Rockies—in 1810. Henry H. Spalding planted Idaho's first potatoes in 1836, though agriculture wouldn't be the leading industry until after 1900.

Pioneers began crossing Idaho on the Oregon Trail in 1843 and then, with the 1849 gold rush, on the California Trail. After Idaho's mineral riches were discovered in 1860, people started coming to stay. Mining took over as the largest industry and in 1863, Idaho became a territory. The Idaho Territory included all of today's Montana and most of Wyoming.

Jobs in mines drew waves of immigrants—first Chinese, then Welsh and Eastern Europeans. After the Civil War, Idaho also attracted many defeated Confederates. Subsequent migrations brought Scandinavians, Japanese and Basques. They formed a sometimes-uneasy melting pot with the Mormon settlers who'd dominated eastern Idaho since the state's first permanent settlement at Franklin in 1860.

Native tribes—including the Shoshone, Snake, Nez Perce, Bannock and Sheepeater—resisted white settlement, sparking a series of wars from 1863 to 1879. Defeated, the tribes were eventually relocated to reservations. If you have native roots here, records of Idaho's various Indian agencies and schools are available at the state historical society and the National Archives' Pacific-Alaska regional facility in Seattle, as well as on Family History Library (FHL) microfilm.

Idaho had an unusually long road to statehood, finally joining the union in 1890. Its post-statehood settlement was fueled in part by silver mining—the Coeur d'Alene mining district, first tapped in 1884, became the nation's richest source of silver—and by timber, with the United States' largest sawmill opening in Potlatch in 1906. Today Idaho is again enjoying a population boom. A new rush of migration from disenchanted Californians and others attracted to its low-key lifestyle and natural beauty has made Idaho one of the fastest-growing states.

research tips

- In Idaho, it's best to look for information in the county where the event occurred—contact county clerks and read through old newspapers.
- The Western States Historical Marriage Record Index **<abish.byui.edu/specialCollections/westernStates/search.cfm>** includes nearly all recorded pre-1900 Idaho marriages.
- The Idaho Death Index, which covers the years 1911-1951, can be found free on the Idaho GenWeb site **<www.rootsweb.ancestry.com/~idgenweb/deaths/search.htm>**. The actual death records are on microfilm at the Idaho State Historical Library and Archives (1911 through 1937) or can be ordered from the Idaho Vital Records Office in Boise.
- Most Idaho land records are kept by the National Archives in Seattle and by the Bureau of Land Management in Boise **<www.vitalrec.com/id.html>**

CENSUS RECORDS

- Federal census: 1850 (Oregon Territory), 1860 (Washington Territory), 1870, 1880, 1900, 1910, 1920, 1930
- Federal mortality schedules: 1870, 1880

RECORD HIGHLIGHTS

Idaho's protracted territorial period meant it was covered by the 1850 Oregon Territory census, the 1860 Washington Territory census (in Spokane County), and 1870 and 1880 Idaho Territory enumerations. Parts of southern Idaho were also included in the 1860 and 1870 censuses of Cache County, Utah. The earliest extant US census as a state is that of 1900.

Be aware of shifting county boundaries—and even disappearing counties, such as Alturas. Juvanne Martin, CGRS, owner of the Research Network and Idaho Connections and Southwest Coordinator of the Idaho Chapter of the Association of Professional Genealogists, advises, "Know when each of the 44 Idaho counties were formed, including the counties that no longer exist. For instance, Canyon County started March 7, 1891. Before that time, it was part of Ada County. Thus, records for the Caldwell/Nampa area would be filed in Boise." She recommends several web sites for tracing Idaho's counties: Idaho State Homepage **<accessidaho.org/aboutidaho/county>**, Idaho GenWeb **<rootsweb.ancestry.com/~idgenweb>**, and a page on her site **<researchnetwork.net/idaho/idaholinks.shtml>**.

Idaho was also a latecomer to statewide vital records. Birth and death registrations were first required on the county level in 1907, switching to a state responsibility in 1911. Statewide marriage and divorce records didn't commence until 1947. Earlier records were sometimes kept by churches, midwives or physicians, and mortuaries or, for marriages, the person performing the ceremony or making a marriage contract.

Cemetery records may offer clues when death records are unavailable: Volunteers from the Church of Jesus Christ of Latter-day Saints have transcribed records for cemeteries representing most Idaho counties. These are available in a set of 12 books or on five microfilm reels from the FHL.

Land records can also be useful in this public-lands state. Records from the land offices in Boise, Blackfoot, Hailey, Lewiston, Coeur d'Alene and Oxford (later known as Blackfoot) are at the National Archives in Seattle and the Bureau of Land Management in Boise. The FHL has microfilmed land records covering 1868 to 1913 on 23 reels. A patent search is available through the Bureau of Land Management's web site **<glorecords.blm.gov>**. For county land records, she says, you can consult microfilm at the state historical society library or contact the assessor's office at each county courthouse.

The biggest challenge facing Idaho researchers, Martin warns, is documenting sources prior to the state's requirement to file vital records. Her suggestion is to look for information in the county where the event occurred. In addition to contacting county clerks, use old newspapers as a source. Fortunately, Idaho enjoys well-preserved collections of early newspapers in both the Idaho State Historical Society Library and Archives and the University of Idaho's library. You can borrow microfilm of these historic newspapers via interlibrary loan. For a list of early Idaho newspapers on microfilm, see **<db.lib.uidaho.edu/news/microfilm.php3>**.

The Internet can also help with vital records, Martin notes. The Idaho Death Index, covering 1911 to 1951, with deaths listed by surname, is the Idaho GenWeb site **<rootsweb.ancestry.com/~idgenweb/deaths/search.htm>** and on subscription site Ancestry.com. Once you've found an ancestor, you can view the death records on microfilm at the Idaho State Historical Library and Archives (1911 through 1937) or order copies from the Idaho Vital Records Office in Boise.

Another useful site, Martin adds, is the Western States Historical Marriage Record Index **<abish.byui.edu/specialCollections/westernStates/search.cfm>**, which covers an enormous collection of early marriage records housed at Brigham Young University-Idaho's library in Rexburg. Virtually all pre-1900 Idaho marriages with available records are included, and many Idaho counties have been extracted into the 1930s or later. Once you've identified an ancestor in the index, look for the record on microfilm at the Idaho State Historical Society Library or by contacting the county clerk where the marriage was recorded.

☞ ARCHIVES, LIBRARIES, AND SOCIETIES

Adams County Historical Society
Box 352, New Meadows, ID 83654

Albertson College Library
2112 Cleveland Blvd., Caldwell, ID 83605, (208) 459-5505, **<collegeofidaho.edu>**

Bannock County Historical Society
300 Alvord Loop, Box 253, Pocatello, ID 83204, (208) 233-0434

Bonner County Genealogical Society
611 South Ella Ave., Sandpoint, ID 83864, **<bonnercountyhistory.org>**

Bonneville County Historical Society
200 N. Eastern Ave., Idaho Falls, ID 83402, (208) 522-1400, **<.museumofidaho.org/BCHS.php>**

Boundary County Historical Society
7229 Main St., Bonners Ferry, ID 83805, **<bonnersferrymuseum.org>**

Caldwell Genealogical Group
3504 S. Illinois St., Caldwell, ID 83605

Camas County Historical Society
General Delivery, Fairfield, ID 83327

Canyon County Historical Society and Museum
1200 Front St., Box 595, Nampa, ID 83651, (208) 467-7611

Caribou County Historical Society
290 W. Third S., Soda Springs, ID 83276, (208) 547-3506

Cascade Public Library
105 Front St., Box 10, Cascade, ID 83611, (208) 382-4757

Cassis County Historical Society
Box 331, Burley, ID 83318, (208) 678-7172

Clearwater County Historical Society
315 College Ave., Box 1154, Orofino, ID 83544, (208) 476-5033

Eagle Rock Railroad Historical Society
Box 2685, Idaho Falls, ID 83404, (208) 522-3125, **<ida.net/org/errhsi>**

Elmore County Historical Foundation
180 S. Third E., Box 204, Mountain Home, ID 83647, (208) 587-9041

Gem County Historical Society
501 E. First, Box 312, Emmett, ID 83617, (208) 365-9530

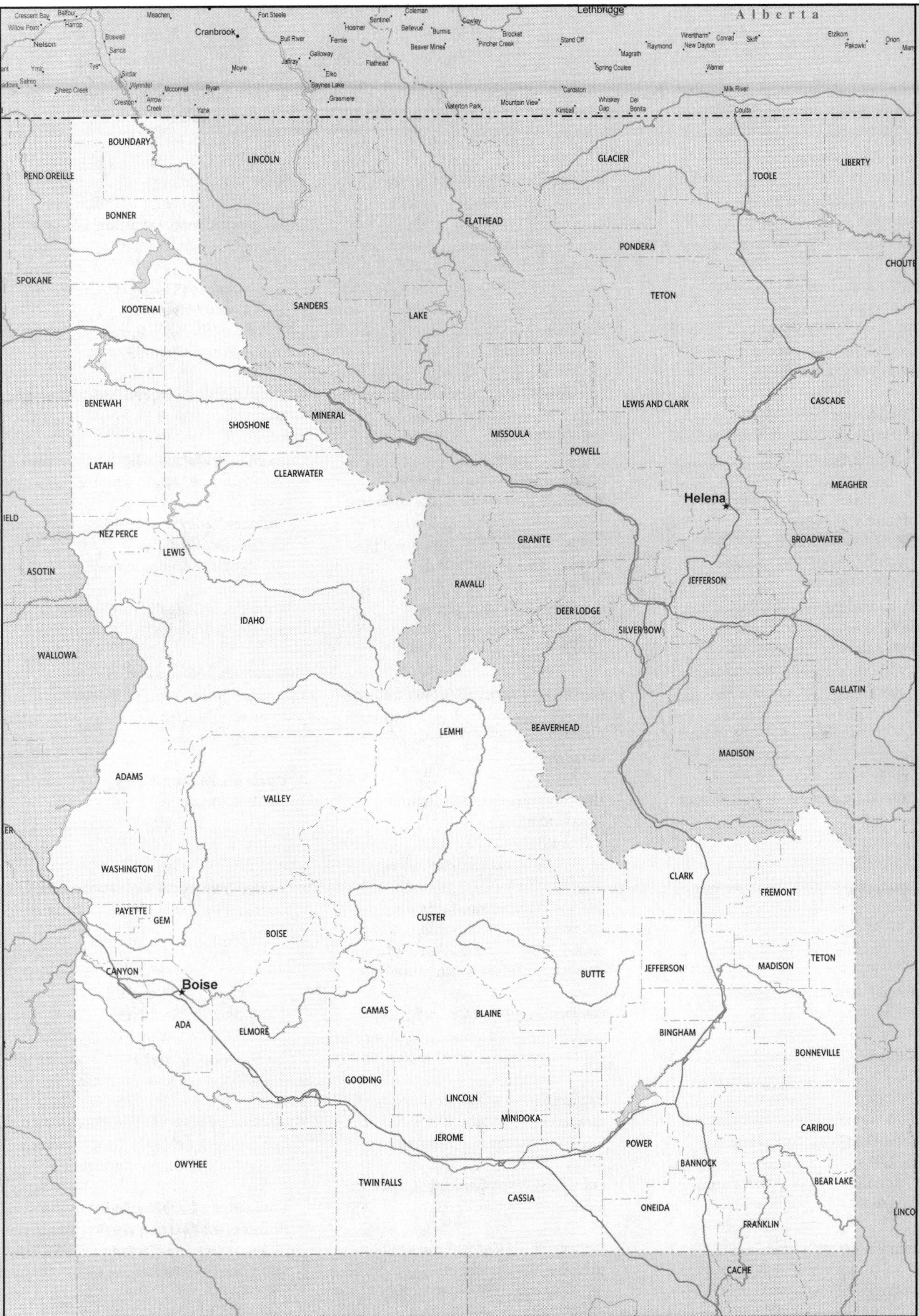
Lethbridge
Alberta
Cranbrook
Nelson
Helena
Boise
BOUNDARY
PEND OREILLE
BONNER
SPOKANE
KOOTENAI
LINCOLN
SANDERS
LAKE
FLATHEAD
GLACIER
TOOLE
LIBERTY
PONDERA
TETON
CHOUTE
BENEWAH
SHOSHONE
MINERAL
MISSOULA
POWELL
LEWIS AND CLARK
CASCADE
MEAGHER
LATAH
CLEARWATER
NEZ PERCE
LEWIS
ASOTIN
GRANITE
RAVALLI
JEFFERSON
BROADWATER
IDAHO
DEER LODGE
SILVER BOW
WALLOWA
GALLATIN
LEMHI
BEAVERHEAD
MADISON
ADAMS
VALLEY
WASHINGTON
CLARK
FREMONT
PAYETTE
GEM
CUSTER
BOISE
CANYON
BUTTE
JEFFERSON
MADISON
TETON
ADA
CAMAS
BLAINE
ELMORE
BINGHAM
BONNEVILLE
GOODING
LINCOLN
MINIDOKA
JEROME
POWER
CARIBOU
OWYHEE
BANNOCK
BEAR LAKE
TWIN FALLS
CASSIA
ONEIDA
FRANKLIN
CACHE
LINCO

Idaho Department of Health and Welfare
450 W. State St., Box 83720,
Boise, ID 83720, (208) 334-5500,
<healthandwelfare.idaho.gov>

Idaho Genealogical Society
Box 1854, Boise, ID 83701,
(208) 384-0542, **<idahogenealogy.org>**

Idaho State Historical Society and Library
1109 Main St., Suite 250, Boise, ID 83702,
(208) 334-2682 , **<idahohistory.net/index.html>**

Idaho State Library
325 W. State St., Boise, ID 83702, (208)
334-2150, **<lili.org>**

Idaho State Office of the Bureau of Land Management
1387 S. Vinnell Way, Boise, ID 83709,
(208) 373-4000, **<id.blm.gov>**

Idaho State University, Eli M. Oboler Library
850 S. Ninth St., Pocatello, ID 83209, (208)
282-2958, **<isu.edu/library/home.htm>**

Ilo-Volmer Historical Society
Box 61, Craigmont, ID 83523, (208) 924-5474

Jefferson County Historical Society
Box 284, Rigby, ID, 83442, (208) 745-8423

Jerome County Historical Society
220 N. Lincoln, Box 50, Jerome,
ID 83338, (208) 324-2711,
<historicaljeromecounty.com>

Kamiah Genealogical Society
Box 322, Kamiah, ID 83536

Kootenai County Genealogical Society
8385 N. Government Way, Hayden, ID
83835

Latah County Historical Society
327 E. Second St., Moscow, ID 83843,
(208) 882-1004, **<users.Moscow.com/lchs>**

Lemhi County Historical Society
Box 645, Salmon, ID 83467, (208) 756-3342, **<lemhimuseum.org>**

Lewis-Clark State College Library
500 Eighth Ave., Lewiston, ID 83501, (208)
792-2396, **<lcsc.edu/library>**

Lewis County Historical Society
Route 2, Box 10, Kamiah, ID 83536

Luna House Historical Museum, and Nez Perce County Historical Society
0306 Third St., Lewiston, ID 83501, (208)
743-2535, **<lctoday.net/cultural/Museums/nez_perce_county_museum.htm>**

Minidoka County Historical Society
Box 21, Rupert, ID 83350, (208) 436-0336,
<minidoka.id.us>

National Archives and Records Administration, Pacific Alaska Region
6125 Sand Point Way NE, Seattle, WA
98115, (206) 336-5115, **<archives.gov/pacific-alaska/seattle>**

Nez Perce Historical Society
0306 Third St., Lewiston, ID 83501,
<npchistsoc.org>

North Idaho College, Molstead library
1000 W. Garden Ave., Coeur d'Alene, ID
83814, (208) 769-3355, **<nic.edu/library>**

Northwest Nazarene College, John E. Riley Library
623 Holly, Nampa, ID 83686, (208) 467-8607, **<nnu.edu/academics/library>**

Old Fort Boise Historical Society
Old Fort Boise Park, Box 608, Parma, ID
83660, (208) 722-8181, **<stepintohistory.com/states/id/ft_boise.htm>**

Owyhee County Historical Society
Box 67, Murphy, ID 83660, (208) 495-2319, **<owyhee.county.net/museum>**

Payette County Historical Society
90 S. Ninth St., Payette, ID 83661, (208)
642-4883, **<payette.govoffice.com>**

Pocatello Branch Genealogical Society
Box 4272, Pocatello, ID 83201

Pullman, Washington Branch Genealogical Library
865 Bitterroot, Moscow, ID 84843

Roman Catholic Chancery Office, Diocese of Boise
1501 S. Federal Way, Ste. 400,
Boise, ID 83705, (208) 342-1311 ,
<catholicidaho.org>

Shoshone County Genealogical Society
Box 183, Kellogg, ID 83837

South Bannock County Historical Society and Museum
110 E. Main St., Box 387, Lava Hot Springs,
ID 83246, (208) 776-5254

South Custer County Historical Society
Box 355, Mackay, ID 83251

Spirit Lake Historical Society
Box 186, Spirit Lake, ID 83869

Treasure Valley Chapter of the Idaho Genealogical Society
325 W. State St., Boise, ID 83702

Twin Rivers Genealogical Society
Box 386, Lewiston, ID 83501

University of Idaho Library
Rayburn St., Box 442350, Moscow,
ID 83844, (208) 885-6584,
<lib.uidaho.edu>

Upper Snake River Valley Historical Society
51 N. Center St., Box 244, Rexburg, ID
83440, (208) 356-9101

Valley County Genealogical Society
Box 697, Cascade, ID 83611, (208) 382-4757

GENERAL RESOURCES

The Basques in Idaho by Pat Bieter (Idaho State Historical Society, ca. 1970)

Blackrobes Journey, 1840-1990 compiled by Joan Drexler, et al. (Holy Rosary Parish, Historical Committee, ca. 1990)

The Brethren Along the Snake River: A History of the Church of the Brethren in Idaho and Western Montana by Roger E. Sappington (Brethren Press, 1966)

Citizens of North Idaho, 2 vols., by Barbera V. Powell (B.V. Powell, ca. 1986-)

Cumulative Baptism Index to the Catholic Church Records of the Pacific Northwest indexed by Sharon E. Osborn-Ryan (Oregon Heritage Press, ca. 1999)

Directory of Churches and Religious Organizations of Idaho prepared by the Idaho Historical Records Survey (Historical Records Survey, 1940)

Directory of Oral History Resources in Idaho compiled and edited by Madeline Buckendorf and Elizabeth P. Jacox (Idaho Oral History Center, Idaho State Historical Society, 1982)

Discovering Idaho, a History by Dwight William Jensen (Caxton Printers, 1977)

Early Methodism in Idaho compiled by Lila Hill, edited by John and Charlotte Hook (United Methodist Church, Oregon-Idaho Conference, Commission on Archives and History, 1996)

Education in the Upper Snake River Valley: the Public Schools, 1880-1950 by Harold S. Forbush (H.S. Forbush, Ricks College Press, ca. 1992)

The First One Hundred Years: Cassia-Oakley Idaho Stake, 1887-1987 by the Church of Jesus Christ of Latter-day Saints, Cassia and Cassia-Oakley Stakes (Burley Reminder, 1987)

Footprints Through Idaho: a Centennial Tribute to the Pioneer by their Descendents, 3 vols., (Idaho Genealogical Society, 1989)

Ghost Towns of Idaho by Donald C. Miller (Pruett Publishing Co., ca. 1976)

The Gold Seekers: a 200 Year History of Mining in Washington, Idaho, Montana and Lower British Columbia by Pauline Battien (P. Battien, ca. 1989)

Guide to the Idaho Folklore Archives by Elaine J. Lawless (Idaho Folklife Center, Idaho State Historical Society, ca. 1983)

A History of the Catholic Church in the Pacific Northwest, 1743-1983 by Wilfred P. Schoenberg (Pastoral Press, ca. 1987)

History of Idaho, 2 vols., by Leonard J. Arrington (University of Idaho Press, 1994)

History of Idaho, 3 vols., by Merrill D. Beal and Merle W. Wells (Lewis Historical Publishing Co., 1959)

The History of Idaho by John Hailey (Press of Syms-York Co., 1910)

History of Idaho, the Gem of the Mountains, 4 vols., by James Henry Hawley (The S. J. Clarke Publishing Co., 1920)

History of the Jews in Utah and Idaho by Juanita Brooks (Western Epics, 1973)

History of Idaho: a Narrative Account of its Historical Progress, its People and its Principal Interests, 3 vols., by Hiram T. French (Lewis Publishing Co., 1914)

A History of Magic Valley by Larry Quinn (Publishing West Associates, 1996)

A History of Southeastern Idaho: an Intimate Narrative of Peaceful Conquest by Empire Builders by M.D. Beal (The Caxton Printers, 1942)

Idaho 100: Stories from Idaho Century Citizens by John Ohara Kirk (Falcon Press, ca. 1989)

The Idaho Encyclopedia compiled by the Federal Writers' Project of the Works Progress Administration (Caxton Printers, 1938)

Idaho Ethnic Heritage, 3 vols., by Laurie Mercier and Carole Simon-Smolinski (Idaho Centennial Commission and Idaho State Historical Society, 1990)

Idaho Folk Life: Homesteads to Headstones edited by Louie W. Attebery, contributions by Brian Attebery, et al. (Idaho State Historical Society, ca. 1985)

Idaho History: a Bibliography by Richard W. Etulain and Merwin Swanson (Idaho State University Press, ca. 1975)

Idaho Local History: a Bibliography with a Checklist of Library Holdings edited by Milo G. Nelson and Charles A. Webbert (University Press of Idaho, 1976)

Idaho; the Place and its People; a History of the Gem State from Prehistoric to Present Days, 3 vols., by Byron Defenbach (The American Historical Society, Inc., 1933)

Idaho Research Outline by the Church of Jesus Christ of Latter-Day Saints (online at **<www.familysearch.org/eng/search/RG/guide/idaho.asp>**)

Idaho Surname Index compiled by Judy Schmick (Idaho Genealogical Society, 1989)

Idaho Women in History: Big and Little Biographies and Other Gender Stories by Betty Penson-Ward (Legendary Publishing Co., ca. 1991)

An Illustrated History of North Idaho, Embracing Nez Perces, Idaho, Latah, Kootenai and Shoshone Counties State of Idaho (Western Publishing Company, 1903)

An Illustrated History of the State of Idaho, 4 vols., (Lewis Publishing Co., 1899)

Indian Peoples of Idaho, 2nd edition (Boise State University Press, 1979)

Indian Wars of Idaho by R. Ross Arnold (The Caxton Printers, 1932)

Indians of Idaho by Deward E. Walker Jr. (University Press of Idaho, ca. 1978)

Lineages of the Members, Past and Present, 1909 through 1961, Sons of the American Revolution, Idaho Society by John Robert Gobble (J.R. Gobble, ca. 1962)

Lives of the Saints in Southeast Idaho: an Introduction to Mormon Pioneer Life Story Writing by Susan Hendricks Swetnam (Idaho State Historical Society, ca. 1991)

Methodism in the Northwest by Erle Howell, edited by Chapin D. Foster (Parthenon Press, Printers, 1966)

The Mining Industry in Idaho: a Short Bibliography of Sources on Mines and Mining in the Idaho State Historical Society Library and Archives (Idaho State Historical Society, 1992)

Mormons and their Neighbors: an Index to Over 75,000 Biographical Sketches from 1820 to the Present, 2 vols., compiled by Marvin E. Wiggins (Harold B. Lee Library, Brigham Young University, ca. 1984)

Newspapers in the Idaho Historical Society Microfilm Collection by the Idaho State Historical Society (Idaho State Historical Society ca. 1999)

Panhandle Personalities, Biographies from the Idaho Panhandle compiled by Claude Simpson and Catherine Simpson (University Press of Idaho, ca. 1984)

Roman Catholic Diocese of Boise, Catholic Chancery Records of Idaho, Master Index, 26 vols. (Idaho Genealogical Society, ca. 1980)

Sketches of the Inter-mountain States: Together with Biographies of Many Prominent and Progressive Citizens who have Helped in the Development and History-making of this Marvelous Region: 1847-1909: Utah, Idaho, Nevada (Salt Lake Tribune, 1909)

Steamboats in the Timber by Ruby El Hult (Caxton Printers, 1952)

Thousands of Idaho Surnames: Abstracted from Rejected Federal Land Applications, 5 vols., (Genealogical Forum of Portland, Oregon, 1980-1987)

Zest for Living: Southern Idaho Senior Profiles by Lorayne Orton Smith (Taylor Publishing, ca. 1991)

CENSUS RECORDS

The 1863 Census of Some Prominent Men of the Idaho Territory by Sherman Lee Pompey (Pacific Specialties, 1974)

1910 Idaho Census Index compiled by Upper Snake River Valley Family History Center volunteers and McKay Library employees at Ricks College (Heritage Quest, 1998)

Idaho Territorial Voters Poll Lists, 1863 transcribed, edited, and indexed by Gene F. Williams (Williams Printing, ca. 1996)

Reconstructed 1890 Census by Idaho State Historical Society Library and Archives, ongoing project

IMMIGRATION RECORDS

Emigrant Trails of Southeastern Idaho by the US Bureau of Land Management (US Department of the Interior, Bureau of Land Management, 1976)

LAND RECORDS

Idaho State Brand Records and Indexes, 4 vols. (Idaho Genealogical Society, ca. 1988)

Stockman's Guide compiled by J.A. Avery (Downey Idahoan, 1913)

Thousands of Idaho Surnames: Abstracted from Rejected Federal Land Applications, 5 vols., (Genealogical Forum of Oregon, 1980-1987)

MAPS

An Atlas of Idaho Territory, 1863-1890 annotated by Merle W. Wells (Idaho Historical Society, 1978)

A Checklist of Idaho Post Offices by Alan H. Patera and John S. Gallagher (The Depot, ca. 1984)

Gazetteer of Cities, Villages, Unincorporated Communities, and Landmark Sites in the State of Idaho, 3rd edition, Idaho Highway Planning Survey, prepared in cooperation with US Bureau of Public Roads (1966)

Ghost Towns and Live Ones: A Chronology of the Post Office Dept. in Idaho, 1861-1973 by Frank R. Schell (1973)

Idaho Place Names: A Geographical Dictionary by Lalia Boone (University of Idaho Press, ca. 1988)

"Idaho Town Names" by Fritz L. Kramer, published in the Idaho State Historical Department Bienneal Report 23, 1951-1952

Maps of Early Idaho: Old Gold Mines, Indian Battle Grounds, Old Military Roads, Old Forts, Overland Stage Routes, Early Towns prepared by R.N. Preston (Western Guide Publishers, 1972)

Route of the Oregon Trail in Idaho Idaho Department of Highways (1963)

A Short History and Postal Record of Idaho Towns: Ada County Thru Washington County by Art Randall (A. Randall, 1994)

PROBATE RECORDS

Justice for the Times: A Centennial History of the Idaho State Courts edited by Carl F. Bianchi (Idaho Law Foundation, ca. 1990)

VITAL RECORDS

AZ, CA, ID, NV, 1850-1951 (Broderbund, ca. 1996. CD-ROM)

Cemetery Records of Idaho, 12 vols., (The Genealogical Society of Utah, 1952-1968)

Guide to Public Vital Statistics Records in Idaho, State and County prepared by the Idaho Historical Records Survey Projects (Idaho Historical Records Survey Projects, 1942)

Western States Historical Marriage Index Online compiled by the Brigham Young University-Idaho Family History Center, **<abish.byui.edu/specialCollections/westernStates/search.cfm>**

•-COUNTY DETAILS-•

ADA
190 E. Front St., Boise, ID 83702, (208) 577-3135, **<adaweb.net>**
- **INCORPORATED:** Dec. 22, 1864
- **PARENT COUNTY:** Boise
- **MARRIAGE RECORDS:** start in 1890, kept by County Clerk/Auditor/Recorder
- **DIVORCE:** unknown, County Clerk/Auditor/Recorder
- **LAND:** 1864, County Clerk/Auditor/Recorder
- **PROBATE:** unknown, County Clerk/Auditor/Recorder
- **COURT:** unknown, County Clerk/Auditor/Recorder

ADAMS
Box 48, Council, ID 83612, (208) 253-4561, **<co.adams.id.us>**
- **INCORPORATED:** March3, 1911
- **PARENT COUNTY:** Washington
- **MARRIAGE RECORDS:** start in 1911, kept by County Clerk/Auditor/Recorder
- **DIVORCE:** 1911, County Clerk/Auditor/Recorder
- **LAND:** 1911, County Clerk/Auditor/Recorder
- **PROBATE:** 1911, County Clerk/Auditor/Recorder
- **COURT:** 1911, County Clerk/Auditor/Recorder

ALTURAS
- **INCORPORATED:** Feb. 4, 1864
- **PARENT COUNTY:** Original county
- **NOTES:** See Blaine County. Abolished March 5, 1896 to create Blaine County.

BANNOCK
624 E. Center St., Pocatello, ID 83201, (208) 236-7340, **<co.bannock.id.us>**
- **INCORPORATED:** March 6, 1893
- **PARENT COUNTY:** Bingham
- **MARRIAGE RECORDS:** start in 1893, keptby County Clerk
- **DIVORCE:** 1893, County Archives
- **LAND:** 1893, County Clerk
- **PROBATE:** 1893, County Archives
- **COURT:** 1893, County Archives
- **NOTES:** County Clerk has birth and death records 1893-1912.

BEAR LAKE
Box 190, Paris, ID 83261, (208) 945-2212, **<bearlakecounty.info>**
- **INCORPORATED:** Jan. 5, 1875
- **PARENT COUNTY:** Oneida
- **MARRIAGE RECORDS:** start in 1875, kept by County Clerk
- **LAND:** 1875, County Clerk
- **DIVORCE:** 1875, County Clerk
- **COURT:** 1875, County Clerk
- **PROBATE:** 1875, County Clerk
- **NOTES:** County Clerk has birth and death records 1907-1911.

BENEWAH
701 College Ave., Saint Maries, ID 83861, (208) 245-3212, **<state.id.us/aboutidaho/county/benewah.html>**
- **INCORPORATED:** Jan. 23, 1915
- **PARENT COUNTY:** Kootenai
- **MARRIAGE:** unknown start, kept by County Clerk
- **DIVORCE:** unknown, County Clerk
- **LAND:** unknown, County Clerk
- **COURT:** unknown, District Court Clerk
- **PROBATE:** unknown, District Court Clerk

BINGHAM
501 N. Maple St., Blackfoot, ID 83221, (208) 785-8040, **<co.bingham.id.us>**
- **INCORPORATED:** Jan. 13, 1885
- **PARENT COUNTY:** Oneida
- **MARRIAGE RECORDS:** start in 1885, kept by County Clerk
- **LAND:** 1885, County Clerk
- **DIVORCE:** 1885, County Clerk
- **COURT:** 1885, County Clerk
- **PROBATE:** 1885, County Clerk
- **NOTES:** County Clerk has birth and death records 1907-1911.

BLAINE
206 First Ave. S., Box 400, Hailey, ID 83333, (208) 788-5505, **<co.blaine.id.us>**
- **INCORPORATED:** March 5, 1895
- **PARENT COUNTIES:** Alturas, Logan
- **MARRIAGE:** start in 1895, kept by County Auditor/Recorder
- **DIVORCE:** 1921, District Court Clerk
- **PROBATE:** 1921, District Court Clerk
- **COURT:** 1921, District Court Clerk
- **LAND:** 1895, County Auditor/Recorder

BOISE
420 Main St., Box 1300, Idaho City, ID 83631, (208) 392-4431, **<co.boise.id.us>**
- **INCORPORATED:** Feb. 4, 1864
- **PARENT COUNTY:** Original county
- **MARRIAGE:** 1868, County Clerk
- **DIVORCE:** ca. 1930, District Court Clerk
- **LAND:** 1864, County Clerk
- **PROBATE:** 1862, State Archives
- **COURT:** 1862, State Archives
- **NOTES:** County Clerk has few birth and death records prior to 1911. Some records are not complete due to fires.

BONNER
215 S. First Ave., Sandpoint, ID 83864, (208) 265-1432, **<co.bonner.id.us>**
- **INCORPORATED:** Feb. 21, 1907
- **PARENT COUNTY:** Kootenai
- **BIRTH RECORDS:** start in unknown, kept at the County Clerk
- **MARRIAGE:** unknown, County Clerk
- **DIVORCE:** unknown, County Clerk
- **DEATH:** unknown, County Clerk
- **LAND:** unknown, County Clerk
- **PROBATE:** 1890, County Clerk
- **COURT:** unknown, County Clerk

BONNEVILLE
605 N. Capital Ave., Idaho Falls, ID 83402,
(208) 529-1350 ext. 1355, **<co.bonneville.id.us>**
- **INCORPORATED:** Feb. 7, 1911
- **PARENT COUNTY:** Bingham
- **MARRIAGE RECORDS:** start in 1911, kept by County Clerk
- **DIVORCE:** 1911, Court Archives
- **LAND:** 1911, County Clerk
- **PROBATE:** 1911, Court Archives
- **COURT:** 1911, Court Archives

BOUNDARY
Box 419, Bonners Ferry, ID 83805, (208) 267-5504,
<boundarycountyid.org>
- **INCORPORATED:** Jan. 23, 1915
- **PARENT COUNTY:** Bonner
- **MARRIAGE:** start in ca. 1890, kept by County Clerk
- **DIVORCE:** 1915, District Court Clerk
- **LAND:** ca. 1890, County Clerk
- **PROBATE:** 1915, District Court Clerk
- **COURT:** 1915, District Court Clerk

BUTTE
248 W. Corand, Box 737, Arco, ID 83213, (208) 527-3021,
<state.id.us/aboutidaho/county/butte.html>
- **INCORPORATED:** Feb. 6, 1917
- **PARENT COUNTIES:** Bingham, Blaine, Jefferson
- **MARRIAGE RECORDS:** start in 1917, kept by County Clerk
- **DIVORCE:** 1930, District Court Clerk
- **LAND:** 1890, County Clerk
- **PROBATE:** 1930, District Court Clerk
- **COURT:** 1930, District Court Clerk

CAMAS
501 Soldier Rd., Box 430, Fairfield, ID 83327, (208) 764-2242,
<idaho.gov/aboutidaho/county/camas.html>
- **INCORPORATED:** Feb. 6, 1917
- **PARENT COUNTY:** Blaine
- **MARRIAGE:** start in ca. 1917, kept by County Clerk
- **DIVORCE:** ca. 1917, County Clerk
- **LAND:** ca. 1917, County Clerk
- **PROBATE:** ca. 1927, County Clerk
- **COURT:** ca. 1927, County Clerk

CANYON
1115 Albany, Caldwell, ID 83605, (208) 454-7337,
<canyoncounty.org>
- **INCORPORATED:** March7, 1891
- **PARENT COUNTY:** Ada
- **MARRIAGE RECORDS:** start in 1895, kept by County Recorder
- **LAND:** 1892, County Recorder
- **DIVORCE:** ca. 1900, County Clerk
- **PROBATE:** ca. 1900, County Clerk
- **COURT:** ca. 1900, County Clerk

CARIBOU
159 S. Main St., Box 775, Soda Springs, ID 83276, (208) 547-4324,
<co.caribou.id.us>
- **INCORPORATED:** Feb. 11, 1919
- **PARENT COUNTY:** Bannock
- **MARRIAGE RECORDS:** start in 1919, kept by County Clerk
- **DIVORCE:** 1919, District Court Magistrate
- **LAND:** 1919, County Clerk
- **PROBATE:** 1919, District Court Magistrate
- **COURT:** 1919, District Court Magistrate

CASSIA
1459 Overland Ave., Burley, ID 83318, (208) 878-5231,
<cassiacounty.org>
- **INCORPORATED:** Feb. 20, 1879
- **PARENT COUNTY:** Owyhee
- **MARRIAGE RECORDS:** start in 1878, kept by County Recorder
- **DIVORCE:** 1879, County Recorder
- **LAND:** 1878, County Recorder
- **PROBATE:** 1878, County Recorder
- **COURT:** 1878, County Recorder
- **NOTES:** County Clerk/Recorder has birth and death records 1907-1911.

CLARK
320 W. Main St., Box 205, Dubois, ID 83423, (208) 374-5304,
<idaho.gov/aboutidaho/county/clark.html>
- **INCORPORATED:** Feb. 1, 1919
- **PARENT COUNTY:** Fremont
- **MARRIAGE RECORDS:** start in 1919, kept by County Clerk
- **DIVORCE:** 1919, County Clerk
- **LAND:** 1919, County Clerk
- **COURT:** 1919, County Clerk

CLEARWATER
150 Michigan Ave., Box 586, Orofino, ID 83544, (208) 476-5615,
<clearwatercounty.org>
- **INCORPORATED:** Feb. 27, 1911
- **PARENT COUNTY:** Nez Perce
- **MARRIAGE RECORDS:** start in 1911, kept by County Auditor/Recorder
- **DIVORCE:** 1911, County Auditor/Recorder
- **LAND:** 1911, County Auditor/Recorder
- **PROBATE:** 1911, County Auditor/Recorder
- **COURT:** 1911, County Auditor/Recorder

CUSTER
Box 385, Challis, ID 83226, (208) 879-2360, **<co.custer.id.us>**
- **INCORPORATED:** Jan. 8, 1881
- **PARENT COUNTIES:** Alturas, Lemhi
- **DIVORCE RECORDS:** start in1872, kept by Office of the Court
- **LAND:** 1881, County Clerk
- **PROBATE:** 1881, Officer of the Court
- **COURT:** 1881, Officer of the Court
- **NOTES:** County Clerk has marriage records from the late 1800s.

ELMORE

150 S. Fourth E St., Ste. 3, Mountain Home, ID 83647
(208) 587-2130, **<elmorecounty.org>**

- **INCORPORATED:** Feb. 7, 1889
- **PARENT COUNTY:** Alturas
- **MARRIAGE RECORDS:** start in 1889, kept by County Auditor/Recorder
- **DIVORCE:** 1889, County Auditor/Recorder
- **LAND:** 1889, County Auditor/Recorder
- **PROBATE:** 1889, County Auditor/Recorder
- **COURT:** 1889, County Auditor/Recorder
- **NOTES:** County Auditor/Recorder has birth and death records 1907-1911.

FRANKLIN

39 W. Oneida St., Preston, ID 83263, (208) 852-1090, **<franklincountyidaho.org>**

- **INCORPORATED:** an. 20, 1913
- **PARENT COUNTY:** Oneida
- **MARRIAGE:** start in 1913, kept by County Clerk
- **DIVORCE:** 1913, County Court Clerk
- **LAND:** ca. 1890, County Clerk
- **PROBATE:** 1913, County Court Clerk
- **COURT:** 1913, County Court Clerk
- **NOTES:** Clerk of District Court has naturalization records 1913-1928.

FREMONT

151 W. First St. N. Room 12, St. Anthony, ID 83445, (208) 624-7332, **<co.fremont.id.us>**

- **INCORPORATED:** March 4, 1893
- **PARENT COUNTIES:** Bingham, Lemhi
- **MARRIAGE RECORDS:** start in 1893, kept by County Clerk
- **DIVORCE:** 1893, Magistrate Court Clerk
- **LAND:** 1893, County Clerk
- **PROBATE:** 1893, Magistrate Court Clerk
- **COURT:** 1893, Magistrate Court Clerk
- **NOTES:** County Clerk has birth and death records 1907-1911.

GEM

415 E. Main St., Emmett, ID 83617, (208) 365-4561, **<co.gem.id.us>**

- **INCORPORATED:** March 15, 1915
- **PARENT COUNTIES:** Boise, Canyon
- **MARRIAGE RECORDS:** start in 1915, kept by County Clerk
- **DIVORCE:** ca. 1915, Magistrate Court Clerk
- **PROBATE:** ca. 1915, Magistrate Court Clerk
- **COURT:** ca. 1915, Magistrate Court Clerk
- **NOTES:** County Clerk has land records from the late 1800s.

GOODING

145 7th Ave E., Box 417, Gooding, ID 83330, (208) 934-4221, **<goodingcounty.org>**

- **INCORPORATED:** Jan. 28, 1913
- **PARENT COUNTY:** Lincoln
- **MARRIAGE RECORDS:** start in 1913, kept by County Clerk
- **DIVORCE:** 1913, County Clerk
- **LAND:** 1913, County Clerk
- **PROBATE:** 1913, County Clerk
- **COURT:** 1913, County Clerk

IDAHO

320 W. Main St., Grangeville, ID 83530, (208) 983-2751, **<idahocounty.org>**

- **INCORPORATED:** Feb. 4, 1864
- **PARENT COUNTY:** Original county
- **MARRIAGE RECORDS:** start in ca. 1890, kept by County Clerk/Auditor/Recorder
- **DIVORCE:** unknown, District Court Clerk
- **LAND:** ca. 1860, County Clerk/Auditor/Recorder
- **PROBATE:** unknown, District Court Clerk
- **COURT:** unknown, District Court Clerk
- **NOTES:** County Clerk/Auditor/Recorder has Birth and Death records 1907-1911.

JEFFERSON

210 Courthouse Way, Ste. 100, Rigby, ID 83442, (208) 745-7756, **<co.jefferson.id.us>**

- **INCORPORATED:** Feb. 18, 1913
- **PARENT COUNTY:** Fremont
- **MARRIAGE:** start in 1914, kept by County Clerk
- **DIVORCE:** 1914, Magistrate Court Clerk
- **LAND:** 1914, County Clerk
- **PROBATE:** 1914, Magistrate Court Clerk
- **COURT:** 1914, Magistrate Court Clerk

JEROME

300 N. Lincoln Ave., Jerome, ID 83338, (208) 644-2700, **<jeromecounty.org>**

- **INCORPORATED:** Feb. 8, 1919
- **PARENT COUNTIES:** Gooding, Lincoln
- **MARRIAGE:** start in 1919, kept by County Clerk
- **DIVORCE:** 1919, Magistrate Court Clerk
- **LAND:** 1919, County Clerk
- **PROBATE:** 1919, Magistrate Court Clerk
- **COURT:** 1919, Magistrate Court Clerk

KOOTENAI

451 N. Government Way, Coeur d'Alene, ID 83814, (208) 446-100, **<co.kootenai.id.us>**

- **INCORPORATED:** Dec. 22, 1864
- **PARENT COUNTY:** Nez Perce
- **MARRIAGE:** start in 1881, kept by County Recorder
- **DIVORCE:** 1895 District Court Clerk
- **PROBATE:** 1895, District Court Clerk
- **COURT:** 1895, District Court Clerk
- **LAND:** 1881, County Recorder
- **NOTES:** County Recorder has birth and death records 1907-1912. Created in 1864, but not organized until 1881.

LATAH

Box 8068, Moscow, ID 83843, (208) 882-8580, **<latah.id.us>**

- **INCORPORATED:** May 14, 1888
- **PARENT COUNTY:** Nez Perce
- **MARRIAGE RECORDS:** start in 1888, kept by County Clerk/Auditor/Recorder
- **LAND:** 1888, County Clerk/Auditor/Recorder
- **NOTES:** County Clerk/Auditor/Recorder has birth and death records 1907-1911. Clerk of District Court has court and probate records from the early 1900s.

LEMHI

206 Courthouse Dr., Salmon, ID 83467, (208) 756-2815, **<lemhicountyidaho.org>**

- **INCORPORATED:** Jan. 9, 1869
- **PARENT COUNTY:** Idaho
- **MARRIAGE RECORDS:** start in 1869, kept by County Recorder
- **DIVORCE:** 1869, Magistrate Court Clerk
- **LAND:** 1869, County Recorder
- **PROBATE:** 1869, Magistrate Court Clerk
- **COURT:** 1869, Magistrate Court Clerk
- **NOTES:** County Clerk/Recorder has birth and death records 1907-1911.

LEWIS

510 Oak St., Nezperce, ID 83543, (208) 937-2661, **<lewiscountyid.us>**

- **INCORPORATED:** March 3, 1911
- **PARENT COUNTY:** Nez Perce
- **MARRIAGE RECORDS:** start in 1911, kept by County Auditor
- **DIVORCE:** 1911, District Court Clerk
- **LAND:** 1911, County Auditor
- **PROBATE:** 1911, District Court Clerk
- **COURT:** 1911, District Court Clerk

LINCOLN

Drawer A, 111 W. B St., Shoshone, ID 83352, (208) 886-7641 **<idaho.gov/aboutidaho/county/lincoln.html>**

- **INCORPORATED:** March 18, 1895
- **PARENT COUNTIES:** Alturas, Blaine
- **MARRIAGE RECORDS:** start in 1895, kept by County Clerk
- **DIVORCE:** 1895, County Clerk
- **LAND:** 1895, County Clerk
- **PROBATE:** 1895, County Clerk
- **COURT:** 1895, County Clerk
- **NOTES:** Fire destroyed many early records. Some 19th-century records are kept in Blaine and Gooding counties.

LOGAN

- **INCOPORATED:** Feb. 7, 1889
- **NOTES:** Combined with Alturas County to form Blaine County March 5, 1895.

MADISON

134 E. Main, Box 389, Rexburg, ID 83440, (208) 359-6200, **<co.madison.id.us>**

- **INCORPORATED:** Feb. 18, 1913
- **PARENT COUNTY:** Fremont
- **MARRIAGE RECORDS:** start in 1919, kept by County Clerk
- **DIVORCE:** 1914, District Court Magistrate Clerk
- **LAND:** 1919, County Clerk
- **PROBATE:** 1914, District Court Magistrate Clerk
- **COURT:** 1914, District Court Magistrate Clerk

MINIDOKA

715 G St., Box 368, Rupert, ID 83350, (208) 436-9511, **<minidoka.id.us>**

- **INCORPORATED:** Jan. 28, 1913
- **PARENT COUNTY:** Lincoln
- **MARRIAGE RECORDS:** start in 1915, kept by County Recorder
- **DIVORCE:** 1913, Magistrate Court Clerk
- **LAND:** 1915, County Recorder
- **PROBATE:** 1913, Magistrate Court Clerk
- **COURT:** 1913, Magistrate Court Clerk

NEZ PERCE

1230 Main St., Box 896, Lewiston, ID 83501, (208) 799-3020, **<co.nezperce.id.us>**

- **INCORPORATED:** Feb. 4, 1864
- **PARENT COUNTY:** Original County
- **MARRIAGE RECORDS:** start in 1860, kept by County Auditor
- **DIVORCE:** 1874, District Court Clerk
- **LAND:** 1860, County Auditor
- **PROBATE:** 1890, District Court Clerk
- **COURT:** 1874, District Court Clerk
- **NOTES:** County Auditor has birth and death records 1900-1911. Organized while part of Washington Territory in 1861.

ONEIDA

10 Court St., Malad, ID 83252, (208) 766-4116, **<idaho.gov/aboutidaho/county/oneida.html>**

- **INCORPORATED:** Jan. 22, 1864
- **PARENT COUNTY:** Original County
- **MARRIAGE RECORDS:** start in 1866, kept by County Recorder
- **LAND:** unknown, County Recorder
- **NOTES:** County Recorder has birth and death records 1907-1911. Magistrate Court Clerk has court, divorce, and probate records from the late 1800s.

OWYHEE

Box 128, Murphy, ID 83650, (208) 495-2421, **<owyheecounty.net>**

- **INCORPORATED:** Dec.31, 1863
- **PARENT COUNTY:** Original County
- **MARRIAGE RECORDS:** start in 1895, kept by County Clerk
- **DIVORCE:** unknown, County Court Clerk
- **LAND:** 1895, County Court Clerk
- **PROBATE:** unknown, County Court Clerk
- **COURT:** unknown, County Court Clerk
- **NOTES:** County Clerk has birth and death records 1907-1913 and naturalization records 1893-1911. Organized while part of Washington Territory.

PAYETTE
1130 Third Ave. N., Drawer D, Payette, ID 83661, (208) 642-6000, **<payettecounty.org>**
- **INCORPORATED:** Feb. 28, 1917
- **PARENT COUNTY:** Canyon
- **MARRIAGE RECORDS:** start in 1917, kept at the County Clerk
- **DIVORCE:** 1917, County Clerk
- **LAND:** 1865, County Clerk
- **PROBATE:** 1917, County Clerk
- **COURT:** 1917, County Clerk
- **NATURALIZATION:** 1930, County Clerk

POWER
543 Bannock Ave., American Falls, ID 83211, (208) 226-7610, **<co.power.id.us>**
- **INCORPORATED:** Jan. 30, 1913
- **PARENT COUNTIES:** Bingham, Blaine, Oneida
- **MARRIAGE RECORDS:** start in 1913. kept by County Clerk
- **DIVORCE:** 1913, District Court Clerk
- **LAND:** 1913, unknown
- **PROBATE:** 1913, Magistrate Court Clerk
- **COURT:** 1913, Magistrate Court Clerk

SHOSHONE
700 Bank St., Wallace, ID 83873, (208) 752-1264, **<state.id.us/aboutidaho/county/shoshone.html>**
- **INCORPORATED:** Feb. 4, 1864
- **PARENT COUNTY:** Original county
- **MARRIAGE RECORDS:** start ca. 1890, kept by County Recorder
- **DIVORCE:** 1887, County Clerk
- **LAND:** ca. 1890, County Recorder
- **PROBATE:** 1885, County Clerk
- **COURT:** 1885, County Clerk
- **NOTES:** County Recorder has birth and death records 1907-1911. Organized while part of Washington Territory in 1861.

TETON
150 Courthouse Dr., Driggs, ID 83422, (208) 354-2905, **<tetoncountyidaho.gov>**
- **INCORPORATED:** Jan. 26, 1915
- **PARENT COUNTY:** Madison
- **MARRIAGE RECORDS:** start in 1924, kept by County Clerk
- **DIVORCE:** 1916, Magistrate Court Clerk
- **LAND:** 1924, County Clerk
- **PROBATE:** 1916, Magistrate Court Clerk
- **COURT:** 1916, Magistrate Court Clerk

TWIN FALLS
425 Shoshone St. N., Box 126, Twin Falls, ID 83303, (208) 736-4004, **<twinfallscounty.org>**
- **INCORPORATED:** Feb. 21, 1907
- **PARENT COUNTY:** Cassia
- **MARRIAGE RECORDS:** start in 1907, kept by County Recorder
- **DIVORCE:** 1907, Court Records
- **LAND:** 1907, County Recorder
- **PROBATE:** 1907, Court Records
- **COURT:** 1907, Court Records

VALLEY
219 N. Main St., Box 1350, Cascade, ID 83611, (208) 382-7126, **<co.valley.id.us>**
- **INCORPORATED:** Feb. 26, 1917
- **PARENT COUNTIES:** Boise, Idaho
- **MARRIAGE RECORDS:** start in 1917, kept by County Recorder
- **DIVORCE:** ca. 1960, Court Clerk
- **LAND:**1917, County Recorder
- **PROBATE:** ca. 1960, Court Clerk
- **COURT:** ca. 1960, Court Clerk

WASHINGTON
256 E. Court St., Weiser, ID 83672, (208) 414-2092, **<co.washington.id.us>**
- **INCORPORATED:** Feb. 20, 1879
- **PARENT COUNTY:** Boise
- **MARRIAGE RECORDS:** start in1879, kept by County Clerk
- **DIVORCE:** 1879, Magistrate Court Clerk
- **LAND:** 1879, County Clerk
- **PROBATE:** 1879, Magistrate Court Clerk
- **COURT:** 1879, Magistrate Court Clerk
- **NOTES:** County Clerk has birth and death records 1907-1911.

ILLINOIS

» BY JAMES W. WARREN

HISTORICAL OVERVIEW

The land on which Chicago's glittering Michigan Avenue stands was a quiet wilderness 300 years ago. Illinois' non-Indian beginnings were along the state's southern waterways. In 1699, French priests founded a mission at Cahokia, in what is now St. Clair County. In 1703, the French also founded Kaskaskia, now in Randolph County; it eventually became the British seat of government. In 1763, France ceded the area to the British after the French and Indian War.

In 1778, the longtime home of the Winnebago, Miami, Illinois, Kickapoo, Pottawatomie, Fox and Sac Indians became part of the United States. Illinois became a county of Virginia after Americans captured Kaskaskia from the British. Virginia relinquished its claim in 1784, and three years later, Congress made Illinois part of the Northwest Territory. In 1800, Illinois became part of Indiana Territory. Illinois Territory was formed from it in 1809. Settlers were primarily from Virginia, Tennessee, Kentucky, and the Carolinas by way of the Ohio River. In 1818 Illinois became the 21st state. Most of the population lived near the state's southern waterways.

The Black Hawk War of 1832 saw the Sauk and Fox Indians driven from the state and the last remaining Indian lands relinquished. Migration to Illinois during the 1830s was largely from New York and New England via the National Road or the Erie Canal to the Great Lakes. In the 1840s, that migration continued, and large numbers of German and Irish also began to arrive. While many soon moved farther west, many remained in Illinois. So did many of the Poles, Italians, Austrians, Hungarians, Russians, and Scandinavians who arrived after the Civil War. More than a quarter-million Illinois troops served the Union during the Civil War.

In the decades after the Civil War, Illinois and the rapidly growing Chicago area drew many African-Americans. Newcomers from around the world continued to migrate to Illinois throughout the 20th century.

RECORD HIGHLIGHTS

Available federal census for Illinois begins with 1820. (The exception is Randolph County, for which the 1810 census survived.) Mortality schedules exist for 1850, 1860, 1870

research tips

- The Illinois State Archives and the Illinois State Genealogical Society have compiled an Illinois Marriage Records Index, 1763–1900, online at **<www.sos.state.il.us/departments/archives/marriage.html>**.
- Search an index to Illinois death certificates from 1916 to 1950 at **<www.sos.state.il.us/departments/archives/idphdeathindex.html>**. Search the pre-1916 Statewide Death Index at **<www.sos.state.il.us/departments/archives/death.html>**.
- The Illinois State Historical Library has a biographical index of over 10,000 Illinois individuals in local histories and other sources.
- The Illinois Regional Archives Depository (IRAD) system houses older county and local government records at seven regional archives and is online at **<www.sos.state.il.us/departments/archives/irad/iradhome.html>**.

CENSUS RECORDS

- Federal census: 1810 (Randolph County), 1820, 1830, 1840, 1850, 1860, 1870, 1880, 1890, 1900, 1910, 1920, 1930
- Federal mortality schedules: 1850, 1860, 1870 (partial), 1880
- State/territorial census: 1810, 1818, 1820 (Edwards County missing), 1825 (Edwards, Fulton Randolph counties only), 1830 (Morgan), 1835, 1840, 1845, 1855, 1865
- 1835 (Fayette, Fulton, Jasper, Morgan), 1840 (35 of 87 counties), 1845 (Cass, Putnam, Tazewell), 1855, 1865 (all counties except Gallatin, Mason, Monroe; for Tazewell, only Elm Grove Township)

(partial), and 1880. Various territorial and state censuses exist, as well. The 1810, 1818, and 1820 territorial censuses have been indexed and published. State censuses for 1825, 1835, 1845, 1855, and 1865 are at the Illinois State Archives and on subscription site Ancestry.com, but many counties are missing or incomplete for the censuses through 1845.

Illinois county-level court records include probate, civil, and criminal cases, divorce, adoption, naturalizations and guardianship. The records are held by the clerks of the county court and the circuit court for each county. Older court and vital records are often available on microfilm through the Family History Library (FHL), or may have been transferred to an Illinois Regional Archives Depository (IRAD) location.

Illinois law required the filing of vital records beginning in 1877, but statewide registration didn't begin until 1916. Compliance wasn't always immediate. Post-1916 birth and death records are available from the State Department of Public Health in Springfield. Earlier records (sometimes including pre-1877 records) can be obtained from the county clerk.

Marriages are all at the county level. For divorces, a statewide index exists only from 1962. Pre-1877 marriage records provide little information. But in 1877, preprinted marriage books included columns for such details as ages, residences, birthplaces, and often the names of the parents of the bride and groom. Couples were required to obtain a marriage license, and marriage returns filed by the minister or justice of the peace indicated where the marriage took place and may provide the couple's religious denomination. Divorce records are part of the civil court records at the county level.

In 1871, the Great Chicago Fire destroyed much of the city and its local records. This makes thorough research in alternate records important for those with early Chicago ancestors. A helpful guide for locating such records is *Chicago and Cook County: Guide to Research* by Loretto Dennis Szucs.

Another useful statewide resource provided by the Illinois State Genealogical Society is their Cemetery Location Project. It is available online at **<rootsweb.ancestry.com/~ilsgs/ilcemetery.html>** The Illinois USGen web site includes a county-by-county list of cemeteries, as well as an index to tombstone transcriptions and abstracts.

Church records can provide vital information. Sacramental records to 1915 for the Roman Catholic Archdiocese of Chicago are available through the FHL. The Evangelical Lutheran Church in America Archives in Chicago is the central archive for American Lutheran Church records research.

Online help for Illinois research is abundant. The Illinois State Archives and the Illinois State Genealogical Society have worked for years to compile the Illinois Marriage Records Index, 1763-1900. The most up-to-date edition of this enormous ongoing project is available at **<cyberdriveillinois.com/departments/archives/marriage.html>**. The State Archives also provides two online indexes to death records: The index to death certificates from 1916 to 1950 is at **<sos.state.il.us/departments/archives/idphdeathindex.html>**. The pre-1916 Statewide Death Index is at **<os.state.il.us/departments/archives/death.html>**.

Many 19th- and early 20th-century Chicago immigrants later migrated farther west. The FHL's strong microfilm holdings for Chicago and Cook County ease the burden of big-city research. Chicago vital records begin in 1871 and include births to 1933, deaths to 1945, and marriages to 1920. Chicago voting records, which can serve as a substitute for the missing 1890 census, are indexed for 1888, 1888 to 1890, and 1892. The Chicago Historical Society is also an important resource for those with ancestors from the Chicago area.

The Illinois State Historical Library has a biographical index of more than 10,000 Illinois individuals in local histories and other sources. The Newberry Library is a private library in downtown Chicago with extensive reference materials and special collections for Illinois and beyond.

The IRAD system houses older county and local government records at seven regional archives, located at various Illinois university campuses. The website, **<cyberdriveillinois.com/departments/archives/irad/iradhome.html>**, provides a searchable database of the records available at each IRAD location, as well as a county-by-county listing.

ARCHIVES, LIBRARIES, AND SOCIETIES

Addison Historical Society and Museum
One Friendship Plaza, Addison, IL 60101, (630) 628-1433, **<addisonadvantage.org/History/HistoricalSite.htm>**

Afro-American Historical and Genealogical Society of Chicago
Box 974, Carbondale, IL 62903, **<aahgs.org/chapters.htm>**

Archdiocese of Chicago Cardinal Joseph Bernardin Archives and Records Center
711 W. Monroe St., Chicago, IL 60661, (312) 831-0711, **<archives.archchicago.org>**

Arlington Heights Memorial Library
500 N. Dunton Ave., Arlington Heights, IL 60004, (847) 392-0100, **<ahml.info>**

Assumption Public Library
205 N. Oak St., Assumption, IL 62510, (217) 226-3915, **<assumptionpubliclibrary.com>**

Augustana Historical Society
7th Ave and 35th St., Rock Island, IL 61201 (309) 794-7266

Aurora Historical Society
Box 905, Aurora, IL 60507, (630) 906-0650, **<aurorahistoricalsociety.org>**

Balzekas Museum of Lithuanian Culture
6500 S. Pulaski Rd., Chicago, IL 60629, (773) 582-6500, **<lithuanianmuseum.org>**

Barrington Area Historical Society
212 W. Main St., Barrington, IL 60010, (847) 381-1730, **<bahsil.org>**

Bartlett Historical Society
228 S. Main St., Bartlett, IL 60103, (630) 837-0800

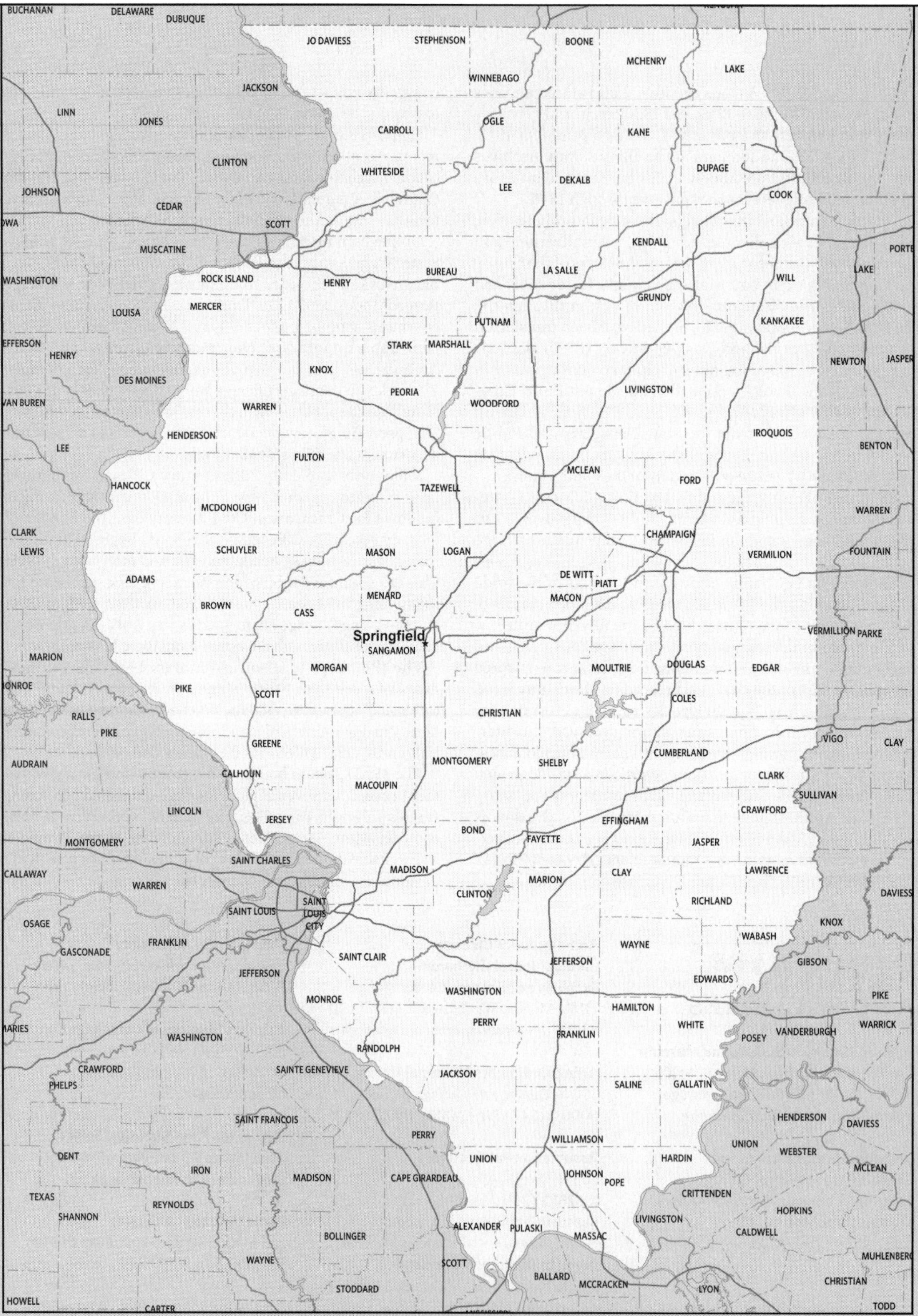
BUCHANAN
DELAWARE
DUBUQUE
JO DAVIESS
STEPHENSON
BOONE
MCHENRY
LAKE
WINNEBAGO
JACKSON
LINN
JONES
CARROLL
OGLE
KANE
CLINTON
WHITESIDE
DEKALB
DUPAGE
LEE
COOK
JOHNSON
CEDAR
SCOTT
KENDALL
MUSCATINE
BUREAU
LA SALLE
WILL
LAKE
ROCK ISLAND
HENRY
GRUNDY
WASHINGTON
MERCER
LOUISA
PUTNAM
KANKAKEE
HENRY
STARK
MARSHALL
NEWTON
KNOX
DES MOINES
PEORIA
WOODFORD
LIVINGSTON
WARREN
HENDERSON
IROQUOIS
BENTON
LEE
FULTON
MCLEAN
FORD
HANCOCK
TAZEWELL
MCDONOUGH
WARREN
CLARK
CHAMPAIGN
LEWIS
SCHUYLER
MASON
LOGAN
VERMILION
FOUNTAIN
DE WITT
PIATT
ADAMS
MENARD
MACON
BROWN
CASS
VERMILLION
PARKE
Springfield
SANGAMON
MARION
MORGAN
MOULTRIE
DOUGLAS
EDGAR
PIKE
SCOTT
COLES
RALLS
CHRISTIAN
PIKE
GREENE
CUMBERLAND
VIGO
CLAY
AUDRAIN
MONTGOMERY
SHELBY
CALHOUN
CLARK
MACOUPIN
SULLIVAN
CRAWFORD
LINCOLN
JERSEY
EFFINGHAM
BOND
FAYETTE
JASPER
MONTGOMERY
SAINT CHARLES
MADISON
LAWRENCE
CALLAWAY
CLAY
WARREN
MARION
CLINTON
SAINT LOUIS CITY
SAINT LOUIS
RICHLAND
DAVIESS
OSAGE
KNOX
FRANKLIN
WAYNE
WABASH
GASCONADE
SAINT CLAIR
JEFFERSON
GIBSON
JEFFERSON
EDWARDS
WASHINGTON
MONROE
PIKE
HAMILTON
PERRY
WHITE
WARRICK
POSEY
VANDERBURGH
FRANKLIN
WASHINGTON
RANDOLPH
CRAWFORD
SAINTE GENEVIEVE
JACKSON
SALINE
GALLATIN
PHELPS
SAINT FRANCOIS
HENDERSON
DAVIESS
PERRY
WILLIAMSON
UNION
DENT
UNION
HARDIN
WEBSTER
IRON
MADISON
CAPE GIRARDEAU
JOHNSON
MCLEAN
POPE
TEXAS
CRITTENDEN
REYNOLDS
SHANNON
HOPKINS
LIVINGSTON
ALEXANDER
PULASKI
MASSAC
BOLLINGER
CALDWELL
WAYNE
SCOTT
MUHLENBERG
BALLARD
MCCRACKEN
CHRISTIAN
STODDARD
LYON
HOWELL
CARTER
TODD

Batavia Historical Society
155 Houston St., Batavia, IL 60510, (630) 406-5274, **<bataviahistoricalsociety.org>**

Belleville Public Library
121 E. Washington St., Belleville, IL 62220, (618) 234-0441, **<bellevillepubliclibrary.org>**

Bellflower Genealogical and Historical Society
Route 1, Box 17, Bellflower, IL 61724, (309) 722-3467

Blackhawk Genealogical Society
Box 3912, Rock Island, IL 61204

Blue Island Historical Society
31018 Maple St., Blue Island, IL, 60406, (708) 371-8546, **<blueisland.org/historical>**

Bond County Genealogical Society
Box 172, Greenville, IL 62246, **<greenvilleusa.org/bcgs>**

Bond County Historical Society
Box 327, Greenville, IL 62246, (618) 664-1590, **<bondcountyhistorical.org>**

Boone County Historical Society and Museum
311 Whitney Blvd., Belvidere, IL 61008, (815) 544-8391, **<boonecountyhistoricalmuseum.org>**

Gail Borden Public Library
2751 W Bowes Rd., Elgin, IL 60120, (847) 742-2411, **<gailborden.info>**

C.E. Brehm Memorial Public Library District
101 S. Seventh St., Mt. Vernon, IL 62864, (618) 242-6322, **<mtvbrehm.lib.il.us>**

Brethren Historical Library and Archives
1451 Dundee Ave., Elgin, IL 60120, (847) 742-6103, **<brethren.org>**

Brookfield Historical Society
Box 342, Brookfield, IL 60513, (708) 485-3420, **<brookfieldcthistory.org>**

Bryan-Bennett Library
Box 864, Salem, IL 62881, (618) 548-3006, **<salembbl.lib.il.us>**

Bureau County Genealogical Society
629 S. Main St., Princeton, IL 61356, (815) 879-3133, **<rootsweb.ancestry.com/~ilbcgs>**

Bureau County Historical Society and Museum
109 Park Ave., West Princeton, IL 61356, (815) 875-2184, **<bureaucountymuseum.com>**

Bushnell Area Historical Society
300 Miller St., Bushnell, IL 61422, (309) 772-3612

Cairo Historical Association
2700 Washington Ave., Cairo IL 62914

Calhoun County Historical Society
Box 46, Hardin, IL 62047, **<calhounhistoricalsociety.i8.com>**

Calumet City Historical Society Museum
760 Wentworth Ave., Calumet City, IL 60409, (708) 832-9390, **<lakenetnwi.net/member/cchs>**

Cambridge Historical Society
RR2, Box 96, Cambridge, IL 61238, **<carolstreamhistorical.com>**

Carol Stream Historical Society
391 Illini Dr., Gretna Museum, Carol Stream, IL 60188, (630) 665-0686, **<carolstreamhistorical.com>**

Carroll County Genealogical Society
326 Third St., Savannah, IL 61074, (815) 273-3714, **<internetni.com/~ahaliotis>**

Carroll County Historical Society
Box 65, Mounty Carroll, IL 61053

Cass County Historical and Genealogical Society
Box 11, Virginia, IL 62691, **<www.rootsweb.ancestry.com/~ilcchgs>**

Catlin Historical Society
210 N. Paris St., Catlin, IL 61817, (217) 427-5766, **<rootsweb.ancestry.com/~ilchs>**

Champaign Genealogical Society
c/o Champaign County Historical Archives 201 W. Green St., Urbana, IL 61801, (217) 367-4025, **<rootsweb.ancestry.com/~ilccgs>**

Chatsworth Historical Society
424 E. Locust St., Box 755, Chatsworth, IL 60921, (815) 635-3124

Chicago Genealogical Society
Box 1160, Chicago, IL 60690, **<chicagogenealogy.org>**

Chicago Heights Historical Society
3893 Merioneth Dr., Crete, IL 60417, (708) 672-5543

Chicago Historical Society
Clark St. at North Ave., Chicago, IL 60614, (312) 642-4600, **<chicagohs.org>**

Chicago Public Library, Harold Washington Library Research Center
400 S. State St., Chicago, IL 60605, (312) 747-4526, **<chipublib.org/001hwlc/001hwlc.html>**

Chillicothe Historical Society
Box 181, Chillicothe, IL 61523, (309) 274-9076, **<chillicothehistorical.org>**

Christian County Genealogical Society
Box 28, Taylorville, IL 62568, **<homepage.Macomb.com/~tkuntz/christianco.htm>**

Christian County Historical Society
Box 254, Taylorville, IL 62568, (217) 824-6922, **<taylorville.net/Historical_Society.htm>**

Clark County Genealogical Society
309 Maple, Box 153, Marshall, IL 62441, (217) 826-2864

Clay County Genealogical Society
Box 94, Louisville, IL 62858, (618) 665-4544, **<clayrootsillinois.com>**

Clinton County Historical Society
1091 Franklin St., Carlyle, IL 62231

Coles County Historical Society
1320 Lafayette, Mattoon, IL 61938, (217) 235-6744 , **<coleshistory.net>**

Coles County Genealogical Society
Box 592, Charleston, IL 61920, **<rootsweb.ancestry.com/~iltccgs>**

Columbia Historical Society
11562 Bluff Road, Columbia, IL 62236 , (618) 281-5734

Cook Memorial Library
413 N. Milwaukee Ave., Libertyville, IL 60048, (847) 362-2330, **<cooklib.org>**

Crawford County Genealogical Society
803 N. Madison, Robinson, IL 62454

Crawford County Historical Society and Museum
Box 554, Robinson, IL 62454, (618) 544-3087, **<rootsweb.ancestry.com/~ilcchs>**

Cumberland County Historical Society of Illinois
213 E. Cumberland St., Greenup, IL 62428, (217) 923-9306

Czech and Slovak American Genealogy Society of Illinois
Box 313, Sugar Grove, IL 60554, **<csagsi.org>**

Danville Public Library
319 N. Vermilion St., Danville, IL 61832, (217) 447-5220, **<danville.lib.il.us>**

Darien Historical Society
7422 Cass Ave., Darien, IL 60559, (630) 969-6171

Decatur Genealogical Library
1255 W. South Side Dr., Decatur, IL 62523, (217) 429-0135, **<rootsweb.ancestry.com/~ildecgs>**

DeKalb County Historical and Genealogical Society
Box 295, Sycamore, IL 60178, **<dekalb.ilgenweb.net/DekCoHistSoc/DekCoHistSoc.htm>**

DeLavan Community Historical Society
Locust St., DeLavan, IL 61734

Des Plaines Historical Society
781 Pearson St., Des Plaines, IL 60016, (847) 391-5399, **<desplaineshistory.org>**

DeWitt County Genealogical Society
Box 632, Clinton, IL 61727, **<dewitt.ilgenweb.net/dewitt-genealogical-society.htm>**

Douglas County Genealogical Society
Box 113, Tuscola, IL 61953

Downers Grove Historical Society
831 Maple Ave., Downers Grove, IL 60515, (630) 963-1309

Dundee Township Historical Society
426 Highland Ave., Dundee, IL 60118, (847) 428-6996, **<dundeetownshiphistorical.org>**

Dunton Genealogical Society
500 N. Dunton, Arlington Heights, IL 60004

DuPage County Genealogical Society
Box 3, Wheaton, IL 60187, **<dcgs.org>**

DuPage County Historical Museum
Box 1460 Wheaton, IL 60189, (630) 407-2888, **<dupagehistory.org>**

Eastern Illinois University, Booth Library
600 Lincoln Ave., Charleston, IL 61920, (217) 581-6061, **<library.eiu.edu>**

Edgar County Genealogical Society
408 N. Main St., Paris, IL 61944, (217) 463-4209, **<comwares.net/ecgl>**

Edgar County Historical Society
414 N. Main St., Paris, IL 61944, (217) 463-5305

Edgewater Historical Society
5358 N. Ashland, Chicago IL 60640, (773) 506-4849, **<edgewaterhistory.org>**

Edwards County Historical Society
414 N. Main St., Albion, IL 62806, (618) 445-2631, **<edwards.ilgenweb.net/ehistsoc.html>**

Edwardsville Public Library
112 S. Kansas, Edwardsville, IL 62025, (618) 692-7556, **<edwardsvillelibrary.org>**

Effingham County Genealogical and Historical Society
Box 1166, Effingham, IL 62401, (217) 342-2210, **<rootsweb.ancestry.com/~ileffing/lookups.htm>**

Ela Historical Society
95 E. Main St., Lake Zurich, IL 60047, **<rootsweb.ancestry.com/~illake/genhistsoc.htm>**

Elgin Area Historical Society
360 Park St., Elgin, IL 60120, (847) 742-4248, **<elginhistory.org>**

Elgin Genealogical Society
Box 1418, Elgin, IL 60121, (630) 833-1457, **<rootsweb.ancestry.com/~ilegs/v3>**

Elk Grove Historical Society
499 Biesterfield Rd., Elk Grove Village, IL 60007, **<elkgroveparks.org/historicalSociety.asp>**

Ellwood House Museum
509 N. First St., DeKalb, IL 60115, (815) 756-4609, **<ellwoodhouse.org>**

Elmwood Historical Society
302 N. Magnolia, Elmwood, IL 61529, (309) 742-7791

Elmwood Park Historical Society
4 Conti Pkwy., Elmwood Park, IL 60635, (630) 453-7645

Mercer County Historical Society
1406 SE Second Ave., Aledo, IL 61231, (309) 582-2280, **<mchsil.org>**

Evangelical Lutheran Church in America Archives
321 Bonnie Lane, Elk Grove Village, IL 60007, (800) 638.3522, **<elca.org>**

Evangelical Lutheran Church in America Library
8765 W. Higgins Rd., Chicago, IL 60631, (773) 380-2811, **<elca.org>**

Evans Public Library
215 S. Fifth St., Vandalia, IL 62471, (618) 283-2824, **<epl.lib.il.us>**

Evanston Historical Society
225 Greenwood, Evanston, IL 60201, (847) 475-3410, **<evanstonhistorycenter.org>**

Fayette County Genealogical and Historical Society
100 N. Walnut, West Union, IA 52175, (563) 422-5797, **<rootsweb.ancestry.com/~iafayett/iafirst6.htm>**

Fern Dell Historic Association
9 E. Front St., Box 254, Newark, IL 60541, (815) 695-5240, **<ferndell.org>**

Ford County Historical Society
Box 115, Paxton, IL 60957, **<rootsweb.ancestry.com/~ilfchs>**

Forest Park Historical Society
c/o Forest Park Library, 7555 Jackson Blvd., Forest Park, IL 60130, (708) 366-7171, **<fppl.org>**

Fox Lake-Grant Township Area Historical Society
411 Washington St., Box 224, Ingleside, IL 60041, (847) 587-0544, **<rootsweb.ancestry.com/~ilflahs>**

Fox Valley Genealogical Society
Box 5435, Nashville, IL 60567, **<ilfvgs.org>**

Frankfort Area Genealogical Society
2000 E. St. Louis St., Box 427, West Frankfort, IL 62896, (618) 932-6159, **<usgennet.org/usa/il/county/franklin/frankfortarea.html>**

Franklin County Historical Society
304 E. Webster, St., Benton, IL 62812, (618) 435-6947

Freeburg Historical and Genealogical society
Box 69, Freeburg, IL 62243, (618) 539-5771

Freeport Public Library
314 W. Stephenson St., Freeport, IL 61032, (815) 233-3000, **<freeportpubliclibrary.org>**

Fulton County Historical and Genealogical Society
Box 583, Canton, IL 61520, (309) 647-0771

Galena/Jo Daviess County Historical Society and Museum
211 S. Bench St., Galena, IL 61036, (815) 777-9129, **<galenahistorymuseum.org>**

Galewood-MontClare Historical Society
1705 N. Nashville Ave., Chicago, IL 60707, (312) 237-8960

Gallatin County Historical Society
Box 693, Shawneetown, IL 62984, (618) 269-3716

Garrett-Evangelical Theological Seminary
2121 Sheridan Rd., Evanston, IL 60201, (800) 736-4627, **<garrett.northwestern.edu>**

Genealogical Forum of Elmhurst
c/o Elmhurst Historical Museum, 120 E. Park Ave., Elmhurst, IL 60126, **<elmhurstespress.com/FORUM>**

Genealogical Society of Southern Illinois
c/o John A. Logan College, Rte. 2, Box 145, Carterville, IL 62918-9599, (618) 985-6213

Genealogy Society of White County
Box 142, Carmi, IL 6281-0142, **<rootsweb.ancestry.com/~ilgswc/index.html>**

Geneseo Historical Association
205 S. State St., Geneseo, IL 61254, (309) 944-3043, **<geneseohistoricalmuseum.com>**

Geneva Historical Society
113 S. 3rd St., Geneva, IL 60134, (630) 262-1086, **<genevahistorycenter.org>**

Glen Ellyn Historical Society
Box 283, Glen Ellyn, IL 60138, (630) 858-8696, **<gehistoricalsociety.homestead.com>**

Glencoe Historical Society at the Eklund History Center and Garden
Box 457, Glencoe, IL 60022, (847) 835-0040, **<glencoehistoricalsociety.org>**

Glenview Area Historical Society
1121 Waukegan Rd., Glenview, IL 60025, (847) 724-2235, **<glenviewhistory.org>**

Glenview Public Library
1930 Glenview Rd., Glenview, IL 60025, (847) 729-7500, **<glenviewpl.org>**

Great River Genealogical Society
c/o Quincy Public Library, 526 Jersey St., Quincy, IL 62301, (217) 222-0226, **<gr-gs.org>**

Greater Harvard Area Historical Society
308 N. Hart St., Box 505, Harvard, Il 60033, (815) 943-6141, **<harvard-history.com>**

Green Hills Genealogical Society
c/o Green Hills Public Library, 8611 W. 103rd, Palos Hills, IL 60465, (708) 598-8446

Greene County Historical and Genealogical Society
Box 137, Carrollton, IL 62016, (217) 942-6013, **<rootsweb.ancestry.com/~ilgreene/gcgs.htm>**

Greenville Public Library
414 W. Main St., Greenville, IL 62246, (618) 664-3115, **<greenvillepubliclibrary.org>**

Griggsville Area Genealogical and Historical Society
Box 75, Griggsville, IL 62340

Hancock County Historical Society
306 Walnut St., Carthage, IL 62321, (217) 357-0043, **<carthage.lib.il.us/community/clubs/historical>**

Hardin County Historical and Genealogical Society
Box 72, Elizabethtown, IL 62931, (618) 287-2361, **<rootsweb.ancestry.com/~ilhardin/hci.htm>**

Henry County Genealogical Society
Box 346, Kewanee, IL 61443, **<rootsweb.ancestry.com/~ilhcgs>**

Henry Historical and Genealogical Society
610 N. St., Henry, IL 61537, (309) 364-3272

Henry County Historical Society
Box 48, Bishop Hill, IL 61419, (309) 927-3528

Highland Park Historical Society
326 Central Ave., Box 56, Highland Park, IL, 60035, (847) 432-7090, **<highlandparkhistory.com>**

Hinsdale Historical Society
Box 336, Hinsdale, IL 60522, (630) 789-2600, **<hinsdalehistory.org>**

Historical Society of the Fort Hill Country
Box 582, Mundelein, IL 60060, (847) 526-7566

Historical Society of Greater Peotone
213 W. North St., Peotone, IL 60468, (708) 258-3436

Historical Society of Montgomery County
904 S. Main St., Hilsboro, IL 62049, **<history.montgomeryco.com>**

Historical Society of Oak Park and River Forest
217 Home Ave., Oak Park, IL 60303, (708) 848-6755, **<oprf.com/OPRFHIST>**

Historical Society of Quincy and Adams County
425 S. Twelfth, Quincy, IL 62301, (217) 222-1835, **<adamscohistory.org>**

Homer Historical Society
105 N. Main St., Homer, IL 61849

Hutsonville Historical and Genealogical Society
10953 E. 1825th Ave., Hutsonville, IL 62433

Hyde Park Historical Society
5529 S. Lake Park Ave., Chicago, IL 60637, (773) 493-1893, **<hydeparkhistory.org>**

Ida Public Library
320 N. State St., Belvidere, IL 61008, (815) 544-3838, **<idapubliclibrary.org>**

Illiana Genealogical and Historical Society
215 W. North St., Danville, IL 61832, (217) 431-8733, **<illianaghs.org>**

Illiana Jewish Genealogical Society
Box 384, Flassmoor, IL 60422, **<lincolnnet.net/ijgs>**

Illinois Department of Public Health Division of Vital Records
605 W. Jefferson St., Springfield, IL 62702, (217) 782-6553, **<www.idph.state.il.us/vitalrecords>**

Illinois Great Rivers Area Conference Archives and Special Collections
Henry Pfeiffer Library, MacMurray College, 447 E. Jackson Ave., Jacksonville, IL 62650, (217) 479-7694, **<archives.gcah.org/exist/Conference/umac/igrc.htm>**

Illinois Heritage Association
602 E. Green St., Champaign, IL 61820, (217) 359-5600, **<illinoisheritage.org>**

Illinois Historic Preservation Society
<illinoishistory.gov>

Illinois Mennonite Historical and Genealogical Society
675 State Rte. 116, Metamora, IL 61548, (309) 367-2551, **<imhgs.org>**

Illinois Regional Archives Depository
Illinois State Archives, Springfield, IL 62756, (217) 782-4682, **<cyberdriveillinois.com/departments/archives/irad/iradhome.html>**

Illinois State Archives
Norton Building, Capitol Complex, Springfield, IL 627566, (217) 524-7216, **<statearchives.us/illinois.htm>**

Illinois State Genealogical Society
Box 10195, Springfield, IL 62791, (217) 789-1968, **<rootsweb.ancestry.com/~ilsgs>**

Illinois State Historical Society
Box 1800, Springfield, IL 62701, (217) 525-2781, **<historyillinois.org>**

Illinois Veterans Home
1707 N. Twelfth St., Quincy, IL 62301, (217) 222-8641 ext. 248, **<quincynet.com/ivh>**

Iroquois County Genealogical Society Old Courthouse Museum
103 W. Cherry St., Watseka, IL, 60970, (815) 432-3730, **<rootsweb.ancestry.com/~ilicgs>**

Jackson County Historical Society
1616 Edith St., Murphysboro IL 62966, (618) 684-6989, **<mysite.ncnetwork.net/resolawr/index.htm>**

Jacksonville Area Genealogical and Historical Society
416 S. Main St., Jacksonville, IL 62650, (217) 245-5911, **<orgsites.com/il/jaghs>**

Jasper County Historical and Genealogical Society
c/o Newton Public Library, 100 S. Van Buren St., Newton, IL 62448, (618) 783-8141

Jefferson County Genealogical Society
1411 N. 27th St., Mt. Vernon, IL 62864, (618) 246-8141, **<jchs.mvn.net>**

Jersey County Genealogical Society
Box 12, Jerseyville, IL 62052

Jersey County Historical Society
601 N. State, Jerseyville, IL 62052, (618) 498-3514, **<jerseyusa.net>**

Jewish Genealogical Society of Illinois
Box 515, Northbrook, IL 60065, (312) 666-0100, **<jewishgen.org/jgsi>**

John Mosser Public Library
106 W. Meek St., Abingdon, IL 61410 (309) 462-3129

Johnson County Genealogical and Historical Society
Box 1207, Vienna, IL 62995, **<johnsoncountyil.net>**

Kanakee County Historical Society
Eighth Ave. and Water St., Kanakee, IL 60901, (815) 932-5279, **<kankakeecountymuseum.com>**

Kanakee Valley Genealogical Society
Box 442, Bourbonnais, IL 60914, **<kvgs.org>**

Kane County Genealogical Society
Box 509, Geneva, IL 60134, **<rootsweb.ancestry.com/~ilkcgs>**

Kendall County Genealogical Society
Box 1086, Oswego, IL 60543, (630) 554-8342

Kendall County Historical Society
Box 123, Yorkville, IL 60560, (630) 553-6777, **<kchs.us>**

Kenilworth Historical Society
415 Kenilworth Ave., Kenilworth, IL 60043, (847) 251-2565, **<kenilworthhistory.org>**

Kewanee Historical Society
211 N. Chestnut St., Kewanee, IL 61443, (309) 854-9701, **<kewaneehistory.com>**

Kishwaukee Valley Heritage Society
622 W. Park Ave, Genoa, IL 60135, (815) 784-5559, **<dekalb.ilgenweb.net/KVHS/KVHS_homepage.htm>**

Knox County Genealogical Society
Box 13, Galesburg, IL 61402, (309) 343-1466, **<knox.ilgenweb.net/home/kcgs.htm>**

Knox County Historical Society
Box 1757, Galesburg, IL 61402, **<knoxchs.homestead.com>**

LaGrange Public Library
10 W. Cossitt, LaGrange, IL 60525, (708) 352-0576, **<lagrangelibrary.org>**

LaHarpe Historical and Genealogical Society
Box 289, LaHarpe, IL 61450, (217)659-3635, **<outfitters.com/illinois/hancock/laharpe/lhgs>**

Lake County Genealogical Society
1170 N. Midlothian Rd., Mendelein, IL 60060, (847) 918-3208, **<rootsweb.ancestry.com/~illcgs>**

Lansing Historical Society
2750 Indiana Ave., Lansing, IL 60438, (708) 474-2447, **<lansing.lib.il.us/historical.html>**

LaSalle County Genealogical Guild
115 W. Glover St., Ottawa, IL 61350, (815) 433-5261, **<lscgg.org>**

Lawrence County Genealogical Society
RR1, Box 44, Bridgeport, IL 62417, (618) 945-7181

Lawrence County Historical Society
Box 511, Lawrenceville, IL 62439, (618) 943-2300, **<lawrencecountyillinois.com/history/index.html>**

Lebanon Historical Society
309 W. St. Louis St., Lebanon, IL 62254, (618) 537-4498, **<lebanon-history.org>**

Lee County Genealogical Society
111 S. Hennepin Ave., Dixon, IL 61021, (815) 288-6702, **<leecoilgen.org>**

Lemont Area Historical Society
Box 126, Lemont, IL 60439, (630) 257-2972, **<township.com/lemont/historical>**

LeRoy Historical Society
301 E. Cedar, LeRoy, IL 61752

Lewis and Clark Genealogical Society
Box 485, Godfrey, IL 62035

Lexington Genealogical and Historical Society
318 W. Main St., Lexington, IL 61753, (309) 365-4591, **<lexingtonillinois.org/fort>**

Libertyville-Mundelein Historical Society
413 N. Milwaukee Ave., Libertyville, IL 60048, (847) 362-2330

Litchfield Carnegie Library
400 N. State St., Litchfield, IL 62056, (217) 324-3866, **<litchfieldpubliclibrary.org>**

Lithuanian American Genealogical Society
c/o Balzekas Museum, 6500 S. Pulaski Rd., Chicago, IL 60629, (773) 582-6500, **<balzekasmuseum.org>**

Logan County Genealogical and Historical Society
114 N. Chicago St., Lincoln, IL 62656, (217) 732-3200, **<www.rootsweb.ancestry.com/~illcghs>**

Lombard Historical Society
23 W. Maple St., Lombard, IL 60148, (630) 629-1885, **<lombardhistory.org>**

Long Grove Historical Society
348 Old McHenry Rd., Long Grove, IL 60047, (847) 634-6155, **<longgrovehistory.com>**

Lyndon Historical Society
405 First St., Lyndon, IL 61261

Lyons Public Library
4209 Joliet Ave., Lyons, IL 60534, (708) 447-3577, **<lyonslibrary.org>**

Macon County Historical Society
5580 N. Fork Rd., Decatur, IL 62521, (217) 422-4919, **<mchsdecatur.org>**

Macoupin County Genealogical Society
Box 95, Staunton, IL 62088, (618) 635-3852, **<macoupinctygenealogy.org/mcgs/index.html>**

Macoupin County Historical Society
Box 432, Carlinville, IL 62626, (217) 854-8916, **<macsociety.org>**

Madison County Genealogical Society
Box 631, Edwardsville, IL 62025, **<www.rootsweb.ancestry.com/~ilmadcgs>**

Madison County Historical Museum
715 N. Main St., Edwardsville, IL 62025, (618) 656-7562, **<madisoncountymuseum.org>**

Manhattan Township Historical Society
240 Whitson, Manhattan, IL 60442, (815) 478-3374

Manito Historical Society
Box 304, Manito, IL 61546, (309) 968-6416

Marion County Genealogical and Historical Society
Box 342, Salem, IL 62881, **<marioncountyil.angelfire.com/iMarionCoGenHistSociety.html>**

Marissa Historical and Genealogical Society
Box 245, Marissa, IL 62257, **<marissahgs.org>**

Marshall County Historical Society
314 Fifth St., Lacon, IL 61540, (309) 246-2349, **<il-mchs.org>**

Mascoutah Historical Society
306 W. Main St., Mascoutah, IL 62258, (618) 566-9774, **<mascoutahheritagemuseum.org/society.htm>**

Mason County Genealogical and Historical Society
Box 446, Havana, IL 62644, **<havana.lib.il.us/community/mcghs.html>**

Massac County Genealogical Society
Box 1043, Metropolis, IL 62960, **<www.rootsweb.ancestry.com/~ilmcgs>**

Massac County Historical Society
Box 1245, Brookport, IL 62910, **<rootsweb.ancestry.com/~ilmcgs>**

Matteson Historical Society
813 School Ave., Matteson, IL 60443, (708) 748-3033

Mattoon Public Library
1600 Charleston Ave., Box 809, Mattoon, IL 61938, (217) 234-2621 **<mattoonlibrary.org>**

McDonough County Genealogical Society
Box 202, Macomb, IL 61455, (309) 255-5161, **<mcdcgs.com>**

McHenry County Historical Society
6422 Main St., Box 434, Union, IL 60180, (815) 923-2267, **<mchsonline.org>**

McHenry County Genealogical Society
Box 184, Crystal Lake, IL 60039, **<mcigs.org>**

McLean County Genealogical Society
Box 488, Normal, IL 61761-0488, **<mcgs.org>**

McLean County Genealogical Society
c/o McLean County Museum of History, 200 N. Main St., Bloomington, IL 61701, (309) 827-0428 ext. 28, **<mchistory.org>**

Melrose Park Historical Society
Box 1453, Melrose Park, IL 60161

Menard County Historical Society
125 S. Seventh St., Petersburg, IL 62675, (217) 632-7363

Mercer County Historical Society
c/o Essley-Noble Museum, 1406 SE Second Ave., Aledo, IL 61231, (309) 582-2280, **<aledomainstreet.com>**

Meredosia Area Historical and Genealogical Society
Box 304, Meredosia, IL 62265

Metropolis Public Library
317 Metropolis St., Metropolis, IL 62960, (618) 524-4312, **<metropolis.lib.il.us>**

Monroe County Genealogical Society
Box 381, Columbia, IL 62236, **<www.rootsweb.ancestry.com/~ilmcghs>**

Montgomery County Genealogical Society
Box 212, Litchfield, IL 62056-0212, **<mcgsil.com>**

Morgan County Historical Society
Box 1033, Jacksonville, IL 62651, (217) 245-5390

Morris Library, Southern Illinois University Carbondale
Special Collections Research Center, 605 Agriculture Dr., Mailcode 6632, Carbondale, IL 62901, (618) 453-2516, **<lib.siu.edu/spcol>**

Moultrie County Historical and Genealogical Society
Box 588, Sullivan, IL 61951, (217) 728-4085, **<354.com/bethany/genealogy.htm>**

Mount Prospect Historical Society
101 S. Maple, Mount Prospect, IL 60056, (847) 392-9006, **<mtphistory.org>**

Mount Pulaski Township Historical Society
104 E. Cooke St., Mount Pulaski, IL 62548, (217) 792-3719, **<www.rootsweb.ancestry.com/~ilmpths>**

Mount Vernon Genealogical Society
101 S. Seventh, Mount Vernon, IL 62864, (618) 242-6322

Mulkeytown Area Historical Society
7570 Mulkeytown Rd., Mulkeytown IL 62865, (618) 724-1156

National Archives Records Administration, Great Lakes Region
7358 S. Pulaski Rd., Chicago, IL 60629, (773) 948-9019, **<archives.gov/great-lakes>**

Nauvoo Historical Society
1380 Mulholland St., Box 69, Nauvoo, IL 62354, (217) 453-2528, **<nauvoohistoricalsociety.org>**

Newberry Library
60 W. Walton St., Chicago, IL 60610, (312) 943-9090, **<www.newberry.org>**

Newport Township Historical Society
Box 98, Wadsworth, IL 60083

North Central Illinois Genealogical Society
Box 4635, Rockford, IL 61110, **<www.rootsweb.ancestry.com/~ilwinneb/ncengen.htm>**

North Suburban Genealogical Society
c/o Winnetka Public Library, 768 Oak St., Winnetka, IL 60093, (847) 446-7220

Northbrook Historical Society
1776 Walter's Ave., Northbrook, IL 60062, (847) 498-3404, **<northbrookhistory.org>**

Northeastern Illinois University Ronald Williams Library
5500 N. St. Louis Ave., Chicago, IL 60625, (773) 442-4400, **<library.neiu.edu>**

Northern Illinois Chapter, American Historical Society of Germans from Russia
847 S. Home Ave., Oak Park, IL 60304, **<ahsgr.org/northern_illinois_chapter.htm>**

Northwest Suburban Council of Genealogists
Box AC, Mount Prospect, IL 60056, **<eresamcmillin.com>**

Norwood Park Historical Society
5624 N. Newark Ave., Chicago, IL 60631, (312) 631-4633, **<norwoodparkhistoricalsociety.org>**

Oak Lawn Historical Society
4332 W. 109th St., Oak Lawn, IL 60453, (708) 425-3424

Odell Prairie Trails Genealogical and Historical Society
Box 82, Odell, IL 60460, (815) 998-2324

O'Fallon Historical Society
101 W. State St., Box 344, O'Fallon, IL 62269, (618) 624-8409, **<www.ofallon.com/apex/museum.shtml>**

Ogle County Genealogical Society
Box 251, Oregon, IL 61061, **<www.rootsweb.ancestry.com/~ilogle>**

Ogle County Historical Society
111 N. Sixth St., Box 183, Oregon, IL 61061, (815) 732-7545, **<www.rootsweb.ancestry.com/~ilogle/historical.htm>**

Oglesby Historical Society
100 Oak St., Oglesby, IL 61348

Old Six Mile Historical Society
3279 Maryville Road, Box 483, Granite City, IL 62040

Orland Historical Society
Box 324, Orland Park, IL 60543, (708) 349-0065, **<orlandhistory.org>**

Ostfriesian Heritage Society of East Central Illinois
3154 CR 2000E, Rantoul, IL 61866, (217) 892-4776

Oswego Roots Genealogical Society
Box 726, Oswego, IL 60543

Palatine Historical Society
Box 134, Palatine, IL 60078, (847) 991-6460, **<palatine.il.us>**

Palatines to America, Illinois Chapter
Box 3884, Quincy, IL 62305, **<palam.org/chapters.php?chapter=2>**

Palestine Historical Society
413 S. Lincoln, Palestine, IL 62451

Palos Historical Society
12021 S.93rd Ave.., Palos Park, IL 60464, (708) 361-3118

Park Forest Historical Society
400 Lakewood Blvd., Park Forest, IL 60466, (708) 748-3731, **<lincolnnet.net/users/lrpfhs>**

Park Ridge Historical Society and Museum
41 Prairie, Park Ridge, IL 60068, (847) 696-1973

Peoria County Genealogical Society
Box 1489, Peoria, IL 61655, **<usgennet.org/usa/il/county/peoria1>**

Peoria Historical Society and Museum
611 SW Washington St., Peoria, IL 61602, (309) 674-1921, **<peoriahistoricalsociety.org>**

Peoria Public Library
107 NE Monroe St., Peoria, IL 61602, (309) 497-2000, **<peoriapubliclibrary.org>**

Perry County Historical Society
108 W. Jackson St., Pickneyville, IL 62274., **<perrycountyillinois.net>**

Piatt County Historical and Genealogical Society
Box 111, Monticello, IL 61856, **<rootsweb.ancestry.com/~ilpchgs>**

Pike and Calhoun Counties Genealogical Society
Box 104, Pleasant Hill, IL 62366, (217) 734-2221

Pike County Historical Society and Museum
Box 44, Pittsfield, IL 62363, (217) 285-4618

Polish Genealogical Society and Museum of America
984 N. Milwaukee Ave., Chicago, IL 60642, (773) 384-3352, **<pgsa.org>**

Pontiac Public Library
211 E. Madison, Pontiac, IL 61764, (815) 844-7229, **<pontiacpubliclibrary.org>**

Pope County Historical Society
Box 837, Golconda, IL 62938, **<pope.ilgenweb.net/pchs.htm>**

Putnam County Historical Society
Box 74, Hennepin, IL 61327, (815) 925-7560, **<rootsweb.ancestry.com/~ilpchs>**

Randolph County Genealogical Society
Box 328, Chester, IL 62233, (618) 826-3807, **<rootsweb.ancestry.com/~ilrcgs>**

Ravenswood-Lakeview Historical Association
c/o Conrad Sulzer Regional Library
4455 N. Lincoln Ave., Chicago, IL 60625, (312) 744-7616, **<ravenswoodlakeview.com/2006/02/index.html>**

Richland County Genealogical and Historical Society
Box 202, Olney, IL 62450, (618) 869-2425

Ridge Historical Society
10621 S. Seeley Ave., Chicago, IL 60643, (773) 881-1675, **<ridgehistoricalsociety.org>**

Riverside Historical Commission and Museum
27 Riverside Rd., Riverside Village, IL 60546, (630) 447-2700, **<riversidemuseum.net>**

Rock Island County Historical Society
822 Eleventh Ave., Moline, IL 61265, (309) 764-8590, **<richs.cc>**

Rockford Historical Society
Box 4387, Rockford, IL 61101

Rockford Public Library
215 N. Wyman St., Rockford, IL 61101, (815) 965-7606, **<rockfordpubliclibrary.org>**

Rogers Park/West Ridge Historical Society
7344 N. Western, Chicago, IL 60645, (773) 764-4078 , **<rpwrhs.org>**

Roselle Public Library
40 S. Park St., Roselle, IL 60172, (630) 529-1641, **<roselle.lib.il.us>**

Rossville Historical Museum
108 W. Attica St., Rossville, Il 60933, (217) 748-4080, **<rossvilleshops.com/society.html>**

Saint Charles Heritage Center
215 E. Main St., St. Charles, IL 60174, (630) 584-6967, **<stcmuseum.org>**

Saint Clair County Genealogical Society
Box 431, Belleville, IL 62222, **<stclair-ilgs.org/stchome.htm>**

Saint Clair County Historical Society
701 E. Washington St., Belleville, IL 62220, (618) 234-0600, **<stcchs.org>**

Saline County Genealogical Society
Box 4, Harrisburg, IL 62946, **<rootsweb.ancestry.com/~ilsaline>**

Sangamon County Genealogical Society
Box 1829, Springfield, IL 62705-1829, **<rootsweb.ancestry.com/~ilscgs2>**

Sangamon County Historical Society
308 E. Adams St., Springfield, IL 62701, (217) 522-2500, **<sancohis.org>**

Schuyler-Brown County Genealogical Society
200 S. Congress, Ruchville, IL 62681

Shelby County Illinois Historical and Genealogical Society
151 S. Washington, Box 286, Shelbyville, IL 62565, (217) 774 2260, **<shelbycounty-il.com/historicalandgenealogicalsociety.htm>**

Skokie Historical Society
8031 Floral Ave., Skokie, IL 60077, (847) 673-1888, **<skokiehistory.info>**

Society of Colonial Wars in the State of Illinois
Box 350, Kenilworth, IL 60043, (857) 251-1400, **<m-mpartners.com/ilscw>**

South Holland Historical Society
Box 48, South Holland, IL 60473, (708) 596-2722, **<southholland.org>**

South Suburban Genealogical and Historical Society
3000 W. 170th Place, Hazel Crest, IL 60429, (708) 335-3340, **<ssghs.org>**

Stark County Genealogical Society
Box 83, Toulon, IL 61483, **<rootsweb.ancestry.com/~ilscgs>**

Staunton Public Library
306 W. Main St., Staunton, IL 62088, (618) 635-3852, **<stauntonil.com>**

Stephenson County Genealogical Society
Box 514, Freeport, IL 61032, **<rootsweb.ancestry.com/~ilstephe/HISTORYandMUSEUMS/GenSociety.html>**

Stephenson County Historical Society
1440 S. Carroll Ave., Freeport, IL 61032, (800) 369-2955 , **<stephcohs.org>**

Sterling-Rock Falls Historical Society and Museum
Box 65, Sterling, IL 61081, (815) 622-6215, **<svonline.net/~srfhs>**

Streatorland Historical Society
306 S. Vermillion St., Streator, IL 61364, (815) 672-2443

Swedish-American Historical Society
3225 W. Foster Ave., Box 48, Chicago, IL 60625, (773) 583-5722, **<swedishamericanhist.org>**

Swenson Swedish Immigration Research Center
Augustana College, 3520 Seventh Ave., Rock Island, Il 61201, (309) 794-7204 **<www.augustana.edu/x13856.xml >**

Sycamore Public Library
103 E. State St., Sycamore, IL 60178, (815) 895-2500, **<sycamorelibrary.org>**

Tazewell County Genealogical and Historical Society
Box 312, Pekin, IL 61555, (309) 477-3044, **<tcghs.org>**

Thorton Township Historical Society
154 E. 154th St., Harvey, IL 60426, (708) 331-4247

Three Rivers Public Library District, Minooka Branch
109 N. Wabena, Minooka, IL 60447, (815) 467-1600, **<three-rivers-library.org>**

Tinely Moraine Genealogists
Box 521, Tinley Park, IL 60477, (708) 532-6594, **<tmgenealogists.org>**

Tinley Park Historical Society
Box 325, Tinley Park, IL 60477, (708) 429-4210

Tri-County Genealogical Society
Box 355, Augusta, IL 62311

Union County Genealogical and Historical Research Committee
101 E. First St., Box 92, Versailles, IL 62378, (217) 225-9094

University of Illinois at Springfield
One University Plaza, MS BRK 140, Springfield, IL 62703-5407, (217) 206-6520, **<uis.edu/archives>**

Urbana Free Library Archives
210 W. Green St., Urbana, IL 61801, (217) 367-4057, **<urbanafreelibrary.org>**

Vandalia Historical Society
307 N. Sixth, Vandalia, IL 62471, (618) 283-0024

Vermilion County Museum
116 N. Gilbert, Danville, IL 61832, (217) 442-2922, **<vermilioncountymuseum.org>**

Versailles Area Genealogical and Historical Society
113 W. First St., IL 62378, (217) 225-3401, **<vaghs.tripod.com>**

Villa Park Historical Society Museum
220 S. Villa Ave., Villa Park, IL 60181, (630) 941-0223, **<vphistoricalsociety.com>**

Village of Thornton Historical Society
114 N. Hunter St., Thorton, IL 60476, (708) 877-6569, **<thornton60476.com>**

Vogel Genealogical Research Library
305 First St., Box 132, Holcomb, IL 61043, (815) 393-4110

Wabash County Historical Society
Box 911, Mount Carmel, IL 62863, **<wabashmuseum.org>**

Warren County Genealogical Society
Box 761, Monmouth, IL 61462, (309) 734-2763, **<usgennet.org/usa/il/county/warren>**

Warren County Historical Society
RR 2, Avon, IL, 61415, (309) 465-3361, **<warrencountyhistoricalsociety.net>**

Warren County Library
60-62 Public Square, Monmouth, IL 61462, (309) 734-3166, **<www.wcplibrary.org>**

Warsaw Historical Society and Museum
401 Main St., Warsaw, IL 62379

Washington County Genealogical Society
Rt. 1, Nashville, IL 62263

Wauconda Township Historical Society
711 N. Main St., Box 256, Wauconda, IL 60084, (847) 526-9303, **<waucondaarea.info/Wauconda_Township_Historical_Society.htm>**

Waukegan Historical Society, J. L. Raymond Memorial Research Library
1911 N. Sheridan Rd., Box 857, Waukegan, IL 60087, (847) 360-4772, **<waukeganhistorical.org>**

Waverly Genealogical and Historical Society
359 E. Tremont St., Waverly, IL 62692, (217) 435-4961, **<waverly.lib.il.us/community/genealogy.html>**

West Chicago Historical Society Kruse House Museum
527 Main St., Box 246, West Chicago, IL 60186, (630) 231-2329

Western Illinois University Library Illinois Regional Archives Depository
1 University Circle, Macomb, IL 61455, (309) 298-2716, **<wiu.edu/users/milibo/wiu/units/archives/irad>**

Westmont Historical Society W.L. Gregg Museum
117 S. Linden, Westmont, IL 60559

Wheaton Public Library
225 N. Cross St., Wheaton, IL 60187, (630) 668-1374, **<wheatonlibrary.org>**

Wheeling Historical Society
Box 3, Wheeling, IL 60090, (847) 537-3119, **<wheelinghistoricalsociety.com>**

White County Historical Society
Box 121, Carmi, IL 62821, (618) 382-8425, **<rootsweb.ancestry.com/~ilwcohs>**

Will County Historical Society
803 S. State St., Lockport, IL 60441, (815) 838-5080, **<willcountyhistory.org>**

Will-Grundy Counties Genealogical Society
Box 24, Wilmington, IL 60481, **<wggs.org>**

Williamson County Historical Society
105 S. Van Buren St., Marion, IL 62959, (618) 997-5863, **<thewchs.com>**

Wilmette Historical Museum and Society
609 Ridge Rd., Wilmette, IL 60091, (847) 853-7666, **<wilmettehistory.org>**

Winfield Historical Society
Box 315, Winfield, IL 60190, (630) 653-1489

Winnebago and Boone Counties Genealogical Society
Box 10166, Rockford, IL 61131, **<rootsweb.ancestry.com/~ilwinneb/winbngen.htm>**

Winnetka Historical Society
Box 365, Winnetka, IL 60093, (847) 501-6025, **<winnetkahistory.org>**

Winnetka-Northfield Public Library
768 Oak St., Winnetka, IL 60093, (847) 446-7220, **<wpld.alibrary.com>**

Withers Public Library
202 E. Washington, Bloomington, IL 61701

Woodford County Historical Society
112 N. Main St., Eureka, IL 61530, (309) 467-4525, **<eureka.lib.il.us/community/wchs>**

Wyanet Historical Society
109 E. Main St., Box 169, Wyanet, IL 61379, (815) 699-2531

Zion Genealogical Society
c/o Zion Public Library, 2400 Gabriel Ave., Zion, IL 60099, **<rootsweb.ancestry.com/~ilzgs>**

Zion Historical Society
1300 Shiloh Blvd., Zion, IL 60099, (847) 746-2427, **<zionhs.com>**

☞ GENERAL RESOURCES

The Biographical Encyclopedia of Illinois of the Nineteenth Century (Galaxy Publishing Company, 1875)

Brethren in Northern Illinois and Wisconsin by John Heckman (Brethren Publishing House, 1941)

A Brief History of the Regular Baptists, Principally of Southern Illinois by Achilles Coffey (Martin Steam Printers and Binders, 1877)

Chicago and Cook County: A Guide to Research by Loretto Dennis Szucs (Ancestry, ca. 1996)

A Complete History of Illinois from 1673-1968 by Alexander Davidson (Illinois Journal Company, 1874)

Descriptive Inventory of the Archives of the State of Illinois, 2nd edition, edited by Robert E. Bailey and Elaine Shemoney Evans (Illinois State Archives, 1997)

Encyclopedia of Biography of Illinois, 3 vols. (Century Publishing and Engraving Co., 1892-1902)

Finding Your Chicago Ancestors by Grace DuMelle (Lake Claremont Press, 2005)

The Frontier State, 1818-1848 by Theodore Calvin Pease (Centennial Commission, 1918)

Genealogical Sources in Chicago, Illinois, 1835-1900 compiled by the Bicentennial Committee, Virginia M. Meyer, chairman (Chicago Genealogical Society, 1982)

Guide to Church Vital Statistics Records in Illinois, preliminary edition prepared by Illinois Historical Records Survey (Illinois Historical Records Survey, 1942)

A Guide to County Records in the Illinois Regional Archives by Roy C. Turnbaugh, Jr. (Illinois State Archives, ca. 1983)

Guide to Depositories of Manuscript Collection in Illinois, preliminary edition prepared by the Illinois Historical Records Survey (Illinois Historical Records Survey, 1940)

A Guide to the History of Illinois edited by John Hoffman (Greenwood Press, 1991)

A Guide to Illinois Area Genealogical Societies and Illinois Researchers (Illinois State Genealogical Society, 1986)

Historical Encyclopedia of Illinois, 3 vols., edited by Newton Bateman, et al. (Brookhaven Press, ca. 2001)

A History of Illinois from its Commencement as a State in 1818 to 1847 by Thomas Ford (S.C. Griggs and Co., 1854)

History of Illinois and Her People, 6 vols., by Professor George W. Smith (American Historical Society, Inc., 1927)

History of the Presbyterian Church in the State of Illinois by A.T. Norton (W.S. Bryan, 1879)

How to Research a Family with Illinois Roots by Lowell M. Volkel and Marjorie Smith (Heritage House, ca. 1977)

Illinois Biographical Dictionary (Somerset, ca. 1993)

Illinois: Crossroads of a Continent by Lois Carrier (University of Illinois Press, ca. 1993)

The Illinois Fact Book and Historical Almanac, 1673-1968 by John Clayton (Southern Illinois University Press, 1970)

Illinois Genealogical Research by George K. Schweitzer (G.K. Scweitzer, ca. 1997)

Illinois, the Heart of the Nation by Edward F. Dunne (Lewis Publishing Co., 1933)

Illinois: A History of the Prairie State by Robert P. Howard (W.B. Eerdmans Publishing Co., 1972)

Illinois Libraries with Genealogical Collections edited by Lowell M. Volkel (Illinois State Genealogical Society, 1992)

Illinois Quaker Meeting Records (Shelby Publishing and Printing, ca. 1996)

Illinois Research Outline by the Church of Jesus Christ of Latter-day Saints (online at **<www.familysearch.org/eng/search/RG/guide/illinois.asp>**)

Illinois State Genealogical Society Surname Index, 1981 compiled by Mrs. O.B. Lunde (Illinois State Genealogical Society, 1982)

The Indians of Illinois: A History and Genealogy by Helen Cox Tregillis (H.C. Tregillis, ca. 1983)

Log Cabins to Steeples: The Complete Story of the United Methodist Way in Illinois by J. Gordon Melton (Commissions on Archives and History, Northern, Central, and Southern Illinois Conferences, 1974)

Manual for Illinois Genealogical Research by Pat and Ray Gooldy (Ye Olde Genealogie Shoppe, ca. 1994)

Men of Illinois (H. Witherspoon, 1902)

Mennonites in Illinois by Willard H. Smith (Herald Press, 1983)

The Methodist Movement in Northern Illinois by Almer M. Pennewell (The Sycamore Tribune, 1942)

Newspapers in the Illinois State Historical Library by the Illinois State Historical Library (1964)

Newspapers and Periodicals of Illinois, 1814-1879, revised edition, by Franklin Wiliiam Scott (Illinois State Historical Library, 1910)

The Patriotism of Illinois. A Record of the Civil and Military History of the State in the War for the Union, 2 vols., by T. M. Eddy (Clarke and Co., 1865-1866)

Plains People; the Midwest (Indiana, Illinois, Iowa, Missouri): Research Sources and Bibliographies (Fiske Genealogical Foundation, 1990)

Prairie Pioneers of Illinois, 2 vols., edited by Beth Rochefort (Illinois State Genealogical Society, 1986-1988)

A Reference Guide for Genealogical and Historical Research in Illinois by Joseph C. Wolf (Detroit Society for Genealogical Research, 1963)

Searching in Illinois: A Reference Guide to Public and Private Records by Gayle Beckstead and Mary Lou Kozub (ISC Publications, ca. 1984)

Sources of Mormon History in Illinois, 1839-48; an Annotated Catalog of the Microfilm Collection at Southern Illinois University, 2nd edition, compiled by Stanley B. Kimball (Southern Illinois University, 1966)

A Summary Guide to Local Government Records in the Illinois Regional Archives edited by Robert E. Bailey, et al. (Illinois State Archives, Office of the Secretary of State, ca. 1992)

The United States Biographical Dictionary and Portrait Gallery of Eminent and Self-made Men, Illinois Volume (American Publishing Co., 1883)

We Were There: An Oral History of the Illinois Baptist State Association, 1907-1976 edited by Robert J. Hastings (Illinois Baptist State Association, 1976)

Who's Who in Illinois, Women, Makers of History by Agness Geneva Gilman and Gertrude Marcelle Gilman (The Electric Publishers, 1927)

The Women of Illinois by Henry McCormick (Pantagraph Printing and Stationery Company, 1913)

☞LAND RECORDS

The Illinois Military Tract; a Study of Land Occupation, Utilization, and Tenure by Theodore Leonard Carlson (University of Illinois Press, 1951)

Original Land Grants, 1824-1870 compiled by Charla Murphy et al. (Williamson County Historical Society, 1997)

Record of the Services of Illinois Soldiers in the Black Hawk War, 1831-32, and in the Mexican War, 1846-48 prepared by Issac H. Elliott (H.W. Rokker, State Printer, 1882)

War of 1812 Bounty Lands in Illinois indexed by James D. Walker with an introduction by Lowell M. Volkel (Heritage House, 1977)

☞MAPS

Counties of Illinois compiled by Edward J. Hughes (E.J. Hughes, 1941)

County and Township Gazetteer; Notes on the Location of Illinois County Seats compiled by Sheila Kelly, notes by Lori Lovett (Illinois State Archives, 1988)

A Gazetteer of the States of Illinois and Missouri by Lewis C. Beck (C.R. and G. Webster, 1823)

Illinois Atlas and Gazetteer (DeLorme Mapping Company, ca. 1991)

Illinois Place Names compiled by James N. Adams, edited by William E. Keller with an addendum by Lowell M. Volkel (Illinois State Historical Society, 1989)

Indian Place Names in Illinois by Virgil Vogel Jr. (1963)

Maps of Illinois Counties in 1876, Together with the Plat of Chicago and other Cities (Mayhill Publications, 1972)

Origin and Evolution of Illinois Counties by Jessie White, Secretary of State (The State, 2000)

☞MILITARY RECORDS

Biographical Sketches of Illinois Officers Engaged in the War Against the Rebellion of 1861 by James Grant Wilson (J. Barnet, 1862)

Fighting Men of Illinois edited by Publishers Subscription Co. (W.C. Cox, 1974)

Illinois in the Civil War, 2nd edition by Victor Hicken, foreword by E.B. Long (University of Illinois Press, ca. 1991)

Illinois Soldier's and Sailor's Home at Quincy, 2 vols., indexed by Lowell M. Volkel (Heritage House, 1975-1980)

Index to War of 1812 Pension Files, revised edition, 2 vols., transcribed by Virgil D. White (National Historical Publishing Co., 1992)

The Martyrs and Heroes of Illinois in the Great Rebellion, edited by James Barnet (Press of J. Barnet, 1865)

Record of the Service of Illinois Soldiers in the Black Hawk War, 1831-32, and the Mexican War, 1846-48 by the Illinois Military and Naval Department (H.W. Rokker, State printer, 1882)

Remembering Illinois Veterans (Illinois State Archives, 1992)

Report of the Adjutant General of the State of Illinois, 9 vols. revised by J. N. Reece (Phillips Brothers, 1900-1902)

Revolutionary Soldiers buried in Illinois by Harriett J. Walker (Genealogical Publishing Co., 1967)

Soldiers of the American Revolution Buried in Illinois (Illinois State Genealogical Society, 1976)

☞PROBATE RECORDS

The Bench and Bar of Illinois: Historical and Reminiscent, 2 vols., edited by John M. Palmer (Lewis Publishing, 1899)

The Illinois Fact Book and Historical Almanac, 1673-1968 by John Clayton (Southern Illinois University Press, 1970)

☞VITAL RECORDS

1850 Illinois Mortality Schedule, 3 vols. transcribed by Lowell M. Volkel (1972-ca. 1973)

1860 Illinois Mortality Schedule, 3 vols. transcribed by Lowell M. Volkel (Heritage House, ca. 1979)

The Era of the Civil War: 1848-1870 by Arthur Charles Cole, introduction by John Y. Simon (University of Illinois Press, ca. 1987)

Guide to Public Vital Statistics Records in Illinois prepared by Illinois Historical Records Survey (Heritage House, 1976)

Index of Illinois Marriages, earliest to 1900, CD-ROMs (Illinois State Genealogical Society)

Marriages from Illinois Counties, 6 vols., by Walter R. Sanders (W.R. Sanders, 1976)

Vital Records from Chicago Newspapers compiled by the Newspaper Research Committee, Mrs. Edward Rickie, Chairman (Chicago Genealogical Society, 1971-1981

•-COUNTY DETAILS-•

ADAMS
521 Vermont St., Quincy, IL 62301, (217) 277-2100, **<co.adams.il.us>**
- **INCORPORATED:** Jan. 13, 1825
- **PARENT COUNTY:** Pike
- **BIRTH RECORDS:** start in 1878, kept by County Clerk
- **MARRIAGE:** 1825, County Clerk
- **DIVORCE:** unknown, Circuit Court Clerk
- **DEATH:** 1878, County Clerk
- **PROBATE:** 1826, Circuit Court Clerk
- **COURT:** 1825, Circuit Court Clerk

ALEXANDER
2000 Washington Ave., Cairo, IL 62914, (618) 734-7000, **<www.myillinoisgenealogy.com/il-county-alexander.html>**
- **INCORPORATED:** March 4, 1819
- **PARENT COUNTY:** Union
- **BIRTH RECORDS:** start in 1851, kept by County Clerk
- **MARRIAGE:** 1819, County Clerk
- **DEATH:** 1851, County Clerk
- **DIVORCE:** unknown, Circuit Court Clerk
- **LAND:** 1818, County Recorder
- **PROBATE:** 1819, Circuit Court Clerk
- **COURT:** 1821, Circuit Court Clerk

BOND
200 W. College, Greenville, IL 62246, (618) 664-3208, **<bondcountyil.com>**
- **INCORPORATED:** Jan. 4, 1817
- **PARENT COUNTY:** Madison
- **BIRTH RECORDS:** start in 1877, kept by County Clerk
- **MARRIAGE:** 1817, County Clerk
- **DIVORCE:** unknown, Circuit Court Clerk
- **DEATH:** 1877, County Clerk
- **LAND:** unknown, County Recorder
- **PROBATE:** unknown, Circuit Court Clerk
- **COURT:** unknown, Circuit Court Clerk
- **MILITARY:** unknown, County Clerk

BOONE
601 N. Main St., Belvidere, IL 61008, (815) 544-3103, **<boonecountyil.org>**
- **INCORPORATED:** March 4, 1837
- **PARENT COUNTY:** Winnebago
- **BIRTH RECORDS:** start in 1877, kept by County Clerk
- **MARRIAGE:** 1838, County Clerk
- **DIVORCE:** unknown, Circuit Court Clerk
- **DEATH:** 1877, County Clerk
- **LAND:** 1838, County Recorder
- **PROBATE:** 1840, Circuit Court Clerk
- **COURT:** 1838, Circuit Court Clerk

BROWN
Courthouse Bldg., 200 E. Court, Mount Sterling, IL 62353, (217) 773-3421, **<browncountyil.com>**
- **INCORPORATED:** Feb. 1, 1839
- **PARENT COUNTY:** Schuyler
- **BIRTH RECORDS:** start in 1878, kept by County Clerk
- **MARRIAGE:** 1839, County Clerk
- **DIVORCE:** unknown, Circuit Court Clerk
- **DEATH:** 1878, County Clerk
- **LAND:** 1817, County Recorder
- **PROBATE:** 1839, Circuit Court Clerk
- **COURT:** 1837, Circuit Court Clerk
- **MILITARY:** 1918, County Clerk

BUREAU
700 S. Main St., Princeton, IL 61356, (815) 872-2001, **<bureaucounty.us>**
- **INCORPORATED:** Feb. 28, 1837
- **PARENT COUNTY:** Putnam
- **BIRTH RECORDS:** start in 1878, kept by County Clerk
- **MARRIAGE:** 1837, County Clerk
- **DEATH:** 1878, County Clerk
- **LAND:** 1817, County Recorder
- **PROBATE:** 1837, Circuit Court Clerk
- **COURT:** 1837, Circuit Court Clerk

CALHOUN

Box 187, Hardin, IL 62047, (618) 576-2451,
<www.myillinoisgenealogy.com/il-county-calhoun.html>
- **INCORPORATED:** Jan. 20, 1825
- **PARENT COUNTY:** Pike
- **BIRTH RECORDS:** start in 1878, kept by County Clerk
- **MARRIAGE:** 1825, County Clerk
- **DEATH:** 1878, County Clerk
- **LAND:** 1825, County Recorder
- **PROBATE:** 1833, Circuit Court Clerk
- **COURT:** 1825, Circuit Court Clerk

CARROLL

301 N. Main, Mount Carroll, IL 61053, (815) 244-0230,
<carroll-county.net>
- **INCORPORATED:** Feb. 22, 1839
- **PARENT COUNTY:** Jo Daviess
- **BIRTH RECORDS:** start in 1877, kept by County Clerk
- **MARRIAGE:** 1839, County Clerk
- **DEATH:** 1877, County Clerk
- **LAND:** 1837, County Recorder
- **PROBATE:** 1839, Circuit Court Clerk
- **COURT:** 1837, Circuit Court Clerk

CASS

100 E. Springfield St., Virginia, IL 62691, (217) 452-7225,
<www.rootsweb.ancestry.com/~ilcass/cass.htm>
- **INCORPORATED:** March 30, 1837
- **PARENT COUNTY:** Morgan
- **BIRTH RECORDS:** start in 1878, kept by County Clerk
- **MARRIAGE:** 1837, County Clerk
- **DEATH:** 1878, County Clerk
- **LAND:** 1826, County Recorder
- **PROBATE:** 1837, Circuit Court Clerk
- **COURT:** 1837, Circuit Court Clerk

CHAMPAIGN

1776 E. Washington St., Urbana, IL 61802, (217) 384-3725,
<co.champaign.il.us>
- **INCORPORATED:** Feb. 20, 1833
- **PARENT COUNTY:** Vermilion
- **BIRTH RECORDS:** start in 1878, kept by County Clerk
- **MARRIAGE:** 1833, County Clerk
- **DEATH:** 1878, County Clerk
- **LAND:** 1833, County Recorder
- **PROBATE:** 1833, Circuit Court Clerk
- **COURT:** 1836, Circuit Court Clerk

CHRISTIAN

101 S. Main St., Taylorville, IL 62568, (217) 824-4966,
<www.rootsweb.ancestry.com/~ilchrist>
- **INCORPORATED:** Feb. 15, 1839
- **PARENT COUNTIES:** Montgomery, Sangamon, Shelby
- **BIRTH RECORDS:** start in 1877, kept by County Clerk
- **MARRIAGE:** 1839, County Clerk
- **DEATH:** 1877, County Clerk
- **LAND:** 1828, County Recorder
- **PROBATE:** 1839, Circuit Court Clerk
- **COURT:** 1839, Circuit Court Clerk
- **NOTES:** Formerly Dane County. Name changed to Christian in 1840.

CLARK

501 Archer Ave., Marshall, IL 62441, (217) 826-2811,
<clarkcountyil.org>
- **INCORPORATED:** March 23, 1819
- **PARENT COUNTY:** Crawford
- **BIRTH:** 1865, County Clerk
- **MARRIAGE:** 1819, County Clerk
- **DEATH:** 1865, County Clerk
- **LAND:** 1816, County Recorder
- **PROBATE:** 1820, Circuit Court Clerk
- **COURT:** 1821, Circuit Court Clerk

CLAY

Box 160, Louisville, IL 62858, (618) 665-3523,
<claycountyillinois.org>
- **INCORPORATED:** Dec. 23, 1824
- **PARENT COUNTIES:** Wayne, Fayette, Crawford
- **BIRTH RECORDS:** start in 1877, kept by County Clerk
- **MARRIAGE:** 1825, County Clerk
- **DEATH:** 1877, County Clerk
- **LAND:** 1825, County Recorder
- **PROBATE:** 1827, Circuit Court Clerk
- **COURT:** 1825, Circuit Court Clerk

CLINTON

850 Fairfax St., Carlyle, IL 62231, (618) 594-2464,
<clintonco.illinois.gov>
- **INCORPORATED:** Dec. 27, 1824
- **PARENT COUNTIES:** Washington, Bond
- **BIRTH RECORDS:** start in 1877, kept by County Clerk
- **MARRIAGE:** 1825, County Clerk
- **DEATH:** 1877, County Clerk
- **LAND:** 1818, County Recorder
- **PROBATE:** 1825, Circuit Court Clerk
- **COURT:** 1825, Circuit Court Clerk

COLES

651 Jackson Ave., Charleston, IL 61920, (217) 348-0501,
<www.co.coles.il.us>
- **INCORPORATED:** Dec. 25, 1830
- **PARENT COUNTIES:** Clark, Edgar
- **BIRTH RECORDS:** started in 1877, kept by County Clerk
- **MARRIAGE:** 1831, County Clerk
- **DEATH:** 1877, County Clerk
- **LAND:** 1830, County Recorder
- **PROBATE:** 1830, Circuit Court Clerk
- **COURT:** 1830, Circuit Court Clerk

COOK

69 W. Washington St., 5th floor, Chicago, IL 60602,
(312) 443-5500, **<co.cook.il.us>**
- **INCORPORATED:** Jan. 15, 1831
- **PARENT COUNTY:** Putnam
- **BIRTH RECORDS:** start in 1871, kept by County Clerk
- **MARRIAGE:** 1856, County Clerk

- **DEATH:** 1871, County Clerk
- **LAND:** 1871, County Recorder
- **PROBATE:** 1871, Circuit Court Clerk
- **COURT:** 1871, Circuit Court Clerk

CRAWFORD

One Courthouse Sq., Box 655, Robinson, IL 62454, (618) 544-2590, **<crawfordcountycentral.com/circuitclerk/index.htm>**

- **INCORPORATED:** Dec. 31, 1816
- **PARENT COUNTY:** Edwards
- **BIRTH RECORDS:** start in 1877, kept by County Clerk
- **MARRIAGE:** 1817, County Clerk
- **DEATH:** 1877, County Clerk
- **LAND:** 1816, County Recorder
- **PROBATE:** 1818, Circuit Court Clerk
- **COURT:** 1817, Circuit Court Clerk

CUMBERLAND

Box 146, Toledo, IL 62468, (217) 849-2631, **<rr1.net/users/ourlocal/html/cumberland.html>**

- **INCORPORATED:** March 2, 1843
- **PARENT COUNTY:** Coles
- **BIRTH RECORDS:** start in 1885, kept by County Clerk
- **MARRIAGE:** 1880, County Clerk
- **DEATH:** 1885, County Clerk
- **LAND:** 1885, County Recorder
- **PROBATE:** 1884, Circuit Court Clerk
- **COURT:** 1885, Circuit Court Clerk

DANE

- **INCORPORATED:** Feb. 15, 1839
- **PARENT COUNTIES:** Montgomery, Sangamon, Shelby
- **NOTES:** See Christian County. Name changed to Christian in 1840.

DE KALB

133 W. State St., Sycamore, IL 60178, (815) 895-7138, **<dekalbcounty.org>**

- **INCORPORATED:** March 4, 1837
- **PARENT COUNTY:** Kane
- **BIRTH RECORDS:** start in 1877, kept by County Clerk
- **MARRIAGE:** 1837, County Clerk
- **DEATH:** 1877, County Clerk
- **LAND:** 1838, County Recorder
- **PROBATE:** 1837, Circuit Court Clerk
- **COURT:** 1838, Circuit Court Clerk

DE WITT

201 W. Washington St., Box 439, Clinton, IL 61727, (217) 935-2195, **<dewittcountyill.com>**

- **INCORPORATED:** March 1, 1839
- **PARENT COUNTIES:** Macon, McLean
- **BIRTH RECORDS:** start in 1877, kept by County Clerk
- **MARRIAGE:** 1839, County Clerk
- **DEATH:** 1877, County Clerk
- **LAND:** 1828, County Recorder
- **PROBATE:** 1839, Circuit Court Clerk
- **COURT:** 1839, Circuit Court Clerk

DOUGLAS

401 S. Center St., Box 50, Tuscola, IL 61953, (217) 253-2352, **<www.douglascountyil.com>**

- **INCORPORATED:** Feb. 8, 1859
- **PARENT COUNTY:** Coles
- **BIRTH RECORDS:** start in 1851, kept by County Clerk
- **MARRIAGE:** unknown, County Clerk
- **DEATH:** 1851, County Clerk
- **LAND:** unknown, County Recorder
- **PROBATE:** unknown, Circuit Court Clerk
- **COURT:** unknown, Circuit Court Clerk

DU PAGE

550 N. County Farm Rd., Wheaton, IL 60189, (630) 407-5500, **<co.dupage.il.us>**

- **INCORPORATED:** Feb. 9, 1839
- **PARENT COUNTY:** Cook
- **BIRTH RECORDS:** start in 1877, kept by County Clerk
- **MARRIAGE:** 1839, County Clerk
- **DEATH:** 1877, County Clerk
- **LAND:** 1828, County Recorder
- **PROBATE:** 1839, Circuit Court Clerk
- **COURT:** 1839, Circuit Court Clerk

EDGAR

115 W. Court St., Paris, IL 61944, (217) 466-7433, **<edgarcounty-il.gov>**

- **INCORPORATED:** Jan. 3, 1823
- **PARENT COUNTY:** Clark
- **BIRTH RECORDS:** start in 1877, kept by County Clerk
- **MARRIAGE:** 1823, County Clerk
- **DEATH:** 1877, County Clerk
- **LAND:** 1823, County Recorder
- **PROBATE:** 1823, Circuit Court Clerk
- **COURT:** 1823, Circuit Court Clerk

EDWARDS

50 E. Main St., Albion, IL 62806, (618) 445-2016, **<www.kindredtrails.com/IL_Edwards.html>**

- **INCORPORATED:** Nov. 28, 1814
- **PARENT COUNTIES:** Madison, Gallatin
- **BIRTH RECORDS:** start in 1877, kept by County Clerk
- **MARRIAGE:** 1815, County Clerk
- **DEATH:** 1877, County Clerk
- **LAND:** 1815, County Clerk
- **PROBATE:** 1815, Circuit Court Clerk
- **COURT:** 1815, Circuit Court Clerk

EFFINGHAM

Box 628, Effingham, IL 62401, (217) 342-6535, **<co.effingham.il.us>**

- **INCORPORATED:** Feb. 15, 1831
- **PARENT COUNTIES:** Fayette, Crawford
- **BIRTH RECORDS:** start in 1877, kept by County Clerk
- **MARRIAGE:** 1833, County Clerk
- **DEATH:** 1871, County Clerk
- **LAND:** 1833, County Recorder
- **PROBATE:** 1838, Circuit Court Clerk
- **COURT:** 1833, Circuit Court Clerk

FAYETTE
221 S. Seventh, Vandalia, IL 62471, (618) 283-5009,
<fayettecountyclerk.com>
- **INCORPORATED:** Feb. 14, 1821
- **PARENT COUNTIES:** Bond, Clark, Crawford, Jefferson
- **BIRTH RECORDS:** start in 1877, kept by County Clerk-Recorder
- **MARRIAGE:** 1821, County Clerk-Recorder
- **DEATH:** 1877, County Clerk-Recorder
- **LAND:** 1816, County Recorder
- **PROBATE:** 1821, Circuit Court Clerk
- **COURT:** 1821, Circuit Court Clerk

FORD
200 W. State St., Box 80, Paxton, IL 60957, (217) 379-2641,
<fordcountycourthouse.com>
- **INCORPORATED:** Feb. 17, 1859
- **PARENT COUNTY:** Vermilion
- **BIRTH RECORDS:** start in 1877, kept by County Clerk
- **MARRIAGE:** 1859, County Clerk
- **DEATH:** 1877, County Clerk
- **LAND:** 1834, County Recorder
- **PROBATE:** 1850, Circuit Court Clerk
- **COURT:** 1859, Circuit Court Clerk

FRANKLIN
Box 485, Benton, IL 62812, (618) 439-2011, **<franklincountyil.org>**
- **INCORPORATED:** Jan. 2, 1818
- **PARENT COUNTIES:** White, Gallatin
- **BIRTH RECORDS:** start in 1877, kept by County Clerk
- **MARRIAGE:** 1837, County Clerk
- **DEATH:** 1877, County Clerk
- **LAND:** 1835, County Recorder
- **PROBATE:** 1837, Circuit Court Clerk
- **COURT:** 1836, Circuit Court Clerk

FULTON
100 N. Main St., Box 152, Lewistown, IL 61542, (309) 547-3041,
<www.fultonco.org>
- **INCORPORATED:** Jan. 28, 1823
- **PARENT COUNTY:** Pike
- **BIRTH RECORDS:** start in 1877, kept by County Clerk
- **MARRIAGE:** 1824, County Clerk
- **DEATH:** 1877, County Clerk
- **LAND:** 1817, County Recorder
- **PROBATE:** 1827, Circuit Court Clerk
- **COURT:** 1824, Circuit Court Clerk

GALLATIN
Box 249, Shawneetown, IL 62984, (618) 269-3140,
<rootsweb.com/~ilgalla2>
- **INCORPORATED:** Sept. 14, 1812
- **PARENT COUNTY:** Randolph
- **BIRTH RECORDS:** start in 1877, kept by County Clerk
- **MARRIAGE:** 1813, County Clerk
- **DEATH:** 1877, County Clerk
- **LAND:** 1813, County Recorder
- **PROBATE:** 1814, Circuit Court Clerk
- **COURT:** 1813, Circuit Court Clerk

GREENE
519 N. Main St., Carrollton, IL 62016-1033, (217) 942-6412,
<greene-county.com>
- **INCORPORATED:** Jan. 20, 1821
- **PARENT COUNTY:** Madison
- **BIRTH RECORDS:** start in 1877, kept by County Clerk
- **MARRIAGE:** 1821, County Clerk
- **DEATH:** 1877, County Clerk
- **LAND:** 1821, County Recorder
- **PROBATE:** 1821, Circuit Court Clerk
- **COURT:** 1821, Circuit Court Clerk

GRUNDY
1320 Union St., Morris, IL 60450, (815) 941-3400, **<grundyco.org>**
- **INCORPORATED:** Feb. 17, 1841
- **PARENT COUNTY:** LaSalle
- **BIRTH RECORDS:** start in 1877, kept by County Clerk
- **MARRIAGE:** 1841, County Clerk
- **DEATH:** 1877, County Clerk
- **LAND:** 1832, County Recorder
- **PROBATE:** 1841, Circuit Court Clerk
- **COURT:** 1837, Circuit Court Clerk

HAMILTON
100 S. Jackson St., McLeansboro, IL 62859, (618) 643-3224,
<www.rootsweb.ancestry.com/~ilhamilt>
- **INCORPORATED:** Feb. 8, 1821
- **PARENT COUNTY:** White
- **BIRTH RECORDS:** start in 1877, kept by County Clerk
- **MARRIAGE:** 1821, County Clerk
- **DEATH:** 1877, County Clerk
- **LAND:** 1823, County Recorder
- **PROBATE:** 1821, Circuit Court Clerk
- **COURT:** 1821, Circuit Court Clerk

HANCOCK
Box 189, Carthage, IL 62321, (217) 357-2616,
<www.hancockcountyclerk.org>
- **INCORPORATED:** Jan. 13, 1825
- **PARENT COUNTY:** Pike
- **BIRTH RECORDS:** start in 1877, kept by County Clerk
- **MARRIAGE:** 1829, County Clerk
- **DEATH:** 1877, County Clerk
- **LAND:** 1817, County Recorder
- **PROBATE:** 1830, Circuit Court Clerk
- **COURT:** 1829, Circuit Court Clerk

HARDIN
Box 308, Elizabethtown, IL 62931, (618) 287-2735,
<hardincountyil.org>
- **INCORPORATED:** March 2, 1839
- **PARENT COUNTIES:** Gallatin, Pope
- **BIRTH RECORDS:** start in 1877, kept by County Clerk
- **MARRIAGE:** 1884, County Clerk
- **DEATH:** 1877, County Clerk
- **LAND:** 1814, County Recorder
- **PROBATE:** 1884, Circuit Court Clerk
- **COURT:** 1841, Circuit Court Clerk

HENDERSON
Box 308, Oquawka, IL 61469, (309) 867-3121,
<www.usgennet.org/usa/il/county/henderson>
- **INCORPORATED:** Jan. 20, 1841
- **PARENT COUNTY:** Warren
- **BIRTH RECORDS:** start in 1877, kept by County Clerk
- **MARRIAGE:** 1841, County Clerk
- **DEATH:** 1877, County Clerk
- **LAND:** 1818, County Recorder
- **PROBATE:** 1839, Circuit Court Clerk
- **COURT:** 1841, Circuit Court Clerk

HENRY
307 W. Center St., Cambridge, IL 61238, (309) 937-3578,
<henrycty.com>
- **INCORPORATED:** Jan. 13, 1825
- **PARENT COUNTY:** Fulton
- **BIRTH RECORDS:** start in 1877, kept by County Clerk
- **DEATH:** 1877, County Clerk
- **MARRIAGE:** 1837, County Clerk
- **DIVORCE:** 1880, Circuit Court Clerk
- **LAND:** 1835, County Clerk
- **PROBATE:** 1880, Circuit Court Clerk
- **COURT:** 1880, Circuit Court Clerk

IROQUOIS
550 S. Tenth St., Watseka, IL 60970, (815) 432-6950,
<co.iroquois.il.us>
- **INCORPORATED:** Feb. 26, 1833
- **PARENT COUNTY:** Vermilion
- **BIRTH RECORDS:** start in 1877, kept by County Clerk
- **MARRIAGE:** 1866, County Clerk
- **DEATH:** 1877, County Clerk
- **LAND:** 1834, County Recorder
- **PROBATE:** 1834, Circuit Court Clerk
- **COURT:** 1834, Circuit Court Clerk

JACKSON
1001 Walnut St., Box 730, Murphysboro, IL 62966, (618) 687-7300,
<co.jackson.il.us>
- **INCORPORATED:** Jan. 10, 1816
- **PARENT COUNTIES:** Randolph, Johnson
- **BIRTH RECORDS:** start in 1877, kept by County Clerk
- **MARRIAGE:** 1843, County Clerk
- **DEATH:** 1877, County Clerk
- **BURIAL:** 1872, County Clerk
- **LAND:** 1814, County Recorder
- **PROBATE:** 1840, Circuit Court Clerk
- **COURT:** 1843, Circuit Court Clerk

JASPER
100 W. Jourdan St., Newton, IL 62448, (618) 783-2524,
<jaspercountyillinois.org>
- **INCORPORATED:** Feb. 15, 1831
- **PARENT COUNTIES:** Clay, Crawford
- **BIRTH RECORDS:** start in 1877, kept by County Clerk
- **MARRIAGE:** 1835, County Clerk
- **DEATH:** 1877, County Clerk
- **LAND:** 1835, County Recorder
- **PROBATE:** 1835, Circuit Court Clerk
- **COURT:** 1835, Circuit Court Clerk

JEFFERSON
100 S. Tenth St., Mount Vernon, IL 62864, (618) 244-8007,
<jeffil.us>
- **INCORPORATED:** March 26, 1819
- **PARENT COUNTIES:** Edwards, White
- **BIRTH RECORDS:** start in 1851, kept by County Clerk
- **MARRIAGE:** unknown, County Clerk
- **DEATH:** 1851, County Clerk
- **LAND:** unknown, County Recorder
- **PROBATE:** unknown, Circuit Court Clerk
- **COURT:** unknown, Circuit Court Clerk

JERSEY
201 W. Pearl St., Jerseyville, IL 62052, (618) 498-5571,
<jerseycounty-il.us>
- **INCORPORATED:** Feb. 28, 1839
- **PARENT COUNTY:** Greene
- **BIRTH RECORDS:** start in 1877, kept by County Clerk
- **MARRIAGE:** 1839, County Clerk
- **DEATH:** 1877, County Clerk
- **LAND:** 1822, County Recorder
- **PROBATE:** 1839, Circuit Court Clerk
- **COURT:** 1839, Circuit Court Clerk

JO DAVIESS
330 N. Bench St., Galena, IL 61036, (815) 777-0037, **<jodaviess.org>**
- **INCORPORATED:** Feb. 17, 1827
- **PARENT COUNTIES:** Henry, Putnam
- **BIRTH RECORDS:** start in 1877, kept by County Clerk
- **MARRIAGE:** 1830, County Clerk
- **DEATH:** 1877, County Clerk
- **LAND:** 1828, County Recorder
- **PROBATE:** 1828, Circuit Court Clerk
- **COURT:** 1827, Circuit Court Clerk

JOHNSON
Box 517, Vienna, IL 62995, (618) 658-4751, **<johnsoncountyil.com>**
- **INCORPORATED:** Sep. 14, 1812
- **PARENT COUNTY:** Randolph
- **BIRTH RECORDS:** start in 1877, kept by County Clerk
- **MARRIAGE:** 1835, County Clerk
- **DEATH:** 1877, County Clerk
- **LAND:** 1809, County Recorder
- **PROBATE:** 1821, Circuit Court Clerk
- **COURT:** 1827, Circuit Court Clerk

KANE
540 S. Randall Rd., St. Charles, IL 60174, (630) 232-3413,
<countyofkane.org>
- **INCORPORATED:** Jan. 16, 1836
- **PARENT COUNTIES:** Cook, LaSalle
- **BIRTH RECORDS:** start in 1877, kept by County Clerk
- **MARRIAGE:** 1836, County Clerk
- **DEATH:** 1877, County Clerk

- **LAND:** 1836, County Recorder
- **PROBATE:** 1836, Circuit Court Clerk
- **COURT:** 1836, Circuit Court Clerk

KANKAKEE
189 E. Court St., Kankakee, IL 60901, (815) 937-2990,
<co.kankakee.il.us>
- **INCORPORATED:** Feb.11, 1853
- **PARENT COUNTY:** Ford, Iroquois, Will
- **BIRTH RECORDS:** start in 1851, kept by County Clerk
- **MARRIAGE:** unknown, County Clerk
- **DEATH:** 1851, County Clerk
- **LAND:** unknown, County Recorder
- **PROBATE:** unknown, Circuit Court Clerk
- **COURT:** unknown, Circuit Court Clerk

KENDALL
111 W. Fox St., Yorkville, IL 60560, (630) 553-4104,
<co.kendall.il.us>
- **INCORPORATED:** Feb. 19, 1841
- **PARENT COUNTIES:** LaSalle, Kane
- **BIRTH RECORDS:** start in 1877, kept by County Clerk
- **MARRIAGE:** 1837, County Clerk
- **DEATH:** 1877, County Clerk
- **LAND:** 1839, County Recorder
- **PROBATE:** 1847, Circuit Court Clerk
- **COURT:** 1841, Circuit Court Clerk

KNOX
200 S. Cherry St., Galesburg, IL 61401, (309) 345-3121,
<knoxcountyil.com>
- **INCORPORATED:** Jan. 13, 1825
- **PARENT COUNTIES:** Fulton, Henry
- **BIRTH RECORDS:** start in 1877, kept by County Clerk
- **MARRIAGE:** 1830, County Clerk
- **DEATH:** 1877, County Clerk
- **LAND:** 1878, County Recorder
- **PROBATE:** 1830, Circuit Court Clerk
- **COURT:** 1836, Circuit Court Clerk

LA SALLE
707 Etna Rd., Ottawa, IL 61350, (815) 434-8202,
<www.lasallecounty.org>
- **INCORPORATED:** Jan. 15, 1831
- **PARENT COUNTIES:** Putnam, Tazewell
- **BIRTH RECORDS:** start in 1877, kept by County Clerk
- **MARRIAGE:** 1831, County Clerk
- **DEATH:** 1877, County Clerk
- **LAND:** unknown, Recorder of Deeds
- **PROBATE:** unknown, Probate Office
- **COURT:** unknown, Circuit Court Clerk

LAKE
18 N. County St., Waukegan, IL 60085, (847) 377-2000,
<lakecountyil.gov>
- **INCORPORATED:** March 1, 1839
- **PARENT COUNTY:** McHenry
- **BIRTH RECORDS:** start in 1877, kept by County Clerk
- **MARRIAGE:** 1839, County Clerk
- **DEATH:** 1877, County Clerk
- **LAND:** 1839, County Recorder
- **PROBATE:** 1839, Circuit Court Clerk
- **COURT:** 1840, Circuit Court Clerk

LAWRENCE
718 11th St.., Lawrenceville, IL 62439, (618) 943-5219,
<lawrencecountyillinois.com>
- **INCORPORATED:** Jan. 16, 1821
- **PARENT COUNTIES:** Crawford, Edwards
- **BIRTH RECORDS:** start in 1877, kept by County Clerk
- **MARRIAGE:** 1821, County Clerk
- **DEATH:** 1877, County Clerk
- **LAND:** 1818, County Recorder
- **PROBATE:** 1821, Circuit Court Clerk
- **COURT:** 1820, Circuit Court Clerk

LEE
309 Galena Ave., Dixon, IL 61021, (815) 288-3309,
<countyoflee.org>
- **INCORPORATED:** Feb. 27, 1839
- **PARENT COUNTY:** Ogle
- **BIRTH RECORDS:** start in 1877, kept by County Clerk
- **MARRIAGE:** 1839, County Clerk
- **DEATH:** 1877, County Clerk
- **LAND:** 1838, County Clerk
- **PROBATE:** 1839, Circuit Court Clerk
- **COURT:** 1840, Circuit Court Clerk

LIVINGSTON
112 W. Madison St., Pontiac, IL 61764, (815) 844-3664,
<livingstoncounty-il.org>
- **INCORPORATED:** Feb. 27, 1837
- **PARENT COUNTIES:** La Salle, McLean
- **BIRTH RECORDS:** start in 1877, kept by County Clerk
- **MARRIAGE:** 1837, County Clerk
- **DEATH:** 1877, County Clerk
- **LAND:** 1835, County Recorder
- **PROBATE:** 1837, Circuit Court Clerk
- **COURT:** 1839, Circuit Court Clerk

LOGAN
Box 278., Lincoln, IL 62656, (217) 732-4148, **<co.logan.il.us>**
- **INCORPORATED:** Feb. 15, 1839
- **PARENT COUNTIES:** McLean, Sangamon, Tazewell
- **BIRTH RECORDS:** start in 1877, kept by County Clerk
- **MARRIAGE:** 1857, County Clerk
- **DEATH:** 1877, County Clerk
- **LAND:** 1829, County Recorder
- **PROBATE:** 1855, Circuit Court Clerk
- **COURT:** 1857, Circuit Court Clerk

MACON
141 W. Main St., Decatur, IL 62523, (217) 424-1405,
<maconcounty-il.gov>
- **INCORPORATED:** Jan. 19, 1829
- **PARENT COUNTY:** Shelby

- **BIRTH RECORDS:** start in 1877, kept by County Clerk
- **MARRIAGE:** 1839, County Clerk
- **DEATH:** 1877, County Clerk
- **PROBATE:** 1831, Circuit Court Clerk
- **COURT:** 1829, Circuit Court Clerk

MACOUPIN

21480 B IL Rte. 4, Carlinville, IL 62626, (217) 854-7727,
<macoupincountyil.gov>

- **INCORPORATED:** Jan. 17, 1829
- **PARENT COUNTIES:** Madison, Greene
- **BIRTH RECORDS:** start in 1877, kept by County Clerk
- **MARRIAGE:** 1829, County Clerk
- **DEATH:** 1877, County Clerk
- **LAND:** 1829, County Recorder
- **PROBATE:** 1829, Circuit Court Clerk
- **COURT:** 1829, Circuit Court Clerk

MADISON

157 N. Main St, Ste. 165, Edwardsville, IL 62025, (618) 269-4580,
<www.co.madison.il.us>

- **INCORPORATED:** Sep. 14, 1812
- **PARENT COUNTY:** St. Clair
- **BIRTH RECORDS:** start in 1877, kept by County Clerk
- **MARRIAGE:** 1813, County Clerk
- **DEATH:** 1877, County Clerk
- **PROBATE:** 1813, Circuit Court Clerk
- **COURT:** 1803, Circuit Court Clerk
- **LAND:** 1802, County Recorder

MARION

101 E. Broadway, Salem, IL 62881, (618) 548-3400,
<sos.state.il.us/departments/archives/irad/marion.html>

- **INCORPORATED:** Jan. 1816
- **PARENT COUNTIES:** Fayette, Jefferson
- **BIRTH:** start in 1851, kept by County Clerk
- **MARRIAGE:** unknown, County Clerk
- **DEATH:** 1851, County Clerk
- **LAND:** unknown, County Recorder
- **PROBATE:** unknown, Circuit Court Clerk
- **COURT:** unknown, Circuit Court Clerk

MARSHALL

122 N. Prairie St., Lacon, IL 61540, (309) 246-6435,
<co.marshall.il.us>

- **INCORPORATED:** Jan. 19, 1839
- **PARENT COUNTIES:** La Salle, Putnam
- **BIRTH RECORDS:** start in 1877, kept by County Clerk
- **MARRIAGE:** 1830, County Clerk
- **DEATH:** 1877, County Clerk
- **LAND:** 1839, County Recorder
- **PROBATE:** 1830, Circuit Court Clerk
- **COURT:** 1840, Circuit Court Clerk

MASON

125 N. Plum, Havana, IL 62644, (309) 543-6661,
<masoncountyil.org>

- **INCORPORATED:** Jan. 20, 1841
- **PARENT COUNTIES:** Tazewell, Menard
- **BIRTH RECORDS:** start in 1877, kept by County Clerk
- **MARRIAGE:** 1841, County Clerk
- **DEATH:** 1878, County Clerk
- **LAND:** 1827, County Recorder
- **PROBATE:** 1841, Circuit Court Clerk
- **COURT:** 1841, Circuit Court Clerk

MASSAC

Box 429, Metropolis, IL 62960, (618) 524-5213,
<sos.state.il.us/departments/archives/irad/massac.html>

- **INCORPORATED:** Feb. 8, 1843
- **PARENT COUNTIES:** Pope, Johnson
- **BIRTH RECORDS:** start in 1877, kept by County Clerk
- **MARRIAGE:** 1843, County Clerk
- **DEATH:** 1877, County Clerk
- **LAND:** 1843, County Recorder
- **PROBATE:** 1843, Circuit Court Clerk
- **COURT:** 1843, Circuit Court Clerk

MCDONOUGH

1 Courthouse Sq., Macomb, IL 61455, (309) 837-4889,
<macomb.com/government.html>

- **INCORPORATED:** Jan. 25, 1826
- **PARENT COUNTY:** Schuyler
- **BIRTH RECORDS:** start in 1877, kept by County Clerk
- **MARRIAGE:** 1830, County Clerk
- **DEATH:** 1877, County Clerk
- **LAND:** 1817, County Recorder
- **PROBATE:** 1833, Circuit Court Clerk
- **COURT:** unknown, Circuit Court Clerk

MCHENRY

2200 N. Seminary Ave., Woodstock, IL 60098, (815) 334-4000,
<co.mchenry.il.us>

- **INCORPORATED:** Jan. 16, 1836
- **PARENT COUNTY:** Cook
- **BIRTH RECORDS:** start in 1877, kept by County Clerk
- **MARRIAGE:** 1837, County Clerk
- **DEATH:** 1877, County Clerk
- **LAND:** 1839, County Recorder
- **PROBATE:** 1840, Circuit Court Clerk
- **COURT:** 1836, Circuit Court Clerk

MCLEAN

104 W. Front St., Bloomington, IL 61701, (309) 888-5001,
<co.mchenry.il.us>

- **INCORPORATED:** Dec. 25, 1830
- **PARENT COUNTIES:** Tazewell, Unorganized Territory
- **BIRTH RECORDS:** start in 1887, kept by County Clerk
- **MARRIAGE:** 1831, County Clerk
- **DEATH:** 1877, County Clerk
- **LAND:** 1931, County Recorder
- **PROBATE:** 1831, Circuit Court Clerk
- **COURT:** 1831, Circuit Court Clerk

MENARD

Box 465, Petersburg, IL 62675, (217) 632-3201, **<menardcountyil.com>**

- **INCORPORATED:** Feb. 15, 1839
- **PARENT COUNTY:** Sangamon
- **BIRTH RECORDS:** start in 1877, kept by County Clerk
- **MARRIAGE:** 1839, County Clerk
- **DEATH:** 1877, County Clerk
- **LAND:** 1821, County Recorder
- **PROBATE:** 1839, Circuit Court Clerk
- **COURT:** 1839, Circuit Court Clerk

MERCER

Box 66, Aledo, IL 61231, (309) 582-7122, **<mercercountyil.org>**

- **INCORPORATED:** 13 Jan. 13, 1825
- **PARENT COUNTY:** Pike
- **BIRTH RECORDS:** start in 1877, kept by County Clerk
- **MARRIAGE:** 1835, County Clerk
- **DEATH:** 1877, County Clerk
- **LAND:** 1834, County Recorder
- **PROBATE:** 1837, Circuit Court Clerk
- **COURT:** 1836, Circuit Court Clerk

MONROE

100 S. Main St., Waterloo, IL 62298, (618) 939-8681, **<monroecountyil.org/directory.aspx>**

- **INCORPORATED:** Jan. 6, 1816
- **PARENT COUNTIES:** Randolph, St. Clair
- **BIRTH RECORDS:** start in 1878, kept by County Clerk
- **MARRIAGE:** 1816, County Clerk
- **DEATH:** 1877, County Clerk
- **LAND:** 1816, County Recorder
- **PROBATE:** 1820, Circuit Court Clerk
- **COURT:** 1816, Circuit Court Clerk

MONTGOMERY

120 N. Main St., Box C., Hillsboro, IL 62049, (217) 532-9546, **<montgomeryco.com/index.php>**

- **INCORPORATED:** Feb. 21, 1821
- **PARENT COUNTIES:** Bond, Madison
- **BIRTH RECORDS:** start in 1877, kept by County Clerk
- **MARRIAGE:** 1821, County Clerk
- **DEATH:** 1877, County Clerk
- **LAND:** 1819, County Recorder
- **PROBATE:** 1821, Circuit Court Clerk
- **COURT:** 1821, Circuit Court Clerk

MORGAN

300 W. State St., Box 1120, Jacksonville, IL 62650, (217) 243-5419, **<morgancounty-il.com>**

- **INCORPORATED:** Jan. 31, 1823
- **PARENT COUNTIES:** Greene, Sangamon
- **BIRTH RECORDS:** start in 1851, kept by County Clerk
- **MARRIAGE:** 1827, County Clerk
- **DEATH:** 1851, County Clerk
- **LAND:** 1824, County Recorder
- **PROBATE:** 1824, County Clerk
- **COURT:** 1827, County Clerk

MOULTRIE

10 S. Main St., Sullivan, IL 61951, (217) 728-4622, **<www.kindredtrails.com/IL_Moultrie.html>**

- **INCORPORATED:** Feb. 16, 1843
- **PARENT COUNTIES:** Shelby, Macon
- **BIRTH RECORDS:** start in 1877, kept by County Clerk
- **MARRIAGE:** 1843, County Clerk
- **DEATH:** 1877, County Clerk
- **LAND:** 1831, County Recorder
- **PROBATE:** 1845, Circuit Court Clerk
- **COURT:** 1840, Circuit Court Clerk

OGLE

106 S. 5th, Ste. 104, Oregon, IL 61061, (815) 732-9093, **<oglecounty.org>**

- **INCORPORATED:** Jan.16, 1836
- **PARENT COUNTIES:** Jo Daviess, La Salle
- **BIRTH RECORDS:** start in 1878, kept by County Clerk
- **MARRIAGE:** 1837, County Clerk
- **DEATH:** 1878, County Clerk
- **LAND:** 1836, County Recorder
- **PROBATE:** 1836, Circuit Court Clerk
- **COURT:** 1837, Circuit Court Clerk

PEORIA

324 Main St. Room G22, Peoria, IL 61602, (309) 672-6989, **<www.co.peoria.il.us>**

- **INCORPORATED:** Jan. 13, 1825
- **PARENT COUNTY:** Fulton
- **BIRTH RECORDS:** start in 1877, kept by County Clerk
- **MARRIAGE:** 1825, County Clerk
- **DEATH:** 1877, County Clerk
- **LAND:** 1818, County Recorder
- **PROBATE:** 1825, Circuit Court Clerk
- **COURT:** 1825, Circuit Court Clerk

PERRY

Box 219, Pinckneyville, IL 62274, (618) 357-6726, **<perrycountyil.org>**

- **INCORPORATED:** Jan. 29, 1827
- **PARENT COUNTIES:** Randolph, Jackson
- **BIRTH RECORDS:** start in 1878, kept by County Clerk
- **MARRIAGE:** 1827, County Clerk
- **DEATH:** 1878, County Clerk
- **LAND:** 1817, County Recorder
- **PROBATE:** 1828, Circuit Court Clerk
- **COURT:** 1827, Circuit Court Clerk

PIATT
101 W. Washington St., Monticello, IL 61856, (217) 762-4966, **<piattcounty.org>**
- **INCORPORATED:** Jan. 27, 1841
- **PARENT COUNTIES:** DeWitt, Macon
- **BIRTH RECORDS:** start in 1877, kept by County Clerk
- **MARRIAGE:** 1841, County Clerk
- **DEATH:** 1877, County Clerk
- **LAND:** 1840, County Recorder
- **PROBATE:** 1843, Circuit Court Clerk
- **COURT:** 1841, Circuit Court Clerk

PIKE
100 E. Washington St., Pittsfield, IL 62363, (217) 285-6612, **<pikeil.org>**
- **INCORPORATED:** Jan. 31, 1821
- **PARENT COUNTY:** Madison
- **BIRTH RECORDS:** start in 1877, kept by County Clerk
- **MARRIAGE:** 1827, County Clerk
- **DEATH:** 1877, County Clerk
- **LAND:** 1818, County Recorder
- **PROBATE:** 1821, Circuit Court Clerk
- **COURT:** 1819, Circuit Court Clerk

POPE
Box 438, Golconda, IL 62938, (618) 683-3941, **<popeco.net>**
- **INCORPORATED:** Jan. 10, 1816
- **PARENT COUNTIES:** Gallatin, Johnson
- **BIRTH RECORDS:** start in 1877, kept by County Clerk
- **MARRIAGE:** 1813, County Clerk
- **DEATH:** 1877, County Clerk
- **LAND:** 1816, County Recorder
- **PROBATE:** 1816, Circuit Court Clerk
- **COURT:** 1817, Circuit Court Clerk

PULASKI
500 Illinois Ave., Box 88, Mound City, IL 62963, (618) 748-9300, **<pulaskicountyil.net/index.php>**
- **INCORPORATED:** March 3, 1843
- **PARENT COUNTIES:** Alexander, Johnson
- **BIRTH RECORDS:** start in 1882, kept by County Clerk
- **MARRIAGE RECORDS:** start in 1861, kept by County Clerk
- **DEATH:** 1882, County Clerk
- **PROBATE:** 1862, Circuit Court Clerk
- **COURT:** 1857, Circuit Court Clerk
- **LAND:** 1843, County Recorder

PUTNAM
120 N. Fourth St., Hennepin, IL 61327, (815) 925-7016, **<putnamcountyil.com>**
- **INCORPORATED:** Jan. 13, 1825
- **PARENT COUNTY:** Fulton
- **BIRTH RECORDS:** start in 1877, kept by County Clerk
- **MARRIAGE:** 1831, County Clerk
- **DEATH:** 1877, County Clerk
- **LAND:** 1831, County Recorder
- **PROBATE:** 1831, Circuit Court Clerk
- **COURT:** 1831, Circuit Court Clerk

RANDOLPH
1 Taylor St., Chester, IL 62233, (618) 826-3116, **<randolphco.org>**
- **INCORPORATED:** Oct. 5, 1795
- **PARENT COUNTIES:** NW Territory, St. Clair
- **BIRTH RECORDS:** start in 1877, kept by County Clerk
- **MARRIAGE:** 1824, County Clerk
- **DEATH:** 1877, County Clerk
- **LAND:** 1724, County Recorder
- **PROBATE:** 1722, Circuit Court Clerk
- **COURT:** 1722, Circuit Court Clerk

RICHLAND
103 W. Main St., Box 21, Olney, IL 62450, (618) 392-2151, **<www.rootsweb.ancestry.com/~ilrichla>**>
- **INCORPORATED:** Feb. 24, 1841
- **PARENT COUNTIES:** Clay, Lawrence
- **BIRTH RECORDS:** start in 1877, kept by County Clerk
- **MARRIAGE:** 1841, County Clerk
- **DEATH:** 1877, County Clerk
- **LAND:** 1836, County Recorder
- **PROBATE:** 1841, Circuit Court Clerk
- **COURT:** 1842, Circuit Court Clerk

ROCK ISLAND
210 15th St., Box 5230, Rock Island, IL 61201, (309) 786-3029, **<co.rock-island.il.us>**
- **INCORPORATED:** Feb. 9, 1831
- **PARENT COUNTY:** Jo Daviess
- **BIRTH RECORDS:** start in 1877, kept by County Clerk
- **MARRIAGE:** 1833, County Clerk
- **DEATH:** 1877, County Clerk
- **LAND:** 1835, County Recorder
- **PROBATE:** 1835, Circuit Court Clerk
- **COURT:** 1834, Circuit Court Clerk

SALINE
10 E. Poplar St., Harrisburg, IL 62946, (618) 253-5096, **<rootsweb.ancestry.com/~ilsaline>**
- **INCORPORATED:** Feb.25, 1847
- **PARENT COUNTY:** Gallatin
- **BIRTH RECORDS:** start in 1877, kept the at County Clerk
- **MARRIAGE:** 1845, County Clerk
- **DEATH:** 1877, County Clerk
- **LAND:** 1817, County Recorder
- **PROBATE:** 1847, Circuit Court Clerk
- **COURT:** 1848, Circuit Court Clerk

SANGAMON
200 S. Ninth St., Springfield, IL 62701, (217) 753-6674, **<co.sangamon.il.us>**
- **INCORPORATED:** Jan. 30, 1821
- **PARENT COUNTIES:** Bond, Madison
- **BIRTH RECORDS:** start in 1877, kept by County Clerk
- **MARRIAGE:** 1821, County Clerk
- **DEATH:** 1877, County Clerk
- **LAND:** 1822, County Recorder
- **PROBATE:** 1821, Circuit Court Clerk
- **COURT:** 1821, Circuit Court Clerk

SCHUYLER
Box 80, Rushville, IL 62681, (217) 322-4633,
<schuylercountyillinois.com>
- **INCORPORATED:** Jan.13, 1825
- **PARENT COUNTY:** Pike
- **BIRTH RECORDS:** start in 1877, kept by County Clerk
- **MARRIAGE:** 1825, County Clerk
- **DEATH:** 1877, County Clerk
- **LAND:** 1817, County Recorder
- **PROBATE:** 1825, Circuit Court Clerk
- **COURT:** 1825, Circuit Court Clerk

SCOTT
35 E. Market St., Winchester, IL 62694, (217) 742-5217,
<sos.state.il.us/departments/archives/irad/scott.html>
- **INCORPORATED:** Feb. 16, 1839
- **PARENT COUNTY:** Morgan
- **BIRTH RECORDS:** start in 1877, kept by County Clerk
- **MARRIAGE:** 1839, County Clerk
- **DEATH:** 1877, County Clerk
- **LAND:** 1823, County Recorder
- **PROBATE:** 1839, Circuit Court Clerk
- **COURT:** 1839, Circuit Court Clerk

SHELBY
Box 469 Shelbyville, IL 62565, (217) 774-4212,
<shelbycounty-il.com>
- **INCORPORATED:** Jan. 23, 1827
- **PARENT COUNTY:** Fayette
- **BIRTH RECORDS:** start in 1877, kept by County Clerk
- **MARRIAGE:** 1827, County Clerk
- **DEATH:** 1877, County Clerk
- **LAND:** 1827, County Recorder
- **PROBATE:** 1831, Circuit Court Clerk
- **COURT:** 1827, Circuit Court Clerk

ST. CLAIR
10 Public Sq., Belleville, IL 62220, (618) 277-6932, **<co.st-clair.il.us>**
- **INCORPORATED:** April 27, 1790
- **PARENT COUNTY:** Northwest Territory
- **BIRTH RECORDS:** start in 1823, kept by County Clerk
- **MARRIAGE:** 1763, County Clerk
- **DEATH:** 1832, County Clerk
- **LAND:** 1786, County Recorder
- **PROBATE:** 1772, Circuit Court Clerk
- **COURT:** 1778, Circuit Court Clerk

STARK
130 W. Main St., Box 426, Toulon, IL 61483, (309) 286-5941,
<starkco.illinois.gov>
- **INCORPORATED:** March 2, 1839
- **PARENT COUNTIES:** Knox, Putnam
- **BIRTH RECORDS:** start in 1877, kept by County Clerk
- **MARRIAGE:** 1839, County Clerk
- **DEATH:** 1878, County Clerk
- **LAND:** 1817, County Recorder
- **PROBATE:** 1839, Circuit Court Clerk
- **COURT:** 1839, Circuit Court Clerk

STEPHENSON
15 N. Galena Ave., Freeport, IL 61032, (815) 235-8266,
<www.co.stephenson.il.us>
- **INCORPORATED:** March 4, 1837
- **PARENT COUNTIES:** Jo Daviess, Winnebago
- **BIRTH RECORDS:** start in 1877, kept by County Clerk
- **MARRIAGE:** 1837, County Clerk
- **DEATH:** 1877, County Clerk
- **LAND:** 1837, County Recorder
- **PROBATE:** 1837, County Clerk
- **COURT:** 1837, County Clerk

TAZEWELL
324 Court St., Pekin IL 61554, (309) 477-2214, **<tazewell.com>**
- **INCORPORATED:** Jan. 31, 1827
- **PARENT COUNTIES:** Fayette, Peoria
- **BIRTH RECORDS:** start in 1877, kept by County Clerk
- **MARRIAGE:** 1827, County Clerk
- **DEATH:** 1877. County Clerk
- **LAND:** 1825, County Recorder
- **PROBATE:** 1827, Circuit Court Clerk
- **COURT:** 1827, Circuit Court Clerk

UNION
309 W. Market St., Jonesboro, IL 62952, (618) 833-5711,
<unioncountyil.net>
- **INCORPORATED:** Jan. 2, 1818
- **PARENT COUNTIES:** Johnson, Jackson
- **BIRTH RECORDS:** start in 1877, kept by County Clerk
- **MARRIAGE:** 1818, County Clerk
- **DEATH:** 1877, County Clerk
- **LAND:** 1818, County Recorder
- **PROBATE:** 1818 Circuit Court Clerk
- **COURT:** 1817, Circuit Court Clerk

VERMILION
6 N. Vermilion St., Danville, IL 61832-5879, (217) 431-2540,
<co.vermilion.il.us>
- **INCORPORATED:** Jan. 18, 1826
- **PARENT COUNTY:** Edgar
- **BIRTH RECORDS:** start in 1877, kept by County Clerk
- **MARRIAGE:** 1826, County Clerk
- **DEATH:** 1877,County Clerk
- **LAND:** 1826, County Recorder
- **PROBATE:** 1826, Circuit Court Clerk
- **COURT:** 1826, Circuit Court Clerk

WABASH
401 Market St., Box 277, Mount Carmel, IL 62863, (618) 262-4561,
<wabashcountychamber.com>
- **INCORPORATED:** Dec. 27, 1824
- **PARENT COUNTY:** Edwards
- **BIRTH RECORDS:** start in 1877, kept by County Clerk
- **MARRIAGE:** 1857, County Clerk
- **DEATH:** 1877, County Clerk
- **LAND:** 1857, County Recorder
- **PROBATE:** 1851, Circuit Court Clerk
- **COURT:** 1851, Circuit Court Clerk

WARREN
100 W. Broadway, Monmouth, IL 61462, (309) 734-8592,
<warrencountyil.com>
- **INCORPORATED:** Jan. 13, 1825
- **PARENT COUNTY:** Pike
- **BIRTH RECORDS:** start in 1877, kept by County Clerk
- **MARRIAGE:** 1831, County Clerk
- **DEATH:** 1877, County Clerk
- **LAND:** 1800, County Recorder
- **PROBATE:** 1830, Circuit Court Clerk
- **COURT:** 1832, Circuit Court Clerk

WASHINGTON
101 E. St. Louis St., Nashville, IL 62263, (618) 327-4800,
<washington.ilgenweb.net>
- **INCORPORATED:** Jan. 2, 1818
- **PARENT COUNTY:** St. Clair
- **BIRTH RECORDS:** start in 1877, kept by County Clerk
- **MARRIAGE:** 1831, County Clerk
- **DEATH:** 1877, County Clerk
- **LAND:** 1815, County Recorder
- **PROBATE:** 1818, Circuit Court Clerk
- **COURT:** 1818, Circuit Court Clerk

WAYNE
Box 187, Fairfield, IL 62837, (618) 842-5182,
<wayne.ilgenweb.net>
- **INCORPORATED:** March 26, 1819
- **PARENT COUNTY:** Edwards
- **BIRTH RECORDS:** start in 1886, kept by the County Clerk
- **MARRIAGE:** 1850, County Clerk
- **DEATH:** 1886, County Clerk
- **LAND:** 1865, County Recorder
- **PROBATE:** 1886, Circuit Court Clerk
- **COURT:** 1819, Circuit Court Clerk

WHITE
Box 339, Carmi, IL 62821, (618) 382-7211, **<whitecounty-il.gov>**
- **INCORPORATED:** Dec. 9, 1815
- **PARENT COUNTY:** Madison
- **BIRTH RECORDS:** start in 1877, kept by County Clerk
- **MARRIAGE:** 1816, County Clerk
- **DEATH:** 1877, County Clerk
- **PROBATE:** 1816, Circuit Court Clerk
- **COURT:** 1816, County Recorder
- **LAND:** 1816, County Recorder

WHITESIDE
200 E. Knox St., Morrison, IL 61270, (815) 740-4615
<whiteside.org>
- **INCORPORATED:** Jan. 16, 1836
- **PARENT COUNTIES:** Jo Daviess, Henry
- **BIRTH RECORDS:** start in 1877, kept by County Clerk
- **MARRIAGE:** 1857, County Clerk
- **DEATH:** 1877, County Clerk
- **LAND:** 1838, County Recorder
- **PROBATE:** 1839, Circuit Court Clerk
- **COURT:** 1838, Circuit Court Clerk

WILL
302 W. Jefferson St., Joliet, IL 60432, (815) 740-4615,
<willcountyillinois.com>
- **INCORPORATED:** Jan. 12, 1836
- **PARENT COUNTIES:** Cook, Iroquois
- **BIRTH RECORDS:** start in 1877, kept by the County Clerk
- **MARRIAGE:** 1836, County Clerk
- **DEATH:** 1877, County Clerk
- **LAND:** 1853, County Recorder
- **PROBATE:** 1837, Circuit Court Clerk
- **COURT:** 1836, Circuit Court Clerk

WILLIAMSON
200 W. Jefferson St., Box 1108, Marion, IL 62959, (618) 997-1301,
<williamsoncountycourthouse.com>
- **INCORPORATED:** Feb. 28, 1839
- **PARENT COUNTY:** Franklin
- **BIRTH RECORDS:** start in 1877, kept a the County Clerk
- **MARRIAGE:** 1839, County Clerk
- **DEATH:** 1877, County Clerk
- **LAND:** 1818, County Recorder
- **PROBATE:** 1836, Circuit Court Clerk
- **COURT:** 1840, Circuit Court Clerk

WINNEBAGO
401 Division St., Rockford, IL 61104, (815) 987-3050,
<co.winnebago.il.us>
- **INCORPORATED:** Jan.1 , 1836
- **PARENT COUNTIES:** Jo Daviess, La Salle
- **BIRTH RECORDS:** start in 1877, kept by County Clerk
- **MARRIAGE:** 1836, County Clerk
- **DEATH:** 1877, County Clerk
- **LAND:** 1836, County Recorder
- **PROBATE:** 1837, Circuit Court Clerk
- **COURT:** 1836, Circuit Court Clerk

WOODFORD
115 N. Main St., Eureka, IL 61530, (309) 467-2822,
<woodford-county.org>
- **INCORPORATED:** Feb. 27, 1841
- **PARENT COUNTIES:** Tazewell, McLean
- **BIRTH RECORDS:** start in 1877, kept by County Clerk
- **MARRIAGE:** 1841, County Clerk
- **DEATH:** 1877, County Clerk
- **LAND:** 1831, County Recorder
- **PROBATE:** 1841, Circuit Court Clerk
- **COURT:** 1841, Circuit Court Clerk

INDIANA

» BY JAMES W. WARREN

HISTORICAL OVERVIEW

The Miami, Wyandot, Wea, Potawatomis, and Delaware Indians gave Indiana its name. The earliest European settlers in Indiana were the French, who established trading outposts at Fort Wayne, Vincennes, and Lafayette in the early 1700s. The British took control of the area in 1763. In 1764, Clarksville (across the Ohio from present-day Louisville, Ky.) was established, Indiana's first authorized American settlement. Indiana became part of Northwest Territory in 1787.

In 1800, Indiana Territory was organized. It was reduced in 1805 when Michigan Territory was created, and again in 1809 with the creation of Illinois Territory. After the War of 1812, Indiana settlement increased, with people who migrated from the Carolinas, Virginia, Kentucky, Tennessee, and Maryland.

Indiana became the 19th state in 1816. The National Road reached Indianapolis in 1834, bringing an influx of settlers from Ohio, Pennsylvania, and New York. Until 1850, most of the settlement was in the southern half of the state, and Indiana did not draw the large numbers of overseas immigrants that other midwest states did in the mid-19th century. But in the last half of the century, the development of roads, canals, and railroads brought more settlers from the east. The industrial growth of northern towns began to attract foreign immigrants. Inexpensive farmland drew many immigrants as well. Quakers fro Tennessee and the Carolinas came to Indiana, away from slavery. During the Civil War, Indiana provided more than 224,000 Union troops.

RECORD HIGHLIGHTS

The first extant federal population census for the State of Indiana is 1820. All of the 1800 and most of the 1810 censuses for Indiana were lost. Most of the 1890 census was destroyed in a fire, and the 1890 Veterans' Schedule for Indiana was also lost. Mortality schedules exist for 1850, 1860, 1870, and 1880. Other territorial and state censuses (including 1807, 1853, 1866, 1871, and 1877) are incomplete or their content is sparse. Those enumerations are at the Indiana State Archives.

Indiana birth and death records were to be recorded by the counties beginning in 1882. Statewide death registration began in 1899; births followed in 1907. Marriage records have been kept by the clerk of the circuit court since 1807, and there was no statewide registration until 1958.

Birth and death certificates can be ordered from the Vital Records Office in Indianapolis. Marriage records can be ordered from the clerk of circuit court in the county where

research tips

- The Indiana State Library has two divisions important to researchers. The Genealogy Division has an extensive reference library, and the Indiana Division houses manuscripts, state documents, newspapers, photographs and oral history collections **<www.statelib.lib.in.us>**.
- The Indiana State Archives is the official repository of Indiana government records **<www.state.in.us/icpr/archives>**.
- The Allen County Public Library in Fort Wayne has one of the largest genealogical collections in the country.
- Another important repository is the Indiana Historical Society, which houses a large collection of published materials as well as many photographs and important manuscripts.

CENSUS RECORDS

- Territorial census: 1807 (Dearborn, Knox, and Randolph counties)
- Federal censuses: 1820, 1830, 1840, 1850, 1860, 1870, 1880, 1900, 1910, 1920, 1930
- State/territorial censuses: 1820, 1830, 1840, 1850, 1860 (enumerations of eligible voters only)
- Mortality schedules: 1850, 1860, 1870, 1880

the marriage took place. Divorces were handled by different courts over time. You may find a ledger book of divorces, or they may be incorporated with other civil case files or in order books.

The Indiana State Library's Genealogy Division has a searchable database of Indiana marriages, originally created by the Works Progress Administration (WPA), through 1850 on its website. Be aware it's not without errors and omissions, though **<208.119.72.68/INMarriages1850/marriages_search.asp>**. WPA-extracted birth, marriage and death records through 1920 are available through the Family History Library (FHL).

In territorial times, there were three courts: Common Pleas, General Court, and Quarter Sessions of the Peace. Circuit court replaced all three in 1814. In 1814, the circuit court became the basic county-level court in Indiana, and still is today. Superior Courts were established around 1871 as case loads became heavier. The court of common pleas appeared again from roughly 1849-1873 and handled probate cases and sometimes divorces and naturalizations. The records of these courts will usually be in court order books and case files, many of which are available through the FHL.

Copies of deeds and mortgages can be ordered from the county recorder's office. Because research in land records can be time-consuming and indexes are often incomplete, whenever possible make use of microfilmed indexes and records. The FHL has filmed the county land records for more than two-thirds of the 92 Indiana counties. Probate records are in the custody of the circuit court in almost all Indiana counties. Many are on microfilm at the Genealogy Division of the Indiana State Library hand the FHL.

During most time periods, naturalization could take place in any court of record. Naturalization records from many of Indiana's counties have been transferred to the Indiana State Archives and microfilmed there. The FHL has many Indiana counties' naturalization records, and the archives' website includes a Naturalization Database Search at **<www.in.gov/serv/icpr_naturalization>**. The largest newspaper collection in the state is at the Indiana Division of the Indiana State Library. The microfilmed newspapers circulate on interlibrary loan. A county-by-county listing of the 16,500 reels of newspaper microfilm is accessible at **<www.in.gov/library/newspapers.htm>**.

The Indiana State Archives has an interesting array of online databases, such as the Indiana Soldier's and Sailor's Children's Home **<www.in.gov/icpr/2547.htm>**. Search all databases at **<www.indianadigitalarchives.org>**.

Indiana's religious history is richly varied and can be important in researching Indiana ancestors. Church records are abundant, and the best capsule description of where and how to look for them is in John Beatty's *Research in Indiana*, a publication of the National Genealogical Society.

The Indiana State Library, Indiana Division manages manuscript and state document collections, as well as photographs, newspapers, and oral history collections. The Indiana Biography Index is a finding aid to books, periodicals, newspaper clippings, obituaries, and other sources. You can search is at **<208.119.72.68/INBiopre1990/bio_cards_search.asp>** (for materials published before 1990) and **<208.119.72.68/INBio1990/biography_search.asp>**.

Another branch of the Indiana State Library, the Genealogy Division, has an excellent reference library for Indiana research and beyond. Their collection includes more than 40,000 printed items, electronic resources, and microfilm. Their website offers an array of information and some online databases as well **<www.in.gov/library/databases.htm>**.

The Indiana Historical Society **<www.indianahistory.org>** is one more repository that should not be overlooked. In addition to its published reference and historical material, it has a huge collection of photographs and manuscript materials. The Allen County Public Library Genealogy Center goes beyond Indiana to cover all 50 states and Canada.

ARCHIVES, LIBRARIES, AND SOCIETIES

Alexandria-Monroe Township Historical Society
313 N. Harrison St., Alexandria, IN 46001 (765) 724-2993,**<www.rootsweb.ancestry.com/~inmadiso/alexandria.htm>**

Allen County Genealogical Society of Indiana
Box 12003, Fort Wayne, IN 46862 **<www.acgsi.org>**

Allen County Public Library
200 E. Berry St., Fort Wayne, IN 46801, (260) 421-1200, **<www.acpl.lib.in.us>**

Anderson Public Library
111 E. Twelfth St., Anderson, IN 46016, (765) 641-2456, **<www.and.lib.in.us>**

Bartholomew County Genealogical Society
Box 2455, Columbus, IN 47202

Bartholomew County Historical Society
524 Third St., Columus, IN 47201, (812) 372-3541, **<barthist.com>**

Blackford County Historical Society
321 North High St., Box 264, Hartford City, IN 47348, **<www.bchs-in.org>**

Boone County Historical Society
404 W. Main St., Box 141, Lebanon, IN 46052, (765) 483-9414, **<www.bccn.boone.in.us/bchs>**

Brown County Genealogical Society
Box 1202, Nashville, IN 47448, **<www.rootsweb.ancestry.com/~inbcgs/title.htm>**

Brown County Historical Society
Box 668, Nashville, IN 47448, (812) 988-6089, **<browncountyhistory.info>**

Carroll County Historical Society
Ground Floor Court House, Box 277, Delphi, IN 46923, (765) 564-3152, **<www.carrollcountymuseum.org>**

Cass County Genealogical Society
Box 373, Logansport, IN 46947

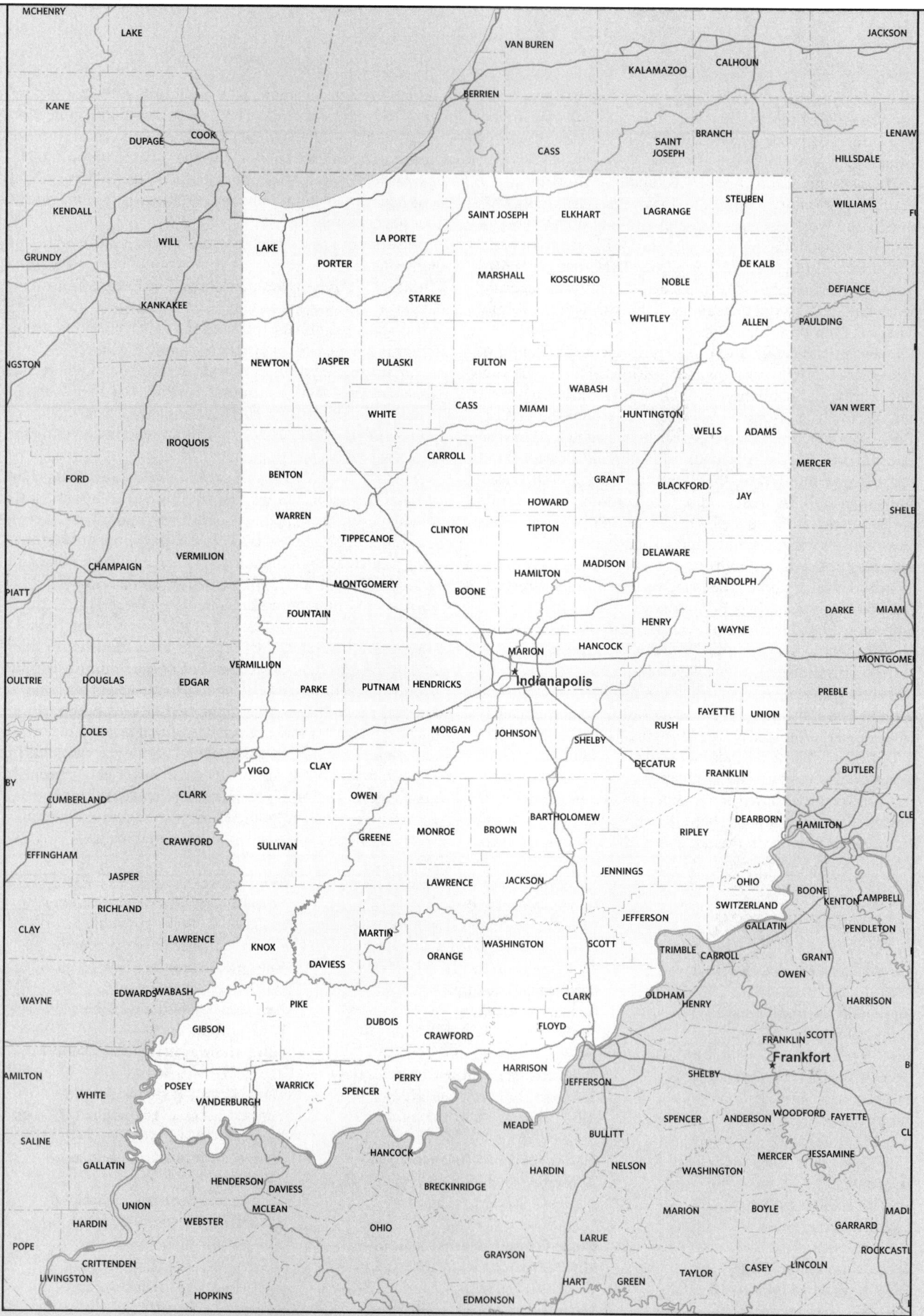
MCHENRY
LAKE
VAN BUREN
JACKSON
KALAMAZOO
CALHOUN
BERRIEN
KANE
DUPAGE
COOK
CASS
SAINT JOSEPH
BRANCH
LENAW
HILLSDALE
KENDALL
STEUBEN
WILLIAMS
SAINT JOSEPH
ELKHART
LAGRANGE
WILL
LAKE
LA PORTE
GRUNDY
PORTER
DE KALB
MARSHALL
KOSCIUSKO
NOBLE
DEFIANCE
STARKE
KANKAKEE
WHITLEY
ALLEN
PAULDING
NGSTON
NEWTON
JASPER
PULASKI
FULTON
WABASH
CASS
MIAMI
VAN WERT
WHITE
HUNTINGTON
WELLS
ADAMS
IROQUOIS
CARROLL
MERCER
BENTON
GRANT
BLACKFORD
FORD
JAY
HOWARD
WARREN
SHELB
CLINTON
TIPTON
TIPPECANOE
DELAWARE
VERMILION
MADISON
CHAMPAIGN
HAMILTON
RANDOLPH
MONTGOMERY
PIATT
BOONE
FOUNTAIN
DARKE
MIAMI
HENRY
WAYNE
HANCOCK
MARION
VERMILLION
MONTGOME
OULTRIE
DOUGLAS
EDGAR
Indianapolis
PARKE
PUTNAM
HENDRICKS
PREBLE
FAYETTE
UNION
RUSH
COLES
MORGAN
JOHNSON
SHELBY
DECATUR
VIGO
CLAY
FRANKLIN
BUTLER
BY
CLARK
OWEN
CUMBERLAND
CLE
BARTHOLOMEW
DEARBORN
HAMILTON
MONROE
BROWN
CRAWFORD
RIPLEY
SULLIVAN
GREENE
EFFINGHAM
JENNINGS
JASPER
LAWRENCE
JACKSON
OHIO
BOONE
RICHLAND
KENTON
CAMPBELL
SWITZERLAND
JEFFERSON
GALLATIN
CLAY
PENDLETON
LAWRENCE
MARTIN
WASHINGTON
KNOX
SCOTT
TRIMBLE
CARROLL
GRANT
ORANGE
DAVIESS
OWEN
OLDHAM
WAYNE
EDWARDS
WABASH
CLARK
HENRY
HARRISON
PIKE
DUBOIS
GIBSON
FLOYD
FRANKLIN
SCOTT
CRAWFORD
Frankfort
AMILTON
HARRISON
SHELBY
PERRY
POSEY
WARRICK
WHITE
SPENCER
JEFFERSON
VANDERBURGH
SPENCER
ANDERSON
WOODFORD
FAYETTE
MEADE
BULLITT
SALINE
HANCOCK
MERCER
JESSAMINE
GALLATIN
HARDIN
NELSON
WASHINGTON
HENDERSON
DAVIESS
BRECKINRIDGE
UNION
MCLEAN
MARION
BOYLE
WEBSTER
HARDIN
OHIO
GARRARD
POPE
LARUE
CRITTENDEN
GRAYSON
ROCKCASTL
LIVINGSTON
CASEY
LINCOLN
TAYLOR
HART
GREEN
HOPKINS
EDMONSON

Cass County Historical Society
1004 East Market St., Logansport, IN 46947, (575) 753-3866, **<casscountyin.tripod.com>**

Clark County Historical Society
Box 606, Jeffersonville, IN 47130

Clay County Genealogical Society
Box 56, Center Point, IN 47840, (812) 835-5005, **<www.ccgsilib.org>**

Clinton County Genealogical Society
c/o Frankfort Community Public Library, 208 W. Clinton St., Frankfort, IN 46041, **<fcpl.accs.net/gen.htm>**

Clinton County Historical Society
301 E. Clinton St., Frankfort, IN 46041 (765) 659-2030, **<www.geetel.net/~cchsm>**

Danville Public Library
101 S. Indiana St., Danville, IN 46122, (317) 745-2604, **<www.dpl.lib.in.us>**

DeKalb County Indiana Genealogy Society
Box 6085, Auburn, IN 46706, **<www.rootsweb.ancestry.com/~indkigs/main_page.html>**

Delaware County Historical Society
120 E. Washington St., Muncie, IN 47305, (765) 282-1550, **<www.the-dchs.org>**

Dubois County Genealogical Society
Box 84, Ferdinand, IN 47532, **<www.rootsweb.ancestry.com/~indubois/dubges.htm>**

Elkhart County Genealogical Society
Box 1031, Elkhart, IN 46515, **<www.rootsweb.ancestry.com/~inelkhar/ecgs.htm>**

Elwood Pipecreek Genealogy Society
1600 Main St., Elwood, IN 46036, **<www.freewebs.com/genealogysocietyelwoodindiana>**

Fountain County Genealogical Society
Box 273, Veedersburg, IN 47987, (765) 294-4954, **<www.focogensoc.org/fcgs.html>**

Fountain County Historical Society
Box 148, Kingman, IN 47952

Frankfort Community/Clinton County Contractual Public Library
208 W. Clinton St, Frankfort, IN 46041, (765) 654-8746, **<www.accs.net/fcpl>**

Fulton County Historical Society
37 E. 375 N., Rochester, IN 46975, (574) 223-4436, **<www.htctech.net/~fchs>**

Fulton Library
514 State Road 25, Box 206, Fulton, IN 46931, (574) 857-3895, **<www.fulco.lib.in.us>**

Genealogical Society of Marion County
Box 2292, Indianapolis, IN 46206, **<www.rootsweb.ancestry.com/~ingsmc>**

Genealogical Society of Whitley County
Box 224, Columbia City, IN 46725, **<genealogy.whitleynet.org>**

Gibson County Historical Society
Box 516, Princeton, IN 47670

Greene County Genealogical Society
Box 164, Bloomfield, IN 47424

Hamilton County Historical Society
Box 397, Noblesville, IN 46061, (317) 770-0775

Hancock County Historical Society
Box 375, Greenfield, IN 46140, (317) 462-7780

Harrison County Historical Society
117 W. Beaver St., Corydon, IN 47112

Henry County Historical Society
606 S. Fourteenth St., New Castle, IN 47362, **<www.kiva.net/~hchisoc/museum.htm>**

Howard County Genealogical Society
Box 176, Kokomo, IN 46903 **<www.ingenweb.org/inhoward/hcgs>**

Huntington City-Township Public Library
200 W. Market St., Huntington, IN 46750 (260) 356-0824, **<www.huntingtonpub.lib.in.us>**

Indiana African-American Historical and Genealogical Society
502 Clover Terrace, Bloomington, IN 47404

Indiana Genealogical Society
Box 10507, Fort Wayne, IN 46852, **<www.indgensoc.org>**

Indiana Historical Society
450 W. Ohio St., Indianapolis, IN 46202, (317) 232-1882, **<www.indianahistory.org>**

Indiana State Archives
6440 E. 30th St., Indianapolis, IN 46219, (317) 591-5222, **<www.in.gov/icpr/2358.htm>**

Indiana State Library
315 W. Ohio St., Indianapolis, IN 46202, (317) 232-3689, **<www.in.gov/library>**

Jackson County Genealogical Society
415 S. Poplar St., Brownstown, IN 47220 (812) 358-2118. **<www.jacksoncountyhistory.org>**

Jasper County Historical Society
479 N. Van Rensselaer, Rensselaer, IN 47978

Jay County Genealogy Society
109 S. Commerce St., Portland, IN 47371 (260) 726-4323, **<www.rootsweb.ancestry.com/~injay/research/jaygene.htm>**

Jay County Historical Society
903 E. Main St., Portland, IN 47371, (260) 726-7168, **<www.jaycountyhistory.org>**

Jefferson County Historical Society
615 W. First St., Madison, IN 47250, (812) 265-2335, **<www.jchshc.org>**

Kokomo-Howard County Public Library
220 N. Union St., Kokomo, IN 46901, (765) 457-3242, **<www.kokomo.lib.in.us>**

Kosciusko County Historical Society
Box 1071, Warsaw, IN 46580, (574) 269-1078, **<culture.kconline.com/kchs>**

LaGrange County Historical Society
<www.rootsweb.ancestry.com/~inlgchs>

LaPorte County Genealogical Society
c/o LaPorte County Public Library, 904 Indiana Ave., LaPorte, IN 46350, **<www.rootsweb.ancestry.com/~inlcigs>**

LaPorte County Historical Society
2405 Indiana Ave., Ste. 1, LaPorte, IN 46350, (219) 324-6767, **<www.laportecountyhistory.org>**

Lexington Historical Society
Box 238, Lexington, IN 47138

Logansport-Cass County Public Library
616 E. Broadway, Logansport, IN 46947, (574) 753-6383, **<www.logan.lib.in.us>**

Madison-Jefferson County Public Library
420 W. Main St., Madison, IN 47250, (812) 265-2744, **<www.madison-jeffco.lib.in.us>**

Marion Public Library
600 S. Washington St., Marion, IN 46953, (765) 668-2900, **<www.marion.lib.in.us>**

Marshall County Historical Society
123 N. Michigan St., Plymouth, IN 46563, (574) 936-2306, **<www.mchistoricalsociety.org>**

Mennonite Church Historical Committee and Archives
Goshen College, 1700 S. Main St., Goshen, IN 46526, (574) 523-3080, **<www.mcusa-archives.org>**

Mennonite Historical Library
Goshen College, 1700 S. Main St., Goshen, IN 46526, (574) 535-7418, **<www.goshen.edu/mhl>**

Merrillville-Ross Township Historical Museum
13 W. 73rd Ave., Merrillville, IN 46410 (219) 756-2042, **<www.rootsweb.ancestry.com/~inlake/ross.htm>**

Miami County Historical Society and Museum
51 N. Broadway, Peru, IN 46970, (765) 473-9183,**<www.miamicountymuseum.com>**

Michigan City Public Library
100 E. Fourth St., Michigan City, IN 46360, **<www.mclib.org>**

Middletown Public Library
780 High St., Middletown, IN 47356, (765) 354-4071

Mishawaka-Penn-Harris Public Library
209 Lincoln Way E., Mishawaka, IN 46544, (574) 259-5277, **<www.mphpl.org>**

Monroe County Historical Society
202 E. Sixth St., Bloomington, IN 47408 (812) 332-2517,**<www.monroehistory.org>**

Monroe County Public Library
303 E. Kirkwood Ave., Bloomington, IN 47408, (812) 349-3050, **<www.monroe.lib.in.us>**

Montgomery County Historical Society
212 S. Water St., Crawfordsville, IN 47933, (765) 362-3416, **<www.lane-mchs.org>**

Morgan County History and Genealogy Association
Box 1012, Martinsville, IN 46151, **<www.rootsweb.ancestry.com/~inmchaga/mchagai.html>**

Morgan County Public Library
110 S. Jefferson St., Martinsville, IN 46151, (765) 342-3451, **<morg.lib.in.us>**

National Archives, Great Lakes Region
7358 S. Pulaski Road, Chicago, IL 60629, (773) 948-9001, **<www.archives.gov/great-lakes>**

Noble County Genealogical Society
Box 162, Albion, IN 46701, **<www.rootsweb.ancestry.com/~inncgs>**

Noblesville-Southeastern Public Library
One Library Plaza, Noblesville, IN 46060 (317) 773-1384

North Central Indiana Genealogical Society
2300 Canterbury Dr., Kokomo, IN 46901

Northern Indiana Historical Society
112 S. Lafayette Blvd., South Bend, IN 46601

Northwest Indiana Genealogical Society
Box 595, Griffith, IN 46319, **<www.rootsweb.ancestry.com/~innwigs>**

Northwest Territory Genealogical Society
c/o Knox County Public Library, 502 N. Seventh St., Vincennes, IN 47591, (812) 885-4380

University of Notre Dame Archives
607 Hesburgh Library, Notre Dame, IN 46556, (574) 631-6448, **<www.nd.edu/~archives>**

Ohio County Indiana Historical Society
212 S. Walnut, Rising Sun, IN 47040, (812) 438-4915, **<www.ohiocountymuseum.org>**

Orange County Genealogical Society
Box 344, Paoli, IN 47454, **<www.usgennet.org/usa/in/county/orange/gensoc.htm>**

Owen County Historical and Genealogical Society
Box 569, Spencer, IN 47460, **<www.owen.in.us/owenhist/owen.htm>**

Owen County Public Library
10 S. Montgomery St., Spencer, IN 47460 (812) 829-3392, **<www.owenlib.org>**

Palatines to America, Indiana Chapter
<www.palam.org/printchap.php?chapter=7>

Paoli Public Library
30 E Court St., Paoli IN 47454, (812) 723-2841, **<paoli.lib.in.us>**

Plainfield-Guilford Township Public Library
1120 Stafford Rd., Plainfield, IN 46168, (317) 839-6602, **<www.plainfieldlibrary.net>**

Plymouth Public Library
201 N. Center St, Plymouth, IN 46563, (574) 936-2324, **<www.plymouth.lib.in.us>**

Porter County Public Library System
103 Jefferson St., Valparaiso, IN 46383, (219) 462-0524, **<www.pcpls.lib.in.us>**

Posey County Historical Society
Box 171, Mt. Vernon, IN 47620, **<www.rootsweb.ancestry.com/~inposey/society.htm>**

Pulaski County Genealogical Society
c/o Pulaski County Library, 121 S. Riverside Dr., Winamac, IN 46996

Pulaski County Public Library
121 S. Riverside Dr., Winamac, IN 46996, (574) 946-3432

Randolph County Historical Society
416 S. Meridian St., Winchester, IN 47394, (765) 584-1334, **<www.randolphcountyindiana historicalsociety.org>**

Ripley County Historical Society
Box 525, Versailles, IN 47042, (812) 689-3031, **<rchslib.org>**

Rockville Public Library
106 N. Market St., Rockville, IN 47872 (765) 569-5544, **<rockvillepl.lib.in.us/index.htm>**

St. Joseph County Public Library
304 S. Main St., South Bend, IN 46601, (574) 282-4646, **<sjcpl.lib.in.us>**

Scott County Genealogical Society
Box 23, Scottsburg, IN 47170, (812) 752-0023, **<www.scgsi.com>**

Shelby County Historical Society
52 W. Broadway St, Shelbyville, IN 46176, (317) 392-4634, **<www.grover museum.org>**

Shelbyville-Shelby County Public Library
57 W. Broadway, Shelbyville, IN 46176, (317) 398-7121 or (317) 835-2653, **<www.sscpl.lib.in.us>**

Society of Indiana Pioneers
140 N. Senate Ave., Indianapolis, IN 46204 (317) 233-6588, **<www.indianapioneers.com>**

South Bend Area Genealogical Society
c/o The Mishawaka-Penn Public Library, 209 Lincoln Way E., Mishawaka, IN 46544, **<www.rootsweb.ancestry.com/~insbags>**

Southern Indiana Genealogical Society
Box 665, New Albany, IN 47151, **<www.rootsweb.ancestry.com/~insigs>**

Spencer County Historical Society
c/o Spencer County Public Library, 210 Walnut St., Rockport, IN 47635, (812) 649-4866, **<www.psci.net/rdawson/history>**

Starke County Genealogical Society
152 W. Culver Rd., Knox, IN 46534, (574) 772-7323, **<www.rootsweb.ancestry.com/~inscgs>**

Steuben County Genealogical Society
Box 884, Angola, IN 46703, **<www.ingenweb.org/insteuben/scgs>**

Sullivan County Historical Society
10 S. Court St., Sullivan, IN 47882, (812) 268-6253, **<www.sctb.net>**

SullivanMunce Cultural Center
225 W. Hawthorne St., Zionsville, IN 46077, (317) 873-4900, **<www.sullivanmunce.org>**

Switzerland County Public Library
205 Ferry St., Vevay, IN 47043, (812) 427-3363, **<scpl.us>**

Tippecanoe County Area Genealogical Society
Box 2464, West Lafayette, IN 47996, **<www.rootsweb.ancestry.com/~intcags>**

Tippecanoe County Historical Association
1001 South St., Lafayette, IN 47901, (765) 476-8411, **<www.tcha.mus.in.us>**

Tipton County Public Library
127 E. Madison St., Tipton, IN 46072, (765) 675-8761, **<www.tiptonpl.lib.in.us>**

Tri-State Genealogical Society
c/o Willard Library, 21 First Ave., Evansville, IN 47710, (812) 425-4309, **<www.rootsweb.ancestry.com/~intsgs>**

Union City Public Library
408 N. Columbia St., Union City, IN 47390, (765) 964-4748

Union County Historical Society
Box 143, Liberty, IN 47353

Union County Public Library
2 E. Seminary, Liberty, IN 47353, (765) 458-5355, **<www.union-county.lib.in.us>**

Valparaiso Public Library
103 Jefferson St., Valparaiso, IN 46383, (219) 462-0524, **<www.pcpls.lib.in.us>**

Vigo County Historical Society
1411 S. Sixth St., Terre Haute, IN 47802, (812) 235-9717, **<web.indstate.edu/vchs/index.php>**

Wabash Carnegie Public Library
188 W. Hill St., Wabash, IN 46992, (260) 563-2972, **<www.wabash.lib.in.us>**

Wabash County Genealogical Society
Box 825, Wabash, IN 46992, **<www.rootsweb.ancestry.com/~inwcgs>**

Wabash Valley Genealogical Society
Box 236, Terre Haute, IN 47808, **<www.inwvgs.org/index2.htm>**

Warren County Historical Society
Box 176, Williamsport, IN 47993

Warsaw Community Public Library
310 E. Main St., Warsaw, IN 46580, (574) 267-6011, **<www.wcpl.lib.in.us>**

Washington Township Public Library
107 N. Main St., Lynn, IN 47355, (765) 874-1488

Wayne County Genealogical Society
Box 2599, Richmond IN 47375, **<www.waynet.org/nonprofit/wcgs.htm>**

Wells County Historical Society
Box 143, Bluffton, IN 46714, **<www.wchs-museum.org>**

White County Genealogical Society
101 S. Bluff St., Monticello, IN 47960, (574) 583-3998

Willard Library of Evansville
21 First Ave., Evansville, IN 47710, (812) 425-4309, **<www.willard.lib.in.us>**

Winchester Community Library
125 N. East St, Winchester, IN 47394, (765) 584-4824, **<www.wincomlib.org>**

GENERAL RESOURCES

Abstracts of the Records of the Society of Friends in Indiana by Ruth Dorrel (Indiana Historical Society, ca. 1996-1999)

Biographical and Historical Sketches of Early Indiana by William Wesley Woollen (W.C. Cox, 1974)

A Biographical History of Eminent and Selfmade Men of the State of Indiana (Western Biographical Publishing Co., 1880)

The Black Women in the Middle West Project: A Comprehensive Resource Guide, Illinois and Indiana by Darlene Clark Hine (Indiana Historical Bureau, 1986)

A Directory of Churches and Religious Organizations in Indiana by the Historical Records Survey (Indiana Historical Records Survey, 1941-)

Executive Journal of Indiana Territory, 1800-1816 by William Wesley Woollen et al. (Indiana Historical Society, Family History Section, 1985)

Finding Indiana Ancestors: A Guide to Historical Research (Indiana Historical Society)

Genealogical Sources: Reprinted from the Genealogy Section, Indiana Magazine of History by Dorothy L. Riker (Indiana Historical Society, 1979)

A Genealogist's Guide to the Ft. Wayne, Indiana, Public Library by Karen B. Cavanaugh (McDowell Publications, ca. 1980)

A Guide to the Manuscript Collections of the Indiana Historical Society and the Indiana State Library by Eric Pumroy and Paul Brockman (Indiana Historical Society, ca. 1986)

History of the Catholic Church in Indiana by Charles Blanchard (A.W. Bowen & Co., 1898)

A History of Indiana: From its Earliest Exploration by Europeans to the Close of the Territorial Government, in 1816 by John B. Dillon (Bingham & Doughty, 1859)

Hoosier Faiths: A History of Indiana Churches and Religious Groups by L.C. Rudolph (Indiana University Press, ca. 1995)

Illiana Ancestors: Genealogy Column in the Commercial-news, Danville, Illinois by Joan A. Griffis (J. Griffis, ca. 1984-1996)

Index to Encyclopedia of American Quaker Genealogy by William Wade Hinshaw (Genealogical Publishing Co., ca. 1999)

Index, Indiana Source Books by Dorothy Riker (Indiana Historical Society, 1983)

Index to Indiana Wills: Phase 1, through 1850; Phase 2, 1850 through 1880 by Charles M. Franklin (Heritage House, ca. 1986-1987)

Indiana Friends Heritage, 1821-1996: The 175th Anniversary History of Indiana Yearly Meeting of Friends (Quakers) by Gregory P. Hinshaw (Indiana Yearly Meeting, 1996)

Indiana Genealogical Resource by George K. Schweitzer (G.K. Schweitzer, ca. 1996)

Indiana Genealogy and Local History Sources Index by Stuart Harter (Stuart Harter, ca. 1985)

Indiana and Indianans: A History of Aboriginal and Territorial Indiana and the Century of Statehood by Jacob Piatt Dunn (American Historical Society, 1919)

Indiana Negro Registers, 1852-1865 by Coy D. Robbins (Heritage Books, ca. 1994)

Indiana Newspaper Bibliography: Historical Accounts of All Indiana Newspapers Published from 1804 to 1980 and Locational Information for All Available Copies, Both Original and Microfilm by John W. Miller (Indiana Historical Society, 1982)

Indiana Research Outline by the Church of Jesus Christ of Latter-day Saints (online at <www.familysearch.org/eng/search/RG/guide/illinois.asp>)

Indiana Source Book: Genealogical Material from The Hoosier Genealogist by Willard Heiss, et al. (Indiana Historical Society, 1977-)

Indiana Sources for Genealogical Research in the Indiana State Library by Carolynne L. Wendel Miller (Indiana Historical Society, ca. 1984)

Indiana Territorial Pioneer Records, 1801-1820 by Charles M. Franklin (Heritage House, ca. 1983-1985)

Indiana's African-American Heritage: Essays from Black History News and Notes by Wilma L. Gibbs (Indiana Historical Society, ca. 1993)

The Negro in Indiana before 1900: A Study of a Minority by Emma Lou Thornbrough (Indiana University Press, 1993)

The Old Northwest: Pioneer Period, 1815-1840 by R. Carlyle Buley (Indiana University Press in association with the Indiana Historical Society, ca. 1978)

The Old Northwest: Studies in Regional History, 1787-1910 by Harry N. Scheiber (University of Nebraska Press, ca. 1969)

The Origin and Development of the Missionary Baptist Church in Indiana by John Frank Cady (Franklin College, 1942)

Peopling Indiana: The Ethnic Experience by Robert M. Taylor, Jr., and Connie A. McBirney (Indiana Historical Society, ca. 1996)

Pioneer Ancestors of Members of the Society of Indiana Pioneers by Ruth Dorrel (Indiana Historical Society, ca. 1983)

Preliminary Checklist of Archives and Manuscripts in Indiana Repositories by Donald E. Thompson (Indiana Historical Society, 1980)

Religion in Indiana: A Guide to Historical Resources by L.C. Rudolph and Judith E. Endelman (Indiana University Press, ca. 1986)

Searching in Indiana: A Reference Guide to Public and Private Records by Mickey Dimon Carty (ISC Publications, ca. 1985)

Who's Your Hoosier Ancestor: Genealogy for Beginners by Mona Robinson (Indiana University Press, ca. 1992)

CENSUS RECORDS

1820 Federal Census for Indiana by Willard Heiss (Indiana Historical Society, Genealogical Section, 1966)

Census of Indiana Territory for 1807 (Indiana Historical Society, 1980)

Indiana Territorial Pioneer Records, 1801-1820 by Charles M. Franklin (Heritage House, ca. 1983-1985)

☞ IMMIGRATION RECORDS

An Index to Indiana Naturalization Records Found in Various Order Books of the Ninety-two Local Courts Prior to 1907 by John J Newman (Indiana Historical Society, 1981)

The National Road in Indiana by Lee Burns (C.E. Pauley, ca. 1920)

☞ LAND RECORDS

French and British Land Grants in the Post Vincennes (Indiana) District, 1750-1784 by Clifford Neal Smith (Westland, 1996)

Indiana Land Entries by Margaret R. Waters (The Bookmark, 1977-1979)

Jeffersonville Land Entries, 1808-1818 by Janet C. Cowen (J.C. Cowen, ca. 1984)

This Land of Ours: The Acquisition and Disposition of the Public Domain; Papers Presented at an Indiana American Revolution Bicentennial Symposium Indiana Historical Society (The Society, ca. 1978)

The Vincennes Donation Lands by Leonard Lux (Indiana Historical Society, 1949)

☞ MAPS

Early Indiana Trails and Surveys by George R. Wilson (C.E. Pauley, 1919)

Genealogical Atlas of Indiana by Charles M. Franklin (Heritage House, ca. 1985)

Illustrated Historical Atlas of the State of Indiana (Indiana Historical Society, 1968)

Indiana: Atlas of Historical County Boundaries by Peggy Tuck Sinko (Charles Scribner's Sons, Simon & Schuster Macmillan, ca. 1996)

Indiana Boundaries: Territory, State and County by George Pence (Indiana Historical Bureau, 1967, ca. 1933)

The Indiana Gazetteer, or, Topographical Dictionary by John Scott (Indiana Historical Society, 1954)

Indiana Place Names by Ronald L. Baker (Indiana University Press, ca. 1975)

Maps of Indiana Counties in 1876 (Indiana Historical Society, 1979)

New Topographical Atlas and Gazetteer of Indiana: Comprising a Topographical View of the Several Counties of the State. . . . (Unigraphic, 1975)

Northwestern Indiana from 1800 to 1900, or, A View of Our Region through the Nineteenth Century by Timothy Horton (W.C. Cox, 1974)

☞ MILITARY RECORDS

Enrollment of the Late Soldiers, Their Widows & Orphans, of the Late Armies of the United States Residing in the State of Indiana, Kosciusko County, 1886, 1890, 1894 by Anne Laurie Austin Smith (Kosciusko County Historical Society, 1992)

Index to Admission Book, Indiana Soldiers and Sailors Home, 1868 through 1995 by Ruth Dorrel (Indiana Historical Society, 1997)

Index to the Report of the Adjutant General of the State of Indiana: An Every Name Index to Volumes I, II and III by Glenda K. Trapp (Trapp Publishing Service, ca. 1986)

Index to Revolutionary Soldiers of Indiana and Other Patriots by Barbara Schull Wolfe (Ye Olde Genealogie Shoppe, ca. 1983)

Indiana, War of 1812 Soldiers: Militia by Charles M. Franklin (Ye Olde Genealogie Shoppe, 1984)

☞ PROBATE RECORDS

Biographical Sketches and Review of the Bench and Bar of Indiana. by Charles W. Taylor (Bench and Bar Pub. Co., 1895)

Directory, Wills and Estates Information in Genealogy Dept., Indiana State Library by Vera Mae (Ginder) Moudy (Ye Olde Genealogie Shoppe, 1981)

Index to Indiana Wills: Phase 1, through 1850; Phase 2, 1850 through 1880 by Charles M. Franklin (Heritage House, ca. 1986-1987)

The Laws and Courts of Northwest and Indiana Territories by Daniel Wait Howe (Bowen-Merrill Co., 1886)

The Laws of Indiana Territory, 1801-1809 (Trustees of the Ill. State Historical Library, ca. 1930)

Preliminary Inventory, Records of the United States Courts for the District of Indiana by the National Archives and Warren B. Griffin (Federal Records Center, 1967)

Research in Indiana Courthouses: Judicial and Other Records by John J. Newman (Indiana Historical Society, 1981)

☞ VITAL RECORDS

1850 Indiana Mortality Schedule by Lowell M. Volkel (L.M. Volkel, ca. 1971)

1870 Illinois Mortality Schedules by Lowell M. Volkel (Heritage House, ca. 1985-1987)

Guide to Public Vital Statistics Records in Indiana by the Historical Records Survey (Indiana Historical Records Survey, 1941)

Illinois Mortality Schedule, 1860 by Lowell M. Volkel (Heritage House, 1979)

Indiana, 1851-1900 (Br¿derbund, ca. 1998. CD-ROM)
Indiana Marriages, Early to 1825: A Research Tool by Jordan R. Dodd and Norman L. Moyes (Precision Indexing, Inc., ca. 1991)

Miscellaneous Records of Indiana, 1827-1922 by the Historical Records Survey (Indiana, 1968)

Pre-1882 Indiana Births, from Secondary Sources by Dawne Slater-Putt (Heritage Pathways, Inc., ca. 1999)

Southern Seed, Northern Soil: African-American Farm Communities in the Midwest 1765-1900 by Stephen A. Vincent (Indiana University Press, ca. 1999)

•-COUNTY DETAILS-•

ADAMS
112 S. Second St., Decatur, IN 46733, (219) 724-2600,
<www.co.adams.in.us>
- **INCORPORATED:** March 1, 1836
- **PARENT COUNTY:** Adam's New Purchase
- **MARRIAGE RECORDS:** start in 1836, kept by County Clerk
- **DIVORCE:** unknown, County Clerk
- **PROBATE:** 1838, County Clerk
- **COURT:** unknown, County Clerk
- **NOTES:** Formed 1829 as Delaware New Purchase, renamed 1827 and abolished 1844.

ALLEN
715 S. Calhoun St., Fort Wayne, IN 46802, (260) 449-7424,
<www.allencounty.us>
- **INCORPORATED:** April 1, 1824
- **PARENT COUNTY:** Delaware New Purchase
- **BIRTH RECORDS:** start in 1882, kept by Department of Health
- **MARRIAGE:** 1824, County Clerk
- **DIVORCE:** 1823, Circuit Court
- **DEATH:** 1882, Department of Health
- **LAND:** 1824, County Recorder
- **PROBATE:** 1825, County Clerk
- **COURT:** 1824, County Clerk
- **BURIAL:** unknown, County Board of Health
- **NOTES:** Formed 1829 as Delaware New Purchase, renamed 1827 and abolished 1844.

BARTHOLOMEW
234 Washington St., Columbus, IN 47202, (812) 379-1600,
<www.bartholomewco.com>
- **INCORPORATED:** Jan. 8, 1821
- **PARENT COUNTIES:** Delaware New Purchase, Jackson
- **BIRTH RECORDS:** start in 1882, kept by Department of Health
- **MARRIAGE:** 1821, County Clerk
- **DIVORCE:** 1821, County Clerk
- **DEATH:** 1882, Department of Health
- **LAND:** 1822, County Recorder
- **PROBATE:** 1821, County Clerk
- **COURT:** 1821, County Clerk
- **MILITARY:** unknown, County Clerk
- **NATURALIZATION.:** unknown, County Clerk

BENTON
706 E. Fifth St. Room 23, Fowler, IN 47944, (765) 884-0370,
<ingenweb.org/inbenton>
- **INCORPORATED:** Feb. 18, 1840
- **PARENT COUNTY:** Jasper
- **BIRTH RECORDS:** start in 1882, kept by Department of Health
- **MARRIAGE:** 1840, County Clerk
- **DIVORCE:** ca. 1800, Circuit Court
- **DEATH:** 1882, Department of Health
- **LAND:** 1840, County Recorder
- **PROBATE:** 1840, County Clerk
- **COURT:** 1840, County Clerk
- **MILITARY:** unknown, County Recorder
- **NATURALIZATION:** unknown, Circuit Court

BLACKFORD
110 W. Washington St., Hartford City, IN 47348, (765)348-1130,
<www.blackfordcounty.com>
- **INCORPORATED:** Feb. 18, 1839
- **PARENT COUNTY:** Jay
- **BIRTH RECORDS:** start in 1882, kept by Department of Health
- **MARRIAGE:** 1839, County Clerk
- **DIVORCE:** 1839, County Clerk
- **DEATH:** 1882, Department of Health
- **LAND:** unknown, County Recorder
- **PROBATE:** 1839, County Clerk
- **COURT:** 1839, County Clerk
- **BURIAL:** unknown, County Coroner

BOONE
212 Courthouse Sq., Lebanon, IN 46052, (765) 482-3510,
<www.boonecounty.in.gov>
- **INCORPORATED:** April 1, 1830
- **PARENT COUNTIES:** Adams New Purchase, Wabash New Purchase
- **BIRTH RECORDS:** start in 1882, kept by Department of Health
- **MARRIAGE:** 1831, County Clerk
- **DIVORCE:** 1830, County Clerk
- **DEATH:** 1882, Department of Health
- **LAND:** 1856, County Recorder
- **PROBATE:** 1846, County Clerk
- **COURT:** 1846, County Clerk

BROWN
Box 85, 20 E. Main St., Nashville, IN 47448, (812) 988-5510,
<www.browncounty.com>
- **INCORPORATED:** Feb. 4, 1836
- **PARENT COUNTIES:** Monroe, Bartholomew, Jackson
- **BIRTH RECORDS:** start in 1882, kept by Department of Health
- **MARRIAGE:** 1836, County Clerk
- **DIVORCE:** 1850, County Clerk
- **DEATH:** 1882, Department of Health
- **LAND:** 1873, County Recorder
- **PROBATE:** 1837, County Clerk
- **COURT:** 1837, County Clerk
- **NOTES:** Some records lost in 1873 fire. County Clerk has court-ordered birth records from 1942.

CARROLL
101 W. Main St., Delphi, IN 46923, (765) 564-4485,
<www.carrollcountyindiana.com>
- **INCORPORATED:** Jan. 7, 1828
- **PARENT COUNTIES:** Adam's New Purchase, Wabash New Purchase, Unorganized Land
- **BIRTH RECORDS:** start in 1882, kept by Department of Health
- **MARRIAGE:** 1828, County Clerk

- **DIVORCE:** 1828, County Clerk
- **DEATH:** 1882, Department of Health
- **LAND:** 1829, County Recorder
- **PROBATE:** 1829, County Clerk
- **COURT:** 1829, County Clerk
- **BURIAL:** 1882, Department of Health

CASS

200 Park Ave., Logansport, IN 46947, (574) 753-7740,
<www.co.cass.in.us>

- **INCORPORATED:** April 13, 1829
- **PARENT COUNTY:** Unorganized Land
- **BIRTH RECORDS:** start in 1882, kept by Department of Health
- **MARRIAGE:** 1829, County Clerk
- **DIVORCE:** 1894, County Clerk
- **DEATH:** 1882, Department of Health
- **LAND:** 1830, County Auditor
- **PROBATE:** 1829, County Clerk
- **COURT:** 1829, County Clerk

CLARK

501 E. Court Ave., Room 105, Jeffersonville, IN 47130,
(812) 285-6235, **<www.co.clark.in.us>**

- **INCORPORATED:** Feb. 3, 1801
- **PARENT COUNTY:** Knox
- **BIRTH RECORDS:** start in 1882, kept by Department of Health
- **MARRIAGE:** 1807, County Clerk
- **DEATH:** 1882, Department of Health
- **LAND:** 1801, County Recorder
- **PROBATE:** 1801, County Clerk
- **COURT:** 1801, County Clerk

CLAY

609 E. National Ave., Brazil, IN 47834, (812) 448-9006,
<www.claycountyin.gov>

- **INCORPORATED:** April 1, 1825
- **PARENT COUNTIES:** Owen, Putnam, Vigo, Sullivan
- **BIRTH RECORDS:** start in 1882, kept by Department of Health
- **MARRIAGE:** 1851, County Clerk
- **DIVORCE:** 1851, County Clerk
- **DEATH:** 1882, Department of Health
- **LAND:** 1825, County Recorder
- **PROBATE:** 1873, County Clerk
- **COURT:** unknown, County Clerk
- **NOTES:** County Recorder has some burial and naturalization records.

CLINTON

265 Courthouse Sq., Frankfort, IN 46041, (765) 659-6335,
<www.rootsweb.ancestry.com/~inclinto>

- **INCORPORATED:** March 1, 1830
- **PARENT COUNTIES:** Adams New Purchase, Wabash New Purchase
- **BIRTH RECORDS:** start in 1882, kept by Department of Health
- **MARRIAGE:** 1830, County Clerk
- **DIVORCE:** 1888, County Clerk
- **DEATH:** 1882, Department of Health
- **LAND:** 1829, County Recorder
- **PROBATE:** 1830, County Clerk
- **COURT:** 1830, County Clerk

CRAWFORD

Box 375, 316 Court St., English, IN 47118, (812) 338-2565,
<www.rootsweb.ancestry.com/~incrawfo>

- **INCORPORATED:** Jan. 29, 1818
- **PARENT COUNTIES:** Orange, Harrison, Perry
- **BIRTH RECORDS:** start in 1882, kept by Department of Health
- **MARRIAGE:** 1818, County Clerk
- **DIVORCE:** 1860, County Clerk
- **DEATH:** 1882, Department of Health
- **LAND:** 1818, County Recorder
- **PROBATE:** 1818, County Clerk
- **COURT:** 1818, County Clerk

DAVIESS

Box 739, 200 E. Walnut St., Washington, IN 47501, (812) 254-8664, **<www.daviesscounty.net>**

- **INCORPORATED:** Feb. 15, 1817
- **PARENT COUNTY:** Knox
- **MARRIAGE RECORDS:** start in 1817, kept by County Clerk
- **DIVORCE:** 1817, County Clerk
- **PROBATE:** 1817, County Clerk
- **COURT:** 1817, County Clerk

DEARBORN

215 W. High St., Lawrenceburg, IN 47025, (812) 537-8867,
<www.dearborncounty.org>

- **INCORPORATED:** March 7, 1803
- **PARENT COUNTY:** Clark
- **BIRTH RECORDS:** start in 1882, kept by Department of Health
- **MARRIAGE:** 1806, County Clerk
- **DIVORCE:** unknown, Circuit Court
- **DEATH:** 1882, Department of Health
- **LAND:** 1824, County Recorder
- **PROBATE:** 1824, County Clerk
- **COURT:** 1824, County Clerk

DECATUR

150 Courthouse Sq., Suite 1, Greensburg, IN 47240, (812) 663-8455, **<www.decaturcounty.in.gov>**

- **INCORPORATED:** Dec. 31, 1821
- **PARENT COUNTIES:** Unorganized Land, Delaware New Purchase
- **BIRTH RECORDS:** start in 1882, kept by Department of Health
- **MARRIAGE:** 1822, County Clerk
- **DIVORCE:** unknown, County Clerk
- **DEATH:** 1882, Department of Health
- **PROBATE:** 1822, County Clerk
- **COURT:** 1822, County Clerk

DELAWARE

100 W. Main St., Muncie, IN 47305, (765) 747-7726,
<www.co.delaware.in.us>

- **INCORPORATED:** April 1, 1827
- **PARENT COUNTY:** Delaware New Purchase
- **MARRIAGE RECORDS:** start in 1827, kept by County Clerk
- **DIVORCE:** 1827, County Clerk

- **PROBATE:** 1830, County Clerk
- **COURT:** unknown, County Clerk
- **NOTES:** Delaware New Purchase formed 1820 from Unorganized Land, renamed Adams New Purchase 1827. Some records may exist in Fayette, Franklin, Jackson, Jennings, Randolph, Ripley, Wayne, and Bartholomew counties.

DEKALB

100 S. Main St., Box 810, Auburn, IN 46706,
<www.co.dekalb.in.us>

- **INCORPORATED:** May 1, 1837
- **PARENT COUNTY:** Unorganized Land
- **BIRTH RECORDS:** start in 1882, kept by Department of Health
- **MARRIAGE:** 1837, County Clerk
- **DEATH:** 1882, Department of Health
- **LAND:** 1837, County Recorder
- **PROBATE:** 1847, County Clerk
- **COURT:** unknown, County Clerk
- **NOTES:** County Clerk has School records for 1903-1932.

DUBOIS

One Courthouse Sq., Jasper, IN 47546, (812) 481-7035,
<www.duboiscountyin.org>

- **INCORPORATED:** Feb. 1, 1818
- **PARENT COUNTY:** Pike
- **BIRTH RECORDS:** start in 1882, kept by Department of Health
- **MARRIAGE:** 1839, County Clerk
- **DIVORCE:** 1839, Records Library
- **DEATH:** 1882 Department of Health
- **LAND:** 1839, County Recorder
- **PROBATE:** 1840, County Clerk
- **COURT:** unknown, County Clerk
- **MILITARY:** 1864, Records Library
- **NATURALIZATION:** 1839, Records Library

ELKHART

101 N. Main St., Goshen, IN 46526, (574) 535-6430,
<www.elkhartcountyindiana.com>

- **INCORPORATED:** April 1, 1830
- **PARENT COUNTY:** Unorganized Land
- **BIRTH RECORDS:** start in 1882, kept by Department of Health
- **MARRIAGE:** 1830, County Clerk
- **DIVORCE:** 1830, County Clerk
- **DEATH:** 1882, Department of Health
- **LAND:** 1831, County Recorder
- **PROBATE:** 1830, County Clerk
- **COURT:** unknown, County Clerk

FAYETTE

401 N. Central Ave., Connersville, IN 47331, (765) 825-1813,
<www.co.fayette.in.us>

- **INCORPORATED:** Dec. 28, 1818
- **PARENT COUNTIES:** Wayne, Franklin, Unorganized Land
- **MARRIAGE RECORDS:** start in 1819, kept by County Clerk
- **DIVORCE:** 1819, Circuit Court
- **PROBATE:** 1819, County Clerk
- **COURT:** unknown, County Clerk
- **NATURALIZATION:** 1924, Circuit Court

FLOYD

311 Hauss Square, New Albany, IN 47150, (812) 948-5430,
<www.floydcounty.in.gov>

- **INCORPORATED:** Jan. 2, 1819
- **PARENT COUNTIES:** Harrison, Clark
- **BIRTH RECORDS:** start in 1882, kept by Department of Health
- **MARRIAGE:** 1819, County Clerk
- **DIVORCE:** 1863, County Clerk
- **DEATH:** 1882, Department of Health
- **PROBATE:** 1819, County Clerk
- **COURT:** unknown, County Clerk

FOUNTAIN

301 Fourth St., Box 183, Covington, IN 47932, (765) 793-2192,
<www.ingenweb.org/fountain>

- **INCORPORATED:** April 1, 1826
- **PARENT COUNTIES:** Montgomery, Wabash New Purchase
- **BIRTH RECORDS:** start in 1882, kept by Department of Health
- **MARRIAGE:** 1826, County Clerk
- **DIVORCE:** 1830, County Clerk
- **DEATH:** 1882, Department of Health
- **LAND:** 1827, County Recorder
- **PROBATE:** 1827, County Clerk
- **COURT:** unknown, County Clerk

FRANKLIN

459 Main St., Brookville, IN 47012, (765) 647-5111,
<www.franklincounty.in.gov>

- **INCORPORATED:** 1811
- **PARENT COUNTIES:** Clark, Dearborn
- **BIRTH RECORDS:** start in 1882, kept by Department of Health
- **MARRIAGE:** 1811, County Clerk
- **DIVORCE:** 1811, County Clerk
- **DEATH:** 1882, Department of Health
- **LAND:** 1811, County Recorder
- **PROBATE:** 1811, County Clerk
- **COURT:** 1811, County Clerk
- **NATURALIZATION:** 1820, Public Library
- **CEMETERY:** 1817, Public Library

FULTON

815 Main St., Rochester, IN 46975, (574) 223-4824,
<www.co.fulton.in.us>

- **INCORPORATED:** 1835
- **PARENT COUNTY:** Unorganized Land
- **BIRTH RECORDS:** start in 1882, kept by Department of Health
- **MARRIAGE:** 1836, County Clerk
- **DIVORCE:** 1836, County Clerk
- **DEATH:** 1882, Department of Health
- **LAND:** 1826, County Recorder
- **PROBATE:** 1828, County Clerk
- **COURT:** 1826, County Clerk

GIBSON

101 N. Main St., Princeton, IN 47670, (812) 386-8401,
<www.gibsoncountyin.org>

- **INCORPORATED:** April 1, 1813
- **PARENT COUNTY:** Knox

- **BIRTH RECORDS:** start in 1882, kept by Department of Health
- **MARRIAGE:** unknown, County Clerk
- **DIVORCE:** 1820, County Clerk
- **DEATH:** 1882, Department of Health
- **PROBATE:** unknown, County Clerk
- **COURT:** unknown, County Clerk

GRANT

101 E. Fourth St., Marion, IN 46952, (765) 668-8121,
<www.grantcounty.net>

- **INCORPORATED:** April 1, 1832
- **PARENT COUNTIES:** Madison, Adams New Purchase, Unorganized Land
- **BIRTH RECORDS:** start in 1882, kept by Department of Health
- **MARRIAGE:** 1831, County Clerk
- **DIVORCE:** 1831, County Clerk
- **DEATH:** 1882, Department of Health
- **LAND:** 1831, County Recorder
- **PROBATE:** 1831, County Clerk
- **COURT:** unknown, County Clerk

GREENE

Box 229, Bloomfield, IN 47424, (812) 384-8532,
<greenecountyindiana.com>

- **INCORPORATED:** Feb. 5, 1821
- **PARENT COUNTIES:** Sullivan, Unorganized Land
- **BIRTH RECORDS:** start in 1882, kept by Department of Health
- **MARRIAGE:** 1821, County Clerk
- **DIVORCE:** 1821, County Clerk
- **DEATH:** 1882, Department of Health
- **LAND:** 1822, County Recorder
- **PROBATE:** 1823, County Clerk
- **COURT:** unknown, County Clerk
- **MILITARY:** unknown, County Recorder
- **NOTES:** County Clerk has Naturalization records 1854-1906. County Recorder has some Cemetery records.

HAMILTON

One Hamilton Sq., Suite 106, Noblesville, IN 46060
(317) 776-9629, **<www.hamiltoncounty.in.gov/Default.asp>**

- **INCORPORATED:** April 7, 1823
- **PARENT COUNTY:** Delaware New Purchase
- **BIRTH RECORDS:** start in 1882, kept by Department of Health
- **MARRIAGE:** 1833, County Clerk
- **DIVORCE:** 1833, County Clerk
- **DEATH:** 1882, Department of Health
- **LAND:** 1825, County Recorder
- **PROBATE:** 1823, County Clerk
- **COURT:** unknown, County Clerk

HANCOCK

9 E. Main St., Greenfield, IN 46140, (317) 477-1107,
<www.hancockcoingov.org>

- **INCORPORATED:** March 1, 1828
- **PARENT COUNTY:** Madison
- **BIRTH RECORDS:** start in 1882, kept by Department of Health
- **MARRIAGE:** 1828, County Clerk
- **DIVORCE:** 1828, County Clerk
- **DEATH:** 1882, Department of Health
- **LAND:** 1827, County Recorder
- **PROBATE:** 1828, County Clerk
- **COURT:** 1828, County Clerk

HARRISON

300 N. Capitol Ave., Corydon, IN 47112, (812) 738-4289,
<harrisoncounty.in.gov>

- **INCORPORATED:** Dec. 1, 1808
- **PARENT COUNTIES:** Knox, Clark
- **BIRTH RECORDS:** start in 1882, kept by Department of Health
- **MARRIAGE:** 1809, County Clerk
- **DIVORCE:** 1815, County Recorder
- **DEATH:** 1882, Department of Health
- **LAND:** 1807, County Clerk
- **PROBATE:** 1809, County Clerk
- **COURT:** unknown, County Clerk

HENDRICKS

355 S. Washington St., Danville, IN 46122, (317) 745-9224,
<www.co.hendricks.in.us>

- **INCORPORATED:** Dec. 28, 1823
- **PARENT COUNTIES:** Delaware New Purchase, Wabash New Purchase
- **BIRTH RECORDS:** start in 1882, kept by Department of Health
- **MARRIAGE:** 1824, County Clerk
- **DIVORCE:** 1823, County Clerk
- **DEATH:** 1882, Department of Health
- **LAND:** 1823, County Auditor
- **PROBATE:** 1822, County Clerk
- **COURT:** unknown, County Clerk

HENRY

Box B, New Castle, IN 47362, (765) 529-6401, **<www.hcgs.net>**

- **INCORPORATED:** June 1, 1822
- **PARENT COUNTY:** Delaware New Purchase
- **BIRTH RECORDS:** start in 1882, kept by Department of Health
- **MARRIAGE:** 1823, County Clerk
- **DIVORCE:** 1822, County Clerk
- **DEATH:** 1882, Department of Health
- **LAND:** 1824, County Recorder
- **PROBATE:** 1822, County Clerk
- **COURT:** unknown, County Clerk
- **CEMETERY DEEDS:** 1925, County Recorder

HOWARD

104 N. Buckeye St. #114, Kokomo, IN 46904, (765) 456-2204,
<co.howard.in.us>

- **INCORPORATED:** May 1, 1844
- **PARENT COUNTY:** Unorganized Land
- **BIRTH RECORDS:** start in 1882, kept by Department of Health
- **MARRIAGE:** 1844, County Clerk
- **DIVORCE:** 1844, County Clerk
- **DEATH:** 1882, Department of Health
- **LAND:** 1846, County Recorder
- **PROBATE:** 1844, County Clerk
- **COURT:** unknown, County Clerk
- **BURIAL:** unknown, Department of Health

- **NOTES:** Formerly Richardville County. Name changed to Howard Dec. 28, 1846.

HUNTINGTON
201 N. Jefferson St., Huntington, IN 46750, (260) 358-4819,
<www.huntington.in.us>
- **INCORPORATED:** Dec. 2, 1834
- **PARENT COUNTIES:** Adams New Purchase, Unorganized Land
- **BIRTH RECORDS:** start in 1882, kept by Department of Health
- **MARRIAGE:** 1837, County Clerk
- **DIVORCE:** 1850, County Clerk
- **DEATH:** 1882, Department of Health
- **LAND:** 1834, County Recorder
- **PROBATE:** 1841, County Clerk
- **COURT:** unknown, County Clerk

JACKSON
111 S. Main St., Brownstown, IN 47220, (812) 358-6117,
<www.jacksoncountyin.com>
- **INCORPORATED:** Jan. 1, 1816
- **PARENT COUNTIES:** Washington, Clark, Jefferson
- **BIRTH RECORDS:** start in 1882, kept by Department of Health
- **MARRIAGE:** 1816, County Clerk
- **DIVORCE:** 1816, County Clerk
- **DEATH:** 1882, Department of Health
- **LAND:** 1815, County Recorder
- **PROBATE:** 1817, County Clerk
- **COURT:** unknown, County Clerk

JASPER
115 W. Washington, Rensselaer, IN 47978, (219) 866-4927,
<www.jaspercountyin.gov>
- **INCORPORATED:** March 15, 1838
- **PARENT COUNTIES:** Wabash New Purchase, Unorganized Land
- **BIRTH RECORDS:** 1882, Department of Health
- **MARRIAGE:** 1850, County Clerk
- **DIVORCE:** 1865, County Clerk
- **DEATH:** 1882, Department of Health
- **PROBATE:** 1864, County Clerk
- **COURT:** unknown, County Clerk
- **NOTES:** Courthouse burned in 1862, all records destroyed.

JAY
120 N. Court St., Portland, IN 47371, (260) 726-6915,
<www.co.jay.in.us>
- **INCORPORATED:** March 1, 1836
- **PARENT COUNTY:** Adams New Purchase
- **BIRTH RECORDS:** start in 1882, kept by Department of Health
- **MARRIAGE:** 1837, County Clerk
- **DIVORCE:** 1882, County Clerk
- **DEATH:** 1882, Department of Health
- **LAND:** 1836, County Recorder
- **PROBATE:** unknown, County Clerk
- **COURT:** unknown, County Clerk

JEFFERSON
300 E. Main St. #203, Madison, IN 47250, (812) 265-8924,
<ingenweb.org/injefferson/indextwo.html>
- **INCORPORATED:** Nov. 23, 1810
- **PARENT COUNTIES:** Dearborn, Clark
- **BIRTH RECORDS:** start in 1882, kept by Department of Health
- **MARRIAGE:** 1811, County Clerk
- **DIVORCE:** unknown, County Clerk
- **DEATH:** 1882, Department of Health
- **LAND:** 1811, County Recorder
- **PROBATE:** 1811, County Clerk
- **COURT:** 1811, County Clerk
- **BURIAL:** unknown, Department of Health

JENNINGS
Box 385, Vernon, IN 47282, (812) 352-3070,
<www.jenningscounty-in.gov>
- **INCORPORATED:** Feb. 1, 1817
- **PARENT COUNTIES:** Jefferson, Jackson
- **BIRTH RECORDS:** start in 1882, kept by Department of Health
- **MARRIAGE:** 1818, County Clerk
- **DEATH:** 1882, Department of Health
- **LAND:** 1817, County Recorder
- **PROBATE:** 1818, County Clerk

JOHNSON
5 E. Jefferson St., Franklin, IN 46131, (317) 346-4450,
<www.co.johnson.in.us>
- **INCORPORATED:** May 5, 1823
- **PARENT COUNTY:** Delaware New Purchase
- **BIRTH RECORDS:** start in 1882, kept by Department of Health
- **MARRIAGE:** 1830, County Clerk
- **DIVORCE:** 1830, County Clerk
- **DEATH:** 1882, Department of Health
- **LAND:** 1825, County Recorder
- **PROBATE:** 1821, County Clerk
- **COURT:** unknown, County Clerk
- **BURIAL:** 1882, Department of Health

KNOX
111 N. Seventh St., Vincennes, IN 47591, (812) 885-2521,
<ingenweb.org/inknox/index.htm>
- **INCORPORATED:** June 20, 1790
- **PARENT COUNTY:** Indiana Territory
- **BIRTH RECORDS:** start in 1882, kept by Department of Health
- **MARRIAGE:** 1806, County Clerk
- **DIVORCE:** 1806, County Clerk
- **DEATH:** 1882, Department of Health
- **LAND:** 1783, County Recorder
- **PROBATE:** 1790, County Clerk
- **COURT:** 1801, County Clerk

KOSCIUSKO
121 N. Lake St., Warsaw, IN 46580, (574) 372-2376,
<www.kcgov.com>
- **INCORPORATED:** June 1, 1837
- **PARENT COUNTY:** Unorganized Land
- **BIRTH RECORDS:** start in 1882, kept by Department of Health
- **MARRIAGE:** 1830, County Clerk
- **DIVORCE:** 1836, County Clerk
- **DEATH:** 1882, Department of Health

- **LAND:** 1834, County Recorder
- **PROBATE:** 1836, County Clerk
- **COURT:** unknown, County Clerk
- **BURIAL:** unknown, Township Trustees

LA PORTE

813 Lincoln Way, La Porte, IN 46350, (219) 326-6808,
<www.laportecounty.org>

- **INCORPORATED:** Jan. 9, 1832
- **PARENT COUNTIES:** St. Joseph, Unorganized Land
- **BIRTH RECORDS:** start in 1882, kept by Department of Health
- **MARRIAGE:** 1832, County Clerk
- **DIVORCE:** 1834, County Clerk
- **DEATH:** 1882, Department of Health
- **LAND:** 1831, County Recorder
- **PROBATE:** 1832, County Clerk
- **COURT:** unknown, County Clerk
- **BURIAL:** unknown, Department of Health

LAGRANGE

105 N. Detroit St., La Grange, IN 46761, (260) 499-6371,
<www.lagrangecounty.org>

- **INCORPORATED:** April 1, 1832
- **PARENT COUNTY:** Unorganized Land
- **BIRTH RECORDS:** start in 1882, kept by Department of Health
- **MARRIAGE:** 1832, County Clerk
- **DIVORCE:** 1832, County Clerk
- **DEATH:** 1882, Department of Health
- **LAND:** 1832, County Recorder
- **PROBATE:** 1832, County Clerk
- **COURT:** unknown, County Clerk

LAKE

2293 N. Main St., Crown Point, IN 46307, (219) 755-3461,
<www.lakecountyin.org>

- **INCORPORATED:** Feb. 15, 1837
- **PARENT COUNTIES:** Porter, Newton
- **BIRTH RECORDS:** 1882, Department of Health
- **MARRIAGE:** 1837, County Clerk
- **DIVORCE:** 1837, Circuit Court
- **DEATH:** 1882, Department of Health
- **LAND:** 1837, County Recorder
- **PROBATE:** 1854, County Clerk
- **COURT:** unknown, County Clerk

LAWRENCE

916 Fifteenth Street, # 31, Bedford, IN 47421, (812) 275-7543,
<www.ingenweb.org/inlawrence>

- **INCORPORATED:** March 1, 1818
- **PARENT COUNTY:** Orange
- **BIRTH RECORDS:** start in 1882, kept by Department of Health
- **MARRIAGE:** 1818, County Clerk
- **DIVORCE:** 1818, County Clerk
- **DEATH:** 1882, Department of Health
- **PROBATE:** 1819, County Clerk
- **COURT:** unknown, County Clerk
- **MILITARY:** unknown, County Recorder
- **LAND:** 1819, County Recorder

MADISON

16 E. Ninth, Anderson, IN 46016, (765) 641-9443,
<www.madisoncountyindiana.org>

- **INCORPORATED:** July 1, 1823
- **PARENT COUNTY:** Delaware New Purchase
- **BIRTH RECORDS:** start in 1882, kept by Department of Health
- **MARRIAGE:** 1853, County Clerk
- **DIVORCE:** 1880, County Clerk
- **DEATH:** 1882, Department of Health
- **LAND:** 1822, County Recorder
- **PROBATE:** 1879, County Clerk
- **COURT:** unknown, County Clerk
- **NOTES:** County Board of Health has school records 1904-1932.

MARION

200 E. Washington St., Indianapolis, IN 46204, (317) 327-4740,
<www.indygov.org>

- **INCORPORATED:** April 1, 1822
- **PARENT COUNTY:** Delaware New Purchase
- **BIRTH RECORDS:** start in 1882, kept by Department of Health
- **MARRIAGE:** 1822, County Clerk
- **DIVORCE:** unknown, County Clerk
- **DEATH:** 1882, Department of Health
- **LAND:** 1822, County Recorder
- **PROBATE:** 1822, County Clerk

MARSHALL

211 W. Madison St., Plymouth, IN 46563, (574) 936-8922,
<www.co.marshall.in.us>

- **INCORPORATED:** Feb. 7, 1835
- **PARENT COUNTIES:** St. Joseph, Unorganized Land
- **BIRTH RECORDS:** start in 1882, kept by Department of Health
- **MARRIAGE:** 1836, County Clerk
- **DIVORCE:** 1836, County Clerk
- **DEATH:** 1882, Department of Health
- **LAND:** 1834, County Recorder
- **PROBATE:** 1834, County Clerk
- **COURT:** unknown, County Clerk
- **BURIAL:** 1882, Department of Health

MARTIN

Box 120, Shoals, IN 47581, (812) 247-3651,
<www.rootsweb.ancestry.com/~inmartin>

- **INCORPORATED:** Feb. 1, 1820
- **PARENT COUNTIES:** Daviess, Dubois
- **BIRTH RECORDS:** start in 1882, kept by Department of Health
- **MARRIAGE:** 1820, County Clerk
- **DIVORCE:** 1842, County Clerk
- **DEATH:** 1882, Department of Health
- **LAND:** 1820, County Recorder
- **PROBATE:** 1821, County Clerk
- **COURT:** unknown, County Clerk

MIAMI

Box 184, Peru, IN 46970, (756) 472-3901,
<www.miamicountyin.gov>

- **INCORPORATED:** March 1, 1834
- **PARENT COUNTIES:** Cass, Unorganized Land

- **BIRTH RECORDS:** start in 1882, kept by Department of Health
- **MARRIAGE:** 1843, County Clerk
- **DIVORCE:** 1843, County Clerk
- **DEATH:** 1882, Department of Health
- **PROBATE:** 1843, County Clerk
- **COURT:** unknown, County Clerk
- **BURIAL:** unknown, Department of Health

MONROE

Box 547, Bloomington, IN 47402, (812) 349-2600,
<www.co.monroe.in.us>

- **INCORPORATED:** April 10, 1818
- **PARENT COUNTY:** Orange
- **BIRTH RECORDS:** start in 1882, Department of Health
- **MARRIAGE:** 1818, County Clerk
- **DIVORCE:** 1818, County Clerk
- **DEATH:** 1882, Department of Health
- **LAND:** 1817, County Recorder
- **PROBATE:** 1818, County Clerk
- **COURT:** 1854, County Clerk
- **BURIAL:** 1882, Department of Health

MONTGOMERY

Box 768, Crawfordsville, IN 47933, (765) 364-6430,
<www.montgomeryco.net>

- **INCORPORATED:** March 1, 1823
- **PARENT COUNTY:** Wabash New Purchase
- **BIRTH RECORDS:** start in 1882, kept by Department of Health
- **MARRIAGE:** 1823, County Clerk
- **DIVORCE:** 1823, County Clerk
- **DEATH:** 1882, Department of Health
- **LAND:** 1821, County Recorder
- **PROBATE:** 1822, County Clerk
- **COURT:** unknown, County Clerk
- **NOTES:** County Clerk has some naturalization records.

MORGAN

Box 1556, Martinsville, IN 46151, (765) 342-1025,
<www.morgancounty.in.gov>

- **INCORPORATED:** Feb. 15, 1822
- **PARENT COUNTIES:** Delaware New Purchase, Wabash New Purchase
- **BIRTH RECORDS:** start in 1882, kept by Department of Health
- **MARRIAGE:** 1822, County Clerk
- **DEATH:** 1882, Department of Health
- **LAND:** 1822, County Recorder
- **PROBATE:** 1822, County Clerk
- **COURT:** unknown, County Clerk

NEWTON

Box 49, Kentland, IN 47951, (219) 474-6081,
<www.newtoncountyin.com>

- **INCORPORATED:** Dec. 9, 1859
- **PARENT COUNTY:** Jasper
- **BIRTH RECORDS:** start in 1882, kept by Department of Health
- **MARRIAGE:** 1860, County Clerk
- **DIVORCE:** 1860, County Clerk
- **DEATH:** 1882, Department of Health
- **LAND:** 1838, County Recorder
- **PROBATE:** 1860, County Clerk
- **COURT:** unknown, County Clerk
- **NOTES:** Attached to St. Joseph, Warren, and White Counties before re-creation and organization from Jasper County 8 December 1859. Old Newton County was formed in 1835 from Unorganized land and abolished in 1839.

NOBLE

101 N. Orange St., Albion, IN 46701, (260) 636-2736,
<www.nobleco.org>

- **INCORPORATED:** March 1, 1836
- **PARENT COUNTY:** Unorganized Land
- **BIRTH RECORDS:** start in 1882, kept by Department of Health
- **MARRIAGE:** 1859, County Clerk
- **DIVORCE:** 1859, County Clerk
- **DEATH:** 1882, Department of Health
- **LAND:** 1834, County Recorder
- **PROBATE:** 1854, County Clerk
- **COURT:** unknown, County Clerk
- **BURIAL:** unknown, City Clerk

OHIO

413 Main St., Rising Sun, IN 47040, (812) 438-2610,
<www.rootsweb.ancestry.com/~inohio>

- **INCORPORATED:** Jan. 15, 1844
- **PARENT COUNTY:** Dearborn
- **MARRIAGE RECORDS:** start in 1844, kept by County Clerk
- **DIVORCE:** 1844, County Clerk
- **PROBATE:** 1844, County Clerk
- **COURT:** unknown, County Clerk

ORANGE

1 Court St., Paoli, IN 47454, (812) 723-2649,
<www.usgennet.org/usa/in/county/orange>

- **INCORPORATED:** Feb. 1, 1816
- **PARENT COUNTIES:** Washington, Knox, Gibson
- **BIRTH RECORDS:** start in 1882, kept by Department of Health
- **MARRIAGE:** 1816, County Clerk
- **DIVORCE:** 1816, County Clerk
- **DEATH:** 1882, Department of Health
- **LAND:** 1816, County Recorder
- **PROBATE:** 1816, County Clerk
- **COURT:** unknown, County Clerk
- **BURIAL:** unknown, Department of Health

OWEN

Box 146, Spencer, IN 47460, (812) 829-5015,
<www.owencounty.org>

- **INCORPORATED:** Jan. 1, 1819
- **PARENT COUNTIES:** Daviess, Sullivan
- **BIRTH RECORDS:** start in 1882, kept by Department of Health
- **MARRIAGE:** 1819, County Clerk
- **DIVORCE:** 1832, County Clerk
- **DEATH:** 1882, Department of Health
- **LAND:** 1819, County Recorder
- **PROBATE:** 1819, County Clerk
- **COURT:** unknown, County Clerk

PARKE

116 W. High St. #204, Rockville, IN 47872, (765) 569-5132,
<www.parkecounty.net>

- **INCORPORATED:** April 2, 1821
- **PARENT COUNTIES:** Unorganized Land, Vigo, Wabash New Purchase
- **BIRTH RECORDS:** start in 1882, kept by Department of Health
- **MARRIAGE:** 1829, County Auditor
- **DIVORCE:** 1833, County Clerk
- **DEATH:** 1882, Department of Health
- **LAND:** 1816, County Recorder
- **PROBATE:** 1833, County Clerk
- **COURT:** unknown, County Clerk

PERRY

2219 Payne St., Tell City, IN 47586, (812) 547-3741,
<www.perrycountyindiana.org>

- **INCORPORATED:** Nov. 1, 1814
- **PARENT COUNTIES:** Warrick, Gibson
- **BIRTH RECORDS:** start in 1882, kept by Department of Health
- **MARRIAGE:** 1814, County Clerk
- **DIVORCE:** 1813, County Clerk
- **DEATH:** 1882, Department of Health
- **LAND:** 1815, County Recorder
- **PROBATE:** 1813, County Clerk
- **COURT:** 1815, County Clerk

PIKE

Box 125, Petersburg, IN 47567, (812) 354-6025,
<www.rootsweb.ancestry.com/~inpike/Pikegen.htm>

- **INCORPORATED:** Feb. 1, 1817
- **PARENT COUNTIES:** Gibson, Perry, Knox
- **BIRTH RECORDS:** start in 1882, kept by Department of Health
- **MARRIAGE:** 1817, County Clerk
- **DIVORCE:** 1817, County Clerk
- **DEATH:** 1882, Department of Health
- **LAND:** 1817, County Recorder
- **COURT:** 1817, County Clerk
- **NOTES:** County Clerk has probate records from early 1805.

PORTER

16 Lincolnway, Suite 211, Valparaiso, IN 46383, (219) 465-3450,
<www.porterco.org>

- **INCORPORATED:** Feb. 1, 1836
- **PARENT COUNTY:** Unorganized Land
- **BIRTH RECORDS:** start in 1882, kept by Department of Health
- **MARRIAGE:** 1836, County Clerk
- **DIVORCE:** 1836, County Clerk
- **DEATH:** 1882, Department of Health
- **LAND:** 1833, County Recorder
- **PROBATE:** 1839, County Clerk
- **COURT:** unknown, County Clerk
- **NOTES:** Attached to St. Joseph County prior to organization Feb. 6, 1836.

POSEY

Box 606, Mt. Vernon, IN 47620, (812) 838-1306,
<www.poseycounty.org>

- **INCORPORATED:** Nov. 1, 1814
- **PARENT COUNTY:** Warrick
- **BIRTH RECORDS:** start in 1882, kept by Department of Health
- **MARRIAGE:** 1814, County Clerk
- **DEATH:** 1882, Department of Health
- **DIVORCE:** 1815, County Clerk
- **LAND:** 1812, County Recorder
- **PROBATE:** 1815, County Clerk
- **COURT:** 1815, County Clerk
- **NOTES:** County Recorder has some military discharge records.

PULASKI

112 E. Main St., Winamac, IN 46996, (574) 946-6038,
<www.pulaskionline.org>

- **INCORPORATED:** May 6, 1840
- **PARENT COUNTY:** Unorganized Land
- **BIRTH RECORDS:** start in 1882, kept by Department of Health
- **MARRIAGE:** 1839, County Clerk
- **DIVORCE:** 1839, County Clerk
- **DEATH:** 1882, Department of Health
- **LAND:** 1840, County Recorder
- **PROBATE:** 1839, County Clerk
- **COURT:** unknown, County Clerk

PUTNAM

One Courthouse Sq., Greencastle, IN 46135, (765) 653-2648,
<www.co.putnam.in.us>

- **INCORPORATED:** April 1, 1822
- **PARENT COUNTIES:** Vigo, Owen, Wabash New Purchase
- **BIRTH RECORDS:** start in 1882, kept by Department of Health
- **MARRIAGE:** 1820, County Clerk
- **DIVORCE:** 1825, County Clerk
- **DEATH:** 1882, Department of Health
- **LAND:** 1824, County Recorder
- **PROBATE:** 1825, County Clerk
- **COURT:** unknown, County Clerk

RANDOLPH

100 S. Main St., Winchester, IN 47394, (765) 584-4214,
<www.rootsweb.ancestry.com/~inrandol>

- **INCORPORATED:** Aug. 10, 1818
- **PARENT COUNTY:** Wayne
- **BIRTH RECORDS:** start in 1882, kept by Department of Health
- **MARRIAGE:** 1819, County Clerk
- **DIVORCE:** unknown, County Clerk
- **DEATH:** 1882, Department of Health
- **LAND:** 1820, County Recorder
- **PROBATE:** 1819, County Clerk
- **COURT:** unknown, County Clerk
- **NOTES:** Formed from St. Clair County. Became part of Indiana Territory 1800, absorbed by Illinois Territory 1809.

RICHARDVILLE

- **INCORPORATED:** Jan. 15, 1844
- **PARENT COUNTY:** Unorganized Land
- **NOTES:** Name changed to Howard Dec. 28, 1846.

RIPLEY

Box 177, Versailles, IN 47042, (812) 689-6115,
<www.ripleycounty.com>

- **INCORPORATED:** April 10, 1818
- **PARENT COUNTY:** Dearborn, Jefferson
- **BIRTH RECORDS:** start in 1882, kept by Department of Health
- **MARRIAGE:** 1818, County Clerk
- **DIVORCE:** 1818, County Clerk
- **DEATH:** 1882, Department of Health
- **LAND:** 1818, County Recorder
- **PROBATE:** 1818, County Clerk
- **COURT:** 1818, County Clerk

RUSH

101 E. Second St., Rushville, IN 46173, (765) 932-2086,
<www.rushcounty.in.gov>

- **INCORPORATED:** April 1, 1822
- **PARENT COUNTY:** Delaware New Purchase
- **BIRTH RECORDS:** start in 1882, Department of Health
- **MARRIAGE:** 1822, County Clerk
- **DIVORCE:** 1822, County Clerk
- **DEATH:** 1882, Department of Health
- **LAND:** 1822, County Recorder
- **PROBATE:** 1822, County Clerk
- **COURT:** 1822, County Clerk
- **BURIAL:** 1882, Department of Health

SCOTT

1 E. McClain Ave., Scottsburg, IN 47170, (812) 752-8420,
<www.greatscottindiana.org>

- **INCORPORATED:** Feb. 1, 1820
- **PARENT COUNTIES:** Clark, Jefferson, Jennings, Jackson, Washington
- **BIRTH RECORDS:** start in 1882, kept by Department of Health
- **MARRIAGE:** 1820, County Clerk
- **DIVORCE:** 1820, County Clerk
- **DEATH:** 1882, Department of Health
- **LAND:** 1819, County Recorder
- **PROBATE:** unknown, County Clerk
- **COURT:** unknown, County Clerk

SHELBY

407 S. Harrison St., Shelbyville, IN 46176, (317) 392-6320,
<www.co.shelby.in.us>

- **INCORPORATED:** April 1, 1822
- **PARENT COUNTY:** Delaware New Purchase
- **BIRTH RECORDS:** start in 1882, kept by Department of Health
- **MARRIAGE:** 1822, County Clerk
- **DIVORCE:** unknown, County Clerk
- **DEATH:** 1882, Department of Health
- **LAND:** 1822, County Auditor
- **PROBATE:** 1822, County Clerk
- **COURT:** unknown, County Clerk
- **BURIAL:** unknown, Department of Health

SPENCER

200 Main St., Rockport, IN 47635, (812) 649-6027,
<spencercounty.in.gov>

- **INCORPORATED:** Feb. 1, 1818
- **PARENT COUNTIES:** Warrick, Perry
- **BIRTH RECORDS:** start in 1882, kept by Department of Health
- **MARRIAGE:** 1818, County Clerk
- **DIVORCE:** 1883, County Clerk
- **DEATH:** 1882, Department of Health
- **LAND:** 1818, County Recorder
- **PROBATE:** 1818, County Clerk
- **COURT:** unknown, County Clerk
- **BURIAL:** unknown, Cemetery Trustees
- **NOTES:** County Clerk has naturalization records 1852-1929.

ST. CLAIR

- **PARENT COUNTY:** Unorganized Land
- **NOTES:** Became part of Indiana Territory in 1800, absorbed by Illinois Territory 1809.

ST. JOSEPH

101 S. Main St., South Bend, IN 46601, (574) 235-9635,
<www.stjosephcountyindiana.com>

- **INCORPORATED:** Jan. 29, 1830
- **PARENT COUNTY:** Unorganized Land
- **BIRTH RECORDS:** start in 1882, kept by Department of Health
- **MARRIAGE:** 1830, County Clerk
- **DIVORCE:** unknown, County Clerk
- **DEATH:** 1882, Department of Health
- **LAND:** 1830, County Recorder
- **PROBATE:** 1830, County Clerk
- **COURT:** unknown, County Clerk
- **BURIAL:** unknown, Department of Health

STARKE

Box 395, Knox, IN 46534, (574) 772-9128,
<www.co.starke.in.us>

- **INCORPORATED:** Jan. 15, 1844
- **PARENT COUNTIES:** St. Joseph, Unorganized Land
- **BIRTH RECORDS:** start in 1882, kept by Department of Health
- **MARRIAGE:** 1840, County Clerk
- **DIVORCE:** 1850, County Clerk
- **DEATH:** 1882, Department of Health
- **LAND:** 1850, County Recorder
- **PROBATE:** 1850, County Clerk
- **COURT:** unknown, County Clerk

STEUBEN

55 S. Public Sq., Angola, IN 46703, (260) 668-1000,
<www.steubencounty.com>

- **INCORPORATED:** May 1, 1837
- **PARENT COUNTY:** Unorganized Land
- **BIRTH RECORDS:** start in 1882, kept by Department of Health
- **MARRIAGE:** 1832, County Clerk
- **DIVORCE:** 1837, County Clerk
- **DEATH:** 1882, Department of Health
- **PROBATE:** 1845, County Clerk
- **COURT:** unknown, County Clerk
- **NOTES:** County Clerk has land records from mid-1800s.

SULLIVAN
100 Courthouse Sq., Sullivan, IN 47882, (812) 268-4657,
<www.sctb.net>
- **INCORPORATED:** Jan. 15, 1817
- **PARENT COUNTY:** Knox
- **MARRIAGE RECORDS:** start in 1850, kept by County Clerk
- **DIVORCE:** 1850, County Clerk
- **PROBATE:** 1844, County Clerk
- **COURT:** unknown, County Clerk

SWITZERLAND
212 W. Main St., Vevay, IN 47043, (812) 427-3175
<www.vevayin.com>
- **INCORPORATED:** Oct. 1, 1814
- **PARENT COUNTIES:** Dearborn, Jefferson
- **BIRTH RECORDS:** start in 1882, kept by Department of Health
- **MARRIAGE:** 1814, County Clerk
- **DIVORCE:** 1814, County Clerk
- **DEATH:** 1882, Department of Health
- **LAND:** 1814, County Recorder
- **PROBATE:** 1814, County Clerk
- **COURT:** unknown, County Clerk
- **BURIAL:** unknown, Department of Health

TIPPECANOE
301 Main St., Lafayette, IN 47901, (765) 423-9326,
<www.county.tippecanoe.in.us>
- **INCORPORATED:** March 1, 1826
- **PARENT COUNTIES:** Unorganized Land, Wabash New Purchase
- **MARRIAGE RECORDS:** start in 1826, kept by County Clerk
- **DIVORCE:** 1850, Circuit Court
- **DEATH:** 1882, Department of Health
- **PROBATE:** 1825, County Clerk
- **COURT:** unknown, County Clerk
- **NATURALIZATION:** unknown, Circuit Court

TIPTON
101 E. Jefferson, Tipton, IN 46072, (765) 675-2795,
<www.tiptongenweb.org>
- **INCORPORATED:** May 1, 1844
- **PARENT COUNTIES:** Adams New Purchase, Unorganized Land
- **MARRIAGE RECORDS:** start in 1844, kept by County Clerk
- **DIVORCE:** 1850, County Clerk
- **PROBATE:** 1844, County Clerk
- **COURT:** unknown, County Clerk

UNION
26 W. Union St., Liberty, IN 47353, (765) 458-6121,
<www.union-county.lib.in.us/USGenwebpage1.htm>
- **INCORPORATED:** Feb. 1, 1821
- **PARENT COUNTIES:** Wayne, Franklin, Fayette
- **BIRTH RECORDS:** start in 1882, kept by Department of Health
- **MARRIAGE:** 1821, Circuit Court
- **DIVORCE:** 1821, Circuit Court
- **DEATH:** 1882, Department of Health
- **PROBATE:** 1821, County Clerk
- **COURT:** unknown, County Clerk

VANDERBURGH
Box 3356, Evansville, IN 47732, (812) 435-5160,
<www.vanderburghgov.org>
- **INCORPORATED:** Feb. 1, 1818
- **PARENT COUNTIES:** Gibson, Posey, Warrick
- **BIRTH RECORDS:** start in 1882, kept by Department of Health
- **MARRIAGE:** 1818, County Clerk
- **DIVORCE:** 1969, County Clerk
- **DEATH:** 1882, Department of Health
- **LAND:** 1818, County Recorder
- **PROBATE:** 1821, County Clerk
- **COURT:** 1825, County Clerk
- **MILITARY:** 1865, County Recorder
- **NOTES:** Willard Library has many older records.

VERMILLION
Box 10, 255 S. Main, Newport, IN 47966, (765) 492-3500,
<www.vermilliongov.us>
- **INCORPORATED:** Jan. 2, 1824
- **PARENT COUNTIES:** Parke, Unorganized Land, Wabash New Purchase
- **BIRTH RECORDS:** start in 1882, kept by Department of Health
- **MARRIAGE:** 1824, County Clerk
- **DIVORCE:** 1824, County Clerk
- **DEATH:** 1882, Department of Health
- **LAND:** 1824, County Recorder
- **PROBATE:** 1827, County Clerk
- **COURT:** 1825, County Clerk

VIGO
33 S. Third St., Terre Haute, IN 47807, (812) 462-3211,
<www.vigocounty.in.gov>
- **INCORPORATED:** March 21, 1818
- **PARENT COUNTY:** Sullivan
- **MARRIAGE RECORDS:** start in 1818, kept by County Clerk
- **DIVORCE:** 1825, County Clerk
- **PROBATE:** 1818, County Clerk
- **COURT:** unknown, County Clerk

WABASH
69 W. Hill St., Wabash, IN 46992, (260) 563-0661,
<www.wabashcounty.in.gov>
- **INCORPORATED:** March 1, 1835
- **PARENT COUNTIES:** Adams New Purchase, Unorganized Land
- **BIRTH RECORDS:** start in 1882, kept by Department of Health
- **MARRIAGE:** 1835, County Clerk
- **DIVORCE:** 1835, County Clerk
- **DEATH:** 1882, Department of Health
- **PROBATE:** 1847, County Clerk
- **COURT:** unknown, County Clerk
- **BURIAL:** unknown, Co. Rec./Museum
- **NOTES:** Formed from territorial Knox County and Unorganized Land abolished 1835. Some early records may be found in Monroe, Owen, Vigo, and Parke counties.

WARREN
125 N. Monroe St., Williamsport, IN 47993, (765) 762-3510,
<www.rootsweb.ancestry.com/~inwarren>
- **INCORPORATED:** March 1, 1827
- **PARENT COUNTIES:** Wabash New Purchase, Unorganized Land
- **BIRTH RECORDS:** start in 1882, kept by Department of Health
- **MARRIAGE:** 1827, County Clerk
- **DIVORCE:** 1827, County Clerk
- **DEATH:** 1882, Department of Health
- **LAND:** 1830, County Recorder
- **PROBATE:** 1829, County Clerk
- **COURT:** unknown, County Clerk

WARRICK
One County Sq., Boonville, IN 47601, (812) 897-6160,
<www.warrickcounty.gov>
- **INCORPORATED:** March 9, 1813
- **PARENT COUNTY:** Knox
- **BIRTH RECORDS:** start in 1882, kept by Department of Health
- **MARRIAGE:** 1813, County Clerk
- **DIVORCE:** 1813, County Clerk
- **DEATH:** 1882, Department of Health
- **LAND:** 1813, County Recorder
- **PROBATE:** 1814, County Clerk
- **COURT:** 1813, County Clerk
- **BURIAL:** unknown, Department of Health

WASHINGTON
99 Public Sq., Salem, IN 47167, (812) 883-5748,
<www.washingtoncountyindiana.com>
- **INCORPORATED:** Dec. 21, 1813
- **PARENT COUNTIES:** Clark, Harrison
- **BIRTH RECORDS:** start in 1882, kept by Department of Health
- **MARRIAGE:** 1815, County Clerk
- **DIVORCE:** 1814, County Clerk
- **DEATH:** 1882, Department of Health
- **LAND:** 1814, County Recorder
- **PROBATE:** 1814, County Clerk
- **COURT:** 1814, County Clerk
- **NOTES:** County Historical Society has many family records.

WAYNE
301 E. Main St., Richmond, IN 47374, (765) 973-9224,
<www.co.wayne.in.us>
- **INCORPORATED:** Nov. 27, 1810
- **PARENT COUNTIES:** Clark, Dearborn, Knox
- **BIRTH RECORDS:** start in 1882, kept by Department of Health
- **MARRIAGE:** 1811, County Clerk
- **DIVORCE:** 1873, County Clerk
- **DEATH:** unknown, Department of Health
- **PROBATE:** 1812, County Clerk
- **COURT:** 1811, County Clerk
- **BURIAL:** unknown, Department of Health
- **NOTES:** Wayne (old) formed from Unorganized Land in the Northwest Territory which included parts of modern Illinois, Michigan, Ohio, and Wisconsin.

WELLS
102 W. Market St., Bluffton, IN 46714, (219) 824-6482,
<www.wellscounty.org>
- **INCORPORATED:** Feb. 17, 1837
- **PARENT COUNTY:** Adams New Purchase
- **BIRTH RECORDS:** start in 1882, kept by Department of Health
- **MARRIAGE:** 1837, County Clerk
- **DIVORCE:** 1837, County Clerk
- **DEATH:** 1882, Department of Health
- **LAND:** 1838, County Recorder
- **PROBATE:** 1838, County Clerk
- **COURT:** unknown, County Clerk

WHITE
Box 350, Monticello, IN 47960, (219) 583-1530,
<www.whitecountyindiana.org>
- **INCORPORATED:** April 1, 1834
- **PARENT COUNTY:** Wabash New Purchase
- **BIRTH RECORDS:** start in 1882, kept by Department of Health
- **MARRIAGE:** 1834, County Clerk
- **DIVORCE:** 1834, County Clerk
- **DEATH:** 1882, Department of Health
- **LAND:** 1834, County Recorder
- **PROBATE:** 1835, County Clerk
- **COURT:** unknown, County Clerk
- **BURIAL:** unknown, Department of Health

WHITLEY
101 W. Van Buren St., Columbia City, IN 46725, (260) 248-3102,
<www.whitleynet.org>
- **INCORPORATED:** Jan. 29, 1839
- **PARENT COUNTY:** Unorganized Land
- **BIRTH RECORDS:** start in 1882, kept by Department of Health
- **MARRIAGE:** 1835, County Clerk
- **DIVORCE:** 1853, County Clerk
- **DEATH:** 1882, Department of Health
- **LAND:** 1813, County Recorder
- **PROBATE:** 1839, County Clerk
- **COURT:** unknown, County Clerk

IOWA

» BY JAMES W. WARREN

HISTORICAL OVERVIEW

Early French explorers who traveled through Iowa in the late 1600s encountered the Fox, Sauk, and Pottawatomie Indians. Julien Dubuque began mining lead in 1798. Though his fellow French-Canadians abandoned the settlement upon Dubuque's 1810 death, a city bearing his name would rise there.

The United States acquired the land in 1803 as part of the Louisiana Purchase. In 1808, Iowa became part of Illinois Territory; in 1812, it became part of Missouri Territory. From 1821 to 1834, Iowa was not attached to any territory.

The Black Hawk War broke out in 1832. When it was over, the Fox and Sauk Indians were forced to relocate to Kansas, leaving Iowa open for legal settlement. The first settlements were in Eastern Iowa in 1833. After Indian claims to the land were extinguished in 1851, settlers poured into the area. The southern part of the state saw arrivals mostly from Kentucky and Tennessee. Settlers in the north were primarily from New England and the Mid- Atlantic, Ohio, Indiana and Illinois.

Iowa became part of Michigan Territory in 1834 and Wisconsin Territory in 1836. In 1838, Iowa Territory was formed; it included what would become Minnesota and parts of the Dakotas. In 1846, Iowa was the 29th state with Iowa City as its capital. In 1857, Des Moines became the capital.

During the 1850s, more people moved into Iowa from Ohio and Indiana, and many immigrants from Germany, Britain, and Ireland arrived. Iowa's population tripled. The Amana colonists settled in Iowa. The last part of the 19th century saw heavy immigration from the Scandinavian countries.

research tips

- Birth, death, and marriage records are with the district court clerk in the county where they were created.
- The Iowa Genealogical Society Library in Des Moines has published local record abstracts, transcriptions and indexes.
- Indexes and collections of Bible records, individuals in local histories, and other resources are available from the State Historical Society of Iowa.

CENSUS RECORDS

- Federal census: 1850, 1860, 1870, 1880, 1900, 1910 and 1920
- Mortality schedules: 1850, 1860, 1870, and 1880
- Territorial and state censuses: 1836 and 1838 (as part of Wisconsin Territory), 1844 (Keokuk), 1846 (Louisa, Polk, Wapello), 1847, 1849, 1851, 1852, 1853 (part of Warren County), 1854, 1856, 1859, 1863 and 1869 (Henry County), 1881 and 1882 (fragments), 1885, 1888, 1889, 1891–1893 (fragments), 1895–1897 (fragments), 1905, 1915, 1925

RECORD HIGHLIGHTS

The first available US census for the state of Iowa is 1850. Subsequent federal censuses through 1930 are available, except 1890, which was destroyed by fire. Mortality schedules exist for 1850, 1860, 1870 and 1880. Many territorial and state censuses taken between 1836 and 1854 don't give much detail; only a few counties' records have survived. The same is true of state censuses taken between 1881 and 1893. But there are exceptions: The 1856, 1885, 1895, 1905, 1915 and 1925 Iowa state censuses list every household member. These are at the State Historical Society in Des Moines and, except for 1905, at the State Historical Society in Iowa City.

Iowa marriage records begin just after county formation, some as early as 1830. Birth and death registration became mandatory in 1880, with most counties complying by 1924. County birth, death, and marriage records are with the clerk of the district court. State birth and marriage records begin in July 1880; deaths, in January 1881. Request them from the Iowa Department of Public Health, Vital Records Bureau **<www.idph.state.ia.us/apl/health_statistics.asp#vital>**.

The State Historical Society of Iowa has collections of cemetery transcriptions. Local cemetery, church, and funeral home records can provide clues not easily found elsewhere.

Iowa county-level courts are district courts, operating under that name as early as 1836. Other courts were also active: County courts (1851-1868) handled probate, marriage licenses, liquor permits, and other lesser civil and criminal cases. Circuit courts (1868-1887) had county-level jurisdiction over juvenile, criminal, civil, and probate cases. When circuit courts were abolished in 1887, district courts assumed their jurisdiction. The Family History Library (FHL) has microfilmed court records for many Iowa counties.

Divorce records are civil court cases recorded in the proceedings of each county's district court. Starting in 1906, a copy of each divorce record was sent to the state. Many divorces from 1906 to the mid-1950s are at the FHL.

Land records are with the county recorder in each county. The FHL has microfilmed many counties' deeds.

Probate courts were created in each county when Iowa Territory was organized, but were later discontinued. Some county and circuit courts handled probate matters until 1887. After that, probate matters normally go through district court. Many probate records are available on FHL microfilm.

Naturalization could be performed during most time periods in any court of law. Local district courts usually handled them; the records are available from the clerk of the district court. The FHL has microfilmed most Iowa county naturalizations. While most people used their local courthouse, some went to the federal courthouse. The FHL and the National Archives have microfilm of thousands of naturalizations processed in Federal District Court, including those for people in Illinois, Wisconsin, and 44 counties in Eastern Iowa. Many naturalization records are digitized on subscription sites Ancestry.com and Footnote.

The State Historical Society of Iowa **<www.iowahistory.org>** has collections including biographical indexes, Bible records, Iowa individuals in local histories, and other resources. The society has two locations: Iowa City and Des Moines. Some material is duplicated in the two facilities, but most is not. The largest collection of Iowa newspapers on microfilm is at the Iowa City location.

Usually dating to the creation of a county, County Board of Supervisors records document the functioning of county boards, whose responsibilities include roads; care of the poor, blind and elderly; levying taxes; and setting salaries for county officials. The FHL has some copies of such records.

School records for many Iowa school districts are on microfilm at the FHL. They often include school censuses that identify birth dates and places as well as parents. Coroner's records for some counties are also on film at the FHL, some starting as early as 1855.

The Iowa Genealogical Society (IGS) has worked with local genealogical societies to publish records, such as tombstone transcriptions, courthouse record abstracts or index to local records. The publications are at the IGS library in downtown Des Moines,.

ARCHIVES, LIBRARIES, AND SOCIETIES

Adair County Anquestors Genealogy Society
c/o Greenfield Public Library, Box 328, Greenfield, IA 50849, **<www.rootsweb.ancestry.com/~iaaags>**

Adams County Genealogical Society
Box 177, Prescott, IA 50859

Allamakee County Historical Society
121 Allamakee St., Box 95, Waukon, IA 52172, (563) 568-2954, **<www.allamakeehistory.org>**

American/Schleswig-Holstein Heritage Society
121 W. Bryant St., Walcott, IA 52773, **<www.ashhs.org/index.html>**

Ankeny Genealogical Society
Box 136, Ankeny, IA 50021

Appanoose County Genealogical Society
1601 S. Sixteenth St., Centerville, IA 52544

Audubon County Genealogical Society
505 Brayton St., Audubon, IA 50025, **<www.auduboncounty.net/acgs>**

Benton County Genealogical Society
1808 Ninth Ave., Belle Plaine, IA 52208, **<iagenweb.org/benton/bcgs>**

Benton County Historical Society
Box 22, Vinton, IA 52349, (319) 477-6370, **<iagenweb.org/benton/bchs/bchs.htm>**

Boone County Genealogical Society
Box 453, Boone, IA 50036, **<www.rootsweb.ancestry.com/~iabcgs>**

Boone County Historical Center
602 Story St., Boone, IA 50036, (515) 432-1907, **<www.boonecountyhistory.org>**

Botna Valley Genealogical Society
Box 633, Oakland, IA 51560

Bremer County Genealogical Society
426 Washington St., Denver, IA 50622, **<iagenweb.org/bremer>**

Buchanan County Genealogical Society
103 Fourth Ave SE, Independence, IA 50644, (319) 334-9333, **<www.rootsweb.ancestry.com/~iabcgs2>**

Buena Vista County Genealogical Society and Library
221 W. Railroad, Storm Lake, IA 50588, (712) 732-7111, **<www.stormlake-ia.com/bvchs/gen1.htm>**

Buena Vista County Historical Society
214 W. Fifth St., Storm Lake, IA 50588, (712) 732-4955, **<www.stormlake-ia.com/bvchs>**

Burlington Public Library
210 N. Court St., Burlington, IA 52601, (319) 753-1647, **<www.burlington.lib.ia.us>**

Butler County Genealogy Society
Box 731, Allison, IA 50602, **<iagenweb.org/butler/BCGS.htm>**

Carroll County Genealogical Society
Box 21, Carroll, IA 51401, **<www.rootsweb.ancestry.com/~iacarrol/ccgs.htm>**

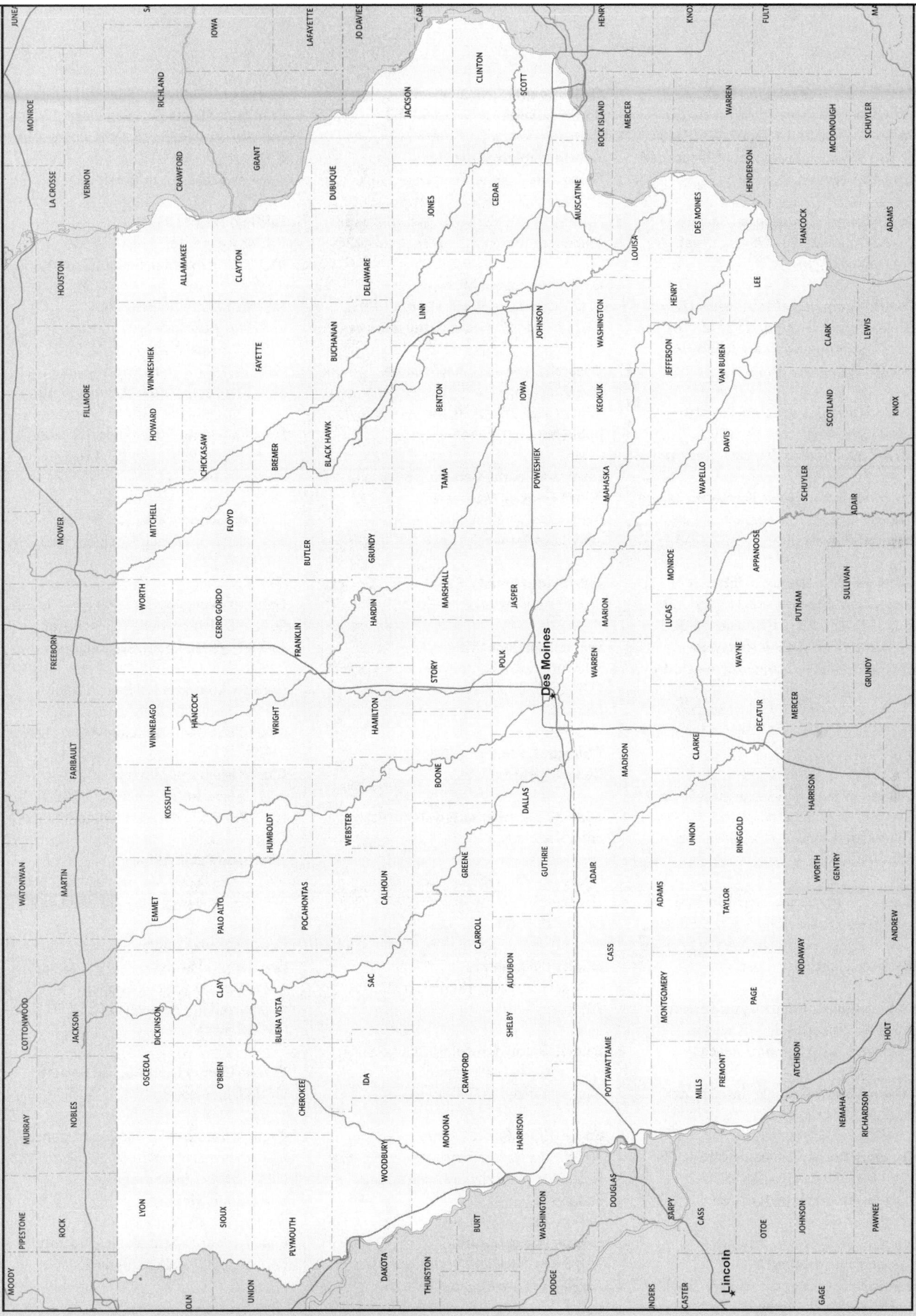
Des Moines
Lincoln
LYON
OSCEOLA
DICKINSON
EMMET
KOSSUTH
WINNEBAGO
WORTH
MITCHELL
HOWARD
WINNESHIEK
ALLAMAKEE
SIOUX
O'BRIEN
CLAY
PALO ALTO
HANCOCK
CERRO GORDO
FLOYD
CHICKASAW
FAYETTE
CLAYTON
PLYMOUTH
CHEROKEE
BUENA VISTA
POCAHONTAS
HUMBOLDT
WRIGHT
FRANKLIN
BUTLER
BREMER
BLACK HAWK
BUCHANAN
DELAWARE
DUBUQUE
WOODBURY
IDA
SAC
CALHOUN
WEBSTER
HAMILTON
HARDIN
GRUNDY
MONONA
CRAWFORD
CARROLL
GREENE
BOONE
STORY
MARSHALL
TAMA
BENTON
LINN
JONES
JACKSON
CLINTON
HARRISON
SHELBY
AUDUBON
GUTHRIE
DALLAS
POLK
JASPER
POWESHIEK
IOWA
JOHNSON
CEDAR
SCOTT
MUSCATINE
POTTAWATTAMIE
CASS
ADAIR
MADISON
WARREN
MARION
MAHASKA
KEOKUK
WASHINGTON
LOUISA
MILLS
MONTGOMERY
ADAMS
UNION
CLARKE
LUCAS
MONROE
WAPELLO
JEFFERSON
HENRY
DES MOINES
FREMONT
PAGE
TAYLOR
RINGGOLD
DECATUR
WAYNE
APPANOOSE
DAVIS
VAN BUREN
LEE
PIPESTONE
ROCK
MURRAY
NOBLES
COTTONWOOD
JACKSON
WATONWAN
MARTIN
FARIBAULT
FREEBORN
MOWER
FILLMORE
HOUSTON
LA CROSSE
VERNON
MONROE
CRAWFORD
RICHLAND
GRANT
IOWA
LAFAYETTE
JO DAVIESS
ROCK ISLAND
MERCER
WARREN
HENDERSON
HANCOCK
MCDONOUGH
SCHUYLER
ADAMS
CLARK
LEWIS
SCOTLAND
KNOX
SCHUYLER
ADAIR
PUTNAM
SULLIVAN
MERCER
GRUNDY
HARRISON
WORTH
GENTRY
NODAWAY
ANDREW
ATCHISON
HOLT
NEMAHA
RICHARDSON
PAWNEE
JOHNSON
GAGE
OTOE
CASS
SARPY
DOUGLAS
WASHINGTON
BURT
THURSTON
DAKOTA
DODGE
UNION
MOODY

Cass County Genealogical Society
c/o Atlantic Carnegie Public Library, 507 Poplar St., Atlantic, IA 50022, (712) 243-5466, **<www.rootsweb.com/~iacassgs/cassgen1.html>**

Cedar County Genealogical Society
Box 52, Tipton, IA 52772, **<iagenweb.org/cedar/ccgs>**

Central Community Historical Society
628 Sixth Ave., DeWitt, IA 52742, (563) 659-3686, **<iagenweb.org/clinton/resources/central.htm>**

Central Iowa Genealogical Society
Box 945, Marshalltown, IA 50158, **<www.manorweb.com/cigs/cigs.html>**

Chadwick Library, Iowa Wesleyan College
107 W. Broad St., Mt. Pleasant, IA 52641, **<chadwick.iwc.edu>**

Charter-Pierce Memorial Internet Genealogical Society and Library
3221 Villa Vista Dr., Des Moines, IA 50316, (515) 266-5326, **<www.rootsweb.ancestry.com/~iapcmigs/cpmigsl.htm>**

Cherokee County Historical Society
Box 247, Cleghorn, IA 51014, (712) 436-2624

Chickasaw County Genealogical Society
Box 434, New Hampton, IA 50659, **<www.chickasawcoia-geniesoc.org/CK_CCGS.htm>**

Clarke County Genealogical Society
c/o Osceola Public Library, 300 S. Fillmore, Osceola, IA 50213, **<iagenweb.org/clarke/ccgs.html>**

Clayton County Genealogical Society
Box 846, Elkader, IA 52043, **<www.rootsweb.ancestry.com/~iaccgs>**

Clinton County Genealogical Chapter
Box 2062, Clinton, IA 52732

Crawford County Genealogical Society
2704 Hwy. 59, Denison, IA 51442, **<iagenweb.org/crawford/xcrgsoc.html>**

Cresco Public Library
320 N. Elm St., Cresco, IA 52136, (563) 547-2540, **<www.cresco.lib.ia.us>**

Dallas County Genealogical Society
Box 264, Dallas Center, IA 50063

Danish Immigrant Archives
Grand View College, Third Floor West, Old Main, 1200 Grandview Ave., Des Moines, IA 50316, **<www.gvc.edu/aspx/audience/audience.aspx?pageid=420>**

Danish Immigrant Museum
2212 Washington St., Elk Horn, IA 51531, (712) 764-7001, **<www.dkmuseum.org>**

Decorah Genealogy Association
202 Winnebago (Lower Level), Decorah, IA 52101, (563) 382-8559, **<www.harveyshobbyhut.com/genealogy>**

Delaware County Genealogical Society
304 N. Franklin, Manchester, IA 52057, **<www.rootsweb.ancestry.com/~iadelawa/gensociety.htm>**

Des Moines County Genealogical Society
Box 493, Burlington, IA 52601

Donnellson Public Library
500 Park, Box 290, Donnellson IA 52625, (319) 835-5545, **<www.donnellson.lib.ia.us>**

Dubuque County-Key City Genealogical Society
Box 13, Dubuque, IA 52004, (563) 663-5303, **<www.rootsweb.ancestry.com/~iadckcgs>**

Dyersville Area Historical Society
120 Third St. SW, Dyersville, IA 52040, (563) 875-2504

Elliott Public Library
401 Main St., Elliott, IA 51532, (712) 767-2355

Emmet County Genealogical Society
c/o Estherville Public Library, 613 Central Ave., Estherville, IA 51334

Emmetsburg Public Library
707 N. Superior, Emmetsburg, IA 50536, (712) 852-4009, **<www.emmetsburg.lib.ia.us>**

Ericson Public Library
702 Greene St, Boone, IA 50036, (515) 432-3727, **<www.boone.lib.ia.us>**

Evangelical Lutheran Church of America, Wartburg Theological Seminary
333 Wartburg Pl., Box 5004, Dubuque, IA 52004, (563) 589-0200, **<www.wartburgseminary.edu>**

Fairfield Public Library
104 W. Adams, Fairfield, IA 52556, (641) 472-6551, **<www.fairfield.lib.ia.us>**

Fayette County Helpers Club and Historical Society
100 N. Walnut, West Union, IA 52175, (563) 422-5797, **<www.rootsweb.ancestry.com/~iafayett/iafirst6.htm>**

Franklin County Genealogical Society
c/o Hampton Public Library, 4 Federal St., Hampton, IA 50441

Fremont County Historical Society
801 Indiana St., Sidney, IA 51652, (712) 374-3248

Gateway Genealogical Society
Box 2256, Clinton, IA 52733, **<clintongatewaygensoc.homestead.com>**

German American Heritage Center
712 W. Second St., Davenport, IA 52802, (563) 322-8844, **<gahc.org>**

Gibson Memorial Library
200 W. Howard St., Creston, IA 50801, (641) 782-2277, **<www.creston.lib.ia.us>**

Glenwood Public Library
109 N. Vine St., Glenwood, IA 51534, (712) 527-5252, **<www.glenwood.lib.ia.us>**

Greater Sioux County Genealogical Society
102 S. Main Ave., Sioux Center, IA 51250, **<iagenweb.org/sioux/GSCGS/GSCGS.htm>**

Greene County Genealogical Society
Box 133, Jefferson, IA 50129

Grout Museum of History and Science
503 South St., Waterloo, IA 50701, (319) 234-6357, **<www.groutmuseumdistrict.org>**

Grundy County Genealogical Society
708 West St., Reinbeck, IA 50668

Guthrie County Genealogical Society
Box 96B, Jamaica, IA 50128, **<www.panora.org/museum/index_files/genealogical_society.htm>**

Hamilton Heritage Hunters Genealogical Society
943 First St., Webster City, IA 50595, **<iagenweb.org/hamilton/HHH.htm>**

Hampton Public Library
4 Federal S., Hampton, IA 50441, (641) 456-4451, **<www.hampton.lib.ia.us>**

Harrison County Genealogical Society
<iagenweb.org/harrison/hcgs>

Howard-Winneshiek Genealogy Society
Box 362, Cresco, IA 52136

Humboldt County Genealogical Society
30 Sixth St. N., Humboldt, IA 50548

Ida County Genealogical Society
1111 S. Main St., Ida Grove, IA 51445

Iowa City Genealogical Society
Box 822, Iowa City, IA 52244, **<iagenweb.org/johnson/ICGSmemberData.htm>**

Iowa County Historical Society
c/o Pioneer Heritage Museum, Box 288, Marengo, IA 52301, (319) 642-7018

Iowa Department of Public Health, Bureau of Vital Statistics
Lucas State Office Building, 321 E. Twelfth St., Des Moines, IA 50319, (515) 281-4944, **<www.idph.state.ia.us/apl/health_statistics.asp>**

Iowa Genealogical Society
628 E. Grand Ave., Des Moines, IA 50309, (515) 276-0287, **<www.iowagenealogy.org>**

Iowa Lakes Genealogical Society
c/o Spencer Public Library, 21 E. Third St., Spencer, IA 51301, (712) 580-7290, **<spencerlibrary.com/genealogy.htm>**

Jackson County Genealogical Chapter
Box 1065, Maquoketa, IA 52060, (563) 652-5020, **<iagenweb.org/jackson/JCGenie.html>**

Jasper County Genealogical Society
113 W. Second St., Newton, IA 50208, **<iagenweb.org/jasper/jcgs>**

Jefferson County Genealogical Society
2791 240th St., Fairfield, IA 52556, **<www.rootsweb.com/~iajeffer/JCGS.htm>**

Johnson County Historical Society
860 Quarry Rd., Box 5081, Coralville, IA 52241, (319) 351-5738, **<www.jchsiowa.org>**

Jones County Genealogical Society
Box 174, Anamosa, IA 52205, **<iowajones.org/research/resources.htm#jcgs>**

KeoMah Genealogical Society
209 A Ave. E., Oskaloosa, IA 52577, (641) 673-9373, **<www.keo-mah.com>**

Keosauqua Public Library
First and Van Buren, Keosauqua, IA 52565, (319) 293-3766, **<www.keopublib.com>**

Lee County Genealogical Society
Box 303, Keokuk, IA 52632, **<www.rootsweb.com/~ialeecgs>**

Le Mars Public Library
46 First St. SW, Le Mars, IA 51031, (712) 546-5004, **<www.lemars.lib.ia.us>**

Linn County Genealogical Society
Box 175, Cedar Rapids, IA 52406, (319) 369-0022, **<www.usgennet.org/usa/ia/county/linn/gen_soc.htm>**

Louisa County Genealogical Society
Box 202, Wapello, IA 52653, **<www.rootsweb.ancestry.com/~ialcgs>**

Lucas County Genealogical Society
c/o Chariton Public Library, 803 Braden Ave., Chariton, IA 50049, (641) 774-5514 **<lucascountygenealogy.blogspot.com>**

Madison County Genealogical Society
Box 26, Winterset, IA 50273, **<www.rootsweb.ancestry.com/~iamadcgs>**

Mamie Doud Eisenhower Birthplace
709 Carroll St., Boone, IA 50036, (515) 432-1907, **<www.mamiesbirthplace.homestead.com>**

Marion County Genealogical Society
Box 385, Knoxville, IA 50138, **<www.rootsweb.ancestry.com/~iamcgs/index.html>**

Marshalltown Public Library
105 W. Boone St., Marshalltown, IA 50158, (641) 754-5738, **<www.marshalltownlibrary.org>**

Mason City Public Library
225 Second St. SE, Mason City, IA 50401, (641) 421-3668, **<www.mcpl.org>**

Mid-America Genealogical Society
Box 316, Davenport, IA 52801

Monona County Genealogical Society
Box 16, Onawa, IA 51040

Monroe County Genealogical Society
c/o Albia Public Library, 203 Benton Ave. E., Albia, IA 52531, **<www.iamonroe.org/monroeco.htm>**

Montgomery County Genealogical Society
705 Washington Ave., Red Oak, IA 51566

Muscatine County Genealogical Society
323 Main St., Muscatine, IA 52761

National Archives, Central Plains Region
400 W. Pershing Rd., Kansas City, MO 64131, (816) 268-8000, **<www.archives.gov/central-plains/kansas-city>**

Nishnabotna Genealogical Society
847 Rd. M56, Harlan, IA 51537, **<iagenweb.org/shelby/scgs.htm>**

North Central Iowa Genealogy Society
Box 237, Mason City, IA 50402, **<ncigs.org>**

Northeast Iowa Genealogical Society
Box 2274, Waterloo, IA 50704, (515) 276-0287, **<www.rootsweb.ancestry.com/~iablackh/neigsbooklist.html>**

Northwest Iowa Genealogical Society
46 First St. SW, LeMars, IA 51031, **<genealogynwia.homestead.com/gen.html>**

Oelwein Area Genealogical Society
Box 389, Oelwein, IA 50662, **<www.rootsweb.ancestry.com/~iaoags>**

Oelwein Area Historical Society Museum
Box 445, Oelwein, IA 50662, (319) 283-4203, **<www.rootsweb.ancestry.com/~iaoahs>**

Old Fort Genealogical Society
Box 1, Fort Madison, IA 52627, **<freepages.genealogy.rootsweb.ancestry.com/~oldfort>**

Oskaloosa Public Library
301 S. Market St., Oskaloosa, IA 52577, (641) 673-0441, **<www.oskaloosalibrary.org>**

Ostfriesen Heritage Society
905 East Ave., Grundy Center, IA 50638, (319) 824-6321, **<iagenweb.org/grundy/ostfriesian_heritage_society.htm>**

Page County Genealogical Society
RR 2, Box 236, Shenandoah, IA 51610

Palo Alto County Genealogical Society
c/o Emmetsburg Public Library, 707 N. Superior St., Emmetsburg, IA 50536, **<www.rootsweb.ancestry.com/~iapaloal>**

Pocahontas County Genealogical Society
14 Second Ave. NW, Pocahontas, IA 50574

Pottawattamie County Genealogical Society
Box 394, Council Bluffs, IA 51502, **<www.rootsweb.ancestry.com/~iapottaw/PCGS.htm>**

Poweshiek County Historical and Genealogical Society
Box 280, Montezuma, IA 50171, (641) 623-3322, **<showcase.netins.net/web/powshk>**

Sac County Genealogical Society
Box 54, Sac City, IA 50583, **<www.rootsweb.ancestry.com/~iasac/gensociety/gensoc.htm>**

Scott County Genealogical Society
Box 3132, Davenport, IA 52808, **<www.rootsweb.ancestry.com/~iascott/scigs.htm>**

Sioux City Public Library
529 Pierce St., Sioux City, IA 51101, (712) 255-2933, **<www.siouxcitylibrary.org>**

Spencer Public Library
21 E. Third St., Spencer, IA 51301, (712) 580-7290, **<spencerlibrary.com/libinfo.htm>**

State Historical Society of Iowa
600 E. Locust, Des Moines, IA 50319, (515) 281-5111, **<www.iowahistory.org>**

Story County Genealogical Society
Box 692, Ames, IA 50010, **<sites.google.com/site/storygenealogy>**

Tama County Tracers Genealogical Society
200 N. Broadway, Toledo, IA 52342

Taylor County Genealogical Society
Box 8, Gravity, IA 50848, **<iagenweb.org/taylor/genhist/tci130.htm>**

Union County Genealogical Society
200 W. Howard, Creston, IA 50801, **<iagenweb.org/union/ucgs/genpage.html>**

Urbandale Public Library
3520 86th St., Urbandale, IA 50322, (515) 278-3945, **<www.urbandalelibrary.org>**

Van Buren County Genealogical Society
Box 160, Keosauqua, IA 52565, **<www.rootsweb.ancestry.com/~iavbcgs/app.htm>**

Vesterheim Norwegian-American Museum
Box 379, Decorah, IA 52101, (563) 382-9681, **<www.vesterheim.org>**

Wapello County Genealogical Society
Box 163, Ottumwa, IA 52501, **<wapellocountygs.org>**

Warren County Genealogical Society
Box 151, Indianola, IA 50125

Wayne County Genealogical Society
c/o LeCompte Memorial Library, 110 S. Franklin St., Corydon, IA 50060, (515) 872-1621, **<freepages.history.rootsweb.ancestry.com/~rkross/wayne_gen_society.html>**

Webster County Genealogical Society
Box 1584, Fort Dodge, IA 50501, **<iagenweb.org/webster/webgenso.htm>**

Woodbury County Genealogical Society
Box 624, Sioux City, IA 51102, **<www.rootsweb.ancestry.com/~iawoodbu/WCGS.htm>**

Wright County Genealogical Searchers
Box 225, Clarion, IA 50525, **<iagenweb.org/wright/WrightCountyGenealogicalSearchers.htm>**

GENERAL RESOURCES

A Bibliography of Iowa Newspapers, 1836-1976 (Iowa State Historical Dept., Division of the State Historical Society, 1979)

Biographical Index to the County Histories of Iowa by Charles Morford (Gateway Press, ca. 1979)

Biographies and Portraits of the Progressive Men of Iowa by B.F. Gue and Benjamin Franklin Shambaugh (Conaway & Shaw, 1899)

The First Century of Congregationalism in Iowa, 1840-1940 by P. Adelstein Johnson (Congregational Christian Conference of Iowa, ca. 1945)

German Settlers of Iowa by Margaret Krug Palen (Heritage Books, ca. 2000)

Guide to Depositories of Manuscript Collections in the United States, Iowa by the Historical Records Survey (Iowa Historical Records Survey, 1940)

Guide to Manuscripts by Katherine Harris (State Historical Society of Iowa, 1973)

A History of the Danes in Iowa by Thomas Peter Christensen (Arno Press, 1979)

History of Iowa from the Earliest Times to the Beginning of the Twentieth Century by Benjamin F. Gue (Century History Co., ca. 1903)

History of Western Iowa: Its Settlement and Growth (W.C. Cox, 1974)

Iowa Biographical Dictionary (Somerset, ca. 1996)

Iowa County Records Manual by Becki Peterson (State Historical Society of Iowa, ca. 1987)

Iowa History and Culture: A Bibliography of Materials Published between 1952

and 1986 by Patricia Dawson (Iowa State University Press, ca. 1989)

Iowa History Reference Guide by William J. Petersen (State Historical Society of Iowa, ca. 1952)

Iowa Research Outline by the Church of Jesus Christ of Latter-day Saints (online at **<www.familysearch.org/eng/search/RG/guide/iowa.asp>**)

A Memorial and Biographical Record of Iowa by Merrill D. Anthony (Walsworth Publishing Co., 1978)

The Mennonites in Iowa by Melvin Gingerich (State Historical Society of Iowa, 1939)

A Narrative History of the People of Iowa by Edgar Rubey Harlan (W.C. Cox, 1974)

Personal Name Index to the 1856 City Directories of Iowa by Elsie L. Sopp (Gale Research Co., 1980)

The Story of Iowa: The Progress of an American State by William John Petersen (Lewis Historical Publishing Co., 1952)

Swedish Settlements in Iowa and Western Illinois by Norma Goedeke and Shirley Graham (Knox County Genealogical Society, 1992)

Upper Midwest German Biographical Index by Don Heinrich Tolzmann (Heritage Books, ca. 1993)

The William Wade Hinshaw Index to Iowa Quaker Meeting Records by William Wade Hinshaw (Selby Publishing and Print., ca. 1990

IMMIGRATION RECORDS

Amsterdamse Emigranten: Onbekende Brieven uit de Prairie van Iowa, 1846-1873 by J. Stellingwerff (Buijten & Schipperheijn, 1975)

German Settlers of Iowa by Margaret Krug Palen (Heritage Books, ca. 2000)

LAND RECORDS

Iowa, Public Land Disposal by Roscoe L. Lokken (State Historical Society of Iowa, ca. 1942)

Pioneers and Profits: Land Speculation on the Iowa Frontier by Robert P. Swierenga (Iowa State University Press, ca. 1968)

MAPS

Abandoned Towns, Villages and Post Offices of Iowa by David C. Mott (J.W. Hoffman & S.L. Purington Publishing, 1973)

From Ackley to Zwingle: The Origins of Iowa Place Names by Harold E. Dilts (Iowa State University Press, ca. 1993)

Iowa Post Offices, 1833-1986 by Alan H. Patera (The Depot, ca. 1986)

Iowa State Gazetteer by James T. Hair (Bailey & Hair, 1865)

Postmarked Iowa: A List of Discontinued and Renamed Post Offices by Guy Reed Ramsey (J-B Publishing, ca. 1976)

MILITARY RECORDS

Iowa in the Civil War by James J. Robertson Jr. (State Historical Society of Iowa, ca. 1970)

The Iowa Department of the Grand Army of the Republic by Jacob A. Swisher (State Historical Society of Iowa, ca. 1936)

List of Ex-Soldiers, Sailors and Marines Living in Iowa by William L. Alexander (Decorah Genealogy Association, 1997)

Roster and Record of Iowa Soldiers in the War of the Rebellion by the Iowa Adjutant General's Office (E.H. English, 1908-1911)

VITAL RECORDS

Guide to Public Records of Iowa Counties by John P. Dolan Jr. (Connie Wimer, ca. 1986)

Guide to Public Vital Statistics Records in Iowa by the Historical Records Survey (Iowa Historical Records Survey, 1941)

Iowa Marriages Before Statehood, 1835-1846 by Shela S. Fretwell (1985)

Iowa Marriages, Early to 1850: A Research Tool by Liahona Research (Liahona Research, Inc., ca. 1990)

COUNTY DETAILS

ADAIR

400 Public Sq., Box L, Greenfield, IA 50849, (641) 743-2445, **<iagenweb.org/adair>**

- **INCORPORATED:** Jan. 15, 1851
- **PARENT COUNTY:** Pottawattamie
- **BIRTH RECORDS:** start in 1880, kept by District Court
- **MARRIAGE:** 1854, District Court
- **DIVORCE:** 1852, District Court
- **DEATH:** 1880, District Court
- **PROBATE:** 1852, District Court
- **COURT:** 1852, District Court
- **NOTES:** Attached to Pottawattamie and Cass counties prior to organization May 6, 1854.

ADAMS

500 Ninth St., Box 484, Corning, IA 50841, (641) 322-4711, **<www.adamscountyia.com>**

- **INCORPORATED:** Jan. 15, 1851
- **PARENT COUNTY:** Pottawattamie
- **BIRTH RECORDS:** start in 1880, kept by District Court

- **MARRIAGE:** 1855, District Court
- **DIVORCE:** 1910, District Court
- **DEATH:** 1880, District Court
- **LAND:** 1853, County Recorder
- **PROBATE:** 1868, District Court
- **COURT:** 1857, District Court
- **NOTES:** Organized March 7, 1853.

ALLAMAKEE

110 Allamakee St., Box 248, Waukon, IA 52172, (563) 568-3813,
<www.co.allamakee.ia.us>

- **INCORPORATED:** Feb. 20, 1847
- **PARENT COUNTY:** Unorganized Territory
- **BIRTH RECORDS:** start in 1880, kept by County Recorder
- **MARRIAGE:** 1845, County Recorder
- **DIVORCE:** 1852, Clerk of Courts
- **DEATH:** 1880, County Recorder
- **LAND:** 1851, County Recorder
- **PROBATE:** 1854, Clerk of Courts
- **COURT:** 1852, Clerk of Courts
- **NATURALIZATION:** 1849, Clerk of Courts
- **NOTES:** Attached to Clayton County prior to March 6, 1849.

APPANOOSE

Box 400, Centerville, IA 52544, (641) 856-6101,
<www.appanoosecounty.net>

- **INCORPORATED:** Feb. 17, 1843
- **PARENT COUNTY:** Unorganized Territory
- **BIRTH RECORDS:** start in 1880, kept by District Court
- **MARRIAGE:** 1846, District Court
- **DIVORCE:** 1847, District Court
- **DEATH:** 1880, District Court
- **LAND:** 1850, County Recorder
- **PROBATE:** 1847, District Court
- **COURT:** 1847, District Court
- **MILITARY:** 1850, County Recorder
- **NOTES:** Attached to Davis and Van Buren counties prior to Aug. 3, 1846. Clerk of District Court has Naturalization records 1868-1953.

AUDUBON

318 Leroy St. #6, Audubon, IA 50025, (712) 563-4275,
<www.auduboncounty.com>

- **INCORPORATED:** Jan. 15, 1851
- **PARENT COUNTY:** Pottawattamie
- **BIRTH RECORDS:** start in 1880, kept by District Court
- **MARRIAGE:** 1856, District Court
- **DIVORCE:** 1867, District Court
- **DEATH:** 1880, District Court
- **LAND:** 1853, County Recorder
- **PROBATE:** 1855District Court
- **COURT:** 1861, District Court
- **BURIAL:** 1880,District Court
- **NOTES:** Attached to Cass County prior to July 9, 1855.

BANCROFT

- **INCORPORATED:** Jan. 15, 1851
- **PARENT COUNTY:** Unorganized Territory
- **NOTES:** Attached to Boone County. Eliminated Jan. 24, 1855 and absorbed by Kossuth County.

BENTON

111 E. Fourth St., Box 719, Vinton, IA 52349, (319) 472-2766,
<www.bentoncountyiowa.com>

- **INCORPORATED:** Dec. 21, 1837
- **PARENT COUNTY:** Dubuque
- **BIRTH RECORDS:** start in 1880, kept by District Court
- **MARRIAGE:** 1851, District Court
- **DIVORCE:** 1900, District Court
- **DEATH:** 1880, District Court
- **LAND:** 1846, District Court
- **PROBATE:** 1872, District Court
- **COURT:** 1850, District Court
- **BURIAL:** 1880, District Court
- **NOTES:** Attached to Jackson and Linn counties before March 1, 1846.

BLACK HAWK

316 E. Fifth St., Waterloo, IA 50703, (319) 833-3331,
<www.co.black-hawk.ia.us>

- **INCORPORATED:** Feb. 17, 1843
- **PARENT COUNTY:** Buchanan
- **BIRTH RECORDS:** start in 1880, kept by District Court
- **MARRIAGE:** 1853, District Court
- **DEATH:** 1880, District Court
- **LAND:** 1853, District Court
- **PROBATE:** 1880, District Court
- **NOTES:** Attached to Buchanan, Benton and Delaware counties prior to Aug. 17, 1853.

BOONE

201 State St., Boone, IA 50036, (515) 433-0561,
<www.co.boone.ia.us>

- **INCORPORATED:** Jan. 13, 1846
- **PARENT COUNTY:** Unorganized Territory
- **BIRTH RECORDS:** start in 1880, kept by District Court
- **MARRIAGE:** 1851, District Court
- **DIVORCE:** 1900, District Court
- **DEATH:** 1880, District Court
- **LAND:** 1849, County Recorder
- **PROBATE:** 1850, District Court
- **COURT:** 1851, District Court
- **NATURALIZATION:** 1867, District Court
- **SCHOOL:** 1889, District Court
- **NOTES:** Attached to Polk and Linn counties prior to Oct. 1, 1849.

BREMER

415 E. Bremer Ave., Box 328, Waverly, IA 50677, (319) 352-5661,
<iagenweb.org/bremer>

- **INCORPORATED:** Jan. 15, 1851
- **PARENT COUNTY:** Unorganized Territory
- **BIRTH RECORDS:** start in 1800, kept by County Recorder
- **MARRIAGE:** 1853, County Recorder
- **DIVORCE:** 1852, Clerk of Courts
- **DEATH:** 1800, County Recorder
- **LAND:** 1852, County Recorder

- **PROBATE:** N/A, Clerk of Courts
- **COURT:** 1853, Clerk of Courts
- **NOTES:** Attached to Buchanan County prior to Aug. 15, 1853.

BUCHANAN
210 Fifth Ave. NE, Box 259, Independence, IA 50644, (319) 334-2196, **<www.co.buchanan.ia.us>**
- **INCORPORATED:** Dec. 21, 1837
- **PARENT COUNTY:** Dubuque
- **BIRTH RECORDS:** start in 1880, kept by District Court
- **MARRIAGE:** 1848, District Court
- **DIVORCE:** 1845, District Court
- **DEATH:** 1880, District Court
- **PROBATE:** 1845, District Court
- **COURT:** 1845, District Court
- **NOTES:** Attached to Dubuque and Delaware counties prior to Oct. 4, 1847.

BUENA VISTA
215 E. Fifth St., Box 1186, Storm Lake, IA 50588, (712) 749-2546, **<www.co.buena-vista.ia.us>**
- **INCORPORATED:** Jan. 15, 1851
- **PARENT COUNTY:** Unorganized Territory
- **BIRTH RECORDS:** start in 1880, kept by District Court
- **MARRIAGE:** 1877, District Court
- **DIVORCE:** 1877, District Court
- **DEATH:** 1880, District Court
- **LAND:** 1869, District Court
- **PROBATE:** 1880, District Court
- **COURT:** 1877, District Court
- **NOTES:** Attached to Woodbury County prior to Nov. 20, 1858.

BUNCOMBE
- **INCORPORATED:** Jan. 15, 1851
- **PARENT COUNTY:** Unorganized Territory
- **NOTES:** See Lyon County. Name changed to Lyon Sept. 11, 1862.

BUTLER
428 Sixth St., Box 307, Allison, IA 50602, (319) 267-2487, **<www.butlercoiowa.org>**
- **INCORPORATED:** Jan. 15, 1851
- **PARENT COUNTY:** Unorganized Territory
- **BIRTH RECORDS:** start in 1880, kept by District Court
- **MARRIAGE:** 1854, District Court
- **DIVORCE:** 1861, District Court
- **DEATH:** 1880, District Court
- **LAND:** 1854, District Court
- **PROBATE:** 1864, District Court
- **COURT:** 1861, District Court
- **NOTES:** Attached to Buchanan and Black Hawk counties prior to Oct. 2, 1854.

CALHOUN
Box 273, Rockwell City, IA 50579, (712) 297-8122, **<www.calhouncountyiowa.com>**
- **INCORPORATED:** Jan. 15, 1851
- **PARENT COUNTY:** Unorganized Territory
- **BIRTH RECORDS:** start in 1880, kept by District Court
- **MARRIAGE:** 1857, District Court
- **DIVORCE:** 1906, District Court
- **DEATH:** 1880, District Court
- **PROBATE:** 1880, District Court
- **COURT:** 1872, District Court
- **BURIAL:** 1900, District Court
- **NOTES:** Formerly Fox County. Name changed to Calhoun Jan. 22, 1853. Attached to Greene and Boone counties before Nov. 7, 1855.

CARROLL
Sixth and Main Streets, Box 867, Carroll, IA 51401, (712)792-4327, **<www.co.carroll.ia.us>**
- **INCORPORATED:** Jan. 15, 1851
- **PARENT COUNTY:** Pottawattamie
- **BIRTH RECORDS:** start in 1880, kept by District Court
- **MARRIAGE:** 1855, District Court
- **DIVORCE:** 1923, District Court
- **DEATH:** 1880, District Court
- **PROBATE:** 1858, District Court
- **TAX:** 1934, District Court
- **COURT:** 1871, District Court
- **NATURALIZATION:** 1873, District Court
- **NOTES:** Attached to Shelby and Guthrie counties prior to Aug. 17, 1855.

CASS
5 W. Seventh St., Atlantic, IA 50022, (712) 243-2105, **<www.casscountyiowa.us>**
- **INCORPORATED:** Jan. 15, 1851
- **PARENT COUNTY:** Pottawattamie
- **BIRTH RECORDS:** start in 1880, kept by District Court
- **MARRIAGE:** 1853, District Court
- **DIVORCE:** 1906, District Court
- **DEATH:** 1880, District Court
- **PROBATE:** 1870, District Court
- **COURT:** 1865, District Court
- **NOTES:** Organized March 7, 1853.

CEDAR
400 Cedar St., Box 111, Tipton, IA 52772, (563) 886-2101, **<www.cedarcounty.org>**
- **INCORPORATED:** Dec. 21, 1837
- **PARENT COUNTY:** Dubuque
- **BIRTH RECORDS:** start in 1880, kept by County Recorder
- **MARRIAGE:** 1841, County Recorder
- **DIVORCE:** 1850, District Court
- **DEATH:** 1880, County Recorder
- **LAND:** 1838, County Recorder
- **PROBATE:** 1839, District Court
- **COURT:** 1839, District Court
- **BURIAL:** 1880, County Recorder

CERRO GORDO
220 N. Washington Ave., Mason City, IA 50401, (641) 424-6431, **<www.co.cerro-gordo.ia.us>**
- **INCORPORATED:** Jan. 15, 1851
- **PARENT COUNTY:** Unorganized Territory
- **BIRTH RECORDS:** start in 1880, kept by County Recorder

- **MARRIAGE:** 1855, County Recorder
- **DEATH:** 1880, County Recorder
- **LAND:** 1882, County Recorder
- **PROBATE:** 1857, Clerk of Courts
- **COURT:** 1880, Clerk of Courts
- **NOTES:** Attached to Floyd County prior to Dec. 29, 1855.

CHEROKEE

520 W. Main St., Cherokee, IA 51012, (712) 225-6744, **<www.cherokeecountyiowa.com>**

- **INCORPORATED:** Jan. 15, 1851
- **PARENT COUNTY:** Unorganized Territory
- **BIRTH RECORDS:** start in 1880, kept by District Court
- **MARRIAGE:** 1859, District Court
- **DEATH:** 1880, District Court
- **PROBATE:** 1859, District Court
- **COURT:** 1872, District Court
- **LAND:** 1856, District Court
- **NOTES:** Attached to Woodbury County prior to Oct. 2, 1858. Clerk of District Court has some cemetery records.

CHICKASAW

8 E. Prospect St., Box 467, New Hampton, IA 50659, (641) 394-2106, **<www.chickasawcoia.org>**

- **INCORPORATED:** Jan. 15, 1851
- **PARENT COUNTY:** Unorganized Territory
- **BIRTH RECORDS:** start in 1880, kept by County Recorder
- **MARRIAGE:** 1853, County Recorder
- **DEATH:** 1880, County Recorder
- **LAND:** 1851, County Recorder
- **PROBATE:** 1854, Clerk of Courts
- **COURT:** 1865, Clerk of Courts
- **NATURALIZATION:** 1880, Clerk of Courts
- **NOTES:** Attached to Fayette County prior to Sept. 12, 1853.

CLARKE

100 S. Main, Osceola, IA 50213, (641) 342-6096, **<www.clarkecountyia.org>**

- **INCORPORATED:** Jan. 13, 1846
- **PARENT COUNTY:** Unorganized Territory
- **BIRTH RECORDS:** start in 1880, kept by District Court
- **MARRIAGE:** 1852, District Court
- **DIVORCE:** 1905, District Court
- **DEATH:** 1880, District Court
- **LAND:** 1849, County Recorder
- **PROBATE:** 1865, District Court
- **COURT:** 1865, District Court
- **NOTES:** Attached to Lucas and Kishkekosh counties prior to Aug. 21, 1851.

CLAY

215 W. Fourth St., Spencer, IA 51301, (712) 262-4335, **<www.co.clay.ia.us>**

- **INCORPORATED:** Jan. 15, 1851
- **PARENT COUNTY:** Unorganized Territory
- **BIRTH RECORDS:** start in 1880, kept by District Court
- **MARRIAGE:** 1864, District Court
- **DIVORCE:** 1906, District Court
- **DEATH:** 1880, District Court
- **LAND:** 1858, District Court
- **PROBATE:** 1871, District Court
- **COURT:** 1869, District Court
- **NOTES:** Attached to Woodbury County prior to Oct. 15, 1858.

CLAYTON

111 High St. NE, Elkader, IA 52043, (563) 245-2204, **<www.claytoncountyiowa.net>**

- **INCORPORATED:** Dec. 21, 1837
- **PARENT COUNTY:** Dubuque
- **BIRTH RECORDS:** start in 1880, kept by District Court
- **MARRIAGE:** 1850, District Court
- **DIVORCE:** 1880, District Court
- **LAND:** 1839, County Recorder
- **PROBATE:** 1840, District Court
- **COURT:** 1840, District Court
- **NATURALIZATION:** 1858, District Court
- **DEATH:** 1880, District Court
- **NOTES:** Clerk of District Court has death records 1880-1921 and from 1941.

CLINTON

612 N. Second St., Box 2957, Clinton, IA 52732, (563) 243-6210, **<www.clintoncounty-ia.gov>**

- **INCORPORATED:** Dec. 21, 1837
- **PARENT COUNTY:** Dubuque
- **BIRTH RECORDS:** start in 1880, kept by District Court
- **MARRIAGE:** 1840, District Court
- **DEATH:** 1880, District Court
- **LAND:** 1840, County Recorder
- **PROBATE:** 1840, District Court
- **COURT:** 1851, District Court
- **NOTES:** Attached to Scott County prior to Jan. 5, 1841. Clerk of District Court has divorce records from mid-1800s.

COOK

- **INCORPORATED:** Dec. 7, 1836
- **PARENT COUNTY:** Des Moines
- **NOTES:** Attached to Muscatine. Absorbed Jan. 18, 1838 into Muscatine.

CRAWFORD

1202 Broadway, Denison, IA 51442, (712) 263-2242, **<www.crawfordcounty.org>**

- **INCORPORATED:** Jan. 15, 1851
- **PARENT COUNTIES:** Pottawattamie, Unorganized Territory
- **BIRTH RECORDS:** start in 1880, kept by County Recorder
- **MARRIAGE:** 1853, County Recorder
- **DIVORCE:** 1906, Clerk of Courts
- **DEATH:** 1880, County Recorder
- **LAND:** 1859, County Recorder
- **PROBATE:** 1869, Clerk of Courts
- **COURT:** 1866, Clerk of Courts
- **NOTES:** Attached to Shelby County prior to organization Sept. 3, 1855. Clerk of Courts has some naturalization records.

CROCKER
- **INCORPORATED:** May 12, 1870
- **PARENT COUNTY:** Kossuth
- **NOTES:** Absorbed Dec. 11, 1871, into Kossuth.

DALLAS
801 Court St., Adel, IA 50003, (515) 993-5816,
<www.co.dallas.ia.us>
- **INCORPORATED:** Jan. 13, 1846
- **PARENT COUNTY:** Unorganized Territory
- **BIRTH RECORDS:** start in 1880, kept by District Court
- **MARRIAGE:** 1851, District Court
- **DIVORCE:** 1881, District Court
- **DEATH:** 1880, District Court
- **LAND:** 1859, County Recorder
- **PROBATE:** 1863, District Court
- **COURT:** 1866, District Court
- **NOTES:** Attached to Polk and Mahaska counties prior to March 1, 1847.

DAVIS
100 Courthouse Square, Bloomfield, IA 52537, (641) 664-2011,
<www.daviscountyiowa.org>
- **INCORPORATED:** Feb. 17, 1843
- **PARENT COUNTY:** Unorganized Territory
- **BIRTH RECORDS:** start in 1880, kept by District Court
- **MARRIAGE:** 1844, District Court
- **DIVORCE:** 1844, District Court
- **DEATH:** 1880, District Court
- **PROBATE:** 1844, District Court
- **COURT:** 1844, District Court
- **NOTES:** Attached to Van Buren County prior to March 1, 1844.

DECATUR
207 N. Main St., Leon, IA 50144, (641) 446-4331,
<iagenweb.org/decatur>
- **INCORPORATED:** Jan. 13, 1846
- **PARENT COUNTY:** Unorganized Territory
- **BIRTH RECORDS:** start in 1880, kept by County Clerk
- **MARRIAGE:** 1874, County Clerk
- **DIVORCE:** 1880, County Clerk
- **DEATH:** 1880, County Clerk
- **LAND:** 1874, County Clerk
- **PROBATE:** 1880, County Clerk
- **COURT:** 1871, County Clerk
- **NOTES:** Attached to Davis County prior to May 6, 1850. Courthouse burned in 1874. County Clerk has some military discharge records.

DELAWARE
301 E. Main St., Box 527, Manchester, IA 52057, (563) 927-4942,
<www.delawarecountyia.com>
- **INCORPORATED**: Dec. 21, 1837
- **PARENT COUNTY:** Dubuque
- **BIRTH RECORDS:** start in 1880, kept by District Court
- **MARRIAGE:** 1861, District Court
- **DIVORCE:** 1851, District Court
- **DEATH:** 1880, District Court
- **PROBATE:** 1849, District Court
- **COURT:** 1851, District Court
- **NOTES:** Organized Nov. 19, 1841.

DES MOINES
513 Main St., Box 158, Burlington, IA 52601, (319) 753-8262,
<www.co.des-moines.ia.us>
- **INCORPORATED:** Oct. 1, 1834
- **PARENT COUNTY:** Michigan Territory
- **BIRTH RECORDS:** start in 1880, kept by District Court
- **MARRIAGE:** 1835, District Court
- **DIVORCE:** 1835, District Court
- **PROBATE:** 1835, District Court
- **COURT:** 1835, District Court
- **NATURALIZATION:** 1840, District Court

DICKINSON
1802 Hill Ave., Spirit Lake, IA 51360, (712) 336-1138, **<
www.co.dickinson.ia.us>**
- **INCORPORATED:** Jan. 15, 1851
- **PARENT COUNTY:** Unorganized Territory
- **BIRTH RECORDS:** start in 1880, kept by District Court
- **MARRIAGE:** 1871, District Court
- **DIVORCE:** 1880, District Court
- **DEATH:** 1880, District Court
- **PROBATE:** 1880, District Court
- **COURT:** 1880, District Court
- **BURIAL:** 1880, District Court
- **NOTES:** Attached to Woodbury County prior to Aug. 3, 1857.

DUBUQUE
720 Central Ave., Dubuque, IA 52001, (563) 589-4418,
<www.dubuquecounty.org>
- **INCORPORATED:** Oct. 1, 1834
- **PARENT COUNTY:** Michigan Territory
- **BIRTH RECORDS:** start in 1880, kept by District Court
- **MARRIAGE:** 1840, District Court
- **DIVORCE:** 1900, District Court
- **DEATH:** 1880, District Court
- **LAND:** 1836, County Recorder
- **PROBATE:** 1835, District Court
- **COURT:** 1836, District Court

EMMET
609 First Ave. N., Estherville, IA 51334, (712) 362-3325,
<www.emmetcountyia.com>
- **INCORPORATED:** Jan. 15, 1851
- **PARENT COUNTY:** Unorganized Territory
- **BIRTH RECORDS:** start in 1880, kept by District Court
- **MARRIAGE:** 1876, District Court
- **DIVORCE:** 1915, District Court
- **DEATH:** 1880, District Court
- **PROBATE:** 1885, District Court
- **NOTES:** Attached to Boone and Webster counties prior to Feb. 7, 1859.

FAYETTE
114 N. Vine St., West Union, IA 52175, (563) 422-5694,
<www.fayettecountyiowa.org>
- **INCORPORATED:** Dec. 21, 1837
- **PARENT COUNTY:** Dubuque
- **BIRTH RECORDS:** start in 1880, kept by County Recorder
- **MARRIAGE:** 1861, County Recorder
- **DIVORCE:** 1897, Clerk of Courts
- **DEATH:** 1880, County Recorder
- **LAND:** 1855, County Recorder
- **PROBATE:** 1869, Clerk of Courts
- **COURT:** 1852, Clerk of Courts
- **NOTES:** Attached to Clayton County prior to Aug. 26, 1850.

FLOYD
101 S. Main St., Charles City, IA 50616, (641) 257-6122,
<www.floydcoia.org>
- **INCORPORATED:** Jan. 15, 1851
- **PARENT COUNTY:** Unorganized Territory
- **BIRTH RECORDS:** start in 1880, kept by District Court
- **MARRIAGE:** 1854, District Court
- **DIVORCE:** 1860, District Court
- **DEATH:** 1880, District Court
- **PROBATE:** 1854, District Court
- **COURT:** 1854, District Court
- **NOTES:** Attached to Fayette and Chickasaw counties prior to Sept. 4, 1854.

FOX
- **INCORPORATED:** Jan. 15, 1851
- **PARENT COUNTY:** Unorganized Territory
- **NOTES:** See Calhoun County. Name changed to Calhoun Jan. 22, 1853.

FRANKLIN
12 First Ave. NW, Hampton, IA 50441, (641) 456-5626, **<co.franklin.ia.us>**
- **INCORPORATED:** Jan. 15, 1851
- **PARENT COUNTY:** Unorganized Territory
- **BIRTH RECORDS:** start in 1880, kept by Circuit Court
- **MARRIAGE:** 1855, Circuit Court
- **DIVORCE:** 1869, Circuit Court
- **DEATH:** 1880, Circuit Court
- **PROBATE:** 1864, Circuit Court
- **COURT:** 1869, Circuit Court
- **NOTES:** Attached to Chickasaw, Fayette and Hardin counties prior to March 3, 1856.

FREMONT
Box 549, Sidney, IA 51652, (712) 374-2232,
<www.co.fremont.ia.us>
- **INCORPORATED:** Feb. 24, 1847
- **PARENT COUNTY:** Unorganized Territory
- **BIRTH RECORDS:** start in 1880, kept by District Court
- **DEATH:** 1880, District Court
- **LAND:** 1849, County Recorder
- **PROBATE:** 1880, District Court
- **COURT:** 1850, District Court
- **NOTES:** Attached to Appanoose County prior to Sept. 10, 1849. Clerk of District Court has limited marriage records from 1948.

GREENE
114 N. Chestnut, Jefferson, IA 50129, (515) 386-2516,
<www.co.greene.ia.us>
- **INCORPORATED:** Jan. 15, 1851
- **PARENT COUNTY:** Unorganized Territory
- **BIRTH RECORDS:** start in 1880, kept by District Court
- **MARRIAGE:** 1855, District Court
- **DEATH:** 1880, District Court
- **LAND:** 1854, District Court
- **PROBATE:** 1854, District Court
- **COURT**: 1880, District Court
- **NOTES:** Attached to Dallas County prior to Aug. 25, 1853.

GRUNDY
706 G Ave., Box 345, Grundy Center, IA 50638, (319) 824-5229,
<www.grundycounty.org>
- **INCORPORATED:** Jan. 15, 1851
- **PARENT COUNTY:** Unorganized Territory
- **BIRTH RECORDS:** start in 1880, kept by District Court
- **MARRIAGE:** 1856, District Court
- **DIVORCE:** 1881, District Court
- **DEATH:** 1880, District Court
- **LAND:** 1863, County Recorder
- **PROBATE:** 1870, District Court
- **COURT:** 1871, District Court
- **NOTES:** Attached to Buchanan and Black Hawk counties prior to Dec. 25, 1856.

GUTHRIE
200 N. Fifth St., Guthrie Center, IA 50115, (641) 747-3415,
<www.guthriecounty.org>
- **INCORPORATED:** Jan. 15, 1851
- **PARENT COUNTY:** Unorganized Territory
- **BIRTH RECORDS:** start in 1880, kept by District Court
- **MARRIAGE:** 1852, District Court
- **DIVORCE:** 1883, District Court
- **DEATH:** 1880, District Court
- **PROBATE:** 1881, District Court
- **COURT:** 1916, District Court

HAMILTON
Box 845, Webster City, IA 50595, (515) 832-9600,
<www.hamiltoncounty.org>
- **INCORPORATED:** Jan. 8, 1857
- **PARENT COUNTY:** Webster
- **BIRTH RECORDS:** start in 1880, kept by District Court
- **MARRIAGE:** 1857, District Court
- **DIVORCE:** 1880, District Court
- **DEATH:** 1880, District Court
- **PROBATE:** 1880, District Court
- **COURT:** 1880, District Court

HANCOCK
855 State St., Box 70, Garner, IA 50438, (641) 923-2532,
<www.hancockcountyia.org>

- **INCORPORATED:** Jan. 15, 1851
- **PARENT COUNTY:** Unorganized Territory
- **BIRTH RECORDS:** start in 1880, kept by District Court
- **MARRIAGE:** 1861, District Court
- **DIVORCE:** 1880, District Court
- **DEATH:** 1880, District Court
- **PROBATE:** 1856, District Court
- **COURT:** 1856, District Court
- **BURIAL:** 1880, District Court
- **NOTES:** Attached to Boone and Webster counties prior to Nov. 25, 1858.

HARDIN

Pioneer Plaza, Box 495, Eldora, IA 50627, (515) 858-2328, **<www.co.hardin.ia.us>**

- **INCORPORATED:** Jan. 15, 1851
- **PARENT COUNTY:** Unorganized Territory
- **BIRTH RECORDS:** start in 1880, kept by District Court
- **MARRIAGE:** 1853, District Court
- **DIVORCE:** 1889, District Court
- **DEATH:** 1880, District Court
- **LAND:** 1853, District Court
- **PROBATE:** 1853, District Court
- **COURT:** 1853, District Court
- **NOTES:** Attached to Marshall County prior to March 2, 1853.

HARRISON

111 N. Second Ave., Logan, IA 51546, (712) 644-2665, **<www.harrisoncountyia.org>**

- **INCORPORATED:** Jan. 15, 1851
- **PARENT COUNTY:** Pottawattamie
- **BIRTH RECORDS:** start in 1880, kept by District Court
- **MARRIAGE:** 1853, District Court
- **DIVORCE:** 1853, District Court
- **DEATH:** 1880, District Court
- **PROBATE:** 1869, District Court
- **COURT:** 1850, District Court
- **NOTES:** Organized March 7, 1853. Clerk of District Court has some burial records.

HENRY

100 E. Washington St., Box 176, Mt. Pleasant, IA 52641, (319) 385-2632, **<www.henrycountyiowa.us>**

- **INCORPORATED:** Dec. 7, 1836
- **PARENT COUNTY:** Des Moines
- **BIRTH RECORDS:** start in 1880, kept by District Court
- **MARRIAGE:** 1836, District Court
- **DEATH:** 1880, District Court
- **LAND:** 1836, County Recorder
- **PROBATE:** 1836, District Court
- **ADOPTION:** 1836, District Court
- **COURT:** 1836, District Court

HOWARD

137 N. Elm St., Cresco, IA 52136, (563) 547-2661, **<www.co.howard.ia.us>**

- **INCORPORATED:** Jan. 15, 1851
- **PARENT COUNTY:** Unorganized Territory
- **BIRTH RECORDS:** start in 1880, kept by District Court
- **MARRIAGE:** 1875, District Court
- **DEATH:** 1880, District Court
- **DIVORCE:** 1876, District Court
- **LAND:** 1855, County Recorder
- **PROBATE:** 1877, District Court
- **COURT:** 1876, District Court
- **NOTES:** Attached to Floyd County prior to Sept. 15, 1855.

HUMBOLDT

Box 100, Dakota City, IA 50529, (515) 332-1806, **<www.humboldtcountyia.org>**

- **INCORPORATED:** Aug. 31, 1857
- **PARENT COUNTIES:** Webster, Kossuth
- **BIRTH RECORDS:** start in 1880, kept by District Court
- **MARRIAGE:** 1858, District Court
- **DIVORCE:** 1890, District Court
- **DEATH:** 1885, District Court
- **PROBATE:** 1873, District Court
- **COURT:** 1892, District Court

HUMBOLDT, OLD

- **INCORPORATED:** Jan. 15, 1851
- **PARENT COUNTY:** Unorganized Territory
- **NOTES:** Attached to Boone. Abolished Jan. 24, 1855 and absorbed by Kossuth and Webster counties.

IDA

401 Moorehead St., Ida Grove, IA 51445, (712) 364-2628, **<iagenweb.org/ida>**

- **INCORPORATED:** Jan. 15, 1851
- **PARENT COUNTY:** Unorganized Territory
- **BIRTH RECORDS:** start in 1880, kept by District Court
- **MARRIAGE:** 1868, District Court
- **DIVORCE:** 1880, District Court
- **DEATH:** 1880, District Court
- **PROBATE:** 1880, District Court
- **COURT:** 1880, District Court
- **NOTES:** Attached to Woodbury County prior to Jan. 1, 1859.

IOWA

Box 266, Marengo, IA 52301, (319) 642-3914, **<www.co.iowa.ia.us>**

- **INCORPORATED:** Feb. 17, 1843
- **PARENT COUNTY:** Keokuk
- **BIRTH RECORDS:** start in 1880, kept by County Recorder
- **MARRIAGE:** 1847, County Recorder
- **DEATH:** 1880, County Recorder
- **CEMETERY:** 1867, County Recorder
- **NOTES:** Attached to Poweshiek and Johnson counties prior to July 1, 1845.

JACKSON

201 W. Platt St., Maquoketa, IA 52060, (563) 652-4946, **<www.jacksoncountyiowa.com/index.cfm>**

- **INCORPORATED:** Dec. 21, 1837
- **PARENT COUNTY:** Dubuque
- **BIRTH RECORDS:** start in 1880, kept by District Court

- **MARRIAGE:** 1847, District Court
- **DIVORCE:** 1906, District Court
- **DEATH:** 1890, District Court
- **PROBATE:** 1869, District Court
- **COURT:** 1858, District Court

JASPER

101 First St. N. Room 104, Newton, IA 50208, (641) 792-3255, **<iagenweb.org/jasper>**

- **INCORPORATED:** Jan. 13, 1846
- **PARENT COUNTY:** Unorganized Territory
- **BIRTH RECORDS:** start in 1880, kept by County Recorder
- **MARRIAGE:** 1846, County Recorder
- **DEATH:** 1880, County Recorder
- **LAND:** 1855, County Recorder
- **PROBATE:** 1882, District Court
- **COURT:** 1857, District Court
- **MILITARY:** 1855, County Recorder
- **NOTES:** Attached to Mahaska County prior to March 1, 1846.

JEFFERSON

51 W. Briggs Ave., Box 984, Fairfield, IA 52556, (641) 472-3454, **<www.jeffersoncountyiowa.com>**

- **INCORPORATED:** Jan. 21, 1839
- **PARENT COUNTIES:** Henry, Unorganized Territory
- **BIRTH RECORDS:** start in 1880, kept by District Court
- **MARRIAGE:** 1839, District Court
- **DIVORCE:** 1880, District Court
- **DEATH:** 1880, District Court
- **PROBATE:** 1850, District Court
- **COURT:** 1880, District Court

JOHNSON

417 S. Clinton St., Box 2510, Iowa City, IA 52240, (319) 356-6060, **<www.johnson-county.com>**

- **INCORPORATED:** Dec. 21, 1837
- **PARENT COUNTIES:** Dubuque, Cook, Muscatine
- **BIRTH RECORDS:** start in 1880, kept by County Recorder
- **MARRIAGE:** 1839, County Recorder
- **DEATH:** 1880, County Recorder
- **NOTES:** Attached to Cedar County prior to July 4, 1838.

JONES

Main St., Box 19, Anamosa, IA 52205, (319) 462-4341, **<jonescountyiowa.org>**

- **INCORPORATED:** Dec. 21, 1837
- **PARENT COUNTY:** Dubuque
- **BIRTH RECORDS:** start in 1880, kept by District Court
- **MARRIAGE:** 1833, District Court
- **DIVORCE:** 1895, District Court
- **DEATH:** 1880, District Court
- **MILITARY:** 1864, County Recorder
- **NOTES:** Attached to Jackson County prior to June 1, 1839.

KEOKUK

101 S. Main St., Sigourney, IA 52591, (641) 622-2210, **<www.keokukcountyia.com>**

- **INCORPORATED:** Dec. 21, 1837
- **PARENT COUNTY:** Dubuque
- **BIRTH RECORDS:** start in 1880, kept by District Court
- **MARRIAGE:** 1844, District Court
- **DIVORCE:** 1845, District Court
- **DEATH:** 1880, District Court
- **PROBATE:** 1845, District Court
- **COURT:** 1845, District Court
- **NOTES:** Attached to Johnson, Washington and Cedar counties prior to March 1, 1844.

KISHKEKOSH

- **INCORPORATED:** Feb. 17, 1843
- **PARENT COUNTY:** Unorganized Territory
- **NOTES:** See Monroe County. Name changed to Monroe Aug. 1, 1846.

KOSSUTH

114 W. State St., Algona, IA 50511, (515) 295-3240, **<www.co.kossuth.ia.us>**

- **INCORPORATED:** Jan. 15, 1851
- **PARENT COUNTY:** Unorganized Territory
- **BIRTH RECORDS:** start in 1880, kept by District Court
- **MARRIAGE:** 1857, District Court
- **DEATH:** 1880, District Court
- **PROBATE:** 1877, District Court
- **BURIAL:** 1880, District Court
- **NOTES:** Attached to Boone and Webster counties prior to organization March 1, 1856.

LEE

Box 1443, Fort Madison, IA 52627, (319) 372-3523, **<www.leecounty.org>**

- **INCORPORATED:** Dec. 7, 1836
- **PARENT COUNTY:** Des Moines
- **BIRTH RECORDS:** start in 1880, kept by District Court in Ft. Madison
- **BIRTH:** 1880, District Court in Keokuk
- **MARRIAGE:** 1837, District Court in Ft. Madison
- **DIVORCE:** 1906, District Court in Keokuk
- **DEATH:** 1867, District Court in Keokuk; 1880, District Court in Ft. Madison
- **PROBATE:** 1838, District Court in Keokuk; 1873, District Court in Ft. Madison
- **COURT:** 1898, District Court in Keokuk

LINN

Third Ave. Bridge, Box 1468, Cedar Rapids, IA 52406, (319) 398-3411, **<www.linncounty.org>**

- **INCORPORATED:** Dec. 21, 1837
- **PARENT COUNTY:** Dubuque
- **BIRTH RECORDS:** start in 1880, kept by District Court
- **MARRIAGE:** 1840, District Court
- **DIVORCE:** 1860, District Court
- **DEATH:** 1880, District Court
- **PROBATE:** 1860, District Court
- **COURT:** 1860, District Court
- **NOTES:** Attached to Jackson County prior to June 1, 1839.

LOUISA
Box 268, Wapello, IA 52653, (319) 523-4541,
<www.louisacountyiowa.org>
- **INCORPORATED:** Dec. 7, 1836
- **PARENT COUNTY:** Des Moines
- **BIRTH RECORDS:** start in 1880, kept by District Court
- **MARRIAGE:** 1842, District Court
- **DEATH:** 1880, District Court

LUCAS
916 Braden Ave., Chariton, IA 50049, (641) 774-4421,
<iagenweb.org/lucas>
- **INCORPORATED:** Jan. 13, 1846
- **PARENT COUNTY:** Unorganized Territory
- **BIRTH RECORDS**: start in 1880, kept by District Court
- **MARRIAGE:** 1849, District Court
- **DIVORCE:** 1900, District Court
- **DEATH:** 1880, District Court
- **PROBATE:** 1850, District Court
- **COURT:** 1900, District Court
- **NATURALIZATION:** 1900, District Court
- **NOTES:** Attached to Monroe County prior to July 4, 1849.

LYON
206 S. Second Ave., Rock Rapids, IA 51246, (712) 472-2623,
<www.lyoncountyiowa.com>
- **INCORPORATED:** Jan. 15, 1851
- **PARENT COUNTY:** Unorganized Territory
- **BIRTH RECORDS:** start in 1880, kept by District Court
- **MARRIAGE:** 1872, District Court
- **DIVORCE:** 1880, District Court
- **DEATH:** 1880, District Court
- **LAND:** 1880, District Court
- **PROBATE:** 1880, District Court
- **COURT:** 1880, District Court
- **NOTES:** Formerly Buncombe County. Name changed to Lyon Sept. 11, 1862. Attached to Woodbury County prior to Jan. 1, 1872.

MADISON
Box 152, Winterset, IA 50273, (515) 462-4451,
<www.madisoncoia.us>
- **INCORPORATED:** Jan. 13, 1846
- **PARENT COUNTY:** Unorganized Territory
- **BIRTH RECORDS:** start in 1880, kept by District Court
- **MARRIAGE:** 1855, District Court
- **DIVORCE:** 1861, District Court
- **DEATH:** 1880, District Court
- **PROBATE:** 1852, District Court
- **COURT:** 1861, District Court
- **BURIAL:** 1849, District Court
- **NOTES:** Attached to Mahaska County prior to Feb. 19, 1849.

MAHASKA
106 S. First St., Oskaloosa, IA 52577, (641) 673-7786,
<www.mahaskacounty.org>
- **INCORPORATED:** Feb. 17, 1843
- **PARENT COUNTY:** Unorganized Territory
- **BIRTH RECORDS:** start in 1880, kept by District Court
- **MARRIAGE:** 1844, District Court
- **DIVORCE:** 1844, District Court
- **DEATH:** 1880, District Court
- **PROBATE:** 1844, District Court
- **COURT:** 1844, District Court
- **NOTES:** Attached to Washington County prior to March 1, 1844.

MARION
Box 497, Knoxville, IA 50138, (641) 828-2207, **<co.marion.ia.us>**
- **INCORPORATED**: Aug. 4, 1845
- **PARENT COUNTY:** Unorganized Territory
- **BIRTH RECORDS:** start in 1880, kept by District Court
- **MARRIAGE:** 1845, District Court
- **DIVORCE:** 1845, District Court
- **DEATH:** 1880, District Court
- **PROBATE:** 1845, District Court

MARSHALL
17 E. Main St., Marshalltown, IA 50158, (641) 754-1606, **< www.co.marshall.ia.us>**
- **INCORPORATED:** Jan. 13, 1846
- **PARENT COUNTY:** Unorganized Territory
- **BIRTH RECORDS:** start in 1880, kept by District Court
- **MARRIAGE:** 1850, District Court
- **DIVORCE:** 1850, District Court
- **DEATH:** 1880, District Court
- **PROBATE:** 1850, District Court
- **COURT:** 1850, District Court
- **NOTES:** Attached to Jasper and Linn counties prior to Oct. 1, 1849.

MILLS
418 Sharp St., Glenwood, IA 51534, (712) 527-4880,
<www.millscoia.us>
- **INCORPORATED:** Jan. 15, 1851
- **PARENT COUNTY:** Pottawattamie
- **BIRTH RECORDS:** start in 1880, kept by County Recorder
- **MARRIAGE:** 1852, County Recorder
- **DEATH:** 1880, County Recorder

MITCHELL
508 Eighth St., Osage, IA 50461, (641)732-3726,
<www.mitchellcoia.us >
- **INCORPORATED:** Jan. 15, 1851
- **PARENT COUNTY:** Unorganized Territory
- **BIRTH RECORDS:** start in 1880, kept by County Recorder
- **MARRIAGE:** 1885, County Recorder
- **DIVORCE:** 1880, Clerk of Courts
- **DEATH:** 1880, County Recorder
- **PROBATE:** 1880, Clerk of Courts
- **COURT:** 1880, Clerk of Courts
- **NOTES:** Attached to Chickasaw and Fayette counties prior to Oct. 2, 1854.

MONONA
610 Iowa Ave., Onawa, IA 51040, (712) 423-2491,
<www.iagenweb.org/monona>
- **INCORPORATED:** Jan. 15, 1851
- **PARENT COUNTY:** Pottawattamie

- **BIRTH RECORDS:** start in 1880, kept by District Court
- **MARRIAGE:** 1856, District Court
- **DEATH:** 1880, District Court
- **DIVORCE:** 1856, District Court
- **PROBATE:** 1858, District Court
- **COURT:** 1856, District Court
- **BURIAL:** 1950, District Court
- **NOTES:** Attached to Harrison County prior to April 3, 1854.

MONROE

10 Benton Ave. E., Albia, IA 52531, (641) 932-5212,
<iagenweb.org/monroe/Resources/local.htm>

- **INCORPORATED:** Feb. 17, 1843
- **PARENT COUNTY:** Unorganized Territory
- **BIRTH RECORDS:** start in 1880, kept by District Court
- **MARRIAGE:** 1845, District Court
- **DIVORCE:** 1845, District Court
- **DEATH:** 1880, District Court
- **PROBATE:** 1845, District Court
- **COURT:** 1845, District Court
- **NOTES:** Formerly Kishkekosh County. Name changed to Monroe Aug. 1, 1846. Attached to Wapello and Jefferson counties prior to July 1, 1845.

MONTGOMERY

105 Coolbaugh St., Box 469, Red Oak, IA 51566, (712) 623-4986,
<montgomerycountyiowa.com>

- **INCORPORATED:** Jan. 15, 1851
- **PARENT COUNTY:** Pottawattamie
- **BIRTH RECORDS:** start in 1880, kept by District Court
- **MARRIAGE:** 1855, District Court
- **DIVORCE:** 1873, District Court
- **DEATH:** 1880, District Court
- **PROBATE:** 1860, District Court
- **COURT:** 1873, District Court
- **NOTES:** Attached to Adams County prior to Aug. 5, 1853.

MUSCATINE

401 E. Third St., Box 8010, Muscatine, IA 52761, (563) 263-6511,
<www.co.muscatine.ia.us>

- **INCORPORATED:** Dec. 7, 1836
- **PARENT COUNTY:** Des Moines
- **BIRTH RECORDS:** start in 1880, kept by County Recorder
- **MARRIAGE:** 1837, County Recorder
- **DEATH:** 1880, County Recorder

O'BRIEN

155 S. Hayes Ave., Primghar, IA 51245, (712) 757-3255,
<www.obriencounty.com>

- **INCORPORATED:** Jan. 15, 1851
- **PARENT COUNTY:** Unorganized Territory
- **BIRTH RECORDS:** start in 1880, kept by County Recorder
- **MARRIAGE:** 1860, County Recorder
- **DIVORCE:** 1880, Clerk of Courts
- **DEATH:** 1880, County Recorder
- **LAND:** 1857, County Recorder
- **PROBATE:** 1880, Clerk of Courts
- **COURT:** 1880, Clerk of Courts
- **MILITARY:** 1917, County Recorder
- **NOTES:** Attached to Woodbury County prior to April 7, 1860.

OSCEOLA

300 Seventh Ave., Box 156, Sibley, IA 51249, (712) 754-3595,
<www.osceolacountyia.com>

- **INCORPORATED:** Jan. 15, 1851
- **PARENT COUNTY:** Unorganized Territory
- **BIRTH RECORDS:** start in 1880, kept by District Court
- **MARRIAGE:** 1872, District Court
- **DIVORCE:** 1880, District Court
- **DEATH:** 1880, District Court
- **PROBATE:** 1880, District Court
- **COURT:** 1880, District Court
- **NOTES:** Attached to Woodbury County prior to Jan. 1, 1872.

PAGE

112 E. Main St., Box 263, Clarinda, IA 51632, (712) 542-3214,
<www.co.page.ia.us>

- **INCORPORATED:** Feb. 24, 1847
- **PARENT COUNTY:** Unorganized Territory
- **BIRTH RECORDS:** start in 1880, kept by County Recorder
- **MARRIAGE:** 1852, County Recorder
- **DEATH:** 1880, County Recorder
- **NOTES:** Attached to Appanoose County prior to organization March 22, 1852.

PALO ALTO

1010 Broadway, Box 387, Emmetsburg, IA 50536, (712) 852-3603,
<www.paloaltoiowa.com>

- **INCORPORATED:** Jan. 15, 1851
- **PARENT COUNTY:** Unorganized Territory
- **BIRTH RECORDS:** start in 1880, kept by District Court
- **MARRIAGE:** 1860, District Court
- **DEATH:** 1880, District Court
- **NOTES:** Attached to Boone and Webster counties prior to Dec. 29, 1858.

PLYMOUTH

215 Fourth Ave. SE, Le Mars, IA 51031, (712) 546-4215,
<www.co.plymouth.ia.us>

- **INCORPORATED:** Jan. 15, 1851
- **PARENT COUNTY:** Unorganized Territory
- **BIRTH RECORDS:** start in 1880, kept by District Court
- **MARRIAGE:** 1871, District Court
- **DEATH:** 1880, District Court
- **COURT:** 1869, District Court
- **NOTES:** Attached to Woodbury County prior to Oct. 27, 1858.

POCAHONTAS

99 Court Sq., Pocahontas, IA 50574, (712) 335-4208,
<iagenweb.org/pocahontas>

- **INCORPORATED:** Jan. 15, 1851
- **PARENT COUNTY:** Unorganized Territory
- **BIRTH RECORDS:** start in 1880, kept by County Recorder
- **MARRIAGE:** 1859, County Recorder
- **DIVORCE:** 1860, District Court
- **DEATH:** 1880, County Recorder

- **PROBATE:** 1872, District Court
- **NOTES:** Attached to Boone and Webster counties prior to May 11, 1859.

POLK

500 Mulberry St. #201, Des Moines, IA 50309, (515) 286-3772, **<www.polkcountyiowa.gov>**

- **INCORPORATED:** Jan. 13, 1846
- **PARENT COUNTY:** Unorganized Territory
- **BIRTH RECORDS:** start in 1880, kept by County Recorder
- **MARRIAGE:** 1846, County Recorder
- **DIVORCE:** 1870, Clerk of Courts
- **DEATH:** 1880, County Recorder
- **PROBATE:** 1855, Clerk of Courts
- **COURT:** 1850, Clerk of Courts
- **NATURALIZATION:** 1870, Clerk of Courts

POTTAWATTAMIE

227 S. Sixth St., Council Bluffs, IA 51501, (712) 328-5604, **<www.pottcounty.com>**

- **INCORPORATED:** Sept. 21, 1848
- **PARENT COUNTY:** Unorganized Territory
- **BIRTH RECORDS:** start in 1880, kept by Clerk of Courts
- **MARRIAGE:** 1848, Clerk of Courts
- **DIVORCE:** 1907, Clerk of Courts
- **DEATH:** 1882, Clerk of Courts
- **PROBATE:** 1898, Clerk of Courts

POWESHIEK

302 E. Main St., Box 218, Montezuma, IA 50171, (641) 623-5644, **<www.poweshiekcounty.org>**

- **INCORPORATED:** Feb. 17, 1843
- **PARENT COUNTY:** Keokuk
- **BIRTH RECORDS:** start in 1880, kept by District Court
- **DIVORCE:** 1880, District Court
- **MARRIAGE:** 1848, District Court
- **DEATH:** 1880, District Court
- **PROBATE:** 1860, District Court
- **NOTES:** Attached to Mahaska and Iowa counties prior to April 3, 1848.

RINGGOLD

109 W. Madison, Box 523, Mount Ayr, IA 50854, (641) 464-3234, **<www.ringgoldcounty.us>**

- **INCORPORATED:** Feb. 24, 1847
- **PARENT COUNTY:** Unorganized Territory
- **BIRTH RECORDS:** start in 1880, kept by District Court
- **MARRIAGE:** 1855, District Court
- **DIVORCE:** 1880, District Court
- **DEATH:** 1880, District Court
- **PROBATE:** 1880, District Court
- **COURT:** 1880, District Court
- **NOTES:** Attached to Taylor and Appanoose counties prior to Jan. 31, 1855.

RISLEY

- **INCORPORATED:** Jan. 15, 1851
- **PARENT COUNTY:** Unorganized Territory
- **NOTES:** See Webster County. Lost to Webster County Jan. 22, 1853.

SAC

Box 368, Sac City, IA 50583, (712) 662-7791, **<www.saccounty.org>**

- **INCORPORATED:** Jan. 15, 1851
- **PARENT COUNTY:** Unorganized Territory
- **BIRTH RECORDS:** start in 1880, kept by District Court
- **MARRIAGE:** 1863, District Court
- **DIVORCE:** 1880, District Court
- **PROBATE:** 1888, District Court
- **COURT:** 1888, District Court
- **BURIAL:** 1888, District Court
- **NOTES:** Attached to Woodbury and Greene counties prior to April 7, 1856. Courthouse burned 1888; some records recovered.

SCOTT

416 W. Fourth St., Davenport, IA 52801, (563) 326-8787, **<www.scottcountyiowa.com>**

- **INCORPORATED:** Dec. 21, 1837
- **PARENT COUNTIES:** Dubuque, Cook, Muscatine
- **BIRTH RECORDS:** start in 1880, kept by District Court
- **MARRIAGE:** 1840, District Court
- **DIVORCE:** 1838, District Court
- **DEATH:** 1880, District Court
- **PROBATE:** 1838, District Court
- **COURT:** 1851, District Court

SHELBY

612 Court St., Box 431, Harlan, IA 51537, (712) 755-5543, **<www.shco.org>**

- **INCORPORATED:** Jan. 15, 1851
- **PARENT COUNTY:** Pottawattamie
- **BIRTH RECORDS:** start in 1880, kept by County Recorder
- **MARRIAGE:** 1853, County Recorder
- **DIVORCE:** 1869, Clerk of Courts
- **DEATH:** 1880, County Recorder
- **LAND:** 1854, County Recorder
- **PROBATE:** 1869, Clerk of Courts
- **COURT:** 1869, Clerk of Courts
- **MILITARY:** 1919, County Recorder
- **NOTES:** Organized March 7, 1853.

SIOUX

Box 47, Orange City, IA 51041, (712) 737-2286, **<www.siouxcounty.org>**

- **INCORPORATED:** Jan. 15, 1851
- **PARENT COUNTY:** Unorganized Territory
- **BIRTH RECORDS:** start in 1880, kept by District Court
- **MARRIAGE:** 1871, District Court
- **DIVORCE:** 1908, District Court
- **DEATH:** 1880, District Court
- **PROBATE:** 1870, District Court
- **NOTES:** Attached to Woodbury County prior to Jan. 1, 1860.

SLAUGHTER
- **INCORPORATED:** Jan. 18, 1838
- **PARENT COUNTIES:** Henry, Louisa, Muscatine
- **NOTES:** See Washington County. Name changed to Washington Jan. 25, 1839.

STORY
1315 S. B Ave., Box 408, Nevada, IA 50201, (515) 382-7410, **<www.storycounty.com>**
- **INCORPORATED:** Jan. 13, 1846
- **PARENT COUNTY:** Unorganized Territory
- **BIRTH RECORDS:** start in 1880, kept by District Court
- **MARRIAGE:** 1854, District Court
- **DIVORCE:** 1854, District Court
- **DEATH:** 1880, District Court
- **PROBATE:** 1854, District Court
- **COURT:** 1854, District Court
- **NOTES:** Attached to Boone, Polk, and Linn counties prior to June 1, 1853.

TAMA
100 W. High St., Box 306, Toledo, IA 52342, (641) 484-3721, **<www.tamacounty.org>**
- **INCORPORATED:** Feb. 17, 1843
- **PARENT COUNTY:** Benton
- **BIRTH RECORDS:** start in 1880, kept by District Court
- **MARRIAGE:** 1853, District Court
- **DIVORCE:** 1908, District Court
- **DEATH:** 1880, District Court
- **PROBATE:** 1895, District Court
- **COURT:** 1859, District Court
- **NOTES:** Attached to Benton and Linn counties prior to July 4, 1853.

TAYLOR
403 Jefferson St., Bedford, IA 50833, (712) 523-2095, **<iagenweb.org/taylor>**
- **INCORPORATED:** Feb. 24, 1847
- **PARENT COUNTY:** Unorganized Territory
- **BIRTH RECORDS:** start in 1880, kept by District Court
- **MARRIAGE:** 1851, District Court
- **DIVORCE:** 1858, District Court
- **DEATH:** 1880, District Court
- **PROBATE:** 1863, District Court
- **COURT:** 1858, District Court
- **NOTES:** Attached to Appanoose County prior to Feb. 26, 1851.

UNION
300 N. Pine St., Creston, IA 50801, (641) 782-7315, **<www.unioncountyiowa.org>**
- **INCORPORATED:** Jan. 15, 1851
- **PARENT COUNTY:** Pottawattamie
- **BIRTH RECORDS:** start in 1880, kept by District Court
- **MARRIAGE:** 1864, District Court
- **DEATH:** 1880, District Court
- **PROBATE:** 1880, District Court
- **COURT:** 1880, District Court
- **NOTES:** Organized March 1, 1853.

VAN BUREN
Box 475, Keosauqua, IA 52565, (319) 293-3108, **<iavanburen.org>**
- **INCORPORATED:** Dec. 7, 1836
- **PARENT COUNTY:** Des Moines
- **BIRTH RECORDS:** start in 1880, kept by District Court
- **MARRIAGE**: 1837, District Court
- **DIVORCE:** 1837, District Court
- **DEATH**: 1880, District Court
- **PROBATE:** 1837, District Court
- **COURT:** 1837, District Court

WAHKAW
- **INCORPORATED:** Jan. 15, 1851
- **PARENT COUNTY:** Unorganized Territory
- **NOTES:** See Woodbury County. Name changed to Woodbury Jan. 22, 1853.

WAPELLO
101 W. Fourth St., Ottumwa, IA 52501, (641) 683-0060, **<www.wapellocounty.org>**
- **INCORPORATED:** 17 Feb. 1843
- **PARENT COUNTY**: Unorganized Territory
- **BIRTH RECORDS:** start in 1880, kept by County Recorder
- **MARRIAGE:** 1844, County Recorder
- **DIVORCE:** 1844, Clerk of Courts
- **DEATH:** 1880, County Recorder
- **PROBATE:** 1844, Clerk of Courts
- **COURT:** 1844, Clerk of Courts
- **NOTES:** Attached to Jefferson County prior to March 1, 1844.

WARREN
Box 379, Indianola, IA 50125, (515) 961-1033, **<www.co.warren.ia.us>**
- **INCORPORATED:** Jan. 13, 1846
- **PARENT COUNTY:** Unorganized Territory
- **BIRTH RECORDS:** start in 1880, kept by District Court
- **MARRIAGE:** 1850, District Court
- **DIVORCE:** 1880, District Court
- **DEATH:** 1880, District Court
- **PROBATE:** 1880, District Court
- **COURT:** 1880, District Court
- **NOTES:** Attached to Mahaska County prior to Feb. 10, 1849.

WASHINGTON
Box 391, Washington, IA 52353, (319) 653-7741, **<co.washington.ia.us>**
- **INCORPORATED:** Jan. 18, 1838
- **PARENT COUNTIES:** Henry, Louisa, Muscatine
- **BIRTH RECORDS:** start in 1880, kept by District Court
- **MARRIAGE:** 1844, District Court
- **DIVORCE:** 1836, District Court
- **DEATH:** 1880, District Court
- **PROBATE:** 1836, District Court
- **COURT:** 1836, District Court
- **NOTES:** Formerly Slaughter County. Name changed to Washington Jan. 25, 1839. Clerk of District Court has some naturalization records.

WAYNE

Box 424, Corydon, IA 50060, (641) 872-2264,
<iagenweb.org/wayne>
- **INCORPORATED:** Jan. 13, 1846
- **PARENT COUNTY:** Unorganized Territory
- **BIRTH RECORDS:** start in 1880, kept by District Court
- **MARRIAGE:** 1851, District Court
- **DIVORCE:** 1906, District Court
- **DEATH:** 1880, District Court
- **PROBATE:** 1891, District Court
- **COURT**: 1875, District Court
- **NOTES:** Attached to Davis County prior to Jan. 27, 1851.

WEBSTER

701 Central Ave., Fort Dodge, IA 50501, (515) 576-7115,
<www.webstercountyia.org>
- **INCORPORATED:** Jan. 15, 1851
- **PARENT COUNTIES:** Yell, Risley
- **BIRTH RECORDS:** start in 1880, kept by District Court
- **MARRIAGE**: 1853, District Court
- **DIVORCE:** 1870, District Court
- **DEATH:** 1880, District Court
- **PROBATE:** 1855, District Court
- **COURT:** 1860, District Court
- **NOTES:** Formerly Risley and Yell counties. Name changed to Webster Jan. 22, 1853.

WINNEBAGO

126 S. Clark, Box 468, Forest City, IA 50436, (641) 585-4520,
<www.winnebagocountyiowa.org>
- **INCORPORATED:** Jan. 15, 1851
- **PARENT COUNTY:** Unorganized Territory
- **BIRTH RECORDS:** start in 1880, kept by Clerk of Courts
- **MARRIAGE:** 1868, Clerk of Courts
- **DIVORCE:** 1865, Clerk of Courts
- **DEATH:** 1880, Clerk of Courts
- **PROBATE:** 1865, Clerk of Courts
- **COURT:** 1865, Clerk of Courts
- **NOTES:** Attached to Boone and Webster counties prior to Nov. 1, 1857.

WINNESHIEK

201 W. Main St., Decorah, IA 52101, (563) 382-2469,
<iagenweb.org/winneshiek>
- **INCORPORATED:** Feb. 20, 1847
- **PARENT COUNTY:** Unorganized Territory
- **BIRTH RECORDS:** start in 1880, kept by District Court
- **MARRIAGE:** 1851, District Court
- **DEATH:** 1880, District Court
- **DIVORCE:** 1855, District Court
- **PROBATE:** 1853, District Court
- **COURT:** 1855, District Court
- **NOTES:** Attached to Clayton County prior to March 1, 1851.

WOODBURY

620 Douglas #101, Sioux City, IA 51101, (712) 279-6611,
<www.woodburyiowa.com>
- **INCORPORATED:** Jan. 15, 1851
- **PARENT COUNTY:** Unorganized Territory
- **BIRTH RECORDS:** start in 1880, kept by District Court
- **DIVORCE:** 1857, District Court
- **DEATH:** 1880, District Court
- **PROBATE:** 1868, District Court
- **COURT:** 1850, District Court
- **ADOPTION**: 1920, District Court
- **MARRIAGE:** 1854, District Court
- **NOTES:** Formerly Wahkaw County. Name changed to Woodbury Jan. 22, 1853. Organized March 7, 1853.

WORTH

1000 Central Ave., Northwood, IA 50459, (641) 324-2840,
<www.worthcounty.org>
- **INCORPORATED:** Jan. 15, 1851
- **PARENT COUNTY:** Unorganized Territory
- **BIRTH RECORDS:** start in 1880, kept by District Court
- **MARRIAGE:** 1853, District Court
- **DEATH:** 1880, District Court
- **LAND:** 1879, District Court
- **PROBATE**: 1857, District Court
- **COURT:** 1857, District Court
- **NOTES:** Attached to Fayette, Chickasaw, Floyd and Mitchell counties prior to Oct. 13, 1857.

WRIGHT

115 N. Main St., Box 306, Clarion, IA 50525, (515) 532-3113,
<iagenweb.org/wright>
- **INCORPORATED:** Jan. 15, 1851
- **PARENT COUNTY:** Unorganized Territory
- **BIRTH RECORDS:** start in 1880, kept by District Court
- **MARRIAGE:** 1855, District Court
- **DEATH:** 1880, District Court
- **DIVORCE:** 1873, District Court
- **NATURALIZATION**: 1857, District Court
- **PROBATE:** 1880, District Court
- **COURT:** 1873, District Court
- **NOTES:** Attached to Boone and Webster counties prior to Oct. 1, 1855.

YELL

- **INCORPORATED:** Jan. 15, 1851
- **PARENT COUNTY:** Unorganized Territory
- **NOTES:** See Webster County. Lost to Webster Jan. 22, 1853.

KANSAS

» BY MAUREEN A. TAYLOR

HISTORICAL OVERVIEW

Kansas, once part of land claimed in 1682 by Frenchman Rene-Robert Cavelier, Sieur de La Salle, became part of the United States through the Louisiana Purchase in 1803. At the time, Omaha, Pawnee, Apache, and Wichita tribes populated the area. The state derives its name from the Kansa tribe.

In the 1820s, steamboats traveled rivers in the area and thousands passed through on the Sante Fe and Oregon Trails. The only permanent settlements were military outposts at forts Riley, Scott and Leavenworth; religious missions; and trading posts. Then the Kansas-Nebraska Act of 1854 opened the area to settlers, conveyed territorial status and let citizens vote on slavery. Antislavery Free Soilers opened a territorial government at Lawrence in 1855, while proslavers founded another government in southeastern Kansas. Resulting conflicts earned the region the nickname Bleeding Kansas.

Kansas became a state in 1861 with Topeka as the capital and a constitution that prohibited slavery. Settlement increased with the 1862 Homestead Act, which gave citizens and those intending to become citizens a chance to claim 160 acres if they stayed five years. Germans, Swedes, English, Mexicans, and African-Americans "Exodusters" settled the area. Mennonites from Russia arrived in the 1870s.

During the 1800s, towns grew along the Chisholm Trail from Texas to Abilene, Kansas. Residents relied on farming or cattle, and stayed despite extreme weather and insect plagues. The Kansas Dust Bowl epitomized the misery of the rest of the country during the Great Depression. In the late 1800s and early 1900s, the state's economy relied on farming, oil production, mineral mines, and aircraft manufacturing.

Kansans made many military contributions. Members of the Kansas 23rd Colored Regiment fought in the Spanish-American War. During the 20th century, camps Funston and Leavenworth became key training facilities. Kansas manufacturing plants supplied aircraft during World War II.

RECORD HIGHLIGHTS

Researchers with Kansas ancestors during the territorial period will have to rely on federal and state census records for 1855, 1859, and 1860. State censuses also were taken between 1865 and 1925. They're available through the Kansas State Historical Society (KSHS) **<www.kshs.org>** and the Family History LIbrary (FHL).

Statewide recording of births and deaths didn't occur until July 1911, but earlier births and deaths may have been recorded in the town or county clerk's office. KSHS has an index to marriage licenses before 1867. Statewide marriage registration began in 1913. Order birth and death records after 1911 and marriages after 1913 from the Office of Vital Statistics.

KSHS has records from the Kansas Adjutant General's Office, including muster rolls, and is collecting war letters of people in the military from the Civil War to the present.

research tips

- The Kansas State Historical Society has an extensive collection of newspapers you can borrow through interlibrary loan. See **<www.kshs.org>** for titles.
- ATLAS, the Associated Topeka Libraries Automated System **<topekalibraries.info>**, is an online catalog covering the holdings of seven libraries, including the Kansas State Historical Society. It contains maps, directories, county and family histories and organizational papers.

CENSUS RECORDS

- Federal censuses: 1870, 1880, 1900, 1910, 1920, 1930
- Territory/state censuses: 1865, 1875, 1885, 1895, 1905, 1915, 1925
- Mortality schedules: 1860, 1870, 1880

Because Kansas is a public domain state, the federal government handled initial land sales and grants. Initial land transfers appear in Kansas Tract Books and are available on microfilm from the National Archives and Records Administration (NARA). Other land records occur on the county level and can be found at the Register of Deeds. Originals of all federal land records for Kansas are at the National Archives.

In 1875, a group of Kansas newspaper publishers sought a repository to preserve papers printed in the state. This led to the founding of KSHS, which has an almost comprehensive collection of unindexed Kansas newspapers (listed on the website). Look in particular for obituaries, which may predate vital records. You'll need an approximate death date.

KSHS also collects microfilm of county materials filmed by the FHL, as well as federal records that document the state's history. You can search the KSHS and other Topeka-area library holdings at **<www.kshs.org/research/collections/documents/opac/opac1.htm>**. You'll find maps, directories, published and unpublished family histories, organizational papers, and county histories in their library. Additional details on the holdings appear on the society's website.

Most of Kansas' 105 counties have groups that participate in the Kansas Council of Genealogical Societies. Their volunteers undertake indexing projects for local records. Once you've determined where your ancestors lived, contact that county's society to see what local materials are available.

ARCHIVES, LIBRARIES, AND SOCIETIES

Anderson County Genealogical Society
Box 194, Garnett, KS 66032

Arkansas City Public Library
120 E. Fifth Ave., Arkansas City, KS 67005, (620) 442-1280, **<www.acpl.org>**

Atchison County Genealogical Society
Box 303, Atchison, KS 66002, **<skyways.lib.ks.us/genweb/society/atchison/ackgs.htm>**

Barton County Genealogical Society
Box 425, Great Bend, KS 67530

Bluestem Genealogical Society
Box 582, Eureka, KS 67045

Branches and Twigs Genealogical Society c/o Kingman Carnegie Library, 455 N. Main, Kingman, KS 67068, (620) 532-3061

Brown County Genealogical Society
116 S. Seventh St., Hiawatha, KS 66434, (785) 742-7511, **<skyways.lib.ks.us/genweb/society/hiawatha>**

Chanute Genealogical Society
607 S. Ashby, Chanute, KS 66720, **<www.rootsweb.ancestry.com/~kscgs>**

Chautauqua County Historical and Genealogical Society
115 W. Main, Sedan, KS 67361, (620) 725-3408, **<freida-wells.tripod.com/chautauquacountykansas>**

Cherokee County Genealogical-Historical Society
Box 33, Columbus, KS 66725, (620) 429-2992

Cloud County Genealogical Society
<skyways.lib.ks.us/genweb/cloud/society.htm>

Cowley County Genealogical Society
1518 E. 12th, Winfield, KS 67156, (620) 221-4591

Crawford County Genealogy Society
308 N. Walnut, Pittsburg, KS 66762, (620) 230-5558, **<skyways.lib.ks.us/genweb/crawford/society.html>**

Decatur County Genealogical Society
c/o The Decatur County Museum, 258 S. Penn Ave., Oberlin, KS

Douglas County Genealogical Society
Box 3664, Lawrence, KS 66046, **<skyways.lib.ks.us/genweb/douglas/dckgs.html>**

Douglas County Historical Society
c/o The Watkins Community Museum of History, 1047 Massachusetts St., Lawrence, KS 66044, (785) 841-4109, **<www.watkinsmuseum.org>**

Finney County Genealogical Society
Box 592, Garden City, KS 67846, **<skyways.lib.ks.us/genweb/society/finney>**

Flint Hills Genealogical Society
Box 555, Emporia, KS 66801, **<skyways.lib.ks.us/genweb/society/emporia>**

Franklin County Genealogical Society
Box 353, Ottawa, KS 66067, **<www.franklincountykansas.net>**

Garden City Public Library
210 N. Seventh, Garden City, KS 67846

Girard Public Library
128 W. Prairie Ave., Girard, KS 66743, (620) 724-4317, **<www.girardpubliclibrary.net>**

Golden Wheat Chapter, American Historical Society of Germans from Russia
928 Spruce, Newton, KS 67114, (316) 283-3129, **<www.ahsgr.org/GoldenWheatChapter/golden_wheat_chapter.htm>**

Greenwood County Historical Society
120 W. Fourth St., Eureka, KS 67045, (620) 583-6682, **<skyways.lib.ks.us/genweb/greenwoo/gchs.htm>**

Halstead Historical Society
Box 88, Halstead, KS 67056, (316) 835-2267, **<historicalsociety.halsteadkansas.com>**

Hamilton County Historical Society
108 E. Hwy. 50, Syracuse, KS 67878, (620) 384-7496

Hamilton County Library
Box 1307, Syracuse, KS 67878, (620) 384-5622, **<skyways.lib.ks.us/library/hamilton>**

Harper County Genealogical Society
c/o Harper Public Library, 1002 Oak St., Harper, KS 67058, **<skyways.lib.ks.us/kansas/genweb/society/harper>**

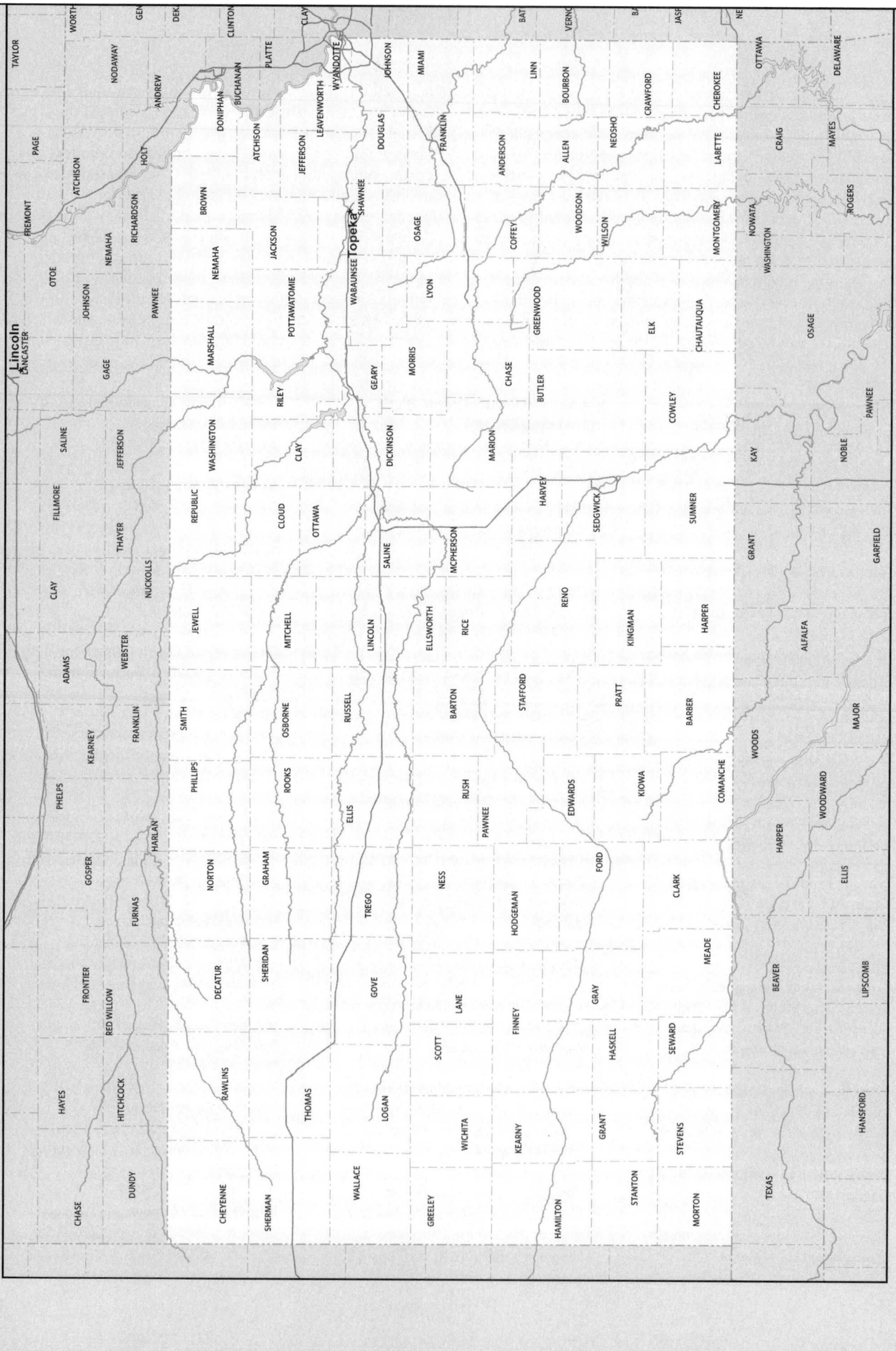
TAYLOR
WORTH
CLINTON
CLAY
NODAWAY
ANDREW
PAGE
ATCHISON
HOLT
FREMONT
RICHARDSON
NEMAHA
OTOE
JOHNSON
PAWNEE
Lincoln
LANCASTER
GAGE
SALINE
JEFFERSON
FILLMORE
THAYER
CLAY
NUCKOLLS
ADAMS
WEBSTER
KEARNEY
FRANKLIN
PHELPS
HARLAN
GOSPER
FURNAS
FRONTIER
RED WILLOW
HAYES
HITCHCOCK
CHASE
DUNDY
DONIPHAN
BUCHANAN
PLATTE
LEAVENWORTH
WYANDOTTE
JOHNSON
MIAMI
LINN
BOURBON
CRAWFORD
CHEROKEE
ATCHISON
JEFFERSON
DOUGLAS
FRANKLIN
ANDERSON
ALLEN
NEOSHO
LABETTE
BROWN
SHAWNEE
Topeka
OSAGE
COFFEY
WOODSON
WILSON
MONTGOMERY
NEMAHA
JACKSON
WABAUNSEE
LYON
GREENWOOD
ELK
CHAUTAUQUA
MARSHALL
POTTAWATOMIE
GEARY
MORRIS
CHASE
BUTLER
COWLEY
RILEY
WASHINGTON
CLAY
DICKINSON
MARION
HARVEY
SEDGWICK
SUMNER
REPUBLIC
CLOUD
OTTAWA
SALINE
MCPHERSON
RENO
KINGMAN
HARPER
JEWELL
MITCHELL
LINCOLN
ELLSWORTH
RICE
SMITH
OSBORNE
RUSSELL
BARTON
STAFFORD
PRATT
BARBER
PHILLIPS
ROOKS
ELLIS
RUSH
PAWNEE
EDWARDS
KIOWA
COMANCHE
NORTON
GRAHAM
TREGO
NESS
HODGEMAN
FORD
CLARK
DECATUR
SHERIDAN
GOVE
LANE
FINNEY
GRAY
MEADE
RAWLINS
THOMAS
LOGAN
SCOTT
HASKELL
SEWARD
WICHITA
KEARNY
GRANT
STEVENS
CHEYENNE
SHERMAN
WALLACE
GREELEY
HAMILTON
STANTON
MORTON
OTTAWA
DELAWARE
CRAIG
MAYES
NOWATA
ROGERS
WASHINGTON
OSAGE
PAWNEE
KAY
NOBLE
GRANT
GARFIELD
ALFALFA
WOODS
MAJOR
HARPER
WOODWARD
ELLIS
BEAVER
LIPSCOMB
TEXAS
HANSFORD

Heart of America Chapter, American Historical Society of Germans from Russia 117 E. Minneapolis St., Salina, KS 67401, (785) 827-0782, **<www.ahsgr.org/heart_of_america_chapter.htm>**

Heritage Seekers of SW Kansas Chapter, American Historical Society of Germans from Russia 411 Sunnydell Circle, South Hutchinson, KS 67505, **<www.ahsgr.org/heritage_seekers_of_sw_kansas_ch.htm>**

Historical Society of the Downs Carnegie Library
S. Morgan Ave., Downs, KS 67437

Hodgeman County Genealogical Society
Box 608, Jetmore, KS 67854, (620) 357-6594

Iola Public Library
218 E. Madison, Iola, KS 66749, (620) 365-3262, **<iola.mykansaslibrary.org>**

Jefferson County Genealogical Society
Box 174, Oskaloosa, KS, 66066, (785) 863-2070, **<skyways.lib.ks.us/kansas/genweb/jefferso/jfcogen.html>**

Johnson County Genealogical Society
Box 12666, Shawnee Mission, KS 66282, (913) 780-4764, **<www.johnsoncountykansasgenealogy.org>**

Kansas City Area Chapter, American Historical Society of Germans from Russia
4441 W. 52nd Terrace, Roeland Park, KS 66205, **<www.ahsgr.org/kansas_city_area_chapter.htm>**

Kansas Council of Genealogical Societies
Box 3858, Topeka, KS 66604
<skyways.lib.ks.us/genweb/kcgs>

Kansas Department of Health and Environment, Office of Vital Statistics
1000 SW Jackson, Topeka, KS 66612, (785) 296-1400, **<www.kdheks.gov/vital>**

Kansas Genealogical Society Library
Village Square Mall, 2601 Central Ave., Dodge City, KS 67801, **<www.kgs-genlibrary.com>**

Kansas Public Library
625 Minnesota Ave., Kansas City, KS 66101

Kansas State Historical Society
6425 SW Sixth Ave., Topeka, KS 66615, (785) 272-8681, **<www.kshs.org>**

Kansas State Library
State Capitol Building, Room 343-N, 300 SW 10th Ave., Topeka, KS 66612, (800) 432-3919, **<skyways.lib.ks.us/KSL>**

Labette County Genealogical Society
Box 544, Parsons, KS 67357, **<skyways.lib.ks.us/genweb/society/parsons>**

Nora E. Larabee Memorial Library
108 N. Union St., Stafford, KS 67578, (620) 234-5762, **<skyways.lib.ks.us/towns/Stafford/library>**

Liberal Area Genealogical Society
Box 1094, Liberal, KS 67905

Marion County Genealogical Society
401 S. Cedar, Marion, KS 66961

Marshall County Historical Society
1207 Broadway, Marysville, KS 66508, (785) 562-5012, **<skyways.lib.ks.us/museums/mchc>**

Mennonite Library and Archives
c/o Bethel College, 300 E. 27th St., North Newton, KS 67117, (316) 284-5304, **<www.bethelks.edu/mla>**

Miami County Genealogy Society
Box 123, Paola, KS 66071, (913) 294-4940, **<www.miamicountykansashistory.org>**

Midwest Historical and Genealogical Society
Box 1121, Wichita, KS 67201, (316) 264-3611, **<skyways.lib.ks.us/kansas/genweb/mhgs>**

Montgomery County Genealogical Society
Box 444, Coffeyville, KS 67333, **<skyways.lib.ks.us/genweb/society/coffeyville>**

Nemaha County Genealogical Society
Sixth and Nemaha, Seneca, KS 66538, **<www.kansasheritage.org/seneca/gensoc.html>**

North Central Kansas Genealogical Society Box 251, Cawker City, KS 67430, **<skyways.lib.ks.us/towns/Cawker/library.html>**

Northeastern Kansas Chapter, American Historical Society of Germans from Russia
2938 SE Peck Rd., Topeka, KS 66605, **<www.ahsgr.org/northeastern_kansas_chapter.htm>**

Northwest Kansas Genealogical and Historical Society
700 W. Third, Oakley, KS 67748

Norton County Historical Society
Box 303, Norton, KS 67654, (785) 877-5107, **<nchistory.hosted.nex-tech.com>**

Old Fort Genealogical Society of Southeastern Kansas
Box 786, Fort Scott, KS 66701, (620) 223-3300, **<skyways.lib.ks.us/genweb/society/ftscott>**

Osage County Historical Society and Hawley Genealogical Research Center
Box 361, Lyndon, KS 66451, (785) 828-3477, **<www.osagechs.org>**

Phillips County Genealogical Society
Box 114, Phillipsburg, KS 67661, **<skyways.lib.ks.us/genweb/phillips/plgensoc.html>**

Pittsburg Public Library
308 N. Walnut, Pittsburg, KS 66762, (620) 231-8110, **<skyways.lib.ks.us/library/pittsburg>**

Post Rock Chapter, American Historical Society of Germans from Russia
18350 Homer Rd., Russell, KS 67665, (785) 483-3976, **<www.ahsgr.org/post_rock_chapter.htm>**

Rawlins County Genealogical Society
<skyways.lib.ks.us/genweb/rawlins/rawgenesoc.html>

Reno County Genealogical Society
Box 5, Hutchinson, KS 67504, **<www.rootsweb.ancestry.com/~ksrcgs>**

Riley County Genealogical Society
2005 Claflin, Manhattan, KS 66502, **<www.rileycgs.com>**

Santa Fe Trail Genealogical Society
Box 528, Syracuse, KS 67878

Smoky Valley Genealogical Society
211 W. Iron, Suite 205, Salina, KS 67401, (785) 825-7573, **<skyways.lib.ks.us/genweb/saline/society>**

Southeast Kansas Genealogy Society
Box 393, Iola, KS 66749, **<skyways.lib.ks.us/orgs/sekgs>**

Southwestern College Memorial Library
100 College St., Winfield, KS 67156, (800) 846-1543, **<www.sckans.edu/library>**

Kenneth Spencer Research Library
1450 Poplar Lane, The University of Kansas, KS 66045, (785) 864-4334, **<spencer.lib.ku.edu/kc>**

St. Mary's Historical Society
106 E. Mission, St. Marys, KS 66536

Stanton County Historical Society
Box 806, Johnson, KS 67855

Sumner County Historical and Genealogical Society
Box 402, Wellington, KS 67152, **<www.rootsweb.com/~ksscgs>**

Topeka Genealogical Society
Box 4048, Topeka, KS 66604, **<www.tgstopeka.org>**

Topeka Public Library
1515 SW 10th Ave., Topeka, KS 66604, **<www.tscpl.org>**

Wichita County Genealogical Society
Box 1561, Leoti, KS 67861, (620) 375-2316, **<www.wichitacountymuseum.org/gensociety.htm>**

Wichita Genealogical Society
Box 3705, Wichita, KS 67201, **<www.wichitagensoc.org>**

Wichita Public Library
223 S. Main, Wichita, KS 67202, (316) 721-8500, **<www.wichita.lib.ks.us>**

Wyandotte County Genealogical Society
Box 4228, Kansas City, KS 66104

Wyandotte County Historical Society
631 N. 126th St., Bonner Springs, KS 66012, (913) 573-5002, **<wycomuseum.wordpress.com>**

GENERAL RESOURCES

The Beginning of the West: Annals of the Kansas Gateway to the American West, 1540-1854 by Louise Barry (Kansas State Historical Society, ca. 1972)

A Biographical History of Central Kansas (Lewis Publishing Co., 1902)

Black, Buckskin and Blue: African American Scouts and Soldiers on the Western Frontier by Arthur T. Burton (Eaton Press, ca. 1999)

A Century of Congregationalism in Kansas, 1854-1954 by Charles M. Correll (The Kansas Congregational and Christian Conference, ca. 1953)

Early Kansas Churches by Edward Robert DeZurko (The College, 1949)

The First Protestant Osage Missions, 1820-1837 by William Whites Graves (Carpenter Press, ca. 1949)

Guide to the Microfilm Collections of the Kansas State Historical Society by David A. Haury (Kansas State Historical Society, 1991)

History of Kansas by the Kansas State Historical Society (Kansas State Printing Plant, 1916)

Illustriana Kansas: Biographical Sketches of Kansas Men and Women of Achievement Who Have Been Awarded Life Membership in Kansas Illustriana Society by Robert Morton Baldwin and Sara Mullin Baldwin (W.C. Cox, 1974)

The Kansa Indians, A History of the Wind People, 1673-1873 by William E. Unrau (University of Oklahoma Press, 1971)

Kansas Biographical Index: State-Wide and Regional by Patricia Douglass Smith (P.D. Smith, ca. 1994)

Kansas: A Cyclopedia of State History by Frank Wilson Blackmar (Standard Publishing Co., ca. 1912)

Kansas, the First Century by John D. Bright (Lewis Historical Publishing Co., ca. 1956)

Six Generation Ancestor Tables by Doris Dockstader Rooney (Kansas Genealogical Society, 1976)

Kansas Newspapers: A Directory of Newspaper Holdings in Kansas by Eileen Anderson (The Board, 1984)

Kansas Orphan Train Riders by Robert A. Hodge (R.A. Hodge, 1996)

Kansas Research Outline by the Church of Jesus Christ of Latter-day Saints (online at **<www.familysearch.org/eng/search/rg/guide/kansas.asp>**)

Kansas Territorial Settlers of 1860 Who Were Born in Tennessee, Virginia, North Carolina and South Carolina by Clara Hamlett Robertson (Genealogical Publishing Co., ca. 1976)

Narratives of African Americans in Kansas, 1870-1992: Beyond the Exodust Movement by Jacob U. Gordon (E. Mellen Press, 1993)

A New Centennial History of the State of Kansas by Charles Richard Tuttle (Inter-state Book Co., 1876)

Peopling the Plains: Who Settled Where in Frontier Kansas by James R. Shortridge (University Press of Kansas, ca. 1995)

Pioneer Women: Voices from the Kansas Frontier by Joanna L. Stratton (Simon and Schuster, ca. 1981)

The Sod House Frontier, 1854-1890 by Everett Dick (University of Nebraska, 1979)

A Standard History of Kansas and Kansans by William Elsey Connelley (Lewis Publishing Co., 1918)

Territorial Papers of Kansas, 1854-1861 by the US Department of State (The National Archives, 1953)

West of Wichita: Settling the High Plains of Kansas, 1865-1890 by Craig Miner (University Press of Kansas, ca. 1986)

The William Wade Hinshaw Index to Kansas Quaker Meeting Records by William Wade Hinshaw (Selby Publishing & Printing, ca. 1991)

☞MAPS

Historical Atlas of Kansas by Homer E. Socolofsky and Huber Self (University of Oklahoma Press, 1988)

Kansas in Maps by Robert W. Baughman (Kansas State Historical Society, 1961)

Kansas Place Names by John Rydjord (University of Oklahoma Press, ca. 1972)

Kansas Post Offices, May 29, 1828-Aug 3, 1961 by Robert W. Baughman (Kansas Postal History Society, ca. 1961)

Kansas Towns & Cities as of 1912 by Debra Graden (Grey Ink, ca. 1997)

The Official State Atlas of Kansas (Kansas Council of Genealogical Societies, 1982)

☞MILITARY RECORDS

Fighting Twentieth, History and Official Souvenir: An Account of the Kansas Volunteers in the Spanish American War, 1898-1899 (John A. Ostertag, 1989)

The History of the Kansas Department of the American Legion by Richard J. Loosbrock (Kansas Department of the American Legion, ca. 1968)

An Honor Roll of Kansas Civil War Veterans by Sherman Lee Pompey (Pacific Specialties, 1972)

Records of Indians in World War I by the US Bureau of Indian Affairs, Potawatomi Agency (Federal Archives and Records Center, 1977)

☞VITAL RECORDS

Abandoned and Semi-Active Cemeteries of Kansas by Don L. Ford (Anundsen, ca. 1983-1985)

Births, Marriages, Deaths and Other News Items and Events by John Ostertag and Enid Ostertag (J.A. Ostertag, 1989-1999)

Guide to Public Vital Statistics Records in Kansas by the Historical Records Survey (The Survey, 1942)

Mortality Schedule, Kansas, volumes for 1860, 1870 and 1880, edited by Ronald Vern Jackson (Accelerated Indexing Systems, 1979)

COUNTY DETAILS

ALLEN
1 N. Washington St., Iola, KS 66749, (620) 365-1407,
<www.allencounty.org>
- **INCORPORATED:** May 7, 1856
- **PARENT COUNTY:** Original county
- **MARRIAGE RECORDS:** start in 1856, kept by County Clerk
- **LAND:** 1861, Registrar of Deeds
- **PROBATE:** 1858, Probate Court
- **COURT:** 1858, Probate Court
- **MILITARY:** 1860, Registrar of Deeds
- **NATURALIZATION:** 1871, District Court
- **NOTES:** Clerk of District Court has divorce records for late 1800s.

ANDERSON
100 E. Fourth St., Box 305, Garnett, KS 66032, (785) 448-6841,
<www.andersoncountyks.org>
- **INCORPORATED:** Jan. 7, 1856
- **PARENT COUNTY:** Original county
- **MARRIAGE RECORDS:** start in 1856, kept by County Clerk
- **LAND:** 1857, Registrar of Deeds
- **PROBATE:** 1855, Probate Court
- **COURT:** 1860, District Court
- **WILLS:** 1869, Probate Court
- **NATURALIZATION:** 1903, District Court

ARAPAHOE
- **INCORPORATED:** 1873
- **PARENT COUNTY:** Original county
- **NOTES:** See Haskell County. Arapahoe County was absorbed by Finney County in 1883 and name changed to Haskell County 1887.

ATCHISON
423 N. Fifth St., Atchison, KS 66002, (913) 367-1653,
<www.atchisoncountyks.org>
- **INCORPORATED:** Sep. 17, 1855
- **PARENT COUNTY:** Original county
- **MARRIAGE RECORDS:** start in 1855, kept by County Clerk
- **DIVORCE:** 1859, District Court
- **LAND:** 1855, Registrar of Deeds
- **PROBATE:** 1855, Probate Court
- **COURT:** 1858, District Court
- **NOTES:** County Clerk has birth and death records 1891-1911. Registrar of Deeds has military discharges 1943-1990. Kansas Genealogical Society has naturalizations 1858-1953, 1914-1929.

BARBER
120 E. Washington St., Medicine Lodge, KS 67104, (620) 886-3961,
<skyways.lib.ks.us/genweb/barber>
- **INCORPORATED:** July 7, 1873
- **PARENT COUNTY:** Marion
- **MARRIAGE RECORDS:** start in 1874, kept by County Clerk
- **COURT:** 1874, District Court
- **LAND:** 1867, Registrar of Deeds
- **PROBATE:** 1867, Probate Court
- **NOTES:** County Clerk has birth and death records 1891-1911.

BARTON
Box 1089, Great Bend, KS 67530, (620) 793-1835,
<www.bartoncounty.org>
- **INCORPORATED:** May 16, 1872
- **PARENT COUNTY:** Marion
- **MARRIAGE RECORDS:** start in 1872, kept by County Clerk

- **LAND:** 1872, County Clerk
- **PROBATE:** 1872, County Clerk
- **COURT:** 1873, County Clerk
- **NOTES:** County Clerk has birth and death records 1892-1911.

BILLINGS

- **INCORPORATED:** March 20, 1873
- **PARENT COUNTY:** Original county
- **NOTES:** See Norton County. Created in 1859 as Oro County, name changed to Norton County in 1867. In 1873 name changed to Billings and changed back to Norton in 1874.

BOURBON

210 S. National Ave., Fort Scott, KS 66701, (316) 223-3800, **<www.bourboncountyks.org>**

- **INCORPORATED:** Sep. 12, 1855
- **PARENT COUNTY:** Original county
- **MARRIAGE RECORDS:** start in 1855, kept by Probate Court
- **LAND:** 1856, Registrar of Deeds
- **PROBATE:** 1864, Probate Court
- **COURT:** 1864, Probate Court
- **NOTES:** District Court has naturalization records 1868-1933. Probate Court has wills 1858-1925.

BRECKENRIDGE

- **INCORPORATED:** Aug. 25, 1855
- **PARENT COUNTY:** Original county
- **NOTES:** See Lyon County. Name changed to Lyon Feb. 5, 1862. Was attached to Madison County for civil and criminal purposes. In 1861 Madison County was abolished and the northern part given to Breckenridge.

BROWN

601 Oregon St., Hiawatha, KS 66434, (785) 742-2581, **<skyways.lib.ks.us/genweb/brown>**

- **INCORPORATED:** Aug. 25, 1855
- **PARENT COUNTY:** Original county
- **BIRTH RECORDS:** start in 1885, kept by County District Ct.
- **MARRIAGE:** 1857, Probate Court
- **DEATH:** 1895, County District Court
- **LAND:** 1857, Registrar of Deeds
- **PROBATE:** 1857, Probate Court
- **COURT:** 1859, District Court
- **NOTES:** District Court has naturalization records 1873-1954.

BUFFALO

- **INCORPORATED:** March 20, 1873
- **PARENT COUNTY:** Unorganized Territory
- **NOTES:** (See Gray, old) In 1881 the northern tier of Buffalo County was added to Lane County. The remainder was added to Gray County and later to Finney County.

BUTLER

205 W. Central Ave., El Dorado, KS 67042, (316) 322-4232, **<www.bucoks.com>**

- **INCORPORATED:** Aug. 25, 1855
- **PARENT COUNTY:** Original county
- **MARRIAGE RECORDS:** start in 1861, kept by District Court
- **LAND:** 1868, Registrar of Deeds
- **NOTES:** Registrar of Deeds has Military Discharge records 1943-1950. County Clerk has birth and death records.

CALHOUN

- **INCORPORATED:** Sep. 24, 1855
- **PARENT COUNTY:** Original county
- **NOTES:** See Jackson County. Name changed to Jackson Feb. 11, 1859. Early marriage records are in Molton and Jackson counties.

CHASE

Courthouse Sq., Box 547, Cottonwood Falls, KS 66845, (620) 273-6423, **<www.chasecountyks.org>**

- **INCORPORATED:** March 15, 1859
- **PARENT COUNTIES:** Butler, Wise
- **MARRIAGE RECORDS:** start in 1860, kept by District Court
- **LAND:** 1859, Registrar of Deeds
- **PROBATE:** 1864, Probate Court
- **COURT:** 1861, District Court
- **NOTES:** Military records 1861-1865 are available. Circuit Court has naturalization records 1872-1941.

CHAUTAUQUA

215 N. Chautauqua St., Sedan, KS 67361, (620) 725-5800, **<skyways.lib.ks.us/genweb/chautauq>**

- **INCORPORATED:** June 1, 1875
- **PARENT COUNTIES:** Howard, Godfrey
- **MARRIAGE RECORDS:** start in 1870, kept by Probate Judge
- **LAND:** 1871, Registrar of Deeds
- **COURT:** 1871, District Court
- **NOTES:** Clerk of District Court has divorce records 1884-1949. Probate Judge has probate records 1871-1900.

CHEROKEE

100 W. Maple, Box 14, Columbus, KS 66725, (620) 429-2042, **<skyways.lib.ks.us/genweb/cherokee>**

- **INCORPORATED:** Aug. 3, 1866
- **PARENT COUNTY:** Unorganized Territory
- **BIRTH RECORDS:** start in 1894, kept by County Clerk
- **MARRIAGE:** 1867, Probate Court
- **DEATH:** 1894, County Clerk
- **NATURALIZATION:** 1870, Probate Court
- **LAND:** 1866, Registrar of Deeds
- **PROBATE:** 1870, Probate Court
- **WILLS:** 1870, Probate Court
- **NOTES:** Formerly McGee County. Name changed to Cherokee Feb. 18, 1860.

CHEYENNE

Box 985, St. Francis, KS 67756, (785) 332-8800, **<www.cheyennecounty.org>**

- **INCORPORATED:** 1886
- **PARENT COUNTY:** Unorganized Territory
- **MARRIAGE RECORDS:** start in 1886, kept by District Court
- **DIVORCE:** 1892, District Court
- **PROBATE:** 1892, District Court
- **COURT:** 1892, District Court
- **LAND:** 1873, Registrar of Deeds

CLARK
913 Highland St., Ashland, KS 67831, (620) 635-2813,
<www.clarkcountyks.com>
- **INCORPORATED:** May 5, 1885
- **PARENT COUNTIES:** Marion, Ford
- **MARRIAGE RECORDS:** start in 1885, kept by Probate Judge
- **DIVORCE:** 1885, Probate Judge
- **LAND:** 1872, Registrar of Deeds
- **PROBATE:** 1885, Probate Judge
- **COURT:** 1885, Probate Judge

CLAY
712 Fifth St., Box 98, Clay Center, KS 67432 , (785) 632-2552,
<www.claycountykansas.org>
- **INCORPORATED:** 1866
- **PARENT COUNTY:** Original county
- **MARRIAGE RECORDS:** start in 1867, kept by Probate Court
- **LAND:** 1866, Registrar of Deeds
- **PROBATE:** 1872, Probate Court
- **COURT:** 1868, District Court
- **WILLS:** 1867, Probate Court
- **NATURALIZATION:** 1868, District Court
- **NOTES:** Registrar of Deeds has military discharge records 1919-1957. Probate Court has birth and death records 1885-1911.

CLOUD
811 Washington St., Concordia, KS 66901 , (785) 243-8110,
<www.cloudcountyks.org>
- **INCORPORATED:** March 27, 1867
- **PARENT COUNTY:** Shirley
- **MARRIAGE RECORDS:** start in 1867, kept by Probate Judge
- **DIVORCE:** ca. 1860, District Court
- **LAND:** 1869, Registrar of Deeds
- **PROBATE:** ca. 1860, Clerk/Circuit Ct.
- **COURT:** ca. 1860, District Court
- **NOTES:** County Clerk has birth and death records 1885-1911. Formerly Shirley County, name changed to Cloud March 27, 1867.

COFFEY
110 S. Sixth St., Burlington, KS 66839, (620) 364-2191,
<www.coffeycountyks.org>
- **INCORPORATED:** Aug. 25, 1855
- **PARENT COUNTY:** Original county
- **BIRTH RECORDS:** start in 1892, kept by County Clerk
- **MARRIAGE:** 1856, County Clerk
- **DIVORCE:** 1861, District Court
- **DEATH:** 1886, County Clerk
- **LAND:** 1857, Registrar of Deeds
- **PROBATE:** 1857, Probate Court
- **COURT:** 1861, District Court
- **NATURALIZATION:** 1869, District Court
- **WILLS:** 1861, Probate Court
- **NOTES:** Registrar of Deeds has military discharges 1869-1885.

COMANCHE
201 S. New York St., Box 776, Coldwater, KS 67029, (620) 582-2361, **<www.comanchecounty.com>**
- **INCORPORATED:** 1885
- **PARENT COUNTY:** Marion
- **DIVORCE RECORDS:** start in 1867, kept by District Court
- **LAND:** 1885, Registrar of Deeds
- **PROBATE:** 1867, District Court
- **COURT:** 1867, District Court
- **NOTES:** County Clerk has birth records 1891-1911, death records 1891-1908, and marriage records 1891-1913.

COWLEY
311 E. Ninth Ave., Box 472, Winfield, KS 67156, (620) 221-5470,
<www.cowleycounty.org>
- **INCORPORATED:** Feb. 28, 1870
- **PARENT COUNTY:** Butler
- **BIRTH RECORDS:** start in 1911, kept by State Vital Records
- **DIVORCE:** 1870, Registrar of Deeds
- **DEATH:** 1911, State Vital Records
- **LAND:** 1871, Registrar of Deeds
- **PROBATE:** 1870, District Court
- **COURT:** 1870, District Court
- **NOTES:** Registrar of Deeds has marriage records 1870-1911. Name was Hunter and changed to Cowley in 1870.

CRAWFORD
Box 249, Girard, KS 66743-0249, (620) 724-6115,
<www.crawfordcountykansas.org>
- **INCORPORATED:** Feb. 13, 1867
- **PARENT COUNTIES:** Bourbon, Cherokee
- **MARRIAGE RECORDS:** start in 1867, kept by Probate Court
- **DIVORCE:** 1867, District Court
- **LAND:** 1867, Registrar of Deeds
- **PROBATE:** 1868, Probate Court
- **COURT:** 1867, District Court
- **NATURALIZATION:** 1868, District Court
- **NOTES:** County Clerk has birth and death records 1887-1911.

DAVIS
- **INCORPORATED:** Aug. 25, 1855
- **PARENT COUNTY:** Original county
- **NOTES:** See Geary County. Name changed March 7, 1889.

DECATUR
Box 28, Oberlin, KS 67749, (785) 475-8102,
<skyways.lib.ks.us/genweb/decatur>
- **INCORPORATED:** Dec. 15, 1879
- **PARENT COUNTY:** Unorganized Territory
- **DIVORCE RECORDS:** start in 1881, kept by District Court
- **LAND:** 1855, Registrar of Deeds
- **PROBATE:** 1891, District Court
- **COURT:** 1881, District Court
- **NATURALIZATION:** 1880, District Court
- **NOTES:** Clerk of District Court has birth and death records 1885-1911 and marriage records 1881-1912, 1917-1926.

DICKINSON
109 E. First St., Box 248, Abilene, KS 67410, (785) 263-3774,
<www.dkcoks.org>
- **INCORPORATED:** Feb. 20, 1857
- **PARENT COUNTIES:** Davis, Unorganized Territory

- **LAND RECORDS:** start in 1859, kept by Registrar of Deeds
- **COURT:** 1882, District Clerk
- **PROBATE:** 1882, District Clerk
- **NOTES:** County Clerk has birth, death, marriage records 1895-1911.

DONIPHAN

Box 278, Troy, KS 66087, (785) 985-3513,
<www.dpcountyks.com>

- **INCORPORATED:** Sep. 18, 1855
- **PARENT COUNTY:** Original county
- **BIRTH RECORDS:** start in 1898, kept by County Health Officer
- **MARRIAGE:** 1856, Probate Court
- **DEATH:** 1898, County Health Officer
- **LAND:** 1856, Registrar of Deeds
- **PROBATE:** 1852, Probate Court
- **COURT:** 1858, District Court
- **NATURALIZATION:** 1868, District Court
- **NOTES:** A yearly county census is taken.

DORN

- **INCORPORATED:** Aug. 25, 1855
- **PARENT COUNTY:** Original county
- **NOTES:** See Neosho County. Name changed June 3, 1861.

DOUGLAS

1100 Massachusetts, Lawrence, KS 66044, (785) 832-5281,
<www.douglas-county.com>

- **INCORPORATED:** Sep. 24, 1855
- **PARENT COUNTY:** Original county
- **DIVORCE RECORDS:** start in 1864, kept by District Court
- **LAND:** 1856, Registrar of Deeds
- **PROBATE:** 1855, District Court
- **COURT:** 1863, District Court
- **NOTES:** Genealogical Society has marriages 1854-1884, Clerk of District Court has naturalizations 1867-1954. Records destroyed Aug. 21, 1863, in Quantrill's raid. Some marriages reconstructed.

EDWARDS

312 Massachusetts Ave., Kinsley, KS 67547, (620) 659-3000,
<www.edwardscounty.org>

- **INCORPORATED:** March 18, 1874
- **PARENT COUNTY:** Kiowa
- **DIVORCE RECORDS:** start in 1874, kept by District Court
- **LAND:** 1874, Registrar of Deeds
- **PROBATE:** 1874, District Court
- **COURT:** 1874, District Court

ELK

127 N. Pine St., Box 606, Howard, KS 67349, (620) 374-2490,
<ks-elk.manatron.com>

- **INCORPORATED:** March 25, 1875
- **PARENT COUNTY:** Howard
- **NOTES:** Clerk of District Court has birth and death records 1885-1889, 1892-1911. Courthouse burned in 1906.
- **MARRIAGE RECORDS:** start in 1878, kept by Registrar of Deeds
- **LAND:** 1871, Registrar of Deeds
- **PROBATE:** 1906, Probate Judge
- **COURT:** 1906, District Court

ELLIS

1204 Fort St., Box 720, Hays, KS 67601, (785) 628-9410,
<www.ellisco.org>

- **INCORPORATED:** Feb. 26, 1867
- **PARENT COUNTY:** Unorganized Territory
- **DIVORCE RECORDS:** start in 1871, kept by District Court
- **LAND:** ca. 1880, Registrar of Deeds
- **PROBATE:** 1871, District Court
- **COURT:** 1871, District Court
- **NOTES:** County Clerk has birth, death, marriage records 1886-1912.

ELLSWORTH

210 N. Kansas Ave., Box 396, Ellsworth, KS 67439, (785) 472-4161,
<www.ellsworthcounty.org>

- **INCORPORATED:** Feb. 26, 1867
- **PARENT COUNTIES:** Marion, Unorganized Territory, Peketon
- **DIVORCE RECORDS:** start in 1868, kept by District Court
- **LAND:** 1867, Registrar of Deeds
- **PROBATE:** 1868, District Court
- **COURT:** 1868, District Court

FINNEY

Box M, Garden City, KS 67846, (620) 272-3500,
<www.finneycounty.org>

- **INCORPORATED:** Feb. 22, 1883
- **PARENT COUNTY:** Marion
- **MARRIAGE RECORDS:** start in 1885, kept by District Court
- **DIVORCE:** 1885, District Court
- **PROBATE:** 1885, District Court
- **COURT:** 1885, District Court
- **NATURALIZATION:** 1885, District Court
- **NOTES:** Formerly Sequoyah County. Name changed Feb. 21, 1883.

FOOTE

- **INCORPORATED:** March 20, 1873
- **PARENT COUNTY:** Marion
- **NOTES:** See Gray County, old. Became Gray 1881, disappeared 1883.

FORD

100 Gunsmoke, Dodge City, KS 67801, (620) 227-4550,
<www.fordcounty.net>

- **INCORPORATED:** April 5, 1873
- **PARENT COUNTY:** Marion
- **DIVORCE RECORDS:** start in 1873, kept by District Court
- **LAND:** 1873, Registrar of Deeds
- **PROBATE:** 1873, Probate Judge
- **COURT:** 1873, Probate Judge
- **NOTES:** County Clerk has birth, death, and marriage records 1905-1911. Probate Judge has naturalization records 1874-1906.

FRANKLIN

315 S. Main, Ottawa, KS 66067, (785) 229-3410,
<www.franklincoks.org>

- **INCORPORATED:** Aug. 25, 1855
- **PARENT COUNTY:** Original county
- **MARRIAGE RECORDS:** start in 1858, kept by District Court
- **DIVORCE:** 1860, District Court
- **LAND:** 1857, Registrar of Deeds

- **PROBATE:** 1859, District Court
- **COURT:** 1859, District Court
- **WILLS:** 1863, Probate Court
- **NATURALIZATION:** 1869, District Court

GARFIELD
- **INCORPORATED:** March 23, 1889
- **PARENT COUNTIES:** Finney, Hodgeman
- **NOTES:** Annexed to Finney March 18, 1893.

GEARY
200 E. Eighth St., Box 927, Junction City, KS 66441, (785) 238-3912, **<ks-geary.manatron.com>**
- **INCORPORATED:** March 7, 1889
- **PARENT COUNTY:** Original county
- **MARRIAGE RECORDS:** start in 1860, kept by Probate Court
- **DIVORCE:** 1867, District Court
- **LAND:** 1858, Registrar of Deeds
- **PROBATE:** 1856, Probate Court
- **COURT:** 1861, District Court
- **NATURALIZATION:** 1865, District Court
- **NOTES:** Formerly Davis County. Name changed Feb. 28, 1889

GODFREY
Aug. 30, 1855
- **PARENT COUNTY:** Original county
- **NOTES:** (See Seward, old) Name changed to Seward June 3, 1861.

GOVE
520 Washington St., Box 128, Gove, KS 67736, (785) 938-2300, **<skyways.lib.ks.us/genweb/gove>**
- **INCORPORATED:** 1886
- **PARENT COUNTY:** Unorganized Territory
- **LAND RECORDS:** start in 1885, kept by Registrar of Deeds
- **PROBATE:** 1886, District Court
- **COURT:** 1886, District Court

GRAHAM
410 N. Pomeroy, Hill City, KS 67642, (785) 421-3453, **<www.grahamcountyks.com>**
- **INCORPORATED:** 1880
- **PARENT COUNTY:** Unorganized Territory
- **DIVORCE RECORDS:** 1887, District Court
- **LAND:** 1886, Registrar of Deeds
- **PROBATE:** 1887, District Court
- **COURT:** 1887, District Court
- **NOTES:** County Clerk has birth, death, marriage records 1892-1904.

GRANT
108 S. Glenn, Ulysses, KS 67880, (620) 356-1335, **<www.grantcoks.org>**
- **INCORPORATED:** 1889
- **PARENT COUNTY:** Unorganized Territory
- **MARRIAGE RECORDS:** start date unknown, kept by District Court
- **DIVORCE:** unknown, District Court
- **LAND:** 1887, Registrar of Deeds
- **PROBATE AND COURT:** unknown, District Court
- **NOTES:** Local census taken every year.

GRAY
300 S. Main, Box 487, Cimarron, KS 67835, (620) 855-3618, **<grayco.org>**
- **INCORPORATED:** July 20, 1887
- **PARENT COUNTIES:** Finney, Ford
- **MARRIAGE RECORDS:** start in 1887, kept by District Court
- **DIVORCE:** 1887, District Court
- **LAND:** 1887, Registrar of Deeds
- **PROBATE:** 1885, District Court

GRAY, OLD
- **INCORPORATED:** March 13, 1881
- **PARENT COUNTIES:** Foote, Buffalo
- **NOTES:** Disappeared in 1883; reorganized July 20, 1887.

GREELEY
208 Harper St., Box 277, Tribune, KS 67879, (620) 376-4256, **<www.greeleycountygovernment.org>**
- **INCORPORATED:** July 9, 1888
- **PARENT COUNTY:** Unorganized Territory
- **MARRIAGE RECORDS:** start in 1888, kept by Probate Judge
- **LAND:** 1886, Registrar of Deeds
- **PROBATE:** 1887, District Court
- **COURT:** 1888, District Court

GREENWOOD
311 N. Main, Box 268, Eureka, KS 67045, (620) 583-8121, **<www.greenwoodcounty.org>**
- **INCORPORATED:** Aug. 25, 1855
- **PARENT COUNTY:** Original county
- **DIVORCE RECORDS:** start in unknown, kept by District Court
- **LAND:** 1858, Registrar of Deeds
- **PROBATE:** 1911, District Court
- **COURT:** unknown, District Court
- **NOTES:** County Historical Society has marriages 1856-1985.

HAMILTON
Box 1167, Syracuse, KS 67878, (620) 384-5629, **<www.hamiltoncountyks.com>**
- **INCORPORATED:** March 20, 1873
- **PARENT COUNTY:** Unorganized Territory
- **DIVORCE RECORDS:** start in 1886, kept by District Court
- **COURT:** 1886, District Court
- **LAND:** 1884, Registrar of Deeds
- **PROBATE:** 1886, District Court

HARPER
201 N. Jennings Ave., Anthony, KS 67003, (620) 842-5555, **<www.harpercountyks.gov>**
- **INCORPORATED:** 1873
- **PARENT COUNTY:** Marion
- **MARRIAGE RECORDS:** start in 1878, kept by District Court
- **LAND:** 1878, Registrar of Deeds
- **PROBATE:** 1883, District Court
- **COURT:** 1883, District Court

HARVEY
800 N. Main, Box 687, Newton, KS 67114, (316) 284-6842,
<www.harveycounty.com>
- **INCORPORATED:** March 7, 1872
- **PARENT COUNTIES:** McPherson, Sedgwick, Marion
- **LAND RECORDS:** start in 1862, kept by Registrar of Deeds
- **PROBATE:** 1872, District Court
- **COURT:** 1877, District Court
- **NOTES:** Clerk of District Court has divorce records 1877-1917 and marriage records 1872-1951. Registrar of Deeds has military discharge records 1919-1945.

HASKELL
Box 518, Sublette, KS 67877, (620) 675-2263,
<www.haskellcounty.org>
- **INCORPORATED:** Jul. 1, 1887
- **PARENT COUNTY:** Finney
- **MARRIAGE RECORDS:** start in 1887, kept by Probate Judge
- **DIVORCE:** 1887, District Court
- **COURT:** 1875, District Court
- **PROBATE:** 1875, District Court

HODGEMAN
500 Main St., Box 247, Jetmore, KS 67854, (620) 357-6421,
<www.hodgemancountyks.com>
- **INCORPORATED:** Feb. 26, 1867
- **PARENT COUNTY:** Marion
- **DIVORCE RECORDS:** start in 1887, kept by District Court
- **LAND:** 1879, Registrar of Deeds
- **PROBATE:** 1887, District Court
- **COURT:** 1887, District Court

HOWARD
- **INCORPORATED:** Feb. 26, 1867
- **PARENT COUNTY:** Original county
- **NOTES:** See Elk and Chautauqua. Originated as Godfrey County. Name changed to Seward, old in 1861 and to Howard in 1867. Howard divided to form Elk and Chautauqua counties in 1875.

HUNTER
- **INCORPORATED:** 1855
- **PARENT COUNTY:** Original county
- **NOTES:** Annexed into Butler County 1864.

JACKSON
400 New York Ave., Holton, KS 66436, (785) 364-2891,
<ks-jackson.manatron.com>
- **INCORPORATED:** Feb. 11, 1859
- **PARENT COUNTY:** Original county
- **MARRIAGE RECORDS:** start in 1855, kept by County Clerk
- **DIVORCE:** 1859, District Court
- **LAND:** 1857, Registrar of Deeds
- **PROBATE:** 1855, Probate Court
- **COURT:** 1858, District Court
- **NATURALIZATION:** 1868, District Court
- **NOTES:** County Clerk has birth and death records 1902-1911. Registrar of Deeds has military discharge records 1862-1965. Formerly Calhoun County. Name changed to Jackson Feb. 11, 1859.

JEFFERSON
300 W. Jefferson St., Box 321, Oskaloosa, KS 66066 , (785) 863-2272, **<www.jfcountyks.com>**
- **INCORPORATED:** Aug. 25, 1855
- **PARENT COUNTY:** Original county
- **MARRIAGE RECORDS:** start in 1856, kept by County Clerk
- **DIVORCE:** unknown, District Court
- **LAND:** 1856, Registrar of Deeds
- **PROBATE:** 1855, District Court

JEWELL
307 N. Commercial, Mankato, KS 66956, (785) 378-4020
skyways.lib.ks.us/counties/JW
- **INCORPORATED:** Feb. 1870
- **PARENT COUNTY:** Unorganized Territory
- **MARRIAGE RECORDS:** start in 1871, kept by District Court
- **DIVORCE:** 1813, District Court
- **LAND:** 1871, Registrar of Deeds
- **PROBATE:** 1813, District Court
- **COURT:** 1813, District Court
- **NOTES:** Registrar of Deeds has birth, death records 1886-1908.

JOHNSON
111 S. Cherry, Suite 1200, Olathe, KS 66061, (913) 715-0780,
<www.jocogov.org>
- **INCORPORATED:** Aug. 25, 1855
- **PARENT COUNTY:** Original county
- **MARRIAGE RECORDS:** start in 1857, kept by Probate Court
- **DIVORCE:** 1860, District Court
- **PROBATE:** 1857, Probate Court
- **COURT:** 1861, District Court
- **LAND:** 1857, Registrar of Deeds
- **NATURALIZATION:** 1870, District Court

KANSAS
- **INCORPORATED:** 1873
- **PARENT COUNTY:** Unorganized Territory
- **NOTES:** Created in 1873 from unorganized lands, absorbed into Seward County in 1883. Reorganized in 1886 as Morton County.

KEARNY
304 N. Main St., Box 86, Lakin, KS 67860, (620) 355-6422,
<www.kearnycountykansas.com>
- **INCORPORATED:** March 27, 1888
- **PARENT COUNTY:** Unorganized Territory
- **DIVORCE RECORDS:** start in 1894, kept by District Court
- **LAND:** 1894, Registrar of Deeds
- **PROBATE:** 1895, District Court
- **COURT:** 1894, District Court
- **LOCAL CENSUS:** 1913, County Appraiser
- **NOTES:** County Clerk has birth, marriage, death records 1900-1910. Find newspapers with County Clerk and Historical Society. Created in 1873 from unorganized lands. Absorbed by Finney and Hamilton in 1883. Re-created in 1887 with same boundaries and formally organized in 1889. A 1904 fire destroyed many county records.

KINGMAN
138 N. Spruce St., Kingman, KS 67068, (620) 523-2521, **<www.kingmancoks.com>**
- **INCORPORATED:** March 7, 1872
- **PARENT COUNTY:** Reno
- **MARRIAGE RECORDS:** start in 1875, kept by District Court
- **DIVORCE:** 1874, District Court
- **LAND:** 1874, Registrar of Deeds
- **PROBATE:** 1874, District Court
- **COURT:** 1874, District Court

KIOWA
211 E. Florida, Greensburg, KS 67054, (620) 723-3366, **<www.kiowacountyks.org>**
- **INCORPORATED:** March 25, 1886
- **PARENT COUNTIES:** Comanche, Edwards
- **LAND RECORDS:** start in 1886, kept by Registrar of Deeds
- **PROBATE:** 1886, District Court
- **COURT:** 1886, District Court

KIOWA, OLD
- **INCORPORATED:** Feb. 26, 1867
- **PARENT COUNTY:** Marion
- **NOTES:** Absorbed by Edwards and Comanche in 1875. Kiowa re-created Feb. 10, 1886 from parts of Edwards and Comanche.

LABETTE
517 Merchant St., Box 387, Oswego, KS 67356, (620)795-2138, **<www.labettecounty.com>**
- **INCORPORATED:** Feb. 26, 1867
- **PARENT COUNTY:** Neosho
- **DIVORCE RECORDS:** start in 1870, kept by District Court
- **PROBATE AND WILLS:** 1868, Probate Court
- **COURT:** 1870, District Court
- **NOTES:** County Clerk has birth records 1885-1891 and death 1885-1889. Registrar of Deeds has land records 1868-1919. Probate Court has marriages 1867-1920. Yearly county census taken 1915-1979.

LANE
144 S. Lane, Box 788, Dighton, KS 67839, (620) 397-5356, **<skyways.lib.ks.us/genweb/lane>**
- **INCORPORATED:** June 3, 1886
- **PARENT COUNTIES:** Unorganized Territory, Pekedon Territory
- **DIVORCE RECORDS:** start in 1887, kept by District Court
- **LAND:** 1887, Registrar of Deeds
- **PROBATE:** 1887, District Court
- **COURT:** 1887, District Court

LEAVENWORTH
300 Walnut, Leavenworth, KS 66048, (913) 684-0422, **<www.leavenworthcounty.org>**
- **INCORPORATED:** Aug. 25, 1855
- **PARENT COUNTY:** Original county
- **MARRIAGE RECORDS:** start in 1855, kept by Probate Judge
- **LAND:** 1857, Registrar of Deeds
- **PROBATE:** 1855, Probate Court
- **COURT:** 1855, District Court
- **WILLS:** 1857, Probate Court

LINCOLN
216 E. Lincoln, Lincoln, KS 67455, (785) 524-4757, **<www.lincolncoks.com>**
- **INCORPORATED:** 1870
- **PARENT COUNTY:** Unorganized Territory
- **BIRTH RECORDS:** start in 1886, kept by Lincoln City Hall
- **DIVORCE:** 1880, District Court
- **MARRIAGE:** 1871, District Court
- **LAND:** 1871, Registrar of Deeds
- **PROBATE:** 1880, District Court
- **COURT:** 1880, District Court
- **NOTES:** Lincoln City Hall has death records 1886-1989.

LINN
315 Main St., Box 350, Mound City, KS 66056, (913) 795-2668, **<www.linncountyks.com>**
- **INCORPORATED:** Aug. 30, 1855
- **PARENT COUNTY:** Original county
- **BIRTH RECORDS:** start in 1885, kept by County Clerk
- **MARRIAGE:** 1855, County Clerk/Probate Judge
- **DEATH:** 1885, County Clerk
- **DIVORCE:** 1856, County Clerk
- **PROBATE:** 1856, Probate Court
- **COURT:** 1856, County Clerk
- **LAND:** 1857, Registrar of Deeds
- **NATURALIZATION:** 1868, District Court
- **WILLS:**1866, Probate Court
- **NOTES:** Registrar of Deeds has military records 1919-1960.

LOGAN
710 W. Second, Oakley, KS 67748, (785) 672-4244, **<skyways.lib.ks.us/genweb/logan>**
- **INCORPORATED:** Sep. 17, 1887
- **PARENT COUNTY:** St. John
- **MARRIAGE RECORDS:** start in 1888, kept by District Court
- **DIVORCE:** 1887, District Court
- **LAND:** 1885, Registrar of Deeds
- **PROBATE:** 1887, District Court
- **COURT:** 1887, District Court
- **NOTES:** Clerk of District Court has naturalization records 1908-1926. Formerly St. John County. Name changed Feb. 24, 1887.

LYKINS
- **INCORPORATED:** Aug. 25, 1855
- **PARENT COUNTY:** Original county
- **NOTES:** See Miami County. Name changed to Miami June 3, 1861.

LYON
430 Commercial St., Emporia, KS 66801, (620) 341-3245, **<www.lyoncounty.org>**
- **INCORPORATED:** 1858
- **PARENT COUNTY:** Original county
- **BIRTH RECORDS:** start in 1885, kept by County Historical Society
- **MARRIAGE:** 1856, District Court
- **DIVORCE:** 1860, District Court
- **DEATH:** 1885, County Historical Society
- **LAND:** 1856, Registrar of Deeds
- **PROBATE:** 1859, District Court

- **COURT:** 1858, District Court
- **NOTES:** Formerly Breckenridge County. Name changed Feb. 5, 1862.

MADISON

- **INCORPORATED:** 1855
- **PARENT COUNTY:** Original county
- **NOTES:** Created in 1855. In 1861 it was divided between Greenwood and and Breckenridge (now Lyon).

MARION

Box 219, Madison, KS 66861, (620) 382-2185,
<www.marioncoks.net>

- **INCORPORATED:** Aug. 30, 1855
- **PARENT COUNTY:** Original county
- **MARRIAGE RECORDS:** start in 1866, kept by Probate Court
- **DIVORCE:** unknown, District Court
- **LAND:** 1870, Registrar of Deeds
- **PROBATE:** 1870, Probate Court
- **COURT:** 1867, District Court
- **NATURALIZATION:** 1870, District Court
- **NOTES:** County Clerk has birth and death records 1885-1902. Created Aug. 30, 1855 as original county but later disappeared. Organized in 1860 as smaller county and enlarged in 1865 to include Peketon area. Reduced in area as other counties formed from it.

MARSHALL

1201 Broadway, Marysville, KS 66508, (785) 562-5361,
<www.marshall.kansasgov.com>

- **INCORPORATED:** Aug. 25, 1855
- **PARENT COUNTY:** Original county
- **MARRIAGE RECORDS:** start in 1857, kept by Probate Court
- **DIVORCE:** 1863, District Court
- **LAND:** 1859, Probate Court
- **PROBATE:** 1857, Probate Court
- **COURT:** 1858, District Court
- **NOTES:** County Clerk has birth records 1885-1911 and death records 1889-1911.

MCGEE

- **INCORPORATED:** Aug. 30, 1855
- **PARENT COUNTY:** Unorganized Territory
- **NOTES:** Created Aug. 25, 1855 as an original county. Name changed to Cherokee County Feb. 18, 1860.

MCPHERSON

Box 425, McPherson, KS 67460, (620) 241-3656,
<www.mcphersoncountyks.us>

- **INCORPORATED:** March 1, 1870
- **PARENT COUNTIES:** Peketon, Marion
- **DIVORCE RECORDS:** start in 1871, kept by District Court
- **LAND:** 1870, Registrar of Deeds
- **COURT:** 1871, District Court
- **NOTES:** County Clerk has birth and death records 1874-1911. Clerk of District Court has marriage records 1870-1951, naturalization records 1908-1929, and Probate records 1859-1923. Originally part of Peketon County. Became a township of Marion County when Peketon was abolished. Organized as a county in 1870.

MEADE

200 N. Fowler St., Box 278, Meade, KS 67864, (620) 873-8700,
<www.meadeco.org>

- **INCORPORATED:** March 30, 1873
- **PARENT COUNTY:** Unorganized Territory
- **BIRTH RECORDS:** start in ca. 1900, kept by District Court
- **MARRIAGE:** ca. 1900, Probate Judge
- **DIVORCE:** ca. 1900, District Court
- **LAND:** 1884, Registrar of Deeds
- **PROBATE:** ca. 1900, District Court
- **COURT:** ca. 1900, District Court
- **NOTES:** Created March 30, 1873 from unorganized lands. Divided in 1883 between Seward, Finney, and Ford counties. Reorganized in the same area but with slightly different boundaries Nov. 3, 1885.

MIAMI

201 S. Pearl St., Suite 102, Paola, KS 66071, (913) 294-3976,
<www.miamicountyks.org>

- **INCORPORATED:** Aug. 30, 1855
- **PARENT COUNTY:** Original county
- **BIRTH RECORDS:** start in 1885, kept by Probate Court
- **MARRIAGE:** 1857, Probate Court
- **DIVORCE:** 1857, District Court
- **DEATH:** 1885, Probate Court
- **LAND:** 1857, Registrar of Deeds
- **PROBATE:** 1857, Probate Court
- **COURT:** 1858, District Court
- **NATURALIZATION:** 1867, District Court
- **WILLS:** 1857, Probate Court
- **NOTES:** Formerly Lykins County. Name changed June 3, 1861.

MITCHELL

111 S. Henry, Box 190, Beloit, KS 67420, (785) 738-3652,
<www.mcks.org>

- **INCORPORATED:** Feb. 26, 1867
- **PARENT COUNTY:** Unorganized Territory
- **MARRIAGE RECORDS:** start in 1870, kept by District Court
- **DIVORCE:** 1875, District Court
- **LAND:** 1871, Registrar of Deeds
- **PROBATE:** ca. 1870, District Court
- **COURT:** ca. 1875, District Court

MONTGOMERY

217 E. Myrtle, Box 446, Independence, KS 67301, (620) 330-1200,
<www.mgcountyks.org>

- **INCORPORATED:** Feb. 26, 1867
- **PARENT COUNTY:** Wilson
- **DIVORCE RECORDS:** start in 1871, kept by District Court
- **PROBATE:** 1870, District Court
- **COURT:** 1871, District Court
- **WILLS:**1870 District Court
- **NOTES:** County Clerk has birth records 1888-1911 and death records 1887-1911. Registrar of Deeds has land records 1870-1886. Clerk of District Court has marriage records 1870-1918 and naturalization records 1870-1917.

MORRIS

501 W. Main St., Council Grove, KS 66846, (620) 767-5518,
<www.morriscountyks.org>

- **INCORPORATED:** Aug. 30, 1855
- **PARENT COUNTY:** Original county
- **MARRIAGE RECORDS:** start in 1859, kept by District Court
- **DIVORCE:** 1860, District Court
- **LAND:** 1858, Registrar of Deeds
- **PROBATE:** 1856, Probate Court
- **COURT:** 1860, District Court
- **NOTES:** County Clerk has military discharge records 1917-1999. Clerk of District Court has naturalization records 1907-1929. Formerly Wise County, name changed to Morris Feb. 11, 1859.

MORTON

1025 Morton St., Box 1116, Elkhart, KS 67950, (620) 697-2157,
<www.mtcoks.com>

- **INCORPORATED:** Feb. 18, 1886
- **PARENT COUNTY:** Seward
- **MARRIAGE RECORDS:** start in 1887, kept by District Court
- **DIVORCE AND PROBATE:** ca. 1900, District Court
- **LAND:** 1886, Registrar of Deeds
- **COURT:** ca. 1900, County Clerkt

NEMAHA

607 Nemaha, Box 186, Seneca, KS 66538, (785) 336-2170,
<www.nemaha.kansasgov.com>

- **INCORPORATED:** Aug. 30, 1855
- **PARENT COUNTY:** Original county
- **MARRIAGE RECORDS:** start in 1861, kept by Probate Court
- **DIVORCE:** 1857, District Court
- **LAND:** 1858, Registrar of Deeds
- **PROBATE:** 1857, Probate Court
- **COURT:** 1859, District Court
- **NATURALIZATION:** 1859, District Court
- **NOTES:** County Clerk has birth, marriage, and death records 1885-1911. Courthouse burned in 1876. Some records were destroyed.

NEOSHO

100 S. Main St., Box 138, Erie, KS 66733, (620) 244-3811,
<www.neoshocountyks.org>

- **INCORPORATED:** June 3, 1861
- **PARENT COUNTY:** Dorn
- **BIRTH RECORDS:** start in 1892, kept by County Clerk
- **MARRIAGE:** 1864, Probate Court
- **DEATH:** 1892, County Clerk
- **LAND:** 1866, Registrar of Deeds
- **PROBATE AND WILLS:** 1867, Probate Court
- **NATURALIZATION:** 1868, District Court
- **COURT:** 1867, Probate Court
- **NOTES:** Registrar of Deeds has military discharges 1883-1947. Formerly Dorn County. Name changed in 1861; organized in 1864.

NESS

202 W. Sycamore St., Ness City, KS 67560, (785) 798-2401,
<www.nesscountyks.com>

- **INCORPORATED:** Feb. 26, 1867
- **PARENT COUNTIES:** Unorganized Territory, Peketon Territory
- **MARRIAGE RECORDS:** start in 1876, kept by District Court
- **DIVORCE:** 1876, District Court
- **LAND:** 1874, Registrar of Deeds
- **PROBATE:** 1876, District Court
- **COURT:** 1876, District Court
- **NOTES:** Created in 1867 from unorganized lands. First organized in 1873, disorganized in 1874, and reorganized April 14, 1880.

NORTON

105 S. Kansas, Box 70, Norton, KS 67654, (785) 877-5710,
<www.nortoncounty.net>

- **INCORPORATED:** Feb. 26, 1867
- **PARENT COUNTY:** Unorganized Territory
- **BIRTH RECORDS:** start in 1874, kept by County Clerk
- **MARRIAGE:** 1875, District Court
- **DIVORCE:** 1874, District Court
- **DEATH:** 1874, County Clerk
- **LAND:** 1874, Registrar of Deeds
- **PROBATE:** 1872, District Court
- **COURT:** 1874, District Court
- **NOTES:** Name changed to Billings March 6, 1873 and back to Norton Feb. 19, 1874. Registrar of Deeds has some cemetery records. Courthouse destroyed by fire Dec. 1, 1926; prior records incomplete.

OLD ARAPAHOE

- **INCORPORATED:** 1855
- **PARENT COUNTY:** Original county
- **NOTES:** Was under the territory of Kansas. Became part of the Colorado territory in 1861.

ORO

- **INCORPORATED:** Feb. 7, 1859
- **PARENT COUNTY:** Original county
- **NOTES:** Now part of Colorado.

OSAGE

717 Topeka Ave., Box 226, Lyndon, KS 66451, (785) 828-4812,
<www.osageco.org>

- **INCORPORATED:** Feb. 11, 1859
- **PARENT COUNTY:** Original County
- **MARRIAGE RECORDS:** start in 1889, kept by District Court
- **DIVORCE:** 1861, District Court
- **LAND:** 1858, Registrar of Deeds
- **COURT:** 1861, District Court
- **NATURALIZATION:** 1870, District Court
- **PROBATE:** 1859, Probate Court
- **WILLS:** 1861, Probate Court
- **NOTES:** County Clerk has birth records 1886-1921 and death records 1885-1909. Formerly Weller County. Name changed to Osage Feb. 11, 1859.

OSBORNE

423 W. Main , Box 160, Osborne, KS 67473, (785) 346-2431,
<www.osbornecounty.org>

- **INCORPORATED:** Feb. 26, 1867
- **PARENT COUNTY:** Unorganized Territory
- **MARRIAGE RECORDS:** start in 1872, kept by Probate Judge
- **DIVORCE:** 1872, Probate Judge

- **LAND:** 1872, Registrar of Deeds
- **PROBATE:** 1872, Probate Judge
- **COURT:** 1872, Probate Judge
- **NOTES:** Created in 1867 from unorganized lands; organized in 1871.

OTOE
- **INCORPORATED:** Feb. 17, 1860
- **PARENT COUNTY:** Marion
- **NOTES:** Became part of Butler County Feb. 24, 1864.

OTTAWA
307 N. Concord, Minneapolis, KS 67467, (785) 392-2279,
<www.ottawacounty.org>
- **INCORPORATED:** Feb. 27, 1860
- **PARENT COUNTY:** Unorganized Territory
- **BIRTH RECORDS:** start in 1890, kept by District Court
- **DIVORCE:** 1890, District Court
- **DEATH:** 1890, District Court
- **LAND:** 1867, Registrar of Deeds
- **PROBATE:** 1890, District Court
- **NOTES:** Clerk of District Court has marriage records 1868-1890. Created in 1860 from unorganized lands; formally organized in 1866.

PAWNEE
715 Broadway, Larned, KS 67550, (620) 285-3721,
<www.pawneecountykansas.com>
- **INCORPORATED:** Feb. 26, 1867
- **PARENT COUNTY:** Marion
- **MARRIAGE RECORDS:** start in 1873, kept by District Court
- **DIVORCE:** ca. 1867, District Court
- **LAND:** 1867, Registrar of Deeds
- **PROBATE:** ca. 1867, District Court
- **COURT:** ca. 1867, District Court

PEKETON
- **INCORPORATED:** 1854
- **PARENT COUNTY:** Original territory
- **NOTES:** Abolished in 1867.

PHILLIPS
301 State St., Phillipsburg, KS 67661, (785) 543-6825,
<www.phillipscounty.org>
- **INCORPORATED:** Feb. 26, 1867
- **PARENT COUNTY:** Unorganized Territory
- **DIVORCE RECORDS:** start in 1867, kept by District Court
- **LAND:** 1867, Registrar of Deeds
- **PROBATE:** 1867, District Court
- **COURT:** 1867, District Court
- **NOTES:** Clerk of District Court has birth, death, marriage records 1872-1924, and naturalizations 1876-1906. County genealogical society has military records 1861-1865. Formally organized in 1872.

POTTAWATOMIE
207 N. First, Box 187, Westmoreland, KS 66549, (785) 457-3314,
<www.pottcounty.org>
- **INCORPORATED:** Feb. 20, 1857
- **PARENT COUNTY:** Riley
- **MARRIAGE RECORDS:** start in 1858, kept by Probate Court
- **DIVORCE:** unknown, Unified Court System
- **LAND:** 1858, Registrar of Deeds
- **PROBATE:** 1857, Probate Court
- **COURT:** 1861, County Court
- **NATURALIZATION:** 1866, District Court
- **NOTES:** County Clerk has birth and death records 1885-1911. Registrar of Deeds has military discharge records 1919-1970.

PRATT
300 S. Ninnescah St., Box 885, Pratt, KS 67124, (620) 672-4110,
<www.prattcounty.org>
- **INCORPORATED:** Feb. 26, 1867
- **PARENT COUNTY:** Marion
- **DIVORCE RECORDS:** start in ca. 1879, kept by District Court
- **LAND:** ca. 1879, Registrar of Deeds
- **PROBATE:** ca. 1979, District Court
- **COURT:** ca. 1879, District Court
- **NOTES:** Clerk of District Court has marriage records 1878-1911.

RAWLINS
607 Main St., Atwood, KS 67730, (785) 626-3351,
<www.rawlinscounty.info>
- **INCORPORATED:** March 20, 1873
- **PARENT COUNTY:** Unorganized Territory
- **LAND RECORDS:** start in 1881, kept by Registrar of Deeds
- **PROBATE:** 1881, District Court
- **COURT:** 1881, District Court
- **NOTES:** Clerk of District Court has marriage records 1880-1920.

RENO
206 W. First, Hutchinson, KS 67501, (620) 694-2514,
<www.renogov.org>
- **INCORPORATED:** 1873
- **PARENT COUNTY:** Marion
- **MARRIAGE RECORDS:** start in 1872, kept by County Clerk
- **DIVORCE:** 1872, District Court
- **PROBATE:** 1872, District Court
- **COURT:** 1872, District Court
- **LAND:** 1872, Registrar of Deeds
- **NOTES:** County Clerk has birth and death records 1890-1911 and cemetery records 1865-1978.

REPUBLIC
Box 429, Belleville, KS 66935, (785) 527-5691,
<www.republiccounty.org>
- **INCORPORATED:** 1867
- **PARENT COUNTIES:** Original county, unorganized land
- **LAND RECORDS:** start in 1865, kept by Registrar of Deeds
- **PROBATE:** ca. 1868, District Court
- **COURT:** ca. 1868, District Court
- **MARRIAGE:** 1872, District Court

RICE
101 W. Commercial St., Lyons, KS 67554, (620) 257-2232,
<www.ricecounty.us>
- **INCORPORATED:** 1871
- **PARENT COUNTY:** Marion
- **MARRIAGE RECORDS:** start in 1872, kept by District Court

- **DIVORCE:** 1898, District Court
- **LAND:** 1872, Registrar of Deeds
- **PROBATE:** 1898, Clerk of Probate Court
- **COURT:** 1898, District Court
- **NOTES:** Lyons City Clerk has birth records 1890-1911. Clerk of District Court has naturalization records 1907-1929.

RICHARDSON

- **INCORPORATED:** Aug. 25, 1855
- **PARENT COUNTY:** Original county
- **NOTES:** Name changed to Wabaunsee Feb. 11, 1859.

RILEY

110 Courthouse Plaza, Manhattan, KS 66502, (785) 537-6300,
<rileyco-ks.genweb.us>

- **INCORPORATED:** Aug. 25, 1855
- **PARENT COUNTY:** Original county
- **MARRIAGE RECORDS:** start in 1856, kept by Probate Court
- **DIVORCE:** 1859, District Court
- **COURT:** 1859, District Court
- **LAND:** 1859, Registrar of Deeds
- **PROBATE:** 1857, Probate Court
- **NATURALIZATION:** 1859, District Court
- **NOTES:** County Clerk has birth and death records 1892-1909. Registrar of Deeds has military discharge records 1919-1953.

ROOKS

115 N. Walnut St., Stockton, KS 67669, (785) 425-6391,
<www.rookscounty.net>

- **INCORPORATED:** 1872
- **PARENT COUNTY:** Unorganized Territory
- **MARRIAGE RECORDS:** start in 1874, kept by District Court
- **DIVORCE:** 1872, District Court
- **LAND:** 1872, Registrar of Deeds
- **PROBATE:** 1872, District Court
- **COURT:** 1872, District Court
- **NOTES:** Clerk of District Court has birth, death records 1888-1901.

RUSH

715 Elm, Box 220, La Crosse, KS 67548, (785) 222-2731,
<www.rushcounty.org>

- **INCORPORATED:** 1874
- **PARENT COUNTY:** Unorganized Territory
- **MARRIAGE RECORDS:** start in ca. 1876, District Court
- **DIVORCE:** 1874, District Court
- **LAND:** 1874, Registrar of Deeds
- **PROBATE:** 1874, District Court
- **COURT:** 1874, District Court

RUSSELL

Box 113, Russell, KS 67665, (785) 483-4641,
<www.russell.kansasgov.com>

- **INCORPORATED:** 1872
- **PARENT COUNTY:** Unorganized Territory
- **MARRIAGE RECORDS:** start in 1873, kept by District Court
- **DIVORCE:** 1872, District Court
- **PROBATE:** 1872, District Court
- **COURT:** 1872, District Court

SALINE

300 W. Ash, Salina, KS 67401, (785) 309-5820,
<www.saline.org>

- **INCORPORATED:** Feb. 15, 1860
- **PARENT COUNTY:** Unorganized land
- **MARRIAGE RECORDS:** start in 1860, kept by District Court
- **LAND:** ca. 1860, Registrar of Deeds
- **PROBATE:** ca. 1860, District Court
- **COURT:** 1870, District Court

SCOTT

303 Court St., Scott City, KS 67871, (620) 872-2420,
<www.scott.kansasgov.com>

- **INCORPORATED:** 1886
- **PARENT COUNTY:** Unorganized Territory
- **MARRIAGE RECORDS:** start in 1886, kept by Probate Judge
- **DIVORCE:** 1886, District Court
- **PROBATE:** 1886, District Court
- **COURT:** 1886, District Court
- **LAND:** 1886, Registrar of Deeds

SEDGWICK

515 N. Main, Suite 211, Wichita, KS 67203, (316) 383-7666,
<www.sedgwickcounty.org>

- **INCORPORATED:** 1870
- **PARENT COUNTIES:** Butler, Marion
- **MARRIAGE RECORDS:** start in 1870, kept by District Court
- **LAND:** 1870, Registrar of Deeds
- **PROBATE:** 1870, District Court
- **COURT:** 1870, District Court
- **NOTES:** Clerk of District Court has naturalization records 1870-1926.

SEQUOYAH

- **INCORPORATED:** 1873
- **PARENT COUNTY:** Marion
- **NOTES:** (See Finney) Name changed to Finney Feb. 21, 1883.

SEWARD

415 N. Washington, Liberal, KS 67901, (620) 626-3204,
<www.sewardcountyks.org>

- **INCORPORATED:** Jan. 17, 1886
- **PARENT COUNTY:** Unorganized land
- **MARRIAGE RECORDS:** start in ca. 1886, kept by District Court
- **DIVORCE:** ca. 1886, District Court
- **LAND:** 1886, Registrar of Deeds
- **PROBATE:** ca. 1886, District Court
- **COURT:** ca. 1886, District Court
- **NOTES:** Created in 1873 from unorganized lands in southwestern Kansas (not old Seward County in eastern Kansas). It was absorbed in 1883 by Kansas, Stevens and part of Meade counties. In 1886 it was organized and reduced in area as counties were divided from it.

SEWARD, OLD

- **INCORPORATED:** Aug. 30, 1855
- **PARENT COUNTY:** Original county
- **NOTES:** Created in 1855 as Godfrey County. In 1861 name changed to Seward (not the modern county of Seward), and again in 1867 to Howard. In 1875 Howard divided into Elk and Chautauqua counties.

SHAWNEE
200 E. Seventh, Room 107, Topeka, KS 66603, (785) 233-8200,
<www.co.shawnee.ks.us>
- **INCORPORATED:** Aug. 25, 1855
- **PARENT COUNTY:** Original county
- **LAND RECORDS:** start in 1859, kept by Registrar of Deeds
- **PROBATE:** 1859, Probate Court
- **NATURALIZATION:** 1865, District Court
- **NOTES:** County Clerk has birth, marriage, and death records 1894-1911. Third Judicial District Court has marriage records 1856-1913.

SHERIDAN
925 Ninth St., Box 899, Hoxie, KS 67740, (785) 675-3361,
<www.accesskansas.org/sheridan>
- **INCORPORATED:** 1880
- **PARENT COUNTY:** Unorganized Territory
- **MARRIAGE RECORDS:** start in ca. 1885, kept by District Court
- **DIVORCE:** ca. 1885, District Court
- **LAND:** 1880, Registrar of Deeds
- **PROBATE:** 1881, District Court
- **COURT:** ca. 1885, District Court

SHERMAN
813 Broadway, Room 102, Goodland, KS 67735, (785) 899-4802,
<www.sherman.kansasgov.com>
- **INCORPORATED:** 1886
- **PARENT COUNTY:** Unorganized Territory
- **DIVORCE RECORDS:** start in 1887, kept by District Court
- **LAND:** 1886, Registrar of Deeds
- **PROBATE:** 1886, District Court
- **COURT:** 1887, District Court
- **NOTES:** County Clerk has birth and death records 1888-1892 and marriage records 1886-1923.

SHIRLEY
- **INCORPORATED:** Sep. 6, 1866
- **PARENT COUNTY:** Original county
- **NOTES:** Shirley County was previously attached to Marshall County for judicial purposes. Name changed to Cloud Feb. 26, 1867.

SMITH
218 S. Grant St., Smith Center, KS 66967, (785) 282-5110,
<www.smithcoks.com>
- **INCORPORATED:** 1872
- **PARENT COUNTY:** Unorganized Territory
- **MARRIAGE RECORDS:** start in 1875, kept by Probate Judge
- **DIVORCE:** 1875, District Court
- **LAND:** 1872, County Clerk
- **PROBATE:** 1875, Probate Judge
- **COURT:** 1875, District Court

ST. JOHN
- **INCORPORATED:** March 13, 1881
- **PARENT COUNTY:** Wallace
- **NOTES:** Name changed to Logan Feb. 25, 1887.

STAFFORD
209 N. Broadway St., St. John, KS 67576, (620) 549-3509,
<www.staffordcounty.org>
- **INCORPORATED:** 1879
- **PARENT COUNTY:** Marion
- **MARRIAGE RECORDS:** start in 1879, kept by Probate Judge
- **LAND:** 1879, Registrar of Deeds
- **PROBATE:** 1879, Probate Judge
- **COURT:** 1879, Probate Judge
- **NOTES:** County Court has birth and death records 1885-1894.

STANTON
Box 190, Johnson, KS 67855, (620) 492-2140,
<www.stantoncountyks.com>
- **INCORPORATED:** 1887
- **PARENT COUNTY:** Unorganized Territory
- **MARRIAGE RECORDS:** start in 1887, kept by District Court
- **DIVORCE:** 1887, District Court
- **LAND:** 1887, Registrar of Deeds
- **PROBATE:** 1887, District Court
- **COURT:** 1887, District Court
- **NOTES:** Absorbed by Hamilton 1883. Reorganized Feb. 1887.

STEVENS
200 E. Sixth St., Hugoton, KS 67951, (620) 544-2541,
<www.stevenscoks.org>
- **INCORPORATED:** 1886
- **PARENT COUNTY:** Unorganized land
- **LAND RECORDS:** start in 1888, kept by Registrar of Deeds
- **PROBATE:** 1887, Probate Court
- **COURT:** 1887, District Court
- **NATURALIZATION:** 1887, District Court
- **NOTES:** Registrar of Deeds has military records 1914-1918. Stevens County was absorbed by Seward County in 1883. In 1886 it was reorganized with the same boundaries as it had in 1873.

SUMNER
501 N. Washington, Wellington, KS 67152, (620) 326-3395,
<www.co.sumner.ks.us>
- **INCORPORATED:** 1871
- **PARENT COUNTY:** Butler, Marion
- **LAND RECORDS:** start in 1873, kept by Registrar of Deeds
- **PROBATE:** 1871, District Court
- **COURT:** 1871, District Court
- **NOTES:** County Court has birth records 1887-1911 and death records 1893-1911. Clerk of District Court has marriage records 1871-1899.

THOMAS
300 N. Court St., Colby, KS 67701, (785) 462-4500,
<www.thomascountyks.com>
- **INCORPORATED:** March 6, 1873
- **PARENT COUNTY:** Unorganized Territory
- **DIVORCE RECORDS:** start in 1885, kept by District Court
- **LAND:** 1885, Registrar of Deeds
- **PROBATE:** 1885, District Court
- **COURT:** 1885, District Court
- **NOTES:** County Clerk has birth and death records 1885-1910. Probate Court has marriage records 1885-1910.

TREGO

216 Main St., WaKeeney, KS 67672, (785) 743-5773,
<www.tregocountyks.com>

- **INCORPORATED:** Feb. 26, 1867
- **PARENT COUNTY:** Unorganized Territory
- **MARRIAGE RECORDS:** start in 1878, kept by District Court
- **DIVORCE:** ca. 1900, District Court
- **LAND:** 1879, Registrar of Deeds
- **PROBATE:** ca. 1900, District Court
- **COURT:** ca. 1900, District Court

WABAUNSEE

215 Kansas St., Alma, KS 66401, (785) 765-3414,
<www.wabaunsee.kansasgov.com>

- **INCORPORATED:** Aug. 30, 1855
- **PARENT COUNTY:** Original county
- **COURT RECORDS:** start in 1860, kept by District Court
- **LAND:** 1858, Registrar of Deeds
- **NOTES:** County Clerk has birth and death records 1892-1911. Clerk of District Court has divorce records 1857-1917 and probate records 1857-1937. Created in 1855 as Richardson County and was an original county. Name changed to Wabaunsee in 1859.

WALLACE

Box 70, Sharon Springs, KS 67758, (785) 852-4282,
<www.wallacecounty.net>

- **INCORPORATED:** March 2, 1868
- **PARENT COUNTY:** Unorganized Territory
- **MARRIAGE RECORDS:** start in 1887, kept by District Court
- **DIVORCE:** 1889, District Court
- **LAND:** 1889, Registrar of Deeds
- **PROBATE:** 1889, District Court
- **COURT:** 1889, District Court
- **NOTES:** Clerk of District Court has birth, death records 1889-1911.

WASHINGTON

214 C St., Washington, KS 66968, (785) 325-2974,
<www.washingtoncountyks.net>

- **INCORPORATED:** 1859
- **PARENT COUNTY:** Unorganized Territory
- **LAND RECORDS:** start in 1870, kept by Registrar of Deeds
- **PROBATE:** 1862, Probate Court
- **COURT:** 1872, District Court
- **NOTES:** County Clerk has birth records 1887-1911 and death records 1885-1911. Clerk of District Court has marriage records 1862-1955 and naturalization records 1907-1928.

WASHINGTON, OLD

- **INCORPORATED:** 1855
- **PARENT COUNTY:** Original county
- **NOTES:** County absorbed by Peketon in 1860.

WELLER

- **INCORPORATED:** Aug. 30, 1855
- **PARENT COUNTY:** Original county
- **NOTES:** See Osage County. Name changed to Osage Feb. 11, 1859.

WICHITA

206 S. Fourth St., Drawer 968, Leoti, KS 67861, (620) 375-2731,
<www.wichitacounty.org>

- **INCORPORATED:** March 6, 1873
- **PARENT COUNTY:** Indian lands
- **MARRIAGE RECORDS:** start in 1887, kept by District Court
- **DIVORCE:** 1887, District Court
- **LAND:** 1886, Registrar of Deeds
- **PROBATE:** 1887, District Court
- **COURT:** 1887, District Court

WILSON

615 Madison St., Fredonia, KS 66736, (626) 378-2186,
<www.wilson.kansasgov.com>

- **INCORPORATED:** 1867
- **PARENT COUNTY:** Original county
- **NOTES:** Probate Judge has probate records 1869-1918.
- **MARRIAGE RECORDS:** start in 1864, kept by Probate Court
- **DIVORCE:** 1869, District Court
- **LAND:** 1868, Registrar of Deeds
- **COURT:** 1869, Probate Court

WISE

- **INCORPORATED:** Aug. 30, 1855
- **PARENT COUNTY:** Original county
- **NOTES:** See Morris County. Name changed to Morris Feb.11, 1859.

WOODSON

105 W. Rutledge, Yates Center, KS 66783, (620) 625-8605,
<www.woodsoncounty.net>

- **INCORPORATED:** Aug. 30, 1855
- **PARENT COUNTY:** Original county
- **MARRIAGE RECORDS:** start in 1860, kept by Probate Court
- **LAND:** 1858, Registrar of Deeds
- **PROBATE:** 1864, Probate Court
- **COURT:** 1864District Court
- **NOTES:** County Clerk has birth and death records 1853-1926.

WYANDOTTE

710 N. Seventh St., Kansas City, KS 66101, (913) 573-2901, **<www.wycokck.org>**

- **INCORPORATED:** Jan. 29, 1859
- **PARENT COUNTY:** Leavenworth, Johnson
- **COURT RECORDS:** start in 1871, kept by District Court
- **LAND:** unknown, Registrar of Deeds
- **PROBATE:** 1857, Probate Court Clerk
- **NOTES:** Clerk of District Court has divorce records 1871-1918. District Court and Probate Court have marriage records 1859-1917. Registrar of Deeds has military discharge records 1919-1929. District Court has naturalization records 1859-1947.

KENTUCKY

» BY EMILY ANNE CROOM

HISTORICAL OVERVIEW

Long home to Indians, Kentucky lay within territory claimed by France in 1682. In the 1750s, British colonials began exploring west of the Appalachian Mountains, moving down the Ohio River or through the Cumberland Gap into Kentucky. Britain's Proclamation of 1763 forbidding settlement west of the Appalachians was largely ignored by land speculators and adventurous North Carolinians and Virginians, who began building stockaded settlements in Kentucky in the 1770s. The region fell within the jurisdiction of Fincastle County, Va., in 1772 and became Kentucky County, Va., in 1776. During the American Revolution, Indians allied with the British raided the western frontiers, driving out many Kentucky settlers.

After the Revolution, bounty land for military veterans and cheap, fertile soil attracted settlers from the east, especially the worn-out tobacco lands of Virginia, North Carolina and Maryland. They often came via the Ohio River from Maryland, Pennsylvania, Virginia, and later from Ohio and Indiana. Thousands from Virginia and the Carolinas traveled along the Wilderness Trail to the Cumberland Gap. Others arrived from neighboring Tennessee, and a few from Europe. After several calls for separation from Virginia, Kentucky became the 15th state in 1792.

The Ohio River became a commercial avenue, with towns springing up along its banks. Some textile, timber and mining industries developed in Kentucky, but most of the state's residents were farmers and planters. Tobacco was king, and corn and wheat were staple crops of smaller farmers.

By 1860, the state's population included about 20 percent slaves, 5 percent foreign-born, and less than 1 percent free blacks. Despite its slave-state status, Kentucky had a large anti-slavery population. Choosing not to secede, the state furnished troops to both sides during the Civil War. In this border state, many Kentuckians preferred neutrality, but military engagements took place within its boundaries.

Railroads, coal mining, and tobacco farming invigorated the economy after the war. The development of the Tennessee Valley Authority in the 1930s and the coming of World War II encouraged manufacturing growth in Kentucky. While coal and tobacco remained the leading industries, others gaining importance since World War II include lumber, whiskey and food processing. By 1970, Kentucky's urban population surpassed its rural population by a small margin.

research tips

- Someone reportedly born in Virginia before 1792 may have been born in what is now Kentucky.
- The state archives, state historical society, and Filson History Society hold Kentucky research materials including censuses, county records and newspapers.
- Kentucky was never public domain land; land grants originated with colonial and state governments. But the process of acquiring land was confusing and inconsistent before statehood. Microfilm of many Kentucky land grant records is at the state archives and the Kentucky Historical Society. Subsequent land transactions between individuals were recorded at any court of record. Some colonial Kentucky land entries are in Fincastle County records, with records of Montgomery County, Va., after Fincastle was abolished in 1777. No records of Kentucky County, Va., are known to survive.

CENSUS RECORDS

- Federal census population schedules: 1810, 1820, 1830, 1840, 1850, 1860, 1870, 1880, 1900, 1910, 1920, 1930
- Federal mortality schedules: 1850, 1860, 1870, 1880
- Federal slave schedules: 1850, 1860. Schedules name slaveholders but rarely name slaves.
- Special census of Civil War Union veterans and widows: 1890 (incomplete)

RECORD HIGHLIGHTS

Kentucky first attempted statewide vital registration from 1852 to 1862, but some cities and counties again created these records in the late 19th century. The Office of Vital Statistics maintains birth and death records from 1911 forward and marriage and divorce certificates after mid-1958. Options for obtaining record copies are online **<chs.ky.gov/publichealth/vital.htm>**. The Kentucky Historical Society in Frankfort **<history.ky.gov>** and the Filson Historical Society in Louisville **<filsonhistorical.org>** hold microfilm of 19th and early 20th century vital records. Link to searchable indexes at **<www.kygenweb.net/vitals>**.

Until 1809, only the General Assembly could grant divorces; between 1809 and 1849 both the legislature and circuit courts had jurisdiction in these cases. The legislature was prohibited from handling divorces after 1849.

More than half of Kentucky's counties have suffered some record loss from fires and storms. Alternate sources can't replace all the information lost, but check for surviving records, resources of parent and neighboring counties, and records created in local, state and federal jurisdictions.

Kentucky has not taken state censuses. Although the 1790, 1800 and 1890 federal enumerations for Kentucky are lost, tax rolls provide important household data from 1782 forward. Besides some published abstracts in libraries, microfilmed tax records are available at the Kentucky Historical Society, Kentucky Department for Libraries and Archives **<kdla.ky.gov/collections.htm>**, Filson Historical Society, Family History Library (FHL) and Clayton Library in Houston **<houstonlibrary.org/clayton-library>**.

Other Kentucky-specific records found at Kentucky and other research libraries include these:

- Draper manuscripts at the State Historical Society of Wisconsin and other major libraries, especially "Series CC, Kentucky Papers," described in *Calendar of the Kentucky Papers of the Draper Collection of Manuscripts,* edited by Mabel Clare Weaks (State Historical Society of Wisconsin, 1925).
- Shane manuscripts, other than those in the Draper collection, at the Presbyterian Historical Society in Philadelphia and on microfilm at major libraries; described in *The Shane Manuscript Collection: A Genealogical Guide to the Kentucky and Ohio Papers* by William K. Hall (Frontier Press, 1990).
- *Index of Economic Material in Documents of the States of the United States: Kentucky, 1792-1904* edited by Adelaide R. Hasse (Carnegie Institution of Washington, 1910). This book can help identify material in state government documents.
- Kentucky militia records, 1786-1864
- School censuses from 1888 forward
- Confederate pensions to veterans or their widows from 1912 forward
- Records of depositors in Kentucky's two branches of the Freedman's Savings and Trust Company, on FHL microfilm

ARCHIVES, LIBRARIES, AND SOCIETIES

Adair County Genealogical Society
Box 613, Columbia, KY 42728

Adair County Public Library
307 Greensburg St., Columbia, KY 42728, (270) 384-2472

Ancestral Trails Historical Society
Box 573, Vine Grove, KY 40175, **<www.aths.com>**

Ballard-Carlisle Historical-Genealogical Society
Box 279, Wickliffe, KY 42087, **<www.ballard-carlisle-ky-genealogy.com>**

Bell County Historical Society
Box 1344, Middlesboro, KY 40965, **<www.bellcountymuseum.com>**

Boyd County Public Library
1740 Central Ave., Ashland, KY 41101, (606) 329-0090, **<www.thebookplace.org>**

Breathitt County Public Library
1024 College Ave., Jackson, KY 41339, (606) 666-5541, **<www.breathittcountylibrary.com>**

Breckinridge County Public Library
112 S. Main St., Box 248, Hardinsburg, KY 40143, (270) 756-2323, **<www.bcplibrary.org>**

Bullitt County Genealogical Society
Box 960, Shepherdsville, KY 40165

Butler County Historical and Genealogical Society
Box 435, Morgantown KY 42261

Campbell County Historical and Genealogical Society
8352 E. Main St., Alexandria KY, 41001, (859) 635-6407, **<www.rootsweb.ancestry.com/~kycchgs>**

Christian County Genealogical Society
1101 Bethel St., Hopkinsville, KY 42240, **<www.westernkyhistory.org/christian/ccgsbks.htm>**

Clay County Public Library
211 Bridge St., Manchester, KY, 40962, **<www.claycountypubliclibrary.org>**

Corbin Genealogical Society
99 Boone Ave., Corbin, KY 40701

Crittenden County Genealogical Society
Box 61, Marion, KY 42054, **<westernkyhistory.org/crittenden/gensoc.html>**

Cynthiana-Harrison County Public Library
104 N. Main St., Cynthiana, KY 41031, (859) 234-4881, **<www.cynthianalibrary.org>**

Daviess County Public Library
2020 Frederica St., Owensboro, KY 42301, (270) 684-0211, **<www.dcplibrary.org>**

Department for Health Services, Office of Vital Statistics
275 E. Main St. 1E-A, Frankfort, KY 40621, (502) 564-4212, **<chfs.ky.gov/dph/vital>**

Eastern Kentucky Genealogical Society
Box 1544, Ashland, KY 41105, **<www.deliverancefarm.com/eastern_kentucky_genealogical_so.htm>**

Eastern Kentucky University Libraries
521 Lancaster Ave., 103 Libraries Complex, Richmond, KY 40475, (859) 622-1790, **<www.library.eku.edu>**

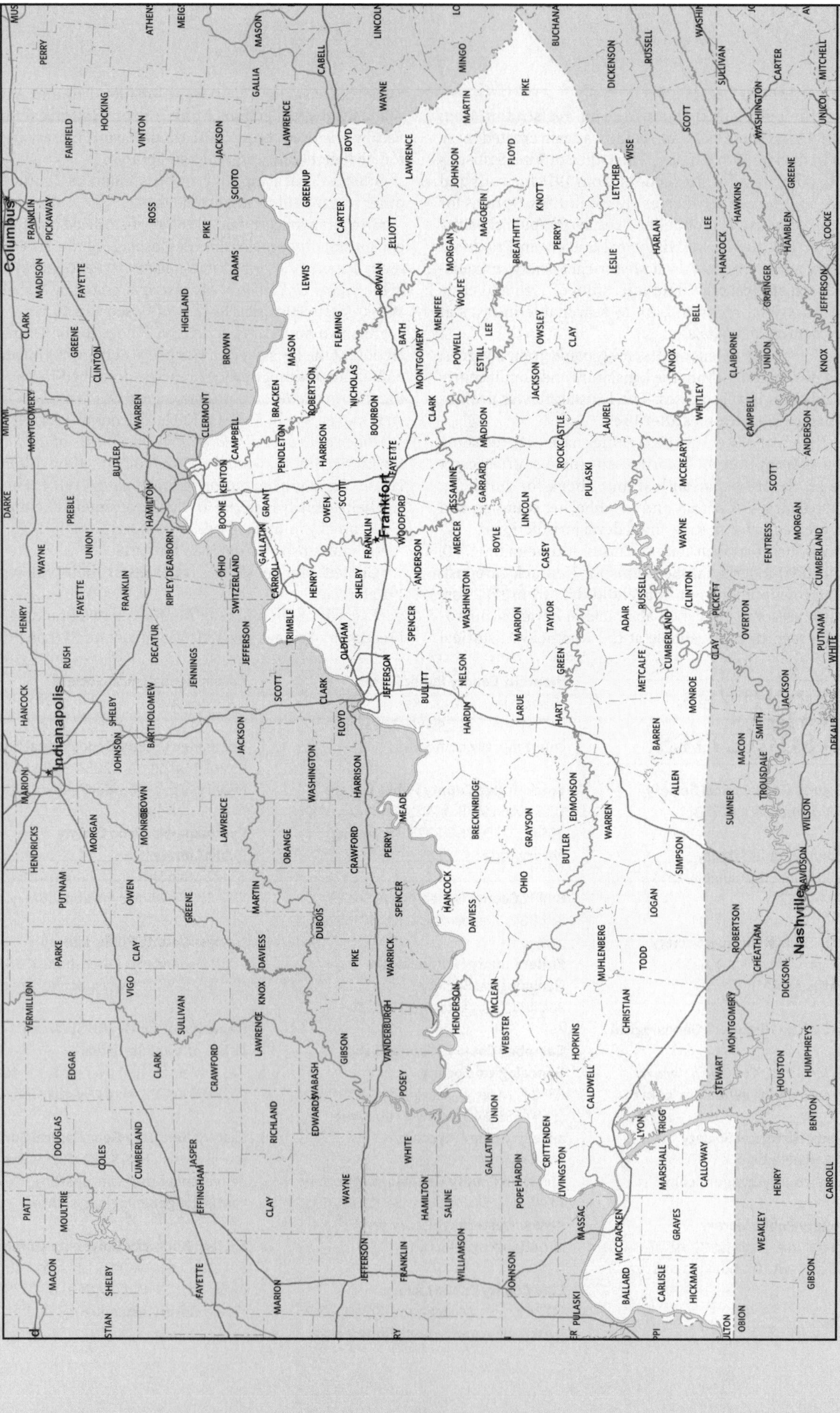
Columbus
Indianapolis
Frankfort
Nashville

Fayette County Genealogical Society
Box 8113, Lexington, KY 40533, **<www.rootsweb.ancestry.com/~kyekg/fayette.htm>**

Filson Historical Society
1310 S. Third St., Louisville, KY 40208, (502) 635-5083, **<www.filsonhistorical.org>**

Fulton County Genealogical Society
Box 1031, Fulton, KY 42041, **<www.rootsweb.ancetsry.com/~kyfulcgs>**

Fulton County Public Library
312 Main St., Fulton, KY 42041, (270) 472-3439, **<www.fultonlibrary.com>**

Gallatin County Public Library
209 W. Market St., Box 848, Warsaw, KY 41095, (859) 567-2786, **<gallatincountylibrary.org>**

Genealogical Society of Hancock County
Box 667, Hawesville, KY 42348, (270) 927-8095

George Coon Public Library
114 S. Harrison St., Box 230, Princeton, KY 42445, (270) 365-2884, **<www.youseemore.com/georgecoon/default.asp>**

Grant County Public Library
201 Barnes Rd., Williamstown, KY 41097, (859) 824-2080, **<www2.youseemore.com/grantcounty>**

Graves County Genealogical Society
Box 245, Mayfield, KY 42066, **<www.gravesgenealogy.org>**

Grayson County Historical Society
Box 84, Leitchfield, KY 42755, **<www.graysoncokyhistsoc.org>**

Green County Genealogical Society
Box 273, Greensburg, KY 42743, **<www.rootsweb.ancestry.com/~kygcgs>**

Greenup Public Library
614 Main St., Greenup, KY 41144, (606) 473-6514, **<www2.youseemore.com/Greenup>**

Harlan County Genealogical Society
Box 1498, Harlan, KY 40831

Harlan Heritage Seekers
Box 853, Harlan, KY 40831

Harrodsburg Historical Society
220 S. Chiles St., Box 316, Harrodsburg, KY 40330, (859) 734-5985, **<www.harrodsburghistorical.org>**

Hart County Historical Society
Box 606, Munfordville, KY 42765, (270) 524-0101, **<www.feenerty.com/history.htm>**

Henderson County Historical and Genealogical Society
Box 303, Henderson, KY 42419, (270) 830-7514, **<www.hendersonkyhistory.com/HCHGS>**

Henderson County Public Library
101 S. Main St., Henderson, KY 42420, (270) 826-3712, **<www.hcpl.org>**

Hickman County Historical Society
Route 3, Box 255, Clinton, KY 42031, **<www.rootsweb.ancestry.com/~kyhickma/hickman_historical.htm>**

Hopkins County Genealogical Society
Box 51, Madisonville, KY 42431, **<hopkinscounty.tripod.com/Genealogical_Society.htm>**

Jewish Genealogical Society of Louisville
3304 Furman Blvd., Louisville, KY 40220

John Fox Jr. Genealogical Library
323 High St., Paris, KY 40361, (859) 987-1786, **<www.kentuckydar.org/johnfoxjrlibrary>**

John L. Street Library
244 Main St., Cadiz, KY 42211, (270) 522-6301, **<www.tclibrary.org>**

Johnson County Historical and Genealogical Society
444 Main St., Box 788, Paintsville, KY 41240, (606) 789-4355, **<www.rootsweb.ancestry.com/~kyjchs/johnson.html>**

Kenton County Public Library
502 Scott Blvd., Covington, KY 41011, (859) 962-4060, **<www.kentonlibrary.org/genealogy>**

Kentucky Department for Libraries and Archives
300 Coffee Tree Rd., Frankfort, KY 40601, **<www.kdla.ky.gov>**

Kentucky Genealogical Society
Box 153, Frankfort, KY 40602, **<www.kygs.org>**

Kentucky Historical Society
100 W. Broadway, Frankfort, KY 40601, (502) 564-1792, **<history.ky.gov>**

Knott County Historical and Genealogical Society
Box 1023, Carew Dr., Duke's Branch, Hindman, KY 41822, (606) 785-5751, **<www.rootsweb.ancestry.com/~kyknott>**

Knox County Historical Society
Box 528, Barbourville, KY 40906

Laurel County Historical Society
Box 816, London, KY 40743, (606) 864-0607, **<laurelcountyhistoricalsociety.org>**

Laurel County Public Library
120 College Park Dr., London, KY 40741, (606) 864-5759, **<laurellibrary.org>**

Leslie County Public Library
22065 Main St, Hyden, KY 41749, (606) 672-2460, **<www.leslielibrary.com>**

Letcher County Historical and Genealogical Society
Box 312, Whitesburg, KY 41858, **<www.rootsweb.ancestry.com/~kyletch/lchgs>**

Lewis County Historical Society
318 Lexington Ave., Box 212, Vanceburg, KY 41179, **<www.rootsweb.ancestry.com/~kylewis/society.htm>**

Lexington Public Library Central Library
140 E. Main St., Lexington, KY 40507, (859) 231-5520, **<www.lexpublib.org>**

Logan County Genealogical Society
Box 853, Russellville, KY 42276, **<www.logancountygenealogicalsociety.org>**

Louisville Free Public Library
301 York St., Louisville, KY 40203, (502) 574-1611, **<www.lfpl.org>**

Louisville Genealogical Society
Box 5164, Louisville, KY 40255, **<www.rootsweb.ancestry.com/~kylgs>**

Louisville Presbyterian Theological Seminary
1044 Alta Vista Rd., Louisville, KY 40205, (800) 264-1839, **<www.lpts.edu/default.asp>**

Magoffin County Historical Society
191 S. Church St., Box 222, Salyersville, KY 41465, (606) 349-1607, **<www.rootsweb.ancestry.com/~kymhs>**

Marshall County Genealogical and Historical Society
1101 Main St., Box 373, Benton, KY 42025, (502) 527-4749, **<www.marshallcounty.ky.gov/index1.html>**

Mason County Genealogical Society
Box 266, Maysville, KY 41056

Mason County Museum and Library
215 Sutton St., Maysville, KY 41056, (606) 564-5865

McCracken County Genealogical Society
4640 Buckner Lane, Paducah, KY 42001

Metcalfe County Historical Society
Box 910, Edmonton, KY 42129

Muhlenberg County Genealogical Society
c/o Central City Public Library, Broad St., Central City, KY 42330

National Archives, Southeast Region
5780 Jonesboro Road, Morrow, GA 30260, (770) 968-2100, **<www.archives.gov/southeast>**

Nelson County Genealogical Roundtable
Box 409, Bardstown, KY 40004, (502) 348-3714, **<www.rootsweb.com/~kyncgr>**

Pendleton County Historical and Genealogical Society
Box 130, Falmouth, KY 41040, **<www.rootsweb.ancestry.com/~kypendle>**

Perry County Public Library
289 Black Gold Blvd., Hazard, KY 41701, (606) 436-2475, **<www.perrycountylibrary.org>**

Pike County Public Library District
119 College St, Pikeville, KY 41502, (606) 432-9977, **<www.pikelibrary.org>**

Pike County Society for Historical and Genealogical Research
Box 97, Pikesville, KY 41502

Pikesville College, Frank M. Allard Library
214 Sycamore, Pikeville, KY 41501, (606) 432-9698, **<www.rootsweb.ancestry.com/~kypike2/pikeaddys.html>**

Pulaski County Historical Society
Box 36, Somerset, KY 42502, (606) 679-8401, **<www.rootsweb.ancestry.com/~kypchs>**

Rowan County Historical Society
Box 60, Morehead, KY 40351

Russell County Historical Society
Box 544, Jamestown, KY 42629

Scott County Genealogical Society
c/o Scott County Public Library, 104 S. Bradford Lane, Georgetown, KY 40324, **<www.rootsweb.ancestry.com/~kyscgs/index.htm>**

Simpson County Archives and Museum
206 N. College St., Franklin, KY 42134, (270) 586-4228, **<www.rootsweb.ancestry.com/~kyschs>**

Southern Kentucky Genealogical Society
Box 1782, Bowling Green, KY 42102, **<www.kytnresearch.com/sokygen/meet.htm>**

Spencer County Historical Society
Box 266, Taylorsville, KY 40071

Van Lear Historical Society
Box 369, Van Lear, KY 41265, (606) 789-8540, **<www.vanlear.org>**

Wayne County Public Library District
159 S. Main St., Monticello, KY 42633, (606) 348-8565, **<www.waynecountylibrary.org>**

Webster County Historical and Genealogical Society
Box 215, Dixon, KY 42409, **<www.rootsweb.com/~kywebste/wch_gs.htm>**

West-Central Kentucky Family Research Association
Box 1932, Owensboro, KY 42302, **<www.rootsweb.com/~kywckfra>**

Western Kentucky University Libraries
1906 College Heights Blvd., #11067, Bowling Green, KY 42101, (270) 745-6125, **<www.wku.edu/Library>**

Woodford County Historical Society
121 Rose Hill Ave., Versailles, KY 40383, (859) 873-6786, **<www.woodfordkyhistory.org>**

GENERAL RESOURCES

Bibliography of County Resources by the Kentucky Historical Society (Kentucky Historical Society, 1990)

A Bibliography of Kentucky History by John Winston Coleman (University of Kentucky Press, 1949)

Biographical Cyclopedia of the Commonwealth of Kentucky by Eileene Sandlin (Southern Historical Press, ca. 1980)

The Biographical Encyclopaedia of Kentucky of the Dead and Living Men of the Nineteenth Century (J.M. Armstrong, 1878)

The Centenary of Catholicity in Kentucky by Ben. J. Webb (McDowell Publications, ca. 1980)

Early Families of Eastern and Southeastern Kentucky and their Descendants by William C. Kozee (Genealogical Publishing Co., 1973)

Early Kentucky Tax Records, from the Register of the Kentucky Historical Society (Genealogical Publishing Co., 1984)

The Fascinating Story of Black Kentuckians: Their Heritage and Traditions by Alice Allison Dunnigan (Associated Publishing, 1982)

Genealogies of Kentucky Families: From the Register of the Kentucky Historical Society by James C. Klotter (Genealogical Publishing Co., 1981)

Guide to Kentucky Archival and Manuscript Collections by Barbara Teague and Jane A. Minder (Kentucky Department for Libraries and Archives, ca. 1988)

A History of Kentucky Baptists: from 1769 to 1885 by John H. Spencer (J.R. Baumes, 1886)

The History of Kentucky by Zachariah Frederick Smith (Prentice Press, 1886; reprint, Courier-Journal Job Printing Co., 1980)

A History of Kentucky, Embracing Gleanings, Reminiscences, Antiquities, Natural Curiosities, Statistics, and Biographical Sketches by William B. Allen (Bradley and Gilbert, 1872; reprint, Green County Historical Society, 1972)

A History of Kentucky and Kentuckians, 3 vols., by E. Polk Johnson (Lewis, 1912)

Kentucky Bible Records from the Files of the Genealogical Records Committee, Kentucky Society, Daughters of the American Revolution (Kentucky Society, Daughters of the American Revolution, ca. 1962-1981)

Kentucky Family Records edited by Mrs. Edgar L. Cox (West Central Kentucky Family Research Association, 1969; reprint; McDowell Publications, 1991)

Kentucky Genealogical Research by George K. Schweitzer (The Author, 1981)

Kentucky; A History of the State by W.H. Perrin, et al. (Reprint: Southern Historical Press, 1979)

Kentucky Index of Biographical Sketches in State, Regional and County Histories by Michael L. Cook (Cook Publications, 1986)

Kentucky Research Outline by the Church of Jesus Christ of Latter-day Saints (online at **<www.familysearch.org/eng/search/rg/guide/kentucky.asp>**)

A Sesqui-Centennial History of Kentucky by Frederick A. Wallis (Historical Record Association, 1945)

☞CENSUS RECORDS

The 1787 Census of Virginia by Netti Schreiner-Yantis (Genealogical Books in Print, 1987)

☞LAND RECORDS

A Calendar of the Warrants for Land in Kentucky, Granted for Service in the French and Indian War by Philip Fall Taylor (Clearfield Co., 1995)

Index for Old Kentucky Survey's and Grants; Index for Tellico Surveys and Grants (Kentucky Historical Society, ca. 1975)

Kentucky Court of Appeals Deed Books by Michael L. Cook (Cook Publications, 1985)

The Kentucky Land Grants: A Systematic Index to All of the Land Grants Recorded in the State Land Office at Frankfort, Kentucky, 1782-1924 by Willard Rouse Jillson (Standard Printing Co., 1925)

Old Kentucky Entries and Deeds by Willard Rouse Jillson (1926; reprint, Genealogical Publishing Co., 1999)

☞MAPS

Atlas of Historical County Boundaries, Kentucky by John H. Long and Gordon DenBoer (Charles Scribner's Sons, ca. 1995)

Atlas of Kentucky by Richard Ulack (University of Kentucky Press, ca. 1998)

A Checklist of Kentucky Post Offices by Alan H. Patera and John S. Gallaher (The Depot, ca. 1989)

A Guide to Kentucky Place Names by Thomas P. Field (University of Kentucky, 1961)

Historic Maps of Kentucky by Thomas D. Clark (University Press of Kentucky, 1979)

An Historical Atlas of Kentucky and Her Counties by Wendell H. Rone Sr. (Progress Printing Co., 1965)

The Kentucky Encyclopedia by John E. Kleber (University Press of Kentucky, ca. 1992)

Kentucky Geographic Names by the US Office of Geographic Research (US Branch of Geographic Names, 1981)

Kentucky Place Names by Robert M. Rennick (University Press of Kentucky, 1984)
Kentucky Post Offices, 1794-1819 by Thelma M. Murphy (The Author, 1975)

Kentucky State Gazetteer and Business Directory for 1895-96 by R.L. Polk and Company (1895; reprint, Ancestral Trails Historical Society, 2000)

Kentucky's Bluegrass: A Survey of the Post Offices by Robert M. Rennick (Depot, 1993)

Pioneer Kentucky by Willard Rouse Jillson (State Journal, 1934)

☞MILITARY RECORDS

Compendium of the War of the Revolution by Frederick H. Dyer (1908; reprint, Morningside Bookshop, 1978)

The Corn Stalk Militia of Kentucky, 1792-1800 by Garrett Gleen Clift (Kentucky Historical Society, 1957)

Index to Veterans of American Wars from Kentucky (Kentucky Historical Society, 1966)

Kentucky Confederate Veteran and Widows Pension Index by Michael L. Cook and Alicia Simpson (Cook & McDowell Publications, ca. 1979)

Kentucky Soldiers of the War of 1812 by Minnie S. Wilder (Genealogical Publishing Co., 1969)

Kentucky in the War of 1812 by Anderson Chenault Quisenberry (Genealogical Publishing Co., 1969)

Kentucky's Revolutionary War Pensioners, Under Acts 1818-1832 by Kenneth Gene Lindsay (Kenma Publishing Co., ca. 1977)

List of the Revolutionary Soldiers of Virginia by H.J. Eckenrode (Virginia State Library, Archives Division, 1912)

Report of the Adjutant General of the State of Kentucky, Confederate Kentucky Volunteers, War 1861-1865 by the Kentucky Adjutant General (1915; reprint, Cook and McDowell, 1980)

Report of the Adjutant General of the State of Kentucky: Kentucky Volunteers, War With Spain, 1898-1899 by the Kentucky Adjutant General (Globe Print Co., 1908)

Revolutionary Soldiers in Kentucky by Anderson Chenault Quisenberry (Southern Book Co., 1959)

The Union Regiments of Kentucky by Thomas Speed and Alfred Pirtle (1897; reprint, Morningside House, ca. 1984)

PROBATE RECORDS

Abstract of Early Kentucky Wills and Inventories by J. Estelle Stewart King (Clearfield Co., 1993)

The County Courts in Antebellum Kentucky by Robert M. Ireland (University Press of Kentucky, ca. 1972)

Federal Courts in the Early Republic: Kentucky 1789-1816 by Mary K. Bonsteel Tachau (Princeton University Press, 1978)
Index to Kentucky Wills to 1851, the Testators by Ronald Vern Jackson and David Schaefermeyer (Accelerated Indexing Systems, ca. 1977)

Kentucky Pioneer and Court Records by Ednah Wilson McAdams (1929; reprint, Genealogical Publishing Co., 1975)

Virgina Supreme Court; District of Kentucky, Order Books, 1783-1792 by Michael L. Cook (Cook Publishing, ca. 1988)

VITAL RECORDS

Cemetery Records of Kentucky by Robert C. Jobson (the author, 1988)

Guide to Public Vital Statistics Records in Kentucky by the Historical Records Survey (Kentucky Historical Records Survey, 1942)

Inventory of Kentucky Birth, Marriage, and Death Records 1852-1910 by Jeffrey Michael Duff (Department of Library and Archives, 1980)
The Kentucky Gazette: Genealogical and Historical Abstracts by Karen Mauer Green (Gateway Press, 1983)

Kentucky Marriage Records, From the Register of the Kentucky Historical Society (Genealogical Publishing Co., 1983)

Kentucky Marriages, 1797-1865 by G. Glenn Clift (Genealogical Publishing Co., 1974)

Kentucky Obituaries, 1787-1854 by Garrett Glenn Clift (Genealogical Publishing Co., ca. 1977)

Kentucky Records: Early Wills and Marriages by Julia Spencer Ardery (1926; reprint, Genealogical Publishing Co., 1965)

Wilderness Road Cemeteries in Kentucky, Tennessee and Virginia by Robert Foster Johnson (McDowell Publications, 1981)

COUNTY DETAILS

ADAIR
424 Public Sq., Suite 1, Columbia, KY 42728, (270) 384-4703,
<www.adairconnection.com>
- **INCORPORATED:** Dec. 11, 1801
- **PARENT COUNTY:** Green
- **MARRIAGE RECORDS:** start in 1802, kept by the County Clerk
- **DIVORCE:** unknown, Circuit Court
- **LAND:** 1801, County Clerk
- **PROBATE:** 1804, Circuit Court
- **COURT:** 1802, Circuit Court
- **MILITARY:** 1802, County Clerk

ALLEN
201 W. Main St., Scottsville, KY 42164, (270) 237-3706,
<www.allencountykentucky.com>
- **INCORPORATED:** Jan. 11, 1815
- **PARENT COUNTIES:** Barren, Warren
- **MARRIAGE:** start in 1815, kept by the County Clerk
- **DIVORCE:** 1902, Circuit Court
- **PROBATE:** 1815, Circuit Court

ANDERSON
137 S. Main St., Lawrenceburg, KY 40342, (502) 839-3471,
<www.lawrenceburgky.org/Local_Govt.html>
- **INCORPORATED:** Jan. 16, 1827
- **PARENT COUNTIES:** Franklin, Mercer, Washington
- **MARRIAGE:** start in 1831, kept by the County Clerk
- **LAND:** 1827, County Clerk
- **PROBATE:** 1827, Circuit Court
- **COURT:** 1827, Circuit Court
- **SCHOOL:** unknown, County Clerk

BALLARD
Box 276, Wickliffe, KY 42087, (270) 335-5176,
<ballardcounty.ky.gov>
- **INCORPORATED:** Feb. 15, 1842
- **PARENT COUNTIES:** Hickman, McCracken
- **MARRIAGE:** start in 1852, kept by County Clerk
- **DIVORCE:** unknown, Circuit Court
- **LAND:** 1873, County Clerk
- **PROBATE:** 1879, Circuit Court
- **NOTES:** Courthouse burned in 1880.

BARREN
117 N. Public Square, Suite 1A, Glasgow, KY 42141, (270) 651-3783,
<www.barrenco-ky.com>
- **INCORPORATED:** Dec. 20, 1798
- **PARENT COUNTIES:** Green, Warren
- **MARRIAGE:** start in 1799, kept by County Clerk
- **DIVORCE:** unknown, Circuit Court
- **LAND:** 1795, County Clerk
- **PROBATE:** 1799, Circuit Court
- **COURT:** 1799, Circuit Court

BATH
Box 39, Owingsville, KY 40360, (606) 674-6346,
<www.bathcounty.ky.gov>
- **INCORPORATED:** Jan. 15, 1811
- **PARENT COUNTY:** Montgomery
- **BIRTH:** start in 1911, kept by state Office of Vital Statistics
- **MARRIAGE:** 1811, County Clerk
- **DIVORCE:** unknown, Circuit Court
- **DEATH:** 1911, state Office of Vital Statistics
- **LAND:** 1811, County Clerk
- **PROBATE:** 1811, Circuit Court
- **COURT:** 1811, Circuit Court
- **MILITARY:** unknown, County Clerk

BELL
Box 339, Pineville, KY 40977, (606) 337-3076,
<www.bellcounty.ky.gov>
- **INCORPORATED:** Aug. 1, 1867
- **PARENT COUNTIES:** Knox, Harlan
- **MARRIAGE:** start in 1867, County Clerk
- **LAND:** 1867, County Clerk

BOONE
2950 E. Washington Sq., Burlington, KY 41005, (859) 334-2112,
<www.boonecountyky.org>
- **INCORPORATED:** Dec. 13, 1799
- **PARENT COUNTY:** Campbell
- **MARRIAGE:** start in 1798, kept by County Clerk
- **PROBATE:** 1800, Circuit Court

BOURBON
Box 312, Paris, KY 40361, (859) 987-2142,
<www.bourboncountyclerk.ky.gov>
- **INCORPORATED:** 1786
- **PARENT COUNTY:** Fayette
- **MARRIAGE:** start in 1786, kept by County Clerk
- **DIVORCE:** unknown, Circuit Court
- **PROBATE:** 1786, Circuit Court
- **COURT:** 1786, Circuit Court

BOYD
Box 523, Catlettsburg, KY 41129, (606) 739-4131,
<www.boydcountyky.net>
- **INCORPORATED:** 1860
- **PARENT COUNTIES:** Carter, Lawrence, Greenup
- **MARRIAGE:** start in 1860, kept by County Clerk
- **DIVORCE:** unknown, Circuit Court
- **LAND:** 1860, County Clerk
- **PROBATE:** 1860, Circuit Court
- **COURT:** 1860, Circuit Court
- **MILITARY:** 1860, County Clerk

BOYLE
321 W. Main St., Room 111, Danville, KY 40422, (859) 238-1100,
<www.boyleky.com>
- **INCORPORATED:** Feb. 15, 1842
- **PARENT COUNTIES:** Mercer, Lincoln
- **MARRIAGE:** start in 1842, kept by County Clerk
- **DIVORCE:** unknown, Circuit Court
- **LAND:** 1842, County Clerk
- **PROBATE:** 1842, Circuit Court
- **COURT:** 1842, Circuit Court
- **MILITARY:** 1797, County Clerk

BRACKEN
Box 147, Brooksville, KY 41004, (606) 735-2952,
<resources.rootsweb.ancestry.com/USA/KY/Bracken>
- **INCORPORATED:** Dec. 14, 1796
- **PARENT COUNTIES:** Campbell, Mason
- **MARRIAGE:** start in 1797, kept by County Clerk
- **LAND:** 1797, County Clerk
- **PROBATE:** 1797, Circuit Court

BREATHITT
1137 Main St., Jackson, KY 41339, (606) 666-3800,
<www.breathittcounty.ky.gov>
- **INCORPORATED:** 1839
- **PARENT COUNTIES:** Clay, Estill, Perry
- **MARRIAGE:** start in 1852, kept by County Clerk
- **DIVORCE:** unknown, Circuit Court
- **LAND:** 1850, County Clerk
- **PROBATE:** 1884, Circuit Court
- **COURT:** 1873, Circuit Court

BRECKINRIDGE
Box 227, Hardinsburg, KY 40143, (270) 756-2269,
<www.breckinridgecountyky.com>
- **INCORPORATED:** Dec. 7, 1799
- **PARENT COUNTY:** Hardin
- **LAND:** start in 1800, kept in County Archives
- **PROBATE:** 1800, Circuit Court
- **COURT:** 1800, Circuit Court
- **NOTES:** County Archives has some marriage records from 1800, some birth records 1853-1969, some death records 1853-1993.

BULLITT
Box 768, 300 S. Buckman St., Shepherdsville, KY 40165, (502) 543-2262, **<www.bullittcounty.ky.gov>**
- **INCORPORATED:** 1797
- **PARENT COUNTIES:** Jefferson, Nelson
- **MARRIAGE:** start in 1797, kept by County Clerk
- **DIVORCE:** unknown, Circuit Court
- **LAND:** 1797, County Clerk
- **PROBATE:** 1796, Clerk/District Court
- **COURT:** 1797, Circuit Court
- **NOTES:** County Clerk has military discharge records 1921-1997.

BUTLER
Box 626, Morgantown, KY 42261, (270) 526-3433,
<www.butlercounty.ky.gov>
- **INCORPORATED:** 1810
- **PARENT COUNTIES:** Logan, Ohio
- **MARRIAGE:** start in 1814, kept by County Clerk
- **DIVORCE:** unknown, Circuit Court
- **LAND:** 1809, County Clerk
- **COURT:** 1810, Circuit Court

CALDWELL

100 E. Market St., Room 27, Princeton, KY 42445, (270) 365-6660,
<www.caldwellcounty.ky.gov>

- **INCORPORATED:** 1809
- **PARENT COUNTY:** Livingston
- **MARRIAGE:** start in 1809, kept by County Clerk
- **DIVORCE:** unknown, Circuit Court
- **LAND:** 1809, County Clerk
- **PROBATE:** 1809, Circuit Court
- **COURT:** 1809, Circuit Court
- **MILITARY:** unknown, County Clerk

CALLOWAY

101 S. Fifth St., Murray, KY 42071, (270) 753-2920,
<www.callowaycounty-ky.gov>

- **INCORPORATED:** 1821
- **PARENT COUNTY:** Hickman
- **MARRIAGE:** start in 1823, kept by County Clerk
- **DIVORCE:** unknown, Circuit Court
- **LAND:** 1823, County Clerk
- **PROBATE:** 1836, Circuit Court
- **MILITARY:** unknown, County Clerk
- **MINISTER BONDS:** unknown, County Clerk
- **ELECTION:** unknown, County Clerk

CAMPBELL

1098 Monmouth St., Newport, KY 41071,
<www.campbellcounty.ky.gov>

- **INCORPORATED:** Dec. 17, 1794
- **PARENT COUNTIES:** Harrison, Mason, Scott
- **MARRIAGE:** start in 1795, kept by County Clerk
- **LAND:** 1795, County Clerk
- **PROBATE:** 1794, Circuit Court

CARLISLE

Box 279, Bardwell, KY 42023, (270) 628-5451,
<carlislecounty.ky.gov>

- **INCORPORATED:** May 3, 1886
- **PARENT COUNTY:** Ballard
- **MARRIAGE:** start in 1886, kept by County Clerk
- **LAND:** 1886, County Clerk
- **PROBATE:** 1886, Circuit Court

CARROLL

440 Main St., Carrollton, KY 41008, (502) 732-7005,
<www.rootsweb.ancestry.com/~kycarro2>

- **INCORPORATED:** 1838
- **PARENT COUNTIES:** Gallatin, Henry, and Trimble
- **MARRIAGE:** start in 1837, kept by County Clerk
- **DIVORCE:** unknown, Circuit Court
- **LAND:** 1795, County Clerk
- **PROBATE:** 1838, Circuit Court
- **COURT:** 1838, Circuit Court

CARTER

300 W. Main St., Grayson, KY 41143, (606) 474-5188,
<www.cartercounty.ky.gov>

- **INCORPORATED:** April 10, 1838
- **PARENT COUNTIES:** Greenup, Lawrence
- **MARRIAGE:** start in 1838, kept by County Clerk
- **DIVORCE:** unknown, Circuit Court
- **PROBATE:** 1835, Circuit Court
- **COURT:** 1838, Circuit Court
- **NOTES:** County Clerk has birth and death records 1911-1954.

CASEY

Box 306, 625 Courthouse Sq., Liberty, KY 42539, (606) 787-8311,
<www.caseycounty.ky.gov>

- **INCORPORATED:** Nov. 14, 1806
- **PARENT COUNTY:** Lincoln
- **BIRTH:** start in 1911, kept by state Office of Vital Statistics
- **MARRIAGE:** 1807, kept by County Clerk
- **DIVORCE:** unknown, Circuit Court
- **DEATH:** 1911, kept by state Office of Vital Statistics
- **LAND:** 1807, County Clerk
- **COURT:** 1807, Circuit Court
- **NOTES:** Probate records can be found with County Clerk (1806) and Clerk of Circuit Court (1978).

CHRISTIAN

515 Weber St., Hopkinsville, KY 42240, (270) 887-4100,
<www.christiancountyky.gov/QCMS/Home.asp>

- **INCORPORATED:** March 1, 1797
- **PARENT COUNTY:** Logan
- **MARRIAGE:** start in 1797, kept by County Clerk
- **DIVORCE:** unknown, Circuit Court
- **LAND:** 1797, County Clerk
- **PROBATE:** 1797, Circuit Court
- **COURT:** 1797, Circuit Court

CLARK

Box 4060, 34 S. Main St., Winchester, KY 40392, (859) 745-0280,
<www.rootsweb.ancestry.com/~kyclark>

- **INCORPORATED:** 1793
- **PARENT COUNTIES:** Bourbon, Fayette
- **MARRIAGE:** start in 1793, kept by County Clerk
- **DIVORCE:** unknown, Circuit Court
- **LAND:** 1793, County Clerk
- **PROBATE:** 1793, Circuit Court
- **COURT:** 1993, Circuit Court

CLAY

102 Richmond Road, Suite 101, Manchester, KY 40962, (606) 598-2544, **<www.claycounty.ky.gov>**

- **INCORPORATED:** April 1, 1807
- **PARENT COUNTIES:** Madison, Floyd, Knox
- **MARRIAGE:** start in 1806, kept by County Clerk
- **DIVORCE:** 1955, Circuit Court
- **LAND:** 1807, County Clerk
- **PROBATE:** 1826, Circuit Court

CLINTON

100 S. Cross Street, Albany, KY 42602, (606) 387-5943,
<www.clintoncounty.ky.gov>

- **INCORPORATED:** Feb. 20, 1835
- **PARENT COUNTIES:** Wayne, Cumberland

- **MARRIAGE:** start in 1852, kept by County Clerk
- **LAND:** 1853, County Clerk
- **PROBATE:** 1863, Circuit Court

CRITTENDEN

107 S. Main St., Suite 203, Marion, KY 42064, (270) 965-3403, **<www.westernkyhistory.org/crittenden>**

- **INCORPORATED:** April 1, 1842
- **PARENT COUNTY:** Livingston
- **MARRIAGE:** start in 1842, kept by County Clerk
- **DIVORCE:** unknown, Circuit Court
- **LAND:** 1842, Circuit Court
- **PROBATE:** 1843, County Clerk
- **COURT:** 1843, Circuit Court

CUMBERLAND

Box 275, Burkesville, KY 42717, (270) 864-3726, **<www.cumberlandcounty.ky.gov>**

- **INCORPORATED:** Dec. 14, 1798
- **PARENT COUNTY:** Green
- **MARRIAGE:** start in 1927, County Clerk
- **DIVORCE:** start date unknown, kept by Circuit Court
- **LAND:** 1799, County Clerk
- **PROBATE:** 1815, Circuit Court
- **COURT:** 1820, Circuit Court
- **NOTES:** County Clerk has some marriage records 1882-1923

DAVIESS

Box 609, Owensboro, KY 42302, (270) 685-8434, **<www.daviessky.org>**

- **INCORPORATED:** Jan. 14, 1815
- **PARENT COUNTY:** Ohio
- **MARRIAGE:** start in 1815, kept by County Clerk
- **DIVORCE:** unknown, Circuit Court
- **LAND:** 1815, County Clerk
- **PROBATE:** 1815, Circuit Court
- **COURT:** 1815, Circuit Court

EDMONSON

Box 830, Brownsville, KY 42210, (270) 597-2624, **<www.edmonsoncounty.ky.gov>**

- **INCORPORATED:** Jan. 12, 1825
- **PARENT COUNTY:** Grayson, Hart, Warren
- **MARRIAGE:** start in 1825, kept by County Clerk

ELLIOTT

Main St., Box 225, Sandy Hook, KY 41171, (606) 738-5421, **<www.elliottcounty.ky.gov>**

- **INCORPORATED:** April 1, 1869
- **PARENT COUNTY:** Carter, Lawrence, Morgan
- **BIRTH:** start in 1911, kept by state Office of Vital Statistics
- **MARRIAGE:** 1874, County Clerk
- **DIVORCE:** 1957, Circuit Court
- **DEATH:** 1911, state Office of Vital Statistics
- **LAND:** 1869, County Clerk
- **PROBATE:** 1966, Circuit Court
- **COURT:** 1858, Circuit Court

ESTILL

Box 59, Irvine, KY 40336, (606) 723-5156, **<www.estillky.com>**

- **INCORPORATED:** Feb. 19, 1808
- **PARENT COUNTY:** Clark, Madison
- **MARRIAGE:** 1808, County Clerk
- **DIVORCE:** unknown, Circuit Court
- **LAND:** 1808, County Clerk
- **PROBATE:** 1808, Circuit Court
- **COURT:** 1808, Circuit Court
- **BURIAL:** 1808, County Clerk

FAYETTE

162 E. Main St., Lexington, KY 40507, (859) 253-3344, **<www.fayettecountyclerk.com>**

- **INCORPORATED:** June 30, 1780
- **PARENT COUNTY:** Kentucky County, Va.
- **MARRIAGE:** start in 1785, kept by County Clerk
- **DIVORCE:** unknown, Circuit Court
- **LAND:** 1782, County Clerk
- **PROBATE:** 1793, Circuit Court
- **COURT:** 1782, Circuit Court

FLEMING

100 Court Square, Flemingsburg, KY 41041 , (606) 845-8461, **<www.flemingcountyky.org>**

- **INCORPORATED:** 1798
- **PARENT COUNTY:** Mason
- **MARRIAGE:** start in 1798, kept by County Clerk
- **LAND:** 1798, County Clerk
- **PROBATE:** 1798, Circuit Court

FLOYD

Box 1089, Prestonburg, KY 41653, (606) 886-3816, **<www.rootsweb.ancestry.com/~kyfloyd/floyd.htm>**

- **INCORPORATED:** June 1, 1800
- **PARENT COUNTIES:** Fleming, Mason, Montgomery
- **MARRIAGE:** 1808, County Clerk
- **LAND:** 1810, County Clerk

FRANKLIN

Box 338, Frankfort, KY 40602, (502) 875-8702, **<www.franklincounty.ky.gov>**

- **INCORPORATED:** Dec. 7, 1794
- **PARENT COUNTIES:** Woodford, Mercer, Shelby
- **MARRIAGE:** start in 1795, kept by County Clerk
- **DIVORCE:** unknown, Circuit Court
- **LAND:** 1794, County Clerk
- **PROBATE:** 1795, Circuit Court
- **COURT:** 1795, Circuit Court

FULTON

Box 126, Hickman, KY 42050, (270) 236-2727, **<www.fultoncounty.ky.gov>**

- **INCORPORATED:** Jan. 15, 1845
- **PARENT COUNTY:** Hickman
- **MARRIAGE:** start in 1845, kept by County Clerk
- **DIVORCE:** unknown, Circuit Court
- **LAND:** 1845, County Clerk

- **PROBATE:** 1845, Circuit Court
- **COURT:** 1845, Circuit Court

GALLATIN

Box 1309, Warsaw, KY 41095, (859) 567-5411,
<www.rootsweb.ancestry.com/~kygalla2>

- **INCORPORATED:** Dec. 14, 1798
- **PARENT COUNTY:** Franklin, Shelby
- **MARRIAGE:** start in 1799, kept by County Clerk
- **DIVORCE:** unknown, Circuit Court
- **LAND:** 1798, County Clerk
- **PROBATE:** 1800, Circuit Court
- **COURT:** 1799, Circuit Court

GARRARD

15 Public Sq., Suite 5, Lancaster, KY 40444, (859) 792-3071,
<www.garrardcounty.ky.gov>

- **INCORPORATED:** Dec. 17, 1796
- **PARENT COUNTIES:** Madison, Lincoln, Mercer
- **MARRIAGE:** start in 1797, kept by County Clerk
- **LAND:** 1797, County Clerk
- **PROBATE:** 1797, Circuit Court
- **COURT:** 1797, Circuit Court

GRANT

107 N. Main St., Williamstown, KY 41097, (859) 824-3321,
<grantcounty.ky.gov>

- **INCORPORATED:** 1820
- **PARENT COUNTY:** Pendleton
- **MARRIAGE:** start in 1820, kept by County Clerk
- **LAND:** 1820, County Clerk
- **PROBATE:** 1820, Circuit Court

GRAVES

101 E. South St., Suite 2, Mayfield, KY 42066, (270) 247-1676,
<www.gravescounty.ky.gov>

- **INCORPORATED:** 1824
- **PARENT COUNTY:** Hickman
- **MARRIAGE:** start in 1852, kept by County Clerk
- **DIVORCE:** unknown, Circuit Court
- **LAND:** 1887, County Clerk
- **PROBATE:** 1887, Circuit Court
- **COURT:** 1853, Circuit Court

GRAYSON

10 Public Sq., Leitchfield, KY 42754, (270) 259-3201,
<www.graysoncounty.ky.gov>

- **INCORPORATED:** Jan. 25, 1810
- **PARENT COUNTIES:** Hardin, Ohio
- **MARRIAGE:** start in 1852, kept by County Clerk
- **DIVORCE:** unknown, Circuit Court
- **LAND:** 1896, County Clerk
- **PROBATE:** 1896, Circuit Court
- **COURT:** 1906, Circuit Court
- **MILITARY:** 1896, County Clerk

GREEN

203 W. Court St., Greensburg, KY 42743, (270) 932-5386,
<www.greencounty.ky.gov>

- **INCORPORATED:** Dec. 20, 1792
- **PARENT COUNTIES:** Lincoln, Nelson
- **BIRTH:** start in 1911, kept by state Office of Vital Statistics
- **MARRIAGE:** 1793, County Clerk
- **DEATH:** 1911, state Office of Vital Statistics
- **DIVORCE:** unknown, Circuit Court
- **LAND:** 1793, County Clerk
- **PROBATE:** 1793, Circuit Court
- **COURT:** 1794, Circuit Court

GREENUP

Box 686, Greenup, KY 41144, (606) 473-7394,
<www.greenupcounty.ky.gov>

- **INCORPORATED:** 1803
- **PARENT COUNTY:** Mason
- **BIRTH:** start in 1911, kept by state Office of Vital Statistics
- **MARRIAGE:** 1803, kept by County Clerk
- **DEATH:** 1911, state Office of Vital Statistics
- **DIVORCE:** 1803, Circuit Court
- **PROBATE:** 1822, Circuit Court
- **COURT:** 1838, Circuit Court

HANCOCK

Box 146, Hawesville, KY 42348, (270) 927-6117,
<www.hancockky.us>

- **INCORPORATED:** Jan. 3, 1829
- **PARENT COUNTIES:** Daviess, Ohio, Breckinridge
- **MARRIAGE:** start in 1829, kept by County Clerk
- **DIVORCE:** unknown, Circuit Court
- **LAND:** 1829, County Clerk
- **PROBATE:** 1830, Circuit Court
- **COURT:** 1834, Circuit Court

HARDIN

Box 1030, Elizabethtown, KY 42701, (270) 765-2171,
<www.hcky.org>

- **INCORPORATED:** Nov. 1792
- **PARENT COUNTY:** Nelson
- **MARRIAGE:** start in 1793, kept by County Clerk
- **LAND:** 1793, County Clerk

HARLAN

Box 670, Harlan, KY 40831, (606) 573-3636,
<www.rootsweb.ancestry.com/~kyharlan>

- **INCORPORATED:** 1819
- **PARENT COUNTY:** Knox
- **MARRIAGE:** start in 1820, kept by County Clerk
- **DIVORCE:** unknown, Circuit Court
- **LAND:** 1820, County Clerk
- **COURT:** 1820, Circuit Court

HARRISON

313 Oddville Ave., Cynthiana, KY 41031, (859) 234-7130,
<www.harrisoncounty.ky.gov>

- **INCORPORATED:** Dec. 21, 1793

- **PARENT COUNTIES:** Bourbon, Scott
- **MARRIAGE:** start in 1794, kept by County Clerk
- **DIVORCE:** unknown, Circuit Court
- **LAND:** 1794, County Clerk
- **PROBATE:** 1794, Circuit Court
- **COURT:** 1794, Circuit Court

HART

Box 277, Munfordville, KY 42765, (270) 524-2751,
<hartcounty.ky.gov>

- **INCORPORATED:** Jan. 28, 1819
- **PARENT COUNTIES:** Hardin, Barren
- **BIRTH:** start in 1911, kept by state Office of Vital Statistics
- **MARRIAGE:** 1852, County Clerk
- **DEATH:** 1911, state Office of Vital Statistics
- **LAND:** 1819, County Clerk
- **PROBATE:** 1819, Circuit Court
- **COURT:** 1819, Circuit Court

HENDERSON

Box 374, Henderson, KY 42420, (270) 826-3906,
<www.hendersonky.us>

- **INCORPORATED:** 1798
- **PARENT COUNTY:** Christian
- **MARRIAGE:** start in 1808, kept by County Clerk
- **DIVORCE:** unknown, Circuit Court
- **LAND:** 1797, County Clerk
- **COURT:** 1816, Circuit Court
- **PROBATE:** 1800, County Clerk; 1979, District Court
- **NOTES:** County Clerk has birth and death records 1911-1949.

HENRY

Box 615, New Castle, KY 40050, (502) 845-5705,
<www.henrycountygov.com>

- **INCORPORATED:** 1799
- **PARENT COUNTY:** Shelby
- **MARRIAGE:** start in 1800, kept by County Clerk
- **DIVORCE:** unknown, Circuit Court
- **LAND:** 1799, County Clerk
- **PROBATE:** 1800, Circuit Court
- **COURT:** 1800, Circuit Court

HICKMAN

110 E. Clay St., Suite E, Clinton, KY 42031, (270) 653-2131,
<www.rootsweb.com/~kyhickma>

- **INCORPORATED:** 1821
- **PARENT COUNTY:** Caldwell, Livingston
- **DIVORCE:** unknown start, kept by Circuit Court
- **LAND:** 1822, County Clerk
- **PROBATE:** 1822, Circuit Court
- **COURT:** 1822, Circuit Court
- **NOTES:** County Clerk has some birth records 1854-1909, some death records 1856-1909, and tax lists 1825-1829.

HOPKINS

24 Union St., Madisonville, KY 42431, (270) 821-7361,
<hopkinscounty.ky.gov>

- **INCORPORATED:** 1806
- **PARENT COUNTY:** Henderson
- **MARRIAGE:** start in 1807, kept by County Clerk
- **LAND:** 1807, County Clerk
- **PROBATE:** 1806, Circuit Court
- **COURT:** 1807, Circuit Court

JACKSON

Box 339, McKee, KY 40447, (606) 287-7800,
<www.jacksoncounty.ky.gov>

- **INCORPORATED:** 1858
- **PARENT COUNTIES:** Rockcastle, Owsley, Madison, Clay, Estill, Laurel
- **BIRTH:** start in 1911, kept by state Office of Vital Statistics
- **MARRIAGE:** 1858, County Clerk
- **DEATH:** 1911, state Office of Vital Statistics
- **LAND:** 1858, County Clerk

JEFFERSON

527 W. Jefferson St., Site 105, Louisville, KY 40202, (502) 574-5700, **<www.rootsweb.ancestry.com/~kyjeffer>**

- **INCORPORATED:** May 1780
- **PARENT COUNTIES:** Kentucky County, Va.
- **MARRIAGE:** start in 1780, kept by County Clerk
- **DIVORCE:** 1850, Circuit Court
- **PROBATE:** 1784, Circuit Court
- **COURT:** 1780, Circuit Court

JESSAMINE

100 N. Main St., Nicholasville, KY 40356, (859) 887-4121,
<www.jessamineco.com>

- **INCORPORATED:** Dec. 19, 1798
- **PARENT COUNTY:** Fayette
- **MARRIAGE:** start in 1799, kept by County Clerk
- **DIVORCE:** unknown, Circuit Court
- **LAND:** 1799, County Clerk
- **PROBATE:** 1799, Circuit Court

JOHNSON

230 Court St., Suite 124, Paintsville, KY 41240, (606) 789-2557,
<www.rootsweb.ancestry.com/~kyjohnso/johnson.htm>

- **INCORPORATED:** 1843
- **PARENT COUNTY:** Floyd, Morgan, Lawrence
- **BIRTH:** start in 1911, kept by state Office of Vital Statistics
- **MARRIAGE:** 1843, County Clerk
- **DEATH:** 1911, state Office of Vital Statistics
- **LAND:** 1843, County Clerk
- **PROBATE:** 1859, Circuit Court
- **COURT:** 1843, Circuit Court

KENTON

Box 1109, Covington, KY 41012, (859) 392-1620,
<www.kentoncounty.org>

- **INCORPORATED:** Jan. 29, 1840
- **PARENT COUNTY:** Campbell
- **MARRIAGE:** 1840, County Clerk
- **DIVORCE:** unknown, Circuit Court
- **LAND:** 1840, County Clerk
- **PROBATE:** 1840, Circuit Court
- **COURT:** 1840, Circuit Court

KNOTT

Box 446, Hindman, KY 41822, (606) 785-5651,
<www.rootsweb.ancestry.com/~kyknott2>
- **INCORPORATED:** 1884
- **PARENT COUNTIES:** Perry, Breathitt, Floyd, Letcher
- **MARRIAGE:** start in 1844, kept by County Clerk
- **LAND:** 1883, County Clerk
- **COURT:** 1888, Circuit Court

KNOX

401 Court Sq., Suite 102, Barbourville, KY 40906, (606) 546-3568,
<knoxcountyky.com>
- **INCORPORATED:** Dec. 19, 1799
- **PARENT COUNTY:** Lincoln
- **MARRIAGE:** start in 1800, kept by County Clerk
- **LAND:** 1800, County Clerk

LARUE

209 W. High St., Suite 3, Hodgenville, KY 42748, (270) 358-3544,
<www.laruecounty.org>
- **INCORPORATED:** March 4, 1843
- **PARENT COUNTY:** Hardin
- **MARRIAGE:** start in 1843, kept by County Clerk
- **DIVORCE:** 1979, Circuit Court
- **LAND:** 1843, County Clerk
- **NOTES:** Clerk of Circuit Court has probate records 1843-1979.

LAUREL

101 S. Main St., Room 203, London, KY 40741, (606) 864-5158,
<www.rootsweb.ancestry.com/~kylaurel>
- **INCORPORATED:** Dec. 12, 1825
- **PARENT COUNTIES:** Whitley, Clay, Knox, Rockcastle
- **MARRIAGE:** start in 1826, kept by County Clerk
- **LAND:** 1826, County Clerk
- **PROBATE:** 1826, Circuit Court
- Court: 1826, Circuit Court

LAWRENCE

122 S. Main Cross St., Louisa, KY 41230, (606) 638-4108,
<www.lawrencecounty.ky.gov>
- **INCORPORATED:** 1822
- **PARENT COUNTIES:** Floyd, Greenup
- **MARRIAGE:** start in 1822, kept by County Clerk
- **DIVORCE:** unknown, Circuit Court
- **LAND:** 1822, County Clerk
- **NOTES:** Clerk of Circuit Court has probate records 1822-1977.

LEE

Box 551, Beattyville, KY 41311, (606) 464-4115,
<www.leecounty.ky.gov>
- **INCORPORATED:** 1870
- **PARENT COUNTY:** Owsley, Breathitt, Wolfe, Estill
- **MARRIAGE:** start in 1870, kept by County Clerk
- **DIVORCE:** unknown, Circuit Court
- **LAND:** 1870, County Clerk
- **PROBATE:** 1873, Circuit Court
- **COURT:** 1870, Circuit Court

LESLIE

Box 916, Hyden, KY 41749, (606) 672-2193,
<www.lesliecounty.ky.gov>
- **INCORPORATED:** March 29, 1878
- **PARENT COUNTIES:** Clay, Harlan, Perry
- **MARRIAGE:** start in 1878, kept by County Clerk
- **DIVORCE:** unknown, Circuit Court
- **LAND:** 1879, County Clerk
- **PROBATE:** 1884, Circuit Court
- **COURT:** 1878, Circuit Court

LETCHER

156 Main St., Suite Whitesburg, KY 41858, (606) 633-2432,
<www.rootsweb.ancestry.com/~kyletch/letcher.htm>
- **INCORPORATED:** 1842
- **PARENT COUNTIES:** Perry, Harlan
- **MARRIAGE:** start in 1842, kept by County Clerk
- **LAND:** 1844, County Clerk
- **PROBATE:** 1871, County Clerk

LEWIS

Box 129, Vanceburg, KY 41179, (606) 796-3062,
<lewiscounty.ky.gov>
- **INCORPORATED:** 1807
- **PARENT COUNTY:** Mason
- **MARRIAGE:** start in 1807, kept by County Clerk
- **LAND:** 1807, County Clerk
- **PROBATE:** 1807, Circuit Court
- **COURT:** 1807, Circuit Court

LINCOLN

102 E. Main St., Suite 3, Stanford, KY 40484, (606) 365-4570,
<www.lincolnky.com>
- **INCORPORATED:** 1780
- **PARENT COUNTIES:** Kentucky County, Virginia
- **MARRIAGE:** start in 1781, kept by County Clerk
- **DIVORCE:** 1792, County Clerk
- **PROBATE:** 1781, Circuit Court
- **COURT:** 1781, Circuit Court

LIVINGSTON

Box 400, Smithland, KY 42081, (270) 928-2162,
<www.livingstonco.ky.gov>
- **INCORPORATED:** 1798
- **PARENT COUNTY:** Christian
- **MARRIAGE:** start in 1799, kept by County Clerk
- **DIVORCE:** unknown, Circuit Court
- **LAND:** 1800, County Clerk
- **PROBATE:** 1799, Circuit Court
- **COURT:** 1799, Circuit Court
- **NOTES:** Records through 1865 have been microfilmed.

LOGAN

Box 358, Russellville, KY 42276, (270) 726-6061,
<www.logancounty.ky.gov>
- **INCORPORATED:** 1792
- **PARENT COUNTY:** Lincoln
- **MARRIAGE:** start in 1790, kept by County Clerk

- **LAND:** 1792, County Clerk
- **PROBATE:** 1795, Circuit Court
- **COURT:** 1793, Circuit Court

LYON

Box 310, Eddyville, KY 42038, (270) 388-2331,
<www.lyoncounty.ky.gov>

- **INCORPORATED:** 1854
- **PARENT COUNTY:** Caldwell
- **BIRTH:** start in 1912, kept by state Office of Vital Statistics
- **MARRIAGE:** 1854, County Clerk
- **DIVORCE:** unknown, Circuit Court
- **LAND:** 1854, County Clerk

MADISON

101 W. Main St., Richmond, KY 40475, (859) 624-4703,
<www.madisoncountyky.us>

- **INCORPORATED:** Dec. 15, 1785
- **PARENT COUNTY:** Lincoln
- **MARRIAGE:** start in 1786, kept by County Clerk
- **DIVORCE:** unknown, Circuit Court
- **LAND:** 1787, County Clerk
- **COURT:** 1787, Circuit Court
- **PROBATE:** 1787, Circuit Court

MAGOFFIN

Box 1535, Salyersville, KY 41465, (606) 349-2216,
<magoffincounty.ky.gov>

- **INCORPORATED:** Feb. 22, 1860
- **PARENT COUNTIES:** Floyd, Johnson, Morgan
- **MARRIAGE:** start in 1860, kept by County Clerk

MARION

223 N. Spalding Ave., Suite 102, Lebanon, KY 40033, (270) 692-2651, **<www.marioncounty.ky.gov>**

- **INCORPORATED:** Jan. 25, 1834
- **PARENT COUNTY:** Washington
- **BIRTH:** start in 1911, kept by state Office of Vital Statistics
- **MARRIAGE:** 1852, County Clerk
- **DIVORCE:** unknown, Circuit Court
- **DEATH:** 1911, state Office of Vital Statistics
- **LAND:** 1863, County Clerk
- **COURT:** 1863, Circuit Court
- **PROBATE:** 1863, Circuit Court

MARSHALL

1101 Main St., Benton, KY 42025, (270) 527-4740,
<www.marshallcounty.ky.gov>

- **INCORPORATED:** June 1, 1842
- **PARENT COUNTY:** Calloway
- **MARRIAGE:** start in 1848, kept by County Clerk
- **LAND:** 1848, County Clerk

MARTIN

Box 460, Inez, KY 41224, (606) 298-2810,
<martincounty.ky.gov>

- **INCORPORATED:** Sept. 1, 1870
- **PARENT COUNTIES:** Lawrence, Floyd, Pike, Johnson
- **MARRIAGE:** start in 1871, kept by County Clerk
- **DIVORCE:** unknown, Circuit Court
- **PROBATE:** 1861, Circuit Court
- **COURT:** 1870, Circuit Court
- **NOTES:** County Clerk has birth records 1911-1949 and death records 1911-1949.

MASON

Box 234, Maysville, KY 41056, (606) 564-3341,
<www.masoncountykentucky.com>

- **INCORPORATED:** 1789
- **PARENT COUNTY:** Bourbon
- **MARRIAGE:** start in 1789, kept by County Clerk
- **DIVORCE:** 1929 Circuit Court
- **LAND:** 1789, County Clerk
- **PROBATE:** 1791, Circuit Court
- **COURT:** 1789, Circuit Court

MCCRACKEN

Box 609, Paducah, KY 42002, (270) 444-4700, **<www.co.mccracken.ky.us>**

- **INCORPORATED:** Jan. 15, 1825
- **PARENT COUNTY:** Hickman
- **MARRIAGE:** start in 1825, kept by County Clerk
- **LAND:** 1825, County Clerk
- **PROBATE:** 1826, Circuit Court

MCCREARY

Box 699, Whitley City, KY 42653, (606) 376-2411,
<www.mccrearycounty.com>

- **INCORPORATED:** 1912
- **PARENT COUNTIES:** Wayne, Pulaski, Whitley
- **MARRIAGE:** start in 1912, kept by County Clerk
- **LAND:** 1912, County Clerk
- **NOTES:** Records from 1923-1927 burned.

MCLEAN

Box 57, Calhoun, KY 42327, (270) 273-3082,
<www.mcleancounty.ky.gov>

- **INCORPORATED:** Jan. 28, 1854
- **PARENT COUNTY:** Muhlenberg, Daviess, Ohio
- **MARRIAGE:** start in 1854, kept by County Clerk
- **DIVORCE:** unknown, Circuit Court
- **LAND:** 1854, County Clerk
- **PROBATE:** 1854, Circuit Court
- **COURT:** 1854, Circuit Court
- **MILITARY:** 1854, County Clerk

MEADE

Box 614, Brandenburg, KY 40108, (270) 422-2152,
<www.visitmeadecounty.org>

- **INCORPORATED:** Dec. 17, 1823
- **PARENT COUNTIES:** Hardin, Breckinridge
- **DIVORCE:** unknown start, kept by Circuit Court
- **PROBATE:** 1824, Circuit Court
- **NOTES:** County Clerk has some marriage and land records from 1824.

MENIFEE
Box 123, Frenchburg, KY 40322, (606) 768-3512,
<www.menifeecounty.ky.gov>
- **INCORPORATED:** May 29, 1869
- **PARENT COUNTIES:** Powell, Wolfe, Bath, Morgan, Montgomery
- **MARRIAGE:** start in 1869, kept by County Clerk
- **DIVORCE:** 1869, Circuit Court

MERCER
Box 426, Harrodsburg, KY 40330, (859) 734-6310,
<www.mercercounty.ky.gov>
- **INCORPORATED:** Dec. 15, 1785
- **PARENT COUNTY:** Lincoln
- **MARRIAGE:** start in 1786, kept by County Clerk
- **DIVORCE:** unknown, Circuit Court
- **LAND:** 1786, County Clerk
- **PROBATE:** 1786, Circuit Court
- **COURT:** 1786, Circuit Court
- **MILITARY:** 1919, County Clerk

METCALFE
Box 25, Edmonton, KY 42129, (270) 432-4821,
<metcalfecounty.ky.gov>
- **INCORPORATED:** May 1, 1860
- **PARENT COUNTIES:** Monroe, Adair, Barren, Cumberland, Green
- **MARRIAGE:** start in 1867, kept by County Clerk
- **LAND:** 1868, County Clerk

MONROE
200 N. Main St., Suite D, Tompkinsville, KY 42167, (270) 487-5471,
<www.monroecounty.ky.gov>
- **INCORPORATED:** Jan. 19, 1820
- **PARENT COUNTY:** Barren, Cumberland
- **MARRIAGE:** start in 1863, kept by County Clerk
- **DIVORCE:** unknown, Circuit Court
- **LAND:** 1863, County Clerk
- **PROBATE:** 1863, County Clerk
- **COURT:** unknown, Circuit Court

MONTGOMERY
1 Court St., Suite 2, Mount Sterling, KY 40353, (859) 498-8700,
<www.montgomerycounty.ky.gov>
- **INCORPORATED:** Dec. 14, 1796
- **PARENT COUNTY:** Clark
- **BIRTH:** start in 1911, kept by state Office of Vital Statistics
- **MARRIAGE:** 1864, County Clerk
- **DIVORCE:** unknown, Circuit Court
- **DEATH:** unknown, Dept./Health
- **LAND:** unknown, County Clerk
- **PROBATE:** 1797, County Clerk
- **COURT:** unknown, Circuit Court

MORGAN
Box 26, West Liberty, KY 41472, (606) 743-3949,
<www.morgancounty.ky.gov>
- **INCORPORATED:** 1823
- **PARENT COUNTIES:** Floyd, Bath
- **BIRTH:** start in 1911, Kentucky Office of Vital Statistics
- **MARRIAGE:** start in 1823, kept by County Clerk
- **LAND:** 1823, County Clerk
- **PROBATE:** 1866, Circuit Court

MUHLENBERG
Box 525, Greenville, KY 42345, (270) 338-1441,
<www.muhlenbergcounty.ky.gov>
- **INCORPORATED:** 1799
- **PARENT COUNTIES:** Christian, Logan
- **MARRIAGE:** start in 1799, kept by County Clerk
- **DIVORCE:** unknown, Circuit Court
- **LAND:** 1798, County Clerk
- **PROBATE:** 1801, Circuit Court

NELSON
Box 312, Bardstown, KY 40004, (502) 348-1820,
<www.nelsoncountyky.com>
- **INCORPORATED:** Nov. 29, 1784
- **PARENT COUNTY:** Jefferson
- **MARRIAGE:** start in 1785, kept by County Clerk
- **PROBATE:** 1784, Circuit Court

NICHOLAS
Box 227, Carlisle, KY 40311, (859) 289-3730,
<www.nicholascounty.ky.gov>
- **INCORPORATED:** 1799
- **PARENT COUNTY:** Bourbon, Mason
- **MARRIAGE:** start in 1800, kept by County Clerk
- **DIVORCE:** unknown, Circuit Court
- **LAND:** 1800, County Clerk
- **PROBATE:** 1800, Circuit Court
- **COURT:** 1800, Circuit Court

OHIO
301 S. Main St., Suite 201, Hartford, KY 42347, (270) 298-4422,
<www.ohiocounty.ky.gov>
- **INCORPORATED:** Dec. 17, 1798
- **PARENT COUNTY:** Hardin
- **MARRIAGE:** start in 1808, kept by County Clerk
- **DIVORCE:** unknown, Circuit Court
- **DEATH:** 1911, state Office of Vital Statistics
- **LAND:** 1799, County Clerk
- **PROBATE:** 1801, Circuit Court
- **MILITARY:** 1861, County Clerk

OLDHAM
100 W. Jefferson St., La Grange, KY 40031, (502) 222-0047,
<oldhamcounty.Kentucky.ky.us>
- **INCORPORATED:** Dec. 15, 1823
- **PARENT COUNTIES:** Henry, Shelby, Jefferson
- **MARRIAGE:** start in 1824, kept by County Clerk
- **DIVORCE:** unknown, Circuit Court
- **LAND:** 1824, County Clerk
- **PROBATE:** 1824, Circuit Court
- **COURT:** 1824, Circuit Court

OWEN
135 W. Bryan St., Owenton, KY 40359, (502) 484-2213,
<www.owencounty.ky.gov>
- **INCORPORATED:** Feb. 6, 1819
- **PARENT COUNTIES:** Scott, Franklin, Gallatin, Pendleton
- **BIRTH:** start in 1911, Kentucky Office of Vital Statistics
- **MARRIAGE:** start in 1819, kept by County Clerk
- **DEATH:** 1911, Kentucky Office of Vital Statistics
- **DIVORCE:** unknown, Kentucky Archives-Frankfort
- **LAND:** 1819, County Clerk
- **PROBATE:** 1820, Circuit Court
- **COURT:** 1819, Circuit Court

OWSLEY
Box 500, Booneville, KY 41314, (606) 593-5735,
<www.usgennet.org/usa/ky/county/owsley>
- **INCORPORATED:** 1843
- **PARENT COUNTIES:** Clay, Estill, Breathitt
- **MARRIAGE:** start in 1852, kept by County Clerk
- **DIVORCE:** unknown, Circuit Court
- **LAND:** 1929, County Clerk
- **PROBATE:** 1929, Circuit Court
- **COURT:** 1923, Circuit Court

PENDLETON
- Box 112, Falmouth, KY 41040, (859) 654-3380, **<www.pendletoncounty.ky.gov>**
- **INCORPORATED:** Dec. 13, 1798
- **PARENT COUNTY:** Bracken, Campbell
- **MARRIAGE:** start in 1799, kept by County Clerk
- **DIVORCE:** unknown, Circuit Court
- **LAND:** 1798, County Clerk
- **PROBATE:** 1841, Circuit Court
- **COURT:** 1799, Circuit Court

PERRY
Box 150, Hazard, KY 41702, (606) 436-4614,
<www.perrycountyky.org>
- **INCORPORATED:** Nov. 2, 1820
- **PARENT COUNTIES:** Clay, Floyd
- **MARRIAGE:** start in 1821, kept by County Clerk
- **DIVORCE:** unknown, Circuit Court
- **LAND:** 1821, County Clerk
- **PROBATE:** 1901, Clerk/District Court
- **COURT:** 1822, Clerk/District Court

PIKE
Box 631, Pikeville, KY 41501, (606) 432-6211,
<www.rootsweb.ancestry.com/~kypike>
- **INCORPORATED:** Dec. 19, 1821
- **PARENT COUNTY:** Floyd
- **BIRTH:** start in 1911, kept by state Office of Vital Statistics
- **MARRIAGE:** 1822, County Clerk
- **DEATH:** 1911, state Office of Vital Statistics
- **LAND:** 1820, County Clerk
- **PROBATE:** 1839, Circuit Court
- **NOTES:** County Clerk has school records 1895-1934.

POWELL
Box 548, Stanton, KY 40380, (606) 663-6444,
<www.powellcounty.ky.gov>
- **INCORPORATED:** Jan. 7, 1852
- **PARENT COUNTIES:** Clark, Estill, Montgomery
- **MARRIAGE:** start in 1852, kept by County Clerk
- **DIVORCE:** unknown, Circuit Court
- **LAND:** 1864, County Clerk
- **PROBATE:** 1864, Circuit Court
- **COURT:** 1864, Circuit Court
- **MILITARY:** 1864, County Clerk

PULASKI
Box 739, Somerset, KY 42501, (606) 679-2042,
<www.rootsweb.ancestry.com/~kypulask>
- **INCORPORATED:** 1799
- **PARENT COUNTIES:** Green, Lincoln
- **MARRIAGE:** start in 1799, kept by County Clerk
- **DIVORCE:** unknown, Circuit Court
- **LAND:** 1799, County Clerk
- **PROBATE:** 1801, Circuit Court
- **COURT:** 1799, Circuit Court

ROBERTSON
Box 75, Mount Olivet, KY 41064, (606) 724-5212,
<www.robertsoncounty.ky.gov>
- **INCORPORATED:** Aug. 1, 1867
- **PARENT COUNTIES:** Nicholas, Bracken, Mason, Harrison
- **MARRIAGE:** start in 1867, kept by County Clerk
- **DIVORCE:** 1867, Circuit Court
- **LAND:** 1868, County Clerk
- **PROBATE:** 1864, Circuit Court
- **COURT:** 1867, Circuit Court

ROCKCASTLE
205 E. Main St. #6, Mount Vernon, KY 40456, (606) 256-2831,
<www.rockcastlecountyky.com>
- **INCORPORATED:** 1810
- **PARENT COUNTIES:** Pulaski, Lincoln, Madison, Knox
- **MARRIAGE:** start in 1852, kept by County Clerk
- **DIVORCE:** 1873, Circuit Court
- **LAND:** 1865, County Clerk
- **PROBATE:** 1855, Circuit Court
- **COURT:** 1873, Circuit Court

ROWAN
627 E. Main St., Morehead, KY 40351, (606) 784-5212,
<www.moreheadrowan.org/rowancounty>
- **INCORPORATED:** 1856
- **PARENT COUNTY:** Fleming, Morgan
- **MARRIAGE:** start in 1881, County Clerk
- **DIVORCE:** unknown, Circuit Court
- **LAND:** 1880, County Clerk
- **PROBATE:** 1853, Circuit Court
- **COURT:** 1880, Circuit Court

RUSSELL

Box 579, Jamestown, KY 42629, (270) 343-2125,
<www.russellcounty.ky.gov>

- **INCORPORATED:** Dec. 14, 1825
- **PARENT COUNTIES:** Cumberland, Adair, Wayne
- **MARRIAGE:** start in 1826, kept by County Clerk
- **DIVORCE:** unknown, Circuit Court
- **LAND:** 1826, County Clerk
- **PROBATE:** 1826, Circuit Court
- **COURT:** 1826, Circuit Court

SCOTT

101 E. Main St., Georgetown, KY 40324, (502) 863-7875

- **<www.scottky.com>**
- **INCORPORATED:** June 1, 1792
- **PARENT COUNTY:** Woodford
- **MARRIAGE:** start in 1837, kept by County Clerk
- **DIVORCE:** unknown, Circuit Court
- **LAND:** 1783, County Clerk
- **PROBATE:** 1792, Circuit Court
- **COURT:** 1792, Circuit Court

SHELBY

501 Main St., Box 819, Shelbyville, KY 40065, (502) 663-4410,
<www.shelbycountykentucky.com>

- **INCORPORATED:** June 23, 1792
- **PARENT COUNTY:** Jefferson
- **BIRTH:** start in 1911, kept by state Office of Vital Statistics
- **MARRIAGE:** 1792, County Clerk
- **PROBATE:** 1792, Circuit Court

SIMPSON

Box 268, Franklin, KY 42134, (270) 586-8161,
<www.simpsoncounty.us>

- **INCORPORATED:** Jan. 28, 1819
- **PARENT COUNTIES:** Allen, Logan, Warren
- **MARRIAGE:** start in 1852, kept by County Clerk
- **LAND:** 1822, County Clerk

SPENCER

Box 544, Taylorsville, KY 40071, (502) 477-3215,
<www.spencercountyky.gov>

- **INCORPORATED:** Jan. 7, 1824
- **PARENT COUNTIES:** Shelby, Bullitt, Nelson
- **MARRIAGE:** start in 1824, kept by County Clerk
- **DIVORCE:** unknown, Circuit Court
- **LAND:** 1824, County Clerk
- **PROBATE:** 1824, Circuit Court
- **COURT:** 1824, Circuit Court

TAYLOR

203 N. Court St., Campbellsville, KY 42718, (270) 465-6677,
<www.taylorcounty.ky.gov>

- **INCORPORATED:** March 1, 1848
- **PARENT COUNTY:** Green
- **BIRTH:** start in 1911, kept by state Office of Vital Statistics
- **MARRIAGE:** 1848, County Clerk
- **DEATH:** 1911, state Office of Vital Statistics
- **LAND:** 1848, County Clerk
- **PROBATE:** 1848, Circuit Court
- **COURT:** 1848, Circuit Court

TODD

Box 307, Elkton, KY 42220, (270) 265-2363,
<www.toddcounty.ky.gov>

- **INCORPORATED:** Dec. 30, 1819
- **PARENT COUNTIES:** Christian, Logan
- **MARRIAGE:** start in 1820, kept by County Clerk
- **DIVORCE:** unknown, County Clerk
- **LAND:** 1820, County Clerk
- **PROBATE:** 1820, Circuit Court
- **COURT:** 1820, Circuit Court

TRIGG

Box 1310, Cadiz, KY 42211, (270) 552-6661,
<www.triggcounty.ky.gov>

- **INCORPORATED:** Jan. 27, 1820
- **PARENT COUNTIES:** Christian, Caldwell
- **BIRTH:** start in 1911, kept by state Office of Vital Statistics
- **MARRIAGE:** 1820, County Clerk
- **DEATH:** 1911, state Office of Vital Statistics
- **DIVORCE:** unknown, Circuit Court
- **LAND:** 1820, County Clerk
- **COURT:** 1820, Circuit Court
- **PROBATE:** 1820, Circuit Court

TRIMBLE

Box 262, Bedford, KY 40006, (502) 255-7174,
<www.trimblecounty.ky.gov>

- **INCORPORATED:** Feb. 9, 1837
- **PARENT COUNTY:** Henry, Oldham, Gallatin
- **BIRTH:** start in 1911, kept by state Office of Vital Statistics
- **DEATH:** 1911, state Office of Vital Statistics
- **MARRIAGE:** 1837, County Clerk
- **LAND:** 1837, County Clerk

UNION

Box 119, Morganfield, KY 42437, (270) 389-1334,
<www.rootsweb.ancestry.com/~kyunion>

- **INCORPORATED:** Jan. 15, 1811
- **PARENT COUNTY:** Henderson
- **MARRIAGE:** start in 1811, kept by County Clerk
- **LAND:** 1811, County Clerk
- **PROBATE:** 1811, Circuit Court

WARREN

Box 478, Bowling Green, KY 42101, (270) 842-1535,
<www.warrencounty.Kentucky.ky.us>

- **INCORPORATED:** Dec. 19, 1796
- **PARENT COUNTY:** Logan
- **BIRTH:** start in 1911, state Office of Vital Statistics
- **MARRIAGE:** 1797, County Clerk
- **LAND:** 1797, County Clerk
- **MILITARY:** 1917, County Clerk
- **PROBATE:** 1796, Circuit Court

WASHINGTON
Box 446, Springfield, KY 40069, (859) 336-5425
- **<www.washingtoncountyky.com>**
- **INCORPORATED:** June 2, 1792
- **PARENT COUNTY:** Nelson
- **MARRIAGE:** start in 1792, kept by County Clerk
- **DIVORCE:** 1792, Circuit Court
- **LAND:** 1792, County Clerk
- **PROBATE:** 1792, Circuit Court
- **COURT:** 1792, Circuit Court
- **NOTES:** County Clerk has school census 1893-1917. Clerk of Circuit Court has some naturalization and military discharge records.

WAYNE
55 N. Main St., Suite 106, Monticello, KY 42633, (606) 348-5721, **<www.waynecounty.ky.gov>**
- **INCORPORATED:** Dec. 13, 1800
- **PARENT COUNTY:** Pulaski, Cumberland
- **MARRIAGE:** start in 1801, kept by County Clerk
- **LAND:** 1800, County Clerk
- **PROBATE:** 1801, Circuit Court

WEBSTER
Box 19, Dixon, KY 42409, (270) 639-7006, **<www.rootsweb.ancestry.com/~kywebste/index.htm>**
- **INCORPORATED:** July 1, 1860
- **PARENT COUNTIES:** Hopkins, Union, Henderson
- **MARRIAGE:** start in 1860, kept by County Clerk
- **DIVORCE:** unknown, Circuit Court
- **LAND:** 1860, County Clerk
- **PROBATE:** 1860, Circuit Court
- **COURT:** 1860, Circuit Court

WHITLEY
Box 8, Williamsburg, KY 40769, (606) 549-6002, **<resources.rootsweb.ancestry.com/USA/KY/Whitley>**
- **INCORPORATED:** Jan. 17, 1818
- **PARENT COUNTY:** Knox
- **BIRTH:** start in 1911, kept by state Office of Vital Statistics
- **MARRIAGE:** 1860, County Clerk
- **DEATH:** 1911, state Office of Vital Statistics
- **LAND:** 1818, County Clerk
- **PROBATE:** 1818, Circuit Court

WOLFE
Box 400, Campton, KY 41301, (606) 668-3515, **<www.rootsweb.ancestry.com/~kywolfe>**
- **INCORPORATED:** 1860
- **PARENT COUNTIES:** Owsley, Breathitt, Powell, Morgan
- **MARRIAGE:** start in 1861, kept by County Clerk
- **DIVORCE:** unknown, Circuit Court
- **LAND:** 1887, County Clerk
- **PROBATE:** 1887, Circuit Court
- **COURT:** 1818, Circuit Court

WOODFORD
103 S. Main St., Suite 120, Versailles, KY 40383, (859) 873-3421, **<www.woodfordcounty.ky.gov>**
- **INCORPORATED:** Nov. 12, 1788
- **PARENT COUNTY:** Fayette
- **MARRIAGE:** start in 1789, kept by County Clerk
- **DIVORCE:** unknown, Circuit Court
- **LAND:** 1789, County Clerk
- **PROBATE:** 1789, Circuit Court
- **COURT:** 1789, Circuit Court

LOUISIANA

» BY EMILY ANNE CROOM

HISTORICAL OVERVIEW

Louisiana's history is a mix of American Indian, Spanish, French, German, English and African cultures. Although Spaniards reached the area in 1541, the earliest European claim came from French explorers at the mouth of the Mississippi River in 1682, and settlements at Biloxi (1699), Natchitoches (1714) and New Orleans (1718). France ceded to Spain its vast land west of the Mississippi plus New Orleans in a secret treaty in 1762. French territory east of the Mississippi River, except for New Orleans, went to Britain at the end of the Seven Years War in 1763. Descendants of European and African colonists, called Creoles, still live in the region. Acadians, exiles from French Canada and ancestors of today's Cajuns, settled in southern Louisiana in the mid-1700s. Other 18th-century European immigrants included Palatinate Germans and Canary Islanders.

President Jefferson sent envoys to try to buy New Orleans, a port of growing commercial importance. Instead, the United States bought the entire territory of Louisiana in 1803. After several years as Orleans Territory, the southern portion of this Louisiana Purchase became the 18th state—Louisiana—in 1812.

Agriculture using slave labor dominated the early economy, from coastal sugar cane and rice plantations to cotton farms and plantations throughout most of the rest of the state. By 1860, the state's 708,000 people included about 47 percent slaves. Of the free inhabitants, about 11 percent were foreign-born and just over 2 percent were free blacks.

Louisiana seceded in January 1861, and numerous Civil War engagements took place on its soil. After winning New Orleans and Baton Rouge, the Union controlled the eastern portion of the state. Louisiana was readmitted to the Union in 1868. After the Civil War, farm labor was largely comprised of tenant farmers and sharecroppers. Urban Louisiana grew during the early 20th century and by 1950, was almost 55 percent of the state's population. Especially after World War II, petrochemical, timber, fishing, and related industries became major economic factors, along with food processing based on agricultural diversity. But cotton, sugar cane and rice farming, as well as the related manufacturing, remained important cornerstones in the state's economy. The port of New Orleans has been a significant commercial and immigration center for more than 200 years.

research tips

- Louisiana's federal land patents are searchable online at **<www.glorecords.blm.gov>**. Land transactions between individuals are filed at parish courthouses.
- Some courthouses have lost records to fires or storms; check for surviving records, resources in neighboring or parent parishes, and local, state, and federal records.

CENSUS RECORDS

- Federal census population schedules: 1810, 1820, 1830, 1840, 1850, 1860, 1870, 1880, 1900, 1910, 1920, 1930
- Federal mortality schedules: 1850, 1860, 1870, 1880
- Federal slave schedules: 1850, 1860 (schedules named slaveholders but rarely named slaves)
- Special census of Civil War Union veterans and widows: 1890
- Colonial censuses: 1699-1796, various years and places

RECORD HIGHLIGHTS

Louisiana began statewide birth and death registration in 1914. Information on obtaining copies is on the Office of Public Health website, **<www.dhh.louisiana.gov/offices/?ID=252>**. The state archives houses early 19th-century vital records from New Orleans. For more information, see **<www.sec.state.la.us/archives/archives/archives-library.htm>** under Vital Records. Also check the Family History Library (FHL) catalog **<www.familysearch.org>**, running a place search for Louisiana and the parish name. Then look under Vital Records. Consult Catholic church registers for ecclesiastical vital records.

Because of its French and Spanish roots, southern Louisiana has been strongly Roman Catholic, and civil records are based on French Napoleonic civil law practices. The state is divided into parishes rather than counties. Deed records are called conveyances; probate records are successions. Important components of succession papers are records of "family meetings" during the probate process.

Notaries wrote legal documents for individuals and businesses; thus, notarial records are important sources. Most were in French in the 18th and early 19th centuries. After US acquisition, records are more consistently in English. The FHL has microfilm and indexes of numerous notarial records. New Orleans notarial records are in the New Orleans Notarial Archives **<www.notarialarchives.org>**. No master index exists, but many volumes have internal indexes.

Try to identify the notary who created your ancestor's records. For example, a land transaction filed in the parish courthouse may name the notary the family hired for that document; check that notary's records for other family documents. An alphabetical list of New Orleans notaries and their dates of service is at **<www.notarialarchives.org/Notaries/lista.htm>**. Additional Louisiana research materials include:

- Colonial civil and ecclesiastical archives (original, microform, and published abstracts) in repositories including the Louisiana State Archives; Historic New Orleans Collection; Louisiana State Museum/Louisiana Historical Center Library; New Orleans Public Library; Louisiana State University; Tulane University; the University of Texas, Center for American History, Austin; and Clayton Library, Houston.
- American State Papers: Public Lands, 8 vols., online at **<memory.loc.gov/ammem/amlaw/lwsp.html>**
- Territorial Papers of the United States, Territorial Papers of the United States Senate, and State Department Territorial Papers for Orleans Territory.
- Confederate pensions from 1898; online index at **<www.sos.louisiana.gov/tabid/53/Default.aspx>**.
- City archives for New Orleans, at the New Orleans Public Library **<nutrias.org/~nopl/spec/speclist.htm>**.

☞ ARCHIVES, LIBRARIES, AND SOCIETIES

Alexandria Historical and Genealogical Library
503 Washington St., Alexandria, LA 71301, (318) 487-8556

Allen Genealogical and Historical Society
Box 789, Kinder, LA 70648

Amite Genealogical Club
739 W. Oak, Amite, LA 70422

Archdiocese of New Orleans Archives
7887 Walmsley Ave. New Orleans, LA 70125, (504) 861-6241, **<www.archdiocese-no.org/archives>**

Archives of the Diocese of Shreveport
3500 Fairfield Ave., Shreveport, LA 71104, (318) 868-4441, **<www.dioshpt.org/archives/archives.html>**

Ark-La-Tex Genealogical Association
Box 4463, Shreveport, LA 71134, **<www.rootsweb.ancestry.com/~laaltga>**

Association for Preservation and Promotion of Iberville
602 Main St., Plaquemine, LA 70764

Attakapas Historical Association
Box 43010 USL, Lafayette, LA 70504

Baton Rouge Genealogical and Historical Society
Box 80565, Southeast Station, Baton Rouge, LA 70898, **<brghs.blogspot.com>**

Beauregard Historical Society
Box 658, De Ridder, LA 70634

Bienville Historical Society
Rt. 1, Box 9, Bienville, LA 71008

Bluebonnet Regional Branch Library
9200 Bluebonnet Blvd., Baton Rouge, LA 70810, (225) 763-2283, **<www.ebr.lib.la.us/branch/Bluebonnet.htm>**

Bossier Restoration Foundation
Box 1481, Benton, LA 71006, (318) 965-4610

Brimstone Historical Society
900 S. Huntington St., Sulphur LA, 70663, (337) 527-0357, **<www.brimstonemuseum.org>**

Calcasieu Historical Preservation Society
Box 1214, Lake Charles, LA 70602 , **<calcasieupreservation.org>**

Cameron Parish Historical and Genealogical Society
Box 1107, Cameron, LA 70631

Centenary College, Magale Library
2911 Centenary Blvd., Box 41188, Shreveport, LA 71134, (318) 869-5462, **<www.centenary.edu/library/archives>**

Central Louisiana Genealogical Society
Box 12206, Alexandria, LA 71301, **<www.rootsweb.ancestry.com/~laclgs/>**

Claiborne Historical Association
931 N. Main St., Homer, LA 71040

Le Cercle Historique
734 Main St., New Roads, LA 70760

Le Comite des Archives de la Louisiane
Box 1547, Baton Rouge, LA 70821, **<www.sec.state.la.us/archives/archives/archives-comite.htm>**

Commission des Avoyelles
Box 28, Hamburg, LA 71339

Diocese of Baton Rouge Archives
Box 2028, Baton Rouge, LA 70821, (225) 387-0561 ext. 226, **<www.diobr.org/archives/archives-main.htm>**

Dorcheat Historical Association
116 Pearl St., Minden, LA 71055, (318) 377-3002, **<museuminminden.blogspot.com>**

East Ascension Genealogical and Historical Society
Box 1006, Gonzales, LA 70707

East Baton Rouge Parish Library
7711 Goodword Blvd., Baton Rouge, LA 70806, (225) 231-3750, **<www.ebr.lib.la.us>**

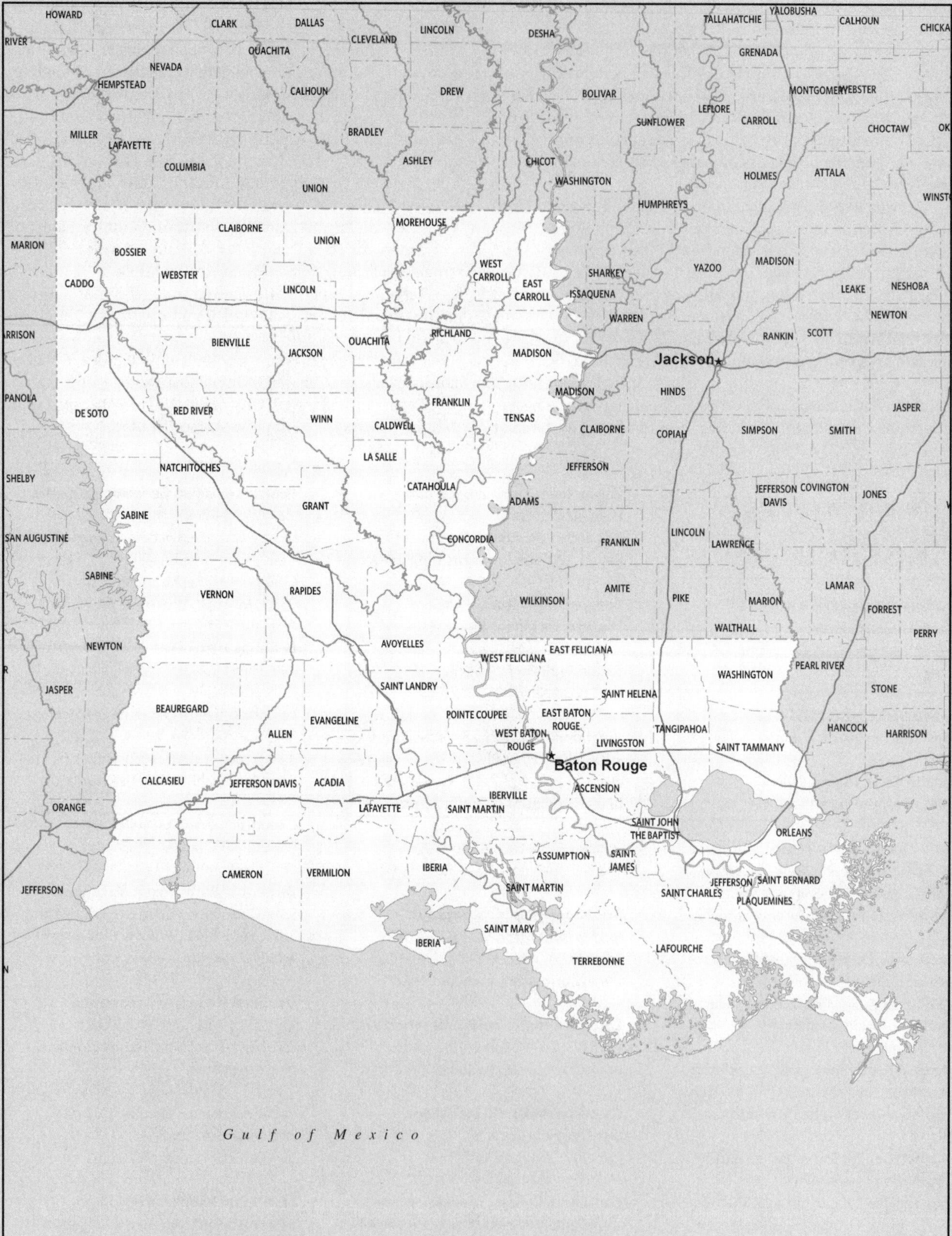
HOWARD
CLARK
DALLAS
LINCOLN
DESHA
YALOBUSHA
TALLAHATCHIE
CALHOUN
RIVER
CLEVELAND
OUACHITA
NEVADA
GRENADA
HEMPSTEAD
CALHOUN
DREW
BOLIVAR
MONTGOMERY
WEBSTER
LEFLORE
SUNFLOWER
CARROLL
MILLER
BRADLEY
CHOCTAW
LAFAYETTE
ASHLEY
CHICOT
COLUMBIA
WASHINGTON
HOLMES
ATTALA
UNION
HUMPHREYS
MOREHOUSE
CLAIBORNE
UNION
MARION
BOSSIER
WEST CARROLL
SHARKEY
YAZOO
MADISON
WEBSTER
EAST CARROLL
ISSAQUENA
CADDO
LINCOLN
LEAKE
NESHOBA
WARREN
NEWTON
RICHLAND
RANKIN
SCOTT
BIENVILLE
OUACHITA
JACKSON
MADISON
Jackson
MADISON
HINDS
PANOLA
FRANKLIN
DE SOTO
RED RIVER
TENSAS
JASPER
WINN
CALDWELL
CLAIBORNE
COPIAH
SIMPSON
SMITH
LA SALLE
NATCHITOCHES
JEFFERSON
SHELBY
CATAHOULA
JEFFERSON DAVIS
COVINGTON
JONES
GRANT
ADAMS
SABINE
LINCOLN
SAN AUGUSTINE
CONCORDIA
FRANKLIN
LAWRENCE
SABINE
AMITE
LAMAR
VERNON
RAPIDES
WILKINSON
PIKE
MARION
FORREST
WALTHALL
PERRY
AVOYELLES
NEWTON
EAST FELICIANA
WEST FELICIANA
WASHINGTON
PEARL RIVER
SAINT LANDRY
JASPER
SAINT HELENA
STONE
BEAUREGARD
POINTE COUPEE
EAST BATON ROUGE
EVANGELINE
TANGIPAHOA
HANCOCK
HARRISON
ALLEN
WEST BATON ROUGE
LIVINGSTON
SAINT TAMMANY
Baton Rouge
CALCASIEU
JEFFERSON DAVIS
ACADIA
ASCENSION
IBERVILLE
ORANGE
LAFAYETTE
SAINT MARTIN
SAINT JOHN THE BAPTIST
ORLEANS
ASSUMPTION
SAINT JAMES
CAMERON
VERMILION
IBERIA
JEFFERSON
SAINT BERNARD
JEFFERSON
SAINT MARTIN
SAINT CHARLES
PLAQUEMINES
SAINT MARY
IBERIA
LAFOURCHE
TERREBONNE
Gulf of Mexico

Edward Livingston Historical Association
Box 67, Livingston, LA 70754

Evangeline Genealogical and Historical Society
Box 664, Ville Platte, LA 70586

Foundation for Historical Louisiana
Box 908, Baton Rouge, LA 70821, (225) 387-2464, **<www.fhl.org>**

Francaise Comite Louisiana
2717 Massachusetts, Matairie, LA 70003

Franklin Parish Genealogical and Historical Society
Rt. 4, Box 150, Winnsboro, LA 71295

French Settlement Historical Society
Box 365, French Settlement, LA 70733

Genealogical Research Society of New Orleans
Box 51791, New Orleans, LA 70151, **<www.rootsweb.ancestry.com/~lagrsno>**

Genealogy West
5644 Abbey Dr., New Orleans, LA 70131

German-Acadian Coast Historical and Genealogical Society
Box 517, Destrehan, LA 70047, **<www.rootsweb.ancestry.com/~lastjohn/geracadn.htm>**

Germantown Commission Association
Box 389, Minden, LA 71055

Grant Genealogical Society
300 Main St., Colfax, LA 71417

Gretna Historical Society
205 Lafayette St., Gretna, LA 70053 , (504) 362-3854

Historic New Orleans Collection
Williams Research Center, 410 Chartres St., New Orleans, LA 70130, (504) 523-4662, **<www.hnoc.org>**

Historical Society of Grand Isle
Box 275, Grand Isle, LA 70358

Iberia Cultural Resources
924 E. Main St., New Iberia, LA 70560

Jackson Assembly of the Felicianas
Box 494, Jackson, LA 70748

Jefferson Genealogical Society
Box 961, Metairie, LA 70004, **<www.jgs25.com>**

Jefferson Parish Library
4747 W. Napoleon Ave., Metairie, LA 70001, (504) 838-1100, **<www.jefferson.lib.la.us>**

Jefferson Parish Library
2751 Manhattan Blvd., Harvey, LA 70058, (504) 364-2660, **<www.jefferson.lib.la.us>**

Jennings Genealogical Society
136 Greenwood Dr., Jennings, LA 70546

Jewish Genealogical Society of New Orleans
Box 7811, Metairie, LA 70010, (504) 836-2720, **<www.jewishgen.org/jgsno>**

Lafayette Genealogical Society
Box 52041, Lafayette, LA 70505, **<www.rootsweb.ancestry.com/~lalgs>**

Lafourche Heritage Society
Box 567, Thibodaux, LA 70393

Lake Providence Historical Society
1002 S. Lake St., Lake Providence, LA 71254

Lincoln Parish Library
910 N. Trenton, Ruston, LA 71270, (318) 251-5030, **<www.mylpl.org>**

Louisiana Czech Heritage Association
14 Locker Rd., DeVille, LA 71328

Louisiana Genealogical and Historical Society
Box 82060, Baton Rouge, LA 70884, **<www.rootsweb.ancestry.com/~la-lghs>**

Louisiana State Museum Historical Center
Old US Mint, 400 Esplanade Ave., New Orleans, LA 70116, (504) 568- 6968, **<lsm.crt.state.la.us/collections/hcenter.htm>**

Louisiana Historical Society
5615 Perrier St., New Orleans, LA 70115 , (504) 866-3049, **<www.louisianahistoricalsociety.org>**

Louisiana Office of Cultural Development
(225) 342-8200, **<www.crt.state.la.us/culture>**

Louisiana State Archives
Box 94125, 3851 Essen Lane, Baton Rouge, LA 70804, (225) 922-1208, **<www.sos.louisiana.gov/tabid/88/Default.aspx>**

Louisiana State University, Hill Memorial Library
Baton Rouge, LA 70803, (225) 578-6544, **<www.lib.lsu.edu/special/>**

Madison Parish Historical Society
Box 268, Tallulah, LA 71284, (318) 574-0082

Mount Lebanon Historical Society
12801 Hwy. 154, Gibsland, LA 71028, **<mountlebanonlouisiana.com/historicmountlebanonlouisiana>**

Natchitoches Genealogical and Historical Association Library
Box 1349, Natchitoches, LA 71458, (318) 357-2235, **<www.rootsweb.ancestry.com/~lanatchi/ngl.htm>**

National Archives, Southwest Region
1400 John Burgess Dr., Fort Worth, TX 76140, (817) 831-5620, **<www.archives.gov/southwest>**

New Orleans Notarial Archives
1340 Poydras St., Suite 360, New Orleans, LA 70112, (504) 680-9604, **<www.notarialarchives.org>**

New Orleans Public Library
219 Loyola Ave., New Orleans, LA 70112, (504) 529-7323, **<nutrias.org>**

North Louisiana Genealogical Society
Box 324, Ruston, LA 71273

North Louisiana Historical Association
Box 6701, Shreveport, LA 71136, **<northlouisianahistory.org>**

Office of Public Health, Vital Records Registry
Box 60630, New Orleans, LA 70160, (504) 219-4500, **<www.oph.dhh.louisiana.gov>**

Ouachita Genealogical Society
221 Riverbend, West Monroe, LA 71292

Plaquemines Deep Delta Genealogical Society
c/o Plaquemines Parish Library, 203 Hwy. 11, South Buras, LA 70041, (504) 657-7121

Plaquemines Public Library
35572 Hwy. 11, Buras, LA 70041, (985) 657-7121, **<plaqueminesppl.booksys.net/opac/plaqueminesppl/index.html>**

Pointe Coupee Historical Society
Box 462, New Roads, LA 70760, **<www.pointecoupeehistoricalsociety.org>**

Pointe Coupee Parish, Le Circle Historique
734 Main St., New Roads, LA 70760

Pointe Coupee Parish Museum
8348 False River Road (State Hwy. 1), New Roads, LA 70760, (225) 638-7788, **<www.nps.gov/history/nr/travel/louisiana/ptc.htm>**

Pointe de l'Eglise: Acadia Genealogical and Historical Society
Box 497, Crowley, LA 70527, **<www.rootsweb.ancestry.com/~lapehgs/aboutsociety.htm>**

Rapides Parish Library
411 Washington St., Alexandria, LA 71301, (318) 442-1858, **<www.rpl.org>**

Red River Heritage Association
Box 117, Colfax, LA 71417, **<www.redriverha.org>**

River Road Historical Society
Box 5, Destrehan, LA 70047, (504) 764-9315

St. Bernard Genealogical Society
107 Rickford Dr., Slidell, LA 70458, (504) 554-1716, **<www.ccugpc.org/sbgs/sbgs.htm>**

Saint Domingue Special Interest Group
1514 Saint Roch Ave., New Orleans, LA 70117, **<freepages.genealogy.rootsweb.ancestry.com/~saintdomingue/SIG%20Info.htm>**

St. Helena Historical Association
Rt. 1, Box 131, Amite, LA 70422

St. Mary Genealogical and Historical Society
Box 662, Morgan City, LA 70381

St. Tammany Genealogical Society
Box 1904, Covington, LA 70434, **<www.sttammanygs.org>**

St. Tammany Historical Society
Box 1001, Mandeville, LA 70470

St. Tammany Parish Library
310 W. 21st Ave., Covington, LA 70433, (985) 871-1219, **<www.sttammany.lib.la.us>**

Shreve Memorial Library, Broadmoor Branch Genealogy Dept.
1212 Captain Shreve Dr., Shreveport, LA 71105, (318) 219-3468, **<www.shreve-lib.org/images/genealogy.htm>**

La Societe Des Cajuns
Box 433, Larose, LA 70373, **<www.vienici.com/lasociete>**

Southeast Louisiana Historical Society
Box 789, Hammond, LA 70401

Southwest Louisiana Genealogical and Historical Library
411 Pujo St., Lake Charles, LA 70601, (337) 721-7110, **<calcasieulibrary.org/genealogy>**

Southwest Louisiana Genealogical Society
Box 5652, Lake Charles, LA 70606, **<www.rootsweb.ancestry.com/~laslgs/swlgs.htm>**

Southwest Louisiana Historical Association
4201 Alma Lane, Lake Charles, LA 70605, **<www.swlahistory.org>**

State Land Office
Box 44124, Baton Rouge, LA 70804, (225) 342-4586, **<www.doa.la.gov/slo>**

State Library of Louisiana
Box 131, Baton Rouge, LA 70821, (225) 342-4923, **<www.state.lib.la.us>**

Tangipahoa Parish Historical Society
200 E. Mulberry Street, Amite, LA 70422

Tangipahoa Parish Library
200 E. Mulberry St., Amite, LA 70422, (985) 748-7559, **<www.tangilibrary.com>**

Terrebonne Genealogical Society
Box 20295, Houma, LA 70360, **<www.rootsweb.ancestry.com/~laterreb/tgs.htm>**

Tulane University, Special Collections
Jones Hall, New Orleans, LA 70118, (504) 865-5685, **<specialcollections.tulane.edu>**

University of Louisiana-Lafayette, Dupre Library, Center for Louisiana Studies
Box 40831, 302 St. Bary Blvd., Lafayette, LA 70504, (337) 482-6027, **<library.louisiana.edu/Spec>**

University of New Orleans, Earl K. Long Library
2000 Lakeshore Dr., New Orleans, LA 70148, (504) 280-6556, **<library.uno.edu>**

Vermillion Genealogical Society
Box 117, Abbeville, LA 70511

Vermillion Historical Society
Box 877, Abbeville, LA 70511, (337) 898-4114, **<www.vermilionhistorical.com>**

Vernon Historical and Genealogical Society and Library
Box 159, Anacoco, LA 71403

West Bank Genealogy Society
Box 872, Harvey, LA 70059

West Baton Rouge Genealogical Society
Box 1126, Port Allen, LA 70767

West Baton Rouge Historical Society
845 N. Jefferson Ave., Port Allen, LA 70767

West Feliciana Historical Society
Box 338, St. Francisville, LA 70775, (225) 635-6330, **<www.audubonpilgrimage.info/museum_hs.htm>**

Winn Parish Genealogical and Historical Association
Box 1357, Winnfield, LA 71483, **<www.rootsweb.ancestry.com/~lawpgha/>**

GENERAL RESOURCES

Acadian-Cajun Genealogy: Step by Step by Timothy Hebert (Center for Louisiana Studies, University of Southwestern Louisiana, ca. 1993)

Acadian to Cajun: Transformation of a People, 1803-1877 by Carl A. Brasseaux (University Press of Mississippi, ca. 1992)

Acadian Odyssey by Oscar William Winzerling (Louisiana State University Press, 1955)

Africans in Colonial Louisiana: The Development of Afro-Creole Culture in the Eighteenth Century by Gwendolyn Midlo Hall (Louisiana State University Press, ca. 1992)

An Atlas of Louisiana Surnames of French and Spanish Origin by Robert C. West (Geoscience Publications, Louisiana State University, 1986)

Biographical and Historical Memoirs of Louisiana, 2 vols., (The Goodspeed Publishing Co., 1892)

Black Names in Louisiana by Mary Eleanor Williams (M. E. Williams, ca. 1992)

The Canary Islanders of Louisiana by Gilbert C. Din (Louisiana State University Press, ca. 1988)

The Catholic Church in Louisiana by Roger Baudier (A.W. Hyatt Stationery Manufacturing Co., Ltd., 1939)

Cajun Sketches from the Prairies of Southwest Louisiana by Lauren C. Post (Louisiana State University Press, 1990)

Creoles of Color in the Bayou Country by Carl A. Brasseaux, Keith P. Fontenot, and Claude F. Oubre, (University Press of Mississippi, ca. 1994)

Creole New Orleans: Race and Americanization edited by Arnold R. Hirsch and Joseph Logsdon (Louisiana State University Press, ca. 1992)

A Dictionary of Louisiana Biography, 2 vols., edited by Glenn R. Conrad (Louisiana Historical Association, ca. 1988)

Dictionnaire Genealogique des Familles Canadiennes Depuis la Fondation de la Colonie jusqu'a nos jours, 7 vols., by Cyprien Tanguay (E. Senecal, 1871-1890)

Down the Old Spanish Trail by Kitty Courts (K. Courts, ca. 1999)

Forgotten People: Cane River's Creoles of Color by Gary B. Mills (Louisiana State University Press, ca. 1977)

Founding of New Acadia: The Beginning of Acadian Life in Louisiana, 1765-1803 by Carl A. Brasseaux (Louisiana State University Press, ca. 1987)

The Free Negro in Ante-Bellum Louisiana by H. E. Sterkc (Fairleigh Dickinson University Press, 1972)

The French Experience in Louisiana edited by Glenn R. Conrad (University of Southwestern Louisiana, 1995)

French and Spanish Records of Louisiana: A Bibliographical Guide to Archive and Manuscript Sources by Henry Putney Beers (Louisiana State University Press, 1989)

Genealogical Materials in the New Orleans Public Library by Collin B. Hamer, Jr. (Friends of the New Orleans Public Library, 1984)

German Coast Families: European Original and Settlement in Colonial Louisiana by Albert J. Robichaux, Jr. (Hebert Publications, ca. 1997)

A Guide to the Acadians in Maryland in the Eighteenth and Nineteenth Centuries by Gregory A. Wood (Gateway Press, 1995)

A Guide to Church Records in Louisiana, 1720-1975 by Donald J. Hebert (1975)

A Guide to the History of Louisiana edited by Light Townsend Cummins and Glen Jeansonne (Greenwood Press, 1982)

Guide to the Microfilm Edition of the Records of the Diocese of Louisiana and the Floridas, 1576-1803 by Thomas T. McAvoy and Lawrence J. Bradley (University of Notre Dame Archives, 1967)

A Guide to Printed Sources for Genealogical and Historical Research in the Louisiana Parishes compiled by Yvette Guillot Boling (Y. G. Boling with the Louisiana Genealogical and Historical Society, ca. 1985)

Gulf Coast Colonials; A Compendium of French Families in Early Eighteenth Century Louisiana by Winston De Ville (Genealogical Publishing Co., 1968)

The Historic Indian Tribes of Louisiana: From 1542 to the Present by Fred B. Kniffen, et al. (Louisiana State University Press, 1987)

A History of the German Churches in Louisiana by J. Hanno Deiler, translated and edited by Marie Stella Condo (Center for Louisiana Studies, University of Southwest Louisiana, ca. 1983)

A History of Louisiana, 4 vols., by Alcee Fortier (Goupil & Co. of Paris, Manzi, Joyant, and Co., 1904)

The History of Louisiana, from the Earliest Period, 2 vols., by Francois Xavier Martin (Lyman and Beardslee, 1827-29)

Index to the Archives of Spanish West Florida, 1782-1810 introduction by Stanley Clisby Arthur (Polyanthos, 1975)

Indians, Settlers & Slaves in a Frontier Exchange Economy: The Lower Mississippi Valley Before 1783 by Daniel H. Usner Jr. (University of North Carolina Press, 1992)

The Large Slaveholders of the Deep South, 1860 by Joseph Karl Menn (UMI Dissertation Services, 1964)

Louisiana Colonials: Soldiers and Vagabonds translated and compiled by Winston De Ville (W. De Ville, 1963)

Louisiana History: The Journal of the Louisiana Historical Association, 42 vols., (Louisiana Historical Association, 1968)

Louisiana, The Land and Its People by Sue Eakin and Manie Culbertson (Pelican Publishing Co., 1986)

Louisiana, A Narrative History, 3rd ed. by Edwin Adams Davis (Claitor's Publishing Division, 1971)

The Louisiana Purchase and Its Aftermath, 1800-1830 edited by Dolores Egger Labbe (University of Southwestern Louisiana, 1998)

Louisiana Research Outline by the Church of Jesus Christ of Latter-day Saints (online at **<www.familysearch.org/eng/search/RG/guide/louisiana.asp>**)

Louisianans and Their State: A Historical And Biographical Text Book of Louisiana by the Louisiana Historical and Biographical Association (ca. 1919)

Newspaper Files in Louisiana State University Library (Louisiana State University Library, 1961)

Old Families of Louisiana, 1608-1929 by Stanley Clisby Arthur (Harmanson, 1931)

Old Louisiana Plantation Homes and Family Trees, 2 vols., by Herman Boehm de Bachelle Seebold (Pelican Press, Inc., ca. 1941)

South Louisiana Records: Church and Civil Records of Lafourche-Terrebonne Parishes, 12 vols., by Donald J.Hebert (D.J. Hebert, ca. 1978-ca. 1985)

A Southern Catholic Heritage by Charles E. Nolan (Archdiocese of New Orleans, 1976)

Southwest Louisiana: Biographical And Historical edited by William Henry Perry (Gulf Publishing Co., 1891)

Southwest Louisiana Records: Church and Civil Records, revised edition, 4 vols., by Donald J. Hebert (Hebert Publications, ca. 1996-ca. 1997)

The Spanish Borderlands: A Chronicle of Old Florida and the Southwest by Herbert Eugene Bolton (Yale University Press, 1921)

Sweet Chariot: Slave Family and Household Structure in Nineteenth-Century Louisiana by Ann Patton Malone (University of North Carolina Press, ca. 1992)

Vignettes of Louisiana Church History by George C. Poret (G. C. Poret, ca. 1985)

Who's Who in Colored Louisiana edited by A. E. Perkins (Douglas Loan Co., Inc., 1930)

Who's Who in Louisiana and Mississippi (Times-Picayune, 1918)

Women in the Florida Parishes, 2 vols., by Donna Burge Adams (1985-1986)

☞CENSUS RECORDS

The Census Tables for the French Colony of Louisiana from 1699 Through 1732 compiled and translated by Charles R. Maduell Jr. (Genealogical Publishing Co., 1972)

Louisiana Census and Militia Lists 1770-1789 compiled, translated and edited by Albert J. Robichaux Jr. (1973)

☞IMMIGRATION RECORDS

The Acadian Exiles in the American Colonies, 1755-1768 compiled, translated, and edited by Milton P. Reider Jr., and Norma Gaudet Rieder (Reider, ca. 1977)

The Canary Islands Migration to Louisiana, 1778-1783: The History and Passenger Lists of the Islenos Volunteer Recruits and Their Families by Sidney Louis Viller'ae (Genealogical Publishing Co., 1972)

The First Families of Louisiana translated and compiled by Glenn R. Conrad (Claitor's Publishing Division, 1970)

The "Foreign French:" Nineteenth-Century French Immigration into Louisiana, 3 vols., by Carl A. Brasseaux (University of Southwestern Louisiana, 1990-1993)

From Palermo to New Orleans compiled by Mary Ann Riviere (M. A. Riviere, ca. 1987)

Immigration Files of Southwest Louisiana, 1840-1929: Naturalization Records by Donald J. Hebert (Hebert Publications, 1990)

A Refuge For All Ages, Immigration In Louisiana History edited by Carl A. Brasseaux (University of Southwestern Louisiana, 1996)

☞LAND RECORDS

English Land Grants in West Florida: A Register for the States of Alabama, Mississippi, and Parts of Florida and Louisiana, 1766-1776 by Winston De Ville (Winston De Ville, 1986)

Federal Land Grants in the Territory of Orleans: The Delta Parishers, by Charles R. Maudell, Jr. (Polyanthose, 1975)

First Settlers of the Louisiana Territory: Orleans Territory Grants from American State Papers, Class VIII, Public Lands (Ericson Books; Ingmire Publications, 1983)

Index To US Tract Books, Northwestern Land District, Old Natchitoches District, In The Louisiana State Land Office compiled by Ennis Mayfield Tipton (Tipton Printing & Publishing Co., 1980)

Land Claims in the Eastern District of the Orleans Territory by Walter Lowrie (Southern Historical Press, 1986)

Louisiana Land Titles: An Inventory of State Land Office Records from the Early Nineteenth Century on File at the State Archives of Louisiana compiled by Orgy G. Poret and John Spencer Howell (Provincial Press, 1998)

Papers of Vicente Sebastian Pintado, 1781-1842 by Vicente Sebastian Pintado

Survey of Federal Archives in Louisiana: From US Land Office Archives by the Historical Records Survey (Work Progress Administration of Louisiana, 1930)

☞MAPS

County-Parish Boundaries in Louisiana prepared by the Historical Records Survey (Louisiana State University, 1939)

Historical Atlas of Louisiana by Charles Robert Goins and John Michael Caldwell (University of Oklahoma Press, ca. 1995)

Index to Louisiana Place Names Mentioned in the War of the Rebellion edited by Dennis A. Gibson, indexed by Jeffrey A. Baker, et al. (University of Southwestern Louisiana, 1975)

Louisiana, A Geographical Portrait by M.B. Newton, Jr. (Geoforensics, 1987)

Louisiana: A Guide to the State, revised edition, edited by Harry Hansen (Hastings House, ca. 1971)

Louisiana Post Offices by John J. Germann et al. (The Depot, ca. 1990)

☞MILITARY RECORDS

The Confederate Cherokees: John Drew's Regiment of Mounted Rifles by W. Craig

Gaines (Louisiana State University Press, ca. 1989)

Doctors in Gray: The Confederate Medical Service, Louisiana by H.H. Cunningham (Louisiana State University Press, 1993)

Guide to Louisiana Confederate Military Units, 1861-1865 by Arthur W. Bergeron Jr. (Louisiana State University Press, ca. 1989)

Louisiana Soldiers in the War of 1812 by Marion John Bennett Pierson (Louisiana Genealogical and Historical Society, 1963)

Louisiana Troops, 1720-1770 by Winston De Ville (Fort Worth American Reference Publishers, ca. 1965, 1967)

Louisiana Volunteers In The War of 1898 compiled by Nancy Lowrie Wright and Cathy Dantin Shannon (Wright Shannon Publications, 1989)

Louisiana in the War of 1812 by Powell A. Casey (1963)

Military Records of Louisiana by Napier Bartlett (L. Graham & Co., Printers, 1875)

More Generals in Gray by Bruce S. Allardice (Louisiana State University Press, ca. 1995)

Records of Louisiana Confederate Soldiers and Louisiana Confederate Commands, 3 vols., compiled by Andrew B. Booth (Reprint Co., 1984)

☞ PROBATE RECORDS

The Calendar of Louisiana Colonial Documents, 3 vols., by Elizabeth Becker Gianelloni and Winston De Ville (Louisiana State Archives and Records Comission, 1961-ca. 1967)

☞ VITAL RECORDS

Be It Known and Remembered: Bible Records by the Louisiana Genealogical and Historical Society (1960)

Death Notices from Louisiana Newspapers, 4 vols., compiled by LaGroue Mayers and Gloria Lambert Kerns (Folk Finders, 1984)

Guide to Public Vital Statistics Records in Louisiana prepared by the Historical Records Survey and the War Services Program, Work Projects Administration (Louisiana State Board of Health, 1942)

Guide to Vital Statistics Records of Church Archives in Louisiana, 2 vols., prepared by War Service Program, Works Projects Administration (Louisiana State Board of Health, 1942)

Louisiana Marriage Contracts: A Compilation of Abstracts From Records of the Superior Council of Louisiana During the French Regime, 1725-1769, 2 vols., by Alice Daly Forsyth et al., index by Yvette Guillot Boling (Polyanthos, 1980-1989)

Marriage Dispensations in the Diocese of Louisiana and the Floridas: 1786-1803 by Shiley Chaisson Gourgard (Polyanthose, 1980)

The New Orleans French, 1720-1733, A Collection of Marriage Records Relating to the First Colonists of the Louisiana Province by Winston De Ville (Genealogical Publishing Co., 1973)

Southwest Louisiana Records: Church and Civil Records, revised edition, 4 vols., by Donald J. Hebert (Herbert Publications, ca. 1996-ca. 1997)

Tombstone Inscriptions of Northwest Louisiana Cemeteries compiled by John Purnell Frazier (John Purnell Frazier, 1986)

COUNTY DETAILS

ACADIA PARISH

- **INCORPORATED:** April 10, 1805
- **PARENT PARISH:** Original parish
- **NOTES:** Discontinued. Became Ascension and St. James parishes March 31, 1807.

ACADIA PARISH

Box 922, Crowley, LA 70527, (337) 788-8881, **<www.rootsweb.com/~lapehgs>**

- **INCORPORATED:** June 30, 1886
- **PARENT PARISH:** St. Landry
- **MARRIAGE:** 1886, Parish Clerk
- **DIVORCE:** 1886, Parish Clerk
- **PROBATE:** start in 1886, kept by Parish Clerk
- **COURT:** 1886, Parish Clerk

ALLEN PARISH

Box 248, Oberlin, LA 70655, (337) 639-4351, **<www.allenparish.com>**

- **INCORPORATED:** Jan. 12, 1912
- **PARENT PARISH:** Calcasieu
- **MARRIAGE:** start in 1913, kept by Parish Clerk
- **DIVORCE:** 1913, Parish Clerk
- **PROBATE:** 1913, Parish Clerk
- **COURT:** 1913, Parish Clerk

ASCENSION PARISH

300 Houmas St., Box 192, Donaldsonville, LA 70346, (225) 773-9866, **<www.ascensionparish.net>**

- **INCORPORATED:** March 31, 1807
- **PARENT PARISHES:** Acadia, St. James
- **MARRIAGE:** start in 1763, kept by Parish Clerk
- **DIVORCE:** 1800, Parish Clerk
- **LAND:** 1770, Parish Clerk
- **PROBATE:** 1800, Parish Clerk
- **COURT:** 1800, Parish Clerk

ASSUMPTION PARISH

4809 Hwy. 1, Box 249, Napoleonville, LA 70390, (985) 369-6653, **<www.assumptionla.com>**

- **INCORPORATED:** March 1807
- **PARENT PARISH:** Original parish

- **MARRIAGE:** start in 1800, kept by Parish Clerk
- **DIVORCE:** 1868, Parish Clerk
- **LAND:** 1788, Parish Clerk
- **COURT:** 1868, Parish Clerk
- **PROBATE:** 1841, Parish Clerk

ATTAKAPAS PARISH

- **INCORPORATED:** April 10, 1805
- **PARENT PARISH:** Original parish
- **NOTES:** Discontinued and divided into St. Martin and St. Mary April 17, 1811; Lafayette, Feb. 17, 1823; and Vermilion March 25, 1844.

AVOYELLES PARISH

Box 219, Marksville, LA 71351, (318) 253-7523, **<www.avoyellesclerk.com>**

- **INCORPORATED:** March 31, 1807
- **PARENT PARISH:** Original parish
- **MARRIAGE:** start in 1908, kept by Parish Clerk
- **DIVORCE:** 1939, Parish Clerk
- **LAND:** 1908, Parish Clerk
- **PROBATE:** 1925, Parish Clerk
- **COURT:** 1925, Parish Clerk
- **MILITARY:** 1886, Parish Clerk

BATON ROUGE PARISH

- **INCORPORATED:** March 31, 1807
- **PARENT PARISH:** Pointe Coupee
- **NOTES:** See East Baton Route and West Baton Rouge. Became East and West Baton Rouge parishes in 1810.

BEAUREGARD PARISH

- 214 W. First St., Box 100, De Ridder, LA 70634, (337) 463-8595, **<www.beauparish.org>**
- **INCORPORATED:** Jan. 12, 1913
- **PARENT PARISH:** Calcasieu
- **MARRIAGE:** start in 1913, kept by Parish Clerk
- **DIVORCE:** 1913, Parish Clerk
- **LAND:** 1913, Parish Clerk
- **PROBATE:** 1913, Parish Clerk
- **COURT:** 1913, Parish Clerk

BIENVILLE PARISH

100 Courthouse Dr., Room 100, Arcadia, LA 71001, (318) 263-2123, **<www.bienvilleparish.org>**

- **INCORPORATED:** March 14, 1848
- **PARENT PARISH:** Claiborne
- **MARRIAGE:** start in 1848 kept by Parish Clerk
- **DIVORCE:** 1848, Parish Clerk
- **PROBATE:** 1848, Parish Clerk
- **COURT:** 1848, Parish Clerk

BOSSIER PARISH

Box 430, Benton, LA 71006, (318) 965-2336, **<www.bossierparishla.gov>**

- **INCORPORATED:** Feb. 24, 1843
- **PARENT PARISH:** Claiborne
- **MARRIAGE:** 1843, Parish Clerk
- **DIVORCE:** 1843, Parish Clerk
- **LAND:** 1843, Parish Clerk
- **PROBATE:** 1843, Parish Clerk
- **COURT:** 1843, Parish Clerk
- **MILITARY:** 1917, Parish Clerk

CADDO PARISH

501 Texas St., Room 103, Shreveport, LA 71101, (318) 226-6780, **<www.caddo.org>**

- **INCORPORATED:** Jan. 18, 1838
- **PARENT PARISH:** Natchitoches
- **MARRIAGE:** start in 1835, kept by Parish Clerk
- **DIVORCE:** 1835, Parish Clerk
- **PROBATE:** 1835, Parish Clerk
- **LAND:** 1835, Parish Clerk
- **COURT:** 1835, Parish Clerk

CALCASIEU PARISH

1000 Ryan St., Box 1030, Lake Charles, LA 70601, (337) 437-3550, **<www.calclerkofcourt.com>**

- **INCORPORATED:** March 24, 1840
- **PARENT PARISH:** St. Landry
- **MARRIAGE:** start in 1910, kept by Parish Clerk
- **DIVORCE:** 1910, Parish Clerk
- **LAND:** 1910, Parish Clerk
- **PROBATE:** 1910, Parish Clerk
- **COURT:** 1910, Parish Clerk

CALDWELL PARISH

Box 1327, Columbia, LA 71418, (318) 649-2273, **<www.rootsweb.ancestry.com/~lacaldwe>**

- **INCORPORATED:** March 6, 1838
- **PARENT PARISHES:** Catahoula, Ouachita
- **MARRIAGE:** start in 1838, kept by Parish Clerk
- **DIVORCE:** 1838, Parish Clerk
- **LAND:** 1838, Parish Clerk
- **PROBATE:** 1838, Parish Clerk
- **COURT:** 1838, Parish Clerk

CAMERON PARISH

Box 549, Cameron, LA 70631, (337) 775-5316, **<theusgenweb.org/la/cameron>**

- **INCORPORATED:** March 15, 1870
- **PARENT PARISHES:** Calcasieu, Vermilion
- **MARRIAGE:** start in 1870, kept by Parish Clerk
- **DIVORCE:** 1870, Parish Clerk
- **LAND:** 1870, Parish Clerk
- **PROBATE:** 1870, Parish Clerk
- **COURT:** 1870, Parish Clerk
- **MILITARY:** 1918, Parish Clerk

CARROLL PARISH

- **INCORPORATED:** March 14, 1832
- **PARENT PARISH:** Concordia, Ouachita
- **NOTES:** See East and West Carroll parishes. Divided into East and West Carroll March 28, 1877.

CATAHOULA PARISH

Box 198, Harrisonburg, LA 71340, (318) 744-5222,
<www.rootsweb.ancestry.com/~lacataho/catahoula.htm>

- **INCORPORATED:** March 23, 1808
- **PARENT PARISH:** Rapides
- **MARRIAGE:** start in 1830, kept by Parish Clerk
- **DIVORCE:** ca. 1800, Parish Clerk
- **LAND:** 1808, Parish Clerk
- **PROBATE:** ca. 1800, Parish Clerk
- **MILITARY:** unknown, Parish Clerk
- **BURIAL:** ca. 1800, Parish Clerk

CLAIBORNE PARISH

Box 330, Homer, LA 71040, (318) 927-9601,
<www.rootsweb.ancestry.com/~laclaib2/claibla.htm>

- **INCORPORATED:** March 13, 1828
- **PARENT PARISH:** Natchitoches
- **MARRIAGE:** start in 1850, kept by Parish Clerk
- **DIVORCE:** 1850, Parish Clerk
- **LAND:** 1850, Parish Clerk
- **PROBATE:** 1850, Parish Clerk
- **COURT:** 1850, Parish Clerk
- **NOTES:** Courthouse burned in 1849.

CONCORDIA PARISH

Box 790, Vidalia, LA 71373, (318) 336-4204,
<www.rootsweb.ancestry.com/~laconcor>

- **INCORPORATED:** April 10, 1805
- **PARENT PARISH:** Original parish (Ayoelles)
- **MARRIAGE:** start in 1840, kept by Parish Clerk
- **DIVORCE:** 1850, Parish Clerk
- **LAND:** 1850, Parish Clerk
- **PROBATE:** 1850, Parish Clerk
- **COURT:** 1850, Parish Clerk

DESOTO PARISH

Box 1206, Mansfield, LA 71052, (318) 872-3110,
<www.rootsweb.ancestry.com/~ladesoto>

- **INCORPORATED:** April 1, 1843
- **PARENT PARISHES:** Natchitoches, Caddo
- **MARRIAGE:** start in 1843, kept by Parish Clerk
- **DIVORCE:** unknown, Parish Clerk
- **LAND:** 1843, Parish Clerk
- **PROBATE:** unknown, Parish Clerk
- **COURT:** unknown, Parish Clerk

EAST BATON ROUGE PARISH

Box 1991, Baton Rouge, LA 70802, (225) 389-3960, **<brgov.com>**

- **INCORPORATED:** Dec. 22, 1810
- **PARENT PARISH:** Baton Rouge
- **MARRIAGE:** start in 1840, kept by Parish Clerk
- **DIVORCE:** 1782, Parish Clerk
- **LAND:** 1782, Parish Clerk
- **PROBATE:** 1782, Parish Clerk
- **COURT:** 1782, Parish Clerk

• EAST CARROLL PARISH

400 First St., Lake Providence, LA 71254, (318) 559-2399,
<www.rootsweb.ancestry.com/~laeastca>

- **INCORPORATED:** March 28, 1877
- **PARENT PARISH:** Carroll
- **MARRIAGE:** unknown start, kept by Parish Clerk
- **LAND:** unknown, Parish Clerk
- **PROBATE:** unknown, Parish Clerk

EAST FELICIANA PARISH

Box 599, Clinton, LA 70722, (225) 683-5145,
<www.eastfelicianaclerk.org>

- **INCORPORATED:** Feb. 17, 1824
- **PARENT PARISH:** Feliciana
- **MARRIAGE:** start in 1824, kept by Parish Clerk
- **DIVORCE:** 1824, Parish Clerk
- **LAND:** 1824, Parish Clerk
- **PROBATE:** 1824, Parish Clerk
- **COURT:** 1824, Parish Clerk

EVANGELINE PARISH

Drawer 347, Ville Platte, LA 70586, (337) 363-5671,
<theusgenweb.org/la/evangeline>

- **INCORPORATED:** June 15, 1911
- **PARENT PARISH:** St. Landry Parish
- **MARRIAGE:** start in 1911, kept by Parish Clerk
- **DIVORCE:** 1911, Parish Clerk
- **PROBATE:** 1911, Parish Clerk
- **LAND:** 1911, Parish Clerk
- **COURT:** 1911, Parish Clerk

FELICIANA PARISH

- **INCORPORATED:** Dec. 7, 1810
- **PARENT PARISH:** Spanish West Florida
- **NOTES:** (See East and West Feliciana) Dissolved to form East and West Feliciana Feb. 17, 1824.

FRANKLIN PARISH

Box 1564, Winnsboro, LA 71295, (318) 435-9429,
<www.rootsweb.ancestry.com/~lafrankl>

- **INCORPORATED:** March 1, 1843
- **PARENT PARISHES:** Catahoula, Ouachita, Madison
- **MARRIAGE:** start in 1843, kept by Parish Clerk
- **DIVORCE:** 1843, Parish Clerk
- **LAND:** 1843, Parish Clerk
- **PROBATE:** 1843, Parish Clerk
- **COURT:** 1843, Parish Clerk

GERMAN COAST COUNTY

- **INCORPORATED:** April 10, 1805
- **PARENT PARISH:** Original parish
- **NOTES:** Discontinued. Divided to form parishes of St. Charles and St. John the Baptist March 31, 1807.

GRANT PARISH

Box 263, Colfax, LA 71417, (318) 627-3246,
<www.rootsweb.ancestry.com/~lagrant>

- **INCORPORATED:** March 4, 1869
- **PARENT PARISHES:** Rapides, Winn
- **MARRIAGE:** start in 1878, kept by Parish Clerk

- **DIVORCE:** 1878, Parish Clerk
- **LAND:** 1878, Parish Clerk
- **PROBATE:** 1878, Parish Clerk
- **COURT:** 1878, Parish Clerk
- **MILITARY:** 1878, Parish Clerk

IBERIA PARISH

Drawer 12010, New Iberia, LA 70562, (337) 365-7282,
<www.iberiaparishgovernment.com>

- **INCORPORATED:** Oct. 30, 1868
- **PARENT PARISHES:** St. Martin, St. Mary
- **MARRIAGE:** start in 1868, kept by Parish Clerk
- **DIVORCE:** 1868, Parish Clerk
- **LAND:** 1868, Parish Clerk
- **PROBATE:** 1868, Parish Clerk
- **COURT:** 1868, Parish Clerk

IBERVILLE PARISH

Box 423, Plaquemine, LA 70764, (225) 687-5160,
<www.ibervilleparish.com>

- **INCORPORATED:** April 10, 1805
- **PARENT PARISH:** Original parish
- **MARRIAGE:** start in 1770, kept by Parish Clerk
- **DIVORCE:** 1807, Parish Clerk
- **LAND:** 1770, Parish Clerk
- **PROBATE:** 1807, Parish Clerk
- **COURT:** 1807, Parish Clerk

JACKSON PARISH

Box 730, Jonesboro, LA 71251, (318) 259-2424,
<www.rootsweb.ancestry.com/~lajackso/jacksonIndex.htm>

- **INCORPORATED:** Feb. 27, 1845
- **PARENT PARISHES:** Claiborne, Ouachita, Union
- **MARRIAGE:** start in 1880, kept by Parish Clerk
- **DIVORCE:** 1880, Parish Clerk
- **LAND:** 1880, Parish Clerk
- **PROBATE:** 1880, Parish Clerk
- **COURT:** 1880, Parish Clerk
- **MILITARY:** 1880, Parish Clerk

JEFFERSON DAVIS PARISH

Box 799, Jennings, LA 70546, (337) 824-1160,
<www.rootsweb.ancestry.com/~lajeffda>

- **INCORPORATED:** June 12, 1912
- **PARENT PARISH:** Calcasieu
- **MARRIAGE:** start in 1913, kept by Parish Clerk
- **DIVORCE:** 1913, Parish Clerk
- **LAND:** 1913, Parish Clerk
- **PROBATE:** 1913, Parish Clerk
- **COURT:** 1913, Parish Clerk

JEFFERSON PARISH

Box 10, Gretna, LA 70054, (504) 364-2900,
<www.jeffparish.net>

- **INCORPORATED:** 11 Feb. 1825
- **PARENT PARISH:** Orleans
- **MARRIAGE:** start in 1863, kept by Parish Clerk
- **DIVORCE:** 1825, Parish Clerk
- **LAND:** 1827, Parish Clerk
- **PROBATE:** 1825, Parish Clerk
- **COURT:** 1825, Parish Clerk

LAFAYETTE PARISH

Box 2009, Lafayette, LA 70502, (337) 291-6400,
<www.lafayettegov.org/>

- **INCORPORATED:** Jan. 17, 1823
- **PARENT PARISHES:** St. Martin, Attakapas
- **MARRIAGE:** start in 1823, kept by Parish Clerk
- **DIVORCE:** 1823, Parish Clerk
- **LAND:** 1823, Parish Clerk
- **PROBATE:** 1823, Parish Clerk
- **COURT:** 1823, Parish Clerk

LAFOURCHE PARISH

Box 818, Thibodaux, LA 70302, (985) 447-4841,
<www.lapage.com/parishes/lafou.htm>

- **INCORPORATED:** April 10, 1805
- **PARENT PARISH:** Original parish
- **BIRTH:** start in 1808, kept by Parish Clerk
- **MARRIAGE:** 1808, Parish Clerk
- **DIVORCE:** 1808, Parish Clerk
- **LAND:** 1808, Parish Clerk
- **PROBATE:** 1808, Parish Clerk
- **COURT:** 1808, Parish Clerk

LASALLE PARISH

Box 1316, Jena, LA 71342, (318) 992-2158,
<theusgenweb.org/la/lasalle/index.htm>

- **INCORPORATED:** July 3, 1908
- **PARENT PARISH:** Catahoula
- **MARRIAGE:** start in 1910, kept by Parish Clerk
- **DIVORCE:** 1910, Parish Clerk
- **LAND:** 1910, Parish Clerk
- **PROBATE:** 1910, Parish Clerk
- **COURT:** 1910, Parish Clerk

LINCOLN PARISH

Box 924, Ruston, LA 71273, (318) 251-5130,
<www.lincolnparish.org>

- **INCORPORATED:** Feb. 27, 1873
- **PARENT PARISHES:** Bienville, Jackson, Union, Claiborne
- **MARRIAGE:** start in 1873, kept by Parish Clerk
- **DIVORCE:** 1873, Parish Clerk
- **PROBATE:** 1873, Parish Clerk
- **COURT:** 1873, Parish Clerk

LIVINGSTON PARISH

Box 1150, Livingston, LA 70754, (225) 686-2216,
<www.lapage.com/parishes/livin.htm>

- **INCORPORATED:** Feb. 10, 1832
- **PARENT PARISH:** St. Helena
- **MARRIAGE:** start in 1875, kept by Parish Clerk
- **DIVORCE:** 1875, Parish Clerk
- **LAND:** 1875, Parish Clerk
- **PROBATE:** 1875, Parish Clerk
- **COURT:** 1875, Parish Clerk

MADISON PARISH

Box 1710, Tallulah, LA 71282, (318) 574-0655,
<www.rootsweb.ancestry.com/~lamadiso>
- **INCORPORATED:** Jan. 19, 1838
- **PARENT PARISH:** Concordia
- **MARRIAGE:** start in 1866, kept by Parish Clerk
- **DIVORCE:** 1839, Parish Clerk
- **LAND:** 1839, Parish Clerk
- **PROBATE:** 1850, Parish Clerk
- Court: 1882, Parish Clerk

MOREHOUSE PARISH

Box 1543, Bastrop, LA 71221, (318) 281-3343,
<www.rootsweb.ancestry.com/~lamoreho>
- **INCORPORATED:** March 25, 1844
- **PARENT PARISH:** Ouachita
- **MARRIAGE:** start in 1870, kept by Parish Clerk
- **DIVORCE:** 1870, Parish Clerk
- **LAND:** 1844, Parish Clerk
- **PROBATE:** 1870, Parish Clerk
- **COURT:** 1870, Parish Clerk
- **NOTES:** Parish Clerk has Cemetery Abstracts 1867-1957.

NATCHITOCHES PARISH

Box 476, Natchitoches, LA 71458, (318) 352-8152,
<www.rootsweb.ancestry.com/~lanatchi>
- **INCORPORATED:** April 10, 1805
- **PARENT PARISH:** Original parish
- **MARRIAGE:** start in 1780, kept by Parish Clerk
- **DIVORCE:** unknown, Parish Clerk
- **PROBATE:** unknown, Parish Clerk
- **COURT:** unknown, Parish Clerk

OPELOUSAS COUNTY

- **INCORPORATED:** 1807
- **PARENT PARISH:** Original parish
- **NOTES:** See St. Landry Parish. St. Landry formed from Opelousas County March 31, 1807.

ORLEANS PARISH

421 Loyola Ave., Room 402, New Orleans, LA 70112, (504) 592-9105, **<www.orleanscdc.com>**
- **INCORPORATED:** April 10, 1805
- **PARENT PARISH:** Original parish
- **DIVORCE:** start in 1805, kept by Clerk/Civil District Court
- **LAND:** 1832, Register/Conveyances
- **PROBATE:** 1805, Clerk/Civil District Court
- **COURT:** 1805, Clerk/Civil District Court
- **CITY:** 1805, Public Library
- **NOTES:** Public library has voter registration records 1895-1941 and precinct books 1895-1952.

OUACHITA PARISH

Box 1862, Monroe, LA 71201, (318) 327-1444,
<www.bayou.com/~suelynn/ouachita.html>
- **INCORPORATED:** April 10, 1805
- **PARENT PARISH:** Original parish
- **NOTES:** Parish Clerk has some Military records.
- **MARRIAGE:** start in ca. 1800, kept by Parish Clerk
- **DIVORCE:** 1900, Parish Clerk
- **LAND:** ca. 1790, Parish Clerk
- **PROBATE:** 1900, Parish Clerk
- **COURT:** 1900, Parish Clerk

PLAQUEMINES PARISH

Box 40, Belle Chasse, LA 70037, (504) 297-5180,
<www.rootsweb.ancestry.com/~laplaque/laplaque.htm>
- **INCORPORATED:** March 31, 1807
- **PARENT PARISH:** Orleans
- **MARRIAGE:** start in 1809, kept by Parish Clerk
- **DIVORCE:** 1800, Parish Clerk
- **LAND:** 1800, Parish Clerk
- **PROBATE:** 1800, Parish Clerk
- **COURT:** 1800, Parish Clerk

POINTE COUPEE PARISH

Box 38, New Roads, LA 70760, (225) 638-9596,
<www.rootsweb.ancestry.com/~lapointe>
- **INCORPORATED:** April 10, 1805
- **PARENT PARISH:** Original parish
- **MARRIAGE:** start in 1735, kept by Clerk of Courts
- **DIVORCE:** 1800, Clerk of Courts
- **LAND:** 1780, Clerk of Courts
- **PROBATE:** 1780, Clerk of Courts
- **COURT:** 1780, Clerk of Courts

RAPIDES PARISH

Box 952, Alexandria, LA 71309, (318) 473-8153, **<www.rppj.com>**
- **INCORPORATED:** April 10, 1805
- **PARENT PARISH:** Original parish
- **MARRIAGE:** start in 1864, kept by Parish Clerk
- **DIVORCE:** 1864, Parish Clerk
- **LAND:** 1864, Parish Clerk
- **PROBATE:** 1864, Parish Clerk
- **COURT:** 1864, Parish Clerk

RED RIVER PARISH

Box 485, Coushatta, LA 71019, (318) 932-6741,
<www.rootsweb.ancestry.com/~laredriv>
- **INCORPORATED:** March 2, 1871
- **PARENT PARISHES:** Caddo, Bienville, Bossier, DeSoto, Natchitoches
- **MARRIAGE:** start in 1871, kept by Clerk of Courts
- **DIVORCE:** 1904, Clerk of Courts
- **PROBATE:** 1871, Clerk of Courts
- **COURT:** 1904, Clerk of Courts

RICHLAND PARISH

Box 119, Rayville, LA 71269, (318) 728-4171,
<www.rootsweb.ancestry.com/~larichla/home.html>
- **INCORPORATED:** Sept. 29, 1868
- **PARENT PARISHES:** Ouachita, Carroll, Franklin, Morehouse
- **MARRIAGE:** start in 1869, kept by Parish Clerk
- **DIVORCE:** 1869, Parish Clerk
- **LAND:** 1869, Parish Clerk
- **PROBATE:** 1869, Parish Clerk
- **COURT:** 1869, Parish Clerk

SABINE PARISH
Box 419, Many, LA 71449, (318) 256-6223,
<www.sabineparish.com>
- Incorporated: March 7, 1843
- Parent Parish: Natchitoches
- Marriage: start in 1843, kept by Parish Clerk
- Divorce: 1843, Parish Clerk
- Land: 1843, Parish Clerk
- **PROBATE:** 1843, Parish Clerk
- **COURT:** 1843, Parish Clerk

ST. BERNARD PARISH
Box 1746, Chalmette, LA 70044, (504) 271-3434, **<www.sbpg.net>**
- **INCORPORATED:** March 31, 1807
- **PARENT PARISH:** Original parish
- **MARRIAGE:** unknown start, kept by Clerk of Courts
- **LAND:** unknown, Clerk of Courts
- **PROBATE:** unknown, Clerk of Courts
- **COURT:** unknown, Clerk of Courts

ST. CHARLES PARISH
Box 424, Hahnville, LA 70057, (985) 783-6632,
<www.stcharlesparish-la.gov>
- **INCORPORATED:** March 31, 1807
- **PARENT PARISH:** German Coast
- **MARRIAGE:** unknown start, kept by Parish Clerk
- **LAND:** unknown, Parish Clerk
- **PROBATE:** unknown, Parish Clerk
- **COURT:** unknown, Parish Clerk

ST. HELENA PARISH
Box 308, Greensburg, LA 70441, (225) 222-4514,
<www.rootsweb.ancestry.com/~lasthele>
- **INCORPORATED:** Oct. 27, 1810
- **PARENT PARISH:** Spanish West Florida
- **NOTES:** Parish Clerk has records from 1804.

ST. JAMES PARISH
Box 63, Convent, LA 70723, (225) 562-2270,
<www.stjamesla.com>
- **INCORPORATED:** March 31, 1807
- **PARENT PARISH:** Original parish
- **MARRIAGE:** start in 1846, kept by Parish Clerk
- **DIVORCE:** 1809, Parish Clerk
- **PROBATE:** 1809, Parish Clerk
- **COURT:** 1809, Parish Clerk

ST. JOHN THE BAPTIST PARISH
Box 280, Edgard, LA 70049, (985) 497-3331,
<www.sjbparish.com>
- **INCORPORATED:** March 31, 1807
- **PARENT PARISH:** German Coast
- **MARRIAGE:** unknown start, kept by Parish Clerk
- **DIVORCE:** unknown, Parish Clerk
- **LAND:** unknown, Parish Clerk
- **PROBATE:** unknown, Parish Clerk
- **COURT:** unknown, Parish Clerk

ST. LANDRY PARISH
Box 750, Opelousas, LA 70571, (337) 942-5606,
<www.stlandryparishgovernment.org>
- **INCORPORATED:** March 31, 1807
- **PARENT PARISH:** Opelousas
- **MARRIAGE:** start in 1808, kept by Parish Clerk
- **DIVORCE:** 1813, Parish Clerk
- **PROBATE:** 1809, Parish Clerk
- **COURT:** 1813, Parish Clerk

ST. MARTIN PARISH
County Courthouse, Box 9, Saint Martinville, LA 70582, (337) 332-4136, **<www.intersurf.com/~johnjanr/stmartin.htm>**
- **INCORPORATED:** April 17, 1811
- **PARENT PARISH:** Attakapas
- **MARRIAGE:** unknown start, kept by Parish Clerk
- **LAND:** unknown, Parish Clerk
- **PROBATE:** unknown, Parish Clerk
- **COURT:** unknown, Parish Clerk

ST. MARY PARISH
Box 1231, Franklin, LA 70538, (337) 828-4100,
<www.parish.st-mary.la.us/>
- **INCORPORATED:** April 17, 1811
- **PARENT PARISH:** Attakapas
- **MARRIAGE:** start in 1800, kept by Parish Clerk
- **DIVORCE:** 1800, Parish Clerk
- **LAND:** 1800, Parish Clerk
- **PROBATE:** 1800, Parish Clerk
- **COURT:** 1800, Parish Clerk

ST. TAMMANY PARISH
Box 1090, Covington, LA 70434, (985) 809-8700,
<www.rootsweb.ancestry.com/~lasttamm>
- **INCORPORATED:** Oct. 27, 1810
- **PARENT PARISH:** Spanish West Florida
- **MARRIAGE:** start in 1812, kept by Parish Clerk
- **DIVORCE:** 1812, Parish Clerk
- **LAND:** 1810, Parish Clerk
- **PROBATE:** 1812, Parish Clerk
- **COURT:** 1812, Parish Clerk
- **TAX:** 1810, Parish Clerk
- **MILITARY:** unknown, Parish Clerk

TANGIPAHOA PARISH
Box 667, Amite, LA 70422, (985) 748-8015,
<www.tangipahoa.org>
- **INCORPORATED:** March 6, 1869
- **PARENT PARISHES:** Livingston, St. Tammany, St. Helena, Washington
- **MARRIAGE:** start in 1869, kept by Parish Clerk
- **DIVORCE:** 1869, Parish Clerk
- **LAND:** 1869, Parish Clerk
- **PROBATE:** 1869, Parish Clerk
- **COURT:** 1869, Parish Clerk

TENSAS PARISH
Box 78, Saint Joseph, LA 71366, (318) 766-3921,
<www.rootsweb.ancestry.com/~latensas>
- **INCORPORATED:** March 17, 1843
- **PARENT PARISH:** Concordia
- **MARRIAGE:** start in 1843, kept by Parish Clerk
- **DIVORCE:** 1843, Parish Clerk
- **PROBATE:** 1843, Parish Clerk
- **COURT:** 1843, Parish Clerk

TERREBONNE PARISH
Box 1569, Houma, LA 70361, (985) 868-5660,
<www.terrebonneparish.com>
- **INCORPORATED:** March 22, 1822
- **PARENT PARISH:** Lafourche
- **MARRIAGE:** unknown start, kept by Parish Clerk
- **LAND:** unknown, Parish Clerk
- **PROBATE:** unknown, Parish Clerk

UNION PARISH
100 E. Bayou St., Suite 105, Farmerville, LA 71241, (318) 368-3055,
<usgwarchives.net/la/union.htm>
- **INCORPORATED:** March 13, 1839
- **PARENT PARISH:** Ouachita
- **MARRIAGE:** start in 1839, kept by Parish Clerk
- **DIVORCE:** 1839, Parish Clerk
- **PROBATE:** 1839, Parish Clerk
- **COURT:** unknown, Parish Clerk

VERMILION PARISH
100 N. State St., Suite 101, Abbeville, LA 70510, (337) 898-1992,
<www.vermilion.org>
- **INCORPORATED:** March 25, 1844
- **PARENT PARISH:** Lafayette
- **MARRIAGE:** start in 1885, kept by Parish Clerk
- **DIVORCE:** 1885, Parish Clerk
- **LAND:** 1885, Parish Clerk
- **PROBATE:** 1885, Parish Clerk
- **COURT:** 1885, Parish Clerk

VERNON PARISH
Box 40, Leesville, LA 71496, (337) 238-1384,
<www.vernonclerk.com>
- **INCORPORATED:** March 30, 1871
- **PARENT PARISHES:** Natchitoches, Rapides, Sabine
- **MARRIAGE:** start in 1890, kept by Parish Clerk
- **DIVORCE:** 1871, Parish Clerk
- **PROBATE:** 1871, Parish Clerk
- **COURT:** 1871, Parish Clerk

WASHINGTON PARISH
Box 607, Franklinton, LA 70438, (985) 839-4663,
<www.wpgov.org>
- Incorporated: March 6, 1819
- **PARENT PARISH:** St. Tammany
- **MARRIAGE:** start in 1897, kept by Parish Clerk
- **DIVORCE:** 1897, Parish Clerk
- **LAND:** 1897, Parish Clerk
- **PROBATE:** 1897, Parish Clerk
- **COURT:** 1897, Parish Clerk

WEBSTER PARISH
Box 370, Minden, LA 71058, (318) 371-0366,
<www.rootsweb.ancestry.com/~lawebste>
- **INCORPORATED:** Feb. 27, 1871
- **PARENT PARISHES:** Claiborne, Bienville, Bossier
- **MARRIAGE:** start in 1871, kept by Parish Clerk
- **DIVORCE:** 1871, Parish Clerk
- **LAND:** 1871, Parish Clerk
- **PROBATE:** 1871, Parish Clerk
- **COURT:** 1871, Parish Clerk

WEST BATON ROUGE PARISH
Box 107, Port Allen, LA 70767, (225) 383-0378,
<www.wbrcouncil.org>
- **INCORPORATED:** March 31, 1807
- **PARENT PARISH:** Baton Rouge
- **BIRTH:** unknown start, kept by Clerk of Courts
- **MARRIAGE:** unknown, Clerk of Courts
- **LAND:** unknown, Clerk of Courts
- **PROBATE:** unknown, Clerk of Courts

WEST CARROLL PARISH
Box 1078, Oak Grove, LA 71263, (318) 428-3281,
<www.rootsweb.ancestry.com/~lawestca>
- **INCORPORATED:** March 28, 1877
- **PARENT PARISH:** Carroll
- **MARRIAGE:** start in 1877, kept by Parish Clerk
- **DIVORCE:** 1833, Parish Clerk
- **LAND:** 1833, Parish Clerk
- **PROBATE:** 1833, Parish Clerk
- **COURT:** 1833, Parish Clerk

WEST FELICIANA PARISH
Box 1843, St., Francisville, LA 70775, (225) 635-3794, **<www.mylouisianagenealogy.com/la-county-west-feliciana.html>**
- **INCORPORATED:** Feb. 17, 1824
- **PARENT PARISH:** Feliciana
- **MARRIAGE:** start in 1879, kept by Parish Clerk
- **DIVORCE:** 1900, Parish Clerk
- **LAND:** 1811, Parish Clerk
- **PROBATE:** 1900, Parish Clerk
- **COURT:** 1900, Parish Clerk

WINN PARISH
Box 137, Winnfield, LA 71483, (318) 628-3515,
<www.rootsweb.ancestry.com/~lawinn>
- **INCORPORATED:** Feb. 24, 1852
- **PARENT PARISHES:** Natchitoches, Catahoula, Rapides
- **MARRIAGE:** start in 1886, kept by Parish Clerk
- **DIVORCE:** 1886, Parish Clerk
- **LAND:** 1886, Parish Clerk
- **PROBATE:** 1886, Parish Clerk
- **COURT:** 1886, Parish Clerk

MAINE

» BY MAUREEN A. TAYLOR

HISTORICAL OVERVIEW

Maine is both the largest New England state and the most sparsely populated. In 1622, England's King Charles I gave John Mason and Sir Fernando Gorges land encompassing part of modern Maine and New Hampshire. Gorges established the region's first Colonial government. He sold his land to Massachusetts in 1677, which it belonged to until 1820.

Emigrants from Massachusetts Bay established the first permanent communities along Maine's coast, while the French inhabited the area near the Penobscot River. Colonial conflicts between the French, English and native populations resulted in Massachusetts declaring war on all American Indians in Maine in 1703. After the French and Indian War (1754-1763) France had to give up its claim to the region. Although early settlers were primarily English, French Canadians, Scots-Irish, Acadians, and African-Americans all populated the area along with the native people.

Maine became a state in 1820 under the Missouri Compromise: Missouri entered the Union as a slave state; Maine became a free state. Boundary disputes with Canada in 1839 resulted in the Aroostook War, which was eventually settled by the Webster-Ashburton Treaty of 1842.

Farming, fishing, logging, shipbuilding, and fur trading supported Maine for much of its early history. But employment opportunities changed in the 1800s: Steamship production began at Maine's shipyards, followed by battleships. Textile mills attracted women from all over, while urban dwellers escaped the cities to enjoy the state's natural charms—creating the tourism industry that is still thriving today.

research tips

- The Massachusetts State Archives and Massachusetts Historical Society contain early records for Maine, which was a part of their state for more than 100 years.
- Conduct most of your Maine research on the state level. Working in town records can be disappointing.
- The Maine State Archives **<www.state.me.us/sos/arc>** and the Maine Historical Society **<www.mainehistory.org>** are the best places to begin your Maine research.

CENSUS RECORDS

- Federal census: 1790, 1800, 1810, 1820, 1830, 1840, 1850, 1860, 1870, 1880, 1900, 1910, 1920, 1930
- Federal mortality schedules: 1850, 1860, 1870,1880
- Special census of Civil War Union veterans and widows: 1890
- State census: 1837 (fragments for Bangor, Portland, Eliot and unincorporated towns)

RECORD HIGHLIGHTS

Historical recording practices in Maine lack the completeness found in other New England states, due to a late start to civil registration and the remoteness of some towns. Only five towns (Biddeford, Kittery, Kennebunkport, York, and Wells) have vital records from the 17th century. State legislation in 1864 required town clerks to provide the state with birth, marriage and death records, but total compliance didn't happen until 1892 with the establishment of the State Board of Vital Statistics. Marriage records from 1892 to 1996 are online **<portal.maine.gov/marriage/archdev.marriage_archive.search_form>**. Still, "as late as 1944, as many as one out of 10 births were not recorded," says Art Dostie, research room supervisor at the Maine State Archives. "You have a 50/50 chance of finding a birth record before 1892, and only a 20 percent chance of locating a death record." The Maine Historical Society **<www.mainehistory.org>** has published compilations of births, marriages, and deaths extracted from diaries, church records, newspapers, gravestones, and vital records for 18 towns. Their library has vital records for 1892-1955 on microfilm, and has an index to the towns listed in the vital records pre-1892. Picton Press **<www.pictonpress.com>** has published vital records for many Maine towns.

Deaths records are being supplemented by the cemetery transcription project of the Maine Old Cemetery Association **<www.rootsweb.ancestry.com/~memoca/moca.htm>**.

Start by identifying when your ancestor was in Maine, determine what type of record you need and visit the appropriate repository. The lack of centralized records means you'll have to look for resources in a various places: Deeds and probates—wills, adoptions and guardianships—are on the county level; court documents are mostly at the Maine State Archives; and military records prior to statehood are in the Massachusetts State Archives or National Archives.

Church records require much effort to locate and use. Most are unpublished and unindexed. The Maine Historical Society has manuscript and published records for Baptist, Congregational, Methodist, Quaker and Unitarian denominations.

The Maine State Archives **<www.state.me.us/sos/arc>** has one of the largest collections in the state. Availability and completeness depend on the time period. The Maine Historical Society has manuscripts, indexed vital records and Bible records, as well as an online guide to genealogical holdings. Of particular note are the more than 2 million unpublished items, especially "the early records of the Kennebec Purchase, the Pejepscot Proprietors and the Pownalborough Courthouse collection." About half the book collection and less than half the manuscript collection is cataloged online, so consult card catalogs or call to verify additional holdings.

The New England Historic Genealogical Society (NEHGS) in Boston has many manuscripts relating to Maine families, including record of the Direct Tax of 1798. See the website **<www.americanancestors.org>** for online databases relating to Maine research (membership required). Of course, because Maine was part of Massachusetts for close to 150 years, you'll need to look outside Maine for records pre-statehood. Both the Massachusetts State Archives and Massachusetts Historical Society contain material on Maine.

Exhaust the materials at these libraries and archives before seeking records at the town level. Researching on the town level usually requires traveling through Maine's 16 counties. And "Maine is the worst New England state for town hall fires," says David Allen Lambert, NEHGS online genealogist. "Success is possible by creating a comprehensive ancestral sketch with the careful searching of vital records, records of the Maine Old Cemetery Association, probates, and deeds. The many other printed and manuscript sources on the state and local level will aid you in rounding out any and all Maine problems."

☞ ARCHIVES, LIBRARIES, AND SOCIETIES

Acton-Shapleigh Historical Society
122 Emery Mills Road, Shapleigh, ME 04076 , **<actonshapleigh.com>**

Albion Historical Society
Box 68, Albion, ME 04910

Allagash Historical Society
<aroostook.me.us/allagash/historical.html>

Androscoggin Historical Society
Court Street Door, County Building, Auburn, ME 04210, (207) 784-0586, **<www.rootsweb.ancestry.com/~meandrhs>**

The Archives of the Diocese of Portland (Roman Catholic)
510 Ocean Ave., Box 11559, Portland, ME 04104, (207) 773-6471, **<www.portlanddiocese.net/info.php?info_id=59>**

Arnold Expedition Historical Society
599 Shapleigh Corner Road, Shapleigh, ME 04076, **<arnoldsmarch.com>**

Auburn Public Library
49 Spring St., Auburn, ME 04210, (207) 333-6640, fax (207) 333-6644 , **<www.auburn.lib.me.us>**

Bangor Public Library
145 Harlow St., Bangor, ME 04401, (207) 947-8336, fax: (207) 945-6694, **<www.bpl.lib.me.us>**

Bath Historical Society
Patten Free Library, 33 Summer St., Bath, ME 04530, (207) 443-5141, **<www.patten.lib.me.us/historicalsociety.html>**

Bethel Historical Society
Box 12, Bethel, ME 04217, (207) 824-2908, **<www.bethelhistorical.org>**

Bridgton Historical Society
Box 44, Bridgton, ME 04009, (207) 647-3699, **<www.bridgtonhistory.org>**

Buckfield Historical Society
R.R. 4, Box 780, Turner, ME 04282

Camden Historical Society
80 Mechanic St., Camden, ME 04843

Camden-Rockport Historical Society
Box 747, Rockport, ME 04856, (207) 236-2257, **<www.crmuseum.org>**

Cherryfield-Narraguagus Historical Society
88 River Road, Box 96, Cherryfield, ME 04622, (207) 546-2076, **<www.cherryfieldhistorical.com>**

Cushing Historical Society
Box 110, Cushing, ME 04563, **<www.rootsweb.com/~usgenweb/me/knox/cushing.htm>**

Dexter Historical Society
Box 481, Dexter, ME 04930, **<dexterhistoricalsociety.com>**

Episcopal Archives of the Diocesan House
143 State St., Portland, ME 04101, (207) 772-1953, **<www.episcopalmaine.org>**

Falmouth Historical Society
Box 367, 190 US Route 1, Falmouth, ME 04105, (207) 781-4727, **<www.falmouthmehistory.org>**

Finnish American Heritage Society of Maine
Box 294, 8 Maple St., West Paris, ME 04289, **<www.mainefinns.org>**

Finnish American Society of Mid-Coast Maine
Box 488, Warren, ME 04864

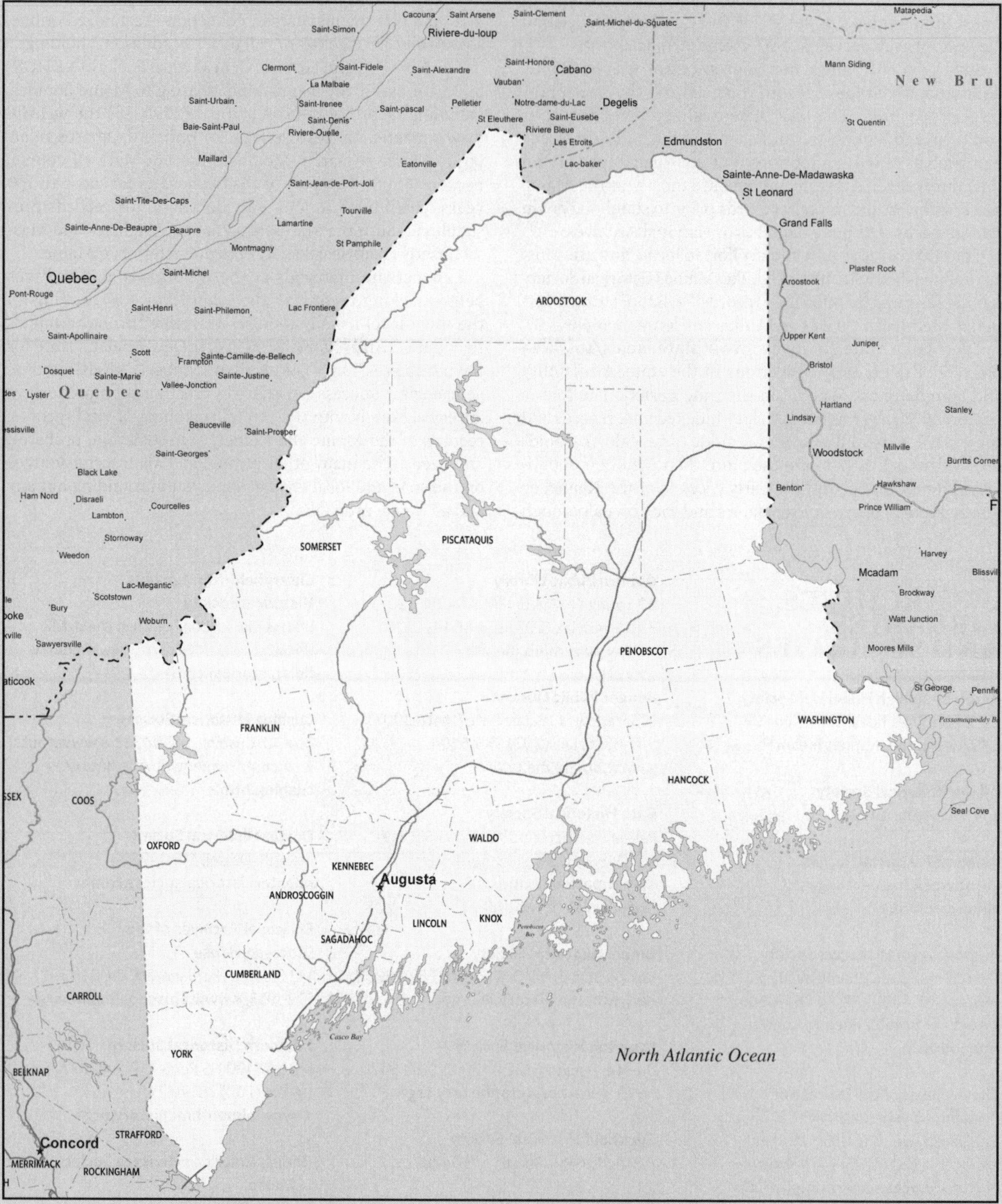
Cacouna
Saint Arsene
Saint-Clement
Matapedia
Saint-Michel-du-Squatec
Saint-Simon
Riviere-du-loup
Clermont
Saint-Fidele
Saint-Alexandre
Saint-Honore
Cabano
Mann Siding
La Malbaie
Vauban
Saint-Urbain
Saint-Irenee
Saint-pascal
Pelletier
Notre-dame-du-Lac
Degelis
Saint-Denis
St Eleuthere
Saint-Eusebe
St Quentin
Baie-Saint-Paul
Riviere-Ouelle
Riviere Bleue
Les Etroits
Edmundston
Maillard
Eatonville
Lac-baker
Saint-Jean-de-Port-Joli
Sainte-Anne-De-Madawaska
St Leonard
Saint-Tite-Des-Caps
Tourville
Lamartine
Grand Falls
Sainte-Anne-De-Beaupre
Beaupre
St Pamphile
Montmagny
Plaster Rock
Quebec
Saint-Michel
Pont-Rouge
Aroostook
AROOSTOOK
Saint-Henri
Saint-Philemon
Lac Frontiere
Saint-Apollinaire
Upper Kent
Juniper
Scott
Sainte-Camille-de-Bellech
Frampton
Bristol
Dosquet
Sainte-Marie
Sainte-Justine
Lyster
Quebec
Vallee-Jonction
Hartland
Stanley
Lindsay
Beauceville
Saint-Prosper
Woodstock
Millville
Saint-Georges
Black Lake
Benton
Hawkshaw
Ham Nord
Disraeli
Courcelles
Prince William
Lambton
Stornoway
SOMERSET
PISCATAQUIS
Weedon
Harvey
Lac-Megantic
Mcadam
Scotstown
Brockway
Bury
Woburn
Watt Junction
Sawyersville
PENOBSCOT
Moores Mills
St George
WASHINGTON
Passamaquoddy Bay
FRANKLIN
COOS
HANCOCK
Seal Cove
OXFORD
WALDO
KENNEBEC
Augusta
ANDROSCOGGIN
LINCOLN
KNOX
Penobscot Bay
SAGADAHOC
CUMBERLAND
CARROLL
Casco Bay
YORK
North Atlantic Ocean
BELKNAP
Concord
STRAFFORD
MERRIMACK
ROCKINGHAM

Gorham Historical Society
28 School St., Gorham, ME 04038, **<www.gorhamhistorical.com>**

Gray Historical Society
Box 544, Gray, ME 04039, (207) 657-2235, **<grayhistorical.org>**

Hancock Genealogical Society
Box 1355, Ellsworth, ME 04605, **<ellsworthme.org/hcgs>**

Hiram Historical Society
158 Sebago Rd., Hiram, ME 04041, (207) 625-4795

Kennebeck Historical Society
Box 5582, Augusta, ME 04332, (207) 622-7718, **<www.kennebechistorical.org>**

Kennebunk Free Library
112 Main St., Kennebunk, ME 04043, (207) 985-2173, **<kennebunklibrary.org>**

Kennebunkport Historical Society
Box 1173, Kennebunkport, ME 04046, (207) 967-2751, **<kporthistory.org>**

Madison Historical and Genealogical Society
165 Main St., Madison, ME 04950

Maine Department of Health and Human Services
Office of Vital Statistics, 244 Water St., 11 State House Station, Augusta, ME 04333, (207) 287-5500, **<www.maine.gov/dhhs>**

Maine Franco-American Genealogical Society
Box 2125, Lewiston, ME 04240, (207) 786-3327 , **<www.ancestors-genealogy.com/mfgs>**

Maine Genealogical Society
Box 221, Farmington, ME 04938, **<www.rootsweb.ancestry.com/~megs>**

Maine Historical Society
489 Congress St., Portland, ME 04101, (207) 774-1822, **<www.mainehistory.org>**

Maine State Archives
84 State House Station, Augusta, ME 04333, (207) 287-5790, **<www.state.me.us/sos/arc/>**

Maine State Library
64 State House Station, Augusta, ME 04333, (207) 289-5600, **<www.state.me.us/msl>**

Milo Historical Society
12 High St., Milo, ME 04463, (207) 943-2268, **<www.milohistorical.org>**

Mount Desert Island Historical Society
373 Sound Drive (Route 3/198), Box 653, Mount Desert, ME 04660, (207) 276-9323, **<www.mdihistory.org>**

National Archives-New England Region Frederick C. Murphy Federal Center
380 Trapelo Road, Waltham, MA 02452, (781) 663-0130, fax: (781) 663-0154, **<www.archives.gov/northeast/boston/>**

New England Historic Genealogical Society
99 Newbury St., Boston, MA 02116, (888) 296-3447, fax: (617) 536-7307, **<www.americanancestors.org>**

Old Broad Bay Family History Association
Box 1242, Waldoboro, ME 04572, **<www.rootsweb.com/~meobbfha/>**

Old York Historical Society Library
Box 312, 207 York St., York, ME 03909, (207) 363-4974, **<www.oldyork.org>**

Otisfield Historical Society
877 State Route 121, Otisfield, ME 04270, **<www.rootsweb.ancestry.com/~mecotisf/otis8.htm>**

Patten Free Library
33 Summer St., Bath, ME 04530, (207) 443-5141, **<www.patten.lib.me.us>**

Pejepscot Historical Society
159 Park Row, Brunswick, ME 04011, (207) 729-6606, **<community.curtislibrary.com/pejepscot.htm>**

The Sandy River Valley Chapter of the Maine Genealogical Society
<www.rootsweb.ancestry.com/~mesrvmgs/mgsindex.htm>

Scarborough Historical Society
Box 156, Scarborough, ME 04070, **<www.scarboroughmaine.com/historical>**

Stephen Phillips Memorial Library Penobscot Marine Museum
Box 498, Searsport, ME 04974, (207) 548-2529, **<www.penobscotmarinemuseum.org/libraryandresearch.html>**

Sullivan and Sorrento Historical Society
Box 44, Sullivan, ME 04664, (207) 422-6277, **<ellsworthme.org/sshs>**

Thomaston Historical Society
Box 384, Thomaston, ME 04861, **<www.thomastonhistoricalsociety.com>**

Union Historical Society
Box 154, Union, ME 04862, (207) 785-5444, **<www.midcoast.com/comespring>**

University of Maine at Orono, Raymond H. Fogler Library
Box 5729, Orono, ME 04469, (207) 581-1661, **<www.library.umaine.edu>**

Vinalhaven Historical Society
Box 339, 41 High St., Vinalhaven, ME 04863, (207) 863-4410, **<vinalhavenhistoricalsociety.org>**

Walker Memorial Library
800 Main St., Westbrook, ME 04092, (207) 854-0630, **<www.walker.lib.me.us>**

Windham Historical Society
<www.rootsweb.com/~mewhs/>

Woolwich Historical Society
Box 98, Woolwich, ME 04579, (207) 443-4833, **<woolwichhistoricalsociety.org>**

GENERAL RESOURCES

Agencies of the State Government, 1820-1971 from the Maine State Archives (Maine State Archives)

Ancient Dominions of Maine: Embracing the Earliest Facts by R.K. Sewall (Heritage Books, 1998)

Bibliographical Reference List of Manuscripts Relating to the History of Maine by Elizabeth Ring (Higginson Books, 1992)

Bibliography of the State of Maine, 2 vols., (Picton Press, 1985)

A Bibliography of the State of Maine from the Earliest Period to 1891, 2 vols., by Joseph Williamson (Thurston Print, 1896)

Brief Biographies, Maine: A Biographical Dictionary of Who's Who in Maine, Vol. 1 by Theodore Roosevelt Hodgkins (Lewiston Journal, 1926-1927)

Directory of Churches and Religious Organizations in Maine from the Historical Records Survey (Historical Records Survey Project, 1940)

English Origins of New England Families: From the New England Historical and Genealogical Register, Second Series, 3 vols., (Genealogical Publishing Co., 1985)

Franco-Americans of the State of Maine, U.S.A., and Their Achievements by R.J. Lawton (H.F. Roy, 1915)

Genealogical Dictionary of Maine and New Hampshire by Sybil Noyes, Charles T. Libby, and Walter G. Davis (Genealogical Publishing Co., 1996)

Genealogical and Family History of the State of Maine, 4 vols., edited by George Thomas Little (Lewis Historical Publishing, 1909)

The Greenlaw Index of the New England Historic Genealogical Society, 2 vols., by William Prescott Greenlaw (G.K. Hall, 1979)

Historic Trails and Waterways of Maine by William Otis Sawtelle (Maine Development Commission, 1932)

A History of the Discovery of Maine by J.G. Kohl (Maine Historical Society, 1869)

An Index and Guide to the Microfilm Edition of the Massachusetts and Maine Direct Tax Census of 1798 edited by Michael H. Gorn (New England Historic Genealogical Society, 1979)

The Indians of Maine and the Atlantic Provinces: A Bibliographical Guide by Roger B. Ray (Maine Historical Society, 1977)

Liberty Men and Great Proprietors: The Revolutionary Settlement on the Maine Frontier, 1760-1820 by Alan Taylor (Frontier Press, 1990)

Maine Becomes a State: The Movement to Separate Maine from Massachusetts, 1785-1820 by Ronald F. Banks (Wesleyan University Press, 1970)

Maine, A Bibliography of Its History from the Committee for a New England Bibliography, edited by John D. Haskell Jr. (G.K. Hall, 1977)

Maine Families in 1790, 6 vols., (Picton Press, 1988-1998)

The Maine Frontier, 1607 to 1763 by Robert Earle Moody (University Microfilms, 1980)

Maine Genealogy: A Bibliography Guide, revised edition, by John Eldridge Frost (Maine Historical Society, 1985)

Maine Historical Sketches by Augustus F. Moulton (Printed for the State by the Lewiston Journal Printshop, 1929)

Maine: A History, 5 vols., edited by Louis Clinton Hatch (American Historical Society, 1919)

Maine & New Hampshire Settlers, 1600s-1900s (Broderbund, 2000. CD-ROM)

Maine Pioneer Settlements, 5 vols., by Herbert Milton Sylvester (W.B. Clark, 1909)

Maine Research Outline by the Church of Jesus Christ of Latter-day Saints (online at **<www.familysearch.org/eng/search/RG/guide/maine.asp>**)

Massachusetts and Maine Families by Walter Goodwin David (Genealogical Publishing Co., 1996)

Men of Progress: Biographical Sketches and Portraits of Leaders in Business and Professional Life in and of the State of Maine by Richard Herdon, et al. (New England Magazine, 1897)

Name Index to Maine Local Histories by Marie Estes (Maine Historical Society, 1985)

New England Families: Genealogical and Memorial, 4 vols., by William Richard Cutter (Lewis Historical Publishing, 1914)

New England Family Histories: States of Maine and Rhode Island by LuVerne V. Hall (Heritage Books, 2000)

Penobscot Pioneers, 4 vols., by Philip Howard Gray (Penobscot Press, 1992-1994)

The Pioneers of Maine and New Hampshire, 1623-1660 by Charles Henry Pope (Clearfield Co., 1997)

Public Record Repositories in Maine from the Maine State Archives (Maine State Archives, 1976)

Representative Men of Maine by Henry Chase (Lakeside Press, 1893)

Sketches of the Ecclesiastical History of the State of Maine from the Earliest Settlement to the Present Time by Jonathan Greenleaf (H. Gray, 1821)

CENSUS RECORDS

1790 Census of Maine from the Maine Genealogical Society (The Society, 1995)

IMMIGRATION RECORDS

The Complete Book of Emigrants, 1607-1776, and Emigrants in Bondage, 1614-1775 by Peter Wilson Coldham (Broderbund, 1996. CD-ROM)

Immigrants to New England, 1700-1775 by Ethel Stanwood Bolton (Essex Institute, 1931)

LAND RECORDS

Black House Papers—A Guide to Certain Microfilmed Land Records from the Maine State Archives (Maine State Archives)

Names of Soldiers of the American Revolution Who Applied for State Bounty, 1893 by Charles J. House (Genealogical Publishing Co., 1967)

☞MAPS

Connecticut, Maine, Massachusetts, and Rhode Island Atlas of Historical County Boundaries edited by John H. Long (Simon & Schuster, 1994)

Counties, Cities, Towns, and Plantations of Maine from the Historical Records Survey (The Survey, 1940)

The Dictionary of Maine Place-Names by Phillip R. Rutherford (Bond Wheelwright Co., 1970)

A Gazetteer of the State of Maine: With Numerous Illustrations by George J. Varney (Heritage Books, 1991)

Indian Place Names of the Penobscot Valley and the Maine Coast by Fannie Hardy Eckstorm (University of Maine, 1978)

Maine County Subdivisions, Towns, Plantations, Unorganized Territories, and Places (Government Printing Office, 1977)

Maine Geographic Names: Alphabetical Finding List from US Office of Geographic Research (US Geological Survey, 1985)

Maine Place Names and the Peopling of its Towns by Ava Harrie Shadbourne (Bond Wheelwright Co., 1955)

Map Exhibiting the Principal Original Grants and Sales of Lands in the State of Maine by Moses Greenleaf (Ellsworth American, 1977)

☞MILITARY RECORDS

An Alphabetical Index of Revolutionary Pensioners Living in Maine by Charles A. Flagg (Genealogical Publishing Co., 1967)

The American Civil War: the Service Records of Atlantic Canadians with the State of Maine Volunteers, 2 vols., by Daniel F. Johnson (D.F. Johnson, 1995)

Aroostook War: Historical Sketch and Roster of Commissioned Officers and Enlisted Men (Kennebec Journal Print, 1904)

Dubros Times: Depositions of Revolutionary War Veterans from the Maine State Archives (Maine State Archives)

Maine in the Civil War: A Bibliographical Guide compiled by William B. Jordan (Maine Historical Society, 1976)

Military Records and Related Sources from the Maine State Archives (Maine State Archives, 2000)

Names of Soldiers of the American Revolution Who Applied for State Bounty under the Resolves of March 17, 1835, March 24, 1836, and March 20, 1838, as Appears of Record in Land Office compiled by Charles L. House (Genealogical Publishing Co., 1967)

Red Diamond Regiment: The 17th Maine Infantry, 1862-1865 by William B. Jordan (Frontier Press, 1995)

Soldiers, Sailors, and Patriots of the Revolutionary War, Maine by Carleton E. Fisher (National Society of the Sons of the American Revolution, 1982)

☞PROBATE RECORDS

History of the Court System of the State of Maine by David Q. Whittier (Maine State Archives, ca. 1980)

Maine Probate Abstracts. Vol. 1, 1687-1775; vol. 2, 1775-1800 by John Eldridge Frost (Picton Press, 1991)

Maine Wills, 1640-1760 by William M. Sargent (Clearfield Co., 1996)

Province and Court Records of Maine, 6 vols., edited by Charles T. Libby, Robert E. Moody, and Neal W. Allen (Maine Historical Society, 1928-1975)

York County, Maine Wills Abstracts 1801-1858, 2 vols., from the Maine Genealogical Society (Picton Press, 1997)

☞TAX RECORDS

An Index and Guide to the Microfilm Edition of the Massachusetts and Maine Direct Tax Census of 1798 by Michael H. Gorn (New England Historic Genealogical Society, 1979)

Massachusetts and Maine Direct Tax Census of 1798 from the US Secretary of the Treasury (New England Historic Genealogical Society, 1978)

The Massachusetts Tax Valuation List of 1771 edited by Betty Hobbs Pruitt (G.K. Hall, 1978)

☞VITAL RECORDS

Cemetery Inscriptions and Odd Information of Various Towns in the State of Maine edited by Charles D. Townsend (Aceto Bookmen, 1995)

Index to Maine Deaths, 1960-1996 from the Maine State Archives (Maine State Archives, 2002)

Index to Maine Marriages, 1892-1966, 1976-1996 from the Maine State Archives (Maine State Archives, 2002)

The Maine Historical and Genealogical Recorder, 9 vols., (S.M. Watson, 1884-98)

Maine Marriages 1892-1966: A Complete List edited by Lewis Bunker Rohrbach (Picton Press, 1996. CD-ROM)

Maine Old Cemetery Association Cemetery Inscription Project: Series One, Two and Three by Katherine W. Trickey (Northeast Reprographics, 1982)

Maine Town Microfilm List: Town and Vital Records, and Census Reports from the Maine State Archives

Vital Records (Births, Marriages, Deaths) Before 1892 and ***Vital Records from 1892-1922*** from the Maine State Archives (Maine State Archives, 2002)

Vital Records, 1923-Present from the Maine State Archives (Maine State Archives, 2002)

Vital Records from Maine Newspapers 1785-1820, 2 vols., by David C. Young and Elizabeth Keene Young (Heritage Books, 1993)

•-COUNTY DETAILS-•

ANDROSCOGGIN

2 Turner St., Auburn, ME 04210, (207) 784-8390, **<www.maine.gov/local/androscoggin>**

- **INCORPORATED:** March 18, 1854
- **PARENT COUNTIES:** Cumberland, Oxford, Kennebec, Lincoln
- **BIRTH:** unknown start, kept by City Clerk
- **MARRIAGE:** unknown, City Clerk
- **DIVORCE:** 1854, Clerk/District Court
- **DEATH:** unknown, City Clerk
- **LAND:** 1854, Registrar of Deeds
- **PROBATE AND WILLS:** 1854, Probate Court
- **COURT:** 1854, County Comm. Office
- **NOTES:** Androscoggin Historical Society has military records 1775-1785. Towns organized before 1800: Durham 1789, Greene 1788, Lewiston 1795, Lisbon 1799, Livermore 1795, Turner 1786.

AROOSTOOK

County Courthouse, 144 Sweden St., Box 846, Caribou, ME 04736, (207) 532-7317, **<www.aroostook.me.us>**

- **INCORPORATED:** March 16, 1839
- **PARENT COUNTIES:** Washington, Penobscot
- **BIRTH:** unknown start, kept by Town Clerks
- **MARRIAGE:** unknown, Town Clerks
- **DIVORCE:** 1839, Clerk/District Court
- **DEATH:** unknown, kept by Town Clerks
- **LAND:** 1839, Registrar of Deeds
- **PROBATE AND COURT:** 1839, Probate Court

CUMBERLAND

142 Federal St., Portland, ME 04101, (207) 871-8380, **<cumberlandcounty.org>**

- **INCORPORATED:** May 28, 1760
- **PARENT COUNTY:** York
- **BIRTH:** unknown start, kept by City/Town Clerks
- **MARRIAGE:** unknown, City/Town Clerks
- **DEATH:** unknown, City/Town Clerks
- **LAND:** 1760, Registrar of Deeds
- **PROBATE:** 1908, Registrar of Probate
- **COURT:** 1760, Court/County Commissioner
- **NOTES:** Towns organized before 1800: Bridgton 1794, Brunswick 1739, Cape Elizabeth 1765, Falmouth 1718, Freeport, 1789, Gorham 1764, Gray 1778, Harpswell 1758, New Gloucester 1774, North Yarmouth 1732, Otisfield 1798, Portland 1786, Scarborough 1658, Standish 1785, Windham 1762.

FRANKLIN

140 Main St., Farmington, ME 04938, (207) 778-6614, **<www.maine.gov/local/franklin>**

- **INCORPORATED:** March 20, 1838
- **PARENT COUNTIES:** Kennebec, Oxford, Somerset
- **BIRTH:** unknown start, kept by Town Clerks
- **MARRIAGE:** unknown, Town Clerks
- **DIVORCE:** 1852, Clerk/District Ct.
- **DEATH:** unknown, Town Clerks
- **LAND:** 1838, Registrar of Deeds
- **PROBATE:** 1838, Probate Court
- **NOTES:** Towns organized before 1800: Farmington 1794, Jay 1795, New Sharon 1794.

HANCOCK

50 State St., Suite 7, Ellsworth, ME 04605, (207) 667-9542, **<www.co.hancock.me.us>**

- **INCORPORATED:** Jun. 25, 1789
- **PARENT COUNTY:** Lincoln
- **BIRTH:** unknown start, kept by Town Clerks
- **MARRIAGE:** unknown, Town Clerks
- **DIVORCE:** unknown, Clerk/District Ct.
- **DEATH:** unknown, Town Clerks
- **LAND:** 1791, Registrar of Deeds
- **PROBATE:** 1791, Probate Court
- **NOTES:** Towns organized before 1800: Bar Harbor 1796; Penobscot 1787; Blue Hill, Deer Isle, Gouldsboro, Mount Desert, Sedgwick, Sullivan, Trenton 1789; Bucksport 1792; Castine 1796,

KENNEBEC

125 State St., Augusta, ME 04330, (207) 622-0971, **<www.kennebeccounty.org>**

- **INCORPORATED:** Feb. 20 1799
- **PARENT COUNTIES:** Lincoln, Cumberland
- **BIRTH:** unknown start, kept by Town Clerks
- **MARRIAGE:** unknown, Town Clerks
- **DEATH:** unknown, Town Clerks
- **LAND:** 1799, Registrar of Deeds
- **PROBATE:** 1799 Probate Court
- **NOTES:** Towns organized before 1800: Hallowell, Vassalboro, Winslow, Winthrop 1771; Pittsdon 1779; Readfield 1791; Monmouth, Mount Vernon, Sidney 1792; Clinton, Fayette 1795; Belgrade, China 1796; Augusta 1797; Litchfield 1798; Wayne 1798.

KNOX

62 Union St., Rockland, ME 04841, (207) 594-9379, **<knoxcounty.midcoast.com>**

- **INCORPORATED:** March 9, 1860
- **PARENT COUNTIES:** Lincoln, Waldo
- **BIRTH:** unknown start, kept by Town Clerks
- **MARRIAGE:** unknown, Town Clerks
- **DIVORCE:** unknown, Clerk/District Court
- **DEATH:** unknown, Town Clerks
- **PROBATE:** 1860 Probate Court
- **COURT:** 1860, Court/County Comm.
- **LAND:** 1860, Registrar of Deeds
- **NOTES:** Towns organized before 1800: Camden 1791, Cushing 1789, Thomaston 1777, Union 1786, Vinalhaven 1789, Warren 1776.

LINCOLN

County Courthouse, High St., Box 249, Wiscasset, ME 04578, (207) 882-6311, **<co.lincoln.me.us>**

- **INCORPORATED:** Jun. 21, 1760

- **PARENT COUNTY:** York
- **MARRIAGE:** unknown start, kept by Clerk of Courts
- **LAND:** 1761, Registrar/Deeds
- **PROBATE:** 1769, Probate Court
- **COURT:** 1761, Court/County Comm.
- **NOTES:** Supreme Judicial Court has military discharge records 1866-1890. Towns organized before 1800: Alna 1794, Boothbay 1764, Bristol 1765, Dresden 1794, Newcastle 1753, Nobleboro 1788, Waldoboro 1773, Wiscasset 1760.

OXFORD

26 Western Ave., Box 179, South Paris, ME 04281, (207) 743-6359, **<www.oxfordcounty.org>**

- **INCORPORATED:** March 4, 1805
- **PARENT COUNTIES:** York, Cumberland
- **BIRTH:** unknown start, kept by Town Clerks
- **MARRIAGE:** unknown, Town Clerks
- **DIVORCE:** 1930, Clerk/District Ct.
- **DEATH:** unknown, Town Clerks
- **PROBATE:** 1805, Probate Court
- **LAND:** 1805, Registrar of Deeds
- **NOTES:** Towns organized before 1800: Bethel 1796, Buckfield 1793, Buxton 1762, Fryeburg 1777, Hartford 1798, Hebron 1792, Norway 1797, Paris 1793, Sumner 1798, Waterford 1797.

PENOBSCOT

97 Hammond St., Bangor, ME 04401, (207) 942-8535, **<www.maine.gov/local/Penobscot>**

- **INCORPORATED:** Feb. 15, 1816
- **PARENT COUNTY:** Hancock
- **DIVORCE:** start in 1900, kept by Clerk/District Court
- **LAND:** 1814, Registrar of Deeds
- **PROBATE:** 1816, Probate Court
- **NATURALIZATION:** 1821, Clerk of Courts
- **NOTES:** Towns before 1800: Hampden 1794, Orrington 1788.

PISCATAQUIS

159 E. Main St., Dover-Foxcroft, ME 04426, (207) 564-2161, **<www.maine.gov/local/piscataquis>**

- **INCORPORATED:** March 23, 1838
- **PARENT COUNTY:** Penobscot, Somerset
- **BIRTH:** unknown start, kept by Town Clerks
- **MARRIAGE:** unknown, Town Clerks
- **DIVORCE:** unknown, Clerk/District Court
- **DEATH:** unknown, Town Clerks
- **LAND:** 1838, Registrar of Deeds
- **PROBATE:** 1838, Probate Court
- **COURT:** 1838, Clerk/District Court

SAGADAHOC

752 High, Box 246, Bath, ME 04530, (207) 443-9332, **<www.rootsweb.ancestry.com/~mesagada>**

- **INCORPORATED:** Apr. 4, 1854
- **PARENT COUNTY:** Lincoln
- **BIRTH:** unknown start, kept by Town Clerks
- **MARRIAGE:** unknown, Town Clerks
- **DIVORCE:** unknown, Clerk/District Court
- **DEATH:** unknown, Town Clerks
- **LAND:** 1826, Registrar of Deeds
- **PROBATE:** 1854, Probate Court
- **NOTES:** Towns before 1800: Bath 1781, Bowdoin 1788, Bowdoinham 1762, Georgetown 1716, Topsham 1764, Woolwich 1759.

SOMERSET

41 Court St., Skowhegan, ME 04976, (207) 474-9861, **<www.somersetcounty-me.org/index.htm>**

- **INCORPORATED:** March 1, 1809
- **PARENT COUNTY:** Kennebec
- **PROBATE:** start in 1830, kept by Probate Court
- **LAND:** 1804, Registrar of Deeds
- **NOTES:** Towns organized before 1800: Canaan 1788, Cornville 1798, Fairfield 1788, Norridgewock 1788, Starks 1795.

WALDO

39-B Spring St., Belfast, ME 04915, (207) 338-3282, fax: (207) 338-6788, **<www.waldocountyme.gov>**

- **INCORPORATED:** Feb. 7, 1827
- **PARENT COUNTY:** Hancock
- **BIRTH:** unknown start, kept by City/Town Clerks
- **MARRIAGE:** unknown, City/Town Clerks
- **DIVORCE:** 1828, Clerk/District Court
- **DEATH:** unknown, City/Town Clerks
- **LAND:** 1789, Registrar of Deeds
- **PROBATE:** 1827, Probate Court
- **NOTES:** Towns organized before 1800: Belfast 1773, Frankfort 1789, Northport 1796, Prospect 1794.

WASHINGTON

- Box 297, 85 Court Street, Machias, ME 04654, (207) 255-3127, **<www.washingtoncountymaine.com>**
- **INCORPORATED:** Jun. 25, 1789
- **PARENT COUNTY:** Lincoln
- **BIRTH AND MARRIAGE:** unknown start, kept by Town Clerks
- **DEATH:** unknown, Town Clerks
- **DIVORCE:** unknown, Clerk of Courts
- **LAND:** 1784, Registrar of Deeds
- **PROBATE:** 1785, Probate Court
- **NOTES:** Towns organized before 1800: Addison 1797, Columbia 1796, Eastport 1798, Harrington 1797, Machias 1784, Steuben 1795.

YORK

45 Kennebunk Rd., Alfred, ME 04002, (207) 324-1571, **<www.yorkcountyme.gov>**

- **INCORPORATED:** Nov. 20, 1652
- **PARENT COUNTY:** Original county
- **BIRTH AND MARRIAGE:** unknown start, Town Clerks
- **DIVORCE:** unknown,Clerk/District Court
- **DEATH:** unknown, Town Clerks
- **LAND:** 1642, Registrar of Deeds
- **PROBATE:** 1689, Probate Court
- **NOTES:** Established in 1652 as Yorkshire County; renamed in 1668. Towns organized before 1800: Berwick 1713, Biddeford 1718, Cornish 1794, Hollis 1798, Kennebunkport 1653, Kittery 1652, Lebanon 1767, Limington 1792, Lyman 1778, Newfield 1794, Parsonfield 1785, Saco 1762, Sanford 1768, Shapleigh 1785, Waterboro 1787, Wells 1653, York 1652.

MARYLAND

» BY RHONDA R. MCCLURE

HISTORICAL OVERVIEW

Like many colonial American territories, Maryland was a giant land-grant, given to Cecil Calvert, Second Baron of Baltimore, in 1632. Cecil was the son of George Calvert, who was the secretary of state under King James I of England—a title he was stripped of when he converted to Catholicism. The grant was given to Cecil after his father passed away. But another son, Leonard, led the first colonists—Catholic and Protestant English—to what became St. Mary's, the first capital. Maryland, or "Terra Mary," was named for the wife of King Charles I, Henrietta Maria, and was also known as Maria's Land and Mariland.

Of particular note in Maryland's history is the Act of Toleration that was passed in 1649. The act encouraged settlement by "nonconformists" including Catholics, Virginian dissenters, and Quakers by guaranteeing that those who were intolerant would be fined, and if they couldn't pay the fine, jailed. Unfortunately, this did not last long—the government of Maryland was overthrown in 1689 in a Protestant coup and the Anglican church became the state church of Maryland. In 1715 Lord Baltimore converted to Protestantism and the proprietary government was restored, though the Catholics found themselves disfranchised in 1781.

Germans from Pennsylvania began to enter the counties of Baltimore and Frederick in the 1730s. Quakers migrated from New Jersey at about the same time. Not all of those coming into the state were from other colonies, however—in the mid-1700s there was an influx of Jacobites, servants and felons from England. As these people were coming into Maryland, many Catholics were heading for Kentucky and Moravians for North Carolina. And don't forget that once the National Road was completed from Cumberland to Wheeling it gave Marylanders a route to the recently opened West.

RECORD HIGHLIGHTS

Don't assume you're out of luck for census records before 1790. Maryland took a colonial census in 1776 for most counties. Unlike many other early censuses, this one lists the name, age, and race of each family member for some counties. In 1778, almost all the males 18 years and older took an oath of fidelity. This list has been published in Bettie Stirling Carothers' *Maryland Oaths of Fidelity*, two vols. (B.S. Carothers, 1971). Males who did not take the oath were primarily Friends (Quakers) and others who objected on religious basis. Some records survive of adult males who did not take the oath; these have also been compiled by Bettie Stirling Carothers in *1778 Census of Maryland* (B.S. Carothers, 1975).

From 1633 to 1683, the Calverts—who originally owned all of Maryland—issued headrights or land grants to encourage immigrants to settle in Maryland. A valuable resource is Gust Skordas' *Early Settlers of Maryland: An Index to Names of Immigrants Compiled from Records of Land Patents, 1633-1680* (Genealogical Publishing Co., 1968). A continuation of

research tips

- Baltimore is an independent city,. It began keeping court, land, and probate records separate from Baltimore County in 1851.
- Check both Union and Confederate Civil War records—Maryland residents fought on both sides.
- Check all trepositories when it comes to records in Maryland. Many county records are now housed at the state archive.

CENSUS RECORDS

- Federal Census: 1790, 1800, 1810, 1820, 1830, 1840, 1850, 1860, 1870, 1880, 1900, 1910, 1920, 1930
- Federal Mortality Schedules: 1850. 1860, 1870, 1880
- Special census of Civil War Union veterans and widows: 1890

this work is Peter Wilson Coldham's *Settlers of Maryland, 5 vols.* (Genealogical Publishing Co., 1995-1996).

Birth records in Maryland from 1898 until 1950, and those for Baltimore City from 1875 until 1941, are on microfilm at the Maryland State Archives. Death records begin in 1898 for the state and 1875 for the city of Baltimore, and go through 1982. While birth records for the last 100 years are restricted, you can write to the Maryland State Archives, 350 Rowe Boulevard, Annapolis, MD 21401. The Archives can supply:

- Copies of death records through 1978 for the state and 1942 for the City of Baltimore
- Unofficial transcripts of genealogical information from birth and death records that are restricted
- Copies of restricted birth and death records to individuals who are entitled to them

Marriage records from 1914 to 1950 are also at the archives. Records from the late 1700s through 1919 may be found at the county court clerks' offices, but the state archives may have what you need. The Family History Library has marriages from the 1850s on microfilm, though it does not have the indexes.

Divorces were not granted before the American Revolution, and after, that they were granted only by the state legislature until 1842. Divorce records can be found at the circuit court in the county where the divorce was granted, or they may be in the state archives.

ARCHIVES, LIBRARIES, AND SOCIETIES

Allegany County Historical Society
219 Washington St., Cumberland, MD 21502

Anne Arundel Genealogical Society
Box 221, Pasadena, MD 21123, **<www.aagensoc.org>**

Appalachian Collection, Allegany Community College Library
12401 Willowbrook Rd. SE, Cumberland, MD 21502, (301) 784-5005

Afro-American Historical and Genealogical Society
Box 9366, Catonsville, MD 21228, **<baahgs.typepad.com>**

Archives of the Archdiocese of Baltimore
St. Mary's Seminary and University, 5400 Roland Ave., Baltimore, MD 21210 (410) 864-4074, **<www.archbalt.org/ministries-offices/archives.cfm>**

Baltimore City Archives
211 E. Pleasant St., Room 201, Baltimore, MD 21202, (410) 396-4861

Baltimore County Genealogical Society
Box 10085, Towson, MD 21285, **<www.serve.com/bcgs/bcgs.html>**

Historical Society of Baltimore County
9811 Van Buren Lane, Cockeysville, MD 21030, (410) 666-1878, **<www.hsobc.org>**

Baptist Convention of Maryland/Delaware
10255 Old Columbia, Columbia, MD 21046, (800) 466-5290, **<bcmd.org>**

Calvert County Genealogical Committee and Historical Society
Box 358, Prince Frederick, MD, 20678, (410) 535-2452, **<www.calverthistory.org>**

Historical Society of Carroll County
210 E. Main St., Westminster, MD 21157 (410) 848-6494, **<hscc.carr.org>**

Carroll County Genealogical Society
Box 1752, Westminster, MD 21158, **<www.carr.org/ccgs/ccgs.html>**

Catonsville Historical Society
Box 9311, Catonsville, MD 21228, (410) 744-3034, **<www.catonsvillehistory.org>**

Central Maryland Afro-American Historical and Genealogical Society
Box 648, Columbia, MD 21045

Crisfield Heritage Foundation
Somers Cover Marina, Crisfield, MD **<www.crisfieldheritagefoundation.org>**

Dorchester Co. Public Library
305 Gay St., Cambridge, MD 21613

Dorchester County Historical Society
Meredith House, 902 LaGrange St., Cambridge, MD 21613, (410) 228-2947 **<www.bluecrab.org/dchs>**

Dundalk Patapsco Neck Historical Society
Box 9235, Dundalk, MD 21222

Enoch Pratt Free Library
400 Cathedral St., Baltimore, MD 21201, (410) 396-5430

Frederick County Genealogical Society
Box 234, Monrovia, MD 21770

Friend Family Association of America Library National Headquarters
Box 86, Friendsville, MD 21531

Garrett County Historical Society
Box 28, Oakland, MD 21550, **<www.deepcreektimes.com/gchs.html>**

Genealogical Council of Maryland
3603 Monterey Rd., Baltimore, MD 21218

Genealogical Society of Allegany County
Box 3103, LaVale, MD 21502

Genealogical Society of Cecil County
Box 11, Charlestown, MD 21914

Germantown Historical Society
Box 475, Germantown, MD 20875, **<www.clark.net/pub/soderber/ghs>**

Granite Historical Society
Box 43, Granite, MD 21163, **<www.bcpl.net/~granhist>**

Harford County Historical Society
Box 366, Bel Air, MD 21014, (410) 838-7691, **<www.harfordhistory.net>**

Harford County Genealogical Society
Box 15, Aberdeen, MD 21001, **<www.rtis.com/reg/md/org/hcgs/default/htm>**

Harford County Historical Society
324 Kenmore Ave., The Hayes House, Bel Air, MD 21014, **<www.rtis.com/reg/md/org/hcgs/default.htm>**

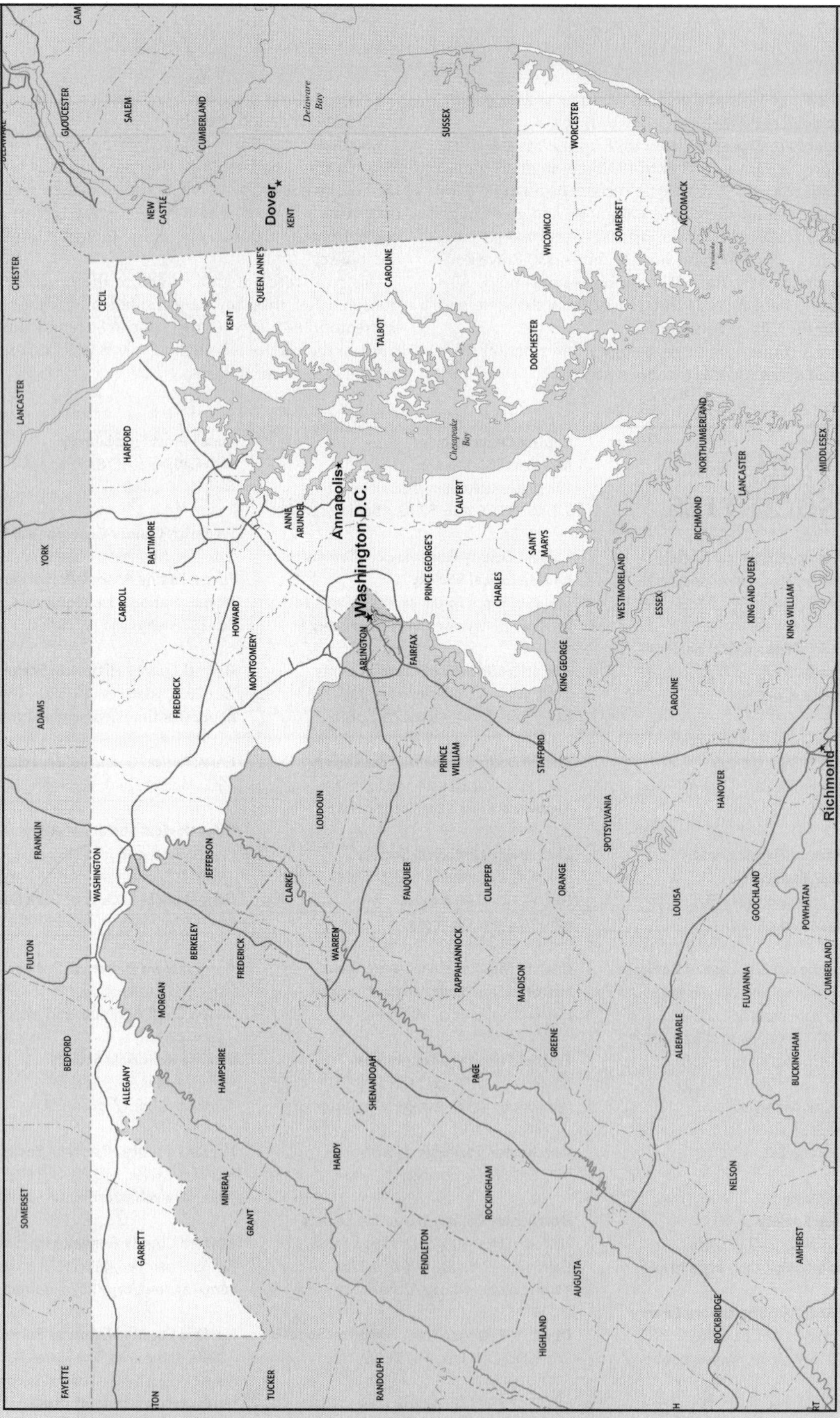
Dover
Annapolis
Washington D.C.
Richmond
Delaware Bay
Chesapeake Bay
Pocomoke Sound
GLOUCESTER
SALEM
CUMBERLAND
SUSSEX
NEW CASTLE
KENT
CHESTER
CECIL
QUEEN ANNE'S
CAROLINE
WICOMICO
WORCESTER
SOMERSET
ACCOMACK
TALBOT
DORCHESTER
LANCASTER
HARFORD
NORTHUMBERLAND
MIDDLESEX
YORK
BALTIMORE
ANNE ARUNDEL
CALVERT
SAINT MARYS
RICHMOND
CARROLL
HOWARD
PRINCE GEORGE'S
CHARLES
WESTMORELAND
ESSEX
KING AND QUEEN
KING WILLIAM
MONTGOMERY
ARLINGTON
FAIRFAX
KING GEORGE
ADAMS
FREDERICK
CAROLINE
PRINCE WILLIAM
STAFFORD
HANOVER
LOUDOUN
SPOTSYLVANIA
FRANKLIN
WASHINGTON
JEFFERSON
CLARKE
FAUQUIER
CULPEPER
ORANGE
LOUISA
GOOCHLAND
POWHATAN
FULTON
BERKELEY
WARREN
RAPPAHANNOCK
MADISON
FLUVANNA
CUMBERLAND
MORGAN
BEDFORD
ALLEGANY
HAMPSHIRE
SHENANDOAH
PAGE
GREENE
ALBEMARLE
BUCKINGHAM
HARDY
MINERAL
ROCKINGHAM
NELSON
SOMERSET
GARRETT
GRANT
PENDLETON
AUGUSTA
AMHERST
ROCKBRIDGE
HIGHLAND
FAYETTE
TUCKER
RANDOLPH

Historic Annapolis Foundation
18 Pinkney St., Annapolis, MD 21401, **<www.annapolis.org>**

Historical and Genealogical Society of Somerset County
10649 Somerset Pike, Somerset, PA 15501, (814) 445-6077

Historical Society of Carroll County
210 E. Main St., Westminster, MD 21157, **<hscc.carr.org>**

Historical Society of Cecil County
135 East Main St., Elkton, MD 21921, **<cchistory.org>**

Historical Society of Frederick County
24 E. Church St., Frederick, MD 21701, **<www.fwp.net/hsfc>**

Historical Society of Talbot County
29 S. Washington St., Easton, MD 21601 (410) 822-7911, **<www.hstc.org>**

Howard County Genealogical Society
Box 274, Columbia, MD 21045

Jewish Genealogical Society of Greater Washington DC
Box 31122, Bethesda, MD 20824-1122, **<www.jewishgen.org/jgsgw>**

Jewish Historical Society Library of Maryland
15 Lloyd St., Baltimore, MD 21202, (410) 732-6400, **<www.ohwy.com/md/j/jehisoma.htm>**

Jewish Special Interest Group, Gesher Galicia
3128 Brooklawn Ter., Chevy Chase, MD 20815

John Hopkins University, George Peabody Library
17 E. Mount Vernon Pl., Baltimore, MD 21202, (410) 659-8179

Lower Delmarva Genealogical Society
Box 3602, Salisbury, MD 21802, **<bay.intercom.net/ldgs/index.html>**

Archives of the Delaware-Maryland Synod, Evangelical Lutheran Church of America
7604 York Rd., Towson, MD 21204, (410) 825-9520, (410) 825-6745

Maryland Genealogical Society
201 W. Monument St., Baltimore, MD 21201, (410) 685-3750, **<www.mdgensoc.org>**

Maryland Historical Society Library
201 W. Monument St., Baltimore, MD 21201, (410) 685-3750, **<www.mdhs.org>**

Maryland State Archives
4201 Patterson Ave., Box 13146, Baltimore, MD 2120, (800) 832-3277, **<www.msa.md.gov>**

Division of Vital Records
6550 Reisterstown Road, Reisterstown Road Plaza, Baltimore, MD 21215, (410) 764-3038, **<vsa.maryland.gov>**

Maryland State Law Library Robert C. Murphy Courts of Appeal
Building, 361 Rowe Blvd., Annapolis, MD 21401, (410) 260-1430, **<www.courts.state.md.us/lawlib>**

Mid-Atlantic Germanic Society
725 Fir Spring Dr., Waynesboro, PA 17268, **<www.magsgen.com>**

Montgomery County Historical Society
111 W. Montgomery Ave., Rockville, MD 20850, (301) 340-2825, **<www.montgomeryhistory.org>**

National Archives , Mid-Atlantic Region
900 Market St., Philadelphia, PA 19107, (215) 606-0100, **<archives.gov/midatlantic>**

Prince George's County Genealogical Society
Box 819, Bowie, MD 20718, (301) 262-2063, **<rootsweb.ancestry.com/~mdpgcgs>**

Prince George's County Afro-American Historical and Genealogical Society
Box 44252, Fort Washington, MD 20749, **<pgcm.aahgs.org>**

Prince George's County Historical Society
Box 14, Riverdale, MD 20738, **<www.pghistory.org>**

Saint Mary's City Historical Society
11 Courthouse Dr., Box 212, Leonardtown, MD 20650

Saint Mary's County Genealogical Society
Box 1109, Leonardtown, MD 20650, **<smcgsmd.com>**

Silver Spring Historical Society
Box 1160, Silver Spring, MD 20910, **<www.homestead.com/silverspringhistory>**

Society for the History of the Germans in Maryland
Box 22595, Baltimore, MD 22585, **<www.shgm.org>**

Theodore R. McKeldin Library, University of Maryland
College Park, MD 20742, (301) 485-0800 **<www.lib.umd.edu/MCK>**

United Baptist Missionary Convention
940 Madison Ave., Baltimore, MD 21201 (410) 523-2950, **<www.ubmcofmd.org>**

United Methodist Historical Society Lovely Lane Museum and Archives
2200 St. Paul St., Baltimore, MD 21218, (410) 889-4458, **<www.lovelylanemuseum.com>**

Upper Shore Genealogical Society
Box 275, Easton, MD 21601, **<www.usgsmd.org>**

Washington County Historical Society
Box 1281, Hagerstown, MD 21741, (301) 797-8782, **<www.rootsweb.ancestry.com/~mdwchs>**

Worcester County Library Snow Hill Branch
307 N. Washington St., Snow Hill, MD 21863, (410) 632-3495, **<www.worcesterlibrary.org/location-snow-hill.shtml>**

GENERAL RESOURCES

Anglican Maryland, 1692-1792 by Canon Arthur Pierce Middleton (The Donning Co./Publishers, 1992)

Archives of Maryland, New Series, Vol. 1 (Maryland State Archives Publications, 1990)

Baltimore County Families, 1659-1759 by Robert W. Barnes (Genealogical Publishing Co., 1989)

Biographical Cyclopedia of Representative Men of Maryland and District of Columbia (National Biographical Publishing Co., 1879)

A Biographical Dictionary of the Maryland Legislature, 1635-1789, 2 vols. by Edward C. Papenfuse, et al. (Johns Hopkins University Press, 1985)

British Roots of Maryland Families by Robert Barnes (Genealogical Publishing Co., 1999)

Calendar of Maryland State Papers: No. 1—The Black Books from the Maryland Hall of Records (Clearfield Co., 1995)

The Calvert Papers: Calendar and Guide to the Microfilm Edition by Donna M. Ellis and Karen A. Stuart (Maryland Historical Society, 1973)

Captains and Mariners of Early Maryland by Raphael T. Semmes (The John Hopkins Press, 1937)

Chronicles of Colonial Maryland by James Walter Thomas (Clearfield Co., 1995)

Church Records at the Maryland State Archives (Maryland State Archives, 2002)

Colonial Chesapeake Society by Lois Green Carr, et al. (Frontier Press, 1988)

Colonial Families of the Eastern Shore of Maryland, Vol., 2. by Robert W. Barnes and F. Edward Wright (Family Line Publications, 1996)

Directory of Maryland Church Records compiled by Edna Agatha Kanely (Family Line Publications, 1987)

Directory of Ministers and the Maryland Churches They Served, 1634-1990, 2 vols. by Edna Agatha Kanely (Family Line Publications, 1991)

Early Families of Southern Maryland, 5 vols. by Elise Greenup Jordan (Family Line Publications, 1995)

The First Parishes of the Province of Maryland by Percy G. Skirven (Clearfield Company, 1997)

The Flowering of the Maryland Palatinate by Harry Wright Newman (Clearfield Co., 1985)

The Free State of Maryland: A History of the State and Its People, 1634-1941, 4 vols. by Frederic Arnold Kummer (Allen County Public Library, ca. 1980)

Genealogical and Memorial Encyclopedia of the State of Maryland by Richard Henry Spencer (Clearfield Co., 1992)

Genealogical Research in Maryland: A Guide, 4th edition, by Mary Keysor Meyer (Maryland Historical Society, 1992)

General History Section Index of Scharf's History of Western Maryland by Helen R. Long (Helen R. Long, 1992)

A Guide to Government Records at the Maryland State Archives (Maryland State Archives, 1992)

A Guide to Historic Episcopal Churches of Southern Maryland, 1634-1984 (Printing Press, ca. 1990)

A Guide to the Maryland Hall of Records: Local, Judicial and Administrative Records on Microfilm by Edward C. Papenfuse, et al. (Hall of Records Commission, 1978)

A Guide to the Microfilm Collection of Newspapers at the Maryland State Archives by Les White (MD State Archives, 1990)

Guide to the Research Collections of the Maryland Historical Society edited by Richard J. Cox and Larry E. Sullivan (Maryland Historical Society, 1981)

Guide to State Agency Records: Histories and Series Descriptions (Maryland State Archives Publications, 1994)

A History of Baltimore Yearly Meeting of Friends by Bliss A. Forbush (Baltimore Yearly Meeting of Friends, 1972)

History of the Church of the Brethren in Maryland by J. Maurice Henry (Brethren Publishing, 1936)

History of Maryland, 3 vols. (Tradition Press, 1967, reprint)

The History of Maryland, from Its First Settlement in 1633 to the Restoration in 1660, Vol., 1 by John Leeds Bozeman (Baltimore: Heritage Books, 1990)

History of Western Maryland by John T. Scharf (Regional Publishing Co., 1968)

An Index to the Source Records of Maryland: Genealogical, Historical by Eleanor P. Passano (Genealogical Publishing Co., 1984)

Inside the Great House: Planter Family Life in Eighteenth-Century Chesapeake Society by Daniel Blake Smith (Frontier Press, 1994)

Inventory of the Church Archives of Maryland: Protestant Episcopal Diocese of Maryland (Historical Records Survey, 1940)

Inventory of Maryland Bible Records from the Genealogical Council of Maryland (Family Line Publications, 1989)

The Manuscript Collections of the Maryland Historical Society compiled by Avril J.M. Pedley (Maryland Historical Society, 1969)

Maryland Biographical Sketch Index by Samuel M. Andrusko (Samuel M. Adrusko, 1983)

Maryland and Delaware Genealogies and Family Histories: A Bibliography by Donald Odell Virdin (Heritage Books, 1993)

Maryland Deponents, 1634-1799 by Henry C. Peden Jr. (Family Line Publications, 1991)

The Maryland Gazette, 1727-1761: Genealogical and Historical Abstracts by Karen M. Green (Frontier Press, 1990)

Maryland Genealogical Library Guide by John W. Heisey (Masthof Press, 1998)

Maryland Genealogical Research by George K. Schweitzer (George K. Schweitzer, 1991)

Maryland: A History, 1632-1974 edited by Richard Walsh and William Lloyd Fox (Maryland Historical Society, 1974)

Maryland, A History of Its People edited by Suzanne Ellery Greene Chapelle (Johns Hopkins University Press, 1986)

Maryland Lost and Found: People and Places from Chesapeake to Appalachia by Eugene L. Meyer (John Hopkins University Press, 1986)

Maryland: A Middle Tempermant, 1634-1980 by Robert J. Brugger (Frontier Press, 1990)

Maryland Records: Colonial Revolutionary, County and Church from Original Sources, 2 vols., by Gaius Marcus Brumbaugh (Genealogical Publishing Co., 1993)

Maryland Research Guide by John W. Heisey (Heritage House, 1986)

Maryland Research Outline by the Church of Jesus Christ of Latter-day Saints (online at **<www.familysearch.org/eng/searcg/RG/guide/maryland>**)

Marylanders to Kentucky, 1775-1825 by Henry C. Peden Jr. (Family Line Publications, 1991)

Men of Mark in Maryland: Biographies of Leading Men in the State, 4 vols. (Johnson-Wynne Co., 1907-12)

Mistress of Riversdale: The Plantation Letters of Rosalie Stier Calvert, 1795-1821 by Margaret L. Callcott (Frontier Press, 1991)

More Maryland Deponents, 1716-1799 by Henry C. Peden Jr. (Family Line Publications, 1992)

Newspapers in Maryland Libraries: A Union List by Eleanor O. Hofstetter (Division of Library Development Services, Maryland State Department of Education, 1977)

Newspapers at the Maryland State Archives (Maryland State Archives, 2002)

Obituaries, Bible Records, Church Records, Family Genealogies, County Records, etc. for Frederick County, Maryland, 1800-1977 by Jacob Mehrling Holdcraft (filmed by the Genealogical Society of Utah, 1975, 1977)

Old Kent: The Eastern Shore of Maryland by George A. Hanson (Clearfield Company, 1996)

The Old Line State: A History of Maryland by Morris Leon Radoff (Hall of Records Commission, 1971)

Old Somerset on the Eastern Shore of Maryland by Clayton Torrence (Clearfield Company, 1996)

The Pennsylvania-German in the Settlement of Maryland by Daniel Wunderlich Nead (Genealogical Publishing Co., 1975)

Pioneers of Old Monocacy: The Early Settlement of Frederick County, Maryland, 1721-1743 by Grace L. Tracey and John P. Dern (Genealogical Publishing Co., 1987)

Portrait and Biographical Record of the Eastern Shore of Maryland (Chapman, 1898)

Portrait and Biographical Record of the Sixth Congressional District, Maryland: Containing Portraits and Biographies (Chapman, 1898)

The Price of Freedom: Slavery and Manumission in Baltimore and Early National Maryland by T. Stephen Whitman (University Press of Kentucky, 1997)

Quaker Records in Maryland by Phebe R. Jacobsen (Hall of Records Commission, 1966)

Quaker Records of Southern Maryland, 1658-1800 by Henry C. Peden Jr. (Family Line Publications, 1992)

Register of Maryland's Heraldic Families 1634-1935, 2 vols., by Alice Parran (Parran, 1937)

Robert Cole's World: Agriculture & Society in Early Maryland by Lois Green Carr, et al. (Frontier Press, 1991)

Scots on the Chesapeake, 1607-1830 by David Dobson (Genealogical Publishing Co., 1985)

Selected Maryland Bibliography and Resources, 2 vols., by Barbara S. Giles (B.S. Giles, ca. 1988-1989)

Side-lights on Maryland History with Sketches of Early Maryland Families, 2 vols., by Hester Dorsey Richardson (Genealogy Publishing Co., 1995)

Sketches of Maryland Eastern Shoremen (Family Line Publications, 1992)

Sources of Genealogical Help in Maryland (Southern California Genealogical Society)

Sources for Genealogical Searching in Maryland by Betty L. McCay (B.L. McCay, 1972)

To Maryland from Overseas by Harry Wright Newman (Genealogical Publishing Co., 1991)

MAPS

Atlas of Maryland edited by Derek Thompson (University of Maryland, 1977)

The Counties of Maryland and Baltimore City from the Maryland State Planning Department (Staff Planning Commission, 1968)

A Gazetteer of Maryland and Delaware by Henry Gannett (Clearfield Co., 1994)

Gazetteer of the State of Maryland by Richard Swainson Fisher (J.H. Colton, 1852)

The Hammond-Harwood House Atlas of Historical Maps of Maryland, 1608-1908 by Edward C. Pappenfuse and Joseph M. Coale (John Hopkins University Press, 1982)

Historical Atlas and Chronology of County Boundaries, 1788-1980 edited by John H. Long (G.K. Hall, 1984)

An Illustrated Genealogy of the Counties of Maryland and the District of Columbia as a Guide to Locating Records by Mary R. Brown (French Bray Printing, 1967)

Maryland A to Z: A Topographical Dictionary by Marion J. Kaminkow (Magna Carta Book Co., 1985)

Maryland-Delaware Atlas & Gazetteer (DeLorme Mapping, 1993)

Place Names of the Eastern Shore of Maryland by J. Kenneth Keatley (Queen Anne Press, 1987)

The Place Names of Maryland: Their Origin and Meaning by Hamill Kenny (Maryland Historical Society)

The Postal History of Maryland, the Delmarva Peninsula and the District of Columbia: The Post Offices and First Postmasters from 1775 To 1984 by Chester M. Smith (The Depot, 1984)

Topographic Maps of the United States from the US Geological Survey (National Archives, 1976)

CENSUS RECORDS

1776 Census of Maryland compiled by Bettie Stirling Carothers (Family Line Publications, 1989)

1778 Census of Maryland by Bettie Stirling Carothers (B.S. Carothers, 1975)

IMMIGRATION RECORDS

Citizens of the Eastern Shore of Maryland, 1659-1750 by F. Edward Wright (Family Line Publications, 1986)

Colonial Maryland Naturalizations by Jeffrey A. Wyand and Florence L. Wyand (Genealogical Publishing Co., 1986)

Copies of Lists of Passengers Arriving at Miscellaneous Ports on the Atlantic and Gulf Coasts and at Ports on the Great Lakes, 1820-1873 from the US Bureau of Customs (National Archives, 1964)

A Guide to the Acadians in Maryland in the 18th and 19th Centuries by Gregory A. Wood (Maryland Acadian Studies, 1995)

Index (Soundex) to Passenger Lists of Vessels Arriving At Baltimore, 1897-1952 from the US Bureau of Customs (National Archives, 1956)

Indexes to Naturalization Petitions to the US Circuit and District Courts for Maryland: 1797-1951 from the US Circuit Court (National Archives, 1982)

The King's Passengers To Maryland And Virginia by Peter Wilson Coldham (Family Line, 1997)

Maryland in Africa: The Maryland State Colonization Society, 1831-1857 by Penelope Campbell (University of Illinois Press, 1971)

Maryland Naturalization Abstracts, Vol., 2. by Robert A. Oszakiewski (Family Line Publications, 1996)

Marylanders to Carolina: Migrations of Marylanders to North and South Carolina Prior to 1800 by Henry C. Peden (Family Line Publications, 1994)

Passenger Lists of Vessels Arriving At Baltimore, 1820-1921; Quarterly Abstracts of Passenger Lists of Vessels Arriving At Baltimore, 1820-1869 from the US Bureau of Customs (National Archives, 1956, 1959, 1969)

LAND RECORDS

The Early Settlers of Maryland by Gust Skordas (Genealogical Publishing Co., Inc., 1995)

Land Office and Prerogative Court Records of Colonial Maryland by Elisabeth Hartsook and Gust Skordas (Clearfield Co., 1968, 1996

Land Records at the Maryland State Archives (Maryland State Archives, 2002)

Patents Series: of the Maryland Land Office from the Hall of Records, Annapolis, Maryland (filmed by the Family History Library, 1947)

Old Manors in the Colony of Maryland, 2 vols., by Annie Middleton Sioussat (Allen County Public Library, ca. 1980)

Settlers of Maryland, 1679-1783, 5 vols., by Peter Wilson Coldham (Genealogical Publishing Co., 1995-1996)

MILITARY RECORDS

The British Invasion of Maryland: 1812-1815 by William M. Marine (Genealogical Publishing Co., 1977)

Colonial Soldiers of the South, 1732-1774 by Murtie June Clark (Genealogical Publishing Co., 1983)

Colored Volunteers of Maryland Civil War, 7th Regiment, United States Colored Troops, 1863-1866 by Agnes Kane Callum (Mullac Publishers, 1990)

Compendium of the Confederate Armies: Kentucky, Maryland, Missouri, the Confederate Units and the Indian Units, 10 vols., by Stewart Sifakis (Facts on File, ca. 1992-1995)

Compiled Service Records of Confederate Soldiers Who Served in Organizations from the State of Maryland from the US Record and Pension Office (National Archives, 1960)

Compiled Service Records of Volunteer Union Soldiers Who Served in Organizations from the State of Maryland from the US Record and Pension Office (National Archives, 1962)

Dartmoor Prison by Thomas V. and Joanne M. Huntsberry (J. Mart Publishers, 1984)

German Regiment of Maryland and Pennsylvania by Henry J. Retzler (Family Line Publications, 1996)

History and Roster of Maryland Volunteers, War of 1861-5 by L. Allison Wilmer (Family Line Publications, 1987)

Index to Compiled Service Records of Volunteer Union Soldiers Who Served in Organizations from the State of Maryland from the US Adjutant General's Office (National Archives, 1962)

A List of Invalid Pensioners from the Maryland Treasurer's Office (J. Hughes, Printer, 1822)

Loyalists in the Southern Campaign of the Revolutionary War by Murtie June Clark (Genealogical Publishing Co., 1981)

Maryland in the Civil War, 2 vols., by Thomas V. and Joanne M. Huntsberry (J. Mart Publishers, 1985)

Maryland and District of Columbia Volunteers in the Mexican War by Charles J. Wells (Family Line Publications, 1991)

The Maryland Line in the Confederate Army, 1861-1865 by William W. Goldborough (Olde Soldier Books, 1987)

The Maryland Militia in the Revolutionary War by S. Eugene Clements (Family Line Publications, 1987)

Maryland Militia, War of 1812, 8 vols. by F. Edward Wright (Family Line Publications, 1979-92)

Maryland Muster Rolls, Fort Cumberland, 1757-58 (filmed by the Genealogical Society of Utah, 1949)

Maryland Revolutionary Records by Harry Wright Newmand (Genealogical Publishing Co., 1993)

Maryland Revolutionary War Pensions, Revolutionary, 1812, and Indian Wars by Lucy K. McGhee (Library of Congress Photoduplication Service, 1987)

Maryland in the World War I, 1917-19. Military and Naval Service Records, 2 vols., (Maryland War Records Commission, 1933)

Maryland, World War I Selective Service System Draft Registration Cards, 1917-1918 from the US Selective Service System (National Archives, 1987-1988)

Marylanders in the Confederacy by Daniel D. Hrtzler (Family Line Publications, 1986)

Marylanders Who Served the Nation by Gerson G. Eisenberg (Maryland State Archives Publications, 1992)

Muster Rolls and Other Records of Service of Maryland Troops in the American Revolution, 1775-1783 from the Maryland Historical Society (Genealogical Publishing Co., 1972)

Revolutionary Records of Maryland by Gaius Marcus Brumbaugh (Clearfield Co., 1996)

Roster of the Soldiers and Sailors Who Served in Organizations from Maryland During the Spanish-American War (Family Line Publications, 1990)

A Short History of the Maryland Line in the Continental Army by John Dwight Kilbourne (Society of the Cincinnati of Maryland, 1992)

Westward of Fort Cumberland Military Lots Set Off for Maryland's Revolutionary Soldiers by Mary K. Meyer (Pipe Creek Publication, 1993)

☞ PROBATE RECORDS

Abstracts of Chancery Court Records of Maryland, 1669-1782 by Debbie Hooper (Family Line Publications, 1996)

Abstracts of the Inventories and Accounts of the Prerogative Court of Maryland by Vernon L. Skinner (Family Line Publications, 1988-91)

The County Courthouses and Records of Maryland, Part Two: The Records by Morris Leon Radoff, et al. (Hall of Records Commission, 1963)

Courts of Admiralty in Colonial America: The Maryland Experience, 1634-1776 by David R. Owen and Michael C. Tolley (Maryland Historical Society)

First Laws of the State of Maryland (Scholarly Resources, 1787, 1981)

Index To Chancery Notes, Chancery Dispositions And Testamentary Proceedings by William F. Cregar, from the Maryland Historical Society (filmed by the Genealogical Society of Utah, 1949)

Index to Inventories of Estates, 1718-1777 (Hall of Records Commission, 1947)

Index to Wills of the Colonial Period, Books 1-41, 1634-1777 by Jane Baldwin Cotton (Hall of Records Commission, 1947)

Judgements and Decrees from the Maryland Court of Appeals (Hall of Records Commission, 1947)

Judicial and Testamentary Business of the Provincial Court: 1637-1683 from the Maryland Provincial Court (Maryland Historical Society, 1887-1964)

The Maryland Calendar of Wills, 16 vols., by Jane Baldwin Cotton (Family Line Publications, 1988)

Maryland Calendar of Wills: From 1744-1779, 8 vols., by F. Edward. Wright (Family Line Publications, 1988)

Maryland Probate Records by Jane Baldwin Cotton (Broderbund, 1998. CD-ROM)

Orderly Book of the "Maryland Loyalists Regiment," June 18, 1778 to October 12, 1778 compiled by Caleb Jones (Clearfield Co., 1891, 1996)

Provincial Court Judgements from the Maryland Provincial Court (Hall of Records Commission, 1947)

☞ VITAL RECORDS

Cemetery Records, 1853-1986 from the Loudon Park Cemetery, Baltimore (filmed by the Genealogical Society of Utah, 1986)

Directory of Maryland Burial Grounds (Family Line Publications, 1996)

Divorces And Names Changes In Maryland: By Act Of The Legislature, 1634-1867 by Mark K. Meyer (Pipe Creek Pub., 1991)

Historic Graves of Maryland and the District of Columbia: With Inscriptions Appearing on the Tombstones in Most of the Counties of the State and in Washington and Georgetown edited by Helen West Ridgely (Genealogical Publishing Co., 1967)

An Illustrated Genealogy of the Counties of Maryland and the District of Columbia as a Guide to Locating Records by Mary Ross Brown (French-Bray Printing Co., 1967)

Marriages and Deaths from the Maryland Gazette, 1727-1839 by Robert W. Barnes (Genealogical Publishing Co., 1973)

Maryland Eastern Shore Vital Records: 1648-1825, 5 vols., by F. Edward Wright (Family Line Publications, 1986)

Maryland Genealogies And Marriages, 1634-1820 (Genealogical Publishing Co., ca. 1998)

Maryland Marriage Records, 23 vols., by Annie W.B. Bell (Annie W.B. Bell, 1938-39)

Maryland Records of Deaths, 1718-1777 by Annie W.B. Bell (Annie W.B. Bell, 1936)

Names in Stone: 75,000 Cemetery Inscriptions from Frederick County, Maryland, 2 vols., by Jacob Mehrling Holdcraft (Genealogical Publishing Co., 1985)

Vital and Probate Records at the Maryland State Archives (Maryland State Archives, 2002)

COUNTY DETAILS

ALLEGANY

701 Kelly Rd. Suite 407, Cumberland, MD 21502
(301) 777-5911, **<gov.allconet.org>**

- **INCORPORATED:** Dec. 25, 1789
- **PARENT COUNTY:** Washington
- **MARRIAGE RECORDS:** start in 1987, kept by Circuit Court
- **NOTES:** State Archives has birth records 1898-1972, court records 1791-1954, death records 1865-1882, 1898-1972, marriage records 1791-1972, and probate records 1790-1964. Department of Health and Mental Hygiene, Division of Vital Records has birth records 1973-1978, death records 1972-1987, and marriage records 1973-1987. Clerk of Circuit Court has naturalization records 1854-1904.

ANNE ARUNDEL

44 Calvert St., Annapolis, MD 21401
(410) 222-7000, **<www.aacounty.org>**

- **INCORPORATED:** April 9, 1650
- **PARENT COUNTY:** Original county
- **MARRIAGE RECORDS:** start in 1987, kept by Circuit Court
- **DIVORCE:** 1851, Circuit Court
- **LAND:** 1653, Circuit Court
- **NOTES:** State Archives has birth records 1804-1877, 1898-1972, court records 1775-1910, death records 1865-1880, 1898-1972, marriage records 1777-1972, and probate records 1777-1980. Clerk of Circuit Court has naturalization records 1899-1929. Department of Health and Mental Hygiene, Division of Vital Records has birth records 1973-1978, death records 1972-1987, and marriage records 1973-1987.

BALTIMORE

400 Washington Ave., Towson, MD 21204,
(410) 887-2601 **<www.baltimorecountymd.gov>**

- **INCORPORATED:** June 30, 1659
- **PARENT COUNTY:** Anne Arundel
- **MARRIAGE RECORDS:** start in 1987, kept by Circuit Court
- **NOTES:** State Archives has birth records 1865-1883, 1898-1972, court records 1755-1964, death records 1898-1972, divorce records 1851-1973, marriage records 1777-1851, 1865-1972, naturalization records 1796-1851, 1868-1906, probate records 1664-1979 and land records starting in 1659. Department of Health and Mental Hygiene, Division of Vital Records has birth records 1973-1978, death records 1972-1987, and marriage records 1973-1987.

BALTIMORE CITY

111 N. Calvert St., Baltimore, MD 21202,
(410) 396-3100, **<baltimorecity.gov>**

- **INCORPORATED:** July 4, 1851
- **PARENT COUNTY:** Baltimore
- **MARRIAGE RECORDS:** start in 1987, kept by Circuit Court
- **NOTES:** State Archives has birth records 1875-1972, court records 1821-1849, 1852-1959, death records 1875-1972, divorce records 1851-1982, marriage records 1851-1972, naturalization records 1845-1906, 1911-1933, probate records 1850-1970 and land records starting in 1851. Department of Health and Mental Hygiene, Division of Vital Records has birth records 1973-1978, death records 1972-1987, and marriage records 1973-1987.

CALVERT

175 Main St., Prince Frederick, MD 20678,
(410) 535-1600, **<www.co.cal.md.us>**

- **INCORPORATED:** July 1654
- **PARENT COUNTY:** Original county
- **MARRIAGE RECORDS:** start in 1987, kept by Circuit Court
- **NOTES:** Called Patuxent County until 1658. Courthouse burned in 1882, destroying most county records. State Archives has birth records 1898-1972, court records 1882-1966, death records 1898-1972, divorce records 1881-1993, marriage records 1812-1972, military discharge records 1954-1972, naturalization records 1908-1920, probate records 1882-1983 and land records starting in 1812. Department of Health and Mental Hygiene, Division of Vital Records has birth records 1973-1978, death records 1972-1987, and marriage records 1973-1987.

CAROLINE

Box 458, Denton, MD 21629,
(410) 479-2303, **<www.carolinemd.org>**

- **INCORPORATED:** December 1773
- **PARENT COUNTIES:** Dorchester, Queen Anne
- **MARRIAGE RECORDS:** start in 1987, Circuit Court
- **NOTES:** State Archives has birth and death records 1865-1884, 1898-1972, court records 1775-1947, divorce records 1969-1984, marriage records 1774-1972, probate records 1685-1981 and land records starting in 1774. Department of Health and Mental Hygiene, Division of Vital Records has birth records 1973-1978, death records 1972-1987, and marriage records 1973-1987.

CARROLL
225 N. Court St., Westminster, MD 21157,
(410) 386-2026, **<ccgovernment.carr.org>**
- **INCORPORATED:** December 1837
- **PARENT COUNTIES:** Baltimore, Frederick
- **MARRIAGE RECORDS:** start in 1987, kept by Circuit Court
- **NOTES:** State Archives has birth records 1865-1891, 1898-1972, court records 1842-1905, death records 1898-1972, divorce records 1837-1983, marriage records 1837-1972, probate records 1837-1975 and land records starting in 1812. Department of Health and Mental Hygiene, Division of Vital Records has birth records 1973-1978, death records 1972-1987, and marriage records 1973-1987.

CECIL
129 E. Main St., Elkton, MD 21921, (410) 996-5376,
<www.ccgov.org>
- **INCORPORATED:** December 1674
- **PARENT COUNTIES:** Baltimore, Kent
- **MARRIAGE RECORDS:** start in 1987, kept by Circuit Court
- **NOTES:** State Archives has birth records 1865-1891, 1898-1972, court records 1750-1856, death records 1898-1972, divorce records 1972-1976, marriage records 1777-1972, probate records 1674-1977 and land records starting in 1674. Department of Health and Mental Hygiene, Division of Vital Records has birth records 1973-1978, death records 1972-1987, and marriage records 1973-1987.

CHARLES
200 Charles St., Box 970, La Plata, MD 20646, (301) 932-3201,
<www.charlescounty.org>
- **INCORPORATED:** July 1658
- **PARENT COUNTY:** Original county
- **MARRIAGE RECORDS:** start in 1987, kept by Circuit Court
- **NOTES:** State Archives has birth records 1654-1706, 1865-1877, 1898-1972, court records 1658-1780, death records 1654-1706, 1865-1866, 1898-1972, divorce records 1829-1885, 1949-1992, marriage records 1654-1706, 1865-1921, military discharge records 1957-1995, probate records 1665-1981 and land records starting in 1658. Department of Health and Mental Hygiene, Division of Vital Records has birth records 1973-1978, death records 1972-1987, and marriage records 1973-1987.

CHARLES, OLD
- **INCORPORATED:** 1650
- **NOTES:** Abolished in 1653.

DORCHESTER
206 High St., Box 150, Cambridge, MD 21613, (410) 228-0480,
<www.msa.md.gov/msa/mdmanual/36loc/do/html/do.html>
- **INCORPORATED:** Feb. 16, 1669
- **PARENT COUNTIES:** Somerset, Talbot
- **MARRIAGE RECORDS:** start in 1987, kept by Circuit Court
- **NATURALIZATION:** 1860, Circuit Court
- **NOTES:** State Archives has birth records 1898-1972, court records 1743-1902, divorce records 1820-1827, 1852-1948, marriage records 1780-1841, 1851-1972, probate records 1688-1976 and land records starting in 1669.

FREDERICK
100 W. Patrick St., Frederick, MD 21701, (301) 600-2570,
<www.frederickcountymd.gov>
- **INCORPORATED:** June 10, 1748
- **PARENT COUNTIES:** Prince George's, Baltimore
- **MARRIAGE RECORDS:** start in 1987, kept by Circuit Court
- **NOTES:** State Archives has birth records 1865-1873, 1898-1972, court records 1748-1936, death records 1865-1881, 1898-1972, divorce records 1807-1988, marriage records 1779-1975, naturalization records 1785-1836, 1854-1958, probate records 1745-1963 and land records starting in 1748. Department of Health and Mental Hygiene, Division of Vital Records has birth records 1973-1978, death records 1972-1987, and marriage records 1976-1987.

GARRETT
203 S. Fourth St. Room 301, Oakland, MD 21550, (301) 334-1941,
<www.garrettcounty.org>
- **INCORPORATED:** April 1, 1872
- **PARENT COUNTY:** Allegany
- **MARRIAGE RECORDS:** start in 1987, kept by Circuit Court
- **NOTES:** State Archives has birth and death records 1898-1972, divorce records 1874-1904, marriage records 1873-1972, probate records 1873-1996 and land records starting in 1872. Department of Health and Mental Hygiene, Division of Vital Records has birth records 1973-1978, death records 1972-1987, and marriage records 1973-1987.

HARFORD
20 W. Courtland: St., Bel Air, MD 21014, (410) 838-6000,
<www.harfordcountymd.gov>
- **INCORPORATED:** March 1773
- **PARENT COUNTY:** Baltimore
- **MARRIAGE RECORDS:** start in 1987, kept by Circuit Court
- **NOTES:** State Archives has birth and death records 1898-1972, court records 1774-1788, divorce records 1851-1972, marriage records 1782-1886, 1914-1972, probate records 1774-1976 and land records starting in 1774. Department of Health and Mental Hygiene, Division of Vital Records has birth records 1973-1978, death records 1972-1987, and marriage records 1973-1987.

HOWARD
9250 Bendix Road, Columbia, MD 21045, (410) 313-5850,
<co.ho.md.us>
- **INCORPORATED:** July 4, 1851
- **PARENT COUNTY:** Anne Arundel
- **MARRIAGE RECORDS:** start in 1987, kept by Circuit Court
- **LAND:** 1839, kept by State Archives
- **NOTES:** Howard District formed in 1838, didn't become a county until 1851. State Archives has birth records 1898-1972, court records 1851-1933, death records 1865-1878, 1898-1972, marriage records 1840-1972, military discharge records 1957-1978, naturalization records 1903-1945, and probate records 1840-1976. Department of Health and Mental Hygiene has vital records has birth records 1973-1978, death records 1972-1987, and marriage records 1973-1987.

KENT

103 N. Cross St., Chestertown, MD 21620, (410) 778-7460,
<www.kentcounty.com>

- **INCORPORATED:** Aug. 2, 1642
- **PARENT COUNTY:** Original county
- **MARRIAGE RECORDS:** start in 1987, kept by Circuit Court
- **NOTES:** State Archives has birth records 1865-1873, 1898-1972, court records 1654-1850, death records 1865-1871, 1898-1972, marriage records 1675-1707, 1796-1792, probate records 1669-1977 and land records starting in 1648. Department of Health and Mental Hygiene, Division of Vital Records has birth records 1973-1978, death records 1972-1987, and marriage records 1973-1987.

MONTGOMERY

50 Maryland Ave., Rockville, MD 20850, (240) 777-9466,
<www.montgomerycountymd.gov>

- **INCORPORATED:** Sept. 6, 1776
- **PARENT COUNTY:** Frederick
- **MARRIAGE RECORDS:** start in 1993, kept by State Archives
- **NOTES:** State Archives has birth records 1865-1972, court records 1779-1820, death records 1898-1972, divorce records 1851-1940, marriage records 1798-1839, 1867-1899, 1939-1980, probate records 1777-1953 and land records starting in 1777. Department of Health and Mental Hygiene, Division of Vital Records has birth records 1973-1978, death records 1972-1987, and marriage records 1973-1987.

PATUXENT

- **INCORPORATED:** July 1654
- **PARENT COUNTY:** Original county
- **NOTES:** See Calvert County. Name changed back to Calvert in 1658.

PRINCE GEORGE'S

14735 Main St., Upper Marlboro, MD 20772, (301) 952-3352,
<www.princegeorgescountymd.gov>

- **INCORPORATED:** May 20, 1695
- **PARENT COUNTIES:** Charles, Calvert
- **MARRIAGE RECORDS:** start in 1987, kept by Circuit Court
- **NOTES:** State Archives has birth records 1865-1867, 1898-1972, court records 1696-1870, death records 1865-1866, 1898-1972, divorce records 1851-1868, 1965-1969, marriage records 1777-1972, naturalization records 1799-1845, 1865-1910, probate records 1698-1984 and land records starting in 1696. Department of Health and Mental Hygiene, Division of Vital Records has birth records 1973-1978, death records 1972-1987, and marriage records 1973-1987.

QUEEN ANNE'S

100 Court House Sq., Centreville, MD 21617, (410) 758-1773,
<www.qac.org>

- **INCORPORATED:** April 18, 1706
- **PARENT COUNTIES:** Kent, Dorchester, Talbot
- **MARRIAGE RECORDS:** start in 1987, kept by Circuit Court
- **NOTES:** State Archives has birth records 1865-1881, 1898-1972, court records 1734-1905, death records 1898-1972, marriage records 1817-1972, military discharge records 1966-1984, probate records 1667-1984 and land records starting in 1707. Department of Health and Mental Hygiene, Division of Vital Records has birth records 1973-1978, death records 1972-1987, and marriage records 1973-1987.

SOMERSET

30512 Prince William St., Princess Anne, MD 21853,
(410) 845-4840, **<www.somersetmd.us>**

- **INCORPORATED:** Aug. 22, 1666
- **PARENT COUNTY:** Original county
- **MARRIAGE RECORDS:** start in 1987, kept by Circuit Court
- **NOTES:** State Archives has birth records 1649-1720, 1865-1870, 1894, 1898-1972, court records 1698-1899, death records 1649-1720, 1898-1972, divorce records 1816-1983, marriage records 1649-1720, 1796-1972, military discharge records 1956-1973, probate records 1664-1977 and land records starting in 1665. Department of Health and Mental Hygiene, division or vital records has birth records 1973-1978, death records 1972-1987, and marriage records 1973-1987.

ST. MARY'S

41605 Courthouse Dr., Box 676, Leonardtown, MD 20650,
(301) 475-7844, **<www.co.saint-marys.md.us>**

- **INCORPORATED:** Feb. 9, 1637
- **PARENT COUNTY:** Original county
- **MARRIAGE RECORDS:** start in 1987, kept by Circuit Court
- **DIVORCE:** 1815, State Archives
- **LAND:** 1777, Registrar of Wills
- **MILITARY:** 1944, State Archives
- **NOTES:** State Archives has birth and death records 1865-1867, 1898-1972, court records 1795-1949, marriage records 1794-1863, 1865-1972, and probate records 1658-1976. Department of Health and Mental Hygiene, Division of Vital Records has birth records 1973-1978, death records 1972-1987, and marriage records 1973-1987.

TALBOT

11 N. Washington St., Easton, MD 21601, (410) 770-8010,
<www.talbgov.org>

- **INCORPORATED:** Feb. 18, 1662
- **PARENT COUNTY:** Original county
- **MARRIAGE RECORDS:** start in 1987, kept by Circuit Court
- **NOTES:** State Archives has birth and death records 1657-1691, 1898-1972, court records 1662-1916, divorce records 1870-1973, marriage records 1657-1691, 1794-1972, military discharge records 1959-1976, probate records 1665-1990 and land records starting in 1662. Department of Health and Mental Hygiene, Division of Vital Records has birth records 1973-1978, death records 1972-1987, and marriage records 1973-1987.

WASHINGTON

24 Summit Ave., Hagerstown, MD 21740, (301) 733-8660,
<www.washco-md.net>

- **INCORPORATED:** Sept. 6, 1776
- **PARENT COUNTY:** Frederick
- **MARRIAGE RECORDS:** start in 1987, kept by Circuit Court
- **NOTES:** State Archives has birth and death records 1865-1867, 1898-1972, court records 1782-1818, marriage records 1799-1981, divorce records starting in 1815, probate records 1749-1977 and

land records starting in 1777. Department of Health and Mental Hygiene, Division of Vital Records has birth records 1973-1978, death records 1972-1987, and marriage records 1973-1987.

WICOMICO

Box 198, Salisbury, MD 21803, (410) 543-6551,
<www.wicomicocounty.org>

- **INCORPORATED:** Aug. 17, 1867
- **PARENT COUNTIES:** Somerset, Worcester
- **MARRIAGE RECORDS:** start in 1987, kept by Circuit Court
- **NOTES:** State Archives has birth and death records 1898-1972, court records 1868-1984, divorce records 1908-1988, marriage records 1868-1981, naturalization records 1912-1975, probate records 1867-1984 and land records starting in 1867. Department of Health and Mental Hygiene, Division of Vital Records has birth records 1973-1978, death records 1972-1987, and marriage records 1973-1987.

WORCESTER

1 W. Market St., Snow Hill, MD 21863, (401) 632-1194,
<www.co.worcester.md.us>

- **INCORPORATED:** Oct. 29, 1742
- **PARENT COUNTY:** Somerset
- **MARRIAGE RECORDS:** start in 1987, kept by Circuit Court
- **NOTES:** State Archives has birth records 1865-1889, 1898-1972, court records 1825-1900, 1959-1969, death records 1898-1972, marriage records 1795-1972, divorce records starting in 1818, probate records 1777-1963 and land records starting in 1742. Department of Health and Mental Hygiene, Division of Vital Records has birth records 1973-1978, death records 1972-1987, and marriage records 1973-1987.

MASSACHUSETTS

» BY MAUREEN A. TAYLOR

HISTORICAL OVERVIEW

Massachusetts is one of the earliest US settlements, but it was actually two separate colonies for most of the 17th century. Plymouth Colony was founded by Pilgrims in 1620, and it eventually expanded to include Plymouth, Barnstable and Bristol counties. Reverend John White and his New England Co. arrived at Cape Ann in 1628 and established the Massachusetts Bay Colony, which consisted of the towns north of the Merrimack River, plus New Hampshire and Suffolk Counties. In 1691, a charter united the two colonies and added parts of Maine and Nova Scotia. Those following religions different from the original settlers left voluntarily or were banished to other parts of New England.

Military conflicts characterize Massachusetts' colonial period, from King Philip's War (1675 to 1676) between settlers and the Narragansett Indians, to European campaigns fought on American soil, such as the French and Indian War. Massachusetts residents sparked the American Revolution with the Boston Tea Party; they also hosted first skirmish of the war. Massachusetts became the sixth state in 1788.

Trade for goods produced in Massachusetts was a critical part of the economy throughout the colonial period, but the state's economy became global in the 19th century with markets including South America and the Orient. The Industrial Revolution gave rise to textile and shoe factories that employed farm girls and later, immigrants from Europe, especially Ireland, Italy and Germany. By the 20th century, newcomers from all over the world sought business, educational and cultural opportunities in Massachusetts.

research tips

- Before delving into local records, explore major research repositories, such as the Massachusetts State Archives **<www.state.ma.us/sec/arc/arcidx.htm>**.
- Take advantage of the wealth of published histories, genealogies and records of Massachusetts before venturing into unpublished manuscripts in state and local collections.
- Boundary and land disputes can affect where your ancestor's records are. They may even be in a neighboring state.

CENSUS RECORDS

- Federal census: 1790, 1800, 1810, 1820, 1830, 1840, 1850, 1860, 1870, 1880, 1900, 1910, 1920, 1930
- Federal mortality schedules: 1850, 1860, 1870, 1880
- State census: 1855 and 1865
- Special census of Civil War Union veterans and widows: 1890

RECORD HIGHLIGHTS

Massachusetts records are a tremendous resource. "Because of the excellent quality and abundance of its records, Massachusetts is, arguably, the best place from which to have ancestors," says David Dearborn, librarian at the New England Historic Genealogical Society. Not everything is in print, though. Many genealogies, vital records, court documents and colonial documents appear in books or periodicals, but state and local repositories have manuscripts that await publication. Start your research by looking at print sources, then survey repositories for relevant unpublished material. The sheer abundance of records, combined with the fact that no single agency is responsible for all the records, means you'll need to be organized and methodical.

As in other New England states, you'll find most Massachusetts records on the town level, rather than in county offices. Puritan leaders modeled their record keeping after those in England, so early records are orderly and plentiful. Town clerks kept books of meeting records, earmarks, tax rolls and vital records. Vital records date from the founding of the colony and many are in print up to 1850. An exception is Boston, where births were not recorded from 1800 to 1849.

Unfortunately, no statewide index exists for those records. Lists of freemen, males of legal age (16 to 21) and church members who participated in government and the military can also be found on the town level, on microfilm or in print.

Between 1620 and 1642, more than 20,000 people migrated to New England in what is known as the Great Migration. Robert Charles Anderson has compiled his research of this event in a series of books, The Great Migration Begins, published by the New England Historic Genealogical Society. The Massachusetts Society of *Mayflower* Descendants is publishing material on *Mayflower* passengers. It is estimated that a quarter of today's US population can trace their ancestry back to these early immigrants.

Whether you're looking for early Massachusetts residents or those from the 19th century, be aware of boundary and land disputes where your ancestor lived. Records might be in an adjacent state: Massachusetts records contain material on early settlers in Maine, which was part of the state until 1820, and, due to boundary changes, the adjacent states of Rhode Island and New Hampshire.

Several Massachusetts cities served as immigration ports in the 19th century. Passenger lists and naturalization papers are at the National Archives in Washington, DC, with some originals at the archives' Northeast regional facility in Waltham, Mass.

US census records start in 1790 with two exceptions: the 1800 census lacks Boston and parts of Suffolk County, and only the veterans enumeration exists from the destroyed 1890 census. State enumerations took place in 1855 and 1865; a partial index exists.

Start at one of the major research facilities in Boston, such as the Massachusetts State Archives **<www.state.ma.us/sec/arc/arcidx.htm>** or the New England Historic Genealogical Society (NEHGS) **<www.americanancestors.org>**. The state archives collects public records such as judicial records, state papers, and materials on state institutions. It has land grants, early divorces, military records from 1643 through 1775, and tax valuations for 1738-1786.

The holdings of the NEHGS are more varied, containing unpublished family genealogies, private letters and diaries, records transcriptions, the papers of leading genealogists and more. The organization also has an extensive research library in Boston's Back Bay.

Once you've exhausted the resources kept in centralized locations, venture to the town or city from which your ancestor hailed. You'll find more than you can imagine in the town clerk's office, at the local historical society and even the public library. Most probate and land records are archives in county offices.

☞ARCHIVES, LIBRARIES, AND SOCIETIES

American-Portuguese Genealogical Society
Box 644, Taunton, MA 02780, (508) 823-3330, **<www.apghs.org>**

Andover-Harvard Theological Library
Harvard Divinity School, 45 Francis Ave., Cambridge, MA 02138, (617) 495-5788, **<www.hds.harvard.edu/library/bms>**

Andover Historical Society
97 Main St., Andover, MA 01810, (978) 475-2236, **<www.andoverhistorical.org>**

Berkshire Historical Society
780 Holmes Rd., Pittsfield, MA 01201, (413) 442-1793, **<www.berkshirehistory.org>**

Beverly Historical Society
117 Cabot St., Beverly, MA 01915, (978) 922-1186, **<www.beverlyhistory.org>**

Boston Public Library
700 Boylston St., Boston MA 02116, (617) 536-5400, **<www.bpl.org>**

Boston University School of Theology Library
745 Commonwealth Ave., Boston, MA 02215, (617) 353-3034, **<www.bu.edu/sthlibrary>**

Braintree Historical Society
31 Tenney Road, Braintree, MA 02184, (617) 848-1640, **<www.braintreehistorical.org>**

Brockton Historical Society
216 Pearl St., Brockton, MA 02301, (508) 583-1039, **<www.brocktonhistoricalsociety.org>**

Canton Historical Society
1400 Washington St., Canton, MA 02021, **<www.canton.org>**

Cape Cod Genealogical Society
Box 1394, Harwich, MA 02645, **<www.capecodgensoc.org>**

Danvers Historical Society
11 Page St., Box 381, Danvers, MA 01923, (978) 777-1666, **<www.danvershistory.org>**

Dedham Historical Society
612 High St., Dedham, MA 02027, (781) 326-1385, **<dedhamhistorical.org>**

Eastham Historical Society
Box 8, Eastham, MA 02642, **<www.easthamhistorical.org>**

Easton Historical Society
80 Mechanic St., North Easton, MA 02356, (508) 238-7774, **<www.eastonhistoricalsociety.org>**

Episcopal Diocese of Massachusetts
138 Tremont St., Boston MA 02111, (617) 482-5800, **<www.diomass.org>**

Essex Society of Genealogists
Box 313, Lynnfield, MA 01940, **<www.esog.org>**

Falmouth Genealogical Society
Box 2107, Falmouth, MA 02536, **<www.falgen.org>**

Finlandia Foundation-Boston
Box 308, Arlington, MA 02474, **<sites.google.com/site/finlandiafoundationboston/Home>**

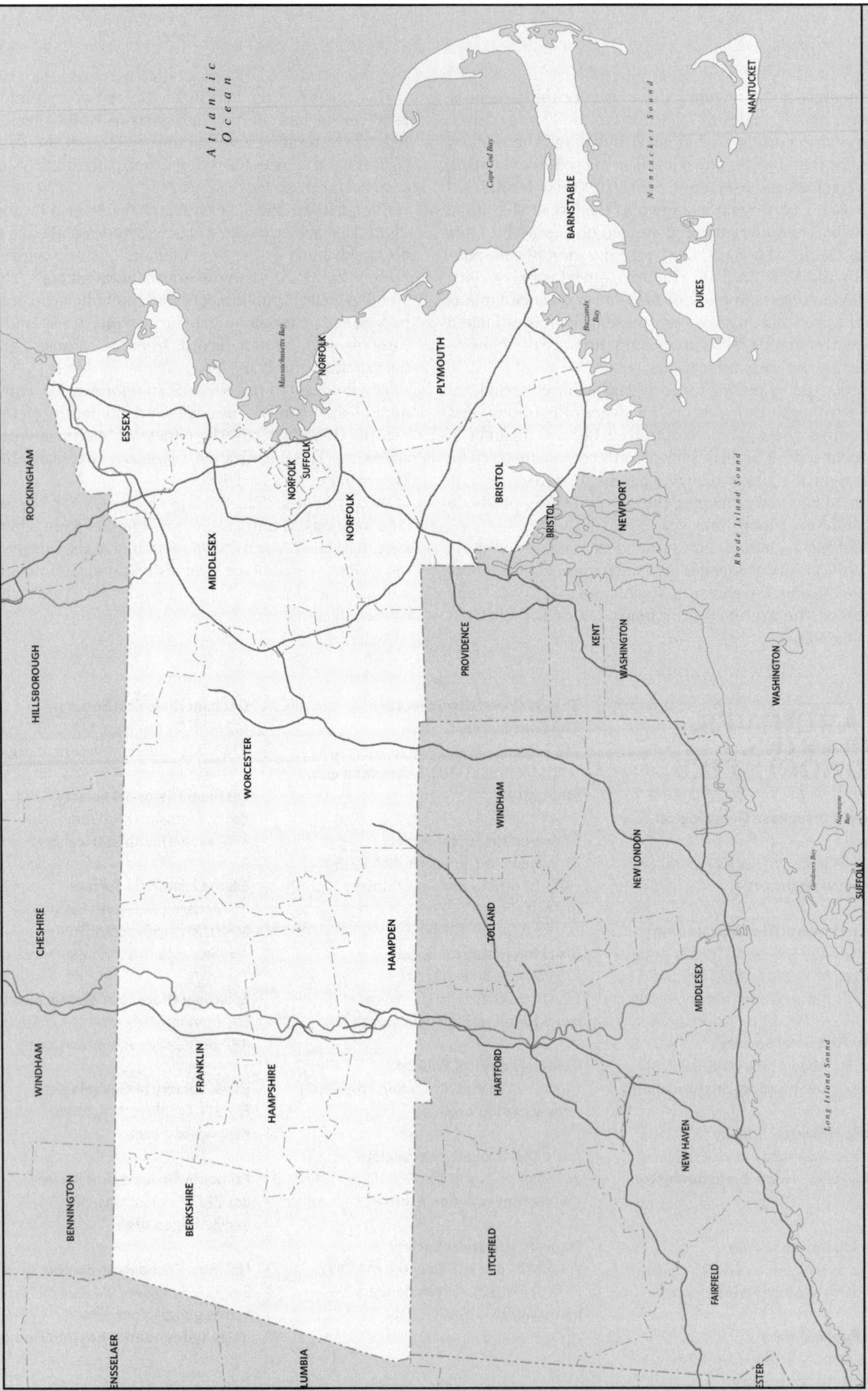

Atlantic Ocean
Massachusetts Bay
Cape Cod Bay
Nantucket Sound
Buzzards Bay
Rhode Island Sound
Long Island Sound
Gardiners Bay
Napeague Bay
ROCKINGHAM
HILLSBOROUGH
CHESHIRE
WINDHAM
BENNINGTON
ENSSELAER
LUMBIA
ESSEX
MIDDLESEX
NORFOLK
SUFFOLK
NORFOLK
NORFOLK
WORCESTER
FRANKLIN
HAMPSHIRE
BERKSHIRE
HAMPDEN
PLYMOUTH
BRISTOL
BRISTOL
BARNSTABLE
DUKES
NANTUCKET
NEWPORT
PROVIDENCE
KENT
WASHINGTON
WASHINGTON
WINDHAM
TOLLAND
HARTFORD
LITCHFIELD
NEW LONDON
MIDDLESEX
NEW HAVEN
FAIRFIELD
SUFFOLK
ESTER

Finnish American Society of Cape Cod
Box 220, West Barnstable, MA 02668

General Society of Colonial Wars
Langsdale Library, 1420 Maryland Ave., Baltimore, MD 21201, **<www.gscw.org>**

General Society of *Mayflower* Descendants
Box 3297, Plymouth, MA 02361, (508) 746-3188, **<www.themayflower society.com>**

Harwich Historical Society
80 Parallel St., Harwich, MA 02645, (508) 432-8089, **<www. harwichhistoricalsociety.org>**

Jamaica Plain Historical Society
Box 302924, Jamaica Plain, MA 02130, **<www.jphs.org>**

Jewish Genealogical Society of Greater Boston
Box 610366, Newton, MA 02461, (617) 796-8522, **<www.jgsgb.org>**

Knights and Ladies of Kaleva
Box 620, Maynard, MA 01752

New England Lutheran Archives,
Trinity Lutheran Church, 292 Orange St., New Haven, CT 06510, (203) 787-6521, **<www.trinitylutherannh.org>**

Martha's Vineyard Historical Society
Box 1310, Edgartown, MA 02539, (508) 627-4441, **<www.marthasvineyard history.org>**

Massachusetts State Archives
220 Morrissey Blvd., Boston, MA 02125, (617) 727-2816, **<www.sec.state.ma.us/ arc>**

Massachusetts Genealogical Council
Box 5393, Cochituate, MA 01778, **<home. comcast.net/~massgencouncil>**

Massachusetts Historical Society
1154 Boylston St., Boston, MA 02215, (617) 536-1608, **<www.masshist.org/ welcome>**

Massachusetts Society of Genealogists
Box 215, Ashland, MA 01721, (508) 892-1225, **<www.massachusettssocietyof genealogists.org>**

Massachusetts Society of *Mayflower* Descendants
150 Wood Road, Suite 103, Braintree, MA 02184, (781) 535-6159, **<www. massmayflower.org>**

Massachusetts Society, Sons of the American Revolution
255 Main St., Marlborough, MA 01752, (508) 229-1776, **<www.massar.org>**

Medford Historical Society
10 Governors Ave., Medford, MA 02155, **<www.medfordhistorical.org>**

Middleborough Historical Association
18 Jackson St., Middleborough, MA 2346, (508) 947-3394

Natick Historical Society and Museum
58 Eliot St., South Natick, MA 01760, (508) 647-4841, **<www.natickhistorical society.org>**

National Archives, New England Region
380 Trapelo Rd., Waltham, MA 02452, (781) 663-0130, **<www.archives.gov/ northeast/boston>**

Needham Historical Society
1147 Central Ave., Needham, MA 02492, (781) 455-8860, **<greisnet.com/ needhist.nsf>**

New England Historic Genealogical Society
99 Newbury St. Boston, MA 02116, (888) 296-3447, **<www.newengland ancestors.org>**

Old Colony Historical Society
66 Church Green, Taunton, MA 02780, (508) 822-1622, **<www. oldcolonyhistoricalsociety.org>**

Peabody Essex Museum
East India Square, 161 Essex St, Salem, MA 01970, (978) 745-9500, **<www.pem.org>**

Peabody Historical Society
35 Washington St., Peabody, MA 01960, (978) 531-0805, **<www.peabody historical.org>**

Pilgrim Society
75 Court St., Plymouth, MA 02360, (508) 746-1620, **<www.pilgrimhall.org>**

Plymouth County Genealogists
Box 1766, Brockton, MA 02303, **<plymouthcolony.net/pcgi>**

Plympton Historical Society
189 Main St., Plympton, MA 02367, (781) 585-2725

Quincy Historical Society
8 Adams St., Quincy, MA 02169, (617) 773-1144, **<quincyhistory.org>**

Massachusetts Registry of Vital Records and Statistics
150 Mount Vernon St., 1st Fl., Dorchester, MA 02125, (617) 740-2600, **<www.mass. gov/dph/rvrs>**

Roman Catholic Archives of the Archdiocese of Boston
66 Brooks Dr., Braintree, MA 02184 **<www.bostoncatholic.org/ Archives.aspx>**

Saugus Historical Society
Box 1209, Saugus, MA 01906, (781) 233-7232, **<www.saugus.org/ HistoricalSociety>**

Sheffield Historical Society
137-161 Main St., Box 747, Sheffield, MA 01257, (413) 229-2694, **<www. sheffieldhistory.org>**

Shirley Historical Society and Museum
182 Center Rd., Box 217, Shirley, MA 01464, (978) 425-9328, **<www.shirleyhistory.org>**

Rhode Island Historical Society
110 Benevolent St., Providence, RI 02906, (401) 331-8575, **<www.rihs.org>**

South Shore Genealogical Society
Box 396, Norwell, MA 02061, **<www. rootsweb.ancestry.com/~massgs>**

Southborough Historical Society
Box 364, 25 Common St., Southborough, MA 01772, **<www.southboroughhistory. org>**

State Library of Massachusetts
State House, Room 341, Boston, MA 02133, (617) 727-2590, **<www.mass.gov/lib>**

Supreme Lodge Knights of Pythias
25 S. Morton Ave., Morton, PA 19070, (610) 544-3500, **<www.pythias.org>**

Swedish Ancestry Research Association
Box 70603, Worcester, MA 01607, **<sarassociation.tripod.com>**

Walpole Historical Society
Box 100, Walpole MA 02081, **<www.walpolehistoricalsociety.org>**

War Records Office of the Adjutant General
239 Causeway St., Boston, MA 02114, (617) 727-2964

Western Massachusetts Genealogical Society
Box 206, Springfield, MA 01108, **<www.rootsweb.ancestry.com/~mawmgs>**

Winchester Historical Society
175 High St., Winchester, MA 01890, (781) 721-0135, **<www.winchesterhistoricalsociety.org>**

☞ GENERAL RESOURCES

Baptists in Massachusetts by John Woolman Brush (Judson Press, 1970)

The Bay Colony: A Civil, Religious and Social history of the Massachusetts Colony and its Settlements from the landing at Cape Ann in 1624 to the Death of Governor Withrop in 1650 by William Dummer Northend (filmed by the Library of Congress Photoduplication Service, 1988)

Bibliography of the Local History of Massachusetts by Jeremiah Colburn (University Microfilms, 1989)

Biographical History of Massachusetts by Samuel Atkins Eliot (Massachusetts Biographical Society, 1911-1918)

Card Index to the Massachusetts Archives by the Massachusetts State Archives (filmed by the Genealogical Society of Utah, 1972-1973)

Catalog of Manuscripts of the Massachusetts Historical Society (G.K. Hall, 1969)

Chronicles of the First Planters of the Colony of Massachusetts Bay from 1623 to 1636 by Alexander Young (C.C. Little and J. Brown, 1846)

Chronicles of the Pilgrim Fathers of the Colony of Plymouth, from 1602 to 1625 by Alexander Young (C.C. Little and J. Brown, 1844)

Commonwealth History of Massachusetts: Colony, Province, and State; with the Cooperation of an Advisory Board of forty-two learned bodies, 5 vols., by Albert Bushnell Hart (States History, ca. 1927-ca. 1930)

Encyclopedia of Massachusetts, Biographical-Genealogical (American Historical Society, ca. 1916)

The English Ancestry and Homes of the Pilgrim Fathers: Who Came to Plymouth on the "Mayflower" in 1620, the "Fortune" in 1621, and the "Anne" and the "Little James" in 1623 by Charles Edward Banks (Genealogical Publishing Co., 1962)

English Origins of New England Families: From The New England Historical and Genealogical Register, first series by Gary Boyd Roberts (Genealogical Publishing Co., 1984)

The Episcopal Diocese of Massachusetts, 1784-1984 by Mark J. Duffy (Episcopal Diocese of Massachusetts, 1984)

Families of the Pilgrims by Huber Kinney Shaw (The Society, ca. 1956)

A Genealogical Dictionary of the First Settlers of New England by James Savage (filmed by the Genealogical Society of Utah, 1961)

Genealogical and Personal Memoirs Relating to the Families of the State of Massachusetts by William F. Adams and William R. Cutter (Lewis Historical Publishing Co., 1910)

Genealogical Research in New England by Ralph J. Crandall (Genealogical Publishing Co., ca. 1984)

Genealogies of Mayflower Families: From The New England Historical and Genealogical Register by Gary Boyd Roberts (Genealogical Publishing Co., ca. 1985)

Genealogist's Handbook for New England Research by Marcia Wiswall Lindberg (New England Historic Genealogical Society, ca. 1993)

A Guide to the History of Massachusetts by Martin Kaufman et al. (Greenwood Press, ca. 1988)

A Guide to Massachusetts Local History by Charles A. Flagg (Salem Press Co., ca. 1907)

Historical Collections by John Warner Barber (Dorr, Howland, 1839)

John Winthrop and the Great Colony, or, Sketches of the Settlement of Boston, and of the more prominent persons connected with the Massachusetts Colony by Charles K. True (filmed by the Library of Congress Photoduplication Service, 1989)

King and People in Provincial Massachusetts by Richard L. Bushman (University of North Carolina Press, ca. 1985)

Massachusetts, 1620-1930 (Broderbund, ca. 1998, CD-ROM)

Massachusetts Bay Connections: Historical and Biographical Sketches of the Towns and Communities of the Massachusetts Bay Colony by Judy Jacobson (Clearfield Co., ca. 1992)

Massachusetts, A Bibliography of its History by John D. Haskell (University Press of New England, ca. 1983)

Massachusetts Biographical Dictionary (American Historical Publications, 1988)

Massachusetts Episcopalians, 1607-1957 by Dudley Tyng (Episcopal Diocese of Massachusetts, ca. 1960)

Massachusetts Genealogical Research by George K. Schweitzer (G.K. Schweitzer, ca. 1990)

Massachusetts and Maine Families: In the Ancestry of Walter Goodwin Davis

(1885-1966) by Walter Goodwin Davis (Genealogical Publishing Co., ca. 1996)

Massachusetts Research Outlines by the Church of Jesus Christ of Latter-day Saints (online at **<www.familysearch.org/eng/search/RG/guide/massachusetts.asp>**)

Massachusetts Society of Mayflower Descendants: the Bowman files by George Ernest Bowman (Massachusetts Society of *Mayflower* Descendants, 1983)

The Mayflower Reader: A selection of articles from The Mayflower Descendant by George Ernest Bowman (Genealogical Publishing Co., 1996)

Pilgrim Genealogies and Histories (Broderbund, ca. 1999, CD-ROM)

The Pilgrim Republic: An Historical Review of the Colony of New Plymouth by John A. Goodwin (filmed by the Library of Congress Photoduplication Service, 1986)

The Pioneers of Massachusetts: by Charles Henry Pope (filmed by the Genealogical Society of Utah, 1973)

Plymouth Colony, Its History & People 1620—1691 by Eugene Aubrey Stratton (Ancestry Publishing, ca. 1986)

The Plymouth Scrap Book: The Oldest Original Documents Extant in Plymouth Archives Printed Verbatim, Some Reproduced, with a Review of Bradford's History of Plymouth Plantation by Charles Henry Pope (C.E. Goodspeed, 1918)

Preliminary Edition of Guide to Depositories of Manuscript Collections in Massachusetts by the Historical Records Survey (The Survey, 1939)

Publications of the Colonial Society of Massachusetts by the Colonial Society of Massachusetts (The Society, 1895)

The Quaker Invasion of Massachusetts by Richard P. Hallowell (Heritage Books, 1987)

Records of the Colony of New Plymouth in New England edited by Nathaniel B. Shurtleff (Heritage Books, 1998)

Report on the Custody and Condition of the Public Records of Parishes, Towns, and Counties by the Massachusetts Commissioner of Public Records (Wright & Potter Printing Company, 1889)

The Rich Men of Massachusetts by Abner Forbes (filmed by the Library of Congress Photoduplication Service, 1989)

A Surname Guide to Massachusetts Town Histories by Phyllis O. Longver (Heritage Books, ca. 1993)

☞ CENSUS RECORDS

List of Freemen of Massachusetts, 1630-1691 by Lucius R. Paige (Genealogical Publishing Co., 1978)

A Research Aid for the Massachusetts 1910 Federal Census by Mary Lou Craver Mariner (Genealogical Publishing Co., ca. 1992)

☞ MAPS

Atlas of Historical County Boundaries: Connecticut, Maine, Massachusetts, Rhode Island edited by John H. Long (Simon & Schuster, 1994)
Directory of Massachusetts Place Names by Charlotte Pease Davis (Bay State News, ca. 1987)

A Gazetteer of Masachusetts by John Hayward (Library of Congress Photoduplication Service, 1989)

A Gazetteer of the State of Massachusetts by Elias Nason (B.B. Russell, 1874)

Genealogist's Handbook for New England Research by Marcia Wiswall Lindberg (New England Historic Genealogical Society, ca. 1993)

A Geographic Dictionary of Massachusetts by Henry Gannett (Genealogical Publishing Co., 1978)

Historical Atlas of Massachusetts by Richard W. Wilkie, Jack Tager, and Roy Doyon (University of Massachusetts Press, ca. 1991)

A Historical and Statistical Gazetteer of Massachusetts by Jeremiah Spofford (Library of Congress Photoduplication Service, 1989)

Massachusetts Town Boundary Atlases, 1898-1916 by the Massachusetts Harbor and Land Commission (filmed by the Genealogical Society of Utah, 1974)

Search for the Passengers of the Mary & John, 1630 by Burton W. Spear (B.W. Spear, ca. 1985)

Topographic Maps of Massachusetts, Rhode Island and Connecticut by the US Geological Survey (US Geological Survey, 1950, 1964-1965)

☞ PROBATE RECORDS

Abstracts of Bristol County, Massachusetts, Probate Records by H. L. Peter Rounds (Genealogical Publishing Co., 1987-1988)

Essex County, Massachusetts, Probate Index, 1638-1840 by Melinde Lutz Sanborn (M.L. Sanborn, ca. 1987)

Index to the Probate Records of the County of Middlesex, Massachusetts: first series, from 1648 to 1871 by the Massachusetts Probate Court (1914)

Law in Colonial Massachusetts, 1630-1800 by the Colonial Society of Massachusetts (The Society, 1984)

List of Freemen of Massachusetts, 1630-1691 by Lucius R. Paige (Genealogical Publishing Co., 1978)

List of Persons Whose Names Have Been Changed in Massachusetts, 1780-1892 (Genealogical Publishing Co., 1972)

Mayflower Deeds & Probates: From the Files of George Ernest Bowman at the Massachusetts Society of Mayflower Descendants by Susan E. Roser (Genealogical Publishing Co., ca. 1994)

Mayflower Source Records by Gary Boyd Roberts (Genealogical Publishing Co., ca. 1986)

Miscellaneous Index and Records (1659-1692) Prior to the Appointment of a Judge of Probate in 1692 by Alice E. Busiel (filmed by the Genealogical Society of Utah, 1964)

Plymouth Colony Probate Guide: Where to Find Wills and Related Data for 800 people of Plymouth Colony, 1620-1691 by Ruth Wilder Sherman (Plymouth Colony Research Group, 1983)

Plymouth County, Massachusetts Probate Index, 1686-1881 by Ralph V. Wood (Picton Press, ca. 1988)

Plymouth Court Records, 1686-1859 by David Thomas Konig and William E. Nelson (Michael Glazier, , in association with the Pilgrim Society, 1978-1981)

Probate Records of Essex County, Massachusetts by the Massachusetts Probate Court (Parker River Researchers, 1988)

Records of the County of Norfolk, in the Colony of Massachusetts by David Pulsifer (filmed by the Genealogical Society of Utah, 1971)

Suffolk County (Mass.) Court Files, 1629-1797 by the Massachusetts County Court (filmed by the Genealogical Society of Utah, 1972)

Suffolk County Wills: Abstracts of the Earliest Wills upon Record in the County of Suffolk, Massachusetts by Judith McGhan (Genealogical Publishing Co., 1984)

☞ IMMIGRATION RECORDS

The Complete Book of Emigrants, 1661-1699 by Peter Wilson Coldham (Genealogical Publishing Co., ca. 1990)

The Complete Book of Emigrants, 1700-1750 by Peter Wilson Coldham (Genealogical Publishing Co., ca. 1992)

Founders of Early American Families: Emigrants from Europe, 1607-1657 by Meredith B. Colket (General Court of the Order of Founders and Patriots of America, ca. 1985)

The Great Migration Begins: Immigrants to New England, 1620-1633 by Robert Charles Anderson (New England Historic Genealogical Society, ca. 1995)

Immigrants to New England, 1700-1775 by Ethel Stanwood Bolton (The Essex Institute, 1931)

Index to New England Naturalization Petitions, 1791-1906 by the US Immigration and Naturalization Service (National Archives and Records Service, 1983)

Indexes to Returns of Naturalizations, 1920-1923, 1924-1925, 1920-1925 by the Massachusetts Secretary of the Commonwealth (filmed by the Genealogical Society of Utah, 1994)

Passenger Lists of Vessels Arriving at Boston, 1820-1891 by the US Bureau of Customs (National Archives Record Service, 1959-1960)

Passenger Lists of Vessels Arriving at Boston, Aug. 1, 1891-1935; Book Indexes to Boston Passenger Lists, 1899-1940; Index to Passenger Lists of Vessels Arriving at Boston, Jan. 1, 1902- Dec. 31, 1920 by the US Immigration and Naturalization Service (National Archives, 1944-1945, 1956)

The Planters of the Commonwealth: A Study of the Emigrants and Emigration in Colonial Times by Charles Edward Banks (Genealogical Publishing Co., 1961)

Port Arrivals and Immigrants to the City of Boston, 1715-1716 and 1762 and 1769 by William H. Whitmore (Genealogical Publishing Co., 1973)

Returns of Naturalization Before Various Massachusetts Courts, 1885-1931 by the Massachusetts Secretary of the Commonwealth (filmed by the Genealogical Society of Utah, 1993)

The Search for Missing Friends: Irish Immigrant Advertisements Placed in The Boston Pilot by Ruth-Ann M. Harris, Donald M. Jacobs, and B.E. O'Keeffe (New England Historic Genealogical Society, 1989-1997)

St. Albans District Manifest Records of Aliens Arriving from Foreign Contiguous Territory: Records of Arrivals Through Small Ports in Vermont, 1895-1924 by the US Immigration and Naturalization Service (National Archives, ca. 1950)

A Supplemental Index to Passenger Lists of Vessels Arriving at Atlantic & Gulf Coast Ports (excluding New York) 1820-1874 by the US Bureau of Customs (filmed by the National Archives Record Services, 1960)

The Winthrop Fleet of 1630: An account of the vessels, the voyage, the passengers and their English home from original authorities by Charles Edward Banks (Genealogical Publishing Co., 1961)

☞ LAND RECORDS

Judd Manuscript, Records of Northampton by Sylvester Judd (filmed by the Genealogical Society of Utah, 1958)

Mayflower Deeds & Probates: From the Files of George Ernest Bowman at the Massachusetts Society of Mayflower Descendants by Susan E. Roser (Genealogical Publishing Co., c1994)

Records of the Colony of New Plymouth, in New England by the New Plymouth (William White, 1855-61)

Records of the Governor and Company of the Massachusetts Bay in New England: Printed by Order of the Legislature by Nathaniel Bradstreet Shurtleff (W. White, 1853-1854)

Registry of Deeds, etc. from the Various Counties of Massachusetts, A Register of Contents by Church of Jesus Christ of Latter-day Saints Genealogical Society Cataloging Section (filmed by the Genealogical Society of Utah, 1969)

☞ MILITARY RECORDS

An Historical Account of the Settlements of Scotch Highlanders in America Prior to the Peace of 1783 by John Patterson MacLean (filmed by the Genealogical Society of Utah, 1968)

Index to War of 1812 Pension Application Files by the US Veterans Administration (National Archives, 1960)

Index to War of 1812 Pension Files by Virgil D. White (National Historical Publishing Co., ca. 1992)

The Loyalists of Massachusetts and the Other Side of the American Revolution by James H. Stark (Heritage Books, 1988)

The Loyalists of Massachusetts: Their Memorials, Petitions and Claims by E. Alfred Jones (Genealogical Publishing Co., 1969)

Massachusetts in the Army and Navy During the War of 1861-65 by Thomas Wentworth Higginson (Wright & Potter Printing, 1895-1896)

Massachusetts Officers in the French and Indian Wars, 1748-1763 by Nancy S. Voye (Society of Colonial Wars in the Commonwealth of Massachusetts, ca. 1975)

Massachusetts Officers and Soldiers, 1702-1722: Queen Anne's War to Dummer's War by Mary E. Donahue (Society of Colonial Wars in the Commonwealth of Massachusetts, ca. 1980)

Massachusetts Officers and Soldiers, 1723-1743: Dummer's War to the War of Jenkins' Ear by Myron O. Stachiw (Society of Colonial Wars in the Commonwealth of Massachusetts, ca. 1979)

Massachusetts Officers and Soldiers in the Seventeenth Century Conflicts by Carole Doreski (Society of Colonial Wars in the Commonwealth of Massachusetts, New England Historic Genealogical Society, ca. 1982)

Massachusetts Privateers of the Revolution by Gardner Weld Allen (Massachusetts Historical Society, 1927)

Massachusetts Soldiers in the French and Indian Wars, 1744-1755 by Robert E. MacKay (Society of Colonial Wars in the Commonwealth of Massachusetts, ca. 1978)

Massachusetts Soldiers, Sailors, and Marines in the Civil War by Charles H. Cole (University Publications of America, ca. 1991)

Massachusetts, World War I Selective Service System Draft Registration Cards, 1917-1918 by the US Selective Service System (National Archives, 1987-1988)

Peirce's Colonial Lists: Civil, military and professional lists of Plymouth and Rhode Island colonies ... 1621-1700 by Ebenezer W. Peirce (Genealogical Publishing Co., 1968)

Record of the Massachusetts Volunteers, 1861-1865 by the Massachusetts Adjutant General (University Publications of America, ca. 1991)

☞ TAX RECORDS

Massachusetts and Maine Direct Tax Census of 1798 by the US Secretary of the Treasury (New England Historic Genealogical Society, 1978)

The Massachusetts Tax Valuation List of 1771 by Bettye Hobbs Pruitt (Picton Press, ca. 1998)

☞ VITAL RECORDS

Bibliography of Massachusetts Vital Records 1620-1905: An Inventory of the Original Volumes of Births, Marriages, and Deaths by Jay Mack Holbrook (Holbrook Research Institute, 1999)

Births, Marriages (1841-1895), and Deaths (1841-1899); Indexes to Births and Marriages (1841-1905), Deaths (1841-1971), 1841-1905 by the Massachusetts Secretary of the Commonwealth (filmed by the Genealogical Society of Utah, 1974, 1985)

Divorce Index, 1952-1970 by the Massachusetts Secretary of the Commonwealth (filmed by the Genealogical Society of Utah, 1974)

Early Massachusetts Marriages Prior to 1800 by Frederic W. Bailey (Genealogical Publishing Co., 1968)

Grave Locations of Revolutionary Soldiers and Sailors of Maine and Massachusetts by the Massachusetts Daughters of the American Revolution (filmed by the Genealogical Society of Utah, 1991)

Index of Marriages in Massachusetts Centinel and Columbian Centinel, 1784 to 1840 by the American Antiquarian Society (G. K. Hall, 1961)

The Massachusetts Magazine: Marriage and Death Notices, 1789-1796 by CJ Stevens (Polyanthos, , ca. 1978)

Mayflower Descendants and Their Marriages for Two Generations After the Landing by John T. Landis (Southern Book Company, 1956)

New England Marriages Prior to 1700 by Clarence Almon Torrey (Northeast Document Conservation Center, ca. 1983)

•-COUNTY DETAILS-•

BARNSTABLE

3195 Main St., Box 427, Barnstable, MA 02630, (508) 362-2511,
<www.barnstablecounty.org>

- **INCORPORATED:** June 2, 1685
- **PARENT COUNTY:** New Plymouth Colony
- **BIRTH RECORDS:** start in 1911, kept by state Registry of Vital Records
- **MARRIAGE:** 1911, state Registry of Vital Records
- **DIVORCE:** 1922, County Probate/Family Courts
- **DEATH:** 1911, state Registry of Vital Records
- **LAND:** 1783, Registrar of Deeds
- **PROBATE:** 1674, Register of Probate
- **COURT:** 1827, Court of Common Pleas/Superior Court
- **NATURALIZATION:** 1907, Superior Court
- **WILLS:** 1637, Register of Probate
- **NOTES:** State Archives has birth, death, and marriage records 1841-1910 (contact City and Town Clerks for records prior to 1841), divorce records 1639-1887. Clerk of Superior Court has divorce records 1872-1922. Towns organized before 1800: Barnstable 1639, Chatham 1712, Dennis 1793, Eastham 1646, Falmouth 1686, Harwich 1694, Mashpee 1763, Orleans 1797, Provincetown 1727, Truro 1709, Wellfleet 1763, Yarmouth 1639. Fire destroyed nearly all early deed books and probate files, but probate books survived. The official deed books only begin in 1827. Many deeds were rerecorded back to 1783, though these are far from complete.

BERKSHIRE

76 East St., Pittsfield, MA 01201, (413) 499-7487,
<www.rootsweb.ancestry.com/~maberksh>

- **INCORPORATED:** May 28, 1760
- **PARENT COUNTY:** Hampshire
- **BIRTH RECORDS:** start in 1911, kept by state Registry of Vital Records
- **MARRIAGE:** 1911, state Registry of Vital Records
- **DIVORCE:** 1847, Clerk/Superior Court
- **DEATH:** 1911, state Registry of Vital Records
- **LAND:** 1761, Registrar of Deeds
- **PROBATE:** 1761, Probate Court
- **COURT:** 1760, Court of Common Pleas
- **NATURALIZATION:** 1815, Court of Common Pleas/Superior Court
- **NOTES:** State Archives has birth, death, and marriage records 1841-1910 (for records prior to 1841 contact City/Town Clerks), divorce records 1639-1887. Clerk of Superior Court has divorce records 1887-1922. Court of Common Pleas has Revolutionary War records 1775-1783. Towns organized before 1800: Adams 1778, Alford 1773, Becket 1765, Chasire 1793, Clarksburg 1798, Dalton 1784, Egremont 1775, Great Barrington 1761, Hancock 1776, Lanesborough 1765, Lee 1777, Lenox 1767, Mount Washington 1779, New Ashford 1781, New Marlborough 1759, Otis 1773, Peru 1771, Pittsfield 1761, Richmond 1765, Savoy 1797, Sheffield 1733, Sandisfield 1762, Stockbridge 1739, Tyringham 1762, Washington 1777, West Stockbridge 1774, Williamstown 1765.

BRISTOL

9 Court St., Taunton, MA 02780, (508) 823-6588,
<www.countyofbristol.net>

- **INCORPORATED:** June 2, 1685
- **PARENT COUNTY:** New Plymouth Colony
- **BIRTH RECORDS:** start in 1911, kept by state Registry of Vital Records
- **MARRIAGE:** 1911, state Registry of Vital Records
- **DIVORCE:** 1862, Supreme Judicial Court
- **DEATH:** 1911, state Registry of Vital Records
- **LAND:** 1686, Registrar's Office
- **PROBATE:** 1687, Probate Court
- **COURT:** 1696, Court of Common Pleas
- **NATURALIZATION:** 1805, Court of Common Pleas/Superior Court
- **NOTES:** State Archives has birth, death, and marriage records 1841-1910 (for records prior to 1841 contact City/Town Clerks, and divorce records 1639-1887. Clerk of Superior Court has divorce records 1887-1922. Towns organized before 1800: Attleboro 1694, Berkley 1735, Dartmouth 1652, Dighton 1712, Easton 1725, Freetown 1683, Mansfield 1775, New Bedford 1787, Norton 1710, Raynham 1731, Rehoboth 1645, Sandwich 1639, Somerset 1790, Swansea 1667, Taunton 1639, Westport 1787.

DUKES

- Box 190, Edgartown, MA 02539, (508) 696-3840, **<www.dukescounty.org>**
- **INCORPORATED:** June 22, 1695
- **PARENT COUNTY:** Martha's Vineyard
- **BIRTH RECORDS:** start in 1911, kept by state Registry of Vital Records
- **MARRIAGE:** 1911, state Registry of Vital Records
- **DIVORCE:** 1922, County Probate/Family Courts
- **DEATH:** 1911, state Registry of Vital Records
- **LAND:** 1641, Registrar of Deeds
- **PROBATE:** 1790, Probate Court
- **NOTES:** State Archives has birth, death, and marriage records 1841-1911 (for records prior to 1841 contact City/Town Clerks), divorce records 1639-1887, and probate records 1690-1938. Clerk of Superior Court has divorce records 1887-1922. Towns organized before 1800: Chilmark 1694, Edgartown 1671, Tisbury 1671.

ESSEX

34 Federal St., Salem, MA , (978) 741-5500, **<www.essexma.org>**

- **INCORPORATED:** May 10, 1643
- **PARENT COUNTY:** Original county
- **BIRTH RECORDS:** start in 1911, state Registry of Vital Records
- **MARRIAGE:** 1911, state Registry of Vital Records
- **DIVORCE:** 1922, County Probate/Family Courts
- **DEATH:** 1911, state Registry of Vital Records
- **LAND:** 1639, Registrar of Deeds
- **PROBATE:** 1638, Probate Court
- **COURT:** 1636, Quarterly Court
- **NATURALIZATION:** 1794, Superior Court

- **NOTES:** County Court has birth, marriage, and death records 1636-1795. State Archives has birth, death, and marriage records 1841-1910 (for records prior to 1841 contact City/Town Clerks), divorce records 1639-1887. Clerk of Superior Court has divorce records 1887-1922. Essex Institute has military records 1755-1761. Towns organized before 1800: Amesbury 1668, Andover 1646, Beverly 1668, Boxford 1694, Danvers 1752, Hamilton 1793, Haverhill 1641, Ipswich 1634, Lynn 1635, Lynnfield 1782, Manchester 1645, Marblehead 1633, Methuen 1725, Middleton 1728, Newbury 1635, Newburyport 1764, Rowley 1639, Salem 1630, Salisbury 1639, Topsfield 1648, Wenham 1643.

FRANKLIN

425 Main St, Greenfield, MA 01301, (413) 774-3167, **<www.frcog.org>**

- **INCORPORATED:** June 24, 1811
- **PARENT COUNTY:** Hampshire
- **BIRTH RECORDS:** start in 1911, kept by state Registry of Vital Records
- **MARRIAGE:** 1911, state Registry of Vital Records
- **DIVORCE:** 1922, County Probate/Family Courts
- **DEATH:** 1911, state Registry of Vital Records
- **LAND:** 1787, Registrar of Deeds
- **PROBATE:** 1810, Probate Court
- **COURT:** 1823, Court of Common Pleas
- **NATURALIZATION:** 1811, Superior Court
- **NOTES:** State Archives has birth, death, and marriage records 1841-1910 (for records prior to 1841 contact City/Town Clerks), and divorce records 1639-1887. Clerk of Superior Court has divorce records 1887-1922. Supreme Judicial Court has court records 1816-1823. Towns organized before 1800: Ashfield 1765, Bernardston 1762, Buckland 1779, Charlemont 1765, Colrain 1761, Conway 1767, Deerfield 1677, Gil 1793, Greenfield 1753, Hawley 1792, Heath 1785, Leverett 1774, Leyden 1784, Montague 1754, New Salem 1753, Northfield 1714, Orange 1783, Rowe 1785, Shelburne 1768, Shuetesbury 1761, Sunderland 1714, Warwick 1763, Wendell 1781, Whately 1771, Williamsburg 1771.

HAMPDEN

625 Main St., Hampden, MA 01036 , (413) 781-8100, **<www.hampden.org>**

- **INCORPORATED:** Feb. 25, 1812
- **PARENT COUNTY:** Hampshire
- **BIRTH RECORDS:** start in 1911, kept by state Registry of Vital Records
- **MARRIAGE:** 1911, state Registry of Vital Records
- **DIVORCE:** 1831, Clerk/Superior Court
- **DEATH:** 1911, state Registry of Vital Records
- **LAND:** 1628, Registrar of Deeds
- **PROBATE:** 1812, Probate Court
- **COURT:** 1812, Court of Common Pleas
- **WILLS:** 1812, Probate Court
- **NOTES:** State Archives has birth, death, and marriage records 1841-1910 (for records prior to 1841 contact City/Town Clerks), and divorce records 1639-91887. Clerk of Superior Court has divorce records 1887-1922. Court of General Sessions of the Peace has court records 1638-1812. Towns organized before 1800: Blandford 1741, Brimfield 1714, Chester 1765, Granville 1754, Holland 1783, Longmeadow 1783, Monson 1760, Montgomery 1780, Palmer 1752, Southwick 1770, Springfield 1641, Wales 1645, West Springfield 1636, Westfield 1669, Wilbraham 1763.

HAMPSHIRE

33 King St., Northampton, MA 01060, (413) 586-8500, **<www.rootsweb.ancestry.com/~mahampsh>**

- **INCORPORATED:** May 7, 1662
- **PARENT COUNTY:** Middlesex
- **BIRTH RECORDS:** start in 1911, kept by state Registry of Vital Records
- **MARRIAGE:** 1758, Court of Sessions, North Hampton
- **DIVORCE:** 1758, Clerk/Superior Court
- **DEATH:** 1911, state Registry of Vital Records
- **LAND:** 1628, Registrar of Deeds
- **PROBATE:** 1660, Probate Court
- **COURT:** 1638, Court of General Sessions of the Peace
- **NATURALIZATION:** 1836, Superior Court
- **NOTES:** State Archives has birth, death, and marriage records 1841-1910 (for records prior to 1841 contact City/Town Clerks), and divorce records 1639-1887. Clerk of Superior Court has divorce records 1887-1922. Towns organized before 1800: Amherst 1759, Belchertown 1761, Chesterfield 1762, Cummington 1779, Easthampton 1785, Goshen 1781, Granby 1768, Hadley 1661, Middlefield 1783, Northampton 1656, Pelham 1743, Plainfield 1785, Russell 1792, South Hadley 1753, Southampton 1753, Ware 1761, Westhampton 1778, Worthington 1768.

MIDDLESEX

208 Cambridge St., East Cambridge, MA 02141, (617) 536-4533, **<www.rootsweb.ancestry.com/~mamiddle>**

- **INCORPORATED:** May 10, 1643
- **PARENT COUNTY:** Original county
- **DIVORCE RECORDS:** start in 1851, kept by Supreme Judicial Court
- **LAND:** 1649, Registrar of Deeds
- **PROBATE:** 1648, Probate Court
- **NATURALIZATION:** 1800, Clerk of Courts
- **NOTES:** Clerk of Courts has birth, death records, and wills 1600-1799, and court records 1648-1798. Superior Court has birth, death, and marriage records 1651-1793. City Clerk has proprietors records 1634-1697, 1751-1773, and 1784-1829. Towns organized before 1800: Acton 1735, Ashby 1767, Bedford 1729, Billerica 1655, Boxborough 1783, Burlington 1799, Cambridge 1638, Carlisle 1754, Chelmsford 1655, Concord 1635, Dracut 1702, Dunstable 1673, Everett 1630, Framingham 1700, Groton 1655, Holliston 1724, Hopkinton 1715, Lexington 1713, Lincoln 1754, Littleton 1716, Malden 1649, Marlborough 1660, Medford 1630, Natick 1651, Newton 1688, Pepperell 1753, Reading 1644, Sherborn 1674, Shirley 1786, Stoneham 1725, Stow 1683, Sudbury 1639, Tewksbury 1734, Townsend 1732, Tyngsboro 1789, Waltham 1738, Watertown 1630, Wayland 1780, Westford 1729, Weston 1713, Wilmington 1730, Woburn 1642.

NANTUCKET

16 Broad St., Nantucket, MA 02554, (508) 228-7250, **<www.nantucket-ma.gov>**

- **INCORPORATED:** June 22, 1695
- **PARENT COUNTY:** Original county

- **BIRTH RECORDS:** start in 1911, kept by state Registry of Vital Records
- **MARRIAGE:** 1911, state Registry of Vital Records
- **DIVORCE:** 1922, Probate/Family Court
- **DEATH:** 1911, state Registry of Vital Records
- **LAND:** 1657, Registrar of Deeds
- **PROBATE:** 1706, Probate Court
- **COURT:** 1721, Court of Common Pleas
- **NATURALIZATION:** 1908, State Archives
- **NOTES:** State Archives has birth, marriage, and death records 1841-1910 (for records prior to 1841 contact City/Town Clerks, and divorce records 1639-1887. Clerks of Superior Courts has divorce records 1887-1922. Towns organized before 1800: Nantucket 1687.

NORFOLK

649 High St., Dedham, MA 02026, (781) 326-7200,
<www.norfolkcountymagen.info>

- **INCORPORATED:** March 26, 1793
- **PARENT COUNTY:** Suffolk
- **BIRTH RECORDS:** start in 1911, kept by state Registry of Vital Records
- **MARRIAGE:** 1911, state Registry of Vital Records
- **DIVORCE:** 1887, Superior Court
- **DEATH:** 1911, state Registry of Vital Records
- **LAND:** 1793, Registrar of Deeds
- **PROBATE:** 1793, Probate Court
- **COURT:** 1793, Court of Common Pleas
- **NATURALIZATION:** 1806, Superior Court
- **NOTES:** Town Clerk has birth, death, and marriage records 1635-1845. State Archives has birth, death, and marriage records 1841-1910, and divorce records 1639-1887. Towns organized before 1800: Bellingham 1719, Braintree 1640, Brookline 1705, Canton 1797, Cohasset 1770, Dedham 1636, Dover 1784, Franklin 1778, Medfield 1651, Milton 1662, Needham 1711, Quincy 1792, Randolph 1793, Sharon 1765, Walpole 1724, Weymouth 1635, Wrentham 1673.

PLYMOUTH

50 Obery St., Plymouth MA 02360 , (508) 830-9200,
<plymouthdeeds.org>

- **INCORPORATED:** June 2, 1685
- **PARENT COUNTY:** New Plymouth Colony
- **BIRTH RECORDS:** start in 1911, kept by state Registry of Vital Records
- **MARRIAGE:** 1911, state Registry of Vital Records
- **DIVORCE:** 1922, County Probate/Family Courts
- **DEATH:** 1911, state Registry of Vital Records
- **LAND:** 1664, Registrar of Deeds
- **NOTES:** Registrar of Deeds has Plymouth Colony birth, death, and marriage records 1636-1686 and 1699-1756. State Archives has birth, death and marriage records 1841-1910. Court of General Sessions has court records 1686-1817. Court of Common Pleas has court records 1702-1859. State Archives has divorce records 1639-1887. Clerk of Superior Court has divorce records 1887-1922. Inferior Court of Common Please and Court of General Sessions of the Peace has marriage records 1692-1746. Fourth District Court, District Court Clerk, Wareham has naturalization records and applications 1885-1906. Superior Court, Massachusetts State Archives, Boston has naturalization declarations and petitions 1907-1945. Superior Court records at Massachusetts State Archives has Plymouth County declarations of intention index 1906-1984. Towns organized before 1800: Abington 1712, Bridgewater 1656, Brockton 1700, Carver 1790, Duxbury 1637, Halifax 1734, Hanover 1727, Hingham 1635, Hull 1644, Kingston 1726, Marshfield 1640, Middleborough 1669, Pembroke 1712, Plymouth 1620, Plympton 1707, Rochester 1686, Scituate 1636, Wareham 1739.

SUFFOLK

24 New Chardon St., Boston, MA 02114, (617) 788-8575,
<www.suffolkdeeds.com>

- **INCORPORATED:** May 10, 1643
- **PARENT COUNTY:** Original county
- **BIRTH RECORDS:** start in 1911, kept by state Registry of Vital Records
- **MARRIAGE:** 1911, state Registry of Vital Records
- **DIVORCE:** 1922, County Probate/Family Courts
- **DEATH:** 1911, state Registry of Vital Records
- **LAND:** 1639, Registrar of Deeds
- **PROBATE:** 1636, Probate Court
- **NATURALIZATION:** 1782, Court of Common Pleas
- **NOTES:** State Archives has birth, death, marriage records 1841-1910 (for records prior to 1841 contact City and Town Clerks), and divorce records 1639-1887. County Court, Court of Common Pleas, Court of General Sessions of Peace, Superior Court of Judicature, and Supreme Judicial Court have court records spanning 1629-1827. Clerk of Superior Court has divorce records 1887-1922. Towns organized before 1800: Boston 1630, Chelsea 1739, Dorchester 1630, Roxbury 1630.

WORCESTER

90 Front St., Worcester, MA 01608 , (508) 798-7717,
<www.worcesterdeeds.com>

- **INCORPORATED:** April 5, 1731
- **PARENT COUNTY:** Suffolk, Middlesex
- **BIRTH RECORDS:** start in 1911, kept by state Registry of Vital Records
- **MARRIAGE:** 1911, state Registry of Vital Records
- **DEATH:** 1911, state Registry of Vital Records
- **LAND:** 1722, Registrar of Deeds
- **PROBATE:** 1731, Probate Court
- **NOTES:** State Archives has birth, death, marriage records 1841-1910, divorce records 1639-1887, and naturalization records 1885-1949. Superior Court has divorce records 1887-1936. Towns organized before 1800: Ashburnham 1765, Athol 1762, Auburn 1778, Barre 1753, Berlin 1784, Bolton 1738, Boylston 1786, Brookfield 1673, Charlton 1755, Douglas 1746, Fitchburg 1764, Gardner 1785, Grafton 1735, Greenwich 1754, Hardwick 1739, Harvard 1732, Hubbardston 1767, Lancaster 1653, Leicester 1722, Leominister 1740, Lunenburg 1726, Mendon 1667, Milford 1780, New Braintree 1751, Northborough 1766, Northbridge 1772, Oakham 1762, Oxford 1713, Paxton 1765, Petersham 1754, Phillipston 1786, Princeton 1759, Royalston 1763, Rutland 1713, Shrewsbury 1727, Southborough 1727, Spencer 1753, Sterling 1781, Sturbridge 1738, Sutton 1716 Templeton 1762, Upton 1735, Uxbridge 1727 Warren 1741 Westbourough 1717, Westminister 1759, Winchendon 1764 Worcester 1722.

MICHIGAN

» BY JAMES W. WARREN

HISTORICAL OVERVIEW

French explorers were the first Europeans into the area that's now Michigan, which the Ojibway, Saginaw, Menominee, Wyandot, Ottawa and other Indian tribes had long occupied. In 1688, Jacques Marquette organized the first permanent settlement at Sault Ste. Marie. Fort Pontchartrain, established in 1701, would later be renamed Detroit. The French gave up possession of the area in 1763 to the British, who discouraged settlement just as the French had.

In 1787, the United States acquired the area and added it to the Northwest Territory, but the British retained control of Detroit and Mackinac. In 1796, when Gen. Anthony Wayne took Detroit, all of Michigan was in US hands.

Michigan became part of Indiana Territory in 1800. In 1805, Michigan territory was formed. In 1836, the disputed "Toledo Strip" of land five to seven miles wide on Michigan's southern border was granted to Ohio

Early settlers came mainly from Canada, New York, Ohio and the New England states. Michigan became the 26th state in 1837, and the population continued to expand. By 1850, large numbers of German and Dutch immigrants were arriving. In subsequent years immigrants continued to pour into Michigan, especially Scandinavian, Irish, Cornish, Polish and Italians, many working in mining and lumbering camps. Eventually, the growth of Detroit and its auto industry would pace the industrial growth of the country.

RECORD HIGHLIGHTS

Except for a few surviving fragments of the 1810 census, the first available federal population census for Michigan is 1820. The 1890 census was destroyed in a fire, but the 1890 Veterans' schedule for Michigan survived. More than 20 territorial censuses were taken in various parts of Michigan Territory, but for many, records for only a few counties survive. Territorial and state censuses were taken in 1827, 1834, 1837, 1845, 1854, 1864, 1874, 1884, 1894 and 1904. Indexes to the 1827, 1837 and 1845 have been published. The most complete collections are the 1884 and 1894 censuses, which list every member of the household and are a good substitute for the lost 1890 federal census. These schedules are available at the Archives of Michigan, and for many counties, on Family History Library (FHL) **<www.familysearch.org>** microfilm.

County registration of births and deaths began in 1867, and state recordkeeping requirements were generally complied with by 1915. Laws required registration of marriages in 1805; most counties kept marriage records from formation. You can order birth, death and marriage records from the county clerk or from the Michigan Department of Community Health (MDCH), which has copies of county records from 1867. The MDCH Website **<www.michigan.gov/mdch/0,1607,7-132-4645---,00.html>** allows online ordering

research tips

- The Michigan Library and Historical Center in Lansing houses both the Library of Michigan **<www.michigan.gov/hal/0,1607,7-160-17449_18635---,00.html>** and the State Archives of Michigan **<www.michigan.gov/hal/0,1607,7-160-17445_19273_19313---,00.html>**. Check both institutions' websites on holdings details.
- Find digitized records and indexes at the library's and archives' Seeking Michigan **<seekingmichigan.org>** and on Michigan GenWeb **<www.migenweb.net>**.
- Try the Michigan Genealogical Death Index, 1867-1882 **<www.mdch.state.mi.us/pha/osr/gendisx/search2.tm>**.

CENSUS RECORDS

- Federal census: 1820, 1830, 1840, 1850, 1860, 1870, 1880, 1900, 1910, 1920, 1930
- Federal mortality schedules: 1850, 1860, 1870, 1880
- Special census of Civil War Union veterans and widows: 1890
- State/territorial census: 1827, 1834, 1837, 1845, 1854, 1864, 1874, 1884, 1894, 1904

of records and provides additional information on restrictions. The FHL has microfilm of birth, death and marriage records for most counties into the 20th century. The Library of Michigan has statewide indexes to births from 1867 to 1915 and deaths from 1867 to 1914.

Early divorces were handled by the Michigan Supreme Court. Later divorce records are usually in circuit courts' civil case files. MCDH has copies of divorce records from about 1897; those can also be ordered on the MDCH website.

Michigan's county-level courts are district courts, but have jurisdiction over only minor matters. Circuit courts, which serve one to four counties, handle most matters. See a list of circuit court records that have been turned over to the Archives of Michigan at **<www.michigan.gov/documents/mhc_sa_circular37_49972_7.pdf>**.

The county clerk in each county holds naturalization records. Indexes to records for 13 Michigan counties are online (PDF format) at **<www.michigan.gov/hal/0,1607,7-160-17449_18635_20684---,00.html>**. The FHL also has 188 rolls of National Archives microfilm of federal district court naturalizations for Michigan.

Probate records are handled by the probate court in each county and date either from the formation of the county or from 1817. Wayne County's records start in 1797. See a finding aid for the Michigan archives' records at **<www.michigan.gov/documents/mhc_sa_circular06_49689_7.pdf>**. Probates from most Michigan counties through roughly 1900 are on microfilm at the FHL.

The Michigan Cemetery Sources website is a compilation of published cemetery transcriptions located at the Library of Michigan; it also has links to cemetery websites. This database identifies the location of more than 3,700 cemeteries in Michigan. It was not intended to include a list of personal names, but now individual burials are being included in the database. This is an ongoing project, so check back regularly **<www.hal.state.mi.us/cemeteries>**.

The Library of Michigan's record collection includes many church and cemetery abstracts, transcriptions and indexes, as well as original records or microfilm copies. The FHL has microfilmed records from some Michigan churches. Most churches and cemeteries still have their original records.

ARCHIVES, LIBRARIES, AND SOCIETIES

Albion Historical Society
Gardner House Museum, 509 S. Superior St., Albion, MI 49224

Archdiocese of Detroit
1234 Washington Blvd., Detroit, MI 48226, (313) 237-5800

Bay City Branch Library
500 Center Ave., Bay City, MI 48708

Bay County Genealogical Society
Box 1366, Bay City, MI 48706, **<www.baymigensociety.org>**

Bergen County Genealogical Society
Box 8808, Benton Harbor, MI 49023, **<w3.qtm.net/bcgensoc>**

Branch County Historical Society
Box 107, Coldwater, MI 49036

Calhoun County Genealogical Society
Box 879, Marshall, MI 49068, **<www.rootsweb.ancestry.com/~micalhou/ccgs.htm>**

Cass River Genealogy Society
359 S. Franklin, Frankenmuth, MI 48734, **<www.rootsweb.ancestry.com/~micrgs>**

Cedar Springs Historical Society
60 Cedar St., Box 296, Cedar Springs, MI 49319, (616) 696-3335

Central Archives of Polonia
The Orchard Lake Schools, 3535 Indian Trail, Orchard Lake, MI 48324

Central Michigan University Library
250 E. Preston St., Mount Pleasant, MI 48859, (989) 774-1100, **<library.cmich.edu>**

Charlevoix County Genealogical Society
201 E. Main St., Boyne City, MI 49712

Charter Township of Redford Genealogical Society
12259 Beech Daly, Redford, MI 48239

Cheboygan County Genealogical Society
Box 51, Cheboygan, MI 49721, **<www.rootsweb.ancestry.com/~miccgs/infopage.htm>**

Chippewa County Genealogical Society
Box 219, Trout Lake, MI 49793, **<www.rootsweb.ancestry.com/~michcgs/index.html>**

Chippewa County Historical Society
Box 342, Sault Ste. Marie, MI 49783

Dearborn Genealogical Society
Box 1112, Dearborn, MI 48121, **<www.rootsweb.ancestry.com/~midgs/dgs_a14.htm>**

Delta County Genealogical Society
Box 442, Escanaba, MI 49829, **<grandmastree.com/society>**

Detroit Health Department
1151 Taylor St., Detroit, MI 48202, (313) 876-4000

Detroit Public Library, Burton Historical Collection
5201 Woodward Ave., Detroit, MI 48202, (313) 833-1480, **<detroit.lib.mi.us>**

Detroit Society for Genealogical Research
c/o Burton Historical Collection, Detroit Public Library, 5201 Woodward Ave., Detroit, MI 48202, **<dsgr.org>**

Dickinson County Genealogical Society
c/o Dickinson County Library, 401 Iron Mountain St., Iron Mountain, MI 48901

Diocese of Grand Rapids
660 Burton St. S.E., Grand Rapids, MI 49507, (616) 243-0491

Diocese of Lansing
300 West Ottawa, Lansing, MI 48933, (517) 342-2440

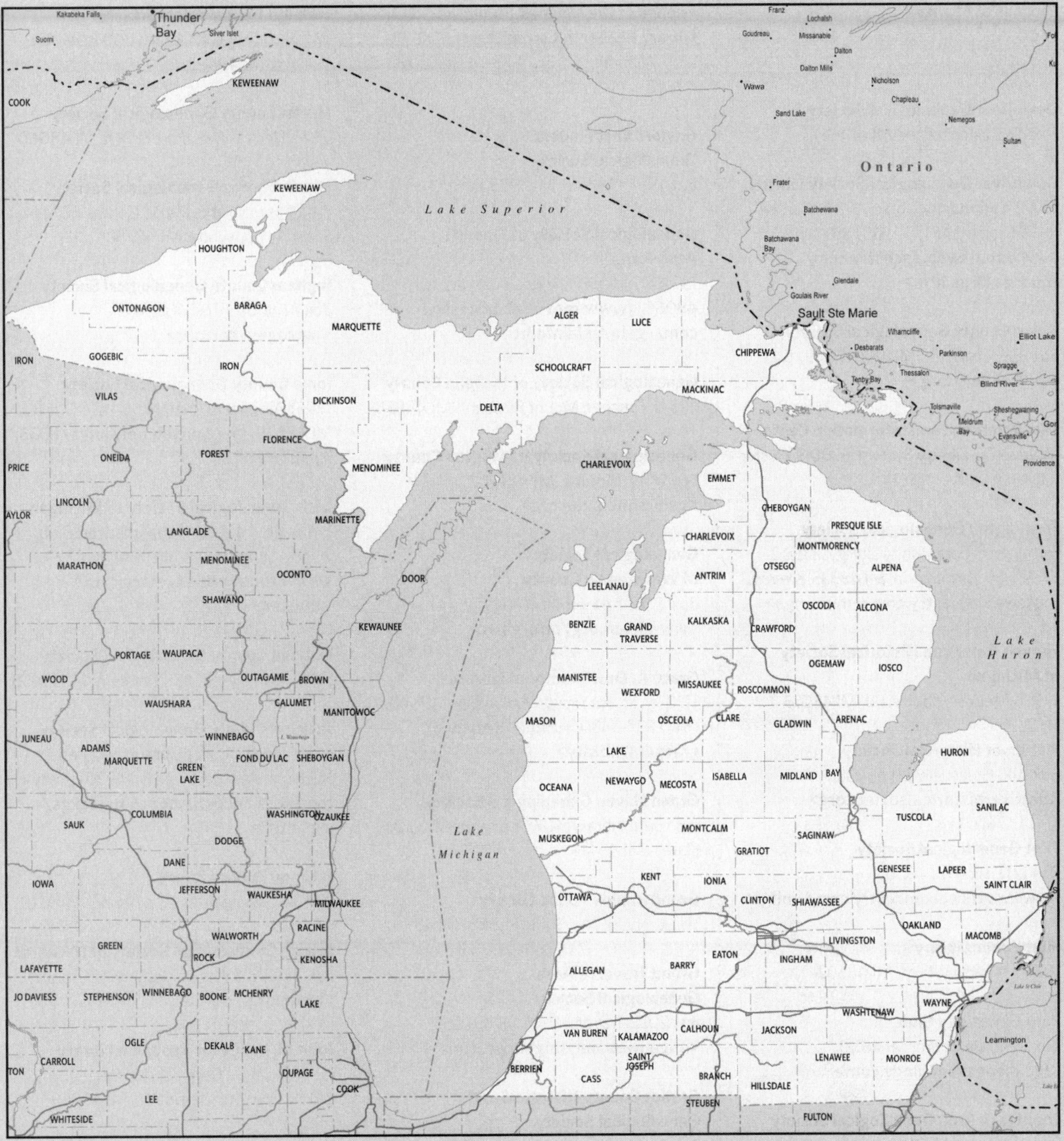
Thunder Bay
Lake Superior
Ontario
Sault Ste Marie
Lake Huron
Lake Michigan
KEWEENAW
HOUGHTON
ONTONAGON
BARAGA
GOGEBIC
IRON
MARQUETTE
ALGER
LUCE
SCHOOLCRAFT
CHIPPEWA
MACKINAC
DELTA
DICKINSON
MENOMINEE
CHARLEVOIX
EMMET
CHEBOYGAN
PRESQUE ISLE
MONTMORENCY
OTSEGO
ALPENA
ANTRIM
LEELANAU
OSCODA
ALCONA
BENZIE
GRAND TRAVERSE
KALKASKA
CRAWFORD
OGEMAW
IOSCO
MANISTEE
WEXFORD
MISSAUKEE
ROSCOMMON
MASON
OSCEOLA
CLARE
GLADWIN
ARENAC
LAKE
HURON
OCEANA
NEWAYGO
MECOSTA
ISABELLA
MIDLAND
BAY
TUSCOLA
SANILAC
MUSKEGON
MONTCALM
GRATIOT
SAGINAW
KENT
IONIA
GENESEE
LAPEER
OTTAWA
CLINTON
SHIAWASSEE
SAINT CLAIR
OAKLAND
MACOMB
LIVINGSTON
EATON
INGHAM
ALLEGAN
BARRY
WASHTENAW
WAYNE
VAN BUREN
KALAMAZOO
CALHOUN
JACKSON
BERRIEN
CASS
SAINT JOSEPH
BRANCH
HILLSDALE
LENAWEE
MONROE
STEUBEN
FULTON
COOK
VILAS
ONEIDA
FOREST
FLORENCE
MARINETTE
PRICE
LINCOLN
LANGLADE
MARATHON
OCONTO
DOOR
SHAWANO
KEWAUNEE
PORTAGE
WAUPACA
WOOD
OUTAGAMIE
BROWN
WAUSHARA
CALUMET
MANITOWOC
JUNEAU
ADAMS
WINNEBAGO
MARQUETTE
GREEN LAKE
FOND DU LAC
SHEBOYGAN
SAUK
COLUMBIA
WASHINGTON
OZAUKEE
DODGE
DANE
IOWA
JEFFERSON
WAUKESHA
MILWAUKEE
RACINE
WALWORTH
GREEN
ROCK
KENOSHA
LAFAYETTE
JO DAVIESS
STEPHENSON
WINNEBAGO
BOONE
MCHENRY
LAKE
OGLE
DEKALB
KANE
CARROLL
DUPAGE
LEE
WHITESIDE
Wawa
Sand Lake
Nemegos
Chapleau
Nicholson
Dalton Mills
Dalton
Missanabie
Lochalsh
Goudreau
Franz
Sultan
Frater
Batchewana
Batchawana Bay
Glendale
Goulais River
Wharncliffe
Desbarats
Parkinson
Thessalon
Spragge
Blind River
Elliot Lake
Tenby Bay
Tolsmaville
Sheshegwaning
Evansville
Providence
Leamington
Kakabeka Falls
Suomi
Silver Islet

Diocese of Saginaw
5800 Weiss St., Saginaw, MI 48603, (989) 799-7910

Downriver Genealogical Society
Box 476, Lincoln Park, MI 48146

Downriver Genealogical Society Library
Taylor Community Library, 12303 Pardee Rd., Taylor, MI 48180, (313) 381-0507, **<www.rootsweb.ancestry.com/~midrgs/drgs.htm>**

Eaton County Genealogical Society
Box 337, Charlotte, MI 48813, (517) 543-6999, **<miegs.org>**

Ellis Reference and Information Center
Monroe Co. Library System, 3700 S. Custer Rd., Monroe, MI 48161

Farmington Genealogical Society
Farmington Community Library, 23500 Liberty St., Farmington, MI 48335, **<www.rootsweb.ancestry.com/~mifarmgs>**

Finnish American Historical Society of Michigan
19995 Melrose, Southfield, MI 48075

Flat River Historical Society
Box 19R, Greenville, MI 49838, **<flatriverhistoricalsociety.org>**

Flint Genealogical Society
Box 1217, Flint, MI 48501, **<www.rootsweb.ancestry.com/~mifgs>**

Flint Public Library
1026 E. Kearsley, Flint, MI 48502

Ford Genealogy Club
Box 1652, Dearborn, MI 48121, **<fgc.dianesgenealogy.com>**

Four Flags Area Genealogical Society
Box 414, Niles, MI 49120

Fred Hart Williams Genealogical Society
c/o Burton Historical Collection, Detroit Public Library, 5201 Woodward Ave., Detroit, MI 48202, **<www.fhwgs.org>**

French Canadian Heritage Society of Michigan
9513 Whipple Shores Dr., Clarkston, MI 48348, **<fchsm.habitant.org>**

Friends of the Mitchell Public Library Research Committee
22 N. Manning St., Box 873, Hillsdale, MI 49242

Gaylord Fact Finders Genealogical Society
Box 1524, Gaylord, MI 49734

Genealogical Society of Flemish Americans
18740 Thirteen Mile Rd., Roseville, MI 48066, **<www.rootsweb.ancestry.com/~gsfa/gsfainfo.html>**

Genealogical Society of Isabella County
523 N. Fancher, Mount Pleasant, MI 48858

Genealogical Society of Monroe County
Box 1428, Monroe, MI 48161, **<gsmc-michigan.org>**

Genealogical Society of Washtenaw County
Box 7155, Ann Arbor, MI 48107, **<www.hvcn.org/info/gswc>**

Grace A. Dow Memorial Library
1710 W. St. Andrews, Midland, MI 48640, (517) 837-3430, **<midland-mi.org/gracedowlibrary>**

Grand Haven Genealogical Society
c/o Loutit Library, 407 Columbus St., Grand Haven, MI 49417

Grand Rapids Public Library
111 Library St, NE, Grand Rapids, MI 49502

Grand Traverse Area Genealogical Society
Box 2015, Traverse City, MI 49685, **<migenweb.net/migensoc.htm>**

Gratiot County Historical and Genealogical Society
Box 73, Ithaca, MI 48847, **<gchgs.org>**

Harrison Area Genealogy Society
Box 796, Harrison, MI 48625, **<harrisongenealogy.com>**

Herrick Public Library
300 S. River Ave., Holland, MI 49423

Hillsdale County Genealogical Society
22 N. Manning St., Hillsdale, MI 49242

Holland Genealogical Society
c/o Herrick Public Library, 300 River Ave., Holland, MI 49423

Huron County Genealogical Society
2843 Electric Ave., Port Huron, MI 48060

Huron Shores Genealogical Society
c/o Robert J. Parks Public Library, 6010 N. Skeel Ave., Oscoda, MI 48750

Ingham County Genealogical Society
Box 85, Mason, MI 48854, **<ingcogenesoc.org>**

Ionia County Genealogical Society
13051 Ainsworth Road, Rt. 3, Lake Odessa, MI 48849, **<migenweb.net/ionia/ICGS/icgshome.htm>**

Irish Genealogical Society of Michigan
c/o Gaelic League/Irish-American Club, 2068 Michigan Ave., Detroit, MI 48216, **<www.rootsweb.ancestry.com/~miigsm>**

Isabella County Genealogical Society
523 N. Fancher St., Mt. Pleasant, MI 48858

Jackson County Genealogical Society
c/o Jackson District Library, 244 W. Michigan Ave., Jackson, MI 49201, **<www.rootsweb.ancestry.com/~mijackgs/jcgs.htm>**

Jackson Public Library
244 W. Michigan Ave., Jackson, MI 49201

Jewish Genealogical Society of Michigan
Box 251693, West Bloomfield, MI 48325, **<jgsmi.org>**

John M. Longyear Research Library
c/o Marquette County Historical Society, 213 N. Front St., Marquette, MI 49855

Kalamazoo College Upjohn Library
1200 Academy St., Kalamazoo, MI 49006, (616) 337-7153

Kalamazoo Valley Genealogical Society
Box 405, Comstock, MI 49041, **<mikvgs.org>**

Kalkaska Genealogical Society
Box 353, Kalkaska, MI 49646, **<www.rootsweb.ancestry.com/~mikgs/index.htm>**

Kinseekers
Box 184, Grawn, MI 49637

Lapeer County Genealogical Society
Box 353, Lapeer, MI 48446

Lapeer County Library
201 Village West Dr., Lapeer, MI 48446

Lenawee County Genealogical Society
Box 511, Adrian, MI 49221

Library of Michigan
717 West Allegan St., Box 30007, Lansing, MI 48909, (517) 373-1300

Livingston County Genealogical Society
Box 1073, Howell, MI 48844, **<www.rootsweb.ancestry.com/~milcgs>**

Livonia Historical Society
20501 Newburgh, Livonia, MI 48152

Log Cabin Genealogical Society
103 North Third St., Manistique, MI 49854

Luce-Mackinac County Genealogical Society
Box 113, Engadine, MI 49827, **<luce.migenweb.net/luce-mac.htm>**

Lyon Township Genealogical Society
c/o Lyon Township Public Library, 27025 Milford Rd., New Hudson, MI 48165

Macomb County Genealogical Group
c/o Mt. Clemens Public Library, 150 Cass Ave., Mt. Clemens, MI 48043, **<www.rootsweb.ancestry.com/~mimcgg/publicationsmcgg.html>**

Marquette County Genealogical Society
217 N. Front St., Marquette, MI 49855, **<www.rootsweb.ancestry.com/~mimarqgs/mcgs.html>**

Mason County Historical Society
c/o Rose Hawley Museum, 1687 S. Lakeshore Dr., Ludington, MI 49431, (231) 843-4808, **<www.historicwhitepinevillage.org>**

Mecosta County Genealogical Society
Box 1068, Big Rapids MI 49307

Michigan Department of Public Health
3423 North Logan St., Box 30035, Lansing, MI 48909, (517) 335-8000

Michigan Genealogical Council
Box 80953, Lansing, MI 48908

Michigan Historical Commission
505 State Office Bldg., Lansing, MI 48913

Michigan Society, Order of Founders and Patriots of America
2961 Woodcreek Way, Bloomfield Hills, MI 48304

Midland County Historical Society
c/o Midland Center for the Arts, 1801 W. St. Andrews Dr., Midland, MI 48640, **<mcfta.org>**

Mt. Clemens Public Library
150 Cass Ave., Mt. Clemens, MI 48043, **<www.libcoop.net/mountclemens>**

Muskegon County Genealogical Society
c/o Hackley Library, 316 W. Webster Ave., Muskegon, MI 49440, **<genealogymuskegon.com>**

National Archives and Records Administration, Great Lakes Region
7358 S. Pulaski Road, Chicago, IL 60629, (773) 948-9019, **<archives.gov/great-lakes>**

Newaygo County Society of History and Genealogy
Box 68, White Cloud, MI 49349, (616) 689-6631, **<ncshg.org>**

North Oakland Genealogical Society
c/o Orion Township Library, 825 Joslyn Rd., Lake Orion, MI 48362, **<www.pontiac.lib.mi.us/genealog.htm>**

Northeast Michigan Genealogical Society
c/o Jesse Besser Museum, 491 Johnson St., Alpena, MI 49707, **<www.rootsweb.ancestry.com/~minemgs/NEMGS_home_page.htm>**

Northville Genealogical Society
Box 932, Northville, MI 48167, **<www.rootsweb.ancestry.com/~mings>**

Northwest Oakland County Historical Society
306 S. Saginaw St., Holly, MI 48442

Northwestern Michigan Genealogical Society
Mark Osterlin Library, 1704 E. Front St., Traverse City, MI 49686

Oakland County Genealogical Society
Box 1094, Birmingham, MI 48012, **<rhpl.org/OCGS>**

Oceana County Historical and Genealogical Society
114 Dryden St., Hart, MI 49420, (231) 873-2600

Ogemaw District Library
107 W. Main, Box 427, Rose City, MI 48654

Ogemaw Genealogical and Historical Society
c/o West Branch Public Library, 119 N. 4th St., West Branch, MI 48661

Onaway Library
Box 742, Onaway, MI 49765

Orion Township Public Library
825 Joslyn, Lake Orion, MI 48362

Osceola County Genealogical Society
Box 27, Reed City, MI 49677

Polish Archives
St. Mary's College, Orchard Lake, MI 48033

Polish Genealogical Society of Michigan
c/o Burton Historical Collection, Detroit Public Library, 201 Woodward Ave., Detroit, MI 48202, **<www.pgsm.org>**

Pontiac Area Historical and Genealogical Society
Box 901, Pontiac, MI 48056

Presque Isle County Genealogical Society
c/o Onaway Library, Box 742, Onaway, MI 49765

Reed City Area Genealogical Society
4918 Park St., Box 27, Reed City, MI 49677

Rockwood Area Historical Society
Box 68, Rockwood, MI 48173

Roman Catholic Diocese of Marquette
444 South Fourth St., Box 550, Marquette, MI 49855, (906) 225-1141, **<www.dioceseofmarquette.org>**

Rose City Area Historical Society
c/o Ogemaw District Library, 107 W. Main, Box 427, Rose City, MI 48654

Roseville Historical and Genealogical Society
c/o Roseville Public Library, 29777 Gratiot Ave., Roseville, MI 48066

Sage Branch Library
100 E. Midland St., Bay City, MI 48706

Saginaw Genealogical Society
c/o Saginaw Public Library, 505 Janes Ave., Saginaw, MI 48607

Saginaw Valley Chapter, American Historical Society of Germans From Russia
2876 N. Michigan Ave., Saginaw, MI 48604, (989) 752-0441, **<ahsgr.org/saginaw_valley_chapter.htm>**

Shiawassee County Genealogical Society
Box 841, Owosso, MI 49967, **<shianet.org/community/orgs/scgs>**

Sons of the American Revolution, Michigan Society
<missar.org>

South Side Branch Library
307 Lafayette St., Bay City, MI 48708

Southern Michigan Genealogical Society
239 E. Chicago Rd., Allen, MI 49227

Southwest Michigan Chapter, American Historical Society of Germans From Russia
3829 E. Bundy Rd., Coloma, MI 49038, **<ahsgr.org/southwest_michigan_chapter.htm>**

St. Clair County Family History Group
c/o St. Clair County Library, Box 611483, Port Huron, MI 48061

St. Clair County Library
Box 611493, 210 McMorran Blvd., Port Huron, MI 48061

St. Joseph Genealogical Society
Box 486, White Pigeon, MI 49099

State Archives of Michigan Michigan Library and Historical Center
717 West Allegan St., Lansing, MI 48918, **<michigan.gov/dnr/0,1607,7-153-54463_19313---,00.html>**

Sterling Heights Genealogical and Historical Society
Box 1154, Sterling Heights, MI 48311, **<ole.net/~maggie/macomb/sterling.htm>**

Sturgis Public Library
255 North St., Sturgis, MI 49091

Then and Now Historical and Genealogical Society of East Allegan County
532 N. Main, Wayland, MI 49348

Three Oaks Township Library
3 N. Elm St., Three Oaks, MI 49128, (269) 756-5621

Three Rivers Genealogical Society
13724 Spence Rd., Three Rives, MI 49093

Tri-State Genealogical Society
c/o Sturgis Public Library, 130 N. Nottawa St., Sturgis, MI 49091

Union City Genealogical Society
510 St. Joseph St., Union City, MI 49094

University of Michigan
1150 Beal Ave., Ann Arbor, MI 48109, (313) 764-3482, **<umich.edu>**

Van Buren District Library
200 N. Phelps St., Decatur, MI 49045, (269) 423-4771

Van Buren Regional Genealogical Society
Box 143, Decatur, MI 49045, **<www.woodlands.lib.mi.us/van/vbrgs.htm>**

Vicksburg Historical Society
Box 103, Vicksburg, MI 49097

Waterford Township Public Library
5168 Civic Center Dr., Waterford, MI 48329, (248) 674-4831, **<waterford.lib.mi.us>**

Webster Memorial Library
200 N. Phelps St., Decatur, MI 49047

Western Michigan Genealogical Society
c/o Grand Rapids Public Library, 111 Library St. NE, Grand Rapids, MI 49503, **<wmgs.org>**

Western Wayne County Genealogical Society
Box 530063, Livonia, Michigan 48153

Westland Michigan Public Library
6123 Central City Pkwy., Westland, MI 48185, (734) 326-6123, **<westland.lib.mi.us>**

White Pine Library Cooperative
3210 Davenport Ave., Saginaw, MI 48602

Willard Library
7 W. Van Buren St., Battle Creek, MI 49017, (269) 968-8166

Ypsilanti Historical Society Museum
220 N. Huron St., Ypsilanti, MI 48197

GENERAL RESOURCES

American Biographical History of Eminent and Self-Made Men: Michigan Volume (Western Biographical Publishing Co., 1878)

Church Record Index, 2 vols. (The Society, 1993)

County Evolution in Michigan, 1790-1897 by Richard Warren Welch (Department of Education, 1972)

Directory of Historical Collections and Societies in Michigan by Wystan Stevens (Historical Society of Michigan, 1973)

Genealogical Materials in the Eddy Historical Collection of the Public Libraries of Saginaw by Nelda M. Hinz (Public Libraries, 1975)

Genealogist's Guide to the Capitol Region of Michigan compiled by Victoria Wilson (Kinseeker Publications, 1987)

Genealogist's Guide to the Middle of Michigan compiled by Victoria Wilson (Kinseeker Publications, 1987)

Genealogist's Guide to Northeastern Michigan compiled by Victoria Wilson (Kinseeker Publications, 1987)

Genealogist's Guide to Southwestern Michigan compiled by Victoria Wilson (Kinseeker Publications, 1987)

Genealogist's Guide to the Thumb Area of Michigan compiled by Victoria Wilson (Kinseeker Publications, 1987)

Genealogist's Guide to Upper Penninsula Michigan compiled by Victoria Wilson (Kinseeker Publications, 1987)

Genealogy in Michigan: What, When, Where, 2nd edition, by Alloa Caviness Anderson (A. Anderson, P. Bender, 1978)

General History of the State of Michigan: With Biographical Sketches, Portrait Engraving and Numerous Illustrations by Charles Richard Tuttle (R.D.S. Tyler, 1873)

A Guide to Ancestral Trails in Michigan, 4th edition, by Lucy Mary Kellogg (Detroit Society for Genealogical Research, 1975)

Guide to the Manuscripts in the Burton Historical Collection by Bernice Cox Sprenger (Detroit Public Library, 1985)

Guide to the Michigan Genealogical and Historical Collections at the Library of Michigan and the State Archives of Michigan (Michigan Genealogical Council, 1996)

History of Michigan, 4 vols., by Charles Moore (Lewis Publishing Co., 1915)

A History of Northern Michigan and Its People, 3 vols., by Perry F. Powers (Lewis Publishing Co, 1912)

A History of the Northern Peninsula of Michigan and Its People, Its Mining, Lumber and Agricultural Industries, 3 vols., by Alvah Littlefield Sawyer (Lewis Publishing Co., 1911)

Inventory of the Church Archives of Michigan, The Roman Catholic Church, Archdiocese of Detroit from the Historical Records Survey (Michigan Historical Records Survey, 1941)

Men of Progress: Embracing Biographical Sketches of Representative Michigan Men, With an Outline History of the State (Evening New Assoc., 1900)

Michigan Biographies from the Library of Michigan (filmed by Microform Systems Inc., ca. 1980)

Michigan Biographies (Clearfield Co., 1924, 1999)

Michigan Centennial File Index from the Library of Michigan (filmed by Microform Systems Inc., ca. 1980)

Michigan, A Centennial History of the State and Its People, 5 vols., by George Newman Fuller (Lewis Publishing Co., 1939)

Michigan County Histories: A Bibliography (Michigan Bureau of Library Services, 1978)

Michigan Genealogy Sources and Resources by Carol McGinnis (Genealogical Publishing Co., 1987)

Michigan's German Heritage, John Russell's History of the German Influence in the Making of Michigan by Don Heinrich Tolzman (Heritage Books, 1994)

Michigan Historical Collections, 40 vols., from the Michigan State Historical Society (W.S. George & Co., 1877-1929)

Michigan Pioneer Records, 1800-1900 (Genealogical Society of Utah, 1973, 1974, 1976)

Michigan Research Outline by the Church of Jesus Christ of Latter-Day Saints (online at <www.familysearch.org/eng/search/RG/guide/Michigan.asp>)

Michigan Sesquicentennial Pioneer Files and Indexes, ca. 1986-1988 (filmed by the Genealogical Society of Utah, 1994)

The Michigan Surname Index edited by Donald J. DeZeeuw (Michigan Genealogical Council, 1984)

Midwest Pioneers, 1600s-1800s (Broderbund, 1999, CD-ROM)

Portrait and Biographical Records of Northern Michigan by Rev. E.H. Pilcher (Record Publishing, 1895)

The Red Book of Michigan; A Civil, Military and Biographical History by Charles Lanman (E. B. Smith, 1871)

Settling the Great Lakes Frontier: Immigration to Michigan, 1837-1924 by C. Warren Vander Hill (Michigan Historical Commission, 1970)

Sourcebook of Michigan Census, County Histories and Vital Records edited by Carole Callard (Library of Michigan, 1986)

Surname Index, 1600s-1900s from the Western Michigan Genealogical Society (filmed by the Family History Library, 1976)

☞MAPS

Along the Tracks: A Directory of Named Places on Michigan Railroads by Graydon M. Meints (Central Michigan University, Clarke Historical Library, 1987)

Bowen's Michigan State Atlas by F. F. Bowen (B.F. Bowen, 1916)

Gazetteer of the State of Michigan by John T. Blois (S.L. Rood, 1939)

Historical Atlas and Chronology of County Boundaries, 1788-1980, 5 vols., edited by John H., Long (G.K. Hall, 1984)

Indian Names in Michigan by Virgil J. Vogel (University of Michigan Press, 1986)

Michigan; Atlas of Historical County Boundaries by Peggy Tuck Sinko (Charles Scribner's Sons, 1997)

Michigan Atlases and Plat Books: A Checklist, 1872-1973 by William Miles (State Library Service, 1975)

Michigan County Map Guide by C. J. Puetz (Thomas Publications, 1990)

Michigan Gazetteer (American Historical Publications, 1991)

Michigan Place Names by Walter Romig (Romig, ca. 1970)

Michigan Postal History: The Post Offices, 1805-1986 by David M. Ellis (The Depot, 1993)

Upper Michigan Postal History and Postmarks by William J. Taylor (The Depot, 1988)

☞CENSUS RECORDS

Index to 1840 Federal Population Census of Michigan edited by Estelle A. McGlynn (Detroit Society for Genealogical Research, 1977)

Internal Revenue Assessment Lists of Michigan, 1862-1866 from the Bureau of Internal Revenue (National Archives, 1973)

Michigan Censuses 1710-1830 Under the French, British and Americans by Donna Valley Russell (Detroit Society for Genealogical Research, 1982)

Michigan Veterans Serving with Allied Forces, 1917-1919: Census of World War I Veterans from the Michigan State Archives (filmed by the Family History Library, 1996)

☞PROBATE RECORDS

Bench and Bar of Michigan: A Volume of History and Biography by George Irving Reed (Century Publishing and Engraving, ca. 1897)

Court Records, 1819-1857: Index to Cases, 1805-1857 from the Michigan Supreme Court (filmed by the Family History Library, 1974)

Records of the Territorial Court, Michigan, 1816-1836 from the Michigan Territorial Court (National Archives, 1988)

☞IMMIGRATION RECORDS

Early Michigan Settlements, 3 vols., by Warren Washburn Florer (W. W. Florer, ca. 1941-1953)

Declarations of Intentions, 1911-1930 from the US District Court (filmed by the Family History Library, 1986)

LAND RECORDS

Land Records: AL, AR, FL, LA, MI, MN, OH, WI (Broderbund, 1996. CD ROM)

Michigan Cash and Homestead Entries from the US Department of the Interior and the Bureau of Land Management (BLM Eastern States, 1994)

Private Land Claims, Illinois, Indiana, Michigan and Wisconsin by Fern Ainsworth (Fern Ainsworth, 1985)

☞MILITARY RECORDS

Annual Report of the Adjutant General 1865-1866, 3 vols., from the Michigan Adjutant General's Office (John A. Kerr & Co., 1866)

Index to Compiled Service Records of Volunteer Soldiers Who Served from the State of Michigan for the Patriot War, 1838-1839 from the US Adjutant General's Office (National Archives, 1965)

Michigan Military Records by Sue Silliman (Genealogical Publishing Co., 1969)

Michigan in the War by John Robertson (W.S. George, 1882)

Michigan in the World War: Military and Naval Honors of Michigan Men and Women by Charles H. Landrum (Michigan Historical Commission, 1924)

Record of Service of Michigan Volunteers in the Civil War from the Michigan Adjutant General's Office (Michigan Secretary of State, 1915)

Soldiers of the War of 1812, Who Died in Michigan by Alice Turner Miller (Alice Turner Miller, 1962)

United States Civil War Soldiers Living in Michigan in 1894 (Genealogists of Clinton County Historical Society, 1988)

United States Spanish War Veterans Master Index, ca. 1890-1984 from the Michigan State Archives (filmed by the Genealogical Society of Utah, 1991)

World War II Honor List of Dead and Missing, State of Michigan (War Dept. Bureau of Public Relations, 1946)

☞VITAL RECORDS

Cemetery Inscriptions, Michigan, 3 vols., by Edward H. Mohnecke (Edward H. Mohnecke, 1939-44)

Michigan Cemetery Compendium from Har-AlInc. (Har-Al, 1979)

Michigan Cemetery Source Book from the State Library of Michigan (State Library of Michigan, 1994)

Michigan Death Index, 1867-1874, 3 vols., (Michigan Department of Community Health, ca. 1997)

Michigan Quakers, Abstracts of Fifteen Meetings of the Society of Friends 1831-1860 by Ann and Conrad Burton (Glyndwr Resources, 1989)

Obituaries Index, 1933-1948 by Muriel Link (Genealogical Society of Utah, 1976)

Vital Statistics Holdings by Government Agencies in Michigan; Birth Records from the Historical Records Survey (The Project, 1941)

Vital Statistics Holdings by Government Agencies in Michigan; Death Records from the Historical Records Survey (The Project, 1942)

Vital Statistics Holdings by Government Agencies in Michigan; Marriage Records from the Historical Records Survey (The Project, 1941)

•-COUNTY DETAILS-•

AISHCUM
- **INCORPORATED:** April 1, 1840
- **PARENT COUNTY:** Mackinac
- **NOTES:** See Lake County. Name changed to Lake March 8, 1843.

ALCONA
106 Fifth St., Harrisville, MI 48740, (517) 724-5374, **<alconacountymi.com>**
- **INCORPORATED:** April 1, 1840
- **PARENT COUNTIES:** Mackinac, Unorganized Territory
- **BIRTH RECORDS:** start in1869, kept by County Clerk
- **MARRIAGE:** 1869, County Clerk
- **DIVORCE:** 1869, County Clerk
- **DEATH:** 1869, County Clerk
- **LAND:** unknown start, Registrar of Deeds
- **PROBATE:** unknown start, Probate Court
- **COURT:** 1869, County Clerk
- **MILITARY:** 1900, County Clerk
- **NATURALIZATION:** 1869, County Clerk
- **NOTES:** Formerly Neewago County. Name changed to Alcona March 8, 1843. Attached to Mackinac, Cheboygan, Iosco and Alpena counties prior to organization March 12, 1869.

ALGER
101 Court St., Munising, MI 49862, (906) 387-2076, **<algercounty.com>**
- **INCORPORATED:** March 17, 1885
- **PARENT COUNTIES:** Schoolcraft
- **BIRTH RECORDS:** start in 1884, kept by County Clerk
- **MARRIAGE:** 1887, County Clerk
- **DIVORCE:** 1885, County Clerk
- **DEATH:** 1884, County Clerk
- **LAND:** 1884, County Clerk
- **PROBATE:** unknown start, Probate Court
- **COURT:** 1885, County Clerk

ALLEGAN
113 Chestnut St., Allegan, MI 49010, (616) 673-0450, **<allegancounty.org>**
- **INCORPORATED:** March 2, 1831
- **PARENT COUNTY:** Barry
- **BIRTH RECORDS:** start in 1867, kept by County Clerk
- **MARRIAGE:** 1835, County Clerk
- **DIVORCE:** 1836, County Clerk
- **DEATH:** 1867, County Clerk
- **LAND:** 1836, County Clerk
- **PROBATE:** 1836, Probate Court
- **COURT:** 1836, County Clerk
- **MILITARY:** unknown start, County Clerk
- **NOTES:** Organized Sept. 7, 1835.

ALPENA
720 W. Chisholm St., Alpena, MI 49707, (517) 356-0115, **<alpenacounty.org>**
- **INCORPORATED:** April 1, 1840
- **PARENT COUNTIES:** Mackinac, Unorganized Territory
- **BIRTH RECORDS:** start in1869, kept in County Clerk
- **MARRIAGE:** 1871, County Clerk
- **DIVORCE:** 1871, County Clerk
- **DEATH:** 1871, County Clerk
- **LAND:** unknown start, Registrar of Deeds
- **PROBATE:** unknown start, Probate Judge
- **COURT:** 1871, County Clerk
- **NOTES:** Formerly Anamickee County. Name changed to Alpena March 8, 1843. Attached to Mackinac and Cheboygan counties prior to organization Feb. 7, 1857.

ANAMICKEE
- **INCORPORATED:** April 1, 1840
- **PARENT COUNTIES:** Mackinac, Unorganized Territory
- **NOTES:** See Alpena County. Name changed to Alpena March 8, 1843.

ANTRIM
208 E. Cayugoa St., Box 520, Bellaire, MI 49615, (616) 533-8607, **<antrimcounty.org>**
- **INCORPORATED:** April 1, 1840
- **PARENT COUNTY:** Mackinac
- **BIRTH RECORDS:** start in 1867, kept by County Clerk
- **MARRIAGE:** 1867, County Clerk
- **DIVORCE:** 1867, County Clerk
- **DEATH:** 1867, County Clerk
- **LAND:** unknown start, Registrar of Deeds
- **PROBATE:** 1863, Probate Judge
- **COURT:** 1867, County Clerk
- **MILITARY:** unknown start, County Clerk
- **NOTES:** Formerly Meegisee County. Name changed to Antrim March 8, 1843. Attached to Mackinac and Grand Traverse counties prior to organization March 11, 1863.

ARENAC
120 N. Grove St., Box 747, Standish, MI 48658, (517) 846-4626, **<arenaccountygov.com>**
- **INCORPORATED:** April 21, 1883
- **PARENT COUNTY:** Bay
- **BIRTH RECORDS:** start in1883, kept by County Clerk
- **MARRIAGE:** 1883, County Clerk
- **DIVORCE:** 1883, County Clerk
- **DEATH:** 1883, County Clerk
- **COURT:** 1883, County Clerk
- **BURIAL:** 1952, County Clerk

ARENAC, OLD
- **INCORPORATED:** March 2, 1831
- **PARENT COUNTY:** Unorganized Territory
- **NOTES:** Attached to Saginaw. Absorbed by Bay County April 20, 1857. Re-created April 21, 1883.

BARAGA

16 N. Third St., L'Anse, MI 49946, (906) 524-6183,
<baragacounty.org>

- **INCORPORATED:** Feb. 19, 1875
- **PARENT COUNTY:** Houghton
- **BIRTH RECORDS:** start in 1875, kept by County Clerk
- **MARRIAGE:** 1875, County Clerk
- **DIVORCE:** 1875, County Clerk
- **DEATH:** 1875, County Clerk
- **LAND:** 1875, County Clerk
- **COURT:** 1875, County Clerk
- Burial: 1950, County Clerk

BARRY

220 W. State St., Hastings, MI 49058, (616) 948-4810,
<barrycounty.org>

- **INCORPORATED:** Oct. 29, 1829
- **PARENT COUNTY:** Unorganized Territory
- **BIRTH RECORDS:** start in 1867, kept by County Clerk
- **MARRIAGE:** 1839, County Clerk
- **DIVORCE:** 1869, County Clerk
- **DEATH:** 1867, County Clerk
- **LAND:** unknown start, Registrar of Deeds
- **PROBATE:** unknown start, Probate Court
- **COURT:** 1845, County Clerk
- **NOTES:** Attached to St. Joseph and Kalamazoo counties prior to organization March 15, 1839.

BAY

515 Center Ave., Bay City, MI 48708, (517) 892-3528,
<baycounty-mi.gov>

- **INCORPORATED:** April 20, 1857
- **PARENT COUNTIES:** Saginaw, Midland, Arenac
- **BIRTH RECORDS:** start in 1868, kept by County Clerk
- **MARRIAGE:** 1857, County Clerk
- **DIVORCE:** 1883, County Clerk
- **DEATH:** 1867, County Clerk
- **LAND:** unknown start, Registrar of Deeds
- **PROBATE:** unknown start, Probate Court
- **COURT:** 1965, County Clerk

BENZIE

448 Court Place, Box 398, Beulah, MI 49617, (616) 882-9671
<benzieco.net>

- **INCORPORATED:** Feb. 27, 1863
- **PARENT COUNTY:** Leelanau
- **BIRTH RECORDS:** start in 1868, kept by County Clerk
- **MARRIAGE:** 1869, County Clerk
- **DIVORCE:** 1870, County Clerk
- **DEATH:** 1868, County Clerk
- **PROBATE:** 1870, County Clerk
- **COURT:** 1869, County Clerk
- **BURIAL:** 1934, County Clerk
- **NATURALIZATION:** 1871, County Clerk
- **NOTES:** Attached to Grand Traverse County prior to organization March 30, 1869.

BERRIEN

701 Main St., St. Joseph, MI 49085, (616) 983-7111
<berriencounty.org>

- **INCORPORATED:** Oct. 29, 1829
- **PARENT COUNTY:** Unorganized Territory
- **BIRTH RECORDS:** start in 1867, kept by County Clerk
- **MARRIAGE:** 1831, County Clerk
- **DIVORCE:** 1835, Circuit Court
- **DEATH:** 1867, County Clerk
- **LAND:** 1831, Registrar of Deeds
- **PROBATE:** 1832, Probate Court
- **COURT:** 1835, Circuit Court
- **MILITARY:** 1918, County Clerk
- **NOTES:** Clerk has naturalization records 1835-1985. Attached to Cass County prior to organization Sept. 1, 1831.

BLEEKER

- **INCORPORATED:** March 15, 1861
- **PARENT COUNTY:** Unorganized Territory
- **NOTES:** See Menominee County. Name changed to Menominee March 19, 1863.

BRANCH

31 Division St., Coldwater, MI 49036, (517) 279-4306, **<co.branch.mi.us>**

- **INCORPORATED:** Oct. 29, 1829
- **PARENT COUNTIES:** Lenawee, Unorganized Territory
- **BIRTH RECORDS:** start in 1867, kept by County Clerk
- **MARRIAGE:** 1833, County Clerk
- **DIVORCE:** unknown start, County Clerk
- **DEATH:** 1867, County Clerk
- **LAND:** unknown start, Registrar of Deeds
- **PROBATE:** unknown start, Probate Court
- **COURT:** 1848, County Clerk
- **BURIAL:** unknown start, City/Town Clerks
- **NATURALIZATION:** 1847, County Clerk
- **NOTES:** Attached to St. Joseph County prior to organization March 1, 1833.

CALHOUN

315 W. Green St., Marshall, MI 49068, (616) 781-0730
<calhouncountymi.org>

- **INCORPORATED:** Oct. 29, 1829
- **PARENT COUNTY:** Unorganized Territory
- **BIRTH RECORDS:** start in 1867, kept by County Clerk
- **MARRIAGE:** 1867, County Clerk
- **DIVORCE:** 1867, County Clerk
- **DEATH:** 1867, County Clerk
- **PROBATE:** unknown start, Probate Court
- **COURT:** 1867, County Clerk
- **BURIAL:** 1952, County Clerk
- **NATURALIZATION:** 1918, County Clerk
- **MILITARY:** 1919, County Clerk
- **ELECTION:** 1972, County Clerk
- **NOTES:** Attached to St. Joseph and Kalamazoo counties prior to organization April 1, 1833.

CASS

120 N. Broadway, Box 355, Cassopolis, MI 49031, (616) 445-8621,
<casscountymi.org>

- **INCORPORATED:** Oct. 29, 1829
- **PARENT COUNTY:** Unorganized Territory
- **BIRTH RECORDS:** start in 1867, kept by County Clerk/Registrar
- **MARRIAGE:** 1837, County Clerk/Registrar
- **DIVORCE:** 1831, County Clerk/Registrar
- **DEATH:** 1867, County Clerk/Registrar
- **LAND:** 1832, County Clerk/Registrar
- **PROBATE:** 1829, Probate Court
- **COURT:** 1831, County Clerk/Registrar
- **NOTES:** County Clerk/Registrar has naturalization records 1924-1941.

CHARLEVOIX

203 W. Antrim St., Charlevoix, MI 49720, (616) 547-7200,
<charlevoixcounty.org>

- **INCORPORATED:** April 2, 1869
- **PARENT COUNTIES:** Emmet, Antrim, Otsego
- **BIRTH RECORDS:** start in 1867, kept by County Clerk
- **MARRIAGE:** 1868, County Clerk
- **DIVORCE:** 1869, County Clerk
- **DEATH:** 1868, County Clerk
- **LAND:** 1869, County Clerk
- **PROBATE:** 1881, County Clerk
- **COURT:** 1869, County Clerk

CHARLEVOIX, OLD

- **INCORPORATED:** April 1, 1840
- **PARENT COUNTY:** Mackinac
- **NOTES:** Formerly Keskkauko County. Name changed to Charlevoix March 8, 1843. Attached to Mackinac. Eliminated Jan. 29, 1853. Recreated April 2, 1869.

CHEBOYGAN

870 S. Main St., Box 70, Cheboygan, MI 49721, (616)627-8808
<cheboygancounty.net>

- **INCORPORATED:** April 1, 1840
- **PARENT COUNTY:** Mackinac
- **BIRTH RECORDS:** start in 1867, kept by County Clerk
- **MARRIAGE:** 1867, County Clerk
- **DIVORCE:** 1884, County Clerk
- **DEATH:** 1867, County Clerk
- **LAND:** 1854, Registrar of Deeds
- **PROBATE:** 1854, Registrar of Probate
- **COURT:** 1884, County Clerk
- **NOTES:** Attached to Mackinac County prior to organization Jan. 29, 1853.

CHEONOQUET

- **INCORPORATED:** April 1, 1840
- **PARENT COUNTY:** Mackinac
- **NOTES:** See Montmorency County listing. Name changed to Montmorency March 8, 1843.

CHIPPEWA

319 Court St., Sault Sainte Marie, MI 49783, (906) 635-6300,
<chippewacountymi.gov>

- **INCORPORATED:** Feb. 1, 1827
- **PARENT COUNTY:** Mackinac
- **BIRTH RECORDS:** start in 1869, kept by County Clerk
- **MARRIAGE:** 1868, County Clerk
- **DIVORCE:** 1891, County Clerk
- **DEATH:** 1870, County Clerk
- **LAND:** unknown start, Registrar of Deeds
- **PROBATE:** unknown start, Probate Court
- **COURT:** unknown start, County Clerk

CLARE

225 W. Main St., Box 438, Harrison, MI 48625, (517) 539-7131,
<clareco.net>

- **INCORPORATED:** April 1, 1840
- **PARENT COUNTY:** Mackinac
- **BIRTH RECORDS:** unknown start, kept by County Clerk
- **MARRIAGE:** unknown start, County Clerk
- **DIVORCE:** unknown start, County Clerk
- **DEATH:** unknown start, County Clerk
- **LAND:** unknown start, County Clerk
- **COURT:** unknown start, County Clerk
- **BURIAL:** unknown start, County Clerk
- **NOTES:** Formerly Kaykakee County. Name changed to Clare March 8, 1843. Attached to Saginaw, Isabelle and Mecosta counties prior to organization March 13, 1871.

CLINTON

100 E. State St., Box 69, St. Johns, MI 48879, (517) 224-5140,
<clinton-county.org>

- **INCORPORATED:** March 2, 1831
- **PARENT COUNTY:** Unorganized Territory
- **BIRTH RECORDS:** start in 1867, kept by County Clerk
- **MARRIAGE:** 1839, County Clerk
- **DIVORCE:** ca. 1800, County Clerk
- **DEATH:** 1867, County Clerk
- **COURT:** unknown start, County Clerk
- **NOTES:** Attached to Kent and Shiawassee counties prior to organization March 12, 1839.

CRAWFORD

200 W. Michigan Ave., Grayling, MI 49738, (517) 348-3200,
<crawfordco.org>

- **INCORPORATED:** April 1, 1840
- **PARENT COUNTY:** Mackinac
- **BIRTH RECORDS:** start in 1879, kept by County Clerk
- **MARRIAGE:** 1878, County Clerk
- **DIVORCE:** 1878, County Clerk
- **DEATH:** 1878, County Clerk
- **LAND:** 1863, County Clerk
- **PROBATE:** 1879, County Clerk
- **COURT:** 1881, County Clerk
- **NOTES:** Formerly Shawano County. Name changed to Crawford March 8, 1843. Attached to Mackinac, Cheboygan, Iosco, Antrim and Kalkaska counties prior to organization March 22, 1879.

DELTA

310 Ludington St., Escanaba, MI 49829, (906) 789-5105, **<deltacountymi.org>**

- **INCORPORATED:** March 9, 1843
- **PARENT COUNTIES:** Mackinac, Unorganized Territories
- **BIRTH RECORDS:** start in 1867, kept by County Clerk
- **MARRIAGE:** 1867, County Clerk
- **DIVORCE:** 1867, County Clerk
- **DEATH:** 1867, County Clerk
- **LAND:** 1867, County Clerk
- **PROBATE:** 1867, County Clerk
- **COURT:** 1867, County Clerk
- **NOTES:** Attached to Mackinac County prior to organization March 12, 1861.

DES MOINES

- **INCORPORATED:** Oct. 1, 1834
- **PARENT COUNTY:** Unorganized Territory
- **NOTES:** Disorganized July 3, 1836, to Wisconsin Territory.

DICKINSON

705 S. Stephenson Ave., Box 609, Iron Mountain, MI 49801, (906) 774-0988, **<dickinsoncountymi.gov>**

- **INCORPORATED:** March 21, 1891
- **PARENT COUNTIES:** Marquette, Menominee, Iron
- **BIRTH RECORDS:** start in 1891, kept by County Clerk
- **MARRIAGE:** 1891, County Clerk
- **DIVORCE:** 1891, County Clerk
- **DEATH:** 1891, County Clerk
- **LAND:** unknown start, Registrar of Deeds
- **PROBATE:** unknown start, Probate Court
- **COURT:** 1891, County Clerk
- **NATURALIZATION:** 1891, County Clerk

EATON

1045 Independence Blvd., Charlotte, MI 48813, (517) 543-7500, **<eatoncounty.org>**

- **INCORPORATED:** Oct. 29, 1829
- **PARENT COUNTY:** Unorganized Territory
- **BIRTH RECORDS:** start in 1867, kept by County Clerk
- **MARRIAGE:** 1838, County Clerk
- **DIVORCE:** 1847, County Clerk
- **DEATH:** 1867, County Clerk
- **LAND:** unknown start, Registrar of Deeds
- **PROBATE:** unknown start, Probate Court
- **COURT:** 1847, County Clerk
- **NOTES:** County Clerk has some naturalization records. Attached to St. Joseph and Kalamazoo counties prior to organization Dec. 29, 1837.

EMMET

200 Division St., Petoskey, MI 49770, (616) 348-1744, **<emmetcounty.org>**

- **INCORPORATED:** April 1, 1840
- **PARENT COUNTY:** Mackinac
- **BIRTH RECORDS:** start at 1867, kept by County Clerk
- **MARRIAGE:** 1867, County Clerk
- **DIVORCE:** 1875, County Clerk
- **DEATH:** 1867, County Clerk
- **COURT:** ca. 1800, County Clerk
- **NATURALIZATION:** ca. 1800, County Clerk
- **NOTES:** County Clerk has some military records. Formerly Tonedagana County. Name changed to Emmet March 8, 1843. Attached to Mackinac prior to organization Jan. 29, 1853.

GENESEE

1101 Beach St., Flint, MI 48502, (810) 257-3225, **<co.genesee.mi.us>**

- **INCORPORATED:** March 28, 1835
- **PARENT COUNTIES:** Lapeer, Saginaw, Shiawassee
- **BIRTH RECORDS:** start at 1867, kept by County Clerk
- **MARRIAGE:** 1835, County Clerk
- **DIVORCE:** 1890, County Clerk
- **DEATH:** 1867, County Clerk
- **PROBATE:** unknown start, Probate Judge
- **COURT:** 1835, County Clerk

GLADWIN

401 W. Cedar Ave., Gladwin, MI 48624, (517) 426-7351, **<gladwinco.com>**

- **INCORPORATED:** March 2, 1831
- **PARENT COUNTY:** Unorganized Territory
- **BIRTH RECORDS:** start in 1875, kept by County Clerk
- **MARRIAGE:** 1875, County Clerk
- **DIVORCE:** 1875, County Clerk
- **DEATH:** 1875, County Clerk
- **LAND:** unknown start, Registrar of Deeds
- **PROBATE:** 1875, Probate Court
- **COURT:** 1875, County Clerk
- **MILITARY:** 1917, County Clerk
- **NOTES:** Attached to Saginaw and Midland counties prior to organization April 8, 1875.

GOGEBIC

200 N. Moore St., Bessemer, MI 49911, (906) 663-4518, **<gogebic.org>**

- **INCORPORATED:** Feb. 7, 1887
- **PARENT COUNTY:** Ontonagon
- **BIRTH RECORDS:** start in 1887, kept by County Clerk
- **MARRIAGE:** 1887, County Clerk
- **DIVORCE:** 1887, County Clerk
- **DEATH:** 1887, County Clerk
- **LAND:** 1887, Registrar of Deeds
- **PROBATE:** 1887, Probate Court
- **COURT:** 1887, County Clerk
- **MILITARY:** unknown start, County Clerk

GRAND TRAVERSE

400 Boardman Ave., Traverse City, MI 49684, (231) 922-4760, **<co.grand-traverse.mi.us>**

- **INCORPORATED:** April 7, 1851
- **PARENT COUNTY:** Omeena
- **BIRTH RECORDS:** start in 1867, kept by County Clerk
- **MARRIAGE:** 1853, County Clerk
- **DEATH:** 1867, County Clerk

- **DIVORCE:** 1882, County Clerk
- **LAND:** unknown start, Registrar of Deeds
- **COURT:** 1882, County Clerk

GRATIOT

214 E. Center St., Ithaca, MI 48847, (517) 875-5215,
<co.gratiot.mi.us>

- **INCORPORATED:** March 2, 1831
- **PARENT COUNTY:** Unorganized Territory
- **BIRTH RECORDS:** start in 1867, kept by County Clerk
- **MARRIAGE:** 1855, County Clerk
- **DIVORCE:** 1867, County Clerk
- **DEATH:** 1867, County Clerk
- **LAND:** unknown start, Registrar of Deeds
- **PROBATE:** unknown start, Probate Court
- **COURT:** 1867, County Clerk
- **NOTES:** Attached to Saginaw and Clinton counties prior to organization Feb. 3, 1855.

HILLSDALE

29 N. Howell St., Hillsdale, MI 49242, (517) 437-3391,
<co.hillsdale.mi.us>

- **INCORPORATED:** Oct. 29, 1829
- **PARENT COUNTY:** Unorganized Territory
- **BIRTH RECORDS:** start in 1867, kept by County Clerk
- **MARRIAGE:** 1835, County Clerk
- **DIVORCE:** 1845, County Clerk
- **DEATH:** 1867, County Clerk
- **LAND:** unknown start, Registrar of Deeds
- **PROBATE:** unknown start, Probate Court
- **COURT:** 1845, County Clerk
- **NOTES:** Attached to Lenawee County prior to organization Feb. 11, 1835.

HOUGHTON

401 E. Houghton Ave., Houghton, MI 49931, (906) 482-1150,
<houghtoncounty.net>

- **INCORPORATED:** March 19, 1845
- **PARENT COUNTIES:** Marquette, Ontonagon
- **BIRTH RECORDS:** start in 1867, kept by County Clerk
- **MARRIAGE:** 1855, County Clerk
- **DIVORCE:** 1853, County Clerk
- **DEATH:** 1867, County Clerk
- **LAND:** 1847, County Clerk
- **PROBATE:** unknown start, Probate Judge
- **COURT:** 1853, County Clerk
- **MILITARY:** unknown start, County Clerk
- **NATURALIZATION:** 1848, County Clerk
- **NOTES:** Attached to Chippewa County prior to organization May 18, 1846.

HURON

250 E. Huron Ave., Bad Axe, MI 48413, (517) 269-9942,
<co.huron.mi.us>

- **INCORPORATED:** April 1, 1840
- **PARENT COUNTY:** Sanilac
- **BIRTH RECORDS:** start in 1867, kept by County Clerk
- **MARRIAGE:** 1867, County Clerk
- **DEATH:** 1867, County Clerk
- **DIVORCE:** 1867, County Clerk
- **LAND:** unknown start, Registrar of Deeds
- **PROBATE:** unknown start, Probate Judge
- **COURT:** 1867, County Clerk
- **NOTES:** Attached to Saginaw, St. Clair and Sanilac counties prior to organization Jan. 25, 1859.

INGHAM

315 S. Jefferson St., Mason, MI 48854, (517) 676-7201,
<ingham.org>

- **INCORPORATED:** Oct. 29, 1829
- **PARENT COUNTIES:** Washtenaw, Shiawassee, Unorganized Territory
- **BIRTH RECORDS:** start in 1867, kept by County Clerk
- **MARRIAGE:** 1838, County Clerk
- **DIVORCE:** 1839, County Clerk
- **DEATH:** 1867, County Clerk
- **PROBATE:** unknown start, Probate Court
- **COURT:** 1839, County Clerk
- **BURIAL:** unknown start, City/Town Clerks
- **NOTES:** Attached to Washtenaw County prior to organization June 4, 1838.

IONIA

100 E. Main St., Ionia, MI 48846, (616) 527-5322,
<ioniacounty.org>

- **INCORPORATED:** March 2, 1831
- **PARENT COUNTY:** Mackinac
- **BIRTH RECORDS:** start in 1867, kept by County Clerk
- **MARRIAGE:** 1837, County Clerk
- **DIVORCE:** 1890, County Clerk
- **DEATH:** 1867, County Clerk
- **COURT:** 1890, County Clerk
- **NOTES:** Attached to Kent County prior to organization April 3, 1837.

IOSCO

422 W. Lake St., Box 838, Tawas City, MI 48763, (517) 362-3497,
<iosco.m33access.com>

- **INCORPORATED:** April 1, 1840
- **PARENT COUNTY:** Unorganized Territory
- **BIRTH RECORDS:** start in 1867, kept by County Clerk
- **MARRIAGE:** 1862, County Clerk
- **DIVORCE:** 1859, County Clerk
- **DEATH:** 1868, County Clerk
- **COURT:** 1859, County Clerk
- **NOTES:** County Clerk has burial records 1961-1978, and naturalization records 1859-1906. Formerly Kanotin County. Name changed to Iosco March 8, 1843. Attached to Mackinac, Saginaw and Cheboygan counties prior to organization Feb. 16, 1857.

IRON

2 S. Sixth St., Crystal Falls, MI 49920, (906) 875-3301, **<iron.org>**

- **INCORPORATED:** April 3, 1885
- **PARENT COUNTIES:** Marquette, Menominee
- **BIRTH RECORDS:** start in 1895, kept by County Clerk
- **MARRIAGE:** 1895, County Clerk
- **DIVORCE:** 1895, County Clerk
- **DEATH:** 1895, County Clerk

- **LAND:** unknown start, Registrar of Deeds
- **PROBATE:** unknown start, Probate Court
- **COURT:** 1895, County Clerk
- **BURIAL:** unknown start, Towns and Cities

ISABELLA

200 N. Main St., Mount Pleasant, MI 48858, (517) 772-0911, **<isabellacounty.org>**

- **INCORPORATED:** March 2, 1831
- **PARENT COUNTY:** Mackinac, Unorganized Territory
- **BIRTH RECORDS:** start in 1880, kept by County Clerk
- **MARRIAGE:** 1880, County Clerk
- **DIVORCE:** 1880, County Clerk
- **DEATH:** 1880, County Clerk
- **COURT:** 1880, County Clerk
- **NOTES:** Attached to Saginaw, Ionia and Midland counties prior to organization Feb. 11, 1859.

ISLE ROYAL

- **INCORPORATED:** March 4, 1875
- **PARENT COUNTY:** Keweenaw
- **NOTES:** Attached to Houghton March 13, 1885. Absorbed by Keweenaw April 9, 1897.

JACKSON

312 S. Jackson St., Jackson, MI 49201, (517) 788-4265, **<co.jackson.mi.us>**

- **INCORPORATED:** Oct. 29, 1829
- **PARENT COUNTIES:** Washtenaw, Unorganized Territory
- **BIRTH RECORDS:** start in 1867, kept by County Clerk
- **MARRIAGE:** ca. 1830, County Clerk
- **DIVORCE:** ca. 1800, County Clerk
- **DEATH:** 1867, County Clerk
- **LAND:** unknown start, Registrar of Deeds
- **PROBATE:** unknown start, Probate Court
- **COURT:** unknown start, Clerk/District Court
- **NATURALIZATION:** unknown start, County Clerk
- **NOTES:** Attached to Washtenaw County prior to organization Aug. 1, 1832.

KALAMAZOO

201 W. Kalamazoo Ave., Kalamazoo, MI 49007, (616) 383-8840, **<kalcounty.com>**

- **INCORPORATED:** Oct. 29, 1829
- **PARENT COUNTY:** Unorganized Territory
- **BIRTH RECORDS:** start in 1867, kept by County Clerk
- **MARRIAGE:** 1831, County Clerk
- **DIVORCE:** ca. 1800, County Clerk
- **DEATH:** 1867, County Clerk
- **LAND:** unknown start, Registrar of Deeds
- **PROBATE:** unknown start, Probate Judge
- **COURT:** ca. 1800, Probate Judge
- **NOTES:** Attached to St. Joseph County prior to organization Oct. 1, 1830.

KALKASKA

605 N. Birch St., Kalkaska, MI 49646, (616) 258-3300, **<kalkaskacounty.net>**

- **INCORPORATED:** April 1, 1840
- **PARENT COUNTY:** Mackinac
- **BIRTH RECORDS:** start in 1871, kept by County Clerk
- **MARRIAGE:** 1871, County Clerk
- **DIVORCE:** 1871, County Clerk
- **DEATH:** 1871, County Clerk
- **LAND:** unknown start, Registrar of Deeds
- **PROBATE:** unknown start, Probate Judge
- **COURT:** 1871, County Clerk
- **BURIAL:** unknown start, County Clerk
- **NOTES:** Formerly Wabassee County. Name changed to Kalkaska March 8, 1843. Attached to Mackinac, Grand Traverse and Antrim counties prior to organization Jan. 27, 1871.

KANOTIN

- **INCORPORATED:** April 1, 1840
- **PARENT COUNTY:** Unorganized Territory
- **NOTES:** See Iosco County. Name changed to Iosco March 8, 1843.

KAUTAWAUBET

- **INCORPORATED:** April 1, 1840
- **PARENT COUNTY:** Mackinac
- **NOTES:** See Wexford County. Name changed to Wexford March 8, 1843.

KAYKAKEE

- **INCORPORATED:** April 1, 1840
- **PARENT COUNTY:** Mackinac
- **NOTES:** See Clare County. Name changed to Clare March 8, 1843.

KENT

300 Monroe Ave. NW, Grand Rapids, MI 49503, (616) 336-3550, **<www.accesskent.com>**

- **INCORPORATED:** March 2, 1831
- **PARENT COUNTIES:** Mackinac, Unorganized Territory
- **BIRTH RECORDS:** start in 1867, kept by County Clerk
- **MARRIAGE:** 1845, County Clerk
- **DIVORCE:** 1867, Circuit Court
- **DEATH:** 1867, County Clerk
- **LAND:** unknown start, Registrar of Deeds
- **PROBATE:** unknown start, Probate Court
- **COURT:** 1867, Circuit Court
- **BURIAL:** 1959, County Clerk
- **NOTES:** Organized April 4, 1836.

KESKKAUKO

- **INCORPORATED:** April 1, 1840
- **PARENT COUNTY:** Mackinac
- **NOTES:** See Charlevoix, old. Name changed to Clarlevoix March 8, 1843.

KEWEENAW

County Courthouse, Fourth St., Eagle River, MI 49924, (906) 337-2229, **<keweenawcountyonline.org>**

- **INCORPORATED:** March 11, 1861
- **PARENT COUNTY:** Houghton
- **BIRTH RECORDS:** start in 1867, kept by County Clerk
- **MARRIAGE:** 1867, County Clerk

- **DIVORCE:** unknown start, County Clerk
- **DEATH:** 1867, County Clerk
- **LAND:** 1848, County Clerk
- **PROBATE:** unknown start, Probate Court
- **COURT:** unknown start, County Clerk

LAKE

800 10th St., Box B, Baldwin, MI 49304, (616) 745-4641,
<lakecountymichigan.com>

- **INCORPORATED:** April 1, 1840
- **PARENT COUNTY:** Mackinac
- **BIRTH RECORDS:** start in 1870, kept by County Clerk
- **MARRIAGE:** 1872, County Clerk
- **DIVORCE:** 1874, Trial Court
- **DEATH:** 1870, County Clerk
- **LAND:** 1880, Registrar of Deeds
- **PROBATE:** unknown start, Trial Court
- **COURT:** 1874, Trial Court
- **MILITARY:** unknown start, County Clerk
- **NOTES:** Formerly Aishcum County. Name changed to Lake March 8, 1843. Attached to Ottawa, Mason and Newaygo counties prior to organization May 1, 1871.

LAPEER

255 Clay St., Lapeer, MI 48446, (810) 667-0356,
<lapeercountyweb.org>

- **INCORPORATED:** Sept. 10, 1822
- **PARENT COUNTY:** Oakland, St. Clair, Unorganized Territory
- **BIRTH RECORDS:** start in 1867, kept by County Clerk
- **MARRIAGE:** 1835, County Clerk
- **DIVORCE:** 1835, County Clerk
- **DEATH:** 1867, County Clerk
- **COURT:** 1835, County Clerk
- **NOTES:** Attached to Oakland County prior to organization Feb. 2, 1835.

LEELANAU

301 E. Cedar St., Box 467, Leland, MI 49654, (231) 256-9824,
<leelanau.cc>

- **INCORPORATED:** April 1, 1840
- **PARENT COUNTY:** Mackinac
- **BIRTH RECORDS:** start in 1867, kept by County Clerk
- **MARRIAGE:** 1867, County Clerk
- **DIVORCE:** 1870, County Clerk
- **DEATH:** 1867, County Clerk
- **PROBATE:** unknown start, Probate Judge
- **COURT:** unknown start, County Clerk
- **NOTES:** Attached to Mackinac and Grand Traverse counties prior to organization Feb. 27, 1863.

LENAWEE

425 N. Main St., Adrian, MI 49221, (517) 264-4606,
<lenawee.mi.us>

- **INCORPORATED:** Sept. 10, 1822
- **PARENT COUNTY:** Monroe
- **BIRTH RECORDS:** start in 1867, kept by County Clerk
- **MARRIAGE:** 1867, County Clerk
- **DIVORCE:** 1870, County Clerk
- **DEATH:** 1867, County Clerk
- **COURT:** 1870, County Clerk
- **NOTES:** Attached to Monroe County prior to organization Dec. 31, 1826. Courthouse burned 1852.

LIVINGSTON

200 E. Grand River Ave., Howell, MI 48843, (517) 546-0500,
<co.livingston.mi.us>

- **INCORPORATED:** March 21, 1833
- **PARENT COUNTIES:** Shiwassee, Washtenaw
- **BIRTH RECORDS:** start in 1867, kept by County Clerk
- **MARRIAGE:** 1836, County Clerk
- **DIVORCE:** 1867, County Clerk
- **DEATH:** 1867, County Clerk
- **LAND:** unknown start, Registrar of Deeds
- **PROBATE:** unknown start Probate Judge
- **COURT:** 1867, County Clerk
- **NOTES:** Attached to Shiawassee and Washtenaw counties prior to organization April 4, 1836.

LUCE

407 W. Harrie St., Newberry, MI 49868, (906) 293-5521

- **INCORPORATED:** March 1, 1887
- **PARENT COUNTIES:** Chippewa, Mackinac
- **BIRTH RECORDS:** start in 1887, kept by County Clerk
- **MARRIAGE:** 1887, County Clerk
- **DIVORCE:** 1887, County Clerk
- **DEATH:** 1887, County Clerk
- **LAND:** 1887, County Clerk
- **PROBATE:** unknown start, Probate Judge
- **COURT:** 1887, County Clerk

MACKINAC

100 S. Marley St., St. Ignace, MI 49781, (906) 643-7300,
<mackinaccounty.net>

- **INCORPORATED:** Oct. 26, 1818
- **PARENT COUNTY:** Wayne
- **BIRTH RECORDS:** start in 1873, kept by County Clerk
- **MARRIAGE:** 1867, County Clerk
- **DIVORCE:** 1808, County Clerk
- **DEATH:** 1873, County Clerk
- **COURT:** 1808, County Clerk
- **NOTES:** Formerly Michilimackinac County. Name changed to Mackinac Jan. 26, 1837.

MACOMB

40 N. Main, Mount Clemens, MI 48043, (810) 469-5120,
<macombcountymi.gov>

- **INCORPORATED:** Jan. 15, 1818
- **PARENT COUNTY:** Wayne
- **BIRTH RECORDS:** start in 1867, kept by County Clerk
- **MARRIAGE:** 1819, County Clerk
- **DIVORCE:** 1847, County Clerk
- **DEATH:** 1867, County Clerk
- **LAND:** unknown start, Registrar of Deeds
- **PROBATE:** unknown start, Probate Court
- **MILITARY:** unknown start, County Clerk

MANISTEE

415 Third St., Manistee, MI 49660, (231) 723-3331,
<manisteecountymi.gov>

- **INCORPORATED:** April 1, 1840
- **PARENT COUNTY:** Mackinac
- **BIRTH RECORDS:** start in 1867, kept by County Clerk
- **MARRIAGE:** 1856, County Clerk
- **DIVORCE:** 1856, County Clerk
- **DEATH:** 1867, County Clerk
- **LAND:** unknown start, Registrar of Deeds
- **PROBATE:** unknown start, Probate Court
- **COURT:** 1855, County Clerk
- **NOTES:** Attached to Mackinac, Ottawa and Grand Traverse counties prior to organization Feb. 13, 1855.

MANITOU

- **INCORPORATED:** Feb. 12, 1855
- **PARENT COUNTIES:** Emmet, Leelanau
- **NOTES:** Attached to Mackinac and Leelanau counties. Disorganized March 16, 1861. Eliminated April 4, 1895 and absorbed by Charlevoix and Leelanau counties.

MARQUETTE

234 W. Baraga Ave., Marquette, MI 49855, (906) 225-8330,
<co.marquette.mi.us>

- **INCORPORATED:** March 9, 1843
- **PARENT COUNTIES:** Chippewa, Mackinac
- **BIRTH RECORDS:** start in 1867, kept by County Clerk
- **MARRIAGE:** 1851, County Clerk
- **DIVORCE:** 1852, County Clerk
- **DEATH:** 1867, County Clerk
- **COURT:** 1852, County Clerk
- **NOTES:** Attached to Chippewa and Houghton counties prior to organization Dec. 1, 1851.

MASON

304 E. Ludington Ave., Ludington, MI 49431, (231) 843-8202,
<masoncounty.net>

- **INCORPORATED:** April 1, 1840
- **PARENT COUNTY:** Mackinac
- **BIRTH RECORDS:** start in 1867, kept by County Clerk
- **MARRIAGE:** 1867, County Clerk
- **DIVORCE:** 1867, County Clerk
- **DEATH:** 1867, County Clerk
- **LAND:** unknown start, Registrar of Deeds
- **PROBATE:** unknown start, Probate Court
- **COURT:** 1867, County Clerk
- **BURIAL:** unknown start, City Clerk
- **NOTES:** Formerly Notipekago County. Name changed to Mason March 8, 1843. Attached to Ottawa County prior to organization Feb. 13, 1855.

MECOSTA

400 Elm St., Big Rapids, MI 49307, (616) 592-0783,
<co.mecosta.mi.us>

- **INCORPORATED:** April 1, 1840
- **PARENT COUNTIES:** Mackinac, Oceana
- **BIRTH RECORDS:** start in 1867, kept by County Clerk
- **MARRIAGE:** 1859, County Clerk
- **DIVORCE:** 1859, County Clerk
- **DEATH:** 1867, County Clerk
- **LAND:** 1859, Registrar of Deeds
- **PROBATE:** 1864, Probate Court
- **COURT:** 1859, County Clerk
- **NOTES:** Attached to Newaygo and Kent counties prior to organization Feb. 11, 1858.

MEEGISEE

- **INCORPORATED:** April 1, 1840
- **PARENT COUNTY:** Mackinac
- **NOTES:** See Antrim County. Name changed to Antrim March 8 1843.

MENOMINEE

839 10th Ave., Menominee, MI 49858, (906) 863-9968,
<www.menomineecounty.com>

- **INCORPORATED:** March 15, 1861
- **PARENT COUNTY:** Unorganized Territory
- **BIRTH RECORDS:** start in 1861, kept by County Clerk
- **MARRIAGE:** 1861, County Clerk
- **DIVORCE:** 1861, County Clerk
- **DEATH:** 1861, County Clerk
- **LAND:** unknown start, Registrar of Deeds
- **PROBATE:** unknown start, Probate Judge
- **COURT:** 1861, County Clerk
- **NOTES:** Formerly Bleeker County. Name changed to Menominee March 19, 1863.

MICHILIMACKINAC

- **INCORPORATED:** Oct. 26, 1818
- **PARENT COUNTY:** Wayne
- **NOTES:** See Mackinac County. Name changed to Mackinac Jan. 26 1837.

MIDLAND

220 W. Ellsworth St., Midland, MI 48640, (517) 832-6739,
<co.midland.mi.us>

- **INCORPORATED:** March 2, 1831
- **PARENT COUNTIES:** Saginaw, Unorganized Territory
- **BIRTH RECORDS:** start in 1867, kept by County Clerk
- **MARRIAGE:** 1867, County Clerk
- **DIVORCE:** ca. 1800, Circuit Court
- **DEATH:** 1867, County Clerk
- **LAND:** 1855, Registrar of Deeds
- **PROBATE:** unknown start, Probate Court
- **COURT:** ca. 1800, Circuit Court
- **MILITARY:** 1918, County Clerk
- **NOTES:** County Clerk has naturalization records 1853-1948, and burial records from mid 1800s. Attached to Saginaw County prior to organization Dec. 31, 1850.

MIKENAUK

- **INCORPORATED:** April 1, 1840
- **PARENT COUNTY:** Mackinac
- **NOTES:** See Roscommon County. Name changed to Roscommon March 8, 1843.

MISSAUKEE
111 S. Canal St., Box 800, Lake City, MI 49651, (231) 839-4967,
<missaukee.org>
- **INCORPORATED:** April 1, 1840
- **PARENT COUNTY:** Mackinac
- **BIRTH RECORDS:** start in 1871, kept by County Clerk
- **MARRIAGE:** 1871, County Clerk
- **DIVORCE:** 1871, County Clerk
- **DEATH:** 1871, County Clerk
- **LAND:** 1871, County Clerk
- **PROBATE:** unknown start, Probate Judge
- **COURT:** 1871, County Clerk
- **BURIAL:** 1871, County Clerk
- **NOTES:** Attached to Mackinac, Grand Traverse, Manistee and Wexford counties prior to organization March 11, 1871. Some records were destroyed by fire in 1944.

MONROE
106 E. First St., Monroe, MI 48161, (734) 240-7020,
<co.monroe.mi.us>
- **INCORPORATED:** Jul. 14, 1817
- **PARENT COUNTY:** Wayne
- **BIRTH RECORDS:** start in 1874, kept by County Clerk
- **MARRIAGE:** 1818, County Clerk
- **DIVORCE:** 1945, County Clerk
- **DEATH:** 1867, County Clerk
- **LAND:** unknown start, Registrar of Deeds
- **PROBATE:** unknown start, Probate Court
- **COURT:** 1945, County Clerk

MONTCALM
617 N. State St., Stanton, MI 48888, (517) 831-7339,
<montcalm.org>
- **INCORPORATED:** March 2, 1831
- **PARENT COUNTY:** Mackinac
- **BIRTH RECORDS:** start in 1867, kept by County Clerk
- **MARRIAGE:** 1858, County Clerk
- **DIVORCE:** 1865, County Clerk
- **DEATH:** 1867, County Clerk
- **LAND:** unknown start, Registrar of Deeds
- **PROBATE:** unknown start, Probate Court
- **COURT:** 1865, County Clerk
- **NOTES:** Attached to Ionia County prior to organization March 20, 1850.

MONTMORENCY
Box 789, Atlanta, MI 49709, (517) 785-4794,
<montmorencycountymichigan.us>
- **INCORPORATED:** April 1, 1840
- **PARENT COUNTY:** Mackinac
- **BIRTH RECORDS:** start in 1881, kept by County Clerk
- **MARRIAGE:** 1881, County Clerk
- **DIVORCE:** 1940, County Clerk
- **DEATH:** 1881, County Clerk
- **COURT:** 1940, County Clerk
- **MILITARY:** 1920, County Clerk
- **NOTES:** Formerly Cheonoquet County. Name changed to Montmorency March 8, 1843. Attached to Mackinac, Cheboygan and Alpena counties prior to organization May 21, 1881. Most records lost in 1942 fire.

MUSKEGON
990 Terrace St., Muskegon, MI 49442, (616) 724-6221,
<co.muskegon.mi.us>
- **INCORPORATED:** Feb. 4, 1859
- **PARENT COUNTY:** Ottawa
- **BIRTH RECORDS:** start in 1859, kept by County Clerk
- **MARRIAGE:** 1859, County Clerk
- **DIVORCE:** 1859, County Clerk
- **DEATH:** 1859, County Clerk
- **LAND:** unknown start, Registrar of Deeds
- **PROBATE:** unknown start, Probate Court
- **COURT:** 1859, County Clerk

NEGWEON
- **INCORPORATED:** April 1, 1840
- **PARENT COUNTIES:** Mackinac, Unorganized Territory
- **NOTES:** See Alcona County. Name changed to Alcona March 8, 1843.

NEWAYGO
1087 Newell St., White Cloud, MI 49349, (616) 689-7235,
<countyofnewaygo.com>
- **INCORPORATED:** April 1, 1840
- **PARENT COUNTIES:** Mackinac, Oceana
- **BIRTH RECORDS:** start in 1867, kept by County Clerk
- **MARRIAGE:** 1851, County Clerk
- **DIVORCE:** unknown start, Circuit Court
- **DEATH:** 1867, County Clerk
- **LAND:** unknown start, Registrar of Deeds
- **PROBATE:** unknown start, Probate Court
- **COURT:** unknown start, Circuit Court
- **MILITARY:** unknown start, County Clerk
- **NATURALIZATION:** unknown start, Circuit Court
- **NOTES:** Attached to Kent and Ottawa counties prior to organization Jan. 27, 1851.

NOTIPEKAGO
- **INCORPORATED:** April 1, 1840
- **PARENT COUNTY:** Mackinac
- **NOTES:** See Mason County. Name changed to Mason March 8, 1843.

OAKLAND
1200 N. Telegraph Rd., Pontiac, MI 48341, (248) 858-0572,
<oakgov.com>
- **INCORPORATED:** Jan. 12, 1819
- **PARENT COUNTY:** Macomb
- **BIRTH RECORDS:** start in 1867, kept by County Clerk
- **MARRIAGE:** 1827, County Clerk
- **DEATH:** 1867, County Clerk
- **NATURALIZATION:** 1827, County Clerk
- **NOTES:** Attached to Macomb County prior to organization March 28, 1820.

OCEANA

100 Store St., Hart, MI 49420, (231) 873-4328, **<oceana.mi.us>**

- **INCORPORATED:** March 2, 1831
- **PARENT COUNTY:** Mackinac
- **BIRTH RECORDS:** start in 1867, kept by County Clerk
- **MARRIAGE:** 1867, County Clerk
- **DIVORCE:** unknown start, Circuit Court
- **DEATH:** 1868, County Clerk
- **LAND:** unknown start, Registrar of Deeds
- **PROBATE:** unknown start, Probate Court
- **COURT:** unknown start, Circuit Court
- **NOTES:** Attached to Kent and Ottawa counties prior to organization April 7, 1851.

OGEMAW

806 W. Houghton Ave., West Branch, MI 48661, (517) 345-0215, **<ogemawcountymi.gov>**

- **INCORPORATED:** April 1, 1840
- **PARENT COUNTY:** Unorganized Territory
- **BIRTH RECORDS:** start in 1879, kept by County Clerk
- **MARRIAGE:** 1887, County Clerk
- **DIVORCE:** 1902, County Clerk
- **DEATH:** 1876, County Clerk
- **LAND:** 1860, Registrar of Deeds
- **PROBATE:** 1873, Probate Court
- **COURT:** 1902, County Clerk
- **MILITARY:** 1919, County Clerk
- **NATURALIZATION:** 1876, County Clerk
- **NOTES:** Attached to Mackinac, Cheboygan and Iosco counties prior to organization. Eliminated March 7, 1867, to Iosco. Re-created March 28, 1873, from Iosco and organized April 27, 1875.

OKKUDDO

- **INCORPORATED:** April 1, 1840
- **PARENT COUNTY:** Mackinac
- **NOTES:** See Otsego County. Name changed to Otsego March 8, 1843.

OMEENA

- **INCORPORATED:** April 1, 1840
- **PARENT COUNTY:** Mackinac
- **NOTES:** See Grand Traverse. Absorbed by Grand Traverse County Feb. 3, 1853.

ONTONAGON

725 Greenland Rd., Ontonagon, MI 49953, (906) 884-4255, **<ontonagonmi.org>**

- **INCORPORATED:** March 9, 1843
- **PARENT COUNTIES:** Chippewa, Mackinac
- **BIRTH RECORDS:** start in 1868, kept by County Clerk
- **MARRIAGE:** 1861, County Clerk
- **DIVORCE:** 1854, County Clerk
- **DEATH:** 1868, County Clerk
- **LAND:** 1850, County Clerk
- **PROBATE:** unknown start, Probate Court
- **COURT:** 1854, County Clerk
- **BURIAL:** unknown start, Cemetery Associations
- **NOTES:** Attached to Chippewa and Houghton counties prior to organization Jan. 1, 1853.

OSCEOLA

301 W. Upton Ave., Box 208, Reed City, MI 49677, (231) 832-6104, **<osceola-county.org>**

- **INCORPORATED:** April 1, 1840
- **PARENT COUNTY:** Mackinac
- **BIRTH RECORDS:** start in 1869, kept by County Clerk
- **MARRIAGE:** 1869, County Clerk
- **DIVORCE:** 1870, County Clerk
- **DEATH:** 1870, County Clerk
- **LAND:** unknown start, County Treasurer
- **PROBATE:** unknown start, Probate Judge
- **COURT:** 1963, County Clerk
- **BURIAL:** unknown start, County Clerk
- **NOTES:** Formerly Unwattin County. Name changed to Osceola March 8, 1843. Attached to Ottawa, Mason, Newaygo and Mecosta counties prior to organization March 17, 1869.

OSCODA

311 Morenci, Box 399, Mio, MI 48647, (517) 826-1110, **<oscodacountymi.com>**

- **INCORPORATED:** April 1, 1840
- **PARENT COUNTY:** Mackinac
- **BIRTH RECORDS:** start in 1881, kept by County Clerk
- **MARRIAGE:** 1881, County Clerk
- **DIVORCE:** 1881, County Clerk
- **DEATH:** 1881, County Clerk
- **LAND:** 1850, County Clerk
- **PROBATE:** unknown start, Probate Judge
- **COURT:** 1881, County Clerk
- **BURIAL:** 1881, County Clerk
- **NOTES:** Attached to Cheboygan, Alpena, Alcona, Iosco and Mackinac counties prior to organization March 10, 1881.

OTSEGO

225 W. Main St., Gaylord, MI 49735, (517) 732-6484, **<otsegocountymi.gov>**

- **INCORPORATED:** April 1, 1840
- **PARENT COUNTY:** Mackinac
- **BIRTH RECORDS:** start in 1875, kept by County Clerk
- **MARRIAGE:** 1875, County Clerk
- **DIVORCE:** 1875, County Clerk
- **DEATH:** 1875, County Clerk

- **LAND:** unknown start, County Treasurer
- **COURT:** 1875, County Clerk
- **NOTES:** Formerly Okkuddo County. Name changed to Otsego March 8, 1843. Attached to Alpena, Mackinac, Cheboygan, Alpena and Antrim counties prior to organization March 12, 1875.

OTTAWA

12220 Fillmore St., West Olive, MI 49460, (616) 738-4000,
<co.ottawa.mi.us>

- **INCORPORATED:** March 2, 1831
- **PARENT COUNTIES:** Mackinac, Unorganized Territory
- **BIRTH RECORDS:** start in 1867, kept by County Clerk
- **MARRIAGE:** 1847, County Clerk
- **DIVORCE:** 1863, County Clerk
- **DEATH:** 1867, County Clerk
- **COURT:** 1847, County Clerk
- **NOTES:** Attached to Kent County prior to organization Dec. 29, 1837.

PRESQUE ISLE

151 E. Huron Ave., Box 110, Rogers City, MI 49779, (517) 734-3288,
<presqueislecounty.org>

- **INCORPORATED:** April 1, 1840
- **PARENT COUNTY:** Mackinac
- **BIRTH RECORDS:** start in 1871, kept by County Clerk
- **MARRIAGE:** 1842, County Clerk
- **DIVORCE:** 1900, County Clerk
- **DEATH:** 1871, County Clerk
- **NOTES:** Attached to Cheboygan and Alpena counties prior to organization March 31, 1871.

ROSCOMMON

500 Lake St., Roscommon, MI 48653, (517) 275-5923,
<roscommon.genwebsite.net>

- **INCORPORATED:** April 1, 1840
- **PARENT COUNTY:** Mackinac
- **BIRTH RECORDS:** start in 1874, kept by County Clerk
- **MARRIAGE:** 1875, County Clerk
- **DIVORCE:** 1875, County Clerk
- **DEATH:** 1874, County Clerk
- **LAND:** 1875, County Clerk
- **PROBATE:** 1875, County Clerk
- **COURT:** 1875, County Clerk
- **NOTES:** Formerly Mikenauk County. Name changed to Roscommon March 8, 1843. Attached to Mackinac, Cheboygan and Midland counties prior to organization March 20, 1875.

SAGINAW

111 S. Michigan Ave., Saginaw, MI 48602, (517) 790-5251,
<saginawcounty.com>

- **INCORPORATED:** Sept. 10, 1822
- **PARENT COUNTIES:** St. Clair, Unorganized Territory
- **BIRTH RECORDS:** start in 1867, kept by County Clerk
- **MARRIAGE:** 1867, County Clerk
- **DIVORCE:** 1886, County Clerk
- **DEATH:** 1868, County Clerk
- **LAND:** unknown start, Equalization Department
- **PROBATE:** unknown start, Probate Court
- **COURT:** 1843, County Clerk
- **NOTES:** Attached to Oakland County prior to organization Feb. 9, 1835.

SANILAC

60 W. Sanilac Rd. Room 203, Sandusky, MI 48471, (810) 648-3212,
<sanilaccounty.net>

- **INCORPORATED:** Sept. 10, 1822
- **PARENT COUNTIES:** St. Clair, Unorganized Territory
- **BIRTH RECORDS:** start in 1860, kept by County Clerk
- **MARRIAGE:** 1849, County Clerk
- **DIVORCE:** 1854, County Clerk
- **DEATH:** 1867, County Clerk
- **LAND:** unknown start, Registrar of Deeds
- **PROBATE:** unknown start, Probate Court
- **COURT:** 1854, County Clerk
- **NOTES:** Attached to Oakland, St. Clair and Lapeer counties prior to organization Dec. 31, 1849.

SCHOOLCRAFT

300 Walnut St. #164, Manistique, MI 49854, (906) 341-3618,
<schoolcraftcounty.net>

- **INCORPORATED:** March 9, 1843
- **PARENT COUNTIES:** Chippewa, Mackinac
- **BIRTH RECORDS:** start in 1870, kept by County Clerk
- **MARRIAGE:** 1870, County Clerk
- **DIVORCE:** 1870, County Clerk
- **DEATH:** 1870, County Clerk
- **LAND:** 1870, County Clerk
- **PROBATE:** 1870, Probate Court
- **COURT:** 1870, County Clerk
- **NOTES:** Attached to Chippewa, Houghton and Marquette counties prior to organization March 23 1871.

SHAWANO

- **INCORPORATED:** April 1, 1840
- **PARENT COUNTY:** Mackinac
- **NOTES:** See Crawford County. Name changed to Crawford March 8, 1843.

SHIAWASSEE

208 N. Shiawassee St., Corunna, MI 48817, (517) 743-2242,
<shiawassee.net>

- **INCORPORATED:** Sept. 10, 1822
- **PARENT COUNTIES:** Oakland, St. Clair, Unorganized Territory
- **BIRTH RECORDS:** start in 1867, kept by County Clerk
- **MARRIAGE:** 1867, County Clerk
- **DIVORCE:** 1848, County Clerk
- **DEATH:** 1867, County Clerk
- **LAND:** unknown start, Registrar of Deeds
- **PROBATE:** unknown start, Probate Judge
- **COURT:** 1848, County Clerk
- **NOTES:** Attached to Genesee and Oakland counties prior to organization March 18, 1837.

ST. CLAIR

201 McMorran Blvd., Port Huron, MI 48060, (810) 985-2200, **<stclaircounty.org>**

- **INCORPORATED:** March 28, 1820
- **PARENT COUNTY:** Macomb
- **BIRTH RECORDS:** start in 1867, kept by County Clerk
- **MARRIAGE:** 1834, County Clerk
- **DIVORCE:** 1849, County Clerk
- **DEATH:** 1868, County Clerk
- **COURT:** 1849, County Clerk
- **NOTES:** Attached to Macomb County prior to organization May 8, 1821.

ST. JOSEPH

125 W. Main St., Box 189, Centreville, MI 49032, (616) 467-5500, **<stjosephcountymi.org>**

- **INCORPORATED:** Oct. 29, 1829
- **PARENT COUNTY:** Unorganized Territory
- **BIRTH RECORDS:** start in 1867, kept in County Clerk
- **MARRIAGE:** 1832, County Clerk
- **DIVORCE:** 1900, County Clerk
- **DEATH:** 1867, County Clerk
- **LAND:** unknown start, Registrar of Deeds
- **PROBATE:** unknown start, Probate Court
- **COURT:** 1900, County Clerk
- **NATURALIZATION:** unknown start, County Clerk

TONEDAGANA

- **INCORPORATED:** April 1, 1840
- **PARENT COUNTY:** Mackinac
- **NOTES:** See Emmet County. Name changed to Emmet March 8, 1843.

TUSCOLA

440 N. State St., Caro, MI 48723, (517) 672-3780, **<tuscolacounty.org>**

- **INCORPORATED:** April 1, 1840
- **PARENT COUNTY:** Sanilac
- **BIRTH RECORDS:** start in 1867, kept by County Clerk
- **MARRIAGE:** 1851, County Clerk
- **DIVORCE:** 1878, County Clerk
- **DEATH:** 1867, County Clerk
- **COURT:** 1878, County Clerk
- **NOTES:** Attached to Saginaw County prior to organization March 2, 1850.

UNWATTIN

- **INCORPORATED:** April 1, 1840
- **PARENT COUNTY:** Mackinac
- **NOTES:** See Osceola County. Name changed to Osceola March 8, 1843.

VAN BUREN

212 E. Paw Paw St., Paw Paw, MI 49079, (616) 657-8218, **<vbco.org>**

- **INCORPORATED:** Oct. 29, 1829
- **PARENT COUNTY:** Unorganized Territory
- **BIRTH RECORDS:** start in 1867, kept by County Clerk
- **MARRIAGE:** 1836, County Clerk
- **DIVORCE:** 1837, County Clerk
- **DEATH:** 1867, County Clerk
- **LAND:** unknown start, Registrar of Deeds
- **PROBATE:** unknown start, Probate Court
- **COURT:** 1837, County Clerk
- **NOTES:** Attached to Cass and Lenawee counties prior to organization April 3, 1837.

WABASSEE

- **INCORPORATED:** April 1, 1840
- **PARENT COUNTY:** Mackinac
- **NOTES:** See Kalkaska County. Name changed to Kalkaska March 8, 1843.

WASHTENAW

101 E. Huron St., Box 8645, Ann Arbor, MI 48107, (734) 222-6700, **<ewashtenaw.org>**

- **INCORPORATED:** Sept. 10, 1822
- **PARENT COUNTY:** Wayne, Oakland
- **BIRTH RECORDS:** start in 1867, kept in County Clerk
- **MARRIAGE:** 1867, County Clerk
- **DIVORCE:** unknown start, County Clerk
- **DEATH:** 1867, County Clerk
- **LAND:** unknown start, County Clerk
- **COURT:** unknown start,County Clerk
- **NATURALIZATION:** 1835, County Clerk
- **SUPERVISOR:** 1835, County Clerk
- **NOTES:** Attached to Wayne County prior to organization Dec. 31, 1826.

WAYNE

500 Griswold St., Detroit, MI 48226, (313) 224-6262, **<waynecounty.com>**

- **INCORPORATED:** Nov. 21, 1815
- **PARENT COUNTY:** Original county
- **BIRTH RECORDS:** unknown start, kept by County Clerk
- **MARRIAGE:** unknown start, County Clerk
- **DEATH:** unknown start, County Clerk
- **LAND:** unknown start, Registrar of Deeds
- **PROBATE:** unknown start, Probate Court

WEXFORD

437 E. Division St., Cadillac, MI 49601, (231) 779-9450, **<www. rootsweb.ancestry.com/~miwxfor>**

- **INCORPORATED:** April 1, 1840
- **PARENT COUNTY:** Mackinac
- **BIRTH RECORDS:** start in 1868, kept by County Clerk
- **MARRIAGE:** 1869, County Clerk
- **DIVORCE:** 1869, County Clerk
- **DEATH:** 1869, County Clerk
- **COURT:** 1869,County Clerk
- **NOTES:** Formerly Kautawaubet county. Name changed to Wexford March 8, 1843. Attached to Mackinac, Manistee and Grand Traverse counties prior to organization March 30, 1869.

MINNESOTA

» BY JAMES W. WARREN

HISTORICAL OVERVIEW

Centuries before Bob Dylan, Sinclair Lewis or Betty Crocker could claim Minnesota as their birthplace, the area was inhabited by the Dakota (Sioux) and Ojibway (Chippewa) Indians. Early French traders and missionaries arrived by 1680, including Father Hennepin, who discovered the headwaters of the Mississippi River at Lake Itasca. The trading area came under English control in 1763.

The eastern part of what would become Minnesota was acquired from the British in 1783. It was part of the Northwest Territory from 1787 until 1800, and of Indiana Territory until 1809. In 1803, the United States acquired western Minnesota from the French with the Louisiana Purchase. All of present-day Minnesota was subsequently part of Illinois, Michigan and Wisconsin territories. After the government established Fort Snelling in 1820 and purchased Indian lands east of the Mississippi in 1837, large-scale settlement began. Minnesota itself became a territory in 1849. In the early 1850s, the Dakota and Ojibway sold almost all their lands west of the Mississippi and the railroads reached the territory. Immigrants flocked to the area.

After becoming the 32nd state in 1858, Minnesota was the first to answer Lincoln's 1861 call for Civil War volunteers. A year later, war erupted within Minnesota. Broken treaties and starvation pushed Dakota Indians to attack several settlements. With hundreds of casualties on both sides, the Dakota Conflict caused panic among settlers across the Midwest.

Early pioneers had come mostly from New England, New York, Pennsylvania or French Canada. After statehood there were large waves of Irish and German immigration, followed by Swedes, Norwegians and Danes in the last third of the 19th century. Discovery of the rich iron ore deposits brought many Eastern Europeans to Minnesota's northern "Iron Range" towns. New arrivals may have come up the Mississippi by steamboat from Iowa, Illinois, St. Louis or New Orleans. For many Irish, English and Scandinavians, the cheapest ocean passage was to Quebec or another Canadian port. From there, they traveled up the Great Lakes and by train or wagon to Minnesota. Today, half of the state's population lives in the Twin Cities region of St. Paul and Minneapolis.

research tips

- The Minnesota Historical Society **<www.mnhs.org>** is the official state archives; it contains many records from state agencies and local governments.
- Minnesota GenWeb **<www.rootsweb.ancestry.com/~mngenweb>** offers links and indexes for records and resources across the state.

CENSUS RECORDS

- Federal census: 1850, 1860, 1870, 1880, 1900, 1910, 1920, 1930
- Federal mortality schedules: 1850, 1860, 1870, 1880, 1900
- Special census of Civil War Union Veterans and widows: 1890
- State/territorial census: 1836, 1838, 1849, 1853, 1857, 1865, 1875, 1885, 1895, 1905

RECORD HIGHLIGHTS

Federal censuses start in 1850 (as a territory) and 1860 (as a state). Only fragments of the 1890 federal census have survived for Minnesota, but the full 1890 Veterans Census is available for the state. Mortality schedules exist for 1850, 1860, 1870 and 1880, and a portion of the 1900 Mortality Schedule survives. The 1856 territorial census and state censuses for 1865, 1875, 1885, 1895 and 1905 are available on microfilm. Partial indexes to some state censuses are online at the Minnesota Historical Society website **<www.mnhs.org>**.

The district court for each Minnesota county has civil and criminal cases, including divorce. Divorce proceedings are usually indexed with other civil cases for that county. The Minnesota Department of Health has a statewide index to divorces that begins with 1970. Each county's probate court handles probate, guardianship, incompetency and sometimes juvenile cases. Land and vital records are usually found in the recorder's office. WPA inventories were completed for a number of Minnesota counties and serve as a shopping list for other, lesser-used court records.

While some county-level records start earlier, statewide birth registration began in 1900 and deaths in 1908. Any Minnesota courthouse can provide any post-1900/1908 Minnesota birth or death record, as each county courthouse has online access to the Minnesota Department of Health's birth and death record database and indexes. The documents that result, however, don't necessarily include all the detail from the original document. Access to Minnesota marriages is a different story, as there's no statewide registration and no central index except to marriages after 1957. You'll need to know the county where the marriage likely took place to find the record. MHS has an online index to births and deaths.

For later immigrants, alien registration records from February 1918 list non-US citizens residing in Minnesota with their name, place of birth, port of entry and date of arrival, names of children and occupation. They're indexed and microfilmed, available at the MHS.

The MHS offers a wealth of resources, including the state archives collections. Minnesota law requires counties, state agencies, local governments and school districts, to offer records they no longer use or plan to retain to the state archives. Older land, probate and other court records from many county courthouses have been transferred to MHS. For example, naturalization records (with indexes) from all 87 Minnesota counties have been transferred to MHS and microfilmed. Those films are available on interlibrary loan (look for copies at the Family History Library, too). Examples of state agency records at MHS are the records of Stillwater State Prison, various state hospitals, the Minnesota Veterans Home and applications for military service bonuses.

Minnesota Genealogical Society (MGS) resources include the MGS Cemetery Project, which lists many cemetery locations in Minnesota, and identifying who holds any records, transcriptions or indexes.

Don't overlook local libraries, county historical societies and museums, and genealogical societies. They may hold unique resources, including helpful staff.

Other resources in specialized collections include Celtic and Luxembourg materials at the University of St. Thomas in St. Paul, the Roberg Collection of Norwegian materials at St. Olaf University in Northfield, the Swedish Institute in Minneapolis, and mining and northern Minnesota history at the Iron Range Research Center in Chisholm. The Immigration History Research Center **<www.ihrc.umn.edu>** in Minneapolis is a major repository for American immigration research, containing manuscripts, books, newspapers and serials.

The Minnesota USGenWeb Project **<www.rootsweb.ancestry.com/~mngenweb>** is an indispensable resource for the resources, indexes and links it provides at both the state and county levels. The Family History Library in Salt Lake City holds microfilmed records for a number of Minnesota counties, primarily in the southern tier of the state, as well as some for Ramsey (St. Paul) and Hennepin (Minneapolis) counties. Active microfilming continues in Minnesota.

ARCHIVES, LIBRARIES, AND SOCIETIES

Aitkin County Historical Society
Box 215, Aitkin, MN 56431, **<www.aitkin.com/achs>**

American Swedish Institute
2600 Park Ave., Minneapolis, MN 55407, (612) 871-8682

Anoka County Historical and Genealogical Society
2135 Third Ave., No., Anoka, MN 55303, **<ac-hs.org>**

Archives of the American Lutheran Church
2481 Como Ave., Saint Paul, MN 55108-1496, (651) 641-3205

Becker County Historical Society
714 Summit, Box 622, Detroit Lakes, MN 56502, (218) 847-5048, **<www.beckercountyhistory.org>**

Benton County Historical Society
Box 312, Sauk Rapids, MN 56379

Blue Earth County Historical Society
415 E. Cherry St., Mankato, MN 56001, **<bushelboy.qwestoffice.net>**

Brown County Historical Society
2 N. Broadway, New Ulm, MN 56073, (507) 354-1068, **<75.146.162.52/bchs>**

Bureau of Land Management Eastern States Office
7450 Boston Blvd., Springfield, VA 22153, (703) 440-1523

Carl B. Ylvisaker Library
Concordia College, 901 Eighth St. S., Moorhead, MN 56562, (218) 299-4000, **<cord.edu/Academics/Library>**

Carver County Historical Society
555 W. First St., Waconia, MN, 55387, (952) 442-4234, **<carvercountyhistoricalsociety.org>**

Chippewa County Genealogical Society
151 Pioneer Dr., Box 303, Montevideo, MN 56265

Chippewa County Historical Society
Box 342, Sault Ste. Marie, MI 49783, (906) 635-7082, **<www.rootsweb.ancestry.com/~micchs>**

Clearwater County Historical Society
Box 241, Bagley, MN 56621, **<www.mnhistoricnw.org/clearwaterchs.htm>**

Crow River Genealogical Society
380 School Rd. N., Hutchinson, MN 55350

Crow Wing County Historical Society
Box 722, Brainerd, MN 56401, **<crowwinghistory.org>**

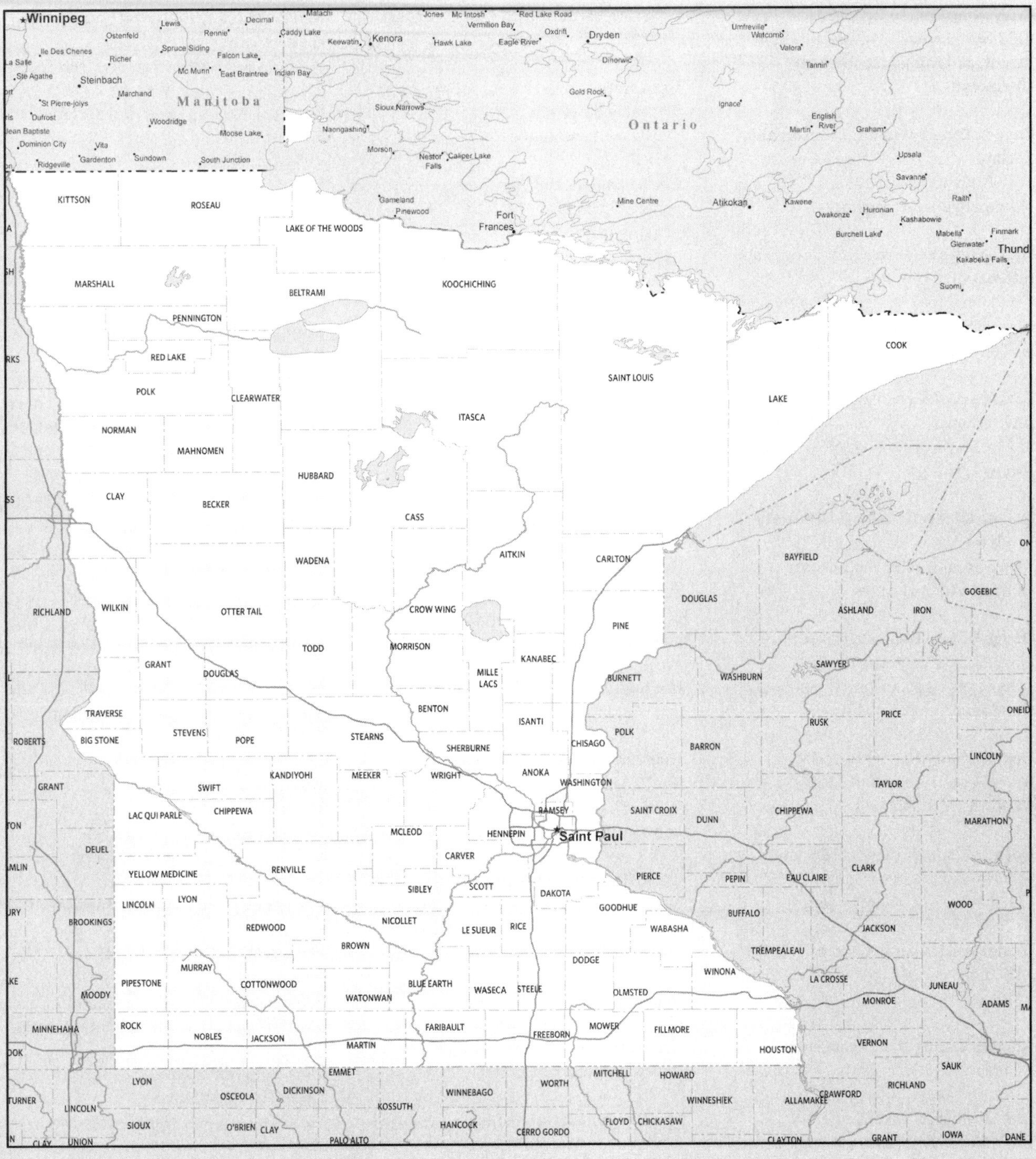
Winnipeg
Manitoba
Ontario
Kenora
Dryden
Fort Frances
Atikokan
Saint Paul
KITTSON
ROSEAU
LAKE OF THE WOODS
MARSHALL
BELTRAMI
KOOCHICHING
PENNINGTON
RED LAKE
COOK
SAINT LOUIS
LAKE
POLK
CLEARWATER
ITASCA
NORMAN
MAHNOMEN
HUBBARD
CLAY
BECKER
CASS
WADENA
AITKIN
CARLTON
WILKIN
OTTER TAIL
CROW WING
PINE
TODD
MORRISON
KANABEC
GRANT
DOUGLAS
MILLE LACS
TRAVERSE
BENTON
ISANTI
BIG STONE
STEVENS
POPE
STEARNS
SHERBURNE
CHISAGO
ANOKA
KANDIYOHI
MEEKER
WRIGHT
WASHINGTON
SWIFT
CHIPPEWA
RAMSEY
LAC QUI PARLE
MCLEOD
HENNEPIN
CARVER
YELLOW MEDICINE
RENVILLE
SIBLEY
SCOTT
DAKOTA
LINCOLN
LYON
NICOLLET
GOODHUE
REDWOOD
LE SUEUR
RICE
WABASHA
BROWN
DODGE
WINONA
MURRAY
PIPESTONE
COTTONWOOD
BLUE EARTH
WASECA
STEELE
WATONWAN
OLMSTED
ROCK
NOBLES
JACKSON
MARTIN
FARIBAULT
FREEBORN
MOWER
FILLMORE
HOUSTON
DOUGLAS
BAYFIELD
ASHLAND
IRON
GOGEBIC
WASHBURN
SAWYER
BURNETT
PRICE
RUSK
BARRON
SAINT CROIX
DUNN
TAYLOR
CHIPPEWA
PIERCE
PEPIN
EAU CLAIRE
CLARK
BUFFALO
TREMPEALEAU
JACKSON
LA CROSSE
MONROE
JUNEAU
VERNON
RICHLAND
ROBERTS
GRANT
DEUEL
BROOKINGS
MOODY
MINNEHAHA
RICHLAND
EMMET
WORTH
MITCHELL
HOWARD
WINNESHIEK
ALLAMAKEE
CRAWFORD
LYON
OSCEOLA
DICKINSON
WINNEBAGO
KOSSUTH
HANCOCK
CERRO GORDO
FLOYD
CHICKASAW
SIOUX
O'BRIEN
CLAY
PALO ALTO
LINCOLN
UNION
WOOD
MARATHON
LINCOLN
ADAMS
SAUK
GRANT
IOWA
DANE
CLAYTON

Crow Wing County Genealogical Society
2103 Graydon Ave., Brainerd, MN 56401, **<www.rootsweb.ancestry.com/~mncwcghs>**

Cuyuna Country Heritage Preservation Society
Box 68, Ironton, MN 56455, **<www.cuyunaheritage.org>**

Czechoslovak Genealogical Society and International Library
c/o Minnesota Genealogical Society Library, 5768 Olson Memorial Hwy., Golden Valley, MN 55422, (612) 595-7799

Czechoslovak Genealogical Society International
Box 16225, St. Paul, MN 55116, **<www.cgsi.org>**

Dakota County Genealogical Society
130 Third Ave. N., St. Paul, MN 55075, **<www.rootsweb.ancestry.com/~mndcgs/index.html>**

Dodge County Genealogical Society
Box 683, Dodge Center, MN 55927, **<www.rootsweb.ancestry.com/~mndodge/resources.htm>**

Dodge County Historical Society
Box 433, Mantorville, MN 55955, **<www.dodgecohistorical.addr.com>**

Douglas County Historical Society
1219 Nokomis St., Alexandria, MN 56308, (320) 762-9062, **<dchsmn.org>**

Evangelical Lutheran Church of America
2481 Como Ave., St. Paul, MN 55108, (612) 641-3205

Fillmore County Historical Center
Fountain, MN 55935

Fort Snelling National Cemetery
7601 34th Ave. S., Fort Snelling, MN 55111, (612) 726-1127

Freeborn County Historical Society
1031 No. Bridge Ave., Albert Lea, MN 56007, (507) 373-8003, **<www.smig.net/fchm>**

Freeborn County Genealogical Society
1033 Bridge Ave., Albert Lee, MN 56007

Genealogical Society of Carlton County
Box 204, Cloquet, MN 55720

German-Bohemian Heritage Society
311 Linden St., New Ulm, MN 56073, **<www.rootsweb.ancestry.com/~gbhs>**

Germanic Genealogy Society
Box 16312, Saint Paul, MN 55116, **<ggsmn.org>**

Goodhue County Family Tree Club
c/o Goodhue County Historical Society, 1166 Oak St., Red Wing, MN 55066

Great Northern Railway Historical Society
<www.gnrhs.org>

Gustavus Adolphus College
800 W. College Ave., Saint Peter, MN 56082, (507) 933-8000, **<www.gustavus.edu>**

Heart O'Lakes Genealogical Library
Box 622, 7114 Summit Ave., Detroit Lakes, MN 56502, **<www.rootsweb.ancestry.com/~mnholgs>**

Heritage Searchers of Kandiyohi County
Box 175, Willmar, MN 56201

Hubbard County Historical Society
Box 327, Park Rapids, MN 56470, (218) 732-5237, **<www.rootsweb.ancestry.com/~mnhchs>**

Icelandic Genealogy Group
c/o Minnesota Genealogical Society 5769 Olson Memorial Hwy., Golden Valley, MN 55422

Iron Range Historical Society
Box 786, Gilbert, MN 55741, **<gilbertmn.homestead.com/files/ironrangehistoricalsociety.html>**

Iron Range Research Center
801 SW Hwy. 169, Ste. 1, Chisholm, MN 55719, (800) 372-6437, **< www.ironrangeresearchcenter.org>**

Itasca Genealogical Club
Box 261, Bovey, MN 55709

Jewish Historical Society of the Upper Midwest
4330 S. Cedar Lake Rd., St. Louis Park, MN 55416, **<jhsum.org>**

Kanabec County Historical Society and History Center
Box 113, West Forest Ave., Mora, MN 55051

Kandiyohi County Historical Society
610 Hwy 71 Srv Rd., Willman, MN 56201, **<kandimuseum.com>**

Le Sueur County Historical Society
Box 240, Elysian, MN 56028, **<lesueurcountyhistory.org>**

Maplewood Area Historical Society
2516 E. Idaho St., Maplewood, MN 55109, **<www.maplewoodhistoricalsociety.org>**

Martin County Genealogical Society
208 W. Second St., Room 104B, Fairmont, MN 56031, **<www.rootsweb.ancestry.com/~flmcgs>**

McLeod County Historical Society
380 School Rd. N., Hutchinson, MN 55350, (320) 587-2107

Military Historical Society of Minnesota
15000 Hwy. 115, Little Falls, MN 56345, (320) 632-7702, **<www.minnesotanationalguard.org/camp_ripley/museum>**

Minneapolis Public Library
300 Nicolet Ave., Minneapolis, MN 55401

Minnesota Department of Health
Box 9441, 717 Delaware St. S.E., Minneapolis, MN 55440, (612) 623-5121

Minnesota Genealogical Society and Library
1185 Concord St. N., Ste. 218, South St. Paul, MN 55075, (651) 455-9057, **<mngs.org>**

Minnesota Historical Depository, United Methodist Conference
122 W. Franklin Ave., Minneapolis, MN 55404, (612) 870-0058

Minnesota Historical Society Research Center
345 Kellogg Blvd. W., St. Paul, MN 55102, (612) 296-2143

Minnesota State Archives
345 W. Kellogg Blvd., St. Paul, MN 55102, (612) 295-9961, **<www.mnhs.org/preserve/records>**

Minnetonka Historical Society
13209 E. McGinty Rd., Minnetonka, MN 55305, **<www.minnetonka.history.org>**

Minnkota Genealogical Society
Box 126, East Grand Forks, MN 56721, **<www.rootsweb.ancestry.com/~minnkota>**

Morrison County Historical Society
2151 S. Lindberg Drive, Little Falls, MN 56345, **<morrisoncountyhistory.org>**

Mower County Genealogical Society
Box 145, Austin, MN 55912

Mower County Historical Society
Box 804, Austin, MN 55912, **<mowercountyhistory.org>**

National Archives Central Plains Region, Kansas City
400 West Pershing Road, Kansas City, MO 64108, (816) 268-8000, **<www.archives.gov/central-plains/kansas-city>**

National Bygdelag Council
10129 Goodrich Circle, Bloomington, MN 55437, (612) 831-4409

National Danish-American Genealogy Society
c/o The Danish American Center at Danebo, 3030 W. River Parkway S., Minneapolis, MN 55406, **<www.danishgenealogy.org>**

Nicollet County Historical Society and Museum
Box 153, St. Peter, MN 56082

Nobles County Genealogical Society
407 Twelfth St., Suite 2, Worthington, MN 56187

Nobles County Historical Society
219 Eleventh Ave., Worthington, MN 56187

Norman County Genealogical Society
100 First St. E., Apt. 202, Ada, MN 56510, **<www.rootsweb.ancestry.com/~mnnorman/NCGenSoc.html>**

North Star of Minnesota Chapter, American Historical Society of Germans from Russia
2479 Churchill St., Roseville, MN 55113, (612) 787-0408, **<northstarchapter.org>**

Northwest Territory Canadian and French Heritage Center
Box 29397, Brooklyn Center, MN 55429

Norwegian-American Genealogical Association
c/o Minnesota Genealogical Society
5768 Olson Memorial Hwy., Golden Valley, MN 55422

Norwegian-American Historical Association
1510 St. Olaf Ave., Northfield, MN 55057, **<www.naha.stolaf.edu>**

Olmsted County Historical Society Library
1195 County Rd. SW, #22, Rochester, MN 55902

Olmsted County Genealogical Society
Box 6411, Rochester, MN 55903, **<www.olmstedhistory.com/ocgs.htm>**

Ostfriesen Genealogical Society of Minnesota
1185 Concord St., S. St. Paul, MN 55075, **<ogsa.us>**

Otter Tail County Genealogical Society
1110 Lincoln Ave. W., Fergus Falls, MN 56537

Pennington County Historical Society
Box 127, Thief River Falls, MN 56701

Pipestone County Genealogical Society
113 S. Hiawatha, Pipestone, MN 56164

Polish Genealogical Society of Minnesota
2217 Wight Bay, Brooklyn Park, MN 55443, **<www.rootsweb.ancestry.com/~mnpolgs/pgs-mn.html>**

Prairieland Genealogical Society
History Center, Room 141, Social Science Building, Southwest State University, Marshall, MN 56258, **<freepages.genealogy.rootsweb.ancestry.com/~cmolitor>**

Ramsey County Historical Society
323 Landmark Center, 75 West Fifth St., Saint Paul, MN 55102, (651) 223-8539, **<www.rchs.com>**

Range Genealogical Society
Box 388, Chisholm, MN 55768

Redwood County Genealogical Society
217 W. Flynn St., Redwood Falls, MN 56283, **<freepages.genealogy.rootsweb.ancestry.com/~corder/RCGS>**

Renville County Genealogical Society
Box 331, 22 N. Main St., Renville, MN 56284, **<www.rootsweb.ancestry.com/~mnrenvil/renville.htm>**

Renville County Historical Society and Museum
411 N. Park Dr., Box 266, Morton, MN 56270, **<renvillecountyhistory.com>**

Rice County Genealogical Society
408 Division St., Northfield, MN 55057

Rice County Historical Museum and Genealogical Research Center
1814 Second Ave., Faribault, MN 55021

Rochester Public Library
Broadway at First St., S.E, Rochester, MN 55901

Rolvaag Memorial Library
St. Olaf College, Northfield, MN 55057

Roman Catholic Archdiocese of St. Paul
226 Summit Ave., St. Paul, MN 55102, (612) 291-4400

Roman Catholic Diocese of Duluth
2830 East Forth St., Duluth, MN 55812, (218) 724-9111

Roman Catholic Diocese of New Ulm
1400 6th St. N., New Ulm, MN 56073-2099, (507) 359-2966

Roman Catholic Diocese of St. Cloud
214 S. Third Ave., Box 1248, St. Cloud, MN 56302, (320) 251-2340

Roman Catholic Diocese of Winona
55 W. Sanborn St., Box 588, Winona, MN 55987, (507) 454-4643

Roseau County Historical Society
110 Second Ave NE, Roseau, MN 56751, (218) 463-3795, **<www.roseaucohistoricalsociety.org>**

Sherburne County Historical Society
10775 27th Ave. S.E., Becker, MN 55308, (763) 251-4437, **<sherburnehistorycenter.org>**

Sibley County Historical Society
Box 407, Henderson, MN 56044, **<history.sibley.mn.us/index.htm>**

Sons of Norway
1455 W. Lake St., Minneapolis, MN 55408, (800) 945-8851

Sons of the American Revolution Minneapolis Society
2546 Cedar Ave., Minneapolis, MN 55404

St. Cloud Area Genealogists
Box 213, St. Cloud, MN 56302-0213, **<www.rootsweb.ancestry.com/~mnscag/SCAG>**

St. Paul Public Library
90 West Forth, St. Paul, MN 55102

Stearns County Historical Society
235 33rd Ave. S., St. Cloud, MN 56301, (320) 253-8424, **<www.stearns-museum.org>**

Swedish Genealogical Society of Minnesota
5768 Olson Memorial Hwy., Golden Valley, MN 55422, **<www.rootsweb.ancestry.com/~mnsgsm>**

Swift County Historical Society
Box 39, Benson, MN 56215

Twin Ports Genealogical Society
Box 16895, Duluth, MN 55816-0895

Upsala Area Historical Society
Box 35, Upsala, MN 56384

Verndale Historical Society
Verndale, MN 56481

Waseca Area Genealogical Society
Box 314, Waseca, MN 56093

Waseca Area Historical Society
Box 314, Waseca, MN 56093, **<www.historical.waseca.mn.us>**

Washington County Historical Society
Box 167, Stillwater, MN 55082, **<wchsmn.org>**

Watertown Area Historical Society
309 Lewis Ave. S., Box 836, Watertown, MN 55388

White Bear Lake Genealogical Society
Box 10555, White Bear Lake, MN 55110

Winona County Genealogical Roundtable
Box 363, Winona, MN 55987

Winona County Historical Society
160 Johnson St., Winona, MN 55987, (507) 454-0006, **<winonahistory.org>**

Wright County Genealogical Society
911 Second Ave. South, Buffalo, MN 55313

Winona County Historical Society Archives
Laird Lucas Library, Archives Library, 160 Johnson St., Winona, MN 55987, (507) 454-2723, **<www.winonahistory.org/archives>**

Yankee Genealogical Society of Minnesota
5768 Olson Memorial Hwy., Golden Valley, MN 55422, **<mngs.org/yankee.html>**

GENERAL RESOURCES

A Bibliography of Books and Pamphlets Held in the Northeast Minnesota Historical Center by D. Gaynon (St. Louis County Historical Society, 1981)

A Bibliography of Minnesota Territorial Documents by Esther Jerabek (Minnesota Historical Society, 1936)

Blacks in Minnesota: A Preliminary Guide to Historical Sources by David Vassar Taylor (Minnesota Historical Society, 1976)

The Book of Minnesotans: A Biographical Dictionary of Leading Living Men of the State of Minnesota by Albert Nelson Marquis (A.N. Marquis, 1907)

Check List of Minnesota State Documents, 1858-1923 by Esther Jerabek (Minnesota Historical Society, 1972)

Chippewa and Dakota Indians: A Subject Catalog of Books, Pamphlets, Periodical Articles and Manuscripts in the Minnesota Historical Society (Minnesota Historical Society, 1969)

Commemorative Biographical Record of the Upper Lake Region (J. H. Beers, 1905)

Compendium of History and Biography of Central and Northern Minnesota (Higginson Books, 1904, 1995)

Continuing Your Genealogical Research in Minnesota by Marilyn Lind (The Linden Tree, 1986)

Directory of Churches and Religious Organizations in Minnesota edited by Antona Hawkins Richardson (Paduan Press, 1977)

Early Presbyterian Church Records from Minnesota 1835-1871 by Mary Hawker Bakeman (Park Genealogical Books, 1992)

Every Name Index to Pioneer Chronicles, Stories of Minnesota Territorial Pioneers by Ann H. Peterson (Warren Research and Marketing, 1990)

Fifty Years in the Northwest (Higginson Books, 1888, 1994)

French-Canadian Families of the North Central States: A Genealogical Dictionary, 8 vols., by Paul J. Lareau and Elmer Courteau (Northwest Territory French and Canadian Heritage Institute, 1980)

Genealogical Resources of the Minnesota Historical Society: A Guide, 2nd edition, (Minnesota Historical Society Press, 1989, 1993)

Guide to Depositories of Manuscript Collections in the United States: Minnesota from the Historical Records Survey (Historical Records Survey, 1941)

Guide to the Northwest Minnesota Historical Center Collections from the Northwest Minnesota Historical Center (Livingston Lord Library, Moorhead State University, 1988)

Guide to the Public Affairs Collection of the Minnesota Historical Society by Lucille M. Kane (Minnesota Historical Society, 1968)

Guide to Public Vital Statistics Records in Minnesota from the Historical Records Survey (Historical Records Survey, 1941)

Historic Resources in Minnesota: A Report on Their Extent, Location and Need for Preservation (Minnesota Historical Society, 1979)

History of the Church of the Brethren on the Northern Plains by Maryanna Hamer (1977)

History of the Finns in Minnesota by Hans R. Wasasjerna (Minnesota Finnish-American Historical Society, 1957)

History of the Great Northwest and Its Men of Progress by C. W. G. Hyde (Minneapolis Journal, 1901)

History of Methodism in Minnesota by Chauncey Hobart (Park Genealogical Books, 1887, 1992)

The History of Minnesota, 4 vols., by Val Bjornson (Lewis Historical Publishing Co., 1969)

History of the St. Croix Valley, 2 vols., edited by Augustus B. Easton, et al. (Higginson Books, 1996)

History of the Swedish-Americans of Minnesota, 3 vols., by A.E. Strand (Higginson Books, 1910, 1994)

History of the Synod of Minnesota—Presbyterian Church USA by Rev. Maurice Dwight Edwards (Park Genealogical Books, 1924, 1993)

History of the Upper Mississippi Valley, Including Explorers and Pioneers of Minnesota, Outlines of the History of Minnesota, Exploration and Development Above the Falls of St. Anthony by Rev. Edward D. Neill (Higginson Books, 1881, 1994)

Holdings of Genealogical Value in Minnesota's County Museums by Lucille L. Kirkeby (L. Kirkeby, 1986)

How to Trace Your Minnesota Ancestors by Robert B. Porter (Porter Publishing Co., 1985)

Illustrated Album of Biography of the Famous Valley of the Red River of the North and the Park Regions (Higginson Books, 1889, 1996)

Illustrated Historical Atlas of the State of Minnesota (A.T. Andreas, 1874)

An Introduction to Minnesota Research Sources by Paula Stewart Warren (Minnesota Genealogical Society, 1988)

Memorial Record of Southwestern Minnesota (Higginson Books, 1897, 1994)

Minnesota: A Bicentennial History by William E. Lass (W.W. Norton & Co., 1977)

Minnesota Biographies, 1655-1912 compiled by Warren Upham (Minnesota Historical Society, 1912)

Minnesota in a Century of Change: The State and Its People Since 1900 by Clifford Edward Clark (Minnesota Historical Society Press, 1989)

Minnesota Genealogical Index by Wiley R. Pope (Minnesota Family Trees, 1984)

Minnesota Genealogical Reference Guide by Paula Stewart Warren (Warren Research & Publishing, 1994)

Minnesota: A History of the State, 2nd edition, by Theodore C. Blegen (University of Minnesota Press, 1975)

Minnesota and Its People, 4 vols., by Joseph Alfred Arner Barnquist (S.J. Clarke, 1924)

Minnesota Research Outline by the Church of Jesus Christ of Latter-day Saints (online at **<www.familysearch.org/eng/search/RG/guide/minnesota.asp>**)

Minnesota State Archives Preliminary Checklist (Minnesota Historical Society, Division of Archives and Manuscripts, 1979)

Minnesota: Its Story and Biography, 3 vols., by Henry Anson Castle (Lewis Publishing Co., 1915)

Minnesota in Three Centuries, 1655-1908, 4 vols., by Lucius Frederick Hubbard (Society of Minnesota, 1908)

The Oral History Collections of the Minnesota Historical Society (Minnesota Historical Society Press, 1984)

Progressive Men of Minnesota by Marion Daniel Shutter (The Minnesota Journal, 1897)

Reference Guide to Minnesota History by Michael Brook (Minnesota Historical Society, 1974)

Research in Minnesota by Paula Stewart Warren (National Genealogical Society, 1992)

They Chose Minnesota: A Survey of the State's Ethnic Groups by June Drenning Holmquist (Minnesota Historical Society, 1981)

Tracing Your Ancestors in Minnesota, A Guide to Sources by Wiley R. Pope and Aliss L. Wiener. (Minnesota Family Trees, 1984)

The United States Biographical Dictionary and Portrait Gallery of Eminent and Self-Made Men: Minnesota Volume (American Biographical Publishing Co., 1879)

Women's History in Minnesota: A Survey of Published Sources and Dissertations by Jo Blatti (Minnesota Historical Society Press, 1993)

Women of Minnesota: Selected Biographical Essays by Barbara Stuhler (Minnesota Historical Society Press, ca.1977, 1979)

☞ CENSUS RECORDS

Guide to the Minnesota State Census Microfilm by Mary Hawker Bakeman (Park Genealogical Books, 1992)

☞ IMMIGRATION RECORDS

Declarations of Intention (1847-1852) of 262 Minnesota Pioneers by James E. Erickson (Park Genealogical Books, 1997)

For Sale—Minnesota: Organized Promotion of Scandinavian Immigration, 1866-1873 by Lars Ljungmark (Swedish Pioneer Historical Society, 1971)

☞LAND RECORDS

Federal Land Grants to the States with Special Reference to Minnesota by Matthias N. Orfield (Matthias N. Orfield, 1915)

A Guide to the Records of Minnesota's Public Lands by Gregory Kinney (Minnesota Historical Society, 1985)

Land Records: AL, AR, FL, LA, MI, MN, OH, WI (Broderbund, 1996. CD-ROM)

Minnesota, 1820-1908: Cash and Homestead Entries from the US Department of the Interior, Bureau of Land Management (BLM Eastern States, 1995, CD-ROM and at **<www.glorecords.blm.gov>**)

Minnesota Land Owner Maps and Directories by Mary Hawker Bakeman (Park Genealogical Books, 1994)

☞MAPS

Atlas of the State of Minnesota compiled by the Thomas O. Nelson Co. (MN: Thomas O. Nelson Co., 1971)

Comprehensive Index to A.T. Andreas' Illustrated Historical Atlas of Minnesota—1874 by Mary Hawker Bakeman (Park Genealogical Books, 1992)

The Establishment of County Boundaries in Minnesota by Mary Ellen Lewis (Master' Thesis, University of Minnesota, 1946)

Every Person's Name Index to An Illustrated Atlas of the State of Minnesota by Paul J. Ostendorf (St. Mary's College, 1979)

Gazetteer of Minnesota Railroad Towns, 1861-1997 by Hudson Leighton (Park Genealogical Books, 1992)

German Place Names in Minnesota—Deutsche Ortsnamen in Minnesota by LaVern J. Rippley (St. Olaf College, 1989)

Illustrated Historical Atlas of the State of Minnesota by Alfred T. Andreas (Unigraphic, 1874, 1976)

Minnesota Atlas and Gazetteer, 2nd edition, (DeLorme Mapping Co., 1995)

Minnesota's Boundary with Canada: Its Evolution since 1783 by William E. Lass (Minnesota Historical Society Press, 1980)

Minnesota Genealogical Periodical Index by Arthur Louis Finnell (Finnell Richter and Assoc., 1980)

Minnesota Geographic Names: Their Origin and Historic Significance by Warren Upham (Minnesota Historical Society, 1920, 1969)

Newspapers on the Minnesota Frontier, 1849-1860 by George Sigrud Hage (Minnesota Historical Society, 1967)

The Post Offices of Minnesota by Alan H. Patera and John S. Gallagher (The Depot, 1978)

Windows to the Past: A Bibliography of Minnesota County Atlases by Mai Treude (Center for Urban and Regional Affairs, University of Minnesota, 1980)

☞MILITARY RECORDS

History of the Fourth Regiment of Minnesota Infantry Volunteers During the Great Rebellion by Alonzo L. Brown (Higginson Books, 1892, 1995)

Known War of 1812 Veterans Buried in Minnesota by Arthur Louis Finnell (A.L. Finnell, 1996)

Minnesota in the Civil and Indian Wars, 1861-1865 (Pioneer Press, 1890-93)

Minnesota in the Spanish-American War and the Philippine Insurrection by Franklin F. Holbrook (Minnesota War Records Commission, 1923)

Minnesotans in the Spanish-American War and the Philippine Insurrection, April 21, 1898-July 4, 1902 by Antona Hawkins Richardson (Paduan Press, 1998)

Minnesota's World War II Army Dead (Park Genealogical Books, 1994)

Minnesota's WWII Combat connected Naval Casualties (Navy, Marine Corps, Coast Guard) from the US Navy (Park Genealogical Books, 1996)

Pensioners on the Rolls as of 1 January 1883 (living in Minnesota) (Park Genealogical Books, 1883, 1994)

☞PROBATE RECORDS

Adoptions & Name Changes: Minnesota Territory & State, 1851-1881 by Stina B. Green (Park Genealogical Books, 1994)

☞VITAL RECORDS

Church Records in Minnesota: Guide to Parish Records of Congregational, Evangelical, Reformed & United Church of Christ Churches 1851-1891 by Anne A. Hage (Park Genealogical Books, 1983)

Early Presbyterian Church Records from Minnesota 1825-1871 by the Pond Brothers, transcribed by Mary Hawker Bakeman (Park Genealogical Books, 1992)

Guide to Church Vital Statistics Records in Minnesota: Baptisms, Marriages, Funerals (Historical Records Survey, 1942)

Guide to Public Vital Statistics Records in Minnesota (Historical Records Survey, 1941)

Minnesota Cemeteries in Print: A Bibliography of Minnesota Published Cemetery Inscriptions, Burials, Etc. by Wiley R. Pope (Minnesota Family Trees, 1986)

•-COUNTY DETAILS-•

AITKIN
209 Second St. NW, Aitkin, MN 56431, (218) 927-7276,
<co.aitkin.mn.us>
- **INCORPORATED:** May 23, 1857
- **PARENT COUNTIES:** Pine, Ramsey
- **BIRTH RECORDS:** start in 1883, kept by District Court
- **MARRIAGE:** 1885, District Court
- **DIVORCE:** 1886, District Court
- **DEATH:** 1887, District Court
- **LAND:** unknown, County Recorder
- **PROBATE:** 1885, District Court
- **COURT:** 1885, District Court
- **NATURALIZATION:** 1885, District Court
- **NOTES:** Attached to Crow Wing and Morrison counties prior to organization Feb. 6, 1885.

ANDY JOHNSON
- **INCORPORATED:** March 18, 1858
- **PARENT COUNTY:** Pembina
- **NOTES:** See Wilkin County. Formerly Toombs County. Name changed to Andy Johnson March 8, 1862, and to Wilkin March 6, 1868.

ANOKA
2100 Third Ave., Anoka, MN 55303, (763) 421-4760,
<co.anoka.mn.us>
- **INCORPORATED:** May 23, 1857
- **PARENT COUNTY:** Ramsey
- **BIRTH RECORDS:** start in 1870, kept by District Court
- **MARRIAGE:** 1865, District Court
- **DIVORCE:** 1866, District Court
- **DEATH:** 1870, District Court
- **LAND:** 1866, District Court
- **PROBATE:** unknown, Probate Judge
- **COURT:** 1866, District Court

BECKER
913 Lake Ave., Box 702, Detroit Lakes, MN 56501, (218) 846-7300,
<co.becker.mn.us>
- **INCORPORATED:** March 18, 1858
- **PARENT COUNTIES:** Cass, Pembina
- **BIRTH RECORDS:** start in 1871, kept by County Recorder
- **MARRIAGE:** 1871, County Recorder
- **DIVORCE:** 1940, County Recorder
- **DEATH:** 1871, County Recorder
- **PROBATE:** 1940, County Recorder
- **COURT:** 1940, County Recorder
- **NOTES:** Attached to Stearns, Crow Wing and Douglas counties prior to organization March 1, 1871.

BELTRAMI
701 Minnesota Ave. NW, Bemidji, MN 56601, (218) 759-4174,
<co.beltrami.mn.us>
- **INCORPORATED:** Feb. 28, 1866
- **PARENT COUNTIES:** Unorganized Territory, Itasca, Pembina, Polk
- **BIRTH RECORDS:** start in 1896, Court Administrator of Customer Service
- **MARRIAGE:** 1896, Court Administrator of Customer Service
- **DIVORCE:** 1951, Clerk of Courts
- **DEATH:** 1896, Court Administrator of Customer Service
- **PROBATE:** unknown, Clerk of Courts
- **COURT:** unknown, Clerk of Courts
- **MILITARY:** unknown, Recorder Office
- **NOTES:** Attached to Becker County prior to organization April 6, 1897. Historical Society has land records prior to 1969.

BENTON
531 Dewey St., Box 129, Foley, MN 56329, (320) 968-5000,
<co.benton.mn.us>
- **INCORPORATED:** Oct. 27, 1849
- **PARENT COUNTY:** St. Croix
- **BIRTH RECORDS:** start in 1870, kept by County Recorder
- **MARRIAGE:** 1887, County Recorder
- **DIVORCE:** 1900, Court Administrator
- **DEATH:** 1871, County Recorder
- **LAND:** 1850, County Recorder
- **PROBATE:** 1850, Court Administrator
- **COURT:** 1900, Court Administrator

BIG SIOUX
- **INCORPORATED:** May 23, 1857
- **PARENT COUNTY:** Brown
- **NOTES:** See South Dakota state chapter. Attached to Pipestone County. Eliminated May 11, 1858, when Minnesota was created.

BIG STONE
20 S.E. Second St., Ortonville, MN 56278, (320) 839-2308,
<bigstonecounty.org>
- **INCORPORATED:** Feb. 20, 1862
- **PARENT COUNTY:** Pierce
- **BIRTH RECORDS:** start in 1881, kept by County Recorder
- **MARRIAGE:** 1881, County Recorder
- **DIVORCE:** 1885, County Recorder
- **DEATH:** 1881, County Recorder
- **LAND:** 1881, County Recorder
- **PROBATE:** unknown, Court Judge
- **COURT:** 1885, County Recorder
- **NOTES:** Attached to Renville and Stevens counties prior to organization Feb. 8, 1881.

BLUE EARTH
204 S. Fifth St., Box 3524, Mankato, MN 56001, (507) 389-8343,
<co.blue-earth.mn.us>
- **INCORPORATED:** March 5, 1853
- **PARENT COUNTIES:** Unorganized Territory, Dakota

- **BIRTH RECORDS:** start in 1870, kept by District Court
- **MARRIAGE:** 1865, District Court
- **DIVORCE:** 1854, District Court
- **DEATH:** 1870, District Court
- **LAND:** unknown, Registrar of Deeds
- **PROBATE:** 1858, District Court
- **COURT:** 1854, District Court

BRECKENRIDGE

- **INCORPORATED:** March 18, 1858
- **PARENT COUNTY:** Pembina
- **NOTES:** See Clay County. Name changed to Clay March 6, 1862.

BROWN

15 S. State St., New Ulm, MN 56073, (507) 233-6657, **<co.brown.mn.us>**

- **INCORPORATED:** Feb. 20, 1855
- **PARENT COUNTY:** Blue Earth
- **BIRTH RECORDS:** start in1870, kept by County Recorder
- **MARRIAGE:** 1857, County Recorder
- **DIVORCE:** 1856, District Court
- **DEATH:** 1870, County Recorder
- **LAND:** unknown, County Recorder
- **PROBATE:** 1856, District Court
- **COURT:** 1885, District Court
- **NATURALIZATION:** unknown, Minnesota Historical Society
- **NOTES:** Organized Feb. 11, 1856.

BUCHANAN

- **INCORPORATED:** May 23, 1857
- **PARENT COUNTY:** Pine
- **NOTES:** See Pine County. Attached to Chisago and St. Louis counties. Eliminated and absorbed by Pine County Oct. 8, 1861.

CARLTON

301 Walnut Ave., Carlton, MN 55718, (218) 384-9195, **<co.carlton.mn.us>**

- **INCORPORATED:** May 23, 1857
- **PARENT COUNTIES:** Pine, St. Louis
- **BIRTH RECORDS:** start in 1872, kept by District Court
- **MARRIAGE:** 1872, District Court
- **DIVORCE:** 1872, District Court
- **DEATH:** 1872, District Court
- **LAND:** 1872, District Court
- **PROBATE:** 1872, District Court
- **COURT:** 1872, District Court
- **NATURALIZATION:** 1872, District Court
- **BURIAL:** 1872, District Court
- **NOTES:** Organized Feb. 18, 1870.

CARVER

600 E. Fourth St., Chaska, MN 55318, (612) 361-1930, **<co.carver.mn.us>**

- **INCORPORATED:** Feb. 20, 1855
- **PARENT COUNTIES:** Hennepin, Sibley
- **BIRTH RECORDS:** start in 1870, kept by County Recorder
- **MARRIAGE:** 1870, County Recorder
- **DIVORCE:** 1856, Court Administrator
- **DEATH:** 1870, County Recorder
- **LAND:** 1870, County Recorder
- **PROBATE:** 1856, Court Administrator
- **COURT:** 1856, Court Administrator

CASS

303 Minnesota Ave. W., Box 3000, Walker, MN 56484, (218) 547-7247, **<co.cass.mn.us>**

- **INCORPORATED:** March 31, 1851
- **PARENT COUNTIES:** Dakota, Pembina, Mahkato, Wahrahta
- **NOTES:** Attached to Benton, Stearns, Crow Wing and Morrison counties prior to organization May 4, 1872.
- **BIRTH RECORDS:** start in 1896, kept by County Treasurer
- **MARRIAGE:** 1897, County Treasurer
- **DIVORCE:** 1899, District Court
- **DEATH:** 1896, County Treasurer
- **PROBATE:** unknown, District Court
- **COURT:** 1898, District Court
- **BURIAL:** unknown, Town/City Clerks
- **NATURALIZATION:** unknown, District Court

CHIPPEWA

629 N. Eleventh St., Montevideo, MN 56265, (320) 269-9431, **<co.chippewa.mn.us>**

- **INCORPORATED:** Feb. 20, 1862
- **PARENT COUNTIES:** Pierce, Davis
- **BIRTH RECORDS:** start in 1870, kept by District Court
- **MARRIAGE:** 1870, District Court
- **DIVORCE:** 1870, District Court
- **DEATH:** 1870, District Court
- **LAND:** 1870, County Recorder
- **PROBATE:** 1870, District Court
- **COURT:** 1870, District Court
- **BURIAL:** unknown, City Clerk
- **NOTES:** Attached to Renville County prior to organization Jan. 9, 1869.

CHISAGO

313 N. Main St., Center City, MN 55012, (612) 213-0438, **<co.chisago.mn.us>**

- **INCORPORATED:** March 31, 1851
- **PARENT COUNTIES:** Washington, Ramsey
- **BIRTH RECORDS:** start in 1870, kept by District Court
- **MARRIAGE:** 1852, District Court
- **DIVORCE:** unknown, District Court
- **DEATH:** 1870, District Court
- **LAND:** unknown, Registrar of Deeds
- **PROBATE:** unknown, Probate Judge
- **COURT:** 1880, District Court
- **NOTES:** Organized Jan. 1, 1852.

CLAY

807 11th St., Moorhead, MN 56560, (218) 299-5031, **<co.clay.mn.us>**

- **INCORPORATE:** March 18, 1858
- **PARENT COUNTY:** Pembina
- **BIRTH RECORDS:** start in 1872, kept by County Recorder
- **MARRIAGE:** 1872, County Recorder

- **DIVORCE:** 1931, Court Administrator
- **DEATH:** 1872, County Recorder
- **LAND:** 1872, County Recorder
- **PROBATE:** 1885, Court Administrator
- **COURT:** 1931, Court Administrator
- **MILITARY:** 1917, County Recorder
- **NOTES:** Formerly Breckenridge County. Name changed to Clay March 6, 1862. Attached to Stearns, Crow Wing, Douglas and Becker counties prior to organization Feb. 27, 1872.

CLEARWATER

213 Main Ave. N., Bagley, MN 56621, (218) 694-6129, **<co.clearwater.mn.us>**

- **INCORPORATE:** Dec. 20, 1902
- **PARENT COUNTY:** Beltrami
- **BIRTH RECORDS:** start in 1903, kept by County Recorder
- **MARRIAGE:** 1903, County Recorder
- **DIVORCE:** unknown, Court Administrator
- **DEATH:** 1903, County Recorder
- **LAND:** 1903, County Recorder
- **PROBATE:** unknown, Court Administrator
- **COURT:** unknown, Court Administrator
- **MILITARY:** 1903, County Recorder
- **NATURALIZATION:** unknown, Court Administrator

COOK

Box 1150, Grand Marais, MN 55604, (218) 387-3000, **<co.cook.mn.us>**

- **INCORPORATED:** Nov. 3, 1874
- **PARENT COUNTY:** Lake
- **BIRTH RECORDS:** start in 1900, kept by County Recorder
- **MARRIAGE:** 1901, County Recorder
- **DIVORCE:** unknown, Court Administrator
- **DEATH:** 1900, County Recorder
- **LAND:** 1886, County Recorder
- **PROBATE:** unknown, Court Administrator
- **COURT:** unknown, Court Administrator
- **MILITARY:** 1919, County Recorder
- **NOTES:** Attached to Lake and St. Louis counties prior to organization April 5, 1897.

COTTONWOOD

900 Third Ave., Windom, MN 56101, (507) 831-1458, **<co.cottonwood.mn.us>**

- **INCORPORATED:** May 23, 1857
- **PARENT COUNTY:** Brown
- **BIRTH RECORDS:** start in 1871, kept by District Court
- **MARRIAGE:** 1871, District Court
- **DIVORCE:** 1871, District Court
- **DEATH:** 1871, District Court
- **COURT:** 1871, District Court
- **NOTES:** Attached to Brown, Redwood and Watonwan counties prior to organization July 4, 1873.

CROW WING

326 Laurel St., Brainerd, MN 56401, (218) 824-1300, **<co.crow-wing.mn.us>**

- **INCORPORATED:** May 23, 1857
- **PARENT COUNTY:** Ramsey
- **BIRTH RECORDS:** start in 1873, kept by County Treasurer
- **MARRIAGE:** 1871, County Treasurer
- **DIVORCE:** unknown, Court Administrator
- **DEATH:** 1874, County Treasurer
- **LAND:** 1867, County Recorder
- **PROBATE:** unknown, Court Administrator
- **COURT:** unknown, Court Administrator
- **MILITARY:** 1919, County Recorder

DAKOTA

1560 Hwy. 55 W., Hastings, MN 55033, (612) 438-4313, **<co.dakota.mn.us>**

- **INCORPORATED:** Oct. 27, 1849
- **PARENT COUNTY:** Unorganized Territory
- **BIRTH RECORDS:** start in 1870, kept by District Court
- **MARRIAGE:** 1857, District Court
- **DIVORCE:** 1853, District Court
- **DEATH:** 1870, District Court
- **COURT:** 1853, District Court
- **NOTES:** Attached to Ramsey County prior to organization March 5, 1853.

DAVIS

- **INCORPORATED:** Feb. 20, 1855
- **PARENT COUNTIES:** Cass, Nicollet, Pierce, Sibley
- **NOTES:** Attached to Stearns County. Eliminated Feb. 20, 1862. Lost to Chippewa and Lac Qui Parle counties.

DODGE

22 E. Sixth St., Box 128, Mantorville, MN 55955, (507) 635-6250, **<co.dodge.mn.us>**

- **INCORPORATED:** Feb. 20, 1855
- **PARENT COUNTIES:** Rice, Unorganized Territory
- **BIRTH RECORDS:** start in 1870, kept by District Court
- **MARRIAGE:** 1865, District Court
- **DIVORCE:** 1870, District Court
- **DEATH:** 1870, District Court
- **PROBATE:** 1858, District Court
- **COURT:** 1870, District Court
- **SCHOOL:** 1917, District Court

DOTY

- **INCORPORATED:** Feb. 20, 1855
- **PARENT COUNTY:** Itasca
- **NOTES:** See St. Louis County. Name changed to Newton March 3, 1855, then to St. Louis County March 1, 1856.

DOUGLAS

305 Eighth Ave. W., Alexandria, MN 56308, (320) 762-3877, **<co.douglas.mn.us>**

- **INCORPORATED:** March 8, 1858
- **PARENT COUNTY:** Cass, Pembina
- **BIRTH RECORDS:** start in 1890, kept by County Recorder
- **MARRIAGE:** 1890, County Recorder
- **DEATH:** 1890, County Recorder
- **DIVORCE:** unknown, Clerk of Courts
- **PROBATE:** unknown, Clerk of Courts

- **COURT:** unknown, Clerk of Courts
- **MILITARY:** unknown, County Recorder
- **NOTES:** County Recorder has land records late 1800s.

FARIBAULT

415 N. Main St., Box 130, Blue Earth, MN 56013, (507) 526-6252, **<www.rootsweb.ancestry.com/~mnfariba>**

- **INCORPORATED:** Feb. 20 1855
- **PARENT COUNTY:** Blue Earth
- **BIRTH RECORDS:** start in 1870, kept by Court Administrator
- **MARRIAGE:** 1870, Court Administrator
- **DIVORCE:** 1870, Court Administrator
- **DEATH:** 1870, Court Administrator
- **LAND:** unknown, Registrar of Deeds
- **PROBATE:** 1870, Court Administrator
- **COURT:** 1950, Court Administrator
- **NATURALIZATION:** N/a, Court Administrator
- **NOTES:** Attached to Blue Earth County prior to organization May 1, 1857.

FILLMORE

101 Fillmore St., Preston, MN 55965, (507) 765-4701, **<www.rootsweb.ancestry.com/~mnfillmo>**

- **INCORPORATED:** March 5, 1853
- **PARENT COUNTY:** Wabasha
- **BIRTH RECORDS:** start in 1870, kept byCourt Administrator
- **MARRIAGE:** 1865, Court Administrator
- **DIVORCE:** 1885, Court Administrator
- **DEATH:** 1870, Court Administrator
- **LAND:** unknown, County Recorder
- **PROBATE:** 1858, Court Administrator
- **COURT:** 1885, Court Administrator

FREEBORN

411 S. Broadway Ave., Albert Lea, MN 56007, (507) 377-5299, **<co.freeborn.mn.us>**

- **INCORPORATED:** Feb. 20, 1855
- **PARENT COUNTIES:** Blue Earth, Rice
- **BIRTH RECORDS:** start in 1870, kept by District Court
- **MARRIAGE:** 1857, District Court
- **DEATH:** 1870, District Court
- **LAND:** 1854, County Recorder
- **PROBATE:** 1866, Probate Office
- **COURT:** 1857, District Court
- **NOTES:** Organized March 6, 1857.

GOODHUE

509 Fifth St. W., Red Wing, MN 55066, (651) 385-3148, **<co.goodhue.mn.us>**

- **INCORPORATED:** March 5, 1853
- **PARENT COUNTIES:** Wabasha, Dakota
- **BIRTH RECORDS:** start in 1870, kept by Court Administrator
- **MARRIAGE:** 1854, Court Administrator
- **DIVORCE:** 1951, Court Administrator
- **DEATH:** 1870, Court Administrator
- **PROBATE:** 1854, Court Administrator
- **COURT:** 1951, Court Administrator
- **NOTES:** Attached to Wabasha County prior to organization June 15, 1854. Minnesota Historical Society has divorce and court records from 1854-1950.

GRANT

County Courthouse, Elbow Lake, MN 56531, (218) 685-4520, **<co.grant.mn.us>**

- **INCORPORATED:** March 6, 1868
- **PARENT COUNTIES:** Stevens, Wilkin, Traverse
- **BIRTH RECORDS:** start in 1877, kept by District Court
- **MARRIAGE:** 1869, District Court
- **DIVORCE:** 1883, District Court
- **DEATH:** 1877, District Court
- **LAND:** unknown, Registrar of Deeds
- **PROBATE:** unknown, Probate Judge
- **COURT:** 1883, District Court
- **NOTES:** Attached to Douglas County prior to organization March 1, 1883.

HENNEPIN

300 S. Sixth St., Minneapolis, MN 55487, (612) 348-8241, **<co.hennepin.mn.us>**

- **INCORPORATED:** March 6, 1852
- **PARENT COUNTY:** Dakota
- **BIRTH RECORDS:** start in 1870, kept by District Court
- **MARRIAGE:** 1853, District Court
- **DIVORCE:** 1853, District Court
- **DEATH:** 1870, District Court
- **COURT:** 1853, District Court

HOUSTON

304 S. Marshall St., Caledonia, MN 55921, (507) 724-5813, **<www.houstoncounty.govoffice2.com>**

- **INCORPORATED:** April 4, 1854
- **PARENT COUNTY:** Fillmore
- **BIRTH RECORDS:** start in 1870, kept by District Court
- **MARRIAGE:** 1854, District Court
- **DIVORCE:** unknown, District Court
- **DEATH:** 1870, District Court
- **LAND:** unknown, Registrar of Deeds
- **PROBATE:** unknown, Probate Judge
- **COURT:** 1856, District Court

HUBBARD

301 Court St., Park Rapids, MN 56470, (218) 732-3552, **<co.hubbard.mn.us>**

- **INCORPORATED:** Feb. 26, 1883
- **PARENT COUNTY:** Cass
- **BIRTH RECORDS:** start in unknown, kept by County Recorder
- **MARRIAGE:** unknown, License Center
- **DIVORCE:** unknown, District Court
- **DEATH:** unknown, County Recorder
- **LAND:** unknown, County Recorder
- **PROBATE:** unknown, District Court
- **COURT:** unknown, District Court
- **NOTES:** Attached to Wadena County prior to organization March 3, 1887.

ISANTI

555 Eighteenth Ave. SW, Cambridge, MN 55008, (763) 689-1191, **<co.isanti.mn.us>**

- **INCORPORATED:** Feb. 13, 1857
- **PARENT COUNTY:** Ramsey
- **BIRTH RECORDS:** start in 1869, kept by District Court
- **MARRIAGE:** 1871, District Court
- **DIVORCE:** 1872, District Court
- **DEATH:** 1873, District Court
- **LAND:** unknown, County Recorder
- **PROBATE:** 1892, District Court
- **COURT:** 1872, District Court
- **NOTES:** Clerk of District Court has burial records from 1900-1908 and 1941-1979.

ITASCA

123 Fourth St. NE, Grand Rapids, MN 55744, (218) 327-2856, **<co.itasca.mn.us>**

- **INCORPORATED:** Oct. 27, 1849
- **PARENT COUNTY:** Unorganized Territories
- **BIRTH RECORDS:** start in 1891, kept by County Recorder/Registrar
- **MARRIAGE:** 1891, County Recorder/Registrar
- **DIVORCE:** 1950, Court Administrator
- **DEATH:** 1894, County Recorder/Registrar
- **LAND:** 1883, County Recorder/Registrar
- **PROBATE:** 1896, Court Administrator
- **COURT:** 1950, Court Administrator
- **BURIAL:** 1900, County Recorder/Registrar
- **MILITARY:** 1919, County Recorder/Registrar
- **NOTES:** Attached to Washington, Benton and Chisago counties prior to organization March 6, 1857. Minnesota Historical Society has divorce and court records to 1950.

JACKSON

405 Fourth St., Box 209, Jackson, MN 56143, (507) 847-2580, **<co.jackson.mn.us>**

- **INCORPORATED:** May 23, 1857
- **PARENT COUNTY:** Brown
- **BIRTH RECORDS:** start in 1870, kept by Court Administrator
- **MARRIAGE:** 1868, Court Administrator
- **DEATH:** 1870, Court Administrator
- **DIVORCE:** 1870, Court Administrator
- **LAND:** 1870, County Recorder
- **PROBATE:** 1870, Court Administrator
- **COURT:** 1870, Court Administrator

KANABEC

18 Vine St. N., Mora, MN 55051, (320) 679-6466, **<kanabeccounty.org>**

- **INCORPORATED:** Oct. 12, 1858
- **PARENT COUNTY:** Pine
- **BIRTH RECORDS:** start in 1883, kept by District Court
- **MARRIAGE:** 1882, District Court
- **DIVORCE:** 1882, District Court
- **DEATH:** 1883, District Court
- **LAND:** unknown, County Recorder
- **PROBATE:** 1891, District Court
- **COURT:** 1882, District Court
- **BURIAL:** unknown, Mora City Hall
- **NOTES:** Attached to Pine County prior to organization Nov. 4, 1881.

KANDIYOHI

400 Benson Ave. SW, Willmar, MN 56201-3281, (320) 231-6532, **<co.kandiyohi.mn.us>**

- **INCORPORATED:** March 20, 1858
- **PARENT COUNTIES:** Meeker, Renville, Pierce, Davis, Stearns
- **BIRTH RECORDS:** start in1870, kept by District Court
- **MARRIAGE:** 1870, District Court
- **DIVORCE:** 1870, District Court
- **DEATH:** 1870, District Court
- **COURT:** 1870, District Court

KITTSON

410 S. Fifth St., Box 39, Hallock, MN 56728, (218) 843-3632, **<co.kittson.mn.us>**

- **INCORPORATION:** Oct. 27, 1849
- **PARENT COUNTY:** Unorganized Territory
- **BIRTH RECORDS:** start in ca. 1880, kept by District Court
- **MARRIAGE:** ca. 1880, District Court
- **DIVORCE:** ca. 1880, District Court
- **LAND:** unknown, County Recorder
- **PROBATE:** ca. 1880, District Court
- **COURT:** ca. 1880, District Court
- **NATURALIZATION:** unknown, Minnesota Historical Society
- **DEATH:** ca. 1880, District Court
- **NOTES:** Formerly Pembina County. Name changed to Kittson March 9, 1878. Attached to Benton prior to organization March 4, 1852. Disorganized March 5, 1853. Recreated April 24, 1862, from Benton. Attached to Benton, Morrison, Crow Wing, Douglas Becker, Clay and Polk counties prior to organization April 6, 1897.

KOOCHICHING

715 Fourth St., International Falls, MN 56649, (218) 283-6260, **<co.koochiching.mn.us>**

- **INCORPORATION:** Dec. 19, 1906
- **PARENT COUNTY:** Itasca
- **BIRTH RECORDS:** start in 1907, kept by District Court
- **MARRIAGE:** 1907, District Court
- **DIVORCE:** 1907, District Court
- **DEATH:** 1907, District Court
- **PROBATE:** 1907, District Court
- **COURT:** 1907, District Court
- **NOTES:** Attached to Redwood County prior to organization Jan. 7, 1873.

LAC QUI PARLE

600 Sixth St., Madison, MN 56256, (320) 598-3724, **<www.lqpco.com>**

- **INCORPORATION:** Nov. 7, 1871
- **PARENT COUNTY:** Redwood
- **BIRTH RECORDS:** start in unknown, kept by County Recorder
- **MARRIAGE:** unknown, County Recorder
- **DIVORCE:** unknown, Court Administrator
- **DEATH:** unknown, County Recorder
- **LAND:** unknown, County Assessor

- **PROBATE:** unknown, Court Administrator
- **COURT:** unknown, Court Administrator
- **MILITARY:** unknown County Recorder
- **NOTES:** Attached to Redwood County prior to organization Jan. 7, 1873.

LAC QUI PARLE, OLD
- **INCORPORATED:** Feb. 20, 1862
- **PARENT COUNTIES:** Davis, Pierce
- **NOTES:** Attached to Renville County. Eliminated Nov. 3, 1868, and absorbed by Chippewa County.

LAKE
601 Third Ave., Two Harbors, MN 55616, (218) 834-8300, **<co.lake.mn.us>**
- **INCORPORATED:** Feb. 20, 1855
- **PARENT COUNTY:** Itasca
- **BIRTH RECORDS:** start in 1898, kept by County Registrar
- **MARRIAGE:** 1891, County Registrar
- **DIVORCE:** 1892, County Registrar
- **DEATH:** 1891, County Registrar
- **PROBATE:** unknown, Probate Judge
- **COURT:** 1892, County Registrar
- **BURIAL:** unknown, City Clerk
- **NOTES:** Formerly Superior County. Name changed to St. Louis (old) March 3, 1855. Name changed to Lake March 1, 1856. Attached to Benton and St. Louis counties prior to organization Feb. 27, 1891.

LAKE OF THE WOODS
206 SE Eighth Ave., Box 808, Baudette, MN 56623, (218) 634-1902, **<co.lake-of-the-woods.mn.us>**
- **INCORPORATED:** Nov. 28, 1922
- **PARENT COUNTY:** Beltrami
- **BIRTH RECORDS:** start in 1923, kept by Court Administrator
- **MARRIAGE:** 1923, Court Administrator
- **DIVORCE:** 1923, Court Administrator
- **DEATH:** 1923, Court Administrator
- **PROBATE:** 1923, Court Administrator
- **COURT:** 1923, Court Administrator

LE SUEUR
88 S. Park Ave., Le Center, MN 56057, (507) 357-2251, **<co.le-sueur.mn.us>**
- **INCORPORATED:** March 5, 1853
- **PARENT COUNTY:** Dakota
- **BIRTH RECORDS:** start in 1870, kept by District Court
- **MARRIAGE:** 1854, District Court
- **DIVORCE:** 1880, District Court
- **DEATH:** 1870, District Court
- **LAND:** 1850, Registrar of Deeds
- **PROBATE:** 1855, Probate Judge
- **COURT:** 1880, District Court
- **NOTES:** Clerk of District Court has some school records from 1920-1945.

LINCOLN
319 N. Rebecca, Box 29, Ivanhoe, MN 56142, (507) 694-1360, **<co.lincoln.mn.us>**
- **INCORPORATED:** Nov. 4, 1873
- **PARENT COUNTY:** Lyon
- **BIRTH RECORDS:** start in 1879, kept by District Court
- **MARRIAGE:** 1879, District Court
- **DIVORCE:** 1891, District Court
- **DEATH:** 1880, District Court
- **LAND:** 1873, Registrar of Deeds
- **PROBATE:** 1877, Probate Judge
- **COURT:** 1880, District Court
- **NOTES:** Attached to Lyon and Redwood counties prior to organization Feb. 9, 1881.

LINCOLN, OLD
- **INCORPORATED:** Oct. 8, 1861
- **PARENT COUNTY:** Renville
- **NOTES:** Attached to McLeod County. Eliminated Nov. 3, 1868, for Renville County.

LYON
607 W. Main, Marshall, MN 56258, (507) 537-6722, **<www.lyonco.org>**
- **INCORPORATED:** Nov. 2, 1869
- **PARENT COUNTY:** Redwood
- **BIRTH RECORDS:** start in 1874, kept by District Court
- **MARRIAGE:** 1872, District Court
- **DEATH:** 1874, District Court
- **DIVORCE:** 1880, District Court
- **LAND:** unknown, County Recorder
- **PROBATE:** 1880, District Court
- **COURT:** 1880, District Court
- **NOTES:** Organized April 12, 1870.

MAHNOMEN
Box 379, Mahnomen, MN 56557, (218) 935-2251, **<www.rootsweb.ancestry.com/~mnmahnom>**
- **INCORPORATED:** Dec. 27, 1906
- **PARENT COUNTY:** Norman
- **BIRTH RECORDS:** start in 1908, kept by District Court
- **MARRIAGE:** 1908, District Court
- **DIVORCE:** 1908, District Court
- **DEATH:** 1908, District Court
- **COURT:** 1908, District Court

MANKAHTO
- **INCORPORATED:** Oct. 27, 1849
- **PARENT COUNTY:** Unorganized Territories
- **NOTES:** Attached to Ramsey. Eliminated Sept. 1, 1851. Lost to Cass and Pembina counties.

MANOMIN
- **INCORPORATED:** May 23, 1857
- **PARENT COUNTY:** Ramsey
- **NOTES:** Eliminated Nov. 2, 1869, for Anoka County.

MARSHALL
208 E. Colvin Ave., Warren, MN 56762, (218) 745-4816, **<co.marshall.mn.us>**
- **INCORPORATED:** Feb. 25, 1879
- **PARENT COUNTY:** Kittson
- **BIRTH RECORDS:** start in1882, kept by Court Administrator
- **MARRIAGE:** 1882, Court Administrator
- **DIVORCE:** 1891, Court Administrator
- **DEATH:** 1882, Court Administrator
- **LAND:** 1883, County Recorder
- **PROBATE:** 1891, Court Administrator
- **COURT:** unknown, Court Administrator
- **MILITARY:** 1919, County Recorder
- **NOTES:** Attached to Polk County prior to organization March 11, 1881.

MARTIN
201 Lake Ave., Fairmont, MN 56031, (507) 238-3213, **<co.martin.mn.us>**
- **INCORPORATED:** May 23, 1857
- **PARENT COUNTIES:** Faribault, Brown
- **BIRTH RECORDS:** start in 1874, kept by County Recorder
- **MARRIAGE:** 1864, County Recorder
- **DIVORCE:** unknown, Court Administrator
- **DEATH:** 1879, County Recorder
- **LAND:** unknown, County Recorder
- **PROBATE:** unknown, Court Administrator
- **COURT:** unknown,Court Administrator

MCLEOD
830 Eleventh St., Box 127, Glencoe, MN 55336, (320) 864-1216, **<co.mcleod.mn.us>**
- **INCORPORATED:** March 1, 1856
- **PARENT COUNTIES:** Carver, Sibley
- **BIRTH RECORDS:** start in 1870, kept by County Recorder
- **MARRIAGE:** 1865, County Recorder
- **DIVORCE:** unknown, County Administrator
- **DEATH:** 1870, County Recorder
- **LAND:** unknown, County Recorder
- **PROBATE:** unknown, County Administrator
- **COURT:** unknown, County Administrator
- **MILITARY:** unknown, Veterans Service
- **SCHOOL CENSUS:** unknown, County Recorder

MEEKER
325 N. Sibley Ave., Litchfield, MN 55355, (320) 693-5345, **<co.meeker.mn.us>**
- **INCORPORATED:** Feb. 23, 1856
- **PARENT COUNTY:** Davis
- **BIRTH RECORDS:** start in1870, kept by District Court
- **MARRIAGE:** 1870, District Court
- **DIVORCE:** 1870, District Court
- **DEATH:** 1870, District Court
- **LAND:** unknown, County Recorder
- **PROBATE:** 1858, District Court
- **COURT:** 1870, District Court
- **NATURALIZATION:** 1884, District Court
- **SCHOOL:** 1884, District Court

MILLE LACS
635 Second St. SE, Milaca, MN 56353, (320) 983-8308, **<co.mille-lacs.mn.us>**
- **INCORPORATED:** May 23, 1857
- **PARENT COUNTY:** Ramsey
- **BIRTH RECORDS:** start in unknown, kept by County Recorder
- **MARRIAGE:** unknown, County Recorder
- **DIVORCE:** unknown, Court Administrator
- **DEATH:** unknown, County Recorder
- **LAND:** unknown, County Recorder
- **PROBATE:** unknown, Court Administrator
- **COURT:** unknown, Court Administrator
- **NOTES:** Attached to Morrison County prior to organization April 30, 1860.

MONONGALIA
- **INCORPORATED:** March 8, 1861
- **PARENT COUNTIES:** Davis, Pierce
- **NOTES:** Discontinued Nov. 8, 1870; became part of Kandyohi County.

MORRISON
213 Fist Ave. SE, Little Falls, MN 56345, (320) 632-1045, **<co.morrison.mn.us>**
- **INCORPORATED:** Feb. 25, 1856
- **PARENT COUNTY:** Benton
- **BIRTH RECORDS:** start in unknown, kept by County Recorder
- **MARRIAGE:** unknown, County Recorder
- **DIVORCE:** unknown, Court Administrator
- **DEATH:** unknown, County Recorder
- **LAND:** unknown, County Recorder
- **PROBATE:** unknown, Court Administrator
- **COURT:** unknown, Court Administrator
- **MILITARY:** unknown, County Recorder
- **NOTES:** County Recorder has some cemetery records.

MOWER
201 First St. NE, Austin, MN 55912, (507) 437-9456, **<co.mower.mn.us>**
- **INCORPORATED:** Feb. 25, 1855
- **PARENT COUNTY:** Rice
- **BIRTH RECORDS:** start in1870, kept by District Court
- **MARRIAGE:** 1865, District Court
- **DIVORCE:** 1900, District Court
- **DEATH:** 1870, District Court
- **LAND:** unknown, County Recorder
- **PROBATE:** 1856, District Court
- **COURT:** 1900, District Court
- **NOTES:** Organized March 1, 1856.

MURRAY
2500 28th St., Slayton, MN 56172, (507) 836-6148, **<murray-countymn.com>**
- **INCORPORATED:** May 23, 1857
- **PARENT COUNTY:** Brown
- **BIRTH RECORDS:** start in unknown, kept by District Court
- **MARRIAGE:** unknown, District Court
- **DIVORCE:** unknown, District Court

- **DEATH:** unknown, District Court
- **LAND:** unknown, County Recorder
- **PROBATE:** unknown, District Court
- **COURT:** unknown, District Court
- **NOTES:** Attached to Brown, Redwood, Watonwan and Cottonwood counties prior to organization March 5, 1879.

NEWTON
- **INCORPORATED:** Feb. 20, 1855
- **PARENT COUNTY:** Itasca
- **NOTES:** Formerly Doty County. Name changed to Newton March 3, 1855, then to St. Louis County March 1, 1856.

NICOLLET
501 S. Minnesota Ave., Box 493, St. Peter, MN 56082, (507) 931-6800, **<co.nicollet.mn.us>**
- **INCORPORATED:** March 5 1853
- **PARENT COUNTY:** Dakota
- **BIRTH RECORDS:** start in1870, kept by District Court
- **MARRIAGE:** 1856, District Court
- **DIVORCE:** 1853, District Court
- **DEATH:** 1870, District Court
- **LAND:** unknown, County Recorder
- **PROBATE:** 1853, District Court
- **COURT:** 1853, District Court

NOBLES
315 10th St., Worthington, MN 56187, (507) 372-8263, **<co.nobles.mn.us>**
- **INCORPORATED:** May 23, 1857
- **PARENT COUNTY:** Brown
- **BIRTH RECORDS:** start in 1872, kept by County Recorder
- **MARRIAGE:** 1872, County Recorder
- **DIVORCE:** 1882, Court Administrator
- **DEATH:** 1872, County Recorder
- **LAND:** unknown, County Recorder
- **PROBATE:** unknown Court Administrator
- **COURT:** 1874, Court Administrator
- **NOTES:** Attached to Brown and Martin counties prior to organization Oct. 19, 1870.

NORMAN
16 E. Third Ave., Ada, MN 56510, (218) 784-7131, **<co.norman.mn.us>**
- **INCORPORATED:** Nov. 8, 1881
- **PARENT COUNTY:** Polk
- **BIRTH RECORDS:** start in 1881, kept by District Court
- **MARRIAGE:** 1882, District Court
- **DEATH:** 1881, District Court
- **PROBATE:** unknown, Probate Judge
- **NOTES:** Clerk of District Court has some divorce and court records.

OLMSTED
151 SE Fourth St., Rochester, MN 55904, (507) 287-1444, **<co.olmsted.mn.us>**
- **INCORPORATED:** Feb. 20, 1855
- **PARENT COUNTIES:** Fillmore, Wabasha, Rice
- **MARRIAGE:** 1855, District Court
- **DIVORCE:** 1860, District Court
- **PROBATE:** unknown, County Court
- **COURT:** 1858, District Court
- **BURIAL:** unknown, Coroner and Department of Health
- **NOTES:** Clerk of District Court has incomplete birth and death records from 1871.

OTTER TAIL
121 W. Junis Ave., Fergus Falls, MN 56537, (218) 739-2271, **<co.otter-tail.mn.us>**
- **INCORPORATED:** March 18, 1858
- **PARENT COUNTIES:** Pembina, Cass
- **BIRTH RECORDS:** start in1870, kept by District Court
- **MARRIAGE:** 1869, District Court
- **DIVORCE:** 1897, District Court
- **DEATH:** 1870, District Court
- **PROBATE:** 1872, District Court
- **COURT:** 1872, District Court
- **NOTES:** Attached to Stearns, Crow Wing and Douglas counties prior to organization Feb. 28, 1870.

PEMBINA
- **INCORPORATED:** Oct. 27, 1849
- **PARENT COUNTY:** Unorganized Territory
- **NOTES:** See Kittson County listing. Name changed to Kittson March 9, 1878.

PENNINGTON
101 Main Ave., Box 616, Thief River Falls, MN 56701, (218) 681-2522, **<www.rootsweb.ancestry.com/~mnpennin/mnpennin.htm>**
- **INCORPORATED:** Nov. 23, 1910
- **PARENT COUNTY:** Red Lake
- **BIRTH RECORDS:** start in 1910, kept by County Recorder
- **MARRIAGE:** 1910, County Recorder
- **DIVORCE:** unknown, Court Administrator
- **DEATH:** 1910, County Recorder
- **LAND:** 1910, County Recorder
- **PROBATE:** unknown, Court Administrator
- **COURT:** unknown, Court Administrator
- **BURIAL:** 1910, County Recorder
- **MILITARY:** 1910, County Recorder

PIERCE
- **INCORPORATED:** March 5, 1853
- **PARENT COUNTY:** Dakota
- **NOTES:** Eliminated Feb. 20, 1862, for Big Stone, Chippewa, Lac Qui Parle, Pope, Stevens and Traverse counties.

PINE
635 Northridge Drive NW, Pine City, MN 55063, (320) 591-1400, **<co.pine.mn.us>**
- **INCORPORATED:** March 1, 1856
- **PARENT COUNTIES:** Chisago, Ramsey
- **BIRTH RECORDS:** start in 1874, kept by District Court
- **MARRIAGE:** 1871, District Court
- **DIVORCE:** 1871, District Court

- **DEATH:** 1879, District Court
- **LAND:** unknown, Registrar of Deeds
- **PROBATE:** unknown, Probate Judge
- **COURT:** 1871, District Court
- **NOTES:** Organized April 1, 1857.

PIPESTONE

416 S. Hiawatha, Pipestone, MN 56164, (507) 825-6755, **<www.pipestone-county.com>**

- **INCORPORATED:** May 23, 1857
- **PARENT COUNTY:** Brown
- **BIRTH RECORDS:** start in 1877, kept by District Court
- **MARRIAGE:** 1877, District Court
- **DIVORCE:** 1877, District Court
- **DEATH:** 1877, District Court
- **LAND:** unknown, County Recorder
- **PROBATE:** 1877, District Court
- **COURT:** 1877, District Court
- **NOTES:** Attached to Big Sioux, Brown, Redwood, Watonwan, Rock and Cottonwood counties prior to organization Jan. 27, 1879.

POLK

612 N. Broadway, Crookston, MN 56716, (218) 281-3464, **<co.polk.mn.us>**

- **INCORPORATED:** Jul. 20, 1858
- **PARENT COUNTY:** Pembina
- **BIRTH RECORDS:** start in 1875, kept by Court Administrator
- **MARRIAGE:** 1875, Court Administrator
- **DEATH:** 1875, Court Administrator
- **LAND:** unknown, County Recorder
- **PROBATE:** 1875, Court Administrator
- **COURT:** 1875, Court Administrator
- **NOTES:** Attached to Crow Wing, Douglas, Becker and Clay counties prior to organization Feb. 27, 1879.

POPE

130 E. Minnesota Ave., Glenwood, MN 56334, (320) 634-5727, **<co.pope.mn.us>**

- **INCORPORATED:** Feb. 20, 1862
- **PARENT COUNTIES:** Pierce, Cass, Unorganized Territory
- **BIRTH RECORDS:** start in 1870, kept by District Court
- **MARRIAGE:** 1870, District Court
- **DIVORCE:** 1880, District Court
- **DEATH:** 1870, District Court
- **PROBATE:** 1867, District Court
- **COURT:** 1880, District Court
- **NOTES:** Organized Feb. 28, 1866.

RAMSEY

15 Kellogg Blvd. W., St. Paul, MN 55102, (651) 266-4444, **<co.ramsey.mn.us>**

- **INCORPORATED:** Oct. 27, 1849
- **PARENT COUNTY:** St. Croix
- **BIRTH RECORDS:** start in 1870, kept by District Court
- **MARRIAGE:** 1850, District Court
- **DIVORCE:** 1900, District Court
- **DEATH:** 1870, District Court
- **LAND:** unknown, Historical Society
- **PROBATE:** 1849, District Court
- **COURT:** 1900, District Court
- **NOTES:** The historical society has court records from 1858-1899.

RED LAKE

124 Langevin Ave., Box 3, Red Lake Falls, MN 56750, (218) 253-2997, **<www.rootsweb.ancestry.com/~mnredlak/mnredlak.htm>**

- **INCORPORATED:** Dec. 24, 1896
- **PARENT COUNTY:** Polk
- **BIRTH RECORDS:** start in 1897, kept by Court Administrator
- **MARRIAGE:** 1897, Court Administrator
- **DIVORCE:** 1897, Court Administrator
- **DEATH:** 1897, Court Administrator
- **LAND:** unknown, County Recorder
- **PROBATE:** 1897, Court Administrator
- **COURT:** 1897, Court Administrator
- **NOTES:** Organized April 6, 1897. Court Administrator has school records from 1900-1955.

REDWOOD

Box 130, Redwood Falls, MN 56283, (507) 637-4032, **<www.rootsweb.ancestry.com/~mnredwoo/rwindex.htm>**

- **INCORPORATED:** Nov. 4, 1862
- **PARENT COUNTY:** Brown
- **BIRTH RECORDS:** start in 1865, kept by Court Administrator
- **MARRIAGE:** 1865, Court Administrator
- **DIVORCE:** 1871, Court Administrator
- **DEATH:** 1865, Court Administrator
- **LAND:** unknown, County Recorder
- **PROBATE:** 1877, Court Administrator
- **COURT:** 1867, Court Administrator
- **NOTES:** Attached to Brown County prior to organization Feb. 23, 1865.

RENVILLE

500 DePue Ave. E., Olivia, MN 56277, (320) 523-3669, **<co.renville.mn.us>**

- **INCORPORATED:** Feb. 20, 1855
- **PARENT COUNTIES:** Nicollet, Pierce, Sibley
- **BIRTH RECORDS:** start in 1870, kept by District Court
- **MARRIAGE:** 1870, District Court
- **DIVORCE:** unknown, District Court
- **DEATH:** 1870, District Court
- **LAND:** unknown, County Recorder
- **PROBATE:** unknown, District Court
- **COURT:** unknown, District Court
- **NOTES:** Attached to Nicollet County prior to organization July 31, 1866.

RICE

320 NW Third St., Faribault, MN 55021, (507) 332-6114, **<co.rice.mn.us>**

- **INCORPORATED:** March 5, 1853
- **PARENT COUNTIES:** Dakota, Wabasha
- **BIRTH RECORDS:** start in 1870, kept by District Court
- **MARRIAGE:** 1856, District Court
- **DIVORCE:** 1870, District Court

- **DEATH:** 1870, District Court
- **LAND:** unknown, County Recorder
- **PROBATE:** 1870, District Court
- **COURT:** 1870, District Court
- **BURIAL:** unknown, District Court
- **NOTES:** Attached to Dakota County prior to organization Oct. 9, 1855.

ROCK

204 E. Brown, Box 509, Luverne, MN 56156, (507) 283-5060, **<co.rock.mn.us>**

- **INCORPORATED:** May 23, 1857
- **PARENT COUNTY:** Brown
- **BIRTH RECORDS:** start in1875, kept by County Auditor/Treasurer
- **MARRIAGE:** 1875, County Auditor/Treasurer
- **DIVORCE:** 1872, District Court
- **DEATH:** 1875, County Auditor/Treasurer
- **COURT:** 1872, District Court
- **NOTES:** Attached to Brown, Martin and Nobles counties prior to organization Feb. 7, 1874.

ROSEAU

606 Fifth Ave. SW Room 20, Roseau, MN 56751, (218) 463-2541, **<co.roseau.mn.us>**

- **INCORPORATED:** Feb. 28, 1894
- **PARENT COUNTIES:** Kittson, Beltrami
- **BIRTH RECORDS:** start in 1895, kept by District Court
- **MARRIAGE:** 1895, District Court
- **DIVORCE:** 1895, District Court
- **DEATH:** 1895, District Court
- **LAND:** unknown, Registrar of Deeds
- **PROBATE:** 1895, District Court
- **COURT:** 1895, District Court
- **NOTES:** Organized April 6, 1896.

SCOTT

428 S. Holmes St., Shakopee, MN 55379, (952) 496-8150, **<co.scott.mn.us>**

- **INCORPORATED:** March 5, 1853
- **PARENT COUNTY:** Dakota
- **BIRTH RECORDS:** start in 1871, kept for County Recorder
- **MARRIAGE:** 1856, County Recorder
- **DIVORCE:** ca. 1850, Clerk of Courts
- **DEATH:** 1871, County Recorder
- **LAND:** ca. 1850, County Recorder
- **PROBATE:** ca. 1850, Clerk of Courts
- **COURT:** 1880, Clerk of Courts
- **MILITARY:** 1950, County Recorder

SHERBURNE

13880 Hwy. 10, Elk River, MN 55330, (763) 241-2915, **<co.sherburne.mn.us>**

- **INCORPORATED:** Feb. 25, 1856
- **PARENT COUNTY:** Benton
- **BIRTH RECORDS:** start in 1870, kept by Court Administrator
- **MARRIAGE:** 1858, Court Administrator
- **DIVORCE:** 1884, Court Administrator
- **DEATH:** 1870, Court Administrator
- **LAND:** unknown, County Recorder
- **PROBATE:** 1893, Court Administrator
- **COURT:** 1877, Court Administrator
- **NOTES:** Attached to Benton County prior to organization March 6, 1862.

SIBLEY

400 Court St., Box 44, Gaylord, MN 55334, (507) 237-4080, **<www.rootsweb.ancestry.com/~mnsibley>**

- **INCORPORATED:** March 5, 1853
- **PARENT COUNTY:** Dakota
- **BIRTH RECORDS:** start in 1860, kept by Court Administrator
- **MARRIAGE:** 1856, Court Administrator
- **DIVORCE:** 1860, Court Administrator
- **DEATH:** 1860, Court Administrator
- **LAND:** 1855, County Recorder
- **PROBATE:** 1870, Court Administrator
- **COURT:** 1870, Court Administrator
- **NOTES:** Attached to Hennepin County prior to organization Oct. 10, 1854.

ST. CROIX

- **INCORPORATED:** Aug. 3, 1840
- **PARENT COUNTY:** Wisconsin Territories
- **NOTES:** Eliminated to Benton, Ramsey and Washington counties Oct. 27, 1849.

ST. LOUIS

100 N. Fifth Ave. W., Duluth, MN 55802, (218) 726-2559, **<co.st-louis.mn.us>**

- **INCORPORATED:** March 1, 1856
- **PARENT COUNTIES:** Itasca, Newton
- **BIRTH RECORDS:** start in 1870, kept from District Court
- **MARRIAGE:** 1870, District Court
- **DIVORCE:** 1859, District Court
- **DEATH:** 1870, District Court
- **LAND:** 1859, District Court
- **PROBATE:** unknown, County Court
- **COURT:** 1859, District Court
- **BURIAL:** 1938, District Court
- **NOTES:** Attached to Benton County prior to organization May 23, 1857.

ST. LOUIS, OLD

- **INCORPORATED:** Feb. 20, 1855
- **PARENT COUNTY:** Itasca
- **NOTES:** Formerly Superior County. Name changed to St. Louis (old) March 3, 1855. Abolished March 1, 1856, and became part of Lake County.

STEARNS

705 Courthouse Sq., St. Cloud, MN 56303, (320) 656-3855, **<co.stearns.mn.us>**

- **INCORPORATED:** Feb. 20, 1855
- **PARENT COUNTIES:** Cass, Nicollet, Pierce, Sibley
- **BIRTH RECORDS:** start in unknown, kept by License Center
- **MARRIAGE:** unknown, License Center
- **DIVORCE:** unknown, Court Administrator

- **DEATH:** unknown, License Center
- **LAND:** unknown, County Recorder
- **PROBATE:** unknown, Court Administrator
- **COURT:** unknown, Court Administrator

STEELE

111 E. Main St., Owatonna, MN 55060, (507) 444-7450, **<co.steele.mn.us>**

- **INCORPORATED:** Feb. 20, 1855
- **PARENT COUNTIES:** Rice, Blue Earth, Le Sueur
- **BIRTH RECORDS:** start in 1870, kept by District Court
- **MARRIAGE:** 1855, District Court
- **DIVORCE:** 1858, District Court
- **DEATH:** 1870, District Court
- **LAND:** 1858, County Recorder
- **PROBATE:** 1858, District Court
- **COURT:** 1858, District Court
- **NOTES:** Organized Feb. 29, 1856.

STEVENS

400 Colorado Ave., Box 530, Morris, MN 56267, (320) 589-7414, **<co.stevens.mn.us>**

- **INCORPORATED:** Feb. 20, 1862
- **PARENT COUNTIES:** Pierce, Unorganized Territory
- **BIRTH RECORDS:** start in1872, kept by District Court
- **MARRIAGE:** 1869, District Court
- **DEATH:** 1872, District Court
- **DIVORCE:** 1873, District Court
- **LAND:** 1871, County Recorder
- **PROBATE:** 1901, District Court
- **COURT:** 1873, District Court
- **NOTES:** Attached to Stearns, Douglas and Pope counties prior to organization Dec. 31, 1871.

SUPERIOR

- **INCORPORATED:** Feb. 20, 1855
- **PARENT COUNTY:** Itasca
- **NOTES:** See Lake County listing. Name changed to St. Louis (old) March 3, 1855. Name changed to Lake March 1, 1856.

SWIFT

301 14th St. N., Box 50, Benson, MN 56215, (320) 843-3377, **<swiftcounty.com>**

- **INCORPORATED:** Nov. 8, 1870
- **PARENT COUNTY:** Chippewa
- **BIRTH RECORDS:** start in 1870, kept by County Treasurer
- **MARRIAGE:** 1871, County Treasurer
- **DIVORCE:** unknown, Clerk of Courts
- **DEATH:** 1872, County Treasurer
- **LAND:** unknown, County Recorder
- **PROBATE:** unknown, Clerk of Courts
- **COURT:** unknown, Clerk of Courts
- **NOTES:** Attached to Pope and Chippewa counties prior to organization April 6, 1897.

TODD

215 First Ave. S., Long Prairie, MN 56347, (320) 732-4428, **<co.todd.mn.us>**

- **INCORPORATED:** Feb. 20, 1855
- **PARENT COUNTY:** Cass
- **BIRTH RECORDS:** start in 1870, kept by County Recorder
- **MARRIAGE:** 1867, County Recorder
- **DIVORCE:** 1880, District Court
- **DEATH:** 1870, County Recorder
- **LAND:** unknown, County Recorder
- **PROBATE:** unknown, District Court
- **COURT:** 1874, District Court
- **SCHOOL CENSUS:** 1914, County Recorder
- **NOTES:** Attached to Stearns and Morrison counties prior to organization Feb. 21, 1873.

TOOMBS

- **INCORPORATED:** March 18, 1858
- **PARENT COUNTY:** Pembina
- **NOTES:** See Wilkin County listing. Name changed to Andy Johnson March 8, 1862. Name changed to Wilkin March 6, 1868.

TRAVERSE

702 Second Ave. N., Box 487, Wheaton, MN 56296, (320) 563-4266, **<co.traverse.mn.us>**

- **INCORPORATED:** Feb. 20, 1862
- **PARENT COUNTIES:** Pierce, Unorganized Territory
- **BIRTH RECORDS:** start in 1881, kept by District Court
- **MARRIAGE:** 1881, District Court
- **DIVORCE:** 1881, District Court
- **DEATH:** 1881, District Court
- **LAND:** 1881, District Court
- **PROBATE:** 1881, District Court
- **COURT:** 1881, District Court
- **NOTES:** Attached to Stearns, Douglas, Pope and Stevens counties prior to organization Feb. 14, 1881.

WABASHA

625 Jefferson Ave., Wabasha, MN 55981, (651) 565-3018, **<co.wabasha.mn.us>**

- **INCORPORATED:** Oct. 27, 1849
- **PARENT COUNTY:** Unorganized Territory
- **BIRTH RECORDS:** start in 1870, kept by County Recorder
- **MARRIAGE:** 1865, County Recorder
- **DIVORCE:** 1858, Court Administrator
- **DEATH:** 1870, County Recorder
- **LAND:** 1855, County Recorder
- **PROBATE:** 1858, Court Administrator
- **COURT:** 1858, Court Administrator
- **MILITARY:** unknown, Veteran Service Office
- **NOTES:** Attached to Washington County prior to organization March 5, 1853.

WADENA

415 S. Jefferson, Box 415, Wadena, MN 56482, (218) 631-7622, **<co.wadena.mn.us>**

- **INCORPORATED:** Jun. 11, 1858
- **PARENT COUNTIES:** Cass, Todd

- **BIRTH RECORDS:** start in 1873, kept by District Court
- **MARRIAGE:** 1873, District Court
- **DIVORCE:** 1881, District Court
- **DEATH:** 1873, District Court
- **COURT:** 1881, District Court
- **NOTES:** Attached to Crow Wing and Morrison counties prior to organization Feb. 17, 1881.

WAHNATA
- **INCORPORATED:** Oct. 4, 1849
- **PARENT COUNTY:** Unorganized Territory
- **NOTES:** Eliminated Sept. 1, 1851 to Cass, Dakota and Pembina counties.

WASECA
307 N. State St., Waseca, MN 56093, (507) 835-0670,
<co.waseca.mn.us>
- **INCORPORATED:** Feb. 27, 1857
- **PARENT COUNTY:** Steele
- **BIRTH RECORDS:** start in 1870, kept by District Court
- **MARRIAGE:** 1858, District Court
- **DIVORCE:** 1858, District Court
- **DEATH:** 1870, District Court
- **PROBATE:** 1870, District Court
- **COURT:** 1870, District Court

WASHINGTON
14949 N. 62nd St., Stillwater, MN 55082, (651) 430-6755,
<co.washington.mn.us>
- **INCORPORATED:** Oct. 27, 1849
- **PARENT COUNTY:** St. Croix
- **BIRTH RECORDS:** start in 1870, kept by District Court
- **MARRIAGE:** 1845, District Court
- **DEATH:** 1870, District Court
- **DIVORCE:** 1847, District Court
- **PROBATE:** 1850, District Court
- **COURT:** 1847, District Court

WATONWAN
710 Second Ave. S., Box 518, St. James, MN 56081, (507) 375-1216,
<co.watonwan.mn.us>
- **INCORPORATED:** Nov. 6, 1860
- **PARENT COUNTY:** Brown
- **BIRTH RECORDS:** start in 1863, kept by District Court
- **MARRIAGE:** 1863, District Court
- **DIVORCE:** 1865, District Court
- **DEATH:** 1863, District Court
- **LAND:** unknown, Registrar of Deeds
- **PROBATE:** unknown, Probate Judge
- **COURT:** 1865, District Court
- **NOTES:** Attached to Brown and Blue Earth counties to organization June 15, 1871.

WILKIN
300 S. Fifth St., Breckenridge, MN 56520, (218) 643-5112,
<co.wilkin.mn.us>
- **INCORPORATE:** March 18, 1858
- **PARENT COUNTY:** Cass, Pembina
- **BIRTH RECORDS:** start in 1874, kept by District Court
- **MARRIAGE:** 1890, District Court
- **DIVORCE:** 1890, District Court
- **DEATH:** 1875, District Court
- **PROBATE:** unknown, Probate Judge
- **COURT:** 1858, District Court
- **NOTES:** Formerly Toombs and Andy Johnson counties. Name changed to Andy Johnson March 8, 1862. Name changed to Wilkin March 6, 1868. Attached to Stearns, Crow Wing, Douglas and Otter Tail counties prior to organization March 4, 1872.

WINONA
171 W. Third St., Winona, MN 55987, (507) 457-6340,
<co.winona.mn.us>
- **INCORPORATE:** April 4, 1854
- **PARENT COUNTY:** Fillmore, Wabasha
- **BIRTH RECORDS:** start in 1870, kept by District Court
- **MARRIAGE:** 1854, District Court
- **DIVORCE:** 1854, District Court
- **DEATH:** 1870, District Court
- **PROBATE:** 1871, District Court
- **COURT:** 1854, District Court
- **NOTES:** Clerk of District Court has school records 1909-1939.

WRIGHT
10 Second St. NW, Buffalo, MN 55313, (763) 682-7357,
<co.wright.mn.us>
- **INCORPORATED:** Feb. 20, 1855
- **PARENT COUNTIES:** Cass, Sibley
- **BIRTH RECORDS:** start in 1871, kept by License Bureau
- **MARRIAGE:** 1866, License Bureau
- **DIVORCE:** 1870, Court Administrator
- **DEATH:** 1871, License Bureau
- **LAND:** unknown, Registrar of Deeds
- **PROBATE:** unknown, Court Administrator
- **COURT:** 1870, Court Administrator

YELLOW MEDICINE
415 Ninth Ave., Granite Falls, MN 56241, (320) 564-2529,
<yellowmedicine.govoffice.com>
- **INCORPORATED:** Nov. 7, 1871
- **PARENT COUNTY:** Redwood
- **BIRTH RECORDS:** start in 1872, kept by District Court
- **MARRIAGE:** 1872, District Court
- **DIVORCE:** unknown, District Court
- **DEATH:** unknown, District Court
- **LAND:** unknown, County Recorder
- **PROBATE:** unknown, District Court
- **COURT:** unknown, District Court
- **NATURALIZATION:** 1872, District Court
- **NOTES:** Organized Feb. 25, 1874.

MISSISSIPPI

» BY EMILY ANNE CROOM

HISTORICAL OVERVIEW

For more than two centuries, Spain, France and Britain vied for a foothold in Mississippi—control of the Mississippi River valley meant dominance in much of North America. Although Spaniards explored Mississippi in 1540, France founded the first European settlement in 1699 near present-day Biloxi. At the end of the Seven Years War (1763), France ceded its territory east of the Mississippi River to Britain. Spain occupied the coastal area in the last years of the American Revolution. After that war, the 1783 Treaty of Paris gave to the new United States the British territory north of the 31st parallel.

Though largely Indian lands, much of present Mississippi and Alabama became Mississippi Territory in 1798. In 1802, Georgia gave up her claim to the northernmost Mississippi-Alabama land along the Tennessee boundary, and the War of 1812 brought the coastal area under US control. From all directions, by road, river and sea, land-hungry settlers flocked to the fertile coastal plains, and Mississippi became the 20th state in 1817. Forced Indian removal in the early 1830s opened the northern part of the state to white settlement. Early residents came mostly from older Southern states.

Along with river commerce, cotton agriculture on farms and plantations—worked largely with slave labor—dominated Mississippi's pre-Civil War economy. By 1860, the state's population was just over 55 percent slaves. Of the free population, 1 percent were foreign-born and less than a tenth of 1 percent were free blacks.

In January 1861, Mississippi became the second state to secede from the United States. The state witnessed numerous Civil War engagements, including the year-long siege of Vicksburg that ended in July 1863 with the Union controlling the Mississippi River corridor. Mississippi was readmitted to the Union in 1870. In this agricultural state, sharecropping replaced slavery and included numerous poor white farmers. The state remained impoverished long after Reconstruction.

Manufacturing grew during the 1900s, especially in the food processing, textile, timber and petroleum industries. In 1900, the state's urban population was 8 percent of the total; by 2000, city-dwellers were still the minority at 49 percent.

research tips

- Ancestors reporting their birthplace as Florida or West Florida before about 1813 could have been born in what is now Mississippi. Someone reportedly born in Mississippi before 1817 may have been born in what is now Alabama.
- Before US censuses began or when schedules are missing, investigate surviving census fragments, state or territorial censuses, and county tax lists.
- The Mississippi Department of Archives and History **<www.mdah.state.ms.us>** is the state's major genealogical research site.
- The University of Southern Mississippi, Hattiesburg, has a large genealogy collection with family and historical manuscripts, and oral histories collection. The University of Mississippi holds collections for state history.

CENSUS RECORDS

- Federal census: 1820, 1830, 1840, 1850, 1860, 1870, 1880, 1900, 1910, 1920, 1930
- Federal mortality schedules: 1850, 1860, 1870, 1880
- Federal slave schedules: 1850, 1860 (schedules name slaveholders but rarely name slaves)
- Special census of Civil War Union veterans and widows: 1890
- State census: 1822-1825, 1837, 1841, 1845, 1853, 1866
- Territorial census: 1805, 1808, 1810, 1813, 1816

RECORD HIGHLIGHTS

The Mississippi Department of Health keeps statewide birth and death records from November 1912. Statewide marriage records and a divorce index date from 1926, except for 1938 to 1941, when only county circuit courts kept marriage records.

In the counties, check circuit and chancery courts for earlier marriage records. The state legislature handled early divorce cases. Check county chancery courts for divorces after the mid-1800s. Pre-1955 adoption records are open; check courts in the county where the adopting parents lived.

More than a third of Mississippi's 82 counties have experienced record losses due to storms or fires, few of which occurred during the Civil War. Since such disasters rarely destroy everything, look for surviving records and those of parent and neighboring counties. Also consult records created in the family and in colonial, territorial, local, state and federal jurisdictions. Mississippi is a federal land state, with land patents searchable at **<www.glorecords.blm.gov>**.

Mississippi began granting Confederate pensions in 1888 to indigent Civil War veterans or their widows. The state archives website **<mdah.state.ms.us>** contains information on requesting copies.

Other helpful Mississippi-specific records include:

- Natchez Trace Papers, primarily for early Mississippi, Louisiana and Arkansas, at the University of Texas, Center for American History, Austin.
- Territorial Papers of the United States (includes some early censuses) and Territorial Papers of the US Senate for Mississippi Territory.
- State censuses, various counties, various years (1822-1825, 1837, 1841, 1845, 1853, 1866). See FHL microfilms 899868-70 for censuses between 1792 and 1866; some are statistical only. Some state censuses of the 1820s contain statistics on births and deaths among slaves and white family members.
- Records of antebellum plantations, on microfilm at the University of Mississippi and the University of Southern Mississippi.
- Records of the three Mississippi branches of the Freedman's Savings and Trust Company, 1865-1874; see FHL microfilm 928584.
- Indentures, marriages, and labor contracts in the records of the Freedmen's Bureau (Family History Library microfilm, beginning with film 491557 and film 1616481).
- Enumerations of Confederate soldiers and widows, 1907, 1925-1933.
- School censuses for the late-19th and early-20th centuries, at the state archives for various counties and years.

ARCHIVES, LIBRARIES, AND SOCIETIES

Alcorn County Genealogical Society
Box 1808, Corinth, MS 38835, **<www.avsia.com/acgs>**

Attala County Library
328 Goodman St., Kosciusko, MS 39090, **<www.mmrls.lib.ms.us/Attala.htm>**

Batesville Public Library
106 College St., Batesville, MS 38606, **<www.firstregional.org/page3.html>**

Biloxi Public Library
Box 467, Biloxi, MS 39533

Bolivar County Historical Society
1615 Terrace Rd., Cleveland, MS 38732, **<www.mymississippigenealogy.com/ms-county-bolivar.html>**

Carnegie Public Library
114 Delta Ave., Box 280, Clarksdale, MS 38614, (601) 624-4461, **<www.youseemore.com/carnegie>**

Chickasaw County Historical and Genealogical Society
Box 42, Houston, MS 38851, **<www.rootsweb.ancestry.com/~mschchgs>**

Claiborne-Jefferson Genealogical Society
Box 1017, Port Gibson, MS 39150

Columbus and Lowndes County Historical Society
916 College St., Columbus, MS 39701

Columbus Public Library
314 N. Seventh St., Columbus, MS 39701, **<www.lowndes.lib.ms.us>**

Evans Memorial Library
105 North Long St., Aberdeen, MS 39730, (601) 369-4601, **<www.tombigbee.lib.ms.us/evans>**

Family Research Association of Mississippi
Box 13334, Jackson, MS 39236, (601) 372-2959

Genealogical Society of Desoto County
Box 607, Hernando, MS 38632, **<www.rootsweb.ancestry.com/~msdesoto>**

Greenville Public Library
341 Main St., Greenville, MS 38701

Greenwood-Leflore Public Library
408 W. Washington, Greenwood, MS 38930

Gulfport Public Library
1300 21st Ave., Gulf Port, MS 39501

Hancock County Historical Society
113 Citizen St., Box 1340, Bay Saint Louis, MS 39520, **<www.hancockcountyhistoricalsociety.com>**

Harriette Person Memorial Library
Port Gibson, MS 39150, **<www.win.net/~kudzu/library.html>**

Hattiesburg Area Historical Society
127 W Front St., Hattiesburg, MS 39401, **<www.hahsmuseum.org>**

Historical and Genealogical Society of Panola County
105 Church St., Batesville, MS 38606, **<www.pangens.com>**

Homochitto Valley Historical Society
Box 337, Crosby, MS 39633

Itawamba County Historical Society
Box 7, Mantachie, MS 38855, **<itawambahistory.org>**

Jackson County Genealogical Society
Box 994, Pascagoula, MS 39567

J.B. Cain Archives of Misissippi Methodism
Millsaps-Wilson Library, Millsaps College, 1701 N. State St., Jackson, MS 39210, (601) 974-1073, **<library.millsaps.edu/index.php/archives/jb-cain-archives-of-mississippi-methodism>**

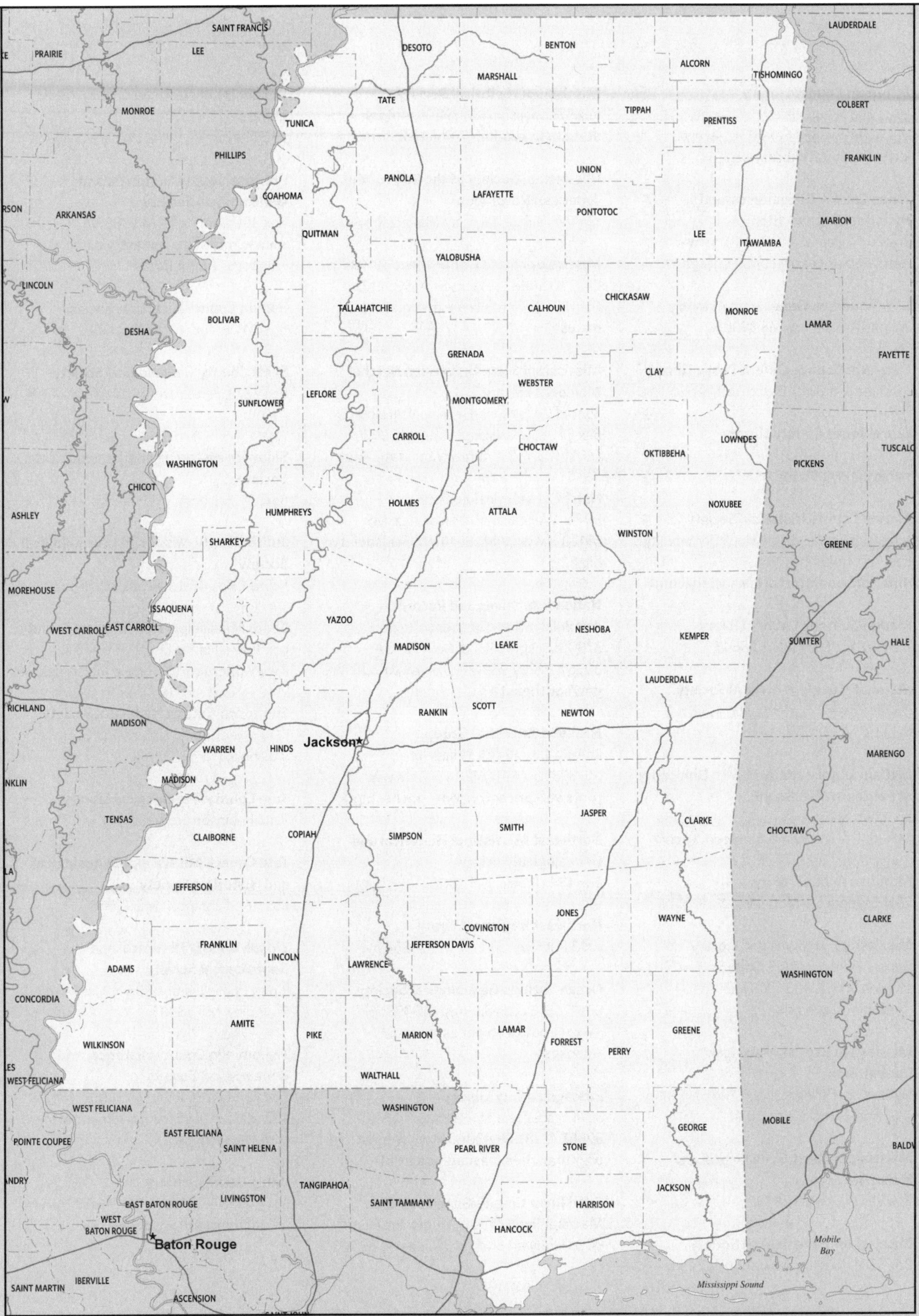
DESOTO
BENTON
MARSHALL
ALCORN
TISHOMINGO
TATE
TIPPAH
PRENTISS
TUNICA
UNION
PANOLA
LAFAYETTE
PONTOTOC
LEE
ITAWAMBA
COAHOMA
QUITMAN
YALOBUSHA
CHICKASAW
TALLAHATCHIE
CALHOUN
MONROE
BOLIVAR
GRENADA
CLAY
WEBSTER
SUNFLOWER
LEFLORE
MONTGOMERY
CARROLL
CHOCTAW
LOWNDES
OKTIBBEHA
WASHINGTON
HOLMES
HUMPHREYS
ATTALA
NOXUBEE
WINSTON
SHARKEY
ISSAQUENA
YAZOO
NESHOBA
KEMPER
MADISON
LEAKE
LAUDERDALE
RANKIN
SCOTT
NEWTON
WARREN
HINDS
Jackson
JASPER
CLARKE
SMITH
CLAIBORNE
COPIAH
SIMPSON
JEFFERSON
JONES
WAYNE
COVINGTON
FRANKLIN
JEFFERSON DAVIS
LINCOLN
LAWRENCE
ADAMS
AMITE
PIKE
MARION
LAMAR
FORREST
PERRY
GREENE
WILKINSON
WALTHALL
WASHINGTON
GEORGE
PEARL RIVER
STONE
JACKSON
HARRISON
HANCOCK
Mississippi Sound
SAINT FRANCIS
PRAIRIE
LEE
MONROE
PHILLIPS
ARKANSAS
LINCOLN
DESHA
CHICOT
ASHLEY
MOREHOUSE
WEST CARROLL
EAST CARROLL
RICHLAND
MADISON
MADISON
TENSAS
CONCORDIA
WEST FELICIANA
WEST FELICIANA
EAST FELICIANA
SAINT HELENA
POINTE COUPEE
TANGIPAHOA
LIVINGSTON
EAST BATON ROUGE
WEST BATON ROUGE
Baton Rouge
SAINT TAMMANY
SAINT MARTIN
IBERVILLE
ASCENSION
LAUDERDALE
COLBERT
FRANKLIN
MARION
LAMAR
FAYETTE
PICKENS
GREENE
SUMTER
HALE
MARENGO
CHOCTAW
CLARKE
WASHINGTON
MOBILE
Mobile Bay

Jefferson County Library
3033 High Ridge Blvd., High Ridge, MS 63049, (636) 677-8186, **<www.jeffersoncountylibrary.org>**

Jones County Genealogical and Historical Organization
Box 2644, Laurel, MS 39442, **<www.rootsweb.ancestry.com/~msjcgho>**

L.W. Anderson Genealogical Library
Box 1647, Gulf Port, MS 39502

Lafayette County-Oxford Public Library
401 Bramlett Blvd., Oxford, MS 38655

Laurel Jones County Library
530 Commerce St., Laurel, MS 39440, **<www.laurel.lib.ms.us>**

Marion County Historical Society
John Ford Home, Sandy Hook Community, Box 430, Columbia, MS 39429, **<marioncountyhistoricalsociety.com>**

Marks-Quitman County Library
315 E. Main, Marks, MS 38646

Marshall County Historical Society
220 E. College Ave., Box 806, Holly Springs, MS 38635

McCain Library and Archives, University of Southern Mississippi
Southern Station, Box 5148, Hattiesburg, MS 39406, **<www.lib.usm.edu/spcol>**

Meridian Public Library
2517 Seventh St., Meridian, MS 30301

Mississippi Archives and Library
Capers Building, 100 S. State St., Box 571, Jackson, MS 39205, (610) 359-6964, **<mdah.state.ms.us>**

Mississippi Baptist Historical Commission
Mississippi College Library, Box 51, Clinton, MS 39060, (601) 924-3434

Mississippi Coast Genealogical and Historical Society
Box 513, Biloxi, MS 39530

Mississippi Genealogical Society
Box 5301, Jackson, MS 39216

Mississippi Historical Society
Box 571, Jackson, MS 39205, **<mdah.state.ms.us/admin/mhistsoc.html>**

Mississippi Society of the Sons of the American Revolution
12 Avery Circle, Jackson, MS 39211

Mississippi State Department of Health
2423 N. State St., Jackson, MS 39216, (601) 960-7981, **<www.msdh.state.ms.us>**

Mississippi State University, Mitchel Memorial Library
Special Collections-Genealogical Library, Box 5408, Mississippi State, MS 39762, (601) 325-7679, **<library.msstate.edu>**

Natchez Historical Society
307 S. Wall St., Box 49, Natchez, MS 39120, **<www.natchezhistoricalsociety.org>**

National Archives and Records Administration-Southeast Region
5780 Jonesboro Road, Morrow, GA 30260, (770) 968-2100, **<www.archives.gov/southeast>**

Neshoba Ancestral Group
Route 1, Box 284 D, Philadelphia, MS 39350, (601) 656-4787, **<www.rootsweb.ancestry.com/~msneshgg>**

Northeast Mississippi Historical and Genealogical Society
Box 434, Tupelo, MS 38802

Northeast Regional Library
1023 Fillmore, Corinth, MS 38834

Ocean Springs Genealogical Society
Box 1765, Ocean Springs, MS 39566, **<www.rootsweb.ancestry.com/~msosgs>**

Pascagoula City Library
3214 Pascagoula St., Pascagoula, MS 39567, (228) 769-3060, **<www.jgrls.org/branches/pascagoula.html>**

Pearl River County Genealogy Club
Margaret Reed Crosby Memorial Library, 900 Goodyear Blvd., Picayune, MS 39466

Philadelphia-Neshoba County Public Library
230 Beacon St., Philadelphia, MS 39350

Prentiss County Historical and Genealogical Society
Box 491, Booneville, MS 38829, **<www.rootsweb.ancestry.com/~mspcgs/Index.html>**

Rankin County Historical Society
Box 841, Brandon, MS 39042

Scott County Genealogical Society
Box 7373, Forest, MS 39074, (601) 469-4799

Skipwith Historical and Genealogical Society
Box 1392, Oxford, MS 38655

Smith County Mississippi Genealogical Society
Route 1, Box 4B-1, Raleigh, MS 39153

South Mississippi Genealogical Society
Box 15271, Hattiesburg, MS 39404, **<www.members.tripod.com/smsghs>**

Sunflower County Historical Society
Sunflower County Library, 201 Cypress Dr., Indianola, MS 38751

Tate County Genealogical Library
102B Robinson St., Senatobia, MS 38668

Tate County Mississippi Genealogical and Historical Society
Box 974, Senatobia, MS 38668

Tippah County Historical and Genealogical Society
Ripley Public Library, 308 N. Commerce St., Ripley, MS 38663

Tishomingo County Historical and Genealogical Society
204 N. Main St, Iuka, MS 38852, (662) 423-2543, **<www.rootsweb.ancestry.com/~mstchgs>**

Union County Library
Box 846, New Albany, MS 38652, **<www.unioncountylibrary.org>**

Vicksburg Genealogical Society
Box 1161, Vicksburg, MS 39181, **<www.rootsweb.ancestry.com/~msvgs>**

Wayne County Genealogical Organization
712 Wayne St., Waynesboro, MS 39367, **<www.wwcls.lib.ms.us/Genealogy.htm>**

Webster County Historical Society
Rt. 3, Box 14, Elepora, MS 39744

West Chickasaw County Genealogical and Historical Society
Box 42, Houston, MS 38851, **<www.rootsweb.ancestry.com/~mschchgs>**

Wilkinson County Museum
Box 1055, Woodville, MS 39669, (601) 888-3998, **<msgw.org/wilkinson/museum.htm>**

Winston County Historical and Genealogical Society
Box 428, Louisville, MS 39339

Yalobusha County Historical Society
Box 258, Coffeeville, MS 38922

Yazoo Historical Society
332 N. Main St., Box 575, Yazoo City, MS 39194, (601) 746-2273, **<www.rootsweb.ancestry.com/~msyazoo>**

GENERAL SOURCES

Abstract History of the Mississippi Baptist Association, 1806-1906 by T.C. Schilling (J. G. Hauser, 1908)

Biographical and Historical Memoirs of Mississippi, 2 vols., (Goodspeed Publishing Co, 1891, Reprint Company, 1996)

Choctaws And Missionaries In Mississippi, 1818-1918 by Clara Sue Kidwell (University of Oklahoma Press, 1995)

The Episcopal Church in Mississippi (Episcopal Diocese of Mississippi, 1992)

First Settlers of the Mississippi Territory by Frances Terry Ingmire (Ingmire Publications, ca. 1982)

Forgotten Time: The Yazoo-Mississippi Delta after the Civil War by John C. Willis (University Press of Virginia, 2000)

Four Centuries on the Pascagoula, 2 vols., by Cyril Edward Cain (C.E. Cain, 1953-1962)

Guide to Official Records in the Mississippi Department of Archives and History compiled by Thomas W. Henderson and Ronald E. Tomlin (Mississippi Department of Archives and History, 1975)

History of Mississippi from the Discovery of the Great River by Hernando Desoto, Including the Earliest Settlement made by The French, Under Iberville, to the Death of Jefferson Davis by Robert Lowry and William H. McCardle (Goodspeed Publishing Co., 1891, Reprint Company, 1978)

History of Mississippi, the Heart of the South, 2 vols., by Dunbar Rowland (1925, Reprint Co., 1978)

History of the Primitive Baptists of Mississippi by Benjamin Griffin (Sammons Printing, 1853, 1958)

The Large Slaveholders of the Deep South, 1860 by Joseph Karl Menn (Ph.D Thesis: University of Texas, 1964)

Lutheranism In the Southeaster State, 1860-1886: A Social History by Hugh George Anderson (Mouton, 1969)

Methodism in the Mississippi Conference by J. Allen Lindsey (Hawkins Foundation, Mississippi Conference Historical Society, 1964)

Mississippi, 4 vols., by Dunbar Rowland (1907; The Reprint Co., 1976)

Mississippi Biographical Abstracts by Jean Strickland (J. Strickland, 1990)

Mississippi: Comprising Sketches of Counties, Towns, Events, Institutions, and Persons, Arranged in Cyclopedic Form, 4 vols., by Dunbar Rowland (1907; The Reprint Co., 1976)

Mississippi Newspapers, 1805-1940: A Preliminary Union List (Mississippi Historical Records Survey, 1942)

Mississippi as a Province, Territory, and State, with Biographical Notices of Eminent Citizens by J.F.H. Claiborne (Goodspeed Publishing Co., 1880; The Reprint Co., 1996)

Mississippi Provincial Archives, 1612-1763, French Dominion edited by Dunbar Rowland and A. G. Sanders (Department of Archives and History, 1968)

Mississippi Research Outline by the Church of Jesus Christ of Latter-Day Saints (online at **<www.familysearch.org/eng/search/RG/guide/mississippi.asp>**)

Mississippi, United Methodist Churches: 200 years of Heritage and Hope by William L. Jenkins (Providence House Publishing, 1998)

The Order of the First Families of Mississippi 1699-1818 edited by Charles Owen Johnson (Edwards Brothers Inc., 1981)

The Removal of the Choctaw Indians by Arthur H. DeRosier (University of Tennessee Press, 1989)

Research In The Mississippi Department of Archives And History from the Mississippi Department of Archives and History (filmed by the Family History Library, 1972)

Redskins, Ruffleshirts and Rednecks: Indian Allotments in Alabama and Mississippi, 1830-1860 by Mary Elizabeth Young (University of Oklahoma Press, 1961)

Residents of the Southeastern Mississippi Territory, 5 vols., by Jean Strickland (J. Strickland, 1996)

A Southern Catholic Heritage by Charles E. Nolan (Archdiocese of New Orleans, 1976)

Steamboats and the Cotton Economy: River Trade in the Yazoo-Mississippi Delta by Harry P. Owens (University Press of Mississippi, 1990)

Tracing Your Mississippi Ancestors by Anne S. Lipscomb and Kathleen S. Hutchison Jackson (University Press of Mississippi, 1994)

Who's Who In Mississippi by Thomas E. Kelly (Tucker Printing House, 1914)

Women in the Florida Parishes, 5 vols., by Donna Burge Adams (D.B. Adams, 1985-1991)

☞CENSUS RECORDS

Anglo-Americans in Spanish Archives: Lists of Anglo-American Settlers in the Spanish Colonies of America; A Finding Aid by Lawrence H. Feldman (Genealogical Publishing Co., 1991)

☞IMMIGRATION RECORDS

Index to Naturalization Records, Mississippi Courts, 1798-1906 (Old Law Naturalization Records Project, 1942)

☞LAND RECORDS

Early Settlers of Mississippi as Taken from Land Claims in the Mississippi Territory by Walter Lowrie (1834; Southern Historical Press, 1986)

English Land Grants in West Florida: A Register for the States of Alabama, Mississippi, and Parts of Florida and Louisiana, 1766-1776 by Winston DeVille (Winston DeVille, 1986)

Mississippi Pre-1908 Patents, Cash, Homestead, Chickasaw Indian Treaty And Choctaw Indian Scrip from the US Department of the Interior, Bureau of Land Management (BLM Eastern States, 1997)

Private Land Claims of Mississippi and Missouri by Fern Ainsworth (Fern Ainsworth)

Spanish And British Land Grants In Mississippi Territory, 1750-1784, 3 vols., by Clifford Neal Smith (Westland, 1996)

☞MAPS

Hometown, Mississippi, 2nd edition, by James Brieger (Town Square Books, 1997)

Mississippi Atlas of Historical County Boundaries compiled by John H. Long and Peggy Tuck Sinko (Simon & Schuster, 1993)

Mississippi, 4 vols., by Dunbar Rowland (Southern Historical Publishing Association 1907; Reprint Co., 1976)

Mississippi Maps, 1816-1873 (Mississippi Department of Archives and History, 1970)

Mississippi Post Offices by John S. Gallagher (The Depot, 1996)

A Postal History of Mississippi—Stampless Period, 1799-1860 by Bruce C. Oakley (Magnolia Publishers, 1969)

☞MILITARY RECORDS

Compiled Service Records of Volunteer Union Soldiers Who Served in Organizations from the State of Mississippi from the US Record and Pension Office (National Archives, 1962)

Military Annals of Mississippi: Military Organizations Which Entered the Service of the Confederate States of America from the State of Mississippi by John C. Rietti (1976; Reprint Co., 1976)

Military History of Mississippi, 1803-1898 by Dunbar Rowland (1908; Reprint Co., 1996)

Mississippi Confederate Grave Registrations, 2 vols., by Betty Crouch Wiltshire (Heritage Books, 1991)

Mississippi Confederate Pension Applications, 3 vols., by Betty Crouch Wiltshire (Pioneer Publishing Co., 1994)

Mississippi Territory in the War of 1812 by Eron Opha Rowland (1921; Clearfield Co., 1996)

Official & Statistical Register of the State of Mississippi, Military History Only by Dunbar Rowland (1908; Higginson Co., 1995)

Residents of the Mississippi Territory, 3 vols., by Jean Strickland and Patricia N. Edwards (Ben Strickland)

Roster of Mississippi Men Who Served in the War of 1812 and Mexican War (Department of Archives and History)

United States Adjutant General's Office Compiled Service Records of Volunteer Soldiers Who Served During the Mexican War in Organizations from the State of Mississippi (National Archives, 1971)

United States Adjutant General's Office Compiled Service Records of Volunteer Soldiers Who Served During the War of 1812 in Organizations from the Territory of Mississippi (National Archives, 1967)

☞PROBATE RECORDS

Mississippi County Court Records by May Wilson McBee (1858; Clearfield Co., 1994)

Mississippi Court Records 1799-1835 by J. Estelle King (1936; Genealogical Publishing Co., 1969)

Mississippi Index of Wills, 1800-1900, compiled by Betty Couch Wiltshire (Heritage Books, 1989)

The Natchez Court Records, 1767-1805 by May Wilson McBee (1953; Clearfield Co., 1994)

☞VITAL RECORDS

Early Mississippi Records by Betty Crouch Wiltshire (Heritage Books, 1996)

Guide to Vital Statistics in Mississippi: Volume 1, Public Archives (Historical Records Survey, 1942)

Mississippi Cemetery and Bible Records, 3 vols., (Mississippi Genealogical Society, 1954)

Mississippi Marriages, Early To 1825 by Jordan R. Dodd (Precision Indexing Publishers, ca. 1990)

•-COUNTY DETAILS-•

ADAMS

115 S. Wall St., Box 1008, Natchez, MS 39120, (601) 446-6684, **<adamscountyms.net>**
- **INCORPORATED:** April 2, 1799
- **PARENT COUNTY:** Natchez District
- **MARRIAGE RECORDS:** unknown start, kept by Circuit Court
- **DEATH:** unknown start, Circuit Court
- **LAND:** unknown start, Chancery Court
- **PROBATE:** unknown start, Chancery Court
- **COURT:** unknown start, Chancery Court

ALCORN

Box 112, Corinth, MS 38834, (601) 286-7702, **<alcorncounty.org>**
- **INCORPORATED:** April 15, 1870
- **PARENT COUNTIES:** Tippah, Tishomingo
- **DIVORCE RECORDS:** start in 1913, kept by Chancery Court
- **COURT:** 1860, Circuit Court

AMITE

243 W. Main St., Liberty, MS 39645, (601) 657-8022, **<www.amitecounty.ms>**
- **INCORPORATED:** Feb. 24, 1809
- **PARENT COUNTY:** Wilkinson
- **MARRIAGE RECORDS:** unknown start, kept by Circuit Court
- **LAND:** 1809, Chancery Court
- **PROBATE:** 1809, Chancery Court
- **COURT:** 1809, Chancery Court

ATTALA

230 W. Washington St., Kosciusko, MS 39090, (662) 289-2921, **<www.attalacounty.net>**
- **INCORPORATED:** Dec. 23, 1833
- **PARENT COUNTY:** Choctaw Cession
- **MARRIAGE RECORDS:** unknown start, kept by Circuit Court
- **DIVORCE:** unknown start, Chancery Court
- **LAND:** unknown start, Chancery Court
- **PROBATE:** unknown start, Chancery Court

BAINBRIDGE

- **INCORPORATED:** Jan. 17, 1823
- **PARENT COUNTIES:** Lawrence, Wayne
- **NOTES:** Discontinued Jan. 1, 1824; became Covington County.

BENTON

Box 218, Ashland, MS 38603, (662) 224-6300, **<www.rootsweb.ancestry.com/~msbenton>**
- **INCORPORATED:** Jul. 12, 1870
- **PARENT COUNTIES:** Marshall, Tippah
- **DIVORCE RECORDS:** start in 1871, kept by Chancery Court
- **LAND:** 1871, Chancery Court
- **PROBATE:** 1871, Chancery Court

BOLIVAR

401 S. Court St., Cleveland, MS 38732, (601) 846-5877, **<co.bolivar.ms.us>**
- **INCORPORATED:** Feb. 9, 1836
- **PARENT COUNTY:** Choctaw Cession
- **MARRIAGE RECORDS:** unknown start, kept by Circuit Court in Cleveland
- **MARRIAGE:** 1866, Circuit Court in Rosedale
- **DIVORCE:** unknown start, Chancery Court in Cleveland
- **DIVORCE:** unknown start, Chancery Court in Rosedale
- **LAND:** unknown start, Chancery Court in Cleveland
- **LAND:** unknown start, Chancery Court in Rosedale
- **PROBATE:** unknown start, Chancery Court in Cleveland
- **PROBATE:** unknown start, Chancery Court in Rosedale
- **COURT:** unknown start, Circuit Court in Cleveland
- **COURT:** 1870, Circuit Court in Rosedale
- **NOTES:** Chancery and Circuit Clerks Office in both courthouses. Rosedale records go back about 20 years earlier than Cleveland.

CALHOUN

Box 8, Pittsboro, MS 38951, (662) 983-3122, **<www.rootsweb.ancestry.com/~mscalhou>**
- **INCORPORATED:** March 8, 1852
- **PARENT COUNTIES:** Lafayette, Yalobusha
- **MARRIAGE RECORDS:** start in 1922, kept by Chancery Court
- **DIVORCE:** 1922, Chancery Court
- **LAND:** 1922, Chancery Court; Abstracts: 1852, Chancery Court
- **PROBATE:** 1922, Chancery Court
- **COURT:** 1922, Chancery Court
- **NOTES:** Courthouse burned in 1922.

CARROLL

Lexington St., Box 60, Carrollton, MS 38917, (662) 237-9274, **<www.msgen.net/co/carroll/index.html>**
- **INCORPORATED:** Dec. 23, 1833
- **PARENT COUNTY:** Choctaw Cession
- **MARRIAGE RECORDS:** start in 1870, kept by County Clerk
- **DIVORCE:** 1870, County Clerk
- **LAND:** 1870, County Clerk
- **PROBATE:** 1870, County Clerk
- **COURT:** 1870, County Clerk

CHICKASAW

101 N. Jefferson, Houston, MS 38851, (662) 456-2531, **<chickasawcoms.com>**
- **INCORPORATED:** Feb. 9, 1836
- **PARENT COUNTY:** Choctaw Cession, 1832
- **MARRIAGE RECORDS:** unknown start, kept by Circuit Court in Houston
- **MARRIAGE:** 1877, Circuit Court in Okolona
- **DIVORCE:** unknown start, Circuit Court in Houston
- **DIVORCE:** 1886, Chancery Court in Okolona
- **LAND:** unknown start, Circuit Court in Houston
- **PROBATE:** unknown start, Circuit Court in Houston
- **PROBATE:** 1886, Chancery Court in Okolona
- **COURT:** unknown start, Circuit Court in Houston
- **COURT:** unknown start, Circuit Court in Okolona
- **NOTES:** Chickasaw County has courthouses in two locations.

CHOCTAW
112 Quinn St., Box 250, Ackerman, MS 39735, (662) 285-6329, **<www.rootsweb.ancestry.com/~mschocta>**
- **INCORPORATED:** Dec. 23, 1833
- **PARENT COUNTY:** Chickasaw Cession, 1832
- **MARRIAGE RECORDS:** start in 1881, kept by Circuit Court
- **DIVORCE:** 1881, Circuit Court
- **LAND:** 1881, Circuit Court
- **PROBATE:** 1881, Circuit Court
- **COURT:** 1881, Circuit Court

CLAIBORNE
Box 449, Port Gibson, MS 39150, (601) 437-4992, **<www.rootsweb.ancestry.com/~msclaib2>**
- **INCORPORATED:** Jan. 27, 1802
- **PARENT COUNTY:** Jefferson
- **MARRIAGE RECORDS:** start in 1816, kept by Chancery Court
- **DIVORCE:** 1856, Chancery Court
- **PROBATE:** 1802, Chancery Court
- **COURT:** 1802, Chancery Court

CLARKE
Box 689, Quitman, MS 39355, (662) 776-2126, **<genealogytrails.com/miss/clarke>**
- **INCORPORATED:** Dec. 10, 1812
- **PARENT COUNTY:** Washington
- **DIVORCE RECORDS:** start in 1875, kept by Chancery Court
- **PROBATE:** 1875, Chancery Court

CLAY
Box 815, West Point, MS 39773, (662) 494-3124, **<www.rootsweb.ancestry.com/~msclay>**
- **INCORPORATE:** May 12, 1871
- **PARENT COUNTIES:** Chickasaw, Lowndes, Monroe, Oktibbeha
- **MARRIAGE RECORDS:** unknown start, kept by Circuit Court
- **DIVORCE:** 1872, Chancery Court
- **LAND:** 1872, Chancery Court
- **PROBATE:** 1872, Chancery Court
- **COURT:** unknown start, Circuit Court
- **NOTES:** Formerly Colfax County. Name changed to Clay April 10, 1876.

COAHOMA
115 First St., Box 98, Clarksdale, MS 38614, (662) 624-3000, **<coahomacounty.net>**
- **INCORPORATED:** Feb. 9, 1836
- **PARENT COUNTY:** Chickasaw Cession, 1836
- **MARRIAGE RECORDS:** start in 1848, kept by Circuit Court
- **DIVORCE:** unknown start, Chancery Court
- **LAND:** unknown start, Chancery Court
- **PROBATE:** unknown start, Chancery Court
- **COURT:** 1848, Circuit Court
- **VOTER:** 1949, Circuit Court

COLFAX
- **INCORPORATED:** May 12, 1871
- **PARENT COUNTIES:** Chickasaw, Lowndes, Monroe, Oktibbeha
- **NOTES:** See Clay County. Name changed to Clay April 10, 1876.

COPIAH
Box 507, Hazlehurst, MS 39083, (601) 894-3021, **<copiahcounty.org>**
- **INCORPORATED:** Jan. 21, 1823
- **PARENT COUNTY:** Hinds
- **MARRIAGE RECORDS:** start in 1825, kept by Circuit Court
- **DIVORCE:** 1840, Chancery Court
- **LAND:** 1825, Chancery Court
- **PROBATE:** 1825, Chancery Court
- **COURT:** unknown start, Circuit Court
- **CONFEDERATE VETERANS:** unknown start, Chancery Court

COVINGTON
Box 1679, Collins, MS 39428, (601) 765-4242, **<msgw.org/covington>**
- **INCORPORATED:** Feb. 5, 1819
- **PARENT COUNTIES:** Lawrence, Wayne
- **MARRIAGE RECORDS:** start in 1900, kept by Chancery Court
- **DIVORCE:** 1900, Chancery Court
- **LAND:** 1860, Chancery Court
- **PROBATE:** 1900, Chancery Court
- **COURT:** 1860, Chancery Court

DE SOTO
2535 Hwy. 51 S., Courthouse Sq., Hernando, MS 38632, (662) 429-1317, **<desotoms.com>**
- **INCORPORATED:** Feb. 9, 1836
- **PARENT COUNTY:** Indian lands
- **DIVORCE RECORDS:** unknown start, kept by Chancery Court
- **LAND:** unknown start, Chancery Court
- **PROBATE:** unknown start, Chancery Court

FORREST
641 Main St., Box 951, Hattiesburg, MS 39401, (601) 545-6014, **<forrestcountyms.us>**
- **INCORPORATED:** April 19, 1906
- **PARENT COUNTY:** Perry
- **MARRIAGE RECORDS:** start in 1893, kept by Circuit Court
- **DIVORCE:** unknown start, Chancery Court
- **LAND:** unknown start, Chancery Court
- **PROBATE:** unknown start, Chancery Court
- **COURT:** 1906, Circuit Court
- **MILITARY:** unknown start, Chancery Court

FRANKLIN
Box 297, Meadville, MS 39653, (601) 384-2330, **<franklincountyms.com>**
- **INCORPORATED:** Dec. 21, 1809
- **PARENT COUNTY:** Adams
- **MARRIAGE RECORDS:** unknown start, kept by Circuit Court
- **LAND:** unknown start, Chancery Court
- **PROBATE:** unknown start, Chancery Court
- **COURT:** unknown start, Chancery Court

GEORGE
320 Cox St., Lucedale, MS 39452, (601) 947-4801, **<www.rootsweb.ancestry.com/~msgeorge>**
- **INCORPORATED:** March 16, 1910

- **PARENT COUNTIES:** Greene, Jackson
- **MARRIAGE:** start in 1911, kept by Circuit Court
- **DIVORCE:** 1911, Chancery Court
- **LAND:** 1911, Chancery Court
- **PROBATE:** 1911, Chancery Court
- **COURT:** 1911, Circuit Court

GREENE

Box 610, Leakesville, MS 39451, (601) 394-2377, **<www.rootsweb.ancestry.com/~msgreene>**

- **INCORPORATED:** Dec. 9, 1811
- **PARENT COUNTIES:** Amite, Franklin, Wayne
- **MARRIAGE RECORDS:** unknown start, kept by Circuit Court
- **LAND:** unknown start, Chancery Court
- **PROBATE:** unknown start, Chancery Court
- **COURT:** unknown start, Chancery Court

GRENADA

Box 1208, Grenada, MS 38902, (662) 226-1821, **<www.rootsweb.ancestry.com/~msgrenad>**

- **INCORPORATED:** May 9, 1870
- **PARENT COUNTY:** unknown start
- **MARRIAGE RECORDS:** start in 1870, kept by Circuit Court
- **DIVORCE:** 1870, Circuit Court
- **LAND:** 1835, Circuit Court
- **PROBATE:** 1870, Circuit Court

HANCOCK

3068 Longfellow, Bay St. Louis, MS 39520, (601) 467-5404, **<hancockcountyms.gov>**

- **INCORPORATED:** Dec. 18, 1812
- **PARENT COUNTY:** Mobile District
- **MARRIAGE RECORDS:** unknown start, kept by Circuit Court
- **DIVORCE:** unknown start, Chancery Court
- **LAND:** unknown start, Chancery Court
- **PROBATE:** unknown start, Chancery Court
- **COURT:** unknown start, Circuit Court

HARRISON

1801 23rd Ave., Drawer CC, Gulfport, MS 39502, (228) 865-4118, **<co.harrison.ms.us>**

- **INCORPORATED:** Feb. 5, 1841
- **PARENT COUNTIES:** Hancock, Jackson
- **MARRIAGE RECORDS:** start in 1841, kept by Circuit Court
- **DIVORCE:** unknown start, Chancery Court
- **LAND:** unknown start, Chancery Court
- **PROBATE:** unknown start, Chancery Court
- **COURT:** unknown start, Circuit Court

HINDS

Box 686, Jackson, MS 39205, (601) 968-6237, **<co.hinds.ms.us>**

- **INCORPORATED:** Feb. 12, 1821
- **PARENT COUNTY:** Choctaw Cession, 1820
- **MARRIAGE RECORDS:** start in 1823, kept by Circuit Court
- **DIVORCE:** unknown start, Chancery Court
- **LAND:** unknown start, Chancery Court
- **PROBATE:** unknown start, Chancery Court
- **COURT:** 1930, Circuit Court

HOLMES

Box 239, Lexington, MS 39095, (662) 834-2281, **<holmescountymississippi.com>**

- **INCORPORATED:** Feb. 19, 1833
- **PARENT COUNTY:** Yazoo
- **MARRIAGE RECORDS:** unknown start, kept by Circuit Court
- **DIVORCE:** 1894, Chancery Court
- **LAND:** 1833, Chancery Court
- **PROBATE:** 1833, Chancery Court
- **COURT:** unknown start, Circuit Court
- **BURIAL:** unknown start, Chancery Court

HUMPHREYS

Box 696, Belzoni, MS 39038, (601) 247-1740, **<www.rootsweb.ancestry.com/~mshumphr>**

- **INCORPORATED:** March 28, 1918
- **PARENT COUNTIES:** Holmes, Washington, Yazoo, Sunflower
- **BIRTH:** unknown start, kept in Circuit Court
- **MARRIAGE:** unknown start, Circuit Court
- **DIVORCE:** 1918, Chancery Court
- **LAND:** 1918, Chancery Court
- **PROBATE:** 1918, Chancery Court

ISSAQUENA

129 Court St., Box 27, Mayersville, MS 39113, (662) 873-2761, **<www.rootsweb.ancestry.com/~msissaq2>**

- **INCORPORATED:** Jan. 23, 1844
- **PARENT COUNTY:** Washington
- **MARRIAGE RECORDS:** start in 1866, kept by Chancery Court
- **DIVORCE:** 1850, Chancery Court
- **LAND:** 1850, Chancery Court
- **PROBATE:** 1850, Chancery Court
- **COURT:** 1850, Chancery Court

ITAWAMBA

Box 577, Fulton, MS 38843, (662) 862-4571, **<itawamba.com>**

- **INCORPORATED:** Feb. 9, 1836
- **PARENT COUNTY:** Chickasaw Cession, 1832
- **MARRIAGE RECORDS:** unknown start, kept by Chancery Court
- **DIVORCE:** unknown start, Chancery Court
- **LAND:** unknown start, Chancery Court
- **PROBATE:** unknown start, Chancery Court
- **COURT:** unknown start, Chancery Court

JACKSON

3104 Magnolia St., Box 998, Pascagoula, MS 39568, (228) 769-3131, **<www.co.jackson.ms.us>**

- **INCORPORATED:** Dec. 18, 1812
- **PARENT COUNTY:** Mobile District
- **MARRIAGE RECORDS:** start in 1875, kept by Circuit Court
- **DIVORCE:** unknown start, Chancery Court
- **PROBATE:** unknown start, Chancery Court
- **JUSTICE OF THE PEACE DOCKETS:** 1875, Chancery Court

JASPER

Court St., Box 1047, Bay Springs, MS 39422, (601) 764-3368, **<www.co.jasper.ms.us>**

- **INCORPORATED:** Dec. 23, 1833

- **PARENT COUNTY:** Choctaw Cession, 1832
- **MARRIAGE RECORDS:** unknown start, kept by Circuit Court
- **DIVORCE:** 1906, County Clerk
- **PROBATE:** 1906, County Clerk
- **COURT:** 1906, County Clerk

JEFFERSON

307 S. Main St., Box 145, Fayette, MS 39069, (601) 786-3021, **<jeffersoncountyms.org>**

- **INCORPORATED:** April 2, 1799
- **PARENT COUNTY:** Natchez District
- **MARRIAGE RECORDS:** start in 1798, kept by Chancery Court
- **DIVORCE:** 1860, Chancery Court
- **LAND:** 1798, Chancery Court
- **PROBATE:** 1798, Chancery Court
- **NOTES:** Formerly Pickering County. Name changed to Jefferson Jan. 11, 1802.

JEFFERSON DAVIS

1025 Third St., Box 1137, Prentiss, MS 39474, (601) 792-4204, **<www.rootsweb.ancestry.com/~msjdavis>**

- **INCORPORATED:** March 31, 1906
- **PARENT COUNTIES:** Covington, Lawrence
- **MARRIAGE RECORDS:** unknown start, kept by Circuit Court
- **LAND:** unknown start, Chancery Court
- **PROBATE:** unknown start, Circuit Court
- **COURT:** unknown start, Chancery Court

JONES

415 N. Fifth Ave., Box 1468, Laurel, MS 39441, (601) 428-0527, **<www.jonescounty.com>**

- **INCORPORATED:** Jan. 24, 1826
- **PARENT COUNTIES:** Covington, Wayne
- **MARRIAGE RECORDS:** start in 1882, kept by Circuit Court
- **DIVORCE:** unknown start, Chancery Court at Laurel and Ellisville
- **LAND:** unknown start, Chancery Court at Laurel and Ellisville
- **COURT:** 1907, Circuit Court

KEMPER

102 Industrial Park, De Kalb, MS 39328, (601) 743-2754, **<www.kempercounty.com>**

- **INCORPORATED:** Dec. 23, 1833
- **PARENT COUNTY:** Choctaw Cession, 1832
- **MARRIAGE RECORDS:** start in 1912, kept by Circuit Court
- **DIVORCE:** 1912, Chancery Court
- **LAND:** 1912, Chancery Court
- **PROBATE:** 1912, Chancery Court
- **COURT:** 1912, Chancery Court

LAFAYETTE

Town Square, Box 1240, Oxford, MS 38655, (662) 234-7563, **<www.lafayettecoms.com>**

- **INCORPORATED:** Feb. 9, 1836
- **PARENT COUNTY:** Chickasaw Cession
- **MARRIAGE RECORDS:** unknown start, kept by Chancery Court
- **DIVORCE:** unknown start, Chancery Court
- **PROBATE:** unknown start, Chancery Court
- **COURT:** unknown start, Chancery Court

LAMAR

203 Main St., Purvis, MS 39475, (601) 794-8504, **<www.lamarcounty.com>**

- **INCORPORATED:** Feb. 19, 1904
- **PARENT COUNTY:** Marion, Pearl River
- **MARRIAGE RECORDS:** unknown start, kept by Circuit Court
- **DIVORCE:** ca.1900, Chancery Court
- **LAND:** ca.1900, Chancery Court
- **PROBATE:** ca.1900, Chancery Court
- **COURT:** unknown start, Justice of the Peace

LAUDERDALE

500 Constitution Ave., Box 1587, Meridian, MS 39302, (601) 482-9704, **<www.lauderdalecounty.org>**

- **INCORPORATED:** Dec. 23, 1833
- **PARENT COUNTY:** Choctaw Cession
- **BIRTH RECORDS:** unknown start, kept by Department of Health
- **MARRIAGE:** unknown start, Circuit Court
- **DIVORCE:** unknown start, Chancery Court
- **DEATH:** unknown start, Dept. of Health
- **LAND:** unknown start, Chancery Court
- **PROBATE:** unknown start, Chancery Court
- **COURT:** unknown start Circuit Court

LAWRENCE

517 E. Broad St., Box 40, Monticello, MS 39654, (601) 587-7162, **<www.mississippigenealogy.com/lawrence>**

- **INCORPORATED:** Dec. 22, 1814
- **PARENT COUNTY:** Marion
- **MARRIAGE RECORDS:** unknown start, kept by Circuit Court
- **DIVORCE:** 1815, Chancery Court
- **LAND:** 1815, Chancery Court
- **PROBATE:** 1815, Chancery Court
- **COURT:** unknown start, Circuit Court

LEAKE

103 N. Pearl, Box 209, Carthage, MS 39051, (601) 267-7371, **<www.leakems.com>**

- **INCORPORATED:** Dec. 23, 1833
- **PARENT COUNTY:** Choctaw Cession
- **MARRIAGE RECORDS:** unknown start, kept by Chancery Court
- **DIVORCE:** 1871, Chancery Court
- **LAND:** 1833, Chancery Court
- **PROBATE:** 1840, Chancery Court
- **COURT:** unknown start, Chancery Court
- **MILITARY:** 1918, Chancery Court

LEE

200 W. Jefferson St., Box 7127, Tupelo, MS 38802, (662) 841-9100, **<www.rootsweb.ancestry.com/~mslee>**

- **INCORPORATED:** Oct. 26, 1866
- **PARENT COUNTIES:** Itawamba, Pontotoc
- **MARRIAGE RECORDS:** unknown start, kept by Circuit Court
- **DIVORCE:** unknown start, Chancery Court
- **LAND:** unknown start, Chancery Court
- **PROBATE:** unknown start, Chancery Court
- **COURT:** unknown start, Justice Court

LEFLORE
317 W. Market St., Box 250, Greenwood, MS 38935, (662) 453-1041, **<www.rootsweb.ancestry.com/~msleflor>**
- **INCORPORATED:** March 15, 1871
- **PARENT COUNTIES:** Carroll, Sunflower, Tallahatchie
- **MARRIAGE RECORDS:** unknown start, kept by Circuit Court
- **DIVORCE:** 1871, Chancery Court
- **LAND:** 1834, Chancery Court
- **PROBATE:** 1871, Chancery Court
- **COURT:** unknown start, Circuit Court

LINCOLN
300 S. Second St., Box 555, Brookhaven, MS 39601, (601) 835-3479, **<lincolnmississippi.com>**
- **INCORPORATED:** April 7, 1870
- **PARENT COUNTIES:** Franklin, Lawrence, Copiah, Pike, Amite
- **MARRIAGE RECORDS:** start in 1893, kept by Clerk/District Ct.
- **DIVORCE:** 1893, Chancery Court
- **PROBATE:** 1893, Chancery Court
- **COURT:** 1893, Chancery Court

LOWNDES
52100 Second Ave. N., Box 684, Columbus, MS 39703, (662) 329-5800, **<www.lowndescountygov.com>**
- **INCORPORATED:** Jan. 30, 1830
- **PARENT COUNTY:** Monroe
- **NOTES:** Department of Archives and History has marriage, divorce, probate, court and land records 1830-1900.

MADISON
Box 404, Canton, MS 39046, (601) 859-1177, **<madison-co.com>**
- **INCORPORATED:** Jan. 29, 1828
- **PARENT COUNTY:** Yazoo
- **MARRIAGE RECORDS:** start in 1828, kept by Chancery Court
- **DIVORCE:** 1828, Chancery Court
- **LAND:** 1828, Chancery Court
- **PROBATE:** 1828, Chancery Court
- **COURT:** 1828, Chancery Court

MARION
250 Broad St. Suite 2, Columbia, MS 39429, (601) 736-2691, **<marioncounty-ms.us>**
- **INCORPORATED:** Dec. 9, 1811
- **PARENT COUNTIES:** Amite, Wayne, Franklin
- **MARRIAGE RECORDS:** unknown start, kept by Chancery Court
- **DIVORCE:** unknown start, Chancery Court
- **LAND:** unknown start, Chancery Court
- **PROBATE:** unknown start, Chancery Court
- **COURT:** unknown start, Chancery Court

MARSHALL
Box 459, Holly Springs, MS 38635, (662) 252-3434, **<marshallcoms.org>**
- **INCORPORATED:** Feb. 9, 1836
- **PARENT COUNTY:** Chickasaw Cession, 1832
- **DIVORCE RECORDS:** start in 1836, kept by Chancery Court
- **LAND:** 1836, Chancery Court
- **PROBATE:** 1836, Chancery Court

MONROE
201 W. Commerce St., Box 578, Aberdeen, MS 39730, (662) 369-8143, **<monroecountyms.org>**
- **INCORPORATED:** Feb. 9, 1821
- **PARENT COUNTY:** Chickasaw Cession, 1821
- **MARRIAGE RECORDS:** unknown start, kept by Circuit Court
- **DIVORCE:** unknown start, Chancery Court
- **LAND:** 1821, Chancery Court
- **PROBATE:** 1821, Chancery Court
- **COURT:** unknown start, Circuit Court

MONTGOMERY
614 Summit St., Box 71, Winona, MS 38967, (662) 283-2333, **<www.rootsweb.ancestry.com/~msmontgo>**
- **INCORPORATED:** May 13, 1871
- **PARENT COUNTIES:** Carroll, Choctaw
- **MARRIAGE RECORDS:** unknown start, kept by Circuit Court
- **DIVORCE:** 1871, Chancery Court
- **LAND:** 1871, Chancery Court
- **PROBATE:** 1871, Chancery Court
- **COURT:** 1871, Chancery Court

NESHOBA
401 E. Beacon St. Suite 107, Philadelphia, MS 39350, (601) 656-3581, **<www.neshoba.org>**
- **INCORPORATED:** Dec. 23, 1833
- **PARENT COUNTY:** Chocktaw Cession, 1830
- **MARRIAGE RECORDS:** start in 1912, kept by Circuit Court
- **DIVORCE:** 1890, Chancery Court
- **PROBATE:** 1890, Chancery Court

NEWTON
92 W. Broad St., Box 68, Decatur, MS 39327, (601) 635-2367, **<nchgs.org>**
- **INCORPORATED:** Feb. 25, 1836
- **PARENT COUNTY:** Neshoba
- **MARRIAGE RECORDS:** unknown start, kept by Circuit Court
- **DIVORCE:** 1876, Chancery Court
- **LAND:** 1876, Chancery Court
- **PROBATE:** 1876, Chancery Court
- **COURT:** 1876, Chancery Court

NOXUBEE
505 S. Jefferson St., Box 147, Macon, MS 39341, (662) 726-4243, **<www.rootsweb.ancestry.com/~msnoxube>**
- **INCORPORATED:** Dec. 23, 1833
- **PARENT COUNTY:** Choctaw Cession, 1830
- **MARRIAGE RECORDS:** start in 1834, kept by Circuit Court
- **DIVORCE:** 1834, Chancery Court
- **LAND:** 1834, Chancery Court
- **PROBATE:** 1834, Chancery Court
- **COURT:** 1834, Circuit Court

OKTIBBEHA
101 W. Main St., Starkville, MS 39759, (662) 323-5834, **<www.gtpdd.com/counties/oktibbeha>**
- **INCORPORATED:** Dec. 23, 1833
- **PARENT COUNTY:** Choctaw Cession, 1830

- **MARRIAGE RECORDS:** unknown start, kept by Circuit Court
- **DIVORCE:** 1880, Chancery Court
- **LAND:** 1834, Chancery Court
- **PROBATE:** 1880, Chancery Court
- **COURT:** 1880, Chancery Court

PANOLA

151 Public Sq., Batesville, MS 38606, (601) 563-6205,
<www.panolacoms.com>

- **INCORPORATED:** Feb. 9, 1836
- **PARENT COUNTY:** Chickasaw Cession, 1832
- **MARRIAGE RECORDS:** start in 1885, kept by Circuit Court
- **DIVORCE:** 1836, Chancery Court
- **PROBATE:** 1836, Chancery Court
- **COURT:** 1836, Circuit Court

PEARL RIVER

200 S. Main St., Box 431, Poplarville, MS 39470, (601) 795-2237,
<pearlrivercounty.net>

- **INCORPORATED:** Feb. 22, 1890
- **PARENT COUNTIES:** Hancock, Marion
- **MARRIAGE RECORDS:** unknown start, kept by Circuit Court
- **DIVORCE:** 1890, Chancery Court
- **PROBATE:** 1890, Chancery Court
- **COURT:** 1890, Chancery Court

PERRY

Box 198, New Augusta, MS 39462-0198, (601) 964-8398,
<www.perrycountyms.com>

- **INCORPORATED:** Feb. 3, 1820
- **PARENT COUNTY:** Greene
- **MARRIAGE RECORDS:** start in 1877, kept by Circuit Court
- **DIVORCE:** 1878, Chancery Court
- **LAND:** 1878, Chancery Court
- **PROBATE:** 1878, Chancery Court
- **COURT:** 1878, Chancery Court

PICKERING

- **INCORPORATED:** April 2, 1799
- **PARENT COUNTY:** Natchez District
- **NOTES:** See Jefferson County. Name changed to Jefferson Jan. 11, 1802.

PIKE

200 E. Bay St., Box 309, Magnolia, MS 39652, (601) 783-3362,
<co.pike.ms.us>

- **INCORPORATED:** Dec. 9, 1815
- **PARENT COUNTY:** Marion
- **MARRIAGE RECORDS:** unknown start, kept by Circuit Court
- **DIVORCE:** 1882, Chancery Court
- **LAND:** 1882, Chancery Court
- **PROBATE:** 1882, Chancery Court
- **COURT:** 1882, Chancery Court

PONTOTOC

11 E. Washington St., Box 209, Pontotoc, MS 38863, (662) 489-3900, **<www.rootsweb.ancestry.com/~mspontot>**

- **INCORPORATED:** Feb. 9, 1836
- **PARENT COUNTY:** Chickasaw Cession, 1832
- **MARRIAGE RECORDS:** unknown start, kept by Circuit Court
- **DIVORCE:** unknown start, Chancery Court
- **LAND:** 1836, Chancery Court
- **PROBATE:** unknown start, Chancery Court
- **COURT:** unknown start, Chancery Court

PRENTISS

100 W. Main St., Box 477, Booneville, MS 38829, (662) 728-8151,
<www.msgen.net/co/prentiss/index.html>

- **INCORPORATED:** April 15, 1870
- **PARENT COUNTY:** Tishomingo
- **MARRIAGE RECORDS:** unknown start, kept by Circuit Court
- **DIVORCE:** 1870, Chancery Court
- **LAND:** 1836, Chancery Court
- **PROBATE:** 1870, Chancery Court
- **COURT:** 1870, Chancery Court

QUITMAN

Box 100, Marks, MS 38646, (662) 326-2661, **<msghn.org>**

- **INCORPORATED:** Feb. 1, 1877
- **PARENT COUNTIES:** Panola, Coahoma, Tunica, Tallahatchie
- **MARRIAGE RECORDS:** unknown start, kept by Circuit Court
- **DIVORCE:** 1877, Chancery Court
- **PROBATE:** 1877, Chancery Court
- **COURT:** unknown start, Circuit Court

RANKIN

301 E. Government St., Brandon, MS 39042, (601) 825-2217,
<rankincounty.org>

- **INCORPORATED:** Feb. 4, 1828
- **PARENT COUNTY:** Hinds
- **DIVORCE RECORDS:** start in 1829, kept by Chancery Court
- **LAND:** 1829, Chancery Court
- **PROBATE:** 1829, Chancery Court

SCOTT

100 E. Main St., Box 630, Forest, MS 39074, (601) 469-1922,
<msgen.net/co/scott>

- **INCORPORATED:** Dec. 23, 1833
- **PARENT COUNTY:** Choctaw Cession, 1832
- **MARRIAGE RECORDS:** unknown start, kept by Circuit Court
- **DIVORCE:** 1900, Chancery Court
- **LAND:** 1835, Chancery Court
- **PROBATE:** 1835, Chancery Court
- **COURT:** 1900, Chancery Court
- **CEMETERY:** unknown start, Chancery Court
- **NOTES:** Clerk of Chancery Court has old church records.

SHARKEY

400 Locust St., Box 218, Rolling Fork, MS 39159, (662) 873-2755
<www.rootsweb.ancestry.com/~mssharke>

- **INCORPORATED:** March 29, 1876
- **PARENT COUNTIES:** Warren, Washington, Issaquena
- **MARRIAGE RECORDS:** start in 1876, kept by Circuit Court
- **LAND:** 1876, Chancery Court
- **PROBATE:** 1876, Chancery Court
- **COURT:** 1876, Chancery Court

SIMPSON

109 W. Pine Ave., Box 367, Mendenhall, MS 39114, (601) 847-2626, **<msgen.net/co/simpson/index.html>**

- **INCORPORATED:** Jan. 23, 1824
- **PARENT COUNTY:** Choctaw Cession, 1820
- **MARRIAGE RECORDS:** unknown start, kept by Circuit Court
- **DIVORCE:** 1880, Chancery Court
- **COURT:** unknown start, Circuit Court
- **NOTES:** Clerk of Chancery Court has some land and probate records.

SMITH

123 Main St., Box 39, Raleigh, MS 39153, (601) 782-9811, **<www.smithcounty.ms.gov>**

- **INCORPORATED:** Dec. 23, 1833
- **PARENT COUNTY:** Choctaw Cession, 1820
- **MARRIAGE RECORDS:** start in 1912, kept by Circuit Court
- **DIVORCE:** 1892, Chancery Court
- **LAND:** 1892, Chancery Court
- **PROBATE:** 1892, Chancery Court
- **COURT:** unknown start, Circuit Court
- **MILITARY:** 1892, Chancery Court

STONE

Box 7, Wiggins, MS 39577, (601) 928-5266, **<www.stonecounty.com>**

- **INCORPORATED:** April 3, 1916
- **PARENT COUNTY:** Harrison
- **MARRIAGE RECORDS:** unknown start, kept by Circuit Court
- **DIVORCE:** 1916, Chancery Court
- **LAND:** 1916, Chancery Court
- **PROBATE:** 1916, Chancery Court
- **COURT:** unknown start, Circuit Court
- **MILITARY:** 1916, Chancery Court

SUMNER

- **INCORPORATED:** April 6, 1874
- **PARENT COUNTIES:** Montgomery, Chickasaw, Choctaw, Okitbbeha
- **NOTES:** See Webster County. Name changed to Webster Jan. 30, 1882.

SUNFLOWER

200 Main St., Box 988, Indianola, MS 38751, (662) 887-4703, **<msgen.net/co/sunflower/index.html>**

- **INCORPORATED:** Feb. 15, 1844
- **PARENT COUNTIES:** Bolivar, Washington
- **MARRIAGE RECORDS:** start in 1871, kept by Chancery Court
- **DIVORCE:** 1871, Chancery Court
- **LAND:** 1871, Chancery Court
- **PROBATE:** 1871, Chancery Court
- **COURT:** 1871, Chancery Court

TALLAHATCHIE

1 Court Sq., Box Drawer 350, Charleston, MS 38921, (662) 647-5551, **<www.rootsweb.ancestry.com/~mstallah>**

- **INCORPORATED:** Dec. 23, 1833
- **PARENT COUNTY:** Choctaw Cession, 1820
- **MARRIAGE RECORDS:** start in 1909, kept by Circuit Court
- **DIVORCE:** 1909, Chancery Court
- **LAND:** 1858, Chancery Court
- **PROBATE:** 1909, Chancery Court

TATE

201 Ward St., Senatobia, MS 38668, (662) 647-5661, **<msghn.org>**

- **INCORPORATED:** April 15, 1873
- **PARENT COUNTIES:** Marshall, Tunica, DeSoto
- **MARRIAGE RECORDS:** start in 1873, kept by Circuit Court
- **DIVORCE:** 1873, Chancery Court
- **LAND:** 1873, Chancery Court
- **PROBATE:** 1873, Chancery Court
- **COURT:** 1873, Chancery Court

TIPPAH

Box 99, Ripley, MS 38663, (662) 837-7374, **<www.rootsweb.ancestry.com/~mstippah>**

- **INCORPORATED:** Feb. 9, 1836
- **PARENT COUNTY:** Chickasaw Cession, 1832
- **NOTES:** Courthouse burned in 1864. Clerk of Chancery Court or Clerk of Circuit Court has divorce, probate and court records from 1856 and marriage records from 1858.

TISHOMINGO

1008 Battleground Dr., Iuka, MS 38852, (662) 423-7010, **<tishomingo.org>**

- **INCORPORATED:** Feb. 9, 1836
- **PARENT COUNTY:** Chickasaw Cession, 1832
- **MARRIAGE RECORDS:** unknown start, kept by Circuit Court
- **DIVORCE:** unknown start, Chancery Court
- **LAND:** unknown start, Chancery Court
- **PROBATE:** unknown start, Chancery Court
- **COURT:** unknown start, Chancery Court

TUNICA

Box 217, Tunica, MS 38676, (662) 363-2451, **<tunicacounty.com>**

- **INCORPORATED:** Feb. 9, 1836
- **PARENT COUNTY:** Chickasaw Cession, 1832
- **MARRIAGE RECORDS:** unknown start, kept by Circuit Court
- **DIVORCE:** unknown start, Chancery Court
- **LAND:** unknown start, Chancery Court
- **PROBATE:** unknown start, Chancery Court
- **COURT:** unknown start, Chancery Court

UNION

109 Main St., Box 847, New Albany, MS 38652, (662) 534-1900, **<www.rootsweb.ancestry.com/~msunion>**

- **INCORPORATED:** Jul. 7, 1870
- **PARENT COUNTIES:** Pontotoc, Tippah
- **MARRIAGE RECORDS:** unknown start, kept by Circuit Court
- **DIVORCE:** unknown start, Chancery Court
- **PROBATE:** unknown start, Chancery Court
- **COURT:** unknown start, Chancery Court

WALTHALL

Box 351, Tylertown, MS 39667, (601) 876-3553, **<www.rootsweb.ancestry.com/~mswaltha/waltmain.html>**

- **INCORPORATED:** March 16, 1910

- **PARENT COUNTIES:** Marion, Pike
- **MARRIAGE RECORDS:** start in 1914, kept by Circuit Court
- **DIVORCE:** 1914, Chancery Court
- **LAND:** 1914, Chancery Court
- **PROBATE:** 1914, Chancery Court
- **COURT:** 1914, Chancery Court

WARREN
1009 Cherry St., Box 351, Vicksburg, MS 39181, (601) 636-4415, **<co.warren.ms.us>**
- **INCORPORATED:** Dec. 22, 1809
- **PARENT COUNTY:** Natchez District
- **MARRIAGE RECORDS:** unknown start, kept by Circuit Court
- **DIVORCE:** unknown start, Chancery Court
- **LAND:** unknown start, Chancery Court
- **PROBATE:** unknown start, Chancery Court
- **COURT:** unknown start Chancery Court

WASHINGTON
900 Washington Ave., Box 309, Greenville, MS 38702, (662) 332-1595, **<co.washington.ms.us>**
- **INCORPORATED:** Jan. 29, 1827
- **PARENT COUNTIES:** Warren, Yazoo
- **MARRIAGE RECORDS:** start in 1858, kept by Circuit Court
- **DIVORCE:** 1856, Chancery Court
- **LAND:** 1831, Chancery Court
- **PROBATE:** 1831, Chancery Court
- **COURT:** 1890, Circuit Court

WASHINGTON, OLD
- **INCORPORATED:** Jun. 4, 1800
- **PARENT COUNTY:** Unorganized Territory
- **NOTES:** Now in Alabama

WAYNE
609 Azalea Dr., Waynesboro, MS 39367, (601) 735-2873, **<wayne.msgen.info>**
- **INCORPORATED:** Dec. 21, 1809
- **PARENT COUNTY:** Washington, old
- **MARRIAGE RECORDS:** unknown start, kept by Chancery Court
- **DIVORCE:** unknown start, Chancery Court
- **LAND:** unknown start, Chancery Court
- **PROBATE:** unknown start, Chancery Court
- **COURT:** unknown start, Chancery Court
- **BURIAL:** unknown start, Chancery Court

WEBSTER
Hwy. 9 N., Box 398, Walthall, MS 39771, (662) 258-4131, **<www.rootsweb.ancestry.com/~mswebst1>**
- **INCORPORATED:** April 6, 1874
- **PARENT COUNTIES:** Montgomery, Chickasaw, Choctaw, Oktibbeha
- **MARRIAGE RECORDS:** unknown start, kept by Circuit Court
- **DIVORCE:** ca. 1800, Chancery Court
- **LAND:** ca. 1800, Chancery Court
- **PROBATE:** ca. 1800, Chancery Court
- **COURT:** unknown start, Circuit Court
- **NOTES:** Formerly Sumner County. Name changed to Webster Jan. 30, 1882.

WILKINSON
Box 516, Woodville, MS 39669, (601) 888-4381, **<msgen.net/co/wilkinson>**
- **INCORPORATED:** Jan. 30, 1802
- **PARENT COUNTY:** Adams
- **MARRIAGE RECORDS:** unknown start, kept by Chancery Court
- **DIVORCE:** unknown start, Chancery Court
- **LAND:** unknown start, Chancery Court
- **PROBATE:** unknown start, Chancery Court
- **COURT:** unknown start, Chancery Court

WINSTON
115 S. Court Ave., County Courthouse, Box Drawer 69, Louisville, MS 39339, (662) 773-3631, **<winstoncounty.com>**
- **INCORPORATED:** Dec. 23, 1833
- **PARENT COUNTY:** Choctaw Cession, 1830
- **MARRIAGE RECORDS:** unknown start, kept by Circuit Court
- **LAND:** 1834, Chancery Court
- **PROBATE:** 1834, Chancery Court
- **COURT:** 1834, Chancery Court

YALOBUSHA
Box 664, Water Valley, MS 38965, (662) 473-2091, **<msgen.net/co/yalobusha>**
- **INCORPORATED:** Dec. 23, 1833
- **PARENT COUNTY:** Choctaw Cession, 1830
- **MARRIAGE RECORDS:** unknown start, kept by Circuit Court in Coffeyville
- **DIVORCE:** unknown start, Chancery Court in Coffeyville
- **LAND:** unknown start, Chancery Court in Coffeyville
- **PROBATE:** unknown start, Chancery Court in Coffeyville
- **COURT:** unknown start Chancery Court in Coffeyville
- **DIVORCE:** unknown start, Chancery Court in Water Valley
- **LAND:** unknown start, Chancery Court in Water Valley
- **PROBATE:** unknown start, Chancery Court in Water Valley
- **COURT:** unknown start, Chancery Court in Water Valley
- **NOTES:** Note records are found in two areas.

YAZOO
332 N. Main St., Yazoo City, MS 39194, (601) 746-2213, **<yazoo.org>**
- **INCORPORATED:** Jan. 21, 1823
- **PARENT COUNTY:** Hinds
- **MARRIAGE RECORDS:** start in 1845, kept by Chancery Court
- **DIVORCE:** 1823, Chancery Court
- **LAND:** 1823, Chancery Court
- **PROBATE:** 1823, Chancery Court
- **COURT:** 1823, Chancery Court

MISSOURI

» BY JAMES W. WARREN

HISTORICAL OVERVIEW

It was the Gateway to the West—the jumping-off point for Lewis and Clark's expedition, the Santa Fe and Oregon trails and gold-hungry 49ers. Missouri was well-known as a stopping point en route to a final destination, but many adventurers made it their home. Whether your ancestors passed through or stayed, Missouri offers wonderful records and resources to help you find their stories.

The area was home to the Missouri, Osage, Delaware and Shawnee Indians long before Europeans ventured there. Early explorers were DeSoto in 1541, Marquette and Joliet in 1673, and Robert Cavelier, Sieur de la Salle, who claimed the Mississippi River Valley for France in 1682. French lead miners established the first permanent white settlement in 1735 at Ste. Genevieve. In 1763, France ceded the area to Spain. French fur traders founded St. Louis the following year, word of the cession to Spain not having reached them.

Settlement by Americans began as early as 1787 in Ste. Genevieve County. Spain offered free land, and after 1795, large numbers of Americans arrived from Kentucky, Tennessee, Virginia and the Carolinas. In 1800 Spain returned the area to France, and in 1803 the United States acquired the land as part of the Louisiana Purchase.

Missouri became part of Louisiana Territory in 1805. In 1812 Congress created Missouri Territory. Migration continued, but many left due to earthquakes, Indian raids and other problems. When Missouri became the 24th state in 1821, the population was approximately 57,000. Descendants of the early French and American settlers were joined by immigrants from Ireland, Switzerland, Italy, Poland, England, Switzerland and Czechoslovakia. In the 1840s large numbers of Germans continued to arrive, as did Irish fleeing the Potato Famine. Many of the new arrivals settled in Missouri's growing cities. During the rest of the century, Missouri's cities saw increasing immigration from Greece, Poland, Italy and Eastern Europe.

Missouri provided soldiers to both the Union and Confederacy during the Civil War, and many critical battles were fought in the state. A slave state, it never officially seceded but had separate governments representing each side.

research tips

- The Missouri State Archives in Jefferson City is the state's official repository for historical records. Many records are online at **<www.sos.mo.gov/mdh>**.
- The St. Louis Genealogical Society website **<www.stlgs.org>** provides details on its many resources and projects .
- The State Historical Society of Missouri has a major collection of Missouri newspapers, as well as indexes, maps and more **<www.umsystem.edu/shs>**.
- The Missouri Historical Society in St. Louis has holdings related to colonial, territorial, and state history **<www.mohistory.org/lrc-home>**. Search an index to many records on its website.
- The Mercantile Library at the University of Missouri—St. Louis specializes in Mississippi Valley history.

CENSUS RECORDS

- Federal censuses: 1830, 1840, 1850, 1860, 1870, 1880, 1900, 1910, 1920, 1930
- Federal mortality schedules: 1850, 1860, 1870, 1880
- Special census of Civil War Union veterans and widows: 1890
- State censuses: 1844, 1852, and 1856 (Callaway and Greene counties), 1876

RECORD HIGHLIGHTS

The first federal census available for the state of Missouri is the 1830. The 1890 census was destroyed, but the 1890 Union Veterans' Schedule survives. The 1850, 1860, 1870 and 1880 Mortality Schedules are also extant.

Statewide registration of births and deaths began in 1863, but it was not mandatory until 1910 (except for 1883-1893, when it was required, but repealed when no one was complying.) Pre-1910 records are available from the county clerk, while later records can be ordered from the Bureau of Vital Records in Jefferson City. In addition, the Missouri State Archives website has a birth and death records database of 185,000 pre-1910 birth and death records from 87 counties you can search (along with many other types of records) at **<www.sos.mo.gov/mdh/browse.asp?id=8>**.

Marriage records are kept by county clerks. Statewide registration of marriages began in 1881. The Bureau of Vital Records in Jefferson City has an index to marriages starting July 1, 1948, and issues certificates of proof of marriage. Copies of actual marriage licenses can be obtained from the county recorder of deeds or from microfilm at the Missouri State Archives. The Family History Library (FHL) has microfilm of marriage licenses from each Missouri county, often up to the 1920s. Divorce records are available from the circuit court clerk for each county, and the Bureau of Vital Records has copies of divorce records from 1948 to the present.

Two county-level courts exist today in Missouri: probate and county. (County courts usually have records for past county-level courts that went by other names: chancery, common-pleas and justice-of-the-peace.) At the district level is the circuit court; 45 judicial circuits cover Missouri's 114 counties. Missouri has had an excellent state archives microfilming program for many years. More than 55,000 rolls of microfilmed county-level records, circuit court civil case files and other significant collections are available for use at the State Archives. The microfilm is available for sale, and much of it is also available through the FHL. You can view the listing of filmed records for any county at the Archives website **<www.sos.mo.gov/archives/resources/county/croll.asp>**.

Naturalization records are generally held by the circuit courts; request them from the clerk's office at the courthouse. You can search an index at **<www.sos.mo.gov/archives/naturalization>**. Some county naturalization records are available through the FHL.

Land records are held by the recorder of deeds in each county. Pre-1900 deeds for almost all Missouri counties are available through the FHL. Probate records are generally maintained by the clerk of the probate court in each county. The FHL has films of probate records for many Missouri counties from the date the county was created to about 1925.

Many Missouri cemetery and church records have been abstracted, indexed or microfilmed, and many original records and church histories are available at archives, historical societies or from the church or cemetery association where they originated. Check the websites and catalogs of major repositories in Missouri, as well as the FHL catalog. For example, the FHL holds microfilmed parish registers of the Roman Catholic Archdiocese of St. Louis, and has alphabetized parish register transcripts from the Roman Catholic Archdiocese of Kansas City covering the years 1830 to 1900.

Newspapers are available at many large libraries, historical societies and colleges. The largest newspaper collection is at the State Historical Society of Missouri in Columbia.

ARCHIVES, LIBRARIES, AND SOCIETIES

Adair County Historical Society
211 S. Elson St., Kirksville, MO 63501, (660) 665-6502, **<www.adairchs.org>**

Afro-American Historical and Genealogical Society
3700 Blue Pkwy., Kansas City, MO 64130

Afro-American Historical and Genealogical Society, Landon Creek Chapter
Box 231804, St. Louis, MO 63121

Andrew County Historical Society
c/o Andrew County Museum, Box 12, Savannah, MO 64485, **<www.rootsweb.ancestry.com/~moandrew/and-society.html>**

Archdiocese of Saint Louis Archives
20 Archbishop May Drive, St. Louis, MO 63119, (314) 792-7020, **<archstl.org/archives>**

Audrain County Area Genealogical Society
c/o Mexico-Audrain County Library, 305 W. Jackson St., Mexico, MO 65265, **<members.socket.net/~macld/genealogy.htm>**

Audrain County Historical Society
501 S. Muldrow, Mexico, MO 65265, (573) 581-3910, **<www.audrain.org>**

Barry County Missouri Genealogical and Historical Society
Box 291, Cassville, MO 65625, **<www.rootsweb.ancestry.com/~mobarry/barrycogen/society.html>**

Boone County Historical Society
3801 Ponderosa St., Columbia, MO 65201, (573) 443-8936, **<boonehistory.org>**

Camden County Museum and Historical Society
Box 19, 204 Locust St., Linn Creek, MO 65052, (573) 346-7191

Cape Girardeau County Archive Center
112 East Washington, Jackson, MO 63755, (573) 204-2331, **<www.capecounty.us/ArchiveCenter/Archive%20Center.aspx>**

Cape Girardeau County Genealogical Society
Box 389, Jackson, MO 63755, **<www.rootsweb.ancestry.com/~mocgcgs>**

Carroll County Genealogical Association
Box 354, Carrollton, MO 64633, **<www.freepages.genealogy.rootsweb.ancestry.com/~pattiejo/carroll>**

Carthage Genealogical Society and Southwest Missouri Genealogical Library
Rt. 3, Box 117, Carthage, MO 64836, (417) 358-6494

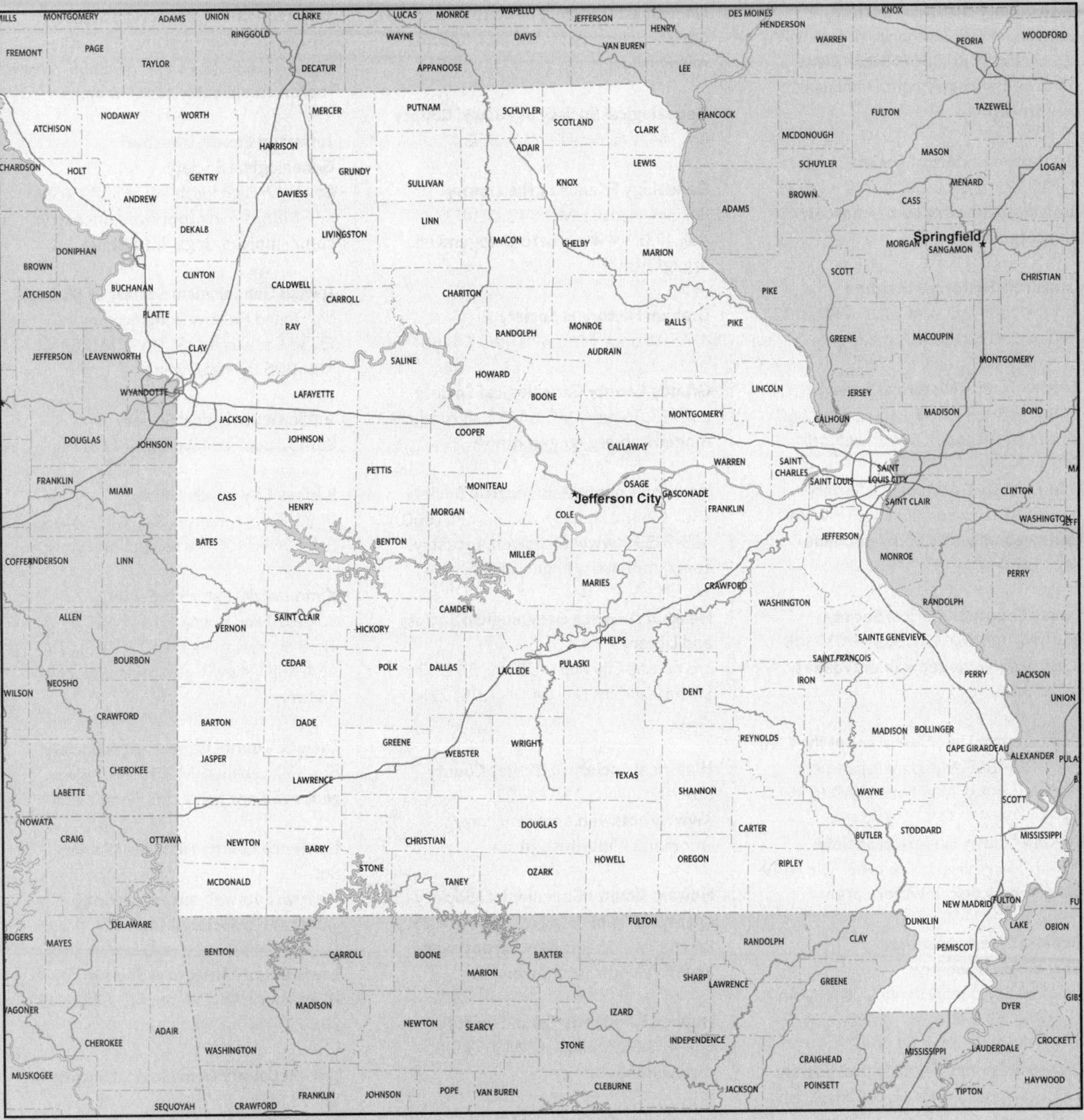
MONTGOMERY
ADAMS
UNION
CLARKE
LUCAS
MONROE
WAPELLO
JEFFERSON
HENRY
DES MOINES
HENDERSON
KNOX
RINGGOLD
WAYNE
DAVIS
VAN BUREN
WARREN
PEORIA
WOODFORD
FREMONT
PAGE
TAYLOR
DECATUR
APPANOOSE
LEE
NODAWAY
WORTH
MERCER
PUTNAM
SCHUYLER
SCOTLAND
CLARK
HANCOCK
FULTON
TAZEWELL
ATCHISON
HARRISON
ADAIR
MCDONOUGH
MASON
LEWIS
HOLT
GRUNDY
SULLIVAN
KNOX
SCHUYLER
LOGAN
GENTRY
DAVIESS
BROWN
MENARD
ANDREW
ADAMS
CASS
LINN
DEKALB
LIVINGSTON
MACON
SHELBY
Springfield
MORGAN
SANGAMON
DONIPHAN
MARION
BROWN
CLINTON
SCOTT
CHRISTIAN
BUCHANAN
CALDWELL
ATCHISON
CARROLL
CHARITON
PIKE
PLATTE
RAY
RANDOLPH
MONROE
RALLS
PIKE
GREENE
MACOUPIN
JEFFERSON
LEAVENWORTH
CLAY
AUDRAIN
MONTGOMERY
SALINE
HOWARD
WYANDOTTE
LAFAYETTE
BOONE
LINCOLN
JERSEY
MADISON
BOND
JACKSON
MONTGOMERY
CALHOUN
DOUGLAS
JOHNSON
JOHNSON
COOPER
CALLAWAY
WARREN
SAINT CHARLES
SAINT LOUIS CITY
SAINT LOUIS
PETTIS
FRANKLIN
MONITEAU
OSAGE
MIAMI
CASS
Jefferson City
GASCONADE
CLINTON
HENRY
MORGAN
COLE
FRANKLIN
SAINT CLAIR
WASHINGTON
BATES
BENTON
JEFFERSON
MILLER
MONROE
ANDERSON
LINN
MARIES
PERRY
CRAWFORD
CAMDEN
WASHINGTON
RANDOLPH
ALLEN
SAINT CLAIR
VERNON
HICKORY
PHELPS
SAINTE GENEVIEVE
BOURBON
CEDAR
POLK
DALLAS
LACLEDE
PULASKI
SAINT FRANCOIS
NEOSHO
IRON
PERRY
JACKSON
WILSON
DENT
UNION
CRAWFORD
BARTON
DADE
REYNOLDS
MADISON
BOLLINGER
GREENE
WEBSTER
WRIGHT
CAPE GIRARDEAU
ALEXANDER
CHEROKEE
JASPER
TEXAS
LAWRENCE
SHANNON
LABETTE
WAYNE
SCOTT
NOWATA
DOUGLAS
CARTER
CRAIG
OTTAWA
NEWTON
CHRISTIAN
BUTLER
STODDARD
MISSISSIPPI
BARRY
HOWELL
OREGON
RIPLEY
STONE
OZARK
MCDONALD
TANEY
NEW MADRID
FULTON
DELAWARE
FULTON
DUNKLIN
LAKE
OBION
ROGERS
MAYES
RANDOLPH
CLAY
BENTON
CARROLL
BOONE
BAXTER
PEMISCOT
MARION
SHARP
LAWRENCE
GREENE
MADISON
IZARD
DYER
NEWTON
SEARCY
CHEROKEE
ADAIR
INDEPENDENCE
STONE
MISSISSIPPI
LAUDERDALE
CROCKETT
WASHINGTON
CRAIGHEAD
MUSKOGEE
HAYWOOD
CLEBURNE
JACKSON
POINSETT
FRANKLIN
JOHNSON
POPE
VAN BUREN
TIPTON
SEQUOYAH
CRAWFORD

Cass County Historical Society
Box 406, 400 E. Mechanic, Harrisonville, MO 64701, (816) 380-4396, **<www.rootsweb.ancestry.com/~mocass/cashist.html>**

Commerce Historical Society
Box 93, Commerce, MO 63742, **<www.rootsweb.ancestry.com/~moscott/moscotgn.htm>**

Concordia Historical Institute
801 DeMun Ave., Saint Louis, MO 63105, (314) 505-7900, **<chi.lcms.org>**

Cooper County Historical Society
111 Roe St., Pilot Grove, MO 65276, (660) 834-3582, **<cooper.mogenweb.org>**

Dade County Genealogical Society
Box 155, Greenfield, MO 65661, **<www.rootsweb.ancestry.com/~modade/dcgs.htm>**

Dallas County Historical Society
Box 594, Buffalo, MO 65622, (417) 345-8694, **<www.mogenweb.org/dallas/DCHS.html>**

Daughters of Union Veterans of the Civil
War, 1861-1865, Missouri Department
2615 Porter Ave., Brentwood, MO 63144

DeKalb County Historical Society
Box 467, Maysville, MO 64469, (816) 449-5451, **<www.dekalbhistory.org>**

Dunklin County Missouri Genealogical Society
c/o Dunklin County Library, 209 N. Main, Kennett, MO 63857, (573) 888-3561

Excelsior Springs Genealogical Society
1000 Magnolia W., Excelsior Springs, MO 64024

Family Tree Climbers
Box 422, Lawson, MO 64062

Four Rivers Genealogy Society
Box 146, Washington, MO 63090, **<washmohistorical.org/Four_Rivers_Genealogical_Society.htm>**

Genealogical Society of Butler County
Box 426, Poplar Bluff, MO 63902, **<www.rootsweb.ancestry.com/~mobcgs>**

Genealogical Society of Central Missouri
Box 26, Columbia, MO 65205, **<gscm.missouri.org>**

Genealogical Society of Pulaski County
Box 144, Waynesville, MO 65583

Genealogy Friends of the Library
Box 314, Neosho, MO 64850, (417) 451-4231, **<www.newton.mogenweb.org/gf.html>**

Graham Historical Society
417 S. Walnut, Marysville, MO 64468

Grundy County Genealogical Society
Box 223, Trenton, MO 64683, **<grundy.mogenweb.org/gcgen.html>**

Harrison County Genealogical Society
2307 Central Bethany, MO 64424, (660) 425-2459, **<www.rootsweb.ancestry.com/~moharris/hcgen.html>**

Heart of America Genealogical Society and Library
c/o Kansas City Public Library, 311 E. 12th St., Kansas City, MO 64106, (816) 221-2685

Historical Society of Maries County
Box 289, Vienna, MO 65582, **<www.rootsweb.ancestry.com/~momaries/marihiso.htm>**

Howard County Genealogical Society
c/o Fayette Public Library, 201 S. Main St., Fayette, MO 65248, **<www.rootsweb.ancestry.com/~mohoward>**

Hubbell Family Historical Society
Box 3813 GS, Springfield, MO 65808, **<www.hubbell.org>**

Iron County Genealogical Society
Box 343, Arcadia, MO 63621, **<www.rootsweb.ancestry.com/~moicgs/icgs_home.html>**

Jackson County Genealogical Society
420 S. Main St., Box 1133, Independence, MO 64055

Jackson County Historical Society
129 W. Lexington, Independence, MO 64050, (816) 461-1897, **<www.jchs.org>**

Jefferson County Historical Society
c/o De Soto Public Library, 712 S. Main, De Soto, MO 63020, (636) 586-3858, **<www.rootsweb.ancestry.com/~mojchs>**

Jefferson County Missouri Genealogical Society
Box 1342, High Ridge, MO 63049, (636) 677-8186, **<www.rootsweb.ancestry.com/~mojcgs/Jcgs_Info.html>**

Jewish Genealogical Society of St. Louis
c/o United Hebrew Congregation, 13788 Conway Rd., St. Louis, MO 63141, **<mo005.urj.net/jgsstl>**

Joplin Genealogical Society
Box 152, Joplin, MO 64801

Kansas City Public Library
14 W. 10th St., Kansas City, MO 64105, (816) 701-3400, **<www.kclibrary.org>**

Kimmswick Historical Society
Burgess-How House, Box 41, 6000 Third St., Kimmswick, MO 63053, (314) 464-8687, **<www.gokimmswick.com/history>**

Laclede County Genealogical Society
Box 350, Lebanon, MO 65536, **<www.rootsweb.ancestry.com/~molacled>**

Lawrence County Historical Society
Box 406, Mt. Vernon, MO 65712, **<www.rootsweb.ancestry.com/~molawre2/society.htm>**

Lewis County Historical Society
112 N. Fourth St., Canton, MO 63435, (573) 288-5713

Lincoln County Genealogical Society
125 W. Second, St., Moscow Mills, MO 63362, **<lincoln.mogenweb.org/research/lcsociety.htm>**

Genealogical Researchers of Linn County
771 Tomahawk, Brookfield, MO 64628

Livingston County Genealogical Society
c/o Livingston County Library, 450 Locust St., Chillicothe, MO 64601, (816) 646-0547, **<www.livingstoncountylibrary.org/history.htm>**

Mercer County Genealogical and Historical Society
Box 97, Princeton, MO 64673, **<www.rootsweb.ancestry.com/~momercer/mcghs.html>**

Mid-Continent Public Library
15616 E. 24 Hwy., Independence, MO 64050, (816) 836-5200, **<www.mcpl.lib.mo.us>**

Mid-Missouri Genealogical Society
Box 387, Jefferson City, MO 65101

Midwest Genealogy Center
3440 S. Lee's Summit Road, Independence, MO 64055, (816) 252-7228, **<www.mcpl.lib.mo.us/genlh/mgc.htm>**

Mine Au Breton Historical Society
10205 Weber Lane, Potosi, MO 63664, **<www.mogenweb.org/washington/mabhs.html>**

Mississippi County Genealogical Society
Box 5, Charleston, MO 63834

Missouri Baptist Historical Commission
William E. Partee Center, William Jewel College, 500 College Hill, Liberty, MO 64068, (816) 781-7700

Missouri Bureau of Vital Records
930 Wildwood, Box 570, Jefferson City, MO 65102, (314) 613-3016, **<www.dhss.mo.gov/BirthAndDeathRecords>**

Missouri Historical Society
Box 11940, St. Louis, MO 63112, (314) 746-4511, **<www.mohistory.org>**

Missouri State Archives
600 W. Main St., Box 1747, Jefferson City, MO 65102, (573) 751-3280, **<www.sos.mo.gov/archives>**

Missouri State Genealogical Association
Box 833 Columbia, MO 65205, **<mosga.org>**

Missouri Territorial Pioneers
3929 Milton Dr., Independence, MO 64055, **<kinnexions.com/ancestries/pioneer/mo.htm>**

Missouri United Methodist Archives
Central Methodist University, 411 Central Methodist Sq., Fayette, MO 65248, **<www.centralmethodist.edu/cmlibrary/archive.html>**

Moniteau County Historical Society
201 N. High, California, MO 65018, (573) 796-3563

Montgomery County Genealogical Society
112 W. Second St., Montgomery City, MO 63361

Morgan County Historical Society
Box 181, Versailles, MO 65084

National Archives and Records Administration, Central Plains Region, Kansas City
400 W. Pershing Rd., Kansas City, MO 64108, (816) 268-8000, **<archives.gov/central-plains/kansas-city>**

Newton County Historical Society/ Genealogical Study Group
Box 675, Neosho, MO 64850

Nodaway County Genealogical Society
Box 214, Maryville, MO 64468, **<www.mogenweb.org/nodaway/histsocity/ncgs.htm>**

Northland Genealogical Society
Box 14121, Parkville, MO 64152, **<homepages.rootsweb.ancestry.com/~kcngs>**

Northwest Missouri Genealogical Society
Box 382, St. Joseph, MO 64502, (816) 233-0524, **<www.rootsweb.ancestry.com/~monwmgs>**

Office of the Adjutant General
2302 Militia Dr., Jefferson City, MO 65101

Old Mines Area Historical Society
Rt. 1, Box 1466, Old Mines, MO 63630, **<www.rootsweb.ancestry.com/~moomahs>**

Oregon County Genealogical Society
c/o Courthouse, Box 324, Alton, MO 65606, (417) 778-6414, **<www.rootsweb.ancestry.com/~mooregon/ocgs.htm>**

Osage County Historical Society
Box 402, Linn, MO 65051, **<www.rootsweb.ancestry.com/~moosage/vosage.htm>**

Ozark County Genealogical and Historical Society
HCR 2, Box 88, Gainsville, MO 65655

Ozarks Genealogical Society
Box 3945, Springfield, MO 65808, **<ozarksgs.org>**

Perry County Historical Society
Box 97, Perryville, MO 63775, **<www.perrycountyhistoricalsociety.org>**

Phelps County Genealogical Society
Box 571, Rolla, MO 65402, **<www.rollanet.org/~pcgs>**

Phelps County Historical Society
Box 1861, Rolla, MO 65402, (573) 364-5977, **<web.mst.edu/~whmcinfo/pchs>**

Pike County Historical Society
304 W. Georgia St., Louisiana, MO 63353

Pike County Genealogical Society
Box 313, Bowling Green, MO 63334, **<pcgenweb.com/pcgs/index.html>**

Platte County Historical and Genealogical Society
Box 103, Platte City, MO 64079, **<www.rootsweb.ancestry.com/~mopchgs>**

Polk County Genealogical Society
Box 632, Bolivar, MO 65613, (417) 777-2820, **<www.rootsweb.ancestry.com/~mopolkgs>**

Randolph County Historical Society
223 N. Clark, Moberly, MO 65270, (660) 263-9396, **<www.randolphhistory.com>**

Ray County Genealogical Association
901 W. Royle St., Richmond, MO 64085, **<www.rootsweb.ancestry.com/~morcga>**

Ray County Historical Society
Box 2, Richmond, MO 64085, (816) 776-2305

Reynolds County Genealogy and Historical Society
Box 281, Ellington, MO 63638, (573) 663-7289

Ripley County Historical Society
101 Washington St., Doniphan, MO 63935, (573) 996-5298

Scotland County Historical Society
Box 263, Memphis, MO 63555, **<www.rootsweb.ancestry.com/~moscotla>**

Scott County Historical and Genealogy Society
Box 151, Benton, MO 63736, **<www.scottcountygenealogy.org>**

South Vernon Genealogical Society
Rt. 2, Box 280, Sheldon, MO 64784

South Central Missouri Genealogical Society
1043 W. Fifth St., West Plains, MO 65775

St. Charles County Genealogical Society
Box 715, St. Charles, MO 63302, **<www.rootsweb.ancestry.com/~mosccgs>**

St. Louis Genealogical Society
Box 43010, St. Louis MO 63143, (314) 647-8547, **<www.stlgs.org>**

St. Louis Public Library
1301 Olive St., St. Louis, MO 63103, (314) 241-2288, **<slpl.org>**

State Historical Society of Missouri
1020 Lowry St., Columbia, MO 65201, (573) 882-7083, **<shs.umsystem.edu>**

Stone County Missouri Historical and Genealogical Society
Box 63, Galena, MO 65656, **<www.rootsweb.ancestry.com/~mostone/society/society.html>**

Texas County Genealogical and Historical Society
Box 12, 300 S. Grand Ave., Houston, MO 65483, (417) 967-3126

Thrailkill Genealogical Society
2018 Gentry, North Kansas City, MO 64116

Tri-County Genealogical Society
Box B, 218 W. Walnut St., Nevada, MO 64772

Union Cemetery Historical Society
227 E. 28th Terrace, Kansas City, MO 64108, (816) 472-4990

United Centenary Methodist Church
55 Plaza Sq., Saint Louis, MO 63103, (314) 588-1450

Vernon County Historical Society
231 N. Main St., Nevada, MO 64772, **<www.bushwhacker.org>**

Warren County Historical Society
Box 12, Warrenton, MO 63383

Webb City Area Genealogical Society
101 S. Liberty St., Webb City, MO 64870, (417) 673-4326

West Central Missouri Genealogical Society
Box 4, Warrensburg, MO, 64093, **<www.rootsweb.ancestry.com/~mojohnso/library/Society.htm>**

Westport Historical Society
4000 Baltimore, Kansas City, MO, 64111, (816) 561-1821, **<www.westporthistory.org>**

White River Valley Historical Society
Box 555, Pt. Lookout, MO 65726, **<www.wrvhs.org>**

Wright County Historical and Genealogical Society
Box 66, Hartville MO 65667

☞ GENERAL RESOURCES

Bible Records of Missouri by Elizabeth B. Langley (Langley, 1968)

A Bibliography of Missouri County Histories and Atlases by Paul O. Selby (Northeast Missouri State Teachers College, 1966)

Bibliography of the Ozarks Books (filmed by the Family History Library, 1977)

The Book of Missourians by M.L. Van Nada (filmed by the Library of Congress Photoduplication Service, 1989)

Campbell's Gazetteer of Missouri by Robert Allen Campbell (filmed by the Genealogical Society of Utah, 1972)

A Centennial History of the State Historical Society of Missouri, 1898-1998 by Alan R. Havig (University of Missouri Press, ca. 1998)

1806-1906, The Centennial Volume of Missouri Methodism, Methodist Episcopal Church, South by Marcus L. Gray (filmed by the Genealogical Society of Utah, 1988)

Directory of Local Historical, Museum, and Genealogical Agencies in Missouri (State Historical Society of Missouri, ca. 1993)

Early Missourians and Kin by Roy Burgess (R. Burgess, ca. 1984-ca. 1987)

Encyclopedia of the History of Missouri by Howard Louis Conard (Southern History Co., 1901)

Genealogical Material and Local Histories in the St. Louis Public Library (St. Louis Public Library, 1953)

A Guide to County Records on Microfilm (Missouri State Archives, 1990)

A Guide to Genealogical Research in St. Louis by Edward E. Steele (St. Louis Genealogical Society, 1995)

Guide to Public Vital Statistics Records in Missouri by the Historical Records Survey (Historical Records Survey, 1941)

Historical and Biographical Sketches of the Early Churches and Pioneer Preachers of the Christian Church in Missouri by T.P. Haley (J.H. Smart, ca. 1888)

Historic Missouri, A Pictorial Narrative of Our State (State Historical Society, ca. 1959)

A History of the Baptists in Missouri by R.S. Duncan (Scammell, 1882)

A History of Missouri from the Earliest Explorations and Settlements until the Admission of the State into the Union by Louis Houck (R.R. Donnelley, ca. 1908)

A History of the Pioneer Families of Missouri by William S. Bryan (Bryan Brand, 1876)

History of Southeast Missouri (filmed by the Genealogical Society of Utah, 1973)

History of the United Methodist Churches of Missouri by Richard A. Seaton (Missouri Methodist Historical Society, 1984)

An Illustrated History of Missouri by Walter Bickford Davis (filmed by the Genealogical Society of Utah, 1976)

A List of Manuscript Collections in the Archives of the Missouri Historical Society by Beverly D. Biship (Missouri Historical Society, ca. 1982)

The Methodist Church in Missouri: 1798-1939, A Brief History by Frank C. Tucker (F.C. Tucker, ca. 1966)

Midwest Pioneers, 1600s-1800s (Broderbund, ca. 1999. CD-ROM)

Missouri, The Center State, 1821-1915 by Walter B. Stevens (filmed by the Library of Congress Photoduplication Service, 1990)

Missouri Family Histories and Genealogies: A Bibliography by Donald M. Hehir (Heritage Books, ca. 1996)

Missouri, A History of the Crossroads State by Edwin C. McReynolds (University of Oklahoma Press, ca. 1962)

Missouri, Mother of the West by Walter Williams (American Historical Society, 1930)

Missouri Pioneers, County and Genealogical Records compiled by Nadine Hodges et al. (N. Hodges, 1967-1976)

Missouri Research Outline by the Church of Jesus Christ of Latter-day Saints (online at **<www.familysearch.org/eng/search/RG/guide/missouri.asp>**)

Officers License and Related Records, 1905-1942 by the US Bureau of Marine Inspection and Navigation, Missouri (filmed by the Family History Library, 1991)

Opening the Ozarks 1835-1839: First Families in Southwest Missouri by Marsha Hoffman Rising (American Society of Genealogists, 2005)

The Organization of Missouri Counties by the Historical Records Survey (Historical Records Survey, 1941)

Orphan Trains to Missouri by Michael D. Patrick (University of Missouri Press, ca. 1997)

Parish Register Transcripts, ca. 1830-1900 by the Catholic Church Archdiocese of Kansas City and St. Joseph (filmed by the Genealogical Society of Utah)

People of Color: Black Genealogical Records and Abstracts from Missouri Sources by Teresa Blattner (Heritage Books, ca. 1993, ca. 1998)

Pioneer Kentuckians with Missouri Cousins by Linda Barber Brooks (Ingmire Publications, ca. 1985)

The Refiner's Fire: The Significance of Events Transpiring in Missouri by Alvin R. Dyer (Deseret Book, 1968)

A Reminiscent History of the Ozark Region (Southern Historical Press, 1978)

Robert E. Parkin's Guide to Tracing Your Family Tree in Missouri by Robert E. Parkin (Genealogical Research and Productions, ca. 1979)

Southeast Missouri by Robert Sidney Douglass (Lewis Publishing Co., 1912)
The Spanish Regime in Missouri by Louis Houck (filmed by the Library of Congress Photoduplication Service, 1990)

The Trail of Tears Across Missouri by Joan Gilbert (University of Missouri Press, ca. 1996)

Zion's Camp 1834: Prelude to the Civil War by James L. Bradley (J.L. Bradley, ca. 1990)

Who's What and Why in Missouri by the Jefferson City, Mo., Chamber of Commerce (Historical Record Association, 1959)

☞ CENSUS RECORDS

Anglo-Americans in Spanish Archives by Lawrence H. Feldman (Genealogical Publishing Co., ca. 1991)

Internal Revenue Assessment Lists for the State of Missouri, 1862-1866 by the US Bureau of Internal Revenue (National Archives, 1984)

Missouri Taxpayers, 1819-1826 by Lois Stanley (Southern Historical Press, ca. 1990)

Ten Thousand Missouri Taxpayers by Sherida K. Eddlemon (Heritage Books, ca. 1996)

☞ IMMIGRATION RECORDS

Declarations of Intention, ca. 1849-1985 by the US Circuit Court (filmed by the Family History Library, 1991)

German Settlement in Missouri: New Land, Old Ways by Robyn Burnett (University of Missouri Press, ca. 1996)

Immigrants in the Ozarks: A Study in Ethnic Geography by Russel L. Gerlach (University of Missouri Press, ca. 1976)

Naturalization Petitions, Depositions, Certificate Stubs, and Miscellaneous Papers, 1907-1937 by the US Circuit Court (filmed by the Genealogical Society of Utah, 1991)

Pioneer Kentuckians with Missouri Cousins by Linda Barber Brooks (Ingmire Publications, ca. 1985)

Settlement Patterns in Missouri, A Study of Population Origins, with a Wall Map by Russel L. Gerlach (University of Missouri Press, ca. 1986)

Virginia Settlers in Missouri by A. Maxim Coppage (Cook & McDowell Publishing, 1979)

The Westfalians: from Germany to Missouri by Walter D. Kamphoefner (Princeton University Press, ca. 1987)

☞LAND RECORDS

Citizens of Missouri by Frances Terry Ingmire (F. T. Ingmire, ca. 1984)

Early Settlers of Missouri as Taken from Land Claims in the Missouri Territory by Walter Lowrie (Southern Historical Press, 1986)

First Settlers of the Missouri Territory (Ericson Books, ca. 1983)

Land Patents, 1800s-early 1900s by the Missouri Governor (State of Missouri, 1971)

Land Proceedings, 1824-1884 by the US District Court (filmed by the Family History Library, 1991)

Miscellaneous Records Relating to Missouri Lands, 1700s, 1800s, 1900s by the Missouri State Archives (State of Missouri, 1969-1972)

Missouri Land Claims (Polyanthos, Inc., 1976)

Missouri Land Plats, 1800s by the United States General Land Office (State of Missouri, 1969)

Missouri Military Land Warrants, War of 1812 by Maxine Dunaway (M. Dunaway, ca. 1985)

Missouri Plat Books in the State Historical Society of Missouri by Laurel Boeckman (State Historical Society of Missouri, 1989)

Record Books, 1795-1808; Index to French and Spanish Land Grants, 1795-1812 by the Louisiana Territory Recorder of Land Titles (State of Missouri, 1970)

Records of Missouri Swamp Lands: Original Selections, New Selections, and Sales, 1800s by the US General Land Office (State of Missouri, 1969)

Tax Deeds, 1847-1878 by the Missouri Register of Lands (State of Missouri, 1970)

United States Land Sales in Missouri, 1827-1903; Index to Land Sales, 1818-1893 by the US General Land Office (State of Missouri, 1969)

War of 1812, Military Bounty Land Warrants, 1815-1858 by the US Veterans Administration (National Archives, 1971)

☞MAPS

A Bibliography of Missouri County Histories and Atlases by Paul O. Selby (Northeast Missouri State Teachers College, 1966)

Campbell's Gazetteer of Missouri by Robert Allen Campbell (filmed by the Genealogical Society of Utah, 1972)

Campbell's New Atlas of Missouri with Descriptions Historical, Scientific and Statistical by Robert Allen Campbell (filmed by the Genealogical Society of Utah, 1976)

A Gazetteer of the States of Illinois and Missouri by Lewis Caleb Beck (Arno Press, Inc., 1975)

Gazetteer of the State of Missouri by Alphonso Wetmore (Arno Press, Inc., 1975)

Historical Atlas of Missouri by Milton D. Rafferty (University of Oklahoma Press, ca. 1982)

Interesting Missouri Place Names by Gerald Leonard Cohen (G. Cohen, ca. 1982)

Missouri Atlas and Gazetteer by the DeLorme Mapping Company (DeLorme Mapping Co., ca. 1998)

Our Storehouse of Missouri Place Names by Robert Lee Ramsay (University of Missouri, 1952)

☞MILITARY RECORDS

Confederate Pension Applications and Soldiers' Home Admission Applications by the Missouri Adjutant General's Office (filmed by the Genealogical Society of Utah, 1977)

The Forgotten Men: Missouri State Guards by Carolyn M. Bartels (Two Trails Publishing, ca. 1995)

Grand Army of the Republic, Missouri Division, Index to Death Rolls 1882-1940 by Marie Concannon (State Historical Society of Missouri, 1995)

Index to Compiled Service Records of Volunteer Union Soldiers who Served in Organizations from the State of Missouri by the US Adjutant General's Office (National Archives, 1962)

Index of Residents State Federal Soldiers' Home of Missouri, St. James, Missouri, 1899-1946 by Marie C. Concannon (State Historical Society of Missouri, 1998)

Military Records, 1812-1904 by the Missouri Adjutant General's Office (filmed by the Family History Library, 1977-1978)

Military Records, 1861-1866 by the Missouri Adjutant General's Office (filmed by the Family History Library, 1977)

Military Records, Spanish-American War, 1897-1898 by the Missouri Adjutant General's Office (filmed by the Family History Library, 1977)

Missouri Confederate Pensions and Confederate Home Applications Index by Peggy Barnes Fox (Hill College Press, ca. 1996)

Missouri, World War I Selective Service System Draft Registration Cards, 1917-1918 by the US Selective Service System (National Archives, 1987-1988)

The 24th Missouri Volunteer Infantry "Lyon's Legion" by J. Randall Houp (J.R. Houp, ca. 1997)

Revolutionary Soldiers Buried in Missouri by Alice Kinyoun Houts (Houts, ca. 1966)

☞PROBATE RECORDS

A Digest of all the Decisions of the Supreme Court of the State of Missouri, Contained in the First 15 Volumes of the Missouri Reports by Evans Casselberry (Fisher & Bennett, 1853)

French and Spanish Archives, 1766-1816 by the St. Louis, Missouri Archival Library (City of St. Louis, 1962)

Gentry County, Missouri Probate Index, 1885-1902 (Northwest Missouri Genealogy Society, ca. 1980)

☞VITAL RECORDS

Cemetery Records in Missouri (filmed by the Family History Library, 1958)

Death Records from Missouri Newspapers: the Civil War Years, January 1861-December 1865 by Lois Stanley (Anundsen, 1983)

Death Records from Missouri Newspapers: January 1854-December 1860 by Lois Stanley (Anundsen, 1982)

Death Records of Pioneer Missouri Women, 1808-1853 by Lois Stanley (Southern Historical Press, ca. 1990)

Divorces, Separations and Annulments in Missouri 1769 to 1850 by Teresa Blattner (Heritage Books, ca. 1993)

Divorces and Separations in Missouri: 1808-1853 by Lois Stanley (Southern Historical Press, ca. 1990)

Early Bibles and Graveyard Records by Kathryn H. Campbell (1972)

Early Missouri Ancestors: From Newspapers by George F. Wilson (The Anundsen Publishing Co., 1986-1987)

East Central Missouri Cemetery and Bible Records by the Daughters of the American Revolution, John Sappington Chapter (1974)

Guide to Public Vital Statistics Records in Missouri by the Historical Records Survey (Historical Records Survey, 1941)

Master List of Missouri Civil War Veteran Burials by Sherman Lee Pompey (filmed by the Genealogical Society of Utah, 1967)

1300 "Missing" Missouri Marriage Records from Newspapers, 1812-1853 by George F. Wilson (Anundsen, 1982)

Missouri, 1851-1900 by the Liahona Research, Orem, Utah (Broderbund, ca. 1998. CD-ROM)

Missouri Birth and Death Records by Sherida K. Eddlemon (Heritage Books, ca. 1995, ca. 1999, ca.2001)

Missouri Cemetery Inscriptions Sources; Print and Microform by Elizabeth Gorrell Kot (Indices Publishing, ca. 1995)

Missouri Cemetery Records (filmed by the Family History Library, 1977)

Missouri Marriages to 1850 by Linda Barber Brooks (Distributed by Ingmire Publications, ca. 1983)

Missouri Marriages Before 1840 by Susan Ormesher (Genealogical Publishing Co., ca. 1982)

Missouri Marriages, Early (ca. 1754) to 1825: A Research Tool by Jordon R. Dodd (Precision Indexing, ca. 1990)

Missouri Taxpayers, 1819-1826 by Lois Stanley (Southern Historical Press, ca. 1990)

More Death Records from Missouri Newspapers, 1810-1857 by Lois Stanley (Anundsen, 1985)

Selected Union Burials, Missouri Units by Edward Parker (The State Historical Society of Missouri, 1988, 1993)

•-COUNTY DETAILS-•

ADAIR

Box 690, Kirksville, MO 63501, (660) 665-2552, **<www.rootsweb.ancestry.com/~moadair>**

- **INCORPORATED:** Jan. 29, 1841
- **PARENT COUNTY:** Macon
- **MARRIAGE RECORDS:** start in 1841, kept by County Recorder
- **DIVORCE:** unknown start, Circuit Court
- **LAND:** 1841, County Recorder
- **PROBATE:** 1841, Probate Clerk
- **COURT:** 1841, County Clerk
- **SCHOOL ENUMERATION:** unknown start, County Clerk
- **NOTES:** County Clerk has birth records 1883-1893.

ALLEN

- **INCORPORATED:** Feb. 23, 1843
- **PARENT COUNTY:** Holt
- **NOTES:** See Atchison County. Name changed to Atchison Feb. 14, 1845.

ANDREW

Box 208, Savannah, MO 64485, (816) 324-4221, **<andrewcounty.org>**

- **INCORPORATED:** Jan. 29, 1841
- **PARENT COUNTY:** Platte Purchase
- **MARRIAGE RECORDS:** start in 1841, kept in County Recorder
- **DIVORCE:** 1841, Circuit Court
- **LAND:** 1841, County Recorder
- **PROBATE:** 1841, Probate Clerk
- **COURT:** 1841, Circuit Court
- **MILITARY:** unknown start, Circuit Court
- **NOTES:** County Clerk has birth records 1883-1895, and death records 1883-1893.

ARKANSAS

- **INCORPORATED:** 1813
- **PARENT COUNTY:** New Madrid
- **NOTES:** Abolished 1819 when Territory of Arkansas was formed.

ASHLEY
- **INCORPORATED:** Feb. 17, 1843
- **PARENT COUNTIES:** Shannon, Wright
- **NOTES:** See Texas county. Name changed to Texas Feb. 14, 1845.

ATCHISON
Box 280, Rock Port, MO 64482, (660) 744-2707,
<atchisoncounty.org>
- **INCORPORATED:** Feb. 23, 1845
- **PARENT COUNTIES:** Holt, Platte Purchase
- **MARRIAGE RECORDS:** start in 1845, kept by County Recorder
- **DIVORCE:** unknown start, Circuit Court
- **LAND:** 1845, County Recorder
- **PROBATE:** 1845, Probate Clerk
- **COURT:** 1845, County Clerk
- **NOTES:** Formerly Allen County. Name changed to Atchison Feb. 14, 1845; part of Platte Purchase; attached to Holt County until 1854; lost 10-mile strip to Iowa in 1848. County Clerk has birth and death records 1883-1893.

AUDRAIN
101 N. Jefferson, Mexico, MO 65265, (573) 473-5840,
<audraincounty.org>
- **INCORPORATED:** Jan. 12, 1831
- **PARENT COUNTY:** Ralls
- **MARRIAGE RECORDS:** start in 1837, kept by County Recorder
- **DIVORCE:** unknown start, Circuit Court
- **LAND:** 1837, County Recorder
- **PROBATE:** 1837, Probate Clerk
- **COURT:** 1837, County Clerk
- **NOTES:** Created in 1831, but remained attached to Callaway, Monroe and Ralls counties until 1836. In 1842 gained an additional 31 square miles from Monroe County. County Clerk has birth and death records 1883-1886.

BARRY
102 West St. #1, Cassville, MO 65625, (417) 847-2361, **<www.rootsweb.ancestry.com/~mobarry/barry.htm>**
- **INCORPORATED:** Jan. 5, 1835
- **PARENT COUNTY:** Greene
- **MARRIAGE RECORDS:** start in 1837, kept by County Recorder
- **DIVORCE:** unknown start, Circuit Court
- **LAND:** 1835, County Recorder
- **PROBATE:** 1835, Probate Clerk
- **COURT:** 1872, County Clerk
- **NOTES:** Fire in 1872 destroyed many records in Circuit Clerk's office. County Clerk has birth and death records 1883-1885.

BARTON
1007 Broadway, Lamar, MO 64759, (417) 682-2444,
<bartoncounty.com>
- **INCORPORATED:** Dec. 12, 1855
- **PARENT COUNTY:** Jasper
- **MARRIAGE RECORDS:** start in 1866, kept by County Recorder
- **DIVORCE:** unknown start, Circuit Court
- **LAND:** 1857, County Recorder
- **PROBATE:** 1866, Probate Clerk
- **COURT:** 1866, County Clerk
- **NOTES:** Courthouse burned in 1860. County Clerk has birth records 1883-1896, and death records 1883-1899.

BATES
1 N. Delaware, Butler, MO 64730, (660) 679-5171,
<batescounty.net>
- **INCORPORATED:** Jan. 29, 1841
- **PARENT COUNTY:** Cass
- **MARRIAGE RECORDS:** start in 1860, kept by County Recorder
- **DIVORCE:** 1860, Circuit Court
- **LAND:** 1839, County Recorder
- **PROBATE:** 1845, Probate Clerk
- **COURT:** 1858, County Clerk
- **NOTES:** Feb. 22, 1855, the three southern tiers of townships in Cass County were added to Bates. Courthouse burned in 1861. County Clerk has birth records 1883-1907, and death records 1883-1893.

BENTON
Box 37, Warsaw, MO 65355, (660) 428-2900,
<bentoncomo.com>
- **INCORPORATED:** Jan. 3, 1835
- **PARENT COUNTY:** Pettis/Greene
- **MARRIAGE RECORDS:** start in 1839, kept by County Recorder
- **DIVORCE:** unknown start, Circuit Court
- **LAND:** 1837, County Recorder
- **PROBATE:** 1836, Probate Clerk
- **COURT:** 1835, County Clerk
- **NOTES:** Benton remained unorganized until Jan. 1837; in 1845, 24 sq. miles of northwest part of Benton became part of Pettis County and Hickory County was created, reducing Benton to its present size. County Clerk has birth and death records 1883-1890.

BOLLINGER
Box 949, Marble Hill, MO 63764, (573) 238-1900, **<www.rootsweb.ancestry.com/~mobollin/bcgenweb.htm>**
- **INCORPORATED:** March 1, 1851
- **PARENT COUNTIES:** Cape Girardeau, Stoddard, Wayne/Madison
- **MARRIAGE RECORDS:** start in 1865, kept by County Recorder
- **DIVORCE:** unknown start, Circuit Court
- **LAND:** 1851, County Recorder
- **PROBATE:** 1866, Probate Clerk
- **COURT:** 1866, County Clerk
- **NOTES:** Courthouse burned in 1866; courthouse burned in 1884 while occupied only by the County Clerk's office. County Clerk has birth records 1883-1891 and death records 1883-1892.

BOONE
705 E. Walnut St., Columbia, MO 65201, (573) 886-4000,
<www.showmeboone.com>
- **INCORPORATED:** Nov. 16, 1820
- **PARENT COUNTY:** Howard
- **MARRIAGE RECORDS:** start in 1821, kept by County Recorder
- **DIVORCE:** 1821, Circuit Court
- **LAND:** 1821, County Recorder
- **PROBATE:** 1821, Probate Clerk
- **COURT:** 1821, County Clerk

BUCHANAN
411 Jules St. Room 331, St. Joseph, MO 64501, (816) 271-1462, **<buchcomo.phpwebhosting.com>**
- **INCORPORATED:** Dec. 31, 1838
- **PARENT COUNTY:** Platte Purchase
- **MARRIAGE RECORDS:** start in 1839, kept by Recorder of Deeds
- **PROBATE:** 1839, Probate Clerk
- **COURT:** 1839, County Clerk
- **LAND:** 1839, County Recorder
- **NOTES:** County Clerk has death records 1883-1893.

BUTLER
100 N. Main, Poplar Bluff, MO 63901, (573) 686-8082, **<www.rootsweb.ancestry.com/~mobutle2/index.html>**
- **INCORPORATED:** Feb. 27, 1849
- **PARENT COUNTY:** Wayne
- **MARRIAGE RECORDS:** start in 1878, kept by Recorder of Deeds
- **LAND:** 1849, County Recorder
- **PROBATE:** 1849, Probate Clerk
- **COURT:** 1849, County Clerk
- **NOTES:** County Clerk has birth and death records 1883-1893.

CALDWELL
49 E. Main St., Box 68, Kingston, MO 64650, (816) 586-2581, **<www.rootsweb.ancestry.com/~mocaldwe>**
- **INCORPORATED:** Dec. 29, 1836
- **PARENT COUNTY:** Ray
- **MARRIAGE RECORDS:** start in 1860, kept by County Recorder
- **LAND:** 1835, County Recorder
- **PROBATE:** 1856, Probate Clerk
- **COURT:** 1859, County Clerk
- **NOTES:** April 19, 1860, courthouse destroyed by fire; all records destroyed except those of the Probate Court. Nov. 28. 1896, courthouse destroyed by fire.

CALLAWAY
10 E. Fifth St., Fulton, MO 65251, (573) 642-0780, **<callaway.county.missouri.org>**
- **INCORPORATED:** Nov. 25, 1820
- **PARENT COUNTIES:** Montgomery, Boone, Howard
- **MARRIAGE RECORDS:** start in 1821, kept by County Recorder
- **LAND:** 1821, County Recorder
- **PROBATE:** 1821, Probate Clerk
- **COURT:** 1821, County Clerk
- **NOTES:** County Clerk has birth and death records 1883-1888.

CAMDEN
1 Court Circle Suite 8, Camdenton, MO 65020, (573) 346-4440, **<camdenmo.org>**
- **INCORPORATED:** Jan. 29, 1841
- **PARENT COUNTIES:** Benton, Pulaski, Morgan
- **MARRIAGE RECORDS:** start in 1902, kept by County Recorder
- **LAND:** 1849, County Recorder
- **PROBATE:** 1902, Probate Clerk
- **COURT:** 1902, County Clerk
- **NOTES:** Formerly Kinderhook County. Name changed to Camden Feb. 23, 1843. Line between Camden and Miller changed 1845. Courthouse burned 1902.

CAPE GIRARDEAU
44 N. Lorimier, Box 2047, Cape Girardeau, MO 63702, (573) 335-8253, **<capecounty.us>**
- **INCORPORATED:** Oct. 1, 1812
- **PARENT COUNTY:** Original District
- **MARRIAGE RECORDS:** start in 1805, kept by County Recorder
- **LAND:** 1805, County Recorder
- **COURT:** 1815, County Clerk
- **PROBATE:** 1805, Probate Clerk
- **NOTES:** Present size of county since March 5, 1849. Courthouse burned in 1870. County Clerk has birth and death records 1883-1893. Riverside Regional Library has all records on microfilm.

CARROLL
County Courthouse, Carrollton, MO 64633, (816) 542-0615, **<carroll.mogenweb.org>**
- **INCORPORATED:** Jan. 3, 1833
- **PARENT COUNTY:** Ray
- **MARRIAGE RECORDS:** start in 1833, kept by Recorder of Deeds
- **DIVORCE:** 1833, Circuit Court
- **LAND:** 1833, County Recorder
- **PROBATE:** 1833, Probate Clerk
- **COURT:** 1833, County Clerk
- **NOTES:** County Clerk has birth records 1883-1885, and death records 1883-1890.

CARTER
Box 578, Van Buren, MO 63965, (573) 323-4513, **<www.rootsweb.ancestry.com/~mocarter>**
- **INCORPORATED:** March 10 1859
- **PARENT COUNTIES:** Oregon, Reynolds, Ripley, Shannon
- **MARRIAGE RECORDS:** start in 1861, kept by Recorder of Deeds
- **LAND:** 1845, County Recorder
- **PROBATE:** 1859, Probate Clerk
- **COURT:** 1866, County Clerk

CASS
102 E. Wall, Harrisonville, MO 64701, (816) 380-8226, **<casscounty.com>**
- **INCORPORATED:** March 3, 1835
- **PARENT COUNTY:** Jackson
- **MARRIAGE RECORDS:** start in 1836, kept by Recorder of Deeds
- **LAND:** 1837, County Recorder
- **PROBATE:** 1835, Probate Clerk
- **COURT:** 1835, County Clerk
- **NOTES:** Formerly Van Buren County. Named changed to Cass Feb. 19, 1949; three southern tiers of townships were relinquished to Bates County Feb. 22, 1855. County Clerk has birth records 1883-1903.

CEDAR
Box 665, Stockton, MO 65785, (417) 276-6700, **<www.rootsweb.ancestry.com/~mocedar>**
- **INCORPORATED:** Feb. 14, 1845
- **PARENT COUNTIES:** Dade, St. Clair
- **MARRIAGE:** start in 1845, kept by County Recorder
- **DIVORCE:** 1845, County Clerk
- **LAND:** 1845, County Recorder

- **PROBATE:** 1845, Probate Clerk
- **COURT:** 1845, County Clerk
- **NOTES:** County Clerk has birth records 1883-1889, death records 1883-1886.

CHARITON

605 Jackson St., Box 112, Keytesville, MO 65261, (660) 288-3602, **<www.rootsweb.ancestry.com/~mocharit>**

- **INCORPORATED:** Nov. 16, 1820
- **PARENT COUNTY:** Howard
- **MARRIAGE RECORDS:** start in 1821, kept by County Recorder
- **COURT:** 1820, County Clerk
- **LAND:** 1826, County Recorder
- **PROBATE:** 1861, Probate Clerk
- **NOTES:** Courthouse burned Sept. 20, 1864; only a few records lost. County Clerk has birth and death records 1883-1887.

CHRISTIAN

100 W. Church, Box 278, Ozark, MO 65721, (417) 581-6372, **<christiancountymo.gov>**

- **INCORPORATED:** March 8, 1859
- **PARENT COUNTIES:** Greene, Taney, Webster
- **MARRIAGE RECORDS:** start in 1866, kept by County Recorder
- **DIVORCE:** unknown start, Circuit Court
- **LAND:** 1861, County Recorder
- **PROBATE:** 1864, Probate Clerk
- **COURT:** 1865, County Clerk
- **NOTES:** Courthouse burned 1865. County Clerk has birth records 1840-1904, death records 1883-1884.

CLARK

111 E. Court St. #2, Kahoka, MO 63445, (660) 727-3292, **<www.rootsweb.ancestry.com/~moclark/clarkcotownship.htm>**

- **INCORPORATED:** Dec. 16, 1836
- **PARENT COUNTY:** Lewis
- **MARRIAGE RECORDS:** start in 1836, kept by County Recorder
- **DIVORCE:** 1836, Circuit Court
- **LAND:** 1833, County Recorder
- **PROBATE:** 1836, Probate Clerk
- **COURT:** 1837, County Clerk
- **NOTES:** County Clerk has birth records 1830-1840 and 1883-1892, death records 1883-1892.

CLARK (OLD)

- **INCORPORATED:** 1818
- **PARENT COUNTY:** Arkansas
- **NOTES:** Never organized; abolished in 1819 when territory of Arkansas was created.

CLAY

11 S. Water St., Box 218, Liberty, MO 64069, (816) 792-7706, **<www.claycogov.com>**

- **INCORPORATED:** Jan. 2, 1822
- **PARENT COUNTY:** Ray
- **MARRIAGE RECORDS:** start in 1822, kept by Recorder of Deeds
- **DIVORCE:** 1822, Circuit Court
- **LAND:** 1822, County Recorder
- **PROBATE:** 1821, Probate Clerk
- **COURT:** 1822, County Clerk
- **NOTES:** County Clerk has birth and death records 1883-1884.

CLINTON

207 N. Main St., Box 275, Plattsburg, MO 64477, (816) 539-3731, **<www.rootsweb.ancestry.com/~moclinto>**

- **INCORPORATED:** Jan. 2, 1833
- **PARENT COUNTY:** Clay
- **MARRIAGE RECORDS:** start in 1847, kept by County Recorder
- **DIVORCE:** 1833, Circuit Court
- **LAND:** 1833, County Recorder
- **PROBATE:** 1833, Parish Clerk
- **COURT:** 1836, County Clerk
- **MILITARY:** 1919, County Clerk
- **NOTES:** County Clerk has birth records 1863-1879; 1883-1888, death records 1883-1888.

COLE

301 E. High St., Box 1870, Jefferson City, MO 65101, (573) 634-9100, **<www.colecounty.org>**

- **INCORPORATED:** Nov. 16, 1820
- **PARENT COUNTY:** Cooper
- **MARRIAGE RECORDS:** start in 1821, kept by Recorder of Deeds
- **DIVORCE:** 1821, Circuit Court
- **LAND:** 1821, County Recorder
- **PROBATE:** 1834, Probate Clerk
- **COURT:** 1821, County Clerk
- **NOTES:** County Clerk has birth and death records 1883-1906.

COOPER

200 Main St., Booneville, MO 65233, (660) 882-2232, **<www.coopercountymo.org>**

- **INCORPORATED:** Dec. 17, 1818
- **PARENT COUNTY:** Howard
- **MARRIAGE RECORDS:** start in 1819, kept by County Recorder
- **DIVORCE:** 1819, Circuit Court
- **LAND:** 1819, County Recorder
- **PROBATE:** 1819, Probate Clerk
- **COURT:** 1821, County Clerk
- **BURIAL:** unknown start, County Clerk
- **NATURALIZATION:** 1819, Circuit Clerk and Recorder
- **NOTES:** County Clerk has birth records 1883-1894, death records 1883-1889.

CRAWFORD

302 W. Main St., Steelville, MO 65565, (573) 775-2376, **<www.rootsweb.ancestry.com/~mocrawfo>**

- **INCORPORATED:** Jan. 23, 1829
- **PARENT COUNTY:** Gasconade
- **MARRIAGE RECORDS:** start in 1829, kept by County Recorder
- **DIVORCE:** 1832, Circuit Court
- **LAND:** 21832, County Recorder
- **PROBATE:** 1832, Probate Clerk
- **COURT:** 1831, County Clerk
- **NOTES:** County Court records lost 1829-1835. Courthouse burned Feb. 15, 1873 and Jan. 5, 1884. County Clerk has birth records 1879-1903, death records 1883-1891 and 1941-1943.

DADE

Main St., Greenfield, MO 65661, (417) 637-2724, **<www.rootsweb.ancestry.com/~modade/modade.htm>**

- **INCORPORATED:** Jan. 29, 1841
- **PARENT COUNTIES:** Barry, Polk
- **MARRIAGE RECORDS:** start in 1863, kept by County Recorder
- **DIVORCE:** 1867, Circuit Court
- **LAND:** 1841, County Recorder
- **PROBATE:** 1841, Probate Clerk
- **COURT:** 1846, County Clerk
- **NOTES:** Lost 10-mile strip on northern boundary to Cedar County and 9-mile strip on southern boundary to Lawrence, reducing it to its present size March 28, 1845. Courthouse burned in 1863, but no records lost. County Clerk has birth and death records 1883-1885.

DALLAS

107 Maple St.; Box 436, Buffalo, MO 65622, (417) 345-2632, **<www.rootsweb.ancestry.com/~modallas>**

- **INCORPORATED:** Jan. 29, 1841
- **PARENT COUNTY:** Polk
- **MARRIAGE RECORDS:** start in 1867, kept by County Recorder
- **DIVORCE:** unknown start, Circuit Court
- **LAND:** 1867, County Recorder
- **PROBATE:** 1867, Probate Clerk
- **COURT:** 1867, County Clerk
- **BURIAL:** unknown start, County Recorder
- **NOTES:** Formerly Niangua County. Name changed to Dallas Dec. 16, 1844. Courthouse burned Oct. 18, 1863; second courthouse burned July 30, 1864 and records destroyed; the replaced records burned Sept. 3, 1867. County Clerk has Birth records 1883-1908, death records 1883-1924.

DAVIESS

Hwy. 13, Box 337, Gallatin, MO 64640, (660) 663-2641, **<www.rootsweb.ancestry.com/~modavies/daviess.htm>**

- **INCORPORATED:** Dec. 29, 1836
- **PARENT COUNTY:** Ray
- **MARRIAGE RECORDS:** start in 1837, kept by County Recorder
- **COURT:** 1837, County Clerk
- **LAND:** 1838, County Recorder
- **PROBATE:** 1890, Probate Clerk
- **LOCAL CENSUS:** 1876, County Library
- **NOTES:** County Library has birth and death records on microfilm 1883-1893. County Clerk has birth and death records 1883-1891.

DE KALB

Box 248, Maysville, MO 64469, (816) 449-2602, **<www.dekalbcountymo.org>**

- **INCORPORATED:** Feb. 25, 1845
- **PARENT COUNTY:** Clinton
- **MARRIAGE RECORDS:** start in 1845, kept by County Recorder
- **DIVORCE:** unknown start, Circuit Court
- **LAND:** 1836, County Recorder
- **PROBATE:** 1877, Probate Clerk
- **COURT:** 1856, County Clerk
- **NOTES:** Courthouse burned in 1878; many records lost, but records of circuit clerk's office were preserved along with a few records from other offices. County clerk has birth records 1883-1893, death records 1883-1891 and 1942-1943.

DENT

112 E. Fifth St., Salem, MO 65560, (573) 729-3931, **<www.rootsweb.ancestry.com/~modent/index.html>**

- **INCORPORATED:** Feb. 10, 1851
- **PARENT COUNTY:** Crawford, Shannon
- **MARRIAGE RECORDS:** start in 1851, kept by County Recorder
- **DIVORCE:** unknown start, Circuit Court
- **LAND:** 1851, County Recorder
- **PROBATE:** 1866, Probate Clerk
- **COURT:** 1866, County Clerk
- **NOTES:** Courthouse burned in 1864, destroying some records. County Clerk has birth and death records 1883-1884.

DODGE

- **INCORPORATED:** Dec. 18, 1846
- **PARENT COUNTY:** Putnam
- **NOTES:** Discontinued in 1853. Lost territory when Iowa boundary was established Feb. 13, 1849, bringing its area below the constitutional limit of 400 sq. miles. Its territory was added to Putnam County March 16, 1853.

DOUGLAS

Box 249, Ava, MO 65608, (417) 683-4713, **<www.rootsweb.ancestry.com/~modougla/doug.htm>**

- **INCORPORATED:** Oct. 29, 1857
- **PARENT COUNTY:** Ozark
- **MARRIAGE RECORDS:** start in 1877, kept by County Recorder
- **DIVORCE:** unknown start, Circuit Court
- **LAND:** 1858, County Recorder
- **PROBATE:** 1886, Probate Clerk
- **COURT:** 1886, County Clerk
- **NOTES:** Territory increased in 1864 by addition of portions of Taney and Webster counties. County Clerk has death records 1886-1894.

DUNKLIN

Box 567, Kennett, MO 63857, (573) 888-2456, **<www.rootsweb.ancestry.com/~modunkl2/dcgenweb.htm>**

- **INCORPORATED:** Feb. 14, 1845
- **PARENT COUNTY:** Stoddard
- **MARRIAGE RECORDS:** start in 1872, kept by Recorder of Deeds
- **DIVORCE:** unknown start, Circuit Court
- **LAND:** 1859, County Recorder
- **PROBATE:** 1865, Probate Clerk
- **COURT:** 1872, County Clerk
- **NOTES:** In 1853, a mile-wide strip from Stoddard County was added to Dunklin County. Courthouse burned in 1872, all records lost.

FRANKLIN

400 E. Locust, Union, MO 63084, (636) 583-6303, **<franklinmo.org>**

- **INCORPORATED:** Dec. 11, 1818
- **PARENT COUNTY:** St. Louis
- **MARRIAGE RECORDS:** start in 1819, kept by Recorder of Deeds
- **DIVORCE:** unknown start, Circuit Court
- **LAND:** 1819, County Recorder
- **PROBATE:** 1819, Probate Clerk
- **NOTES:** Boundaries not accurately defined until 1845. County clerk has birth records 1862-1892, and death records 1883-1887.

GASCONADE

119 E. First St. Room 6, Hermann, MO 65041, (573) 486-2632, **<www.gscnd.com>**

- **INCORPORATED:** Nov. 25, 1820
- **PARENT COUNTY:** Franklin
- **MARRIAGE:** start in 1822, kept by County Recorder
- **LAND:** 1821, County Recorder
- **PROBATE:** 1825, Probate Clerk
- **COURT:** 1821, County Clerk
- **NOTES:** In 1869 relinquished 36 square miles to Crawford County. County Clerk has birth records 1867-1896, and death records 1883-1896.

GENTRY

200 Clay St., Albany, MO 64402, (660) 726-3525, **<www.mogenweb.org/gentry>**

- **INCORPORATED:** Feb. 12, 1845
- **PARENT COUNTY:** Clinton
- **MARRIAGE:** start in 1859, kept by County Recorder
- **DIVORCE:** 1885, Circuit Court
- **LAND:** 1885, County Recorder
- **PROBATE:** 1885, Probate Clerk
- **COURT:** 1885, County Clerk
- **NOTES:** Organization completed 1843. Courthouse burned 1885. County Clerk has birth records 1867-1893, and death records 1883-1893.

GREENE

1010 Boonville, Springfield, MO 65802, (417) 868-4074, **<www.greenecountymo.org>**

- **INCORPORATED:** Jan. 2, 1833
- **PARENT COUNTY:** Crawford
- **MARRIAGE RECORDS:** start in 1833, kept by County Recorder
- **LAND:** 1833, County Recorder
- **PROBATE:** 1832, Probate Clerk
- **TAX:** 1833, County Archives and Record Center
- **COURT:** 1833, County Clerk
- **LOCAL CENSUS:** 1876, County Archives and Record Center
- **MILITARY:** unknown start, County Archives and Record Center
- **NOTES:** Courthouse burned 1861; few records lost. County clerk has birth records 1883-1901, and death records 1883-1902. Clerk of circuit court has divorce records 1837-1950.

GRUNDY

700 Main St., Box 196, Trenton, MO 64683, (660) 359-6605, **<www.grundycountymo.com>**

- **INCORPORATED:** Jan. 29, 1841
- **PARENT COUNTY:** Livingston
- **MARRIAGE RECORDS:** start in 1841, kept by County Recorder
- **DIVORCE:** unknown start, Circuit Court
- **LAND:** 1841, County Recorder
- **PROBATE:** 1863, Probate Clerk
- **COURT:** 1841, County Clerk
- **NOTES:** County clerk has birth records 1847-1866, birth and death records 1883-1893.

HARRISON

Box 189, Bethany, MO 64424, (660) 425-6425, **<www.rootsweb.ancestry.com/~moharris>**

- **INCORPORATED:** Feb. 14, 1845
- **PARENT COUNTY:** Daviess
- **LAND:** start in 1845, kept by County Recorder
- **MARRIAGE:** 1845, County Recorder
- **DIVORCE:** 1858, Circuit Court
- **PROBATE:** 1853, Probate Clerk
- **COURT:** 1845, County Clerk
- **NOTES:** Courthouse burned Jan. 1874, most records saved, tax records destroyed. County Clerk has birth records 1883-1889, and death records 1883-1893.

HEMPSTEAD

- **INCORPORATED:** 1818
- **PARENT COUNTY:** New Madrid
- **NOTES:** Abolished 1819 when territory of Arkansas was created.

HENRY

100 W. Franklin St., Box 478, Clinton, MO 64735, (660) 885-7200, **<www.henrycomo.com>**

- **INCORPORATED:** Dec. 13, 1834
- **PARENT COUNTY:** Lillard
- **MARRIAGE RECORDS:** start in 1835, kept by County Recorder
- **DIVORCE:** unknown start, Circuit Court
- **LAND:** 1835, County Recorder
- **PROBATE:** 1834, Probate Clerk
- **COURT:** 1835, County Clerk
- **BURIAL:** unknown start, County Museum
- **MILITARY:** unknown start, County Recorder
- **NOTES:** Formerly Rives County. Name changed to Henry Feb. 15, 1841. Death records are scattered. County Clerk has birth records 1883-1890.

HICKORY

Box 101, Hermitage, MO 65668, (417) 745-6421, **<www.hickorycountymo.com>**

- **INCORPORATED:** Feb. 14, 1845
- **PARENT COUNTIES:** Benton, Polk
- **MARRIAGE RECORDS:** start in 1872, kept by County Recorder
- **DIVORCE:** 1858, Circuit Court
- **PROBATE:** 1845, Probate Clerk
- **COURT:** 1845, County Clerk
- **LAND:** 1846, County Recorder
- **NOTES:** Courthouse burned 1852 and 1881, many records lost. County Clerk has birth and death records 1883-1898.

HOLT

100 W. Nodaway St., Oregon, MO 64473, (660) 446-3303, **<www.rootsweb.ancestry.com/~mohchs>**

- **INCORPORATED:** Jan. 29, 1841
- **PARENT COUNTY:** Platte Purchase
- **MARRIAGE RECORDS:** start in 1841, kept by County Recorder
- **DIVORCE:** 1841, Circuit Court
- **LAND:** 1841, County Recorder
- **PROBATE:** 1837, Probate Clerk
- **COURT:** 1841, County Clerk

- **NOTES:** Formerly Nodaway County. Name changed to Holt Feb. 15, 1841. Courthouse burned Jan. 30 1965, most records undamaged. County Clerk has birth and death records 1883-1889.

HOWARD

1 Courthouse Sq., Fayette, MO 65248, (660) 248-2194,
<www.rootsweb.ancestry.com/~mohoward>

- **INCORPORATED:** Jan. 13, 1816
- **PARENT COUNTIES:** St. Charles, St. Louis
- **MARRIAGE RECORDS:** start in 1816, kept by County Recorder
- **DIVORCE:** 1900, Circuit Court
- **LAND:** 1816, County Recorder
- **PROBATE:** 1816, Parish Clerk
- **COURT:** 1816, County Clerk
- **BURIAL:** 1820, Circuit Court
- **MILITARY:** 1900, Circuit Court
- **NOTES:** Courthouse burned 1887; few records lost. County Clerk has birth records 1883-1893, and death records 1883-1888.

HOWELL

Box 967, West Plains, MO 65775, (417) 256-3741,
<www.howellcounty.net>

- **INCORPORATED:** March 2, 1857
- **PARENT COUNTY:** Oregon
- **MARRIAGE RECORDS:** start in 1867, kept by County Recorder
- **DIVORCE:** unknown start, Circuit Court
- **LAND:** 1866, County Recorder
- **PROBATE:** 1862, Probate Clerk
- **COURT:** 1857, County Clerk
- **NOTES:** Courthouse destroyed during Civil War. County Clerk has birth and death records 1883-1895.

IRON

Box 424, Ironton, MO 63650, (573) 546-2811, **<www.rootsweb.ancestry.com/~moicgs/icgs_home.html>**

- **INCORPORATED:** Feb. 17, 1857
- **PARENT COUNTIES:** Madison, Reynolds, St. Francis, Washington, Wayne
- **MARRIAGE RECORDS:** start in 1857, kept by County Recorder
- **DIVORCE:** unknown start, Circuit Court
- **LAND:** 1814, County Recorder
- **PROBATE:** 1857, Probate Clerk
- **COURT:** 1857, County Clerk
- **NOTES:** County Clerk has birth records 1883-1896, and death records 1883-1887.

JACKSON

415 E. 12th St. 3rd Floor, Kansas City, MO 64106, (816) 881-3926,
<www.jacksongov.org>

- **INCORPORATED:** Dec. 15, 1826
- **PARENT COUNTY:** Lillard
- **MARRIAGE RECORDS:** start in 1827, kept by County Recorder
- **DIVORCE:** unknown start, Circuit Court
- **LAND:** 1827, County Recorder
- **PROBATE:** 1828, Probate Clerk
- **COURT:** 1828, County Clerk
- **NOTES:** Nearly all its territory was acquired from Osage and Kansas Indians June 2, 1825. County Clerk has birth records 1883-1895, and death records 1883-1893.

JASPER

302 S. Main St. Room 303, Carthage, MO 64836, (417) 358-0441,
<www.jaspercounty.org>

- **INCORPORATED:** Jan. 29, 1841
- **PARENT COUNTY:** Barry
- **MARRIAGE RECORDS:** start in 1841, kept by Recorder of Deeds
- **LAND:** 1841, County Recorder
- **PROBATE:** 1841, Probate Clerk
- **COURT:** 1841, County Clerk
- **NOTES:** Courthouse destroyed in 1863, records had been removed and were returned in 1865. Courthouse burned in 1883. County Clerk has birth records 1883-1900, and death records 1883-1897.

JEFFERSON

Box 100, Hillsboro, MO 63050, (636) 797-5443,
<www.jeffcomo.org>

- **INCORPORATED:** Dec. 8, 1818
- **PARENT COUNTIES:** St. Genevieve, St. Louis
- **MARRIAGE RECORDS:** start in 1825, kept by Recorder of Deeds
- **LAND:** 1819, County Recorder
- **PROBATE:** 1820, Probate Clerk
- **COURT:** 1819, County Clerk
- **NOTES:** County Clerk has birth and death records 1883-1892.

JOHNSON

101 W. Market, Warrensburg, MO 64093, (660) 422-7413,
<www.rootsweb.ancestry.com/~mojohnso>

- **INCORPORATED:** Dec. 13, 1834
- **PARENT COUNTY:** Lillard
- **MARRIAGE:** start in 1835, kept by Recorder of Deeds
- **DIVORCE:** ca. 1860, Circuit Court
- **LAND:** 1832, County Recorder
- **PROBATE:** 1835, Probate Clerk
- **COURT:** 1835, County Clerk
- **NOTES:** County Clerk has birth and death records 1883-1894.

KINDERHOOK

- **INCORPORATED:** Jan. 29, 1841
- **PARENT COUNTY:** Benton, Pulaski, Morgan
- **NOTES:** Name changed to Camden Feb. 23, 1843.

KNOX

107 N. Fourth St., Box 116, Edina, MO 63537, (660) 397-2688,
<knoxcountymo.org>

- **INCORPORATED:** Feb. 14, 1845
- **PARENT COUNTY:** Scotland
- **MARRIAGE RECORDS:** start in 1845, kept by County Recorder
- **DIVORCE:** unknown start, Circuit Court
- **LAND:** 1845, County Recorder
- **PROBATE:** 1845, Probate Clerk
- **COURT:** 1845, County Clerk
- **NOTES:** County Clerk has birth records 1883-1939, and death records 1883-1893.

LACLEDE
200 N. Adams St., Lebanon, MO 65536, (417) 532-2471, **<www.lacledecountymissouri.org>**
- **INCORPORATED:** Feb. 24, 1849
- **PARENT COUNTIES:** Camden, Pulaski, Wright
- **MARRIAGE RECORDS:** start in 1855, kept by County Recorder
- **DIVORCE:** unknown start, Circuit Court
- **LAND:** 1849, County Recorder
- **PROBATE:** 1848, Probate Clerk
- **COURT:** 1845, County Clerk
- **NOTES:** County Clerk has birth records 1883-1893.

LAFAYETTE
1001 Main St., Box 357, Lexington, MO 64067, (660) 259-4315, **<www.lafayettecountymo.com>**
- **INCORPORATED:** Nov. 16, 1820
- **PARENT COUNTY:** Cooper
- **MARRIAGE RECORDS:** start in 1821, kept by County Recorder
- **DIVORCE:** 1821, Circuit Court
- **LAND:** 1820, County Recorder
- **PROBATE:** 1821, County Clerk
- **COURT:** 1821, County Recorder
- **NOTES:** Formerly Lillard County. Name changed to Lafayette Feb. 16, 1825.

LAWRENCE
1 Courthouse Sq. Suite 201, Mount Vernon, MO 65712, (417) 466-2471, **<www.rootsweb.ancestry.com/~molawre2>**
- **INCORPORATED:** Feb. 14, 1845
- **PARENT COUNTIES:** Barry, Dade
- **MARRIAGE RECORDS:** start in 1845, kept by Recorder of Deeds
- **DIVORCE:** 1846, Circuit Court
- **LAND:** 1845, County Recorder
- **PROBATE:** 1843, Probate Clerk
- **COURT:** 1845, County Clerk
- **NOTES:** County Clerk has birth and death records 1883-1893.

LAWRENCE, OLD
- **INCORPORATED:** March 1, 1815
- **PARENT COUNTY:** New Madrid
- **NOTES:** Lost territory to Wayne Feb. 1, 1819. Abolished Feb. 16, 1825.

LEWIS
Box 97, Monticello, MO 63457, (573) 767-5352, **<www.rootsweb.ancestry.com/~molewis>**
- **INCORPORATED:** Jan. 2, 1833
- **PARENT COUNTY:** Marion
- **MARRIAGE RECORDS:** start in 1833, kept by County Recorder
- **DIVORCE:** unknown start, Circuit Court
- **LAND:** 1833, County Recorder
- **PROBATE:** 1833, Probate Clerk
- **COURT:** 1833, County Clerk
- **NOTES:** County Clerk has birth and death records 1883-1887.

LILLARD
- **INCORPORATED:** Nov. 16, 1820
- **PARENT COUNTY:** Cooper
- **NOTES:** See Lafayette County. Name changed to Lafayette Feb. 16, 1825.

LINCOLN
201 Main St., Troy, MO 63379, (636) 528-6300, **<www.lcmo.us>**
- **INCORPORATED:** Dec. 14, 1818
- **PARENT COUNTY:** St. Charles
- **MARRIAGE RECORDS:** start in 1825, kept by County Recorder
- **DIVORCE:** unknown start, Circuit Court
- **LAND:** 1819, County Recorder
- **PROBATE:** 1820, Probate Clerk
- **BURIAL:** unknown start, County Recorder
- **COURT:** 1819, County Clerk
- **NOTES:** County Clerk has death records 1883-1884.

LINN
108 N. High, Box 84, Linneus, MO 64653, (660) 895-5409, **<www.rootsweb.ancestry.com/~molinn>**
- **INCORPORATED:** Jan. 6, 1837
- **PARENT COUNTY:** Chariton
- **MARRIAGE RECORDS:** start in 1857, kept by County Recorder
- **DIVORCE:** 1837, Circuit Court
- **LAND:** 1836, County Recorder
- **PROBATE:** 1840, Probate Clerk
- **COURT:** 1857, County Clerk
- **NOTES:** County Clerk has birth records 1822-1888, and death records 1883-1887.

LIVINGSTON
700 Webster St., Chillicothe, MO 64601, (660) 646-1718, **<www.livingstoncountymo.com>**
- **INCORPORATED:** Jan. 6, 1837
- **PARENT COUNTY:** Carroll
- **MARRIAGE RECORDS:** start in 1837, kept by Recorder of Deeds
- **LAND:** 1837, County Recorder
- **PROBATE:** 1837, Probate Clerk
- **COURT:** 1837, County Clerk
- **NOTES:** County Clerk has birth records 1883-1891, and death records 1883-1890.

MACON
101 E. Washington St., Box 382, Macon, MO 63552, (660) 385-4631, **<www.maconcountymo.com>**
- **INCORPORATED:** Jan. 6, 1837
- **PARENT COUNTIES:** Randolph, Chariton
- **MARRIAGE RECORDS:** start in 1837, kept by County Recorder
- **DIVORCE:** unknown start, Circuit Court
- **LAND:** 1837, County Recorder
- **PROBATE:** 1838, Probate Clerk
- **COURT:** 1837, County Clerk
- **NOTES:** County Clerk has birth and death records 1883-1893.

MADISON
1 Courthouse Square., Fredericktown, MO 63645, (573) 783-2176,
<www.rootsweb.ancestry.com/~momadiso>
- **INCORPORATED:** Dec. 14, 1818
- **PARENT COUNTIES:** Cape Giradeau, St. Genevieve
- **MARRIAGE RECORDS:** 1821, Circuit Court
- **DIVORCE:** 1821, Circuit Court
- **LAND:** 1819, County Recorder
- **PROBATE:** 1821, Probate Clerk
- **COURT:** 1827, County Clerk
- **MILITARY:** 1943, Circuit Court
- **LOCAL CENSUS:** 1876, County Clerk
- **NOTES:** County Clerk has birth and death records 1883-1900.

MARIES
211 Fourth St., Box 213, Vienna, MO 65582, (573) 422-3338,
<www.rootsweb.ancestry.com/~momaries/maries.htm>
- **INCORPORATED:** March 2, 1855
- **PARENT COUNTIES:** Osage, Pulaski
- **MARRIAGE RECORDS:** start in 1869, kept by County Recorder
- **DIVORCE:** 1866, Circuit Court
- **LAND:** 1855, County Recorder
- **PROBATE:** 1866, Probate Clerk
- **COURT:** 1866, County Clerk
- **SCHOOL:** 1911, Circuit Court
- **NOTES:** In 1859 and 1868, small tracts of land were exchanged with Phelps County. Courthouse burned Nov. 6, 1868; nearly all records destroyed. County Clerk has birth records 1883-1884, and death records for 1883 only.

MARION
100 S. Main St., Box 392, Palmyra, MO 63461, (573) 769-2318,
<www.rootsweb.ancestry.com/~momarion>
- **INCORPORATED:** Dec. 14, 1826
- **PARENT COUNTY:** Ralls
- **MARRIAGE RECORDS:** start in 1827, kept by County Recorder
- **DIVORCE:** 1827, Circuit Court
- **LAND:** 1827, County Recorder
- **PROBATE:** 1827, Probate Clerk
- **COURT:** 1827, County Clerk
- **MILITARY:** unknown start, Circuit Court
- **NOTES:** County Clerk has birth records 1883-1890, death records 1883-1889, and birth and death records 1927-1930.

MCDONALD
Box 157, Pineville, MO 64856, (417) 223-7515,
<www.mcdonaldcountygov.com>
- **INCORPORATED:** March 3, 1849
- **PARENT COUNTY:** Newton
- **MARRIAGE RECORDS:** start in 1865, kept by Recorder of Deeds
- **DIVORCE:** unknown start, Circuit Court
- **LAND:** 1853, County Recorder
- **PROBATE:** 1865, Probate Clerk
- **COURT:** 1855, County Clerk
- **NOTES:** Name changed from Seneca to McDonald in 1849. In 1876 a survey error was corrected, establishing a new eastern line, annexing a 2.5-mile strip from Barry County. Courthouse and records burned in 1863. County Clerk has birth records 1856-1894.

MERCER
802 E. Main St., Princeton, MO 64673, (660) 748-3425,
<www.rootsweb.ancestry.com/~momercer>
- **INCORPORATED:** Feb. 14, 1845
- **PARENT COUNTY:** Grundy
- **MARRIAGE RECORDS:** start in 1898, kept by County Recorder
- **DIVORCE:** unknown start, Circuit Court
- **COURT:** 1868, County Clerk
- **LAND:** 1846, County Recorder
- **PROBATE:** 1849, Probate Clerk
- **NOTES:** Courthouse burned March 24, 1898; nearly all records of the Circuit Clerk and Recorder, Treasurer and Sheriff were destroyed or damaged. Records in office of Probate Judge and County Clerk were saved, but many were damaged. County Clerk has birth records 1883-1894 and records 1883-1894.

MILLER
2001 Highway 52, Tuscumbia, MO 65082, (573) 369-1900,
<millercountymissouri.org>
- **INCORPORATED:** Feb. 6, 1837
- **PARENT COUNTIES:** Cole, Pulaski
- **MARRIAGE RECORDS:** start in 1837, kept by County Recorder
- **DIVORCE:** unknown start, Circuit Court
- **LAND:** 1837, County Recorder
- **PROBATE:** 1837, Probate Clerk
- **COURT:** 1837, County Clerk
- **NOTES:** Line between Camden and Miller changed 1845. Territory from Morgan County annexed 1860. Minor changes in 1868. County Clerk has birth records 1883-1891, and death records 1883-1904.

MISSISSIPPI
200 N. Main St., Box 369, Charleston, MO 63834, (573) 683-2146,
<www.misscomo.net>
- **INCORPORATED:** Feb. 14, 1845
- **PARENT COUNTY:** Scott
- **MARRIAGE RECORDS:** start in 1845, kept by County Recorder
- **DIVORCE:** NA, Circuit Court
- **COURT:** 1845, County Clerk
- **PROBATE:** 1845, Probate Clerk
- **LAND:** 1823, County Recorder

MONITEAU
200 E. Main, California, MO 65018, (573) 796-2071,
<www.moniteau.net>
- **INCORPORATED:** Feb. 14, 1845
- **PARENT COUNTIES:** Cole, Morgan
- **COURT:** 1845, County Clerk
- **MARRIAGE:** start in 1845, kept by Recorder of Deeds
- **LAND:** 1845, County Recorder
- **PROBATE:** 1845, Probate Clerk
- **NOTES:** County Clerk has birth records 1883-1894, and death records 1883-1887.

MONROE
Box 227, Paris, MO 65275, (660) 327-5204, **<www.rootsweb.ancestry.com/~momonroe>**
- **INCORPORATED:** Jan. 6, 1831

- **PARENT COUNTY:** Ralls
- **MARRIAGE RECORDS:** start in 1831, kept by County Recorder
- **DIVORCE:** unknown start, Circuit Court
- **COURT:** 1831, County Clerk
- **PROBATE:** 1832, Probate Clerk
- **LAND:** 1831, County Recorder
- **NOTES:** County Clerk has birth and death records 1883-1885.

MONTGOMERY

211 E. Third St., Montgomery City, MO 63361, (573) 564-3341,
<www.montgomerycountymo.org>

- **INCORPORATED:** Dec. 14, 1818
- **PARENT COUNTY:** St. Charles
- **MARRIAGE RECORDS:** start in 1864, kept by County Recorder
- **DIVORCE:** 1886, Circuit Court
- **LAND:** 1839, County Recorder
- **COURT:** 1886, County Clerk
- **PROBATE:** 1889, Probate Clerk
- **NOTES:** County records burned 1864.

MORGAN

100 E. Newton St., Versailles, MO 65084, (573) 378-5436,
<morgan-county.org>

- **INCORPORATED:** Jan. 5, 1833
- **PARENT COUNTY:** Cooper
- **MARRIAGE RECORDS:** start in 1833, kept by Recorder of Deeds
- **LAND:** 1837, County Recorder
- **PROBATE:** 1834, Probate Clerk
- **COURT:** 1833, County Clerk
- **NOTES:** Courthouse burned 1887, no records lost. County Clerk has birth records 1841-1863, and birth and death records 1883-1886.

NEW MADRID

450 Main St., New Madrid, MO 63869, (573) 748-2228, **<www.rootsweb.ancestry.com/~monewmad/nmgenweb.htm>**

- **INCORPORATED:** Oct. 1, 1812
- **PARENT COUNTY:** Original district
- **MARRIAGE RECORDS:** start in 1847, kept by Recorder of Deeds
- **DIVORCE:** unknown start, Circuit Court
- **LAND:** 1805, County Recorder
- **PROBATE:** 1800, Probate Clerk
- **COURT:** 1805, County Clerk

NEWTON

Box 130, Neosho, MO 64850, (417) 451-8257, **<www.rootsweb.ancestry.com/~monewton/newton.html>**

- **INCORPORATED:** Dec. 30, 1838
- **PARENT COUNTY:** Barry
- **MARRIAGE RECORDS:** start in 1865, kept by County Recorder
- **DIVORCE:** unknown start, County Clerk
- **PROBATE:** 1839, Probate Clerk
- **COURT:** 1839, County Clerk
- **LAND:** 1839, County Recorder
- **NOTES:** In 1846 a strip two miles wide from Newton County was attached to Jasper County. Courthouse burned 1862. County Clerk has birth and death records 1883-1885.

NIANGUA

- **INCORPORATED:** Jan. 29, 1841
- **PARENT COUNTY:** Polk
- **NOTES:** See Dallas County. Boundaries slightly changed and name changed to Dallas Dec. 16, 1844.

NODAWAY

305 N. Main St., Maryville, MO 64468, (660) 582-2251,
<www.nodawaycountymo.com>

- **INCORPORATED:** Jan. 2, 1845
- **PARENT COUNTY:** Andrew
- **MARRIAGE RECORDS:** start in 1845, kept by County Recorder
- **DIVORCE:** 1845, Circuit Court
- **LAND:** 1845, County Recorder
- **PROBATE:** 1845, Probate Clerk
- **COURT:** 1845, County Clerk
- **NOTES:** Attached to Andrew County until organization Feb. 14, 1845. County Clerk has birth records 1883-1890, and death records 1883-1893.

OREGON

Box 406, Alton, MO 65606, (417) 778-7460,
<www.mooregon.org>

- **INCORPORATED:** Feb. 14, 1845
- **PARENT COUNTY:** Ripley
- **MARRIAGE RECORDS:** start in 1877, kept by County Recorder
- **DIVORCE:** unknown start, Circuit Court
- **LAND:** 1845, County Recorder
- **PROBATE:** 1854, Probate Clerk
- **COURT:** 1872, County Clerk
- **NOTES:** Courthouse burned during Civil War; records were removed and most saved. County Clerk has birth records 1883-1890, court records 1845-1859, and death records 1883-1889. County Recorder has marriage records 1845-1861.

OSAGE

Box 825, Linn, MO 65051, (573) 897-3114, **<osagecountygov.com>**

- **INCORPORATED:** Jan. 29, 1841
- **PARENT COUNTY:** Gasconade
- **MARRIAGE:** start in 1841, kept by Recorder of Deeds
- **LAND:** 1841, County Recorder
- **PROBATE:** 1841, Probate Clerk
- **NOTES:** March 1, 1855, boundaries between Osage and Pulaski defined. Courthouse burned Nov. 15, 1880, records saved. County Clerk has birth records 1883-1898, and death records 1883-1894.

OZARK

Box 416, Gainesville, MO 65655, (417) 679-3516,
<www.ozarkcounty.net>

- **INCORPORATED:** Jan. 29, 1841
- **PARENT COUNTY:** Taney
- **MARRIAGE RECORDS:** start in 1858, kept by County Recorder
- **DIVORCE:** unknown start, Circuit Court
- **LAND:** 1858, County Recorder
- **PROBATE:** 1865, Probate Clerk
- **COURT:** 1858, County Clerk
- **COMMISSIONER MINUTES:** unknown start, County Clerk
- **NOTES:** Name changed to Decatur Feb. 22, 1843. Name changed

back to Ozark March 24 1845. County Clerk has birth records 1884-1890, and death records 1887-1889.

PEMISCOT

610 Ward Ave., Box 34, Caruthersville, MO 63830, (573) 333-0182, **<www.rootsweb.ancestry.com/~mopemis2>**

- **INCORPORATED:** Feb. 19, 1851
- **PARENT COUNTY:** New Madrid
- **MARRIAGE RECORDS:** 1882, Recorder of Deeds
- **LAND:** 1881, County Recorder
- **PROBATE:** 1865, Probate Clerk
- **DIVORCE:** 1890, Circuit Court
- **COURT:** 1883, County Clerk
- **NOTES:** Courthouse and records burned 1883. County Clerk has birth records 1883-1884.

PERRY

15 W. Saint Maries St. #2, Perryville, MO 63775, (573) 547-6581, **<perrycountymo.us>**

- **INCORPORATED:** Nov. 16, 1820
- **PARENT COUNTY:** St. Genevieve
- **MARRIAGE RECORDS:** start in 1830, kept by County Recorder
- **DIVORCE:** unknown start, Circuit Court
- **LAND:** 1821, County Recorder
- **PROBATE:** 1821, Probate Clerk
- **COURT:** 1821, County Clerk
- **MILITARY:** unknown start, County Recorder
- **NATURALIZATION:** 1821, County Clerk
- **NOTES:** County Clerk has birth and death records 1883-1894.

PETTIS

415 S. Ohio Ave., Sedalia, MO 65301, (660) 826-0617, **<www.pettiscomo.com>**

- **INCORPORATED:** Jan. 26, 1833
- **PARENT COUNTIES:** Cooper, Saline
- **MARRIAGE RECORDS:** 1833, Recorder of Deeds
- **LAND:** 1833, County Recorder
- **PROBATE:** 1833, Probate Clerk
- **COURT:** 1833, County Clerk
- **NOTES:** County Clerk has birth and death records 1883-1885.

PHELPS

200 N. Main, Rolla, MO 65401, (573) 364-1891, **<phelpscounty.org>**

- **INCORPORATED:** Nov. 13, 1857
- **PARENT COUNTIES:** Crawford, Pulaski, Maries
- **MARRIAGE RECORDS:** start in 1857, kept by County Recorder
- **DIVORCE:** 1857, Circuit Court
- **LAND:** 1857, County Recorder
- **PROBATE:** 1858, Probate Clerk
- **COURT:** 1857, County Clerk
- **NOTES:** County Clerk has birth and death records 1883-1890.

PIKE

115 W. Main, Bowling Green, MO 63334, (573) 324-3112, **<www.pcgenweb.com>**

- **INCORPORATED:** Dec. 14, 1818
- **PARENT COUNTY:** St. Charles
- **MARRIAGE RECORDS:** start in 1825, kept by Recorder of Deeds
- **LAND:** 1819, County Recorder
- **PROBATE:** 1825, Probate Clerk
- **COURT:** 1819, County Clerk
- **NOTES:** Courthouse burned 1864, no mention of fate of records. County Clerk has birth records 1883-1884.

PLATTE

415 Third St., Platte City, MO 64079, (816) 858-2232, **<co.platte.mo.us>**

- **INCORPORATED:** Dec. 31, 1838
- **PARENT COUNTY:** Platte Purchase
- **MARRIAGE RECORDS:** start in 1839, kept by Recorder of Deeds
- **DIVORCE:** unknown start, Circuit Court
- **LAND:** 1839, County Recorder
- **PROBATE:** 1839, Probate Clerk
- **COURT:** 1839, County Clerk
- **NOTES:** Attached to Clay County for civil and military purposes from Dec. 1836 to Dec. 1838. County Clerk has birth and death records 1883-1887.

POLK

102 E. Broadway Room 14, Bolivar, MO 65613, (417) 326-4912, **<www.rootsweb.ancestry.com/~mopolk>**

- **INCORPORATED:** Jan. 5, 1835
- **PARENT COUNTY:** Greene
- **MARRIAGE RECORDS:** start in 1836, kept by County Recorder
- **DIVORCE:** 1857, Circuit Court
- **LAND:** 1837, County Recorder
- **PROBATE:** 1835, Probate Clerk
- **COURT:** 1836, County Clerk
- **NOTES:** County Clerk has birth records 1872-1900, and death records 1883-1890.

PULASKI

301 Historic Rt. 66 E. Room 202, Waynesville, MO 65583, (573) 774-4755, **<www.pulaskicountyweb.com>**

- **INCORPORATED:** Jan. 19, 1833
- **PARENT COUNTY:** Crawford
- **MARRIAGE RECORDS:** start in 1903, kept by County Recorder
- **DIVORCE:** 1903, Circuit Court
- **LAND:** 1903, County Recorder
- **PROBATE:** 1833, Probate Clerk
- **COURT:** 1903, County Clerk

PULASKI, OLD

- **INCORPORATED:** 1818
- **PARENT COUNTY:** Franklin
- **NOTES:** Organization not perfected and much of its territory became Gasconade in 1820. Abolished 1819 when territory of Arkansas was created.

PUTNAM

1601 W. Main St., Unionville, MO 63565, (660) 947-2071, **<putnam.mogenweb.org>**

- **INCORPORATED:** Feb. 22, 1845
- **PARENT COUNTIES:** Adair, Sullivan
- **MARRIAGE RECORDS:** start in 1849, kept by County Recorder

- **DIVORCE:** 1855, Circuit Court
- **LAND:** 1847, County Recorder
- **PROBATE:** 1853, Probate Clerk
- **COURT:** 1855, County Clerk
- **NOTES:** When the Iowa boundary was established, the areas of both Putnam and Dodge counties were below the constitutional limit. Dodge disorganized in 1853 and its territory was regained by Putnam. County Clerk has birth records 1878-1907, and death records 1887-1907.

RALLS

Box 444, New London, MO 63459, (573) 985-5633, **<www.rallscounty.org>**

- **INCORPORATED:** Nov. 16, 1820
- **PARENT COUNTY:** Pike
- **MARRIAGE RECORDS:** start in 1821, kept by County Recorder
- **DIVORCE:** 1821, Circuit Court
- **LAND:** 1821, County Recorder
- **PROBATE:** 1821, Probate Clerk
- **COURT:** 1821, County Clerk
- **NOTES:** County Clerk has birth records 1883-1893, and death records 1883-1886.

RANDOLPH

23 N. Williams, Moberly, MO 65270, (660) 263-4474, **<www.randolphcounty-mo.gov>**

- **INCORPORATED:** Jan. 22, 1829
- **PARENT COUNTIES:** Chariton, Ralls
- **MARRIAGE RECORDS:** start in 1829, kept by County Recorder
- **DIVORCE:** unknown start, Circuit Court
- **LAND:** 1841, County Recorder
- **PROBATE:** 1829, Probate Clerk
- **COURT:** 1858, County Clerk
- **NOTES:** Courthouse burned 1880, few records lost. County Clerk has birth and death records 1883-1889.

RAY

100 W. Main St., Richmond, MO 64085, (816) 776-3377, **<ray.mogenweb.org >**

- **INCORPORATED:** Nov. 14, 1820
- **PARENT COUNTY:** Howard
- **MARRIAGE RECORDS:** start in 1820, kept by Recorder of Deeds
- **DIVORCE:** unknown start, Circuit Court
- **LAND:** 1820, County Recorder
- **COURT:** 1821, County Clerk
- **PROBATE:** 1821, Probate Clerk
- **NOTES:** County Clerk has birth records 1883-1890, and death records 1883-1889. Records of interest to genealogists obtainable from Ray County Historical Society, Richmond, MO 64085.

REYNOLDS

Box 76, Centerville, MO 63633, (573) 648-2494, **<www.rootsweb.ancestry.com/~moreynol>**

- **INCORPORATED:** Feb. 25, 1845
- **PARENT COUNTY:** Shannon
- **MARRIAGE RECORDS:** start in 1872, kept by County Recorder
- **DIVORCE:** 1872, Circuit Court
- **LAND:** 1872, County Recorder
- **PROBATE:** 1872, Probate Clerk
- **COURT:** 1872, County Clerk
- **NOTES:** Courthouse burned 1872, all records lost. County Clerk has birth and death records 1883-1886.

RIPLEY

100 Courthouse Sq. Suite 3, Doniphan, MO 63935, (573) 996-2818, **<ripleycountymissouri.org>**

- **INCORPORATED:** Jan. 5, 1833
- **PARENT COUNTY:** Wayne
- **MARRIAGE RECORDS:** start in 1833, kept by Recorder of Deeds
- **LAND:** 1833, County Recorder
- **PROBATE:** 1856, Probate Clerk
- **COURT:** 1867, County Clerk
- **NOTES:** County clerk has birth records 1883-1897, and death records 1883-1893.

RIVES

- **INCORPORATED:** Dec. 13, 1834
- **PARENT COUNTY:** Lafayette
- **NOTES:** See Henry County. Name changed to Henry Feb. 15, 1841.

SALINE

101 E. Arrow St., Marshall, MO 65340, (660) 886-3331, **<saline.mogenweb.org>**

- **INCORPORATED:** Nov. 25, 1820
- **PARENT COUNTIES:** Cooper, Howard
- **MARRIAGE RECORDS:** start in 1835, kept by County Recorder
- **LAND:** 1821, County Recorder
- **PROBATE:** 1821, Probate Clerk
- **COURT:** 1821, County Clerk
- **CEMETERY:** unknown start, Marshall Public Library
- **NOTES:** Courthouse burned 1864, but records were saved. County Clerk has birth and death records 1883-1885.

SCHUYLER

Hwy. 136, Lancaster, MO 63548, (660) 457-3842, **<www.rootsweb.ancestry.com/~moschuy2>**

- **INCORPORATED:** Feb. 14, 1845
- **PARENT COUNTY:** Adair
- **MARRIAGE RECORDS:** start in 1845, kept by County Recorder
- **DIVORCE:** unknown start, Circuit Court
- **LAND:** 1845, County Recorder
- **PROBATE:** 1845, Probate Clerk
- **COURT:** 1846, County Clerk
- **NOTES:** County Clerk has birth records 1883-1893, and death records 1883-1891.

SCOTLAND

117 S. Market St. #106, Memphis, MO 63555, (660) 465-8605, **<www.scotlandcounty.net>**

- **INCORPORATED:** Jan. 29, 1841
- **PARENT COUNTIES:** Lewis, Clark, Shelby
- **MARRIAGE RECORDS:** start in 1841, kept by County Recorder
- **DIVORCE:** 1841, Circuit Court
- **LAND:** 1836, County Recorder
- **PROBATE:** 1842, Probate Clerk
- **COURT:** 1841, County Clerk
- **NOTES:** County Clerk has birth and death records 1883-1889.

SCOTT

Box 277, Benton, MO 63736, (573) 545-3596, **<scottcountymo.com>**
- **INCORPORATED:** Dec. 28, 1821
- **PARENT COUNTY:** New Madrid
- **MARRIAGE RECORDS:** start in 1840, kept by Recorder of Deeds
- **DIVORCE:** unknown start, Circuit Court
- **LAND:** 1822, County Recorder
- **PROBATE:** 1825, Probate Clerk
- **COURT:** 1822, County Clerk
- **NOTES:** County Clerk has birth and death records 1883-1886.

SHANNON

Box 148, Eminence, MO 65466, (573) 226-3315, **<www.rootsweb.ancestry.com/~moshanno>**
- **INCORPORATED:** Jan. 29, 1841
- **PARENT COUNTY:** Ripley
- **MARRIAGE RECORDS:** start in 1881, kept by County Recorder
- **DIVORCE:** 1872, Circuit Court
- **LAND:** 1859, County Recorder
- **PROBATE:** 1869, Probate Clerk
- **COURT:** 1872, County Clerk
- **NOTES:** Courthouse destroyed during Civil War. Courthouse burned 1863, 1871 and 1938. Recorder Office burned 1893. Some land records in Ironton, MO, prior to 1872.

SHELBY

Box 176, Shelbyville, MO 63469, (573) 633-2151, **<shelby-mo.com>**
- **INCORPORATED:** Jan. 2, 1835
- **PARENT COUNTY:** Marion
- **MARRIAGE RECORDS:** start in 1835, kept by Recorder of Deeds
- **DIVORCE:** unknown start, Circuit Court
- **LAND:** 1835, County Recorder
- **PROBATE:** 1836, Probate Clerk
- **COURT:** 1835, County Clerk
- **NOTES:** County Clerk has birth and death records 1883-1887.

ST. CHARLES

300 N. Second St., St. Charles, MO 63301, (636) 949-7900, **<sccmo.org>**
- **INCORPORATED:** Oct. 1, 1812
- **PARENT COUNTY:** Original district
- **MARRIAGE RECORDS:** start in 1807, kept by Recorder of Deeds
- **LAND:** 1804, County Recorder
- **PROBATE:** 1805, Probate Clerk
- **COURT:** 1808, County Clerk
- **NOTES:** County Clerk has birth records 1867-1890.

ST. CLAIR

655 Second St., Box 493, Osceola, MO 64776, (417) 646-2315, **<stclaircountymissouri.com>**
- **INCORPORATED:** Jan. 16, 1833
- **PARENT COUNTY:** Lafayette
- **MARRIAGE RECORDS:** start in 1855, kept by County Recorder
- **DIVORCE:** unknown start, Circuit Court
- **LAND:** 1841, County Recorder
- **PROBATE:** 1865, Probate Clerk
- **COURT:** 1841, County Clerk
- **NOTES:** Lost land to Pettis Jan. 26, 1833, and attached to Rives until formally organized from Rives County Jan. 29, 1841. County Clerk has birth records 1883-1903, and death records 1883-1890.

ST. FRANCOIS

1 N. Washington St., Farmington, MO 63640, (573) 756-4511, **<sfcgov.org>**
- **INCORPORATED:** Dec. 19, 1821
- **PARENT COUNTIES:** Jefferson, St. Genevieve, Washington
- **MARRIAGE RECORDS:** start in 1836, kept by County Recorder
- **DIVORCE:** unknown start, Circuit Court
- **LAND:** 1822, County Recorder
- **PROBATE:** 1822, Probate Clerk
- **NOTES:** County Clerk has birth records 1883-1893, and death records 1883-1890.

ST. GENEVIEVE

55 S. Third St., St. Genevieve, MO 63670, (573) 883-2705, **<stegenevievemissouri.com>**
- **INCORPORATED:** Oct. 1, 1812
- **PARENT COUNTY:** Original district
- **MARRIAGE RECORDS:** start in 1807, kept by County Recorder
- **DIVORCE:** unknown start, District Court
- **LAND:** 1804, County Recorder
- **PROBATE:** 1807, Probate Clerk
- **COURT:** 1804, County Clerk
- **NOTES:** County Clerk has birth and death records 1883-1892.

ST. LOUIS

7900 Carondelet, Clayton, MO 63105, (314) 615-8029, **<co.st-louis.mo.us>**
- **INCORPORATED:** Oct. 1, 1876
- **PARENT COUNTIES:** Original district, St. Louis City
- **BIRTH RECORDS:** start in 1876, kept by County Clerk
- **MARRIAGE:** 1876, Recorder of Deeds
- **DIVORCE:** unknown start, Circuit Court
- **DEATH:** 1883, County Clerk
- **LAND:** 1876, County Recorder
- **COURT:** 1876, County Clerk
- **PROBATE:** 1876, Probate Clerk

ST. LOUIS CITY

10 N. Tucker, Cibil Courts Bldg., St. Louis, MO 63101, (314) 622-4405, **<stlouis.missouri.org/government>**
- **INCORPORATED:** March 5, 1804
- **PARENT COUNTY:** Original county
- **BIRTH RECORDS:** start in 1825, kept by County Clerk
- **MARRIAGE:** 1766, County Recorder
- **DEATH:** 1825, County Clerk
- **LAND:** 1766, County Recorder
- **PROBATE:** 1766, Probate Clerk
- **TAX:** unknown start, Assessor
- **COURT:** 1766, County Clerk

STODDARD

Box 30, Bloomfield, MO 63825, (573) 568-4640, **<www.rootsweb.ancestry.com/~mostodd2/index.html>**
- **INCORPORATED:** Jan. 2, 1835

- **PARENT COUNTY:** New Madrid
- **MARRIAGE RECORDS:** start in 1863, kept by Recorder of Deeds
- **DIVORCE:** unknown start, Circuit Court
- **LAND:** 1835, County Recorder
- **PROBATE:** 1835, Probate Clerk
- **COURT:** 1835, County Clerk
- **MILITARY:** unknown start, County Clerk
- **NOTES:** Courthouse burned 1864, but records had been removed safely. County Clerk has birth records 1883-1887 and 1883-1886.

STONE

Box 45, Galena, MO 65656, (417) 357-6127, **<stoneco-mo.us>**

- **INCORPORATED:** Feb. 10, 1851
- **PARENT COUNTY:** Taney
- **MARRIAGE RECORDS:** start in 1851, kept by County Recorder
- **LAND:** 1854, County Recorder
- **PROBATE:** 1848, Probate Clerk
- **COURT:** 1851, County Clerk
- **MILITARY:** 1918, County Clerk

SULLIVAN

109 N. Main, Milan, MO 63556, (660) 265-4717, **<www.sullivancountymissouri.com>**

- **INCORPORATED:** Feb. 14, 1845
- **PARENT COUNTY:** Linn
- **MARRIAGE RECORDS:** start in 1845, kept by Recorder of Deeds
- **DIVORCE:** 1845, Circuit Court
- **LAND:** 1845, County Recorder
- **PROBATE:** 1849, Probate Clerk
- **COURT:** 1845, County Clerk
- **NOTES:** Recorder of Deeds has birth records 1835-1871 and 1883-1892, and death records 1883-1899.

TANEY

132 David St., Forsyth, MO 65653, (417) 546-7200, **<taneycounty.org>**

- **INCORPORATED:** Jan. 6, 1837
- **PARENT COUNTY:** Greene
- **MARRIAGE RECORDS:** start in 1885, kept by County Recorder
- **DIVORCE:** unknown start, Circuit Court
- **LAND:** 1881, County Recorder
- **PROBATE:** 1888, Probate Clerk
- **COURT:** 1887, County Clerk
- **VOTER REGISTRATION:** 1961, County Clerk
- **NOTES:** Courthouse burned 1885.

TEXAS

210 N. Grand, Houston, MO 65483, (417) 967-3742, **<texascountymissouri.org>**

- **INCORPORATED:** Feb. 14, 1845
- **PARENT COUNTY:** Shannon, Wright
- **MARRIAGE RECORDS:** start in 1855, kept by Recorder of Deeds
- **DIVORCE:** 1855, Circuit Court
- **LAND:** 1843, County Recorder
- **PROBATE:** 1870, Probate Clerk
- **COURT:** 1858, County Clerk
- **NOTES:** Formerly Ashley County. Name changed to Texas Feb. 14, 1845. County Clerk has birth records 1883-1887, and death records 1883-1890.

VAN BUREN

- **INCORPORATED:** March 3, 1835
- **PARENT COUNTY:** Jackson
- **NOTES:** See Cass County. Name changed to Cass Feb. 19, 1849.

VERNON

100 W. Cherry St., Nevada, MO 64772, (417) 448-2550, **<vernoncountymo.org>**

- **INCORPORATED:** Feb. 17, 1851
- **PARENT COUNTY:** Bates
- **MARRIAGE RECORDS:** start in 1855, kept by Recorder of Deeds
- **DIVORCE:** unknown start, Circuit Court
- **LAND:** 1855, County Recorder
- **PROBATE:** 1855, Probate Clerk
- **COURT:** 1856, County Clerk
- **BURIAL:** unknown start, County Historical Society
- **NOTES:** Created Feb. 17, 1851, but was declared unconstitutional because its territory was exactly that of Bates County; legally created Feb. 27, 1855. Reorganized Oct. 17, 1865 after suspension of civil order during Civil War. Courthouse destroyed during that period, but clerk had taken records when he joined the army and all except the deed book were later recovered. County Clerk has birth records 1883-1897, and death records 1883-1904.

WARREN

104 W. Main St., Warrenton, MO 63383, (636) 456-3363, **<warrencountymo.org>**

- **INCORPORATED:** Jan. 5, 1833
- **PARENT COUNTY:** Montgomery
- **MARRIAGE RECORDS:** start in 1833, kept by Recorder of Deeds
- **LAND:** 1833, County Recorder
- **PROBATE:** 1833, Probate Clerk
- **COURT:** 1833, County Clerk
- **NOTES:** County Clerk has birth records 1883-1889, and death records 1883-1894.

WASHINGTON

102 N. Missouri St., Potosi, MO 63664, (573) 438-4171, **<www.mogenweb.org/washington/index.html>**

- **INCORPORATED:** Aug. 21, 1813
- **PARENT COUNTY:** St. Genevieve
- **MARRIAGE RECORDS:** start in 1815, kept by Circuit Court
- **DIVORCE:** 1825, Circuit Court
- **LAND:** 1813, County Recorder
- **PROBATE:** 1813, Probate Clerk
- **COURT:** 1819, County Clerk
- **NOTES:** County Clerk has birth records 1883-1895, death records 1883-1895 and 1974-1976.

WAYNE

Box 47, Greenville, MO 63944, (573) 224-3052, **<www.rootsweb.ancestry.com/~mowayne>**

- **INCORPORATED:** Dec. 11, 1818
- **PARENT COUNTIES:** Cape Girardeau, Lawrence
- **MARRIAGE RECORDS:** start in 1892, kept by Circuit Court
- **DIVORCE:** unknown start, Circuit Court
- **LAND:** 1849, County Recorder
- **PROBATE:** 1869, Probate Clerk

- **COURT:** 1893, County Clerk
- **NOTES:** Courthouse and all records burned 1854 and 1892. County Clerk has birth and death records 1914-1940.

WEBSTER

Box 529, Marshfield, MO 65706, (417) 859-2006,
<webstercountymo.gov>

- **INCORPORATED:** March 3, 1855
- **PARENT COUNTIES:** Greene, Wright
- **MARRIAGE RECORDS:** start in 1855, kept by County Recorder
- **DIVORCE:** unknown start, Circuit Court
- **LAND:** 1854, County Recorder
- **PROBATE:** 1855, Probate Clerk
- **COURT:** 1855, County Clerk
- **NOTES:** Courthouse burned 1863, but records were saved, except tax rolls and election returns. County Clerk has birth records 1883-1893, and death records 1883-1884.

WORTH

4th and Front St., Grant City, MO 64456, (660) 564-2210,
<worthcounty.us>

- **INCORPORATED:** Feb. 8, 1861
- **PARENT COUNTY:** Gentry
- **MARRIAGE RECORDS:** start in 1861, kept by County Recorder
- **DIVORCE:** 1861, Circuit Court
- **LAND:** 1849, County Recorder
- **PROBATE:** 1861, Probate Clerk
- **COURT:** 1861, County Clerk
- **NOTES:** County clerk has birth and death records 1883-1893.

WRIGHT

Box 39, Hartville, MO 65667, (417) 741-7121,
<wrightcountymo.com>

- **INCORPORATED:** Jan. 29, 1841
- **PARENT COUNTY:** Pulaski
- **MARRIAGE RECORDS:** start in 1897, kept by County Recorder
- **DIVORCE:** unknown start, Circuit Court
- **LAND:** 1853, County Recorder
- **PROBATE:** 1853, Probate Clerk
- **COURT:** 1895, County Clerk
- **NOTES:** Courthouse burned in 1864, destroying many records. Courthouse and records destroyed in 1897.

MONTANA

» BY RHONDA R. MCCLURE

HISTORICAL OVERVIEW

Montana's American roots begin in the early 1800s, when the United States acquired the part of Montana east of the mountains from France. It was another 40 years before Britain relinquished its claim to the western section of the state.

Established in 1846, Fort Benton was the only trading post to become a permanent settlement. Steamboats brought early travelers there after a trip that took months on the Missouri River from St. Louis or Sioux City.

During the 1850s, Native Americans, adventurous explorers, fur trappers and some missionaries lived there. Jesuit priests founded St. Mary's, the first mission, in 1841; it would become the center for ranching in the Bitterroot Valley. This early influx of settlers came from all over the world. Homesteaders appeared from the East, the South, and even the West, including Chinese and others who had originally settled in California and Oregon. The discovery of gold in 1862 brought the first major migration to Montana. Gold miners also began to farm. Their earliest settlements include Missoula, Deer Lodge and Bozeman.

The territory of Montana was established in 1864. Railroads reached it in the 1880s, and in 1889, it became a state. In the early 1900s, many homesteaders moved into the eastern part of the state, but drought in the late 1920s and 1930 prompted some to move out.

research tips

- The Montana Historical Society **<www.his.state.mt.us>** has a large collection of church, military, prison and institution records, territorial censuses and poll lists.
- In the 1860s, western Montana was in Missoula County, Wash.; eastern Montana was in Nebraska Territory.
- Those living on land now in Yellowstone National Park during the 1880 census were recorded in Wyoming.

CENSUS RECORDS

- Federal census: 1870, 1880, 1900, 1910, 1920, 1930
- Federal mortality schedules: 1870, 1880
- Special census of Civil War Union veterans and widows: 1890
- Territorial censuses: 1860 (see Washington Territory for western Montana and Nebraska Territory for eastern Montana)

RECORD HIGHLIGHTS

Montana was a public-domain state, meaning initial land purchases were made from the government. Homesteading was another way to obtain land: After 1862, the law allowed people to earn free land by living on it for a certain length of time and making improvements. You can search these initial land patents through the Bureau of Land Management General Land Office Records site **<www.glorecords.blm.gov>**. If the entry is anything other than a cash sale, you'll want to order a copy of the land entry case file from the National Archives and Records Administration (see **<www.archives.gov/genealogy/land>** for information. Once land was transferred to individuals, sales were recorded in deeds of the county where the sale took place. Patents on timber and mining claims also are at the county level in the office of the county recorder.

Federal census records for Montana begin in 1870, though early residents of the area may be listed in Washington or Nebraska. A list of early settlers, mostly miners, is in "List of Early Settlers: A List of All Persons (Except Indians) Who Were in What is Now Montana During the Winter of 1862-1863," in *Contributions to the Historical Society of Montana*, vol. 1 (Rocky Mountain Publishing Co., 1902).

Vital records for Montana are not as complete as researchers would like. Births and deaths were not recorded until 1895. Statewide registration began only in 1907, and it was 1932 before 90 percent of births were being reported. Death records fared a little better, with reporting more than 90 percent complete by 1915.

Probate records were kept by probate courts for the years 1864 to 1889. These courts handled marriages, minor civil and criminal matters, adoptions and probate. Once they were disbanded, their functions and records were transferred to district courts. District courts now serve as the major trial courts; each covers cases from one to seven counties, with court sessions held in each county and most records dating to the year the county was founded.

During the 1880 census, those who lived in the area that was set aside in 1872 as Yellowstone National Park were recorded in Wyoming. Another early census you'll want to check is the 1864 Montana poll list, which lists eligible voters residing in the area.

The Montana Historical Society, 225 N. Roberts in Helena **<www.his.state.mt.us>**, has been amassing records since 1969. Records include governors' papers, prison and institution records, church and military records, territorial censuses, poll lists, and manuscripts. The society has compiled indexes by subject, name and place to aid researchers in using the records. You can search the society's catalog online, and many of the records can also be found in the National Union Catalog of Manuscript Collections **<loc.gov/coll/nucmc>**.

☞ ARCHIVES, LIBRARIES, AND SOCIETIES

Beaverhead County Museum
15 S. Montana St., Dillon, MT 59725, (406) 683-5027

Beaverhead Hunters Genealogical Society
15 S. Montana, Dillon, MT 59725, **<www.rootsweb.ancestry.com/~mtmsgs/soc_bhh.htm>**

Big Horn County Genealogical Society
Box 51, Hardin, MT 59034, **<www.rootsweb.ancestry.com/~mtmsgs/soc_bhcgs.htm>**

Bitterroot Genealogical Society
Box 941, Corvallis, MT 59828, **<www.rootsweb.ancestry.com/~mtbgs>**

Broken Mountain Genealogical Society
Box 261, Chester, MT 59522, **<www.rootsweb.ancestry.com/~mtmsgs/soc_bmgs.htm>**

Bureau of Land Management, Montana State Office
5001 Southgate Dr., Billings, MT 59101, (406) 896-5000, **<blm.gov/mt/st/en.html>**

Butte-Silver Bow Public Library
226 W. Broadway, Butte, MT 59701, (406) 723-3361

Cascade County Historical Museum
1400 First Ave. N., Great Falls, MT 59401, (406) 452-3462

Central Montana Genealogical Society
c/o Lewistown Public Library, 701 W. Main, Lewistown, MT 59457, (406) 538-5212, **<www.lewistownlibrary.org>**

Fort Assiniboine Genealogical Society
Box 321, Havre, MT 59531, **<www.rootsweb.ancestry.com/~mtmsgs/soc_fags.htm>**

Gallatin Genealogical Society
c/o Bonnie Whittimore, Box 1783, Bozeman, MT 59771, **<www.rootsweb.ancestry.com/~mtmsgs/soc_ggs.htm>**

Glasgow Root Diggers
c/o Charlotte Furhman, 102 Bonnie St., Glasgow, MT 59230, **<www.rootsweb.ancestry.com/~mtmsgs/soc_grd.htm>**

Glendive Public Library
200 . Kendrick Ave., Glendive, MT 59330, (406) 377-3633, **<www.dawsoncountymontana.org/library.htm>**

Great Falls Genealogy Society
301 Second Ave. N., Great Falls, MT 59401, (406) 727-3922, **<www.mt.net/~gfgs>**

Havre-Hill County Library
402 Third St., Havre, MT 59501, (406) 265-2123, **<www.mtha.mt.lib.org>**

Historian Archivist, Diocese of Helena
515 N. Ewing, Helena, MT 59624, (406) 442-5820

Lewis and Clark County Genealogical Society
120 Last Chance Gulch, Helena, MT 59601, (406) 447-1690, **<www.lewisandclarklibrary.org>**

Liberty County Library
100 E. First St., Box 458, Chester, MT 59522, (406) 759-5445

Mansfield Library, University of Montana-Missoula
32 Campus Dr., Missoula, MT 59812, (406) 243-6800, **<www.lib.umt.edu>**

Miles City Genealogical Society
Box 711, Miles City, MT 59301

Miles City Public Library
One S. Tenth St., Miles City, MT 59301, **<milescitypubliclibrary.org>**

Milk River Genealogical Society
Box 1000, Chinook, MT 59523, **<www.rootsweb.ancestry.com/~mtmsgs/soc_mrgs.htm>**

Missoula Public Library
301 E. Main, Missoula, MT 59802, (406) 721-2665, **<www.missoula.lib.mt.us>**

Montana Historical Society
225 N. Roberts, Box 201201, Helena, MT 59620, (406) 444-2694, **<www.his.state.mt.us>**

Montana Society, Sons of the American Revolution
Box 1218, Ennis, Mt. 59729, **<www.sar.org/mtssar>**

Montana State Genealogical Society
Box 555, Chester, MT 59522, **<www.rootsweb.ancestry.com/~mtmsgs>**

Montana State Library
1515 E. Sixth Ave., Box 201800, Helena, MT 59620, (406) 444-3004, **<msl.state.mt.us>**

Montana State University Libraries
Box 173320, Bozeman, MT 59717, (406) 994-3119, **<www.lib.montana.edu>**

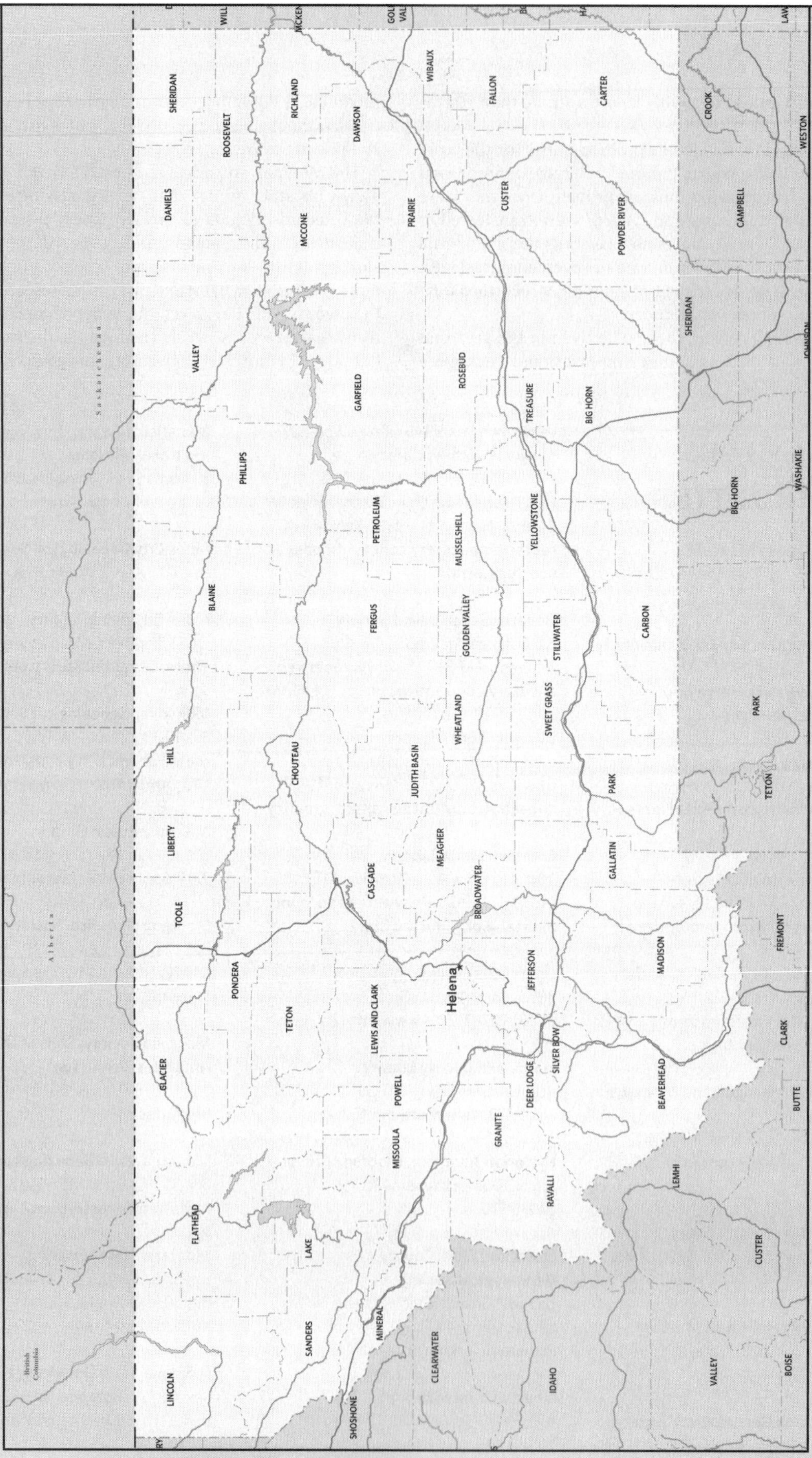
Saskatchewan
Alberta
British Columbia
SHERIDAN
DANIELS
ROOSEVELT
RICHLAND
DAWSON
MCCONE
WIBAUX
FALLON
PRAIRIE
CUSTER
CARTER
POWDER RIVER
CROOK
WESTON
CAMPBELL
SHERIDAN
JOHNSON
VALLEY
GARFIELD
ROSEBUD
TREASURE
BIG HORN
PHILLIPS
PETROLEUM
MUSSELSHELL
YELLOWSTONE
WASHAKIE
BIG HORN
BLAINE
FERGUS
GOLDEN VALLEY
STILLWATER
CARBON
WHEATLAND
SWEET GRASS
PARK
HILL
CHOUTEAU
JUDITH BASIN
PARK
TETON
LIBERTY
CASCADE
MEAGHER
GALLATIN
TOOLE
BROADWATER
FREMONT
PONDERA
TETON
LEWIS AND CLARK
Helena
JEFFERSON
MADISON
GLACIER
POWELL
DEER LODGE
SILVER BOW
BEAVERHEAD
CLARK
BUTTE
MISSOULA
GRANITE
LEMHI
FLATHEAD
LAKE
RAVALLI
CUSTER
SANDERS
MINERAL
CLEARWATER
IDAHO
VALLEY
BOISE
LINCOLN
SHOSHONE

Montana State Vital Records Office
Box 4210 Helena, MT 59604, (406) 444-2685, **<www.vitalrec.com/mt.html>**

National Archives and Record Administration, Rocky Mountain Region
Box 25307, Denver, CO 80225, (303) 407-5751, **<archives.gov/rocky-mountain>**

Parmly Billings Library
510 N. Broadway, Billings, MT 59101, (406) 657-8257, **<www.billings.lib.mt.us>**

Phillips County Genealogical Society
c/o Delores Messerly
Box 334, Malta, MT 59538, **<www.rootsweb.ancestry.com/~mtmsgs/soc_phcgs.htm>**

Powell County Genealogical Society
501 Missouri Ave., Deer Lodge, MT 59722, **<www.rootsweb.ancestry.com/~mtmsgs/soc_pcgs.htm>**

Roman Catholic Archives, Diocese of Great Falls-Billings
<www.dioceseofgfb.org>

Sheridan County Daybreakers Genealogical Society
<www.rootsweb.ancestry.com/~mtscdgs>

Tangled Roots Genealogical Society
Box 1992, Cut Bank, MT 59427, **<www.rootsweb.ancestry.com/~mtmsgs/soc_trgs.htm>**

The Tree Branches
Box 1275, Glendive, MT 59330, **<www.cheyenneancestors.com/dawson/dwsgens.html>**

Western Montana Genealogical Society
Box 2714, Missoula, MT 59806, **<www.rootsweb.ancestry.com/~mtwmgs>**

Yellowstone Genealogy Forum
c/o Parmly Billings Library, 510 N. Broadway, Billings, MT 59101, **<www.rootsweb.ancestry.com/~mtygf>**

Yellowstone Valley Chapter, American Historical Society of Germans from Russia
715 W. Fifth St., Laurel, MT 59044, (406) 628-6795, **<www.ahsgr.org/yellowstone_valley_chapter.htm>**

GENERAL RESOURCES

Bibliography of Montana Local Histories by Coburn Johnson (Montana Library Association, 1977)

Bicentennial Tapestry of the Yellowstone Conference compiled by Doris Whithorn (Meagher County News; Order from D. Whithorn, 1984)

The Bloody Bozeman: The Perilous Trail to Montana's Gold by Dorothy M. Johnson (Mountain Press, 1983)

The Bridger Trail: A Viable Alternative to the Gold Fields of Montana Territory in 1864 by James A. Lowe (Arthur H. Clark Co., 1999)

A Directory of Churches & Religious Organizations in Montana prepared by the Historical Records Survey (1941)

First Families of Montana and Early Settlers by Al Stoner (Montana State Genealogical Society, 2000)

Golden Opportunities: A Biographical History of Montana's Jewish Communities by Julie L. Coleman (SkyHouse Publishers, ca. 1994)

Go With Haste Into the Mountains: A History of the Diocese of Helena by Cornelia M. Flaherty (Catholic Diocese of Helena, 1984)

A History of Montana, 3 vols., edited by Merrill G. Burlingame et al. (Lewis Historical Publishing Co., 1957)

A History of the Catholic Church in the Pacific Northwest, 1743-1983 by Wilfred P. Schoenberg (Pastoral Press, 1987)

History of the Great Northwest and Its Men of Progress edited by C.W.G. Hyde and William Stoddard (Minneapolis Journal, 1901)

Indian and White in the Northwest, or, A History of Catholicity in Montana by L.B. Palladino (J. Murphy, 1894)

Jesuits in Montana 1840-1960 by Wilfred P. Schoenberg (Jesuits, 1960)

Men and Trade on the Northwest Frontier as Shown by the Fort Owen Ledger edited by George Ferdinand Weisel (Montana State University Press, 1955)

Montana Data Index: A Reference Guide to Historical and Genealogical Resources compiled by Paulette K. Parpart and Donald E. Spritzer (Montana Library Association, 1992)

Montana, Its Story and Biography, 3 vols., edited by Tom Stout (American Historical Society, 1921)

Montana Legislators, 1864-1979: Profiles and Biographical Directory by Ellis Waldron (Bureau of Government Research, University of Montana, 1980)

The Montana Locator: A Directory of Public Records for Locating People Dead or Alive in Montana by Laurie Nicklas (L. Nicklas, 1999)

Montana Pay Dirt: A Guide to Mining Camps of the Treasure State by Muriel Vincent Sibell Wolle (Sage, 1963)

Montana Research Outline by the Church of Jesus Christ of Latter-day Saints (online at **<www.familysearch.org/eng/search/RG/guide/montana.asp>**)

Montana's Genealogical and Local History Records by Dennis L. Richards (Gale Research Co., 1981)

More Than Petticoats: Remarkable Montana Women by Gayle C. Shirley (Falcon Press, 1995)

Names on the Face of Montana: the Story of Montana's Place Names by Roberta Carkeek Cheney (Mountain Press Publishing Co., 1984)

The Pioneer Work of the Presbyterian Church in Montana edited by Rev. George Edwards (Independent Publishing Co., 1907)

Plains, Peaks, and Pioneers: 80 Years of Methodism in Montana by Edward Laird Mills (Binford & Mort, 1947)

Speaking of Montana: A Guide to the Oral History Collection at the Montana Historical Society compiled by Patricia Borneman, et al, edited by Jodie Foley and Dave Walter (Montana Historical Society Press, 1997)

Territorial Papers of Montana, 1864-1872 by US Department of State (National Archives, 1963)

Twentieth-Century Montana: A State of Extremes by K. Ross Toole (University of Oklahoma Press, 1972)

☞IMMIGRATION RECORDS

Declaration of Intent, 1891-1929; Petition for Naturalization, 1891-1929; Citizenship Records, 1894-1906; Certificates, 1907-1927 by the US District Court, Montana Southern District (filmed by the Genealogical Society of Utah, 1988)

Indexes to Naturalization Records of the Montana Territorial and Federal Courts, 1868-1929 by the US Immigration and Naturalization Service (National Archives, 1987)

Swedish Immigrants Living in Montana, 1900 by Diane Fuhrman (D. Fuhrman, 1989)

☞LAND RECORDS

After Barbed Wire: A Pictorial History of the Homestead Rush Into the Northern Great Plains, 1900-1919 by Marie Peterson MacDonald (Frontier Gateway Museum, 1983)

☞MAPS

Atlas of the Pacific Northwest edited by Richard M. Highsmith and A. Jon Kimerling (University of Oregon Press, 1979)

Catalog of the Map Collection (Montana Historical Society, 1983)

Military Posts in Montana by Michael J. Koury (Old Army Press, 1970)

☞MILITARY RECORDS

Men With Custer: Biographies of the 7th Cavalry, 25 June, 1876 by Kenneth Hammer (Old Army Press, 1972)

Montana, World War I Selective Service System Draft Registration Cards (1917-1918) by the US Selective Service System (National Archives, 1987-1988)

Roll Call on the Little Big Horn, 28 June 1876 compiled by John M. Carroll and Byron Price (Old Army Press, 1974)

☞VITAL RECORDS

Cemetery Inscriptions and Church Records From Hingham, Rudyard, Inverness, Whitlash, Lothair, Joplin, and Chester, Montana compiled by Una Moog (Broken Mountains Genealogical Society, 1986)

Cemetery Records of Montana copied by members of the L.D.S. Church (1947-1961)

Inventory of the Vital Statistics Records of Church and Religious Organizations in Montana, 1942 (Montana Historical Records Survey, 1942)

Montana Cemetery Records prepared by the Lewistown Genealogy Society (filmed by the Genealogical Society of Utah, 1982)

●COUNTY DETAILS●

BEAVERHEAD
2 S. Pacific St. Cluster #3, Dillon, MT 59725, (406) 683-2642, <beaverheadcounty.org>
- INCORPORATED: Feb. 2, 1865
- PARENT COUNTY: Original county
- BIRTH RECORDS: start in 1901, kept by County Clerk
- MARRIAGE: 1877, County Clerk
- DEATH: 1901, County Clerk
- LAND: 1876, County Clerk
- PROBATE: 1865, District Court
- COURT: 1865, District Court

BIG HORN
Box 908, Hardin, MT 59034, (406) 665-1506, <bighorn.mt.gov>
- INCORPORATED: Jan. 13, 1913
- PARENT COUNTIES: Rosebud, Yellowstone
- MARRIAGE RECORDS: start in 1913, kept by District Court
- LAND: 1913, County Clerk
- PROBATE: 1913, District Court
- COURT: 1913, District Court

BLAINE
Box 908, Chinook, MT 59523, (406) 357-3240, <blaine.mtgenweb.org>
- INCORPORATED: Feb. 29, 1912
- PARENT COUNTY: Chouteau
- MARRIAGE RECORDS: start in 1912, kept by District Court
- LAND: 1912, County Clerk
- PROBATE: 1912, District Court
- COURT: 1912, District Court

BROADWATER
515 Broadway St., Townsend, MT 59644, (406) 266-3443, <www.rootsweb.ancestry.com/~mtbroadw>
- INCORPORATED: Feb. 9, 1897
- PARENT COUNTIES: Jefferson, Meagher
- BIRTH RECORDS: start in 1894, kept by County Recorder
- MARRIAGE: 1897, Clerk of Courts
- DEATH: 1903, County Recorder
- LAND: 1866, County Recorder
- PROBATE: 1897, Clerk of Courts
- COURT: 1897, Clerk of Courts

CARBON
Box 887, Red Lodge, MT 59068, (406) 446-1220, **<co.carbon.mt.us>**
- **INCORPORATED:** March 4, 1895
- **PARENT COUNTIES:** Park, Yellowstone, Custer
- **BIRTH RECORDS:** start in 1904, County Clerk
- **MARRIAGE:** 1895, County Clerk
- **DEATH:** 1895, County Clerk
- **LAND:** 1888, County Clerk
- **PROBATE:** 1895, County Clerk
- **COURT:** 1895, County Clerk

CARTER
Box 315, Ekalaka, MT 59324, (406) 775-8749, **<www.cartercountymt.info>**
- **INCORPORATED:** Feb. 22, 1917
- **PARENT COUNTY:** Custer
- **MARRIAGE RECORDS:** start in 1917, kept by Clerk of Courts
- **LAND:** 1917, County Clerk
- **PROBATE:** 1917, Clerk of Courts
- **COURT:** 1917, Clerk of Courts

CASCADE
415 N. Second Ave. Room 203, Box 2305, Great Falls, MT 59401, (406) 454-6801, **<co.cascade.mt.us>**
- **INCORPORATED:** Sep. 12, 1887
- **PARENT COUNTIES:** Chouteau, Meagher, Lewis and Clark
- **BIRTH RECORDS:** start in 1892, kept by County Recorder
- **MARRIAGE:** 1888, Clerk of Courts
- **DEATH:** 1893, County Recorder
- **LAND:** 1889, County Recorder
- **PROBATE:** 1889, Clerk of Courts
- **COURT:** 1889, Clerk of Courts

CHOUTEAU
1308 Franklin St., Box 459, Fort Benton, MT 59442, (406) 622-5151, **<co.chouteau.mt.us>**
- **INCORPORATED:** Feb. 2, 1865
- **PARENT COUNTY:** Original county
- **BIRTH RECORDS:** start in 1895, kept by County Clerk
- **MARRIAGE:** 1882, Clerk of Courts
- **DEATH:** 1895, County Clerk
- **LAND:** 1872, County Clerk
- **PROBATE:** 1880, Clerk of Courts
- **COURT:** 1895, Clerk of Courts

CUSTER
1010 Main St., Miles City, MT 59301, (406) 233-3457, **<www.rootsweb.ancestry.com/~mtcuster>**
- **INCORPORATED:** Feb. 2, 1865
- **PARENT COUNTY:** Original county
- **BIRTH RECORDS:** start in 1895, kept by County Clerk
- **MARRIAGE:** 1887, District Court
- **DIVORCE:** unknown start District Court
- **DEATH:** 1895, County Clerk
- **LAND:** 1877, County Clerk
- **PROBATE:** 1883, District Court
- **COURT:** 1879, Justice of the Peace
- **NOTES:** Formerly Big Horn County. Name changed to Custer Feb. 16, 1877.

DANIELS
Box 247, Scobey, MT 59263, (406) 487-5561, **<www.rootsweb.ancestry.com/~mtdaniel>**
- **INCORPORATED:** Aug. 30, 1920
- **PARENT COUNTIES:** Valley, Sheridan
- **MARRIAGE RECORDS:** start in 1920, kept in Clerk of Courts
- **LAND:** 1920, County Recorder
- **PROBATE:** 1920, Clerk of Courts
- **COURT:** 1910, District Court

DAWSON
207 W. Bell St., Glendive, MT 59330, (406) 377-3058, **<dawsoncountymontana.org>**
- **INCORPORATED:** Jan. 15, 1869
- **PARENT COUNTY:** Original county
- **BIRTH RECORDS:** start in 1895, kept by County Clerk
- **MARRIAGE:** 1882, Clerk of Courts
- **DEATH:** 1895, County Clerk
- **LAND:** 1881, County Clerk
- **PROBATE:** 1883, Clerk of Courts
- **COURT:** 1883, Clerk of Courts

DEER LODGE
800 S. Main St., Anaconda, MT 59711, (406) 563-4060, **<anacondadeerlodge.mt.gov>**
- **INCORPORATED:** Feb. 2, 1865
- **PARENT COUNTY:** Original county
- **BIRTH RECORDS:** start in 1903, kept by County Clerk
- **MARRIAGE:** 1865, Clerk of Courts
- **DEATH:** 1895, County Clerk
- **LAND:** 1864, County Clerk
- **PROBATE:** 1871, Clerk of Courts
- **COURT:** 1865, Clerk of Courts

EDGERTON
- **INCORPORATED:** Feb. 2, 1865
- **PARENT COUNTY:** Original county
- **NOTES:** See Lewis and Clark County. Name changed to Lewis and Clark Dec. 20, 1867.

FALLON
10 W. Fallon Ave., Box 846, Baker, MT 59313, (406) 788-7106, **<falloncounty.net>**
- **INCORPORATED:** Dec. 9, 1913
- **PARENT COUNTY:** Custer
- **MARRIAGE RECORDS:** start in 1912, kept by Clerk of Courts
- **LAND:** 1889, County Recorder
- **PROBATE:** 1914, Clerk of Courts
- **COURT:** 1914, Clerk of Courts

FERGUS
712 W. Main St., Lewistown, MT 59457, (406) 538-5242, **<co.fergus.mt.us>**
- **INCORPORATED:** March 12, 1885
- **PARENT COUNTIES:** Meagher, Chouteau

- **BIRTH RECORDS:** start in 1904, kept by County Clerk
- **MARRIAGE:** 1885, Clerk of Courts
- **DEATH:** 1904, County Clerk
- **LAND:** 1888, County Assessor
- **PROBATE:** 1888, Clerk of Courts
- **COURT:** 1888, Clerk of Courts

FLATHEAD

800 S. Main St., Kalispell, MT 59901, (406) 758-5526, **<flathead.mt.gov>**
- **INCORPORATED:** Feb. 6, 1893
- **PARENT COUNTY:** Missoula
- **BIRTH RECORDS:** start in 1896, kept by County Recorder
- **MARRIAGE:** 1892, District Court
- **LAND:** 1884, County Recorder
- **PROBATE:** 1893, District Court
- **COURT:** 1893, District Court

GALLATIN

311 W. Main St., Box 204, Bozeman, MT 59715, (406) 582-3050, **<www.gallatin.mt.gov>**
- **INCORPORATED:** Feb. 2, 1865
- **PARENT COUNTY:** Original county
- **BIRTH RECORDS:** start in 1895, kept by County Recorder
- **MARRIAGE:** 1865, District Court
- **DEATH:** 1895, County Recorder
- **LAND:** 1862, County Recorder
- **PROBATE:** 1886, District Court
- **COURT:** 1886, District Court

GARFIELD

Box 7, Jordan, MT 59337, (406) 557-2760, **<garfieldcounty.com>**
- **INCORPORATED:** Feb. 7, 1919
- **PARENT COUNTY:** Dawson
- **MARRIAGE RECORDS:** start in 1919, kept by Clerk of Courts
- **LAND:** 1919, County Clerk
- **PROBATE:** 1919, Clerk of Courts
- **COURT:** 1919, Clerk of Courts

GLACIER

512 E. Main St., Cut Bank, MT 59427, (406) 873-5063, **<glaciercountygov.com>**
- **INCORPORATED:** Feb. 17, 1919
- **PARENT COUNTY:** Teton
- **MARRIAGE RECORDS:** start in 1910, kept by Clerk of Courts
- **LAND:** 1919, County Clerk
- **PROBATE:** 1919, Clerk of Courts
- **COURT:** 1919, Clerk of Courts

GOLDEN VALLEY

107 Kemp St., Box 10, Ryegate, MT 59074, (406) 568-2231, **<co.golden-valley.mt.us>**
- **INCORPORATED:** Oct. 4, 1920
- **PARENT COUNTIES:** Musselshell, Sweet Grass
- **LAND:** 1920, County Recorder
- **PROBATE:** 1920, County Recorder
- **COURT:** 1920, County Recorder

GRANITE

Box 925, Phillipsburg, MT 59858, (406) 859-3771, **<co.granite.mt.us>**
- **INCORPORATED:** March 2, 1893
- **PARENT COUNTY:** Deer Lodge
- **BIRTH RECORDS:** start in 1895, kept by County Recorder
- **MARRIAGE:** 1893, Clerk of Courts
- **DEATH:** 1895, County Recorder
- **LAND:** 1866, County Recorder
- **PROBATE:** 1893, Clerk of Courts
- **COURT:** 1893, Clerk of Courts

HILL

315 Fourth St., Havre, MT 59501, (406) 265-5481, **<co.hill.mt.us>**
- **INCORPORATED:** Feb. 28, 1912
- **PARENT COUNTY:** Chouteau
- **BIRTH RECORDS:** start in 1898, kept by County Recorder
- **MARRIAGE:** 1912, Clerk of Courts
- **DEATH:** 1897, County Recorder
- **LAND:** 1912, County Recorder
- **PROBATE:** 1912, Clerk of Courts
- **COURT:** 1912, Clerk of Courts

JEFFERSON

Box H, Boulder, MT 59632, (406) 225-4020, **<jeffco.mt.gov>**
- **INCORPORATED:** Feb. 2, 1865
- **PARENT COUNTY:** Original county
- **BIRTH RECORDS:** start in 1895, kept by County Clerk
- **MARRIAGE:** 1887, District Court
- **DEATH:** 1895, District Court
- **LAND:** 1865, County Clerk
- **PROBATE:** 1869, District Court
- **COURT:** 1869, District Court

JUDITH BASIN

Box 427, Stanford, MT 59479, (406) 566-2277, **<www.rootsweb.ancestry.com/~mtjudith>**
- **INCORPORATED:** Dec. 10, 1920
- **PARENT COUNTIES:** Fergus, Cascade
- **MARRIAGE RECORDS:** start in 1920, kept by Clerk of Courts
- **LAND:** 1921, County Recorder
- **PROBATE:** 1921, Clerk of Courts
- **COURT:** 1921, Clerk of Courts

LAKE

106 Fourth Ave., Polson, MT 59860, (406) 883-7215, **<lakecounty-mt.org>**
- **INCORPORATED:** May 11, 1923
- **PARENT COUNTIES:** Flathead, Missoula
- **MARRIAGE RECORDS:** start in 1923, kept by Clerk of Courts
- **LAND:** 1923, County Recorder
- **PROBATE:** 1923, Clerk of Courts
- **COURT:** 1923, Clerk of Courts

LEWIS AND CLARK

316 N. Park, Box 1721, Helena, MT 59601, (406) 447-8334, **<co.lewis-clark.mt.us>**
- **INCORPORATED:** Feb. 2, 1865

- **PARENT COUNTY:** Original county
- **BIRTH RECORDS:** start in 1895, kept by County Clerk
- **MARRIAGE:** 1865, District Court
- **DEATH:** 1895, County Clerk
- **LAND:** 1865, County Clerk
- **PROBATE:** 1895, District Court
- **COURT:** 1867, District Court
- **NOTES:** Formerly Edgerton County. Name changed to Lewis and Clark Dec. 20, 1867.

LIBERTY
Box 459, Chester, MT 59522, (406) 759-5365, **<co.liberty.mt.us>**
- **INCORPORATED:** Feb. 11, 1920
- **PARENT COUNTIES:** Chouteau, Hill
- **MARRIAGE RECORDS:** start in 1920, kept by District Court
- **LAND:** 1920, County Clerk
- **PROBATE:** 1920, District Court
- **COURT:** 1920, District Court

LINCOLN
512 California Ave., Libby, MT 59923, (406) 293-7781, **<lincolncountymt.us>**
- **INCORPORATED:** March 9, 1909
- **PARENT COUNTY:** Flathead
- **BIRTH RECORDS:** start in 1897, kept by County Clerk
- **MARRIAGE:** 1896, District Court
- **DEATH:** 1897, County Clerk
- **LAND:** 1909, County Clerk
- **PROBATE:** 1909, District Court
- **COURT:** 1909, District Court

MADISON
110 W. Wallace St., Box 366, Virginia City, MT 59755, (406) 843-4270, **<madison.mt.gov>**
- **INCORPORATED:** Feb. 2, 1865
- **PARENT COUNTY:** Original county
- **BIRTH RECORDS:** start in 1903, kept by County Recorder
- **MARRIAGE:** 1887, Clerk of Courts
- **DEATH:** 1903, County Recorder
- **LAND:** 1863, County Recorder
- **PROBATE:** 1864, Clerk of Courts
- **COURT:** 1864, Clerk of Courts

MCCONE
Box 199, Circle, MT 59215, (406) 485-3505, **<www.rootsweb.ancestry.com/~mtmccone>**
- **INCORPORATED:** Feb. 20, 1919
- **PARENT COUNTIES:** Dawson, Richland
- **MARRIAGE RECORDS:** start in 1919, kept by Clerk of Courts
- **LAND:** 1919, County Recorder
- **PROBATE:** 1919, Clerk of Courts
- **COURT:** 1919, Clerk of Courts

MEAGHER
15 W. Main St., Box 309, White Sulphur Springs, MT 59645, (406) 547-3612, **<meaghercounty.org>**
- **INCORPORATED:** Nov. 16, 1867
- **PARENT COUNTY:** Original county
- **BIRTH RECORDS:** start in 1895, kept by County Recorder
- **MARRIAGE:** 1866, Clerk of Courts
- **LAND:** 1866, County Recorder
- **PROBATE:** 1866, Clerk of Courts
- **COURT:** 1867, Clerk of Courts

MINERAL
Box 550, Superior, MT 59872, (406) 822-3521, **<co.mineral.mt.us>**
- **INCORPORATED:** Aug. 7, 1914
- **PARENT COUNTY:** Missoula
- **MARRIAGE RECORDS:** start in 1887, kept by District Court
- **LAND:** 1914, County Recorder
- **PROBATE:** 1914, District Court
- **COURT:** 1914, District Court

MISSOULA
200 W. Broadway, Missoula, MT 59802, (406) 721-5700, **<co.missoula.mt.us>**
- **INCORPORATED:** Feb. 2, 1865
- **PARENT COUNTY:** Original county
- **BIRTH RECORDS:** start in 1895, kept by County Clerk
- **MARRIAGE:** 1865, Clerk of Courts
- **DEATH:** 1895, County Clerk
- **LAND:** 1868, County Clerk
- **PROBATE:** 1867, Clerk of Courts
- **COURT:** 1865, Clerk of Courts

MUSSELSHELL
506 S. Main St., Box 686, Roundup, MT 59072, (406) 323-1104, **<www.rootsweb.ancestry.com/~mtmussel>**
- **INCORPORATED:** Feb. 11, 1911
- **PARENT COUNTIES:** Fergus, Yellowstone
- **MARRIAGE RECORDS:** start in 1895, kept by Clerk of Courts
- **LAND:** 1911, County Recorder
- **PROBATE:** 1911, Clerk of Courts
- **COURT:** 1911, Clerk of Courts

PARK
414 E. Callender, Livingston, MT 59047, (406) 222-4110, **<parkcounty.org>**
- **INCORPORATED:** Feb. 23, 1887
- **PARENT COUNTY:** Gallatin
- **BIRTH RECORDS:** start in 1889, kept by County Clerk
- **MARRIAGE:** 1887, District Court
- **DEATH:** 1892, County Clerk
- **LAND:** 1887, County Clerk
- **PROBATE:** 1886, District Court
- **COURT:** 1886, District Court

PETROLEUM
201 E. Main St., Box 226, Winnett, MT 59087, (406) 429-5311, **<petroleum.mtgenweb.org>**
- **INCORPORATED:** Nov. 24, 1924
- **PARENT COUNTY:** Fergus
- **MARRIAGE RECORDS:** start in 1925, kept by Director of Records
- **LAND:** 1925, Director of Records
- **PROBATE:** 1925, Director of Records

- **COURT:** 1925, Director of Records
- **BURIAL:** 1925, Director of Records

PHILLIPS
314 Second Ave. W., Box 306, Malta, MT 59538, (406) 654-2423, **<www.rootsweb.ancestry.com/~mtphilli>**
- **INCORPORATED:** Feb. 5, 1915
- **PARENT COUNTIES:** Valley, Blaine
- **MARRIAGE RECORDS:** start in 1915, kept by Clerk of Courts
- **LAND:** 1915, County Clerk
- **PROBATE:** 1915, Clerk of Courts
- **COURT:** 1915, Clerk of Courts

PONDERA
20 Fourth Ave. SW, Conrad, MT 5942, (406) 278-4000, **<ponderacountymontana.org>**
- **INCORPORATED:** Feb. 17, 1919
- **PARENT COUNTIES:** Chouteau, Teton
- **MARRIAGE RECORDS:** start in 1919, kept by Clerk of Courts
- **LAND:** 1919, County Clerk
- **PROBATE:** 1919, Clerk of Courts
- **COURT:** 1919, Clerk of Courts

POWDER RIVER
Box 270, Broadus, MT 59317, (406) 436-2361, **<prco.mt.gov>**
- **INCORPORATED:** March 7, 1919
- **PARENT COUNTY:** Custer
- **MARRIAGE RECORDS:** start in 1919, kept by District Court
- **LAND:** 1919, County Clerk
- **PROBATE:** 1919, District Court
- **COURT:** 1919, District Court

POWELL
409 Missouri Ave., Box 125, Deer Lodge, MT 59722, (406) 846-3680, **<powellcountymontana.com>**
- **INCORPORATED:** Jan. 31, 1901
- **PARENT COUNTY:** Deer Lodge
- **MARRIAGE RECORDS:** start in 1901, kept by Clerk of Courts
- **LAND:** 1901, County Clerk
- **PROBATE:** 1901, Clerk of Courts
- **COURT:** 1901, Clerk of Courts

PRAIRIE
Box 125, Terry, MT 59349, (406) 637-5575, **<prairie.mt.gov>**
- **INCORPORATED:** Feb. 5, 1915
- **PARENT COUNTY:** Custer
- **MARRIAGE RECORDS:** start in 1915, kept by Clerk of Courts
- **LAND:** 1915, County Clerk
- **PROBATE:** 1915, Clerk of Courts
- **COURT:** 1915, Clerk of Courts

RAVALLI
205 Bedford St., Hamilton, MT 59840, (406) 375-6213, **<ravallicounty.mt.gov>**
- **INCORPORATED:** Feb. 16, 1893
- **PARENT COUNTY:** Missoula
- **MARRIAGE RECORDS:** start in 1893, kept by Clerk of Courts
- **LAND:** 1866, County Clerk
- **PROBATE:** 1893, Clerk of Courts
- **COURT:** 1893, Clerk of Courts

RICHLAND
201 W. Main St., Sidney, MT 59270, (406) 482-1708, **<richland.org>**
- **INCORPORATED:** May 27, 1914
- **PARENT COUNTY:** Dawson
- **MARRIAGE RECORDS:** start in 1914, kept by District Court
- **LAND:** 1914, County Clerk
- **PROBATE:** 1914, District Court
- **COURT:** 1914, District Court

ROOSEVELT
400 Second Ave. S, Wolf Point, MT 59201, (406) 653-6229, **<www.rootsweb.ancestry.com/~mtroosev>**
- **INCORPORATED:** Feb. 18, 1919
- **PARENT COUNTY:** Sheridan
- **MARRIAGE RECORDS:** start in 1913, kept by District Court
- **LAND:** 1919, County Recorder
- **PROBATE:** 1919, District Court
- **COURT:** 1919, District Court

ROSEBUD
Box 48, Forsyth, MT 59327, (406) 356-7318, **<rosebudcountymt.com>**
- **INCORPORATED:** Feb. 11, 1901
- **PARENT COUNTY:** Custer
- **BIRTH RECORDS:** start in 1893, kept by County Clerk
- **MARRIAGE:** 1901, District Court
- **DEATH:** 1909, County Clerk
- **LAND:** 1877, County Clerk
- **PROBATE:** 1901, District Court
- **COURT:** 1901, District Court

SANDERS
Box 519, Thompson Falls, MT 59873, (406) 827-4392, **<co.sanders.mt.us>**
- **INCORPORATED:** Feb. 7, 1905
- **PARENT COUNTY:** Missoula
- **MARRIAGE RECORDS:** start in 1906, kept by County Recorder
- **LAND:** 1885, County Recorder
- **PROBATE:** 1906, County Recorder
- **COURT:** 1906, County Recorder

SHERIDAN
100 W. Laurel Ave., Plentywood, MT 59254, (406) 765-2310, **<co.sheridan.mt.us>**
- **INCORPORATED:** March 24, 1913
- **PARENT COUNTY:** Valley
- **MARRIAGE RECORDS:** start in 1913, kept by Clerk of Courts
- **DEATH:** 1913, County Clerk
- **LAND:** 1913, County Clerk
- **PROBATE:** 1913, Clerk of Courts
- **COURT:** 1913, Clerk of Courts

SILVER BOW

155 W. Granite St., Box 585, Butte, MT 59701, (406) 723-6335, **<co.silverbow.mt.us>**

- **INCORPORATED:** Feb. 16, 1881
- **PARENT COUNTY:** Deer Lodge
- **BIRTH RECORDS:** start in 1878, kept by County Recorder
- **MARRIAGE:** 1881, Clerk of Courts
- **DEATH:** 1890, County Recorder
- **LAND:** 1881, County Recorder
- **PROBATE:** 1881, Clerk of Courts
- **COURT:** 1881, Clerk of Courts
- **NOTES:** May 2, 1977, the city of Butte and county of Silver Bow were unified to form the Butte-Silver Bow government.

STILLWATER

400 E. Third Ave. N., Box 149, Columbus, MT 59019, (406) 322-8000, **<co.stillwater.mt.us>**

- **INCORPORATED:** March 24, 1913
- **PARENT COUNTIES:** Sweet Grass, Yellowstone, Carbon
- **BIRTH RECORDS:** start in 1887, kept by County Recorder
- **MARRIAGE:** 1913, Clerk of Courts
- **LAND:** 1913, County Recorder
- **PROBATE:** 1913, Clerk of Courts
- **COURT:** 1913, Clerk of Courts

SWEET GRASS

200 W. First Ave., Box 460, Big Timber, MT 59011, (406) 932-5152, **<co.sweetgrass.mt.us>**

- **INCORPORATED:** March 5, 1895
- **PARENT COUNTIES:** Meagher, Park, Yellowstone
- **BIRTH RECORDS:** start in 1895, kept by County Recorder
- **MARRIAGE:** 1895, District Court
- **DEATH:** 1895, County Recorder
- **LAND:** 1895, County Recorder
- **PROBATE:** 1895, District Court
- **COURT:** 1895, District Court

TETON

Box 610, Choteau, MT 59422, (406) 466-2693, **<tetoncomt.org>**

- **INCORPORATED:** Feb. 7, 1893
- **PARENT COUNTY:** Chouteau
- **BIRTH RECORDS:** start in 1897, kept by County Clerk
- **MARRIAGE:** 1893, District Court
- **LAND:** 1893, County Clerk
- **PROBATE:** 1890, District Court
- **COURT:** 1895, District Court

TOOLE

226 First St. S., Shelby, MT 59474, (406) 434-2232, **<toolecountymt.gov>**

- **INCORPORATED:** May 7, 1914
- **PARENT COUNTIES:** Teton, Hill
- **MARRIAGE RECORDS:** start in 1914, kept by Clerk of Courts
- **LAND:** 1914, County Recorder
- **PROBATE:** 1914, Clerk of Courts
- **COURT:** 1914, Clerk of Courts
- **BURIAL:** 1914, County Recorder

TREASURE

Box 392, Hysham, MT 59038, (406) 342-5547. **<www.rootsweb.ancestry.com/~mttreasu>**

- **INCORPORATED:** Feb. 7, 1919
- **PARENT COUNTY:** Rosebud
- **MARRIAGE RECORDS:** start in 1919, kept by District Court
- **LAND:** 1879, County Recorder
- **PROBATE:** 1919, District Court
- **COURT:** 1919, District Court

VALLEY

501 Court Sq. #2, Glasgow, MT 59230, (406) 228-8221, **<valley.mtgenweb.org>**

- **INCORPORATED:** Feb. 6, 1893
- **PARENT COUNTY:** Dawson
- **MARRIAGE RECORDS:** start in 1893, kept by Clerk of Courts
- **LAND:** 1893, County Recorder
- **PROBATE:** 1893, Clerk of Courts
- **COURT:** 1893, Clerk of Courts

WHEATLAND

Box 1903, Harlowton, MT 59036, (406) 632-4891, **<www.rootsweb.ancestry.com/~mtwheatl>**

- **INCORPORATED:** Feb. 22, 1917
- **PARENT COUNTIES:** Meagher, Sweet Grass
- **MARRIAGE RECORDS:** start in 1917, kept by Clerk of Courts
- **LAND:** 1917, County Recorder
- **PROBATE:** 1917, Clerk of Courts
- **COURT:** 1917, Clerk of Courts

WIBAUX

200 S. Wibaux St., Box 199, Wibaux, MT 59353, (406) 796-2481, **<wibaux.mtgenweb.org>**

- **INCORPORATED:** Aug. 17, 1914
- **PARENT COUNTIES:** Dawson, Fallon
- **MARRIAGE RECORDS:** start in 1914, kept by District Court
- **LAND:** 1914, County Recorder
- **PROBATE:** 1914, District Court
- **COURT:** 1914, District Court

YELLOWSTONE

Box 35002, Billings, MT 59107, (406) 256-2785, **<co.yellowstone.mt.us>**

- **INCORPORATED:** Feb. 26, 1883
- **PARENT COUNTIES:** Gallatin, Custer
- **BIRTH RECORDS:** start in 1884, kept by County Recorder
- **MARRIAGE:** 1895, District Court
- **DEATH:** 1884, County Recorder
- **LAND:** 1881, County Recorder
- **PROBATE:** 1890, District Court
- **COURT:** 1884, District Court

NEBRASKA

» BY MAUREEN A. TAYLOR

HISTORICAL OVERVIEW

The United States acquired the area that's now Nebraska with the Louisiana Purchase in 1803. American Indians from the Cheyenne, Dakota, Omaha, Oto, Pawnee and Ponca tribes inhabited the plains of the future state. Fort Atkinson, a military outpost, was established in 1819. Fur traders and missionaries moved into the area during the ensuing decades. Emigrants following the Oregon and Mormon Trails along the Platte River traversed the area's plains.

The Kansas-Nebraska Act of 1854 gave those regions territorial status. Nebraska territory included the state's present boundaries as well as Montana and parts of Wyoming, Colorado and the Dakotas. Omaha was the territorial capital.

The promise of free land and the emergence of railroads encouraged immigrants and settlers from the eastern United States to move to Nebraska. The Homestead Act of 1862 gave 160 acres to families who farmed and lived on the land for five years. Settlers were mostly European immigrants, Civil War veterans and some African-Americans. Nebraska became the 37th state in 1867.

Indian conflicts and harsh living conditions caused many settlers to move on, but others arrived to take their place. By 1900, half of the state's population was foreign-born.

Agriculture and cattle ranching became mainstays of the state's economy. During World Wars I and II, much of the grain produced in the United States came from Nebraska.

research tips

- The Nebraska State Historical Society **<www.nebraskahistory.org>** became the official repository of state and local public records in 1905. It also serves as the state archives. Holdings cover records from 1854 to the present, including all census records.
- Newspapers from the territorial period to the present are on microfilm at the Nebraska Historical Society. These can help fill in the gaps when vital records do not exist.
- County clerks' offices hold a variety of helpful documents, including motor vehicle registrations, school registers, probate files, wills and guardianships.

CENSUS RECORDS

- Federal census: 1860, 1870, 1880, 1900, 1910, 1920, 1930
- State and territorial censuses: 1854, 1855, 1856, 1885
- Special census of Civil War Union veterans and widows: 1890

RECORD HIGHLIGHTS

Birth and death records in Nebraska were not mandated until 1904; marriages and divorces followed in 1909. Recording errors and a lack of compliance characterize the first decades after civil registration. Copies are available from the state Bureau of Vital Records. Marriages and divorces before and after 1909 are on file with individual counties.

You can fill in the vital records gaps with church records, but completeness varies depending on the denomination. Most church records are still at the church, but you'll need to track down registers of churches that moved, merged or disbanded. Check first with the church, then contact the denominational headquarters on the state or regional level. The Nebraska State Historical Society (NSHS) lists its church record holdings by county at **<www.nebraskahistory.org/lib-arch/research/manuscripts/church>**.

Newspaper obituaries and marriages also may fill in gaps left by missing vital records. Since the 1890s, the Nebraska Press Association has sent copies of papers to NSHS. Newspapers from the territorial period to the present are on microfilm at the society, and most can be borrowed via interlibrary loan through public libraries.

All existing state and federal Nebraska census records also are available at the NSHS. Territorial census originals and transcriptions (1854, 1855, and 1856) are there as well. County census records exist for some counties during the

1860s, 1870s and 1880s, as well as a special census of Germans from Russia living in Lincoln in 1913 to 1914. School censuses, taken annually from the 1870s to the present, can supply data for families prior to the recording of vital records. Surviving records are either at the county level or at NSHS.

County clerks' offices have a variety of helpful documents, including motor vehicle registrations, military discharges, voter registrations and school registers. Also on the county level are probate documents, including wills and guardianships. District court proceedings cover civil and criminal cases, divorces and naturalizations. In some cases, certain county records have been transferred to NSHS.

Between 1854 and 1863, the most common type of land entry in Nebraska was the pre-emption claim under the Act of 1841, which was followed by the Homestead Act of 1862. NSHS has General Land Office (GLO) tract books for Nebraska on microfilm, as well as indexes for some counties. Search land patents on the GLO website **<www.glorecords.blm.gov>**. Homestead records from Nebraska's Broken Bow Land Office are on subscription genealogy site Footnote **<www.footnote.com>**. See **<www.archives.gov/genealogy/land>** for details on requesting land entry case files from the National Archives and Records Administration.

After the initial sale from the federal government, land records are with the county registers of deeds. County boundaries have changed over the years, so be sure to verify county borders at the time of the land transaction.

You probably won't find much published material about Nebraska's many small cemeteries. For volunteer transcriptions of cemeteries, visit Nebraska GenWeb **<www.usgennet.org/usa/ne/topic/cemeteries>** and websites such as Interment.net **<interment.net>**.

ARCHIVES, LIBRARIES, AND SOCIETIES

Adams County Genealogical Society
Box 424, Hastings, NE 68902, (402) 463-5838, **<www.adamshistory.org/acgs.html>**

Adams County Historical Society
Box 102, Hastings, NE 68902, (402) 463-5838, **<www.adamshistory.org>**

Alliance Public Library
1750 Sweetwater Ave., Alliance, NE 69301, (308) 762-1387, **<alliancelibrary.org>**

American Historical Society of Germans from Russia
631 D St., Lincoln, NE 68502, (402) 474-3363, **<ahsgr.org>**

Boone-Nance Genealogical Society
Box 231, Belgrade, NE 68623, **<usgennet.org/usa/ne/county/boone/bngs.html>**

Buffalo County Historical Society
Box 523, Kearney, NE 68848, (308) 234-3041, **<bchs.kearney.net>**

Bureau of Land Management, Wyoming
5353 Yellowstone Rd., Cheyenne, WY 82009, (307) 775-6256, **<www.wy.blm.gov>**

Butler County Historical Society
200 D St., David City, NE 68632

Cairo Roots
Route 1, Box 42, Cairo, NE 68824

Chase County Genealogical Society
Box 303, Imperial, NE 69033

Chase County Historical Society
73989 320th Ave., Imperial, NE 69033, **<freepages.genealogy.rootsweb.ancestry.com/~chasecountyne>**

Cherry County Genealogical Society
Box 1380, Valentine, NE 69201, **<www.rootsweb.ancestry.com/~bwo/nebraska.html>**

Cheyenne County Genealogical Society
Box 802, Sidney, NE 69162

Cravath Memorial Library
Box 309, Hay Springs, NE 69347, (308) 638-4541

Cuming County Historical Society
130 N. River, West Point, NE 68788

Custer County Historical Society
Box 334, Broken Bow, NE 68822, (308) 872-2203, **<www.rootsweb.ancestry.com/~necuster>**

Dakota County Genealogical Society
Box 18, Dakota City, NE 68850, **<www.dakotacountyhistoricalsociety.com>**

Danish Immigrant Archive
Dana College, 2848 College Dr., Blair, NE 68008, (402) 426-7300, **<danishamericanarchive.com>**

Dawson County Genealogical Society
514 E. 8th St., Cozad, NE 69130

Dawson County Historical Society
Box 369, Lexington NE 68850, (308) 324-5340

Denton Community Historical Society
Box 405, Denton, NE 68339, **<denton.ancestralwhispers.com>**

Dixon County Historical Society
Box 95, Allen, NE 68710, **<dixonconegenwebproject.homestead.com/dixoncomuseum.html>**

Eastern Nebraska Genealogical Society
Box 541, Fremont, NE 68026, **<www.usgennet.org/usa/ne/county/dodge/ENGS.HTM>**

Elkhorn Valley Genealogical Society
341 E. Walnut, West Point, NE 68788, **<www.rootsweb.ancestry.com/~necuming/evgs.html>**

Fillmore Heritage Genealogical Society
Rt. 2, Box 28, Exeter, NE 68351

Fort Kearney Genealogical Society
Box 22, Kearney, NE 68847, **<www.rootsweb.ancestry.com/~nebuffal/fkgs.htm>**

Frontier County Historical Society
Box 242, Curtis, NE 69025

Furnas County Genealogical Society
Box 391, Beaver City, NE 68926

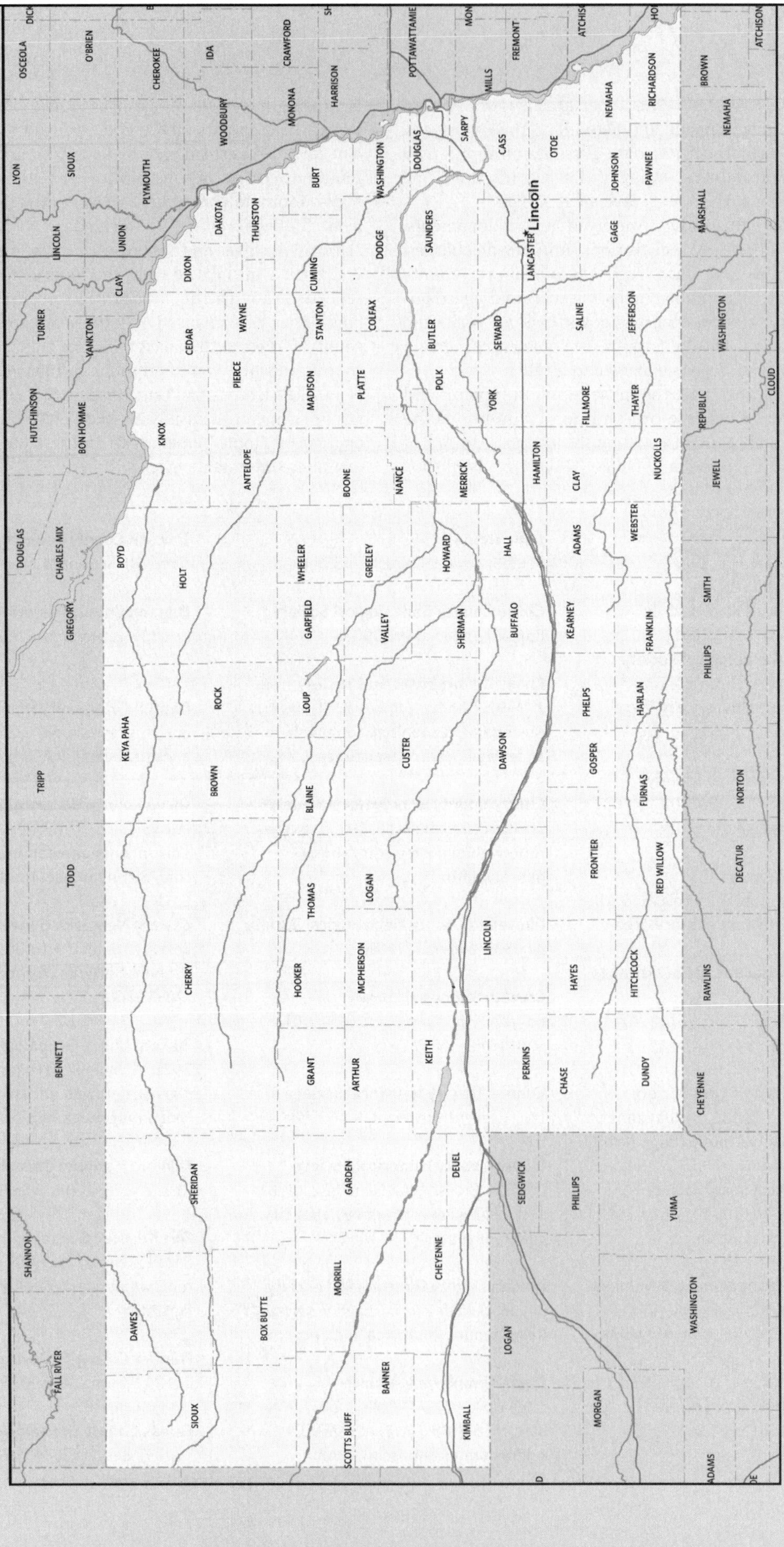

Lincoln
SIOUX
DAWES
SHERIDAN
CHERRY
KEYA PAHA
BOYD
BROWN
ROCK
HOLT
KNOX
CEDAR
DIXON
DAKOTA
THURSTON
WAYNE
PIERCE
ANTELOPE
BOX BUTTE
GRANT
HOOKER
THOMAS
BLAINE
LOUP
GARFIELD
WHEELER
BOONE
MADISON
STANTON
CUMING
BURT
SCOTTS BLUFF
BANNER
MORRILL
GARDEN
ARTHUR
MCPHERSON
LOGAN
CUSTER
VALLEY
GREELEY
NANCE
PLATTE
COLFAX
DODGE
WASHINGTON
KIMBALL
CHEYENNE
DEUEL
KEITH
LINCOLN
DAWSON
BUFFALO
SHERMAN
HOWARD
HALL
MERRICK
POLK
BUTLER
SAUNDERS
DOUGLAS
SARPY
PERKINS
CHASE
HAYES
FRONTIER
GOSPER
PHELPS
KEARNEY
ADAMS
CLAY
HAMILTON
YORK
SEWARD
LANCASTER
CASS
OTOE
DUNDY
HITCHCOCK
RED WILLOW
FURNAS
HARLAN
FRANKLIN
WEBSTER
NUCKOLLS
THAYER
FILLMORE
SALINE
JEFFERSON
GAGE
JOHNSON
PAWNEE
NEMAHA
RICHARDSON
FALL RIVER
SHANNON
BENNETT
TODD
TRIPP
GREGORY
CHARLES MIX
DOUGLAS
BON HOMME
HUTCHINSON
YANKTON
TURNER
CLAY
UNION
LINCOLN
SIOUX
LYON
OSCEOLA
O'BRIEN
CHEROKEE
PLYMOUTH
IDA
WOODBURY
MONONA
CRAWFORD
HARRISON
POTTAWATTAMIE
MILLS
FREMONT
LOGAN
MORGAN
SEDGWICK
PHILLIPS
YUMA
WASHINGTON
ADAMS
CHEYENNE
RAWLINS
DECATUR
NORTON
PHILLIPS
SMITH
JEWELL
REPUBLIC
WASHINGTON
MARSHALL
NEMAHA
BROWN
CLOUD
ATCHISON

Gage County Historical Society
101 2nd St., Beatrice, NE 68310, (402) 228-1679, **<www.byjake.com/gagecountymuseum>**

Genealogical Seekers
462 East 13th St., Wahoo, NE 68066

Genealogical Society of Wayne
1108 Walnut St., Wayne, NE 68787

Grand Island Public Library
211 N. Washington St., Grand Island, NE 68801, (308) 385-5333, **<www.gi.lib.ne.us>**

Greater Omaha Genealogical Society
Box 4011, Omaha, NE 68104, **<gogsmembers.wordpress.com>**

Kilgore Memorial Library
520 Nebraska Ave., York, NE 68467, (402) 362-2620, **<www.yorklib.org>**

Holdrege Area Genealogical Club
Box 164, Holdrege, NE 68949, **<www.rootsweb.ancestry.com/~nephelps/phelpsgen.html>**

Holt County Genealogical Society
Box 376, O'Neill, NE 68763

Holt County Historical Society
402 E Douglas, O'Neill, NE 68763, **<www.usgennet.org/usa/ne/county/holt1>**

Hooker County Genealogical Society
Box 280, Mullen, NE 69152, **<www.mullen.bravepages.com>**

Howard County Historical Society
Box 1, Saint Paul, NE 68873, (308) 754-4901, **<www.historichc.us>**

Howard County Kinquesters
317 7th St., ST Paul, NE 68873

Leila Stahl Buffet Genealogy Center
330 N. Colfax St., West Point, NE 68788, (402) 372-3831, **<www.rootsweb.ancestry.com/~necuming/lsbuffet.html>**

Jefferson County Genealogical Society
Box 163, Fairbury, NE 68352, **<www.rootsweb.ancestry.com/~nejeffgs>**

Jensen Memorial Library
443 North Kearney, Minden, NE 68959, (308) 832-2648

Johnson County Historical Society
860 Quarry Road, Box 5081, Tecumseh, NE 68450, **<jchsiowa.org>**

Lexington Genealogical Society
Box 778, Lexington, NE 68850, **<www.usgennet.org/usa/ne/county/dawson1/lexsoc.html>**

Lincoln City Library
136 S. 14th St., Lincoln, NE 68508, (402) 441-8500

Lincoln Nebraska Chapter American Historical Society of Germans from Russia
9439 Benziger Drive, Lincoln, NE 68526, (402) 438-3814, **<www.ahsgr.org/lincoln_nebraska_chapter.htm>**

Lincoln-Lancaster County Genealogical Society
Box 30055, Lincoln, NE 68503, **<llcgs.info>**

Nebraska Synod, Evangelical Lutheran Church of America
4980 S. 118th St., Ste. D, Omaha, NE 68137, (402) 896-5311, **<site.nebraskasynod.org>**

Madison County Genealogical Society
Box 1031, Norfolk, NE 68702, **<www.rootsweb.ancestry.com/~nemadiso>**

Nebraska Wesleyan University
5000 St. Paul Ave., Lincoln, NE 68504, (800) 541-3818, **<nebrwesleyan.edu>**

Midlands Chapter, American Historical Society of Germans from Russia
9373 Maplewood Blvd., Omaha, NE 68134, (402) 572-8871, **<www.ahsgr.org/midlands_chapter.htm>**

Nancy Fawcett Memorial Library
Box 318, Lodgepole, NE 69149, (308) 483-5714

Naponee Historical Society
Box 128, Naponee, NE 68960, (308) 269-2791, **<users.atcjet.net/p/psdesigns/naponeehist.html>**

Nebraska Department of Health and Human Services
301 Centennial Mall South, Lincoln, NE 68509, (402) 471-3121, **<hhs.state.ne.us>**

Nebraska Panhandle Chapter American Historical Society of Germans from Russia
2430 Ave. C, Scottsbluff, NE 69361, (308) 632-2459, **<www.ahsgr.org/nebraska_panhandle_chapter.htm>**

Nebraska State Historical Society and Archives
Box 82554, Lincoln, NE 68501, **<www.nebraskahistory.org>**

Nebraska State Genealogical Society
Box 5608, Lincoln, NE 68505, **<nesgs.org>**

Nemaha Valley Genealogical Society
Box 25, Auburn, NE 68305, **<www.rootsweb.ancestry.com/~nenemaha/nvgs.html>**

Norfolk Public Library
127 N. First St., Norfolk, NE 68701, (402) 844-2000, **<www.ci.norfolk.ne.us/library>**

North Platte Genealogical Society
Box 1452, North Platte, NE 69101

Northeast Nebraska Chapter, American Historical Society of Germans from Russia
314 So 13th Place, Norfolk, NE 68701, (402) 371-0693, **<www.ahsgr.org/northeast_nebraska_chapter.htm>**

Northeastern Nebraska Genealogical Society
Box 169, Lyons, NE 68038

Northern Antelope County Genealogical Society
Box 56, Orchard, NE 68764

Northern Nebraska Genealogical Society
Box 362, O'Neill, NE 68763

Northwest Genealogical Society
Box 6, Alliance, NE 69301, (308) 762-1387, **<usgennet.org/usa/ne/county/boxbutte/northwestgensociety.html>**

Nuckolls County Genealogical Society
Box 441, Superior, NE 68978

Omaha Nebraska Family History Center
11027 Martha St., Omaha, NE 68144, (402) 393-7641

Omaha Public Library
215 S. 15th St., Omaha, NE 68102, (402) 444-4833, **<www.omaha.lib.ne.us>**

Pastfinders Library, Saline County
730 E. 13th St, Crete, NE 68333, (402) 826-3462

Pawnee Genealogy Scouters
Box 112, Albion, NE 68620

Perkins County Genealogical Society
Box 418, Grant, NE 69140

Phelps County Museum Library
Box 164, Holdrege, NE 68949

Plains Genealogical Society
208 South Walnut St., Kimball, NE 69145

Platte Valley Kin Seekers
2916 16th St., Columbus, NE 68602, **<www.megavision.net/pvks>**

Potter Public Library
Box 317, Potter, NE 69156, (308) 879-4345

Prairie Pioneer Genealogical Society
Box 1122, Grand Island, NE 68802, **<hall.ancestralwhispers.com/societies/ppg_society.html>**

Rebecca Winters Genealogical Society
Box 323, Scottsbluff, NE 69363

Saline County Genealogical Society
Box 24, Crete, NE 68333, (402) 821-2430, **<www.rootsweb.ancestry.com/~netpl>**

Sarpy County Genealogical Society
2402 Sac Pl., Bellevue, NE 68005

Saunders Co. Genealogy Seekers
462 E. 13, Wahoo, NE 68066

Saunders County Historical Society
240 N. Walnut, Wahoo, NE 68066, (402) 443-3090, **<www.visitsaunderscounty.org/attractions/museum>**

Schuyler Historical Society and Museum
1005 B St., Schuyler, NE 68661, (402) 352-3219

Seward County Genealogical Society
Box 72, Seward, NE 68434

South Central Genealogical Society
Rte. 2, Box 57, Minden, NE 68959

Southeast Nebraska Genealogical Society
Box 562, Beatrice, NE 68301

Southwest Nebraska Genealogical Society
Box 156, McCook, NE 69001, **<nesgs.org/~swngs>**

Thayer County Genealogical Society
Box 388, Belvidere, NE 68315

Thomas County Genealogical Society
Box 136, Thedford, NE 69166

United Methodist Historical Center, Nebraska Conference
Box 4553, Lincoln, NE 68504, (402) 464-5994, **<www.umcneb.org>**

Valley County Genealogical Society
619 S. 10th, Ord, NE 68862

Wahoo Genealogical Seekers
871 W. 6th, Wahoo, NE 68066

Washington County Genealogical Society
c/o Blair Public Library, 210 S. 17th St., Blair, NE 68008, (402) 426-2013, **<www.blairpubliclibrary.com/cemetery>**

Washington County Historical Association
Box 25, Fort Calhoun, NE 68023, (402) 468-5740, **<www.newashcohist.org>**

Wayne Public Library
410 Pearl St., Wayne, NE 68787, (402) 375-3135, **<library.waynene.org>**

Wilson Public Library
910 Meridian Ave., Cozad, NE 69130, (308) 784-2019

GENERAL RESOURCES

Compendium of History, Reminiscence and Biography of Nebraska (W.C. Cox Co., 1974)

Early Pioneers of Nebraska by Beth Haring (Nebraska State Genealogical Society, ca. 1980)

Germans and German-Russians in Nebraska by Janet Warkentin Rife (Nebraska Curriculum Development Center, University of Nebraska—Lincoln, 1980)

A Guide to the Manuscript Division of the State Archives, Nebraska State Historical Society (Nebraska State Historical Society, 1974)

A Guide to the Newspaper Collection of the State Archives (Nebraska State Historical Society, 1969)

Historical Resources for Genealogists in the Nebraska State Historical Society (Nebraska State Historical Society, 1986)

History of the Catholic Church in Nebraska by Henry Weber Casper (Catholic Life Publications, 1960-1966)

A History of Czechs (Bohemians) in Nebraska by Rose Rosicky (Unigraphic, Inc., 1977)

History of Nebraska by James C. Olson: (University of Nebraska Press, 1966)

Illustrated History of Nebraska by J. Sterling Morton, et al. (Jacob North & Co., ca. 1905-1913)

The Nebraska Conference of the Augustana Synod by Charles Frederick Sandahl (filmed by the Genealogical Society of Utah, 1978)

Nebraska, A Guide to Genealogical Research by Georgene Morris Sones (Nebraska State Genealogical Society, 1984)

Nebraska, Kansas Czech Settlers by Margie Sobotka (Whipporwill, ca. 1980)

Nebraska: the Land and the People by Addison Erwin Sheldon (Lewis Publishing Co., 1931)

Nebraska Local History and Genealogy Reference Guide: A Bibliography of County Research Materials in Selected Repositories by Sylvia Nimmo and Mary Cutler (S. Nimmo, 1987)

Nebraska Newspaper Abstracts: A Computer Index to Names and Events (Nebraska State Genealogical Society, 1983)

Nebraska: Research Outline by the Church of Jesus Christ of Latter-day Saints (online at <www.familysearch.org/eng/search/RG/guide/nebraska.asp>)

Nebraskana, Biographical Sketches of Nebraska Men and Women of Achievement Who Have Been Awarded Life Membership in the Nebraskana Society edited by Sara Mullin Baldwin and Robert Morton Baldwin (The Baldwin Company, 1932)

Preliminary Edition of Guide to Depositories of Manuscript Collections in the United States-Nebraska prepared by the Nebraska Historical Records Survey Project (Nebraska Historical Records Survey Project, 1940)

Sittler Index of Surnames by Melvin Sittler (Lincoln-Lancaster County Genealogical Society, 1983-1984,1993)

☞CENSUS RECORDS

1854, 1855, 1856 Nebraska Territory Censuses compiled by E. Evelyn Cox (1977)

111 days to Zion by Hal Knight and Dr. Stanley B. Kimball (Deseret News, 1978)

Czech Immigrant Passenger List (for Nebraska) 1879 compiled by Margie Sobotka (Eastern Nebraska Genealogical Society, 1982)

☞LAND RECORDS

Homestead Guide of Kansas and Nebraska (University Microfilms International, 1970)

☞MAPS

Maps Showing County Boundaries of Nebraska, 1854-1925 by Sylvia L. Nimmo (1978)

Nebraska Atlas by N.D. Searcy and A.R. Longwell (Nebraska Atlas Publishing Co., 1964)

Nebraska Atlas and Gazetteer (DeLorme, 1996)

Nebraska Place-Names by Lilian L. Fitzpatrick (University of Nebraska Press, 1960)

The Official State Atlas of Nebraska: Compiled From Government Surveys, County Records and Personal Investigations (filmed by the Genealogical Society of Utah, 1978)

Perkey's Nebraska Place-Names by Elton Perkey (Nebraska State Historical Society, 1982)

The Post Offices of Nebraska: Part 1, Territorial Post Offices by William F. Rapp and Janet L. C. Rapp (J-B Pub., 1992)

☞MILITARY RECORDS

Nebraska Born Veterans Buried in Colorado, 1862-1949 by Gerald E. Sherard (G.E. Sherard, 1997)

A Nebraska Civil War Ancestor by Gerald E. Sherard (G.M.E. Sherard, 1994)

Nebraska's Militia: the History of the Army and Air National Guard, 1854-1991 by Douglas R. Hartman (Donning, 1994)

Nebraska, World War I Selective Service System Draft Registration Cards, 1917-1918 by the US Selective Service System (National Archives, 1987-1988)

Roster and Indexes of Soldiers, 1911 by Grand Army of the Republic (Nebraska State Historical Society, 1974)

Roster of Nebraska Soldiers (filmed by the Genealogical Society of Utah, 1958)

Roster of Nebraska Volunteers from 1861 to 1869 compiled by Edgar S. Dudley (filmed by the Genealogical Society of Utah, 1963)

Roster of Soldiers, Sailors and Marines of the War of 1812, the Mexican War, and the War of the Rebellion, Residing in Nebraska as of June 1, 1891, Who Enlisted from the State of Illinois by John C. Allen (Nebraska State Genealogical Society, 2000)

Roster of Soldiers, Sailors and Marines who Served in the War of the Rebellion, Spanish-American War and World War: Nebraska (filmed by the Genealogical Society of Utah, 1995)

☞PROBATE RECORDS

Preliminary Inventory Records of the United States District Court for the District of Nebraska: Record Group 21 compiled by Fred W. Hons and Delbert A. Bishop (Federal Records Center, 1967)

☞VITAL RECORDS

Eighth Census of the United States 1860 Nebraska Territory Mortality Schedules by Jane Emerson James (Century Enterprises, 1972)

Guide to Public Vital Statistics Records in Nebraska by the Historical Records Survey (Historical Records Survey, 1941)

Nebraska 1870 Mortality Schedule by Ronald Vern Jackson (Accelerated Indexing Systems, 1980)

Nebraska 1880 Mortality Schedule by Ronald Vern Jackson, et al. (Accelerated Indexing Systems, 1981)

Nebraska Cemeteries and Burial Sites: in Two Parts by Georgene Morris Sones, et al. (Nebraska State Genealogical Society, 1996)

•-COUNTY DETAILS-•

ADAMS

500 W. Fifth, Hastings, NE 68901, (402) 461-7107,
<adamscounty.org>

- **INCORPORATED:** Feb. 16, 1867
- **PARENT COUNTY:** Unorganized territory
- **MARRIAGE RECORDS:** unknown start, kept by County Judge
- **DIVORCE:** unknown, District Court
- **LAND:** unknown, District Court
- **PROBATE:** unknown, County Judge

ANTELOPE

501 Main St., Neligh, NE 68756, (402) 887-4410,
<co.antelope.ne.us>

- **INCORPORATED:** March 1, 1871
- **PARENT COUNTY:** L'Eau Qui Court, unorganized territory
- **MARRIAGE RECORDS:** unknown start, kept by County Judge
- **LAND:** unknown, County Clerk
- **PROBATE:** unknown, County Judge

ARTHUR

Main St., Arthur, NE 69121, (308) 764-2203,
<www.rootsweb.ancestry.com/~nearthur>

- **INCORPORATED:** March 31, 1887
- **PARENT COUNTY:** Unorganized territory
- **MARRIAGE RECORDS:** start in 1913, kept by County Court
- **DIVORCE:** 1913, District Court
- **LAND:** 1913, County Clerk
- **PROBATE:** 1913, County Court
- **COURT:** 1913, County Court
- **BURIAL:** unknown, County Cemetery Sexton
- **SCHOOL CENSUS:** 1913, County Superintendent of Schools
- **NOTES:** Arthur County was formed in 1887, but did not have county officials until 1913. Before 1913, records were kept in McPherson County.

BANNER

Box 67, Harrisburg, NE 69345, (308) 436-5265,
<bannercounty-gov.us>

- **INCORPORATED:** Nov. 6, 1888
- **PARENT COUNTY:** Cheyenne
- **BIRTH RECORDS:** start in 1920, kept by County Clerk
- **MARRIAGE:** 1890, County Court
- **DIVORCE:** unknown, Department of Health
- **LAND:** 1890, County Clerk
- **PROBATE:** 1890, County Court
- **COURT:** 1890, County Court
- **BURIAL:** unknown, Department of Health

BLACKBIRD

- **INCORPORATED:** Nov. 7, 1855
- **PARENT COUNTY:** Burt
- **NOTES:** See Thurston County. Name changed to Thurston March 28, 1889.

BLAINE

Box 136, Brewster, NE 68821, (308) 547-2222,
<blainecounty.ne.gov>

- **INCORPORATED:** March 5, 1885
- **PARENT COUNTY:** Custer
- **DIVORCE RECORDS:** start in 1887, kept by County Clerk
- **LAND:** 1887, County Clerk
- **PROBATE:** unknown, County Judge
- **COURT:** unknown, County Judge

BOONE

222 S. Fourth St., Albion, NE 68620, (402) 395-2055,
<www.co.boone.ne.us>

- **INCORPORATED:** March 1, 1871
- **PARENT COUNTY:** Unorganized territory
- **MARRIAGE RECORDS:** start in 1932, kept by County Clerk
- **DIVORCE:** unknown, County Clerk
- **LAND:** unknown, Recorder of Deeds
- **PROBATE:** unknown, County Clerk
- **COURT:** unknown, County Clerk
- **NOTES:** State archives has marriage records to 1932.

BOX BUTTE

515 Box Butte Ave. #203, Alliance, NE 69301, (308) 762-6565,
<co.box-butte.ne.us>

- **INCORPORATED:** March 23, 1887
- **PARENT COUNTY:** Dawes
- **MARRIAGE RECORDS:** unknown start, kept by County Clerk
- **DIVORCE:** unknown, District Court
- **LAND:** unknown, County Clerk
- **PROBATE:** unknown, County Judge
- **COURT:** unknown, County Judge

BOYD

401 Thayer St., Butte, NE 68722, (402) 775-2391,
<www.rootsweb.ancestry.com/~neboyd>

- **INCORPORATED:** April 20, 1891
- **PARENT COUNTY:** Holt
- **MARRIAGE RECORDS:** unknown start, kept by County Clerk
- **DIVORCE:** unknown, County Clerk
- **LAND:** unknown, County Clerk
- **PROBATE:** unknown, Clerk of County Court
- **COURT:** unknown, District Court
- **NATURALIZATION:** unknown, County Clerk
- **MILITARY:** unknown, County Clerk

BROWN

148 W. Fourth St., Ainsworth, NE 69210, (402) 387-2705,
<co.brown.ne.us>

- **INCORPORATED:** Feb. 19, 1883
- **PARENT COUNTY:** Unorganized territory
- **MARRIAGE RECORDS:** start in 1883, kept by County Clerk
- **DIVORCE:** unknown, District Court
- **LAND:** 1883, County Clerk
- **PROBATE:** unknown, County Judge

- **COURT:** unknown, District Court
- **NATURALIZATION:** 1884-1922, County Clerk
- **MILITARY:** 1919, County Clerk
- **SCHOOL CENSUS:** 1883, County Superintendent of Schools
- **NOTES:** Attached to Holt County prior to 1883.

BUFFALO

Box 1270, Kearney, NE 68848, (308) 236-1226, **<buffalogov.org>**
- **INCORPORATED:** March 14, 1855
- **PARENT COUNTY:** Original county
- **MARRIAGE RECORDS:** start in 1872, kept by County Clerk
- **DIVORCE:** unknown, District Court
- **LAND:** unknown, Registrar of Deeds
- **PROBATE:** 1872, County Judge
- **COURT:** 1872, County Judge

BURT

111 N. 13 St., Tekamah, NE 68061, (402) 374-2955, **<burtcounty.ne.gov>**
- **INCORPORATED:** Nov. 23, 1854
- **PARENT COUNTY:** Original county
- **MARRIAGE RECORDS:** unknown start, kept by County Clerk
- **DIVORCE:** unknown, District Court
- **LAND:** unknown, County Clerk
- **PROBATE:** unknown, County Judge
- **COURT:** unknown, County Judge

BUTLER

451 Fifth St., David City, NE 68632, (402) 367-7430, **<co.butler.ne.us>**
- **INCORPORATED:** Jan. 26, 1856
- **PARENT COUNTY:** Greene
- **MARRIAGE RECORDS:** unknown start, kept by County Court
- **DIVORCE:** unknown, District Court
- **LAND:** 1869, County Clerk
- **PROBATE:** unknown, County Court
- **COURT:** unknown, District Court

CALHOUN

- **INCORPORATED:** Jan. 26, 1856
- **PARENT COUNTIES:** Lancaster, Douglas
- **NOTES:** See Saunders County. Name changed to Saunders Jan. 8, 1862.

CASS

346 Main St. #202, Plattsmouth, NE 68048, (402) 296-9300, **<cassne.org>**
- **INCORPORATED:** Nov. 23, 1854
- **PARENT COUNTY:** Original county
- **MARRIAGE RECORDS:** start in 1855, kept by County Clerk
- **DIVORCE:** 1855, District Court
- **LAND:** unknown, Registrar of Deeds
- **PROBATE:** 1854, County Court
- **COURT:** 1854, County Court
- **BURIAL:** unknown, Cemetery Board

CEDAR

101 S. Broadway Ave., Box 47, Hartington, NE 68739, (402) 254-7411, **<co.cedar.ne.us>**
- **INCORPORATED:** Feb. 12, 1857
- **PARENT COUNTIES:** Dixon, Pierce
- **MARRIAGE RECORDS:** unknown start, kept by County Clerk
- **DIVORCE:** unknown, District Court
- **LAND:** unknown, County Clerk
- **PROBATE:** unknown, County Judge
- **COURT:** unknown, County Judge

CHASE

921 Broadway, Imperial, NE 69033, (308) 882-5266, **<co.chase.ne.us>**
- **INCORPORATED:** Feb. 27. 1873
- **PARENT COUNTY:** Unorganized territory
- **MARRIAGE RECORDS:** start in 1886, kept by County Judge
- **DIVORCE:** 1886, District Court
- **LAND:** 1886, County Clerk
- **PROBATE:** 1886, County Judge
- **COURT:** 1886, County Judge

CHERRY

365 N. Main St., Box 120, Valentine, NE 69201, (402) 376-2771, **<co.cherry.ne.us>**
- **INCORPORATED:** Feb. 23, 1883
- **PARENT COUNTY:** Unorganized territory
- **MARRIAGE RECORDS:** unknown start, kept by County Clerk
- **DIVORCE:** unknown, District Court
- **LAND:** unknown, County Clerk
- **PROBATE:** unknown, County Court
- **COURT:** unknown, County Court

CHEYENNE

1000 10th Ave., Box 217, Sidney, NE 69162, (308) 254-2141, **<co.cheyenne.ne.us>**
- **INCORPORATED:** Jun. 22, 1867
- **PARENT COUNTY:** Unorganized territory
- **MARRIAGE RECORDS:** unknown start, kept by County Clerk
- **DIVORCE:** unknown, District Court
- **LAND:** unknown, County Clerk
- **PROBATE:** unknown, County Court

CLAY

111 W. Fairfield St., Clay Center, NE 68933, (402) 762-3463, **<claycounty.ne.gov>**
- **INCORPORATED:** Feb. 16, 1867
- **PARENT COUNTY:** Unorganized territory
- **MARRIAGE RECORDS:** start in 1871, kept by County Clerk
- **DIVORCE:** unknown, District Court
- **LAND:** 1871, County Clerk
- **PROBATE:** unknown, County Court
- **COURT:** unknown, District Court
- **MILITARY:** 1921, County Clerk
- **NATURALIZATION:** unknown, District Court
- **NOTES:** County Clerk has birth and death records 1917-1918.

CLAY, OLD
- **INCORPORATED:** March 7, 1855
- **PARENT COUNTY:** Original county
- **NOTES:** Absorbed by Gage County in 1864.

COLFAX
411 E. 11th St., Schuyler, NE 68661, (402) 352-3434,
<colfaxcounty.ne.gov>
- **INCORPORATED:** Feb. 15, 1869
- **PARENT COUNTY:** Platte
- **MARRIAGE RECORDS:** start in 1869, kept by County Judge
- **DIVORCE:** 1881, District Court
- **LAND:** 1860, County Clerk
- **PROBATE:** 1886, County Judge
- **COURT:** 1885, County Judge

CUMING
200 S. Lincoln St., West Point, NE 68788, (402) 372-6002,
<co.cuming.ne.us>
- **INCORPORATED:** March 16, 1855
- **PARENT COUNTY:** Burt
- **MARRIAGE RECORDS:** start in 1866, kept by County Judge
- **DIVORCE:** 1869, District Court
- **PROBATE:** 1866, County Judge
- **COURT:** 1960, County Judge
- **SCHOOL CENSUS:** unknown, County Judge

CUSTER
431 S. 10th Ave., Broken Bow, NE 68822, (308) 872-5701,
<co.custer.ne.us>
- **INCORPORATED:** Feb. 17, 1877
- **PARENT COUNTY:** Unorganized territory
- **BIRTH RECORDS:** start in 1910, kept by County Clerk
- **MARRIAGE:** 1878, County Judge
- **DIVORCE:** 1881, District Court
- **DEATH:** 1915, County Clerk
- **LAND:** 1880, Registrar of Deeds
- **PROBATE:** 1887, County Judge
- **COURT:** 1887, County Judge
- **OBITUARIES:** 1877, County Clerk
- **PIONEER BIOGRAPHICAL DATA:** unknown, County Clerk
- **NOTES:** County historical society has many other records.

DAKOTA
1601 Broadway St., Dakota City, NE 68731, (402) 987-2126,
<www.dakotacountyne.org>
- **INCORPORATED:** March 7, 1855
- **PARENT COUNTY:** Burt
- **MARRIAGE RECORDS:** start in 1856, kept by County Clerk
- **DIVORCE:** 1862, District Court
- **LAND:** 1856, Registrar of Deeds
- **PROBATE:** 1858, County Court
- **COURT:** 1862, Court
- **NATURALIZATION:** unknown, District Court
- **MILITARY:** 1921, County Clerk

DAWES
451 Main St., Chadron, NE 69337, (308) 432-0100,
<co.dawes.ne.us>
- **INCORPORATED:** Feb. 19, 1885
- **PARENT COUNTY:** Sioux
- **MARRIAGE RECORDS:** unknown start, kept by County Judge
- **DIVORCE:** unknown, District Court
- **LAND:** 1880, County Clerk
- **PROBATE:** unknown, County Judge

DAWSON
Box 370, Lexington, NE 68850, (308) 324-2127,
<www.dawsoncountyne.net>
- **INCORPORATED:** Jan. 11, 1860
- **PARENT COUNTY:** Unorganized territory
- **MARRIAGE RECORDS:** start in 1873, kept by County Clerk
- **DIVORCE:** unknown, District Court
- **LAND:** unknown, Registrar of Deeds
- **PROBATE:** unknown, County Court
- **COURT:** unknown, County Court
- **NATURALIZATION:** unknown, District Court
- **MILITARY:** unknown, Veterans Service Office

DEUEL
Third & Vincent, Chappell, NE 69129, (308) 874-3308,
<co.deuel.ne.us>
- **INCORPORATED:** Nov. 6, 1888
- **PARENT COUNTY:** Cheyenne
- **MARRIAGE RECORDS:** unknown start, kept by County Judge
- **DIVORCE:** unknown, County Clerk
- **LAND:** unknown, County Clerk
- **PROBATE:** unknown, County Judge
- **COURT:** 1890, County Clerk
- **BURIAL:** unknown, County Clerk

DIXON
302 Third St., Ponca, NE 68770, (402) 755-2208,
<co.dixon.ne.us>
- **INCORPORATED:** Jan. 26, 1856
- **PARENT COUNTIES:** Blackbird, Izard, unorganized territory
- **BIRTH RECORDS:** start in 1919, kept by County Clerk
- **DEATH:** 1919, County Clerk
- **LAND:** 1871, County Clerk
- **BURIAL:** 1919, County Clerk

DODGE
435 N. Park Ave., Fremont, NE 68025, (402) 727-2767,
<dodgecounty.ne.gov>
- **INCORPORATED:** Nov. 23, 1854
- **PARENT COUNTY:** Original county
- **MARRIAGE RECORDS:** unknown start, kept by County Clerk
- **DIVORCE:** unknown, District Court
- **LAND:** unknown, Registrar of Deeds
- **PROBATE:** unknown, County Judge

DOUGLAS

1819 Farman St., Omaha, NE 68102, (402) 444-7143,
<douglascounty-ne.gov>

- **INCORPORATED:** Nov. 23, 1854
- **PARENT COUNTY:** Original county
- **MARRIAGE RECORDS:** unknown start, kept by County Judge
- **DIVORCE:** unknown, District Court
- **PROBATE:** unknown, County Judge
- **MILITARY:** unknown, County Clerk

DUNDY

Box 506, Benkelman, NE 69021, (308) 423-2058,
<co.dundy.ne.us>

- **INCORPORATED:** Feb. 27, 1873
- **PARENT COUNTY:** Unorganized territory
- **BIRTH RECORDS:** start in 1907, kept by County Clerk
- **DEATH:** 1904, County Clerk
- **DIVORCE:** unknown, County Clerk
- **PROBATE:** unknown, County Judge
- **COURT:** unknown, County Clerk
- **BURIAL:** unknown, County Clerk

EMMET

- **INCORPORATED:** Feb. 10, 1857
- **PARENT COUNTIES:** Pierce, unorganized territory
- **NOTES:** See Knox County. Formerly L'Eau Qui Court County. Name changed to Emmet Feb. 18, 1867, and to Knox Feb. 21, 1873.

FILLMORE

900 G St., Geneva, NE 68361, (402) 759-4931,
<fillmorecounty.org>

- **INCORPORATED:** Jan. 26, 1856
- **PARENT COUNTY:** Unorganized territory
- **MARRIAGE RECORDS:** start in 1872, kept by County Clerk
- **DIVORCE:** unknown, District Court
- **LAND:** 1872, County Clerk
- **PROBATE:** unknown, County Court
- **COURT:** unknown, County Court
- **SCHOOL CENSUS:** unknown, County Superintendent of Schools
- **NOTES:** County Clerk has delayed birth records.

FORNEY

- **INCORPORATED:** Nov. 23, 1854
- **PARENT COUNTY:** Original county
- **NOTES:** See Nemaha County. Name changed to Nemaha March 7, 1855.

FRANKLIN

405 15th Ave., Box 146, Franklin, NE 68939, (308) 425-6202,
<co.franklin.ne.us>

- **INCORPORATED:** Feb. 16, 1867
- **PARENT COUNTY:** Kearney
- **MARRIAGE RECORDS:** start in 1872, kept by County Clerk
- **DIVORCE:** unknown, County Clerk
- **LAND:** unknown, County Clerk

FRONTIER

1 Wellington St., Box 40, Stockville, NE 69042, (308) 367-8641,
<co.frontier.ne.us>

- **INCORPORATED:** Jan. 17, 1872
- **PARENT COUNTY:** Unorganized territory
- **MARRIAGE RECORDS:** unknown start, kept by County Clerk
- **DIVORCE:** unknown, County Judge
- **LAND:** unknown, Registrar of Deeds
- **PROBATE:** unknown, County Judge
- **COURT:** unknown, County Judge
- **NATURALIZATION:** unknown, County Judge
- **MILITARY:** unknown, County Clerk
- **BURIAL:** unknown, Clerk and Treasurer
- **SCHOOL CENSUS:** unknown, Superintendent of Schools

FURNAS

912 R St., Box 387, Beaver City, NE 68926, (308) 268-4145,
<furnascounty.ne.gov>

- **INCORPORATED:** Feb. 27, 1873
- **PARENT COUNTY:** Unorganized territory
- **MARRIAGE RECORDS:** unknown start, kept by County Judge
- **DIVORCE:** unknown, District Court
- **LAND:** 1873, County Clerk
- **PROBATE:** unknown, County Judge
- **COURT:** unknown, County Judge

GAGE

612 Grant St., Box 429, Beatrice, NE 68310, (402) 223-1300,
<co.gage.ne.us>

- **INCORPORATED:** March 16 1855
- **PARENT COUNTY:** Original county
- **MARRIAGE RECORDS:** start in 1860, kept in County Judge
- **DIVORCE:** unknown, District Court
- **PROBATE:** 1860, County Judge

GARDEN

611 Main St., Box 486, Oshkosh, NE 69154, (308) 772-3924,
<co.garden.ne.us>

- **INCORPORATED:** Nov. 6, 1909
- **PARENT COUNTY:** Deuel
- **MARRIAGE RECORDS:** unknown start, kept by County Clerk
- **DIVORCE:** unknown, District Court
- **LAND:** unknown, County Clerk
- **PROBATE:** unknown, County Judge
- **COURT:** unknown, County Judge

GARFIELD

250 S. Eighth St., Box 218, Burwell, NE 68823, (308) 346-4161,
<www.garfieldcounty.ne.gov>

- **INCORPORATED:** Nov. 8, 1884
- **PARENT COUNTY:** Wheeler
- **MARRIAGE RECORDS:** unknown start, kept by County Judge
- **DIVORCE:** unknown, County Judge
- **PROBATE:** unknown, County Judge

GOSPER

507 Smith Ave., Box 136, Elwood, NE 68937, (308) 785-2611,
<co.gosper.ne.us>

- **INCORPORATED:** Nov. 26, 1873
- **PARENT COUNTY:** Unorganized territory, Kearney
- **MARRIAGE RECORDS:** start in 1891, kept by County Judge
- **DIVORCE:** 1880, County Clerk
- **LAND:** unknown, County Clerk
- **PROBATE:** 1891, County Judge
- **COURT:** 1920, County Judge

GRANT

Box 139, Hyannis, NE 69350, (308) 458-2488,
<www.usgennet.org/usa/ne/county/sioux>

- **INCORPORATED:** March 31, 1887
- **PARENT COUNTY:** Unorganized territory
- **MARRIAGE RECORDS:** start in 1888, kept by County Clerk
- **DIVORCE:** 1890, County Clerk
- **LAND:** 1888, County Clerk
- **PROBATE:** unknown, County Judge
- **COURT:** 1897, County Clerk
- **MILITARY:** 1921, County Clerk
- **NOTES:** County Clerk has naturalization records 1891-1912.

GREELEY

Box 287, Greeley, NE 68842, (308) 428-3625,
<greeleycounty.ne.gov>

- **INCORPORATED:** March 1, 1871
- **PARENT COUNTY:** Unorganized territory
- **MARRIAGE RECORDS:** unknown start, kept by County Clerk
- **DIVORCE:** unknown, District Court
- **LAND:** unknown, County Clerk
- **PROBATE:** unknown, County Court
- **COURT:** unknown, District Court
- **NATURALIZATION:** unknown, County Clerk
- **MILITARY:** unknown, County Clerk

GREENE

- **INCORPORATED:** March 6, 1855
- **PARENT COUNTIES:** Cass, Pierce (old)
- **NOTES:** See Seward County. Name changed to Seward Jan. 3, 1862.

HALL

121 S. Pine St., Grand Island, NE 68801, (308) 385-5080,
<hallcountyne.gov>

- **INCORPORATED:** Nov. 4, 1858
- **PARENT COUNTY:** Original county
- **MARRIAGE RECORDS:** start in 1869, kept by County Clerk
- **DIVORCE:** unknown, District Court
- **LAND:** unknown, Registrar of Deeds
- **PROBATE:** unknown, County Judge
- **COURT:** unknown, District Court

HAMILTON

1111 13th St. Suite 1, Aurora, NE 68818, (402) 694-3443,
<co.hamilton.ne.us>

- **INCORPORATED:** Feb. 16, 1867
- **PARENT COUNTY:** Unorganized territory
- **MARRIAGE RECORDS:** 1870, County Clerk
- **DIVORCE:** unknown, District Court
- **LAND:** 1870, County Clerk
- **PROBATE:** unknown, County Judge
- **COURT:** unknown, County Judge

HARLAN

706 W. Second St., Alma, NE 68920, (308) 928-2173,
<www.rootsweb.ancestry.com/~neharlan>

- **INCORPORATED:** Jun. 3, 1871
- **PARENT COUNTY:** Kearney
- **MARRIAGE RECORDS:** unknown start, kept by County Clerk
- **DIVORCE:** unknown, District Court
- **LAND:** unknown, County Clerk and Registrar of Deeds
- **PROBATE:** unknown, County Judge
- **COURT:** unknown, County Judge

HARRISON

- **INCORPORATED:** 2003
- **PARENT COUNTY:** unknown
- **NOTES:** Never organized county in southwest corner of state. With Lincoln County in 1870 Census.

HAYES

502 Troth St., Box 370, Hayes Center, NE 69032, (308) 286-3413,
<hayescounty.ne.gov>

- **INCORPORATED:** Feb. 19, 1877
- **PARENT COUNTY:** Unorganized territory
- **DEATH:** unknown start, kept by County Clerk
- **LAND:** unknown, County Clerk
- **BURIAL:** unknown, County Clerk

HITCHCOCK

229 E. D St., Box 248, Trenton, NE 69044, (308) 334-5646,
<co.hitchcock.ne.us>

- **INCORPORATED:** Feb. 27, 1873
- **PARENT COUNTY:** Unorganized territory
- **MARRIAGE RECORDS:** unknown start, kept by County Clerk
- **DIVORCE:** unknown, County Clerk
- **LAND:** unknown, County Clerk
- **PROBATE:** unknown, County Judge
- **COURT:** unknown, County Clerk

HOLT

204 N. Fourth St., Box 329, O'Neill, NE 68763, (402) 336-1762,
<co.holt.ne.us>

- **INCORPORATED:** Jan. 13, 1860
- **PARENT COUNTY:** Unorganized territory
- **MARRIAGE RECORDS:** start in 1878, kept by County Clerk
- **DIVORCE:** 1879, District Court
- **LAND:** 1879, Registrar of Deeds
- **PROBATE:** 1882, County Judge
- **COURT:** 1882, County Judge
- **NOTES:** Formerly West County. Name changed to Holt Jan. 9, 1862.

HOOKER
303 NE First St., Box 184, Mullen, NE 69152, (308) 546-2244,
<co.hooker.ne.us>
- **INCORPORATED:** March 29, 1889
- **PARENT COUNTY:** Unorganized territory
- **BIRTH RECORDS:** start in 1919, kept by County Clerk
- **MARRIAGE:** unknown, County Judge
- **DEATH:** 1919, County Clerk
- **LAND:** 1889, County Clerk
- **PROBATE:** unknown, County Judge

HOWARD
612 Indian S., Box 25, St. Paul, NE 68873, (308) 754-4343,
<howardcounty.ne.gov>
- **INCORPORATED:** March 1, 1871
- **PARENT COUNTY:** Hall
- **MARRIAGE RECORDS:** start in 1872, kept by County Judge
- **DIVORCE:** 1873, County Judge
- **LAND:** 1872, County Judge
- **PROBATE:** 1872, County Judge
- **COURT:** 1872, County Judge
- **NATURALIZATION:** 1872, County Judge

IZARD
- **INCORPORATED:** March 6, 1855
- **PARENT COUNTY:** Unorganized territory
- **NOTES:** See Stanton County. Name changed to Stanton Jan. 10, 1862.

JACKSON
- **INCORPORATED:** 1855
- **PARENT COUNTY:** Unorganized territory
- **NOTES:** See Fillmore County. Never organized. Changed to Fillmore Jan. 26, 1856.

JEFFERSON
411 Fourth St., Fairbury, NE 68352, (402) 729-2323,
<co.jefferson.ne.us>
- **INCORPORATED:** Jan. 26, 1856
- **PARENT COUNTY:** Unorganized territory
- **MARRIAGE RECORDS:** unknown start, kept by County Clerk
- **DIVORCE:** unknown, District Court
- **LAND:** unknown, Registrar of Deeds
- **PROBATE:** unknown, County Judge
- **COURT:** unknown, County Judge
- **NOTES:** Formerly Jones County. Name changed to Jefferson 1864. Boundaries redefined 1867 and 1871.

JOHNSON
Box 416, Tecumseh, NE 68450, (402) 335-3246,
<co.johnson.ne.us>
- **INCORPORATED:** March 2, 1855
- **PARENT COUNTY:** Nemaha
- **MARRIAGE RECORDS:** start in 1858, kept by County Clerk
- **DIVORCE:** 1858, District Court
- **LAND:** 1858, County Clerk
- **PROBATE:** unknown, County Judge
- **COURT:** unknown, County Judge

JONES
- **INCORPORATED:** Jan. 26, 1856
- **PARENT COUNTY:** Unorganized territory
- **NOTES:** See Jefferson County. Absorbed by Jefferson in 1867.

KEARNEY
424 N. Colorado, Minden, NE 68959, (308) 832-2723,
<kearneycounty.ne.gov>
- **INCORPORATED:** Jan. 10, 1860
- **PARENT COUNTY:** Unorganized territory
- **MARRIAGE RECORDS:** start in 1872, kept by County Clerk
- **DIVORCE:** unknown, District Court
- **LAND:** unknown, County Clerk
- **PROBATE:** unknown, County Judge
- **COURT:** unknown, County Judge

KEITH
511 N. Spruce St., Box 149, Ogallala, NE 69153, (308) 284-4726,
<co.keith.ne.us>
- **INCORPORATED:** Feb. 27, 1873
- **PARENT COUNTY:** Unorganized territory
- **BIRTH RECORDS:** unknown start, kept by County Clerk
- **MARRIAGE:** unknown, County Judge
- **DIVORCE:** unknown, District Court
- **DEATH:** unknown, County Clerk
- **LAND:** unknown, County Clerk
- **PROBATE:** unknown, District Court
- **COURT:** unknown, District Court

KEYA PAHA
Box 349, Springview, NE 68778, (402) 497-3791,
<co.keya-paha.ne.us>
- **INCORPORATED:** Nov. 4, 1884
- **PARENT COUNTY:** Brown
- **MARRIAGE RECORDS:** start in 1886, kept by County Clerk
- **DIVORCE:** 1886, County Clerk
- **LAND:** 1886, County Clerk
- **PROBATE:** 1886, County Clerk
- **COURT:** 1886, County Clerk
- **SCHOOL CENSUS:** unknown, County Clerk

KIMBALL
114 E. Third St., Kimball, NE 69145, (308) 235-2241,
<co.kimball.ne.us>
- **INCORPORATED:** Nov. 6, 1888
- **PARENT COUNTY:** Cheyenne
- **MARRIAGE RECORDS:** unknown start, kept by County Judge
- **DIVORCE:** unknown, County Clerk
- **PROBATE:** unknown, County Clerk
- **COURT:** unknown, County Judge

KNOX
Box 166, Center, NE 68724, (402) 288-4282,
<co.knox.ne.us>
- **INCORPORATED:** Feb. 10, 1857
- **PARENT COUNTIES:** Pierce, unorganized territory
- **MARRIAGE RECORDS:** unknown start, kept by County Clerk
- **DIVORCE:** unknown, District Court

- **LAND:** unknown, Registrar of Deeds
- **PROBATE:** unknown, County Judge
- **COURT:** unknown, County Judge
- **NOTES:** Formerly L'Eau Qui Court and Emmet counties. Created as L'Eau Qui Court County. Name changed to Emmet Feb. 18, 1867. Name changed to Knox Feb. 21, 1873.

L'EAU QUI COURT
- **INCORPORATED:** Feb. 10, 1857
- **PARENT COUNTIES:** Pierce, Unorganized territory
- **NOTES:** See Knox County. Name changed to Emmet Feb. 18, 1867. Name changed to Knox Feb. 21, 1873.

LANCASTER
555 S. 10th St., Lincoln, NE 68508, (402) 441-7484, **<lancaster.ne.gov>**
- **INCORPORATED:** March 6, 1855
- **PARENT COUNTIES:** Cass, Pierce (old)
- **MARRIAGE RECORDS:** unknown start, kept by County Judge
- **LAND:** unknown, County Clerk
- **PROBATE:** unknown, County Judge

LINCOLN
301 N. Jeffers, North Platte, NE 69101, (308) 532-4051, **<lincoln.ne.gov>**
- **INCORPORATED:** Jan. 7, 1860
- **PARENT COUNTY:** Unorganized territory
- **MARRIAGE RECORDS:** unknown start, kept by County Clerk
- **DIVORCE:** unknown, District Court
- **LAND:** unknown, Registrar of Deeds
- **PROBATE:** unknown, County Court
- **COURT:** unknown, County Court
- **NOTES:** Formerly Shorter County. Name changed to Lincoln Dec. 11, 1861.

LOGAN
317 Main St., Box 8, Stapleton, NE 69163, (308) 636-2311, **<www.rootsweb.ancestry.com/~nelogan>**
- **INCORPORATED:** Feb. 24, 1885
- **PARENT COUNTY:** Unorganized territory
- **MARRIAGE RECORDS:** start in 1885, kept by County Judge
- **DIVORCE:** 1885, County Judge
- **LAND:** unknown, County Clerk
- **PROBATE:** 1885, County Judge
- **COURT:** 1885, County Judge
- **NOTES:** County Judge has partial burial records.

LOUP
Box 187, Taylor, NE 68879, (308) 942-3135, **<co.loup.ne.us>**
- **INCORPORATED:** Feb. 23, 1883
- **PARENT COUNTY:** Unorganized territory
- **MARRIAGE RECORDS:** unknown start, kept by County Judge
- **DIVORCE:** 1887, County Clerk
- **LAND:** 1887, County Clerk
- **PROBATE:** unknown, County Judge
- **COURT:** 1887, County Clerk

LOUP, OLD
- **INCORPORATED:** March 6, 1855
- **PARENT COUNTY:** Burt
- **NOTES:** Disorganized in 1856; became part of Izard, Madison, Monroe and Platte counties.

LYON
- **INCORPORATED:** 2003
- **PARENT COUNTY:** unknown
- **NOTES:** Never organized county in southwest corner of state. With Lincoln County in 1870 Census.

MADISON
110 Clara Davis Dr., Box 290, Madison, NE 68748, (402) 454-3311, **<co.madison.ne.us>**
- **INCORPORATED:** Jan. 26, 1856
- **PARENT COUNTIES:** McNeale, Loup (old)
- **MARRIAGE RECORDS:** start in 1868, kept by County Clerk
- **DIVORCE:** 1907, County Clerk
- **LAND:** 1868, County Clerk
- **PROBATE:** 1863, County Clerk
- **COURT:** 1907, County Clerk

MCNEALE
- **INCORPORATED:** 1855
- **PARENT COUNTY:** Burt
- **NOTES:** Absorbed by Madison and Izard (now Stanton) counties in 1856.

MCPHERSON
Box 122, Tryon, NE 69167, (308) 587-2363, **<www.rootsweb.ancestry.com/~nemcpher>**
- **INCORPORATED:** March 31, 1887
- **PARENT COUNTIES:** Lincoln, Keith, Logan
- **MARRIAGE RECORDS:** unknown start, kept by County Clerk
- **DIVORCE:** unknown, County Clerk
- **LAND:** unknown, County Clerk
- **PROBATE:** unknown, County Judge
- **COURT:** unknown, County Judge

MERRICK
1510 18th St., Box 27, Central City, NE 68826, (308) 946-2881, **<merrickcounty.ne.gov>**
- **INCORPORATED:** Nov. 4, 1858
- **PARENT COUNTY:** Unorganized territory
- **BIRTH RECORDS:** unknown start, kept by County Clerk
- **MARRIAGE:** unknown, County Judge
- **DIVORCE:** unknown, County Judge
- **DEATH:** unknown, County Clerk
- **LAND:** 1873, Registrar of Deeds
- **PROBATE:** unknown, County Judge
- **COURT:** unknown, County Judge

MONROE
- **INCORPORATED:** 1856
- **PARENT COUNTY:** Loup (old)
- **NOTES:** Absorbed by Platte County in 1860.

MORRILL
Box 610, Bridgeport, NE 69336, (308) 262-0860,
<morrillcounty.ne.gov>
- **INCORPORATED:** Nov. 12, 1908
- **PARENT COUNTY:** Cheyenne
- **BIRTH RECORDS:** start in 1917, kept by County Clerk
- **MARRIAGE RECORDS:** unknown, County Judge
- **DEATH:** 1917, County Clerk
- **LAND:** 1909, County Clerk
- **PROBATE:** unknown, County Judge
- **BURIAL:** 1917, County Clerk

NANCE
209 Esther St., Fullerton, NE 68638, (308) 536-2331,
<co.nance.ne.us>
- **INCORPORATED:** Feb. 13, 1879
- **PARENT COUNTY:** Pawnee Indian Reservation
- **MARRIAGE RECORDS:** start in 1890, kept by County Clerk
- **DIVORCE:** 1882, District Court
- **LAND:** 1879, County Clerk
- **PROBATE:** unknown, County Judge
- **COURT:** 1882, District Court

NEMAHA
1824 N St., Auburn, NE 68305, (402) 274-4213,
<nemahacounty.ne.gov>
- **INCORPORATED:** Nov. 23, 1854
- **PARENT COUNTY:** Original county
- **MARRIAGE RECORDS:** start in 1856, kept by County Clerk
- **DIVORCE:** unknown, District Court
- **LAND:** unknown, County Clerk
- **PROBATE:** unknown, County Judge
- **COURT:** unknown, County Judge
- **MILITARY:** unknown, County Clerk
- **NOTES:** Formerly Forney County. Name changed to Nemaha March 7, 1855.

NUCKOLLS
150 S. Main St., Box 366, Nelson, NE 68961, (409) 225-4361,
<nuckollscounty.ne.gov>
- **INCORPORATED:** Jan. 13, 1860
- **PARENT COUNTY:** Unorganized territory
- **MARRIAGE RECORDS:** unknown start, kept by County Judge
- **DIVORCE:** unknown, District Court
- **LAND:** 1900, County Clerk
- **PROBATE:** unknown, County Judge
- **COURT:** unknown, District Court

OTOE
1021 Central Ave., Box 249, Nebraska City, NE 68410, (402) 873-9505, **<co.otoe.ne.us>**
- **INCORPORATED:** Nov. 23, 1854
- **PARENT COUNTIES:** Cass, Pierce (old)
- **NOTES:** Formerly Pierce (old). Name changed to Otoe.
- **MARRIAGE RECORDS:** unknown start, kept by County Clerk
- **DIVORCE:** unknown, County Clerk
- **LAND:** unknown, Registrar of Deeds
- **PROBATE:** unknown, County Judge
- **COURT:** unknown, County Clerk

PAWNEE
625 Sixth St., Box 431, Pawnee City, NE 68420, (402) 852-2962,
<co.pawnee.ne.us>
- **INCORPORATED:** March 6, 1855
- **PARENT COUNTY:** Richardson
- **MARRIAGE RECORDS:** start in 1858, kept by County Clerk
- **DIVORCE:** unknown, County Clerk
- **LAND:** unknown, County Clerk
- **PROBATE:** unknown, County Judge
- **COURT:** unknown, County Clerk

PERKINS
200 Lincoln Ave., Box 156, Grant, NE 69140, (308) 352-4643,
<co.perkins.ne.us>
- **INCORPORATED:** Nov. 8, 1887
- **PARENT COUNTY:** Keith
- **MARRIAGE RECORDS:** unknown start, kept by County Clerk
- **DIVORCE:** unknown, County Clerk
- **LAND:** unknown, County Clerk
- **PROBATE:** unknown, County Judge
- **COURT:** unknown, County Clerk

PHELPS
Box 404, Holdrege, NE 68949, (308) 995-4469, **<phelpsgov.org>**
- **INCORPORATED:** Feb. 11, 1873
- **PARENT COUNTY:** Kearney
- **MARRIAGE RECORDS:** unknown start, kept by County Clerk
- **DIVORCE:** unknown, District Court
- **LAND:** unknown, County Clerk
- **PROBATE:** unknown, County Judge

PIERCE
111 W. Court St. Room 1, Pierce, NE 68767, (402) 329-4225,
<co.pierce.ne.us>
- **INCORPORATED:** Jan. 26, 1856
- **PARENT COUNTY:** Izard, unorganized territory
- **MARRIAGE RECORDS:** unknown start, kept by County Clerk
- **DIVORCE:** unknown, District Court
- **LAND:** unknown, County Clerk
- **PROBATE:** unknown, County Court
- **NATURALIZATION:** unknown, District Court
- **MILITARY:** unknown, County Clerk
- **SCHOOL CENSUS:** unknown, School Superintendent
- **NOTES:** Formerly Otoe County

PIERCE, OLD

- **INCORPORATED:** 1854
- **PARENT COUNTY:** Original County
- **NOTES:** See Otoe County. Became part of Otoe County in 1855.

PLATTE

2610 14th St., Columbus, NE 68601, (402) 563-4904, **<plattecounty.net>**

- **INCORPORATED:** Jan. 26, 1856
- **PARENT COUNTY:** Loup (old)
- **MARRIAGE RECORDS:** unknown start, kept by County Judge
- **DIVORCE:** unknown, District Court
- **LAND:** unknown, County Assessor
- **PROBATE:** unknown, County Judge
- **COURT:** unknown, District Court

POLK

400 Hawkeye St., Box 276, Osceola, NE 68651, (402) 747-5431, **<polkcounty.ne.gov>**

- **INCORPORATED:** Jan. 26, 1856
- **PARENT COUNTY:** York, unorganized territory
- **MARRIAGE RECORDS:** unknown start, kept by County Judge
- **LAND:** unknown, County Clerk
- **PROBATE:** unknown, County Judge

RED WILLOW

502 Norris Ave., McCook, NE 69001, (308) 345-1552, **<co.red-willow.ne.us>**

- **INCORPORATED:** Feb. 27, 1873
- **PARENT COUNTY:** Unorganized territory
- **MARRIAGE RECORDS:** start in 1874, kept by County Clerk
- **DIVORCE:** unknown, District Court
- **LAND:** 1888, County Clerk
- **PROBATE:** unknown, County Court
- **COURT:** unknown, District Court
- **MILITARY:** unknown, Veteran Service Office
- **SCHOOL CENSUS:** unknown, School Superintendent

RICHARDSON

1700 Stone St., Falls City, NE 68355, (402) 245-2911, **<co.richardson.ne.us>**

- **INCORPORATED:** Nov. 23, 1854
- **PARENT COUNTY:** Original county
- **BIRTH RECORDS:** start in 1918, kept by County Clerk
- **MARRIAGE:** ca. 1800, County Judge
- **DEATH:** 1918, County Clerk
- **DIVORCE:** unknown, District Court
- **LAND:** unknown, Registrar of Deeds
- **PROBATE:** unknown, County Judge
- **COURT:** unknown, County Judge

ROCK

400 State St., Box 367, Bassett, NE 68714, (402) 684-3933, **<co.rock.ne.us>**

- **INCORPORATED:** Nov. 6, 1888
- **PARENT COUNTY:** Brown
- **MARRIAGE RECORDS:** unknown start, kept by County Judge
- **DIVORCE:** 1889, County Clerk
- **LAND:** 1889, County Clerk
- **PROBATE:** 1889, County Clerk
- **COURT:** 1889, County Clerk

SALINE

215 S. Court St., Box 865, Wilber, NE 68465, (402) 821-2374, **<co.saline.ne.us>**

- **INCORPORATED:** March 6, 1855
- **PARENT COUNTY:** Original county
- **BIRTH RECORDS:** start in 1976, kept by County Clerk
- **MARRIAGE:** 1886, County Court
- **DIVORCE:** 1886, District Court
- **DEATH:** 1976, County Clerk
- **LAND:** 1886, County Clerk
- **PROBATE:** 1870, County Court
- **COURT:** 1886, District Court

SARPY

1210 Golden Gate Dr., Papillion, NE 68046, (402) 593-2100, **<www.sarpy.com>**

- **INCORPORATED:** Feb. 7, 1857
- **PARENT COUNTY:** Douglas
- **MARRIAGE RECORDS:** unknown start, kept by County Judge
- **LAND:** unknown, County Clerk
- **PROBATE:** unknown, County Judge

SAUNDERS

Box 61, Wahoo, NE 68066, (402) 443-8101, **<saunderscounty.ne.gov>**

- **INCORPORATED:** Jan. 26, 1856
- **PARENT COUNTIES:** Lancaster, Douglas
- **MARRIAGE RECORDS:** unknown start, kept by County Clerk
- **DIVORCE:** unknown, County Clerk
- **LAND:** unknown, County Clerk
- **PROBATE:** unknown, County Clerk
- **COURT:** unknown, County Clerk
- **BURIAL:** unknown, County Clerk
- **NOTES:** Formerly Calhoun County. Name changed to Saunders Jan. 8, 1862.

SCOTTS BLUFF

1825 10th St., Gering, NE 69341, (308) 436-6600, **<scottsbluffcounty.org>**

- **INCORPORATED:** Nov. 6, 1888
- **PARENT COUNTY:** Cheyenne
- **MARRIAGE RECORDS:** unknown, County Clerk
- **DIVORCE:** unknown, County Judge
- **PROBATE:** unknown, County Judge
- **COURT:** unknown, County Judge

SEWARD

529 Seward St., Box 190, Seward, NE 68434, (402) 643-2883, **<www.connectseward.org/cgov>**

- **INCORPORATED:** March 6, 1855
- **PARENT COUNTY:** Cass, Pierce (old)
- **MARRIAGE RECORDS:** start in 1866, kept by County Clerk
- **DIVORCE:** 1868, District Court
- **LAND:** 1866, County Clerk

- **PROBATE:** 1869, County Court
- **COURT:** 1869, District Court
- **NOTES:** Formerly Greene County. Name changed to Seward Jan. 3, 1862.

SHERIDAN

301 E. Second St., Box 39, Rushville, NE 69360, (308) 327-2633, **<www.sheridancountynebraska.com>**

- **INCORPORATED:** Feb. 25, 1885
- **PARENT COUNTY:** Sioux
- **MARRIAGE RECORDS:** unknown start, kept by County Judge
- **DIVORCE:** unknown, District Court
- **PROBATE:** unknown, County Judge
- **COURT:** unknown, County Judge

SHERMAN

630 O St., Box 456, Loup City, NE 68853, (308) 745-1513, **<co.sherman.ne.us>**

- **INCORPORATED:** March 1, 1871
- **PARENT COUNTIES:** Buffalo, unorganized territory
- **NOTES:** County Clerk has naturalization records 1882-1920.
- **MARRIAGE RECORDS:** start in 1883, kept by County Clerk
- **DIVORCE:** 1882, County Clerk
- **LAND:** 1873, County Clerk
- **PROBATE:** unknown, County Clerk Magistrate
- **COURT:** 1882, County Clerk

SHORTER

- **INCORPORATED:** Jan. 7, 1860
- **PARENT COUNTY:** Unorganized territory
- **NOTES:** See Lincoln County. Name changed to Lincoln Dec. 11, 1861.

SIOUX

325 Main St., Box 158, Harrison, NE 69346, (308) 668-2443, **<co.sioux.ne.us>**

- **INCORPORATED:** Feb. 19, 1877
- **PARENT COUNTY:** Unorganized territory
- **MARRIAGE RECORDS:** unknown start, kept by County Judge
- **DIVORCE:** unknown, District Court
- **LAND:** unknown, County Clerk
- **PROBATE:** unknown, County Judge
- **COURT:** unknown, County Judge

STANTON

804 Ivy St., Box 347, Stanton, NE 68779, (402) 439-2222, **<co.stanton.ne.us>**

- **INCORPORATED:** March 6, 1855
- **PARENT COUNTY:** Unorganized territory
- **MARRIAGE RECORDS:** start in 1869, kept by County Clerk
- **DIVORCE:** 1875, District Court
- **LAND:** 1868, County Clerk
- **PROBATE:** unknown, County Court
- **COURT:** 1875, District Court
- **NATURALIZATION:** unknown, County Clerk
- **MILITARY:** unknown, County Clerk
- **NOTES:** Formerly Izard County. Name changed to Stanton Jan. 20, 1862.

TAYLOR

- **INCORPORATED:** 2003
- **PARENT COUNTY:** unknown
- **NOTES:** Never organized county in southwest corner of state. Became part of Cheyenne County. With Lincoln County in 1870 Census.

THAYER

225 N. Fourth St., Box 208, Hebron, NE 68370, (402) 768-6126, **<thayercounty.ne.gov>**

- **INCORPORATED:** Jan. 26, 1871
- **PARENT COUNTY:** Jefferson
- **MARRIAGE RECORDS:** unknown start, kept by County Judge
- **DIVORCE:** unknown, District Court
- **LAND:** unknown, County Clerk
- **PROBATE:** unknown, County Judge
- **COURT:** unknown, County Judge

THOMAS

503 Main St., Thedford, NE 69166, (308) 645-2261, **<thomascountynebraska.us>**

- **INCORPORATED:** March 31, 1887
- **PARENT COUNTY:** Unorganized territory
- **MARRIAGE RECORDS:** start in 1887, kept by County Clerk
- **DIVORCE:** unknown, District Court
- **LAND:** unknown, County Clerk
- **PROBATE:** unknown, County Judge
- **COURT:** unknown, District Court

THURSTON

106 S. Fifth St., Box G, Pender, NE 68047, (402) 385-2343, **<www.thurstoncountynebraska.us>**

- **INCORPORATED:** March 28, 1889
- **PARENT COUNTY:** Burt
- **MARRIAGE RECORDS:** start in 1889, kept by County Judge
- **DIVORCE:** 1889, District Court
- **LAND:** 1885, County Clerk
- **PROBATE:** 1889, County Judge
- **COURT:** 1889, District Court
- **NOTES:** Thurston County was originally an Indian reservation. Prior to organization, it was Blackbird County, created March 7, 1855. From 1884-1889 it was administered by Dakota County. Name changed to Thurston March 28, 1889.

VALLEY

125 S. 15th St., Ord, NE 68862, (308) 728-3700, **<co.valley.ne.us>**

- **INCORPORATED:** March 1, 1871
- **PARENT COUNTY:** Unorganized territory
- **MARRIAGE RECORDS:** start in 1883, kept by County Clerk
- **DIVORCE:** unknown, District Court
- **LAND:** 1883, County Clerk
- **PROBATE:** unknown, County Judge
- **COURT:** unknown, District Court

WASHINGTON

1555 Colfax St., Blair, NE 68008, (402) 426-6822, **<co.washington.ne.us>**

- **INCORPORATED:** Nov. 23, 1854

- **PARENT COUNTY:** Original County
- **BIRTH RECORDS:** unknown start, kept by County Clerk
- **MARRIAGE:** unknown, County Judge
- **DIVORCE:** unknown, District Court
- **DEATH:** unknown, County Clerk
- **LAND:** unknown, County Clerk
- **PROBATE:** unknown, County Judge
- **COURT:** unknown, County Judge
- **BURIAL:** unknown, County Clerk

WAYNE

510 N. Pearl St., Box 248, Wayne, NE 68787, (402) 375-2288, **<www.waynecountyne.org>**

- **INCORPORATED:** March 4, 1871
- **PARENT COUNTY:** Unorganized territory
- **MARRIAGE RECORDS:** start in 1871, kept by County Judge
- **DIVORCE:** unknown, District Court
- **LAND:** 1870, County Clerk
- **PROBATE:** 1871, County Judge
- **COURT:** 1871, County Judge

WEBSTER

621 N. Cedar St., Red Cloud, NE 68970, (402) 746-2716, **<co.webster.ne.us>**

- **INCORPORATED:** Feb. 16, 1867
- **PARENT COUNTY:** Unorganized territory
- **MARRIAGE RECORDS:** start in 1871, kept by County Clerk
- **DIVORCE:** 1871, County Clerk
- **LAND:** 1871, County Clerk
- **PROBATE:** 1871, County Clerk
- **COURT:** 1871, County Clerk
- **NATURALIZATION:** 1874, County Clerk

WEST

- **INCORPORATED:** 13 Jan. 1860
- **PARENT COUNTY:** Unorganized territory
- **NOTES:** See Holt County. Name changed to Holt Jan. 9, 1862.

WHEELER

Box 127, Bartlett, NE 68622, (308) 654-3235, **<www.rootsweb.ancestry.com/~newheele>**

- **INCORPORATED:** Feb. 17, 1877
- **PARENT COUNTY:** Unorganized territory
- **LAND:** unknown, County Clerk
- **COURT:** unknown, County Clerk

YORK

510 Lincoln Ave., York, NE 68467, (402) 362-7759, **<yorkcounty.ne.gov>**

- **INCORPORATED:** March 13, 1855
- **PARENT COUNTIES:** Cass, Pierce (old)
- **MARRIAGE RECORDS:** unknown start, kept by County Clerk
- **DIVORCE:** unknown, District Court
- **LAND:** unknown, Registrar of Deeds
- **PROBATE:** unknown, County Court
- **MILITARY:** unknown, Veteran Service Office

NEVADA

» BY DAVID A. FRYXELL

HISTORICAL OVERVIEW

Nevada's history is far more compressed than that of its Southwestern neighbors. The outside world didn't pay much attention to Nevada until the 1833-to-1834 expedition of John C. Fremont, in which he discovered Lake Tahoe. But that began to change with the 1847 arrival of Brigham Young in Utah and the 1849 discovery of gold in California. Nevada came under US control with the 1848 Treaty of Guadalupe Hidalgo. Most of Nevada became part of the new Utah Territory in 1850, with the southern tip assigned to the New Mexico Territory. The first permanent European-American settlement in Nevada was established in 1851 at Mormon Station, 13 miles south of what would soon become Carson City. That same year, gold was discovered at Dalton.

With the 1859 gold and silver find, dubbed the Comstock Lode, Nevada jumped onto the fast track to settlement and statehood. Virginia City sprang up almost overnight. A separate Nevada Territory was established in 1861, the same year journalist Mark Twain arrived in Carson City, beginning an adventure he'd dramatize in *Roughing It* (1872). Statehood came in 1864.

But bust soon followed boom, and Nevada slid into a depression that saw its population decline by a third from 1880 to 1900, when gold was found at Tonopah.

What most think of as modern Nevada began in 1927 with the re-legalization of gambling and the six-week divorce law. Soon Reno and Las Vegas were "wide open" cities. In 1941, the first hotel opened on what became the Las Vegas Strip.

RECORD HIGHLIGHTS

Nevada's records essentially begin with the 1860 census, in which the counties of Carson, Humboldt and St. Mary's were enumerated with Utah Territory. There were partial territorial censuses in 1862 and 1863. Note that post-statehood, in 1866, Arizona Territory ceded lands to Nevada that, along with land from Utah Territory, became Lincoln County. In addition to the regular federal census in 1870, Nevada took a state census in 1875. Nevada census researchers are unusually fortunate: The Nevada State Historic Preservation Office has put 310,000 entries, the state's entire 1860, 1870, 1880, 1900, 1910, and 1900 censuses, online at **<nvshpo.org/index.php?option=com_content&view=article&id=1278&Itemid=382>**.

Keep in mind that because Nevadans moved so often, they can be found in various locations. Always check the history and formation of a county when you are looking for an ancestor. Your ancestor may live in the same spot, but it will now be a different county. In a state like Nevada, 10 years between censuses is a long time.

Nevada didn't begin statewide records of births and deaths until 1911 and marriages until 1968. Some Nevada counties have birth and death records beginning in 1887 in their county recorder's office. Nevada is a tough state to research in, warns genealogist and author Patricia A. Hall Scott, in

research tips

- *The Nevada Guide to Genealogical Records* by Diane E. Greene can point you to the sources of records.
- In Nevada, it's important to check the history and formation of the counties where you're researching; county names and boundaries changed often.
- State censuses from 1860 through 1910 are online at **<nvshpo.org/index.php?option=com_content&view=article&id=1278&Itemid=382>**.

CENSUS RECORDS

- Federal census: 1870, 1880, 1900, 1910, 1920, 1930
- Statewide and territorial censuses: 1860 (Carson, Humboldt, and St. Mary's counties), 1862 (Douglas, Humboldt, Lyon, Ormsby, Storey, and Washoe counties), 1863 (Lander county), 1875
- Mortality schedules: 1870, 1880
- Mortality schedules for Utah Territory: 1850, 1860

part because death records are not open to the public. Obituary files are being posted online; see the Nevada Obituary Project at **<usgwarchives.net/obits/nv/obitsnv.htm>**.

If your ancestors went to Nevada for a "quickie divorce," you can obtain those records from the clerk of the district court in the county.

With the transient nature of mining work and out-of-the-way desert locales, Scott adds, your ancestors' final resting place may be equally tricky to find. Volunteers are also working to put data on "lost" Nevada cemeteries online, she says. Extant cemetery records from almost every county can be accessed on microfilm from the Family History Library.

On the bright side, miners left records because of the nature of their work. They traveled from boom to boom, each of which lasted from a few months to decades, but most only a few years, explains David A. Davis, newsletter editor of the Nevada State Genealogical Society. After the Comstock Lode, more than 200 mining districts were established to record deeds and claims. These records, along with mining corporation papers and state mine inspection records, are at the state archives. Your ancestor also might be mentioned in lists of mine supervisors, hoist operators or accident victims.

Records of the massive irrigation projects began in 1902, and though scattered among several archives they can also prove useful, according to professional researcher, Barbara L. Hodges, CGRS.

And don't forget military records. Nevada joined the Union during the Civil War—hence its motto, "Battle Born"—and a dozen Army companies were raised there even before statehood, though they served only locally.

ARCHIVES, LIBRARIES, AND SOCIETIES

Bureau of Land Management
Box 12000, Reno, NV 89520, (775) 861-6400, **<www.blm.gov/nv/st/en.html>**

Carson City Historical Society
1207 North Carson St., Carson City, NV 89702, (775) 882-5694, **<cchistorical.org>**

Carson Valley Historical Society
c/o Carson Valley Museum, 1477 Hwy. 395 N., Gardnerville, NV 89410, (775) 782-2555, **<historicnevada.org>**

Churchill County Historical and Genealogical Society
c/o Churchill County Museum, 1050 South Maine St., Fallon, NV 89406, (775) 423-3677, **<ccmuseum.org>**

Clark County Heritage Museum
1830 S. Boulder Hwy., Henderson, NV 89015, (702) 455-7955, **<accessclarkcounty.com>**

Clark County Genealogical Society
Box 1929, Las Vegas, NV 89125, (702) 225-5838, **<www.rootsweb.ancestry.com/~nvccngs>**

Elko Genealogical Society
3001 N. Fifth St., Elko, NV 89801, (775) 738-4565, **<www.rootsweb.ancestry.com/~nvelko>**

Goldfield Historical Society
Box 393, Goldfield, NV 89013, (775) 485-9560, **<goldfieldhistoricalsociety.com>**

Humboldt County Genealogical Society
c/o Humboldt County Library, 85 E. Fifth St., Winnemucca, NV 89445, (775) 623-6388, **<www.clan.lib.nv.us/polpac/library/clan/HCL/humtest.htm>**

Las Vegas Family History Center
509 S. Ninth St., Las Vegas, NV 89101, (702) 382-9695, **<www.familyhistorylv.org>**

Las Vegas Public Library
833 Las Vegas Blvd. N., Las Vegas, NV 89101, (702) 734-7323, **<lvccld.org>**

Lincoln County Historical Museum
69 Main St., Pioche, NV 89043, (775) 962-5207

Nevada Historical Society
1650 N. Virginia St., Reno, NV 89503, (775) 688-1190, **<museums.nevadaculture.org>**

Nevada State Genealogical Society
Box 20666, Reno, NV 89515, **<www.rootsweb.ancestry.com/~nvsgs>**

Nevada State Library and Archives
100 N. Stewart St., Carson City, NV 89701 Archives: (775) 684-3313; Library: (775) 684-3365, **<clan.lib.nv.us>**

Nevada State Museum and Historical Society
700 Twin Lakes Dr., Las Vegas, NV 89107, (702) 486-5205, **<nevadaculture.org>**

North Las Vegas Library
2300 Civic Center Dr., North Las Vegas, NV 89030, (702) 633-1070, **<www.cityofnorthlasvegas.com/Departments/Library/Library.shtm>**

Northeastern Nevada Historical Society
1515 Idaho St., Elko, NV 89801, (775) 738-3418, **<museumelko.org>**

Office of Vital Records and Statistics
4150 Technology Way, Suite 104, Carson City, NV 89706, (775) 684-4242, **<health.nv.gov/VS.htm>**

Sparks Heritage Society
c/o Sparks Heritage Museum, 814 Victorian Ave., Sparks, NV 89431, (775) 355-1144, **<sparksmuseum.org>**

University of Nevada-Las Vegas, Department of Special Collections
Box 457010, 4505 Maryland Parkway, Las Vegas, NV 89154, (703) 895-2234, **<library.unlv.edu/speccol>**

University of Nevada-Reno
3rd floor, Mathewson-IGT Knowledge Center, 1664 N. Virginia St. Reno, NV 89503, (775) 682-5665, **<knowledgecenter.unr.edu/specoll>**

Valley of Fire Chapter of the Daughters of the American Revolution
<www.rootsweb.ancestry.com/~nvvfcdar>

Washoe County Library
Downtown Reno Branch, 301 South Center St., Reno, NV 89507, (775) 327-8300, **<www.washoe.lib.nv.us>**

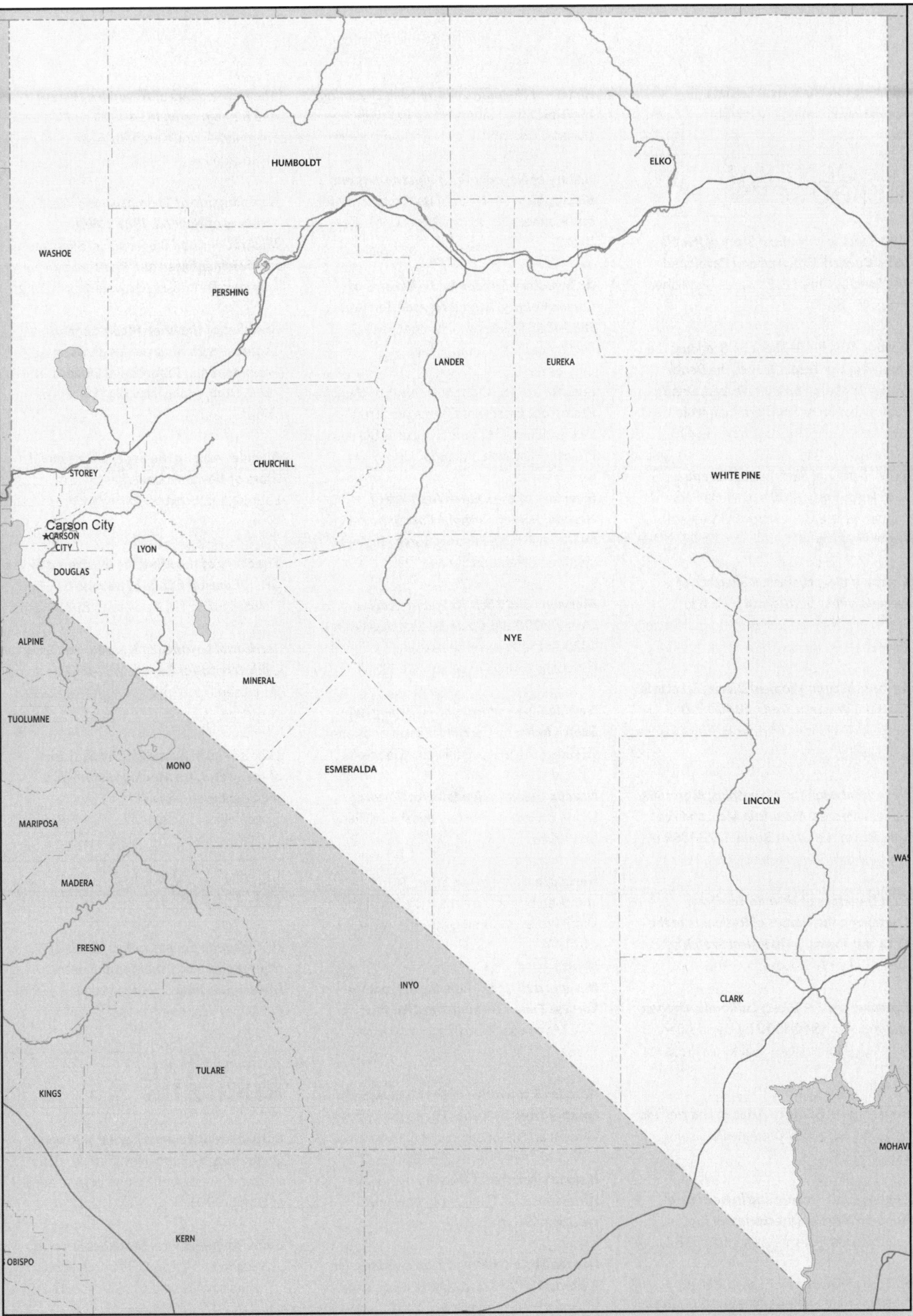
HUMBOLDT
ELKO
WASHOE
PERSHING
LANDER
EUREKA
CHURCHILL
STOREY
WHITE PINE
Carson City
CARSON CITY
LYON
DOUGLAS
NYE
ALPINE
MINERAL
TUOLUMNE
MONO
ESMERALDA
LINCOLN
MARIPOSA
WAS
MADERA
FRESNO
INYO
CLARK
TULARE
KINGS
MOHAVE
KERN
OBISPO

Wellington Historical Society
Box 36, Wellington, NV 89444

☞GENERAL RESOURCES

200 Years in Nevada: a Story of People Who Opened, Explored and Developed the Land by Elbert B. Edwards (Publishers Press, 1978)

Beyond This Place There Be Dragons: the Routes of the Tragic Trek of the Death Valley 1849ers Through Nevada, Death Valley, and on to Southern California by George Koenig (Arthur Clark, 1984)

Brief Historical Sketches of Nevada Residents, Early 1900's by Nona Parkin (filmed by the Genealogical Society of Utah, 1997)

Carson Valley: Historical Sketches of Nevada's First Settlement by Grace Dangberg (Carson Valley Historical Society, 1972)

Covered Wagon Women: Diaries & Letters from the Western Trails, 1840-1890 by Kenneth L. Holmes (Arthur H. Clark Co., ca. 1983-1991)

Desert Between the Mountains: Mormons, Miners, Padres, Mountain Men, and the Opening of the Great Basin, 1772-1869 by Michael S. Durham (Henry Holt, 1997)

First Directory of Nevada Territory: Containing the Names of Residents in the Principal Towns, a Historical Sketch by J. Wells Kelly (W.C. Cox Co., 1974)

Founding the Far West; California, Oregon, and Nevada, 1840-1890 by David Allen Johnson (University of California Press, ca. 1992)

Genealogical Guide to Arizona and Nevada by Joyce V. Hawley (Verlene Publishing, ca. 1983)

Genealogical Prospecting in Nevada: a Guide to Nevada Directories by Joyce C. Lee (Nevada Library Association, 1984)

History of Nevada by Russell R Elliott (University of Nebraska Press, 1984, 1973)

History of Nevada, Colorado and Wyoming, 1540-1888 by Hubert Howe Bancroft (History Co., 1890)

History of Nevada: With Illustrations and Biographical Sketches of its Prominent Men and Pioneers by Myron Angel (W.C. Cox, 1974)

An Inventory & Index to the Records of Carson County, Utah & Nevada Territories, 1855-1861 by Ellison, Marion (Grace Dangberg Foundation, 1984)

Inventory of the Church Archives of Nevada, Protestant Episcopal Church prepared by the Nevada Historical Records Survey Project (Historical Records Survey, 1941)

Inventory of the Church Archives of Nevada, Roman Catholic Church prepared by the Historical Records Survey Project (Historical Records Survey, 1939)

Mormons and Their Neighbors: an Index to Over 75,000 Biographical Sketches From 1820 To the Present by Marvin E. Wiggins (Brigham Young University, ca. 1984)

Nevada Biographical and Genealogical Sketch Index by Carlyle J. Parker and Janet G. Parker (Marietta Publishing Co., ca. 1986)

Nevada Guide to Genealogical Records by Diane E. Greene (Genealogical Publishing Co., 1998)

Nevada, a Guide to the Silver State compiled by the Writer's Program of the Work Projects Administration (W.C. Cox Co., 1974)

Nevada: a History of the State From the Earliest Times Through the Civil War by Effle Mona Mack (Arthur H. Clark Co., 1936)

Nevada: A Narrative of the Conquest of a Frontier Land by James Graves Scrugham (American Historical Society, 1935)

Nevada's Northeast Frontier by Edna B. Patterson, et al. (University of Nevada Press, ca. 1991)

Nevada State Children's Home, Admission Records, 1870-1920 by Doreen Robinson (Quintin Publications, ca. 2000)

The Newspapers of Nevada: a History and Bibliography, 1854-1979 by Richard E Lingenfelter and Karen Rix Gash (University of Nevada Press, 1984)

Reproduction of Thompson and West's "History of Nevada, 1881": With Illustrations and Biographical Sketches of its Prominent Men and Pioneers by Thomas Hinckley Thompson (Howell-North, 1958)

Sketches of the Inter-Mountain States: Together with Biographies of Many Prominent and Progressive Citizens, 1847, 1909, Utah, Idaho, Nevada (Salt Lake Tribune, 1909)

Steeples Among the Sage, a Centennial Story of Nevada's Churches by Leonidas Latimer Loofbourow (Lake Park Press, ca. 1964)

The Story of the Mine: As Illustrated by the Great Comstock Lode of Nevada by Charles Howard Shinn (D. Appleton, 1897)

Territorial Lawmen of Nevada: Vol. One, the Utah Territorial Period, 1851-1861 by Robert W. Ellison (Hot Springs Mountain Press, ca. 1999)

Who's Who in Nevada: Brief Sketches of Men Who Are Making History in the Sagebrush State (filmed by the Genealogical Society of Utah, 1968)

☞CENSUS RECORDS

1910 Nevada Census Index: Heads of Households and Other Surnames in Households Index by Bryan Lee Dilts (Index Publishing, 1984)

☞VITAL RECORDS

Card Index of Persons Buried in Nevada Cemeteries by Reno, Nev., Family History Center (filmed by the Genealogical Society of Utah, 1990)

Guide To Public Vital Statistics Records in Nevada by Historical Records Survey (University of Nevada, Las Vegas, 1941)

Index to Marriage Licenses and Marriage Notices in Miscellaneous Nevada Newspapers, 1906-1968 by Edna E. Ostrander (filmed by the Genealogical Society of Utah, 1986)

Nevada Cemeteries: Tombstone Inscriptions of Nevada Cemeteries Collected by Local DAR Chapters Throughout Nevada by Verna S. Paterson (filmed by the Genealogical Society of Utah, 1995)

Nevada State Cemeteries by Jean Winters Ferral and Roger Ferrel (ca. 1997)

The Nevada Tombstone Record Book by Richard B. Taylor (Nevada Families Project, ca. 1986)

☞IMMIGRATION RECORDS

The Basques in the Northwest: A Dissertation by Flavina Maria McCullough (R and E Research Associates, 1974)

The Mormons in Nevada by Leonard J. Arrington (Las Vegas Sun, 1979)

☞MILITARY RECORDS

Annual Reports, 1865-1930 Compiled by the Nevada State Library and Archives (filmed by Nevada Printing and Micrographics Division, 1991)

Index to Compiled Service Records of Volunteer Union Soldiers Who Served in Organizations From the State of Nevada by US Adjutant General's Office (National Archives, 1964)
Nevada's Golden Stars by Maurice J. Sullivan (W.C. Cox, 1974)

Nevada, World War I Selective Service System Draft Registration Cards, 1917-1918 by US Selective Service System (National Archives, 1987-1988)

Records of Early Nevada Military Units and Personnel by J.S. Thompson (filmed by the Genealogical Society of Utah, 1995)

Revised and Complete Roster of Nevada Veterans, Civil War, Spanish American War, Nevada National Guards to 1914, State Militia, Home Guards by the Nevada Historical Society (filmed by the Genealogical Society of Utah, 1994)

☞MAPS

Directory of Southern Nevada Place Names by Walter R. Averett (W.R. Averett, ca. 1962)

Nevada Atlas & Gazetteer (DeLorme, ca. 1996)

Nevada Ghost Towns & Mining Camps by Stanley W. Paher (Nevada Publications, ca. 1970)

Nevada Place Names: A Geographical Dictionary by Helen S. Carlson (University of Nevada Press, 1974)

Nevada Place Names: Their Origin and Significance by Rufus Wood Leigh (Deseret News Press, ca. 1964)

Nevada Post Offices: An Illustrated History by James Gamett (Nevada Publications, ca. 1983)

Nevada Postal History, 1861 to 1972 by Robert P. Harris (Bonanza Press, 1973)

COUNTY DETAILS

CARSON

- **INCORPORATED:** Jan. 17, 1854
- **PARENT COUNTY:** Original county
- **NOTES:** Organized as a county in Utah Territory. Discontinued March 2, 1861, when Nevada Territory was created. Became part of Douglas, Lyon, Ormsby, Storey, Churchill, Pershing, Humboldt and Washoe Counties.

CARSON CITY

885 E. Musser St., Carson City, NV 89701, (775) 887-2260, **<www.carson-city.nv.us>**
- **INCORPORATED:** Nov. 25, 1861
- **PARENT COUNTIES:** Original County
- **BIRTH RECORDS:** Start in 1887, kept by County Recorder
- **MARRIAGE:** 1855, County Clerk
- **DIVORCE:** 1864, County Clerk
- **DEATH:** 1891, County Recorder
- **LAND:** 1862, County Recorder
- **PROBATE:** 1864, County Clerk
- **COURT:** 1864, County Clerk
- **NATURALIZATION:** 1864, County Clerk
- **MILITARY:** 1919, County Recorder
- **NOTES:** Organized as Ormsby County. Consolidated into Carson City 1969 and Ormsby County discontinued.

CHURCHILL

155 N. Taylor St. 110, Fallon, NV 89406, (775) 423-5136, **<churchillcounty.org>**
- **INCORPORATED:** Nov. 25, 1861
- **PARENT COUNTY:** Original county
- **BIRTH RECORDS:** Start in 1888, kept by the County Clerk
- **MARRIAGE:** 1864, County Clerk
- **DIVORCE:** 1905, County Clerk
- **DEATH:** 1888, County Clerk
- **LAND:** 1864, County Clerk
- **PROBATE:** 1904, County Clerk
- **COURT:** 1904, County Clerk

CLARK

500 S. Grand Central Pkwy., 2nd Floor, Las Vegas, NV 89106, (702) 455-3156, **<accessclarkcounty.com>**
- **INCORPORATED:** Feb. 5, 1909

- **PARENT COUNTY:** Lincoln
- **BIRTH RECORDS:** start in 1909, kept by Department of Health
- **MARRIAGE:** 1909, County Recorder
- **DIVORCE:** unknown, County Clerk
- **DEATH:** 1909, Department of Health
- **LAND:** 1909, County Recorder
- **PROBATE:** 1909, County Clerk
- **COURT:** 1909, County Clerk

DOUGLAS

1616 8th St., Box 218, Minden, NV 89423, (775) 782-9025,
<www.douglascountynv.gov>

- **INCORPORATED:** Nov. 25, 1861
- **PARENT COUNTY:** Original county
- **BIRTH RECORDS:** Start in 1887, kept by County Clerk
- **MARRIAGE:** 1802, County Clerk
- **DIVORCE:** unknown, County Clerk
- **DEATH:** 1887, County Clerk
- **LAND:** 1855, County Clerk
- **PROBATE:** 1887, County Clerk
- **COURT:** 1887, County Clerk

ELKO

571 Idaho St. Room 103, Elko, NV 89801, (775) 738-6526,
<elkocountynv.net>

- **INCORPORATED:** March 5, 1869
- **PARENT COUNTY:** St. Mary's
- **BIRTH RECORDS:** Start in 1887, kept by County Recorder
- **MARRIAGE RECORDS:** 1869, County Clerk
- **MARRIAGE APPLICATIONS:** 1876, County Clerk
- **DIVORCE:** 1876, County Clerk
- **DEATH:** 1887, County Recorder
- **LAND:** 1869, County Recorder
- **PROBATE:** 1869, County Clerk
- **COURT:** 1869, County Clerk
- **BURIAL:** unknown, County Recorder

ESMERALDA

233 Crook Ave., Goldfield, NV 89013, (775) 485-6337,
<accessesmeralda.com>

- **INCORPORATED:** Nov. 25, 1861
- **PARENT COUNTIES:** Original County
- **BIRTH RECORDS:** Start in 1907, kept by County Clerk/Treasurer
- **MARRIAGE:** 1898, County Clerk/Treasurer
- **DIVORCE:** 1908, County Clerk/Treasurer
- **DEATH:** 1907, County Clerk/Treasurer
- **LAND:** 1863, County Clerk/Treasurer
- **PROBATE:** 1881, County Clerk/Treasurer
- **COURT:** 1908, County Clerk/Treasurer
- **NATURALIZATION:** 1904, County Clerk/Treasurer

EUREKA

Box 556, Eureka, NV 89316, (775) 237-5263,
<www.co.eureka.nv.us>

- **INCORPORATED:** March 1, 1873
- **PARENT COUNTY:** Lander
- **BIRTH RECORDS:** Start in 1873, kept by County Recorder
- **MARRIAGE:** 1873, County Recorder
- **DIVORCE:** 1874, County Clerk
- **DEATH:** 1887, County Recorder
- **LAND:** 1873, County Recorder
- **PROBATE:** 1873, County Clerk
- **COURT:** 1873, County Clerk
- **BURIAL:** unknown, County Recorder

HUMBOLDT

25 West Fourth St., Winnemucca, NV 89445, (775) 623-6412,
<www.hcnv.us/recorder/recorder.htm>

- **INCORPORATED:** Nov. 25, 1861
- **PARENT COUNTY:** Original County
- **BIRTH RECORDS:** Start in 1888, kept by County Clerk
- **MARRIAGE:** 1862, County Clerk
- **DIVORCE:** 1863, County Clerk
- **DEATH:** 1888, County Clerk
- **LAND:** 1861, County Assessor
- **PROBATE:** 1863, County Clerk
- **COURT:** 1862, County Clerk
- **NATURALIZATION:** 1864, County Clerk
- **NOTES:** See 1860 Utah census.

LANDER

315 S. Humboldt St., Battle Mountain, NV 89820, (775) 635-5173,
<landercountynv.org>

- **INCORPORATED:** Dec. 19, 1862
- **PARENT COUNTY:** Original County
- **MARRIAGE:** 1867, County Clerk
- **DIVORCE:** 1865, County Clerk
- **LAND:** 1862, County Auditor
- **PROBATE:** 1862, County Clerk
- **COURT:** 1862, County Clerk
- **NOTES:** County Auditor has some birth records

LINCOLN

Box 218, Pioche, NV 89043, (775) 962-5180,
<www.lincolncountynv.org>

- **INCORPORATED:** Feb. 26, 1866
- **PARENT COUNTY:** Nye
- **BIRTH RECORDS:** Start in 1887, kept by County Clerk
- **MARRIAGE:** 1872, County Clerk
- **DIVORCE:** 1873, County Clerk
- **DEATH:** 1887, County Clerk
- **LAND:** 1865, County Clerk
- **PROBATE:** 1855, County Clerk
- **COURT:** 1873, County Clerk
- **NOTES:** See 1860 Utah census.

LYON

27 S. Main St., Yerington, NV 89447, (775) 463-6581,
<lyon-county.org>

- **INCORPORATED:** Nov. 25, 1861
- **PARENT COUNTY:** Original County
- **BIRTH RECORDS:** Start in 1887, kept by County Recorder
- **MARRIAGE:** 1862, County Recorder
- **DIVORCE:** 1890, County Clerk
- **DEATH:** 1887, County Recorder
- **LAND:** 1862, County Recorder

- **PROBATE:** 1867, County Clerk
- **COURT:** 1867, County Clerk

MINERAL

314 5th St., Box 2250, Hawthorne, NV 89415, (775) 945-3676, **<mineralcountychamber.com/HTML/MineralCountyInfo/mcphonedirectory.html>**

- **INCORPORATED:** Feb. 10, 1911
- **PARENT COUNTY:** Esmeralda
- **BIRTH RECORDS:** Start in 1911, kept by County Clerk
- **MARRIAGE RECORDS:** 1911, County Clerk
- **MARRIAGE APPLICATIONS:** 1911, County Recorder
- **DIVORCE:** 1911, County Clerk
- **DEATH:** 1911, County Clerk
- **LAND:** 1911, County Treasurer
- **PROBATE:** 1911, County Clerk
- **COURT:** 1911, County Clerk
- **MILITARY:** 1911, County Recorder
- **BURIAL:** unknown, County Recorder
- **NOTES:** County Clerk has some divorce, probate and court records before 1911, and naturalization records 1911-1956.

NYE

101 Radar Rd., Box 1111, Tonopah, NV 89049, (775) 482-8116, **<nyecounty.net>**

- **INCORPORATED:** Feb. 16, 1864
- **PARENT COUNTY:** Esmeralda
- **BIRTH RECORDS:** Start in 1887, kept by County Clerk
- **MARRIAGE:** 1864, County Clerk
- **DIVORCE:** 1860, County Clerk
- **DEATH:** 1887, County Clerk
- **LAND:** 1864, County Recorder
- **PROBATE:** 1865, County Clerk
- **COURT:** 1864, County Clerk

ORMSBY

- **INCORPORATED:** Nov. 25, 1861
- **PARENT COUNTY:** Original County
- **NOTES:** Consolidated with Carson City 1969 and discontinued.

PAHUTE

- **INCORPORATED:** 1864
- **PARENT COUNTY:** unknown
- **NOTES:** Discontinued. See Lincoln County, now Clark.

PERSHING

398 Main St., Lovelock, NV 89419, (775) 273-2208, **<pershingcounty.net/recorderauditor.htm>**

- **INCORPORATED:** March 18, 1919
- **PARENT COUNTY:** Humboldt
- **BIRTH RECORDS:** Start in 1919, kept by County Clerk
- **MARRIAGE:** 1919, County Clerk
- **DIVORCE:** 1919, County Clerk
- **DEATH:** 1919, County Clerk
- **LAND:** 1919, County Clerk
- **PROBATE:** 1919, County Clerk
- **COURT:** 1919, County Clerk

ROOP

- **INCORPORATED:** 1860
- **PARENT COUNTY:** Original County
- **NOTES:** Discontinued after a boundary dispute with California. Territory absorbed by Plumas County, Calif., and Washoe County.

ST. MARY'S

- **INCORPORATED:** 1856
- **PARENT COUNTY:** Original County
- **NOTES:** Organized as a county in Utah Territory. Discontinued March 2, 1861, when Nevada Territory was created.

STOREY

26 B St., Virginia City, NV 89440, (755) 847-0967, **<storeycounty.org>**

- **INCORPORATED:** Nov. 25, 1861
- **PARENT COUNTY:** Original County
- **BIRTH RECORDS:** Start in 1887, kept by County Recorder
- **MARRIAGE:** 1874, County Recorder
- **DIVORCE:** 1861, County Clerk
- **DEATH:** 1887, County Recorder
- **LAND:** 1876, County Recorder
- **PROBATE:** 1886, County Clerk
- **COURT:** 1861, County Clerk

WASHOE

1001 E. 9th St., Box 11130, Reno, NV 89520, (775) 328-3361, **<www.co.washoe.nv.us/recorder/>**

- **INCORPORATED:** Nov. 25, 1861
- **PARENT COUNTY:** Original County
- **BIRTH RECORDS:** Start in 1887, kept by Department of Health
- **MARRIAGE:** 1861, County Recorder
- **DIVORCE:** 1862, Department of Health
- **DEATH:** 1887, County Clerk
- **LAND:** 1870, County Recorder
- **PROBATE:** 1870, County Clerk
- **COURT:** 1870, County Clerk
- **NATURALIZATION:** 1862, County Clerk
- **BURIAL:** 1900, Department of Health

WHITE PINE

801 Clark St., Box 68 Ely, NV 89301, (775) 289-4567, **<www.whitepinecounty.net>**

- **INCORPORATED:** March 2, 1869
- **PARENT COUNTIES:** Millard, Utah Territory
- **BIRTH RECORDS:** Start in 1887, kept by County Clerk
- **MARRIAGE:** 1869, County Clerk
- **DIVORCE:** 1907, County Clerk
- **DEATH:** 1887, County Clerk
- **LAND:** 1885, County Recorder
- **PROBATE:** 1885, County Clerk
- **COURT:** 1885, County Clerk
- **NATURALIZATION:** unknown, County Clerk

NEW HAMPSHIRE

» BY MAUREEN TAYLOR

HISTORICAL OVERVIEW

Four towns founded by migrants from Essex County, Massachusetts—Portsmouth, Dover, Exeter, and Hampton—clustered near the New Hampshire shoreline. Massachusetts governed the area from 1642 to 1679 and again during 1690 to 1692, even though the area became a royal province in 1679. New Hampshire's border disputes with adjacent states weren't settled until the mid-18th century, when its present boundaries were established.

More than 18,000 men from New Hampshire joined forces to fight the British in the American Revolution. Shortly thereafter, in 1781, 36 towns declared themselves part of Vermont, not New Hampshire, but the rift was temporary. New Hampshire ratified the Constitution in 1788 to become the ninth state.

In the 17th century residents settled in the area to fish, farm, and trade furs, with Portsmouth being the center of trade, shipbuilding, and logging. Textile manufacturing became a major industry in the 19th and early 20th century with Amoskeag Manufacturing Co. of Manchester. European immigrants came to New Hampshire from many countries, including England, France, Germany, Greece, Ireland, Poland, Russia, Scotland and Sweden to work in the fabric and shoe industries, as did laborers from French Canada. During the 20th century, World War I and II kept these factories and the Portsmouth Navy Yard busy producing goods for the war effort.

research tips

- Start your New Hampshire research in Concord, the state capitol—it's home to the New Hampshire Historical Society's Tuck Library, the New Hampshire State Library, and the New Hampshire Division of Records Management and Archives.
- Town reports, unpublished genealogies, city directories, letters, diaries, some church manuscripts and more are at the New Hampshire Historical Society **<nhhistory.library.net>**.
- The New England Historic Genealogical Society **<www.americanancestors.org>** has material on New Hampshire families, as well as some town documents and cemetery transcriptions.

CENSUS RECORDS

- Federal census: 1790, 1800, 1810, 1820, 1830, 1840, 1850, 1860, 1870, 1880, 1900, 1910, 1920, 1930
- Veterans schedules: 1840, 1890
- Mortality schedules: 1850, 1860, 1870, 1880
- Colonial census: 1732, 1742, 1776

RECORD HIGHLIGHTS

New Hampshire's records date from the early colonial period. Town and city clerks kept track of vital records, but coverage is spotty. An every-name index to early vital records exists, but doesn't include 17 towns. Microfilm copies can be found at the New Hampshire State Library, the New England Historic Genealogical Society in Boston, and through the Family History LIbrary (FHL) **<www.familysearch.org>**.

Civil Registration in 1866 required cities and towns to send copies of their birth and death records to the state, but total compliance didn't occur until 1905, with the establishment of the Bureau of Vital Records. Originals remain in most town and city halls. Births prior to 1901 and marriages, divorces, and deaths before 1949 are open to the public.

Colonial resources include provincial tax lists for 1732, 1744, 1767, and 1776. With the exception of 1732, they all appear in the 40-volume *Documents and Records Relating to New Hampshire, 1623-1800*, known as the New Hampshire State Papers. The State Papers are a good resource for lists of Revolutionary War soldiers and probate documents prior to statehood.

Land records provide clues to early families, but recording was inconsistent and didn't always occur at the time of the transaction. After the establishment of counties in 1769, land records reside in the registrar's office of each county. Some land transactions appear in probate records (also kept in the county seat), especially if the transfer occurred between family members.

Researchers with families in the southern part of the state will find a greater variety of records to search than those in the north. Individuals with ancestors in southern New Hampshire and Northern Massachusetts should look for records on both sides of the border for families in the area prior to boundary decisions.

New Hampshire resources are plentiful, so preparing for your research trip beforehand will help you identify facilities to visit. The small size of the state makes it easy to visit multiple facilities. The state capital, Concord, is the center for New Hampshire research, with three major repositories: the New Hampshire Historical Society's Tuck Library, the New Hampshire State Library, and the New Hampshire Division of Records Management and Archives.

At the New Hampshire Historical Society, discover town reports, unpublished genealogies, city directories, newspapers, letters, diaries, and papers for the state's residents. The society also has a collection of manuscripts for many New Hampshire churches, it only represents a small number of congregations. Papers for the rest might be at the church, with descendants of the ministers, or in libraries or historical societies. Search the online catalog for resources relevant to your research **<nhhistory.library.net>**.

Fill in gaps in the vital records by consulting probate and land records on the county level. Probate records on the county level offer additional genealogical clues for some families by listing children and wives.

Court records can be found at the New Hampshire Division of Records Management and Archives. Provincial records from the period before 1771 are organized and indexed; some appear in the New Hampshire State Papers.

Also at the state archives are legislative petitions beginning in the 17th century. They contain an assortment of material, including petitions for release from prison, divorces, and name changes. Organized by year, they are being indexed. Approximately 20 percent of them appear in the New Hampshire State Papers. The state archives also has military papers, including indexes for the Revolutionary War and War of 1812, and Civil War enlistment cards.

Town histories are in print for most communities and often include genealogies of founding families. The largest collection of these is at the New Hampshire Historical Society's Tuck Library **<www.nhhistory.org>**.

Not all New Hampshire material is located in-state. The New England Historic Genealogical Society's manuscript department contains material on New Hampshire families, as well as some town documents and cemetery transcriptions. The website <**www.americanancestors.org**> features databases and research information.

☞ ARCHIVES, LIBRARIES, AND SOCIETIES

Acadian Genealogical and Historical Association
Box 497, Crowley, LA 70527, **<www.rootsweb.ancestry.com/~lapehgs/index.htm>**

American Baptist Churches of Vermont and New Hampshire
1 Oak Ridge Rd., B3, #4A, West Lebanon, NH 03784, (603) 643-4201 or (888) 262-3223, **<www.abcvnh.org>**

American-Canadian Genealogical Society
Box 6478, Manchester, NH 03108, (603) 622-1554, **<www.acgs.org>**

Baker-Berry Library, Dartmouth College
Hanover, NH 03755, (603) 646-2560, **<www.dartmouth.edu/~library/bakerberry>**

Berlin and Coos County Historical Society
119 High St., Box 52, Berlin, NH 03570, (603) 752-7337, **<www.aannh.org/heritage/coos/moffett.php>**

Bureau of Vital Records, Health and Welfare Building
29 Hazen Dr., Concord, NH 03301, **<www.statearchives.us/public/new-hampshire.htm>**

Conway Historical Society
100 Main St., Box 1949, Conway, NH 03818, (603) 447-5551, **<www.conwayhistory.org>**

Dover Public Library
73 Locust St., Dover, NH 03820, (603) 516-6050, **<www.dover.lib.nh.us>**

Exeter Public Library
4 Chestnut St., Exeter, NH 03833, (603) 772-3101, **<www.exeterpl.org>**

Hancock Historical Society
Box 138, 7 Main St., Hancock, NH 03449, (603) 525-9379, **<www.hancocknh.org/hhs>**

Historical Society of Cheshire County
Box 803, 246 Main St., Keene, NH 03431, (603) 352-1895, **<www.hsccnh.org>**

Hollis Historical Society
Box 754, Hollis, NH 03079, (603) 465-3935, **<www.hollis-history.org>**

Manchester City Library
405 Pine St., Manchester, NH 03104, (603) 624-6550, **<www.manchesternh.gov/CityGov/LIB/Home.html>**

Massachusetts Society of Genealogists
Box 215, Ashland, MA 01721, (508) 799-1670, **<www.massog.org>**

Merrimack Historical Society
520 Boston Post Rd., Merrimack, NH 03054, (603) 880-4343, **<www.merrimackhistory.org>**

National Archives and Records Administration, Northeast Region
Frederick C. Murphy Federal Center, 380 Trapelo Rd., Waltham, MA 02452, (781) 663-0130, **<www.archives.gov/northeast/boston>**

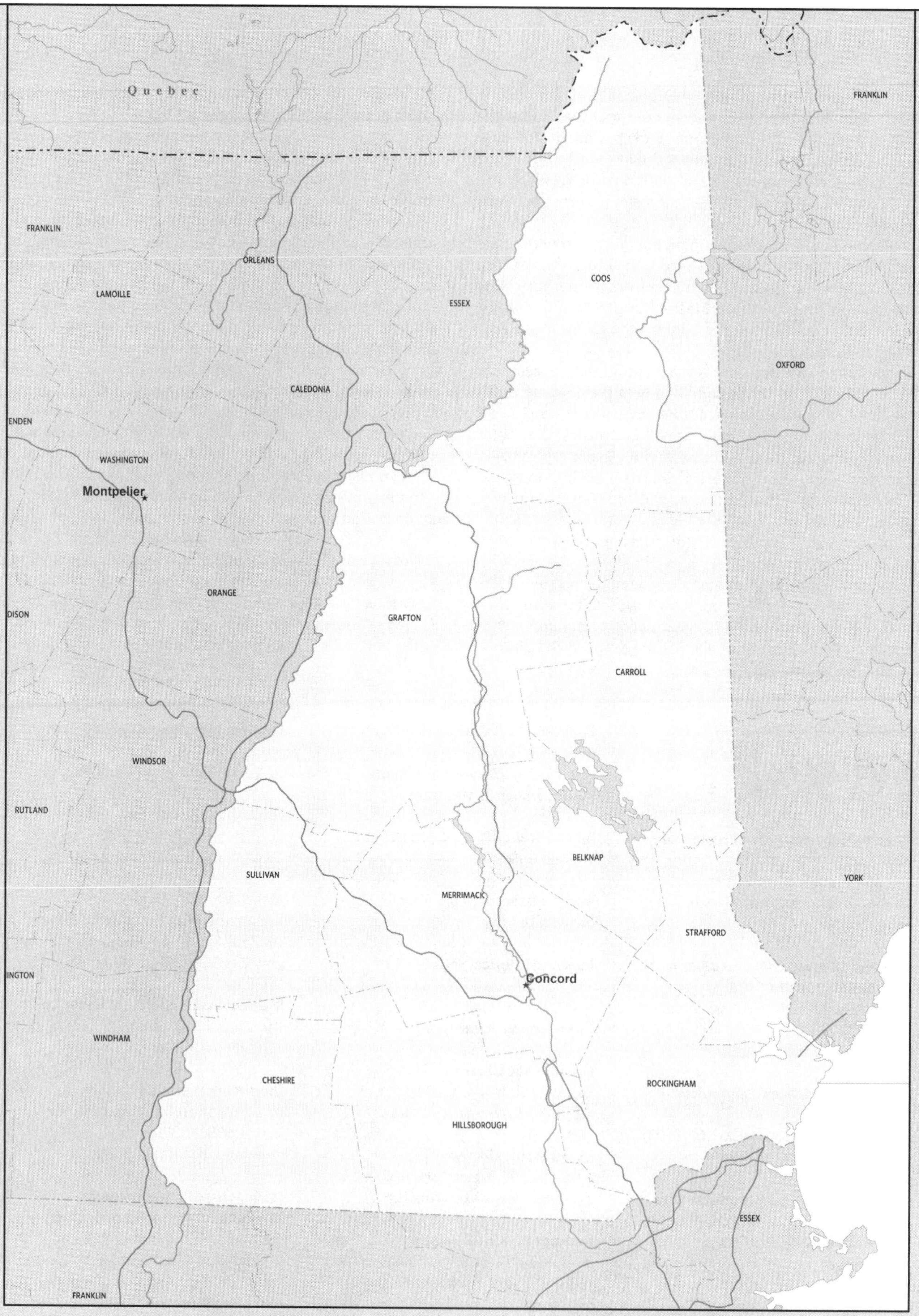
Quebec
FRANKLIN
FRANKLIN
ORLEANS
LAMOILLE
COOS
ESSEX
OXFORD
CALEDONIA
ENDEN
WASHINGTON
Montpelier
ORANGE
DISON
GRAFTON
CARROLL
WINDSOR
RUTLAND
BELKNAP
SULLIVAN
YORK
MERRIMACK
STRAFFORD
INGTON
Concord
WINDHAM
CHESHIRE
ROCKINGHAM
HILLSBOROUGH
ESSEX
FRANKLIN

New Hampshire Division of Archives and Records Management
71 South Fruit St., Concord, NH 03301, (603) 271-2236, **<www.sos.nh.gov/archives>**

New Hampshire Historical Society
30 Park St., Concord, NH 03301, (603) 228-6688, **<www.nhhistory.org>**

New Hampshire Old Graveyard Association
Box 1016, Goshen, NH 03752, **<www.rootsweb.ancestry.com/~nhoga>**

New Hampshire Society of Genealogists
Box 2316, Concord, NH 03302, **<www.nhsog.org>**

New Hampshire State Library
20 Park St., Concord, NH 03301, (603) 271-2144, **<www.state.nh.us/nhsl>**

Northwood Historical Society
Box 114, Northwood, NH 03261, **<www.rootsweb.ancestry.com/~nhnhs>**

Portsmouth Athenaeum
9 Market Sq., Third Floor, Portsmouth, NH 03801, (603) 431-2538, **<www.portsmouthathenaeum.org/about.html>**

Rindge Historical Society
24 School St., Rindge, NH 03461, **<www.town.rindge.nh.us/History.cfm>**

Roman Catholic Diocese of Manchester
153 Ash St., Box 310, Manchester, NH 03105, (603) 669-3100, **<www.catholicchurchnh.org>**

University of New Hampshire Library
18 Library Way, Durham, NH 03824, (603) 862-1535, **<www.library.unh.edu>**

GENERAL RESOURCES

The Baptists of New Hampshire by William Hurlin (Printed by the John B. Clarke Company, 1902)

Bent's Bibliography of the White Mountains by Allen H. Bent, edited by E.J. Hanrahan (New Hampshire Publishing Co., 1971)

Biographical Sketches of Representative Citizens of the State of New Hampshire (New England Historical Publishing, 1902)

Card Index to Genealogies, by the New Hampshire Historical Society (filmed by the Genealogical Society of Utah, 1975)

Check List of New Hampshire History by Otis Grant Hammond, edited by E.J. Hanrahan (New Hampshire Publishing Co., 1971)

Descriptive Inventory of the New Hampshire Collection by Randall C. Carpenter (University of Utah Press, 1983)

Directory of Repositories of Family History in New Hampshire by Scott E. Green (S.l.: Clearfield Company, 1993)

The First Laws of the State of New Hampshire (Michael Glazier, 1981)

Gathered Sketches From the Early History of New Hampshire and Vermont: Containing Vivid and Interesting Accounts of a Great Variety of the Adventures of our Forefathers, and of Other Incidents of Olden Time, Original and Selected edited by Francis Chase (Heritage Books, ca. 1987)

Genealogical and Family History of the State of New Hampshire: A Record of the Achievements of Her People in the Making of a Commonwealth and the Founding of a Nation, 4 vols., by Ezra S. Stearns, et al. (Lewis Publishing Company, 1908)

Genealogical Collection by the Daughters of the American Revolution, New Hampshire (filmed by the Genealogical Society of Utah, 1971)

Genealogical Dictionary of Maine and New Hampshire by Sybil Noyes, Charles T. Libby, and Walter Goodwin Davis (Genealogical Publishing Co., 1983)

Genealogical Research in New England edited by Ralph J. Crandall (Genealogical Publishing Co., 1984)

God, Grace, and Granite: The History of Methodism in New Hampshire, 1768-1988 by Charles W. Kern (Published for the New Hampshire United Methodist Conference by Phoenix Publishing, 1988)

Guide to Church Vital Statistics Records in New Hampshire by the Historical Records Survey, New Hampshire (The Survey, 1942)

Guide to Depositories of Manuscript Collections in the United States, New Hampshire by the Historical Records Survey, New Hampshire (The Survey, 1940)

Guide to Early Documents (c. 1680-c. 1900) at the New Hampshire Records Management and Archives Center compiled by Frank C. Mevers (Division of Records Management and Archives, 1981)

The Heart of the White Mountains by Samuel Adams Drake (Harper & Brothers, 1882)

The History of New Hampshire by Jeremy Belknap (Arno Press, 1972)

History of New Hampshire, 4 vols.by Everett S. Stackpole (American Historical Society, 1916)

History of New Hampshire, From its First Discovery to the Year 1830 by Edwin David Sanborn (J.B. Clarke, 1875)

History of the White Mountains: From the First Settlement of Upper Coos and Pequaket by Lucy Crawford (filmed by the Genealogical Society of Utah, 1992)

Index to Genealogies in New Hampshire Town Histories by William Copeley (New Hampshire Historical Society, ca. 1988)

Inhabitants of New Hampshire, 1776 by Emily S. Wilson (Genealogical Publishing Co., 1993)

Inventory of the Church Archives of New Hampshire, Protestant Episcopal Diocese of New Hampshire by the Historical Records Survey, New Hampshire (The Survey, 1942)

Inventory of the Roman Catholic Church Records in New Hampshire by the Historical Records Survey, New Hampshire (Diocese of Manchester, 1938)

Manuscript Church Records at the New Hampshire Historical Society, August, 1981 by William Copeley (Genealogical Society of Utah, 1985)

The Native Ministry of New Hampshire by Rev. N.F. Carter (Rumford Printing Co., 1906)

New Hampshire, a Bibliography of Its History prepared by the Committee for a New England Bibliography edited by John D. Haskell, Jr., and T.D. Seymour Bassett (G.K. Hall, 1979)

New Hampshire Churches by Robert F. Lawrence (1856)

New Hampshire Family Histories by Rich Rollock (Family Histories Directory; Capital Copy, 1993)

New Hampshire Family Records, 2 vols.by William Copeley (Heritage Books, 1994)

New Hampshire Genealogical Digest, 1623-1900 by Glenn C. Towle (Heritage Books, 1986-)

New Hampshire Genealogical Research Guide by Laird C. Towle and Ann N. Brown (Heritage Books, 1983)

New Hampshire Men. A Collection of Biographical Sketches, With Portraits, of Sons and Residents of the State who Have Become Known in Commercial, Professional, and Political Life compiled and edited by George H. Moses (The New Hampshire Publishing Company, 1893)

New Hampshire Name Changes, 1768-1923 by Richard P. Roberts (Heritage Books, 1996)

New Hampshire Notables Card File by the New Hampshire Historical Society (filmed by the Genealogical Society of Utah, 1988)

New Hampshire Research Outline by the Church of Jesus Christ of Latter-day Saints (online at **<www.familysearch.org/eng/search/RG/guide/new_hampshire.asp>**)

New Hampshire Women: A Collection of Portraits and Biographical Sketches of Daughters and Residents of the Granite State, who are Worthy Representatives of Their Sex in the Various Walks and Conditions of Life by Henry Harrison Metcalf (The New Hampshire Publishing Co., 1895)

The Pastors of New Hampshire, Congregational and Presbyterian by Henry Allen Hazen (Printed by R.W. Musgrove, 1878)

The Pioneers of Maine and New Hampshire, 1623 to 1660: A Descriptive List, Drawn From Records of the Colonies, Towns, Churches, Courts and Other Contemporary Sources by Charles Henry Pope (Genealogical Publishing Co., 1965)

The Records of American Baptists in New Hampshire and Related Organizations by the American Baptist Historical Society and Susan M. Eltscher (American Baptist Historical Society, 1981)

Sketches of the History of New Hampshire, From Its Settlement in 1623 to 1833: Comprising Notices of the Memorable Events and Interesting Incidents of a Period of Two Hundred and Ten Years by John M. Whiton (filmed by the Genealogical Society of Utah, 1973)

State Builders; an Illustrated Historical and Biographical Record of the State of New Hampshire at the Beginning of the Twentieth Century edited by George Franklyn Willey (The New Hampshire Publishing Corporation, 1903)

The Statistics and Gazetteer of New-Hampshire Containing Descriptions of all the Counties, Towns, and Villages . . . Statistical Tables . . . With a List of State Officers, etc. compiled by Alonzo J. Fogg (D.L. Guernsey, 1874)

They Paved the Way: A History of N.H. Women by Olive Tardiff (Women for Women Weekly Publishing, 1980)

The Yankee Pioneers: A Saga of Courage by Samuel B. Pettengill (Regional Center for Educational Training, 1977)

☞ CENSUS RECORDS

Census of New Hampshire, for the Years 1767 and 1775 (filmed by the Genealogical Society of Utah, 1975)

New Hampshire 1732 Census by Jay Mack Holbrook (Holbrook Research Institute, 1981)

New Hampshire 1776 Census by Jay Mack Holbrook (Holbrook Research Institute, 1976)

New Hampshire Residents, 1633-1699 by Jay Mack Holbrook (Holbrook Research Institute, 1979)

☞ IMMIGRATION RECORDS

Immigrants to New England, 1700-1775 by Ethel Bolton (Genealogical Publishing Co., 1966)

Index to New England Naturalization Petitions, 1791-1906 by the US Immigration and Naturalization Service (National Archives, 1983)

☞ LAND RECORDS

Proprietors' Records, 1748-1846 by the New Hampshire Proprietors (filmed by the Genealogical Society of Utah, 1975)

☞ MAPS

Atlas of Historical County Boundaries: New Hampshire, Vermont edited by John H. Long, compiled by Gordon DenBoer and George E. Goodridge Jr. (Simon & Schuster, 1993)

Communities, Settlements, and Neighborhood Centers in the State of New Hampshire: An Inventory (New Hampshire State Planning and Development Commission, 1937)

A Gazetteer of the State of New-Hampshire by John Farmer and Jacob B. Moore (Heritage Books, 1997)

New Hampshire As It Is compiled by Edwin A. Charlton (Tracy and Sanford, 1855)

The New Hampshire Atlas and Gazetteer (DeLorme Mapping Company, 1987)

New Hampshire Maps to 1900: An Annotated Checklist by David A. Cobb (New Hampshire Historical Society, 1981)

New Hampshire Post Offices, 1775-1978 by L.W. Simonds (N.H.: Simonds, 1978)

New Hampshire Town Names and Whence They Came by Elmer Munson Hunt (Noone House, 1971, ca. 1970)

The Place Names of the White Mountains: History and Origins by Robert and Mary Hixon (Down East Books, 1980)

The Postal History of New Hampshire: The Post Offices and First Postmasters From 1775 to 1985 by Chester M. Smith, Jr. and John L. Kay (Depot, 1986)

Town and City Atlas of the State of New Hampshire (D.H. Hurd Company, 1892)

☞MILITARY RECORDS

Indian and French Wars and Revolutionary Papers: Collection of 1880 (filmed by the Genealogical Society of Utah, 1975)

Military History of New Hampshire, From its Settlement, in 1623, to the Year 1861 by Chandler Eastman Potter (1868)

New Hampshire in the Great Rebellion: Containing Histories of the Several New Hampshire Regiments, and a Biographical Notices of Many of the Prominent Actors in the Civil War of 1861-65 by Otis F.R. Waite (Tracy, Chase & Co., 1870)

New Hampshire's Role in the American Revolution, 1763-1789: A Bibliography (New Hampshire American Revolution Bicentennial Commission, 1974)

New Hampshire, World War I Selective Service System Draft Registration Cards, 1917-1918 by the US Selective Service System (National Archives, 1987-1988)

Revised Register of the Soldiers and Sailors of New Hampshire in the War of the Rebellion, 1861-1866 by the New Hampshire Adjutant General's Office and Augustus D. Ayling (Ira C. Evans, 1895)

State of New Hampshire. Rolls of the Soldiers in the Revolutionary War, 4 vols., by Isaac Weare Hammond (AMS Press, 1973)

☞PROBATE RECORDS

The Bench and Bar of New Hampshire, Including Biographical Notices of Deceased Judges of the Highest Court, and Lawyers of the Province and State, and a List of Names of Those now Living by Charles H. Bell (Houghton, Mifflin and Company, 1894)

Colonial Court Records, Names of Those now Living by Charles H. Bell (filmed by the Genealogical Society of Utah, 1975)

New Hampshire Provincial and State Papers, 40 vols. (George E. Jenks, 1867-1943)

Probate Records of the Province of New Hampshire, 9 vols., by Albert Stillman Batchellor (Rumford Printing Co., 1907-41)

Province Deeds and Probate Records From 1623-1772 by the Colony of New Hampshire (filmed by the Genealogical Society of Utah, 1975)

☞VITAL RECORDS

Bride's Index, 1640-1900 by (New Hampshire Division of Vital Statistics, ca. 1970)

Card File Index to Bible Records by the New Hampshire Historical Society (filmed by the Genealogical Society of Utah, 1975)

Card File Index to Publishments of Marriage Intention Prior to 1900 by the New Hampshire Historical Society (filmed by the Genealogical Society of Utah, 1975)

Colonial Gravestone Inscriptions in the State of New Hampshire compiled by Winifred Lane Goss (Genealogical Publishing Co., 1974)

Guide to Church Vital Statistics Records in New Hampshire by the New Hampshire Historical Records Survey (The Survey, 1942)

Index to Births, Early to 1900 by the New Hampshire Registrar of Vital Statistics (filmed by the Genealogical Society of Utah, 1974)

Index to Deaths, Early to 1900 by the New Hampshire Registrar of Vital Statistics (filmed by the Genealogical Society of Utah, 1974)

Index to Divorces and Annulments Prior to 1938 by the New Hampshire Registrar of Vital Statistics (filmed by the Genealogical Society of Utah, 1975)

Index to Early Town Records, New Hampshire, Early to 1850 by the New Hampshire Secretary of State (filmed by the Genealogical Society of Utah, 1950)

New Hampshire Marriage Licenses and Intentions, 1709-1961 by Pauline Johnson Oesterlin (Heritage Books, 1991)

Northern New Hampshire Graveyards and Cemeteries: Transcriptions and Indexes of Burial Sites in the Towns of Clarksville, Colebrook, Columbia, Dixville, Pittsburg, Stewartstown, and Stratford by Nancy L. Dodge (Higginson Books, 1985)

•-COUNTY DETAILS-•

BELKNAP

34 County Dr., Laconia, NH 03246, (603) 524-5400,
<www.belknapcounty.org>

- **INCORPORATED:** Dec 22, 1840
- **PARENT COUNTIES:** Strafford, Merrimac
- **BIRTH RECORDS:** unknown start, kept by Town or City Clerk
- **MARRIAGE:** unknown start, Town or City Clerk
- **DIVORCE:** 1808, Bureau of Vital Records
- **DEATH:** unknown start, Town or City Clerk
- **LAND:** 1862, Registrar of Deeds
- **PROBATE:** 1841, Probate Court
- **COURT:** 1841, Clerk of Superior Court
- **NATURALIZATION:** 1842, County Courthouse
- **NOTES:** Towns organized before 1800: Alton 1796, Barnstead 1727, Centre Harbor 1797, Gilmanton 1727, Meredith 1768, New Hampton 1777, Sanbornton 1770.

CARROLL

95 WaterVillage Rd., Ossipee, NH 03864, (603) 539-7751,
<www.carrollcountynh.net>

- **INCORPORATED:** Dec 22, 1840
- **PARENT COUNTY:** Strafford
- **BIRTH RECORDS:** unknown start, kept by Town or City Clerk
- **MARRIAGE:** unknown start, Town or City Clerk
- **DIVORCE:** 1808, Bureau of Vital Records
- **DEATH:** unknown start, Town or City Clerk
- **LAND:** 1841, Registrar of Deeds
- **PROBATE:** 1840, Probate Court
- **COURT:** 1861, County Courthouse
- **NATURALIZATION:** 1871, County Courthouse
- **NOTES:** Towns organized before 1800: Albany 1766, Brookfield 1794, Chatham 1767, Conway 1765, Eaton 1766, Effingham 1778, Moultonborough 1777, Ossipee 1785, Sandwich 1763, Tamworth 1766, Tuftonborough 1795, Wakefield 1774, Wolfeborough 1770.

CHESHIRE

12 Court St., Keene, NH 03431, (603) 352-6902,
<wwwco.cheshire.nh.us>

- **INCORPORATED:** April 29, 1769
- **PARENT COUNTY:** Original County
- **BIRTH RECORDS:** unknown start, kept by Town or City Clerk
- **MARRIAGE:** unknown start, Town or City Clerk
- **DIVORCE:** 1808, Bureau of Vital Records
- **DEATH:** unknown start, Town or City Clerk
- **LAND:** 1770, Registrar of Deeds
- **PROBATE:** 1769, Probate Court
- **WILLS:** 1771, Probate Court
- **COURT:** 1871, County Courthouse
- **NATURALIZATION:** 1860, County Courthouse
- **NOTES:** Towns organized before 1800: Alstead 1763, Chesterfield 1752, Dublin 1771, Fitzwilliam 1773, Gilsum 1787, Hinsdale 1753, Jaffrey 1773, Keene 1753, Marlborough 1776, Marlow 1761, Nelson 1774, Richmond 1752, Rindge 1768, Stoddard 1774, Sullivan 1787, Surry 1769, Swanzey 1753, Walpole 1752, Winchester 1753.

COOS

Box 309, Lancaster, NH 03584, (603) 788-4900,
<www.cooscountynh.us>

- **INCORPORATED:** Dec. 24, 1803
- **PARENT COUNTY:** Grafton
- **BIRTH RECORDS:** unknown start, kept by Town or City Clerk
- **MARRIAGE:** unknown start, Town or City Clerk
- **DIVORCE:** 1808, Bureau of Vital Records
- **DEATH:** unknown start, Town or City Clerk
- **LAND:** 1772, Registrar of Deeds
- **PROBATE:** 1885, Registrar of Probate
- **COURT:** 1886, County Courthouse
- **NATURALIZATION:** 1888, Supreme Court
- **NOTES:** Towns organized before 1800: Bartlett 1790, Cambridge 1773, Colebrook 1790, Columbia 1797, Dalton 1784, Dummer 1773, Jefferson 1796, Kilkenny 1774, Lancaster 1763, Millsfield 1774, Northumberland 1779, Stratford 1773, Stewartstown 1799, Success 1773, Whitefield 1774.

GRAFTON

3855 Dartmouth College Hwy., North Haverhill, NH 03774, (603) 787-6941, **<www.graftoncountynh.us>**

- **INCORPORATED:** April 29, 1769
- **PARENT COUNTY:** Original County
- **BIRTH RECORDS:** unknown start, kept by Town or City Clerk
- **MARRIAGE:** unknown start, Town or City Clerk
- **DIVORCE:** 1773, State Archives
- **DEATH:** unknown start, Town or City Clerk
- **LAND:** 1773, Registrar of Deeds
- **PROBATE:** 1873, Probate Court
- **COURT:** 1773, County Courthouse
- **NATURALIZATION:** 1840, Superior Court
- **NOTES:** Towns organized before 1800: Alexandria 1782, Bath 1761, Benton 1764, Bethlehem 1799, Bridgewater 1788, Campton 1761, Canaan 1761, Danbury 1795, Dorchester 1761, Enfield 1761, Franconia 1764, Grafton 1778, Groton 1796, Hanover 1761, Haverhill 1763, Hebron 1792, Hill 1778, Holderness 1761, Landaff 1764, Lebanon 1761, Lisbon 1768, Lincoln 1764, Littleton 1784, Lyman 1761, Lyme 1761, Orange 1780, Orford 1761, Plymouth 1763, Rumney 1761, Thornton 1781, Warren 1763, Wentworth 1766, Woodstock 1784.

HILLSBOROUGH

Ste 1, 30 Spring St., Nashua, NH 03060, (603) 883-6461,
<www.hillsboroughcounty.org>

- **INCORPORATED:** April 29, 1769
- **PARENT COUNTY:** Original County
- **BIRTH RECORDS:** unknown start, kept by Town or City Clerk
- **MARRIAGE:** unknown start, Town or City Clerk
- **DEATH:** unknown start, Town or City Clerk
- **LAND:** 1771, Registrar of Deeds
- **PROBATE:** 1771, Probate Court
- **COURT:** 1772, Superior Court
- **NATURALIZATION:** 1842, Superior Court
- **NOTES:** State Archives has divorce records 1783-ca. 1836. Towns

organized before 1800: Amherst 1760, Antrim 1777, Bedford 1750, Brookline 1789, Deering 1774, Francestown 1772, Goffstown 1761, Greenfield 1791, Hancock 1779, Hillsborough 1772, Hollis 1746, Hudson 1746, Litchfield 1749, Lyndeborough 1764, Manchester 1751, Mason 1768, Merrimack 1746, Milford 1794, Nashua 1746, New Ipswich 1762, New Boston 1763, Pelham 1746, Peterborough 1760, Sharon 1791, Temple 1769, Weare 1764, Wilton 1762, Windsor 1798.

MERRIMACK

163 N Main St., Concord, NH 03301, (603) 225-5501, **<www.ci.concord.nh.us>**

- **INCORPORATED:** July 1, 1823
- **PARENT COUNTIES:** Rockingham, Hillsborough
- **BIRTH RECORDS:** unknown start, kept by Town or City Clerk
- **MARRIAGE:** unknown start, Town or City Clerk
- **DIVORCE:** 1840, County Clerk
- **DEATH:** unknown start, Town or City Clerk
- **LAND:** 1823, Registrar of Deeds
- **PROBATE:** 1823, Probate Court
- **COURT:** 1840, County Courthouse
- **NATURALIZATION:** 1846, County Courthouse
- **BURIAL:** unknown start, Town or City Clerk
- **NOTES:** State Archives has divorce records 1824-1880. Towns organized before 1800: Andover 1779, Bradford 1771, Bow 1727, Boscawen 1760, Canterbury 1727, Chichester 1727, Concord 1765, Dunbarton 1765, Epsom 1727, Henniker 1768, Hopkinton 1765, Loudon 1773, New Bradford 1787, Newbury 1778, New London 1779, Northfield 1780, Pembroke 1759, Pittsfield 1782, Salisbury 1768, Sutton 1784, Warner 1774.

ROCKINGHAM

119 North Rd., Brentwood, NH 03833, (603) 679-9350, **<www.co.rockingham.nh.us>**

- **INCORPORATED:** April 29, 1769
- **PARENT COUNTY:** Original County
- **BIRTH RECORDS:** unknown start, kept by Town or City Clerk
- **MARRIAGE:** unknown start, Town or City Clerk
- **DIVORCE:** ca 1920, State Archives
- **DEATH:** unknown start, Town or City Clerk
- **LAND:** 1770, Registrar of Deeds
- **PROBATE:** 1771, Probate Court
- **COURT:** 1772, Common Pleas Court
- **NATURALIZATION:** 1771, Superior Court
- **NOTES:** Towns organized before 1800: Atkinson 1767, Brentwood 1742, Candia 1763, Chester 1722, Danville 1760, Deerfield 1766, East Kingston 1738, Epping 1741, Exeter 1638, Gosport 1715, Greenland 1704, Hampstead 1749, Hampton 1639, Hampton Falls 1723, Kensington 1737, Kingston 1694, Londonderry 1722, New Castle 1693, Newington 1764, New Market 1727, Newton 1749, North Hampton 1742, Northwood 1773, Nottingham 1722, Plaistow 1749, Poplin 1764, Portsmouth 1653, Raymond 1764, Rye 1726, Salem 1750, Sandown 1756, Seabrook 1768, South Hampton 1742, Stratham 1716, Windham 1741.

STRAFFORD

279 County Farm Rd., Box 799, Dover, NH 03820, (603) 742-3065, **<co.strafford.nh.us>**

- **INCORPORATED:** April 29, 1769
- **PARENT COUNTY:** Original County
- **BIRTH RECORDS:** unknown start, kept by Town or City Clerk
- **MARRIAGE:** unknown start, Town or City Clerk
- **DEATH:** unknown start, Town or City Clerk
- **LAND:** 1773, Registrar of Deeds
- **PROBATE:** 1773, Probate Court
- **COURT:** 1773, Superior Court
- **NATURALIZATION:** 1842, Common Pleas Court
- **NOTES:** State Archives has divorce records 1780-1859, 1870-1874. Towns organized before 1800: Barrington 1722, Dover 1623, Durham 1732, Farmington 1798, Lee 1766, Madbury 1755, Middleton 1778, New Durham 1762, Rochester 1722, Somersworth 1754.

SULLIVAN

22 Main St., Box 45, Newport, NH 03773, (603) 863-3450, **<courts.state.nh.us/index.htm>**

- **INCORPORATED:** July 5, 1827
- **PARENT COUNTY:** Cheshire
- **BIRTH RECORDS:** unknown start, kept by Town or City Clerk
- **MARRIAGE:** unknown start, Town or City Clerk
- **DIVORCE:** 1827, Superior Court
- **DEATH:** unknown start, Town or City Clerk
- **LAND:** 1827, Registrar of Deeds
- **PROBATE:** 1827, Probate Court
- **COURT:** 1827, Superior Court
- **NATURALIZATION:** 1838, Supreme Court
- **NOTES:** State Archives has divorce records 1828-1919. Towns organized before 1800: Acworth 1766, Charlestown 1753, Claremont 1764, Cornish 1763, Croydon 1763, Goshen 1791, Grantham 1761, Langdon 1787, Lempster 1761, Newport 1761, Plainfield 1761, Springfield 1794, Unity 1764, Washington 1776, Wendell 1781.

NJ NEW JERSEY

» BY RHONDA R. MCCLURE

HISTORICAL OVERVIEW

The Dutch attempted to settle the area that became New Jersey in the early 1600s, but it wasn't until the Swedes and Finns settled New Sweden along the Delaware River that things began to take hold. Some of those living in New Netherland (eventually New York) gained control, and Dutch farmers began to move into New Jersey.

Official New Jersey history is generally accepted to have started in 1664, when the British conquered New Netherland, and New Jersey was divided and granted to two proprietors. The king granted East Jersey to Sir George Carteret and West Jersey went to Lord John Berkeley. Within a year, there was a major influx of settlers from New England and New York, specifically Long Island.

You will also find a number of Quakers in New Jersey. William Penn and other early Quakers purchased the proprietorships from Berkeley and Carteret between 1672 and 1682.

RECORD HIGHLIGHTS

Mug books—so named because of the photos that accompanied biographies of those who subscribed to the publication—were popular in the late 19th century, and New Jersey has many at state and county repositories. Mug books should always be used with caution. Because people paid to be included, the facts are sometimes suspiciously complete, with maiden names for all the females and complete dates of events. They can be great places to begin, but remember, they usually only include prosperous members of the community.

New Jersey took state censuses decennially from 1855 to 1915, times conveniently between federal censuses. Like early federal census records, the 1855 and 1865 censuses only name the head of household, with all others enumerated by gender. In addition, some counties are missing in the 1855 and 1865 censuses, and enumerations of other counties are partial. The 1875 census only has two counties that survived, Sussex and Essex. All counties' records are available for the 1885, 1895, 1905 and 1915 censuses. Considering the destruction of the 1890 federal census, the 1885 and 1895 state censuses—which name everyone in the household—are a blessing. State census records are available on microfilm through the Family History Library (FHL); the 1895 count is on subscription site Ancestry.com.

Land sales before 1785 were recorded in the capitals of East and West Jersey—Perth Amboy and Burlington, respectively. In 1795, records were transferred to Trenton; look into the Secretary of State's Deeds. Mortgages can be found in county court records from 1766; and other deeds, from 1785. Proprietary records, the first distribution of land by the proprietors, were handled differently. Some have been

research tips

- Some of the state's earliest records were destroyed during the American Revolution.
- New Jersey was a natural migration route to other New England states, especially East Jersey, in the latter 1600s.
- New Englanders brought their record-keeping practices with them to East Jersey. Town records may contain vital records and other documents with genealogical value.
- Some marriage records are hiding in deed books. These books are indexed in *Index of Names to Various Records in Various New Jersey Counties, 1600–1800s*, on microfilm at the Family History Library.

CENSUS RECORDS

- Federal census: 1830, 1840, 1850, 1860, 1870, 1880, 1900, 1910, 1920, 1930
- Federal mortality schedules: 1850, 1860, 1870, 1880
- Special census of Civil War Union veterans and widows: 1890
- State/territorial census: 1855 (incomplete), 1865 (incomplete), 1875 (Essex and Sussex counties only), 1885, 1895, 1905, 1915

published; others are available on microfilm or in transcriptions of land surveys. The records were kept separately by individual boards of proprietors for East and West Jersey.

New Jersey required statewide registration of births and deaths beginning in 1848, though it wasn't until 1920 that county clerks recorded them consistently. The state archives has microfilm of birth certificates from 1878 to 1900, as well as birth registers. The FHL has only the registers. You can get birth and death records for the years 1901 to 1940 from the state archives. Death returns from May 1, 1848 to May 31, 1878 are on microfilm at the New Jersey State Archives, 225 West State Street, Box 307, Trenton, NJ 08625, **<www.state.nj.us/state/darm/links/archives.html>**, as well as from the FHL.

Provincial marriage records were supposed to begin in 1673, though they are incomplete in the early years. Marriage licenses or publishing banns for three weeks was required from 1719 until 1795, when the marriage license requirement was eliminated. After 1795, marriage certificates were moved to the county courts of common pleas. Unfortunately, these records seldom mention the couples' parents' names, but the good news is that you can access the marriages from 1795 to 1900 on microfilm through the FHL and its branch Family History Centers.

ARCHIVES, LIBRARIES, AND SOCIETIES

Atlantic Heritage Center
907 Shore Rd., Box 301, Somers Point, NJ 08244, (609) 927-5218, **<www.atlanticheritagecenternj.org>**

Atlantic Highlands Historical Society
Box 108, Atlantic Highlands, NJ 07716, **<www.atlantichighlandshistory.com>**

Bergen County Historical Society
1201 Main St., River Edge, NJ 07661, (201) 343-9492, **<bergencountyhistory.org>**

The Boonton Historical Society
The John Taylor Building, 210 Main St., Boonton, NJ 07005, (973) 402-8840, **<www.boonton.org/historical>**

Bureau of Vital Statistics, Department of Health and Senior Services
Box 370, Trenton, NJ 08625, (866) 649-8726, **<www.state.nj.us/health/vital/vital.shtml>**

Burlington County Historical Society
451 High St., Burlington City, NJ 08016, (609) 386-4773, **<08016.com/bchs.html>**

Camden County Historical Society
Box 378, Collingswood, NJ 08108, (856) 964-3333, **<www.cchsnj.com>**

Central Jersey Genealogy Club
Box 9903, Hamilton, NJ 08650, **<www.rootsweb.com/~njcjgc>**

Cranford Historical Society
The Hanson House, 38 Springfield Ave., Cranford, NJ 07016, (908) 276-0489, **<www.bobdevlin.com/crhissoc.html>**

Cumberland County Historical Society
Box 16, Greenwich, NJ 08323, (856) 455-4055, **<www.cchistsoc.org>**

Diocese of New Jersey
808 W. State St., Trenton, NJ 08618, (609) 394-5281, **<newjersey.anglican.org>**

Genealogical Society of Bergen County
Box 432, Midland Park, NJ 07432, **<www.rootsweb.com/~njgsbc>**

Genealogical Society of New Jersey
Box 1476, Trenton, NJ 08607, **<www.gsnj.org>**

Genealogical Society of the West Fields
c/o Westfield Memorial Library, 550 E. Broad St., Westfield, NJ 07090, **<www.westfieldnj.com/gswf>**

Gloucester County Historical Society
17 Hunter St., Woodbury, NJ 08096, (856) 845-7881, **<www.rootsweb.ancestry.com/~njglouce/gchs>**

Greater Cape May Historical Society
Box 495, Cape May, NJ 08204, (609) 884-9100, **<www.capemayhistory.org>**

Highland Park Historical Society
228 Donaldson St., Highland Park, NJ 08904, (732) 220-6618, **<mysite.verizon.net/reswf4oi/highlandparkhistoricalsociety222>**

Historical Society of Moorestown
12 High St., Box 477, Moorestown, NJ 08057, (856) 235-0353, **<www.moorestown.com/community/history>**

Holland Society of New York
20 W. 44th St., New York, NY 10036, (212) 758-1675, **<www.hollandsociety.com>**

Howell Historical Society
427 Lakewood-Farmingdale Rd., Howell, NJ 07731, (732) 938-2212, **<www.howellnj.com/historic>**

Hunterdon County Historical Society
114 Main St., Flemington, NJ 08822, (908) 782-1091, **<www.rootsweb.ancestry.com/~njhunter/hchs.htm>**

Jewish Genealogical Society of North Jersey
YM-YWHA of Wayne, 1 Pike Dr., Wayne, NJ 07470, (973) 595-0100, **<mysite.verizon.net/vze2gnpn>**

Jewish Historical Society of Central Jersey
222 Livingston Ave., New Brunswick, NJ 08901, (732) 249-4894, **<www.jewishgen.org/jhscj>**

Jewish Historical Society of Metrowest
901 Route 10, Whippany, NJ 07981, (973) 929-2995, **<www.jhsmw.org>**

Metuchen-Edison Historical Society
Box 61, Metuchen, NJ 08840, **<www.jhalpin.com/mehs>**

Monmouth County Genealogy Society
Box 5, Lincroft, NJ 07738, **<www.rootsweb.ancestry.com/~njmcgs>**

Monmouth County Historical Association
70 Court St., Freehold, NJ 07728, (732) 462-1466, **<www.monmouthhistory.org>**

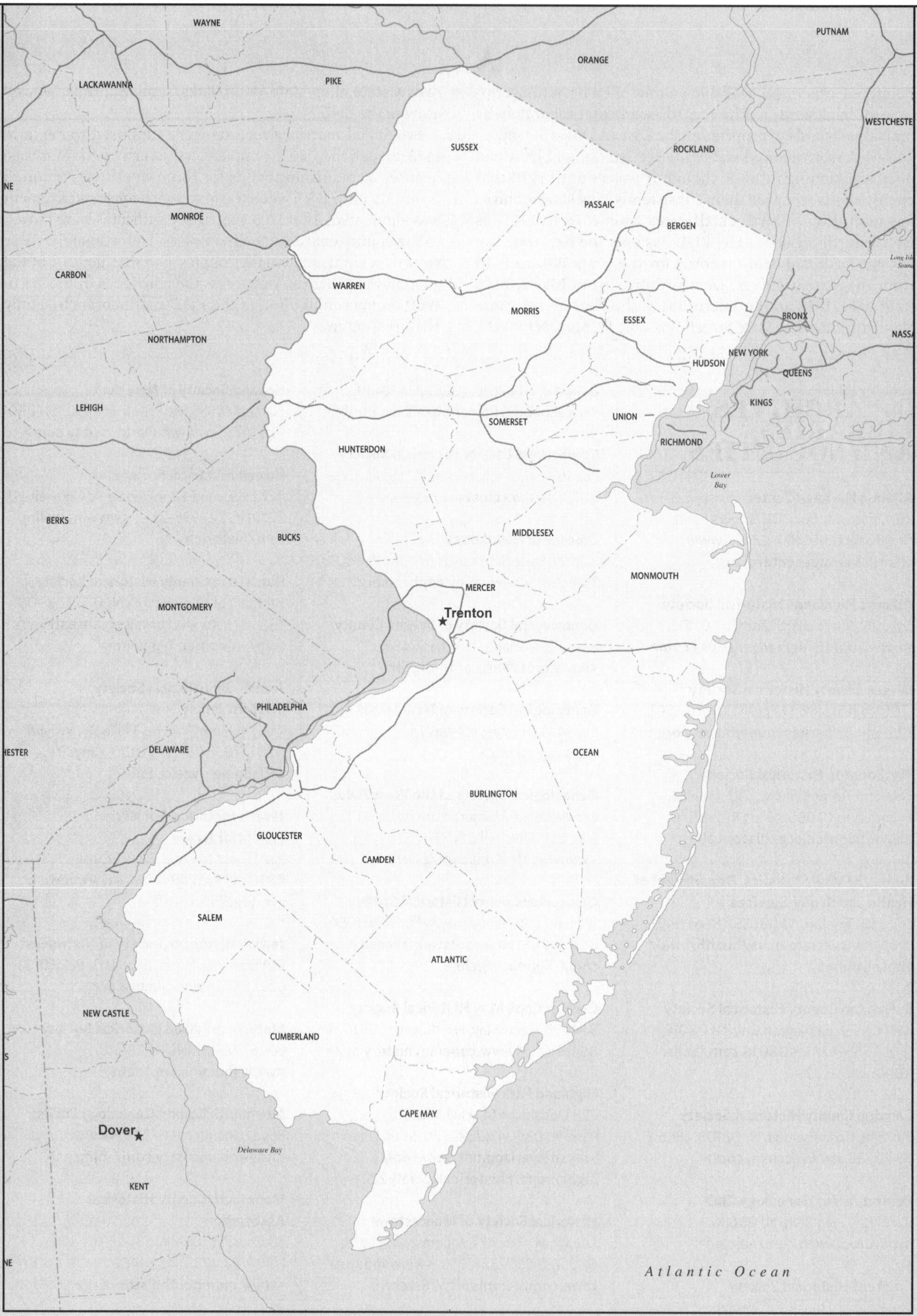
WAYNE
PUTNAM
ORANGE
LACKAWANNA
PIKE
WESTCHESTE
SUSSEX
ROCKLAND
NE
PASSAIC
MONROE
BERGEN
CARBON
Long Isl
Sound
WARREN
MORRIS
ESSEX
BRONX
NASSA
NORTHAMPTON
NEW YORK
HUDSON
QUEENS
KINGS
LEHIGH
UNION
SOMERSET
RICHMOND
HUNTERDON
Lower
Bay
BERKS
MIDDLESEX
BUCKS
MONMOUTH
MERCER
MONTGOMERY
Trenton
PHILADELPHIA
HESTER
DELAWARE
OCEAN
BURLINGTON
GLOUCESTER
CAMDEN
SALEM
ATLANTIC
NEW CASTLE
CUMBERLAND
CAPE MAY
Dover
Delaware Bay
KENT
Atlantic Ocean

Morris Area Genealogy Society
Box 105, Convent Station, NJ 07961, **<www.rootsweb.ancestry.com/~njmags>**

National Archives and Records Administration, Northeast Region
201 Varick St., 12th Floor, New York, NY 10014, (866) 840-1752, **<www.archives.gov/northeast/nyc>**

Navy Lakehurst Historical Society
Box 328, Lakehurst, NJ 08733, (732) 244-8861, **<www.nlhs.com>**

New Jersey Historical Society
52 Park Pl., Newark, NJ 07102, (973) 596-8500, **<www.jerseyhistory.org>**

New Jersey State Archives
225 W. State St., Box 307, Trenton, NJ 08625, (609) 292-6260, **<www.state.nj.us/state/darm/links/archives.html>**

New Jersey State Library
Box 520, Trenton, NJ 08625, (609) 278-2640, **<www.njstatelib.org>**

Newark Public Library
5 Washington St., Box 630, Newark, NJ 07101, (973) 733-7784, **<www.npl.org>**

Ocean County Historical Society
26 Hadley Ave., Toms River, NJ 08753, (732) 341-1880, **<www.oceancountyhistory.org>**

Old Mill Hill Society
<www.trentonmillhill.org/history.html>

Passaic County Historical Society
Lambert Castle, 3 Valley Rd., Paterson, NJ 07503, (973) 247-0085, **<www.lambertcastle.org>**

Plainsboro Historical Society
641 Plainsboro Rd., Plainsboro, NJ 08536, (609) 799-9040, **<www.plainsborohistory.org>**

Rutgers University Libraries
169 College Ave., New Brunswick, NJ 08901, (732) 932-7851, **<www.libraries.rutgers.edu/rul/libs>**

Salem County Historical Society
79-83 Market St., Salem, NJ 08079, (856) 935-5004, **<www.salemcountyhistoricalsociety.com>**

Scandinavian American Heritage Society of New Jersey
<www.sahsnj.org>

Seton Hall University Libraries
400 S. Orange Ave., South Orange, NJ 07079, (973) 761-9000, **<library.shu.edu>**

Township of Neptune Historical Society
c/o Neptune Township Public Library, 25 Neptune Blvd., Neptune, NJ 07754

Vineland Historical and Antiquarian Society
108 S. 7th St., Box 35, Vineland, NJ 08360, (856) 691-1111, **<www.vineland.org/history/society>**

Westfield Historical Society
Box 613, Westfield, NJ 07091, (908) 654-1794, **<www.westfieldhistoricalsociety.org>**

GENERAL RESOURCES

The Biographical Encyclopedia of New Jersey of the Nineteenth Century (Microfilming Corporation of America, 1983)

The Catholic Church in New Jersey by Joseph M. Flynn (1904)

Church Records in New Jersey by William Nelson (filmed by the Genealogical Society of Utah, 1985)

Collection of Family Data by Gilbert Cope (filmed by the Genealogical Society of Utah, 1966)

Collection, Family File by John Pickens Dornan (filmed by the Genealogical Society of Utah, 1971)

The Complete Public Records Guide: Central and Northern New Jersey Region by Fred D. Knapp (Reyn, 1993)

Cyclopedia of New Jersey Biography: Memorial and Biographical compiled with the assistance of the Advisory Committee (American Historical Society, 1923)

Directory of Churches in New Jersey, 10 vols., prepared by the New Jersey Historical Records Survey (Historical Records Survey, 1940-1941)

Directory of New Jersey Newspapers, 1765-1970 edited by William C. Wright and Paul A. Stellhorn (New Jersey Historical Commission, 1977)

Documents Relating to the Colonial History of the State of New Jersey (The Daily Journal Establishment, 1880-1949)

Documents Relating to the Colonial History of the State of New Jersey, Marriage Records, 1665-1800 edited by William Nelson (Archives of the State of New Jersey, vol. 22, 1900)

Dutch Systems in Family Naming, New York-New Jersey by Rosalie Fellows Bailey (National Genealogical Society Bookstore, 1965)

The Early Germans of New Jersey; Their History, Churches, and Genealogies by Theodore Frelinghuysen Chambers (Genealogical Publishing Co., 1969)

Family Records: Or, Genealogies of the First Settlers of Passaic Valley (and Vicinity) by John Littell (General Publishing Co., 1976)

The First Laws of the State of New Jersey edited by John D. Cushing (Michael Glazier, Inc., 1981)

First Settlers of Ye Plantations of Piscataway and Woodbridge, olde East New Jersey, 1664-1714, a Period of Fifty Years by Orra Eugene Monette (The Leroy Carman Press, 1930)

Genealogical Collection by the Genealogical Society of New Jersey (filmed by the Genealogical Society of Utah, 1971)

Genealogical and Memorial History of the State of New Jersey compiled and edited by Francis Bazley Lee (filmed by the Genealogical Society of Utah, 1967)

Genealogical Resources in Southern New Jersey by Edith Hoelle (Gloucester County Historical Society, 1989)

Genealogy of Early Settlers in Trenton and Ewing, "Old Hunterdon County," New Jersey by Eli F. and William Cooley (Genealogical Publishing Co., 1977)

General Index to the Documents Relating to the Colonial History of the State of New Jersey: First in Series, in Ten Volumes prepared by Frederick W. Ricord (Genealogical Research Society of New Orleans, 1994)

Guide to Family History Sources in the New Jersey State Archives, 2nd edition, compiled by Bette Marie Barker, et al. (Division of Archives and Records Management, 1990)

Guide to Local Church Records in the Archives of the Reformed Church in America and to Genealogical Resources in the Gardner Sage Library: New Brunswick Theological Seminary edited by Russell L. Gasero (Historical Society of the Reformed Church in America, 1979)

Guide to the Manuscript Collections of the New Jersey Historical Society compiled by Don C. Skemer and Robert C. Morris (The Society, 1979)

Guide to the Manuscript Collection of the Rutgers University Library compiled by Herbert F. Smith (Rutgers University Library, 1964)

Guide to Vital Statistics Records in New Jersey, 2 vols., prepared by the New Jersey Historical Records Survey (1941)

Historical Collections of New Jersey: Historical and Genealogical Files, 1600's to 1900's by the Gloucester County Historical Society by John Warner Barber, assisted by Henry Howe (Reprint, 1966) (filmed by the Genealogical Society of Utah, 1976)

Historical and Genealogical Miscellany; Data Relating to the Settlement and Settlers of New York and New Jersey, 5 vols., by John E. Stillwell (Genealogical Publishing Co., 1970)

Historical Organizations in New Jersey: A Directory compiled by Mary Alice Quigley, et al. (New Jersey Historical Commission, 1983)

History and Genealogy of Fenwick's Colony by Thomas Shourds (Genealogical Publishing Co., 1976)

The Huguenots or Early French in New Jersey by Albert F. Koehler (University Microfilms International, 1985)

Indentures Collection Containing Deeds, Bonds, Commissions, etc. of New Jersey Individuals: And Other States, 1600-1900 (Genealogical Society of Utah, 1970)

Index of Names to Various Records in Various New Jersey Counties, 1600s-1800s (filmed by the Genealogical Society of Utah, 1972)

The Judicial and Civil History of New Jersey by John Whitehead (Lawbook Exchange, 2004)

Memorial Cyclopedia of New Jersey, 3 vols., by Mary Depue Ogden (Memorial History Co., 1915-17)

A Narrative and Descriptive Bibliography of New Jersey by Nelson R. Burr (Van Nostrand, 1964)

Nelson's Biographical Cyclopedia of New Jersey edited by William Nelson (Eastern Historical Publishing Society, 1913)

New Jersey Bible Records, 1700's to 1800's, vols., 3-5, 13, compiled by Martha Knowles Collins (filmed by the Genealogical Society of Utah, 1971)

New Jersey Biographical Card Index, 1790-1900 by Trinity Episcopal Church (filmed by the Genealogical Society of Utah, 2000)

New Jersey Biographical and Genealogical Notes From the Volumes of the New Jersey Archives, With Additions and Supplements by William Nelson (The Society, 1916)

A New Jersey Biographical Index compiled by Donald Arleigh Sinclair (Genealogical Publishing Co., 1993)

New Jersey: Digging for Ancestors in the Garden State by Kenn Stryker-Rodda (Detroit Society for Genealogical Research, 1984)

New Jersey Ethnic History: A Bibliography compiled by David Steven Cohen (New Jersey Historical Commission, 1986)

New Jersey from Colony to State, 1609-1789 by Richard Patrick McCormick (Rutgers, 1964)

New Jersey Historical Manuscripts: A Guide to Collections in the State compiled by Mary R. Murrin (New Jersey Historical Commission, 1987)

New Jersey, a History, 6 vols., edited by Irving S. Kull (American Historical Society, 1930-1932)

New Jersey Research Outline by the Church of Jesus Christ of Latter-day Saints (online at **<www.familysearch.org/eng/search/RG/guide/new_jersey.asp>**)

New Jersey Tax Lists, 1772-1822, 4 vols., edited by Ronald Vern Jackson (Accelerated Indexing Systems, 1981)

Northwest New Jersey: A History of Somerset, Morris, Hunterdon, Warren and Sussex Counties, 4 vols., by Abraham Van Doren Honeyman (Lewis Publishing Company, Inc., 1927)

Notices From New Jersey Newspapers, 2 vols., by Thomas B. Wilson and Dorothy Agans Stratford (Hunterdon House, ca. 1988, ca. 2002)

Old Farm by Andrew D. Mellick (Rutgers University Press, 1961, ca. 1948)

Pennsylvania and Middle Atlantic States Genealogical Manuscripts compiled by Carlyle J. Parker (Marietta Publishing Co., 1986)

Pioneer Families of Northwestern New Jersey by William C. Armstrong (Hunterdon House, 1979)

Register of New Jersey County Tax Ratables, Abstracts and Exempt Lists, 1773 to About 1889 (filmed by the Genealogical Society of Utah, 1969)

South Jersey, a History, 1664-1924, 5 vols., by Alfred Miller Heston (Lewis Historical Publishing Company, Inc., 1924)

The Stockton Genealogy: Plate 1, Generations 1-4 by Elias Boudinot Stockton (L.C. Photoduplication Service, 1986)

The Story of New Jersey, 5 vols., edited by William Starr Myers (Lewis Historical Publishing Company, Inc., 1945)

The Story of New Jersey's Civil Boundaries 1606-1968 by John P. Snyder (Bureau of Geology and Topography, 1969).

Year Book of the Holland Society of New York by Henricus Selyns and the Holland Society of New York (The Society, 1886)

☞CENSUS RECORDS

Census of New Jersey, 1850-1880; Third Series (of Persons who Died During the Years Ending 30 June, 1850; 1 June, 1860; 1 June, 1870; 31 May, 1880) by the US Census Office (State Library of Archives and History, 1966)

The 1693 Census of the Swedes on the Delaware: Family Histories of the Swedish Lutheran Church Members Residing in Pennsylvania, Delaware, West New Jersey and Cecil County, Maryland, 1638-1693 by Peter Stebbins Craig (SAG Publications, 1993)

New Jersey 1850 Mortality Schedule Index compiled by Shirley J. George and Sandra E. Glenn (G. & G. Genealogical Book Co., 1982)

New Jersey 1890 edited by Ronald Vern Jackson (Accelerated Indexing Systems, 1990)

Revolutionary Census of New Jersey by Kenn Stryker-Rodda (Polyanthos, 1972)

☞VITAL RECORDS

Card Index to Civil War Soldiers' Graves, 1862 (filmed by the Genealogical Society of Utah, 2000)

County File of Miscellaneous New Jersey Information (filmed by the Genealogical Society of Utah, 1971)

Guide to Vital Statistics Records in New Jersey by the New Jersey Historical Records Survey (1941)

An Historical Records Survey of a Miscellany of New Jersey Vital Statistics Records, 1753-1870 (filmed by the Genealogical Society of Utah, 2000)

Index to Inquisitions on the Dead, 1700's-1800's by the New Jersey Bureau of Archives and History (Genealogical Society of Utah, 1972)

New Jersey Catholic Baptismal Records From 1759 to 1781 by Janet Drumm Dirnberger (Brambles, 1981)

New Jersey Cemetery Inscriptions (Genealogical Society of Utah, 1976)

New Jersey Marriage Bonds, W.P.A. Marriage Records, 1670-1800 (filmed by the Genealogical Society of Utah, 1969)

New Jersey Marriage Records, 1665-1800 edited by William Nelson (Genealogical Publishing Co., 1967, 1973, 1982)

New Jersey Tombstone Inscriptions (filmed by the Genealogical Society of Utah, 1969)

☞LAND RECORDS

East Jersey Deeds, 1667-1783 by the New Jersey State Library (filmed by the Genealogical Society of Utah, 1967)

Estates and Partitions, 1712-1866 by the New Jersey Supreme Court (filmed by the Genealogical Society of Utah, 1993)

Index to Deeds, Grantee and Grantor by the New Jersey State Library (filmed by the Genealogical Society of Utah, 1967-1968)

Minutes of the Board of Proprietors of the Eastern Division of New Jersey, 4 vols., by the Board of Proprietors of the Eastern Division of New Jersey (The Board, 1949-1985)

Patents and Deeds and Other Early Records of New Jersey, 1664-1703 edited by William Nelson (Genealogical Publishing Co., 1976)

Perth Amboy Surveys, 1678-1814 by the New Jersey Surveyor General (filmed by the Genealogical Society of Utah, 1973)

☞PROBATE RECORDS

Calendar of New Jersey Wills, 7 vols., by William Nelson and Abraham Van Doren Honeyman (Heritage Books, 1994-1997)

Chancery Court Cases, 1743-1845 by the New Jersey Chancery Court (filmed by the Genealogical Society of Utah, 1978)

Chancery Docket Books, 1824-1900; Index to Chancery Records, 1824-1904 by the New Jersey Court of Chancery (filmed by the Genealogical Society of Utah, 1978)

Chancery Register, 1781-1894 by the New Jersey Court of Chancery (filmed by the Genealogical Society of Utah, 1977)

The Courts of Chancery in New Jersey, 1684-1696 by George Julius Miller (H.E. Pickersgill, 1934)

Court Tickler, 1858-1896 by the New Jersey Court of Chancery (filmed by the Genealogical Society of Utah, 1977)

Early Index to Supreme Court Minutes, 1681-1842 by the New Jersey Supreme Court (Bibliofilm, 1938)

Enrolled Decrees, 1825-1850; Index to Enrolled Decrees, 1825-1854 by the New Jersey Chancery Court (filmed by the Genealogical Society of Utah, 1979)

Genealogical Research: A Guide to Source Materials in the Archives and History Bureau of the New Jersey State Library by the New Jersey Bureau of Archives and History (filmed by the Genealogical Society of Utah, 1989)

Index to New Jersey Wills, 1689-1890: The Testators edited by Lee Smeal and Ronald Vern Jackson (Accelerated Indexing Systems, 1979)

Index to Supreme Court Cases Before and After the Revolution by the New Jersey Supreme Court (filmed by the Genealogical Society of Utah, 1978)

The Law and Practice of New Jersey From the Earliest Times: Concerning the Probate of Wills, the Administration of Estates, the Protection of Orphans and Minors, and the Control of Their Estates by William Nelson (Paterson History Club, 1909)

New Jersey Index to Wills, 3 vols., by the New Jersey Secretary of State (Genealogical Publishing Co., 1969)

Parchment Rolls, 1755-1806 by the New Jersey Court of Chancery (filmed by the Genealogical Society of Utah, 1977)

Religion in New Jersey: A Brief History by Wallace N. Jamison (D. Van Nostrand, 1964)

Records of the US District Court of New Jersey and Predecessor Courts: 1789-1950 by the US District Court, New Jersey (National Archives, ca. 1950)

☞IMMIGRATION RECORDS

The Complete Book of Emigrants, 4 vols., by Peter Wilson Coldham (Genealogical Publishing Co., 1987-1993)

The Early Germans of New Jersey: Their History, Churches and Genealogies by Theodore Frelinghuysen Chambers (Genealogical Publishing Co., 1969)

Guide to Naturalization Records in New Jersey prepared by the New Jersey Historical Records Survey (Microfilming Corporation of America, 1983)

Index to Naturalization Records, 1703-1862 by the New Jersey Bureau of Archives and History (Genealogical Society of Utah, 1972)

Index to Powers of Attorney, Surveyors Reports, Commissions, etc., Referring to Deeds, ca. 1703-1856 by the New Jersey Bureau of Archives and History (Genealogical Society of Utah, 1969)

Mayflower Pilgrim Descendants in Cape May County, New Jersey by Paul Sturtevant Howe (Genealogical Publishing Co., 1977)

More Palatine Families: Some Immigrants to the Middle Colonies, 1717-1776, and Their European Origins by Henry Z. Jones (H.Z. Jones, 1991)

Naturalization Records, 1749-1873; Card Index, 1761-1860 by the New Jersey Supreme Court (filmed by the Genealogical Society of Utah, 1978)

☞MILITARY RECORDS

Alphabetical Roll of New Jersey Volunteers in the Civil War (filmed by the Genealogical Society of Utah, 1969)

A Bibliography: The Civil War and New Jersey by Donald A. Sinclair (Friends of the Rutgers University Library for the New Jersey Civil War Centennial Commission, 1968)

Certificates and Receipts of Revolutionary New Jersey by Dorothy Agans Stratford and Thomas B. Wilson (Hunterdon House, 1996)

Civil War Pension Claims, New Jersey Soldiers Alphabetical (filmed by the Genealogical Society of Utah, 1969)

Genealogical Abstracts of Revolutionary War Pension Files, 4 vols., abstracted by Virgil D. White (National Historical Publishing Co., 1990-1992)

Index to Military Men of New Jersey, 1775-1815 edited by Ronald Vern Jackson, et al. (Accelerated Indexing Systems, 1977)

Index to Records of Spanish-American War, Books 1-122 by the New Jersey State Library (Genealogical Society of Utah, 1969)

Index to Revolutionary War Service Records, 4 vols., transcribed by Virgil D. White (National Historical Publishing Company, 1995)

Lineage Records, no. 1-14199, 1607-1967; Supplemental Records, 1-13850, 1607-1967; Register of Members by the General Society of Colonial Wars (filmed by the Genealogical Society of Utah, 1967)

The Loyalists of New Jersey, Their Memorials, Petitions, Claims, etc., From English Records by Edward Alfred Jones (New Jersey Historical Society, 1927)

Military Officers Recorded in the Office of the Secretary of State, Trenton, New Jersey; Colonial Wars, 1668-1774 by the New Jersey State Library (Genealogical Society of Utah, 1969)

New Jersey in 1793: An Abstract and Index to the 1793 Militia Census of the State of New Jersey by James S. Norton (1973)

New Jersey Civil War Records, Books 1-829 by the New Jersey State Library (State Library of Archives and History, 1969)

New Jersey Records; French and Indian War, 1757-1764 by the New Jersey State Library (Genealogical Society of Utah, 1969)

New Jersey and the Revolutionary War by Alfred Hoyt Bill (Rutgers University, 1964)

"New Jersey Volunteers" (Loyalists) In the Revolutionary War by William Scudder Stryker (Naar, Day & Naar, printers, 1887)

New Jersey in the War of 1812; Books 1-52 by the New Jersey State Library (Genealogical Society of Utah, 1969)

New Jersey, World War I Selective Service System Draft Registration Cards, 1917-1918 by the US Selective Service System (National Archives, 1987-1988)

Official Register of the Officers and Men of New Jersey in the Revolutionary War compiled by James W.S. Campbell (Genealogical Publishing Co., 1967)

Record of Officers and Men of New Jersey in the Civil War, 1861-1865 by the New Jersey Adjutant General's Office (J.L. Murphy, 1876)

Records of Officers and Men of New Jersey in Wars 1791-1815 by the New Jersey Adjutant General's Office (filmed by the Genealogical Society of Utah, 1972)

Register of the Commissioned Officers and Privates of the New Jersey Volunteers in the Service of the United States by the New Jersey Adjutant General's Office (University Publications of America, 1991)

Revolutionary War Pensioners Living in New Jersey Before 1834 by Inez Raney Waldenmaier (Inez Waldenmaier, 1983)

Revolutionary War Records of New Jersey (filmed by the Genealogical Society of Utah, 1969)

Revolutionary War Slips, Single Citations of the New Jersey Department of Defense Materials (filmed by the Genealogical Society of Utah, 1968)

Soldiers and Sailors of New Jersey in the Spanish-American War by Bernard McNally (Library of Congress Photoduplication Service, 1989)

☞MAPS

An Alphabetical Listing of Local Places and Incorporated Municipalities in the State of New Jersey by the New Jersey Department of Transportation Office of Information Services (University Microfilms International, 1985)

A Gazetteer of the State of New Jersey by Thomas F. Gordon (D. Fenton, 1834)

A Geographic Dictionary of New Jersey by Henry Gannett (Genealogical Publishing Co., 1978)

Historical Atlas and Chronology of County Boundaries, 1788-1980, 5 vols., edited John H. Long (G.K. Hall, 1984)

The National Gazetteer of the United States of America—New Jersey, 1983 prepared by the US Geological Survey and the US Board on Geographic Names (US Government Printing Office, 1983)

New Jersey Historic Map Portfolio edited by Don C. Skemer (Afton Publishing, 1983)

New Jersey Postal History: The Post Offices and First Postmasters, 1776-1976 by John L. Kay and Chester Smith, Jr. (Quarterman Publications, 1977)

The Origin of New Jersey Place Names compiled by workers of the Federal Writer's Program (New Jersey Public Library Commission, 1945)

The Story of New Jersey's Civil Boundaries, 1606-1968 by John P. Snyder (New Jersey Geological Survey, 1988)

•-COUNTY DETAILS-•

ATLANTIC

5901 Main St., Mays Landing, NJ 08330, (609) 641-6867,
<www.atlanticcountyclerk.org>

- **INCORPORATED:** Feb. 7, 1837
- **PARENT COUNTY:** Gloucester
- **BIRTH RECORDS:** Start in 1878, kept by Department of Health and Vital Statistics
- **MARRIAGE:** 1878, Department of Health and Vital Statistics
- **DIVORCE:** 1878, Department of Health and Vital Statistics
- **DEATH:** 1878, Department of Health and Vital Statistics
- **NOTES:** State Archives has birth and death records 1848-1878, court records 1838-1905, land records 1837-1900, marriage records 1875-1897 and microfilm records of marriage records 1837-1876, naturalization records 1837-1951, and probate records and wills 1837-1922. County Clerk has marriage records 1837-1876. Superior Court Public Information Center has divorce records 1901-1992.

BERGEN

1 Bergen County Plaza, Hackensack, NJ 07601, (201) 336-7000,
<www.co.bergen.nj.us>

- **INCORPORATED:** March 7, 1683
- **PARENT COUNTY:** East Jersey
- **BIRTH RECORDS:** Start in 1878, kept by Department of Health and Vital Statistics
- **MARRIAGE:** 1878, Department of Health and Vital Statistics
- **DIVORCE:** 1992, County Court
- **DEATH:** 1878, Department of Health and Vital Statistics
- **COURT:** unknown, County Clerk
- **NOTES:** State Archives has birth and death records 1848-1878, land records 1715-1901, marriage records 1795-1877, naturalization records 1804-1906, probate records 1785-1962, and wills 1698-1900. Superior Court Public Information Center has divorce records 1901-1992.

BURLINGTON

49 Rancocas Rd., Mount Holly, NJ 08060, (609) 265-5000,
<co.burlington.nj.us>

- **INCORPORATED:** May 17, 1694
- **PARENT COUNTY:** Province of West Jersey
- **BIRTH RECORDS:** Start in 1878, kept by Department of Health and Vital Statistics
- **MARRIAGE:** 1878, Department of Health and Vital Statistics
- **DIVORCE:** 1992, County Court
- **DEATH:** 1878, Department of Health and Vital Statistics
- **NOTES:** State Archives has birth and death records 1848-1878, court records 1681-1937, land records 1718-1901, marriage records 1795-1878, naturalization records 1790-1956, probate records 1785-1970, and wills 1688-1900. Superior Court Public Information Center has divorce records 1901-1992.

CAMDEN

Camden County Courthouse, Room 102, 520 Market St., Camden, NJ 08102, (856) 225-5300, **<www.co.camden.nj.us>**

- **INCORPORATED:** March 13, 1844
- **PARENT COUNTY:** Gloucester
- **BIRTH RECORDS:** Start in 1878, kept by Department of Health and Vital Statistics
- **MARRIAGE:** 1878, Department of Health and Vital Statistics
- **DIVORCE:** 1992, County Court
- **DEATH:** 1878, Department of Health and Vital Statistics
- **NOTES:** State Archives has birth and death records 1848-1878, court records 1844-1961, land records 1759-1840, 1844-1900, marriage records 1848-1878, and probate records 1844-1946. Superior Court Public Information Center has divorce records 1901-1992. Land records prior to 1844 are from parts of Gloucester County that became Camden County.

CAPE MAY

7 N. Main St. DN 109, Box 5000, Cape May Court House, NJ 08210, (609) 465-1010, **<www.capemaycountygov.net>**

- **INCORPORATED:** Nov. 12, 1692
- **PARENT COUNTY:** West Jersey
- **BIRTH RECORDS:** Start in 1878, kept by Department of Health and Vital Statistics
- **MARRIAGE:** 1878, Department of Health and Vital Statistics
- **DIVORCE:** 1992, County Court
- **DEATH:** 1878, Department of Health and Vital Statistics
- **NOTES:** State Archives has birth and death records 1848-1878, court records 1790-1964, land records 1692-1926, marriage records 1795-1878, probate records 1786-1980, and wills 1704-1900. Superior Court Public Information Center has divorce records 1901-1992.

CUMBERLAND

60 W. Broad St., Bridgeton, NJ 08302, (856) 451-4860, **<www.co.cumberland.nj.us>**

- **INCORPORATED:** Jan. 19, 1748
- **PARENT COUNTY:** Salem
- **BIRTH RECORDS:** Start in 1878, kept by Department of Health and Vital Statistics
- **MARRIAGE:** 1878, Department of Health and Vital Statistics
- **DIVORCE:** 1992, County Court
- **DEATH:** 1878, Department of Health and Vital Statistics
- **NOTES:** State Archives has birth and death records 1848-1878, court records 1745-1937, land records 1785-1952, marriage records 1795-1878, naturalization records 1802-1931, probate records 1785-1904, and wills 1747-1900. Superior Court Public Information Center has divorce records 1901-1992.

ESSEX

465 Martin Luther King Blvd., Room 247 Newark, NJ 07101, (973) 621-4921, **<www.essexclerk.com>**

- **INCORPORATED:** March 1, 1683
- **PARENT COUNTY:** Province of East Jersey
- **BIRTH RECORDS:** Start in 1878, kept by Department of Health and Vital Statistics
- **MARRIAGE:** 1878, Department of Health and Vital Statistics
- **DIVORCE:** 1992, County Court
- **DEATH:** 1878, Department of Health and Vital Statistics
- **NOTES:** State Archives has birth and death records 1848-1878, court records 1709-1911, land records 1728-1909, marriage records 1795-1893, naturalization records 1698-1931, probate records 1793-1907, and wills 1697-1900. Superior Court Public Information Center has divorce records 1901-1992.

GLOUCESTER

1 N. Broad St., Box 129, Woodbury, NJ 08096, (856) 853-3237, **<www.co.gloucester.nj.us>**

- **INCORPORATED:** May 17, 1694
- **PARENT COUNTY:** Province of West Jersey
- **BIRTH RECORDS:** Start in 1878, kept by Department of Health and Vital Statistics
- **MARRIAGE:** 1878, Department of Health and Vital Statistics
- **DIVORCE:** 1992, County Court
- **DEATH:** 1878, Department of Health and Vital Statistics
- **NOTES:** State Archives has birth and death records 1848-1878, court records 1686-1887, land records 1650-1703, 1714-1779, 1786-1901, naturalization records 1808-1932, probate records 1785-1897, and wills 1691-1922. Superior Court Public Information Center has divorce records 1901-1992. County Historical Society has marriage records 1686-1939. Courthouse burned 1786, early records preserved at Surveyor General's Office, Burlington and Secretary of State Office, Trenton.

HUDSON

257 Cornelison Ave., 4th Floor, Jersey City, NJ 07302, (201) 369-3470, **<www.hudsoncountyclerk.org>**

- **INCORPORATED:** Feb. 22, 1840
- **PARENT COUNTY:** Bergen
- **BIRTH RECORDS:** Start in 1878, kept by Department of Health and Vital Statistics
- **MARRIAGE:** 1878, Department of Health and Vital Statistics
- **DIVORCE:** 1992, County Court
- **DEATH:** 1878, Department of Health and Vital Statistics
- **LAND:** unknown, Registrar of Deeds
- **NOTES:** State Archives has birth and death records 1848-1878, court records 1842-1927, land records 1805-1901, marriage records 1848-1878, and probate records 1840-1953. Superior Court Public Information Center has divorce records 1901-1992.

HUNTERDON

71 Main St., Box 2900, Flemington, NJ 08822, (908) 788-1221, **<www.co.hunterdon.nj.us>**

- **INCORPORATED:** March 13, 1714
- **PARENT COUNTY:** Burlington
- **BIRTH RECORDS:** Start in 1878, kept by Department of Health and Vital Statistics
- **MARRIAGE:** 1878, Department of Health and Vital Statistics
- **DIVORCE:** 1992, County Court
- **DEATH:** 1878, Department of Health and Vital Statistics
- **NOTES:** State Archives has birth and death records 1848-1878, court records 1712-1916, land records 1705-1955, marriage records 1795-1900, naturalization records 1803-1906, probate records 1785-1906, and wills 1704-1919. Superior Court Public Information Center has divorce records 1901-1992.

MERCER

209 S. Broad St., Trenton, NJ 08650, (609) 989-6464,
<www.mercercounty.org>

- **INCORPORATED:** Feb. 22, 1838
- **PARENT COUNTIES:** Somerset, Middlesex, Hunterdon, Burlington
- **BIRTH RECORDS:** Start in 1878, kept by Department of Health and Vital Statistics
- **MARRIAGE:** 1878, Department of Health and Vital Statistics
- **DIVORCE:** 1992, County Court
- **DEATH:** 1878, Department of Health and Vital Statistics
- **COURT:** 1838, County Clerk
- **NOTES:** State Archives has birth and death records 1848-1878, land records 1795-ca. 1930s, marriage records 1815-1832, 1841-1887, naturalization records 1838-1940, and probate records 1838-1939. Superior Court Public Information Center has divorce records 1901-1992

MIDDLESEX

75 Bayard St., New Brunswick, NJ 08901, (732) 745-3005,
<co.middlesex.nj.us>

- **INCORPORATED:** March 7, 1683
- **PARENT COUNTY:** East Jersey
- **BIRTH RECORDS:** Start in 1878, kept by Department of Health and Vital Statistics
- **MARRIAGE:** 1878, Department of Health and Vital Statistics
- **DIVORCE:** 1992, County Court
- **DEATH:** 1878, Department of Health and Vital Statistics
- **LAND:** 1683, County Clerk
- **NOTES:** State Archives has birth and death records 1848-1878, court records 1792-1871, naturalization records 1794-1906, probate records 1786-1971, and wills 1683-1913. Superior Court Public Information Center has divorce records 1901-1992.

MONMOUTH

1 East Main St., Freehold, NJ 07728, (732) 431-7324,
<shore.co.monmouth.nj.us>

- **INCORPORATED:** March 1, 1683
- **PARENT COUNTY:** Province of East Jersey
- **BIRTH RECORDS:** Start in 1878, kept by Department of Health and Vital Statistics
- **MARRIAGE:** 1878, Department of Health and Vital Statistics
- **DIVORCE:** 1992, County Court
- **DEATH:** 1878, Department of Health and Vital Statistics
- **NOTES:** State Archives has birth and death records 1848-1878, land records 1665-1899, marriage records 1789-1880, naturalization records 1824-1908, probate records 1785-1969, and wills 1695-1900. Superior Court Public Information Center has divorce records 1901-1992.

MORRIS

Hall of Records Administration Bldg., Court St., Box 315, Morristown, NJ 07963, (973) 829-8219, **<www.co.morris.nj.us>**

- **INCORPORATED:** March 15, 1739
- **PARENT COUNTY:** Hunterdon
- **BIRTH RECORDS:** Start in 1878, kept by Department of Health and Vital Statistics
- **MARRIAGE:** 1878, Department of Health and Vital Statistics
- **DIVORCE:** 1992, County Court
- **DEATH:** 1878, Department of Health and Vital Statistics
- **PROBATE:** unknown, County Surrogate
- **NOTES:** State Archives has birth and death records 1848-1878, court records 1740-1866, land records 1785-1962, marriage records 1795-1919, naturalization records 1816-1906, and wills 1740-1900. Superior Court Public Information Center has divorce records 1901-1992.

OCEAN

Box 2191, Toms River, NJ 08754, (732) 929-2018,
<www.co.ocean.nj.us>

- **INCORPORATED:** Feb. 15, 1850
- **PARENT COUNTY:** Monmouth
- **BIRTH RECORDS:** Start in 1878, kept by Department of Health and Vital Statistics
- **MARRIAGE:** 1878, Department of Health and Vital Statistics
- **DIVORCE:** 1992, County Court
- **DEATH:** 1878, Department of Health and Vital Statistics
- **COURT:** 1850, County Clerk
- **NOTES:** State Archives has birth and death records 1848-1878, land records 1850-1960, marriage records 1850-1908, probate records 1850-1955, and wills 1850-1900. Superior Court Public Information Center has divorce records 1901-1992.

PASSAIC

401 Grand St., Paterson, NJ 07505, (973) 225-3632,
<www.passaiccountynj.org>

- **INCORPORATED:** Feb. 7, 1837
- **PARENT COUNTIES:** Bergen, Essex
- **BIRTH RECORDS:** Start in 1878, kept by Department of Health and Vital Statistics
- **MARRIAGE:** 1878, Department of Health and Vital Statistics
- **DIVORCE:** 1992, County Court
- **DEATH:** 1878, Department of Health and Vital Statistics
- **NOTES:** State Archives has birth and death records 1848-1878, court records 1837-1946, land records 1837-1901, marriage records 1847-1902, naturalization records 1837-1906, probate records 1835-1919, and wills 1837-1902. Superior Court Public Information Center has divorce records 1901-1992.

SALEM

92 Market St., Salem, NJ 08079, (856) 935-7510,
<salemcountyclerk.org>

- **INCORPORATED:** May 17, 1694
- **PARENT COUNTY:** Salem Tenth
- **BIRTH RECORDS:** Start in 1878, kept by Department of Health and Vital Statistics
- **MARRIAGE:** 1878, Department of Health and Vital Statistics
- **DIVORCE:** 1992, County Court
- **DEATH:** 1878, Department of Health and Vital Statistics
- **NOTES:** State Archives has birth and death records 1848-1878, court records 1706-1953, land records 1664-1710, 1786-1900, marriage records 1680-1956, naturalization records 1800-1929, and wills 1678-1703, 1712, 1923. Superior Court Public Information Center has divorce records 1901-1992. County Surrogate has probate records 1748-1908.

SOMERSET

20 Grove St., Box 3000, Somerville, NJ 08876, (908) 231-7006, **<www.co.somerset.nj.us>**

- **INCORPORATED:** May 14, 1688
- **PARENT COUNTY:** Middlesex
- **DIVORCE RECORDS:** Start in 1992, kept by County Court
- **LAND:** 1785, County Clerk
- **PROBATE:** unknown, County Surrogate
- **COURT:** 1777, County Clerk
- **DEATH:** 1878, Department of Health and Vital Statistics
- **NOTES:** State Archives has birth and death records 1848-1878, court records 1776-1926, land records 1779-1901, marriage records 1778-1887, naturalization records 1805-1922, probate records 1794-1972, and wills 1702-1900. Superior Court Public Information Center has divorce records 1901-1992.

SUSSEX

Hall of Records, 83 Spring St., Ste. 304, Newton, NJ 07860, (973) 579-0900, **<www.sussex.nj.us>**

- **INCORPORATED:** June 8, 1753
- **PARENT COUNTY:** Morris
- **BIRTH RECORDS:** Start in 1878, kept by Department of Health and Vital Statistics
- **MARRIAGE:** 1878, Department of Health and Vital Statistics
- **DIVORCE:** 1992, County Court
- **DEATH:** 1878, Department of Health and Vital Statistics
- **NOTES:** State Archives has birth and death records 1848-1878, court records 1798-1907, land records 1785-1901, marriage records 1795-1878, naturalization records 1855-1902, probate records 1779-1924, and wills 1754-1905. Superior Court Public Information Center has divorce records 1901-1992.

UNION

2 Broad St., Elizabeth, NJ 07207, (908) 527-4360, **<www.unioncountynj.org>**

- **INCORPORATED:** March 19, 1857
- **PARENT COUNTY:** Essex
- **BIRTH RECORDS:** Start in 1878, kept by Department of Health and Vital Statistics
- **MARRIAGE:** 1878, Department of Health and Vital Statistics
- **DIVORCE:** 1992, County Court
- **DEATH:** 1878, Department of Health and Vital Statistics
- **LAND:** 1857, County Clerk
- **NOTES:** State Archives has birth and death records 1848-1878, court records 1819-1933, marriage records 1850-1878, naturalization records 1845-1945, probate records 1854-1902, and wills 1854-1911. Superior Court Public Information Center has divorce records 1901-1992.

WARREN

413 Second St., Belvidere, NJ 07823, (908) 475-6211, **<www.co.warren.nj.us>**

- **INCORPORATED:** Nov. 20, 1824
- **PARENT COUNTY:** Sussex
- **BIRTH RECORDS:** Start in 1878, kept by Department of Health and Vital Statistics
- **MARRIAGE:** 1878, Department of Health and Vital Statistics
- **DIVORCE:** 1992, County Court
- **DEATH:** 1878, Department of Health and Vital Statistics
- **NOTES:** State Archives has birth and death records 1848-1878, court records 1824-1941, land records 1823-1901, marriage records 1825-1902, naturalization records 1825-1906, probate records 1825-1956, and wills 1824-1901. Superior Court Public Information Center has divorce records 1901-1992.

NEW MEXICO

» BY DAVID A. FRYXELL

HISTORICAL OVERVIEW

New Mexico's is among the most recent stars on the American flag, gaining statehood in 1912. Yet New Mexico's history, both native and European, is among the longest on the continent. Evidence of habitation by the Sandia people dates to 25,000 BC. Other native cultures there include the Mogollon, the Anasazi, and around 1130 to 1180, the Pueblo Indians, who were here when Coronado came in 1540. Don Juan de Oñate founded the first Spanish settlements in 1598. Santa Fe was founded in 1610; Albuquerque marked its tricentennial in 2006. Except for Pueblo Indian revolts in 1680 and 1696, which briefly sent colonists fleeing, the Spanish held sway in this area for centuries. For a brief period following Mexican independence in 1821, Mexico's flag replaced Spain's.

With the outbreak of the Mexican-American War in 1846, the Stars and Stripes arrived in New Mexico. In 1848, the Treaty of Guadalupe Hidalgo ended the war and fixed the boundaries between the US and Mexico at the Rio Grande, the Gila River, and the Colorado River. The Gadsden Purchase, signed in Mesilla, NM, in 1854, added the rest of southwestern New Mexico and southern Arizona.

The Compromise of 1850 created New Mexico Territory from today's New Mexico plus southern Nevada and Arizona, which split off in 1863. The arrival of the telegraph in 1877 and the joining of the second transcontinental railroad at Deming, NM, in 1881, began to bring the rough-and-tumble territory into the American family. New Mexico attracted miners and ranchers. Some of the latter battled in the Lincoln County Wars, which made a legend of Billy the Kid.

New Mexico's soldiers formed Teddy Roosevelt's Rough Riders in the Spanish-American War. During World War II, the atomic age was born at Los Alamos and Alamogordo, beginning a new, high-tech era for this ancient land.

RECORD HIGHLIGHTS

If your roots go back to the Spanish and Mexican era, you can find colonial censuses from 1750 to 1830 at the state archives, and in a collection published by the New Mexico Genealogical Society. The archives also has Spanish land records from 1693 to 1821 and Mexican records from 1821 to 1845. Catholic church records from the Archdiocese of Santa Fe, now at the archives, also extend to this time; the Family History Library (FHL) has microfilmed these back to 1726.

Ancestors during the territorial period may be in territorial censuses, taken along with the regular federal enumeration beginning in 1850. Note that the 1860 head count covered only the area south of the Gila River. Also check the 1885 state census (actually federally administered), which listed all household members; it's available on microfilm through the FHL.

New Mexico was the last state to adopt statewide vital records and health statistics—not until 1920, when prompted by war and the flu epidemic. Access to records is restricted

research tips

- Many early records are in Spanish. Translations may contain inaccuracies or gaps.
- The key to successful New Mexico research is knowing the history of the records for which you are searching. Read up on the many phases of the state's past.
- Rocky Mountain Online Archives **<rmoa.unm.edu>** is a guide to several of the state's major archival holdings.
- The New Mexico Genealogical Society's site **<www.nmgs.org>** contains tons of helpful tips and tools.

CENSUS RECORDS

- Federal census: 1820, 1860, 1870, 1880, 1900, 1910, 1920, 1930
- Special Census of Civil War Union veterans and widows: 1890
- Spanish/Mexican census: 1790, 1823, 1845
- State/territorial census: 1885

to immediate family. For pre-1920 vital records, look at the county level; church records may substitute.

The state archives contain a wide variety of helpful records, such as land grants, early probates, and pre-1912 court papers. Military records here include the Spanish and Mexican era, the Indian Wars, and the Civil War (including Confederate data). See the archives' online guide for genealogists at **<www.nmcpr.state.nm.us/archives/ancestors.htm>**.

According to Karen Stein Daniel, CG, editor of the *New Mexico Genealogist*, another key repository is Albuquerque's Special Collections Library, a branch of the Rio Grande Valley Library System. This library holds the Spanish Archives of New Mexico I and II, the Mexican Archives of New Mexico, land grant records, and portions of the territorial records, all on microfilm. You'll also find a large collection of family genealogies, territorial newspapers, city directories, vital records and indexes, obituary indexes, and materials from the Archives of the Archdiocese of Santa Fe.

New Mexico's long history represents both a challenge and an opportunity for researchers, spanning Native American, Spanish, Mexican, territorial, and statehood periods. Daniel says the most valuable tip for beginning researchers is to read about the history of the area. Records are typically divided and catalogued according to the period in which they fall, meaning you must know the history to know where to look.

Finally, Daniel advises, if at first you don't succeed, don't give up—look somewhere else. You may have to scour several locations for the records you need. For example, some county records are now housed in the archives in Santa Fe. The best chance of success, says Daniel, comes from doing your homework, preparing a research plan, and establishing the location of records you seek prior to setting out.

☞ARCHIVES, LIBRARIES, AND SOCIETIES

Albuquerque Genealogical Society
Box 25512 Albuquerque, NM 87125, **<abqgen.swnet.com>**

Albuquerque Special Collections Library
423 East Central Ave., Albuquerque, NM 87101, (505) 848-1376, **<cabq.gov/library/specol.html>**

Albuquerque Public Library
501 Copper Ave. NW, Albuquerque, NM 87102, (505) 768-5170, **<cabq.gov/library>**

Artesia Public Library
306 West Richardson, Artesia, NM 88210, (505) 746-4252, **<www.pvtnetworks.net/~apublib>**

Bureau of Land Management, New Mexico State Office
Box 27115, Santa Fe, NM 87502, (505) 954-2000, **<www.blm.gov/nm/st/en.html>**

Chaves County Genealogy
Box 1085, Roswell, NM 88201, (505) 623-6864

Genealogy Club of Angel Fire
Box 503, Angel Fire, NM 87710, (505) 377-2535

Historical Society of New Mexico
Box 1912, Santa Fe, NM 87504, **<www.hsnm.org>**

History Library Museum of New Mexico
Palace of the Governors, 105 West Palace Ave., Santa Fe, NM 87501, (505) 476-5100, **<www.palaceofthegovernors.org>**

Los Alamos Historical Society
1050 Bathtub Row, Box 43, Los Alamos, NM 87544, (505) 662-6272, **<www.losalamoshistory.org>**

Lovington Public Library
115 S. Main Ave., Lovington, NM 88260, (575) 396-3144, **<lovingtonpublib.leaco.net>**

New Mexico Genealogical Society
Box 27559, Albuquerque, NM 87125, **<www.nmgs.org>**

New Mexico Health Services
1190 St. Francis Dr., Santa Fe, NM 87502, (505) 827-2613, **<www.health.state.nm.us>**

New Mexico Records Center and Archives
1205 Camino Carlos Rey, Santa Fe, NM 87507, (505) 476-7000, **<www.nmcpr.state.nm.us>**

New Mexico State Library
1209 Camino Carlos Rey, Santa Fe, NM 87507, (505) 476-9700, **<www.nmstatelibrary.org>**

New Mexico State University Library
Box 30006, Department 3475, Las Cruces, NM 88003, (575) 646-2932, **<lib.nmsu.edu>**

Portales Public Library
218 S. Ave. B, Portales, NM 88130, (575) 356-3940, **<www.portalesnm.org>**

Roman Catholic Archdiocese of Santa Fe
4000 St. Joseph Place NW, Albuquerque, NM 87120, (505) 831-8100, **<www.archdiocesesantafe.org>**

Roman Catholic Diocese of Gallup
P.O. Box 1338, Gallup, NM 87305, (505) 863-4406, **<www.dioceseofgallup.org>**

Roman Catholic Diocese of Las Cruces
1280 Med Park, Las Cruces, NM 88005, (505) 523-7577, **<www.dioceseoflascruces.org>**

Roswell Public Library
301 N. Pennsylvania Ave., Roswell, NM 88201, (575) 622-7101, **<www.roswellpubliclibrary.org/colls.htm>**

Sierra County Genealogical Society
c/o Truth or Consequences Public Library 325 Library Lane, Truth or Consequences, NM 87901, **<www.rootsweb.ancestry.com/~nmscgs2>**

Socorro County Historical Society
Box 923, Socorro, NM 87801, (575) 835-3437, **<www.rootsweb.ancestry.com/~nmschs>**

Sons of the American Revolution, New Mexico Society
905 Santa Ana SE, Albuquerque, NM 87123, (505) 296-0446, **<www.sar.org/Committees/Genealogy>**

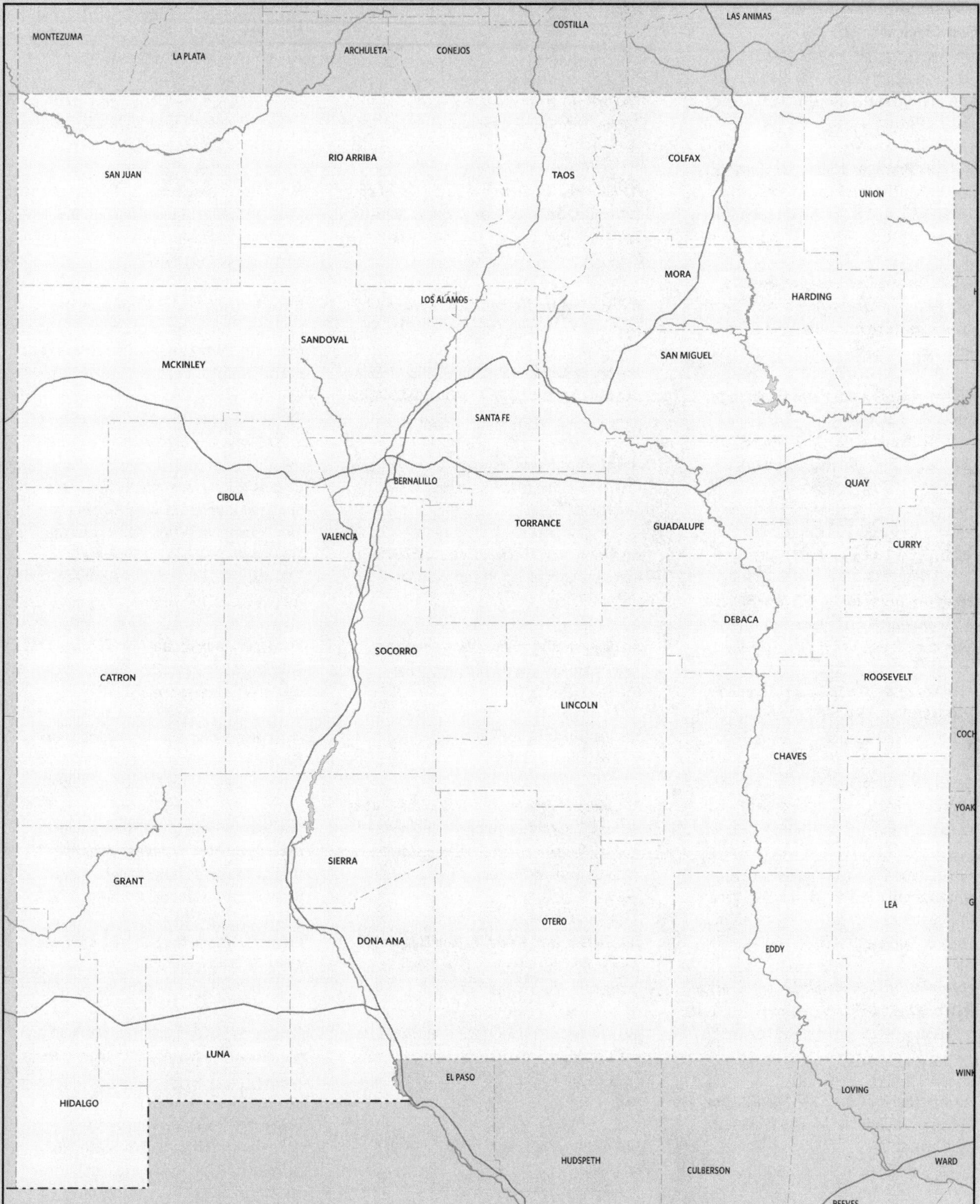
MONTEZUMA
LA PLATA
ARCHULETA
CONEJOS
COSTILLA
LAS ANIMAS
SAN JUAN
RIO ARRIBA
TAOS
COLFAX
UNION
MORA
HARDING
LOS ALAMOS
SANDOVAL
MCKINLEY
SAN MIGUEL
SANTA FE
CIBOLA
BERNALILLO
QUAY
VALENCIA
TORRANCE
GUADALUPE
CURRY
DEBACA
SOCORRO
CATRON
ROOSEVELT
LINCOLN
CHAVES
SIERRA
GRANT
LEA
OTERO
DONA ANA
EDDY
LUNA
EL PASO
HIDALGO
LOVING
HUDSPETH
CULBERSON
WARD
REEVES

Southeastern New Mexico Genealogical Society
c/o Agnes Kastner Head Center, 200 E. Park St., Hobbs, NM 88240, **<genealogytrails.com/newmex/lea/senmgs.htm>**

Thomas Branigan Memorial Library
200 E. Picacho Ave., Las Cruces, NM 88001, (575) 528-4000, **<library.las-cruces.org>**

Totah Tracers Genealogical Society
1412 Anna Lane, Farmington, NM 87401 **<www.rootsweb.ancestry.com/~nmttgs>**

Wilson-Cobb History and Genealogy Research Library
301 S. Richardson, Roswell, NM 88202, (575) 622-3322, **<wilsoncobb.org>**

GENERAL RESOURCES

20,000 Years of History: A New Mexico Bibliography by Frances Leon Swadesh (Sunstone Press, 1973)

Archives of the Archdiocese of Santa Fe, 1678-1900 by Angelico Chavez (Academy of American Franciscan History, 1957)

Caronado's Land: Daily Life in Colonial New Mexico by Marc Simons (Frontier Press, 1996)

Directory of Churches and Religious Organizations in New Mexico, 1940 from the Historical Records Survey (Historical Records Survey, 1940)

Foreigners in their Native Land: Historical Roots of the Mexican Americans by David J. Weber (University of New Mexico Press, 1972)

A Forgotten Kingdom: The Spanish Frontier In Colorado and New Mexico 1540-1821 by, Frederic J. Athern (Bureau of Land Management, Colorado State Office, 1989)

Genealogical Resources in New Mexico by Robert E. Esterly (Genealogical Society, 1997)

Handy Genealogical Guide to New Mexico by Joyce V. Hawley Spiros (Verlene Publishing, 1981)

The Historical Encyclopedia of New Mexico, 2 vols. (New Mexico Historical Association, 1945)

A History of the Church of Jesus Christ of Latter-Day Saints in New Mexico, 1876-1989 by Lyle K. Porter (L.K. and W.H. Porter, 2001)

A History of the Italians in New Mexico by Frederick G. Bohme (Arno Press, 1975)

History of Mormon Settlements in Mexico and New Mexico by H. Mannie Foster (Utah State Agricultural College, 1955)

A History of New Mexico, 3 vols., by Charles F. Coan (American Historical Society, 1925)

History of New Mexico: Its Resources and People, 2 vols., (Pacific States Publishing Co., 1907)

An Illustrated History of New Mexico by Thomas E. Chavez (University of New Mexico Press, 2002)

An Illustrated History of New Mexico (Lewis Pub. Co., 1895)

Inventory of Federal Archives in the States, Series 03, Department of the Treasury, No. 30, New Mexico from the Historical Records Survey (Historical Records Survey 1941)

Leading Facts of New Mexican History, 2 vols., by Ralph Emerson Twitchell (Higginson Book Co., 1994)

Los Primeros Pobladores: Antecesores De Los Chicanos En Nuevo Mexico by Frances Leon Swadesh (*Fondo de Cultura Economica*, 1977)

The Missions of New Mexico, 1776 by Francisco A. Dominquez (University of New Mexico Press, 1956)

Mormons and Their Neighbors: an Index to Over 75,000 Biographical Sketches from 1820 to the Present, 2 vols., by Marvin E. Wiggins (Brigham Young University, 1984)

Navajos in the Catholic Church Records of New Mexico, 1694-1875 by David M. Brugge (Parks and Recreation Department, 1968)

The Navajos: The Past and Present of a Great People by John Upton Terrell (Weybright and Talley, 1970)

New Mexico Newspapers: A Comprehensive Guide to Bibliographical Entries and Locations by Pearce S. Grove (University of New Mexico Press, 1975)

New Mexico Research Outline by the Church of Jesus Christ of Latter-day Saints (online at **<www.familysearch.org/eng/search/RG/guide/new_mexico.asp>**)

The Old Ones of New Mexico by Robert Coles (University of New Mexico Press, 1973)

Origins of New Mexico Families in the Spanish Colonial Period in Two Parts: The Seventeenth (1598-1693) and the Eighteenth (1693-1821) Centuries by Fray Angelico Chavez (University of Albuquerque, 1973)

The Plains Indians and New Mexico, 1751-1778 by Alfred Barnaby Thomas (University Microfilms International, 1978)

Pobladores: Hispanic Americans of the Ute Frontier by Frances. Leon Quintant (University of Notre Dame Press, 1991)

Preliminary Inventory of the Pueblo Records Created by Field Offices of the Bureau of Indian Affairs by Robert Svenningsen (National Archives, 1980)

Protestantism in the Sangre De Cristos, 1850-1920 by Randi Jones Walker (University of New Mexico Press, 1991)

Sanctuaries of Spanish New Mexico by Marc Treib (University of California Press, 1933)

Soldiers of the Cross: Notes on the Ecclesiastical History of New Mexico, Arizona and Colorado by Jean Baptiste Salpionte (St. Boniface's Industrial School, 1898)

Sources for New Mexican History, 1821-1848 by Daniel Tyler (Museum of New Mexico Press, 1984)

The Southern Utes: A Tribal History by James Jefferson (Southern Ute Tribe, ca. 1972)

Southwestern Indian Tribes by Tom Bahti (KC Publications, 1968)

The Spanish Archives of New Mexico by Ralph Emerson Twitchell (Torch Press, 1914)

The Spanish Borderlands: A Chronicle of Old Florida and the Southwest by Herbert E. Bolton (Frontier Press, 1996)

Spanish and Mexican Records of the American Southwest: A Bibliographic Guide to Archive and Manuscript Sources by Henry P. Beers (University of Arizona Press, 1979)

Spanish Mission Churches of New Mexico by Le Baron Bradford Prince (Rio Grande Press, 1977)

The Taos Indians by Blanche Chloe Grant (Rio Grande Press, 1976)

The Territorial press of New Mexico, 1834-1912 by Porter A. Stratton (University of New Mexico Press, 1969)

The Ute Mountain Utes by Robert W. Delaney (University of New Mexico Press, 1989)

Victoria and the Mimbres Apaches by Dan L. Thrapp (University of Oklahoma Press, 1974)

Voices of the Territory of New Mexico: and Oral History of People of Spanish Descent and Early Settlers born During the Territorial Days by Alfonso Griego (Griego, 1985)

Women of the New Mexico Frontier; 1846-1912 by Cheryl J. Foote (University Press of Colorado, 1990)

☞CENSUS RECORDS

Internal Revenue Assessment Lists for the Territory of New Mexico, 1862-1874 from the US Bureau of Internal Revenue (National Archives, 1988)

Latin American Census Records, 2nd edition, by Lyman D. Platt (*Instituto Genealogico e Historico Latinoamericano*, 1992)

Spanish and Mexican Censuses of New Mexico: 1750-1830 by Virginia L. Olmsted (New Mexico Genealogical Society, 1981)

Spanish and Mexican Colonial Censuses of New Mexico: 1790, 1823, 1845 by Virginia L. Olmsted (New Mexico Genealogical Society, 1975)

☞VITAL RECORDS

Cemetery Records from Southern New Mexico by Lee Myers (Lee Myers, 1982)

Certificates and Records of Death, 1889-1942 from the New Mexico Department of Health (filmed by the Genealogical Society Of Utah, 1996)

Delayed Certificates of Birth from the New Mexico Department of Health (filmed by the Genealogical Society of Utah, 1995)

Guide to Public Vital Statistics Records in New Mexico (Historical Records Survey, 1942)

New Mexico Roots LTD: A Demographic Perspective from Genealogical, Historical, and Geographical Data Found in the Diligencia Matrimoniales or Pre-nuptial Investigations (1678-1869) of the Archives of the Archdiocese of Santa Fe by Angelico Chavez (Angelico Chavez, 1982)

Some Marriages of the State of New Mexico, ca. 1880-1920, 2 vols. (New Mexico Chapter, Daughters of the American Revolution, 1971-73)

☞LAND RECORDS

A Guide to the Microfilm of Papers Relating to New Mexico Land Grants by Albert James Diaz (University of New Mexico Press, 1960)

Miscellaneous Archives Relating to New Mexico Land Grants, 1695-1842 (University of New Mexico Library, 1955-1957)

Press Copies of Grant Papers from the Surveyor General's office of the New Mexico Territory (University of New Mexico Library, 1955-57)

The Public Domain in New Mexico, 1854-1891 by Victor Westphall (University of New Mexico, 1965)

Records of Land Titles, 1847-1852 from the secretary's office of the New Mexico Territory (University of New Mexico Library, 1955-1957)

Record of Private Land Claims Adjudicated By the U.S. Surveyor General, 1855-1890 from the Surveyor General's office of the New Mexico Territory (University of New Mexico Library, 1955-1957)

Researching New Mexico Land Grants from the New Mexico Commission of Public Records (State Records Center and Archives, 2002)

Spanish & Mexican Land Grants in New Mexico and Colorado by John R. Van Ness and Christine M. Van Ness (AG Press, ca. 1980)

Vigil's Index, 1681-1846 by Donaciano Vigil (University of New Mexico Library, 1955-1957)

☞PROBATE RECORDS

Inventory of Federal Archives in the States, Series 02, Federal Courts, No. 30, New Mexico from the Historical Records Survey (Historical Records Survey, 1941)

List of New Mexico County Courthouses from the New Mexico Commission of Public Records, State Records Center and Archives (State Records Center and Archives, 2002)

☞IMMIGRATION RECORDS

The Juan Paez Hurtado Expedition of 1865: Fraud in Recruiting colonists for New Mexico by John B. Colligan (University of New Mexico Press, 1995)

Let There be Towns: Spanish Municipal Origins in the American Southwest, 1610-1810 by Gilberto Rafael Cruz (Texas A&M University Press, 1988)

Mexican Immigrant: His Life-Story by Manuel Gamio (Arno Press and the *New York Times*, 1969)

Mexican Immigration to the United States: A Study of Human Migration and Adjustment by Manuel Gamio (Arno Press and the *New York Times*, 1969)

Over 1,400 Naturalization Records for Various Courts of New Mexico: 1882-1917, Denver Federal Archives (Foothills Genealogical Society of Colorado, 1998)

☞MILITARY RECORDS

The History of the Military Occupation of the Territory of New Mexico from 1846 to 1851 by Ralph E. Twitchell (W.C. Cox, 1974)

Inventory of Federal Archives in the States, Series 04, Department of the Navy, No. 30, New Mexico from the Historical Records Survey (Historical Records Survey, 1940)

It Tolled for New Mexico: New Mexicans Captured by the Japanese, 1941-1945 by Eva Jane Matson (Yucca Tree Press, 1994)

New Mexico's Buffalo Soldiers, 1866-1900 by Monroe Lee Billington (University Press of Colorado, 1991)

Soldiers of the Great War, 3 vols. by W.M. Haulsee, F.C. Hoe, and A.C. Doyle (Soldiers Records Publishing Association, 1920)

Soldiers and Settlers: Military Supply in the Southwest, 1861-1885 by Darlis A. Miller (University of New Mexico Press, 1989)

☞MAPS

The County Boundaries of New Mexico by Charles F. Coan (1922; Legislative Council Service, 1965)

Historical Atlas of New Mexico by Warren A. Beck and Ynez D. Haase (University of Oklahoma Press, 1969)

New Mexico in Maps edited by Jerry L. Williams (University of New Mexico Press, 1986)

New Mexico Place Names: A Geographical Dictionary by T.M. Pearce (University of New Mexico Press, 1985)

The Place Names of New Mexico, 2nd edition, by Robert Hixson Julyan (University of New Mexico Press, 1998)

Post Offices of New Mexico by Richard W. Helbock (R.W. Helbock, 1981)

The Territorial Post Offices of New Mexico by Sheldon H. Dike (New Mexico Historical Review, October 1958)

•-COUNTY DETAILS-•

BERNALILLO
1 Civic Plaza, Room 6029, Albuquerque, NM 87102, (505) 468-1290, **<eagleweb.bernco.gov:8080/recorder/web>**
- **INCORPORATED:** Jan. 9, 1852
- **PARENT COUNTY:** Original county
- **MARRIAGE:** Start in 1885, kept by County Clerk
- **LAND:** 1873, County Clerk

CATRON
101 Main St., Reserve, NM 87830, (575) 533-6400, **<catroncountynm.com>**
- **INCORPORATED:** Feb. 25, 1921
- **PARENT COUNTY:** Socorro
- **MARRIAGE:** Start in 1921, kept by County Clerk
- **LAND:** 1921, County Clerk
- **PROBATE:** 1921, County Clerk

CHAVES
1 St. Mary's Place Ste #110, Roswell, NM 88203, (575) 624-6600, **<www.co.chaves.nm.us/county/Departments/Clerk>**
- **INCORPORATED:** Feb. 25, 1889
- **PARENT COUNTY:** Lincoln
- **PROBATE RECORDS:** Start in 1900, kept by Clerk/District Court?

CIBOLA
515 West High St., Grants, NM 87020, (505) 285-5434, **<www.co.cibola.nm.us>**
- **INCORPORATED:** 1981
- **PARENT COUNTY:** Valencia
- **MARRIAGE RECORDS:** Start in 1981, kept by County Clerk
- **LAND:** 1981, County Clerk
- **PROBATE:** 1981, County Clerk

COLFAX
226 East 4th St., 159, Raton, NM 87740, (575) 445-3601, **<www.co.colfax.nm.us/clerk.htm>**
- **INCORPORATED:** Jan. 25, 1869
- **PARENT COUNTY:** Mora
- **LAND:** Start in 1864, kept by County Clerk

CURRY
700 N. Main St., Clovis, NM 88101, (505) 763-5591, **<currycounty.org>**
- **INCORPORATED:** Feb. 25, 1909
- **PARENT COUNTIES:** Quay, Roosevelt

DE BACA
Box 347, Fort Sumner, NM 88119, (505) 355-2601
- **INCORPORATED:** Feb. 28, 1917
- **PARENT COUNTIES:** Chaves, Guadalupe, Roosevelt

DONA ANA
845 N. Motel Blvd., Las Cruces, NM 88007, (575) 647-7421, **<www.co.dona-ana.nm.us>**
- **INCORPORATED:** Jan. 9, 1852
- **PARENT COUNTY:** Original County

EDDY
101 W. Greene St., Carlsbad, NM 88220, (575) 885-3383, **<www.co.eddy.nm.us>**
- **INCORPORATED:** Feb. 25, 1889
- **PARENT COUNTY:** Lincoln

GRANT
1400 Highway 180 East, Silver City, NM 88061, (575) 574-0000, **<www.grantcountynm.com>**
- **INCORPORATED:** Jan. 30,1868
- **PARENT COUNTY:** Dona Ana

GUADALUPE
420 Parker Ave., Santa Rosa, NM 88435, (505) 472-3306
- **INCORPORATED:** Feb. 26, 1891
- **PARENT COUNTIES:** Lincoln, San Miguel

HARDING
Box 1002, Mosquero, NM 87733, (575) 673-2301, **<www.hardingcounty.org>**
- **INCORPORATED:** March 4, 1921
- **PARENT COUNTIES:** Mora, Union

HIDALGO
300 S. Shakespeare St., Lordsburg, NM 88045, (575) 542-3414, **<www.hidalgocounty.org/gene.html>**
- **INCORPORATED:** Feb. 25, 1919
- **PARENT COUNTY:** Grant

LEA
100 North Main, Lovington, NM 88260, (575) 396-8521, **<www.leacounty.net/clerk.htm>**
- **INCORPORATED:** March 7, 1917
- **PARENT COUNTIES:** Chaves, Eddy

LINCOLN
300 Central Ave., Box 338, Carrizozo, NM 88301, (575) 648-2394, **<www.lincolncountynm.net>**
- **INCORPORATED:** Jan. 16, 1869
- **PARENT COUNTIES:** Socorro, Dona Ana

LOS ALAMOS
Box 30, Los Alamos, NM 87544, (505) 662-8010, **<www.losalamosnm.us/clerk>**
- **INCORPORATED:** March 16, 1949
- **PARENT COUNTIES:** Sandoval, Santa Fe

LUNA
700 South Silver Box 1838, Deming, NM 88030, (575) 546-0491, **<www.lunacountynm.us/clerk.html>**
- **INCORPORATED:** March 16, 1901
- **PARENT COUNTIES:** Dona Ana, Grant

MCKINLEY
207 W. Hill St., Gallup, NM 87301, (505) 722-3868, **<www.co.mckinley.nm.us>**
- **INCORPORATED:** Feb. 23, 1899
- **PARENT COUNTIES:** Bernalillo, Valencia, San Juan, Rio Arriba

MORA
1 Courthouse Dr., Mora, NM 87732, (575) 387-2448, **<www.moravalley.com>**
- **INCORPORATED:** Feb. 1, 1860
- **PARENT COUNTY:** Taos

OTERO
1000 New York Ave. #108, Alamogordo, NM 88310, (575) 437-4942, **<www.co.otero.nm.us>**
- **INCORPORATED:** Jan. 30, 1899
- **PARENT COUNTIES:** Dona Ana, Lincoln, Socorro

QUAY
300 S. 3rd St., Tucumcari, NM 88401, (575) 461-0510, **<quaycounty-nm.gov/clerk.html>**
- **INCORPORATED:** Feb. 28, 1903
- **PARENT COUNTIES:** Guadalupe, Union

RIO ARRIBA
Box 158, Tierra Amarilla, NM 87575, (575) 588-7724, **<www.rio-arriba.org>**
- **INCORPORATED:** Jan. 9, 1852
- **PARENT COUNTY:** Original county

ROOSEVELT
109 W. 1st St., Portales, NM 88130, (575) 356-8562, **<www.rooseveltcounty.com>**
- **INCORPORATED:** Feb. 28, 1903
- **PARENT COUNTIES:** Chaves, Guadalupe

SAN JUAN
Box 550, Aztec, NM 87410, (505) 334-9471, **<www.sjcclerk.net>**
- **INCORPORATED:** Feb., 24, 1887
- **PARENT COUNTY:** Rio Arriba

SAN MIGUEL
500 W. National St., Ste. 200, Las Vegas, NM 87701, (505) 425-9331, **<www.smcounty.net/clerk.htm>**
- **INCORPORATED:** Jan. 9, 1852
- **PARENT COUNTY:** Original county

SANDOVAL
711 S. Camino Del Pueblo, Bernalillo, NM 87004, (505) 867-7572, **<www.sandovalcounty.com>**
- **INCORPORATED:** March 10, 1903
- **PARENT COUNTY:** Bernalillo
- **MARRIAGE RECORDS :** Start in 1903, kept by County Clerk
- **DEATH:** 1925, Bureau of Public Health
- **LAND:** 1903, County Clerk
- **PROBATE:** 1903, County Clerk

SANTA ANA

- **INCORPORATED:** 1850
- **PARENT COUNTY:** Original County
- **NOTES:** Became part of Bernalillo County in 1876

SANTA FE

102 Grant Ave., Santa Fe, NM 87501, (505) 986-6200, **<www.santafecounty.org>**

- **INCORPORATED:** Jan. 9, 1852
- **PARENT COUNTY:** Original County

SIERRA

100 N. Date St., Truth or Consequences, NM 87901, (575) 894-2840, **<mylocalgov.com/sierracountynm>**

- **INCORPORATED:** April 3, 1884
- **PARENT COUNTIES:** Socorro, Grant, Dona Ana

SOCORRO

200 Church St., Box 1, Socorro, NM 87801, (575) 835-3263, **<www.socorronm.gov>**

- **INCORPORATED:** Jan. 9, 1852
- **PARENT COUNTY:** Original county
- **DEATH:** Start in 1907, kept by Bureau of Public Health
- **LAND:** 1851, County Clerk
- **PROBATE:** 1974, County Clerk
- **COURT:** 1851, County Recorder

TAOS

105 Albright St. Suite D, Taos, NM 87571, (575) 737-6380, **<www.taoscounty.org>**

- **INCORPORATED:** Jan. 9, 1852
- **PARENT COUNTY:** Original county

TORRANCE

205 9th St., Box 767, Estancia, NM 87016, (505) 246-4735, **<www.torrancecountynm.org>**

- **INCORPORATED:** March 16, 1903
- **PARENT COUNTIES:** San Miguel, Socorro, Santa Fe, Valencia, Bernalillo
- **NOTES:** Courthouse burned in 1910

UNION

Box 430, Clayton, NM 88415, (505) 374-9491

- **INCORPORATED:** Feb. 23, 1893
- **PARENT COUNTIES:** Colfax, Mora, San Miguel

VALENCIA

444 Luna Ave., Los Lunas, NM 87031, (505) 866-2021, **<www.co.valencia.nm.us>**

- **INCORPORATED:** Jan. 9, 1852
- **PARENT COUNTY:** Original county
- **DEATH RECORDS:** Started in 1907, kept by City Clerk
- **LAND:** 1873, County Clerk
- **PROBATE:** 1871, County Clerk

NEW YORK

» BY RHONDA R. MCCLURE

HISTORICAL OVERVIEW

Originally called New Netherland, New York was founded by the Dutch West India Co., a merchant company founded in 1621, and chartered by the Dutch government. The colony remained New Netherland until 1664, when the English separated it into what became the British colonies of New York and New Jersey.

After the American Revolutionary War ended in 1783, Loyalists from New York were relocated to Nova Scotia, New Brunswick and the British West Indies. If your ancestor seems to have disappeared about this time, you may want to investigate these areas.

The Reorganization Act of 1788 divided the state into 120 towns, which became the level at which many records are kept. Cities are not part of towns. In fact, New York City is in many ways almost a separate entity, exempt from some of the state laws, that can affect record keeping.

New York began to grow in many different ways after the American Revolutionary War. Shipping lines chose its port, as a major stop, increasing immigrants and cargo traffic and giving New York City an opportunity to become a thriving metropolis. The completion of the Erie Canal in 1825 further enhanced travel through the state of New York.

RECORD HIGHLIGHTS

The state's land records have gone through numerous systems. The first Dutch owners enacted patroonship (manorial) records, which was changed to patents and surveys by the British, and finally to the more modern system of deeds and mortgages. To get a true sense of all these different records and what exists, see the Land Records section of the Church of Jesus Christ of Latter-Day Saints New York Research Outline (see General Resources).

Probate records for New York can offer a wealth of information. Instead of just concentrating on wills—though you certainly want to locate them—look for probate packets, handled by the Surrogate Court in each county. Probate packets have many documents generated during the estate settlement process that can offer you insight into where heirs lived, married names of women and much more.

research tips

- When working with state census records, look for a published index for the county of interest.
- Border disputes with Connecticut, New Jersey, Massachusetts and Vermont during the 1700s may affect where you search for records. Some records from this time may be in one of these states.
- New York has town and county historians. See the Association of Public Historians of New York State website **<www.aphnys.org>** for their contact information.

CENSUS RECORDS

- Federal census: 1790, 1800, 1810, 1820, 1830, 1840, 1850, 1860, 1870, 1880, 1890 (only Eastchester, Westchester, Brookhaven and Suffolk counties), 1900, 1910, 1920
- Federal mortality schedules: 1850, 1860, 1870,1880
- Civil War Union veterans and widows: 1890
- Agricultural, industrial (manufacturing) and social schedules: 1850, 1860, 1870, 1880

State census records for New York offer lots of useful information and are available from 1825 through 1855 for some counties, with many more counties available from 1865 through 1925. Those taken from 1855 to 1875 not only list where the person was born, but if they were born in the state of New York, the enumerator listed the county of birth. Some offer insight into how long the family or individual had been living in the given county. Records are available on microfilm through the Family History Library and at the New York state archives. Subscription site Ancestry.com has information from three New York state censuses.

Vital records for New York are not as encompassing as some other states. Not until the mid-19th century did the state first attempt to enforce the keeping of vital records. In the latter 1800s, the state tried again. Towns originated the records and sent copies to the New York Department of Health. Look for vital records both on the state and the town levels, as well as on FHL microfilm. You can request copies from the Department of Health by writing to the Genealogy Unit, Vital Records Section, Box 2602, Albany, NY 12220 **<www.health.state.ny.us/vital_records/genealogy.htm>**. Be prepared to be patient, as requests to this unit can take up to 10 months to process. The state suggests contacting the local town registrar if you know the exact place of birth, death, or marriage.

Vital records for New York City's boroughs are filed in the New York City Municipal Archives, 31 Chambers St., New York, NY 10007. Record availability varies from borough to borough. Many of them have been microfilmed and are available through the Family History Library.

You may need to use vital record substitutes such as tombstones, newspapers, and church records to get the dates of births, marriages or deaths.

ARCHIVES, LIBRARIES, AND SOCIETIES

Adirondack Genealogical and Historical Society
100 Main St., Saranac Lake, NY 12983, **<freepages.genealogy.rootsweb.ancestry.com/~adkghs>**

Adirondack History Center Museum
Box 428, 7590 Court St., Elizabethtown, NY 12932, (518) 873-6466, **<www.adkhistorycenter.org>**

Adriance Memorial Library
93 Market St., Poughkeepsie, NY 12601, (845) 485-3445, **<www.poklib.org>**

African-Atlantic Genealogical Society
144 W. Merrick Rd., Freeport, NY 11520, **<www.aagsinc.net>**

Albany County Hall of Records
95 Tivoli St., Albany, NY 12207, (518) 436-3663, **<www.albanycounty.com/ACHOR>**

Allegany Area Historical Association
Box 162, Allegany, NY 14706, **<aaha.bfn.org>**

Almond Historical Society
7 Main St., Almond, NY 14804, **<www.rootsweb.ancestry.com/~nyahs/AlmondHS.html>**

Archdiocese of New York
1011 First Ave., New York, NY 10022, (212) 371-1000, **<www.ny-archdiocese.org>**

Bethlehem Historical Association
Box 263, 1003 River Rd., Selkirk, NY 12158, (513) 767-9432, **<bha1965.webs.com>**

Blauvelt Free Library
541 Western Hwy., Blauvelt, NY 10913, (845) 359-2811, **<www.rcls.org/blv>**

Bronx County Historical Society
3309 Bainbridge Ave., The Bronx, NY 10467, (718) 881-8900, **<www.bronxhistoricalsociety.org>**

Brooklyn Historical Society
128 Pierrepont St., Brooklyn, NY 11201, (718) 222-4111, **<www.brooklynhistory.org>**

Buffalo Irish Genealogical Society
GAAA Library Buffalo Irish Center, 245 Abbott Rd., Buffalo, NY 14220, (716) 627-2417, **<www.buffaloirishcenter.com>**

Capital District Genealogical Society
Empire State Plaza Station, Box 2175, Albany, NY 12220, (518) 439-5160

Cayuga County Historian's Office
Historic Old Post Office Bldg., 3rd Floor, 157 Genesee St., Auburn, NY 13021, (315) 253-1300, **<www.co.cayuga.ny.us/history/index.html>**

Cayuga-Owasco Lakes Historical Society
Box 247, 14 W. Cayuga St., Moravia, NY 13118, **<www.rootsweb.ancestry.com/~nycayuga/colhs.htm>**

Central New York Genealogical Society
Box 104, Colvin Station, Syracuse, NY 13205, **<www.rootsweb.ancestry.com/~nycnygs>**

Cheektowaga Historical Association
3329 Broadway, Cheektowaga, NY 14227, (716) 683-5589, **<www.cheektowagahistory.com/page9.php>**

Chemung Valley History Museum and Historical Society
415 E. Water St., Elmira, NY 14901, (607) 734-4167, **<www.chemungvalleymuseum.org>**

Chenango Historical Society
45 Rexford St., Norwich, NY 13815, (607) 334-9227, **<www.chenango.history.museum>**

Columbia County Historical Society
5 Albany Ave., Box 311, Kinderhook, NY 12106, (518) 758-9265, **<www.berkshire.net/OnlineArchives/columbia/cchs.html>**

Columbia University, Journalism Library
204 Journalism, 2950 Broadway, New York, NY 10027, (212) 854-0390, **<www.columbia.edu/cu/lweb/indiv/jour>**

Cortland County Historical Society
25 Homer Ave., Cortland, NY 13045, (607) 756-6071, **<www.rootsweb.ancestry.com/~nycortla/chsfe.htm>**

Cow Neck Peninsula Historical Society
336 Port Washington Blvd., Port Washington, NY 11050, (516) 365-9074, **<www.cowneck.org>**

Creole-American Genealogical Society
Box 2666, Church Street Station, New York, NY 10008

East Greenbush Community Library
10 Community Way, East Greenbush, NY 12061, (518) 447-7476, **<www.eastgreenbushlibrary.org>**

East Hampton Library
159 Main St., East Hampton, NY 11937, (631) 324-0222, **<www.easthamptonlibrary.org>**

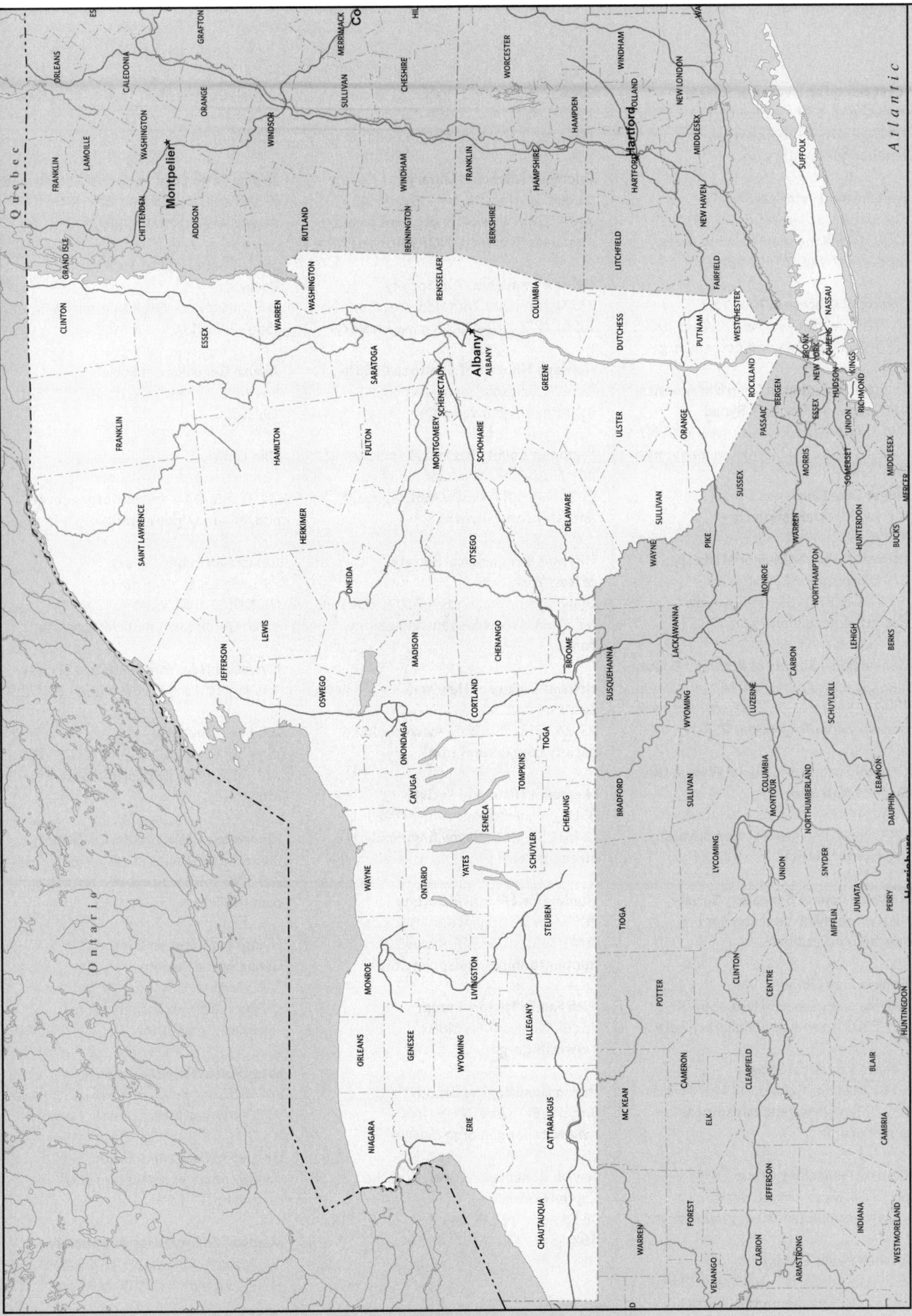
Quebec
Ontario
Atlantic
Montpelier
Hartford
Albany
FRANKLIN
ORLEANS
LAMOILLE
CALEDONIA
WASHINGTON
ORANGE
GRAFTON
CHITTENDEN
GRAND ISLE
ADDISON
WINDSOR
RUTLAND
SULLIVAN
MERRIMACK
CHESHIRE
WINDHAM
BENNINGTON
WORCESTER
FRANKLIN
HAMPSHIRE
BERKSHIRE
HAMPDEN
TOLLAND
WINDHAM
HARTFORD
LITCHFIELD
NEW LONDON
MIDDLESEX
NEW HAVEN
FAIRFIELD
SUFFOLK
NASSAU
CLINTON
ESSEX
WARREN
WASHINGTON
RENSSELAER
COLUMBIA
DUTCHESS
PUTNAM
WESTCHESTER
FRANKLIN
HAMILTON
SARATOGA
SCHENECTADY
ALBANY
GREENE
ULSTER
ORANGE
ROCKLAND
BRONX
NEW YORK
QUEENS
KINGS
RICHMOND
HUDSON
BERGEN
ESSEX
PASSAIC
UNION
MORRIS
SOMERSET
MIDDLESEX
SUSSEX
FULTON
MONTGOMERY
SCHOHARIE
DELAWARE
SULLIVAN
SAINT LAWRENCE
HERKIMER
OTSEGO
WAYNE
PIKE
WARREN
HUNTERDON
MERCER
BUCKS
ONEIDA
NORTHAMPTON
MONROE
LEWIS
MADISON
CHENANGO
BROOME
SUSQUEHANNA
LACKAWANNA
LEHIGH
BERKS
JEFFERSON
OSWEGO
CORTLAND
WYOMING
LUZERNE
CARBON
SCHUYLKILL
ONONDAGA
TIOGA
TOMPKINS
CAYUGA
SENECA
CHEMUNG
BRADFORD
SULLIVAN
COLUMBIA
MONTOUR
NORTHUMBERLAND
LEBANON
DAUPHIN
WAYNE
ONTARIO
YATES
SCHUYLER
LYCOMING
UNION
SNYDER
JUNIATA
PERRY
MIFFLIN
STEUBEN
TIOGA
MONROE
LIVINGSTON
POTTER
CLINTON
CENTRE
HUNTINGDON
ALLEGANY
ORLEANS
GENESEE
WYOMING
CAMERON
CLEARFIELD
BLAIR
NIAGARA
ERIE
CATTARAUGUS
MC KEAN
ELK
CAMBRIA
JEFFERSON
CHAUTAUQUA
WARREN
FOREST
CLARION
ARMSTRONG
INDIANA
WESTMORELAND
VENANGO

East Hampton Historical Society
101 Main St., East Hampton, NY 11937, (631) 324-6850, <www.easthamptonhistory.org>

Eastchester Historical Society
Box 37, Eastchester, NY 10709, (914) 793-1900, <www.museumsusa.org/data/museums/NY/22461.htm>

Episcopal Diocese of New York
1047 Amsterdam Ave., New York, NY 10025, (212) 316-7400, <www.dioceseny.org>

Evangelical Lutheran Church in America, Metropolitan New York Synod
475 Riverside Dr., Ste. 1620, New York, NY 10115, (212) 665-0732, <www.mnys.org>

Finger Lake Finns
<www.fingerlakesfinns.org>

Roswell P. Flower Memorial Library
229 Washington St., Watertown, NY 13601, (315) 785-7705, <www.flowermemoriallibrary.org>

Genealogical Society of Rockland County
New City Library, Box 444, New City, NY 10956, (845) 942-0577, <www.rootsweb.ancestry.com/~nyrockla/GSRC>

General Society of Colonial Wars in the State of New York
20 W. 44th St., New York, NY 10036, (212) 755-7082, <www.colonialwarsny.org/contact.htm>

Genesse County Genealogy Society
<www.rootsweb.ancestry.com/~nygags/index.htm>

Geneva Free Library
244 Main St., Geneva, NY 14456, (315) 789-5303, <genevapubliclibrary.net>

Geneva Historical Society
543 S. Main St., Geneva, NY 14456, (315) 789-5151, <www.genevahistoricalsociety.com>

German Genealogy Group
Box 1004, Kings Park, NY 11754, <www.germangenealogygroup.com>

Goshen Public Library
203 Main St., Goshen, NY 10924, (845) 294-6606, <goshenpubliclibrary.org>

Greater Ridgewood Historical Society
1820 Flushing Ave., Ridgewood, NY 11385, (718) 456-1776, <onderdonkhouse.org>

Guernsey Memorial Library
3 Court St., Norwich, NY 13815, (607) 334-4034, <www.4cls.org/webpages/members/Norwich/NORWICH.HTML>

Hebrew Immigrant Aid Society
333 Seventh Ave., 16th Floor, New York, NY 10001, (212) 967-4100, <www.hias.org>

Heritage Hunters of Saratoga County
Box 270, Sarasota Springs, NY 12866, <saratoganygenweb.com>

Herkimer County Historical Society
400 N. Main St., Herkimer, NY 13350, (315) 866-6413, <www.rootsweb.ancestry.com/~nyhchs>

Hispanic Genealogical Society of New York
Grand Central Station, Box 3009, New York, NY 10163, <www.hispanicgenealogy.com>

Holland Society of New York
20 W. 44th St, 5th Floor, New York, NY 10036, (212) 758-1675, <www.hollandsociety.com/index1.html>

Huguenot Historical Society
81 Huguenot St.,, New Paltz, NY 12561, (845) 255-1660, <www.huguenotstreet.org>

Huntington Historical Society
209 Main St., Huntington, NY 11743, (631) 427-7045, <www.huntingtonhistoricalsociety.org>

Irish Family History Forum
Box 67, Plainview, NY 11803, <www.ifhf.org>

Italian Genealogical Group
Box 626, Bethpage, NY 11714, <www.italiangen.org>

Jewish Genealogical Society of the Capital District
58 Edgecomb St., Albany, NY 12209, (518) 462-4815

Jewish Genealogical Society of Buffalo
3700 Main St., Amherst, NY 14226, (716) 833-0743

Jewish Genealogy Society of Long Island
37 Westcliff Dr., Dix Hills, NY 11746, <www.jewishgen.org/jgsli>

Jewish Genealogical Society of Rochester
265 Viennawood Dr., Rochester, NY 14618, (585) 271-2118

Jewish Genealogical Society
Box 286398, New York, NY 10128, (212) 294-8326

Olin Library
Cornell University, Ithaca, NY 14853, (607) 255-4144, <www.library.cornell.edu/olinuris/index.html>

Johnstown Public Library
38 S. Market St., Johnstown, NY 12095, (518) 762-8317, <www.johnstownpubliclibrary.info>

Lancaster New York Historical Society
40 Clark St., Lancaster, NY, (716) 681-7719

Leo Baeck Institute
15 W. 16th St., New York, NY 10011, (212) 744-6400, <www.lbi.org/fellowships.html>

Livingston County Historical Society
30 Center St., Geneseo, NY 14454, (716) 243-9147, <www.rootsweb.ancestry.com/~nylchs>

Livingston-Steuben County Genealogical Society
5 Elizabeth St., Dansville, NY 14437, <www.rootsweb.ancestry.com/~nyliving/lscgs.htm>

Long Beach Historical Society
Box 286, Long Beach, NY 11561, (516) 432-1192, <www.longbeachhistory.org>

Longwood Genealogy Group
<www.rootsweb.ancestry.com/~nygglshp/

Madison County Historical Society
435 Main St., Oneida, NY 13421, (315) 363-4136, <www.mchs1900.org>

Malverne Historical and Preservation Society
Box 393, Malverne, NY 11565, (516) 792-1910, **<www.malvernehistoricalsociety.org>**

Manlius Historical Society
109 Pleasant St., Box 28, Manlius, NY 13104, (315) 682-6660, **<www.manliushistory.org>**

Margaret Reaney Memorial Library
19 Kingsbury Ave., St. Johnsville, NY 13452, (518) 568-7822, **<www2.telenet.net/community/mvla/stjo>**

Minisink Valley Historical Society
125-133 W. Main St., Port Jervis, NY 12771, (845) 856-2375, **<www.minisink.org>**

Montgomery County Department of History and Archives
Old Courthouse, Box 1500, Fonda, NY 12068, (518) 853-8186, **<www.amsterdam-ny.com/mcha>**

Moore Memorial Library
59 Genesee St., Greene, NY 13778, (607) 656-9349, **<www.4cls.org/Greene/Greene.html>**

New Castle Historical Society
100 King St., Chappaqua, NY 10514, (914) 238-4666, **<www.newcastlehistoricalsociety.org>**

New City Library
220 N. Main St., New City, NY 10956, (845) 634-4997, **<www.newcitylibrary.org>**

New-York Historical Society
170 Central Park West, New York, NY 10024, (212) 873-3400, **<www.nyhistory.org>**

New York City Board of Elections
32 Broadway, 7th Floor, New York, NY 10004, (212) 487-2170, **<www.vote.nyc.ny.us>**

New York City Department of Records, Municipal Archives
31 Chambers St., Room 103, New York, NY 10007, (212) 639-9675, **<www.nyc.gov/html/records/html/about/archives.shtml>**

New York Family History Center
125 Columbus Ave., 1st Floor, New York, NY 10023, (212) 799-2414, **<www.familysearch.org>**

New York Foundling Hospital
590 Avenue of the Americas, New York, NY 10011, (212) 633-9300, **<www.nyfoundling.org>**

New York Genealogical and Biographical Society
36 W. 44th St., 7th Floor, New York, NY 10036, (212) 755-8532, **<www.newyorkfamilyhistory.org>**

New York Historical Association
Box 800, Cooperstown, NY 13326, (888) 547-1400, **<www.nysha.org/about/index.htm>**

New York Public Library, Dorot Jewish Division
Fifth Ave. and 42nd St., New York, NY 10018, (212) 930-0601, **<www.nypl.org/research/chss/jws/jewish.html>**

New York Public Library, Irma and Paul Milstein Division of US History, Local History and Genealogy
Fifth Avenue and 42nd St., Room 121, New York, NY 10018, (212) 930-0828, **<www.nypl.org/research/chss/lhg/genea.html>**

New York State Archives
Cultural Education Center, Albany, NY 12230, (518) 474-6926, **<www.archives.nysed.gov/aindex.shtml>**

New York State Library
Cultural Education Center, Albany, NY 12230, (518) 474-5355, **<www.nysl.nysed.gov>**

New York State Museum
Cultural Education Center, Albany, NY 12230, (518) 474-5877, **<www.nysm.nysed.gov>**

Newburgh Free Library
124 Grand St., Newburgh, NY 12550, (845) 563-3600, **<www.newburghlibrary.org>**

Niagara County Genealogical Society
215 Niagara St., Lockport, NY 14094, (716) 433-1033, **<www.niagaracounty.org/genealogical_society_home.htm>**

Northern New York American-Canadian Genealogical Society
Box 1256, Plattsburgh, NY 12901, **<www.nnyacgs.org>**

Ogdensburg Public Library
312 Washington St., Ogdensburg, NY 13669, (315) 393-4325, **<www.nc3r.org/ogdensburg>**

Olive Free Library Association
4033 Rte. 28-A, West Shokan, NY 12494, (845) 657-2482, **<olive.westshokan.lib.ny.us>**

Oneida County Historical Society
1608 Genesee St., Utica, NY 13502, (315) 735-3642, **<www.midyork.org/ochs>**

Oneida Public Library
220 Broad St., Oneida, NY 13421, (315) 363-3050, **<www.midyork.org/oneida>**

Onondaga County Public Library
447 S. Salina St., Syracuse, NY 13202, (315) 435-1900, **<www.onlib.org>**

Onondaga Historical Association
321 Montgomery St., Syracuse, NY 13202, (315) 428-1864, **<www.cnyhistory.org>**

Ontario County Genealogical Society
55 N. Main St., Canandaigua, NY 14424, **<www.ochs.org/Genealogy/Ocgs>**

Ontario County Historical Society
55 N. Main St., Canandaigua, NY 14424, (585) 394-4975, **<www.ochs.org>**

Orange County Genealogical Society
Attn: Gen Research, 101 Main St., Goshen, NY 10924, **<www.ocgsny.org>**

Oyster Bay Historical Society
Box 297, 20 Summit St., Oyster Bay, NY 11771, (516) 922-5032, **<www.oysterbayhistory.org>**

Polish Genealogical Society of New York State
12645 Rt. 78, East Aurora, NY 14052, **<www.pgsnys.org>**

Port Chester Public Library
1 Haseco Ave., Port Chester, NY 10573, (914) 939-6710, **<www.portchesterlibrary.org>**

Puerto Rican/Hispanic Genealogical Society
Box 260118, Bellerose, NY 11426, **<www.rootsweb.ancestry.com/~prhgs>**

Queens Borough Public Library
89-11 Merrick Blvd., Jamaica, NY 11432, (718) 990-0700, **<www.queenslibrary.org>**

Queens Historical Society
143-135 37th Ave., Flushing, NY 11354, (718) 939-0647, **<www.queenshistoricalsociety.org>**

Registrar, City of Albany Vital Statistics
Room 254M, City Hall, Albany, NY 12207, (518) 434-5045, **<www.albanyny.org/Government/Departments/VitalStatistics.aspx>**

Rennsselaer County Historical Society
57 Second St., Troy, NY 12180, (518) 272-7232, **<www.rchsonline.org>**

Richmond Memorial Library
19 Ross St., Batavia, NY 14020, (585) 343-9550, **<www.batavialibrary.org>**

Rochester Genealogical Society
1050 East Ave., Rochester, NY 14610, **<nyrgs.org>**

Rochester Public Library
115 South Ave., Rochester, NY 14604, (585) 428-8370, **<www.rochester.lib.ny.us/rochimag/lochist.html>**

St. Lawrence County Historical Association
3 E. Main St., Box 8, Canton, NY 13617, (315) 386-8133, **<www.slcha.org>**

Scarsdale Historical Society
937 Post Rd., Scarsdale, NY 10583, (914) 723-1744, **<www.scarsdalehistory.org>**

Schenectady County Historical Society
32 Washington Ave., Schenectady, NY 12305, (518) 374-0263, **<www.schist.org>**

Schuyler County Historical Society
108 N. Catharine St., Box 651, Montour Falls, NY 14865, (607) 535-9741, **<www.schuylerhistory.org>**

Shaker Heritage Society
25 Meeting House Rd., Albany, NY 12211, (518) 456-7890, **<www.shakerheritage.org>**

Slovak Heritage and Folklore Society International
151 Colebrook Dr., Rochester, NY 14617, (716) 342-9383, **<www.iarelative.com/shfsinfo.htm>**

Southern Tier Genealogical Society
Box 680, Vestal, NY 13850, **<www.rootsweb.ancestry.com/~nybroome/stgs/stgs.htm>**

Southold Historical Society
Box 1, Southold, NY 11971, (631) 765-5500, **<www.southoldhistoricalsociety.org>**

St. George's Society of New York
216 E. 45th St., Ste. 901, New York, NY 10017, (212) 682-6110, **<www.stgeorgessociety.org>**

Staten Island Historical Society
Historic Richmond Town, 441 Clarke Ave., Staten Island, NY 10306, (718) 351-1611, **<www.newyorkled.com/Staten-Island-Historical.htm>**

Steele Memorial Library
101 E. Church St., Elmira, NY 14901, (607) 733-9173, **<www.steele.lib.ny.us>**

Suffolk County Historical Society
300 W. Main St., Riverhead, NY 11901, (631) 727-2881, **<www.riverheadli.com/rmuseum.html>**

Sullivan County Historical Society
Box 247, Hurleyville, NY 12747, (845) 434-8044, **<www.sullivancountyhistory.org>**

Three Village Historical Society
93 North Country Rd., Setauket, NY 11733, (631) 751-3730, **<www.threevillagehistoricalsociety.org>**

Tioga County Historical Society
110 Front St., Owego, NY 13827, (607) 687-2460, **<www.tiogahistory.org>**

Troy Public Library
100 Second St., Troy, NY 12180, (518) 274-7071, **<www.thetroylibrary.org>**

Ulster County Elting Memorial Library
93 Main St., New Paltz, NY 12561, (845) 255-5030, **<elting.newpaltz.lib.ny.us>**

Ulster County Genealogical Society
Box 536, Hurley, NY 12443, **<www.ucgsny.org>**

Utica Public Library
303 Genesee St., Utica, NY 13501, (315) 735-2279, **<uticapubliclibrary.org>**

Wayne County Historical Society
21 Butternut St., Lyons, NY 14489, (315) 946-4943, **<www.waynehistory.org>**

Westchester County Historical Society
2199 Saw Mill River Rd., Elmsford, NY 10523, (914) 592-4323, **<www.westchesterhistory.com>**

Western New York Genealogical Society
Box 338, Hamburg, NY 14075, **<www.wnygs.org>**

Yates County Genealogical and Historical Society
107 Chapel St., Penn Yan, NY 14527, (315) 536-7318, **<www.yatespast.com>**

YIVO Institute for Jewish Research, The Center for Jewish History
15 W. 16th St., New York, NY 10011, (212) 246-6080, **<www.yivoinstitute.org>**

Yorktown Historical Society
Box 355, Yorktown Heights, NY 10598, (914) 962-5722 ext. 440, **<www.yorktownhistory.org>**

GENERAL RESOURCES

A Bibliography of New York State Communities, 3rd edition, compiled by Harold Nestler (Heritage Books, 1990)

The Book of Names Especially Relating to the Early Palatines and the First Settlers

in the Mohawk Valley compiled by Lou D. MacWethy (Genealogical Publishing Co., 1981)

Colonial Families of Long Island, New York and Connecticut, 5 vols., by Herbert Furman Seversmith (H.F. Seversmith, 1939-1958)

Contributions for the Genealogies of the Descendants of the First Settlers of the Patent and City of Schenectady, From 1662 to 1800 by Jonathan Pearson (Genealogical Publishing Co., 1976)

Cutter Index: A Consolidated Index of Cutter's 9 Genealogy Series by Norma Olin Ireland and Winifred Irving (Ireland Indexing Service, ca. 1970)

Documentary History of the State of New York, 4 vols., arranged by E.B. O'Callaghan (Weed, Parson, Public Printers, 1849)

Documents Relative to the Colonial History of the State of New York: Procured in Holland, England, and France, 15 vols., by John Romeyn Brodhead, edited by E.B. O'Callaghan (Weed, Parsons & Co., 1853-1887)

Dutch Houses in the Hudson Valley Before 1776 by Helen Wilkinson Reynolds (Dover Publications, 1965)

Encyclopedia of Biography of New York, 4 vols., by Charles Elliot Fitch (American Historical Society, 1916)

Famous Families of New York, 2 vols., by Margherita Arlina Hamm (G.P. Putnam's Sons, 1902)

Genealogical Data from Colonial New York Newspapers compiled by Kenneth Scott (Genealogical Publishing Co., 1977)

Genealogical Data from New York Administration Bonds, 1753-1799 and Hithero Unpublished Letters of Administration abstracted by Kenneth Scott (Genealogical and Biographical Society, 1969)

Genealogical Data from the New York Post-Boy, 1743-1773 by Kenneth Scott (National Genealogical Society, 1970)

Genealogical and Family History of Central New York, 3 vols. (Reprinted for Clearfield Co. by the Genealogical Publishing Co., 1994)

Genealogical and Family History of Southern New York and the Hudson River Valley, 3 vols. (Lewis Historical Publishing Co., 1914)

Genealogical Notes of New York and New England Families by S.V. Talcott (Genealogical Publishing Co., 1973)

Genealogical Resources in New York edited by Estelle M. Guzik (Jewish Genealogical Society, 2003)

Genealogical Resources in the New York Metropolitan Area edited by Estelle M. Guzik (Jewish Genealogical Society, 1989)

Genealogies of Long Island Families: From the New York Genealogical and Biographical Record, 2 vols., selected by Henry B. Hoff (Genealogical Publishing Co., 1987)

Genealogy of the French Settlers of New Paltz by Louis Bevier (Genealogical Publishing Co., 1965)

Guide to Genealogical and Biographical Sources for New York City (Manhattan) 1783-1898 by Rosalie Fellows Bailey (1954)

A Guide to the Manuscript Collections of the New-York Historical Society, 2 vols., by Arthur J. Breton (Greenwood Press, 1972)

The Guide to NYC Public Records by Barbara Kronman (Public Interest Clearing House, 1992)

History of the Mohawk Valley: Gateway to the West, 1614-1925, Covering the six Counties of Schenectady, Schoharie, Montgomery, Fulton, Herkimer, and Oneida, 4 vols., edited by Nelson Greene (S.J. Clarke, 1925)

A History of New York State by David M. Ellis. et al. (Cornell University Press, 1983)

History of the Valley of the Hudson: River of Destiny, 1609-1930, Covering the Sixteen New York State Hudson River Counties, 5 vols., edited by Nelson Greene (Genealogical Society of Utah, 2000)

Inhabitants of New York, 1774-1776 by Thomas B. Wilson (Genealogical Publishing Co., 1993)

Land Papers translated and edited by Charles T. Gehring (Genealogical Publishing Co., 1980)

Lists of Inhabitants of Colonial New York by E.B. O'Callaghan (Edmund Bailey) (Genealogical Publishing Co., 1979)

Long Island Genealogical Source Material, a Bibliography by Herbert F. Seversmith and Kenn Stryker-Rodda (National Genealogical Society, 1962)

New Netherland Roots by Gwen F. Epperson (Genealogical Publishing Co., 1994)

New York Area Key: A Guide to the Genealogical Records of the State of New York by Florence Clint (Keyline Publishers, 1979)

The New York Genealogical and Biographical Record: Master Index, 113 Years, 1870-1982 by Jean D. Worden (J.D. Worden, 1983)

New York Genealogical Research by George K. Schweitzer (Schweitzer, 1988)

New York Research Outline by the Church of Jesus Christ of Latter-Day Saints Family History Library (online at **<www.familysearch.org/eng/search/RG/guide/new_york.asp>**)

New York State Probate Records: A Genealogist's Guide to Testate and Intestate Records by Gordon L. Remington (New England Historic Genealogical Society, 2002)

New York State Towns, Villages, and Cities: A Guide to Genealogical Sources by Gordon L. Remington (New England Historic Genealogical Society, 2002)

Obituary Index . . . edited by Ellen S. Wasserman (Meckler Publishing, 1989)

Personal Name Index to "The New York Times Index," 1851-1974, 25 vols., by Byron A. Falk, Jr. and Valerie R. Falk (Roxbury Data Interface, 1976-1985)

Personal Name Index to "The New York Times Index," 1975-1996 Supplement, 7 vols., by Byron A. Falk, Jr. and Valerie R. Falk (Roxbury Data Interface, 1998-1999)

Proceedings of the Commissioners of Indian Affairs Appointed by Law for the Extinguishment of Indian Title in the State of New York by the New York Commissioners of Indian Affairs (filmed by the Genealogical Society of Utah, 1973)

Searching in New York: A Reference Guide to Public and Private Records by Kate Burke (ISC Publications, 1987)

☞ CENSUS RECORDS

Early New York State Census Records. 1663-1772 by Carol M. Meyers (RAM Publishers, 1965)

☞ VITAL RECORDS

7,000 Hudson-Mohawk Valley (NY) Vital Records, 1808-1850 by Fred Q. Bowman (Genealogical Publishing Co., 1997)

8,000 More Vital Records of Eastern New York State, 1804-1805 by Fred Q. Bowman (Kinship, 1991)

10,000 Vital Records of Central New York, 1813-1850 by Fred Q. Bowman (Genealogical Publishing Co., 1986)

10,000 Vital Records of Eastern New York, 1777-1834 by Fred Q. Bowman (Genealogical Publishing Co., 1987)

10,000 Vital Records of Western New York, 1809-1850 by Fred Q. Bowman (Genealogical Publishing Co., 1985)

Directory to Collections of New York Vital Records, 1726-1989, With Rare Gazetteer by Fred Q. Bowman (Heritage Books, 1995)

Genealogical Records; Manuscript Entries of Births, Deaths and Marriages, Taken From Family Bibles, 1581-1917 edited by Jeannie F. J. Robison and Henrietta C. Bartlett (Genealogical Publishing Co., 1972)

Guide to Vital Statistics in the City of New York, Borough of Manhattan: Churches by the Historical Records Survey, New York City (Historical Records Survey, 1942)

Guide to Vital Statistics Records of Churches in New York State, Exclusive of New York City prepared by the Historical Records Survey (The Survey, 1942)

Marriages and Deaths From the New Yorker (Double Quarto Edition), 1836-1841 by Kenneth Scott (National Genealogical Society, 1980)

Names of Persons for Whom Marriage Licences Were Issued by the Secretary of the Province of New York, Previous to 1784 by the New York Secretary of State (filmed by the Genealogical Society of Utah, 1967)

1890 New York Census Index of Civil War Veterans or Their Widows compiled by Bryan Lee Dilts (Index Publishing, 1984)

New York State Cemeteries Name/Location Inventory, 1995-1997, 3 vols., compiled by the Association of Municipal Historians of New York State (Heritage Books, 1999)

New York State Cemetery Inscriptions: Albany Co., Herkimer Co., Montgomery Co., Saratoga Co., Schenectady Co. compiled by Marie Noll Cormack and Katherine Furman (filmed by the Genealogical Society of Utah, 1967)

Vital Records File by the New York State Library (New York State Library, ca. 1979)

☞ LAND RECORDS

Calender of N.Y. Colonial Manuscripts, Indorsed Land Papers: In the Office of the Secretary of State of New York, 1643-1803 compiled by E.B. O'Callaghan (Harbor Hill Books, 1987)

Denizations, Naturalizations, and Oaths of Allegiance in Colonial New York by Kenneth Scott and Kenn Stryker-Rodda (Genealogical Publishing Co., 1975)

The Disposition of Loyalist Estates in the Southern District of the State of New York by Harry Beller Yoshpe (Columbia University, 1999)

Dutch New York by Esther Singleton (B. Blom, 1968)

Early New York Naturalizations: Abstracts of Naturalization Records From Federal, State, and Local Courts, 1792-1840 compiled by Kenneth Scott (Genealogical Publishing Co., 1981)

Inventory of the Archives of the Holland Land Company by Wilhelmina C. Pierterse, English translation by Sytha Hart (Municipal Print. Office, 1976)

Patents of the State of New York, 1649-1912 by the New York Secretary of State (filmed by the Genealogical Society of Utah, 1973)

Western New York Land Transactions, 1825-1835: Extracted From the Archives of the Holland Land Company by Karen E. Livsey (Genealogical Publishing Co., 1996)

☞ PROBATE RECORDS

Abstracts of Albany Co., N.Y. Probate and Family Records transcribed by William Burt Cook (filmed by the Genealogical Society of Utah, 1971)

Calender of Wills on File and Recorded in the Offices of the Clerk of the Court of Appeals, of the County Clerk at Albany, and of the Secretary of State, 1626-1836 by Berthold Fernow (Genealogical Publishing Co., 1967)

Genealogical Data From Further New York Administration Bonds, 1791-1798 abstracted by Kenneth Scott (New York Genealogical and Biographical Society, 1971)

Genealogical Data From Inventories of New York Estates, 1666-1825 by Kenneth Scott and James A. Owre (New York Genealogical and Biographical Society, 1970)

Genealogical Data From New York Administration Bonds, 1753-1799 and Hithero Unpublished Letters of Administration abstracted by Kenneth Scott (New York Genealogical and Biographical Society, 1969)

Index of Wills for New York County (New York City), From 1662-1850 compiled by Ray C. Sawyer (filmed by the Genealogical Society of Utah, 1941)

Index of Wills for New York County, New York, From 1851-1875 compiled by Ray C. Sawyer (filmed by the Genealogical Society of Utah, 1971)

List of pre-1847 Court Records in the State Archives by the New York State Archives (Office of Cultural Education, New York State Education Department, 1984)

New York Alien Residents, 1825-1848 compiled by Kenneth Scott and Rosanne Conway (Genealogical Publishing Co., 1978)

Records of the Court of Assizes for the Colony of New York, 1665-1682 edited by Peter R. Christoph and Florence A. Christoph (Genealogical Publishing Co., 1983)

The Records of New Amsterdam From 1653 to 1674 Anno Domini, 7 vols., edited by Berthold Fernow (Genealogical Publishing Co., 1976)

☞IMMIGRATION RECORDS

Landholders of Northeastern New York, 1739-1802 by Fred Q. Bowman (Genealogical Publishing Co., 1983)

Lists of Patents of Lands, etc. to be Sold in January, 1822, for Arrears of Quit Rent by Elijah Ellsworth Brownell (filmed by the Genealogical Society of Utah, 1973)

New York State—Confiscations of Loyalists copied by H.C. Burleigh (United Empire Loyalists' Association of Canada, 1970)

The Palatine Families of New York: A Study of the German Immigrants who Arrived in Colonial New York in 1710, 2 vols., by Henry Z. Jones (H.Z. Jones, 1985)

Palatine Roots: The 1710 German Settlement in New York as Experienced by Johann Peter Wagner by Nancy Wagoner Dixon (Picton Press, 1994)

Reports of Joseph Ellicott as Chief of Survey (1797-1800): and as Agent (1800-1821) of the Holland Land Company's Purchases in Western New York, 2 vols., edited by Robert Warwick Bingham (The Buffalo Historical Society, 1937-41)

Ship Passenger Lists, New York and New Jersey, 1600-1825 edited and indexed by Carl Boyer (C. Boyer, 1978)

☞MILITARY RECORDS

A Guide to the Revolutionary War Manuscripts in the New York State Library edited by Stefan Bielinski (New York State American Revolution Bicentennial Commission, 1976)

A History of the 134th New York Volunteer Infantry Regiment in the American Civil War, 1862-1865 by Charles H. Cosgrove (E. Mellen Press, 1997)

Index of Awards on Claims of the Soldiers of the War of 1812 by the New York Adjutant General's Office (Genealogical Publishing Co., 1969)

Inhabitants of New York, 1774-1776 by Thomas B. Wilson (Genealogical Publishing Co., 1993)

Military Minutes of the Council of Appointment of the State of New York, 1783-1821, 4 vols., compiled and edited by Hugh Hastings (J.B. Lyon, State Printer, 1901-02)

New York in the American Revolution: A Bibliography by Milton M. Klein (New York State American Revolution Bicentennial Commission, 1974)

New York in the Revolution by Berthold Fernow (Polyanthos, 1972)

New York in the Revolution as Colony and State by James A. Roberts (Genealogical Publishing Co., 1996)

New York, World War I Selective Service System Draft Registration Cards, 1917-1918 by the US Selective Service System (National Archives, 1987-1988)

A Record of the Commissioned Officers, Non-Commissioned Officers and Privates, of the Regiments Which Were Organized in the State of New York and Called Into the Service of the United States to Assist in Suppressing the Rebellion by the New York Adjutant General's Office (filmed by the Genealogical Society of Utah, 1971)

☞ MAPS

Atlas of Historical County Boundaries. New York edited by John H. Long and compiled by Kathryn Ford Thorne (Simon & Schuster, 1993)

Gazetteer of the State of New York by John Homer French (Genealogical Publishing Co., 1995)

Gazetteer of the State of New York by Thomas Francis Gordon (Printed for the Author, 1836)

COUNTY DETAILS

ALBANY

95 Tivoli St., Albany, NY 12207, (518) 436-3663,
<www.albanycounty.com/achor>

- **INCORPORATED:** Nov. 1, 1683
- **PARENT COUNTY:** Original County
- **LAND RECORDS:** Start in 1630, kept by Hall of Records
- **PROBATE:** 1629, Surrogate Court
- **COURT:** 1652, County Clerk
- **NATURALIZATION:** 1895, County Court
- **TAX:** 1850, Hall of Records

ALLEGANY

7 Court St., Belmont, NY 14813, (585) 268-9270,
<www.alleganyco.com>
- **INCORPORATED:** April 7, 1806
- **PARENT COUNTY:** Genesee
- **LAND RECORDS:** Start in 1807, kept by County Clerk
- **PROBATE:** 1807, Clerk of Surrogate Court
- **COURT:** 1807, County Clerk
- **NATURALIZATION:** 1866, Supreme Court
- **NOTES:** County Clerk has marriage records 1908-1935.

BRONX

851 Grand Concourse Room 118, Bronx, NY 10451, (866) 797-7214,
<bronxcountyclerksoffice.com>
- **INCORPORATED:** April 19, 1912
- **PARENT COUNTY:** New York
- **BIRTH RECORDS:** Start in 1898, kept by Department of Health
- **MARRIAGE:** 1897, Department of Health
- **DEATH:** 1898, Department of Health
- **NATURALIZATION:** 1914, County Clerk

BROOME

44 Hawley St., Box 2062, Binghamton, NY 13902, (607) 778-2451,
<www.gobroomecounty.com>
- **INCORPORATED:** March 28, 1806
- **PARENT COUNTY:** Tioga
- **BIRTH RECORDS:** Start in 1847, kept by Town or City Clerks
- **MARRIAGE:** 1847, Town or City Clerks
- **DEATH:** 1847, Town or City Clerks
- **LAND:** 1791, County Clerk
- **PROBATE:** 1806, Surrogate Court
- **COURT:** 1808, County Court
- **NATURALIZATION:** 1820, Supreme Court

CATTARAUGUS

303 Court St., Little Valley, NY 14755, (716) 938-9111,
<www.cattco.org>
- **INCORPORATED:** March 11, 1808
- **PARENT COUNTY:** Genesee
- **MARRIAGE RECORDS:** Start in 1808, kept by Town or City Clerks
- **LAND:** 1800, County Clerk
- **PROBATE:** 1800, County Clerk
- **COURT:** 1817, County Clerk
- **NATURALIZATION:** 1847, Supreme Court

CAYUGA

160 Genesee St. 1st Floor, Auburn, NY 13021, (315) 253-1271,
<co.cayuga.ny.us/clerk>
- **INCORPORATED:** March 8, 1799
- **PARENT COUNTY:** Onondaga
- **MARRIAGE RECORDS:** Start in 1908, kept by Town or City Clerks
- **LAND:** 1794, County Clerk
- **PROBATE:** 1799, Surrogate Court
- **COURT:** 1794, County Clerk
- **NATURALIZATION:** 1879, County Court

CHARLOTTE ,

- **INCORPORATED:** March 12, 1772
- **PARENT COUNTY:** Albany
- **NOTES:** Name changed to Washington April 2, 1784.

CHAUTAUQUA

1 N. Erie St., Box 170, Mayville, NY 14757, (716) 753-4331,
<www.co.chautauqua.ny.us>
- **INCORPORATED:** March 11, 1808
- **PARENT COUNTY:** Genesee
- **MARRIAGE RECORDS:** Start in 1908, kept by County Clerk
- **LAND:** 1811, County Clerk
- **PROBATE:** 1811, Surrogate Court
- **COURT:** 1794, County Clerk
- **NATURALIZATION:** 1837, Supreme Court

CHEMUNG

210 Lake St., Box 588, Elmira , NY 14902, (607) 737-2920,
<www.chemungcounty.com>
- **INCORPORATED:** March 29, 1836
- **PARENT COUNTY:** Tioga
- **MARRIAGE RECORDS:** Start in 1908, kept by Town or City Clerks
- **LAND:** 1791, County Clerk
- **PROBATE:** 1836, Surrogate Court
- **COURT:** 1836, County Clerk

CHENANGO

5 Court St., Norwich, NY 13815, (607) 337-1450, **<www.co.chenango.ny.us/CountyClerk/CountyClerk.htm>**
- **INCORPORATED:** March 15, 1798
- **PARENT COUNTY:** Tioga
- **MARRIAGE RECORDS:** Start in 1908, kept by Town Clerk
- **LAND:** 1798, County Clerk
- **PROBATE:** 1792, Surrogate Court
- **COURT:** 1799, County Clerk
- **NATURALIZATION:** 1859, Supreme Court

CLINTON

137 Margaret St., Plattsburgh, NY 12901, (518) 565-4700,
<www.clintoncountygov.com>
- **INCORPORATED:** March 7, 1788
- **PARENT COUNTY:** Washington
- **MARRIAGE RECORDS:** Start in 1908, kept by Town or City Clerk
- **LAND:** 1788, County Clerk
- **PROBATE:** 1790, Surrogate Court
- **COURT:** 1789, Court of Common Pleas
- **NATURALIZATION:** 1820, County Court

COLUMBIA

560 Warren St., Hudson, NY 12534, (518) 828-3339,
<www.columbiacountyny.com/depts/ctyclerk>
- **INCORPORATED:** April 4, 1786
- **PARENT COUNTY:** Albany
- **MARRIAGE RECORDS:** Start in 1908, kept by Town Clerk
- **LAND:** 1786, County Clerk
- **PROBATE:** 1786, Surrogate Court
- **COURT:** 1830, Surrogate Clerk
- **NATURALIZATION:** 1835, County Court

CORTLAND

46 Greenbush St. Ste. 105, Cortland, NY 13045, (607) 753-5021, **<www.cortland-co.org/cc/index.htm>**

- **INCORPORATED:** April 8, 1808
- **PARENT COUNTY:** Onandaga
- **MARRIAGE RECORDS:** Start in 1908, kept by Town or City Clerk
- **LAND:** 1808, County Clerk
- **PROBATE:** 1809, Surrogate Court
- **COURT:** 1808, County Clerk
- **NATURALIZATION:** 1816, County Court

DELAWARE

Box 426, Delhi, NY 13753, (607) 746-2123, **<www.co.delaware.ny.us/departments/clerk/clerk.htm>**

- **INCORPORATED:** March 10, 1797
- **PARENT COUNTIES:** Ulster, Otsego
- **BIRTH RECORDS:** Start in 1847, kept by Town Clerks
- **MARRIAGE:** 1847, Town Clerks
- **DEATH:** 1847, Town Clerks
- **LAND:** 1792, County Court
- **PROBATE:** 1797, Surrogate Court
- **COURT:** 1797, Court of Common Pleas
- **NATURALIZATION:** 1810, Court of Common Pleas

DUTCHESS

22 Market St., Poughkeepsie, NY 12601, (866) 694-4700, **<www.co.dutchess.ny.us>**

- **INCORPORATED:** Nov. 1, 1683
- **PARENT COUNTY:** Original County
- **LAND RECORDS:** Start in 1697, kept by County Clerk
- **PROBATE:** 1721, County Court
- **COURT:** 1721, County Clerk
- **NATURALIZATION:** 1802, County Court

ERIE

92 Franklin St., Buffalo, NY 14202, (716) 858-8865, **<www.erie.gov/depts/government/clerk.phtml>**

- **INCORPORATED:** April 2, 1821
- **PARENT COUNTY:** Niagra
- **LAND RECORDS:** Start in 1808, kept by County Clerk
- **COURT:** 1808, County Clerk
- **NATURALIZATION:** 1831, County Court

ESSEX

7559 Court St., Box 247, Elizabethtown, NY 12932, (518) 873-3600, **<www.co.essex.ny.us/cclerk.asp>**

- **INCORPORATED:** March 1, 1799
- **PARENT COUNTY:** Clinton
- **MARRIAGE RECORDS:** Start in 1908, kept by Town or City Clerks
- **LAND:** 1799, County Clerk
- **PROBATE:** 1799, Surrogate Court
- **COURT:** 1799, Supreme Court
- **NATURALIZATION:** 1856, County Court

FRANKLIN

355 W. Main St., Box 70, Malone, NY 12953, (518) 481-1681, **<www.franklincony.org>**

- **INCORPORATED:** March 11, 1808
- **PARENT COUNTY:** Clinton
- **LAND RECORDS:** Start in 1808, kept by County Clerk
- **PROBATE:** 1809, Surrogate Court
- **COURT:** 1808, County Clerk
- **NATURALIZATION:** 1832, County Court

FULTON

223 W. Main St., Johnstown, NY 12095, (518) 736-5555, **<www.fultoncountyny.gov>**

- **INCORPORATED:** April 18, 1838
- **PARENT COUNTY:** Montgomery
- **BIRTH RECORDS:** Start in 1847, kept by County Clerk
- **MARRIAGE:** 1847, County Clerk
- **DEATH:** 1847, County Clerk
- **LAND:** 1772, County Clerk
- **PROBATE:** 1789, Surrogate Court

GENESEE

Co. Bldg. #1, Box 379, Batavia, NY 14021, (585) 344-2550, **<www.co.genesee.ny.us>**

- **INCORPORATED:** March 30, 1802
- **PARENT COUNTY:** Ontario
- **MARRIAGE RECORDS:** Start in 1908, kept by Town or City Clerks
- **LAND:** 1792, County Clerk
- **PROBATE:** 1805, Surrogate Court
- **COURT:** 1865, Supreme Court
- **NATURALIZATION:** 1849, Supreme Court

GREENE

411 Main St., Catskill, NY 12414, (518) 719-3255, **<www.greenegovernment.com>**

- **INCORPORATED:** March 25, 1800
- **PARENT COUNTIES:** Ulster, Albany
- **MARRIAGE RECORDS:** Start in 1908, kept by Town Clerks
- **LAND:** 1800, County Clerk
- **PROBATE:** 1800, Surrogate Court
- **NATURALIZATION:** 1850, Clerk of County Court

HAMILTON

Rt. 8, Box 204, Lake Pleasant, NY 12108, (518) 548-7111

- **INCORPORATED:** April 12, 1816
- **PARENT COUNTY:** Montgomery
- **MARRIAGE RECORDS:** Start in 1908, kept by Town or City Clerks
- **LAND:** 1797, County Clerk
- **PROBATE:** 1861, Surrogate Court
- **COURT:** 1880, Supreme Court
- **NATURALIZATION:** 1854, County Court

HERKIMER

109 Mary St. Ste. 1111, Herkimer, NY 13350, (315) 867-1129, **<www.herkimercounty.org>**

- **INCORPORATED:** Feb. 16, 1791
- **PARENT COUNTY:** Montgomery
- **MARRIAGE RECORDS:** Start in 1908, kept by County Clerk
- **LAND:** 1791, County Clerk
- **PROBATE:** 1792, Surrogate Court
- **NATURALIZATION:** 1818, Court of Common Pleas
- **NOTES:** County Clerk has vital records 1847-1849.

JEFFERSON

175 Arsenal St., Watertown, NY 13601, (315) 785-5149,
<www.co.jefferson.ny.us>

- **INCORPORATED:** March 28, 1805
- **PARENT COUNTY:** Oneida
- **MARRIAGE RECORDS:** Start in 1908, kept by Town or County Clerk
- **LAND:** 1805, County Clerk
- **PROBATE:** 1805, Surrogate Court
- **COURT:** 1817, Court of Common Pleas
- **NATURALIZATION:** 1896, County Clerk
- **CORONER'S REPORT:** 1878, County Coroner

KINGS

360 Adams St. Room 189, Brooklyn, NY 11201, (347) 404-9772,
<www.nycourts.gov/courts/2jd/kingsclerk>

- **INCORPORATED:** Nov. 1, 1683
- **PARENT COUNTY:** Original County
- **BIRTH RECORDS:** Start in 1866 kept by Department of Health, Brooklyn Borough Office
- **MARRIAGE:** 1866, Board of Health
- **DEATH:** 1898, Department of Health, Brooklyn Borough Office
- **LAND:** 1724, County Registrar
- **PROBATE:** 1787, Surrogate Court
- **NATURALIZATION:** 1792, County Court

LEWIS

7660 N. State St., Lowville, NY 13367, (315) 377-2000,
<www.lewiscountyny.org>

- **INCORPORATED:** March 28, 1805
- **PARENT COUNTY:** Oneida
- **LAND RECORDS:** Start in 1788, kept by County Clerk
- **PROBATE:** 1805, Surrogate Court
- **COURT:** 1805, Supreme Court
- **NATURALIZATION:** 1808, County Court
- **NOTES:** County Clerk has birth and death records 1848-1851.

LIVINGSTON

5 Murray Hill Dr., Mt Moris, NY 14510, (585) 243-7955,
<www.co.livingston.state.ny.us>

- **INCORPORATED:** Feb. 23, 1821
- **PARENT COUNTIES:** Genesee, Ontario
- **MARRIAGE RECORDS:** Start in 1908, kept by County Clerk
- **LAND:** 1820, County Clerk
- **PROBATE:** 1821, Surrogate Court
- **COURT:** 1821, Court of Common Pleas
- **NATURALIZATION:** 1821, Supreme Court

MADISON

138 N. Court St., Box 668, Wampsville, NY 13163, (315) 366-2261,
<www.madisoncounty.org>

- **INCORPORATED:** March 21, 1806
- **PARENT COUNTY:** Chenango
- **MARRIAGE RECORDS:** Start in 1806 kept by Town Clerks
- **LAND:** 1806, County Clerk
- **PROBATE:** 1806, Surrogate Court
- **COURT:** 1808, County Clerk
- **NATURALIZATION:** 1819–1950, County Court

MONROE

101 County Office Bldg., 39 W. Main St., Rochester, NY 14614, (585) 753-1600, **<www.monroecounty.gov>**

- **INCORPORATED:** Feb. 23, 1821
- **PARENT COUNTIES:** Genesee, Ontario
- **LAND RECORDS:** Start in 1821, kept by County Clerk
- **PROBATE:** 1826, Surrogate Court
- **COURT:** 1821, County Clerk
- **NATURALIZATION:** 1821, County Court

MONTGOMERY

Box 1500, Fonda, NY 12010, (518) 853-8115,
<www.co.montgomery.ny.us>

- **INCORPORATED:** March 12, 1772
- **PARENT COUNTY:** Albany
- **MARRIAGE RECORDS:** Start in 1908, kept by Town or City Clerks
- **LAND:** 1772, County Clerk
- **COURT:** 1772, Court of General Session
- **NATURALIZATION:** 1810, Supreme Court

NASSAU

240 Old Country Rd., Mineola, NY 11501, (516) 571-2664,
<www.nassaucountyny.gov>

- **INCORPORATED:** April 27, 1898
- **PARENT COUNTY:** Queens
- **MARRIAGE:** Start in 1908, kept by Town Clerks
- **NATURALIZATION:** 1899, County Court

NEW YORK

60 Centre St., Room 161, New York , NY 10007, (646) 386-5955,
<www.nyc.gov>

- **INCORPORATED:** Nov. 1, 1683
- **PARENT COUNTY:** Original County
- **BIRTH RECORDS:** Start in 1866, kept by Department of Health
- **MARRIAGE:** 1830, County Clerk
- **DEATH:** 1795, Department of Health
- **LAND:** 1680, County Registrar
- **PROBATE:** 1787, Surrogate Court
- **COURT:** 1665, Court of Assizes
- **NATURALIZATION:** 1784, Court of Common Pleas

NIAGARA

Niagara County Courthouse, 1st Floor, Box 461, Lockport, NY 14095, (716) 439-7025, **<www.niagaracounty.com/about.asp>**

- **INCORPORATED:** March 11, 1808
- **PARENT COUNTY:** Genesee
- **MARRIAGE RECORDS:** Start in 1908, kept by Town or City Clerks
- **LAND:** 1800, County Clerk
- **PROBATE:** 1820, Surrogate Court
- **COURT:** 1831, Supreme Court
- **NATURALIZATION:** 1830, County Court

ONEIDA

800 Park Ave., Utica, NY 13501, (315) 798-5794, **<ocgov.net/oneida/countyclerk>**

- **INCORPORATED:** March 15, 1798
- **PARENT COUNTY:** Herkimer
- **MARRIAGE RECORDS:** Start in 1908, kept by Town Clerks

- **LAND:** 1791, County Clerk
- **PROBATE:** 1798, Surrogate Court
- **COURT:** 1830, Surrogate Court
- **NATURALIZATION:** 1805, Court of Common Pleas

ONONDAGA

401 Montgomery St., Room 200, Syracuse, NY 13202, (315) 435-2227, **<www.ongov.net>**

- **INCORPORATED:** March 5, 1794
- **PARENT COUNTY:** Herkimer
- **MARRIAGE RECORDS:** unknown start, kept by Town or City Clerks
- **LAND:** 1794, County Clerk
- **PROBATE:** 1796, Surrogate Court
- **COURT:** 1807, Court of Common Pleas
- **NATURALIZATION:** 1802, County Court

ONTARIO

20 Ontario St., Canandaigua, NY 14424, (585) 396-4200, **<www.co.ontario.ny.us>**

- **INCORPORATED:** Jan. 27, 1789
- **PARENT COUNTY:** Montgomery
- **MARRIAGE RECORDS:** Start in 1908, kept by Records Management Officer
- **LAND:** 1789, Records Management Officer
- **NATURALIZATION:** 1803, Court of Common Pleas

ORANGE

255 Main St., Goshen, NY 10924, (845) 291-2690, **<www.orangecountygov.com>**

- **INCORPORATED:** Nov. 1, 1683
- **PARENT COUNTY:** Original County
- **MARRIAGE RECORDS:** Start in 1908, kept by County Clerk
- **LAND:** 1703, County Clerk
- **PROBATE:** 1785, Surrogate Court
- **COURT:** 1727, Court of Common Pleas

ORLEANS

3 S. Main St., Albion, NY 14411, (585) 589-4457, **<orleansny.com>**

- **INCORPORATED:** Nov. 12, 1824
- **PARENT COUNTY:** Genesee
- **MARRIAGE RECORDS:** Start in 1908, kept by Town or City Clerks
- **LAND:** 1810, County Clerk
- **PROBATE:** 1825, Surrogate Court
- **COURT:** 1864, Supreme Court
- **NATURALIZATION:** 1830, County Court
- **NOTES:** Town or City Clerks have birth, marriage and death records 1847-1849.

OSWEGO

46 E. Bridge St., Oswego, NY 13126, (315) 349-8621, **<www.co.oswego.ny.us>**

- **INCORPORATED:** March 1, 1816
- **PARENT COUNTIES:** Oneida, Onondaga
- **LAND RECORDS:** Start in 1791, kept by County Clerk
- **PROBATE:** 1816, Surrogate Court
- **COURT:** 1816, County Clerk
- **NATURALIZATION:** 1830, County Court

OTSEGO

197 Main St., Box 710, Cooperstown, NY 13326, (607) 547-4276, **<www.otsegocounty.com/depts/clk>**

- **INCORPORATED:** Feb. 16, 1791
- **PARENT COUNTY:** Montgomery
- **MARRIAGE RECORDS:** Start in 1908, kept by Town or City Clerks
- **LAND:** 1791, County Clerk
- **PROBATE:** 1781, Surrogate Court
- **COURT:** 1791, Court of Common Pleas
- **NATURALIZATION:** 1806, Court of Common Pleas

PUTNAM

40 Gleneida Ave., Carmel, NY 10512, (845) 808-1142, **<www.putnamcountyny.com/countyclerk/about.htm>**

- **INCORPORATED:** June 12, 1812
- **PARENT COUNTY:** Dutchess
- **MARRIAGE RECORDS:** Start in 1908, kept by Town Clerks
- **LAND:** 1812, County Clerk
- **COURT:** 1824, Supreme Court
- **NATURALIZATION:** 1861, County Court

QUEENS

88-11 Sutphin Blvd., Jamaica, NY 11435, (718) 520-0499, **<www.nycourts.gov/courts/11jd/index.shtml>**

- **INCORPORATED:** Nov. 1, 1683
- **PARENT COUNTY:** Original County
- **BIRTH RECORDS:** Start in 1898, kept by New York City Municipal Archives
- **MARRIAGE:** 1881, NYC Municipal Archives
- **DEATH:** 1898, NYC Municipal Archives
- **LAND:** 1686, County Registrar
- **PROBATE:** 1787, Surrogate Court
- **COURT:** 1701, Chancery Court Clerk
- **NATURALIZATION:** 1794, County Court

RENSSELAER

105 Third St., Troy, NY 12180, (518) 270-4080, **<www.rensco.com/departments_countyclerk.asp>**

- **INCORPORATED:** Feb. 7, 1791
- **PARENT COUNTY:** Albany
- **LAND RECORDS:** Start in 1791, kept by County Clerk
- **PROBATE:** 1791, Surrogate Court
- **COURT:** 1843, Court of Common Pleas
- **NATURALIZATION:** 1827, Justice Court

RICHMOND

130 Stuyvesant Place, Staten Island, NY 10301, (718) 390-5389, **<www.richmondcountyclerk.com>**

- **INCORPORATED:** Nov. 1, 1683
- **PARENT COUNTY:** Original County
- **BIRTH RECORDS:** Start in 1847 kept by Town Clerks
- **MARRIAGE:** 1897, Department of Health
- **DEATH:** 1847, Town Clerks
- **LAND:** 1683, County Clerk
- **PROBATE:** 1664, Surrogate Court
- **COURT:** 1711, Court of Common Pleas
- **NATURALIZATION:** 1820, County Court
- **NOTES:** Town Clerks have marriage records 1847-1897.

ROCKLAND

1 S. Main St. Ste. 100, New City, NY 10956, (845) 638-5070,
<www.rocklandcountyclerk.com>
- **INCORPORATED:** Feb. 23, 1798
- **PARENT COUNTY:** Orange
- **MARRIAGE RECORDS:** Start in 1908, kept by County Clerk
- **LAND:** 1703, County Clerk
- **PROBATE:** 1798, Surrogate Court
- **COURT:** 1798, Surrogate Court
- **NATURALIZATION:** 1817, County Clerk

SARATOGA

40 McMasters St., Ballston Spa, NY 12020, (518) 885-2213,
<www.saratogacountyny.gov>
- **INCORPORATED:** Feb. 7, 1791
- **PARENT COUNTY:** Albany
- **MARRIAGE RECORDS:** Start in 1908, kept by County Clerk
- **LAND:** 1774, County Clerk
- **PROBATE:** 1791, Surrogate Court
- **COURT:** 1791, Court of Oyer and Terminer
- **NATURALIZATION:** 1791, County Court

SCHENECTADY

620 State St. 3rd Floor, Schenectady, NY 12305, (518) 388-4220,
<www.schenectadycounty.com>
- **INCORPORATED:** March 7, 1809
- **PARENT COUNTY:** Albany
- **MARRIAGE RECORDS:** Start in 1908, kept by County Clerk
- **LAND:** 1809, County Clerk
- **PROBATE:** 1809, Surrogate Court
- **COURT:** 1809, Court of Common Pleas
- **NATURALIZATION:** 1810, Court of Common Pleas

SCHOHARIE

300 Main St., Box 549, Schoharie, NY 12157, (518) 295-8316,
<www.schohariecounty-ny.gov>
- **INCORPORATED:** April 6, 1795
- **PARENT COUNTIES:** Albany, Otsego
- **MARRIAGE RECORDS:** Start in 1908, kept by Town Clerks
- **LAND:** 1795, County Clerk
- **PROBATE:** 1795, Surrogate Court
- **COURT:** 1796, Court of Common Pleas
- **NATURALIZATION:** 1810, County Court
- **NOTES:** Town Clerks have marriage records 1847-1852.

SCHUYLER

105 Ninth St., Unit 8, Watkins Glen, NY 14891, (607) 535-8133,
<www.schuylercounty.us/coclerk.htm>
- **INCORPORATED:** April 17, 1854
- **PARENT COUNTIES:** Tompkins, Steuben, Chemung
- **MARRIAGE RECORDS:** Start in 1908, kept by Town Clerks
- **LAND:** 1799, County Clerk
- **PROBATE:** 1829, Surrogate Court
- **COURT:** 1855, Supreme Court
- **NATURALIZATION:** 1864, Supreme Court

SENECA

1 DiPronio Dr., Waterloo, NY 13165, (315) 539-1771,
<www.co.seneca.ny.us>
- **INCORPORATED:** March 24, 1804
- **PARENT COUNTY:** Cayuga
- **MARRIAGE RECORDS:** Start in 1908, kept by Town or City Clerks
- **LAND:** 1804, County Clerk
- **PROBATE:** 1804, Surrogate Court
- **COURT:** 1804, County Clerk
- **NATURALIZATION:** 1827, Supreme Court

ST. LAWRENCE

48 Court St., Canton, NY 13617, (315) 379-2276,
<www.co.st-lawrence.ny.us>
- **INCORPORATED:** March 3, 1802
- **PARENT COUNTIES:** Clinton, Herkimer, Montgomery
- **MARRIAGE RECORDS:** Start in 1908, kept by County Clerk
- **LAND:** 1787, County Clerk
- **PROBATE:** 1830, Surrogate Court
- **COURT:** 1802, Court of General Session
- **NATURALIZATION:** 1816, Surrogate Court
- **NOTES:** County Clerk has birth, marriage and death records 1847-1949.

STEUBEN

3 Pulteney Sq., Bath, NY 14810, (607) 776-9631,
<www.steubencony.org>
- **INCORPORATED:** March 18, 1796
- **PARENT COUNTY:** Ontario
- **BIRTH RECORDS:** Start in 1908 kept by Town or City Clerks
- **LAND:** 1796, County Clerk
- **PROBATE:** 1796, Surrogate Court
- **COURT:** 1841, Surrogate Court
- **NATURALIZATION:** 1820, Court of Common Pleas

SUFFOLK

310 Center Dr., Riverhead, NY 11901, (631) 852-2000,
<www.co.suffolk.ny.us>
- **INCORPORATED:** Nov. 1, 1683
- **PARENT COUNTY:** Original County
- **BIRTH RECORDS:** Start in 1847 kept by County Clerk
- **MARRIAGE:** 1847, County Clerk
- **DEATH:** 1847, County Clerk
- **LAND:** 1660, County Clerk
- **PROBATE:** 1669, County Clerk
- **COURT:** 1669, County Clerk
- **NATURALIZATION:** 1853, County Court

SULLIVAN

100 North St., Monticello, NY 12701, (845) 794-3000 ext. 3,
<co.sullivan.ny.us>
- **INCORPORATED:** March 27, 1809
- **PARENT COUNTY:** Ulster
- **MARRIAGE RECORDS:** Start in 1908, kept by Town Clerks
- **LAND:** 1809, County Clerk
- **COURT:** 1835, Court of Oyer and Terminer
- **NATURALIZATION:** 1835, Court of Oyer and Terminer

TIOGA
16 Court St., Owego, NY 13827, (607) 687-8660, **<www.tiogacountyny.com>**
- **INCORPORATED:** Feb. 16, 1791
- **PARENT COUNTY:** Montgomery
- **LAND RECORDS:** Start in 1796, kept by County Clerk
- **PROBATE:** 1798, Surrogate Court
- **COURT:** 1790, Circuit Court
- **NATURALIZATION:** 1854, County Clerk
- **NOTES:** Town Clerks have marriage records 1847-1850.

TOMPKINS
320 N. Tioga St., Ithaca, NY 14850, (607) 273-7187, **<www.tompkins-co.org/cclerk>**
- **INCORPORATED:** April 7, 1817
- **PARENT COUNTY:** Cayuga, Seneca
- **MARRIAGE RECORDS:** Start in 1908, kept by County Clerk
- **LAND:** 1799, County Clerk
- **COURT:** 1817, County Clerk
- **NATURALIZATION:** 1818, Supreme Court

TRYON
- **INCORPORATED:** March 12, 1772
- **PARENT COUNTY:** Albany
- **NOTES:** See Montgomery County. Name changed to Montgomery April 2, 1784.

ULSTER
244 Fair St., Kingston, NY 12401, (845) 340-3288, **<www.co.ulster.ny.us/countyclerk/reach.html>**
- **INCORPORATED:** Nov. 1, 1683
- **PARENT COUNTY:** Original County
- **MARRIAGE RECORDS:** Start in 1908, kept by County Clerk
- **LAND:** 1685, County Clerk
- **PROBATE:** 1662, Surrogate Court
- **COURT:** 1844, Circuit Court
- **NATURALIZATION:** 1844, County Clerk

WARREN
1340 State Rt. 9, Lake George, NY 12845, (518) 761-6484, **<www.co.warren.ny.us>**
- **INCORPORATED:** March 12, 1813
- **PARENT COUNTY:** Washington
- **MARRIAGE RECORDS:** Start in 1908, kept by Town or City Clerks
- **LAND:** 1813, County Clerk
- **PROBATE:** 1813, Surrogate Court
- **COURT:** 1813, County Clerk
- **NATURALIZATION:** 1821, Supreme Court

WASHINGTON
383 Broadway Bldg. A, Fort Edward, NY 12828, (518) 746-2170, **<www.co.washington.ny.us>**
- **INCORPORATED:** March 12, 1772
- **PARENT COUNTY:** Albany
- **MARRIAGE RECORDS:** Start in 1908, kept by Town Clerks
- **LAND:** 1773, County Clerk
- **PROBATE:** 1798, Surrogate Court
- **COURT:** 1830, Surrogate Court
- **NATURALIZATION:** 1793, Court of Common Pleas
- **NOTES:** Town Clerks have birth, death and marriage records 1847-1849.

WAYNE
9 Pearl St., Box 608, Lyons , NY 14489, (315) 946-7470, **<www.co.wayne.ny.us>**
- **INCORPORATED:** April 11, 1823
- **PARENT COUNTIES:** Ontario, Seneca
- **MARRIAGE RECORDS:** Start in 1908, kept by Town Clerks
- **LAND:** 1823, County Clerk
- **PROBATE:** 1823, Surrogate Court
- **COURT:** 1836, Supreme Court
- **NATURALIZATION:** 1855, County Court

WESTCHESTER
110 Dr. Martin Luther King Jr. Blvd., White Plains, NY 10601, (914) 995-3080, **<www.westchesterclerk.com>**
- **INCORPORATED:** Nov. 1, 1683
- **PARENT COUNTY:** Original County
- **MARRIAGE RECORDS:** Start in 1908, kept by Town Clerks
- **LAND:** 1684, County Archives
- **PROBATE:** 1775, Surrogate Court
- **COURT:** 1657, Court of Sessions
- **NATURALIZATION:** 1844, County Court

WYOMING
143 N. Main St., Warsaw, NY 14569, (585) 786-8810, **<www.wyomingco.net>**
- **INCORPORATED:** May 19, 1841
- **PARENT COUNTY:** Genesee
- **MARRIAGE RECORDS:** Start in 1908, kept by Town Clerks
- **LAND:** 1841, County Clerk
- **PROBATE:** 1841, Surrogate Court
- **COURT:** 1841, County Clerk
- **NATURALIZATION:** 1841, County Court

YATES
417 Liberty St. Suite 1107, Penn Yan, NY 14527, (315) 536-5120, **<www.yatescounty.org>**
- **INCORPORATED:** Feb. 5, 1823
- **PARENT COUNTY:** Ontario
- **BIRTH RECORDS:** Start in 1908, kept by Town Clerks
- **LAND:** 1823, County Clerk
- **PROBATE:** 1823, Surrogate Court
- **COURT:** 1823, County Clerk
- **NATURALIZATION:** 1823, County Court

NORTH CAROLINA

» BY EMILY ANNE CROOM

HISTORICAL OVERVIEW

In the 1650s, before Carolina was an official colony, Virginians began seeking new tobacco-farming land around Albemarle Sound in the northeast corner of what is now North Carolina. Ten years later, the British king granted eight proprietors the region south of Virginia. By 1691, when the northern part of the province settled by the proprietors had acquired the name North Carolina, it had developed a different economy and society from its southern counterpart and was, in effect, a separate colony. Official separation occurred in 1712, and Parliament made both Carolinas royal colonies in 1729.

Many early settlers came from Barbados, Virginia, and Europe, including Swiss, German, French (Huguenots), and English immigrants. Along with tobacco and rice, North Carolina farmers produced foodstuffs for neighboring colonies and the West Indies, and a naval stores industry developed. Because barrier islands and lack of natural harbors discouraged ocean-going vessels, trade and passengers generally went through the harbors at Charles Town and Norfolk. Slavery, though present, developed more slowly in North Carolina than elsewhere. Most of the Indians eventually died of disease or in war with the newcomers, or were forced westward.

As a royal colony, North Carolina saw its population mushroom. From the 1730s, Ulster Scots, Germans, Virginians, and other British colonists arrived in large numbers, many coming via the Great Philadelphia Wagon Road through Maryland and Virginia and settling in the Piedmont. By the 1760s, North Carolinians were spilling over the mountains into eastern Tennessee.

North Carolina's Continental Congress delegates voted for independence, but during the Revolution, conflict raged between the colony's patriots and loyalists, who included many Highland Scots. Wary of a strong central government, North Carolina did not ratify the new Constitution until late 1789, after the Bill of Rights was proposed. North Carolina permanently relinquished claim to Tennessee in 1790.

As cotton production increased and farmland wore out, many North Carolinians moved west and southwest to newer states. But in spite of large emigrations, by 1860 North Caro-

research tips

- Due to its colonial beginnings, North Carolina is a state land state.
- Marriage license applications, often made by a friend or relative of the groom, may not be completely accurate.
- The boundaries of North Carolina were established after settlement began: the Virginia border about 1728; the South Carolina border, 1772. Researchers should consult land records from adjoining states when studying ancestors from border counties.
- Although numerous church records exist for North Carolina research, no 18th-century Anglican parish registers survive.
- Someone reporting a North Carolina birth prior to 1796 may have been born in what is now Tennessee.
- Major archival collections are housed at the North Carolina Division of Archives and History; University of North Carolina, Chapel Hill; and Duke University, Durham.

CENSUS RECORDS

- Federal census population schedules: 1790 (incomplete), 1800, 1810 (incomplete), 1820 (incomplete), 1830, 1840, 1850, 1860, 1870, 1880, 1890 (fragments of Gaston and Cleveland counties), 1900, 1910, 1920, 1930
- Federal census soundex or miracode: 1880, 1900, 1910, 1920, 1930
- Federal mortality schedules: 1850, 1860, 1870, 1880
- Federal slave schedules: 1850, 1860
- State census: 1784–1787
- Special census of Civil War Union veterans and widows: 1890

lina had almost one million residents, of whom one-third were slaves, about 3 percent were free blacks, and about three-tenths of 1 percent were foreign-born immigrants.

North Carolina did not secede until after Civil War hostilities began. Sending and losing large numbers of men to the war, the state saw limited engagements but experienced a significant peace movement. The state was readmitted to the Union in 1868.

From the Civil War forward, industries developed around natural resources and dominant crops—forests (especially the furniture industry), minerals, commercial fishing, tobacco, and cotton. The 1990 census was the first to show the urban population barely surpassing the rural.

RECORD HIGHLIGHTS

North Carolina began statewide registration of births and deaths in October 1913, marriages in 1962, and divorces in 1958. Records of these events are also kept in the county where the event occurred: birth (before 1960), death, and marriage records with the register of deeds; divorces with the superior court clerk. Before the 20th century, legislative divorces (before 1835) or court-granted divorces (after 1814) were rare. The state archives holds surviving pre-1868 marriage bonds; few early marriage licenses exist.

For vital records copies, try the county office first. The Vital Records Registrar website **<vitalrecords.nc.gov/vital-records>** contains information on obtaining copies from the state Vital Records Unit.

The state archives site **<www.archives.ncdcr.gov>** contains information on its genealogical holdings. For detailed guides to manuscripts and county records held at the archives, see **<www.archives.ncdcr.gov/ead>**. Other records include:

- Colonial records, including some abstracted or microfilmed tax lists and estate records
- Early North Carolina papers in several series, especially series KK, of the Draper Manuscripts, which are housed at the State Historical Society of Wisconsin and available on microfilm at major research libraries
- 1785-1787 state census, various counties, not complete; no state censuses after 1787
- Pre-Civil War records of ante-bellum plantations and industries (see Witcher's book cited below)
- Post-Civil War African-American cohabitation (marriage) records and slave narratives
- Records of the three North Carolina branches of the Freedman's Savings and Trust Company (FHL film 928586)
- North Carolina Confederate pension records from 1885, at the state archives

ARCHIVES, LIBRARIES, AND SOCIETIES

Alamance County Genealogical Society
Box 3052, Burlington, NC 27215, **<www.rootsweb.ancestry.com/~ncacgs>**

Alexander County Genealogical Society
Box 545, Hiddenite, NC 28636

Alleghany Historical-Genealogical Society
Box 817, Sparta, NC 28675, **<www.ahgs.org>**

Ashe County Historical Society
Box 1361, Jefferson, NC 28640, **<www.ashehistoricalsociety.org>**

Baptist Historical Collection
Z. Smith Reynolds Library, Wake Forest University, Box 7777, Winston-Salem, NC 27109, (336) 758-3978, **<zsr.wfu.edu/collections/special/Baptist>**

Beaufort County Genealogical Society
Box 1089, Washington, NC 27889, **<www.ncroots.com/Beaufort/bcgs.htm>**

Bladen County Historical Society
Box 848, Elizabethtown, NC 28337

Braswell Memorial Library
727 N. Grace St., Rocky Mount, NC 27804, (252) 442-1951, **<www.braswell-library.org>**

Broad River Genealogical Society
Box 2261, Shelby, NC 28151, **<www.rootsweb.ancestry.com/~ncbrgs>**

Burke County Genealogical Society
Box 661, Morganton, NC 28680, **<www.ncgenweb.us/burke/burkegs.htm>**

Burke County Public Library, Morganton Branch
204 S. King St., Morganton, NC 28655, (828) 437-5638, **<www.bcpls.org>**

Cabarrus Genealogy Society
Box 2981, Concord, NC 28025, **<www.rootsweb.ancestry.com/~nccgs>**

Carolinas Genealogical Society
Box 397, Monroe, NC 28111, **<www.rootsweb.ancestry.com/~ncunion/Genealogical_society.htm>**

Carteret County Historical Society
1008 Arendell St., Morehead City, NC 28557, **<www.thehistoryplace.org>**

Catawba County Genealogical Society
Box 2406, Hickory, NC 28603, **<www.ncgenweb.us/catawba/ccgsmain.htm>**

Charles R. Jonas Public Library
306 W. Main St., Lincolnton, NC 28092, (704) 735-8044, **<www.glrl.lib.nc.us/index.htm>**

Chatham County Historical Association
Box 93, Pittsboro, NC 27312, **<chathamhistory.org>**

Cumberland County Genealogical Society
Box 53299, Fayetteville, NC 28305, **<www.ncgenweb.us/cumberland/society.htm>**

Davidson County Public Library
602 S. Main St., Lexington, NC 27292, (336) 242-2040, **<www.co.davidson.nc.us/library>**

Davie County Historical and Genealogical Society
371 N. Main St., Mocksville, NC 27028, **<www.rootsweb.ancestry.com/~ncdavhgs>**

Durham-Orange Genealogical Society
Box 4703, Chapel Hill, NC 27515, **<www.ncgenweb.us/dogsnc>**

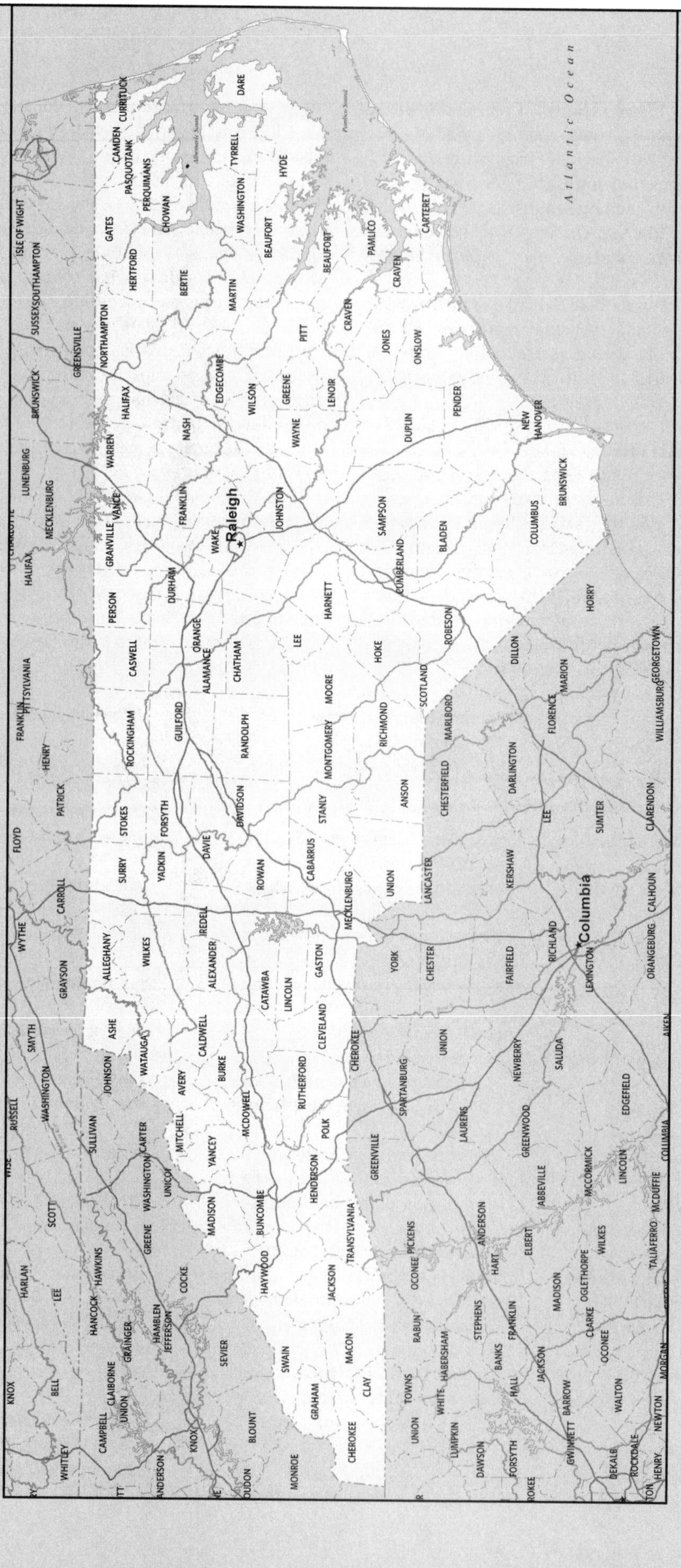
Atlantic Ocean
Raleigh
Columbia
Albemarle Sound
Pamlico Sound
CURRITUCK
CAMDEN
PASQUOTANK
PERQUIMANS
CHOWAN
GATES
DARE
TYRRELL
WASHINGTON
HYDE
BEAUFORT
HERTFORD
BERTIE
MARTIN
PAMLICO
CARTERET
CRAVEN
NORTHAMPTON
HALIFAX
EDGECOMBE
PITT
JONES
ONSLOW
WILSON
GREENE
LENOIR
NASH
WAYNE
DUPLIN
PENDER
NEW HANOVER
WARREN
FRANKLIN
JOHNSTON
SAMPSON
BRUNSWICK
VANCE
GRANVILLE
WAKE
CUMBERLAND
BLADEN
COLUMBUS
PERSON
DURHAM
HARNETT
ROBESON
ORANGE
CASWELL
ALAMANCE
CHATHAM
LEE
HOKE
MOORE
SCOTLAND
ROCKINGHAM
GUILFORD
RANDOLPH
MONTGOMERY
RICHMOND
STOKES
FORSYTH
DAVIDSON
STANLY
ANSON
SURRY
YADKIN
DAVIE
ROWAN
CABARRUS
UNION
MECKLENBURG
ALLEGHANY
WILKES
IREDELL
ALEXANDER
CATAWBA
LINCOLN
GASTON
ASHE
WATAUGA
CALDWELL
CLEVELAND
AVERY
BURKE
RUTHERFORD
MITCHELL
YANCEY
MCDOWELL
POLK
MADISON
BUNCOMBE
HENDERSON
HAYWOOD
TRANSYLVANIA
JACKSON
SWAIN
MACON
GRAHAM
CHEROKEE
CLAY

Family Research Society of Northeastern North Carolina
Box 1425, Elizabeth City, NC 27906, (252) 333-1640, <www.rootsweb.ancestry.com/~ncfrsnnc>

Forsyth County Genealogical Society
Box 5715, Winston-Salem, NC 27113, <www.rootsweb.ancestry.com/~ncfcgs>

Free Will Baptist Collection, Moye Library
Mount Olive College, 634 Henderson St., Mount Olive, NC 28365, (800) 653-0854, <www.moc.edu/?moyelibrary/Library%20Homepage>

Friends Historical Collection, Guilford College
5800 W. Friendly Ave., Greensboro, NC 27410, (336) 316-2000, <www.guilford.edu>

Gaston Lincoln Genealogical Society
Box 584, Mount Holly, NC 28120, <www.rootsweb.ancestry.com/~ncglgs/Index.htm>

Gates County Historical Society
Box 98, Gates, NC 27937, <www.throughwire.net/gchs>

Genealogical Society of Davidson County
Box 1665, Lexington, NC 27293, <www.rootsweb.ancestry.com/~ncgsdc>

Genealogical Society of Iredell County
Box 946, Statesville, NC 28687, (704) 878-5384, <www.kindredtrails.com/NC_Iredell.html>

Genealogical Society of Old Tryon County
Box 938, Forest City, NC 28043, (828) 247-8700

Genealogical Society of Rockingham and Stokes Counties
Box 152, Mayodan, NC 27027, <gsrsnc.com>

Genealogical Society of Rowan County
Box 4305, Salisbury, NC 28145, <www.lib.co.rowan.nc.us/HistoryRoom/html/gsrc.htm>

Granville County Genealogical Society
Box 1746, Oxford, NC 27565, <www.gcgs.org>

Guilford County Genealogical Society
Box 49104, Greensboro, NC 27419, <www.rootsweb.ancestry.com/~ncgcgs>

Haywood County Genealogical Society
Box 1331, Waynesville, NC 28786, <www.rootsweb.ancestry.com/~nchcgs>

Henderson County Genealogical and Historical Society
400 N. Main St., Hendersonville, NC 28792, (828) 693-1531, <www.hcghs.com>

Hyde County Historical and Genealogical Society
<www.ncgenweb.us/hyde/HCHGS.HTM>

Jackson County Genealogical Society
Box 2108, Cullowhee, NC 28723, <www.jcncgs.com>

Johnston County Genealogical and Historical Society
Box 2373, Smithfield, NC 27577, <www.rootsweb.ancestry.com/~ncjohnst>

Moravian Archives
457 S. Church St., Winston-Salem, NC 27101, <www.moravianarchives.org>

National Archives and Record Administration, Southeast Region
5780 Jonesboro Road, Morrow, GA 30260, (770) 968-2100, <www.archives.gov/southeast>

North Carolina African-American Historical Society
Box 26334, Raleigh, NC 27611

North Carolina Department of Health and Human Services, Vital Records
1903 Mail Service Center, Raleigh, NC 27699, (919) 733-3000, <vitalrecords.dhhs.state.nc.us/vr/index.html>

North Carolina Genealogical Society
Box 30815, Raleigh, NC 27622, <www.ncgenealogy.org>

North Carolina State Archives
4614 Mail Service Center, Raleigh, NC 27699, (919) 807-7310, <www.archives.ncdcr.gov>

State Library of North Carolina
109 E. Jones St., Raleigh, NC 27601, (919) 807-7430, <statelibrary.ncdcr.gov>

North Carolina Synod Archives, Evangelical Lutheran Church in America
1988 Lutheran Synod Dr., Salisbury, NC 28144, (704) 633-4861

Old Buncombe County Genealogical Society
Box 2122, Asheville, NC 28802, (828) 253-1894, <obcgs.com>

Old Dobbs County Genealogical Society
Box 617, Goldsboro, NC 27533, <www.rootsweb.ancestry.com/~ncodcgs>

Old Mecklenburg Genealogical Society
Box 32453, Charlotte, NC 28232, <www.rootsweb.ancestry.com/~ncomgs>

Old New Hanover Genealogical Society
Box 2536, Wilmington, NC 28402, <www.onhgs.org>

Pack Memorial Public Library
67 Haywood St., Asheville, NC 28801, (828) 255-5203, <www.buncombecounty.org/governing/depts/Library>

PAF-Finders Genealogy Club
Box 17494, Raleigh, NC 27619, (919) 876-6456, <freepages.genealogy.rootsweb.ancestry.com/~paffinders>

Pitt County Family Researchers
Box 2608, Greenville, NC 27836, <www.rootsweb.ancestry.com/~ncpcfr>

Presbyterian Church, Montreat Office
Box 849, Montreat, NC 28757, (828) 669-7061, <www.history.pcusa.org>

Public Library of Charlotte and Mecklenburg County
310 N. Tryon St., Charlotte, NC 28202, (704) 416-0100, <www.plcmc.org>

Rare Books, Manuscript, and Special Collections Library
Duke University, Durham, NC 27708, (919) 660-5822, <scriptorium.lib.duke.edu>

Richard H. Thornton Library
Box 339, Oxford, NC 27565, (919) 693-1121, <www.granville.lib.nc.us>

Rowan Public Library
201 W. Fisher St., Salisbury, NC 28144, (704) 638-3001, <www.lib.co.rowan.nc.us>

Southeastern North Carolina Genealogical Society
Box 463, Lake Waccamaw, NC 28450, **<www.sencgs.org>**

Southport Historical Society
Box 10014, Southport, NC 28461, **<www.southporthistoricalsociety.com>**

Toe Valley Genealogical Society
491 Beaver Creek Rd., Spruce Pine, NC 28777, **<www.rootsweb.ancestry.com/~ncmitche/tvgs.html>**

Union County Public Library
316 E. Windsor St., Monroe, NC 28112, (704) 283-8184, **<www.union.lib.nc.us>**

Wake County Genealogical Society
Box 17713, Raleigh, NC 27619, **<www.rootsweb.ancestry.com/~ncwcgs>**

Wayne County Historical Association
116 N. William St., Goldsboro, NC 27533, (919) 734-5023, **<www.waynecountyhistoricalnc.org>**

Western North Carolina Conference Archives (Methodist)
3400 Shamrock Dr., Charlotte, NC 28215, (704) 535-2260, **<www.wnccumc.org>**

Wilkes Genealogical Society
Box 1629, North Wilkesboro, NC 28659, **<www.wilkesgensoc.org>**

Wilson County Genealogical Society
<www.wcgs.org>

Wilson Library, University of North Carolina
Chapel Hill, NC 27514, (919) 962-1172, **<www.lib.unc.edu/ncc>**

GENERAL RESOURCES

The American Indian in North Carolina by Douglas L. Rights (J.F. Blair, 1957)

Archival and Manuscript Repositories in North Carolina: A Directory (Society of North Carolina Archivists, 1993)

Biographical History of North Carolina From Colonial Times to the Present edited by Samuel A'Court Ashe (C.L. Van Noppen, 1905-1917)

A Bibliography of North Carolina, 1589-1956 by Mary Lindsay Thornton (Greenwood Press, 1973, ca. 1958)

The Carolina Backcountry on the Eve of the Revolution by Charles Woodmason (Published for the Institute of Early American History and Culture at Williamsburg, Va., by University of North Carolina Press, 1953)

Carolina Cradle; Settlement of the Northwest Carolina Frontier, 1747-1762 by Robert W. Ramsey (University of North Carolina Press, 1964)

Carolina Families: A Bibliography of Books About North and South Carolina Families by Donald M. Hehir (Heritage Books, 1994)

Colonial Families of Virginia and North Carolina compiled by Motte Alston Read (filmed by the Genealogical Society of Utah, 1952)

The Colonial Records of North Carolina, 10 vols., collected and edited by William L. Saunders (P.M. Hale State Printer, 1886-90)

The Country Church in North Carolina by Jesse Marvin Ormond (Duke University Press, 1931)

Dictionary of North Carolina Biography, 6 vols., by William Stevens Powell (University of North Carolina Press, ca. 1979-1996)

Directory of Scots in the Carolinas, 1680-1830 by David Dobson (Genealogical Publishing Co., 1986)

Early Methodism in the Carolinas by A.M. Chreitzberg (Reprint Co., 1972)

Encyclopedia of American Quaker Genealogy by William Wade Hinshaw, compiled by Thomas W. Marshall (Genealogical Publishing Co., 1969)

The Episcopal Church in North Carolina, 1701-1959 edited by Lawrence Foushee London and Sarah McCulloh Lemmon (Episcopal Diocese of North Carolina, 1987)

Exploring Your Cherokee Ancestry: A Basic Genealogical Research Guide by Thomas G. Mooney (Cherokee National Historical Society, 1988, ca. 1990)

The Flowering of Methodism in Western North Carolina by George William Bumgarner and James Elwood Carroll (Commission on Archives and History of the Western North Carolina Conference of the United Methodist Church, 1984)

The Formation of North Carolina Counties, 1663-1943 by David Leroy Corbitt (State Department of Archives and History, 1969)

Guide to Genealogical Research in North Carolina by Wendy L. Elliott (W.L. Elliott, ca. 1988)

Guide to Manuscripts in the Archives of the Moravian Church in America, Southern Province by the Historical Records Survey (Historical Records Survey, 1942)

Guide to Manuscripts in the Southern Historical Collection of the University of North Carolina by the Historical Records Survey (University of North Carolina Press, 1941)

Guide to North Carolina Newspapers on Microfilm: Titles Available From the Division of Archives and History compiled by Roger C. Jones (North Carolina Division of Archives and History, 1984)

Guide to Private Manuscript Collections in the North Carolina State Archives compiled and edited by Barbara T. Cain et al. (North Carolina Division of Archives and History, 1981)

Guide to Research Materials in the North Carolina State Archives: County Records (North Carolina Division of Archives and History)

Guide to Research Materials in the North Carolina State Archives (North Carolina Division of Archives and History, 1995)

The Heritage of Blacks in North Carolina by Linda Simmons-Henry; edited by Phillip N. Henry and Carol M. Speas (North Carolina African-American Heritage Foundation and the Delmar Co., 1990)

The Historical Records of North Carolina edited by Charles Christopher Crittenden and Dan Lacy (North Carolina Historical Commission, 1938-39)

Historical Sketches of North Carolina, From 1584 to 1851, Compiled From Original Records, Official Documents and Traditional Statements by John H. Wheeler (filmed by the Genealogical Society of Utah, 1980)

A History of African Americans in North Carolina by Jeffrey J. Crow et al. (North Carolina Divions of Archives and History, 1992)

History of the German Settlements and of the Lutheran Church in North and South Carolina, From the Earliest Period of the Colonization of the Dutch, German and Swiss Settlers to the Close of the First Half of the Present Century by Gotthardt Dellmann Bernheim (The Lutheran Book Store, 1872)

History of North Carolina, 4 vols., by Hugh Talmage Leffer (Lewis Historical Publishing Co., 1956)

History of the North Carolina Baptists by George Washington Paschal (Church History Research and Archives, 1990, 1955)

History of the Protestant Episcopal Church in North Carolina by the Prostestant Episcopal Church (North Carolina Division of Archives and History, 1961)

I Have Called You Friends; the Story of Quakerism in North Carolina by Francis Charles Anscombe (Christopher Publishing House, 1959)

Index to the North Carolina Historical and Genealogical Register: Hathaway's Register by David O. Hamrick (D.O. Hamrick, 1983)

An Index to North Carolina Newspapers, 1784-1789 by Alan D. Watson (North Carolina Division of Archives and History, 1992)

An Intermediate Short, Short Course in the Use of Some North Carolina Records in Genealogical Research by Margaret M. Hofmann (Copy-It-Print, 1990)

Introductory Guide to Indian-Related Records (to 1876) in the North Carolina State Archives by Donna Spindel (North Carolina Division of Archives and History, 1977)

Inventory of the State Archives of North Carolina (filmed by the Genealogical Society of Utah, 1986)

King's Mountain and Its Heroes; History of the Battle of King's Mountain, October 7th, 1780, and the Events Which Led to It by Lyman Copeland Draper (Reprint Co., 1967)

Lawson's History of North Carolina: Containing the Exact Description and Natural History of That Country, Together With the Present State Thereof and a Journal of a Thousand Miles Traveled Through Several Nations of Indians by John Lawson and Frances Latham Harriss (Garrett and Massie, 1937)

Lost Tribes of North Carolina. Where did They Come From? Where did They go? by Worth Stickley Ray (1947)

"A Master Plan for North Carolina Research" by Helen F.M. Leary in *National Genealogical Society Quarterly* vol. 75 (March 1987), pages 15-36

McCubbin's Collection by Mamie McCubbins et al. (filmed by the Genealogical Society of Utah, 1956)

The Melungeons: Notes on the Origin of a Race by Bonnie Ball (Overmountain Press, 1992)

Melungeons Yesterday and Today by Jean Patterson Bible (J.P. Bible, 1975)

More Than Petticoats. Remarkable North Carolina Women by Scotti Kent (TwoDot, 2000)

North Carolina Bible Records; Dating From the Early Eighteenth Century to the Present Day, Including Genealogical Notes and Letters Found in Some Bibles compiled by Wilma Cartwright Spence and Edna Morrisette Shannonhouse (Unique Print Service, ca. 1973)

North Carolina Disciples of Christ: A History of Their Rise and Progress, and of Their Contribution to Their General Brotherhood by Charles Crossfield Ware (University of Microfilms International, 1982)

The North Carolina Experience, an Interpretive and Documentary History edited by Lindley S. Butler and Alan D. Watson (University of North Carolina Press, 1984)

North Carolina Genealogical Reference: A Research Guide for all Genealogists, Both Amateur and Professional compiled and edited by Wallace R. Draughon and William Perry Johnson (s.n., 1966)

North Carolina Genealogical Research by George K. Schweitzer (G.K. Schweitzer, 1984)

North Carolina Higher Court Records edited by Mattie Erma Parker (State Dept. of Archives and History, 1968-1981)

North Carolina Lives: The Tar Heel Who's Who; a Reference Edition Recording the Biographies of Contemporary Leaders in North Carolina With Special Emphasis on Their Achievements in Making it one of America's Greatest States by William Stevens Powell (Historical Records Association, 1962)

North Carolina Local History, a Select Bibliography compiled by George Stevenson (North Carolina Division of Archives and History, 1984)

North Carolina Portraits of Faith: A Pictorial History of Religions by Anne Russell and Marjorie Megivern (Donning Co., 1986)

North Carolina Research: Genealogy and Local History, 2nd edition, by Helen F.M. Leary, ed. (North Carolina Genealogical Society, 1996)

North Carolina Research Outline by the Church of Jesus Christ of Latter-Day Saints (online at **<www.familysearch.org/eng/search/RG/guide/north_carolina.asp>**)

North Carolina Through Four Centuries by William Stevens Powell (University of North Carolina Press, ca. 1989)

Old Cherokee Families: Notes of Dr. Emmet Starr, 3 vols., edited and annotated by Jack D. Baker and David Keith Hampton (Baker Pub. Co., 1987)

One Dozen Pre-Revolutionary War Families of Eastern North Carolina, and Some of Their Descendants by Primrose Watson Fisher (New Bern Historical Society Foundation, 1958)

Paths Towards Freedom: A Biographical History of Blacks and Indians in North Carolina by Frank Emory (Center for Urban Affairs, North Carolina State University, 1976)

Quaker Women of Carolina: Freedom, Achievement by Seth B. Hinshaw and Mary Edith Hinshaw (North Carolina United Society of Friends Women, 1994)

Records of the Executive Council, 1644-1734 edited by Robert J. Cain (North Carolina Division of Archives and History, 1984)

Records of the Executive Council, 1735-1754 edited by Robert J. Cain (North Carolina Division of Archives and History, 1988)

Records of the Executive Council, 1755-1775 edited by Robert J. Cain (North Carolina Division of Archives and History, 1994)

Reminiscences and Memoirs of North Carolina and Eminent North Carolinians by John H. Wheeler (Genealogical Publishing Co., 1966)

A Selective Guide to Women-Related Records in the North Carolina State Archives by Catherine E. Thompson (North Carolina Division of Archives and History, 1977)

Sketches of North Carolina, Historical and Biographical, Illustrative of the Principles of a Portion of Her Early Settlers by William Henry Foote (filmed by the Library of Congress, ca. 1980)

Sketches of the Pioneers of Methodism in North Carolina and Virginia by M.H. Moore (Southern Methodist Publishing House, 1884)

Sketches of Western North Carolina, Historical and Biographical; Illustrating Principally the Revolutionary Period of Mecklenburg, Rowan, Lincoln, and Adjoining Counties, Accompanied With Miscellaneous Information by C.L. Hunter (Regional Publishing Co., 1970)

Slavery in the State of North Carolina by John Spencer Bassett (AMS Press, 1972)

Sojourners no More: The Quakers in the New South, 1865-1920 by Damon D. Hickey (North Carolina Friends Historical Society, 1997)

Some Colonial and Revolutionary Families of North Carolina, 3 vols., by Marilu Burch Smallwood (1964-1976)

The Southern Historical Collection; a Guide to Manuscripts by Susan Sokol Blosser and Clyde Norman Wilson, Jr. (1970)

Union Lists of North Carolina Newspapers, 1751-1900 edited by H.G. Jones and Julius H. Avant (State Department of Archives and History, 1963)

☞ CENSUS RECORDS

An Abstract of North Carolina Wills From About 1760 to About 1800 by Fred A. Olds (Genealogical Publishing. Co., 1965)

Catalogue, North Carolina Federal Court Records, National Archives—Atlanta Branch edited by William D. Bennett (W.D. Bennett, 1987)

Colonial Estate Papers, 1669-1759 by the North Carolina Division of Archives and History (filmed by the Genealogical Society of Utah, 1996)

The County Court in North Carolina Before 1750 by Paul Moffatt McCain (Duke University Press, 1954)

The Eastern Cherokees, a Census of the Cherokee Nation in North Carolina, Tennessee, Alabama and Georgia in 1851 compiled by David W. Siler (Polyanthos, 1972)

The First Laws of the State of North Carolina, 2 vols., by John D. Cushing (M. Clazier, 1984)

Internal Revenue Assessment Lists for North Carolina, 1864-1866 by the US Bureau of Internal Revenue (filmed by the Genealogical Society of Utah, 1988)

North Carolina Extant Voter Registrations of 1867 by Frances Holloway Wynne (Heritage Books, 1992)

North Carolina Higher-court Records, 5 vols. (State Department of Archives and History, 1968-1981)

North Carolina Taxpayers compiled by Clarence E. Ratcliff (Genealogical Publishing. Co., 1987-1989)

North Carolina Wills and Court Records, 1679-1775 (filmed by the Genealogical Society of Utah, 1941)

North Carolina Wills and Inventories, Copied From Original and Recorded Wills and Inventories in the Office of the Secretary of State by J. Bryan Grimes (Genealogical Publishing. Co., 1967)

North Carolina Wills, a Testator Index 1665-1900, 2 vols., by Thornton W. Mitchell (T.W. Mitchell, 1987)

The State Records of North State Census Records by Ann S. Lainhart (AMS, 1970)

☞ IMMIGRATION RECORDS

Explorations, Descriptions and Attempted Settlements of Carolina, 1584-1590 by Richard Hakluyt, edited by David Leroy Corbitt (State Department. of Archives and History, 1948)

The Highland Scots of North Carolina by Duane Gilbert Meyer (Carolina Charter Tercentenary Commission, 1963)

The Loyalists in North Carolina During the Revolution by Robert O. DeMond (Genealogical Publishing Co., 1979, ca. 1940)

Marylanders to Carolina: Migration of Marylanders to North Carolina and South Carolina Prior to 1800 by Henry C. Peden, Jr. (Family Line Publications, 1994)

The Moravians in North Carolina; an Authentic History by Levin Theodore Reichel (Genealogical Publishing Co., 1968)

North Carolina Naturalization Index, 1792-1862 by Betty J. Camin (B.J. Camin, 1989)

Record of Emigrants From England and Scotland to North Carolina, 1774-1775 edited by Albert Ray Newsome (North Carolina Division of Archives and History, ca. 1989)

Roster of Soldiers From North Carolina in the American Revolution by the Daughters of the American Revolution (North Carolina) (Genealogical Publishing Co., 1977)

Westward From Virginia: The Exploration of the Virginia-Carolina Frontier, 1650-1710 by Alan Vance Briceland (University Press of Virginia, 1987)

☞LAND RECORDS

Colonial Land Entries in North Carolina, 3 vols., by A.B. Pruitt (A.B. Pruitt, 1994-1995)

Colony of North Carolina: Abstracts of Land Patents, 2 vols., by Margaret M. Hofmann (Roanoke News Co., 1982-1984)

The Granville District of North Carolina, 1748-1763: Abstracts of Land Grants, 4 vols., by Margaret M. Hofmann (Roanoke News Co., 1986-1993)

The History of Land Titles in Western North Carolina: A History of the Cherokee Land Laws Affecting the Title to Land Lying West of the Meigs and Freeman Line, and Laws Affecting the Title of Land Lying East of the Meigs and Freeman Line Back to the Top of Blue Ridge by George Henry Smathers (Miller Printing Co., 1938)

Land Grants, Land Entries and Warrants and List of Grants for Various Counties of North Carolina, 1764-1853 by the North Carolina Secretary of State (filmed by the Genealogical Society of Utah, 1941)

Land Records, 1600 Thru 1957; Indexes, 1693-1959 by the North Carolina Secretary of State Land Grant Office (North Carolina State Archives, 1980-2003)

North Carolina Land Grants in Tennessee, 1778-1791 compiled by Goldene Fillers Burgner (Southern Historical Press, 1981)

North Carolina Land and Property Records: A Register of the Several Counties, Alphabetically Arranged, Being a Listing of Deed Records, Mortgages, Trusts, etc. by the Jesus Christ Church of Latter-Day Saints Genealogical Department (filmed by the Genealogical Society of Utah, 1969)

The Proprietors of Carolina by William Stevens Powell (Carolina Charter Tercentenary Commission, 1963)

Province of North Carolina, 1663-1729: Abstracts of Land Patents by Margaret M. Hofmann (Roanoke News Co., 1979)

☞MAPS

The Formation of North Carolina Counties, 1663-1943 by David Leroy Corbitt (North Carolina Division of Archives and History, 1950)

Index to Maps of North Carolina in Books and Periodicals Illustrating the History of the State From the Voyage of Verrazzano in 1524 to 1975 by David Sanders Clark (Clark, 1976)

The National Post Road by Virginia Greene DePriest (V.G. DePriest, 1990)

North Carolina Atlas and Gazetteer: Topo Maps of the Entire State (Delorme, 1997)

North Carolina Atlas: Portrait of a Changing Southern State edited by James W. Clay et al. (University of North Carolina Press, 1975)

North Carolina County Maps compiled by C.J. Puetz (Puetz Place, ca. 1980)

North Carolina, Her Counties, Her Townships, and Her Towns compiled by Joan Colbert Gioe (Researchers, 1981)

North Carolina in Maps by William P. Cumming (State Department of Archives and History, 1966)

Statistical Gazetteer of the States of Virginia and North Carolina: Embracing Important Topographical and Historical Information, From Recent and Original Sources Together With the Results of the Last Census, Population and Statistics in Many Cases to 1855 edited by Richard Edwards (Published for the Proprietor, 1856)

☞MILITARY RECORDS

Abstracts and Letters of Resignations of Militia Officers in North Carolina, 1779-1840 compiled and abstracted by Timothy Kearney (North Carolina Genealogical Society, 1992, Walsworth Pub.)

Abstracts of Pensions of North Carolina Soldiers of the Revolution, War of 1812 & Indian Wars by Annie W. Burns (ca. 1960)

The Black Experience in Revolutionary North Carolina by Jeffrey J. Crow (North Carolina Division of Archives and History, 1977)

Compendium of the Confederate Armies, 11 vols., by Stewart Sifakis (Facts on File, 1992-1995)

Histories of the Several Regiments and Battalions From North Carolina in the Great War, 1861-'65, 5 vols., edited by Walter Clark (Broadfoot Publishing., 1996)

The King's Mountain Men; the Story of the Battle, With Sketches of the American Soldiers who Took Part by Katherine Keogh White (Genealogical Publishing Co., 1966)

Muster Roles of the Soldiers of the War of 1812 Detached From the Militia of North Carolina in 1812 and 1814 by Maurice S. Toler (Genealogical Publishing Co., 1976)

North Carolina Civil War Documentary edited by W. Buck Yearns and John G. Barrett (University of North Carolina, 2002)

North Carolina Confederate Militia Officers Roster as Contained in the Adjutant-General's Officers Roster edited by Stephen E. Bradley, Jr. (Broadfoot Pub. Co., 1992)

North Carolina Revolutionary Soldiers, Sailors, Patriots & Descendants compiled by Joseph T. Maddox and Mary Carter (Georgia Pioneers Publications, ca. 1970)

North Carolina's Role in the First World War by Sarah McCulloh Lemmon (State Department. of Archives and History, 1966)

North Carolina's Role in the Spanish-American War by Joseph S. Steelman (North Carolina Division of Archives and History, 1975)

North Carolina Troops, 1861-1865: A Roster, 15 vols., compiled by Louis H. Manarin (State Department of Archives and History, 1966-2003)

North Carolina, World War I Selective Service System Draft Registration Cards, 1917-1918 by the US Selective Service System (National Archives, 1987-1988)

Roster of Soldiers From North Carolina in the American Revolution: With an Appendix Containing a Collection of Miscellaneous Records by the Daughters of the American Revolution, North Carolina (Genealogical Publishing Co., 1977)

This Destructive War: The British Campaign in the Carolinas, 1780-1782 by John S. Pancake (University of Alabama Press, 2003)

Volunteer Soldiers in the Cherokee War, 1836-39 by James L. Douthat (Mountain Press, 1995)

☞ VITAL RECORDS

Abstracts of Vital Records From Raleigh, North Carolina Newspapers compiled by Lois Smathers Neal (Reprint Co., 1979-1995)

Cemetery Records of North Carolina, 8 vols., copied by the Church of Jesus Christ of Latter-Day Saints Genealogical Society (The Society, 1947-1961)

Death Certificates, 1906-1994; Still Births, 1914-1953; Fetal Deaths, 1960-1974; Index, 1906-1967, 1906-1974 by the North Carolina Department of Public Health, Vital Records Section (filmed by the Genealogical Society of Utah, 1993-1995)

Gravestone Records, 10 vols., by Leora Hiatt McEachern (L.H. McEachern, 1971-1981)

Guide to Vital Statistics Records in North Carolina by the Historical Records Survey (The Survey, 1942)

Index to Death Certificates, 1968-1994 (North Carolina Department of Public Health Vital Records Section, ca. 1994)

An Index to Marriage Bonds Filed in the North Carolina State Archives (North Carolina Division of Archives and History, 1977)

Marriage and Death Notices in Raleigh Register and North Carolina State Gazette (1799-1867), 4 vols., compiled by Carrie L. Broughton (Genealogical Publishing Co., 1949)

Master File Relocation Card Index for Grave and Cemetery Removal and Relocation, 1934-1954 by the Tennessee Valley Authority (filmed by the Genealogical Society of Utah, 1996)

North Carolina Marriage Records: Early to 1800 edited by Jordan R. Dodd (Precision Indexing, 1990)

Post-1914 Cemetery Inscription Card Index by the Historical Records Survey (North Carolina Department. of Archives and History, 1972)

Pre-1914 Cemetery Inscription Card Index by the Historical Records Survey (North Carolina Department. of Archives and History, 1972)

Somebody Knows My Name: Marriages of Freed People in North Carolina County by County, 3 vols., compiled by Barnetta McGee White (Iberian Publishing Co., 1995)

Tar Heel Tombstones and the Tales They Tell by Henry King (Down Home Press, 1990)

•-COUNTY DETAILS-•

ALAMANCE

Box 837, 118 W. Harden St., Graham, NC 27253, (336) 570-6565,
<www.alamance-nc.com>

- **INCORPORATED:** April 1849
- **PARENT COUNTY:** Orange
- **BIRTH RECORDS:** start in 1913, kept by Registrar of Deeds
- **MARRIAGE:** 1849, Registrar of Deeds
- **DIVORCE:** 1917, Superior Court
- **DEATH:** 1913, Registrar of Deeds
- **LAND:** 1905, Registrar of Deeds
- **PROBATE:** 1949, Superior Court
- **COURT:** 1920, Superior Court
- **NOTES:** State Archives has court records 1849-1920, divorce records 1889-1917, land records 1793-1905, probate records 1856-1949, and wills 1832-1900.

ALBEMARLE

- **INCORPORATED:** 1664
- **PARENT COUNTY:** Original county
- **NOTES:** County divided into Chowan, Currituck, Pasauotark, and Perauimans Precincts in 1668. County discontinued in 1689.

ALEXANDER

201 First St. SW Suite 1, Taylorsville, NC 28681, (828) 632-3152,
<www.co.alexander.nc.us>

- **INCORPORATED:** Jan. 15, 1847
- **PARENT COUNTIES:** Iredell, Caldwell, Wilkes
- **BIRTH RECORDS:** start in 1913, kept by Registrar of Deeds
- **MARRIAGE:** 1866, Registrar of Deeds
- **DIVORCE:** 1905, Superior Court
- **DEATH:** 1913, Registrar of Deeds
- **LAND:** 1847, Registrar of Deeds
- **PROBATE:** 1939, Superior Court
- **COURT:** 1900, Superior Court
- **NOTES:** State Archives has court records 1866-1900, divorce records 1867-1905, probate records 1858-1939, and wills 1847-1949. Courthouse burned in 1865, destroying many records.

ALLEGHANY
12 N. Main St., Box 186, Sparta, NC 28675, (336) 372-4342,
<www.alleghanycounty-nc.gov>
- **INCORPORATED:** 1859
- **PARENT COUNTY:** Ashe
- **BIRTH RECORDS:** start in 1913, kept by Registrar of Deeds
- **MARRIAGE:** 1859, Registrar of Deeds
- **DIVORCE:** 1932, Superior Court
- **DEATH:** 1913, Registrar of Deeds
- **LAND:** 1908, Registrar of Deeds
- **PROBATE:** 1928, Superior Court
- **COURT:** 1928, Superior Court
- **NOTES:** State Archives has court records 1862-1928, divorce records 1862-1932, land records 1837-1908, probate records 1859-1928, and wills 1859-1912. Courthouse fire in 1932 destroyed some records.

ANSON
Box 352, Wadesboro, NC 28170, (704) 694-3212,
<www.co.anson.nc.us>
- **INCORPORATED:** March 1750
- **PARENT COUNTY:** Bladen
- **BIRTH RECORDS:** start in 1914, kept by Registrar of Deeds
- **MARRIAGE:** 1869, Registrar of Deeds
- **DIVORCE:** 1925, Superior Court
- **DEATH:** 1914, Registrar of Deeds
- **LAND:** 1838, Registrar of Deeds
- **PROBATE:** 1953, Superior Court
- **COURT:** 1905, Superior Court
- **NOTES:** State Archives has court records 1771-1777, 1848-1905, divorce records 1872-1925, land records 1749-1838, naturalization records 1913-1924, probate records 1805-1953, and wills 1754-1946. Courthouse burned 1868.

ARCHDALE
- **INCORPORATED:** Dec. 3, 1705
- **PARENT COUNTY:** Bath
- **NOTES:** See Craven County. Name changed to Craven, 1712.

ASHE
150 Government Circle Suite 2300, Jefferson, NC 28640, (336) 219-2540, **<www.ashecountygov.com>**
- **INCORPORATED:** Nov. 18, 1799
- **PARENT COUNTY:** Wilkes
- **BIRTH RECORDS:** start in 1913, kept by Registrar of Deeds
- **MARRIAGE:** 1853, Superior Court
- **DIVORCE:** 1912, Superior Court
- **DEATH:** 1913, Registrar of Deeds
- **LAND:** 1954, Registrar of Deeds
- **PROBATE:** 1935 Superior Court
- **COURT:** 1938, Superior Court
- **NOTES:** State Archives has court records 1807-1938, divorce records 1822-1912, land records 1778-1954, probate records 1819-1935 and wills 1801-1912. Fire in 1865 destroyed many court records.

AVERY
200 Montezuma St., Newland, NC 28657, (828) 733-8260,
<www.averycountync.gov>
- **INCORPORATED:** February 1911
- **PARENT COUNTIES:** Caldwell, Mitchell, Watauga
- **BIRTH RECORDS:** start in 1913, kept by Registrar of Deeds
- **MARRIAGE:** 1859, Registrar of Deeds
- **DIVORCE:** 1911, Superior Court
- **DEATH:** 1913, Registrar of Deeds
- **LAND:** 1911, Registrar of Deeds
- **PROBATE:** 1911, Superior Court
- **COURT:** 1911, Superior Court

BATH
<www.usgennet.org/usa/nc/county/bath>
- **INCORPORATED:** 1696
- **PARENT COUNTY:** Original county
- **NOTES:** Divided into Archdale, Pamptecough and Wickham Precincts 1705; County discontinued in 1724.

BEAUFORT
112 W. Second St., Washington, NC 27889, (252) 946-2323,
<www.beaufort-county.com>
- **INCORPORATED:** December 1705
- **PARENT COUNTY:** Bath
- **BIRTH RECORDS:** start in 1913, kept by Registrar of Deeds
- **MARRIAGE:** 1850, Registrar of Deeds
- **DIVORCE:** 1923, State Archives
- **DEATH:** 1913, Registrar of Deeds
- **LAND:** 1881, Registrar of Deeds
- **PROBATE:** 1949, Superior Court
- **COURT:** 1902, Superior Court
- **NOTES:** State Archives has court records 1756-1902, divorce records 1868-1902, land records 1695-1881, probate records 1760-1949, and wills 1720-1903.

BERKELEY
- **INCORPORATED:** 1668
- **PARENT COUNTY:** Precinct in Albemarle County
- **NOTES:** See Perquimans County. Perquimans County known as Berkeley Precinct from 1670 to 1682.

BERTIE
Box 340, Windsor, NC 27983, (252) 794-5309,
<www.co.bertie.nc.us>
- **INCORPORATED:** August 1722
- **PARENT COUNTY:** Chowan
- **BIRTH RECORDS:** start in 1913, kept by Registrar of Deeds
- **MARRIAGE:** 1902, Registrar of Deeds
- **DIVORCE:** unknown start, Superior Court
- **DEATH:** 1913, Registrar of Deeds
- **LAND:** 1820, Registrar of Deeds
- **PROBATE:** 1920, Superior Court
- **COURT:** 1915, Superior Court
- **NOTES:** State Archives has court records 1724-1915, land records 1723-1820, marriage records 1762-1868, 1870-1903, probate records 1728-1920, and wills 1749-1897.

BLADEN
106 E. Broad St., Elizabethtown, NC 28337, (910) 862-6710,
<www.bladeninfo.org>

- **INCORPORATED:** 1734
- **PARENT COUNTY:** New Hanover
- **BIRTH RECORDS:** start in 1913, kept by Registrar of Deeds
- **MARRIAGE:** 1904, Superior Court
- **DIVORCE:** 1955, Superior Court
- **DEATH:** 1913, Registrar of Deeds
- **LAND:** 1804, Registrar of Deeds
- **PROBATE:** 1956, Superior Court
- **COURT:** 1956, Superior Court
- **NOTES:** State Archives has court records 1866-1890, 1893-1956, divorce records 1893-1955, land records 1738-1804, marriage records 1892-1904, and probate records 1761, 1862, and 1868-1956. Courthouse burned 1800 and 1893.

BRUNSWICK

Box 87, 76 Courthouse Dr., Bolivia, NC 28422, (910) 253-2690, **<www.brunsco.net>**

- **INCORPORATED:** January 1764
- **PARENT COUNTIES:** New Hanover, Bladen
- **BIRTH RECORDS:** start in 1913, kept by Registrar of Deeds
- **MARRIAGE:** 1804, Registrar of Deeds
- **DIVORCE:** 1905, Superior Court
- **DEATH:** 1913, Registrar of Deeds
- **LAND:** 1764, Registrar of Deeds
- **PROBATE:** 1920, Superior Court
- **COURT:** 1912, Superior Court
- **NOTES:** State Archives has court records 1782-1912, divorce records 1849, 1866, 1869-1905, probate records 1783-1920, and wills 1765-1912. Many records were destroyed in 1865.

BUNCOMBE

60 Court Plaza, Room 110, Asheville, NC 28801, (828) 250-4300, **<www.buncombecounty.org>**

- **INCORPORATED:** December 1791
- **PARENT COUNTIES:** Burke, Rutherford
- **BIRTH RECORDS:** start in 1913, kept by Registrar of Deeds
- **MARRIAGE:** 1868, Registrar of Deeds
- **DIVORCE:** 1919, Superior Court
- **DEATH:** 1913, Registrar of Deeds
- **LAND:** 1919, Registrar of Deeds
- **PROBATE:** 1924, Superior Court
- **COURT:** 1892, Superior Court
- **NOTES:** State Archives has court records 1792-1892, divorce records 1830-1918, land records 1789-1919, marriage records 1842-1867, probate records 1815-1924, and wills 1826-1909. Courthouse burned 1830 and 1835.

BURKE

201 S. Green St., Box 219, Morganton, NC 28680, (828) 438-5450,**<www.co.burke.nc.us>**

- **INCORPORATED:** June 1, 1777
- **PARENT COUNTY:** Rowan
- **BIRTH RECORDS:** start in 1913, kept by Registrar of Deeds
- **MARRIAGE:** 1865, Registrar of Deeds
- **DIVORCE:** 1911, Superior Court
- **DEATH:** 1913, Registrar of Deeds
- **LAND:** 1865, Registrar of Deeds
- **PROBATE:** 1935, Superior Court
- **COURT:** 1908, Superior Court
- **NOTES:** State Archives has court records 1791-1907, divorce records 1828-1911, marriage records 1780-1865, probate records 1776-1934, and wills 1790-1905. Many records prior to 1865 were destroyed during the Civil War.

BUTE

<www.rootsweb.ancestry.com/~ncbute>

- **INCORPORATED:** 1764
- **PARENT COUNTY:** Granville
- **NOTES:** Became Warren and Franklin counties in 1779.

CABARRUS

65 Church St. SE, Concord, NC 28025, (704) 920-2112, **<www.co.cabarrus.nc.us>**

- **INCORPORATED:** November 1792
- **PARENT COUNTY:** Mecklenburg
- **BIRTH RECORDS:** start in 1913, kept by Registrar of Deeds
- **MARRIAGE:** 1856, Registrar of Deeds
- **DIVORCE:** 1931, Superior Court
- **DEATH:** 1913, Registrar of Deeds
- **LAND:** 1792, Registrar of Deeds
- **PROBATE:** 1954, Superior Court
- **COURT:** 1943, Superior Court
- **NOTES:** State Archives has court records 1793-1943, divorce records 1866, 1868, and 1783-1930, probate records 1793-1953, and wills 1794-1921. Courthouse burned 1874.

CALDWELL

905 West Ave. NW, Lenoir, NC 28645, (828) 757-1310, **<www.co.caldwell.nc.us>**

- **INCORPORATED:** January 1841
- **PARENT COUNTIES:** Burke, Wilkes
- **BIRTH RECORDS:** start in 1914, kept by Registrar of Deeds
- **MARRIAGE:** 1850, Registrar of Deeds
- **DIVORCE:** 1926, Superior Court
- **DEATH:** 1914, Registrar of Deeds
- **LAND:** 1840, Registrar of Deeds
- **PROBATE:** 1935, Superior Court
- **COURT:** 1911, Superior Court
- **NOTES:** State Archives has court records 1841-1911, divorce records 1850-1925, probate records 1841-1934, and wills 1830-1925.

CAMDEN

117 North NC343, Camden, NC 27921, (252) 331-4851, **<www.camdencountync.gov>**

- **INCORPORATED:** April 1777
- **PARENT COUNTY:** Pasquotank
- **BIRTH RECORDS:** start in 1913, kept by Registrar of Deeds
- **MARRIAGE:** 1848, Registrar of Deeds
- **DIVORCE:** unknown start, Superior Court
- **DEATH:** 1913, Registrar of Deeds
- **LAND:** 1913, Registrar of Deeds
- **PROBATE:** 1930, Superior Court
- **COURT:** 1912, Superior Court
- **NOTES:** State Archives has court records 1853-1911, land records 1739-1912, and probate records 1790-1929.

CARTERET
Courthouse Sq., Beaufort, NC 28516, (252) 728-8474,
<www.carteretcountygov.org>
- **INCORPORATED:** 1722
- **PARENT COUNTY:** Craven
- **BIRTH RECORDS:** start in 1913, kept by Registrar of Deeds
- **MARRIAGE:** 1873, Registrar of Deeds
- **DIVORCE:** 1940, Superior Court
- **DEATH:** 1913, Registrar of Deeds
- **LAND:** 1953, Registrar of Deeds
- **PROBATE:** 1958, Superior Court
- **COURT:** 1908, Superior Court
- **NOTES:** State Archives has court records 1723-1907, divorce records 1877-1939, land records 1721-1952, marriage records 1746-1872, probate records 1744-1957, and wills 1744-1921.

CASWELL
Box 98, 139 E. Church St., Yanceyville, NC 27379, (336) 694-4197,
<www.caswellcountync.gov>
- **INCORPORATED:** April 8, 1777
- **PARENT COUNTY:** Orange
- **BIRTH RECORDS:** start in 1913, kept by Registrar of Deeds
- **MARRIAGE:** 1869, Registrar of Deeds
- **DIVORCE:** 1929, Superior Court
- **DEATH:** 1913, Registrar of Deeds
- **LAND:** 1885, Registrar of Deeds
- **PROBATE:** 1942, Superior Court
- **COURT:** 1925, Superior Court
- **NOTES:** State Archives has court records 1777-1924, divorce records 1818-1928, land records 1780-1884, marriage records 1778-1868, and probate records 1772-1941.

CATAWBA
Box 65, Newton, NC 28658, (828) 465-1573,
<www.catawbacountync.gov>
- **INCORPORATED:** December 1842
- **PARENT COUNTY:** Lincoln
- **BIRTH RECORDS:** start in 1913, kept by Registrar of Deeds
- **MARRIAGE:** 1842, Registrar of Deeds
- **DIVORCE:** 1928, Superior Court
- **DEATH:** 1913, Registrar of Deeds
- **LAND:** 1842, Registrar of Deeds
- **PROBATE:** 1923, Superior Court
- **COURT:** 1887, Superior Court
- **NOTES:** State Archives has court records 1843-1886, divorce records 1869-1927, probate records 1843-1922, and wills 1843-1966.

CHATHAM
12 East Rd., Pittsboro, NC 27312, (919) 542-8235,
<www.chathamnc.org>
- **INCORPORATED:** December 1771
- **PARENT COUNTY:** Orange
- **BIRTH RECORDS:** start in 1913, kept by Registrar of Deeds
- **DIVORCE:** 1935, Superior Court
- **DEATH:** 1913, Registrar of Deeds
- **LAND:** 1771, Registrar of Deeds
- **PROBATE:** 1949, Superior Court
- **COURT:** 1932, Superior Court
- **NOTES:** State Archives has court records 1774-1931, divorce records 1829-1934, marriage records 1778-1876, probate records 1771-1948, and wills 1771-1964.

CHEROKEE
53 Peachtree, Murphy, NC 28906, (828) 837-2613,
<www.cherokeecounty-nc.gov>
- **INCORPORATED:** Jan. 4, 1839
- **PARENT COUNTY:** Macon
- **BIRTH RECORDS:** start in 1913, kept by Registrar of Deeds
- **MARRIAGE:** 1865, Registrar of Deeds
- **DIVORCE:** 1915, Superior Court
- **DEATH:** 1913, Registrar of Deeds
- **LAND:** 1838, Registrar of Deeds
- **PROBATE:** 1941, Superior Court
- **COURT:** 1914, Superior Court
- **NOTES:** State Archives has court records 1865-1913, divorce records 1869-1914, and 1942, probate records 1843-1940, and wills 1857-1941. A portion of Cherokee County lies in Cherokee land. For information regarding the genealogy of the Eastern band of the Cherokee of North Carolina contact the Qualla Public Library, Acauoni Road, Cherokee, NC.

CHOWAN
101 S. Broad St., Edenton, NC 27932, (252) 482-2619,
<www.chowancounty-nc.gov>
- **INCORPORATED:** 1670
- **PARENT COUNTY:** Albemarle
- **BIRTH RECORDS:** start in 1913, kept by Registrar of Deeds
- **MARRIAGE:** 1869, Registrar of Deeds
- **DIVORCE:** 1910, Superior Court
- **DEATH:** 1913, Registrar of Deeds
- **LAND:** 1678, Registrar of Deeds
- **PROBATE:** 1694, Superior Court
- **COURT:** 1911, Superior Court
- **NOTES:** State Archives has court records 1714-1910, divorce records 1823-1909, and marriage records 1747-1868.

CLARENDON
- **INCORPORATED:** 1664
- **PARENT COUNTY:** Original county
- **NOTES:** Abandoned in 1667.

CLAY
Box 118, Hayesville, NC 28904, (828) 389-0087,
<www.clayconc.com>
- **INCORPORATED:** February 1861
- **PARENT COUNTY:** Cherokee
- **BIRTH RECORDS:** start in 1913, kept by Registrar of Deeds
- **MARRIAGE:** 1877, Registrar of Deeds
- **DEATH:** 1913, Registrar of Deeds
- **LAND:** 1838, Registrar of Deeds
- **PROBATE:** 1944, Superior Court
- **COURT:** 1903, Superior Court
- **NOTES:** State Archives has court records 1870-1902, land records 1845-1937, probate records 1862-1943, and wills 1870-1928.

CLEVELAND

311 E. Marion St., Box 1210, Shelby, NC 28150, (704) 484-4834, <www.clevelandcounty.com>

- **INCORPORATED:** January 1841
- **PARENT COUNTIES:** Rutherford, Lincoln
- **BIRTH RECORDS:** start in 1913, kept by Registrar of Deeds
- **MARRIAGE:** 1851, Registrar of Deeds
- **DIVORCE 1908, SUPERIOR COURT**
- **DEATH:** 1913, Registrar of Deeds
- **LAND:** 1899, Registrar of Deeds
- **PROBATE:** 1916, Superior Court
- **COURT:** 1911, Superior Court
- **NOTES:** State Archives has court records 1841-1910, divorce records 1842-1907, land records 1775-1898, probate records 1795-1915, and wills 1841-1919.

COLUMBUS

612 N. Madison St., Whiteville, NC 28472, (910) 640-6625, <www.columbusco.org>

- **INCORPORATED:** December 1808
- **PARENT COUNTIES:** Bladen, Brunswick
- **BIRTH RECORDS:** start in 1913, kept by Registrar of Deeds
- **MARRIAGE:** 1867, Registrar of Deeds
- **DIVORCE:** 1817, Superior Court
- **DEATH:** 1913, Registrar of Deeds
- **LAND:** 1802, Registrar of Deeds
- **PROBATE:** 1924, Superior Court
- **COURT:** 1969, Superior Court
- **NOTES:** State Archives has court records 1817-1968, probate records 1812-1923, and wills 1808-1917.

CRAVEN

226 Pollock St., New Bern, NC 28560, (252) 636-6617, <www.cravencounty.com>

- **INCORPORATED:** December 1705
- **PARENT COUNTY:** Archdale Precinct of Bath County
- **BIRTH RECORDS:** start in 1914, kept by Registrar of Deeds
- **MARRIAGE:** 1740, Registrar of Deeds
- **DIVORCE:** 1898, Superior Court
- **DEATH:** 1914, Registrar of Deeds
- **LAND:** 1710, Registrar of Deeds
- **PROBATE:** 1946, Superior Court
- **COURT:** 1915, Superior Court
- **NOTES:** State Archives has court records 1712-1715, 1730-1914, divorce records 1828-1897, probate records 1745-1945, and wills 1737-1868. Formerly Archdale Precinct of Bath County. Named changed to Craven, 1712.

CUMBERLAND

117 Dick St. Room 114, Fayetteville, NC 28301, (910) 678-7775, <www.co.cumberland.nc.us>

- **INCORPORATED:** February 1754
- **PARENT COUNTY:** Bladen
- **BIRTH RECORDS:** start in 1913, kept by Registrar of Deeds
- **MARRIAGE:** 1907, Registrar of Deeds
- **DIVORCE:** unknown start, Superior Court
- **DEATH:** 1913, Registrar of Deeds
- **LAND:** 1754, Registrar of Deeds
- **PROBATE:** 1931, Superior Court
- **COURT:** 1914, Superior Court
- **NOTES:** State Archives has court records 1755-1913, marriage records 1868-1906, probate records 1758-1930, and wills 1757-1955.

CURRITUCK

Box 71, Currituck, NC 27929, (252) 232-3297, <www.co.currituck.nc.us>

- **INCORPORATED:** 1668
- **PARENT COUNTY:** Albemarle
- **BIRTH RECORDS:** start in 1913, kept by Registrar of Deeds
- **MARRIAGE:** 1850, Registrar of Deeds
- **DIVORCE:** unknown start, Superior Court
- **DEATH:** 1913, Registrar of Deeds
- **LAND:** 1696, Registrar of Deeds
- **PROBATE:** 1927, Superior Court
- **COURT:** 1908, Superior Court
- **NOTES:** State Archives has court records 1799-1907, probate records 1812-1926, and wills 1841-1924.

DARE

962 Marshall C. Collins Dr., Manteo, NC 27954, (252) 475-5970, <www.co.dare.nc.us>

- **INCORPORATED:** February 1870
- **PARENT COUNTIES:** Currituck, Tyrell, Hyde
- **BIRTH RECORDS:** start in 1913, kept by Registrar of Deeds
- **MARRIAGE:** 1880, Registrar of Deeds
- **DIVORCE:** 1970, Superior Court
- **DEATH:** 1913, Registrar of Deeds
- **LAND:** 1880, Registrar of Deeds
- **PROBATE:** 1965, Superior Court
- **COURT:** 1967, Superior Court
- **NOTES:** State Archives has court records 1870-1966, divorce records 1882-1969, probate records 1832-1964, and wills 1872-1959.

DAVIDSON

Box 464, Lexington, NC 27293, (336) 242-2150, <www.co.davidson.nc.us>

- **INCORPORATED:** December 1822
- **PARENT COUNTY:** Rowan
- **BIRTH RECORDS:** start in 1822, kept by Registrar of Deeds
- **MARRIAGE:** 1822, Registrar of Deeds
- **DIVORCE:** 1944, Superior Court
- **DEATH:** 1823, Registrar of Deeds
- **LAND:** 1923, Registrar of Deeds
- **PROBATE:** 1949, Superior Court
- **COURT:** 1911, Superior Court
- **NOTES:** State Archives has court records 1823-1910, divorce records 1831-1944, land records 1808-1922, probate records 1817-1948, and wills 1823-1940. Courthouse fire in 1866 destroyed some records.

DAVIE

123 S. Main St., Mocksville, NC 27028, (336) 751-2513, <www.co.davie.nc.us>

- **INCORPORATED:** December 1836
- **PARENT COUNTY:** Rowan
- **BIRTH RECORDS:** start in 1913, kept by Registrar of Deeds

- **MARRIAGE:** 1836, Registrar of Deeds
- **DIVORCE:** 1909, Superior Court
- **DEATH:** 1913, Registrar of Probate
- **LAND:** 1836, Registrar of Deeds
- **PROBATE:** 1937, Superior Court
- **COURT:** 1906, Superior Court
- **NOTES:** State Archives has court records 1837-1905, divorce records 1849-1908, probate records 1809-1936, and wills 1808-1902.

DOBBS

- **INCORPORATED:** 1759
- **PARENT COUNTY:** Johnston
- **NOTES:** Discontinued and became part of Wayne County in 1779 and Glasgow and Lenoir Counties in 1791.

DUPLIN

118 Duplin St., Kenansville, NC 28349, (910) 296-2108, **<www.duplincountync.com>**

- Incorporated: April 7, 1750
- **PARENT COUNTY:** New Hanover
- **BIRTH RECORDS:** start in 1913, kept by Registrar of Deeds
- **MARRIAGE:** 1870, Registrar of Deeds
- **DIVORCE:** 1953, Superior Court
- **DEATH:** 1913, Registrar of Deeds
- **LAND:** 1749, Registrar of Deeds
- **PROBATE:** 1931, Superior Court
- **COURT:** 1909, Superior Court
- **NOTES:** State Archives has court records 1784-1908, divorce records 1869-1952, marriage records 1755-1869, probate records 1752-1930, and wills 1759-1913.

DURHAM

200 E. Main St., Durham, NC 27707, (919) 560-0480, **<www.co.durham.nc.us>**

- **INCORPORATED:** February 1881
- **PARENT COUNTIES:** Orange, Wake
- **BIRTH RECORDS:** start in 1913, kept by Dept. of Health
- **MARRIAGE:** 1881, Registrar of Deeds
- **DIVORCE:** 1881, Superior Court
- **DEATH:** 1913, Dept. of Health
- **LAND:** 1881, Registrar of Deeds
- **PROBATE:** 1927, Superior Court
- **COURT:** 1925, Superior Court
- **NOTES:** State Archives has court records 1887-1924, naturalization records 1882-1904, and probate records 1875-1926.

EDGECOMBE

301 Saint Andrews St., Box 386, Tarboro, NC 27886, (252) 641-7924, **<www.edgecombecountync.gov>**

- **INCORPORATED:** April 1741
- **PARENT COUNTY:** Bertie
- **BIRTH RECORDS:** start in 1913, kept by Registrar of Deeds
- **MARRIAGE:** 1866, Registrar of Deeds
- **DIVORCE:** 1902, Superior Court
- **DEATH 1913, REGISTRAR OF DEEDS**
- **LAND:** 1759, Registrar of Deeds
- **PROBATE:** 1911, Superior Court
- **COURT:** unknown start, Superior Court
- **NOTES:** State Archives has court records 1744-1746, 1757-1910, divorce records 1835-1901, land records 1732-1741, probate records 1748-1917, and wills 1750-1945. Records prior to 1759 are found in Halifax County.

FORSYTH

102 W. Third St., Box 20639, Winston-Salem, NC 27120, **<www.co.forsyth.nc.us>**

- **INCORPORATED:** January 1849
- **PARENT COUNTY:** Stokes
- **BIRTH RECORDS:** start in 1913, kept by Registrar of Deeds
- **MARRIAGE:** 1849, Registrar of Deeds
- **DIVORCE:** 1930, Superior Court
- **DEATH:** 1913, Registrar of Deeds
- **LAND:** 1849, Registrar of Deeds
- **PROBATE:** 1957, Superior Court
- **COURT:** 1942, Superior Court
- **NOTES:** State Archives has court records 1848-1941, divorce records 1871-1929, probate records 1845-1956, and wills 1840-1900.

FRANKLIN

113 S. Main St., Box 545, Louisburg, NC 27549, (919) 496-3500, **<www.co.franklin.nc.us>**

- **INCORPORATED:** April 1779
- **PARENT COUNTY:** Bute
- **BIRTH RECORDS:** start in 1913, kept by Registrar of Deeds
- **MARRIAGE:** 1869, Registrar of Deeds
- **DIVORCE:** 1929, Superior Court
- **DEATH:** 1913, Registrar of Deeds
- **LAND:** 1776, Registrar of Deeds
- **PROBATE:** 1935, Superior Court
- **COURT:** 1884, Superior Court
- **NOTES:** State Archives has court records 1785-1883, divorce records 1820-1928, marriage records 1789-1868, probate records 1781-1934, and wills 1787-1929.

GASTON

325 N. Marietta St., Box 1578, Gastonia, NC 28053, (704) 862-7680, **<www.co.gaston.nc.us>**

- **INCORPORATED:** December 1846
- **PARENT COUNTY:** Lincoln
- **BIRTH RECORDS:** start in 1913, kept by Registrar of Deeds
- **MARRIAGE:** 1948, Registrar of Deeds
- **DIVORCE:** 1911, Superior Court
- **DEATH:** 1913, Registrar of Deeds
- **LAND:** 1846, Registrar of Deeds
- **PROBATE:** 1929, Superior Court
- **COURT:** 1942, Superior Court
- **NOTES:** State Archives has court records 1847-1941, divorce records 1859-1910, probate records 1839-1928, and wills 1849-1924. Many records were destroyed in courthouse in 1874.

GATES

Box 471, Gatesville, NC 27938, (252) 357-0850, **<www.gatescounty.govoffice2.com>**

- **INCORPORATED:** April 1779
- **PARENT COUNTIES:** Chowan, Hertford, Perquimans
- **BIRTH RECORDS:** start in 1913, kept by Registrar of Deeds

- **MARRIAGE:** 1869, Registrar of Deeds
- **DIVORCE:** 1912, Superior Court
- **DEATH:** 1913, Registrar of Deeds
- **LAND:** 1779, Registrar of Deeds
- **PROBATE:** 1921, Superior Court
- **COURT:** 1869, Superior Court
- **NOTES:** State Archives has court records 1779-1868, divorce records 1817-1911, marriage records 1779-1868, probate records 1765-1920, and wills 1762-1904.

GLASGOW

- **INCORPORATED:** December 1791
- **PARENT COUNTY:** Dobbs
- **NOTES:** Name changed to Greene County in 1799.

GRAHAM

Box 406, Robbinsville, NC 28771, (828) 479-7971, **<www.grahamcounty.org>**

- **INCORPORATED:** Janurary 1872
- **PARENT COUNTY:** Cherokee
- **BIRTH RECORDS:** start in 1913, kept by Registrar of Deeds
- **MARRIAGE:** 1950, Registrar of Deeds
- **DIVORCE:** 1872, Superior Court
- **DEATH:** 1913, Registrar of Deeds
- **LAND:** 1922, Superior Court
- **PROBATE:** 1931, Superior Court
- **COURT:** 1909, Superior Court
- **NOTES:** State Archives has court records 1873-1908, land records 1789-1921, marriage records 1873-1926, and probate records 1847-1930. A portion of Graham County lies in Cherokee land. Contact Eastern Band of the Cherokee at Cherokee Qualla Public Library, Acauoni Road, Cherokee, NC for genealogy information.

GRANVILLE

101 Main St., Oxford, NC 27565, (919) 693-6314, **<www.granvillecounty.org>**

- **INCORPORATED:** June 1746
- **PARENT COUNTY:** Edgecombe
- **BIRTH RECORDS:** start in 1913, kept by Registrar of Deeds
- **MARRIAGE:** 1869, Registrar of Deeds
- **DIVORCE:** 1896, Superior Court
- **DEATH:** 1913, Registrar of Deeds
- **LAND:** 1746, Registrar of Deeds
- **PROBATE:** 1920, Superior Court
- **COURT:** 1901, Superior Court
- **NOTES:** State Archives has court records 1754-1900, divorce records 1819-1895, probate records 1746-1919, and wills 1749-1968.

GREENE

Box 86, Snow Hill, NC 28580, (252) 747-3620, **<www.co.greene.nc.us>**

- **INCORPORATED:** November 1791
- **PARENT COUNTY:** Glasgow
- **BIRTH RECORDS:** start in 1913, kept by Registrar of Deeds
- **MARRIAGE:** 1875, Registrar of Deeds
- **DIVORCE:** 1960, Superior Court
- **DEATH:** 1913, Registrar of Deeds
- **LAND:** 1875, Registrar of Deeds
- **PROBATE:** 1963, Superior Court
- **COURT:** 1960, Superior Court
- **NOTES:** State Archives has court records 1868-1959, divorce records 1875-1959, probate records 1809-1962, and wills 1846-1944. Established as Glasgow County in 1791. Name changed to Greene County in 1799. Courthouse burned in 1876.

GUILFORD

201 S. Eugene St., Box 3427, Greensboro, NC 27402, (336) 641-7556, **<www.co.guilford.nc.us>**

- **INCORPORATED:** December 1771
- **PARENT COUNTIES:** Rowan, Orange
- **BIRTH RECORDS:** start in 1913, kept by Registrar of Deeds
- **MARRIAGE:** 1865, Registrar of Deeds
- **DIVORCE:** 1930, Superior Court
- **DEATH:** 1913, Registrar of Deeds
- **LAND:** 1771, Registrar of Deeds
- **PROBATE:** 1943, Superior Court
- **COURT:** 1925, Superior Court
- **NOTES:** State Archives has court records 1781-1924, divorce records 1820-1929, probate records 1778-1942, and wills 1771-1968. Courthouse burned 1872; many older records still available.

HALIFAX

King St., Box 67, Halifax, NC 27839, (252) 583-2101, **<www.halifaxnc.com>**

- **INCORPORATED:** December 1758
- **PARENT COUNTY:** Edgecombe
- **BIRTH RECORDS:** start in 1913, kept by Registrar of Deeds
- **MARRIAGE:** 1825, Registrar of Deeds
- **DIVORCE:** 1923, Superior Court
- **DEATH:** 1913, Registrar of Deeds
- **LAND:** 1732, Registrar of Deeds
- **PROBATE:** 1925, Superior Court
- **COURT:** 1903, Superior Court
- **NOTES:** State Archives has court records 1759-1902, divorce records 1870-1922, naturalization records 1916-1925, probate records 1762-1924, and wills 1772-1916.

HARNETT

305 W. Cornelius Harnett Blvd. Suite 200, Lillington, NC 27546, (910) 893-7542, **<www.harnett.org>**

- **INCORPORATED:** February 1855
- **PARENT COUNTY:** Cumberland
- **BIRTH RECORDS:** start in 1913, kept by Registrar of Deeds
- **MARRIAGE:** 1862, Registrar of Deeds
- **DIVORCE:** unknown start, Superior Court
- **DEATH:** 1913, Registrar of Deeds
- **LAND:** 1855, Registrar of Deeds
- **PROBATE:** 1884, Superior Court
- **COURT:** 1892, Superior Court
- **NOTES:** Many Court and land records were destroyed in courthouse fires in 1892 and 1894.

HAYWOOD

215 N. Main St., Waynesville, NC 28786, (828) 452-6635, **<www.haywoodnc.net>**

- **INCORPORATED:** December 1808

- **PARENT COUNTY:** Buncombe
- **BIRTH RECORDS:** start in 1913, kept by Registrar of Deeds
- **MARRIAGE:** 1869, Registrar of Deeds
- **DEATH:** 1913, Registrar of Deeds
- **LAND:** 1949, Registrar of Deeds
- **PROBATE:** 1943, Superior Court
- **COURT:** 1914, Superior Court
- **NOTES:** State Archives has court records 1815-1913, divorce records 1829-1944, land records 1801-1942, marriage records 1808-1868, probate records 1809-1942, and wills 1803-1937.

HENDERSON
200 N. Grove St. Suite 129, Hendersonville, NC 28792, (828) 697-4901, **<www.hendersoncountync.org>**
- **INCORPORATED:** December 1838
- **PARENT COUNTY:** Buncombe
- **BIRTH RECORDS:** start in 1914, kept by Registrar of Deeds
- **MARRIAGE:** 1968, Registrar of Deeds
- **DIVORCE:** 1932, Superior Court
- **DEATH:** 1914, Registrar of Deeds
- **LAND:** 1893, Registrar of Deeds
- **PROBATE:** 1969, Superior Court
- **COURT:** 1960, Superior Court
- **NOTES:** State Archives has court records 1808-1959, divorce records 1842-1931, marriage records 1838-1967, probate records 1838-1968, and wills 1797, 1817, and 1835-1969

HERTFORD
701 N. King St., Box 36, Winton, NC 27986, (252) 358-7850, **<www.co.hertford.nc.us>**
- **INCORPORATED:** May. 1, 1760
- **PARENT COUNTIES:** Bertie, Chowan, Northampton
- **BIRTH RECORDS:** start in 1913, kept by Registrar of Deeds
- **MARRIAGE:** 1868, Registrar of Deeds
- **DIVORCE:** 1914, Superior Court
- **DEATH:** 1913, Registrar of Deeds
- **LAND:** 1941, Registrar of Deeds
- **PROBATE:** 1915, Superior Court
- **COURT:** 1916, Superior Court
- **MILITARY:** 1928, Registrar of Deeds
- **NOTES:** State Archives has court records 1830-1915, divorce records 1871-1914, land records 1775-1940, probate records 1830-1914, and wills 1763, and 1861-1903. Courthouse burned in 1832 and 1862.

HOKE
304 N. Main St., Raeford, NC 28376, (910) 875-2035, **<www.hokecounty.net>**
- **INCORPORATED:** February 1911
- **PARENT COUNTIES:** Cumberland, Robeson
- **BIRTH RECORDS:** start in 1913, kept by Registrar of Deeds
- **MARRIAGE:** 1911, Registrar of Deeds
- **DIVORCE:** 1911, Superior Court
- **DEATH:** 1913, Registrar of Deeds
- **LAND:** 1911, Registrar of Deeds
- **PROBATE:** 1911, Superior Court
- **COURT:** 1911, Superior Court

HYDE
Box 294, Swan Quarter, NC 27885, (252) 926-4181, **<www.hydecounty.org/government>**
- **INCORPORATED:** December 1705
- **PARENT COUNTY:** Bath
- **BIRTH RECORDS:** start in 1913, kept by Registrar of Deeds
- **MARRIAGE:** 1850, Registrar of Deeds
- **DIVORCE:** 1915, Superior Court
- **DEATH:** 1913, Registrar of Deeds
- **LAND:** 1736, Registrar of Deeds
- **PROBATE:** 1934, Superior Court
- **COURT:** 1915, Superior Court
- **NOTES:** State Archives has court records 1736-1914, divorce records 1829-1914, probate records 1735-1933, and wills 1760-1908. Formerly Wickham, Precinct of Bath County. Name changed to Hyde, 1712.

IREDELL
201 E. Water St., Box 904, Statesville, NC 28677, (704) 872-7468, **<www.co.iredell.nc.us>**
- **INCORPORATED:** Nov. 3, 1788
- **PARENT COUNTY:** Rowan
- **BIRTH RECORDS:** start in 1913, kept by Registrar of Deeds
- **MARRIAGE:** 1869, Registrar of Deeds
- **DIVORCE:** 1935, Superior Court
- **DEATH:** 1913, Registrar of Deeds
- **LAND:** 1788, Registrar of Deeds
- **PROBATE:** 1971, Superior Court
- **COURT:** 1910, Superior Court
- **NOTES:** State Archives has court records 1788-1909, divorce records 1855-1934, marriage records 1788-1868, probate records 1790-1970, and wills 1787-1917. Courthouse burned in 1854.

JACKSON
401 Grindstaff Cove Rd., Room 103, Sylva, NC 28779, (828) 586-7592, **<www.jacksonnc.org>**
- **INCORPORATED:** January 1851
- **PARENT COUNTIES:** Haywood, Macon
- **BIRTH RECORDS:** start in 1913, kept by Registrar of Deeds
- **MARRIAGE:** ca. 1890 Registrar of Deeds
- **DIVORCE:** 1853, Superior Court
- **DEATH:** 1913, Registrar of Deeds
- **LAND:** 1890, Registrar of Deeds
- **PROBATE:** 1880, Superior Court
- **COURT:** 1911, Superior Court
- **NOTES:** A portion of Jackson County lies in Cherokee land. Contact Cherokee Qualla Public Library, Acauoni Road, Cherokee, NC for genealogy information. State Archives has court records 1853-1910 and probate records 1853-1879.

JOHNSTON
Box 118, Smithfield, NC 27577, (919) 989-5160, **<www.co.johnston.nc.us>**
- **INCORPORATED:** June 1746
- **PARENT COUNTY:** Craven
- **BIRTH RECORDS:** start in 1913, kept by Registrar of Deeds
- **MARRIAGE:** 1869, Registrar of Deeds
- **DEATH:** 1913, Registrar of Deeds

- **LAND:** 1940, Registrar of Deeds
- **PROBATE:** 1963, Superior Court
- **COURT:** 1914, Superior Court
- **NOTES:** State Archives has court records 1759-1913, land records 1748-1939, marriage records 1746-1868, and probate records 1771-1962.

JONES

Box 189, Trenton, NC 28585, (252) 448-2551, **<www.co.jones.nc.us>**

- **INCORPORATED:** Jan. 19, 1779
- **PARENT COUNTY:** Craven
- **BIRTH RECORDS:** start in 1913, kept by Registrar of Deeds
- **MARRIAGE:** 1875, Registrar of Deeds
- **DIVORCE:** 1906, Superior Court
- **DEATH:** 1913, Registrar of Deeds
- **LAND:** 1779, Registrar of Deeds
- **PROBATE:** 1855, Superior Court
- **COURT:** 1933, Superior Court
- **NOTES:** State Archives has court records 1807-1932, marriage records 1851-1874, probate records 1780-1854, and wills 1779-1935. Courthouse burned in 1862.

LEE

Box 2040, Sanford, NC 27331, (919) 774-4821, **<www.leecountync.com>**

- **INCORPORATED:** April 1, 1908
- **PARENT COUNTIES:** Chatham, Moore
- **BIRTH RECORDS:** start in 1913, kept by Registrar of Deeds
- **MARRIAGE:** 1908, Registrar of Deeds
- **DIVORCE:** 1908, Superior Court
- **DEATH:** 1913, Registrar of Deeds
- **LAND:** 1908, Registrar of Deeds
- **PROBATE:** 1908, Superior Court
- **COURT:** 1908, Superior Court

LENOIR

Box 3289, Kinston, NC 28502, (252) 559-6420, **<www.co.lenoir.nc.us>**

- **INCORPORATED:** December 1791
- **PARENT COUNTY:** Dobbs
- **BIRTH RECORDS:** start in 1913, kept by Registrar of Deeds
- **MARRIAGE:** 1896, Registrar of Deeds
- **DIVORCE:** 1915, Superior Court
- **DEATH:** 1913, Registrar of Deeds
- **LAND:** 1896, Registrar of Deeds
- **PROBATE:** 1957, Superior Court
- **COURT:** 1940, Superior Court
- **NOTES:** State Archives has court records 1866-1939, divorce records 1880-1914, marriage records 1791-1868, and probate records 1830-1956. Registrar of Deeds has Wills 1824-1916. Courthouse burned in 1878 and 1880.

LINCOLN

115 W. Main St., Box 218, Lincolnton, NC 28093, (704) 736-8530, **<www.co.lincoln.nc.us>**

- **INCORPORATED:** April 1779
- **PARENT COUNTY:** Tryon
- **BIRTH RECORDS:** start in 1913, kept by Registrar of Deeds
- **MARRIAGE:** 1869, Registrar of Deeds
- **DIVORCE:** 1922, Superior Court
- **DEATH:** 1913, Registrar of Deeds
- **LAND:** 1763, Registrar of Deeds
- **PROBATE:** 1926, Superior Court
- **COURT:** 1912, Superior Court
- **NOTES:** State Archives has court records 1781-1911, divorce records 1811-1921, marriage records 1779-1868, and probate records 1779-1925.

MACON

5 W. Main St., Franklin, NC 28734, (828) 349-2095, **<www.maconnc.org>**

- **INCORPORATED:** 1828
- **PARENT COUNTY:** Haywood
- **BIRTH RECORDS:** start in 1913, kept by Registrar of Deeds
- **MARRIAGE:** 1892, Registrar of Deeds
- **DIVORCE:** 1914, Superior Court
- **DEATH:** 1913, Registrar of Deeds
- **LAND:** 1820, Registrar of Deeds
- **PROBATE:** 1921, Superior Court
- **COURT:** 1915, Superior Court
- **NOTES:** State Archives has court records 1829-1914, divorce records 1835-1913, marriage records 1828-1891, probate records 1831-1920, and wills 1830-1905, and 1933.

MADISON

Box 66, 75 Blannahasset Island, Marshall, NC 28753, (828) 649-3131, **<www.madisoncountync.org>**

- **INCORPORATED:** January 1851
- **PARENT COUNTIES:** Buncombe, Yancey
- **BIRTH RECORDS:** start in 1913, kept by Registrar of Deeds
- **MARRIAGE:** 1946, Registrar of Deeds
- **DIVORCE:** 1927, Superior Court
- **DEATH:** 1913, Registrar of Deeds
- **LAND:** 1851, Registrar of Deeds
- **PROBATE:** 1944, Superior Court
- **COURT:** 1926, Superior Court
- **NOTES:** State Archives has court records 1837-1925, divorce records 1854-1926, marriage records 1851-1945, probate records 1833-1943, and wills 1851-1912.

MARTIN

Box 348, Williamston, NC 27892, (252) 792-1683, **<www.martincountyncgov.com>**

- **INCORPORATED:** March 1774
- **PARENT COUNTIES:** Halifax, Tyrrell
- **BIRTH RECORDS:** start in 1913, kept by Registrar of Deeds
- **MARRIAGE:** 1872, Registrar of Deeds
- **DIVORCE:** 1904, Superior Court
- **DEATH:** 1913, Registrar of Deeds
- **LAND:** 1776, Registrar of Deeds
- **PROBATE:** 1907, Superior Court
- **COURT:** 1913, Superior Court
- **NOTES:** State Archives has court records 1838-1912, divorce records 1882-1903, and probate records 1820-1906. Courthouse burned in 1884.

MCDOWELL
21 S. Main St. Suite A, Marion, NC 28752, (828) 652-4727, **<www.mcdowellgov.com>**
- **INCORPORATED:** December 1842
- **PARENT COUNTIES:** Burke, Rutherford
- **BIRTH RECORDS:** start in 1913, kept by Registrar of Deeds
- **MARRIAGE:** 1869, Registrar of Deeds
- **DIVORCE:** 1942, Superior Court
- **DEATH:** 1913, Registrar of Deeds
- **LAND:** 1917, Registrar of Deeds
- **PROBATE:** 1940, Superior Court
- **COURT:** 1926, Superior Court
- **NOTES:** State Archives has court records 1843-1925, divorce records 1849-1941, land records 1813-1916, marriage records 1842-1868, and probate records 1830-1832, 1842-1939, and wills 1841-1920.

MECKLENBURG
720 E. Fourth St., Charlotte, NC 28202, (704) 336-2443, **<www.charmeck.org>**
- **INCORPORATED:** Feb. 1, 1763
- **PARENT COUNTY:** Anson
- **BIRTH RECORDS:** start in 1913, kept by Dept. of Health
- **MARRIAGE:** 1869, Registrar of Deeds
- **DIVORCE:** 1970, Superior Court
- **DEATH:** 1913, Dept. of Health
- **LAND:** 1763, Registrar of Deeds
- **PROBATE:** 1958, Superior Court
- **COURT:** 1886, Superior Court
- **NOTES:** State Archives has court records 1774-1885, divorce records 1846-1969, marriage records 1783-1868, naturalization records 1822, 1886-1927, probate records 1762-1957, and wills 1749-1918.

MITCHELL
26 Crimson Laurel Circle Suite #4, Bakersville, NC 28705, (828) 688-2139 ext. 1, **<www.mitchellcounty.org>**
- **INCORPORATED:** February 1861
- **PARENT COUNTIES:** Burke, Caldwell, McDowell, Watauga, Yancey
- **BIRTH RECORDS:** start in 1913, kept by Registrar of Deeds
- **MARRIAGE:** 1861, Registrar of Deeds
- **DIVORCE:** 1916, Superior Court
- **DEATH:** 1913, Registrar of Deeds
- **LAND:** 1952, Registrar of Deeds
- **PROBATE:** 1947, Superior Court
- **COURT:** 1911, Superior Court
- **NOTES:** State Archives has court records 1861-1910, divorce records 1867-1915, land records 1846-1951, probate records 1826-1946, and wills 1823-1927.

MONTGOMERY
102 E. Main St., Troy, NC 27371, (910) 576-4271, **<www.montgomeryrod.net>**
- **INCORPORATED:** April 1779
- **PARENT COUNTY:** Anson
- **BIRTH RECORDS:** start in 1913, kept by Registrar of Deeds
- **MARRIAGE:** 1869, Registrar of Deeds
- **DIVORCE:** 1908, Superior Court
- **DEATH:** 1913, Registrar of Deeds
- **LAND:** 1843, Registrar of Deeds
- **PROBATE:** 1970, Superior Court
- **COURT:** 1913, Superior Court
- **NOTES:** State Archives has court records 1843-1912, divorce records 1856-1907, marriage records 1779-1868, probate records 1818-1970, and wills 1785-1970. Courthouse burned in 1835.

MOORE
Box 1210, Carthage, NC 28327, (910) 947-6370, **<www.moorecountync.gov>**
- **INCORPORATED:** April 1784
- **PARENT COUNTY:** Cumberland
- **BIRTH RECORDS:** start in 1913, kept by Registrar of Deeds
- **MARRIAGE:** 1889, Registrar of Deeds
- **DIVORCE:** 1916, Superior Court
- **DEATH:** 1913, Registrar of Deeds
- **LAND:** 1924, Registrar of Deeds
- **PROBATE:** 1922, Superior Court
- **COURT:** 1874, Superior Court
- **NOTES:** State Archives has court records 1784-1873, divorce records 1887-1915, land records 1797-1923, naturalization records 1887-1914, probate records 1828-1921, and wills 1831, 1859-1921. Courthouse burned in 1889.

NASH
Box 974, Nashville, NC 27856, (252) 459-9836, **<www.co.nash.nc.us>**
- **INCORPORATED:** November 1777
- **PARENT COUNTY:** Edgecombe
- **BIRTH RECORDS:** start in 1913, kept by Registrar of Deeds
- **MARRIAGE:** 1867, Registrar of Deeds
- **DIVORCE:** 1867, Registrar of Deeds
- **DEATH:** 1913, Registrar of Deeds
- **LAND:** 1777, Registrar of Deeds
- **PROBATE:** 1910, Superior Court
- **COURT:** 1916, Superior Court
- **NOTES:** State Archives has court records 1778-1915, divorce records 1818-1866, marriage records 1777-1868, probate records 1770-1909, and wills 1778-1922.

NEW HANOVER
216 N. Second St. Room 4, Wilmington, NC 28401, (910) 341-4530, **<www.nhcgov.com>**
- **INCORPORATED:** November 1729
- **PARENT COUNTY:** Craven
- **BIRTH RECORDS:** start in 1913, kept by Registrar of Deeds
- **MARRIAGE:** 1869, Registrar of Deeds
- **DIVORCE:** 1946, Superior Court
- **DEATH:** 1913, Registrar of Deeds
- **LAND:** 1729, Registrar of Deeds
- **PROBATE:** 1940, Superior Court
- **COURT:** 1911, Superior Court
- **NOTES:** State Archives has court records 1738-1910, divorce records 1858-1945, marriage records 1741-1868, probate records 1746-1939, and wills 1732-1961.

NORTHAMPTON

Box 128, Jackson, NC 27845, (252) 534-2511,
<www.northamptonnc.com>

- **INCORPORATED:** 1741
- **PARENT COUNTY:** Bertie
- **BIRTH RECORDS:** start in 1913, kept by Registrar of Deeds
- **MARRIAGE:** 1869, Registrar of Deeds
- **DIVORCE:** 1952, Superior Court
- **DEATH:** 1913, Registrar of Deeds
- **LAND:** 1741, Registrar of Deeds
- **PROBATE:** 1930, Superior Court
- **COURT:** 1909, Superior Court
- **NOTES:** State Archives has court records 1792-1908, divorce records 1818-1951, marriage records 1811-1868, probate records 1781-1929, and wills 1764-1950.

ONSLOW

109 Old Bridge St., Jacksonville, NC 28540, (910) 347-3451,
<www.co.onslow.nc.us>

- **INCORPORATED:** 1734
- **PARENT COUNTY:** New Hanover
- **BIRTH RECORDS:** start in 1914, kept by Registrar of Deeds
- **MARRIAGE:** 1869, Registrar of Deeds
- **DIVORCE:** 1907, Superior Court
- **DEATH:** 1914, Registrar of Deeds
- **LAND:** 1734, Registrar of Deeds
- **PROBATE:** 1915, Superior Court
- **COURT:** 1910, Superior Court
- **NOTES:** State Archives has court records 1732-1909, divorce records 1866-1906, marriage records 1745-1868, probate records 1735-1914, and wills 1746-1968. Many records were destroyed in storms in 1752 and 1786.

ORANGE

200 S. Cameron St., Box 8181, Hillsborough, NC 27278, (919) 245-2675, **<www.co.orange.nc.us>**

- **INCORPORATED:** March 1752
- **PARENT COUNTIES:** Bladen, Granville, Johnston
- **BIRTH RECORDS:** start in 1913, kept by Registrar of Deeds
- **MARRIAGE:** 1752, Registrar of Deeds
- **DIVORCE:** 1909, Superior Court
- **DEATH:** 1913, Registrar of Deeds
- **LAND:** 1752, Registrar of Deeds
- **PROBATE:** 1945, Superior Court
- **COURT:** 1890, Superior Court
- **NOTES:** State Archives has court records 1752-1889, divorce records 1824-1908, probate records 1754-1944, and wills 1753-1968. Courthouse burned in 1789.

PAMLICO

Box 433, Bayboro, NC 28515, (252) 745-4421,
<www.co.pamlico.nc.us>

- **INCORPORATED:** Feb. 8, 1872
- **PARENT COUNTIES:** Beaufort, Craven
- **BIRTH RECORDS:** start in 1913, kept by Registrar of Deeds
- **MARRIAGE:** 1872, Registrar of Deeds
- **DIVORCE:** 1916, Superior Court
- **DEATH:** 1913, Registrar of Deeds
- **LAND:** 1872, Registrar of Deeds
- **PROBATE:** 1940, Superior Court
- **COURT:** 1969, Superior Court
- **NOTES:** State Archives has court records 1872-1968, divorce records 1874-1915, probate records 1872-1939, and wills 1872-1921.

PAMPTECOUGH

- **INCORPORATED:** December 1705
- **PARENT COUNTY:** Bath
- **NOTES:** See Beaufort County. Name changed to Beaufort in 1712.

PASQUOTANK

206 E. Main, Box 154, Elizabeth City, NC 27909, (252) 335-4367,
<www.co.pasquotank.nc.us>

- **INCORPORATED:** 1668
- **PARENT COUNTY:** Albemarle
- **BIRTH RECORDS:** start in 1913, kept by Registrar of Deeds
- **MARRIAGE:** 1869, Registrar of Deeds
- **DIVORCE:** 1911, Superior Court
- **DEATH:** 1913, Registrar of Deeds
- **LAND:** 1948, Registrar of Deeds
- **PROBATE:** 1932, Superior Court
- **COURT:** 1923, Superior Court
- **NOTES:** State Archives has court records 1737-1922, divorce records 1838-1910, land records 1666-1947, marriage records 1741-1868, probate records 1712-1931, and wills 1709-1917.

PENDER

300 E. Fremont St., Box 43, Burgaw, NC 28425, (910) 259-1225,
<www.pender-county.com>

- **INCORPORATED:** February 1875
- **PARENT COUNTY:** New Hanover
- **BIRTH RECORDS:** start in 1913, kept by Registrar of Deeds
- **MARRIAGE:** 1937, Registrar of Deeds
- **DIVORCE:** 1875, Superior Court
- **DEATH:** 1913, Registrar of Deeds
- **LAND:** 1873, Registrar of Deeds
- **PROBATE:** 1970, Superior Court
- **COURT:** 1875, Superior Court
- **NOTES:** State Archives has marriage records 1875-1936, probate records 1866-1969, and wills 1832, 1875-1969.

PERQUIMANS

Box 74, Hertford, NC 27944, (252) 426-5660,
<www.co.perquimans.nc.us>

- **INCORPORATED:** 1668
- **PARENT COUNTY:** Albemarle
- **MARRIAGE RECORDS:** start in 1869, kept by Registrar of Deeds
- **DIVORCE:** 1913, Superior Court
- **LAND:** 1681, Registrar of Deeds
- **PROBATE:** 1931, Superior Court
- **COURT:** 1909, Superior Court
- **NOTES:** State Archives has court records 1688-1908, divorce records 1824-1912, marriage records 1742-1868, probate records 1714-1930, and wills 1711-1909. Perquimans County was known as Berkeley Precinct 1670-1682.

PERSON

105 S. Main St., Roxboro, NC 27573, (336) 597-1733,
<www.personcounty.net>

- **INCORPORATED:** December 1791
- **PARENT COUNTY:** Caswell
- **BIRTH RECORDS:** start in 1913, kept by Registrar of Deeds
- **MARRIAGE:** 1913, Registrar of Deeds
- **DIVORCE:** 1940, Superior Court
- **DEATH:** 1913, Registrar of Deeds
- **LAND:** 1919, Registrar of Deeds
- **PROBATE:** 1952, Superior Court
- **COURT:** 1910, Superior Court
- **NOTES:** State Archives has court records 1792-1909, divorce records 1821-1939, land records 1777-1918, marriage records 1791-1868, probate records 1791-1951, and wills 1790-1943.

PITT

W. Third St., Box 35, Greenville, NC 27835, (252) 902-1650,
<www.co.pitt.nc.us>

- **INCORPORATED:** April 1760
- **PARENT COUNTY:** Beaufort
- **BIRTH RECORDS:** start in 1913, kept by Registrar of Deeds
- **MARRIAGE:** 1913, Registrar of Deeds
- **DIVORCE:** 1907, Superior Court
- **DEATH:** 1913, Registrar of Deeds
- **LAND:** 1762, Registrar of Deeds
- **PROBATE:** 1948, Superior Court
- **COURT:** 1922, Superior Court
- **NOTES:** State Archives has court records 1858-1921, divorce records 1861, 1866, 1870-1906, marriage records 1826-1833, 1867-1875, probate records 1791, 1827-1947, and wills 1805, 1808, 1817, 1836-1930, and 1938. Courthouse burned 1857.

POLK

Box 308, Columbus, NC 28722, (828) 894-8450,
<www.polkcounty.org>

- **INCORPORATED:** January 1847
- **PARENT COUNTIES:** Henderson, Rutherford
- **BIRTH RECORDS:** start in 1913, kept by Registrar of Deeds
- **MARRIAGE:** 1855, Registrar of Deeds
- **DIVORCE:** 1910, Superior Court
- **DEATH:** 1913, Registrar of Deeds
- **LAND:** 1855, Registrar of Deeds
- **PROBATE:** 1914, Superior Court
- **COURT:** 1943, Superior Court
- **NOTES:** State Archives has court records 1847-1848, 1855-1942, divorce records 1856-1909, and probate records 1851-1913. Polk County was originally established in 1847 from Henderson and Rutherford Counties. In 1848 the act was appealed. Polk was reestablished in 1855.

RANDOLPH

158 Worth St., Asheboro, NC 27203, (336) 318-6960,
<www.co.randolph.nc.us>

- **INCORPORATED:** April 1779
- **PARENT COUNTY:** Guilford
- **BIRTH RECORDS:** start in 1913, kept by Registrar of Deeds
- **MARRIAGE:** 1913, Registrar of Deeds
- **DIVORCE:** 1928, Superior Court
- **DEATH:** 1913, Registrar of Deeds
- **LAND:** 1779, Registrar of Deeds
- **PROBATE:** 1929, Superior Court
- **COURT:** 1940, Superior Court
- **NOTES:** State Archives has court records 1783-1939, divorce records 1804-1927, marriage records 1779-1868, probate records 1781-1928, and wills 1775-1902.

RICHMOND

114 E. Franklin St. #101, Rockingham, NC 28379, (910) 997-8250,
<www.co.richmond.nc.us>

- **INCORPORATED:** April 14, 1779
- **PARENT COUNTY:** Anson
- **BIRTH RECORDS:** start in 1913, kept by Registrar of Deeds
- **MARRIAGE:** 1900, Registrar of Deeds
- **DIVORCE:** 1911, Superior Court
- **DEATH:** 1913, Registrar of Deeds
- **LAND:** 1784, Registrar of Deeds
- **PROBATE:** 1934, Superior Court
- **COURT:** 1914, Superior Court
- **NOTES:** State Archives has court records 1779-1913, divorce records 1816-1910, marriage records 1791-1872, probate records 1772-1933, and wills 1779-1915.

ROBESON

500 N. Elm St., Box 22, Lumberton, NC 28358, (910) 671-3044,
<www.co.robeson.nc.us>

- **INCORPORATED:** Jan. 6, 1787
- **PARENT COUNTY:** Bladen
- **BIRTH RECORDS:** start in 1913, kept by Registrar of Deeds
- **MARRIAGE:** 1869, Registrar of Deeds
- **DIVORCE:** 1921, Superior Court
- **DEATH:** 1916, Registrar of Deeds
- **LAND:** 1787, Registrar of Deeds
- **PROBATE:** 1936, Superior Court
- **COURT:** 1913, Superior Court
- **NOTES:** State Archives has court records 1797-1912, divorce records 1841-1920, marriage records 1803-1868, probate records 1801-1935, and wills 1783-1918, 1930, 1933, and 1935.

ROCKINGHAM

371 NC 65 #212, Box 56, Wentworth, NC 27320, (336) 342-8100,
<www.co.rockingham.nc.us>

- **INCORPORATED:** Dec. 29, 1785
- **PARENT COUNTY:** Guilford
- **BIRTH RECORDS:** start in 1913, kept by Registrar of Deeds
- **MARRIAGE:** 1869, Registrar of Deeds
- **DIVORCE:** 1922, Superior Court
- **DEATH:** 1913, Registrar of Deeds
- **LAND:** 1787, Registrar of Deeds
- **PROBATE:** 1927, Superior Court
- **COURT:** 1869, Superior Court
- **NOTES:** State Archives has court records 1786-1868, divorce records 1824-1921, marriage records 1785-1868, probate records 1780-1926, and wills 1772-1925, 1936, and 1938.

ROWAN

Box 2568, Salisbury, NC 28145, (704) 638-3102,
<www.co.rowan.nc.us>

- **INCORPORATED:** March 27, 1753
- **PARENT COUNTY:** Anson
- **BIRTH RECORDS:** start in 1913, kept by Registrar of Deeds
- **MARRIAGE:** 1753, Registrar of Deeds
- **DIVORCE:** 1901, Superior Court
- **DEATH:** 1913, Registrar of Deeds
- **LAND:** 1755, Registrar of Deeds
- **PROBATE:** 1930, Superior Court
- **COURT:** 1911, Superior Court
- **NOTES:** State Archives has court records 1753-1910, divorce records 1805-1900, naturalization records 1823-1915, probate records 1753-1929, and wills 1743-1900. Federal troops destroyed some records in 1865.

RUTHERFORD

229 N. Main St., Box 551, Rutherfordton, NC 28139, (828) 287-6155,
<www.rutherfordcountync.gov>

- **INCORPORATED:** April 14, 1779
- **PARENT COUNTY:** Tryon
- **BIRTH RECORDS:** start in 1913, kept by Registrar of Deeds
- **MARRIAGE:** 1779, Registrar of Deeds
- **DIVORCE:** 1941, Superior Court
- **DEATH:** 1913, Registrar of Deeds
- **LAND:** 1779, Registrar of Deeds
- **PROBATE:** 1969, Superior Court
- **COURT:** 1912, Superior Court
- **NOTES:** State Archives has court records 1783-1911, divorce records 1870-1940, probate records 1802-1968, and wills 1784-1968. Courthouse burned in 1907.

SAMPSON

Sampson County Courthouse, Room 107, Main St., Clinton, NC 28328, (910) 592-8026, **<www.sampsonnc.com>**

- **INCORPORATED:** April 1784
- **PARENT COUNTY:** Duplin
- **BIRTH RECORDS:** start in 1913, kept by Registrar of Deeds
- **MARRIAGE:** 1865, Registrar of Deeds
- **DIVORCE:** 1922, Superior Court
- **DEATH:** 1913, Registrar of Deeds
- **LAND:** 1784, Registrar of Deeds
- **PROBATE:** 1924, Superior Court
- **COURT:** 1926, Superior Court
- **NOTES:** State Archives has court records 1794-1925, divorce records 1869-1921, probate records 1784-1923, and wills 1778-1953. Courthouse burned 1921.

SCOTLAND

212 Biggs St., Box 769, Laurinburg, NC 28353, (910) 277-2577,
<www.scotlandcounty.org>

- **INCORPORATED:** Feb. 20, 1899
- **PARENT COUNTY:** Richmond
- **BIRTH RECORDS:** start in 1913, kept by Registrar of Deeds
- **MARRIAGE:** 1900, Registrar of Deeds
- **DIVORCE:** 1949, Superior Court
- **DEATH:** 1913, Registrar of Deeds
- **LAND:** 1900, Registrar of Deeds
- **PROBATE:** 1952, Superior Court
- **COURT:** 1900, Superior Court
- **NOTES:** State Archives has divorce records 1901-1948, probate records 1887-1951, and wills, 1893, 1896, and 1900-1937.

STANLY

201 S. Second St., Albemarle, NC 28001, (704) 983-3640,
<www.co.stanly.nc.us>

- **INCORPORATED:** Jan. 11, 1841
- **PARENT COUNTY:** Montgomery
- **BIRTH RECORDS:** start in 1913, kept by Registrar of Deeds
- **MARRIAGE:** 1865, Registrar of Deeds
- **DIVORCE:** 1921, Superior Court
- **DEATH:** 1913, Registrar of Deeds
- **LAND:** 1841, Registrar of Deeds
- **PROBATE:** 1953, Superior Court
- **NOTES:** State Archives has divorce records 1854-1920 and probate records 1820, 1839-1952.

STOKES

1014 Main St., Danbury, NC 27016, (336) 593-2811,
<www.co.stokes.nc.us>

- **INCORPORATED:** Nov. 2, 1789
- **PARENT COUNTY:** Surry
- **BIRTH RECORDS:** start in 1913, kept by Registrar of Deeds
- **MARRIAGE:** 1869, Registrar of Deeds
- **DIVORCE:** 1942, Superior Court
- **DEATH:** 1913, Registrar of Deeds
- **LAND:** 1930, Registrar of Deeds
- **PROBATE:** 1942, Superior Court
- **COURT:** 1913, Superior Court
- **NOTES:** State Archives has court records 1790-1912, divorce records 1816-1941, land records 1760-1929, marriage records 1790-1868, probate records 1753-1941, and wills 1775-1925.

SURRY

201 E. Kapp St., Box 303, Dobson, NC 27017, (336) 401-8150,
<www.co.surry.nc.us>

- **INCORPORATED:** April 1, 1771
- **PARENT COUNTY:** Rowan
- **BIRTH RECORDS:** start in 1913, kept by Registrar of Deeds
- **MARRIAGE:** 1771, Registrar of Deeds
- **DIVORCE:** 1928, Superior Court
- **DEATH:** 1913, Registrar of Deeds
- **LAND:** 1771, Registrar of Deeds
- **PROBATE:** 1944, Superior Court
- **COURT:** 1911, Superior Court
- **BURIAL:** unknown start, Registrar of Deeds
- **NOTES:** State Archives Court records 1778-1910, divorce records 1826-1927, probate records 1771-1943, and wills 1770-1970.

SWAIN

101 Mitchell St., Box 1183, Bryson, NC 28713, (828) 488-9273,
<www.swaincountync.gov>

- **INCORPORATED:** February 1871
- **PARENT COUNTIES:** Jackson, Macon
- **BIRTH RECORDS:** start in 1913, kept by Registrar of Deeds

- **MARRIAGE:** 1871, Registrar of Deeds
- **DIVORCE:** 1871, Superior Court
- **DEATH:** 1913, Registrar of Deeds
- **LAND:** 1871, Registrar of Deeds
- **PROBATE:** 1871, Superior Court
- **COURT:** 1908, Superior Court
- **NOTES:** State Archives has court records 1871-1907. A portion of Swain County lies in Cherokee land. For genealogy information on the Eastern Band of the Cherokee contact the Cherokee Qualla Public Library, Acauoni Road, Cherokee, NC. Many records were destroyed in a courthouse fire in 1879.

TRANSYLVANIA

12 E. Main St., Brevard, NC 28712, (828) 884-3162,
<www.transylvaniacounty.org>

- **INCORPORATED:** February 1861
- **PARENT COUNTIES:** Henderson, Jackson
- **BIRTH RECORDS:** start in 1913, kept by Registrar of Deeds
- **MARRIAGE:** 1885, Registrar of Deeds
- **DIVORCE:** 1922, Superior Court
- **DEATH:** 1913, Registrar of Deeds
- **LAND:** 1924, Registrar of Deeds
- **PROBATE:** 1952, Superior Court
- **COURT:** 1911, Superior Court
- **NOTES:** State Archives has court records 1861-1910, divorce records 1866-1921, land records 1827-1923, marriage records 1861-1872, probate records 1810-1951, and wills 1838-1926.

TRYON

- **INCORPORATED:** 1768
- **PARENT COUNTY:** Mecklenburg
- **NOTES:** See Lincoln and Rutherford Counties. Discontinued 1779. Split into Lincoln and Rutherford Counties.

TYRRELL

Box 449, Columbia, NC 27925, (252) 796-2901,
<www.ncgenweb.us/tyrrell/TYRRELL.HTM>

- **INCORPORATED:** Nov. 27, 1729
- **PARENT COUNTIES:** Chowan, Currituck, Pasquotank
- **BIRTH RECORDS:** start in 1913, kept by Registrar of Deeds
- **MARRIAGE:** 1742, Registrar of Deeds
- **DIVORCE:** 1926, Superior Court
- **DEATH:** 1913, Registrar of Deeds
- **LAND:** 1736, Registrar of Deeds
- **PROBATE:** 1936, Superior Court
- **COURT:** 1884, Superior Court
- **NOTES:** State Archives has court records 1735-1883, divorce records 1815-1925, probate records 1738-1935, and wills 1744-1925.

UNION

Box 248, Monroe, NC 28111, (704) 283-3727,
<www.co.union.nc.us>

- **INCORPORATED:** December 1842
- **PARENT COUNTIES:** Anson, Mecklenburg
- **BIRTH RECORDS:** start in 1913, kept by Registrar of Deeds
- **MARRIAGE:** 1842, Registrar of Deeds
- **DIVORCE:** 1929, Superior Court
- **DEATH:** 1913, Registrar of Deeds
- **LAND:** 1842, Registrar of Deeds
- **PROBATE:** 1970, Superior Court
- **COURT:** 1921, Superior Court
- **NOTES:** State Archives has court records 1843-1920, divorce records 1865-1928, probate records 1818-1969, and wills 1837-1968, 1977, 1978.

VANCE

122 Young St. Suite F, Henderson, NC 27536, (252) 738-2110,
<www.vancecounty.org>

- **INCORPORATED:** March 1881
- **PARENT COUNTIES:** Franklin, Granville, Warren
- **BIRTH RECORDS:** start in 1913, kept by Registrar of Deeds
- **MARRIAGE:** 1881, Registrar of Deeds
- **DIVORCE:** 1881, Superior Court
- **DEATH:** 1913, Registrar of Deeds
- **LAND:** 1881, Registrar of Deeds
- **PROBATE:** 1881, Superior Court
- **COURT:** 1881, Superior Court

WAKE

St. Garland James Bldg., Box 1897, Raleigh, NC 27602, (919) 856-5460, **<www.wakegov.com>**

- **INCORPORATED:** Dec. 5, 1770
- **PARENT COUNTIES:** Cumberland, Johnston, Orange
- **BIRTH RECORDS:** start in 1913, kept by Registrar of Deeds
- **MARRIAGE:** 1866, Registrar of Deeds
- **DIVORCE:** 1953, Superior Court
- **DEATH:** 1913, Registrar of Deeds
- **LAND:** 1774, Registrar of Deeds
- **PROBATE:** 1953, Superior Court
- **COURT:** 1942, Superior Court
- **NOTES:** State Archives has court records 1777-1941, Death records 1900-1909, divorce records 1831-1952, marriage records 1790-1865, naturalization records 1821-1908, probate records 1771-1952, and wills 1771-1966. Fire at the Registrar's office in 1832 destroyed some deed books.

WARREN

Box 506, Warrenton, NC 27589, (252) 257-3265,
<www.warrencountync.com>

- **INCORPORATED:** Jan. 20, 1779
- **PARENT COUNTY:** Bute
- **BIRTH RECORDS:** start in 1914, kept by Registrar of Deeds
- **MARRIAGE:** 1869, Registrar of Deeds
- **DIVORCE:** 1923, Superior Court
- **DEATH:** 1914, Registrar of Deeds
- **LAND:** 1778, Registrar of Deeds
- **PROBATE:** 1941, Superior Court
- **COURT:** 1932, Superior Court
- **NOTES:** State Archives has court records 1780-1931, divorce records 1874-1914, 1922, marriage records 1779-1868, probate records 1772-1940, and wills 1779-1931.

WASHINGTON

120 Adams St., Box 1007, Plymouth, NC 27962, (252) 793-2325,
<www.washconc.org>

- **INCORPORATED:** Nov. 1799

- **PARENT COUNTY:** Tyrrell
- **BIRTH RECORDS:** start in 1913, kept by Registrar of Deeds
- **MARRIAGE:** 1851, Registrar of Deeds
- **DIVORCE:** 1904, Superior Court
- **DEATH:** 1913, Registrar of Deeds
- **LAND:** 1799, Registrar of Deeds
- **PROBATE:** 1934, Superior Court
- **COURT:** 1922, Superior Court
- **NOTES:** State Archives has court records 1822-1921, divorce records 1851, 1873-1903, probate records 1795-1933, and wills 1856-1964. Courthouse burned 1862, 1869 and 1873.

WATAUGA

842 W. King St. Suite 9, Boone, NC 28607, (828) 265-8052, **<www.wataugacounty.org>**

- **INCORPORATED:** January 1849
- **PARENT COUNTIES:** Ashe, Caldwell, Wilkes, Yancey
- **BIRTH RECORDS:** start in 1914, kept by Registrar of Deeds
- **MARRIAGE:** 1872, Registrar of Deeds
- **DIVORCE:** 1949, Superior Court
- **DEATH:** 1914, Registrar of Deeds
- **LAND:** 1977, Registrar of Deeds
- **PROBATE:** 1949, Superior Court
- **COURT:** 1925, Superior Court
- **NOTES:** State Archives has court records 1873-1924, divorce records 1874-1948, land records 1858-1976, probate records 1858-1948, and wills 1859, 1872-1947. A courthouse fire in 1873 destroyed all of the land records and most of the Court records.

WAYNE

224 E. Walnut St., Box 267, Goldsboro, NC 27533, (919) 731-1449, **<www.waynegov.com>**

- **INCORPORATED:** October 1779
- **PARENT COUNTY:** Dobbs
- **BIRTH RECORDS:** start in 1913, kept by Registrar of Deeds
- **MARRIAGE:** 1860, Registrar of Deeds
- **DIVORCE:** 1931, Superior Court
- **DEATH:** 1913, Registrar of Deeds
- **LAND:** 1779, Registrar of Deeds
- **PROBATE:** 1938, Superior Court
- **COURT:** 1969, Superior Court
- **NOTES:** State Archives has court records 1787-1968, divorce records 1822-1930, marriage records 1790-1859, probate records 1782-1937. Clerk of Superior Court has Wills 1776-1927.

WICKHAM

- **INCORPORATED:** December 1705
- **PARENT COUNTY:** Bath
- **NOTES:** See Hyde County. Name changed to Hyde, 1712.

WILKES

110 North St., Wilkesboro, NC 28697, (336) 651-7351, **<www.wilkescounty.net>**

- **INCORPORATED:** Feb. 15, 1778
- **PARENT COUNTIES:** Surry, District of Washington
- **BIRTH RECORDS:** start in 1913, kept by Registrar of Deeds
- **MARRIAGE:** 1778, Registrar of Deeds
- **DIVORCE:** 1913, Superior Court
- **DEATH:** 1913, Registrar of Deeds
- **LAND:** 1778, Registrar of Deeds
- **PROBATE:** 1946, Superior Court
- **COURT:** 1932, Superior Court
- **NOTES:** State Archives has court records 1778-1931, divorce records 1820-1912, probate records 1777-1945, and wills 1778-1948.

WILSON

101 N. Goldsboro St., Wilson, NC 27893, (252) 399-2935, **<www.wilson-co.com>**

- **INCORPORATED:** February 1855
- **PARENT COUNTIES:** Edgecombe, Johnston, Nash, Wayne
- **BIRTH RECORDS:** start in 1913, kept by Registrar of Deeds
- **MARRIAGE:** 1855, Registrar of Deeds
- **DIVORCE:** 1913, Superior Court
- **DEATH:** 1913, Registrar of Deeds
- **LAND:** 1855, Registrar of Deeds
- **PROBATE:** 1960, Superior Court
- **COURT:** 1915, Superior Court
- **NOTES:** State Archives has court records 1855-1914, divorce records 1859-1912, probate records 1854-19159, and wills 1840-1925.

YADKIN

Box 211, 101 State St., Yadkinville, NC 27055, (336) 679-4225, **<www.yadkincounty.gov>**

- **INCORPORATED:** December 1850
- **PARENT COUNTY:** Surry
- **BIRTH RECORDS:** start in 1913, kept by Registrar of Deeds
- **MARRIAGE:** 1850, Registrar of Deeds
- **DIVORCE:** 1932, Superior Court
- **DEATH:** 1913, Registrar of Deeds
- **LAND:** 1952, Registrar of Deeds
- **PROBATE:** 1921, Superior Court
- **COURT:** 1899, Superior Court
- **NOTES:** State Archives has court records 1851-1898, divorce records 1851-1931, land records 1793-1951, probate records 1850-1920, and wills 1836-1942.

YANCEY

County Courthouse, Burnsville, NC 28714, (828) 682-2174, **<www.yanceycountync.gov>**

- **INCORPORATED:** 1833
- **PARENT COUNTIES:** Buncombe, Burke
- **BIRTH RECORDS:** start in 1913, kept by Registrar of Deeds
- **MARRIAGE:** 1855, Registrar of Deeds
- **DIVORCE:** 1915, Superior Court
- **DEATH:** 1913, Registrar of Deeds
- **LAND:** 1833, Registrar of Deeds
- **PROBATE:** 1916, Superior Court
- **COURT:** 1916, Superior Court
- **NOTES:** State Archives has court records 1834-1915, divorce records 1866-1914, probate records 1853-1915, and wills 1885-1909.

NORTH DAKOTA

» BY JAMES W. WARREN

HISTORICAL OVERVIEW

Teddy Roosevelt loved the state, Lawrence Welk was born here, and Lewis and Clark wintered here during their great expedition. From the plains along the Red River on its eastern border, North Dakota's lands gradually rise to the spectacular badlands on its western border. The area's original settlers were the Dakota (Sioux), Arapaho, Cheyenne, Mandan, Hidatsa, and Assiniboine Indians.

Fur traders from the Missouri Fur Company paved the way for settlers to come to the area. TheUnited States acquired half of the state in the Louisiana Purchase in 1803, and the other half from Britain in 1818. The first settlement was along the Red River, made by Scottish settlers from Canada on what became the Red River Ox Cart Trail. Early white settlers were primarily from Canada, states directly to the east (Minnesota, Iowa or Wisconsin), New York and Norway.

Dakota Territory was created in 1861 and included what would become North Dakota, South Dakota, Montana, and Wyoming. In 1864, Montana Territory was split off, as was Wyoming Territory in 1868.

In 1871, railroads extending across Minnesota reached the Dakotas' eastern boundary. Settlement boomed, and through 1888, large numbers of immigrants poured into the eastern part of the state. They included many Norwegians, Germans, and Germans from Russia, as well as smaller numbers of people from the British Isles and other European countries. Cycles of boom and bust, fueled partly by land speculators and partly by the inherent risks of farm yields, weather and prices, saw many settlers leave the area after a few years. The temporary successes of the Bonanza Farms, huge tracts of land owned by eastern speculators and worked by immigrant laborers, fueled some speculation. In 1889, North and South Dakota were admitted to the Union. Homesteaders again moved into the state in large numbers through 1915.

RECORD HIGHLIGHTS

The federal censuses for the state of North Dakota start with 1900. Territorial censuses and mortality schedules were taken in 1860, 1870, 1880 and 1885 for Dakota Territory. State censuses for 1905, 1915, and 1925 are available at the State Historical Society of North Dakota **<history.nd.gov>**. The 1915 and 1925 enumerations are on Ancestry.com.

The Division of Vital Records in Bismarck holds statewide birth certificates from 1870, death certificates from 1881, and marriages from July 1925. Online ordering is available at **<www.ndhealth.gov/vital>**. Earlier marriages, if registered,

research tips

- The three most important repositories containing North Dakota records are the University of North Dakota in Grand Forks, North Dakota State University in Fargo, and the State Historical Society in Bismarck.
- Local county resources such as church records and newspapers are particularly important to North Dakota research, due to late settlement of the state and the relatively few record resources available. Genealogical society publications can also be helpful.
- The web can be useful for North Dakota researchers—look for links to county sources on Cyndi's List and the North Dakota GenWeb.

CENSUS RECORDS

- Federal census: 1900, 1910, 1920
- Special census of Civil War Union veterans and widows: 1890
- State censuses: 1836 (included in the Wisconsin census), 1840 (Iowa), 1850 (Minnesota)
- Dakota territory census: 1860, 1870, 1880, 1885, 1905, 1915, 1925 (records are located at the State Historical Society of North Dakota)
- Mortality schedules: 1860, 1870, 1880, 1885

will be found with the county recorder in the county in which the marriage license was issued. Divorces are also in the hands of the pertinent county recorder. The legal requirement to register vital events was generally complied with by the mid-1920s.

Compared to the rest of the country, North Dakota was settled and populated relatively late, and is rather lacking in record resources. County courthouse records include land, naturalization, probate, guardianship, and civil and criminal cases. Most of these records and their indexes remain in the county, and little has been microfilmed. This makes local research key to success. While some counties are starting to put a few indexes online, in most cases you'll need to contact the courthouse or plan to have research done on-site.

Local church and cemetery records may be important to fill the research gaps. Local or church newspapers may provide details or clues not recorded elsewhere. Newspapers that at the State Historical Society in Bismarck have largely been microfilmed.

Some church, cemetery, and newspaper abstracts and indexes have been published or posted online. Genealogical society publications may also hold clues and provide contacts to put you on the right track. Check for links to such resources at Cyndi's List **<www.cyndislist.com>** and the USGenWeb site for North Dakota **<www.rootsweb.ancestry.com/~ndgenweb>**. The North Dakota State Genealogical Society's Web site is another contact point **<www.rootsweb.ancestry.com/~ndsgs/index.html>**.

By the time the State Historical Society of North Dakota was founded in Bismarck, significant historical and genealogical resources had already been gathered at both the University of North Dakota in Grand Forks and North Dakota State University (NDSU) in Fargo. All three facilities have excellent published genealogy and manuscript collections, much of which is not duplicated by the other institutions. None of these repositories should be overlooked when researching North Dakota ancestors.

The State Historical Society of North Dakota's website **<history.nd.gov>** includes information about the society's holdings, which includes library, newspaper, and manuscript collections, as well as the State Archives. The society also holds important collections of oral history interviews. Also available online is the North Dakota Naturalization Records Database. It lists the 212,000 name entries for the first and second naturalization papers recorded at the county level and is complete for all North Dakota counties. The records themselves have all been transferred from the counties to the historical society.

The University of North Dakota's Department of Special Collections at the Chester Fritz Library holds the genealogy and history collections. Online information and some useful indexes are available at **<www.library.und.edu/Collections/spk.html>**. For example, recently added databases include an index to the Grand Forks County Coroner Records, 1881-1989, and a keyword-searchable index to the student newspaper covering 1888 to the present.

The North Dakota Institute for Regional Studies collection at NDSU in Fargo has North Dakota county, town, and church histories. All those volumes acquired prior to 1980 are indexed by every name, and available online at the North Dakota Biography Index **<library.ndsu.edu/db/biography>**. The collection also focuses on Germans from Russia, an active historical and genealogical society for descendants of an important portion of the North Dakota settlers.

ARCHIVES, LIBRARIES, AND SOCIETIES

Bismarck Mandan Historical and Genealogical Society
Box 485, Bismarck, ND 58502,
<bmhgs.com>

Dakotas Conference of the United Methodist Church
Box 460, 1331 W. University Ave., Mitchell, SD 57301, (605) 996-6552, **<www.dakotasumc.nonprofitoffice.com>**

Chester Fritz Library, University of North Dakota
Box 9000, Grand Forks, ND 58202, (701) 777-2617, **<www.library.und.edu>**

Germans from Russia Heritage Society
1125 W. Turnpike Ave., Bismark, ND 58501, (701) 223-6167, **<www.grhs.com>**

Institute for Regional Studies, North Dakota State University
Box 5599, Fargo, ND 58105, (701) 231-8914, **<library.ndsu.edu/archives/collections-institute>**

Minot Public Library
516 Second Ave. SW, Minot, ND 58701, (701) 852-1045, **<www.minotlibrary.org>**

Mouse River Loop Genealogical Society
Box 1391, Minot, ND 58702, **<www.rootsweb.ancestry.com/~ndmrlgs>**

National Archives and Records Administration, Central Plains Region
400 W. Pershing Rd., Kansas City, MO 64108, (816) 268-8000, **<www.archives.gov/central-plains/kansas-city>**

National Archives and Records Administration, Rocky Mountain Region
Box 25307, Denver, CO 80225, (303) 407-5700, **<www.archives.gov/rocky-mountain>**

North Dakota Division of Vital Records
600 E. Boulevard Ave., Bismarck, ND 58505, (701) 328-2360, **<www.ndhealth.gov/vital>**

North Dakota Genealogical Society
<www.rootsweb.ancestry.com/~ndsgs>

North Dakota State Archives and Library
612 E. Boulevard Ave., Bismarck, ND 58505, (701) 328-2091, **<www.statearchives.us/north-dakota.htm>**

North Dakota State Water Commission
900 E. Boulevard Ave., Bismarck, ND 58505, (701) 328-2750, **<www.swc.state.nd.us>**

Red River Valley Genealogical Society
Box 9284, Fargo, ND 58106,
<www.redrivergenealogy.com>

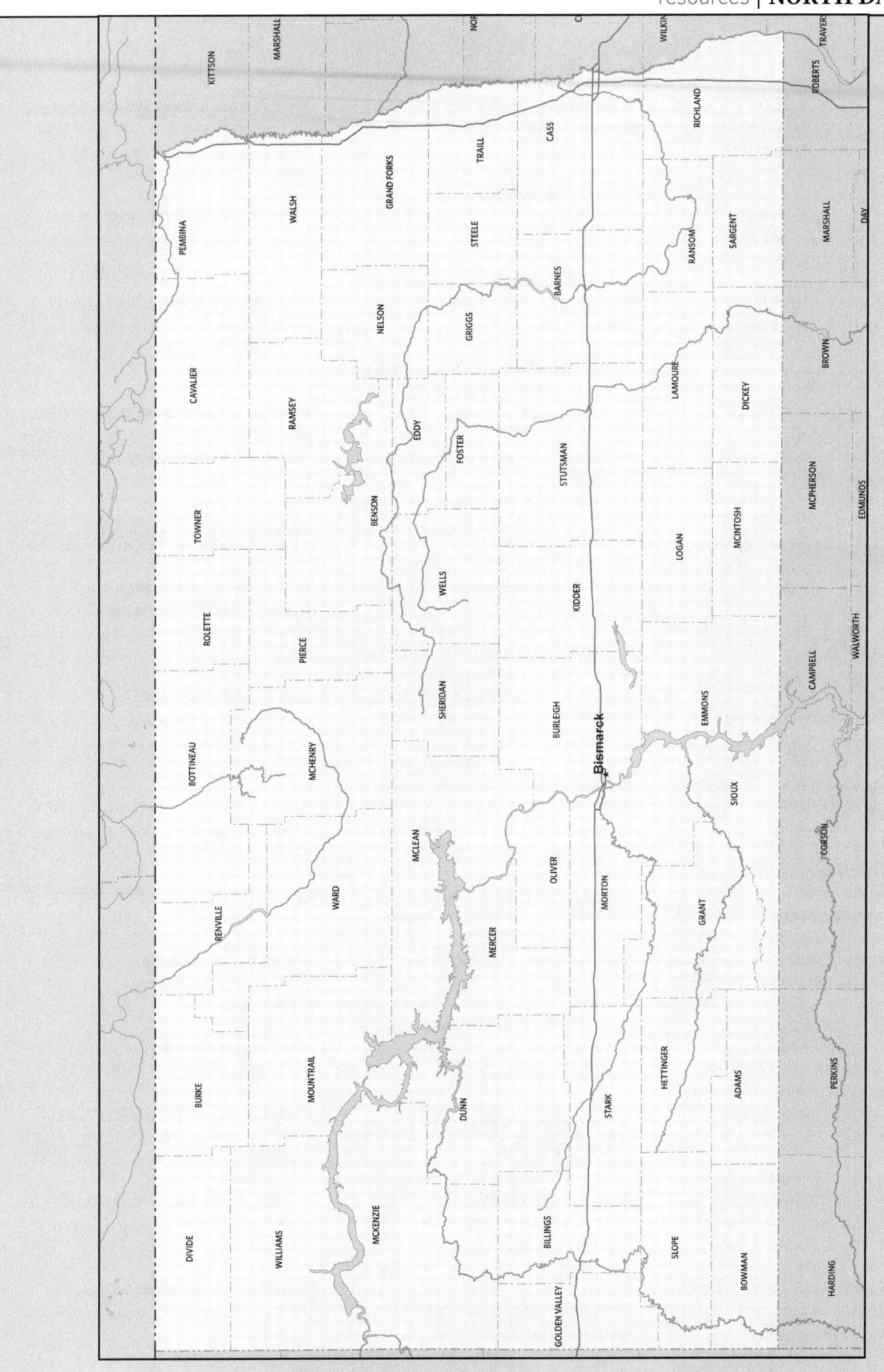

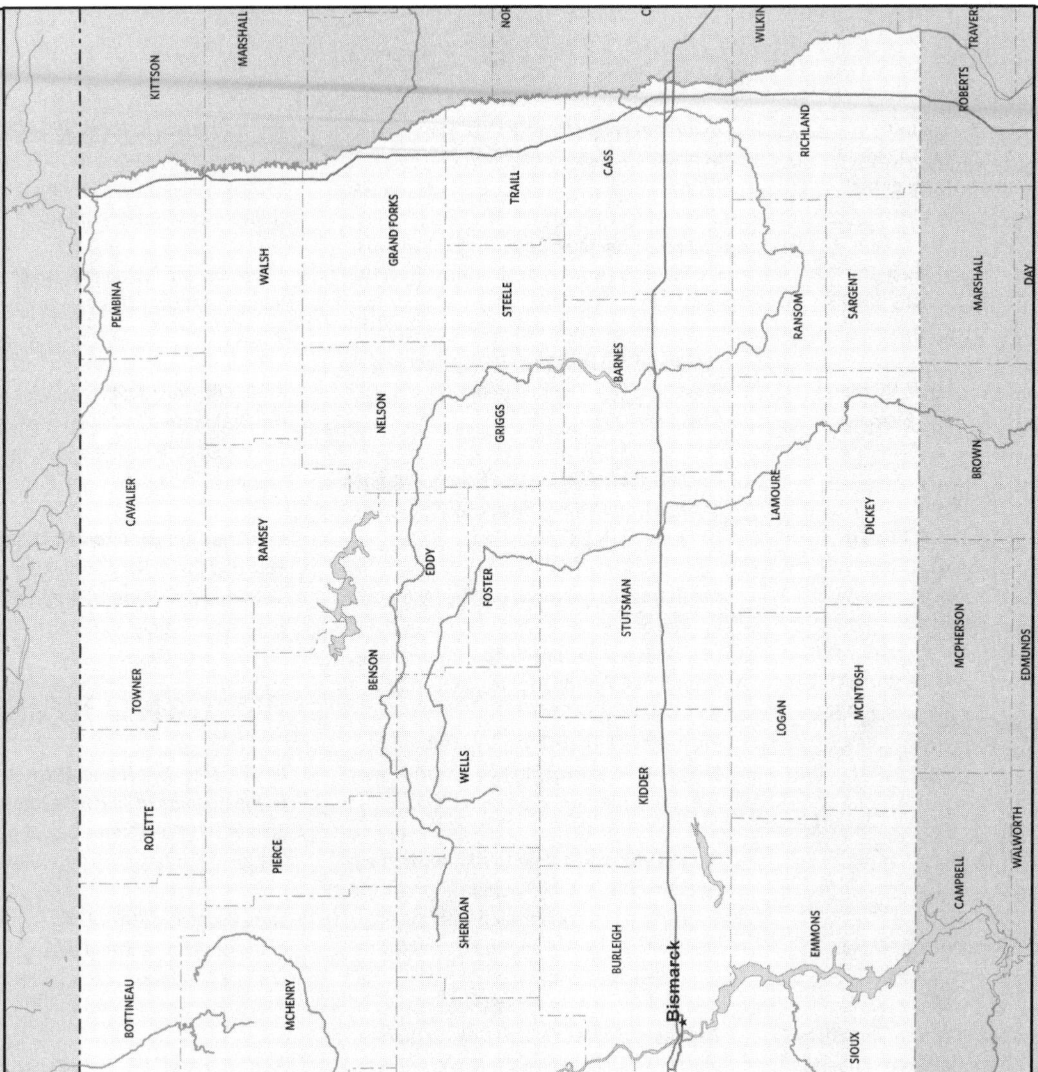

Bismarck
DIVIDE
BURKE
RENVILLE
BOTTINEAU
ROLETTE
TOWNER
CAVALIER
PEMBINA
WILLIAMS
MOUNTRAIL
WARD
MCHENRY
PIERCE
RAMSEY
WALSH
MCKENZIE
DUNN
MERCER
MCLEAN
SHERIDAN
WELLS
BENSON
EDDY
FOSTER
NELSON
GRAND FORKS
GRIGGS
STEELE
TRAILL
BILLINGS
GOLDEN VALLEY
STARK
OLIVER
MORTON
BURLEIGH
KIDDER
STUTSMAN
BARNES
CASS
SLOPE
BOWMAN
HETTINGER
ADAMS
GRANT
SIOUX
EMMONS
LOGAN
MCINTOSH
LAMOURE
DICKEY
RANSOM
SARGENT
RICHLAND
KITTSON
MARSHALL
WILKIN
ROBERTS
TRAVERS
MARSHALL
DAY
BROWN
MCPHERSON
EDMUNDS
CAMPBELL
WALWORTH
CORSON
PERKINS
HARDING

James River Genealogy Club
651 Fourth St., Carrington, ND 58421, **<www.rootsweb.ancestry.com/~ndjrgc>**

Pioneer Trails Regional Museum
12 First Ave. NE, Bowman, ND 58623, (701) 523-3600, **<www.ptrm.org>**

Roman Catholic Diocese of Bismarck
Chancery Office, Box 1575, Bismarck, ND 58502, (701) 223-1347, **<bismarckdiocese.com>**

Roman Catholic Diocese of Fargo
5201 Bishops Blvd., Suite A, Fargo, ND 58104, (701) 356-7900, **<www.fargodiocese.org>**

State Historical Society of North Dakota
612 E. Boulevard Ave., Bismark, ND 58505, (701) 328-2666, **<www.state.nd.us/hist>**

GENERAL RESOURCES

The Black Sea Germans in the Dakotas by George Rath (Pine Hills Press, 1977)

Chronology and Documentary Handbook of the State of North Dakota by Robert I. Vexler (Oceana Publications, 1978)

Compendium of History and Biography of North Dakota Containing a History of North Dakota: Embracing an Account of Early Explorations, Early Settlement, Indian Occupancy . . . and a Concise History of Growth and Development of the State Also a Compendium of Biography of North Dakota (Geo. A. Ogle & Co., 1900)

French-Canadian Families of the North Central States: A Genealogical Dictionary, 8 vols., compiled by Paul J. Lareau and Elmer Courteau (1980-1981)

Guide to the Orin G. Libby Manuscript Collection & Related Research Collections, 3 vols., compiled by John B. Davenport, et al. (University of North Dakota, 1975-1985)

Historical Data Project; Pioneer Biography Files (State Historical Society of North Dakota, 1988-1989)

History of North Dakota by Elwyn B. Robinson (University of Nebraska Press, 1966)

History of North Dakota, 3 vols., by Lewis F. Crawford (American Historical Society, 1931)

History of the Red River Valley Past and Present, 2 vols. (Herald Printing Co., C.F. Cooper, 1909)

North Dakota History and People, Outlines of American History, 3 vols. by C.A. Lounsberry (S.J. Clarke, 1916)

North Dakota Research Outline by the Church of Jesus Christ of Latter-Day Saints (online at **<www.familysearch.org/eng/search/RG/guide/north_dakota.asp>**)

Pioneers and Their Sons: One Hundred Sixty Five Family Histories, 2 vols. by George P. Aberle (Tumbleweed Press, 1980)

Plains Folk: North Dakota's Ethnic History edited by Playford V. Thorson and William C. Sherman (in cooperation with the ND Humanities Council and the University of North Dakota, 1988)

Reference Guide to North Dakota History and North Dakota Literature compiled by Dan Rylance and J.F.S. Smeall (Chester Fritz Library, University of North Dakota, 1979)

Steppes to Neu Odessa: Germans From Russia who Settled in Odessa Township, Dakota Territory, 1872-1876 by Cynthia Anne Frank Stupnik (Heritage Books, 2002)

The Way it Was: The North Dakota Frontier Experience: Book Four: Germans From Russia Settlers edited by Everett C. Albers (Grass Roots Press, 1999)

IMMIGRATION RECORDS

Declarations of Intention, 1890-1924 by the US Circuit Court, Southeastern Division (filmed by the Genealogical Society of Utah, 1991)

Ethnic Group Files, ca. 1935-1942 by the Writers' Program, North Dakota(State Historical Society of North Dakota, 1989)

Naturalization Records, 1906-1924 by the US District Court and the US Circuit Court, Southeastern Division, (filmed by the Genealogical Society of Utah, 1991)

North Dakota Pioneers From the Banat by John M. Michels (University of Mary Press, 1992)

Prairie Mosaic: An Ethnic Atlas of Rural North Dakota by William C. Sherman (North Dakota Institute for Regional Studies, 1983)

Red River Trails: Oxcart Routes Between St. Paul and the Selkirk Settlement, 1820-1870 by Rhoda R. Gilman, et al. (Minnesota Historical Society, 1979)

LAND RECORDS

Land in Her Own Name: Women as Homesteaders in North Dakota by H. Elaine Lindgren (North Dakota Institute for Regional Studies, 1991)

Land Records, 1906-1921 by the US Bureau of Indian Affairs, Standing Rock Agency (Federal Archives and Records Center, 1977)

Sioux Personal Property Claims: From the Original Ledger by Ruth Brown (Rogue Valley Genealogical Society, 1987)

MAPS

The Atlas of North Dakota by L.R. Goodman and R.J. Eidem (North Dakota Studies, 1976)

North Dakota Place Names by Douglas A. Wick (Hedemarken Collectibles, 1988)

North Dakota Post Offices, 1850-1982 by Alan H. Patera and John S. Gallagher (The Depot, 1982)

Origins of North Dakota Place Names by Mary Ann Barnes Williams (Bismark Tribune, 1966)

Postoffices and Postmarks of Dakota ***Territory*** by George H. Phillips (J-B Pub. Co., 1973)

MILITARY RECORDS

General Index to Pension Files, 1861-1934 by the US Veterans Administration (Veterans Administration, Publications Service, 1953)

Index to Compiled Service Records of Volunteer Union Soldiers who Served in Organizations From the Territory of Dakota by the US General Adjutant's Office (National Archives, 1964)

North Dakota, World War I Selective Service System Draft Registration Cards, 1917-1918 by the US Selective Service System (National Archives, 1987-1988)

VITAL RECORDS

Births, Marriages and Deaths, 1880-1942 [Standing Rock Agency] by the US Bureau of Indian Affairs, Standing Rock Agency (Federal Archives and Records Center, 1977)

Guide to Public Vital Statistics Records in North Dakota by the Historical Records Survey, North Dakota (The Survey, 1941)

North Dakota Cemeteries, 32 vols., by the Fargo Genealogical Society (Fargo Genealogical Society, 1972-1977, 1986-1998)

COUNTY DETAILS

ADAMS
602 Adams Ave., Hettinger, ND 58639, (701) 567-2460,
<www.rootsweb.ancestry.com/~ndadams>
- **INCORPORATED:** April 17, 1907
- **PARENT COUNTY:** Hettinger
- **MARRIAGE RECORDS:** start in 1907, kept by Clerk of District Court
- **DIVORCE:** 1907, Clerk of District Court
- **LAND:** 1907, Clerk of District Court
- **PROBATE:** 1907, Clerk of District Court
- **COURT:** 1907, Clerk of District Court
- **NOTES:** State Department-Division of Vital Statistics or records in Bismarck, ND, has birth and death records 1907 to present.

ALLRED
- **INCORPORATED:** March 9, 1883
- **PARENT COUNTY:** Howard
- **NOTES:** See McKenzie County. Eliminated March 16, 1905 and absorbed by McKenzie.

BARNES
230 Fourth St. NW, Valley City, ND 58072, (701) 845-8512,
<www.co.barnes.nd.us>
- **INCORPORATED:** Jan. 4, 1873
- **PARENT COUNTY:** Pembina
- **BIRTH RECORDS:** unknown start, kept by Clerk of District Court
- **MARRIAGE:** 1880, County Judge
- **DEATH:** unknown start, Clerk of District Court
- **PROBATE:** unknown start, County Judge
- **COURT:** unknown start, Clerk of District Court
- **BURIAL:** unknown start, Clerk of District Court
- **NOTES:** Formerly Burbank County. Name changed to Barnes Jan. 14, 1875. Organized Aug. 5, 1878.

BENSON
311 B Ave. S, Box 213, Minnewaukan, ND 58351, (701) 473-5345,
<www.rootsweb.ancestry.com/~ndbenson>
- **INCORPORATED:** March 9, 1883
- **PARENT COUNTIES:** De Smet, Ramsey
- **BIRTH RECORDS:** start in 1890, kept by Clerk of District Court
- **MARRIAGE:** 1889, Clerk of District Court
- **DIVORCE:** 1895, Clerk of District Court
- **DEATH:** 1895, Clerk of District Court
- **LAND:** 1885, Registrar of Deeds
- **PROBATE:** 1895, Clerk of District Court
- **COURT:** 1895, Clerk of District Court
- **BURIAL:** 1930, Clerk of District Court

BILLINGS
495 Fourth St., Box 138, Medora, ND 58645, (701) 623-4492,
<www.billingscountynd.gov>
- **INCORPORATED:** Feb. 10, 1879
- **PARENT COUNTIES:** Unorganized Territory, Howard
- **MARRIAGE RECORDS:** start in 1893, kept by Clerk of District Court
- **DIVORCE:** 1895, Clerk of District Court
- **LAND:** 1886, Clerk of District Court
- **PROBATE:** 1895, Clerk of District Court
- **COURT:** 1890, Clerk of District Court
- **BURIAL:** 1922, Clerk of District Court
- **NOTES:** Organized April 30, 1886.

BOTTINEAU
314 W. Fifth St., Bottineau, ND 58318, (701) 228-3983,
<www.kindredtrails.com/ND_Bottineau.html>
- **INCORPORATED:** Jan. 4, 1873
- **PARENT COUNTY:** Buffalo
- **BIRTH RECORDS:** start in 1943, kept by Clerk of District Court
- **MARRIAGE:** 1887, Clerk of District Court
- **DIVORCE:** 1889, Clerk of District Court
- **DEATH:** 1943, Clerk of District Court
- **LAND:** 1889, Registrar of Deeds
- **PROBATE:** 1889, Clerk of District Court
- **COURT:** 1889, Clerk of District Court
- **NATURALIZATION:** 1884, State Historical Society
- **BURIAL:** 1943, Clerk of District Court
- **NOTES:** Organized July 22, 1884.

BOWMAN

104 First St. NW, Bowman, ND 58623, (701) 523-3450,
<www.rootsweb.ancestry.com/~ndbowman>

- **INCORPORATED:** March 8, 1883
- **PARENT COUNTY:** Billings
- **MARRIAGE RECORDS:** start in 1907, kept by Clerk of District Court
- **DIVORCE:** 1908, Clerk of District Court
- **LAND:** 1896, Clerk of District Court
- **PROBATE:** 1908, Clerk of District Court
- **COURT:** 1908, Clerk of District Court
- **BURIAL:** 1950, Clerk of District Court
- **NOTES:** Eliminated Nov. 30, 1896. Recreated May 24, 1901. Attached to Stark County prior to organization April 17, 1907.

BUFFALO

- **INCORPORATED:** Jan. 6, 1864
- **PARENT COUNTIES:** Brugier, Charles Mix and Unorganized Territory, South Dakota
- **NOTES:** Now in South Dakota. See Burleigh, Kidder, Logan, McHenry, Rolette and Sheridan counties.

BUFORD

- **INCORPORATED:** March 9, 1883
- **PARENT COUNTY:** Wallette
- **NOTES:** See Williams County. Eliminated Nov. 30, 1892 and added to Williams.

BURBANK

- **INCORPORATED:** Jan. 4, 1873
- **PARENT COUNTY:** Pembina
- **NOTES:** See Barnes County. Name changed to Barnes Jan. 14, 1875. Lost to Trail County Jan. 12, 1875, and Griggs County Feb. 18, 1881, and discontinued.

BURKE

Box 219, Bowbells, ND 58721, (701) 377-2718,
<www.rootsweb.ancestry.com/~ndburke/burke2.htm>

- **INCORPORATED:** Feb. 8, 1910
- **PARENT COUNTY:** Ward
- **MARRIAGE RECORDS:** start in 1910, kept by Clerk of District Court
- **DIVORCE:** 1910, Clerk of District Court
- **LAND:** 1910, Clerk of District Court
- **PROBATE:** 1910, Clerk of District Court
- **COURT:** 1910, Clerk of District Court
- **BURIAL:** 1910, Clerk of District Court
- **NOTES:** Vital Statistics in Bismarck has birth and death records.

BURLEIGH

514 E. Thayer Ave., Box 1055, Bismarck, ND 58502, (701) 222-6690, **<www.rootsweb.ancestry.com/~ndburlei>**

- **INCORPORATED:** Jan. 4, 1873
- **PARENT COUNTY:** Buffalo
- **MARRIAGE RECORDS:** start in 1898, kept by Clerk of District Court
- **DIVORCE:** 1876, Clerk of District Court
- **PROBATE:** 1873, Clerk of District Court
- **COURT:** 1873, Clerk of District Court
- **BURIAL:** 1950, Recorder's Office
- **NOTES:** Recorder's Office has land and marriage records from late 1800s.

CASS

211 Ninth St. S., Fargo, ND 58103, (701) 241-5646,
<www.co.cass.nd.us>

- **INCORPORATED:** Jan. 4, 1873
- **PARENT COUNTY:** Pembina
- **MARRIAGE RECORDS:** start in 1945, kept by Treasurer's Office
- **DIVORCE:** 1940, Clerk of District Court
- **COURT:** 1940, Clerk of District Court
- **NOTES:** Recorder's Office has land records back to Dakota Territory days.

CAVALIER

901 Third St., Langdon, ND 58249, (701) 256-2124,
<www.ccjda.org>

- **INCORPORATED:** Jan. 4, 1873
- **PARENT COUNTY:** Pembina
- **MARRIAGE RECORDS:** start in 1890, kept by Clerk of District Court
- **DIVORCE:** 1900, Clerk of District Court
- **LAND:** 1883, Recorder's Office
- **PROBATE:** 1900, Clerk of District Court
- **COURT:** 1900, Clerk of District Court
- **MILITARY:** 1943, Clerk of District Court
- **BURIAL:** 1920, Clerk of District Court
- **NOTES:** Clerk of District has township books from late 1800s-1940s. Organized July 8, 1884.

CHIPPEWA

- **INCORPORATED:** April 24, 1862
- **PARENT COUNTY:** Unorganized Territory
- **NOTES:** Eliminated Dec. 17, 1863 to Unorganized Territory.

CHURCH

- **INCORPORATED:** March 11, 1887
- **PARENT COUNTIES:** McHenry; Sheridan, old
- **NOTES:** See Sheridan County. Attached to McHenry. Lost to McHenry, McLean and Pierce counties. Eliminated Nov. 30, 1892 to Sheridan.

DE SMET

- **INCORPORATED:** Jan. 4, 1873
- **PARENT COUNTY:** Buffalo
- **NOTES:** (See Pierce) Formerly French County. Name changed to De Smet Jan. 14, 1875. Eliminated March 11, 1887 to Pierce.

DICKEY
309 N. Second St., Ellendale, ND 58436, (701) 349-3249,
<www.dickeynd.com>
- **INCORPORATED:** March 5, 1881
- **PARENT COUNTIES:** La Moure, Ransom, Unorganized Territory
- **MARRIAGE RECORDS:** start in 1887, kept by Clerk of District Court
- **DIVORCE:** 1881, Clerk of District Court
- **LAND:** 1882, Recorder's Office
- **PROBATE:** 1881, Clerk of District Court
- **COURT:** 1881, Clerk of District Court
- **NATURALIZATION:** unknown start, State Historical Society
- **MILITARY:** unknown start, Clerk of District Court
- **BURIAL:** unknown start, Clerk of District Court
- **NOTES:** "The Oakes Times" newspaper has birth announcements 1888-1921, 1932, and 1934. Organized Aug. 31, 1882.

DIVIDE
300 N. Main St., Box 68, Crosby, ND 58730, (701) 965-6831,
<www.rootsweb.ancestry.com/~nddivide/divide97.htm>
- **INCORPORATED:** Nov. 8, 1910
- **PARENT COUNTY:** Williams
- **BIRTH RECORDS:** start in 1910, kept by Clerk of District Court
- **MARRIAGE:** 1910, Clerk of District Court
- **DIVORCE:** 1910, Clerk of District Court
- **DEATH:** 1910, Clerk of District Court
- **LAND:** 1910, Registrar of Deeds
- **PROBATE:** 1910, Clerk of District Court
- **COURT:** 1910, Clerk of District Court
- **NATURALIZATION:** unknown start, State Historical Society
- **MILITARY:** 1919, Clerk of District Court
- **BURIAL:** 1910, Clerk of District Court
- **NOTES:** Township birth and death records turned over to the county in 1943. Divide County Library has county newspapers (obituaries, birth announcements etc.) back to 1916, tombstone records back to 1909, and family history books compiled in 1964 and 1974.

DUNN
205 Owens St., Manning, ND 58642, (701) 573-4447,
<www.rootsweb.ancestry.com/~nddunn2>
- **INCORPORATED:** May 24, 1901
- **PARENT COUNTY:** Stark
- **MARRIAGE RECORDS:** start in 1908, kept by Clerk of District Court
- **DIVORCE:** 1914, Clerk of District Court
- **LAND:** 1900, Registrar of Deeds
- **PROBATE:** 1931, Clerk of District Court
- **COURT:** 1914, Clerk of District Court
- **NATURALIZATION:** unknown start, State Historical Society
- **TAX:** 1908, Auditor's Office
- **MILITARY:** 1919, Clerk of District Court
- **NOTES:** Recorder's Office has land records from late 1800s. Organized Jan. 17, 1908. Dunn County Historical Museum has Homestead records, old city records books, county family history books, Voting records, Service records, etc.

DUNN, OLD
<www.rootsweb.ancestry.com/~nddunn>
- **INCORPORATED:** March 9, 1883
- **PARENT COUNTY:** Howard
- **NOTES:** Discontinued and annexed to Stark Nov. 30, 1896.

EDDY
524 Central Ave., New Rockford, ND 58356, (701) 947-2813,
<www.rootsweb.ancestry.com/~ndeddy>
- **INCORPORATED:** March 31, 1885
- **PARENT COUNTY:** Foster
- **MARRIAGE RECORDS:** start in 1887, kept by Clerk of District Court
- **DIVORCE:** 1887, Clerk of District Court
- **LAND:** 1880, Recorder's Office
- **PROBATE:** 1887, Clerk of District Court
- **COURT:** 1887, Clerk of District Court
- **MILITARY:** 1919, Clerk of District Court
- **BURIAL:** unknown start, Clerk of District Court
- **NOTES:** Burial permits can be destroyed after one year.

EMMONS
100 Fourth St. NW, Linton, ND 58552, (701) 254-4812,
<emmonscounty.tripod.com>
- **INCORPORATED:** Feb. 10, 1879
- **PARENT COUNTIES:** Unorganized Territory, Burleigh, Campbell
- **BIRTH RECORDS:** start in 1889, kept by Clerk of District Court
- **MARRIAGE:** 1888, Clerk of District Court
- **DIVORCE:** 1890, Clerk of District Court
- **DEATH:** 1890, Clerk of District Court
- **LAND:** 1890, Recorder's Office
- **PROBATE:** 1885, Clerk of District Court
- **COURT:** 1930, Clerk of District Court
- **NATURALIZATION:** unknown start, State Historic Center
- **BURIAL:** 1950, Clerk of District Court
- **NOTES:** Military records are not open to public. Would need to go through veteran service officer. Court records (not probate) are destroyed after so many years. Organized Nov. 9, 1883.

FLANNERY
- **INCORPORATED:** March 9, 1883
- **PARENT COUNTY:** Wallette
- **NOTES:** See Williams County. Eliminated Nov. 30, 1892 and added to Williams.

FOSTER
1000 Fifth St. N., Carrington, ND 58421, (701) 652-1001,
<www.rootsweb.ancestry.com/~ndfoster>
- **INCORPORATED:** Jan. 4, 1873
- **PARENT COUNTY:** Pembina
- **BIRTH RECORDS:** start in 1900, kept by Clerk of District Court
- **MARRIAGE:** 1896, Clerk of District Court
- **DIVORCE:** 1896, Clerk of District Court
- **DEATH:** 1900, Clerk of District Court
- **LAND:** 1890, Registrar of Deeds
- **PROBATE:** 1896, Clerk of District Court
- **COURT:** 1896, Clerk of District Court
- **NATURALIZATION:** 1883, Clerk of District Court

- **MILITARY:** 1917, Clerk of District Court
- **NOTES:** Auditor's office keeps the old county newspapers in a basement vault. Organized Oct. 11, 1883.

FRENCH
- **INCORPORATED:** Jan. 4, 1873
- **PARENT COUNTY:** Buffalo
- **NOTES:** See Pierce County. Name changed to De Smet Jan. 14, 1875. Eliminated March 11, 1887 to Pierce.

GARFIELD
- **INCORPORATED:** March 13, 1885
- **PARENT COUNTY:** Mountrail, Stevens
- **NOTES:** Eliminated Nov. 30, 1892 to McLean and Ward.

GINGRAS
- **INCORPORATED:** Jan. 4, 1873
- **PARENT COUNTY:** Buffalo
- **NOTES:** See Wells County. Name changed to Wells Feb. 26, 1881.

GOLDEN VALLEY
150 First Ave. SE, Box 9, Beach, ND 58621, (701) 872-3713, **<www.rootsweb.ancestry.com/~ndgolden>**
- **INCORPORATED:** Nov. 19, 1912
- **PARENT COUNTY:** Billings
- **MARRIAGE RECORDS:** start in 1912, kept by Clerk of District Court
- **DIVORCE:** 1912, Clerk of District Court
- **LAND:** 1912, Recorder's Office
- **PROBATE:** 1912, Clerk of District Court
- **COURT:** 1912, Clerk of District Court
- **BURIAL:** 1912, Clerk of District Court

GRAND FORKS
Box 5939, Grand Forks, ND 58206, (701) 780-8221, **<www.gfcounty.nd.gov>**
- **INCORPORATED:** Jan. 4, 1873
- **PARENT COUNTY:** Pembina
- **MARRIAGE RECORDS:** start in 1887, kept by County Judge
- **DIVORCE:** 1878, Clerk of District Court
- **LAND:** 1880, Recorder's Office
- **PROBATE:** 1880, County Judge
- **COURT:** unknown start, Clerk of District Court
- **NOTES:** Organized Jan. 12, 1875. Lost many older records in flood of 1997.

GRANT
N. Main St., Box 258, Carson, ND 58529, (701) 622-3615, **<www.rootsweb.ancestry.com/~ndgrant>**
- **INCORPORATED:** Nov. 7, 1916
- **PARENT COUNTY:** Morton
- **BIRTH RECORDS:** start in 1945, kept by Clerk of District Court
- **MARRIAGE:** 1916, Clerk of District Court
- **DIVORCE:** 1916, Clerk of District Court
- **LAND:** 1916, Recorder's Office
- **PROBATE:** 1916, Clerk of District Court
- **COURT:** 1916, Clerk of District Court
- **BURIAL:** 1916, Clerk of District Court

GRIGGS
808 Rollin Ave. SW, Box 326, Cooperstown, ND 58425, (701) 797-2772, **<www.cooperstownnd.com>**
- **INCORPORATED:** Feb. 18, 1881
- **PARENT COUNTIES:** Foster, Burbank, Traill
- **BIRTH RECORDS:** start in 1901, kept by Clerk of District Court
- **MARRIAGE:** 1884, Clerk of District Court
- **DIVORCE:** 1887, Clerk of District Court
- **DEATH:** 1901, Clerk of District Court
- **LAND:** 1880, Recorder's Office
- **PROBATE:** 1883, Clerk of District Court
- **COURT:** 1887, Clerk of District Court
- **NOTES:** Organized June 16, 1882.

HETTINGER
336 Pacific Ave., Mott, ND 58646, (701) 824-2645, **<www.hettingernd.com>**
- **INCORPORATED:** May 24, 1901
- **PARENT COUNTY:** Stark
- **BIRTH RECORDS:** start in 1907, kept by Clerk of District Court
- **MARRIAGE:** 1907, Clerk of District Court
- **DIVORCE:** 1907, Clerk of District Court
- **DEATH:** 1907, Clerk of District Court
- **LAND:** 1907, Recorder's Office
- **PROBATE:** 1907, Clerk of District Court
- **COURT:** 1907, Clerk of District Court
- **BURIAL:** 1943, Clerk of District Court
- **NOTES:** Attached to Stark County prior to organization April 17, 1907.

HETTINGER, OLD
- **INCORPORATED:** March 29, 1883
- **PARENT COUNTY:** Stark
- **NOTES:** Eliminated Nov. 30, 1896 to Stark.

HOWARD
- **INCORPORATED:** Jan. 8, 1873
- **PARENT COUNTY:** Unorganized Territory
- **NOTES:** Eliminated March 9, 1883 to Allred, Dunn, McKenzie, old and Wallace.

KIDDER
Box 66, Steele, ND 58482, (701) 475-2632, **<www.rootsweb.ancestry.com/~ndkidder>**
- **INCORPORATED:** Jan. 4, 1873
- **PARENT COUNTY:** Buffalo
- **BIRTH RECORDS:** start in 1943, kept by Clerk of District Court
- **MARRIAGE:** 1887, Clerk of District Court
- **DIVORCE:** 1885, Clerk of District Court
- **DEATH:** 1943, Clerk of District Court
- **LAND:** 1881, Recorder's Office
- **PROBATE:** 1883, Clerk of District Court
- **COURT:** 1885, Clerk of District Court
- **BURIAL:** 1943, Clerk of District Court
- **NOTES:** Organized March 22, 1881.

KITTSON
- **INCORPORATED:** April 24, 1862
- **PARENT COUNTY:** Unorganized Territory
- **NOTES:** Organized June 1, 1862. Eliminated Dec. 17, 1863 to Unorganized Territory.

LAMOURE
202 Fourth Ave. NE, Box 128, LaMoure, ND 58458, (701) 883-5301, **<www.lamourecountynd.com>**
- **INCORPORATED:** Jan. 4, 1873
- **PARENT COUNTY:** Pembina
- **BIRTH RECORDS:** start in 1881, kept by Clerk of District Court
- **MARRIAGE:** 1881, Clerk of District Court
- **DIVORCE:** 1881, Clerk of District Court
- **DEATH:** 1881, Clerk of District Court
- **LAND:** 1890, Recorder's Office
- **PROBATE:** 1881, Clerk of District Court
- **COURT:** 1881, Clerk of District Court
- **BURIAL:** 1930, Clerk of District Court
- **NOTES:** Organized Oct. 27, 1881.

LOGAN
301 Broadway, Napoleon, ND 58561, (701) 754-2751, **<www.rootsweb.ancestry.com/~ndlogan>**
- **INCORPORATED:** Jan. 4, 1873
- **PARENT COUNTY:** Buffalo
- **MARRIAGE RECORDS:** start in 1890, kept by Clerk of District Court
- **DIVORCE:** 1920, Clerk of District Court
- **LAND:** 1884, Recorder's Office
- **MILITARY:** 1920, Clerk of District Court
- **BURIAL:** 1950, Clerk of District Court
- **NOTES:** Clerk of District Court has incomplete birth and death records from 1893, court probate records from late 1800s, and marriage records from 1890 or 1900. Organized Sept. 1, 1884.

MCHENRY
407 Main St., Towner, ND 58788, (701) 537-5729, **<www.rootsweb.ancestry.com/~ndmchenr>**
- **INCORPORATED:** Jan. 4, 1873
- **PARENT COUNTY:** Buffalo
- **MARRIAGE RECORDS:** start in 1920, kept by Clerk of District Court
- **DIVORCE:** 1920, Clerk of District Court
- **PROBATE:** 1900, Clerk of District Court
- **COURT:** 1910, Clerk of District Court
- **NOTES:** Recorder's Office has land records from late 1800s. Organized May 14, 1885.

MCINTOSH
112 NE First St., Ashley, ND 58413, (701) 288-3450, **<www.rootsweb.ancestry.com/~ndmcinto>**
- **INCORPORATED:** March 9, 1883
- **PARENT COUNTIES:** Logan, Unorganized Territory, McPherson
- **BIRTH RECORDS:** start in 1899, kept by Clerk of District Court
- **MARRIAGE:** 1885, Clerk of District Court
- **DIVORCE:** 1937, Clerk of District Court
- **DEATH:** 1899, Clerk of District Court
- **LAND:** unknown start, Recorder's Office
- **PROBATE:** 1889, Clerk of District Court
- **COURT:** 1883, Clerk of District Court
- **NATURALIZATION:** unknown start, State Historical Society
- **MILITARY:** 1943, Clerk of District Court
- **NOTES:** Organized Oct. 4, 1884.

MCKENZIE
201 Fifth St. NW, Box 524, Watford City, ND 58854, (701) 444-3452, **<www.4eyes.net>**
- **INCORPORATED:** May 24, 1901
- **PARENT COUNTY:** Billings
- **BIRTH RECORDS:** start in 1910, kept by Clerk of District Court
- **MARRIAGE:** 1905, Clerk of District Court
- **DIVORCE:** 1905, Clerk of District Court
- **DEATH:** 1910, Clerk of District Court
- **LAND:** 1905, Recorder's Office
- **PROBATE:** 1905, Clerk of District Court
- **COURT:** 1905, Clerk of District Court
- **MILITARY:** unknown start Recorder's Office
- **NOTES:** Attached to Stark County prior to organization March 16, 1905.

MCKENZIE, OLD
- **INCORPORATED:** March 9, 1883
- **PARENT COUNTY:** Howard
- **NOTES:** Annexed to Billings Nov. 30, 1896.

MCLEAN
712 Fifth Ave., Washburn, ND 58577, (701) 462-8541, **<www.visitmcleancounty.com/officials/officialsindex.html>**
- **INCORPORATED:** March 8, 1883
- **PARENT COUNTIES:** Stevens, Burleigh, Sheridan, old
- **MARRIAGE RECORDS:** start in 1898, kept by Clerk of District Court
- **DIVORCE:** 1900, Clerk of District Court
- **LAND:** 1883, Recorder's Office
- **PROBATE:** 1900, Clerk of District Court
- **COURT:** 1900, Clerk of District Court
- **BURIAL:** 1920, Clerk of District Court

MERCER
1021 Arthur St., Stanton, ND 58571, (701) 745-3262, **<www.mercercountynd.com>**
- **INCORPORATED:** Jan. 14, 1875
- **PARENT COUNTY:** Unorganized Territory
- **MARRIAGE RECORDS:** start in 1894, kept by Clerk of District Court
- **DIVORCE:** 1940, Clerk of District Court
- **DEATH:** 1942, Clerk of District Court
- **LAND:** 1908, Recorder's Office
- **PROBATE:** 1898, Clerk of District Court
- **COURT:** 1906, Clerk of District Court
- **NATURALIZATION:** unknown start, State Historical Society
- **BURIAL:** unknown start, State Historical Society
- **NOTES:** Organized Aug. 22, 1884.

MORTON
210 Second Ave. NW, Mandan, ND 58554, (701) 667-3355, **<www.co.morton.nd.us>**
- **INCORPORATED:** Jan. 8, 1873
- **PARENT COUNTY:** Unorganized Territory

- **MARRIAGE RECORDS:** start in 1882, kept by Recorder's Office
- **DIVORCE:** 1900, Clerk of District Court
- **PROBATE:** 1900, Clerk of District Court
- **BURIAL:** unknown start, Recorder's Office
- **NOTES:** Clerk of District Court has court records from late 1800s. Recorder's Office has land records from late 1800s. Organized Feb. 28, 1881.

MOUNTRAIL

Box 69, Stanley, ND 58784, (701) 628-2915, **<www.rootsweb.ancestry.com/~ndmountr>**

- **INCORPORATED:** Jan. 4, 1873
- **PARENT COUNTY:** Buffalo
- **BIRTH RECORDS:** start in 1909, kept by Clerk of District Court
- **MARRIAGE:** 1909, Clerk of District Court
- **DIVORCE:** 1909, Clerk of District Court
- **DEATH:** 1909, Clerk of District Court
- **LAND:** 1908, Records Office
- **PROBATE:** 1909, Clerk of District Court
- **COURT:** 1909, Clerk of District Court
- **NATURALIZATION:** 1909, State Historical Society
- **MILITARY:** 1919, Clerk of District Court
- **NOTES:** Clerk of District Court has incomplete burial records. Annexed to Ward in 1891 and eliminated Nov. 30, 1892. Recreated Jan. 29, 1909 from Ward.

NELSON

210 B Ave. W, Box 565, Lakota, ND 58344, (701) 247-2462, **<www.nelsonco.org>**

- **INCORPORATED:** March 2, 1883
- **PARENT COUNTIES:** Foster, Grand Forks, Ramsey, Unorganized Territory
- **BIRTH RECORDS:** start in 1903, kept by Clerk of District Court
- **MARRIAGE:** 1883, Clerk of District Court
- **DIVORCE:** 1883, Clerk of District Court
- **DEATH:** 1903, Clerk of District Court
- **LAND:** 1880, Clerk of District Court
- **PROBATE:** 1880, Clerk of District Court
- **COURT:** unknown start, Clerk of District Court
- **NOTES:** Clerk of District Court has burial records from mid-1900s.

OLIVER

115 W. Main St., Center, ND 58530, (701) 794-8777, **<www.rootsweb.ancestry.com/~ndoliver>**

- **INCORPORATED:** April 14, 1885
- **PARENT COUNTY:** Mercer
- **MARRIAGE RECORDS:** start in 1915, kept by Clerk of District Court
- **DEATH:** 1920, Clerk of District Court
- **LAND:** 1900, Recorder's Office
- **PROBATE:** 1900, County Judge
- **COURT:** 1900, County Judge

PEMBINA

301 Dakota St. W. #10, Cavalier, ND 58220, (701) 265-4275, **<pembinacountynd.gov>**

- **INCORPORATED:** Jan. 9, 1867
- **PARENT COUNTY:** Unorganized Territory
- **BIRTH RECORDS:** start in 1893, kept by Clerk of District Court
- **MARRIAGE:** 1881, Clerk of District Court
- **DIVORCE:** 1883, Clerk of District Court
- **DEATH:** 1893, Clerk of District Court
- **LAND:** 1880, Recorder's Office
- **PROBATE:** 1883, Clerk of District Court
- **COURT:** 1883, Clerk of District Court
- **MILITARY:** 1945, Veterans Service Officer
- **BURIAL:** 1943, Clerk of District Court

PIERCE

240 SE Second St., Rugby, ND 58368, (701) 776-6161, **<www.rootsweb.ancestry.com/~ndpierce>**

- **INCORPORATED:** March 11, 1887
- **PARENT COUNTIES:** De Smet, Bottineau, McHenry, Rolette
- **BIRTH RECORDS:** start in 1945, kept by Clerk of District Court
- **MARRIAGE:** 1890, Clerk of District Court
- **DIVORCE:** 1910, Clerk of District Court
- **DEATH:** 1945, Clerk of District Court
- **LAND:** 1884, Recorder's Office
- **PROBATE:** 1898, Clerk of District Court
- **COURT:** 1900, Clerk of District Court
- **MILITARY:** 1940, Veterans Service Officer
- **BURIAL PERMITS:** 1943, Clerk of District Court
- **NOTES:** Organized April 11, 1889.

RAMSEY

524 Fourth Ave. #4, Devils Lake, ND 58301, (701) 662-1039, **<www.co.ramsey.nd.us>**

- **INCORPORATED:** Jan. 4, 1873
- **PARENT COUNTY:** Pembina
- **BIRTH RECORDS:** start in 1900, kept by Recorder's Office
- **MARRIAGE:** 1887, Recorder's Office
- **DEATH:** 1900, Recorder's Office
- **LAND:** 1885, Recorder's Office
- **MILITARY:** unknown start, Recorder's Office
- **BURIAL PERMITS:** unknown start, Recorder's Office
- **NOTES:** Clerk of District Court has court and divorce records from late 1800s. County Judge has probate records from late 1800s. Organized Jan. 25, 1885.

RANSOM

204 Fifth Ave. W., Box 626, Lisbon, ND 58054, (701) 683-5823 ext. 1, **<www.ransomcountynd.com>**

- **INCORPORATED:** Jan. 4, 1873
- **PARENT COUNTY:** Pembina
- **MARRIAGE RECORDS:** start in 1908, kept by Clerk of District Court
- **DIVORCE:** 1908, Clerk of District Court
- **LAND:** 1870, Recorder's Office
- **PROBATE:** 1908, Clerk of District Court
- **COURT:** 1908, Clerk of District Court
- **MILITARY:** 1919, Clerk of District Court
- **NOTES:** Organized April 4, 1881.

RENVILLE

205 Main St. E., Box 68, Mohall, ND 58761, (701) 756-6398, **<renvillecountynd.org>**

- **INCORPORATED:** June 3, 1910
- **PARENT COUNTY:** Ward

- **MARRIAGE RECORDS:** start in 1910, kept by Clerk of District Court
- **DIVORCE:** 1910, Clerk of District Court
- **LAND:** 1910, Registrar of Deeds
- **PROBATE:** 1910, Clerk of District Court
- **COURT:** 1910, Clerk of District Court
- **MILITARY:** 1910, Clerk of District Court
- **NOTES:** Clerk of District Court has incomplete birth and death records.

RENVILLE, OLD

- **INCORPORATED:** Jan. 4, 1873
- **PARENT COUNTY:** Buffalo
- **NOTES:** Part taken to form Ward County April 14, 1885. Attached to Ward. Eliminated Nov. 30, 1892 to Bottineau and Ward. Recreated June 3, 1910.

RICHLAND

418 Second Ave. N., Wahpeton, ND 58075, (701) 671-1524
<www.rootsweb.ancestry.com/~ndrichla>

- **INCORPORATED:** Jan. 4, 1873
- **PARENT COUNTY:** Pembina
- **DIVORCE RECORDS:** unknown start, kept by County Recorder
- **LAND:** unknown start, County Recorder
- **PROBATE:** unknown start, County Judge
- **COURT:** unknown start, Clerk of District Court
- **BURIAL:** unknown start, County Recorder
- **NOTES:** County Recorder has Marriage records from late 1800s. Organized Nov. 25, 1875.

ROLETTE

102 Second St. NE, Rolla, ND 58367, (701) 477-3816,
<www.rolettecounty.com>

- **INCORPORATED:** Jan. 4, 1873
- **PARENT COUNTY:** Buffalo
- **MARRIAGE RECORDS:** 1887, Clerk of District Court
- **DIVORCE:** start in 1889, kept by Clerk of District Court
- **LAND:** 1884, Recorder's Office
- **PROBATE:** 1896, Clerk of District Court
- **COURT:** 1889, Clerk of District Court
- **MILITARY:** 1944, Clerk of District Court
- **BURIAL PERMITS:** unknown start, Clerk of District Court
- **NOTES:** Clerk of District Court has Death from late 1800s. Organized Oct. 14, 1884.

SARGENT

355 Main St., Box 176, Forman, ND 58032, (701) 724-6241,
<theusgenweb.org/nd/sargent>

- **INCORPORATED:** April 9, 1883
- **PARENT COUNTY:** Ransom
- **BIRTH RECORDS:** start in 1900, kept by Clerk of District Court
- **MARRIAGE:** 1886, Clerk of District Court
- **DIVORCE:** unknown start, Clerk of District Court
- **DEATH:** 1903, Clerk of District Court
- **LAND:** 1886, Recorder's Office
- **PROBATE:** 1883, Clerk of District Court
- **COURT:** unknown start, Clerk of District Court
- **MILITARY:** unknown start, Recorder's Office
- **BURIAL:** 1948, Clerk of District Court

SHERIDAN

215 E. Second St., Box 409, McClusky, ND 58463, (701) 363-2207,
<www.rootsweb.ancestry.com/~ndsherid>

- **INCORPORATED:** Dec. 24, 1908
- **PARENT COUNTY:** McLean
- **BIRTH RECORDS:** start in 1943, kept by Clerk of District Court
- **MARRIAGE:** 1909, Clerk of District Court
- **DIVORCE:** 1909, Clerk of District Court
- **DEATH:** 1943, Clerk of District Court
- **LAND:** 1909, Registrar of Deeds
- **PROBATE:** 1909, Clerk of District Court
- **COURT:** 1909, Clerk of District Court
- **MILITARY:** 1918, Clerk of District Court
- **BURIAL:** unknown start, Clerk of District Court
- **NOTES:** Birth and death records prior to 1908 are held by townships.

SHERIDAN, OLD

- **INCORPORATED:** Jan. 4, 1873
- **PARENT COUNTY:** Buffalo
- **NOTES:** Part taken to form part of Church March 11, 1887. Eliminated Nov. 30, 1892 to McLean.

SHEYENNE

- **INCORPORATED:** April 24, 1862
- **PARENT COUNTY:** Unorganized Territory
- **NOTES:** Eliminated Dec. 17, 1863 to Unorganized Territory.

SIOUX

303 Second Ave., Fort Yates, ND 58538, (701) 854-3853,
<www.rootsweb.ancestry.com/~ndsioux>

- **INCORPORATED:** Sept. 3, 1914
- **PARENT COUNTY:** Standing Rock Reservation
- **MARRIAGE RECORDS:** start in 1916, kept by Clerk of District Court
- **DIVORCE:** unknown start, Clerk of District Court
- **LAND:** unknown start, Clerk of District Court
- **PROBATE:** unknown start, Clerk of District Court
- **COURT:** unknown start, Clerk of District Court
- **MILITARY:** 1880, Clerk of District Court
- **BURIAL:** unknown start, Clerk of District Court
- **NOTES:** This county is an Indian reservation. The Tribal Court has been keeping records since 1970s. Bureau of Indian Affairs has reservation birth and death records.

SLOPE

206 S. Main St., Amidon, ND 58620, (701) 879-6275,
<www.slopecountynd.com>

- **INCORPORATED:** Nov. 3, 1914
- **PARENT COUNTY:** Billings
- **MARRIAGE RECORDS:** start in 1915, kept by Clerk of District Court
- **DIVORCE:** 1915, Clerk of District Court
- **DEATH:** 1915, Clerk of District Court
- **LAND:** 1915, Clerk of District Court
- **PROBATE:** 1915, Clerk of District Court
- **COURT:** 1915, Clerk of District Court
- **BURIAL:** 1915, Clerk of District Court
- **NOTES:** Organized Jan. 14, 1915.

STARK

51 Third St. E., Dickinson, ND 58602, (701) 456-7645,
<hometownchronicles.com/nd/stark>

- **INCORPORATED:** Feb. 10, 1879
- **PARENT COUNTIES:** Unorganized Territory; Howard; William, old
- **BIRTH RECORDS:** start in 1898, kept by Recorder's Office
- **DIVORCE:** 1950, Clerk of District Court
- **DEATH:** 1898, Recorder's Office
- **LAND:** unknown start, Registrar of Deeds
- **COURT:** unknown start, Clerk of District Court
- **NOTES:** Recorder's Office has Land records from late 1800s. State Historical Center has Divorce records prior to 1950. Clerk of District Court has Naturalization records 1887-1963. Organized May 30, 1883.

STEELE

201 W. Washington Ave., Box 296, Finley, ND 58230, (701) 524-2152, **<www.rootsweb.ancestry.com/~ndsteele>**

- **INCORPORATED:** June 2, 1883
- **PARENT COUNTY:** Griggs, Traill
- **BIRTH RECORDS:** unknown start, kept by Clerk of District Court
- **MARRIAGE:** 1883, County Judge
- **DIVORCE:** 1886, Clerk of District Court
- **DEATH:** unknown start, Clerk of District Court
- **LAND:** unknown start, Registrar of Deeds
- **PROBATE:** 1886, County Judge
- **COURT:** 1886, Clerk of District Court

STEVENS

- **INCORPORATED:** Jan. 4, 1873
- **PARENT COUNTY:** Buffalo
- **NOTES:** Eliminated Nov. 30, 1892 to McLean and Ward.

STEVENS, OLD

- **INCORPORATED:** April 24 1862
- **PARENT COUNTY:** Unorganized Territory
- **NOTES:** Eliminated Dec. 17, 1863 to Unorganized Territory.

STUTSMAN

511 Second Ave. SE, Jamestown, ND 58401, (701) 252-9042,
<www.co.stutsman.nd.us>

- **INCORPORATED:** Jan. 4, 1873
- **PARENT COUNTIES:** Pembina, Buffalo
- **BIRTH RECORDS:** unknown start, kept by Clerk of District Court
- **MARRIAGE:** 1884, Recorder's Office
- **DIVORCE:** unknown start, Clerk of District Court
- **DEATH:** unknown start, Clerk of District Court
- **LAND:** 1874, Recorder's Office
- **PROBATE:** unknown start, Clerk of Courts
- **COURT:** unknown start, Clerk of District Court
- **BURIAL:** unknown start, Clerk of District Court
- **NOTES:** The state has birth and death records.

TOWNER

315 Second St., Box 517, Cando, ND 58324, (701) 968-4343,
<www.rootsweb.ancestry.com/~ndtowner>

- **INCORPORATED:** March 8, 1883
- **PARENT COUNTIES:** Rolette, Cavalier
- **BIRTH RECORDS:** start in 1940, kept by Clerk of Courts
- **MARRIAGE:** 1889, Clerk of District Court
- **DIVORCE:** 1884, Clerk of District Court
- **DEATH:** 1940, Clerk of Courts
- **LAND:** 1884, Clerk of District Court
- **PROBATE:** 1886, Clerk of District Court
- **COURT:** 1884, Clerk of District Court
- **NOTES:** Organized Jan. 24, 1884.

TRAILL

13 First St. NW, Hillsboro, ND 58045, (701) 636-4454,
<www.co.traill.nd.us>

- **INCORPORATED:** Jan. 12, 1875
- **PARENT COUNTIES:** Grand Forks, Burbank, Cass
- **MARRIAGE RECORDS:** start in 1872, kept by Clerk of District Court
- **DIVORCE:** 1890, Clerk of District Court
- **LAND:** unknown start, Registrar of Deeds
- **PROBATE:** 1882, Clerk of District Court
- **NOTES:** Recorder's Office has Land records from mid-1800s.

VILLARD

- **INCORPORATED:** March 8, 1883
- **PARENT COUNTY:** Billings
- **NOTES:** Eliminated March 10, 1887 to Billings and Stark.

WALLACE

- **INCORPORATED:** March 9, 1883
- **PARENT COUNTY:** Howard
- **NOTES:** See McKenzie County. Eliminated Nov. 30, 1896 to Billings and Stark. Recreated May 24, 1901 from Billings and Stark and attached to Stark County. Eliminated March 16, 1905 to McKenzie.

WALLETTE

- **INCORPORATED:** Jan. 4, 1873
- **PARENT COUNTY:** Buffalo
- **NOTES:** Eliminated March 9, 1883 to Buford and Flannery.

WALSH

600 Cooper Ave., Grafton, ND 58237, (701) 352-0350,
<www.rootsweb.ancestry.com/~ndwalsh/walsh.htm>

- **INCORPORATED:** May 20, 1881
- **PARENT COUNTIES:** Grand Forks, Pembina
- **MARRIAGE RECORDS:** start in 1884, kept by Clerk of District Court
- **DIVORCE:** unknown start, Clerk of District Court
- **LAND:** 1878, County Recorder
- **PROBATE:** unknown start, Clerk of District Court
- **COURT:** unknown start, Clerk of District Court

WARD

315 Third St. SE, Minot, ND 58701, (701) 857-6460,
<www.co.ward.nd.us>

- **INCORPORATED:** April 14, 1885
- **PARENT COUNTIES:** Stevens; Wynn; Renville, old
- **MARRIAGE RECORDS:** unknown start, kept by County Judge
- **DIVORCE:** unknown start, Clerk of District Court
- **PROBATE:** unknown start, County Judge
- **MILITARY:** 1930, County Recorder
- **BURIAL:** unknown start, County Recorder
- **NOTES:** County Recorder has land records from late 1800s.

WELLS

700 Railway St. N., Fessenden, ND 58438, (701) 547-3122,
<mylocalgov.com/wellscountynd>

- **INCORPORATED:** Jan. 4, 1873
- **PARENT COUNTY:** Buffalo
- **MARRIAGE RECORDS:** start in 1890, kept by Clerk of District Court
- **DIVORCE:** unknown start, Clerk of District Court
- **LAND:** 1884, Recorder's Office
- **COURT:** unknown start, Clerk of District Court
- **NOTES:** Clerk of District Court has Probate records from late 1800s. Formerly Gingras County. Name changed to Wells Feb. 26, 1881. Organized Aug. 24, 1884.

WILLIAMS

Box 2047, Williston, ND 58802, (701) 774-4374,
<www.williamsnd.com>

- **INCORPORATED:** Nov. 30, 1892
- **PARENT COUNTIES:** Buford, Flannery
- **MARRIAGE RECORDS:** start in 1892, kept by Auditor's Office
- **DIVORCE:** 1926, Clerk of Courts
- **LAND:** 1900, County Treasurer
- **PROBATE:** 1903, Clerk of Courts
- **COURT:** 1903, Clerk of District Court
- **NOTES:** Divorce records prior to 1926 are held in Bismark. Superintendent of Schools has township books. Organized March 10, 1903.

WILLIAMS, OLD

- **INCORPORATED:** Jan. 8, 1873
- **PARENT COUNTY:** Unorganized Territory
- **NOTES:** Eliminated Nov. 30, 1892 to Mercer.

WYNN

- **INCORPORATED:** March 9, 1883
- **PARENT COUNTY:** Bottineau; Renville, old
- **NOTES:** Eliminated March 11, 1887 to Bottineau, McHenry, Renville (old) and Ward.

OHIO

» BY RHONDA R. MCCLURE

HISTORICAL OVERVIEW

While many consider the 1787 establishment of Northwest Territory to be responsible for the foundation of Ohio, the state's history can be traced even further back. In 1747, the Ohio Co. of Virginia was organized to settle in the Ohio River Valley. Among the members of this land speculation firm was Lawrence Washington, brother of George, the future US president. Because of Lawrence's involvement, George Washington was recruited to take some soldiers to the area to warn off the French who had settled there. This incident launched the French and Indian War, which ignited the Seven Years War in Europe. When it was all over, the British had possession of what would become Ohio, though they did not encourage settlement.

After the American Revolution, states possessing land west of the Appalachian Mountains were encouraged to "donate" this land to the newly formed government to aid in creating revenue, thus avoiding the need for taxes. The Northwest Territory and the Ordinance of 1787 established how all other territories and states would be created. The Northwest Territory was eventually divided into the states of Ohio (1803), Indiana (1816), Illinois (1818), Michigan (1837), Wisconsin (1848) and Minnesota (1858).

Maps of early Ohio show land that was set aside for bounties and other promised entitlements. In addition to bounty land given to soldiers for fighting in the American Revolution, areas were also reserved for repaying individuals who lost land in support of the patriots.

research tips

- Ohio has eight regional research centers, each responsible for records concerning the counties in their district. Visit **<www.ohiohistory.org/resource/lgr/networkl.html>** to find the center you need.
- The best place to begin Ohio research is the Ohio Historical Society in Columbus, where you'll find primary resources and research tools to help you find the records you need **<www.ohiohistory.org>**.
- The Ohio Genealogical Society **<www.ogs.org>** in Mansfield has published many Ohio records and offers searchable online databases to members.

CENSUS RECORDS

- Federal census: 1820, 1830, 1840, 1850, 1860, 1870, 1880, 1900, 1910, 1920, 1930
- Federal mortality schedules: 1850, 1860, 1870
- Special census of Civil War Union veterans and widows: 1890

RECORD HIGHLIGHTS

County-level registration of births and deaths began in 1867 and was the responsibility of the probate court. Statewide vital registration would not begin until the end of 1908. Marriage records generally exist from statehood, though they often list only the names of the bride and groom, the marriage date, and the officiant.

Indexes to death records from 1908 to 1937 are available online through the Ohio Historical Society's Web site **<www.ohiohistory.org>**. The Society has copies of death certificates from 1908 to 1944, and you can request them for a fee (you also can find Ohio death certificates from 1908 to 1953 free on FamilySearch **<www.familysearch.org>**). Births after 1908 and deaths after 1953 must be requested from the Ohio Department of Health, Division of Vital Statistics, Box 15098, Columbus, OH 43215, **<www.odh.ohio.gov/vitalstatistics/vitalstats.aspx>**.

Remember that which land tract your ancestor settled affects where you will find early land records. The federal government sold some Ohio land, while other tracts were used to satisfy federal and state bounty lands. In all, 13 tracts were earmarked for dispersal. Understanding where a given tract lay and the counties formed from it is a clue to where your ancestors may have lived before Ohio. An excellent resource for Ohio history and the division of land is the *Official Ohio Lands Book* by Dr. George W. Knepper (Auditor of State, 2002). This book is available online at **<www.auditor.state.oh.us/Publications/General/OhioLandsBook.pdf>**.

From 1797 until 1851, probate records were the responsibility of courts of common pleas. In 1852, separate probate courts were created. Look for both the will and the estate file, sometimes called a case file or probate packet, which includes much more than the will. You may find settlement papers, inventories and receipts. For estates before 1850, a valuable statewide resource is Carol Willsey Bell's *Ohio Wills and Estates to 1850: An Index* (Carol Willsey Bell, 1981).

The Ohio Historical Society, 1982 Velma Ave., Columbus, OH 43211, which serves as the state archives, is an excellent place to begin your Ohio research. Also visit the Ohio Genealogical Society, which has published many Ohio records and offers members databases on its website **<www.ogs.org>**.

The Western Reserve Historical Society, 10825 East Blvd., Cleveland, OH 44106, **<www.wrhs.org>**, has an extensive manuscript collection, as well as Revolutionary War Pension records.

Ohio has established eight research centers, each responsible for collecting records for the counties in its region. To find out more about each center and the counties it is responsible for, visit the Ohio Historical Society's website **<www.ohiohistory.org/resource/lgr/networkl.html>**.

ARCHIVES, LIBRARIES, AND SOCIETIES

Adams Genealogical Society
Box 231, West Union, OH 45693

Allen County Genealogical Society
Box 1104, Lima, OH 45802, **<www.rootsweb.ancestry.com/~ohallcgs>**

Allen County Historical Society
620 W. Market St., Lima, OH 45801, **<www.allencountymuseum.org>**

African-American Genealogical Society of Cleveland
Box 201476, Cleveland, OH 44120, **<www.aagsclev.org>**

Akron-Summit County Public Library
60 S. High St., Akron, OH 44326, (330) 643-9000, **<www.akronlibrary.org>**

Archives of Ohio Methodism, Ohio Wesleyan University
Beeghly Library, 43 Rowland Ave., Delaware, OH 43015 **<library.owu.edu/spuma.htm>**

Ashland County Genealogical Society
Box 681, Ashland, OH 44805, **<ashlandohiogenealogy.org>**

Ashtabula County Genealogical Society, Geneva Public Library
860 Sherman St., Geneva, OH 44041, **<www.ashtabulagen.org>**

Athens County Genealogical Society, Historical Society and Museum
65 N. Court St., Athens, OH 45701, (740) 592-2280, **<www.athenshistory.org>**

Auglaize County Genealogical Society
Box 2021, Wapakoneta, OH 45895, **<www.rootsweb.ancestry.com/~ohaugogs>**

Bedford Historical Society
Box 46282, Bedford, OH 44146, (440) 232-0796, **<www.bedfordohiohistory.org>**

Belmont County Genealogical Society
Box 285, Barnesville, OH 43713, **<www.rootsweb.ancestry.com/~ohbelogs>**

Bowling Green State University, Center for Archival Collections
Jerome Library, Bowling Green, OH 43403, (419) 372-2411

Brookville Historical Society
Box 82, Brookville, OH 45309, **<www.dcoweb.org/brookville>**

Brown County Genealogical Society
Box 83, Georgetown, OH 45121

Butler County Genealogical Society
Box 224, Middletown, OH 45042, **<www.butlercountyogs.org>**

Carnegie Public Library
127 S. North St., Washington Courthouse, OH 43160, (740) 335-2540, **<www.cplwcho.org>**

Carroll County Genealogical Society
Box 36, Carrollton, OH 44615, (330) 627-9411, **<www.rootsweb.ancestry.com/~ohcarcgs>**

Champaign County Genealogical Society
Box 682, Urbana, OH 43078, **<www.rootsweb.ancestry.com/~ohchampa/society.htm>**

Champaign County Historical Museum
809 E. Lawn, Urbana, OH 43078, **<www.champaigncountyhistoricalmuseum.org>**

Champaign County Library
1060 Scioto St., Urbana, OH 43078, (937) 653-3811, **<www.champaign.lib.oh.us>**

Chillicothe and Ross County Public Library
140 S. Paint St., Chillicothe, OH 45601, **<www.crcpl.org>**

Cincinnati Historical Society Library
Museum Center at Cincinnati Union Terminal, 1301 Western Ave., Cincinnati, OH 45203, **<library.cincymuseum.org>**

Clark County Friends of the Library Genealogical Research Group
2757 S. Burnett Ave., Springfield, OH 45505, **<www.rootsweb.ancestry.com/~ohflgrg>**

Clark County Genealogical Society
Box 2524, Springfield, OH 45501, (937) 324-0657, **<www.heritagecenter.us/genealogy.cfm>**

Clark County Public Library
201 S. Fountain Ave., Box 1080, Springfield, OH 45506, **<www.ccpl.lib.oh.us>**

Clermont County Genealogical Society
Box 394, Batavia, OH 45103, **<www.rootsweb.ancestry.com/~ohclecgs>**

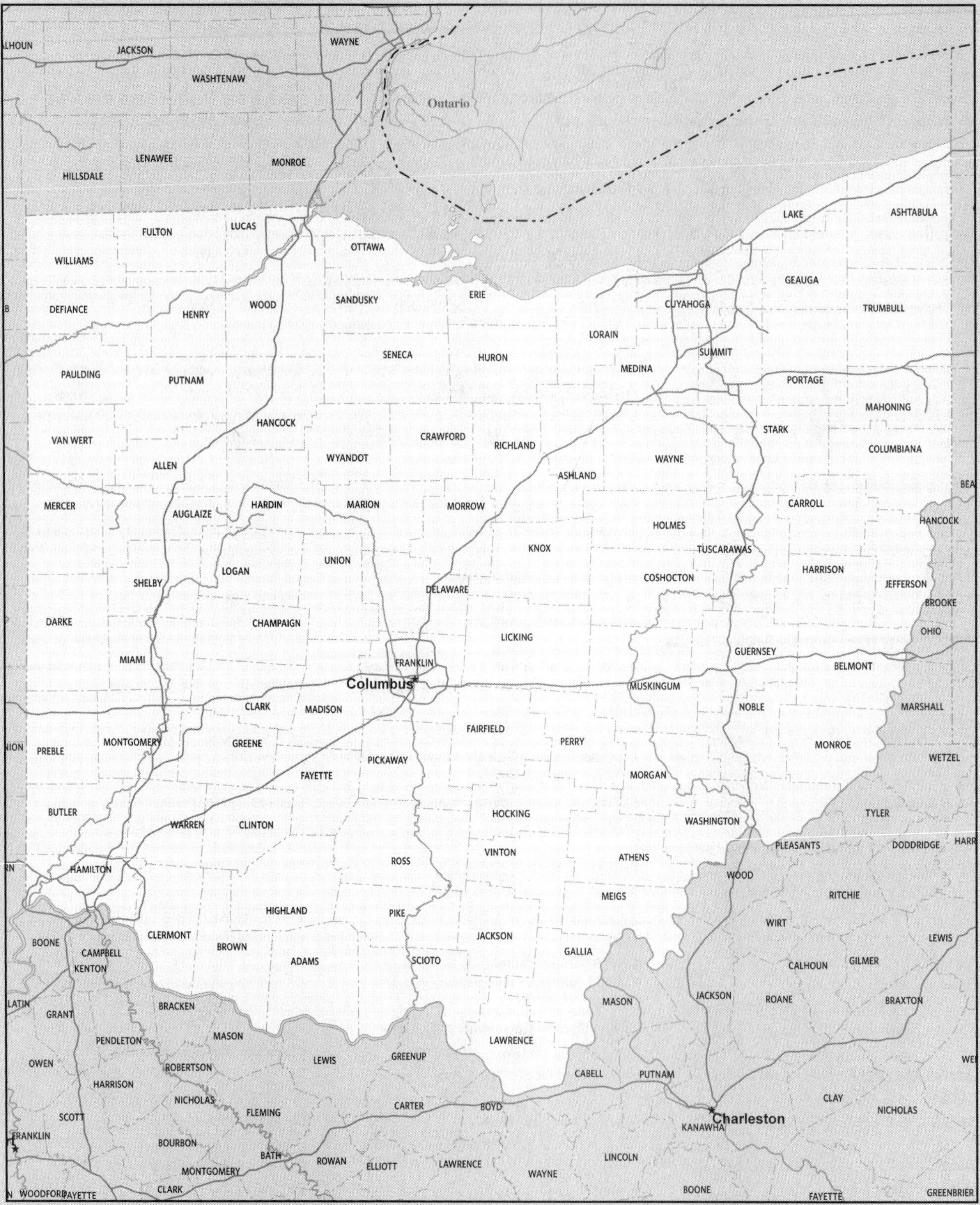
WAYNE
JACKSON
WASHTENAW
Ontario
LENAWEE
MONROE
HILLSDALE
LUCAS
FULTON
WILLIAMS
OTTAWA
LAKE
ASHTABULA
GEAUGA
DEFIANCE
HENRY
WOOD
SANDUSKY
ERIE
CUYAHOGA
TRUMBULL
LORAIN
SUMMIT
SENECA
HURON
MEDINA
PAULDING
PUTNAM
PORTAGE
MAHONING
HANCOCK
STARK
VAN WERT
CRAWFORD
RICHLAND
COLUMBIANA
WYANDOT
WAYNE
ALLEN
ASHLAND
MERCER
HARDIN
MARION
MORROW
CARROLL
AUGLAIZE
HOLMES
HANCOCK
KNOX
TUSCARAWAS
UNION
LOGAN
HARRISON
COSHOCTON
SHELBY
JEFFERSON
DELAWARE
BROOKE
DARKE
CHAMPAIGN
LICKING
OHIO
MIAMI
GUERNSEY
FRANKLIN
BELMONT
Columbus
MUSKINGUM
CLARK
MADISON
NOBLE
MARSHALL
PREBLE
MONTGOMERY
GREENE
FAIRFIELD
PERRY
MONROE
PICKAWAY
WETZEL
FAYETTE
MORGAN
BUTLER
HOCKING
WASHINGTON
TYLER
WARREN
CLINTON
PLEASANTS
DODDRIDGE
VINTON
ROSS
ATHENS
HAMILTON
WOOD
RITCHIE
MEIGS
HIGHLAND
PIKE
WIRT
CLERMONT
JACKSON
LEWIS
BOONE
BROWN
GALLIA
CAMPBELL
ADAMS
SCIOTO
CALHOUN
GILMER
KENTON
MASON
JACKSON
ROANE
BRAXTON
GRANT
BRACKEN
PENDLETON
MASON
LAWRENCE
OWEN
LEWIS
GREENUP
ROBERTSON
CABELL
PUTNAM
HARRISON
NICHOLAS
CLAY
FLEMING
CARTER
BOYD
NICHOLAS
SCOTT
Charleston
KANAWHA
FRANKLIN
BOURBON
BATH
ROWAN
ELLIOTT
LAWRENCE
LINCOLN
MONTGOMERY
WAYNE
CLARK
BOONE
WOODFORD
FAYETTE
FAYETTE
GREENBRIER

Cleveland Public Library
325 Superior Ave., Cleveland, OH 44114, (216) 623-2800, **<cpl.org>**

Clinton County Historical Society
149 E. Locust St., Wilmington, OH 45177, (937) 382-4684, **<www.clintoncountyhistory.org>**

Columbiana County Genealogical Society
Box 861, Salem OH 44460, **<www.rootsweb.ancestry.com/~ohcolumb>**

Columbiana County Historical Society
Box 221, Lisbon, OH 44432

Columbus Jewish Historical Society
1175 College Ave., Columbus, OH 43209, **<www.columbusjewishhistoricalsociety.org>**

Columbus Metropolitan Library,
96 S. Grant Ave., Columbus, OH 43215 **<www.columbuslibrary.org>**

Coshocton County Genealogical Society
Box 128, Coshocton, OH 43812, **<www.coshoctongenealogy.org>**

Coshocton Public Library
655 Main St., Coshocton, OH 43812, (740) 622-0956

Crawford County Genealogical Society
Box 92, Galion, OH 44833, **<www.rootsweb.ancestry.com/~ohccgs>**

Cumberland Trail Genealogical Society
Box 576, St. Clairesville, OH 43905

Cuyahoga-Parma Chapter, Ohio Genealogical Society
Box 29509, Parma, OH 44129

Cuyahoga Valley Genealogical Society
Box 311074, Independence, OH 44131, **<www.rootsweb.ancestry.com/~ohcvgs>**

Cuyahoga West Genealogical Society
Box 45607, Westlake, Ohio 44145, **<www.rootsweb.ancestry.com/~ohcwogs>**

Darke County Genealogical Society
Box 908, Greenville, OH 45331, **<dcgs.dcoweb.org>**

Dayton Metro Library
215 E. Third St., Dayton, OH 45402, (937) 463-2665, **<www.daytonmetrolibrary.org>**

Defiance County Genealogical Society
Box 7006, Defiance, OH 43512, **<www.rootsweb.ancestry.com/~ohdcgs>**

Delaware County Genealogical Society
84 E. Winter St., Delaware, OH 43015, (740) 369-4375, **<www.rootsweb.ancestry.com/~ohdchs>**

Delaware County Historical Society
157 E. William St. Delaware, OH 43015

Division of Vital Statistics, Ohio Department of Health
Box 15098, Columbus, OH 43215, (614) 446-2531, **<www.odh.ohio.gov/vitalstatistics/vitalstats.aspx>**

East Cuyahoga County Genealogical Society
Box 24182, Lyndhurst, OH 44124, **<www.rootsweb.ancestry.com/~ohcdrt/members/eccgs.html>**

East Liverpool Historical Society
Box 476, East Liverpool, OH 43920, **<www.eastliverpoolhistoricalsociety.org>**

East Palestine Historical Society
555 Bacon Ave., East Palestine, OH 44413

Ebenezer Zane Chapter, Ohio Society, Sons of the American Revolution
2101 County Rd. 1, Rayland, OH 43943, (740) 769-7906, **<mysite.ncnetwork.net/resrjk8x>**

Erie County Genealogical Society
Box 1301, Sandusky, OH 44871, **<www.rootsweb.ancestry.com/~oheccogs>**

Evangelical Friends Church, Eastern Division
5350 Broadmoor Circle NW, Canton, OH 44709, (330) 493-1660, **<www.efcer.org>**

Ewing Chapter, Ohio Society, Sons of the American Revolution
18660 State Rt. 550, Amesville, OH 45711, (740) 448-7269, **<sar-ewing.org>**

Fairfield County Genealogical Society
503 Lenwood Dr., Lancaster, OH 43130, **<www.fairfieldgenealogy.org>**

Fairfield County District Library
219 N. Broad St., Lancaster, OH 43130, **<www.fairfield.lib.oh.us>**

Fayette County Genealogical Society
Box 342, Washington Courthouse, OH 43160, **<www.fayettecogs.org>**

Firelands Historical Society Library
4 Case Ave., Norwalk, Ohio 44857, **<www.firelandsmuseum.org>**

Franklin County Genealogical and Historical Society
3378 Park St., Suite D, Columbus, OH 43123, (614) 871-2110, **<www.rootsweb.ancestry.com/~ohfcghs>**

Fulton County Genealogical Society
Box 337, Swanton, OH 43558, **<www.rootsweb.ancestry.com/~ohfulton>**

Gallia County Genealogical Society
Box 1007, Gallipolis, OH 45631, (740) 446-4242, **<www.galliagenealogy.org>**

Garst Museum Genealogical Library
205 N. Broadway, Greenville, OH 45331, **<www.garstmuseum.org>**

Geauga County Genealogical Society
110 E. Park St., Chardon, OH 44024, **<www.rootsweb.ancestry.com/~ohgeauga>**

Geauga West Library
13445 Chillicothe Rd., Chesterland, OH 44026

George Rogers Clark Chapter, Ohio Society, Sons of the American Revolution
<www.grccsar.org>

Glendower Warren County Museum
105 S. Broadway, Lebanon, OH 45036

Granville Public Library
217 E. Broadway, Granville, OH 43023, **<www.granvillelibrary.org>**

Greater Cleveland Genealogical Society
Box 24182, Lyndhurst, OH 44124

Greene Count Genealogical Society
Box 706, Xenia, Ohio 45385, **<www.rootsweb.ancestry.com/~ohgccogs>**

Greene County Public Library
76 E. Market St., Xenia, Ohio 45385, **<www.greenelibrary.info>**

Greenville Carnegie Library
520 Sycamore St., Greenville, OH 45331

Guernsey County Genealogical Society
Box 661, Cambridge, OH 43725, (614) 432-9249, **<www.rootsweb.ancestry.com/~ohguerns/resources.html>**

Guernsey County District Public Library
800 Steubenville Ave., Cambridge, OH 43725

Hamilton County Genealogical Society
Box 15865, Cincinnati, OH 45215, (513) 956-7078, **<hcgsohio.org>**

Hancock County Genealogical Society
Box 672, Findlay, OH 45839, **<www.rootsweb.ancestry.com/~ohhccogs>**

Hanover Township Historical Society
Box 381, Hanoverton, OH 44423

Hardin County Historical Museums
223 N. Main St., Kenton, OH 43326, (419) 673-7147, **<www.hardinmuseums.org>**

Hardin County Genealogy Society
Box 520, Kenton, OH 43326, (419) 674-4088, **<www.kenton.com/users/chuck/soc.htm>**

Harrison County Genealogical Society
168 E. Market St., Cadiz, OH 43907, **<www.rootsweb.ancestry.com/~ohharris/hcgs.htm>**

Hayes Presidential Center Library
1337 Hayes Ave., Fremont, OH 43420, **<www.rbhayes.org/hayes>**

Henry County Genealogical Society
Box 231, Deshler, OH 43516, **<www.henrycountyohiogenealogy.org>**

Highland County Genealogical Society
713 S. Main St., Mansfield, OH 44907, (419) 756-7294

Historical Society of Columbiana and Fairfield Townships
10 Park Ave., Columbiana, OH 44408

Hocking County Genealogical Society
Box 115, Rockbridge, Ohio 43149

Holmes County Genealogical Society
Box 136, Millersburg, OH 44654, **<www.rootsweb.ancestry.com/~ohholmes/hcgs.htm>**

Hudson Genealogical Study Group
Hudson Library and Historical Society, 96 Library St., Hudson, Ohio 44236, (330) 653-6658, **<www.rootsweb.ancestry.com/~ohhudogs/hudson.htm>**

Huron County Genealogical Society
Box 923, Norwalk, OH 44857, **<www.rootsweb.ancestry.com/~ohhuron/member.html>**

Jackson County Genealogical Society
Box 807, Jackson, OH 45640, **<www.jacksoncountyohiogen.com>**

Jefferson County Genealogical Society
Box 2367, Wintersville, OH 43953, (740) 346-2820, **<www.jeffcochapter.com>**

Jefferson County Historical Society
426 Franklin Ave., Steubenville, OH 43952, **<www.rootsweb.ancestry.com/~ohjcha/library.htm>**

Knox County Genealogical Society
Box 1098, Mt. Vernon, OH 43050, **<www.rootsweb.ancestry.com/~ohkcgs>**

Lafayette Chapter, Ohio Society, Sons of the American Revolution
1044 Tuscarawas Ave., Akron, OH 44203, **<www.lafayette-ohssar.org>**

Lake County Genealogical Society
184 Phelps St., Painesville, OH 44077, **<www.morleylibrary.org/genealogy_lcgs.htm>**

Lakewood Public Library
15425 Detroit Ave., Lakewood, Ohio 44107, (216) 226-8275, **<www.lkwdpl.org>**

Lawrence County Genealogical Society
Box 1035, Proctorville, OH 45669

Lisbon Historical Society
Box 221, Lisbon, OH 44432

Licking County Genealogical Society
101 W. Main St., Newark, OH 43055, (740) 349-5510, **<www.npls.org/lcgs>**

Logan County Genealogical Society
Box 36, Bellefontaine, OH 43311, (937) 593-7811, **<www.logangs.embarqspace.com>**

Lorain County Genealogical Society
Box 865, Elyria, OH 44036, **<www.centuryinter.net/lorgen>**

Lorain Public Library
351 W. Sixth St., Lorain, OH 44052, (440) 244-1192, **<www.lorain.lib.oh.us>**

Lucasville Historical Society
Box 761, Lucasville, OH 45648

Madison County Genealogical Society
Box 102, London, OH 43140

Mahoning County Genealogical Society
Box 9333, Youngstown, OH 44513, **<www.mahoningcountychapterogs.org>**

Mansfield/Richland County Public Library
43 W. Third St., Mansfield, OH 44902, (419) 521-3100, **<www.mrcpl.org>**

Marion Area Genealogical Society
Box 844, Marion, OH 43301, **<www.rootsweb.ancestry.com/~ohmags>**

Medina County Genealogical Society
Box 804, Medina, OH 44258, **<www.rootsweb.ancestry.com/~ohmcogs2>**

Meigs County Genealogical Society
Box 346, Pomeroy, OH 45769

Meigs County Historical Society
Box 145, Pomeroy, OH 45769, **<meigscohistorical.org/422.html>**

Mennonite Historical Library
Bluffton College, Bluffton, OH 45817

Mercer County Genealogical Society
Box 437, Celina, OH 45822, **<mercerogs.com>**

Miami County Historical and Genealogical Society
Box 305, Troy, OH 45373, **<www.rootsweb.ancestry.com/~ohmchgs>**

Miami Valley County Genealogical Society
Box 1364, Dayton, OH 45401

Miamisburg Historical Society
Box 774, Miamisburg, Ohio 45343, **<miamisburg.org/miamisburg_historical_society.htm>**

Middletown Public Library
125 S. Broad St., Middletown, OH 45044, (513) 424-1251, **<www.middletownlibrary.org>**

Milan Public Library
Box 1550, Milan, OH 44846, (419) 499-4117, **<www.milan-berlin.lib.oh.us>**

Monroe County Genealogical Society
Box 641, Woodsfield, OH 43793, **<www.rootsweb.ancestry.com/~ohmccogs>**

Montgomery County Genealogical Society
Box 1584, Dayton, OH 45401, **<www.rootsweb.ancestry.com/~ohmontgs>**

Morgan County Genealogical Society
Box 418, McConnelsville, OH 43756, **<www.morgancountyogs.org>**

Morley Library
184 Phelps St., Painesville, OH 44077, (440) 352-3383, **<www.morleylibrary.org>**

Morrow County Genealogical Society
Box 401, Mt. Gilead, OH 43338, (419) 947-5866, **<www.rootsweb.ancestry.com/~ohmorrow>**

Muskingum County Genealogical Society
Box 2427, Zanesville, OH 43702, **<www.rootsweb.ancestry.com/~ohmuskin/mccogs>**

National Archives, Great Lakes Region
7358 S. Pulaski Rd., Chicago, IL 60629, (773) 948-9050, **<www.archives.gov/great-lakes>**

Noble County Genealogical Society
Box 174, Caldwell, OH 43724

North American Baptist, General Conference
7308 Madison St., Forest Park, IL 60130

Northeastern Chapter #12, SAR
1659 Chapel Rd., Jefferson, OH 44047

Norwalk Public Library
46 W. Main St., Norwalk, OH 44857, **<www.norwalk.lib.oh.us>**

Ohio Genealogical Society
713 Main St., Mansfield, Ohio 44907, (419) 756-7294, **<www.ogs.org>**

Ohio Historical Society Archives/Library
Ohio Historical Center, 1982 Velma Ave., Columbus, OH 43211, (614) 297-8300, **<www.ohiohistory.org/resource/archlib>**

Ohio Land Office, Auditor of State
Box 1140, 88 E. Broad St., Columbus, OH 43266, (614) 466-4514

Ohio University, Mahn Center for Archives and Special Collections
Alden Library, Athens, OH 45701, (740) 593-2710, **<www.library.ohiou.edu/archives>**

Old Northwest Historical Society
Box 62635, Cincinnati, OH 45262, (513) 530-9543, **<home.fuse.net/rrowan>**

Ottawa County Genealogical Society
Box 193, Port Clinton, OH 43452, **<www.rootsweb.ancestry.com/~ohoccgs>**

Palatines to America German Genealogy Society, Ohio Chapter
Box 302, Worthington, OH 43085, **<www.oh-palam.org>**

Palatines to America
Box 141260, Columbus, OH 43214, (614) 267-4700, **<www.palam.org>**

Paulding County Genealogy Society
205 E. Main St., Paulding, OH 45879, **<pauldingcountylibrary.org/geneaolgysociety.htm>**

Paulding County Carnegie Library
205 S. Main St., Paulding, OH 45879

Pemberville Public Library
375 E. Front St., Pemberville, Ohio 43450, (419) 287-4012, **<www.pembervillelibrary.org>**

Perry County Genealogical Society
Box 275, Junction City, OH 43748, **<perrycountychapterogs.org>**

Pickaway County Historical and Genealogical Society
410 N. Court St., Circleville, OH 43113, (740) 474-9144, **<www.pchgl.org>**

Pike County Genealogy Society
Box 224, Waverly, OH 45690, **<www.rootsweb.ancestry.com/~ohpcgs>**

Piqua Public Library
116 W. High St., Piqua, OH 45356, (937) 773-6753, **<www.youseemore.com/piqua>**

Polish Genealogical Society of Greater Cleveland
1901 Wexford Ave., Parma, OH 44134, **<www.rootsweb.ancestry.com/~ohcdrt/members/polish.html>**

Portage County Genealogical Society
Box 821, Ravenna, OH 44266, **<www.rootsweb.ancestry.com/~ohportag>**

Portsmouth Public Library
1220 Gallia St., Portsmouth, OH 45662, (740) 354-5688, **<www.portsmouth.lib.oh.us>**

Preble County District Library, Eaton Branch
301 N. Barren St., Eaton, OH 45320, (937) 456-4331, **<www.pcdl.lib.oh.us/locations/eaton.html>**

Preble County Genealogical Society
Preble County District Library, 450 S. Barron St., Eaton, OH 45320, **<www.pcdl.lib.oh.us/pcgs>**

Preble County Historical Society
7693 Swartsel Rd., Easton, Ohio 45320, (937) 787-4256, **<www.pchs.preblecounty.com>**

Presbyterian Historical Society
425 Lombard St., Philadelphia, PA 19147, (215) 627-1852, **<www.history.pcusa.org>**

Public Library of Cincinnati and Hamilton County
800 Vine St., Cincinnati, OH 45202, (513) 369-6900, **<www.cincinnatilibrary.org>**

Putnam County Genealogical Society
Box 403, Ottawa, OH 45875,
<www.putnamgenealogy.com>

Randolph Township Historical Society
114 Valleyview Dr., Englewood, OH 45322

Richland County Genealogical Society
Box 3823, Mansfield, OH 44907, **<www.rootsweb.ancestry.com/~ohrichgs>**

Roman Catholic Archdiocese of Cincinnati
100 E. Eighth St., Cincinnati, OH 45202, (513) 421-3131, **<www.catholiccincinnati.org>**

Roman Catholic Diocese of Cleveland
Chancery Building, 1027 Superior Ave., Cleveland, OH 44114, (216) 696-6525, **<www.dioceseofcleveland.org>**

Roman Catholic Diocese of Columbus
198 E. Broad St., Columbus, OH 43215, (614) 224-2251

Roman Catholic Diocese of Toledo
Chancery Office, Box 985, Toledo, OH 43697, (419) 244-6711

Roman Catholic Diocese of Youngstown
Chancery Office, 144 W. Wood St., Youngstown, OH 44503, (330) 744-8451

Roman Catholic Diocese of Steubenville
422 Washington St., Box 969, Steubenville, OH 43952,(740) 282-3631

Ross County Genealogical Society
Box 6352, Chillicothe, OH 45601, (740) 773-2715, **<www.rootsweb.ancestry.com/~ohrcgs>**

Salem Historical Society
208 S. Broadway Ave., Salem, OH 44460, **<www.salemhistoricalsociety.org>**

Samuel Huntington Chapter, Ohio Society, Sons of the American Revolution
6366 Indian Point Rd., Painesville, OH 44077, **<www.ohssar.org/samuel_huntington_chapter.htm>**

Sandusky County Kin Hunters
Spiegel Grove, Fremont, OH 43420, **<www.kinhunters.org>**

Schiappa Branch Library
4141 Mall Dr., Steubenville, OH 43952

Scioto County Genealogical Society
Box 812, Portsmouth, OH 45662, **<www.sccogs.com>**

Seneca County Genealogical Society
Box 157, Tiffin, Ohio 44883, **<www.senecasearchers.org>**

Shelby Genealogical Society
Box 766, Shelby, OH 44875, **<www.rootsweb.ancestry.com/~ohscogs>**

Sidney Public Library
230 E. North St., Sidney, OH 45365

Society of Friends, Olney Friends School
61830 Sandy Ridge Rd., Barnesville, OH 43713, (740) 425-3655

Southern Ohio Genealogical Society
Box 414, Hillsboro, OH 45133

Southwest Cuyahoga County Genealogical Society
19176 Wheeler Ln., Strongville OH 44149, **<www.rootsweb.ancestry.com/~ohcdrt/members/swcuy.html>**

Stark County District Library
715 Market Ave., North Canton, OH 44702, **<www.starklibrary.org>**

Stark County Genealogical Society
1950 Market Ave. N., Apt. B2, Canton, OH 44714, **<www.starkcountyogs.org>**

State Library of Ohio
274 E. First Ave., Suite 100, Columbus, OH 43201, (614) 644-7061, **<www.library.ohio.gov>**

St. Paris Public Library
E. Main St., St. Paris, Ohio 43072, (937) 663-4349, **<www.stparispubliclibrary.org>**

Summit County Genealogical Society
<www.acorn.net/gen>

Toledo Area Genealogical Society
Box 352258, Toledo, OH 43635, **<www.tagsohio.org>**

Toledo-Lucas County Public Library
325. Michigan St., Toledo, OH 43604, (419) 259-5207, **<www.toledolibrary.org>**

Trumbull County Genealogical Society
Box 309, Warren, OH 44482

Tuscarawas County Genealogical Society
Box 141, New Philadelphia, OH 44633, **<web.tusco.net/tcgs/index.htm>**

Union County Genealogical Society
Box 438, Marysville, OH 43040, **<www.rootsweb.ancestry.com/~ohuniogs>**

University of Cincinnati, Archives and Rare Books
8th Floor Blegen Library, 2602 McMicken Circle, Cincinnati, OH 45221, (513) 556-1959, **<www.libraries.uc.edu/libraries/arb>**

Van Wert County Genealogical Society
Box 485, Van Wert, Ohio 45891, **<www.rootsweb.ancestry.com/~ohvwogs>**

Vinton County Historical and Genealogical Society
Box 306, Hamden, OH 45634, **<www.rootsweb.ancestry.com/~ohvinton/ogschapt.htm>**

Warder Public Library
137 E. High St., Springfield, OH 45502, **<www.clarkcountyliteracy.org>**

Warren County Genealogical Society
406 Justice Dr., Lebanon, OH 45036, **<www.rootsweb.ancestry.com/~ohwarren>**

Warren County Genealogy Resource Center
300 E. Silver St., Lebanon, OH 45036

Warren-Trumbull County Public Library
444 Mahoning Ave. NW, Warren, OH 44483, **<www.wtcpl.org>**

Washington County Genealogical Society
Box 2174, Marietta, Ohio 45750, **<www.washogs.org>**

Washington County Public Library
615 Fifth St., Marietta, OH 45750, (740) 373-1057, **<www.wcplib.lib.oh.us>**

Wayne County Genealogical Society
Box 856, Wooster, OH 44691, **<www.rootsweb.ancestry.com/~ohwayne/wcgs.htm>**

Wayne County Public Library
220 W. Libaray St., Wooster, OH 44691, (330) 262-0916, **<www.wayne.lib.oh.us>**

Wellsville Historical Society
1003 Riverside Ave., Wellsville, OH 43968, **<www.wellsvilleohio.net/historicalsociety.html>**

Western Reserve Historical Society
10825 East Blvd., Cleveland, OH 44106, (216) 721-5722, **<www.wrhs.org>**

Williams County Genealogical Society
Box 293, Bryan, OH 43506, **<www.wcgs-ogs.com>**

Wood County Genealogical Society
Box 722, Bowling Green, OH 43402, **<www.rootsweb.ancestry.com/~ohwood>**

Wright State University, Special Collections and Archives
Paul Laurence Dunbar Library, Dayton, OH 45435, (937) 775-2092

Youngstown Historical Center of Industry and Labor Archives-Library
151 W. Wood St., Youngstown, OH 44503, (330) 743-5934

Youngstown and Mahoning Counties Public Library
305 Wick Ave., Youngstown, OH 44503, (330) 744-8636, **<www.libraryvisit.org>**

GENERAL RESOURCES

The Henry R. Baldwin Genealogy Records, 67 vols., by Henry R. Baldwin (Allen County Public Library, 1983)

Bench and Bar of Ohio: A Compendium of History and Biography, 2 vols., by George Irving Reed (Century Publishing and Engraving Co., 1897)

Bibliography of the State of Ohio, Being a Catalog of the Books and Pamphlets Relating to the History of the State, the West and Northwest by Peter G. Thomson (Higginson Book Co., 1993)

The Biographical Encyclopedia of Ohio of the Nineteenth Century by Charles Robson (Galaxy Pub. Co., 1876)

Black Ohio and the Color Line, 1860-1915 by David Allison Gerber (University of Illinois Press, 1976)

Card Catalog to the Manuscripts Collection in the Library of the Western Reserve Historical Society by the Western Reserve Historical Society (filmed by the Genealogical Society of Utah, 1974)

Early History of the Disciples in the Western Reserve 1875 by A.S. Hayden (Reprint. The Bookmark, 1979)

Early Ohio Tax Records, 2 vols., by Esther Weygandt Powell (Genealogical Publishing Co., 1993)

The Encyclopedia Of Quaker Genealogy 1750-1930 (Broderbund, 1998, CD-ROM)

First Families of Ohio, Official Roster (Ohio Genealogical Society, 1988)

Frontier Republic: Ideology and Politics in the Ohio Country 1780-1825 by Andrew Cayton (Frontier Press, 1986)

Gateway to the West, 2 vols., by Ruth Bowers and Anita Short (Genealogical Publishing Co., 1989)

Genealogical Data Relating to Women in the Western Reserve Before 1840 (1850) compiled by the Cleveland Centennial Commission (Ohio Historical Society, 1973)

Genealogical Research in Ohio, 2nd edition, by Kip Sperry (Genealogical Publishing Co., 2003)

Genealogical Researcher's Manual: With Special References for Using the Ohio Historical Society Library compiled by Suzanne Wolfe Mettle and Nova Anderson Weller (Ohio Genealogical Society, 1981)

Guide to the Manuscript Collection of Early Ohio Methodism by Frances D. Harter (United Methodist Archives Center, 1980)

Guide to Manuscript Collections and Institutional Records in Ohio edited by David R. Larson (Society of Ohio Archivists, 1974)

A Guide to Manuscripts at the Ohio Historical Society edited by Sara S. Fuller and Andrea D. Lentz (The Society, 1972)

A Guide to the Manuscripts and Archives of the Western Reserve Historical Society by Kermit J. Pike (Western Reserve Historical Society, 1972)

Guide to Ohio County and Municipal Records for Urban Research by Paul D. Yon (Ohio Historical Society, 1973)

A Guide to Shaker Manuscripts in the Library of The Western Reserve Historical Society, with an Inventory of its Shaker Photographs (Western Reserve Historical Society, 1974)

Historical Collections of Ohio, 2 vols., by Henry Howe (Higginson Book Co., 1994)

A History of the Diocese of Ohio Until the Year 1918 by George Franklin Smythe (The Diocese, ca. 1931)

History of Ohio, 5 vols., by Charles Burleigh Galbreath (American Historical Society, 1925)

A History of the Ohio Conference of the Churches of God, General Conferences, 1836-1986 by Richard Kern (Richard Kern, 1986)

The History of the State of Ohio, 6 vols., edited by Carl F. Wittke (The Society, 1941-1944)

History of West Central Ohio, 3 vols., by Orton G. Rust (Historical Publishing Co., 1934)

History of the Western Reserve, 3 vols., by Harriet T. Upton (Higginson Book Co., 1995)

Inventory Of The Church Archives Of Ohio Presbyterian Churches by the Historical Records Survey (filmed by the Family History Library, 1972)

Inventory of the State Archives Of Ohio by the Historical Records Survey (Ohio Historical Records Survey Project, 1940)

Local History And Genealogy Resources Guide To Southeastern Ohio by Linda L. Harfst (Ohio Valley Area Libraries, 1984)

Log Construction in the Ohio Country, 1750-1850 by Donald A. Hutslar (Frontier Press, 1992)

Memoirs of the Early Pioneer Settlers of Ohio, with Narratives of Incidents and Occurrences in 1775 by S.P. Hildreth (Reprint, Clearfield Co., 1995)

Memoirs of the Lower Ohio Valley: Personal and Genealogical with Portraits, 2 vols., (Federal Publishing, 1905)

Memoirs of the Miami Valley, 3 vols., by John Calvin Hover (R.O. Law Co., 1919)

Methodist Ministers Card Index: All Ohio Conferences, 1797-1981 by the United Methodist Archives, Ohio (Ohio Historical Society, 1982)

Newspapers: Microfilm Available from the Ohio Historical Society (The Society, 1987)

Ohio Bible Records, 2 vols., by Mrs. Don R. Short and Mrs. Denver Eller (Allen County Public Library, 1983)

Ohio County Records Manual (Ohio Historical Society, 1983)

Ohio Families: A Bibliography of Books About Ohio Families by Donald M. Hehir (Heritage books, 1993)

Ohio; The Future Great State: Her Manufacturers and a History of Her Commercial Cities, Cincinnati and Cleveland with Portraits and Biographies of Some of the Old Settlers, and Many of The Most Prominent Business Men by W.J. Comley and W. D'Eggville (Comley Brothers Manufacturing and Publishing Co., 1875)

Ohio Genealogical Guide, 6th edition, by Carol Willsey Bell (Carol Willsey Bell, 1993)

Ohio Genealogical Research by George K. Schweitzer (George K. Schweitzer, 1995)

Ohio Genealogical Research Guide by John W. Heisey (Heritage House, 1987)

Ohio Genealogy and Local History Sources Index by Stuart Herter (CompuGen Systems, 1986)

Ohio Guide to Genealogical Sources (Genealogical Publishing Co., Reprint, 1993)

The Ohio Hundred Year book: A Hand-Book of the Public Men and Public Institutions of Ohio from the Formation of the North-West Territory (1787) to July 1, 1901 by Elliot Howard Gilkey (F.J. Heer, 1901)

Ohio Newspaper Index (Ohio Historical Society, 1996-2001)

Ohio Research Outline by the Church of Jesus Christ of Latter-day Saints (online at <www.familysearch.org/eng/search/RG/guide/ohio.asp>)

The Ohio River: A Course of Empire by Archer Butler Hulbert (Higginson Book Co., 1996)

Ohio Source Records from The Ohio Genealogical Quarterly (1937-1944, 1986) by Ohio Genealogical Society (Genealogical Publishing Co., 1993)

Ohio Valley German Biographical Index by Don Heinrich Tolzmann (Heritage Books, 1992)

Ohio's Progressive Sons, A History of the State (Queen City Publishing, 1905)

The Old Northwest: Pioneer Period, 1815-1840, 2 vols., by R. Carlyle Buley (Indiana University Press with the Indiana Historical Society, 1978)

Pioneer Ohio Newspapers, 1793-1810 and 1802-1818, 2 vols., by Karen Mauer Green (Frontier Press, 1988)

Pioneer Sketches: Scenes and Incidents of Former Days by M.P. Sargent (Higginson Book Co., 1993)

Progressive Men Of Northern Ohio (Plain Dealer Publishing Co., 1906)

The Records of American Baptists in Ohio, and Related Organizations compiled by Susan M. Eltscher (American Baptist Historical Society, 1981)

Shane Manuscript Collection (filmed by the Genealogical Society of Utah, 1966-1967)

The Shane Manuscript Collection: A Genealogical Guide to the Kentucky and Ohio Papers by William K. Hall (Frontier Press, 1990)

Six Thousand Country Churches by Charles Otis Gill and Gifford Pinchot (Macmillan, 1919)

Sketches of Western Methodism: Biographical, Historical & Miscellaneous, Illustrative Of Pioneer Life by James Bradley Finley (Methodist Book Concern, 1856)

Southern Ohio And Its Builders (Southern Ohio Biographical Association, 1927)

State Centennial History of Ohio, Covering The Period of Indian, French and British Dominion, the Territory Northwest, and the Hundred Years of Statehood by Rowland H. Rerick (Higginson Book Co., 1995)

The Western Reserve: The Story of New Connecticut in Ohio by Harlan Hatcher (Frontier Press, 1991)

CENSUS RECORDS

Federal Non-Population Census Schedules, Ohio 1850-1880, in The Custody of the State Library of Ohio: Products of Agriculture, And Products of Industry (National Archives, 1988)

IMMIGRATION RECORDS

County Naturalizations Held by OHS (Ohio Historical Society, 1996-2001)

Gone to Ohio: Ashland, Brown, Columbiana, Harrison, Jefferson, Richland, Champaign, Crawford, Wood, Logan, Mahoning, Stark and Trumbull Counties, From the Pennsylvania Counties: Adams, Cumberland, Dauphin, Franklin, Lancaster, and York, 3 vols., by Gloria L. Aughenbaugh (South Central Pennsylvania Genealogical Society, 1990-1996)

Mountain People in a Flat Land: A Popular History of Appalachian Migration to Northeast Ohio 1940-1965 by Carl E. Feather (Ohio University Press, 1998)

Naturalization Index 1852-1991 from the US District Court Records, Southern District of Ohio (filmed by the Genealogical Society of Utah, 1992)

Ohio, Trailways to Highways 1776-1976 (Genealogical Society of Utah, 1977)

The Origin and Distribution of Settlement Groups by Hubert G.H. Wilhelm (Ohio University, 1982)

The Politics of Community: Migration and Politics in Antebellum Ohio by Kenneth J. Winkle (Press Syndicate of the University of Cambridge, 1988)

☞LAND RECORDS

The Bounty Lands of the American Revolution in Ohio by William Thomas Hutchinson (Arno Press, 1979)

Canal Lands by the Ohio Auditor of State, Ohio Historical Society (filmed by the Genealogical Society of Utah, 1959)

Early Ohio Settlers Purchasers of Land in Southwestern Ohio, 1800-1840 by Ellen T. Berry and David Berry (Genealogical Publishing Co., 1993)

Early Ohioans' Residences From the Land Grant Records by Mayburt Stephenson Riegel (Ohio Genealogical Society, 1976)

First Ownership of Ohio Lands by Albion Morris Dyer (Genealogical Publishing Co., 1982)

Governor's Deeds Card Index, 1833-1994 from the Ohio Historical Society (filmed by the Genealogical Society of Utah, 1995)

Miscellaneous Lands Ohio Auditor of State Records (Columbus Microfilm, Inc., 1954-1958, 1995)

Ohio, 1787-1840 (Broderbund, 1999, CD-ROM)

Ohio Lands: A Short History, 6th edition, by Thomas E. Ferguson (Auditor's Office, State of Ohio, 1995)

Ohio Lands South of the Indian Boundary Line (Marie Taylor Clark, 1984)

Ohio Lands and Their History by William Edwards Peters (W.E. Peters, 1930)

Ohio Lands and Their Subdivision, 2nd edition, by William Edwards Peters (W.E. Peters, 1918)

Original Ohio Land Subdivision Being Volume III: Final Report Ohio Cooperative Topographic Survey by C.E. Sherman (State Reformatory Press, 1925)

US Revolutionary War Bounty Land Warrants Used in the U.S. Military District of Ohio and Related Papers, Acts of 1788, 1803, 1806 from the US General Land Office (National Archives, 1971)

Virginia Military District Lands of Ohio; Indexes from the State Auditor's Office in Columbus, OH (filmed by the Genealogical Society of Utah, 1995, 1958)

☞MAPS

Atlas of Ohio (American Publishing Co., 1975)

Atlas of the State of Ohio by H.F. Walling (The Bookmark, 1868, reprint 1995)

The Development of Ohio's Counties and Their Historic Courthouses by Lawrence J. Marzulli (County Commissioners Association of Ohio, ca. 1980)

Early Maps of the Ohio Valley by Lloyd Arnold Brown (University of Pittsburgh Press, 1959)

Historical Atlas and Chronology of County Boundaries, 1788-1980 by John H. Long (G.K. Hall, 1984)

Jurisdictional Histories For Ohio's Eighty-Eight Counties, 1788-1985 by W. Louis Phillips (Heritage Books, 1986)

Maps Of Ohio Showing The Development Of Its Counties (W.L. Howison & Assoc., 1980)

Ohio Atlas and Gazetteer, 4th edition, (DeLorme Mapping Co., 1996)

Ohio County Maps compiled by C.J Puetz (Thomas Publishing Co., 1992)

The Ohio Gazetteer by John Kilbourn (The Bookmark, 1981)

The Ohio Gazetteer And Traveler's Guide by Warren Jenkins (Isaac N. Whiting, 1837)

Ohio Lands: A Short History, 3rd edition, by Thomas A. Burke (State Auditor, 1991)

Ohio Place Names by Larry L. Miller (Indiana University Press, 1996)

Ohio Town Names by William D. Overman (Atlantic Press, 1958)

The Post Offices Of Ohio by John S. Gallagher (The Depot, 1979)

☞MILITARY RECORDS

Annotated Bibliography of Ohio Patriots: Revolutionary War & War of 1812 by William Louis Phillips (Heritage Books, 1985)

Civil War Documents (Ohio Historical Society, 1996-2001)

Genealogical Abstracts of the Revolutionary War Pension Files, 4 vols., by Virgil D. White (National Historical Publishing, 1990)

History of the 21st Regiment, Ohio Volunteer Infantry, in the War of the Rebellion (Higginson Book Co., 1893, reprint 1995)

Index to the Official Roster of Ohio Soldiers in The War with Spain by Jana Sloan Broglin (Ohio Genealogical Society, 1990)

Index to Roster of Ohio Soldiers, War of 1812 by Grace Garner (Eastern Washington Genealogical Society, 1974)

Middle Western Section Records from the Daughters of the American Revolution, Ohio (Allen County Public Library, 1983)

The Official Roster of Ohio Soldiers, Sailors, and Marines in the World War, 1917-1918, 22 vols., from the Ohio Adjutant General's Office (F.J. Heer Printing Co., 1926-1929)

The Official Roster of Ohio Soldiers in the War with Spain 1898-1899 from the Ohio Adjutant General's Office (Edward T. Miller, Co., 1916)

The Official Roster of the Soldiers of the American Revolution Buried in the State of Ohio, 3 vols., from the Ohio Adjutant General's Office (F.J. Heer Printing, 1929-59)

The Official Roster of the Soldiers of the American Revolution Who Lived in the State of Ohio: Vol. 2, A-Z by Mrs. Orville D. Dailey (Daughters of the American Revolution, Ohio, ca. 1938)

Official Roster of the Soldiers of the State of Ohio in the War of the Rebellion, 1861-1866 from the Ohio Roster Commission (Werner Co., 1886-1895)

Ohio Indian, Revolutionary War, and War of 1812 Trails by Fay Maxwell (Ohio Genealogy Center, 1974)

Ohio Revolutionary War Soldiers 1840 Census and Grave Locations by Fay Maxwell (Ohio Genealogy Center, 1985)

Ohio, World War I Selective Service System Draft Registration Cards, 1917-1918 from the US Selective Service System (National Archives, 1987-1988)

Ohio's Virginia Military Tract Settlers, Also 1801 Tax List by Fay Maxwell (Ohio Genealogy Center, 1991)

Revolutionary War Pension and Bounty-Land-Warrant Application Files from the US Veterans Administration (National Archives, 1969)

Roster of Ohio Soldiers in The War of 1812 from the Ohio Adjutant General's Department (Clearfield Co., 1968, reprint 1989)

Roster of the Soldiers of the State of Ohio in the War with Mexico 1846-1848 (Ohio Genealogical Society, 1897, reprint 1991)

State Summary of War Casualties (Ohio), U.S. Navy, 1946: (Includes Navy, Marine, And Coast Guard) from the US Navy Department (filmed by the Genealogical Society of Utah, 1960)

Two Hundred Years the Military History of Ohio (H.H. Hardesty, 1886)

War of 1812, Roster of Ohio Soldiers (Ohio Historical Society, 1996-2001)

World War II Honor List of Dead and Missing—State of Ohio, June 1946 from the US War Department (filmed by the Genealogical Society of Utah, 1960)

Young American Patriots: The Youth of Ohio in World War II (National Publishing Co., 1947)

☞PROBATE RECORDS

Abstracts and Extracts of the Legislative Acts And Resolutions of the State of Ohio: 1803-1821 by Mary L. Bowman (Ohio Genealogical Society, 1994)

Guide to Local Government Records at the Ohio University Library by the Ohio Historical Society (Ohio University Library, 1986)

A History of the Courts and Lawyers of Ohio, 4 vols., edited by Carrington Tanner Marshall (American Historical Society, 1934)

Inventory of the State Archives of Ohio by the Historical Records Survey (Ohio Historical Records Survey Project, 1940)

Ohio Circuit Court Records (National Archives)

Ohio Federal Court Orders, 1803-1807 (TLC Genealogy, 1998)

Ohio Marriages Recorded in County Courts Through 1820: An Index by Jean Nathan (The Society, 1996)

Ohio Wills and Estates to 1850: An Index by Carol Willsey Bell (Bell Books, 1981)

Wills, 1655-1871, 1917 by (Daughters of the American Revolution, Ohio, 1970-1971)

☞VITAL RECORDS

Certificates of Death, 1908-1944; Index, 1908-1911 from the Ohio Department of Health (Ohio Historical Society, 1983, 1994-1995)

Death Certificate Index, 1913-1937 (Ohio Historical Society, 1992)

Early Vital Records of Ohio, 1750-1970 from the Daughters of the American Revolution, Ohio (Genealogical Society of Utah, 1972)

Index of Death and Other Notices Appearing In the Cincinnati Free Press 1874-1920 indexed by Jeffrey G. Herbert (Heritage Books, 1993)

Index to Grave Records of Servicemen in the War of 1812 edited by Phyllis Miller (Society of the US Daughters of 1812)

Marriage Notices From the Ohio Observer Series 1827-1855 by James F. Caccamo (Closson Press, 1994)

Marriage Records (Automated Archives, 1994, CD-ROM)

Ohio Birth and Death Records by County (State Library of Ohio, 2001)

Ohio Cemeteries edited by Maxine Hartmann Smith (Ohio Genealogical Society, 1978)

Ohio Cemetery Records (filmed by the Genealogical Society of Utah, 1972)

Ohio Cemetery Records: Extracted from the "Old Northwest" Genealogical Quarterly (Genealogical Publishing Co., 1989)

Ohio Divorces: The Early Years by Carol Willsey Bell (Bell Books, ca. 1994)

Ohio Marriages: Extracted form the Old Northwest Genealogical Quarterly edited by Marjorie Smith (Genealogical Publishing Co., 1980)

Veteran's Records, 1941-1964 from the Ohio Department of Health (filmed by the Genealogical Society of Utah, 1974)

•-COUNTY DETAILS-•

ADAMS
110 W. Main St., West Union, OH 45693, (937) 544-5547, **<www.adamscountyoh.com>**
- **INCORPORATED:** July 10, 1797
- **PARENT COUNTY:** Hamilton
- **MARRIAGE RECORDS:** start in 1910, kept by Probate Court
- **DIVORCE:** 1910, Clerk of Courts
- **LAND:** 1797, County Recorder
- **PROBATE:** 1910, Probate Court
- **COURT:** 1910, Clerk of Courts
- **NOTES:** Probate Court has non-certifiable township birth and death records 1888-1893, marriage records 1803-1833, Wills 1849-1860, and a book by the genealogy society of marriages 1834-1910. Courthouse burned in 1910, some records saved, some as early as 1796; records of several adjacent counties prior to their formation included.

ALLEN
301 N. Main St., Lima, OH 45802, (419) 223-8513, **<www.co.allen.oh.us>**
- **PARENT COUNTY:** Shelby
- **INCORPORATED:** Feb. 12, 1820
- **MARRIAGE RECORDS:** start in 1831, kept by Probate Court
- **DIVORCE:** 1831, Clerk of Courts
- **PROBATE:** 1831, Probate Court
- **COURT:** 1831, Clerk of Courts
- **NOTES:** Probate Court has birth and death records 1867-1908. County Museum has naturalization records 1830s-1870s.

ASHLAND
142 W. Second St., Ashland, OH 44805, (419) 282-4235, **<www.ashlandcounty.org>**
- **INCORPORATED:** Feb. 24, 1846
- **PARENT COUNTIES:** Wayne, Richland, Huron, Lorain
- **MARRIAGE RECORDS:** start in 1846, kept by Probate Court
- **LAND:** 1847, County Recorder
- **PROBATE:** 1846, Probate Court
- **NOTES:** Probate Court has birth records 1879-1908 and death records 1867-1908. Clerk of Courts has court and divorce records from mid 1800s.

ASHTABULA
25 W. Jefferson St., Jefferson, OH 44047, (440) 576-3637, **<www.co.ashtabula.oh.us>**
- **INCORPORATED:** Feb. 10, 1807
- **PARENT COUNTIES:** Trumbull, Geauga
- **MARRIAGE RECORDS:** start in 1812, kept by Probate Court
- **DIVORCE:** 1811, Clerk of Courts
- **LAND:** 1800, County Recorder
- **PROBATE:** 1811, Probate Court
- **COURT:** 1811, Clerk of Courts
- **NOTES:** Probate Court has birth and death records 1867-1908.

ATHENS
Court & Washington Sts., Box 290, Athens, OH 45701, (614) 592-3242, **<www.athenscountygovernment.com>**
- **INCORPORATED:** Feb. 20, 1805
- **PARENT COUNTY:** Washington
- **MARRIAGE RECORDS:** start in 1800, kept by Probate Court
- **DIVORCE:** 1800, Alden Library Archives
- **LAND:** 1790, County Recorder
- **PROBATE:** unknown, Probate Court
- **COURT:** ca. 1800, Alden Library Archives
- **NOTES:** Probate Court has birth and some death records 1867-1908.

AUGLAIZE
201 Willipie St. Suite 103, Wapakoneta, OH 45895, (419) 738-7710, **<www2.auglaizecounty.org>**
- **INCORPORATED:** Feb. 14, 1848
- **PARENT COUNTIES:** Allen, Mercer, Darke, Hardin, Logan, Shelby, Van Wert
- **MARRIAGE:** start in 1848, kept by Probate Court
- **DIVORCE:** 1848, Clerk of Courts
- **LAND:** ca. 1830, County Recorder
- **PROBATE:** 1848, Probate Court
- **COURT:** 1848, Clerk of Courts
- **NOTES:** Probate Court has birth and death records 1867-1908.

BELMONT
101 W. Main St., St. Clairsville, OH 43950, (740) 699-2169, **<www.belmontcountyohio.org>**
- **INCORPORATED:** Sep. 7, 1801
- **PARENT COUNTIES:** Jefferson, Washington
- **MARRIAGE RECORDS:** start ca. 1800, kept by Probate Court
- **PROBATE:** ca. 1800, Probate Court
- **COURT:** 1803, Clerk of Courts
- **NOTES:** Probate Court has birth and death records 1867-1908. Divorce records will be in journals from 1803-1897. St. Clairsville Library has cemetery/tombstone records.

BROWN
101 S. Main St., Georgetown, OH 45121, (937) 378-3100, **<www.browncountyohio.gov>**
- **INCORPORATED:** Dec. 27, 1817
- **PARENT COUNTIES:** Adams, Clermont
- **MARRIAGE RECORDS:** start in 1818, kept by Probate Court
- **DIVORCE:** 1800, Clerk of Courts
- **LAND:** 1818, County Recorder
- **PROBATE:** 1818, Probate Court
- **COURT:** ca. 1800, Clerk of Courts
- **NOTES:** Probate Court has birth and death records 1867-1908.

BUTLER
315 High St., Hamilton, OH 45011, (513) 887-3278, **<www.butlercountyohio.org>**
- **INCORPORATED:** March 24, 1803

- **PARENT COUNTY:** Hamilton
- **MARRIAGE RECORDS:** start in 2000, kept by Probate Court
- **DIVORCE:** 1976, Clerk of Courts
- **LAND:** 1978, County Auditor
- **PROBATE:** unknown, Probate Court
- **NOTES:** Butler County Health Department has birth and death records 1914-present, City of Hamilton Health Department 1913-present, and City of Middletown 1885-present. City of Hamilton and County birth and death records 1909-1912 were lost in a flood. Archive building has birth and death records 1867-1908 plus other record types prior to 1976.

CARROLL

119 Lisbon St., Carrollton, OH 44615, (330) 627-4869, **<pages.eohio.net/carrcomm>**

- **INCORPORATED:** Dec. 25, 1832
- **PARENT COUNTIES:** Columbiana, Stark, Harrison, Jefferson, Tuscarawas
- **MARRIAGE RECORDS:** start in 1936, kept by Probate Court
- **DIVORCE:** 1833, Clerk of Courts
- **LAND:** 1831, County Recorder
- **PROBATE:** 1947, Probate Court
- **COURT:** 1833, Clerk of Courts
- **NOTES:** Probate Court has birth and death records 1867-1909. All public records other than land records prior to years noted are housed at the Genealogy Building on Second Street.

CHAMPAIGN

200 N. Main St., Urbana, OH 43078, (937) 653-2746, **<www.co.champaign.oh.us>**

- **INCORPORATED:** Feb. 20, 1805
- **PARENT COUNTIES:** Greene, Franklin
- **MARRIAGE RECORDS:** start in 1802, kept by Probate Court
- **DIVORCE:** ca. 1800, Clerk of Courts
- **LAND:** 1805, County Recorder
- **PROBATE:** 1800, Probate Court
- **COURT:** 1800, Clerk of Courts
- **NOTES:** Probate Court has birth and death records 1867-1908.

CLARK

101 N. Limestone St., Springfield, OH 45502, (937) 328-2458, **<www.clarkcountyohio.gov>**

- **INCORPORATED:** Dec. 26, 1817
- **PARENT COUNTIES:** Champaign, Madison, Greene
- **MARRIAGE RECORDS:** start in 1818, kept by Probate Court
- **DIVORCE:** 1991, Common Pleas Court
- **LAND:** 1818, County Recorder
- **PROBATE:** 1818, Probate Court
- **COURT:** 1850, Clerk of Courts
- **NOTES:** Probate Court has birth and death records 1867-1908 and naturalization records 1861-1904. Clerk of Courts has divorce records late 1880s-1990. The Heritage Center houses the Clark County Historical Society, a genealogy department and library.

CLERMONT

270 Main St., Batavia, OH 45103, (513) 732-7308, **<www.clermontcountyohio.gov >**

- **INCORPORATED:** Dec. 6, 1800
- **PARENT COUNTIES:** Hamilton
- **MARRIAGE RECORDS:** start in 1800, kept by Probate Court
- **DIVORCE:** 1861, Clerk of Courts
- **LAND:** 1800, County Recorder
- **PROBATE:** 1800, Probate Court
- **COURT:** 1803, Clerk of Courts
- **NATURALIZATION:** 1860, Probate Court
- **NOTES:** Probate Court has birth and death records 1867-1908.

CLINTON

46 S. South St., Wilmington, OH 45177, (937) 382-2316, **<co.clinton.oh.us>**

- **INCORPORATED:** Feb. 19, 1810
- **PARENT COUNTIES:** Highland, Warren
- **BIRTH RECORDS:** start in 1908, kept by Department of Health
- **MARRIAGE:** 1817, Probate Court
- **DIVORCE:** 1810, Clerk of Courts
- **DEATH:** 1908, Department of Health
- **LAND:** 1806, County Recorder
- **PROBATE:** 1810, Probate Court
- **COURT:** 1810, Clerk of Courts
- **NOTES:** Probate Court has birth and death records 1867-1908. Many original birth, death and marriage records are kept at the Records Center on Nelson Avenue.

COLUMBIANA

105 S. Market St., Lisbon, OH 44432, (330) 424-9511, **<www.columbianacounty.org>**

- **INCORPORATED:** March 25, 1803
- **PARENT COUNTIES:** Jefferson, Washington
- **MARRIAGE RECORDS:** start in 1803, kept by Probate Court
- **DIVORCE:** unknown, Clerk of Courts
- **LAND:** 1798, County Recorder
- **PROBATE:** 1803, Probate Court
- **COURT:** 1803, Clerk of Courts
- **NOTES:** Probate has birth and death records 1867-1908. Birth and death records from 1909 to the present are at the City or County Health Departments of Salem City, East Liverpool City, or East Palestine City. Clerk of Courts has naturalization records 1840-1970.

COSHOCTON

318 Main St., Coshocton, OH 43812, (740) 622-1456, **<www.coshoctoncounty.net >**

- **INCORPORATED:** Jan. 31, 1810
- **PARENT COUNTIES:** Tuscarawas, Muskingum
- **MARRIAGE RECORDS:** start in 1811, kept by Probate Court
- **DIVORCE:** 1811, Clerk of Courts
- **LAND:** 1800, County Recorder
- **PROBATE:** 1811, Probate Court
- **COURT:** 1811, Clerk of Courts
- **NOTES:** Probate has birth and death records 1867-1908. Common Pleas has some naturalization records from 1912.

CRAWFORD

112 E. Mansfield St., Bucyrus, OH 44820, (419) 562-2766, **<www.crawford-co.org>**

- **INCORPORATED:** Feb. 12, 1820
- **PARENT COUNTY:** Delaware

- **MARRIAGE RECORDS:** start in 1831, kept by Probate Court
- **NOTES:** Probate Court has birth and death records 1867-1908. Galion City Health Department has birth and death records for the city only from 1909 to the present. The County Health Department has all others.

CUYAHOGA

2905 Franklin Blvd., Cleveland, OH 44113, (216) 443-7250, **<www.cuyahogacounty.us>**

- **INCORPORATED:** Feb. 10, 1808
- **PARENT COUNTY:** Geauga
- **LAND RECORDS:** start in 1810, kept by County Administration Building
- **PROBATE:** 1810, Probate Court
- **NOTES:** Probate Court has birth and death records 1868-1908. Western Reserve Historical Society has marriage records 1810-1941 and tax records 1819-1869. County Archives has naturalization records 1818-1971. Clerk of Courts has divorce records 1837-1925.

DARKE

504 S. Broadway St., Greenville, OH 45331, (937) 547-7335, **<ohdarke.ohgenweb.net>**

- **INCORPORATED:** Jan. 3, 1809
- **PARENT COUNTY:** Miami
- **MARRIAGE RECORDS:** start in 1817, kept by Probate Court
- **DIVORCE:** ca. 1800, Clerk of Courts
- **LAND:** 1816, County Recorder
- **PROBATE:** 1800, Probate Court
- **COURT:** 1800, Clerk of Courts
- **NOTES:** Probate Court has birth and death records 1867-1908. County Recorder has burial records (veterans graves) from 1832.

DEFIANCE

510 Court St., Defiance, OH 43512, (419) 782-8918, **<www.defiance-county.com>**

- **INCORPORATED:** March 4, 1845
- **PARENT COUNTIES:** Williams, Henry, Paulding
- **MARRIAGE RECORDS:** start in 1845, kept by County Records Center
- **DIVORCE:** 1845, County Records Center
- **LAND:** 1823, County Recorder
- **NOTES:** County Records Center has birth and death records 1867-1908, naturalization records 1872-1903, military discharge records 1865-1974, and circuit court probate and court records of closed cases from 1845 to the present.

DELAWARE

91 N. Sandusky St., Delaware, OH 43015, (740) 833-2500, **<www.co.delaware.oh.us>**

- **INCORPORATED:** Feb. 10, 1808
- **PARENT COUNTY:** Franklin
- **DIVORCE RECORDS:** start in 1825, kept by Records Center
- **LAND:** 1803, County Records Center
- **PROBATE:** 1812, County Records Center
- **NOTES:** Records Center has birth and death records 1867-1908, marriage records 1835-1995. Genealogical society has court records 1835-1883.

ERIE

323 Columbus Ave., Sandusky, OH 44870, (419) 627-7705, **<www.erie-county-ohio.net>**

- **INCORPORATED:** March 15, 1838
- **PARENT COUNTIES:** Huron, Sandusky
- **MARRIAGE RECORDS:** start in 1838, kept by Probate Court
- **DIVORCE:** 1838, Clerk of Courts
- **LAND:** 1838, County Recorder
- **PROBATE:** 1841, Probate Court
- **COURT:** 1838, Clerk of Courts
- **NOTES:** Probate Court has birth and death records 1856-1908.

FAIRFIELD

224 E. Main St., Box 370, Lancaster, OH 43130, (740) 687-7030, **<www.co.fairfield.oh.us>**

- **INCORPORATED:** Dec. 9, 1800
- **PARENT COUNTIES:** Ross, Washington
- **MARRIAGE RECORDS:** start in 1803, kept by Probate Court
- **DIVORCE:** 1803, Clerk of Courts
- **LAND:** 1800, County Recorder
- **PROBATE:** 1802, Probate Court
- **COURT:** 1803, Clerk of Courts
- **NOTES:** Probate Court has birth records 1867-1909.

FAYETTE

110 E. Court St., Washington Court House, OH 43160, (740) 335-6371, **<www.fayette-co-oh.com>**

- **INCORPORATED:** Feb. 19, 1810
- **PARENT COUNTIES:** Ross, Highland
- **DIVORCE RECORDS:** unknown start, kept by County Archives
- **LAND:** 1810, County Archives
- **PROBATE:** 1828, County Archives
- **COURT:** 1828, County Archives
- **NOTES:** Probate court has birth and death records 1867-1908. Some records lost in 1828 courthouse fire.

FRANKLIN

373 S. High St., Columbus, OH 43215, (614) 462-3600, **<www.co.franklin.oh.us>**

- **INCORPORATED:** March 30, 1803
- **PARENT COUNTY:** Ross
- **MARRIAGE RECORDS:** start in 1803, kept by Probate Court
- **DIVORCE:** 1820, Clerk of Courts
- **LAND:** 1803, County Recorder
- **COURT:** unknown, Clerk of Courts
- **NOTES:** Probate Court has birth and death records from before 1867 to 1908 and probate records 1803-1944.

FULTON

210 S. Fulton St., Wauseon, OH 43567, (419) 337-9230, **<www.fultoncountyoh.com>**

- **INCORPORATED:** Feb. 28, 1850
- **PARENT COUNTIES:** Lucas, Henry, Williams
- **MARRIAGE RECORDS:** start in 1864, kept by Probate Court
- **DIVORCE:** 1850, Clerk of Courts
- **LAND:** 1850, County Recorder
- **PROBATE:** 1864, Probate Court
- **COURT:** 1850, Clerk of Courts

- **NOTES:** Probate Court has birth and death records 1867-1908 and naturalization records ca. 1867-1908.

GALLIA
18 Locust St., Gallipolis, OH 45631, (740) 446-4612, **<www.gallianet.net/Gallia/index.htm >**
- **INCORPORATED:** March 25, 1803
- **PARENT COUNTIES:** Washington, Adams
- **DIVORCE RECORDS:** start in 1870, kept by Clerk of Courts
- **LAND:** 1795, County Recorder
- **PROBATE:** 1803, Probate Court
- **COURT:** 1870, Clerk of Courts
- **NOTES:** Probate Court has birth and death records 1867-1908.

GEAUGA
100 Short Court St., Ste. 300, Chardon, OH 44024, (440) 285-2222, **<www.co.geauga.oh.us>**
- **INCORPORATED:** Dec. 31, 1805
- **PARENT COUNTY:** Trumbull
- **MARRIAGE RECORDS:** start in 1806, kept by Probate Court
- **DIVORCE:** 1806, Clerk of Courts
- **LAND:** 1798, County Recorder
- **PROBATE:** 1806, Probate Court
- **COURT:** 1806, Clerk of Courts
- **NOTES:** Probate Court has birth and death records 1867-1908.

GREENE
45 N. Detroit St., Xenia, OH 45385, (937) 562-5290, **<www.co.greene.oh.us>**
- **INCORPORATED:** March 24, 1803
- **PARENT COUNTIES:** Hamilton, Ross
- **MARRIAGE RECORDS:** start in 1803, kept by Probate Court
- **DIVORCE:** 1802, Clerk of Courts
- **LAND:** 1803, County Recorder
- **PROBATE:** 1803, Probate Court
- **COURT:** 1803, Clerk of Courts
- **TAX:** 1803, County Auditor
- **NOTES:** Probate Court has Birth records 1869-1908. Greene County Library has obituaries, birth and death records 1869-1908, marriage records 1803-1968, wills and estates 1803-1950, and land records 1803-1940.

GUERNSEY
801 Wheeling Ave., Cambridge, OH 43725, (740) 432-9230, **<www.guernseycounty.org >**
- **INCORPORATED:** Jan. 31, 1810
- **PARENT COUNTIES:** Belmont, Muskingum
- **MARRIAGE RECORDS:** start in 1812, kept by Probate Court
- **DIVORCE:** 1850, Clerk of Courts
- **LAND:** 1802, County Recorder
- **PROBATE:** 1812, Probate Court
- **COURT:** 1810, Clerk of Courts
- **NOTES:** Probate Court has birth and death records 1867-1909.

HAMILTON
1000 Main St., Cincinnati, OH 45202, (513) 946-5635, **<www.hamilton-co.org>**
- **INCORPORATED:** Jan. 2, 1790
- **PARENT COUNTY:** Original county
- **MARRIAGE RECORDS:** start in 1817, kept by Probate Court
- **DIVORCE:** 1830, Clerk of Courts
- **LAND:** 1789, County Recorder
- **PROBATE:** 1791, Probate Court
- **NOTES:** Probate Court has birth records 1864-1908 and death records 1822-1908. Clerk of Courts has court records from mid 1800s. Records 1791-1884 incomplete due to fire and other losses.

HANCOCK
300 S. Main St., Findlay, OH 45840, (419) 424-7037, **<www.co.hancock.oh.us>**
- **INCORPORATED:** Feb. 12, 1820
- **PARENT COUNTY:** Logan
- **MARRIAGE RECORDS:** start in 1828, kept by Probate Court
- **DIVORCE:** 1830, Clerk of Courts
- **LAND:** 1830, County Recorder
- **PROBATE:** 1828, Probate Court
- **COURT UNKNOWN, CLERK OF COURTS**
- **NOTES:** Probate Court has birth and death records 1867-1908.

HARDIN
1 Courthouse Sq. Suite 310, Kenton, OH 43326, (419) 674-2278, **<www.hardincountyoh.com >**
- **INCORPORATED:** Feb. 12, 1820
- **PARENT COUNTY:** Logan
- **MARRIAGE RECORDS:** start in 1833, kept by Probate Court
- **DIVORCE:** 1864, Clerk of Courts
- **DEATH:** unknown, Probate Court
- **LAND:** 1831, County Recorder
- **PROBATE:** 1830, Probate Court
- **COURT:** 1833, Clerk of Courts
- **NOTES:** Probate Court has birth and death records 1867-1908. Clerk of Courts has court and divorce records from mid 1800s.

HARRISON
100 W. Market St., Cadiz, OH 43907, (740) 942-8863, **<harrisoncountyohio.org>**
- **INCORPORATED:** Jan. 2, 1813
- **PARENT COUNTIES:** Jefferson, Tuscarawas
- **MARRIAGE RECORDS:** unknown start, kept by Probate Court
- **DIVORCE:** 1819, Clerk of Courts
- **LAND:** unknown, County Recorder
- **PROBATE:** unknown, Probate Court
- **COURT:** unknown, Clerk of Courts
- **NOTES:** Probate Court has birth and death records 1867-1990.

HENRY
660 N. Perry St., Napoleon, OH 43545, (419) 592-5886, **<www.henrycountyohio.com>**
- **INCORPORATED:** Feb. 12, 1820
- **PARENT COUNTY:** Shelby
- **MARRIAGE RECORDS:** start in 1847, kept by Probate Court
- **DIVORCE:** 1860, Clerk of Courts
- **DEATH:** 1909, Department of Health
- **LAND:** 1847, County Recorder
- **PROBATE:** 1847, Probate Court
- **COURT:** 1860, Clerk of Courts

- **NOTES:** Probate Court has birth and death records 1867-1908. Henry County was attached to Wood and Williams counties from 1820-1834; check these counties for early court records.

HIGHLAND

105 N. High St., Hillsboro, OH 45133, (937) 393-9957,
<www.co.highland.oh.us>

- **INCORPORATED:** Feb. 18, 1805
- **PARENT COUNTIES:** Ross, Adams, Clermont
- **BIRTH RECORDS:** start in 1909, kept by Department of Health
- **MARRIAGE:** 1830, Probate Court
- **DIVORCE:** 1805, Clerk of Courts
- **DEATH:** 1909, Department of Health
- **LAND:** 1805, County Recorder
- **COURT:** 1805, Clerk of Courts
- **NOTES:** Probate Court has birth and death records 1867-1908. Clerk of Courts has some naturalizations. Recorder's office has some military discharge and burial records. Probate Court has probate records ca. 1800-ca. 1810.

HOCKING

1 E. Main St., Logan, OH 43138, (740) 385-2616,
<www.co.hocking.oh.us>

- **INCORPORATED:** Jan. 3, 1818
- **PARENT COUNTIES:** Athens, Ross, Fairfield
- **DIVORCE RECORDS:** start in 1873, kept by Clerk of Courts
- **LAND:** 1818, County Recorder
- **PROBATE:** 1813, Probate Court
- **COURT:** 1820, Clerk of Courts
- **NOTES:** Probate Court has birth records 1867-1909, death records 1867-1908, and marriage records 1818-1990.

HOLMES

1 E. Jackson St., Millersburg, OH 44654, (330) 674-1876,
<www.co.holmes.oh.us>

- **INCORPORATED:** Jan. 20, 1824
- **PARENT COUNTIES:** Coshocton, Wayne, Tuscarawas
- **MARRIAGE RECORDS:** 1825, Probate Court
- **LAND:** 1825, County Recorder
- **PROBATE:** 1825, Probate Court
- **COURT:** 1850, Clerk of Courts
- **MILITARY:** 1825, County Recorder
- **BURIAL:** 1825, County Library
- **NOTES:** Probate Court has birth and death records 1867-1908.

HURON

2 E. Main St., Norwalk, OH 44857, (419) 668-5113,
<www.huroncountyclerk.com>

- **INCORPORATED:** Feb. 7, 1809
- **PARENT COUNTIES:** Portage, Cuyahoga
- **MARRIAGE RECORDS:** start in 1815, kept by Probate Court
- **LAND:** 1808, County Recorder
- **PROBATE:** 1815, Probate Court
- **COURT:** 1815, County Clerk
- **TAX:** 1820, County Auditor
- **MILITARY:** 1865, County Recorder
- **NOTES:** Probate Court has birth and death records 1867-1908, name changes and clergy records 1823-1976, and naturalization records 1859-1899. County Recorder has Connecticut Fire Sufferers records 1792-1808. County Auditor has infirmary records 1848-1974, tax records 1815-1825, land partition records 1815-1920, county militia lists 1864-1865, and Indigent Soldier Burial records 1880-1920. County Clerk has divorce records 1815-1859.

JACKSON

226 E. Main St., Jackson, OH 45640, (740) 286-2006,
<www.jcclerk.com>

- **INCORPORATED:** Jan. 12, 1816
- **PARENT COUNTIES:** Scioto, Gallia, Athens, Ross
- **MARRIAGE RECORDS:** start in 1817, kept by Probate Court
- **DIVORCE:** 1800, Clerk of Courts
- **LAND:** 1816, County Recorder
- **PROBATE:** 1867, Probate Court
- **COURT:** 1800, Clerk of Courts
- **NOTES:** Probate Court has birth and death records 1867-1908.

JEFFERSON

301 Market St., Steubenville, OH 43952, (740) 283-8583,
<www.jeffersoncountyoh.com>

- **INCORPORATED:** July 27, 1797
- **PARENT COUNTY:** Washington
- **MARRIAGE RECORDS:** start in 1803, kept by Probate Court
- **DIVORCE:** 1797, Clerk of Courts
- **LAND:** 1796, County Recorder
- **PROBATE:** 1798, Probate Court
- **COURT:** 1797, Clerk of Courts
- **NOTES:** Probate Court has birth and death records 1867-1908 and naturalization records 1863-1903. Kent State University Library has naturalization records 1800-1863. Clerk of Courts has naturalization records 1903-1939.

KNOX

117 E. High St., Mount Vernon, OH 43050, (740)393-6788,
<www.co.knox.oh.us >

- **INCORPORATED:** Jan. 30, 1808
- **PARENT COUNTY:** Fairfield
- **MARRIAGE RECORDS:** start in 1808, kept by Probate Court
- **DIVORCE:** 1808, Clerk of Courts
- **LAND:** 1807, County Recorder
- **PROBATE:** 1808, Probate Court
- **COURT:** 1808, Clerk of Courts
- **NOTES:** Probate Court has birth and death records 1867-1908.

LAKE

25 N. Park Pl., Painesville, OH 44077, (440) 350-2657,
<www.lakecountyohio.org >

- **INCORPORATED:** March 6, 1840
- **PARENT COUNTIES:** Geauga, Cuyahoga
- **MARRIAGE RECORDS:** start in 1840, kept by Probate Court
- **DIVORCE:** 1840, Clerk of Courts
- **LAND:** 1840, County Recorder
- **PROBATE:** 1840, Probate Court
- **COURT:** 1840, Clerk of Courts
- **NOTES:** Probate Court has birth and death records 1867-1908.

LAWRENCE

111 N. Fourth St., Ironton, OH 45638, (740) 533-4355,
<www.lawrenceclerk.com >

- **INCORPORATED:** Dec. 21, 1815
- **PARENT COUNTIES:** Gallia, Scioto
- **MARRIAGE RECORDS:** start in 1817, kept by Briggs Library
- **LAND:** 1818, County Recorder
- **PROBATE:** 1817, Probate Court
- **COURT:** 1817, Clerk of Courts
- **NOTES:** Probate Court has birth records 1868-1938 and death records 1868-1933.

LICKING

Box 4370, Newark, OH 43058, (740) 670-5791,
<www.lcounty.com>

- **INCORPORATED:** Jan. 30, 1808
- **PARENT COUNTY:** Fairfield
- **DIVORCE RECORDS:** start in 1876, kept by Clerk of Courts
- **LAND:** 1809, County Recorder
- **PROBATE:** 1875, Probate Court
- **COURT:** 1872, Clerk of Courts
- **NOTES:** Probate Court has birth records 1875-1903 and marriage records 1808-1828. County Health Department has death records 1882-1908.

LOGAN

101 S. Main St., Bellefontaine, OH 43311, (937) 599-7275,
<www.co.logan.oh.us>

- **INCORPORATED:** Dec. 30, 1817
- **PARENT COUNTY:** Champaign
- **MARRIAGE RECORDS:** start in 1818, kept by Probate Court
- **DIVORCE:** 1942, Domestic Court
- **LAND:** 1818, County Recorder
- **PROBATE:** 1930, Probate Court
- **COURT:** 1942, Domestic Court
- **NOTES:** Probate Court has birth and death records 1867-1909.

LORAIN

225 Court St., Elyria, OH 44036, (440) 329-5000,
<www.loraincounty.com >

- **INCORPORATED:** Dec. 26, 1822
- **PARENT COUNTIES:** Huron, Cuyahoga, Medina
- **MARRIAGE RECORDS:** start in 1824, kept by Probate Court
- **DIVORCE:** 1854, Clerk of Courts
- **LAND:** 1824, County Recorder
- **PROBATE:** 1824, Probate Court
- **COURT:** 1854, Clerk of Courts
- **NOTES:** Probate Court has birth and death records 1867-1908 and indigent soldier burial records 1926-1927.

LUCAS

700 Adams St., Toledo, OH 43604, (419) 213-4484,
<co.lucas.oh.us>

- **INCORPORATED:** Jun. 20, 1835
- **PARENT COUNTIES:** Wood, Sandusky, Henry
- **MARRIAGE RECORDS:** 1835, Probate Court
- **DIVORCE:** 1835, Clerk of Courts
- **LAND:** 1835, County Recorder
- **PROBATE:** 1835, Probate Court
- **COURT:** 1835, Clerk of Courts
- **NOTES:** Probate Court has birth records 1865-1908 and death records 1867-1908.

MADISON

1 N. Main St., Box 557, London, OH 43140, (740) 852-9776,
<www.co.madison.oh.us>

- **INCORPORATED:** Feb. 16, 1810
- **PARENT COUNTY:** Franklin
- **MARRIAGE RECORDS:** start in 1810, kept by Probate Court
- **DIVORCE:** unknown, Clerk of Courts
- **LAND:** 1810, County Recorder
- **PROBATE:** 1810, Probate Court
- **COURT:** unknown, Clerk of Courts
- **NATURALIZATION:** 1860, Probate Court
- **MILITARY:** 1865, County Recorder
- **NOTES:** Probate Court has birth and death records 1865-1908.

MAHONING

120 Market St., Youngstown, OH 44503, (330) 740-2104,
<www.mahoningcountyoh.gov>

- **INCORPORATED:** Feb. 16, 1846
- **PARENT COUNTIES:** Columbiana, Trumbull
- **MARRIAGE RECORDS:** start in 1846, kept by Probate Court
- **DIVORCE:** 1846, Clerk of Courts
- **LAND:** 1846, County Recorder
- **PROBATE:** 1846, Probate Court
- **COURT:** 1846, Clerk of Courts
- **NOTES:** Probate has birth and death records 1847-1908.

MARION

100 N. Main St., Marion, OH 43302, (740) 223-4270,
<www.co.marion.oh.us>

- **INCORPORATED:** Feb. 12, 1820
- **PARENT COUNTY:** Delaware
- **DIVORCE RECORDS:** unknown start, kept by Clerk of Courts
- **LAND:** 1821, County Recorder
- **PROBATE:** 1820, Probate Court
- **COURT:** unknown, Clerk of Courts
- **NOTES:** Probate Court has birth and death records 1867-1908 and marriage certificates 1824-1920. Ohio Historical Society in Columbus has original marriage certificates.

MEDINA

93 Public Sq., Medina, OH 44256, (330) 725-9722,
<www.co.medina.oh.us>

- **INCORPORATED:** Feb. 18, 1812
- **PARENT COUNTY:** Portage
- **MARRIAGE RECORDS:** start in 1818, kept by Probate Court
- **DIVORCE:** 1818, Clerk of Courts
- **LAND:** 1800, County Recorder
- **PROBATE:** 1818, Probate Court
- **COURT:** 1818, Clerk of Courts
- **NOTES:** Probate Court has birth and death records 1867-1908.

MEIGS
100 E. Second St., Pomeroy, OH 45769, (740) 992-5290,
<www.rootsweb.ancestry.com/~ohmeigs/meigs.html>
- **INCORPORATED:** Jan. 21, 1819
- **PARENT COUNTIES:** Gallia, Athens
- **DIVORCE RECORDS:** start ca. 1800, kept by Clerk of Courts
- **LAND:** 1820, County Recorder
- **PROBATE:** 1824, Probate Court
- **COURT:** 1800, Clerk of Courts
- **NOTES:** Probate Court has birth and death records 1865-1909 and marriage records 1819-1930.

MERCER
101 N. Main St., Box 28, Celina, OH 45822, (419) 586-6461,
<www.mercercountyohio.org>
- **INCORPORATED:** Feb. 12, 1820
- **PARENT COUNTY:** Darke
- **MARRIAGE RECORDS:** start in 1838, kept by Probate Court
- **DIVORCE:** 1850, Clerk of Courts
- **LAND:** 1824, County Recorder
- **PROBATE:** 1850, Probate Court
- **COURT:** 1850, Clerk of Courts
- **NOTES:** Probate Court has birth and death records 1867-1908. Wright State University in Dayton has some naturalization records 1852-1930 and some Supreme Court cases 1825-1873.

MIAMI
201 W. Main St., Troy, OH 45373, (937) 440-6010,
<www.co.miami.oh.us>
- **INCORPORATED:** Jan. 16, 1807
- **PARENT COUNTY:** Montgomery
- **MARRIAGE RECORDS:** start in 1807, kept by Probate Court
- **DIVORCE:** 1807, Clerk of Courts
- **LAND:** 1809, County Recorder
- **PROBATE:** 1807, Probate Court
- **COURT:** 1807, Clerk of Courts
- **NOTES:** Probate Court has birth and death records 1853-1908. City of Piqua Health Department has birth and death records for the city of Piqua.

MONROE
101 N. Main St., Woodsfield, OH 43793, (740) 472-0761,
<www.rootsweb.ancestry.com/~ohmonroe>
- **INCORPORATED:** Jan. 29, 1813
- **PARENT COUNTIES:** Belmont, Washington, Guernsey
- **MARRIAGE RECORDS:** start in 1866, kept by Probate Court
- **LAND:** 1836, County Recorder
- **PROBATE:** unknown, Probate Court
- **NOTES:** Probate Court has birth and death records 1867-1908.

MONTGOMERY
41 N. Perry St., Dayton, OH 45402, (937) 496-7213,
<www.mcohio.org>
- **INCORPORATED:** March 24, 1803
- **PARENT COUNTIES:** Hamilton; Wayne, old
- **MARRIAGE RECORDS:** start in 1803, kept by Probate Court
- **DIVORCE:** 1991, Clerk of Courts
- **LAND:** 1805, County Recorder
- **PROBATE:** 1803, Probate Court
- **COURT:** 1803, Clerk of Courts
- **NOTES:** The Records Center in the Riebold Building in Dayton has all old records. Probate Court has birth and death records 1867-1908.

MORGAN
19 E. Main St., McConnelsville, OH 43756, (740) 962-4752,
<www.rootsweb.ancestry.com/~ohmorgan>
- **INCORPORATED:** Dec. 29, 1817
- **PARENT COUNTIES:** Washington, Guernsey, Muskingum
- **MARRIAGE RECORDS:** start in 1819, kept by Probate Court
- **LAND:** 1795, County Recorder
- **PROBATE:** 1819, Probate Court
- **NOTES:** Probate Court has birth and death records 1867-1908.

MORROW
48 E. High St., Mount Gilead, OH 43338, (419) 947-2085,
<www.rootsweb.ancestry.com/~ohmorrow>
- **INCORPORATED:** Feb. 24, 1848
- **PARENT COUNTIES:** Knox, Marion, Delaware, Richland
- **MARRIAGE RECORDS:** start in 1848, kept by Probate Court
- **DIVORCE:** ca. 1850, Common Pleas Court
- **LAND:** 1848, County Recorder
- **PROBATE:** 1848, Probate Court
- **COURT:** 1848, Common Pleas Court
- **MILITARY:** 1846, County Recorder
- **NOTES:** Probate Court has birth and death records 1867-1908 and some naturalization records. Request Common Pleas Court records prior to February 1970 ahead of time, as they are stored off-site.

MUSKINGUM
401 Main St., Zanesville, OH 43701, (740) 455-7104,
<www.muskingumcounty.org>
- **INCORPORATED:** Jan. 7, 1804
- **PARENT COUNTIES:** Washington, Fairfield
- **MARRIAGE RECORDS:** start in 1804, kept by Probate Court
- **DIVORCE:** 1846, Clerk of Courts
- **LAND:** 1800, County Recorder
- **PROBATE:** 1804, Probate Court
- **COURT:** 1804, Clerk of Courts
- **MILITARY:** 1864, County Recorder
- **NOTES:** Probate Court has birth and death records 1867-1908. Probate Court has naturalization records 1860-1940.

NOBLE
350 Courthouse Sq., Caldwell, OH 43724, (740) 732-4045,
<www.rootsweb.ancestry.com/~ohnoble>
- **INCORPORATED:** March 11, 1851
- **PARENT COUNTIES:** Monroe, Washington, Morgan, Guernsey
- **MARRIAGE RECORDS:** start in 1851, kept by Probate Court
- **DIVORCE:** 1851, Clerk of Courts
- **LAND:** 1851, County Recorder
- **PROBATE:** 1851, Probate Court
- **COURT:** 1851, Clerk of Courts
- **NOTES:** Probate Court has birth and death records 1867-1908.

OTTAWA
315 Madison St. Room 304, Port Clinton, OH 43452, (419) 734-6755, **<www.co.ottawa.oh.us>**
- **INCORPORATED:** March 6, 1840
- **PARENT COUNTIES:** Erie, Sandusky, Lucas
- **MARRIAGE RECORDS:** start in 1840, kept by Probate Court
- **DIVORCE:** 1840, Clerk of Courts
- **LAND:** 1820, County Recorder
- **PROBATE:** 1840, Probate Court
- **COURT:** 1840, Clerk of Courts
- **NOTES:** Probate Court has birth and death records 1867-1908. Ohio Historical Society has death records 1908-1944. Clerk of Courts has naturalization records 1905-1929.

PAULDING
115 N. Williams St., Paulding, OH 45879, (419) 399-8210, **<www.rootsweb.ancestry.com/~ohpauldi>**
- **INCORPORATED:** Feb. 12, 1820
- **PARENT COUNTY:** Darke
- **MARRIAGE RECORDS:** start in 1839, kept by Probate Court
- **DIVORCE:** 1820, Clerk of Courts
- **LAND:** 1835, County Recorder
- **PROBATE:** 1842, Probate Court
- **COURT:** 1839, Clerk of Courts
- **NOTES:** Probate Court has birth and death records 1867-1908. County Recorder has some Civil War military discharge records.

PERRY
105 N. Main St., New Lexington, OH 43764, (740) 342-1022, **<www.ohgen.net/ohperry>**
- **INCORPORATED:** Dec. 26, 1817
- **PARENT COUNTIES:** Washington, Fairfield, Muskingum
- **MARRIAGE RECORDS:** start in 1818, kept by Probate Court
- **DIVORCE:** ca. 1800, Clerk of Courts
- **LAND:** 1818, County Recorder
- **PROBATE:** 1817, Probate Court
- **COURT:** 1800, Clerk of Courts
- **NOTES:** Probate Court has birth and death records 1867-1908.

PICKAWAY
207 S. Court St., Box 270, Circleville, OH 43113, (740) 474-5231, **<www.rootsweb.ancestry.com/~ohpickaw>**
- **INCORPORATED:** Jan. 12, 1810
- **PARENT COUNTIES:** Ross, Fairfield, Franklin
- **MARRIAGE RECORDS:** start in 1810, kept by Probate Court
- **LAND:** 1810, County Recorder
- **PROBATE:** 1810, Probate Court
- **NOTES:** Probate Court has birth and death records 1867-1908. Civil Clerk of Courts has court and divorce records from late 1800s.

PIKE
100 E. Second St., Waverly, OH 45690, (740) 947-2715, **<ohgenealogy.com/pikeco>**
- **INCORPORATED:** Jan. 4, 1815
- **PARENT COUNTIES:** Ross, Scioto, Adams
- **BIRTH RECORDS:** start in 1908, kept by Department of Health
- **MARRIAGE:** 1815, Probate Court
- **DIVORCE:** 1815, Clerk of Courts
- **DEATH:** 1919, Department of Health
- **LAND:** 1799, County Recorder
- **PROBATE:** 1815, Probate Court
- **COURT:** 1815, Clerk of Courts
- **NOTES:** Probate has birth and death records 1867-1909. Ohio Department of Health/Vital Statistics Department has birth and death records 1909-ca. 1932.

PORTAGE
203 W. Main St., Box 1035, Ravenna, OH 44266, (330) 297-3644, **<www.portageworkforce.org/portagecountydirectory>**
- **INCORPORATED:** Feb. 10, 1807
- **PARENT COUNTY:** Trumbull
- **MARRIAGE RECORDS:** start in 1808, kept by Probate Court
- **DIVORCE:** 1885, Clerk of Courts
- **LAND:** 1795, County Recorder
- **PROBATE:** 1803, Probate Court
- **COURT:** 1809, Clerk of Courts
- **NOTES:** Probate Court has birth and death records 1867-1908.

PREBLE
100 Main St., Eaton, OH 45320, (937) 456-8160, **<www.preblecountyohio.net>**
- **INCORPORATED:** Feb. 15, 1808
- **PARENT COUNTIES:** Montgomery, Butler
- **MARRIAGE RECORDS:** start in 1808, kept by Probate Court
- **DIVORCE:** ca. 1853, Clerk of Courts
- **LAND:** 1805, County Recorder
- **PROBATE:** 1808, Probate Court
- **COURT:** 1808, Clerk of Courts
- **NOTES:** Probate Court has birth and death records 1867-1908.

PUTNAM
245 E. Main St., Ottawa, OH 45875, (419) 523-3110, **<www.putnamcountyohio.com>**
- **INCORPORATED:** Feb. 12, 1820
- **PARENT COUNTY:** Shelby
- **MARRIAGE RECORDS:** start in 1867, kept by Probate Court
- **DIVORCE:** 1834, Clerk of Courts
- **LAND:** 1830, County Recorder
- **PROBATE:** 1804, Probate Court
- **COURT:** 1809, Clerk of Courts
- **NOTES:** Probate Court has birth and death records 1867-1920.

RICHLAND
50 Park Ave. E., Mansfield, OH 44902, (419) 774-5543, **<www.richlandcountyoh.us>**
- **INCORPORATED:** Jan. 30, 1808
- **PARENT COUNTY:** Fairfield
- **MARRIAGE RECORDS:** start in 1813, kept by Probate Court
- **DIVORCE:** 1920, Clerk of Courts
- **LAND:** 1814, County Recorder
- **PROBATE:** 1813, Probate Court
- **COURT:** 1819, Clerk of Courts
- **NOTES:** Probate Court has birth and death records 1867-1908.

ROSS
2 N. Paint St., Chillicothe, OH 45601, (740) 702-3010,
<www.co.ross.oh.us>
- **INCORPORATED:** Aug. 20, 1798
- **PARENT COUNTIES:** Adams, Washington
- **MARRIAGE RECORDS:** start in 1798, kept by Probate Court
- **DEATH:** 1909, County Board of Health
- **LAND:** 1796, County Recorder
- **PROBATE:** 1798, Probate Court
- **COURT:** 1803, Clerk of Courts
- **NOTES:** Probate Court has birth and death records 1867-1908.

SANDUSKY
100 N. Park Ave., Fremont, OH 43420, (419) 334-6161,
<www.sandusky-county.org>
- **INCORPORATED:** Feb. 12, 1820
- **PARENT COUNTY:** Huron
- **MARRIAGE RECORDS:** start in 1820, kept by Probate Court
- **DIVORCE:** 1868, Clerk of Courts
- **DEATH:** 1908, County Board of Health
- **LAND:** 1822, County Recorder
- **PROBATE:** 1820, Probate Court
- **COURT:** 1820, Clerk of Courts
- **NOTES:** Probate Court has birth and death records 1867-1908.

SCIOTO
602 Seventh St., Portsmouth, OH 45662, (740) 355-8226,
<www.sciotocountyohio.com>
- **INCORPORATED:** March 24, 1803
- **PARENT COUNTY:** Adams
- **MARRIAGE RECORDS:** start in 1804, kept by Probate Court
- **DIVORCE:** 1835, Clerk of Courts
- **LAND:** 1803, County Recorder
- **PROBATE:** 1804, Probate Court
- **COURT:** 1809, Clerk of Courts
- **NOTES:** Probate Court has birth and death records 1856-1908. Portsmouth Board of Health has birth and death records for the city from 1909. County Board of Health has birth and death records for the rest of the county from 1909.

SENECA
117 E. Market St., Tiffin, OH 44883, (419) 447-0671,
<www.senecaco.org>
- **INCORPORATED:** Feb. 12, 1820
- **PARENT COUNTY:** Huron
- **MARRIAGE RECORDS:** start in 1841, kept by Probate Court
- **DIVORCE:** ca. 1800, Clerk of Courts
- **LAND:** 1821, County Recorder
- **PROBATE:** 1836, Probate Court
- **COURT:** 1824, Clerk of Courts
- **NOTES:** Probate Court has birth and death records 1867-1908.

SHELBY
Box 809, Sidney, OH 45365, (937) 498-7221,
<www.co.shelby.oh.us>
- **INCORPORATED:** Jan. 7, 1819
- **PARENT COUNTY:** Miami
- **MARRIAGE RECORDS:** start in 1824, kept by Probate Court
- **LAND:** 1819, County Recorder
- **PROBATE:** 1825, Probate Court
- **COURT:** 1819, Clerk of Courts

STARK
115 Central Plaza S., Canton, OH 44702, (330) 451-7801,
<www.co.stark.oh.us>
- **INCORPORATED:** Feb. 13, 1808
- **PARENT COUNTY:** Columbiana
- **MARRIAGE RECORDS:** start in 1809, kept by Probate Court
- **LAND:** 1809, County Recorder
- **PROBATE:** 1810, Probate Court
- **COURT:** 1809, Clerk of Courts
- **NOTES:** Probate Court has birth and death records 1867-1908.

SUMMIT
205 S. High St., Akron, OH 44308, (330) 643-2211,
<www.co.summit.oh.us>
- **INCORPORATED:** March 3, 1840
- **PARENT COUNTIES:** Portage, Medina, Stark
- **MARRIAGE RECORDS:** start in 1840, kept by Probate Court
- **DIVORCE:** 1902, Domestic Court
- **LAND:** 1840, County Recorder
- **PROBATE:** 1839, Probate Court
- **NOTES:** Probate Court has birth and death records 1869-1908. Clerk of Court has Court records from late 1800s.

TRUMBULL
161 High St., Warren, OH 44481, (330) 675-2557,
<www.co.trumbull.oh.us>
- **INCORPORATED:** July 10, 1800
- **PARENT COUNTIES:** Jefferson; Wayne, old
- **MARRIAGE:** start in 1803, kept by Probate Court
- **DIVORCE:** 1800, Clerk of Courts
- **DEATH:** 1908, Warren Health Department
- **LAND:** 1795, County Recorder
- **PROBATE:** 1803, Probate Court
- **COURT:** 1807, Clerk of Courts
- **NATURALIZATION:** 1800, Clerk of Courts
- **NOTES:** Trumbull Records Center has birth and death records 1867-1908.

TUSCARAWAS
125 E. High Ave., New Philadelphia, OH 44663, (330) 365-3243,
<www.co.tuscarawas.oh.us>
- **INCORPORATED:** Feb. 13, 1808
- **PARENT COUNTY:** Muskingum
- **MARRIAGE RECORDS:** unknown start, kept by Probate Court
- **DIVORCE:** 1808, Clerk of Courts
- **LAND:** unknown, County Recorder
- **PROBATE:** unknown, Probate Court
- **COURT:** 1808, Clerk of Courts

- **NOTES:** Probate Court has birth and death records 1867-1908. Clerk of Courts has naturalization records 1908-1980. Probate Court has earlier naturalization records.

UNION

215 W. Fifth St., Marysville, OH 43040, (937) 645-3006,
<www.co.union.oh.us>

- **INCORPORATED:** Jan. 10, 1820
- **PARENT COUNTIES:** Franklin, Madison, Logan, Delaware
- **MARRIAGE RECORDS:** start in 1820, kept by Probate Court
- **DIVORCE:** 1821, Clerk of Courts
- **LAND:** 1811, County Recorder
- **PROBATE:** 1820, Probate Court
- **COURT:** 1820, Clerk of Courts
- **NOTES:** Probate Court has birth and death records 1867-1908

VAN WERT

121 E. Main St. 3rd Floor, Van Wert, OH 45891, (419) 238-1022,
<www.rootsweb.ancestry.com/~ohvanwer>

- **INCORPORATED:** Feb. 12, 1820
- **PARENT COUNTY:** Darke
- **MARRIAGE RECORDS:** start in 1840, kept by Probate Court
- **DIVORCE:** unknown, Clerk of Courts
- **LAND:** 1824, County Recorder
- **PROBATE:** 1840, Probate Court
- **COURT:** 1837, Clerk of Courts
- **NOTES:** Probate Court has birth and death records 1867-1908.

VINTON

100 E. Main St., McArthur, OH 45651, (740) 596-3001,
<www.vintoncounty.com>

- **INCORPORATED:** March 23, 1850
- **PARENT COUNTIES:** Gallia, Athens, Ross, Jackson, Hocking
- **NOTES:** Probate Court has birth and death records 1867-1908.
- **MARRIAGE RECORDS:** start in 1850, kept by Probate Court
- **DIVORCE:** 1850, Clerk of Courts
- **LAND:** 1850, County Recorder
- **PROBATE:** 1852, Probate Court
- **COURT:** 1850, Clerk of Courts

WARREN

500 Justice Dr., Box 238, Lebanon, OH 45036, (513) 695-1120,
<www.co.warren.oh.us>

- **INCORPORATED:** March 24, 1803
- **PARENT COUNTY:** Hamilton
- **MARRIAGE RECORDS:** start in 1803, kept by Probate Court
- **DIVORCE:** 1803, Clerk of Courts
- **LAND:** 1795, County Recorder
- **PROBATE:** 1803, Probate Court
- **COURT:** 1803, Clerk of Courts
- **NOTES:** Probate Court has birth and death records 1867-1908.

WASHINGTON

205 Putnam St., Marietta, OH 45750, (740) 373-6623,
<www.washingtongov.org>

- **INCORPORATED:** July 27, 1788
- **PARENT COUNTY:** Original county
- **MARRIAGE RECORDS:** start in 1789, kept by Probate Court
- **DIVORCE:** 1787, Clerk of Courts
- **LAND:** 1788, County Recorder
- **PROBATE:** 1789, Probate Court
- **COURT:** 1787, Clerk of Courts
- **NOTES:** Probate Court has birth and death records 1867-1908

WAYNE

107 W. Liberty St., Wooster, OH 44691, (330) 287-5590,
<www.wayneohio.org>

- **INCORPORATED:** Feb. 13, 1808
- **PARENT COUNTY:** Columbiana
- **NOTES:** Probate Court has birth and death records 1867-1908.
- **MARRIAGE RECORDS:** start in 1813, kept by Probate Court
- **DIVORCE:** 1812, Clerk/Common Pleas Ct.
- **LAND:** 1813, County Recorder
- **PROBATE:** 1817, Probate Court
- **COURT:** 1812, Clerk/Common Pleas Ct.

WAYNE, OLD

- **INCORPORATED:** Aug. 15, 1786
- **PARENT COUNTY:** Original county
- **NOTES:** This county disappeared from Ohio in 1803 when Ohio became a state. It ultimately became Wayne County, Mich.

WILLIAMS

1 Courthouse Sq., Bryan, OH 43506, (419) 636-1551,
<www.co.williams.oh.us>

- **INCORPORATED:** Feb. 12, 1820
- **PARENT COUNTY:** Darke
- **NOTES:** Probate Court has birth and death records 1867-1908; Civil Court, domestic court and divorce records 1824-1980; criminal court records 1824-1999; Marriage and Probate records 1824-1996; and naturalization records 1835-1877.

WOOD

1 Courthouse Sq., Bowling Green, OH 43402, (419) 354-9280,
<www.co.wood.oh.us>

- **INCORPORATED:** Feb. 12, 1820
- **PARENT COUNTY:** Logan
- **NOTES:** Probate Court has birth and death records 1867-1908.
- **MARRIAGE RECORDS:** start in 1820, kept by Probate Court
- **DIVORCE:** 1851, Clerk of Courts
- **LAND:** 1821, County Recorder
- **PROBATE:** 1820, Probate Court
- **COURT:** 1823, Clerk of Courts

WYANDOT

109 S. Sandusky Ave., Upper Sandusky, OH 43351, (419) 294-1432,
<www.co.wyandot.oh.us>

- **INCORPORATED:** Feb. 3, 1845
- **PARENT COUNTIES:** Marion, Crawford, Hardin, Hancock
- **MARRIAGE RECORDS:** start in 1845, kept by Probate Court
- **DIVORCE:** 1848, Clerk of Courts
- **LAND:** 1845, County Recorder
- **PROBATE:** 1845, Probate Court
- **COURT:** 1848, Clerk of Courts
- **NOTES:** Probate Court has birth and death records 1867-1908.

OKLAHOMA

» BY RHONDA R. MCCLURE

HISTORICAL OVERVIEW

Oklahoma has the distinction of being the only state that was originally two separate territories. The land that became Oklahoma was among the acres Thomas Jefferson acquired in the Louisiana Purchase, though the panhandle was still under Spanish control in 1803. Oklahoma was then part of Missouri Territory in 1812 and Arkansas Territory in 1819.

In 1830, the western part of the Louisiana Purchase, which included Arkansas Territory, was set aside as Indian Territory. There, the Indian Removal Act resulted in the resettlement of many Native Americans from the south and southeast, with the promise that it would be their home. Of course, after the Civil War, partly in response to the Five Civilized Tribes' support of the Confederacy, the treaties were renegotiated, and approximately 2 million acres were designated as "Unassigned Lands." In 1889, the federal government purchased these lands from the Native Americans and opened them up for white settlement, the birth of Oklahoma Territory. From 1890 to 1906, Oklahoma Territory began to absorb a number of reservations and other Native American lands, and in 1907, the "twin territories" were combined to form the new state of Oklahoma.

Though the "Unassigned Lands" were not open for white settlement until 1889, many whites settled in Indian Territory from 1865 to 1889, using loopholes in the law that allowed artisans and professionals to contract with the Native Americans for labor.

RECORD HIGHLIGHTS

Though Oklahoma required statewide registration of births and death from 1908, many counties did not comply until 1930. You may discover some county vital records from before 1930, but they are highly incomplete. To request births and deaths from the state, contact the Vital Records Section, Vital Records Service, State Department of Health, 1000 Northeast 10th Street, Oklahoma City, OK 73117 **<www.ok.gov/health/Birth_and_Death_Certificates>**.

Marriage records began around 1890 for existing counties, and at the date of creation in counties established later. In the territorial years (1890-1907), many marriages were not recorded, and you will need to check county courthouses in Arkansas, Texas and Kansas as well.

Land records for whites who settled in the territory before 1889 (the year it became legal for whites to own land there) will be found in the Bureau of Indian Affairs in the land records for the Five Civilized Tribes nation from whom the individual leased the land.

research tips

- Your white ancestorsmay have been in Indian Territory during the 1900 census. Examine records for both of the "twin territories."
- When researching Native American ancestry, consult the Indian Archives Division of the Oklahoma Historical Society, 2100 N. Lincoln Blvd., Oklahoma City, OK 73105, **www.okhistory.org/research/collections/indian_archives.html>** . Knowing the tribe is the first step.
- The Dawes Rolls Database-Final Rolls of Cherokee tribe members is searchable online at **<www.accessgenealogy.com/native/dawes.php>**. You can get the necessary identifying information to find the enrollment cards (from the National Archives or the subscription website Footnote), which will then take you to census and other records.

CENSUS RECORDS

- Federal census: 1860 (with Arkansas), 1900, 1910, 1920, 1930
- Special census of Civil War Union veterans and widows: 1890
- Territorial census: 1890 (Unassigned lands, not Indian territory)

In April 1889, the first "land run" offered people the opportunity to race to claim a surveyed section of land on a first-come basis. It is estimated that 50,000 people settled tracts the first day of the run. Additional land runs followed in September 1891, April 1892, September 1893, and May 1895. You can search homestead records through the Bureau of Land Management General Land Office Records website **<www.glorecords.blm.gov>**, which supplies you with a digitized image of the final patent and the information necessary to order the land case file from the National Archives. Later land records of transactions between individuals are found in county courthouses.

When researching Native American ancestry in Oklahoma, it is important to know your ancestor's tribe. Tribes were self-governing entities for years, though the US government did conduct censuses. Other records include land allotments, which required the applicant to prove Native American descent. The Dawes Commission was established in 1898 to enroll those Indian Territory residents in one of the five tribes. When the US government began to grant land after the governments of the Five Civilized Tribes dissolved in 1908, many whites were entitled to receive land because of intermarriage with Indians. Dawes Commission records were used to establish the right to receive land.

ARCHIVES, LIBRARIES, AND SOCIETIES

American Heritage Library
Box 176, Davis, OK 73030

Arbuckle Historical Society
201 S. Fourth St., Davis, OK 73030, **<www.ahsmc.org>**

Atoka County Library
215 E. A St., Atoka, OK 74525

Atoka County Genealogical Society
Box 245, Atoka, OK 74525

Bartlesville Genealogical Society
c/o Bartlesville Public Library, 600 S. Johnstone Ave., Bartlesville, OK 74003

Bartlesville Public Library
600 S. Johnstone, Bartlesville, OK 74003, **<www.bartlesville.lib.ok.us>**

Beaver River Genealogical and Historical Society
Rt. 1, Box 79, Hooker, OK 73945

Broken Arrow Genealogical Society
Box 1244, Broken Arrow, OK 74013, **<www.rootsweb.ancestry.com/~okbags>**

Bryan County Heritage Society
Box 153, Calera, OK 74730

Bureau of Land Management, New Mexico Office
Federal Building, 1474 Rodeo Rd., Box 27115, Santa Fe, NM 87502, (505) 438-7400

Canadian County Genealogical Society
Box 866, El Reno, OK 73036, **<www.rootsweb.ancestry.com/~okccgs>**

Carter County Genealogical Society
Box 1014, Ardmore, OK 73402

Central Oklahoma Chapter, American Historical Society of Germans from Russia
<www.ahsgr.org/central_oklahoma_chapter.htm>

Cherokee City-County Public Library
123 S. Grand Ave., Cherokee, OK 73728

Chickasha Public Library
527 Iowa Ave., Chickasha, OK 73018, **<www.chickashapl.okpls.org>**

Choctaw County Genealogical Society
703 E. Jackson St., Hugo, OK 74743, **<www.okgenweb.org/~ccgs2>**

Cleveland County Genealogical Society
Box 6176, Norman, OK 73070, **<www.rootsweb.ancestry.com/~okccogs>**

Coal County Genealogical Society
115 W. Ohio, Coalgate, OK 74538, **<www.coalcounty.org>**

Craig County Genealogical Society
Box 484, Vinita, OK 74301, **<www.okgenweb.org/~okcraig>**

Cushing Genealogical Society
c/o Cushing Public Library, Box 551, 215 N. Steele, Cushing, OK 74203

Delaware County Genealogical Society
Grove Public Library, 206 S. Elk St., Grove, OK 74344, **<www.rootsweb.ancestry.com/~okdelawa>**

Delaware County Historical Society
Box 855, Jay, OK 74346

Edmond Genealogical Society
Box 1984, Edmond, OK 73083, **<www.rootsweb.ancestry.com/~okegs>**

Federation of Oklahoma Genealogical Societies
Box 26151, Oklahoma City, OK 73126

Five Civilized Tribes Museum
1101 Honor Heights Dr., Muskogee, OK 74401, (918) 683-1701, **<www.fivetribes.org>**

Fort Gibson Genealogical and Historical Society
Box 416, Fort Gibson, OK 74434

Garfield County Genealogists
Box 1106, Enid, OK 73702, **<www.garfieldokgen.org>**

Golden Spread Chapter, American Historical Society of Germans from Russia
Box 307, Shattuck, OK 73858, **<www.ahsgr.org/golden_spread_chapter.htm>**

Grady County Genealogical Society
Box 792, Chickasha, OK 73023

Grant County Historical Society
Box 127, Medford, OK 73759

Greer County Genealogical and Historical Society
201 W. Lincoln, Mangum, OK 73554

Haskell County Genealogical Society
402 NE Sixth St., Stigler, OK 74462

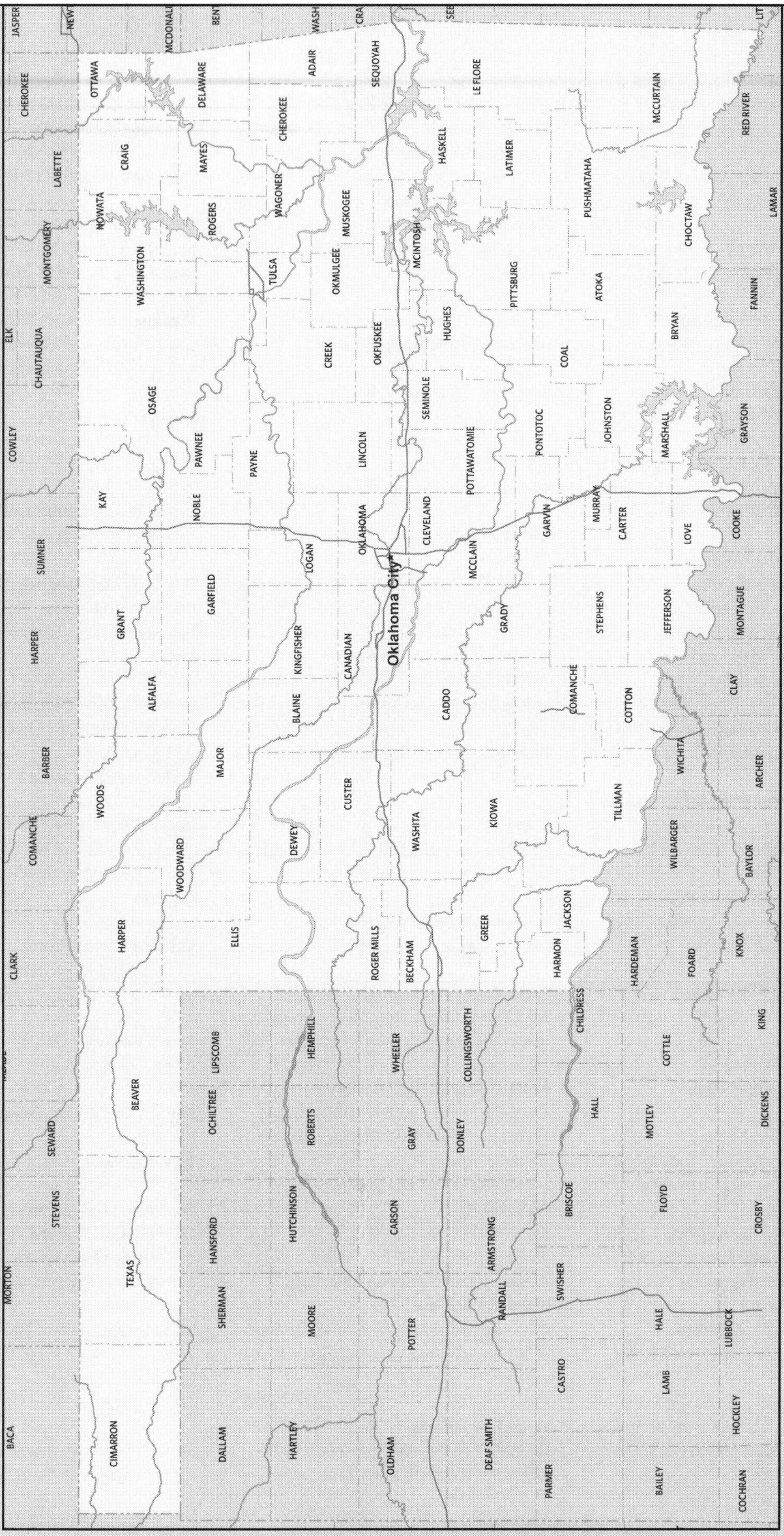
Oklahoma City
JASPER
CHEROKEE
LABETTE
MONTGOMERY
ELK
CHAUTAUQUA
COWLEY
SUMNER
HARPER
BARBER
COMANCHE
CLARK
SEWARD
STEVENS
MORTON
BACA
OTTAWA
CRAIG
NOWATA
WASHINGTON
OSAGE
KAY
GRANT
ALFALFA
WOODS
HARPER
BEAVER
TEXAS
CIMARRON
MCDONALD
DELAWARE
MAYES
ROGERS
PAWNEE
NOBLE
GARFIELD
MAJOR
WOODWARD
ELLIS
BENT
ADAIR
CHEROKEE
WAGONER
TULSA
CREEK
PAYNE
LOGAN
KINGFISHER
BLAINE
DEWEY
SEQUOYAH
MUSKOGEE
OKMULGEE
OKFUSKEE
LINCOLN
OKLAHOMA
CANADIAN
CUSTER
ROGER MILLS
BECKHAM
LE FLORE
HASKELL
MCINTOSH
HUGHES
SEMINOLE
POTTAWATOMIE
CLEVELAND
MCCLAIN
CADDO
WASHITA
KIOWA
GREER
LATIMER
PITTSBURG
COAL
PONTOTOC
GARVIN
GRADY
COMANCHE
JACKSON
HARMON
MCCURTAIN
PUSHMATAHA
ATOKA
JOHNSTON
MURRAY
CARTER
STEPHENS
COTTON
TILLMAN
CHOCTAW
BRYAN
MARSHALL
LOVE
JEFFERSON
WICHITA
WILBARGER
RED RIVER
LAMAR
FANNIN
GRAYSON
COOKE
MONTAGUE
CLAY
ARCHER
BAYLOR
KNOX
KING
DICKENS
CROSBY
LUBBOCK
HOCKLEY
COCHRAN
HARDEMAN
FOARD
COTTLE
MOTLEY
FLOYD
HALE
LAMB
BAILEY
CHILDRESS
HALL
BRISCOE
SWISHER
CASTRO
PARMER
COLLINGSWORTH
DONLEY
ARMSTRONG
RANDALL
DEAF SMITH
WHEELER
GRAY
CARSON
POTTER
OLDHAM
HEMPHILL
ROBERTS
HUTCHINSON
MOORE
HARTLEY
LIPSCOMB
OCHILTREE
HANSFORD
SHERMAN
DALLAM

Kiowa County Genealogical Society
Box 191, Hobart, OK 73651

Lawton Public Library
110 SW Fourth St., Lawton, OK 73501, (580) 581-3450

Logan County Genealogical Society
Box 1419, Guthrie, OK 73044, **<www.rootsweb.ancestry.com/~oklcgs/lib.htm>**

Love County Historical Society
Box 134, Marietta, OK 73448

Major County Genealogical Society
Box 74, Fairview OK 73737, **<www.okgenweb.org/~okmajor/mcgs.htm>**

Mayes County Genealogical Society
Box 924, Chouteau, OK 74337, **<www.okgenweb.org/~okmayes>**

McClain County Oklahoma Historical and Genealogical Society
203 W. Washington St., Purcell, OK 73080, **<www.rootsweb.ancestry.com/~okmchgs/mchgs.htm>**

McCurtain County Genealogical Society
Box 1832, Idabel, OK 74745, **<www.rootsweb.ancestry.com/~okmcgs>**

Metropolitan Library System
131 Dean McGee Ave., Oklahoma City, OK 73102, **<www.mls.lib.ok.us>**

Muldrow Genealogical Society
Box 1253, Muldrow, OK 74938

Muldrow Public Library
Box 449, Muldrow, OK 74948

Museum of the Great Plains
601 Ferris, Lawton, OK 73507, (580) 581-3460, **<www.museumgreatplains.org>**

Muskogee County Genealogical Society
801 W. Okmulgee, Muskogee, OK 74401, **<www.okgenweb.org/~mcgs>**

National Archives and Records Administration, Central Plains Region, Kansas City
400 W. Pershing Rd., Kansas City, MO 64108, (816) 268-8000, **<www.archives.gov/central-plains/kansas-city>**

Noble County Genealogical Society
Box 785, Perry, OK 73077, **<www.okgenweb.org/~oknoble>**

Northwest Oklahoma Genealogical Society
<www.rootsweb.ancestry.com/~oknwgs>

Oklahoma Department of Libraries, Legislative Reference Division
Capitol Building, 2300 N. Lincoln Blvd., Room B-8, Oklahoma City, OK 73105

Oklahoma Genealogical Society
Box 12986, Oklahoma City, OK 73157, **<www.rootsweb.ancestry.com/~okgs>**

Oklahoma Historical Society
800 Nazih Zuhdi Dr., Oklahoma City, OK 73105, (405) 521-2491, **<www.ok-history.mus.ok.us>**

Oklahoma State Archives
200 NE 18th St., Oklahoma City, OK 73105, **<www.odl.state.ok.us/oar>**

Okmulgee County Genealogical Society
Box 805, Okmulgee, OK 74447

Ottawa County Genealogical Society
Box 1383, Miami, OK 74355, **<www.rootsweb.ancestry.com/~okottawa>**

Pawhuska Genealogical Society
Box 807, Pawhuska, OK 74056

Payne County Genealogical Society
Box 2708, Stillwater, OK 74076, **<www.rootsweb.ancestry.com/~okpcgs>**

Pioneer Genealogical Society
Box 1965, Ponca City, OK 74602, **<www.kaycounty.info/PGS/frtpage.html>**

Pioneer Sons and Daughters of the Cherokee Strip
Box 465, Enid, OK 73702

Pittsburg County Genealogical and Historical Society
113 E. Carol Albert Pkwy., McAlester, OK 74501, **<www.pittsburgcogenealogical.org>**

Ponca City Library
515 E. Grand Ave., Ponca, OK 74601, **<www.poncacitylibrary.com>**

Pontotoc County Historical and Genealogical Society
221 W. 16th St., Ada, OK 74820, **<www.rootsweb.ancestry.com/~okpontgs>**

Poteau Valley Genealogical Society
Box 1031, Poteau, OK 74953, **<www.rootsweb.ancestry.com/~okleflor/pvgs.htm>**

Pushmataha County Historical Society
Box 285, Antler, OK 74523, **<www.okgenweb.org/~okpushma>**

Ralph Ellison Library
2000 NE 23d St., Oklahoma City, OK 73111, (405) 424-1437

Roger Mills County Genealogical Society
<www.okgenweb.org/~okrogerm>

Rogers County Genealogical Society
Box 2493, Claremore, OK 74018, **<www.okgenweb.org/~okrogers/resources.htm>**

Roman Catholic Diocese of Oklahoma City
7501 NW Expressway, Oklahoma City, OK 73123, (405) 721-5651, **<www.catharchdioceseokc.org>**

Rudisill North Regional Library
1520 N. Hartford, Tulsa, OK 74106, (918) 596-7280, **<www.tulsalibrary.org/rudisill>**

Sapulpa Public Library
27 W. Dewey Ave., Sapulpa, OK 74066, **<www.sapulpalibrary.com>**

Seminole Public Library
424 N. Main St., Seminole, OK 74868

Sons of Confederate Veterans
Box 57312, Oklahoma City, OK 73157, **<www.scv.org>**

Southwest Oklahoma Genealogical Society
Box 148, Lawton, OK 73502, **<www.sirinet.net/~lgarris/swogs>**

State Department of Health
1000 NE 10th St., Box 53551, Oklahoma City, OK 73152, (405) 271-4040, **<www.ok.gov/health>**

Stanley Tubbs Memorial Library
101 E. Cherokee St., Sallisaw, OK 74955

Stephens County Genealogical Society
301 N. Eighth St., Duncan, OK 73533, (580) 255-8718, **<stephenscogen.org>**

Swink Historical Preservation Association
Box 165, Swink, OK 74716

Talbot Library and Museum
500 S. Colcord Ave., Box 349, Colcord, OK 74338, **<www.talbotlibrary.com>**

Thomas Gilcrease Institute of American History and Art
1400 N. Gilcrease Museum Rd., Tulsa, OK 74127, (918) 596-2700, **<www.gilcrease.org>**

Three Forks Genealogical Society
102 S. State St., Wagoner, OK 74467, **<www.rootsweb.ancestry.com/~ok3fgs>**

Tulsa County Public Library, Schusterman-Benson Branch
3333 E. 32nd Pl., Tulsa, OK 74135, **<www.tulsalibrary.org/schustermanbenson>**

Tulsa Genealogical Society Library
9136 E. 31st, Tulsa, OK 74105, (918) 627-4224, **<www.tulsagenealogy.org/library>**

Tulsa Public Library
400 Civic Center, Tulsa, OK 74103, **<www.tulsalibrary.org>**

University of Oklahoma American Indian Institute
1639 Cross Center Dr., Norman, OK 73019, (405) 325-7757, **<aii.ou.edu>**

University of Oklahoma Libraries
630 Parrington, Oval Room 452, Norman, OK 73019, **<libraries.ou.edu>**

Vinita Public Library
215 W. Illinois, Vinita, OK 74301, **<www.vinitapl.okpls.org>**

Weatherford Public Library
219 E. Franklin Ave., Weatherford, OK 73096

Western Trails Genealogy Library
Southern Prairie Library, 421 Hudson St., Box 70, Altus, OK 73521

Woods County Genealogical Society
Box 234, Alva, OK 73717, **<www.rootsweb.ancestry.com/~okwoods>**

☞ GENERAL RESOURCES

All Along the Chisholm Trail, 2 vols., by James W. Parker (J.W. Parker, 1988)

American Indian Resource Materials in the Western History Collections, University Of Oklahoma by Donald L. Dewitt (University of Oklahoma Press, 1990)

An Annotated Guide to the Chronicles of Oklahoma, 1921-1994 by Carol Welsh (Oklahoma Historical Society, 1996)

Applications for Enrollment of the Commission to the Five Civilized Tribes, 1898-1914 from the United States Commission to the Five Civilized Tribes (National Archives, 1983)

Bible Belt Catholicism: A History of the Roman Catholic Church in Oklahoma, 1905-1945 by Thomas E. Brown (US Catholic Historical Society, 1977)

Black Indian Genealogy Research: African-American Ancestors Among the Five Civilized Tribes by Angela Y. Walton-Raji (Heritage Books, 1993)

Boundaries of Oklahoma edited by John W. Morris (Oklahoma Historical Society, 1980)

Catalog Of Microfilm Holdings in the Archives & Manuscripts Division of the Oklahoma Historical Society 1976-1989: Native American Tribal Records and Special Collections from the Oklahoma Historical Society, Indian Archives Division (Oklahoma Historical Society, 1976-1989)

Cherokee Notes by James Manford Carselowey (Yesterdays Publications, 1980)

Cherokee Pioneers by James Manford Carselowey (J.M. Carselowey, 1961)

The Cherokee Strip of Oklahoma: A Hundred Yesteryears by Robert N. Gray (Sons and Daughters of the Cherokee Strip Pioneers Museum, 1992)

The Chickasaw Freemen: A People Without A Country by Daniel F. Littlefield (Greenwood Press, 1980)

The Chisholm Trail by Wayne Gard (University Of Oklahoma Press, 1976)

The Czechs in Oklahoma by Karel D. Bicha (University of Oklahoma Press, 1980)

Directory of Oklahoma Sources (Federation of Oklahoma Genealogical Societies, 1993)

Establishing of Churches in the Cherokee Nation, 1866-1908 from the Oklahoma Historical Society, Indian Archives Division (Oklahoma Historical Society, 1976-)

Exploring Your Cherokee Ancestry: A Basic Genealogical Research Guide by Thomas G. Mooney (Cherokee National Historical Society, 1990)

Family History: A Bibliography of the Collection In the Oklahoma Historical Society by Mary Huffman (the Oklahoma Historical Society, 1992)

First Families of the Twin Territories: Our Ancestors in Oklahoma Before Statehood (the Oklahoma Genealogical Society, 1997)

The Five Civilized Tribes: A Bibliography by Mary Huffman (Oklahoma Historical Society, Library Resources Division, 1991)

Genealogy of Old and New Cherokee Indian Families by George Bell (George Bell, 1972)

Growing Faith: General Conference Mennonites In Oklahoma by Wilma McKee (Faith and Life Press, 1988)

Guide to Cherokee Indian Records Microfilm Collection: Archives and Manuscripts Division, Oklahoma Historical Society by Sharron Standifer Aston (Ashton Books, 1996)

Guide to the Historical Records of Oklahoma by Bradford Koplowitz (Heritage Books, 1990, 1997)

A Guide to the Indian Tribes of Oklahoma by Muriel Hazel Wright (University of Oklahoma Press, 1951, 1986)

Guide to Manuscript Collections Western History Collections University of Oklahoma by Donald L. Dewitt (Heritage Books, 1994)

Guide to Records in the National Archives Relating to American Indians compiled by Edward E. Hill (National Archives, 1981)

A Guide to Regional Manuscript Collections in the Division of Manuscripts, University of Oklahoma Library by Arrell M. Gibson (University of Oklahoma Press, 1960)

A History of the Church of Jesus Christ of Latter-day Saints in Eastern Oklahoma by Lynetta K. Bingha (Tulsa, Okla., Stake, 1980)

History of Oklahoma, 4 vols., by Gatson Litton (Lewis Historical Publishing Co., 1957)

A History of the State of Oklahoma, 2 vols., by Luther B. Hill (Lewis Publishing Co., 1908)

Index to Oklahoma Newspapers (Oklahoma Historical Society 2002)

Indian Leaders: Oklahoma's First Statesmen by H. Glenn Jordan (Oklahoma Historical Society, 1979)

The Indian Territory: Its Chiefs, Legislators and Leading Men by Harry F. and Edward S. O'Beirne (C.B. Woodward Co., 1892)

The Intruders: The Illegal Residents of Cherokee Nation, 1866-1907 by Nancy Hope Sober (Cherokee Books, 1991)

The Jews in Oklahoma by Henry J. Tobias (University of Oklahoma Press, 1980)

Journey Toward Hope: A History of Blacks In Oklahoma by Jimmie L. Franklin (University of Oklahoma Press, 1982)

The Kiowa Indians: Their History & Life Stories by Hugh D. Corwin (H.D. Corwin, 1958)

Leaders and Leading Men of the Indian Territory by Harry F. O'Beirne (American Publishers Association, 1891)

Like A Prairie Fire: A History of the Assemblies of God in Oklahoma by Bob Burke (Oklahoma District Council of the Assemblies of God, 1994)

A List of the Records of the State of Oklahoma from the Historical Records Survey (Historical Records Survey, 1938)

Missions and Missionaries of Indian Territory by C.W. West (Muscogee Publishing, 1990)

Oklahoma Christians: A History of Christian Churches and of the Start of the Christian Church (Disciples of Christ) in Oklahoma by Stephen J. England (Bethany Press, 1975)

Oklahoma Genealogical Research by Mary Metzger O'Brien (M. O'Brien Bookshop, 1986)

Oklahoma: A History of Five Centuries, 2nd edition, by Arrell Morgan Gibson (1965; Harlow Publishing Corporation, 1981)

Oklahoma, A History of the State and its People, 4 vols., by Joseph Bradfield Thorburn (Lewis Historical Publishing Co., 1929)

The Oklahoma Land Rush of 1889 by Stan Hoig (Oklahoma Historical Society, 1984)

Oklahoma Marriages: A Bibliography by Laura Martin (Library Resources Division, 1996)

Oklahoma: Records and Archives by Patrick J. Blessing (Universitory of Tulsa Publications, 1978)

Oklahoma Research Outline by the Church of Jesus Christ of Latter-day Saints (online at <www.familysearch.org/eng/search/RG/guide/oklahoma.asp>)

Oklahoma Research: The Twin Territories by Jean C. Brown (Jean C. Brown, 1975)

The Oklahoma Spirit of '17: Biographical Volume by W.E. Welch (Historical Publishing, 1920)

Oklahoma State, County and Town Records (Oklahoma Historical Society, 2002)

Oklahoma: A Student's Guide to Localized History by Arrell M. Gibson (Columbia University, 1965)

The Poles in Oklahoma by Richard M. Bernard (University of Oklahoma Press, 1980)

Portraits and Biographical Record of Oklahoma (Chapman Publishing Co., 1901)

Prairie Fire: A Pioneer History of Western Oklahoma from the Western Oklahoma Historical Society (Western Oklahoma Historical Society, 1978)

Preliminary List of Churches and Religious Organizations in Oklahoma by James W. Parker (Historical Records Survey, 1942)

A Seminole Sourcebook by William C. Sturtevant (Garland Publishing, 1987)

Smith's First Directory of Oklahoma Territory, for the Year Commencing August 1st, 1890 (Oklahoma Historical Society, 1986)

The Souls of the Just: A Necrology of the Catholic Church in Oklahoma by James D. White (Sarto Press, 1983)

Southwest Oklahoma Keys by Willie Reeves Hardin Bivins (Southwest Oklahoma Genealogical Society, 1982)

A Standard History of Oklahoma, 5 vols., by Joseph Bradfield Thorburn (American Historical Society, 1916)

State Records, Manuscripts, and Newspapers at the Oklahoma State Archives and Oklahoma Historical Society by John Stewart and Kenny A. Franks (State Department Of Libraries and Oklahoma Historical Society, 1975)

The Story of Oklahoma by W. David Baird (University of Oklahoma Press, 1994)

The Story of Oklahoma Baptists by E. C. Routh (Baptist General Convention, 1932)

They Carried the Torch: the Story of Oklahoma's Pioneer Newspapers by Mrs. Tom B. Ferguson (Levite Of Apache, 1989)

Tracing Indian Family Histories by Duane Kendall Hale (OCCE Copy Service, University of Oklahoma, 1983)

Where Are My Cherokees by Sandi Garrett (Cherokee Woman Publishing, 1997)

Women of Oklahoma, 1890-1920 by Linda Williams Reese (University of Oklahoma, 1997)

☞IMMIGRATION RECORDS

Choctaw Emigration Records, 2 vols., by Monty Olsen (Bryan County Heritage Association, 1990)

German-Russian Heritage, Steppes to America by the American Historical Society of Germans from Russia, Oklahoma Harvester Chapter (AHSGR, 1991)

☞LAND RECORDS

Boundaries of Oklahoma edited by John W. Morris (Oklahoma Historical Society, 1980)

Containing Grants in Present States of Missouri, Arkansas and Oklahoma by Frances Terry Ingmire (F.T. Ingmire, 1984)

El Reno District 1901 Land Lottery: Index to Names of Homesteaders Filings by Julie Peterson Hinton and Louise F. Wilcox (J.P. Hinton, 1985)

Oklahoma Land Records (Oklahoma Historical Society)

The Oklahoma Land Rush of 1889 by Stan Hoig (Oklahoma Historical Society, 1984)

☞MAPS

Boundaries of Oklahoma by John W. Morris (Oklahoma Historical Society, 1980)

A Gazetteer of Indian Territory by Henry A. Gannett (US Government Printing Office, 1905; Oklahoma Yesterday Publishing, 1980)

Ghost Towns of Oklahoma by John W. Morris (University of Oklahoma Press, 1977)

Historical Atlas of Oklahoma by John W. Morris and Edwin C. McReynolds (University of Oklahoma Press, 1976)

Oklahoma Place Names, 2nd edition, by George H. Shirk (University of Oklahoma Press, 1974)

Town and Place Locations (Oklahoma Department of Transportation, 1991)

☞MILITARY RECORDS

Black, Buckskin And Blue: African American Scouts And Soldiers On The Western Frontier by Arthur T. Burton (Eaton Press, 1999)

Early Military Forts and Posts in Oklahoma edited by Odie B. Faulk, et al. (Oklahoma Historical Society, 1978)

A History of the Second World War: A Remembrance, An Appreciation, A Memorial (Victory Publishing Co., 1946)

Index to Applications for Pensions From the State of Oklahoma Submitted by Confederate Soldiers, Sailors and their Widows (Oklahoma Genealogical Society, 1969)

Muster Lists of the Cherokee Confederate Indians by Sherman Lee Pompey (Historical and Genealogical Publishing Co., 1965)

Muster Lists of the Creek and Other Confederate Indians by Sherman Lee Pompey (Historical and Genealogical Publishing Co., 1996)

Oklahoma Air National Guard Pilots in the Korean War by Stanley Newman (45th Infantry Division Museum, 1990)

☞PROBATE RECORDS

Abstracts of Wills from Oklahoma Chapters N.S.D.A.R. from the Daughters of the American Revolution, Black Beaver Chapter (filmed by the Family History Library, 1970)

Abstracts of Wills of Our Forefathers from the Daughters of the American Revolution, Enid Chapter (filmed by the Genealogical Society of Utah, 1972)

Collection of Old Wills Assembled by D.A.R. Chapters of Oklahoma by Mrs. John P. Cook (filmed by the Family History Library, 1970)

Probate Records, 1808-1812 from the Louisiana Territory Probate Court (filmed by the Family History Library, 1975)

Probate Records, 1892-1908, Northern District Cherokee Nation, 3 vols., by Orpha Jewell Wever (Northeast Oklahoma Genealogical Society, 1982-83)

☞VITAL RECORDS

Birth and Death Notices In Oklahoma and Indian Territories From 1871 by N. Dale Talkington (N.D. Talkington, 1999)

Cherokee National Births and Deaths, 1884-1901 by Dixie Bogle (Cook and McDowell Publishers, 1980)

Cherokee Nation Marriages, 1884-1901 by Dixie Bogle (Cook and McDowell Publishers, 1980)

Guide to Public Vital Statistics Records in Oklahoma (Historical Records Survey, 1941)

Oklahoma Cemeteries: A Bibliography of the Collections in the Oklahoma Historical Society by Barbara Pierce and Brian Basore (The Society, 1993)

Oklahoma Marriage Records, Choctaw Nation, Indian Territory, 10 vols., by Ellen Tifee and Gloryann Hankins Young (University of Oklahoma, 1969-78)

Oklahoma Territory Weddings by Frances M. Bode (Pioneer Book Committee, 1983)

Our People and Where They Rest, 12 vols., by James W. Tyner and Alice Tyner Timmons (University of Oklahoma, 1969-78)

Relocated Cemeteries in Oklahoma and Parts of Arkansas, Kansas, Texas by Madeline S. Mills and Helen R. Mullenax (Mills and Mullenax, 1974)

Union List of Oklahoma Cemeteries (Oklahoma Genealogical Society, 1969)

•-COUNTY DETAILS-•

A
- **INCORPORATED:** 1891
- **PARENT COUNTIES:** Iowa-Sac-Fox and Pottawatomie-Shawnee Lands
- **NOTES:** See Lincoln County. Name changed to Lincoln.

ADAIR
Second and Division Sts., Box 169, Stilwell, OK 74960, (918) 696-7633, **<www.rootsweb.ancestry.com/~okadair/adaircty.htm>**
- **INCORPORATED:** July 16, 1907
- **PARENT COUNTY:** Cherokee Lands
- **MARRIAGE RECORDS:** start in 1907, kept by Clerk of Court
- **DIVORCE:** 1907, Clerk of Court
- **LAND:** 1906, County Clerk
- **PROBATE:** 1907, Clerk of Court
- **COURT:** 1907, Clerk of Court
- **MILITARY:** 1906, County Clerk

ALFALFA
County Courthouse 300 S. Grand St., Cherokee, OK 73728, (580) 596-3523, **<www.rootsweb.ancestry.com/~okalfalf/main-alfalfa.htm>**
- **INCORPORATED:** Julyy 16, 1907
- **PARENT COUNTY:** Woods
- **MARRIAGE RECORDS:** unknown start, kept by Clerk of Court
- **DIVORCE:** 1893, Clerk of Court
- **LAND:** 1893, County Clerk
- **PROBATE:** 1893, Clerk of Court
- **COURT:** 1893, Clerk of Court
- **MILITARY (WWI):** unknown start, County Clerk

ATOKA
200 E. Court St., Atoka, OK 74525, (580) 889-5157, **<www.rootsweb.ancestry.com/~okatoka/atoka.htm>**
- **INCORPORATED:** July 16, 1907
- **PARENT COUNTY:** Choctaw Lands
- **MARRIAGE RECORDS:** start in 1897, kept by Clerk of Court
- **DIVORCE:** unknown start, Clerk of Court
- **LAND:** 1903, County Clerk
- **PROBATE:** unknown start, Clerk of Court
- **COURT:** unknown start, Clerk of Court
- **MILITARY (WWI):** unknown start, County Clerk

B
- **INCORPORATED:** 1891
- **PARENT COUNTY:** Original county from Pottawatomie-Shawnee Lands
- **NOTES:** See Pottawatomie County. Name changed to Pottawatomie.

BEAVER
111 W. Second St., Box 338, Beaver, OK 73932, (580) 625-3191, **<beaver.okcounties.org>**
- **INCORPORATED:** 1890
- **PARENT COUNTY:** Original county (Public Lands)
- **MARRIAGE RECORDS:** start in 1890, kept by Clerk of Court
- **DIVORCE:** 1890, Clerk of Court
- **LAND:** 1890, County Clerk
- **PROBATE:** 1891, Clerk of Court
- **COURT:** 1890, Clerk of Court
- **MILITARY:** 1917, County Clerk

BECKHAM
302 E. Main St., Box 428, Sayre, OK 73662, (580) 928-3330, **<www.rootsweb.ancestry.com/~okbeckha>**
- **INCORPORATED:** July 16, 1907
- **PARENT COUNTIES:** Roger Mills, Greer Territory
- **MARRIAGE RECORDS:** start in 1907, kept by Clerk of Court
- **LAND:** 1907, County Clerk
- **PROBATE:** 1907, Clerk of Court
- **COURT:** unknown start, Clerk of Court
- **MILITARY (WWI):** unknown start, County Clerk

BLAINE
212 N. Weigle Ave., Box 138, Watonga, OK 73772, (580) 623-5970, **<blainecountyok.com>**
- **INCORPORATED:** 1892
- **PARENT COUNTY:** Original county
- **MARRIAGE RECORDS:** start in 1892, kept by Clerk of Court
- **DIVORCE:** 1892, Clerk of Court
- **LAND:** 1892, County Clerk
- **PROBATE:** 1892, Clerk of Court
- **COURT:** 1892, Clerk of Court
- **MILITARY:** 1918, County Clerk
- **NOTES:** Formerly C County. Name changed to Blaine.

BRYAN
402 W. Evergreen St., Durant, OK 74701, (580) 924-1446, **<www.rootsweb.ancestry.com/~okbryan>**
- **INCORPORATED:** July 16, 1907
- **PARENT COUNTY:** Choctaw Lands
- **MARRIAGE RECORDS:** start in 1907, kept by Clerk of Court
- **DIVORCE:** 1907, Clerk of Court
- **LAND:** 1903, County Clerk
- **PROBATE:** 1907, Clerk of Court
- **COURT:** 1907, Clerk of Court
- **MILITARY:** 1919, County Clerk

C
- **INCORPORATED:** 1892
- **PARENT COUNTY:** Original county
- **NOTES:** See Blaine County. Name changed to Blaine.

CADDO
SW Second St. & Oklahoma Ave., Anadarko, OK 73005, (405) 247-3393, **<www.rootsweb.ancestry.com/~okcaddo/ccpage.htm>**
- **INCORPORATED:** 1901
- **PARENT COUNTY:** Original Lands
- **MARRIAGE RECORDS:** start in 1901, kept by Clerk of Court
- **DIVORCE:** 1901, Clerk of Court

- **LAND:** 1907, County Clerk
- **PROBATE:** 1901, Clerk of Court
- **COURT:** 1901, Clerk of Court
- **MILITARY (WWI):** unknown start, County Clerk
- **NOTES:** Formerly I County. Name changed to Caddo Nov. 8, 1902.

CANADIAN

201 N. Choctaw Ave., Box 458, El Reno, OK 73036, (405) 262-1070, **<www.canadiancounty.org>**

- **INCORPORATED:** 1889
- **PARENT COUNTY:** Original county
- **MARRIAGE RECORDS:** start in 1890, kept by Clerk of Court
- **DIVORCE:** 1890, Clerk of Court
- **LAND:** 1889, County Clerk
- **PROBATE:** 1890, Clerk of Court
- **COURT:** 1890, Clerk of Court
- **MILITARY:** 1919, County Clerk

CARTER

First and B St. SW, Box 1236, Ardmore, OK 73401, (580) 223-8162, **<www.brightok.net/cartercounty>**

- **INCORPORATED:** July 16, 1907
- **PARENT COUNTY:** Chickasaw Lands
- **MARRIAGE RECORDS:** start in 1895, kept by Clerk of Court
- **DIVORCE:** 1907, Clerk of Court
- **LAND:** 1907, County Clerk
- **PROBATE:** 1907, Clerk of Court
- **COURT:** 1907, Clerk of Court
- **MILITARY:** unknown start, County Clerk

CHEROKEE

213 W. Delaware St., Tahlequah, OK 74464, (918) 456-3171, **<www.rootsweb.ancestry.com/~okchero2>**

- **INCORPORATED:** July 16, 1907
- **PARENT COUNTY:** Cherokee Lands
- **MARRIAGE RECORDS:** start in 1907, kept by Clerk of Court
- **DIVORCE:** 1907, Clerk of Court
- **LAND:** 1907, County Clerk
- **PROBATE:** 1907, Clerk of Court
- **COURT:** 1907, Clerk of Court
- **MILITARY:** 1918, County Clerk

CHOCTAW

300 E. Duke St., Hugo, OK 74743, (580) 326-7554, **<www.rootsweb.ancestry.com/~okchocta>**

- **INCORPORATED:** July 16, 1907
- **PARENT COUNTY:** Choctaw Lands
- **MARRIAGE RECORDS:** start in 1907, kept by Clerk of Court
- **DIVORCE:** 1907, Clerk of Court
- **LAND:** 1907, County Clerk
- **PROBATE:** 1907, Clerk of Court
- **COURT:** 1907, Clerk of Court
- **MILITARY (WWI):** unknown start, County Clerk

CIMARRON

Box 145, Boise City, OK 73933, (580) 544-2251, **<www.rootsweb.ancestry.com/~okcimarr/cimarron.htm>**

- **INCORPORATED:** July 16, 1907
- **PARENT COUNTY:** Beaver
- **MARRIAGE RECORDS:** start in 1908, kept by Clerk of Court
- **DIVORCE:** 1908, Clerk of Court
- **LAND:** 1907, County Clerk
- **PROBATE:** 1908, Clerk of Court
- **COURT:** 1908, Clerk of Court
- **MILITARY (WWI):** unknown start, County Clerk

CLEVELAND

641 E. Robinson, Norman, OK 73071, (405) 366-0240, **<www.ccok.us>**

- **INCORPORATED:** 1890
- **PARENT COUNTY:** Unassigned Lands
- **MARRIAGE RECORDS:** start in 1890, kept by Clerk of Court
- **DIVORCE:** unknown start, Clerk of Court
- **LAND:** 1889, County Clerk
- **PROBATE:** unknown start, Clerk of Court
- **COURT:** unknown start, Clerk of Court
- **MILITARY:** unknown start, County Clerk

COAL

4 N. Main St., Suite 1, Coalgate, OK 74538, (580) 927-2103, **<www.rootsweb.ancestry.com/~okcoal>**

- **INCORPORATED:** July 16, 1907
- **PARENT COUNTY:** Cherokee Lands
- **MARRIAGE RECORDS:** start in 1907, kept by Clerk of Court
- **DIVORCE:** 1907, Clerk of Court
- **LAND:** 1907, County Clerk
- **PROBATE:** 1907, Clerk of Court
- **COURT:** 1907, Clerk of Court
- **MILITARY (WWI):** 1917, County Clerk

COMANCHE

315 SW Fifth St., Lawton, OK 73501, (580) 355-5214, **<www.comanchecounty.us>**

- **INCORPORATED:** 1901
- **PARENT COUNTIES:** Kiowa-Comanche-Apache and Wichita-Caddo Lands
- **MARRIAGE RECORDS:** start in 1900, kept by Clerk of Court
- **DIVORCE:** 1900, Clerk of Court
- **LAND:** 1901, County Clerk
- **PROBATE:** 1900, Clerk of Court
- **COURT:** 1900, Clerk of Court
- **MILITARY:** 1918, County Clerk

COTTON

301 N. Broadway St., Walters, OK 73572, (580) 875-3029, **<www.rootsweb.ancestry.com/~okcotton>**

- **INCORPORATED:** Aug. 22 1912
- **PARENT COUNTIES:** Comanche, Oklahoma Territory
- **MARRIAGE RECORDS:** start in 1912, kept by Clerk of Court
- **DIVORCE:** 1912, Clerk of Court
- **DEATH:** 1912, Clerk of Court
- **LAND:** 1912, County Clerk
- **PROBATE:** 1912, Clerk of Court
- **COURT:** 1912, Clerk of Court
- **NOTES:** County Clerk has birth records 1912-1945.

CRAIG
301 W. Canadian Ave., Vinita, OK 74301, (918) 256-6451, **<www.rootsweb.ancestry.com/~okcraig>**
- **INCORPORATED:** July 16, 1907
- **PARENT COUNTY:** Cherokee Lands
- **MARRIAGE RECORDS:** start in 1902, kept by Clerk of Court
- **DIVORCE:** 1907, Clerk of Court
- **LAND:** 1907, County Clerk
- **PROBATE:** 1907, Clerk of Court
- **COURT:** 1907, Clerk of Court

CREEK
222 E. Dewey Suite 201, Sapulpa, OK 74067, (918) 227-2525, **<www.creekcountyonline.com>**
- **INCORPORATED:** July 16, 1907
- **PARENT COUNTY:** Creek Lands
- **MARRIAGE RECORDS:** start in 1907, kept by Clerk of Court
- **DIVORCE:** 1907, Clerk of Court
- **LAND:** 1907, County Clerk
- **PROBATE:** 1907, Clerk of Court
- **COURT:** 1907, Clerk of Court
- **NOTES:** District Court in Bristow and County Clerk of Court in Drumright have marriage and divorce records for their respective towns.

CUSTER
Seventh & B Sts., Arapaho, OK 73620, (580) 323-3233, **<www.custercountyok.org/otheroffices.htm>**
- **INCORPORATED:** 1892
- **PARENT COUNTY:** Cheyenne-Arapaho Lands
- **MARRIAGE RECORDS:** start in 1895, kept by Clerk of Court
- **DIVORCE:** 1899, Clerk of Court
- **LAND:** 1896, Clerk of Court
- **PROBATE:** 1900, Clerk of Court
- **COURT:** 1896, Clerk of Court
- **MILITARY:** 1892, County Clerk
- **SCHOOL CENSUS:** 1913, County Clerk
- **COUNTY REGISTER OF ELECTORS:** 1916, County Clerk
- **NOTES:** Formerly G County. Name changed to Custer Nov. 8, 1892. Cemetery Association has burial records for each city.

D
- **INCORPORATED:** 1892
- **PARENT COUNTY:** Original county (Cheyenne-Arapaho Lands)
- **NOTES:** See Dewey County. Name changed to Dewey Nov. 8, 1898.

DAY
- **INCORPORATED:** April 19, 1892
- **PARENT COUNTY:** Cheyenne-Arapaho Lands
- **NOTES:** Formerly E County. Name changed to Day. Discontinued Nov. 16, 1907 and became part of Ellis and Roger Mills counties.

DELAWARE
Box 309, Jay, OK 74346, (918) 253-4420, **<www.delawareclerk.org>**
- **INCORPORATED:** July 16, 1907
- **PARENT COUNTY:** Cherokee Lands
- **MARRIAGE RECORDS:** start in 1907, kept by Clerk of Court
- **LAND:** 1907, County Clerk
- **PROBATE:** 1906, Clerk of Court

DEWEY
Box 278, Taloga, OK 73667, (580) 328-5521, **<www.rootsweb.ancestry.com/~okdewey/okdewey.htm>**
- **INCORPORATED:** 1892
- **PARENT COUNTY:** Original county (Cheyenne-Arapaho Lands)
- **MARRIAGE RECORDS:** start in 1893, kept by Clerk of Court
- **DIVORCE:** 1894, Clerk of Court
- **LAND:** 1892, County Clerk
- **PROBATE:** 1893, Clerk of Court
- **COURT:** 1893, Clerk of Court
- **NOTES:** Formerly D County. Name changed to Dewey Nov. 8, 1898.

E
- **INCORPORATED:** 1892
- **PARENT COUNTY:** Cheyenne-Arapaho Lands
- **NOTES:** See Day County. Name changed to Day.

ELLIS
Courthouse Sq., 100 S. Washington, Arnett, OK 73832, (580) 885-7301, **<www.rootsweb.ancestry.com/~okellis/ellis.htm>**
- **INCORPORATED:** July 16, 1907
- **PARENT COUNTIES:** Day, Woodward
- **MARRIAGE RECORDS:** start in 1892, kept by Clerk of Court
- **LAND:** 1898, County Clerk
- **DIVORCE:** 1893, Clerk of Court
- **PROBATE:** 1908, Clerk of Court
- **COURT:** 1896, Clerk of Court

F
- **INCORPORATED:** 1892
- **PARENT COUNTY:** Cheyenne-Arapaho Lands
- **NOTES:** See Roger Mills County. Name changed to Roger Mills Nov. 8, 1892.

G
- **INCORPORATED:** 1892
- **PARENT COUNTY:** Cheyenne-Arapaho Lands
- **NOTES:** See Custer County. Name changed to Custer Nov. 8, 1892.

GARFIELD
County Courthouse Room 101, Enid, OK 73701, (580) 237-0232, **<www.rootsweb.ancestry.com/~okgarfie/gar.htm>**
- **INCORPORATED:** 1893
- **PARENT COUNTY:** Original county (Cherokee Outlet)
- **MARRIAGE RECORDS:** start in 1893, kept by Clerk of District Court
- **DIVORCE:** 1893, Clerk of District Court
- **LAND:** 1893, Registrar of Deeds
- **PROBATE:** 1893, Clerk of District Court

- **COURT:** 1893, Clerk of District Court
- **NOTES:** Originally O County. Name changed to Garfield Nov. 6, 1894.

GARVIN
Box 239, Pauls Valley, OK 73075, (405) 238-5596, **<www.rootsweb.ancestry.com/~okgarvin/garvin.htm>**
- **INCORPORATED:** July 16, 1907
- **PARENT COUNTY:** Chickasaw Lands
- **MARRIAGE RECORDS:** start in 1907, kept by Clerk of Court
- **DIVORCE:** 1907, Clerk of Court
- **LAND:** 1907, County Clerk
- **PROBATE:** 1907, Clerk of Court
- **COURT:** 1907, Clerk of Court

GRADY
320 E. Choctaw, Chickasha, OK 73018, (405) 224-7446, **<www.gradycountyok.com>**
- **INCORPORATED:** July 16, 1907
- **PARENT COUNTY:** Chickasaw Lands
- **MARRIAGE RECORDS:** start in 1907, kept by Clerk of Court
- **DIVORCE:** 1907, Clerk of Court
- **LAND:** 1907, Clerk of Court
- **PROBATE:** 1907, Clerk of Court
- **COURT:** 1907, Clerk of Court
- **MILITARY:** 1907, County Clerk
- **BURIAL:** 1907, County Clerk

GRANT
Grant County Courthouse, Box 167, Medford, OK 73759, (580) 395-2828, **<www.rootsweb.ancestry.com/~okgrant/okgrant.htm>**
- **INCORPORATED:** 1893
- **PARENT COUNTY:** Original county (Cherokee Outlet)
- **MARRIAGE RECORDS:** start in 1893, kept by Clerk of Court
- **DIVORCE:** 1893, Clerk of Court
- **LAND:** 1894, County Clerk
- **PROBATE:** 1893, Clerk of Court
- **COURT:** 1893, Clerk of Court
- **MILITARY:** unknown start, County Clerk
- **NOTES:** Formerly L County. Name changed to Grant Nov. 6, 1894.

GREER
Greer County Courthouse, Box 216, Mangum, OK 73554, (580) 782-3665, **<www.rootsweb.ancestry.com/~okgreer>**
- **INCORPORATED:** 1886
- **PARENT COUNTY:** Organized by Texas, transferred to Oklahoma by court decision
- **MARRIAGE RECORDS:** start in 1901, kept by Clerk of Court
- **DIVORCE:** 1901, Clerk of Court
- **LAND:** 1898, County Clerk
- **PROBATE:** 1901, Clerk of Court
- **COURT:** 1901, Clerk of Court
- **NOTES:** Organized as Greer County, Texas in 1886; an act of Congress on May 4, 1896 declared it Greer County, Okla. A fire in 1901 destroyed the county records.

H
- **INCORPORATED:** 1892
- **PARENT COUNTY:** Cheyenne-Arapaho Lands
- **NOTES:** See Washita County. Name changed to Washita Nov. 8, 1892.

HARMON
County Courthouse 114 W. Hollis, Hollis, OK 73550, (580) 688-3617, **<www.rootsweb.ancestry.com/~okharmon/harmon.htm>**
- **INCORPORATED:** June 2, 1909
- **PARENT COUNTY:** Greer
- **MARRIAGE RECORDS:** start in 1909, kept by Clerk of Court
- **DIVORCE:** 1909, Clerk of Court
- **LAND:** 1909, County Clerk
- **PROBATE:** 1909, Clerk of Court
- **COURT:** 1909, Clerk of Court

HARPER
311 SE First St., Box 347, Buffalo, OK 73834, (580) 735-2012, **<www.rootsweb.ancestry.com/~okharper>**
- **INCORPORATED:** July 16, 1907
- **PARENT COUNTIES:** Woodward, Woods, Indian Lands
- **MARRIAGE RECORDS:** start in 1907, kept by Clerk of Court
- **DIVORCE:** 1907, Clerk of Court
- **LAND:** 1907, County Clerk
- **PROBATE:** unknown start, Clerk of Court
- **COURT:** 1907, Clerk of Court
- **NOTES:** County Clerk has School records 1907-1963.

HASKELL
202 E. Main St., Stigler, OK 74462, (918) 967-3323, **<www.rootsweb.ancestry.com/~okhaskel/index.htm>**
- **INCORPORATED:** July 16, 1907
- **PARENT COUNTY:** Choctaw Lands
- **MARRIAGE RECORDS:** start in 1907, kept by Clerk of Court
- **DIVORCE:** 1907, Clerk of Court
- **LAND:** 1905, County Clerk
- **PROBATE:** 1907, Clerk of Court
- **COURT:** 1907, Clerk of Court

HUGHES
Hughes County Courthouse, Box 32, Holdenville, OK 74848, (405) 379-3384, **<www.rootsweb.ancestry.com/~okhughes>**
- **INCORPORATED:** July 16, 1907
- **PARENT COUNTY:** Creek Lands (Creek & Choctaw Lands)
- **MARRIAGE RECORDS:** start in 1907, kept by Clerk of Court
- **DIVORCE:** 1907, Clerk of Court
- **LAND:** 1907, County Clerk
- **PROBATE:** 1907, Clerk of Court
- **COURT:** 1907, Clerk of Court

I
- **INCORPORATED:** 1901
- **PARENT COUNTY:** Original Lands
- **NOTES:** See Caddo County. Name changed to Caddo Nov. 8, 1902.

JACKSON
101 N. Main St., Altus, OK 73521, (580) 482-0448, **<www.jacksoncountyok.com>**
- **INCORPORATED:** July 16, 1907
- **PARENT COUNTY:** Greer
- **MARRIAGE RECORDS:** start in 1907, kept by Clerk of Court
- **DIVORCE:** 1907, Clerk of Court
- **LAND:** 1907, County Clerk
- **PROBATE:** 1907, Clerk of Court
- **COURT:** 1907, Clerk of Court

JEFFERSON
Chourthouse 220 N. Main St. Room 101, Waurika, OK 73573, (580) 228-2961, **<www.jeffcoinfo.org>**
- **INCORPORATED:** July 16, 1907
- **PARENT COUNTY:** Comanche (Chickasaw Lands)
- **MARRIAGE RECORDS:** start in 1907, kept by Clerk of Court
- **DIVORCE:** 1907, Clerk of Court
- **LAND:** 1907, County Clerk
- **PROBATE:** 1907, Clerk of Court
- **COURT:** 1907, Clerk of Court

JOHNSTON
403 W. Main Suite 201, Tishomingo, OK 73460, (580) 371-3281, **<www.rootsweb.ancestry.com/~okjohnst/index.htm>**
- **INCORPORATED:** July 16, 1907
- **PARENT COUNTY:** Chickasaw Lands
- **MARRIAGE RECORDS:** start in 1907, kept by Clerk of Court
- **DIVORCE:** 1907, Clerk of Court
- **LAND:** 1907, County Clerk
- **PROBATE:** 1907, Clerk of Court
- **COURT:** 1907, Clerk of Court
- **MILITARY:** 1917, County Clerk

K
- **INCORPORATED:** 1893
- **PARENT COUNTY:** Original county
- **NOTES:** (See Kay) Name changed to Kay.

KAY
Box 450, Newkirk, OK 74647, (580) 362-3350, **<www.courthouse.kay.ok.us>**
- **INCORPORATED:** 1893
- **PARENT COUNTY:** Original county (Cherokee Outlet)
- **MARRIAGE RECORDS:** start in 1893, kept by Clerk of Court
- **DIVORCE:** 1893, Clerk of Court
- **LAND:** 1893, County Clerk
- **PROBATE:** 1893, Clerk of Court
- **COURT:** 1893, Clerk of Court
- **NOTES:** Formerly K County. Name changed to Kay.

KINGFISHER
Box 328, Kingfisher, OK 73750, (405) 375-3813, **<www.rootsweb.ancestry.com/~okkingfi>**
- **INCORPORATED:** 1890
- **PARENT COUNTY:** Original county
- **MARRIAGE RECORDS:** start in 1900, kept by Clerk of Court
- **DIVORCE:** 1900, Clerk of Court
- **LAND:** 1890, County Clerk
- **PROBATE:** 1900, Clerk of Court
- **COURT:** 1900, Clerk of Court

KIOWA
316 S. Main, Box 73, Hobart, OK 73651, (580) 726-5125, **<www.rootsweb.ancestry.com/~okkiowa>**
- **INCORPORATED:** 1901
- **PARENT COUNTY:** Kiowa-Comanche-Apache and Caddo-Wichita Lands
- **MARRIAGE RECORDS:** start in 1901, kept by Clerk of Court
- **DIVORCE:** 1901, Clerk of Court
- **LAND:** 1901, County Clerk
- **PROBATE:** 1901, Clerk of Court
- **COURT:** 1901, Clerk of Court
- **MILITARY:** 1901, County Clerk
- **BURIAL:** 1901, County Clerk
- **SCHOOL CENSUS:** 1916, County Clerk

L
- **INCORPORATED:** 1893
- **PARENT COUNTY:** Chickasaw Lands
- **NOTES:** See Grant County. Name changed to Grant Nov. 6, 1894.

LATIMER
109 N. Central St. Room 200, Wilburton, OK 74578, (918) 465-2011, **<www.rootsweb.ancestry.com/~oklatime>**
- **INCORPORATED:** 1902
- **PARENT COUNTY:** Choctaw Lands
- **MARRIAGE RECORDS:** start in 1906, kept by Clerk of Court
- **DIVORCE:** 1907, Clerk of Court
- **PROBATE:** 1907, Clerk of Court
- **COURT:** 1907, Clerk of Court

LE FLORE
Courthouse, Box 218, Poteau, OK 74953, (918) 647-3181, **<www.rootsweb.ancestry.com/~okleflor>**
- **INCORPORATED:** July 16, 1907
- **PARENT COUNTY:** Choctaw Lands
- **MARRIAGE RECORDS:** start in 1897, kept by Clerk of Court
- **DIVORCE:** 1907, Clerk of Court
- **LAND:** 1907, County Clerk
- **PROBATE:** 1907, Clerk of Court
- **COURT:** 1907, Clerk of Court
- **NOTES:** Clerk of Court has some Probate records as early as 1895.

LINCOLN
Box 307, Manvel Ave., Chandler, OK 74834, (405) 258-1309, **<www.rootsweb.ancestry.com/~oklincol>**
- **INCORPORATED:** 1891
- **PARENT COUNTY:** Iowa-Sac-Fox and Pottawatomie-Shawnee Lands
- **MARRIAGE RECORDS:** start in 1892, kept by Clerk of District Court
- **DIVORCE:** 1892, Clerk of District Court
- **LAND:** 1892, County Clerk
- **PROBATE:** 1892, Clerk of District Court
- **COURT:** 1892, Clerk of District Court
- **NOTES:** Formerly A County. Name changed to Lincoln.

LOGAN
301 E. Harrison Ave., Guthrie, OK 73044, (405) 282-0123, **<www.logancountyok.com>**
- **INCORPORATED:** May 1890
- **PARENT COUNTY:** Original county
- **MARRIAGE RECORDS:** start in 1889, kept by Clerk of Court
- **DIVORCE:** unknown start, Clerk of Court
- **LAND:** 1889, County Clerk
- **PROBATE:** 1900, Clerk of Court
- **COURT:** 1900, Clerk of Court

LOVE
405 W. Main St., Marietta, OK 73448, (580) 276-2235, **<www.rootsweb.ancestry.com/~oklove>**
- **INCORPORATED:** July 16, 1907
- **PARENT COUNTY:** Chickasaw Lands
- **BIRTH RECORDS:** start in 1908, kept by County Clerk
- **MARRIAGE:** 1907, Clerk of Court
- **DIVORCE:** 1907, Clerk of Court
- **DEATH:** 1908, County Clerk
- **LAND:** 1903, County Clerk
- **PROBATE:** 1907, Clerk of Court
- **COURT:** 1907, Clerk of Court

M
- **INCORPORATED:** 1893
- **PARENT COUNTY:** Cherokee Outlet
- **NOTES:** See Woods County. Name changed to Woods Nov. 6, 1894.

MAJOR
Box 379, E. Broadway, Fairview, OK 73737, (580) 227-4712, **<www.rootsweb.ancestry.com/~okmajor/major.htm>**
- **INCORPORATED:** July 16, 1907
- **PARENT COUNTY:** Woods
- **DIVORCE RECORDS:** start in 1907, kept by Clerk of Court
- **LAND:** 1907, County Clerk
- **PROBATE:** 1907, Clerk of Court
- **COURT:** 1907, Clerk of Court
- **NOTES:** Clerk of Court has marriage records from late 1800's.

MARSHALL
Box 58, Madill, OK 73446, (580) 795-3278, **<marshall.okcounties.org>**
- **INCORPORATED:** July 16, 1907
- **PARENT COUNTY:** Chickasaw Lands
- **MARRIAGE RECORDS:** start in 1907, kept by Clerk of Court
- **DIVORCE:** 1907, Clerk of Court
- **LAND:** 1907, County Clerk
- **PROBATE:** 1907, Clerk of Court
- **COURT:** 1907, Clerk of Court
- **MILITARY:** unknown start, County Clerk
- **SCHOOL:** unknown start, County Superintendent

MAYES
Courthouse, Pryor, OK 74361, (918) 825-2426, **<www.rootsweb.ancestry.com/~okmayes>**
- **INCORPORATED:** July 16, 1907
- **PARENT COUNTY:** Cherokee Lands
- **MARRIAGE RECORDS:** start in 1907, kept by Clerk of Court
- **DIVORCE:** 1907, Clerk of Court
- **LAND:** 1907, County Clerk
- **PROBATE:** 1907, Clerk of Court
- **COURT:** 1907, Clerk of Court
- **TAX:** unknown start, County Treasurer

MCCLAIN
121 N. Second St. Suite 231, Purcell, OK 73080, (405) 527-3221, **<www.rootsweb.ancestry.com/~okmcclai/okmcclain.html>**
- **INCORPORATED:** July 16, 1907
- **PARENT COUNTY:** Chickasaw Lands
- **MARRIAGE RECORDS:** start in 1907, kept by Clerk of Court
- **DEATH:** 1883, Clerk of Court
- **LAND:** unknown start, County Clerk
- **PROBATE:** 1895, Clerk of Court
- **COURT:** 1895, Clerk of Court

MCCURTAIN
Box 1378, Idabel, OK 74745, (580) 286-3693, **<backwardbranch.com/okmccurt>**
- **INCORPORATED:** July 16, 1907
- **PARENT COUNTY:** Choctaw Lands
- **BIRTH RECORDS:** start in 1908, kept by County Clerk
- **MARRIAGE:** 1907, Clerk of Court
- **DIVORCE:** 1907, Clerk of Court
- **DEATH:** 1908, County Clerk
- **LAND:** 1907, County Clerk
- **PROBATE:** 1907, Clerk of Court
- **COURT:** 1907, Clerk of Court

MCINTOSH
Box 426, Eufaula, OK 2282, (918) 689-2741, **<www.rootsweb.ancestry.com/~okmcinto/index.htm>**
- **INCORPORATED:** July 16, 1907
- **PARENT COUNTIES:** Creek Lands, Cherokee Nations
- **BIRTH RECORDS:** unknown start, kept by State Health Department
- **MARRIAGE:** 1907, Clerk of Court
- **DIVORCE:** 1907, Clerk of Court
- **DEATH:** unknown start, State Health Department
- **LAND:** 1907, County Clerk
- **PROBATE:** 1907, Clerk of Court
- **COURT:** 1907, Clerk of Court

MURRAY
Box 578, Sulphur, OK 73086, (580) 622-3223, **<www.murrayok.com/murray-county-government.asp>**
- **INCORPORATED:** July 16, 1907
- **PARENT COUNTY:** Chickasaw Lands
- **MARRIAGE RECORDS:** start in 1907, kept by Clerk of Court
- **DIVORCE:** 1907, Clerk of Court
- **LAND:** 1908, County Clerk
- **PROBATE:** 1907, Clerk of Court
- **COURT:** 1907, Clerk of Court

MUSKOGEE

Box 1008, Muskogee, OK 7873, (918) 682-7781, **<www.rootsweb.ancestry.com/~okmuskog/index.html>**

- **INCORPORATED:** 1898
- **PARENT COUNTIES:** Creek Lands, Cherokee Nations
- **MARRIAGE RECORDS:** start in 1890, kept by Clerk of Court
- **DIVORCE:** 1907, Clerk of Court
- **LAND:** 1907, County Clerk
- **NOTES:** Clerk of Court has court and probate records 1890-1907.

N

- **INCORPORATED:** 1893
- **PARENT COUNTY:** Cherokee Outlet
- **NOTES:** See Woodward County. Name changed to Woodward Nov. 6, 1894.

NOBLE

300 Courthouse Dr. #14, Perry, OK 73077, (580) 336-5187, **<www.rootsweb.ancestry.com/~oknoble>**

- **INCORPORATED:** 1893
- **PARENT COUNTY:** Cherokee Outlet
- **MARRIAGE RECORDS:** start in 1893, kept by Clerk of Court
- **DIVORCE:** 1893, Clerk of Court
- **LAND:** 1893, County Clerk
- **PROBATE:** 1893, Clerk of Court
- **COURT:** 1893, Clerk of Court
- **NOTES:** Formerly P County. Name changed to Noble Nov. 6, 1893.

NOWATA

229 N. Maple St., Nowata, OK 74048, (918) 273-0127, **<www.rootsweb.ancestry.com/~oknowata>**

- **INCORPORATED:** July 16, 1907
- **PARENT COUNTY:** Cherokee Lands
- **MARRIAGE RECORDS:** start in 1907, kept by Clerk of District Court
- **DIVORCE:** 1907, Clerk of District Court
- **LAND:** 1911, County Clerk
- **PROBATE:** 1907, Clerk of District Court
- **COURT:** 1907, Clerk of District Court

O

- **INCORPORATED:** 1893
- **PARENT COUNTY:** Cherokee Outlet
- **NOTES:** See Garfield County. Name changed to Garfield Nov. 6, 1894.

OKFUSKEE

Third & Atlanta, Box 30, Okemah, OK 74859, (918) 623-0525, **<www.rootsweb.ancestry.com/~okokfusk>**

- **INCORPORATED:** July 16, 1907
- **PARENT COUNTY:** Creek Lands
- **MARRIAGE RECORDS:** start in 1907, kept by Clerk of Court
- **DIVORCE:** 1907, Clerk of Court
- **LAND:** 1907, County Clerk
- **PROBATE:** 1907, Clerk of Court
- **COURT:** 1907, Clerk of Court
- **NOTES:** County Historical Society has incomplete birth records 1909-1923 and incomplete death records 1911-1923.

OKLAHOMA

320 Robert S. Kerr Ave. Office 409, Oklahoma City, OK 73102, (405) 713-1708, **<www.oklahomacounty.org>**

- **INCORPORATED:** May 1890
- **PARENT COUNTY:** Original county
- **MARRIAGE RECORDS:** start in 1890, kept by Clerk of Court
- **DIVORCE:** 1907, Clerk of Court
- **PROBATE:** 1920, Clerk of Court
- **COURT:** 1890, Clerk of Court

OKMULGEE

314 W. Seventh St., Okmulgee, OK 74447, (918) 756-3042, **<www.rootsweb.ancestry.com/~okokmulg>**

- **INCORPORATED:** July 16, 1907
- **PARENT COUNTY:** Creek Lands
- **MARRIAGE RECORDS:** start in 1907, kept by Clerk of Court
- **DIVORCE:** 1907, Clerk of Court
- **LAND:** 1900, County Clerk
- **PROBATE:** 1907, Clerk of Court
- **COURT:** 1907, Clerk of Court

OSAGE

600 Grandview Ave., Pawhuska, OK 74056, (918) 287-4104, **<www.rootsweb.ancestry.com/~okosage2>**

- **INCORPORATED:** July 16, 1907
- **PARENT COUNTY:** Osage Indian Lands
- **MARRIAGE RECORDS:** start in 1907, kept by Clerk of Court
- **DIVORCE:** 1907, Clerk of Court
- **LAND:** 1907, County Clerk
- **PROBATE:** 1907, Clerk of Court
- **COURT:** 1907, Clerk of Court

OTTAWA

102 E. Central, Miami, OK 74354, (918) 542-2801, **<www.rootsweb.ancestry.com/~okottawa>**

- **INCORPORATED:** July 16, 1907
- **PARENT COUNTY:** Cherokee Lands
- **MARRIAGE RECORDS:** start in 1907, kept by Clerk of Court
- **DIVORCE:** 1907, Clerk of Court
- **LAND:** 1890, County Clerk
- **PROBATE:** 1907, Clerk of Court
- **COURT:** 1907, Clerk of Court

P

- **INCORPORATED:** 1893
- **PARENT COUNTY:** Cherokee Outlet
- **NOTES:** See Noble County. Name changed to Noble Nov. 6, 1894.

PAWNEE

500 Harrison St. Room 300, Pawnee, OK 74058, (918) 762-2547, **<www.rootsweb.ancestry.com/~okpawnee/pawnee.htm>**

- **INCORPORATED:** 1893
- **PARENT COUNTIES:** Pawnee Lands, Cherokee Outlet
- **MARRIAGE RECORDS:** start in 1893, kept by Clerk of Court
- **DIVORCE:** 1893, Clerk of Court
- **LAND:** 1893, County Clerk
- **PROBATE:** 1893, Clerk of Court

- **COURT:** 1893, Clerk of Court
- **NOTES:** Formerly Q County. Name changed to Pawnee.

PAYNE
308 Payne County Courthouse, Stillwater, OK 74074, (405) 372-4744, **<www.paynecounty.org>**
- **INCORPORATED:** May 1890
- **PARENT COUNTIES:** Unassigned lands, Oklahoma
- **MARRIAGE RECORDS:** start in 1894, kept by Clerk of Court
- **DIVORCE:** 1894, Clerk of Court
- **LAND:** 1894, County Clerk
- **PROBATE:** 1894, Clerk of Court
- **COURT:** 1894, Clerk of Court

PITTSBURG
Box 460, McAlester, OK 74502, (918) 423-4859, **<www.rootsweb.ancestry.com/~okpitts2>**
- **INCORPORATED:** July 16, 1907
- **PARENT COUNTY:** Choctaw Lands
- **BIRTH RECORDS:** start in 1908, kept by State Health Department
- **MARRIAGE:** 1907, Clerk of Court
- **DIVORCE:** 1907, Clerk of Court
- **DEATH:** 1908, State Health Department
- **LAND:** 1907, County Clerk
- **PROBATE:** 1907, Clerk of Court
- **COURT:** 1907, Clerk of Court
- **NOTES:** Clerk of Court has naturalization records 1890-1908.

PONTOTOC
Box 427, Ada, OK 74820, (580) 332-5763, **<www.rootsweb.ancestry.com/~okpontotoc.htm>**
- **INCORPORATED:** July 16, 1907
- **PARENT COUNTY:** Chickasaw Lands
- **MARRIAGE RECORDS:** start in 1907, kept by Clerk of Court
- **DIVORCE:** 1907, Clerk of Court
- **LAND:** 1907, Clerk of Court
- **PROBATE:** 1907, Clerk of Court
- **COURT:** 1907, Clerk of Court

POTTAWATOMIE
325 N. Broadway St., Shawnee, OK 74801, (405) 273-3624, **<www.usgennet.org/usa/ok/county/pottawatomie>**
- **INCORPORATED:** 1891
- **PARENT COUNTY:** Original county from Pottawatomie-Shawnee lands
- **BIRTH RECORDS:** start in 1908, kept by Clerk of Court
- **MARRIAGE:** 1892, Clerk of Court
- **DIVORCE:** 1892, Clerk of Court
- **DEATH:** 1908, Clerk of Court
- **LAND:** 1895, County Clerk
- **PROBATE:** 1892, Clerk of Court
- **COURT:** 1892, Clerk of Court
- **NOTES:** Formerly B County. Name changed to Pottawatomie.

PUSHMATAHA
302 SW "B", Antlers, OK 74523, (580) 298-2274, **<www.rootsweb.ancestry.com/~okpushma>**
- **INCORPORATED:** July 16, 1907
- **PARENT COUNTY:** Choctaw Lands
- **MARRIAGE RECORDS:** start in 1907, kept by Clerk of Court
- **LAND:** 1907, County Clerk
- **PROBATE:** 1907, Clerk of Court
- **COURT:** 1907, Clerk of Court

Q
- **INCORPORATED:** 1893
- **PARENT COUNTIES:** Pawnee Lands, Cherokee Outlet
- **NOTES:** See Pawnee County. Name changed to Pawnee in 1893.

ROGER MILLS
Box 409, Cheyenne, OK 73628, (580) 497-3361, **<www.rogermills.org>**
- **INCORPORATED:** 1892
- **PARENT COUNTY:** Cheyenne-Arapaho Lands
- **MARRIAGE RECORDS:** start in 1897, kept by Clerk of Court
- **DIVORCE:** 1892, Clerk of Court
- **LAND:** 1892, County Clerk
- **PROBATE:** 1892, Clerk of Court
- **COURT:** 1892, Clerk of Court
- **NOTES:** Formerly F County. Name changed to Roger Mills Nov. 8, 1892.

ROGERS
Box 839, 219 S. Missouri Ave., Claremore, OK 74018, (918) 341-5711, **<www.rogerscounty.org>**
- **INCORPORATED:** Jan. 26, 1907
- **PARENT COUNTY:** Cherokee Nation
- **MARRIAGE RECORDS:** start in 1907, kept by Clerk of Court
- **DIVORCE:** 1907, Clerk of Court
- **PROBATE:** 1907, Clerk of Court
- **COURT:** 1907, Clerk of Court

SEMINOLE
120 S. Wewoka Ave., Box 130, Wewoka, OK 74884, (405) 257-6236, **<www.usgennet.org/usa/ok/county/seminole>**
- **INCORPORATED:** July 16, 1907
- **PARENT COUNTY:** Seminole Indian Lands
- **MARRIAGE RECORDS:** start in 1907, kept by Clerk of Court
- **DIVORCE:** 1907, Clerk of Court
- **LAND:** 1907, County Recorder
- **PROBATE:** 1907, Clerk of Court
- **COURT:** 1907, Clerk of Court

SEQUOYAH
120 E. Chickasaw Ave., Sallisaw, OK 74955, (918) 775-4411, **<www.rootsweb.ancestry.com/~oksequo2>**
- **INCORPORATED:** July 16, 1907
- **PARENT COUNTY:** Cherokee Indian Lands
- **MARRIAGE RECORDS:** start in 1907, kept by Clerk of Court
- **DIVORCE:** 1907, Clerk of Court
- **LAND:** 1907, County Clerk
- **PROBATE:** 1907, Clerk of Court
- **COURT:** 1907, Clerk of Court

STEPHENS

101 S. 11th St. #203, Duncan, OK 73533, (580) 470-2000, **<www.rootsweb.ancestry.com/~okstephe/stephens.htm>**

- **INCORPORATED:** July 16, 1907
- **PARENT COUNTIES:** Comanche, Chickasaw Lands, Oklahoma Territory
- **MARRIAGE RECORDS:** start in 1907, kept by Clerk of Court
- **LAND:** 1907, County Clerk
- **PROBATE:** 1907, Clerk of Court
- **COURT:** 1907, Clerk of Court

TEXAS

Box 1081, Guymon, OK 73942, (580) 338-3003, **<www.txcountyok.com>**

- **INCORPORATED:** July 1907
- **PARENT COUNTIES:** Beaver, Oklahoma Territory
- **MARRIAGE RECORDS:** start in 1907, kept by Clerk of Court
- **DIVORCE:** 1907, Clerk of Court
- **LAND:** 1889, County Clerk
- **PROBATE:** 1907, Clerk of Court
- **COURT:** 1907, Clerk of Court
- **NOTES:** Part of the panhandle area known as No Man's Land 1850-1890.

TILLMAN

Box 116, Frederick, OK 73542, (580) 335-3023, **<www.tillmancounty.org>**

- **INCORPORATED:** July 16, 1907
- **PARENT COUNTIES:** Comanche, Kiowa
- **MARRIAGE RECORDS:** start in 1907, kept by Clerk of Court
- **DIVORCE:** 1907, Clerk of Court
- **LAND:** 1907, County Clerk
- **PROBATE:** 1907, Clerk of Court
- **COURT:** 1907, Clerk of Court

TOBUCKSY

- **INCORPORATED:** 1876
- **PARENT COUNTY:** Choctaw Lands, part of the Moshulatubee District
- **NOTES:** See Pittsburgh and Atoka counties. Became extinct after Oklahoma statehood in 1907. For more information on Choctaw lands, visit **<www.rootsweb.ancestry.com/~itchocta>**.

TULSA

500 S. Denver Ave. Room 200, Tulsa, OK 74103, (918) 596-5000, **<www.tulsacounty.org>**

- **INCORPORATED:** 1905
- **PARENT COUNTIES:** Creek Lands, Cherokee Lands
- **MARRIAGE RECORDS:** start in 1907, kept by Clerk of Court
- **DIVORCE:** 1907, Clerk of Court
- **PROBATE:** 1907, Clerk of Court
- **COURT:** 1907, Clerk of Court

WAGONER

Box 249, Wagoner, OK 74477, (918) 485-4508, **<www.wagonercountyclerk.com>**

- **INCORPORATED:** July 1908
- **PARENT COUNTY:** Creek Nation Lands
- **BIRTH RECORDS:** start in 1908, kept by Clerk of Court
- **MARRIAGE:** 1908, Clerk of Court
- **DIVORCE:** 1907, Clerk of Court
- **DEATH:** 1908, Clerk of Court
- **LAND:** 1906, County Clerk
- **PROBATE:** 1907, Clerk of Court
- **COURT:** 1907, Clerk of Court

WASHINGTON

420 S. Johnstone Ave., Bartlesville, OK 74003, (918) 337-2870, **<www.co.washington.ok.us>**

- **INCORPORATED:** 1907
- **PARENT COUNTY:** Cherokee Lands
- **MARRIAGE RECORDS:** start in 1907, kept by Clerk of Court
- **DIVORCE:** 1907, Clerk of Court
- **LAND:** 1907, County Clerk
- **PROBATE:** 1907, Clerk of Court
- **COURT:** 1907, Clerk of Court

WASHITA

Box 397, Cordell, OK 73632, (580) 832-3836, **<www.rootsweb.ancestry.com/~okwashit>**

- **INCORPORATED:** 1900
- **PARENT COUNTY:** Cheyenne-Arapaho Lands
- **MARRIAGE RECORDS:** start in 1900, kept by Clerk of Court
- **DIVORCE:** 1900, Clerk of Court
- **PROBATE:** 1900, Clerk of Court
- **COURT:** 1900, Clerk of Court
- **NOTES:** Formerly H County. Name changed to Washita after statehood.

WOODS

Box 924, Alva, OK 73717, (580) 327-3119, **<www.rootsweb.ancestry.com/~okwoods/main-woods.html>**

- **INCORPORATED:** 1893
- **PARENT COUNTY:** Cherokee Outlet
- **MARRIAGE RECORDS:** start in 1894, kept by Clerk of Court
- **DIVORCE:** 1893, Clerk of Court
- **LAND:** 1893, County Clerk
- **PROBATE:** 1901, Clerk of Court
- **COURT:** 1893, Clerk of Court
- **NOTES:** Formerly M County. Name changed to Woods Nov. 6, 1894.

WOODWARD

1600 Main St., Woodward, OK 73801, (580) 256-3413, **<www.woodwardcounty.org>**

- **INCORPORATED:** 1893
- **PARENT COUNTY:** Cherokee Outlet
- **MARRIAGE RECORDS:** start in 1897, kept by Clerk of Court
- **LAND:** 1894, County Clerk
- **PROBATE:** 1900, Clerk of Court
- **COURT:** 1894, Clerk of Court
- **NOTES:** Formerly N County. Name changed to Woodward Nov. 6, 1894.

OREGON

» BY DAVID A. FRYXELL

HISTORICAL OVERVIEW

Spanish mariners, Sir Francis Drake, and, two centuries later, Captain James Cook and Russian fur traders all had eyes for Oregon in its earliest history. The arrival of the first American, Robert Gray, in 1792 set off a 54-year tussle with the British over Oregon. Lewis and Clark came in 1805, soon followed by agents of John Jacob Astor's fur company, who in 1811 founded Astoria, the first permanent American settlement on the Pacific Coast. Dr. John McLoughlin of the Hudson's Bay Company established Willamette Falls, later renamed Oregon City, in 1829. The same year, missionaries began to encourage farmers from the Mississippi, Missouri and Ohio River valleys to move to Oregon. That trickle became a flood with the wagon trains of the Oregon Trail starting in 1842: 53,000 newcomers arrived between 1840 and 1860.

The boundary disputes with the British were finally settled in 1846. Oregon Territory was established in 1848, partly in response to the massacre of settlers by Indians. The territory originally included everything west of the Rockies and north of the 42nd parallel, but a separate Washington Territory was carved out in 1853. Oregon became a state in 1859.

Gold strikes, railroads, farming and ranching, and then logging drove subsequent waves of settlement. Chinese came to work the mines and the railroads. In the 1870s, Scandinavians began to arrive, with many Finns settling in Astoria. Swiss immigrants to Tillamook began the state's cheese industry. Basques settled in southeast Oregon in the late 1800s and early 1900s.

By 1880, Indian uprisings had been quelled and the state's tribes—including the Chinookan, Shahaptian, Athapascan, Molala, Klamath, Umpqua, Kalapooian, Salishan, Kusan, Yakonan, Modoc and Northern Paiutes—were exiled to reservations in Oregon, Washington, and as far away as Oklahoma. If you have Native American roots in Oregon, seek records of Indian agencies and the Chemawa Indian School.

RECORD HIGHLIGHTS

Oregon's boom years were tracked by a succession of territorial censuses beginning in 1842 and repeated almost annually until statehood; the Family History Library (FHL) has indexes to the surviving schedules. These and subsequent state censuses in 1865, 1875 and 1885, typically name only heads of households. State censuses in 1895 and 1905 list all family members. The first federal census to include Oregon Territory was in 1850; it was enumerated as a state beginning in 1860.

research tips

- Many Oregon records can only be found at the county level, so it's crucial to pinpoint where your ancestors lived in order to find the documents you need.
- Search the Oregon Death Index, part of subscription site Ancestry.com, and the Oregon State Archives' Historical Records Index **<arcweb.s os.state.or.us/banners/genealogy.htm>**.
- The Oregon State Archives in Salem is the best research repository in the state, but you'll also want to search the Genealogical Forum of Oregon collection.

CENSUS RECORDS

- Federal census: 1850, 1860, 1870, 1880, 1900, 1910, 1920, 1930
- Federal mortality schedules: 1850, 1860, 1870, 1880
- Special census of Civil War Union Veterans and Widows: 1890
- State/territorial census: 1842-1846 (a few counties), 1849 (males over age 21), 1850- 1859 (various counties), 1865 (Benton, Columbia, Marion, Umatilla counties), 1870 and 1875 (Umatilla county), 1885 (Linn and Umatilla counties), 1895 (Linn, Morrow, Multnomah, Marion counties), 1905 (Baker, Lane, Linn, Marion counties)

Oregon didn't begin statewide birth and death registration until 1903, marriages in 1906 and divorces in 1925. Many of these records, along with earlier local vital records, are at the state archives. The online Oregon Historical Records Index **<arcweb.sos.state.or.us/banners/genealogy.htm>** totals more than half a million entries, including Portland births (1881–1902) and deaths (1881–1917). The archives also has some early probate records, though these largely remain at county courthouses.

Land records can also provide clues to ancestors who joined the rush to Oregon. Territorial land records have been indexed and are kept in the state archives. Look for Donation Land Claims, which document those who arrived by 1855 and contain records rich in details about the settler family. Federal land records are available on microfilm from the FHL; post-1908 records are in the Bureau of Land Management's database at **<www.glorecords.blm.gov>**.

Don't forget that Oregon had joined the Union by the time of the Civil War, so its military records go back to that conflict. The FHL has microfilms of service and burial records of Oregon soldiers in the Civil War.

The biggest challenge for Oregon researchers, according to Connie Lenzen, a member of the Genealogical Forum of Oregon, is that many of the records you'll seek are still in courthouses, archives and libraries. Generally, she warns, they are not published or online. But the Oregon Death Index, included in the Ancestry.com subscription service, and the aforementioned Oregon State Archives' Historical Records Index, can help you get started long-distance.

Because so many Oregon records are located at the county level, Lenzensays it's crucial to first locate your ancestors in censuses so you know where they lived. Records in county courthouses may be difficult to access from a distance, she adds: "Most offices are short-staffed. The day-to-day business of running a county government takes precedence over answering queries by mail."

Ferne Kellow, president of the Oregon Genealogical Society, adds that many records may not be filed where you might expect. For example, Kellow found the pioneer cemetery records for a Josephine County-owned cemetery in the county's Parks and Recreation Department. The Oregon Historical County Records Guide **<arcweb.sos.state.or.us/county/cphome.html>** can help you figure out what's where.

The number-one research repository, according to Lenzen, is the Oregon State Archives in Salem. You may not even have to leave home to tap the archives' holdings: The FHL has microfilmed many records at the Oregon State Archives and other state repositories **<www.familysearch.org>**.

For published resources, she adds, the holdings of the Genealogical Forum of Oregon (GFO) are among the best in the state. The GFO will look up materials in its library for a nominal fee. See the research policy at **<www.gfo.org/respol.htm>**. The largest collection of Oregon historical materials belongs to the Oregon Historical Society Library in Portland, which holds books, photographs, maps and original documents. You can search its catalog of book and serial holdings online at **<librarycatalog.ohs.org/eosweb/opac>**.

For more advice on getting started with Oregon research, consult Lenzen's online guide Oregon Records for Genealogists **<www.lenzenresearch.com/oregonguide.html>**. This will give you details on the type of records you can expect to find and information about where they are located.

ARCHIVES, LIBRARIES, AND SOCIETIES

Alsi Historical and Genealogical Society
c/o Waldport Heritage Museum, 320 NE Grant St., Box 822, Waldport, OR 97394, (541) 563-7092

American Baptist Historical Society
3001 Mercer University Dr., Atlanta, GA 30341, (678) 547-6680, **<www.abhsarchives.org>**

American Historical Society of Germans From Russia, Oregon Chapter
<www.ahsgroregon.com>

Archdiocese of Portland in Oregon
2838 E. Burnside St., Portland, OR 97214, (503) 234-5334, **<www.archdpdx.org>**

Astoria Public Library
450 Tenth St., Astoria, OR 97103, **<www.astorialibrary.org>**

Baker County Genealogical Group
c/o Baker County Public Library, 2400 Resort St., Baker City, OR 97814

Bend Genealogical Society
Box 8254, Bend, OR 97708, (541) 317-9553, **<www.rootsweb.ancestry.com/~ordeschu/bend-gs>**

Benton County Genealogical Society
Box 1646, Philomath, OR 97370, (541) 752-6425, **<www.rootsweb.ancestry.com/~orbentgs>**

Blue Mountain Genealogical Society
Box 1801, Pendleton, OR 97801, **<www.rootsweb.ancestry.com/~orbmgs>**

Bureau of Land Management, Oregon State Office
333 SW First Ave., Box 2965, Portland, OR 97208, (503) 808-6001, **<www.blm.gov/or>**

Center for Health Statistics, Oregon
Box 14050, Portland, OR 97293, (971) 673-1190, **<www.oregon.gov/DHS/ph/chs>**

Clackamas County Family History Society
211 Tumwater Dr., Box 995, Oregon City, OR 97045, (503) 655-5574, **<www.rootsweb.ancestry.com/~genepool/ccfhs.htm>**

Clatsop County Genealogical Society
Box 1299, Astoria, OR 97103, **<www.pacifier.com/~karenl>**

Clatsop County Historical Society
Box 88, Astoria, OR 97103, (503) 325-2203, **<www.cumtux.org>**

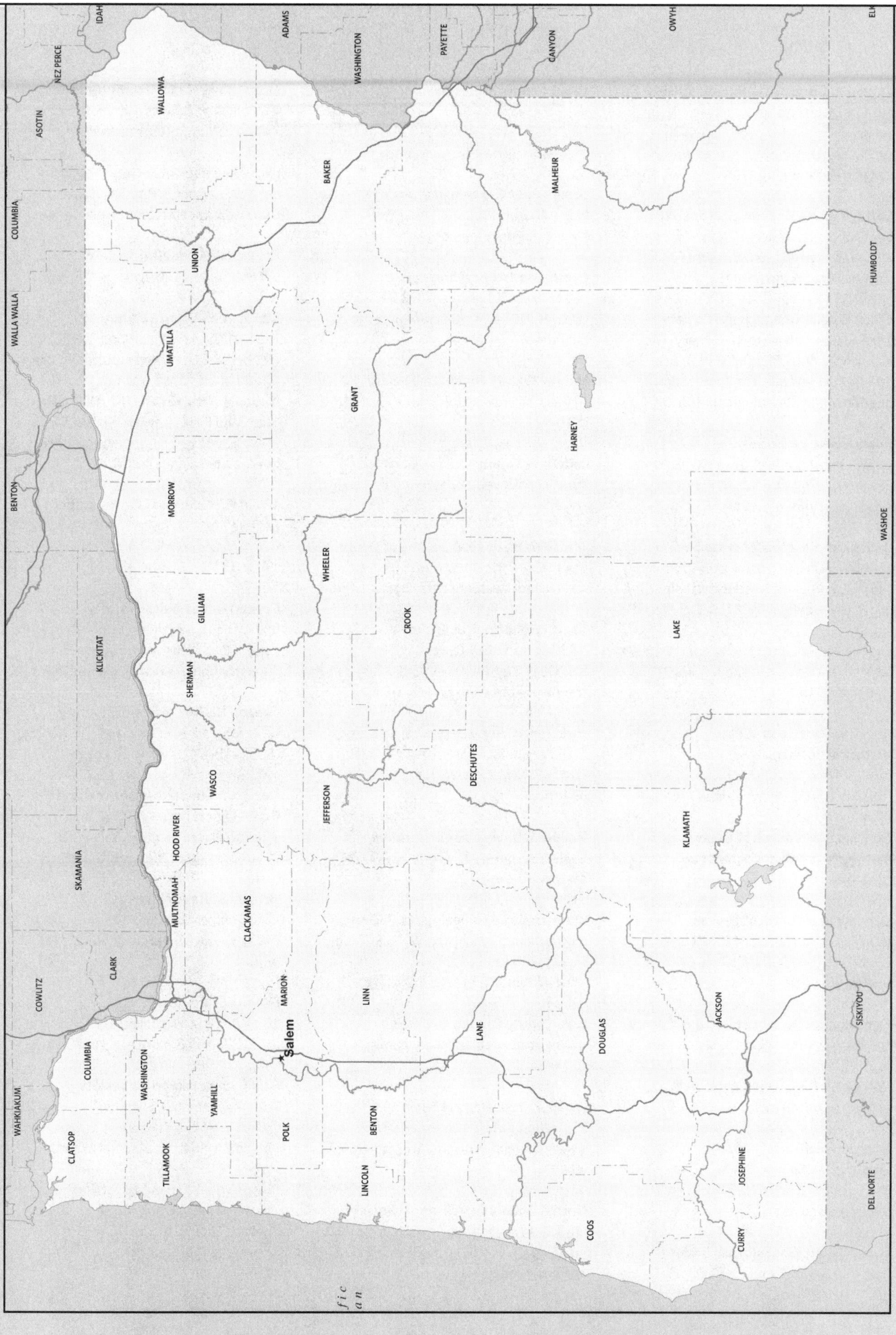
ADAMS
WASHINGTON
PAYETTE
CANYON
NEZ PERCE
ASOTIN
WALLOWA
COLUMBIA
BAKER
MALHEUR
WALLA WALLA
UNION
UMATILLA
HUMBOLDT
GRANT
HARNEY
BENTON
MORROW
WHEELER
WASHOE
GILLIAM
CROOK
LAKE
KLICKITAT
SHERMAN
WASCO
DESCHUTES
JEFFERSON
HOOD RIVER
SKAMANIA
KLAMATH
MULTNOMAH
CLACKAMAS
CLARK
COWLITZ
MARION
LINN
JACKSON
LANE
Salem
SISKIYOU
COLUMBIA
DOUGLAS
WASHINGTON
WAHKIAKUM
YAMHILL
CLATSOP
POLK
BENTON
TILLAMOOK
JOSEPHINE
LINCOLN
DEL NORTE
COOS
CURRY

Columbia Gorge Genealogical Society
c/o The Dalles-Wasco County Public Library, 722 Court St., The Dalles, OR 97058, (541) 296-2815, **<community.gorge.net/genealogy>**

Cottage Grove Genealogical Society
Box 388, Cottage Grove, OR 97424, **<www.rootsweb.ancestry.com/~orlane/links/cggs.htm>**

Crook County Genealogical Society
c/o A.R. Bowman Memorial Library, 246 N. Main St., Prineville, OR 97754, (541) 447-5449, **<www.bowmanmuseum.org/BowmanGenealogical.html>**

Curry Historical Society
29410 Ellensburg Ave., Box 1598, Gold Beach, OR 97444, (541) 247-9396, **<www.curryhistory.com>**

Deschutes County Historical Society
129 NW Idaho Ave., Bend, OR 97701, (541) 389-1813, **<www.deschuteshistory.org/the+society>**

Eugene Public Library
100 W. Tenth Ave., Eugene, OR 97401, (541) 682-5450

Fairview-Rockwood-Wilkes Historical Society
Box 946, Fairview, OR 97024, (503) 261-8078, **<www.frwhs.org>**

Genealogical Council of Oregon
<www.rootsweb.ancestry.com/~orgco2>

Genealogical Forum of Oregon
1505 SE Gideon St., Box 42567, Portland, OR 97242, (503) 963-1932, **<www.gfo.org>**

Genealogical Society of Douglas County
c/o Douglas County Courthouse, Room 111, 1036 SE Douglas Ave., Roseburg, OR 97470 (541) 440-6178, **<www.rootsweb.ancestry.com/~orgsdc>**

Genealogical Society of Washington County
Box 2123, Hillsboro, OR 97123, **<www.gswco.org>**

Grant County Genealogical Society
Box 418, Canyon City, OR 97820

Grant County Museum
101 S. Canyon City Blvd., Box 464, Canyon City, OR 97820, (541) 575-0362, **<www.ortelco.net/~museum>**

Grants Pass Genealogical Society
Box 214, Grants Pass, OR 97528, **<www.gpgenealogy.org>**

Gresham Historical Society
410 N. Main St., Gresham, OR 97030, (503) 661-0347, **<community.gorge.net/ghs>**

Harney County Historical Society
18 W. D. St., Box 388, Burns, OR 97720, (541) 573-5618

Jefferson County Oregon GenWeb
<www.rootsweb.ancestry.com/~orjeffer>

Jewish Genealogical Society of Oregon
Box 19736, Portland, OR 97280, **<www.rootsweb.ancestry.com/~orjgs>**

Jewish Genealogical Society of Willamette Valley Oregon
Box 71681, Eugene, OR 97401, **<www.nwfam.com/jgswvo.html>**

Josephine County Historical Society
512 SW Fifth St., Grants Pass, OR 97526 (541) 479-7827, **<www.josephinehistorical.org>**

Juniper Branch of Family Finders
21 SE D St., Box 652, Madras, OR 97741 **<www.jbff.org>**

Klamath Basin Genealogical Society
c/o Klamath County Library, 126 S. Third St., Klamath Falls, OR 97601, **<www.klamathlibrary.plinkit.org>**

Lake County Oregon GenWeb
<www.rootsweb.ancestry.com/~orlake>

Lebanon Genealogical Society
55 Academy St., Lebanon, OR 97355, **<www.usgennet.org/usa/or/town/lebanon>**

Lincoln County Genealogical Society
c/o Toledo Public Library, 173 NW Seventh St., Toledo, OR 97391, **<www.rootsweb.ancestry.com/~orygs>**

Linn County Historical Museum
101 Park Ave., Brownsville, OR 97327, **<www.co.linn.or.us/museum>**

Linn Genealogical Society
Box 1222, Albany, OR 97321, **<www.rootsweb.ancestry.com/~orlinngs>**

Madras Genealogical Society
671 SW Fairgrounds, Madras, OR 97741

Multnomah County Library
801 SW Tenth Ave., Portland, OR 97205, (503) 988-5123, **<www.multcolib.org>**

National Archives, Pacific Alaska Region
6125 Sand Point Way NE, Seattle, WA 98115, (206) 336-5115, **<www.archives.gov/pacific-alaska/seattle>**

Jereld R. Nicholson Library, Linfield College
900 S. Baker St., McMinnville, OR 97128 (503) 883-2261

Oregon Genealogical Society
955 Oak Alley, Eugene, OR 97401, (541) 345-0399, **<www.rootsweb.ancestry.com/~orlncogs/ogsinfo.htm>**

Oregon Historical Society Library
1200 SW Park Ave., Portland, OR 97205, (503) 222-1741, **<www.ohs.org>**

Oregon Mennonite Historical and Genealogical Society
9045 Wallace Road NW, Salem, OR 97304, **<mhgsor.mennonite.net>**

Oregon State Archives
800 Summer St. NE, Salem, OR 97310, (503) 373-0701, **<arcweb.sos.state.or.us>**

Oregon State Library
250 Winter St. NE, Salem, OR 97301, (503) 378-4243, **<oregon.gov/OSL>**

Polk County Historical Society
Box 67, Monmouth, OR 97361, (503) 623-6251, **<www.polkcountyhistoricalsociety.com>**

Rogue Valley Genealogical Society
95 Houston Road, Box 1468, Phoenix, OR 97535, (541) 512-2340, **<www.rvgslibrary.org>**

Sherman County Historical Society
200 Dewey St., Box 173, Moro, OR 97039, (541) 565-3232, **<www.shermanmuseum.org>**

Siuslaw Genealogical Society
Box 1540, Florence, OR 97439, **<www.rootsweb.ancestry.com/~orsgs>**

Southern Ohio Historical Society
Box 1570, Jacksonville, OR 97530, **<www.sohs.org>**

St. Paul Mission Historical Society
Box 158, St. Paul, OR 97137, **<www.rootsweb.ancestry.com/~orspmhs/stpaulindex.html>**

Sweet Home Genealogical Society
Box 279, Sweet Home, OR 97386, (541) 367-5034, **<shgenealogy.com>**

Tillamook County Historical Society
c/o Tillamook County Pioneer Museum, 2106 Second St., Tillamook, OR 97801, **<www.tcpm.org/tchs.htm>**

Troutdale Historical Society
104 SE Kibling, Troutdale, OR 97060, (503) 661-2164, **<www.troutdalehistory.org>**

Umatilla County Historical Society
c/o Heritage Station Museum, 108 SW Frazer St., Box 253, Pendleton, OR 97801, (541) 276-0012, **<www.heritagestationmuseum.org>**

Waldport Heritage Museum
320 NE Grant St., Box 822, Waldport, OR 97394, (541) 563-7092

Willamette Heritage Center
260 12th St. SW, Salem, OR 97301, (503) 364-2128, **<www.marionhistory.org>**

Willamette Valley Genealogical Society
Box 2083, Salem, OR 97308, **<www.osl.state.or.us/home/Gen/wvgs.html>**

Yamhill County Genealogical Society
Box 1713, McMinnville, OR 97128, **<yamhillcountygenealogicalsociety.org>**

Yamhill County Historical Society
605 Market St., Box 484, Lafayette, OR 97127, (503) 864-2308, **<yamhillcountyhistory.org>**

GENERAL RESOURCES

Apart and Together: Mennonites in Oregon and Neighboring States, 1876-1976 by Hope Kauffman Lind (Herald Press, 1990)

Baptist Annals of Oregon, 1844-1900, 2 vols., by Charles Hiram Mattoon (Telephone Register Publishing Co., 1913)

Capitol Names: Individuals Woven Into Oregon's History by Philip Cogswell (Oregon Historical Society, 1977)

Capitol's Who's Who For Oregon, 1936-1944, 2 vols., (Capitol Publishing Co., 1936-1942)

Catholic Church Records of the Pacific Northwest: Grand Ronde Register I (1860-1885), Grand Ronde Register II (1886-1898): St. Michael the Archangel Parish, Grand Ronde Indian Reservation, Grand Ronder, Oregon; St. Patrick's Parish, Muddy Valley, Oregon by Harriet Duncan Munnick (Binford & Mort, 1987)

Catholic Church Records of the Pacific Northwest: Missions of St. Ann and St. Rose of the Cayuse, 1847-1888; Walla Walla and Frenchtown, 1858-1872, Frenchtown, 1872-1888 by Harriet Duncan Munnick (Binford & Mort, 1989)

The Centennial History of Oregon, 1811-1912, 4 vols., by Joseph Gaston (S.J. Clarke Publishing Co., 1912)

Christians on the Oregon Trail: Churches of Christ and Christian Churches in Early Oregon, 1842-1882 by Jerry Rushford (College Press Publishing Co., 1997)

Covered Wagon Women: Diaries & Letters From the Western Trails, 1840-1890, 11 vols., by Kenneth L. Holmes (Arthur H. Clark Co., 1983-1991)

Directory of Churches and Religious Organizations, State of Oregon (Historical Records Survey, 1940)

Give All to Oregon: Missionary Pioneers of the Far West by Cecil Pearl Dryden (Hastings House, 1968)

Guide to Depositories of Manuscript Collections in the United States: Oregon-Washington (Oregon Historical Records Survey, 1940)

Guide to Genealogical Sources by Connie Miller Lenzen (Genealogical Forum of Oregon, 1994)

Guide to the Manuscript Collections of the Oregon Historical Society (Oregon Historical Records Survey, 1940)

A Guide to the State of Jefferson: A Union List of Historical Materials Relating to Northern California and Southern Oregon From the Southern Oregon Library Federation (filmed by the Oregon Historical Society, ca. 1970)

History of the Columbia River Valley From the Dalles to the Sea, 3 vols., by Fred Lockley (S.J. Clarke Publishing Co., 1928)

History of Oregon, 2 vols., by Hubert Howe Bancroft (The History Co., 1886-1888)

History of Oregon, 3 vols., by Charles Henry Carey (Pioneer History Publishing Co., 1922)

History of Oregon: The Growth of an American State by Horace Sumner Lyman (North Pacific Publishing Society, 1903)

A History of Oregon Methodism by Thomas D. Yarnes (Oregon Methodist Conference Historical Society, 1957)

A History of the Oregon Trail, Santa Fe Trail, and Other Trails by Jacob Ray Gregg (Binfords & Mort, ca. 1955)

History of the Pacific Northwest: Oregon and Washington, 2 vols., by Elwood Evans (North Pacific History Co., 1889)

An Illustrated History of Central Oregon: Embracing Wasco, Sherman, Gilliam, Wheeler, Crook, Lake, and Klamath Counties by F.A. Shaver, Arthur P. Rose, R.F. Steele, and A.E. Adams (Western Historical Publishing Co., 1905)

An Illustrated History of the State of Oregon by Harvey K. Hines (Lewis Publishing Co., 1893)

Index to Oregon Newspaper Clippings, 1895-1952 by Alice Stansfield Herzberg (Rogue Valley Genealogical Society, 1995)

Indians of Oregon Bibliography, 1966-1983 in Oregon State Library by Betty Book (Genealogical Council of Oregon, 1991)

The Mantle of Elias: The Story of Fathers Blanchet and Demers in Early Oregon by M. Leona Nichols (Binfords & Mort, 1941)

Oregon Biography Index edited by Patricia Brandt and Nancy Guilford (Oregon State University, 1976)

Oregon: Comprising a Brief History and Full Description of the Territories of Oregon and Washington: Together With Remarks Upon the Social Position, Productions, Resources and Prospects of the Country a Dissertation Upon the Climate, and a Full Description of the Indian Tribes of the Pacific Slope by A.N. Armstrong (Library of Congress, 1989)

Oregon History and Early Literature: A Pictorial Narrative of the Pacific Northwest by John B. Horner (J.K. Gill Co., 1931)

Oregon Pioneers by the Oregon Genealogical Society (Oregon Historical Society, ca. 1980)

Oregon Research Outline by the Church of Jesus Christ of Latter-day Saints (online at **<www.familysearch.org/eng/search/RG/guide/oregon.asp>**)

Oregon Trail: Last of the Pioneers by Rick Steber (Bonanza Publishing, 1993)

Paths to the Northwest: A Jesuit History of the Oregon Province by Wilfred P. Schoenberg (Loyola University Press, 1982)

Portrait and Biographical Record of the Willamette Valley, Oregon (Chapman Publishing Co., 1903)

Portrait and Biographical Record of Western Oregon: (Chapman Publishing Co., 1904)

Presbyterianism in Southern Oregon: A History of the Presbytery of Southwest Oregon and Its Forebears, 1851-1949 by Lawrence H. Mitchelmore (L.H. Mitchelmore, 1949)

Research in Oregon by Connie Miller Lenzen (National Genealogical Society, 1992)

Rolls of Certain Indian Tribes in Oregon and Washington by Charles E. McChesney (Ye Galleon Press, 1969)

Saints to the Columbia: A History of the Church of Jesus Christ of Latter-day Saints in Oregon and Southwestern Washington, 1850-1990 by Louis G. Gassawy Kullberg (L-K Publications, 1991)

The Story of Oregon: A History With Portraits and Biographies, 2 vols., by Julian Hawthorne (American Historical Publishing Co., 1892)

Terrible Trail: The Meek Cutoff, 1845 by Keith Clark (Caxton Printers, 1966)

These Valiant Women: History of the Sisters of St. Mary of Oregon, 1886-1986 by Wilfred P. Schoenberg (Sisters of St. Mary of Oregon, 1986)

Who's Who for Idaho, Combined With Who's Who for Oregon and Who's Who for the Western States (Capitol Publishing Co., 1970)

☞CENSUS RECORDS

Oregon Memorial of Citizens of the U.S. and Miscellaneous Information: Census Records for 1843. (filmed by the Genealogical Society of Utah, 1966)

☞IMMIGRATION RECORDS

How to Find Oregon Naturalization Records by Connie Lenzen (C. Lenzen, 1990)

Oregon Naturalization Records Index: Declaration of Intention, 2 vols., by W. David Samuelsen (Sampubco, 1995)

Overland Passages: A Guide to Overland Documents in the Oregon Historical Society by Kris White (Oregon Historical Society Press, 1993)

The Willamette Valley: Migration and Settlement on the Oregon Frontier by William Adrian Bowen (University of Washington Press, 1978)

☞LAND RECORDS

The Frontier: The Agricultural Opening of the Oregon Country, 1786-1846 by James R. Farming Gibson (University of British Columbia Press, 1985)

Genealogical Material in Oregon Donation Land Claims, 5 vols., (Genealogical Forum of Portland, 1957-1975)

Index of Oregon Donation Land Claims, 2nd edition, compiled by the Oregon State Archives (Genealogical Forum of Portland, 1987)

Preliminary Inventory of the Land-Entry Papers of the General Land Office compiled by Harry P. Yoshpe and Philip P. Brower (National Archives, 1949)

☞MAPS

Historical Maps of Oregon: Overland Stage Routes, Old Military Roads, Indian Battle Grounds, Old Forts, and Old Gold Mines by Ralph N. Preston (Western Guide Publishers, 1972)

Oregon Atlas and Gazetteer, 2nd edition (DeLorme Mapping Co., 1995)

Oregon County Boundary Change Maps, 1843-1916 by Erma Skyles Brown (End of Trail Researchers, 1970)

Oregon Geographic Names, 6th edition, by Lewis A. McArthur (Oregon Historical Society, 1992)

Oregon Post Offices, 1847-1982 by Richard W. Helbock (La Posta, ca. 1982)

Places Names of the Pacific Northwest Coast by Lynn Middleton (Superior Publishing Co, 1969)

A Preliminary Atlas of Oregon by William G. Loy (Geography Department, University of Oregon, 1972)

R.L. Polk & Co., Oregon and Washington Gazetteer and Business Directory, 1909-1910 (R.L. Polk, 1909)

☞MILITARY RECORDS

An Account of the Origin and Early Prosecution of the Indian War in Oregon by Charles S. Drew (Ye Galleon Press, 1972)

Honor Roll of Oregon Grand Army of the Republic, 1881-1935 by Jane Myers (Cottage Grove Genealogical Society, 1980)

The Official Records of the Oregon Volunteers in the Spanish War and Philippine Insurrection, 2nd edition, by C.U. Gantenbein (J.R. Whitney, 1903)

Oregon Combined Military Alphabetical Index, 1837-1933 (filmed by the Family History Library, 2000)

A Partial List of Military Casualties and MIA's From the State of Oregon During World War II by Spencer Leonard (Genealogical Forum of Oregon., 1993)

Soldiers Who Served in the Oregon Volunteers: Civil War Period, Infantry and Cavalry by M.A. Pekar (Genealogical Forum of Portland, 1961)

☞VITAL RECORDS

Cumulative Baptism Index to the Catholic Church Records of the Pacific Northwest by Sharon E. Osborn-Ryan (Oregon Heritage Press, 1999)

Cumulative Death Index to the Catholic Church Records of the Pacific Northwest by Sharon E. Osborn-Ryan (Oregon Territorial Press, 1998)

Cumulative Marriage Index to the Catholic Church Records of the Pacific Northwest by Sharon E. Osborn-Ryan (Oregon Heritage Press, 1998)

Episcopal Marriages of the Southern Oregon Coast, 1884-1940 by Barbara Brown Eakley (Bayview Publishers, 1997)

Guide to Public Vital Statistics Records in Oregon (Historical Records Survey, 1942)

Oregon Cemetery Directory (Oregon Heritage Council, 1976)

COUNTY DETAILS

BAKER

1995 Third St., Baker City, OR 97814, (541) 523-8200, **<www.bakercounty.org>**

- **INCORPORATED:** Sept. 22, 1862
- **PARENT COUNTY:** Wasco
- **MARRIAGE RECORDS:** start in 1862, kept by County Clerk
- **DIVORCE:** from 1862-1988
- **LAND:** 1865, County Clerk
- **MILITARY:** 1891, County Clerk
- **NOTES:** Oregon State Archives has birth records 1871-1929 and Death records 1905-1944. County Clerk has Circuit Court records 1862-1988, divorce records 1862-1988, Nauturalization records 1897-1928, and probate records 1863-1984. Since 1965, marriage records and military discharge records have been recorded in the Baker County Records. Since 1987, County Probate Court records have been filed in the Oregon Judicial Information Network.

BENTON

408 SW Monroe Ave., Suite 111, Corvallis, OR 97333, (541) 766-6800, **<www.co.benton.or.us>**

- **INCORPORATED:** Dec. 23, 1847
- **PARENT COUNTY:** Polk
- **PROBATE RECORDS:** start in 1880, kept at Benton County Courthouse
- **MILITARY:** 1920, County Clerk
- **NOTES:** County Clerk has birth records ca. 1868-ca. 1950, Benton County Historical Museum has birth records 1907-1916, and Oregon State Archives has birth records 1907-1929. County Clerk has Circuit Court records 1853-1984, death records 1907-1948, divorce records 1853-1984, land records ca. 1865-1971, marriage records 1852-1878, and naturalization records ca. 1864-ca. 1950.

CLACKAMAS

2051 Kaen Road, 2nd floor, Oregon City, Oregon 97045, (503) 655-8551, **<www.co.clackamas.or.us>**

- **INCORPORATED:** July 5, 1843
- **PARENT COUNTY:** original county
- **LAND RECORDS:** ca. 1851, Oregon State Archives; 1906-1972, County Clerk
- **PROBATE:** 1850, County Clerk
- **MILITARY:** start in 1920, County Clerk
- **NOTES:** County Clerk has birth and death records 1902-1920, land records 1906-1972, marriage records 1853-1966, and naturalization records 1890-1905. Oregon State Archives has birth and death records 1915-1945, Circuit Court records 1846-1986, divorce records 1850-1949, marriage records 1848-1948, and naturalization records 1887-1926. From 1967-1977 Military discharges were entered by the County Clerk in the Recording Instruments. Since 1977, the County Clerk has filed military discharges in the Recording Index.

CLARK

- **INCORPORATED:** June 27, 1844
- **PARENT COUNTY:** original county
- **NOTES:** Now part of the state of Washington.

CLATSOP

820 Exchange St., Suite 220, Box 178, Astoria, OR 97103, (503) 325-8511, **<www.co.clatsop.or.us>**

- **INCORPORATED:** June 22, 1844
- **PARENT COUNTY:** Twality
- **LAND RECORDS:** start in 1860, County Clerk
- **PROBATE:** ca. 1850, County Clerk

- **NOTES:** Comments/research tips: County Clerk has birth records 1894-1937, Circuit Court and divorce records 1855-1987, death records 1903-1937, marriage records 1851-1985, military records 1892-1900 and from 1919, and naturalization records 1907-1924, Clatsop County Historical Society has birth records 1915-1949 and Death records 1915-1949. Oregon State Archives has Circuit Court and divorce records 1849-1858 and 1860-1935, Naturalization records 1907-1970, and probate records 1848-1930.

COLUMBIA

230 Strand St., St. Helens, OR 97051, (503) 397-3796, **<www.co.columbia.or.us>**

- **INCORPORATED:** Jan. 16, 1854
- **PARENT COUNTY:** Washington
- **PROBATE RECORDS:** start in 1874, County Clerk
- **NOTES:** County Clerk has birth records 1907-1929, Circuit Court and divorce records 1854-1987, death records 1907-1929, land records 1854-1860 and 1872-1991, marriage records 1854-1961, military records 1887-1900 and 1919-1958, and naturalization records 1891-1926. Oregon State Archives has probate records 1850-1930. In 1987, Columbia County started filing county probate cases with the Oregon Judicial Information Network.

COOS

250 N. Baxter St., Coquille, OR 97423, (541) 396-3121, **<www.co.coos.or.us>**

- **INCORPORATED:** Dec. 22, 1853
- **PARENT COUNTIES:** Umpqua, Jackson
- **LAND RECORDS:** start in 1854, County Clerk
- **NOTES:** County Clerk has birth and death records 1906-1929, Circuit Court records 1854-1983, divorce records 1854-1983, marriage records 1853-1968, military records 1875-1906 and from 1946, Naturalization records 1907-1929, and probate records 1852-1989 and from 1990. Prior to 1946 Military Discharges were filed by the County Clerk in the Miscellaneous Record. Since 1965, the County Clerk has filed Military Discharges in the Clerk's Book of Records. After 1987, all Coos County Probate Court cases have been filed in Oregon Judicial Information Network.

CROOK

300 NE Third St., Prineville, OR 97754, (541) 447-6553, **<www.co.crook.or.us>**

- **INCORPORATED:** Oct. 24, 1882
- **PARENT COUNTY:** Wasco
- **LAND RECORDS:** 1883, County Clerk
- **PROBATE:** start in 1883, Trial Court Administrator
- **MILITARY:** start in 1883, County Clerk
- **NOTES:** Comments/research tips: County Clerk has birth and death records 1907-1939, Circuit Court records 1882-1919, and divorce records 1882-1919, marriage records 1882-1975, Naturalization records 1903-1925, and probate records 1882-1943 and 1971-1982. Trial Court Administrator has Circuit Court and divorce records 1883-1985. A.R. Bowman Museum has Land records 1869-1997. The County Clerk has recorded military discharges in the clerk's Microfiche Records since 1982. After 1986, all Crook County probate court cases have been filed in Oregon Judicial Information Network.

CURRY

29821 Ellensburg Ave., Box 746, Gold Beach, OR 97444, (541) 247-7011, **<www.co.curry.or.us>**

- **INCORPORATED:** Dec. 18, 1855
- **PARENT COUNTY:** Coos
- **LAND RECORDS:** 1865, County Clerk
- **PROBATE:** 1888, Curry County Courthouse
- **NOTES:** Comments/research tips: Oregon State Archives has Circuit Court records 1872-1939 and naturalization records from 1904, 1909-1913, and 1916-1928. Oregon Historical Records Index has Divorce records 1866-1929. State Courts Civil-Domestic-Probate Office has Divorce records 1903-1987. County Clerk has Marriage records 1856-1964 and military records 1887-1902 and from 1920. The County Clerk has recorded military discharges in the clerk's Book of Records since 1966. After 1987, all Curry County probate court cases have been filed in Oregon Judicial Information Network.

DESCHUTES

1300 NW Wall St., Bend, OR 97701, (541) 388-6549, **<www.deschutes.org>**

- **INCORPORATED:** Dec. 13, 1916
- **PARENT COUNTY:** Crook
- **LAND RECORDS:** 1900, County Clerk
- **PROBATE:** 1916, Circuit Court Clerk; 1986, Oregon Judicial Information Network
- **MILITARY:** start in 1916, County Clerk
- **NOTES:** Circuit Court Clerk has Circuit Court records 1917-1985 and divorce records 1917-1986. County Clerk has Marriage records 1916-1975. Oregon State Archives has naturalization records 1917-1969. The Crook County surveyor's office has provided a computer database of subdivision plats dating from 1904 to the present, and partition plats dating from 1977 to the present. The clerk's Miscellaneous Record contains Military Discharge records before 1945. After 1983 the County Clerk has military discharge records. After 1986, all Deschutes County Probate Court cases have been filed in Oregon Judicial Information Network.

DOUGLAS

1036 SE Douglas Ave., Room 221, Roseburg, OR 97470, (541) 440-4324, **<www.co.douglas.or.us>**

- **INCORPORATED:** Jan. 7, 1852
- **PARENT COUNTY:** Umpqua
- **LAND RECORDS:** 1851, County Clerk
- **MILITARY:** start in 1887, County Clerk
- **NOTES:** County Clerk has birth records 1903-1933, Circuit Court records 1852-1978, death records 1903-1933, divorce records 1852-1978, marriage records 1852-1969, and naturalization records 1907-1927. Trial Court Administrator has Circuit Court records 1852-1983, divorce records 1852-1983, and probate records 1852-1989. Oregon State Archives has Marriage records 1852-1983. Absorbed by Umpqua County 1862.

GILLIAM

221 S. Oregon St., Box 427, Condon, OR 97823, (541) 384-2311, **<www.co.gilliam.or.us>**

- **INCORPORATED:** Oct. 14, 1864
- **PARENT COUNTY:** Wasco

- **LAND RECORDS:** 1882, County Clerk
- **PROBATE:** 1885, County Clerk
- **MILITARY:** start in 1871, County Clerk
- **NOTES:** County Clerk has birth records 1903-1920, Circuit Court and divorce records 1885-1985, death records for 1914 only, marriage records 1885-1984, and naturalization records 1885-1928. Oregon State Archives has birth records 1913-1933 and Death records 1912-1933. Miscellaneous Record has military records before 1945.

GRANT

201 S. Humboldt St., Canyon City, OR 97820, (541) 575-1675, **<www.gcoregonlive2.com>**

- **INCORPORATED:** Oct. 14, 1864
- **PARENT COUNTIES:** Wasco, Umatilla
- **LAND RECORDS:** start in ca. 1877, County Clerk
- **PROBATE:** 1864, County Clerk
- **MILITARY:** 1920, County Clerk
- **NOTES:** County Clerk has birth records 1894-1929, 1940-1941, death records 1915-1929, marriage records 1864-1970, military records 1887-1901, and naturalization records 1862-1948. Circuit Court Clerk has Circuit Court records 1887-1888 and 1893-1986. Oregon State Archives has Circuit Court records 1864-1923 and military records 1872-1898. Oregon Historical Records Index has Divorce records 1872-1922.

HARNEY

450 N. Buena Vista Ave. #14, Burns, OR 97720, (541) 573-6641, **<www.co.harney.or.us>**

- **INCORPORATED:** Feb. 25, 1889
- **PARENT COUNTY:** Grant
- **LAND RECORDS:** 1885, 1902, start in 1911, County Clerk
- **PROBATE:** start in 1898, County Clerk
- **MILITARY:** 1942, County Clerk
- **NOTES:** County Clerk has Circuit Court and divorce records 1886-1976, land records for 1885 and 1902, marriage records 1889-1966, military records 1889-1900, and naturalization records 1889-1929. Circuit Courtroom Cabinet has Circuit Court records 1947-1985.

HOOD RIVER

601 State St., Hood River, OR 97031, (541) 386-1442, **<www.co.hood-river.or.us>**

- **INCORPORATED:** June 23, 1908
- **PARENT COUNTY:** Wasco
- **LAND RECORDS:** start in 1890, County Clerk
- **PROBATE:** 1868, Trial Court Clerk
- **MILITARY:** start in 1919, County Clerk
- **NOTES:** Oregon State Archives has birth and death records 1907-1921 and naturalization records 1913-1928. Hood River County Trial Court Clerk has Circuit Court and divorce records 1896-1898, 1908-1983. Hood River County Assessment Office has Marriage records 1908-1961. Oregon Historical Records Index has naturalization records 1880-1940. Probate, land and Circuit Court case records from Wasco County prior to the creation of Hood River County are included.

JACKSON

10 S. Oakdale Ave., Room 114, Medford, OR 97501, (541) 774-6147, **<www.co.jackson.or.us>**

- **INCORPORATED:** 12 Jan. 12, 1852
- **PARENT COUNTY:** Lane
- **PROBATE RECORDS:** ca. 1853-1987, Circuit Court Clerk; start in 1988, Oregon Judicial Information Network
- **CIRCUIT COURT:** start in 1983, Oregon Judicial Information Network
- **MILITARY:** 1966, Clerk's Official Records
- **NOTES:** County Clerk has birth records 1907-1929, death records 1906-1929, land records for 1887 and 1905-1971, and Marriage records 1855-1964. Oregon State Archives has birth records 1906-1915, Circuit Court records 1856-1914, military records 1868-1873, and naturalization records 1859-1981. Circuit Court Clerk has Circuit Court records 1860-1983, divorce records 1856-1978, and probate records ca. 1853-1987. University or Oregon, Knight Library has Circuit Court records 1858-1918, land records ca. 1867-1892, and military records for 1864 and 1874. Southern Oregon Historical Society has Marriage records 1854-1930. Oregon Historical Society has military records 1863, 1868-1875, 1877, 1879-1880, and 1883-1883. County Court Clerk has naturalization records 1907-1929. Military discharges were recorded in the clerk's Miscellaneous Record before 1966.

JEFFERSON

66 SE D St., Madras, OR 97741, (541) 475-4451, **<www.co.jefferson.or.us>**

- **INCORPORATED:** Dec. 12, 1914
- **PARENT COUNTY:** Crook
- **LAND RECORDS:** start in 1870, Jefferson County Historical Society Museum;
- **PROBATE:** 1893, Trial Court Administrator
- **MILITARY:** 1983, County Clerk
- **NOTES:** County Clerk has birth records 1886-1944, death records 1915-1944, marriage records 1882-1961, military records 1920-1982, and naturalization records 1915-1928. Trial Court Administrator has Circuit Court and divorce records 1915-1984, and probate records 1893-1985. Jeffercon County Public Works Department has Land records 1918-1949. Jefferson County Probate records have been filed on Oregon Judicial Information Network since 1985.

JOSEPHINE

500 NW Sixth St., Grants Pass, OR 97526, (541) 474-5240, **<www.co.josephine.or.us>**

- **INCORPORATED:** Jan. 22, 1856
- **PARENT COUNTY:** Jackson
- **LAND RECORDS:** start in 1854, County Clerk
- **PROBATE:** 1987, Oregon Judicial Information Network
- **MILITARY:** start in 1919, County Clerk
- **NOTES:** Josephine County Public Health Department has birth and death records 1906-1925. County Clerk has Circuit Court records 1958-1981, divorce records 1925-1949 and 1959-1978, marriage records 1857-1971, and military records 1863-1893 and 1896-1900. Oregon State Archives has naturalization records 1907-1936 and Probate records 1848-1944. Josephine County Court Civil Unit Office has probate records 1939-1986.

KLAMATH

305 Main St., Klamath Falls, OR 97601, (541) 883-5134, <www.co.klamath.or.us>

- **INCORPORATED:** Oct. 17, 1882
- **PARENT COUNTY:** Lake County
- **MARRIAGE RECORDS:** from 1882–1990, kept by County Clerk
- **DIVORCE:** 1883–1988,Clerk of Circuit Court
- **LAND:** start in ca. 1870, Klamath County Surveyor; 1875, County Clerk
- **PROBATE:** ca. 1882–1987, Clerk of County Court; start in 1988, Oregon Judicial Information Network
- **COURT:** 1883–1987, Clerk of Circuit Court
- **NATURALIZATION:** 1889–1981, Clerk of County Court
- **MILITARY:** 1887–1888, start in 1919, County Clerk
- **NOTES:** Clerk of Circuit Court has Circuit Court records 1883-1987 and divorce records 1883-1988. County Clerk has Marriage records 1882-1990 and military records 1887-1888. Clerk of County Court has naturalization records 1889-1981. Military Discharge records were recorded in the Miscellaneous Record before 1920 and filed in the clerk's Book of Records since 1965. Clerk of County Court has probate records ca. 1882-1987.

LAKE

513 Center St., Lakeview, OR 97630, (541) 947-6051, <www.lakecountyor.org>

- **INCORPORATED:** Oct. 24, 1874
- **PARENT COUNTIES:** Jackson, Wasco
- **LAND RECORDS:** start in ca. 1879, County Clerk
- **PROBATE:** start in ca. 1892, Trial Court Administrator
- **MILITARY:** start in 1944, County Clerk
- **NOTES:** Trial Court Administrator has Circuit Court records 1875-1983 and divorce records 1875-1984. County Clerk has Marriage records 1875-1968, Naturalization records ca. 1882-1957, and probate records 1875-1930. Lake County Museum has military records 1887-1888. Planning and Building Department has naturalization records ca. 1875-1940.

LANE

125 E. Eighth Ave., Eugene, OR 97401, (541) 682-3654, <www.co.lane.or.us>

- **INCORPORATED:** Jan. 28, 1851
- **PARENT COUNTIES:** Benton, Linn
- **LAND RECORDS:** 1856, Deeds and Records Archives
- **PROBATE:** 1853–1982, start in 1988, Court Archives
- **MILITARY:** 1905, Lane County Historical Museum
- **NOTES:** Deeds/Records Research Library has birth and death records 1882-1915, marriage records 1852-1965, military records 1918-1966, and naturalization records 1926-1980. State Archives has birth and death records 1915-1928. Court Archives has Circuit Court records 1854-1989, divorce records 1854-1989, and probate records 1853-1982. Lane County Historical Museum has military records 1858-1894.

LEWIS

- **INCORPORATED:** Dec. 21, 1845
- **PARENT COUNTY:** original county
- **NOTES:** Now part of the state of Washington.

LINCOLN

225 W. Olive St., Room 201, Newport, OR 97365, (541) 265-4131, <www.co.lincoln.or.us>

- **INCORPORATED:** Feb. 20, 1893
- **PARENT COUNTIES:** Benton, Polk
- **LAND RECORDS:** 1869, County Clerk
- **PROBATE:** 1992, Trial Court Administrator
- **NOTES:** County Clerk has birth and death records 1907-1920, marriage records 1893-1989. Trial Court Administrator has Circuit Court and divorce records 1893-1983, military records 1945-1986, and probate records 1893-1989. Community Corrections Clerk has military records 1894-1899. Public Service Building Clerk has naturalization records 1903-1929. Military discharge records after 1968 filed in the Book of Records. Circuit and Probate Court records after 1983 filed on Oregon Judicial Information Network.

LINN

300 SW Fourth Ave., Room 205, Box 100, Albany, OR 97321, (541) 967-3829, <www.co.linn.or.us>

- **INCORPORATED:** Dec. 28, 1847
- **PARENT COUNTY:** Marion
- **DIVORCE RECORDS:** start in 1983, Circuit Court Clerk
- **LAND:** 1856, County Surveyor
- **PROBATE:** 1863, Circuit Court Clerk
- **COURT:** 1983, Circuit Court Clerk
- **NOTES:** State Archives has birth and death records 1903-1949, military records 1874-1893, and naturalization records 1891-1956. Circuit Court Clerk has Circuit Court and divorce records 1861-1974. County Clerk has Marriage records 1850-1969 and military records 1888-1901 and 1919-1970. Historical Records Index has naturalization records 1850-1856.

MALHEUR

251 B St. W, Suite 4, Vale, OR 97918, (541) 473-5151, <www.malheurco.org>

- **INCORPORATED:** Feb. 17, 1887
- **PARENT COUNTY:** Baker
- **LAND RECORDS:** start in 1887, County Clerk
- **PROBATE:** 1886, County Clerk
- **MILITARY:** 1983, County Clerk
- **NOTES:** Trial Court Administrator has birth and death records 1907-1939 and Circuit Court ahd Divorce records. State Archives has Circuit Court and divorce records 1886-1930. County Clerk has Marriage records 1880-1986, military records 1944-1973, and naturalization records 1861-1908.

MARION

100 High St. NE, Room 1331, Salem, OR 97301, (503) 588-5225, <www.co.marion.or.us>

- **INCORPORATED:** July 5, 1843
- **PARENT COUNTY:** original county
- **LAND RECORDS:** 1850, County Clerk
- **PROBATE:** 1843, Circuit Court Clerk
- **MILITARY:** 1913, County Clerk
- **NOTES:** County Clerk has birth records 1871-1932, death records 1907-1929, and Marriage records 1849-1967. Circuit Court Clerk has Circuit Court records 1848-1984 and divorce records 1848-1984. State Archives has military records 1891-1893, 1896-1902,

1917, and 1940. Probate Court records after 1987 filed on Oregon Judicial Information Network. Originally Champooick District. Name changed to Marion 3 September 1849.

MORROW

100 S. Court St., Suite 102, Box 338, Heppner, OR 97836, (541) 676-9061, **<www.morrowcountyoregon.com>**

- **INCORPORATED:** 16 Feb. 16, 1885
- **PARENT COUNTIES:** Umatilla, Wasco
- **LAND RECORDS:** start in 1935, County Clerk
- **PROBATE:** 1885, Circuit Court Clerk
- **MILITARY:** 1945, County Clerk
- **NOTES:** County Clerk has birth and death records 1905-1929, land records 1861-1915, marriage records 1885-1901 and 1905-1988, military records 1887-1898, and naturalization records 1906-1953. Circuit Court Clerk has Circuit Court and divorce records 1885-1985.

MULTNOMAH

1021 SW Fourth Ave., Portland, OR 97204, (503) 988-3957, **<www.multco.us>**

- **INCORPORATED:** Dec. 22, 1854
- **PARENT COUNTIES:** Washington, Clackamas
- **LAND RECORDS:** start in 1851, Assessment and Taxation
- **PROBATE:** start in 1855, Circuit Court Clerk
- **MILITARY:** 1909, Assessment and Taxation
- **NOTES:** Circuit Court, public access has Circuit Court records 1855-1860, 1906-1929, 1972-1982, and divorce records 1855-1860, 1906-1929, 1972-1983. County Assessment/Taxation Division has Marriage records 1855-1968 and military records for 1893. Circuit Court Clerk has naturalization records 1887-1940. Oregon Historical Society has probate records 1850-1873 and 1896. Book of Records has military discharge records before 1964.

POLK

850 Main St., Dallas, OR 97338, (503) 623-9217, **<www.co.polk.or.us>**

- **INCORPORATED:** Dec. 22, 1845
- **PARENT COUNTY:** Yamhill
- **LAND RECORDS:** start in 1890, County Clerk
- **PROBATE:** start in 1986, Circuit Court Clerk
- **MILITARY:** start in 1919, County Clerk
- **NOTES:** State Archives has birth records 1903-1915, death records 1903-1906, military records 1892-1901, Naturalization records 1872-1906 and 1908-1925, and probate records 1847-1921. County Clerk has birth records 1915-1921, death records 1907-1921, and Marriage records 1848-1980. Circuit Court Clerk has Circuit Court records 1846-1983, divorce records 1846-1983, and probate records 1921-1971. Public Works Department has military records for 1877.

SHERMAN

500 Court St., Box 365, Moro, OR 97039, (541) 565-3606, **<www.sherman-county.com>**

- **INCORPORATED:** Feb. 25, 1889
- **PARENT COUNTY:** Wasco
- **LAND RECORDS:** start in 1885, County Clerk
- **PROBATE:** 1889, County Clerk
- **MILITARY:** 1987, County Clerk
- **NOTES:** County Clerk has birth records 1904-1941, Circuit Court records 1889-1933, death records 1905-1952, divorce records 1889-1933, marriage records 1889-1977 and 1982-1987, military records 1921-1955, 1960-1977, and for 1982, and naturalization records 1889-1901 and 1907-1929. Circuit Court Clerk has Circuit Court and divorce records 1933-1987.

TILLAMOOK

201 Laurel Ave., Tillamook, OR 97141, (503) 842-3402, **<www.co.tillamook.or.us>**

- **INCORPORATED:** Dec. 15, 1853
- **PARENT COUNTIES:** Clatsop, Polk, Yamhill
- **LAND RECORDS:** start in 1860, County Clerk
- **PROBATE:** start in 1988, Oregon Judicial Information Network
- **MILITARY:** start in 1918, County Clerk
- **NOTES:** State Archives has birth and death records 1903-1943, Circuit Court records 1862-1969, divorce records 1862-1969, and naturalization records 1907-1927. Tillamook County Pioneer Museum has Death records 1918-1945. Trial Court Administrator has Divorce records ca. 1868-1983 and Probate records 1859-1987. County Clerk has Marriage records 1854-1964. Circuit Court civil and criminal records dating before 1904 were recorded separately. Recorded Instruments has military discharge records before 1968. Direct and Indirect Alpha Indexes has as part of the recorded instruments Military Discharge records after 1994.

TWALITY

- **INCORPORATED:** July 5, 1843
- **PARENT COUNTY:** original county
- **NOTES:** See Washington County. Name changed to Washington Sept. 3, 1849.

UMATILLA

216 SE Fourth St., Pendleton, OR 97801, (541) 276-7111, **<www.co.umatilla.or.us>**

- **INCORPORATED:** Sept. 27, 1862
- **PARENT COUNTY:** Wasco
- **LAND RECORDS:** start in 1862, County Clerk
- **PROBATE:** 1987, Oregon Judicial Information Network
- **MILITARY:** 1910, County Clerk
- **NOTES:** County Clerk has birth records 1890-1897, 1914-1926, death records 1892-1897, 1914-1926, marriage records 1862-1962, and naturalization records ca. 1863-1974. State Archives has birth records 1906-1945 and Death records 1907-1944. Trial Court Administrator has Circuit Court records 1863-ca. 1997, divorce records 1863-ca. 1997, and probate records 1863-1986. County Surveyor's office has military records 1889-1902 and 1942-1976. The clerk's Miscellaneous Record has military discharge records before 1942.

UMPQUA

- **INCORPORATED:** Jan. 24, 1851
- **PARENT COUNTIES:** Benton, Linn
- **NOTES:** See Douglas County. Absorbed by Douglas County Oct. 16, 1862.

UNION

1106 K Ave., La Grande, OR 97850, (541) 963-1001, **<www.union-county.org>**

- **INCORPORATED:** Oct. 14, 1864
- **PARENT COUNTY:** Baker
- **LAND RECORDS:** start in 1865, County Clerk
- **PROBATE:** 1987, Oregon Judicial Information Network
- **MILITARY:** 1989, County Clerk
- **NOTES:** County Clerk has birth and death records 1905-1906, marriage records 1864-1968, military records 1864-1991, military Discharge records 1919-1944, and Naturalization records 1865-1926. Trial Court Administrator has Circuit Court records 1864-1986, divorce records 1864-1986, and probate records 1865-1986.

WALLOWA

101 S. River St., Room 100, Enterprise, OR 97828, (541) 426-4543, **<www.co.wallowa.or.us>**

- **INCORPORATED:** Feb. 11, 1887
- **PARENT COUNTY:** Union
- **LAND RECORDS:** start in 1906, County Clerk
- **PROBATE:** 1987, Oregon Judicial Information Network
- **MILITARY:** 1990, County Clerk
- **NOTES:** County Clerk has birth and death records 1905-1944, Circuit Court and divorce records 1887-1983, marriage records 1887-1970, military records for 1878, 1888-1900, 1919-1990, Naturalization records 1897-1906, and probate records 1886-1995

WASCO

511 Washington St., The Dalles, OR 97058, (541) 506-2530, **<www.co.wasco.or.us>**

- **INCORPORATED:** Jan. 11, 1854
- **PARENT COUNTIES:** Clackamas, Marion, Linn, Lane
- **LAND RECORDS:** start in 1854, County Clerk
- **PROBATE:** 1854, Court Operations and Filing Office
- **NOTES:** County Clerk has birth and death records 1865-1891, marriage records 1854-1962, and military records 1855-1856, 1889-1905, 1918-1962, and 1975-1986. Oregon State Archives has birth and death records 1915-1941, Circuit Court records 1848-1963, divorce records 1848-1963, and naturalization records 1885-1962. Circuit Court Clerk has Circuit Court and divorce records 1854-1989.

WASHINGTON

155 N. First Ave., Suite 130, Hillsboro, OR 97124, (503) 846-8741, **<www.co.washington.or.us>**

- **INCORPORATED:** July 5, 1843
- **PARENT COUNTY:** original county
- **LAND RECORDS:** start in 1868, Assessment and Taxation
- **PROBATE:** 1987, Oregon Judicial Information Network
- **MILITARY:** 1964, Book of Records
- **NOTES:** Assessment/Taxation Department has birth and death records 1907-1946, marriage records 1842-1961, military records 1895-1917, 1919-1977, and naturalization records 1903-1906. Clerk of Circuit Court has Circuit Court and divorce records 1850-1982, and probate records 1848-1986. State Archives has Circuit Court and divorce records 1844-1939, military records for 1864, 1867-1873, 1884-1900, 1917-1918, naturalization records 1907-1927, and probate records 1842-1921. Washington County Historical Museum has land records ca. 1850-1985. Formerly named Twality County. Name changed to Washington Sept. 3, 1849.

WHEELER

701 Adams St., Suite 204, Box 327, Fossil, OR 97830, (541) 763-2400, **<www.wheelercounty-oregon.com>**

- **INCORPORATED:** Feb. 17, 1889
- **PARENT COUNTIES:** Crook, Gilliam, Grant
- **LAND RECORDS:** start in 1884, County Clerk
- **PROBATE:** 1887, County Clerk
- **MILITARY:** 1899, County Clerk
- **NOTES:** State Archives has birth and death records 1915-1930. Trial Court Coordinator has Circuit Court and divorce records 1898-1988. County Clerk has Marriage records 1896-1977 and naturalization records 1899-1927.

YAMHILL

414 NE Evans St., McMinnville, OR 97128, (503) 434-7518, **<www.co.yamhill.or.us>**

- **INCORPORATED:** July 5, 1843
- **PARENT COUNTIES:** original county
- **LAND RECORDS:** ca. 1858, County Clerk
- **PROBATE:** 1852, Trial Court Administrator
- **MILITARY:** start in 1919, County Clerk
- **NOTES:** State Archives has birth records 1871-1944, Circuit Court and divorce records 1854-1943, death records 1907-1928, and naturalization records 1853-1959. County Clerk has birth records 1903-1906 and 1908-1925, and Marriage records 1856-1978. Trial Court Administrator has Circuit Court and divorce records 1894-1979. Yamhill County Museum has Death records ca. 1919-ca. 1928. Yamhill Public Works/Surveyor's office has Land records 1852-1899. Oregon Historical Society has military records 1864-1870.

PENNSYLVANIA

» BY MAUREEN A. TAYLOR

HISTORICAL OVERVIEW

William Penn received a Royal Charter in 1681 to establish a colony on land taken from the Dutch. Initially known as Penn's Woods, the official name of the colony would become Pennsylvania. Penn opened the area to individuals of diverse religious beliefs and published advertisements in European newspapers encouraging immigration. By the early 18th century, Philadelphia was already a bustling city.

In 1749, the Ohio Co. claimed land from Virginia north through the Ohio valley, including what is now western Pennsylvania. Pennsylvania had land disputes with Maryland and Connecticut that lasted through the Revolutionary War. Many early immigrants to the western part of the colony came from the eastern Pennsylvania settlements and other colonies, generally not from other countries.

Philadelphia became a center of the Revolutionary War when other colonies sent representatives to the First Continental Congress held there. The city was the site of the first public reading of the Declaration of Independence July 8, 1776. In 1787, representatives again met in Philadelphia for a Constitutional Convention to establish the US government. Philadelphia served as the US capital from 1790 to 1800.

Canals—including the 300-mile Pennsylvania Main Line Canal—traversed the state during the early 1800s. Philadelphia and Pittsburgh were shipping hubs due to their access to major transportation routes and waterways. Philadelphia merchants imported goods from foreign ports and shipped them west to Pittsburgh. In the 19th century, multiple railroad lines encouraged transportation and trade between the eastern and western parts of the state.

Ulster Scots, Dutch, Finns, Germans, French and Swedes brought religious denominations including the Amish, Mennonites, Moravians, Schwenkfelders, Reformed and Lutherans, taking advantage of the religious freedom encouraged by William Penn. In the 19th century, immigrants from southern and eastern Europe established residence. Today, people from all over the world, including Asia and Latin America, call Pennsylvania home.

Pennsylvania is known for agriculture, tourism, and manufacturing, including Hershey's chocolate and Pittsburgh's Heinz Co. pickles and ketchup. Manufactured goods include steel, chemicals, clothing and petroleum products.

research tips

- Start your Pennsylvania research from your living room with the websites of the Genealogical Society of Pennsylvania **<www.libertynet.org/gspa>** and the Historical Society of Pennsylvania **<www.hsp.org>**.
- Before chasing your ancestors in county records across this large state, know where they lived and when.
- If you're researching in Western Pennsylvania, visit the Carnegie Library of Pittsburgh **<www.clpgh.org>** and the Blair County Genealogical Society in Hollidaysburg **<www.rootsweb.ancestry.com/~pabcgs>**. But these regional resources do not thoroughly cover the entire state—you'll need to delve into the collections of local public libraries and societies.

CENSUS RECORDS

- Federal census: 1790, 1800, 1810, 1820, 1830, 1840, 1850, 1860, 1870, 1880, 1900, 1910, 1920, 1930
- Federal mortality schedules: 1850, 1860, 1870, 1880
- Special census of Civil War Union veterans and widows: 1890
- Septennial census: 1779–1863

RECORD HIGHLIGHTS

Aside from what exists in the published Pennsylvania Archives series (free on historical records site Footnote **<www.footnote.com/documents/185749/pennsylvania_archives>**), few vital records are extant before the mid-19th century. It wasn't until Jan. 1, 1906, that the state officially recorded birth and death records. From 1852 to 1854, the Register of Wills in each county recorded births, marriages and deaths, but records are not complete. According to the Pennsylvania State Archives website **<www.phmc.state.pa.us>**, the Clerk of the Orphan's Court in each county recorded vital records: births and deaths from 1893–1906 and marriages from 1885. Compliance varied by county. Because of the lack of civil registration in the 19th century, church records are the main source for vital information, especially for German and Quaker congregations.

Many types of records are available on the county level, including estate papers (wills, orphan court records, inventories, and affidavits of death); land records (deeds, mortgages, and tax records); and court records (criminal and civil cases, naturalization, and divorces).

Land records date from 1682. Transactions between individuals and the Commonwealth of Pennsylvania are at the Pennsylvania State Archives. Deeds can also be found in the Office of the Recorder of Deeds for each county. The State Archives website states that a 1706 law required that, within six months, every deed or conveyance of real property had to be acknowledged by two witnesses before a justice of the peace or the recorder of deeds or his deputy.

Tax records are particularly good for Pennsylvania and can substitute for state census records and missing vital records. Every seven years, a taxpayer list known as the Septennial Census was compiled, but only a small percentage of the documents have survived. The information enumerated depends on the county and time period, but usually includes taxable inhabitants, freemen, and starting in 1800, details about slaves and occasionally the name of the owner. In addition to the Septennial Census, Pennsylvania counties compiled yearly tax rolls, available at county courthouses or historical societies. Tax records generally cover from the mid-1700s through the present day (in one form or another), depending upon the county. Many early county tax lists are in the published Pennsylvania Archives series.

The Pennsylvania State Archives has military papers from 1775 to 1985, but its website cautions that "most records of military service created prior to 1861 contain scant genealogical or descriptive data." A listing of pre-Civil War service is in the Pennsylvania Archives series. The State Archives has online information about service in various wars.

"Finding genealogical records depends on establishing an ancestor's place of residence in a particular county," says Jane Addams Clark of the Genealogical Society of Pennsylvania. Many counties were carved out of the three original counties: Philadelphia, Bucks and Chester. Also, the counties of Bedford, Cumberland, Westmoreland and Northumberland, served as mother counties for many western and northern counties.

The websites of the Genealogical Society of Pennsylvania (GSP) **<www.genpa.org>** and the Historical Society of Pennsylvania (HSP) **<www.hsp.org>** contain helpful information. Researchers can start their search in Philadelphia at either of these two major research libraries. Volunteers of the GSP have abstracted wills for Philadelphia County and other counties in southeastern Pennsylvania to create an every-name online index. Researchers can access the HSP catalog online as well. Peruse the collections of these institutions before proceeding to the county level. For western Pennsylvania, visit the Carnegie Library of Pittsburgh and the Blair County Genealogical Society in Hollidaysburg. Even these regional libraries do not cover all areas of this large state. Thus, you will need to look into the holdings of local public libraries and historical societies.

ARCHIVES, LIBRARIES, AND SOCIETIES

Adams County Pennsylvania Historical Society
Box 4325, Gettysburg, PA 17325, (717) 334-4723, **<www.achs-pa.org>**

African-American Genealogical Group
Box 27356, Philadelphia, PA 19118, (215) 572-6063, **<www.aagg.org>**

Allegheny Foothills Historical Society
c/o Boyce Park Administration Building, 675 Old Frankstown Road, Pittsburgh, PA 15239, (412) 832-0685, **<www.plumhistory.org>**

Allegheny-Kiski Valley Historical Society
224 E. Seventh Ave., Tarentum, PA 15084, (724) 224-7666, **<www.akvhs.org>**

Altoona Area Public Library
1600 Fifth Ave., Altoona, PA 16602, (814) 946-0417, **<www.altoonalibrary.org>**

Ancient Order of Hibernians
<www.paaoh.org>

Armstrong County Historical Museum and Genealogical Society
300 N. McKean St., Box 735, Kittanning, PA 16201, (724) 548-5707, **<www.armstronghistory.org/armco>**

Baltzer Meyer Historical Society
642 Baltzer Meyer Pike, Greensburg, PA 15601, (724) 836-6915, **<www.pa-roots.com/baltzermeyer>**

Beaver County Genealogy and History Center
Carnegie Library, 1301 S. 7th Ave., Beaver Falls, PA 15010, (724) 847-9253, **<www.rootsweb.ancestry.com/~pabecgs>**

Bedford County Historical Society
Pioneer Library, 6441 Lincoln Highway, Bedford, PA 15522, (814) 623-2011, **<www.bedfordpahistory.com>**

Berks County Genealogical Society
201 Washington St., Room 413, Reading, PA 19601, (610) 921-4970, **<www.berksgenes.org>**

Berwick Historical Society
102 E. Second St., Box 301, Berwick, PA 18603, (570) 759-8020, **<www.berwickhistoricalsociety.org>**

Blair County Genealogical Society
431 Scotch Valley Road, Hollidaysburg, PA 16648, (814) 696-3492, **<www.bcgslibrary.org>**

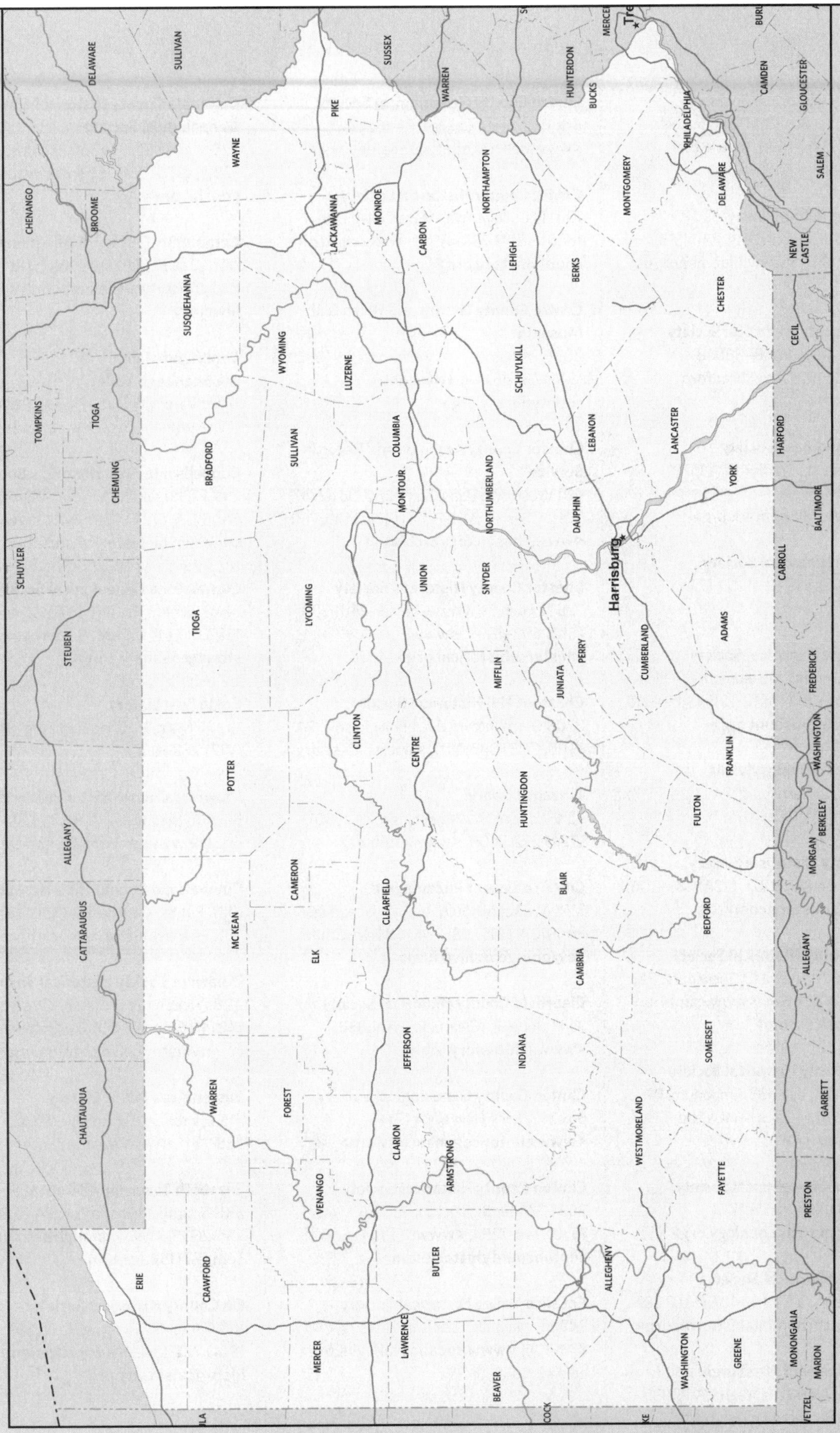
SULLIVAN
DELAWARE
CHENANGO
BROOME
TOMPKINS
TIOGA
CHEMUNG
SCHUYLER
STEUBEN
ALLEGANY
CATTARAUGUS
CHAUTAUQUA
ERIE
CRAWFORD
WARREN
MC KEAN
POTTER
TIOGA
BRADFORD
SUSQUEHANNA
WAYNE
PIKE
SUSSEX
WARREN
HUNTERDON
BUCKS
CAMDEN
GLOUCESTER
SALEM
NEW CASTLE
DELAWARE
PHILADELPHIA
MONTGOMERY
NORTHAMPTON
MONROE
LACKAWANNA
CARBON
LEHIGH
BERKS
CHESTER
CECIL
SCHUYLKILL
LUZERNE
WYOMING
SULLIVAN
COLUMBIA
MONTOUR
LEBANON
LANCASTER
HARFORD
YORK
NORTHUMBERLAND
DAUPHIN
Harrisburg
BALTIMORE
CARROLL
UNION
SNYDER
LYCOMING
ADAMS
CUMBERLAND
PERRY
JUNIATA
MIFFLIN
FREDERICK
CLINTON
CENTRE
HUNTINGDON
FRANKLIN
WASHINGTON
FULTON
BERKELEY
MORGAN
CAMERON
CLEARFIELD
BLAIR
BEDFORD
ELK
CAMBRIA
ALLEGANY
SOMERSET
INDIANA
JEFFERSON
FOREST
GARRETT
CLARION
ARMSTRONG
WESTMORELAND
VENANGO
FAYETTE
PRESTON
BUTLER
ALLEGHENY
MERCER
LAWRENCE
BEAVER
WASHINGTON
GREENE
MONONGALIA
MARION

Blair County Historical Society
3419 Oak Lane, Box 1083, Altoona, PA 16603, (814) 942-3916, **<www.blairhistory.org>**

Bloomsburg Public Library
225 Market St., Bloomsburg, PA 17815, (570) 784-0883, **<www.bloomsburgpl.org>**

Bradford County Historical Society
109 Pine St., Towanda, PA 18848, (570) 265-2240, **<www.bradfordhistory.com>**

Bradford Landmark Society
45 E. Corydon St., Bradford, PA 16701, (814) 362-3906, **<www.bradfordlandmark.org>**

Brownsville Historical Society
Box 24, Brownsville, PA 15417, (724) 785-6882

Bucks County Historical Society
Mercer and Fonthill Museums, 84 S. Pine St., Doylestown, PA 18901, (215) 345-0210, **<www.mercermuseum.org>**

State Library of Pennsylvania
333 Market St., Harrisburg, PA 17126, (717) 783-5950

Butler County Historical Society
Box 414, Butler, PA 16003, (724) 283-8116, **<www.butlerhistory.com>**

Cambria County Historical Society
615 N. Center St., Box 278, Ebensburg, PA 15931, (814) 472-6674, **<www.cambriacountyhistorical.com>**

Cameron County Historical Society
139 E. Fourth St., Box 433, Emporium, PA 15834, (814) 486-0213, **<www.thelittlemuseum.org>**

Capital Area Genealogical Society
Box 4502, Harrisburg, PA 17111, **<www.capitalareagenealogy.org>**

Carbondale Historical Society
Box 151, Carbondale, PA 18407, (570) 282-0385,**<www.carbondalehistorical.org>**

Carnegie Library of Pittsburgh
4400 Forbes Ave., Pittsburgh, PA 15213, (412) 622-3114, **<www.clpgh.org>**

Centre County Genealogical Society
Box 1135, State College, PA 16804, **<www.centrecountygenealogy.org>**

Centre County Historical Society
1001 E. College Ave., State College, PA 16801, (814) 234-4779, **<www.centrecountyhistory.org>**

Centre County Library and Historical Museum
203 N. Allegheny St., Bellefonte, PA 16823, (814) 355-1516, **<www.centrecountylibrary.org>**

Chester County Archives and Records Service
601 Westtown Road, Suite 080, Box 2747, West Chester, PA 19380, (610) 344-6760, **<www.chesco.org/archives>**

Chester County Historical Society
225 N. High St., West Chester, PA 19380, (610) 692-4800, **<www.chestercohistorical.org>**

Chestnut Hill Historical Society
8708 Germantown Ave., Philadelphia, PA 19118, (215) 247-0417, **<www.chhist.org>**

Citizens Library
55 S. College St., Washington, PA 15301, (724) 222-2400, **<www.citlib.org>**

City Archives of Philadelphia
3101 Market St., Suite 150, Philadelphia, PA 19104, (215) 685-9401, **<www.phila.gov/phils/carchive.htm>**

Clearfield County Historical Society
104 E. Pine St., Clearfield, PA 16830, **<www.clfdhistory.org>**

Clinton County Genealogical Society
Box 393, Lock Haven, PA 17745, **<www.clintoncogensociety.org>**

Clinton County Historical Society
362 E. Water St., Lock Haven, PA 17745, (570) 748-7254, **<www.clintoncountyhistory.com>**

Cocalico Valley Historical Society
249 W. Main St., Ephrata, PA 17522, (717) 733-1616, **<www.cocalicovalleyhs.org>**

Columbia County Historical and Genealogical Society
225 Market St., Box 360, Bloomsburg, PA 17815, (570) 784-1600, **<www.colcohist-gensoc.org>**

Community Library of Allegheny Valley
400 Lock St., Tarentum, PA 15084, (724) 226-0770, **<www.einpgh.org/ein/alvalley>**

Community Library of the Shenango Valley
11 N. Sharpsville Ave., Sharon, PA 16146, (724) 981-4360, **<www.clsv.net>**

Connellsville Area Historical Society
299 S. Pittsburgh St., Connellsville, PA 15425, (724) 628-5640, **<www.connellsvillehistoricalsociety.com>**

Cornerstone Genealogical Society
144 E. Greene St., Box 547, Waynesburg, PA 15370, (724) 627-5653, **<www.cornerstonegenealogy.com>**

Coyle Free Library
102 N. Main St., Chambersburg, PA 17201, (717) 263-1054

Crawford County Historical Society
Box 411, Meadville, PA 16335, (814) 724-6080, **<www.crawfordhistorical.org>**

Cumberland County Historical Society
21 N. Pitt St., Carlisle, PA 17013, (717) 249-7610, **<www.historicalsociety.com>**

Delaware County Historical Society
408 Avenue of the States, Chester, PA 19014, (610) 872-0502, **<delawarecountyhistoricalsociety-pa.org>**

Easton Area Public Library
515 Church St., Easton, PA 18042, (610) 258-2917, **<www.eastonpl.org>**

Elizabeth Township Historical Society
5811 Smithfield St., Boston, PA 15135, (412) 754-2030, **<www.familytreetracer.com/ETHSpage.htm>**

Elk County Historical Society
109 Center St., Ridgway, PA 15853, (814) 776-1032, **<www.elkcountyhistoricalsociety.org>**

Episcopal Diocese of Pennsylvania
240 S. Fourth St., Philadelphia, PA 19106, (215) 627-6434, **<www.diopa.org>**

Erie County Historical Society
419 State St., Erie, PA 16501, (814) 454-1813, **<www.eriecountyhistory.org>**

Erie County Public Library
160 E. Front St., Erie, PA 16507, (814) 451-6900, **<www.erielibrary.org>**

Erie Society for Genealogical Research
Box 1403, Erie, PA 16512, **<erie.pa-roots.com>**

Evangelical and Reformed Historical Society
555 W. James St., Lancaster, PA 17603, (717) 290-8734, **<www.erhs.info>**

Fayette County Genealogical Society of Pennsylvania
24 Jefferson St., Uniontown, PA 15401, **<www.fcgspa.org>**

Ford City Public Library
1136 Fourth Ave., Ford City, PA 16226, (724) 763-3591, **<www.armstronglibraries.org/fordcity.php>**

Forest County Historical Society
206 Elm St., Box 546, Tionesta, PA 16353, (814) 755-4422, **<forestcounty.com/historyhouse.html>**

Franklin County Historical Society-Kittochtinny
75 E. King St., Chambersburg, PA 17201, (717) 264-1667, **<pafch.tripod.com>**

Franklin Public Library
421 Twelfth St., Franklin, PA 16323, (814) 432-5062, **<www.franklinlibrary.org>**

Free Library of Philadelphia
1901 Vine St., Philadelphia, PA 19103, (215) 686-5322, **<www.library.phila.gov>**

Friends Historical Library
Swarthmore College, 500 College Ave., Swarthmore, PA 19081, (610) 328-8496, **<www.swarthmore.edu/fhl.xml>**

Fulton County Historical Society
Box 115, McConnellsburg, PA 17233, **<www.fultonhistory.org>**

Genealogical Research Society of Northeastern Pennsylvania
Box 1, Olyphant, PA 18447, (570) 383-7661, **<www.grsnp.org>**

Genealogical Society of Pennsylvania
2207 Chestnut St., Philadelphia, PA 19103, (215) 545-0391, **<www.genpa.org>**

Genealogical Society of Southwestern Pennsylvania
c/o Citizens Library, 55 S. College St., Washington, PA 15301,**<www.genealogicalsocietyswpa.com>**

German Society of Pennsylvania
611 Spring Garden St., Philadelphia, PA 19123, (215) 627-2332, **<www.germansociety.org>**

Greene County Historical Society
918 Rolling Meadow Road, Waynesburg, PA 15370, (724) 627-3204, **<www.greenecountyhistory.com>**

Green Free Library
134 Main St., Wellsboro, PA 16901, (570) 724-4876, **<www.greenfreelibrary.org>**

Hanover Area Historical Society
105 High St., Hanover, PA 17331, (717) 632-3207, **<www.hanoverareahistoricalsociety.org>**

Historical and Genealogical Society of Indiana County
621 Wayne Ave., Indiana, PA 15701, (724) 463-9600, **<www.rootsweb.ancestry.com/~paicgs>**

Historical Society of Berks County
940 Centre Ave., Reading, PA 19601, (610) 375-4375, **<www.berkshistory.org>**

Historical Society of Dauphin County
219 S. Front St., Harrisburg, PA 17104, (717) 233-3462, **<www.dauphincountyhistory.org>**

Historical Society of Green Tree
c/o Green Tree Public Library, 10 W. Manilla Ave., Pittsburgh, PA 15220, (412) 921-8013, **<www.einpgh.org/ein/greentree/histsoc.html>**

Historical Society of Montgomery County
1654 Dekalb St., Norristown, PA 19401, (610) 272-0297, **<www.hsmcpa.org>**

Historical Society of Pennsylvania
1300 Locust St., Philadelphia, PA 19107, (215) 732-6200, **<www.hsp.org>**

Historical Society of Perry County
129 N. Second St., Box 81, Newport, PA 17074, (717) 567-9011, **<hsofpc.org>**

Historical Society of Schuylkill County
305 N. Centre St., Pottsville, PA 17901, (570) 622-7540, **<schuylkillhistory.org>**

Historical Society of St. Marys and Benzinger Township
99 Eric Ave., St. Marys, PA 15857, (814) 834-6525, **<www.smhistoricalsociety.com>**

Historical Society of Trappe, Collegeville, Perkiomen Valley
Box 26708, Collegeville, PA 19426, (610) 489-7560, **<www.trappehistoricalsociety.org>**

Historic Schaefferstown
Box 307, Schaefferstown, PA 17088, (717) 949-2244, **<www.hsimuseum.org>**

Hummelstown Area Historical Society
28 W. Main St., Hummelstown, PA 17036, (717) 566-6314, **<www.hummelstownhistorical.org>**

Huntingdon County Historical Society
106 Fourth St., Box 305, Huntingdon, PA 16652, (814) 643-5449, **<www.huntingdonhistory.org>**

James V. Brown Library
19 E. Fourth St., Williamsport, PA 17701, (570) 326-0536, **<www.jvbrown.edu>**

Jefferson County Historical Society
172-176 Main St., Brookville, PA 15825, (814) 849-0077, **<www.jchconline.org>**

Jewish Genealogical Society of Greater Philadelphia
Box 335, Exton, PA 19341, **<www.jewishgen.org/jgsp>**

Jewish Genealogical Society of Pittsburgh
<www.jewishgen.org/jgs-Pittsburgh>

Johnstown Area Genealogical and Historical Society
Box 5048, Johnstown, PA 15904, **<www.pennhighlands.edu/library/Gensoc/genealogy.htm>**

Juniata County Historical Society
498B Jefferson St., Mifflintown, PA 17059, (717) 436-5152, **<www.rootsweb.ancestry.com/~pajchs>**

Kutztown Area Historical Society
Box 307, Kutztown, PA 19530, (610) 683-7697, **<www.kutztownhistory.org>**

Lackawanna Historical Society
The Catlin House, 232 Monroe Ave., Scranton, PA 18510, (570) 344-3841, **<www.lackawannahistory.org>**

Lancaster County Historical Society
230 N. President Ave., Lancaster, PA 17603, (717) 392-4633, **<www.lancasterhistory.org>**

Lancaster Mennonite Historical Society
2215 Millstream Road, Lancaster, PA 17602, (717) 393-9745, **<www.lmhs.org>**

Latrobe Area Historical Society
1501 Ligonier St., Latrobe, PA 15650, (724) 539-8889, **<www.greaterlatrobe.net/history>**

Lawrence County Historical Society
408 N. Jefferson St., Box 1745, New Castle, PA 16103, (724) 658-4022, **<www.lawrencechs.com>**

Lebanon County Historical Society
924 Cumberland St., Lebanon, PA 17042, (717) 272-1473, **<lebanoncountyhistoricalsociety.org>**

Lehigh County Historical Society
c/o Lehigh Valley Heritage Museum, 432 W. Walnut St., Allentown, PA 18102, (610) 435-1074, **<www.lchs.museum>**

Ligonier Valley Historical Society
Box 167, Laughlintown, PA 15655, (724) 238-6818, **<www.compassinn.com/lvhs.asp>**

Lutheran Theological Seminary at Philadelphia
Northeast Regional Archives of the Evangelical Lutheran Church in America, 7301 Germantown Ave., Philadelphia, PA 19119, (215) 248-4616, **<www.ltsp.edu/lutheran-archives-philadelphia>**

Luzerne County Historical Society
49 S. Franklin St., Wilkes-Barre, PA 18701, (570) 823-6244, **<www.luzernecountyhistory.com>**

Lycoming County Genealogical Society
Box 3625, Williamsport, PA 17701, (570) 326-3326, **<lycominglineage.com>**

Lycoming County Historical Society and Museum
Thomas T. Taber Museum, 858 W. Fourth St., Williamsport, PA 17701, (570) 326-3326, **<www.tabermuseum.org>**

Magill Library, Haverford College
370 Lancaster Ave., Haverford, PA 19041, (610) 896-1161, **<www.haverford.edu/library >**

Mahanoy and Mahantongo Historical and Preservation Society
Box 143, Dalmatia, PA 17017, **<www.mahantongo.org>**

Martinsburg Community Library
201 S. Walnut St., Martinsburg, PA 16662, (814) 793-3335, **<www.nbcsd.org/2023108129939433/site/default.asp>**

McKean County Genealogical Society
c/o Hanley Library, University of Pittsburgh at Bradford, 300 Campus Dr., Bradford, Pa. 16701, (814) 362-7610, **<www.library.pitt.edu/brad/hanley.html>**

McKean County Historical Society
Old Jail Museum, 502 W. King St., Smethport, PA 16749, (814) 887-5142, **<www.smethportchamber.com/old_jail_museum.htm>**

Mennonite Heritage Center
565 Yoder Road, Box 82, Harleysville, PA 19438, (215) 256-3020, **<www.mhep.org>**

Mercer County Genealogical Society
<www.rootsweb.ancestry.com/~pamercer/PA/index.htm>

Mercer County Historical Society
119 S. Pitt St., Mercer, PA 16137, (724) 662-3490, **<www.mchspa.org>**

Mifflin County Historical Society
1 W. Market St., Suite 1, Lewistown, PA 17044, (717) 242-1022, **<www.rootsweb.ancestry.com/~pamchs/home.htm>**

Mifflin Township Historical Society
3000 Lebanon Church Road, Suite 202, West Mifflin, PA 15122, (412) 600-0229, **<www.mifflintownship.org>**

Monroe County Historical Association
900 Main St., Stroudsburg, PA 18360, (570) 421-7703, **<www.monroehistorical.org>**

Montgomery County Archival Records Department
2000 Old Arch Road, Norristown, PA 19401, (610) 278-3441, **<www.montcopa.org>**

Montour County Genealogical Society
205 Ferry St., Danville, PA 17821, (570) 275-6177, **<www.rootsweb.ancestry.com/~pamcgs/>**

Montour County Historical Society
1 Bloom St., Box 8, Danville, PA 17821, (570) 271-0830

Mt. Lebanon Public Library
16 Castle Shannon Blvd., Pittsburgh, PA 15228, (412) 531-1912,**<www.mtlebanonlibrary.org>**

Muncy Historical Society
40 N. Main St., Box 11, Muncy, PA 17756, (570) 546-5917, **<www.muncyhistoricalsociety.org>**

Myerstown Community Library
199 N. College St., Myerstown, PA 17067, (717) 866-2800, **<www.lclibs.org/myerstown/index.php>**

National Archives, Mid-Atlantic Region
900 Market St., Philadelphia, PA 19107, (215) 606-0100, **<www.archives.gov/midatlantic>**

New Castle Public Library
207 E. North St., New Castle, PA 16101, (724) 658-6659, ext. 107, **<www.ncdlc.org>**

North Hills Genealogists
Box 304, Ingomar, PA 15127, **<www.northhillsgenealogists.org>**

Northampton County Historical and Genealogical Society
101 S. Fourth St., Easton, PA 18042, (610) 253-1222, **<www.northamptonctymuseum.org>**

Northeast Pennsylvania Genealogical Society
Box 1776, Shavertown, PA 18708, **<www.rootsweb.ancestry.com/~panepgs>**

Northland Public Library
300 Cumberland Rd., Pittsburgh, PA 15237, (412) 366-8100, **<www.northlandlibrary.org>**

Northumberland County Historical Society
1150 N. Front St., Sunbury, PA 17801, (570) 286-4083, **<www.northumberlandcountyhistoricalsociety .org>**

Oil City Library
2 Central Ave., Oil City, PA 16301, (814) 678-3077, **<www.oilcitylibrary.org>**

Old York Road Genealogical Society
c/o Abington Free Library, 1030 Old York Road, Abington, PA 19001, **<www.oyrgs.org>**

Osterhout Free Public Library
71 S. Franklin St., Wilkes-Barre, PA 18701, (570) 823-0156, **<www.osterhout.lib.pa.us>**

Palatines to America, Pennsylvania Chapter
Box 280, Strasburg, PA 17579, **<www.pa-palam.org>**

Palmer Theological Seminary, The Seminary of Eastern University
6 E. Lancaster Ave., Wynnewood, PA 19096, (610) 896-5000, **<www.palmerseminary.edu>**

Palmyra Area Genealogical Society
Box 544, Palmyra, PA 17078

Penns Valley Area Historical Museum
244 W. Aaron Square, Aaronsburg, PA 16820, (814) 349-8960, **<www.pennsvalleymuseum.org>**

Pennsylvania Department of Health
625 Forster St., 8th floor West, Harrisburg, PA 17120, (877) 724-3258, **<www.health.state.pa.us>**

Pennsylvania German Society
Box 244, Kutztown, PA 19530, (717) 597-7940, **<www.pgs.org>**

Pennsylvania Heritage Society
Commonwealth Keystone Building, 400 North St., Harrisburg, PA 17120, (717) 787-2407 or (866) 823-6539, **<www.paheritage.org>**

Pennsylvania Historical and Museum Commission
State Museum Building, 300 North St., Harrisburg, PA 17120, (717) 787-3362, **<www.phmc.state.pa.us>**

Pennsylvania State Archives
350 North St., Harrisburg, PA 17120, **<www.phmc.state.pa.us>**

Perry Historians
Box 73, Newport, PA 17074, **<www.theperryhistorians.org>**

Pike County Historical Society
The Columns, 608 Broad St., Milford, PA 18337, (570) 296-8126, **<www.pikecountyhistoricalsociety.org>**

Pinegrove Historical Society
Box 65, Pine Grove, PA 17963, (570) 345-0157, **<www.rootsweb.ancestry.com/~papghs>**

Pioneer Library
6441 Lincoln Highway, Bedford, PA 15522, (814) 623-2011, **<www.bedfordpahistory.com>**

Potter County Historical Society
308 N. Main St., Box 605, Coudersport, PA 16915, (814) 274-4410, **<history.pottercountypa.net>**

Presbyterian Historical Society
425 Lombard St., Philadelphia, PA 19147, (215) 627-1852, **<www.history.pcusa.org>**

Punxsutawney Area Historical and Genealogical Society
401 W. Mahoning St., Box 286, Punxsutawney, PA 15767, (814) 938-2555, **<www.punxsyhistory.org>**

Reading Public Library
100 S. Fifth St., Reading, PA 19602, (610) 655-6350, **<www.reading.lib.pa.us>**

Annie Halenbake Ross Library
232 W. Main St., Lock Haven, PA 17745, (570) 748-3321, **<www.rosslibrary.org>**

Schlow Centre Region Library
211 S. Allen St., State College, PA 16801, (814) 237-6236, **<www.schlowlibrary.org>**

Scottish Historic and Research Society
102 St. Paul's Road, Ardmore, PA 19003, **<www.shrs.org>**

Sewickley Valley Historical Society
200 Broad St., Sewickley, PA 15143, (412) 741-5315, **<www.sewickleyhistory.org>**

Shippensburg Historical Society
73 W. King St., Box 539, Shippensburg, PA 17257, (717) 532-6727, **<www.shippensburghistory.org**

Snyder County Historical Society
30 E. Market St., Box 276, Middleburg, PA 17842, (570) 837-6191, **<www.snydercounty.org>**

Solebury Township Historical Society
3020 N. Sugan Road, Box 525, Solebury, PA 18963, (215) 297-5091, **<www.soleburyhistory.org>**

Somerset Historical Center
10649 Somerset Pike, Somerset, PA 15501, (814) 445-6077, **<www.somersethistoricalcenter.org>**

Springs Historical Society of the Casselman Valley
Box 62, Springs, PA 15562, (814) 662-2625, **<www.springspa.org>**

Strasburg Heritage Society
Box 81, Strasburg, PA 17579, (717) 687-3534, **<www.strasburgheritagepa.org**

Sullivan County Historical Society
Courthouse Square, LaPorte, PA 18626, (570) 946-5020, **<www.rootsweb.ancestry.com/~pasulliv/SullivanCountyHistoricalSociety/SCHS.html>**

Susquehanna County Historical Society
2 Monument Square, Montrose, PA 18801, (570) 278-1881, **<www.susqcohistsoc.org>**

Tarentum Genealogical Society
Box 66, Tarentum, PA 15084, **<www.rootsweb.ancestry.com/~patgs>**

Tri-County Heritage Society
Box 352, Morgantown, PA 19543, (610) 286-7477, **<www.tricountyheritage.org>**

Tulpehocken Settlement Historical Society
116 N. Front St., Box 53, Womelsdorf, PA 19567, (610) 589-2527, **<www.tulpehockenroots.org>**

Tyrone Area Historical Society
Box 1850, Tyrone, PA 16686, (814) 684-5141, **<www.tyronehistory.org>**

Union County Historical Society
c/o Union County Court House, St. Louis and S. Second streets, Lewisburg, PA 17837, (570) 524-8666, **<www.unioncountyhistoricalsociety.org>**

Venango County Genealogy Club
c/o Oil City Library, 2 Central Ave., Oil City, PA 16301, (814) 678-3077, **<www.csonline.net/vengen>**

Venango County Historical Society
301 S. Park St., Franklin, PA 16323, (814) 437-2275, **<venango.pa-roots.com/venangohistoricalsociety.html>**

Warren County Historical Society
210 Fourth Ave., Warren, PA 16365, (814) 723-1795, **<www.warrenhistory.org>**

Warren Public Library
205 Market St., Warren, PA 16365, (814) 723-4650, **<www.warrenlibrary.org>**

Washington County Historical Society
LeMoyne House, 49 E. Maiden St., Washington, PA 15301, (724) 225-6740, **<www.wchspa.org>**

Wattsburg Area Historical Society
14438 Main St., Box 240, Wattsburg, PA 16442, (814) 739-2952

Wayne County Historical Society
810 Main St., Box 446, Honesdale, PA 18431, (570) 253-3240, **<www.waynehistorypa.org>**

Waynesboro Historical Society
138 W. Main St., Waynesboro, PA 17268, (717) 762-1747, **<www.waynesborohistory.com>**

A.R. Wentz Library, Lutheran Theological Seminary at Gettysburg
66 Seminary Ridge, Gettysburg, PA 17325, (717) 338-3014, **<www.ltsg.edu/Resources/Wentz-Library>**

Western Pennsylvania Genealogical Society
4400 Forbes Ave., Pittsburgh, PA 15213, (412) 687-6811, **<www.wpgs.org>**

Westmoreland Historical Society
41 W. Otterman St., Suite 310, Greensburg, PA 15601, (724) 836-1800, **<www.starofthewest.org>**

Wyoming County Historical Society
Box 309, Tunkhannock, PA 18657, (570) 836-5303, **<www.rootsweb.ancestry.com/~pawyomin/WCHS.html>**

Yardley Historical Association
The Old Library by Lake Afton, 46 West Afton Ave, Box 212, Yardley, PA 19067, (215) 493-9883 , **<www.yardleyhistory.org>**

York County Archives
150 Pleasant Acres Road, York, PA 17402, (717) 840-7222, **<www.yorkcountyarchives.org>**

York County Heritage Trust
250 E. Market St., York, PA 17403, (717) 848-1587, **<www.yorkheritage.org>**

Zelienople Historical Society
243 S. Main St., Zelienople, PA 16063, (742) 452-9457, **<www.zelienoplehistoricalsociety.com>**

☞ GENERAL RESOURCES

African Americans in Pennsylvania: A History and Guide by Charles L. Blockson (Black Classic Press, 1994)

Applications for Membership in Alphabetical Order by Member With a Complete Genealogy from the Colonial Society of Pennsylvania (filmed by the Family History Library, 1968)

The Biographical Encyclopedia of Pennsylvania of the Nineteenth Century edited by Charles Robson (Galaxy, 1874)

Bibliography of Pennsylvania History, 2nd edition, compiled by Norman B. Wilkinson, edited by Sylvester Kirby Stevens and Donald H. Kent (Pennsylvania Historical and Museum Commission, 1957)

Bibliography on the Colonial Germans of North American: Especially the Pennsylvania Germans and Their Descendants by Emil Meyen (Reprint: Genealogical Publishing Co., 1982)

A Checklist of Pennsylvania Newspapers, Philadelphia County from the Pennsylvania Historical Survey (Pennsylvania Historical Commission, 1944)

Church and Pastoral Records in the Archives of the United Church of Christ and the Evangelical and Reformed Historical Society, Lancaster Pennsylvania by Florence M. Bricker (The Society, 1982)

Colonial and Revolutionary Families of Pennsylvania, 11 vols., by John W. Jordan, et al. (Lewis Publishing, 1911-65)

A Country Between: The Upper Ohio Valley and Its Peoples, 1724-1774 by Michael N. McConnell (University of Nebraska Press, 1992)

County Government and Archives in Pennsylvania from the Pennsylvania Historical Survey (Pennsylvania Historical and Museum Commission, 1947)

Directory of Museums and Historical Organizations in Pennsylvania by Jean H. Cutler (The Federation, 1991)

Encyclopedia of Pennsylvania Biography, 32 vols., by John W. Jordan, et al. (Lewis Historical Publishing Co, 1914-67)

Every Name Index to Egle's Notes and Queries, 2 vols., by Eva Draegert Schory (Decatur Genealogical Society, 1982-1986)

Genealogical Abstracts From Newspapers of the German Reformed Church, 1830-

1839 by Barbara Manning (Heritage Books, 1992)

Genealogical Abstracts From Newspapers of the German Reformed Church 1840-1843 by Barbara Manning (Heritage Books, 1995)

Genealogical and Personal History of the Allegheny Valley, Pennsylvania, 3 vols., by John W. Jordan (Lewis Historical Publishing, 1913)

Genealogical and Personal History of Northern Pennsylvania, 3 vols., edited by John W. Jordan (Lewis Historical Publishing, 1913)

Genealogical Collections: Families of Pennsylvania, New Jersey, Etc., 1700-1950 from the Pennsylvania Historical Society (filmed by the Family History Library, 1966)

The Genealogical Records of the Schwenkfelder Families: Seekers of Religious Liberty Who Fled From Silesia to Saxony and Thence to Pennsylvania in the Years 1731 to 1737 by Samuel Kriebel Brecht (Rand McNally, printed for the Board of Publication of the Schwenkfelder Church, Pennsburg, PA, 1923)

Genealogies of Pennsylvania Families: From the Pennsylvania Genealogical Magazine, 3 vols., (Genealogical Publishing Co., 1982)

A Genealogist's Guide to Pennsylvania Records compiled by Helen Hutchison Woodroofe (Reprinted from the *Pennsylvania Genealogical Magazine*; Genealogical Society of Pennsylvania, 1995)

Guide to Depositories of Manuscript Collections in Pennsylvania by Margaret Sherburne Elliot (Pennsylvania Historical Commission, 1939)

Guide to Genealogical and Historical Research in Pennsylvania by Floyd G. Hoenstine (Floyd G. Hoenstine, 1978)

A Guide to the History of Pennsylvania by Dennis B. Downey and Francis J. Bremer (Greenwood Press, 1993)

Guide to the Microfilm of the Records of Pennsylvania's Revolutionary Governments, 1775-1790 (Record Group 27) in the Pennsylvania State Archives by Roland M. Baumann (Pennsylvania Historical and Museum Commission, 1978)

Guide to the Records Groups in the Pennsylvania State Archives by Frank M. Suran (Pennsylvania Historical and Museum Commission, 1980)

Handbook for Genealogical Research in Pennsylvania by John W. Heisey (Heritage House, 1985)

Historical Manuscript Depositories in Pennsylvania by Irwin Richman (The Pennsylvania Historical and Museum Commission, 1965)

Historic Background and Annals of the Swiss and German Pioneer Settlers of Southeastern Pennsylvania and of Their Remote Ancestors From the Middle of the Dark Ages, Down to the Time of the Revolutionary War ... With Particular Reference to the German-Swiss Mennonites or Anabaptists, the Amish and Other Non-resistant Sects by Frank Eshleman (1917; Genealogical Publishing Co., 1969)

An Illustrated History of the Commonwealth of Pennsylvania by William Henry Egle (E.M. Gardner, 1880)

Index to the Encyclopedia of Pennsylvania Biography by Frederic Antes Godcharles (W.D. Stock, 1996)

Memorials of the Huguenots in America, With Special Reference to Their Emigration [sic] to Pennsylvania by Ammon Stapleton (1901; Genealogical Publishing Co., 1969)

Merion in the Welsh Tract: With Sketches of the Townships of Haverford and Radnor, Historical and Genealogical Collections Concerning the Welsh Barony in the Province of Pennsylvania, Settled by the Cymric Quaker in 1682 by Thomas Allen Glenn (Herald Press, 1896)

The Negro in Pennsylvania: Slavery-Servitude-Freedom, 1639-1861 by Edward Raymond Turner (Negro Universities Press, 1969)

Notes and Queries: Historical, Biographical, and Genealogical, Relating Chiefly to Interior Pennsylvania. 1894-1904 edited by William Henry Egle (Reprint: Genealogical Publishing Co., 1971)

Penn's Example to the Nations: 300 Years of the Holy Experiment by Robert Grant Crist (Pennsylvania Council of Churches, for the Pennsylvania Religious Tercentenary Committee, 1987)

Pennsylvania: A History, 9 vols., by George P. Donehoo (Lewis Historical Publishing Co., 1926-1931)

Pennsylvania and Middle Atlantic States Genealogical Manuscripts: A User's Guide to the Manuscript Collections of the Genealogical Society of Pennsylvania by J. Carlyle Parker (Marietta Publishing, 1986)

Pennsylvania Archives by J. Severns (J. Severns, 1852-1856, 1874-1935)

Pennsylvania Area Key: A Guide to the Genealogical Records of the State of Pennsylvania, 2nd edition, by Florence Clint (Area Keys, 1976)

Pennsylvania Biographical Dictionary by William T. Parsons (American Historical Publications, 1989)

Pennsylvania Directory of Historical Organizations, 1970 by Gail M. Gibson (Pennsylvania Historical and Museum Commission, 1970)

The Pennsylvania Dutch: A Persistent Minority by William T. Parsons (Twayne Publishers, 1976)

Pennsylvania Family Histories and Genealogies by Donald Odell Virdin (Heritage Books, 1992)

Pennsylvania Genealogical Research by George K. Schweitzer (G. Schweitzer, 1986)

Pennsylvania Genealogies, Chiefly Scotch-Irish and German by William Henry Egle (Reprint: Genealogical Publishing Co., 1969)

The Pennsylvania Germans, 1891-1965, Frequently Known as the "Pennsylvania Dutch" by Homer Tope Rosenberger (H.T. Rosenberger, 1966)

Pennsylvania Historical Bibliography, vols., 1-6, by John B. Trussell Jr. (Pennsylvania Historical and Museum Commission, 1979-1989)

Pennsylvania Line: A Research Guide to Pennsylvania Genealogy and Local History, 4th ed., edited by William L. Iscrupe and Shirley G.M. Iscrupe (Southwest Pennsylvania Genealogical Services, 1990)

Pennsylvania Newspapers, a Bibliography and Union List edited by (Pennsylvania Library Association, 1969)

Pennsylvania Research Outline by the Church of Jesus Christ of Latter-day Saints (online at **<www/familysearch.org/eng/search/RG/guide/pennsylvania.asp>**)

Pennsylvania: The Heritage of a Commonwealth, 4 vols., by Sylvester Kirby Stevens (The American Historical Company, 1968)

Record of Eligibility of Ladies of the Grand Army of the Republic, Department of Pennsylvania 1883-1992 (filmed by the Family History Library, 1993)

The Scotch-Irish of Colonial Pennsylvania by Wayland Fuller Dunaway (University of North Carolina Press, 1944)

Summary Guide to the Pennsylvania State Archives edited by Frank B. Evans and Martha L. Simonetti (Pennsylvania Historical and Museum Commission, 1970)

Welsh Founders of Pennsylvania, 2 vols., by Thomas Allen Glenn (Fox, Jones and Co., 1911-1913)

Welsh Settlement of Pennsylvania by Charles Henry Browning (William J. Campbell, 1912)

The William Hinshaw Index to Quaker Meeting Records in the Friends Library in Swarthmore College, Pennsylvania by William Wade Hinshaw (filmed by the Genealogical Society of Utah, 1957)

Writing on Pennsylvania History: A Bibliography by Arthur C. Bining (Pennsylvania Historical and Museum Commission, 1946)

☞ CENSUS RECORDS

Non-Population Census Schedules For Pennsylvania: Agricultural Schedules, 1850-1880 from the US Census Office (filmed by the National Archives, 1970)

☞ IMMIGRATION RECORDS

Declarations of Intentions, 1810-1932; Index, 1810-1887 from the Pennsylvania Court of Quarter Sessions (filmed by the Family History Library, 1974, 1991)

Emigrants to Pennsylvania, 1641-1819: A Consolidation of Ship Passenger Lists from the *Pennsylvania Magazine of History and Biography* (Genealogical Publishing Co., 1975)

Immigrants to Pennsylvania, 1600's-1800's (Broderbund, 1999, CD-ROM)

Index to the Names of 30,000 Immigrants—German, Swiss, Dutch and French—Into Pennsylvania, 1727-1776 by M.V. Koger (filmed by Genealogical Society of Utah, 1972)

Names of Foreigners Who Took the Oath of Allegiance to the Province and State of Pennsylvania, 1727-1775, with Foreign Arrivals, 1786-1808 by William Henry Egle (Genealogical Publishing Co., 1967)

Names of Persons Who Took the Oath of Allegiance to the State of Pennsylvania Between the Years 1777 and 1789 by Thompson Westcott (1865; Genealogical Publishing Co., 1965)

Passenger Arrivals at the Port of Philadelphia, 1800-1819 by Elizabeth P. Bentley and Michael H. Tepper (Genealogical Publishing Co., 1986)

Pennsylvania German Pioneers: A Publication of the Original Lists of Arrivals in The Port of Philadelphia from 1727 to 1808 by Ralph Beaver Strassburger and William John Hinke (Pennsylvania German Society, 1934)

Petitions for Naturalization 1793-1906; Indexes 1793-1930 from the Pennsylvania Court of Common Pleas (filmed by the Family History Library, 1974)

Philadelphia Naturalization Records, and Index to Records of Aliens 'Declarations of Intentions and/or Oaths of Allegiance, 1789-1880 by P. William Filby and Mary K. Meyer (Gale Research, 1982)

Ship Passenger Lists, Pennsylvania and Delaware, 1641-1825 by Carl Boyer (C. Boyer, 1980)

The Trail of the Black Walnut by George Elmore Reaman (Genealogical Publishing Co., 1993)

☞ LAND RECORDS

Early Pennsylvania Land Records: Minutes of the Board of Property edited by William Henry Egle (Genealogical Publishing Co., 1976)

Pennsylvania Land Records: A History and Guide for Research by Donna Bingham Munger (Scholarly Resources, 1991)

Susquehanna Company Papers, 11 vols., by Julian P. Boyd and Robert J. Taylor (Cornell University Press, 1962-71)

Warrantees of Land in the Several Counties of the State of Pennsylvania, 1730-1898, 3 vols., edited by William Henry Egle (W.S. Ray, State Printer, 1897)

Warrant Register, 1682-1950 from the Bureau of Land Records in Harrisburg, Pa. (filmed by the Family History Library, 1976)

Warrants and Surveys of the Province of Pennsylvania Including the Three Lower Counties, 1759 by Allen Weinberg and Thomas E. Slatterly (City of Philadelphia, Department of Records, 1965)

☞ MAPS

Atlas of Pennsylvania (Temple University, 1989)

Atlas of the State of Pennsylvania: From Original Surveys and Various Loval Surveys

revised and corrected by Joseph R. Bien (Julius Bein & Co., 1900)

Descriptive List of the Map Collection in the Pennsylvania State Archives compiled by Martha L. Simonetti, edited by Donald H. Kent and Harry E. Whipkey (Pennsylvania Historical and Museum Commission, 1976)

A Gazetteer of the State of Pennsylvania by Thomas F. Gordon (Philadelphia: T. Belknap, 1932)

Historical Atlas and Chronology of County Boundaries, 1788-1980, vol. 1., edited by John H. Long (G.K. Hall, 1984)

Historical Topographical Atlas of the State of Pennsylvania by H.F. Walling and O.W. Gray (1872; Bookmark, 1977)

How Pennsylvania County Maps by William A. Russ Jr. (Pennsylvania Historical Association, 1966)

Pennsylvania: Atlas of Historical County Boundaries by John H. Long (Charles Scribner's Sons, Simon and Schuster Macmillan, 1996)

Pennsylvania Gazetteer (American Historical Publications, 1989)

Pennsylvania: Index to Topographic and Other Map Coverage from the United States Geological Survey (The Survey, ca. 1983)

Pennsylvania Place Names by Abraham H. Espenschade (1925; Genealogical Publishing Co., 1970)

Pennsylvania Postal History by John L. Kay and Chester M. Smith Jr. (Quarterman Publications, 1976)

☞MILITARY RECORDS

History of Pennsylvania Volunteers by Samuel P. Bates (State Printer, 1869-71)

Muster Rolls of the Pennsylvania Volunteers in the War of 1812-1814 (Genealogical Publishing Co., 1967)

Officers and Soldiers in the Service of the Province of Pennsylvania, 1744-1764 by James B. Nolan (University of Pennsylvania, 1936)

Pennsylvania and the War of 1812 by Harold L. Myers (Pennsylvania Historical and Museum Commission, 1964)

Pennsylvania Archives, 138 vols., from the State of Pennsylvania (Pennsylvania Historical and Museum Commission, 1857-1914)

Pennsylvania in the War of the Revolution, Battalions and Line 1775-1783 by John Blair Linn (State printer, 1880)

Pennsylvania in the War with Mexico by Randy W. Hackenburg (White Mane Publishing Co., 1992)

The Pennsylvania Line, Regimental Organization and Operations, 1776-1783 by John B. Trussell Jr. (Pennsylvania Historical and Museum Commission, 1977)

Pennsylvania Military History: A Bibliography; Part II, The Civil War by Dan A. Nettling (US Army Military History Institute, 1992)

Pennsylvania's Second Year at War: December 7, 1942-December 7, 1943 by S.K. Stevens, et al. (Pennsylvania Historical and Museum Commission, 1945)

Record of Pennsylvania Volunteers in the Spanish-American War, 1898, 2nd edition, by Thomas J. Stewart (William Stanley Ray, 1901)

☞PROBATE RECORDS

Documents Relative to the Colonial History of the State of New York: Procured in Holland, England, and France edited by E.B. O'Callaghan (Weed, Parsons & Co., Print, 1853-1887)

Guide to Records of the Court of Common Pleas, Chester County, Pennsylvania, 1681-1900 by Lynn Ann Catanese (Chester County Historical Society, 1987)

Guide to Records of the Court of Quarter Sessions, Chester County, Pennsylvania, 1681-1969 by Lynn Ann Catanese (Chester County Historical Society, 1988)

Pennsylvania in the 1700's: An Index to Who Was There and Where by Donna Beers (D. Beers, 1998)

Registrar's Book of Governor Keith's Court of Chancery of the Province of Pennsylvania, 1720-1735 (Pennsylvania Bar Association, 1941)

☞VITAL RECORDS

Abstracts (Mainly Deaths) From the Pennsylvania Gazette, 1775-1783 by Kenneth Scott (Genealogical Publishing Co., 1976)

Catholic Vital Records of Central Pennsylvania, 4 vols., by Albert H. Ledoux (A.H. Ledoux, 1993-1996)

Cemetery Records of Pennsylvania, 9 vols., (filmed by the Genealogical Society of Utah, 1946-1968)

Coroner's Views and Inquisitions, 1710-1906; Index, 1722-1946 from the Bucks County, Pa., Coroner (filmed by the Family History Library, 1973)

Early Pennsylvania Births: 1675-1875 by Charles Adam Fisher (1947; Genealogical Publishing Co., 1979)

Inventory of Vital Statistics Within Each County (Historical Records Survey)

Pennsylvania Marriages Prior to 1790 (Reprint: Genealogical Publishing Co., 1968)

Pennsylvania Vital Records From the Pennsylvania Genealogical Magazine and the Pennsylvania Magazine of History and Biography, 3 vols., (Genealogical Publishing Co., 1983)

•-COUNTY DETAILS-•

ADAMS
111 Baltimore St., Gettysburg, PA 17325, (717) 334-6781, **<www.adamscounty.us>**
- **INCORPORATED:** Jan. 22, 1800
- **PARENT COUNTY:** York
- **MARRIAGE RECORDS:** start in 1893, Clerk of Court
- **DIVORCE:** start in 1800, Prothonotary Office
- **PROBATE:** 1800, Register of Wills
- **COURT:** 1800, Prothonotary Office
- **NOTES:** Clerk of Courts has birth and death records 1852-1855, 1893-1905, and marriage records 1852-1855, 1893. Register/Recorder has land records 1800-1937.

ALLEGHENY
414 Grant St., Pittsburgh, PA 15219, (412) 350-4188 **<www.county.allegheny.pa.us>**
- **INCORPORATED:** Sept. 24, 1788
- **PARENT COUNTIES:** Westmoreland, Washington
- **DIVORCE RECORDS:** Prothonotary Office
- **LAND:** start in 1787, Recorder of Deeds
- **PROBATE:** 1789, Registrar of Wills
- **COURT:** Clerk of Court
- **NOTES:** Pennsylvania Room of the Carnegie Main Library has birth records 1852-1854. Registrar of Wills has birth records 1893-1905, death records 1870-1905, naturalization records 1798-1891, and marriage records 1885-1925. Pennsylvania State Archives has land records 1788-1904.

ARMSTRONG
500 E. Market St., Kittanning, PA 16201, (724) 543-2500, **<co.armstrong.pa.us>**
- **INCORPORATED:** March 12, 1800
- **PARENT COUNTIES:** Allegheny, Lycoming, Westmoreland
- **MARRIAGE RECORDS:** start in 1885, County Recorder/Registrar
- **LAND:** 1805, County Recorder/Registrar
- **PROBATE:** 1805, County Recorder/Registrar
- **NOTES:** County Recorder/Registrar has birth and death records 1893-1905.

BEAVER
810 Third St., Beaver, PA 15009, (724) 728-5700, **<www.beavercountypa.gov>**
- **INCORPORATED:** March 12, 1800
- **PARENT COUNTIES:** Allegheny, Washington
- **DIVORCE:** start in 1802, Clerk of Courts
- **LAND:** 1800, Recorder of Deeds
- **PROBATE:** 1800, Registrar of Wills
- **COURT:** 1802, Clerk of Courts
- **NATURALIZATION:** 1800, Prothonotary
- **MILITARY:** 1862, Veterans Office
- **NOTES:** Registrar of Wills has birth records 1893-1906, marriage records 1852-1854, 1886, and death records 1893-1906, 1893-1906.

BEDFORD
203 S. Juliana St., Bedford, PA 15522, (814) 623-4833, **<www.bedfordcounty.net>**
- **INCORPORATED:** March 9, 1771
- **PARENT COUNTY:** Cumberland
- **DIVORCE:** start in 1804, Prothonotary
- **LAND:** 1771, Recorder of Deeds
- **COURT:** 1771, Prothonotary
- **MILITARY:** 1777, Prothonotary
- **NOTES:** Prothonotary has birth and death records 1852-1854, 1894-1906, marriage records 1852-1854, 1885-1963, and naturalization records 1802-1934. State Archives has military records 1775-1791.

BERKS
633 Court St., Reading, PA 19601, (610) 478-6136, **<www.co.berks.pa.us>**
- **INCORPORATED:** March 11, 1752
- **PARENT COUNTIES:** Lancaster, Philadelphia, Chester
- **MARRIAGE RECORDS:** start in 1885, Registrar of Wills
- **LAND:** 1752, Recorder of Deeds
- **NATURALIZATION:** 1795, Prothonotary
- **NOTES:** Registrar of Wills has birth records 1876-1906, death records 1852-1855, 1876-1906, and probate records 1752-1914. Prothonotary Office has divorce records 1754-1950 and court records 1754-1950, 1770-1956.

BLAIR
423 Allegheny St., Hollidaysburg, PA 16648, (814) 695-5541, **<blair.pacounties.org>**
- **INCORPORATED:** Feb. 20, 1848
- **PARENT COUNTIES:** Huntingdon, Bedford
- **MARRIAGE RECORDS:** start in 1885, Prothonotary
- **DIVORCE:** 1846, Prothonotary
- **PROBATE:** 1846, Prothonotary
- **COURT:** 1846, Prothonotary
- **NATURALIZATION:** 1848, Prothonotary
- **NOTES:** Prothonotary Office has birth and death records 1893-1905.

BRADFORD
301 Main St., Towanda, PA 18848, (570) 265-1727, **<www.bradfordcountypa.org>**
- **INCORPORATED:** Feb. 21, 1810
- **PARENT COUNTIES:** Luzerne, Lycoming
- **MARRIAGE RECORDS:** start in 1885, Registrar/Recorder
- **DIVORCE:** 1878, Prothonotary/Clerk of Courts
- **LAND:** 1812, Registrar/Recorder
- **PROBATE:** 1812, Registrar/Recorder
- **COURT:** 1812, Prothonotary/Clerk of Courts
- **MILITARY:** 1940, Registrar/Recorder
- **NOTES:** Registrar/Recorder has birth and death records 1893-1905. Prothonotary/Clerk of Courts has naturalization records 1832-1960. Formerly Ontario County. Name changed to Bradford March 24, 1812.

BUCKS
55 E. Court St., Doylestown, PA 18901, (215) 348-6000,
<www.buckscounty.org>
- **INCORPORATED:** March 10, 1682
- **PARENT COUNTY:** original county
- **NOTES:** Registrar of Wills/Orphan's Court has birth records 1893-1906, 1852-1854, death records 1852-1855, 1893-1906, marriage records 1812-1842, 1852-1859, 1885-1906, military records 1776-1802, and probate records 1682-1906. Prothonotary has court records 1733-1923, divorce records 1733-1923, and naturalization records 1802-1906. Recorder of Deeds has land records 1684-1866.

BUTLER
124 W. Diamond St., Box 1208, Butler, PA 16001, (724) 285-4731,
<www.co.butler.pa.us>
- **INCORPORATED:** March 12, 1800
- **PARENT COUNTY:** Allegheny
- **DIVORCE RECORDS:** start in 1805, Prothonotary
- **LAND:** 1804, Recorder of Deeds
- **NOTES:** Registrar of Wills has birth and death records 1893-1906, marriage records 1885, 1893-1905, and probate records 1800-1971. Prothonotary has court records 1804-1866 and naturalization records 1804-1903.

CAMBRIA
200 S. Center St., Box 298, Edensburg, PA 15931, (814) 472-1440,
<www.co.cambria.pa.us>
- **INCORPORATED:** March 26, 1804
- **PARENT COUNTIES:** Somerset, Bedford, Huntingdon
- **MARRIAGE RECORDS:** start in 1885, Registrar of Wills
- **DIVORCE:** 1866, Prothonotary
- **LAND:** 1804, Recorder of Deeds
- **PROBATE:** 1805, Registrar of Wills
- **COURT:** 1849, Clerk of Courts
- **NOTES:** Registrar of Wills has birth and death records 1893-1906. Prothonotary has naturalization records 1835-1906.

CAMERON
20 E. Fifth St., Emporium, PA 15834, (814) 486-2315,
<www.cameroncountypa.com>
- **INCORPORATED:** March 29, 1860
- **PARENT COUNTIES:** Clinton, Elk, McKean, Potter
- **MARRIAGE RECORDS:** start in 1860, County Clerk
- **DIVORCE:** 1860, County Clerk
- **LAND:** 1860, County Clerk
- **PROBATE:** 1860, County Clerk
- **COURT:** 1860, County Clerk
- **NATURALIZATION:** 1860, County Clerk
- **NOTES:** County Clerk has birth records 1894-1906 and death records 1860-1905.

CARBON
Box 129, Jim Thorpe, PA 18229, (570) 325-3637,
<www.carboncounty.com>
- **INCORPORATED:** March 13, 1843
- **PARENT COUNTIES:** Northampton, Monroe
- **MARRIAGE RECORDS:** start in 1885, Courthouse Archivist/Records Coordinator
- **DIVORCE:** 1843, Courthouse Archivist/Records Coordinator
- **LAND:** 1843, Recorder of Deeds
- **PROBATE:** 1843, County Clerk
- **COURT:** 1843, Courthouse Archivist/Records Coordinator
- **NOTES:** Courthouse Archivist/Records Coordinator has birth records 1892-1905, death records 1894-1905, naturalization records 1843-1958, and probate records 1843-1990.

CENTRE
County Courthouse, Bellefonte, PA 16823, (814) 355-6724,
<www.co.centre.pa.us>
- **INCORPORATED:** Feb. 13, 1800
- **PARENT COUNTIES:** Lycoming, Mifflin, Northumberland
- **MARRIAGE RECORDS:** 1885, Registrar of Wills/Clerk of Orphans' Court
- **DIVORCE:** 1890, Prothonotary
- **LAND:** 1801, Recorder of Deeds
- **PROBATE:** 1800, Registrar of Wills
- **COURT:** 1800, Prothonotary
- **NATURALIZATION:** 1800, Prothonotary
- **NOTES:** Registrar of Wills/Clerk of Orphan's Court has birth and death records 1893-1905.

CHESTER
2 N. High St., Box 2748, West Chester, PA 19380, (610) 344-6000,
<www.chesco.org>
- **INCORPORATED:** March 10, 1682
- **PARENT COUNTY:** original county
- **MARRIAGE RECORDS:** start in 1931, Clerk of Orphans' Court
- **PROBATE:** 1923, Registrar of Wills
- **NOTES:** County Archives has birth and death records 1852-1855, 1893-1906, court records 1681-1900, divorce records 1681-1900, land records 1688-1905, marriage records 1852-1855, 1885-1930, naturalization records 1798-1989, probate records 1714-1923, and tax records 1715-1939.

CLARION
421 Main St., Clarion, PA 16214, (814) 226-4000,
<www.co.clarion.pa.us>
- **INCORPORATED:** March 11, 1839
- **PARENT COUNTIES:** Venango, Armstrong
- **MARRIAGE RECORDS:** start in 1885, Registrar/Recorder
- **DIVORCE:** start in 1880, Prothonotary
- **LAND:** 1840, Registrar/Recorder
- **PROBATE:** 1840, Registrar/Recorder
- **COURT:** 1874, Prothonotary
- **NOTES:** Registrar/Recorder has birth records 1893-1906, death records 1852-1854, 1893-1906, and marriage records 1852-1854.

CLEARFIELD
230 Market St., Box 549, Clearfield, PA 16830, (814) 765-2641,
<www.clearfieldco.org>
- **INCORPORATED:** March 26, 1804
- **PARENT COUNTY:** Huntingdon, Lycoming
- **MARRIAGE RECORDS:** start in 1885, County Registrar/Recorder
- **DIVORCE:** 1828, Prothonotary

- **LAND:** 1805, County Commissioner
- **PROBATE:** 1875, County Recorder
- **COURT:** 1828, Prothonotary
- **NOTES:** County Registrar/Recorder have birth and death records 1893-1905.

CLINTON

230 E. Water St., Lock Haven, PA 17745, (570) 893-4010, **<www.clintoncountypa.com>**

- **INCORPORATED:** June 21, 1839
- **PARENT COUNTIES:** Lycoming, Centre
- **MARRIAGE RECORDS:** start in 1885, County Registrar/Recorder
- **DIVORCE:** 1839, Prothonotary
- **LAND:** County Registrar/Recorder
- **PROBATE:** County Registrar/Recorder
- **COURT:** Prothonotary
- **NOTES:** County Registrar/Recorder has birth and death records 1893-1905. Prothonotary has naturalization records 1839-1982.

COLUMBIA

35 W. Main St., Box 380, Bloomsburg, PA 17815, (570) 389-5614, **<www.columbiapa.org>**

- **INCORPORATED:** March 22, 1813
- **PARENT COUNTY:** Northumberland
- **DIVORCE:** start in 1814, Prothonotary
- **COURT:** 1814, Prothonotary
- **NOTES:** Prothonotary has birth and death records 1893-1905 and marriage records 1885-1907. Columbia County Genealogy Society has death and marriage records 1837-1870.

CRAWFORD

903 Diamond Park, Meadville, PA 16335, (814) 333-7300, **<www.crawfordcountypa.net>**

- **INCORPORATED:** March 12, 1800
- **PARENT COUNTY:** Allegheny
- **MARRIAGE RECORDS:** start in 1885, Clerk of Courts
- **DIVORCE:** start in 1800, Prothonotary
- **LAND:** 1800, Registrar/Recorder
- **PROBATE:** 1800, Registrar/Recorder
- **COURT:** 1800, County Clerk
- **NOTES:** Clerk of Courts has birth records 1893-1905, court records 1800-1859, death records 1852-1854, 1893-1905, and marriage records 1852-1854.

CUMBERLAND

1 Courthouse Sq., Carlisle, PA 17013, (717) 240-6100, **<www.ccpa.net>**

- **INCORPORATED:** Jan. 27, 1750
- **PARENT COUNTY:** Lancaster
- **MARRIAGE RECORDS:** start in 1885, Registrar of Wills
- **DIVORCE:** 1751, Prothonotary
- **LAND:** 1751, Recorder of Deeds
- **PROBATE:** 1750, Registrar of Wills
- **COURT:** 1750, Registrar of Wills
- **NOTES:** Registrar of Wills has birth and death records 1894-1906.

DAUPHIN

101 Market St., Room 103, Harrisburg, PA 17101, (717) 255-6323, **<www.dauphincounty.org>**

- **INCORPORATED:** March 4, 1785
- **PARENT COUNTY:** Lancaster
- **DIVORCE RECORDS:** start in 1785, Prothonotary
- **LAND:** 1785, Recorder of Deeds
- **PROBATE:** 1785, Registrar of Wills/Orphans' Court
- **COURT:** 1785, Prothonotary
- **NOTES:** Registrar of Wills/Clerk of Orphan's Court has birth records 1852-1854, 1893-1906, death records 1852-1855, 1893-1906, and marriage records 1852-1855.

DELAWARE

201 W. Front St., Media, PA 19063, (610) 891-4000, **<www.co.delaware.pa.us>**

- **INCORPORATED:** Sept. 26, 1789
- **PARENT COUNTY:** Chester
- **MARRIAGE RECORDS:** start in 1885, Registrar of Wills/Orphans' Court
- **DIVORCE:** 1927, Prothonotary
- **LAND:** 1789, Recorder of Deeds
- **PROBATE:** 1790, Registrar of Wills/Orphans' Court
- **COURT:** 1897, Prothonotary
- **ORPHANS' COURT:** 1865, County Clerk
- **NOTES:** Registrar of Wills/Clerk of Orphan's Court has birth and death records 1893-1906. County Clerk has delayed birth records 1875-1900.

ELK

240 Main St., Box 314, Ridgway, PA 15853, (814) 776-5349, **<www.co.elk.pa.us>**

- **INCORPORATED:** April 18, 1843
- **PARENT COUNTIES:** Jefferson, McKean, Clearfield
- **MARRIAGE RECORDS:** start in 1885, Registrar/Recorder
- **DIVORCE:** 1844, Prothonotary
- **LAND:** 1844, Registrar/Recorder
- **PROBATE:** 1844, Registrar/Recorder
- **COURT:** 1844, Prothonotary
- **NOTES:** Registrar/Recorder has birth and death records 1893-1906.

ERIE

140 W. Sixth St., Erie, PA 16501, (814) 451-6000, **<www.eriecountygov.org>**

- **INCORPORATED:** March 12, 1800
- **PARENT COUNTY:** Allegheny
- **MARRIAGE RECORDS:** start in 1885, Clerk of Records
- **DIVORCE:** 1823, Prothonotary
- **LAND:** 1823, Recorder of Deeds
- **PROBATE:** 1823, Registrar of Wills
- **COURT:** 1823, Prothonotary
- **NOTES:** Clerk of Records has birth and death records 1893-1906. Courthouse burned in 1823; all records destroyed.

FAYETTE

61 E. Main St., Uniontown, PA 15401, (724) 430-1206, **<www.co.fayette.pa.us>**

- **INCORPORATED:** Sept. 26, 1783

- **PARENT COUNTY:** Westmoreland
- **MARRIAGE RECORDS:** start in 1885, Clerk of Orphans' Court
- **DIVORCE:** 1784, Prothonotary
- **LAND:** 1784, Recorder of Deeds
- **PROBATE:** 1784, Registrar of Wills
- **COURT:** 1784, Prothonotary
- **NOTES:** Clerk of Orphans Court has birth and death records 1893-1905.

FOREST
526 Elm St., Box 2, Tionesta, PA 16353, (814) 755-3526,
<www.forestcounty.com>
- **INCORPORATED:** April 11, 1848
- **PARENT COUNTY:** Jefferson
- **MARRIAGE RECORDS:** start in 1885, Prothonotary
- **DIVORCE:** 1857, Prothonotary
- **LAND:** 1857, Prothonotary
- **NOTES:** Prothonotary has birth records 1893-1906 and death records 1893-1907.

FRANKLIN
157 Lincoln Way E, Chambersburg, PA 17201, (717) 261-3810,
<www.co.franklin.pa.us>
- **INCORPORATED:** Sept. 9, 1784
- **PARENT COUNTY:** Cumberland
- **MARRIAGE RECORDS:** 1885, County Clerk
- **DIVORCE:** 1884, County Clerk
- **LAND:** 1785, Registrar/Recorder
- **PROBATE:** 1785, Registrar/Recorder
- **NOTES:** County Clerk has birth and death records 1894-1906.

FULTON
201 N. Second St., McConnellsburg, PA 17233, (717) 485-4212,
<www.co.fulton.pa.us>
- **INCORPORATED:** April 19, 1851
- **PARENT COUNTY:** Bedford
- **MARRIAGE RECORDS:** start in 1885, Clerk of Orphans' Court
- **DIVORCE:** start in 1850, Prothonotary
- **LAND:** 1850, Recorder of Deeds
- **PROBATE:** 1850, Registrar of Wills
- **COURT:** 1850, Prothonotary
- **ORPHANS' COURT:** 1850, Clerk of Orphans' Court
- **NOTES:** Clerk of Orphans Court has birth records 1895-1905, death records 1852-1854, 1895-1905, and marriage records 1852-1854.

GREENE
93 E. High St., Waynesburg, PA 15370, (724) 852-5281,
<www.co.greene.pa.us>
- **INCORPORATED:** Feb. 9, 1796
- **PARENT COUNTY:** Washington
- **MARRIAGE RECORDS:** start in 1885, Registrar/Recorder
- **DIVORCE:** 1816, Prothonotary
- **LAND:** 1796, Registrar/Recorder
- **PROBATE:** 1796, Registrar/Recorder
- **COURT:** 1797, Prothonotary
- **NOTES:** Prothonotary has birth and death records 1893-1915.

HUNTINGDON
223 Penn St., Box 39, Huntingdon, PA 16652, (814) 643-3091,
<www.huntingdoncounty.net>
- **INCORPORATED:** Sept. 20. 1787
- **PARENT COUNTY:** Bedford
- **MARRIAGE RECORDS:** start in 1885, Registrar/Recorder
- **DIVORCE:** 1787, Prothonotary
- **PROBATE:** 1787, Registrar/Recorder
- **COURT:** 1787, Prothonotary
- **NOTES:** Registrar/Recorder Clerk has birth records 1894-1906 and death records 1894-1905.

INDIANA
825 Philadelphia St., Indiana, PA 15701, (724) 465-3860,
<www.countyofindiana.org>
- **INCORPORATED:** March 30, 1803
- **PARENT COUNTIES:** Westmoreland, Lycoming
- **MARRIAGE RECORDS:** start in 1887, Registrar/Recorder
- **DIVORCE:** start in 1807, Prothonotary
- **LAND:** 1807, Registrar/Recorder
- **PROBATE:** 1807, Registrar/Recorder
- **COURT:** 1807, Prothonotary
- **NOTES:** Registrar/Recorder has birth and death records 1852-1855, 1893-1906, marriage records 1852-1855. Prothonotary has naturalization records 1807-1959.

JEFFERSON
155 Main St., Brookville, PA 15825, (814) 849-1610,
<www.jeffersoncountypa.com>
- **INCORPORATED:** March 26, 1804
- **PARENT COUNTY:** Lycoming
- **MARRIAGE RECORDS:** start in 1885, Registrar/Recorder
- **DIVORCE:** start in 1885, Prothonotary/Clerk of Courts
- **LAND:** 1828, Registrar/Recorder
- **PROBATE:** 1830, Registrar/Recorder
- **COURT:** 1940, Prothonotary/Clerk of Courts
- **NOTES:** Registrar/Recorder has birth and death records 1893-1906, and marriage records 1852-1855.

JUNIATA
Bridge and Main streets, Box 68, Mifflintown, PA 17059, (717) 436-8991, **<www.co.juniata.pa.us>**
- **INCORPORATED:** March 2, 1831
- **PARENT COUNTY:** Mifflin
- **MARRIAGE RECORDS:** start in 1885, County Clerk
- **DIVORCE:** 1900, County Clerk
- **LAND:** 1831, County Clerk
- **PROBATE:** 1831, County Clerk
- **COURT:** 1831, County Clerk
- **NOTES:** County Clerk has birth records 1893-1907, death records 1852-1878, 1893-1907, naturalization records early 1800-1930. Juniata County Historical Society has marriage records 1800-1995.

LACKAWANNA
200 N. Washington Ave., Scranton, PA 18503, (570) 963-6723,
<www.lackawannacounty.org>
- **INCORPORATED:** Aug. 21, 1878
- **PARENT COUNTY:** Luzerne

- **MARRIAGE RECORDS:** start in 1885, marriage License Bureau
- **DIVORCE:** 1878, Clerk of Judicial Records
- **LAND:** 1878, Recorder of Deeds
- **PROBATE:** 1878, Registrar of Wills
- **COURT:** 1878, Clerk of Judicial Records
- **NOTES:** Registrar of Wills has birth and death records 1893-1905. Clerk of Judicial Records has naturalization records.

LANCASTER

50 N. Duke St., Box 3480, Lancaster, PA 17603, (717) 299-8319,
<www.co.lancaster.pa.us>

- **INCORPORATED:** May 10, 1729
- **PARENT COUNTY:** Chester
- **MARRIAGE RECORDS:** start in 1885, Office of Records
- **DIVORCE:** Office of Records
- **LAND:** 1729, Office of Records
- **PROBATE:** 1729, Office of Records
- **COURT:** 1729, Office of Records
- **ORPHANS' COURT:** 1742, Office of Records
- **NOTES:** Registrar of Wills has birth records 1881-1906. Office of Records has death records 1894-1927.

LAWRENCE

430 Court St., New Castle, PA 16101, (724) 656-2541,
<www.co.lawrence.pa.us>

- **INCORPORATED:** March 20, 1849
- **PARENT COUNTIES:** Beaver, Mercer
- **MARRIAGE RECORDS:** start in 1885, Prothonotary
- **DIVORCE:** 1885, Prothonotary
- **LAND:** 1849, Registrar/Recorder
- **PROBATE:** 1849, Registrar/Recorder
- **COURT:** 1855, Prothonotary
- **NOTES:** Prothonotary has birth and death records 1893-1905.

LEBANON

400 S. Eighth St., Lebanon, PA 17042, (717) 274-2801,
<www.lebcounty.org>

- **INCORPORATED:** Feb. 16, 1813
- **PARENT COUNTIES:** Lancaster, Dauphin
- **MARRIAGE RECORDS:** start in 1885, Registrar of Wills
- **DIVORCE:** 1888, Prothonotary
- **PROBATE:** 1813, Registrar of Wills
- **NOTES:** Registrar of Wills has birth records 1893-1906.

LEHIGH

455 W. Hamilton St., Allentown, PA 18101, (610) 782-3148,
<www.lehighcounty.org>

- **INCORPORATED:** March 6, 1812
- **PARENT COUNTY:** Northampton
- **MARRIAGE RECORDS:** start in 1885, Clerk of Orphans' Court
- **DIVORCE:** 1812, Clerk of Courts
- **LAND:** 1812, Recorder of Deeds
- **PROBATE:** 1812, Registrar of Wills
- **COURT:** 1812, Clerk of Courts
- **NOTES:** Clerk of Orphans Court has birth records 1895-1905, death records 1893-1904.

LUZERNE

200 N. River St., Wilkes-Barre, PA 18702, (570) 825-1585,
<www.luzernecounty.org>

- **INCORPORATED:** Sept. 25, 1786
- **PARENT COUNTY:** Northumberland
- **MARRIAGE RECORDS:** start in 1885, Registrar of Wills
- **DIVORCE:** 1878, Prothonotary
- **LAND:** 1876, Recorder of Deeds
- **PROBATE:** 1786, Registrar of Wills
- **COURT:** 1878, Prothonotary
- **NOTES:** Registrar of Wills has birth and death records 1890-1906.

LYCOMING

48 W. Third St., Williamsport, PA 17701, (570) 327-2200,
<www.lyco.org>

- **INCORPORATED:** April 13, 1795
- **PARENT COUNTY:** Northumberland
- **MARRIAGE RECORDS:** start in 1885, Registrar/Recorder
- **DIVORCE:** 1795, Prothonotary
- **LAND:** 1795, Registrar/Recorder
- **PROBATE:** 1850, Registrar/Recorder
- **COURT:** 1795, Prothonotary
- **NOTES:** Registrar/Recorder has birth records 1893-1905 and death records 1893-1898. Prothonotary has naturalization records 1804-1956. The James V. Brown Library, 19 E. Fourth St., Williamsport, Pa., is the major source of Lycoming County genealogical information.

MCKEAN

500 W. Main St., Box 273, Smethport, PA 16749, (814) 887-3270,
<www.mckeancountypa.org>

- **INCORPORATED:** March 26, 1804
- **PARENT COUNTY:** Lycoming
- **MARRIAGE RECORDS:** start in 1885, Registrar of Wills
- **DIVORCE:** 1804, Prothonotary
- **LAND:** 1804, Recorder of Deeds
- **PROBATE:** 1827, Registrar of Wills
- **COURT:** 1804, Prothonotary
- **NOTES:** Registrar of Wills has birth and death records 1892-1905.

MERCER

112 Mercer County Courthouse, Mercer, PA 16137, (724) 662-3800,
<www.mcc.co.mercer.pa.us>

- **INCORPORATED:** March 12, 1800
- **PARENT COUNTY:** Allegheny
- **MARRIAGE RECORDS:** start in 1885, County Clerk
- **DIVORCE:** Prothonotary No dates
- **LAND:** 1800, Recorder of Deeds
- **PROBATE:** 1800, Registrar of Wills
- **COURT:** Prothonotary No dates
- **NOTES:** Clerk of Orphan's Court has birth records 1893-1905. Registrar of Wills has death records 1893-1905. County courthouse does not research records.

MIFFLIN

20 N. Wayne St., Lewistown, PA 17044, (717) 248-6733,
<www.co.mifflin.pa.us>

- **INCORPORATED:** Sept. 19, 1789

- **PARENT COUNTIES:** Cumberland, Northumberland
- **MARRIAGE RECORDS:** start in 1885, Registrar/Recorder
- **NOTES:** Registrar/Recorder has birth records 1853,1854, 1893-1905, 1941-1969, death records 1852-1855, 1896-1905, land records 1789-1953, marriage records 1852-1853, and probate records 1789-1899. Prothonotary Office has court and divorce records 1792-1809, 1826-1834.

MONROE

7 Monroe St., Stroudsburg, PA 18360, (570) 517-3370, **<www.co.monroe.pa.us>**

- **INCORPORATED:** April 1, 1836
- **PARENT COUNTIES:** Pike, Northampton
- **MARRIAGE RECORDS:** start in 1885, County Clerk
- **DIVORCE:** 1900, County Clerk
- **LAND:** 1836, Recorder of Deeds
- **PROBATE:** Registrar of Wills No dates
- **COURT:** 1845, County Clerk
- **NOTES:** Prothonotary has birth records 1892-1905.

MONTGOMERY

County Court House, Airy and Swede streets, Box 311, Norristown, PA 19404, (610) 278-3360, **<www.montcopa.org>**

- **INCORPORATED:** Sept. 10, 1784
- **PARENT COUNTY:** Philadelphia
- **MARRIAGE RECORDS:** start in 1885, County Records
- **DIVORCE:** start in 1784, Prothonotary
- **LAND:** 1784, County Records
- **PROBATE:** 1784, County Records
- **COURT:** 1784, Prothonotary Office
- **NOTES:** County Records Department has birth and death records 1852-1855, 1893-1913 and marriage records 1852-1855.

MONTOUR

29 Mill St., Danville, PA 17821, (570) 271-3012, **<www.montourco.org>**

- **INCORPORATED:** May 3, 1850
- **PARENT COUNTY:** Columbia
- **MARRIAGE RECORDS:** start in 1885, Prothonotary
- **DIVORCE:** 1850, Prothonotary
- **LAND:** 1850, Recorder of Deeds
- **PROBATE:** 1850, Registrar/Recorder
- **COURT:** 1850, Prothonotary/Clerk of Courts
- **NOTES:** Prothonotary has birth and death records 1893-1905 and naturalization records 1850-1940.

NORTHAMPTON

669 Washington St., Easton, PA 18042, (610) 559-3000, **<www.northamptoncounty.org>**

- **INCORPORATED:** Oct. 14, 1751
- **PARENT COUNTY:** Bucks
- **MARRIAGE RECORDS:** start in 1885, County Archives
- **DIVORCE:** 1752, Prothonotary
- **LAND:** 1752, County Archives
- **PROBATE:** 1752, Registrar of Wills
- **COURT:** 1752, Prothonotary
- **NOTES:** Clerk of Orphans Court has birth and death records 1893-1936.

NORTHUMBERLAND

201 Market St., Sunbury, PA 17801, (570) 988-4100, **<www.northumberlandco.org>**

- **INCORPORATED:** March 21, 1772
- **PARENT COUNTIES:** Lancaster, Berks, Cumberland, Bedford, Northampton
- **MARRIAGE RECORDS:** start in 1885, Registrar/Recorder
- **DIVORCE:** 1772, Prothonotary
- **LAND:** 1772, Registrar/Recorder
- **PROBATE:** 1772, Registrar/Recorder
- **COURT:** 1772, Prothonotary Office
- **NOTES:** Registrar/Recorder has birth and death records 1893-1905.

ONTARIO

- **INCORPORATED:** Feb. 21, 1810
- **PARENT COUNTIES:** Luzerne, Lycoming
- **NOTES:** See Bradford County. Name changed to Bradford March 24, 1812.

PERRY

25 W. Main St., Box 37, New Bloomfield, PA 17068, (717) 582-2131, **<www.perryco.org>**

- **INCORPORATED:** March 22, 1820
- **PARENT COUNTY:** Cumberland
- **LAND RECORDS:** start in 1820, Registrar/Recorder
- **PROBATE:** 1820, Registrar/Recorder
- **NOTES:** Registrar/Recorder has birth records 1893-1918, death records 1894-1914, and marriage records 1870-1885.

PHILADELPHIA

3101 Market St., 19104, (215) 685-9400, **<www.phila.gov/Records/Archives/Archives.html>**

- **INCORPORATED:** March 10, 1682
- **PARENT COUNTY:** original county
- **MARRIAGE RECORDS:** start in 1885, Clerk of Orphans' Court
- **PROBATE:** Registrar of Wills
- **NOTES:** Philadelphia City Archives has birth records 1860-1915, court records 1810-1811, 1819-1874, divorce records 1851-1875, land records 1683-1952, and naturalization records 1793-1930.

PIKE

412 Broad St., Milford, PA 18337, (570) 296-7231, **<www.pikepa.org>**

- **INCORPORATED:** March 26, 1814
- **PARENT COUNTY:** Wayne
- **MARRIAGE RECORDS:** start in 1664, Prothonotary
- **DIVORCE:** 1814, Prothonotary
- **LAND:** 1814, Prothonotary
- **PROBATE:** 1814, Prothonotary
- **COURT:** 1814, Prothonotary
- **NOTES:** Prothonotary has birth and death records 1893-1905.

POTTER

1 E. Second St., Coudersport, PA 16915, (814) 274-9740, **<www.pottercountypa.net>**

- **INCORPORATED:** March 26, 1804
- **PARENT COUNTY:** Lycoming
- **MARRIAGE RECORDS:** start in 1885, Prothonotary

- **DIVORCE:** 1885, Prothonotary
- **LAND:** Registrar/Recorder No dates
- **PROBATE:** Registrar/Recorder No dates
- **NOTES:** Prothonotary has birth, death, and burial records 1893-1905.

SCHUYLKILL

401 N. Second St., Pottsville, PA 17901, (570) 622-5570, **<www.co.schuylkill.pa.us>**

- **INCORPORATED:** March 1, 1811
- **PARENT COUNTIES:** Berks, Northampton
- **MARRIAGE RECORDS:** start in 1885, Registrar of Wills
- **DIVORCE:** 1878, County Archives
- **LAND:** 1811, Recorder of Deeds
- **PROBATE:** 1811, Registrar of Wills
- **COURT:** 1811, County Archives
- **NOTES:** Registrar of Wills has birth and death records 1893-1905. County Archives has naturalization records 1828-1988.

SNYDER

9 W. Market St., Box 217, Middleburg, PA 17842, (570) 837-4208, **<www.snydercounty.org>**

- **INCORPORATED:** March 2, 1855
- **PARENT COUNTY:** Union
- **MARRIAGE RECORDS:** start in 1885, Prothonotary
- **DIVORCE:** 1855, Prothonotary
- **LAND:** 1855, County Registrar/Recorder
- **PROBATE:** 1855, County Registrar/Recorder
- **COURT:** 1855, Prothonotary
- **NOTES:** Prothonotary has birth and death records 1893-1905. Susquehanna University Library in Selinsgrove has Census records for 1910 and 1920.

SOMERSET

111 E. Union St., Somerset, PA 15501, (814) 445-1428, **<www.co.somerset.pa.us>**

- **INCORPORATED:** April 17, 1795
- **PARENT COUNTY:** Bedford
- **MARRIAGE RECORDS:** start in 1885, Registrar of Wills
- **DIVORCE:** 1795, Prothonotary Office
- **LAND:** 1795, Recorder of Deeds
- **PROBATE:** 1795, Registrar of Wills
- **COURT:** 1795, Prothonotary
- **MILITARY:** 1865, Recorder of Deeds
- **NOTES:** Registrar of Wills has birth and death records 1893-1906. Prothonotary Office has naturalization records 1795-1955.

SULLIVAN

Main and Muncy streets, Laporte, PA 18626, (570) 946-5201, **<www.sullivancounty-pa.us>**

- **INCORPORATED:** March 15, 1847
- **PARENT COUNTY:** Lycoming
- **MARRIAGE RECORDS:** start in 1874, Prothonotary
- **DIVORCE:** 1847, Prothonotary
- **LAND:** 1847, Prothonotary
- **PROBATE:** 1847, Prothonotary
- **COURT:** 1847, Prothonotary
- **NOTES:** Prothonotary has birth and death records 1893-1905.

SUSQUEHANNA

11 Maple St., Box 218, Montrose, PA 18801, (570) 278-4600, **<www.susqco.com>**

- **INCORPORATED:** Feb. 21, 1810
- **PARENT COUNTY:** Luzerne
- **MARRIAGE RECORDS:** start in 1885, Registrar/Recorder
- **DIVORCE:** 1877, Prothonotary
- **LAND:** 1810, Registrar/Recorder
- **PROBATE:** 1810, Registrar/Recorder
- **COURT:** 1812, Prothonotary
- **MILITARY:** 1918, Registrar/Recorder
- **NOTES:** Registrar/Recorder have birth and death records 1893-1905. Prothonotary has naturalization records 1844-1956.

TIOGA

118 Main St., Wellsboro, PA 16901, (717) 723-8191, **<www.seda-cog.org/tioga>**

- **INCORPORATED:** March 26, 1804
- **PARENT COUNTY:** Lycoming
- **MARRIAGE RECORDS:** start in 1885, Registrar/Recorder
- **DIVORCE:** 1813, Prothonotary
- **LAND:** 1807, Registrar/Recorder
- **PROBATE:** 1803, Registrar/Recorder
- **COURT:** 1813, Prothonotary
- **NATURALIZATION:** 1818, Prothonotary
- **MILITARY:** 1868, Registrar/Recorder
- **ORPHANS' COURT:** 1812, Registrar/Recorder
- **NOTES:** Registrar/Recorder has birth and death records 1893-1905.

UNION

103 S. Second St., Lewisburg, PA 17837, (570) 524-8751, **<www.unioncountypa.org>**

- **INCORPORATED:** March 22, 1813
- **PARENT COUNTY:** Northumberland
- **MARRIAGE RECORDS:** start in 1885, Prothonotary
- **DIVORCE:** 1813, Prothonotary
- **LAND:** 1813, Registrar/Recorder
- **PROBATE:** 1813, Registrar/Recorder
- **COURT:** 1813, Prothonotary
- **NOTES:** Prothonotary has birth records 1893-1905.

VENANGO

1168 Liberty St., Franklin, PA 16323, (814) 432-9577, **<www.co.venango.pa.us>**

- **INCORPORATED:** March 12, 1800
- **PARENT COUNTIES:** Allegheny, Lycoming
- **MARRIAGE RECORDS:** start in 1885, Clerk of Courts/Recorder of Deeds
- **DIVORCE:** Clerk of Courts/Recorder of Deeds
- **LAND:** 1806, Clerk of Courts/Recorder of Deeds
- **PROBATE:** 1806, Clerk of Courts/Recorder of Deeds
- **COURT:** Clerk of Courts/Recorder of Deeds
- **NOTES:** Clerk of Courts/Recorder of Deeds have birth and death records 1893-1905.

WARREN
204 Fourth Ave., Warren, PA 16365, (814) 728-3440, **<www.warren-county.net>**
- **INCORPORATED:** March 12, 1800
- **PARENT COUNTIES:** Allegheny, Lycoming
- **MARRIAGE RECORDS:** start in 1885, Registrar/Recorder
- **DIVORCE:** ca. 1800, Prothonotary
- **LAND:** 1819, Registrar/Recorder
- **PROBATE:** 1819, Registrar/Recorder
- **COURT:** ca. 1800, Prothonotary
- **NOTES:** Registrar/Recorder has birth and death records 1893-1906.

WASHINGTON
1 S. Main St., Washington, PA 15301, (724) 228-6787, **<www.co.washington.pa.us>**
- **INCORPORATED:** March 28, 1781
- **PARENT COUNTY:** Westmoreland
- **MARRIAGE RECORDS:** start in 1885, Registrar of Wills
- **DIVORCE:** 1781, Prothonotary/Clerk of Courts
- **LAND:** 1781, Recorder of Deeds
- **PROBATE:** 1785, Registrar of Wills
- **COURT:** 1781, Prothonotary
- **MILITARY:** 1781, Recorder of Deeds
- **NOTES:** Registrar of Wills has birth and death records 1893-1906. Prothonotary has naturalization records 1802-1905, 1918-1984.

WAYNE
925 Court St., Honesdale, PA 18431, (570) 253-5970, **<www.co.wayne.pa.us>**
- **INCORPORATED:** March 21, 1798
- **PARENT COUNTY:** Northampton
- **MARRIAGE RECORDS:** start in 1885, Prothonotary
- **DIVORCE:** 1900, Prothonotary
- **LAND:** 1798, Recorder of Deeds
- **PROBATE:** 1798, Registrar of Wills
- **COURT:** 1798, Prothonotary
- **NOTES:** Prothonotary has birth and death records 1893-1906.

WESTMORELAND
2 N. Main St., Suite 203, Greensburg, PA 15601, (724) 830-3734, **<www.co.westmoreland.pa.us>**
- **INCORPORATED:** Feb. 26, 1773
- **PARENT COUNTY:** Bedford
- **MARRIAGE RECORDS:** start in 1885, County Clerk
- **DIVORCE:** 1893–1905, Registrar of Wills; Prothonotary Office
- **LAND:** 1773, Recorder of Deeds
- **PROBATE:** 1773, Registrar of Wills
- **COURT:** 1773, Clerk of Courts
- **NATURALIZATION:** 1804, Prothonotary
- **NOTES:** Registrar of Wills has birth and divorce records 1893-1905.

WYOMING
1 Courthouse Square, Tunkhannock, PA 18657, (570) 836-3200, **<www.adamscounty.us/wyoming>**
- **INCORPORATED:** April 4, 1842
- **PARENT COUNTY:** Luzerne
- **MARRIAGE RECORDS:** start in 1885, Prothonotary
- **DIVORCE:** 1842, Prothonotary
- **LAND:** 1842, Registrar of Wills/Recorder of Deeds
- **PROBATE:** 1842, Registrar of Wills/Recorder of Deeds
- **COURT:** 1842, Prothonotary
- **NOTES:** Prothonotary has birth and death records 1893-1906.

YORK
28 E. Market St., York, PA 17401, (717) 771-9675, **<www.york-county.org>**
- **INCORPORATED:** Aug. 19, 1749
- **PARENT COUNTY:** Lancaster
- **MARRIAGE RECORDS:** start in 1885, County Clerk
- **DIVORCE:** 1749, County Clerk; 1749-1989, County Archives
- **LAND:** 1749, Recorder of Deeds
- **PROBATE:** 1967, Registrar of Wills
- **COURT:** start in 1749, County Clerk; 1749–1989, County Archives
- **NOTES:** Clerk of Orphan's Court has birth and death records 1893-1906. County Archives has court and divorce records 1749-1989 and probate records 1749-1967. Prothonotary has naturalization records 1795-1992.

RHODE ISLAND

» BY MAUREEN A. TAYLOR

HISTORICAL OVERVIEW

Rhode Island is a small state with a long name—State of Rhode Island and Providence Plantations. The original four towns were clustered around Narragansett Bay. Roger Williams, a minister banished from Massachusetts Bay, established Providence. Another religious free thinker, Samuel Gorton, founded Warwick; Anne Hutchinson's followers settled in Portsmouth; and Thomas Coddington's devotees populated Newport. The colony became a haven for those seeking freedom to worship, attracting Baptists, French Huguenots and Calvinists, Jews and Quakers. King Philip's War of 1675 to 1676 devastated the colony and local Native Americans. At war's end, only a small tribe remained in what is now Charlestown. Both Massachusetts and Connecticut claimed ownership of parts of the colony in the 17th century.

In the 18th century, the close proximity of Narragansett Bay enabled Rhode Island traders to lead the Colonies in imports and exports. Many Rhode Island families today have connections in the West Indies due to the colony's prominence in the Triangle Trade of slaves, rum and sugar. Many inhabitants of coastal areas participated in whaling and fishing.

The American Industrial Revolution began with Samuel Slater, an English immigrant who built the first US factory for manufacturing cotton thread. Textile manufacturing attracted immigrants to towns such as Slatersville in waves—Irish, Scots, French-Canadians and Italians. Germans found employment in the jewelry and silver trades.

As the factories left, Rhode Islanders turned their coastline into a playground for the rich and famous. Today, tourism attracts visitors from all over the world.

RECORD HIGHLIGHTS

Rhode Island is a gold mine for genealogical research. Records date back to 1636, with most material located in two major repositories—the Rhode Island State Archives and the Rhode Island Historical Society.

Town governments maintained town meeting minutes, vital records, land transactions, and probate and tax valuations. Originals are located in town clerk's offices, but researchers also can find vital records on microfilm, transcribed in print, or online. Civil registration occurred in 1853, but discrepancies exist between those kept by the town and those submitted to the state. Prior to total compliance, cover-

research tips

- Know the history of your ancestral town or village. Town boundaries act as political divisions for record-keeping purposes, but individuals usually claim allegiance to one of the more than 100 villages in Rhode Island, not the town where they were born. Orientation is possible by using a gazetteer of place names for the state.
- Start your research at the Rhode Island Historical Society for the broadest possible selection of resources. Reference materials are open to the public, but use of the manuscript and photo departments requires an appointment.
- Once you've covered the resources in the major repositories, take your search to your ancestors' town. Outside the major cities, towns are small and you can easily connect with a town historian.
- Regardless of the time period you're researching, you'll discover basic sources and little-known collections to trace your family through Rhode Island's colorful past. This tiny state can be traversed in a day, enabling genealogists to visit town clerks, public libraries, and state repositories.

CENSUS RECORDS

- Federal census: 1790, 1800, 1810, 1820, 1830, 1840, 1850, 1860, 1870, 1880, 1900, 1910, 1920, 1930
- Special census of Civil War Union veterans and widows: 1890
- State census: 1865, 1875, 1885, 1905, 1915, 1925, 1935

age is spotty in the rural parts of the state, but you can fill the gaps with other types of documents.

You'll find a wealth of census material in print for the colonial period. Check out *Rhode Island Freemen, 1747–1755: A Census of Registered Voters* edited by Bruce C. MacGunnigle (Genealogical Publishing Co., 1977), and the other books listed in the Census Records section of this guie. State censuses were taken every 10 years from 1865 to 1935 and are available at the state archives. These can supplement US population and special schedules—except for the 1890 census, for which only the veterans schedule exists.

Volunteers for the Rhode Island Cemetery Transcription Project have created a database **<ricemeteries.tripod.com>** of all known stones. They're looking for transcriptions and additional cemeteries.

The Rhode Island Historical Society **<www.rihs.org>** holds the largest manuscript, map, and photograph collections in the state. The library also contains unpublished manuscripts and all newspapers published in the state.

Church records are spread throughout the state in archives and churches. The records of the Episcopal Diocese are at the University of Rhode Island. The Rhode Island Historical Society has the New England Yearly Meeting collection of Quaker records. The manuscript department also contains church registers for miscellaneous denominations.

Rhode Islanders participated in every military conflict, with record coverage varying depending on the war. Original military records are at the Rhode Island State Archives and the Rhode Island Historical Society, as well as the National Archives. For the American Revolution, muster rolls, pay rosters and hospital records are available but not indexed. The State Archives Civil War materials include enlistment rosters. It also has records relating to colonial militia and the National Guard.

Court records—civil and criminal—are stored in the Judicial Records Center in Pawtucket. A guide to its holdings and the accessibility of those materials is online at **<www.judicial-records.state.ri.us>**.

ARCHIVES, LIBRARIES, AND SOCIETIES

Clerk of Family Court
1 Dorrance Plaza, Providence, RI 02903

East Greenwich Free Library
82 Pierce St., East Greenwich, RI 02818, (401) 884-9510, **<www.eastgreenwichlibrary.org>**

Episcopal Diocese of Connecticut
1335 Asylum Ave., Hartford, CT 06105, (860) 233-4481, **<www.ctdiocese.org>**

John Hay Library, Brown University
20 Prospect St., Box A, Providence, RI 02912, (401) 863-3723, **<dl.lib.brown.edu/libweb/about/hay>**

Knight Memorial Library
275 Elmwood Ave., Providence, RI 02907, (401) 467-2625, **<www.provcomlib.org>**

National Archives, New England Region
Frederick C. Murphy Federal Center, 380 Trapelo Road, Waltham, MA 02452, (781) 663-0130, **<archives.gov/northeast/boston>**

New England Historic Genealogical Society
99-101 Newbury St., Boston, MA 02116, (888) 296-3447, **<www.newenglandancestors.org>**

Newport Historical Society
82 Touro St., Newport, RI 02840, (401) 846-0813, **<www.newporthistorical.org>**

Pettaquamscutt Historical Society
2636 Kingstown Road, Kingston, RI 02881, (401) 783-1328, **<www.pettaquamscutt.org>**

Phillips Memorial Library, Providence College
549 River Ave., Providence, RI 02918, (401) 865-2578, **<www.providence.edu/archives>**

Providence Public Library
150 Empire St., Providence, RI 02903, (401) 455-8000, **<www.provlib.org>**

Rhode Island Black Heritage Society
65 Weybosset St. at the Arcade, Ste. 29, Providence, RI 02903, (401) 751-3490, **<www.providenceri.com/RI_BlackHeritage>**

Rhode Island Department of Health
3 Capitol Hill, Providence, RI 02908, (401) 222-5960, **<www.health.ri.gov>**

Rhode Island Genealogical Society
Box 211, Hope, RI 02831, **<www.rigensoc.org>**

Rhode Island Historical Society
121 Hope St., Providence, RI 02906, (401) 273-8107 ext. 10, **<www.rihs.org>**

Rhode Island Jewish Historical Association
130 Sessions St., Providence, RI 02906, (401) 331-1360, **<www.rijha.org>**

Rhode Island State Archives
337 Westminster St., Providence, RI 02903, (401) 222-2353, **<www.sos.ri.gov>**

Rhode Island State Library
State House, 2nd floor, 82 Smith St., Providence, RI 02903, (401) 222-2473, **<www.sos.ri.gov>**

Roman Catholic Diocese of Providence
The Chancery Office, 34 Fenner St., Providence, RI 02903, (401) 278-4500, **<www.dioceseofprovidence.org>**

Westerly Public Library
44 Broad St., Westerly, RI 02891, (401) 596-2877, **<www.westerlylibrary.org>**

GENERAL RESOURCES

An Album of Rhode Island History, 1636–1986 by Patrick T. Conley (Donning, 1986)

Bibliography of Rhode Island: A Catalogue of Books and Other Publications Relating to the State of Rhode Island by John Russell Bartlett (filmed by University Microfilms, 1987)

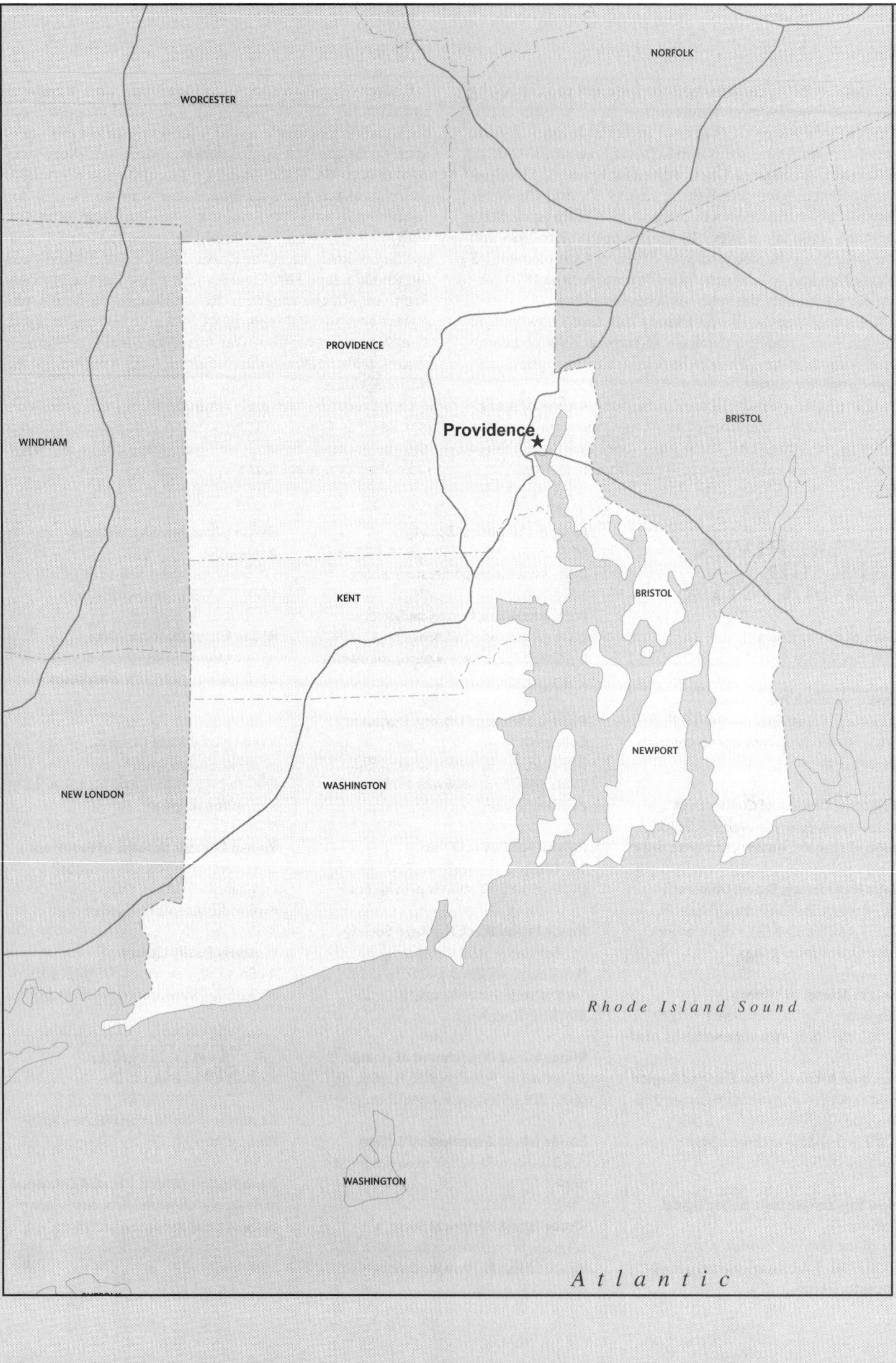
NORFOLK
WORCESTER
PROVIDENCE
Providence
BRISTOL
WINDHAM
KENT
BRISTOL
NEWPORT
NEW LONDON
WASHINGTON
Rhode Island Sound
WASHINGTON
Atlantic

Biographical Cyclopedia of Representative Men of Rhode Island, 2 vols. (National Biographical Publishing Co., 1881)

The Catholic Church in Rhode Island by Thomas F. Cullen (Franciscan Missionaries of Mary, 1936)

Civil, Military and Professional Lists of Plymouth and Rhode Island Colonies: Comprising Colonial, County, and Town Officers, Clergymen, Physicians and Lawyers by Ebenezer Weaver Pierce (1881; Genealogical Publishing Co., 1968)

Documentary History of Rhode Island, 2 vols., by Howard Millar Chapin (Preston and Rounds, 1916, 1919)

The Early Records of the Town of Providence, 21 vols. (Snow and Farnham, 1892-1915)

English Origins of New England Families: From the New England Historical and Genealogical Register, 3 vols., from the New England Historic Genealogical Society (Genealogical Publishing Co., 1985)

The Genealogical Dictionary of Rhode Island: Comprising Three Generations of Settlers Who Came Before 1690 by John Osborne Austin (Genealogical Publishing Co., 1978)

A Genealogical Dictionary of the First Settlers of New England, 4 vols., by James Savage (ca. 1860; Genealogical Publishing Co., 1965)

Genealogies of Rhode Island Families: From Rhode Island Periodicals, 2 vols. (Genealogical Publishing Co., 1983)

History of the State of Rhode Island and Providence Plantations: 1636-1790, 2 vols., by Samuel Green Arnold (Reprint Co., 1970)

Inventory of Church Archives in Rhode Island: Baptist Bodies from the Works Projects Administration (Historical Records Survey, 1939)

Inventory of the Church Archives of Rhode Island by Society of Friends (Historical Records Survey, 1939)

Memorial Encyclopedia of the State of Rhode Island by Wilfred H. Munro (American Historical Society, 1916)

Men of Progress: Biographical Sketches and Portraits of Leaders in Business and Professional Life in the State of Rhode Island and Providence Plantations by Richard Herndon (*New England Magazine*, 1896)

New England Families: Genealogical and Memorial, 4 vols., by William Richard Cutter (1913; Lewis Historical Publishing Co., 1914)

New England Family Histories: States of Maine and Rhode Island by Lu Verne V. Hall (Heritage Books, 2000)

The Records of American Baptists in Rhode Island and Related Organizations (American Baptist Historical Society, 1981)

Representative Men and Old Families of Rhode Island, 3 vols. (J.H. Beers & Co., 1908)

Rhode Island: A Bibliography of Its History edited by Roger Parks (University Press of New England, 1983)

Rhode Island Biographical and Genealogical Sketch Index by J. Carlyle Parker (Marietta Publishing Co., 1991)

Rhode Island Genealogies (Broderbund, 1996, CD-ROM)

Rhode Island Research Outline by the Church of Jesus Christ of Latter-day Saints (online at **<www.familysearch.org/eng/search/RG/guide/rhode_island.asp>**)

Rhode Island Sources for Family Historians and Genealogists by Kip Sperry (Everton Publishers, 1986)

State of Rhode Island and Providence Plantations at the End of the Century, 3 vols., edited by Edward Feld (Mason Publishing Co., 1902)

CENSUS RECORDS

Atlas of the State of Rhode and Providence Plantations by Daniel G. Beers (Pomeroy & Beers, 1870)

Census of the Inhabitants of the Colony of Rhode Island and Providence Plantations, 1774 compiled by John R. Bartlett (Genealogical Publishing Co., 1969)

The Rhode Island 1777 Military Census by Mildred M. Chamberlain (Genealogical Publishing Co., 1985)

Rhode Island 1782 Census edited by Jay Mack Holbrook (Holbrook Research Institute, 1979)

Rhode Island Freemen, 1747-1755: A Census of Registered Voters edited by Bruce C. MacGunnigle (Genealogical Publishing Co., 1985)

IMMIGRATION RECORDS

Immigrants to New England, 1700-1775 by Ethel Stanwood Bolton (The Essex Institute, 1931)

Rhode Island Passenger Lists: Port of Providence 1798-1808: 1820-1872 and Port of Bristol and Warren 1820-1871 by Maureen A. Taylor (Genealogical Publishing Co., 1993)

LAND RECORDS

The Records of the Properties of the Narragansett, Otherwise Called the Fones Record by James N. Arnold (Narragansett Historical Publishing, 1894)

Rhode Island Land Evidences, vol. I, 1648-96, compiled by Dorothy Worthington (Rhode Island Historical Society, 1921; Genealogical Publishing Co., 1970)

Rhode Island Miscellaneous Records, ca. 1600-1900 (filmed by the Genealogical Society of Utah, 1992)

MAPS

Connecticut, Maine, Massachusetts, Rhode Island, Atlas of Historical County Boundaries by John H. Long (Simon & Schuster, 1994)

A Gazetteer of the State of Connecticut and Rhode Island by John Chauncey Pease and John M. Niles (Heritage Books, 1991)

A Geographic Dictionary of Connecticut and Rhode Island by Henry Gannett (1894; Genealogical Publishing Co., 1978)

The Post Offices of Rhode Island by Johns S. Gallagher (The Depot, 1977)

Rhode Island—A Guide to the Smallest State (Houghton Mifflin Co., 1937)

Rhode Island Atlas by Marion I. Wright and Robert J. Sullivan (Rhode Island Publications Society, 1982)

Rhode Island Boundaries, 1636-1936 by John H. Cady (State of Rhode Island and Providence Plantations, 1936)

Rhode Island Postal History: The Post Office by Lawrence M. Merolla, et al. (Rhode Island Postal History Society, 1977)

☞MILITARY RECORDS

Civil and Military List of Rhode Island, 1647-1800, 3 vols., by Joseph J. Smith (Preston and Rounds, 1901)

Rhode Island in the Colonial Wars: A List of Rhode Island Soldiers and Sailors in King George's War, 1740-1748 by Howard Miller Chapin (Rhode Island Historical Society, 1920)

Rhode Island in the Colonial Wars: A List of Rhode Island Soldiers and Sailors in the Old French and Indian Wars, 1755-1762 by Howard Miller Chapin (Rhode Island Historical Society, 1918)

So Few the Brave: Rhode Island Continentals, 1775-1783 by Anthony Walker (Seafield, 1981)

Spirit of '76 in Rhode Island by Benjamin Cowell (A.J. Wright, 1850)

☞PROBATE RECORDS

Index of Wills, 1636-1850 by Nellie M.C. Beaman (Rhode Island Families Association, 1992)

Index to the Probate Records of the Municipal Court of the City of Providence, Rhode Island: From 1646 to and Including the Year 1899 edited by Edward Field (Providence Press, 1902)

Index to Wills in Rhode Island Genealogical Register, 4 vols., by Robert S. Wakefield (Plymouth Colony Research Group, 1982)

The Providence Probate Records to 1775 With Index by Frank T. Calef (filmed by the Family History Library, 1950)

Records of the Colony of Rhode Island and Providence Plantations in New England, 10 vols., by John R. Bartlett (A.C. Green, 1856-1865)

Records of the Vice-Admiralty Court of Rhode Island: 1716-1752 (Kraus Reprint, 1975)

Rhode Island Court Records: Records of the Court of Trails of the Colony of Providence Plantations, 1647-1670, 2 vols. (Rhode Island Historical Society, 1920-1922)

Rhode Island General Court of Trials, 1671-1704 (J.F. Fiske, 1998)

☞VITAL RECORDS

Coventry R.I. Headstone Inscriptions by James N. Arnold (filmed by the Family History Library, 1950)

Guide to the Public Vital Statistics Records (Births, Marriages, Deaths) in the State of Rhode Island and Providence Plantations from the Rhode Island Department of State (Historical Records Survey, 1941)

Miscellaneous Vital Records, 1700-1850 From Records in James Arnold's Family Notes (filmed by the Family History Library, 1992)

New England Marriages Prior to 1700 by Clarence Almon Torrey (Genealogical Publishing Co., 1985)

Rhode Island Burial Grounds by Nellie Brownell Potter (filmed by the Genealogical Society of Utah, 1950)

Vital Records of Rhode Island, 1636-1850, 20 vols., by James N. Arnold (Narragansett Historical Publishing Co., 1891-1912)

Vital Records of Rhode Island, New Series, 13 vols., compiled by Alden G. Beaman (Alden G. Beaman, 1975-87)

•-COUNTY DETAILS-•

BRISTOL

1 Dorrance Plaza, Bristol, RI 02809, (508) 823-6588, **<www.kindredtrails.com/RI_Bristol.html>**

- **INCORPORATED:** Feb. 17, 1747
- **PARENT COUNTY:** created from Bristol, MA
- **BIRTH RECORDS:** unknown, kept by town and city clerks
- **MARRIAGE:** unknown, town clerks
- **DEATH:** unknown, town clerks
- **PROBATE:** unknown, town clerks
- **COURT:** unknown, District Court Clerk
- **BURIAL:** unknown, town clerks
- **NOTES:** There is no County Clerk in Bristol County. Each of the four towns in Bristol County keeps its own records. Towns organized before 1800: Barrington, 1717; Bristol, 1681; and Warren, 1746-1747. Block Island was transferred from Newport County to Washington County on May 6, 1963.

KENT

222 Quaker Lane, Warwick, RI 02886, (401) 822-6750, **<www.kindredtrails.com/RI_Kent.html>**

- **INCORPORATED:** June 11, 1750
- **PARENT COUNTY:** Providence
- **BIRTH RECORDS:** kept by town clerks
- **MARRIAGE:** town clerks
- **DEATH:** town clerks
- **LAND:** town clerks
- **PROBATE:** town clerks
- **BURIAL:** town clerks
- **NOTES:** There is no county government in Kent County. Each of the five towns in Kent County keeps its own records. Towns organized before 1800: Coventry, 1741; East Greenwich, 1677; Warwick, 1642-1643; and West Greenwich, 1741.

KING'S

- **INCORPORATED:** June 3, 1729
- **PARENT COUNTY:** Providence Plantations
- **NOTES:** See Washington County. Name changed to Washington Oct. 29, 1781.

NEWPORT

Washington Square, Newport, RI 02840, (401) 841-8350, **<www.kindredtrails.com/RI_Newport.html>**

- **INCORPORATED:** June 16, 1729
- **PARENT COUNTY:** Rhode Island
- **BIRTH RECORDS:** unknown, kept by town and city clerks
- **MARRIAGE:** unknown, town and city clerks
- **DIVORCE:** Family and Superior Court
- **DEATH:** unknown, town and city clerks
- **LAND:** unknown, start in 1780, town and city clerks
- **PROBATE:** unknown, 1784, Probate Court
- **COURT:** unknown, District Court
- **BURIAL:** unknown, town and city clerks
- **NOTES:** Formerly Rhode Island County. Name changed to Newport June 16, 1729. The eastern boundary was adjusted in 1746-1747 under decree of the King of England. There is no county government in Newport County. Each of the five towns and one city in Newport County keeps its own records. Towns organized before 1800: Jamestown, 1678; Little Compton, 1746-1747; Middletown, 1743; part of Washington County; Portsmouth, 1638; Newport, 1939; and Tiverton, 1746-1747. Newport Historical Society has early church, land, and probate records.

PROVIDENCE

250 Benefit St., Providence, RI 02903, (401) 277-6710, **<www.kindredtrails.com/RI_Providence.html>**

- **INCORPORATED:** June 22, 1703
- **PARENT COUNTY:** Providence Plantations
- **BIRTH RECORDS:** unknown, kept by town clerks
- **MARRIAGE:** unknown, town clerks
- **DIVORCE:** Funknown, amily Court
- **DEATH:** unknown, town clerks
- **LAND:** unknown, Recorder of Deeds
- **PROBATE:** unknown, Probate Judge
- **COURT:** unknown, Municipal Court
- **NOTES:** Formerly Providence Plantations County. Name changed to Providence County June 16, 1729. There is no county government in Providence County. Each of the 22 towns in Providence County keeps its own records. Towns organized before 1800: Cranston, 1754; Cumberland, 1746-1747; Foster, 1781; Gloucester, 1730-1731; Johnston, 1759; North Providence, 1765; Providence, 1636; Scituate, 1730-1731; and Smithfield, 1730-1731.

PROVIDENCE PLANTATIONS

- **INCORPORATED:** June 22, 1703
- **PARENT COUNTY:** original county
- **NOTES:** See Providence County. Name changed to Providence County June 16, 1729.

RHODE ISLAND

- **INCORPORATED:** June 22, 1703
- **PARENT COUNTY:** original county
- **NOTES:** See Newport County. Name changed to Newport June 16, 1729.

WASHINGTON

4800 Tower Hill Road, Wakefield, RI 02879, (401) 841-8350, **<www.kindredtrails.com/RI_Washington.html>**

- **INCORPORATED:** Oct. 29, 1781
- **PARENT COUNTY:** Newport
- **BIRTH RECORDS:** unknown, kept by town clerks
- **MARRIAGE:** unknown, town clerks
- **DEATH:** unknown, town clerks
- **LAND:** unknown, town clerks
- **PROBATE:** unknown, town clerks
- **NOTES:** Formerly King's County. Name changed to Washington County Oct. 29, 1781. There is no county government in Washington County. Each of the 20 towns in Washington County keeps its own records. Towns organized before 1800: Charlestown, 1738; Exeter, 1742-1743; Hopkinton, 1757; North Kingstown, 1641; Richmond, 1747; South Kingstown (Pettaquamscutt), 1656-1657; and Westerly, 1669.

SOUTH CAROLINA

» BY EMILY ANNE CROOM

HISTORICAL OVERVIEW

Spain, France, and England all desired a permanent foothold along the Atlantic coast in the early 16th century. In 1663, Britain's Charles II granted a charter to eight proprietors to colonize between 31° and 36° north latitude from sea to sea. English colonists built Charles Town near present-day Charleston in 1670. Early settlers—mostly from Virginia, British Caribbean and New England colonies, the British Isles, and France (Huguenots)—created an economy based on fur and deer-skin trade and production of foodstuffs and forest products. In 1712, North and South Carolina became separate provinces. Parliament to established both Carolinas as royal colonies in 1729.

South Carolina experienced remarkable growth in its first century. In the coastal lowcountry, plantations growing rice (after 1700) and indigo (from the 1740s) using slave labor began to dominate the economy. In the 1750s, settlement in the upcountry—the inland area and highlands in the northwest—began with yeomen farmers, some recruited from Europe and others moving overland from or through Pennsylvania, Virginia and North Carolina.

During the American Revolution, the British occupied Charleston from May 1780 to late 1782. More than 200 engagements took place in South Carolina, including conflicts between its numerous loyalists and its patriots.

By the 1820s, cotton culture dominated the state's economy and slaves were the majority of the population. By 1860, the state had almost 704,000 residents; more than 57 percent were slaves. Free black and the foreign-born populations were each about 1.4 percent. Decades of economic and political tension came to a head after Lincoln's election in 1860, when South Carolina seceded. The Civil War began in April 1861 as Confederate forces fired on Fort Sumter in Charleston Harbor. The city was under siege during much of the war. Sherman's march to the sea in 1865 destroyed most of the capital, Columbia, and left the state impoverished. South Carolina was readmitted to the Union in June 1868.

Between the Civil War and World War II, agricultural domination declined, and the state's economy diversified to include textile mills, food and forest products, fishing, and mineral industries. Poverty still gripped much of the state. By 1922, large numbers of African Americans had migrated to northern cities, leaving the black population a minority.

research tips

- The state archives is South Carolina's major research facility **<www.archives.sc.gov>**. Other important research locations are the South Caroliniana Library of the University of South Carolina in Columbia and the South Carolina Historical Society, Charleston.
- In the 18th century, parishes registered life events and provided aid to the poor. Many parish records have been published or placed at the South Carolina Historical Society.
- Before 1785, most legal documents were recorded in Charleston. Between 1785 and 1800 and since 1868, South Carolina's civil divisions have been counties. Between 1800 and 1868, records were created in districts. Be sure to identify the ancestral parish, district, and/or county.
- The late establishment of the North-South Carolina boundary (1772) suggests that researchers consult records on both sides of the current line.

CENSUS RECORDS

- Federal census: 1790, 1800, 1810, 1830, 1840, 1850, 1860, 1870, 1880, 1900, 1910, 1920, 1930
- Federal slave schedules: 1850, 1860 (schedules name slaveholders but rarely name slaves)
- Federal mortality schedules: 1850, 1860, 1870, 1880
- Special census of Civil War Union veterans and widows: 1890
- State census: (all incomplete) 1829, 1839, 1869, 1875

RECORD HIGHLIGHTS

South Carolina began statewide registration of births and deaths in 1915, marriages in July 1950, and divorces in July 1962. The Division of Vital Records **<www.scdhec.gov/administration/vr>** can supply copies of all four records. Vital records offices in the county health departments handle birth and death records only. Several county health departments or courthouses hold birth and death records from the late 19th century. Vital records at the state archives are listed at **<archives.sc.gov/information/vital>**.

The state did not require marriage licenses until July 1911. Some pre-1911 marriage records and settlements (prenuptial agreements) exist, and evidence of marriages can be found in other county records and newspapers. For marriage records from 1911 to July 1950, contact the county probate office that issued the license. Before 1949, divorce was illegal and rarely granted. For divorce records since April 1949, contact the county clerk where the case was filed. Records available at the state archives and/or other research facilities include the following:

- Mills' *Atlas of the State of South Carolina*, 1825
- Several series of the Draper Manuscripts, especially V, TT, and UU, dealing with South Carolina, kept at the State Historical Society of Wisconsin and on microfilm at major libraries
- Voter registrations, 1867-1868
- Records of depositors in South Carolina's two branches of the Freedman's Savings and Trust Company (FHL microfilm 928587-89)
- Confederate pension applications, 1919-1938
- Indexes to various records series, including Confederate pensions, online at **<www.archivesindex.sc.gov>**
- Agricultural censuses (1868, 1875) and state censuses (1829, 1839, 1869, 1875), various counties, various years

ARCHIVES, LIBRARIES, AND SOCIETIES

Aiken-Barnwell Genealogical Society
Box 45, Aiken, SC 29802, **<www.aikenbarnwellgenealogy.net>**

Allendale County Historical Society
Box 523, Allendale, SC 29810, **<sciway3.net/clark/allendale/histsoc.html>**

Anderson County Chapter of the South Carolina Genealogical Society
Box 74, Anderson, SC 29622, **<www.andersoncounty.scgen.org>**

Bluffton Historical Preservation Society
(843) 757-6293, **<www.heywardhouse.org>**

Calhoun County Museum Archives
313 Butler St., St. Matthews, SC 29135, Catawba Wateree Genealogical Society

Camden Archives and Museum
1314 Broad St., Camden, SC 29020, (803) 425-6050, **<camdenarchives.org>**

Charleston Chapter of the South Carolina Genealogical Society
Box 20266, Charleston, SC 29413, **<www.charleston.scgen.org>**

Charleston Roman Catholic Diocesan Archives
119 Broad St., Box 818, Charleston, SC 29402, (803) 723-3488

Charleston Library Society
164 King St., Charleston, SC 29401, (843) 723-9912, **<charlestonlibrarysociety.org>**

Chester County Genealogical Society
Box 336, Richburg SC 29729, **<www.rootsweb.ancestry.com/~scchest2/scchester.htm>**

Chesterfield District Chapter of the South Carolina Genealogical Society
Box 167, Chesterfield, SC 29709, (843) 623-2244, **<chesterfield.scgen.org/links.html>**

Clarendon County Archives
211 N. Brooks St., Manning, SC 29102, (803) 435-0328, **<www.clarendoncounty.sc.gov/archives>**

Columbia Chapter of the South Carolina Genealogical Society
Box 11353, Columbia, SC 29211, **<www.rootsweb.ancestry.com/~scccscgs>**

Darlington County Historical Commission
104 Hewitt St., Darlington, SC 29532, (843) 398-4710, **<www.darcosc.com/HistoricalCommission>**

Edgefield County Historical Society
Box 486, Edgefield, SC 29824,

Greenville County Library
300 College St., Greenville, SC 29601, (864) 242-5000, **<www.greenvillelibrary.org>**

Greenville County Historical Society
Box 10472, Greenville, SC 29603, (864) 233-4103, **<www.greenvillehistory.org>**

Horry County Historical Society
606 Main St., Conway, SC 29526, (843) 488-1966, **<www.hchsonline.org>**

Huguenot Society of South Carolina
138 Logan St., Charleston, SC 29401, (843) 723-3235, **<www.huguenotsociety.org>**

Jasper County Historical Society
Box 2111, Ridgeland, SC 29936, (843) 726-8136, **<www.state.sc.us/scdah/historgs/rptlistorgs_1Page30.html>**

Kershaw County Historical Society
811 Fair St., Box 501, Camden, SC 29020, (803) 425-1123, **<www.kershawcountyhistoricalsociety.org>**

Laurens County Library
1017 W. Main St., Laurens, SC 29360, (864) 681-7323, **<www.lcpl.org>**

Laurens District Chapter of the South Carolina Genealogical Society
Box 1217, Laurens, SC 29360, **<www.laurens.scgen.org>**

Lexington Genealogical Association
Box 1442, Lexington, SC 29071, **<lexingtongenealogy.homestead.com/main.html>**

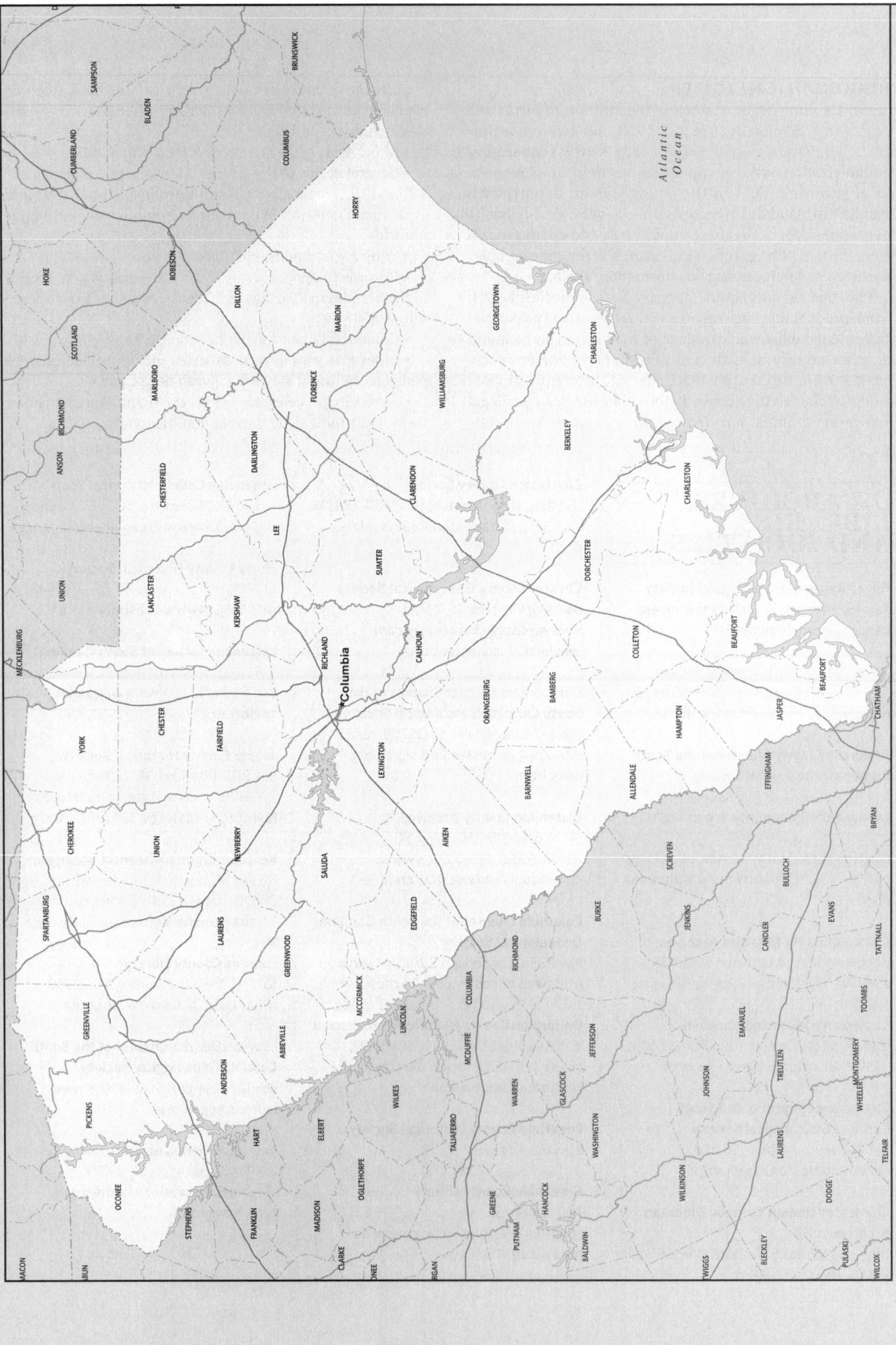
Atlantic Ocean
Columbia
MECKLENBURG
YORK
CHESTER
LANCASTER
CHESTERFIELD
MARLBORO
DILLON
HORRY
MARION
FLORENCE
DARLINGTON
LEE
KERSHAW
FAIRFIELD
RICHLAND
SUMTER
CLARENDON
WILLIAMSBURG
GEORGETOWN
CHARLESTON
BERKELEY
DORCHESTER
CALHOUN
ORANGEBURG
LEXINGTON
SALUDA
NEWBERRY
UNION
CHEROKEE
SPARTANBURG
GREENVILLE
PICKENS
OCONEE
ANDERSON
ABBEVILLE
LAURENS
GREENWOOD
MCCORMICK
EDGEFIELD
AIKEN
BARNWELL
BAMBERG
COLLETON
ALLENDALE
HAMPTON
JASPER
BEAUFORT
CHATHAM
EFFINGHAM
BRYAN
SCREVEN
BULLOCH
JENKINS
BURKE
RICHMOND
COLUMBIA
MCDUFFIE
LINCOLN
WILKES
ELBERT
HART
FRANKLIN
STEPHENS
MADISON
OGLETHORPE
CLARKE
TALIAFERRO
WARREN
GLASCOCK
JEFFERSON
WASHINGTON
HANCOCK
GREENE
PUTNAM
BALDWIN
WILKINSON
JOHNSON
EMANUEL
CANDLER
EVANS
TATTNALL
TOOMBS
MONTGOMERY
WHEELER
TREUTLEN
LAURENS
DODGE
TELFAIR
BLECKLEY
PULASKI
WILCOX
TWIGGS
MACON
HOKE
ROBESON
SCOTLAND
RICHMOND
ANSON
UNION
CUMBERLAND
BLADEN
SAMPSON
COLUMBUS
BRUNSWICK

National Archives and Records Administration, Southeast Region
5780 Jonesboro Road, Morrow, GA 30260, (770) 968-2100, **<www.archives.gov/southeast>**

Office of Vital Records and Public Health Statistics
2600 Bull St., Columbia, SC 29201, (803) 898-3668, **<health.state.ga.us/programs/vitalrecords>**

Old Darlington District Chapter of the South Carolina Genealogical Society
114 South Fourth St., Box 175, Hartsville, SC 29551, (843) 857-0300, **<www.olddarlington.scgen.org>**

Old Pendleton District Chapter of the South Carolina Genealogical Society
228 Ivydale Dr., Greenville, SC 29609, **<www.oldpendleton.scgen.org/resources.html>**

Old St. Bartholomew Chapter of the South Carolina Genealogical Society
418 Wichman St., Walterboro, SC 29488, **<www.bartholomew.scgen.org>**

Orangeburg German-Swiss Genealogical Society
Box 974, Orangeburg, SC 29119, **<www.ogsgs.org>**

Pee Dee Chapter of the South Carolina Genealogical Society
Box 1428, Marion, SC 29571, **<www.peedee.scgen.org>**

Piedmont Historical Society
Box 127, Campobello, SC 29322, **<www.piedmont-historical-society.org>**

Pinckney District Chapter of the South Carolina Genealogical Society
Box 5281, Spartanburg, SC 29304, **<www.pinckney.scgen.org>**

Richland County Public Library
1431 Assembly St., Columbia, SC 29201, (803) 799-9084, **<www.richland.lib.sc.us>**

Rickman Library, Southern Wesleyan University
Box 1020, Central, SC 29630, (864) 644-5088, **<www.swu.edu/library/about/claytonroom.htm>**

Saluda County Historical Society
Box 22, Saluda, SC 29138, (864) 445-8550, **<saludacountyhistoricalsociety.org>**

South Carolina Baptist Historical Collection
c/o James B. Duke Library, Furman University, 3300 Poinsett Hwy., Greenville, SC 29613, (864) 294-2194, **<library.furman.edu/specialcollections>**

South Carolina Department of Archives and History
8301 Parklane Rd. Columbia, SC 29223, (803) 896-6100, **<scdah.sc.gov>**

South Carolina Division of the Sons of Confederate Veterans
<www.scscv.com>

South Carolina Genealogical Society
Old Edgefield District Genealogical Research Library, 104 Courthouse Square, Edgefield, SC, 29824, **<scgen.org>**

South Carolina Historical Society
100 Meeting St., Charleston, SC 29401, (843) 723-3225, **<www.southcarolinahistoricalsociety.org>**

South Carolina Methodist Conference
c/o Wofford College, 429 N. Church St., Spartanburg, SC 29303, (864) 597-4000, **<www.wofford.edu/library/archives>**

South Carolina State Library
Box 11469, Columbia, SC 29211, (803) 734-8666, **<www.statelibrary.sc.gov>**

Spartanburg County Historical Association
Box 887, Spartanburg, SC 29304, (864) 596-3501, **<spartanburghistory.org>**

Thomas Cooper Library, University of South Carolina
1322 Greene St., University of South Carolina, Columbia, SC 29208, (803) 777-3142, **<www.sc.edu/library>**

Three Rivers Historical Society
414 N. Main St., Hemingway, SC 29554, (843) 558-2355, **<threeriversshistoricalsociety.org>**

York County Library
138 East Black St., Rock Hill, SC 29730, (803) 981-5858, **<www.yclibrary.org>**

GENERAL RESOURCES

Books and Articles on South Carolina History by Leis P. Jones (University of South Carolina Press, 1991)

Carolina Families: A Bibliography of Books About North and South Carolina Families by Donald M. Hehir (Heritage Books, 1994)

A Checklist of South Carolina State Publications, 3 vols., by M. Hayes Mizell (Archives of South Carolina, 1962)

A Collection of Upper South Carolina Genealogical and Family Records, 3 vols., edited by James E. Wooley (Southern Historical Press, 1979-82)

Colonial Families of South Carolina compiled by Motte Alston Read (filmed by the Genealogical Society of Utah, 1952)

Correct Mispronunciations of Some South Carolina Names by Claude Neuffer (University of South Carolina Press, 1983)

Cyclopedia of Eminent and Representative Men of the Carolina of the Nineteenth Century (Brant & Fuller, 1892)

Dictionary of South Carolina Biography, vol. 1., by Richard N. Cote and Patricia H. Williams (Southern Historical Press, 1985)

The Growth and Distribution of Population in South Carolina by Julian J. Petty (Reprint Co., 1975)

A Guide To Local Government Records in the South Carolina Archives by South Carolina Department of Archives and History (University of South Carolina Press, 1988)

A Guide to the Manuscript Collection of the South Caroliniana Library by Allen H. Stokes (South Caroliniana Library, 1982)

A Guide to South Carolina Genealogical Research and Records by Brent Howard Holcomb (Brent Howard Holcomb, 1998)

Guide to the Study and Reading of South Carolina History, 2 vols., by James H. Easterby (Historical Commission of South Carolina, 1949-1950)

History of South Carolina, 5 vols. by Yates Snowden and Harry G. Cutler (Lewis Publishing Co., 1920)

Journal of the Commons House of Assemble, 1736-1754 (Historical Commission of South Carolina, 1951-)

Lineage Charts South Carolina Genealogical Society Chapters, 4 vols., (Greenville Chapter, South Carolina Genealogical Society, ca. 1976-1987)

Local and Family History in South Carolina: A Bibliography by Richard N. Cote (Southern Historical Press, 1981)

Men of Mark in South Carolina, 4 vols., by James C. Hemphill (Men of Mark Publishing Co., 1907-1909)

North Carolina-South Carolina Bible Records by Jeannette H. Austin (J.H. Austin, 1987)

Records in the British Public Records Office Relating to South Carolina, 1663-1782 by Helen C. Carson (South Carolina Department of Archives and History, 1973)

Research Materials in South Carolina by John Hammond Moore (University of South Carolina Press, 1967)

A Sketch of the History of South Carolina to the Close of the Proprietary Government by the Revolution of 1719 by William James Rivers (McCarter & Co., 1856)

The South Carolina Archives:, 2nd edition, by Marion C. Chandler (Department of Archives and History, 1976)

South Carolina Genealogical Research by George K. Schweitzer (George K. Schweitzer, 1985)

South Carolina Genealogies: Articles from the South Carolina Historical and Genealogical Magazine, 5 vols. (Reprint Co., 1983)

South Carolina: A Guide for Genealogists by Theresa Hicks (Columbian Chapter, South Carolina Genealogical Society, 1996)

South Carolina Newspapers by John Hammond Moore (University of South Carolina Press, 1988)

South Carolina Research Outline by the Church of Jesus Christ of Latter-Day Saints (online at **<www.familysearch.org/eng/search/RG/guide/south_carolina.asp>**)

South Carolina Women, 2nd ed. by Idella Bodie (Sandlapper Pub., 1991)

The Story of the South Carolina Lowcountry, 3 vols., by Herbert Ravenel Sass (J.F. Hyer Pub., ca. 1956)

☞IMMIGRATION RECORDS

Citizens and Immigrants—South Carolina, 1768 by Mary Bondurant Warren (Heritage Papers, ca.1980)

A Compilation of the Original Lists of Protestant Immigrants to South Carolina, 1763-1773 by Janie Revill (1939; Genealogical Publishing Co., 1968)

First Settlers of South Carolina 1670-1700 by Agnes Lelans Bladwin (Southern Historical Press, 1985)

Scotch-Irish Migration to South Carolina, 1772 by Jean Stephenson (Shenandoah Publishing House, 1971)

South Carolina Immigrants, 1760 to 1770 by Jack Moreland Jones and Mary Bondurant Warren (Heritage Papers, 1988)

South Carolina Naturalizations, 1783-1850 by Brent H. Holcomb (Genealogical Publishing Co., 1985)

☞LAND RECORDS

Early South Carolina Settlers, 1600's-1800's (Broderbund CD-ROM, 2000)

An Index to Deeds of the Province and State of South Carolina 1719-1785 and Charleston District 1785-1800 by Silas Emmett Lucas Jr. (Southern Historical Press, 1977)

Index to South Carolina Land Grants, 1784-1800 by Ronald Vern Jackson (Accelerated Indexing Systems, 1977)

Miscellaneous Land Records, 1731-1882 from the South Carolina Secretary of State's Office (filmed by the Genealogical Society of Utah, 1951)

North Carolina Land Grants in South Carolina, 2 vols., by Brent H. Holcomb (Brent H. Holcomb, 1975, 1976)

Petitions for Land from the South Carolina Council Journals by Brent H. Holcomb (South Carolina Magazine of Ancestral Research, ca. 1996-ca. 1999)

The Promised Land: The History of The South Carolina Land Commission 1869-1890 by Carol K. Rothrock Bleser (University of South Carolina Press, 1969)

Records of the Secretary of the Province and The Register of the Province of South Carolina, 1671-1675 by Alexander S. Salley (Historical Commission of South Carolina, 1944)

South Carolina Deed Abstracts, 3 vols. by Brent H. Holcomb (South Carolina Magazine of Ancestral Research, 1996)

South Carolina Memorials, Abstracts of Land Titles by Jesse Hogan Motes (Southern Historical Press, 1996)

South Carolina Memorials, 1731-1776: Abstracts of Selected Land Records from a Collection in the Department of Archives and History, 2 vols., by Katie-Prince Ward Esker (Polyanthos, 1973-1977)

South Carolina as a Royal Province, 1719-1776 by William Roy Smith (Macmillan, 1903)

Warrants for Land in South Carolina 1672-1711 edited by A.S. Salley Jr. and R.N. Oldsberg (University of South Carolina Press, 1973)

☞MAPS

Atlas of the State of South Carolina, 1825 by Robert Mills (Southern Historical Press, 1980)

Names of South Carolina, vols. 1-12, edited by Claude H. Neuffer (University of South Carolina, 1967; Reprint Co., 1976)

Palmetto Place Names from the Work Projects Administration (1941; Reprint Co., 1975)

Post Offices of Yesteryear by Olin J. Salley (filmed by the Family History Library, 1974)

South Carolina County Maps compiled by C.J Puetz (Thomas Publishing Co., 1989)

South Carolina Waterways As They Appear in Mill's Atlas by Mariam D. Cropper (Accelerated Indexing Systems, 1977)

MILITARY RECORDS

Colonial Soldiers of the South, 1732-1774 compiled by Murtie June Clark (Genealogical Publishing Co., 1983)

A Copy of the Original Index book Showing the Revolutionary Claims Filed in South Carolina Between August 20, 1783 and August 31, 1786 by Janie Revill (1941; Genealogical Publishing Co., 1969)

The Militia in Antebellum South Carolina Society by Jean Martin Flynn (Reprint Co., ca. 1991)

Records of the Regiments of the South Carolina Line compiled by Alexander S. Salley (Genealogical Publishing Co., 1977)

Roster of South Carolina Patriots in the American Revolution by Bobby Gilmer Moss (Genealogical Publishing Co., 1983)

South Carolina in the Mexican War by Jack Allen Myer (South Carolina Dept. of Archives and History, 1996)

South Carolinians in the Revolution, with Service Records and Miscellaneous Data 1775-1855 edited by Sara A. Ervin (1959, Genealogical Publishing Co., 1971)

South Carolina Revolutionary Records, Selected Final Pension Payment Vouchers, 1818-1864 by Alycon Trubey Pierce (Iberian Pub. Co., 1996)

South Carolina Troops in Confederate Service by A.S. Salley Jr. (R.L. Bryan, 1913-30)

Stub Entries to Indents Issues in Payment of Claims Against South Carolina Growing Out of the Revolution, 12 vols., from the South Carolina Department of Archives and History (1919-57)

PROBATE RECORDS

Abstracts of the Wills of the State of South Carolina, 3 vols., by Carolina T. Moore and Agatha Aimar Simmons (the compilers, 1960-69)

A Genealogical Collection of South Carolina Wills and Records, 2 vols., by Willie Pauline Young (1955; Southern Historical Press, 1981)

Indexes to the County Wills of South Carolina compiled by Martha Lou Houston (1939; Genealogical Publishing Co., 1964)

Probate Records of South Carolina, 3 vols. by Brent H. Holcomb (Southern Historical Press, 1977)

Records of the Secretary of the Province of South Carolina, 1692-1721 by Caroline T. Moore (R.L. Bryan Co., 1978)

South Carolina Begins: The Records of a Proprietary Colony, 1663-1721 by Charles H. Lesser (South Carolina Department of Archives and History, 1995)

South Carolina Jury Lists, 1718 through 1783 by Mary B. Warren (Heritage Papers, 1977)

South Carolina Wills, 1670-1853, or Later (Heritage Papers, 1981)

South Carolina Wills and Other Court Records by Katie-Prince Ward Esker (filmed by the Genealogical Society Of Utah, 1998)

VITAL RECORDS

Cemetery Records of Confederate Soldiers Buried in South Carolina (filmed by the Genealogical Society of Utah, 1947)

North and South Carolina Marriage Records by William M. Dlemens (Genealogical Publishing Co., 1981)

South Carolina Marriages: 1688-1799, 3 vols., by Brent H. Holcomb (Genealogical Publishing Co., 1980-81, 1984)

South Carolina Marriage Settlements, 1785-1889 (filmed by the Genealogical Society of Utah, 1950)

Supplement to South Carolina Marriages, 1688-1820 by Brent H. Holcomb (Genealogical Publishing Co., 1984)

COUNTY DETAILS

ABBEVILLE

Box 99, Abbeville, SC 29620, (864) 366-5312, **<www.abbevillecountysc.com>**

- **INCORPORATED:** March 12, 1785
- **PARENT COUNTY:** District 96
- **BIRTH RECORDS:** 1915, Department of Health
- **DIVORCE:** start in 1873, kept by Clerk of Court
- **DEATH:** 1915, Department of Health
- **COURT:** 1873, Clerk of Court
- **NOTES:** Probate Judge has land records 1840-1875, marriage records 1911-1950, and probate records 1782-1950. Fire destroyed most pre-1872 county records.

AIKEN

828 Richland Ave. W., Aiken, SC 29801, (803) 642-1715, **<www.aikencounty.net>**

- **INCORPORATED:** March 10, 1871
- **PARENT COUNTIES:** Edgefield, Orangeburg, Barnwell, Lexington

- **BIRTH RECORDS:** start in 1901, kept by Department of Health
- **MARRIAGE:** 1911, Probate Judge
- **DIVORCE:** 1873, Clerk of Court
- **DEATH:** 1999, Department of Health
- **PROBATE:** 1872, Probate Judge
- **COURT:** 1873, Clerk of Court
- **LAND:** 1872, Registrar Mesne Conveyance

ALLENDALE

292 Barnwell Highway, Box 126, Allendale, SC 29810, (803) 584-2737, **<www.allendalecounty.com>**

- **INCORPORATED:** Feb. 6, 1919
- **PARENT COUNTIES:** Barnwell, Hampton
- **LAND RECORDS:** 1919, Clerk of Courts
- **COURT:** start in 1919, kept by Clerk of Courts
- **NOTES:** County Board of Health has birth and death records 1915-1958. Probate Judge has marriage records 1919-2000 and probate records 1919-1951. Pre 1919 birth and death records include Barnwell County births and deaths.

ANDERSON

101 S. Main St., Box 8002, Anderson, SC 29622, (864) 260-1052, **<www.andersoncountysc.org>**

- **INCORPORATED:** Dec. 20, 1826
- **PARENT COUNTY:** Pendleton District
- **BIRTH RECORDS:** start in 1915, kept by Department of Health
- **DIVORCE:** 1949, Clerk of Court
- **DEATH:** 1915, Department of Health
- **COURT:** 1828, Clerk of Court
- **NOTES:** Anderson County Public Library has land records 1719-1772. Registrar of Deeds has land records 1828-1942. Probate Judge has marriage records 1911-1955 and probate records 1828-1907.

BAMBERG

Box 150, Bamberg, SC 29003, (803) 245-3025, **<www.bambergcountysc.gov>**

- **INCORPORATED:** Feb. 25, 1897
- **PARENT COUNTY:** Barnwell
- **BIRTH RECORDS:** 1915, Department of Health
- **MARRIAGE:** 1904, Probate Judge
- **DIVORCE:** start in 1898, kept by Clerk of Court
- **DEATH:** 1915, Department of Health
- **LAND:** 1898, Clerk of Court
- **PROBATE:** 1904, Probate Judge
- **COURT:** 1898, Clerk of Court

BARNWELL

Box 723, Barnwell, SC 29812, (803) 541-1020, **<www.barnwellcounty.sc.gov>**

- **INCORPORATED:** 1800
- **PARENT COUNTY:** Orangeburg District
- **DIVORCE RECORDS:** ca. 1800, County Clerk
- **LAND RECORDS:** start in 1779, kept by County Clerk
- **COURT:** ca. 1800, County Clerk
- **NOTES:** Probate Judge has marriage records 1911-1959 and probate records 1787-1932. Probate records 1781-1787 and Clerk of Courts records 1791-1799 were destroyed with Orangeburg County records in February 1865.

BEAUFORT

Drawer 1228, Beaufort, SC 29901, (843) 470-5218, **<www.bcgov.net>**

- **INCORPORATED:** 1769
- **PARENT COUNTY:** Beaufort District (name changed 1785)
- **BIRTH RECORDS:** 1915, Department of Health
- **MARRIAGE:** unknown start, Probate Judge
- **DEATH:** 1915, Department of Health
- **LAND RECORDS:** start in 1885, Registrar of Deeds
- **PROBATE:** unknown start, Probate Judge
- **NOTES:** Records prior to 1785 are filed in Charleston. Many records dating before 1865 were lost during reconstruction.

BERKELEY

Box 6122, Moncks Corner, SC 29461, (843) 719-4234, **<www.berkeleycountysc.gov>**

- **INCORPORATED:** Jan. 31, 1882
- **PARENT COUNTY:** Charleston
- **BIRTH RECORDS:** 1915, Department of Health
- **MARRIAGE:** 1920, Probate Judge
- **DIVORCE:** unknown start, kept by Clerk of Court
- **DEATH:** 1915, Department of Health
- **COURT:** unknown start, Clerk of Court
- **BURIAL:** unknown start, Department of Health
- **NOTES:** Registrar of Deeds has land records 1885-1926. Probate Judge has probate records 1883-1939.

BERKELEY, OLD

- **INCORPORATED:** 1682
- **PARENT COUNTY:** Original county
- **NOTES:** One of four original counties. Discontinued, 1769. Became part of Charleston District.

CALHOUN

Box 709, St. Matthews, SC 29135, (803) 874-3524, **<www.calhouncounty.sc.gov>**

- **INCORPORATED:** Feb. 14, 1908
- **PARENT COUNTIES:** Lexington, Orangeburg
- **BIRTH RECORDS:** start in 1915, kept by Department of Health
- **MARRIAGE:** 1911, Probate Judge
- **DIVORCE:** 1949, Clerk of Court
- **DEATH:** 1915, Department of Health
- **LAND:** 1735, Historical Commission
- **PROBATE:** 1908, Probate Judge
- **COURT:** 1908, Clerk of Court
- **BIBLE:** 1735, Historical Commission
- **OTHER GENEALOGICAL:** 1735, Historical Commission
- **NOTES:** Probate Judge has marriage records 1911-1956 and probate records 1908-1950.

CAMDEN DISTRICT

- **INCORPORATED:** 1769
- **PARENT COUNTIES:** Craven, Berkeley, old
- **NOTES:** Created as one of seven original judicial districts. Discontinued in 1798 to form Chester, Claremont, Clarendon, Fairfield, Kershaw, and Lancaster counties.

CARTERET DISTRICT
- **INCORPORATED:** 1685
- **PARENT COUNTY:** unknown
- **NOTES:** name changed to Granville 1708.

CHARLESTON
100 Broad Street, Suite 106, Charleston, SC 29401, (843) 958-5000, **<www.charlestoncounty.org>**
- **INCORPORATED:** 1769
- **PARENT COUNTY:** Colleton, Berkeley, old
- **MARRIAGE RECORDS:** start in 1879, kept by Probate Judge
- **DIVORCE:** unknown start, Clerk of Court
- **COURT:** 1867, Clerk of Courts
- **NOTES:** County Health Department has birth records 1877-1926 and death records 1866-1914. Registrar of Mense Conveyance has land records 1680-1929. Probate Judge has probate records 1671-1874. Created in 1769 from portions of Colleton and Berkeley, old, as one of seven original judicial districts; split in 1798 to form Charleston and Colleton counties.

CHERAWS
- **INCORPORATED:** 1769
- **PARENT COUNTY:** Original district
- **NOTES:** Created in 1769 as one of seven original judicial districts. Discontinued in 1798 to form Chesterfield, Darlington and Marlboro counties.

CHEROKEE
125 E. Floyd Baker Blvd., Drawer 2289, Gaffney, SC 29342, (864) 487-2571, **<www.cherokeecountysc.com>**
- **INCORPORATED:** Feb. 25, 1897
- **PARENT COUNTIES:** Union, York, Spartanburg
- **BIRTH RECORDS:** start in 1915, kept by Department of Health
- **DEATH:** 1915, Department of Health
- **LAND:** 1897, Clerk of Court
- **NOTES:** Clerk of Courts has court and divorce records 1897-1937. Probate Judge has marriage records 1911-1950 and probate records 1897-1950.

CHESTER
140 Main St., Box 580, Chester, SC 29706, (803) 385-2605, **<www.chestercounty.org>**
- **INCORPORATED:** 1785
- **PARENT COUNTY:** Camden District
- **BIRTH RECORDS:** 1915, Department of Health
- **DIVORCE:** 1962, Clerk of Court
- **DEATH:** start in 1915, kept by Department of Health
- **LAND:** 1776, Clerk of Court
- **COURT:** 1785, Clerk of Court
- **NOTES:** Probate Judge has marriage records 1911-1962 and probate records 1787-1950.

CHESTERFIELD
Box 529, Chesterfield, SC 29709, (843) 623-2574, **<www.chesterfieldcountysc.com>**
- **INCORPORATED:** 1785
- **PARENT COUNTY:** Cheraws District
- **BIRTH RECORDS:** 1915, Department of Health
- **DEATH:** 1915, Department of Health
- **COURT:** start in 1865, kept by Clerk of Courts
- **NOTES:** Probate Judge has marriage records 1911-1962 and probate records 1787-1950. Sherman's army burned the county courthouse along with almost all public records in March 1865.

CLAREMONT
- **PARENT COUNTY:** unknown
- **NOTES:** See Sumter County.

CLARENDON
Box 136, Manning, SC 29102, (803) 435-4443, **<www.clarendoncountygov.org>**
- **INCORPORATED:** 1785
- **PARENT COUNTY:** Camden District
- **BIRTH RECORDS:** 1915, Department of Health
- **DIVORCE:** 1947, Clerk of Court
- **DEATH:** 1915, Department of Health
- **LAND:** 1908, Registrar Mesne Conveyance
- **NOTES:** Clerk of Courts has court records 1840-1964. Probate Judge has marriage records 1911-1950 and probate records 1875-1915. Absorbed by Sumter District 1800, then recreated from Sumter 1855. Census schedules missing for 1820, 1830, 1840 and 1850. Clarendon's loose probate records begin in 1875.

COLLETON
Box 620, Walterboro, SC 29488, (843) 549-5791, **<www.colletoncounty.org>**
- **INCORPORATED:** 1798
- **PARENT COUNTY:** Charleston District
- **BIRTH RECORDS:** start in 1915, kept by Dept of Health
- **DIVORCE:** 1949, Clerk of Court
- **DEATH:** 1915, Department of Health
- **LAND:** 1865, Registrar of Deeds
- **MILITARY:** 1865, Veterans Affairs Office
- **NOTES:** Clerk of Courts has court records 1824-1861. Probate Court has marriage records 1911-1973 and probate records 1865-1972. Most pre-1865 records destroyed in 1865 fire.

COLLETON, OLD
- **INCORPORATED:** 1683
- **PARENT COUNTY:** Original county
- **NOTES:** One of four original counties. Discontinued, 1769.

CRAVEN, OLD
- **INCORPORATED:** 1683
- **PARENT COUNTY:** Original county
- **NOTES:** One of four original counties. Discontinued, 1769.

DARLINGTON
1 Public Sq., Darlington, SC 29532, (843) 398-4330, **<www.darcosc.com>**
- **INCORPORATED:** 1785
- **PARENT COUNTY:** Cheraws District
- **BIRTH RECORDS:** 1915, Department of Health
- **DIVORCE:** 1950, County Clerk
- **DEATH:** 1915, Department of Health
- **LAND:** 1910, County Clerk

- **PROBATE:** start in 1900, kept by Probate Judge
- **NOTES:** County Historical Commission has court records 1841-1875, land records 1806-1900, and probate records 1840-1895. Probate Judge has marriage records 1911-1941.

DILLON

Drawer 1220, Dillon, SC 29536, (843) 774-1425,
<www.dilloncounty.sc.gov>

- **INCORPORATED:** Feb. 5, 1910
- **PARENT COUNTY:** Marion
- **BIRTH RECORDS:** 1915, Department of Health
- **MARRIAGE:** 1913, Probate Judge
- **DEATH:** start in 1915, Department of Health
- **LAND:** 1910, Clerk of Courts
- **COURT:** 1910, Clerk of Courts
- **NOTES:** Probate Judge has probate records 1910-1950.

DORCHESTER

5200 E. Jim Bilton Blvd., St. George, SC 29477, (843) 563-0120,
<www.dorchestercounty.net>

- **INCORPORATED:** Feb. 25, 1897
- **PARENT COUNTIES:** Berkeley, Colleton
- **BIRTH RECORDS:** start in 1915, kept by Department of Health
- **DEATH:** 1915, Department of Health
- **NOTES:** County Clerk has court records 1897-1960. Registrar of Mesne Conveyances has land records 1847-1920. Probate Judge has marriage records 1911-1957 and probate records 1897-1915.

EDGEFIELD

124 Courthouse Sq., Edgefield, SC 29824, (803) 637-4000,
<www.edgefieldcounty.sc.gov>

- **INCORPORATED:** 1795
- **PARENT COUNTY:** District 96
- **BIRTH RECORDS:** start in 1915, kept by Department of Health
- **DIVORCE:** unknown start, County Clerk
- **DEATH:** 1915, Department of Health
- **LAND:** 1839, County Clerk
- **NOTES:** County Clerk has court records 1800-1922. Probate Judge has marriage records 1911-1976 and probate records 1787-1905. Small portion of Aiken County added to Edgefield in 1966.

FAIRFIELD

Drawer 299, Winnsboro, SC 29180, (803) 712-6526,
<www.fairfieldsc.com>

- **INCORPORATED:** 1785
- **PARENT COUNTY:** Camden District
- **BIRTH RECORDS:** 1915, Department of Health
- **DIVORCE:** unknown start, kept by Clerk of Courts
- **DEATH:** 1915, Department of Health
- **LAND:** 1918, Clerk of Courts
- **NOTES:** Clerk of Courts has court records 1800-1907. Probate Judge has marriage records 1911-1993 and probate records 1840-1904.

FLORENCE

180 N. Irby St., Florence, SC 29501, (843) 665-3031,
<www.florenceco.org>

- **INCORPORATED:** Dec. 22, 1888
- **PARENT COUNTIES:** Marion, Darlington, Clarendon, Williamsburg
- **BIRTH RECORDS:** start in 1915, kept by Department of Health
- **DIVORCE:** unknown start, Clerk of Court
- **DEATH:** 1915, Department of Health
- **LAND:** 1889, Clerk of Courts
- **NOTES:** Clerk of Courts has court records 1889-1965. Probate Judge has marriage records 1911-1955 and probate records 1888-1916.

GEORGETOWN

401 Cleland Street, Georgetown, SC 29440, (843) 545-3036,
<www.georgetowncountysc.org>

- **INCORPORATED:** 1800
- **PARENT COUNTIES:** Craven, Georgetown District
- **BIRTH RECORDS:** start in 1915, kept by Department of Health
- **MARRIAGE:** 1911, Probate Judge
- **DIVORCE:** 1949, Clerk of Court
- **DEATH:** 1915, Department of Health
- **LAND:** 1866, Registrar of Deeds
- **PROBATE:** 1865, Probate Judge
- **NOTES:** Clerk of Courts has court records 1850-1984. Created in 1769 from Craven County as one of seven original judicial districts. Records prior to 1785 are filed in Charleston. Georgetown County records destroyed in Civil War in March 1865.

GRANVILLE

- **INCORPORATED:** 1686
- **PARENT COUNTY:** Original county
- **NOTES:** Discontinued, 1769.

GREENVILLE

305 East N. St., Greenville, SC 29601, (864) 467-8551,
<www.greenvillecounty.org>

- **INCORPORATED:** 1786
- **PARENT COUNTY:** Cherokee lands
- **BIRTH RECORDS:** start in 1915, kept by Department of Health
- **MARRIAGE:** 1911, Probate Judge
- **DIVORCE:** unknown start, Clerk of Court
- **DEATH:** 1915, Department of Health
- **NOTES:** Registrar of Deeds has land records 1787-1940. Probate Judge has probate records 1787-1951. From 1791-1800 Greenville County was part of Washington District.

GREENWOOD

528 Monument St., Greenwood, SC 29646, (864) 942-8546,
<www.co.greenwood.sc.us>

- **INCORPORATED:** March 2, 1897
- **PARENT COUNTIES:** Abbeville, Edgefield
- **BIRTH RECORDS:** start in 1915, kept by Department of Health
- **DIVORCE:** 1937, Clerk of Courts
- **DEATH:** 1915, Department of Health
- **PROBATE:** 1897, Probate Judge
- **COURT:** 1897, Clerk of Courts
- **NOTES:** Clerk of Courts has land records 1899-1945. Probate Judge has marriage records 1911-1970.

HAMPTON

Box 7, Hampton, SC 29924, (803) 914-2250,
<www.hamptoncountysc.org>

- **INCORPORATED:** Feb. 18, 1878
- **PARENT COUNTY:** Beaufort
- **BIRTH RECORDS:** start in 1915, kept by Department of Health
- **DEATH:** 1915, Department of Health
- **PROBATE:** 1878, Probate Judge
- **COURT:** unknown start, Clerk of Court
- **NOTES:** Clerk of Courts has land records 1918-1930. Probate Judge has marriage records 1911-1951.

HORRY

1301 Second Ave., Conway, SC 29526, (843) 915-5000,
<www.horrycounty.org>

- **INCORPORATED:** Dec. 19, 1801
- **PARENT COUNTY:** Georgetown District
- **BIRTH RECORDS:** start in 1915, kept by Department of Health
- **DIVORCE:** 1947, Clerk of Court
- **DEATH:** 1915, Department of Health
- **LAND:** 1803, Registrar of Deeds
- **NOTES:** Clerk of Courts has court records 1803-1944. Probate Judge has marriage records 1911-1950 and probate records 1819-1907.

JASPER

Box 248, Ridgeland, SC 29936, (843) 726-7710,
<www.jaspercountysc.org>

- **INCORPORATED:** Jan. 30, 1912
- **PARENT COUNTIES:** Beaufort, Hampton
- **BIRTH RECORDS:** 1915, Department of Health
- **DIVORCE:** unknown start, Clerk of Courts
- **DEATH:** 1915, Department of Health
- **LAND:** 1912, Clerk of Courts
- **COURT:** start in 1912, kept by Clerk of Courts
- **NOTES:** Probate Judge has marriage records 1912-1950 and probate records 1912-1967. A majority of equity (old criminal court) records were lost pre-1829.

KERSHAW

Box 1557, Camden, SC 29020, (803) 425-1500,
<www.kershaw.sc.gov>

- **INCORPORATED:** 1791
- **PARENT COUNTIES:** Claremont, Fairfield, Lancaster and Richland counties
- **BIRTH RECORDS:** 1915, Department of Health
- **DIVORCE:** start in 1949, kept by Clerk of Court
- **DEATH:** 1915, Department of Health
- **NOTES:** Clerk of Courts has court records 1783-1908 and land records 1791-1934. Probate Judge has marriage records 1911-1960 and probate records 1791-1911. Camden Archives and Museum has wills 1775-1853.

LANCASTER

Box 1809, Lancaster, SC 29721, (803) 285-1581,
<www.lancastercountysc.net>

- **INCORPORATED:** 1798
- **PARENT COUNTY:** Camden District
- **BIRTH RECORDS:** start in 1915, Department of Health
- **MARRIAGE:** unknown start, Probate Judge
- **DIVORCE:** 1977, Family Court Clerk
- **DEATH:** 1915, Department of Health
- **LAND:** 1719, Registrar of Deeds
- **PROBATE:** unknown start, Probate Judge
- **NOTES:** Clerk of Courts has court records 1800-1962 and divorce records 1958-1976. Probate Judge has marriage records 1911-1950 and probate records 1865-1919. Most of Lancaster County's loose equity papers and probate records were destroyed during the Civil War.

LAURENS

Box 287, Laurens, SC 29360, (864) 984-3538,
<www.laurenscounty.org>

- **INCORPORATED:** 1795
- **PARENT COUNTY:** District 96
- **BIRTH RECORDS:** 1915, Department of Health
- **DIVORCE:** unknown start, Clerk of Court
- **DEATH:** 1915, Department of Health
- **LAND:** 1785, Clerk of Court
- **PROBATE:** start in 1901, kept by Probate Judge
- **NOTES:** Clerk of Courts has court records 1800-1937. County library has death records 1915-1944 and probate records 1785-1900. Probate Judge has marriage records 1911-1951.

LEE

Box 387, Bishopville, SC 29010, (803) 484-5341,
<www.rootsweb.ancestry.com/~sclee/index.html>

- **INCORPORATED:** Feb. 25, 1902
- **PARENT COUNTIES:** Darlington, Sumter, Kershaw
- **BIRTH RECORDS:** start in 1915, kept by Department of Health
- **MARRIAGE:** 1902, Probate Judge
- **DEATH:** 1915, Department of Health
- **LAND:** 1902, Clerk of Court
- **PROBATE:** 1902, Probate Judge
- **COURT:** 1902, Clerk of Court

LEXINGTON

205 E. Main St., Lexington, SC 29072, (803) 785-8212,
<www.lex-co.com>

- **INCORPORATED:** 1785
- **PARENT COUNTY:** Orangeburg District
- **BIRTH RECORDS:** start in 1915, kept by Department of Health
- **DIVORCE:** 1949, Clerk of Courts
- **DEATH:** 1915, Department of Health
- **LAND:** 1839, Registrar of Deeds
- **NOTES:** Clerk of Courts has court records 1806-1954. Probate Judge has marriage records 1911-1973 and probate records 1865-1908. Formed from Orangeburg District 1785. 1791 county was re-absorbed into Orangeburg District. In 1804 Lexington became a separate county. Union troops destroyed Clerk of Courts' records dating prior to 1839. Destroyed records included deeds and almost all probate records.

LIBERTY

- **PARENT COUNTY:** unknown
- **NOTES:** See Marion County. Used briefly as a subdivision of Marion County.

MARION
Box 295, Marion, SC 29571, (843) 423-8240, **<www.sccounties.org/directory/Marion/Marion.aspx>**
- **INCORPORATED:** 1798
- **PARENT COUNTY:** Georgetown District
- **BIRTH RECORDS:** start in 1915, kept by Department of Health
- **MARRIAGE:** unknown start, Probate Judge
- **DIVORCE:** 1948, Clerk of Courts
- **DEATH:** 1915, Department of Health
- **LAND:** 1907, Clerk of Courts
- **PROBATE:** 1900, Probate Judge
- **NOTES:** Clerk of Courts has court records 1800-1873. County Archives/History Center has land records 1800-1906 and probate records 1800-1900. Probate Judge has marriage records 1800-1859 and 1911-1950.

MARLBORO
Drawer 996, Bennettsville, 29512, (843) 479-5613, **<www.marlborocounty.sc.gov>**
- **INCORPORATED:** 1785
- **PARENT COUNTY:** Cheraws District
- **BIRTH RECORDS:** start in 1915, kept by Department of Health
- **DIVORCE:** 1950, County Clerk
- **DEATH:** 1915, Department of Health
- **LAND:** 1786, County Clerk
- **NOTES:** County Clerk has court records 1800-1933. Probate Judge has marriage records 1788-1950 and probate records 1787-1902.

MCCORMICK
133 S. Mine St., McCormick, SC 29835, (864) 852-2195, **<www.mccormickcountysc.org>**
- **INCORPORATED:** Feb. 19, 1916
- **PARENT COUNTIES:** Greenwood, Abbeville, Edgefield
- **BIRTH RECORDS:** 1916, Department of Health
- **MARRIAGE:** 1916, Probate Judge
- **DIVORCE:** start in 1950, kept by Clerk of Courts
- **DEATH:** 1916, Department of Health
- **LAND:** 1916, Clerk of Courts
- **NOTES:** Clerk of Courts has court records 1917-1960. Probate Judge has probate records 1917-1966.

NEWBERRY
Box 278, Newberry, SC 29108, (803) 321-2110, **<www.sccounties.org/directory/Newberry/Newberry.aspx>**
- **INCORPORATED:** 1785
- **PARENT COUNTY:** District 96
- **BIRTH RECORDS:** start in 1915, kept by Department of Health
- **MARRIAGE:** 1911, Probate Court
- **DIVORCE:** 1950, Clerk of Courts
- **DEATH:** 1915, Department of Health
- **LAND:** 1785, Clerk of Courts
- **PROBATE:** 1776, Clerk of Court
- **COURT:** 1776, Clerk of Court
- **NOTES:** Clerk of Courts has court records 1785-1798, 1816-1956. County library has land records 1785-1834. Probate Court has probate records 1787-1913. Pre 1818 equity rolls, pre 1881 general sessions indictments, and pre 1870 judgement rolls were lost.

NINETY-SIX
- **INCORPORATED:** 1769
- **PARENT COUNTIES:** Original district, area NW of Camden District
- **NOTES:** One of seven original judicial districts. Discontinued in 1785 to form Abbeville, Edgefield, Newberry, Laurens, Spartanburg, and Union counties.

OCONEE
Box 678, Walhalla, SC 29691, (864) 638-4280, **<www.sccounties.org/directory/Oconee/Oconee.aspx>**
- **INCORPORATED:** Jan. 29, 1868
- **PARENT COUNTY:** Pickens
- **BIRTH RECORDS:** start in 1915, kept by Department of Health
- **MARRIAGE:** 1911, Probate Judge
- **DIVORCE:** 1950, Clerk of Court
- **DEATH:** 1915, Department of Health
- **NOTES:** Clerk of Courts has court records 1868-1976. Registrar of Deeds has land records 1868-1926. Probate Judge has probate records 1868-1928.

ORANGE
- **INCORPORATED:** 1785
- **PARENT COUNTY:** Orangeburg District
- **NOTES:** Former County in Orangeburg District abolished 1791. Pre 1865 public records were burned by Sherman's troops.

ORANGEBURG
Drawer 9000, Orangeburg, SC 29116, (803) 533-6243, **<www.orangeburgcounty.org>**
- **INCORPORATED:** 1769
- **PARENT COUNTY:** Orangeburg District
- **BIRTH RECORDS:** 1915, Department of Health
- **MARRIAGE:** 1911, Probate Judge
- **DIVORCE:** start in 1950, kept by Clerk of Court
- **DEATH:** 1915, Department of Health
- **COURT:** 1865, Clerk of Court
- **NOTES:** Clerk of Courts has court records 1824-1837. Recorder of Deeds has land records 1865-1957, 1974-1978. Probate Judge has probate records 1864-1957. Created as one of seven original judicial districts.

PENDLETON
- **INCORPORATED:** 1789
- **PARENT COUNTY:** Cherokee Lands
- **NOTES:** Pendleton County was known as Washington District 1791-1800. (See Pickens and Anderson) Discontinued in 1826 to form Pickens and Anderson counties.

PICKENS
Box 215, Pickens, SC 29671, (864) 898-5866, **<www.co.pickens.sc.us>**
- **INCORPORATED:** Dec. 20, 1826
- **PARENT COUNTY:** Pendleton District
- **BIRTH RECORDS:** start in 1915, kept by Department of Health
- **MARRIAGE:** 1911, Probate Judge
- **DIVORCE:** 1950, Clerk of Court
- **DEATH:** 1915, Department of Health
- **LAND:** 1826, Registrar of Deeds

- **NOTES:** Clerk of Court has court records 1828-1907. Probate Judge has probate records 1828-1884. Anderson County Registrar of Deeds office has Pickens area land records 1789-1826.

PICKNEY DISTRICT

- **INCORPORATED:** 1795
- **PARENT COUNTY:** 96 District
- **NOTES:** Discontinued in 1800 to form Union and York counties.

RICHLAND

Box 2766, Columbia, 29202, (803) 576-1929, **<www.rcgov.us>**

- **INCORPORATED:** 1785
- **PARENT COUNTY:** Camden District
- **BIRTH RECORDS:** 1915, Department of Health
- **DEATH:** start in 1915, kept by Department of Health
- **PROBATE:** 1787, Probate Judge
- **NOTES:** County Clerk has court records 1781-1957. Registrar of Deeds has land records 1865-1951. Probate Judge has marriage records 1911-1965. Fire of February 1865 destroyed the courthouse and most public records. However, most equity and probate records were removed prior to the fire. 1800 census schedules missing.

SALEM

- **INCORPORATED:** 1791
- **PARENT COUNTIES:** Parts of Claremont and Clarendon
- **NOTES:** In 1800 Claremont, Clarendon, and Salem counties were combined to create Sumter District. Clarendon (1857), Lee (1902), and Sumter counties were created out of Sumter District.

SALUDA

100 E. Church St., Saluda, SC 29138, (864) 445-4500, **<www.sccounties.org/directory/Saluda/Saluda.aspx>**

- **INCORPORATED:** February 1895
- **PARENT COUNTY:** Edgefield
- **BIRTH RECORDS:** 1915, Department of Health
- **DIVORCE:** unknown start, kept by Clerk of Court
- **DEATH:** 1915, Department of Health
- **NOTES:** Clerk of Courts has court records 1929-1964 and land records 1896-1928. Probate Judge has marriage records 1911-1950 and probate records 1896-1963.

SPARTANBURG

Box 3483, Spartanburg, 29304, (864) 596-2591, **<www.spartanburgcounty.org>**

- **INCORPORATED:** 1785
- **PARENT COUNTY:** 96 District
- **BIRTH RECORDS:** start in 1915, kept by Department of Health
- **MARRIAGE:** 1911, Probate Judge
- **DIVORCE:** unknown start, Clerk of Court
- **DEATH:** 1915, Department of Health
- **NOTES:** Clerk of Courts has court records 1785-1960. Registrar of Deeds has land records 1785-1911. Probate Judge has probate records 1787-1968. Spartanburg County Public Library has South Carolina census records 1790-1930, county estate papers (probate) 1787-1900, county land records 1785-1900, and Death register 1895-1896, 1903-1914.

SUMTER

141 N Main St., Sumter, SC 29150, (803) 436-2227, **<www.sumtercountysc.org>**

- **INCORPORATED:** 1798
- **PARENT COUNTY:** Camden District
- **BIRTH RECORDS:** unknown start, kept by Department of Health
- **MARRIAGE:** 1910, Probate Judge
- **DIVORCE:** unknown start, Clerk of Court
- **DEATH:** unknown start, Department of Health
- **LAND:** unknown start, Clerk of Court
- **PROBATE:** 1900, Probate Judge
- **COURT:** unknown start, Clerk of Court

UNION

Box 703, Union, SC 29379, (864) 429-1630, **<www.countyofunion.org>**

- **INCORPORATED:** 1798
- **PARENT COUNTY:** Pickney District
- **MARRIAGE RECORDS:** unknown start, Probate Judge
- **DIVORCE:** unknown start, Clerk of Court
- **LAND:** unknown start, Clerk of Court
- **PROBATE:** unknown start, Probate Judge
- **COURT:** start in 1785, kept by Clerk of Court

WILLIAMSBURG

147 W. Main St., Kingstree, SC 29556, (843) 355-9321, **<www.williamsburgsc.com>**

- **INCORPORATED:** 1804
- **PARENT COUNTY:** Georgetown District
- **BIRTH RECORDS:** 1915, Department of Health
- **DIVORCE:** start in 1948, kept by Clerk of Court
- **DEATH:** 1915, Department of Health
- **NOTES:** Clerk of Courts has court records 1806-1909 and land records 1806-1929. Probate Judge has marriage records 1911-1950 and probate records 1802-1915.

WINYAH

- **INCORPORATED:** 1785
- **PARENT COUNTY:** unknown
- **NOTES:** Formerly a county in Georgetown District, later became Georgetown County.

YORK

Box 649, York, SC 29745, (803) 628-3039, **<www.yorkcountygov.com>**

- **INCORPORATED:** 1785
- **PARENT COUNTY:** Camden District
- **BIRTH RECORDS:** start in 1915, kept by Department of Health
- **DIVORCE:** 1942, Clerk of Court
- **DEATH:** 1915, Department of Health
- **COURT:** 1786, Clerk of Court
- **NOTES:** Clerk of Courts has court records 1786-1797, 1800-1950, and land records 1786-1950. Probate Judge has marriage records 1911-1950 and probate records 1787-1977. Historical Center of York County has court records 1750-1979. From 1791-1800 York County was part of Pickney District.

SOUTH DAKOTA

» BY JAMES W. WARREN

HISTORICAL OVERVIEW

Pioneers to South Dakota hoped to be rewarded at the end of their arduous journey there, but instead they found the challenge of surviving life on its unforgiving, endless plains. The area's original settlers were the Dakota, Arapaho, Cheyenne, Mandan, Hidatsa, and Assiniboine Indians. The worst of the land was eventually made reservation land for Indians.

South Dakota became part of the United States with the Louisiana Purchase in 1803. Shortly after, Lewis and Clark traveled through the region. Throughout the first half of the 19th century, South Dakota was inhabited primarily by Dakota (Sioux) Indians, and there was relatively little white settlement. The land at various times was part of the territories of Missouri, Michigan, Wisconsin, Iowa, Minnesota and Nebraska.

Army posts were established in the 1850s, and in 1858 the Yankton Sioux ceded lands to the United States. Settlement between the Big Sioux and Missouri rivers began with towns at Yankton and Vermillion. Dakota Territory was created in 1861, including what would become North Dakota, South Dakota, Montana and Wyoming. (Montana Territory was split off in 1864; and Wyoming, in 1868.)

After the Homestead Act of 1863, newcomers from Iowa, Minnesota, Illinois and Wisconsin, largely of Norwegian descent, began to settle southern Dakota Territory. Migrations from Midwestern and Eastern states continued, as well as Czechs, Danes, Swedes and Germans from Russia. In 1875, gold was discovered in the sacred Indian land of the Black Hills and thousands of settlers poured in. Between 1877 and 1887, the influx of settlers peaked as railroads tracked through the northeast and central part of what would become South Dakota.

In 1889 Dakota Territory was split into South Dakota and North Dakota, and both states were admitted to the Union. During the first decade of the 20th century, western South Dakota was settled after the railroads were extended there.

research tips

- South Dakota was settled late and is relatively recordless, making it important to track down local resources. While some local church and cemetery records have been published, you will likely need to contact these organizations. Newspapers as well as county, town, church and organizational histories can provide clues.
- The South Dakota Genealogical Society website **<www.rootsweb.ancestry.com/~sdgs>** and the South Dakota GenWeb site **<www.rootsweb.ancestry.com/~sdgenweb>** are good places to begin your research.
- Because the State Archives was founded recently, state university, college and town libraries; local museums; and historical societies are important resources.
- American Indians make up a significant percentage of South Dakota's population. The State Archives holds Indian census rolls, microfilmed federal records and correspondence. Also consult collections at the Center for Western Studies at Augustana College in Sioux Falls, and the Institute of American Indian Studies at the University of South Dakota at Vermillion.

CENSUS RECORDS

- Federal census: 1860, 1870, 1880, 1900, 1910, 1920, 1930
- Federal mortality schedules: 1860, 1870, 1880
- Special census of Civil War Union veterans and widows: 1890
- State/territorial census: 1836, 1885, 1895, 1905, 1915, 1925, 1935, 1945

RECORD HIGHLIGHTS

The first available federal census for the state of South Dakota is the 1900 census. Dakota Territory censuses and mortality schedules were taken in 1860, 1870, 1880 and 1885. South Dakota's state censuses are true research gems. Taken every 10 years beginning in 1895, they are available through 1945 and include details not usually found on other enumerations.

For example, the 1925 through 1945 censuses gathered the following information: name; county; post office where person received mail; town or township name; if in a town, ward number; age; occupation; owner or renter; place of birth; years lived in South Dakota; years living in United States; if naturalized; birthplace of father and mother; and more. These censuses, recorded primarily on index cards, are available at the South Dakota State Historical Society **<history.sd.gov>** and on Family History Library microfilm. The 1895 census is on subscription site Ancestry.com.

South Dakota began keeping birth, death, marriage and divorce records on a statewide basis in 1905. This registration requirement was usually complied with by the early 1930s. Some records prior to 1905 may be found at county courthouses with the registrar of deeds.

Vital records 1905 and later are on file with the State Health Department at the Office of Vital Records in Pierre. When South Dakota's Vital Records System was started in July of 1905, individuals born before then were given the opportunity to file delayed birth records. Nearly 200,000 birth records more than 100 years old can be searched online at **<www.state.sd.us/applications/PH14Over100-BirthRec/index.asp>**.

Marriages prior to 1905 recorded in a town or county are available from that county's treasurer. Pre-1905 divorces will be on file with the clerk of courts in the county where the divorce case was tried.

County-level courts in South Dakota include District County Court and Circuit Court. Their records include probate, guardianship, and civil and criminal cases. Land records are held by the registrar of deeds in the individual counties. Most of these records and their indexes remain in county courthouses, and few records are available on microfilm.

The state archives, part of the South Dakota State Historical Society, has naturalization records from South Dakota county courts except Brule and Campbell. It also holds Territorial Probate Court records and some local and county records. Its newspaper microfilm is available through interlibrary loan.

The archives holds book, periodical, manuscript, map, and sound recording collections for the State Historical Society, as well as government documents. But because the State Archives was not created until 1975, the collections are not as extensive as those of many state archives. For a fee, you can request searches of the archives' naturalization records, newspapers, and federal and state census collections.

ARCHIVES, LIBRARIES, AND SOCIETIES

Aberdeen Area Genealogical Society
Box 493, Aberdeen, SD 57402, **<www.rootsweb.ancestry.com/~sdgs/affiliates.html>**

Alexander Mitchell Public Library
519 S. Kline St., Aberdeen, SD 57401, (605) 626-7097, **<ampl.sdln.net>**

Bennett County Genealogical Society
<www.kindredtrails.com/SD_Bennett.html>

Brookings Area Genealogical Society
515 Third St., Brookings, South Dakota 57006, **<www.rootsweb.ancestry.com/~sdbags>**

Bureau of Land Management, South Dakota Field Office
310 Roundup St., Belle Fourche, SD 57717, (605) 892-7000, **<www.blm.gov/mt/st/en/fo/south_dakota_field.html>**

Center for Western Studies
2001 S. Summit Ave., Sioux Falls, SD 57197, (800) 727-2844, **<www.augie.edu/cws>**

Center of the Nation, American Historical Society of Germans from Russia
21850 Custer Peak Rd., Deadwood, SD 57732, (605) 584-2178, **<www.ahsgr.org/center_of_the_nation_chapter.htm>**

East River Genealogical Forum
20084-387th Ave., Wolsey, SD 57384, (605) 352-6849, **<freepages.genealogy.rootsweb.ancestry.com/~eastrivergenforum>**

Family Tree Genealogical Society
SD Genealogical Society, Box 1101, Pierre, SD 57501, **<www.rootsweb.ancestry.com/~sdgs/affiliates.html>**

Heritage Club-Platte
Rt. 2, Box 128, Platte, SD 57369, **<daddezio.com/society/hill/SH-SD-001.html>**

Homestead Chapter, American Historical Society of Germans from Russia
<www.cyndislist.com/germruss.htm>

Hyde County Historical and Genealogical Society
Box 392, Highmore, SD 57345, (605) 852-3148, **<www.travelsd.com/Attractions/Hyde-County-Historical-and-Genealogical-Society.dr>**

I.D. Weeks Library, University of South Dakota
414 E. Clark St., Vermillion, SD 57069, (877)COYOTES or (877) 269-6837, **<www.usd.edu/library>**

Kingsbury Genealogical Society
Box 305, De Smet, SD 57231, **<sdgenweb.com/kingsbury/Society.html>**

Lake County Genealogical Society
<www.rootsweb.ancestry.com/~sdlake>

Lyman-Brule Genealogical Society
110 E. Lawler, Chamberlain, SD 57325, **<www.rootsweb.ancestry.com/~sdlbgs>**

Methodist Archives and History Library
1331 W. University Blvd., Mitchell, SD 57301, (605) 996-6552, **<wiki.familysearch.org/en/ South_Dakota_Church_ Records>**

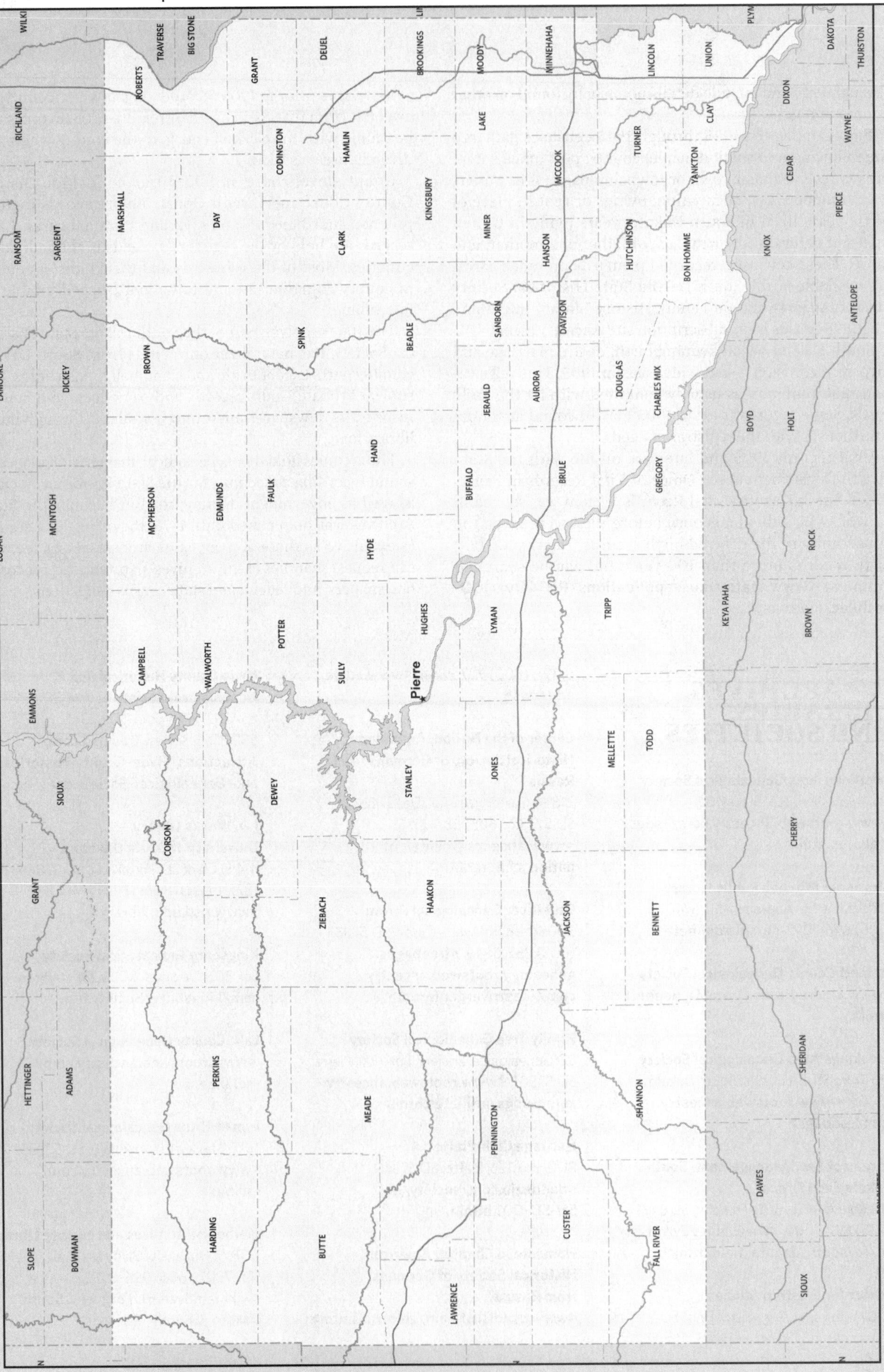
Pierre
RICHLAND
ROBERTS
TRAVERSE
BIG STONE
GRANT
DEUEL
BROOKINGS
MOODY
MINNEHAHA
LINCOLN
UNION
RANSOM
SARGENT
MARSHALL
DAY
CODINGTON
HAMLIN
CLARK
KINGSBURY
LAKE
MINER
MCCOOK
HANSON
TURNER
HUTCHINSON
YANKTON
CLAY
BON HOMME
LAMOURE
DICKEY
BROWN
SPINK
BEADLE
SANBORN
JERAULD
AURORA
DAVISON
DOUGLAS
CHARLES MIX
LOGAN
MCINTOSH
MCPHERSON
EDMUNDS
FAULK
HAND
BUFFALO
BRULE
GREGORY
EMMONS
CAMPBELL
WALWORTH
POTTER
HYDE
HUGHES
SULLY
LYMAN
TRIPP
SIOUX
CORSON
DEWEY
STANLEY
JONES
MELLETTE
TODD
GRANT
ZIEBACH
HAAKON
JACKSON
BENNETT
HETTINGER
ADAMS
PERKINS
MEADE
PENNINGTON
SHANNON
SLOPE
BOWMAN
HARDING
BUTTE
LAWRENCE
CUSTER
FALL RIVER
DAKOTA
THURSTON
DIXON
WAYNE
CEDAR
PIERCE
KNOX
ANTELOPE
BOYD
HOLT
ROCK
KEYA PAHA
BROWN
CHERRY
SHERIDAN
DAWES
SIOUX

Mitchell Area Genealogical Society
620 N. Edmunds, Mitchell, SD 57301, **<daddezio.com/society/hill/SH-SD-001.html>**

Moody County Genealogical Society
501 W. First Ave., Flandreau, SD 57028, **<www.rook.org/places/sd/moodycosd.html>**

Murdo Genealogical Society
Box 441, Murdo, SD 57559, **<genealogytrails.com/sdak/mellette/links.htm>**

National Archives and Records Administration, Rocky Mountain Region
Box 25307, Denver, Colorado 80225, (303) 407-5740, **<www.archives.gov/rocky-mountain>**

North Central South Dakota Genealogical Society
178 Southshore Dr., Mina, SD 57462, **<genealogytrails.com/sdak/mellette/links.htm>**

Pierre-Ft. Pierre Genealogical Society
Box 925, Pierre, SD 57501, **<www.rootsweb.ancestry.com/~sdgs/affiliates.html>**

Platte Heritage Club
Box 517, Platte, SD 57369, **<history.sd.gov/Aboutus/organizations/heritage.aspx>**

Rapid City Society for Genealogical Research
<www.rootsweb.ancestry.com/~sdrcsgr/rapid_city_society.htm>

Roman Catholic Diocese of Rapid City
Chancery Office, 606 Cathedral Dr., Rapid City, SD 57701, (605) 343-3541, **<www.rapidcitydiocese.org>**

Roman Catholic Diocese of Sioux Falls
523 N Duluth Ave Sioux Falls SD 57104, (800) 700-7867, **<sfcatholic.org>**

Sioux Valley Genealogical Society
200 W. Sixth S., Sioux Falls, SD 57104, **<www.siouxvalleygenealogicalsociety.org>**

South Dakota Genealogical Society
Box 1101, Pierre, SD 57501, **<www.rootsweb.ancestry.com/~sdgs>**

South Dakota State Historical Society
900 Governors Dr., Pierre, SD 57501, (605) 773-3458, **<history.sd.gov>**

State Department of Health
600 E. Capitol, Pierre, SD 57501, (605) 773-3361 or (800) 738-2301

Tri-State Genealogical Society
c/o Public Library, 905 Fifth St., Belle Fourche, SD 57717, **<freepages.genealogy.rootsweb.ancestry.com/~tristate>**

Union County Historical Society
Box 552, Elk Point, SD 57025, **<www.acsnet.com/~jkjar>**

Watertown Genealogical Society
611 NE B Ave., Watertown, SD 57201, **<www.rootsweb.ancestry.com/~sdcoding>**

Yankton Genealogical Society
1803 Douglas Ave., Yankton 57078

GENERAL RESOURCES

Daughters of Dakota, 6 vols., by Sally Roesch Wagner (Daughters of Dakota, ca. 1989)

Fox's Who's Who Among South Dakotans, 2 vols., (Fox Kindley, 1929)

Historical Data Project; Pioneer Biography Files (State Historical Society of North Dakota, 1988-1989)

History of Dakota Territory and South Dakota: Its History and Its People, 5 vols., by George Martin Smith (S.J. Clarke Co., 1915)

History of South Dakota by Herbert S. Schell (University of Nebraska Press, 1968)

Once Their Home: or Our Legacy From the Dahkotahs by Frances Chamberlain Holley (Donohue & Henneberry, 1892)

Prairie Progress in West Central South Dakota (Historical Society of Old Stanley County, South Dakota, 1968)

South Dakota: Changing, Changeless, 1889-1989 compiled by Ruth A. Alexander, et al. (South Dakota Library Association, 1985)

South Dakota Research Outline by the Church of Jesus Christ of Latter-day Saints (online at **<www.familysearch.org/eng/search/RG/guide/south_dakota.asp>**)

IMMIGRATION RECORDS

French-Canadian Families of the North Central Sates: A Genealogical Dictionary, 8 vols., Paul J. Lareau and Elmer Courteau (Northwest Territory French and Canadian Heritage Institute, 1980)

LAND RECORDS

The Administration of the Public Domain in South Dakota by Charles L. Green (Hipple Printing, 1939)

Fifty Million Acres: Conflicts Over Kansas Land Policy, 1854-1890 by Paul Wallace Gates (University of Oklahoma Press, 1997)

A History of the Public Land Policies by Benjamin Horace Hibbard (University of Wisconsin Press, 1965)

Indian Depredation Claims, 1796-1920 by Larry C. Skogen (University of Oklahoma Press, ca. 1996)

MAPS

Northwestern Gazetteer: Minnesota, North and South Dakota and Montana Gazetteer and Business Directory from R.L. Polk & Company (R.L. Polk & Company, 1914)

Postoffices and Postmarks of Dakota Territory by George H. Phillips (J-B Publishing, 1973)

The Post Offices of South Dakota, 1861-1930 by George H. Phillips (J-B Publishing, 1975)

South Dakota Place Names from the Federal Writer's Project (University of South Dakota, 1940)

VITAL RECORDS

Some Black Hills Area Cemeteries, South Dakota, 6 vols., from the Rapid City Society for Genealogical Research (Rapid City Society for Genealogical Research, 1993)

South Dakota Cemeteries, 1990 by Maurice Krueger and Florence Krueger (Maurice and Florence Krueger, 1990)

South Dakota Grave Registration Project; Cemetery Information from the US Work Projects Administration (filmed by the Family History Library, 1980)

South Dakota Graves Registration Service; Field Data-Veterans from the US Work Projects Administration (filmed by the Family History Library, 1980)

COUNTY DETAILS

ARMSTRONG
- **INCORPORATED:** March 1895
- **PARENT COUNTY:** Pratt
- **NOTES:** See Dewey County. Formerly Pyatt County. Eliminated 1952 to Dewey, Haakon, and Ziebach.

ARMSTRONG, OLD
- **INCORPORATED:** January 1873
- **PARENT COUNTY:** Dakota territory
- **NOTES:** See Hutchinson County. Eliminated 1879 to Hutchinson.

ASHMORE
- **INCORPORATED:** January 1875
- **PARENT COUNTY:** Buffalo
- **NOTES:** See Potter County. Name changed to Potter 1877.

AURORA
Box 397, Plankinton, SD 57368, (605) 942-7752, **<www.rootsweb.ancestry.com/~sdaurora>**
- **INCORPORATED:** October 1879
- **PARENT COUNTY:** Brule
- **BIRTH RECORDS:** 1905, Registrar of Deeds
- **MARRIAGE:** 1905, Registrar of Deeds
- **DIVORCE:** start in 1883, kept by Clerk of Courts
- **DEATH:** 1905, Registrar of Deeds
- **LAND:** 1882, Registrar of Deeds
- **PROBATE:** 1882, Clerk of Courts
- **COURT:** 1882, Clerk of Courts
- **BURIAL:** 1941, Registrar of Deeds
- **NOTES:** Registrar of Deeds has incomplete marriage records dating from 1883 to 1904. State Archives has naturalization records 1882-1953.

BEADLE
450 3rd St SW, Huron, SD 57350, (605) 353-8400, **<www.beadlecounty.org>**
- **INCORPORATED:** October 1879
- **PARENT COUNTIES:** Spink, Clark
- **BIRTH RECORDS:** 1905, Registrar of Deeds
- **MARRIAGE:** 1880, Registrar of Deeds
- **DIVORCE:** start in 1881, kept by Clerk of Courts
- **DEATH:** 1905, Registrar of Deeds
- **LAND:** 1886, Registrar of Deeds
- **PROBATE:** 1882, Clerk of Courts
- **COURT:** 1882, Clerk of Courts
- **BURIAL:** 1925, Registrar of Deeds
- **NOTES:** Organized 1880. State Archives has naturalization records 1880-1956.

BEADLE, OLD
- **INCORPORATED:** January 1873
- **PARENT COUNTY:** Hanson
- **NOTES:** See Brown County. Eliminated 1879 to Brown.

BENNETT
Box 460, Martin, SD 57551, (605) 685-6969, **<www.rootsweb.ancestry.com/~sdbennet>**
- **INCORPORATED:** June 1909
- **PARENT COUNTY:** Indian land
- **BIRTH RECORDS:** 1912, Registrar of Deeds
- **MARRIAGE:** 1912, Registrar of Deeds
- **DIVORCE:** Start in 1912, kept by Clerk of Courts
- **DEATH:** 1912, Registrar of Deeds
- **LAND:** 1907, Registrar of Deeds
- **PROBATE:** 1912, Clerk of Courts
- **COURT:** 1912, Clerk of Courts
- **BURIAL:** 1940, Registrar of Deeds
- **NOTES:** Attached to Fall River County prior to organization 1912. State Archives has naturalization records 1912-1952.

BON HOMME
300 W 18th Ave., Tyndall, SD 57066, (605) 589-4212, **<www.rootsweb.ancestry.com/~sdbonhom>**
- **INCORPORATED:** April 1862
- **PARENT COUNTY:** Charles Mix
- **BIRTH RECORDS:** 1905, Registrar of Deeds
- **MARRIAGE:** 1885, Registrar of Deeds
- **DIVORCE:** 1870, Clerk of Courts
- **DEATH:** 1905, Registrar of Deeds
- **LAND:** 1890, Registrar of Deeds
- **PROBATE:** start in 1877, kept by Clerk of Courts
- **COURT:** 1871, Clerk of Courts
- **BURIAL:** 1940, Registrar of Deeds
- **NOTES:** State Archives has naturalization records 1871-1944.

BOREMAN
- **INCORPORATED:** January 1873
- **PARENT COUNTY:** Unorganized Territory
- **NOTES:** See Corson County. Attached to Campbell County. Eliminated 1909 to Corson.

BRAMBLE

- **INCORPORATED:** January 1873
- **PARENT COUNTY:** Hanson
- **NOTES:** Eliminated 1879 to Miner.

BROOKINGS

314 Sixth Ave., Brookings, SD 57006, (605) 696-8205,
<www.brookingscountysd.gov>

- **INCORPORATED:** April 1862
- **PARENT COUNTY:** Unorganized Territory
- **BIRTH RECORDS:** 1905, Registrar of Deeds
- **MARRIAGE:** 1905, Registrar of Deeds
- **DIVORCE:** start in 1870s, kept by Clerk of Courts
- **DEATH:** 1905, Registrar of Deeds
- **LAND:** 1871, Registrar of Deeds
- **PROBATE:** 1870s, Clerk of Courts
- **COURT:** 1870s, Clerk of Courts
- **NOTES:** Organized July 3, 1871. Registrar of Deeds has incomplete marriage records 1887-1905. State Archives has naturalization records 1880-1954.

BROWN

25 Market St., Aberdeen, SD 57401, (605) 626-7109,
<www.brown.sd.us>

- **INCORPORATED:** July 20, 1880
- **PARENT COUNTIES:** Mills, Stone, Beadle, old
- **BIRTH RECORDS:** 1905, Registrar of Deeds
- **MARRIAGE:** 1905, Registrar of Deeds
- **DIVORCE:** start in 1884, kept by Clerk of Courts
- **DEATH:** 1905, Registrar of Deeds
- **LAND:** 1880, Registrar of Deeds
- **PROBATE:** ca. 1880, Clerk of Courts
- **COURT:** ca. 1880, Clerk of Courts
- **MILITARY:** 1917, Registrar of Deeds
- **BURIAL:** 1885, Registrar of Deeds
- **NOTES:** Registrar of Deeds has incomplete marriage records 1892-1905. State Archives has naturalization records 1881-1954.

BRUGUIER

- **INCORPORATED:** May 1862
- **PARENT COUNTY:** Unorganized Territory
- **NOTES:** Attached to Charles Mix. Eliminated 1864 to Buffalo and Charles Mix.

BRULE

300 S. Courtland St., Chamberlain, SD 57325, (605) 234-4430,
<brulecounty.org>

- **INCORPORATED:** January 1875
- **PARENT COUNTY:** Charles Mix
- **BIRTH RECORDS:** 1905, Registrar of Deeds
- **MARRIAGE:** 1882, Registrar of Deeds
- **DIVORCE:** 1883, Clerk of Courts
- **DEATH:** 1905, Registrar of Deeds
- **LAND:** 1879, Registrar of Deeds
- **PROBATE:** ca. 1875, Clerk of Courts
- **COURT:** start in ca. 1875, kept by Clerk of Courts
- **NATURALIZATION:** 1882, Clerk of Courts
- **BURIAL:** 1941, Registrar of Deeds
- **NOTES:** Registrar of Deeds has incomplete burial records 1888-1941.

BUFFALO

Box 146, Gann Valley, SD 57341, (605) 293- 3217,
<genealogytrails.com/sdak/buffalo>

- **INCORPORATED:** January 1864
- **PARENT COUNTIES:** Brugier, Charles Mix, Unorganized Territory
- **BIRTH RECORDS:** 1905, Registrar of Deeds
- **MARRIAGE:** 1887, Registrar of Deeds
- **DIVORCE:** start in 1889, kept by Clerk of Courts
- **DEATH:** 1905, Registrar of Deeds
- **LAND:** 1885, Registrar of Deeds
- **PROBATE:** 1884, Clerk of Courts
- **COURT:** 1890, Clerk of Courts
- **MILITARY:** 1919, Registrar of Deeds
- **BURIAL:** 1941, Registrar of Deeds
- **NOTES:** Attached to Bon Homme County prior to organization 1871. State Archives has naturalization records 1885-1938.

BURCHARD

- **INCORPORATED:** January 1873
- **PARENT COUNTY:** Hanson
- **NOTES:** Eliminated 1879 to Beadle and Hand.

BURDICK

- **INCORPORATED:** March 1883
- **PARENT COUNTY:** Dakota territory
- **NOTES:** Eliminated 1889 to Harding.

BUTTE

839 Fifth Ave., Belle Fourche, SD 57717, (605) 892- 4485,
<www.buttecountysd.org>

- **INCORPORATED:** May 1883
- **PARENT COUNTIES:** Lawrence, Mandan
- **BIRTH RECORDS:** 1905, Registrar of Deeds
- **MARRIAGE:** 1890, Registrar of Deeds
- **DIVORCE:** start in 1893, kept by Clerk of Courts
- **DEATH:** 1905, Registrar of Deeds
- **LAND:** 1883, Registrar of Deeds
- **PROBATE:** ca. 1883, Clerk of Courts
- **COURT:** ca. 1883, Clerk of Courts
- **BURIAL:** 1907, Registrar of Deeds
- **NOTES:** State Archives has naturalization records 1876-1955.

CAMPBELL

Box 37, Mound City, SD 57646, (605) 955-3366,
<genealogytrails.com/sdak/campbell>

- **INCORPORATED:** January 1873
- **PARENT COUNTY:** Buffalo
- **BIRTH RECORDS:** 1905, Registrar of Deeds
- **MARRIAGE:** 1888, Registrar of Deeds
- **DIVORCE:** 1884, Clerk of Courts
- **DEATH:** 1905, Registrar of Deeds
- **LAND:** 1898, Registrar of Deeds
- **PROBATE:** 1884, Clerk of Courts
- **COURT:** 1884, Clerk of Courts

- **NATURALIZATION:** start in 1884, kept by Clerk of Courts
- **BURIAL:** 1941, Registrar of Deeds
- **NOTES:** Organized 1884. Registrar of Deeds has incomplete burial records 1923-1934.

CHARLES MIX

Box 490, Lake Andes, SD 57356, (605) 487-7131,
<www.charlesmixcountysd.org>

- **INCORPORATED:** May 1862
- **PARENT COUNTY:** Unorganized Territory
- **BIRTH RECORDS:** 1905, Registrar of Deeds
- **MARRIAGE:** 1883, Registrar of Deeds
- **DIVORCE:** start in 1886, kept by Clerk of Courts
- **DEATH:** 1905, Registrar of Deeds
- **LAND:** late 1800s, Registrar of Deeds
- **PROBATE:** ca. 1875, Clerk of Courts
- **COURT:** ca. 1875, Clerk of Courts
- **NOTES:** County was dissolved in 1864 and was attached to Bon Homme county. County was reorganized in 1879. State Archives has naturalization records 1879-1955.

CHEYENNE

- **INCORPORATED:** January 1875
- **PARENT COUNTIES:** Pratt, Rusk, Stanley, Unorganized Territory
- **NOTES:** Eliminated 1883 to Jackson, Nowlin, Pyatt and Sterling.

CHOTEAU

- **INCORPORATED:** March 1883
- **PARENT COUNTY:** Martin
- **NOTES:** Attached to Lawrence County. Eliminated 1898 to Butte and Meade.

CLARK

Box 294, Clark, SD 57225, (605) 532-5921, **<www.clarksd.com>**

- **INCORPORATED:** January 1873
- **PARENT COUNTY:** Hanson
- **BIRTH RECORDS:** 1905, Registrar of Deeds
- **MARRIAGE:** 1905, Registrar of Deeds
- **DIVORCE:** start in 1882, kept by Clerk of Courts
- **DEATH:** 1905, Registrar of Deeds
- **LAND:** 1881, Registrar of Deeds
- **PROBATE:** 1882, Clerk of Courts
- **COURT:** 1885, Clerk of Courts
- **BURIAL:** 1940, Registrar of Deeds
- **NOTES:** Organized 1881. Registrar of Deeds has incomplete marriage records 1883-1905. State Archives has naturalization records 1881-1945.

CLAY

211 W Main St., Vermillion, SD 57069, (605) 677-7120,
<www.claycountysd.org>

- **INCORPORATED:** April 1862
- **PARENT COUNTY:** Unorganized Territory
- **BIRTH RECORDS:** 1905, Registrar of Deeds
- **MARRIAGE:** 1860, Registrar of Deeds
- **DIVORCE:** 1866, Clerk of Courts
- **DEATH:** 1905, Registrar of Deeds
- **LAND:** 1863, Registrar of Deeds
- **PROBATE:** ca. 1862, Clerk of Court
- **COURT:** start in ca. 1862, kept by Clerk of Courts
- **NOTES:** Burial records are kept by individual cemeteries. State Archives has naturalization records 1867-1929.

CODINGTON

14 First Ave. SE, Watertown, SD 57201, (605) 882-6297,
<www.codington.org>

- **INCORPORATED:** February 1877
- **PARENT COUNTIES:** Clark, Grant, Hamlin
- **BIRTH RECORDS:** 1905, Registrar of Deeds
- **MARRIAGE:** 1905, Registrar of Deeds
- **DIVORCE:** start in 1887, kept by Clerk of Courts
- **DEATH:** 1905, Registrar of Deeds
- **LAND:** 1877, Registrar of Deeds
- **PROBATE:** 1878, Clerk of Courts
- **COURT:** 1878 Clerk of Courts
- **MILITARY:** 1919, Registrar of Deeds
- **BURIAL:** 1892, Registrar of Deeds
- **NOTES:** Organized 19 July 1878. Registrar of Deeds has incomplete birth records 1884-1905, and marriage records 1887-1905. State Archives has naturalization records 1879-1930.

COLE

- **INCORPORATED:** April 1862
- **PARENT COUNTY:** Unorganized Territory
- **NOTES:** See Union County. Name changed to Union 1864.

CORSON

Box 255, McIntosh, SD 57641, (605) 273-4229, **<www.rootsweb.ancestry.com/~sdcorson>**

- **INCORPORATED:** March 1909
- **PARENT COUNTIES:** Boreman, Dewey, Schnasse
- **BIRTH RECORDS:** 1909, Registrar of Deeds
- **MARRIAGE:** 1909, Registrar of Deeds
- **DIVORCE:** start in 1909, kept by Clerk of Courts
- **DEATH:** 1909, Registrar of Deeds
- **LAND:** 1909, Registrar of Deeds
- **PROBATE:** ca. 1909, Clerk of Courts
- **COURT:** ca. 1909, Clerk of Courts
- **NOTES:** State Archives has naturalization records 1909-1951.

CRAGIN

- **INCORPORATED:** January 1873
- **PARENT COUNTY:** Hanson
- **NOTES:** Eliminated 1879 to Aurora.

CUSTER

420 Mt. Rushmore Rd., Custer, SD 57730, (605) 673-8100,
<www.custercountysd.com>

- **INCORPORATED:** January 1875
- **PARENT COUNTY:** Unorganized Territory
- **BIRTH RECORDS:** 1905, Registrar of Deeds
- **MARRIAGE:** 1890, Registrar of Deeds
- **DIVORCE:** start in 1880, kept by Clerk of Courts
- **DEATH:** 1905, Registrar of Deeds
- **LAND:** 1875, Registrar of Deeds
- **PROBATE:** ca. 1877, Clerk of Courts

- **COURT:** ca. 1877, Clerk of Courts
- **NOTES:** Organized 1877. State Archives has naturalization records 1880-1942.

DAVISON

200 E. Fourth Ave., Mitchell, SD 57301, (605) 995-8608, **<www.davisoncounty.org>**

- **INCORPORATED:** January 1873
- **PARENT COUNTY:** Hanson
- **BIRTH RECORDS:** 1905, Registrar of Deeds
- **MARRIAGE:** 1887, Registrar of Deeds
- **DIVORCE:** start in 1882, kept by Clerk of Courts
- **DEATH:** 1905, Registrar of Deeds
- **LAND:** 1873, Registrar of Deeds
- **PROBATE:** ca. 1873, Clerk of Courts
- **COURT:** ca. 1833, Clerk of Courts
- **NOTES:** Organized 1874. State Archives has naturalization records 1878-1956.

DAY

711 W. First St., Webster, SD 57274, (605) 345-3102, **<www.daycountysd.org>**

- **INCORPORATED:** October 1879
- **PARENT COUNTIES:** Greeley, Stone
- **BIRTH RECORDS:** 1905, Registrar of Deeds
- **MARRIAGE:** 1882, Registrar of Deeds
- **DIVORCE:** start in 1881, kept by Clerk of Courts
- **DEATH:** 1905, Registrar of Deeds
- **LAND:** 1879, Registrar of Deeds
- **PROBATE:** ca. 1882, Clerk of Courts
- **COURT:** ca. 1882, Clerk of Courts
- **BURIAL:** 1905, Registrar of Deeds
- **NOTES:** Organized 1882. State Archives has naturalization records 1882-1942.

DELANO

- **INCORPORATED:** January 1875
- **PARENT COUNTY:** Unorganized Territory
- **NOTES:** Attached to Lawrence County. Eliminated 1898 to Meade.

DEUEL

Box 616, Clear Lake, SD 57226, (605) 874-2321, **<www.deuelcountysd.com>**

- **INCORPORATED:** April 1862
- **PARENT COUNTY:** Unorganized Territory
- **BIRTH RECORDS:** 1905, Registrar of Deeds
- **MARRIAGE:** 1879, Registrar of Deeds
- **DIVORCE:** start in 1879, kept by Clerk of Courts
- **DEATH:** 1905, Registrar of Deeds
- **LAND:** 1885, Registrar of Deeds
- **PROBATE:** ca. 1878, Clerk of Courts
- **COURT:** ca. 1878, Clerk of Courts
- **BURIAL:** 1941, Registrar of Deeds
- **NOTES:** Organized 1878. Registrar of Deeds has incomplete birth records 1880-1905, and burial records 1930-1941. State Archives has naturalization records 1878-1930.

DEWEY

Box 277, Timber Lake, SD 57656, (605) 865-3672, **<www.rootsweb.ancestry.com/~sddewey>**

- **INCORPORATED:** January 1873
- **PARENT COUNTY:** Unorganized Territory
- **BIRTH RECORDS:** 1905, Registrar of Deeds
- **MARRIAGE:** 1910, Registrar of Deeds
- **DIVORCE:** start in 1910, kept by Clerk of Courts
- **DEATH:** 1905, Registrar of Deeds
- **LAND:** 1912, Registrar of Deeds
- **PROBATE:** ca. 1910, Clerk of Courts
- **COURT:** ca. 1910, Clerk of Courts
- **BURIAL:** 1941 Registrar of Deeds
- **NOTES:** Formerly Rusk County. Name changed to Dewey 1883. Attached to Walworth County prior to organized 1910. State Archives has naturalization records 1911-1955.

DOUGLAS

Box 159, Armour, SD 57313, (605) 724-2423, **<www.rootsweb.ancestry.com/~sddougla>**

- **INCORPORATED:** January 1873
- **PARENT COUNTY:** Charles Mix
- **BIRTH RECORDS:** 1905, Registrar of Deeds
- **MARRIAGE:** 1883, Registrar of Deeds
- **DIVORCE:** 1885, Clerk of Courts
- **DEATH:** 1905, Registrar of Deeds
- **LAND:** 1882, Registrar of Deeds
- **PROBATE:** ca. 1882, Clerk of Courts
- **COURT:** start in ca. 1882, kept by Clerk of Courts
- **NOTES:** Organized 1882. State Archives has naturalization records 1882-1943.

EDMUNDS

Box 97, Ipswich, SD 57451, (605) 426-6762, **<www.rootsweb.ancestry.com/~sdedmund>**

- **INCORPORATED:** January 1873
- **PARENT COUNTY:** Buffalo
- **BIRTH RECORDS:** 1905, Registrar of Deeds
- **MARRIAGE:** 1887, Registrar of Deeds
- **DIVORCE:** start in 1884, kept by Clerk of Courts
- **DEATH:** 1905, Registrar of Deeds
- **LAND:** 1883, Registrar of Deeds
- **PROBATE:** 1884, Clerk of Courts
- **COURT:** 1884, Clerk of Courts
- **BURIAL:** 1941, Registrar of Deeds
- **NOTES:** Organized 1883. State Archives has naturalization records 1884-1954.

EWING

- **INCORPORATED:** March 1883
- **PARENT COUNTY:** Harding
- **NOTES:** Attached to Butte County. Eliminated 1894 to Harding.

FALL RIVER

906 N. River St., Hot Springs, SD 57747, (605) 745-5130, **<www.fallrivercounty.org>**

- **INCORPORATED:** April 1883
- **PARENT COUNTY:** Custer

- **BIRTH RECORDS:** 1905, Registrar of Deeds
- **MARRIAGE:** 1905, Registrar of Deeds
- **DIVORCE:** start in 1882, kept by Clerk of Courts
- **DEATH:** 1905, Registrar of Deeds
- **LAND:** 1907, Registrar of Deeds
- **PROBATE:** ca. 1883, Clerk of Courts
- **COURT:** ca. 1883, Clerk of Courts
- **NOTES:** State Archives has naturalization records 1905-1954.

FAULK

Box 309, Faulkton, SD 57438, (605) 598-6224, **<www.rootsweb.ancestry.com/~sdfaulk/findex.htm>**

- **INCORPORATED:** January 1873
- **PARENT COUNTY:** Buffalo
- **BIRTH RECORDS:** 1905, Registrar of Deeds
- **MARRIAGE:** 1890, Registrar of Deeds
- **DIVORCE:** start in 1883, kept by Clerk of Courts
- **DEATH:** 1905, Registrar of Deeds
- **LAND:** 1888, Registrar of Deeds
- **PROBATE:** 1884, Clerk of Courts
- **COURT:** 1883, Clerk of Courts
- **BURIAL:** 1890, Registrar of Deeds
- **NOTES:** Organized 1883. Registrar of Deeds has incomplete marriage records 1883-1887. State Archives has naturalization records 1884-1944.

FORSYTHE

- **INCORPORATED:** January 1875
- **PARENT COUNTY:** Unorganized Territory
- **NOTES:** Eliminated 1881 to Custer.

GRANT

210 E. Fifth Ave., Milbank, SD 57252, (605) 432-6711, **<www.rootsweb.ancestry.com/~sdgrant>**

- **INCORPORATED:** January 1873
- **PARENT COUNTIES:** Deuel, Hanson
- **BIRTH RECORDS:** 1905, Registrar of Deeds
- **MARRIAGE:** 1905, Registrar of Deeds
- **DIVORCE:** start in 1895, kept by Clerk of Courts
- **DEATH:** 1905, Registrar of Deeds
- **LAND:** 1878, Registrar of Deeds
- **PROBATE:** 1878, Clerk of Courts
- **COURT:** 1878, Clerk of Courts
- **NOTES:** Organized 1878. Fire in early 1900s destroyed many records. State Archives has naturalization records 1881-1955.

GREELY

- **INCORPORATED:** January 1873
- **PARENT COUNTY:** Hanson
- **NOTES:** Eliminated 1879 to Day.

GREGORY

Box 437, Burke, SD 57523, (605) 775-2664, **<genealogytrails.com/sdak/gregory>**

- **INCORPORATED:** May 1862
- **PARENT COUNTY:** Unorganized Territory
- **BIRTH RECORDS:** 1905, Registrar of Deeds
- **MARRIAGE:** 1898, Registrar of Deeds
- **DIVORCE:** start in 1899, kept by Clerk of Courts
- **DEATH:** 1905, Registrar of Deeds
- **LAND:** 1862, Registrar of Deeds
- **PROBATE:** 1862, Clerk of Courts
- **COURT:** 1862, Clerk of Courts
- **BURIAL:** 1905, Registrar of Deeds
- **NOTES:** Attached to Todd and Charles Mix counties prior to organization 1898. State Archives has naturalization records 1898-1952.

HAAKON

Box 698, Philip, SD 57567, (605) 859-2800, **<www.rootsweb.ancestry.com/~sdhaakon>**

- **INCORPORATED:** November 1914
- **PARENT COUNTY:** Stanley
- **BIRTH RECORDS:** 1915, Registrar of Deeds
- **MARRIAGE:** 1915, Registrar of Deeds
- **DIVORCE:** start in 1915, kept by Clerk of Courts
- **DEATH:** 1915, Registrar of Deeds
- **LAND:** 1893, Registrar of Deeds
- **PROBATE:** 1915, Clerk of Courts
- **COURT:** 1915, Clerk of Courts
- **BURIAL:** 1941, Registrar of Deeds
- **NOTES:** Organized 1915.

HAMLIN

Box 237, Hayti, SD 57241, (605) 783-3201, **<sdgenweb.com/hamlin>**

- **INCORPORATED:** January 1873
- **PARENT COUNTIES:** Deuel, Hanson
- **BIRTH RECORDS:** 1905, Registrar of Deeds
- **MARRIAGE:** 1887, Registrar of Deeds
- **DIVORCE:** 1885, Clerk of Courts
- **DEATH:** 1905, Registrar of Deeds
- **LAND:** 1885, Registrar of Deeds
- **PROBATE:** ca. 1878, Clerk of Courts
- **COURT:** start in ca. 1878, kept by Clerk of Courts
- **NOTES:** Organized 1878. State Archives has naturalization records 1880-1945.

HAND

415 W. First Ave., Miller, SD 57362, (605) 853-2182, **<www.handcountysd.org>**

- **INCORPORATED:** January 1873
- **PARENT COUNTY:** Buffalo
- **BIRTH RECORDS:** 1905, Registrar of Deeds
- **MARRIAGE:** 1883, Registrar of Deeds
- **DIVORCE:** start in 1882, kept by Clerk of Courts
- **DEATH:** 1905, Registrar of Deeds
- **LAND:** 1881, Registrar of Deeds
- **PROBATE:** 1873, Clerk of Courts
- **COURT:** 1873, Clerk of Courts
- **BURIAL:** 1932, Registrar of Deeds
- **NOTES:** Organized 1882. State Archives has naturalization records 1882-1945.

HANSON

Box 500, Alexandria, SD 57311, (605) 239-4714, **<www.rootsweb.ancestry.com/~sdhanson>**

- **INCORPORATED:** January 1871
- **PARENT COUNTIES:** Buffalo, Deuel, Brookings, Charles Mix, Hutchinson, Jayne, Minnehaha, unorganized land
- **BIRTH RECORDS:** 1905, Registrar of Deeds
- **MARRIAGE:** 1901, Registrar of Deeds
- **DIVORCE:** start in 1896, kept by Clerk of Courts
- **DEATH:** 1905, Registrar of Deeds
- **PROBATE:** ca. 1873, Clerk of Courts
- **COURT:** ca. 1873, Clerk of Courts
- **NOTES:** Organized 1873. State Archives has naturalization records 1901-1946.

HARDING

Box 26, Buffalo, SD 57720, (605) 375-3313, **<www.rootsweb.ancestry.com/~sdhardin>**

- **INCORPORATED:** March 1881
- **PARENT COUNTY:** Unorganized Territory
- **BIRTH RECORDS:** 1909, Registrar of Deeds
- **MARRIAGE:** 1909, Registrar of Deeds
- **DIVORCE:** start in 1909, kept by Clerk of Courts
- **DEATH:** 1909, Registrar of Deeds
- **LAND:** 1909, Registrar of Deeds
- **PROBATE:** ca. 1911, Clerk of Courts
- **COURT:** ca. 1911, Clerk of Courts
- **MILITARY:** 1917, Registrar of Deeds
- **NOTES:** Attached to Butte County 1881-1898. Eliminated 1898 to Butte. Recreated 1908 from Butte. Organized 1911. State Archives has naturalization records 1909-1944.

HUGHES

104 E. Capitol Ave., Pierre, SD 57501, (605) 773-7477, **<www.hughescounty.org>**

- **INCORPORATED:** January 1873
- **PARENT COUNTY:** Buffalo
- **BIRTH RECORDS:** 1905, Registrar of Deeds
- **MARRIAGE:** 1905, Registrar of Deeds
- **DIVORCE:** start in 1909, kept by Clerk of Courts
- **DEATH:** 1905, Registrar of Deeds
- **LAND:** 1885, Registrar of Deeds
- **PROBATE:** ca. 1880, Clerk of Courts
- **COURT:** ca. 1880, Clerk of Courts
- **BURIAL:** 1951, Registrar of Deeds
- **NOTES:** Organized 1880. State Archives has naturalization records 1881-1956.

HUTCHINSON

140 Euclid St. Room 128, Olivet, SD 57052, (605) 387-4217, **<www.rootsweb.ancestry.com/~sdhutchi>**

- **INCORPORATED:** May 1862
- **PARENT COUNTY:** Unorganized Territory
- **BIRTH RECORDS:** 1905, Registrar of Deeds
- **MARRIAGE:** 1887, Registrar of Deeds
- **DEATH:** 1905, Registrar of Deeds
- **LAND:** 1876, Registrar of Deeds
- **PROBATE:** ca. 1871, Clerk of Courts
- **COURT:** start in ca. 1871, kept by Clerk of Courts
- **NOTES:** Organized 1871. State Archives has naturalization records 1876-1948.

HYDE

Box 379, Highmore, SD 57345, (605) 852-2519, **<www.rootsweb.ancestry.com/~sdhyde>**

- **INCORPORATED:** January 1873
- **PARENT COUNTY:** Buffalo
- **BIRTH RECORDS:** 1905, Registrar of Deeds
- **MARRIAGE:** 1890, Registrar of Deeds
- **DEATH:** 1905, Registrar of Deeds
- **LAND:** ca. 1883, Registrar of Deeds
- **PROBATE:** ca. 1883, Clerk of Courts
- **COURT:** start in ca. 1883, kept by Clerk of Courts
- **NOTES:** Organized 1883. State Archives has naturalization records 1883-1944.

JACKSON

Box 280, Kadoka, SD 57543, (605) 837-2422, **<www.rootsweb.ancestry.com/~sdjackso>**

- **INCORPORATED:** March 1883
- **PARENT COUNTIES:** Cheyenne, Lugenbeel, White River
- **BIRTH RECORDS:** 1915, Registrar of Deeds
- **MARRIAGE:** 1915, Registrar of Deeds
- **DEATH:** 1915, Registrar of Deeds
- **LAND:** 1907, Registrar of Deeds
- **PROBATE:** start in 1915, kept by Clerk of Courts
- **COURT:** 1915, Clerk of Courts
- **BURIAL:** 1915, Registrar of Deeds
- **NOTES:** Attached to Pennington County. Eliminated 1909 to Mellette and Washabaugh. Recreated 1914 from Stanley. Organized 1915. State Archives has naturalization records 1916-1948.

JAYNE

- **INCORPORATED:** May 1862
- **PARENT COUNTY:** Unorganized Territory
- **NOTES:** Attached to Yankton County. Eliminated 1871 to Hanson, Hutchinson and Turner counties.

JERAULD

Box 422, Wessington Springs, SD 57382, (605) 539-9301, **<www.rootsweb.ancestry.com/~sdjeraul>**

- **INCORPORATED:** April 1883
- **PARENT COUNTIES:** Aurora, Buffalo
- **BIRTH RECORDS:** 1905, Registrar of Deeds
- **MARRIAGE:** 1888, Registrar of Deeds
- **DEATH:** 1905, Registrar of Deeds
- **LAND:** early 1900s, Registrar of Deeds
- **PROBATE:** start in ca. 1883, kept by Clerk of Courts
- **COURT:** ca. 1883, Clerk of Courts
- **NOTES:** Registrar of Deeds has incomplete marriage records 1884-1887. State Archives has naturalization records 1906-1947.

JONES

Box 307, Murdo, SD 57559, (605) 669-2242, **<www.rootsweb.ancestry.com/~sdjones>**

- **INCORPORATED:** January 1916
- **PARENT COUNTY:** Lyman
- **BIRTH RECORDS:** 1917, Registrar of Deeds
- **MARRIAGE:** 1917, Registrar of Deeds
- **DEATH:** 1917, Registrar of Deeds
- **LAND:** 1906, Registrar of Deeds
- **PROBATE:** start in ca. 1917, kept by Clerk of Courts
- **COURT:** ca. 1917, Clerk of Courts
- **BURIAL:** 1917, Registrar of Deeds
- **NOTES:** State Archives has naturalization records 1903-1959.

KINGSBURY

Box 196, De Smet, SD 57231, (605) 854-3832, **<sdgenweb.com/kingsbury>**

- **INCORPORATED:** January 1873
- **PARENT COUNTY:** Hanson
- **BIRTH RECORDS:** 1905, Registrar of Deeds
- **MARRIAGE:** 1887, Registrar of Deeds
- **DEATH:** 1905, Registrar of Deeds
- **LAND:** ca. 1880, Registrar of Deeds
- **PROBATE:** ca. 1880, Clerk of Courts
- **COURT:** start in ca. 1880, kept by Clerk of Courts
- **BURIAL:** 1941, Registrar of Deeds
- **NOTES:** Organized 1880. State Archives has naturalization records 1883-1945.

LAKE

200 E Center St., Madison, SD 57042, (605) 256-7600, **<www.lakecountysd.com>**

- **INCORPORATED:** January 1873
- **PARENT COUNTIES:** Brookings, Hanson, Minnehaha
- **BIRTH RECORDS:** 1905, Registrar of Deeds
- **MARRIAGE:** 1880, Registrar of Deeds
- **DEATH:** 1905, Registrar of Deeds
- **LAND:** 1878, Registrar of Deeds
- **PROBATE:** ca. 1880, Clerk of Courts
- **COURT:** start in ca. 1880, kept by Clerk of Courts
- **BURIAL:** 1941, Registrar of Deeds
- **NOTES:** State Archives has naturalization records 1881-1944.

LAWRENCE

Box F, Deadwood, SD 57732, (605) 578-1941, **<www.lawrence.sd.us>**

- **INCORPORATED:** January 1875
- **PARENT COUNTY:** Unorganized Territory
- **BIRTH RECORDS:** 1905, Registrar of Deeds
- **MARRIAGE:** 1880, Registrar of Deeds
- **DEATH:** 1877, Registrar of Deeds
- **LAND:** 1880s, Registrar of Deeds
- **PROBATE:** start in ca. 1877, kept by Clerk of Courts
- **COURT:** ca. 1877, Clerk of Courts
- **MILITARY:** 1921, Registrar of Deeds
- **NOTES:** Organized 1877. Registrar of Deeds has incomplete burial records dating from 1870 to the present. State Archives has naturalization records 1879-1954.

LINCOLN

100 E. Fifth St., Carton, SD 57013, (605) 764-2581, **<www.lincolncountysd.org>**

- **INCORPORATED:** April 1862
- **PARENT COUNTY:** Unorganized Territory
- **BIRTH RECORDS:** 1905, Registrar of Deeds
- **MARRIAGE:** 1905, Registrar of Deeds
- **DEATH:** 1905, Registrar of Deeds
- **LAND:** 1870s, Registrar of Deeds
- **PROBATE:** start in ca. 1867, kept by Clerk of Courts
- **COURT:** ca. 1867, Clerk of Courts
- **BURIAL:** 1941 Registrar of Deeds
- **NOTES:** Organized 1867. Registrar of Deeds has incomplete marriage records 1873-1905. State Archives has naturalization records 1871-1945.

LUGENBEEL

- **INCORPORATED:** January 1875
- **PARENT COUNTIES:** Meyer, Pratt, unorganized land
- **NOTES:** See Washabaugh County. Eliminated 1909 to Bennett and Todd.

LYMAN

Box 38, Kennebec, SD 57544, (605) 869-2247, **<www.lymancounty.org>**

- **INCORPORATED:** January 1873
- **PARENT COUNTIES:** Gregory, Unorganized Territory
- **BIRTH RECORDS:** 1905, Registrar of Deeds
- **MARRIAGE:** 1893, Registrar of Deeds
- **DEATH:** 1905, Registrar of Deeds
- **LAND:** 1893, Registrar of Deeds
- **PROBATE:** start in ca. 1893, kept by Clerk of Courts
- **COURT:** ca. 1893, Clerk of Courts
- **BURIAL:** 1944, Registrar of Deeds
- **NOTES:** Organized 1893. State Archives has naturalization records 1893-1950.

MANDAN

- **INCORPORATED:** January 1875
- **PARENT COUNTY:** Unorganized Territory
- **NOTES:** Eliminated 1887 to Lawrence.

MARSHALL

Box 130, Britton, SD 57430, (605) 448-2401, **<www.rootsweb.ancestry.com/~sdmarsha>**

- **INCORPORATED:** May 1885
- **PARENT COUNTY:** Day
- **BIRTH RECORDS:** 1905, Registrar of Deeds
- **MARRIAGE:** 1887, Registrar of Deeds
- **DEATH:** 1905, Registrar of Deeds
- **LAND:** ca. 1885, Registrar of Deeds
- **PROBATE:** start inca. 1885, kept by Clerk of Courts
- **COURT:** ca. 1885, Clerk of Courts
- **NOTES:** State Archives has naturalization records 1885-1944.

MARTIN

- **INCORPORATED:** March 1881
- **PARENT COUNTY:** Unorganized Territory
- **NOTES:** Attached to Lawrence County. Eliminated 1898 to Butte.

MCCOOK
Box 190, Salem, SD 57058, (605) 425-2791, **<www.rootsweb.ancestry.com/~sdmccook>**
- **INCORPORATED:** January 1873
- **PARENT COUNTY:** Hanson
- **BIRTH RECORDS:** 1880, Registrar of Deeds
- **MARRIAGE:** 1887, Registrar of Deeds
- **DEATH:** 1905, Registrar of Deeds
- **LAND:** 1878, Registrar of Deeds
- **PROBATE:** ca. 1878, Clerk of Courts
- **COURT:** start in ca. 1878, kept by Clerk of Courts
- **NOTES:** Organized 1878. State Archives has naturalization records 1870-1945.

MCPHERSON
Box L, Leola, SD 57456, (605) 439-3314, **<www.rootsweb.ancestry.com/~sdmcpher>**
- **INCORPORATED:** January 1873
- **PARENT COUNTY:** Buffalo
- **BIRTH RECORDS:** 1905, Registrar of Deeds
- **MARRIAGE:** 1884, Registrar of Deeds
- **DEATH:** 1905, Registrar of Deeds
- **LAND:** late 1800s, Registrar of Deeds
- **PROBATE:** start in ca. 1884, kept by Clerk of Courts
- **COURT:** ca. 1884, Clerk of Courts
- **NOTES:** Organized 1884. State Archives has naturalization records 1884-1944.

MEADE
1425 Sherman St., Sturgis, SD 57785, (605) 347-2360, **<www.meadecounty.org>**
- **INCORPORATED:** February 1889
- **PARENT COUNTY:** Lawrence
- **BIRTH RECORDS:** 1905, Registrar of Deeds
- **MARRIAGE:** 1905, Registrar of Deeds
- **DEATH:** 1905, Registrar of Deeds
- **LAND:** 1889, Registrar of Deeds
- **PROBATE:** start in ca. 1889, kept by Clerk of Courts
- **COURT:** ca. 1889, Clerk of Courts
- **BURIAL:** 1905, Registrar of Deeds
- **NOTES:** State Archives has naturalization records 1889-1943.

MELLETTE
Box C, White River, SD 57579, (605) 259-3291, **<genealogytrails.com/sdak/mellette>**
- **INCORPORATED:** June 1909
- **PARENT COUNTIES:** Jackdon, Meyer, Washabaugh, Unorganized Territory
- **BIRTH RECORDS:** 1912, Registrar of Deeds
- **MARRIAGE:** 1912, Registrar of Deeds
- **DEATH:** 1912, Registrar of Deeds
- **LAND:** 1907, Registrar of Deeds
- **PROBATE:** start in 1912, kept by Clerk of Courts
- **COURT:** 1912, Clerk of Courts
- **NOTES:** Organized 1911. State Archives has naturalization records 1912-1946.

MEYER
- **INCORPORATED:** January 1873
- **PARENT COUNTY:** Unorganized Territory
- **NOTES:** Eliminated 1909 to Mellette and Todd.

MINER
Box 86, Howard, SD 57349, (605) 772-4671, **<www.minercountysd.org>**
- **INCORPORATED:** January 1873
- **PARENT COUNTY:** Hanson
- **BIRTH RECORDS:** 1905, Registrar of Deeds
- **MARRIAGE:** 1887, Registrar of Deeds
- **DEATH:** 1905, Registrar of Deeds
- **LAND:** 1881, Registrar of Deeds
- **PROBATE:** start in 1883, kept by Clerk of Courts
- **COURT:** 1881, Clerk of Courts
- **NOTES:** Organized 1880. State Archives has naturalization records 1881-1944.

MINNEHAHA
415 N. Dakota Ave., Sioux Falls, SD 57104, (605) 367-4206, **<www.minnehahacounty.org>**
- **INCORPORATED:** April 1862
- **PARENT COUNTY:** Unorganized Territory
- **BIRTH RECORDS:** 1856, Registrar of Deeds
- **MARRIAGE:** 1872, Registrar of Deeds
- **DEATH:** 1867, Registrar of Deeds
- **LAND:** 1870, Registrar of Deeds
- **PROBATE:** start in 1873, kept by Clerk of Courts
- **COURT:** 1862, Clerk of Courts
- **BURIAL:** 1941, Registrar of Deeds
- **NOTES:** Attached to Union County prior to organization 1868. State Archives has naturalization records 1868-1954.

MOODY
101 E Pipestone Ave. Suite D, Flandreau, SD 57028 (605) 997-3161, **<www.moodycounty.net>**
- **INCORPORATED:** January 1873
- **PARENT COUNTIES:** Brookings, Minnehaha
- **BIRTH RECORDS:** 1905, Registrar of Deeds
- **MARRIAGE:** 1887, Registrar of Deeds
- **DIVORCE:** start in 1891, kept by Clerk of Courts
- **DEATH:** 1905, Registrar of Deeds
- **LAND:** 1873, Registrar of Deeds
- **PROBATE:** ca. 1873, Clerk of Courts
- **COURT:** ca. 1873, Clerk of Courts
- **BURIAL:** 1941, Registrar of Deeds
- **NOTES:** State Archives has naturalization records 1877-1944.

NOWLIN
- **INCORPORATED:** March 1883
- **PARENT COUNTY:** Dakota territory
- **NOTES:** Eliminated 1898 to Haakon and Jackson.

PENNINGTON
315 St. Joseph St., Rapid City, SD 57701, (605) 394-2171, **<www.co.pennington.sd.us>**
- **INCORPORATED:** January 1875

- **PARENT COUNTY:** Unorganized Territory
- **BIRTH RECORDS:** 1905, Registrar of Deeds
- **MARRIAGE:** 1887, Registrar of Deeds
- **DIVORCE:** start in 1877, kept by Clerk of Courts
- **DEATH:** 1905, Registrar of Deeds
- **LAND:** 1883, Registrar of Deeds
- **PROBATE:** ca. 1877, Clerk of Courts
- **COURT:** ca. 1877, Clerk of Courts
- **NOTES:** Organized April 19 1877. State Archives has naturalization records 1879-1975.

PERKINS

Box 126, Bison, SD 57620, (605) 244-5624, **<sdgenweb.com/perkins>**

- **INCORPORATED:** November 1908
- **PARENT COUNTY:** Butte
- **BIRTH RECORDS:** 1909, Registrar of Deeds
- **MARRIAGE:** 1909, Registrar of Deeds
- **DIVORCE:** 1909, Clerk of Courts
- **DEATH:** 1909, Registrar of Deeds
- **LAND:** 1908, Registrar of Deeds
- **PROBATE:** start in ca. 1909, kept by Clerk of Courts
- **COURT:** ca. 1909, Clerk of Courts
- **NOTES:** Organized 1909. State Archives has naturalization records 1909-1955.

POTTER

201 S. Exene St., Gettysburg, SD 57442, (605) 765-9408, **<www.rootsweb.ancestry.com/~sdpotter/potterindex.htm>**

- **INCORPORATED:** January 1873
- **PARENT COUNTY:** Buffalo
- **BIRTH RECORDS:** 1905, Registrar of Deeds
- **MARRIAGE:** 1890, Registrar of Deeds
- **DIVORCE:** 1884, Clerk of Courts
- **DEATH:** 1905, Registrar of Deeds
- **LAND:** ca. 1875, Registrar of Deeds
- **PROBATE:** start in ca. 1883, kept by Clerk of Courts
- **COURT:** ca. 1883, Clerk of Courts
- **BURIAL:** 1941, Registrar of Deeds
- **NOTES:** Formerly Ashmore County. Name changed to Potter 1875. Organized 1883. State Archives has naturalization records 1884-1943.

PRATT

- **INCORPORATED:** January 1883
- **PARENT COUNTY:** Unorganized Territory
- **NOTES:** Eliminated 1895 to Jones, Lyman, Mellette and Stanley.

PYATT

- **INCORPORATED:** March 1883
- **PARENT COUNTIES:** Cheyenne, Rusk, Stanley
- **NOTES:** See Dewey County. Attached to Lawrence county. Name changed to Armstrong 1895. Armstrong eliminated 1952 to Dewey.

RINEHART

- **INCORPORATED:** March 1883
- **PARENT COUNTY:** unorganized territory
- **NOTES:** Eliminated 1897 to Perkins.

ROBERTS

411 Second Ave. E., Sisseton, SD 57262, (605) 698-3395, **<www.rootsweb.ancestry.com/~sdrobert>**

- **INCORPORATED:** March 1883
- **PARENT COUNTIES:** Grant, Sisseton/Wahpeton Indian Reserve
- **BIRTH RECORDS:** 1905, Registrar of Deeds
- **MARRIAGE:** 1887, Registrar of Deeds
- **DIVORCE:** start in 1884, kept by Clerk of Courts
- **DEATH:** 1905, Registrar of Deeds
- **LAND:** late 1800s, Registrar of Deeds
- **PROBATE:** ca. 1883, Clerk of Courts
- **COURT:** ca. 1883, Clerk of Courts
- **BURIAL:** 1941, Registrar of Deeds
- **NOTES:** State Archives has naturalization records 1884-1946.

RUSK

- **INCORPORATED:** January 1873
- **PARENT COUNTY:** Unorganized Territory
- **NOTES:** See Dewey County. Name changed to Dewey 1883.

SANBORN

Box 7, Woonsocket, SD 57385, (605) 796-4513, **<www.rootsweb.ancestry.com/~sdsanbor>**

- **INCORPORATED:** May 1883
- **PARENT COUNTY:** Miner
- **BIRTH RECORDS:** 1905, Registrar of Deeds
- **MARRIAGE:** 1887, Registrar of Deeds
- **DIVORCE:** start in 1884, kept by Clerk of Courts
- **DEATH:** 1905, Registrar of Deeds
- **LAND:** 1883, Registrar of Deeds
- **PROBATE:** ca. 1883, Clerk of Courts
- **COURT:** ca. 1883, Clerk of Courts
- **BURIAL:** 1894, Registrar of Deeds
- **NOTES:** State Archives has naturalization records 1885-1930.

SCHNASSE

- **INCORPORATED:** March 1883
- **PARENT COUNTIES:** Boreman, Unorganized Territory
- **NOTES:** Eliminated 1911 to Ziebach.

SCOBEY

- **INCORPORATED:** March 1883
- **PARENT COUNTY:** Dakota territory
- **NOTES:** Eliminated 1897 to Meade.

SHANNON

900 N. River St., Hot Springs, SD 57747, (605) 745-3996, **<www.rootsweb.ancestry.com/~sdshanno>**

- **INCORPORATED:** January 1875
- **PARENT COUNTY:** Unorganized Territory
- **BIRTH RECORDS:** 1905, Registrar of Deeds
- **MARRIAGE:** 1905, Registrar of Deeds
- **DEATH:** 1905, Registrar of Deeds
- **LAND:** 1907, Registrar of Deeds
- **PROBATE:** start in ca. 1883, kept by Clerk of Courts
- **COURT:** ca. 1883, Clerk of Courts
- **NOTES:** Attached to Fall River County.

SPINK
210 E. Seventh Ave., Redfield, SD 57469, (605) 472-1825, **<www.spinkcounty-sd.org>**
- **INCORPORATED:** January 1873
- **PARENT COUNTY:** Hanson
- **BIRTH RECORDS:** 1905, Registrar of Deeds
- **MARRIAGE:** 1880, Registrar of Deeds
- **DIVORCE:** start in 1882, kept by Clerk of Courts
- **DEATH:** 1905, Registrar of Wills
- **LAND:** ca. 1883, Registrar of Deeds
- **PROBATE:** ca. 1879, Clerk of Courts
- **COURT:** ca. 1879, Clerk of Courts
- **BURIAL:** 1941, Registrar of Deeds
- **NOTES:** Organized 1879. State Archives has naturalization records 1879-1945.

STANLEY
Box 595, Ft. Pierre, SD 57532, (605) 223-2673, **<www.rootsweb.ancestry.com/~sdstanle>**
- **INCORPORATED:** January 1873
- **PARENT COUNTY:** Unorganized Territory
- **BIRTH RECORDS:** 1905, Registrar of Deeds
- **MARRIAGE:** 1905, Registrar of Deeds
- **DIVORCE:** start in 1890, kept by Clerk of Courts
- **DEATH:** 1905, Registrar of Deeds
- **LAND:** na, Registrar of Deeds
- **PROBATE:** ca. 1890, Clerk of Courts
- **COURT:** ca. 1890, Clerk of Courts
- **NOTES:** Organized 1890. Registrar of Deeds has incomplete Marriage records 1892-1905. State Archives has naturalization records 1892-1927.

STERLING
- **INCORPORATED:** March 1883
- **PARENT COUNTY:** Cheyenne
- **NOTES:** Attached to Lawrence County. Eliminated 1911 to Ziebach.

STONE
- **INCORPORATED:** January 1873
- **PARENT COUNTY:** Hanson
- **NOTES:** Eliminated 1879 to Brown, and Day counties

SULLY
Box 265, Onida , SD 57564, (605) 258-2541, **<www.sullycounty.net>**
- **INCORPORATED:** January 1873
- **PARENT COUNTY:** Buffalo
- **BIRTH RECORDS:** 1905, Registrar of Deeds
- **MARRIAGE:** 1883, Registrar of Deeds
- **DIVORCE:** start in 1885, kept by Clerk of Courts
- **DEATH:** 1905, Registrar of Deeds
- **LAND:** 1883, Registrar of Deeds
- **PROBATE:** ca. 1883, Clerk of Courts
- **COURT:** ca. 1883, Clerk of Courts
- **NOTES:** Organized 1883.

TODD
200 E. Third St., Winner, SD 57580, (605) 842-1700, **<www.rootsweb.ancestry.com/~sdtodd>**
- **INCORPORATED:** March 1909
- **PARENT COUNTIES:** Lugenbeel, Meyer, Washabaugh, Unorganized Territory
- **BIRTH RECORDS:** 1905, Registrar of Deeds
- **MARRIAGE:** 1905, Registrar of Deeds
- **DIVORCE:** start in1928, kept by Clerk of Courts
- **DEATH:** 1905, Registrar of Deeds
- **LAND:** 1909, Registrar of Deeds
- **PROBATE:** ca. 1909, Clerk of Courts
- **COURT:** ca. 1909, Clerk of Courts
- **NOTES:** Though created by legislative act 1909, Todd has never been fully organized. Attached to Lyman and Trip counties.

TODD, OLD
- **INCORPORATED:** May 1862
- **PARENT COUNTY:** Unorganized Territory
- **NOTES:** Disorganized 1890 and attached to Charles Mix County. Eliminated 1897 to Gregory.

TRIPP
200 E. Third St., Winner, SD 57580, (605) 842-3727, **<www.rootsweb.ancestry.com/~sdtripp>**
- **INCORPORATED:** January 1873
- **PARENT COUNTIES:** Unorganized Territory, Gregory, Todd, old
- **BIRTH RECORDS:** 1905, Registrar of Deeds
- **MARRIAGE:** 1905, Registrar of Deeds
- **DIVORCE:** start in 1909, kept by Clerk of Courts
- **DEATH:** 1905, Registrar of Deeds
- **LAND:** 1909, Registrar of Deeds
- **PROBATE:** ca. 1909, Clerk of Courts
- **COURT:** ca. 1909, Clerk of Courts
- **NOTES:** Organized 1909. State Archives has naturalization records 1908-1952.

TURNER
Box 370, Parker, SD 57053, (605) 297-3153, **<www.turnercountysd.com>**
- **INCORPORATED:** January 1871
- **PARENT COUNTY:** Lincoln, Jayne
- **BIRTH RECORDS:** 1905, Registrar of Deeds
- **MARRIAGE:** 1905, Registrar of Deeds
- **DIVORCE:** start in 1880, kept by Clerk of Courts
- **DEATH:** 1905, Registrar of Deeds
- **LAND:** 1871, Registrar of Deeds
- **PROBATE:** ca. 1871, Clerk of Courts
- **COURT:** ca. 1871, Clerk of Courts
- **NOTES:** Registrar of Deeds has incomplete marriage records 1872-1905, and Burial records 1941 to the present. State Archives has naturalization records 1873-1945.

UNION
209 East Main St., Elk Point, SD 57025, (605) 356-2041, **<www.unioncountysd.org>**
- **INCORPORATED:** April 1862
- **PARENT COUNTY:** Unorganized Territory

- **BIRTH RECORDS:** 1905, Registrar of Deeds
- **MARRIAGE:** 1866, Registrar of Deeds
- **DIVORCE:** 1875, Clerk of Courts
- **DEATH:** 1905, Registrar of Deeds
- **LAND:** 1862, Registrar of Deeds
- **PROBATE:** ca. 1862, Clerk of Court
- **COURT:** start in ca. 1862, kept by Clerk of Courts
- **BURIAL:** 1962, Registrar of Deeds
- **NOTES:** Formerly Cole County. Name changed to Union 1864. State Archives has naturalization records 1873-1946.

WAGNER
- **INCORPORATED:** March 1883
- **PARENT COUNTY:** Dakota Territory
- **NOTES:** Eliminated 1897 to Perkins.

WALWORTH
Box 199, Selby, SD 57472, (605) 649-7878, **<www.rootsweb.ancestry.com/~sdwalwor>**
- **INCORPORATED:** January 1873
- **PARENT COUNTY:** Buffalo
- **BIRTH RECORDS:** 1905, Registrar of Deeds
- **MARRIAGE:** 1890, Registrar of Deeds
- **DIVORCE:** start in 1889, kept by Clerk of Courts
- **DEATH:** 1905, Registrar of Deeds
- **LAND:** ca. 1873, Registrar of Deeds
- **PROBATE:** ca. 1883, Clerk of Courts
- **COURT:** ca. 1883, Clerk of Courts
- **BURIAL:** 1941, Registrar of Deeds
- **NOTES:** Organized 1883. State Archives has naturalization records 1883-1954.

WASHABAUGH
- **INCORPORATED:** March 1883
- **PARENT COUNTY:** Lugenbeel
- **NOTES:** Unorganized; Attached to Custer and Jackson counties.

WASHINGTON
- **INCORPORATED:** March 1883
- **PARENT COUNTIES:** Shannon, Lugenbeel
- **NOTES:** Unorganized; Attached to Custer county. Eliminated 1943 to Shannon.

WETMORE
- **INCORPORATED:** January 1873
- **PARENT COUNTY:** Hanson
- **NOTES:** Eliminated 1879 to Aurora and Miner.

WHITE RIVER
- **INCORPORATED:** January 1875
- **PARENT COUNTIES:** Pratt, Unorganized Territory
- **NOTES:** Eliminated 1883 to Jackson.

YANKTON
Box137, Yankton, SD 57078, (605) 665-2143, **<www.co.yankton.sd.us>**
- **INCORPORATED:** April 1862
- **PARENT COUNTY:** Unorganized Territory
- **BIRTH RECORDS:** 1905, Registrar of Deeds
- **MARRIAGE:** 1905, Registrar of Deeds
- **DIVORCE:** start in 1874, kept by Clerk of Courts
- **DEATH:** 1905, Registrar of Deeds
- **LAND:** 1862, Registrar of Deeds
- **PROBATE:** ca. 1862, Clerk of Courts
- **COURT:** ca. 1862, Clerk of Courts
- **BURIAL:** 1950, Registrar of Deeds
- **NOTES:** Registrar of Deeds has incomplete marriage records 1889-1905. State Archives has naturalization records 1874-1955.

ZIEBACH
Box 68, Dupree, SD 57623, (605) 365-5157, **<www.rootsweb.ancestry.com/~sdziebac>**
- **INCORPORATED:** February 1911
- **PARENT COUNTIES:** Schnasse, Sterling, Armstrong
- **BIRTH RECORDS:** 1910, Registrar of Deeds
- **MARRIAGE:** 1910, Registrar of Deeds
- **DIVORCE:** start in 1911, kept by Clerk of Courts
- **DEATH:** 1910, Registrar of Deeds
- **LAND:** 1911, Registrar of Deeds
- **PROBATE:** ca. 1911, Clerk of Courts
- **COURT:** ca. 1911, Clerk of Courts
- **BURIAL:** 1910, Registrar of Deeds
- **NOTES:** Within limits of Cheyenne River Indian Reservation. State Archives has naturalization records 1911-1951.

ZIEBACH, OLD
- **INCORPORATED:** February 1877
- **PARENT COUNTY:** Pennington
- **NOTES:** Eliminated 1898 to Pennington.

TENNESSEE

» BY EMILY ANNE CROOM

HISTORICAL OVERVIEW

Spaniards explored the fringes of Tennessee in the 1540s, but the French claimed the region in 1673, established trade with Indians, and built Fort Assumption at present-day Memphis in 1739. French lands east of the Mississippi became British in the 1763 Treaty of Paris. Thus, while technically still Indian land, Tennessee became British on European maps and by the king's proclamation was off-limits to settlement from the east-coast colonies.

Ignoring the ban, pioneers from North Carolina and Virginia settled along the Watauga River in the northeastern Tennessee highlands in the 1770s. In 1777, Tennessee came under the jurisdiction of Washington County, NC. North Carolinians established a settlement in 1779-1780 at a trading spot on the Cumberland River called French Lick, now Nashville. In 1783, that area became Davidson County, NC.

After several years of turbulence from Indian raids, lack of stable local government, and apparent lack of concern from national and state governments, Tennesseans wanted to govern themselves. In 1788, North Carolina ceded its claim to the area. Two years later, Congress established the Territory South of the River Ohio, commonly called the Southwest Territory, and Tennessee became the 16th state in 1796.

Via rivers and trails and through the Cumberland Gap, settlers flocked into Tennessee, especially from the Carolinas and Virginia. Considerable numbers came also from Georgia, Kentucky, Maryland, and Pennsylvania. Indian land cessions and forced removal had opened all of Tennessee to white settlement by the 1830s.

Farmers and planters grew tobacco and cotton, often with slave labor, while the Mississippi, Cumberland and Tennessee rivers encouraged commerce. By 1860, Tennessee had over 1 million residents, of whom 25 percent were slaves, less than 1 percent were free blacks, and nearly 2 percent were foreign-born.

Tennessee seceded after hostilities began in 1861, sent soldiers to both sides during the Civil War, and saw numerous battles. The Union army occupied much of the state early in the war and virtually all of the state by 1863. In 1866, impoverished but without going through Reconstruction, Tennes-

research tips

- Tax lists and other contemporary records can help replace lost census schedules and identify early residents. Partial substitutes for the lost 1890 census are the 1891 enumerations of males over 21, available for most counties at the state archives and on microfilm elsewhere.
- Tennessee is not a federal land state, but some North Carolina Revolutionary War veterans or their heirs received bounty land in the state.
- Because Tennessee was considered an offshoot of North Carolina, people reporting they were born in North Carolina before 1796 might have been born in what is now Tennessee.
- The Tennessee State Library and Archives participates in interlibrary loan of some materials. See **<www.tennessee.gov/tsla/history/mailill.htm>** for information.
- Visit **<www.gbmuseum.tn.org/books/GEN_HIST.htm>** and **<www.tn.gov/tsla/history/bibliographies/bibindex.htm>** for extensive Tennessee bibliographies.

CENSUS RECORDS

- Federal census population schedules: 1810 (Rutherford and Grainger counties only), 1820 (26 counties), 1830, 1840, 1850, 1860, 1870, 1880, 1900, 1910, 1920, 1930
- Federal mortality schedules: 1850, 1860, 1880
- Federal slave schedules: 1850, 1860 (schedules name slaveholders but rarely name slaves.)
- Special census of Civil War Union veterans and widows: 1890

see was the first former Confederate state readmitted to the Union. Until the 1940s, the state remained largely agricultural, dedicated to cotton and tobacco, but with growing industries for food, wood, textile, mineral and chemical products. By 1960, the urban population surpassed the rural with 52 percent of the state's total.

RECORD HIGHLIGHTS

More than 50 Tennessee counties have lost some records in fires or storms. County-by-county lists of the disasters record losses are at the state archives website, **<www.state.tn.us/tsla/history/county/lost.htm>**, along with indexes and information about other holdings. Courthouse disasters rarely destroy all records. Investigate surviving materials, resources of parent and neighboring counties, and family, local, state, and federal records.

Tennessee first tried statewide birth and death registration between 1908 and 1912, but some counties and cities have 19th-century records. For information on pre-1908 records and death, marriage, and divorce records more than 50 years old, see **<www.tn.gov/tsla/history/vital/vital.htm>**. The state Department of Health **<health.state.tn.us/vr>** holds birth records from 1914 and death, marriage, and divorce records less than 50 years old. Usually, county clerks hold marriage records dating from the formation of their counties. County circuit courts have handled divorces since 1834, and the legislature had jurisdiction to grant earlier divorces. Birth and death indexes and records, 1908-1912, and death records, 1914-1950, are available on microfilm from the Family History Library (FHL), but there are no records for 1913. Other Tennessee-specific records include:

- Several series of the Draper Manuscripts, especially series XX, Tennessee Papers, housed at the State Historical Society of Wisconsin and on microfilm at research libraries.
- Territorial Papers of the United States and Territorial Papers of the US Senate for the Territory South of the River Ohio.
- Confederate pensions; index to applications for pensions and the Confederate Soldiers Home, and list of Tennessee Confederate physicians at **<tennessee.gov/tsla/history/military/pension.htm>**; pension indexes and applications are available on microfilm from the FHL.
- *Civil War Veterans Questionnaires, 1914-1920* are at the Tennessee State Library and Archives and have been compiled into five volumes by Gustavus W. Dyer and John Trotwood Moore (Southern Historical Press, 1985). You can see an online index at **<www.tennessee.gov/tsla/history/military/quest.htm>**.
- County tax lists; available at the state archives, **<www.tennessee.gov/tsla/history/county/taxlist.htm>**.
- School censuses for various counties, most from the 20th century; see a list at **<www.censusfinder.com/tennessee.htm>**.
- Records of depositors in Tennessee's two branches of the Freedman's Savings and Trust Company (FHL microfilm 928590).
- 1869 and 1897 censuses of Memphis (FHL microfilm 375237).

ARCHIVES, LIBRARIES, AND SOCIETIES

Art Circle Public Library
3 East St., Crossville, TN 38555, (931) 484-6790, **<www.artcirclelibrary.info>**

Bedford County Historical Society
Box 141, Shelbyville, TN 37162, **<home.flash.net/~coley/bedford_society.html>**

Blount County Public Library
508 N. Cusick St., Maryville, TN 37804, (865) 982-0981, **<www.blountlibrary.org>**

Blount County Genealogical and Historical Society
Box 4986, Maryville, TN 37902, **<blountcountytngenealogy.org>**

Bradley County Genealogical Society
Box 1384, Cleveland, TN 37364, **<www.tngenweb.org/bradley/society.html>**

Campbell County Historical Society
101 Sixth St., LaFollette, TN 37766, **<www.tngennet.org/scott/genealogy_societies.htm>**

Carroll County Library
625 High St., Huntingdon, TN 38344, (731) 986-1919, **<www.librarytechnology.org/lwc-displaylibrary.pl?RC=6195>**

Central of Georgia Railway Historical Society
<www.cofg.org>

Chattanooga-Hamilton County Bicentennial Library
1001 Broad St. Chattanooga, TN 37402, (423) 757-5310, **<www.lib.chattanooga.gov>**

Civil War Plymouth Pilgrims Descendants Society
10106 Champions Circle, Franklin, TN 37064

Claiborne County Historical Society
Box 32, Tazewell, TN 37879, (423) 526-5737, **<www.rootsweb.ancestry.com/~tnccths>**

Cleveland Public Library History Branch
833 N. Ocoee St., Cleveland, TN 37311, (423) 722-2163, **<www.librarytechnology.org/lwc-displaylibrary.pl?RC=11122>**

Clyde W. Roddy Library
371 First Ave., Dayton, TN 37321, (423) 775-8406, **<www.daytontn.net/library.php>**

Coffee County Historical Society
101 W. Fort St., Box 2, Manchester, TN 37355, (931) 728-0145, **<bellsouthpwp.net/C/a/CanCofHist/coffee/pubs.htm>**

Cossitt-Goodwyn Library
33 S. Front St., Memphis, TN 38103, (901) 526-1712, **<www.memphislibrary.org/about/libraries/cossitt.htm>**

Dandridge Memorial Library
Box 339, Dandridge, TN 37725, (865) 397-9758

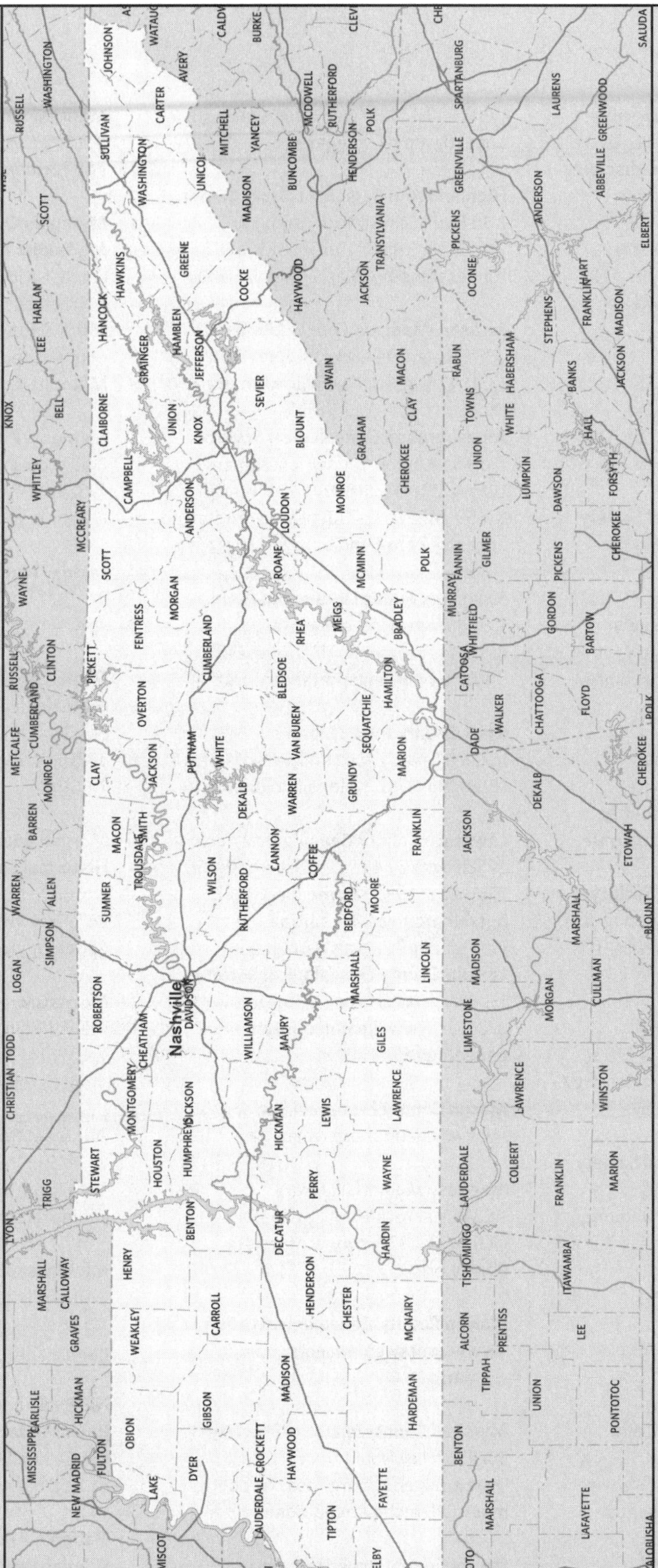
Nashville
DAVIDSON
SHELBY
TIPTON
FAYETTE
HARDEMAN
HAYWOOD
LAUDERDALE
CROCKETT
MADISON
DYER
LAKE
OBION
GIBSON
WEAKLEY
CARROLL
HENRY
BENTON
DECATUR
HENDERSON
CHESTER
MCNAIRY
HARDIN
WAYNE
PERRY
HUMPHREYS
HOUSTON
STEWART
MONTGOMERY
DICKSON
HICKMAN
LEWIS
LAWRENCE
GILES
MAURY
WILLIAMSON
CHEATHAM
ROBERTSON
SUMNER
TROUSDALE
MACON
SMITH
WILSON
RUTHERFORD
MARSHALL
BEDFORD
LINCOLN
MOORE
FRANKLIN
COFFEE
CANNON
DEKALB
WARREN
GRUNDY
MARION
SEQUATCHIE
VAN BUREN
WHITE
PUTNAM
JACKSON
CLAY
OVERTON
PICKETT
FENTRESS
CUMBERLAND
BLEDSOE
HAMILTON
RHEA
MEIGS
BRADLEY
POLK
MCMINN
MONROE
LOUDON
ROANE
MORGAN
SCOTT
CAMPBELL
ANDERSON
KNOX
BLOUNT
SEVIER
UNION
CLAIBORNE
GRAINGER
JEFFERSON
HAMBLEN
COCKE
HANCOCK
HAWKINS
GREENE
SULLIVAN
WASHINGTON
UNICOI
CARTER
JOHNSON
STODDARD
PEMISCOT
DUNKLIN
MISSISSIPPI
NEW MADRID
CARLISLE
HICKMAN
FULTON
GRAVES
CALLOWAY
MARSHALL
LYON
TRIGG
CHRISTIAN
TODD
LOGAN
SIMPSON
WARREN
ALLEN
BARREN
MONROE
METCALFE
CUMBERLAND
RUSSELL
CLINTON
WAYNE
MCCREARY
WHITLEY
KNOX
BELL
LEE
HARLAN
SCOTT
RUSSELL
WASHINGTON
AVERY
WATAUGA
MITCHELL
YANCEY
MADISON
BUNCOMBE
MCDOWELL
RUTHERFORD
HENDERSON
POLK
HAYWOOD
JACKSON
TRANSYLVANIA
SWAIN
GRAHAM
MACON
CLAY
CHEROKEE
SPARTANBURG
GREENVILLE
PICKENS
OCONEE
ANDERSON
LAURENS
ABBEVILLE
GREENWOOD
ELBERT
RABUN
TOWNS
UNION
FANNIN
GILMER
MURRAY
WHITFIELD
CATOOSA
DADE
WALKER
CHATTOOGA
GORDON
BARTOW
FLOYD
HABERSHAM
WHITE
LUMPKIN
DAWSON
PICKENS
CHEROKEE
FORSYTH
HALL
BANKS
STEPHENS
FRANKLIN
HART
MADISON
JACKSON
POLK
CHEROKEE
DEKALB
JACKSON
MADISON
LIMESTONE
LAUDERDALE
COLBERT
LAWRENCE
MORGAN
MARSHALL
ETOWAH
BLOUNT
CULLMAN
WINSTON
FRANKLIN
MARION
TISHOMINGO
ALCORN
PRENTISS
ITAWAMBA
LEE
TIPPAH
UNION
PONTOTOC
BENTON
MARSHALL
LAFAYETTE
DESOTO
TATE
PANOLA
YALOBUSHA

Disciples of Christ Historical Society
1101 Nineteenth Ave. S., Nashville, TN 37212, (866) 834-7563, **<www.discipleshistory.org/about/default.htm>**

East Tennessee Historical Society
601 S. Gay St., Box 1629, Knoxville, TN 37901, (865) 215-8824, **<www.easttnhistory.org>**

Fayetteville-Lincoln County Public Library
400 Rocky Knob Lane, Fayetteville, TN 37334, (931) 433-3286

Fentress County Genealogical Society
<www.rootsweb.ancestry.com/~tnfentre/fent.htm>

Franklin County Historical Society
Box 130, Winchester, TN 37398, (931) 962-1476, **<www.tngenweb.org/franklin/society.htm>**

Giles County Historical Society
Box 693, Pulaski, TN 38478, (931) 363-2720, **<www.gilescountylibrary.org/Library/Historical.html>**

Greene County Genealogical Society
T. Elmer Cox Historical and Genealogical Library, 229 N. Main St., Greeneville, TN 37745, (423)638-5034

H.B. Stamps Memorial Library
407 W. Main St., Rogersville, TN 37857, (423) 272-8710, **<hawkinslibraries.org/HB_Stamps_Memorial_Library>**

Hamblen County Genealogical Society
Box 1213, Morristown, TN 37816, (423) 586-1961, **<www.tngenweb.org/hamblen>**

Hancock County Historical and Genealogical Society
Box 307, Sneedville, TN 37869, **<overhomesneedville.com>**

Hawkins County Genealogical and Historical Society
Box 429, Rogersville, TN 37857, **<www.rootsweb.ancestry.com/~tnhcghs>**

Henry County Archive and Genealogy Library
W. O. Inman Genealogy Room
400 W. Washington St., Paris, TN 38242, (731) 642-1702, **<www.rootsweb.ancestry.com/~tnhenry2>**

Highland Rim Regional Library Center
2118 East Main St., Murfreesboro, TN 37130, (615) 893-3380, **<www.tennessee.gov/tsla/regional/HRRL>**

Jackson-Madison County Library
433 E. Lafayette, Jackson, TN 38301, (731) 425-8600, **<www.jmcl.tn.org>**

Jonesborough Genealogical Society
c/o Washington County-Jonesborough Library, 200 Sabine Dr., Jonesborough, TN 37659, (423) 753-1800, **<www.rootsweb.ancestry.com/~tncjones/JGS>**

Kingsport Public Library and Archives
J. Fred Johnson Memorial Library, 400 Broad St., Kingsport, TN 37660, (423) 229-9489, **<www.kingsportlibrary.org>**

Knox County Public Library
500 W. Church Ave., Knoxville, TN 37902, (865) 215-8742, **<blogs.knoxlib.org>**

Lawrence County Genealogical Society
2258 Highway 43 S., Leoma, TN 38468, (931) 852-4091, **<home.lorettotel.net/~lcarchives/lcgs.htm>**

Lincoln County Genealogical Society
1508 W. Washington St., Fayetteville, TN 37334, **<www.lincolncountytn.com/genealogy>**

Macon County Historical Society
<www.tngennet.org/macon>

Magness Memorial Library
118 W. Main St., McMinnville, TN 37110, (931) 473-2428, **<www.magnesslibrary.org>**

Marion County Genealogical Group
<www.rootsweb.ancestry.com/~tnmario2>

Marshall County Historical Society
Box 1352, Lewisburg, TN 37901, **<www.usgennet.org/usa/tn/county/marshall/mchq/mchqindex.htm>**

Maury County Public Library
211 W. Eighth St., Columbia, TN 38401, (931) 375-6501, **<www.maurycountylibrary.org>**

Maury County Historical Society
Box 147, Columbia, TN 38402, **<historicmaury.org>**

Memphis Conference United Methodist Archives
Luther L. Gobbel Library, Lambuth College, 705 Lambuth Blvd., Jackson, TN 38301, (800) 526-2884, **<www.lambuth.edu/academics/library/MemphisConferenceArchives.html>**

Memphis Public Library
3030 Poplar Ave., Memphis, TN 38111, (901) 415-2700, **<www.memphislibrary.org>**

Middle Tennessee Genealogical Society
Box 330948, Nashville, TN 37203, **<www.mtgs.org>**

Mid-West Tennessee Genealogical Society
Box 3343, Murray Station, Jackson, TN 38303, **<www.jmcl.tn.org/Mid-West_Tn.htm>**

Morgan County Genealogical and Historical Society
Box 684, Wartburg, TN 37887, (423) 346-2479, **<www.tngenweb.org/morgan/genealogyroom.html>**

Morristown-Hamblen Library
417 W. Main St., Morristown, TN 37814, (423) 586-6410, **<morristownhamblenlibrary.org>**

Mt. Juliet Public Library
Box 319, 2765 N. Mt. Juliet Rd., Mt. Juliet, TN 37122, (615) 758-7051, **<www.youseemore.com/MtJuliet/directory.asp>**

Mt. Pleasant Public Library
200 Hay Long Ave., Mt. Pleasant, TN 38474, (931) 379-3752, **<www.maurycountylibrary.org>**

Nashville and Davidson County Public Library
615 Church St., Nashville, TN 37219, (615) 862-5800, **<www.library.nashville.org>**

National Archives and Records Administartion, Southeast Region
5780 Jonesboro Road, Morrow, GA 30260, (770) 968-2100, **<www.archives.gov/southeast>**

Obion County Genealogical Society
Box 241, Union City, TN 38261, **<www.tngenweb.org/obion/library/hsociety.htm>**

James County, Tenn., Genealogy
<www.tngenweb.org/james>

Pellissippi Genealogical and Historical Society
c/o Clinton Public Library, 118 S. Hicks, Clinton, TN 37716, (865) 457-0519, **<www.pellissippi-society.home.comcast.net>**

Polk County Historical and Genealogical Society Library
Box 636, Benton, TN 37307, **<www.tngenweb.org/polk/pchgs>**

Public Library of Nashville and Davidson County
615 Church St., Nashville, TN 37219, (615) 862-5800, **<www.library.nashville.org>**

Shelby County Health Department, Office of Vital Records
814 Jefferson St., Memphis, TN 38105, (901) 544- 7608, **<www.shelbycountytn.gov/FirstPortal/dotShowDoc/Government/CountyServices/HealthServices/AdministrativeServices/birth_cert.htm>**

Southern Baptist Historical Library and Archives
901 Commerce St., # 400, Nashville, TN 37203, (615) 224-0344, **<www.sbhla.org/info.htm>**

Tennessee State Library and Archives
403 7th Avenue North, Nashville, TN 37243, (615) 741-2764, **<www.state.tn.us/tsla>**

Sumner County Archives
365 North Belvedere Dr., Gallatin, TN 37066, (615) 452-0037, **<www.sumnertn.org/archives>**

Tennessee Department of Health
425 Fifth Ave., Cordell Hull Building, 3rd Floor, Nashville, TN 37243, (615) 741-3111, **<www.state.tn.us/health>**

Tennessee Genealogical Society
7779 Poplar Pike, Germantown, TN 38138, (901) 757-8480, **<www.tngs.org>**

Trousdale County Historical Society
4233 Green Grove Rd., Hartsville, TN 37074, **<www.tngennet.org/trousdale/t-tchs.html>**

Union County Historical Society
Box 95, Maynardville, TN 37807, (865) 992-2136, **<www.unioncountytn.com/history>**

University of Memphis Library, Special Collections
126 Ned R. McWherter Library, Memphis, TN 38152, (901) 678-8242, **<www.memphis.edu/specialcollections>**

University of Tennessee, Knoxville, Hoskins Library
1015 Volunteer Blvd., Knoxville, TN 37996, (865) 974-4351, **<www.lib.utk.edu/special>**

Upper Cumberland Genealogical Association
Box 575, Cookeville, TN 38503, **<www.rootsweb.ancestry.com/~tnucga/index.htm>**

Upper Cumberland Genealogical Support Group
Art Circle Public Library, 306 E. First St., Crossville, TN 38555, (931) 484-6790, **<www.tngenweb.org/cumberland/page7.html>**

Van Buren County Historical Society
Burritt Memorial Library, Box 18, Spencer, TN 38585, (931) 946-2575, **<www.rootsweb.ancestry.com/~tnvanbur>**

Vardy Community Historical Society
Box 554, Sneedville, TN 37869, (423) 733-2305, **<vardyhistoricalsociety.org/vardyhistoricalsociety_009.htm>**

Watauga Association of Genealogists, Upper East Tennessee
Box 70295, Johnson City, TN 37614, (423) 439-4338, **<www.etsu.edu/cass/Archives/Collections/afindaid/a295.html>**

Weakley County Genealogy Society
Box 894, Martin, TN 38237, **<www.rootsweb.ancestry.com/~tnweakle/genealogical_society.htm>**

White County Genealogical-Historical Society
Box 721, Sparta, TN 38583, (931) 837-4066

Williamson County Public Library, Special Collections and Genealogy
1314 Columbia Ave., Franklin, TN 37064, (615) 595-1246, **<lib.williamson-tn.org/Special_Collections/Gen.htm>**

GENERAL RESOURCES

Bible Records of Families of East Tennessee And Their Connections From Other Areas, 3 vols., by Adele Weiss Sneed (Knoxville Chapter of the Daughters of the American Colonists and James White Chapter of the Daughters of the American Revolution, 1959-60)

Check List of Tennessee Imprints, 1841-1850 from the Historical Records Survey (Tennessee Historical Records Survey, 1941)

Early Times in Middle Tennessee by John Carr (R.H. Horsley and Associates, 1958)

Genealogy Research Sources in Tennessee by Beverly W. Hathaway (Allstates Research Co., 1972)

Guide to County Records and Genealogical Resources in Tennessee by Richard Carlton Fulcher (Genealogical Publishing Co., 1987)

Guide to Microfilmed Manuscript Holdings of the Tennessee State Library and Archives, 3rd edition (Tennessee State Library and Archives, 1983)

History of Tennessee, 4 vols., by Stanley John Folmsbee (Lewis Historical Publishing Co., 1960)

A History of Tennessee And Tennesseans, 8 vols., by William T. Hale and Dixon L. Merritt (Lewis Publishing Co., 1913)

Inventory of the Church Archives of Tennessee: Nashville Baptist Association from the Historical Records Survey (Historical Records Survey, WPA, 1939)

List of Tennessee Imprints, 1793-1840, in Tennessee Libraries from the Historical Records Survey (Tennessee Historical Records Survey, 1941)

Notable Men of Tennessee: Personal and Genealogical With Portraits, 2 vols., by John Roy V. Allison (Southern Historical Association, 1905)

Sketches of Prominent Tennesseans by William S. Speer (A.B. Tavel, 1888)

Tennessee County Records Manual (Tennessee State Library and Archives, ca. 1968)

Tennessee Cousins: A History of Tennessee People by Worth Stickley Ray (1950; Genealogical Publishing Co., 1968)

Tennessee Genealogical Records: Records Of Early Settlers from State and County Archives by Edythe Rucker Whitley (Genealogical Publishing Co., 1981)

Tennessee Genealogical Research by George K. Schweitzer (George K. Schweitzer, 1986)

Tennessee History: A Bibliography compiled and edited by Sam B. Smith and Luke H. Banker (University of Tennessee Press, 1974)

Tennessee Newspapers: A Cumulative List of Microfilmed Tennessee Newspapers in the Tennessee State Library (Tennessee State Library and Archives, 1978)

Tennessee Research Outline by the Church of Jesus Christ of Latter-day Saints (online at **<www.familysearch.org/eng/search/RG/guide/tennessee.asp>**)

Tennessee, the Volunteer State, 1760-1923, 4 vols., by John Trotwood Moore and Austin P. Foster (S.J. Clark Publishing Co., 1923)

Timeless Tennesseans by James A. Crutchfield (Strode Publishers, 1984)

CENSUS RECORDS

Eastern Cherokees: A Census of the Cherokee Nation, 1851 by David W. Siler (Polyanthos, 1972)

East Tennessee Tax Lists (Arrow Printing Co., 1964)

LAND RECORDS

Earliest Tennessee Land Records & Earliest Tennessee Land History by Irene M. Griffey (Clearfield Co., 2000)

The Hidden Revolutionary War Land Grants In the Tennessee Military Reservation by Shirley Hollis Rice (Family Tree Press, 1992)

Land Grants, 1775-1905, 1911 (filmed by the Tennessee State Library and Archives)

North Carolina Land Grants in Tennessee, 1778-1791 compiled by Goldene F. Burgner (Southern Historical Press, 1981)

Tennessee Land: Its Early History and Laws by Billie R. McNamara (B.R. McNamara, 1997)

Tennessee Land Entries: John Armstrong's Office, 2 vols., by Albert Bruce Pruitt (Pruitt, A. Bruce, 1995)

Tennessee Land Entries Military Bounty Land (1783-1841), 7 vols., by Albert Bruce Pruitt (Pruitt, A. Bruce, 1997)

Tennessee Land Grants. Surnames, 17 vols., by Byron Sistler (Byron Sistler, 1997)

Tennessee Land Warrants by Albert Bruce Pruitt (Pruitt, A. Bruce, 1999)

MAPS

Counties of Tennessee by Austin P. Foster (Department of Education, Division of History, State of Tennessee, 1923)

Eastin Morris' Tennessee Gazetteer 1834 and Matthew Rhea's Map of the State Of Tennessee, 1832 edited by Robert M. McBride and Owen Meredith (The Gazetteer Press, 1971)

Place Names of Tennessee by Ralph O. Fullerton (Tennessee Department of Conservation, Division of Geology, 1974)

Tennessee Atlas and Gazetteer, 3rd edition, (DeLorme Mapping Co., 1995)

Tennessee County Maps compiled by C.J. Puetz (Thomas Publishing Co., 1992)

MILITARY RECORDS

Confederate Patriot Index (1894-1978), 2 vols., (Tennessee Division, United Daughters of the Confederacy, 1976, 1978)

Index to Tennessee Confederate Pension Applications by Samuel Sistler (Byron Sistler, 1995)

"List of North Carolina Revolutionary Soldiers Given Land in Tennessee, by the Act of 1782-83" by John Haywood (In *The History of Tennessee*; Reprint; Arno Press, 1971)

Record of Commissions of Officers in the 1796-1815 Tennessee Militia by Mrs. J.T. Moore (Genealogical Publishing Co., 1977)

Republic of Texas Pension Application Abstracts by John C. Barron, et al. (Austin Genealogical Society, 1987)

Roll Call at the Alamo by Phil Rosenthal and Bill Groneman (Old Army Press, 1985)

Soldiers of the War of 1812 Buried in Tennessee by M.H. McCown and I.E. Burns (Society of US Daughters of 1812, 1959)

Some Tennessee Heroes of the Revolution, Compiled From Pensions of the Republic of Texas compiled by Zella Armstrong (Daughters of the Republic Of Texas, 1986)

Tennesseans in the Civil War (Civil War Commission, 1965)

The Tennessee Civil War Veterans Questionnaires, 5 vols., by Gustavus Dyer (Southern Historical Press, 1985)

Tennessee Confederate Widows and Their Families: Abstracts of 11,190 Confederate Widows' Applications by Edna Wiefering (Cleveland Public Library, 1992)

Tennessee Soldiers in the Revolution by Penelope J. Allen (Genealogical Publishing Co., 1975)

Texas Veterans in the Mexican War by Charles D. Spurlin (Ingmire Pub., 1984)

Texas Volunteers in the Mexican War by Henry W. Barton (Texan Press, 1970)

Twenty-four Hundred Tennessee Pensioners of the Revolution, War of 1812 compiled by Zella Armstrong (Lookout Publishing Co., 1937)

Volunteers: Tennesseans in the War with Mexico, 2 vols., by Reid Brock (Kitchen Table Press, 1986)

☞PROBATE RECORDS

Index to Tennessee Wills and Administrations, 1779-1861 by Byron Sistler and Barbara Sistler (Byron Sistler & Assoc., 1990)

Survey to Tennessee County Court Records, Prior to 1860, in the Second, Third and Fourth Districts (Historical Records Survey, 1943)

Tennessee Tidbits, 1778-1914, 3 vols., by Marjorie Hood Fischer and Ruth Blake Burns (Ram Press, 1988)

☞VITAL RECORDS

Tennessee Records: Bible Records and Marriages Bonds by Jeannette T. Acklen (Clearfield Co., 1997)

Tennessee Records: Tombstone Inscriptions and Manuscripts, Historical and Biographical by Jeannette T. Acklen (Cullom and Ghertner, 1976)

Obituaries and Marriage Notices From the Tennessee Baptists: 1844-1862 by Russell Pierce Baker (Southern Historical Press, 1979)

Tennessee Divorces, 1797-1858 by Gale W. Bamman (G. Bamman, 1985)

Obituaries from Tennessee Newspapers by Jill L. Garrett (Southern Historical Press, 1980)

Guide to Church Vital Statistics in Tennessee (War Services Section, WPA, 1942)

Church, Cemetery, Bible, and Family Records from Tennessee from the Historical Records Project and Historical Records Survey (filmed by the Genealogical Society of Utah, 1943)

35,000 Tennessee Marriage Records and Bonds, 1783-1870, 3 vols., by Silas E. Lucas and Ella L. Sheffield (Southern Historical Press, 1981)

Marriages from Early Tennessee Newspapers, 1794-1851 by Silas E. Lucas (Southern Historical Press, 1978)

Tennessee Ancestors: The Brave and the Dead, Probate and Death Records of Early Middle Tennessee, 1780-1805 by Oveda Meier (O. Meier, 1990)

Early East Tennessee Marriages, 2 vols., by Byron Sistler and Barbara Sistler (Byron Sistler & Assoc., 1987)

Early Middle Tennessee Marriages, 2 vols., (Byron Sistler & Assoc., 1988)

Early West Tennessee Marriages, 2 vols., by Byron Sistler and Barbara Sistler (Byron Sistler & Assoc., 1989)

Miscellaneous Birth, Death, and Marriage Records, 1837-1987 from the Tennessee Division of Vital Records (filmed by the Tennessee State Library and Archives, ca. 1980)

Vital Statistics from Nineteenth Century Tennessee Church Records by Byron Sistler and Barbara Sistler (Byron Sistler & Assoc., 1979)

•-COUNTY DETAILS-•

ANDERSON

100 N. Main St., Clinton, TN 37716, (865) 457-6228,
<www.andersontn.org>

- **INCORPORATED:** Nov. 6, 1801
- **PARENT COUNTIES:** Knox, Grainger
- **MARRIAGE RECORDS:** 1838, County Clerk
- **LAND:** start in 1802, kept by Registrar of Deeds
- **PROBATE:** 1830, County Clerk
- **COURT:** 1811, County Clerk
- **NOTES:** Clerk of Circuit Court had divorce records 1947-1951. Tennessee State Library and Archives or Vital Records Office has birth and death records.

BEDFORD

1 Public Sq., Shelbyville, TN 37160, (931) 684-7944,
<www.bedfordcountytn.org>

- **INCORPORATED:** Dec. 31, 1807
- **PARENT COUNTY:** Rutherford
- **BIRTH RECORDS:** 1949, Dept. of Health
- **DIVORCE:** unknown start, Circuit Court
- **LAND:** start in 1808, kept by Registrar of Deeds
- **COURT:** 1840, Circuit Court
- **NOTES:** County Clerk has marriage records 1861-1987 and probate records 1861-1988. Registrar of Deeds has military discharge records 1919-1988. Courthouse destroyed by tornado in 1830 and fire in 1863.

BENTON

1 E. Court Sq., # 102, Camden, TN 38320, (731) 584-6011,
<www.tennesseeanytime.org/local/benton.html>

- **INCORPORATED:** Dec. 19, 1835
- **PARENT COUNTIES:** Henry, Humphreys
- **BIRTH RECORDS:** start in 1914, kept by Tennessee Vital Records Office
- **DEATH:** 1914, Tennessee State Library and Archives
- **MARRIAGE:** 1838, County Clerk

- **DIVORCE:** unknown start, Circuit Court
- **LAND:** 1836, Registrar of Deeds
- **PROBATE:** 1836, County Court Clerk
- **CIRCUIT COURT:** 1836, Circuit Court
- **NOTES:** County Clerk has birth and death records 1881-1882, 1900-1901.

BLEDSOE

3150 Main St., Pikeville, TN 37367, (423) 447-6855,
<www.pikeville-bledsoe.com>

- **INCORPORATED:** Nov. 30, 1807
- **PARENT COUNTY:** Roane
- **MARRIAGE RECORDS:** 1909, County Clerk
- **LAND:** 1808, Registrar of Deeds
- **PROBATE:** 1909, County Clerk
- **COURT:** start in 1845, kept by Circuit Court
- **NOTES:** Courthouse burned in Dec. 9, 1909. Birth and death records held by state.

BLOUNT

341 Court St., Maryville, TN 37804, (865) 273-5700,
<www.blounttn.org>

- **INCORPORATED:** July 11, 1795
- **PARENT COUNTY:** Knox
- **MARRIAGE RECORDS:** 1795, County Clerk
- **DIVORCE:** unknown start, Clerk & Master
- **LAND:** 1795, Registrar of Deeds
- **PROBATE:** 1795, County Clerk
- **COURT:** start in 1852, kept by Circuit Court
- **NOTES:** County Health Department has birth and death records 1881-1882, 1908-1912, 1925-1938.

BRADLEY

155 Broad St., NW, Cleveland, TN 37311, (423) 728-7141,
<www.bradleyco.net>

- **INCORPORATED:** Feb. 10, 1836
- **PARENT COUNTY:** Cherokee Indian Lands
- **DIVORCE RECORDS:** start in 1864, kept by Clerk & Master
- **LAND:** 1862, Registrar of Deeds
- **PROBATE:** 1859, Clerk & Master
- **COURT:** 1838, Circuit Court
- **MILITARY:** 1864, Registrar of Deeds
- **NOTES:** Courthouse records destroyed by fire in November 1864. Cleveland Public Library has early birth, court, census, Land, probate, marriage, and death records. County Clerk had birth records 1908-1912, death records 1908-1912, 1914-1925, and marriage records 1864-1912, 1914-1957.

CAMPBELL

570 Main St., Jacksboro, TN 37757, (423) 562-2526,
<www.tennesseeanytime.org/local/campbell.html>

- **INCORPORATED:** Sept. 11, 1806
- **PARENT COUNTIES:** Anderson, Claiborne
- **NOTES:** Registrar of Deeds has land records 1806-1986 and military discharge records 1919-1974. County Clerk has marriage records 1838-1986. Clerk and Master has probate records 1806-1841, 1848-1983.

CANNON

200W. Main St., Woodbury, TN 37190, (615) 563-2320,
<www.cannoncounty.net>

- **INCORPORATED:** Jan. 31, 1836
- **PARENT COUNTIES:** Warren, Rutherford, Smith, Wilson
- **NOTES:** Clerk of Circuit Court has court records 1840-1987. Registrar of Deeds has land records 1836-1985 and military discharge records 1917-1987. County Clerk has marriage records 1838-1989. Clerk and Master has probate records 1836-1926, 1935-1970, 1974-1987. Birth and death records at state.

CARROLL

625 High St., Huntingdon, TN 38344, (731) 986-1936,
<carrollcounty-tn-chamber.com>

- **INCORPORATED:** Nov. 7, 1821
- **PARENT COUNTY:** Chickasaw Indian Lands
- **LAND RECORDS:** start in 1822, kept by Registrar of Deeds
- **NOTES:** County Clerk has Court records for 1839 and marriage records 1838-1986. Chancery Court Clerk had divorce records 1826-1900. Registrar of Deeds has land records 1822-1989 and military discharge records 1919-1988. Clerk and Master has probate records 1822-1986. Microfilm of earlier records (except birth and death) are archived at the Gordon Browning Museum.

CARTER

801 E. Elk Ave., Elizabethton, TN 37643, (423) 542-1801,
<cartercountytn.com>

- **INCORPORATED:** April 9, 1796
- **PARENT COUNTY:** Washington
- **DIVORCE RECORDS:** unknown start, kept by Chancery & Circuit Court
- **NOTES:** County Clerk has birth and death records 1907-1962 and marriage records 1790-1993. Chancery and Circuit Court has court records 1848-2000. Registrar of Deeds has land records 1796-1976 and military discharge records 1920-1976. County or Chancery Court has probate records 1794-1985.

CHEATHAM

100 Public Sq., Ashland City, TN 37015, (615) 792-4316,
<www.cheathamcountytn.gov>

- **INCORPORATED:** Feb. 28, 1856
- **PARENT COUNTIES:** Davidson, Dickson, Montgomery, Robertson
- **NOTES:** County Clerk had birth records 1881-1882, 1908-1912, death records 1881-1882, 1908-1912, 1925-1941, and marriage records 1856-1996. Circuit/General Sessions/Juvenile Clerk has court records 1877-1996. Chancery Clerk has marriage records 1856-1996 and probate records 1856-1994. Registrar of Deeds has land records 1856-1996 and military discharge records 1919-1997.

CHESTER

159 E. Main St., Henderson, TN 38340, (731) 989-5672,
<www.tennesseeanytime.org/local/chester.html>

- **INCORPORATED:** March 1879
- **PARENT COUNTIES:** Hardeman, Madison, Henderson, McNairy
- **DIVORCE RECORDS:** unknown start, kept by Chancery Court Clerk

- **NOTES:** Clerk of Circuit Court has court records 1882-1993. Registrar of Deeds has land records 1891-1994 and military discharge records 1945-1987. County Clerk has marriage records 1891-1994. Chancery Court Clerk has probate records 1891-1990.

CLAIBORNE

1740 Main St., Tazewell, TN 37879, (423) 626-5236,
<claibornecounty.com>

- **INCORPORATED:** Oct. 29, 1801
- **PARENT COUNTIES:** Grainger, Hawkins
- **NOTES:** Clerk of Circuit Court has court and divorce records 1837-1842 and 1916-1994. Registrar of Deeds has land records 1801-1994 and military discharge records 1919-1996. County Clerk has marriage records 1838-1995 and vital statistics 1908-1912, 1925-1938. Chancery Court Clerk has probate records 1812-1992.

CLAY

145 Cordell Hull, Celina, TN 38551, (931) 243-2161,
<www.tennesseeanytime.org/local/clay.html>

- **INCORPORATED:** June 24, 1870
- **PARENT COUNTIES:** Jackson, Overton
- **BIRTH RECORDS:** 1914, TN Vital Record
- **MARRIAGE:** start in 1871, kept by County Clerk
- **DIVORCE:** 1871, County Clerk
- **LAND:** 1871, Registrar of Deeds
- **PROBATE:** 1871, County Clerk
- **COURT:** 1871, Circuit Court
- **NOTES:** County Clerk has birth and death records 1908-1912. Tennessee State Library and Archives has death records 1908-1949. Registrar of Deeds has military discharge records 1919-1995.

COCKE

360 East Main St, Newport, TN 37821, (423) 623-8791,
<www.cockecounty.net/index.htm>

- **INCORPORATED:** Oct. 9, 1797
- **PARENT COUNTY:** Jefferson
- **NOTES:** County Clerk has birth 1909-1911, 1925-1938, death records 1909-1911, 1926-1938, and marriage records 1877-1994. Clerk of Circuit Court has court records 1877-1993. Clerk and Master had divorce records 1886-1899, probate records 1877-1996. Registrar of Deeds has land records 1865-1996. Stokely Memorial Library has a genealogical section with birth records 1908-1912, 1925-1938, records of all county courts, probate, deed, etc.

COFFEE

1329 McArthur St., Manchester, TN 37355, (931) 723-5100,
<www.coffeecountytn.org>

- **INCORPORATED:** Jan. 8, 1836
- **PARENT COUNTIES:** Franklin, Warren, Bedford
- **DIVORCE RECORDS:** unknown start, kept by Circuit Court
- **NOTES:** Tennessee State Library and Archives had birth records 1881-1882-1908, 1912. Clerk of Circuit Court has court records 1852-1988. Registrar of Deeds has land records 1836-1973 and military discharge records 1919-1988. County Clerk has marriage records 1853-1989 and probate records 1836-1987. Birth and death records found at Tennessee State Library and Archives and Tennessee Vital Records Office.

CROCKETT

1 S. Bells St., Alamo, TN 38001, (731) 696-5460,
<www.tennesseeanytime.org/local/crockett.html>

- **INCORPORATED:** December 1872
- **PARENT COUNTIES:** Dyer, Madison, Gibson, Haywood
- **DIVORCE RECORDS:** start in 1872, kept by County Clerk
- **NOTES:** County Clerk has birth and death records 1908-1911, 1925-1938, marriage records 1872-1987, and probate records 1872-1980. Clerk of Circuit Court has court records 1872-1986. Registrar of Deeds has land records 1872-1980 and military discharge records 1917-1970. Many early census records of residents of Crockett County are in surrounding counties. Crockett County formed and dissolved several times between Dec. 20, 1845 and 1872.

CUMBERLAND

2 N. Main St. #203, Crossville, TN 38555, (931) 484-6165,
<www.tennesseeanytime.org/local/cumberland.html>

- **INCORPORATED:** Nov. 16, 1855
- **PARENT COUNTIES:** Bledsoe, Morgan, Roane, White, Rhea, Van Buren, Putnam
- **DIVORCE RECORDS:** unknown start, kept by Clerk/Master/Circuit Court
- **NOTES:** Clerk of Circuit Court has court records 1907-1995. Registrar of Deeds has land records 1855-1969 and military discharge records 1920-1992. County Clerk has marriage records 1905-1996. Clerk and Master has probate records 1905-1997. Cumberland Courthouse fire of 1905 destroyed many early records except deeds. The Art Circle Public Library has census and genealogical data (marriages, land records, court and probate records, birth and state records).

DAVIDSON

1 Public Sq., Nashville, TN 37201, (615) 862-6000,
<www.nashville.gov>

- **INCORPORATED:** April 18, 1783
- **PARENT COUNTY:** Washington
- **BIRTH RECORDS:** unknown start, kept by Tennessee State Library and Archives/Tennessee Vital Records Office
- **MARRIAGE:** 1789, County Clerk
- **DIVORCE:** 1803, Circuit Court
- **DEATH:** unknown start, Tennessee State Library and Archives/Tennessee Vital Records Office
- **LAND:** 1784, Registrar of Deeds
- **PROBATE:** 1783, Probate Court Clerk
- **COURT:** 1803, Circuit Court

DEKALB

#1 Public Square, Room 204, Smithville, TN 37166, (615) 597-5175,
<www.smithvilletn.com>

- **INCORPORATED:** Dec. 11, 1837
- **PARENT COUNTIES:** Cannon, Warren, White, and Smith
- **MARRIAGE RECORDS:** start in 1848, kept by County Clerk
- **LAND:** 1838, Registrar of Deeds
- **NOTES:** Clerk of Circuit Court has court and divorce records 1860-1995. Registrar of Deeds has military discharge records 1919-1995. County Clerk has probate records 1846-1995.

DECATUR

22 W. Main St., Decaturville, TN 38329, (731) 852-2131,
<www.decaturcountytn.org>

- **INCORPORATED:** November 1845
- **PARENT COUNTY:** Perry
- **NOTES:** Clerk of Circuit Court has Court records 1927-1994. Registrar of Deeds has land records 1846-1995 and military discharge records 1943-1994. County Clerk has marriage records 1869-1990. Clerk/Master has probate records 1869-1992. In 1927 and on July 3, 1869, fire destroyed the county courthouse and all documents except Registrar of Deeds and Clerk and Masters' records. Birth and death records are kept by the state at Tennessee State Library and Archives and Tennessee Vital Records Office.

DICKSON

2 Court Sq., Charlotte, TN 37036, (615) 789-5093,
<dicksoncounty.net>

- **INCORPORATED:** Oct. 25, 1803
- **PARENT COUNTIES:** Montgomery, Robertson
- **MARRIAGE RECORDS:** start in 1817, kept by County Clerk
- **LAND:** 1804, Registrar of Deeds
- **PROBATE:** 1803, Clerk & Master
- **NOTES:** County Clerk had birth records 1908-1930, death records 1908-1939, and Divorce records 1849-1932. Clerk of Circuit Court has court records 1810-1827, 1839-1996. Registrar of Deeds has military discharge records 1920-1981. Courthouse was destroyed by tornado about 1835; many records were destroyed. County Clerk has birth and death records 1908-1912, 1925-1939.

DYER

1 Veterans Sq., Dyersburg, TN 38025, (731) 286-7800,
<www.tennesseeanytime.org/local/dyer.html>

- **INCORPORATED:** Oct. 16, 1823
- **PARENT COUNTY:** Chickasaw Indian Lands
- **MARRIAGE RECORDS:** start in 1860, kept by County Clerk
- **DIVORCE:** unknown start, Circuit Court
- **COURT:** 1863, Circuit Court
- **NOTES:** County Clerk has birth and death records 1908-1912 and probate records 1850-1976. Registrar of Deeds has land records 1822-1976 and military discharge records 1918-1976.

FAYETTE

13095 N. Main, Box 218, Somerville, TN 38068, (901) 465-5202,
<www.fayettetn.us>

- **INCORPORATED:** Sept. 29, 1824
- **PARENT COUNTIES:** Shelby, Hardeman
- **MARRIAGE RECORDS:** 1926, County Clerk
- **LAND:** 1825, Registrar of Deeds
- **PROBATE:** 1836, Clerk & Master
- **COURT:** start in 1829, kept by Circuit Court
- **NOTES:** County Clerk has birth and death records 1925-1929, marriage records 1838-1917. Registrar of Deeds has military discharge records 1943-1988. Marriage records 1918-1925 lost in fire.

FENTRESS

101 S. Main St., Jamestown, TN 38556, (931) 879-7713,
<www.jamestowntn.org/fentressofficials.htm>

- **INCORPORATED:** Nov. 28, 1823
- **PARENT COUNTIES:** Morgan, Overton, White
- **MARRIAGE RECORDS:** 1905, County Clerk
- **LAND:** 1820, Registrar of Deeds
- **PROBATE:** 1905, Clerk & Master
- **COURT:** start in 1905, kept by Circuit Court
- **NOTES:** County Clerk has birth and death records 1909-1939. For other birth and death records, see the Tennessee State Library and Archives. Registrar of Deeds has military discharge records 1943-1972. Many county records were destroyed in courthouse fire of 1905.

FRANKLIN

1 S. Jefferson St., Winchester, TN 37398, (931) 967-2905,
<www.franklincotn.us>

- **INCORPORATED:** Dec. 3, 1807
- **PARENT COUNTY:** White
- **MARRIAGE RECORDS:** start in 1838, kept by County Clerk
- **LAND:** 1808, Registrar of Deeds
- **PROBATE:** 1808, Clerk & Master
- **COURT:** 1832, Circuit Court
- **NOTES:** County Clerk has birth and death records 1881-1883, 1908-1912, and divorce records 1860-1930. Registrar of Deeds has military records 1917-1919, 1944-1987. County boundaries have changed 13 times since 1807; check neighboring counties for records. Minute books for county court before 1832 have been destroyed or lost. Circuit Court records begin in 1824.

GIBSON

One Court Square, Suite 200, Trenton, TN 38382, (731) 855-7611,
<www.gibsoncountytn.com>

- **INCORPORATED:** Oct. 21, 1823
- **PARENT COUNTY:** Chickasaw Indian Lands
- **MARRIAGE RECORDS:** start in 1824, kept by County Clerk
- **LAND:** 1819, Registrar of Deeds
- **COURT:** 1824, Circuit Court
- **NOTES:** County Clerk has birth records 1881-1882, 1909-1911, death records 1909-1911, and probate records 1824-1981. Registrar of Deeds has military discharge records 1943-1988.

GILES

222 W. Main St., Pulaski, TN 38478, (931) 363-5300,
<www.rackleyhost.com/GilesCounty>

- **INCORPORATED:** Nov. 14, 1809
- **PARENT COUNTY:** Maury
- **BIRTH RECORDS:** 1936, County Clerk
- **MARRIAGE :** 1865, County Clerk
- **DEATH:** start in 1936, kept by County Clerk
- **LAND:** 1790, Registrar of Deeds
- **PROBATE:** 1860, County Clerk
- **COURT:** 1817, Circuit Court
- **NOTES:** County Clerk has marriage records 1818-1862. Registrar has military discharge records 1919-1990. Courthouse burned April 20, 1907.

GRAINGER

8095 Rutledge St., Suite 100, Rutledge, TN 37861, (865) 828-3513,
<graingertn.com>

- **INCORPORATED:** April 22, 1796

- **PARENT COUNTIES:** Hawkins, Knox
- **MARRIAGE RECORDS:** 1796, County Clerk
- **LAND:** 1796, Registrar of Deeds
- **PROBATE:** 1831, County Clerk
- **COURT:** start in 1826, kept by Circuit Court
- **NOTES:** County Clerk has birth and death records 1908-1912. Registrar of Deeds has military discharge records 1943-1982.

GREENE

204 N. Cutler St., Suite 206, Greeneville, TN 37743, (423) 798-1766, **<greenecountytngovt.com>**

- **INCORPORATED:** April 18, 1783
- **PARENT COUNTY:** Washington
- **MARRIAGE RECORDS:** start in 1780, kept by County Clerk
- **LAND:** 1785, Registrar of Deeds
- **NOTES:** County Clerk has birth and death records 1908-1912, 1925-1939, probate records 1780-1986. Clerk of Circuit Court has court records 1809-1986. Registrar of Deeds has military discharge records 1865-1882, 1916-1988. The T. Elmer Cox Library has marriage, death, court, land and probate records.

GRUNDY

Box 177, Altamont, TN 37301, (931) 692-3718, **<www.grundycountytn.net>**

- **INCORPORATED:** Jan. 29, 1844
- **PARENT COUNTIES:** Warren, Franklin
- **MARRIAGE RECORDS:** start in 1850, kept by County Clerk
- **LAND:** 1852, Registrar of Deeds
- **PROBATE:** 1838, County Clerk
- **NOTES:** County Clerk has birth and death records 1908-1912. Clerk of Circuit Court has court records 1848-1986. Registrar of Deeds has military discharge records 1919-1988.

HAMBLEN

511 W. Second N. St., Morristown, TN 37814, (423) 586-1931, **<hamblencountygovernment.us>**

- **INCORPORATED:** June 8, 1870
- **PARENT COUNTIES:** Grainger, Jefferson, and Greene has Hamblen County Census (1830-1880) and marriage records.
- **MARRIAGE RECORDS:** start in 1863, kept by County Clerk
- **LAND:** 1870, Registrar of Deeds
- **PROBATE:** 1870 County Clerk
- **COURT:** 1870, Circuit Court
- **NOTES:** County Clerk has birth records 1909-1912, death records 1909-1912, 1925-1939. The Morristown-Hamblen County Library has Hamblen County census (1830-1880) and marriage records.

HAMILTON

201 E. 7th St., Room 201, Chattanooga, TN 37402, (423) 209-6100, **<www.hamiltontn.gov>**

- **INCORPORATED:** Oct. 25, 1819
- **PARENT COUNTIES:** Cherokee Indian Lands and Rhea County
- **BIRTH RECORDS:** 1949, Dept. of Health
- **MARRIAGE:** 1857, County Clerk
- **DIVORCE:** unknown start, kept by Circuit Court
- **DEATH:** 1972, Department of Health
- **LAND:** 1796, Registrar of Deeds
- **PROBATE:** 1862, Clerk & Master
- **COURT:** 1860, Circuit Court
- **MILITARY:** unknown start, Registrar of Deeds

HANCOCK

1237 Main St., Box 347, Sneedville, TN 37869, (423) 733-4341, **<hancockcountytn.com>**

- **INCORPORATED:** Jan. 7, 1844
- **PARENT COUNTIES:** Claiborne, Hawkins
- **MARRIAGE RECORDS:** start in 1930, kept by County Clerk
- **LAND:** 1879, Registrar of Deeds
- **PROBATE:** 1924, County Clerk
- **COURT:** 1930, Circuit Court
- **NOTES:** Registrar of Deeds has military discharge records 1919-1944.

HARDEMAN

100 N. Main St., Bolivar, TN 38008, (731) 658-3266, **<hardemancountytn.com>**

- **INCORPORATED:** Oct. 16, 1823
- **PARENT COUNTIES:** Chickasaw Indian Lands and Hardin County
- **MARRIAGE RECORDS:** 1823, County Clerk
- **LAND:** 1822, Registrar of Deeds
- **PROBATE:** 1824, Clerk & Master
- **COURT:** start in 1833, kept by Circuit Court
- **MILITARY:** 1919, Registrar of Deeds
- **NOTES:** County Clerk has birth and death records 1828-1939.

HARDIN

465 Main St., Savannah, TN 38372, (901) 925-9078, **<tourhardincounty.org>**

- **INCORPORATED:** Nov. 13, 1819
- **PARENT COUNTY:** Chickasaw Indian Lands
- **MARRIAGE RECORDS:** start in 1874, kept by County Clerk
- **LAND:** 1835, Registrar of Deeds
- **PROBATE:** 1836, County Clerk
- **COURT:** 1840, Circuit Court
- **NOTES:** County Library had birth records 1908-1912, death records 1908-1912, 1914-1939, and marriage records 1863-1958. Registrar of Deeds has military discharge records 1919-1970.

HAWKINS

150 E. Washington St., Rogersville, TN 37645, (423) 272-7359, **<www.hawkinscountytn.gov>**

- **INCORPORATED:** Nov. 18, 1786
- **PARENT COUNTY:** Sullivan
- **MARRIAGE RECORDS:** start in 1789, kept by County Clerk
- **LAND:** 1787, Registrar of Deeds
- **PROBATE:** 1797, County Clerk
- **COURT:** 1837, Circuit Court
- **NOTES:** County Clerk has birth and death records 1925-1938 and military discharge records 1920-1978. Clerk of Circuit Court has Court records 1810-1829.

HAYWOOD

1 N. Washington St., Brownsville, TN 38012, (731) 772-1432, **<haywoodcountybrownsville.com>**

- **INCORPORATED:** Nov. 3, 1823
- **PARENT COUNTY:** Chickasaw Indian Lands

- **NOTES:** County Clerk has birth and death records 1881-1882, 1908-1912, 1937-1939, Divorce records 1941-1965, marriage records 1859-1986, and probate records 1826-1983. Clerk of Circuit Court has Court records 1840-1985. Clerk and Master has divorce records 1860-1936. Registrar of Deeds has land records 1823-1986 and military discharge records 1943-1972.

HENDERSON

17 Monroe St., Suite 4, Lexington, TN 38351, (731) 968-0122, **<www.tennesseeanytime.org/local/henderson.html>**

- **INCORPORATED:** Nov. 7, 1821
- **PARENT COUNTY:** Chickasaw Indian Lands
- **LAND RECORDS:** start in 1895, kept by Registrar of Deeds
- **NOTES:** County Clerk has birth and death records 1908-1912, 1925-1938, marriage records 1893-1991, and probate records 1895-1986. Clerk of Circuit Court has court records 1893-1943. Clerk and Master has divorce records 1896-1950. Registrar of Deeds has land records 1856-1878, 1880-1884, 1892-1894, and military discharge records 1933-1994. Courthouse burned 1863 and 1895; most county records were lost.

HENRY

101 W. Washington St., Paris, TN 38242, (731) 642-5212, **<www.henryco.com>**

- **INCORPORATED:** Nov. 7, 1821
- **PARENT COUNTY:** Chickasaw Indian Lands
- **NOTES:** County Clerk had birth records 1914-1936, death records 1925-1939, marriage records 1838-1987, and probate records 1822-1987. Clerk of Circuit Court has court records 1834-1986. Registrar of Deeds has land records 1822-1986 and military discharge records 1864-1978. Rhea Public Library had birth records 1908-1912, 1914-1946, death records 1908-1939, microfilm copies of Court, Land, and probate records.

HICKMAN

5 Public Sq., Centerville, TN 37033, (931) 729-2492, **<www.hickmanco.com>**

- **INCORPORATED:** Dec. 3, 1807
- **PARENT COUNTY:** Dickson
- **DIVORCE RECORDS:** unknown start, kept by Clerk & Master
- **LAND:** 1808, Registrar of Deeds
- **COURT:** 1841, Circuit Court
- **NOTES:** County Clerk has birth and death records 1908-1912, 1925-1939, marriage records 1868-1992, and probate records 1866-1944. Registrar of Deeds has military discharge records 1967-1990. Courthouse burned in 1865; all records were lost. Hickman County Library has census records for 1850, 1860, 1870, and marriage records 1865-1907.

HOUSTON

4725 Main St., Erin, TN 37061, (931) 289-3633, **<www.houstoncochamber.com>**

- **INCORPORATED:** Jan. 23, 1871
- **PARENT COUNTIES:** Dickson, Stewart, Humphreys, and Montgomery
- **LAND RECORDS:** start in 1871, kept by Registrar of Deeds
- **NOTES:** County Clerk has birth records 1881-1882, marriage records 1871-1991, and probate records 1869-1994. Clerk of Circuit Court has Court records 1871-1994. Registrar of Deeds has military discharge records 1945-1979.

HUMPHREYS

Courthouse Annex Room 1, Waverly, TN 37174, (931) 296-7795, **<www.humphreystn.com>**

- **INCORPORATED:** Oct. 19, 1809
- **PARENT COUNTY:** Stewart
- **MARRIAGE RECORDS:** 1864, County Clerk
- **LAND:** 1810, Registrar of Deeds
- **PROBATE:** 1837, County Clerk
- **COURT:** start in 1898, kept by Circuit Court
- **MILITARY:** 1919, Registrar of Deeds
- **NOTES:** County Clerk had birth records 1908-1912, 1925-1939 and death records 1908-1912, 1925-1935. Courthouse burned in 1876 and 1898; many records were lost; only land records are complete.

JACKSON

101 Hull St., Gainesboro, TN 38562, (931) 268-9888, **<www.jacksonco.com/index.php>**

- **INCORPORATED:** Nov. 6, 1801
- **PARENT COUNTIES:** Smith and Indian Lands
- **MARRIAGE RECORDS:** 1870, County Clerk
- **LAND:** 1872, Registrar of Deeds
- **PROBATE:** 1872 Clerk & Master
- **COURT:** start in 1839, kept by Circuit Court
- **NOTES:** County Clerk has death records 1881-1883, 1909-1912. County, Chancery, and Circuit Courts have divorce records 1839-1915. Birth records are available from Tennessee Vital Records Office and Tennessee State Library and Archives.

JAMES

- **INCORPORATED:** 1871
- **PARENT COUNTIES:** Bradley, Hamilton
- **NOTES:** Abolished in 1919 and absorbed into Hamilton County. All James County records are in Hamilton County.

JEFFERSON

214 W. Main St., Dandridge, TN 37725, (865) 397-3800, **<www.jeffersoncountytn.gov>**

- **INCORPORATED:** June 11, 1792
- **PARENT COUNTIES:** Greene, Hawkins
- **MARRIAGE RECORDS:** start in 1792, kept by County Clerk
- **LAND:** 1792, Registrar of Deeds
- **PROBATE:** 1792, County Clerk
- **COURT:** 1810, Circuit Court
- **NOTES:** County Clerk had birth records 1881-1882, 1908-1909, 1925-1939 and death records 1881-1882, 1925-1939. Registrar of Deeds has military discharge records 1919-1993.

JOHNSON

222 W. Main St., Mountain City, TN 37683, (423) 727-9696, **<johnsoncountytn.org>**

- **INCORPORATED:** Jan. 2, 1836
- **PARENT COUNTY:** Carter
- **MARRIAGE RECORDS:** start in 1838, kept by County Clerk

- **DIVORCE:** unknown start, Chancery Court Clerk
- **LAND:** 1836, Registrar of Deeds
- **PROBATE:** 1836, County Clerk
- **COURT:** 1836, Circuit Court
- **NOTES:** Tennessee State Library and Archives and Vital Records Office have birth and death records.

KNOX

400 Main St., Suite 615, Knoxville, TN 37902, (865) 215-2005, **<www.knoxcounty.org>**

- **INCORPORATED:** June 11, 1792
- **PARENT COUNTIES:** Greene, Hawkins
- **MARRIAGE RECORDS:** start in 1792, kept by County Archives
- **DIVORCE:** 1793, County Archives
- **LAND:** 1932, Registrar of Deeds
- **PROBATE:** 1792, County Archives
- **COURT:** 1792, County Archives
- **TAX:** 1806, County Archives
- **NOTES:** County Archives has birth and death records 1881-1913, and land records 1792-1931. County Archives are at Knoxville Public Library, 300 Main Ave., Knoxville, TN 37902.

LAKE

229 Church St., Box 1, Tiptonville, TN 38079, (731) 253-7382, **<www.tennesseeanytime.org/local/lake.html>**

- **INCORPORATED:** June 24, 1870
- **PARENT COUNTY:** Obion
- **DIVORCE RECORDS:** unknown start, kept by Clerk/Chancery/Circuit Court
- **LAND:** 1870, Registrar
- **NOTES:** County Clerk has birth and death records 1925-1939, marriage records 1883-1953, and probate records 1871-1975. Clerk of Circuit Court has court records 1892-1947. Registrar of Deeds has military discharge records 1945-1953.

LAUDERDALE

100 Court Sq., Ripley, TN 38063, (731) 635-3500, **<lctn.com>**

- **INCORPORATED:** Nov. 24, 1835
- **PARENT COUNTIES:** Dyer, Tipton, Haywood
- **DIVORCE RECORDS:** unknown start, kept by Chancery Court
- **NOTES:** County Clerk has birth and death records 1881-1882, 1908, 1912, 1925, 1938, marriage records 1838-1962, and probate records 1837-1966. Circuit Court has court records 1836-1956. Registrar of Deeds has land records 1835-1952 and military discharge records 1943-1968. Sugarhill Library has a collection of microfilmed records that include census, marriage, probate and land records.

LAWRENCE

240 W. Gaines St., Lawrenceburg, TN 38464, (931) 762-7700, **<www.lawcotn.org>**

- **INCORPORATED:** Oct. 21, 1817
- **PARENT COUNTIES:** Hickman and Indian Lands
- **BIRTH RECORDS:** unknown start, Dept. of Health
- **DIVORCE:** unknown start, Circuit Court
- **LAND:** 1909, Registrar of Deeds
- **PROBATE:** 1847, County Clerk
- **COURT:** 1826, Circuit Court
- **MILITARY:** start in 1919, kept by Registrar of Deeds
- **NOTES:** County Archives had birth records 1908-1912, death records 1908-1938, land records 1818-1909, marriage records 1818-1838, and probate records 1829-1847.

LEWIS

110 N. Park St., Room 107, Hohenwald, TN 38462, (931) 796-3378, **<www.tennesseeanytime.org/local/lewis.html>**

- **INCORPORATED:** Dec. 21, 1843
- **PARENT COUNTIES:** Hickman, Maury, Wayne, Lawrence
- **MARRIAGE RECORDS:** start in 1847, kept by County Clerk
- **DIVORCE:** unknown start, Circuit Court
- **LAND:** 1844, Registrar of Deeds
- **PROBATE:** 1842, County Clerk
- **COURT:** 1844, Circuit Court
- **NOTES:** County Clerk has birth and death records 1908-1912. Registrar of Deeds has military discharge records 1930-1979. County completely abolished for one year following the Civil War, for that year records will be found in Maury, Lawrence, Hickman and Wayne counties.

LINCOLN

112 Main Ave. S., Room 101, Fayetteville, TN 37334, (931) 433-3045, **<www.lincolncountytngov.com>**

- **INCORPORATED:** Nov. 14, 1809
- **PARENT COUNTY:** Bedford
- **MARRIAGE RECORDS:** start in 1838, kept by County Clerk
- **DIVORCE:** unknown start, Circuit Court
- **LAND:** 1810, Registrar of Deeds
- **COURT:** 1941, Circuit Court
- **NOTES:** County Clerk had birth records 1881-1883 and probate records 1809-1986. County Archives has court records 1855-1940. Fayetteville-Lincoln Public Library has death records 1908-1912, 1914-1926. Registrar of Deeds has military discharge records 1921-1988. All unbound records are kept in County Archives.

LOUDON

100 River Road, Suite 106, Loudon, TN 37774, (865) 458-4664, **<www.loudoncounty-tn.gov>**

- **INCORPORATED:** June 2, 1870
- **PARENT COUNTIES:** Blount, Monroe, Roane, and McMinn
- **MARRIAGE RECORDS:** start in 1870, kept by County Clerk
- **LAND:** 1870, County Clerk
- **PROBATE:** 1870, County Clerk
- **COURT:** 1870, Circuit Court
- **NOTES:** County Clerk has birth and death records 1908-1936 and military discharge records 1920-1988. Clerk of Circuit Court had divorce records 1963-1986.

MACON

201 County Courthouse, Lafayette, TN 37083, (615) 666-2363, **<www.maconcountytn.com>**

- **INCORPORATED:** Jan. 18, 1842
- **PARENT COUNTIES:** Smith, Sumner
- **MARRIAGE RECORDS:** start in 1901, kept by County Clerk
- **LAND:** 1901, Registrar of Deeds

- **PROBATE:** 1901, County Clerk
- **NOTES:** County Clerk had birth records 1908-1910 and death records 1920-1939. Clerk of Circuit Court had divorce records 1907-1996 and court records 1901-1996. Registrar of Deeds has military discharge records 1919-1972.

MADISON

100 E. Main St., Suite 302, Jackson, TN 38301, (731) 423-6020, **<www.co.madison.tn.us>**

- **INCORPORATED:** Nov. 7, 1821
- **PARENT COUNTY:** Chickasaw Indian Lands
- **MARRIAGE RECORDS:** start in 1846, kept by County Clerk
- **DIVORCE:** 1846, Clerk/Master/Chancery Court
- **LAND:** 1821, Registrar of Deeds
- **PROBATE:** 1825, Clerk/Master
- **COURT:** 1821, Circuit Court
- **NOTES:** County Clerk has birth and death records 1925-1939 and marriage records 1823-1832.

MARION

24 Courthouse Sq., Jasper, TN 37347, (423) 942-2515, **<www.tennesseeanytime.org/local/marion.html>**

- **INCORPORATED:** Nov. 20, 1817
- **PARENT COUNTY:** Cherokee Indian Lands
- **MARRIAGE RECORDS:** start in 1881, kept by County Clerk
- **LAND:** 1819, Registrar of Deeds
- **PROBATE:** 1875, County Clerk
- **NOTES:** Clerk of Circuit Court has court records 1922-1986. Registrar of Deeds has military discharge records 1919-1969. Courthouse burned in 1822; marriage records destroyed.

MARSHALL

1107 Courthouse Annex, Lewisburg, TN 37091, (931) 359-1072, **<www.tennesseeanytime.org/local/marshall.html>**

- **INCORPORATED:** Feb. 20, 1836
- **PARENT COUNTIES:** Bedford, Lincoln, Maury
- **MARRIAGE RECORDS:** start in 1836, kept by County Clerk
- **LAND:** 1836, Registrar of Deeds
- **PROBATE:** 1835, County Clerk
- **NOTES:** County Clerk had birth records 1909-1912, 1927-1938 and death records 1909-1911. Clerk of Circuit Court has court records 1836-1986. Registrar of Deeds has military discharge records 1920-1967.

MAURY

10 Public Sq., Columbia, TN 38401, (931) 381-3690, **<www.maurycounty-tn.gov>**

- **INCORPORATED:** Nov. 16, 1807
- **PARENT COUNTIES:** Williamson and Indian lands
- **DIVORCE RECORDS:** start in 1810, kept by Circuit Court
- **LAND:** 1808, Registrar of Deeds
- **COURT:** 1810, Circuit Court
- **NOTES:** County Clerk has birth and death records 1908-1910, 1914-1940. County Archives has marriage records 1807-ca. 1950 and probate records 1807-ca. 1900. Registrar of Deeds has military discharge records 1943-1967.

MCMINN

6 E. Madison Ave., Athens, TN 37303, (423) 745-7634, **<www.mcminncounty.org>**

- **INCORPORATED:** Nov. 13, 1819
- **PARENT COUNTY:** Cherokee Indian Lands
- **MARRIAGE RECORDS:** start in 1820, kept by County Clerk
- **LAND:** 1820, Registrar of Deeds
- **PROBATE:** 1819, County Clerk
- **COURT:** 1860, Circuit Court
- **NOTES:** County Clerk has birth and death records 1908-1912, 1914-1925. Registrar of Deeds has military discharge records 1919-1970.

MCNAIRY

170 W. Court Ave., Suite 201, Selmer, TN 38375, (731) 645-3472, **<www.mcnairycountytn.com>**

- **INCORPORATED:** Oct. 8, 1823
- **PARENT COUNTY:** Hardin
- **PROBATE RECORDS:** start in 1861, kept by Circuit Court
- **MARRIAGE:** 1861, County Clerk
- **DEATH:** unknown start, County Clerk
- **DIVORCE:** 1856, Circuit Court
- **LAND:** 1823, Registrar of Deeds
- **COURT:** 1856, Circuit Court
- **NOTES:** County Clerk had birth records 1881-1882. Registrar of Deeds has military discharge records 1919-1994.

MEIGS

17214 State Highway 58 N., Decatur, TN 37322, (423) 334-5850, **<meigscountytnchamber.org>**

- **INCORPORATED:** Jan. 20, 1836
- **PARENT COUNTY:** Rhea
- **MARRIAGE RECORDS:** start in 1838, kept by County Clerk
- **DIVORCE:** 1836, County Clerk
- **LAND:** 1876, Registrar of Deeds
- **PROBATE:** 1836, County Clerk
- **COURT:** 1836, County Clerk
- **NOTES:** County Clerk had birth records 1908-1912, death records 1908-1912, 1925-1937. Registrar of Deeds has military discharge records 1919-1969.

MONROE

105 College St., Madisonville, TN 37354, (423) 442-3981, **<www.monroegovernment.org>**

- **INCORPORATED:** Nov. 13, 1819
- **PARENT COUNTY:** Cherokee Indian Lands
- **MARRIAGE RECORDS:** start in 1838, kept by County Clerk
- **LAND:** 1820, Registrar of Deeds
- **PROBATE:** 1833, County Clerk
- **COURT:** 1827, Circuit Court
- **NOTES:** County Clerk had birth records 1881-1889, 1909-1911, death records 1909-1911. Registrar of Deeds has military discharge records 1919-1956. Wills are filed with the Registrar of Deeds.

MONTGOMERY

1 Millennium Plaza, Suite 205, Clarksville, TN 37040, (931) 648-5787, **<www.montgomerycountytn.org/county/default.aspx>**

- **INCORPORATED:** April 9, 1796
- **PARENT COUNTY:** Tennessee

- **MARRIAGE RECORDS:** start in 1975, kept by County Archives
- **DIVORCE:** 1930, Circuit Court
- **LAND:** 1804, Registrar of Deeds
- **PROBATE:** 1819, County Clerk
- **COURT:** 1825, Clerk of County Court
- **NOTES:** County Archives has Court records 1808-1825, land records 1784-1804, marriage records 1799-1836-1838-1975, military records 1798-1900, and probate records 1796-1819. Tennessee State Library and Archives and Tennessee Vital Records Office have birth and death records.

MOORE

196 Main St., Lynchburg, TN 37352, (931) 759-7076, **<www.tennesseeanytime.org/local/moore.html>**

- **INCORPORATED:** Dec. 14, 1871
- **PARENT COUNTIES:** Bedford, Franklin, Lincoln
- **MARRIAGE RECORDS:** start in 1872, kept by County Clerk
- **LAND:** 1872, Registrar of Deeds
- **PROBATE:** 1872, County Clerk
- **COURT:** 1872, Circuit Court
- **NOTES:** County Clerk has birth and death records 1881-1882, 1908-1912. Registrar of Deeds has military discharge records 1918-1980.

MORGAN

Box 387, Wartburg, TN 37887, (423) 346-6288, **<morgancountychamber.com>**

- **INCORPORATED:** Oct. 15, 1817
- **PARENT COUNTIES:** Anderson and Roane
- **MARRIAGE RECORDS:** start in 1862, kept by County Clerk
- **DIVORCE:** 1905, Circuit Court
- **LAND:** 1818, Registrar of Deeds
- **PROBATE:** 1866, County Clerk
- **COURT:** 1840, Circuit Court
- **NOTES:** County Clerk has birth and death records 1908-1912, 1925-1940. Registrar of Deeds has military discharge records 1945-1984. Fires occurred at county courthouse in 1826, 1870, and 1904.

OBION

1 Bill Burnett Circle, Union City, TN 38261, (731) 885-9611, **<obioncounty.com>**

- **INCORPORATED:** Oct. 24, 1823
- **PARENT COUNTY:** Chickasaw Indian Lands
- **MARRIAGE RECORDS:** start in 1838, kept by County Clerk
- **LAND:** 1824, Registrar of Deeds
- **PROBATE:** 1834, County Clerk
- **COURT:** 1826, Circuit/General Sessions Court
- **NOTES:** County Clerk had birth records 1925-1938 and death records 1881-1882. Circuit Court has divorce records 1823-195. Registrar of Deeds has military discharge records 1920-1968.

OVERTON

317 E. University St., Livingston, TN 38570, (931) 823-5638, **<www.overtoncountytn.com>**

- **INCORPORATED:** Sept. 11, 1806
- **PARENT COUNTIES:** Jackson and Indian lands
- **MARRIAGE RECORDS:** start in 1867, kept by County Clerk
- **DIVORCE:** 1907, Circuit Court
- **LAND:** 1801, Registrar of Deeds
- **PROBATE:** 1870, County Clerk
- **COURT:** 1815, Circuit Court
- **NOTES:** County Clerk has birth and death records 1908-1938. Registrar of Deeds has military discharge records 1943-1966. Almost all pre-1865 records lost in April 1865 courthouse fire.

PERRY

121 E. Main St., Linden, TN 37096, (931) 589-2216, **<perrycountytennessee.com>**

- **INCORPORATED:** Nov. 14, 1818
- **PARENT COUNTY:** Hickman
- **MARRIAGE RECORDS:** start in 1865, kept by County Clerk
- **LAND:** 1841, Registrar of Deeds
- **PROBATE:** 1847, County Clerk
- **COURT:** 1834, Circuit Court
- **NOTES:** County Clerk had birth records 1881-1882, 1908-1912, death records 1881-1882, 1908-1912, 1926-1938. Registrar of Deeds has military discharge records 1920-1988. County courthouse and all county records burned during the Civil War.

PICKETT

1 Courthouse Sq., Suite 100, Byrdstown, TN 38549, (931) 864-3798, **<www.dalehollow.com/Government.htm>**

- **INCORPORATED:** Feb. 27, 1879
- **PARENT COUNTIES:** Fentress, Overton
- **MARRIAGE RECORDS:** start in 1934, kept by County Clerk
- **DIVORCE:** 1934, Circuit Court
- **LAND:** 1934, Registrar of Deeds
- **PROBATE:** 1933, County Clerk
- **COURT:** 1935, Circuit Court
- **NOTES:** County Clerk has birth and death records 1934-1938. Registrar of Deeds has military discharge records 1945-1995.

POLK

Box 128, Benton, TN 37307, (423) 338-4527, **<www.polkgovernment.com>**

- **INCORPORATED:** Nov. 28, 1839
- **PARENT COUNTIES:** Bradley, McMinn
- **MARRIAGE RECORDS:** start in 1894, kept by County Clerk
- **LAND:** 1894, Registrar of Deeds
- **PROBATE:** 1873, County Clerk
- **COURT:** 1886, Circuit Court
- **NOTES:** Registrar of Deeds has military discharge records 1945-1989. Tennessee State Library and Archives and Tennessee Vital Records Office have birth and death records.

PUTNAM

300 E. Spring St., Room 8, Cookeville, TN 38501, (931) 526-2161, **<www.putnamcountytn.gov/index.php>**

- **INCORPORATED:** Feb. 2, 1842
- **PARENT COUNTIES:** White, Jackson, Overton, Smith, Fentress
- **MARRIAGE RECORDS:** start in 1879, kept by County Clerk
- **DIVORCE:** 1900, Clerk & Master
- **LAND:** 1854, Registrar of Deeds
- **PROBATE:** 1876, County Clerk
- **CHANCERY COURT:** 1895, Clerk & Master
- **CIRCUIT COURT:** 1842, Circuit Court
- **NOTES:** County Clerk had birth records 1908-1912, 1925-1931

and death records 1908-1912, 1925-1937. Registrar of Deeds has military discharge records 1918-1994. Courthouse burned in 1899.

RHEA

375 Church St., Suite 215, Dayton, TN 37321, (423) 775-7801, **<www.rheacountyetc.com/government.php>**

- **INCORPORATED:** Nov. 30, 1807
- **PARENT COUNTY:** Roane
- **MARRIAGE RECORDS:** 1808, County Clerk
- **LAND:** 1809, Registrar of Deeds
- **PROBATE:** 1825, County Clerk
- **COURT:** start in 1809, kept by Circuit Court
- **NOTES:** County Clerk had birth records 1908-1912, 1924-1939, death records 1925-1939. Registrar of Deeds has military discharge records 1919-1996.

ROANE

200 E. Race St., Suite 1, Kingston, TN 37763, (865) 376-5578, **<www.roanegov.org>**

- **INCORPORATED:** Nov. 6, 1801
- **PARENT COUNTIES:** Knox and Indian lands
- **MARRIAGE RECORDS:** 1801, County Clerk
- **LAND:** 1801, Registrar of Deeds
- **PROBATE:** 1802, County Clerk
- **COURT:** start in 1810, kept by Circuit Court
- **NOTES:** Registrar of Deeds has military discharge records 1944-1968. Tennessee State Library and Archives and Tennessee Vital Records Office have birth and death records.

ROBERTSON

501 S. Main St., Springfield, TN 37172, (615) 384-2476, **<www.robertsoncountytn.org>**

- **INCORPORATED:** April 9, 1796
- **PARENT COUNTIES:** Tennessee, Sumner
- **MARRIAGE RECORDS:** start in 1980, kept by County Clerk
- **DIVORCE:** 1935, Circuit Court
- **LAND:** 1899, Registrar of Deeds
- **PROBATE:** 1975, County Clerk
- **COURT:** 1993, Circuit Court
- **NOTES:** County Clerk has birth and death records 1908-1912, court records 1832-1993, land records 1796-1899, marriage records 1839-ca. 1980, and probate records 1796-1975. Registrar of Deeds has military discharge records 1922-1989.

RUTHERFORD

101 Courthouse, Murfreesboro, TN 37130, (615) 898-7745, **<www.rutherfordcountytn.gov>**

- **INCORPORATED:** Oct. 25, 1803
- **PARENT COUNTIES:** Davidson, Williamson, Wilson
- **MARRIAGE RECORDS:** 1804 County Clerk
- **LAND:** 1804, Registrar of Deeds
- **PROBATE:** 1804, County Clerk
- **COURT:** start in 1849, kept by Circuit Court
- **NOTES:** County Archives has naturalization records 1922-1924. Tennessee State Library and Archives and Tennessee Vital Records Office have Birth and death records.

SCOTT

2845 Bakers Highway, Huntsville, TN 37756, (423) 663-2000, **<www.scott.tn.us>**

- **INCORPORATED:** Dec. 17, 1849
- **PARENT COUNTIES:** Fentress, Morgan, Anderson, Campbell
- **MARRIAGE RECORDS:** unknown start, kept by County Clerk
- **LAND:** unknown start, Registrar of Deeds
- **PROBATE:** unknown start, County Clerk
- **NOTES:** Scott County Historical Society has court records 1850-1987, death records 1901-1968, land records 1850-1972, marriage records 1854-1972, military discharge records 1919-1987, and probate records 1850-1927.

SEQUATCHIE

22 Cherry St., Dunlap, TN 37327, (423) 949-3479, **<sequatchie.com>**

- **INCORPORATED:** Dec. 9, 1857
- **PARENT COUNTY:** Hamilton
- **BIRTH RECORDS:** start in 1858, kept by County Clerk
- **MARRIAGE:** 1858, County Clerk
- **DIVORCE:** 1898, Circuit Court
- **DEATH:** 1858, County Clerk
- **LAND:** 1858, Registrar of Deeds
- **PROBATE:** 1858, County Clerk
- **COURT:** 1898, Circuit Court
- **NOTES:** County Clerk had birth records 1880-1940 and death records 1881-1938. Registrar of Deeds has military discharge records 1919-1968.

SEVIER

125 Court Ave. #201E, Sevierville, TN 37862, (423) 453-6136, **<www.seviercountytn.org>**

- **INCORPORATED:** Sept. 28, 1794
- **PARENT COUNTY:** Jefferson
- **MARRIAGE RECORDS:** 1856, County Clerk
- **LAND:** 1845, Registrar of Deeds
- **PROBATE:** 1849, County Clerk
- **COURT:** start in 1850, kept by Circuit Court
- **NOTES:** Tennessee State Library and Archives and Tennessee Vital Records Office have birth and death records. Courthouse fire of 1856 destroyed all county records except one surveyor's book.

SHELBY

160 N. Main St., Suite 850, Memphis, TN 38103, (901) 545-4500, **<www.shelbycountytn.gov>**

- **INCORPORATED:** Nov. 24, 1819
- **PARENT COUNTY:** Hardin
- **BIRTH RECORDS:** start in 1914, kept by Dept. of Health
- **MARRIAGE:** 1820, County Clerk
- **DIVORCE:** 1895, Circuit Court
- **DEATH:** 1950, Dept. of Health
- **LAND:** 1788, County Archives
- **PROBATE:** 1900, Probate Court Clerk
- **COURT:** 1828, Circuit Court
- **NOTES:** County Archives has death records 1848-1951, marriage records 1820-1999, naturalization records 1856-1906, and probate records 1820-1900

SMITH
122 Turner High Circle, Suite 100, Carthage, TN 37030, (615) 735-2294, **<smithcounty.org>**
- **INCORPORATED:** Oct. 26, 1799
- **PARENT COUNTIES:** Sumner, Indian Lands
- **MARRIAGE RECORDS:** 1838, County Clerk
- **DEATH:** unknown start, County Clerk
- **LAND:** 1799, Registrar of Deeds
- **PROBATE:** 1805, County Clerk
- **COURT:** start in 1811, kept by Circuit Court
- **NOTES:** County Clerk has birth and death records 1881-1882, 1908-1912. Registrar of Deeds has military discharge records 1919-1988.

STEWART
226 Lakeview Dr., Dover, TN 37058, (931) 232-3100, **<www.stewartcountygovernment.com>**
- **INCORPORATED:** Nov. 1, 1803
- **PARENT COUNTY:** Montgomery
- **MARRIAGE RECORDS:** 1849, County Clerk
- **LAND:** 1796, Registrar of Deeds
- **PROBATE:** 1812, County Clerk
- **COURT:** start in 1821, kept by Circuit Court
- **NOTES:** County Clerk had birth records 1881-1912 and death records 1881-1912, 1914-1925. Registrar of Deeds has military discharge records 1917-1994. Courthouse burned during Civil War.

SULLIVAN
3411 Hwy. 126, Suite 206, Blountville, TN 37617, (423) 323-6417, **<www.sullivancounty.org>**
- **INCORPORATED:** Oct. 18, 1779
- **PARENT COUNTY:** Washington
- **MARRIAGE RECORDS:** 1863, County Clerk
- **LAND:** 1770, Registrar of Deeds
- **PROBATE:** 1867, Chancery Court
- **COURT:** start in 1879, kept by Circuit Court
- **NOTES:** Tennessee State Library and Archives and Tennessee Vital Records Office has birth and death records.

SUMNER
355 North Belvedere Dr., Room 102, Gallatin, TN 37066, (615) 452-3604, **<www.sumnertn.org>**
- **INCORPORATED:** Nov. 18, 1786
- **PARENT COUNTY:** Davidson
- **MARRIAGE RECORDS:** start in 1998, kept by County Clerk
- **LAND:** 1965, Registrar of Deeds
- **PROBATE:** 1985, County Clerk
- **NOTES:** County Archives has death records 1908-1925, land records 1793-1965, loose court papers 1786-1930, marriage records 1787-1998, and probate records 1789-1985.

TENNESSEE
- **PARENT COUNTY:** unknown
- **INCORPORATED:** 1788
- **NOTES:** County surrendered name when state became Tennessee, 1796. Portions of Tennessee County now found in Robertson and Montgomery counties.

TIPTON
1 Liberty Ave., Rm. 101, Covington, TN 38019, (901) 476-0200, **<www.tiptonco.com>**
- **INCORPORATED:** Oct. 29, 1823
- **PARENT COUNTY:** Chickasaw Indian Lands
- **MARRIAGE RECORDS:** start in 1840, kept by County Clerk
- **LAND:** 1824, Registrar of Deeds
- **PROBATE:** 1824, Chancery Court
- **COURT:** 1832, Circuit Court
- **NOTES:** County Clerk had birth records 1908-1912, 1925-1939, death records 1925-1939, and divorce records 1911-1950. Registrar of Deeds has military discharge records 1919-1976.

TROUSDALE
210 Broadway, Room 5, Hartsville, TN 37074, (615) 374-2461, **<www.hartsvilletrousdale.com>**
- **INCORPORATED:** Sept. 5, 1870
- **PARENT COUNTIES:** Macon, Smith, Wilson, Sumner
- **MARRIAGE RECORDS:** start in 1905, kept by County Clerk
- **DIVORCE:** 1906, Circuit Court
- **LAND:** 1905, Registrar of Deeds
- **PROBATE:** 1905, County Clerk
- **COURT:** 1906, Circuit Court
- **NOTES:** County Clerk had birth records 1917-1940. Registrar of Deeds has military discharge records 1917-1919, 1948-1981. Courthouse documents were damaged in fires of 1900 and 1904.

UNICOI
100 N. Main Ave., Unicoi, TN 37692, (423) 743-9391, **<www.unicoicountytn.gov>**
- **INCORPORATED:** March 23, 1875
- **PARENT COUNTIES:** Carter, Washington
- **MARRIAGE RECORDS:** start in 1876, kept by County Clerk
- **DIVORCE:** unknown start, Clerk/Chancery/Circuit Court
- **LAND:** 1876, Registrar of Deeds
- **PROBATE:** 1876, County Clerk
- **COURT:** 1876, Clerk/Chancery/Circuit Court
- **NOTES:** County Clerk has birth and death records 1908-1912, 1924-1939. Registrar of Deeds has military discharge records 1919-1996.

UNION
901 Main Street, Suite 124, Maynardville, TN 37807, (865) 992-3061, **<www.unioncountytn.org>**
- **INCORPORATED:** Jan. 3, 1850
- **PARENT COUNTY:** Anderson, Campbell, Claiborne, Grainger, Knox
- **MARRIAGE RECORDS:** 1864 County Clerk
- **LAND:** 1856, Registrar of Deeds
- **PROBATE:** 1856, County Clerk
- **COURT:** start in 1854, kept by Clerk of County Court
- **NOTES:** County Clerk has birth and death records 1881-1882. Registrar of Deeds has military discharge records 1949-1984.

VAN BUREN
500 College St., Spencer, TN 38585, (931) 946-2314, **<vanburenchamber.com>**
- **INCORPORATED:** Jan. 3, 1840

- **PARENT COUNTIES:** Bledsoe, Warren, White
- **MARRIAGE RECORDS:** start in 1840, kept by County Clerk
- **DIVORCE:** 1840, Circuit Court
- **LAND:** 1840, Registrar of Deeds
- **PROBATE:** 1840, County Clerk
- **COURT:** 1840, Circuit Court
- **NOTES:** County Clerk has birth and death records 1908-1911, 1925-1935. Registrar of Deeds has military discharge records 1919-1968.

WARREN

201 Locust Street, Suite 1, McMinnville, TN 37110, (931) 473-2505,
<www.warrencountytn.gov>

- **INCORPORATED:** Nov. 26, 1807
- **PARENT COUNTY:** White
- **MARRIAGE RECORDS:** start in 1852, kept by County Clerk
- **DIVORCE:** unknown start, Clerk/Chancery/Circuit Court
- **LAND:** 1814, Registrar of Deeds
- **PROBATE:** 1827, County Clerk
- **COURT:** 1842, Circuit Court
- **NOTES:** County Clerk has birth and death records 1881-1912. Registrar of Deeds has military discharge records 1919-1983.

WASHINGTON

Box 219, Jonesborough, TN 37659, (423) 753-1666,
<www.washingtoncountytn.com>

- **INCORPORATED:** June 1, 1796
- **PARENT COUNTY:** Washington County NC
- **LAND RECORDS:** start in 1782, kept by Registrar of Deeds
- **PROBATE:** 1779, County Clerk
- **NOTES:** Tennessee State Library and Archives and Tennessee Vital Records office have birth and death records. East Tennessee State University Archives has Chancery Court records 1836-1886 and Circuit Court records 1810-1886. Circuit Court Clerk had divorce records 1799-1945. County Clerk has marriage records 1787-1945. 18th century court records are kept at the Archives of Appalachia collection at East Tennessee State University. Covered present state. Many counties formed from it. This county also embraced parts of present North Carolina counties. County Clerk had birth records 1908-1912 and 1925-1938.

WAYNE

- **INCORPORATED:** 1785
- **PARENT COUNTY:** State of Franklin
- **NOTES:** Abolished June 1, 1796. This Wayne County was created under the state of Franklin. Included present Carter County and part of Johnson County.

WAYNE

100 Court Circle, Waynesboro, TN 38485, (931) 722-3653,
<www.waynecountytn.org>

- **INCORPORATED:** Nov. 24, 1817
- **PARENT COUNTY:** Hickman
- **MARRIAGE RECORDS:** 1857, County Clerk
- **LAND:** 1821, Registrar of Deeds
- **PROBATE:** 1848, County Clerk
- **COURT:** start in 1848, kept by Clerk of County Court
- **NOTES:** County Clerk has birth and death records 1881-1883, 1908-1921. Registrar of Deeds has military discharge records 1914-1975.

WEAKLEY

116 Main Street, Room 106, Dresden, TN 38225, (731) 364-5413,
<www.weakleycountytn.gov>

- **INCORPORATED:** Oct. 21, 1823
- **PARENT COUNTY:** Chickasaw Indian Lands
- **MARRIAGE RECORDS:** start in 1843, kept by County Clerk
- **DIVORCE:** unknown start, Clerk/Chancery/Circuit Court
- **LAND:** 1822, Registrar of Deeds
- **PROBATE:** 1828 County Clerk
- **COURT:** 1827, Chancery Court
- **NOTES:** County Clerk had birth records 1908-1912. Registrar of Deeds has military discharge records for 1917-1989.

WHITE

Courthouse, Room 205, Sparta, TN 38583, (931) 836-3203,
<www.tennesseeanytime.org/local/white.html>

- **INCORPORATED:** Sept. 11, 1806
- **PARENT COUNTY:** Smith
- **BIRTH RECORDS:** 1881, County Clerk
- **MARRIAGE:** 1809, County Clerk
- **DEATH:** 1881, County Clerk
- **LAND:** start in 1806, kept by Registrar of Deeds
- **PROBATE:** 1806, County Clerk
- **COURT:** 1806, County Clerk
- **NOTES:** Registrar of Deeds has military discharge records 1943-1992.

WILLIAMSON

1320 W. Main, Suite 125, Franklin, TN 37064, (615) 790-5700,
<www.williamsoncounty-tn.gov>

- **INCORPORATED:** Oct. 26, 1799
- **PARENT COUNTY:** Davidson
- **LAND RECORDS:** start in 1950, kept by Registrar of Deeds
- **PROBATE:** 1899, County Clerk
- **NOTES:** County Clerk has birth and death records 1881-1882, 1908-1912. County Archives had divorce records 1900-1950, land records 1800-1950, marriage records 1800-2000, and probate records 1800-1899. Registrar of Deeds has military discharge records 1918-1966.

WILSON

228 E Main Street, Room 104, Lebanon, TN 37087, (615) 444-1383,
<www.wilsoncountytn.com>

- **INCORPORATED:** Oct. 26, 1799
- **PARENT COUNTY:** Sumner
- **MARRIAGE RECORDS:** start in 1953, kept by County Clerk
- **DIVORCE:** unknown start, Clerk/Master/Circuit Court
- **LAND:** 1789, Registrar of Deeds
- **NOTES:** County Archives had birth records 1881-1886, 1907-1912, Court records 1803-1964, death records 1907-1912, 1925-1939, marriage records 1802-1953, and probate records 1802-1964. Registrar of Deeds has military discharge records 1919-1986.

TEXAS

» BY EMILY ANNE CROOM

HISTORICAL OVERVIEW

16th-century Spaniards exploring Texas found indigenous people, but not the gold they sought. Later Spanish missions, presidios and villages were the nuclei for modern cities, including El Paso (1682), San Antonio (1718), and Nacogdoches (1779)—the latter well situated for trade with the Indians and with Natchitoches, La. French settlement on the Texas Gulf coast in 1685 was short-lived. When France ceded greater Louisiana to Spain in 1762, Texas and Louisiana were under the same crown. In 1803, the United States tried to claim Texas as part of the Louisiana Purchase.

Anglo-American settlement had not begun when Mexico gained independence from Spain in 1821. Under a renegotiated Mexican contract, Stephen F. Austin recruited several hundred families to settle river valleys near his San Felipe de Austin headquarters. Other empresarios also settled the Mexican State of Coahuila and Texas. Newcomers had to swear allegiance to Mexico and Catholicism.

Adventurers and would-be land speculators became disgruntled by the centralist Mexican government and its 1830 attempt to halt Anglo-American settlement. Many colonists were alarmed by Mexican preparations to send an army to occupy Texas. After several battles, Texans declared themselves an independent republic on March 2, 1836. The war for independence was short. The Republic of Texas existed for nine years before the US Congress annexed it in late 1845, accepting Texas as the 28th state. After a war with Mexico from 1846 to 1848, Mexico relinquished its claim to Texas and the United States gained most of its Southwest.

Early settlers arrived largely from Alabama, Mississippi, Tennessee, Arkansas, Georgia, Louisiana and Missouri, as well as other US states, Mexico, the British Isles and German states. Czechs, Scandinavians, and Alsatians began arriving in the 1840s; Poles, in the 1850s. Most early settlers were small farmers, but cotton planters with slaves also moved in. By 1860, Texas had about 604,000 residents, of whom 30 percent were slaves, 7 percent were foreign-born immigrants, and only about 350 were free blacks. Not counted in censuses were numerous Indians, many of whom were eventually relocated to Indian Territory reservations.

research tips

- The Texas State Library participates in interlibrary loan of microfilmed county records through a regional historical resource depository' program. See lists of regional depositories and available county records at **<www.tsl.state.tx.us/arc/local>**.
- Besides the state library and archives in Austin, major research facilities include the Center for American History, University of Texas, Austin, **<www.cah.utexas.edu>**; Clayton Library Center for Genealogical Research, a unit of the Houston Public Library, **<www.houstonlibrary.org/clayton>**; the Texas Room, Central Library, Houston Public Library; Dallas Public Library's genealogy department and Texas/Dallas history and archives department, **<www.dallaslibrary.org/central.htm>**; and various academic libraries. Numerous Texas public libraries have genealogy collections.

CENSUS RECORDS

- Federal census: 1850, 1860, 1870, 1880, 1900, 1910, 1920, 1930
- Federal mortality schedules: 1850, 1860, 1870, 1880
- Federal slave schedules: 1850, 1860 (schedules name slaveholders but rarely name slaves)
- Special census of Civil War Union veterans and widows: 1890
- Colonial: 1829–1836

Although divided over the issues of slavery and secession, Texas seceded from the United States in February 1861. The state saw limited military action during the Civil War and was readmitted to the Union in 1870.

From the 1820s to the early 1900s, cotton was the money crop and corn sustained life. After the Civil War, cotton, railroads, and cattle and sheep industries expanded rapidly. The 20th century saw economic diversification in agriculture and development of the petrochemical, timber-related, food-processing and other industries.

RECORD HIGHLIGHTS

Texas began statewide civil registration of births and deaths in 1903, marriages in 1966, and divorces in 1968. Copies of birth and death certificates can be requested from the county clerk's office where the record originated, or the state bureau of vital statistics. The county office is often a good first choice; fees vary. Certified copies of marriage licenses come only from the county clerk's office that issued the license; copies of divorce decrees come only from the district clerk's office where the case was heard. The state vital statistics office issues only a verification of marriage or divorce based on the application the court clerk submitted to that office. The website **<www.dshs.state.tx.us/vs>** provides instructions and fees; allow about three months for a response from the state office. The voluntary Central Adoption Registry is described at **<www.dshs.state.tx.us/vs/reqproc/adoptionregistry.shtm>**. Pre-1903 vital records exist for some locations. Marriage records often survive from the creation of the county; many pre-republic marriages have been published. The Congress of the Republic granted few divorces.

The first federal census for Texas is 1850. Texas has taken no state censuses, but most Spanish and Mexican town censuses and resident lists have been published. Good resources for republic and early state residents are county tax rolls, many dating from 1836.

Never federal public domain, Texas officially retained the land within its current boundaries after statehood. Colonial, republic, and state land grants and related records are at the Texas General Land Office see **<www.glo.state.tx.us/archives.html>**.

In the state library, state archives, general land office, or other repositories, records include the following:

- Colonial collections such as the Bexar, Laredo, and Nacogdoches archives
- 1834-1835 character certificates, mostly for East Texans
- Confederate indigent families list **<www.tsl.state.tx.us/arc/cif/index.html>**
- Confederate pension applications from 1899; an index is available online at **<www.tsl.state.tx.us/arc/pensions/introcpi.html>**
- Republic of Texas claims for payment, reimbursement, or damages that citizens submitted to the Republic government, 1835-1846; republic pensions and claims submitted after 1846; index at **<www2.tsl.state.tx.us/trail/RepublicSearch.jsp>**
- 1854-1855 scholastic censuses of school-age children, various counties
- 1867 voter registrations

ARCHIVES, LIBRARIES, AND SOCIETIES

Abilene Public Library
202 Cedar, Abilene, TX 79606, (915) 676-6029, **<www.abilenetx.com/apl>**

Amarillo Genealogical Society
c/o Amarillo Public Library, 413 East Fourth St., Amarillo, TX 79189, (806) 378-3054

Angelina County Genealogical Society
Box 150631, Lufkin, TX 75915, **<www.rootsweb.ancestry.com/~txacgs>**

Archer County Historical Commission
Rt. 1, Windthorst, TX 76389

Arlington Genealogical Society
4319 Waycross Dr., Arlington, TX 76016, (817) 451-5764, **<www.rootsweb.ancestry.com/~txags/ags.htm>**

Arlington Public Library
101 E. Abram, Arlington, TX 76010, (817) 459-6900, **<arlingtonlibrary.org>**

Atascosa County Genealogical Society
Mummer Memorial Building, Fourth and H Aves., Box 93, Poteet, TX 78065, **<rootsweb.ancestry.com/~txacgsl>**

Athens Genealogical Organization
c/o Henderson Public Library, 121 Prairieville St., Athens, TX 75751, **<txgenweb7.org/txhenderson/ago.htm>**

Atlanta Public Library
101 W. Hiram, Atlanta, TX 75551, (903) 796-2112, www.atlantalib.com

Austin County Historical Commission
206 S. Masonie St, Bellville, TX 77418

Austin Genealogical Society
Box 10010, Austin, TX 78766, (512) 378-4735, **<www.austintxgensoc.org>**

Austin History Center
810 Guadalupe St., Austin, TX 78701, (512) 974-7480, **<www.ci.austin.tx.us/library/ahc>**

Bay Area Genealogical Society
Box 891447, Houston, TX 77289, (281) 486-0406, **<txbayareagen.org>**

Bay Area Heritage Society
220 W. Defee Ave., Baytown, TX 77520, (281) 427-8768

Baylor University Institute for Oral History
Carroll Library, Suite 304, One Bear Place #97271, Waco, TX 76798, (254) 710-3437, **<baylor.edu/oral_history>**

Bear Creek Genealogical Society
Box 842661., Houston, TX 77284, **<www.rootsweb.ancestry.com/~txgcgs>**

Beaumont Heritage Society
3025 French Rd., Beaumont TX 77706, (409) 898-0348, **<beaumontheritage.org>**

Bellville Historical Society
Box 67, Bellville, TX 77418, **<bellvillehistoricalsociety.com>**

Big Bend Genealogy Society
Box 1251, Alpine, TX 79831, **<www.rootsweb.ancestry.com/~txbcgs>**

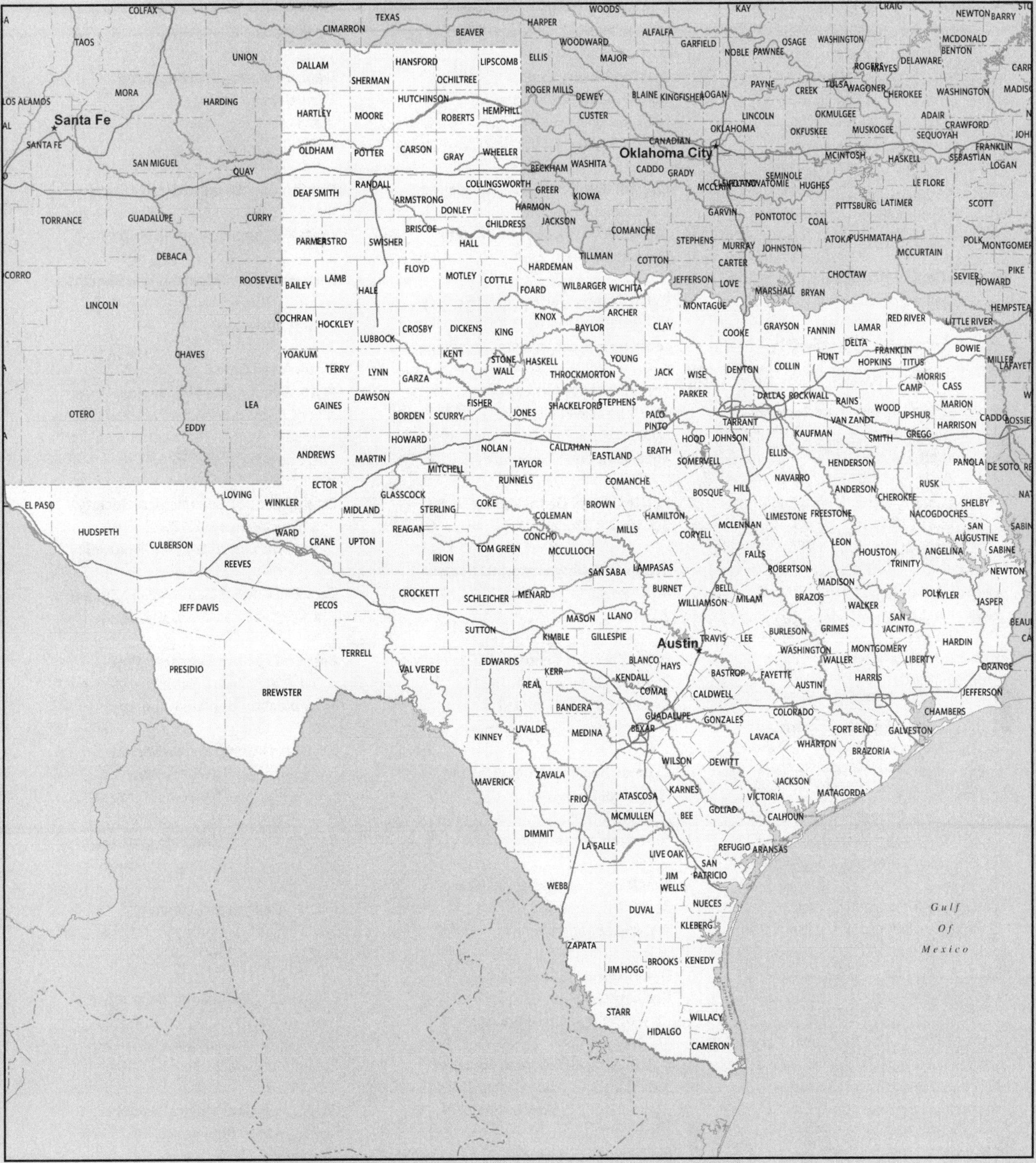
COLFAX
TEXAS
CIMARRON
BEAVER
HARPER
WOODS
ALFALFA
KAY
CRAIG
NEWTON
BARRY
TAOS
UNION
DALLAM
HANSFORD
LIPSCOMB
ELLIS
WOODWARD
MAJOR
GARFIELD
NOBLE
PAWNEE
OSAGE
WASHINGTON
MCDONALD
BENTON
SHERMAN
OCHILTREE
ROGERS
MAYES
DELAWARE
MORA
HARDING
HUTCHINSON
ROGER MILLS
DEWEY
BLAINE
KINGFISHER
LOGAN
PAYNE
CREEK
TULSA
WAGONER
CHEROKEE
WASHINGTON
LOS ALAMOS
HARTLEY
MOORE
ROBERTS
HEMPHILL
CUSTER
LINCOLN
OKMULGEE
ADAIR
Santa Fe
CRAWFORD
OKLAHOMA
OKFUSKEE
MUSKOGEE
SEQUOYAH
SANTA FE
CANADIAN
Oklahoma City
FRANKLIN
OLDHAM
POTTER
CARSON
GRAY
WHEELER
MCINTOSH
HASKELL
SEBASTIAN
LOGAN
SAN MIGUEL
QUAY
BECKHAM
WASHITA
CADDO
GRADY
CLEVELAND
POTTAWATOMIE
SEMINOLE
HUGHES
LE FLORE
DEAF SMITH
RANDALL
COLLINGSWORTH
GREER
MCCLAIN
ARMSTRONG
KIOWA
DONLEY
HARMON
PITTSBURG
LATIMER
SCOTT
TORRANCE
GUADALUPE
CURRY
GARVIN
PONTOTOC
COAL
CHILDRESS
JACKSON
BRISCOE
COMANCHE
ATOKA
PUSHMATAHA
PARMER
CASTRO
SWISHER
HALL
STEPHENS
MURRAY
JOHNSTON
POLK
MONTGOMERY
DEBACA
TILLMAN
MCCURTAIN
COTTON
HARDEMAN
CARTER
FLOYD
MOTLEY
COTTLE
PIKE
SOCORRO
ROOSEVELT
BAILEY
LAMB
HALE
FOARD
WILBARGER
WICHITA
JEFFERSON
LOVE
CHOCTAW
SEVIER
HOWARD
MARSHALL
BRYAN
LINCOLN
MONTAGUE
HEMPSTEAD
ARCHER
COCHRAN
HOCKLEY
CROSBY
DICKENS
KING
KNOX
BAYLOR
CLAY
GRAYSON
FANNIN
LAMAR
RED RIVER
LITTLE RIVER
COOKE
DELTA
LUBBOCK
BOWIE
FRANKLIN
CHAVES
YOAKUM
KENT
STONE WALL
HASKELL
YOUNG
HUNT
HOPKINS
TITUS
MILLER
LAFAYETTE
TERRY
LYNN
GARZA
THROCKMORTON
JACK
WISE
DENTON
COLLIN
MORRIS
CAMP
CASS
PARKER
DALLAS
ROCKWALL
RAINS
DAWSON
FISHER
SHACKELFORD
STEPHENS
WOOD
MARION
OTERO
LEA
GAINES
BORDEN
SCURRY
JONES
PALO PINTO
TARRANT
UPSHUR
VAN ZANDT
HARRISON
CADDO
BOSSIER
EDDY
KAUFMAN
GREGG
HOWARD
NOLAN
CALLAHAN
HOOD
JOHNSON
SMITH
ANDREWS
MARTIN
TAYLOR
EASTLAND
ERATH
ELLIS
HENDERSON
PANOLA
DE SOTO
SOMERVELL
MITCHELL
RUNNELS
NAVARRO
ECTOR
RUSK
LOVING
COMANCHE
GLASSCOCK
COKE
BOSQUE
HILL
ANDERSON
CHEROKEE
EL PASO
WINKLER
STERLING
BROWN
SHELBY
MIDLAND
COLEMAN
HAMILTON
LIMESTONE
FREESTONE
NACOGDOCHES
REAGAN
MCLENNAN
SAN AUGUSTINE
HUDSPETH
WARD
CRANE
UPTON
MILLS
CORYELL
LEON
SABINE
CULBERSON
CONCHO
TOM GREEN
MCCULLOCH
HOUSTON
ANGELINA
REEVES
IRION
FALLS
TRINITY
NEWTON
SAN SABA
LAMPASAS
ROBERTSON
MADISON
CROCKETT
MENARD
BELL
SCHLEICHER
BURNET
MILAM
POLK
TYLER
JASPER
JEFF DAVIS
PECOS
WILLIAMSON
BRAZOS
WALKER
MASON
LLANO
SAN JACINTO
SUTTON
KIMBLE
GILLESPIE
TRAVIS
LEE
BURLESON
GRIMES
HARDIN
Austin
TERRELL
EDWARDS
BLANCO
WASHINGTON
MONTGOMERY
LIBERTY
PRESIDIO
VAL VERDE
KERR
HAYS
BASTROP
FAYETTE
WALLER
HARRIS
ORANGE
KENDALL
AUSTIN
REAL
COMAL
CALDWELL
JEFFERSON
BREWSTER
BANDERA
GUADALUPE
GONZALES
COLORADO
CHAMBERS
KINNEY
UVALDE
MEDINA
BEXAR
LAVACA
FORT BEND
GALVESTON
WHARTON
BRAZORIA
WILSON
DEWITT
MAVERICK
ZAVALA
JACKSON
MATAGORDA
ATASCOSA
KARNES
FRIO
VICTORIA
MCMULLEN
BEE
GOLIAD
CALHOUN
DIMMIT
LA SALLE
REFUGIO
ARANSAS
LIVE OAK
SAN PATRICIO
JIM WELLS
WEBB
NUECES
DUVAL
Gulf Of Mexico
KLEBERG
ZAPATA
BROOKS
KENEDY
JIM HOGG
STARR
WILLACY
HIDALGO
CAMERON

Boerne Area Historical Society
Box 178, Boerne, TX 78006, (830) 249-7277, **<www.rootsweb.ancestry.com/~txbahps>**

Brazos Genealogical Association
Box 5493, Bryan, TX 77805, **<www.brazosgenealogy.org>**

Brazosport Genealogical Society
Box 813, Lake Jackson, TX 77566

Brooks County Historical Commission
604 W. Blucher, Falfurrias, TX 78355

Brown County Historical Society
Box 146, Brownwood, TX 76804

Burkburnett Genealogical Society
c/o Burkburnett Library, 215 E. Fourth St., Burkburnett, TX 76354

Burnet County Genealogical Society
c/o Herman Brown Free Library, 100 Washington St., Burnet, TX 78611

Caldwell County Genealogical and Historical Society
215 S. Pecan Ave., Luling, TX 78648, (830) 875-9466, **<www.txgenweb2.org/txcaldwell/socpage.htm>**

Camp County Genealogical Society
Box 1083, Pittsburg, TX 75686, **<www.rootsweb.ancestry.com/~txccgs>**

Cass County Genealogical Society
Box 880, Atlanta, TX 75551, (903) 796-2107, **<www.atlantalib.com/ccgs>**

Center for American History, University of Texas at Austin
Sid Richardson Hall 2.106, 1 University Station D1100, Austin, TX 78712, (512) 495-4518 **<www.cah.utexas.edu>**

Central Texas Genealogical Society
Waco-McLennan County Library System 1717 Austin Ave., Waco, TX 76701, **<www.rootsweb.ancestry.com/~txctgs>**

Chaparral Genealogical Society
Box 606, Tomball, TX 77377, (281) 516-7417, **<www.chaparralgensoc.org>**

Cherokee County Genealogical Society
Box 1332, Jacksonville, TX 75766, (903) 586-0135

Childress Genealogical Society
117 Ave. B. NE, Childress, TX 79201

Clayton Library Center for Genealogical Research
5300 Caroline, Houston, TX 77004, (832) 393-2600, **<www.hpl.lib.tx.us/clayton>**

Coastal Bend Genealogical Society
Box 2826, Corpus Christi, TX 78403, **<www.rootsweb.ancestry.com/~txcbgs/txcbgs.htm>**

Collin County Genealogical Society
Box 865052, Plano, TX 75086, **<www.rootsweb.ancestry.com/~txcolcgs>**

Coryell County Genealogical Society
c/o Gatesville Public Library, 811 Main St., Gatesville, TX 76528, **<www.rootsweb.ancestry.com/~txcoryel>**

Cottle County Genealogical Society
Box 1005, Paducah, TX 79248

Crockett County Historical Society
404 11th St., Ozona, TX 76943, (915) 392-2837

Cross Timbers Genealogical Society
Box 197, Gainesville, TX 76241, **<www.rootsweb.ancestry.com/~txcooke/ctgs_index.htm>**

Cypress Basin Genealogical and Historical Society
Box 403, Mt. Pleasant, TX 75455, **<www.rootsweb.ancestry.com/~txcypbgs>**

Czech Heritage Society of Texas
Box 1027, La Grange, TX 78945, **<www.czechheritage.org>**

Dallas Genealogical Society
Box 12648, Dallas, TX 7525, **<www.dallasgenealogy.org>**

Dallas Jewish Historical Society
7900 Northaven Rd., Dallas, TX 75230, (214) 239-7120, **<www.djhs.org>**

Dallas Public Library
1515 Young St., Dallas, TX 75201, (214) 670-1400, **<www.dallaslibrary2.org>**

Daughters of the Republic of Texas
Box 1401, San Antonio, TX 78295, (210) 225-1071, **<www.drtl.org>**

Deaf Smith County Genealogical Society
211 E. Fourth St., Hereford, TX 79045

Denison Library Historical and Genealogical Society
300 West Grandy, Denison, TX 75020, (903) 465-9447

Denton County Genealogical Society
Box 424707, Denton, TX 76204, **<www.rootsweb.ancestry.com/~txdcgs>**

Descendants of Mexican War Veterans
Box 830482, Richardson, TX 75083, **<www.dmwv.org>**

Disciples of Christ, Brite Divinity School Collection
Mary Couts Burnett Library, Texas Christian University, 2913 West Lowden, Fort Worth, TX 76129, (817) 921-7117

Donley County Genealogical Society
Box 116, Clarendon, TX 79226, **<.rootsweb.ancestry.com/~txdonley>**

East Bell County Genealogical Society
Box 1493, Temple, TX 76503

East End Historical Association
1501 Post Office St., Galveston TX, 77550, **<www.eastendgalveston.org>**

East Texas Genealogical Society
Box 6967, Tyler, TX 75711, **<www.rootsweb.ancestry.com/~txetgs>**

Eastland County Genealogical Society
609 Marsh St., Eastland, TX 76448

El Paso Genealogical Society
c/o El Paso Public Library, 501 N. Oregon St., El Paso, TX 79901, (915) 543-5474

Ellis County Genealogical Society
Box 479, Waxahachie, TX 75168, Ertah County Genealogical Society, 174 N. Columbia, Stephenville, TX 76401

Fort Brown Genealogical Society
608 E. Adams, Brownsville, TX 78520, (512) 542-4824

Fort Worth Genealogical Society
Box 471789, Fort Worth, TX 76147

Fredericksburg Genealogical Society
Box 164, 108 N. Edison St., Fredericksburg, TX 78624, **<www.fbgtxgensoc.org>**

Freestone County Genealogical Society
Box 14, Fairfield, TX 75840, (903) 389-2292

Galveston County Genealogical Society
Box 1141, Galveston, TX 77553

Genealogical Society of Aransas County
Box 1642, Fulton, TX 78358

Genealogical Society of Big Sprigs
810 E. 12th St., Big Spring TX 79720, (915) 267-7236

Genealogical Society of Kendall County
Box 623, Boerne, TX 78006, **<www.rootsweb.ancestry.com/~txgskc>**

Genealogical Society of Kerrville
505 Water St., Kerrville, TX 78028, (210) 257-8422

German Texas Heritage Society
507 E. Tenth St., Box 684171, Austin, TX 78768, (512) 482-0927

Gillespie County Historical Society
309 W. Main St., Fredericksburg, TX 78624, (210) 997-2835

Golden Spread Chapter, American Historical Society of Germans from Russia
Box 307, Shattuck, OK 73858, (580) 938-2139

Grand Prairie Genealogical Society
Box 532026, Grand Prairie, TX 75053, (972) 237-5700

Grayson County Genealogical Society
421 N. Travis, Sherman, TX 75090, (903) 892-7240

Gregg County Historical and Genealogical Society
222 W. Cotton, Longview, TX 75601, (214) 237-1350

Grimes County Heritage Association
1215 E. Washington Ave., Navasota, TX 77868, (936) 825-6744, **<www.rootsweb.ancestry.com/~txgrimes>**

Guadalupe County Genealogical Society
707 E. College St., Sequin, TX 78155, (830) 3790-1531, **<www.txgenweb2.org/txguadalupe/gensoc.html>**

Gulf Coast Ancestry Researchers
Box 16, Wallisville, TX 77597, (409) 389-2486

Harrison County Historical Old Courthouse Museum
Peter Whetstone Square, Mashall, TX 75670, (903) 938-2680

Heart of Texas Genealogical Society
Box 1837, Rochelle, TX 76872

Hemphill County Historical and Genealogical Society
Rt. 2, Canadian, TX 79014

Henderson County Historical Society
Box 943, Athens, TX 75751, (903) 677-3611

Heritage Association of San Marcos
Box 1806, San Marcos, TX 78666, **<www.heritageassociationsm.org>**

Heritage Society of Washington County
2203 Century Circle, Brenham, TX 77833, (979) 836-1690, **<www.giddingsstonemansion.com>**

High Plains Genealogical Society
825 Austin St., Plainview, TX 79072, (806) 296-1148

Hill County Genealogical Society
Box 636, Hillsboro, TX 76645

Hillsboro Heritage League
Box 2, Hillsboro, TX 76645

Hispanic Genealogical Society
Box 231271, Houston, TX 77223

Hood County Genealogical Society
109 Ewell St., Box 1623, Granbury, TX 76048, (817) 573-2557

Hood County Library
222 N. Travis, Granbury, TX 76048, (817) 573-3569

Hopkins County Genealogical Society
Box 624, Sulphur Springs, TX 75483, (903) 885-8523

Houston Academy of Medicine Historical Research Center
1133 John Freeman Blvd., Houston, TX 77030, (713) 795-4200, **<www.library.tmc.edu>**

Houston Afro-American Historical and Genealogical Society
11100 Braesridge, Ste. 2202, Houston, TX 77062, **<htown.aahgs.org>**

Houston Area Genealogical Association
2507 Tannehill, Houston, TX 77008, (713) 864-6862

Houston Genealogical Forum
Box 271466, Houston, TX 77277, (713) 968-9750, **<www.hgftx.org>**

Houston Public Library, Houston Metropolitan Research Center
500 McKinney St., Houston, TX 77002, (713) 236-1313, **<www2.houstonlibrary.org/hmrc>**

Humble Area Genealogical Society
Box 2723, Humble TX 77338

Hunt County Genealogical Society
Box 398, Greenville, TX 75403, (903) 886-8690

Huntsville Public Library
1216 Fourteenth St., Huntsville, TX 77340, (936) 291-5472, **<www.myhuntsvillelibrary.com>**

Hutchinson County Genealogical Society
625 Weatherly St., Borger TX, 79007

Hutchinson County Library
625 Weatherly St., Borger, TX 79007, (806) 273-0126

Institute of Texas Cultures
Hemisfair Plaza, 801 E. Durango Blvd., San Antonio, TX 78205, (210) 458-2300

Irish Family Names Society
Box 861656, Plano, TX 75086

Irving Public Library
Box 152288, Irving, Texas 75015, (972) 721-2600, **<catalog.cityofirving.org/rooms>**

Jewish Genealogical Society of Houston
11727 Riverview Dr., Houston, TX 77077, **<www.texsys.com/ghjgs>**

Jewish Holocaust Education Center and Memorial Museum of Houston
5401 Caroline, Houston, TX 77004, (713) 789-9898, **<www.hmh.org>**

Johnson County Genealogical Society
Box 1256, Cleburne, TX 76033, **<users.htcomp.net/jcgs>**

Karnes County Historical Society
Box 162, Karnes City, TX 78118

Kaufman County Genealogical Society
Box 337, Terrell, TX 75160

Kent County Genealogical and Historical Society
Box 414, Jayton, TX 79528

Kingsland Genealogical Society
Box 952, Kingsland, TX 78639 **<www.rootsweb.ancestry.com/~txkinggs>**

Kingsland Library
125 W. Polk St., Kingsland, TX 78639, (325) 388-3170, **<www.llano-library-system.net>**

Kurth Memorial Library
706 S. Raquet, Lufkin, TX 75904, (936) 630-0566, **<www.kurthmemoriall ibrary.com>**

La Porte Library
600 South, La Porte, TX 77571, (281) 471-4022, **<www.hcpl.net>**

La Retama Public Library
805 Comanche, Corpus Christi, TX 78401, (361) 826-7000, **<www.cclibraries.com>**

Lake Jackson Historical Association
249 Circle Way, Lake Jackson, TX 77566, (979) 297-1570, **<www.lakejacksonmuseum.org>**

Lamar County Genealogical Society
1125 Bonham St., Paris, TX 75460, (903) 784-5020, **<gen.1starnet.com/lamargen.htm>**

Lamar County Genealogical Society
Box 187, 2400 Clarksville St., Paris, TX 75460

Lamesa Area Genealogical Society
Box 1264, Lamesa, TX 79331

Lee County Genealogical Society
177 South Mason, Giddings, TX 78946

Leon County Genealogical Society
Box 500, Centerville, TX 75833

Liberty County Historical Commission
Box 723, Liberty, TX 77575, **<www.libertycountytexasgenealogy.com>**

Llano County Library
102 Haynie St., Llano, TX 78643, **<www.llano-library-system.net>**

Longview Public Library
222 W. Cotton St., Longview, TX 75601, (903) 237-1350, **<www.longview.lib.tx.us>**

Los Bexarenos Genealogical Society
Box 1935, San Antonio, TX 78297, **<www.losbexarenos.org>**

Lubbock City-County Library
1306 Ninth St., Lubbock, TX 79401, **<library.ci.lubbock.tx.us>**

Lubbock Heritage Society
Box 5443, Lubbock, TX 79417, **<lubbockheritage.org>**

Lufkin Genealogical and Historical Society
Box 150631, Lufkin, TX 75915

Luling Public Library
215 S. Pecan Ave., Luling, TX 78648, (830) 875-2813

Madison County Genealogical Society
Box 26, Madisonville, TX 77864

Marion County Genealogical Society
Box 224, Jefferson, TX 75657

Matagorda County African-American Historical Society
Box 1386, Bay City, TX 77404

Matagorda County Genealogical Society
1100 7th St., Bay City, TX 77404, (979) 245-6931

McKinney Memorial Public Library
101 W. Hunt St., McKinney, TX 75069, (972) 547-7323

McLennan County Library
1717 Austin Ave., Waco, TX 76701, (254) 750-5941, **<www.waco-texas.com/cms-library>**

Menard Genealogical Society
Box 714, Menard, TX 76859

Mesquite Historical and Genealogical Society
Box 850164, Mesquite, TX 75185, **<www.rootsweb.ancestry.com/~txmhgs>**

Mesquite Public Library
300 Grubb Dr., Mesquite, TX 75149, **<www.cityofmesquite.com/library>**, (972) 216-6220

Mid-Cities Genealogical Society
Box 407, Bedford, TX 76095

Midland County Public Library, Redfern Genealogical Research Center
301 W. Missouri, Midland, TX 79701, (915) 688-8991, **<www.rootsweb.ancestry.com/~txmidlan/mcl.htm>**

Midland Genealogical Society
c/o Midland County Public Library, 301 W. Missouri, Midland, TX 79701

Milam County Genealogical Society
c/o Lucy Patterson Memorial Library
201 Ackerman, Rockdale, TX 76567

Montgomery County Library
104 I-45 North, Conroe, TX 77301, (936) 442-7712, **<www.countylibrary.org>**

Montgomery County Genealogical and Historical Society
1500 N. Frazier St., Conroe, TX 77301, (936) 539-1200

Moody Texas Ranger Library
Box 2570, Waco, TX 76702, **<www.texasranger.org/ReCenter/RCenter.htm>**

Moore Memorial Library
1701 Ninth Ave North, Texas City, TX 77590, (409) 643-5979

Mt. Pleasant Municipal Library
Box 1285, 213 N Madison, Mt. Pleasant, TX 75455, (903) 575-4180, **<www.mpcity.net/library_public.htm>**

Nacogdoches Genealogical Society
Box 4634, Nacogdoches, TX 75962, **<www.rootsweb.ancestry.com/~txngs>**

National Archives and Records Administration, Southwest Region
1400 John Burgess Drive, Fort Worth, Texas 76140, (817) 831-5620, **<www.archives.gov/southwest>**

Navarro County Genealogical Society
912 West Park, Corsicana, TX 75110

New Boston Genealogical Society
c/o New Boston Public Library, Box 104, New Boston, TX 75570

Newton County Historical Commission
213 Court St., Newton TX 75988, (409) 379-2109, **<www.newton-texas.com/historical_commission/index.htm>**

Nicholson Memorial Library
625 Austin St., Garland, TX 75040, (972) 205-2500, **<www.ci.garland.tx.us>**

Nolan County Genealogical Association
c/o County City Library, Box 780, Sweetwater, TX 79556

North Texas Genealogical and Historical Association
Box 4602, Wichita Falls, TX 76308, **<northtexasgenealogyassociation.web.officelive.com>**

Orange County Historical Society
Box 1345, Orange, TX 77630

Palestine Public Library
1101 N. Cedar, Palestine, TX 75801, (903) 729-4121

Palo Pinto County Historical Association
Box 42, Palo Pinto, TX 76072, **<www.rootsweb.ancestry.com/~txpalopi/links/county.htm>**

Pampa Genealogical and Historical Society
430 N. Summer St., Pampa, TX 79065

Parker County Genealogical Society
1214 North Summer St., Pampa TX 79065

Permian Basin Genealogical Society
321 W. Fifth St., Odessa, TX 79761, (915) 332-0634

Pilot Point Community Library
324 S. Washington St., Box 969, Pilot Point, TX 76258, (940) 686-5004, **<www.pilotpointlibrary.org>**

Plano Heritage Association
1900 W. Fifteenth St., Plano, TX 75075, (972) 881-0140, **<www.heritagefarmstead.org>**

Polish Genealogical Society of Texas
18123 Campbellford Dr., Tomball, TX 77377, **<pgst.org>**

Polk County Heritage Society
507 W. Church St., Livingston, TX 77351, (936) 327-3336

Quitman Public Library
202 E. Goode St., Box 77, Quitman, TX 75783, (903) 763-4191, **<www.quitmanlibrary.org>**

Randolph Area Genealogical Society
Box 2134, Universal City, TX 78148, (210) 659-7881

Red River County Texas Genealogical Society
Box 516, Clarksville, TX 75426, (903) 427-3991

Refugio County Historical Society
102 West St., Refugio, TX 78377, (361) 526-5555, **<www.refugiocountytx.org/museum.htm>**

Roberts County Historical Commission
c/o Roberts County Museum, Box 306, Miami, TX 79059

Roman Catholic Archives of Texas
Box 13124, Austin, TX 78711, (512) 476-6296, **<www.catholicarchivesoftx.org>**

Root Seekers Genealogical Society
Tri-County Library, Box 1770, Mabank, TX 75147, (903) 451-2213

Rosenberg Library Archives
2310 Sealy Ave., Galveston, TX 77550, (409) 763-8854

Round Rock Public Library
216 E. Main, Round Rock, TX 78664, (512) 218-7003, **<www.roundrocktexas.gov>**

Rusk County Library
106 E. Main St., Henderson, TX 75652, (903) 657-8557

Rusk County Historical Commission
514 N. High St., Henderson, TX 75652, (903) 657-2261

Salado Historical Society
Box 251, Salado, TX 76571, **<www.saladohistoricalsociety.org>**

Sam Houston Regional Library Research Center
1011 Governor's Rd., Box 310, Liberty, TX 77575, (409) 336-8821, **<www.tsl.state.tx.us/shc>**

San Angelo Genealogical and Historical Society
Box 3453, San Angelo, TX 76902

San Antonio Genealogical and Historical Society
Box 17461, San Antonio, TX 78217

San Augustine Public Library
413 E. Columbia, San Augustine, TX 75972, (936) 275-5367, **<www.salibrary.org>**

San Jacinto County Heritage Society
Box 505, Coldspring, TX 77331, (936) 653-2009

San Jacinto Museum of History
300 Park Rd. #1836, La Porte, TX 77571, (281) 497-2421, **<www.sanjacinto-museum.org>**

San Marcos/Hays County Genealogical Society
Box 503, San Marcos, TX 78666, (512) 353-5823

Schleicher County Historical Society
Box 473, Eldorado, TX 76936

Scurry County Library
1916 23rd St., Snyder, TX 79549, (325) 573-5572, **<www.scurrycountylibrary.com>**

Sherman Public Library
Box 1106, 421 N. Travis, Sherman, TX 75090, (903) 892-7240

Smith County Historical Society
624 N. Broadway, Tyler, TX 75702, (214) 597-5304

Somervell County Genealogical and Heritage Society
Box 1097, Glen Rose, TX 76043, **<www.paluxyvalleygenealogy.com>**

Sophienburg Archives
401 W. Coll St., New Braunfels, TX 78130, (830) 629-1572, **<www.sophienburg.com>**

South Plains Genealogical Society
Box 6607, Lubbock, TX 79493, (806) 775-3106, **<www.rootsweb.ancestry.com/~txspgs>**

South Texas Genealogical Society
Box 754, Beeville, TX 78104, (512) 358-1135

Southeast Texas Genealogical & Historical Society
c/o Tyrrell Historical Library, Box 3827, Beaumont, TX 77704, (409) 833-2759, **<www.rootsweb.ancestry.com/~txsetghs/index.htm>**

Southwest Genealogical Society & Library
1300 San Pedro Ave, San Antonio TX 78212

Southwest Texas Genealogical Society
Box 295, Uvalde, TX 78802

Stephens County Genealogical Society
Box 350, Breckenridge, TX 76024, (817) 559-8471

Stephens County Historical Association
201 N. Harding, Breckenridge, TX 76024

Sterling Municipal Library
#1 Mary Elizabeth Wilbanks Ave., Baytown, TX 77520, (281) 427-7331

Tanant County Black History & Genealogical Society
Box 50483, Fort Worth, TX 76105

Taylor Heritage Society
385, Taylor, TX 76574

Temple Public Library
100 W. Adams Ave., Temple, TX 76501, (254) 298-5557, **<www.ci.temple.tx.us>**

Terrell County Historical Commission
Box 7, Sanderson, TX 79848

Texarkana Public Library
600 W. 3rd St., Texarkana, TX 75501, (903) 794-2149, **<www.txar-publib.org>**

Texarkana USA Genealogical Society
Box 5825, Texarkana, TX 75505, **<www.rootsweb.ancestry.com/~txkusa/GenSoc.html>**

Texas City Ancestry Searchers
Box 3301, TX City, TX 77592, **<www.rootsweb.ancestry.com/~txtcas>**

Texas Czech Heritage and Cultural Center
Box 6, La Grange, TX 78945, (409) 968-8373, **<www.czechtx.com>**

Texas Department of Health
1100 W. Forty-ninth St., Austin, TX 78756, (512) 458-7111, **<www.dshs.state.tx.us>**

Texas Land Office
Stephen F. Austin Bldg., 1700 N. Congress, Austin, TX 78701, (512) 364-5277, **<www.glo.state.tx.us>**

Texas State Archives
1201 St., Box 12927, Austin, TX 78711, (512) 463-5480, **<www.tsl.state.tx.us>**

Texas State Genealogical Society
2507 Tannehill, Houston, TX 77008, (713) 864-6862 or (713) 864-3540, **<www.rootsweb.ancestry.com/~txsgs>**

Texas State Library
1201 Brazos, Box 12927, Austin, TX 78711 **<www.tsl.state.tx.us>**

Texas Wendish Heritage Society
1011 County Rd. 212 Giddings, TX 78942, (979) 366-2441, **<wendish.concordia.edu>**

Tex-Ok Panhandle Genealogical Society
5th and Ash, Perryton, TX 79070, (806) 435-5801

Timpson Area Genealogical and Heritage Society
Box 726, Timpson, TX 75975, (409) 254-3344

Tom Burnett Memorial Library
400 W. Alameda, Iowa Park, TX 76367, (940) 592-4981

Tom Green County Historical Preservation League
Box 1625, San Angelo, TX 76902

Tri-County Genealogical Society
Box 107, Leonard, TX 75452, (903) 587-2246

Troup Genealogical/Historical Society
Box 400, Troup, TX 75789

Tyler Public Library
201 S. College Ave., Tyler, TX 75702, (903) 593-7323, **<www.tylerTX.com/cot/departments/library>**

Tyrell Public Library
695 Pearl St., Beaumont, TX 77701, (409) 883-2759

Val Verde County Genealogical Society
1315 Kings Way Del Rio, TX 78840, (830) 775-4511

Van Alstyne Genealogical Society
Box 629, Van Alstyne, TX 75095

Van Zandt County Library of Genealogy and Local History
317 1st Monday Lane, Canton TX, 75103, (903) 567-5012

Van Zandt County Genealogical Society
Box 434, Wills Point, TX 75169

Victoria County Genealogical Society
Box 413, Victoria, TX 77902, **<www.rootsweb.ancestry.com/~txvicto2/vcgs.html>**

Waco Public Library
300 Austin Ave., Waco, TX 76702, **<www.waco-texas.com/cms-library>**

Walker County Genealogical Society
Box 1295, Huntsville, TX 77342, **<www.wcgen.com>**

Wallisville Heritage Library and Museum
Hwy. I-10, Box 16, Wallisville, TX 77597, (409) 389-2252, **<www.wallisville.com>**

Walworth Harrison Public Library
1 Lou Finney Ln., Greenville, TX 75401, (903) 457-2992, **<www2.youseemore.com/harrison/default.asp>**

Ward County Genealogical Society
400 E. Fourth St., Monahans, TX 79756

Weatherford Public Library
1014 Charles St., Weatherford, TX 76086, (817) 598-4150, **<www.ci.weatherford.tx.us>**

Webb County Heritage Foundation
500 Flores Ave., Laredo, TX 78042

West Bell Genealogical Society
Box 851, Killeen, TX 76540, (817) 699-2143

West Texas Genealogical Society
Box 2307, Abilene, TX 79604

Wharton County Chapter of the Texas German Society
Box 1236, El Campo, TX 77457

Wharton County Czech Society
Rt. 1, Box 23, Louise, TX 77455

Whitmeyer Genealogy Library and Heritage Village Museum
Box 2022, Woodville, TX 75979

Williamson County Genealogical Society
Box 585, Round Rock, TX 78680, **<www.rootsweb.ancestry.com/~txwcgs>**

Wise County Genealogical Society
Box 125, Rhome, TX 76078

Wise County Historical Society
Box 427, Decatur, TX 76234, **<www.wisehistory.com/Wise%20County%20Historical%20Society,%20Inc.htm>**

Wood County Genealogical Society
Box 832, Quitman, TX 75783, (903) 763-4191

Yoakum County Historical Commission
Box 960, Plains, TX 79355

Zapata County Historical Commission
Box 6305, Zapata, TX 78076

GENERAL RESOURCES

Bibliography of Texas, 1795-1845 by Archibald Hanna (Fresearch Publishing, 1983)

Biographical Gazetteer of Texas: Publication of the Biographical Sketch File of the Texas Collection At Baylor University, an Ongoing Project, 6 vols., (Morrison Books, 1985-)

Biographical Souvenir of the State of Texas, 1889 (Southern Historical Press, 1978)

Black Churches in Texas: A Guide to Historic Congregations by Clyde McQueen (Texas A & M Univ., 2000)

Catalog of Genealogical Materials in Texas Libraries by John Corbin (Texas State Library and Historical Commission, 1965)

Citizens of the Republic of Texas by Mrs. Harry Joseph Morris (Texas State Genealogical Society, 1977)

Cracker Barrel Chronicles: A Bibliography of Texas Town and County Histories by John Holmes Jenkins (Pemberton Press, 1965)

Founders and Patriots of the Republic of Texas: Lineages of the Members of the Daughters of the Republic of Texas, 3 vols., (Daughters of the Republic of Texas, 1963-85)

Four Decades of Catholicism in Texas 1820-1860 by Mary Angela Fitzmorris (Catholic University of America, 1926)

Genealogical Records in Texas by Imogene Kinard Kennedy and J. Leon Kennedy (Genealogical Publishing Co., 1987)

Genealogical Research in Texas: A Bibliographical Guide by Lloyd DeWitt Bockstruck in *National Genealogical Society Quarterly vol. 75* (Sept. 1987) pages 194-215

Genealogies of Texas Families: Biographical Notes of Pioneer Settlers by James Pylant (Datatrace Systems, 1989)

Guide to Genealogical Resources in the Texas State Archives by Jean Carefoot (Archives Division, Texas State Library, 1984)

A Guide to Texas Research by Carolyn R. Ericson and Joe E. Ericson (Ericson Books, 1994)

A Guide to the Texana Holdings of the Texas History Library of the Daughters of the Republic of Texas, 2 vols. (Daughters of the Republic of Texas, 1978)

The Handbook of Texas, 3 vols., edited by Walter Prescott Webb (Texas State Historical Association, 1952-1976)

The Historical Encyclopedia of Texas, 2 vols., edited by Thomas S. Chamblin (Texas Historical Institute, 1982)

History of Early Methodism in Texas, 1817-1866 by Macum Phelan (Cokesbury Press, 1924)

A History of Texas Baptists by James M. Carroll (Baptist Standard Publishing Co., 1923)

History of Texas and Texans, 5 vols., by Frank W. Johnson (American Historical Society, 1914)

Indian Wars and Pioneers of Texas by John Henry Brown (1880; Southern Historical Press, 1978)

Residents of Texas, 182-1836, 3 vols., (San Antonio: The University of Texas, Institute of Texan Cultures, 1984)

Resources of Texas Libraries by Edward G. Holley (Texas State Library, 1968)

Spanish and Mexican Records of the American Southwest: A Bibliographic Guide to Archive and Manuscript Sources by Henry P. Beers (University of Arizona Press, 1979)

Texas Family Land Heritage Registry, 8 vols., (Texas Department of Agriculture, 1974-)

Texas Historical and Biographical Record with a Genealogical Study of Historical Family Records by Emory E. Bailey (Texas Historical and Biographical Record)

Texas Local History: A Source Book for Available Town and County Histories, Local Memoirs and Genealogical Records by Tom Munnerlyn (Eakin Press, 1983)

Texas Newspapers, 1813-1939: A Union List of Newspaper Files Available in Offices of Publishers, Libraries, and a Number of Private Collections (San Jacinto Museum of History Associations, 1941)

Texas Research Outline by the Church of Jesus Christ of Latter-day Saints (online at <www.familysearch.org/eng/search/RG/guide/texas.asp>)

Who's Who in Texas by Emory E. Bailey, et al. (Who's Who Publishing, 1931)

Who's Who in Texas Today: A New Biographical Survey of Texas by Seymour V. Connor (Pemberton Press, 1968)

CENSUS RECORDS

1830 Citizens of Texas by Gifford E. White (Eakin Press, 1983)

Texas, 1830-1839, Census Index by Ronald Vern Jackson (Accelerated Indexing Systems International, 1981)

IMMIGRATION RECORDS

Comal County, Texas, and New Braunfels, Texas, German Immigrant Ships, 1845-1846 by J. McManus (F.T. Ingmire, 1985)

A New Land Beckoned: German Immigration to Texas, 1844-1847 by Chester W. Geue and Ethel H. Geue (Texian Press, 1972)

Passenger Lists for Galveston 1850-1855 by Albert J. Blaha (A.J. Blaha, 1985)

Ships Passenger Lists, Port of Galveston, Texas, 1846-1871 (Southern Historical Press, 1984)

Stephen F. Austin's Register of Families edited by Villamae Williams (Genealogical Publishing Co., 1989)

Tennesseans in Texas by Helen and Timothy Marsh (Southern Historical Press, 1986)

LAND RECORDS

Abstract of Land Claims, compiled from the records of the Genealogy Land Office (Civilian Book Office, 1852)

Abstract of Land Titles of Texas Comprising the Titled, Parented, and Located Lands in the State (Shaw and Blaylo, 1878)

Bounty and Donation Land Grants of Texas 1835-1888 by Thomas Lloyd Miller (University of Texas Press, 1967)

Character Certificates in the General Land Office of Texas by Gifford White (G. White, 1985)

Claiming Their Land: Women Homesteaders in Texas by Florence C. Gould (Texas Western Press, 1991)

Early Texas Settlers, 1700's-1800's (Broderbund, 2000, CD-ROM)

First Settlers of the Republic of Texas: Headright Land Grants, 1840, 2 vols., by Carolyn Reeves Ericson (1841; Carolyn R. Ericson, ca. 1982)

Index to Spanish and Mexican Land Grants in Texas by Virginia H. Taylor (Lone Star Press, 1974)

The Land Commissioners of Texas: by Garry Mauro (Texas General Land Office, 1986)

The Public Lands of Texas 1519-1970 by Thomas Lloyd Miller (University of Oklahoma Press, 1971)

Residents of Texas, 1782-1836, 3 vols., from the University of Texas (The Institute, 1984)

Spanish and Mexican Land Grants in the Chibuabuan Acquisition by J.J. Bowden (Texas Western Press, 1971)

MAPS

Biographical Gazetteer of Texas, 6 vols., by Virginia H. Ming and William L. Ming (W.M. Morrison Books, 1985-1987)

A Gazetteer of Texas by Henry Gannett (Government Printing Office, 1904)

A Historical Atlas of Texas by William C. Pool (Encino Press, 1975)

How Come It's Called That?: Place Names in the Big Bend Country by Virginia Madison and Hallie Stillwell (Univesity of New Mexico Press, 1958)

Maps of Texas, 1527-1900: The Map Collection of the Texas State Archives compiled by James M. Day (Pemberton Press, 1974)

Maps of Texas and the Southwest, 1513-1900 by James C. Martin and Robert S. Martin (University of New Mexico Press, 1984)

Old Texas Trails by J. W. Williams (Eakin Press, 1979)

Texas Atlas and Gazetteer (DeLorme Mapping, 1995)

800 Texas Ghost Towns by Ed Bartholomew (Frontier Books, 1971)

1001 Texas Place Names by Fred Tarpley (University of Texas Press, 1980)

MILITARY RECORDS

The Heroes of San Jacinto by Sam Houston Dixon and Louise Wiltz Kemp (The Anson Jones Press, 1932)

Index to Applications for Texas Confederate Pensions by John M. Kinney (Archives Division, Texas State Library, 1977)

Index to Texas CSA Pension Files by Virgil D. White (National Historical Publishing Co., 1989)

Lone Stars and State Gazettes: Texas Newspapers Before the Civil War by Marilyn McAdams Sibley (Texas A&M University Press, 1983)

Muster Lists of the Texas Confederate Troops by Sherman L. Pompey (Historical and Genealogical Publishing Co., 1966)

Muster Rolls of the Texas Revolution (Daughters of the Republic of Texas, 1986)

Republic of Texan Pension Application Abstracts by John C. Baron, et al. (Austin Genealogical Society, 1987)

Roll Call at the Alamo (The Old Army Press, 1985)

Texas Frontiersmen, 1839-1860: Minute Men, Militia, Home Guard, Indian Fighters by Frances Terry Ingmire (F.T. Ingmire, 1982)

Texas Newspapers, 1813-1939: A Union List (San Jacinto Museum of History Association, 1951)

Texas Rangers: Frontier Battalion, Minute Men, Commanding Officers, 1847-1900, 6 vols., by Frances Terry Ingmire (F.T. Ingmire, 1982)

Texas Ranger Indian War Pensions by Robert W. Stephens (Nortex Press, 1975)

Texas Volunteers in the Mexican War by Henry W. Barton (Texican Press, 1970)

War of 1812 Veterans in Texas by Mary Smith Fay (Polyanthos, 1979)

☞PROBATE RECORDS

Index to Probate Cases of Texas compiled by the Work Projects Administration for 31 counties (University of Texas, 1980)

☞VITAL RECORDS

4000 Tombstone Inscriptions from Texas. 1745-1870: Along the Old San Antonio Road and the Trail of Austin's Colonists by Mrs. Malcolm B. Biggerstaff (Oklahoma Historical Society, 1952)

Cemetery Records of Texas, 6 vols. (Genealogical Society of Utah, 1956-63)

Early Texas Birth Records, 1838-1878, 2 vols. (Alice D. Gracy, Emma G. S. Gentry, and Jane Sumner, 1969, 1971)

An Index to Texas Probate Birth Records, ca. 1900-1945 (filmed by the Texas State Library, 1988)

Marriage Records of Early Texas, 1826-1846 by Norma R. Grammer (Fort Worth Genealogical Society, 1971)

Northeast Texas Cemeteries by John P. Frazier (S. and W. Enterprises, 1984)

A Reference to Texas Cemetery Records by Kim Parsons (Kim Parsons, 1988)

Texas Cemetery Inscriptions: A Source Index by Sherry Crofford-Gould (Limited Editions, 1977)

8,800 Texas Marriages, 1824-1850, 2 vols., by Helen S. Swenson (Helen S. Swanson, 1981)

Texas Marriages, Early to 1850: A Research Tool by Jordan R. Dodd (Precision Indexing, 1990)

•-COUNTY DETAILS-•

ANDERSON

500 N. Church St., Palestine, TX 75801, (903) 723-7432, **<www.rootsweb.ancestry.com/~txanders>**

- **INCORPORATED:** Mar. 24, 1846
- **PARENT COUNTY:** Houston
- **BIRTH RECORDS:** start in 1903, kept at the District Court
- **MARRIAGE:** 1846, County Clerk
- **DEATH:** 1903, County Clerk
- **DIVORCE:** 1898, District Clerk
- **LAND:** 1846, County Clerk
- **PROBATE:** 1846, County Clerk
- **COURT:** 1846, District Clerk
- **NOTES:** County Clerk has military discharge records 1919-1947. District Clerk has naturalization records 1874-1928.

ANDREWS

215 NW First St., Andrews, TX 79714, (915) 524-1426, **<www.rootsweb.ancestry.com/~txandrew>**

- **INCORPORATED:** Aug. 21, 1876
- **PARENT COUNTIES:** Bexar Land District
- **BIRTH RECORDS:** 1910, County Clerk
- **MARRIAGE:** 1910, County Clerk
- **DIVORCE:** unknown start, District Clerk
- **LAND:** 1884, County Clerk
- **PROBATE:** 1911, County Clerk
- **COURT:** 1910, County Clerk

ANGELINA

Box 908, Lufkin, TX 75902, (936) 634-8339, **<www.angelinacountygenealogy.com>**

- **INCORPORATED:** Apr. 22, 1846
- **PARENT COUNTY:** Nacogdoches
- **BIRTH RECORDS:** start in 1875, kept by the County Clerk
- **DIVORCE:** 1847, District Clerk
- **DEATH:** 1903, County Clerk
- **COURT:** 1847, County Clerk & District Court
- **NOTES:** County Clerk has land records 1846-1887, marriage records 1846-1917, and probate records 1850-1934.

ARANSAS

301 N. Live Oak St., Rockport, TX 78382, (361) 790-0122, **<www.rootsweb.ancestry.com/~txaransa>**

- **INCORPORATED:** Sep. 18, 1871
- **PARENT COUNTY:** Refugio
- **BIRTH RECORDS:** start in 1871, kept by the County Clerk
- **MARRIAGE:** 1871, County Clerk
- **DEATH:** 1871, County Clerk
- **LAND:** 1871, County Clerk
- **PROBATE:** 1860, County Clerk
- **COURT:** 1871, County Clerk
- **NOTES:** District Clerk has naturalization records 1908-1913.

ARCHER
Box 427, Archer City, TX 46351, (940) 574-4302,
<www.rootsweb.ancestry.com/~txarcher>
- **INCORPORATED:** Jan. 22, 1858
- **PARENT COUNTY:** Clay
- **BIRTH RECORDS:** start in 1903, kept by the County Clerk
- **MARRIAGE:** 1927, County Clerk
- **DIVORCE:** 1881, District Clerk
- **DEATH:** 1903, County Clerk
- **NOTES:** County Clerk has court records 1881-1941, land records 1855-1901, naturalization records 1811-1957, and probate records 1875-1936.

ARMSTRONG
Box 309, Claude, TX 79019, (806) 226-2081,
<www.co.armstrong.tx.us>
- **INCORPORATED:** Aug. 21, 1876
- **PARENT COUNTY:** Bexar
- **BIRTH RECORDS:** start in 1903, kept by the County Clerk
- **MARRIAGE:** 1890, County Clerk
- **DIVORCE:** unknown start, District Clerk
- **DEATH:** 1903, County Clerk
- **LAND:** 1883, County Clerk
- **PROBATE:** 1890, County Clerk
- **COURT:** 1898, County Clerk

ATASCOSA
#1 Courthouse Circle, Ste. 102, Jourdanton, TX 78026, (830) 767-2511
- **INCORPORATED:** Jan. 25, 1856
- **PARENT COUNTIES:** Bexar Land District
- **BIRTH RECORDS:** start in 1856, kept by the County Clerk
- **DIVORCE:** 1857, District Clerk
- **DEATH:** 1903, County Clerk
- **NOTES:** District Clerk has court records 1857-1910 and naturalization records 1888-1903. County Clerk has land records 1856-1907, marriage records 1856-1911, and probate records 1873-1910.

AUSTIN
1 E. Main St., Bellville, TX 77418, (979) 865-5911,
<www.austincounty.com>
- **INCORPORATED:** March 27, 1837
- **PARENT COUNTY:** Old Mexican Municipality
- **BIRTH RECORDS:** start in 1903, kept by the County Clerk
- **MARRIAGE:** 1824, County Clerk
- **DIVORCE:** 1839, District Court
- **DEATH:** 1903, County Clerk
- **NOTES:** County Clerk has land records 1837-1920, military discharge records 1918-1951, naturalization records 1849-1936, and probate records 1837-1977. District Clerk has court records 1839-1940.

BAILEY
300 S. First St., Ste. 200, Muleshoe, TX 79347, (806) 272-3044,
<www.co.bailey.tx.us>
- **INCORPORATED:** Aug. 21, 1876
- **PARENT COUNTY:** Bexar Land District
- **BIRTH RECORDS:** start in 1919, kept by the County Clerk
- **MARRIAGE:** 1919, County Clerk
- **DIVORCE:** 1919, District Clerk
- **LAND:** 1919, County Clerk
- **PROBATE:** 1919, County Clerk
- **COURT:** 1919, County Clerk
- **NOTES:** Became an independent county in 1919. Previously Bailey County was attached to Jack County 1876-1881, Baylor County 1881-1887, Hale County 1887-1892 and Castro County 1892-1919.

BANDERA
Box 823, Bandera, TX 78003, (830) 796-3332,
<www.banderacounty.org>
- **INCORPORATED:** Jan. 26, 1856
- **PARENT COUNTIES:** Bexar, Uvalde
- **BIRTH RECORDS:** start in 1926, kept by the County Clerk
- **DIVORCE:** 1856, District Clerk
- **DEATH:** 1904, County Clerk
- **COURT:** 1857, District Clerk
- **NOTES:** County Clerk has birth records 1873-1876, land records 1856-1906, marriage records 1856-1931, and probate records 1856-1970.

BASTROP
Box 577, Bastrop, TX 78602, (512) 332-7234,
<www.co.bastrop.tx.us>
- **INCORPORATED:** Dec. 18, 1837
- **PARENT COUNTY:** Old Mexican Municipality (Municipality of Mina)
- **BIRTH RECORDS:** start in 1853, kept by the County Clerk
- **DEATH:** 1903, County Clerk
- **NOTES:** District Clerk has court records 1837-1952 and divorce records 1901-1942. County Clerk has land records 1837-1920, marriage records 1851-1974, military discharge records 1917-1943, naturalization records 1837-1941, and probate records 1837-1974.

BAYLOR
101 S. Washington, Seymour, TX 76380, (940) 889-3322,
<www.rootsweb.ancestry.com/~txbaylor/baylor.htm>
- **INCORPORATED:** Feb. 1, 1858
- **PARENT COUNTY:** Fannin Land District
- **BIRTH RECORDS:** start in 1903, kept by the County Clerk
- **DIVORCE:** 1881, County Clerk
- **DEATH:** 1903, County Clerk
- **PROBATE:** 1880, County Clerk
- **COURT:** 1880, County Clerk
- **NOTES:** County Clerk has marriage records 1879-1920.

BEE
105 W. Corpus Christi St., Rm. #108, Beeville, TX 78102, (361) 362-3245, **<www.co.bee.tx.us>**
- **INCORPORATED:** Dec. 8, 1857
- **PARENT COUNTIES:** Goliad, Refugio, Live Oak, San Patricio, Karnes
- **BIRTH RECORDS:** 1903, kept by the County Clerk
- **DEATH:** 1903, County Clerk
- **NOTES:** District Clerk has court and divorce records 1858-1895. County Clerk has land records 1858-1892, marriage records 1860-1911, and probate records 1859-1895.

BELL
550 E. Second St., Box 480, Belton, TX 76513, (254) 933-5160, <www.bellcountytx.com>
- **INCORPORATED:** Jan. 22, 1850
- **PARENT COUNTY:** Milam
- **MARRIAGE RECORDS:** start in 1850, kept by the County Clerk
- **DIVORCE:** 1893, District Court Clerk
- **DEATH:** 1903, County Clerk
- **LAND:** 1850, County Clerk
- **PROBATE:** 1850, County Clerk
- **COURT:** 1852, District Court Clerk
- **MILITARY:** unknown start, County Clerk
- **NOTES:** County Clerk has birth records 1873-1876. Clerk of District Court has naturalization records 1886-1920.

BEXAR
100 Dolorosa St. Suite 104, San Antonio, TX 78205, (210) 335-2216, <www.bexar.org>
- **INCORPORATED:** Dec. 20, 1836
- **PARENT COUNTY:** Old Mexican Municipality (established 1731), Department of Bejar
- **MARRIAGE RECORDS:** start in 1837, kept by the County Clerk
- **LAND:** 1736, County Clerk
- **PROBATE:** 1837, County Clerk
- **COURT:** 1836, District Clerk
- **MILITARY:** 1919, County Clerk
- **NOTES:** County Clerk has birth records 1837-1967, death records 1902-1967, and naturalization records 1850-1906. County Clerk also has Spanish Church records from 1737-1859 and Spanish City Council minutes from 1815-1820.

BLANCO
Box 65, Johnson City, TX 78636, (830) 868-7357, <www.co.blanco.tx.us>
- **INCORPORATED:** Feb. 12, 1858
- **PARENT COUNTIES:** Gillespie, Comal, Burnet, Hays
- **BIRTH RECORDS:** start in 1903, kept by the County Clerk
- **DEATH:** 1903, County Clerk
- **PROBATE:** 1876, County Clerk
- **COURT:** 1876, County Clerk
- **NOTES:** County Clerk has divorce and land records 1875-1959, marriage records 1876-1974, military records 1917-1943, and naturalization records 1880-1924.

BORDEN
Box 124, Gail, TX 79738, (806) 756-4312, <www.co.borden.tx.us>
- **INCORPORATED:** Aug. 21, 1876
- **PARENT COUNTY:** Bosque
- **BIRTH RECORDS:** 1900, County Clerk
- **MARRIAGE:** 1891, County Clerk
- **DIVORCE:** 1891, County Clerk
- **DEATH:** 1900, County Clerk
- **LAND:** 1880, County Clerk
- **PROBATE:** 1894, County Clerk
- **COURT:** 1891, County Clerk

BOSQUE
Box 617, Meridian, TX 76665, (254) 435-2201, <www.bosquecounty.us>
- **INCORPORATED:** Feb. 4, 1854
- **PARENT COUNTIES:** McLennan, Milan
- **BIRTH RECORDS:** start in 1903, kept by the County Clerk
- **MARRIAGE:** 1860, County Clerk
- **DIVORCE:** unknown start, District Clerk
- **DEATH:** 1903, County Clerk
- **LAND:** 1860, County Clerk
- **PROBATE:** 1860, County Clerk
- **NOTES:** District Clerk has court records 1856-1980 and naturalization records 1887-1914.

BOWIE
Box 248, New Boston, TX 75570, (903) 628-6742, <www.co.bowie.tx.us>
- **INCORPORATED:** Dec. 17, 1840
- **PARENT COUNTY:** Red River
- **MILITARY RECORDS:** unknown start, County Clerk
- **NOTES:** County Clerk has birth records 1903-1941, death records 1903-1966, land records 1889-1908, marriage records 1889-1952, and probate records 1889-1931. Clerk of District Court has court records 1883-1931 and divorce records 1883-1942.

BRAZORIA
111 E. Locust St. Suite 200, Angleton, TX 77515, (979) 864-1355, <www.brazoria-county.com>
- **INCORPORATED:** March 17, 1836
- **PARENT COUNTY:** Old Mexican Municipality
- **BIRTH RECORDS:** start in 1901, kept by the County Clerk
- **DEATH:** 1903, County Clerk
- **LAND:** 1837, County Clerk
- **MILITARY:** 1919, County Clerk
- **NOTES:** County Clerk has court records 1867-1915, marriage records 1829-1948, and probate records 1826-1916.

BRAZOS
300 E. 26th St. Suite 120, Bryan, TX 77803, (979) 361-4128, <www.co.brazos.tx.us>
- **INCORPORATED:** Jan. 30, 1841
- **PARENT COUNTIES:** Washington, Robertson
- **BIRTH RECORDS:** start in 1900, kept by the County Clerk
- **MARRIAGE:** 1843, County Clerk
- **DEATH:** 1900, County Clerk
- **LAND:** 1841, County Clerk
- **NOTES:** District Clerk has court records 1841-1924. County Clerk has naturalization records 1872-1941; probate records 1844-1947. Formerly Navasota County. Name changed to Brazos Jan. 28, 1842.

BREWSTER
Box 119, Alpine, TX 79831, (432) 837-3366, <brewstercountytx.com>
- **INCORPORATED:** Feb. 2, 1887
- **PARENT COUNTY:** Presidio
- **DIVORCE RECORDS:** 1887, District Court
- **LAND:** 1887, County Clerk
- **PROBATE:** 1887, County Clerk

- **COURT:** 1887, District Clerk
- **MILITARY:** 1900, County Clerk
- **NOTES:** County Clerk has birth records 1903-1912, 1915-1946, death records 1903-1971, and marriage records 1887-1965.

BRISCOE

Box 555, Silverton, TX 79257, (806) 823-2134,
<www.co.briscoe.tx.us>

- **INCORPORATED:** Aug. 21, 1876
- **PARENT COUNTY:** Bexar Land District
- **BIRTH RECORDS:** start in 1903, kept by the County Clerk
- **MARRIAGE:** 1892, County Clerk
- **DIVORCE:** unknown start, County Clerk
- **DEATH:** 1903, County Clerk
- **LAND:** 1892, County Clerk
- **PROBATE:** 1892, County Clerk
- **COURT:** 1892, County Clerk

BROOKS

Box 427, Falfurrias, TX 78355, (361) 325-5604,
<www.co.brooks.tx.us>

- **INCORPORATED:** March 11, 1911
- **PARENT COUNTIES:** Starr, Zapata, Hidalgo
- **BIRTH RECORDS:** start in 1911, kept by the County Clerk
- **LAND:** 1848, County Clerk
- **COURT:** 1911, County Clerk
- **NOTES:** County Clerk has death records 1911-1971, marriage records 1911-1951, military discharge records 1919-1947, and probate records 1911-1990. Land records from 1848-1911 are transcribed from Hidalgo County records.

BROWN

200 S. Broadway St., Brownwood, TX 76801, (325) 643-2594,
<www.browncountytx.org>

- **INCORPORATED:** Aug. 27, 1856
- **PARENT COUNTIES:** Travis, Comanche
- **COURT RECORDS:** 1884, District Clerk
- **MILITARY:** 1880, County Clerk
- **NOTES:** County Clerk has birth records 1903-1969, death records 1903-1987, land records 1880-1919, marriage records 1880-1937, military discharge records 1917-1985, and probate records 1880-1964. District Clerk has divorce records 1906-1938.

BUCHANAN

- **INCORPORATED:** Jan. 22, 1858
- **PARENT COUNTY:** Bosque
- **NOTES:** See Stephens County. Name changed to Stephens Dec. 17, 1861.

BURLESON

100 W. Buck Street, Suite 203, Caldwell, TX 77836, (979) 567-2329, **<www.co.burleson.tx.us>**

- **INCORPORATED:** March 24, 1846
- **PARENT COUNTIES:** Milam, Washington
- **BIRTH RECORDS:** start in 1903, kept by the County Clerk
- **MARRIAGE:** 1846, County Clerk
- **LAND:** 1846, County Clerk
- **PROBATE:** 1847, County Clerk
- **COURT:** 1845, County Clerk
- **NOTES:** County Clerk has death records 1903-1941. District Clerk has divorce records 1856-1891, 1899-1908.

BURNET

220 S. Pierce St., Burnet, TX 78611, (512) 756-5406,
<www.burnetcountytexas.org>

- **INCORPORATED:** Feb. 5, 1852
- **PARENT COUNTIES:** Travis, Bell, Williamson
- **BIRTH RECORDS:** start in 1903, kept by the County Clerk
- **MARRIAGE:** 1852, County Clerk
- **DIVORCE:** 1867, District Clerk
- **PROBATE:** 1852, County Clerk
- **COURT:** 1854, District Clerk
- **BURIAL:** 1852, County Clerk
- **NOTES:** County Clerk has death records 1903-1917, land records 1852-1927, and military discharge records 1919-1968. District Clerk has naturalization records 1852-1906.

CALDWELL

Box 906, Lockhart, TX 78644, (512) 398-1804,
<www.co.caldwell.tx.us>

- **INCORPORATED:** March 6, 1848
- **PARENT COUNTY:** Gonzales
- **BIRTH RECORDS:** start in 1915, kept by the County Clerk
- **MARRIAGE:** 1848, County Clerk
- **DEATH:** 1915, County Clerk
- **LAND:** 1846, County Clerk
- **PROBATE:** 1849, County Clerk
- **COURT:** 1848, County Clerk
- **NOTES:** County Clerk has birth records 1873-1876, 1903-1912, death records 1903-1915, military discharge records 1918-1931, and naturalization records 1853-1925. District Clerk has divorce records 1896-1944.

CALHOUN

211 S. Ann St., Port Lavaca, TX 77979, (361) 553-4411,
<www.calhouncotx.org>

- **INCORPORATED:** April 4, 1846
- **PARENT COUNTIES:** Victoria, Matagorda, Jackson
- **LAND RECORDS:** 1846, County Clerk
- **NOTES:** County Clerk has birth and death records from mid-1800s, marriage records 1846-1919, and probate records 1846-1968. District Clerk has court records 1847-1914 and naturalization records 1851-1914.

CALLAHAN

100 W. 4th St., Suite 104, Baird, TX 79504, (325) 854-5815,
<www.co.callahan.tx.us>

- **INCORPORATED:** Feb. 1, 1858
- **PARENT COUNTIES:** Bexar, Travis, Bosque
- **BIRTH RECORDS:** start in 1903, kept by the County Clerk
- **MARRIAGE:** 1878, County Clerk
- **DIVORCE:** unknown start, District Clerk
- **DEATH:** 1903, District/County Clerk
- **LAND:** 1878, County Clerk
- **PROBATE:** 1879, County Clerk
- **COURT:** 1879, County Clerk

CAMERON

Box 2178, Brownsville, TX 78520, (956) 554-0815, **<www.co.cameron.tx.us>**

- **INCORPORATED:** Feb. 12, 1848
- **PARENT COUNTY:** Nueces
- **BIRTH RECORDS:** 1903, County Clerk
- **DEATH:** 1903, County Clerk
- **COURT:** 1849, District Clerk
- **NOTES:** District Clerk has divorce records 1849-1914. County Clerk has land records 1848-1911, marriage and probate records 1848-1912, and naturalization records 1876-1930.

CAMP

126 Church St., Pittsburg, TX 75686, (903) 856-2731, **<www.co.camp.tx.us>**

- **INCORPORATED:** April 6, 1874
- **PARENT COUNTY:** Upshur
- **BIRTH RECORDS:** start in 1903, kept by the County Clerk
- **MARRIAGE:** 1874, County Clerk
- **DEATH:** 1903, County Clerk
- **LAND:** 1874, County Clerk
- **PROBATE:** 1874, County Clerk
- **NOTES:** District Clerk has court records 1874-1974 and divorce records 1911-1943.

CARSON

Box 487, Panhandle, TX 79068, (806) 537-3873, **<www.co.carson.tx.us>**

- **INCORPORATED:** Aug. 21, 1876
- **PARENT COUNTY:** Bexar Land District
- **BIRTH RECORDS:** start in1903, kept by the County Clerk
- **MARRIAGE:** 1888, County Clerk
- **DIVORCE:** 1902, County Clerk
- **DEATH:** 1903, County Clerk
- **LAND:** 1883, County Clerk
- **PROBATE:** 1907, County Clerk

CASS

Box 449, Linden, TX 75563, (903) 756-5071, **<www.co.cass.tx.us>**

- **INCORPORATED:** April 25, 1846
- **PARENT COUNTY:** Bowie
- **BIRTH RECORDS:** start in 1903, kept by the County Clerk
- **MARRIAGE:** 1847, County Clerk
- **DIVORCE:** 1841, District Court
- **DEATH:** 1903, County Clerk
- **LAND:** 1846, County Clerk
- **PROBATE:** 1846, County Clerk
- **COURT:** 1841, District Clerk
- **NOTES:** Name changed to Davis Dec. 17, 1861; and back to Cass May 16, 1871. County Clerk has delayed birth records from 1873.

CASTRO

100 E. Bedford St., Room 101, Dimmitt, TX 79027, (806) 647-3338, **<www.co.castro.tx.us>**

- **INCORPORATED:** Aug. 21, 1876
- **PARENT COUNTY:** Bexar Land District
- **BIRTH RECORDS:** start in 1903, kept by the County Clerk
- **MARRIAGE:** 1892, County Clerk
- **DIVORCE:** 1892, County Clerk
- **DEATH:** 1903, County Clerk
- **LAND:** 1911, County Clerk
- **PROBATE:** 1948, County Clerk
- **COURT:** 1892, County Clerk
- **MILITARY:** 1917, County Clerk

CHAMBERS

404 Washington Ave., Box 728, Anahuac, TX 77514, (409) 267-2418, **<www.co.chambers.tx.us>**

- **INCORPORATED:** Feb. 12, 1858
- **PARENT COUNTIES:** Jefferson, Liberty
- **BIRTH RECORDS:** 1903, County Clerk
- **DIVORCE:** 1910, County Clerk
- **DEATH:** 1908, County Clerk
- **LAND:** 1875, County Clerk
- **COURT:** 1875, County Clerk
- **NOTES:** County Clerk has land records 1875-1902, marriage records 1876-1916 and probate records 1876-1945.

CHEROKEE

Box 420, Rusk, TX 75785, (903) 683-2350, **<www.co.cherokee.tx.us>**

- **INCORPORATED:** April11, 1846
- **PARENT COUNTY:** Nacogdoches
- **DIVORCE RECORDS:** 1879, County Clerk
- **COURT:** 1867, County Clerk
- **NOTES:** County Clerk has birth records 1903-1987, death records 1903-1935, land records 1846-1901, marriage records 1846-1934, and probate records 1839-1934.

CHILDRESS

Courthouse, Box 4, Childress, TX 79201, (940) 937-6143, **<www.co.childress.tx.us>**

- **INCORPORATED:** Aug. 21, 1876
- **PARENT COUNTY:** Donley
- **BIRTH RECORDS:** start in 1903, kept by the County Clerk
- **MARRIAGE:** 1893, County Clerk
- **DIVORCE:** 1900, County Clerk
- **DEATH:** 1903, County Clerk
- **LAND:** 1895, County Clerk
- **PROBATE:** 1894,County Clerk
- **COURT:** 1900, County Clerk
- **NOTES:** Courthouse fire Oct. 21, 1891 destroyed many documents.

CLAY

100 N. Bridge St., Henrietta, TX 76365, (940) 538-4631, **<www.co.clay.tx.us>**

- **INCORPORATED:** Dec. 24, 1857
- **PARENT COUNTY:** Cooke
- **BIRTH RECORDS:** start in 1903, kept by the County Clerk
- **DEATH:** 1903, County Clerk
- **NOTES:** District Clerk has court records 1874-1945, divorce records 1925-1943, and naturalization records 1879-1917. County Clerk has land records 1873-1891, marriage records 1870-1946, and probate records 1873-1961. County was dissolved in 1862, then reorganized in 1873.

COCHRAN

100 N. Main, Room 102, Morton, TX 79346, (806) 266-5450,
<www.co.cochran.tx.us>

- **INCORPORATED:** Aug. 21, 1876
- **PARENT COUNTY:** Bexar, Young
- **BIRTH RECORDS:** start in 1926, kept by the County Clerk
- **MARRIAGE:** 1924, County Clerk
- **DIVORCE:** 1926, County Clerk
- **DEATH:** 1926, County Clerk
- **LAND:** 1884, County Clerk
- **PROBATE:** 1926, County Clerk
- **COURT:** 1926, County Clerk

COKE

13 E. 7th St., Robert Lee, TX 76945, (325) 453-2631,
<www.co.coke.tx.us>

- **INCORPORATED:** March13, 1889
- **PARENT COUNTY:** Tom Green
- **DIVORCE RECORDS:** 1891, County Clerk
- **DEATH:** 1903, County Clerk
- **LAND:** 1872, County Clerk
- **PROBATE:** 1891, County Clerk
- **COURT:** 1891, County Clerk
- **NOTES:** County Clerk has birth records 1903-1910, 1926-1990, and marriage records 1890-2000.

COLEMAN

100 W. Liveoak St. Suite 105, Coleman, TX 76834, (325) 625-2889,
<www.co.coleman.tx.us>

- **INCORPORATED:** Feb. 1, 1858
- **PARENT COUNTIES:** Travis, Brown
- **BIRTH RECORDS:** start in 1900, kept by the County Clerk
- **MARRIAGE:** 1873, County Clerk
- **DIVORCE:** unknown start, District/County Clerk
- **DEATH:** 1900, County Clerk
- **LAND:** 1846, County Clerk
- **PROBATE:** 1876, County Clerk
- **COURT:** 1976, County Clerk
- **MILITARY:** 1918, County Clerk

COLLIN

2300 Bloomdale Rd., #2104, McKinney, TX 75071, (972) 548-4139,
<www.co.collin.tx.us>

- **INCORPORATED:** April 3, 1846
- **PARENT COUNTY:** Fannin
- **BIRTH RECORDS:** start in 1903, kept by the County Clerk
- **MARRIAGE:** 1846, County Clerk
- **DIVORCE:** 1846, District Clerk
- **DEATH:** 1903, County Clerk
- **LAND:**1846, County Clerk
- **PROBATE:** 1846, County Clerk
- **COURT:** 1846, District Clerk
- **NOTES:** County Clerk has military discharge records 1919-1943. District Clerk has naturalization records 1893-1902.

COLLINGSWORTH

800 W. Ave., Box 10, Wellington, TX 79095, (806) 447-2408,
<www.co.collingsworth.tx.us>

- **INCORPORATED:** Aug. 21, 1876
- **PARENT COUNTY:** Bexar Land District, Young Land District
- **BIRTH RECORDS:** 1891, County Clerk
- **MARRIAGE:** 1890, County Clerk
- **DIVORCE:** 1903, County Clerk
- **DEATH:** 1892, County Clerk
- **LAND:** unknown start, County Clerk
- **COURT:** 1903, County Clerk

COLORADO

400 Spring Street, Suite 103, Columbus, TX 78934, (979) 732-2155,
<www.co.colorado.tx.us>

- **INCORPORATED:** March 17, 1836
- **PARENT COUNTY:** Old Mexican Municipality
- **NOTES:** County Clerk has marriage records 1837-1879.
- **BIRTH RECORDS:** start in 1903, kept by the County Clerk
- **MARRIAGE:** 1966, County Clerk
- **DIVORCE:** 1837, District Clerk
- **DEATH:** 1903, County Clerk
- **LAND:** 1908, County Clerk
- **PROBATE:** 1837, County Clerk
- **COURT:** 1937, District Clerk

COMAL

150 N. Seguin Suite 101, New Braunfels, TX 78130, (830) 221-1230,
<www.co.comal.tx.us>

- **INCORPORATED:** March 24, 1846
- **PARENT COUNTIES:** Bexar, Gonzales, Travis
- **BIRTH RECORDS:** start in 1903, kept by the County Clerk
- **DEATH:** 1903, County Clerk
- **NOTES:** County Clerk has land records 1846-1901, marriage records, military discharge records 1919-1956, naturalization records 1847-1926, and probate records 1846-1981. District Clerk has court records 1946-1944.

COMANCHE

101 West Central, Comanche, TX 76442, (325) 356-2655,
<www.rootsweb.ancestry.com/~txcomanc/comanche.htm>

- **INCORPORATED:** Jan. 25, 1856
- **PARENT COUNTIES:** Bosque, Coryell
- **BIRTH RECORDS:** start in 1903, kept by the County Clerk
- **MARRIAGE:** 1856, County Clerk
- **DEATH:** 1903, County Clerk
- **LAND:** 1859, County Clerk
- **PROBATE:** 1897, County Clerk
- **COURT:** 1858, County Clerk

CONCHO

Box 98, Paint Rock, TX 76866, (325) 732-4322,
<www.co.concho.tx.us>

- **INCORPORATED:** Feb. 1, 1858
- **PARENT COUNTY:** Bexar
- **BIRTH RECORDS:** start in 1800, kept by the County Clerk
- **MARRIAGE:** 1879, County Clerk
- **DIVORCE:** 1907, County Clerk

- **DEATH:** 1903, County Clerk
- **LAND:** 1879, County Clerk
- **PROBATE:** 1879, County Clerk
- **COURT:** 1907, County Clerk

COOKE

100 S. Dixon St., Gainesville, TX 76240, (940) 668-5420,
<www.co.cooke.tx.us>

- **INCORPORATED:** March 20, 1848
- **PARENT COUNTY:** Fannin
- **BIRTH RECORDS:** 1903, County Clerk
- **MARRIAGE:** 1849, County Clerk
- **DIVORCE:** 1850, District Clerk
- **DEATH:** 1903, County Clerk
- **LAND:** 1850, County Clerk
- **PROBATE:** 1848, County Clerk
- **COURT:** 1850, District Clerk

CORYELL

Box 237, Gatesville, TX 76528, (254) 865-5911,
<www.coryellcounty.org>

- **INCORPORATED:** Feb. 4, 1854
- **PARENT COUNTY:** Bell
- **BIRTH RECORDS:** start in 1903, kept by the County Clerk
- **DEATH:** 1903, County Clerk
- **LAND:** 1852, County Clerk
- **NOTES:** District Clerk has court records 1856-1978. County Clerk has marriage records 1854-1956, military discharge records for 1919, naturalization records 1887-1926, and probate records 1854-1934.

COTTLE

Box 717, Paducah, TX 79248, (806) 492-3823,
<www.co.cottle.tx.us>

- **INCORPORATED:** Aug. 21, 1876
- **PARENT COUNTY:** Fannin
- **BIRTH RECORDS:** 1892, County Clerk
- **MARRIAGE:** 1892, County Clerk
- **DIVORCE:** 1892, County Clerk
- **DEATH:** 1892, County Clerk
- **LAND:** 1892, County Clerk
- **PROBATE:** 1892, County Clerk
- **COURT:** 1892, County Clerk

CRANE

Box 578, Crane, TX 79731, (432) 558-3581, **<www.co.crane.tx.us>**

- **INCORPORATED:** Feb. 26, 1887
- **PARENT COUNTY:** Tom Green
- **BIRTH RECORDS:** 1928, County Clerk
- **MARRIAGE:** 1927, County Clerk
- **DIVORCE:** 1927, County Clerk
- **DEATH:** 1927, County Clerk
- **LAND:** 1927, County Clerk
- **PROBATE:** 1927, County Clerk
- **COURT:** 1927, County Clerk

CROCKETT

Drawer C, Ozona, TX 76943, (325) 392-2022,
<www.co.crockett.tx.us>

- **INCORPORATED:** Jul. 1, 1891
- **PARENT COUNTY:** Bexar Land District
- **BIRTH RECORDS:** start in 1903, kept by the County Clerk
- **MARRIAGE:** 1891, County Clerk
- **DIVORCE:** 1892, County Clerk
- **DEATH:** 1903, County Clerk
- **PROBATE:** 1892, County Clerk
- **COURT:** 1892, County Clerk

CROSBY

201 W. Aspen Suite 102, Crosbyton, TX 79322, (806) 675-2334,
<www.co.crosby.tx.us>

- **INCORPORATED:** Aug. 21, 1876
- **PARENT COUNTIES:** Bexar, Young
- **DIVORCE RECORDS:** 1887, District Clerk
- **LAND:** 1886, County Clerk
- **PROBATE:** 1887, County Clerk
- **COURT:** 1887, District Clerk
- **NOTES:** County Clerk has birth records 1903-1946, death records 1903-1971, and marriage records 1886-1953.

CULBERSON

Box 158, Van Horn, TX 79855, (432) 283-2058,
<www.co.culberson.tx.us>

- **INCORPORATED:** March10, 1911
- **PARENT COUNTY:** El Paso
- **BIRTH RECORDS:** start in 1911, kept by the County Clerk
- **MARRIAGE:** 1911, County Clerk
- **DIVORCE:** 1911, County Clerk
- **DEATH:** 1911, County Clerk
- **LAND:** 1911, County Clerk
- **PROBATE:** 1911, County Clerk
- **COURT:** 1911, County Clerk

DALLAM

Box 1352, Dalhart, TX 79022, (806) 244-4751, **<www.dallam.org/county>**

- **INCORPORATED:** Aug. 21, 1876
- **PARENT COUNTY:** Bexar Land District
- **BIRTH RECORDS:** start in 1903, kept by the County Clerk
- **MARRIAGE:** 1891, County Clerk
- **DIVORCE:** 1892, County Clerk
- **DEATH:** 1903, County Clerk
- **LAND:** 1876, County Clerk
- **PROBATE:** 1900, County Clerk
- **COURT:** 1891, County Clerk

DALLAS

509 Main St., Dallas, TX 75202, (214) 653-7099,
<www.dallascounty.org>

- **INCORPORATED:** March 30, 1846
- **PARENT COUNTIES:** Nacogdoches, Robertson
- **BIRTH RECORDS:** start in 1903, kept by the County Clerk
- **MARRIAGE:** 1846, County Clerk
- **DEATH:** 1903, County Clerk

- **LAND:** 1880, County Clerk
- **PROBATE:** 1848, County Clerk
- **NOTES:** District Clerk has court records and divorce records 1846-1939 and naturalization records 1872-1912.

DAWSON

Box 1268, Lamesa, TX 79331, (806) 872-3778,
<www.co.dawson.tx.us>

- **INCORPORATED:** Feb. 13, 1905
- **PARENT COUNTY:** Howard
- **BIRTH RECORDS:** start in1905, kept by the County Clerk
- **DIVORCE:** 1920, District Clerk
- **LAND:** 1905, County Clerk
- **PROBATE:** 1905, County Clerk
- **COURT:** 1920, District Clerk
- **NOTES:** County Clerk has death records 1918-1971 and marriage records 1905-1953.

DE WITT

307 N. Gonzales St., Cuero, TX 77954, (361) 275-0864,
<www.co.dewitt.tx.us>

- **INCORPORATED:** March 24, 1846
- **PARENT COUNTIES:** Goliad, Gonzales, Victoria
- **BIRTH RECORDS:** start in 1903, kept by the County Clerk
- **MARRIAGE:** 1846, County Clerk
- **DEATH:** 1903, County Clerk
- **LAND:** 1846, County Clerk
- **NOTES:** District Clerk has court records 1852-1912. County Clerk has naturalization records 1851-1929; probate records 1846-1938.

DEAF SMITH

235 E. Third, Room 203, Hereford, TX 79045, (806) 363-7077,
<www.co.deaf-smith.tx.us>

- **INCORPORATED:** Aug. 21, 1876
- **PARENT COUNTY:** Bexar Land District
- **BIRTH RECORDS:** start in 1903, kept by the County Clerk
- **MARRIAGE:** 1891, County Clerk
- **DIVORCE:** unknown start, District Clerk
- **DEATH:** 1903, County Clerk
- **LAND:** 1882, County Clerk
- **PROBATE:** 1891, County Clerk
- **COURT:** 1891, District Clerk
- **MILITARY:** 1919, County Clerk

DELTA

200 W. Dallas Ave., Cooper, TX 75432, (903) 395-4400 ext. 222,
<www.co.delta.tx.us>

- **INCORPORATED:** Jul. 29, 1870
- **PARENT COUNTIES:** Hopkins, Lamar
- **BIRTH RECORDS:** start in 1903, kept by the County Clerk
- **DEATH:** ca. 1916, County Clerk
- **NOTES:** County Clerk has court records 1872-1918, land records 1871-1886, marriage records 1871-1970, probate records 1872-1946.

DENTON

1450 E. McKinney Suite 1103, Denton, TX 76209, (940) 349-2012,
<www.co.denton.tx.us>

- **INCORPORATED:** 11 April 11, 1846
- **PARENT COUNTY:** Fannin
- **BIRTH RECORDS:** start in 1904, kept by the County Clerk
- **DEATH:** 1904, County Clerk
- **NOTES:** District Clerk has court records 1877-1954 and divorce records 1876-1931. County Clerk has land records 1854-1902, marriage records 1875-1905, and probate records 1876-1931. Courthouse burned in 1875; a few records were saved.

DICKENS

Box 120, Dickens, TX 79229, (806) 623-5531,
<www.co.dickens.tx.us>

- **INCORPORATED:** Aug. 21, 1876
- **PARENT COUNTY:** Bexar Land District
- **BIRTH RECORDS:** start in 1892, kept by the County Clerk
- **MARRIAGE:** 1891, County Clerk
- **DIVORCE:** 1891, County Clerk
- **DEATH:** 1892, County Clerk
- **LAND:** 1884, County Clerk
- **PROBATE:** 1891, County Clerk
- **COURT:** 1891, County Clerk

DIMMIT

Courthouse, 103 N. 5th St., Carrizo Springs, TX 78834, (830) 876-4209, **<www.dimmitcountytx.com>**

- **INCORPORATED:** Feb. 1, 1858
- **PARENT COUNTIES:** Uvalde, Bexar, Maverick, Webb
- **BIRTH RECORDS:** start in 1903, kept by the County Clerk
- **MARRIAGE:** 1880, County Clerk
- **DEATH:** 1903, County Clerk
- **NOTES:** District Clerk has court records, divorce records, and naturalization records 1881-1931. County Clerk has land records 1880-1912 and probate records 1881-1952.

DONLEY

300 S. Sully, Drawer U, Clarendon, TX 79226, (806) 874-3436,
<www.co.donley.tx.us>

- **INCORPORATED:** Aug. 21, 1876
- **PARENT COUNTY:** Bexar Land District
- **BIRTH RECORDS:** start in 1903, kept by the County Clerk
- **MARRIAGE:** 1882, County Clerk
- **DEATH:** 1903, County Clerk
- **LAND:** 1882, County Clerk
- **PROBATE:** 1882, County Clerk
- **COURT:** 1882, County Clerk

DUVAL

Box 248, San Diego, TX 78384, (361) 279-3322, **<www.rootsweb.ancestry.com/~txduval>**

- **INCORPORATED:** Feb. 1, 1858
- **PARENT COUNTIES:** Live Oak, Starr, Neuces
- **BIRTH RECORDS:** start in 1903, kept by the County Clerk
- **DEATH:** 1903, County Clerk
- **NOTES:** District Clerk has court records 1879-1908. County Clerk has land records 1877-1919, probate records 1877-1883, 1887-1901, and marriage records 1877-1902.

EASTLAND

100 W. Main #102, Box 110, Eastland, TX 76448, (254) 629-1583, **<www.eastlandcountytexas.com>**

- **INCORPORATED:** Feb. 1, 1858
- **PARENT COUNTIES:** Bosque, Coryell, Travis
- **MARRIAGE RECORDS:** 1874, County Clerk
- **DIVORCE:** 1903, District Court
- **LAND:** 1870, County Clerk
- **PROBATE:** 1882, County Clerk
- **MILITARY:** 1919, County Clerk
- **NOTES:** County Clerk has birth records and death records from 1903-1930 and 1940-1950.

ECTOR

300 N. Grant Ave., Room 111, Odessa, TX 79761, (432) 498-4130, **<www.co.ector.tx.us>**

- **INCORPORATED:** Feb. 26, 1887
- **PARENT COUNTY:** Tom Green
- **BIRTH RECORDS:** start in 1903, kept by the County Clerk
- **DIVORCE:** unknown start, District Clerk
- **LAND:** 1896, County Clerk
- **COURT:** 1896, County Clerk
- **NOTES:** County Clerk has death records 1903-1971, marriage records 1891-1994, and probate records 1891-1945.

EDWARDS

Box 184, Rocksprings, TX 78880, (830) 683-2235, **<www.rootsweb.ancestry.com/~txedward>**

- **INCORPORATED:** Feb. 1, 1858
- **PARENT COUNTY:** Bexar Land District
- **BIRTH RECORDS:** start in 1903, kept by the County Clerk
- **MARRIAGE:** 1888, County Clerk
- **DIVORCE:** 1884, County Clerk
- **DEATH:** 1903, County Clerk
- **LAND:** 1888, County Clerk
- **PROBATE:** 1888, County Clerk
- **COURT:** 1888, County Clerk

EL PASO

500 E. San Antonio St., Room 105, El Paso, TX 79901, (915) 546-2071, **<www.co.el-paso.tx.us>**

- **INCORPORATED:** Jan. 3, 1850
- **PARENT COUNTY:** Bexar Land District
- **BIRTH RECORDS:** start in 1903, kept by the County Clerk
- **MARRIAGE:** 1866, County Clerk
- **DEATH:** 1903, County Clerk
- **LAND:** 1856, County Clerk
- **PROBATE:** 1866, County Clerk
- **COURT:** 1861, County Clerk

ELLIS

Box 250, Waxahachie, TX 75168, (972) 923-5070 **<www.co.ellis.tx.us>**

- **INCORPORATED:** Dec. 20, 1849
- **PARENT COUNTY:** Navarro
- **MARRIAGE RECORDS:** 1850, County Clerk
- **NOTES:** County Clerk has birth records 1903-1936, death records 1903-1982, land records 1845-1901, military discharge records 1919-1980, and probate records 1850-1946. District Clerk has court records 1850-1931, divorce records 1899-1936, and naturalization records 1854-1935.

ENCINAL

- **INCORPORATED:** Feb. 1, 1858
- **PARENT COUNTY:** Webb
- **NOTES:** See Webb County. Never organized. Discontinued March 12, 1899 and returned to Webb County.

ERATH

100 W. Washington St., Stephenville, TX 76401, (254) 965-1482, **<co.erath.tx.us>**

- **INCORPORATED:** Jan. 25, 1856
- **PARENT COUNTIES:** Bosque, Coryell
- **NOTES:** County Clerk has birth records 1903-1942, death records 1903-1992, land records 1867-1902, marriage records 1869-1956, naturalization records 1886-1910, and probate records 1866-1934. District Clerk has court records 1866-1977 and divorce records 1866-1985.

FALLS

Box 458, Marlin, TX 76661, (254) 883-1408, **<www.rootsweb.ancestry.com/~txfalls>**

- **INCORPORATED:** Jan. 28, 1850
- **PARENT COUNTIES:** Limestone, Milam
- **BIRTH RECORDS:** start in 1904, kept by the County Clerk
- **DEATH:** 1904, County Clerk
- **NOTES:** District Clerk has court records 1851-1906, divorce records 1869-1950, and naturalization records 1855-1926. County Clerk has land records 1850-1904, marriage records 1854-1946, and probate records 1851-1935.

FANNIN

101 E. Sam Rayburn Dr., #102, Bonham, TX 75418, (903) 583-7488, **<www.co.fannin.tx.us>**

- **INCORPORATED:** Dec. 14, 1837
- **PARENT COUNTY:** Red River
- **BIRTH RECORDS:** start in 1903, kept by the County Clerk
- **NOTES:** County Clerk has birth Records 1874-1876, court records 1840-1889, death records 1903-1973, land records 1838-1886, marriage records 1852-1917, and probate records 1838-1888.

FAYETTE

Box 59, La Grange, TX 78945, (979) 968-3251, **<www.co.fayette.tx.us>**

- **INCORPORATED:** Jan. 18, 1838
- **PARENT COUNTIES:** Colorado, Mina
- **BIRTH RECORDS:** start in 1903, kept by the County Clerk
- **DEATH:** 1903, County Clerk
- **NOTES:** District Clerk has court and divorce records 1838-1936. County Clerk has land records 1838-1901, marriage records 1838-1942, naturalization records 1850-1936, and probate records 1838-1934.

FISHER
Box 368, Roby, TX 79543, (325) 776-2401, **<www.co.fisher.tx.us>**
- **INCORPORATED:** Aug. 21, 1876
- **PARENT COUNTIES:** Bexar Territory, Young Territory
- **BIRTH RECORDS:** start in 1903, kept by the County Clerk
- **MARRIAGE:** 1886, County Clerk
- **DEATH:** 1903, County Clerk
- **LAND:** 1886, County Clerk
- **PROBATE:** 1886, County Clerk
- **COURT:** 1886, County Clerk

FLOYD
105 S. Main St., Room 101, Floydada, TX 79235, (806) 983-4900, **<www.txfloyd.org>**
- **INCORPORATED:** Aug. 21, 1876
- **PARENT COUNTIES:** Bexar Territory, Young Territory
- **DIVORCE RECORDS:** unknown start, District Clerk
- **LAND:** 1890, County Clerk
- **PROBATE:** 1890, County Clerk
- **COURT:** 1890, County Clerk
- **NOTES:** County Clerk has birth records 1903-1946, death records 1903-1971, and marriage records 1890-1955.

FOARD
Box 539, Crowell, TX 79227, (940) 684-1365, **<www.rootsweb.ancestry.com/~txfoard>**
- **INCORPORATED:** March 3, 1891
- **PARENT COUNTIES:** Hardeman, Knox, King, Cottle
- **BIRTH RECORDS:** start in 1903, kept by the County Clerk
- **MARRIAGE:** 1891, County Clerk
- **DIVORCE:** 1891, County Clerk
- **DEATH:** 1903, County Clerk
- **LAND:** 1891, County Clerk
- **PROBATE:** 1891, County Clerk
- **COURT:** 1891, County Clerk

FORT BEND
301 Jackson St., Richmond, TX 77469, (281) 341-8685, **<www.co.fort-bend.tx.us>**
- **INCORPORATED:** Dec. 29, 1837
- **PARENT COUNTIES:** Austin, Harris, Bazoria
- **BIRTH RECORDS:** start in 1903, kept by the County Clerk
- **MARRIAGE:** 1838, County Clerk
- **DEATH:** 1903, County Clerk
- **LAND:** 1838, County Clerk
- **PROBATE:** 1838, County Clerk
- **COURT:** 1838, County Clerk
- **NOTES:** District Clerk has naturalization records 1854-1929.

FRANKLIN
200 N. Kaufman Street, Mount Vernon, TX 75457, (903) 537-4252, **<co.franklin.tx.us>**
- **INCORPORATED:** 6 March 6, 1875
- **PARENT COUNTY:** Titus
- **BIRTH RECORDS:** start in 1903, kept by the County Clerk
- **MARRIAGE:** 1875, County Clerk
- **DIVORCE:** 1875, District Clerk
- **DEATH:** 1903, County Clerk
- **LAND:** 1845, County Clerk
- **PROBATE:** 1875, County Clerk
- **NOTES:** County Clerk also has deeds for Red River County.

FREESTONE
Box 1010, Fairfield, TX 75840, (903) 389-2635, **<www.co.freestone.tx.us>**
- **INCORPORATED:** Sep. 6, 1850
- **PARENT COUNTY:** Limestone
- **BIRTH RECORDS:** 1903, County Clerk
- **MARRIAGE:** 1851, County Clerk
- **DEATH:** 1903, County Clerk
- **LAND:** 1850, County Clerk
- **PROBATE:** 1851, County Clerk
- **COURT:** 1851, County Clerk

FRIO
500 E. San Antonio St., Box #6, Pearsall, TX 78061, (830) 334-2214, **<www.co.frio.tx.us>**
- **INCORPORATED:** Feb. 1, 1858
- **PARENT COUNTIES:** Atascosa, Bexar, Uvalde
- **BIRTH RECORDS:** start in 1903, kept by the County Clerk
- **MARRIAGE:** 1871, County Clerk
- **DEATH:** 1903, County Clerk
- **LAND:** 1871, County Clerk
- **PROBATE:** 1871, County Clerk
- **COURT:** 1873, County Clerk
- **NOTES:** County Clerk has naturalization records 1877-1916.

GAINES
101 S. Main St. Room 107, Seminole, TX 79360, (432) 758-4003, **<www.co.gaines.tx.us>**
- **INCORPORATED:** Aug. 21, 1876
- **PARENT COUNTIES:** Bexar Territory, Young Territory
- **BIRTH RECORDS:** start in 1905, kept by the County Clerk
- **MARRIAGE:** 1905, County Clerk
- **DEATH:** 1905, County Clerk
- **LAND:** 1905, County Clerk
- **PROBATE:** 1905, County Clerk
- **COURT:** 1906, County Clerk

GALVESTON
Box 17253, Galveston, TX 77552, (409) 766-2210, **<www.co.galveston.tx.us>**
- **INCORPORATED:** May.15, 1838
- **PARENT COUNTIES:** Brazoria, Liberty, Harrisburg
- **NOTES:** County Clerk has birth records 1903-1910, land records 1838-1886, marriage records 1838-1907, naturalization records 1876-1906, and probate records 1838-1930. District Clerk has court records 1839-1909.

GARZA
Box 366, Post, TX 79356, (806) 495-4430, **<www.garzacounty.net>**
- **INCORPORATED:** Aug. 21, 1876
- **PARENT COUNTY:** Bexar Land District, Young Territory
- **BIRTH RECORDS:** start in 1903, kept by the County Clerk
- **MARRIAGE:** 1907, County Clerk

- **DIVORCE:** 1907, County Clerk
- **DEATH:** 1903, County Clerk
- **LAND:** 1907, County Clerk
- **PROBATE:** 1907, County Clerk
- **COURT:** 1907, County Clerk

GILLESPIE

101 W. Main St. #13, Fredericksburg, TX 78624, (830) 997-6515,
<www.gillespiecounty.org>
- **INCORPORATED:** Feb. 23, 1848
- **PARENT COUNTIES:** Bexar, Travis
- **BIRTH RECORDS:** start in 1846, kept by the County Clerk
- **DEATH:** 1903, County Clerk
- **LAND:** 1850, County Clerk
- **NOTES:** District Clerk has court records 1849-1946 and divorce records 1850-1940. County Clerk has marriage records 1850-1965, military discharge records 1917-1919, naturalization records 1849-1936, and probate records 1850-1936.

GLASSCOCK

Box 190, Garden City, TX 79739, (432) 354-2371,
<www.co.glasscock.tx.us>
- **INCORPORATED:** April 4, 1887
- **PARENT COUNTY:** Tom Green
- **BIRTH RECORDS:** start in 1903, kept by the County Clerk
- **MARRIAGE:** 1893, County Clerk
- **DIVORCE:** unknown start, County Clerk
- **DEATH:** 1903, County Clerk
- **LAND:** 1893, County Clerk
- **PROBATE:** 1893, County Clerk
- **COURT:** 1893, County Clerk
- **NOTES:** County Judge has recent burial records.

GOLIAD

Box 50, Goliad, TX 77963, (361) 645-3294,
<www.co.goliad.tx.us>
- **INCORPORATED:** March 17, 1836
- **PARENT COUNTY:** Old Mexican Municipality
- **BIRTH RECORDS:** start in 1903, kept by the County Clerk
- **DEATH:** 1903, County Clerk
- **NOTES:** District Clerk has court records 1855-1866 and 1870-1907. County Clerk has divorce records 1855-1866, 1870-1907, land records 1870-1908, marriage records 1876-1911, and probate records 1871-1913.

GONZALES

Box 77, Gonzales, TX 78629, (830) 672-2801,
<www.co.gonzales.tx.us>
- **INCORPORATED:** March 17, 1836
- **PARENT COUNTY:** Old Mexican Municipality
- **NOTES:** County Clerk has birth records and death records 1903-1995, land records 1837-1993, marriage records 1839-1955, and probate records 1838-1935. District Clerk has divorce records 1927-1958 and naturalization records 1887-1929. Archives and Records Center has all older records from County and District clerks, cemetery records and school census. Guadalupe, Caldwell, Comal, Lavaca, Fayette, DeWitt, Victoria, and Jackson counties formed out of Gonzales, contain old county records.

GRAY

Box 1902, Pampa, TX 79065, (806) 669-8004,
<www.co.gray.tx.us>
- **INCORPORATED:** Aug. 21, 1876
- **PARENT COUNTY:** Bexar Land District
- **BIRTH RECORDS:** start in 1903, kept by the County Clerk
- **MARRIAGE:** 1902, County Clerk
- **DIVORCE:** unknown start, District Clerk
- **DEATH:** 1903, County Clerk
- **LAND:** 1902, County Clerk
- **PROBATE:** 1902, County Clerk
- **COURT:** 1903, County Clerk

GRAYSON

100 W. Houston St. Suite 17, Sherman, TX 75090, (903) 813-4243,
<www.co.grayson.tx.us>
- **INCORPORATED:** March 17, 1846
- **PARENT COUNTY:** Fannin Land District
- **BIRTH RECORDS:** start in 1909, kept by the County Clerk
- **MARRIAGE:** 1846, County Clerk
- **DIVORCE:** unknown start, District Clerk
- **DEATH:** 1909, County Clerk
- **LAND:** 1846, County Clerk
- **PROBATE:** 1846, County Clerk
- **NOTES:** District Clerk has court records 1836-1893. County Clerk has naturalization records 1853-1906.

GREGG

Box 3049, Longview, TX 75606, (903) 236-8430,
<www.co.gregg.tx.us>
- **INCORPORATED:** April 12, 1873
- **PARENT COUNTIES:** Rusk, Upshur
- **DEATH RECORDS:** start in 1964, kept by the County Clerk
- **PROBATE:** 1873, County Clerk
- **NOTES:** County Clerk has birth records 1873-1946, death records 1906-1915, land records 1873-1901, and marriage records 1873-1936. District Clerk has court records 1848-1934 and divorce records 1905-1935.

GRIMES

Box 209, Anderson, TX 77830, (936) 873-2111,
<www.co.gray.tx.us>
- **INCORPORATED:** April 6, 1846
- **PARENT COUNTY:** Montgomery
- **DEATH RECORDS:** start in 1903, kept by the County Clerk
- **NOTES:** County Clerk has birth records ca. 1850-1946, land records 1846-1898, marriage records 1848-1960, and probate records 1838-1957. District Clerk has court records 1848-1934 and naturalization records 1890-1925. Four courthouses were destroyed; present courthouse was built in 1894.

GUADALUPE

101 E. Court St. #206, Seguin, TX 78155, (830) 303-4188,
<www.co.guadalupe.tx.us>
- **INCORPORATED:** March 30, 1846
- **PARENT COUNTIES:** Bexar, Gonzales
- **MARRIAGE RECORDS:** start in 1846, kept by the County Clerk
- **DIVORCE:** 1846, District Clerk

- **DEATH:** 1903, County Clerk
- **LAND:** 1840, County Clerk
- **PROBATE:** 1846, County Clerk
- **COURT:** 1848, District Clerk
- **BURIAL:** 1935, County Clerk
- **NOTES:** County Clerk has birth records 1903-1942 and naturalization records 1887-1906.

HALE

500 Broadway #140, Plainview, TX 79072, (806) 291-5205, **<www.rootsweb.ancestry.com/~txhale>**

- **INCORPORATED:** Aug. 21, 1876
- **PARENT COUNTY:** Bexar Land District
- **BIRTH RECORDS:** start in 1903, kept by the County Clerk
- **MARRIAGE:** 1888, County Clerk
- **DIVORCE:** unknown start, District Clerk
- **DEATH:** 1903, County Clerk
- **LAND:** 1888, County Clerk
- **PROBATE:** 1888, County Clerk
- **COURT:** 1888, County Clerk

HALL

512 Main St., Suite 8, Memphis, TX 79245, (806) 259-2627, **<www.hallcountytexas.com>**

- **INCORPORATED:** Aug. 21, 1876
- **PARENT COUNTY:** Bexar Land District, Young
- **BIRTH RECORDS:** start in 1903, kept by the County Clerk
- **MARRIAGE:** 1890, County Clerk
- **DIVORCE:** 1890, County Clerk
- **DEATH:** 1903, County Clerk
- **LAND:** 1890, County Clerk
- **PROBATE:** 1890, County Clerk
- **COURT:** 1890, County Clerk

HAMILTON

102 N. Rice St., Suite 107, Hamilton, TX 76531, (254) 386-3518, **<www.co.hamilton.tx.us>**

- **INCORPORATED:** June 22, 1858
- **PARENT COUNTIES:** Bosque, Comanche, Lampasas
- **DIVORCE RECORDS:** 1870, District Clerk
- **NOTES:** County Clerk has birth records 1903-1985, death records 1903-1941, land records 1866-1844, marriage records 1876-1935, and probate records 1870-1948. District Clerk has court records 1870-1930 and naturalization records 1880-1927.

HANSFORD

15 NW Court, Spearman, TX 79081, (806) 659-4110, **<www.co.hansford.tx.us>**

- **PARENT COUNTY:** Bexar Land District, Young
- **BIRTH RECORDS:** start in 1903, kept by the County Clerk
- **MARRIAGE:** 1889, County Clerk
- **DIVORCE:** unknown start, County Clerk
- **DEATH:** 1903, County Clerk
- **LAND:** 1889, County Clerk
- **PROBATE:** 1889, County Clerk
- **COURT:** 1889, County Clerk

HARDEMAN

Box 30, Quanah, TX 79252, (940) 663-2961, **<www.rootsweb.ancestry.com/~txhardem>**

- **INCORPORATED:** Feb. 1, 1858
- **PARENT COUNTIES:** Fannin Land District
- **BIRTH RECORDS:** start in 1903, kept by the County Clerk
- **MARRIAGE:** 1885, County Clerk
- **DIVORCE:** unknown start, District Clerk
- **DEATH:** 1903, County Clerk
- **LAND:** 1884, County Clerk
- **PROBATE:** 1885, County Clerk
- **COURT:** 1885, County Clerk

HARDIN

Box 38, Kountze, TX 77625, (409) 246-5185, **<www.co.hardin.tx.us>**

- **INCORPORATED:** Jan. 22, 1858
- **PARENT COUNTIES:** Jefferson, Liberty
- **BIRTH RECORDS:** start in 1903, kept by the County Clerk
- **DEATH:** 1903, County Clerk
- **DIVORCE:** unknown start, District Clerk
- **NOTES:** District Clerk has court records 1871, 1879-1925. County Clerk has land records 1858-1894, marriage records 1862-1920, and probate records 1886-1936.

HARRIS

Box 1148, Houston, TX 77251, (713) 755-6411, **<www.co.harris.tx.us>**

- **INCORPORATED:** Dec. 30, 1835
- **PARENT COUNTY:** Old Mexican Municipality
- **BIRTH RECORDS:** start in 1903, kept by the County Clerk
- **MARRIAGE:** 1837, County Clerk
- **DIVORCE:** unknown start, District Clerk
- **DEATH:** 1903, County Clerk
- **NOTES:** District Clerk has court records 1872-1910. County Clerk has land records 1837-1886, naturalization records 1855-1906, and probate records 1837-1891. Name changed to Harrisburg County in 1836. Name changed to Harris Dec. 28, 1839.

HARRISBURG

- **INCORPORATED:** March 17, 1836
- **PARENT COUNTY:** Old Mexican Municipality
- **NOTES:** See Harris County. Name changed to Harris Dec. 28, 1839.

HARRISON

Box 1365, Marshall, TX 75671, (903) 935-8403, **<www.co.harrison.tx.us>**

- **INCORPORATED:** Jan. 28, 1839
- **PARENT COUNTY:** Shelby
- **BIRTH RECORDS:** start in 1903, kept by the County Clerk
- **DEATH:** 1903, County Clerk
- **NOTES:** County Clerk has land records 1840-1886, marriage records 1860-1936, and probate records 1840-1934. District Clerk has court records 1840-1934, divorce records 1903-1943, and naturalization records 1850-1916.

HARTLEY
Box T, Channing, TX 79018, (806) 235-3582,
<www.co.hartley.tx.us>
- **INCORPORATED:** Aug. 21, 1876
- **PARENT COUNTY:** Bexar Land District, Young
- **BIRTH RECORDS:** start in 1903, kept by the County Clerk
- **MARRIAGE:** 1891, County Clerk
- **DIVORCE:** 1891, County Clerk
- **DEATH:** 1903, County Clerk
- **LAND:** 1891, County Clerk
- **PROBATE:** 1891, County Clerk
- **COURT:** 1891, County Clerk

HASKELL
Box 725, Haskell, TX 79521, (817) 864-2451,
<www.co.haskell.tx.us>
- **INCORPORATED:** Feb. 1, 1858
- **PARENT COUNTIES:** Fannin, Milam
- **BIRTH RECORDS:** start in 1903, kept by the County Clerk
- **MARRIAGE:** 1885, County Clerk
- **DIVORCE:** unknown start, District Court
- **DEATH:** 1903, County Clerk
- **LAND:** 1885, County Clerk
- **PROBATE:** 1885, County Clerk
- **COURT:** 1885, County Clerk

HAYS
137 N. Guadalupe St., San Marcos, TX 78666, (512) 393-7330,
<www.co.hays.tx.us>
- **INCORPORATED:** March 1, 1848
- **PARENT COUNTY:** Travis
- **BIRTH RECORDS:** start in 1865, kept by the County Clerk
- **NOTES:** District Clerk has court records 1850-1864, 1874-1876, 1881-1939, divorce records 1896-1929, and naturalization records 1876-1906. County Clerk has death records 1903-1934, land records 1848-1905, marriage records 1848-1931, military discharge records 1908-1944, and probate records 1848-1950.

HEMPHILL
Box 867, Canadian, TX 79014, (806) 323-6212, **<www.rootsweb.ancestry.com/~txhemphi>**
- **INCORPORATED:** Aug. 21, 1876
- **PARENT COUNTIES:** Bexar Territory, Young Territory, Clay County
- **BIRTH RECORDS:** start in 1903, kept by the County Clerk
- **MARRIAGE:** 1887, County Clerk
- **DIVORCE:** 1887, County Clerk
- **DEATH:** 1903, County Clerk
- **LAND:** 1887, County Clerk
- **PROBATE:** 1887, County Clerk
- Court: 1887, County Clerk

HENDERSON
Box 632, Athens, TX 75751, (903) 675-6140,
<www.co.henderson.tx.us>
- **INCORPORATED:** April 27, 1846
- **PARENT COUNTIES:** Houston, Nacogdoches
- **BIRTH RECORDS:** start in 1903, kept by the County Clerk
- **COURT:** 1847, County Clerk
- **NOTES:** County Clerk has death records 1908-1938, 1941-1965, land records 1847-1901, marriage records 1847-1854, 1860-1941, and probate records 1846-1936.

HIDALGO
Box 87, Edinburg, TX 78540, (210) 318-2100,
<www.co.hidalgo.tx.us>
- **INCORPORATED:** Jan. 24, 1852
- **PARENT COUNTY:** Cameron
- **BIRTH RECORDS:** start in 1903, kept by the County Clerk
- **DEATH:** 1903, County Clerk
- **LAND:** 1852, County Clerk
- **NOTES:** District Clerk has court records 1853-1912 and divorce records 1853-1912. County Clerk has land records 1852-1912, marriage records 1852-1957, and probate records 1852-1911.

HILL
Box 398, Hillsboro, TX 76645, (817) 582-2161,
<www.co.hill.tx.us>
- **INCORPORATED:** Feb. 7, 1853
- **PARENT COUNTY:** Navarro
- **NOTES:** County Clerk has birth records 1903-1935, land records 1857-1901, death records 1903-1938, marriage records 1873-1934, and probate records 1853-1934. District Clerk has court records 1867-1932, divorce records 1896-1947, and naturalization records 1896-1913. Courthouse burned between 1874 and 1878.

HOCKLEY
800 Houston St., Levelland, TX 79336, (806) 894-3185,
<www.co.hockley.tx.us>
- **INCORPORATED:** Aug. 21, 1876
- **PARENT COUNTIES:** Bexar Land District, Young
- **BIRTH RECORDS:** start in 1903, kept by the County Clerk
- **MARRIAGE:** 1921, County Clerk
- **DEATH:** 1903, County Clerk
- **LAND:** 1921, County Clerk
- **PROBATE:** 1921, County Clerk
- **COURT:** 1921, County Clerk
- **NOTES:** Attached to Lubbock County from 1891-1921.

HOOD
101 Pearl St., Box 339, Granbury, TX 76048, (817) 579-3222,
<www.co.hood.tx.us>
- **INCORPORATED:** Nov. 3, 1865
- **PARENT COUNTY:** Johnson
- **NOTES:** County Clerk has birth records 1903-1995, death records 1903-1998, divorce records 1908-1946, land records 1875-1910, marriage records 1854-2002, and probate records 173-1936. District Clerk has court records 1875-1943. Hood Public Library in Granbury has many records of the late Judge Henry Davis.

HOPKINS
Box 288, Sulphur Springs, TX 75482, (903) 885-3929,
<www.hopkinscountytx.org>
- **INCORPORATED:** March 25, 1846
- **PARENT COUNTIES:** Lamar, Nacogdoches
- **BIRTH RECORDS:** start in 1903, kept by the County Clerk
- **DEATH:** 1903, County Clerk

- **NOTES:** District Clerk has court records 1846-1911. County Clerk has divorce records 1846-1911, land records 1846-1887, marriage records 1846-1920, and probate records 1846-1946.

HOUSTON

Box 370, Crockett, TX 75835, (936) 544-3255 ext. 2,
<www.co.houston.tx.us>

- **INCORPORATED:** Aug. 21, 1876
- **PARENT COUNTY:** Nacogdoches
- **BIRTH RECORDS:** start in 1903, kept by the County Clerk
- **MARRIAGE:** 1903, County Clerk
- **DIVORCE:** 1920, District Clerk
- **DEATH:** 1903, County Clerk
- **COURT:** 1882, County Clerk
- **NOTES:** County Clerk has land records 1865-1909, probate records 1859-1945. District Clerk has naturalization records 1880-1925.

HOWARD

300 Main St., Box 1468, Big Spring, TX 79721, (915) 369-2301,
<www.co.howard.tx.us>

- **INCORPORATED:** Aug. 21, 1876
- **PARENT COUNTIES:** Bexar Land District, Young
- **BIRTH RECORDS:** start in 1903, kept by the County Clerk
- **MARRIAGE:** 1882, County Clerk
- **DIVORCE:** 1883, County Clerk
- **DEATH:** 1903, County Clerk
- **LAND:** 1882, County Clerk
- **PROBATE:** 1882, County Clerk
- **COURT:** 1882, County Clerk

HUDSPETH

Drawer A, Sierra Blanca, TX 79851, (915) 369-2301,
<www.co.hudspeth.tx.us/ips/cms>

- **INCORPORATED:** Feb. 16, 1917
- **PARENT COUNTY:** El Paso
- **DIVORCE RECORDS:** 1917, County Clerk
- **LAND:** 1836, County Clerk
- **PROBATE:** 1917, County Clerk
- **COURT:** 1917, County Clerk
- **NOTES:** County Clerk has birth records 1917-1937, death records 1917-1971, and marriage records 1917-1960.

HUNT

2500 Lee St., Box 1316, Greenville, TX 75403, (903) 408-4130,
<www.huntcounty.net>

- **INCORPORATED:** April 11, 1846
- **PARENT COUNTIES:** Fannin, Nacogdoches
- **BIRTH RECORDS:** start in 1903, kept by the County Clerk
- **DEATH:** 1903, County Clerk
- **LAND:** 1846, County Clerk
- **MILITARY:** unknown start, County Clerk
- **NOTES:** District Clerk has court and divorce records 1851-1930 and naturalization records 1851-1926. County Clerk has marriage records 1858-1912 and probate records 1847-1927.

HUTCHINSON

Box 1186, Stinnett, TX 79083, (806) 878-4002,
<www.co.hutchinson.tx.us>

- **INCORPORATED:** Aug. 21, 1876
- **PARENT COUNTY:** Bexar Land District
- **BIRTH RECORDS:** start in 1903, kept by the County Clerk
- **MARRIAGE:** 1901, County Clerk
- **DIVORCE:** 1901, County Clerk
- **DEATH:** 1903, County Clerk
- **LAND:** 1901, County Clerk
- **PROBATE:** 1901, County Clerk
- **COURT:** 1901, County Clerk
- **NOTES:** County was attached to Wheeler and Carson County until it was officially organized on 13 May 1901.

IRION

Box 736, Mertzon, TX 76941, (915) 835-2421,
<www.co.irion.tx.us>

- **INCORPORATED:** March 7, 1889
- **PARENT COUNTY:** Tom Green
- **BIRTH RECORDS:** 1901, County Clerk
- **MARRIAGE:** 1889, County Clerk
- **DIVORCE:** 1889, County Clerk
- **DEATH:** 1903, County Clerk
- **LAND:** 1889, County Clerk
- **PROBATE:** 1889, County Clerk
- **MILITARY:** unknown start, County Clerk
- Court: 1889, County Clerk

JACK

100 Main St., Jacksboro, TX 76458, (817) 567-2111,
<www.jackcounty.org>

- **INCORPORATED:** Aug. 27, 1856
- **PARENT COUNTY:** Cooke
- **BIRTH RECORDS:** start in 1903, kept by the County Clerk
- **MARRIAGE:** 1858, County Clerk
- **DIVORCE:** unknown start, County Clerk
- **DEATH:** 1903, County Clerk
- **LAND:** 1858, County Clerk
- **PROBATE:** 1858, County Clerk
- **COURT:** 1858, County Clerk

JACKSON

115 W. Main St. Room 203, Edna, TX 77957, (361) 782-3563,
<www.co.jackson.tx.us>

- **INCORPORATED:** March17, 1836
- **PARENT COUNTY:** Old Mexican Municipality
- **BIRTH RECORDS:** start in 1903, kept by the County Clerk
- **DIVORCE:** unknown start, District Clerk
- **DEATH:** 1903, County Clerk
- **NOTES:** District Clerk has court records 1838-1944 and naturalization records 1903-1906. County Clerk has land records 1837-1886, marriage records 1835-1976, and probate records 1837-1944.

JASPER
Box 2070, Jasper, TX 75951, (409) 384-2632,
<www.co.jasper.tx.us>
- **INCORPORATED:** March 17, 1836
- **PARENT COUNTY:** Old Mexican Municipality known as Municipality of Bevil
- **BIRTH RECORDS:** start in 1903, kept by the County Clerk
- **DIVORCE:** unknown start, District/County Clerk
- **DEATH:** 1903, County Clerk
- **COURT:** 1850, County Clerk
- **NOTES:** County Clerk has land records 1849-1888, marriage records 1849-1921, and probate records 1849-1920. Fire destroyed county courthouse and records in 1849.

JEFF DAVIS
Box 398, Fort Davis, TX 79734, (915) 426-3251,
<www.co.jeff-davis.tx.us>
- **INCORPORATED:** March15, 1887
- **PARENT COUNTY:** Presidio
- **DIVORCE RECORDS:** unknown start, County Clerk
- **LAND:** 1887, County Clerk
- **PROBATE:** 1887, County Clerk
- **COURT:** 1887, County Clerk
- **NOTES:** County Clerk has birth records 1903-1950, death records 1903-1971, and marriage records 1887-1974.

JEFFERSON
Box 1151, Beaumont, TX 77704, (409) 835-8475,
<www.co.jefferson.tx.us>
- **INCORPORATED:** Dec. 21, 1837
- **PARENT COUNTY:** Old Mexican Municipality, Jefferson Municipality
- **BIRTH RECORDS:** start in 1903, kept by the County Clerk
- **DEATH:** 1903, County Clerk
- **MILITARY:** unknown start, County Clerk
- **NOTES:** District Clerk has court records 1844-1896, divorce records 1896-1908, and naturalization records 1894-1906. County Court has land records 1834-1887, marriage records 1837-1926, and probate records 1838-1965.

JIM HOGG
102 E. Tilley, Box 878, Hebbronville, TX 78361, (512) 527-4031,
<www.co.jim-hogg.tx.us>
- Incorporated: March 31, 1913
- **PARENT COUNTIES:** Brooks, Duval
- **BIRTH RECORDS:** start in 1913, kept by the County Clerk
- **MARRIAGE:** 1913, County Clerk
- **DIVORCE:** 1913, County Clerk
- **DEATH:** 1913, County Clerk
- **LAND:** 1913, County Clerk
- **PROBATE:** 1913, County Clerk
- **COURT:** 1913, County Clerk
- **MILITARY:** 1913, County Clerk

JIM WELLS
200 N. Almond St., Box 1459, Alice, TX 78332, (512) 668-5702,
<www.co.jim-wells.tx.us>
- **INCORPORATED:** March 25, 1911
- **PARENT COUNTY:** Nueces
- **BIRTH RECORDS:** start in 1912, kept by the County Clerk
- **MARRIAGE:** 1912, County Clerk
- **DIVORCE:** unknown start, District/County Clerk
- **LAND:** 1912, County Clerk
- **PROBATE:** 1912, County Clerk
- **COURT:** 1912, County Clerk
- **NOTES:** County Clerk has Death records 1900-2003.

JOHNSON
2 Main St., Box 662, Cleburne, TX 76031, (817) 556-6323,
<www.johnsoncountytx.org>
- **INCORPORATED:** Feb. 13, 1854
- **PARENT COUNTIES:** Ellis, Hill, Navarro, McLennan
- **NOTES:** County Clerk has birth records 1903-1985, death records 1903-1966, land records 1853-1911, marriage records 1860-1867, 1870-1942, naturalization records 1898-1904, and probate records 1854-1945. District Clerk has court records 1856-1934 and divorce records 1893-1936.

JONES
Box 552, Anson, TX 79501, (915) 823-3762,
<www.co.jones.tx.us>
- **INCORPORATED:** Feb. 1, 1858
- **PARENT COUNTIES:** Bexar, Bosque
- **BIRTH RECORDS:** start in 1903, kept by the County Clerk
- **MARRIAGE:** 1881, County Clerk
- **DIVORCE:** unknown start, District/County Clerk
- **DEATH:** 1903, County Clerk
- **LAND:** 1881, County Clerk
- **PROBATE:** 1881, County Clerk
- **COURT:** 1881, District/County Clerk

KARNES
101 N. Panna Maria St., Karnes City, TX 78118, (210) 780-3939,
<ww.co.karnes.tx.us>
- **INCORPORATED:** Feb. 4, 1854
- **PARENT COUNTIES:** Bexar, DeWitt, Goliad, San Patricio, Gonzales
- **BIRTH RECORDS:** start in 1903, kept by the County Clerk
- **DIVORCE:** unknown start, District/County Clerk
- **DEATH:** 1903, County Clerk
- **NOTES:** District Clerk has court records 1858-1910. County Clerk has land records 1855-1905, marriage records 1865-1910, naturalization records 1892-1924, and probate records 1865-1907.

KAUFMAN
County Courthouse 100 W. Mulberry St., Kaufman, TX 75142, (214) 932-4331 ext. 2, **<www.kaufmancounty.net>**
- **INCORPORATED:** Feb. 26, 1848
- **PARENT COUNTY:** Henderson
- **BIRTH RECORDS:** 1848, kept by the County Clerk
- **MARRIAGE:** 1848, County Clerk
- **NOTES:** District Clerk has court records 1848-1931, divorce records 1901-1945, naturalization records 1908-1913. County Clerk has Death records 1903-1966, land records 1849-1911, naturalization records 1892-1893, and probate records 1848-1940.

KENDALL
204 E. San Antonio St., Boerne, TX 78006, (210) 249-9343,
<www.co.kendall.tx.us>
- **INCORPORATED:** Jan 10, 1862
- **PARENT COUNTIES:** Kerr, Blanco
- **BIRTH RECORDS:** start in 1903, kept by the County Clerk
- **DEATH:** 1903, County Clerk
- **NOTES:** District Clerk has court records 1869-1939 and naturalization records 1876-1906. County Clerk has land records 1862-1887, marriage records 1862-1956, and probate records 1862-1977.

KENEDY
Box 1519, Sarita, TX 78385, (512) 294-5220,
<www.co.kenedy.tx.us>
- **INCORPORATED:** April 2, 1921
- **PARENT COUNTIES:** Willacy, Hidalgo, Cameron
- **BIRTH RECORDS:** start in 1903, kept by the County Clerk
- **DIVORCE:** 1911, County Clerk
- **DEATH:** 1903, County Clerk
- **COURT:** 1911, County Clerk
- **NOTES:** County Clerk has land records 1845-1911, marriage records 1911-1965, and probate records 1860-1911. 1911-1921 marriages were recorded as Willacy County. Probate records and land records are transcribed from parent counties' land records.

KENT
101 Main St., Box 9, Jayton, TX 79528, (806) 237-3881,
<www.co.kent.tx.us>
- **INCORPORATED:** Aug. 21, 1876
- **PARENT COUNTIES:** Bexar Territory, Young Territory
- **BIRTH RECORDS:** start in 1903, kept by the County Clerk
- **MARRIAGE:** 1892, County Clerk
- **DIVORCE:** 1892, County Clerk
- **DEATH:** 1903, County Clerk
- **LAND:** 1892 ,County Clerk
- **PROBATE:** 1892, County Clerk
- **COURT:** 1892, County Clerk

KERR
700 Main St. Suite 122, Kerrville, TX 78028, (210) 896-2844,
<www.co.kerr.tx.us>
- **INCORPORATED:** Jan. 26, 1856
- **PARENT COUNTY:** Bexar
- **BIRTH RECORDS:** start in 1903, kept by the County Clerk
- **MARRIAGE:** 1856, County Clerk
- **DIVORCE:** 1856, County Clerk
- **DEATH:** 1903, County Clerk
- **LAND:** 1856, County Clerk
- **PROBATE:** 1856, County Clerk
- **COURT:** 1856, County Clerk

KIMBLE
501 Main St., Junction, TX 76849, (915) 446-3353,
<www.co.kimble.tx.us>
- **INCORPORATED:** Jan. 22, 1858
- **PARENT COUNTY:** Bexar Land District
- **BIRTH RECORDS:** start in 1874, kept by the County Clerk
- **MARRIAGE:** 1884, County Clerk
- **DIVORCE:** 1884, County Clerk
- **DEATH:** 1903, County Clerk
- **LAND:** 1884, County Clerk
- **PROBATE:** 1884, County Clerk
- **COURT:** 1884, County Clerk
- **NOTES:** Kimble County was attached to Gillespie County until Sept. 6, 1875.

KING
Box 135, Guthrie, TX 79236, (806) 596-4412,
<www.kingcountytx.com>
- **INCORPORATED:** Aug. 21, 1876
- **PARENT COUNTY:** Bexar Land District
- **BIRTH RECORDS:** start in 1903, kept by the County Clerk
- **MARRIAGE:** 1914, County Clerk
- **DIVORCE:** unknown start, County Clerk
- **DEATH:** 1903, County Clerk
- **LAND:** 1914, County Clerk
- **PROBATE:** 1914, County Clerk
- **COURT:** 1914, County Clerk

KINNEY
Drawer 9, Brackettville, TX 78832, (210) 563-2521,
<www.co.kinney.tx.us>
- **INCORPORATED:** Jan. 28, 1850
- **PARENT COUNTY:** Bexar Land District
- **BIRTH RECORDS:** start in 1903, kept by the County Clerk
- **DIVORCE:** unknown start, District/County Clerk
- **DEATH:** 1903, County Clerk
- **NOTES:** District Clerk has court records 1873-1937 and naturalization records 1887-1906. County Clerk has land records 1872-1887, marriage 1872-1915, and probate records 1874-1913. St. Mary's Catholic Church, Brackettville, Texas has burial records.

KLEBERG
700 E. Kleberg, Box 312, Kingsville, TX 78364, (361) 595-8548,
<www.co.kleberg.tx.us>
- **INCORPORATED:** Feb. 27, 1913
- **PARENT COUNTY:** Nueces
- **BIRTH RECORDS:** start in 1913, kept by the County Clerk
- **MARRIAGE:** 1913, County Clerk
- **DIVORCE:** unknown start, District Clerk
- **DEATH:** 1913, County Clerk
- **LAND:** 1913, County Clerk
- **PROBATE:** 1913, County Clerk
- **COURT:** 1913, County Clerk

KNOX
Box 196, Benjamin, TX 79505, (817) 454-2441,
<www.knoxcountytexas.org>
- **INCORPORATED:** Feb. 1, 1858
- **PARENT COUNTIES:** Young, Bexar
- **BIRTH RECORDS:** start in 1903, kept by the County Clerk
- **MARRIAGE:** 1886, County Clerk
- **DIVORCE:** unknown start, County Clerk
- **DEATH:** 1903, County Clerk
- **LAND:** 1886, County Clerk

- **NOTES:** District Clerk has court records 1886-1937 and naturalization records 1906-1936. County Clerk has probate records 1886-1975.

LA SALLE

Box 340, Cotulla, TX 78014, (210) 780-2117, **<lasallecountytx.org>**

- **INCORPORATED:** Feb. 1, 1858
- **PARENT COUNTY:** Bexar
- **BIRTH RECORDS:** start in 1903, kept at the District/County Clerk
- **DIVORCE:** unknown start, District/County Clerk
- **DEATH:** 1903, District/County Clerk
- **NOTES:** District/County Clerk has court records 1881-1910, land records 1880-1896, marriage records 1880-1940, naturalization records 1882-1906, and probate records 1881-1949.

LAMAR

119 N. Main St., Paris, TX 75460, (903) 737-2420, **<www.co.lamar.tx.us>**

- **INCORPORATED:** Dec. 17, 1840
- **PARENT COUNTY:** Red River
- **BIRTH RECORDS:** 1903, kept by the County Clerk
- **MARRIAGE:** 1841, County Clerk
- **DIVORCE:** unknown start, District/County Clerk
- **DEATH:** 1903, County Clerk
- **PROBATE:** 1841, County Clerk
- **NOTES:** District Clerk has court records 1887-1927, naturalization records 1855-1925. County Clerk has land records 1841-1889.

LAMB

Box 3, Littlefield, TX 79339, (806) 385-5173, **<www.co.lamb.tx.us>**

- **INCORPORATED:** Aug. 21, 1876
- **PARENT COUNTY:** Bexar Land District
- **BIRTH RECORDS:** start in 1908, kept by the County Clerk
- **MARRIAGE:** 1909, County Clerk
- **DEATH:** 1908, County Clerk
- **LAND:** 1908, County Clerk
- **PROBATE:** 1909, County Clerk
- **COURT:** 1909, County Clerk

LAMPASAS

Box 347, Lampasas, TX 76550, (512) 556-8271 ext. 3, **<www.co.lampasas.tx.us>**

- **INCORPORATED:** Feb. 1, 1856
- **PARENT COUNTIES:** Bell, Travis, Coryell
- **BIRTH RECORDS:** start in 1903, kept by the County Clerk
- **DEATH:** 1903, County Clerk
- **LAND:** 1872, County Clerk
- **NOTES:** District Clerk has court records 1877-1926 and naturalization records 1909-1914. County Clerk has marriage records 1886-1937 and probate records 1876-1937.

LAVACA

Box 326, Hallettsville, TX 77964, (512) 798-3612, **<www.co.lavaca.tx.us>**

- **INCORPORATED:** April 6, 1846
- **PARENT COUNTIES:** Colorado, Victoria, Jackson, Gonzales, Fayette
- **BIRTH RECORDS:** start in 1903, kept by the County Clerk
- **DEATH:** 1903, County Clerk
- **NOTES:** County Clerk has birth records 1870-1879, land records 1846-1889, marriage records 1847-1917, naturalization records 1856-1935, and probate records 1846-1916. District Clerk has court records 1847-1974. From 1842-1846 area was known as La Baca County.

LEE

Box 419, Giddings, TX 78942, (409) 542-3684, **<www.co.lee.tx.us>**

- **INCORPORATED:** April14, 1874
- **PARENT COUNTIES:** Bastrop, Burleson, Washington, Fayette
- **NOTES:** County Clerk has birth records 1873-1985, death records 1903-1985, land records 1874-1908, marriage records 1874-1937, and probate records 1874-1936. District Clerk has court records 1874-1932, divorce records 1901-1952, and naturalization records 1876-1936.

LEON

Box 98, Centerville, TX 75833, (903) 536-2352, **<www.co.leon.tx.us>**

- **INCORPORATED:** March 17, 1846
- **PARENT COUNTY:** Robertson
- **BIRTH RECORDS:** start in 1903, kept by the County Clerk
- **DIVORCE:** 1884, District Clerk
- **NOTES:** District Clerk has court records 1846-1937. County Clerk has death records 1903-1934, land records 1846-1903, marriage records 1885-1935, and probate records 1846-1933.

LIBERTY

1923 Sam Houston St., Box 369, Liberty, TX 77575, (409) 336-4670, **<www.co.liberty.tx.us>**

- **INCORPORATED:** March 17, 1836
- **PARENT COUNTY:** Old Mexican municipality called Villa de la Santisima Trinidad de la Libertad
- **BIRTH RECORDS:** start in 1903, kept by the County Clerk
- **DIVORCE:** unknown start, District/County Clerk
- **DEATH:** 1903, County Clerk
- **NOTES:** District Clerk has court records 1874-1910. County Clerk has land records 1875-1886, marriage records 1875-1919, and probate records 1873-1917. Courthouse burned Dec. 11, 1874; records destroyed.

LIMESTONE

200 W. State St., Box 350, Groesbeck, TX 76642, (817) 729-5504, **<www.co.limestone.tx.us>**

- **INCORPORATED:** April 11, 1846
- **PARENT COUNTY:** Robertson
- **BIRTH RECORDS:** start in 1903, kept by the County Clerk
- **DIVORCE:** unknown start, District/County Clerk
- **DEATH:** 1903, County Clerk
- **COURT:** 1873, County Clerk
- **NOTES:** County Clerk has land records 1873-1889, marriage records 1873-1946, probate records 1876-1918, and military records for 1861 and 1936. Original county courthouse along with all county records was burned in 1873.

LIPSCOMB

Box 70, Lipscomb, TX 79056, (806) 862-3091, **<www.co.lipscomb.tx.us>**

- **INCORPORATED:** Aug. 21, 1876
- **PARENT COUNTY:** Bexar Land District
- **BIRTH RECORDS:** start in 1903, kept by the County Clerk
- **DIVORCE:** 1887, County Clerk
- **DEATH:** 1903, County Clerk
- **LAND:** 1887, County Clerk
- **PROBATE:** 1887, County Clerk
- **COURT:** 1887, County Clerk
- **NOTES:** County Clerk has marriage records 1851-1900.

LIVE OAK

Box 280, George West, TX 78022, (512) 449-2733, **<www.co.live-oak.tx.us>**

- **INCORPORATED:** Feb. 2, 1856
- **PARENT COUNTIES:** Nueces, San Patricio
- **BIRTH RECORDS:** , start in 1903, kept by the County Clerk
- **DEATH:** 1903, County Clerk
- **COURT:** 1856, County Clerk
- **NOTES:** County Clerk has divorce records for 1860 and 1867-1868, land records 1856-1886, marriage records 1857-1926, and probate records 1857-1903.

LLANO

109 W. Sandstone, Llano, TX 78643, (915) 247-4455, **<www.co.llano.tx.us>**

- **INCORPORATED:** Feb. 1, 1856
- **PARENT COUNTY:** Bexar, Gillespie
- **BIRTH RECORDS:** start in 1903, kept by the County Clerk
- **NOTES:** District Clerk has court and divorce records 1882-1940 and naturalization records 1882-1925. County Clerk has death records 1903-1966, land records 1880-1928, marriage records 1880-1957, military discharge records 1919-1943, and probate records 1881-1955.

LOVING

Box 194, Mentone, TX 79754, (915) 377-2441, **<www.lovingcountytexas.us>**

- **PARENT COUNTY:** Tom Green
- **BIRTH RECORDS:** start in 1886, kept by the County Clerk
- **DIVORCE:** 1931, County Clerk
- **LAND:** 1931, County Clerk
- **PROBATE:** 1931, County Clerk
- **COURT:** 1931, County Clerk
- **NOTES:** County Clerk has death records 1931-1951 and marriage records 1931-1974. Attached to Reeves County. Organized July 8, 1893; dissolved May 12, 1897; reorganized 1931.

LUBBOCK

904 Broadway, Box 10536, Lubbock, TX 79408, (806) 765-1042, **<www.co.lubbock.tx.us>**

- **INCORPORATED:** Aug. 21, 1876
- **PARENT COUNTY:** Bexar Land District
- **BIRTH RECORDS:** start in 1903, kept by the County Clerk
- **DEATH:** 1903, County Clerk
- **LAND:** 1891, County Clerk
- **PROBATE:** 1891, County Clerk
- **COURT:** 1891, County Clerk
- **NOTES:** County Clerk has marriage records 1891-1975. Attached to Crosby, Young and Baylor counties at one time. Officially formed March 10, 1891.

LYNN

Box 937, Tahoka, TX 79373, (806) 998-4750, **<www.co.lynn.tx.us>**

- **INCORPORATED:** Aug. 21, 1876
- **PARENT COUNTY:** Bexar Land District
- **LAND RECORDS:** 1903, County Clerk
- **PROBATE:** 1903, County Clerk
- **COURT:** 1903, County Clerk
- **NOTES:** County Clerk has birth records 1870-1946, death records 1904-1971, and marriage records 1903-1962.

MADISON

Box 599, Anderson, TX 77830, (936) 348-2638, **<www.co.madison.tx.us>**

- **INCORPORATED:** Jan. 27, 1853
- **PARENT COUNTIES:** Leon, Grimes, Walker
- **BIRTH RECORDS:** start in 1903, kept by the County Clerk
- **DEATH:** 1903, County Clerk
- **LAND:** 1873, County Clerk
- **PROBATE:** 1873, County Clerk
- **NOTES:** District Clerk has court records 1873-1904. County Clerk has marriage records 1874-1940.

MARION

Box F, Jefferson, TX 75657, (903) 665-3971, **<www.co.marion.tx.us>**

- **INCORPORATED:** Feb. 8, 1860
- **PARENT COUNTY:** Cass
- **NOTES:** County Clerk has birth records 1873-1876, 1903-1940, death records 1903-1940, land records 1838-1850, 1860-1900, marriage records 1860-1937, naturalization records 1871-1938,and probate records 1860-1943. District Clerk has court records 1860-1934. 1838-1850 land records transcribed from Bowie, Cass, Harrison, Red River, and Titus counties.

MARTIN

Box 906, Stanton, TX 79782, (915) 756-3412, **<www.rootsweb.ancestry.com/~txmartin>**

- **INCORPORATED:** Aug. 21, 1876
- **PARENT COUNTY:** Bexar Land District
- **DIVORCE RECORDS:** unknown start, District/County Clerk
- **DEATH:** 1910, County Clerk
- **LAND:** 1885, County Clerk
- **PROBATE:** 1885, County Clerk
- **COURT:** 1885, County Clerk
- **NOTES:** County Clerk has birth records 1873-1950 and marriage records 1885-1950. Martin County was attached to Mitchell County for five months after county formation; then, Martin County was attached to Howard County until 1884.

MASON
Box 702, Mason, TX 76856, (915) 347-5253,
<us-gen.com/tx/mason>
- **INCORPORATED:** Jan. 22, 1858
- **PARENT COUNTIES:** Gillespie, Bexar Land District
- **BIRTH RECORDS:** start in 1903, kept by the County Clerk
- **MARRIAGE:** 1877, County Clerk
- **DIVORCE:** unknown start, County Clerk
- **DEATH:** 1903, County Clerk
- **LAND:** 1877, County Clerk
- **PROBATE:** 1877, County Clerk
- **COURT:** 1877, County Clerk

MATAGORDA
Box 69, Bay City, TX 77404, (409) 244-7680,
<www.co.matagorda.tx.us>
- **INCORPORATED:** March 17, 1836
- **PARENT COUNTY:** Old Mexican Municipality called Matagorda
- **BIRTH RECORDS:** start in 1903,kept by the County Clerk
- **DEATH:** 1903, County Clerk
- **NOTES:** District Clerk has court records 1837-1947. County Clerk has land records 1837-1898, marriage records 1837-1927, and probate records 1837-1913.

MAVERICK
500 Quarry St Box 4050, Eagle Pass, TX 78853, (210) 773-2829,
<www.co.maverick.tx.us>
- **INCORPORATED:** Feb. 2, 1856
- **PARENT COUNTY:** Kinney
- **BIRTH RECORDS:** start in 1903, kept by the County Clerk
- **DEATH:** 1903, County Clerk
- **NOTES:** District Clerk has court records 1871-1905. County Clerk has land records 1871-1923, marriage records 1871-1917, naturalization records 1871-1926, and probate records 1876-1913.

MCCULLOCH
County Courthouse Courthouse Sq., Brady, TX 76825, (915) 597-0733, **<www.co.mcculloch.tx.us>**
- **INCORPORATED:** Aug. 27, 1856
- **PARENT COUNTY:** Bexar
- **BIRTH RECORDS:** start in 1903, kept by the County Clerk
- **MARRIAGE:** 1876, County Clerk
- **DEATH:** 1903, County Clerk
- **LAND:** 1876, County Clerk
- **COURT:** 1876, County Clerk
- **PROBATE:** 1876, County Clerk

MCLENNAN
215 N. Fifth, Box 1727, Waco, TX 76703, (817) 757-5078,
<www.co.mclennan.tx.us>
- **INCORPORATED:** Jan. 22, 1850
- **PARENT COUNTIES:** Milam, Limestone, Navarro
- **DEATH RECORDS:** 1903, County Clerk
- **NOTES:** County Clerk has birth records 1908-1917, land records 1850-1906, marriage records 1850-1916, naturalization records 1855-1907, and probate records 1861-1949. District Clerk has court records 1893-1904 and divorce records 1851-1907.

MCMULLEN
Box 235, Tilden, TX 78072, (512) 274-3215, **<www.rootsweb.ancestry.com/~txmcmull>**
- **PARENT COUNTIES:** Bexar, Live Oak, Atascosa
- **BIRTH RECORDS:** start in 1903,kept by the County Clerk
- **DEATH:** 1903, County Clerk
- **NOTES:** District Clerk has court records 1879-1919 and naturalization records 1892-1904. County Clerk has land records 1871-1910, marriage records 1877-1918, and probate records 1877-1925. Officially organized in 1877.

MEDINA
County Courthouse 110 16th St., Hondo, TX 78861, (210) 741-6040,
<www.rootsweb.ancestry.com/~txmedina>
- **INCORPORATED:** Feb. 12, 1848
- **PARENT COUNTY:** Bexar Land District
- **BIRTH RECORDS:** start in 1903, kept by the County Clerk
- **DEATH:** 1903, County Clerk
- **NOTES:** District Clerk has court records 1849-1909. County Clerk has land records 1848-1886, and marriage and probate records 1848-1977.

MENARD
Box 1028, Menard, TX 76859, (915) 396-4682,
<www.menardtexas.com>
- **INCORPORATED:** Jan. 22, 1858
- **PARENT COUNTY:** Bexar Land District
- **BIRTH RECORDS:** start in 1903, kept by the County Clerk
- **MARRIAGE:** 1871, County Clerk
- **DIVORCE:** unknown start, County Clerk
- **DEATH:** 1903, County Clerk
- **LAND:** 1871, County Clerk
- **PROBATE:** 1871, County Clerk
- **COURT:** 1871, County Clerk

MIDLAND
200 W. Wall, Box 211, Midland, TX 79701, (915) 688-1070,
<www.co.midland.tx.us>
- **INCORPORATED:** March 4, 1885
- **PARENT COUNTY:** Tom Green
- **BIRTH RECORDS:** start in 1903, kept by the County Clerk
- **MARRIAGE:** 1885 ,County Clerk
- **DEATH:** 1903, County Clerk
- **LAND:** 1885, County Clerk
- **COURT:** 1886, County Clerk
- **NOTES:** District Clerk has divorce records 1886-1900. County Clerk has Probate records 1886-1893.

MILAM
107 W. Main,. Box 191, Cameron, TX 76520, (254) 697-7049,
<www.milamcounty.org>
- **INCORPORATED:** March 17,1836
- **PARENT COUNTIES:** Old Mexican Municipality, Municipality of Milam
- **BIRTH RECORDS:** start in 1903, kept by the County Clerk
- **MARRIAGE:** 1874, County Clerk
- **DEATH:** 1903, County Clerk
- **LAND:** 1874, County Clerk

- **PROBATE:** 1874, County Clerk
- **COURT:** 1872, County Clerk
- **NOTES:** County Clerk has School Census records 1909-1970.

MILLS
Box 646, Goldthwaite, TX 76844, (915) 648-2711,
<www.co.mills.tx.us>
- **INCORPORATED:** March15, 1887
- **PARENT COUNTIES:** Comanche, Brown, Hamilton, Lampasas
- **BIRTH RECORDS:** 1903, County Clerk
- **MARRIAGE:** 1887, County Clerk
- **DEATH:** 1903, County Clerk
- **DIVORCE:** 1887, County Clerk
- **LAND:** 1887, County Clerk
- **PROBATE:** 1887, County Clerk
- **COURT:** 1887, County Clerk

MITCHELL
349 Oak St. Room 103, Colorado City, TX 79512, (915) 728-3481,
<www.rootsweb.ancestry.com/~txmitche>
- **INCORPORATED:** Aug. 21, 1876
- **PARENT COUNTY:** Bexar Land District
- **BIRTH RECORDS:** start in 1903, kept by the County Clerk
- **MARRIAGE:** 1881, County Clerk
- **DEATH:** 1903, County Clerk
- **LAND:** 1881, County Clerk
- **PROBATE:** 1881, County Clerk
- **COURT:** 1881, County Clerk

MONTAGUE
Box 77, Montague, TX 76251, (817) 894-2461,
<www.co.montague.tx.us>
- **INCORPORATED:** Dec. 24, 1857
- **PARENT COUNTY:** Cooke
- **BIRTH RECORDS:** start in 1903, kept by the County Clerk
- **DEATH:** 1903, County Clerk
- **NOTES:** County Clerk has court records 1876-1985, land records 1873-1926, marriage records 1873-1940, and probate records 1874-1950. District Clerk has divorce records 1921-1946 and naturalization records 1885-1927.

MONTGOMERY
301 N. Main, Box 959, Conroe, TX 77305, (409) 539-7885,
<www.co.montgomery.tx.us>
- **INCORPORATED:** Dec. 14, 1837
- **PARENT COUNTY:** Washington
- **BIRTH RECORDS:** start in 1903, kept by the County Clerk
- **MARRIAGE:** 1838, County Clerk
- **DIVORCE:** unknown start, District Clerk
- **DEATH:** 1903, County Clerk
- **PROBATE:** 1839, County Clerk
- **NOTES:** District Clerk has court records 1839-1912. County Clerk has land records 1838-1887.

MOORE
715 Dumas Ave. Room 105, Dumas, TX 79029, (806) 935-6164,
<www.co.moore.tx.us>
- **INCORPORATED:** Aug. 21, 1876
- **PARENT COUNTY:** Bexar
- **BIRTH RECORDS:** start in 1903, kept by the County Clerk
- **MARRIAGE:** 1892, County Clerk
- **DIVORCE:** unknown start, District/County Clerk
- **DEATH:** 1903, County Clerk
- **LAND:** 1882, County Clerk
- **PROBATE:** 1892, County Clerk
- **COURT:** 1892, County Clerk

MORRIS
500 Broadnax St., Daingerfield, TX 75638, (903) 645-3911,
<www.co.morris.tx.us>
- **INCORPORATED:** March 13, 1875
- **PARENT COUNTY:** Titus
- **BIRTH RECORDS:** start in 1903, kept by the County Clerk
- **DIVORCE:** unknown start, District Clerk
- **DEATH:** 1903, County Clerk
- **NOTES:** District Clerk has court records 1875-1954. County Clerk has land records 1875-1910, marriage records 1875-1940, and probate records 1876-1955.

MOTLEY
701 Dundee, Box 66, Matador, TX 79244, (806) 347-2334,
<www.co.motley.tx.us>
- **INCORPORATED:** Aug. 21, 1876
- **PARENT COUNTY:** Bexar Land District
- **BIRTH RECORDS:** start in 1903, kept by the County Clerk
- **MARRIAGE:** 1891, County Clerk
- **DIVORCE:** 1891, County Clerk
- **DEATH:** 1903, County Clerk
- **PROBATE:** 1891, County Clerk
- **COURT:** 1891. County Clerk
- **NOTES:** Motley County was organized in 1891.

NACOGDOCHES
101 W. Main St., Nacogdoches, TX 75961, (409) 560-7733,
<www.co.nacogdoches.tx.us>
- **INCORPORATED:** March 17, 1836
- **PARENT COUNTY:** Old Mexican Municipality, Municipality of Nacogdoches
- **BIRTH RECORDS:** start in 1903, kept by the County Clerk
- **DIVORCE:** unknown start, District/County Clerk
- **DEATH:** 1903, County Clerk
- **COURT:** 1837, County Clerk
- **NOTES:** County Clerk has land records 1826-1887, marriage records 1820-1918, and probate records 1838-1917. County Archives has military records 1820-1830.

NAVARRO
300 W. Third Ave., Box 423, Corsicana, TX 75151, (903) 654-3035,
<www.co.navarro.tx.us>
- **PARENT COUNTY:** Robertson
- **NOTES:** County Clerk has birth records 1873-1987, death records 1903-1988, land records 1846-1912, marriage records 1846-1942, and probate records 1847-1978. District Clerk has court records 1855-1936, divorce records 1905-1937, and naturalization records 1894-1914.

NEWTON
Box 484, Newton, TX 75966, (409) 379-5341,
<www.co.newton.tx.us>
- **INCORPORATED:** April 22, 1846
- **PARENT COUNTY:** Jasper
- **BIRTH RECORDS:** start in 1903, kept by the County Clerk
- **DEATH:** 1903, County Clerk
- **COURT:** 1846, County Clerk
- **NOTES:** County Clerk has land records 1846-1889, marriage records 1846-1923, and probate records 1846-1920.

NOLAN
Box 98, Sweetwater, TX 79556, (915) 235-2462,
<www.co.nolan.tx.us>
- **INCORPORATED:** Aug. 21, 1876
- **PARENT COUNTY:** Bexar Land District, Young
- **BIRTH RECORDS:** start in 1903, kept by the County Clerk
- **MARRIAGE:** 1881, County Clerk
- **DIVORCE:** unknown start, District/County Clerk
- **DEATH:** 1900, County Clerk
- **LAND:** 1881, County Clerk
- **PROBATE:** 1881, County Clerk
- **COURT:** 1881, County Clerk

NUECES
Box 2627 Corpus Christi, TX 78403, (512) 888-0580,
<www.co.nueces.tx.us>
- **INCORPORATED:** April 18, 1846
- **PARENT COUNTY:** San Patricio
- **BIRTH RECORDS:** start in 1903, kept by the County Clerk
- **DEATH:** 1903, County Clerk
- **NOTES:** District Clerk has court records 1850-1910 and naturalization records 1912-1914. County Clerk has land records 1847-1902, marriage records 1846-1906, naturalization records 1852-1906, and probate records 1846-1907.

OCHILTREE
511 S. Main St., Perryton, TX 79070, (806) 435-8105,
<www.co.ochiltree.tx.us>
- **INCORPORATED:** Aug. 21, 1876
- **PARENT COUNTY:** Bexar Land District
- **BIRTH RECORDS:** start in 1903, kept by the County Clerk
- **DEATH:** 1903, County Clerk
- **MARRIAGE:** 1889, County Clerk
- **PROBATE:** 1889, County Clerk
- **LAND:** 1889, County Clerk
- **COURT:** 1889, County Clerk
- **DIVORCE:** unknown start, District/County Clerk

OLDHAM
Box 360, Vega, TX 79092, (806) 267-2667,
<www.co.oldham.tx.us>
- **INCORPORATED:** Aug. 21, 1876
- **PARENT COUNTY:** Bexar Land District
- **BIRTH RECORDS:** start in 1903, kept by the County Clerk
- **MARRIAGE:** 1881, County Clerk
- **DIVORCE:** 1881, County Clerk
- **DEATH:** 1903, County Clerk
- **LAND:** 1881, County Clerk
- **PROBATE:** 1887, County Clerk
- **COURT:** 1881, County Clerk

ORANGE
801 W. Division St., Box 1536, Orange, TX 77630, (409) 882-7055,
<www.co.orange.tx.us>
- **INCORPORATED:** Jan. 5, 1852
- **PARENT COUNTY:** Jefferson
- **BIRTH RECORDS:** start in 1903, kept by the County Clerk
- **DIVORCE:** unknown start, District Clerk
- **DEATH:** 1903, County Clerk
- **NOTES:** District Clerk has court records 1852-1909. County Clerk has land records 1852-1905, marriage records 1852-1921, naturalization records 1871-1909, and probate records 1852-1942.

PALO PINTO
Box 219, Palo Pinto, TX 76484, (817) 659-1277,
<www.co.palo-pinto.tx.us>
- **INCORPORATED:** Aug. 27, 1856
- **PARENT COUNTIES:** Navarro, Bosque
- **BIRTH RECORDS:** start in 1903, kept by the County Clerk
- **MARRIAGE:** 1858, County Clerk
- **DIVORCE:** unknown start, District/County Clerk
- **DEATH:** 1903, County Clerk
- **LAND:** 1858, County Clerk
- **PROBATE:** 1858, County Clerk
- **COURT:** 1858, County Clerk

PANOLA
110 W. Sycamore St., Carthage, TX 75633, (903) 693-0302,
<www.co.panola.tx.us>
- **INCORPORATED:** March 30, 1846
- **PARENT COUNTIES:** Harrison, Shelby
- **BIRTH RECORDS:** start in 1903, kept by the County Clerk
- **DEATH:** 1903, County Clerk
- **COURT:** 1846, County Clerk
- **NOTES:** County Clerk has land records 1846-1887, marriage records 1846-1950, and probate records 1846-1923.

PARKER
1112 Santa Fe, Box 819, Weatherford, TX 76086, (817) 594-7461,
<www.co.parker.tx.us>
- **INCORPORATED:** Dec. 12, 1855
- **PARENT COUNTIES:** Bosque, Navarro
- **BIRTH RECORDS:** start in 1903, kept by the County Clerk
- **DEATH:** 1903, County Clerk
- **NOTES:** District Clerk has court records 1874-1931 and divorce records 1900-1944. County Clerk has land records 1874-19089, marriage records 1874-1939, naturalization records 1874-1930, and probate records 1860-1935.

PARMER
401 Third St., Box 356, Farwell, TX 79325, (806) 481-3691,
<www.co.parmer.tx.us>
- **INCORPORATED:** Aug. 21, 1876
- **PARENT COUNTY:** Bexar Land District
- **BIRTH RECORDS:** start in 1903, kept by the County Clerk

- **MARRIAGE:** 1907, County Clerk
- **DIVORCE:** unknown start, District/County Clerk
- **DEATH:** 1903, County Clerk
- **LAND:** 1907, County Clerk
- **PROBATE:** 1907, County Clerk
- **COURT:** 1907, County Clerk

PECOS

103 W. Callaghan St., Fort Stockton, TX 79735, (915) 336-7555, **<www.co.pecos.tx.us>**

- **INCORPORATED:** May 3, 1871
- **PARENT COUNTY:** Presidio
- **BIRTH RECORDS:** start in 1903, kept by the County Clerk
- **LAND:** 1875, County Clerk
- **PROBATE:** 1875, County Clerk
- **COURT:** 1825, District Clerk
- **NOTES:** County Clerk has death records 1903-1965 and marriage records for 1875-1951, 1983, 1991, and 1995.

POLK

101 Church St. W., Drawer 2119, Livingston, TX 77351, (409) 327-8210, **<www.co.polk.tx.us>**

- **INCORPORATED:** March 30, 1846
- **PARENT COUNTY:** Liberty Municipality
- **BIRTH RECORDS:** start in 1903, kept by the County Clerk
- **DIVORCE:** unknown start, District/County Clerk
- **DEATH:** 1903, County Clerk
- **NOTES:** District Clerk has court records 1848-1868, 1872-1879, and 1883-1909. County Clerk has land records 1846-1898, marriage records 1846-1937, and probate records 1840-1976.

POTTER

501 S. Filmore, Box 9638, Amarillo, TX 79101, (806) 379-2275, **<www.co.potter.tx.us/home.html>**

- **INCORPORATED:** Aug. 21, 1876
- **PARENT COUNTY:** Bexar Land District
- **MARRIAGE RECORDS:** 1887, County Clerk
- **DIVORCE:** unknown start, District Clerk
- **LAND:** 1887, County Clerk
- **PROBATE:** 1887, County Clerk
- **COURT:** 1889, County Clerk
- **NOTES:** County Clerk has birth and death records 1941-1951.

PRESIDIO

County Courthouse, 320 N. Highland St., Box 789, Marfa, TX 79843, (915) 729-4812, **<www.co.presidio.tx.us>**

- **INCORPORATED:** Jan. 3, 1850
- **PARENT COUNTY:** Bexar Land District
- **BIRTH RECORDS:** start in 1903, kept by the County Clerk
- **MARRIAGE:** 1875, County Clerk
- **DIVORCE:** 1876, County Clerk
- **DEATH:** 1903, County Clerk
- **LAND:** 1876, County Clerk
- **PROBATE:** 1875, County Clerk
- **COURT:** 1876, County Clerk

RAINS

100 Quitman St Box 187, Emory, TX 75440, (903) 473-2461, **<www.co.rains.tx.us>**

- **INCORPORATED:** June 9, 1870
- **PARENT COUNTIES:** Hopkins, Hunt, Wood
- **BIRTH RECORDS:** start in 1903, kept by the County Clerk
- **MARRIAGE:** 1879, County Clerk
- **DIVORCE:** unknown start, District/County Clerk
- **DEATH:** 1903, County Clerk
- **LAND:** 1870, County Clerk
- **PROBATE:** 1880, County Clerk
- **COURT:** 1880, County Clerk

RANDALL

401 Fifteenth St., Box 660, Canyon, TX 79015, (806) 655-6330, **<www.randallcounty.org>**

- **INCORPORATED:** Aug. 21, 1876
- **PARENT COUNTY:** Bexar Land District
- **BIRTH RECORDS:** start in 1903, kept by the County Clerk
- **MARRIAGE:** 1889, County Clerk
- **DIVORCE:** unknown start, District/County Clerk
- **DEATH:** 1903, County Clerk
- **LAND:** 1889, County Clerk
- **PROBATE:** 1889, County Clerk
- **COURT:** 1889, County Clerk
- **NOTES:** County was unorganized until 1889. 1876-1889 Randall County was attached to Jack County (1876-1879), Wheeler County (1879-1881, Oldham County (1881-1883), Donley County (1883-1885), and Oldham (1885-1889).

REAGAN

Box 100, Big Lake, TX 76932, (915) 884-2442, **<www.rootsweb.ancestry.com/~txreagan>**

- **INCORPORATED:** March7, 1903
- **PARENT COUNTY:** Tom Green
- **BIRTH RECORDS:** start in 1903, kept by the County Clerk
- **MARRIAGE:** 1903, County Clerk
- **DIVORCE:** 1903, County Clerk
- **DEATH:** 1903, County Clerk
- **LAND:** 1903, County Clerk
- **PROBATE:** 1903, County Clerk
- **COURT:** 1903, County Clerk
- **NOTES:** Some records from 1883 transferred from Tom Green County.

REAL

Box 656, Leakey, TX 78873, (210) 232-5202, **<www.co.real.tx.us>**

- **INCORPORATED:** April 3, 1913
- **PARENT COUNTIES:** Bandera, Kerr, Edwards
- **BIRTH RECORDS:** start in 1913, kept by the County Clerk
- **MARRIAGE:** 1913, County Clerk
- **DIVORCE:** 1913, County Clerk
- **DEATH:** 1913, County Clerk
- **LAND:** 1913, County Clerk
- **PROBATE:** 1913, County Clerk
- **COURT:** 1913, County Clerk

RED RIVER

Red River County Annex, 200 N. Walnut St., Clarksville, TX 75426, (903) 427-2401, **<www.co.red-river.tx.us>**

- **INCORPORATED:** March 7, 1836
- **PARENT COUNTY:** Red River District
- **BIRTH RECORDS:** start in 1903, kept by the County Clerk
- **DIVORCE:** unknown start, District/County Clerk
- **DEATH:** 1903, County Clerk
- **NOTES:** District Clerk has court records 1840-1910 and naturalization records 1839-1927. County Clerk has land records 1838-1886, marriage records 1846-1934, and probate records 1838-1887.

REEVES

100 E. Fourteenth St., Box 867, Pecos, TX 79772, (915) 445-5467, **<www.rootsweb.ancestry.com/~txreeves>**

- **INCORPORATED:** April14, 1883
- **PARENT COUNTY:** Pecos
- **BIRTH RECORDS:** start in 1903, kept by the County Clerk
- **MARRIAGE:** 1884, County Clerk
- **DEATH:** 1903, County Clerk
- **LAND:** 1884, County Clerk
- **PROBATE:** 1884, County Clerk
- **COURT:** 1885, County Clerk
- **NOTES:** County Clerk has some deferred birth records from the 1800s.

REFUGIO

808 Commerce St. Room 112, Box 736, Refugio, TX 78377, (512) 526-2233, **<www.co.refugio.tx.us>**

- **INCORPORATED:** March17, 1836
- **PARENT COUNTY:** Refugio Municipality
- **BIRTH RECORDS:** start in 1903, kept by the County Clerk
- **DEATH:** 1903, County Clerk
- **NOTES:** County Clerk has court records 1879-1922, land records 1839-1904, marriage records 1851-1956, naturalization records 1854-1904, and probate records 1840-1909.

ROBERTS

Box 477, Miami, TX 79059, (806) 868-2341, **<www.co.roberts.tx.us>**

- **INCORPORATED:** Aug. 21, 1876
- **PARENT COUNTIES:** Bexar County, Clay Land District
- **BIRTH RECORDS:** start in 1903, kept by the County Clerk
- **MARRIAGE:** 1889, County Clerk
- **DIVORCE:** 1889, County Clerk
- **DEATH:** 1903, County Clerk
- **LAND:** 1889, County Clerk
- **PROBATE:** 1889, County Clerk
- **COURT:** 1889, County Clerk
- **NOTES:** County was organized in January 1889. From 1876-1889 Roberts was attached to Wheeler County.

ROBERTSON

Box 1029, Franklin, TX 77856, (409) 828-4130, **<www.co.robertson.tx.us>**

- **INCORPORATED:** Dec. 14, 1837
- **PARENT COUNTIES:** Milam, Bexar, Nacogdoches
- **BIRTH RECORDS:** start in 1903, kept by the County Clerk
- **MARRIAGE:** 1838, County Clerk
- **NOTES:** District Clerk has court records 1838-1972 and divorce records 1903-1972. County Clerk has death records 1903-1934, land records 1838-1901, naturalization records 1874-1941, and probate records 1838-1974.

ROCKWALL

101 E. Rusk St., Rockwall, TX 75087, (214) 771-5141, **<www.rockwallcountytexas.com>**

- **INCORPORATED:** March 1, 1873
- **PARENT COUNTY:** Kaufman
- **BIRTH RECORDS:** start in 1903, kept by the County Clerk
- **MARRIAGE:** 1875, County Clerk
- **DEATH:** 1903, County Clerk
- **NOTES:** District Clerk has court records 1874-1978. County Clerk has land records 1873-1901 and probate records 1877-1938.

RUNNELS

600 Courthouse Sq., Box 189, Ballinger, TX 76821, (915) 365-2720, **<www.co.runnels.tx.us>**

- **INCORPORATED:** Feb. 1, 1858
- **PARENT COUNTIES:** Bexar, Travis
- **BIRTH RECORDS:** start in 1903, kept by the County Clerk
- **MARRIAGE:** 1880, County Clerk
- **DIVORCE:** unknown start, District/County Clerk
- **DEATH:** 1903, County Clerk
- **LAND:** 1880, County Clerk
- **PROBATE:** 1880, County Clerk
- **COURT:** 1881, County Clerk

RUSK

2115 N. Main St., Box 758, Henderson, TX 75653, (903) 657-0330, **<www.co.rusk.tx.us>**

- **INCORPORATED:** Jan. 16, 1843
- **PARENT COUNTY:** Nacogdoches
- **DEATH RECORDS:** 1903, County Clerk
- **DIVORCE:** 1847, District Court
- **NOTES:** County Clerk has birth records 1873-1876, 1903-1917, land records 1843-1845, 1851-1887, marriage records 1839-1917, and probate records 1847-1930. District Clerk has court records 1847-1930. Courthouse fire in 1878 destroyed some records.

SABINE

Drawer 580, Hemphill, TX 75948, (409) 787-3786, **<www.sabinecountytexas.com>**

- **INCORPORATED:** March17, 1836
- **PARENT COUNTY:** Sabine Municipality
- **BIRTH RECORDS:** start in 1903, kept by the County Clerk
- **DIVORCE:** unknown start, District/County Clerk
- **DEATH:** 1903, County Clerk
- **COURT:** 1876, County Clerk
- **NOTES:** County Clerk has land records 1876-1891, marriage records 1875-1919, and probate records 1879-1923. Fire destroyed most pre-1875 records.

SAN AUGUSTINE

100 W. Columbia St., San Augustine, TX 75972, (409) 275-2452, **<www.co.san-augustine.tx.us>**

- **INCORPORATED:** March 17, 1836
- **PARENT COUNTY:** San Augustine Municipality
- **BIRTH RECORDS:** start in 1903, kept by the County Clerk
- **DIVORCE:** unknown start, District/County Clerk
- **DEATH:** 1903, County Clerk
- **COURT:** 1837, District Clerk
- **NOTES:** County Clerk has land records 1833-1901, marriage records 1837-1920, and probate records 1837-1920.

SAN JACINTO

Box 669, Cold Spring, TX 77331, (409) 653-2324, **<www.co.san-jacinto.tx.us>**

- **INCORPORATED:** Aug. 13, 1870
- **PARENT COUNTIES:** Liberty, Polk, Montgomery, Walker
- **BIRTH RECORDS:** start in 1888, kept by the County Clerk
- **DEATH:** 1888, County Clerk
- **NOTES:** District Clerk has court records 1872-1954 and divorce records 1900-1931. County Clerk has land records 1870-1886, marriage records 1870-1965, and probate records 1876-1926.

SAN PATRICIO

400 W. Sinton Room 105, Box 578, Sinton, TX 78387, (512) 364-6290, **<www.co.san-patricio.tx.us>**

- **INCORPORATED:** March 17, 1836
- **PARENT COUNTY:** San Patricio Municipality
- **BIRTH RECORDS:** start in 1903, kept by the County Clerk
- **DEATH:** 1903, County Clerk
- **NOTES:** District Clerk has court records 1848-1896. County Clerk has land records 1846-1896, marriage records 1859-1958, and probate records 1847-1976.

SAN SABA

County Courthouse 502 E. Wallace, San Saba, TX 76877, (915) 372-3614, **<www.sansabacounty.org>**

- **INCORPORATED:** Feb. 1, 1856
- **PARENT COUNTY:** Bexar Land District
- **BIRTH RECORDS:** start in 1903, kept by the County Clerk
- **MARRIAGE:** 1857, County Clerk
- **DIVORCE:** unknown start, District/County Clerk
- **DEATH:** 1903, County Clerk
- **LAND:** 1857, County Clerk
- **PROBATE:** 1868, County Clerk
- **COURT:** 1868, County Clerk

SCHLEICHER

Drawer 580, Eldorado, TX 76936, (915) 853-2833, **<www.co.schleicher.tx.us>**

- **INCORPORATED:** April 1, 1887
- **PARENT COUNTY:** Crockett
- **BIRTH RECORDS:** start in 1903, kept by the County Clerk
- **MARRIAGE:** 1901, County Clerk
- **DIVORCE:** 1901, County Clerk
- **DEATH:** 1903, County Clerk
- **LAND:** 1901, County Clerk
- **PROBATE:** 1901, County Clerk
- **COURT:** 1901, County Clerk
- **NOTES:** Due to its small population, Schleicher County was attached to Kimble, then Menard County. First election of county officials occurred in 1901.

SCURRY

1806 Twenty-Fifth St. Suite 300, Snyder, TX 79549, (915) 573-5332, **<www.co.scurry.tx.us>**

- **INCORPORATED:** Aug. 21, 1876
- **PARENT COUNTY:** Bexar Land District
- **BIRTH RECORDS:** start in 1903, kept by the County Clerk
- **MARRIAGE:** 1884, County Clerk
- **DIVORCE:** unknown start, District/County Clerk
- **DEATH:** 1903, County Clerk
- **LAND:** 1884, County Clerk
- **PROBATE:** 1884, County Clerk
- **COURT:** 1885, County Clerk
- **NOTES:** Scurry County was attached to Mitchell County until 1884.

SHACKELFORD

225 S. Main, Box 247, Albany, TX 76430, (915) 762-2232, **<www.co.shackelford.tx.us>**

- **INCORPORATED:** Feb. 1, 1858
- **PARENT COUNTY:** Bosque
- **BIRTH RECORDS:** start in 1903, kept by the County Clerk
- **MARRIAGE:** 1874, County Clerk
- **DIVORCE:** unknown start, County Clerk
- **DEATH:** 1903, County Clerk
- **LAND:** 1874, County Clerk
- **PROBATE:** 1874, County Clerk
- **COURT:** 1875, County Clerk

SHELBY

Box 498, Center, TX 75935, (409) 598-6361, **<www.co.shelby.tx.us>**

- **INCORPORATED:** March 17, 1836
- **PARENT COUNTIES:** Tenehaw Municipality
- **BIRTH RECORDS:** start in 1903, kept by the County Clerk
- **MARRIAGE:** 1882, County Clerk
- **DIVORCE:** unknown start, District/County Clerk
- **DEATH:** 1903, County Clerk
- **LAND:** 1838, County Clerk
- **PROBATE:** 1881, County Clerk
- **COURT:** 1882, County Clerk
- **NOTES:** County courthouse records were destroyed in fire of 1882.

SHERMAN

701 N. Third, Box 270, Stratford, TX 79084, (806) 396-2371, **<www.co.sherman.tx.us>**

- **INCORPORATED:** Aug. 21, 1876
- **PARENT COUNTY:** Bexar Land District
- **BIRTH RECORDS:** start in 1903, kept by the County Clerk
- **MARRIAGE:** 1889, County Clerk
- **DIVORCE:** 1889, County Clerk
- **DEATH:** 1903, County Clerk
- **LAND:** 1889, County Clerk
- **PROBATE:** 1889, County Clerk
- **COURT:** 1889, County Clerk

SMITH
Box 1018, Tyler, TX 75710, (903) 535-0630,
<www.smith-county.com>
- **PARENT COUNTY:** Nacogdoches District
- **NOTES:** County Clerk has birth records 1873-1876, 1880-1992, death records 1903-1965, land records 1846-1901, marriage records 1848-1951, and probate records 1846-1931. District Clerk has court records 1846-1941, divorce records 1893-1951, and naturalization records ca. 1854-1912.

SOMERVELL
Box 1098, Glen Rose, TX 76043, (254) 897-4427,
<co.somervell.tx.us>
- **INCORPORATED:** March 13, 1875
- **PARENT COUNTY:** Hood
- **BIRTH RECORDS:** 1903, County Clerk
- **MARRIAGE:** 1885, County Clerk
- **DIVORCE:** unknown start, District/County Clerk
- **DEATH:** 1903, County Clerk
- **LAND:** 1875, County Clerk
- **PROBATE:** 1875, County Clerk
- **COURT:** 1875, County Clerk

STARR
County Courthouse 401 N. Britian Room 201, Rio Grande City, TX 78582, (210) 487-2954, **<www.co.starr.tx.us>**
- **INCORPORATED:** Feb. 10, 1848
- **PARENT COUNTY:** Nueces
- **BIRTH RECORDS:** start in 1880, kept by the County Clerk
- **DEATH:** 1903, County Clerk
- **NOTES:** District Clerk has court records 1848-1966. County Clerk has land records 1848-1909, marriage records 1858-1974, naturalization records 1883-1902, and probate records 1848-1939.

STEPHENS
County Courthouse, 200 W. Walker, Breckenridge, TX 76424, (817) 559-3700, **<www.co.stephens.tx.us>**
- **INCORPORATED:** Jan. 22, 1858
- **PARENT COUNTY:** Bosque
- **BIRTH RECORDS:** start in 1903, kept by the County Clerk
- **MARRIAGE:** 1876, County Clerk
- **DIVORCE:** unknown start, District/County Clerk
- **DEATH:** 1903, County Clerk
- **LAND:** 1876, County Clerk
- **PROBATE:** 1876, County Clerk
- **COURT:** 1876, County Clerk
- **NOTES:** Formerly Buchanan County. Name changed to Stephens Dec. 17, 1861.

STERLING
615 Fourth, Box 55, Sterling City, TX 76951, (915) 378-5191,
<www.co.sterling.tx.us>
- **INCORPORATED:** March 4, 1891
- **PARENT COUNTY:** Tom Green
- **BIRTH RECORDS:** start in 1903, kept by the County Clerk
- **MARRIAGE:** 1891, County Clerk
- **DIVORCE:** 1891, County Clerk
- **DEATH:** 1903, County Clerk
- **LAND:** 1891, County Clerk
- **PROBATE:** 1891, County Clerk
- **COURT:** 1891, County Clerk

STONEWALL
Drawer P, Aspermont, TX 79502, (817) 989-2272,
<www.rootsweb.ancestry.com/~txstonew>
- **INCORPORATED:** Aug. 21, 1876
- **PARENT COUNTIES:** Bexar District, Young District
- **BIRTH RECORDS:** 1903, County Clerk
- **MARRIAGE:** 1888, County Clerk
- **DIVORCE:** ca. 1900, District/County Clerk
- **DEATH:** 1903, County Clerk
- **LAND:** 1887, County Clerk
- **PROBATE:** 1888, County Clerk
- **COURT:** 1889, County Clerk

SUTTON
300 E. Oak St. Suite 3, Sonora, TX 76950, (915) 387-3815,
<www.co.sutton.tx.us>
- **INCORPORATED:** April1, 1887
- **PARENT COUNTY:** Crockett
- **BIRTH RECORDS:** start in 1903, kept by the County Clerk
- **MARRIAGE:** 1890, County Clerk
- **DIVORCE:** 1890, County Clerk
- **DEATH:** 1903, County Clerk
- **LAND:** 1890, County Clerk
- **PROBATE:** 1890, County Clerk
- **COURT:** 1890, County Clerk

SWISHER
County Courthouse 119 S. Maxwell, Tulia, TX 79088, (806) 995-4121, **<www.co.swisher.tx.us>**
- **INCORPORATED:** Aug. 21, 1876
- **PARENT COUNTIES:** Bexar District, Young District
- **BIRTH RECORDS:** start in 1903, kept by the County Clerk
- **MARRIAGE:** 1890, County Clerk
- **DIVORCE:** 1890, County Clerk
- **DEATH:** 1903, County Clerk
- **LAND:** 1890, County Clerk
- **PROBATE:** 1890, County Clerk
- **COURT:** 1890, County Clerk

TARRANT
100 W. Weatherford St., Fort Worth, TX 76196, (817) 884-1195,
<www.tarrantcounty.com>
- **INCORPORATED:** Dec. 20, 1849
- **PARENT COUNTY:** Navarro
- **BIRTH RECORDS:** start in 1903, kept by the County Clerk
- **MARRIAGE:** 1876, County Clerk
- **DIVORCE:** 1887, District Clerk
- **DEATH:** 1903, County Clerk
- **LAND:** 1850, County Clerk
- **PROBATE:** 1856, County Clerk
- **COURT:** 1876, County Clerk
- **NOTES:** 1860 census is missing. All early records for Tarrant County were destroyed in courthouse fire of 1876.

TAYLOR

300 Oak St., Abilene, TX 79602, (325) 674-1205, **<www.taylorcountytexas.org>**

- **INCORPORATED:** Feb. 1, 1858
- **PARENT COUNTIES:** Bexar, Travis
- **BIRTH RECORDS:** start in 1908, kept by the County Clerk
- **MARRIAGE:** 1878, County Clerk
- **DEATH:** 1903, County Clerk
- **LAND:** 1878, County Clerk
- **PROBATE:** 1878, County Clerk
- **COURT:** 1878, County Clerk

TERRELL

Drawer 410, Sanderson, TX 79848, (432) 345-2391, **<www.co.terrell.tx.us>**

- **INCORPORATED:** April 8, 1905
- **PARENT COUNTY:** Pecos
- **BIRTH RECORDS:** start in 1905, kept by the County Clerk
- **MARRIAGE:** 1905, County Clerk
- **DEATH:** 1905, County Clerk
- **LAND:** 1905, County Clerk
- **PROBATE:** 1905, County Clerk
- **COURT:** 1905, County Clerk

TERRY

500 W. Main, Brownfield, TX 79316, (806) 637-8551, **<www.co.terry.tx.us>**

- **INCORPORATED:** Aug. 21, 1876
- **PARENT COUNTY:** Bexar Land District
- **BIRTH RECORDS:** start in 1904, kept by the County Clerk
- **MARRIAGE:** 1904, County Clerk
- **DEATH:** 1904, County Clerk
- **LAND:** 1904, County Clerk
- **PROBATE:** 1904, County Clerk
- **COURT:** 1904, County Clerk
- **NOTES:** Attached to Young County 1876-1881, Throckmorton County 1881-1883, Howard County 1883-1889, Martin County 1889-1904.

THROCKMORTON

Box 309, Throckmorton, TX 76483, (940) 849-2501, **<www.co.throckmorton.tx.us>**

- **INCORPORATED:** Jan. 13, 1858
- **PARENT COUNTIES:** Fannin, Bosque
- **BIRTH RECORDS:** start in 1903, kept by the County Clerk
- **MARRIAGE:** 1879, County Clerk
- **DIVORCE:** 1879, County Clerk
- **DEATH:** 1903, County Clerk
- **LAND:** 1879, County Clerk
- **PROBATE:** 1879, County Clerk
- **COURT:** 1879, County Clerk
- **NOTES:** 1870 census is missing. County was organized in 1879.

TITUS

100 W. First St. Suite 204, Mt. Pleasant, TX 75455, (903) 577-6796, **<www.co.titus.tx.us>**

- **INCORPORATED:** May 11, 1846
- **PARENT COUNTIES:** Red River, Bowie
- **DIVORCE RECORDS:** unknown start, District Clerk
- **COURT:** 1895, County Clerk
- **NOTES:** County Clerk has birth records and death records 1903-1984, land records 1846-1906, marriage records 1895-1973, and probate records 1895-1935.

TOM GREEN

124 W. Beauregard Ave., San Angelo, TX 76903, (915) 659-6553, **<www.co.tom-green.tx.us>**

- **INCORPORATED:** March 13, 1874
- **PARENT COUNTY:** Bexar Land District
- **BIRTH RECORDS:** start in 1903, kept by the County Clerk
- **MARRIAGE:** 1875, County Clerk
- **DEATH:** 1903, County Clerk
- **LAND:** 1875, County Clerk
- **PROBATE:** 1875, County Clerk
- **COURT:** 1875, County Clerk

TRAVIS

1000 Guadalupe St. #222, Box 1748, Austin, TX 78767, (512) 854-9188, **<www.rootsweb.ancestry.com/~txtravis>**

- **INCORPORATED:** Jan. 25, 1840
- **PARENT COUNTY:** Bastrop
- **BIRTH RECORDS:** start in 1903, kept by the County Clerk
- **DEATH:** 1903, County Clerk
- **NOTES:** County Clerk has court records 1876-1894, land records 1840-1886, marriage records 1840-1916, naturalization records 1840-1907, and probate records 1840-1918

TRINITY

Box 456, Groveton, TX 75845, (936) 642-1208, **<www.co.trinity.tx.us>**

- **INCORPORATED:** Feb. 11, 1850
- **PARENT COUNTY:** Houston
- **BIRTH RECORDS:** start in 1911, kept by the County Clerk
- **MARRIAGE:** 1876, County Clerk
- **DIVORCE:** unknown start, District/County Clerk
- **DEATH:** 1903, County Clerk
- **NOTES:** District Clerk has court records 1887-1901 and naturalization records 1886-1925. County Clerk has land records 1873-1886 and probate records 1876-1920. Courthouse burned in 1876; some deeds were refiled.

TYLER

116 S. Charlton St., Woodville, TX 75979, (409) 283-2281, **<www.co.tyler.tx.us>**

- **INCORPORATED:** April 3, 1846
- **PARENT COUNTY:** Liberty
- **BIRTH RECORDS:** 1838, County Clerk
- **MARRIAGE:** 1849, County Clerk
- **DIVORCE:** unknown start, District Clerk
- **DEATH:** 1903, County Clerk
- **LAND:** 1846, County Clerk
- **PROBATE:** 1845, County Clerk
- **COURT:** unknown start, District Clerk
- **BURIAL:** 1903, County Clerk

UPSHUR
Box 730, Gilmer, TX 75644, (903) 843-4015,
<www.countyofupshur.com>
- **INCORPORATED:** April 27, 1846
- **PARENT COUNTIES:** Harrison, Nacogdoches
- **BIRTH RECORDS:** start in 1873, kept by the County Clerk
- **MARRIAGE:** 1873, County Clerk
- **DIVORCE:** unknown start, District/County Clerk
- **DEATH:** 1903, County Clerk
- **LAND:** 1846, County Clerk
- **PROBATE:** 1846, County Clerk
- **COURT:** 1846, County Clerk

UPTON
Box 465, Rankin, TX 79778, (432) 693-2861,
<www.co.upton.tx.us>
- **INCORPORATED:** Feb. 26, 1887
- **PARENT COUNTY:** Tom Green
- **BIRTH RECORDS:** start in 1910, kept by the County Clerk
- **MARRIAGE:** 1910, County Clerk
- **DIVORCE:** 1910, County Clerk
- **DEATH:** 1910, County Clerk
- **LAND:** 1910, County Clerk
- **PROBATE:** 1910, County Clerk
- **COURT:** 1910, County Clerk
- **NOTES:** County was organized in 1910.

UVALDE
100 N. Getty St., Box 284, Uvalde, TX 78802, (830) 278-6614,
<www.uvaldecounty.com>
- **INCORPORATED:** Feb. 8, 1850
- **PARENT COUNTY:** Bexar
- **BIRTH RECORDS:** start in 1903, kept by the County Clerk
- **DIVORCE:** unknown start, District/County Clerk
- **DEATH:** 1903, County Clerk
- **NOTES:** District Clerk has court records 1857-1912 and naturalization records 1884-1906. County Clerk has land records 1856-1906, marriage records 1856-1919, and probate records 1857-1920. Recreated and reorganized Feb. 2, 1856.

VAL VERDE
400 Pecan St., Box 1267, Del Rio, TX 78841, (830) 774-7564,
<www.historictexas.net/valverde>
- **INCORPORATED:** Feb. 20, 1885
- **PARENT COUNTIES:** Crockett, Kinney, Pecos
- **DIVORCE RECORDS:** unknown start, District/County Clerk
- **LAND:** 1885, County Clerk
- **PROBATE:** 1885, County Clerk
- **COURT:** 1885, County Clerk
- **NOTES:** County Clerk has birth, death, and marriage records 1882-1995.

VAN ZANDT
121 E. Dallas St. Room 202, Canton, TX 75103, (903) 567-6503,
<www.vanzandtcounty.org>
- **INCORPORATED:** March 20, 1848
- **PARENT COUNTY:** Henderson
- **NOTES:** County Clerk has birth records 1872-1877, 1903-1988, death records 1903-1991, land records 1848-1925, marriage records 1848-1957, and probate records 1848-1936. District Clerk has court records 1848-1935, divorce records 1899-1935, and naturalization records 1907-1920.

VICTORIA
Box 1968, Victoria, TX 77902, (361) 575-1478,
<www.victoriacountytx.org>
- **INCORPORATED:** March 17, 1836
- **PARENT COUNTY:** Guadalupe Victoria Municipality
- **BIRTH RECORDS:** start in 1902, kept by the County Clerk
- **MARRIAGE:** 1838, County Clerk
- **DIVORCE:** 1838, District Clerk
- **DEATH:** 1902, County Clerk
- **LAND:** 1838, County Clerk
- **PROBATE:** 1838, County Clerk
- **COURT:** 1867, County Clerk
- **NOTES:** District Clerk has naturalization records 1849-1887, 1895, 1897, and 1904. County Clerk has naturalization records 1888-1906.

WALKER
1100 University Ave., Box 210, Huntsville, TX 77342, (936) 436-4922, **<www.co.walker.tx.us>**
- **INCORPORATED:** April 6, 1846
- **PARENT COUNTY:** Montgomery
- **BIRTH RECORDS:** start in 1903, kept by the County Clerk
- **MARRIAGE:** 1846, County Clerk
- **DIVORCE:** unknown start, District/County Clerk
- **DEATH:** 1903, County Clerk
- **NOTES:** District Clerk has court records 1847-1902 and naturalization records 1857-1920. County Clerk has land records 1846-1886 and probate records 1846-1948.

WALLER
836 Austin St. Room #103, Hempstead, TX 77445, (979) 826-7643, **<www.co.waller.tx.us>**
- **INCORPORATED:** April 28, 1873
- **PARENT COUNTIES:** Austin, Grimes
- **BIRTH RECORDS:** 1903, kept by the County Clerk
- **MARRIAGE:** 1873, County Clerk
- **DEATH:** 1903, County Clerk
- **LAND:** 1873, County Clerk
- **PROBATE:** 1873, County Clerk
- **COURT:** 1873, County Clerk

WARD
400 S. Allen St., Ste. 101, Monahans, TX 79756, (432) 943-3294,
<www.co.ward.tx.us>
- **INCORPORATED:** Feb. 26, 1887
- **PARENT COUNTY:** Tom Green
- **BIRTH RECORDS:** start in 1882, kept by the County Clerk
- **DIVORCE:** unknown start, District/County Clerk
- **LAND:** 1893, County Clerk
- **PROBATE:** 1893, County Clerk
- **COURT:** 1893, County Clerk
- **NOTES:** County Clerk has death records 1893-1951 and marriage records 1893-1951. County was organized in 1892.

WASHINGTON
100 E. Main St. Suite 102, Brenham, TX 77833, (979) 277-6200,
<www.co.washington.tx.us>
- **INCORPORATED:** March17, 1836
- **PARENT COUNTY:** Texas Municipality
- **COURT:** 1876, County Clerk
- **BIRTH RECORDS:** start in 1903, kept by the County Clerk
- **MARRIAGE:** 1836, County Clerk
- **DEATH:** 1903, County Clerk
- **LAND:** 1831, County Clerk
- **PROBATE:** 1837, County Clerk
- **NOTES:** District Clerk has divorce records 1895-1943. County Clerk has military discharge records 1917-1966 and naturalization records 1850-1940.

WEBB
1110 Victoria St., #210, Laredo, TX 78040, (956) 523-5035,
<www.webbcountytx.gov>
- **INCORPORATED:** Jan. 28, 1848
- **PARENT COUNTY:** Nueces
- **BIRTH RECORDS:** start in 1903, kept by the County Clerk
- **DEATH:** 1903, County Clerk
- **NOTES:** District Clerk has court records 1851-1914. County Clerk has land records 1843-1890, marriage records 1849-1909, naturalization records 1881-1907, and probate records 1851-1945.

WHARTON
309 E. Milam, Ste. 700, Wharton, TX 77488, (979) 532-2381,
<www.co.wharton.tx.us>
- **PARENT COUNTIES:** Matagorda, Jackson, Colorado
- **INCORPORATED:** April 3, 1846
- **BIRTH RECORDS:** start in 1903, kept by the County Clerk
- **DEATH:** 1903, County Clerk
- **NOTES:** District Clerk has court records 1847-1918; naturalization records 1880-1930. County Clerk has land records 1837-1900, marriage records 1847-1909, and probate records 1846-1938.

WHEELER
Box 465, Wheeler, TX 79096, (806) 826-5544,
<www.co.wheeler.tx.us>
- **INCORPORATED:** Aug. 21, 1876
- **PARENT COUNTY:** Bexar District, Young District
- **BIRTH RECORDS:** start in 1903, kept by the County Clerk
- **MARRIAGE:** 1879, County Clerk
- **DIVORCE:** unknown start, District/County Clerk
- **DEATH:** 1903, County Clerk
- **LAND:** 1881, County Clerk
- **PROBATE:** 1879, County Clerk
- **COURT 1879, COUNTY CLERK**

WICHITA
Box 1679, Wichita Falls, TX 76307, (940) 766-8144,
<www.co.wichita.tx.us>
- **INCORPORATED:** Feb. 1, 1858
- **PARENT COUNTY:** Cooke Land District
- **DIVORCE:** unknown start, District Clerk
- **NOTES:** County Clerk has birth records and death records 1860-1949, land records 1873-1917, and marriage and probate records 1882-1934. District Clerk has court records 1882-1943 and naturalization records 1884-1917.

WILBARGER
1700 Wilbarger St. Room 15, Vernon, TX 76384, (940) 552-5486,
<www.co.wilbarger.tx.us>
- **INCORPORATED:** Feb. 1, 1858
- **PARENT COUNTY:** Cooke
- **BIRTH RECORDS:** start in 1900, kept by the County Clerk
- **MARRIAGE:** 1882, County Clerk
- **DIVORCE:** unknown start, District Clerk
- **DEATH:** 1900, County Clerk
- **LAND:** 1900, County Clerk
- **PROBATE:** 1882, County Clerk
- **COURT:** 1900, County Clerk
- **BURIAL:** unknown start, City Secretary
- **NOTES:** Wilbarger County was organized Oct. 10, 1881.

WILLACY
576 W. Main, Raymondville, TX 78580, (956) 689-2710,
<www.co.willacy.tx.us>
- **INCORPORATED:** March 11, 1911
- **PARENT COUNTIES:** Hidalgo, Cameron
- **BIRTH RECORDS:** start in 1903, kept by the County Clerk
- **MARRIAGE:** 1921, County Clerk
- **DEATH:** 1903, County Clerk
- **LAND:** 1891, County Clerk
- **PROBATE:** 1921, County Clerk
- **COURT:** 1921, County Clerk
- **NOTES:** Recreated and reorganized in 1921.

WILLIAMSON
Box 14, Georgetown, TX 78626, (512) 943-1515,
<www.williamson-county.org>
- **INCORPORATED:** March 13, 1848
- **PARENT COUNTY:** Milam
- **BIRTH RECORDS:** start in 1903, kept by the County Clerk
- **MARRIAGE:** 1848, County Clerk
- **DEATH:** 1903, County Clerk
- **LAND:** 1835, County Clerk
- **PROBATE:** 1848, County Clerk
- **COURT:** 1848, District Clerk
- **NOTES:** County Clerk has birth records 1873-1876, military discharge records 1918-1945, and naturalization records 1857-1938. District Clerk has divorce records 1909-1938.

WILSON
1420 Third St., Box 27, Floresville, TX 78114, (830) 393-7308,
<www.co.wilson.tx.us>
- **INCORPORATED:** Feb. 13, 1860
- **PARENT COUNTIES:** Bexar, Karnes
- **BIRTH RECORDS:** start in 1903, kept by the County Clerk
- **DEATH:** 1903, County Clerk
- **NOTES:** District Clerk has court records 1896-1908, divorce records 1893-1985, and naturalization records 1891-1924. County Clerk has land records 1860-1976, marriage records 1860-1908, and probate records 1862-1915. From 1869-1874 Wilson County was called Cibilo County.

WINKLER
Box 1007, Kermit, TX 79745, (432) 586-3401,
<www.co.winkler.tx.us>
- **INCORPORATED:** Feb. 26, 1887
- **PARENT COUNTY:** Tom Green
- **BIRTH RECORDS:** start in 1910, kept by the County Clerk
- **MARRIAGE:** 1910, County Clerk
- **DIVORCE:** unknown start, District Clerk
- **DEATH:** 1910, County Clerk
- **LAND:** 1910, County Clerk
- **PROBATE:** 1910, County Clerk
- **COURT:** 1910, County Clerk
- **NOTES:** Winkler County was organized in 1910.

WISE
Box 359, Decatur, TX 76234, (940) 627-3351,
<www.co.wise.tx.us>
- **INCORPORATED:** Jan. 23, 1856
- **PARENT COUNTY:** Cooke
- **BIRTH RECORDS:** start in 1864, kept by the County Clerk
- **MARRIAGE:** 1881, County Clerk
- **DEATH:** 1902, County Clerk
- **NOTES:** District Clerk has court records 1894-1940, divorce records 1915-1940, and naturalization records 1907-1914. County Clerk has land records 1852-1982, military discharge records 1918-1943, and probate records 1882-1991.

WOOD
1 Main St., Box 1796, Quitman, TX 75783, (903) 763-2711,
<www.co.wood.tx.us>
- **INCORPORATED:** Feb. 5, 1850
- **PARENT COUNTY:** Van Zandt
- **NOTES:** County Clerk has birth records 1903-1995, death records 1903-1999, land records 1878-1909, marriage records 1879-2002, military discharge records 1918-1949, and probate records 1878-1932. District Clerk has court records 1860-1936 and divorce records 1897-1935. County courthouse and records were burned in 1878.

YOAKUM
Box 309, Plains, TX 79355, (806) 456-2721,
<www.co.yoakum.tx.us>
- **INCORPORATED:** Aug. 21, 1876
- **PARENT COUNTY:** Bexar Land District
- **BIRTH RECORDS:** start in 1903, kept by the County Clerk
- **MARRIAGE:** 1907, County Clerk
- **DIVORCE:** unknown start, District/County Clerk
- **DEATH:** 1903, County Clerk
- **LAND:** 1907, County Clerk
- **PROBATE:** 1907, County Clerk
- **COURT:** 1907, County Clerk
- **NOTES:** Attached to Martin County 1904-1907. Yoakum County was organized in 1907.

YOUNG
516 Fourth St. Room 104, Graham, TX 76450, (940) 549-8432,
<www.co.young.tx.us>
- **INCORPORATED:** Feb. 2, 1856
- **PARENT COUNTIES:** Bosque, Fannin
- **BIRTH RECORDS:** start in 1903, kept by the County Clerk
- **MARRIAGE:** 1856, County Clerk
- **DIVORCE:** unknown start, District/County Clerk
- **DEATH:** 1903, County Clerk
- **LAND:** 1858, County Clerk
- **PROBATE:** 1858, County Clerk
- **COURT:** 1858, County Clerk

ZAPATA
Box 789, Zapata, TX 78076, (956) 765-9915,
<www.co.zapata.tx.us>
- **INCORPORATED:** Jan. 22, 1858
- **PARENT COUNTIES:** Starr, Webb
- **BIRTH RECORDS:** start in 1903, kept at the Justice of the Peace
- **DIVORCE:** unknown start, District/County Clerk
- **DEATH:** 1903, County Clerk
- **NOTES:** District Clerk has court records 1874-1881 and 1884-1928. County Clerk has land records 1868-1891, marriage records 1873-1915, naturalization records 1885-1906, and probate records 1886-1944.

ZAVALA
200 E. Uvalde St., Ste. 7 Crystal City, TX 78839, (830) 374-2331,
<www.co.zavala.tx.us>
- **INCORPORATED:** February 1846
- **PARENT COUNTIES:** Uvalde, Maverick
- **BIRTH RECORDS:** start in 1903, kept by the County Clerk
- **MARRIAGE:** 1884, County Clerk
- **DIVORCE:** unknown start, District/County Clerk
- **DEATH:** 1903, County Clerk
- **LAND:** 1884, County Clerk
- **PROBATE:** 1884, County Clerk
- **COURT:** 1885, County Clerk
- **NOTES:** County was organized in 1858. From 1846-1858, county was attached to San Antonio Municipality.

UTAH

» BY RHONDA R. MCCLURE

HISTORICAL OVERVIEW

The first white settlers in Utah were the pioneer Saints—members of the Church of Jesus Christ of Latter-day Saints—who were following Brigham Young, the newly recognized prophet of the church. Brigham Young led the first wagon train of Mormons into the Salt Lake Valley in 1847. Over the next 12 years, some 69,000 Mormons flocked to Utah by wagon and handcart. In 1849, the provisional State of Deseret was organized with a constitution and system of government that was in effect until Utah became a US territory in 1850.

Until statehood was granted in 1896, the federal government and the Mormons—the majority of Utah's settlers—often came to disagreements, mostly as a result of the unique practices of the religion, which included polygamy. Over the years a number of federal anti-polygamy acts had a direct affect on when, where and how the territory's courts worked, in addition to altering record-keeping practices.

Because of the overseas missionary efforts of the church, Utah had a large influx of immigrants as those in Britain, Europe, and Scandinavia began to convert to this new religion and head to "Zion"—Utah.

RECORD HIGHLIGHTS

Though birth and death registration was required beginning in 1905, compliance at the state level took another 12 years. You can contact the Bureau of Vital Records, Utah State Department of Health, Box 141010, Salt Lake City, UT 84114, **<health.utah.gov/vitalrecords>**. The website offers information on how to order certificates and supplies the necessary forms. You'll also want to search at the county level. Some counties began to keep birth and death records as early as 1898. Salt Lake City, Ogden and Logan have also kept birth and death records at the city level.

Marriage records are kept on the county level, with a few existing before 1887 in the justice of the peace or probate court records. The Edmunds-Tucker Act of 1887, an anti-polygamy law, required that all marriages be registered with the office of the probate court. In the 1890s, registration was moved to the county clerk. The Family History Library (FHL) has microfilm copies of county marriages to about 1960.

research tips

- A Church of Jesus Christ of Latter-day Saints Church History Library online database names pioneers who came to Utah from 1847 to 1868 **<www.lds.org/churchhistory/library/pioneercompanysearch/1,15773,3966-1,00.html>**.
- While the Family History Library is under the auspices of the Church of Jesus Christ of Latter-day Saints, it is open to anyone. To get the most from the Family History Library and its branches around the country, read *Your Guide to the Family History Library* by Paula Stuart Warren and James W. Warren (Betterway Books, 2001).
- When it comes to early births, see whether midwives' records exist. The Family History Library is a good place to start, searching on the city and town level.

CENSUS RECORDS

- Federal census: 1850, 1860, 1870, 1880, 1900, 1910, 1920, 1930
- Federal mortality schedules: 1870
- Special census of Civil War Union veterans and widows: 1890
- State/territorial census: 1851, 1856

Divorce records can be found in several places. Early divorces had to be granted by church leaders. During the territorial period (1852–1895) the federal district courts had jurisdiction, although there is overlap with the probate courts, which also had jurisdiction from 1852 to 1887. After statehood, divorces fell under the auspices of state district courts.

In the early years of settlement, LDS Bishops Courts, also known as Ecclesiastical courts, were responsible for criminal and civil cases for individuals in their wards or churches. These records are found in the Church History Library, 50 E. North Temple St., Room 227E, Salt Lake City, UT 84150, **<www.lds.org/churchhistory/library>**.

At the same time Bishops Courts were in effect, there were also civil courts. These included county courts, which were replaced by probate courts in 1851, as well as justice of the peace courts for cases involving less than $300. In 1874, many courts of Utah were restricted, as a result of the attempts to eliminate polygamy. Many civil, criminal, and probate matters were handled in federal district courts until statehood in 1896.

After statehood, Utah was divided into seven districts and state district courts were instituted, though each county has a district court branch. An eighth district was added in 1988. State district courts have jurisdiction over criminal felonies and civil actions, including divorces, custody disputes, adoptions, probate and naturalization.

County-level records for land, probate and court usually begin with the creation of the county, though there are a few exceptions—for instance, Rich County was created in 1864 but its land, probate, and court records begin in 1872.

ARCHIVES, LIBRARIES, AND SOCIETIES

American Historical Society of Germans From Russia, Intermountain Chapter
<intermountainchapterahsgr.blogspot.com>

Bear River District Health Department
655 E. 1300 North, Logan, UT 84341, (435) 792-6500, **<www.brhd.org>**

Brigham City Carnegie Library
26 E. Forest, Brigham City, UT 84302, (435) 723-5850, **<bcpl.lib.ut.us>**

Brigham Young University, Harold B. Lee Library
Box 26800, Provo, UT, 84602, (801) 422-2927, **<www.lib.byu.edu>**

Bureau of Land Management, Utah State Office
440 W. 200 South, Suite 500, Box 45155, Salt Lake City, UT 84101, (801) 539-4001, **<www.blm.gov/ut/st/en.htm>**

Bureau of Vital Records, Utah State Department of Health
288 N. 1460 West, Box 141010, Salt Lake City, UT 84114, (801) 538-6105, **<health.utah.gov/vitalrecords>**

Catholic Diocese of Salt Lake City Pastoral Center
27 C St., Salt Lake City, UT 84103, (801) 328-8641, **<www.dioslc.org>**

Cuban Genealogical Society
Box 2650, Salt Lake City, UT 84110, **<www.rootsweb.ancestry.com/~utcubangs>**

Daughters of Utah Pioneers
300 N. Main St., Salt Lake City, UT 84103, (801) 532-6479, **<www.dupinternational.org>**

Episcopal Diocese of Utah
75 S. 300 East, Box 3090, Salt Lake City, UT 84110, (801) 322-4131, **<www.episcopal-ut.org>**

Genealogical Society of Utah
50 E. North Temple, Salt Lake City, UT 84150, (801) 538-2978, **<www.gensocietyofutah.org>**

Icelandic Association of Utah
84 N. 1120 East, Box 874, Spanish Fork, UT 84660, **<www.utahicelanders.com>**

Institute of Genealogy and History for Latin America
2191 S. 2200 East, Mount Springs, UT 84757, (435) 652-1710, **<www.genealogy.com/00000140.html>**

Logan Public Library
255 N. Main, Logan, UT 84321, (435) 716-9123, **<library.loganutah.org>**

J. Willard Marriott Library, University of Utah
295 S. 1500 East, Salt Lake City, UT 84112, (801) 581-8558, **<www.lib.utah.edu>**

Merrill-Cazier Library, Utah State University
3000 Old Man Hill, Logan, UT 84322, (435) 797-2663, **<library.usu.edu/Specol>**

Mormon Battalion Association
Box 1983, Sandy, UT 84091, (801) 256-0329, **<www.mormonbattalion.com>**

National Archives and Records Administration, Rocky Mountain Region
Box 25307, Denver, CO 80225, (303) 407-5740, **<www.archives.gov/rocky-mountain>**

Presbytery of Utah
699 E. South Temple, Suite 202, Salt Lake City, UT 84102, (801) 539-8446, **<www.pbyutah.org>**

Salt Lake City Public Library
210 E. 400 South, Salt Lake City, UT 84111, (801) 524-8200, **<www.slcpl.lib.ut.us>**

Salt Lake County Archives
4505 S. 5600 West, West Valley City, UT 84120, (801) 963-7330, **<www.archives.slco.org>**

Sons of Utah Pioneers
3301 E. 2920 South, Salt Lake City, UT 84109, (801) 484-4441, **<www.sonsofutahpioneers.org>**

Uintah and Ouray Agency, Bureau of Indian Affairs
988 S. 7500 East, Box 130, Fort Duchesne, UT 84026, (435) 722-4300, **<www.bia.gov>**

Utah Division of Indian Affairs
324 S. State St., Suite 500, Salt Lake City, Utah 84114, (801) 538-8808, **<indian.utah.gov>**

Utah Genealogical Association
Box 1144, Salt Lake City, UT 84110, (888) 463-6842, **<www.infouga.org>**

Utah Jewish Genealogical Society
2450 E. 3700 North, Layton, UT 84040, **<www.ujgs.org>**

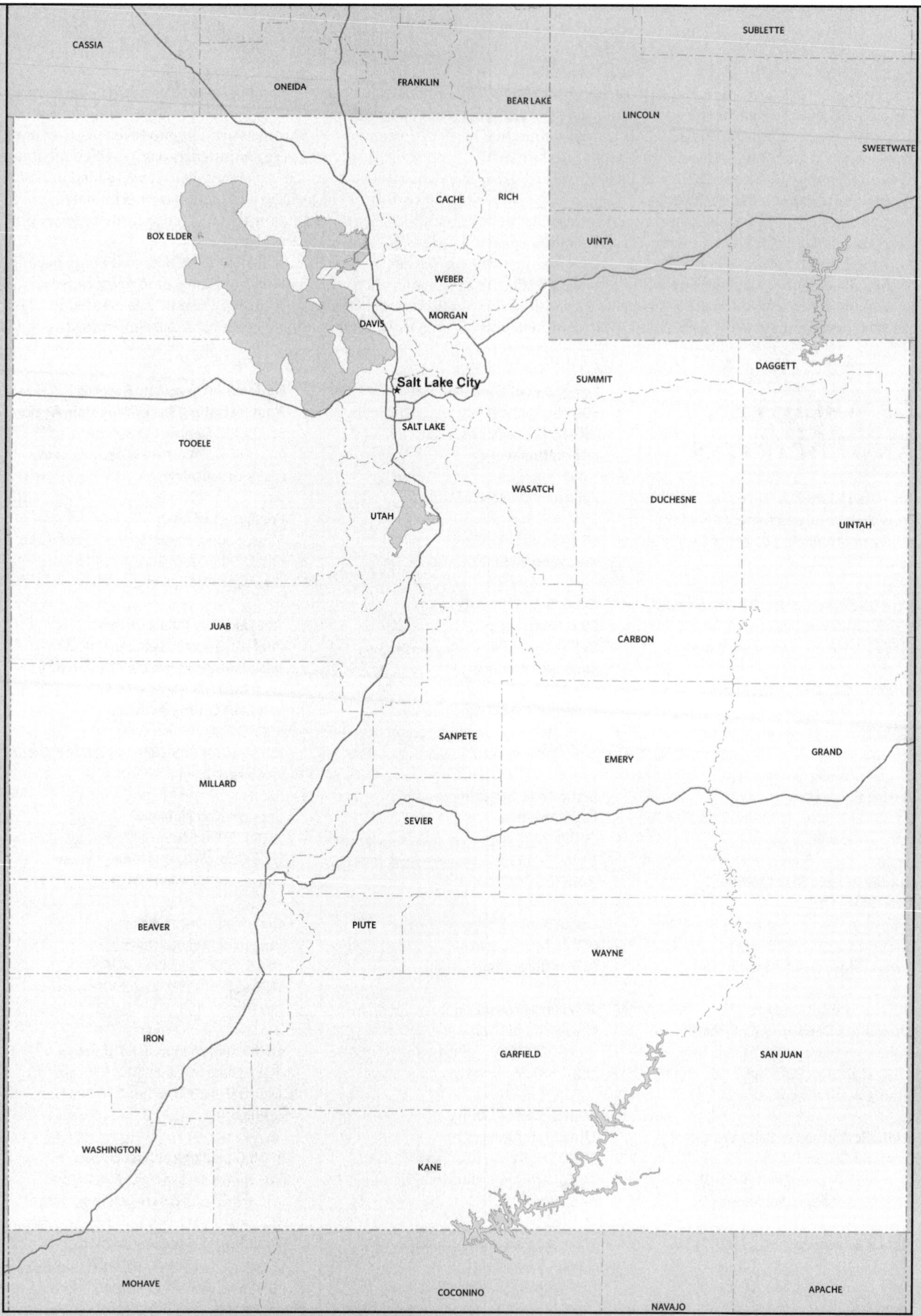
CASSIA
ONEIDA
FRANKLIN
BEAR LAKE
SUBLETTE
LINCOLN
SWEETWATE
CACHE
RICH
BOX ELDER
UINTA
WEBER
MORGAN
DAVIS
Salt Lake City
SUMMIT
DAGGETT
SALT LAKE
TOOELE
WASATCH
DUCHESNE
UINTAH
UTAH
JUAB
CARBON
SANPETE
EMERY
GRAND
MILLARD
SEVIER
PIUTE
BEAVER
WAYNE
IRON
GARFIELD
SAN JUAN
WASHINGTON
KANE
MOHAVE
COCONINO
NAVAJO
APACHE

Utah State Archives and Records Service
300 S. Rio Grande St., Salt Lake City, UT 84101, (801) 533-3535, **<www.archives.utah.gov>**

Utah State Historical Society and Library
300 S. Rio Grande St., Salt Lake City, UT 84101, (801) 533-3500, **<history.utah.gov>**

☞ GENERAL RESOURCES

Church Records, 1868-1940 from the Church of Jesus Christ of Latter-day Saints (filmed by the Family History Library, 1994)

Daughters of the Utah Pioneer Lessons, 31 vols., by Kate B. Carter (Daughters of the Utah Pioneers, 1937-1968)

Early Utah Journalism by J. Cecil Alter (Utah State Historical Society, 1938)

Encyclopedia History of the Church by Andrew Jenson (Deseret News Publishing Co., 1941)

Episcopal Register of the Bishop of Utah (Bishop's Personal Register) 1899-1946, 1951-1967 from the Episcopal Diocese of Utah (filmed by the Genealogical Society of Utah, 1975)

Genealogical Records in Utah by Laureen Richardson Jaussi and Gloria Duncan Chaston (Deseret Book Co., 1974)

Guide to Archives and Manuscript Collections in Selected Utah Repositories (Utah State Historical Society, 1990, CD-ROM)

Guide to Mormon Diaries and Autobiographies by Davis Bitton (Brigham Young University Press, 1977)

Guide to Newspapers Located in the Utah State Historical Society Library by Linda Thatcher (Utah State Historical Society, 1985)

Guide to Official Records of Genealogical Value in the State of Utah (Utah State Archives and Records Service, 1980)

A Guide to the Oral History Collection (Utah State Historical Society Library, 1980)

A Guide to Unpublished Materials at the Utah State Historical Society in Salt Lake City (Utah State Historical Society, 1989)

Heart Throbs of the West, 12 vols., compiled by Kate B. Carter (Daughters of the Utah Pioneers, 1939-)

Here Are the Counties of Utah by Betty R. Cook (Betty R. Cook, 1983)

"The History of Marriage in Utah, 1847-1905" by Lyman D. Platt in *Genealogical Journal* vol. 12 (Spring 1983) pages 28-41

History of the Church of Jesus Christ of Latter-day Saints, 7 vols., by Joseph Smith (1902; Deseret Book Co., 1970)

Inventory of the Church Archives of Utah, 3 vols., from the Historical Records Survey (Utah Historical Records Survey, 1940)

Latter-day Saint Biographical Encyclopedia by Andrew Jenson (A. Jenson History Co., 1901-1936)

The Mormon Experience: A History of the Latter-day Saints by Leonard J. Arrington (Alfred A. Knopf, 1980)

Mormons and Their Neighbors: An Index of Over 75,000 Biographical Sketches From 1820 to the Present, 2 vols., by Marvin E. Wiggins (Brigham Young Univ., 1984)

Municipal Records Manual, 1983 (Utah State Archives and Records Service, 1983)

Name Index to the Library of Congress, *Collection of Mormon Diaries* (Utah State University, 1971)

Our Pioneer Heritage, 20 vols., compiled by Kate B. Carter (Daughters of the Utah Pioneers, 1958-1977)

Pioneers and Prominent Men of Utah by Frank Esshom (1913; Western Epics, 1966)

Portrait, Genealogical and Biographical Record of the State of Utah (National Historical Board, 1902)

Salt of the Earth by Bernice Mooney (Catholic Diocese of Salt Lake City, 1987)

The Story of the Latter-day Saints by James B. Allen and Glen M. Leonard (Deseret Book Co., 1976)

Treasures of Pioneer History, 6 vols., compiled by Kate B. Carter (Daughters of the Utah Pioneers, 1952-1957)

Utah: A Centennial History, 3 vols., edited by Wain Sutton (Lewis Historical Publishing Co., 1949)

Utah: A People's History by Dean L. May (University of Utah Press, 1987)

Utah Research Outline by the Church of Jesus Christ of Latter-day Saints (online at **<www.familysearch.org/eng/search.RG/guide/utah.asp>**)

Utah's Newspapers: Traces of Her Past edited by Robert P. Holley (University of Utah, 1984)

Utah, the Storied Domain: A Documentary History of Utah's Eventful Career, 3 vols., by J. Cecil Alter (American Historical Society, 1932)

☞ CENSUS RECORDS

Church Census Records, 1914-1960 from the Church of Jesus Christ of Latter-day Saints (filmed by the Family History Library, 1962)

Indian Census Rolls, Fort Hall, 1885-1939 from the US Bureau of Indian Affairs (National Archives, 1965)

☞ IMMIGRATION RECORDS

Handcarts to Zion: The Story of a Unique Western Migration, 1856-1860, With Contemporary Journals, Accounts, Reports, and Rosters of Members of the Ten Handcart Companies by LeRoy R. Hafen and Ann W. Hafen (Arthur H. Clark, 1960)

Mormons on the High Seas: Ocean Voyage Narratives to American (1840-1890) by Melvin L. Bashire and Linda L. Haslam

(Historical Department of the Church of Jesus Christ of Latter-day Saints, 1990)

Mormon Pioneer Companies Crossing the Plains (1847-1868) Narratives: Guide to Sources in Utah Libraries and Archives by Melvin Lee Bashire (Historical Department of the Church of Jesus Christ of Latter-day Saints, 1990)

Naturalization Records, 1853-1989 (Utah State Archives and Records Service, 1989)

Saints on the Seas: A Maritime History of Mormon Migration, 1830-1890 by Conway B. Sonne (University of Utah, Press, 1983)

Ships, Saints, and Mariners: A Maritime Encyclopedia of Mormon Migration, 1830-1890 by Conway B. Sonne (University of Utah Press, 1987)

Worldwide LDS Ship Register 1840-1913 by Margery Taylor (Family History Library, 1991)

LAND RECORDS

"Establishing and Maintaining Land Ownership in Utah Prior to 1869" by Lawrence L. Linford in *Utah Historical Society Quarterly*, vol. 42 (1974) pages 126-43

The Mormon Land System: A Study of the Settlement and Utilization of Land Under the Direction of the Mormon Church by Feramorz Young Fox (Utah State Agricultural College, 1955)

The Mormon Village: A Pattern and Technique of Land Settlement by Lowry Nelson (University of Utah Press, 1952)

Preliminary Inventory of Land Management—Utah by Joel Barker (Denver Archives and Records Center, 1979)

MAPS

Atlas of Utah by Deon C. Greer, et al. (Weber State College, 1981)

A Gazetteer of Utah by Henry A. Gannett (U.S. Government Printing Office, 1900)

LDS Place Names Gazetteer by Jill Anderson Ward (Family History Library, 1986)

Origins of Utah Place Names from the Utah Writer's Project (State Department of Instruction, 1940)

Postal History of Utah, 1849-1976 by Ted Gruber (J-B Publishing Co., 1978)

The Post Offices of Utah by John S. Gallagher (The Depot, 1977)

Printed Maps of Utah to 1900: An Annotated Cartobibliography by Riley Moore Moffat (Western Association of Map Librarians, 1981)

Utah Gazetteer and Directory of Logan, Ogden, Provo and Salt Lake City for 1884 by Robert W. Sloan (Herald Printing and Publishing Co., 1884)

Utah: A Guide to the State (Hastings House, 1941)

Utah Place Names: A Comprehensive Guide to the Origins of Geographic Names compiled by John E. Van Cott (University of Utah Press, 1990)

MILITARY RECORDS

A Database of the Mormon Battalion by Carl V. Larson (K.W. Watkins, 1987)

Johnston, Connor and the Mormons: An Outline of Military History in Northern Utah (Irma Watson Hance and Irene Warr, 1962)

Utah and the Civil War by Margaret May Merrill Fisher (Deseret Book Co., 1929)

Utah in the World War by Noble Warrum (Utah State Council of Defense, 1924)

VITAL RECORDS

Cemeteries in Utah by Irvin C. McClay (Utah State Archives and Records Service, 1980)

Cemetery Records of Utah, 13 vols. (Genealogical Society of Utah, 1953)

Guide to Public Vital Statistics of Utah (Utah Historical Records Survey, 1941)

An Inventory and Index to the Records of Carson County, Utah and Nevada Territories, 1855-1861 by Marion Ellison (Grace Dangberg Foundation, 1984)

Marriages in Utah Territory, 1850-1884: From the Deseret News, 1850-1872, and the Elias Smith Journals, 1850-1884 by Judith Woolstenhume Hansen (Utah Genealogical Association, 1998)

Obituary Index File to the Salt Lake Tribune and Deseret News as of 31 December 1970 (filmed by the Family History Library, 1971)

COUNTY DETAILS

BEAVER

105 E. Center, Box 392, Beaver, UT 84713, (435) 438-6463, **<www.beaver.utah.gov>**

- **INCORPORATED:** Jan. 5, 1856
- **PARENT COUNTIES:** Iron, Millard
- **MARRIAGE RECORDS:** 1901, start in 1920, County Clerk
- **LAND:** start in 1878, County Recorder
- **COURT:** 1856, Clerk of 5th District Court
- **NATURALIZATION:** 1846-1902, Clerk of 5th District Court Clerk
- **NOTES:** County Clerk has birth records 1897-1905 and death records 1900-1905, marriage records for 1901, and probate records 1856-1897. Historical Society has burial records 1865-1986. Clerk of 5th District Court Clerk has divorce records 1870-1897 and naturalization records 1846-1902. Index for birth and death records online at Utah State Archives and Records Service **<archives.utah.gov>**.

BOX ELDER
1 S. Main St., Brigham City, UT 84302, (435) 734-3391,
<www.boxeldercounty.org>
- **INCORPORATED:** Jan. 5, 1856
- **PARENT COUNTIES:** unorganized territory, Weber, Green River
- **MARRIAGE RECORDS:** start in 1887, County Recorder
- **LAND:** 1856, County Recorder
- **NOTES:** County Clerk has birth and death records 1898-1905 and Court records 1889-1895. Probate Court has divorce records 1856-1877. County Recorder has military discharge records 1944-1952. County Clerk has naturalization records 1868-1869. Clerk of 1st District Court has has probate records 1856-1877.

CACHE
179 N. Main St., Suite 102, Logan, UT 84321, (435) 755-1460,
<www.cachecounty.org>
- **INCORPORATED:** Jan. 5, 1856
- **PARENT COUNTIES:** unorganized territory, Green River
- **MARRIAGE RECORDS:** start in 1888, County Clerk
- **LAND:** 1856, County Recorder
- **NOTES:** Index for birth records online at Utah State Archives and Records Service. County Clerk has birth and death records 1898-1905. Clerk of 1st District Court has court records 1889-1895, divorce records 1860-1887, and probate records 1876-1906.

CARBON
120 E. Main St., Price, UT 84501, (435) 636-3201,
<www.carbon.utah.gov>
- **INCORPORATED:** March 8, 1894
- **PARENT COUNTY:** Emery
- **MARRIAGE RECORDS:** start in 1894, County Clerk
- **DIVORCE:** 1895, Clerk of 7th District Court
- **LAND:** 1894, County Recorder
- **COURT:** 1896, Clerk of 7th District Court
- **MILITARY:** 1944, County Recorder
- **NOTES:** County Clerk has birth and death records 1898-1905. Index available online at Utah State Archives and Records Service. Clerk of 7th District Court has probate records 1895-1966.

CARSON
- **INCORPORATED:** Jan. 17, 1854
- **PARENT COUNTIES:** Tooele, Juab, Millard, Iron
- **NOTES:** Transferred to Nevada Territory March 2, 1861.

CEDAR
- **INCORPORATED:** Jan. 5, 1856
- **PARENT COUNTY:** unknown
- **NOTES:** Absorbed by Utah County Jan. 17, 1862.

DAGGETT
95 North First St. West, Box 400, Manila, UT 84046, (435) 784-3154, **<www.daggettcounty.org>**
- **INCORPORATED:** Jan. 17, 1918
- **PARENT COUNTY:** Uintah
- **MARRIAGE RECORDS:** start in 1918, kept by County Clerk
- **DIVORCE:** 1918, County Clerk
- **LAND:** 1918, County Recorder
- **PROBATE:** 1918, County Clerk; 1916-1966, District Court
- **COURT:** 1918, County Clerk
- **NOTES:** District Court has probate records 1916-1966. See Unitah County for birth and death records.

DAVIS
28 E. State St., Box 618, Farmington, UT 84025, (801) 451-3324,
<www.co.davis.ut.us>
- **INCORPORATED:** March 3, 1852
- **PARENT COUNTY:** original county
- **MARRIAGE RECORDS:** start in 1887, County Clerk
- **LAND:** 1862, County Recorder
- **COURT:** 1862, Clerk of 2nd District Court
- **NOTES:** County Clerk has birth and death records 1898-1905. Birth index online at Utah State Archives and Records Service. Clerk of 2nd District Court has divorce records 1875-1886 and naturalization records 1902-1938. Probate Court has probate records 1853-1896.

DESERT
- **INCORPORATED:** March 3, 1852
- **PARENT COUNTY:** unknown
- **NOTES:** Absorbed by Tooele and Box Elder counties Jan. 17, 1862.

DUCHESNE
734 N. Center, Box 910, Duchesne, UT 84021, (435) 738-1123,
<www.duchesnegov.net>
- **INCORPORATED:** Jan. 4, 1915
- **PARENT COUNTY:** Wasatch
- **MARRIAGE RECORDS:** unknown start, kept by Clerk/Auditor
- **DIVORCE:** start in 1915, Clerk of 8th District Court
- **LAND:** 1915, County Recorder
- **COURT:** 1915, Clerk of 8th District Court
- **NOTES:** See Wasatch County for birth and death records. Clerk of 8th District Court has probate records 1922-1966.

EMERY
75 E. Main St., Box 907, Castle Dale, UT 84513, (435) 381-5106,
<www.emerycounty.com>
- **INCORPORATED:** Feb. 12, 1880
- **PARENT COUNTIES:** Sanpete, Sevier
- **MARRIAGE RECORDS:** start in 1888, County Clerk
- **LAND:** 1880, County Recorder
- **PROBATE:** 1886, Clerk of 7th District Court
- **NATURALIZATION:** 1904-1942, Clerk of 7th District Court
- **NOTES:** County Clerk has birth and death records 1898-1905. Birth index online at Utah State Archives and Records Service. Clerk of 7th District Court has court and divorce records 1896-1986 and naturalization records 1904-1942. County Recorder has military discharge records 1923-1952.

GARFIELD
55 S. Main St., Panguitch, UT 84759, (435) 676-1100,
<garfield.utah.gov>
- **INCORPORATED:** March 9, 1882
- **PARENT COUNTY:** Iron
- **MARRIAGE RECORDS:** start in 1890, County Clerk
- **DIVORCE:** 1896, County Clerk
- **LAND:** 1882, County Recorder

- **COURT:** 1896, County Clerk
- **NOTES:** County Clerk has birth and death records 1898-1905. Clerk of 6th District Court has probate records 1896-1966.

GRAND
125 E. Center St., Moab, UT 84532, (435) 259-1321,
<www.grandcountyutah.net>
- **INCORPORATED:** March 13, 1890
- **PARENT COUNTY:** Emery
- **MARRIAGE RECORDS:** start in 1890, County Clerk
- **DIVORCE:** 1896, Clerk of 7th District Court
- **LAND:** 1890, County Recorder
- **COURT:** 1896, Clerk of 7th District Court
- **NOTES:** County Clerk has birth and death records 1898-1905. Birth index online at Utah State Archives and Records Service. Clerk of 7th District Court has probate records 1908-1975.

GREASEWOOD
- **INCORPORATED:** Jan. 5, 1856
- **PARENT COUNTY:** unknown
- **NOTES:** Absorbed by Box Elder County Jan. 17, 1862.

GREAT SALT LAKE
- **INCORPORATED:** March 3, 1852
- **PARENT COUNTY:** original county
- **NOTES:** See Salt Lake County. Name changed to Salt Lake Jan. 29, 1868.

GREEN RIVER
- **INCORPORATED:** March 3, 1852
- **PARENT COUNTY:** original county
- **NOTES:** Green River County was dissolved Feb. 16, 1872. Cache, Webber, Morgan, Davis, Wasatch, Summit, Duchesne, Carbon, and Utah counties contain parts of Green River County. Some parts of Green River County went to Wyoming and Colorado territories.

HUMBOLDT
- **INCORPORATED:** Jan. 5, 1856
- **PARENT COUNTIES:** unknown
- **NOTES:** Transferred to Nevada Territory March 2, 1861.

IRON
68 South 100 East, Parowan, UT 84761, (435) 477-8340,
<www.ironcounty.net>
- **INCORPORATED:** March 3, 1850
- **PARENT COUNTY:** original county
- **LAND:** start in 1852, County Recorder
- **NOTES:** County Clerk has birth and death records 1898-1905, and marriage records 1887-1893. Birth index online. Clerk of 5th District Court has court records 1896-1948, divorce records 1852-1896, naturalization records 1853-1868, and probate records 1854-1965. Formerly Little Salt Lake County. Name changed to Iron Dec. 3, 1850.

JUAB
160 N. Main St., Nephi, UT 84648, (435) 623-3410,
<www.co.juab.ut.us>
- **INCORPORATED:** March 3, 1852
- **PARENT COUNTIES:** original county
- **DIVORCE:** start in 1898, County Clerk
- **LAND:** 1852, County Recorder
- **COURT:** 1898, County Clerk
- **NOTES:** County Clerk has birth, death, and marriage records 1898-1905. Clerk of 4th District Court has probate records 1862-1962 and naturalization records 1904-1958. County Recorder has military discharge records 1944-1947.

KANE
76 N. Main St., Kanab, UT 84741, (435) 644-2458,
<kane.utah.gov>
- **INCORPORATED:** Jan. 16, 1864
- **PARENT COUNTY:** Washington
- **LAND:** start in 1864, County Recorder
- **NOTES:** County Clerk has birth records 1900-1905 and death records 1898-1905 and marriage records 1887-1966. Birth index online. Clerk of 6th District Court has court and divorce records 1864-1966. Probate Court has probate records 1864-1896. County Recorder has military discharge records 1945-1994.

LITTLE SALT LAKE
- **INCORPORATED:** Jan. 31, 1850
- **PARENT COUNTY:** original county
- **NOTES:** See Iron County. Name changed to Iron Dec. 3, 1850.

MALAD
- **INCORPORATED:** Jan. 5, 1856
- **PARENT COUNTIES:** unknown
- **NOTES:** Absorbed by Box Elder County Jan. 17, 1862.

MILLARD
765 S. Highway 99, Suite 6, Fillmore, UT 84631, (435) 743-6223,
<www.millardcounty.org>
- **INCORPORATED:** Oct. 4, 1851
- **PARENT COUNTY:** Iron
- **MARRIAGE RECORDS:** start in 1887, kept by County Clerk
- **DIVORCE:** 1852, County Clerk
- **LAND:** 1851, County Recorder
- **COURT:** 1852, County Clerk
- **NOTES:** Clerk of 4th District Court has probate records 1870-1966 and naturalization records 1896-1906. County Recorder has military discharge records 1944-1960. No death registration before 1905.

MORGAN
48 W. Young St., Box 886, Morgan, UT 84050, (801) 845-4022,
<www.morgan-county.net>
- **INCORPORATED:** Jan. 17, 1862
- **PARENT COUNTIES:** Summit, Weber, Cache
- **MARRIAGE RECORDS:** start in 1888, County Clerk
- **DIVORCE:** 1896, County Clerk
- **LAND:** 1862, County Recorder
- **NOTES:** County Clerk has birth and death records 1897-1905 and court records 1889-1895. Clerk of 2nd District Court has probate records 1868-1966. County Recorder has military discharge records 1943-1951.

PIUTE
550 N. Main St., Junction, UT 84740, (435) 577-2840, **<www.piute.org>**
- **INCORPORATED:** Jan. 16, 1865
- **PARENT COUNTY:** Beaver
- **BIRTH RECORDS:** start in 1898, kept by County Clerk
- **MARRIAGE RECORDS:** 1887, County Clerk
- **DIVORCE:** 1872, County Clerk
- **LAND:** 1865, County Recorder
- **NOTES:** Birth index available online. County Clerk has death records for 1898 and 1904, court and probate records 1869-1892. Clerk of 6th District Court has naturalization records 1896-1920, and probate records 1869-1910.

RICH
20 S. Main St., Box 218, Randolph, UT 84064, (435) 793-2415, **<www.richcountyut.org>**
- **INCORPORATED:** Jan. 16, 1864
- **PARENT COUNTY:** Cache
- **MARRIAGE RECORDS:** start in 1888, County Clerk
- **DIVORCE:** 1872, County Clerk
- **LAND:** 1864, County Recorder
- **PROBATE:** 1872, County Clerk
- **NOTES:** County Clerk has birth and death records 1898-1905. Birth index online. County Clerk has court records 1889-1895. Clerk of 1st District Court has naturalization records 1880-1896. Formerly Richland County. Name changed to Rich Jan. 29, 1868.

RICHLAND
- **INCORPORATED:** Jan. 16, 1864
- **PARENT COUNTY:** Cache
- **NOTES:** See Rich County. Name changed to Rich Jan. 29, 1868.

RIO VIRGIN
- **INCORPORATED:** Feb. 18, 1869
- **PARENT COUNTY:** unknown
- **NOTES:** Absorbed by Washington County Feb. 16, 1872. Parts of county went to Nevada and Arizona.

SALT LAKE
2001 S. State St. Room S-2200, Salt Lake City, UT 84190, (801) 468-3439, **<www.slco.org>**
- **INCORPORATED:** March 3, 1852
- **PARENT COUNTY:** original county
- **MARRIAGE RECORDS:** start in 1887, County Clerk
- **DIVORCE:** 1896, County Clerk
- **LAND:** 1852, County Recorder
- **COURT:** 1896, County Clerk
- **NOTES:** County Clerk has birth and death records 1898-1905. Birth index online. Salt Lake City Recorder has death records 1848-1933. County Clerk has death records 1897-1905. Clerk of 3rd District Court has probate records 1852-1966 and naturalization records 1896-1929. Formerly Great Salt Lake County. Name changed to Salt Lake Jan. 29, 1868.

SAN JUAN
117 S. Main St., Box 338, Monticello, UT 84535, (435) 587-3223, **<www.sanjuancounty.org>**
- **INCORPORATED:** Feb. 17, 1880
- **PARENT COUNTIES:** Kane, Iron, Piute
- **MARRIAGE RECORDS:** start in 1888, County Clerk
- **DIVORCE:** 1891, County Clerk
- **LAND:** 1880, County Recorder
- **COURT:** 1891, County Clerk
- **NOTES:** County Clerk has birth and death records 1898-1905. County Recorder has military discharge records 1944-1948. Clerk of 7th District Court has probate records 1888-1975.

SANPETE
Box 100, Manti, UT 84642, (435) 835-2131, **<sanpete.com>**
- **INCORPORATED:** March 3, 1852
- **PARENT COUNTY:** original county
- **MARRIAGE RECORDS:** start in 1888, County Clerk
- **DIVORCE:** 1878, County Clerk
- **LAND:** 1852, County Recorder
- **COURT:** 1878, County Clerk
- **NOTES:** County Clerk has birth and death records 1898-1905. Clerk of 6th District has probate records 1870-1901. County Recorder has military discharge records 1944-1964.

SEVIER
250 N. Main, Richfield, UT 84701, (435) 893-0401, **<www.sevierutah.net>**
- **INCORPORATED:** Jan. 16, 1865
- **PARENT COUNTY:** Sanpete
- **MARRIAGE RECORDS:** start in 1887, County Clerk
- **DIVORCE:** 1865, Clerk of 6th District Court
- **LAND:** 1865, County Recorder
- **PROBATE:** 1865–1985, Clerk of 6th District Court
- **COURT:** 1865–1892, Clerk of 6th District Court
- **MILITARY:** 1942, County Recorder
- **NOTES:** County Clerk has birth and death records 1898-1905, and naturalization records 1850-1898. Clerk of 6th District Court has court records 1869-1892 and probate records 1865-1985. County Recorder has military discharge records 1942-1970.

SHAMBIP
- **INCORPORATED:** Jan. 12, 1856
- **PARENT COUNTY:** unknown
- **NOTES:** Absorbed by Tooele County Jan. 17, 1862.

ST. MARYS
- **INCORPORATED:** Jan. 5, 1856
- **PARENT COUNTY:** unknown
- **NOTES:** Transferred to Nevada Territory March 2, 1861.

SUMMIT
60 N. Main St., Box 128, Coalville, UT 84017, (435) 336-3204, **<www.summitcounty.org>**
- **INCORPORATED:** Jan. 13, 1854
- **PARENT COUNTIES:** Green River, Great Salt Lake
- **MARRIAGE RECORDS:** start in 1888, County Clerk
- **DIVORCE:** 1896, County Clerk

- **LAND:** 1854, County Recorder
- **COURT:** 1896, County Clerk
- **NATURALIZATION:** 1896, Clerk of 3rd District Court
- **NOTES:** County Clerk has birth and death records 1898-1905. Clerk of 3rd District Court has probate records 1866-1963.

TOOELE

47 S. Main St., Tooele, UT 84074, (435) 843-3140,
<www.co.tooele.ut.us>

- **INCORPORATED:** March 3, 1852
- **PARENT COUNTY:** original county
- **MARRIAGE RECORDS:** start in 1887, County Clerk
- **LAND:** 1852, County Recorder
- **COURT:** 1852, Clerk of 3rd District Court
- **NOTES:** County Clerk has birth and death records 1898-1905. Clerk of 3rd District Court has divorce records 1854-1892 and probate records 1896-1966.

UINTAH

147 E. Main St., Vernal, UT 84078, (435) 781-5361,
<www.co.uintah.ut.us>

- **INCORPORATED:** Feb. 18, 1880
- **PARENT COUNTY:** Wasatch
- **DIVORCE RECORDS:** start in 1886, Clerk of 8th District Court
- **LAND:** 1880, County Recorder
- **COURT:** 1886, Clerk of 8th District Court
- **NOTES:** County Clerk has birth records 1898-1905, death records 1900-1901, 1904-1905, and marriage records 1888-1978. County Recorder has military discharge records 1944-1992. Clerk of 8th District Court has probate records 1886-1966.

UTAH

100 E. Center St., Room 3600, Provo, UT 84606, (801) 851-8109,
<www.co.utah.ut.us>

- **INCORPORATED:** March 3, 1852
- **PARENT COUNTY:** original county
- **MARRIAGE RECORDS:** start in 1887, County Clerk
- **DIVORCE:** 1859, County Clerk
- **LAND:** 1852, County Recorder
- **COURT:** 1885, County Clerk
- **NOTES:** County Clerk has birth and death records 1898-1905. Clerk of 4th District Court has naturalization records 1878-1896 and probate records 1852-1900, 1958-1964. County Recorder has military discharge records 1944-1992.

WASATCH

25 N. Main St., Heber City, UT 84032, (435) 657-3190,
<www.co.wasatch.ut.us>

- **INCORPORATED:** Jan. 17, 1862
- **PARENT COUNTIES:** Davis, Green River
- **MARRIAGE RECORDS:** start in 1879, County Clerk
- **DIVORCE:** 1898, County Clerk
- **LAND:** 1862, County Recorder
- **COURT:** 1898, County Clerk
- **NOTES:** County Clerk has birth and death records 1898-1905. Clerk of 4th District Court has naturalization records 1896-1935 and probate records 1862-1964. County Recorder has military discharge records 1919-1954.

WASHINGTON

197 E. Tabernacle St., St. George, UT 84770, (435) 634-5712,
<www.washco.utah.gov>

- **INCORPORATED:** March 3, 1852
- **PARENT COUNTY:** unorganized territory
- **MARRIAGE RECORDS:** 1862-1919, start in 1887, County Clerk
- **DIVORCE:** start in 1878, County Clerk
- **LAND:** 1852, County Recorder
- **PROBATE:** 1874-1981, Clerk of 5th District Court
- **COURT:** 1874, County Clerk
- **NOTES:** County Clerk has birth and death records 1898-1905 and marriage records 1862-1919. Clerk of 5th District Court has naturalization records 1896-1940 and probate records 1877-1981. County Recorder has military discharge records 1923-1967.

WAYNE

18 S. Main, Box 189, Loa, UT 84747, (435) 836-2765,
<www.waynecountyutah.org>

- **INCORPORATED:** March 10, 1892
- **PARENT COUNTY:** Piute
- **MARRIAGE RECORDS:** start in 1892, County Clerk
- **DIVORCE:** 1898, County Clerk
- **LAND:** 1892, County Recorder
- **COURT:** 1892, County Clerk
- **NOTES:** County Clerk has some birth and death records 1898-1905. Clerk of 6th District Court has naturalization records 1896-1902 and probate records 1889-1987. County Recorder has military discharge records 1945-1974.

WEBER

2380 Washington Blvd., Ogden, UT 84401, (801) 399-8400,
<www.co.weber.ut.us>

- **INCORPORATED:** March 3, 1852
- **PARENT COUNTY:** original county
- **MARRIAGE RECORDS:** start in 1887, County Clerk
- **DIVORCE:** Clerk of 2nd District Court
- **LAND:** 1852, County Recorder
- **NATURALIZATION:** 1896, Clerk of 2nd District Court
- **NOTES:** County Clerk has birth and death records 1898-1905. Birth index online. Death records exclude Ogden. Clerk of 2nd District Court records 1889-1895, and probate records 1879-1959 and 1975-1984.

VERMONT

» BY MAUREEN A. TAYLOR

HISTORICAL OVERVIEW

Geography and climate hindered the development of the second-largest New England state: Vermont had no permanent settlements until 1760. Independent-minded Vermonters fought off land claims from New York State and New Hampshire to form their own republic in 1777. In 1791, Vermont became the 14th state. Montpelier was chosen as the capital in 1805. Vermont was the first state to provide voting rights to all males regardless of race or religion, and to abolish the land-ownership requirement.

By the time of the American Revolution, only 22,000 people lived in the area, mostly emigrants from Connecticut (who traveled up the Connecticut River) and Massachusetts. Harsh living conditions and a depressed economy forced many to migrate to the northern part of the state or west into New York. New immigrants arrived to take their place as French Canadians moved down from Quebec. Scottish immigrants came to work Vermont's rock quarries and the Irish built its canals, including the 1823 Champlain Canal connecting Lake Champlain to the Hudson River.

Vermont's waterways provided transportation for goods produced at its paper mills, sawmills and tanneries, as well as agricultural and dairy products. Today, Vermonters can be proud of their rock quarries that supply marble throughout the world, their craftsmen who turn wood into furniture, the dairy products that appear on tables throughout the country, and the tourists who ski the state's mountains.

research tips

- Genealogical research in Vermont begins with knowing the town where your ancestor lived. Then, begin consulting the cemetery records and published histories of that town.
- Visit the Vermont Historical Society Library **<www.vermonthistory.org>** for a large collection of statewide resources such as vital records, census records, and family histories, as well as manuscripts and photographs documenting the history of the state.
- Search for ancestors who left the state for greener pastures—the freezing winters and rough farming environment chased many early settlers away.

CENSUS RECORDS

- Federal census: 1790, 1800, 1810, 1820, 1830, 1840, 1850, 1860, 1870, 1880, 1900, 1910, 1920, 1930
- Federal mortality schedules: 1880
- Special census of Civil War Union veterans and widows: 1890

RECORD HIGHLIGHTS

As in the rest of New England, vital records in Vermont are incomplete before civil registration in 1857. Before 1820, entire families sometimes appear together in the records of the towns where they lived. Vermont's population was mobile, with families looking for economic opportunities in various areas—an additional challenge to your research.

Vermont ratified the Constitution in 1791, missing the first federal census by one year—but there is a 1791 census for the state. The Genealogical Society of Vermont **<www.genealogyvermont.org>** has compiled genealogies of 1791 residents in the series *Vermont Families in 1791* (Picton Press). Jay Mack Holbrook compiled names from land grants and other sources to produce the book *1771 Census* (Holbrook Research, 1982). Examine the original sources cited to verify whether your ancestor actually lived in Vermont or was just awarded land.

Probate records, when they exist, were recorded on the district level. They are indexed, but only by district. Microfilm copies of probate proceedings do not include all the papers found in an original probate file. Use the indexes to locate a record, then track down the originals.

Land disputes in the colonial period mean pre-1777 land transactions could be in New York, New Hampshire or Vermont. The New Hampshire State Papers (see New Hampshire) and Vermont State Papers contain information on original territorial proprietors, and a volume of Vermont State Papers has information on confiscated land. Search the Nye index, which indexes signatories to petitions, on the Vermont State Archives website **<vermont-archives.org/research/database/nye.asp>**. After 1777, land records are in the town clerk's office. Most records have been microfilmed and are available in central repositories such as the Vermont Historical Society **<www.vermonthistory.org>**.

The Vermont Historical Society has an index of veteran's graves from the Civil War through World War I. Microfilms of vital records include cemetery cards serving as a statewide index to grave records.

Unfortunately, a fire destroyed some of Vermont's state-level military records before 1920. Miscellaneous records are available in town clerk's offices or at the Vermont State Archives. Records that were saved from the fire have been preserved and microfilmed by the Vermont Department of Public Records and are available there. A finding aid is online at **<vermont-archives.org/research/genealogy>**.

Church registers provide documentation on Vermont families prior to civil registration. A Works Progress Administration inventory of church records at the Vermont Public Records Office enables you to locate original records, but some listings are out of date.

Vermont's first published newspaper predates statehood. The Vermont Department of Libraries has an extensive collection of papers printed since 1781 on microfilm.

Genealogical research in Vermont is both challenging and rewarding. Incomplete colonial records, the lack of statewide indexes and an extremely mobile population make locating material difficult. However, there are rewards for the persistent researcher willing to patiently search town records and multiple districts.

"Knowing the town is the primary access point for finding information," counsels Marjorie Strong, assistant librarian at the Vermont Historical Society. "Once you have the town you'll be able to consult cemetery records, published histories, and family genealogies."

According to Strong, "start looking at vital records at the Vital Records Office in Montpelier to find life dates and towns of residence for family members." Then, visit the largest genealogical society in the state—the Vermont Historical Society Library **<www.vermonthistory.org>** in Barre. The society has family histories, published vital records, cemetery inscriptions, town histories and censuses, as well as manuscripts and photographs on the history of the state. A guide to its genealogical resources is on the website.

If you're looking for a colonial Vermont ancestor, records of his settlement might be in New York or New Hampshire, depending where he lived and when. Learn the history of his town to determine where materials are found. Remember that many families traveled together from town to town.

Since most early settlers emigrated from Connecticut, following the Connecticut River through Massachusetts and into Vermont, look for pre-Vermont information on the family in the records of towns near the river.

It is quite possible that at least some members of your Vermont family sought opportunities outside the state. During the 1820s, approximately half the state's population left to join communities established by ex-Vermonters. Poor agricultural conditions and harsh winters drove many to New York, lower Canada, Pennsylvania, Ohio, Michigan, Illinois, Wisconsin and elsewhere. Many of these former Vermonters established Sons of Vermont chapters outside the state. Find evidence of their emigration in church removal records and insolvency cases in probate records.

Vermont ancestral research is complicated, but not impossible. Travel from major repositories to small towns looking for your ancestors and don't forget to enjoy the beautiful scenery along the way.

ARCHIVES, LIBRARIES, AND SOCIETIES

Addison Town Historical Society
3968 Rt. 22A, Addison, VT 05491, (802) 759-2380

Alburg Historical Society
Box 453, Alburg, VT 05440, **<www.alburghvt.org/historical.php>**

Archives of the Roman Catholic Diocese of Burlington
351 North Ave., Burlington, VT 05401, (802) 658-6110, **<www.vermontcatholic.org>**

Assemblée des Évêques du Quebec
1225 St. Joseph Blvd. E., Montreal, Quebec, Canada H2J 1L7, **<www.eveques.qc.ca>**

Bailey-Howe Library, University of Vermont
538 Main St., Burlington, VT 05405, (802) 656-2022, **<library.uvm.edu>**

Barnet Historical Society
RR 1, Box 241, Barnet, VT 05821, **<www.rootsweb.ancestry.com/~vtcbarne/barnet.htm>**

Bennington Historical Society
75 W. Main St., Bennington, VT 05201, **<www.benningtonmuseum.org/bennington-historical-society.html>**

Berlin Historical Society
1921 Scott Hill Rd., Berlin, VT 05602, **<www.berlinvt.org/Berlin%20Historical%20Society.htm>**

Bethel Historical Society
Box 25, Bethel, VT 05032, **<www.bethelhistorical.org>**

Bradford Historical Society
Box 301, Bradford, VT 05033, **<www.vmga.org/orange/bradfordhs.html>**

Braintree Historical Society
RFD 1, Thayer Brook Rd., Randolph, VT 05060, **<www.vmga.org/orange/braintree.html>**

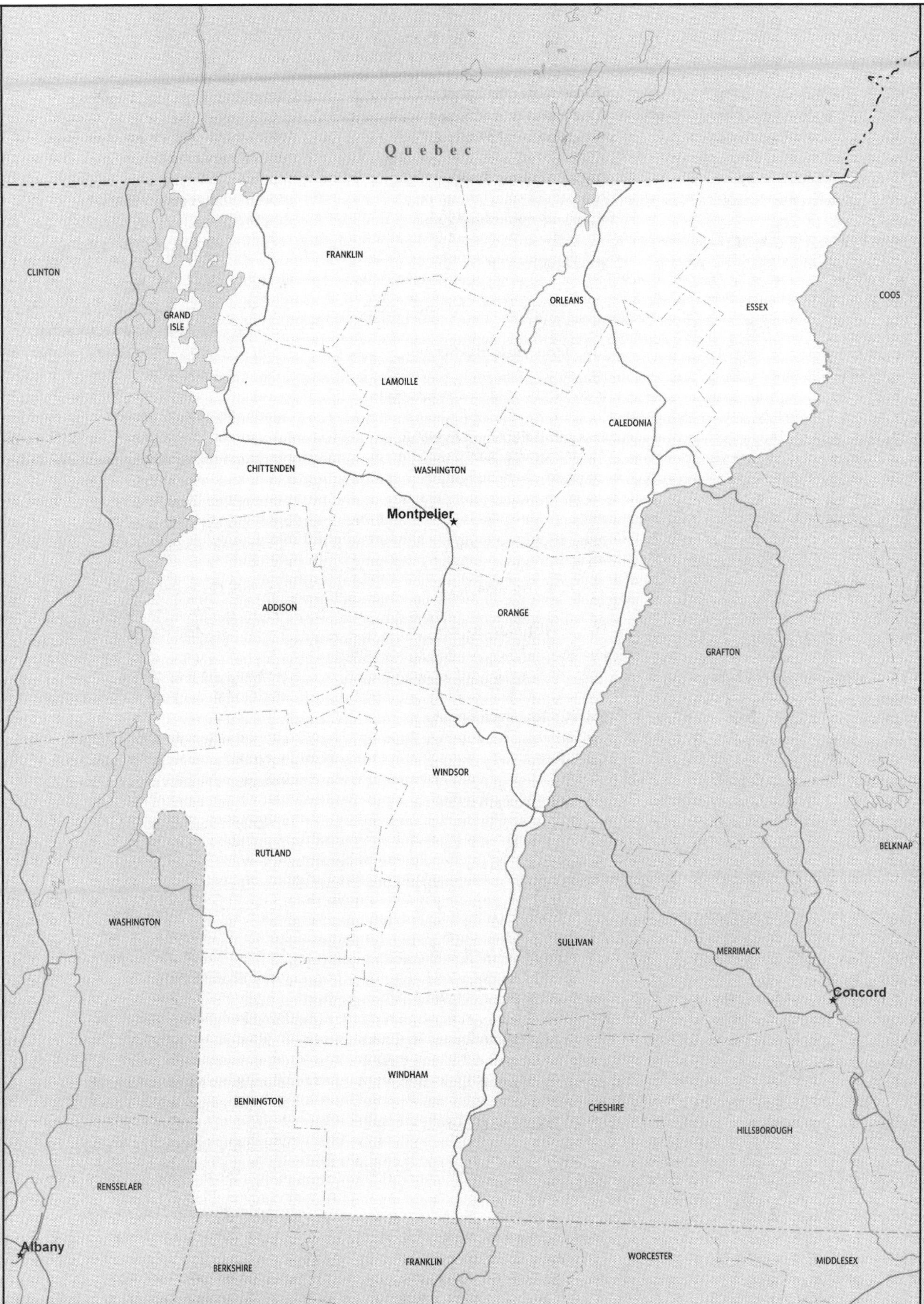
Quebec
CLINTON
FRANKLIN
GRAND ISLE
ORLEANS
ESSEX
COOS
LAMOILLE
CALEDONIA
CHITTENDEN
WASHINGTON
Montpelier
ADDISON
ORANGE
GRAFTON
WINDSOR
BELKNAP
RUTLAND
WASHINGTON
SULLIVAN
MERRIMACK
Concord
WINDHAM
BENNINGTON
CHESHIRE
HILLSBOROUGH
RENSSELAER
Albany
BERKSHIRE
FRANKLIN
WORCESTER
MIDDLESEX

Brattleboro Historical Society
230 Main St., Brattleboro, VT 05301, **<www.brattleborohistoricalsociety.org>**

Bridport Historical Society
2947 Basin Harbor Rd., Bridport, VT 05734

Bristol Historical Society Museum
Howden Hall Community Center, 19 West St., Bristol, VT 05443

Brooks Memorial Library
224 Main St., Brattleboro, VT 05301, **<www.brooks.lib.vt.us>**

Cabot Historical Society
193 McKinstry Road, Marshfield, VT 05647, **<www.cabothistory.org>**

Canaan Historical Society
Box 371, Canaan, VT 05903, **<canaanvthistoricalsociety.org>**

Cavendish Historical Society
Box 110, Cavendish, VT 05142, **<cavendishhistory.org>**

Charleston Historical Society
1896 Vermont Route 105, Box 46, West Charleston, VT 05833, **<www.charlestonvt.org/historical.php>**

Charlotte Historical Society
4205 Ethan Allen HWY, Charlotte, VT 05445

Chelsea Historical Society
Box 206, Chelsea, VT 05038, **<www.usgennet.org/usa/vt/town/chelsea>**

Chester Historical Society
Box 118, Chester, VT 05143, (802) 875-6211, **<www.chesterhistory.org>**

Concord Historical Society
Box 195, Concord, VT 05824

Crystal Lake Falls Historical Association
Box 253, Barton, VT 05822

Derby Historical Society
Box 357, Derby, VT 05829, **<www.derbyvt.org/historical.htm>**

Division of State Papers, Office of the Secretary of State
1078 Route 2, Montpelier, VT 05633, (802) 828-3700

Dorset Historical Society
Box 52, Dorset, VT 05251, **<www.dorsetvthistory.org>**

Dover Historical Society
Box 53, East Dover, VT 05341, **<www.doververmont.com>**

Elmore Historical Society
Box 53, Lake Elmore, VT 05657, **<www.elmorehistoricalsociety.org>**

Enosburgh Historical Society
Box 98, Enosburg Falls, VT 05450, **<www.enosburghvt.org/historical.htm>**

Episcopal Diocesan Center
5 Rock Point Rd., Burlington, VT 05401, (802) 863-3431, **<www.dioceseofvermont.org>**

Essex Historical Society
3 Browns River Rd., Essex Jct., VT 05452, **<www.vermonthistory.org>**

Fairfax Historical Society
Box 145, Fairfax, VT 05454, (802) 849-6638, **<www.vtgrandpa.com/fhs>**

Fairfield Historical Society
1345 Northrup Rd., Enosburg Falls, VT 05450

Fairlee Historical Society
Box 95, Fairlee, VT 05045

Fletcher Free Library
149 Church St., Burlington, VT 05401, **<www.fletcherfree.org>**

Genealogical Society of Vermont
Box 14, Randolph, VT 05060, **<www.genealogyvermont.org>**

Georgia Historical Society Museum
Box 2072, Georgia, VT 05468, **<www.vmga.org/franklin/georgiahs.html>**

Glover Historical Society
Box 208 Glover, VT 05839, (802) 525-8855, **<www.gloverhistoricalsociety.org>**

Grafton Historical Society
Box 202, Grafton, VT 05146, **<www.graftonhistory.org>**

Green Mountain College Library
1 Brennan Circle, Poultney, VT 05764, (802) 287-8000, **<www.greenmtn.edu/library.aspx>**

Greensboro Historical Society
Box 151, Greensboro, VT 05841, **<greensborohistoricalsociety.org>**

Groton Historical Society
Box 89, Groton, VT 05046, (802) 584-3417, **<www.rootsweb.ancestry.com/~vtgenweb/vtcaldon/Groton/GrotonHistSoc.html>**

Guilford Historical Society
236 School Rd., Guilford, VT 05301, **<www.vmga.org/windham/guilfordhs.html>**

Halifax Historical Society
RR 4, Box 531, Brattleboro, VT 05301, **<www.halifaxvthistory.org>**

Hartford Historical Society
Box 547, Hartford, VT 05047, **<www.hartfordhistory.org>**

Historical Society of Peru
Box 73, Peru, VT 05152

Historical Society of Windham County
Box 246, Newfane, VT 05345, **<homepages.sover.net/~histwind>**

Holland Historical Society
RD 1, Box 37, Derby Line, Holland, VT 05830

Huntington Historical Society
Box 147, Huntington, VT 05462, **<www.vmga.org/chittenden/huntingtonhs.html>**

Hyde Park Historical Society
97 Eden St., Hyde Park, VT 05655

Island Pond Historical Society
Box 408, Island Pond, VT 05846

Isle La Motte Historical Society
Box 18, Isle La Motte, VT 05463

Jamaica Historical Foundation
Box 287, Jamaica, VT 05343

Jericho Historical Society
Box 35, Jericho, VT 05465, **<snowflakebentley.com/jhs.htm>**

Lincoln Historical Society
88 Quaker St., Lincoln, VT 05443, (802) 453-3371

Londonderry Historical Society
Box 114, South Londonderry, VT 05155, **<www.londonderryvt.org>**

Lowell Historical Society
636 Irish Hill Rd., Lowell, VT 05847

Lunenburg Historical Society
Box 195, Lunenburg, VT 05906, **<www.lunenburghistoricalsociety.org>**

Lyndon Historical Society
Box 85, Lyndon Center, VT 05850, (802) 626-8746

Manchester Historical Society
Box 363, Manchester, VT 05254, **<www.manchesterhistoricalsociety.org>**

Marlboro Historical Society
Box 131, Marlboro, VT 05344, **<www.marlboro.vt.us/groups/historical_society>**

Memphremagog Historical Society
96 Stagecoach Drive, Newport, VT 05855

Middlesex Historical Society
5 Church St., Middlesex, VT 05602, **<www.middlesex-vt.org/html/historical_society.html>**

Milton Historical Society
Box 2, Milton, VT 05468

Missisquoi Valley Historical Society
Box 237, North Troy, VT 05859, (802) 988-2397

Montgomery Historical Society
Box 47, Montgomery, VT 05470, **<www.montgomeryvt.us/mhs.htm>**

Moretown Historical Society
800 South Hill Rd., Moretown, VT 05660, (802) 496-2090, **<www.johnhilferty.com/history3.html>**

National Archives and Records Administration, Northeast Region
380 Trapelo Rd., Waltham, MA 02452, (781) 663-0130, **<www.archives.gov/northeast/boston>**

New England Historic Genealogical Society
101 Newbury St., Boston, MA 02116, (617) 536-5740, **<www.americanancestors.org>**

New Haven Historical Society
89 North St., New Haven, VT 05472

Northfield Historical Society
Box 88, Northfield, VT 05663

Norwich Historical Society
Box 1680, Norwich, VT 05055, **<www.norwichhistory.org>**

Peacham Historical Association
Box 101, Peacham, VT 05862, **<www.peachamhistorical.org>**

Pittsford Historical Society
3399 Rt. 7, Pittsford, VT 05763, **<www.pittsfordhistorical.com>**

Poultney Historical Society
1499 E. Main St., Poultney, VT 05764, **<www.poultneyhistoricalsociety.org>**

Pownal Historical Society
Box 313, Pownal, VT 05261, **<www.pownal.org>**

Randolph Historical Society
Box 15, Randolph Center, VT 05061, **<www.vmga.org/orange/randolphhs.html>**

Reading Historical Society
Box 252, Reading, VT 05062, (802) 484-5738

Readsboro Historical Society
Box 158, Readsboro, VT 05350, **<www.vmga.org/bennington/readsboro.html>**

Richford Historical Society
186 S. Main St., Richford, VT 05476, **<www.richfordvt.com/history/richford-historical-society>**

Rochester Historical Society
Box 428, Rochester, VT 05767, **<www.rochesterhistorical.org>**

Royalton Historical Society
4184 Route 14, South Royalton, VT 05068, **<www.rootsweb.ancestry.com/~vtcroyal/address.htm>**

Rupert Historical Society
Box 2, Lewis Rd., Rupert, VT 05768

Rutland Historical Society
96 Center St., Rutland, VT 05701, **<www.rutlandhistory.com>**

Salisbury Historical Society
7 Forbes Circle, Middlebury, VT 05753

Saxtons River Historical Society
Box 18, Saxtons River, VT 05154

Shaftsbury Historical Society
Box 401, Shaftsbury, VT 05262

Shoreham Historical Society
Box 235, Shoreham, VT 05770, (802) 897-2600

Shrewsbury Historical Society
RR103, Cuttingsville, VT 05738, (802) 492-2175, **<shrewsburyhistoricalsociety.com>**

Springfield Art and Historical Society
Box 313, Springfield, VT 05156, **<www.millerartcenter.com>**

St. Albans Historical Society
Box 722, St. Albans, VT 05478, **<www.stamuseum.com>**

St. Johnsbury Historical Society
1302 Main St. Johnsbury, VT 05819, (802) 748-8281

Stannard Historical Society
9 Willey Rd., Greensboro Bend, VT 05842, **<www.vmga.org/caledonia/stannard.html>**

Stowe Historical Society
Box 822, Stowe, VT 05672, (802) 253-6360, **<www.stowehistoricalsociety.org>**

Swanton Historical Society
58 S. River Rd., Swanton, VT 05488, **<www.swantonhistoricalsociety.org>**

Thetford Historical Society
Box 33, Thetford, VT 05074, **<www.thetfordhistoricalsociety.org>**

Tinmouth Historical and Genealogical Society
43 Chipmunk Crossing Dr., Tinmouth, VT

05773, **<tinmouthvt.org/MainPages/Organizations/HistoricalSociety.php>**

Townshend Historical Society
Box 95, Townshend, VT 01469, **<www.townsendhistoricalsociety.org>**

Tunbridge Historical Society
24 The Crossroad, Tunbridge, VT 05077

Vermont Department of Libraries
Pavilion Office Bldg., 109 State St., Montpelier, VT 05609, (802) 828-3261, **<libraries.vermont.gov>**

Vermont Finnish Society
RR1, Box 349A, Jamaica, VT 05343

Vermont French Canadian Genealogical Society
Box 65128, Burlington, VT 05406, **<www.vt-fcgs.org>**

Vermont Genealogical Society
Box 423, Pittsford, VT 05763, **<www.genealogyvermont.org>**

Vermont Historical Society
Pavilion Office Bldg., 109 State St., Montpelier, VT 05609, (802) 828-2291, **<www.vermonthistory.org>**

Vermont Public Records Division
Drawer 33, Montpelier, VT 05633, (802) 828-3286, **<vermont-archives.org>**

Vermont State Archives
109 State St. Montpelier, VT 05609, (802) 828-2308, **<vermont-archives.org>**

Vernon Historians
Box 282, Vernon, VT 05354, **<www.vernon-vt.org/historians.html>**

Veterans' Affairs Office, Vermont Adjutant General
120 State St., Montpelier, VT 05620, (802) 828-3379, **<www.vtguard.com/tag/index.htm>**

Vermont Department of Health
108 Cherry St., Burlington, VT 05402, (802) 464-4343, **<healthvermont.gov>**

Waitsfield Historical Society
Box 816, Waitsfield, VT 05673, **<www.waitsfieldhistoricalsociety.com>**

Wallingford Historical Society
Box 327, Wallingford, VT 05773, **<www.wallingfordvt.com/town_info.htm>**

Waterbury Historical Society
28 N. Main St., Box 708, Waterbury, VT 05676, **<www.rootsweb.ancestry.com/~vtwhs>**

Weathersfield Historical Society
Box 126, Weathersfield, VT 05151, **<www.weathersfield.org/pages/histsoc.htm>**

Wells Historical Society
Wells Town Office, Wells, VT 05774, **<www.museumsusa.org/museums/info/1161903>**

Welsh-American Genealogical Society
60 Norton Ave., Poultney, VT 05764, **<www.rootsweb.ancestry.com/~vtwags>**

West Haven Historical Society
834 Main St, West Haven, VT 05743

West Windsor Historical Society
Box 12, Brownsville, VT 05037, (802) 484-7474, **<www.rootsweb.ancestry.com/~vtwindso/wwhs.htm>**

Westford Historical Society
Box 21, Westford, VT 05494

Westminister Historical Society
Box 2, Westminster, VT 05158, **<www.usgennet.org/usa/vt/town/westminster/wrhistsoc.html>**

Whitingham Historical Society
Box 125, Jacksonville, VT 05342

Williamstown Historical Society
498 Boyce Rd., Williamstown, VT 05679, **<www.williamstownvt.org/histsoc.html>**

Williston Historical Society
Box 995, Williston, VT 05495, **<www.whsvt.org>**

Woodstock Historical Society
26 Elm St., Woodstock, VT 05091, **<www.woodstockhistorical.org>**

GENERAL RESOURCES

Basic Sources for Vermont Historical Research (Office of the Secretary of State, ca. 1981)

A Calendar of Manuscripts in Certain Boxes At the Vermont Historical Society by Loriman S. Brigham (Loriman S. Brigham, 1970)

Collecting Vermont Ancestors by Alice Eichholz (New Trails, 1986)

The Congregational Churches of Vermont and Their Ministry by John Moore Comstock (Caledonian Co., 1915)

Cutter Index: A Consolidated Index of Cutter's Nine Genealogy Series by Norma Olin Ireland and Winfred Irving (Ireland Indexing Service, ca. 1970)

A Directory of Churches And Religious Organizations in the State of Vermont from the Historical Records Survey (Historical Records Survey, 1939)

Encyclopedia, Vermont Biography by Prentiss Cutler Dodge (Ullery Publishing Co., 1912)

English Origins of New England Families: From the New England Historical and Genealogical Register, 3 vols., from the New England Historic Genealogical Society (The Society, 1984)

Final Report and Inventory of the Vermont Historical Records Survey, W.P.A. (Works Progress Administration, 1942)

A Genealogical Dictionary of the First Settlers of New England: Showing Three Generations of Those Who Came Before May 1692, 4 vols., by James Savage (Genealogical Publishing Co., 1981)

Genealogical and Family History of the State of Vermont, 2 vols., by Hiram Carleton (Lewis Publishing Co., 1903)

Genealogical Research in New England edited by Ralph J. Crandall (Genealogical Publishing Co., 1984)

Genealogist's Handbook for New England Research, 3rd edition (New England Historic Genealogical Society, 1993)

The Greenlaw Index of the New England Historic Genealogical Society, 2 vols., by William Prescott Greenlaw (G.K. Hall, 1979)

Guide to the "Miscellaneous File" of Uncatalogued Material in the Vermont Historical Society by Loriman S. Brigham (Loriman S. Brigham, 1969)

A Guide to Newspaper Indexes in New England (New England Library Association, 1978)

A Guide to Vermont's Repositories (Vermont State Archives, 1986)

History of the Baptists in Vermont by Henry Crocker (P.H. Gobie Press, 1913)

History of Vermont by Zadock Thompson (Thompson, 1853)

The History of Vermont, from its Discovery to its Administration into the Union in 1791 by Hiland Hall (J. Munsell, 1868)

Index to the Burlington Free Press, 6 vols., (Historical Records Survey, 1941)

Inventory of the Church Archives of Vermont, No. 1 Diocese of Vermont, Protestant Episcopal from the Historical Records Survey (Historical Records Survey, 1940)

Men of Vermont by Jacob G. Ullery (Transcript Publishing Co., 1894)

New England Families, Genealogical and Memorial, 4 vols., by William Richard Cutter (Lewis Historical Publishing Co., 1914)

New England Family Histories and Genealogies: States of New Hampshire and Vermont by Lu Verne V. Hall (Heritage Books, 2000)

Vermont: A Bibliography of Its History edited by T.D. Seymour Bassett (G.K. Hall & Co., 1981)

Vermont's First Settlers by Jay Mack Holbrook (Holbrook Research Institute, 1976)

Vermont Historical Gazetteer: A Magazine Embracing a History of Each Town, Civil, Ecclesiastical, Biographical and Military, 6 vols., edited by Abby Maria Hemenway (A.M. Hemenway, 1868-1891)

Vermont Newspaper Abstract: Vermont Gazette, The Vermont Gazette: Epitome of the World, The World, the Green-Mountain Farmer by Marsh Hoffman Rising (New England Historic Genealogical Society, 2001)

Vermont Research Outline by the Church of Jesus Christ of Latter-day Saints (online at **<www.familysearch.org/eng/search/RG/guide/vermont.asp>**)

Vermonters by Dorman B.E. Kent (Vermont Historical Society, 1937)

CENSUS RECORDS

Vermont 1771 Census by Jay Mack Holbrook (Holbrook Research Institute, 1982)

IMMIGRATION RECORDS

Migration from Vermont by Lewis D. Stillwell (Vermont Historical Society, 1948)

Passenger and Immigration Lists Index, 15 vols., by P. William Filby (Gale Research, 1981)

LAND RECORDS

Charters Granted by the State of Vermont, 1779-1846, 2 vols., (Vermont Public Records Division, 1974)

Index to the Papers of the Surveyors-General (Secretary of State, 1918)

Massachusetts Land Grants in Vermont by Herbert Williams Denio (John Wilson and Son, University Press, 1920)

State Papers of Vermont from the Vermont Secretary of State (Published by authority of the Secretary of State, 1939)

Vermont's First Settlers by Jay Mack Holbrook (Holbrook Research Institute, 1976)

The Vermont Lease Lands by Walter Thompson Bogart (Vermont Historical Society, 1950)

MAPS

A Gazetteer of Vermont: Containing Descriptions Of all the Counties, Towns and Districts in the State, and of its Principal Mountains, Rivers, Waterfalls, Harbors, Islands and Curious Places by John Hayward (Heritage books, 1990)

The Postal History of Vermont by George C. Slawson et al. (Collectors Club, 1969)

The Shaping of Vermont: 1749-1877 by J. Kevin Graffagnino (Vermont Heritage Press, 1983)

Vermont Atlas and Gazetteer (DeLorme Mapping Co., 1996)

Vermont Place-Names: Footprints of History by Ester Munroe Swift (Stephen Green Press, 1977)

MILITARY RECORDS

A List of Pensioners of the War of 1812 [Vermont Claimants] by Byron N. Clark (Genealogical Publishing Co., 1969)

Revised Roster of Vermont Volunteers and Lists Of Vermonters Who Served in the Army and Navy of the United States During the War of the Rebellion, 1861-66 by Theodore S. Peck (Watchman Publishing Co., 1892)

Revolutionary Soldiers Buried in Vermont by Walter Hill Crockett (Genealogical Publishing Co., 1959)

Rolls of Soldiers in the Revolutionary War, 1775-1783 compiled and edited by John E. Goodrich (Tuttle Co., 1904)

Roster of Soldiers in the War Of 1812-1814 from the Vermont Adjutant Generals Office (Herbert T. Johnson, Adjutant General, 1933)

Soldiers, Sailors and Patriots of the Revolutionary War, Vermont by Carleton E. Fisher (Picton Press, 1992)

Vermont in the Spanish-American War by Herbert T. Johnson (Adjutant General, 1929)

☞PROBATE RECORDS

State Papers of Vermont from the Vermont Secretary of State (Published by authority of Secretary of State, 1939)

☞VITAL RECORDS

Burial Grounds of Vermont by Arthur L. Hyde (Vermont Old Cemetery Association, 1991)

Index to Known Cemetery Listings in Vermont by Joann H. Nichols (Joann H. Nichols, 1976)

Vermont Warnings Out, 2 vols., by Alden M. Rollins (Picton Press, 1995-1997)

•-COUNTY DETAILS-•

ADDISON

5 Court St., Middlebury, VT 05753, (802) 388-7741, **<www.addisoncounty.com>**

- **INCORPORATED:** Oct. 18, 1785
- **PARENT COUNTY:** Rutland
- **BIRTH RECORDS:** unknown start, kept by Town Clerks
- **MARRIAGE:** unknown start, Town Clerks
- **DIVORCE:** 1797, Dept. of BGS
- **DEATH:** unknown start, Town Clerks
- **PROBATE:** 1824, Probate Office
- **COURT:** 1797, District/Superior Clerk
- **BURIAL:** unknown start, Town Clerks
- **NOTES:** Towns chartered before 1800: Addison 1761, Bridport 1761, Cornwall 1761, Ferrisburgh 1762, Leicester 1761, Lincoln 1780, Middlebury 1761, Monkton 1762, New Haven 1761, Orwell 1763, Panton 1761, Ripton 1781, Salisbury 1761, Shoreham 1761, Starksboro 1780, Vergennes 1788, Waltham 1796, Weybridge 1761, Whiting 1763.

BENNINGTON

207 South St., Bennington, VT 05201, (802) 442-8528, **<www.bennington.com>**

- **INCORPORATED:** Feb. 11, 1779
- **PARENT COUNTY:** Original county
- **BIRTH RECORDS:** unknown start, Town Clerks
- **MARRIAGE:** unknown start, Town Clerks
- **DIVORCE:** 1899, County Clerk
- **DEATH:** unknown start, Town Clerks
- **COURT:** 1861, District/Superior Clerk
- **NOTES:** Towns chartered before 1800: Arlington 1761, Bennington 1749, Dorset 1761, Glastenbury 1761, Landgrove 1780, Manchester 1761, Peru 1761, Pownal 1760, Rupert 1761, Sandgate 1761, Shaftsbury 1761, Sunderland 1761, Winhall 1761. Bennington County has 2 probate districts: Bennington (Probate Office has records from 1778) and Manchester (Probate Office has records from 1779).

CALEDONIA

1136 Main St., St. Johnsbury, VT 05819, (802) 748-6605, **<www.rootsweb.ancestry.com/~vermont/Caledonia.html>**

- **INCORPORATED:** Nov. 5, 1792
- **PARENT COUNTY:** Orange
- **BIRTH RECORDS:** unknown start, Town Clerks
- **MARRIAGE:** unknown start, Town Clerks
- **DIVORCE:** ca. 1800, Dept. of BGS
- **DEATH:** unknown start, Town Clerks
- **LAND:** unknown start, Town Clerks
- **PROBATE:** unknown start, Probate Office
- **COURT:** ca. 1800, District/Superior Clerk
- **NOTES:** Towns chartered before 1800: Barnet 1763, Burke 1782, Cabot 1780, Danville 1786, Groton 1789, Hardwick 1781, Lyndon 1780, Peacham 1763, Ryegate 1763, Sheffield 1780, St. Johnsbury 1786, Sutton 1782, Walden 1781, Waterford 1780, Wheelock 1785. City of Cabot became part of Washington County in 1855.

CHITTENDEN

175 Main St., Burlington, VT 05402, (802) 863-3467, **<www.ccrpcvt.org>**

- **INCORPORATED:** Oct. 22, 1787
- **PARENT COUNTY:** Addison
- **BIRTH RECORDS:** unknown start, Town Clerks
- **MARRIAGE:** unknown start, Town Clerks
- **DIVORCE:** unknown start, Dept. of BGS
- **DEATH:** unknown start, Town Clerks
- **LAND:** unknown start, Town Clerks
- **PROBATE:** unknown start, Probate Office
- **COURT:** 1969, District/Superior Clerk
- **NOTES:** Towns chartered before 1800: Bolton 1763, Burlington 1763, Charlotte 1762, Colchester 1763, Essex 1763, Hinesburg 1762, Huntington 1763, Jericho 1763, Milton 1763, Richmond 1794, Shelburne 1763, St. George 1763, Underhill 1763, Williston 1763.

ESSEX

75 Courthouse Dr., Box 75, Guildhall, VT 05905, (802) 676-3910, **<www.essex.org>**

- **INCORPORATED:** Nov. 5, 1792
- **PARENT COUNTY:** Orange
- **BIRTH RECORDS:** unknown start, Town Clerks
- **MARRIAGE:** unknown start, Town Clerks
- **DIVORCE:** unknown start, Dept. of BGS
- **DEATH:** unknown start, Town Clerks
- **LAND:** unknown start, Town Clerks

- **PROBATE:** 1791, Probate Office
- **COURT:** unknown start, Dept. of BGS
- **NOTES:** Towns chartered before 1800: Bloomfield 1762, Brunswick 1761, Canaan 1782, Concord 1780, Guildhall 1761, Lunenburg 1763, Maidstone 1761, Victory 1781.

FRANKLIN

Church St., Box 808, St. Albans, VT 05478, (802) 828-3286, **<www.stalbanschamber.com>**

- **INCORPORATED:** Nov. 5, 1792
- **PARENT COUNTY:** Chittenden
- **DIVORCE RECORDS:** 1900, Dept. of BGS
- **LAND:** unknown start, Town Clerks
- **PROBATE:** ca. 1800, Probate Office
- **COURT:** ca. 1940, District/Superior Clerk
- **NOTES:** Town Clerks have birth, death and marriage records 1760-1954. Towns founded before 1800: Bakersfield 1791, Berkshire 1781, Enosburg 1780, Fairfax 1763, Fairfield 1763, Fletcher 1781, Franklin 1789, Georgia 1763, Highgate 1762, Montgomery 1789, Richford 1780, Sheldon 1763, Swanton 1763, St. Albans 1763.

GRAND ISLE

3677 Rt. 2, Box 7, North Hero, VT 05474, (802) 372-8350, **<www.rootsweb.ancestry.com/~vermont/GenWebGrndisleCounty.html>**

- **INCORPORATED:** Nov. 9, 1802
- **PARENT COUNTIES:** Franklin, Chittenden
- **BIRTH RECORDS:** unknown start, Town Clerks
- **MARRIAGE:** unknown start, Town Clerks
- **DEATH:** unknown start, Town Clerks
- **LAND:** unknown start, Town Clerks
- **PROBATE:** 1800, County Clerk
- **COURT:** 1800, County Clerk
- **NOTES:** Towns chartered before 1800: Alburg 1781, Grand Isle 1779, Isles La Motte 1779, North Hero 1779, South Hero 1779.

JEFFERSON

- **INCORPORATED:** Nov. 1 1810
- **PARENT COUNTIES:** Chittenden, Caledonia, Orange
- **NOTES:** See Washington County. Name changed to Washington Nov. 8, 1814.

LAMOILLE

Box 303, Hyde Park, VT 05655, (802) 888-2207, **<www.lcpcvt.org>**

- **INCORPORATED:** Oct. 26, 1835
- **PARENT COUNTIES:** Chittenden, Orleans, Franklin, Washington
- **BIRTH RECORDS:** unknown start, Town Clerks
- **MARRIAGE:** unknown start, Town Clerks
- **DIVORCE:** unknown start, State Dept. of BGS
- **DEATH:** unknown start, Town Clerks
- **LAND:** unknown start, Town Clerks
- **PROBATE:** 1837, Probate Clerk
- **COURT:** 1837, District/County Clerk
- **NOTES:** Towns chartered before 1800: Cambridge 1781, Elmore 1781, Hyde Park 1781, Johnson 1792, Morristown 1781, Stowe 1763, Wolcott 1781.

ORANGE

5 Court St., Chelsea, VT 05038, (802) 685-4610, **<www.usgennet.org/usa/vt/county/orange>**

- **INCORPORATED:** Feb. 22, 1781
- **PARENT COUNTY:** Cumberland
- **BIRTH RECORDS:** unknown start, Town Clerks
- **MARRIAGE:** unknown start, Town Clerks
- **DIVORCE:** unknown start, State Dept. of BGS
- **DEATH:** unknown start, Town Clerks
- **LAND:** unknown start, Town Clerks
- **PROBATE:** 1771, Probate Office
- **COURT:** 1781, District/Superior Clerk
- **NOTES:** Towns chartered before 1800: Bradford 1770, Braintree 1781, Brookfield 1781, Chelsea 1781, Corinth 1764, Fairlee 1761, Newbury 1763, Orange 1781, Randolph 1781, Straford 1761, Thetford 1761, Topsham 1763, Turnbridge 1761, Vershire 1781, Washington 1781, West Fairlee 1779, Williamstown 1781.

ORLEANS

247 Main St., Box 787, Newport, VT 05855, (802) 334-3344, **<www.rootsweb.ancestry.com/~vtorlean/VTGenWeb.SM.htm>**

- **INCORPORATED:** Nov. 5, 1792
- **PARENT COUNTY:** Chittenden
- **BIRTH RECORDS:** unknown start, Town Clerks
- **MARRIAGE:** unknown start, Town Clerks
- **DIVORCE:** unknown start, State Dept. of BGS
- **DEATH:** unknown start, Town Clerks
- **LAND:** unknown start, Town Clerks
- **PROBATE:** 1796, Probate Office
- **COURT:** unknown start, District/Superior Clerk
- **NOTES:** Towns chartered before 1800: Barton 1789, Craftsbury 1781, Derby 1779, Glover 1783, Greensboro 1781, Holland 1779, Jay 1792, Westfield 1780.

RUTLAND

83 Center St., Rutland, VT 05701, (802) 775-4394, **<www.rutlandvermont.com>**

- **INCORPORATED:** Feb. 22, 1781
- **PARENT COUNTY:** Bennington
- **LAND RECORDS:** unknown start, Town Clerks
- **PROBATE:** 1780, Probate Office
- **COURT:** ca. 1775, District/Superior Clerk
- **NOTES:** Rutland County has two probate districts: Fairhaven and Rutland. Towns organized before 1800: Benson 1780, Brandon 1761, Castleton 1761, Chittenden 1780, Clarendon 1761, Danby 1761, Fair Haven 1779, Hubbardton 1764, Ira 1780, Mendon 1781, Middletown Springs 1784, Mt. Holly 1792, Mt. Tabor 1761, Pawlet 1761, Pittsford 1761, Poultney 1761, Rutland 1761, Sherburne 1761, Shrewsbury 1761, Sudbury 1763, Wallingford 1761, Wells 1761, West Haven 1792.

WASHINGTON

Box 426, Montpelier, VT 05602, (802) 223-2091, **<www.rootsweb.ancestry.com/~vtwashin>**

- **INCORPORATED:** Nov. 1, 1810
- **PARENT COUNTIES:** Addison, Orange, Caledonia, Orleans
- **BIRTH RECORDS:** unknown start, Town Clerks

- **MARRIAGE:** unknown start, Town Clerks
- **DIVORCE:** unknown start, Dept. of BGS
- **DEATH:** unknown start, Town Clerks
- **LAND:** unknown start, Town Clerks
- **PROBATE:** 1811, Probate Office
- **COURT:** unknown start, District/Superior Clerk
- **NOTES:** Formerly Jefferson County. Name changed to Washington Nov. 8, 1814. Towns organized before 1800: Barre 1781, Berlin 1763, Cabot 1780, Calais 1781, Duxbury 1763, Marshfield 1782, Middlesex 1763, Montpelier 1781, Moretown 1763, Northfield 1781, Plainfield 1797, Roxbury 1781, Waitsfield 1782, Warren 1780, Waterbury 1763, Worcester 1763.

WINDHAM

555 Vt. Rt. 30, Box 207, Newfane, VT 05345, (802) 365-7979,
<www.rootsweb.ancestry.com/~vtwindha>

- **INCORPORATED:** Feb. 22 1781
- **PARENT COUNTY:** Cumberland
- **BIRTH RECORDS:** unknown start, Town Clerks
- **MARRIAGE:** unknown start, Town Clerks
- **DIVORCE:** unknown start, Dept. of BGS
- **DEATH:** unknown start, Town Clerks
- **LAND:** unknown start, Town Clerks
- **COURT:** unknown start, District/Superior Clerk
- **NOTES:** Windham County has two probate districts: Marlboro and Westminster. Probate Clerk has probate records for Marlboro District from 1790. Probate Office has probate records for Westminster District from 1781. Towns chartered before 1800: Athens 1780, Brattleboro 1753, Brookline 1794, Grafton 1754, Guilford 1754, Halifax 1750, Jamaica 1780, Londonderry 1780, Marlboro 1751, Newfane 1753, Putney 1753, Rockingham 1752, Townshend 1753, Woodbury 1781, Westminster 1752, Whitingham 1770, Wilmington 1751, Windham 1795.

WINDSOR

12 The Green, Woodstock, VT 05091, (802) 457-2121,
<www.rootsweb.ancestry.com/~vtgenweb/Windsor-Co-VT.htm>

- **INCORPORATED:** Feb. 22, 1781
- **PARENT COUNTY:** Cumberland
- **BIRTH RECORDS:** unknown start, Town Clerks
- **MARRIAGE:** unknown start, Town Clerks
- **DIVORCE:** 1782, Dept. of BGS
- **DEATH:** unknown start, Town Clerks
- **LAND:** unknown start, Town Clerks
- **COURT:** 1782, Clerk/District Ct.
- **NOTES:** Windsor has two probate districts: Hartford and Windsor. Probate Offices in Hartford and Windsor have probate records. Towns chartered before 1800: Andover 1761, Baltimore 1793, Barnard 1761, Bethel 1779, Bridgewater 1761, Cavendish 1761, Chester 1754, Hartford 1761, Hartland 1761, Ludlow 1761, Norwich 1761, Plymouth 1761, Pomfret 1761, Reading 1761, Royalton 1769, Sharon 1761, Springfield 1761, Stockbridge 1761, Weathersfield 1761, Weston 1799, Windsor 1761, Woodstock 1761.

VIRGINIA

» BY RHONDA R. MCCLURE

HISTORICAL OVERVIEW

Jamestown is often overshadowed by Plymouth Colony when it comes to the founding of the United States. Jamestown was founded in 1607, making it the second-oldest community in the United States (to St. Augustine, Fla.), but the first permanent English settlement. Unlike St. Augustine and Plymouth, however, Jamestown almost didn't survive its first five years. It took John Rolfe's experiments with tobacco, especially his exportation of it to London, to make Virginia—named after the Virgin Queen, Elizabeth I—economically sustaining.

Early colonization of Virginia was encouraged through the use of headright grants, a method of giving public land—50 acres—to anyone who paid his own way to the new colony. These individuals could earn additional lots of 50 acres per individual for whom they paid passage. The original territory called Virginia was enormous and was eventually was carved up to form the following:

- 1779: a section became part of North Carolina
- 1786: a section became part of Pennsylvania
- 1792: a section became Kentucky and another became a part of Maryland
- 1803: a section became part of Tennessee and another area became Ohio and Indiana Territory
- 1816: a former part became Indiana
- 1818: a former part became Illinois
- 1863: a former part became West Virginia

Some divisions were enacted to settle border disputes. In the case of the Midwest states of Ohio, Indiana and Illinois, the land (known then as the Northwest Territory) was ceded to the United States when Virginia ratified the Constitution and became a state. Finally, West Virginia's counties broke away from Virginia because of their support of the Union during the Civil War.

research tips

- When researching colonial ancestors, records such as tithables lists and quitrent rolls help to establish the head of the household. Tithables were essentially head counts. Those considered tithable changed over the years from every male above age 16 to all males, nonwhite females, and wives of free nonwhite males. Quitrents were annual rents paid to the crown or to the proprietor who had granted a person his land. Many tithables and quitrents have been published.
- Virginia has 41 independent cities that keep their own records, though they reside within a county. In some instances, the county was absorbed by an independent city. Before spending a lot of time digging in county records, verify whether your ancestor lived in one of these cities (indicated in the Virginia county listings). Also visit the Virginia USGenWeb site **<www.rootsweb.ancestry.com/~vagenweb>** and view the county links. Links to the independent cities are with the counties.

CENSUS RECORDS

- Federal census: 1810, 1820, 1830. 1840, 1850, 1860, 1870, 1880, 1900, 1910, 1920, 1930
- Federal mortality schedules: 1850, 1860, 1870, 1880
- Tax lists: 1782-1785

RECORD HIGHLIGHTS

Though Virginia census enumerations were taken in 1790 and 1800, the records have not survived. Part of the 1810 census does exist. This makes it necessary to turn your attention to census alternatives, including Virginia tax lists from 1782 through 1785. Tax lists hold a wealth of information; they include the tithables and quitrents described above. For pre-1783 tax records, see *Virginia Tax Records: From the Virginia Magazine of History and Biography, The William and Mary College Quarterly,* and *Tyler's Quarterly* (Genealogical Publishing Co., 1983).

Researching Virginia court records is a maze of county courts, orphans' court, courts of claim, quarter courts, general courts, a supreme court of appeals, a high court of chancery, a superior court of chancery, district courts, circuit superior courts of law and chancery and circuit courts. Some courts overlap; others replaced earlier courts. To get more information about the different courts and their jurisdictions, refer to *A Preliminary Guide to Pre-1904 County Records in the Archives Branch, Virginia State Library and Archives* by Suzanne Smith Ray, Lyndon H. Hart III and J. Christian Kolbe (Virginia State Library and Archives, 1987).

Virginia began registration of births and deaths early on, requiring counties to register these records beginning in 1853. This continued until 1896, but there is a gap during the Civil War, when most counties abandoned registration. You will find another gap in the records from 1896 until statewide registration began in 1912. Just a few independent cities kept birth and death records during this time.

Before 1853, marriages were handled by posting a bond—a written agreement to forfeit an amount of money should the marriage not take place—or banns, which were announced at three church meetings prior to the ceremony. Banns, therefore, are found in church records rather than county courthouse records.

Since 1853, state law has required counties and independent cities to issue marriage licenses. The application for marriage, which was formalized in 1858, asks for full names, ages, places of birth and residence, proposed marriage date and place, whether divorced or widowed, parents' names, groom's occupation and minister's name. When the officiant gave the license to the state, the clerk was required to enter the marriage in a marriage register. The Division of Vital Records has this marriage register, which dates from January 1853. The clerk of the county or city court has copies of all marriage records kept by that court. The Library of Virginia **<www.lva.virginia.gov>** has many marriage records. The Family History Library has microfilmed copies of marriage bonds and marriage registers up until about 1935.

ARCHIVES, LIBRARIES, AND SOCIETIES

Albemarle Charlottsville Historical Society
McIntire Building, 200 Second St. NE, Charlottesville, VA 22902, (434) 296-1492, **<www.albemarlehistory.org>**

Alderman Library, University of Virginia
Box 400114, Charlottesville VA 22904, (434) 924-3021, **<www2.lib.virginia.edu/alderman>**

Alexandria Library
5005 Duke St., Alexandria, VA 22304

Alleghany Highlands Genealogical Society
1011 N. Rockbridge St., Covington, VA 24426

Arlington Central Library
1015 N. Quincy St., Arlington, VA 22201

Augusta County Genealogical Society
2002 Lyndhurst Rd., Waynesboro, VA 22890

Augusta County Historical Society
Box 686, Staunton, VA 247401, (540) 248-4151, **<www.augustacountyhs.org>**

Bath County Historical Society
Box 180, Warm Springs, VA 24484, **<www.bathcountyhistory.org>**

Bedford Historical Society
Box 602, Bedford, VA 24523

Blue Ridge Regional Library
310 E. Church St., Box 5264, Martinsville, VA 24115

Bristol Public Library
701 Goode St., Bristol, VA 24201

Caroline County Genealogical Society
Box 324, Bowling Green, VA 22427

Carroll County Genealogical Club
Box 395, Hillsville, VA 24343

Carroll County Historical Society
Box 937, Hillsville, VA 24343

Carroll County Historical Society
515 N. Main St., Box 937, Hillsville, VA 24343

Central Virginia Genealogical Association
Box 5583, Charlottesville, VA 22905, **<cvga.avenue.org>**

Chesterfield Historical Society of Virginia
Box 40, Chesterfield, VA 23832, **<www.chesterfieldhistory.com>**

Claiborne County Historical Society
Rt. 1, Box 589, Jonesville, VA 24263

College of William and Mary
Earl Gregg Swem Library, 400 Landrum Drive, Box 8794, Williamsburg, VA 23187, (757) 221-3050, **<www.swem.wm.edu>**

Culpeper Historical Society
Box 785, Culpeper, VA 22701

Culpeper Town and County Library
271 Southgate Shopping Center, Culpeper, VA 22701, (540) 825-8691, **<tlc.library.net/culpeper>**

Cumberland County Historical Society
Box 77, Cumberland, VA 23040

Danville Public Library
511 Patton St., Danville, VA 24541

Fairfax City Regional Library
Fairfax County Public Library System, 10360 North St., Fairfax, VA 22030

Fairfax Genealogical Society
Box 2290, Merrifield, VA 22116, **<www.fxgs.org>**

Fairfax County Historical Society
Box 415, Fairfax, VA 22038, **<www.fairfaxhistoricalsociety.org>**

Fauquier Heritage Society
Box 548, Marshall, VA 22115

Franklin County Genealogical Society
Box 316, Ferrum, VA 24088

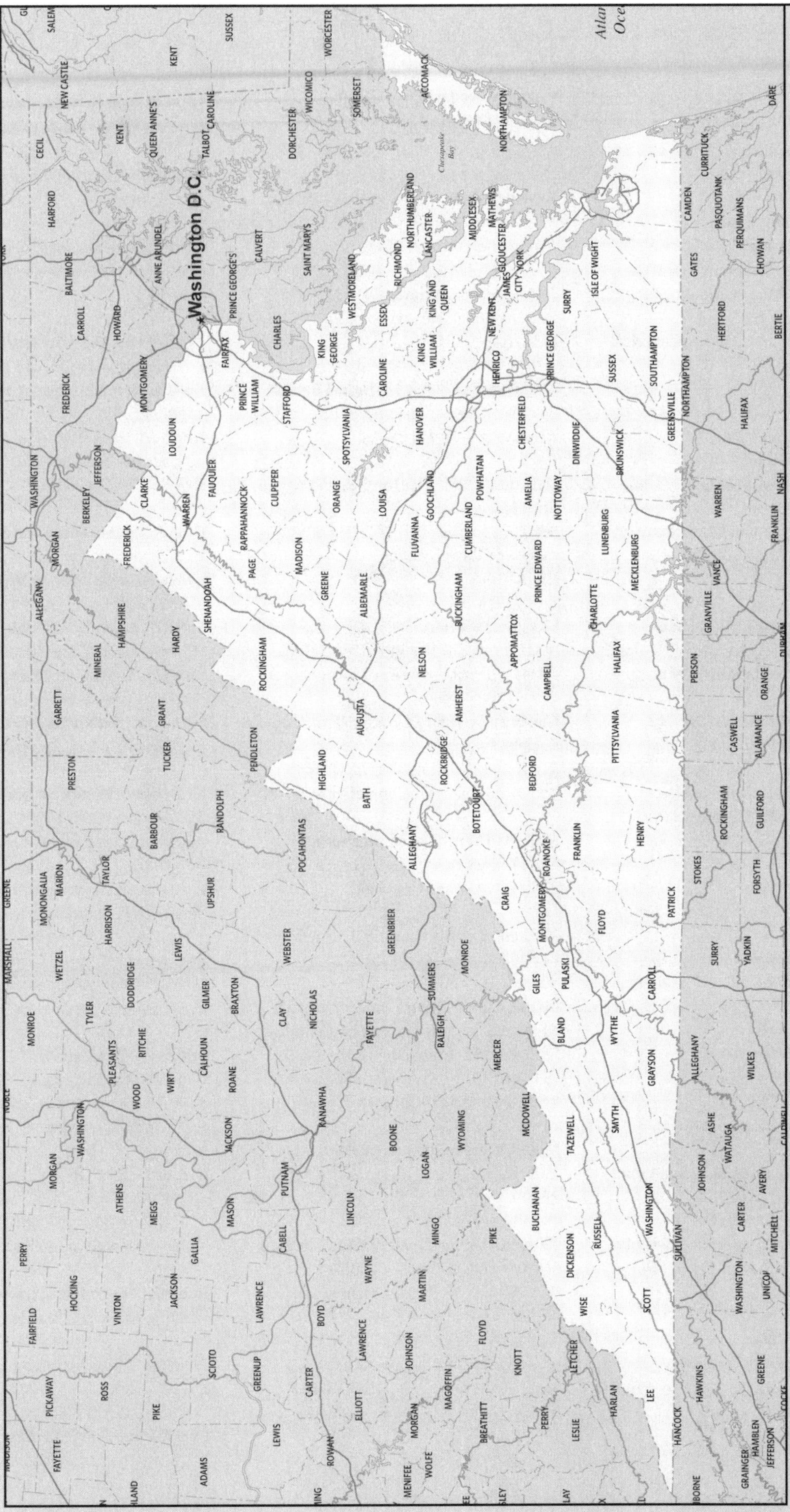
Washington D.C.
Atlantic Ocean
Chesapeake Bay
LOUDOUN
FAIRFAX
PRINCE WILLIAM
STAFFORD
FAUQUIER
CLARKE
WARREN
FREDERICK
SHENANDOAH
PAGE
RAPPAHANNOCK
CULPEPER
MADISON
ORANGE
SPOTSYLVANIA
KING GEORGE
WESTMORELAND
NORTHUMBERLAND
RICHMOND
LANCASTER
ESSEX
CAROLINE
KING AND QUEEN
KING WILLIAM
MIDDLESEX
MATHEWS
GLOUCESTER
JAMES CITY
YORK
NEW KENT
HENRICO
HANOVER
LOUISA
GREENE
ALBEMARLE
FLUVANNA
GOOCHLAND
POWHATAN
CHESTERFIELD
PRINCE GEORGE
SURRY
ISLE OF WIGHT
SUSSEX
SOUTHAMPTON
DINWIDDIE
AMELIA
NOTTOWAY
CUMBERLAND
BUCKINGHAM
PRINCE EDWARD
LUNENBURG
BRUNSWICK
GREENSVILLE
MECKLENBURG
CHARLOTTE
APPOMATTOX
NELSON
ROCKINGHAM
AUGUSTA
HIGHLAND
BATH
ROCKBRIDGE
AMHERST
CAMPBELL
HALIFAX
PITTSYLVANIA
BEDFORD
BOTETOURT
ALLEGHANY
CRAIG
ROANOKE
FRANKLIN
HENRY
PATRICK
FLOYD
MONTGOMERY
PULASKI
GILES
BLAND
WYTHE
CARROLL
GRAYSON
SMYTH
TAZEWELL
BUCHANAN
DICKENSON
RUSSELL
WASHINGTON
WISE
SCOTT
LEE
ACCOMACK
NORTHAMPTON
MONTGOMERY
FREDERICK
CARROLL
HOWARD
BALTIMORE
HARFORD
CECIL
ANNE ARUNDEL
PRINCE GEORGE'S
CHARLES
CALVERT
SAINT MARYS
KENT
QUEEN ANNE'S
TALBOT
CAROLINE
DORCHESTER
WICOMICO
SOMERSET
WORCESTER
NEW CASTLE
SUSSEX
SALEM
WASHINGTON
ALLEGANY
GARRETT
JEFFERSON
BERKELEY
MORGAN
HAMPSHIRE
MINERAL
HARDY
GRANT
PENDLETON
TUCKER
PRESTON
RANDOLPH
BARBOUR
POCAHONTAS
TAYLOR
MONONGALIA
MARION
UPSHUR
HARRISON
GREENBRIER
WEBSTER
LEWIS
WETZEL
MARSHALL
GREENE
DODDRIDGE
TYLER
MONROE
SUMMERS
RALEIGH
FAYETTE
NICHOLAS
CLAY
BRAXTON
GILMER
RITCHIE
PLEASANTS
CALHOUN
WIRT
WOOD
ROANE
KANAWHA
MERCER
MCDOWELL
WYOMING
BOONE
LOGAN
JACKSON
WASHINGTON
MORGAN
ATHENS
MEIGS
MASON
PUTNAM
CABELL
LINCOLN
MINGO
WAYNE
MARTIN
PIKE
GALLIA
PERRY
HOCKING
VINTON
FAIRFIELD
LAWRENCE
BOYD
JOHNSON
FLOYD
KNOTT
LETCHER
HARLAN
LESLIE
PERRY
BREATHITT
MAGOFFIN
MORGAN
WOLFE
MENIFEE
ELLIOTT
CARTER
ROWAN
GREENUP
SCIOTO
LEWIS
ADAMS
PIKE
ROSS
PICKAWAY
FAYETTE
CURRITUCK
CAMDEN
PASQUOTANK
PERQUIMANS
CHOWAN
GATES
HERTFORD
BERTIE
NORTHAMPTON
HALIFAX
NASH
WARREN
FRANKLIN
VANCE
GRANVILLE
DURHAM
PERSON
ORANGE
CASWELL
ALAMANCE
ROCKINGHAM
GUILFORD
STOKES
FORSYTH
SURRY
YADKIN
ALLEGHANY
WILKES
ASHE
WATAUGA
JOHNSON
AVERY
CARTER
MITCHELL
SULLIVAN
WASHINGTON
UNICOI
GREENE
HAWKINS
HANCOCK
HAMBLEN
GRAINGER
JEFFERSON
DARE

Franklin County Historical Society
508 Franklin St., Rocky Mount, VA 24151, **<www.franklincountyvirginia historicalsoc.org>**

Fredericksburg Regional Genealogical Society
Box 42013, Fredericksburg, VA 22404, **<www.fredericksburggenealogy.org>**

Ft. Eustis Historical and Archaeological Association
Box 4408, Ft. Eustis, VA 23604

Genealogical Research Institute of Virginia
Box 29178, Richmond, VA 23242

Genealogical Society of Page County
c/o Page Public Library, 100 Zerkel St., Luray, VA 22835

Goochland County Historical Society
Box 602, Goochland, VA 23063, (804) 556-3966, **<www.goochlandhistory.org>**

Grayson County Historical Society
Box 529, Independence, VA 24348

Green County Historical Society
38 Court St., Box 185, Stanardsville, VA 22973

Hampton Public Library
4207 Victoria Blvd., Hampton, VA 23669

Handley Library
Box 58, Winchester, VA 22601, (540) 662-9041

Harrisonburg-Rockingham Historical Society
Box 716, Dayton, VA 22812, **<www.heritagecenter.com>**

Historical Society of Washington County
Box 484, Abingdon, VA 24212

Isle of Wight County Historical Society
Box 121, Smithfield, VA 23431, **<www.iwchs.com>**

James Monroe Museum and Memorial Library
908 Charles St., Fredericksburg, VA 22401, **<www.umw.edu/ jamesmonroemuseum>**

Jefferson/Madison Regional Library
201 E. Market St., Charlottesville, VA 22902

Jewish Genealogical Society of Tidewater
Jewish Community Center, 7300 Newport Ave., Norfolk, VA 23505

Jones Memorial Library
2311 Memorial Ave., Lynchburg, VA 24501, (434) 846-0501

King George County Historical Society
Box 424, King George, VA 22485, **<www.kghistory.org>**

Lee County Historical and Genealogical Society
Box 231, Jonesville, VA 24263, **<www.rootsweb.ancestry.com/~valee/ lchgs.htm>**

Library of Virginia
800 E. Broad St., Richmond, VA 23219, (804) 692-350, **<www.lva.virginia.gov>**

Martinsville Henry County Historical Society
Drawer 432, Martinsville, VA 24114, **<www.mhchistoricalsociety.com>**

Mary Ball Washington Museum
8346 Mary Ball Rd., Box 97, Lancaster, VA 22503, **<www.mbwm.org>**

Mathews County Historical Society
Box 885, Mathews, VA 23109

Menno Simons Historical Library and Archives, Eastern Mennonite College
1200 Park Rd., Harrisonburg, VA 22801, (540) 432-4177, **<www.emu.edu/ library/historical-library>**

Mount Vernon Genealogical Society
1500 Shenandoah Rd., Alexandria, VA 22308

National Archives, Mid-Atlantic Region
900 Market St., Philadelphia, PA 19107, (215) 606-0100, **<www.archives.gov/ midatlantic>**

New River Historical Society
Box 373, Newborn, VA 24126, **<www. rootsweb.ancestry.com/~vanrhs>**

Norfolk County Historical Society
c/o Chesapeake Public Library, 298 Cedar Road, Chesapeake, VA 23322, **<www.chesapeake.lib.va.us/wallace/ nchs.htm>**

Norfolk Genealogical Society
Box 12813, Thomas Corner Station, Norfolk, VA 23502

Norfolk Historical Society
Box 6367, Norfolk, VA 23508, **<www.norfolkhistorical.org>**

Northern Neck Historical Society
43 Courthouse Square, Box 716, Montross, VA 22520, (804) 493-8440, **<nnvhs.org>**

Orange County Historical Society
130 Caroline St., Orange, VA 22960, **<www.orangecovahist.org>**

Patrick County Genealogical Society
116 W. Blue Ridge St., Stuart, VA 24171, **<www.patcovahistory.org>**

Petersburg Public Library
137 S. Sycamore St., Petersburg, VA 23803

Pittsylvania Historical Society
Box 1146, Chatham, VA 24531, **<www.vintagedesigns.com/phs>**

Portsmouth Genealogical Society
Box 7062, Portsmouth, VA 23707

Presbyterian Church Archives
Union Theological Seminary, 34901 Brook Rd., Richmond, VA 23227, (804) 355-0671

Prince William County Genealogical Society
Box 2019, Manassas, VA 20108, **<www. rootsweb.ancestry.com/~vapwcgs>**

Radford Public Library
30 W. Main St., Radford, VA 24141, (540) 731-3621 or (540) 731-4857, **<www.radford.va.us/library>**

Roanoke City Public Library
706 S. Jefferson St., Roanoke, VA 24016

Roanoke Valley Historical Society
Box 1904, Roanoke, VA 24008

Rockingham Public Library
45 Newman Ave., Harrisonburg, VA 22801

Shenandoah County Library
514 Stoney Creek Blvd., Edinburg, VA 22824, (504) 984-8200, **<www.shenandoah.co.lib.va.us>**

Simpson Library, Mary Washington College
801 College Ave., Fredericksburg, VA 22401, (703) 899-4594, **<www.umw.edu/library/about/simpson_library>**

Surry County Historical Society
Box 262, Surry, VA 23883, **<www.rootsweb.ancestry.com/~vaschsm>**

Thomas Balch Library
208 W. Market St., Leesburg, VA 22075, (703) 777-0132, **<www.leesburgva.gov/index.aspx?page=84>**

Tidewater Genealogical Society
Box 7650, Hampton, VA 23666, **< www.rootsweb.ancestry.com/~vatgs>**

Tidewater Afro-American Historical and Genealogical Society
2200 Crossroad Trail, Virginia Beach, VA 23456

Virginia Baptist Historical Society
c/o Boatwright Memorial Library, Box 34, University of Richmond, Richmond, VA 23173, (804) 289-8434

Virginia Beach Genealogical Society
Box 62901, VA Beach, VA 23466, **<www.rootsweb.ancestry.com/~vavbgs>**

Virginia Office of Vital Records
Box 1000, Richmond, VA 23218, (804) 662-6200, **<www.vdh.state.va.us/vital_records>**

Virginia Genealogical Society
1900 Byrd Ave., Suite 104, Richmond, VA 23230, **<www.vgs.org>**

Virginia Historical Society
428 North Blvd., Richmond, VA 23220, (804) 342-9677, **<www.vahistorical.org>**

Virginia-North Carolina, Piedmont Genealogical Society
Box 2272, Danville, VA 24541, **<www.rootsweb.ancestry.com/~vancpgs/Index.htm>**

Winchester-Frederick County Historical Society
1340 S. Pleasant Valley Road, Winchester, VA 22601, (540) 662-6550, **<www.winchesterhistory.org>**

GENERAL RESOURCES

Adventurers Of Purse and Person, Virginia, 1607-1624/5 by Annie Lash Jester and Martha Woodruff Hiden (Order of the First Families of Virginia, 1987)

Annals of Southwest Virginia, 1769-1800 by Lewis Preston Summers (Genealogical Publishing Co., 1996)

Biographical Sketches of Virginia by S. Bassett French (Virginia State Library, 1942)

Calendar of Virginia State Papers and Other Manuscripts Preserved in the Capitol, 3 vols., edited by William P. Palmer (1875-1883)

A Calendar of the Warrants for Land in Kentucky, Granted for Service in the French and Indian War by Philip F. Taylor (Genealogical Publishing Co., 1967)

The Colonial Church in Virginia by Edward L. Goodwin (Morehouse Pub., 1927)

Early Virginia Families Along the James River, 2 vols., by Louise Pledge Heath Foley (Genealogical Publishing Co., 1990)

Encyclopedia of Virginia Biography, 5 vols., by Lyn Gardiner Tyler (Lewis Historical Publishing, 1915)

English Duplicates of Lost Virginia Records compiled by Louis Des Cognet Jr. (Genealogical Publishing Co., 1981)

Executive Journals of the Council of Colonial Virginia, 6 vols., (Virginia State Library, 1966-1978)

Genealogies of Virginia Families: From Tyler's Quarterly, 4 vols., (Genealogical Publishing Co., 1981)

Genealogies of Virginia Families: From the William and Mary College Quarterly, 5 vols., (Genealogical Publishing Co., 1982)

A Guide to Church Records in the Archives Branch, Virginia State Library by Jewell T. Clark and Elizabeth Terry Long (Virginia State Library, 1981)

A Guide to Episcopal Church Records in Virginia by Edith F. Axelson (Iberian Publishing, 1988)

A Guide to Genealogical Notes and Charts in the Archives Branch, Virginia State Library compiled by Lyndon H. Hart (Virginia State Library, 1983)

A Guide to State Records in the Archives Branch compiled by John S. Salmon (Virginia State Library, 1985)

History of Virginia, 6 vols., (American Historical Society, 1924)

The Hornbook of Virginia History, 4th edition, by Emily J. Salmon and Edward D.C. Campbell (Library of Virginia, 1994)

Index to Printed Virginia Genealogies by Robert Armistead Stewart (Genealogical Publishing Co., 1970)

Journals of the Council of the State of Virginia, 5 vols., (Virginia State Library, 1931-1982)

A Key to Survey Reports and Microfilm of the Virginia Colonial Records Project (Virginia State Library and Archives, 1990)

Men of Mark in Virginia, 5 vols. (Men of Mark Publishing Co., 1906-09)

Old Churches, Ministers and Families of Virginia, 1857 by William Meade (Genealogical Publishing Co., 1966)

A Preliminary Guide to Pre-1904 Municipal Records in the Archives Branch, Virginia State Library and Archives by Lyndon H. Hart and Suzanne Smith Ray (Library and Archives, ca. 1988)

Research in Virginia by Eric Grundset (National Genealogical Society, 1998)

Sketches of Virginia: Historical and Biographical, 2 vols., by William Henry Foote (William S. Marten, 1850-56)

Some Peculiarities of Genealogical Research in Virginia: Colonial by Annie Lash Jester (Church of Jesus Christ of Latter-day Saints, 1969)

Some Peculiarities of Genealogical Research in Virginia: Post-Revolutionary by Virginia Pope Livingston (Church of Jesus Christ of Latter-day Saints, 1969)

Some Prominent Virginia Families, 4 vols., by Louise Pecquet du Bellet (Genealogical Publishing Co., 1976)

State Slavery Statutes: Guide to the Microfiche Collection by Paul Finkelman (University Publications of America, 1989)

3rd Burned County Data 1809-1848: As Found in the Virginia Contested Elected Files by Benjamin B. Weisiger (Benjamin B. Weisiger, 1986)

3rd Guide to Bible Records in the Archives Branch, Virginia State Library by Lyndon H. Hart (Virginia State Library and Archives, 1985)

Timesaving Aid to Virginia-West Virginia Ancestors, 4 vols., by Patrick G. Wardell (Iberian Publishing Co., 1985-1990)

The Virginia Battles and Leaders Series by H.E. Howard (H.E. Howard, 1984)

Virginia Colonial Abstracts, 34 vols., by Beverley Fleet (Genealogical Publishing Co., 1988)

Virginia Genealogical Research by George K. Schweitzer (George K. Schweitzer, 1982)

Virginia Genealogical Resources by Robert Young Clay (Detroit Society of Genealogical Research, 1980)

Virginia Genealogies: A Trial List of Printed Books and Pamphlets, 2 vols., by Stuart E. Brown Jr. (Virginia Book, 1967, 1980)

Virginia Genealogy: A Guide to Resources in the University of Virginia Library (University Press of Virginia, 1983)

Virginia Historical Index, 2 vols., by Earl Gregg Swen (Peter Smith, 1965)

Virginia in the 1600's: An Index to Who Was There!—and Where! compiled and edited by Harold Oliver (D&H Publishing Co., 1992)

Virginia Local History: A Bibliography (Virginia State Library, 1971)

Virginia: The New Dominion by Virginius Dabney (University Press of Virginia, 1971)

Virginia Newspapers 1821-1935: A Bibliography with Historical Introductions and Notes by Lester J. Cappon (D. Appleton Century, 1936)

Virginia Research Outline by the Church of Jesus Christ of Latter-day Saints (online at <www.familysearch.org/eng/search/RG/guide/virginia.asp>)

Virginia and Virginians, 2 vols., by Robert Alonzo Brock (H.H. Hardesty, 1888)

Virginians and West Virginians, 1607-1870, 3 vols., by Patrick G. Wardell (Heritage Books, 1986-1992)

CENSUS RECORDS

The 1787 Census of Virginia, 3 vols., by Netti Schreiner-Yanits and Florence Speakman Love (Genealogical Books in Print, 1987)

State Slavery Statutes: Guide to the Microfiche Collection by Paul Finkelman (University Publications of American, 1989)

A Supplement to the 1810 Census of Virginia: Tax Lists of the counties for Which the Census is Missing by Netti Schreiner-Yanits (Genealogical Books in Print, 1971)

Virginia in 1740: A Reconstructed Census (T.L. C. Genealogy, 1992)

Virginia Taxpayers, 1782-1787 by Augusta B. Fothergill (Genealogical Publishing Co., 1974)

Virginia Tax Records: From the Virginia Magazine of History and Biography, the William and Mary College Quarterly, and Tyler's Quarterly (Genealogical Publishing Co., 1983)

Virginia Tithables from Burned Record Counties by Robert F. and Isobel B. Woodson (Isobel B. Woodson, 1970)

IMMIGRATION RECORDS

The Complete Book of Emigrants, 1607-1776, and Emigrants I Bondage, 1614-1775 by Peter Wilson Coldham (Broderbund Software, 1996, CD-ROM)

Documents, Chiefly Unpublished, Relating to the Huguenot Emigration to Virginia and to the Settlement at Manakintown by Robert A. Brock (Genealogical Publishing Co., 1987)

Early Child Immigrants to Virginia, 1618-1642 by Robert Hume (Magna Carta Book Co., 1986)

Early Virginia Immigrants, 1623-1666 by George C. Greer (Genealogical Publishing Co., 1982)

Some Emigrants to Virginia: Memoranda in Regard to Several Hundred Emigrants to Virginia During the Colonial Periods by William Glover Stanard (Genealogical Publishing Co., 1979)

Virginia Gleanings in England: Abstracts of 17th and 18th-Century English Wills and Administrations Relating to Virginia and Virginians by Lathrop Withington (Genealogical Publishing Co., 1980)

LAND RECORDS

Abstract of Land Grant Surveys, 1761-1791 by Peter Cline Kaylor (Clearfield Co., 1991)

Cavaliers and Pioneers: Abstracts of Virginia Land Patents and Grants, 5 vols., edited by Dennis Hudgins (Virginia Genealogical Society, 1994)

Master Index Virginia Surveys and Grants 1774-1791 by Joan E. Brookes-Smith (Kentucky Historical Society, 1976)

Mother Earth-Land Grants in Virginia, 1607-1699 by W. Stitt Robinson (350th Anniversary Celebration Corp., 1957)

Old Rights, Property Rights, Virginia Entries and Soldiers Entitled to Donation Lands by William Henry Egle (C.M. Busch, State Printer, 1896)

The Quit Rents of Virginia, 1704 compiled by Annie Laurie Wright Smith (Genealogical Publishing Co., 1980)

Turff and Twigg: The French Lands by Priscilla Harriss Cabell (Priscilla Harriss Cabell, 1988)

Virginia Land Patent Books by William Lindsay Hopkins in *Magazine of Virginia Genealogy* (Virginia Genealogical Society, 1984)

Virginia Land Records: From the Virginia Magazine of History and Biography, the William and Mary College Quarterly, and Tyler's Quarterly by Gary Parks (Genealogical Publishing Co., 1982)

Virginia Northern Neck Land Grants, 4 vols., by Gertrude E. Gray (Genealogical Publishing Co., 1993)

Virginia Revolutionary War Land Grant Claims 1783-1850 by William Lindsay Hopkins (Gen-N-Dex, 1988)

War of 1812 Virginia Bounty Land and Pension Applicants by Patrick G. Wardell (Heritage Books, 1987)

☞MAPS

Approved Place Names in Virginia by Mary Topping (University Press of Virginia, 1971)

Atlas of County Boundary Changes in Virginia, 1634-1895 by Michael F. Doran (Iberian Publishing, 1987)

The Cartography of Northern Virginia: Facsimile Reproductions of Maps Dating From 1608 to 1915 by Richard W. Stephenson (Fairfax County, Virginia, 1981)

A Gazetteer of Virginia and West Virginia by Henry Gannett (Genealogical Publishing Co., 1975)

A Historical Atlas of Colonial Virginia by John S. Hale (Old Dominion Publications, 1978)

How Justice Grew: Virginia Counties, and Abstract of Their Formation by Martha W. Hiden (Clearfield Co., 1992)

Index of Kentucky and Virginia Maps, 1562 to 1900 by James W. Sames III (Kentucky Historical Society, 1976)

A New and Comprehensive Gazetteer of Virginia, and the District of Columbia by Joseph Martin (J. Martin, 1835)

Virginia Atlas and Gazetteer (Delorme Mapping Co., 1995)

Virginia Place Names by Raus McDill Hanson (McClure Press, 1969)

Virginia Postmasters and Post Office, 1789-1832 by Edith F. Axelson (Iberian Publishing Co., 1991)

☞MILITARY RECORDS

A Calendar of the Warrants for Land in Kentucky, Granted for Service in the French and Indian War by Philip F. Taylor (Genealogical Publishing Co., 1967)

Catalogue of Revolutionary Soldiers and Sailors of the Commonwealth of Virginia: To Whom Land Bounty Warrants Were Granted By Virginia for Military Service in the War for Independence by Samuel Mackay Wilson (Genealogical Publishing Co., 1967)

Gold Star Honor Roll of Virginians in the Second World War edited by W. Edwin Hemphill (Virginia World War II History Commission, 1947)

A Guide to Virginia Military Organizations, 1860-1865 by Lee A. Wallace (H.E. Howard, 1986)

Guide to Virginia Militia Units in the War of 1812 by Stuart Lee Butler (Iberian Publishing Co. 1988)

Historical Register of Virginians in the Revolution: Soldiers, Sailors, Marines: 1775-1783 by John H. Gwathmey (Genealogical Publishing Co., 1973)

Index to Saffell's List of Virginia Soldiers in the Revolution by Joseph T. McCallister (McAllister Publishing Co., 1913)

List of the Colonial Soldiers of Virginia by H.J. Eckenrod (Genealogical Publishing Co., 1974)

List of the Revolutionary Soldiers of Virginia by H.J. Eckenrod (D. Bottom, 1912)

Old Rights, Property Rights, Virginia Entries and Soldiers Entitled to Donation Lands by William Henry Egle (C.M. Busch, State Printer, 1896)

Revolutionary War Records: Virginia Army And Navy Forces with Bounty Land Warrants for Virginia Military District of Ohio and Virginia Scrip by Gaius M. Brumbaugh (Genealogical Publishing Co., 1967)

Soldiery of West Virginia in the French and Indian War, Lord Dunmore's War, The Revolution, The Later Indian Wars, The Whiskey Insurrection, The Second War with England, The War with Mexico, and Addenda Relating to West Virginians In the Civil War by Virgil A. Lewis (Genealogical Publishing Co., 1967)

Virginia Colonial Militia, 1651-1776 by William Armstrong Crozier (Genealogical Publishing Co., 1982)

Virginia's Colonial Soldiers by Lloyd DeWitt Bockstruck (Genealogical Publishing Co., 1988)

Virginia Military Records: From the Virginia Magazine of History And Biography, the William and Mary College Quarterly, and Tyler's Quarterly (Genealogical Publishing Co., 1983)

Virginia Public Claims, 3 vols., by Janice L. Abercrombie (Iberian Publishing Co., 1992)

Virginia Regimental History Series by H.E. Howard (H.E. Howard, 1982)

Virginia Revolutionary War State Pensions (Southern Historical Press, 1982)

Virginia Soldiers in the United States Army, 1800-1815 by Stuart Lee Butler (Iberian Publishing Co., 1986)

Virginia Soldiers of 1776, 3 vols., compiled and edited by Louis A. Burgess (Reprint Co., 1973)

The War with Mexico, and Addenda Relating to West Virginias in the Civil War (Genealogical Publishing Co., 1967)

War of 1812: Virginia Bounty Land and Pension Applications by Patrick G. Wardell (Heritage Books 1987)

☞PROBATE RECORDS

Chronicles of the Scotch-Irish Settlement in Virginia: Extracted form the Original Court records of Augusta County, 1754-1800, 3 vols., by Lyman Chalkey (Genealogical Publishing Co., 1980)

Hanover County Chancery Wills and Notes: by William Ronald Crocke (Genealogical Publishing Co., 1978)

Minutes of the Council and General Court of Colonial Virginia by H.R. McIlwaine (Virginia State Library, 1979)

Some Wills from Burned Counties of Virginia and Other Wills Not Listed in the Virginia Wills and Administrations, 1632-1800 by William Lindsay Hopkins (W.L. Hopkins, 1987)

Virginia Settlers and English Adventurers: Abstracts of Wills, 1484-1798, and Legal Proceedings, 1560-1700, Relating to Early Virginia Families, 3 vols., by Noel Currier-Briggs (Genealogical Publishing Co., 1970)

Virginia Wills and Administrations 1632-1800 by Clayton Torrence (Genealogical Publishing Co., 1985)

Virginia Wills Before 1799: A Complete Abstract Register of All Names Mentioned in Over 600 Recorded Wills compiled by William Montgomery Clemens (Biblio Co., 1924)

Virginia Will Records by Judith McGhan (Genealogical Publishing Co., 1982)

Will and Estate Records In the Virginia State Library: A Researcher's Guide by John Vogt and T. William Kethley Jr. (Iberian Publishing Co., 1987)

☞VITAL RECORDS

Abstracts of Marriage and Obituary Notices in Virginia Newspapers Before 1820 by Virginius Cornick Hall (Genealogical Society of Utah, 1987)

Early Virginia Marriages by William A. Crozier (Genealogical Publishing Co., 1982)

Index to Obituary Notices in the Richmond Enquirer form May 9, 1804 through 1828, and the Richmond Whig from January 1824 to 1838 by H.R. McIlwaine (Genealogical Publishing Co., 1974)

Marriage Records in the Virginia State Library: A Researcher's Guide by John Vogt and T. William Kethley (Iberian Press, 1984)

Marriages of Some Virginia Residents, 1607-1800, 2 vols., by Dorothy F. Wulfeck (Genealogical Publishing Co., 1986)

Some Marriages in the Burned Record Counties of Virginia (Virginia Genealogical Society, 1979)

Some Virginia Marriages, 1700-1799, 25 vols., by Cecil D. McDonald (Cecil D. McDonald, 1972)

Some Virginia Marriages, 1800-1825, 12 vols., by Cecil D. McDonald (Cecil D. McDonald, 1973)

Some Virginia Marriages, 1826-1850, 2 vols., by Ransom B. True (Cecil D. McDonald, 1975)

Tombstone Inscriptions (Virginia), 9 vols., by Duane L. Borden (Yates Pub. Co., 1986)

Virginia Cemeteries: A Guide to Resources by Anne M. Hogg and Dennis A. Tosh. (University of Virginia, 1986)

Virginia Marriage Records: From the Virginia Magazine of History And Biography, the William and Mary's College Quarterly, and The Tyler's Quarterly (Genealogical Publishing Co., 1982)

Virginia Vital Records: From the Virginia Magazine of History and Biography, the William and Mary's College Quarterly, and the Tyler's Quarterly (Genealogical Publishing Co., 1982)

COUNTY DETAILS

ACCAWMAC

- **INCORPORATED:** 1634
- **PARENT COUNTY:** Original shire
- **NOTES:** See Northampton County. Name changed to Northampton 1642.

ACCOMACK

23296 Courthouse Rd., Box 388, Accomac, VA 23301, (757) 787-5776, **<co.accomack.va.us>**

- **INCORPORATED:** 1663
- **PARENT COUNTY:** Accomac Shire
- **MARRIAGE RECORDS:** start in 1774, kept by Circuit Court
- **DIVORCE:** 1848, Circuit Court
- **LAND:** 1663, Circuit Court
- **PROBATE:** 1663, Circuit Court
- **COURT:** 1666, Circuit Court
- **NOTES:** Clerk of Circuit Court has birth records 1853-1896, death records 1853-1871, and military records 1823-1849, 1861-1865, 1917-1967.

ALBEMARLE

401 McIntire Rd., Charlottesville, VA 22902, (434) 972-4084, **<www.albemarle.org>**

- **INCORPORATED:** May 6, 1744
- **PARENT COUNTIES:** Goochland, Louisa
- **BIRTH RECORDS:** start in 1852, kept by Circuit Court
- **MARRIAGE:** 1780, Circuit Court
- **DIVORCE:** 1848, Circuit Court

- **DEATH:** 1853, Circuit Court
- **LAND:** 1748, Circuit Court
- **PROBATE:** 1748, Circuit Court
- **COURT:** 1744, Circuit Court

ALEXANDRIA (INDEPENDENT CITY)

520 King St. Suite 307, Alexandria, VA 22314, (703) 838-4044, **<alexandriava.gov>**

- **INCORPORATED:** May 11, 1749
- **PARENT COUNTY:** Fairfax
- **BIRTH RECORDS:** start in 1853, kept by Alexandria Health Center
- **MARRIAGE:** start in 1870, kept by Circuit Court
- **DIVORCE:** 1870, Circuit Court
- **DEATH:** 1863, Alexandria Health Center
- **LAND:** 1783, Circuit Court
- **PROBATE:** 1786, Circuit Court
- **COURT:** 1785, Circuit Court
- **NOTES:** Clerk of Circuit Court has naturalization records 1909-1920. Part of Fairfax County 1749-1801. Part of District of Columbia 1801-1847. Incorporated as a city in 1852. Alexandria is an independent city government.

ALLEGHANY

266 W. Main St., Covington, VA 24426, (540) 965-1730, **<co.alleghany.va.us>**

- **INCORPORATED:** Jan. 5, 1822
- **PARENT COUNTIES:** Bath, Botetourt, Monroe, West Virginia
- **BIRTH RECORDS:** start in 1833, kept by Circuit Court
- **MARRIAGE:** 1822, Circuit Court
- **DIVORCE:** 1881, Circuit Court
- **DEATH:** 1853, Circuit Court
- **LAND:** 1822, Circuit Court
- **PROBATE:** 1822, Circuit Court
- **COURT:** 1822, Circuit Court
- **NOTES:** Clerk of Circuit Court has naturalization records 1908-1929.

AMELIA

16441 Court St., Box 237, Amelia Court House, VA 23002, (804) 561-2128, **<www.ameliava.com>**

- **INCORPORATED:** Feb. 1, 1734
- **PARENT COUNTIES:** Brunswick, Prince George
- **BIRTH RECORDS:** start in 1853, kept by Circuit Court
- **MARRIAGE:** 1735, Circuit Court
- **DIVORCE:** 1848, Circuit Court
- **DEATH:** 1853, Circuit Court
- **LAND:** 1734, Circuit Court
- **PROBATE:** 1734, Circuit Court
- **COURT:** 1735, Circuit Court
- **NOTES:** Clerk of Circuit Court has military records 1861-1865, 1918-1966.

AMHERST

113 Taylor St., Box 462, Amherst, VA 24521, (434) 946-9321, **<www.countyofamherst.com>**

- **INCORPORATED:** March 1761
- **PARENT COUNTY:** Albemarle
- **BIRTH RECORDS:** start in 1912, kept by Library of Virginia
- **MARRIAGE:** 1763, Circuit Court
- **DIVORCE:** 1761, Circuit Court
- **DEATH:** 1912, Library of Virginia
- **LAND:** 1761, Circuit Court
- **PROBATE:** 1761, Circuit Court
- **COURT:** 1761, Circuit Court
- **NOTES:** Library of Virginia has birth and death records 1853-1896.

APPOMATTOX

Box 863, Appomattox, VA 24522, (804) 352-2637, **<www.appomattoxcountyva.gov>**

- **INCORPORATED:** Feb. 8, 1845
- **PARENT COUNTIES:** Buckingham, Campbell, Charlotte, Prince Edward
- **MARRIAGE RECORDS:** start in 1854, kept by Circuit Court
- **DIVORCE:** 1892, Circuit Court
- **LAND:** 1892, Circuit Court
- **PROBATE:** 1892, Circuit Court
- **COURT:** 1892, Circuit Court

ARLINGTON

1425 N. Court House Rd., Arlington, VA 22201, (703) 228-7010, **<co.arlington.va.us>**

- **INCORPORATED:** March 13, 1847
- **PARENT COUNTY:** Fairfax
- **BIRTH RECORDS:** start in 1853, kept by Library of Virginia
- **MARRIAGE:** 1801, Circuit Court
- **DEATH:** 1853, Library of Virginia
- **LAND:** 1801, Circuit Court
- **PROBATE:** 1800, Circuit Court
- **COURT:** 1783,Circuit Court
- **NOTES:** Formerly Alexandria County. Founded as Alexandria, Va., in 1789. Became part of District of Columbia in 1802. Rejoined Virginia in 1847. Name changed to Arlington March 16, 1920.

AUGUSTA

6 E. Johnson St., Staunton, VA 24401, (540) 245-5321, **<co.augusta.va.us>**

- **INCORPORATED:** April 1, 1738
- **PARENT COUNTY:** Orange
- **MARRIAGE RECORDS:** start in 1785, kept by Circuit Court
- **LAND:** 1745, Circuit Court
- **PROBATE:** 1745, Circuit Court
- **COURT:** 1745, Circuit Court
- **NOTES:** Clerk of Circuit Court has birth records 1853-1896; death records 1853-1912; military records 1756-1796, 1807-1812, 1861-1865; and naturalization records 1753-1902. Property tax records 1800-1851, and court claims 1782-1785.

BARBOUR

- **PARENT COUNTIES:** Harrison, Lewis, Randolph
- **NOTES:** See West Virginia.

BATH

Box 180, Warm Springs, VA 24484, (540) 839-7226, **<www.bathcountyva.org>**

- **INCORPORATED:** Dec. 14, 1790
- **PARENT COUNTIES:** Augusta, Botetourt, Greenbrier, WV

- **MARRIAGE RECORDS:** start in 1791, kept by Circuit Court
- **DIVORCE:** 1791, Circuit Court
- **LAND:** 1791, Circuit Court
- **PROBATE:** 1791, Circuit Court
- **COURT:** 1791, Circuit Court
- **NOTES:** Clerk of Circuit Court has birth and death records 1853-1870, and military records 1917-1918.

BEDFORD

123 E. Main St., Suite 201, Bedford, VA 24523, (540) 586-7632, **<co.bedford.va.us>**

- **INCORPORATED:** Dec. 13, 1753
- **PARENT COUNTIES:** Albemarle, Lunenburg
- **MARRIAGE RECORDS:** start in 1755, kept by Circuit Court
- **DIVORCE:** 1754, Circuit Court
- **LAND:** 1754, Circuit Court
- **PROBATE:** 1754, Circuit Court
- **COURT:** 1753, Circuit Court
- **NOTES:** Clerk of Circuit Court has birth records 1853-1897, death records 1853-1917, and military records 1861-1865, 1917-1918.

BEDFORD (INDEPENDENT CITY)

123 E. Main St., Bedford, VA 24523, (540) 586-7632, **<www.bedfordva.gov>**

- **INCORPORATED:** 1969
- **PARENT COUNTY:** Bedford
- **MARRIAGE RECORDS:** start in 1969, kept by Circuit Court
- **LAND:** start in 1969, kept by Circuit Court
- **PROBATE:** 1969, Circuit Court
- **COURT:** 1969, Circuit Court
- **NOTES:** Established 1782 as Liberty. Name changed to Bedford City in 1890. Name changed to Bedford in 1912. Incorporated as a city in 1969. County seat of Bedford.

BERKELEY

- **PARENT COUNTY:** Frederick
- **NOTES:** See West Virginia.

BLAND

Box 510, Bland, VA 24315, (540) 688-4622, **<www.bland.org>**

- **INCORPORATED:** March 30, 1861
- **PARENT COUNTIES:** Giles, Tazewell, Wythe
- **MARRIAGE RECORDS:** start in 1861, kept by Circuit Court
- **DIVORCE:** 1900, Circuit Court
- **LAND:** 1861, Circuit Court
- **PROBATE:** 1861, Circuit Court
- **COURT:** 1861, Circuit Court

BOONE

- **PARENT COUNTIES:** Cabell, Kanawha and Logan
- **NOTES:** See West Virginia.

BOTETOURT

1 W. Main St., Box 219, Fincastle, VA 24090, (540) 473-8274, **<co.botetourt.va.us>**

- **INCORPORATED:** Nov. 7, 1769
- **PARENT COUNTIES:** Augusta, Rockbridge
- **MARRIAGE RECORDS:** start in 1770, kept by Circuit Court
- **DIVORCE:** 1770, Circuit Court
- **LAND:** 1770, Circuit Court
- **PROBATE:** 1770, Circuit Court
- **COURT:** 1770, Circuit Court
- **NOTES:** Clerk of Circuit Court has birth and death records 1853-1870.

BRAXTON

- **PARENT COUNTIES:** Kanawha, Lewis, Nicholas, Randolph
- **NOTES:** See West Virginia.

BRISTOL (INDEPENDENT CITY)

497 Cumberland St., Bristol, VA 24201, (276) 645-7321, **<www.bristolva.org>**

- **INCORPORATED:** Feb. 12, 1890
- **PARENT COUNTY:** Washington
- **MARRIAGE RECORDS:** start in 1890, kept by Circuit Court
- **DIVORCE:** 1890, Circuit Court
- **LAND:** 1890, Circuit Court
- **PROBATE:** 1890, Circuit Court
- **COURT:** 1890, Circuit Court
- **MILITARY:** 1890, Circuit Court
- **NOTES:** Bristol, Va., was known as Goodson, Va., 1850-1890. Bristol, Tenn., and Bristol, Va., have separate governments. Bristol, Va., was incorporated as a city Feb. 12, 1890.

BROOKE

- **PARENT COUNTY:** Ohio
- **NOTES:** See West Virginia.

BRUNSWICK

216 N. Main St., Lawrenceville, VA 23868, (434) 848-2215, **<www.brunswickco.com>**

- **INCORPORATED:** Nov. 2, 1720
- **PARENT COUNTIES:** Prince George, Isle of Wight, Surry
- **MARRIAGE RECORDS:** start in 1750, kept by Circuit Court
- **DIVORCE:** unknown start, Circuit Court
- **LAND:** 1732, Circuit Court
- **PROBATE:** 1732, Circuit Court
- **COURT:** 1732, Circuit Court
- **NOTES:** Clerk of Circuit Court has birth records 1867-1896. County was not organized until 1732.

BUCHANAN

Box 849, Grundy, VA 24614, (276) 935-6567, **<www.buchanancountyinfo.org>**

- **INCORPORATED:** Feb. 13, 1858
- **PARENT COUNTIES:** Russell, Tazewell
- **MARRIAGE RECORDS:** start in 1885, kept by Circuit Court
- **DIVORCE:** 1885, Circuit Court
- **LAND:** 1870, Circuit Court
- **PROBATE:** 1874, Circuit Court
- **COURT:** 1885, Circuit Court
- **NOTES:** Courthouse burned in 1885.

BUCKINGHAM
Box 252, Buckingham, VA 23921, (434) 969-4242,
<buckinghamcountyva.org>
- **INCORPORATED:** September 1761
- **PARENT COUNTY:** Albemarle
- **BIRTH RECORDS:** start in 1896, kept by Circuit Court
- **MARRIAGE:** 1869, Circuit Court
- **DIVORCE:** 1869, Circuit Court
- **DEATH:** 1896, Circuit Court
- **PROBATE:** 1869, Circuit Court
- **COURT:** 1869, Circuit Court
- **NOTES:** Courthouse and records were destroyed in 1869 fire.

BUENA VISTA (INDEPENDENT CITY)
2039 Sycamore Ave., Buena Vista, VA 24416, (540) 261-6121,
<www.buenavistavirginia.org>
- **INCORPORATED:** Feb. 15, 1892
- **PARENT COUNTY:** Rockbridge
- **MARRIAGE RECORDS:** start in 1892, kept by Circuit Court
- **DIVORCE:** 1892, Circuit Court
- **LAND:** 1892, Circuit Court
- **PROBATE:** 1892, Circuit Court
- **COURT:** 1892, Circuit Court
- **NOTES:** Clerk of Circuit Court has military records 1926-1970.

CABELL
- **PARENT COUNTY:** Kanawha
- **NOTES:** See West Virginia.

CALHOUN
- **PARENT COUNTY:** Gilmer
- **NOTES:** See West Virginia.

CAMPBELL
Box 100, Rustburg, VA 24588, (434) 332-9517,
<co.campbell.va.us>
- **INCORPORATED:** Nov. 5, 1781
- **PARENT COUNTY:** Bedford
- **MARRIAGE RECORDS:** start in 1782, kept by Circuit Court
- **DIVORCE:** 1782, Circuit Court
- **LAND:** 1782, Circuit Court
- **PROBATE:** 1782, Circuit Court
- **COURT:** 1782, Circuit Court
- **NOTES:** Clerk of Circuit Court has birth records 1853-1865, 1912-1932; death records 1853-1865, 1912-1930; and military records 1854, 1855, 1917-1919, 1953-1980.

CAROLINE
Box 407, Bowling Green, VA 22427, (804) 633-5380,
<co.caroline.va.us>
- **INCORPORATED:** February 1728
- **PARENT COUNTIES:** Essex, King and Queen, King William
- **MARRIAGE RECORDS:** start in 1786, kept by Circuit Court
- **MILITARY:** 1918, Circuit Court
- **DIVORCE:** 1848, Circuit Court
- **LAND:** 1777, Circuit Court
- **PROBATE:** 1742, Circuit Court
- **COURT:** 1732, Circuit Court
- **NOTES:** Clerk of Circuit Court has birth records 1864-1867, and death records 1865-1867.

CARROLL
605 Pine St., Box 218, Hillsville, VA 24343, (276) 728-3117,
<carrollcountyva.org>
- **INCORPORATED:** Jan. 17, 1842
- **PARENT COUNTIES:** Grayson, Patrick
- **MARRIAGE RECORDS:** start in 1853, kept by Circuit Court
- **DIVORCE:** 1848, Circuit Court
- **LAND:** 1842, Circuit Court
- **PROBATE:** 1842, Circuit Court
- **COURT:** 1842, Circuit Court
- **NOTES:** Clerk of Circuit Court has death records 1855-1896.

CHARLES CITY
10900 Courthouse Rd., Box 128, Charles City, VA 23030, (804) 652-4701, **<co.charles-city.va.us>**
- **INCORPORATED:** 1634
- **PARENT COUNTY:** Original shire
- **MARRIAGE RECORDS:** start in 1762, kept by Circuit Court
- **LAND:** 1655, Circuit Court
- **PROBATE:** 1789, Circuit Court
- **COURT:** 1650, Circuit Court
- **NOTES:** Clerk of Circuit Court has birth and death records 1853-1896, and military records 1861-1865. County center for local history has microfilmed vital records (804) 829-5609.

CHARLES RIVER
- **INCORPORATED:** 1634
- **PARENT COUNTY:** Original shire
- **NOTES:** See York County. Name changed to York 1643.

CHARLOTTE
250 LaGrande Ave., Suite A, Box 608, Charlotte Court House, VA 23923, (804) 542-5117, **<www.charlotteva.com>**
- **INCORPORATED:** May 26, 1764
- **PARENT COUNTY:** Lunenburg
- **MARRIAGE RECORDS:** start in 1765, kept by Circuit Court
- **DIVORCE:** 1848, Circuit Court
- **LAND:** 1765, Circuit Court
- **PROBATE:** 1765, Circuit Court
- **COURT:** 1765, Circuit Court
- **NOTES:** Clerk of Circuit Court has military records 1811-1822, 1860-1868.

CHARLOTTESVILLE (INDEPENDENT CITY)
605 E. High St., Charlottesville, VA 22902, (434) 970-3333,
<www.charlottesville.org>
- **INCORPORATED:** 1762
- **PARENT COUNTY:** Albemarle
- **MARRIAGE RECORDS:** unknown start, kept by Circuit Court
- **LAND:** unknown start, Circuit Court
- **PROBATE:** unknown start, Circuit Court
- **NOTES:** Established in 1762, and incorporated as a city in 1888. County seat of Albemarle County.

CHESAPEAKE (INDEPENDENT CITY)

307 Albemarle Dr. Suite 300A, Chesapeake, VA 23322, (757) 382-3000, **<www.chesapeake.va.us>**

- **INCORPORATED:** Jan. 1, 1963
- **PARENT COUNTY:** Norfolk
- **MARRIAGE RECORDS:** start in 1850, kept by Department of Health
- **DIVORCE:** 1850, Circuit Court
- **LAND:** 1637, Circuit Court
- **PROBATE:** 1637, Circuit Court
- **NOTES:** Formerly Norfolk County. Norfolk County merged with city of South Norfolk to create Chesapeake Jan. 1, 1963. Clerk of Circuit Court has birth and death records 1853-1870.

CHESTERFIELD

9500 Courthouse Rd., Box 125, Chesterfield, VA 23832, (804) 748-1241, **<www.chesterfield.gov>**

- **INCORPORATED:** May 1, 1749
- **PARENT COUNTY:** Henrico
- **MARRIAGE RECORDS:** start in 1770, kept by Circuit Court
- **DIVORCE:** 1848, Circuit Court
- **LAND:** 1749, Circuit Court
- **PROBATE:** 1749, Circuit Court
- **COURT:** 1749, Circuit Court
- **NOTES:** Clerk of Circuit Court has military records for 1812 and 1861-1865.

CLARKE

102 N. Church St., Box 189, Berryville, VA 22611, (540) 955-5116, **<www.clarkecounty.gov>**

- **INCORPORATED:** March 8, 1836
- **PARENT COUNTIES:** Frederick, Warren
- **MARRIAGE RECORDS:** start in 1836, kept by Circuit Court
- **DIVORCE:** 1848, Circuit Court
- **LAND:** 1836, Circuit Court
- **PROBATE:** 1836, Circuit Court
- **COURT:** 1836, Circuit Court
- **NOTES:** Clerk of Circuit Court has military records 1861-1865.

CLAY

- **PARENT COUNTIES:** Braxton, Nicholas, Kanawha
- **NOTES:** See West Virginia.

CLIFTON FORGE (INDEPENDENT CITY)

266 W. Main St., Box 670, Covington, VA 24426, (540) 965-1730, **<www.cliftonforge.org>**

- **INCORPORATED:** 1906
- **PARENT COUNTY:** Alleghany
- **MARRIAGE RECORDS:** start in 1906, kept by Circuit Court
- **DIVORCE:** 1906, Circuit Court
- **LAND:** 1906, Circuit Court
- **PROBATE:** 1906, Circuit Court
- **NOTES:** Clifton Forge records are kept in Alleghany County Circuit Court.

COLONIAL HEIGHTS (INDEPENDENT CITY)

401 Temple Ave., Box 3401, Colonial Heights, VA 23834, (804) 520-9364, **<www.colonial-heights.com>**

- **INCORPORATED:** 1960
- **PARENT COUNTY:** Chesterfield
- **MARRIAGE RECORDS:** start in 1961, kept by Circuit Court
- **DIVORCE:** 1961, Circuit Court
- **LAND:** 1961, Circuit Court
- **PROBATE:** 1961, Circuit Court
- **COURT:** 1961, Circuit Court
- **NOTES:** Incorporated as a town in 1926, incorporated as a city in 1948, and became an independent city in 1960.

COVINGTON (INDEPENDENT CITY)

266 W. Main St., Box 670, Covington, VA 24426, (540) 965-1730, **<www.covington.va.us>**

- **INCORPORATED:** 1952
- **PARENT COUNTY:** Alleghany
- **MARRIAGE RECORDS:** unknown start, kept by Circuit Court
- **LAND:** unknown start, Circuit Court
- **PROBATE:** unknown start, Circuit Court
- **NOTES:** Established in 1819. Incorporated as a town 1873. Incorporated as a city 1952. County seat of Alleghany County.

CRAIG

303 Main St., Box 185, New Castle, VA 24127, (540) 864-6141, **<www.craigcountyva.gov>**

- **INCORPORATED:** March 21, 1851
- **PARENT COUNTIES:** Botetourt, Giles, Roanoke, Monroe West Virginia, Montgomery, Alleghany
- **MARRIAGE RECORDS:** start in 1865, kept by Circuit Court
- **DIVORCE:** 1848, Circuit Court
- **LAND:** 1851, Circuit Court
- **PROBATE:** 1851, Circuit Court
- **COURT:** 1851, Circuit Court
- **NOTES:** Clerk of Circuit Court has birth and death records 1864-1869, and military records 1861-1865, 1917-1918.

CULPEPER

101 S. W St., Culpeper, VA 22701, (540) 727-3435, **<web.culpepercounty.gov>**

- **INCORPORATED:** March 23, 1748
- **PARENT COUNTY:** Orange
- **MARRIAGE RECORDS:** start in 1781, kept by Circuit Court
- **LAND:** 1749, Circuit Court
- **PROBATE:** 1749, Circuit Court
- **COURT:** 1763, Circuit Court
- **NOTES:** Clerk of Circuit Court has birth records 1864-1896, 1912-1917, and death records 1864-1896.

CUMBERLAND

1 Courthouse Circle, Box 8, Cumberland, VA 23040, (804) 492-4442, **<www.cumberlandcounty.virginia.gov>**

- **INCORPORATED:** 1748
- **PARENT COUNTY:** Goochland
- **MARRIAGE RECORDS:** start in 1749, kept by Circuit Court
- **DIVORCE:** 1848, Circuit Court
- **LAND:** 1749, Circuit Court
- **PROBATE:** 1749, Circuit Court
- **COURT:** 1749, Circuit Court
- **NOTES:** Clerk of Circuit Court has birth records 1853-1872, and death records 1853-1885.

DANVILLE (INDEPENDENT CITY)
401 Patton St., Box 3300, Danville, VA 24543, (434) 799-5168, **<www.danville-va.gov>**
- **INCORPORATED:** 1890
- **PARENT COUNTY:** Pittsylvania
- **MARRIAGE RECORDS:** start in 1841, kept by Circuit Court
- **DIVORCE:** 1860, Circuit Court
- **LAND:** 1841, Circuit Court
- **PROBATE:** 1841, Circuit Court
- **COURT:** 1859, Circuit Court
- **NOTES:** Established in 1793, incorporated as a town in 1830, and incorporated as a city in 1890.

DICKENSON
293 Clintwood Main St., Box 190, Clintwood, VA 24228, (276) 926-1616, **<www.dickensoncountyvirginia.org>**
- **INCORPORATED:** March 3, 1880
- **PARENT COUNTIES:** Buchanan, Russell, Wise
- **BIRTH RECORDS:** start in 1912, kept by Department of Health and Library of Virginia
- **MARRIAGE:** 1880, Circuit Court
- **DIVORCE:** 1880, Circuit Court
- **DEATH:** 1912, Department of Health and Library of Virginia
- **LAND:** 1880, Circuit Court
- **PROBATE:** 1880, Circuit Court
- **COURT:** 1880, Circuit Court

DINWIDDIE
Box 63, Dinwiddie, VA 23841, (804) 469-4540, **<www.dinwiddieva.us>**
- **INCORPORATED:** Feb. 27, 1752
- **PARENT COUNTY:** Prince George
- **MARRIAGE RECORDS:** start in 1850, kept by Circuit Court
- **DIVORCE:** 1832, Circuit Court
- **LAND:** 1833, Circuit Court
- **PROBATE:** 1758, Circuit Court
- **COURT:** 1819, Circuit Court
- **NOTES:** Clerk of Circuit Court has birth and death records 1865-1896.

DODDRIDGE
- **PARENT COUNTIES:** Harrison, Tyler, Ritchie, Lewis
- **NOTES:** See West Virginia

DUNMORE
- **INCORPORATED:** March 24, 1772
- **PARENT COUNTY:** Frederick
- **NOTES:** See Shenandoah County. Name changed to Shenandoah Feb. 1, 1778.

ELIZABETH CITY
- **INCORPORATED:** 1634
- **PARENT COUNTY:** Original shire
- **NOTES:** See Hampton County. Absorbed by Hampton County July 1952.

ESSEX
305 Prince St., Box 445, Tappahannock, VA 22560, (804) 443-3541, **<www.essex-virginia.org>**
- **INCORPORATED:** April 16, 1692
- **PARENT COUNTY:** Rappahannock, old
- **MARRIAGE RECORDS:** start in 1804, kept by Circuit Court
- **DIVORCE:** 1852, Circuit Court
- **LAND:** 1692, Circuit Court
- **PROBATE:** 1692, Circuit Court
- **COURT:** 1692, Circuit Court
- **NOTES:** Clerk of Circuit Court has birth and death records 1856-1916, military records 1861-1865, and the probate records of Rappahannock 1654-1692.

FAIRFAX
4110 Chain Bridge Rd., Fairfax, VA 22030, (703) 246-4168, **<www.fairfaxcounty.gov>**
- **INCORPORATED:** May 6, 1742
- **PARENT COUNTY:** Prince William
- **MARRIAGE RECORDS:** start in 1853, kept by Circuit Court
- **DIVORCE:** 1852, Circuit Court
- **LAND:** 1742, Circuit Court
- **PROBATE:** 1742, Circuit Court
- **COURT:** 1749, Circuit Court
- **NOTES:** Clerk of Circuit Court has birth records 1853-1897, 1912-1917, and military records 1861-1865.

FAIRFAX (INDEPENDENT CITY)
4110 Chain Bridge Rd., Fairfax, VA 22030, (703) 246-4168, **<www.fairfaxva.gov>**
- **INCORPORATED:** 1961
- **PARENT COUNTY:** Fairfax
- **MARRIAGE RECORDS:** start in 1961, kept by Circuit Court
- **LAND:** 1961, Circuit Court
- **PROBATE:** 1961, Circuit Court
- **NOTES:** Established as Providence in 1805. Name changed to Fairfax in 1859. Incorporated as a town in 1874, and incorporated as a city in 1961. County seat of Fairfax County.

FALLS CHURCH (INDEPENDENT CITY)
300 Park Ave., Falls Church, VA 22046, (703) 241-5014, **<www.fallschurchva.gov>**
- **INCORPORATED:** 1948
- **PARENT COUNTY:** Fairfax
- **BIRTH RECORDS:** unknown start, kept by Circuit Court
- **MARRIAGE:** unknown start, Circuit Court
- **DIVORCE:** unknown start, Circuit Court
- **LAND:** unknown start, Circuit Court
- **PROBATE:** unknown start, Circuit Court
- **COURT:** unknown start, Circuit Court
- **NOTES:** Fairfax County Courthouse has records prior to 1988. Arlington County Courthouse has records after 1988. Established 1850. Incorporated as a town 1875. Incorporated as a city 1948.

FAUQUIER
40 Culpeper St., Warrenton, VA 20186, (540) 347-8610, **<www.fauquiercounty.gov>**
- **INCORPORATED:** May 1, 1759

- **PARENT COUNTY:** Prince William
- **MARRIAGE RECORDS:** start in 1759, kept by Circuit Court
- **DIVORCE:** 1831, Circuit Court
- **LAND:** 1759, Circuit Court
- **PROBATE:** 1759, Circuit Court
- **COURT:** 1759, Circuit Court
- **NOTES:** Clerk of Circuit Court has birth and death records 1853-1896, and military muster records 1861-1865.

FAYETTE

- **INCORPORATED:** 1831
- **PARENT COUNTIES:** Kanawha, Nicholas, Greenbrier, Logan
- **NOTES:** See West Virginia. Two Counties, Fayette 1, split to Kentucky and Fayette 2, split to West Virginia.

FINCASTLE

- **INCORPORATED:** 1772
- **PARENT COUNTY:** Botetourt
- **NOTES:** See Montgomery County. Discontinued 1776. Divided into Kentucky, Montgomery County and Washington County.

FLOYD

100 E. Main St. Room 200, Floyd, VA 24091, (540) 745-9330, **<www.floydcova.org>**

- **INCORPORATED:** Jan. 15, 1831
- **PARENT COUNTIES:** Montgomery, Franklin
- **MARRIAGE RECORDS:** start in 1831, kept by Circuit Court
- **DIVORCE:** 1831, Circuit Court
- **LAND:** 1831, Circuit Court
- **PROBATE:** 1831, Circuit Court
- **COURT:** 1828, Circuit Court
- **NOTES:** Clerk of Circuit Court has military records 1861-1865, 1916-1919.

FLUVANNA

132 Main St., Box 550, Palmyra, VA 22963, (434) 591-1970, **<co.fluvanna.va.us>**

- **INCORPORATED:** May 5, 1777
- **PARENT COUNTY:** Albemarle
- **MARRIAGE RECORDS:** start in 1777, kept by Circuit Court
- **DIVORCE:** 1831, Circuit Court
- **LAND:** 1777, Circuit Court
- **PROBATE:** 1777, Circuit Court
- **COURT:** 1777, Circuit Court
- **NOTES:** Clerk of Circuit Court has birth and death records 1853-1896.

FRANKLIN

275 S. Main St. Suite 212, Box 567, Rocky Mount, VA 24151, (540) 483-3065, **<www.franklincountyva.org>**

- **INCORPORATED:** Oct. 17, 1785
- **PARENT COUNTIES:** Bedford, Henry
- **MARRIAGE RECORDS:** start in 1785, kept by Circuit Court
- **LAND:** 1786, Circuit Court
- **PROBATE:** 1786, Circuit Court
- **COURT:** 1786, Circuit Court
- **NOTES:** Clerk of Circuit Court has birth and death records 1853-1896.

FRANKLIN (INDEPENDENT CITY)

Box 190, 22350 Main St., Courtland, VA 23837, (757) 653-2200, **<www.franklinva.com>**

- **INCORPORATED:** 1961
- **PARENT COUNTY:** Southampton
- **DIVORCE RECORDS:** unknown start, kept by Circuit Court
- **LAND:** unknown start, Circuit Court
- **PROBATE:** unknown start, Circuit Court
- **COURT:** unknown start, Circuit Court
- **NOTES:** Southampton Clerk of Circuit Court has records. All records begin in 1961. Established in 1830s. Incorporated as a town in 1876. Incorporated as a city in 1961.

FREDERICK

5 N. Kent St., Winchester, VA 22601, (540) 667-5770, **<co.frederick.va.us>**

- **INCORPORATED:** Aug. 1, 1738
- **PARENT COUNTIES:** Orange, Augusta
- **MARRIAGE RECORDS:** start in 1773, kept by Circuit Court
- **DIVORCE:** 1852, Circuit Court
- **LAND:** 1743, Circuit Court
- **PROBATE:** 1743, Circuit Court
- **COURT:** 1743, Circuit Court
- **NOTES:** Clerk of Circuit Court has birth records 1853-1912, death records 1853-1896, 1912-1917, and military records 1796-1821, 1861-1865. Nine square miles of Frederick County annexed to city of Winchester. County government established in 1743.

FREDERICKSBURG (INDEPENDENT CITY)

815 Princess Anne St., Box 359, Fredericksburg, VA 22404, (540) 372-1066, **<www.fredericksburgva.gov>**

- **INCORPORATED:** 1879
- **PARENT COUNTY:** Spotsylvania
- **MARRIAGE RECORDS:** start in 1850, kept by Circuit Court
- **LAND:** 1782, Circuit Court
- **PROBATE:** 1782, Circuit Court
- **COURT:** 1782, Circuit Court
- **NOTES:** Library of Virginia has birth and death records 1853-1896. Clerk of Circuit Court has marriage bond and tombstone inscription records 1781-1850. City established in 1728 and incorporated as a town in 1782.

GALAX (INDEPENDENT CITY)

353 N. Main St., Suite 204, Galax, VA 24333, (276) 236-8731, **<www.galaxva.com>**

- **INCORPORATED:** 1954
- **PARENT COUNTIES:** Carroll, Grayson
- **NOTES:** Galax, Va., is on the line between Grayson and Carroll counties; contact both counties for their records of Galax. Previously known as Bonaparte. Incorporated as a town in 1906 and incorporated as a city in 1954. Name changed to Galax in 1905. Established 1903.

GILES

501 Wenonah Ave, Box 502, Pearisburg, VA 24134, (540) 921-1722, **<gilescounty.org>**

- **INCORPORATED:** Jan. 16, 1806
- **PARENT COUNTIES:** Montgomery; Monroe, WV; Tazewell;

Wythe; Mercer, WV; Craig
- **MARRIAGE RECORDS:** start in 1806, kept by Circuit Court
- **DIVORCE:** 1831, Circuit Court
- **LAND:** 1806, Circuit Court
- **PROBATE:** 1806, Circuit Court
- **COURT:** 1806, Circuit Court

GILMER
- **PARENT COUNTIES:** Lewis, Kanawha
- **NOTES:** See West Virginia.

GLOUCESTER
7400 Justice Dr., Suite 327, Gloucester, VA 23061, (804) 693-2502, **<co.gloucester.va.us>**
- **INCORPORATED:** 1651
- **PARENT COUNTY:** York
- **MARRIAGE RECORDS:** start in 1853, kept by Circuit Court
- **DIVORCE:** 1865, Circuit Court
- **LAND:** 1733, Circuit Court
- **PROBATE:** 1862, Circuit Court
- **COURT:** 1820, Circuit Court
- **NOTES:** Clerk of Circuit Court has birth and death records from 1863-1890, and military records from 1946-1976.

GOOCHLAND
2938 River Rd. W., Box 196, Goochland, VA 23063, (804) 556-5353, **<co.goochland.va.us>**
- **INCORPORATED:** Feb. 1, 1728
- **PARENT COUNTY:** Henrico
- **MARRIAGE RECORDS:** start in 1730, kept by Circuit Court
- **DIVORCE:** 1837, Circuit Court
- **LAND:** 1728, Circuit Court
- **PROBATE:** 1728, Circuit Court
- **COURT:** 1728, Circuit Court
- **NOTES:** Clerk of Circuit Court has birth and death records 1852-1901, and military records 1861-1865.

GRAYSON
129 Davis St., Box 130, Independence, VA 24348, (276) 773-2231, **<www.graysoncountyva.com>**
- **INCORPORATED:** Nov. 7, 1792
- **PARENT COUNTIES:** Wythe, Patrick
- **MARRIAGE RECORDS:** start in 1793, kept by Circuit Court
- **DIVORCE:** 1832, Circuit Court
- **LAND:** 1793, Circuit Court
- **PROBATE:** 1796, Circuit Court
- **COURT:** 1793, Circuit Court
- **NOTES:** Clerk of Circuit Court has birth and death records 1853-1870.

GREENBRIER
- **PARENT COUNTIES:** Montgomery, Botetourt
- **NOTES:** See West Virginia.

GREENE
40 Celt Rd., Box 358, Stanardsville, VA 22973, (434) 985-5201, **<www.gcva.us>**
- **INCORPORATED:** Jan. 24, 1838
- **PARENT COUNTY:** Orange
- **MARRIAGE RECORDS:** start in 1838, kept by Circuit Court
- **DIVORCE:** 1838, Circuit Court
- **LAND:** 1838, Circuit Court
- **PROBATE:** 1838, Circuit Court
- **COURT:** 1838, Circuit Court
- **NOTES:** Clerk of Circuit Court has birth records from 1853-1919, and death records from 1853-1917.

GREENSVILLE
Box 631, 337 S. Main St., Emporia, VA 23847, (434) 348-4215, **<www.greensvillecountyva.gov>**
- **INCORPORATED:** Oct. 16, 1780
- **PARENT COUNTIES:** Brunswick, Sussex
- **MARRIAGE RECORDS:** start in 1781, kept by Circuit Court
- **DIVORCE:** 1848, Circuit Court
- **LAND:** 1781, Circuit Court
- **PROBATE:** 1781, Circuit Court
- **COURT:** 1781, Circuit Court
- **NOTES:** Clerk of Circuit Court has birth and death records 1853-1860.

HALIFAX
Box 729, Halifax, VA 24558, (804) 476-6221, **<www.halifaxcountyva.gov>**
- **INCORPORATED:** Feb. 27, 1752
- **PARENT COUNTY:** Lunenburg
- **MARRIAGE RECORDS:** start in 1753, kept by Circuit Court
- **DIVORCE:** 1831, Circuit Court
- **LAND:** 1752, Circuit Court
- **PROBATE:** 1753, Circuit Court
- **COURT:** 1752, Circuit Court
- **NOTES:** Clerk of Circuit Court has birth and death records 1853-1871.

HAMPSHIRE
- **INCORPORATED:** 1754
- **NOTES:** See West Virginia.

HAMPTON (INDEPENDENT CITY)
22 Lincoln St., Hampton, VA 23669, (757) 726-6997, **<www.hampton.va.us>**
- **INCORPORATED:** 1908
- **PARENT COUNTY:** Elizabeth City
- **MARRIAGE RECORDS:** start in ca. 1890, kept by Circuit Court
- **LAND:** ca. 1890, Circuit Court
- **PROBATE:** ca. 1890, Circuit Court
- **COURT:** ca. 1890, Circuit Court
- **NOTES:** Established in 1680, and incorporated as a city in 1908. Merged with Elizabeth City and Phoebus in July 1952.

HANCOCK
- **PARENT COUNTY:** Brooke
- **NOTES:** See West Virginia.

HANOVER

7507 Library Dr., Hanover, VA 23069, (804) 365-6120, **<co.hanover.va.us>**

- **INCORPORATED:** Nov. 2, 1720
- **PARENT COUNTY:** New Kent
- **MARRIAGE RECORDS:** start in 1863, kept by Circuit Court
- **DIVORCE:** 1865, Circuit Court
- **PROBATE:** 1785, Circuit Court
- **COURT:** 1873, Circuit Court
- **NOTES:** Clerk of Circuit Court has birth records 1853-1879; court and land records 1733-1735, 1783-1792; and probate records 1733-1735.

HARDY

- **PARENT COUNTY:** Hampshire
- **NOTES:** See West Virginia.

HARRISON

- **PARENT COUNTIES:** Monongalia, Ohio
- **NOTES:** See West Virginia.

HARRISONBURG (INDEPENDENT CITY)

53 Court Sq., Room 132, Harrisonburg, VA 22801, (540) 564-3130, **<www.harrisonburgva.gov>**

- **INCORPORATED:** 1916
- **PARENT COUNTY:** Rockingham
- **MARRIAGE RECORDS:** start in 1778, kept by Circuit Court
- **LAND:** 1778, Circuit Court
- **PROBATE:** 1778, Circuit Court
- **COURT:** 1778, Circuit Court
- **NOTES:** City Clerk has birth and death records from 1862-1894. Established in 1780, incorporated as a town in 1849, and incorporated as a city in 1916. Many records dating before 1864 were destroyed in the Civil War.

HENRICO

4301 E. Parham Rd., Box 27032, Richmond, VA 23273, (804) 501-4202, **<co.henrico.va.us>**

- **INCORPORATED:** 1634
- **PARENT COUNTY:** Original shire
- **MARRIAGE RECORDS:** start in 1781, kept by Circuit Court
- **DIVORCE:** 1848, Circuit Court
- **LAND:** 1650, Circuit Court
- **PROBATE:** 1650, Circuit Court
- **COURT:** 1650, Circuit Court
- **NOTES:** Clerk of Circuit Court has birth and death records 1853-1870.

HENRY

3160 Kings Mountain Rd. Suite B, Martinsville, VA 24112, (276) 634-4880, **<www.henrycountyva.gov>**

- **INCORPORATED:** Oct. 7, 1776
- **PARENT COUNTY:** Pittsylvania
- **MARRIAGE RECORDS:** start in 1778, kept by Circuit Court
- **DIVORCE:** 1909, Circuit Court
- **LAND:** 1777, Circuit Court
- **PROBATE:** 1777, Circuit Court
- **COURT:** 1777, Circuit Court
- **NOTES:** Clerk of Circuit Court has birth and death records 1853-1871.

HIGHLAND

Box 190, Main St., Monterey, VA 24465, (540) 468-2447, **<www.highlandcova.org>**

- **INCORPORATED:** March 19, 1847
- **PARENT COUNTIES:** Bath, Pendleton
- **MARRIAGE RECORDS:** start in 1853, kept by Circuit Court
- **DIVORCE:** 1848, Circuit Court
- **LAND:** 1847, Circuit Court
- **PROBATE:** 1859, Circuit Court
- **COURT:** 1847, Circuit Court
- **NOTES:** Clerk of Circuit Court has birth records from 1853-1878, and death records 1853-1868.

HOPEWELL (INDEPENDENT CITY)

100 E. Broadway Ave., Room 251, Box 310, Hopewell, VA 23860, (804) 541-2239, **<ci.hopewell.va.us>**

- **INCORPORATED:** 1911
- **PARENT COUNTY:** Prince George
- **MARRIAGE RECORDS:** start in 1916, kept by Circuit Court
- **DIVORCE:** 1916, Circuit Court
- **LAND:** 1916, Circuit Court
- **PROBATE:** 1916, Circuit Court
- **COURT:** 1916, Circuit Court
- **NOTES:** Established in 1613 and incorporated as a city in 1916. Known as Citypoint until 1913.

ILLINOIS

- **INCORPORATED:** 1778
- **PARENT COUNTY:** Augusta
- **NOTES:** Discontinued 1784, and became Northwest Territory.

ISLE OF WIGHT

17110 Monument Circle, Box 122, Isle of Wight, VA 23397, (757) 365-6244, **<co.isle-of-wight.va.us>**

- **INCORPORATED:** 1634
- **PARENT COUNTY:** Original shire
- **MARRIAGE RECORDS:** start in 1772, kept by Circuit Court
- **DIVORCE:** 1853, Circuit Court
- **LAND:** 1936, Circuit Court
- **PROBATE:** 1662, Circuit Court
- **COURT:** 1693, Circuit Court
- **NOTES:** Clerk of Circuit Court has birth and death records from 1853-1900. Formerly Warrosquyoake. Name changed to Isle of Wight 1637.

JACKSON

- **PARENT COUNTIES:** Kanawha, Mason, Wood
- **NOTES:** See West Virginia.

JAMES CITY

5201 Monticello Ave. Suite 6, Williamsburg, VA 23188, (757) 564-2242, **<www.jccegov.com>**

- **INCORPORATED:** 1634
- **PARENT COUNTY:** Original shire
- **MARRIAGE RECORDS:** start in 1865, kept by Circuit Court

- **DIVORCE:** 1865, Circuit Court
- **LAND:** 1854, Circuit Court
- **PROBATE:** 1865, Circuit Court
- **COURT:** 1865, Circuit Court
- **NOTES:** All county court records prior to 1865 were lost.

JEFFERSON

- **PARENT COUNTY:** Berkeley
- **NOTES:** See West Virginia.

KANAWAH

- **INCORPORATED:** 1789
- **PARENT COUNTIES:** Greenbriar, Montgomery
- **NOTES:** See West Virginia.

KENTUCKY

- **INCORPORATED:** 1776
- **PARENT COUNTY:** Fincastle
- **NOTES:** Discontinued 1780, and became Fayette, Jefferson and Lincoln counties, Kentucky.

KING AND QUEEN

234 Allen's Circle, Box 67, King and Queen, VA 23085, (804) 785-5984, **<www.kingandqueenco.net>**

- **INCORPORATED:** April 16, 1691
- **PARENT COUNTY:** New Kent
- **BIRTH RECORDS:** start in 1865, kept by Circuit Court
- **MARRIAGE:** 1867, Circuit Court
- **DIVORCE:** 1831, Circuit Court
- **DEATH:** 1865, Circuit Court
- **LAND:** 1719, Circuit Court
- **PROBATE:** 1864, Circuit Court
- **COURT:** 1831, Circuit Court

KING GEORGE

9483 Kings Hwy. #3, King George, VA 22485, (540) 775-3322, **<www.king-george.va.us>**

- **INCORPORATED:** Nov. 2, 1720
- **PARENT COUNTIES:** Richmond, Westmoreland
- **MARRIAGE RECORDS:** start in 1786, kept by Circuit Court
- **DIVORCE:** 1811, Circuit Court
- **LAND:** 1721, Circuit Court
- **PROBATE:** 1721, Circuit Court
- **COURT:** 1721, Circuit Court
- **NOTES:** Clerk of Circuit Court has birth records 1871-1917, and military records 1824-1860.

KING WILLIAM

Box 216, King William, VA 23086, (804) 769-4936, **<www.kingwilliamcounty.us>**

- **INCORPORATED:** December 1701
- **PARENT COUNTY:** King and Queen
- **MARRIAGE RECORDS:** start in 1944, kept by Circuit Court
- **DIVORCE:** 1885, Circuit Court
- **LAND:** 1702, Circuit Court
- **PROBATE:** 1885, Circuit Court
- **COURT:** 1702, Circuit Court
- **NOTES:** Clerk of Circuit Court has military records 1917-1919 and 1945-1946. Fire in 1855 burned most records, some records to 1702 have been photocopied.

LANCASTER

8311 Mary Ball Rd., Box 99, Lancaster, VA 22503, (804) 462-5611, **<www.lancova.com>**

- **INCORPORATED:** 1651
- **PARENT COUNTIES:** Northumberland, York
- **MARRIAGE RECORDS:** start in 1715, kept by Circuit Court
- **DIVORCE:** 1831, Circuit Court
- **LAND:** 1652, Circuit Court
- **PROBATE:** 1652, Circuit Court
- **COURT:** 1653, Circuit Court
- **NOTES:** Clerk of Circuit Court has birth records 1853-1895, and death records 1853-1885.

LEE

Box 326, Main St., Jonesville, VA 24263, (276) 346-7763, **<www.rootsweb.ancestry.com/~valee>**

- **INCORPORATED:** Oct. 25, 1792
- **PARENT COUNTIES:** Russell, Scott
- **MARRIAGE RECORDS:** start in 1830, kept by Circuit Court
- **DIVORCE:** 1832, Circuit Court
- **LAND:** 1793, Circuit Court
- **PROBATE:** 1794, Circuit Court
- **COURT:** 1808, Circuit Court
- **NOTES:** Clerk of Circuit Court has birth and death records from 1853-1877.

LEWIS

- **PARENT COUNTIES:** Harrison, Randolph
- **NOTES:** See West Virginia.

LEXINGTON (INDEPENDENT CITY)

2 S. Main St., Lexington, VA 24450, (540) 463-2232, **<www.ci.lexington.va.us>**

- **INCORPORATED:** 1965
- **PARENT COUNTY:** Rockbridge
- **MARRIAGE RECORDS:** start in 1778, kept by Circuit Court
- **DIVORCE:** 1831, Circuit Court
- **LAND:** 1778, Circuit Court
- **PROBATE:** 1778, Circuit Court
- **COURT:** 1778, Circuit Court
- **NOTES:** Rockbridge County Clerk of Circuit Court has birth records 1853-1896, and military records 1861-1865. County seat of Rockbridge County. Established in 1778, incorporated as a town in 1874, and incorporated as a city in 1965.

LINCOLN

- **PARENT COUNTIES:** Boone, Cabell, Kanawha
- **NOTES:** See West Virginia.

LOGAN

- **PARENT COUNTIES:** Cabell, Kanawha, Giles, Tazewell
- **NOTES:** See West Virginia.

LOUDOUN

Box 550, 18 E. Market St., Leesburg, VA 20178, (703) 777-0270, **<www.loudoun.gov>**

- **INCORPORATED:** March 25, 1757
- **PARENT COUNTY:** Fairfax
- **MARRIAGE RECORDS:** start in 1760, kept by Circuit Court
- **DIVORCE:** 1831, Circuit Court
- **LAND:** 1757, Circuit Court
- **PROBATE:** 1757, Circuit Court
- **COURT:** 1757, Circuit Court
- **NOTES:** Clerk of Circuit Court has birth records 1853-1859, 1864-1866; death records 1853-1866; military records 1793-1827, 1811-1860, 1861-1865; and naturalization records 1908-1910.

LOUISA

Box 37, Louisa, VA 23093, (540) 967-5312, **<www.louisa-county.com>**

- **INCORPORATED:** May 6, 1742
- **PARENT COUNTY:** Hanover
- **MARRIAGE RECORDS:** start in 1766, kept by Circuit Court
- **DIVORCE:** 1844, Circuit Court
- **LAND:** 1742, Circuit Court
- **PROBATE:** 1745, Circuit Court
- **COURT:** 1742, Circuit Court
- **NOTES:** Clerk of Circuit Court has birth records 1864-1871, death records 1864-1870, and military records for 1814 and 1861-1865.

LOWER NORFOLK

- **INCORPORATED:** 1637
- **PARENT COUNTY:** New Norfolk
- **NOTES:** See Princess Anne and Norfolk counties. Abolished 1691 and divided between Princess Anne and Norfolk counties.

LUNENBURG

11435 Courthouse Rd., Lunenburg, VA 23952, (434) 696-2230, **<lunenburgva.org>**

- **INCORPORATED:** May 6, 1745
- **PARENT COUNTY:** Brunswick
- **MARRIAGE RECORDS:** start in 1746, kept by Circuit Court
- **DIVORCE:** 1842, Circuit Court
- **LAND:** 1746, Circuit Court
- **PROBATE:** 1746, Circuit Court
- **COURT:** 1746, Circuit Court
- **NOTES:** Clerk of Circuit Court has birth records 1853-1889, and death records 1853-1870.

LYNCHBURG (INDEPENDENT CITY)

901 Court St., Lynchburg, VA 24504, (434) 455-6226, **<www.lynchburgva.gov>**

- **INCORPORATED:** 1852
- **PARENT COUNTY:** Campbell
- **MARRIAGE RECORDS:** start in 1805, kept by Circuit Court
- **DIVORCE:** 1814, Circuit Court
- **LAND:** 1805, Circuit Court
- **PROBATE:** 1809, Circuit Court
- **COURT:** 1805, Circuit Court
- **NOTES:** Clerk of Circuit Court has birth and death records 1853-1868, and military records 1861-1865. Established in 1786, incorporated as a town in 1805, and incorporated as a city in 1852.

MADISON

100 Court Sq. Main St., Box 220, Madison, VA 22727, (540) 948-6888, **<www.madison-va.com>**

- **INCORPORATED:** Dec. 4, 1792
- **PARENT COUNTY:** Culpeper
- **MARRIAGE RECORDS:** start in 1793, kept by Circuit Court
- **DIVORCE:** 1831, Circuit Court
- **LAND:** 1793, Circuit Court
- **PROBATE:** 1793, Circuit Court
- **COURT:** 1793, Circuit Court
- **NOTES:** Clerk of Circuit Court has military records for 1812 and 1861-1865.

MANASSAS (INDEPENDENT CITY)

9311 Lee Ave., Manassas, VA 20110, (703) 792-6015, **<www.manassascity.org>**

- **INCORPORATED:** 1975
- **NOTES:** Established in 1852, incorporated as a town in 1874, and incorporated as a city in 1975. County Seat of Prince William County. Clerk of Circuit Court has all records 1975 to the present.

MANASSAS PARK (INDEPENDENT CITY)

9311 Lee Ave., Manassas, VA 20110, (703) 792-6015

- **INCORPORATED:** 1975
- **PARENT COUNTY:** Manassas City
- **MARRIAGE RECORDS:** start in 1975, kept by Circuit Court
- **DIVORCE:** 1975, Circuit Court
- **LAND:** 1975, Circuit Court
- **PROBATE:** 1975, Circuit Court
- **COURT:** 1975, Circuit Court
- **NOTES:** Established in 1955, incorporated as a town in 1957, and as a city in 1975. Cities of Manassas and Manassas Park records are kept by Prince William County Clerk of Circuit Court.

MARION

- **INCORPORATED:** 1842
- **PARENT COUNTIES:** Harrison, Monongalia
- **NOTES:** See West Virginia.

MARSHALL

- **PARENT COUNTY:** Ohio
- **NOTES:** See West Virginia.

MARTINSVILLE (INDEPENDENT CITY)

55 W. Church St., Box 1206, Martinsville, VA 24114, (276) 403-5106, **<www.martinsville-va.gov>**

- **INCORPORATED:** 1928
- **PARENT COUNTY:** Henry
- **MARRIAGE RECORDS:** start in 1942, kept by Circuit Court
- **DIVORCE:** 1942, Circuit Court
- **LAND:** 1942, Circuit Court
- **PROBATE:** 1942, Circuit Court
- **COURT:** 1942, Circuit Court
- **NOTES:** Established in 1791, incorporated as a town in 1873, and incorporated as a city in 1928. County seat of Henry County.

MASON

- **PARENT COUNTY:** Kanawha
- **NOTES:** See West Virginia.

MATHEWS

Box 463, Mathews, VA 23109, (804) 725-2550, **<co.mathews.va.us>**

- **INCORPORATED:** May 1, 1791
- **PARENT COUNTY:** Gloucester
- **MARRIAGE RECORDS:** start in 1827, kept by Circuit Court
- **DIVORCE:** 1805, Circuit Court
- **LAND:** 1814, Circuit Court
- **PROBATE:** 1865, Circuit Court
- **COURT:** 1795, Circuit Court
- **NOTES:** Clerk of Circuit Court has birth and death records 1865-1896.

MCDOWELL

- **PARENT COUNTY:** Tazewell
- **NOTES:** See West Virginia.

MECKLENBURG

1294 Jefferson St., Box 530, Boydton, VA 23917, (434) 738-6191 ext. 4222, **<www.mecklenburgva.com>**

- **INCORPORATED:** May 26, 1764
- **PARENT COUNTY:** Lunenburg
- **MARRIAGE RECORDS:** start in 1765, kept by Circuit Court
- **LAND:** 1765, Circuit Court
- **PROBATE:** 1765, Circuit Court
- **COURT:** 1765, Circuit Court

MERCER

- **INCORPORATED:** 1837
- **PARENT COUNTIES:** Giles, Tazewell
- **NOTES:** See West Virginia.

MIDDLESEX

Rts. 17 and 33, Box 158, Saluda, VA 23149, (804) 758-5317, **<www.co.middlesex.va.us>**

- **INCORPORATED:** September 1669
- **PARENT COUNTY:** Lancaster
- **MARRIAGE RECORDS:** start in 1740, kept by Circuit Court
- **DIVORCE:** 1825, Circuit Court
- **LAND:** 1673, Circuit Court
- **PROBATE:** 1673, Circuit Court
- **COURT:** 1673, Circuit Court
- **NOTES:** Clerk of Circuit Court has birth records 1754-1763, 1853-1896; death records 1758-1763, 1853-1896; marriage records 1663-1719; and military records 1861-1865, 1917-1960.

MONONGALIA

- **PARENT COUNTY:** District of West Augusta
- **NOTES:** See West Virginia.

MONROE

- **PARENT COUNTIES:** Greenbriar, Botetourt
- **NOTES:** See West Virginia.

MONTGOMERY

1 E. Main St. Suite B-5, Box 6309, Christiansburg, VA 24068, (540) 382-5760, **<www.montva.com>**

- **INCORPORATED:** Oct. 7, 1776
- **PARENT COUNTIES:** Fincastle, Botetourt, Pulaski
- **MARRIAGE RECORDS:** start in 1777, kept by Circuit Court
- **DIVORCE:** 1831, Circuit Court
- **LAND:** 1773, Circuit Court
- **PROBATE:** 1773, Circuit Court
- **COURT:** 1773, Circuit Court
- **NOTES:** Clerk of Circuit Court has birth and death records from 1853-1868, and military records 1818-1839.

MORGAN

- **PARENT COUNTIES:** Berkeley, Hampshire
- **NOTES:** See West Virginia.

NANSEMOND

- **INCORPORATED:** 1637
- **PARENT COUNTY:** New Norfolk
- **NOTES:** See Suffolk City. Formerly Upper Norfolk County. Name changed to Nansemond County in 1646. Became an independent city in 1972. Nansemond City absorbed by Suffolk City Jan. 1, 1974.

NELSON

84 Courthouse Sq., Box 10, Lovingston, VA 22949, (434) 263-7020, **<nelsoncounty.com>**

- **INCORPORATED:** Dec. 25, 1807
- **PARENT COUNTY:** Amherst
- **MARRIAGE RECORDS:** start in 1808, kept by Circuit Court
- **DIVORCE:** 1831, Circuit Court
- **LAND:** 1808, Circuit Court
- **PROBATE:** 1808, Circuit Court
- **COURT:** 1808, Circuit Court
- **NOTES:** Clerk of Circuit Court has birth and death records 1853-1872.

NEW KENT

12001 Courthouse Circle, Box 98, New Kent, VA 23124, (804) 966-9520, **<co.new-kent.va.us>**

- **INCORPORATED:** Nov. 20, 1654
- **PARENT COUNTY:** York
- **MARRIAGE RECORDS:** start in 1858, kept by Circuit Court
- **DIVORCE:** 1823, Circuit Court
- **LAND:** 1864, Circuit Court
- **PROBATE:** 1863, Circuit Court
- **COURT:** 1865, Circuit Court
- **NOTES:** Clerk of Circuit Court has birth and death records 1865-1888, court records 1823-1824, and military records 1917-1918, 1941-1977.

NEW NORFOLK

- **INCORPORATED:** 1636
- **PARENT COUNTY:** Elizabeth City
- **NOTES:** Abolished 1637. Divided to Upper Norfolk (now Suffolk) and Lower Norfolk (now Chesapeake).

NEWPORT NEWS (INDEPENDENT CITY)

2500 Washington Ave., Newport News, VA 23607, (757) 926-8561, **<www.nngov.com>**

- **INCORPORATED:** 1896
- **PARENT COUNTY:** Warwick
- **MARRIAGE RECORDS:** start in 1959, kept by Circuit Court
- **LAND:** 1846, Circuit Court
- **PROBATE:** 1922, Circuit Court
- **NOTES:** Clerk of Circuit Court has marriage records 1890-1895. Established in 1880 and incorporated as a city in 1896. Part of Warwick County until 1896 and from 1952-1958. Enlarged due to the addition of Warwick July 1, 1958.

NICHOLAS

- **INCORPORATED:** 1818
- **PARENT COUNTIES:** Greenbriar, Kanawha, Randolph
- **NOTES:** See West Virginia.

NORFOLK

- **INCORPORATED:** 1691
- **PARENT COUNTY:** Lower Norfolk
- **NOTES:** Consolidated with city of South Norfolk to create Chesapeake City Jan. 1, 1963. Records kept by Chesapeake City Clerk of Circuit Court. Norfolk County extinct.

NORFOLK (INDEPENDENT CITY)

100 St. Paul's Blvd., Norfolk, VA 23510, (757) 664-4380, **<www.norfolk.gov>**

- **INCORPORATED:** 1680
- **PARENT COUNTY:** Norfolk
- **MARRIAGE RECORDS:** start in 1797, kept by Circuit Court
- **DIVORCE:** 1833, Circuit Court
- **LAND:** 1784, Circuit Court
- **PROBATE:** 1784, Circuit Court
- **COURT:** 1761, Circuit Court
- **NOTES:** Clerk of Circuit Court has birth records 1792-1896, and death records 1853-1871, 1892-1897. Incorporated as a borough in 1736, incorporated as a city in 1845, and annexed town of Berkeley in 1906.

NORTHAMPTON

522 The Hornes, Box 36, Eastville, VA 23347, (757) 678-0465, **<co.northampton.va.us>**

- **INCORPORATED:** 1634
- **PARENT COUNTY:** Original shire
- **MARRIAGE RECORDS:** start in 1706, kept by Circuit Court
- **DIVORCE:** 1831, Circuit Court
- **LAND:** 1632, Circuit Court
- **PROBATE:** 1632, Circuit Court
- **COURT:** 1632, Circuit Court
- **NOTES:** Clerk of Circuit Court has birth and death records 1853-1870. Formerly Accomac County. Name changed to Northampton 1643.

NORTHUMBERLAND

39 Judicial Place, Box 217, Heathsville, VA 22473, (804) 580-3700, **<co.northumberland.va.us>**

- **INCORPORATED:** Oct. 12, 1648
- **PARENT COUNTY:** Indian District of Chickacoan
- **MARRIAGE RECORDS:** start in 1735, kept by Circuit Court
- **DIVORCE:** 1805, Circuit Court
- **LAND:** 1650, Circuit Court
- **PROBATE:** 1652, Circuit Court
- **COURT:** 1650, Circuit Court
- **NOTES:** Some records were lost during a fire in October 1710.

NORTON (INDEPENDENT CITY)

Box 1248, Wise, VA 24293, (276) 328-6111,

- **INCORPORATED:** 1954
- **PARENT COUNTY:** Wise
- **NOTES:** All records are with Wise County Clerk of Circuit Court. Established in 1787 and incorporated as a town in 1894.

NOTTOWAY

328 W. Courthouse Rd., Box 25, Nottoway, VA 23955, (434) 645-9043, **<www.nottoway.org>**

- **INCORPORATED:** Dec. 22, 1788
- **PARENT COUNTY:** Amelia
- **MARRIAGE RECORDS:** start in 1865, kept by Circuit Court
- **DIVORCE:** 1832, Circuit Court
- **LAND:** 1789, Circuit Court
- **PROBATE:** 1789, Circuit Court
- **COURT:** 1793, Circuit Court
- **NOTES:** Some records were destroyed during the Civil War.

OHIO

- **PARENT COUNTY:** Augusta
- **NOTES:** See West Virginia.

ORANGE

110 N. Madison Rd., Box 230, Orange, VA 22960, (540) 672-4030, **<www.orangecova.com>**

- **INCORPORATED:** Feb. 1, 1734
- **PARENT COUNTY:** Spotsylvania
- **MARRIAGE RECORDS:** start in 1756, kept by Circuit Court
- **DIVORCE:** 1868, Circuit Court
- **LAND:** 1734, Circuit Court
- **PROBATE:** 1734, Circuit Court
- **COURT:** 1736, Circuit Court
- **NOTES:** Clerk of Circuit Court has birth records from 1751-1778, 1886-1895.

PAGE

116 S. Court St. Suite A, Luray, VA 22835, (540) 743-4064, **<www.pagecounty.virginia.gov>**

- **INCORPORATED:** March 30, 1831
- **PARENT COUNTIES:** Rockingham, Shenandoah
- **MARRIAGE RECORDS:** start in 1831, kept by Circuit Court
- **DIVORCE:** 1831, Circuit Court
- **LAND:** 1831, Circuit Court
- **PROBATE:** 1831, Circuit Court
- **COURT:** 1831, Circuit Court
- **NOTES:** Clerk of Circuit Court has birth records 1865-1872, death records 1864-1872, and military records 1917-1918.

PATRICK

Box 148, Stuart, VA 24171, (276) 694-7213, **<co.patrick.va.us>**
- **INCORPORATED:** Nov. 26, 1790
- **PARENT COUNTY:** Henry
- **MARRIAGE RECORDS:** start in 1791, kept by Circuit Court
- **DIVORCE:** 1832, Circuit Court
- **LAND:** 1791, Circuit Court
- **PROBATE:** 1791, Circuit Court
- **COURT:** 1791, Circuit Court
- **NOTES:** Clerk of Circuit Court has birth records 1853-1896, death records 1853-1870, and military records 1861-1865, 1917-1919, 1945-1970.

PENDLETON

- **PARENT COUNTIES:** Hardy, Augusta, Rockingham
- **NOTES:** See West Virginia.

PETERSBURG (INDEPENDENT CITY)

7 Courthouse Ave., Petersburg, VA 23803, (804) 733-2367, **<www.petersburg-va.org>**
- **INCORPORATED:** March 16, 1850
- **PARENT COUNTIES:** Dinwiddie, Prince George, Chesterfield
- **MARRIAGE RECORDS:** start in 1784, kept by Circuit Court
- **DIVORCE:** 1831, Circuit Court
- **LAND:** 1784, Circuit Court
- **PROBATE:** 1784, Circuit Court
- **COURT:** 1784, Circuit Court
- **NOTES:** Clerk of Circuit Court has birth and death records 1853-1896. Established in 1748, incorporated as a town in 1785, and incorporated as a city in 1850. Portions of Prince George and Dinwiddie counties were added in 1972.

PITTSYLVANIA

Drawer 31, 3 N. Main St., Chatham, VA 24531, (434) 432-7887, **<www.pittgov.org>**
- **INCORPORATED:** Nov. 6, 1766
- **PARENT COUNTY:** Halifax
- **MARRIAGE RECORDS:** start in 1767, kept by Circuit Court
- **DIVORCE:** 1831, Circuit Court
- **LAND:** 1767, Circuit Court
- **PROBATE:** 1767, Circuit Court
- **COURT:** 1767, Circuit Court
- **NOTES:** Clerk of Circuit Court has birth and death records 1853-1896.

PLEASANTS

- **PARENT COUNTIES:** Ritchie, Tyler, Wood
- **NOTES:** See West Virginia.

POCAHONTAS

- **PARENT COUNTIES:** Pendleton, Randolph, Greenbrier, Bath
- **NOTES:** See West Virginia.

POQUOSON (INDEPENDENT CITY)

Box 262, Grafton, VA 23690, (757) 890-3508, **<ci.poquoson.va.us>**
- **INCORPORATED:** 1976
- **PARENT COUNTY:** York
- **MARRIAGE RECORDS:** start in 1976, kept by Circuit Court
- **DIVORCE:** 1976, Circuit Court
- **LAND:** 1976, Circuit Court
- **PROBATE:** 1976, Circuit Court
- **NOTES:** York County Clerk of Circuit Court has all Poquoson records. Established ca. 1888, incorporated as a town in 1952, and incorporated as a city in 1976.

PORTSMOUTH (INDEPENDENT CITY)

601 Crawford Pkwy., Box 1217, Portsmouth, VA 23705, (757) 393-8671, **< www.portsmouthva.gov>**
- **INCORPORATED:** 1858
- **PARENT COUNTY:** Norfolk
- **MARRIAGE RECORDS:** start in 1858, kept by Circuit Court
- **DIVORCE:** 1866, Circuit Court
- **LAND:** 1858, Circuit Court
- **PROBATE:** 1858, Circuit Court
- **COURT:** 1858, Circuit Court
- **NOTES:** Library of Virginia has birth and death records from 1853-1896. Established in 1752, incorporated as a town in 1836, and incorporated as a city in 1858. Territory taken from Norfolk County and annexed to Portsmouth in 1848, 1960 and 1968.

POWHATAN

3880 Old Buckingham Rd. Suite C, Box 37, Powhatan, VA 23139, (804) 598-5660, **<www.powhatanva.com>**
- **INCORPORATED:** May 5, 1777
- **PARENT COUNTIES:** Chesterfield, Cumberland
- **MARRIAGE RECORDS:** start in 1777, kept by Circuit Court
- **DIVORCE:** 1809, Circuit Court
- **LAND:** 1777, Circuit Court
- **PROBATE:** 1777, Circuit Court
- **COURT:** 1777, Circuit Court
- **NOTES:** Clerk of Circuit Court has birth and death records 1853-1871.

PRESTON

- **PARENT COUNTIES:** Monongalia, Randolph
- **NOTES:** See West Virginia.

PRINCE EDWARD

Box 304, Farmville, VA 23901, (434) 392-5145, **<co.prince-edward.va.us>**
- **INCORPORATED:** February 1753
- **PARENT COUNTY:** Amelia
- **MARRIAGE RECORDS:** start in 1754, kept by Circuit Court
- **DIVORCE:** 1754, Circuit Court
- **LAND:** 1754, Circuit Court
- **PROBATE:** 1754, Circuit Court
- **COURT:** 1754, Circuit Court
- **NOTES:** Clerk of Circuit Court has birth records 1853-1896, death records 1853-1868, military records 1861-1865, and naturalization records 1901-1925.

PRINCE GEORGE

6601 Courts Dr., Box 98, Prince George, VA 23875, (804) 733-2640, **<www.princegeorgeva.org>**
- **INCORPORATED:** December 1702
- **PARENT COUNTY:** Charles City
- **MARRIAGE RECORDS:** start in 1865, kept by Circuit Court

- **DIVORCE:** 1836, Circuit Court
- **LAND:** 1710, Circuit Court
- **PROBATE:** 1713, Circuit Court
- **COURT:** 1714, Circuit Court
- **NOTES:** Clerk of Circuit Court has birth and death records 1865-1904, and military records 1861-1865.

PRINCE WILLIAM

9311 Lee Ave., Manassas, VA 20110, (703) 792-6015, **<www.co.prince-william.va.us>**

- **INCORPORATED:** February 1730
- **PARENT COUNTIES:** King George, Stafford
- **MARRIAGE RECORDS:** start in 1859, kept by Circuit Court
- **DIVORCE:** 1823, Circuit Court
- **LAND:** 1731, Circuit Court
- **PROBATE:** 1734, Circuit Court
- **COURT:** 1752, Circuit Court
- **NOTES:** Clerk of Circuit Court has birth and death records 1864-1870.

PRINCESS ANNE

- **INCORPORATED:** 1691
- **PARENT COUNTY:** Lower Norfolk
- **NOTES:** See Virginia Beach. Now part of Independent City of Virginia Beach, consolidated 1963.

PULASKI

45 Third St. N.W., Suite 101, Pulaski, VA 24301, (540) 980-7825, **<www.pulaskicounty.org>**

- **INCORPORATED:** March 30, 1839
- **PARENT COUNTIES:** Montgomery, Wythe
- **MARRIAGE RECORDS:** start in 1839, kept by Circuit Court
- **DIVORCE:** 1839, Circuit Court
- **LAND:** 1839, Circuit Court
- **PROBATE:** 1839, Circuit Court
- **COURT:** 1839, Circuit Court
- **NOTES:** Clerk of Circuit Court has birth and death records 1853-1870, and military records 1917-1918.

PUTNAM

- **PARENT COUNTIES:** Kanawha, Mason, Cabell
- **NOTES:** See West Virginia.

RADFORD (INDEPENDENT CITY)

619 Second St., West Radford, VA 24141, (540) 731-3610, **<radford.va.us>**

- **INCORPORATED:** 1887
- **PARENT COUNTY:** Montgomery
- **MARRIAGE RECORDS:** kept by 1892, start in Radford Clerk of Circuit Court
- **DIVORCE:** 1892, Radford Clerk of Circuit Court
- **COURT:** 1892, Radford Clerk of Circuit Court
- **LAND:** 1892, Radford Clerk of Circuit Court
- **PROBATE:** 1892, Radford Clerk of Circuit Court
- **NOTES:** Established in 1885, incorporated as a town in 1887, and incorporated as a city in 1892. Previously named Central City; name changed to Radford in 1890.

RALEIGH

- **INCORPORATED:** 1850
- **PARENT COUNTY:** Fayette
- **NOTES:** See West Virginia.

RANDOLPH

- **INCORPORATED:** 1787
- **PARENT COUNTY:** Harrison
- **NOTES:** See West Virginia.

RAPPAHANNOCK

238 Gay St., Box 517, Washington, VA 22747, (540) 675-5350, **<www.rappahannockcountyva.gov>**

- **INCORPORATED:** Feb. 8, 1833
- **PARENT COUNTY:** Culpeper
- **MARRIAGE RECORDS:** start in 1833, kept by Circuit Court
- **DIVORCE:** 1833, Circuit Court
- **LAND:** 1833, Circuit Court
- **PROBATE:** 1833, Circuit Court
- **COURT:** 1833, Circuit Court
- **NOTES:** Clerk of Circuit Court has birth records 1853-1870, and death records 1853-1891.

RAPPAHANNOCK, OLD

- **INCORPORATED:** 1656
- **PARENT COUNTY:** Lancaster
- **NOTES:** See Essex and Richmond counties. Abolished 1662. Split into Essex and Richmond counties.

RICHMOND

400 N. Ninth St., John Marshall Courts Building, Richmond, VA 23219, (804) 646-6505, **<co.richmond.va.us>**

- **INCORPORATED:** April 16, 1692
- **PARENT COUNTY:** Rappahannock, old
- **MARRIAGE RECORDS:** start in 1824, kept by Circuit Court
- **DIVORCE:** 1815, Circuit Court
- **LAND:** 1692, Circuit Court
- **PROBATE:** 1699, Circuit Court
- **COURT:** 1692, Circuit Court
- **NOTES:** Clerk of Circuit Court has birth records 1853-1895, 1912-1914; death records 1853-1895, 1912-1917; and marriage records 1709-1716.

RICHMOND (INDEPENDENT CITY)

400 N. Ninth St., John Marshall Courts Bldg., Richmond, VA 23219, (804) 780-7970, **<www.richmondgov.com>**

- **INCORPORATED:** 1782
- **PARENT COUNTY:** Henrico
- **MARRIAGE RECORDS:** start in 1797, kept by Circuit Court
- **DIVORCE:** 1815, Circuit Court
- **LAND:** 1782, Circuit Court
- **PROBATE:** 1782, Circuit Court
- **COURT:** 1692, Circuit Court
- **COURT:** 1782, Clerk of Civil Court
- **NOTES:** Clerk of Circuit Court has birth and death records 1870-1954. John Marshall Courts Building has city records. Established in 1742, incorporated as a town in 1782, and as a city in 1842. Richmond Circuit Court has two locations: John Marshall Courts

Building 400 N. Ninth St., Richmond VA 23219, (804) 646-6505 and Manchester Courthouse, 10th and Hull Sts., Richmond VA 23224, (804) 646-8470.

RITCHIE

- **PARENT COUNTIES:** Harrison, Lewis, Wood
- **NOTES:** See West Virginia.

ROANE

- **PARENT COUNTIES:** Kanawha, Jackson, Gilmer
- **NOTES:** See West Virginia.

ROANOKE

305 E. Main St., Box 1126, Salem, VA 24153, (540) 387-6205, **<www.roanokecountyva.gov>**

- **INCORPORATED:** March 30, 1838
- **PARENT COUNTIES:** Botetourt, Montgomery
- **MARRIAGE RECORDS:** start in 1838, kept by Circuit Court
- **DIVORCE:** 1838, Circuit Court
- **LAND:** 1838, Circuit Court
- **PROBATE:** 1838, Circuit Court
- **COURT:** 1838, Circuit Court

ROANOKE (INDEPENDENT CITY)

315 Church Ave. SW, Roanoke, VA 24011, (540) 853-6702, **<www.roanokeva.gov>**

- **INCORPORATED:** 1884
- **PARENT COUNTY:** Roanoke
- **MARRIAGE RECORDS:** start in 1884, kept by Circuit Court
- **DIVORCE:** 1884, Circuit Court
- **LAND:** 1884, Circuit Court
- **PROBATE:** 1884, Circuit Court
- **COURT:** 1884, Circuit Court
- **NOTES:** Clerk of Courts has birth records 1886-1896. Established in 1852, incorporated as a town in 1874, and as a city in 1884. Previous name was Big Lick.

ROCKBRIDGE

20 S. Randolph St., Suite 101, Lexington, VA 24450, (540) 463-2232, **<co.rockbridge.va.us>**

- **INCORPORATED:** Oct. 20, 1778
- **PARENT COUNTY:** Augusta, Botetourt
- **MARRIAGE RECORDS:** start in 1778, kept by Circuit Court
- **DIVORCE:** 1831, Circuit Court
- **LAND:** 1778, Circuit Court
- **PROBATE:** 1778, Circuit Court
- **COURT:** 1778, Circuit Court
- **NOTES:** Clerk of Circuit Court has birth records 1853-1896, death records 1853-1870, and military records 1861-1865.

ROCKINGHAM

Rockingham County Courthouse Courthouse Sq., Harrisonburg, VA 22801, (540) 564-3111, **<www.rockinghamcountyva.gov>**

- **INCORPORATED:** October 1778
- **PARENT COUNTY:** Augusta
- **MARRIAGE RECORDS:** start in 1778, kept by Circuit Court
- **DIVORCE:** 1831, Circuit Court
- **LAND:** 1778, Circuit Court
- **PROBATE:** 1789, Circuit Court
- **COURT:** 1778, Circuit Court
- **NOTES:** Clerk of Circuit Court has birth records 1791-1795, 1862-1894; and death records 1862-1894; and military records 1861-1865, 1917-1919. Some records were burned in 1864 and 1787.

RUSSELL

53 E. Main St., Box 435, Lebanon, VA 24266, (276) 889-8023, **<www.russellcountyva.us>**

- **INCORPORATED:** October 1786
- **PARENT COUNTY:** Washington
- **MARRIAGE RECORDS:** starts in 1853, kept by Circuit Court
- **DIVORCE:** 1831, Circuit Court
- **LAND:** 1786, Circuit Court
- **PROBATE:** 1803, Circuit Court
- **COURT:** 1786, Circuit Court
- **NOTES:** Clerk of Circuit Court has birth and death records 1853-1866, and military records 1917-1918, 1945.

SALEM (INDEPENDENT CITY)

2 E. Calhoun St., Salem, VA 24153, (540) 375-3067, **<ci.salem.va.us>**

- **INCORPORATED:** 1968
- **PARENT COUNTY:** Roanoke
- **MARRIAGE RECORDS:** start in 1968, kept by Circuit Court
- **DIVORCE:** 1968, Circuit Court
- **LAND:** 1968, Circuit Court
- **PROBATE:** 1968, Circuit Court
- **COURT:** 1968, Circuit Court
- **NOTES:** Established in 1806, incorporated as a town in 1836, and incorporated as a city in 1968. County seat of Roanoke County.

SCOTT

202 W. Jackson St. Suite 102, Gate City, VA 24251, (276) 386-3801, **<www.scottcountyva.com>**

- **INCORPORATED:** Nov. 24, 1814
- **PARENT COUNTIES:** Lee, Russell, Washington
- **MARRIAGE RECORDS:** start in 1815, kept by Circuit Court
- **DIVORCE:** 1831, Circuit Court
- **LAND:** 1815, Circuit Court
- **PROBATE:** 1815, Circuit Court
- **COURT:** 1815, Circuit Court
- **NOTES:** Clerk of Circuit Court has birth records 1853-1870, 1874-1895; death records from 1853-1870; and military records 1830-1850, 1917-1918.

SHENANDOAH

112 S. Main St., Box 406, Woodstock, VA 22664, (540) 459-6150, **<www.shenandoahcountyva.us>**

- **INCORPORATED:** March 24, 1772
- **PARENT COUNTY:** Frederick
- **MARRIAGE RECORDS:** start in 1772, kept by Circuit Court
- **DIVORCE:** 1831, Circuit Court
- **LAND:** 1772, Circuit Court
- **PROBATE:** 1772, Circuit Court
- **COURT:** 1772, Circuit Court
- **NOTES:** Clerk of Circuit Court has birth and death records 1853-1871, and military records 1861-1865. Formerly Dunmore County. Name changed to Shenandoah Feb. 1, 1778.

SMYTH
109 W. Main St. Room 144, Marion, VA 24354, (276) 782-4044, **<www.smythcounty.org>**
- **INCORPORATED:** Feb. 23, 1832
- **PARENT COUNTIES:** Washington, Wythe
- **MARRIAGE RECORDS:** 1832, Circuit Court
- **DIVORCE:** 1833, Circuit Court
- **LAND:** 1832, Circuit Court
- **PROBATE:** 1832, Circuit Court
- **COURT:** 1832, Circuit Court
- **NOTES:** Clerk of Circuit Court has birth and death records 1857-1896, and military records 1917-1918, 1940-1980.

SOUTHAMPTON
22350 Main St., Box 190, Courtland, VA 23837, (757) 653-2200, **<www.southamptoncounty.org>**
- **INCORPORATED:** April 30, 1749
- **PARENT COUNTIES:** Isle of Wight, Nansemond
- **MARRIAGE RECORDS:** start in 1750, kept by Circuit Court
- **DIVORCE:** 1859, Circuit Court
- **LAND:** 1749, Circuit Court
- **PROBATE:** 1749, Circuit Court
- **COURT:** 1749, Circuit Court
- **NOTES:** Clerk of Circuit Court has birth records 1853-1872, court records for 1708, death records 1853-1870, and naturalization records 1867-1912.

SPOTSYLVANIA
9115 Courthouse Rd., Box 96, Spotsylvania, VA 22553, (540) 582-7090, **<www.spotsylvania.va.us>**
- **INCORPORATED:** Nov. 2, 1720
- **PARENT COUNTIES:** Essex, King and Queen, King William
- **MARRIAGE RECORDS:** start in 1795, kept by Circuit Court
- **DIVORCE:** 1848, Circuit Court
- **LAND:** 1722, Circuit Court
- **PROBATE:** 1722, Circuit Court
- **COURT:** 1722, Circuit Court

STAFFORD
1300 Courthouse Rd., Box 69, Stafford, VA 22554, (540) 658-8750, **<co.stafford.va.us>**
- **INCORPORATED:** June 5, 1666
- **PARENT COUNTY:** Westmoreland
- **MARRIAGE RECORDS:** start in 1854, kept by Circuit Court
- **DIVORCE:** 1831, Circuit Court
- **LAND:** 1699, Circuit Court
- **PROBATE:** 1699, Circuit Court
- **COURT:** 1664, Circuit Court
- **NOTES:** Clerk of Circuit Court has birth and death records 1853-1873, land records for 1680, and military records 1861-1865, 1917-1918.

STAUNTON (INDEPENDENT CITY)
113 E. Beverley St., Box 1286 Staunton, VA 24402, (540) 332-3874, **<www.staunton.va.us>**
- **INCORPORATED:** January 1871
- **PARENT COUNTY:** Augusta
- **MARRIAGE RECORDS:** start in 1802, kept by Circuit Court
- **DIVORCE:** 1848, Circuit Court
- **LAND:** 1802, Circuit Court
- **PROBATE:** 1802, Circuit Court
- **COURT:** 1802, Circuit Court
- **NOTES:** Clerk of Circuit Court has birth records from 1854-1896, and death records from 1853-1892. Established in 1761, incorporated as a town in 1801, and incorporated as a city in 1871.

SUFFOLK (INDEPENDENT CITY)
Mills E. Godwin Jr. Courts Bldg., 150 N. Main St., Box 1604, Suffolk, VA 23439, (757) 923-2251, **<www.suffolk.va.us>**
- **INCORPORATED:** 1910
- **PARENT COUNTY:** Nansemond
- **MARRIAGE RECORDS:** start in 1866, kept by Circuit Court
- **DIVORCE:** 1866, Circuit Court
- **LAND:** 1866, Circuit Court
- **PROBATE:** 1866, Circuit Court
- **COURT:** 1866, Circuit Court
- **NOTES:** Established in 1742, incorporated as a town in 1808, and as a city in 1910. Nansemond County and Suffolk City merged Jan. 1, 1974.

SURRY
28 Colonial Trail E., Surry, VA 23883, (757) 294-3161, **<www.surrycountyva.gov>**
- **INCORPORATED:** 1652
- **PARENT COUNTY:** James City
- **MARRIAGE RECORDS:** start in 1768, kept by Circuit Court
- **DIVORCE:** 1831, Circuit Court
- **LAND:** 1652, Circuit Court
- **PROBATE:** 1652, Circuit Court
- **COURT:** 1671, Circuit Court
- **NOTES:** Clerk of Circuit Court has birth and death records from 1853-1896, and military records 1840-1861, 1917-1918, 1946-1950.

SUSSEX
15088 Courthouse Rd. Rt. 735, Box 1337, Sussex, VA 23884, (434) 246-5511, **<sussexcounty.govoffice.com>**
- **INCORPORATED:** February 1753
- **PARENT COUNTY:** Surry
- **MARRIAGE RECORDS:** start in 1754, kept by Circuit Court
- **LAND:** 1754, Circuit Court
- **PROBATE:** 1754, Circuit Court
- **COURT:** 1754, Circuit Court
- **NOTES:** Clerk of Circuit Court has birth and death records 1853-1869.

TAYLOR
- **PARENT COUNTIES:** Harrison, Barbour, Marion
- **NOTES:** See West Virginia.

TAZEWELL

101 Main St., Box 968, Tazewell, VA 24651, (276) 988-1222, www.mindspring.com/~ronways/Tazgen.html

- **INCORPORATED:** Dec. 17, 1799
- **PARENT COUNTIES:** Russell, Wythe
- **MARRIAGE RECORDS:** start in 1800, kept by Circuit Court
- **DIVORCE:** 1832, Circuit Court
- **LAND:** 1800, Circuit Court
- **PROBATE:** 1800, Circuit Court
- **COURT:** 1800, Circuit Court
- **NOTES:** Clerk of Circuit Court has birth records 1853-1870, death records 1853-1871, and military records 1915-1918, 1941, 1944.

TUCKER

- **PARENT COUNTY:** Randolph
- **NOTES:** See West Virginia.

TYLER

- **PARENT COUNTY:** Ohio
- **NOTES:** See West Virginia.

UPPER NORFOLK

- **INCORPORATED:** 1637
- **PARENT COUNTY:** New Norfolk
- **NOTES:** See Nansemond County. Name changed to Nansemond 1646.

UPSHUR

- **PARENT COUNTIES:** Randolph, Barbour, Lewis
- **NOTES:** See West Virginia.

VIRGINIA BEACH (INDEPENDENT CITY)

2425 Nimmo Pkwy., Virginia Beach, VA 23456, (757) 385-4181, **<www.vbgov.com>**

- **INCORPORATED:** Jan. 1, 1963
- **PARENT COUNTY:** Princess Anne
- **DIVORCE RECORDS:** start in 1814, kept by Circuit Court
- **LAND:** 1691, Circuit Court
- **PROBATE:** 1691, Circuit Court
- **COURT:** 1691, Circuit Court
- **NOTES:** Clerk of Circuit Court has birth and death records 1864-1894. Marriage records 1822-1852 were destroyed in fire. Incorporated as a town in 1906, and as a city in 1952. Merged with Princess Anne County in 1963. Records before 1963 are for Princess Anne County.

WARREN

1 E. Main St., Front Royal, VA 22630, (540) 635-2435, **<www.warrencountyva.net>**

- **INCORPORATED:** March 9, 1836
- **PARENT COUNTIES:** Frederick, Shenandoah
- **MARRIAGE RECORDS:** start in 1836, kept by Circuit Court
- **DIVORCE:** 1836, Circuit Court
- **LAND:** 1836, Circuit Court
- **PROBATE:** 1836, Circuit Court
- **COURT:** 1836, Circuit Court
- **NOTES:** Clerk of Circuit Court has birth records 1853-1917, death records 1853-1874, and military records 1861-1865.

WARROSQUOYAKE

- **INCORPORATED:** 1634
- **PARENT COUNTY:** Original shire
- **NOTES:** See Isle of Wight County. Name changed to Isle of Wight 1637.

WARWICK

- **INCORPORATED:** 1634
- **PARENT COUNTY:** Original shire
- **NOTES:** See Newport News, Independent City. Formerly Warwick River. Name changed to Warwick 1643. Incorporated as an independent city 1952. Merged with Newport News July 1, 1958.

WARWICK RIVER

- **INCORPORATED:** 1634
- **PARENT COUNTY:** Original shire
- **NOTES:** Name changed to Warwick 1643, merged with Newport News July 1, 1958.

WASHINGTON

189 E. Main St., Box 289, Abingdon, VA 24212, (276) 676-6224, **<www.washcova.com>**

- **INCORPORATED:** Oct. 7, 1776
- **PARENT COUNTIES:** Fincastle, Montgomery (1777)
- **MARRIAGE RECORDS:** start in 1785, kept by Circuit Court
- **DIVORCE:** 1830, Circuit Court
- **LAND:** 1778, Circuit Court
- **PROBATE:** 1777, Circuit Court
- **COURT:** 1777, Circuit Court
- **NOTES:** Clerk of Circuit Court has birth and death records 1853-1892, and military records 1861-1865.

WAYNE

- **PARENT COUNTY:** Cabell
- **NOTES:** See West Virginia.

WAYNESBORO (IND. CITY)

250 S. Wayne Ave., Box 910, Waynesboro, VA 22980, (540) 942-6616, **<www.waynesboro.va.us>**

- **INCORPORATED:** February 1948
- **PARENT COUNTY:** Augusta
- **MARRIAGE RECORDS:** start in 1948, kept by Circuit Court
- **DIVORCE:** 1948, Circuit Court
- **LAND:** 1948, Circuit Court
- **PROBATE:** 1948, Circuit Court
- **COURT:** 1948, Circuit Court
- **NOTES:** Established in 1801, incorporated as a town in 1834, and consolidated with Basic City in 1923.

WEBSTER

- **PARENT COUNTIES:** Braxton, Nicholas, Randolph
- **NOTES:** See West Virginia.

WESTMORELAND

Box 307, Montross, VA 22520, (804) 493-0108, **<www.westmoreland-county.org>**

- **INCORPORATED:** July 5, 1653
- **PARENT COUNTY:** Northumberland

- **MARRIAGE RECORDS:** start in 1772, kept by Circuit Court
- **DIVORCE:** 1851, Circuit Court
- **LAND:** 1653, Circuit Court
- **PROBATE:** 1653, Circuit Court
- **COURT:** 1653, Circuit Court
- **NOTES:** Clerk of Circuit Court has birth records 1858-1895, and death records 1857-1861, 1864-1877, 1881-1889.

WETZEL
- **PARENT COUNTY:** Tyler
- **NOTES:** See West Virginia.

WILLIAMSBURG (IND. CITY)
5201 Monticello Ave. Suite 6, Williamsburg, VA 23188, (757) 564-2242, **<www.williamsburgva.gov>**
- **INCORPORATED:** 1884
- **PARENT COUNTIES:** James City, York
- **MARRIAGE RECORDS:** start in 1854, kept by Circuit Court
- **DIVORCE:** 1865, Circuit Court
- **LAND:** 1865, Circuit Court
- **PROBATE:** 1858, Circuit Court
- **COURT:** 1865, Circuit Court
- **NOTES:** Established in 1633 as Middle Plantation, renamed Williamsburg in 1699, incorporated as a borough in 1772, and as a city in 1884. County seat of James City County. Clerk of Circuit has jurisdiction over Williamsburg and James City County.

WINCHESTER (INDEPENDENT CITY)
5 N. Kent St., Winchester, VA 22601, (540) 667-5770, **<www.winchesterva.gov>**
- **INCORPORATED:** 1874
- **PARENT COUNTY:** Frederick
- **MARRIAGE RECORDS:** start in 1790, kept by City Clerk
- **LAND:** 1789, City Clerk
- **PROBATE:** 1794, City Clerk
- **COURT:** 1856, City Clerk
- **NOTES:** City Clerk has birth records 1865-1891, and death records 1871-1891. Established in 1752, incorporated as a town in 1779, and incorporated as a city in 1874.

WIRT
- **PARENT COUNTIES:** Wood, Jackson
- **NOTES:** See West Virginia.

WISE
206 E. Main St., Box 1248, Wise, VA 24293, (276) 328-6111, **<www.wisecounty.org>**
- **INCORPORATED:** Feb. 16, 1856
- **PARENT COUNTIES:** Lee, Russell, Scott
- **MARRIAGE RECORDS:** 1856, Circuit Court
- **DIVORCE:** 1856, Circuit Court
- **PROBATE:** 1856, Circuit Court
- **LAND:** 1856, Circuit Court
- **COURT:** 1856, Circuit Court
- **NOTES:** Clerk of Circuit Court has birth records 1856-1866, and death records 1856-1894.

WOOD
- **PARENT COUNTIES:** Harrison, Kanawha
- **NOTES:** See West Virginia.

WYOMING
- **PARENT COUNTY:** Logan
- **NOTES:** See West Virginia.

WYTHE
Circuit Court Bldg., 225 S. Fourth St. Room 105, Wytheville, VA 24382, (276) 223-6050, **<www.wytheco.org>**
- **INCORPORATED:** Dec. 1, 1789
- **PARENT COUNTY:** Montgomery
- **MARRIAGE RECORDS:** start in 1790, kept by Circuit Court
- **DIVORCE:** 1831, Circuit Court
- **LAND:** 1790, Circuit Court
- **PROBATE:** 1790, Circuit Court
- **COURT:** 1795, Circuit Court
- **NOTES:** Clerk of Circuit Court has birth records 1853-1872, and death records 1853-1870.

YOHOGANIA
- **INCORPORATED:** 1776
- **PARENT COUNTY:** West Augusta District
- **NOTES:** Discontinued and ceded to Pennsylvania 1780 as Westmoreland County.

YORK
300 Ballard St., Box 371, Yorktown, VA 23690, (757) 890-3350, **<www.yorkcounty.gov>**
- **INCORPORATED:** 1634
- **PARENT COUNTY:** Original shire
- **MARRIAGE RECORDS:** start in 1772, kept by Circuit Court
- **DIVORCE:** 1831, Circuit Court
- **LAND:** 1633, Circuit Court
- **PROBATE:** 1633, Circuit Court
- **COURT:** 1633, Circuit Court
- **NOTES:** Clerk of Circuit Court has birth and death records 1856-1858, and military records 1943-1956. Formerly Charles River County. Name changed to York 1643.

WASHINGTON

» BY DAVID A. FRYXELL

HISTORICAL OVERVIEW

What would become Washington state was the object of a sort of ping-pong match for the first centuries of European exploration: It was first claimed by Spain in 1543, and then by England in 1579, after Sir Francis Drake sighted the coastline. The Spanish actually landed in 1775; Captain Cook claimed the Olympic peninsula for England in 1778. Finally, the Treaty of Nootka in 1790 mostly settled Pacific Northwest claims in favor of England.

But England's claim didn't remain undisputed. Americans Robert Gray and John Kendrick had already visited in 1788; Gray discovered the Columbia River in 1791. Lewis and Clark reached the river's mouth in 1805. American and English fur traders soon established rival forts near present-day Spokane. American missionaries arrived in 1836, and Oregon Trail pioneers came en masse starting in 1843. The conflict came to a head in 1844 with James K. Polk's election-year battle cry of "54-40 or Fight." War was averted and the 49th parallel set as America's northern boundary in 1846.

Throughout this period, Washington was considered part of Oregon, and it was incorporated into Oregon Territory in 1848. Congress included it in the 1850 Donation Land Law, which provided grants of 320 acres per settler. Spurred by the law and a fledgling timber industry, settlement surged. Seattle was founded in 1852. Citizens eventually demanded a separate Washington Territory, which was created in 1853.

Native tribes increased their resistance during this heightened period of colonization. A series of Indian wars filled the 1850s. Ultimately the tribes, including the Puyallup, Kalispell, Bannock, Yakima, Paiute and Nez Perce, were exiled to reservations. Nez Perce Chief Joseph surrendered in 1876, proclaiming, "I will fight no more forever."

The discovery of gold in 1860 and the passage of the Homestead Act in 1862 made Washington irresistible. The transcontinental line of the Northern Pacific Railroad reached Spokane in 1881 and Tacoma in 1887. At last, Washington became a state in 1889.

The early statehood years saw a swarm of immigrants from England, Ireland, Canada, Sweden and Norway. Dutch, Italian, Finnish, Russian and German communities also sprang up. Chinese came to work the mines and railroads; Japanese labored on truck farms. World War II brought many African-Americans to Washington's growing industrial base.

research tips

- The biggest challenge in researching your Washington ancestors is finding marriage records, according to Charles M. Hansen of the Eastern Washington Genealogical Society. Until the state took over in 1967, each county kept these records. But couples don't have to get married in— nor even record their marriage in—their home county. Check surrounding counties, plus nearby Idaho counties.
- Another challenge, according to Hansen, is spotty territorial records. Here it helps that Washington Territory labored long for statehood and thus took many censuses. These can also help substitute for the burned 1890 federal census, Hansen notes. You can search many early census indexes in the Washington Digital Archives **<www.digitalarchives.wa.gov>**.
- The Family History Library has microfilmed all birth and death certificates from when the state started recording them in mid-1907, as well as a wealth of land records, cemetery records, and even many early birth, death, and marriage records extracted from county courthouses.

CENSUS RECORDS

- Federal census: 1860, 1870, 1880, 1900, 1910, 1920, 1930
- Federal mortality schedules: 1850, 1860, 1870, 1880
- Special census of Civil War Union veterans and widows: 1890
- State/territorial census: 1878, 1881, 1883, 1885, 1887, 1889, 1892

RECORD HIGHLIGHTS

Washington was included in the 1850 federal Oregon Territory Census and in several subsequent Washington territorial and state censuses, 1857-1892, which are available on microfilm through the state archives and the Family History Library (FHL). The first federal census enumerating Washington Territory was in 1860; the earliest extant census post-statehood is from 1900. Washington census and naturalization records can be searched on the state archives' website at **<www.digitalarchives.wa.gov>**. The site also includes several other types of records.

Official birth and death records were kept at the county level from 1891 to 1907, and by the state thereafter. Some pre-1891 records exist and have been microfilmed, as have many 1891-to-1907 county records. Indexes of Washington births and deaths are on subscription website Ancestry.com.

Statewide marriage records didn't begin until 1967. You can search many earlier county records from eastern Washington on the Western States Historical Marriage Records Index site at **<abish.byui.edu/specialCollections/westernStates/search.cfm>**.

Land records and related water-rights and mining documents provide crucial clues to Washington's settlement boom. Files from the Donation Land Act (1851-1903) are kept at the National Archives' regional office in Seattle, with indexes and abstracts available at the National Archives and via the FHL. Homestead Act claims are archived at the Bureau of Land Management office in Portland, Ore. Water-rights records dating from 1917 are kept at the Department of Ecology and the state archives. An index to mining surveys covering 1883 to 1964 is available via the FHL; the 66 volumes of surveys have been microfilmed by the state archives. The state archives also has military records from Washington's Indian wars, files from the state's soldiers and veterans homes, and applications for state bonuses to veterans from World War I through the Vietnam War.

The Washington State Library in Olympia maintains an extensive collection of microfilmed state newspapers, accessible through interlibrary loan. For information on the collection, see **<www.sos.wa.gov/library/microfilm.aspx>**; learn more about the newspaper holdings at **<www.sos.wa.gov/library/newspapers_wsl.aspx>**.

ARCHIVES, LIBRARIES, AND SOCIETIES

Anna Lemon Wheelock Library
3722 N. 26th St., Tacoma, WA 98402, (253) 591-5640, **<www.tpl.lib.wa.us/Page.aspx?nid=60>**

Bellevue Regional Library
1111 110th Ave. NE, Bellevue, WA 98004, (425) 450-1765, **<www.kcls.org/bellevue>**

Bellingham Public Library
210 Central Ave. CS-9710, Bellingham, WA 98227, **<www.bellinghampubliclibrary.org>**

Big Bend Chapter, American Historical Society of Germans from Russia
202 W. Second Ave., Ritzville, WA 99169, (509) 659-1537, **<www.ahsgr.org/big_bend_chapter.htm>**

Blue Mountain Chapter, American Historical Society of Germans from Russia
240 Bald Road, Touchet, WA 99360, (509) 525-2048, **<www.ahsgr.org/blue_mountain_chapter.htm>**

Bureau of Land Management, Oregon State Office
333 SW 1st. Ave., Portland, OR 97204, (503) 808-6002, **<www.blm.gov/or>**

Burlington Public Library
820 E. Burlington Ave., Burlington, WA 98233

Central Washington Chapter, American Historical Society of Germans from Russia
403 S. 16th Ave., Toppenish, WA 98902, **<www.ahsgr.org/central_washington_chapter.htm>**

Chehalis Valley Historical Society
268-11 Oak Meadows Rd., Oakville, WA 98568

Chelan Valley Genealogical Society
Box Y, Chelan, WA 98816

Clallam County Genealogical Society
c/o Genealogical Library, Clallam County Museum 223 E. Fourth St., Port Angeles, WA 98362, **<www.olypen.com/ccgs>**

Clark County Genealogical Society
717 Grand Blvd., Vancouver, WA 98661, (360) 750-5688, **<www.ccgs-wa.org>**

Clark County Historical Museum
1511 Main St., Vancouver, WA 98668, **<www.cchmuseum.org>**

Collins Memorial Library, University of Puget Sound
1500 N. Warner, Tacoma, WA 98416, (253) 879-3669, **<www.pugetsound.edu/academics/academic-resources/collins-memorial-library>**

Douglas County Genealogical Society
Box 580, Waterville, WA 98858

Eastern Washington Genealogical Society
Box 1826, Spokane, WA 99210, **<ewgsi.org>**

Eastside Genealogical Society
Box 374, Bellevue, WA 98009

Ellensburg Genealogical Group
413 N. Main, Suites L & M Ellensburg, Washington 98926

Everett Public Library
2702 Hoyt Ave., Everett, WA 98201

Fiske Genealogical Foundation Library
1644 43rd Ave. E., Seattle, WA 98122, (206) 328-2716, **<www.fiskelibrary.org>**

Fort Vancouver Historical Society
Box 1834, Vancouver, WA 98663, **<www.fvrl.org>**

Fort Vancouver Regional Library
1007 E. Mill Plain Blvd., Vancouver, WA 98663

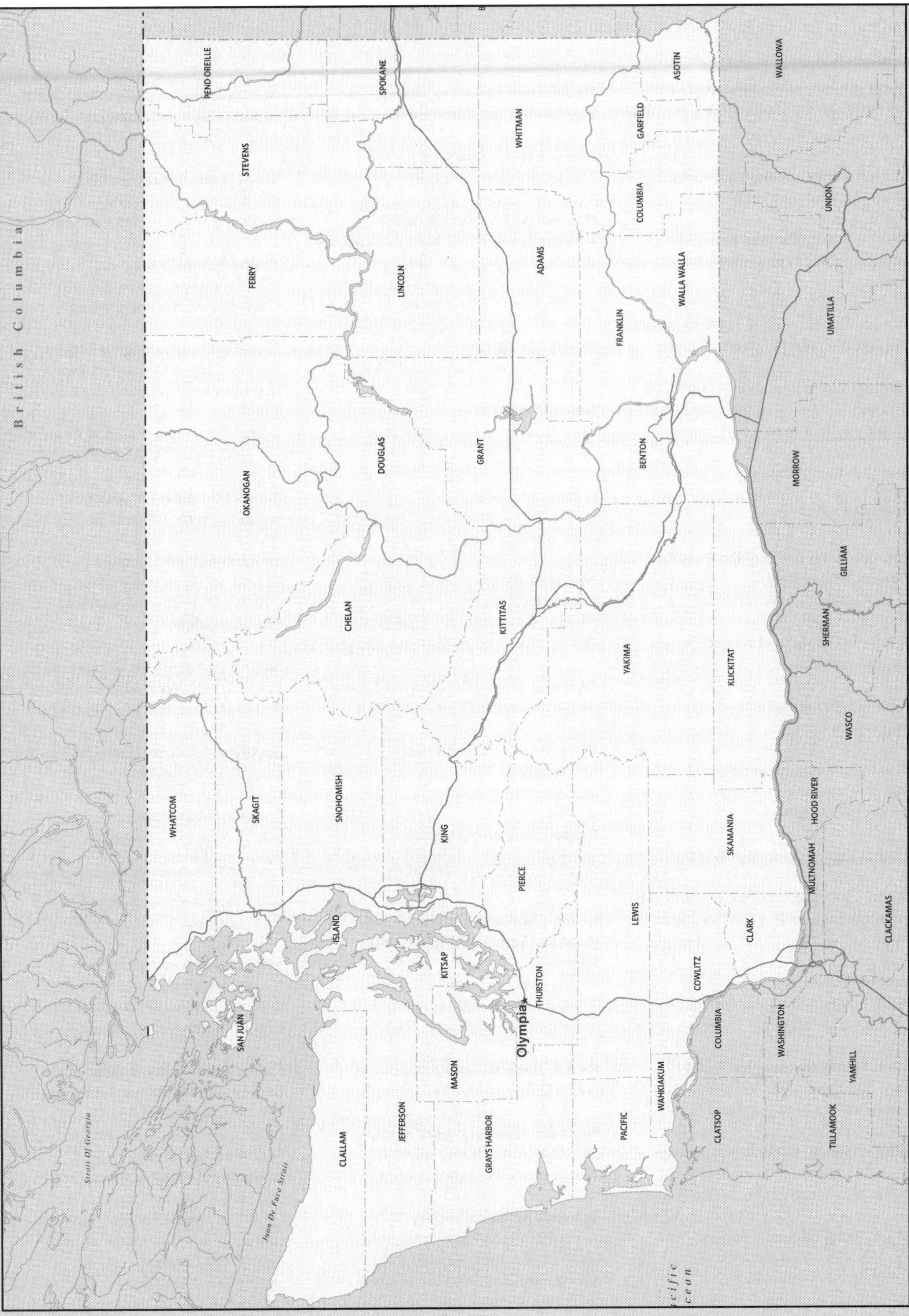
British Columbia
Strait Of Georgia
Juan De Fuca Strait
Pacific Ocean
Olympia
PEND OREILLE
SPOKANE
STEVENS
WHITMAN
ASOTIN
GARFIELD
COLUMBIA
FERRY
LINCOLN
ADAMS
FRANKLIN
WALLA WALLA
OKANOGAN
DOUGLAS
GRANT
BENTON
CHELAN
KITTITAS
YAKIMA
KLICKITAT
WHATCOM
SKAGIT
SNOHOMISH
KING
PIERCE
LEWIS
SKAMANIA
ISLAND
KITSAP
THURSTON
CLARK
COWLITZ
SAN JUAN
MASON
WAHKIAKUM
PACIFIC
CLALLAM
JEFFERSON
GRAYS HARBOR
WALLOWA
UNION
UMATILLA
MORROW
GILLIAM
SHERMAN
WASCO
HOOD RIVER
MULTNOMAH
CLACKAMAS
WASHINGTON
YAMHILL
TILLAMOOK
CLATSOP

Grant County Genealogical Society
c/o Ephrata Public Library, 45 Alder St. NW, Ephrata, WA 98823

Grays Harbor Genealogical Society
Box 867, Cosmopolis, WA 98537

Greater Seattle Chapter, American Historical Society of Germans from Russia
815 South 216th Street C31, Des Moines, WA 98198, (206) 870-2031, **<www.ahsgr.org/greater_seattle_chapter.htm>**

Heritage Quest Research Library
909 Main St., Suite 5, Sumner, WA 98390, (253) 863-1806, **<www.hqrl.com>**

Issaquah Public Library
10 W. Sunset Way, Bellevue, WA 98027, (425) 392-5430

Italian Interest Group of the Eastside Genealogical Society
Box 374, Bellevue, WA 98009

Jefferson County Genealogical Society
13692 Airport Cutoff Road, Box 627, Port Townsend, WA 98368, (360) 385-9495, **<www.rootsweb.ancestry.com/~wajcgs>**

Jewish Genealogical Society of Washington State
<www.jgsws.org>

Kittitas County Genealogical Society
413 N. Main, Suites L & M, Ellensburg, WA 98926, (509) 925-5951, **<www.rootsweb.ancestry.com/~wakcgs/KCGS_index.htm>**

Lake Hills Library
15528 Lake Hills Blvd., Bellevue, WA 98007, (425) 747-3350

Lewis County Genealogical Society
Box 782, Chehalis, WA 98532, **<www.walcgs.org>**

Lower Columbia Genealogical Society
Box 472, Longview, WA 98632, **<www.rootsweb.ancestry.com/~walcolgs>**

Maple Valley Historical Society
Box 123, Maple Valley, WA 98038, **<maplevalleyhistorical.com>**

Mason County Genealogical Society
Box 1535, Shelton, WA 98544

Mid-Columbia Library
405 South Dayton, Kennewick, WA 99336

National Archives and Records Administration, Pacific Northwest Region
6125 Sand Point Way NE, Seattle, WA 98115, (206) 336-5115, **<www.archives.gov/pacific-alaska/seattle>**

Neill Public Library
N. 210 Grand Ave., Pullman, WA 99163

Newport Way Library
14520 SE Newport Way, Bellevue, WA 98006, (425) 747-2390

North Bend Library
115 E. Fourth St., North Bend, WA 98045, (425) 888-0554

Northeast Washington Genealogical Society
c/o Colville Public Library, 195 S. Oak, Colville, WA 99114, **<www.newgs.org>**

Okanogan County Genealogical Society
263 Old Riverside Hwy., Omak, WA 98841

Olympia Genealogical Society
c/o Olympia Public Library, 313 Eighth Ave. SE., Olympia, WA 98501

Olympia Timberland Library
313 Eighth Ave. SE., Olympia, WA 98501, (206) 352-0595

Olympic Peninsula Chapter, American Historical Society of Germans from Russia
2551 Fir Ave., Bremerton, WA 98310, (360) 479-0516, **<www.ahsgr.org/olympic_peninsula_chapter.htm>**

Pacific County Genealogical Society
Box 843, Ocean Park, WA 98640

Puget Sound Genealogical Society
2501 Mile Hill Dr., Port Orchard, WA 98366, **<www.pusogensoc.org>**

Redmond Historical Society
The Old Redmond Schoolhouse, 16600 NE 80 St., Rm. 106, Redmond, WA 98052, **<www.redmondhistoricalsociety.org>**

Roman Catholic Archdiocese of Seattle
Chancery Office, 910 Marion St., Seattle, WA 98104, (206) 382-4560

Seattle Genealogical Society
Box 15329, Seattle, WA 98115, **<www.rootsweb.ancestry.com/~waseags>**

Seattle Public Library
1000 Fourth Ave., Seattle, WA 98104, (206) 386-4629, **<www.spl.org>**

Skagit Valley Genealogical Society
Box 715, Conway, WA 98238, **<www.rootsweb.ancestry.com/~wasvgs>**

Snohomish County Historical Association
Box 5203, Everett, WA 98206

Sno-Isle Genealogical Society
Box 63, Edmonds, WA 98020

Snoqualmie Public Library
7824 Center Blvd. SE, Snoqualmie, WA 98065, (425) 888-1223, **<www.kcls.org/snoqualmie>**

South King County Genealogical Society
Box 3174, Kent, WA 98089, **<www.rootsweb.ancestry.com/~waskcgs>**

South Pierce County Historical Society
Box 1131, Eatonville, WA 98328, V

Spokane Public Library
906 W. Main Ave., Spokane, WA 99201, **<www.spokanelibrary.org>**

State Capitol Historical Association
211 W. 21st Ave., Olympia, WA 98501

State Department of Health
Box 9709, Olympia, WA 98507, (360) 236-4300, **<www.doh.wa.gov/EHSPHL/CHS/Cert.htm>**

Stillaguamish Valley Genealogical Society of North Snohomish County
Box 34, Arlington, WA 98223

Suzzallo-Allen Library, University of Washington
Box 352900, Seattle, WA 98195, (206) 543-9158, **<www.lib.washington.edu>**

Swan Creek Library
3828 Portland Ave., Tacoma, WA 98404, (253) 594-7805

Tacoma Public Library
1102 Tacoma Ave. S., Tacoma, WA 98402, (253) 591-5666, **<www.tpl.lib.wa.us>**

Tacoma-Pierce County Genealogical Society
Box 1952, Tacoma, WA 98401, **<www.rootsweb.ancestry.com/~watpcgs>**

Tonasket Genealogical Society
Box 84, Tonasket, WA 98855

Tri-City Genealogical Society
Box 1410, Richland, WA 99352

Walla Walla Valley Genealogical Society
Box 115, Walla Walla, WA 99362

Washington State Archives
1120 Washington St. SE, Box 40238, Olympia, WA 98504, (360) 586-1492, **<www.sos.wa.gov/archives>**

Washington State Genealogical Society
1901 S. 12th Ave., Union Gap, WA 98903, **<www.rootsweb.ancestry.com/~wasgs>**

Washington State Historical Society and Museum
1911 Pacific Ave., Tacoma, WA 98402, **<www.wshs.org>**

Washington State Library
6880 Capital Blvd. S., Box 42460, Olympia, WA 98504, (360) 704-5200, **<www.secstate.wa.gov/library/libraries>**

Wenatchee Area Genealogical Society
133 S. Mission St., Box 5280, Wenatchee, WA 98807

Whatcom Genealogical Society
Box 1493, Bellingham, WA 98227

Whitman County Genealogical Society
Box 393, Pullman, WA 99163, **<www.rootsweb.ancestry.com/~wawcgs>**

Willapa Harbor Genealogical Society
c/o Raymond Public Library, 507 Duryea St., Raymond, WA 98577

Yakima Valley Genealogical Society
Box 445, Yakima, WA 98907, **<www.yvgs.net>**

GENERAL RESOURCES

Bibliography of Washington State Historical Society Library, 3 vols., (Tacoma-Pierce County Genealogical Society, 1986)

Celebrating the History of the Pioneer Families of Washington, 1853-1889 by Frances Caldwell Miller (Native Daughters of Washington Territorial Pioneers, 1989)

Comprehensive Guide to the Manuscripts Collection and to the Personal Papers in the University Archives by Marilyn Priestly (The Library, 1980)

Cumulative Baptism Index to the Catholic Church Records of the Pacific Northwest by Sharon E. Osborn-Ryan (Oregon Heritage Press, 1999)

The Dictionary Catalog of the Pacific Northwest Collection of the University Of Washington, 6 vols. (G.K. Hall and Co., 1972)

Early Washington: Overland Stage Routes, Old Military Roads, Indian Battle Grounds, Old Forts, Old Gold Mines by Ralph N. Preston (Western Guide Publishers, 1974)

The Evolution of Washington Counties by Newton Carl Abbott and Fred E. Carver, compiled by J.W. Helm (Yakima Valley Genealogical Society and Klickitat County Historical Society, 1978)

Genealogical Resources in Washington State (Secretary Of State, Division Of Archives and Records Management, 1983)

Germans from Russia in the Yakima Valley, Prior to 1940 by Frieda Eickler Brulotte (The Society, 1990)

Historical Records of Washington State: Records and Papers Held at Repositories (Washington State Historical Records Advisory Board, 1981)

A History of the Catholic Church in the Pacific Northwest, 1743-1983 by Wilfred P. Schoenberg (Pastoral Press, 1987)

History of the Pacific Northwest: Oregon and Washington, 2 vols., by Elwood Evans (North Pacific History Co., ca. 1889)

History of the Synod of Washington of the Presbyterian Church in the United States of America 1835-1909 by Robert Boyd (The Synod, ca. 1910)

A History of Washington, 4 vols., by Lancaster Pollard (American Historical Society, 1937)

An Illustrated History of the State of Washington: Containing Biographical Mention of its Pioneers and Prominent Citizens by Harvey K. Hines (Lewis Pub. Co., 1893)

Index to Washington State Daughters of the American Revolution compiled by Shirley Swart (Yakima Valley Genealogical Society, 1983)

Methodism in the Northwest by Erle Howell (Pacific Northwest Conference Historical Society, 1966)

Missionary History of the Pacific Northwest: Containing the Wonderful Story of Jason Lee, with Sketches of Many of his Co-Laborers all Illustrating Life on the Plains and in the Mountains in Pioneer Days (Library of Congress, 1990)

Reminiscences of Washington Territory by Charles Prosch (Ye Galleon Press, 1969)

Sketches of Washington (W.C. Wolfe & Co., 1906)

A Social History of Scandinavian Immigration, Washington State, 1895-1910 by Jorgen Dahlie (Arno Press, 1980)

Washington: A History of the Evergreen State by Mary Williamson Avery (University of Washington Press, 1967)

Washington Research Outline by the Church of Jesus Christ of Latter-day Saints (online at **<www.familysearch.org/eng/search/RG/guide/washington.asp>**)

Washington West of the Cascades: Historical and Descriptive, the Explorers, the Indians, the Modern by Herbert Hunt (S.J. Clarke, 1917)

Who's Who in Washington State (H. Allen Pub., 1927)

☞ LAND RECORDS

Index to Mining Surveys, 1883-1964 by Kathleen Waugh (K. Waugh, 1985)

Washington Territory Donation Land Claims: an Abstract of Information in the Land Claim Papers of Persons Who Settled in Washington Territory Before 1856 (Seattle Genealogical Society, 1980)

☞ MAPS

Early Washington Atlas, 2nd edition (Binford & Mort Publishers, 1974)

The Evolution of Washington Counties by Newton Carl Abbott and Fred E. Carver, compiled by J.W. Helm (Yakima Valley Genealogical Society and Klickitat County Historical Society, 1978)

A Geographic Dictionary of Washington by Henry Landes (F.J. Lamborn, 1917)

Historical Atlas of Washington by James R. Scott and Roland L. DeLorme (University of Oklahoma Press, 1988)

Origin of Washington Geographic Names by Edmond S. Meany (Gale Research Co., 1968)

R.L. Polk & Co. Oregon & Washington Gazetteer and Business Directory, 1909-1910 (R.L. Polk, 1909)

Washington Atlas and Gazetteer (DeLorme Mapping Co., 1996)

Washington: A Centennial Atlas by James R. Scott (Western Washington University, 1989)

Washington State Place Names by James W. Phillips (University of Washington Press, 1971)

☞ MILITARY RECORDS

Burial List of the Members of the 1st Washington Territory Infantry by Sherman Lee Pompey (Pacific Specialties, 1972)

Civil War Veteran Burials from the Arizona Territory, Nebraska, Nevada, New Mexico, Oregon, Utah and the Washington Territory by Sherman Lee Pompey (filmed by the Genealogical Society of Utah, 1975)

Washington National Guard Pamphlet: The Official History of the Washington National Guard, 7 vols., by Virgil F. Field (Office of the Adjutant General, 1961)

☞ PROBATE RECORDS

Frontier Justice: Guide to the Court records of Washington Territory, 1853-1889, 2 vols., from the Frontier Justice Records Project (National Historical Publications and Records Commission, 1987)

A Guide to the Records of Washington Territorial Supreme Court, 1853-1889 by Pat Hopkins (Washington State Archives, 1983)

☞ VITAL RECORDS

A Directory of Cemeteries and Funeral Homes in Washington State from the Washington Interment Association and the Washington State Funeral Directors Association (HeritageQuest, 1990)

Washington's First Marriages of the 39 Counties edited by John D. Carter (Eastern Washington Genealogical Society, 1986)

Cemetery Records of Washington, 6 vols., (Genealogical Society of Utah, ca. 1956-1960)

Guide to Public Vital Statistics Records in Washington (Washington Historical Records Survey, 1941)

Index to Birth Certificates, 1907-1959 (filmed by the Washington Bureau of Vital Statistics, 1960)

Index to Death Certificates, 1907-1959, 1960-1979 (filmed by the Washington Bureau of Vital Statistics, 1954-1960)

Index to Delayed Birth Records, 1900-1980 from the Washington Department of Health (filmed by the Bureau of Vital Statistics, 1996)

•-COUNTY DETAILS-•

ADAMS

210 W. Broadway Ave., Ritzville, WA 99169, (509) 659-3257, **<co.adams.wa.us>**

- **INCORPORATED:** Nov. 28, 1883
- **PARENT COUNTY:** Whitman
- **BIRTH RECORDS:** start in 1909, kept by Department of Health
- **MARRIAGE:** 1887, County Auditor
- **DIVORCE:** 1889, County Clerk
- **DEATH:** 1910, Department of Health
- **LAND:** 1891, County Auditor
- **PROBATE:** 1885, County Clerk
- **COURT:** 1889, County Clerk
- **NOTES:** County Health Department has death records 1891-1907. County Clerk has naturalization records 1890-1956.

ASOTIN

135 Second St., Box 159, Asotin, WA 99402, (509) 243-2081, **<co.asotin.wa.us>**

- **INCORPORATED:** Oct. 27, 1883
- **PARENT COUNTY:** Garfield
- **BIRTH RECORDS:** start in 1907, kept by Center for Health Statistics
- **MARRIAGE:** 1897, County Auditor
- **DIVORCE:** 1890, County Clerk
- **DEATH:** 1907, Center for Health Statistics
- **LAND:** 1891, County Auditor
- **PROBATE:** 1885, County Clerk
- **COURT:** 1890, County Clerk
- **NOTES:** County auditor has military records 1888-1897. County Clerk has naturalization records 1885-1974.

BENTON

620 Market St., Prosser, WA 99350, (509) 786-5710, **<co.benton.wa.us>**

- **INCORPORATED:** March 8, 1905
- **PARENT COUNTIES:** Yakima, Klickitat
- **MARRIAGE RECORDS:** start in 1905, kept by County Auditor
- **DIVORCE:** 1905, County Auditor
- **LAND:** 1874, County Auditor
- **PROBATE:** 1906, County Clerk
- **COURT:** 1906, County Clerk
- **NOTES:** County Auditor has birth records 1905-1907. County Clerk has naturalization records 1905-1954.

CHEHALIS

- **INCORPORATED:** April 26, 1854
- **PARENT COUNTY:** Thurston
- **NOTES:** See Grays Harbor County. Name changed to Grays Harbor March 15, 1915.

CHELAN

350 Orondo St., Wenatchee, WA 98801, (509) 667-6380, **<co.chelan.wa.us>**

- **INCORPORATED:** March 13, 1899
- **PARENT COUNTY:** Kittitas
- **MARRIAGE RECORDS:** start in 1899, kept by County Auditor
- **DIVORCE:** 1900, County Clerk
- **LAND:** 1899, County Auditor
- **PROBATE:** 1888, County Clerk
- **COURT:** 1900, County Clerk
- **NOTES:** County Auditor has birth and death records 1899-1907. County Clerk has naturalization records 1900-1906.

CLALLAM

223 E. Fourth St., Port Angeles, WA 98362, (360) 417-2333, **<www.clallam.net>**

- **INCORPORATED:** April 26, 1854
- **PARENT COUNTY:** Jefferson
- **MARRIAGE RECORDS:** start in 1858, kept by County Auditor
- **LAND:** 1858, County Auditor
- **PROBATE:** 1914, County Clerk
- **COURT:** 1889, County Clerk
- **NOTES:** County Auditor has birth and death records 1891-1906, and military discharge records 1944-1965.

CLARK

1200 Franklin St., Box 5000, Vancouver, WA 98666, (360) 397-2150, **<co.clark.wa.us>**

- **INCORPORATED:** July 27, 1844
- **PARENT COUNTY:** Original county
- **MARRIAGE RECORDS:** start in 1852, kept by County Auditor
- **DIVORCE:** 1890, County Clerk
- **LAND:** 1850, County Auditor
- **PROBATE:** 1889, County Clerk
- **COURT:** 1889, County Clerk
- **NOTES:** County Auditor has birth and death records 1890-1907, and military records 1888-1894. County Clerk has naturalization records 1890-1991. Formerly Vancouver County. Name changed to Clark Sept. 3, 1849.

COLUMBIA

341 E. Main St., Dayton, WA 99328, (509) 382-4321, **<www.columbiaco.com>**

- **INCORPORATED:** Nov. 11, 1875
- **PARENT COUNTY:** Walla Walla
- **MARRIAGE RECORDS:** start in 1879, kept by County Auditor
- **DIVORCE:** 1878, County Clerk
- **LAND:** 1879, County Auditor
- **PROBATE:** 1877, County Clerk
- **COURT:** 1878, County Clerk
- **NOTES:** County Auditor has birth and death records 1891-1906. County Clerk has naturalization records 1890-1941.

COWLITZ

312 SW First Ave., Kelso, WA 98626, (360) 577-3016, **<co.cowlitz.wa.us>**

- **INCORPORATED:** April 22, 1854
- **PARENT COUNTY:** Lewis
- **MARRIAGE RECORDS:** start in 1844, kept by County Auditor
- **DIVORCE:** 1874, County Clerk
- **LAND:** 1858, County Auditor
- **PROBATE:** 1861, County Clerk
- **COURT:** 1874, County Clerk
- **MILITARY:** 1945, County Auditor
- **ADOPTION:** 1895, County Clerk
- **NOTES:** County Auditor has death records 1892-1907. County Clerk has naturalization records 1859-1920.

DOUGLAS

203 S. Rainier, Box 516, Waterville, WA 98858, (509) 745-8529, **<douglascountywa.net>**

- **INCORPORATED:** Nov. 23, 1883
- **PARENT COUNTY:** Lincoln
- **MARRIAGE RECORDS:** start in 1887, kept by County Auditor
- **DIVORCE:** 1888, County Clerk
- **LAND:** 1884, County Auditor
- **PROBATE:** 1887, County Clerk
- **COURT:** 1894, County Clerk
- **NOTES:** County Auditor has birth and death records 1891-1907. County Clerk has naturalization records 1891-1973.

FERRY

350 E. Delaware Ave. Suite 4, Republic, WA 99166, (509) 775-5232, **<www.ferry-county.com>**

- **INCORPORATED:** Feb. 18, 1899
- **PARENT COUNTY:** Stevens
- **MARRIAGE RECORDS:** start in 1898, kept by County Auditor
- **DIVORCE:** 1899, County Clerk
- **LAND:** 1898, County Auditor
- **PROBATE:** 1887, County Clerk
- **COURT:** 1899, County Clerk
- **NOTES:** County Auditor has birth and death records 1898-1911.

FRANKLIN

1016 N. Fourth Ave. Room 306, Pasco, WA 99301, (509) 545-3525, **<co.franklin.wa.us>**

- **INCORPORATED:** Nov. 28, 1883
- **PARENT COUNTY:** Whitman

- **MARRIAGE RECORDS:** start in 1890, kept by County Auditor
- **DIVORCE:** 1920, County Clerk
- **LAND:** 1883, County Auditor
- **PROBATE:** 1913, County Clerk
- **COURT:** 1909, County Clerk
- **NOTES:** County Auditor has birth and death records 1891-1910. County Clerk has naturalization records 1891-1975.

GARFIELD

789 Main St., Box 915, Pomeroy, WA 99347, (509) 843-3731, **<co.garfield.wa.us>**

- **INCORPORATED:** Nov. 29, 1881
- **PARENT COUNTY:** Columbia
- **MARRIAGE RECORDS:** start in ca. 1890, kept by County Auditor
- **DIVORCE:** 1882, County Clerk
- **LAND:** 1891, County Auditor
- **PROBATE:** 1882, County Clerk
- **COURT:** 1882, County Clerk
- **NOTES:** County Auditor has birth and death records ca. 1890-1908.

GRANT

35 C St. NW, Box 37, Ephrata, WA 98823, (509) 754-2011 ext. 444, **<co.grant.wa.us>**

- **INCORPORATED:** Feb. 24, 1909
- **PARENT COUNTY:** Douglas
- **MARRIAGE RECORDS:** start in 1909, kept by County Auditor
- **LAND:** 1909, County Auditor
- **DIVORCE:** 1909, County Clerk
- **PROBATE:** 1909, County Clerk
- **COURT:** 1889, County Clerk
- **NOTES:** Court records prior to 1909 were transcribed from Douglas County Superior Court records.

GRAYS HARBOR

102 W. Broadway Ave. W. Room 203, Montesano, WA 98563, (360) 249-3842, **<co.grays-harbor.wa.us>**

- **INCORPORATED:** April 14, 1854
- **PARENT COUNTY:** Thurston
- **MARRIAGE RECORDS:** start in 1855, kept by County Auditor
- **DIVORCE:** 1884, County Clerk
- **LAND:** 1855, County Auditor
- **COURT:** 1884, County Clerk
- **PROBATE:** 1852, County Clerk
- **NOTES:** County Auditor has birth records 1891-1908, and death records 1891-1907. County Clerk has naturalization records 1884-1980. Formerly Chehalis County. Name changed to Grays Harbor March 15, 1915.

ISLAND

101 NE Sixth St., Box 5000, Coupeville, WA 98239, (360) 679-7359, **<www.islandcounty.net>**

- **INCORPORATED:** Jan. 6, 1853
- **PARENT COUNTY:** Thurston
- **MARRIAGE RECORDS:** start in 1855, kept by County Auditor
- **DIVORCE:** 1889, County Clerk
- **LAND:** 1853, County Auditor
- **PROBATE:** 1854, County Clerk
- **COURT:** 1889, County Clerk
- **NOTES:** County Auditor has birth and death records 1891-1907, and military records 1888-1894. County Clerk has naturalization records 1894-1974.

JEFFERSON

1820 Jefferson St., Box 1220, Port Townsend, WA 98368, (360) 385-9125, **<co.jefferson.wa.us>**

- **INCORPORATED:** Dec. 22, 1852
- **PARENT COUNTY:** Thurston
- **MARRIAGE RECORDS:** start in 1853, kept by County Auditor
- **DIVORCE:** 1890, County Clerk
- **LAND:** 1855, County Auditor
- **PROBATE:** 1853, County Clerk
- **COURT:** 1890, County Clerk
- **NOTES:** County Auditor has birth and death records 1891-1906. County Clerk has naturalization records 1893-1973.

KING

516 Third Ave. Room E609, Seattle, WA 98104, (206) 296-9300, **<www.kingcounty.gov>**

- **INCORPORATED:** Dec. 22, 1852
- **PARENT COUNTY:** Thurston
- **BIRTH RECORDS:** start in 1880, kept by County Department of Public Health and Vital Statistics
- **MARRIAGE:** 1866, Recorder's Office
- **DIVORCE:** 1853, County Clerk
- **DEATH:** 1890, County Department of Public Health and Vital Statistics
- **LAND:** 1853, Recorder's Office
- **PROBATE:** 1854, County Clerk
- **COURT:** 1853, County Clerk

KITSAP

614 Division St. MS34, Port Orchard, WA 98366, (360) 337-7164, **<www.kitsapgov.com>**

- **INCORPORATED:** Jan. 16, 1857
- **PARENT COUNTIES:** King, Jefferson
- **MARRIAGE RECORDS:** start in 1860, kept by County Auditor
- **DIVORCE:** 1888, County Clerk
- **LAND:** 1857, County Auditor
- **PROBATE:** 1860, County Clerk
- **COURT:** 1888, County Clerk
- **ADOPTION:** 1861, County Clerk
- **NOTES:** County Clerk has divorce records 1910-1959, and naturalization records 1892-1906 and 1923-1989. Formerly Slaughter County. Name changed to Kitsap July 13, 1857.

KITTITAS

205 W. Fifth Ave. Suite 210, Ellensburg, WA 98926, (509) 962-7531, **<co.kittitas.wa.us>**

- **INCORPORATED:** Nov. 24 1883
- **PARENT COUNTY:** Yakima
- **MARRIAGE RECORDS:** start in 1884, kept by County Auditor
- **DIVORCE:** 1891, County Clerk
- **LAND:** 1882, County Auditor
- **PROBATE:** 1886, County Clerk
- **COURT:** 1891, County Clerk

- **NOTES:** County Auditor has birth records 1889-1907, death records 1891-1907, and military discharge records 1919-1969. County Clerk has naturalization records 1907-1921.

KLICKITAT
205 S. Columbus Ave. MS CH-3, Room 204, Goldendale, WA 98620, (509) 773-5744, **<www.klickitatcounty.org>**
- **INCORPORATED:** Dec. 20, 1859
- **PARENT COUNTY:** Skamania
- **MARRIAGE RECORDS:** start in 1867, kept by County Auditor
- **DIVORCE:** 1879, County Clerk
- **LAND:** 1864, County Auditor
- **PROBATE:** 1885, County Clerk
- **COURT:** 1879, County Clerk
- **MILITARY:** 1919, County Auditor
- **NOTES:** County Auditor has birth records 1891-1907, and death records 1882-1907. County Clerk has naturalization records 1893-1927.

LEWIS
360 W. Main St. Fourth Floor, Chehalis, WA 98532, (360) 740-1333, **<lewiscountywa.gov>**
- **INCORPORATED:** Dec. 21, 1845
- **PARENT COUNTY:** District of Vancouver
- **MARRIAGE RECORDS:** start in 1858, kept by County Auditor
- **DIVORCE:** 1893, County Clerk
- **LAND:** 1856, County Auditor
- **PROBATE:** 1891, County Clerk
- **COURT:** 1893, County Clerk
- **NOTES:** County Auditor has birth and death records 1856-1906.

LINCOLN
450 Logan St., Box 68, Davenport, WA 99122, (509) 725-1401, **<co.lincoln.wa.us>**
- **INCORPORATED:** Nov. 24, 1883
- **PARENT COUNTY:** Spokane
- **MARRIAGE RECORDS:** start in 1884, kept by County Auditor
- **DIVORCE:** 1907, County Clerk
- **LAND:** 1883, County Auditor
- **PROBATE:** 1907, County Clerk
- **COURT:** 1907, County Clerk
- **NOTES:** County Auditor has birth and death records 1891-1907. County Clerk has naturalization records 1886-1924.

MASON
419 N. Fourth St. 2nd Floor, Box 340, Shelton, WA 98584, (360) 427-9670 ext. 346, **<co.mason.wa.us>**
- **INCORPORATED:** March 13, 1854
- **PARENT COUNTY:** Thurston
- **MARRIAGE RECORDS:** start in 1887, kept by County Auditor
- **DIVORCE:** 1858, County Clerk
- **LAND:** 1856, County Auditor
- **PROBATE:** 1858, County Clerk
- **COURT:** 1858, County Clerk
- **NOTES:** County Auditor has military discharge records 1938-1984. Formerly Sawamish County. Name changed to Mason Jan. 8, 1864.

OKANOGAN
149 Third N., Box 72, Okanogan, WA 98840, (509) 422-7275, **<www.okanogancounty.org>**
- **INCORPORATED:** Feb. 2, 1888
- **PARENT COUNTY:** Stevens
- **MARRIAGE RECORDS:** start in 1888, kept by County Auditor
- **DIVORCE:** 1888, County Clerk
- **LAND:** 1888, County Auditor
- **PROBATE:** 1888, County Clerk
- **COURT:** 1888, County Clerk
- **NOTES:** County Auditor has birth records 1891-1914, death records 1891-1908, and military discharge records 1919-1974. County Clerk has naturalization records 1890-1906.

PACIFIC
300 Memorial Ave., Box 67, South Bend, WA 98586, (360) 875-9320 ext. 2222, **<co.pacific.wa.us>**
- **INCORPORATED:** Feb. 4, 1851
- **PARENT COUNTY:** Lewis
- **MARRIAGE:** start in 1852, kept by County Auditor
- **DIVORCE:** 1851, County Clerk
- **LAND:** 1850, County Auditor
- **PROBATE:** 1851, County Clerk
- **COURT:** 1851, County Clerk
- **MILITARY:** 1919, County Auditor
- **NOTES:** County Auditor has birth records 1891-1915, and death records 1891-1917.

PEND OREILLE
229 S. Garden Ave., Box 5020, Newport, WA 99156, (509) 447-2435, **<www.pendoreilleco.org>**
- **INCORPORATED:** Nov. 11, 1911
- **PARENT COUNTY:** Stevens
- **BIRTH RECORDS:** start in 1911, kept by County Auditor
- **MARRIAGE:** 1911, County Auditor
- **DIVORCE:** 1911, County Clerk
- **LAND:** 1911, County Auditor
- **PROBATE:** 1911, County Clerk
- **COURT:** 1911, County Clerk

PIERCE
930 Tacoma Ave. S. Room 110, Tacoma, WA 98402, (253) 798-7455, **<co.pierce.wa.us>**
- **INCORPORATED:** Dec. 22, 1852
- **PARENT COUNTY:** Lewis
- **MARRIAGE RECORDS:** start in 1859, kept by County Auditor
- **DIVORCE:** 1854, County Clerk
- **LAND:** 1859, County Auditor
- **PROBATE:** 1853, County Clerk
- **COURT:** 1854, County Clerk
- **NOTES:** County Auditor has birth and death records 1891-1907, and military records 1888-1892.

SAN JUAN
350 Court St. Suite #7, Friday Harbor, WA 98250, (360) 378-2163, **<co.san-juan.wa.us>**
- **INCORPORATED:** Oct. 31, 1873
- **PARENT COUNTY:** Whatcom

- **MARRIAGE RECORDS:** start in 1878, kept by County Auditor
- **DIVORCE:** 1890, County Clerk
- **PROBATE:** 1874, County Clerk
- **COURT:** 1890, County Clerk
- **NOTES:** County Auditor has birth records 1892-1907, and death records 1890-1907. County Clerk has naturalization records 1871-1960.

SAWAMISH

- **INCORPORATED:** March 13, 1854
- **PARENT COUNTY:** Thurston
- **NOTES:** See Mason County. Name changed to Mason Jan. 8, 1864.

SKAGIT

205 W. Kincaid St. Suite 103, Mount Vernon, WA 98273, (360) 336-9440, **<www.skagitcounty.net>**

- **INCORPORATED:** Nov. 28, 1883
- **PARENT COUNTY:** Whatcom
- **MARRIAGE RECORDS:** start in 1884, kept by County Auditor
- **DIVORCE:** 1878, County Clerk
- **LAND:** 1884, County Auditor
- **PROBATE:** 1878, County Clerk
- **COURT:** 1878, County Clerk
- **NOTES:** County Auditor has birth records 1891-1907, death records 1891-1910, and military records 1892-1896. County Clerk has naturalization records 1904-1974.

SKAMANIA

240 Vancouver Ave., Box 790, Stevenson, WA 98648, (509) 427-3765, **<www.skamaniacounty.org>**

- **INCORPORATED:** March 9, 1854
- **PARENT COUNTY:** Clark
- **MARRIAGE RECORDS:** start in 1874, kept by County Auditor
- **DIVORCE:** 1854, County Clerk
- **LAND:** 1855, County Auditor
- **PROBATE:** 1854, County Clerk
- **COURT:** 1854, County Clerk
- **MILITARY:** 1945, County Auditor
- **NOTES:** County was dissolved Jan. 14, 1865, and reestablished Jan. 31, 1867.

SLAUGHTER

- **INCORPORATED:** Jan. 16, 1857
- **PARENT COUNTIES:** King, Jefferson
- **NOTES:** See Kitsap County. Name changed to Kitsap July 13, 1857.

SNOHOMISH

3000 Rockefeller Ave. MS 502, Everett, WA 98201, (425) 388-3421, **<www1.co.snohomish.wa.us>**

- **INCORPORATED:** Jan. 20, 1861
- **PARENT COUNTY:** Island
- **MARRIAGE RECORDS:** start in 1891, kept by County Auditor
- **DIVORCE:** 1889, County Clerk
- **PROBATE:** 1866, County Clerk
- **COURT:** 1889, County Clerk
- **NOTES:** County Auditor has birth and death records 1891-1907, and military discharge records 1919-1979.

SPOKANE

1116 W. Broadway Ave., Spokane, WA 99260, (509) 477-2265, **<www.spokanecounty.org>**

- **INCORPORATED:** Jan. 29, 1868
- **PARENT COUNTY:** Walla Walla
- **MARRIAGE RECORDS:** start in 1880, kept by County Auditor
- **DIVORCE:** 1879, County Clerk
- **LAND:** unknown start, County Auditor
- **PROBATE:** 1883, County Clerk
- **COURT:** 1879, County Clerk
- **NOTES:** County Auditor has birth and death records 1886-1907. County Clerk has naturalization records 1885-1923. Spokane County was organized in 1868 from Walla Walla, then disorganized and reorganized in 1879 from Stevens County.

STEVENS

215 S. Oak St. Room 206, Colville, WA 99114, (509) 684-7575, **<co.stevens.wa.us>**

- **INCORPORATED:** Jan. 20, 1863
- **PARENT COUNTY:** Walla Walla
- **MARRIAGE RECORDS:** start in 1864, kept by County Auditor
- **DIVORCE:** 1882, County Clerk
- **LAND:** 1886, County Auditor
- **PROBATE:** 1874, County Clerk
- **COURT:** 1882, County Clerk
- **NOTES:** County Auditor has birth and death records 1891-1907. County Clerk has naturalization records 1888-1970.

THURSTON

2000 Lakeridge Dr. SW Bldg. 2, Olympia, WA 98502, (360) 709-3260, **<co.thurston.wa.us>**

- **INCORPORATED:** Jan. 12, 1852
- **PARENT COUNTY:** Lewis
- **MARRIAGE RECORDS:** start in 1844, kept by County Auditor
- **DIVORCE:** 1889, County Clerk
- **LAND:** 1852, County Auditor
- **PROBATE:** 1848, County Clerk
- **COURT:** 1851, County Clerk
- **NOTES:** County Auditor has birth and death records 1891-1907. County Clerk has naturalization records 1849-1974.

VANCOUVER

- **INCORPORATED:** July 27, 1844
- **PARENT COUNTY:** Original county
- **NOTES:** See Clark County. Name changed to Clark Sept. 3, 1849.

WAHKIAKUM

64 Main St., Box 116, Cathlamet, WA 98612, (360) 795-3558, **<co.wahkiakum.wa.us>**

- **INCORPORATED:** April 24, 1854
- **PARENT COUNTY:** Pacific
- **MARRIAGE RECORDS:** start in 1868, kept by County Auditor
- **DIVORCE:** 1890, County Clerk
- **LAND:** 1858, County Auditor
- **PROBATE:** 1852, County Clerk
- **COURT:** 1890, County Clerk
- **MILITARY:** 1943, County Auditor
- **NOTES:** County Auditor has birth and death records 1891-1984.

WALLA WALLA

315 West Main St., Box 836, Walla Walla, WA 99362, (509) 527-3221, **<co.walla-walla.wa.us>**

- **INCORPORATED:** April 25, 1854
- **PARENT COUNTY:** Skamania
- **DIVORCE RECORDS:** start in 1860, kept by County Clerk
- **PROBATE:** 1860, County Clerk
- **COURT:** 1860, County Clerk
- **NOTES:** County Auditor has land records from late 1800s. County Clerk has naturalization records 1861-1906.

WHATCOM

311 Grand Ave. Room 301, Bellingham, WA 98227, (360) 676-7688, **<co.whatcom.wa.us>**

- **INCORPORATED:** March 9, 1854
- **PARENT COUNTY:** Island
- **BIRTH RECORDS:** start in 1936, kept by County Health and Human Services
- **MARRIAGE:** 1854, County Auditor
- **DIVORCE:** 1883, County Clerk
- **DEATH:** 1936, County Health and Human Services
- **LAND:** 1854, County Auditor
- **PROBATE:** 1872, County Clerk
- **COURT:** 1883, County Clerk

WHITMAN

400 N. Main St., Box 390, Colfax, WA 99111, (509) 397-6240, **<www.whitmancounty.org>**

- **INCORPORATED:** Nov. 29, 1871
- **PARENT COUNTY:** Stevens
- **MARRIAGE RECORDS:** start in 1873, kept by County Auditor
- **DIVORCE:** 1890, County Clerk
- **LAND:** 1874, County Auditor
- **PROBATE:** 1877, County Clerk
- **COURT:** 1890, County Clerk
- **NOTES:** County Auditor has birth and death records 1891-1907.

YAKIMA

128 N. Second St. Room 323, Yakima, WA 98901, (509) 574-1430, **<www.yakimacounty.us>**

- **INCORPORATED:** Jan. 21, 1865
- **PARENT COUNTY:** Ferguson
- **MARRIAGE RECORDS:** start in 1869, kept by County Auditor
- **DIVORCE:** 1890, County Clerk
- **LAND:** 1882, County Auditor
- **PROBATE:** 1879, County Clerk
- **COURT:** 1890, County Clerk
- **MILITARY:** 1882, County Auditor
- **NOTES:** County Auditor has birth records 1891-1907, and death records 1896-1907. Many County Clerk records were lost in 1908 courthouse fire.

WEST VIRGINIA

» BY RHONDA R. MCCLURE

HISTORICAL OVERVIEW

Until 1863, West Virginia's history is Virginia's history. While many of the other states joined the Union as territories created out of nothingness, West Virginia took existing counties—50 in all—and broke away from Virginia. These counties formed the "restored government of Virginia," and Congress admitted West Virginia to the Union on June 20, 1863.

All but the five counties of West Virginia created after June 1863—Grant, Lincoln, Mineral, Mingo, and Summers—were first subject to the laws of the state of Virginia. This affects the types of records that were maintained and the court or clerk who was responsible for them. This also means that, with the exception of those five counties, you may find records for your West Virginia ancestor in Virginia.

RECORD HIGHLIGHTS

Because of the unique way in which West Virginia was created, many of the same problems with Virginia records affect pre-1863 West Virginia records. When it comes to census records, the first true West Virginia enumeration is for 1870. Prior to 1870 you need to turn your attention to census records for Virginia.

While birth and death recording in West Virginia began in 1853, these vital events were recorded until 1900—offering four more years of records than counties remaining in Virginia. Statewide registration began on Jan. 1, 1917, but a fire destroyed many records at the state level through 1921. When requesting vital records, it's better to contact the county clerk for anything recorded before 1921.

Marriages were generally recorded from the inception of each county. You can search birth, marriage and death records from many counties and years at the Division of Culture and History website at **<www.wvculture.org/vrr>**.

Although West Virginia was created long after the United States, it is one of those exception states—called "state-land states"—where the federal government did not get to sell the land first.

This is primarily because the counties trace their origins back to when there were colonies rather than states, and it wasn't until after the end of the American Revolution that the federal government existed and began to have a hand in selling land. Early land grants have been indexed in *Sims' Index to Land Grants in West Virginia*. Edgar Barr Sims was the State Auditor for West Virginia at various times in the 1930s, 1940s, and 1950s, and his index was published in 1952.

research tips

- West Virginia is the only state in which county records greatly predate the existence of the state. In some ways this makes researching easier when dealing with records that remained in the county. But never assume that all the records are in that county. Always turn your attention to records and repositories in Virginia, as well.
- If you know your ancestor's religion, check the holdings of the West Virginia and Regional History Collection at the West Virginia University, Box 6069, 1549 University Ave., Morgantown, WV 26506, **<www.libraries.wvu.edu/wvcollection>**.
- Though West Virginia broke away from Virginia over seceding from the Union, an estimated 10,000 soldiers fought for the Confederacy.
- Newspapers can often be used as a record alternative, and not just for vital records. To learn more about newspapers and where you can find them today, consult *Newspapers in the West Virginia University Library* (West Virginia University Library, 1964).

CENSUS RECORDS

- Federal census: 1870, 1880, 1900, 1910, 1920, 1930
- Federal mortality schedules: 1850, 1860, 1870, 1880
- Special census of Civil War Union veterans and widows: 1890

It includes grants made by Lord Fairfax before the creation of the Virginia Land Office. The index is arranged by county and lists the grantee, number of acres, local description, year, book, and page numbers. Probate and court records, as well as the courts that are responsible for them, have simply carried over from when West Virginia was part of Virginia. Will books are available on microfilm through a number of West Virginia repositories and the Family History Library.

ARCHIVES, LIBRARIES, AND SOCIETIES

Allegheny Regional Family History Society
Box 1804, Elkins, WV 26241, **<www.swcp.com/~dhickman>**

Archives and History Library
The Cultural Center, Capitol Complex, 1900 Kanawha Blvd. E., Charleston, WV 25305, (304) 558-0220, **<www.wvculture.org/history>**

Berkelely County Genealogical-Historical Society
Box 1624, Martinsburg, WV 25402, (304) 267-4713, **<www.bchs.org>**

Boone County Genealogical Society
375 Main St., Madison, WV 25130, (304) 369-7842, **<www.boonewvgen.org>**

Brooke County Genealogical Society
Box 144, Beech Bottom WV 26030, **<www.brookecountywvgenealogy.org>**

Cabell County Public Library
455 Ninth St. Plaza, Huntington, WV 25701, (304) 528-5700, **<cabell.lib.wv.us>**

Cabell-Wayne County Historical Society
Box 9412, Huntington, WV 25704, **<www.kindredtrails.com/WV_Cabell.html>**

Central West Virginia Genealogy & History Library
45 Abbotts Run Road, Horner, WV 26372, (304) 269-7091, **<www.hackerscreek.com/library1.htm>**

Episcopal Diocese of West Virginia
1608 Virginia St. E., Box 5400, Charleston, WV 25361, (304) 344-3597, **<www.wvdiocese.org>**

Genealogical Society of Fayette and Raleigh Counties
Box 68, Oak Hill, WV 25901, **<www.mywestvirginiagenealogy.com/wv-county-raleigh.html>**

Gilmer County Historical Society
Box 235, Glenville, WV 26351, (304) 462-4295, **<www.wvgenweb.org/gilmer>**

Jackson County Historical Society
Box 22, Ripley, WV 25271, (304) 372-5343, **<www.museumsusa.org/museums/info/1164599>**

Kanawha Valley Genealogical Society
Box 8555, South Charleston, WV 25303, (304) 776-1037, **<www.rootsweb.ancestry.com/~wvkvgs>**

Library of Virginia
800 E. Broad St., Richmond, VA 23219, (804) 692-3500, **<www.lva.virginia.gov>**

Lincoln County Genealogical Society
7999 Lynn Ave., Hamlin, WV 25523, (304) 824-5634 or (304) 824-3319, **<www.lincolnwvgen.org>**

Logan County Genealogical Society
Box 1959, Logan, WV 25601 **<www.wvgenweb.org/logan/logan.htm>**

Marion County Genealogical Club
c/o Marion County Library, 321 Monroe St., Fairmont, WV 26554, (304) 366-1210, **<www.marioncountypubliclibrary.org>**

Mason County Genealogical-Historical Society
200 6th St., Point Pleasant WV 25550, (304) 558-9100, **<www.mywestvirginiagenealogy.com/wv-county-mason.html>**

Mercer County Genealogical-Historical Society
Box 5012, Princeton, WV 24740, (304) 425-2697, **<www.wvculture.org/history/histsocs.html>**

Methodist Historical Society, West Virginia Wesleyan College
Annie M. Pfeiffer Library, College Ave., Buckhannon, WV 26201, (304) 473-8013, **<www.wvwc.edu/lib>**

Mineral County Historical Landmark Commission
Box 1325, Keyser, WV 26726, (304) 788-3989, **<mincohistfoundation.org>**

Mingo County Genealogical Society
101 Logan St., Williamson, WV 25661, (304) 235-6029 or (304) 235-6030, **<williamsonlibrary.lib.wv.us/Genealogy/genealogy.htm>**

Monroe County Historical Society
Box 465, Union, WV 24983, **<monroewvhistory.org>**

Morgan County Historical and Genealogical Society
Box 52, Berkeley Springs, WV 25411, **<www.rootsweb.ancestry.com/~wvmorgan>**

Morgantown Public Library
373 Spruce St., Morgantown, WV 26505, (304) 291-7425, **<morgantown.lib.wv.us>**

National Archives and Records Administration, Mid-Atlantic Region
900 Market St., Philadelphia, PA 19107, (215) 606-0100, **<www.archives.gov/midatlantic>**

Palatines to America, West Virginia Chapter
240 Waitman St., Morgantown, WV 26501, (304) 292-2991, **<www.palam.org/chapters.php?chapter=6>**

Pendleton County Historical Society
Main St., Franklin, West VA 26807

Pocahontas County Historical Society
810 2nd Ave., Marlinton, WV 24954, (304) 799-4973

Ritchie County Historical Society
310 Myles Ave., Pennsboro, WV 26415, (304) 659-3962, **<www.rootsweb.ancestry.com/~wvritchi/rchs.htm>**

Roane County Historical Society
Box 161, Spencer, WV 25276, **<www.wvroane.org>**

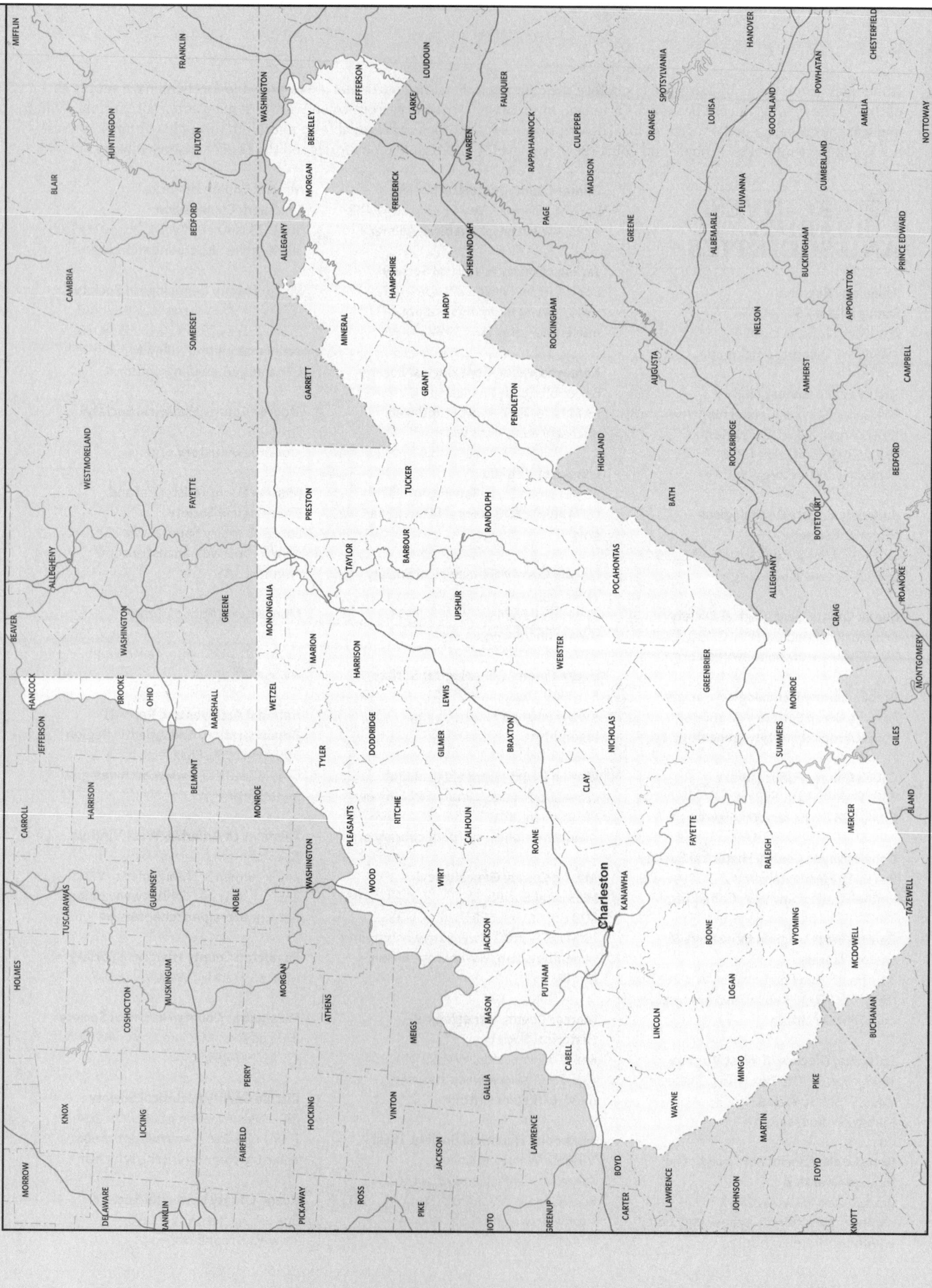
Charleston
MIFFLIN
FRANKLIN
HUNTINGDON
FULTON
WASHINGTON
BLAIR
BEDFORD
CAMBRIA
SOMERSET
WESTMORELAND
FAYETTE
ALLEGHENY
BEAVER
WASHINGTON
GREENE
HANCOCK
BROOKE
OHIO
MARSHALL
WETZEL
MONONGALIA
MARION
PRESTON
TAYLOR
BARBOUR
TUCKER
GARRETT
ALLEGANY
MORGAN
BERKELEY
JEFFERSON
LOUDOUN
CLARKE
FREDERICK
HAMPSHIRE
MINERAL
GRANT
HARDY
WARREN
SHENANDOAH
FAUQUIER
RAPPAHANNOCK
CULPEPER
MADISON
PAGE
ROCKINGHAM
PENDLETON
RANDOLPH
HIGHLAND
ORANGE
SPOTSYLVANIA
GREENE
LOUISA
ALBEMARLE
FLUVANNA
GOOCHLAND
HANOVER
POWHATAN
CHESTERFIELD
AMELIA
CUMBERLAND
NOTTOWAY
BUCKINGHAM
PRINCE EDWARD
APPOMATTOX
NELSON
AUGUSTA
AMHERST
CAMPBELL
ROCKBRIDGE
BEDFORD
BATH
BOTETOURT
POCAHONTAS
ALLEGHANY
ROANOKE
CRAIG
UPSHUR
HARRISON
WEBSTER
GREENBRIER
MONTGOMERY
MONROE
LEWIS
DODDRIDGE
TYLER
GILMER
BRAXTON
NICHOLAS
SUMMERS
GILES
CLAY
PLEASANTS
RITCHIE
CALHOUN
ROANE
FAYETTE
RALEIGH
MERCER
BLAND
WOOD
WIRT
KANAWHA
JACKSON
BOONE
WYOMING
TAZEWELL
PUTNAM
LOGAN
MCDOWELL
MASON
LINCOLN
BUCHANAN
CABELL
MINGO
PIKE
WAYNE
MARTIN
FLOYD
JOHNSON
KNOTT
LAWRENCE
BOYD
CARTER
GREENUP
LAWRENCE
GALLIA
JACKSON
MEIGS
VINTON
HOCKING
ATHENS
MORGAN
WASHINGTON
NOBLE
MONROE
BELMONT
HARRISON
JEFFERSON
CARROLL
TUSCARAWAS
GUERNSEY
MUSKINGUM
COSHOCTON
HOLMES
KNOX
LICKING
PERRY
FAIRFIELD
MORROW
DELAWARE
FRANKLIN
PICKAWAY
ROSS
PIKE
IOTO

Roman Catholic Diocese of Wheeling-Charleston
Box 230, Wheeling, WV 26003, (888) 434-6237, **<www.dwc.org>**

State Auditor
Capitol Building, County Collections Division, Building-1 Room W-100, Charleston, WV 25305, (877) 982-9148, **<www.wvsao.gov/countycollections>**

Taylor County Public Library
200 Beech St., Grafton, WV 26354, (304) 265-6121, **<taylor.clark.lib.wv.us/history.htm>**

Taylor County Historical and Genealogical Society
Box 522, Grafton, WV 26354, **<www.rootsweb.ancestry.com/~wvtaylor/tchgs.htm>**

Tri-State Genealogical and Historical Society
717 Washington St., Newell, WV 26050, (304) 387-2467, **<www.rootsweb.ancestry.com/~wvtsghs/index.html>**

Tyler County Historical Society
Box 317, Dodd St., Middlebourne, WV 26149, (304) 758-4288 or (304) 758-4432, **<www.wvgenweb.org/tyler/Pages/museum.htm>**

Upshur County Historical Society
Box 2082, Buckhannon, WV 26201, **<www.upshurcountyhistoricalsociety.com>**

West Virginia Division of Vital Statistics, Bureau of Public Health
Capitol Complex, Building 3, Room 516, Charleston, WV 25305, (304) 558-2931, **<www.wvdhhr.org/bph/hsc/vital/genealogy.asp>**

West Augusta Historical and Genealogical Society
Box 414, Mannington, WV 26582

West Virginia Midland Trail Genealogical Society
2614 Furlong Ave., St. Albans, WV 25177, (304) 727-5655, **<www.rootsweb.ancestry.com/~wvmtgs>**

West Virginia Baptist Historical Society
Route #2, Box 304, Ripley, WV 25271, **<wvbhs.com>**

West Virginia University Library
Colson Hall, Box 6069, Morgantown, WV 26506, (304) 293-4040, **<www.libraries.wvu.edu>**

West Virginia Genealogical Society
Box 249, Elkview, WV 25071, (304) 965-1179, **<www.rootsweb.ancestry.com/~wvgs>**

Wheeling Area Genealogical Society
Box 6450, Wheeling, WV 26003, **<www.lindapages.com/wags-ohio/index.htm>**

Wyoming County Historical Museum
Box 2041, Oceana, WV 24870, (304) 682-6231, **<wyomingcountymuseum.webs.com>**

☞ GENERAL RESOURCES

A Bibliography of West Virginia, 2 parts, by Innis C. Davis (West Virginia Department of Archives and History, 1939)

Church Records Survey, West Virginia, Episcopal, Protestant, Methodist, Baptist, Presbyterian from the Historical Records Survey (filmed by The Genealogical Society of Utah, 1961)

Finding Your People in the Shenandoah Valley of Virginia and West Virginia by Rebecca H. Good and Rebecca Ebert (The Rebecca Co., 1984)

Genealogical and Personal History of the Upper Monongahela Valley, West Virginia, 3 vols., by Bernard Lee Butcher (Lewis Historical Publishing Co., 1912)

A Guide to Church Records in the Archives Branch of the Virginia State Library by Newell T. Clark and Elizabeth Terry Long (Virginia State Library, 1981)

Guide to Manuscripts and Archives in the West Virginia Collection by James W. Hess (West Virginia University Library, 1974)

Guide to the Study of West Virginia History by Charles Shetler (West Virginia University Library, 1960)

A Handbook for Genealogical Research in West Virginia by Helen S., Stinson (Kanawha Valley Genealogical Society, 1981)

History of the Great Kanawha Valley: With Family History and Biographical Sketches, 2 vols., (Brant, Fuller & Co., 1891)

A History and Record of the Protestant Episcopal Church in the Diocese of West Virginia by George W. Peterkin (Tribune Co., 1902)

History of West Virginia, Old and New, 3 vols., by James Morton Callahan (American Historical Society, 1923)

Index to Printed Virginia Genealogies by Robert Armistead Stewart (Genealogical Publishing Co., 1970)

Loyal West Virginia from 1861 to 1865 by Theodore F. Lang (Deutsch, 1895)

Making a State: Formation of West Virginia, Including Maps, Illustrations, Plates and the Acts of the Virginia Assembly and the Legislature of West Virginia Creating the Counties by Edgar Barr Sims (Edgar Barr Sims, 1956)

Men of West Virginia, 2 vols., (Biographical Publishing Co., 1903)

Obituaries from newspapers of Northern West Virginia, 2 vols., by W. Guy Tetrick (W.G. Tetrick, 1933)

Prominent Men of West Virginia by George Wesley Atkinson (W.L. Callin, 1890)

Timesaving Aid to Virginia-West Virginia Ancestors: A Genealogical Index of Surnames from Published Sources, 4 vols., by Patrick G. Wardell (Iberian Publishing Co., 1990)

Virginia Genealogical Resources by Stuart E. Brown Jr (Detroit Society for Genealogical Research, 1980)

Virginia Genealogies, A Trial List of Printed Books and Pamphlets, 3 vols., by Stuart E. Brown Jr. (Virginia Book Co., 1967-89)

Virginians & West Virginians, 1607-1870 by Patrick G. Wardell (Heritage Books, 1986-1992)

West Virginia Genealogy Sources and Resources by Carol McGinnis (Genealogical Publishing Company, 1988)

The West Virginia Heritage Encyclopedia compiled and edited by Jim Comstock (Comstock, 1976)

West Virginia: A History by Otis K. Rice (University Press of Kentucky, 1985)

West Virginia History: A Guide to Research by Harold M. Forbes (West Virginia University Press, 1981)

West Virginia and Its People, 3 vols., by Thomas Condit Miller and Hu Maxwell (Lewis Historical Publishing Co., 1913)

West Virginia Research Outline by the Church of Jesus Christ of Latter-day Saints (**<www.familysearch.org/eng/search/RG/guide/west_virginia.asp>**)

☞CENSUS RECORDS

The 1787 Census of Virginia: an Accounting of the Names of Every White Male Tithable Over 21 Years, 3 vols., by Netti Schreiner-Yantis and Florence Speakman Love (Genealogical Books-in-Print, 1987)

Heads of Families. . . . Records of the State Enumerations; 1782 to 1785, Virginia, (Southern Book Co., 1952)

Map Guide to the U.S. Federal Census, 1790-1920 by William Thorndale and William Dollarhide (Genealogical Publishing Co., 1987)

A Supplement to the 1810 Census of Virginia: Tax Lists of the Counties for Which the Census is Missing by Netti Schreiner-Yantis (Genealogical Books-in-Print, 1971)

Virginians in 1800; Counties of West Virginia by Steven A. Bridges (Steven A. Bridges, 1987)

Virginia Tax Payers, 1782-87, Other than Those Published by the United States Census Bureau by Augusta B. Fothergill and John Mark Naugle (Genealogical Publishing Co., 1966)

☞IMMIGRATION RECORDS

Chronicles of the Scotch-Irish Settlement in Virginia: Extracted from the Original Court Records of Augusta County, 1754-1800 by Lyman Chalkley (Genealogical Publishing Co., 1980)

☞LAND RECORDS

Dyer's Index to Land Grants in West Virginia by M.H. Dyer (Higginson Book Co., 1996)

Sims' Index to Land Grants in West Virginia by Edgar B. Sims (Auditor's Office, 1952)

Making a State: Formation of West Virginia by Edgar B. Sims (E.B. Sims, 1956)

Misc. Land Records, 1748-1912 from the West Virginia State Auditor (filmed by the Family History Library)

☞MAPS

Gazetteer of West Virginia by Henry Gannett (Genealogical Publishing Co., 1975)

Making a State: Formation of West Virginia by Edgar B. Sims (Edgar B. Sims, 1956)

New Descriptive Atlas of West Virginia, (Clarksburg Publishing Co., 1933)

West Virginia County Formations and Boundary Changes from the West Virginia Historical Records Survey (1938)

West Virginia County Maps compiled by C.J. Puetz (Thomas Publishing Co., 1990)

West Virginia Place Names, Their Origin and Meaning, Including the Nomenclature of the Streams and Mountains by Hamill Kenny (Place Name Press, 1945)

☞MILITARY RECORDS

Military Records of Maryland, Pennsylvania, Virginia and West Virginia, 1775-1920 by Hazel Groves Hansrote (filmed by the Genealogical Society of Utah, 1975)

Reminiscences of Confederate Service, 1861-1865 by Francis Warrington Dawson (University Publications of America, 1990)

The Soldiery of West Virginian the French And Indian War, Lord Dunmore's War, The Revolution, the War with Mexico by Virgil A. Lewis in *Third Biennial Report Of the State Department of Archives and History*, pages 39-118 (Reprint: Genealogical Publishing Co.)

War of 1812: Virginia Bounty Land & Pension Applicants: A Quick Reference Guide to Ancestors Having War of 1812 Service Who Served, Lived, Died, or Married in Virginia or West Virginia by Patrick G. Wardell (Heritage Books, 1987)

West Virginia in the Civil War by Boyd B. Stutler (Educational Foundation, 1963)

West Virginians in the Revolution compiled by Ross B. Johnston (Genealogical Publishing Co., 1977)

West Virginia Revolutionary Ancestors Whose Services Were Non-Military by Anne Waller Reddy (Genealogical Publishing Co., 1963)

☞PROBATE RECORDS

Early West Virginia Wills by K.T.H. McFarland (Closson Press, 1993)

Virginia Wills and Administrations, 1632-1800 by Clayton Torrence (1930; Genealogical Publishing Co., 1965)

☞VITAL RECORDS

Birth Certificates and Delayed Birth Certificates, 1852-1930 from the West Virginia Division of Vital Statistics (filmed by the Family History Library, 1994-1995)

Inventory of Public Vital Statistics Records in West Virginia, 2 vols., from the Historical Record Survey (West Virginia Historical Records Survey, 1941-1942)

Obituaries form Newspapers of Northern West Virginia: Principally from the Counties of Barbour, Braxton, Calhoun,

Doddridge, Gilmer, Harrison, Lewis, Nichols, Pocahontas, Preston, Randolph, Ritchie, Taylor, Tucker, Tyler, Upshur, Webster and parts of Marion, Wetzel and Wirt, 2 vols., by W. Guy Tetrick (W.G. Tetrick, 1933)

Roster of Confederate Graves, 7 vols., from the United Daughters of the Confederacy (United Daughters of the Confederacy, Georgia Division, 1995)

West Virginia, 1863-1900 [Marriages] (Broderbund, 1999. CD-ROM)

COUNTY DETAILS

BARBOUR
8 N. Main St., Philippi, WV 26416, (304) 457-3952, **<www.wv.gov/local/county/Pages/barbour.aspx>**
- **INCORPORATED:** March 3, 1843
- **PARENT COUNTIES:** Harrison, Lewis, Randolph
- **BIRTH RECORDS:** start in 1853, kept by County Clerk
- **MARRIAGE:** 1840, County Clerk
- **DIVORCE:** 1843, Circuit Court
- **DEATH:** 1853, County Clerk
- **LAND:** 1843, County Clerk
- **PROBATE:** 1843, County Clerk
- **COURT:** 1843, Circuit Court

BERKELEY
400 W. Stephen St., Martinsburg, WV 25401, (304) 264-1923, **<www.berkeleycountycomm.org>**
- **INCORPORATED:** Feb. 10, 1772
- **PARENT COUNTY:** Frederick
- **BIRTH RECORDS:** start in 1865, kept by County Clerk
- **MARRIAGE:** 1781, County Clerk
- **DIVORCE:** unknown start, Circuit Court
- **DEATH:** 1865, County Clerk
- **LAND:** 1772, County Clerk
- **PROBATE:** 1772, County Clerk
- **COURT:** 1772, Circuit Court
- **NOTES:** County Clerk has naturalization records 1911-1929.

BOONE
206 Court St., Madison, WV 25130, (304) 369-7301, **<www.boonecountywv.org>**
- **INCORPORATED:** March 11, 1847
- **PARENT COUNTIES:** Kanawha, Cabell, Logan
- **BIRTH RECORDS:** start in 1865, kept by County Clerk
- **MARRIAGE:** 1860, County Clerk
- **DIVORCE:** 1865, Circuit Court
- **DEATH:** 1865, County Clerk
- **LAND:** 1847, County Clerk
- **PROBATE:** 1865, County Clerk
- **COURT:** 1865, Circuit Court
- **NOTES:** County Auditor has military discharge records 1917-1927.

BRAXTON
Courthouse Complex, Sutton, WV 26601, (304) 765-2833, **<www.braxtonwv.org>**
- **INCORPORATED:** Jan. 15, 1836
- **PARENT COUNTIES:** Kanawha, Lewis, Nicholas
- **BIRTH RECORDS:** 1853, County Clerk
- **MARRIAGE:** 1836, County Clerk
- **DIVORCE:** start in 1836, kept by Circuit Court
- **DEATH:** 1853, County Clerk
- **LAND:** 1836, County Clerk
- **PROBATE:** 1836, County Clerk
- **COURT:** 1836, Circuit Court

BROOKE
632 Main St., Wellsburg, WV 26070, (304) 737-4024, **<www.brookewv.org>**
- **INCORPORATED:** May 23, 1797
- **PARENT COUNTY:** Ohio
- **BIRTH RECORDS:** start in 1854, kept by County Clerk
- **MARRIAGE:** 1797, County Clerk
- **DIVORCE:** unknown start, Circuit Court
- **DEATH:** 1889, County Clerk
- **LAND:** 1797, County Clerk
- **PROBATE:** 1797, County Clerk
- **COURT:** unknown start, Circuit Court

CABELL
750 Fifth Ave., Huntington, WV 25701, (304) 526-8634, **<www.cabellcounty.org>**
- **INCORPORATED:** Jan. 2, 1809
- **PARENT COUNTY:** Kanawha
- **BIRTH RECORDS:** start in 1865, kept by County Clerk
- **MARRIAGE:** 1809, County Clerk
- **DIVORCE:** 1809, Circuit Court
- **DEATH:** 1853, County Clerk
- **LAND:** 1809, County Clerk
- **PROBATE:** 1820, County Clerk
- **COURT:** 1809, Circuit Court
- **NOTES:** County Clerk has birth records 1853-1854.

CALHOUN
Box 230, Grantsville, WV 26147, (304) 354-6725, **<www.wv.gov/local/county/Pages/calhoun.aspx>**
- **INCORPORATED:** March 5, 1856
- **PARENT COUNTY:** Gilmer
- **BIRTH RECORDS:** start in 1856, kept by County Clerk
- **MARRIAGE:** 1856, County Clerk
- **DEATH:** 1856, County Clerk
- **LAND:** 1856, County Clerk
- **PROBATE:** 1856, County Clerk
- **COURT:** 1856, Circuit Court
- **NOTES:** County Clerk has military discharge records 1918-1945.

CLAY
207 Main St., Clay, WV 25043, (304) 587-4259,
<www.claywestvirginia.com>
- **INCORPORATED:** March 29, 1858
- **PARENT COUNTIES:** Braxton, Nicholas
- **BIRTH RECORDS:** start in 1858, kept by County Clerk
- **MARRIAGE:** 1858, County Clerk
- **DEATH:** 1858, County Clerk
- **LAND:** 1873, County Clerk
- **PROBATE:** 1858, County Clerk
- **COURT:** 1858, Circuit Court

DODDRIDGE
118 E. Court St., West Union, WV 26456, (304) 873-2631,
<www.wv.gov/local/county/Pages/doddridge.aspx>
- **INCORPORATED:** Feb. 4, 1845
- **PARENT COUNTIES:** Harrison, Tyler, Ritchie, Lewis
- **BIRTH RECORDS:** start in 1853, kept by County Clerk
- **MARRIAGE:** 1846, County Clerk
- **DEATH:** 1853, County Clerk
- **LAND:** 1845, County Clerk
- **PROBATE:** 1887, County Clerk
- **COURT:** 1845, Circuit Court

FAYETTE
100 N Court St., Fayetteville, WV 25840, (304) 574-4249,
<www.wv.gov/local/county/Pages/fayette.aspx>
- **INCORPORATED:** Feb. 28, 1831
- **PARENT COUNTIES:** Kanawha, Greenbrier, Logan, Nicholas
- **BIRTH RECORDS:** start in 1866, kept by County Clerk
- **MARRIAGE:** 1831, County Clerk
- **DIVORCE:** 1832, Circuit Court
- **DEATH:** 1866, County Clerk
- **LAND:** 1831, County Clerk
- **PROBATE:** 1861, County Clerk
- **COURT:** 1832, Circuit Court

GILMER
10 Howard St., Glenville, WV 26351, (304) 462-7641,
<www.gilmerwv.org>
- **INCORPORATED:** Feb. 3, 1845
- **PARENT COUNTIES:** Lewis, Kanawha
- **BIRTH RECORDS:** start in 1853, kept by County Clerk
- **MARRIAGE:** 1845, County Clerk
- **DEATH:** 1853, County Clerk
- **LAND:** 1845, County Clerk
- **PROBATE:** 1845, County Clerk
- **COURT:** 1853, Circuit Court
- **NOTES:** County Clerk has military discharge records 1896-1944.

GRANT
5 Highland Ave., Petersburg, WV 26847, (304) 257-4550,
<www.wv.gov/local/county/Pages/grant.aspx>
- **INCORPORATED:** Feb. 14, 1866
- **PARENT COUNTY:** Hardy
- **BIRTH RECORDS:** start in 1865, kept by County Clerk
- **MARRIAGE:** 1866, County Clerk
- **DEATH:** 1865, County Clerk
- **DIVORCE:** 1866, Circuit Court
- **LAND:** 1866, County Clerk
- **PROBATE:** 1866, County Clerk
- **COURT:** 1866, Circuit Court

GREENBRIER
Box 506, Lewisburg, WV 24901, (304) 647-6602, **<www.greenbriercounty.net>**
- **INCORPORATED:** Oct. 20, 1777
- **PARENT COUNTIES:** Montgomery & Botetourt, VA
- **BIRTH RECORDS:** start in 1853, kept by County Clerk
- **MARRIAGE:** 1780, County Clerk
- **DEATH:** 1853, County Clerk
- **LAND:** 1780, County Clerk
- **PROBATE:** 1777, County Clerk
- **COURT:** 1814, Circuit Court

HAMPSHIRE
66 N. High St., Romney, WV 26757, (304) 822-5112,
<www.hampshirecountywv.org>
- **INCORPORATED:** May 1, 1754
- **PARENT COUNTIES:** Frederick, Augusta
- **BIRTH RECORDS:** start in 1865, kept by County Clerk
- **MARRIAGE:** 1865County Clerk
- **DEATH:** 1866County Clerk
- **LAND:** 1757County Clerk
- **PROBATE:** 1851County Clerk
- **COURT:** 1831Circuit Court
- **NOTES:** County Clerk has marriage records 1824-1828.

HANCOCK
102 N. Court St., New Cumberland, WV 26047, (304) 564-3311,
<hancockcountywv.org>
- **INCORPORATED:** Jan. 15, 1848
- **PARENT COUNTY:** Brooke
- **BIRTH RECORDS:** start in 1853, kept by County Clerk
- **MARRIAGE:** 1854, County Clerk
- **DIVORCE:** 1848, Circuit Court
- **DEATH:** 1853, County Clerk
- **LAND:** 1848, County Clerk
- **PROBATE:** 1848, County Clerk
- **COURT:** 1848, Circuit Court
- **NOTES:** County Clerk has military discharge records 1866-1992 and naturalization records 1907-1956.

HARDY
204 Washington St., Moorefield, WV 26836, (304) 530-0265,
<www.wv.gov/local/county/Pages/hardy.aspx>
- **INCORPORATED:** Oct. 17, 1785
- **PARENT COUNTY:** Hampshire
- **BIRTH RECORDS:** 1853, County Clerk
- **MARRIAGE:** 1795, County Clerk
- **DIVORCE:** 1831, Circuit Court
- **DEATH:** 1853, County Clerk
- **LAND:** 1786, County Clerk
- **PROBATE:** start in 1786, kept by County Clerk
- **COURT:** 1788, Circuit Court
- **NATURALIZATION:** 1916, County Clerk

HARRISON

301 W. Main St., Clarksburg, WV 26301, (304) 624-8673, **<www.harrisoncountywv.com>**

- **INCORPORATED:** May 3, 1784
- **PARENT COUNTY:** Monongalia
- **BIRTH RECORDS:** start in 1853, kept by County Clerk
- **MARRIAGE:** 1784, County Clerk
- **DIVORCE:** 1803, Circuit Court
- **DEATH:** 1853, County Clerk
- **LAND:** 1786, County Clerk
- **PROBATE:** 1788, County Clerk
- **COURT:** 1803, Circuit Court

JACKSON

Box 800, Ripley, WV 25271, (304) 372-2011, **<www.wv.gov/local/county/Pages/jackson.aspx>**

- **INCORPORATED:** March 1, 1831
- **PARENT COUNTIES:** Kanawha, Mason, Wood
- **BIRTH RECORDS:** start in 1853, kept by County Clerk
- **MARRIAGE:** 1831, County Clerk
- **DIVORCE:** 1831, Circuit Court
- **DEATH:** 1853, County Clerk
- **LAND:** 1831, County Clerk
- **PROBATE:** 1831, County Clerk
- **COURT:** 1831, Circuit Court
- **NOTES:** County Clerk has military discharge records 1918-1992.

JEFFERSON

110 E Washington St., Charles Town, WV 25414, (304) 728-2944, **<www.jeffersoncountywv.org>**

- **INCORPORATED:** Jan. 8, 1801
- **PARENT COUNTY:** Berkeley
- **BIRTH RECORDS:** 1853, County Clerk
- **MARRIAGE:** start in 1801, kept by County Clerk
- **DIVORCE:** 1831, Circuit Court
- **DEATH:** 1853, County Clerk
- **LAND:** 1801, County Clerk
- **PROBATE:** 1801, County Clerk
- **COURT:** 1831, Circuit Court

KANAWHA

407 Virginia St. E., Charleston, WV 25331, (304) 357-0101, **<www.kanawha.us>**

- **INCORPORATED:** Nov. 14, 1788
- **PARENT COUNTIES:** Greenbrier, Montgomery
- **BIRTH RECORDS:** start in 1853, kept by County Clerk
- **MARRIAGE:** 1850, County Clerk
- **DIVORCE:** 1831, Circuit Court
- **DEATH:** 1853, County Clerk
- **LAND:** 1790, County Clerk
- **PROBATE:** 1820, County Clerk
- **COURT:** 1832, Circuit Court
- **NOTES:** Clerk of Circuit Court has Court records 1801-1813. County Clerk has marriage records 1794-1843 and military discharge records 1915-1966.

LEWIS

Box 466, Weston, WV 26452, (304) 269-8202, **<www.wv.gov/local/county/Pages/lewis.aspx>**

- **INCORPORATED:** Dec. 18, 1816
- **PARENT COUNTY:** Harrison
- **BIRTH RECORDS:** start in 1853, kept by County Clerk
- **MARRIAGE:** 1817, County Clerk
- **DEATH:** 1853, County Clerk
- **DIVORCE:** unknown start, Circuit Court
- **LAND:** 1817, County Clerk
- **PROBATE:** 1817, County Clerk

LINCOLN

Box 297, Hamlin, WV 25523, (304) 824-7990, **<www.wv.gov/local/county/Pages/lincoln.aspx>**

- **INCORPORATED:** Feb. 23, 1867
- **PARENT COUNTIES:** Boone, Cabell, Kanawha, Putnam
- **BIRTH RECORDS:** start in 1909, kept by County Clerk
- **MARRIAGE:** 1895, County Clerk
- **DIVORCE:** 1909, Circuit Court
- **DEATH:** 1909, County Clerk
- **LAND:** 1909, County Clerk
- **PROBATE:** 1909, County Clerk
- **COURT:** 1909, Circuit Court
- **NOTES:** County Clerk has military discharge records 1919-1980.

LOGAN

300 Stratton St., Logan, WV 25601, (304) 792-9088, **<www.wv.gov/local/county/Pages/logan.aspx>**

- **INCORPORATED:** Jan. 12, 1824
- **PARENT COUNTIES:** Kanawha and Cabell, WV,; Giles and Tazewell, Va.
- **BIRTH RECORDS:** start in 1872, kept by County Clerk
- **MARRIAGE:** 1872, County Clerk
- **DIVORCE:** 1868, Circuit Court
- **DEATH:** 1872, County Clerk
- **LAND:** 1835, County Clerk
- **PROBATE:** 1873, County Clerk
- **COURT:** 1868, Circuit Court
- **NOTES:** County Clerk has military discharge records 1917-1989 and naturalization records 1913-1958.

MARION

217 Adams St., Fairmont, WV 26554, (304) 367-5431, **<www.marioncounty.wv.com>**

- **INCORPORATED:** Jan. 14, 1842
- **PARENT COUNTIES:** Harrison, Monongalia
- **BIRTH RECORDS:** start in 1860, kept by County Clerk
- **MARRIAGE:** 1842, County Clerk
- **DEATH:** 1861, County Clerk
- **LAND:** 1842, County Clerk
- **PROBATE:** 1842, County Clerk
- **NOTES:** County Clerk has naturalization records 1904-1926.

MARSHALL

Drawer B, Moundsville, WV 26041, (304) 845-5891, **<www.marshallcountywv.org>**

- **INCORPORATED:** March 12, 1835
- **PARENT COUNTY:** Ohio
- **BIRTH RECORDS:** start in 1853, kept by County Clerk
- **MARRIAGE:** 1835, County Clerk
- **DIVORCE:** 1835, Circuit Court
- **DEATH:** 1853, County Clerk
- **LAND:** 1835, County Clerk
- **PROBATE:** 1835, County Clerk
- **COURT:** 1835, Circuit Court
- **NOTES:** County Clerk has military discharge records 1919-1942.

MASON

200 Sixth St., Point Pleasant, WV 25550, (304) 675-1110, **<www.wv.gov/local/county/Pages/mason.aspx>**

- **INCORPORATED:** Jan. 2, 1804
- **PARENT COUNTY:** Kanawha
- **BIRTH RECORDS:** start in 1853, kept by County Clerk
- **MARRIAGE:** 1806, County Clerk
- **DIVORCE:** unknown start, Circuit Court
- **DEATH:** 1853, County Clerk
- **LAND:** 1803, County Clerk
- **PROBATE:** 1834, County Clerk
- **COURT:** 1809, Circuit Court
- **NOTES:** County Clerk has military discharge records 1917-1987.

MCDOWELL

90 Wyoming St., Welch, WV 24801, (304) 436-8576, **<www.mcdowellwv.com>**

- **INCORPORATED:** Feb. 20, 1858
- **PARENT COUNTY:** Tazewell
- **BIRTH RECORDS:** start in 1872, kept by County Clerk
- **MARRIAGE:** 1859, County Clerk
- **DIVORCE:** 1858, Circuit Court
- **DEATH:** 1894, County Clerk
- **LAND:** 1868, County Clerk
- **PROBATE:** 1897, County Clerk
- **NOTES:** County Clerk has naturalization records 1908-1926. County seat was first Perryville, moved to Welch in 1892.

MERCER

1501 W. Main St., Princeton, WV 24740, (304) 487-8311, **<www.wv.gov/local/county/Pages/mercer.aspx>**

- **INCORPORATED:** March 17, 1837
- **PARENT COUNTIES:** Giles and Tazewell
- **BIRTH RECORDS:** start in 1853, kept by County Clerk
- **MARRIAGE:** 1854, County Clerk
- **DIVORCE:** 1837, Circuit Court
- **DEATH:** 1853, County Clerk
- **LAND:** 1837, County Clerk
- **PROBATE:** 1838, County Clerk
- **COURT:** 1837, Circuit Court
- **NOTES:** County Clerk has military discharge records 1914-1944.

MINERAL

150 Armstrong St., Keyser, WV 26726, (304) 788-3924, **<www.wv.gov/local/county/Pages/mineral.aspx>**

- **INCORPORATED:** Feb. 1, 1866
- **PARENT COUNTY:** Hampshire
- **BIRTH RECORDS:** start in 1865, kept by County Clerk
- **MARRIAGE:** 1866, County Clerk
- **DIVORCE:** 1866, Circuit Court
- **DEATH:** 1865, County Clerk
- **LAND:** 1866, County Clerk
- **PROBATE:** 1866, County Clerk
- **NOTES:** County Clerk has naturalization records 1908-1911, 1920-1923.

MINGO

75 E. 2nd Ave., Williamson, WV 25661, (304) 235-0378, **<www.mingocountywv.com>**

- **INCORPORATED:** Jan. 30, 1895
- **PARENT COUNTY:** Logan
- **BIRTH RECORDS:** start in 1900, kept by County Clerk
- **MARRIAGE:** 1895, County Clerk
- **DIVORCE:** 1895, Circuit Court
- **DEATH:** 1894, County Clerk
- **LAND:** 1836, County Clerk
- **PROBATE:** 1895, County Clerk
- **COURT:** 1895, Circuit Court
- **NOTES:** County Clerk has military discharge records 1918-1945 and naturalization records 1910-1927.

MONONGALIA

243 High St., Morgantown, WV 26505, (304) 291-7257, **<co.monongalia.wv.us>**

- **INCORPORATED:** Oct. 7, 1776
- **PARENT COUNTY:** District of W. Augusta
- **BIRTH RECORDS:** start in 1853, kept by County Clerk
- **MARRIAGE:** 1796, County Clerk
- **DIVORCE:** 1832, Circuit Court
- **DEATH:** 1852, County Clerk
- **LAND:** 1789, County Clerk
- **PROBATE:** 1819, County Clerk
- **COURT:** 1789, Circuit Court
- **NOTES:** Clerk of Circuit Court has naturalization records 1907-1929.

MONROE

Main St., Union, WV 24983, (304) 772-3096, **<www.wv.gov/local/county/Pages/monroe.aspx>**

- **INCORPORATED:** Jan. 14, 1799
- **PARENT COUNTY:** Botetourt, Greenbrier
- **BIRTH RECORDS:** start in 1853, kept by County Clerk
- **MARRIAGE:** 1799, County Clerk
- **DIVORCE:** 1789, Circuit Court
- **DEATH:** 1853, County Clerk
- **LAND:** 1789, County Clerk
- **PROBATE:** 1799, County Clerk
- **COURT:** 1789, Circuit Court

MORGAN
83 Fairfax St., Berkeley Springs, WV 25411, (304) 258-8541, **<www.morgancounty.wv.gov>**
- **INCORPORATED:** Feb. 9 1820
- **PARENT COUNTIES:** Berkeley, Hampshire
- **BIRTH RECORDS:** start in 1865, kept by County Clerk
- **MARRIAGE:** 1820, County Clerk
- **DIVORCE:** 1831, Circuit Court
- **DEATH:** 1865, County Clerk
- **LAND:** 1820, County Clerk
- **PROBATE:** 1820, County Clerk
- **COURT:** 1820, Circuit Court

NICHOLAS
700 Main St., Summersville, WV 26651, (304) 872-7830, **<www.nicholascountywv.org>**
- **INCORPORATED:** Jan. 30, 1818
- **PARENT COUNTIES:** Greenbrier, Kanawha, Randolph
- **BIRTH RECORDS:** start in 1853, kept by County Clerk
- **MARRIAGE:** 1817, County Clerk
- **DIVORCE:** 1818, Circuit Court
- **DEATH:** 1853, County Clerk
- **LAND:** 1818, County Clerk
- **PROBATE:** 1820, County Clerk
- **COURT:** 1818, Circuit Court

OHIO
1500 Chapline St., Wheeling, WV 26003, (304) 234-3628, **<www.wv.gov/local/county/Pages/ohio.aspx>**
- **INCORPORATED:** Oct. 7, 1776
- **PARENT COUNTY:** District of West Augusta
- **BIRTH RECORDS:** start in 1853, kept by County Clerk
- **MARRIAGE:** 1790, County Clerk
- **DIVORCE:** 1831, Circuit Court
- **DEATH:** 1853, County Clerk
- **LAND:** 1778, County Clerk
- **PROBATE:** 1777, County Clerk
- **COURT:** 1818, Circuit Court
- **NOTES:** County Clerk has military discharge records 1917-1992 and naturalization records 1814-1895.

PENDLETON
Box 187, Franklin, WV 26807, (304) 358-7573, **<www.wv.gov/local/county/Pages/pendleton.aspx>**
- **INCORPORATED:** Dec. 4, 1787
- **PARENT COUNTIES:** Augusta, Hardy and Rockingham
- **BIRTH RECORDS:** start in 1853, kept by County Clerk
- **MARRIAGE:** 1797, County Clerk
- **DIVORCE:** 1789, Circuit Court
- **DEATH:** 1853, County Clerk
- **LAND:** 1788, County Clerk
- **PROBATE:** 1788, County Clerk
- **COURT:** 1788, Circuit Court

PLEASANTS
301 Court Lane, St. Marys, WV 26170, (304) 684-6976, **<www.pleasantscountywv.com>**
- **INCORPORATED:** March 29, 1851
- **PARENT COUNTIES:** Ritchie, Tyler, Wood
- **BIRTH RECORDS:** start in 1853, kept by County Clerk
- **MARRIAGE:** 1853, County Clerk
- **DIVORCE:** 1868, Circuit Court
- **DEATH:** 1853, County Clerk
- **LAND:** 1851, County Clerk
- **PROBATE:** 1851, County Clerk
- **COURT:** 1868, Circuit Court

POCAHONTAS
900C Tenth Ave., Marlinton, WV 24954, (304) 799-6063, **<www.pocahontascountywv.com>**
- **INCORPORATED:** Dec. 21, 1821
- **PARENT COUNTIES:** Pendleton, Randolph, Bath
- **BIRTH RECORDS:** start in 1853, kept by County Clerk
- **MARRIAGE:** 1822, County Clerk
- **DIVORCE:** 1881, Circuit Court
- **DEATH:** 1853, County Clerk
- **LAND:** 1822, County Clerk
- **PROBATE:** 1822, County Clerk
- **COURT:** 1881, Circuit Court

PRESTON
106 W Main St., Kingwood, WV 26537, (304) 329-1805, **<www.prestoncountywv.com>**
- **INCORPORATED:** Jan. 19, 1818
- **PARENT COUNTY:** Monongalia
- **BIRTH RECORDS:** start in 1868, kept by County Clerk
- **MARRIAGE:** 1869, County Clerk
- **DIVORCE:** 1864, Circuit Court
- **DEATH:** 1868, County Clerk
- **LAND:** 1869, County Clerk
- **PROBATE:** 1869, County Clerk
- **COURT:** 1864, Circuit Court

PUTNAM
3389 Winfield Rd., Winfield, WV 25213, (304) 586-0202, **<www.putnamcounty.org>**
- **INCORPORATED:** March 11, 1848
- **PARENT COUNTIES:** Kanawha, Mason, Cabell
- **BIRTH RECORDS:** start in 1853, kept by County Clerk
- **MARRIAGE:** 1848, County Clerk
- **DIVORCE:** 1848, Circuit Court
- **DEATH:** 1853, County Clerk
- **LAND:** 1848, County Clerk
- **PROBATE:** 1847, County Clerk
- **COURT:** 1848, Circuit Court

RALEIGH
County Courthouse, 215 Main St., Beckley, WV 25801, (304) 255-9166, **<www.raleighcounty.com>**
- **INCORPORATED:** Jan. 23, 1850
- **PARENT COUNTY:** Fayette
- **BIRTH RECORDS:** start in 1853, kept by County Clerk
- **MARRIAGE:** 1850, County Clerk
- **DIVORCE:** 1850, Circuit Court
- **DEATH:** 1853, County Clerk
- **LAND:** 1850, County Clerk

- **PROBATE:** 1850, County Clerk
- **COURT:** 1850, Circuit Court
- **NOTES:** County Clerk has military discharge records 1917-1943 and naturalization records 1908-1949.

RANDOLPH

Randolph County Courthouse, Box 2092, Elkins, WV 26241, (304) 636-2114, **<www.wv.gov/local/county/Pages/randolph.aspx>**

- **INCORPORATED:** October 1787
- **PARENT COUNTY:** Harrison
- **BIRTH RECORDS:** start in 1853, kept by County Clerk
- **MARRIAGE:** 1787, County Clerk
- **DEATH:** 1853, County Clerk
- **LAND:** 1787, County Clerk
- **PROBATE:** 1787, County Clerk
- **NOTES:** County Clerk has naturalization records 1907-1929.

RITCHIE

115 E. Main St., Harrisville, WV 26362, (304) 643-2164, **<www.wv.gov/local/county/Pages/ritchie.aspx>**

- **INCORPORATED:** Feb. 18, 1843
- **PARENT COUNTIES:** Harrison, Lewis, Wood
- **BIRTH RECORDS:** start in 1853, kept by County Clerk
- **MARRIAGE:** 1843, County Clerk
- **DIVORCE:** 1843, Circuit Court
- **DEATH:** 1889, County Clerk
- **LAND:** 1843, County Clerk
- **PROBATE:** 1843, County Clerk
- **COURT:** 1843, Circuit Court
- **NOTES:** County Clerk has military discharge records 1918-1975.

ROANE

200 Main St., Spencer, WV 25276, (304) 927-2860, **<www.wv.gov/local/county/Pages/roane.aspx>**

- **INCORPORATED:** March 11, 1856
- **PARENT COUNTIES:** Kanawha, Jackson, Gilmer
- **BIRTH RECORDS:** start in 1856, kept by County Clerk
- **MARRIAGE:** 1856, County Clerk
- **DIVORCE:** 1856, Circuit Court
- **DEATH:** 1856, County Clerk
- **LAND:** 1856, County Clerk
- **PROBATE:** 1857, County Clerk
- **COURT:** 1856, Circuit Court

SUMMERS

Box 97, Hinton, WV 25951, (304) 466-7100, **<summerscountywv.org>**

- **INCORPORATED:** Feb. 27, 1871
- **PARENT COUNTIES:** Greenbrier, Monroe, Mercer, Fayette
- **BIRTH RECORDS:** start in 1871, kept by County Clerk
- **MARRIAGE:** 1871, County Clerk
- **DIVORCE:** 1874, Circuit Court
- **DEATH:** 1871, County Clerk
- **LAND:** 1870, County Clerk
- **PROBATE:** 1854, County Clerk
- **COURT:** 1871, Circuit Court
- **NOTES:** County Clerk has naturalization records 1908-1945.

TAYLOR

214 W. Main St., Grafton, WV 26354, (304) 265-0880, **<www.wv.gov/local/county/Pages/taylor.aspx>**

- **INCORPORATED:** Jan. 19, 1844
- **PARENT COUNTIES:** Barbour, Harrison, Marion
- **BIRTH RECORDS:** start in 1853, kept by County Clerk
- **MARRIAGE:** 1853, County Clerk
- **DIVORCE:** 1881, Circuit Court
- **DEATH:** 1853, County Clerk
- **LAND:** 1844, County Clerk
- **PROBATE:** 1844, County Clerk
- **COURT:** 1881, Circuit Court
- **NOTES:** County Clerk has military discharge records 1918-1946.

TUCKER

215 First St., Parsons, WV 26287, (304) 478-2866, **<www.wv.gov/local/county/Pages/tucker.aspx>**

- **INCORPORATED:** March 7, 1856
- **PARENT COUNTY:** Randolph
- **BIRTH RECORDS:** start in 1856, kept by County Clerk
- **MARRIAGE:** 1856, County Clerk
- **DIVORCE:** 1856, Circuit Court
- **DEATH:** 1852, County Clerk
- **LAND:** 1856, County Clerk
- **PROBATE:** 1852, County Clerk
- **COURT:** 1856, Circuit Court
- **NOTES:** County Clerk has naturalization records 1904-1950.

TYLER

121 Main St., Middlebourne, WV 26149, **<www.wv.gov/local/county/Pages/tyler.aspx>**

- **INCORPORATED:** Dec. 6, 1814
- **PARENT COUNTY:** Ohio
- **BIRTH RECORDS:** start in 1853, kept by County Clerk
- **MARRIAGE:** 1815, County Clerk
- **DIVORCE:** 1873, Circuit Court
- **DEATH:** 1853, County Clerk
- **LAND:** 1815, County Clerk
- **PROBATE:** 1815, County Clerk
- **COURT:** 1815, Circuit Court
- **NOTES:** County Clerk has military discharge records 1917-1970.

UPSHUR

38 W. Main St., Buckhannon, WV 26201, (304) 472-1068, **<www.wv.gov/local/county/Pages/upshur.aspx>**

- **INCORPORATED:** March 26, 1851
- **PARENT COUNTIES:** Randolph, Barbour, Lewis
- **NOTES:** County Clerk has naturalization records 1908-1928.
- **BIRTH RECORDS:** start in 1853, kept by County Clerk
- **MARRIAGE:** 1853, County Clerk
- **DIVORCE:** 1874, Circuit Court
- **DEATH:** 1853, County Clerk
- **LAND:** 1851, County Clerk
- **PROBATE:** 1852, County Clerk
- **COURT:** 1851, Circuit Court

WAYNE

Box 248, Wayne, WV 25570, (304) 272-6350, **<www.waynecountywv.org>**

- **INCORPORATED:** Jan. 18, 1842
- **PARENT COUNTY:** Cabell
- **BIRTH RECORDS:** start in 1853, kept by County Clerk
- **MARRIAGE:** 1853, County Clerk
- **DIVORCE:** 1843, Circuit Court
- **DEATH:** 1853, County Clerk
- **LAND:** 1842, County Clerk
- **PROBATE:** 1843, County Clerk
- **COURT:** 1843, Circuit Court

WEBSTER

2 Court Sq., Webster Springs, WV 26288, (304) 847-5904, **<www.wv.gov/local/county/Pages/webster.aspx>**

- **INCORPORATED:** Jan. 10, 1860
- **PARENT COUNTIES:** Braxton, Nicholas, Randolph
- **BIRTH RECORDS:** start in 1887, kept by County Clerk
- **MARRIAGE:** 1888, County Clerk
- **DIVORCE:** 1875, Circuit Court
- **DEATH:** 1887, County Clerk
- **LAND:** 1877, County Clerk
- **PROBATE:** 1888, County Clerk
- **COURT:** 1875, Circuit Court
- **NOTES:** County Clerk has military discharge records 1918-1945.

WETZEL

Box 156, New Martinsville, WV 26155, (304) 455-8224, **<www.wv.gov/local/county/Pages/wetzel.aspx>**

- **INCORPORATED:** Jan. 10, 1846
- **PARENT COUNTY:** Tyler
- **BIRTH RECORDS:** start in 1845, kept by County Clerk
- **MARRIAGE:** 1845, County Clerk
- **DIVORCE:** 1846, Circuit Court
- **DEATH:** 1845, County Clerk
- **LAND:** 1845, County Clerk
- **PROBATE:** 1845, County Clerk
- **COURT:** 1846, Circuit Court
- **NOTES:** County Clerk has military discharge records 1917-1992 and naturalization records 1913-1920, 1922-1927.

WIRT

Box 53, Elizabeth, WV 26143, (304) 275-4048, **<www.wv.gov/local/county/Pages/wirt.aspx>**

- **INCORPORATED:** Jan. 19, 1848
- **PARENT COUNTIES:** Wood, Jackson
- **BIRTH RECORDS:** start in 1870, kept by County Clerk
- **MARRIAGE:** 1854, County Clerk
- **DIVORCE:** 1849, Circuit Court
- **DEATH:** 1870, County Clerk
- **LAND:** 1848, County Clerk
- **PROBATE:** 1848, County Clerk
- **COURT:** 1849, Circuit Court

WOOD

One Court Square, Parkersburg, WV 26101, (304) 424-1850, **<www.woodcountywv.com>**

- **INCORPORATED:** Dec. 21, 1798
- **PARENT COUNTY:** Harrison
- **BIRTH RECORDS:** start in 1853, kept by County Clerk
- **MARRIAGE:** 1801, County Clerk
- **DIVORCE:** 1831, Circuit Court
- **DEATH:** 1853, County Clerk
- **LAND:** 1802, County Clerk
- **PROBATE:** 1800, County Clerk
- **COURT:** 1803, Circuit Court
- **NOTES:** County Clerk has military discharge records 1917-1966.

WYOMING

Box 309, Pineville, WV 24874, (304) 732-8000, **<www.wyomingcounty.com/government.php?id=8>**

- **INCORPORATED:** Jan. 26, 1850
- **PARENT COUNTY:** Logan
- **BIRTH RECORDS:** start in 1853, kept by County Clerk
- **MARRIAGE:** 1855, County Clerk
- **DIVORCE:** 1850, Circuit Court
- **DEATH:** 1853, County Clerk
- **LAND:** 1850, County Clerk
- **PROBATE:** 1850, County Clerk
- **COURT:** 1850, Circuit Court
- **NOTES:** County Clerk has military discharge records 1917-1945 and naturalization records 1907-1945.

WISCONSIN

» BY JAMES W. WARREN

HISTORICAL OVERVIEW

LaVerne and Shirley bottled beer in Milwaukee, just as one of your German ancestors may have done decades earlier. But long before the first German was spoken on the western shores of Lake Michigan, the area was home to the Winnebago, Ojibway (Chippewa), Menominee, Oneida, Sauk and other Indian tribes driven west by the Iroquois.

The first European in what would become Wisconsin was Jean Nicolet in 1634. In 1690, Catholic missionaries established a mission at Michilimackinac (now Mackinac, Mich.), a focal point for traders. French traders first came to the Green Bay and Prairie du Chien areas in the 1700s. In 1763, the British gained control of the area from the French. The United States acquired it in 1783. It became part of Northwest Territory in 1787, Indiana Territory in 1800, Illinois Territory in 1809, and Michigan Territory in 1818.

Lead mining along the Illinois/Wisconsin border attracted settlers from Southern states beginning about 1820. Migration to the Lake Michigan shoreline increased in the 1830s. Many later settlers were from New York, Vermont, Pennsylvania and Ohio. Lumbering, mining, and farming were major enterprises.

In 1836, the new Wisconsin Territory included lands as far west as the Missouri River. In 1838, much of that western land was transferred to Iowa Territory. Wisconsin became the 30th state in 1848, and the last Indian lands were obtained by treaty.

In the 1840s and 1850s, large numbers of foreign immigrants arrived. Before the Civil War, Germans, Norwegians and Irish were the largest immigrant groups, with substantial numbers from other British Isles countries as well as Canada. Later groups arriving in the state included Poles, Czechs, Austrians, Swedes, Danes, Italians, Greeks, Finns, Russians and Yugoslavs.

Wisconsin sent more than 90,000 soldiers to serve with the Union in the Civil War. Its Great Lakes towns became industrial centers; the northern lakes and woods became a vacation, hunting and fishing mecca; and the southern and western farmlands earned the state its nickname of "America's Dairyland."

research tips

- The Wisconsin Historical Society (WHS) holds Wisconsin newspaper titles, a large collection of city directories, histories, genealogies, indexes, periodicals, WPA inventories, abstracts and reference material on every state and Canadian province. It holds virtually all available US and Canadian censuses, as well as microfilmed immigration passenger lists.
- You can search an index to Wisconsin vital records and other information through the Wisconsin Genealogy Index **<www.wisconsinhistory.org/vitalrecords>**.
- Norwegians were the second-largest immigrant group to Wisconsin. Research them at the Norwegian American Genealogical Center and Naeseth Library in Madison **<nagcnl.org>**.
- WHS is part of a network of 13 area research centers located around the state. See locations at **<www.wisconsinhistory.org/libraryarchives/arcnet>**.

CENSUS RECORDS

- Federal census: 1820 and 1830 (with Michigan), 1840, 1850, 1860, 1870, 1880, 1900, 1910, 1920, 1930
- Federal mortality schedules: 1850, 1880
- Special census of Civil War Union veterans and widows: 1890
- State/territorial census: 1836, 1838, 1842, 1846, 1847, 1855, 1875, 1885, 1895, 1905

RECORD HIGHLIGHTS

Available federal census population schedules for the state of Wisconsin begin with 1850. Earlier censuses record Wisconsin-area residents in 1820 and 1830 in Michigan Territory) and in 1840 in Wisconsin Territory. The 1890 census did not survive, but the Union Veterans and Widows Schedule for Wisconsin did.

Mortality schedules taken with the federal census exist for 1850, 1860, 1870 (partial) and 1880. Special censuses were also taken in Wisconsin Territory in 1836, 1838, 1840, 1842, 1846 and 1847. Wisconsin took state censuses in 1855, 1865, 1875, 1885, 1895 and 1905. These records are available on microfilm at the Wisconsin Historical Society, as are indexes to many of them. Some are also on microfilm at the Family History Library (FHL). State censuses are not especially detailed until 1905, which includes such information as age, marital status, place of birth, parents' place of birth and occupation, and also includes a veterans' enumeration.

Pre-1907 birth, death and marriage records are microfilmed and available through the FHL, the Wisconsin Historical Society, and the 13 Area Research Centers in Wisconsin. Some births and deaths were recorded as early as the 1850s, but most date from the 1870s or later. Marriage records for some counties date from as early as 1816. Statewide registration of vital records began in 1907. You can search a vital records index and order copies online at **<www.wisconsinhistory.org/vitalrecords>**. Birth, death or marriage records 1907 and later can be obtained from the Vital Records Office at 1 West Wilson Street in Madison (Box 309, Madison, WI 53701, (608) 266-1371, **<dhs.wisconsin.gov/vitalrecords>**.

Circuit and County Courts have, at various times, had jurisdiction over all court matters, including civil and criminal cases, divorce, probate, adoption, juvenile cases, dependency and neglect. Naturalization records from about three-fourths of the counties have been transferred to Area Research Centers. For the other counties, the Circuit Clerk Court should still have the records.

Divorce records are held by the County or Circuit Court Clerk. Probate records are held by the Clerk of County Court. Land records at the county courthouse are found with the Register of Deeds. The FHL has filmed naturalizations and probate files, many land grantee-grantor indexes, and some deeds for some counties.

Church and cemetery records for Wisconsin are abundant. The Wisconsin Historical Society **<www.wisconsinhistory.org>** holds church and cemetery abstracts, transcriptions and indexes, as well as original records or microfilm copies. The Wisconsin State Genealogical Society **<wsgs.wetpaint.com>** has published hundreds of cemetery transcriptions, and the Wisconsin State Old Cemetery Society **<my.execpc.com/~dondorf/wsocs.htm>** has card indexes to many burials. A useful guide is *Cemetery Locations in Wisconsin* by Linda M. and Wendy K. Uncapher (Origins). Catholic and Lutheran denominations dominated Wisconsin throughout the 1800s, and the FHL has microfilmed records from many Wisconsin churches, including parish records to about 1920 of the Roman Catholic Archdiocese of Milwaukee. Microfilms of the records of more than 200 Lutheran Wisconsin congregations are held by the Evangelical Lutheran Church in America **<www.elca.org>** archives in Chicago. Most churches and cemeteries still have their original records.

ARCHIVES, LIBRARIES, AND SOCIETIES

African American Genealogical Society of Milwaukee
Martin Luther King Public Library, 310 W. Locust St., Milwaukee, WI 53212, **<www.rootsweb.ancestry.com/~wiaagsm>**

Ancestors of Richland County Hills
325 N. Central Ave., Richland Center, WI 535481, (608) 647-6444, **<www.rootsweb.ancestry.com/~wirichla>**

Archdiocese of Milwaukee
1501 S. Layton Blvd., Milwaukee, WI 53215, (414) 758-2200, **<www.archmil.org>**

Ashland County Historical Society
509 W. Main St., Ashland, WI 54806, (715) 682-4911, **<www.ashlandhistory.com>**

Barron County Genealogical Society
1672-17 1/2 St., Barron, WI 54812, (715) 234-7941, **<www.co.barron.wi.us>**

Bay Area Genealogical Society
Box 283, Green Bay, WI 54305, <bayareagenealogicalsociety.org>

Beaver Dam Community Library
311 N. Spring St., Beaver Dam, WI 53916, (920) 887-4631, **<www.cityofbeaverdam.com/department/?fDD=16-0>**

Black River Falls Public Library
222 Fillmore St., Black River Falls, WI 54615, (715) 284-4112, **<www.blackriverfallslibrary.org>**

Brown County Library
515 Pine St., Green Bay, WI 54301, (920) 448-4400, **<www.co.brown.wi.us/library>**

Bureau of Land Management, Eastern States Office
7450 Boston Blvd., Springfield, VA 22153, (703) 440-1600, **<www.blm.gov/es/st/en.html>**

Chalmer Davee Library, University of Wisconsin River Falls
410 S. Third St., River Falls, WI 54022, (715) 425-3911, **<www.uwrf.edu/library/govdocs>**

Charles and JoAnn Lester Memorial Library
100 Park St., Nekoosa, WI 54457, (715) 886-7879, **<www.nkpl.8m.com>**

Chippewa County Genealogical Society
123 Allen St., Chippewa Falls, WI 54729, (715) 723-4399, **<ccgswi.wetpaint.com>**

Circus World Museum
550 Water St., Baraboo, WI 53913, (866) 693-1500, **<circusworld.wisconsinhistory.org>**

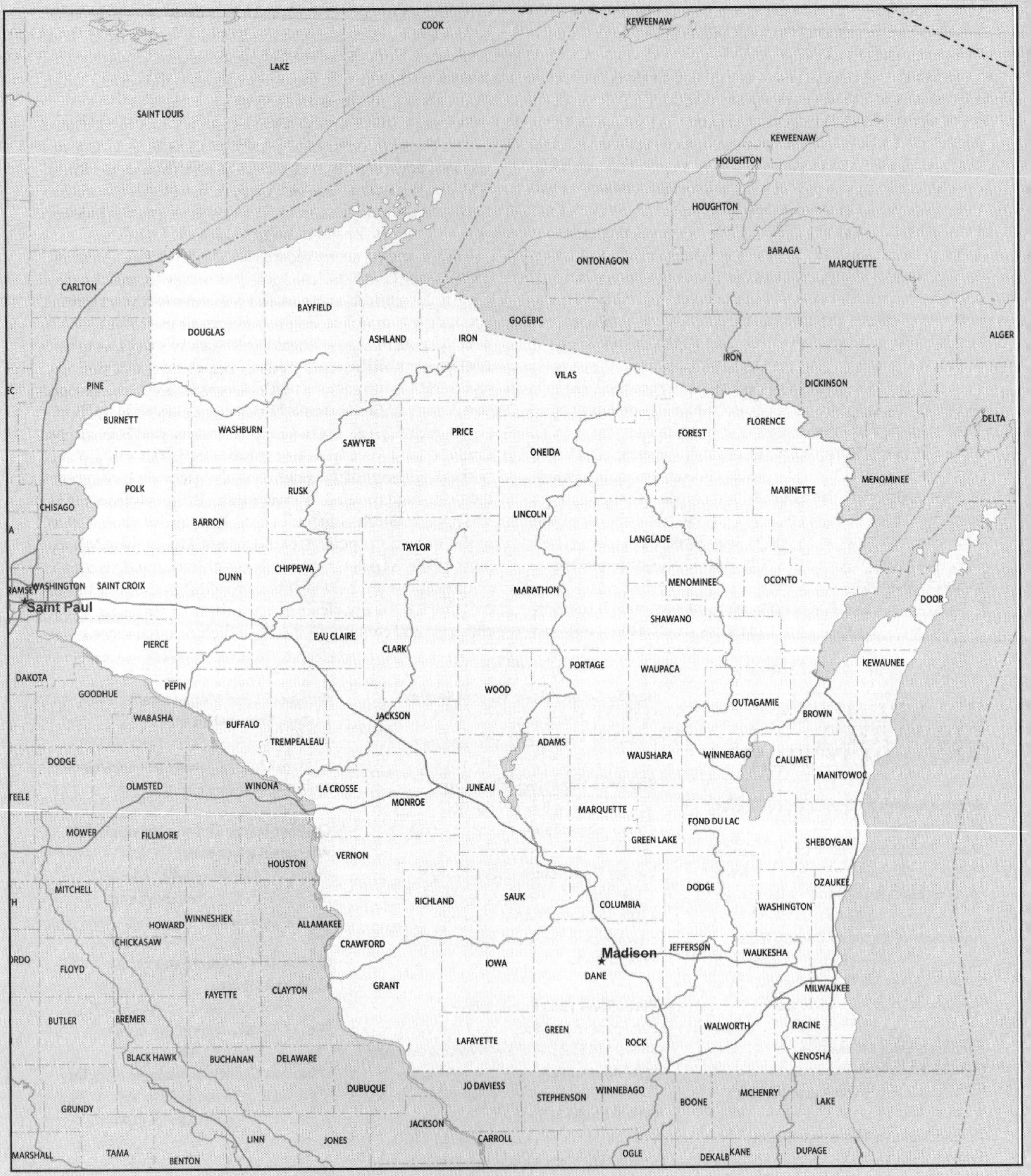
COOK
KEWEENAW
LAKE
SAINT LOUIS
KEWEENAW
HOUGHTON
HOUGHTON
BARAGA
MARQUETTE
ONTONAGON
CARLTON
BAYFIELD
GOGEBIC
ALGER
DOUGLAS
ASHLAND
IRON
IRON
VILAS
DICKINSON
PINE
BURNETT
WASHBURN
SAWYER
PRICE
FOREST
FLORENCE
DELTA
ONEIDA
MENOMINEE
POLK
RUSK
MARINETTE
CHISAGO
LINCOLN
BARRON
LANGLADE
TAYLOR
CHIPPEWA
DUNN
MENOMINEE
OCONTO
WASHINGTON
SAINT CROIX
MARATHON
DOOR
RAMSEY
Saint Paul
SHAWANO
EAU CLAIRE
PIERCE
CLARK
PORTAGE
WAUPACA
KEWAUNEE
DAKOTA
PEPIN
WOOD
GOODHUE
OUTAGAMIE
WABASHA
JACKSON
BROWN
BUFFALO
TREMPEALEAU
ADAMS
WAUSHARA
WINNEBAGO
CALUMET
DODGE
MANITOWOC
OLMSTED
WINONA
LA CROSSE
JUNEAU
MONROE
MARQUETTE
FOND DU LAC
MOWER
FILLMORE
GREEN LAKE
SHEBOYGAN
VERNON
HOUSTON
OZAUKEE
MITCHELL
DODGE
RICHLAND
SAUK
COLUMBIA
WASHINGTON
WINNESHIEK
HOWARD
ALLAMAKEE
CHICKASAW
CRAWFORD
Madison
JEFFERSON
WAUKESHA
IOWA
DANE
FLOYD
GRANT
MILWAUKEE
FAYETTE
CLAYTON
BUTLER
BREMER
GREEN
WALWORTH
RACINE
LAFAYETTE
ROCK
BLACK HAWK
BUCHANAN
DELAWARE
KENOSHA
DUBUQUE
JO DAVIESS
STEPHENSON
WINNEBAGO
BOONE
MCHENRY
LAKE
GRUNDY
JACKSON
LINN
JONES
CARROLL
OGLE
KANE
DUPAGE
DEKALB
MARSHALL
TAMA
BENTON

Commissioner of Public Lands
Box 8943, Madison, WI 53708, (608) 266-1370, **<bcpl.wisconsin.gov>**

Dodge and Jefferson Counties Genealogical Society
Box 91, Watertown, WI 53094, **<www.dodgejeffgen.com>**

Dunn County Genealogical Society
Box 633, Menomonie, WI 54731, (715) 235-0770, **<www.rootsweb.ancestry.com/~widunn/dcgs.htm>**

Eagle River Historical Society
519 Sheridan St., Eagle River, WI 54521, (715) 479-2396

Elton E. Karrmann Library, University of Wisconsin-Platteville
1 University Plaza, Platteville, WI 53818, (608) 342-1668 or (888) 450-4632, **<www.uwplatt.edu/library>**

Eugene W. Murphy Library, University of Wisconsin-La Crosse
1725 State St., La Crosse, WI 54601, (608) 785-8000, **<perth.uwlax.edu/murphylibrary/help.htm>**

Fond du Lac County Genealogical Society
Box 1264, Fond du Lac, WI 54936, (920) 929-8538, **<www.rootsweb.ancestry.com/~wifonddu/resources/organizations/fdlgensoc.htm>**

Fond du Lac County Historical Society
Box 1284, Fond du Lac, WI 54936, (920) 922-0991, **<www.fdlhistory.com>**

Fond du Lac Public Library
32 Sheboygan St., Fond du Lac, WI 54935, (920) 929-7080, **<www.fdlpl.org>**

Forrest R. Polk Library, University of Wisconsin-Oshkosh
800 Algoma Blvd., Oshkosh, WI 54901, (920) 424-4333 or (800) 574-5041, **<www.uwosh.edu/library>**

Fox Valley Genealogical Society
330 E. College Ave., Appleton, Wisconsin 54911, (920) 735-9370, **<www.foxvalleyhistory.org>**

Fox Valley of Wisconsin Chapter, American Historical Society of Germans from Russia
945 Anchorage Court, Oshkosh, WI 54901, (920) 235-7231, **<www.ahsgr.org/fox_valley_of__wisconsin_chapter.htm>**

French Canadian/Acadian Genealogies of Wisconsin
Box 414, Hales Corners, WI 53130, **<fcgw.org>**

Genealogical Research Society of Eau Claire
Chippewa Valley Museum, Box 1204, Eau Claire, WI 54702, (715) 834-7871, **<www.rootsweb.ancestry.com/~wigsec>**

Gilbert Simmons Library
711 59th Place, Kenosha, WI 53140, (262) 564-6100, **<www.mykpl.info>**

Golda Meir Library, University of Wisconsin-Milwaukee
2311 E. Hartford Ave., Milwaukee, WI 53201, (414) 229-4785, **<www4.uwm.edu/libraries>**

Grant County Genealogical Society
Box 281, Dickeyville, WI 53808, **<www.rootsweb.ancestry.com/~wigrant/gcgensoc.htm>**

Harold W. Anderson Library, University of Wisconsin-Whitewater
800 W. Main St., Whitewater, WI 53190, (414) 472-5511, **<library.uww.edu>**

Hartford Genealogical Society
c/o Hartford Public Library, 115 N. Main St., Hartford, WI 53027, (262) 673-8240, **<www.hartfordlibrary.org>**

Heart O'Wisconsin Genealogical Society
Box 516, Wisconsin Rapids, WI 54494, **<howgs.org>**

Huguenot Society of Wisconsin
8920 N. Lake Dr., Bayside, WI 53217, (414) 351-0644, **<my.execpc.com/~drg/wihs.html>**

Iowa County Genealogical Society
Box 321, Dodgeville, WI 53533, **<www.friendsnfamily.net/wiiowagensoc>**

Irish Genealogical Society of Wisconsin
Box 13766, Wauwatosa, WI 53213, **<igswonline.com>**

Jackson County Historical Society
Box 37, Black River Falls, WI 54615, (715) 284-5314

Jackson County Wisconsin Footprints
W11770 City Rd. P, Black River Falls, WI 54615, (715) 284-4807, **<www.rootsweb.ancestry.com/~wijackso>**

Kenosha County Genealogical Society
Box 25, Kenosha, WI 53141, **<www.rootsweb.ancestry.com/~wikenosh/gensoc.htm>**

Kewaunee County Historical Society
<www.rootsweb.ancestry.com/~wikewaun>

La Crosse Area Genealogical Society
Box 1782, La Crosse, WI 54602, **<www.rootsweb.ancestry.com/~wilacgs>**

La Crosse Public Library, Archives and Local History
800 Main St., La Crosse, WI 54601, (608) 789-7136, **<lacrosselibrary.org/genealogy>**

Lafayette County Genealogical Society
Box 186, Shullsburg, WI 53586, (608) 776-2755, **<www.rootsweb.ancestry.com/~wilafcgs>**

Langlade County Genealogical Society
Box 307, Antigo, WI 54409, **<www.rootsweb.ancestry.com/~wilcgs>**

Lower Wisconsin River Genealogical and Historical Research Center
60401 Wachuta Rd., Prairie du Chien, WI 53821, **<home.mchsi.com/~dragonslair>**

Manitowoc County Genealogical Society
c/o Two Rivers Lester Library, 1001 Adams St., Two Rivers, WI 54241, **<www.2manitowoc.com>**

Marathon County Historical Museum
403 McIndoe, Wausau, WI 54403, (715) 842-5750 or (715) 848-0378, **<marathoncountyhistory.com>**

Marathon County Public Library
300 N. First St., Wausau, WI 54403, (715) 261-7200, **<www.mcpl.us>**

Marathon County Genealogical Society
Box 1512, Wausau, WI 54402, **<marathoncountygenealogicalsociety.org>**

Marshfield Area Genealogical Group
500 South Birch, Marshfield, WI 54449, (715) 389-2484

Menomonee Falls Public Library
W156 N8447 Pilgrim Rd., Menomonee Falls, WI 53051, (262) 532-8900, **<www.mf.lib.wi.us>**

Max Kade Institute, German Research
901 University Bay Dr., Madison, WI 53705, (608) 262-7546, **<mki.wisc.edu>**

Menomonee Falls Historical Society
Box 91, Menomonee Falls, WI 53052

Milwaukee County Genealogical Society
Box 270326, Milwaukee, WI 53227, **<www.milwaukeegenealogy.org>**

Milwaukee County Historical Society
910 N. Old World Third St., Milwaukee, WI 53203, (414) 273-8288, **<www.milwaukeehistory.net>**

Milwaukee Public Library
814 W. Wisconsin Ave., Milwaukee, WI 53233, (414) 286-3000, **<mpl.org>**

Monroe County Local History Room
200 W. Main St., Sparta, WI 54656, (608) 269-8680, **<monroecountyhistory.org>**

National Archives, Great Lakes Region
7358 S. Pulaski Rd., Chicago, IL 60629, (773) 948-9001, **<www.archives.gov/great-lakes>**

Northland College, Dexter Library Area Research Center
1411 Ellis Ave., Ashland, WI 54806, (715) 682-1699 or (800) 753-1840, **<www.northland.edu/sustainability-campus-initiatives-dexter-library>**

Northwoods Genealogical Society
Box 1132, Rhinelander, WI 54501, **<www.genealogyforum.rootsweb.ancestry.com/gfaol/resource/WI/GS2.htm>**

Norwegian American Genealogical Center and Naeseth Library
415 W. Main St., Madison, WI 54703, (608) 255-2224, **<nagcnl.org>**

Oconomowoc Genealogical Club of Waukesha County
37198 E. Washington, Oconomowoc, WI 53066

Oshkosh Public Library
106 Washington Ave., Oshkosh, WI 54901, (920) 236-5205, **<www.oshkoshpubliclibrary.org>**

Polish Genealogical Society of Wisconsin
Box 764, Hales Corners, WI 53130

Portage County Library
1001 Main St., Stevens Point, WI 54481, (715) 346-1548, **<library.uwsp.edu/pcl>**

Rock County Genealogical Society
Box 711, Janesville, WI 53547, (608) 756-4509 or (608) 752-5891, **<www.rootsweb.ancestry.com/~wircgs>**

Roman Catholic Diocese of Green Bay
Box 23825, Green Bay, WI 54305, (920) 437-7531, **<www.gbdioc.org>**

Roman Catholic Diocese of LaCrosse
Box 4004, La Crosse, Wisconsin 54602, (608) 788-7700, **<www.dioceseoflacrosse.com>**

Roman Catholic Diocese of Madison
702 S. High Point Rd., Box 44983, Madison, WI 53719, (608) 821-3000, **<www.madisondiocese.org>**

Roman Catholic Diocese of Superior
1201 Hughitt Ave., Superior, WI 54880, (715) 392-2937, **<www.catholicdos.org>**

Saint Croix Valley Genealogical Society
Box 396, River Falls, WI 54022, **<www.pressenter.com/~scvgs>**

Sauk County Historical Society
Box 651, Baraboo, WI 53913, (608) 356-1001, **<www.saukcountyhistory.org>**

Seventh Day Baptist Historical Society
Box 1678, Janesville, WI 53547, (608) 752-5055, **<sdbhistory.org>**

Sheboygan County Historical Research Center
518 Water St., Sheboygan Falls, WI 53085, (920) 467-4667, **<www.schrc.org>**

Southeastern Wisconsin Chapter, American Historical Society of Germans from Russia
W330S7660 Horse Shoe Ct., Mukwonago, WI 53149, (262) 392-2161, **<www.ahsgr.org/southeastern_wisconsin_chapter.htm>**

St. Croix Valley Genealogical Society
Box 396, River Falls, WI 54022, **<www.pressenter.com/~scvgs>**

Stevens Point Area Genealogical Society
c/o Portage County Library, 1001 Main St., Stevens Point, WI 54481, **<www.rootsweb.ancestry.com/~wispags>**

Superior Public Library
1530 Tower Ave., Superior, WI 54880, (715) 394-8860, **<www.ci.superior.wi.us/index.aspx?NID=156>**

Taylor County Genealogical Society
224 S. Second St., Medford, WI 54451 **<www.rootsweb.ancestry.com/~witcgs>**

Village of North Fond du Lac Public Library
719 Wisconsin Ave., North Fond du Lac, WI 54937, (920) 929-3771, **<www.northfonddulaclibrary.org>**

Vital Records Office
1 W. Wilson St., Madison, WI 53703, (608) 266-1371, **<dhs.wisconsin.gov/vitalrecords>**

Walworth County Genealogical Society
Box 159, Delavan, WI 53115, **<walworthcgs.com>**

Washburn County Genealogical Society
Box 366, Shell Lake, WI 54871, **<www.mywisconsingenealogy.com/wi-county-washburn.html>**

Washington County Historical Society
320 S. Fifth Ave., West Bend, WI 53095, (262) 335-4678, **<www.historyisfun.com/index.php>**

Waukesha County Genealogical Society
Box 1541, Waukesha, WI 53187, **<www.rootsweb.ancestry.com/~wiwcgs>**

Waupaca are Genealogical Society
Box 42, King, WI 54946, **<www.wigenweb.org/waupaca/WAGS/WAGS.htm>**

White Pine Genealogical Society
Box 512, Marienette, WI 54143, **<www.wisconline.com/counties/marinette>**

William D. McIntyre Library, University of Wisconsin-Eau Claire
105 Garfield Ave., Eau Claire, WI 54702, (715) 836-3858 or (715) 836-3856, **<www.uwec.edu/Library/gp/govpub2.html>**

Winnebagoland Genealogical Society
Box 2124, Oshkosh, WI 54903, **<winnebagogenealogy.blogspot.com>**

Wisconsin Black Historical Society
2620 West Center St., Milwaukee, WI 53206, (414) 372-7677, **<wbhsm.homestead.com/home.html>**

Wisconsin Conference United Methodist Church
750 Windsor St., Sun Prairie, WI 53590, (608) 837-7328 or (888) 240-7328, **<www.wisconsinumc.org/content/index.php>**

Wisconsin Evangelical Lutheran Synod
Department of Archives and History, 2929 North Mayfair Rd., Milwaukee, WI 53222, (414) 256-3888, **<www.wels.net>**

Wisconsin Genealogical Council
N9307 Abitz Lane, Luxemburg, WI 54217

Wisconsin Historical Society
816 State St., Madison, WI 53706, **<www.wisconsinhistory.org/libraryarchives>**

Wisconsin State Genealogical Society
Box 5106, Madison, WI 53705, **<wsgs.wetpaint.com>**

Wisconsin State Old Cemetery Society
6100 W. Mequon Rd., Mequon, WI 53092, (262) 242-3290, **<my.execpc.com/~dondorf/wsocs.htm>**

Wyllie Library/Learning Center, University of Wisconsin-Parkside
900 Wood Rd., Kenosha, WI 53141, (262) 595-2077 or (262) 595-2411, **<www.wisconsinhistory.org/libraryarchives/arcnet/parkside.asp>**

☞ GENERAL RESOURCES

The Bench and Bar of Wisconsin: History and Biography by Parker McCobb Reed (P.M. Reed, 1882)

Biography Index to the Wisconsin Blue Books by Darlene E. Waterstreet (Badger Infosearch, 1974)

Black Settlers in Rural Wisconsin by Zachary Cooper (State Historical Society of Wisconsin, 1997)

Brethren in Northern Illinois and Wisconsin by John Heckman (Brethren Publishing House, 1941)

The Catholic Church in Wisconsin: A History Of the Catholic Church in Wisconsin from the Earliest Time to the Present Day by Harry H. Heming (Catholic Historical Publishing Co., 1895-1898)

Collections of the State Historical Society of Wisconsin, 24 vols., by Lyman Copeland Draper (State Historical Society of Wisconsin, 1855-)

Columbian Biographical Dictionary and Portrait Gallery by David I. Nelke (Lewis Publishing Co., 1895)

Cross and Flame in Wisconsin: the Story of United Methodism in the Badger State by William Blake (United Methodist Church, Wisconsin Conference, 1973)

Dictionary of Wisconsin Biography (State Historical Society, 1960)

Directory of Churches and Religious Organizations in Wisconsin from the Historical Records Survey (Wisconsin Historical Records Survey, 1941)

French-Canadian Families Of the North Central States: A Genealogical Dictionary, 8 vols., by Paul J. Lareau and Elmer Courteau (Northwest Territory French and Canadian Heritage Institute, 1980)

Genealogical Research: An Introduction to the Resources of the State Historical Society of Wisconsin by Jame P. Danky (State Historical Society of Wisconsin, 1986)

Ghost Towns of Wisconsin by William F. Stark (Zimmermann Press, 1977)

Guide to Church Vital Statistics Records in Wisconsin from the Historical Records Survey (Wisconsin Historical Records Survey, 1942)

Guide to the Manuscripts of the Wisconsin Historical Society edited by Alice E. Smith (State Historical Society of Wisconsin, 1944, 1957)

Guide to Wisconsin Newspapers, 1833-1957 by Donald E. Oehlerts (State Historical Society of Wisconsin, 1958)

History of the Catholic Church in Wisconsin by Leo Rummel (Wisconsin State Council, Knights of Columbus, 1976)

History of Methodism in Wisconsin by Pansy S. Bennett (Cranston & Stowe, 1890)

History of Northern Wisconsin (Western Historical Society, 1881)

History of the Presbyterian and Congregational Churches and Ministers in Wisconsin by Stephen Peet (S. Chapman, 1851)

History of Wisconsin, 6 vols., (State Historical Society, 1973-1988)

An Illustrated History of the State of Wisconsin: Being a Complete Civil, Political and Military History of the State from its First Exploration Down to 1875 by Charles Richard Tuttle (B.B. Russell, 1875)

Index to Green Bay Newspapers, 1833-1840 by Barry Christopher Noonan (Wisconsin State Historical Society, 1987)

Introduction to Wisconsin Indians: Prehistory to Statehood by Carol I. Mason (Sheffield Publishing, 1988)

Men of Progress, Wisconsin by Andrew J. Aikens (Evening Wisconsin Co., 1897)

Newspapers in the State Historical Society ***of Wisconsin: A Bibliography with Holdings***, 2 vols., by Jame P. Danky (Norman Ross, 1994)

Notable Men of Wisconsin (W.C. Cox Co., 1974)

Printed Resources for Genealogical Searching in Wisconsin: A Selective Bibliography by Margaret Gleason (Detroit Society for Genealogical Research, 1964)

Regathering of the Scattered Saints in Wisconsin And Illinois by Pearl Wilcox (P. Wilcox, 1984)

Searching for Your Wisconsin Ancestors in the Wisconsin Libraries by Carol Ward Ryan (Carol Ward Ryan, 1988)

Subject Bibliography of Wisconsin History by Leroy Schlinkert (State Historical Society of Wisconsin, 1947)

United States Biographical Dictionary and Portrait: Gallery of Eminent and Self-made Men: Wisconsin Volume (American Biographical Publishing, 1877)

Wisconsin Doomsday Book: Town Studies from the State Historical Society of Wisconsin (George Santa Publishing Co., 1924)

Wisconsin's Early French by Jo Bartels Alderson (Heritage Books, 1988)

The Wisconsin Fur-Trade People by Les Rentmeester (L & J Rentmeester, 1991)

Wisconsin Genealogical Research by Linda M. Herrick (Origins, 1996)

Wisconsin History: An Annotated Bibliography by Barbara Dotts Paul (Greenwood Press, 1999)
Wisconsin: Its History and Its People, 1634-1924, 4 vols., by Milo Milton Quaife (S.J.Clarke Publishing Co., 1924)

Wisconsin Indians by Nancy Ostrich Lurie (State Historical Society of Wisconsin, 1980)

Wisconsin Research Outline by the Church of Jesus Christ of Latter-day Saints (online at <www.familysearch.org/eng/search/RG/guide/wisconsin.asp>)

Wisconsin: Its Story and Biography, 1848-1913, 8 vols., by Ellis B. Usher (Lewis Publishing Co., 1914)

☞IMMIGRATION RECORDS

A German State? in Wisconsin: A Bicentennial History by Richard Nelson Current (WW Norton & Co., 1977)

Immigration to Wisconsin: A Thesis by Maude Sachtjen (University of Wisconsin, 1928)

Misc. Naturalization Records, 1840-1906 from the Wisconsin Supreme, Circuit, and Municipal Courts, State Historical Society (filmed by the Family History Library)

☞LAND RECORDS

Conquest of the Country Northwest of The River Ohio, 1778-1783, and Life of General George Rogers Clark: With Numerous Sketches of Men Who Served Under Clark and Full List of Those Allotted Lands in Clark's Grant for Service in the Campaigns Against the British Posts, Showing Exact Land Allotted Each, 2 vols., by William Hayden English (Bowen-Merrill, 1896)

Land Records: AL, AR, FL, LA, MI, MN, OH, WI (Broderbund, 1996, CD-ROM)

Wisconsin, 1820-1908 Cash and Homestead Entries, Cadastral Survey Plats from the Bureau of Land Management (BLM Eastern states, 1994)

☞MAPS

Atlas of the State of Wisconsin by H.F. Walling (Walling, Tackabury and Co., 1876)

Atlas of Wisconsin: General Maps and Gazetteers by Arthur Robinson and Jerry B. Culver (University of Wisconsin Press, 1974)

Historical Atlas and Chronology of County Boundaries, 1788-1980, 5 vols., edited by John H. Long (G.K. Hall, 1984)

Historical Atlas of Wisconsin by Van Vechten Snyder & Co. (Origins, 1995)

Maps and Atlases Showing Land Ownership in Wisconsin compiled by Michael J. Fox (State Historical Society of Wisconsin, 1978)

The Romance of Wisconsin Place Names by Robert E. Gard and L.G. Sorden (1968; Heartland Press, 1988)

Wisconsin Atlas & Gazetteer (DeLorme Mapping Co., 1988)

Wisconsin, Atlas of Historical County Boundaries by Gordon DenBoer (Charles Scribner's Sons, 1997)

Wisconsin: Comprising Sketches of Counties, Towns, Events, Institutions and Persons Arranged in Cyclopedic Form edited by George W. Peck (Western Historical Association, 1906)

Wisconsin County Maps compiled by C.J. Puetz (Thomas Publishing Co., 1992)

Wisconsin Post Office Handbook, 1921-1971 compiled by James B. Hale (Wisconsin Postal History Society, 1971)

☞MILITARY RECORDS

Admission Applications, 1867-1872, National Home for Disabled Volunteer Soldiers, Northwestern Branch, Milwaukee, Wisconsin by Leslie Elizabeth Miljat (L.E. Miljat, 1991)

Researching Your Civil War Ancestors in Wisconsin by Denis R. Moore (Bivouac Publications, 1994)

Wisconsin's Gold Star List: Soldiers, Sailors, Marines and Nurses From the Badger State (State Historical Society of Wisconsin, 1925)

☞PROBATE RECORDS

Guide to the Wisconsin State Archives by David J. Delgado (State Historical Society of Wisconsin, 1966)

☞VITAL RECORDS

Bible and Cemetery Records, 1700-1940 from the Daughters of the American Revolution (filmed by the Family History Library, 1970)

Cemetery Locations in Wisconsin by Linda M. Herrick and Wendy K. Uncapher (Origins 1998)

Index to deaths Reported in "The Wisconsin Jewish Chronicle," 1921-1961 by Manning M. Bookstaff (M.M. Bookstaff, 1994)

Registration of Births, 1852-1907 from the Wisconsin Bureau of Health Statistics (Wisconsin State Historical Society, 1979)

Registration of Deaths, ca. 1862-1907 from the Wisconsin Bureau of Health Statistics (filmed by the Genealogical society of Utah, 1981)

•-COUNTY DETAILS-•

ADAMS

100 Main St., Friendship, WI 53934, (608) 339-4200, **<www.co.adams.wi.gov>**

- **INCORPORATED:** March 11, 1848
- **PARENT COUNTY:** Portage
- **BIRTH RECORDS:** 1908, Registrar of Deeds
- **MARRIAGE:** 1908, Registrar of Deeds
- **DIVORCE:** start in 1848, kept by Circuit Court
- **DEATH:** 1908, Registrar of Deeds
- **LAND:** 1853, Registrar of Deeds
- **PROBATE:** 1929, Registrar in Probate
- **COURT:** 1848, Circuit Court
- **NOTES:** The James H. Alberton Library of the University of Wisconsin, Stevens Point has birth records 1857-1907, death records 1876-1907, marriage records 1854-1907, naturalization records 1853-1949, and probate records 1848-1928.

ASHLAND

201 W. Main St., Ashland, WI 54806, (715) 682-7000, **<co.ashland.wi.us>**

- **INCORPORATED:** March 27, 1860
- **PARENT COUNTY:** La Pointe
- **BIRTH RECORDS:** 1908, Registrar of Deeds
- **MARRIAGE:** 1908, Registrar of Deeds
- **DIVORCE:** start in 1905, kept by Circuit Court
- **DEATH:** 1908, Registrar of Deeds
- **LAND:** 1873, Registrar of Deeds
- **PROBATE:** 1890, Registrar in Probate
- **COURT:** 1905, Circuit Court
- **NOTES:** Northern Great Lakes Visitors Center, History Center and Archives has birth records 1852-1907, Court records 1873-1904, death records 1877-1907, divorce records 1873-1904, land records 1856-1872, marriage records 1874-1907, and naturalization records 1879-1992.

BAD AX

- **INCORPORATED:** March 1851
- **PARENT COUNTIES:** Crawford, Richland
- **NOTES:** See Vernon County. Name changed to Vernon 1865.

BARRON

330 E. La Salle Ave., Barron, WI 54812, (715) 537-6200, **<www.barroncountywi.gov>**

- **INCORPORATED:** March 1859
- **PARENT COUNTY:** St. Croix
- **BIRTH RECORDS:** 1908, Registrar of Deeds
- **MARRIAGE:** 1908, Registrar of Deeds
- **DEATH:** 1908, Registrar of Deeds
- **LAND:** 1962, Registrar of Deeds
- **PROBATE:** 1910, Registrar in Probate
- **COURT:** start in 1963, kept by Circuit Court
- **NOTES:** University of Wisconsin-Stout, Library Learning Center has birth records 1877-1907, Court records 1875-1962, death records 1876-1907, land records 1888-1961, naturalization records 1874-1954, marriage records 1871-1907, and probate records 1882-1909. Formerly Dallas County. Name changed to Barron 1869.

BAYFIELD

117 E. Fifth St., Washburn, WI 54891, (715) 373-6138, **<www.bayfieldcounty.org>**

- **INCORPORATED:** February 1845
- **PARENT COUNTY:** St. Croix
- **BIRTH RECORDS:** 1908, Registrar of Deeds
- **MARRIAGE:** 1908, Registrar of Deeds
- **DIVORCE:** start in 1985, kept by Circuit Court
- **DEATH:** 1908, Registrar of Deeds
- **LAND:** 1845, Registrar of Deeds
- **PROBATE:** 1870, Registrar in Probate
- **COURT:** 1985, Circuit Court
- **NOTES:** The Northern Great Lakes Visitors Center, History Center

and Archives has birth records 1852-1907, Court records 1888-1984, death records 1862-1907, divorce records 1889-1984, and naturalization records 1859-1945. Formerly La Pointe County. Name changed to Bayfield in 1866.

BROWN

100 S. Jefferson St., Box 23600, Green Bay, WI 54305, (920) 448-4016, **<www.co.brown.wi.us>**

- **INCORPORATED:** Oct. 26, 1818
- **PARENT COUNTY:** Michigan Territory
- **BIRTH RECORDS:** 1908, Registrar of Deeds
- **MARRIAGE:** 1908, Registrar of Deeds
- **DIVORCE:** start in 1940, kept by Circuit Court
- **DEATH:** 1908, Registrar of Deeds
- **LAND:** 1903, Registrar of Deeds
- **PROBATE:** 1922, Registrar in Probate
- **COURT:** 1940 Circuit Court
- **NOTES:** University of Wisconsin-Green Bay, Cofrin Library has birth records 1746-1907, court records 1823-1939, death records 1834-1907, divorce records 1823-1939, land records 1820-1902, marriage records 1821-1907, naturalization records 1829-1984, and probate records 1821-1921. See Michigan for 1820-1830 census.

BUFFALO

407 S. Second St., Box 28, Alma, WI 54610, (608) 685-6213, **<www.buffalocounty.com>**

- **INCORPORATED:** July 8, 1853
- **PARENT COUNTY:** Jackson
- **BIRTH RECORDS:** 1908, Registrar of Deeds
- **MARRIAGE:** 1908, Registrar of Deeds
- **DIVORCE:** start in 1985, kept by Circuit Court
- **DEATH:** 1908, Registrar of Deeds
- **LAND:** 1893, Registrar of Deeds
- **PROBATE:** 1902, Registrar in Probate
- **COURT:** 1985, Circuit Court
- **NOTES:** University of Wisconsin-Eau Claire, William D. McIntyre Library has birth records 1852-1907, Court records 1854-1984, death records 1874-1907, divorce: records 1854-1984, land records 1854-1892, marriage records 1860-1907, naturalization records 1907-1929, and probate records 1854-1901.

BURNETT

7410 County Rd. K, Siren, WI 54872, (715) 349-2169, **<www.burnettcounty.com>**

- **INCORPORATED:** March 1856
- **PARENT COUNTY:** Polk, Douglas
- **BIRTH RECORDS:** 1908, Registrar of Deeds
- **MARRIAGE:** 1908, Registrar of Deeds
- **DIVORCE:** 1856, University of Wisconsin-River Falls, Chalmer Davee Library
- **DEATH:** 1908, Registrar of Deeds
- **LAND:** start in 1856, kept by Registrar of Deeds
- **PROBATE:** 1856, Registrar in Probate
- **NOTES:** University of Wisconsin-River Falls, Chalmer Davee Library has birth records 1853-1907, death records 1846-1907, marriage records 1869-1907, and naturalization records 1859-1953. Clerk of Circuit Court has court records from early 1900s.

CALUMET

206 Court St., Chilton, WI 53014, (920) 849-1458, **<www.co.calumet.wi.us>**

- **INCORPORATED:** December 1836
- **PARENT COUNTY:** Brown
- **BIRTH RECORDS:** 1908 Registrar of Deeds
- **MARRIAGE:** 1908, Registrar of Deeds
- **DIVORCE:** start in 1880, kept by Circuit Court
- **DEATH:** 1908, Registrar of Deeds
- **LAND:** 1840, Registrar of Deeds
- **PROBATE:** 1868, Registrar in Probate
- **COURT:** 1877, Circuit Court
- **NOTES:** University of Wisconsin-Green Bay, Cofrin Library has birth records 1858-1907, death records 1856-1907, marriage records 1850-1907, and naturalization records 1850-1955.

CHIPPEWA

711 N. Bridge St., Chippewa Falls, WI 54729, (715) 726-7985, **<www.co.chippewa.wi.us>**

- **INCORPORATED:** Feb. 3, 1845
- **PARENT COUNTY:** Crawford
- **BIRTH RECORDS:** 1908, Registrar of Deeds
- **MARRIAGE:** 1908, Registrar of Deeds
- **DIVORCE:** start in 1951, kept by Circuit Court
- **DEATH:** 1858, Registrar of Deeds
- **LAND:** 1886, Registrar of Deeds
- **PROBATE:** 1901, Registrar in Probate
- **NOTES:** University of Wisconsin-Eau Claire, William D. McIntyre Library has birth records 1852-1907, divorce records 1854-1950, land records 1856-1885, marriage records 1869-1907, naturalization records 1871-1923, and probate records 1860-1900. Clerk of Circuit Court has court records 1854-1951.

CLARK

517 Court St., Neillsville, WI 54456, (715) 743-5148, **<www.co.clark.wi.us/ClarkCounty>**

- **INCORPORATED:** July 6, 1853
- **PARENT COUNTY:** Jackson
- **BIRTH RECORDS:** 1908, Registrar of Deeds
- **MARRIAGE:** 1908, Registrar of Deeds
- **DEATH:** 1908, Registrar of Deeds
- **LAND:** start in 1855, kept by Registrar of Deeds
- **PROBATE:** 1919, Registrar in Probate
- **NOTES:** University of Wisconsin-Eau Claire, William D. McIntyre Library has birth records 1852-1907, death records 1879-1907, marriage records 1858-1907, naturalization records 1907-1927, and probate records 1873-1918. Clerk of Circuit Court has divorce records from late 1800s.

COLUMBIA

400 DeWitt St., Portage, WI 53901, (608) 742-2191, **<www.co.columbia.wi.us/ColumbiaCounty>**

- **INCORPORATED:** Feb. 3, 1845
- **PARENT COUNTY:** Portage
- **BIRTH RECORDS:** 1860, Registrar of Deeds
- **MARRIAGE:** 1849, Registrar of Deeds
- **DIVORCE:** unknown start, kept by Circuit Court
- **DEATH:** 1877, Registrar of Deeds

- **LAND:** 1937, Registrar of Deeds
- **PROBATE:** 1856, Registrar in Probate
- **COURT:** unknown start, Circuit Court
- **NOTES:** Wisconsin State Archives, Wisconsin Historical Society has Land records 1826-1936. State Archives has naturalization records 1845-1955.

CRAWFORD

220 N. Beaumont Rd., Prairie du Chien, WI 53821, (608) 326-0201, **<crawfordcountywi.org>**

- **INCORPORATED:** Oct. 26, 1818
- **PARENT COUNTY:** Michigan Territory
- **BIRTH RECORDS:** 1908, Registrar of Deeds
- **MARRIAGE:** 1908, Registrar of Deeds
- **DIVORCE:** 1848 Circuit Court
- **DEATH:** 1908, Registrar of Deeds
- **LAND:** ca. 1700 Registrar of Deeds
- **PROBATE:** start in ca. 1850, kept by County Clerk
- **COURT:** 1848 Circuit Court
- **NOTES:** University of Wisconsin-Platteville, Southwest Wisconsin room, Karrmann Library has birth records 1858-1907, death records 1876-1907, marriage records 1862-1907, and naturalization records 1824-1950. Crawford County was part of Michigan Territory until 1836, when Wisconsin territory was formed.

DALLAS

- **INCORPORATED:** March 1859
- **PARENT COUNTY:** St. Croix
- **NOTES:** Name changed to Barron in 1869.

DANE

215 S. Hamilton St., Madison, WI 53703, (608) 266-4121, **<www.countyofdane.com>**

- **INCORPORATED:** Dec. 7, 1836
- **PARENT COUNTIES:** Crawford, Iowa, Milwaukee
- **BIRTH RECORDS:** 1876, Registrar of Deeds
- **MARRIAGE:** 1839, Registrar of Deeds
- **DIVORCE:** start in 1929, kept by Circuit Court
- **DEATH:** 1876, Registrar of Deeds
- **LAND:** 1979, Registrar of Deeds
- **PROBATE:** 1848, Registrar in Probate
- **COURT:** 1977, Circuit Court
- **NOTES:** The Wisconsin State Archives, Wisconsin Historical Society has court records 1839-1976, divorce records 1839-1928, land records 1835-1978, military discharge records 1918-1994, and naturalization records 1841-1954.

DODGE

127 E. Oak St., Juneau, WI 53039, (920) 386-3600, **<www.co.dodge.wi.us>**

- **INCORPORATED:** December 1836
- **PARENT COUNTIES:** Brown, Milwaukee
- **BIRTH RECORDS:** 1908, Registrar of Deeds
- **MARRIAGE:** 1908, Registrar of Deeds
- **DIVORCE:** start in 1934, kept by Circuit Court
- **DEATH:** 1908, Registrar of Deeds
- **LAND:** 1981, Registrar of Deeds
- **PROBATE:** 1854, Registrar in Probate
- **COURT:** 1934, Circuit Court
- **NOTES:** University of Wisconsin-Oshkosh, Forest R. Polk Library has birth records 1852-1907, death records 1872-1907, marriage records 1854-1907, land records 1877-1980, and naturalization records 1844-1954.

DOOR

421 Nebraska St., Sturgeon Bay, WI 54235, (920) 746-2200, **<www.co.door.wi.gov>**

- **INCORPORATED:** February 1851
- **PARENT COUNTY:** Brown
- **BIRTH RECORDS:** 1852, Registrar of Deeds
- **MARRIAGE:** 1860, Registrar of Deeds
- **DIVORCE:** start in 1979, kept by Circuit Court
- **DEATH:** 1856, Registrar of Deeds
- **LAND:** 1854, Registrar of Deeds
- **PROBATE:** 1954, Registrar in Probate
- **COURT:** 1979, Circuit Court
- **NOTES:** University of Wisconsin-Green Bay, Cofrin Library has court records 1895-1978, divorce records 1895-1978, naturalization records 1850-1955, and probate records 1945-1953.

DOUGLAS

1313 Belknap St., Superior, WI 54880, (715) 395-1586, **<www.douglascountywi.org>**

- **INCORPORATED:** Feb. 9, 1854
- **PARENT COUNTY:** La Pointe
- **BIRTH RECORDS:** 1908, Registrar of Deeds
- **MARRIAGE:** 1908, Registrar of Deeds
- **DIVORCE:** start in 1878, kept by Circuit Court
- **DEATH:** 1908, Registrar of Deeds
- **LAND:** 1854, Registrar of Deeds
- **PROBATE:** 1878, Probate Department
- **COURT:** 1878, Circuit Court
- **NOTES:** Superior Public Library has birth records 1861-1907, death records 1877-1907, and marriage records 1854-1907.

DUNN

800 Wilson Ave., Menomonie, WI 54751, (715) 232-1677, **<dunncountywi.govoffice2.com>**

- **INCORPORATED:** February 1854
- **PARENT COUNTY:** Chippewa
- **BIRTH RECORDS:** 1870, Registrar of Deeds
- **MARRIAGE:** 1858, Registrar of Deeds
- **DIVORCE:** 1930, Circuit Court
- **DEATH:** 1877, Registrar of Deeds
- **LAND:** 1854, Registrar of Deeds
- **PROBATE:** 1945, Registrar in Probate
- **COURT:** start in 1930, kept by Circuit Court
- **NOTES:** University of Wisconsin-Stout, Library Learning Center has court and divorce records 1850-1920, probate records ca. 1868-1944.

EAU CLAIRE
721 Oxford Ave., Eau Claire, WI 54703, (715) 839-4801,
<www.co.eau-claire.wi.us>
- **INCORPORATED:** October 1856
- **PARENT COUNTY:** Chippewa
- **BIRTH RECORDS:** 1908, Registrar of Deeds
- **MARRIAGE:** 1908, Registrar of Deeds
- **DIVORCE:** start in 1973, kept by Circuit Court
- **DEATH:** 1908, Registrar of Deeds
- **LAND:** 1890, Registrar of Deeds
- **PROBATE:** 1954, Registrar in Probate
- **COURT:** 1971, Clerk of Court
- **NOTES:** University of Wisconsin-Eau Claire, William D. McIntyre Library has birth records 1852-1907, Court records 1857-1970, death records 1876-1907, divorce records 1857-1972, land records 1856-1889, marriage records 1864-1907, naturalization records 1857-1928, and probate records 1856-1953.

FLORENCE
501 Lake Ave., Florence, WI 54121, (715) 584-3201,
<www.florencewisconsin.com>
- **INCORPORATED:** March 1882
- **PARENT COUNTIES:** Marinette, Oconto
- **BIRTH RECORDS:** 1908, Registrar of Deeds
- **MARRIAGE:** 1908, Registrar of Deeds
- **DIVORCE:** start in 1882, kept by Circuit Court
- **DEATH:** 1908, Registrar of Deeds
- **LAND:** 1882 Registrar of Deeds
- **PROBATE:** 1882, Registrar in Probate
- **COURT:** 1882, Circuit Court
- **NOTES:** University of Wisconsin-Green Bay, Cofrin Library has birth, death, and marriage records 1882-1907, and naturalization records 1882-1947.

FOND DU LAC
160 S. Macy St., Fond du Lac, WI 54936, (920) 929-3000,
<www.fdlco.wi.gov>
- **INCORPORATED:** December 1836
- **PARENT COUNTY:** Brown
- **BIRTH RECORDS:** 1907, Registrar of Deeds
- **MARRIAGE:** 1907, Registrar of Deeds
- **DIVORCE:** start in 1973, kept by Circuit Court
- **DEATH:** 1907, Registrar of Deeds
- **LAND:** 1981, Registrar of Deeds
- **PROBATE:** 1975, Registrar in Probate
- **COURT:** 1973, Circuit Court
- **NOTES:** University of Wisconsin-Oshkosh, Forest R. Polk Library has birth records 1852-1907, court records 1848-1972, death records 1871-1907, divorce records 1848-1972, land records 1850-1980, marriage records 1844-1907, naturalization records 1844-1974, and probate records 1848-1974.

FOREST
200 E. Madison St., Crandon, WI 54520, (715) 478-2422,
<www.co.forest.wi.gov>
- **INCORPORATED:** April 11, 1885
- **PARENT COUNTIES:** Langlade, Oconto
- **BIRTH RECORDS:** 1908, Registrar of Deeds
- **MARRIAGE:** 1908, Registrar of Deeds
- **DIVORCE:** start in 1906, kept by Circuit Court
- **DEATH:** 1908, Registrar of Deeds
- **LAND:** 1885, Registrar of Deeds
- **PROBATE:** 1885, Registrar in Probate
- **COURT:** 1906, Circuit Court
- **NOTES:** The Northern Great Lakes Visitors Center, History Center and Archives has birth records 1852-1907, Court records 1885-1905, death records 1887-1907, divorce records 1885-1905, marriage records 1885-1907, and naturalization records 1885-1955.

GATES
- **INCORPORATED:** May 1901
- **PARENT COUNTY:** Chippewa
- **NOTES:** See Rusk County. Name changed to Rusk in 1905.

GRANT
111 S. Jefferson, Lancaster, WI 53813, (608) 723-2675,
<www.co.grant.wi.gov>
- **INCORPORATED:** Dec. 1836
- **PARENT COUNTY:** Iowa
- **BIRTH RECORDS:** 1870, Registrar of Deeds
- **MARRIAGE:** 1842, Registrar of Deeds
- **DIVORCE:** start in 1921, kept by Circuit Court
- **DEATH:** 1876, Registrar of Deeds
- **LAND:** 1903, Registrar of Deeds
- **PROBATE:** 1840, Registrar in Probate
- **COURT:** 1921, Circuit Court
- **NOTES:** University of Wisconsin-Plattville Southwest Wisconsin Room, Karrmann Library has court and divorce records 1838-1920 and land records 1837-1902.

GREEN
1016 16th Ave., Monroe, WI 53566, (608) 328-9430,
<www.co.green.wi.gov>
- **INCORPORATED:** Dec. 8, 1836
- **PARENT COUNTY:** Territorial county
- **BIRTH RECORDS:** 1862, Registrar of Deeds
- **MARRIAGE:** 1838, Registrar of Deeds
- **DIVORCE:** start in 1911, kept by Circuit Court
- **DEATH:** 1874, Registrar of Deeds
- **LAND:** 1921, Registrar of Deeds
- **PROBATE:** ca. 1890, County Judge
- **COURT:** 1911, Circuit Court
- **NOTES:** University of Wisconsin-Plattville, Southwest Wisconsin Room, Karrmann Library has court and divorce records 1838-1910, land records 1836-1920, and naturalization records 1837-1945.

GREEN LAKE
492 Hill St., Green Lake, WI 54941, (920) 294-4005,
<www.co.green-lake.wi.us>
- **INCORPORATED:** March 1856
- **PARENT COUNTY:** Marquette
- **BIRTH RECORDS:** 1908, Registrar of Deeds
- **MARRIAGE:** 1908, Registrar of Deeds
- **DIVORCE:** start in ca. 1900, kept by Clerk of Courts
- **DEATH:** 1908, Registrar of Deeds
- **LAND:** 1995, Registrar of Deeds

- **PROBATE:** 1856, Registrar in Probate
- **COURT:** ca. 1900, Clerk of Courts
- **NOTES:** University of Wisconsin-Oshkosh, Forest R. Polk Library has birth records 1852-1907, death records 1876-1907, land records 1843-1994, marriage records 1863-1907, naturalization records 1858-1949.

IOWA

222 N. Iowa St., Dodgeville, WI 53533, (608) 935-0399,
<www.iowacounty.org>

- **INCORPORATED:** October 1839
- **PARENT COUNTY:** Territorial county
- **BIRTH RECORDS:** 1876, Registrar of Deeds
- **MARRIAGE:** 1836, Registrar of Deeds
- **DIVORCE:** start in 1991, kept by Circuit Court
- **DEATH:** 1871, Registrar of Deeds
- **LAND:** 1908, Registrar of Deeds
- **PROBATE:** 1975, Registrar in Probate
- **COURT:** 1991, Circuit Court
- **NOTES:** University of Wisconsin-Plattville, Southwest Wisconsin Room, Karrmann Library has court records 1837-1990, divorce records 1823-1990, land records 1835-1907, naturalization records 1835-1906, and probate records 1837-1974.

IRON

300 Taconite St., Hurley, WI 54534, (715) 561-3375,
<www.co.iron.wi.gov>

- **INCORPORATED:** March 1893
- **PARENT COUNTIES:** Ashland, Oneida
- **BIRTH RECORDS:** 1886, Registrar of Deeds
- **MARRIAGE:** 1858, Registrar of Deeds
- **DIVORCE:** start in 1930, kept by Circuit Court
- **DEATH:** 1887, Registrar of Deeds
- **LAND:** 1893, Registrar of Deeds
- **PROBATE:** 1929, Registrar in Probate
- **COURT:** 1930, Circuit Court
- **NOTES:** The Northern Great Lakes Visitors Center, History Center and Archives has naturalization records 1893-1954.

JACKSON

307 Main St., Black River Falls, WI 54615, (715) 284-0278,
<www.wicounties.org/counties/desc/33>

- **INCORPORATED:** February 1853
- **PARENT COUNTY:** La Crosse
- **BIRTH RECORDS:** 1876, Registrar of Deeds
- **MARRIAGE:** 1858, Registrar of Deeds
- **DIVORCE:** 1926, Clerk of Court
- **DEATH:** 1876, Registrar of Deeds
- **LAND:** start in 1947, kept by Registrar of Deeds
- **PROBATE:** 1901, Registrar in Probate
- **COURT:** 1926, Clerk of Court
- **NOTES:** University of Wisconsin-La Crosse, Murphy Library Resource Center has land records 1854-1946, naturalization records 1853-1963, and probate records 1869-1900.

JEFFERSON

320 S. Main St., Jefferson, WI 53549, (920) 674-7368,
<www.jeffersoncountywi.gov>

- **INCORPORATED:** Dec. 7, 1836
- **PARENT COUNTY:** Milwaukee
- **BIRTH RECORDS:** 1852, Registrar of Deeds
- **MARRIAGE:** 1844, Registrar of Deeds
- **DIVORCE:** start in 1965, kept by Circuit Court
- **DEATH:** 1856, Registrar of Deeds
- **LAND:** 1901, Registrar of Deeds
- **PROBATE:** 1912, Registrar in Probate
- **COURT:** 1955, Circuit Court
- **NOTES:** University of Wisconsin-Whitewater, Harold Andersen Library has court records 1843-1954, divorce records 1851-1964, land records 1838-1900, naturalization records 1842-1950, probate records 1844-1911.

JUNEAU

220 E. State St., Mauston, WI 53948, (608) 847-9300,
<www.co.juneau.wi.gov>

- **INCORPORATED:** Jan. 1, 1857
- **PARENT COUNTY:** Adams
- **BIRTH RECORDS:** 1877, Registrar of Deeds
- **MARRIAGE:** 1844, Registrar of Deeds
- **DIVORCE:** start in 1995, kept by Circuit Court
- **DEATH:** 1876, Registrar of Deeds
- **LAND:** 1842, Registrar of Deeds
- **PROBATE:** 1889, Registrar in Probate
- **COURT:** 1995, Circuit Court
- **NOTES:** University of Wisconsin-Stevens Point, James H. Albertson Library has court and divorce records to 1994, naturalization records 1849-1957, and probate records 1857-1888.

KENOSHA

1010 Fifty-sixth St., Kenosha, WI 53140, (262) 653-2552,
<www.co.kenosha.wi.us/index.html>

- **INCORPORATED:** January 1850
- **PARENT COUNTY:** Racine
- **BIRTH RECORDS:** start in 1876, kept by Registrar of Deeds
- **MARRIAGE:** 1850, Registrar of Deeds
- **LAND:** 1873, Registrar of Deeds
- **PROBATE:** 1850, Registrar in Probate
- **COURT:** 1972, Registrar of Deeds
- **NOTES:** University of Wisconsin-Parkside, University Library and Area Research Center has court records 1850-1971, land records 1838-1872, and naturalization records 1850-1983.

KEWAUNEE

613 Dodge St., Kewaunee, WI 54216, (920) 388-7133,
<www.kewauneeco.org>

- **INCORPORATED:** April 1852
- **PARENT COUNTY:** Manitowoc
- **DEATH RECORDS:** 1873, Registrar of Deeds
- **LAND:** 1852, Registrar of Deeds
- **PROBATE:** 1867, Registrar in Probate
- **COURT:** start in 1943, kept by Circuit Court
- **NOTES:** Registrar of Deeds has birth records 1861-1873 and

marriage records 1857-1874. University of Wisconsin-Green Bay, Cofrin Library has court records 1858-1942 and naturalization records 1850-1950.

LA CROSSE

333 Vine St., La Crosse, WI 54601, (608) 785-9573, **<www.co.la-crosse.wi.us>**

- **INCORPORATED:** March 1851
- **PARENT COUNTY:** Unorganized territory
- **BIRTH RECORDS:** 1877, Registrar of Deeds
- **MARRIAGE:** 1851, Registrar of Deeds
- **DIVORCE:** start in 1859, kept by Circuit Court
- **DEATH:** 1876, Registrar of Deeds
- **LAND:** 1887, Registrar of Deeds
- **PROBATE:** 1982, Registrar in Probate
- **COURT:** 1859, Circuit Court
- **NOTES:** University of Wisconsin-La Crosse, Murphy Library Resource Center has land records 1851-1886, naturalization records 1846-1991, and probate records 1851-1981.

LA POINTE

- **INCORPORATED:** February 1845
- **PARENT COUNTY:** St. Croix
- **NOTES:** See Bayfield County. Name changed to Bayfield in 1866.

LAFAYETTE

626 Main St., Darlington, WI 53530, (608) 776-4850, **<www.co.lafayette.wi.gov>**

- **INCORPORATED:** January 1847
- **PARENT COUNTY:** Iowa
- **BIRTH RECORDS:** 1854, Registrar of Deeds
- **MARRIAGE:** 1847, Registrar of Deeds
- **DIVORCE:** start in 1920, kept by Circuit Court
- **DEATH:** 1877, Registrar of Deeds
- **LAND:** 1928, Registrar of Deeds
- **PROBATE:** 1853, Registrar in Probate
- **COURT:** 1920, Circuit Court
- **NOTES:** University of Wisconsin-Plattville, Southwest Wisconsin Room, Karrman Library has court and divorce records 1846-1919, land records 1835-1927, and naturalization records 1847-1945.

LANGLADE

800 Clermont St., Antigo, WI 54409, (715) 627-6209, **<www.co.langlade.wi.us>**

- **INCORPORATED:** Feb. 1879
- **PARENT COUNTIES:** Oconto, Lincoln
- **BIRTH RECORDS:** 1882, Registrar of Deeds
- **MARRIAGE:** 1881, Registrar of Deeds
- **DIVORCE:** start in ca. 1880, kept by Circuit Court
- **DEATH:** 1868, Registrar of Deeds
- **LAND:** 1879, Registrar of Deeds
- **PROBATE:** ca. 1890, Registrar in Probate
- **COURT:** ca. 1880, Circuit Court
- **NOTES:** University of Wisconsin-Stevens Point, James H. Albertson Library has naturalization records 1881-1957. Formerly New County. Name changed to Langlade in 1880.

LINCOLN

1110 E. Main St., Merrill, WI 54452, (715) 536-0312, **<www.co.lincoln.wi.us>**

- **INCORPORATED:** March 1874
- **PARENT COUNTY:** Marathon
- **BIRTH RECORDS:** 1875, Registrar of Deeds
- **MARRIAGE:** 1875, Registrar of Deeds
- **DIVORCE:** 1926, Circuit Court
- **DEATH:** 1871, Registrar of Deeds
- **LAND:** 1873, Registrar of Deeds
- **PROBATE:** 1925, Registrar in Probate
- **COURT:** start in 1926, kept by Circuit Court
- **NOTES:** University of Wisconsin-Stevens Point, James H. Albertson Library has court and divorce records 1880-1925, naturalization records 1872-1958, and probate records 1886-1924.

MANITOWOC

1010 S. Eighth St., Manitowoc, WI 54220, (920) 683-4007, **<www.co.manitowoc.wi.us>**

- **INCORPORATED:** Dec. 1838
- **PARENT COUNTY:** Brown
- **BIRTH RECORDS:** 1908, Registrar of Deeds
- **MARRIAGE:** 1908, Registrar of Deeds
- **DIVORCE:** start in 1944, kept by Circuit Court
- **DEATH:** 1908, Registrar of Deeds
- **PROBATE:** 1960, Registrar in Probate
- **COURT:** 1944, Circuit Court
- **NOTES:** University of Wisconsin-Green Bay, Cofrin Library has birth records 1858-1907, Court records 1848-1943, divorce records 1849-1943, marriage records 1859-1907, naturalization records 1848-1955, and probate records 1864-1959. Registrar of Deeds has Land records from early 1800s.

MARATHON

500 Forest St., Wausau, WI 54403, (715) 261-1000, **<www.co.marathon.wi.us>**

- **INCORPORATED:** Feb. 1850
- **PARENT COUNTY:** Portage
- **BIRTH RECORDS:** 1870, Registrar of Deeds
- **MARRIAGE:** 1865, Registrar of Deeds
- **DIVORCE:** start in 1945, kept by Clerk of Courts
- **DEATH:** 1868, Registrar of Deeds
- **LAND:** 1850, Registrar of Deeds
- **PROBATE:** 1982, Clerk of Courts
- **COURT:** 1976, Clerk of Courts
- **NOTES:** University of Wisconsin-Stevens Point, James H. Albertson Library has court records 1853-1975, divorce records 1853-1944, naturalization records 1851-1991, and probate records ca. 1851-1981.

MARINETTE

1926 Hall Ave., Marinette, WI 54143, (715) 732-7532, **<www.marinettecounty.com>**

- **INCORPORATED:** Feb. 27, 1879
- **PARENT COUNTY:** Oconto
- **BIRTH RECORDS:** 1874, Registrar of Deeds
- **MARRIAGE:** 1878, Registrar of Deeds
- **DIVORCE:** start in 1940, kept by Circuit Court

- **DEATH:** 1879, Registrar of Deeds
- **LAND:** 1879, Registrar of Deeds
- **PROBATE:** 1917, Registrar in Probate
- **COURT:** 1940, Circuit Court
- **NOTES:** University of Wisconsin-Green Bay, Cofrin Library has court and Divorce records 1879-1939, naturalization records 1879-1980, and probate records 1879-1916.

MARQUETTE

77 West Park St., Montello, WI 53949, (608) 297-3100, **<co.marquette.wi.us>**

- **INCORPORATED:** Dec. 7, 1836
- **PARENT COUNTY:** Brown
- **BIRTH RECORDS:** 1908, Registrar of Deeds
- **MARRIAGE:** 1908, Registrar of Deeds
- **DIVORCE:** start in 1967, kept by Circuit Court
- **DEATH:** 1908, Registrar of Deeds
- **LAND:** 1941, Registrar of Deeds
- **PROBATE:** 1922, Registrar in Probate
- **COURT:** 1967, Circuit Court
- **NATURALIZATION:** 1868-1936, Circuit Court
- **NOTES:** University of Wisconsin-Oshkosh, Forest R. Polk Library has birth records 1852-1907, Court records 1876-1966, death records 1876-1907, divorce records 1876-1966, land records 1892-1940, marriage records 1863-1907, naturalization records 1848-1949, and probate records 1860-1921.

MENOMINEE

W3269 Courthouse Lane, Keshena, WI 54135, (715) 799-3311, **<www.menominee-nsn.gov>**

- **INCORPORATED:** May 2, 1961
- **PARENT COUNTY:** Menominee Indian Reservation
- **BIRTH RECORDS:** 1961, Registrar of Deeds
- **MARRIAGE:** 1961, Registrar of Deeds
- **DIVORCE:** 1961, Circuit Court
- **DEATH:** 1961, Registrar of Deeds
- **LAND:** 1961, Registrar of Deeds
- **PROBATE:** 1961, Registrar in Probate
- **COURT:** start in 1961, kept by Circuit Court

MILWAUKEE

901 N. Ninth St., Milwaukee, WI 53233, (414) 278-4069, **<www.milwaukeecounty.org>**

- **INCORPORATED:** Sept. 1834
- **PARENT COUNTY:** Territorial county
- **BIRTH RECORDS:** 1823, Registrar of Deeds
- **MARRIAGE:** 1830, Registrar of Deeds
- **DIVORCE:** 1946, Circuit Court
- **DEATH:** 1852, Registrar of Deeds
- **LAND:** 1835, Registrar of Deeds
- **PROBATE:** 1989, Registrar in Probate
- **COURT:** start in 1946, kept by Circuit Court
- **NOTES:** University of Wisconsin-Milwaukee, Milwaukee Urban Archives, Golda Meir Library has court and divorce records 1834-1945 and probate records 1815-1988. Milwaukee Historical Society has naturalization records 1836-1941.

MONROE

202 S. K St., Sparta, WI 54656, (608) 269-8705, **<www.co.monroe.wi.us>**

- **INCORPORATED:** March 1854
- **PARENT COUNTY:** La Crosse
- **BIRTH RECORDS:** 1877, Registrar of Deeds
- **MARRIAGE:** 1856, Registrar of Deeds
- **DIVORCE:** start in 1938, kept by Circuit Court
- **DEATH:** 1876, Registrar of Deeds
- **LAND:** 1851, Registrar of Deeds
- **PROBATE:** 1902, Registrar in Probate
- **COURT:** 1938, Circuit Court
- **NOTES:** University of Wisconsin-La Crosse, Murphy Library Research Center has court and divorce records 1855-1937, naturalization records 1854-1946, and probate records 1867-1901.

NEW

- **INCORPORATED:** Feb. 1879
- **PARENT COUNTIES:** Oconto, Lincoln
- **NOTES:** See Lauglade County. Name changed to Langlade in 1880.

OCONTO

301 Washington St., Oconto, WI 54153, (920) 834-6800, **<www.co.oconto.wi.us>**

- **INCORPORATED:** Feb. 1851
- **PARENT COUNTY:** Brown
- **BIRTH RECORDS:** 1876, Registrar of Deeds
- **MARRIAGE:** 1855, Registrar of Deeds
- **DIVORCE:** start in 1974, kept by Circuit Court
- **DEATH:** 1872, Registrar of Deeds
- **LAND:** 1851, Registrar of Deeds
- **PROBATE:** 1924, Registrar in Probate
- **COURT:** 1974, Circuit Court
- **NOTES:** University of Wisconsin-Green Bay, Cofrin Library has court and divorce records 1857-1973, naturalization records 1857-1952, and probate records 1857-1923.

ONEIDA

1 S. Oneida Ave., Rhinelander, WI 54501, (715) 369-6143, **<www.co.oneida.wi.gov>**

- **INCORPORATED:** April 1885
- **PARENT COUNTY:** Lincoln
- **BIRTH RECORDS:** 1908, Registrar of Deeds
- **MARRIAGE:** 1908, Registrar of Deeds
- **DIVORCE:** start in 1984, kept by Circuit Court
- **DEATH:** 1908, Registrar of Deeds
- **PROBATE:** 1984, Circuit Court
- **COURT:** 1984, Circuit Court
- **NOTES:** The Northern Great Lakes Visitors Center, History Center and Archives has birth records 1852-1907, court, divorce, and probate records ca. 1900-1983, death records 1889-1907, naturalization records 1887-1954, and marriage records 1887-1907. Registrar of Deeds has land records from late 1800s.

OUTAGAMIE

410 S. Walnut St., Appleton, WI 54911, (920) 832-5079, **<www.co.outagamie.wi.us>**

- **INCORPORATED:** Feb. 1851

- **PARENT COUNTY:** Brown
- **BIRTH RECORDS:** 1856, Registrar of Deeds
- **MARRIAGE:** 1855, Registrar of Deeds
- **DIVORCE:** start in 1980, kept by Circuit Court
- **DEATH:** 1869, Registrar of Deeds
- **LAND:** 1850, Registrar of Deeds
- **PROBATE:** 1959, Registrar in Probate
- **COURT:** 1980, Circuit Court
- **NOTES:** University of Wisconsin-Green Bay, Cofrin Library has court and divorce records 1852-1979, naturalization records 1852-1963, and probate records 1853-1958.

OZAUKEE

121 W. Main St., Port Washington, WI 53074, (262) 284-8111, **<www.co.ozaukee.wi.us>**

- **INCORPORATED:** March 1853
- **PARENT COUNTY:** Washington
- **BIRTH RECORDS:** 1852, Registrar of Deeds
- **MARRIAGE:** 1855, Registrar of Deeds
- **DIVORCE:** start in 1974, kept by Circuit Court
- **DEATH:** 1849, Registrar of Deeds
- **LAND:** 1890, Registrar of Deeds
- **PROBATE:** 1901, Registrar in Probate
- **COURT:** 1974, Circuit Court
- **NOTES:** University of Wisconsin-Milwaukee, Milwaukee Urban Archives, Golda Meir Library has land records 1835-1889, naturalization records 1842-1906, and probate records 1849-1900.

PEPIN

740 Seventh Ave. W., Durand, WI 54736, (715) 672-8857, **<www.co.pepin.wi.us>**

- **INCORPORATED:** Feb. 1858
- **PARENT COUNTY:** Dunn
- **BIRTH RECORDS:** 1863, Registrar of Deeds
- **MARRIAGE:** 1857, Registrar of Deeds
- **DIVORCE:** start in na, kept by Circuit Court
- **DEATH:** 1877, Registrar of Deeds
- **LAND:** 1856, Registrar of Deeds
- **PROBATE:** 1901, Registrar in Probate
- **COURT:** na, Circuit Court
- **NOTES:** University of Wisconsin-Stout, Library Learning Center has naturalization records 1858-1919, probate records 1856-1900.

PIERCE

414 W. Main St., Ellsworth, WI 54011, (715) 273-3531, **<www.co.pierce.wi.us>**

- **INCORPORATED:** Feb. 1853
- **PARENT COUNTY:** St. Croix
- **BIRTH RECORDS:** start in 1870, kept by County Clerk
- **MARRIAGE:** 1892, Registrar of Deeds
- **DIVORCE:** 1931, Circuit Court
- **DEATH:** 1876, Registrar of Deeds
- **PROBATE:** 1979, Registrar in Probate
- **COURT:** 1931, Circuit Court
- **NOTES:** University of Wisconsin-River Falls, Chalmer Davee Library has court and divorce records ca. 1866-1930, marriage records 1867-1891, naturalization records 1850-1963, and probate records ca. 1875-1978.

POLK

100 Polk County Plaza, Balsam Lake, WI 54810, (715) 485-9226, **<www.co.polk.wi.us>**

- **INCORPORATED:** March 14, 1853
- **PARENT COUNTY:** St. Croix
- **BIRTH RECORDS:** 1867, Registrar of Deeds
- **MARRIAGE:** 1855, Registrar of Deeds
- **DIVORCE:** na, Clerk of Court
- **DEATH:** 1865, Registrar of Deeds
- **LAND:** start in 1853, kept by Registrar of Deeds
- **COURT:** na, Clerk of Court
- **PROBATE:** 1942, Registrar in Probate
- **NOTES:** University of Wisconsin-River Falls, Chalmer Davee Library has naturalization records 1855-1954 and probate records 1855-1941.

PORTAGE

1516 Church St., Stevens Point, WI 54481, (715) 346-1351, **<www.co.portage.wi.us>**

- **INCORPORATED:** Dec. 1836
- **PARENT COUNTY:** Territorial county
- **DIVORCE:** start in 1927, kept by Circuit Court
- **COURT:** 1927, Circuit Court
- **LAND:** 1841, Registrar of Deeds
- **BIRTH RECORDS:** 1898, Registrar of Deeds
- **MARRIAGE:** 1897, Registrar of Deeds
- **DEATH:** 1898, Registrar of Deeds
- **PROBATE:** 1911, Registrar in Probate
- **NOTES:** University of Wisconsin-Stevens Point, James H. Albertson Library has birth records 1876-1897, Court records 1844-1926, death records 1877-1878, 1886, 1888-1897, divorce records 1844-1926, marriage records 1844-1896, naturalization records 1844-1956, and probate records 1837-1910.

PRICE

126 Cherry St., Phillips, WI 54555, (715) 339-4115, **<www.wicounties.org/counties/desc/9>**

- **INCORPORATED:** March 3, 1879
- **PARENT COUNTY:** Chippewa, Lincoln
- **BIRTH RECORDS:** 1908, Registrar of Deeds
- **MARRIAGE:** 1908, Registrar of Deeds
- **DIVORCE:** start in 1937, kept by Circuit Court
- **DEATH:** 1908, Registrar of Deeds
- **LAND:** 1880, Registrar of Deeds
- **PROBATE:** 1900, Registrar in Probate
- **COURT:** 1937, Circuit Court
- **NOTES:** Northern Great Lakes Visitors Center, History Center and Archives has birth records 1852-1907, court records 1880-1936, death records 1881-1907, divorce records 1882-1936, marriage records 1881-1907, naturalization records 1882-1954, and probate records 1881-1899.

RACINE

730 Wisconsin Ave., Racine, WI 53403, (262) 636-3121, **<www.racineco.com>**

- **INCORPORATED:** Dec. 1836
- **PARENT COUNTY:** Milwaukee
- **BIRTH RECORDS:** 1877, Registrar of Deeds

- **MARRIAGE:** 1839, Registrar of Deeds
- **DIVORCE:** start in 1956, kept by Circuit Court
- **DEATH:** 1880, Registrar of Deeds
- **LAND:** 1837, Registrar of Deeds
- **PROBATE:** 1907, Registrar in Probate
- **COURT:** 1954, Circuit Court
- **NOTES:** University of Wisconsin-Parkside, University Archives and Area Research Center has court records 1837-1953, divorce records 1846-1955, naturalization records 1837-1975, and probate records 1849-ca. 1906.

RICHLAND

181 W. Seminary St., Richland Center, WI 53581, (608) 647-2197,
<www.co.richland.wi.us>

- **INCORPORATED:** Feb. 1842
- **PARENT COUNTY:** Iowa
- **BIRTH RECORDS:** 1875, Registrar of Deeds
- **MARRIAGE:** 1864, Registrar of Deeds
- **DIVORCE:** start in 1921, kept by Circuit Court
- **DEATH:** 1876, Registrar of Deeds
- **LAND:** 1850, Registrar of Deeds
- **PROBATE:** 1854, Registrar in Probate
- **COURT:** 1921, Circuit Court
- **NOTES:** University of Wisconsin-Plattville, Southwest Wisconsin Room, Karrmann Library has court and divorce records 1869-1920 and naturalization records 1860-1946.

ROCK

51 S. Main St., Janesville, WI 53545, (608) 757-5660,
<www.co.rock.wi.us>

- **INCORPORATED:** Dec. 7, 1836
- **PARENT COUNTY:** Milwaukee
- **BIRTH RECORDS:** 1849, Registrar of Deeds
- **MARRIAGE:** 1849, Registrar of Deeds
- **DIVORCE:** 1937, Circuit Court
- **DEATH:** 1871, Registrar of Deeds
- **LAND:** 1901, Registrar of Deeds
- **PROBATE:** 1939, Registrar in Probate
- **COURT:** start in 1937, kept by Circuit Court
- **NOTES:** University of Wisconsin-Whitewater, Harold Andersen Library has court and divorce records ca. 1842-1936, land records 1839-1900, and naturalization records 1839-1983. Rock County Historical Society has probate records 1853-1938.

RUSK

311 Miner Ave. E., Ladysmith, WI 54848, (715) 532-2100,
<www.ruskcounty.org>

- **INCORPORATED:** May 1901
- **PARENT COUNTY:** Chippewa
- **BIRTH RECORDS:** 1908, Registrar of Deeds
- **MARRIAGE:** 1908, Registrar of Deeds
- **DIVORCE:** start in 1918, kept by Circuit Court
- **DEATH:** 1908, Registrar of Deeds
- **LAND:** 1868, Registrar of Deeds
- **PROBATE:** 1901, Registrar in Probate
- **COURT:** 1918, Circuit Court
- **NOTES:** University of Wisconsin-Eau Claire, William D. McIntyre Library, Suite 132 N has birth records 1852-1907, Court and divorce records 1901-1917, death and marriage records 1901-1907, and naturalization records 1885-1954. Formerly Gates County. Name changed to Rusk June 19, 1905.

SAUK

505 Broadway, Baraboo, WI 53913, (608) 356-5581,
<www.co.sauk.wi.us>

- **INCORPORATED:** Jan. 1840
- **PARENT COUNTY:** Territorial county
- **BIRTH RECORDS:** 1864, Registrar of Deeds
- **MARRIAGE:** 1852, Registrar of Deeds
- **DIVORCE:** start in 1926, kept by Circuit Court
- **DEATH:** 1876, Registrar of Deeds
- **LAND:** 1843, Registrar of Deeds
- **PROBATE:** 1914, Registrar in Probate
- **COURT:** 1926, Circuit Court
- **NOTES:** State Archives, Wisconsin Historical Society has court and divorce records 1848-1925, naturalization records 1844-1955, and probate records 1847-1913.

SAWYER

10610 Main St., Hayward, WI 54843, (715) 634-4866,
<www.sawyercountygov.org>

- **INCORPORATED:** March 1883
- **PARENT COUNTIES:** Ashland, Chippewa
- **BIRTH RECORDS:** 1852, Registrar of Deeds
- **MARRIAGE:** 1883, Registrar of Deeds
- **DIVORCE:** start in 1977, kept by Circuit Court
- **DEATH:** 1874, Registrar of Deeds
- **LAND:** 1883, Registrar of Deeds
- **PROBATE:** 1883, Registrar in Probate
- **COURT:** 1977, Circuit Court
- **NOTES:** Northern Great Lakes Visitors Center, History Center and Archives has court and divorce records 1876-1976 and naturalization records 1883-1954.

SHAWANO

311 N. Main St., Shawano, WI 54166, (715) 526-9150,
<www.co.shawano.wi.us>

- **INCORPORATED:** Feb. 1853
- **PARENT COUNTIES:** Oconto, Outagamie
- **BIRTH RECORDS:** 1862, Registrar of Deeds
- **MARRIAGE:** 1848, Registrar of Deeds
- **DIVORCE:** 1943, Circuit Court
- **DEATH:** 1873, Registrar of Deeds
- **LAND:** 1853, Registrar of Deeds
- **PROBATE:** ca. 1890, Registrar in Probate
- **COURT:** start in 1943, kept by Circuit Court
- **NOTES:** University of Wisconsin-Green Bay, Cofrin Library has court and divorce records 1860-1942 and naturalization records 1858-1949.

SHEBOYGAN
508 New York Ave., Sheboygan, WI 53081, (920) 459-3003,
<www.co.sheboygan.wi.us>
- **INCORPORATED:** Dec. 17, 1836
- **PARENT COUNTY:** Brown
- **BIRTH RECORDS:** 1852, Registrar of Deeds
- **MARRIAGE:** 1852, Registrar of Deeds
- **DIVORCE:** 1963, District Court Clerk
- **DEATH:** 1854, Registrar of Deeds
- **LAND:** 1881, Registrar of Deeds
- **COURT:** start in 1963, kept by Circuit Court
- **NOTES:** University of Wisconsin-Milwaukee, Milwaukee Urban Archives, Golda Meir Library has court and divorce records 1846-1962, land records 1838-1880, naturalization records 1851-1982, and probate records 1882-1928.

ST. CROIX
1101 Carmichael Rd., Hudson, WI 54016, (715) 386-4610,
<www.co.saint-croix.wi.us>
- **INCORPORATED:** Jan. 1840
- **PARENT COUNTY:** Territorial county
- **BIRTH RECORDS:** 1858, Registrar of Deeds
- **MARRIAGE:** 1852, Registrar of Deeds
- **DIVORCE:** start in 1929, Circuit Court
- **DEATH:** 1876, Registrar of Deeds
- **LAND:** 1854, Registrar of Deeds
- **PROBATE:** na, Registrar in Probate
- **COURT:** 1929, Circuit Court
- **NOTES:** University of Wisconsin-River Falls, Chalmer Davee Library has court and divorce records ca. 1840-1928 and naturalization records 1850-1954.

TAYLOR
224 S. Second St., Medford, WI 54451, (715) 748-1400,
<www.co.taylor.wi.us>
- **INCORPORATED:** March 1848
- **PARENT COUNTIES:** Clark, Lincoln, Marathon, Chippewa
- **BIRTH RECORDS:** 1908, Registrar of Deeds
- **MARRIAGE:** 1908, Registrar of Deeds
- **DIVORCE:** start in 1935, kept by Circuit Court
- **DEATH:** 1908, Registrar of Deeds
- **LAND:** 1900, Registrar of Deeds
- **PROBATE:** 1947, Registrar in Probate
- **COURT:** 1926, Circuit Court
- **NOTES:** University of Wisconsin-Eau Claire, William D. McIntyre Library has birth records 1852-1907, Court records 1877-1925, death records 1877-1907, divorce records 1877-1925, 1931-1934, marriage records 1875-1907, naturalization records 1877-1927, and probate records 1878-1946. Clerk of Circuit Court has divorce records 1926-1930.

TREMPEALEAU
36245 Main St., Whitehall, WI 54773, (715) 538-2311,
<www.tremplocounty.com>
- **INCORPORATED:** Jan. 1854
- **PARENT COUNTY:** La Crosse
- **BIRTH RECORDS:** 1845, Registrar of Deeds
- **MARRIAGE:** 1856, Registrar of Deeds
- **DIVORCE:** start in 1917, kept by Circuit Court
- **DEATH:** 1847, Registrar of Deeds
- **LAND:** 1853, Registrar of Deeds
- **PROBATE:** 1855, Registrar in Probate
- **COURT:** 1917, Circuit Court
- **NOTES:** University of Wisconsin-La Crosse, Murphy Library Resource Center has court and divorce records 1860-1916 and naturalization records 1857-1954.

VERNON
400 Court House Sq., Viroqua, WI 54665, (608) 637-5556,
<www.co.vernon.wi.gov>
- **INCORPORATED:** March 1851
- **PARENT COUNTY:** Crawford
- **BIRTH RECORDS:** 1863, Registrar of Deeds
- **MARRIAGE:** 1855, Registrar of Deeds
- **DIVORCE:** start in 1935, kept by Circuit Court
- **DEATH:** 1878, Registrar of Deeds
- **LAND:** 1851, Registrar of Deeds
- **PROBATE:** 1850, Registrar in Probate
- **COURT:** 1935, Circuit Court
- **NOTES:** University of Wisconsin-La Cross, Murphy Library Resource Center has court and divorce records 1859-1934 and naturalization records 1853-1947. Formerly Bad Ax County. Name changed to Vernon in 1862.

VILAS
330 Court St., Eagle River, WI 54521, (715) 479-3660,
<www.co.vilas.wi.us>
- **INCORPORATED:** April 1893
- **PARENT COUNTY:** Oneida
- **BIRTH RECORDS:** 1889, Registrar of Deeds
- **MARRIAGE:** 1893, Registrar of Deeds
- **DIVORCE:** 1939, Circuit Court
- **DEATH:** 1889, Registrar of Deeds
- **LAND:** 1893, Registrar of Deeds
- **PROBATE:** 1894, Registrar in Probate
- **COURT:** start in 1939, kept by Circuit Court
- **NOTES:** Northern Great Lakes Visitors Center, History Center and Archives has court and divorce records 1893-1938 and naturalization records 1876-1949.

WALWORTH
100 W. Walworth St., Elkhorn, WI 53121, (262) 741-4241,
<www.co.walworth.wi.us>
- **INCORPORATED:** Dec. 1838
- **PARENT COUNTY:** Milwaukee
- **BIRTH RECORDS:** 1872, Registrar of Deeds
- **MARRIAGE:** 1839, Registrar of Deeds
- **DIVORCE:** start in 1963, kept by Circuit Court
- **DEATH:** 1872, Registrar of Deeds
- **LAND:** 1839, Registrar of Deeds
- **PROBATE:** 1993, Registrar in Probate
- **COURT:** 1963, Circuit Court
- **NOTES:** University of Wisconsin-Whitewater, Harold Andersen Library has court records 1839-1962, divorce records 1839-1962, naturalization records 1838-1955, and probate records 1848-1992.

WASHBURN
10 Fourth Ave., Shell Lake, WI 54871, (715) 468-4600, **<www.co.washburn.wi.us>**
- **INCORPORATED:** March 1883
- **PARENT COUNTY:** Burnett
- **BIRTH RECORDS:** 1883, Registrar of Deeds
- **MARRIAGE:** 1883, Registrar of Deeds
- **DIVORCE:** 1977, Circuit Court
- **DEATH:** 1883, Registrar of Deeds
- **LAND:** 1883, Registrar of Deeds
- **PROBATE:** 1883, Registrar in Probate
- **COURT:** start in 1883, kept by Clerk of Courts
- **NOTES:** Northern Great Lakes Visitors Center, History Center and Archives has court and Divorce records 1883-1976 and naturalization records 1878-1954.

WASHINGTON
432 E. Washington St., West Bend, WI 53095, (262) 335-4305, **<www.co.washington.wi.us>**
- **INCORPORATED:** Dec. 1836
- **PARENT COUNTY:** Territorial county
- **BIRTH RECORDS:** 1859, Registrar of Deeds
- **MARRIAGE:** 1846, Registrar of Deeds
- **DIVORCE:** start in 1986, kept by Circuit Court
- **DEATH:** 1873, Registrar of Deeds
- **LAND:** 1935, Registrar of Deeds
- **PROBATE:** 1855, Registrar in Probate
- **COURT:** 1986, Circuit Court
- **NOTES:** University of Wisconsin, Milwaukee Urban Archives, Golda Meir Library has court and divorce records 1845-1985 and naturalization records 1845-1963.

WAUKESHA
515 W. Moreland Blvd., Waukesha, WI 53188, (262) 548-7010, **<www.waukeshacounty.gov>**
- **INCORPORATED:** Jan. 1846
- **PARENT COUNTY:** Milwaukee
- **BIRTH RECORDS:** 1860, Registrar of Deeds
- **MARRIAGE:** 1846, Registrar of Deeds
- **DIVORCE:** na, Circuit Court
- **DEATH:** 1872, Registrar of Deeds
- **LAND:** 1886, Registrar of Deeds
- **PROBATE:** 1855, Registrar in Probate
- **COURT:** unknown start, kept by Clerk of Courts
- **NOTES:** University of Wisconsin-Milwaukee, Milwaukee Urban Archives, Golda Meir Library has land records 1839-1885 and naturalization records 1847-1955.

WAUPACA
811 Harding St., Waupaca, WI 54981, (715) 258-6200, **<public3.co.waupaca.wi.us>**
- **INCORPORATED:** Feb. 1851
- **PARENT COUNTIES:** Brown, Winnebago
- **BIRTH RECORDS:** 1858, Registrar of Deeds
- **MARRIAGE:** 1852, Registrar of Deeds
- **DIVORCE:** start in 1928, kept by Circuit Court
- **DEATH:** 1848, Registrar of Deeds
- **LAND:** 1851, Registrar of Deeds
- **PROBATE:** 1931, Registrar in Probate
- **COURT:** 1928, Circuit Court
- **NOTES:** University of Wisconsin-Stevens Point, James H. Albertsen Library has court and divorce records 1854-1927, naturalization records 1853-1948, and probate records 1860-1930.

WAUSHARA
209 S. St. Marie St., Wautoma, WI 54982, (920) 787-0442, **<www.co.waushara.wi.us>**
- **INCORPORATED:** Feb. 15, 1851
- **PARENT COUNTY:** Marquette
- **BIRTH RECORDS:** 1859, Registrar of Deeds
- **MARRIAGE:** 1852, Registrar of Deeds
- **DIVORCE:** start in 1947, kept by Circuit Court
- **DEATH:** 1876, Registrar of Deeds
- **LAND:** 1852, Registrar of Deeds
- **PROBATE:** 1940, Registrar in Probate
- **COURT:** 1947, Circuit Court
- **NOTES:** University of Wisconsin-Stevens Point, James H. Albertsen Library has court and divorce records 1857-1946, naturalization records 1852-1949, and probate records 1853-1939.

WINNEBAGO
415 Jackson St., Oshkosh, WI 54901, (920) 236-4888, **<www.co.winnebago.wi.us>**
- **INCORPORATED:** Jan. 1840
- **PARENT COUNTY:** Territorial county
- **BIRTH RECORDS:** 1876, Registrar of Deeds
- **MARRIAGE:** 1860, Registrar of Deeds
- **DIVORCE:** 1970, Circuit Court
- **DEATH:** 1876, Registrar of Deeds
- **LAND:** 1860, Registrar of Deeds
- **PROBATE:** 1871, Registrar in Probate
- **COURT:** start in 1970, kept by Circuit Court
- **NOTES:** University of Wisconsin-Oshkosh, Forest R. Polk Library has court and divorce records 1848-1969, naturalization records 1844-1963, and probate records 1838-1870. Attached to Brown and Fond du Lac Counties prior to organization Jan, 1, 1848.

WOOD
400 Market St., Wisconsin Rapids, WI 54495, (715) 421-8808, **<www.co.wood.wi.us>**
- **INCORPORATED:** March 1856
- **PARENT COUNTY:** Portage
- **BIRTH RECORDS:** 1871, Registrar of Deeds
- **MARRIAGE:** 1844, Registrar of Deeds
- **DIVORCE:** start in 1875, kept by Clerk of Courts
- **DEATH:** 1872, Registrar of Deeds
- **LAND:** 1856, Registrar of Deeds
- **PROBATE:** 1875, Registrar in Probate
- **COURT:** 1875, Clerk of Courts
- **NOTES:** University of Wisconsin-Stevens Point, James H. Albertsen Library has naturalization records 1858-1991.

WYOMING

» BY DAVID A. FRYXELL

HISTORICAL OVERVIEW

The first recorded experience of an American in Wyoming was not encouraging to future settlement. In 1807, John Colter, a fur trapper, mountain man, and Lewis and Clark expedition veteran, chanced upon an area of geysers where the earth itself seemed to bubble. He dubbed it "Colter's Hell." Nonetheless, other intrepid explorers followed. For decades, Wyoming was primarily a site of fur-trade rendezvous and a way-station en route to Astoria, Ore. Fort Laramie, the first permanent trading post, was founded in 1834. Mormons established Fort Supply, the first farming settlement, in 1853.

Native Americans were already here, of course. Wyoming's most prominent tribes are the Eastern Shoshone and Northern Arapaho, who were moved onto the Wind River Reservation in 1868 and 1877, respectively. (The Southern Arapaho and Southern Cheyenne were removed to Oklahoma.)

Immigrants came to Wyoming in waves, especially following the 1868 creation of Wyoming Territory (carved largely from Dakota Territory). Chinese laborers worked on the Union Pacific Railroad, whose progress across the state from 1867 to 1869 created the towns of Cheyenne, Evanston, Green River, Laramie, Rawlins and Rock Springs. Many Irish also came to work on the railroad. They and others from the British Isles accounted for half of Wyoming's foreign-born population in 1870. English arrivals were often Mormon converts.

Another early visitor to northwest Wyoming was "Buffalo Bill" Cody. He guided tours through the Yellowstone area, which became America's first national park in 1872.

Germans and Russian-Germans came to Wyoming in the later 1800s, according to a landmark study, *Peopling the High Plains: Wyoming's European Heritage* (Wyoming State Archives, 1977). The Russian-Germans helped found the sugar beet industry in northwestern Wyoming. Other major groups who helped settle Wyoming included Italians, Greeks, Eastern Europeans, and Basques, who helped launch the sheep industry.

Wyoming became the 44th state in 1890. In 1925 it made history by electing America's first woman governor, Nellie Tayloe Ross, continuing a tradition of Wyoming milestones for women begun with the first equal-suffrage vote

research tips

- Wyoming professional researcher and editor of *History of Cheyenne* Sharon Lass Field says that finding where an ancestor is buried can lead to clues such as death certificates, obituaries, probate records, cemetery records, and of course, the gravestone. Field also emphasizes the importance of using land records.
- "We do not have a lot of the old county histories and biographical collections states farther east might have," Field says. "Catching a family on a census record is good—then a search of deeds, mortgages, cemeteries, and newspapers can be invaluable."
- A Wyoming researcher's first stop in the state, according to Field, should be the state archives in Cheyenne. Most court records, biographical files, books, census records, military records, newspapers and some courthouse records are there. The next stop should be the Laramie County Library, which houses the genealogy collection for the state. Also look for local data in county "Wyoming Rooms" or collections, Field says, usually in the county-seat library.
- The web site of the state archives **<wyoarchives.state.wy.us>** lists helpful resources such as school censuses.

CENSUS RECORDS

- Federal census: 1860 (with Nebraska), 1870, 1880, 1900, 1910, 1920, 1930
- Federal mortality schedules: 1870, 1880
- Special census of Civil War Union veterans and widows: 1890
- State/territorial census: 1905

RECORD HIGHLIGHTS

Probably the biggest challenge for Wyoming genealogists, according to Suzanne Leonard, Sheridan County coordinator for Wyoming GenWeb **<wygenweb.org>**, is the lack of early records. There are a few early census enumerations: Fort Bridger was included in Utah Territory in the 1850 US count, some Wyoming inhabitants were counted with Nebraska Territory in 1860, and a First Wyoming Territorial Census in 1869 preceded the territory's inclusion in the 1870 federal tally. A 1905 state census with information on entire households is available at the state archives. Keep in mind that Wyoming's counties evolved rapidly, from just six in 1869 (Albany, Carbon, Laramie, and Carter—renamed Sweetwater—from Dakota Territory; Green from Utah Territory; and the new Uinta County from parts of Idaho and Utah) to 23 counties in 1923.

Births and deaths weren't recorded statewide until 1909, and marriages and divorces not until 1941. Few prior birth and death records were kept by counties, though marriage records dating to 1869 can be accessed at the state archives. The archives also has many probate records, which were kept first by a territorial probate court and then by county district court clerks.

Land records, which date to 1841, can be a good resource if you can't find other early traces of your Wyoming ancestors. Most county land records begin with the territorial era and are at the state archives. The first homestead entry was in 1870, but public-lands settlement was slow until homestead requirements changes in 1912, peaking in the early 1920s.

They state archives' microfilm collection has nearly all newspapers published in Wyoming. Papers from 1849 to 1922 are digitized at **<www.wyonewspapers.org>**.

ARCHIVES, LIBRARIES, AND SOCIETIES

Albany County Genealogical Society
<www.rootsweb.ancestry.com/~wyalbany>

Bureau of Land Management, Wyoming State Office
Box 1828, Cheyenne, WY 82003, (307) 775-6256, **<www.blm.gov/wy/st/en.html>**

Cheyenne Genealogical and Historical Society
Box 2539, Cheyenne, WY 82003, **<cghswyoming.org>**

Fremont County Genealogical Society
c/o Riverton Branch Library, 1330 W. Park Ave., Riverton, WY 82501, (307) 856-3556, **<www.rootsweb.ancestry.com/~wyfremon>**

Goshen County Public Library
2001 East A St., Torrington, WY 82240, (307) 532-3411, **<will.state.wy.us/goshen>**

Land of Goshen Chapter, American Historical Society of Germans from Russia
101 Holly Dr., Torrington, WY 82240, **<www.ahsgr.org/land_of_goshen_chapter.htm>**

Lander Valley Genealogical Society
1015 Black Blvd., lander, WY 85250

Laramie County Public Library
2200 Pioneer Ave., Cheyenne, WY 82001, (307) 634-3561, **<www.lclsonline.org>**

Laramie Peekers Genealogical Society of Platte County
1108 21st St., Wheatland, WY 82201, **<www.rootsweb.ancestry.com/~wyplatte>**

National Archives and Records Administration, Rocky Mountain Region
Box 25307, Denver, CO 80225, (303) 407-5740, **<www.archives.gov/rocky-mountain>**

Natrona County Genealogical Society
Box 50665, Casper, WY 82605, **<www.rootsweb.ancestry.com/~wynatron>**

Park County Genealogical Society
1232 Alpine Ave., Cody, WY 82414

Powell Valley Genealogical Club
Box 184, Powell, WY 82435

Roman Catholic Diocese of Cheyenne
2121 Capitol Ave., Cheyenne, WY 82001, (866) 790-0014, **<dioceseofcheyenne.org>**

Sheridan Genealogical Society
Sheridan County Library, 335 W. Alger St., Sheridan, WY 82801, **<www.rootsweb.ancestry.com/~wyshergs>**

Southeastern Wyoming Chapter, American Historical Society of Germans from Russia
409 E. 7 St., Cheyenne, WY 82007, **<www.ahsgr.org/southeastern_wyoming_chapter.htm>**

Sublette County Genealogical Society
Box 1186, Pinedale, WY 82941

University of Wyoming Library
1000 E. University Ave., Laramie, WY 82071, (307) 766-3190 or (800) 442-6757, **<www-lib.uwyo.edu>**

Vital Records Services
Hathaway Building, Cheyenne, WY 82002, (307) 777-7591, **<www.publicrecordsinfo.com/vital_records/wyoming_vital_records.htm>**

Weston County Genealogical Society
<www.rootsweb.ancestry.com/~wyweston>

Sheridan County, Fulmer Public Library
335 W. Alger St., Sheridan, WY 82801, (307) 674-8585, **<sheridanwyolibrary.org>**

Wyoming State Archives
Barrett Building, 2301 Central Ave., Cheyenne, WY 82002, (307) 777-7826, **<wyoarchives.state.wy.us>**

Wyoming State Historical Society
<wyshs.org>

Wyoming State Library
2800 Central Ave., Cheyenne, WY 82002, (307) 777-6333, **<will.state.wy.us>**

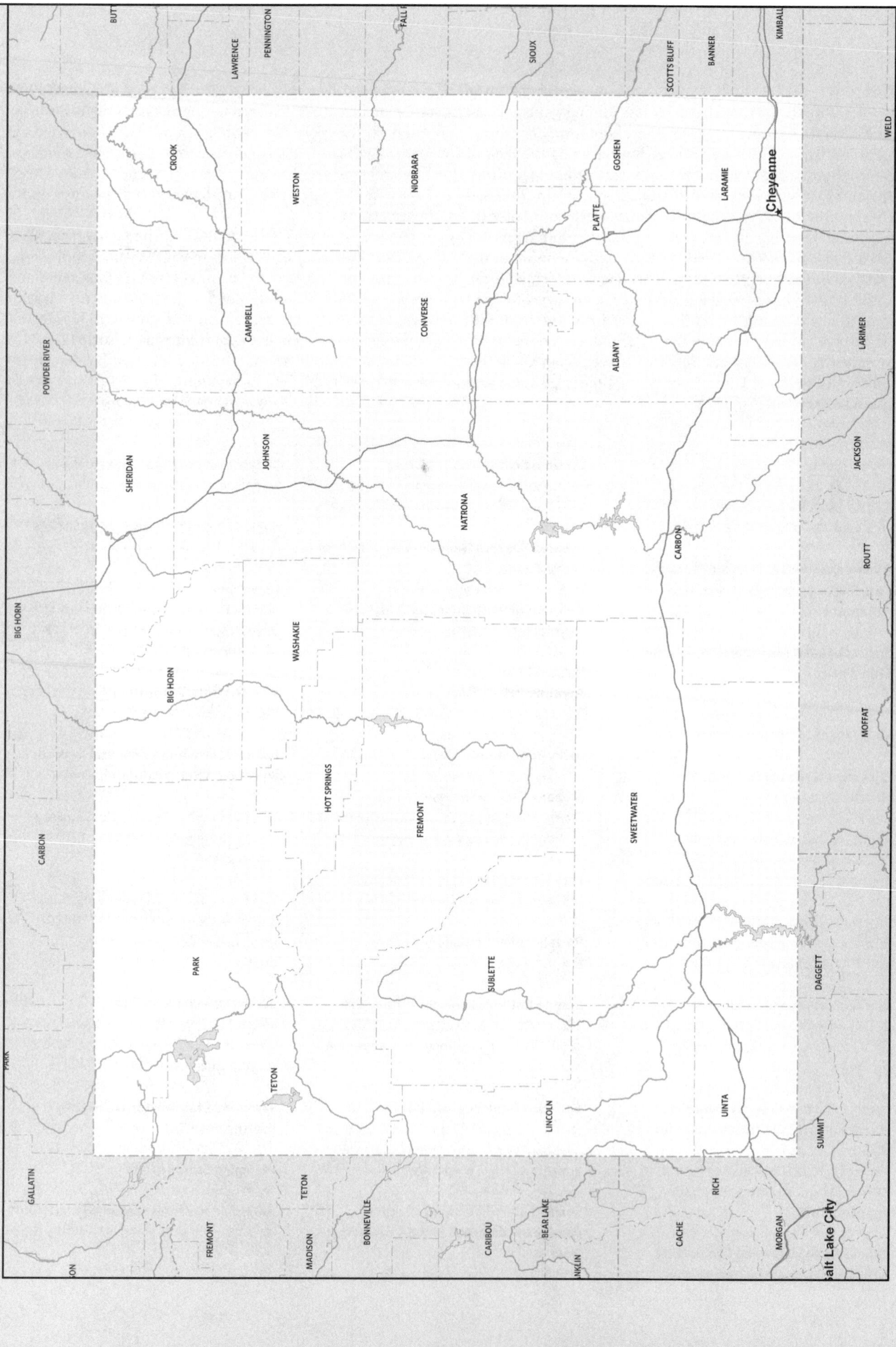
CROOK
WESTON
NIOBRARA
GOSHEN
LARAMIE
Cheyenne
PLATTE
CAMPBELL
CONVERSE
ALBANY
SHERIDAN
JOHNSON
NATRONA
CARBON
WASHAKIE
BIG HORN
HOT SPRINGS
FREMONT
SWEETWATER
PARK
SUBLETTE
TETON
LINCOLN
UINTA
LAWRENCE
PENNINGTON
SIOUX
SCOTTS BLUFF
BANNER
KIMBALL
WELD
LARIMER
JACKSON
ROUTT
MOFFAT
DAGGETT
SUMMIT
Salt Lake City
MORGAN
RICH
CACHE
BEAR LAKE
CARIBOU
BONNEVILLE
MADISON
TETON
FREMONT
GALLATIN
CARBON
PARK
BIG HORN
POWDER RIVER

☞GENERAL RESOURCES

A Directory of Church and Religious Organizations in the State of Wyoming (Historical Records Survey, 1939)

Empty Saddles, Forgotten Names: Outlaws of the Black Hills and Wyoming by Doug Engebretson (North Plains Press, 1982)

Federal Postal Employees and Contractors in Wyoming, 1869-1911 (Medicine Bow Publications, 1985)

From Rags to Riches: A History of Hilliard and Bear River, 1890-1990 by Margaret Moore Lester (First Impressions, 1992)

Genealogical Guide to Wyoming by Joyce V.H. Spiros (Verlene Publisher, 1982)

Guide to the County Archives of Wyoming edited by Jim Donahue (Wyoming State Archives, 1991)

Guide to Public Vital Statistics Records in Wyoming (US Work Projects Administration, 1941)

Guide to the State Government and Municipal Archives of Wyoming by Jim Donahue, et al. (Wyoming State Archives, 1991)

Guide to Vital Statistics Records in Wyoming: Church Archives (Historical Records Survey, 1942)

Guide to Wyoming Frontier Newspapers, in the *Annals of Wyoming*, vols. 33-35, (1961-1963) Wyoming State Archives

Guide to Wyoming Newspapers, 1867-1967 by Lola Homsher (Wyoming State Library, 1971)

The Historical Encyclopedia of Wyoming, 2 vols., by Thomas S. Chamblin (the Wyoming Historical Institute, 1970)

History of Big Horn Basin: by Charles Arthur Welch (Deseret News Press, 1940)

A History of the Covenant Church in the Midwest and Southwest Conferences by Billie Hoy (Arrow Printing Co., 1961)

History of Wyoming, 3 vols., by Ichabod S. Bartlett (S.J. Clarke Publishing Co., 1918)

History of Wyoming by Alfred Larson Taft (University of Nebraska Press, 1965)

Inventory of the Church Archives of Wyoming Presbyterian Churches from the Historical Records Survey (filmed by the Family History Library, 1967)

Mormons and Their Neighbors: An Index to Over 75,000 Biographical Sketches form 1820 to the Present, 2 vols., by Mavin E. Wiggins (Harold B. Lee Library, Brigham Young University, 1984)

Peopling the High Plains: Wyoming's European Heritage by Gordon Olaf Hendrickson (Wyoming State Archives and Historical Department, 1977)

Progressive Men of the State of Wyoming (A.W. Bowen, 1903)

Some of the West: Biographical Accounts of Early-Day Wyoming by Lorah Chaffin (Caxton Printers, 1941)

Women of Wyoming, 2 vols., by Cora May Brown Beach (S.E. Boyer, 1927)

Wyoming Biographies by Lawrence M. Woods (High Plains Publishing Co., 1991)

Wyoming Clue Book, 5 vols., by Virginia Cole Trenholm (Wyoming State Archives and Historical Department, 1991)

Wyoming Research Outline by the Church of Jesus Christ of Latter-day Saints (online at **<www.familysearch.org/eng/search/RG/guide/wyoming>**)

Wyoming from Territorial Days to the Present, 3 vols., by Frances B. Beard (American Historical Society, 1933)

Wyoming's Territorial Sheriffs by Ann Gorzalka (High Plains Press, 1998)

☞IMMIGRATION RECORDS

111 Days to Zion by Al Knight (Deseret News, 1978)

Rescue of the 1856 Handcart Companies by Rebecca Cornwall (Brigham Young University Press, 1981)

☞MAPS

Maps of Wyoming Trails, Roads, Migration Routes and Forts by Loren C. Bishop (Wyoming State Archives & Historical Dept., 1963)

Wyoming Atlas and Gazetteer (DeLorme Mapping Co., 1993)

Wyoming Place Names by Mae B. Urbank (Mountain Press Publishing Co., 1988)

Wyoming Post Offices, 1850-1980 by John S. Gallagher (The Depot, 1980)

☞MILITARY RECORDS

The Bloody Bozeman: The Perilous Trail to Montana's Gold by Dorothy M. Johnson (Mountain Press Pub. Co., 1998)

Military Posts of Wyoming by Robert A. Murray (The Old Army Press, 1974)

Reflections of World War II, 115th U.S. Cavalry Wyoming National Guard by Leo R. Sanchez (The School, ca. 1994)

☞VITAL RECORDS

Burial Records from the Wyoming State Hospital (filmed by the Genealogical Society of Utah, 1969)

Davis Funeral Homes Records for 1918-1951. Riverton, Wyoming: Master Index by Evelyn Lovell and Marlys Albert Bias (Fremont County Genealogical Society, 1987)

Death in Yellowstone: Accidents and Foolhardiness in the First National Park by Lee H. Whittlesey (Roberts Rinehart Pub., 1995)

Uinta County, Wyoming Cemetery Records by Phyllis J. Martin (Phyllis J. Martin, 1982)

•-COUNTY DETAILS-•

ALBANY
525 Grand Ave., Laramie, WY 82070, (307) 721-2541,
<www.co.albany.wy.us>
- **INCORPORATED:** Dec. 16, 1868
- **PARENT COUNTY:** Original County
- **MARRIAGE RECORDS:** start in 1948, kept by County Clerk
- **DIVORCE:** 1980, District Court
- **LAND:** 1948, County Clerk
- **PROBATE:** 1981, District Court
- **COURT:** 1980, District Court
- **NOTES:** State Archives has court and divorce records 1869-1979, Death records 1899-1908, land records 1869-1947, naturalization 1869-1908, and probate records 1869-1980.

BIG HORN
Box 31, Basin, WY 82410, (307) 568-2612,
<www.bighorncountywy.gov>
- **INCORPORATED:** March 1890
- **PARENT COUNTIES:** Fremont, Johnson, Sheridan
- **MARRIAGE RECORDS:** start in 1968, kept by County Clerk
- **DIVORCE:** 1970, District Court
- **LAND:** 1965, County Clerk
- **PROBATE:** 1970, District Court
- **COURT:** 1970, District Court
- **NOTES:** State Archives has court and divorce records 1897-1969, land records 1885-1964, marriage records 1897-1967, military discharge records 1919-1964, naturalization records 1929-1955, and probate records 1897-1969.

CAMPBELL
500 S. Gillette Ave., Gillette, WY 82716, (307) 682-7283,
<www.ccgov.net>
- **INCORPORATED:** February 1911
- **PARENT COUNTIES:** Crook, Weston
- **MARRIAGE RECORDS:** start in 1961, kept by County Clerk
- **DIVORCE:** 1988, District Court
- **LAND:** 1961, County Clerk
- **PROBATE:** 1970, District Court
- **COURT:** 1988, District Court
- **NOTES:** State Archives has court and divorce records 1912-1987, land records 1885-1960, marriage records 1913-1960, military discharge records 1919-1960, naturalization records 1913-1940, and probate records 1915-1969.

CARBON
Box 6, Rawlins, WY 82301, (307) 328-2668,
<www.carbonwy.com>
- **INCORPORATED:** Dec. 16, 1868
- **PARENT COUNTY:** Original County
- **MARRIAGE RECORDS:** start in 1959, kept by County Clerk
- **DIVORCE:** 1988, District Court
- **LAND:** 1948, County Clerk
- **PROBATE:** 1953, District Court
- **COURT:** 1988, District Court
- **NOTES:** State Archives has court and divorce records 1870-1979, land records 1869-1947, marriage records 1870-1958, military discharge records 1919-1951, naturalization records 1908-1936, and probate records 1875-1952. See Nebraska for 1860 census.

CARTER
- **INCORPORATED:** Dec. 27, 1867
- **PARENT COUNTY:** Original County
- **NOTES:** See Sweetwater County. Name changed to Sweetwater 1869.

CONVERSE
107 N. Fifth St., Suite 114, Douglas, WY 82633, (307) 358-2244,
<conversecounty.org>
- **INCORPORATED:** March 1888
- **PARENT COUNTIES:** Laramie, Albany
- **MARRIAGE RECORDS:** start in 1963, kept by County Clerk
- **DIVORCE:** 1963, District Court
- **LAND:** 1963, County Clerk
- **PROBATE:** 1963, District Court
- **COURT:** 1963, District Court
- **NOTES:** State Archives has court and divorce records 1888-1962, land records 1885-1962, marriage records 1888-1962, military discharge records 1919-1962, naturalization records 1888-1940, and probate records 1892-1962.

CROOK
Box 37, Sundance, WY 82729, (307) 283-1323,
<www.crookcounty.wy.gov>
- **INCORPORATED:** December 1875
- **PARENT COUNTIES:** Laramie, Albany
- **MARRIAGE RECORDS:** start in 1970, kept by County Clerk
- **DIVORCE:** 1905, District Court
- **LAND:** 1952, County Clerk
- **PROBATE:** 1929, District Court
- **COURT:** 1905, District Court
- **NOTES:** State Archives has court and divorce records 1886-1904, land records 1885-1951, marriage records 1885-1969, military discharge records 1945-1952, naturalization records 1879-1918, and probate records 1886-1928.

FREMONT
450 N. Second St., lander, WY 82520, (307) 332-2405,
<fremontcountywy.org>
- **INCORPORATED:** March 1884
- **PARENT COUNTY:** Sweetwater
- **MARRIAGE RECORDS:** start in 1969, kept by County Clerk
- **DIVORCE:** 1965, District Court
- **LAND:** 1968, County Clerk
- **PROBATE:** 1977, District Court
- **COURT:** 1965, District Court
- **NOTES:** State Archives has court and divorce records 1888-1964, land records 1884-1967, marriage records 1884-1968, military discharge records 1918-1920, naturalization records 1907-1939, and probate records 1884-1976.

GOSHEN

Box 160, Torrington, WY 82240, (307) 532-4051,
<goshencounty.org>
- **INCORPORATED:** February 1911
- **PARENT COUNTY:** Laramie
- **MARRIAGE RECORDS:** start in 1911, kept by County Clerk
- **DIVORCE:** 1969, District Court
- **LAND:** late 1800s, County Clerk
- **PROBATE:** 1980, District Court
- **COURT:** 1969, District Court
- **NOTES:** State Archives has court and divorce records 1913-1968, and probate records 1913-1979. State Archives has a few early court and divorce records dating from 1868.

HOT SPRINGS

415 Arapahoe St., Thermopolis, WY 82443, (307) 864-3515,
<www.hscounty.com>
- **INCORPORATED:** February 1911
- **PARENT COUNTIES:** Fremont, Park, Big Horn
- **MARRIAGE RECORDS:** start in 1956, kept by County Clerk
- **DIVORCE:** 1936, District Court
- **LAND:** 1950, County Clerk
- **PROBATE:** 1921, District Court
- **COURT:** 1936, District Court
- **NOTES:** State Archives has court and divorce records 1911-1935, land records 1893-1949, marriage records 1913-1955, military discharge records 1919-1948, and probate records 1912-1920.

JOHNSON

76 N. Main St., Buffalo, WY 82834, (307) 684-7555,
<www.johnsoncountywyoming.org>
- **INCORPORATED:** December 1875
- **PARENT COUNTIES:** Carbon and Sweetwater
- **MARRIAGE RECORDS:** start in 1961, kept by County Clerk
- **DIVORCE:** 1964, District Court
- **LAND:** 1961, County Clerk
- **PROBATE:** 1939, District Court
- **COURT:** 1964, District Court
- **NOTES:** State Archives has court and divorce records ca. 1882-1963, land and marriage records 1881-1960, military discharge records 1871, 1884, 1890, 1919-1960, naturalization records 1881-1933, and probate records ca. 1885-1938. Formerly Pease County. Name changed to Johnson 1879.

LARAMIE

310 W. 19th St., Room 400, Cheyenne, WY 82001, (307) 633-4260, **<www.laramiecounty.com>**
- **INCORPORATED:** Jan. 9, 1867
- **PARENT COUNTY:** Original County
- **MARRIAGE RECORDS:** start in 1974, kept by County Clerk
- **DIVORCE:** 1921, District Court
- **LAND:** 1976, County Clerk
- **PROBATE:** 1993, District Court
- **COURT:** 1921, District Court
- **NOTES:** State Archives has court and divorce records 1868-1920, land records 1867-1975, marriage records 1868-1973, military discharges 1945-1963, naturalization records 1868-1943, probate records 1891-1992, wills 1973-1993. See Nebraska for 1860 census.

LINCOLN

925 Sage Ave., Kemmerer, WY 83101, (307) 877-9056,
<www.lcwy.org>
- **INCORPORATED:** February 1911
- **PARENT COUNTY:** Uinta
- **MARRIAGE RECORDS:** start in 1967, kept by County Clerk
- **DIVORCE:** 1974, District Court
- **LAND:** 1967, County Clerk
- **PROBATE:** 1966, District Court
- **COURT:** 1974, District Court
- **NOTES:** State Archives has court and divorce records 1913-1973, land records 1880-1966, marriage records 1913-1966, military discharge records 1919-1968, probate records 1913-1965, and wills 1888-1975.

NATRONA

Box 863, Casper, WY 82602, (307) 235-9202,
<www.natrona.net>
- **INCORPORATED:** March 1888
- **PARENT COUNTY:** Carbon
- **MARRIAGE RECORDS:** start in 1972, kept by County Clerk
- **DIVORCE:** 1959, District Court
- **LAND:** 1979, County Clerk
- **PROBATE:** 1958, District Court
- **COURT:** 1959, District Court
- **NOTES:** State Archives has court and divorce records 1890-1958, land records 1880-1978, marriage records 1890-1971, military discharge records 1919-1978, and probate records 1891-1957.

NIOBRARA

Box 1238, Lusk, WY 82225, (307) 334-2211,
<genealogytrails.com/wyo/niobrara>
- **INCORPORATED:** February 1911
- **PARENT COUNTY:** Converse
- **MARRIAGE RECORDS:** start in 1964, kept by County Clerk
- **DIVORCE:** 1922, District Court
- **LAND:** 1964, County Clerk
- **PROBATE:** 1964, District Court
- **COURT:** 1922, District Court
- **NOTES:** State Archives has court and divorce records 1913-1921, land records 1883-1963, marriage and probate records 1889-1963, and military discharge records 1919-1963.

PARK

1002 Sheridan Ave., Cody, WY 82414, (307) 527-8500,
<www.parkcounty.us>
- **INCORPORATED:** February 1909
- **PARENT COUNTY:** Big Horn
- **MARRIAGE RECORDS:** start in 1965, kept by County Clerk
- **DIVORCE:** 1971, District Court
- **LAND:** 1965, County Clerk
- **PROBATE:** 1956, District Court
- **COURT:** 1971, District Court
- **NOTES:** State Archives has court and divorce records 1911-1970, land and Marriage records 1911-1964, military discharge records 1919-1964, and probate records 1911-1955.

PEASE
- **INCORPORATED:** December 1875
- **PARENT COUNTIES:** Carbon and Sweetwater
- **NOTES:** See Johnson County. Name changed to Johnson 1879.

PLATTE
Box 728, Wheatland, WY 82201, (307) 322-3555,
<plattecountywyoming.com>
- **INCORPORATED:** February 1911
- **PARENT COUNTY:** Laramie
- **MARRIAGE RECORDS:** start in 1966, kept by County Clerk
- **DIVORCE:** 1979, District Court
- **LAND:** 1966, County Clerk
- **PROBATE:** 1969, District Court
- **COURT:** 1979, District Court
- **NOTES:** State Archives has court and divorce records 1913-1978, land records 1873-1965, marriage records 1913-1965, military discharge records 1919-1965, and probate records 1913-1968.

SHERIDAN
224 S. Main St., Sheridan, WY 82801, (307) 674-6722,
<www.sheridancounty.com>
- **INCORPORATED:** March 1888
- **PARENT COUNTY:** Johnson
- **MARRIAGE RECORDS:** start in 1962, kept by County Clerk
- **DIVORCE:** 1956, District Court
- **LAND:** 1972, County Clerk
- **PROBATE:** 1925, District Court
- **COURT:** 1956, District Court
- **NOTES:** State Archives has court and divorce records 1888-1955, land records 1888-1971, marriage records 1888-1961, military discharge records 1922-1971, and probate records 1888-1924.

SUBLETTE
Box 250,, Pinedale, WY 82941, (307) 367-4372,
<www.sublette.com>
- **INCORPORATED:** February 1921
- **PARENT COUNTIES:** Fremont, Lincoln
- **MARRIAGE RECORDS:** start in 1968, kept by County Clerk
- **DIVORCE:** 1923, District Court
- **LAND:** 1968, County Clerk
- **PROBATE:** 1923, District Court
- **COURT:** 1923, District Court
- **NOTES:** State Archives has land records 1922-1967 and marriage records 1923-1967.

SWEETWATER
Box 730, Green River, WY 82935, (307) 872-9360,
<www.sweet.wy.us>
- **INCORPORATED:** Dec. 27, 1867
- **PARENT COUNTY:** Original County
- **MARRIAGE RECORDS:** start in 1967, kept by County Clerk
- **DIVORCE:** 1987, District Court
- **LAND:** 1948, County Clerk
- **PROBATE:** 1960, District Court
- **NOTES:** State Archives has court and divorce records 1870-1986, land records 1868-1947, marriage records 1870-1966, military discharge records 1898-1948, naturalization records 1890-1931, and probate records 1869-1959. Formerly Carter County. Name changed to Sweetwater 1869. See Nebraska for 1860 census.

TETON
Box 3594, Jackson, WY 83001, (307) 733-4430,
<www.tetonwyo.org>
- **INCORPORATED:** February 1921
- **PARENT COUNTY:** Lincoln
- **MARRIAGE RECORDS:** start in 1969, kept by County Clerk
- **DIVORCE:** 1980, District Court
- **LAND:** 1969, County Clerk
- **PROBATE:** 1978, District Court
- **COURT:** 1980, District Court
- **NOTES:** State Archives has court and divorce records 1923-1979, land records 1902-1968, marriage records 1922-1968, military discharge records 1941-1967, and probate records 1922-1977.

UINTA
225 Ninth St., Evanston, WY 82931, (307) 783-0301,
<www.uintacounty.com>
- **INCORPORATED:** December 1869
- **PARENT COUNTY:** Original County
- **MARRIAGE RECORDS:** 1972, County Clerk & Recorder
- **LAND:** 1977, County Clerk & Recorder
- **DIVORCE:** start in 1970, kept by District Court
- **PROBATE:** 1934, District Court
- **COURT:** 1970, District Court
- **NOTES:** State Archives has court and divorce records 1872-1969, land records 1861-1976, marriage records 1872-1971, military discharge records 1919-1965, naturalization records 1872-1941, and probate records 1861-1933. See Nebraska for the 1860 census.

WASHAKIE
Box 260, Worland, WY 82401, (307) 347-3131,
<washakiecounty.net>
- **INCORPORATED:** February 1911
- **PARENT COUNTY:** Big Horn
- **MARRIAGE RECORDS:** start in 1913, kept by County Clerk
- **DIVORCE:** 1979 District Court
- **LAND:** 1953 County Clerk
- **PROBATE:** 1973 District Court
- **COURT:** 1979 District Court
- **NOTES:** State Archives has court and divorce records 1912-1978, land records 1913-1952, and probate records 1913-1972.

WESTON
1 W. Main St., Newcastle, WY 82701, (307) 746-2684,
<www.rootsweb.ancestry.com/~wyweston>
- **INCORPORATED:** March 1890
- **PARENT COUNTY:** Crook
- **MARRIAGE RECORDS:** start in 1970, kept by County Clerk
- **DIVORCE:** 1966, District Court
- **LAND:** 1968, County Clerk
- **PROBATE:** 1970, District Court
- **COURT:** 1966, District Court
- **NOTES:** State Archives has court and divorce records 1890-1965, land records 1886-1967, marriage records 1890-1969, military discharge records 1919-1967, and probate records 1891-1969.

STATE WEBSITES

» BY DAVID A. FRYXELL

The internetization of America also has swept over the nation's state archives, historical and genealogical societies, libraries, vital-records offices and other keepers of genealogical gold. Many of the resources that once gathered dust in state repositories can now be accessed from home, on your computer. These 75 stellar websites—we've included at least one site per state—are worthy of stars on your genealogical research flag.

ALABAMA

Alabama Department of Archives and History
<archives.state.al.us>

Encyclopedia of Alabama
<encyclopediaofalabama.org>

ALASKA

Alaska Libraries, Archives and Museums
<lam.alaska.gov>

ARIZONA

Arizona Genealogy Birth and Death Certificates
<genealogy.az.gov>

Arizona Biographical Database
<lib.az.us/bio/default.aspx>

ARKANSAS

Arkansas History Commission
<www.ark-ives.com>

CALIFORNIA

Online Archive of California
<www.oac.cdlib.org>

California Genealogical Society and Library
<californiaancestors.org>

COLORADO

Colorado Historic Newspapers Collection
<www.coloradohistoricnewspapers.org>

Colorado State Archives
<www.colorado.gov/dpa/doit/archives/geneal.htm>

CONNECTICUT

Connecticut State Library
<cslib.org>

DELAWARE

Delaware Public Archives
<archives.delaware.gov>

FLORIDA

Florida Memory Project
<floridamemory.com>

GEORGIA

Digital Library of Georgia
<dlg.galileo.usg.edu>

Georgia Archives
<sos.georgia.gov/archives>

HAWAII

Hawaii State Archives
<hawaii.gov/dags/archives>

IDAHO

BYU-Idaho Special Collections
<abish.byui.edu/specialCollections/famhist>

ILLINOIS

Illinois State Archives
<www.library.sos.state.il.us/departments/archives/databases.html>

Cook County Clerk of the Circuit Court
<cookcountyclerkofcourt.org/nr>

INDIANA
Indiana State Digital Archives
<indianadigitalarchives.org>

Allen County Public Library
<genealogycenter.info>

IOWA
Iowa Genealogical Society
<iowagenealogy.org>

Iowa GenWeb Project
<iagenweb.org>

KANSAS
Kansas State Historical Society
<kshs.org/genealogists>

KENTUCKY
Kentucky Historical Society
<history.ky.gov>

LOUISIANA
Louisiana State Archives
<sos.louisiana.gov/tabid/88/default.aspx>

Louisiana Biography and Obituary Index
<neworleanspubliclibrary.org/obits/obits.htm>

MAINE
Maine State Archives
<maine.gov/portal/facts_history/genealogy.html>

Maine Memory Network
<www.mainememory.net>

MARYLAND
Archives of Maryland Online
<aomol.net>

Western Maryland Historical Library
<whilbr.org>

MASSACHUSETTS
Massachusetts Archives
<www.sec.state.ma.us/arc/arcidx.htm>

MICHIGAN
Seeking Michigan
<seekingmichigan.org>

MINNESOTA
Minnesota Historical Society
<www.mnhs.org/genealogy>

Minnesota Discovery Center
<mndiscoverycenter.com/research-center>

MISSISSIPPI
Mississippi Department of Archives and History
<mdah.state.ms.us>

MISSOURI
Missouri Digital Heritage Initiative
<sos.mo.gov/mdh>

Missouri History Museum
<mohistory.org/genealogy>

MONTANA
Montana Historical Society Research Center
<mhs.mt.gov/research>

NEBRASKA
Nebraska State Historical Society
<nebraskahistory.org>

NEVADA
Nevada Census Database
<nvshpo.org/index.php?option=com_content&view=article&id=1278&Itemid=391>

NEW HAMPSHIRE
New Hampshire Division of Archives and Records Management
<www.sos.nh.gov/archives>

NEW JERSEY
New Jersey State Library
<www.njstatelib.org/NJ_Information/Digital_Collections>

NEW MEXICO
New Mexico Genealogical Society
<nmgs.org>

NEW YORK
New York State Archives
<www.archives.nysed.gov/a/research/res_topics_genealogy.shtml>

New York State Military Museum and Veterans Research Center
<dmna.state.ny.us/historic/mil-hist.htm>

NORTH CAROLINA
North Carolina State Archives
<archives.ncdcr.gov>

NCGenWeb Project
<www.ncgenweb.us>

NORTH DAKOTA
North Dakota State University Institute for Regional Studies
<library.ndsu.edu/archives/biography-genealogy>

North Dakota Department of Public Health Public Death Index
<secure.apps.state.nd.us/doh/certificates/deathCertSearch.htm>

OHIO
Ohio Historical Society
<www.ohiohistory.org/resource/archlib>

Ohio Memory
<www.ohiomemory.org>

OKLAHOMA
Oklahoma Historical Society
<okhistory.org>

OREGON
Oregon State Archives
<arcweb.sos.state.or.us/banners/genealogy.htm>

PENNSYLVANIA
Pennsylvania State Archives
<www.digitalarchives.state.pa.us/archive.asp>

Historical Society of Pennsylvania
<www.hsp.org>

RHODE ISLAND
Rhode Island Historical Society
<rihs.org>

SOUTH CAROLINA
South Carolina Department of Archives and History
<archives.sc.gov/genealogy>

SOUTH DAKOTA
South Dakota Department of Health
<apps.sd.gov/applications/ph14over100birthrec/index.asp>

South Dakota State Historical Society
<history.sd.gov/archives/genealogists.aspx>

TENNESSEE
Tennessee State Library and Archives
<www.tn.gov/tsla/Collections.htm>

Tennessee Virtual Archive
<teva.contentdm.oclc.org>

TEXAS
Texas State Library and Archives Commission
<tsl.state.tx.us/arc/genfirst.html>

Texas State Historical Association
<tshaonline.org>

UTAH
Utah Death Certificate Index
<archives.utah.gov/research/indexes/20842.htm>

Cemetery and Burial Database
<history.utah.gov/research_and_collections/cemeteries>

Utah Digital Newspapers
<digitalnewspapers.org>

VERMONT
Vermont Historical Society
<vermonthistory.org>

VIRGINIA
Virginia Memory
<www.virginiamemory.com/collections>

Virginia Historical Society
<vahistorical.org>

WASHINGTON
Washington State Digital Archives
<digitalarchives.wa.gov>

Historic Newspapers in Washington
<www.sos.wa.gov/history/newspapers.aspx>

WEST VIRGINIA
West Virginia Archives and History
<www.wvculture.org/history/archivesindex.aspx>

WISCONSIN
Wisconsin Historical Society
<www.wisconsinhistory.org/genealogy>

WYOMING
Wyoming Newspaper Project
<wyonewspapers.org>

NATIONAL RESOURCES

Although the *Family Tree Sourcebook* focuses on helping you access your ancestors' county-level vital, military, land, court, naturalization and other records, national-level resources also are important to your genealogy research. For example, a national church archive could help you find religious records mentioning your ancestor. The Family History Library in Salt Lake City holds microfilm of county records across the country (accessible via its network of local Family History Centers). A reference such as Ann S. Lainhart's *State Census Records* might point you to records that can fill in the years between US censuses. Listed below are libraries, societies, archives, print and online resources *Family Tree Magazine* recommends exploring when tracing your family's roots across state lines.

ARCHIVES, LIBRARIES, AND SOCIETIES

Afro-American Historical and Genealogical Society
Box 73067, Washington, DC 20056, **<www.aahgs.org>**

American Baptist Historical Society
3001 Mercer University Dr., Atlanta, GA 30341, (678) 547-6680, **<www.abhsarchives.org>**

American Baptist-Samuel Colgate Historical Library
1106 S. Goodman St., Rochester, NY 14620, (716) 473-1740

American Catholic Historical Society
263 S. Fourth St., Philadelphia, PA, 19106, (610) 517-0835, **<www.amchs.org>**

American-French Genealogical Society
78 Earle St., Box 830, Woonsocket, RI 02895, (401) 765-6141, **<www.afgs.org>**

American Irish Historical Society
991 Fifth Ave., New York, NY 10028, (212) 288-2263, **<www.aihs.org>**

American Jewish Archives
3101 Clifton Ave., Cincinnati, OH 45220, (513) 221-1875, **<www.americanjewisharchives.org>**

American Jewish Historical Society
160 Herrick Rd., Newton Centre, MA 02459, (617) 559-8880, **<www.ajhs.org>**

American Latvian Association
400 Hurley Ave., Rockville, MD 20850, (301) 340-1914, **<www.alausa.org>**

American Scandinavian Foundation
58 Park Ave., New York, NY 10016 (212) 879-9779, **<www.amscan.org>**

American Swedish Historical Museum
1900 Pattison Ave., Philadelphia, PA 19145 (215) 389-1776, **<www.americanswedish.org>**

Archives of the Episcopal Church
606 Rathervue Place, Box 2247, Austin, TX 78768, (512) 472-6816, **<www.episcopalarchives.org>**

Association for Gravestone Studies
101 Munson St., Suite 108, Greenfield, MA 01301, (413) 772-0836, **<www.gravestonestudies.org>**

Association of Professional Genealogists
Box 350998, Westminster, CO 80035, (303) 465-6980, **<www.apgen.org>**

Boston University School of Theology Library
745 Commonwealth Ave., Boston, MA 02215, (617) 353-3034, **<www.bu.edu/sthlibrary>**

Congregational Library and Archives
14 Beacon St., Boston, MA 02108, (617) 523-0470, **<www.14beacon.org>**

Evangelical Lutheran Church of America Archives
321 Bonnie Lane, Elk Grove Village, IL 60007, (847) 690-9410, **<www.elca.org/Who-We-Are/History/ELCA-Archives.aspx>**

Family History Library
35 NW Temple St., Salt Lake City, UT 84150, (800) 346-6044, **<www.familysearch.org>**

Federation of East European Family History Societies
Box 510898, Salt Lake City, UT 84151, **<www.feefhs.org>**

International Association of Jewish Genealogical Societies
<www.iajgs.org>

Irish Ancestral Research Association
Dept. W, 2120 Commonwealth Ave., Auburndale, MA 02466, **<tiara.ie>**

Irish Genealogical Society International
Box 16585, St. Paul, MN 55116, **<irishgenealogical.org>**

Italian Genealogical Society of America
Box 3572, Peabody, MA 01961, **<www.italianroots.org>**

National Archives and Records Administration, Washington, DC
700 Pennsylvania Avenue, NW Washington, DC 20408, (866) 325-7208 **<www.archives.gov>**

National Archives and Records Administration, College Park, Md.
8601 Adelphi Rd., College Park, MD 20740, (866) 272-6272, **<archives.gov/dc-metro/college-park>**

National Genealogical Society
3108 Columbia Pike, Suite 300, Arlington, Va., 22204, (800) 473-0060, **<www.ngsgenealogy.org>**

National Society, Daughters of the American Revolution
1776 D St. NW, Washington, DC 20006, (202) 628-1776, **<www.dar.org>**

New England Historic Genealogical Society
99 Newbury St., Boston, MA 02116, (888) 296-3447, **<www.americanancestors.org>**

Palatines to America German Genealogy Society
Box 141260, Columbus, OH 43214, (614) 267-4700, **<www.palam.org>**

Philadelphia Jewish Archives Center
615 N. Broad St., Philadelphia, PA 19123, (215) 925-8090, **<library.temple.edu/collections/pjac>**

Presbyterian Historical Society, National Archives of the Presbyterian Church
425 Lombard St., Philadelphia, PA 19147, (215) 627-1852, **<www.history.pcusa.org>**

Reformed Church in America, New Brunswick Theological Seminary
Gardner A. Sage Library, 21 Seminary Pl., New Brunswick, NJ 08901, (732) 246-1779, **<www.rca.org/Page.aspx?pid=230>**

Sons of Union Veterans of the Civil War
Box 1865, Harrisburg, PA 17105, (717) 232-7000, **<suvcw.org>**

United Brethren Historical Library
Church of the Brethren, 1451 Dundee Ave., Elgin, IL 60120, (847) 742-5100, Ext. 294, **<www.cob-net.org/genhis.htm>**

United Daughters of the Confederacy
UDC General Headquarters, 328 North Blvd., Richmond, VA 23220, (804) 353-1636, **<www.hqudc.org>**

United Methodist Archives Center
General Commission on Archives and History, 36 Madison Ave., Box 127, Madison, NJ 07940, (973) 408-3189, **<www.gcah.org>**

GENERAL RESOURCES

African-American Genealogy: A Bibliography and Guide to Sources by Curt Bryan Witcher (Round Tower Books, 2000)

American Forts, Yesterday and Today by Bruce Grant, illustrated by Lorence F. Bjorklund (Dutton, 1965)

The American Genealogical-Biographical Index (Godfrey Memorial Library, 2000-2003)

The American Genealogical Index by Fremont Rider (Published by a committee representing the cooperating subscribing libraries at Wesleyan University Station, 1942-1951)

The American Genealogical and Biographical Index edited by Fremont Rider (Godfrey Memorial Library, 1952-2000)

American Naturalization Records, 1790-1990: What They Are and How to Use Them by John J. Newman (HeritageQuest, 1998)

Assessment Lists of the Federal Bureau of Internal Revenue, 1862-66 by the US Bureau of Internal Revenue (National Archives, 1965)

Genealogical Encyclopedia of the Colonial Americas by Christina K. Schaefer (Genealogical Publishing Co., 1998.)

Genealogical Research: Methods and Sources by various authors, edited by Kenn Stryker-Rodda (American Society of Genealogists, 1983)

The Genealogist's Companion and Sourcebook, 2nd edition, by Emily Anne Croom (Betterway Books, 2003)

A Genealogist's Guide to Discovering Your African-American Ancestors by Franklin Carter Smith and Emily Anne Croom (Betterway Books, 2003)

Guide to Genealogical Research in the National Archives of the United States edited by Anne Bruner Eales and Robert M. Kvasnicka (National Archives, 2000)

A Handy Guide to Record-Searching in the Larger Cities of the United States by E. Kay Kirkham (Everton, 1974)

History and Bibliography of American Newspapers, 1690-1820, 2 vols., by Clarence Saunders Brigham (American Antiquarian Society, 1947, 1975)

Index to Naturalization Records, ca. 1876-1906 by the US Circuit Court (filmed by the Family History Library, 1991)

Key Title Index to the American Genealogical-Biographical Index: Register of Family History Library Call Numbers edited by Patricia L. Clark and Dorothy Huntsman (Family History Library, 1990)

Miscellaneous Records: 1856-1972 by Daughters of the American Revolution (filmed by the Genealogical Society of Utah, 1972)

Naturalization Index Cards, 1790-1926 by the US District Court (filmed by the Genealogical Society of Utah, 1985)

Naturalization Records, 1906-1917 by the US District Court (National Archives, 1988)

They Became Americans: Finding Naturalization Records and Ethnic Origins by Loretto Dennis Szucs (Ancestry, 1998)

CENSUS RECORDS

The American Census Handbook by Thomas Jay Kemp (Scholarly Resources, 2001)

The Census Book: A Genealogist's Guide to Federal Census Facts, Schedules, and Indexes by William Dollarhide (Heritage Quest, 2000)

Finding Answers in US Census Records by Loretto Dennis Szucs and Matthew Wright (Ancestry Publishing, 2002)

Map Guide to the US Federal Censuses, 1790-1920 by William Thorndale and William Dollarhide (Genealogical Publishing Co., 1987)

State Census Records by Ann S. Lainhart (Genealogical Publishing Co., 1992)

Tribal Census Information, 1877-1952 from the US Bureau of Indian Affairs (filmed by the Family History Library, 1978)

Your Guide to the Federal Census by Kathleen W. Hinckley (Betterway Books, 2002)

IMMIGRATION RECORDS

American Passenger Arrival Records by Michael Tepper (Genealogical Publishing Co., 1993)

The Complete Book of Emigrants: 1607-1776 and Emigrants in Bondage, 1614-1775 by Peter Wilson Coldham (Broderbund, 1996)

Declarations of Intentions, Naturalizations, and Petitions, 1855-1960, United States District Court (filmed by the Genealogical Society of Utah, 1987-1989)

Misc. Naturalization Records, 1890-1972 from the US District Court (filmed by the Family History Library, ca. 1984)

A List of Alien Passengers, Bonded, from January 1, 1847 to January 1, 1851 by J.B. Munroe (Genealogical Publishing Co., 1971)

Passenger and Immigration Lists Index by P. William Filby and Mary K. Meyer (Gale Research, ca. 1981-)

They Came in Ships: A Guide to Finding Your Immigrant Ancestor's Arrival Records, 2nd edition, by John P. Colletta (Ancestry, 1993)

LAND RECORDS

Land and Property Research in the United States by Wade E. Hone (Ancestry, 1997)

Land & Property Research in the United States by Wade E. Hone (Ancestry, 1997)

Land Ownership Maps, a Checklist of Nineteenth Century United States County Maps in the Library of Congress compiled by Richard W. Stephenson (1967)

Locating Your Roots: Discover Your Ancestors Using Land Records by Patricia Law Hatcher (Betterway Books, 2003)

Tract Books by the US Bureau of Land Management (Records Improvement, Bureau of Land Management, 1957)

MILITARY RECORDS

Genealogical Abstracts of Revolutionary War Pension Files by Virgil D. White (National Historical Publishing Co., 1990-1992)

Master Alphabetical Index, World War Veterans, Army, 1917-1918 (filmed by the Genealogical Society of Utah, 1972)

Index to Revolutionary War Service Records by Virgil D. White (National Historical Publishing Co., ca. 1995)

General Index to Compiled Military Service Records of Revolutionary War Soldiers by the US Adjutant General's Office (National Archives, 1942)

General index to Pension Files, 1861-1934 by the US Veterans Administration (Veterans Administration, Publications Service, 1953)

The Life of Johnny Reb: The Common Soldier of the Confederacy by Bell Irvin Wiley (Louisiana State University Press, 1978)

Pension Index File, Alphabetical; of the Veterans Administrative Contact and Administrative Services, Administrative Operations Services, 1861-1934 from the US Veterans Administration (Veterans Administration, Publications Service, 1953)

Registers of Enlistments in the United States Army, 1798-1914 from the US Army (filmed by the National Archives, 1956)

Revolutionary War Pension and Bounty-Land-Warrant Application Files by the US Veterans Administration, 1969)

Schedules Enumerating Union Veterans and Widows of Union Veterans of The Civil War from the US Census Office (National Archives, 1948)

Uncle, We Are Ready! Registering America's Men, 1917-1918: A Guide to Researching World War I Draft Registration Cards by John J. Newman (Heritage Quest, 2001)

US Military Records: A Guide to Federal & State Resources, Colonial America to the Present by James C. Neagles (Ancestry, 1994)

World War II: A Family Historian's Guide by Debra Johnson Knox (MIE Publishing, 2003)

VITAL RECORDS

Your Guide to Cemetery Research by Sharon DeBartolo Carmack (Betterway Books, 2002)

WEBSITES

GENERAL RESEARCH

AccessGenealogy
<www.accessgenealogy.com>

AmericanAncestors.org $
<www.americanancestors.org>

Ancestry.com $
<ancestry.com>

Archives $
<archives.com>

Cyndi's List
<cyndislist.com>

Daughters of the American Revolution
<www.dar.org>

DistantCousin.com
<www.distantcousin.com>

FamilySearch
<www.familysearch.org>

Footnote $
<footnote.com>

GenealogyBank $
<www.genealogybank.com>

HeritageQuest Online
<www.heritagequestonline.com>
(available through subscribing libraries)

Library of Congress
<loc.gov>

National Archives and Records Administration
<archives.gov>

Newspaper Abstracts
<www.newspaperabstracts.com>

OliveTreeGenealogy
<olivetreegenealogy.com>

One-Step Web Pages
<stevemorse.org>

RootsWeb
<www.rootsweb.ancestry.com>

USGenWeb
<usgenweb.org>

World Vital Records $
<www.worldvitalrecords.com>

DIGITIZED BOOKS

Internet Archives
<archive.org>

Family History Archive
<www.lib.byu.edu/fhc>

Google Books
<books.google.com>

ETHNIC RESEARCH

AfriGeneas
<www.afrigeneas.com>

AfriQuest
<afriquest.com>

Cherokee Heritage Center
<www.cherokeeheritage.org>

Immigration History Research Center
<www.ihrc.umn.edu>

JewishGen
<www.jewishgen.org>

LowCountry Africana
<lowcountryafricana.net>

Society of Hispanic Historical and Ancestral Research
<shhar.net>

FAMILY TREES

FamilyLink
<www.familylink.com>

Genetree
<www.genetree.com>

Geni
<www.geni.com>

MyFamily.com
<www.myfamily.com>

MyHeritage
<www.myheritage.com>

OneGreatFamily $
<www.onegreatfamily.com>

TribalPages
<www.tribalpages.com>

WeRelate
<www.werelate.org>

IMMIGRATION RECORDS

Castle Garden
<castlegarden.org>

Ellis Island
<ellisisland.org>

Immigrant Ships Transcribers Guild
<www.immigrantships.net>

Information Wanted
<infowanted.bc.edu>

TheShipsList
<www.theshipslist.com>

LAND RECORDS

Bureau of Land Management General Land Office Records
<www.glorecords.blm.gov>

MILITARY RESEARCH

Civil War Soldiers and Sailors System
<www.itd.nps.gov/cwss>

eHistory
<ehistory.osu.edu>

VITAL RECORDS

Find a Grave
<www.findagrave.com>

Nationwide Gravesite Locator
<gravelocator.cem.va.gov>

Western States Historical Marriage Records Index
<abish.byui.edu/specialcollections/westernstates/search.cfm>

$ denotes primarily paid content

ACKNOWLEDGMENTS

★ **AMONG THE FIRST** genealogical reference books of this kind was the ubiquitous *Everton's Handy Book for Genealogists*, first published in 1947. References published since, which include Ancestry's *Red Book* and *The Source*, have relied on that pioneering tome for county record start dates. *The Family Tree Sourcebook for Genealogists* is the only such reference still being published, and we've updated it to be even more helpful to your search.

This book was made possible by numerous contributors, fact checkers, editors and proofreaders. They provided genealogical advice for each state, verified county addresses and other data through phone calls and Google searches, and compiled resources. Naturally, with a work of this magnitude, there will always be discrepancies and errors, despite everyone's best efforts. We hope the reader will take this into consideration and not be overly critical or frustrated when an error is discovered. If you should find an error, please e-mail it to us at **ftmedit@fwmedia.com**.

We extend our appreciation to Jim Cappo, Brad Crawford, Jason Cutler, Karrie Jackson, Nicolas Krupar, Barbara Poe, Matthew Wagner, Kateri Kosta, Rebecca Pittman, Leslie Stroope, Cathy Dyer, Caitlin Saniga, Jamie Royce, Amy Wilson, Megan Milstead, Jeff Suess, Katie Hilbert and others who helped along the way. We'd also like to acknowledge Erin Nevius, who coordinated the first edition of this book.

Finally, we give special thanks to the work of these contributors, who shared their genealogical expertise about researching in US states:

★ **SHARON DEBARTOLO CARMACK** is a certified genealogist and a partner in the Salt Lake City-based genealogical and historical research firm of Warren, Carmack & Associates **<www.warrencarmack.com>**. She's a contributing editor to *Family Tree Magazine* and author of 14 books, including *Your Guide to Cemetery Research, Organizing Your Family History Search, You Can Write Your Family History* and *Finding Your Ellis Island Ancestors*, all from Family Tree Books.

★ **EMILY ANNE CROOM** is a genealogical researcher, lecturer, teacher and writer in Bellaire, Texas. Her genealogy books include *Unpuzzling Your Past, 4th edition, The Unpuzzling Your Past Workbook, A Genealogist's Guide to Discovering Your African-American Ancestors* with coauthor Franklin Smith, *The Sleuth Book for Genealogists* and *The Genealogist's Companion and Sourcebook*, 2nd edition.

★ **DAVID A. FRYXELL** is the founding editor of *Family Tree Magazine*, America's largest-circulation publication for genealogists. He edited *The Family Tree Guide Book* and contributed to *The Family Tree Guide Book to Europe*, both from Betterway Books. Fryxell lives in Silver City, NM, where he edits and publishes a regional periodical, *Desert Exposure*, serves as contributing editor to *Family Tree Magazine*, and works on his Swedish, English and Southern US genealogy lines.

★ **RHONDA R. MCCLURE** is a lecturer, author and staff genealogist at the New England Historic and Genealogical Society. She's written for a variety of genealogical periodicals and is the author of *Digitizing Your Family History* (Family Tree Books), *Finding Your Famous (& Infamous) Ancestors* (Betterway Books), *The Complete Idiot's Guide to Online Genealogy* (Alpha) and other titles.

★ **MAUREEN A. TAYLOR**, of photo research firm **<TaylorandStrong.com>**, is a professional photo historian, contributing editor to *Family Tree Magazine* and author of the books *Preserving Your Family Photographs* (Betterway Books) and *Uncovering Your Ancestry Through Family Photographs*, 2nd edition (Family Tree Books). She's been featured in *The New York Times* and appeared on television shows including "The View" and "Today."

★ **JAMES W. WARREN** is a professional writer, lecturer and researcher, specializing in Midwestern US, American Indian and immigrant ancestors; writing family history narratives; and on-site research in Washington, DC, and Salt Lake City. He's a partner in the Salt Lake City-based genealogical and historical research and publishing firm of Warren, Carmack & Associates. He co-authored books including *Your Guide to the Family History Library* and *Getting the Most Mileage from Genealogical Research Trips*.